Hoover's Handbook of Emerging Companies 2022

Austin, Texas

Hoover's Handbook of Emerging Companies 2022 is intended to provide readers with accurate and authoritative information about the enterprises covered in it. Hoover's researched all companies and organizations profiled, and in many cases contacted them directly so that companies represented could provide information. The information contained herein is as accurate as we could reasonably make it. In many cases we have relied on third-party material that we believe to be trustworthy, but were unable to independently verify. We do not warrant that the book is absolutely accurate or without error. Readers should not rely on any information contained herein in instances where such reliance might cause financial loss. The publisher, the editors, and their data suppliers specifically disclaim all warranties, including the implied warranties of merchantability and fitness for a specific purpose. This book is sold with the understanding that neither the publisher, the editors, nor any content contributors are engaged in providing investment, financial, accounting, legal, or other professional advice.

The financial data (Historical Financials sections) in this book are from a variety of sources. Mergent Inc., provided selected data for the Historical Financials sections of publicly traded companies. For private companies and for historical information on public companies prior to their becoming public, we obtained information directly from the companies or from trade sources deemed to be reliable. Hoover's, Inc., is solely responsible for the presentation of all data.

Many of the names of products and services mentioned in this book are the trademarks or service marks of the companies manufacturing or selling them and are subject to protection under US law. Space has not permitted us to indicate which names are subject to such protection, and readers are advised to consult with the owners of such marks regarding their use. Hoover's is a trademark of Hoover's, Inc.

Copyright © 2022 by Dun & Bradstreet. All rights reserved. No part of this book may be reproduced or transmitted in any form or by any means, electronic or mechanical, including by photocopying, facsimile transmission, recording, rekeying, or using any information storage and retrieval system, without permission in writing from Hoover's, except that brief passages may be quoted by a reviewer in a magazine, in a newspaper, online, or in a broadcast review.

10 9 8 7 6 5 4 3 2 1

Publishers Cataloging-in-Publication Data

Hoover's Handbook of Emerging Companies 2021

    Includes indexes.

    ISBN: 978-1-64972-826-5

    ISSN 1073-6433

    1. Business enterprises — Directories. 2. Corporations — Directories.

HF3010 338.7

U.S. AND WORLD BOOK SALES

Mergent Inc.
580 Kingsley Park Drive
Fort Mill, SC 29715
Phone: 704-559-6961
e-mail: skardon@ftserussell.com
Web: www.mergentbusinesspress.com

Mergent Inc.

Executive Managing Director: John Pedernales

Publisher and Managing Director of Print Products : Thomas Wecera

Director of Print Products: Charlot Volny

Quality Assurance Editor: Wayne Arnold

Production Research Assistant: Davie Christna

Data Manager: Allison Shank

MERGENT CUSTOMER SERVICE-PRINT

Support and Fulfillment Manager: Stephanie Kardon Phone: 704-559-6961
e-mail: skardon@ftserussell.com

ABOUT MERGENT INC.

For over 100 years, Mergent, Inc. has been a leading provider of business and financial information on public and private companies globally. Mergent is known to be a trusted partner to corporate and financial institutions, as well as to academic and public libraries. Today we continue to build on a century of experience by transforming data into knowledge and combining our expertise with the latest technology to create new global data and analytical solutions for our clients. With advanced data collection services, cloud-based applications, desktop analytics and print products, Mergent and its subsidiaries provide solutions from top down economic and demographic information, to detailed equity and debt fundamental analysis. We incorporate value added tools such as quantitative Smart Beta equity research and tools for portfolio building and measurement. Based in the U.S., Mergent maintains a strong global presence, with offices in New York, Charlotte, San Diego, London, Tokyo, Kuching and Melbourne. Mergent, Inc. is a member of the London Stock Exchange plc group of companies. The Mergent business forms part of LSEG's Information Services Division, which includes FTSE Russell, a global leader in indexes.

Abbreviations

AFL-CIO – American Federation of Labor and Congress of Industrial Organizations
AMA – American Medical Association
AMEX – American Stock Exchange
ARM – adjustable-rate mortgage
ASP – application services provider
ATM – asynchronous transfer mode
ATM – automated teller machine
CAD/CAM – computer-aided design/computer-aided manufacturing
CD-ROM – compact disc – read-only memory
CD-R – CD-recordable
CEO – chief executive officer
CFO – chief financial officer
CMOS – complementary metal oxide silicon
COO – chief operating officer
DAT – digital audiotape
DOD – Department of Defense
DOE – Department of Energy
DOS – disk operating system
DOT – Department of Transportation
DRAM – dynamic random-access memory
DSL – digital subscriber line
DVD – digital versatile disc/digital video disc
DVD-R – DVD-recordable
EPA – Environmental Protection Agency
EPS – earnings per share
ESOP – employee stock ownership plan
EU – European Union
EVP – executive vice president
FCC – Federal Communications Commission
FDA – Food and Drug Administration
FDIC – Federal Deposit Insurance Corporation

FTC – Federal Trade Commission
GATT – General Agreement on Tariffs and Trade
GDP – gross domestic product
HMO – health maintenance organization
HR – human resources
HTML – hypertext markup language
ICC – Interstate Commerce Commission
IPO – initial public offering
IRS – Internal Revenue Service
ISP – Internet service provider
kWh – kilowatt-hour
LAN – local-area network
LBO – leveraged buyout
LCD – liquid crystal display
LNG – liquefied natural gas
LP – limited partnership
Ltd. – limited
mips – millions of instructions per second
MW – megawatt
NAFTA – North American Free Trade Agreement
NASA – National Aeronautics and Space Administration
NASDAQ – National Association of Securities Dealers Automated Quotations
NATO – North Atlantic Treaty Organization
NYSE – New York Stock Exchange
OCR – optical character recognition
OECD – Organization for Economic Cooperation and Development
OEM – original equipment manufacturer
OPEC – Organization of Petroleum Exporting Countries
OS – operating system

OSHA – Occupational Safety and Health Administration
OTC – over-the-counter
PBX – private branch exchange
PCMCIA – Personal Computer Memory Card International Association
P/E – price to earnings ratio
RAID – redundant array of independent disks
RAM – random-access memory
R&D – research and development
RBOC – regional Bell operating company
RISC – reduced instruction set computer
REIT – real estate investment trust
ROA – return on assets
ROE – return on equity
ROI – return on investment
ROM – read-only memory
S&L – savings and loan
SEC – Securities and Exchange Commission
SEVP – senior executive vice president
SIC – Standard Industrial Classification
SOC – system on a chip
SVP – senior vice president
USB – universal serial bus
VAR – value-added reseller
VAT – value-added tax
VC – venture capitalist
VoIP – Voice over Internet Protocol
VP – vice president
WAN – wide-area network

Contents

Companies Profiled...vi

About *Hoover's Handbook of Emerging Companies 2022* x

Using Hoover's Handbooks xi

A List-Lover's Compendium 1a

    The 300 Largest Companies by Sales in In *Mergents*

    Data Base for 2022 ....2a

    The 300 Largest Employers in In *Mergents*

    Data Base for 2022 ....3a

    Top 200 Companies by Net Income in In *Mergents*

    Data Base for 2022 13

The Companies...1

The Indexes 459

    Index of Companies by Headquarters Location 461

    Index of Company Executives 493

Companies Profiled

1-800 Flowers.com, Inc. 1
ABIOMED, Inc. 2
ACM Research Inc 3
ACNB Corp 3
Addus HomeCare Corp 4
Advanced Drainage Systems Inc 5
Advanced Energy Industries Inc 5
AeroVironment, Inc. 6
Agree Realty Corp. 8
Air Lease Corp 9
Air Transport Services Group, Inc. 9
Akamai Technologies Inc 10
Alamo Group, Inc. 11
Alarm.com Holdings Inc 12
Alerus Financial Corp. 13
Alexandria Real Estate Equities Inc 13
Align Technology Inc 14
Allegiance Bancshares Inc 15
AllianceBernstein Holding LP 15
Allied Motion Technologies Inc................16
Alpine Banks of Colorado 17
Alpine Income Property Trust Inc 17
Amalgamated Financial Corp. 17
Amedisys, Inc. 17
Ameresco Inc 18
America's Car-Mart Inc 19
American Bank Inc (PA) 20
American Business Bank (Los
    Angeles, CA) 21
American National Bankshares, Inc.
    (Danville, VA) 21
American Outdoor Brands Inc...................22
American Vanguard Corp. 22
American Woodmark Corp. 23
Ameris Bancorp..24
Ames National Corp. 25
Amneal Pharmaceuticals Inc 26
Ansys Inc. 27
Antares Pharma Inc. 28
Antero Midstream Corp............................28
Apollo Medical Holdings Inc 29
AppFolio Inc 29
Arbor Realty Trust Inc..............................29
Ares Management Corp............................30
Arista Networks Inc.................................30
ARKO Corp...30
Armada Hoffler Properties Inc 30
Arrow Financial Corp. 31
ASGN Inc 31
Aspen Technology Inc 33
Atkore Inc 34
Atlantic Union Bankshares Corp...............34
Atlanticus Holdings Corp 35
AtriCure Inc...36
Aura Minerals Inc (British Virgin Islands) .37
Autodesk Inc..37

Avid Bioservices Inc 38
Avidbank Holdings Inc............................39
Axcelis Technologies Inc 39
Axos Financial Inc...................................40
AZEK Co Inc (The)..................................41
B Riley Financial Inc...............................42
B&G Foods Inc..42
BancFirst Corp. (Oklahoma City, Okla).....44
Bank First Corp..45
Bank Of Princeton (The) 45
Bank OZK 45
Bank7 Corp..46
BankFirst Capital Corp.............................46
Bar Harbor Bankshares.............................46
Barnwell Industries, Inc...........................47
BayCom Corp..48
BCB Bancorp Inc.....................................48
BellRing Brands Inc 48
Bio-Techne Corp......................................49
BioDelivery Sciences International Inc.......50
BioMarin Pharmaceutical Inc...................51
Bioqual Inc 51
Blackhawk Bancorp Inc 52
Blackstone Mortgage Trust Inc 52
Blue Ridge Bankshares Inc (Luray, VA) 52
Bluerock Residential Growth REIT Inc 53
BNCCORP Inc..53
BOK Financial Corp.................................53
Boomer Holdings Inc 54
Boot Barn Holdings Inc...........................55
Boston Beer Co Inc (The).........................55
Bridgewater Bancshares Inc 56
BrightView Holdings Inc 56
Broadmark Realty Capital Inc 56
Broadstone Net Lease Inc.........................57
Brown & Brown Inc 57
Business First Bancshares Inc 58
BWX Technologies inc 58
Byline Bancorp Inc..................................59
Cable One Inc 59
Cactus Inc 60
Cadence Bank 61
Cadence Design Systems Inc....................61
California First Leasing Corp....................63
Calloway's Nursery, Inc...........................64
Cambium Networks Corp.........................64
Cambridge Bancorp..................................64
Canandaigua National Corp. 65
Capital Bancorp Inc (MD)........................66
Capital City Bank Group, Inc. 66
CapStar Financial Holdings Inc................67
Cara Therapeutics Inc...............................67
Cardinal Ethanol LLC 68
CareTrust REIT Inc 68
CarGurus Inc 68
Casella Waste Systems, Inc. 68

Cashmere Valley Bank Washington (New) 69
Catalent Inc...70
Cathay General Bancorp..........................70
Cavco Industries Inc (DE)........................71
Cboe Global Markets Inc.........................72
Celsius Holdings Inc................................74
Central Garden & Pet Co 74
Central Valley Community Bancorp 76
Cerence Inc 76
CF Bankshares Inc...................................77
ChampionX Corp.....................................77
ChannelAdvisor Corp...............................77
Charles & Colvard Ltd 78
Charles River Laboratories
    International Inc..................................78
Chart Industries Inc 80
ChoiceOne Financial Services, Inc............81
CIB Marine Bancshares Inc......................82
Citizens & Northern Corp 82
Citizens Community Bancorp Inc (MD).....83
Citizens Financial Services Inc 83
City Holding Co.......................................84
Civista Bancshares Inc 84
Civitas Resources Inc..............................85
Clearfield Inc...86
CNB Bank Shares Inc..............................86
CNB Community Bancorp Inc 87
CNB Financial Corp. (Clearfield, PA) 87
Coastal Financial Corp (WA)....................88
CoastalSouth Bancshares Inc 88
Cognex Corp..88
Cohen & Company Inc (New)....................89
Coherus BioSciences Inc 90
Cohu Inc 90
Collegium Pharmaceuticals Inc................91
Colony Bankcorp, Inc..............................91
Columbia Banking System Inc 92
Columbia Financial Inc 93
Comfort Systems USA Inc 93
Communities First Financial Corp 94
Community Bank System Inc....................94
Community Financial Corp (The) 95
Community Healthcare Trust Inc 96
Community West Bancshares.....................96
Compass Diversified 97
ConnectOne Bancorp Inc (New) 97
Consolidated Communications
    Holdings Inc......................................98
Construction Partners Inc.........................98
Consumers Bancorp, Inc. (Minerva, OH) ...99
Cooper Companies, Inc. (The) 99
Copart Inc..101
Corcept Therapeutics Inc........................102
CoreCard Corp.......................................103
CoStar Group, Inc..................................103
Cousins Properties Inc............................104

vi

Companies Profiled (continued)

Cowen Inc	105	
CRA International Inc	106	
Crawford United Corp	107	
Credit Acceptance Corp (MI)	108	
Crescent Capital BDC Inc	109	
Crexendo Inc	109	
Crocs Inc	110	
CrossFirst Bankshares Inc	111	
Crossroads Systems Inc (New)	111	
CSB Bancorp Inc (OH)	111	
Customers Bancorp Inc	112	
CVB Financial Corp	113	
CW Bancorp	114	
CyrusOne Inc	114	
Dart Financial Corp	114	
Davey Tree Expert Co. (The)	114	
Deckers Outdoor Corp.	115	
DexCom Inc	116	
Digi International Inc	117	
Digital Realty Trust Inc	119	
Digital Turbine Inc	120	
Diodes, Inc.	120	
DLH Holdings Corp	122	
Dorian LPG Ltd.	122	
Dorman Products Inc	122	
Dropbox Inc	123	
Duke Realty Corp	124	
Duluth Holdings Inc	124	
Dynatrace Inc	125	
EACO Corp	125	
Eagle Bancorp Inc (MD)	125	
Eagle Bancorp Montana, Inc.	126	
Eagle Financial Services, Inc.	127	
East West Bancorp, Inc	127	
Easterly Government Properties Inc	128	
EastGroup Properties Inc	128	
Ebix Inc	129	
Educational Development Corp.	130	
eHealth Inc	130	
Ellington Residential Mortgaging Real Estate Investment Trust	132	
Embassy Bancorp Inc	132	
Emclaire Financial Corp.	132	
Emergent BioSolutions Inc	133	
ENB Financial Corp	134	
Encore Capital Group Inc	134	
Encore Wire Corp.	135	
Energizer Holdings Inc (New)	136	
Energy Recovery Inc	136	
Enerkon Solar International Inc	137	
Enova International Inc	137	
Enphase Energy Inc.	138	
Ensign Group Inc	138	
Entegris Inc.	140	
Enterprise Bancorp, Inc. (MA)	141	
Enterprise Financial Services Corp	141	
Envela Corp	142	
Enviva Inc.	143	
Epam Systems, Inc.	143	
Equitrans Midstream Corp	144	
Erie Indemnity Co.	144	
Escalade, Inc.	145	
Esquire Financial Holdings Inc	146	
Essential Properties Realty Trust Inc	147	
Essential Utilities Inc.	147	
Etsy Inc	148	

Evans Bancorp, Inc.	148	
Evercore Inc.	148	
EVI Industries Inc	149	
Exelixis Inc	150	
ExlService Holdings Inc	151	
eXp World Holdings Inc	152	
Extra Space Storage Inc.	152	
Exxe Group Inc.	153	
F & M Bank Corp.	153	
Fair Isaac Corp	154	
Farmers & Merchants Bancorp (Lodi, CA)	155	
Farmers & Merchants Bancorp Inc (OH)	155	
Farmers National Banc Corp. (Canfield,OH)	156	
Farmland Partners Inc	156	
FB Financial Corp	157	
FCN Banc Corp	157	
Federal Agricultural Mortgage Corp	157	
Federal Home Loan Bank New York	158	
Federal Home Loan Bank Of Dallas	158	
Federal Signal Corp.	159	
Fentura Financial Inc	160	
FFD Financial Corp.	160	
Fidelity D&D Bancorp Inc	160	
Finance of America Companies Inc	161	
Finemark Holdings Inc	161	
Finward Bancorp	161	
First Bancorp (NC)	162	
First Bancorp Inc (ME)	162	
First Bancshares Inc (MS)	163	
First Bank (Williamstown, NJ)	164	
First Busey Corp.	164	
First Commonwealth Financial Corp (Indiana, PA)	165	
First Community Corp (SC)	166	
First Farmers Financial Corp	166	
First Financial Bancorp (OH)	166	
First Financial Bankshares, Inc.	167	
First Financial Northwest Inc	168	
First Foundation Inc	169	
First Guaranty Bancshares, Inc.	169	
First Horizon Corp.	169	
First Internet Bancorp	170	
First Interstate BancSystem Inc	171	
First Merchants Corp.	172	
First Mid Bancshares Inc	173	
First Northwest Bancorp	173	
First Reliance Bancshares Inc	174	
First Savings Financial Group Inc	174	
First Western Financial Inc	174	
FirstCash Holdings Inc	175	
Five Below Inc	176	
Flagstar Bancorp, Inc.	177	
Floor & Decor Holdings Inc	178	
FNB Corp	178	
Focus Financial Partners Inc	179	
Forestar Group Inc (New)	179	
FormFactor Inc	180	
Forrester Research Inc.	181	
Fortinet Inc	182	
Founders Bay Holdings	183	
Four Corners Property Trust Inc.	183	
Fox Factory Holding Corp.	183	
Franchise Group Inc	184	
Franklin Wireless Corp.	185	

Friedman Industries, Inc.	185	
FRMO Corp.	186	
Frontdoor Inc	187	
FRP Holdings Inc	187	
FS Bancorp (Indiana)	187	
FS Bancorp Inc (Washington)	188	
Fulgent Genetics Inc	188	
Fuller (HB) Company	188	
FVCBankcorp Inc	190	
Gaming & Leisure Properties, Inc	190	
Generac Holdings Inc	190	
Genie Energy Ltd	191	
German American Bancorp Inc	192	
Glacier Bancorp, Inc.	192	
Gladstone Commercial Corp	193	
Global Net Lease Inc	194	
Globus Medical Inc	194	
GMS Inc	195	
GoDaddy Inc	196	
Goldman Sachs BDC Inc	196	
Good Times Restaurants Inc.	196	
Goosehead Insurance Inc	196	
GrafTech International Ltd	197	
Granite Falls Energy LLC	198	
Gray Television Inc	198	
Green Brick Partners Inc	199	
Green Dot Corp	200	
Green Thumb Industries Inc	201	
Greene County Bancorp Inc	201	
GreenSky Inc	201	
Griffon Corp.	201	
Grocery Outlet Holding Corp	203	
Guaranty Bancshares Inc	203	
Guaranty Federal Bancshares Inc (Springfield, MO)	204	
Halozyme Therapeutics Inc	204	
Hamilton Lane Inc	205	
Hannon Armstrong Sustainable Infrastructure Capital Inc	205	
HarborOne Bancorp Inc (New)	206	
Hawthorn Bancshares Inc	206	
Healthcare Trust Of America Inc	207	
HealthEquity Inc	207	
Heartland BancCorp	207	
Heartland Financial USA, Inc. (Dubuque, IA)	207	
Helios Technologies Inc	209	
Helix Energy Solutions Group Inc	210	
Heritage Commerce Corp.	211	
Heritage Financial Corp (WA)	212	
Hess Midstream LP	212	
Hibbett Inc	213	
Hillenbrand Inc	214	
Hingham Institution for Savings	215	
Home Bancorp Inc	216	
Home BancShares Inc	216	
HomeTrust Bancshares Inc.	217	
Hope Bancorp Inc	218	
Horizon Bancorp Inc	218	
Hostess Brands Inc	219	
Houlihan Lokey Inc	219	
HV Bancorp Inc	219	
IAC/InterActiveCorp (New)	219	
Ichor Holdings Ltd	220	
ICU Medical Inc	220	
Idexx Laboratories, Inc.	221	

Companies Profiled (continued)

IES Holdings Inc 222
II-VI Inc 223
Incyte Corporation 224
Independence Realty Trust Inc 225
Independent Bank Corp (MA) 226
Independent Bank Corporation (Ionia, MI) 226
Independent Bank Group Inc 227
Industrial Logistics Properties Trust 227
InfuSystem Holdings Inc 228
Innovative Industrial Properties Inc 228
Innoviva Inc 228
Inotiv Inc 229
Installed Building Products Inc 230
Insteel Industries, Inc. 231
Insulet Corp 232
Integra LifeSciences Holdings Corp 233
Interactive Brokers Group Inc 234
Investar Holding Corp 235
Investors Title Co. 235
Invitation Homes Inc 236
iRobot Corp 236
Ironwood Pharmaceuticals Inc 237
Janus International Group Inc 238
John Marshall Bancorp Inc 238
Johnson Outdoors Inc 238
Joint Corp (New) 240
Kadant Inc 240
Kearny Financial Corp (MD) 241
Kilroy Realty L.P. 241
Kimball Electronics Inc 241
Kinsale Capital Group Inc 241
Kish Bancorp Inc. 242
KKR Real Estate Finance Trust Inc 242
Lakeland Bancorp, Inc. 242
Lakeland Financial Corp 243
Lakeland Industries, Inc. 244
Landmark Bancorp Inc 245
LCI Industries 245
LCNB Corp 247
Ledyard Financial Group Inc 247
Lee Enterprises, Inc. 247
Legacy Housing Corp 249
LeMaitre Vascular Inc 249
Leslie's Inc 250
Level One Bancorp Inc 251
LGI Homes, Inc. 251
LHC Group Inc 251
Liberty Broadband Corp 252
LICT Corp 252
Limbach Holdings Inc 253
Limestone Bancorp Inc 253
Lincoln Educational Services Corp 253
Littelfuse Inc 254
Live Oak Bancshares Inc 255
Live Ventures Inc 256
Lovesac Co 256
Lumentum Holdings Inc 256
Luther Burbank Corp 256
Lyons Bancorp Inc. 257
M/I Homes Inc 257
Magnolia Oil & Gas Corp 258
MainStreet Bancshares Inc 258
Malibu Boats Inc 258
ManTech International Corp 259
MarineMax Inc 260

MarketAxess Holdings Inc. 261
Masimo Corp. 262
Mastech Digital Inc 263
MasterCraft Boat Holdings Inc 263
MaxLinear Inc 264
Maxus Realty Trust Inc 265
Medical Properties Trust Inc 265
Medifast Inc 266
Medpace Holdings Inc 266
Mercantile Bank Corp. 267
Merchants Bancorp (Indiana) 267
Mercury Systems Inc 268
Meridian Bioscience Inc. 269
Meridian Corp 270
Meritage Hospitality Group Inc 270
Mesabi Trust 271
Meta Financial Group Inc 271
MetroCity Bankshares Inc 272
Metropolitan Bank Holding Corp 272
Mettler-Toledo International, Inc. 272
Mid Penn Bancorp Inc 274
Middlefield Banc Corp. 274
Midland States Bancorp Inc 275
MidWestOne Financial Group, Inc. 276
Mitek Systems, Inc. 276
MKS Instruments Inc 277
Moelis & Co 278
Monolithic Power Systems Inc 278
Morningstar Inc 279
Morris St Bancshares Inc 281
Mountain Commerce Bancorp Inc 281
Mr Cooper Group Inc 281
MSCI Inc 281
Muncy Bank Financial, Inc. (Muncy, PA) 282
MVB Financial Corp 283
MYR Group Inc 283
NASB Financial Inc 284
National Bank Holdings Corp 285
National Rural Utilities Cooperative Finance Corp 286
National Storage Affiliates Trust 286
National Vision Holdings Inc 286
Natural Alternatives International, Inc. 287
Natural Grocers By Vitamin Cottage Inc . 288
Nautilus Inc 288
Nelnet Inc 289
Neurocrine Biosciences, Inc. 290
New Residential Investment Corp 291
Newmark Group Inc 292
Newtek Business Services Corp 292
NexPoint Residential Trust Inc 293
NI Holdings Inc 293
Nicolet Bankshares Inc 293
NMI Holdings Inc 293
Northeast Bank (ME) 294
NorthEast Community Bancorp Inc (MD) 295
Northern Technologies International Corp. 295
Northrim BanCorp Inc 296
Northwest Pipe Co. 296
Norwood Financial Corp. 297
Novanta Inc 298
Nuvera Communications Inc 299
NV5 Global Inc 299
Oak Valley Bancorp (Oakdale, CA) 300
Ocean Bio-Chem, Inc. 301

OceanFirst Financial Corp 301
Old Second Bancorp., Inc. (Aurora, Ill.) ... 302
Ollie's Bargain Outlet Holdings Inc 303
OneMain Finance Corp 303
OneWater Marine Inc 303
Onto Innovation Inc 303
OP Bancorp 305
Oppenheimer Holdings Inc 305
Orange County Bancorp Inc 306
Origin Bancorp Inc 306
Orion Energy Systems Inc 306
Orrstown Financial Services, Inc. 307
OTC Markets Group Inc 308
Otter Tail Corp. 308
Overstock.com Inc (DE) 309
Pacific Premier Bancorp Inc 310
Pacira BioSciences Inc 310
Palomar Holdings Inc 311
Pangaea Logistics Solutions Ltd. 311
Parade Technologies Ltd. 311
Park National Corp (Newark, OH) 312
Parke Bancorp Inc 312
Parkway Acquisition Corp 313
Pathfinder Bancorp Inc. (MD) 313
Patrick Industries Inc 313
Paycom Software Inc 314
Paylocity Holding Corp 314
PBF Logistics LP 315
PCB Bancorp 315
Peapack-Gladstone Financial Corp. 315
Pennant Group Inc 316
PennyMac Financial Services Inc (New) .. 316
Pennymac Mortgage Investment Trust 317
People's United Financial Inc 318
PerkinElmer, Inc. 319
PGT Innovations Inc 321
Phillips 66 Partners LP 321
Phillips Edison & Co Inc 322
Photronics, Inc. 322
Physicians Realty Trust 323
Pinnacle Financial Partners Inc 324
Pinterest Inc 325
Piper Sandler Companies 325
PJT Partners Inc 326
Plumas Bancorp Inc 326
Pool Corp 327
PotlatchDeltic Corp 328
Power Integrations Inc 329
Preferred Bank (Los Angeles, CA) 331
Preformed Line Products Co. 331
Premier Financial Corp. 332
Primerica Inc 333
Primis Financial Corp. 333
Primoris Services Corp 334
Private Bancorp Of America Inc 335
Professional Holding Corp 335
Progyny Inc 335
Prosperity Bancshares Inc. 335
Proto Labs Inc 337
Provident Bancorp Inc (MD) 338
Prudential Bancorp Inc (New) 338
PTC Inc 338
Pure Cycle Corp. 339
QCR Holdings Inc 339
Quaker Houghton 340
Qualys, Inc. 340

viii

Companies Profiled (continued)

Quidel Corp. ...341
QuinStreet, Inc. ...342
R1 RCM Inc ...343
Rand Worldwide Inc ...344
Randolph Bancorp Inc ...344
Rattler Midstream LP ...345
RBB Bancorp ...345
Re/Max Holdings Inc ...345
Ready Capital Corp ...345
Realty Income Corp ...346
Red River Bancshares Inc ...347
Regional Management Corp ...347
Renasant Corp ...348
Repligen Corp. ...349
Republic Bancorp, Inc. (KY) ...350
ResMed Inc. ...351
Retractable Technologies Inc ...352
Revolve Group Inc ...353
Rexford Industrial Realty Inc ...353
RF Industries Ltd. ...354
Rhinebeck Bancorp Inc ...354
Ribbon Communications Inc ...354
Richmond Mutual Bancorporation Inc ...355
Risk George Industries Inc ...355
River Financial Corp ...355
RLI Corp. ...355
RMR Group Inc (The) ...356
Roku Inc ...357
Rollins, Inc. ...357
Royalty Pharma plc ...358
Sachem Capital Corp ...358
Safehold Inc ...359
Saia Inc ...359
Sandy Spring Bancorp Inc ...360
Santa Cruz County Bank (CA) ...360
SB Financial Group Inc ...361
Schnitzer Steel Industries Inc ...361
SciPlay Corp ...362
Scripps (EW) Company (The) ...363
Seacoast Banking Corp. of Florida ...364
Security Federal Corp (SC) ...365
Security National Financial Corp ...365
Selective Insurance Group Inc ...366
SelectQuote Inc ...367
Semler Scientific Inc ...367
ServisFirst Bancshares Inc ...367
Sharps Compliance Corp. ...368
Shell Midstream Partners LP ...368
Shutterstock Inc ...369
Sierra Bancorp ...369
SIGA Technologies Inc ...370
Signature Bank (New York, NY) ...371
Sila Realty Trust Inc ...372
Silvergate Capital Corp ...372
Simmons First National Corp ...372
Simply Good Foods Company (The) ...373
Simpson Manufacturing Co., Inc. (DE) ...374
Simulations Plus Inc ...375
SiteOne Landscape Supply Inc ...375
SJW Group ...375
Skyline Champion Corp ...376
Sleep Number Corp ...377
SLM Corp. ...378
Smart Sand Inc ...379
SmartFinancial Inc. ...379
SolarWinds Corp ...380

Solera National Bancorp Inc ...380
Sonos Inc ...380
Sound Financial Bancorp Inc ...381
South Atlantic Bancshares Inc ...381
South Jersey Industries Inc ...381
South Plains Financial Inc ...382
Southern First Bancshares, Inc. ...382
Southern Michigan Bancorp Inc (United States) ...382
Southern Missouri Bancorp, Inc. ...383
SouthState Corp. ...383
Spirit of Texas Bancshares Inc ...384
Sportsman's Warehouse Holdings Inc ...384
SPS Commerce, Inc. ...384
SStarTrade Tech Inc ...385
St. Joe Co. (The) ...385
Staar Surgical Co. ...387
STAG Industrial Inc ...388
Starwood Property Trust Inc. ...389
StepStone Group Inc ...389
Sterling Construction Co Inc ...390
Stock Yards Bancorp Inc ...390
STORE Capital Corp ...391
Strategic Education Inc ...391
Stride Inc ...393
Sturgis Bancorp Inc ...394
Summit Financial Group Inc ...394
Summit Materials Inc ...395
Summit State Bank (Santa Rosa, CA) ...395
Sun Communities Inc ...395
Sun Country Airlines Holdings Inc ...396
Super Micro Computer Inc ...397
Superior Group of Companies Inc ...397
Supernus Pharmaceuticals Inc ...398
Surface Oncology Inc ...399
Switch Inc ...399
Synovus Financial Corp ...400
Take-Two Interactive Software, Inc. ...401
Teb Bancorp Inc ...402
TechTarget Inc. ...403
Teledyne Technologies Inc. ...404
Teradyne, Inc. ...405
Terreno Realty Corp ...406
Texas Pacific Land Corp ...407
The Bancorp Inc ...407
The Trade Desk Inc. ...408
Thomasville Bancshares, Inc. ...409
Timberland Bancorp, Inc. ...409
TopBuild Corp. ...409
Toro Company (The) ...410
TowneBank ...411
Tradeweb Markets Inc ...412
TransUnion ...412
Trex Co Inc ...412
Tri Pointe Homes Inc. ...413
TriCo Bancshares (Chico, CA) ...413
Trimble Inc ...414
TriState Capital Holdings Inc ...415
Triumph Bancorp Inc ...416
TTEC Holdings Inc ...416
Turning Point Brands Inc ...418
Turtle Beach Corp ...418
Tyler Technologies, Inc. ...418
U&I Financial Corp ...419
Ubiquiti Inc. ...420
Ultra Clean Holdings Inc ...420

UMB Financial Corp ...421
Union Bankshares, Inc. (Morrisville, VT) ...422
United Bancorp, Inc. (Martins Ferry, OH) ...422
United Bancshares Inc. (OH) ...423
United Bankshares Inc. ...423
United Community Banks Inc (Blairsville, GA) ...424
United States 12 Month Oil Fund LP ...425
United States Brent Oil Fund L.P. ...425
United States Gasoline Fund LP ...425
Unity Bancorp, Inc. ...425
Universal Display Corp ...426
Universal Insurance Holdings Inc ...426
University Bancorp Inc. (MI) ...427
Univest Financial Corp ...428
Upstart Holdings Inc ...429
US Global Investors Inc ...429
USA Compression Partners LP ...429
USA Truck, Inc. ...429
Uwharrie Capital Corp. ...430
Valley National Bancorp (NJ) ...431
Valley Republic Bancorp ...431
Valvoline Inc ...432
Vanda Pharmaceuticals Inc ...432
Veeva Systems Inc ...433
Verisk Analytics Inc ...434
Veritex Holdings Inc ...435
Veru Inc ...435
Viavi Solutions Inc ...436
VICI Properties Inc. ...437
Vicor Corp ...437
Victory Capital Holdings Inc (DE) ...439
Viemed Healthcare Inc ...439
Village Bank & Trust Financial Corp ...439
Virginia National Bankshares Corp ...439
VirnetX Holding Corp ...440
Virtu Financial Inc. ...440
Virtus Investment Partners Inc ...441
Vital Farms Inc ...442
Voyager Therapeutics Inc ...442
W.P. Carey Inc ...442
Walker & Dunlop Inc ...443
Waterstone Financial Inc (MD) ...444
Weber Inc ...444
WesBanco Inc. ...444
West Bancorporation, Inc. ...445
West Pharmaceutical Services, Inc. ...446
Western Alliance Bancorporation ...447
Western Midstream Partners LP ...447
Western New England Bancorp Inc ...448
WidePoint Corp ...448
Willis Lease Finance Corp. ...449
Wilson Bank Holding Co. ...450
Wingstop Inc ...450
Winnebago Industries, Inc. ...450
Wintrust Financial Corp (IL) ...451
World Wrestling Entertainment Inc ...452
WSFS Financial Corp. ...454
XOMA Corp ...455
XPEL Inc ...456
Xperi Holding Corp. ...456
Zedge Inc ...457
Ziff Davis Inc ...457
Zoom Video Communications Inc ...457
Zynex Inc ...457

About Hoover's Handbook of Emerging Companies 2022

Hoover's Handbook of Emerging Companies enters its 28th year as one of America's premier sources of business information on younger, growth-oriented enterprises. Given our current economic realities, finding value in the marketplace becomes ever more difficult, and so we are particularly pleased to present this edition of Hoover's Handbook of Emerging Companies 2020 — the result of a search of our extensive database of business information for companies with demonstrated growth and the potential for future gains.

The 600 companies in this book were chosen from the universe of public US companies with sales between $10 million and $2.5 billion. Their selection was based primarily on sales growth and profitability, although in a few cases we made some rather subjective decisions about which companies we chose to include. They all have reported at least three years of sales and have sustained annualized sales growth of at least 7% during that time. Also, they are profitable (through year-end September 2018).

In addition to the companies featured in our handbooks, comprehensive coverage of more than 40,000 business enterprises is available in electronic format on our website, Hoover's Online (www.hoovers.com). Our goal is to provide one site that offers authoritative, updated intelligence on US and global companies, industries, and the people who shape them. Hoover's has partnered with other prestigious business information and service providers to bring you all the right business information, services, and links in one place.

Hoover's Handbook of Emerging Companies is one of our four-title series of handbooks that covers, literally, the world of business. The series is available as an indexed set, and also includes Hoover's Handbook of American Business, Hoover's Handbook of World Business, and Hoover's Handbook of Private Companies. This series brings you information on the biggest, fastest-growing, and most influential enterprises in the world.

We believe that anyone who buys from, sells to, invests in, lends to, competes with, interviews with, or works for a company should know as much as possible about that enterprise. Taken together, Hoover's Handbook of Emerging Companies 2016 and the other Hoover's products represent the most complete source of basic corporate information readily available to the general public.

How to use this book

This book has four sections:

1. "Using Hoover's Handbooks" describes the contents of our profiles.

2. "A List-Lover's Compendium" contains lists of the fastest-growing and most profitable companies. The lists are based on the information in our profiles, or compiled from well-known sources.

3. The company profiles section makes up the largest and most important part of the book — 600 profiles arranged alphabetically. Each profile features an overview of the company; some larger and more visible companies have an additional History section. All companies have up to five years of financial information, product information where available, and a list of company executives and key competitors.

4. At the end of this volume are the combined indexes from our 2021 editions of all Hoover's Handbooks. The information is organized into three separate sections. The first sorts companies by industry groups, the second by headquarters location. The third index is a list of all the executives found in the Executives section of each company profile. For a more thorough description of our indexing style, see page xii.

Using Hoover's Handbooks

ORGANIZATION

The profiles in this volume are presented in alphabetical order. This alphabetization is generally word by word, which means that Bridge Bancorp precedes Bridgepoint Education. You will find the commonly used name of the enterprise at the beginning of the profile; the full, legal name is found in the Locations section. If a company name starts with initials, such as BJ's Restaurants or U.S. Physical Therapy, look for it under the combined initials (in the above example, BJ or US, respectively).

Basic financial data is listed under the heading Historical Financials; also included is the exchange on which the company's stock is traded, the ticker symbol used by the stock exchange, and the company's fiscal year-end. The annual financial information contained in the profiles is current through fiscal year-ends occurring as late as January 2018. We have included certain nonfinancial developments, such as officer changes, through January 2021.

OVERVIEW

In the first section of the profile, we have tried to give a thumbnail description of the company and what it does. The description will usually include information on the company's strategy, reputation, and ownership. We recommend that you read this section first.

HISTORY

This extended section, which is available for some of the larger and more well-known companies, reflects our belief that every enterprise is the sum of its history and that you have to know where you came from in order to know where you are going. While some companies have limited historical awareness, we think the vast majority of the enterprises in this book have colorful backgrounds. We have tried to focus on the people who made the enterprises what they are today. We have found these histories to be full of twists and ironies; they make fascinating reading.

EXECUTIVES

Here we list the names of the people who run the company, insofar as space allows. In the case of public companies, we have shown the ages and pay of key officers. The published data is for the previous fiscal year, although the company may have announced promotions or retirements since year-end. The pay represents cash compensation, including bonuses, but excludes stock option programs.

Although companies are free to structure their management titles any way they please, most modern corporations follow standard practices. The ultimate power in any corporation lies with the shareholders, who elect a board of directors, usually including officers or "insiders," as well as individuals from outside the company. The chief officer, the person on whose desk the buck stops, is usually called the chief executive officer (CEO). Often, he or she is also the chairman of the board.

As corporate management has become more complex, it is common for the CEO to have a "right-hand person" who oversees the day-to-day operations of the company, allowing the CEO plenty of time to focus on strategy and long-term issues. This right-hand person is usually designated the chief operating officer (COO) and is often the president of the company. In other cases one person is both chairman and president.

A multitude of other titles exists, including chief financial officer (CFO), chief administrative officer, and vice chairman. We have always tried to include the CFO, the chief legal officer, and the chief human resources or personnel officer. Our best advice is that officers' pay levels are clear indicators of who the board of directors thinks are the most important members of the management team.

The people named in the Executives section are indexed at the back of the book.

The Executives section also includes the name of the company's auditing (accounting) firm, where available.

LOCATIONS

Here we include the company's full legal name and its headquarters, street address, telephone and fax numbers, and website, as available. The back of the book includes an index of companies by headquarters locations.

In some cases we have also included information on the geographic distribution of the company's business, including sales and profit data. Note that these profit numbers, like those in the Products/Operations section below, are usually operating or pretax profits rather than net profits. Operating profits are generally those before financing costs (interest income and payments) and before taxes, which are considered costs attributable to the whole company rather than to one division or part of the world. For this reason the net income figures (in the Historical Financials section) are usually much lower, since they are after interest and taxes. Pretax profits are after interest but before taxes.

PRODUCTS/OPERATIONS

This section lists as many of the company's products, services, brand names, divisions, subsidiaries, and joint ventures as we could fit. We have tried to include all its major lines and all familiar brand names. The nature of this section varies by company and the amount of information available. If the company publishes sales and profit information by type of business, we have included it.

COMPETITORS

In this section we have listed companies that compete with the profiled company. This feature is included as a quick way to locate similar companies and compare them. The universe of competitors includes all public companies and all private companies with sales in excess of $500 million. In a few instances we have identified smaller private companies as key competitors.

HISTORICAL FINANCIALS

Here we have tried to present as much data about each enterprise's financial performance as we could compile in the allocated space. Although the information varies somewhat from industry to industry, the following is generally present.

A five-year table, with relevant annualized compound growth rates, covers:

- Sales — fiscal year sales (year-end assets for most financial companies)
- Net income — fiscal year net income (before accounting changes)
- Net profit margin — fiscal year net income as a percent of sales (as a percent of assets for most financial firms)
- Employees — fiscal year-end or average number of employees
- Stock price — the fiscal year closing price
- P/E — high and low price/earnings ratio
- Earnings per share — fiscal year earnings per share (EPS)
- Dividends per share — fiscal year dividends per share
- Book value per share — fiscal year-end book value (common shareholders' equity per share)

The information on the number of employees is intended to aid the reader interested in knowing whether a company has a long-term trend of increasing or decreasing employment. As far as we know, we are the only company that publishes this information in print format.

The numbers on the left in each row of the Historical Financials section give the month and the year in which the company's fiscal year actually ends. Thus, a company with a September 30, 2020, year-end is shown as 9/18.

In addition, we have provided in graph form a stock price history for each company. The graphs, covering up to five years, show the range of trading between the high and the low price, as well as the closing price for each fiscal year. Key year-end statistics in this section generally show the financial strength of the enterprise, including:

- Debt ratio (long-term debt as a percent of shareholders' equity)
- Return on equity (net income divided by the average of beginning and ending common shareholders' equity)
- Cash and cash equivalents
- Current ratio (ratio of current assets to current liabilities)
- Total long-term debt (including capital lease obligations)
- Number of shares of common stock outstanding
- Dividend yield (fiscal year dividends per share divided by the fiscal year-end closing stock price)
- Dividend payout (fiscal year dividends divided by fiscal year EPS)
- Market value at fiscal year-end (fiscal year-end closing stock price multiplied by fiscal year-end number of shares outstanding)

Per-share data has been adjusted for stock splits. The data for public companies has been provided to us by Morningstar, Inc. Other public company information was compiled by Hoover's, which takes full responsibility for the content of this section.

Hoover's Handbook of

Emerging Companies

A List-Lover's Compendium

The 300 Largest Public Global Companies by Sales in Mergent's Database

Rank	Company	Sales ($ mil)	Rank	Company	Sales ($ mil)	Rank	Company	Sales $ mil
1	Walmart Inc	$559,151	61	Assicurazioni Generali S.p.A	$101,377	121	Disney (Walt) Co. (The)	$67,418
2	Amazon.com Inc	$469,822	62	United Parcel Service Inc	$97,287	122	Lockheed Martin Corp	$67,044
3	Apple Inc	$365,817	63	Nestle SA	$96,148	123	Xiamen C & D Inc	$66,198
4	China Petroleum & Chemical	$322,004	64	China Communications Constru	$95,958	124	Freddie Mac	$65,898
5	PetroChina Co Ltd	$295,682	65	Hyundai Motor Co., Ltd.	$95,557	125	Raytheon Technologies Corp	$64,388
6	CVS Health Corp	$292,111	66	Chevron Corporation	$94,692	126	China Vanke Co Ltd	$64,082
7	UnitedHealth Group Inc	$287,597	67	Dell Technologies Inc	$94,224	127	China Pacific Insurance (Gro	$64,059
8	Exxon Mobil Corp	$285,640	68	Bank of America Corp	$93,851	128	Aviva Plc (United Kingdom)	$63,553
9	Volkswagen AG	$273,543	69	Johnson & Johnson	$93,775	129	HP Inc	$63,487
10	Toyota Motor Corp	$272,933	70	ITOCHU Corp (Japan)	$93,589	130	Brookfield Asset Management Inc	$62,752
11	Alphabet Inc	$257,637	71	Target Corp	$93,561	131	AUDI AG	$62,516
12	Berkshire Hathaway Inc	$245,510	72	CITIC Ltd	$93,328	132	Boeing Co.	$62,286
13	McKesson Corp	$238,228	73	Koninklijke Ahold Delhaize N	$90,687	133	Unilever Plc (United Kingdom)	$62,253
14	Samsung Electronics Co Ltd	$217,588	74	BNP Paribas (France)	$89,709	134	Zhejiang Material Industrial	$61,766
15	AmerisourceBergen Corp.	$213,989	75	Lowe's Companies Inc	$89,597	135	Airbus SE	$61,256
16	Industrial and Commercial Ba	$201,209	76	Citigroup Inc	$88,839	136	Metallurgical Corp China Ltd	$61,177
17	Costco Wholesale Corp	$195,929	77	Archer Daniels Midland Co.	$85,249	137	BHP Group Ltd	$60,817
18	Hon Hai Precision Industry C	$190,662	78	PJSC Gazprom	$84,927	138	Lenovo Group Ltd	$60,742
19	Mercedes-Benz AG	$189,382	79	FedEx Corp	$83,959	139	Japan Post Insurance Co Ltd	$60,649
20	Shell plc	$183,195	80	Carrefour S.A.	$83,244	140	Panasonic Corp	$60,500
21	China Construction Bank Corp	$180,888	81	Humana, Inc.	$83,064	141	China Telecom Corp Ltd	$60,175
22	BP PLC	$180,626	82	Wells Fargo & Co (New)	$82,407	142	Fortum OYJ	$60,156
23	AT&T Inc	$168,864	83	HSBC Holdings Plc	$82,026	143	Zurich Insurance Group AG	$59,001
24	Microsoft Corporation	$168,088	84	Deutsche Post AG	$81,990	144	HCA Healthcare Inc	$58,752
25	Cardinal Health, Inc.	$162,467	85	Sony Group Corp	$81,277	145	International Business Mach.	$57,350
26	Cigna Corp (New)	$160,401	86	Aeon Co Ltd	$80,922	146	Marubeni Corp.	$57,191
27	China Railway Group Ltd	$149,039	87	Tesco PLC	$80,586	147	Toyota Tsusho Corp	$56,982
28	Exor NV	$146,684	88	T-Mobile US Inc	$80,118	148	AbbVie Inc	$56,197
29	Glencore PLC	$142,338	89	Electricite de France	$80,072	149	Societe Generale	$56,071
30	China Railway Construction	$139,188	90	Enel SpA	$79,755	150	ENI S.p.A.	$55,163
31	Anthem Inc	$138,639	91	PepsiCo Inc	$79,474	151	Xiamen Xiangyu Co Ltd	$55,077
32	Ford Motor Co. (DE)	$136,341	92	Intel Corp	$79,024	152	Dow Inc	$54,968
33	Verizon Communications Inc	$133,613	93	Hitachi, Ltd.	$78,837	153	AEGON NV	$54,877
34	Walgreens Boots Alliance Inc	$132,509	94	Munich Re Group	$78,413	154	LVMH Moet Hennessy Louis Vu	$54,748
35	Kroger Co (The)	$132,498	95	Prudential Plc	$77,092	155	Federal Reserve Bank Of New Y	$54,640
36	Home Depot Inc	$132,110	96	Rosneft Oil Co OJSC (Moscow)	$76,961	156	Seven & i Holdings Co. Ltd.	$54,237
37	Allianz SE	$129,097	97	Banco Santander SA	$76,318	157	PTT Public Co Ltd	$53,967
38	JPMorgan Chase & Co	$127,202	98	Procter & Gamble Co (The)	$76,118	158	Vinci SA	$53,966
39	General Motors Co	$127,004	99	E.ON SE	$75,682	159	LG Electronics Inc	$53,963
40	Centene Corp	$125,982	100	PJSC Lukoil	$75,389	160	Tesla Inc	$53,823
41	AXA SA	$125,786	101	Nippon Life Insurance Co.	$74,447	161	Petroleo Brasileiro SA	$53,683
42	Deutsche Telekom AG	$123,955	102	General Electric Co	$74,196	162	Xiamen International Trade Gr	$53,681
43	Bayerische Motoren Werke AG	$121,489	103	Tencent Holdings Ltd.	$73,707	163	Goldman Sachs Group Inc	$53,498
44	TotalEnergies SE	$119,704	104	BASF SE	$72,593	164	Renault S.A. (France)	$53,355
45	Honda Motor Co Ltd	$118,948	105	Mitsui & Co., Ltd.	$72,344	165	ArcelorMittal SA	$53,270
46	Meta Platforms Inc	$117,929	106	Siemens AG (Germany)	$72,072	166	Korea Electric Power Corp KEP	$53,225
47	China Mobile Limited	$117,437	107	MetLife Inc	$71,080	167	Tokyo Electric Power Company	$52,986
48	Comcast Corp	$116,385	108	Nissan Motor Co., Ltd.	$71,010	168	Novartis AG Basel	$52,877
49	Mitsubishi Corp	$116,366	109	Prudential Financial Inc	$70,934	169	Telefonica SA	$52,867
50	Phillips 66	$114,852	110	Country Garden Holdings Co L	$70,770	170	POSCO (South Korea)	$52,803
51	JD.com, Inc.	$114,033	111	Shanghai Jinfeng Investment C	$69,732	171	State Bank Of India	$52,612
52	Valero Energy Corp	$113,977	112	Albertsons Companies Inc	$69,690	172	American International Group Inc	$52,057
53	SAIC Motor Corp Ltd	$113,472	113	Eneos Holdings Inc	$69,163	173	Morgan Stanley	$52,047
54	Alibaba Group Holding Ltd	$109,499	114	Marathon Petroleum Corp.	$69,032	174	JBS S.A.	$52,027
55	Nippon Telegraph & Telephone	$107,871	115	Reliance Industries Ltd	$68,699	175	Orange	$51,875
56	Stellantis NV	$106,377	116	China Evergrande Group	$68,633	176	Charter Communications Inc	$51,682
57	Japan Post Holdings Co Ltd	$105,852	117	Legal & General Group PLC (U	$68,551	177	Tianjin Tianhai Investment C	$51,480
58	Credit Agricole SA	$105,648	118	Roche Holding AG	$68,514	178	Vodafone Group Plc	$51,391
59	Federal Reserve System	$104,976	119	Engie SA	$68,423	179	Sysco Corp	$51,298
60	Fannie Mae	$101,543	120	Dai-ichi Life Holdings Inc	$67,746	180	America Movil SAB de CV	$51,179

SOURCE: MERGENT INC., DATABASE, FEBRUARY 2022

The 300 Largest Public Global Companies by Sales in Mergent's Database (continued)

Rank	Company	Sales ($ mil.)
181	Caterpillar Inc.	$50,971
182	Power Corp. of Canada	$50,882
183	Bayer AG	$50,810
184	Allstate Corp	$50,588
185	Great-West Lifeco Inc	$50,577
186	Accenture plc	$50,533
187	Wilmar International Ltd	$50,527
188	AIA Group Ltd.	$50,342
189	Cisco Systems Inc	$49,818
190	Jiangxi Copper Co., Ltd.	$48,708
191	Manulife Financial Corp	$48,539
192	Tokio Marine Holdings Inc	$48,519
193	ConocoPhillips	$48,349
194	Mexican Petroleum	$47,997
195	Merck & Co Inc	$47,994
196	KDDI Corp	$47,980
197	Taiwan Semiconductor Manufac.	$47,656
198	Best Buy Inc	$47,262
199	Tyson Foods Inc	$47,049
200	SoftBank Corp (New)	$47,013
201	Anheuser Busch InBev SA/NV	$46,881
202	Royal Bank of Canada (Montreal,	$46,821
203	Compagnie de Saint-Gobain	$46,810
204	GlaxoSmithKline Plc	$46,535
205	China United Network Communi	$46,457
206	China Unicom (Hong Kong) Ltd	$46,457
207	Bristol Myers Squibb Co.	$46,385
208	Continental AG (Germany, Fed	$46,296
209	Lloyds Banking Group Plc	$46,225
210	Sanofi	$45,863
211	Equinor ASA	$45,818
212	Alimentation Couche-Tard Inc	$45,760
213	Hongkong And Shanghai Bankin	$45,692
214	Publix Super Markets, Inc.	$45,204
215	Rio Tinto Plc (United Kingdom)	$44,611
216	Denso Corp	$44,586
217	Intesa Sanpaolo S.P.A.	$44,543
218	NIKE Inc	$44,538
219	Fresenius SE & Co KGaA	$44,522
220	Deere & Co.	$44,024

Rank	Company	Sales ($ mil.)
221	Woolworths Group Ltd	$43,769
222	American Express Co.	$43,663
223	Nippon Steel Corp (New)	$43,615
224	MS&AD Insurance Group Holdin	$43,495
225	Baoshan Iron & Steel Co Ltd	$43,490
226	ACS Actividades de Construcc	$43,349
227	Swiss Re AG	$43,338
228	Abbott Laboratories	$43,075
229	George Weston Ltd	$42,965
230	Sberbank Russia	$42,911
231	Bouygues S.A.	$42,661
232	Progressive Corp. (OH)	$42,658
233	StoneX Group Inc	$42,443
234	Talanx AG	$42,033
235	Sumitomo Corp.	$41,951
236	Pfizer Inc	$41,908
237	Rio Tinto Ltd	$41,848
238	Imperial Brands PLC	$41,773
239	Volvo AB	$41,424
240	Bunge Ltd.	$41,404
241	Loblaw Companies Ltd	$41,379
242	Idemitsu Kosan Co Ltd	$41,153
243	Banco Bilbao Vizcaya Argentaria	$41,041
244	Iberdrola SA	$40,679
245	Oracle Corp	$40,479
246	J.Sainsbury PLC	$40,138
247	Repsol S.A.	$40,081
248	Vale SA	$40,018
249	Casino Guichard Perrachon S.	$39,899
250	A.P. Moller - Maersk A/S	$39,740
251	Mitsubishi UFJ Financial Gro	$39,638
252	Toronto Dominion Bank	$39,609
253	UBS Group AG	$39,106
254	Energy Transfer LP	$38,954
255	Coca-Cola Co (The)	$38,655
256	Suning.com Co Ltd	$38,576
257	Phoenix Group Holdings PLC	$38,513
258	General Dynamics Corp	$38,469
259	CHS Inc	$38,448
260	CK Hutchison Holdings Ltd	$38,401

Rank	Company	Sales ($ mil.)
261	Mitsubishi Electric Corp	$37,855
262	Barclays PLC	$37,706
263	innogy SE	$37,652
264	Brookfield Business Partners LP	$37,635
265	Deutsche Bank AG	$37,329
266	Compal Electronics Inc	$37,326
267	Daiwa House Industry Co Ltd	$37,271
268	Poly Developments and Holdings	$37,186
269	Enbridge Inc	$36,958
270	Cenovus Energy Inc	$36,397
271	Chubb Ltd	$35,994
272	Meiji Yasuda Life Insurance	$35,810
273	Northrop Grumman Corp	$35,667
274	China Shenhua Energy Co., Lt	$35,666
275	Shanghai Construction Group	$35,370
276	3M Co	$35,355
277	Wal-Mart de Mexico S.A.B. de	$35,318
278	British American Tobacco Plc	$35,177
279	Travelers Companies Inc (The)	$34,816
280	CRRC Corp Ltd	$34,808
281	Arrow Electronics, Inc.	$34,477
282	Honeywell International Inc	$34,392
283	L'Oreal S.A.	$34,354
284	Sumitomo Mitsui Financial Tokyo	$34,328
285	Sompo Holdings Inc	$34,248
286	Tata Motors Ltd	$33,917
287	ThyssenKrupp AG	$33,837
288	Dollar General Corp	$33,747
289	Qualcomm Inc	$33,566
290	SAP SE	$33,552
291	Mitsubishi Heavy Industries	$33,416
292	Exelon Corp	$33,039
293	Yankuang Energy Group Co Ltd	$32,872
294	Magna International Inc	$32,647
295	Jardine Matheson Holdings Ltd.	$32,647
296	Fujitsu Ltd	$32,420
297	Thermo Fisher Scientific Inc	$32,218
298	Siemens Energy AG	$32,148
299	TJX Companies, Inc.	$32,137
300	Haier Smart Home Co Ltd	$32,067

HOOVER'S HANDBOOK OF EMERGING COMPANIES 2022

The 300 Largest Public Global Companies by Employees in Mergent's Database

Rank	Company	Employees	Rank	Company	Employees	Rank	Company	Employees
1	Taiwan Semiconductor Manu	29,847,196	62	China Unicom (Hong Kong) Ltd	254,702	123	Darden Restaurants, Inc.	156,883
2	Walmart Inc	2,300,000	63	Alibaba Group Holding Ltd	251,462	124	Alphabet Inc	156,500
3	Amazon.com Inc	1,608,000	64	JBS S.A.	250,000	125	Aptiv PLC	155,000
4	Volkswagen AG	662,600	65	Aramark	248,300	126	Apple Inc	154,000
5	Accenture plc	624,000	66	Wells Fargo & Co (New)	247,848	127	Country Garden Services Holdin	153,585
6	Randstad NV	603,480	67	State Bank Of India	245,652	128	Schneider Electric SE	151,297
7	Deutsche Post AG	571,974	68	Panasonic Corp	243,540	129	LVMH Moet Hennessy Louis Vuin	150,479
8	Compass Group PLC (United Ki	548,143	69	Jardine Cycle & Carriage Ltd	240,000	130	Allianz SE	150,269
9	United Parcel Service Inc	534,000	70	Continental AG (Germany, Fed	236,386	131	Brookfield Asset Management Inc	150,000
10	Home Depot Inc	504,800	71	Reliance Industries Ltd	236,334	132	Unilever Plc (United Kingdom)	150,000
11	ISS	471,056	72	Wal-Mart de Mexico S.A.B. de	231,271	133	Grupo Bimbo SAB de CV (Mexic	148,746
12	PJSC Gazprom	467,000	73	Publix Super Markets, Inc.	227,000	134	Nissan Motor Co., Ltd.	148,559
13	Kroger Co (The)	465,000	74	Deutsche Telekom AG	226,291	135	Prosegur Compania De Segurid	147,231
14	China Mobile Limited	454,332	75	P.T. Astra International TBK	226,105	136	Mitsubishi Electric Corp	145,653
15	Industrial and Commercial Ba	439,787	76	HSBC Holdings Plc	226,059	137	Glencore PLC	145,000
16	Sodexo	422,712	77	Yamato Holdings Co., Ltd.	223,191	138	Johnson & Johnson	144,300
17	Koninklijke Ahold Delhaize N	414,000	78	Loblaw Companies Ltd	220,000	139	Industria De Diseno Textil I	144,116
18	Target Corp	409,000	79	Dairy Farm International Hol	220,000	140	NTT Data Corp	143,081
19	Aeon Co Ltd	408,567	80	Capgemini SE	219,314	141	Shoprite Holdings, Ltd.	142,602
20	Jardine Matheson Holdings Ltd.	403,000	81	Vinci SA	217,731	142	Credit Agricole SA	142,159
21	Japan Post Holdings Co Ltd	390,775	82	Woolworths Group Ltd	215,000	143	Orange	142,150
22	Teleperformance SA	383,233	83	Honda Motor Co Ltd	211,374	144	Boeing Co.	142,000
23	Starbucks Corp.	383,000	84	Citigroup Inc	210,153	145	Hilton Worldwide Holdings Inc	142,000
24	Nippon Telegraph & Telephone	371,816	85	Bank of America Corp	208,000	146	Aisin Corporation	139,832
25	Toyota Motor Corp	370,870	86	AT&T Inc	203,000	147	Atento SA	139,805
26	Securitas AB	370,000	87	Casino Guichard Perrachon S.	202,955	148	Fujitsu Ltd	138,698
27	Tesco PLC	367,321	88	Fareast Islami Life Insuranc	200,288	149	Bridgestone Corp. (Japan)	138,036
28	Berkshire Hathaway Inc	360,000	89	McDonald's Corp	200,000	150	Tyson Foods Inc	137,000
29	Rosneft Oil Co OJSC (Moscow)	355,900	90	Wipro Ltd	200,000	151	Nidec Corp	136,186
30	Kelly Services, Inc.	354,500	91	Dollar Tree Inc	199,327	152	Seven & i Holdings Co. Ltd.	135,332
31	Hitachi, Ltd.	350,864	92	Denso Corp	196,126	153	CITIC Ltd	135,304
32	UnitedHealth Group Inc	350,000	93	BNP Paribas (France)	193,319	154	Empire Co Ltd	134,000
33	China Construction Bank Corp	349,671	94	Half Robert International Inc.	191,600	155	DXC Technology Co	134,000
34	Lowe's Companies Inc	340,000	95	Banco Santander SA	191,189	156	Societe Generale	133,251
35	X5 Retail Group NV	339,716	96	Disney (Walt) Co. (The)	190,000	157	China Evergrande Group	133,123
36	Cognizant Technology Solutions	330,600	97	Stellantis NV	189,512	158	Oracle Corp	132,000
37	Sumitomo Electric Industries	325,011	98	Comcast Corp	189,000	159	Airbus SE	131,349
38	Carrefour S.A.	321,383	99	America Movil SAB de CV	186,851	160	Wendel	130,621
39	Fomento Economico Mexicano,	320,618	100	Ford Motor Co. (DE)	183,000	161	ICICI Bank Ltd (India)	130,170
40	TJX Companies, Inc.	320,000	101	Canon Inc	181,897	162	TDK Corp	129,284
41	Magnit PJSC	316,001	102	ACS Actividades de Construcc	181,699	163	Bouygues S.A.	129,018
42	Walgreens Boots Alliance Inc	315,000	103	Microsoft Corporation	181,000	164	Fast Retailing Co., Ltd.	128,492
43	JD.com, Inc.	314,906	104	J.Sainsbury PLC	180,000	165	Zug Estates Holding AG	128,100
44	Fresenius SE & Co KGaA	311,269	105	Veolia Environnement SA	178,021	166	Associated British Foods Plc	127,912
45	PepsiCo Inc	309,000	106	Raytheon Technologies Corp	174,000	167	Fresenius Medical Care AG & A	125,364
46	International Business Machines.	307,600	107	Engie SA	172,703	168	Nippon Steel Corp (New)	125,038
47	Siemens AG (Germany)	303,000	108	ITOCHU Corp (Japan)	171,829	169	Alimentation Couche-Tard Inc	124,000
48	CVS Health Corp	300,000	109	Renault S.A. (France)	170,158	170	ABM Industries, Inc.	124,000
49	Albertsons Companies Inc	300,000	110	General Electric Co	168,000	171	Cie Generale des Etablisseme	123,642
50	CK Hutchison Holdings Ltd	300,000	111	ArcelorMittal SA	167,743	172	American Airlines Group Inc	123,400
51	Concentrix Corp	290,000	112	Compagnie de Saint-Gobain	167,552	173	Banco Bilbao Vizcaya Argentaria	123,174
52	FedEx Corp	289,000	113	Flex Ltd	167,201	174	Bidvest Group Ltd	121,344
53	Mercedes-Benz AG	288,481	114	Anheuser Busch InBev SA/NV	163,695	175	Intel Corp	121,100
54	Costco Wholesale Corp	288,000	115	Mitsubishi UFJ Financial Gro	163,500	176	Mexican Petroleum	120,936
55	Sberbank Russia	285,600	116	Electricite de France	161,552	177	Bayerische Motoren Werke AG	120,726
56	HCA Healthcare Inc	284,000	117	Lear Corp.	160,100	178	HDFC Bank Ltd	120,093
57	China Telecom Corp Ltd	281,192	118	Royal Mail Plc	158,592	179	Marriott International, Inc.	120,000
58	Jabil Inc	280,000	119	Dell Technologies Inc	158,000	180	GXO Logistics Inc	120,000
59	Nestle SA	273,000	120	Dollar General Corp	158,000	181	KE Holdings Inc	119,658
60	JPMorgan Chase & Co	271,025	121	Magna International Inc	158,000	182	Poste Italiane SpA	118,523
61	Infosys Ltd.	259,619	122	General Motors Co	157,000	183	Verizon Communications Inc	118,400

SOURCE: HOOVER'S, INC., DATABASE, JANUARY 2022

4a

HOOVER'S HANDBOOK OF EMERGING COMPANIES 2022

The 300 Largest Public Global Companies by Employees in Mergent's Database (continued)

Rank	Company	Employees	Rank	Company	Employees	Rank	Company	Employees
184	Cencosud SA	117,638	223	Danone	101,911	262	Outsourcing Inc, Shizuoka	93,028
185	Toshiba Corp	117,300	224	First Pacific Co. Ltd.	101,836	263	Bath & Body Works Inc	92,300
186	Gap Inc	117,000	225	Roche Holding AG	101,465	264	Nokia Corp	92,039
187	Barrett Business Services, Inc.	115,075	226	Bayer AG	101,459	265	Schlumberger Ltd	92,000
188	NEC Corp	114,714	227	Tenet Healthcare Corp.	101,100	266	SGS SA	91,698
189	AXA SA	114,625	228	Leoni AG	101,007	267	Swire (John) & Sons Ltd. (Unit	91,022
190	Lockheed Martin Corp	114,000	229	BRF S.A.	101,002	268	Unicredit SpA	90,836
191	Faurecia SE (France)	113,931	230	Procter & Gamble Co (The)	101,000	269	Jones Lang LaSalle Inc	90,800
192	Abbott Laboratories	113,000	231	Johnson Controls International	101,000	270	AUDI AG	90,640
193	Surgutneftegas PJSC	113,000	232	Ericsson	100,824	271	Mitsubishi Heavy Industries	90,322
194	Telefonica SA	112,797	233	PJSC Lukoil	100,800	272	Medtronic PLC	90,000
195	China Pacific Insurance (Gro	110,940	234	CBRE Group Inc	100,000	273	Kyndryl Holdings Inc	90,000
196	BASF SE	110,302	235	Wilmar International Ltd	100,000	274	Metro Inc	90,000
197	Valeo SE	110,300	236	AutoZone, Inc.	100,000	275	Amphenol Corp.	90,000
198	Lufthansa AG (Germany,	110,065	237	WPP Plc (New)	99,830	276	Pick 'n Pay Stores Ltd.	90,000
199	Kohl's Corp.	110,000	238	BT Group Plc	99,700	277	BAE Systems Plc	89,600
200	Sony Group Corp	109,700	239	Sanofi	99,412	278	Banco Bradesco SA	89,575
201	Steinhoff International Hold	108,361	240	Tesla Inc	99,290	279	Bank Nova Scotia Halifax	89,488
202	Caterpillar Inc.	107,700	241	Honeywell International Inc	99,000	280	Toronto Dominion Bank	89,464
203	WH Group Ltd	107,000	242	Byd Electronic International	99,000	281	British American Tobacco Plc	89,182
204	Wesfarmers Ltd.	107,000	243	Anthem Inc	98,200	282	Shenzhou International Group	89,100
205	Mitsubishi Corp	106,902	244	East Japan Railway Co.	98,158	283	En+ Group Plc	89,075
206	Intesa Sanpaolo S.P.A.	105,615	245	Sumitomo Mitsui Financial Group	98,100	284	FirstGroup Plc	89,053
207	ABB Ltd	105,600	246	SG Holdings Co Ltd	97,774	285	TE Connectivity Ltd	89,000
208	TotalEnergies SE	105,476	247	Chipotle Mexican Grill Inc	97,660	286	Universal Health Services, Inc.	89,000
209	New Oriental Education & Tech	105,212	248	Metro AG (New)	97,639	287	Grupo Elektra S.A. de C.V.	88,883
210	Grupo Aval Acciones Y Valores	104,862	249	Humana, Inc.	96,900	288	Indofood Sukses Makmur TBK	88,704
211	Elior SCA	104,566	250	Vodafone Group Plc	96,506	289	Northrop Grumman Corp	88,000
212	Atos Origin	104,430	251	Genpact Ltd	96,500	290	Lufax Holding Ltd	87,240
213	Novartis AG Basel	104,323	252	Organizacion Soriana, S.A.B.	96,355	291	Nippon Express Holdings Inc	87,041
214	Suzuki Motor Corp.	103,891	253	Volvo AB	96,194	292	Swire Pacific Ltd. (Hong Kon	86,768
215	ThyssenKrupp AG	103,598	254	Falabella SA	96,111	293	Emerson Electric Co.	86,700
216	Sumitomo Corp.	103,443	255	3M Co	95,000	294	Shell plc	86,000
217	Minebea Mitsumi Inc	103,213	256	GlaxoSmithKline Plc	94,066	295	Eaton Corp plc	86,000
218	General Dynamics Corp	103,100	257	Sime Darby Plantation Bhd	94,000	296	Tencent Holdings Ltd.	85,858
219	Haidilao International Holdi	102,793	258	Country Garden Holdings Co L	93,899	297	FIH Mobile Ltd	85,729
220	SAP SE	102,430	259	Charter Communications Inc (New)	93,700	298	L'Oreal S.A.	85,392
221	Best Buy Inc	102,000	260	Ross Stores Inc	93,700	299	Royal Bank of Canada (Montreal,	85,301
222	ASE Technology Holding Co Ltd	101,981	261	Daikin Industries Ltd	93,102	300	Royal Caribbean Group	85,000

The 300 Largest Public Global Companies by Net Income in Mergent's Database

Rank	Company	Net Income ($ mil.)
1	Apple Inc	$94,680
2	Alphabet Inc	$76,033
3	Microsoft Corporation	$61,271
4	JPMorgan Chase & Co	$48,334
5	Industrial and Commercial Ba	$48,302
6	Berkshire Hathaway Inc	$42,521
7	China Construction Bank Corp	$40,583
8	Meta Platforms Inc	$39,370
9	Amazon.com Inc	$33,364
10	Bank of America Corp	$31,978
11	Tencent Holdings Ltd.	$24,441
12	Novartis AG Basel	$24,021
13	Samsung Electronics Co Ltd	$23,973
14	Exxon Mobil Corp	$23,040
15	Alibaba Group Holding Ltd	$22,987
16	Fannie Mae	$22,176
17	Verizon Communications Inc	$22,065
18	Ping An Insurance (Group) Co	$21,880
19	Wells Fargo & Co (New)	$21,548
20	Johnson & Johnson	$20,878
21	AT&T Inc	$20,081
22	Intel Corp	$19,868
23	Taiwan Semiconductor Manufact	$18,429
24	Ford Motor Co. (DE)	$17,937
25	UnitedHealth Group Inc	$17,285
26	Toyota Motor Corp	$17,002
27	China Mobile Limited	$16,489
28	Roche Holding AG	$16,231
29	Sanofi	$15,113
30	Procter & Gamble Co (The)	$14,306
31	Comcast Corp	$14,159
32	Nestle SA	$13,888
33	Oracle Corp	$13,746
34	Walmart Inc	$13,510
35	Hongkong And Shanghai Bankin	$13,382
36	Royal Bank of Canada (Montreal,	$12,983
37	United Parcel Service Inc	$12,890
38	Home Depot Inc	$12,866
39	Visa Inc	$12,311
40	Freddie Mac	$12,109
41	Bank of Japan	$11,933
42	AbbVie Inc	$11,542
43	Toronto Dominion Bank	$11,373
44	BHP Group Ltd	$11,304
45	ThyssenKrupp AG	$11,223
46	Citigroup Inc	$11,047
47	Morgan Stanley	$10,996
48	Cisco Systems Inc	$10,591
49	Sony Group Corp	$10,583
50	Volkswagen AG	$10,228
51	Sberbank Russia	$10,175
52	Mitsubishi UFJ Financial Gro	$10,091
53	General Motors Co	$10,019
54	Surgutneftegas PJSC	$9,931
55	Coca-Cola Co (The)	$9,771
56	Rio Tinto Ltd	$9,769
57	Pfizer Inc	$9,616
58	RWE AG	$9,541
59	Goldman Sachs Group Inc	$9,459
60	American International Group Inc	$9,388

Rank	Company	Net Income ($ mil.)
61	Philip Morris International Inc	$9,109
62	Qualcomm Inc	$9,043
63	Telecom Italia SpA	$8,866
64	British American Tobacco Plc (UK	$8,734
65	Mastercard Inc	$8,687
66	BNP Paribas (France)	$8,673
67	Tesco PLC	$8,552
68	Cigna Corp (New)	$8,458
69	Allianz SE	$8,354
70	Nippon Telegraph & Telephone	$8,274
71	ConocoPhillips	$8,079
72	Regeneron Pharmaceuticals, Inc.	$8,075
73	American Express Co.	$8,060
74	U.S. Bancorp (DE)	$7,963
75	CVS Health Corp	$7,910
76	GlaxoSmithKline Plc	$7,846
77	Texas Instruments, Inc.	$7,769
78	Prudential Financial Inc	$7,724
79	China Life Insurance Co Ltd	$7,686
80	Commonwealth Bank of Australia	$7,642
81	PepsiCo Inc	$7,618
82	Bank Nova Scotia Halifax	$7,602
83	JD.com, Inc.	$7,554
84	PNC Financial Services Group	$7,517
85	Prosus N V	$7,449
86	CITIC Ltd	$7,304
87	Novo-Nordisk AS	$7,268
88	Kweichow Moutai Co., Ltd.	$7,140
89	Siemens AG (Germany)	$7,131
90	Abbott Laboratories	$7,071
91	Merck & Co Inc	$7,067
92	Northrop Grumman Corp	$7,005
93	Bristol Myers Squibb Co.	$6,994
94	HCA Healthcare Inc	$6,956
95	Unilever Plc (United Kingdom)	$6,850
96	Broadcom Inc (DE)	$6,736
97	Reliance Industries Ltd	$6,715
98	ASML Holding NV	$6,659
99	Mercantil Servicios Financie	$6,658
100	UBS Group AG	$6,557
101	MetLife Inc	$6,554
102	Union Pacific Corp	$6,523
103	HP Inc	$6,503
104	Caterpillar Inc.	$6,489
105	DuPont de Nemours Inc	$6,467
106	Investor AB	$6,461
107	Truist Financial Corp	$6,440
108	Danaher Corp	$6,433
109	Thermo Fisher Scientific Inc	$6,375
110	China Vanke Co Ltd	$6,348
111	Lockheed Martin Corp	$6,315
112	SAP SE	$6,314
113	Dow Inc	$6,311
114	Gilead Sciences Inc	$6,225
115	Sumitomo Mitsui Financial Group	$6,209
116	Anthem Inc	$6,104
117	Bank of Montreal (Quebec)	$6,080
118	China Shenhua Energy Co., Lt	$5,989
119	China Overseas Land & Invest	$5,981
120	Deere & Co.	$5,963

Rank	Company	Sales ($ mil.)
121	Honda Motor Co Ltd	$5,937
122	3M Co	$5,921
123	Orange	$5,918
124	Accenture plc	$5,907
125	Amgen Inc	$5,893
126	Applied Materials, Inc.	$5,888
127	KDDI Corp	$5,884
128	Micron Technology Inc.	$5,861
129	Lowe's Companies Inc	$5,835
130	Electricite de France	$5,788
131	AIA Group Ltd.	$5,779
132	LVMH Moet Hennessy Louis Vuitt	$5,771
133	Credit Agricole SA	$5,755
134	International Business Machines	$5,743
135	NIKE Inc	$5,727
136	Progressive Corp. (OH)	$5,705
137	eBay Inc.	$5,667
138	Eli Lilly & Co	$5,582
139	Manulife Financial Corp	$5,578
140	Honeywell International Inc	$5,542
141	Tesla Inc	$5,519
142	Anhui Conch Cement Co Ltd	$5,371
143	Country Garden Holdings Co L	$5,355
144	Naspers Ltd	$5,304
145	FedEx Corp	$5,231
146	Canadian Imperial Bank Of Comm	$5,205
147	ABB Ltd	$5,146
148	HSBC Holdings Plc	$5,139
149	Netflix Inc	$5,116
150	CK Hutchison Holdings Ltd	$5,115
151	Deutsche Telekom AG	$5,103
152	Bombardier Inc.	$5,041
153	China Petroleum & Chemical Corp	$5,034
154	Costco Wholesale Corp	$5,007
155	BlackRock Inc	$4,932
156	Vale SA	$4,881
157	Enbridge Inc	$4,859
158	Adobe Inc	$4,822
159	Fortescue Metals Group Ltd	$4,735
160	McDonald's Corp	$4,731
161	Charter Communications Inc (New)	$4,654
162	Bayerische Motoren Werke AG	$4,633
163	National Australia Bank Ltd	$4,579
164	China Resources Land Ltd	$4,558
165	Paramount Global	$4,543
166	Hitachi, Ltd.	$4,530
167	Ford Motor Credit Company LLC	$4,521
168	Altria Group Inc	$4,467
169	HDFC Bank Ltd	$4,455
170	Mercedes-Benz AG	$4,451
171	SoftBank Corp (New)	$4,437
172	Iberdrola SA	$4,432
173	Lennar Corp	$4,430
174	Poly Developments and Holdings	$4,426
175	NatWest Group PLC	$4,379
176	L'Oreal S.A.	$4,373
177	Target Corp	$4,368
178	Nintendo Co., Ltd.	$4,338
179	NVIDIA Corp	$4,332
180	AFLAC Inc.	$4,325

SOURCE: MERGENT INC., FEBRUARY 2022

The 300 Largest Public Global Companies by Net Income in Mergent's Database (continued)

Rank	Company	Net Income ($ mil.)	Rank	Company	Net Income ($ mil.)	Rank	Company	Sales ($ mil.)
181	AUDI AG	$4,323	221	Medtronic PLC	$3,606	261	Prologis LP	$3,022
182	Freeport-McMoRan Inc	$4,306	222	NextEra Energy Inc	$3,573	262	Japan Tobacco Inc.	$3,010
183	Mondelez International Inc	$4,300	223	DBS Group Holdings Ltd.	$3,572	263	Norfolk Southern Corp	$3,005
184	Bio-Rad Laboratories Inc	$4,246	224	Chubb Ltd	$3,533	264	L'Air Liquide S.A.	$2,989
185	Synchrony Financial	$4,221	225	Sun Hung Kai Properties Ltd	$3,436	265	Cleveland-Cliffs Inc (New)	$2,988
186	Starbucks Corp.	$4,199	226	Baidu Inc	$3,436	266	Carlyle Group Inc (The)	$2,975
187	DR Horton Inc	$4,176	227	Hewlett Packard Enterprise Co	$3,427	267	West Fraser Timber Co Ltd	$2,947
188	United States Steel Corp.	$4,174	228	China Railway Construction Corp	$3,424	268	Cooper Companies, Inc.	$2,945
189	PayPal Holdings Inc	$4,169	229	Boc Hong Kong Holdings Ltd	$3,416	269	Prologis Inc	$2,940
190	Salesforce.Com Inc	$4,072	230	First Abu Dhabi Bank PJSC	$3,409	270	Humana, Inc.	$2,933
191	Intercontinental Exchange Inc	$4,058	231	Takeda Pharmaceutical Co Ltd	$3,396	271	Shopify Inc	$2,915
192	loanDepot Inc	$4,026	232	Gree Electric Appliances Inc	$3,391	272	PetroChina Co Ltd	$2,905
193	Intesa Sanpaolo S.P.A.	$4,022	233	MMC Norilsk Nickel PJSC	$3,385	273	Scout24 SE	$2,905
194	China Yangtze Power Co Ltd	$4,021	234	Charles Schwab Corp	$3,299	274	Prudential Plc	$2,890
195	Publix Super Markets, Inc.	$3,972	235	Qatar National Bank	$3,297	275	Transneft	$2,882
196	Vonovia SE	$3,962	236	Impala Platinum Holdings Ltd	$3,290	276	TPG Partners LLC	$2,878
197	Sempra	$3,933	237	Dai-ichi Life Holdings Inc	$3,285	277	Lauder (Estee) Cos., Inc. (The)	$2,870
198	Westpac Banking Corp	$3,927	238	General Dynamics Corp	$3,257	278	A.P. Moller - Maersk A/S	$2,850
199	Lam Research Corp	$3,908	239	Barclays PLC	$3,252	279	Saudi Telecom Co	$2,844
200	AXA SA	$3,883	240	Dell Technologies Inc	$3,250	280	Newmont Corp	$2,829
201	Raytheon Technologies Corp	$3,864	241	Porsche Automobil Holding SE	$3,219	281	Al Rajhi Banking and Investm	$2,825
202	China Railway Group Ltd	$3,851	242	Enel SpA	$3,203	282	Devon Energy Corp.	$2,813
203	Canadian National Railway Co	$3,841	243	AstraZeneca Plc	$3,196	283	ING Groep NV	$2,761
204	Zurich Insurance Group AG	$3,834	244	China Telecom Corp Ltd	$3,188	284	Nordea Bank ABp	$2,747
205	Aviva Plc (United Kingdom)	$3,818	245	KB Financial Group, Inc.	$3,175	285	Capital One Financial Corp	$2,714
206	CNOOC Ltd	$3,816	246	Sun Life Financial Inc	$3,168	286	Oversea-Chinese Banking Corp	$2,713
207	CSX Corp	$3,781	247	Advanced Micro Devices Inc	$3,162	287	Schneider Electric SE	$2,709
208	Japan Post Holdings Co Ltd	$3,777	248	Marsh & McLennan Companies .	$3,143	288	Archer Daniels Midland Co.	$2,709
209	Enterprise Products Partners L.P.	$3,776	249	Shinhan Financial Group Co. Ltd.	$3,137	289	Alimentation Couche-Tard Inc	$2,706
210	National Westminster Bank Plc	$3,764	250	SSE PLC	$3,134	290	Neles OYJ	$2,698
211	China Pacific Insurance (Gro	$3,759	251	SAIC Motor Corp Ltd	$3,124	291	Illinois Tool Works, Inc.	$2,694
212	CK Asset Holdings Ltd	$3,741	252	State Bank Of India	$3,062	292	State Street Corp.	$2,693
213	Sunac China Holdings Ltd	$3,741	253	Wuliangye Yibin Co Ltd	$3,051	293	Macquarie Infrastructure Holdi	$2,684
214	Diageo Plc	$3,688	254	Banco Bradesco SA	$3,049	294	Dollar General Corp	$2,655
215	Travelers Companies Inc (The)	$3,662	255	Tyson Foods Inc	$3,047	295	Cathay Financial Holding Co	$2,654
216	Deutsche Post AG	$3,656	256	National Commercial Bank	$3,040	296	Shin-Etsu Chemical Co., Ltd.	$2,653
217	Itau Unibanco Holding S.A.	$3,638	257	Credit Suisse Group AG	$3,030	297	Florida Power & Light Co.	$2,650
218	ITOCHU Corp (Japan)	$3,626	258	Mitsui & Co., Ltd.	$3,030	298	Kering SA	$2,639
219	Hon Hai Precision Industry C	$3,622	259	T-Mobile US Inc	$3,024	299	Longfor Group Holdings Ltd	$2,635
220	Bank of New York Mellon Corp	$3,617	260	S&P Global Inc	$3,024	300	KeyCorp	$2,625

HOOVER'S HANDBOOK OF EMERGING COMPANIES 2022

This Page left intentionally blank

Hoover's Handbook of

Emerging Companies

2022

1-800 Flowers.com, Inc.

1-800-FLOWERS.COM sells fresh-cut flowers floral arrangements and plants through its toll-free number and websites; it also markets gifts via catalogs TV and radio ads and online affiliates. Through subsidiaries the company offers gourmet foods (Harry & David) popcorn (The Popcorn Factory) baked goods (Cheryl's) fruit arrangements (FruitBouquets.com) and a host of other products. Its BloomNet service provides products and services to florists. 1-800-FLOWERS operates primarily in the US. Founder and chairman James McCann launched the company in 1976. In 2020 the company has completed its acquisition of PersonalizationMall.com.

Operations

1-800-FLOWERS operates through three segments: Gourmet Foods & Gift Baskets Consumer Floral and BloomNet.

Gourmet Foods & Gift Baskets generates just about 55% its revenue from premium food items and gift boxes and containers. Businesses in this segment include Simply Chocolates (artisan chocolates and confections) and Harry & David (fruit baskets gourmet food gifts); other brands include Wolferman's Cushman's and MooseMunch.

The company's traditional cut flowers and plants business — offered through its namesake business as well as Flowerama Goodsey and others — accounts for about 40% of revenue. The segment also includes edible fruit arrangements from Fruit Bouquets.

Services for florists (clearinghouse marketing communications) account for over 5%% of revenue and are provided through 1-800-FLOWERS' BloomNet business.

Geographic Reach

1-800-FLOWERS operates almost completely in the US. Headquartered in New York it operates its customer service centers in Ohio and Oregon. The company has more than two dozen principal properties in Florida Illinois Nevada New York Ohio Oregon and Tennessee.

Sales and Marketing

1-800-FLOWERS aims to reach customers through online and offline media direct marketing public relations and strategic online and digital relationship. Advertising expense was $171.4 million $147.8 million and $138.2 million for the years ended 2020 2019 and 2018 respectively. E-commerce represents about 80% of total revenue.

Financial Performance

Despite a slight fall in revenue in 2018 the company performance was generally on an upward swing in the last five years.

In fiscal 2020 the company reported revenue of $1.5 billion up 19% from the prior year. The increase reflected strong execution of the company's strategy to engage with its customers and build deeper relationships and thereby drive sustainable long-term growth.

Net income rose 70% in 2020 to $59 million as a result of an increase in revenue.

Cash at the end of fiscal 2020 was $240.5 million an increase of $67.6 million from the prior year. Cash from operations contributed $139.4 million to the coffers while investing and financing activities used $56.4 million and $15.5 million respectively. Main cash uses for the year were for capital expenditures acquisitions and repayment of borrowings.

Strategy

The recent acquisition of PersonalizationMall has added an extensive selection of personalized products to its offerings. This extended line of gift offerings helps its customers with all of their celebratory occasions and will enable the company to increase the number of purchases and the average order value by existing customers who have come to trust the 1-800-FLOWERS.COM brand as well as continue to attract new customers. The company's consolidated customer database and multi-brand website are designed to expose all of its brands to its customers further enhancing the company's position as a leading one-stop destination for all of its customers' gifting and celebratory needs.

As part of the company's continuing effort to serve the thoughtful gifting needs of its customers and leverage its business platform the company continues to execute its vision to build a "Celebratory Ecosystem" including a collection of premium gifting brands and an increasing suite of products and services designed to help its customers deliver smiles to the important people in their lives. The platform that the company has built allows it to expand rapidly into new product categories using a "marketplace" concept providing its customers with a wider selection of solutions to help them express connect and celebrate for all occasions and recipients ? including themselves. The company intends to accomplish this through organic development and where appropriate through acquisition of the complementary businesses.

Mergers and Acquisitions

In mid-2020 1-800-FLOWERS.COM Inc. announced that it has completed its acquisition of PersonalizationMall.com (headquartered in Illinois) a leading ecommerce provider of personalized products that offers thousands of products available with a broad range of innovative personalization options. It cost $245.0 million. The acquisition will increase the company's annual revenue run rate to more than $1.6 billion. It also enhances 1-800-FLOWERS.COM's ability to help its customers engage and stay connected with the important people in their lives

In mid-2019 1-800-FLOWERS.COM Inc. announced that it has completed its purchase of the Shari's Berries brand. The acquisition follows the company's winning bid at the auction held on July 31 2019 for certain assets of FTD's gourmet food business including the Shari's Berries brand which were previously operated by Provide Commerce LLC a division of FTD. The company acquired the Shari's Berries brand and the assets through one of its wholly owned subsidiaries.

Company Background

Social worker Jim McCann bought a New York City florist shop in 1976 to supplement his income from St. John's Home for Boys. By 1986 he had expanded his Flora Plenty chain to 14 shops in the New York metropolitan area and made the floral business his full-time job.

The next year McCann paid $9 million for 1-800-FLOWERS a young struggling Dallas-based floral-delivery company that had been founded by John Davis and Jim Poage. McCann's shops had worked with 1-800-FLOWERS but he had to sell most of his Flora Plenty stores to keep the telemarketing business from wilting altogether. By 1990 however business was blossoming and 1-800-FLOWERS was profitable.

It went public in 1999.

HISTORY

Social worker Jim McCann bought a New York City florist shop in 1976 to supplement his income from St. John's Home for Boys. By 1986 he had expanded his Flora Plenty chain to 14 shops in the New York metropolitan area and made the floral business his full-time job.

The next year McCann paid $9 million for 1-800-FLOWERS a young struggling Dallas-based floral-delivery company that had been founded by John Davis and Jim Poage. McCann's shops had worked with 1-800-FLOWERS but he had to sell most of his Flora Plenty stores to keep the telemarketing business from wilting altogether. By 1990 however business was blossoming and 1-800-FLOWERS was profitable.

In 1992 the company began selling flowers online through Compuserve. 1-800-FLOWERS launched its own website three years later and teamed with online providers such as America Online (now Time Warner Inc.) and Microsoft Network.

1-800-FLOWERS added home and garden merchandise to its offerings — and picked up catalog expertise — when it bought an 80% stake in Plow & Hearth in 1998 (it acquired the remainder in 1999). In May 1999 the company received more than $100 million from Benchmark Capital Japanese technology firm SOFTBANK and luxury goods kingpin LVMH. 1-800-FLOWERS then added ".COM" to its name and went public in August 1999.

In late 1999 the company bought online gourmet foods retailer GreatFood.com for $18.5 million. It added jewelry to its offerings by teaming up with retailer Finlay Enterprises in 2000. It also launched its Spanish language Web site — 1-800-LASFLORES.COM. New additions in 2001 included a partnership with Touchpoint allowing customers to create personalized cards and photos and the addition of children's gifts dolls crafts and other toys and games with the acquisition of The Children's Group.

1-800-FLOWERS.COM continued its acquisitive ways in 2002 by acquiring The Popcorn Factory (direct marketing of premium popcorn chocolates and other food gift products packaged in decorative tins and baskets). That year the firm agreed to cross-promote its goods with American Greetings; under the agreement 1-800-FLOWERS.COM became the exclusive provider of flowers on several American Greetings Web sites. And in 2004 it got into the wine distribution business with its purchase of The Winetasting Network which is now a subsidiary.

In March 2005 the company acquired cookie-and-baked-gifts-maker Cheryl & Co. for an undisclosed price. The company moved its corporate headquarters to Carle Place New York the next year. In mid-2006 the Internet flower company acquired candy maker Fannie May Confections Brands for $85 million.

1-800-FLOWERS.COM bought gourmet gift basket maker DesignPac Gifts in May 2008 for about $36 million. It also purchased Napco Marketing which wholesales and markets products for the floral industry for $9 million.

In March 2009 the company acquired certain assets of online wine seller Geerlings & Wade Inc.

HOOVER'S HANDBOOK OF EMERGING COMPANIES 2022

for about $2 million to complement its Winetasting Network business. It also launched 1-800-BASKETS.com that year.

To focus on its core floral and food units 1-800-FLOWERS.COM sold its home d©cor and children's gift brands to PH International a Virginia-based home d©cor distributor in January 2010. The deal which was worth $17 million included the brands of HearthSong Magic Cabin Plow & Hearth Problem Solvers and Wind & Weather.

EXECUTIVES

Independent Director, Katherine Oliver
Senior Vice President, General Counsel, Corporate Secretary, Michael Manley, $412,404 total compensation
Independent Director, Adam Hanft
President - Bloomnet, Dinesh Popat
Independent Director, Dina Colombo
Independent Director, Stephanie Hofmann
Independent Director, James Cannavino
Group President - Gourmet Foods And Gift Baskets, Steven Lightman, $497,404 total compensation
Executive Chairman Of The Board, Founder, James Mccann, $975,000 total compensation
President, Chief Executive Officer, Director, Christopher McCann, $775,000 total compensation
Chief Financial Officer, Senior Vice President, Treasurer, William Shea, $550,000 total compensation
Group President - Consumer Floral And Gifts, Thomas Hartnett, $497,404 total compensation
Independent Director, Larry Zarin
Independent Director, Geralyn Breig
Senior Vice President, Chief Information Officer, Arnie Leap
Independent Director, Celia Brown
Auditors: BDO USA, LLP

LOCATIONS

HQ: 1-800 Flowers.com, Inc.
Two Jericho Plaza, Suite 200, Jericho, NY 11753
Phone: 516 237-6000
Web: www.1800flowers.com

PRODUCTS/OPERATIONS

2018 Sales

	$ mil.	% of total
1-800-Flowers.com consumer floral	457.0	40
Gourmet food & gift baskets	606.0	52
BloomNet Wire Service	90.0	8
Corporate	1.0	-
Adjustments	(2)	-
Total	**1,152.0**	**100**

2018 Sales

	$ mil.	% of total
E-commerce	922.0	80
Other	230.0	20
Total	**1,152.0**	**100**

Selected Brands

1-800-Flowers.com
1-800-Baskets
Celebrations
Cheryl's
Cushman's
DesignPac
Flowerama
Goodsey
GreatFoods.com
Harry & David
MooseMunch
Mrs. Beasley's

Napco
Personalization Universe
Simply Chocolate
The Popcorn Factory
Wolferman's

COMPETITORS

BED BATH & BEYOND INC.	Otto (GmbH & Co KG)
BEST BUY CO. INC.	PROVELL INC.
BF 2017 INC.	WAYFAIR INC.
ETSY INC.	WINMARK CORPORATION
FLOWERS FOODS INC.	

HISTORICAL FINANCIALS

Company Type: Public

Income Statement

FYE: June 27

	REVENUE ($ mil.)	NET INCOME ($ mil.)	NET PROFIT MARGIN	EMPLOYEES
06/21	2,122.2	118.6	5.6%	4,800
06/20	1,489.6	59.0	4.0%	4,300
06/19*	1,248.6	34.7	2.8%	4,095
07/18	1,151.9	40.7	3.5%	4,785
07/17	1,193.6	44.0	3.7%	4,633
Annual Growth	15.5%	28.1%	—	0.9%

*Fiscal year change

2021 Year-End Financials

Debt ratio: 16.8%	No. of shares (mil.): 65.0
Return on equity: 26.1%	Dividends
Cash ($ mil.): 173.5	Yield: —
Current ratio: 1.50	Payout: —
Long-term debt ($ mil.): 161.5	Market value ($ mil.): 2,189.0

	STOCK PRICE ($) FY Close	P/E High/Low		PER SHARE ($) Earnings	Dividends	Book Value
06/21	33.68	21	11	1.78	0.00	7.83
06/20	19.87	27	12	0.89	0.00	6.22
06/19*	18.88	39	19	0.52	0.00	5.32
07/18	12.55	21	13	0.61	0.00	4.87
07/17	9.75	16	13	0.65	0.00	4.33
Annual Growth	36.3%	—		28.6%	—	15.9%

*Fiscal year change

ABIOMED, Inc.

ABIOMED gives weary hearts a rest. The medical device maker has developed a range of cardiac assist devices and is developing a self-contained artificial heart. Its Impella micro heart pumps can temporarily take over blood circulation during surgery or catheterization. Its Impella CP device provides blood flow of approximately one liter more per minute than the Impella 2.5 device and is primarily used by either interventional cardiologists to support patients in the cath lab or by cardiac surgeons in the heart surgery suite. ABIOMED markets its products through both a direct sales force and distributors. About 85% of the company's revenue is generated from the US.

Operations

ABIOMED operates in one business segment ? the research development and sale of medical devices to assist or replace the pumping function of the failing heart. Its products are used in the cardiac catheterization lab or cath lab by interventional cardiologists the electrophysiology lab the hybrid lab and in the heart surgery suite by cardiac surgeons. The company's products include Impella 2.5 Impella CP Impella 5.0 and Impella LD Impella 5.5 as well as Impella RP Impella SmartAssist and Impella Connect. ABIOMED's product pipeline includes Impella ECP Impella XR Sheath and Impella BTR.

The company generates about 95% of total revenue from Impella products while service and other provide the remaining.

Geographic Reach

Headquartered in Danvers Massachusetts ABIOMED markets and sells its products in certain parts of Europe Asia South America and the Middle East. The company manufactures its products in Danvers Massachusetts and Aachen Germany. Its Aachen facility performs final assembly and manufactures most of the company's disposable Impella devices.

In addition to its locations in Massachusetts and Germany the company has regulatory and clinical affairs marketing and distribution center in Japan.

The US provides nearly 85% of total revenue while international markets account for the remaining.

Sales and Marketing

ABIOMED primarily sells its products to hospitals and distributors. No customer accounts for more than 10% of total revenues.

Financial Performance

Total revenue for fiscal 2020 increased $71.5 million or 9% to $840.9 million from $769.4 million for fiscal 2019 driven by both its Impella product revenue and our service and other revenue as further described below.

The company had a net income of $203 million a 22% decrease from the previous year.

The company's cash for the year ended 2020 totaled $192.3 million. Operating activities generated $314.9 million while investing activities used $125.5 million mainly for purchases of marketable securities. Financing activities used another $117.7 million mainly for repurchases of common stocks.

Strategy

The company's strategic focus and the driver of its revenue growth is the market penetration of its family of Impella heart pumps. The Impella device portfolio which includes the Impella 2.5 Impella CP Impella 5.0 Impella LD Impella 5.5 and Impella RP devices has supported thousands of patients worldwide. The company expects that most of its product and service revenue in the near future will be from the company's Impella devices. Its Impella 2.5 Impella CP Impella 5.0 Impella LD Impella 5.5 and Impella RP devices have U.S Food and Drug Administration or FDA and CE Mark which allows the company to market these devices in the U.S. and European Union.

Mergers and Acquisitions

In early 2020 ABIOMED acquired Breethe Inc. a Maryland company. Breethe is engaged in research and development of a novel extracorporeal membrane oxygenation (ECMO) system that will complement and expand the company's product portfolio to more comprehensively serve the needs of patients whose lungs can no longer provide sufficient oxygenation including some patients suffering from cardiogenic shock or respiratory failure such as ARDS H1N1 SARS or COVID-19. The company acquired Breethe for $55.0 million in cash with additional potential payouts up to a maximum of $55.0 million payable based on the achievement of certain technical regulatory and commercial milestones.

HISTORY

David Lederman founded ABIOMED in 1981 to make products he had designed (such as artificial heart pumps and valves) as well as dental diagnostic products. ABIOMED went public in 1987. In 1988 it got about $1 million from the National Institutes of Health for heart replacement device (HRD) research and development. In 1990 it began working with Canada's World Heart on HRD technology. In 1992 ABIOMED launched BVS-5000.

In 1990 the company formed ABIODENT to consolidate its dental operations. It received FDA clearance to market the PerioTemp device in 1994. In 1996 it voluntarily recalled some of its BVS-5000 blood pumps citing component irregularities (it said no patients were affected).

To fund product development ABIOMED accepted government funding to finish testing its battery-powered HRD (1996) and to develop a laser-based tissue-welding system (1998). Biotech firm Genzyme invested about $15 million in ABIOMED that year acquiring 14% of the firm.

In 1998 ABIOMED again recalled some lots of BVS-5000 this time for electrical problems. The company attributed 1998's losses to an increase in self-funding on the HRD project as well as to red ink in its now-discontinued dental business.

ABIOMED received funding from the National Heart Lung and Blood Institutes in 2000 to support the testing of its AbioCor product an implantable heart replacement device. The following year AbioCor became the first artificial heart implanted in a patient.

The FDA approved the use of the artificial hearts in five patients in 2001 all of whom were considered too sick to receive heart transplants. The first patient died the same year but the cause of death was not attributed to AbioCor.

The fifth patient to receive the device died early in 2002. By late 2002 seven patients had been fitted with the device but only one was living. A moratorium on recruiting new patients was imposed. ABIOMED wanted patients that were healthy enough to live long past the time of implantation but only patients that were extremely ill would be considered candidates for the device.

By January of 2003 the moratorium had been lifted and three more patients had received implants by March. Because of the troubles with finding qualified recipients for its AbioCor product the company began focusing on other products to sustain revenues. It got good news on that front that same year when the FDA approved ABIOMED's AB5000 Circulatory Support System Console a device that temporarily pumps the patient's blood when the heart has failed.

EXECUTIVES

Chairman, President And Chief Executive Officer, Michael Minogue, $608,363 total compensation
Lead Independent Director, Dorothy Puhy
Independent Director, Christopher Van Gorder
Independent Director, Myron Rolle
Independent Director, Paula Johnson
Vice President, Chief Commercial Officer, Andrew Greenfield, $301,454 total compensation

Chief Operating Officer, Senior Vice President, David Weber, $350,363 total compensation
Independent Director, Eric Rose
Independent Director, Paul Thomas
Independent Director, Jeannine Rivet
Chief Financial Officer, Vice President, Todd Trapp, $430,000 total compensation
Vice President, General Counsel, Secretary, Marc Began, $342,656 total compensation
Auditors: DELOITTE & TOUCHE LLP

LOCATIONS

HQ: ABIOMED, Inc.
   22 Cherry Hill Drive, Danvers, MA 01923
Phone: 978 646-1400   **Fax:** 978 777-8411
Web: www.abiomed.com

PRODUCTS/OPERATIONS

2015 Revenues

	$ mil.	% of total
Impella products	212.7	92
Service & other revenue	13.8	6
Other products	3.5	2
Funded research & development	0.3	-
Total	**230.3**	**100**

COMPETITORS

ARTIVION INC.
CAREFUSION CORPORATION
MEDICAL INC.
ESCALON MEDICAL CORP.
HAEMONETICS
CORPORATION
HEARTWARE
INTERNATIONAL INC.

LIVANOVA USA INC.
NXSTAGE
STEREOTAXIS INC.
UTAH MEDICAL PRODUCTS INC.
VIVEVE MEDICAL INC.

HISTORICAL FINANCIALS

Company Type: Public

Income Statement				FYE: March 31
	REVENUE ($ mil.)	NET INCOME ($ mil.)	NET PROFIT MARGIN	EMPLOYEES
03/21	847.5	225.5	26.6%	1,725
03/20	840.8	203.0	24.1%	1,536
03/19	769.4	259.0	33.7%	1,371
03/18	593.7	112.1	18.9%	1,143
03/17	445.3	52.1	11.7%	908
Annual Growth	17.5%	44.2%	—	17.4%

2021 Year-End Financials

Debt ratio: —
Return on equity: 18.8%
Cash ($ mil.): 232.7
Current ratio: 6.11
Long-term debt ($ mil.): —

No. of shares (mil.): 45.2
Dividends
   Yield: —
   Payout: —
Market value ($ mil.): 14,429.0

	STOCK PRICE ($) FY Close	P/E High/Low		PER SHARE ($) Earnings	Dividends	Book Value
03/21	318.73	71	28	4.94	0.00	29.37
03/20	145.16	63	29	4.43	0.00	23.67
03/19	285.59	78	48	5.61	0.00	20.76
03/18	290.99	116	76	2.45	0.00	15.54
03/17	125.20	109	78	1.17	0.00	10.35
Annual Growth	26.3%	—	—	43.3%	—	29.8%

ACM Research Inc

Auditors: BDO China Shu Lun Pan Certified Public Accountants LLP

LOCATIONS

HQ: ACM Research Inc
   42307 Osgood Road, Suite I, Fremont, CA 94539
Phone: 510 445-3700
Web: www.acmrcsh.com

HISTORICAL FINANCIALS

Company Type: Public

Income Statement				FYE: December 31
	REVENUE ($ mil.)	NET INCOME ($ mil.)	NET PROFIT MARGIN	EMPLOYEES
12/20	156.6	18.7	12.0%	543
12/19	107.5	18.8	17.6%	361
12/18	74.6	6.5	8.8%	273
12/17	36.5	(0.3)	—	191
12/16	27.3	1.0	3.8%	187
Annual Growth	54.7%	106.6%	—	30.5%

2020 Year-End Financials

Debt ratio: 13.4%
Return on equity: 15.7%
Cash ($ mil.): 71.7
Current ratio: 2.53
Long-term debt ($ mil.): 17.9

No. of shares (mil.): 18.7
Dividends
   Yield: —
   Payout: —
Market value ($ mil.): 1,519.0

	STOCK PRICE ($) FY Close	P/E High/Low		PER SHARE ($) Earnings	Dividends	Book Value
12/20	81.25	109	17	0.89	0.00	7.55
12/19	18.45	19	8	0.99	0.00	5.39
12/18	10.88	36	11	0.37	0.00	3.27
12/17	5.25	—	—	(0.05)	0.00	2.60
Annual Growth	149.2%	—	—	—	—	42.7%

ACNB Corp

Seven score and a few years ago ACNB Corporation's fathers brought forth a small-town bank. Now ACNB is dedicated to the proposition of being the holding company for Adams County National Bank operating more than 20 branches in the Gettysburg and Newville areas of Pennsylvania. It is altogether fitting and proper that the bank offers traditional retail banking services. The world may long note and remember that the bank also provides residential mortgage (about 60% of the portfolio) commercial real estate consumer and business loans. In addition ACNB gives a full measure of devotion to insurance products; provides trust services; and hopes that community banking shall not perish from the earth.

EXECUTIVES

Independent Vice Chairman Of The Board, Todd Herring
Executive Vice President - Finance, Jason Weber
Independent Director, Kimberly Chaney
Director, D. Arthur Seibel

HOOVER'S HANDBOOK OF EMERGING COMPANIES 2022

Independent Director, Scott Kelley
Independent Director, Donna Newell
President, Chief Executive Officer, Director,
  James Helt, $450,000 total compensation
Independent Director, James Lott
Independent Director, James Williams
Independent Director, Daniel Potts
Chairman, Alan Stock
Chief Financial Officer, Executive Vice President,
  Treasurer, David Cathell, $261,779 total
  compensation
Independent Director, Marian Schultz
Independent Director, Frank Elsner
Chief Governance Officer, Executive Vice
  President, Secretary, Lynda Glass, $276,161 total
  compensation
Independent Director, Thomas Ritter
Auditors: RSM US LLP

LOCATIONS

HQ: ACNB Corp
  16 Lincoln Square, Gettysburg, PA 17325
Phone: 717 334-3161
Web: www.acnb.com

COMPETITORS

BURKE & HERBERT BANK &   M&F BANCORP
  INC.
  TRUST COMPANY
FB FINANCIAL
  CORPORATION

HISTORICAL FINANCIALS

Company Type: Public

Income Statement   FYE: December 31

	ASSETS ($ mil.)	NET INCOME ($ mil.)	INCOME AS % OF ASSETS	EMPLOYEES
12/20	2,555.3	18.3	0.7%	396
12/19	1,720.2	23.7	1.4%	374
12/18	1,647.7	21.7	1.3%	361
12/17	1,595.4	9.7	0.6%	358
12/16	1,206.3	10.8	0.9%	303
Annual Growth	20.6%	14.1%	—	6.9%

2020 Year-End Financials

Return on assets: 0.8%	Dividends
Return on equity: 8.2%	Yield: 4.0%
Long-term debt ($ mil.): —	Payout: 49.0%
No. of shares (mil.): 8.7	Market value ($ mil.): 218.0
Sales ($ mil): 105.2	

	STOCK PRICE ($) FY Close	P/E High/Low		PER SHARE ($) Earnings	Dividends	Book Value
12/20	25.00	17	9	2.13	1.00	29.62
12/19	37.82	12	10	3.36	0.98	26.77
12/18	39.25	13	9	3.09	0.89	23.86
12/17	29.55	21	17	1.50	0.80	21.92
12/16	31.25	18	12	1.80	0.80	19.80
Annual Growth	(5.4%)	—	—	4.3%	5.7%	10.6%

Addus HomeCare Corp

Addus HomeCare doing business through subsidiary Addus HealthCare it serves the elderly and
disabled. Its home and community unit provides

long-term non-medical social services such as
bathing grooming housekeeping meal preparation
and transportation. State and county government
payors generate most of its revenues. Operating
from 215 offices Addus provides its services in
about 20 states primarily in the Midwestern and
western US with its largest markets in Illinois New
York and New Mexico.

Operations

The company operates three segments: personal
care hospice and home health.

Personal care segment provides non-medical assistance with activities of daily living primarily to
persons who are at increased risk of hospitalization
or institutionalization such as the elderly chronically ill or disabled. The services include assistance
with bathing grooming oral care feeding and dress-
ing medication reminders meal planning and
preparation housekeeping and transportation services. The segment accounts the largest for about
90% of total revenue.

The hospice segment (nearly 10%) provides
physical emotional and spiritual care for people
who are terminally ill as well as related services
for their families. The hospice services include palliative nursing care social work spiritual counseling
homemaker services and bereavement counseling.

Home health segment provides services that are
primarily medical in nature to individuals who may
require assistance during an illness or after hospitalization and include skilled nursing and physical
occupational and speech therapy. It generally provides home health services on a short-term inter-
mittent or episodic basis to individuals typically to
assist patients recovering from an illness or injury.
The segment accounts a small portion of the revenue.

Geographic Reach

Headquartered in Frisco Texas Addus derives a
significant amount of its revenue from its operations in Illinois New York and New Mexico.

Sales and Marketing

Addus' payor clients include federal state and
local governmental agencies managed care organizations commercial insurers and private individuals. More than 50% of net service revenues were
derived from state and local government programs
with some 45% derived from managed care organizations while nearly 5% and a small portion
of net service revenues were derived from private
pay consumers and commercial insurance programs respectively. The Illinois Department on
Aging is its largest customer (accounted for 25%
revenues).

Financial Performance

Addus in 2020 had a net service revenue of
$764.8 million an 18% increase from the previous
year. All of the company's segments had a hand in
the said increase.

In 2020 the company had a net income of $33.1
million a 31% increase compared to the previous
year's net income of $25.2 million.

The company's cash at the end of 2020 was
$145.1 million. Operating activities generated
$109.4 million while investing activities used
$214.2 million primarily for acquisition of busi-
nesses. Financing activities provided another
$138.2 million.

Strategy

Addus' continued growth depends on its ability
to provide consistently high quality care maintain
its existing payor relationships establish relationships with new payors and increase its referral

sources. The company's continued growth is also
dependent upon the authorization by state agencies of new consumers to receive its services. The
company believes there are several market opportunities for growth.

Additionally Addus believes the overwhelming
majority of individuals in need of care generally
prefer to receive care in their homes. Finally Addus
believes the provision of personal care services is
more cost-effective than the provision of similar
services in institutional settings for long-term care.

Addus plans to continue its revenue growth and
margin improvement and enhance its competitive
positioning by executing on the following growth
strategies: consistently provide high-quality care;
drive organic growth in existing markets; market
to managed care organizations; and grow through
acquisitions.

In addition to its organic growth Addus has
been growing through acquisitions that have expanded its presence in current markets or facilitated its entry into new markets. In 2020 Addus
completed four acquisitions: A Plus Health Care
Inc. ("A Plus") on July 1 2020 County Homemakers Inc. ("County Homemakers") on November 1
2020 SLHC Inc. d/b/a SunLife Home Care ("Sun-
Life Home Care") on December 1 2020 and Queen
City Hospice on December 4 2020.

Mergers and Acquisitions

In 2020 Addus completed the acquisition of
Queen City Hospice LLC and its affiliate Miracle
City Hospice LLC for a cash purchase price of
$192.0 million. Based in Cincinnati Ohio Queen
City Hospice currently serves an average daily census of approximately 900 patients across the state
of Ohio. This acquisition further advances the company's strategy of providing hospice and home
health care in markets where it already has a significant personal care presence. With this acquisition Ohio becomes the second state where it has
the capability to provide all three levels of home
care.

In mid-2020 Addus announced the purchase of
A Plus Health Care Inc. Based in Kalispell Montana
A Plus Health Care provides home care services
including personal care private duty nursing care
management and medical staffing to approximately 1200 clients through over 650 employees
in seven office locations. The acquisition represents
a significant step forward in its strategy to acquire
providers that strengthen Addus' presence in its
current markets.

EXECUTIVES

Executive Vice President, Chief Legal Officer,
  Sean Gaffney, $320,192 total compensation
Executive Vice President , Chief Strategy Officer,
  Darby Anderson, $351,154 total compensation
Chairman Of The Board, Chief Executive Officer,
  R. Dirk Allison, $725,961 total compensation
Lead Independent Director, Steven Geringer
Independent Director, Michael Earley
Independent Director, Darin Gordon
Independent Director, Susan Weaver
Independent Director, Jean Rush
Executive Vice President, Chief Information
  Officer, Michael Wattenbarger, $245,942 total
  compensation
Executive Vice President And Chief Development
  Officer, David Tucker, $240,919 total
  compensation
Independent Director, Esteban Lopez
Independent Director, Veronica Hill-Milbourne

Chief Human Resource Officer, Executive Vice President, Robby Stevenson
Chief Financial Officer, Executive Vice President, Brian Poff, $405,961 total compensation
President, Chief Operating Officer, W. Bradley Bickham, $433,269 total compensation
Auditors: PricewaterhouseCoopers LLP

LOCATIONS

HQ: Addus HomeCare Corp
6303 Cowboys Way, Suite 600, Frisco, TX 75034
Phone: 469 535-8200
Web: www.addus.com

COMPETITORS

AMERICAN CARESOURCE HOLDINGS INC.
COMPUTER PROGRAMS AND SYSTEMS INC.
Extendicare Real Estate Investment Trust
GENESIS HEALTHCARE INC.
HANGER INC.
OPTION CARE HEALTH INC.
TIVITY HEALTH INC.
UNIVERSAL HEALTH SERVICES INC.
VITAS HEALTHCARE CORPORATION

HISTORICAL FINANCIALS

Company Type: Public

Income Statement				FYE: December 31
	REVENUE ($ mil.)	NET INCOME ($ mil.)	NET PROFIT MARGIN	EMPLOYEES
12/20	764.7	33.1	4.3%	35,139
12/19	648.7	25.2	3.9%	33,238
12/18	518.1	17.5	3.4%	33,153
12/17	425.7	13.6	3.2%	26,097
12/16	400.6	12.0	3.0%	23,070
Annual Growth	17.5%	28.8%	—	11.1%

2020 Year-End Financials

Debt ratio: 21.8%	No. of shares (mil.): 15.8
Return on equity: 6.6%	Dividends
Cash ($ mil.): 145.0	Yield: —
Current ratio: 2.00	Payout: —
Long-term debt ($ mil.): 193.9	Market value ($ mil.): 1,853.0

	STOCK PRICE ($) FY Close	P/E High/Low		PER SHARE ($) Earnings	Dividends	Book Value
12/20	117.09	55	23	2.08	0.00	32.77
12/19	97.22	53	32	1.77	0.00	30.45
12/18	67.88	53	24	1.41	0.00	20.99
12/17	34.80	34	25	1.17	0.00	15.05
12/16	35.05	34	15	1.06	0.00	13.79
Annual Growth	35.2%	—	—	18.4%	—	24.2%

Advanced Drainage Systems Inc

Auditors: DELOITTE & TOUCHE LLP

LOCATIONS

HQ: Advanced Drainage Systems Inc
4640 Trueman Boulevard, Hilliard, OH 43026
Phone: 614 658-0050
Web: www.ads-pipe.com

HISTORICAL FINANCIALS

Company Type: Public

Income Statement				FYE: March 31
	REVENUE ($ mil.)	NET INCOME ($ mil.)	NET PROFIT MARGIN	EMPLOYEES
03/21	1,982.7	224.2	11.3%	5,000
03/20	1,673.8	(193.1)	—	4,950
03/19	1,384.7	77.7	5.6%	4,400
03/18	1,330.3	62.0	4.7%	4,400
03/17	1,257.2	32.9	2.6%	4,500
Annual Growth	12.1%	61.5%	—	2.7%

2021 Year-End Financials

Debt ratio: 34.8%	No. of shares (mil.): 71.5
Return on equity: 24.6%	Dividends
Cash ($ mil.): 195.0	Yield: 0.3%
Current ratio: 2.33	Payout: 14.5%
Long-term debt ($ mil.): 815.1	Market value ($ mil.): 7,400.0

	STOCK PRICE ($) FY Close	P/E High/Low		PER SHARE ($) Earnings	Dividends	Book Value
03/21	103.39	43	10	2.59	0.36	14.67
03/20	29.44	—	—	(3.21)	1.36	11.15
03/19	25.77	27	19	1.22	0.32	8.46
03/18	25.90	27	18	0.99	0.28	7.39
03/17	21.90	55	37	0.50	0.24	6.06
Annual Growth	47.4%	—	—	50.9%	10.7%	24.7%

Advanced Energy Industries Inc

Advanced Energy Industries tames electricity for its high-tech clients. The company's power conversion products transform raw electricity making it uniform enough to ensure consistent production in high-precision manufacturing. Semiconductor and solar manufacturing equipment maker Applied Materials is its top customer. Advanced Energy's gear also is used in the production of solar panels and other thin-film products such as cell phones computers cars and glass panels for windows and electronic devices. The company gets about half of its sales from the US. The company strengthened its portfolio of industrial products in 2019 with the $400 million acquisition of Artesyn Embedded Technologies.

Operations

Advanced Energy sells equipment to companies that make equipment for the fabrication of semiconductors. That business accounts for more than 60% of Advanced Energy's revenue. Sales to industrial customers for machine tools automotive parts and other products accounts for about a quarter of revenue. The company's Global Support unit which makes repairs brings in some 15% of sales.

Geographic Reach

Advanced Energy based in Fort Collins Colorado has operations in the US and about 25 countries in Europe and the Asia/Pacific region.

Customers in the US generate more than half of the company's revenue followed by South Korea and China which each account for about 10% of revenue.

Sales and Marketing

Advanced Energy sells to about 370 OEMs and integrators and directly to about 1500 end users. It uses a direct sales force as well as independent sales representatives and distributors. The company's 10 largest customers account for more than 60% of sales. Advanced Energy relies on two customers for about 50% of its sales with Applied Materials accounting for about 35% and LAM Research supplying about 20%.

Financial Performance

Advanced Energy's revenue has increased five years in a row as the semiconductor market strengthened and with help from acquisitions. The company's profit has risen in the past three years after a net loss in 2015.

Revenue advanced 7% in 2018 to about $719 million up about $48 million from 2017 despite a 4% drop in the company's biggest business semiconductor-related sales. The overall semiconductor industry slumped in 2018 but Advanced Energy's sales to industrial customers ramped up lifted by acquisitions as did its global services sales.

Advanced Energy posted a profit of $147.1 million in 2018 about $9 million higher than the 2017 profit. The company had higher expenses in 2018 due to costs associated with integration of acquisitions but it had a lower tax provision than it did for 2017.

The company's net cash stood at $349.3 million in 2018 compared to $407.3 million the year before. Operating activities provided $151.3 million in 2018 while investing activities used $113.6 million and financing activities used $97.1 million.

Strategy

Advanced Energy went on an acquisition binge in 2017 and 2018 that quickly paid off. The company acquired several companies that strengthened its Industrial Technologies segment and reduced reliance on the semiconductor industry. Semiconductor sales trailed off in 2018 on a general industry downturn and the impact of the US-China trade war. But the acquisitions helped lift sales of the industrial business 43% year-over-year.

The acquisition of LumaSense help drive increases in applied power analytical devices and medical devices; Advanced Energy is the leading power supply provider to the medical lasers market.

The $85 million acquisition of LumaSense was just a warm-up exercise for Advanced Energy. In 2019 the company spent $400 million to buy the embedded power business of Artesyn Embedded Technologies from Platinum Equity. With Artesyn Advanced Energy's sales would total $1.3 billion and its industrial business would leapfrog the semiconductor business as the company's top revenue producer. Artesyn has products for the hyperscale data center 5G wireless industrial and medical technologies markets.

Even as the acquisitions improved revenue integration costs and other related expenses raised operating expenses in 2018 compared to 2017. Advanced Energy took steps to reduce redundant activities and trim costs.

Mergers and Acquisitions

In 2019 Advanced Energy acquired the embedded power business of Artesyn Embedded Technologies from Platinum Equity for about $400 million. The deal helps diversify Advanced Energy's offerings.

In 2018 Advanced Energy made several deals that expanded its product line.

The company acquired LumaSense a provider of temperature and gas sensing devices for about $85 million. The acquisition expanded Advanced Energy's electrostatic chuck offerings and added integrated industrial temperature control and metrology applications in both thin films coating and thermal processing.

Another deal was for Monroe Electronics which develops electrostatic applications.

The $12 million acquisition of Trek and its power supply products strengthened Advanced Energy's portfolio of high voltage applications.

Company Background

Douglas Schatz (chairman) a veteran of Applied Materials and Brent Backman who had worked for Hughes Aircraft founded Advanced Energy Industries in 1981. The company's first product replaced a refrigerator-sized power source with one the size of a bread box. Also during the 1980s the company introduced its first direct-current system for use in semiconductor deposition processes.

HISTORY

Douglas Schatz (chairman) a veteran of Applied Materials and Brent Backman who had worked for Hughes Aircraft (sold to General Motors in 1986) founded Advanced Energy Industries in 1981. The company's first product replaced a refrigerator-sized power source with one the size of a bread box. Also during the 1980s the company introduced its first direct-current system for use in semiconductor deposition processes.

The company went public in 1995. The following year sales growth slowed as the chip industry went through one of its periodic slumps. To cushion its dependence on the volatile semiconductor market in 1997 and 1998 Advanced Energy acquired power supply firms Tower Electronics (products used in the telecommunications medical and non-impact printing industries) and MIK Physics (power supplies used in industrial vacuum coating) among others. Advanced Energy also bought one of its main rivals RF Power Products. In 2000 Advanced Energy bought Noah Holding a privately held maker of temperature control systems.

In 2001 the company acquired Engineering Measurements Company (EMCO) a maker of flow meters and other precision measurement equipment. During 2001 the company twice cut its workforce — by a total of one-fourth — in response to a sharp decline in the worldwide electronics industry.

In 2002 Advanced Energy acquired Aera Japan (mass flow controllers) for about $80 million in cash and debt assumption. Later that year it acquired Germany-based Dressler HF Technik (power systems for plasma-based production equipment) and the e-diagnostics applications of privately held Symphony Systems (Web-based software used to control wafer manufacturing processes).

In 2005 Doug Schatz said he would retire as president and CEO once a successor could be found. Hans-Georg Betz CEO of West STEAG Partners (a German venture capital firm) and a director of Advanced Energy since 2004 was named president and CEO later that year. Schatz remained as nonexecutive chairman of the company.

Later that year Advanced Energy raised around $92 million in a secondary stock offering. The company marked its 25th anniversary in business during 2006.

The company closed its plant in Stolberg Germany in 2007. Manufacturing was shifted to Advanced Energy's high-volume plant in Shenzhen China and to its advanced manufacturing facility in Fort Collins Colorado. The company said the decision came down to deciding whether to expand the plants in Stolberg and Shenzhen with the Chinese facility getting the nod. Advanced Energy acquired the Stolberg location through the acquisition of Dressler HF Technik in 2002. The German plant employed about 65 people.

Bolstering its power conversion products for the solar market in 2010 Advanced Energy acquired PV Powered a maker solar inverters for the commercial residential and utility-scale markets. Later the same year the company sold its Aera mass flow control and related product lines to Hitachi Metals for about $44 million in order to focus on its core power product lines.

EXECUTIVES

Independent Director, Thomas Rohrs
Independent Director, Edward Grady
Executive Vice President Of Corporate Development, Chief Administrative Officer, Corporate Secretary, Thomas McGimpsey, $382,000 total compensation
Chairman Of The Board, Grant Beard
Independent Director, John Roush
Chief Financial Officer, Executive Vice President, Paul Oldham, $460,000 total compensation
Independent Director, Anne DelSanto
Independent Director, Lanesha Minnix
Chief Operating Officer, Executive Vice President, Eduardo Acebedo
Independent Director, David Reed
Independent Director, Frederick Ball
Independent Director, Ronald Foster
Chief Executive Officer, President, And Director, Stephen Kelley
Auditors: Ernst & Young LLP

LOCATIONS

HQ: Advanced Energy Industries Inc
1595 Wynkoop Street, Suite 800, Denver, CO 80202
Phone: 970 407-6626
Web: www.advancedenergy.com

PRODUCTS/OPERATIONS

2018 Sales

	$ mil.	% of total
Semiconductor capital equipment	443.1	62
Industrial technology capital equipment	167.2	23
Global Support	108.6	15
Total	**718.9**	**100**

Selected Products

Inductively coupled plasma sources
Ion sources
Optical fiber thermometers
Photovoltaic (PV) power inverters
  Bipolar transformerless inverters (Solaron)
  Grid-tie PV inverters (PV Powered)
Power control and conversion systems (used with wafer etching and vapor deposition equipment)
  AC power supply
  Direct-current (DC) products
  High-power products
  Low-frequency products
  Mid-frequency power supplies
  Radio-frequency generators

Radio-frequency power systems (cables generators instrumentation power supplies power delivery systems and variable frequency generators)

COMPETITORS

ALPS ALPINE CO. LTD.
AMERICAN SUPERCONDUCTOR CORPORATION
APC TECHNOLOGY GROUP PLC
COHERENT INC.
Conergy AG
ELECTRO SCIENTIFIC INDUSTRIES INC.
FLEX LTD.
NITTO DENKO CORPORATION
TDK CORPORATION
TERADYNE INC.
ULTRALIFE CORPORATION
VICOR CORPORATION

HISTORICAL FINANCIALS

Company Type: Public

Income Statement				FYE: December 31
	REVENUE ($ mil.)	NET INCOME ($ mil.)	NET PROFIT MARGIN	EMPLOYEES
12/20	1,415.8	134.6	9.5%	10,000
12/19	788.9	64.9	8.2%	10,917
12/18	718.8	147.0	20.5%	2,259
12/17	671.0	137.8	20.5%	1,876
12/16	483.7	127.4	26.3%	1,558
Annual Growth	30.8%	1.4%	—	59.2%

2020 Year-End Financials

Debt ratio: 19.5%	No. of shares (mil.): 38.2
Return on equity: 18.0%	Dividends
Cash ($ mil.): 480.3	Yield: —
Current ratio: 3.31	Payout: —
Long-term debt ($ mil.): 304.5	Market value ($ mil.): 3,713.0

	STOCK PRICE ($) FY Close	P/E High/Low	PER SHARE ($) Earnings	Dividends	Book Value
12/20	96.97	29 10	3.50	0.00	21.28
12/19	71.20	42 24	1.69	0.00	17.64
12/18	42.93	21 10	3.74	0.00	15.90
12/17	67.48	27 16	3.43	0.00	13.15
12/16	54.75	18 8	3.18	0.00	9.87
Annual Growth	15.4%	— —	2.4%	—	21.2%

AeroVironment, Inc.

AeroVironment (AV) designs develops produces delivers and supports a technologically-advanced portfolio of intelligent multi-domain robotic systems and related services for government agencies and businesses. The company designs and manufactures a line of small unmanned aircraft systems (UAS) tactical missile systems (TMS) unmanned ground vehicles (UGV) and related services primarily for the Department of Defense (DoD). The business addresses the increasing economic and security value of distributed network-centric intelligence surveillance and reconnaissance (ISR) communications remote sensing and effects delivery with innovative UAS and tactical missile system solutions. AeroVironment was founded in 1971. The company generates around 60% of total sales domestically.

Operations

AV operates its business as two reportable segment: Unmanned Aircraft Systems (UAS; around 95% of sales) and Medium Unmanned Aircraft Systems (MUAS; some 5%). The UAS segment consists of its existing small UAS tactical missile systems and HAPS product lines and the recently acquired ISG business. The MUAS segment consists of its recently acquired Arcturus business. It has major products lines and program such as Small UAS (some 60%) Tactical missile system TMS (over 20%) High-Altitude Pseudo-Satellite HAPS (around 10 20%) medium unmanned aircraft systems (some 5%) and others (about 5%).

Small UAS including Raven Wasp AE Puma AE Puma LE VAPOR and Quantix Recon are designed to operate reliably at very low altitudes in a wide range of environmental conditions providing a vantage point from which to collect and deliver valuable information. Military forces employ the company's small UAS to deliver ISR and communications.

TMS consists of tube-launched aircraft that deploy with the push of a button fly at higher speeds than its small UAS and perform either effects delivery or reconnaissance missions.

AV also has existing solutions such as terrestrial cellular towers and communications. In addition AV provides comprehensive training services to support all of the small UAS and tactical missile systems for defense applications.

Overall the business focuses primarily on the design development production marketing support and operation of innovative UAS and tactical missile systems that provide situational awareness remote sensing multi-band communications force protection and other information and mission effects to increase the safety and effectiveness of our customers' operations. Its products accounts for around 70% of total sales and contract services account for the rest.

Geographic Reach

The company is based in Arlington Virginia. It has facilities located in California Alabama Kansas Massachusetts Minnesota and Virginia. Its domestic sales account for around 70% while international sales accounted for about 40% of its revenue.

Sales and Marketing

AV sells the majority of its UAS and services to organizations within the DoD including the US Army Marine Corps Special Operations Command Air Force and Navy and to allied governments. It sells tactical missile systems to organizations within the US government. It sells its UGV and services to US and allied government military and public safety agencies as well as to commercial entities. It also develops High Altitude Pseudo-Satellite (HAPS) systems for SoftBank Corp. HAPS Mobile Inc. a commercial joint venture of which the company owns over 5%. The US Army and other US government agencies generate about 70% of its total sales. Non-US government is responsible for the remaining 30%.

AV's advertising expenses were approximately $675000 $934000 and $897000 for the years 2021 2020 and 2019 respectively.

Financial Performance

Revenue for the fiscal 2021 was $394.9 million as compared to $367.3 million for the fiscal 2020 representing an increase of $27.6 million or 8%. The increase in revenue was due to an increase in product revenue of $22.1 million and an increase in service revenue of $5.5 million.

Net income for fiscal 2021 decreased to $23.3 million compared from the prior year with $41.3 million.

Cash held by the company at the end of fiscal 2021 decreased to $157.1 million. Cash provided by operations and financing activities were $86.5 million and $194.2 million respectively. Cash used by investing activities was $378.8 million mainly for business acquisitions.

Strategy

AeroVironment intends to grow its business by preserving a leadership position in its core UAS and tactical missile systems markets and by creating new solutions that enable it to create and establish leadership positions in new markets. Key components of this strategy include the following:

Expand the market penetration of existing products and services. The company intends to increase the penetration of its small and medium UAS and UGV products and services within the U.S. military the military forces of allied nations other government agencies and non-government organizations including commercial entities and to increase the penetration of its TMS within the U.S. military and within the military forces of allied nations.

Deliver innovative new solutions into existing and new markets. Customer-focused innovation is the primary driver of its growth. AeroVironment's plan to continue investing in internally-funded research and development projects while expanding its pursuit of customer-funded research and development projects to generate revenue and develop better more capable products services and business models both in response to and in anticipation of emerging customer needs.

Foster its entrepreneurial culture and continue to attract develop and retain highly-skilled personnel. AeroVironment's company culture encourages innovation and entrepreneurialism which helps to attract and retain highly-skilled professionals. AeroVironment intend to preserve this culture to encourage the development of the innovative highly technical system solutions and business models that give the company its competitive advantage.

Preserve its agility and flexibility. AeroVironment respond rapidly to evolving markets solve complicated customer problems and strive to deliver new products services and capabilities quickly efficiently and affordably relative to available alternatives.

Effectively manage its growth portfolio for long-term value creation. AeroVironment's production and development programs and services present numerous investment opportunities that the company believe will deliver long-term growth by providing its customers with valuable new capabilities.

Mergers and Acquisitions

In 2021 AeroVironment was granted clearance from the German government and completed the previously announced acquisition of Telerob Gesellschaft f r Fernhantierungstechnik mbH (Telerob) in a $45.4 million. Telerob now operates as a wholly-owned subsidiary of AeroVironment. Telerob offers one of the industry's most advanced and comprehensive turn-key unmanned ground robotics solutions including the telemax and tEODor EVO family of UGVs fully-equipped transport vehicles and training repair and support services. Its acquisition of Telerob marks a significant expansion to its portfolio of intelligent multi-do-

main robotic systems from small and medium unmanned aircraft systems to tactical missile systems and now unmanned ground vehicles.

In early 2021 AeroVironment has acquired Progeny Systems Corporation's Intelligent Systems Group (ISG) a leader in the development of artificial intelligence-enabled computer vision machine learning and perceptive autonomy technologies and provider of related services to United States government customers. The acquisition will significantly accelerate AeroVironment's development of advanced autonomy capabilities for the company's growing portfolio of intelligent multi-domain robotic systems increase customer-funded research and development revenue and broaden its advanced engineering services offering to defense and commercial customers. Under the terms of the transaction AeroVironment acquired ISG for $30 million in cash.

Also in early 2021 AeroVironment has completed its acquisition of California-based Arcturus UAV Inc. a leading designer and manufacturer of high-performance unmanned aircraft systems (UAS) for approximately $405 million. The acquisition of Arcturus UAV enables the company to accelerate its growth strategy and expand its reach into the more valuable Group 2 and 3 UAS segments.

EXECUTIVES

Independent Director, Catharine Merigold
Independent Director, Stephen Page
Chief Financial Officer, Senior Vice President, Kevin Mcdonnell, $401,543 total compensation
Chief Accounting Officer, Brian Shackley, $241,906 total compensation
Ir Contact Officer, Jonah Teeter-Balin
Chief Compliance Officer, Vice President, General Counsel, Company Secretary, Melissa Brown, $342,003 total compensation
Chairman Of The Board, President, Chief Executive Officer, Wahid Nawabi, $632,319 total compensation
Auditors: Deloitte & Touche LLP

LOCATIONS

HQ: AeroVironment, Inc.
241 18th Street, Suite 415, Arlington, VA 22202
Phone: 805 520-8350
Web: www.avinc.com

PRODUCTS/OPERATIONS

2015 Sales

	$ mil.	% of total
Product sales	205.0	79
Contract services	54.4	21
Total	**259.4**	**100**

2015 Sales

	$ mil.	% of total
UAS	221.0	85
EES	38.4	15
Total	**259.4**	**100**

Selected Products

Efficient Energy Systems
Electric Vehicle Charging Solutions:
Passenger and Fleet Electric Vehicle Charging Systems Installation Service and Data Communications
PosiCharge Industrial Electric Vehicle Fast Charge SystemPower Cycling and Testing

COMPETITORS

BAE SYSTEMS PLC
COMTECH TELECOMMUNICATIONS CORP.
CUBIC CORPORATION
EXELIS INC.
INSITU INC.
KAMAN CORPORATION
KRATOS DEFENSE & SECURITY SOLUTIONS INC.
LEONARDO SPA
MAXAR TECHNOLOGIES INC.
TEXTRON INC.
THE BOEING COMPANY
ULTRA ELECTRONICS HOLDINGS PLC

HISTORICAL FINANCIALS

Company Type: Public

Income Statement

FYE: April 30

	REVENUE ($ mil.)	NET INCOME ($ mil.)	NET PROFIT MARGIN	EMPLOYEES
04/21	394.9	23.3	5.9%	1,177
04/20	367.3	41.0	11.2%	828
04/19	314.2	47.4	15.1%	699
04/18	271.0	20.0	7.4%	697
04/17	264.8	12.4	4.7%	661
Annual Growth	10.5%	16.9%	—	15.5%

2021 Year-End Financials

Debt ratio: 21.2%	No. of shares (mil.): 24.7
Return on equity: 4.1%	Dividends
Cash ($ mil.): 148.7	Yield: —
Current ratio: 4.18	Payout: —
Long-term debt ($ mil.): 187.5	Market value ($ mil.): 2,735.0

	STOCK PRICE ($) FY Close	P/E High/Low	PER SHARE ($) Earnings	Dividends	Book Value
04/21	110.37	142 61	0.96	0.00	24.70
04/20	60.26	42 27	1.71	0.00	21.19
04/19	68.56	58 26	1.97	0.00	19.32
04/18	54.50	68 33	0.84	0.00	17.15
04/17	28.57	60 41	0.54	0.00	16.16
Annual Growth	40.2%		15.5%	—	11.2%

Agree Realty Corp.

Shopping sprees really agree with Agree Realty. The self-managed real estate investment trust (REIT) owns develops and manages retail real estate. It owns around 820 retail properties spanning approximately 14.6 million square feet of leasable space across 45-plus states. Most of its tenants are national retailers with its largest tenants being Sherwin-Williams Wal-Mart and TJX Companies. The REIT typically acquires either property portfolios or single-asset net lease retail properties worth approximately $702.9 million with credit-worthy tenants. It was founded in 1971 by CEO Richard Agree.

Operations

Agree Realty's portfolio is made up of over 820 properties. Approximately all of it are leased and has a weighted average remaining lease term of approximately 10 years. Virtually all of the REIT's revenue is from rental income.

Geographic Reach

Bloomfields hills Michigan-based Agree Realty had properties in about 45 US states. About 10% of its rental revenue came from properties in Michigan while more than 15% came from properties based in Florida Ohio and Texas. All other regions each accounted for less than 5% of its revenue.

Sales and Marketing

The REIT mostly leases properties to retailers such as pharmacies restaurants general merchandisers apparel retailers grocery stores warehouse clubs sporting goods stores health & fitness centers convenience stores and dollar stores among others.

Agree Realty's largest tenant by revenue is Sherwin-Williams which contributed about 5% to the REIT's total rental income during 2019. Its four next largest tenants that year were Wal-Mart (nearly 5% of rental income) TJX (roughly 5%) Walgreens (less than 5%) and Best Buy (less than 5%).

Financial Performance

Agree Realty's annual revenues have almost tripled since 2015 as net income doubled for the same period.

The REIT's revenue climbed 37% to $187.5 million during 2019 mostly as its real estate investment portfolio grew to approximately $2.2 billion in gross investment amount representing 821 properties with 14.6 million square feet of gross leasable space.

Net income increased $22 million or 38% to $80.1 million for fiscal 2019 compared to $58.2 million for 2018. Higher revenues and higher gains on asset mainly contributed to the increase.

Cash at the end of fiscal 2019 was $42.2 million. Net cash provided by operating activities was $126.7 million and financing activities added another $529 million to the coffers. Investing activities used $667.5 million for acquisition of real estate investments and developments.

Strategy

The company's primary business objective is to generate consistent shareholder returns by primarily investing in and actively managing a diversified portfolio of retail properties net leased to industry-leading tenants.

Its investment strategy is to expand and enhance its portfolio by identifying the best risk-adjusted investment opportunities across its development Partner Capital Solutions (PCS) and acquisition platforms. It believes that development and PCS projects have the potential to generate superior risk-adjusted returns on investment in properties that are substantially similar to those it acquires.

Its financing strategy is to maintain a capital structure that provides it with the flexibility to manage its business and pursue its growth strategies while allowing it to service its debt requirements and generate appropriate risk-adjusted returns for its shareholders. The company believes these objectives are best achieved by a capital structure that consists primarily of common equity and prudent amounts of debt financing. However it may raise capital in any form and under terms that it deemed acceptable and in the best interest of its shareholders.

Company Background

In 1971 Richard Agree Executive Chairman of the Board of Directors founded Agree Development Company the predecessor to Agree Realty Corporation. Over its 23 year history Agree developed over 40 community shopping centers primarily throughout the Midwestern and Southeast United States.

With an Initial Public Offering of 2.5 million shares in 1994 Agree Realty Corporation commenced operations as a publicly traded Real Estate Investment Trust (REIT). Agree Realty is listed on the New York Stock Exchange under the ticker symbol ADC.

EXECUTIVES

Executive Chairman Of The Board, Richard Agree, $150,004 total compensation
President, Chief Executive Officer And Director, Joel Agree, $792,788 total compensation
Independent Director, Michael Hollman
Independent Director, Jerome Rossi
Chief Financial Officer And Secretary, Peter Coughenour
General Counsel, Danielle Spehar, $300,961 total compensation
Lead Independent Director, W. Gregory Lehmkuhl
Chief Operating Officer, Craig Erlich, $125,912 total compensation
Independent Director, Karen Dearing
Independent Director, Michael Judlowe
Deputy Chief Accounting Officer, Stephen Breslin
Chief Accounting Officer, David Wolff
Auditors: Grant Thornton LLP

LOCATIONS

HQ: Agree Realty Corp.
70 E. Long Lake Road, Bloomfield Hills, MI 48304
Phone: 248 737-4190 **Fax:** 248 737-9110
Web: www.agreerealty.com

PRODUCTS/OPERATIONS

2015 sales

	$ mil.	% of total
Minimum rents	64.3	92
operating cost reimbursement	5.3	8
Percentage rents	0.2	-
other income	0.2	-
Total	**70.0**	**100**

COMPETITORS

A & J MUCKLOW GROUP LIMITED
CENTERSPACE
COUSINS PROPERTIES INCORPORATED
LXP INDUSTRIAL TRUST
RPT REALTY
WASHINGTON PRIME GROUP
L.P.
WASHINGTON REAL ESTATE INVESTMENT TRUST

HISTORICAL FINANCIALS

Company Type: Public

Income Statement

FYE: December 31

	REVENUE ($ mil.)	NET INCOME ($ mil.)	NET PROFIT MARGIN	EMPLOYEES
12/20	248.5	91.3	36.8%	49
12/19	187.4	80.0	42.7%	41
12/18	148.2	58.1	39.3%	36
12/17	116.5	58.1	49.9%	32
12/16	91.5	45.1	49.3%	24
Annual Growth	28.4%	19.3%	—	19.5%

2020 Year-End Financials

Debt ratio: 31.3%
Return on equity: 4.3%
Cash ($ mil.): 7.9
Current ratio: 0.43
Long-term debt ($ mil.): 1,218.3

No. of shares (mil.): 60.0
Dividends
　Yield: 3.6%
　Payout: 138.2%
Market value ($ mil.): 3,996.0

	STOCK PRICE ($) FY Close	P/E High/Low		Earnings	PER SHARE ($) Dividends	Book Value
12/20	66.58	45	28	1.74	2.41	42.06
12/19	70.17	40	29	1.93	2.28	37.07
12/18	59.12	35	25	1.78	2.16	32.92
12/17	51.44	25	21	2.08	2.03	29.31
12/16	46.05	26	16	1.97	1.92	26.10
Annual Growth	9.7%	—	—	(3.1%)	5.8%	12.7%

Air Lease Corp

Air Lease doesn't really lease air unless of course you include the air inside the cabins of its fleet of airplanes. An aircraft leasing company Air Lease buys new and used commercial aircraft from manufacturers and airlines and then leases to airline carriers in Europe the Asia-Pacific region and the Americas. It owns a fleet of almost 240 aircraft comprised of 181 single-aisle narrowbody jet aircraft 40 twin-aisle widebody jet aircraft and 19 turboprop aircraft. In addition to leasing Air Lease also offers fleet management services such as lease management and sales.

Geographic Reach

Air Lease is based in Los Angeles and has airline customers throughout the world. Europe accounted for 32% of its net sales in 2015. Other markets included China (22%); Asia excluding China (19%); Central America South America and Mexico (10%); the Middle East and Africa (8%); the US and Canada (5%); and the Pacific Australia and New Zealand (4%).

Sales and Marketing

Its customers have included Air Canada; Sunwing Airlines; WestJet; AeroMexico; Aeromar; Interjet; Volaris; Hawaiian Airlines; Southwest Airlines; Spirit Airlines; Sun Country; United Continental Holdings; Liat Airline; and Caribbean-Airlines.

Financial Performance

Air Lease has experienced explosive growth over the years with revenues reaching a record-setting $1.22 billion in 2015. Profits also remained consistent hovering around the $255 million mark for both 2014 and 2015. The static profits for 2015 was attributed to about $72 million it paid in litigation settlement expenses. The company's cash from operating activities has gradually increased the last five years climbing by 9% from 2014 to 2015.

The historic growth for 2015 was fueled by an 18% spike in the rental of flight equipment. This was aided by the delivery of 51 additional aircraft all of which were leased at the time of delivery. Air Lease also enjoyed major growth in the key markets of the Middle East and Africa (89%); the Pacific Australia and New Zealand (52%) and China (21%).

Strategy

Although the largest portion of its fleet is leased to customers in Western Europe Air Lease is setting its sights on markets in the Asia-Pacific region Eastern Europe South America and the Middle East where it predicts the travel industry will grow the fastest in coming years. It has also targeted carriers in stable but slower-growing travel markets such as North America.

One way Air Lease has achieved impressive revenue growth over the years is by adding to its fleet size. In 2015 it purchased and took delivery of 51 aircraft and sold 24 aircraft ending the year with a total of 240 owned aircraft. During 2015 it increased its managed fleet by 12 aircraft ending the year with 29 aircraft in its managed fleet portfolio. (The company typically sells aircraft that are currently operated by an airline with multiple years of lease term remaining on the contract.)

Company Background

Air Lease went public in 2011. Udvar-H ˇzy and other Air Lease used a significant portion of the proceeds raised to acquire additional aircraft and for general corporate purposes. With sufficient capital and financing already in place Air Lease has placed orders for some 150 new aircraft to be delivered by 2017. While most of its fleet will consist of Boeing and Airbus passenger airplanes the company has ordered similar aircraft manufactured by Embraer and turboprops from Avions de Transport R ©gional (ATR).

Udvar-H ˇzy had co-founded ILFC now one of the largest aircraft leasing companies in the industry in the 1970s. He stayed on after AIG bought ILFC in the 1990s and continued to head the company until 2010 when he retired in the wake of the ongoing financial trouble that hit AIG in 2008. Udvar-H ˇzy subsequently founded Air Lease with the help of institutional investors including some that were large shareholders prior to the IPO's filing (Ares Management which held an 11% stake; Leonard Green & Partners 11%; and Commonwealth Bank of Australia 10%). Udvar-H ˇzy maintained a 7% stake in Air Lease in 2013.

EXECUTIVES

Executive Vice President, Alex Khatibi
Executive Vice President Of Marketing And Commercial Affairs, Grant Levy, $820,000 total compensation
Chief Financial Officer, Executive Vice President, Gregory Willis, $666,667 total compensation
Executive Vice President, Managing Director Of Asia, Jie Chen, $930,000 total compensation
Executive Vice President - Aircraft Procurement And Specifications, John Poerschke
President, Chief Executive Officer And Director, John Plueger, $1,000,000 total compensation
Lead Independent Director, Robert Milton
Executive Chairman Of The Board, Steven Udvar-Hazy, $1,800,000 total compensation
Executive Vice President - Marketing, Kishore Korde
Executive Vice President, Chief Compliance Officer, General Counsel, Corporate Secretary, Carol Forsyte
Independent Director, Cheryl Krongard
Independent Director, Matthew Hart
Independent Director, Ian Saines
Independent Director, Susan McCaw
Independent Director, Yvette Clark
Auditors: KPMG LLP

LOCATIONS

HQ: Air Lease Corp
2000 Avenue of the Stars, Suite 1000N, Los Angeles, CA 90067
Phone: 310 553-0555
Web: www.airleasecorp.com

PRODUCTS/OPERATIONS

2015 Sales

	$ mil.	% of total
Rental of flight equipment	1,174.5	96
Aircraft sales trading and other	48.3	4
Total	**1,222.8**	**100**

COMPETITORS

AIRCASTLE LIMITED	RENT-A-CENTER INC.
AQUADRILL CAPRICORN LTD.	SINGAPORE AIRLINES LIMITED
DELTA AIR LINES INC.	UNITED AIRLINES
FLYBE GROUP LIMITED	HOLDINGS INC.
H&E EQUIPMENT SERVICES CORPORATION INC.	WINMARK
	WIZZ AIR HOLDINGS PLC

HISTORICAL FINANCIALS

Company Type: Public

Income Statement

FYE: December 31

	REVENUE ($ mil.)	NET INCOME ($ mil.)	NET PROFIT MARGIN	EMPLOYEES
12/21	2,088.3	436.6	20.9%	129
12/20	2,015.4	516.2	25.6%	120
12/19	2,016.9	587.1	29.1%	117
12/18	1,679.7	510.8	30.4%	97
12/17	1,516.3	756.1	49.9%	87
Annual Growth	8.3%	(12.8%)	—	10.3%

2021 Year-End Financials

Debt ratio: 63.1%
Return on equity: 6.6%
Cash ($ mil.): 1,086.5
Current ratio: 1.47
Long-term debt ($ mil.): 17,022.4

No. of shares (mil.): 113.9
Dividends
　Yield: 1.5%
　Payout: 20.4%
Market value ($ mil.): 5,042.0

	STOCK PRICE ($) FY Close	P/E High/Low		Earnings	PER SHARE ($) Dividends	Book Value
12/21	44.23	15	10	3.57	0.67	61.49
12/20	44.42	11	2	4.39	0.61	53.33
12/19	47.52	9	6	5.09	0.54	49.61
12/18	30.21	10	6	4.60	0.43	43.32
12/17	48.09	7	5	6.82	0.33	39.83
Annual Growth	(2.1%)	—	—	(14.9%)	19.6%	11.5%

Air Transport Services Group, Inc.

Air Transport Services Group (ATSG) leases aircraft and provides airline operations ground handling services aircraft modification and maintenance services and other support services to the air transportation and logistics industries. It is a leading provider of aircraft leasing and air cargo transportation services in the United States and internationally. In addition it is a provider of passenger charter service to the United States Department of Defense ("DoD"). The company has segments ACMI Services provides aircraft crew maintenance and insurance operations to the company's customers DHL and the US military through airline subsidiaries Ohio-based ABX Air Inc. and Arkansas-based ATI. ATSG's Cargo Aircraft Management (CAM) subsidiary leases Boeing 777 767 and 757 aircraft and aircraft engines.. The company was founded in 1980.

Operations

The company has two reportable segments: ACMI Services (nearly 65%) which includes the airlines' operations and "CAM" (more than 15% of the total sales) which includes the cargo and passenger transportation operations of the three airlines.

CAM leases aircraft to ATSG's airlines and to external customers including DHL and ASI usually under multi-year contracts with a schedule of fixed monthly payments. In addition CAM monitors the customer's business and financial status throughout the term of the lease. While ACMI Services consists of the operations of the company's three airline subsidiaries. Through the airlines the company provides airlift operations to DHL ASI the DoD and other transportation customers. A typical operating agreement requires the airline to supply at a specific rate per block hour and/or per month a combination of aircraft crew maintenance and insurance for specified transportation operations. Moreover it offers ACMI (airline provides the aircraft flight crews aircraft maintenance) CMI (customer is responsible for providing the aircraft) and Charter (airline is responsible for providing full service).

Geographic Reach

Based in Ohio the company has its presence in Illinois Florida and Oklahoma.

Sales and Marketing

The business development and marketing activities of its operating subsidiaries are supported by its Airborne Global Solutions Inc. (AGS). ATSG's long-standing strategic customer relationships with Amazon DHL and the DoD in addition to numerous other companies and government agencies that rely on aircraft services in their operations. The DoD accounts for around 30% of sales Amazon with some 30% and DHL with over 10%.

Financial Performance

External customer revenues from continuing operations increased by $118.4 million or 8% to $1.6 billion during 2020 compared to 2019. Customer revenues increased in 2020 for contracted airline services charter flights aircraft leasing and aviation fuel sales compared to the previous year.

The consolidated net earnings from continuing operations were $25.1 million for 2020 compared to $60.0 million for 2019 and $67.9 million for 2018.

Cash held by the company at the end of fiscal 2020 decreased to $39.7 million. Cash provided by operations was $512.3 million while cash used for investing and financing activities were $499.2 million and $19.6 million respectively. Main uses of cash were expenditures for property and equipment; and principal payments on long term obligations.

Strategy

The company's strategy targets opportunities primarily for medium range and medium capacity airlift by investing in the acquisition of used pas-

senger aircraft. ATSG converts most of these aircraft to a freighter configuration where upon the company leases the converted freighters to customers for operations in specific networks and regional geographies. ASTG manages the conversion of passenger aircraft into freighters and brings freighter aircraft to market leveraging its decades of experience as an airline. As a result the aircraft can be deployed into regional markets more economically than larger capacity aircraft newly built aircraft or other competing alternatives. The company customizes the interiors of its passenger aircraft for the DoD and commercial customers. In 2017 ATSG launched a joint venture to convert Airbus A321 passenger aircraft into freighters which is intended to further support its ability to meet the growing demand worldwide for narrow body air freighters. The company modifies its level of investment in growth assets based on its perception of strength in market demand.

Company Background

ATSG was formed as a holding company in late 2007 from the reorganization of ABX.

EXECUTIVES

Chairman Of The Board, Joseph Hete, $430,769 total compensation
Chief Financial Officer, Quint Turner, $464,231 total compensation
Senior Vice President, Corporate General Counsel, Secretary And Chief Legal Officer, W. Joseph Payne, $422,885 total compensation
Independent Director, Richard Baudouin
Chief Commercial Officer, Michael Berger, $386,154 total compensation
Independent Director, Raymond Johns
Independent Director, Laura Peterson
Chief Operating Officer, Edward Koharik, $427,885 total compensation
Independent Director, Phyllis Campbell
Independent Director, Paul Williams
Independent Director, J. Christopher Teets
Vice President - Government Programs, Trisha Frank
President, Chief Executive Officer, Director, Richard Corrado, $650,482 total compensation
Auditors: DELOITTE & TOUCHE LLP

LOCATIONS

HQ: Air Transport Services Group, Inc.
145 Hunter Drive, Wilmington, OH 45177
Phone: 937 382-5591
Web: www.atsginc.com

PRODUCTS/OPERATIONS

2014 Sales

	$ mil.	% of total
ACMI Services	439.9	59
CAM	166.3	22
Other	142.3	19
Adjustments	(158.9)	-
Total	**589.6**	**100**

Services

Aircraft leasing
ACMI services
Support services

COMPETITORS

AAR CORP.	Icelandair ehf.
ASTAR USA LLC	KALITTA AIR L.L.C.
ATLAS AIR WORLDWIDE HOLDINGS INC.	T AIR INC
	THE BOEING COMPANY

AerCap Holdings N.V.
Flugfelagid Atlanta ehf.

HISTORICAL FINANCIALS

Company Type: Public

Income Statement				FYE: December 31
	REVENUE ($ mil.)	NET INCOME ($ mil.)	NET PROFIT MARGIN	EMPLOYEES
12/20	1,570.5	32.1	2.0%	5,305
12/19	1,452.1	61.2	4.2%	4,380
12/18	892.3	69.2	7.8%	3,830
12/17	1,068.2	18.5	1.7%	3,010
12/16	768.8	23.4	3.1%	3,230
Annual Growth	19.6%	8.1%	—	13.2%

2020 Year-End Financials

Debt ratio: 49.2%   No. of shares (mil.): 59.5
Return on equity: 4.8%   Dividends
Cash ($ mil.): 39.7   Yield: —
Current ratio: 0.90   Payout: —
Long-term debt ($ mil.): 1,465.3   Market value ($ mil.): 1,867.0

	STOCK PRICE ($) FY Close	P/E High/Low		PER SHARE ($) Earnings	Dividends	Book Value
12/20	31.34	59 26		0.54	0.00	14.36
12/19	23.46	25 19		0.79	0.00	7.76
12/18	22.81	23 15		0.91	0.00	7.38
12/17	23.14	82 48		0.31	0.00	6.69
12/16	15.96	45 24		0.37	0.00	5.58
Annual Growth	18.4%	— —		9.9%	—	26.7%

Akamai Technologies Inc

Akamai Technologies provides solutions for securing and delivering content and business applications over the internet. The company's cloud services help its customers ? corporations and government agencies ? deliver digital content over the internet at optimal speeds and security. It also offers applications that supply network data feeds and website analytics to customers. With its software working from a network of more than 325000 servers in some 130 countries Akamai analyzes and manages web traffic transmitting content from servers that are geographically closest to end users. Customers include Toshiba the Coca-Cola Company and PayPal. About 55% of the company's total revenue comes from US.

Operations

At the heart of Akamai business is its Intelligent Edge Platform which connects nearly 1400 networks ranging from large backbone network providers to medium and small internet service providers to cable modem and satellite providers to universities and other networks.

Akamai offers products and services that include cloud and enterprise security web and mobile performance media delivery edge compute carrier and services and support.

The company reports revenue in two divisions according to the customers they serve. The Web

Division accounts for more than 50% of revenue and the Media Delivery Solutions account for about 50% of revenue.

Geographic Reach

Akamai is based in Cambridge Massachusetts and has several other sites in the US. Overseas the company has operations in Bangalore India and Krakow Poland.

The share of international revenue has grown to about 40% of Akamai's revenue with about 60% from US customers.

Sales and Marketing

Akamai sells its products through a direct sales force as well as channel partners such as AT&T IBM Orange Business Services Deutsche Telecom and Spain's top telco Telefonica. It also does business with public sector customers.

Other Akamai customers include Autodesk eBay Electronic Arts FedEx Honda Rabobank Spotify Toshiba the US Department of Labor the US Department of State the US Department of Transportation and the US Department of the Treasury the US Census Bureau and the US Department of Defense.

Financial Performance

In 2020 Akamai's revenue increased by 11% to $3.2 billion from $2.9 billion in 2019. The increase in its revenue in 2020 as compared to 2019 was primarily the result of higher media traffic volumes due in part to behavioral changes prompted by the COVID-19 pandemic and continued strong growth in sales of its Cloud Security Solutions.

Net income in 2020 increased to $557.1 million from $478.0 million in 2019.

Cash held by the company at the end of fiscal 2020 decreased to $353.5 million. Operating activities provided $1.2 billion while investing and financing activities used $1.0 billion and $223.6 million respectively. Main cash uses were Purchases of short-and long-term marketable securities and Repurchases of common stock.

Strategy

Akamai's strategy is to meet the needs of this transformation by offering security performance and delivery solutions that give its customers the competitive edge they need. The Akamai Intelligent Edge Platform is central to its approach; positioning the company at the edge of the internet for more than 20 years. Akamai's platform is deployed across approximately 4100 locations around the world tied together with sophisticated software and algorithms. Through this uniquely pervasive presence at the edge Akamai brings applications experiences and business decisions closer to users ? and helps keep attacks and threats away. The company believes the strategic proximity enabled by this distributed approach makes Akamai well situated to empower its customers to cost-effectively deliver superior user experiences that are interactive rich and secure.

Mergers and Acquisitions

In early 2021 Akamai acquired Montreal-based Inverse for approximately $20 million. Inverse provides a robust data repository and world class algorithms capable of identifying an expansive universe of IoT mobile and other device types. The acquisition is intended to enhance Akamai's enterprise security capabilities and expand its portfolio of zero trust and secure access service edge solutions for IoT.

In late 2020 Akamai acquired Asavie whose global platform manages the security performance and access policies for mobile and internet-connected devices for $155.0 million in cash. Asavie's mobile IoT (internet of things) and security solutions will become part of Akamai's Security and Personalization Services (SPS) product line sold to carrier partners that embed the solution within the technology bundle sold to their subscribers.

In early 2020 Akamai closed an asset purchase transaction with Palo Alto California-based Instart to acquire customer contracts and intellectual property (IP) for $36.4 million in cash. Akamai intends to expeditiously transition the acquired customers to Akamai's platform. The acquired IP is expected to benefit the development of Akamai's page integrity solution.

Company Background

Tom Leighton a mathematics professor at MIT developed algorithms to help move traffic in the early days o the World Wide Web. In 1997 Leighton and his partners entered an entrepreneurship contest at MIT and finished in the top six. In 1998 they incorporated Akamai licensing intellectual property from MIT. Most of the company's early employees were students who had worked on the project at MIT.

EXECUTIVES

Independent Director, Monte Ford
Independent Director, Jonathan Miller
Independent Director, Daniel Hesse
Chief Executive Officer, Principal Executive Officer, Director, F. Thomson Leighton, $1 total compensation
Executive Vice President And Chief Technology Officer, Robert Blumofe, $505,000 total compensation
Chief Operating Officer, General Manager - Edge Technology Division, Adam Karon, $475,000 total compensation
Chief Financial Officer, Executive Vice President, Edward McGowan, $462,308 total compensation
Executive Vice President, General Counsel, Corporate Secretary, Aaron Ahola
Executive Vice President - Global Sales, Paul Joseph
Principal Accounting Officer, Laura Howell
Executive Vice President, Chief Marketing Officer, Kim Salem-Jackson
Executive Vice President, General Manager Of The Security Technology Group, Mani Sundaram
Independent Director, William Wagner
Independent Director, Peter Killalea
Chief Human Resource Officer, Executive Vice President, Anthony Williams
Independent Director, Madhu Ranganathan
Independent Director, Marianne Brown
Independent Director, Sharon Bowen
Chief Information Officer, Kate Prouty
Auditors: PricewaterhouseCoopers LLP

LOCATIONS

HQ: Akamai Technologies Inc
145 Broadway, Cambridge, MA 02142
Phone: 617 444-3000   **Fax:** 617 444-3001
Web: www.akamai.com

PRODUCTS/OPERATIONS

2018 Sales

	$ mil.	% of total
Web Division	1,446.1	53
Media Delivery Solutions	1,268.4	47
Total	**2,714.5**	**100**

PRODUCTS

Security
Media Delivery
Network Operator
Services
Web Performance

COMPETITORS

ALTERYX INC.	MCAFEE LLC
BROADSOFT INC.	Open Text Corporation
CA INC.	PROOFPOINT INC.
CIENA CORPORATION	RACKSPACE TECHNOLOGY
CISCO SYSTEMS INC.	GLOBAL INC.
EXTREME NETWORKS INC.	TENABLE INC.
FIVE9 INC.	

HISTORICAL FINANCIALS

Company Type: Public

Income Statement | | | | FYE: December 31

	REVENUE ($ mil.)	NET INCOME ($ mil.)	NET PROFIT MARGIN	EMPLOYEES
12/20	3,198.1	557.0	17.4%	8,368
12/19	2,893.6	478.0	16.5%	7,724
12/18	2,714.4	298.3	11.0%	7,519
12/17	2,503.0	218.3	8.7%	7,650
12/16	2,340.0	316.1	13.5%	6,490
Annual Growth	8.1%	15.2%	—	6.6%

2020 Year-End Financials

Debt ratio: 24.5%	No. of shares (mil.): 162.7
Return on equity: 14.0%	Dividends
Cash ($ mil.): 352.9	Yield: —
Current ratio: 2.54	Payout: —
Long-term debt ($ mil.): 1,906.7	Market value ($ mil.): 17,083.0

	STOCK PRICE ($) FY Close	P/E High/Low		PER SHARE ($) Earnings	Dividends	Book Value
12/20	104.99	35	23	3.37	0.00	26.13
12/19	86.38	31	20	2.90	0.00	22.58
12/18	61.08	46	33	1.76	0.00	19.59
12/17	65.04	56	35	1.26	0.00	19.49
12/16	66.68	39	22	1.79	0.00	18.61
Annual Growth	12.0%	—	—	17.1%	—	8.9%

Alamo Group, Inc.

Alamo Group is a leader in the design and manufacture of high quality agricultural equipment and infrastructure maintenance equipment for governmental and industrial use. Its branded lines Alamo Industrial and Tiger hydraulically powered tractor-mounted mowers serve US government agencies. Rhino Products and M&W Gear subsidiaries sell rotary cutters and other equipment to farmers for pasture upkeep. UK McConnel and Bomford and France's S.M.A. subsidiaries market vegetation maintenance equipment such as hydraulic boom-mounted hedge and grass mowers. The company generates majority of revenue domestically.

Operations

Alamo has two reportable segments: the Industrial Division and the Agricultural Division.

Industrial Division which generates about 70% of its total revenue is comprised of brands including Gradall VacAll Super Products Rivard Morbank

Tenco and RPM Wausau Everest Henke H.P. Fairfield Schwarze ODB Night-Hawk and Dutch Power; while Agricultural Division which comprised of brands including Bush Hog Schulte Dixie Chopper McConnel Bomford Rousseau SMA Forges Gorce and Herder generates around 30% portion of revenue.

Overall the company produces around 75% of total revenue from sales its wholegoods lines followed by sales of replacement parts which accounts for nearly 20% of total revenue.

Geographic Reach

Alamo operates over 25 plants in North America South America Europe and Australia. The US generates about 75% of its sales. Other major markets include France (over 5%) the UK (approximately 5%) Canada (some 5%) and Australia. The company is headquartered in Seguin Texas.

Sales and Marketing

Alamo sells its products primarily through a network of independent dealers and distributors to governmental end-users related independent contractors as well as to the agricultural and commercial turf markets.

The company's advertising and marketing expense for fiscal years 2020 2019 and 2018 were approximately $10.1 million $12.2 million and $11.8 million respectively.

Financial Performance

Alamo's revenue has been rising in the last five years with an overall growth of 38% between 2016 and 2020.

The company's net sales increased by 4% from $1.1 billion in 2019 to $1.2 billion in 2020. The increase in net sales was due to the acquisitions of Morbark and Dutch Power in 2019 which was offset by market declines due to COVID-19.

The company's net income decreased by 10% or $6.3 million from $62.9 million in 2019 to $56.6 million in 2020. The decrease in net income was attributable to the COVID-19 pandemic which began to materially affect the company's operations in March 2020 and continued to negatively impact the company's overall financial performance during the year.

The company's cash and cash equivalents for the end of 2020 was $50.2 million. Operating activities generated $184.3 million while investing activities used $14.2 million mainly for capital expenditures. Financing activities used another $$164.2 million primarily for repayment on bank revolving credit facility.

Strategy

The company believes that within the US it is a leading supplier to governmental markets a leading supplier in the US agricultural market and one of the largest suppliers in the European market for its key niche product offerings. The company's products are sold through the company's various marketing organizations and extensive worldwide dealer and distributor networks under the Gradall VacAll Super Products Rivard Alamo Industrial Terrain King Tiger Herder Conver Roberine Votex Schwarze NiteHawk ODB Henke Tenco Wausau Everest H.P. Fairfield R.P.M. Tech Morbark Rayco Denis Cimaf Boxer Bush Hog Rhino Earthmaster RhinoAg Dixie Chopper Herschel Valu-Bilt CT Farm & Country Schulte Fieldquip Santa Izabel McConnel Bomford Spearhead Twose SMA Forges Gorce Faucheux Rousseau and trademarks (some with related designs) as well as other trademarks and trade names.

The company intends to grow internally and through the acquisition of businesses and assets that will complement its current businesses.

EXECUTIVES

Executive Vice President, Chief Sustainability Officer, Dan Malone, $357,385 total compensation
Executive Vice President - Vegetation Management Division, Richard Raborn, $389,761 total compensation
Vice President, General Counsel, Secretary, Edward Rizzuti, $307,308 total compensation
Independent Director, Tracy Jokinen
Chief Financial Officer, Executive Vice President, Richard Wehrle, $160,746 total compensation
Chairman Of The Board, Roderick Baty
President, Chief Executive Officer And Director, Jeffery Leonard, $445,287 total compensation
Independent Director, Robert Bauer
Independent Director, Eric Etchart
Independent Director, Richard Parod
Vice President - Human Resources, Janet Pollock
Vice President - Internal Audit, Lori Sullivan
Independent Director, Lorie Tekorius
Executive Vice President - Industrial Equipment Division, Michael Haberman
Independent Director, Nina Grooms
Auditors: KPMG LLP

LOCATIONS

HQ: Alamo Group, Inc.
 1627 East Walnut, Seguin, TX 78155
Phone: 830 379-1480   **Fax:** 830 372-9683
Web: www.alamo-group.com

PRODUCTS/OPERATIONS

2014 Sales

	$ mil.	% of total
North American		
Industrial	436.0	52
Agricultural	214.4	26
European	188.7	22
Total	**839.1**	**100**

Selected Products

Boom mowers/power arms
Excavators
Flail mowers
Loader/backhoes
Rotary mowers
Snow removal equipment
Street sweepers
Vacuum trucks

COMPETITORS

ACCO BRANDS CORPORATION
AGCO CORPORATION
Buhler Industries Inc
DEERE & COMPANY
DOUGLAS DYNAMICS INC.
Finning International Inc
HITACHI CONSTRUCTION MACHINERY CO. LTD.
KOBELCO CONSTRUCTION MACHINERY AMERICA LLC
KUBOTA CORPORATION
LINDSAY CORPORATION
MERITOR INC.
METALCRAFT OF MAYVILLE INC.
OXBO INTERNATIONAL CORPORATION
SUMITOMO HEAVY INDUSTRIES LTD.
Sany Heavy Industry Co.Ltd
TENNECO INC.
WELBILT INC.

HISTORICAL FINANCIALS

Company Type: Public

Income Statement

FYE: December 31

	REVENUE ($ mil.)	NET INCOME ($ mil.)	NET PROFIT MARGIN	EMPLOYEES
12/20	1,163.4	56.6	4.9%	3,990
12/19	1,119.1	62.9	5.6%	4,270
12/18	1,008.8	73.4	7.3%	3,470
12/17	912.3	44.3	4.9%	3,280
12/16	844.7	40.0	4.7%	2,900
Annual Growth	**8.3%**	**9.0%**	**—**	**8.3%**

2020 Year-End Financials

Debt ratio: 25.7%
Return on equity: 9.4%
Cash ($ mil.): 50.2
Current ratio: 3.20
Long-term debt ($ mil.): 270.3
No. of shares (mil.): 11.8
Dividends
 Yield: 0.3%
 Payout: 10.8%
Market value ($ mil.): 1,629.0

	STOCK PRICE ($) FY Close	P/E High/Low	PER SHARE ($)		
			Earnings	Dividends	Book Value
12/20	137.95	30 16	4.78	0.52	52.98
12/19	125.55	24 14	5.33	0.48	48.48
12/18	77.32	19 12	6.25	0.44	43.50
12/17	112.87	31 19	3.79	0.40	38.79
12/16	76.10	22 14	3.46	0.36	33.95
Annual Growth	**16.0%**	**— —**	**8.4%**	**9.6%**	**11.8%**

Alarm.com Holdings Inc

Auditors: PricewaterhouseCoopers LLP

LOCATIONS

HQ: Alarm.com Holdings Inc
 8281 Greensboro Drive, Suite 100, Tysons, VA 22102
Phone: 877 389-4033
Web: www.alarm.com

HISTORICAL FINANCIALS

Company Type: Public

Income Statement

FYE: December 31

	REVENUE ($ mil.)	NET INCOME ($ mil.)	NET PROFIT MARGIN	EMPLOYEES
12/20	618.0	77.8	12.6%	1,404
12/19	502.3	53.5	10.7%	1,160
12/18	420.4	21.5	5.1%	884
12/17	338.9	29.2	8.6%	784
12/16	261.1	10.1	3.9%	607
Annual Growth	**24.0%**	**66.4%**	**—**	**23.3%**

2020 Year-End Financials

Debt ratio: 15.0%
Return on equity: 18.8%
Cash ($ mil.): 253.4
Current ratio: 4.40
Long-term debt ($ mil.): 110.0
No. of shares (mil.): 49.4
Dividends
 Yield: —
 Payout: —
Market value ($ mil.): 5,119.0

HOOVER'S HANDBOOK OF EMERGING COMPANIES 2022

STOCK PRICE ($) FY Close	P/E High/Low	PER SHARE ($) Earnings	Dividends	Book Value
12/20	103.45	65 22	1.53	0.00	9.45
12/19	42.97	64 37	1.06	0.00	7.30
12/18	51.87	130 78	0.43	0.00	5.77
12/17	37.75	78 43	0.59	0.00	4.93
12/16	27.83	150 65	0.21	0.00	4.14
Annual Growth 38.9%	—	64.3%	—	22.9%

Alerus Financial Corp

EXECUTIVES

Chb-Pres-Ceo, Randy L Newman
Exec V Pres-Cfo, Katie A Lorenson
Exec V Pres-Csso, Ann M McConn
Exec V Pres-Cro, Karin M Taylor
Exec V Pres-Cro, Ryan S Goldberg
Scs Specialist, Robin Wirth
Education Consultant, Anne Guerriero
Account Manager, Grant Benson
Client Manager, Jamie Lovering
Relationship Manager, Jessica Hoppe
Marketing Research Analyst, Lexie Bakken
Auditors: CliftonLarsonAllen LLP

LOCATIONS

HQ: Alerus Financial Corp
  401 Demers Avenue, Grand Forks, ND 58201
Phone: 701 795-3200   **Fax:** 701 795-3378
Web: www.alerus.com

HISTORICAL FINANCIALS

Company Type: Public

Income Statement   FYE: December 31

	ASSETS ($ mil.)	NET INCOME ($ mil.)	INCOME AS % OF ASSETS	EMPLOYEES
12/20	3,013.7	44.6	1.5%	851
12/19	2,356.8	29.5	1.3%	789
12/18	2,179.0	25.8	1.2%	0
12/17	2,137.0	15.4	0.7%	0
12/16	2,050.5	14.0	0.7%	0
Annual Growth 10.1%	33.6%	—	—

2020 Year-End Financials

Return on assets: 1.6%
Return on equity: 14.4%
Long-term debt ($ mil.): —
No. of shares (mil.): 17.1
Sales ($ mil): 245.4

Dividends
  Yield: 2.1%
  Payout: 25.4%
Market value ($ mil.): 469.0

STOCK PRICE ($) FY Close	P/E High/Low	PER SHARE ($) Earnings	Dividends	Book Value
12/20	27.37	11 6	2.52	0.60	19.28
12/19	22.85	12 10	1.91	0.57	16.76
12/18	19.25	14 10	1.84	0.53	14.30
12/17	20.45	18 15	1.10	0.48	13.18
12/16	17.00	19 16	1.00	0.44	12.47
Annual Growth 12.6%	— —	26.0%	8.1%	11.5%

Alexandria Real Estate Equities Inc

Alexandria Real Estate Equities owns develops and operates offices and labs to life science tenants including biotech and pharmaceutical companies universities research institutions medical office developers and government agencies. A real estate investment trust (REIT) Alexandria owns approximately 340 specialized properties with more than 35.1 million sq. ft. of rentable space in the US and Canada. Its portfolio is largely located in high-tech hotbeds such as Boston greater New York City the San Francisco Bay area San Diego Seattle and Research Triangle.

Operations
The company engaged in the business of providing space for lease to the life science technology and agtech industries. Its properties are similar in that they provide space for lease to the aforementioned industries consist of improvements that are generic and reusable are primarily located in AAA urban innovation cluster locations and have similar economic characteristics. Most of its revenues came from rentals.

Geographic Reach
The company has about 340 properties in North America containing approximately 35.1 million RSF of operating properties and development and redevelopment of new Class A properties (under construction) including about 40 properties that are held by consolidated real estate joint ventures and six properties that are held by unconsolidated real estate joint ventures. Greater Boston is the highest in terms of annual rental which accounts for more than 35%.

Its corporate headquarters is located in Pasadena California.

Sales and Marketing
Bristol-Myers Takeda Facebook Illumina and Sanofi are among the REIT's top largest tenants (though none account for more than 5% of its overall rental revenues). Public Biotechnology accounts for about 25% of the total company tenant mix followed by multinational pharmaceuticals Life Science Product and the rest.

Financial Performance
Alexandria's revenue has been rising in the last five years with an overall increase of $105% between 2016 and 2020. Its net income follows a similar pattern but had a minor dip in 2019.

The company in 2020 had a total revenue of $1.9 billion up 23% for the year ended December 31 2020 compared to $1.5 billion for the year ended December 31 2019. This was due to a higher income from rentals.

In 2020 the company had a net income of $827.2 million a 105% or $423.1 million increase compared to the previous year's net income of $404 million.

The company's cash at the end of 2020 was $597.7 million. Operating activities generated $882.5 million while investing activities used $3.3 billion primarily for purchases of real estate. Financing activities provided another $2.8 billion.

Strategy
The company's primary business objective is to maximize long-term asset value and shareholder returns based on a multifaceted platform of inter-nal and external growth. A key element of its strategy is its unique focus on Class A properties clustered in urban campuses located in AAA innovation cluster locations. These key urban campus locations are characterized by high barriers to entry for new landlords high barriers to exit for tenants and a limited supply of available space. They represent highly desirable locations for tenancy by life science technology and agtech entities because of their close proximity to concentrations of specialized skills knowledge institutions and related businesses.

Its strategy also includes drawing upon its deep and broad real estate life science technology and agtech relationships in order to identify and attract new and leading tenants and to source additional value-creation real estate.

EXECUTIVES

Chairman, Joel Marcus, $1,080,000 total compensation
Chief Development Officer, Vincent Ciruzzi, $530,000 total compensation
Independent Director, Richard Klein
President And Chief Financial Officer, Dean Shigenaga, $640,000 total compensation
Chief Executive Officer, Stephen Richardson, $675,000 total compensation
Co-chief Operating Officer And Regional Market Director – Maryland, Lawrence Diamond
Executive Vice President, Real Estate Legal Affairs, Gary Dean
Executive Vice President And Regional Market Director, New York City, John Cunningham, $525,000 total compensation
Executive Vice President And Regional Market Director, San Francisco, Terezia Nemeth
Co-chief Executive Officer And Co-chief Investment Officer, Peter Moglia, $675,000 total compensation
Independent Director, Maria Freire
Executive Vice President - Finance, Treasurer, Marc Binda
Co-chief Investment Officer And Regional Market Director, San Diego, Daniel Ryan, $635,000 total compensation
Chief Accounting Officer, Andres Gavinet
General Counsel And Secretary, Jackie Clem
Co-chief Operating Officer And Chief Strategic Transactions Officer, Joseph Hakman
Independent Director, Jennifer Goldstein
Executive Vice President, Regional Market Director, Greater Boston, Hunter Kass
Lead Independent Director, Steven Hash
Independent Director, Michael Woronoff
Auditors: Ernst & Young LLP

LOCATIONS

HQ: Alexandria Real Estate Equities Inc
  26 North Euclid Avenue, Pasadena, CA 91101
Phone: 626 578-0777
Web: www.are.com

PRODUCTS/OPERATIONS

2015 Sales

	$ mil.	% of total
Rental	608.8	72
Tenant recoveries	209.1	25
Other	25.6	3
Total	**843.5**	**100**

HOOVER'S HANDBOOK OF EMERGING COMPANIES 2022

2015 Client Tenant Mix by ABR

	% of total
Public Biotechnology	26
Multinational Pharmaceutical	22
Life Science Product Service and Device	22
Institutional	20
Private Biotechnology	7
Office & Tech Office	3
Total	**100**

COMPETITORS

APARTMENT INVESTMENT AND MANAGEMENT COMPANY
Allied Properties Real Estate Investment Trust
CAMDEN PROPERTY TRUST
CORESITE REALTY CORPORATION
COUSINS PROPERTIES INCORPORATED
DOUGLAS EMMETT INC.
DUKE REALTY CORPORATION
JBG SMITH PROPERTIES
PROLOGIS INC.
SAUL CENTERS INC.
UDR INC.
WHITESTONE REIT

HISTORICAL FINANCIALS

Company Type: Public

Income Statement — FYE: December 31

	REVENUE ($ mil.)	NET INCOME ($ mil.)	NET PROFIT MARGIN	EMPLOYEES
12/21	2,114.1	571.2	27.0%	559
12/20	1,885.6	770.9	40.9%	470
12/19	1,531.3	363.1	23.7%	439
12/18	1,327.4	379.3	28.6%	386
12/17	1,128.1	169.0	15.0%	323
Annual Growth	17.0%	35.6%	—	14.7%

2021 Year-End Financials

Debt ratio: 29.0%
Return on equity: 4.0%
Cash ($ mil.): 415.2
Current ratio: 0.18
Long-term debt ($ mil.): 8,791.8
No. of shares (mil.): 158.0
Dividends
Yield: 2.0%
Payout: 66.6%
Market value ($ mil.): 35,237.0

	STOCK PRICE ($) FY Close	P/E High/Low	PER SHARE ($) Earnings	Dividends	Book Value
12/21	222.96	58 41	3.82	4.48	102.44
12/20	178.22	29 19	6.01	4.24	85.78
12/19	161.58	52 36	3.12	4.00	73.39
12/18	115.24	37 31	3.52	3.73	66.14
12/17	130.59	84 68	1.58	3.45	59.63
Annual Growth	14.3%	—	24.7%	6.7%	14.5%

Align Technology Inc

Align Technology is a global medical device company engaged in the design manufacture and marketing of Invisalign clear aligners and iTero intraoral scanners and services for dentistry and exocad computer-aided design and computer-aided manufacturing (CAD/CAM) software for dental laboratories and dental practitioners. Its products are intended primarily for the treatment of malocclusion or the misalignment of teeth and are designed to help dental professionals achieve the clinical outcomes that they expect and the results patients' desire. To date over 9.6 million people worldwide have been treated with Invisalign System. Most of the company's revenues come from the US.

Operations

Align operates into two reportable segments: Clear Aligner segment and Imaging Systems and CAD/CAM services (Systems and Services) segment. The Systems and Services segment was formerly known as the Scanner and Services segment prior to its acquisition of exocad in early 2020.

Clear Aligner segment consists of Comprehensive Products (Invisalign Comprehensive and Invisalign First) Non-Comprehensive Products (Invisalign Moderate Lite and Express packages and Invisalign Go) and Non-Case (Vivera retainers along with its training and ancillary products for treating malocclusion). The segment accounts for about 85% of total revenue.

The Systems and Services segment consists of its iTero intraoral scanning systems which includes a single hardware platform and restorative or orthodontic software options OrthoCAD services and ancillary products as well as exocad's CAD/CAM software solution that integrates workflows to dental labs and dental practices. The segment generates 15% of total revenue.

In 2020 Align trained about 21100 new Invisalign doctors of which about 12025 were trained in the International region and roughly 9100 were trained in the Americas region.

Geographic Reach

San Jose California-based Align has North American regional headquarters in Raleigh North Carolina; European regional headquarters in Rotkreuz Switzerland; and Asia Pacific regional headquarters in Singapore.

Manufacturing facilities are located in Juarez Mexico and Ziyang China where it conducts aligner fabrication distributes and repairs scanners and performs CAD/CAM services. In addition Align produces its handheld intraoral scanner wand perform final scanner assembly and repair its scanners at its facilities in Or Yehuda Israel and Ziyang China. It also perform digital treatment planning and interpretation for restorative cases based on digital scans generated by its iTerointraoral scanners. The digital treatment planning facilities are located worldwide including in Costa Rica China and other in ternational locations.

About 45% of revenues come from the US but the company continues to focus on increasing sales to the Asia Pacific (APAC) and Europe Middle East Africa (EMEA) markets.

Sales and Marketing

Align sells the majority of its products directly through a dedicated and specialized sales force to its customers: orthodontists general practitioner dentists (GPs) restorative and aesthetic dentists including prosthodontists periodontists and oral surgeons and dental laboratories. It also sells through non-inventory carrying sales agents and distributors in certain countries. In addition Align sells directly to Dental Support Organizations (DSOs) who contract with dental practices to provide critical business management and support including non-clinical operations and it sell products used by dental laboratories who manufacture or customize a variety of products used by licensed dentists to provide oral health care.

Because the teenage and younger market makes up to about 75% of the approximately 15 million total orthodontic case starts each year the company continues to target teenage and younger patients through sales and marketing programs. Align has approximately 102000 active Invisalign trained doctors which the company defines as having submitted at least one case in the prior 12-month period.

The cost of advertising and media for 2020 2019 and 2018 was $161.0 million $119.1 million and $88.4 million respectively.

Financial Performance

The company's revenue for fiscal 2020 increased by 3% to $2.5 billion compared from the prior year with $2.4 billion. The increase was primarily as a result of higher Clear Aligner volumes in the International region partially offset by lower average selling prices (ASP) in the Americas region and lower Systems and Services net revenues in most regions.

Net income for fiscal 2020 increased to $1.8 billion compared from the prior year with $442.8 million.

Cash held by the company at the end of fiscal 2020 increased to $961.5 million. Cash provided by operations and financing activities were $662.2 million and $10.5 million respectively. Cash used by investing activities was $231.5 million mainly for acquisition.

Strategy

Align's goal remains to establish the Invisalign System as the standard method for treating malocclusion and its intraoral scanning platform as the preferred scanning protocol for digital dental scans. The company's technology and innovations are designed to meet the demands of today's patients with treatment options that are convenient comfortable affordable while helping to improve overall oral health. Align strive to help its doctors move their practices forward by connecting them with new patients providing digital solutions to help increase practice efficiency and helping them deliver the best possible treatment outcomes and experiences to millions of people around the world. The company achieve this by focusing on and executing to its strategic growth drivers: International Expansion; GP Adoption; Patient Demand & Conversion; and Orthodontist Utilization.

Mergers and Acquisitions

In early 2020 Align Technology completed the acquisition of privately held exocad Global Holdings GmbH (exocad) for approximately ?376 million in cash. exocad is a global leader in the dental CAD/CAM software market and offers fully integrated workflows to dental labs and dental practices via a broad customer base of partners and resellers in over 150 countries. The acquisition of exocad broadens Align's digital platform reach by adding technology that addresses restorative needs in an end-to-end digital platform workflow to facilitate ortho-restorative and comprehensive dentistry.

Company Background

In 1997 five employees in a small duplex in Redwood City California founded Align Technology with a single concept in mind ? how to leverage technology to straighten teeth. In 1999 Align Technology introduced the Invisalign system and sublaunched a large US national advertising campaign. The company went public in 2001 at which point it had manufactured one million unique aligners and trained more than ten thousand doctors.

EXECUTIVES

Senior Vice President, Managing Director, Americas Region, Simon Beard, $517,692 total compensation
Independent Director, Susan Siegel
Independent Director, Kevin Dallas
Senior Vice President, Managing Director - Itero Scanner And Services Business, Yuval Shaked
Independent Director, Anne Myong
Senior Vice President, Chief Legal And Regulatory Officer, Julie Coletti
Senior Vice President, Chief Technology Officer, Zelko Relic, $423,077 total compensation
President, Chief Executive Officer And Director, Joseph Hogan, $1,171,539 total compensation
Senior Vice President Of Global Human Resources, Stuart Hockridge, $375,308 total compensation
Chief Financial Officer, Senior Vice President, Global Finance, John Morici, $536,923 total compensation
Chief Product And Marketing Officer, And Svp And Managing Director, Asia Pacific Region, Raj Pudipeddi, $488,077 total compensation
Senior Vice President, Managing Director, Emea, Markus Sebastian
Senior Vice President - Global Operations, Emory Wright, $463,077 total compensation
Independent Director, Gregory Santora
Senior Vice President And Managing Director, Customer Success, Jennifer Olson
Senior Vice President, Chief Digital Officer, Sreelakshmi Kolli
Independent Chairman Of The Board, Charles Larkin
Senior Vice President - Product Research & Development, Srini Kaza
Auditors: PricewaterhouseCoopers LLP

LOCATIONS

HQ: Align Technology Inc
410 North Scottsdale Road, Suite 1300, Tempe, AZ 85281
Phone: 602 742-2000
Web: www.aligntech.com

PRODUCTS/OPERATIONS

2017 Sales by Segment

	$ mil.	% of total
Clear Align	1,309.3	89
Scanner	164.1	11
Total	**1,473.4**	**100**

COMPETITORS

ACCURAY INCORPORATED
GLOBUS MEDICAL INC.
HANGER INC.
HU-FRIEDY MFG. CO. LLC
MASIMO CORPORATION
MILESTONE SCIENTIFIC INC. HOLDINGS
NATIONAL DENTEX LLC
NUVASIVE INC.
ORMCO CORPORATION
PHILIPS ORAL HEALTHCARE LLC
SYBRON DENTAL SPECIALTIES INC.
ZIMMER BIOMET INC.

HISTORICAL FINANCIALS
Company Type: Public

Income Statement
FYE: December 31

	REVENUE ($ mil.)	NET INCOME ($ mil.)	NET PROFIT MARGIN	EMPLOYEES
12/20	2,471.9	1,775.8	71.8%	18,070
12/19	2,406.8	442.7	18.4%	14,530
12/18	1,966.4	400.2	20.4%	11,660
12/17	1,473.4	231.4	15.7%	8,715
12/16	1,079.8	189.6	17.6%	6,060
Annual Growth	**23.0%**	**74.9%**	**—**	**31.4%**

2020 Year-End Financials

Debt ratio: —
Return on equity: 77.3%
Cash ($ mil.): 960.8
Current ratio: 1.40
Long-term debt ($ mil.): —
No. of shares (mil.): 78.8
Dividends
  Yield: —
  Payout: —
Market value ($ mil.): 42,141.0

	STOCK PRICE ($) FY Close	P/E High/Low	Earnings	Dividends	Book Value
12/20	534.38	24 6	22.41	0.00	41.01
12/19	279.04	59 31	5.53	0.00	17.16
12/18	209.43	79 39	4.92	0.00	15.70
12/17	222.19	91 31	2.83	0.00	14.37
12/16	96.13	42 25	2.33	0.00	12.51
Annual Growth	**53.5%**	**— —**	**76.1%**	**—**	**34.5%**

Allegiance Bancshares Inc

Auditors: Crowe LLP

LOCATIONS

HQ: Allegiance Bancshares Inc
8847 West Sam Houston Parkway, N., Suite 200, Houston, TX 77040
Phone: 281 894-3200
Web: www.allegiancebank.com

HISTORICAL FINANCIALS
Company Type: Public

Income Statement
FYE: December 31

	ASSETS ($ mil.)	NET INCOME ($ mil.)	INCOME AS % OF ASSETS	EMPLOYEES
12/20	6,050.1	45.5	0.8%	598
12/19	4,992.6	52.9	1.1%	588
12/18	4,655.2	37.3	0.8%	569
12/17	2,860.2	17.6	0.6%	375
12/16	2,450.9	22.8	0.9%	327
Annual Growth	**25.3%**	**18.8%**	**—**	**16.3%**

2020 Year-End Financials

Return on assets: 0.8%
Return on equity: 6.1%
Long-term debt ($ mil.): —
No. of shares (mil.): 20.2
Sales ($ mil): 249.9
Dividends
  Yield: 1.1%
  Payout: 19.0%
Market value ($ mil.): 690.0

	STOCK PRICE ($) FY Close	P/E High/Low	Earnings	Dividends	Book Value
12/20	34.13	17 10	2.22	0.40	37.54
12/19	37.60	16 12	2.47	0.00	34.59
12/18	32.37	19 12	2.37	0.00	32.04
12/17	37.65	30 23	1.31	0.00	23.20
12/16	36.15	21 9	1.75	0.00	21.59
Annual Growth	**(1.4%)**	**— —**	**6.1%**	**—**	**14.8%**

AllianceBernstein Holding LP

The raison d'etre of AllianceBernstein Holding is its more than 35% stake in investment manager AllianceBernstein. (French insurer AXA through its AXA Financial unit owns a majority of the subsidiary.) AllianceBernstein which has more than $420 million of client assets under management administers about 200 mutual funds invested in growth and value equities fixed-income securities and index and blended strategies. The subsidiary also offer separately managed accounts closed-end funds structured financial products and alternative investments such as hedge funds. It mainly serves institutional clients such as pension funds corporations and not-for-profits in addition to retail investors.

Auditors: PricewaterhouseCoopers LLP

LOCATIONS

HQ: AllianceBernstein Holding LP
501 Commerce Street, Nashville, TN 37203
Phone: 615 622-0000
Web: www.alliancebernstein.com

HISTORICAL FINANCIALS
Company Type: Public

Income Statement
FYE: December 31

	REVENUE ($ mil.)	NET INCOME ($ mil.)	NET PROFIT MARGIN	EMPLOYEES
12/21	416.3	385.8	92.7%	4,118
12/20	308.4	279.3	90.6%	3,929
12/19	266.2	238.5	89.6%	3,811
12/18	270.6	242.4	89.6%	3,641
12/17	232.3	207.4	89.3%	3,466
Annual Growth	**15.7%**	**16.8%**	**—**	**4.4%**

2021 Year-End Financials

Debt ratio: —
Return on equity: —
Cash ($ mil.): —
Current ratio: —
Long-term debt ($ mil.): —
No. of shares (mil.): 99.2
Dividends
  Yield: 7.3%
  Payout: 100.9%
Market value ($ mil.): 4,848.0

STOCK PRICE ($)		P/E		PER SHARE ($)		
	FY Close	High/Low		Earnings	Dividends	Book Value
12/21	48.84	15	9	3.88	3.58	16.34
12/20	33.77	12	5	2.88	2.79	16.32
12/19	30.26	13	11	2.49	2.32	15.81
12/18	27.32	12	9	2.50	2.88	15.42
12/17	25.05	12	9	2.19	2.13	16.00
Annual Growth	18.2%	—	—	15.4%	13.9%	0.5%

Allied Motion Technologies Inc

Allied Motion Technologies is a global company that designs manufactures and sells precision and specialty controlled motion components and systems. The company makes specialized brush and brushless DC (BLDC) motors and brushless drives used in broad range of industries. Its products are incorporated into a number of end products including high-definition printers scanners surgical tools and equipment surgical robots diagnostic equipment test equipment patient mobility and rehabilitation equipment hospital beds and mobile equipment carts. Allied Motion's target markets include vehicle aerospace and defense industrial and medical. The company was incorporated in 1962. The US was responsible for about 60% of the total sales.

Operations

The company operates in one segment for the manufacture and marketing of controlled motion products for OEM and end user applications. Its target markets are vehicle (nearly 30% of the total sales) industrial (some 30%) medical (nearly 25%) and aerospace and defense (around 10%).

For vehicles it focuses on electronic power steering and drive-by-wire applications to electrically replace or provide power-assist to a variety of mechanical linkages traction / drive systems and pumps automated and remotely guided power steering systems. It includes HVAC systems LPG and others. For medical it centers on surgical robots prosthetics electric powered surgical hand pieces programmable pumps to meter and administer infusions associated with chemotherapy pain control and antibiotics. In Aerospace & Defense it includes inertial guided missiles mid-range smart munitions systems weapons systems on armed personnel carriers unmanned vehicles security and access control camera systems door access control airport screening and scanning devices. Last is the Industrial. The products are used in factory automation specialty equipment material handling equipment commercial grade floor polishers and cleaners commercial building equipment such as welders cable pullers and assembly tools the handling inspection and testing of components and final products such as PCs gaming equipment and cell phone.

In general the company is known worldwide for expertise in electro-magnetic mechanical and electronic motion technology. The products include brush and brushless DC (BLDC) motors brushless servo and torque motors coreless DC motors integrated brushless motor-drives gearmotors gearing modular digital servo drives motion controllers incremental and absolute optical encoders active and passive filters for power quality and harmonic issues and other controlled motion-related products. In addition it operates Allied Motion Solution Centers that apply all Allied Motion products to create integrated controlled motion solutions for the customers. Allied Motion has Solution Centers in China Europe and North America that enable the design and sale of individual component products as well as integrated controlled motion systems that utilize multiple Allied Motion products.

Geographic Reach

The company manufactures its products in the US Canada China Germany Portugal Mexico Czech Republic the Netherlands and Sweden. The US accounts for nearly 60% sales followed by Europe with some 35% and Asia Pacific with over 5%.

The company is headquartered in Amherst New York.

Sales and Marketing

The company sells the products and solutions globally to a broad spectrum of customers through direct sales force and authorized manufacturers' representatives and distributors. The customers include end users and original equipment manufacturers (OEMs). The target markets include Vehicle Medical Aerospace & Defense (A&D) and Industrial.

Financial Performance

The company's revenue for fiscal 2020 increased to $366.7 million compared to $371.1 million in the prior year. Its market position in the Medical market combined with the acquisition of Dynamic Controls nearly offset reductions in the company's other served markets many of which were negatively impacted by the COVID-19 pandemic.

Net income for fiscal 2020 decreased by 20% to $13.6 million compared from the prior year with $17.0 million.

Cash held by the company at the end of fiscal 2020 $23.1 million. Cash provided by operations and financing activities were $24.8 million and $7.5 million respectively. Cash used for investing activities was $24.1 million mainly for consideration paid for acquisitions.

Strategy

The company's growth strategy is focused on becoming the controlled motion solution leader in its selected target markets by further developing its products and services platform to utilize multiple Allied Motion technologies to create increased value solutions for its customers. Its strategy further defines Allied Motion as being a "technology/know-how" driven company and to be successful the company continues to invest in its areas of excellence. Growth targets have been set for the company and it will align and focus its resources to meet those targets. First and foremost the company invests in its people as it believes that attracting and retaining the right people is the most important element in the strategy. The company will continue to invest in applied and design engineering resources which can be leveraged across the entire Allied organization.

One of the company's growth initiatives includes product line platform development to meet the emerging needs of its selected target markets. Platform development emphasizes a combination of technologies to create increased value solutions for customers. The emphasis on new opportunities has evolved from being an individual component provider to becoming a solutions provider whereby the new opportunities utilize multiple company technologies in a system solution approach. The company believes this approach will allow it to provide increased value to its customers and improved margins for the company. Its strong financial condition along with Allied Systematic Tools (AST) continuous improvement initiatives in quality delivery and cost allows for a positive outlook for the continued long-term growth of the company.

Mergers and Acquisitions

In early 2020 Allied Motion Technologies has acquired Dynamic Controls Group (Dynamic Controls) a wholly owned subsidiary of Invacare Corporation a market-leading designer and manufacturer of equipment for the medical mobility and rehabilitation markets based in New Zealand. With the acquisition of Dynamic Controls Allied continues to build out its ability to leverage controlled motion system solutions in a wide range of markets. Terms were not disclosed.

Company Background

Allied Motion was originally incorporated as a public company in 1962.

EXECUTIVES

Chairman, President, And Ceo, Richard Warzala, $570,833 total compensation
Vice President, Operational Excellence, Geoffery Rondeau
Senior Vice President & Group President, Robert Maida, $308,334 total compensation
Independent Director, Robert Engel
Independent Director, Steven Finch
Independent Director, Nicole Tzetzo
Vice President & Group President, Helmut Pirthauer, $285,373 total compensation
Vice President & Group President, Ashish Bendre, $390,993 total compensation
Chief Financial Officer & Senior Vice President, Michael Leach, $340,000 total compensation
Auditors: DELOITTE & TOUCHE LLP

LOCATIONS

HQ: Allied Motion Technologies Inc
495 Commerce Drive, Amherst, NY 14228
Phone: 716 242-8634
Web: www.alliedmotion.com

PRODUCTS/OPERATIONS

Selected Products
Brushless DC motors
Brushless drives
Encoders
Gearmotors
Permanent magnet DC motors
Servo motors
Small precision motors
Torque motors
Transaxles

COMPETITORS

AMERICAN SUPERCONDUCTOR CORPORATION
APPLIED INDUSTRIAL TECHNOLOGIES INC.
DOVER CORPORATION
FRANKLIN ELECTRIC CO. INC.
GENERAC HOLDINGS INC.
HITACHI LTD.
NOVANTA INC.
Nordex SE
VOLEX PLC

HISTORICAL FINANCIALS
Company Type: Public

Income Statement				FYE: December 31
	REVENUE ($ mil.)	NET INCOME ($ mil.)	NET PROFIT MARGIN	EMPLOYEES
12/20	366.6	13.6	3.7%	1,770
12/19	371.0	17.0	4.6%	1,700
12/18	310.6	15.9	5.1%	1,600
12/17	252.0	8.0	3.2%	1,250
12/16	245.8	9.0	3.7%	1,220
Annual Growth	10.5%	10.7%	—	9.7%

2020 Year-End Financials
Debt ratio: 34.3%
Return on equity: 10.3%
Cash ($ mil.): 23.1
Current ratio: 2.71
Long-term debt ($ mil.): 120.0
No. of shares (mil.): 14.6
Dividends
  Yield: 0.2%
  Payout: 8.3%
Market value ($ mil.): 748.0

	STOCK PRICE ($) FY Close	P/E High/Low		PER SHARE ($) Earnings	Dividends	Book Value
12/20	51.10	53	21	0.95	0.08	9.78
12/19	48.50	39	26	1.20	0.08	8.28
12/18	44.69	47	26	1.13	0.08	7.16
12/17	33.09	57	33	0.58	0.07	6.18
12/16	21.39	39	24	0.67	0.07	5.14
Annual Growth	24.3%			9.4%	4.7%	17.4%

Alpine Banks of Colorado

Auditors: Dalby Wendland & Co., P.C.

LOCATIONS

HQ: Alpine Banks of Colorado
2200 Grand Avenue, Glenwood Springs, CO 81601
Phone: 970 384-3257   **Fax:** 970 945-2214
Web: www.alpinebank.com

HISTORICAL FINANCIALS
Company Type: Public

Income Statement				FYE: December 31
	REVENUE ($ mil.)	NET INCOME ($ mil.)	NET PROFIT MARGIN	EMPLOYEES
12/20	214.5	51.1	23.8%	0
12/19	207.4	58.0	28.0%	0
12/18	188.1	54.8	29.2%	730
12/17	163.3	33.6	20.6%	0
12/16	144.1	33.4	23.2%	0
Annual Growth	10.5%	11.2%	—	—

2020 Year-End Financials
Debt ratio: 2.3%
Return on equity: 14.1%
Cash ($ mil.): 864.1
Current ratio: 0.19
Long-term debt ($ mil.): 119.1
No. of shares (mil.): 7.6
Dividends
  Yield: 291.8%
  Payout: 16.4%
Market value ($ mil.): 211.0

	STOCK PRICE ($) FY Close	P/E High/Low		PER SHARE ($) Earnings	Dividends	Book Value
12/20	27.75	1524	8	3.28	81.00	49.50
12/19	4,950.00	10	9	553.00	87.00	3,271.51
Annual Growth	(99.4%)		—	—(99.4%)	(6.9%)	(98.5%)

Alpine Income Property Trust Inc

Auditors: Grant Thornton LLP

LOCATIONS

HQ: Alpine Income Property Trust Inc
1140 North Williamson Blvd. Suite 140, Daytona Beach, FL 32114
Phone: 386 274-2202
Web: www.alpinereit.com

HISTORICAL FINANCIALS
Company Type: Public

Income Statement				FYE: December 31
	REVENUE ($ mil.)	NET INCOME ($ mil.)	NET PROFIT MARGIN	EMPLOYEES
12/21	30.1	9.9	33.1%	0
12/20	19.2	0.9	5.1%	0
12/19*	1.3	(0.0)	—	0
11/19	11.8	3.6	30.7%	0
12/18	11.7	4.0	34.3%	0
Annual Growth	26.6%	25.5%	—	—

*Fiscal year change

2021 Year-End Financials
Debt ratio: 52.9%
Return on equity: 6.1%
Cash ($ mil.): 9.5
Current ratio: 2.16
Long-term debt ($ mil.): 267.7
No. of shares (mil.): 11.4
Dividends
  Yield: 5.0%
  Payout: 597.0%
Market value ($ mil.): 230.0

	STOCK PRICE ($) FY Close	P/E High/Low		PER SHARE ($) Earnings	Dividends	Book Value
12/21	20.04	20	14	0.89	1.02	17.16
12/20	14.99	151	60	0.11	0.82	16.99
12/19*	19.03	—	—	(0.00)	0.06	17.40
11/19	18.65	—	—	(0.00)	0.00	(0.00)
Annual Growth	2.4%			—	—	—

*Fiscal year change

Amalgamated Financial Corp

Auditors: Crowe LLP

LOCATIONS

HQ: Amalgamated Financial Corp
275 Seventh Avenue, New York, NY 10001
Phone: 212 255-6200
Web: www.amalgamatedbank.com

HISTORICAL FINANCIALS
Company Type: Public

Income Statement				FYE: December 31
	REVENUE ($ mil.)	NET INCOME ($ mil.)	NET PROFIT MARGIN	EMPLOYEES
12/20	231.1	46.1	20.0%	370
12/19	215.1	47.2	21.9%	398
12/18	192.2	44.6	23.2%	421
12/17	166.4	6.1	3.7%	401
12/16	158.4	10.5	6.7%	0
Annual Growth	9.9%	44.6%	—	—

2020 Year-End Financials
Debt ratio: —
Return on equity: 8.9%
Cash ($ mil.): 38.7
Current ratio: 0.01
Long-term debt ($ mil.): —
No. of shares (mil.): 31.0
Dividends
  Yield: 0.0%
  Payout: 21.6%
Market value ($ mil.): 427.0

	STOCK PRICE ($) FY Close	P/E High/Low		PER SHARE ($) Earnings	Dividends	Book Value
12/20	13.74	13	5	1.48	0.32	17.25
12/19	19.45	13	10	1.47	0.26	15.56
12/18	19.50	180	11	1.46	0.00	13.82
Annual Growth	(16.1%)		—	0.7%	—	11.7%

Amedisys, Inc.

Through approximately 515 home health care agencies located throughout the US Amedisys provides skilled nursing and home health services primarily to geriatric patients covered by Medicare. It is also a post-acute care partner to over 2900 hospitals and about 78000 physicians across the country. Its range of services includes disease-specific programs that help patients recovering from stroke as well as assistance for those coping with emphysema or diabetes. In addition to home health services Amedisys owns or manages about 180 hospice centers that offer palliative care to terminally ill patients. Amedisys provides home health hospice care and personal care services to more than 418000 patients annually.

Operations

Amedisys operates three reportable business segments: home health hospice and personal care.

Home health segment account for about 60% of total revenue delivers a wide range of services in the homes of individuals who may be recovering from surgery have a chronic disability or terminal illness or need assistance with completing important tasks.

The hospice segment accounts for nearly another more than 35% of revenue provides palliative care and comfort to terminally ill patients and their families.

The personal care segment provides patients with assistance with the essential activities of daily living. It brings less than 5% of total revenue.

The company owns and operates around 320 Medicare-certified home health centers about 180 Medicare-certified hospice care centers and around 15 personal care centers. Due to the demographics of its patient base its services are primarily paid by Medicare.

Geographic Reach

Amedisys operates in about 40 states with the heaviest concentration of home health and hospice operations in the Georgia South Carolina Tennessee Pennsylvania and Alabama. Over the years the company has moved into new markets through acquisitions and organic growth measures.

Its executive office is located in Nashville Tennessee and its corporate headquarters is located in Baton Rouge Louisiana.

Sales and Marketing

Because Amedisys serves predominantly older patients some 75% of its revenue is derived from Medicare. The company promotes its products and

HOOVER'S HANDBOOK OF EMERGING COMPANIES 2022

services through direct contact with customers and through promotional materials. Advertising expense for 2019 was some $8.5 million versus $7.0 million in 2018 and $6.5 million in 2017.

Financial Performance

Amedisys' revenue for the year ended 2020 totaled $2.1 billion a 6% increase from the previous year's revenue.

In 2020 the company had a net income of $185.2 million a 45% increase compared to the previous year's $127.9 million net income.

Amedisys' cash at the end of 2020 was $83.4 million. Operating activities generated $289 million while investing activities used $287.1 million mainly for acquisitions. Financing activities used another $15 million mainly for repayments of borrowings under revolving line of credit.

Strategy

Amedisys' strategy is to be the best choice for care wherever its patients call home. The company accomplishes this by providing clinically distinct care being the employer of choice and delivering operational excellence and efficiency which when combined drive growth. Amedisys' mission is to provide best-in-class home health hospice and personal care services allowing its patients to maintain a sense of independence quality of life and dignity while delivering industry leading outcomes. The company believes that its unwavering dedication to clinical quality and constant focus on both patients and employees differentiates it from its competitors.

Mergers and Acquisitions

In 2020 Amedisys acquired Homecare Preferred Choice Inc. doing business as AseraCare Hospice a national hospice care provider with an executive office in Plano Texas and administrative support center in Fort Smith Arkansas. This acquisition adds greater scale to Amedisys' high-quality nationwide network. The acquisition price was $235 million.

In early 2020 Amedisys completed the acquisition of 100%t ownership interests in Asana Hospice. Asana provides hospice care to approximately 540 patients daily in eight locations in Pennsylvania Ohio Missouri Kansas and Texas. As a result of the acquisition Amedisys adds eight locations in Pennsylvania Ohio Texas Missouri and Kansas to its hospice network the third largest in the country. Terms were not disclosed.

EXECUTIVES

Chief Financial Officer, Executive Vice President, Scott Ginn, $525,000 total compensation
Independent Director, Jeffrey Rideout
Chief Information Officer, Michael North, $325,540 total compensation
Independent Director, Julie Klapstein
Independent Director, Vickie Capps
Independent Director, Teresa Kline
Independent Director, Molly Coye
Chief Compliance Officer, Denise Bohnert
Independent Director, Ivanetta Samuels
Chairman Of The Board, Paul Kusserow, $900,000 total compensation
Chief Legal And Government Affairs Officer, David Kemmerly, $400,000 total compensation
President And Chief Operating Officer, Chris Gerard, $575,000 total compensation
Chief Human Resource Officer, Sharon Brunecz, $400,000 total compensation
Auditors: KPMG LLP

LOCATIONS

HQ: Amedisys, Inc.
3854 American Way, Suite A, Baton Rouge, LA 70816
Phone: 225 292-2031
Web: www.amedisys.com

PRODUCTS/OPERATIONS

2017 Sales by Segment

	$ mil.	% of total
Home Health	1,101.8	72
Hospice	371.0	24
Personal Care	60.9	4
Total	**1,533.7**	**100**

2017 Centers

	No.
Georgia	68
Alabama	37
Massachusetts	29
South Carolina	26
Florida	21
Kentucky	17
West Virginia	17
Louisiana	14
North Carolina	14
Virginia	14
Pennsylvania	13
Maryland	10
Mississippi	9
Indiana	6
Maine	6
Missouri	6
New Hampshire	6
Oklahoma	6
Arkansas	5
Connecticut	5
New York	5
Arizona	4
California	4
Oregon	4
Illinois	3
New Jersey	3
Ohio	3
Rhode Island	3
Delaware	2
Kansas	2
Texas	2
Washington	1
Wisconsin	1
Washington DC	1
Total	**421**

COMPETITORS

ALMOST FAMILY INC.
ENCOMPASS HEALTH CORPORATION
GENESIS HEALTHCARE INC.
NATIONAL HEALTHCARE CORPORATION

OPTION CARE HEALTH INC.
ST. JOSEPH HEALTH SYSTEM
TIVITY HEALTH INC.
VITAS HEALTHCARE CORPORATION

HISTORICAL FINANCIALS

Company Type: Public

Income Statement

FYE: December 31

	REVENUE ($ mil.)	NET INCOME ($ mil.)	NET PROFIT MARGIN	EMPLOYEES
12/20	2,105.8	183.6	8.7%	21,000
12/19	1,955.6	126.8	6.5%	21,300
12/18	1,662.5	119.3	7.2%	21,000
12/17	1,533.6	30.3	2.0%	17,900
12/16	1,437.4	37.2	2.6%	16,000
Annual Growth	**10.0%**	**49.0%**	**—**	**7.0%**

2020 Year-End Financials

Debt ratio: 13.7%	No. of shares (mil.): 32.8
Return on equity: 25.2%	Dividends
Cash ($ mil.): 81.8	Yield: —
Current ratio: 0.79	Payout: —
Long-term debt ($ mil.): 204.5	Market value ($ mil.): 9,625.0

	STOCK PRICE ($) FY Close	P/E High/Low	PER SHARE ($) Earnings	Dividends	Book Value
12/20	293.33	52 24	5.52	0.00	24.66
12/19	166.92	42 27	3.84	0.00	19.84
12/18	117.11	39 14	3.55	0.00	15.06
12/17	52.71	73 47	0.88	0.00	15.17
12/16	42.63	49 28	1.10	0.00	13.70
Annual Growth	**62.0%**	**— —**	**49.7%**	**—**	**15.8%**

Ameresco Inc

Primarily serving commercial and industrial customers along with municipal and federal government agencies Ameresco provides designing engineering and installation services to clients seeking to upgrade and improve the efficiency of their heating and air conditioning ventilation lighting and other building systems. Other services include developing and constructing small-scale on-site (or near-site) renewable energy plants for customers as well as installing solar panels wind turbines and other alternative energy sources. Ameresco operates through more than 70 regional offices in the US Canada and the UK. The US accounts for about 95% of company's revenues.

Operations

Ameresco operates through US Regions (some 40% of revenue) US Federal (about 35%) Canada (around 5%) Non-Solar Distributed Generation (about 10%) and All Other (some 10% of revenue).

The company's US Regions US Federal and Canada segments offer energy efficiency products and services which include the design engineering and installation of equipment and other measures to improve the efficiency and control the operation of a facility's energy infrastructure renewable energy solutions and services which include the construction of small-scale plants that the company owns or develops for customers that produce electricity gas heat or cooling from renewable sources of energy and O&M services.

The company's Non-Solar DG segment sells electricity processed renewable gas fuel heat or cooling produced from renewable sources of energy other than solar and generated by small-scale plants that the company owns and O&M services for customer-owned small-scale plants.

The All Other category offers enterprise energy management services consulting services and the sale of solar PV energy products and systems which the company refers to as integrated-PV. Revenues from projects generate the majority of sales by products and service line followed by energy assets O&M Integrated-PV and other services.

Geographic Reach

Headquartered in Framingham Massachusetts Ameresco occupies nine regional offices in Arizona New York Illinois Maryland North Carolina Tennessee Texas Washington and Ontario. In addition it also has about 75 offices throughout North America and in the UK and about 130 small-scale renewable energy plants in North America and one in Ireland.

Majority of its sales came from the US.

Sales and Marketing

The sales design and construction process for energy efficiency and renewable energy projects recently has been averaging from about 20 to about 55 months. The company identifies project opportunities through referrals requests for proposals ("RFPs") conferences and events website online campaigns telemarketing and repeat business from existing customers. The company's direct sales force develops and follows up on customer leads and had about 135 employees in direct sales.

More than 70% of revenues were derived from federal state provincial or local government entities including public housing authorities and public universities. The US federal government which is considered a single customer for reporting purposes. Its largest 20 customers accounted for about 60% of total revenues.

Financial Performance

Company's revenue for fiscal 2020 increased by 19% to $1 billion compared from the prior year with $866.9 million. The increase was primarily due to a $153.5 million or 25% increase in its project revenue attributed to strong execution of its contracted backlog and a $20.2 million or 21% increase in its energy asset revenue attributed to increased assets in operations and improved output and pricing related to certain of its non-solar distributed generation assets in operation partially offset by a $8.8 million or 18%.

Net income for fiscal 2020 increased to $54.1 million compared from the prior year with $44.4 million.

Cash held by the company at the end of fiscal 2020 increased to $98.8 million. Cash provided by financing activities was $305.2 million while cash used for operations and investing activities were $102.6 million and $181 million respectively.

Strategy

Ameresco's growth is driven by staying ahead of the curve and at the leading edge of innovation taking place in the energy sector offering new products and services to new and existing customers. In 2020 the company launched its first owned and operated wind power project in Ireland that became its first renewable energy asset outside of North America. Strategic acquisitions of complementary businesses and assets have been an important part of the company's growth enabling it to broaden its service offerings and expand its geographical reach. Over the past three years the company has acquired businesses and energy assets under construction in Washington DC Hawaii Massachusetts New York Illinois and Connecticut.

EXECUTIVES

Lead Independent Director, Joseph Sutton
Independent Director, Douglas Foy
Executive Vice President And General Manager - Federal Solutions, Nicole Bulgarino, $380,452 total compensation
Evp, Robert Georgeoff
Chief Accounting Officer, Vice President - Finance, Mark Chiplock, $260,000 total compensation
Independent Director, Thomas Murley

Independent Director, Claire Johnson
Executive Vice President, Louis Maltezos, $336,075 total compensation
Chairman, President And Chief Executive Officer, George Sakellaris, $950,481 total compensation
Executive Vice President, General Counsel, Secretary, Director, David Corrsin, $364,926 total compensation
Executive Vice President - Distributed Energy Systems, Michael Bakas, $366,474 total compensation
Senior Vice President - London Operations, Britta MacIntosh
Auditors: RSM US LLP

LOCATIONS

HQ: Ameresco Inc
111 Speen Street, Suite 410, Framingham, MA 01701
Phone: 508 661-2200
Web: www.ameresco.com

PRODUCTS/OPERATIONS

2018 Sales by Segment

	$ mil.	% of total
US Region	334.3	42
US Federal	246.3	31
Canada	39.0	5
Non-Solar DG	82.7	11
All Other	84.8	11
Total	**787.1**	**100**

2018 Sales

	$ mil.	% of total
Project Revenue	545.1	69
Energy Assets	95.8	12
O&M Revenue	65.3	8
Other	81.1	10
Total	**787.2**	**100**

Selected Subsidiaries

Ameresco Canada Inc.
Ameresco CEPEO Solar Inc.
Ameresco Duffering Solar Inc.
Ameresco Enertech Inc.
Ameresco Federal Solutions Inc.
Ameresco Geothermal Inc.
Ameresco Langstaff Solar Inc.
Ameresco Myles Solar Inc.
Ameresco Planergy Housing Inc.
Ameresco Quantum Inc.
Ameresco Select Inc.
Ameresco Solar - Solutions Inc.
Ameresco Vasco Road LLC
AmerescoSolutions Inc.
EI Fund One Inc.

COMPETITORS

AECOM
CALPINE CORPORATION
CH2M HILL COMPANIES LTD.
COVANTA HOLDING CORPORATION
GIBRALTAR INDUSTRIES INC.
GOOD ENERGY GROUP PLC
Just Energy Group Inc
POWERSECURE INTERNATIONAL INC.
SNC-Lavalin Group Inc
TECNICAS REUNIDAS SA
TUCSON ELECTRIC POWER COMPANY
WILLDAN GROUP INC.

HISTORICAL FINANCIALS

Company Type: Public

Income Statement

FYE: December 31

	REVENUE ($ mil.)	NET INCOME ($ mil.)	NET PROFIT MARGIN	EMPLOYEES
12/20	1,032.2	54.0	5.2%	1,141
12/19	866.9	44.4	5.1%	1,127
12/18	787.1	37.9	4.8%	1,116
12/17	717.1	37.4	5.2%	1,049
12/16	651.2	12.0	1.8%	1,038
Annual Growth	12.2%	45.6%	—	2.4%

2020 Year-End Financials

Debt ratio: 21.7%
Return on equity: 11.7%
Cash ($ mil.): 66.4
Current ratio: 1.28
Long-term debt ($ mil.): 311.6
No. of shares (mil.): 48.2
Dividends
 Yield: —
 Payout: —
Market value ($ mil.): 2,519.0

	STOCK PRICE ($) FY Close	P/E High/Low		PER SHARE ($) Earnings	Dividends	Book Value
12/20	52.24	47	13	1.10	0.00	10.22
12/19	17.50	19	14	0.93	0.00	9.08
12/18	14.10	20	9	0.81	0.00	8.14
12/17	8.60	11	6	0.82	0.00	7.39
12/16	5.50	24	15	0.26	0.00	6.44
Annual Growth	75.6%	—	—	43.4%	—	12.2%

America's Car-Mart Inc

No Credit? Bad Credit? No problem. America's Car-Mart targets car buyers with poor or limited credit histories. The company's subsidiaries operate about 150 used car dealerships in more than 10 states primarily in smaller urban and rural markets throughout the US South Central region. Dealerships focus on selling basic and affordable transportation with an average selling price of about $11795 in 2020. It has facilities in Alabama Tennessee and Mississippi among others. While the company's business plan has focused on cities with up to 50000 in population (about 75% of sales) it sees better collection results among the smaller communities it serves. America's Car-Mart was founded in 1981 as the Crown Group. Most of the company's stores are located in Arkansas.

Operations

America's Car-Mart operates its business through two subsidiaries: one that sells cars (America's Car Mart Inc. also known as Car-Mart of Arkansas) and one that finances them (Colonial Auto Finance Inc.). Substantially all of its customers take advantage of financing offered by Colonial Auto Finance. The company's dealerships operate within a decentralized model. For instance dealers conduct their own collections with support from corporate management.

Nearly 90% of total revenue came from the company's sales while interest income and others accounts for the rest.

Geographic Reach

Arkansas-based Car-Mart has about 150 locations in Alabama Arkansas Georgia Indiana Kentucky Mississippi Missouri Oklahoma Tennessee Illinois Iowa and Texas.

HOOVER'S HANDBOOK OF EMERGING COMPANIES 2022

Sales and Marketing

Selling is done predominantly by the dealership manager assistant manager manager trainee or sales associate. The Company uses an outside marketing firm and has recently hired a director of digital experience in order to broaden and increase the company's usage of digital and social media channels. The company estimates that approximately 10% to 15% of the company's sales result from customer referrals.

Car-Mart spent $3.1 million $3.1 million and $3.8 million for fiscal year 2020 2019 and 2018 respectively for advertising consists of radio print media and digital marketing.

Financial Performance

Total revenues increased $75.5 million or 11% in fiscal 2020 as compared to revenue growth of 9% in fiscal 2019 principally as a result of revenue growth from dealerships that operated a full twelve months in both fiscal years ($61.5 million) and revenue from stores opened or acquired during or after the year ended April 30 2019 ($17.0 million) partially offset by decreased revenue from dealerships closed during or after the year ended April 30 2019 ($3.0 million). The increase in revenue for fiscal 2020 is attributable to a 6% increase in average retail sales price a 5% increase in retail units sold and an 11% increase in interest and other income.

The company's net income increased by $3.7 million to $51.3 million in 2020 compared to $47.6 million in prior year. The increase was due to higher revenues.

Cash held by the company at the end of 2020 increased by $1.8 million to $59.6 million compared to $57.8 million in prior year. Cash provided by operations and financing activities were $20.9 million and $46.8 million respectively. Cash used for investing activities was $10.0 million primarily for purchase of investments and purchases of property and equipment.

Strategy

In general it is the company's objective to continue to expand its business using the same business model that has been developed and used by Car-Mart for over 38 years. This business strategy focuses on collecting customer accounts maintaining a decentralized operation expanding through controlled organic growth and strategic acquisitions selling basic transportation operating in smaller communities enhanced management talent and experience and cultivating customer relationships.

The company focuses on selling basic and affordable transportation to its customers. The company's average retail sales price was $11793 per unit in fiscal 2020. By selling vehicles at this price point the company can keep the terms of its instalment sales contracts relatively short (overall portfolio weighted average of 33.3 months) while requiring relatively low payments.

Mergers and Acquisitions

In late 2019 Car-Mart entered an agreement to acquire dealership assets of Taylor Motor Company and Auto Credit of Southern Illinois for an undisclosed amount. The company will be gaining three dealership locations in Marion Benton and Mount Vernon Illinois as well as a vehicle reconditioning location in Benton Illinois after this acquisition. Illinois will represent the company's 12th state and these locations are near existing Car-Mart dealerships in surrounding states.

Company Background

Car-Mart was started in 1981 when the company's first used-car dealership opened in Rogers Arkansas. The basis of the company's business strategy from the start was to sell automobiles to customers with limited or poor credit. In 1999 Car-Mart was acquired by Crown Group Inc. In 2002 Crown Group changes its name to America's Car-Mart Inc.

EXECUTIVES

Independent Director, Daniel Englander
President, Chief Executive Officer And Director, Jeffrey Williams, $750,000 total compensation
Chief Financial Officer, Vickie Judy, $400,000 total compensation
Chief Operating Officer, Leonard Walthall, $400,000 total compensation
Chairman, Joshua Welch
Independent Director, Dawn Morris
Director, Julian Davis
Auditors: Grant Thornton LLP

LOCATIONS

HQ: America's Car-Mart Inc
  1805 North 2nd Street, Suite 401, Rogers, AR 72756
Phone: 479 464-9944
Web: www.car-mart.com

PRODUCTS/OPERATIONS

2015 Sales

	$ mil.	% of total
Sales	472.6	89
Interest income & other	57.7	11
Total	**530.3**	**100**

Selected Subsidiaries

Auto Finance Investors Inc.
Colonial Auto Finance Inc.
Colonial Underwriting Inc.
Crown Delaware Investments Corp.
Crown Group of Nevada Inc.
Texas Car-Mart Inc.

COMPETITORS

ASBURY AUTOMOTIVE GROUP INC.	COPART INC.
AUTOTRADER.COM INC.	FIRSTCASH INC.
AUTOWEB INC.	MOTORPOINT GROUP PLC
CAR GIANT LIMITED	UNITED ROAD SERVICES INC.

HISTORICAL FINANCIALS

Company Type: Public

Income Statement — FYE: April 30

	REVENUE ($ mil.)	NET INCOME ($ mil.)	NET PROFIT MARGIN	EMPLOYEES
04/21	918.6	104.1	11.3%	1,850
04/20	744.6	51.3	6.9%	1,750
04/19	669.1	47.6	7.1%	1,600
04/18	612.2	36.5	6.0%	1,504
04/17	587.7	20.2	3.4%	1,460
Annual Growth	**11.8%**	**50.7%**	**—**	**6.1%**

2021 Year-End Financials

Debt ratio: 27.4%	No. of shares (mil.): 6.6
Return on equity: 29.3%	Dividends
Cash ($ mil.): 2.8	Yield: —
Current ratio: 6.70	Payout: —
Long-term debt ($ mil.): 225.9	Market value ($ mil.): 999.0

	STOCK PRICE ($) FY Close	P/E High/Low		PER SHARE ($) Earnings	Dividends	Book Value
04/21	150.83	11	4	14.95	0.00	61.39
04/20	65.95	17	5	7.39	0.00	45.78
04/19	99.05	15	8	6.73	0.00	38.93
04/18	53.30	11	7	4.90	0.00	33.70
04/17	37.30	18	8	2.49	0.00	30.66
Annual Growth	**41.8%**	**—**	**—**	**56.5%**	**—**	**19.0%**

American Bank Inc (PA)

American Bank Incorporated is the holding company for American Bank which operates a single branch in Allentown Pennsylvania. It serves customers throughout the US via its pcbanker.com Web site. The bank's products and services include checking and savings accounts money market accounts CDs credit cards and discount brokerage. It primarily originates real estate loans although it also offers commercial mortgages and residential mortgages. The Jaindl family including company president and CEO Mark Jaindl owns a majority of American Bank Incorporated.

EXECUTIVES

Vice President, Treasurer; Senior Vice President And Chief Financial Officer Of American Bank, Harry Birkhimer
Vice President, Secretary; Senior Vice President, Chief Operating Officer And Secretary Of American Bank, Sandra Berg
Senior Vice President, Chief Lending Officer, Chris Persichetti, $115,027 total compensation
Senior Vice President, Chief Technology Officer Of The Bank, Robert Turner, $102,470 total compensation
Director, Phillip Schwartz
Director, Martin Spiro
Director, John Eureyecko
Director, Donald Whiting
Director, Michael Molewski
Director, John Galuchie
Chairman Of The Board, President, Chief Executive Officer, Mark Jaindl, $239,351 total compensation
Auditors: S. R. Snodgrass, P.C.

LOCATIONS

HQ: American Bank Inc (PA)
  4029 West Tilghman Street, Allentown, PA 18104
Phone: 610 366-1800   **Fax:** 610 366-1900
Web: www.ambk.com

COMPETITORS

ARVEST BANK GROUP INC.	FIRST NATIONAL
COMMUNITY SHORES BANK	CORPORATION
CORPORATION	

HISTORICAL FINANCIALS

Company Type: Public

Income Statement

FYE: December 31

	ASSETS ($ mil.)	NET INCOME ($ mil.)	INCOME AS % OF ASSETS	EMPLOYEES
12/20	734.2	8.7	1.2%	0
12/19	641.5	7.8	1.2%	0
12/18	621.9	6.8	1.1%	0
12/17	580.8	5.5	1.0%	0
12/16	557.1	4.4	0.8%	0
Annual Growth	7.1%	18.3%	—	—

2020 Year-End Financials

Return on assets: 1.2%
Return on equity: 13.6%
Long-term debt ($ mil.): —
No. of shares (mil.): 5.5
Sales ($ mil): 29.0

Dividends
Yield: 4.0%
Payout: 35.0%
Market value ($ mil.): 67.0

	STOCK PRICE ($) FY Close	P/E High/Low		PER SHARE ($) Earnings	Dividends	Book Value
12/20	12.00	8	7	1.37	0.48	11.90
12/19	12.00	9	8	1.24	0.46	10.83
12/18	12.50	10	9	1.08	0.40	9.82
12/17	11.45	12	11	0.87	0.36	9.05
12/16	12.40	16	12	0.70	0.36	8.74
Annual Growth	(0.8%)	—	—	18.3%	7.5%	8.0%

American Business Bank (Los Angeles, CA)

Auditors: RSM US LLP

LOCATIONS

HQ: American Business Bank (Los Angeles, CA)
400 South Hope Street, Suite 300, Los Angeles, CA 90071
Phone: 213 430-4000
Web: www.americanbb.bank

HISTORICAL FINANCIALS

Company Type: Public

Income Statement

FYE: December 31

	ASSETS ($ mil.)	NET INCOME ($ mil.)	INCOME AS % OF ASSETS	EMPLOYEES
12/20	3,454.2	28.7	0.8%	0
12/19	2,401.9	22.0	0.9%	0
12/18	2,157.4	16.3	0.8%	0
12/17	1,873.5	8.3	0.4%	0
12/16	1,843.1	12.7	0.7%	0
Annual Growth	17.0%	22.6%	—	—

2020 Year-End Financials

Return on assets: 0.9%
Return on equity: 12.6%
Long-term debt ($ mil.): —
No. of shares (mil.): 8.7
Sales ($ mil): 98.8

Dividends
Yield: —
Payout: —
Market value ($ mil.): 278.0

	STOCK PRICE ($) FY Close	P/E High/Low		PER SHARE ($) Earnings	Dividends	Book Value
12/20	31.83	11	6	3.22	0.00	28.37
12/19	35.65	15	12	2.48	0.00	23.93
12/18	31.55	22	16	1.90	0.00	19.47
12/17	39.40	42	35	0.97	0.00	18.42
12/16	34.95	22	18	1.56	0.00	16.60
Annual Growth	(2.3%)	—	—	19.8%	—	14.3%

American National Bankshares, Inc. (Danville, VA)

American National Bankshares with total assets of around $2.5 billion is the holding company for American National Bank and Trust. Founded in 1909 the bank operates some 30 branches that serve southern and central Virginia and north central North Carolina. Operating through two segments — Community Banking and Trust and Investment Services — it offers checking and savings accounts CDs IRAs and insurance. Lending activities primarily consist of real estate loans: Commercial mortgages account for about 40% of its loan portfolio while residential mortgages bring in another 20%. American National Bankshares' trust and investment services division manages nearly $610 million in assets.

Operations

American National Bankshares operates through two segments: Community Banking which accounts for more than 80% of the company's total revenue and offers deposit accounts and loans to individuals and small and middle-market businesses; and Trust and Investment Services which provides estate planning trust account administration investment management and retail brokerage services.

The bank makes more than 80% of its revenue from interest income. About 68% of its total revenue came from loan interest during 2015 while another 13% came from interest income on investment securities. The rest of its revenue came from trust fees (6% of revenue) deposit account service charges (3%) mortgage banking income (2%) brokerage fees (1%) and other miscellaneous income sources.

Geographic Reach

Danville Virginia-based American National Bankshares has 25 branches mostly in southern Virginia and in North Carolina (including in Alamance and Guilford Counties). It also has two loan production offices in Roanoke Virginia and Raleigh North Carolina.

Sales and Marketing

American National Bankshares has been cutting back on its advertising and marketing spend in recent years. It spent $356000 on advertising and marketing in 2015 up from $453000 and $607000 in 2014 and 2013 respectively.

Financial Performance

The bank group has struggled to consistently grow its revenues and profits over the past several years despite steadily increasing loan business mostly due to shrinking interest margins on loans stemming from the low-interest environment.

American National had a breakthrough year in 2015 however as its revenue jumped 17% to $68.46 million almost entirely thanks to its acquisition of MainStreet BankShares which boosted its loan and other interest-earning assets by double digits and increased its non-interest income by 19% with newly acquired deposit and other fee related income.

Double-digit revenue growth in 2015 drove the group's net income up 18% to $15.04 million. The bank's operating cash levels climbed 16% to $19.26 million for the year thanks to the boost in cash-denominated earnings.

Strategy

American National Bankshares grows its branch reach as well as its loan and deposit business by opening new branch locations or by buying other branches or banks.

The bank continues to have the largest deposit market share in the Dannville Virginia metro area boasting a 32.8% market share in the region as of mid-2015. It also had the second-largest market share in Pittsylvania County Virginia with a 21.1% share.

Mergers and Acquisitions

In 2019 American National Bankshares acquired Roanoke Virginia-based Hometown Bankshares for about $85 million. The acquisition expands American National's network to around 30 branches. The combined company has about $2.5 billion in assets.

Company Background

In 2011 American National acquired bank holding company MidCarolina Financial expanding its presence in North Carolina specifically in both Alamance and Guilford counties.

EXECUTIVES

Non-executive Independent Chairman Of The Board Of The Company And The Bank, Charles Majors
President, Chief Executive Officer Of The Company And The Bank, Director, Jeffrey Haley, $549,314 total compensation
Lead Independent Director, Michael Haley
Independent Director, Dan Pleasant
Independent Director, Joel Shepherd
Executive Vice President And Co-head, Banking - Commercial, Rhonda Joyce
Independent Director, Tammy Finley
Independent Director, Charles Harris
Independent Director, John Love
Independent Director, F. D. Hornaday
Independent Director, Nancy Agee
Director, Susan Still
Chief Information Officer, Anguel Lindarev
Independent Director, Ronda Penn
Executive Vice President, President Of Trust And Investment Services, John Settle, $224,530 total compensation
Executive Vice President, Chief Administrative Officer Of The Company And The Bank And President Of Virginia Banking, Edward Martin, $281,116 total compensation
Chief Financial Officer, Chief Operating Officer, Executive Vice President Of The Company And The Bank, Treasurer, Secretary, Jeffrey Farrar, $348,855 total compensation

HOOVER'S HANDBOOK OF EMERGING COMPANIES 2022

Executive Vice President And Co-head, Banking – Consumer And Financial Services, Alex Jung

Auditors: Yount, Hyde & Barbour, P.C.

LOCATIONS

HQ: American National Bankshares, Inc. (Danville, VA)
628 Main Street, Danville, VA 24541
Phone: 434 792-5111
Web: www.amnb.com

PRODUCTS/OPERATIONS

2015 Sales

	$ mil.	% of total
Interest and Dividend Income		
Interest and fees on loans	46.9	69
Taxable	4.2	6
Tax-exempt	3.9	5
Other	0.1	1
Non-interest income		
Trust fees	3.9	7
Service charges on deposit accounts	2.1	3
Other fees and commissions	2.4	3
Other	4.9	6
Total	**68.4**	**100**

Selected Subsidiaries

American National Bank and Trust Company
AMNB Statutory Trust I A Delaware Statutory Trust
MidCarolina Trust I A Delaware Statutory Trust
MidCarolina Trust II A Delaware Statutory Trust

Selected Services

Business Banking
  Cash Management
  Checking
  Loans
  Savings
Personal Banking
  Checking
  Loans
  Savings
Insurance
  Business
  Personal

COMPETITORS

CAMDEN NATIONAL CORPORATION	CITY HOLDING COMPANY
CAPITAL BANK FINANCIAL FINANCIAL CORP.	MIDSOUTH BANCORP INC.
	PEOPLES
	SERVICES CORP.

HISTORICAL FINANCIALS

Company Type: Public

Income Statement				FYE: December 31
	ASSETS ($ mil.)	NET INCOME ($ mil.)	INCOME AS % OF ASSETS	EMPLOYEES
12/20	3,050.0	30.0	1.0%	342
12/19	2,478.5	20.9	0.8%	355
12/18	1,862.8	22.5	1.2%	305
12/17	1,816.0	15.2	0.8%	328
12/16	1,678.6	16.3	1.0%	320
Annual Growth	16.1%	16.5%	—	1.7%

2020 Year-End Financials

Return on assets: 1.0%	Dividends
Return on equity: 9.1%	Yield: 4.1%
Long-term debt ($ mil.): —	Payout: 41.3%
No. of shares (mil.): 10.9	Market value ($ mil.): 288.0
Sales ($ mil): 112.6	

	STOCK PRICE ($) FY Close	P/E High/Low		PER SHARE ($) Earnings	Dividends	Book Value
12/20	26.21	14	7	2.73	1.08	30.77
12/19	39.57	20	15	1.98	1.04	28.93
12/18	29.31	16	11	2.59	1.00	25.52
12/17	38.30	24	20	1.76	0.97	24.13
12/16	34.80	19	12	1.89	0.96	23.37
Annual Growth	(6.8%)	—	—	9.6%	3.0%	7.1%

American Outdoor Brands Inc

LOCATIONS

HQ: American Outdoor Brands Inc
1800 North Route Z, Suite A, Columbia, MO 65202
Phone: 800 338-9585
Web: www.AOB.com

HISTORICAL FINANCIALS

Company Type: Public

Income Statement				FYE: April 30
	REVENUE ($ mil.)	NET INCOME ($ mil.)	NET PROFIT MARGIN	EMPLOYEES
04/21	276.6	18.4	6.7%	317
04/20	167.3	(96.2)	—	262
04/19	177.3	(9.5)	—	0
04/18	171.6	8.1	4.8%	0
Annual Growth	17.2%	31.1%	—	—

2021 Year-End Financials

Debt ratio: —	No. of shares (mil.): 14.0
Return on equity: 7.3%	Dividends
Cash ($ mil.): 60.8	Yield: —
Current ratio: 4.95	Payout: —
Long-term debt ($ mil.): —	Market value ($ mil.): 363.0

	STOCK PRICE ($) FY Close	P/E High/Low		PER SHARE ($) Earnings	Dividends	Book Value
04/21	25.85	22	10	1.29	0.00	19.91
04/20	0.00	—	—	(0.00)	0.00	161.41
Annual Growth	—	—	—	—	—	—
(87.7%)						

American Vanguard Corp.

American Vanguard Corporation (AVD) is a specialty chemical manufacturer that develops and markets products for agricultural commercial and consumer uses. This California-based specialty chemical manufacturer sells products to protect crops turf and ornamental plants as well as human and animal health. Products include insecticides fungicides herbicides molluscicides growth regu-

lators and soil fumigants. Through its subsidiary AMVAC Chemical Corporation the company pursues new product acquisitions and licensing for US domestic sales and worldwide product distribution. Its products are sold across the US and about 55 countries around the world. The company generates about 60% of sales from the US.

Operations

AVD sells products in two categories: crop and non-crop.

Crop products account for about 50% of total revenue. The non-crop sales account for some 10% of total company sales.

Geographic Reach

In the US AVD has presence across the country including California Texas Idaho and Alabama. Internationally it operates in Mexico Costa Rica the Netherlands China and the Asia Pacific region. The US accounts for about 60% of annual sales.

Headquartered in California AVD's products reach in about 55 countries worldwide.

Sales and Marketing

The company delivers its products through "closed delivery systems" like SmartBox Lock 'n Load and EZ Load systems and is commercializing a precision application technology known as SIMPAS which permits the delivery of multiple products (from AMVAC and/or other companies) at variable rates in a single pass.

AVD primarily sells its products to distribution companies buying groups or co-operatives.

AVD's advertising costs were $4.8 million $5.5 million and $4.9 million in 2020 2019 and 2018 respectively.

Financial Performance

Company net sales for fiscal 2020 decreased by 2% to $458.7 million compared from the prior year with $468.2 million.

Net income for fiscal 2020 increased to $15.2 million compared from the prior year with $13.6 million.

Cash held by the company at the end of fiscal 2020 increased to $15.9 million. Cash provided by operations was $89.2 million while cash used for investing and financing activities were $35.8 million and $43.2 million respectively. Main uses of cash were acquisitions of businesses and product lines; and payments borrowings under line of credit agreement.

Strategy

The company has had a history of investing in technological innovation including with respect to product delivery systems essential oil technology and biologicals as one of its core strategies. These investments are based upon the premise that new technology will allow for safer handling or lower overall toxicity profile of the company's product portfolio appeal to regulatory agencies and the market it serves gain commercial acceptance and command a return that is sufficiently in excess of the investment.

Research product development and regulatory expenses increased by 9% to $26.3 million in 2020 as compared to $24.1 million in 2019. The main drivers were increases in its product defense and product development costs primarily resulting from increased activities in its newly acquired businesses partially offset by the general delays in activities with third-party service providers caused by pandemic related disruption.

Mergers and Acquisitions

In mid-2021 AVD's subsidiary AMVAC Chemical has entered into agreements with Syngenta

Crop Protection to acquire rights to Envoke herbicide. The acquisition includes end-use product registrations and trademarks for Envoke herbicide in the US. Syngenta and AMVAC will work together over the next several months until the US Environmental Protection Agency registration has officially transferred to facilitate an orderly transition to maintain quality customer service in all domestic geographies. The financial terms of the transaction were not disclosed.

In late 2020 AVD's wholly-owned subsidiary American Vanguard Australia acquired all shares of the Australian specialist agrochemical company AgNova Technologies. AgNova is focused on serving customers primarily in the value-added fruit and vegetables segment of the Australian market. It has a growing product portfolio and ample R&D resources to create a pipeline of tailored solutions to meet the needs of Australian growers. Details of the transaction were not disclosed.

Also in 2020 AVD's subsidiary AMVAC Chemical acquired the Agrinos group of companies a privately-owned technology leader in biological crop inputs. Agrinos is a fully integrated biological input supplier with proprietary technology internal manufacturing and global distribution capabilities. The company's high yield technology product platform works in conjunction with other nutritional crop inputs to increase crop yield improve soil health and reduce the environmental footprint of traditional agricultural practices.

EXECUTIVES

Managing Director, Amvac Netherlands Bv, Peter Eilers, $299,800 total compensation
Executive Vice President, Chief Operating Officer Of Amvac Chemical Corporation, Ulrich Trogele, $422,583 total compensation
Independent Director, Scott Baskin
Independent Director, Morton Erlich
Lead Independent Director, John Killmer
Director, Marisol Angelini
Independent Director, Emer Gunter
Senior Vice President - Crop Sales For U.s. & Canada, Anthony Hendrix, $327,014 total compensation
Independent Director, Debra Edwards
Independent Director, Alfred Ingulli
Chief Administrative Officer, General Counsel, Secretary, Timothy Donnelly, $328,107 total compensation
Chief Financial Officer, Vice President, Treasurer, David Johnson, $387,950 total compensation
Chairman Of The Board, Chief Executive Officer, Eric Wintemute, $684,500 total compensation
Auditors: BDO USA, LLP

LOCATIONS

HQ: American Vanguard Corp.
 4695 MacArthur Court, Newport Beach, CA 92660
Phone: 949 260-1200
Web: www.american-vanguard.com

PRODUCTS/OPERATIONS

2016 Sales

	$ mil.	% of total
Crops		
Insecticides	119.2	38
Herbicides	123.6	40
Other	29.4	9
Non-crop	39.9	13
Total	**312.1**	**100**

COMPETITORS

Bayer CropScience AG
EVOQUA WATER TECHNOLOGIES CORP.
EVOQUA WATER TECHNOLOGIES LLC
ICL GROUP LTD
IDEXX LABORATORIES INC.
MARRONE BIO INNOVATIONS INC.
N L INDUSTRIES INC.
NEOGEN CORPORATION
NISSAN CHEMICAL CORPORATION
NUFARM LIMITED
REPLIGEN CORPORATION
SYNGENTA CORPORATION
VALHI INC.
WATERS CORPORATION

HISTORICAL FINANCIALS

Company Type: Public

Income Statement — FYE: December 31

	REVENUE ($ mil.)	NET INCOME ($ mil.)	NET PROFIT MARGIN	EMPLOYEES
12/20	458.7	15.2	3.3%	771
12/19	468.1	13.6	2.9%	671
12/18	454.2	24.2	5.3%	624
12/17	355.0	20.2	5.7%	605
12/16	312.1	12.7	4.1%	395
Annual Growth	10.1%	4.5%	—	18.2%

2020 Year-End Financials

Debt ratio: 15.7%
Return on equity: 4.3%
Cash ($ mil.): 15.9
Current ratio: 1.94
Long-term debt ($ mil.): 107.4
No. of shares (mil.): 30.8
Dividends
 Yield: 0.2%
 Payout: 10.8%
Market value ($ mil.): 479.0

	STOCK PRICE ($) FY Close	P/E High/Low	PER SHARE ($) Earnings	Dividends	Book Value
12/20	15.52	38 22	0.51	0.04	11.69
12/19	19.47	42 27	0.46	0.08	11.41
12/18	15.19	29 17	0.81	0.08	11.03
12/17	19.65	34 22	0.68	0.06	10.24
12/16	19.15	45 23	0.44	0.03	9.61
Annual Growth	(5.1%)	— —	3.8%	7.5%	5.0%

American Woodmark Corp.

American Woodmark offers a wide variety of products that fall into product lines including kitchen cabinetry bath cabinetry office cabinetry home organization and hardware. Its cabinetry products are available in a variety of designs finishes and finish colors and door styles. Styles vary by finish (oak cherry hickory maple as well as laminate) and door design. Brands include American Woodmark Shenandoah Cabinetry Timberlake and Waypoint. Targeting the remodeling and new home construction markets American Woodmark sells its lineup through home centers and independent dealers and distributors; it also sells directly to major builders. American Woodmark was established through a leveraged buyout of Boise Cascade's cabinet division.

Operations

Business is divided between two markets ? remodeling and new home construction. Products are distributed directly from the company's assembly plants and a third-party logistics network.

Through its eight service centers nationwide American Woodmark offers complete turnkey installation services to its direct builder customers.

The company offers products in two categories: made-to-order and stock. Made-to-order products typically utilize higher grade materials with more options as compared to stock and are all special ordered and shipped directly to the home from the factory. Its home organization products are exclusively stock products. Kitchen cabinetry and bath cabinetry are offered across all product categories (made-to-order and stock) and office cabinetry is offered as stock.

Geographic Reach

Virginia-based American Woodmark presently operates more than 15 manufacturing facilities located in Maryland Indiana West Virginia Georgia Arizona Kentucky Virginia California Texas North Carolina and Tijuana Mexico and eight primary service centers across the country and Mexico.

Sales and Marketing

Through three primary channels ? home centers (about 50% of sales) builders (nearly 40%) and independent dealers and distributors (more than 10%) ? American Woodmark services the remodeling and new home construction markets. Its brand names include American Woodmark Timberlake (sold to major home builders) Shenandoah Cabinetry (Lowe's) Villa Bath (Lowe's) Waypoint Living Spaces and others.

Together Lowe's and The Home Depot accounted for about 50% of the company's sales.

Advertising expenses were approximately $34.1 million $33.9 million and $38.9 million in 2021 2020 and 2019 respectively.

Financial Performance

Net sales for fiscal 2021 increased 6% to $1.7 billion from the prior fiscal year. The company experienced growth in the home center builder and independent dealers and distributors channels.

Net income in 2020 decreased to $58.8 million from 74.9 million in 2019.

Cash held by the company at the end of fiscal 2020 decreased to $91.1 million. Operating activities provided $151.8 million while investing and financing activities used $42.4 million and $115.3 million respectively. Main cash uses were payments to acquire property plant and equipment; and payments of long-term debt.

Strategy

The company strategy has been to develop long-term strategic relationships with both Home Depot and Lowe's to distribute its products. Products for R&R projects are predominately purchased through home centers such as Home Depot and Lowe's. The market presence store network and customer reach of these large home centers are why the company wants to maintain its strategic relationship with them.

Company Background

American Woodmark Corporation was incorporated by the four principal managers of the Boise Cascade Cabinet Division executives Bill Brandt Al Graber Jeff Holcomb and Don Mathias through a leveraged buyout of that division in 1980. The company operated privately until it went public in 1986 and moved to a new corporate headquarters in Winchester Virginia and operated a limited-product-line high-inventory business model for rapid order fulfillment. In 2017 American Woodmark acquired RSI a company known for creating exceptional value for customers. This is the largest acquisition in industry history adding more than 10 brands and nearly 4500 employees to the American Woodmark family.

HISTORY

Alvin Goldhush in 1951 started cabinet company Form Laminates which lumber giant Boise Cascade acquired two decades later. Four senior managers of Boise Cascade's cabinet division — William Brandt Jeff Holcomb Al Graber and Donald Mathias — engineered an LBO of the unit in 1980 and named it American Woodmark after a popular line of cabinets. The company started selling cabinets nationwide through distribution centers and went public in 1986.

American Woodmark spent the first half of the 1990s diversifying its product and brands. In 1990 it introduced Timberlake a cabinet line for the construction industry. Other brands including Coventry and Case Crestwood and Scots Pine were added and quintupled its product line.

President and COO Jake Gosa became CEO in 1996. The sales cupboard was rather bare that year from a downturn in the closely linked home centers industry. The market surged in 1997 causing American Woodmark's profits to nearly triple and new equipment and manufacturing techniques boosted output. In 1998 the company began offering hickory cabinets (its first new wood species in a decade) kitchen accessories and high-quality ready-to-assemble framed cabinets (Flat Pack).

In 1999 American Woodmark expanded its hickory cabinet offerings (adding the Newport and Charleston brands). The company began operations at its new assembly facility in Gas City Indiana in 2000. To both preserve and increase market share in a slow-growth economy in 2001 American Woodmark initiated plans to expand two plants and open two more in Kentucky and Oklahoma.

EXECUTIVES

Independent Director, Carol Moerdyk
Independent Director, Daniel Hendrix
Independent Director, Andrew Cogan
Independent Director, James Davis
Independent Chairman Of The Board, Vance Tang
Independent Director, David Rodriguez
Senior Vice President - Manufacturing And Technical Operations, Robert Adams, $376,928 total compensation
Independent Director, Martha Hayes
Senior Vice President, Chief Marketing Officer, Teresa May, $310,788 total compensation
President, Chief Executive Officer, Director, M. Scott Culbreth, $627,584 total compensation
Chief Financial Officer, Vice President, Paul Joachimczyk, $310,447 total compensation
Independent Director, Emily Videtto
Auditors: KPMG LLP

LOCATIONS

HQ: American Woodmark Corp.
  561 Shady Elm Road, Winchester, VA 22602
Phone: 540 665-9100
Web: www.americanwoodmark.com

PRODUCTS/OPERATIONS

Selected Brands
American Woodmark
Potomac
Shenandoah Cabinetry
Timberlake
Waypoint Living Spaces

COMPETITORS

BJT PROPERTIES INC.
BOISE CASCADE COMPANY
DESIGN STUDIO GROUP LTD.
ETHAN ALLEN INTERIORS INC.
HNI CORPORATION
KNOLL INC.

KREAMER CABINET COMPANY
MASCO CORPORATION
REPUBLIC NATIONAL CABINET CORPORATION
THE HOME DEPOT INC
WOODCRAFT INDUSTRIES INC.

HISTORICAL FINANCIALS
Company Type: Public

Income Statement
FYE: April 30

	REVENUE ($ mil.)	NET INCOME ($ mil.)	NET PROFIT MARGIN	EMPLOYEES
04/21	1,744.0	58.7	3.4%	10,000
04/20	1,650.3	74.8	4.5%	9,900
04/19	1,645.3	83.6	5.1%	9,300
04/18	1,250.2	63.1	5.1%	9,400
04/17	1,030.2	71.2	6.9%	5,808
Annual Growth	14.1%	(4.7%)	—	14.5%

2021 Year-End Financials

Debt ratio: 31.8%	No. of shares (mil.): 16.8
Return on equity: 8.1%	Dividends
Cash ($ mil.): 91.0	Yield: —
Current ratio: 1.78	Payout: —
Long-term debt ($ mil.): 513.4	Market value ($ mil.): 1,671.0

	STOCK PRICE ($) FY Close	P/E High/Low		PER SHARE ($) Earnings	Dividends	Book Value
04/21	99.46	31	13	3.45	0.00	44.22
04/20	51.41	26	8	4.42	0.00	41.39
04/19	89.93	22	11	4.83	0.00	36.82
04/18	82.20	37	21	3.77	0.00	33.23
04/17	91.90	21	14	4.34	0.00	21.71
Annual Growth	2.0%	—	—	(5.6%)	—	19.5%

Ameris Bancorp

Ameris Bancorp is a financial holding company whose business is conducted primarily through its wholly owned banking subsidiary Ameris Bank which provides a full range of banking services to its retail and commercial customers who are primarily concentrated in select markets in Alabama Georgia South Carolina and northern Florida. It operates nearly 165 full-service domestic banking offices. Loans secured by commercial real estate and farmland accounted for over 35% of the company's loan portfolio. Ameris Bank opened its doors as American Banking company on 1971.

Operations
The company has five reportable segments; the Banking Division (nearly 50% of sales) the Retail Mortgage Division (over 40%) the Warehouse Lending Division the SBA Division and the Premium Finance Division which generated about 10% combined.

The Banking Division derives its revenues from the delivery of full-service financial services to include commercial loans consumer loans and deposit accounts. The Retail Mortgage Division derives its revenues from the origination sales and servicing of one-to-four family residential mortgage loans. The Warehouse Lending Division derives its revenues from the origination and servicing of warehouse lines to other businesses that are secured by underlying one-to-four family residential mortgage loans and residential mortgage servicing rights. The SBA Division derives its revenues from the origination sales and servicing of SBA loans. The Premium Finance Division derives its revenues from the origination and servicing of commercial insurance premium finance loans.

Overall interest and fees on loans generated about 60% of sales while mortgage banking activity generated more than 30%. In addition its loan portfolio includes real estate - commercial and farmland (over 35% of sales) real estate ? residential (nearly 20%) and commercial financial and agricultural and real estate - construction and development (around 10% each).

Geographic Reach
Headquartered in Atlanta Georgia the company's markets are concentrated primarily in Georgia Alabama Florida and South Carolina. Ameris operates roughly 165 office or branch locations.

Sales and Marketing
Through an acquisition-oriented growth strategy Ameris seeks to grow its brand and presence in the markets it currently serves in Georgia Alabama Florida and South Carolina as well as in neighboring communities.

The company spent $8 million $7.9 million and $5.6 million for the years 2020 2019 and 2018 respectively.

Financial Performance
For the year ended December 31 2020 interest income was $726.5 million an increase of $90.1 million or 14% compared with the same period in 2019. Average earning assets increased $4.24 billion or 32% to $17.4 billion for the year ended December 31 2020 compared with $13.13 billion for 2019.

In 2020 the company had a net income of $262 million a 62% increase from the previous year's net income of $161.4 million.

The company's cash at the end of 2020 was $2.1 billion. Operating activities generated $798.4 million while investing activities used $1.2 billion primarily for net increase in loans. Financing activities provided another $1.9 billion.

Strategy
Ameris seeks to increase its presence and grow the "Ameris" brand in the markets that it currently serves in Georgia Alabama Florida and South Carolina and in neighboring communities that present attractive opportunities for expansion. Management has pursued this objective through an acquisition-oriented growth strategy and a prudent operating strategy. Its community banking philosophy emphasizes personalized service and building broad and deep customer relationships which has provided it with a substantial base of low-cost core deposits. The company's markets are managed by senior level experienced decision makers in a decentralized structure that differentiates the company from its larger competitors.

Management believes that this structure along with involvement in and knowledge of its local markets will continue to provide growth and assist in managing risk throughout the company.

Ameris has maintained focus on a long-term strategy of expanding and diversifying franchise in terms of revenues profitability and asset size. Its growth over the past several years has been enhanced significantly by bank acquisitions. The company expects to continue to take advantage of the consolidation in the financial services industry and enhance its franchise through future acquisitions. The company intends to grow within its existing markets to branch into or acquire financial institutions in existing markets as well as financial institutions in other markets consistent with the company's capital availability and management abilities.

Mergers and Acquisitions

In late 2021 Ameris Bancorp announced that its banking subsidiary Ameris Bank has acquired Balboa Capital Corporation an online provider of business lending solutions to small and mid-sized businesses nationwide based in Costa Mesa California. The acquisition of Balboa Capital and its technology accelerates Ameris Bank's small business and C&I lending initiatives and increases its presence in the fast-growing point-of-sale financing market. The addition of Balboa Capital also diversifies Ameris Bank's already robust portfolio of nationwide lending platforms which includes its premium finance mortgage banking and warehouse lending businesses. Terms were not disclosed.

Company Background

In addition to acquiring several troubled and failing banks with help from the FDIC Ameris merged with Prosperity Bank in 2013 which broadened its reach into Florida through Prosperity's branches in St. Augustine Jacksonville Panama City Lynn Haven Palatka and Ormand Beach.

Georgia's economy was one of the hardest hit in the US during the recession and Ameris has taken advantage of the plethora of banks seized by regulators in the state. Since 2009 the company has acquired about 10 failed banks in Georgia though FDIC-assisted transactions adding some 20 branches to its network. Ameris also snagged the failed First Bank of Jacksonville in Florida which had two locations.

EXECUTIVES

Executive Vice President, Chief Administrative Officer, Corporate Secretary, Cindi Lewis, $145,000 total compensation
Independent Director, Daniel Jeter
Independent Director, Robert Lynch
Executive Vice President, Chief Credit Officer, Jon Edwards, $375,000 total compensation
Independent Director, Rodney Bullard
Executive Vice President, Chief Strategy Officer, James LaHaise, $375,000 total compensation
Independent Director, William Bowen
Executive Vice President, Chief Risk Officer, William McKendry, $362,676 total compensation
Independent Director, William Stern
Chief Financial Officer, Executive Vice President, Nicole Stokes, $440,000 total compensation
Independent Director, Robert Ezzell
Lead Independent Director, Leo Hill
Independent Director, William Choate
Chairman Of The Board, James Miller
Independent Director, Gloria O'Neal

Chief Executive Officer, Director, H. Palmer Proctor, $850,000 total compensation
Executive Vice President, Chief Governance Officer, Michael Pierson
Executive Vice President, Chief Legal Officer, Jody Spencer
Executive Vice President, Chief Innovation Officer - Bank, Ross Creasy
Executive Vice President, Chief Specialty Banking Officer, R. Todd Shutley
Executive Vice President, Chief Banking Officer, President - Bank, Lawton Bassett, $500,000 total compensation
Auditors: KPMG LLP

LOCATIONS

HQ: Ameris Bancorp
3490 Piedmont Rd N.E., Suite 1550, Atlanta, GA 30305
Phone: 404 639-6500
Web: www.amerisbank.com

PRODUCTS/OPERATIONS

2016 sales chart

	$ mil.	% of total
Interest income:		
Interest and fees on loans	218.7	64
Interest on taxable securities	17.9	5
Interest on nontaxable securities	1.8	-
Interest on deposits in other banks	0.9	-
Interest on federal funds sold	-	-
Non Interest income:		
Service charges on deposit accounts	42.8	13
Mortgage banking activity	48.2	14
Other service charges commissions and fees	3.5	1
Net gains on sales of securities	-	-
Gain on sale of SBA loans	3.9	1
Other noninterest income	7.1	2
Total	**344.8**	**100**

2016 sales chart

	% of total
Banking Division	91
Retail Mortgage Division	5
Warehouse Lending Division	3
SBA Division	1
Total	**100**

Selected Acquisitions

American United Bank
Central Bank of Georgia
Darby Bank & Trust
First Bank of Jacksonville
High Trust Bank
Montgomery Bank & Trust
One Georgia Bank
Satilla Community Bank
Tifton Banking Company
United Security Bank

COMPETITORS

BANKUNITED INC.
CASCADE BANCORP
CENTERSTATE BANK CORPORATION
CITIZENS FINANCIAL GROUP INC.
CLIFTON BANCORP INC.
COLUMBIA BANKING SYSTEM INC.
COMMERCE BANCSHARES INC.
GREAT SOUTHERN BANCORP INC.
HANCOCK WHITNEY CORPORATION
MUFG AMERICAS HOLDINGS CORPORATION
NATIONAL BANK HOLDINGS CORPORATION
NEWBRIDGE BANCORP
OLD LINE BANCSHARES INC.
PRIVATEBANCORP INC.
SEACOAST BANKING CORPORATION OF FLORIDA
WINTRUST FINANCIAL CORPORATION

HISTORICAL FINANCIALS

Company Type: Public

Income Statement

FYE: December 31

	ASSETS ($ mil.)	NET INCOME ($ mil.)	INCOME AS % OF ASSETS	EMPLOYEES
12/20	20,438.6	261.9	1.3%	2,671
12/19	18,242.5	161.4	0.9%	2,722
12/18	11,443.5	121.0	1.1%	1,804
12/17	7,856.2	73.5	0.9%	1,460
12/16	6,892.0	72.1	1.0%	1,298
Annual Growth	31.2%	38.1%	—	19.8%

2020 Year-End Financials

Return on assets: 1.3%
Return on equity: 10.2%
Long-term debt ($ mil.): —
No. of shares (mil.): 69.5
Sales ($ mil): 1,173.0
Dividends
Yield: 1.5%
Payout: 17.9%
Market value ($ mil.): 2,647.0

	STOCK PRICE ($) FY Close	P/E High/Low		PER SHARE ($)		
				Earnings	Dividends	Book Value
12/20	38.07	12	5	3.77	0.60	38.06
12/19	42.54	16	12	2.75	0.50	35.53
12/18	31.67	21	11	2.80	0.40	30.66
12/17	48.20	26	21	1.98	0.40	21.59
12/16	43.60	23	12	2.08	0.30	18.51
Annual Growth	(3.3%)	—	—	16.0%	18.9%	19.7%

Ames National Corp.

This company aims to please citizens of Ames... and central Iowa. Ames National Corporation is the multi-bank holding company for flagship subsidiary First National Bank Ames Iowa as well as Boone Bank & Trust Reliance State State Bank & Trust and United Bank & Trust. Boasting over $1 billion in assets and 15 branches the banks provide area individuals and businesses with standard services such as deposit accounts IRAs and credit and debit cards. Commercial-related loans account for about 50% of Ames' loan portfolio while agricultural loans make up another 20%. The banks also write residential construction consumer and business loans and offer trust and financial management services.

Operations

Ames National's five banking subsidiaries consists of two national banks (First National Bank and United Bank & Trust) and three state-chartered banks (Reliance State Bank Boone Bank & Trust Co. and State Bank & Trust Co.).

About 54% of Ames National's total revenue came from loan interest (including fees) in 2014 while another 28% came from interest on its taxable and tax-exempt investment securities. The rest of its revenue came from wealth management income (5%) service fees (3%) merchant and card fees (2%) and other miscellaneous income sources. The bank had a staff of roughly 220 employees at the end of 2014.

Geographic Reach

The company's five commercial banks serve central and north central Iowa through 16 branches in the counties of Boone Hancock Marshall Polk and Story counties.

Financial Performance

Ames National's revenues and profits have been rising over the past few years largely thanks to growing loan business and lower interest expenses on deposits in the low-interest environment.

The company's revenue jumped 9% to $50.22 million in 2014 mostly thanks to real estate loan business growth and higher yields on its taxable investment securities. Its non-interest income rose by 20% largely due to gains made onthe sale of some of its property and equipment and higher wealth management fee income.

Higher revenue a continued decline in interest expenses and lower loan loss provisions drove Ames National's net income higher by 9% to $15.3 million. The bank's operating cash levels fell by 17% to $19.5 million after adjusting its cash for non-cash items mostly related to amortization of mortgage-backed securities asset changes and gains on property and equipment sales.

Strategy

The bank (through its banking subsidiaries) focuses on serving small-to-medium size businesses that traditionally wish to develop and maintain an exclusive relationship with a single bank. It sometimes pursues bank or branch acquisitions in its target markets in Iowa to strengthen its market share expand its reach and grow its loan and deposit business.

Mergers and Acquisitions

In August 2014 subsidiary First National Bank continued to strengthen and expand its market share in Des Moines Iowa after purchasing three bank branches of First Bank located in West Des Moines and Johnston for $4.1 million. The deal added $80 million in new deposits and $49 million in new loan business to First National's books.

Growing its customer base and increasing its presence in north central Iowa in 2012 Ames National's Reliance State Bank (formerly known as Randall-Story State Bank) purchased two bank offices in Garner and Klemme Iowa from Liberty Bank FSB.

EXECUTIVES

Independent Director, Kevin Swartz
Independent Director, Patrick Hagan
Independent Director, Michelle Cassabaum
Chairman Of The Board, thomas Pohlman
President, Chief Executive Officer, Director, John Nelson, $367,605 total compensation
President And Director Of Reliance Bank, Richard Schreier, $152,100 total compensation
Chief Financial Officer, Secretary, Director, John Pierschbacher, $217,350 total compensation
Independent Director, Lisa Eslinger
Auditors: CliftonLarsonAllen LLP

LOCATIONS

HQ: Ames National Corp.
405 5th Street, Ames, IA 50010
Phone: 515 232-6251   **Fax:** 515 663-3033
Web: www.amesnational.com

PRODUCTS/OPERATIONS

2014 Sales

	$ mil.	% of total
Interest income	41.0	82
Non-interest income	9.2	18
Total	**50.2**	**100**

COMPETITORS

AMERICAN NATIONAL BANKSHARES INC.
OLD NATIONAL BANCORP
PEOPLES FINANCIAL SERVICES CORP.

HISTORICAL FINANCIALS

Company Type: Public

Income Statement

FYE: December 31

	ASSETS ($ mil.)	NET INCOME ($ mil.)	INCOME AS % OF ASSETS	EMPLOYEES
12/20	1,975.6	18.8	1.0%	265
12/19	1,737.1	17.1	1.0%	133
12/18	1,455.6	17.0	1.2%	138
12/17	1,375.0	13.7	1.0%	221
12/16	1,366.4	15.7	1.2%	202
Annual Growth	**9.7%**	**4.6%**	**—**	**7.0%**

2020 Year-End Financials

Return on assets: 1.0%
Return on equity: 9.4%
Long-term debt ($ mil.): —
No. of shares (mil.): 9.1
Sales ($ mil): 73.5

Dividends
  Yield: 4.1%
  Payout: 50.5%
Market value ($ mil.): 219.0

	STOCK PRICE ($) FY Close	P/E High/Low		PER SHARE ($) Earnings	Dividends	Book Value
12/20	24.02	13	8	2.06	0.99	22.96
12/19	28.06	16	13	1.86	0.95	20.34
12/18	25.42	17	14	1.83	1.16	18.60
12/17	27.85	23	18	1.47	0.87	18.34
12/16	33.00	21	13	1.69	0.83	17.73
Annual Growth	**(7.6%)**	**—**	**—**	**5.1%**	**4.5%**	**6.7%**

Amneal Pharmaceuticals Inc

Impax Laboratories is betting that its pharmaceuticals will make a positive impact on the world's health. The company makes specialty generic pharmaceuticals which it markets through its Impax Generics division and through marketing alliances with other pharmaceutical firms. It concentrates on controlled-release versions of various generic versions of branded and niche pharmaceuticals that require difficult-to-obtain raw materials or specialized expertise. Additionally the company's branded pharmaceuticals business (Impax Specialty Pharma) is developing and improving upon previously approved drugs that target Parkinson's disease multiple sclerosis and other central nervous system disorders. In 2018 Impax merged with Amneal Pharmaceuticals to create a top generics firm.

Operations

Prior to the merger with Amneal Pharmaceuticals Impax earned the majority (more than 70%) of its revenue through its Impax Generics division which produces dosage variations of about 75 generic compounds including fenofibrate (generic Lofibra for high cholesterol) midodrine HCl (generic ProAmatine) and generic Adderall XR (for attention-deficit hyperactivity disorder or ADHD).

The smaller Impax Pharmaceuticals division which brought in about 30% of revenue develops sells and distributes branded drugs. Its portfolio includes central nervous system products other specialty drugs and development-stage candidates.

Geographic Reach

Impax is headquartered in New Jersey; it has administrative offices in Pennsylvania. The company has other locations in the US India Ireland Germany Switzerland and the UK.

Sales and Marketing

Impax Generics sells the group's generic products to wholesalers chain drug stores and mail order pharmacies. Impax also works through strategic alliances that include co-promotion licensing third-party marketing or manufacturing and supply agreements with other generic and branded pharmaceutical manufacturers.

The company's top three customers are wholesalers Cardinal (about one-third of revenue) McKesson (some 30%) and AmerisourceBergen (about 25%).

Strategy

To expand the operations of its main Impax Generics division Impax works to develop new generic versions of drugs that have lost (or are about to lose) patent protection with a focus on controlled-release and specialty products. It also develops medicines that come in alternative-dosage forms such as nasal sprays inhalers ointments injectables and patches. The company's generic development programs are conducted both independently and through research or licensing partnerships with other drug makers. Impax seeks to gain first-to-file and first-to market status with its new products and in some cases Impax enters agreements with branded pharmaceutical firms to make authorized generic versions of off-patent drugs.

Revenues for the unit fluctuate from year to year due to competitive conditions (how many additional generic versions of a product are on the market) and shifts in consumer demand for certain medications.

The Impax Pharmaceuticals division has products in clinical stages of development including treatments for multiple sclerosis and Parkinson's disease. The division also focuses its development efforts on other central nervous system disorders such as Alzheimer's disease depression epilepsy and migraines. The company hopes to build its portfolio of branded products through internal development acquisitions and licensing agreements with the ultimate goal of selling some products commercially.

Mergers and Acquisitions

In 2018 Impax merged with another generics drug maker Amneal Pharmaceuticals. The combined firm which is 75%-owned by Amneal shareholders is now be the nation's fifth-largest generics manufacturer. It has some 150 pending Abbreviated New Drug Applications.

In 2016 Impax bought a portfolio of generic drugs from Teva and Allergan for $586 million. The deal included about 20 marketed pending and development products as well as the commercial rights to the generic equivalent to Concerta.

Auditors: Ernst & Young LLP

HOOVER'S HANDBOOK OF EMERGING COMPANIES 2022

LOCATIONS

HQ: Amneal Pharmaceuticals Inc
400 Crossing Boulevard, Bridgewater, NJ 08807
Phone: 908 947-3120
Web: www.amneal.com

COMPETITORS

ANI PHARMACEUTICALS INC.
HIKMA PHARMACEUTICALS PUBLIC LIMITED
  COMPANY
HOSPIRA INC.
MYLAN PHARMACEUTICALS INC.
PAR PHARMACEUTICAL COMPANIES INC.
SANDOZ INC.
TELIGENT INC.
VECTURA GROUP SERVICES LIMITED

HISTORICAL FINANCIALS

Company Type: Public

Income Statement   FYE: December 31

	REVENUE ($ mil.)	NET INCOME ($ mil.)	NET PROFIT MARGIN	EMPLOYEES
12/20	1,992.5	91.0	4.6%	6,000
12/19	1,626.3	(361.9)	—	5,500
12/18	1,662.9	(169.7)	—	6,000
12/17	775.7	(469.2)	—	1,257
12/16	824.4	(472.0)	—	1,495
Annual Growth	24.7%	—	—	41.5%

2020 Year-End Financials

Debt ratio: 71.8%	No. of shares (mil.): 299.7
Return on equity: 33.9%	Dividends
Cash ($ mil.): 341.3	Yield: —
Current ratio: 2.29	Payout: —
Long-term debt ($ mil.): 2,831.9	Market value ($ mil.): 1,370.0

	STOCK PRICE ($) FY Close	P/E High/Low		PER SHARE ($) Earnings	Dividends	Book Value
12/20	4.57	9	4	0.61	0.00	1.01
12/19	4.82	—	—	(2.74)	0.00	0.78
12/18	13.53	—	—	(0.16)	0.00	1.69
Annual Growth	(41.9%)	—	—	—	—	(22.6%)

Ansys Inc.

ANSYS develops and globally markets engineering simulation software and services widely used by engineers designers researchers and student across a broad spectrum of industries and academia including aerospace and defense automotive electronics semiconductors energy consumer products healthcare and more. The company focus on development and flexible solutions that enable users to analyze and designs directly to desktop providing a common platform for fast efficient and cost-conscious product development from design concept to final-stage testing and validation. The company products consist of Platform Structures Fluids Electronics Semiconductors Embedded Software and more The company distribute simulation technologies through direct sales offices in strategic global locations and independent resellers and distributors (collectively channel partners).

Operations

ANSYS revenue is derived principally from the licensing of computer software products and from maintenance contracts. About 55% of the company's revenue comes from maintenance and services and the rest comes from licensing.

The company's products include ANSYS Workbench a framework that ties together the entire simulation process guiding the user through multiphysics analyses. It include Structures Fluids Electronics Semiconductors Embedded Software Systems High-Performance Computing and 3-D Design.

Geographic Reach

ANSYS based in Canonsburg Pennsylvania. The company has office facility Pune India Livermore California and Apex North Carolina. The US accounts for about 45% revenue and Japan about 10% and Germany for about 10% of revenue each. European countries other than Germany supply about 15% of revenue.

Sales and Marketing

ANSYS sells its products directly and through channel partners worldwide as well as distribution partners in more than 40 countries. Indirect sales account for about one-fourth of ANSYS' revenue. In addition it collaborates with CAD and electronic design automation (EDA) system providers such as Autodesk and Cadence to provide links between design packages and ANSYS' simulation portfolio. These strategic alliances provide additional marketing opportunities for the company.

Financial Performance

The company had a revenue of $1.7 billion an 11% increase compared to 2019. The growth rate was favorably impacted by the company's continued investments in its global sales support and marketing organizations the timing and duration of its multi-year lease contracts and its 2020 and 2019 acquisitions product sales contributed incremental revenue of $84.9 million.

In 2020 the company had a net income of $433.9 million a 4% decrease from the previous year.

The company's cash for the year ended 2020 was $912 million. Operating activities generated $547.3 million while investing activities used $614.3 million mainly for acquisitions. Financing activities generated another $96.6 million.

Strategy

The company's strategy of Pervasive Engineering Simulation seeks to deepen the use of simulation in its core inject simulation throughout the product lifecycle and embed simulation into its partners' ecosystems. The engineering software simulation market is strong and growing. Its market growth is driven by customers' need for rapid quality innovation in a cost efficient manner enabling faster time to market of new products and lower warranty costs. While the transition away from physical prototyping toward simulation is prevalent through all industries its demand is heightened by investments in high-growth solutions including 5G electrification autonomous and the Industrial Internet of Things (IIoT). The company's strategy of Pervasive Engineering Simulation is aligned with the market growth.

Mergers and Acquisitions

In 2020 ANSYS entered into a definitive agreement to acquired Lumerical Inc. a leading developer of photonic design and simulation tools. The acquisition will add best-in-class photonics products to the Ansys multiphysics portfolio providing customers with a full set of solutions to solve their next-generation product challenges.

In 2020 of same year ANSYS entered into a definitive agreement to acquire Analytical Graphics Inc. (AGI) a premier provider of mission-driven simulation modeling testing and analysis software for aerospace defense and intelligence applications. The acquisition will expand the scope of Ansys' solution offering empowering users to solve challenges by simulating from the chip now all the way to a customers' entire mission ? like tracking an orbiting satellite and its periodic connection to ground stations. The purchase price for the transaction is $700 million of which 67% of the consideration will be paid in cash and 33% will be paid through the issuance of Ansys common stock.

EXECUTIVES

Senior Vice President - Administration, Maria Shields, $420,849 total compensation
Senior Vice President - Products, Shane Emswiler, $312,995 total compensation
President, Chief Executive Officer, Director, Ajei Gopal, $818,750 total compensation
Independent Chairman Of The Board, Ronald Hovsepian
Vice President, General Counsel, Secretary, Janet Lee, $316,975 total compensation
Independent Director, Glenda Dorchak
Cfo And Senior Vice President, Finance, Nicole Anasenes, $74,439 total compensation
Independent Director, Ravi Vijayaraghavan
Independent Director, Robert Calderoni
Independent Director, James Frankola
Director, Anil Chakravarthy
Senior Vice President - Worldwide Sales And Customer Excellence, Richard Mahoney, $401,365 total compensation
Auditors: DELOITTE & TOUCHE LLP

LOCATIONS

HQ: Ansys Inc.
2600 ANSYS Drive, Canonsburg, PA 15317
Phone: 844 462-6797
Web: www.ansys.com

PRODUCTS/OPERATIONS

2018 Sales

	$ mil.	% of total
Software licenses:		
Lease licenses	275.6	21
Perpetual licenses	301.1	23
Maintenance & service:		
Maintenance	676.9	53
Service	40.0	3
Total	**1,293.6**	**100**

COMPETITORS

ASPEN TECHNOLOGY INC.	NETSCOUT SYSTEMS INC.
BENTLEY SYSTEMS INCORPORATED	PDF SOLUTIONS INC.
COGNEX CORPORATION	PROGRESS SOFTWARE CORPORATION
FIVE9 INC.	QAD INC.
KEYSIGHT TECHNOLOGIES INC.	STRATASYS LTD
	VERTEX INC.

HOOVER'S HANDBOOK OF EMERGING COMPANIES 2022

HISTORICAL FINANCIALS
Company Type: Public

Income Statement				FYE: December 31
	REVENUE ($ mil.)	NET INCOME ($ mil.)	NET PROFIT MARGIN	EMPLOYEES
12/21	1,906.7	454.6	23.8%	5,100
12/20	1,681.3	433.8	25.8%	4,800
12/19	1,515.8	451.3	29.8%	4,100
12/18	1,293.6	419.3	32.4%	3,400
12/17	1,095.2	259.2	23.7%	2,900
Annual Growth	14.9%	15.1%	—	15.2%

2021 Year-End Financials

Debt ratio: 11.9%
Return on equity: 10.6%
Cash ($ mil.): 667.6
Current ratio: 2.10
Long-term debt ($ mil.): 753.5

No. of shares (mil.): 87.0
Dividends
　Yield: —
　Payout: —
Market value ($ mil.): 34,929.0

	STOCK PRICE ($) FY Close	P/E High/Low		PER SHARE ($) Earnings	Dividends	Book Value
12/21	401.12	79	56	5.16	0.00	51.49
12/20	363.80	72	40	4.97	0.00	47.33
12/19	257.41	48	26	5.25	0.00	40.28
12/18	142.94	38	27	4.88	0.00	31.68
12/17	147.59	50	31	2.98	0.00	26.68
Annual Growth	28.4%	—	—	14.7%	—	17.9%

Antares Pharma Inc.

Antares Pharma understands antagonism towards needles. The company develops needle-free systems for administering injectable drugs. Its Medi-Jector Vision system for instance injects a thin high-pressure stream of liquid eliminating the need for a needle. The Vision system is used primarily for the delivery of insulin and of human growth hormones (hGH) and Vibex disposable pen injectors carry epinephrine and other products. The products are available in the US and overseas. In addition to its needle-free systems the company develops other drug-delivery platforms including topical gels orally administered disintegrating tablets and mini-needle injection systems.

Operations

Much of the company's revenue particularly for its injection devices comes via agreements with pharmaceutical partners which sell its needle-free injectors along with their drugs. Antares' multi-product deal with manufacturer Teva Pharmaceutical includes hGH and epinephrine delivery systems. Dutch drug firm Ferring which distributes Antares' needle-free device for use with its hGH hormone is another key customer. Teva and Ferring each account for a third of Antares' sales.

Its first topical gel product the Elestrin treatment for menopausal symptoms is marketed by Meda Pharma. Gelnique another menopause-related treatment is marketed by Actavis.

Geographic Reach

Antares has two facilities in the US; it markets its products in the US Canada Europe and Asia through partners. The US accounts for about three-quarters of revenue.

Financial Performance

For 2012 revenue jumped nearly 40% on the strength of its agreements with Teva milestone payments from undisclosed development projects and other partner payouts. R&D spending however lead to an $11 million net loss as the company works on a rheumatoid arthritis treatment. The company issued stock during the year and finished with positive cash flow. Though Antares has been experiencing revenue growth continued R&D and marketing expenses have it operating at an accumulated deficit of $152 million.

Strategy

Going forward Antares just has to keep developing products and finding marketing partners to help sell them. To cut the risk a bit it usually partners with others for R&D which keeps the money flowing in the form of milestone payments.

Company Background

Antares was formed in 2001 when Medi-Ject (the company's former name) completed a reverse acquisition of Permatec a Swiss company with expertise in topical and oral drug delivery technologies. Director Jacques Gonella the founder of Permatec owns about 15% of Antares Pharma.

EXECUTIVES

President, Chief Executive Officer, Director, Robert Apple, $592,020 total compensation
Independent Chairman Of The Board, Leonard Jacob
Independent Director, Robert Roche
Independent Director, Karen Smith
Executive Vice President, Research And Development And Chief Medical Officer, Peter Richardson
Director, Carmen Volkart
Executive Vice President, Chief Compliance Officer - Human Resources, General Counsel, Corporate Secretary, Peter Graham, $408,825 total compensation
Chief Financial Officer, Executive Vice President, Fred Powell, $406,600 total compensation
Auditors: KPMG LLP

LOCATIONS

HQ: Antares Pharma Inc.
　100 Princeton South, Suite 300, Ewing, NJ 08628
Phone: 609 359-3020
Web: www.antarespharma.com

PRODUCTS/OPERATIONS

2015 Sales

	$ mil.	% of total
Product sales	27.5	60
Development revenue	8.9	19
Licensing fees	7.3	16
Royalties	2.0	4
Total	**45.7**	**100**

Selected Products

Elestrin estradiol gel (Meda)
Gelnique 3% (Oxybutynin Gel 3%) (Actavis)
Otrexup (McKesson)
Twin-Jector EZ II (JCR Pharmaceuticals)
ZOMA-Jet for ZOMACTON brand human growth hormone. (Ferring)
ZomaJet 2 Vision (Ferring)

COMPETITORS

ACURA PHARMACEUTICALS PHARMA INC. INC.

HORIZON

LANNETT COMPANY INC.

AKORN INC.
ALLERGAN LIMITED
Bausch Health Companies Inc
CONSORT MEDICAL LIMITED

PARATEK PHARMACEUTICALS INC.
THE MEDICINES COMPANY

HISTORICAL FINANCIALS
Company Type: Public

Income Statement				FYE: December 31
	REVENUE ($ mil.)	NET INCOME ($ mil.)	NET PROFIT MARGIN	EMPLOYEES
12/20	149.6	56.2	37.6%	185
12/19	123.8	(2.0)	—	178
12/18	63.5	(6.5)	—	165
12/17	54.5	(16.7)	—	111
12/16	52.2	(24.3)	—	110
Annual Growth	30.1%	—	—	13.9%

2020 Year-End Financials

Debt ratio: 19.2%
Return on equity: 64.5%
Cash ($ mil.): 53.1
Current ratio: 2.00
Long-term debt ($ mil.): 24.6

No. of shares (mil.): 166.8
Dividends
　Yield: —
　Payout: —
Market value ($ mil.): 666.0

	STOCK PRICE ($) FY Close	P/E High/Low		PER SHARE ($) Earnings	Dividends	Book Value
12/20	3.99	13	5	0.33	0.00	0.71
12/19	4.70	—	—	(0.01)	0.00	0.33
12/18	2.72	—	—	(0.04)	0.00	0.24
12/17	1.99	—	—	(0.11)	0.00	0.21
12/16	2.33	—	—	(0.16)	0.00	0.29
Annual Growth	14.4%	—	—	—	—	25.1%

Antero Midstream Corp

Auditors: KPMG LLP

LOCATIONS

HQ: Antero Midstream Corp
　1615 Wynkoop Street, Denver, CO 80202
Phone: 303 357-7310
Web: www.anteromidstream.com

HISTORICAL FINANCIALS
Company Type: Public

Income Statement				FYE: December 31
	REVENUE ($ mil.)	NET INCOME ($ mil.)	NET PROFIT MARGIN	EMPLOYEES
12/21	898.2	331.6	36.9%	519
12/20	900.7	(122.5)	—	522
12/19	792.5	(355.1)	—	547
12/18	142.9	66.6	46.6%	0
12/17	69.7	2.3	3.3%	0
Annual Growth	89.5%	245.6%	—	—

2021 Year-End Financials

Debt ratio: 56.3%
Return on equity: 14.1%
Cash ($ mil.): —
Current ratio: 0.74
Long-term debt ($ mil.): 3,122.9

No. of shares (mil.): 477.5
Dividends
　Yield: 10.1%
　Payout: 142.3%
Market value ($ mil.): 4,622.0

STOCK PRICE ($) FY Close	P/E High/Low	PER SHARE ($) Earnings	Dividends	Book Value
12/21	9.68	17 11	0.69	0.98	4.79
12/20	7.71	— —	(0.26)	1.23	5.07
12/19	7.59	— —	(0.80)	0.92	6.49
12/18	11.18	67 32	0.33	0.54	0.17
12/17	19.72	752559	0.03	0.00	0.08
Annual Growth	(16.3%) 174.9%	—	—119.0%		—

Apollo Medical Holdings Inc

EXECUTIVES

Director, J. Lorraine Estradas
President, Co-chief Executive Officer, Director, Thomas Lam, $950,000 total compensation
Chief Financial Officer, Secretary, Eric Chin, $300,000 total compensation
Chief Administrative Officer, Albert Young, $366,945 total compensation
Independent Director, David Schmidt
Independent Director, Mark Fawcett
Executive Chairman Of The Board, Kenneth Sim, $950,000 total compensation
Lead Independent Director, Mitchell Kitayama
Independent Director, John Chiang
Director, Linda Marsh
Director, Matthew Mazdyasni
Co-chief Executive Officer, Chief Technology Officer, Vice President - Engineering, Brandon Sim, $124,039 total compensation
Director, Weili Dai
Auditors: Ernst and Young, LLP

LOCATIONS

HQ: Apollo Medical Holdings Inc
1668 S. Garfield Avenue, 2nd Floor, Alhambra, CA 91801
Phone: 626 282-0288
Web: www.apollomed.net

HISTORICAL FINANCIALS

Company Type: Public

Income Statement — FYE: December 31

	REVENUE ($ mil.)	NET INCOME ($ mil.)	NET PROFIT MARGIN	EMPLOYEES
12/20	687.1	37.8	5.5%	630
12/19	560.6	14.1	2.5%	555
12/18	519.9	10.8	2.1%	575
12/17*	357.7	25.8	7.2%	613
03/17	57.4	(8.9)	—	1,149
Annual Growth	86.0%	—	—	(13.9%)

*Fiscal year change

2020 Year-End Financials

Debt ratio: 29.5%
Return on equity: 14.4%
Cash ($ mil.): 193.4
Current ratio: 2.94
Long-term debt ($ mil.): 230.5
No. of shares (mil.): 42.2
Dividends
  Yield: —
  Payout: —
Market value ($ mil.): 772.0

AppFolio Inc

Auditors: PricewaterhouseCoopers LLP

LOCATIONS

HQ: AppFolio Inc
50 Castilian Drive, Santa Barbara, CA 93117
Phone: 805 364-6093

HISTORICAL FINANCIALS

Company Type: Public

Income Statement — FYE: December 31

	REVENUE ($ mil.)	NET INCOME ($ mil.)	NET PROFIT MARGIN	EMPLOYEES
12/20	310.0	158.4	51.1%	1,335
12/19	256.0	36.2	14.2%	1,240
12/18	190.0	19.9	10.5%	916
12/17	143.8	9.7	6.8%	672
12/16	105.5	(8.2)	—	626
Annual Growth	30.9%	—		20.8%

2020 Year-End Financials

Debt ratio: —
Return on equity: 75.6%
Cash ($ mil.): 140.2
Current ratio: 4.00
Long-term debt ($ mil.): —
No. of shares (mil.): 34.3
Dividends
  Yield: —
  Payout: —
Market value ($ mil.): 6,191.0

	STOCK PRICE ($) FY Close	P/E High/Low	PER SHARE ($) Earnings	Dividends	Book Value
12/20	180.04	40 18	4.44	0.00	8.31
12/19	109.95	108 53	1.02	0.00	3.86
12/18	59.22	154 66	0.56	0.00	2.71
12/17	41.50	178 76	0.28	0.00	2.50
12/16	23.85	— —	(0.25)	0.00	2.07
Annual Growth	65.8%	— —	—	—	41.6%

Arbor Realty Trust Inc

Money doesn't grow on trees so Arbor Realty Trust invests in real estate-related assets. The real estate investment trust (REIT) buys structured finance assets in the commercial and multifamily real estate markets. It primarily invests in bridge loans (short-term financing) and mezzanine loans (large and usually unsecured loans) but also invests in discounted mortgage notes and other as-

STOCK PRICE ($) FY Close	P/E High/Low	PER SHARE ($) Earnings	Dividends	Book Value
12/20	18.27	19 9	1.01	0.00	7.83
12/19	18.41	52 34	0.39	0.00	5.33
12/18	19.85	91 40	0.29	0.00	5.22
12/17*	24.00	24 6	0.90	0.00	4.95
03/17	9.00	— —	(1.49)	0.00	(0.06)
Annual Growth	19.4%	— —	—	—	—

*Fiscal year change

sets. The REIT targets lending and investment opportunities where borrowers seek interim financing until permanent financing is attained. Arbor Realty Trust is managed by financing firm Arbor Commercial Mortgage though in early 2016 the REIT agreed to buy Arbor Commercial Mortgage for $250 million to expand into the government-sponsored multi-family real estate loan origination business.

EXECUTIVES

Chairman Of The Board, President, Chief Executive Officer, Ivan Kaufman, $1,000,000 total compensation
Executive Vice President - Structured Finance, Fred Weber, $500,000 total compensation
Executive Vice President - Structured Securitization, Gene Kilgore, $500,000 total compensation
Independent Director, Archie Dykes
Director, Joseph Martello
Chief Financial Officer, Paul Elenio, $500,000 total compensation
Chief Operating Officer — Agency Lending, John Caulfield, $500,000 total compensation
Managing Director And Chief Credit Officer - Structured Finance, Andrew Guziewicz, $300,000 total compensation
Executive Vice President - Treasury And Servicing, John Natalone
Chief Accounting Officer, Thomas Ridings
Independent Director, George Tsunis
Independent Director, Edward Farrell
Independent Director, Elliot Schwartz
Independent Director, Kenneth Bacon
Executive Vice President, Senior Counsel, Corporate Secretary, John Bishar
Executive Vice President - Servicing And Asset Management, Danny Van Der Reis
Auditors: Ernst & Young LLP

LOCATIONS

HQ: Arbor Realty Trust Inc
333 Earle Ovington Boulevard, Suite 900, Uniondale, NY 11553
Phone: 516 506-4200
Web: www.arbor.com

COMPETITORS

ANNALY CAPITAL MANAGEMENT INC.
ARBOR COMMERCIAL MORTGAGE LLC
CHERRY HILL MORTGAGE INVESTMENT CORPORATION
EASTERN LIGHT CAPITAL INCORPORATED
ELLINGTON FINANCIAL INC.
PETRA REAL ESTATE OPPORTUNITY TRUST
RC MERGER SUBSIDIARY LLC
TIS MORTGAGE INVESTMENT COMPANY

HISTORICAL FINANCIALS

Company Type: Public

Income Statement — FYE: December 31

	REVENUE ($ mil.)	NET INCOME ($ mil.)	NET PROFIT MARGIN	EMPLOYEES
12/21	799.2	339.3	42.5%	579
12/20	603.7	170.9	28.3%	522
12/19	535.7	128.6	24.0%	532
12/18	484.9	180.2	37.2%	468
12/17	346.6	121.6	35.1%	445
Annual Growth	23.2%	29.2%	—	6.8%

HOOVER'S HANDBOOK OF EMERGING COMPANIES 2022

2021 Year-End Financials

Debt ratio: 79.9%
Return on equity: 18.0%
Cash ($ mil.): 404.5
Current ratio: 0.19
Long-term debt ($ mil.): 7,575.1

No. of shares (mil.): 151.3
Dividends
  Yield: 7.5%
  Payout: 57.7%
Market value ($ mil.): 2,773.0

	STOCK PRICE ($) FY Close	P/E High/Low		PER SHARE ($) Earnings	Dividends	Book Value
12/21	18.32	9	6	2.28	1.38	15.98
12/20	14.18	11	3	1.41	1.23	10.91
12/19	14.35	12	8	1.27	1.29	10.80
12/18	10.07	8	5	1.50	1.13	10.66
12/17	8.64	8	6	1.12	0.72	11.27
Annual Growth	20.7%	—	—	19.4%	17.7%	9.1%

Ares Management Corp

Auditors: Ernst & Young LLP

LOCATIONS

HQ: Ares Management Corp
2000 Avenue of the Stars, 12th Floor, Los Angeles, CA 90067
Phone: 310 201-4100
Web: www.aresmgmt.com

HISTORICAL FINANCIALS

Company Type: Public

Income Statement
FYE: December 31

	REVENUE ($ mil.)	NET INCOME ($ mil.)	NET PROFIT MARGIN	EMPLOYEES
12/20	1,764.0	152.1	8.6%	1,450
12/19	1,765.4	148.8	8.4%	1,200
12/18	958.4	57.0	5.9%	1,100
12/17	1,415.5	76.1	5.4%	1,000
12/16	1,199.2	111.8	9.3%	925
Annual Growth	10.1%	8.0%	—	11.9%

2020 Year-End Financials

Debt ratio: 70.6%
Return on equity: 15.4%
Cash ($ mil.): 1,062.1
Current ratio: 8.39
Long-term debt ($ mil.): 10,722.9

No. of shares (mil.): 259.6
Dividends
  Yield: 3.4%
  Payout: 296.3%
Market value ($ mil.): 12,216.0

	STOCK PRICE ($) FY Close	P/E High/Low		PER SHARE ($) Earnings	Dividends	Book Value
12/20	47.05	56	26	0.87	1.60	4.60
12/19	35.69	32	15	1.06	1.28	6.67
12/18	17.78	84	56	0.30	1.33	5.79
12/17	20.00	38	28	0.62	1.13	6.97
12/16	19.20	16	9	1.20	0.83	7.32
Annual Growth	25.1%	—	—	(7.7%)	17.8%	(11.0%)

Arista Networks Inc

Auditors: Ernst & Young LLP

LOCATIONS

HQ: Arista Networks Inc
5453 Great America Parkway, Santa Clara, CA 95054
Phone: 408 547-5500
Web: www.arista.com

HISTORICAL FINANCIALS

Company Type: Public

Income Statement
FYE: December 31

	REVENUE ($ mil.)	NET INCOME ($ mil.)	NET PROFIT MARGIN	EMPLOYEES
12/21	2,948.0	840.8	28.5%	2,993
12/20	2,317.5	634.5	27.4%	2,613
12/19	2,410.7	859.8	35.7%	2,300
12/18	2,151.3	328.1	15.3%	2,300
12/17	1,646.1	423.2	25.7%	1,800
Annual Growth	15.7%	18.7%	—	13.6%

2021 Year-End Financials

Debt ratio: —
Return on equity: 23.0%
Cash ($ mil.): 620.8
Current ratio: 4.34
Long-term debt ($ mil.): —

No. of shares (mil.): 307.6
Dividends
  Yield: —
  Payout: —
Market value ($ mil.): 44,229.0

	STOCK PRICE ($) FY Close	P/E High/Low		PER SHARE ($) Earnings	Dividends	Book Value
12/21	143.75	194	44	2.63	0.00	12.93
12/20	290.57	139	75	2.00	0.00	10.90
12/19	203.40	117	66	2.66	0.00	9.47
12/18	210.70	281	172	1.02	0.00	7.08
12/17	235.58	167	60	1.34	0.00	5.64
Annual Growth	(11.6%)	—	—	18.4%	—	23.1%

ARKO Corp

LOCATIONS

HQ: ARKO Corp
8565 Magellan Parkway, Suite 400, Richmond, VA 23227-1150
Phone: 804 730-1568
Web: www.arkocorp.com

HISTORICAL FINANCIALS

Company Type: Public

Income Statement
FYE: December 31

	REVENUE ($ mil.)	NET INCOME ($ mil.)	NET PROFIT MARGIN	EMPLOYEES
12/20	3,910.7	13.1	0.3%	10,380
12/19	4,128.6	(43.5)	—	10,102
12/18	4,064.8	10.9	0.3%	0
12/17	3,041.1	(5.8)	—	0
Annual Growth	8.7%	—	—	—

2020 Year-End Financials

Debt ratio: 35.9%
Return on equity: 6.8%
Cash ($ mil.): 293.6
Current ratio: 1.57
Long-term debt ($ mil.): 935.2

No. of shares (mil.): 124.1
Dividends
  Yield: —
  Payout: —
Market value ($ mil.): 1,117.0

	STOCK PRICE ($) FY Close	P/E High/Low		PER SHARE ($) Earnings	Dividends	Book Value
12/20	9.00	67	56	0.14	0.00	2.56
12/19	0.00	—	—	(0.06)	0.00	0.09
Annual Growth	—	—	—	—	—	2861.8%

Armada Hoffler Properties Inc

EXECUTIVES

Executive Chairman Of The Board Of Directors, Daniel Hoffler
Chief Financial Officer, Treasurer And Corporate Secretary, Michael O'hara, $399,635 total compensation
President, Chief Executive Officer, Vice Chairman Of The Board, Louis Haddad, $861,640 total compensation
President - Asset Management, Shelly Hampton, $324,819 total compensation
President - Construction, Eric Apperson, $374,904 total compensation
Director, A. Russell Kirk
Independent Director, Dorothy McAuliffe
Independent Director, George Allen
Independent Director, James Carroll
Independent Director, John Snow
Independent Director, Eva Hardy
Chief Operating Officer, Shawn Tibbetts, $350,002 total compensation
Auditors: Ernst & Young LLP

LOCATIONS

HQ: Armada Hoffler Properties Inc
222 Central Park Avenue, Suite 2100, Virginia Beach, VA 23462
Phone: 757 366-4000
Web: www.armadahoffler.com

HISTORICAL FINANCIALS

Company Type: Public

Income Statement
FYE: December 31

	REVENUE ($ mil.)	NET INCOME ($ mil.)	NET PROFIT MARGIN	EMPLOYEES
12/20	383.6	29.1	7.6%	158
12/19	257.2	24.0	9.4%	169
12/18	193.3	17.2	8.9%	156
12/17	302.7	21.0	7.0%	160
12/16	258.3	28.0	10.9%	151
Annual Growth	10.4%	0.9%	—	1.1%

2020 Year-End Financials

Debt ratio: 51.2%
Return on equity: 6.2%
Cash ($ mil.): 41.0
Current ratio: 2.76
Long-term debt ($ mil.): 981.8

No. of shares (mil.): 59.0
Dividends
  Yield: 3.9%
  Payout: 115.7%
Market value ($ mil.): 663.0

	STOCK PRICE ($) FY Close	P/E High/Low		PER SHARE ($) Earnings	Dividends	Book Value
12/20	11.22	50	19	0.38	0.44	8.86
12/19	18.35	46	34	0.41	0.84	7.26
12/18	14.06	45	36	0.36	0.80	5.48
12/17	15.53	32	25	0.50	0.76	5.04
12/16	14.57	18	12	0.85	0.72	3.95
Annual Growth	(6.3%)	—	—	(18.2%)	(11.6%)	22.4%

Arrow Financial Corp.

Arrow Financial has more than one shaft in its quiver. It's the holding company for two banks: $2 billion-asset Glens Falls National Bank operates 30 branches in eastern upstate New York while $400 million-asset Saratoga National Bank and Trust Company has around 10 branches in Saratoga County. Serving local individuals and businesses the banks offer standard deposit and loan products as well as retirement trust and estate planning services and employee benefit plan administration. Its subsidiaries include: McPhillips Insurance Agency and Upstate Agency which offer property and casualty insurance; Capital Financial Group which sells group health plans; and North Country Investment Advisors which provides financial planning services.

Operations

Arrow Financial's loan portfolio consisted of residential real estate mortgages and home equity loans (40% of loan assets) commercial and commercial real estate loans (31%) and indirect auto loans (29%) at the end of 2015.

The banking group makes more than 70% of its revenue from interest income. About 58% of Arrow Financial's total revenue came from loan interest (including fees) during 2015 while another 14% came from interest on taxable and tax-exempt investment securities. The rest of its revenue came from insurance commissions (9% of revenue) customer service fees (9%) fiduciary activity income (8%) and other miscellaneous income sources.

Geographic Reach

Glens Falls National Bank has 30 branches in eastern upstate New York (in Warren Washington Saratoga Essex and Clinton Counties). Saratoga Springs-based Saratoga National Bank operates nine branches in Saratoga Albany and Rensselaer Counties.

Financial Performance

Arrow Financial Corporation's revenues and profits have been slowly rising since 2013 mostly as steady — and more creditworthy — loan growth has spurred more interest income.

The group's revenue climbed 4% to $98.86 million during 2015 mostly as 7%-plus growth in loan and other interest-earning assets continued to spur additional interest income.

Revenue growth in 2015 pushed Arrow Financial's net income up 6% to $24.66 million. The banking group's operating cash levels dipped 6% to $28.93 million despite earnings growth mostly due to unfavorable working capital changes.

Strategy

Arrow Financial has been working its loan portfolio quality by implementing smarter lending strategies with stronger underwriting and collateral control procedures and credit review systems.

It's also slowly expanding its business and branch network in the Capital District of New York which has been a key market for the bnak's growth. In September 2015 its Saratoga National Bank subsidiary opened its ninth branch in Troy. In June 2014 it opened a new branch in Colonie after opening two new branches in Queensbury and Clifton Park in 2013.

EXECUTIVES

Independent Chairman Of The Board, Thomas Hoy
Independent Director, David Kruczlnicki
Independent Director, Michael Clarke
Senior Vice President, Chief Credit Officer, David Kaiser, $275,000 total compensation
Independent Director, Colin Read
Independent Director, Elizabeth Miller
Independent Director, Mark Behan
Chief Operating Officer, Senior Vice President, Andrew Wise, $250,000 total compensation
Independent Director, Gary Dake
President, Chief Executive Officer, Director, Thomas Murphy, $560,000 total compensation
Senior Vice President And Chief Banking Officer, David Demarco, $340,000 total compensation
Independent Director, Tenee Casaccio
Independent Director, William Owens
Chief Financial Officer, Senior Vice President, Treasurer, Edward Campanella, $275,000 total compensation
Auditors: KPMG LLP

LOCATIONS

HQ: Arrow Financial Corp.
  250 Glen Street, Glens Falls, NY 12801
Phone: 518 745-1000
Web: www.arrowfinancial.com

PRODUCTS/OPERATIONS

2015 Sales

	$ mil.	% of total
Interest and dividend income		
Interest and Fees on Loans	56.9	58
Fully Taxable	8.0	8
Exempt from Federal Taxes	5.7	6
Non-interest income		
Fees for Other Services to Customers	9.2	9
Insurance Commissions	9.0	9
Income From Fiduciary Activities	7.8	8
Other	2.2	2
Total	**98.8**	**100**

Selected Subsidiaries

Glens Falls National Bank and Trust Company
  Arrow Properties Inc. (real estate investment trust)
  Capital Financial Group Inc.
  Glens Falls National Community Development Corporation
  Glens Falls National Insurance Agencies LLC (dba McPhillips Agency)
  Loomis & LaPann Inc.
  NC Financial Services Inc.
  North Country Investment Advisers Inc.
  Upstate Agency LLC
Saratoga National Bank and Trust Company

COMPETITORS

CAMDEN NATIONAL CORPORATION	FIRST HORIZON CORPORATION
CITY HOLDING COMPANY	FIRSTMERIT CORPORATION
COMMUNITY BANK SYSTEM INC.	

HISTORICAL FINANCIALS

Company Type: Public

Income Statement

FYE: December 31

	ASSETS ($ mil.)	NET INCOME ($ mil.)	INCOME AS % OF ASSETS	EMPLOYEES
12/20	3,688.6	40.8	1.1%	517
12/19	3,184.2	37.4	1.2%	520
12/18	2,988.3	36.2	1.2%	516
12/17	2,760.4	29.3	1.1%	533
12/16	2,605.2	26.5	1.0%	524
Annual Growth	9.1%	11.4%	—	(0.3%)

2020 Year-End Financials

Return on assets: 1.1%
Return on equity: 12.8%
Long-term debt ($ mil.): —
No. of shares (mil.): 15.9
Sales ($ mil): 144.5

Dividends
  Yield: 3.5%
  Payout: 39.6%
Market value ($ mil.): 478.0

	STOCK PRICE ($) FY Close	P/E High/Low		PER SHARE ($) Earnings	Dividends	Book Value
12/20	29.91	15	9	2.56	1.02	20.92
12/19	37.80	16	13	2.36	0.99	18.96
12/18	32.02	17	13	2.29	0.94	17.04
12/17	33.95	22	17	1.87	0.87	15.91
12/16	40.50	24	15	1.70	0.84	14.88
Annual Growth	(7.3%)	—	—	10.8%	4.8%	8.9%

ASGN Inc

ASGN Incorporated (formerly known as On Assignment) is a specialist staffing agency that places professionals from IT consultants to lab assistants with clients in need of temporary (or permanent) help. The firm operates through several divisions: Apex (IT and engineering staffing for temporary temp-to-hire and permanent placements); Oxford (engineering and specialized high-end IT consultants); and ECS (cloud cybersecurity and software). ASGN brands include CyberCoders Cyrus Lab Support Oxford Oxford Global Resources and among other. The company generated majority of its sales in domestic operations.

Operations

ASGN operates three segments that serve different staffing needs Apex ECS and Oxford.

Apex is the company's biggest earner pulling in more than two-thirds of sales. It comprises two units Apex Systems (IT) and Creative Circle (creative marketing advertising and digital). The Apex Segment provides technology digital creative scientific engineering staffing and consulting services.

Oxford generates some 20% of sales and holds ASGN's Oxford Global Resources (IT engineering and regulatory and compliance sectors) and Cyber Coders (tech engineering sales executives accounting scientific and legal).

ECS segment delivers advanced solutions in cloud cybersecurity artificial intelligence machine learning software development IT modernization and science and engineering.

Geographic Reach

Headquartered in Calabasas California ASGN Incorporated operates from about 160 branch offices in US Canada Belgium Ireland the Netherlands Spain and Switzerland). The Oxford division's operational HQ is in Beverly Massachusetts; Apex is based in Richmond Virginia; and ECS is based in Fairfax Virginia.

The domestic accounts for over 95% of ASGN's sales.

Sales and Marketing

ASGN provides staffing services and solutions to several markets including Fortune 1000 companies and mid-market clients and the federal state and local government.

The company places about 63400 contract professionals on assignment contracts with clients. Over 75% of the company's revenue are generated in the through assignment contracts.

Financial Performance

ASGN's revenue has been growing strongly over the last five years.

In 2019 the company grew its sales 15% to $3.9 billion. The year-over-year increase in revenues was attributable to growth in assignment revenues and a full year contribution from ECS which was acquired on April 2 2018. The growth in assignment revenues was mainly from large-volume customers and from consulting services..

ASGN reported net income in 2019 at $174.4 million. A 19% increase in operating profits was offset by a higher interest expense (and an increase in income tax expense.

ASGN's cash balance improved slightly during 2019 ending the year $53.4 million higher at $95.2 million. The company generated $313.2 million from its operating activities and $110.5 million used in financing activities; investing activities used $149.1 million. The company spent $116.4 million on acquisitions while taking on new debt of $653 million. As a result ASGN ended 2019 with net debt of $1 billion.

Strategy

ASGN's strategy is to identify enter and be a significant player in the most attractive subsectors of the IT and professional staffing and consulting services markets through both organic and acquisitive growth. In 2017 the company set a revenue goal of $5.0 billion by 2022 while ensuring that it maintain attractive gross margins earnings before interest taxes depreciation and amortization ("EBITDA") margins and earnings per share ("EPS") growth. To achieve these goals ASGN continue to specialize in the large and growing technology engineering digital creative and life sciences markets reinforce its position as a significant competitor in each advance its pursuit of the IT services market with its professional staffing services invest primarily in domestic markets and pursue additional acquisitions that support its differentiated resource deployment model.

ASGN strategic innovation efforts and technology investments focus on putting the best productivity tools in the hands of its recruiters candidates and clients making it easy for clients and consultants to work with ASGN. The company respond to emerging trends in digitization and candidate sourcing to better position its businesses and improve how it serve clients and consultants.

In addition ASGN invest in leasehold improvements as it expand relocate and rationalize its branch facilities to increase the productivity of its consultants.

Mergers and Acquisitions

In 2020 ASGN acquired Virginia-based Blackstone Federal or $85 million in cash which is now part of ASGN's ECS government IT solutions and services segment. Blackstone Federal will be immediately integrated into ECS' enterprise solutions group which focuses on delivering digital solutions to Federal civilian customers.

In 2019 ASGN acquired Intersys Consulting a Texas-based provider of technology services to the commercial and government sectors. The acquired company will become part of the ASGN Apex Systems division. The company acquired Intersys Consulting for $67 million in cash.

ASGN bought DHA in early 2019 for $46 million in cash. DHA is a provider of mobility cybersecurity cloud and IT services to the Federal Bureau of Investigation (FBI) and other federal customers. DHA will become part of ASGN's ECS Segment.

Company Background

ASGN Incorporated was founded in 1985. Since its IPO in 1992 the company has grown steadily with multiple offices throughout North America and Europe.

HISTORY

Chemists Bruce Culver and Raf Dahlquist concocted the company in 1985. Lab Support (its original name) got off to a good start but the founders were scientists not business strategists; by 1989 the company was losing steam. The firm's venture investors took over installing new management under Tom Buelter who had developed Kelly Services' home care division. He refocused operations to temporary scientific services and turned the company around. It went public in 1992 as On Assignment.

In 1994 On Assignment bought 1st Choice Personnel and Sklar Resource Group which specialized in temporary placement of financial professionals. The next year it started its Advanced Science Professionals unit to place temps in highly skilled scientific positions. With the 1996 purchase of Minneapolis-based EnviroStaff On Assignment also began providing temporary workers in environmental fields. On Assignment crossed the border and started operations in Canada in 1997. In 1999 it established Clinical Lab Staff as its fourth division. Also by 1999 the company had opened the first three of several planned European offices in the UK.

In 2001 Buelter relinquished the CEO position to Joe Peterson. (Buelter resigned as chairman early the following year.) Also in 2002 the company acquired Health Personnel Options Corporation a provider of temporary travel nurses and other health care professionals. The end of 2003 saw the appointment of Peter Dameris as the president and CEO of On Assignment.

In 2007 On Assignment reached new levels of growth with the key acquisitions of IT and engineering staffing provider Oxford Global Resources and physician staffing firm VISTA Staffing Solutions.

As with most players in the staffing sector On Assignment felt the painful effects of the global recession in 2008 and 2009 as it was hurt by high unemployment rates and shrinking demand for its staffing services.

As the economy began to pick up in 2010 On Assignment bought The Cambridge Group Ltd. a staffing services firm placing physicians clinical and scientific personnel and IT professionals. Also that year the company acquired Sharpstream a firm with expertise in search services for executive to middle managers residing in the life sciences

sector. The deal added offices in the US the UK and Shanghai.

Continuing its string of acquisitions in 2011 On Assignment obtained Valesta a provider of clinical research specialized staffing services with headquarters in Belgium and additional offices in Spain and The Netherlands. The company next acquired Apex Systems the sixth largest staffing firm and one of the fastest growing IT staffing firms in the US in 2012.

EXECUTIVES

Chief Financial Officer, Executive Vice President, Edward Pierce, $630,000 total compensation

President, Randolph Blazer, $838,000 total compensation

Independent Director, Jonathan Holman

President, Chief Executive Officer And Director, Theodore Hanson, $930,000 total compensation

Independent Director, Edwin Sheridan

Independent Director, Brian Callaghan

President, Ecs, George Wilson, $530,000 total compensation

Independent Director, Mark Frantz

Independent Director, Joseph Dyer

Independent Director, Carol Lindstrom

Independent Director, Maria Hawthorne

Senior Vice President, Chief Administrative Officer, Treasurer, James Brill, $335,564 total compensation

Independent Director, Marty Kittrell

Senior Vice President, Chief Legal Officer, Secretary, Jennifer Painter, $430,000 total compensation

Auditors: DELOITTE & TOUCHE LLP

LOCATIONS

HQ: ASGN Inc
4400 Cox Road, Suite 110, Glen Allen, VA 23060
Phone: 888 482-8068
Web: www.asgn.com

PRODUCTS/OPERATIONS

2018 Sales

	$ mil.	% of total
Assignment	2,760.5	81
Permanent Placement	146.3	5
ECS	439.0	14
Total	**3,399.8**	**100**

2018 Sales

	$ mil.	% of total
Apex	2,300.3	68
Oxford	606.5	18
ECS	493.0	14
Total	**3,399.8**	**100**

Selected Divisions and Operating Units

Apex (IT staffing)
On Assignment Clinical Research
On Assignment Engineering
On Assignment Healthcare Staffing
On Assignment Health Information Management
On Assignment Lab Support
Oxford Global Resources (IT and engineering staffing)

COMPETITORS

CHG HEALTHCARE SERVICES INC.
CROSS COUNTRY HEALTHCARE INC.
KFORCE INC.
MANPOWERGROUP INC.

ROBERT HALF INTERNATIONAL INC.
TEKSYSTEMS INC.
THE DAY & ZIMMERMANN GROUP INC

HISTORICAL FINANCIALS

Company Type: Public

Income Statement

FYE: December 31

	REVENUE ($ mil.)	NET INCOME ($ mil.)	NET PROFIT MARGIN	EMPLOYEES
12/20	3,950.6	200.3	5.1%	55,200
12/19	3,923.9	174.7	4.5%	67,700
12/18	3,399.7	157.7	4.6%	66,200
12/17	2,625.9	157.6	6.0%	59,200
12/16	2,440.4	97.2	4.0%	55,880
Annual Growth	12.8%	19.8%	—	(0.3%)

2020 Year-End Financials

Debt ratio: 31.5%	No. of shares (mil.): 52.9
Return on equity: 13.4%	Dividends
Cash ($ mil.): 274.4	Yield: —
Current ratio: 2.39	Payout: —
Long-term debt ($ mil.): 1,033.4	Market value ($ mil.): 4,419.0

	STOCK PRICE ($) FY Close	P/E High/Low		PER SHARE ($) Earnings	Dividends	Book Value
12/20	83.53	23	8	3.76	0.00	30.00
12/19	70.97	22	15	3.28	0.00	26.02
12/18	54.50	31	17	2.98	0.00	22.51
12/17	64.27	22	14	2.97	0.00	19.01
12/16	44.16	25	16	1.81	0.00	16.48
Annual Growth	17.3%	—	—	20.1%	—	16.2%

Aspen Technology Inc

Aspen Technology (AspenTech) helps its customers scale mountains of supply chain and engineering challenges. It provides supply chain manufacturing and engineering process optimization software to some 2400 companies in the energy chemical construction and pharmaceutical industries among others. The company's software ? which includes supplier collaboration inventory management production planning and collaborative engineering functions ? is offered under its aspenONE subscription service. AspenTech which generates most of its sales outside the US also provides related technical and professional services such as technical support training and systems implementation and integration.

Operations

AspenTech reports in two segments: subscription and software segment which is engaged in the licensing of process optimization and asset performance management software solutions and associated support services and includes its license and maintenance revenue; and services and other segment which includes professional services and training and includes its services and other revenue. The company's subscription and software segment accounts vast majority of revenue with services accounting for the rest.

In addition AspenTech's revenue by type of performance obligation is divided into three types ? Term Licenses Maintenance and Professional services and other ? which generates around 65% approximately 30% and some 5% of total sales respectively.

Geographic Reach

AspenTech is headquartered in Bedford Massachusetts and has offices in the UK Shanghai Mexico City Singapore Beijing Pune Moscow Tokyo and Bahrain.

The US is the company's largest geographic segment accounting for almost 45% of sales. Europe contributes around 25% of sales. Other markets served include the Asia-Pacific region Canada Latin America and the Middle East.

Sales and Marketing

AspenTech sells directly through Field Sales organization and by licensing to universities to encourage future demand. Using webinars digital communities social media videos email and other digital means the company seeks to engage its extensive user base with targeted messages intended to address the specific needs of each market customer and user. It counts some 2400 customers globally. The company incurred advertising expenses of $3.5 million $4.4 million and $3.2 million during 2020 2019 and 2018 respectively.

Financial Performance

Total revenue increased by $2.0 million during fiscal 2020 as compared to the prior fiscal year. The increase of $2.0 million was due to an increase in maintenance revenue of $14.6 million and an increase in services and other revenue of $3.9 million partially offset by a decrease in license revenue of $(16.4) million as compared to the prior fiscal year.

Cash held by the company at the end of fiscal 2020 increased to $287.8 million while in 2019 was $215.9 million. Cash provided by operations and financing activities were $243.3 million and $49.4 million respectively. Cash used for investing activities was $76.2 million mainly for payments for business acquisitions.

Strategy

Aspen seeks to maintain and extend its position as a leading global provider of process optimization software and related services to the process industries. The company has introduced a new strategy to evolve its scope of optimization from the process units in a plant to the process and the equipment in the plant or entire asset. Aspen has expanded its reach in optimization from conceptualization and design operations and supply chain to the maintenance aspects of the plant. The company plan to continue to build on its expertise in process optimization its installed base and long-term customer relationships to further expand its reach in the maintenance area of the plant. By focusing on asset optimization the company will be able to optimize the design and operations of a plant considering the performance and constraints of process equipment so as to optimize the full asset lifecycle. Aspen's primary growth strategy is to expand organically within its core verticals by leveraging its market leadership position and driving increased usage and product adoption of the broad capabilities in its aspenONE offerings. Additionally Aspen seeks acquisitions to accelerate its overall growth in the design and operations of the process and acquisitions that will expand its maintenance solution to deliver asset optimization.

To accomplish these goals the company will pursue the following activities: continue to provide innovative market-leading solutions; further penetrate existing customer base; adoption and usage in customer base; asset performance management expansion; build an ecosystem; pursue acquisi-

tions; and expand the company's total addressable market.

Mergers and Acquisitions

In late 2020 AspenTech acquired OptiPlant a leading provider of AI Driven 3D Conceptual Design and Engineering Automation software to help owner operators and EPC optimize conceptual designs and estimates and accelerate development of Front-End Engineering Designs (FEED) to save capital improve safety and reduce environmental impact headquartered in Walnut Creek California. The transaction further strengthens the company's solutions for owner-operators and EPC companies in the process industries.

Also in late 2020 AspenTech acquired Camo Analytics AS a leading provider of industrial analytics based in Norway for an undisclosed amount. The technology and expertise acquired with Camo Analytics further strengthens AspenTech's solutions to drive higher levels of performance profitability and consistent quality for industries such as pharmaceuticals and biotech.

In mid-2019 AspenTech acquired Mnubo Inc. a Montreal-based provider of purpose-built artificial intelligence (AI) and analytics infrastructure for the Internet of Things (IoT). The Mnubo technology accelerates the realization of AspenTech's vision for the next generation of asset optimization solutions that combine deep process expertise with AI and machine learning. In addition to deploying AI-powered applications the ability to visualize vast quantities of information and analyzed data is critical to the evolution of the smart enterprise. To further enhance the capabilities AspenTech has acquired Sabisu Ltd. a UK-based company that provides a flexible enterprise visualization and workflow solution to deliver real-time decision support.

HISTORY

Lawrence Evans was a chemical engineering professor at MIT in 1976 when he became the principal investigator for the Energy Department's ASPEN (Advanced System for Process Engineering) project to develop synthetic fuels. He was joined by Joseph Boston and Herbert Britt (both chemical engineers) in 1977. Four years later they formed Aspen Technology to develop and market computer-aided chemical engineering software for process manufacturers.

The company launched its first product in 1982 and introduced process simulation software the following year. Boston became AspenTech's president and Evans became chairman and CEO in 1984.

The company went public in 1994. A series of acquisitions followed — including the purchases of Industrial Systems in 1995 and Dynamic Matrix Control and Setpoint in 1996 — which gave the company operation control software. In 1997 it bought consultant Special Analysis & Simulation Technologies and intelligent software expert NeuralWare.

EXECUTIVES

Independent Director, R. Halsey Wise
Senior Vice President, General Counsel, Secretary, Frederic Hammond, $370,750 total compensation
President, Chief Executive Officer And Director, Antonio Pietri, $600,000 total compensation
Independent Chairman Of The Board, Jill Smith

Independent Chairman Of The Board, Robert Whelan
Independent Director, Georgia Keresty
Independent Director, Thomas Bradicich
Independent Director, Adriana Karaboutis
Independent Director, Amarpreet Hanspal
Independent Director, Karen Golz
Chief Financial Officer, Senior Vice President, Chantelle Breithaupt, $117,420 total compensation
Executive Vice President, Operations, John Hague, $380,000 total compensation
Auditors: KPMG LLP

LOCATIONS

HQ: Aspen Technology Inc
  20 Crosby Drive, Bedford, MA 01730
Phone: 781 221-6400
Web: www.aspentech.com

PRODUCTS/OPERATIONS

2015 Sales

	$ mil.	% of total
Subscription & software	405.6	92
Services	34.8	8
Total	**440.4**	**100**

Selected Products

Aspen Plus
Aspen HYSYS
Aspen Exchanger Design and Rating
Aspen Economic Evaluation
Aspen Basic Engineering
Aspen Info Plus.21
Aspen DMCplus
Aspen Collaborative Demand Manager
Aspen Petroleum Scheduler
Aspen PIMS
Aspen Plant Scheduler
Aspen Supply Chain Planner
Aspen Inventory Management & Operations Scheduling
Aspen Petroleum Supply Chain Planner
Aspen Fleet Optimizer

COMPETITORS

ANSYS INC.	NETSCOUT SYSTEMS INC.
ASITE LIMITED	PROOFPOINT INC.
BENTLEY SYSTEMS INCORPORATED	PROS HOLDINGS INC.
D4T4 SOLUTIONS PLC	Software AG
KBC ADVANCED TECHNOLOGIES LIMITED	

HISTORICAL FINANCIALS

Company Type: Public

Income Statement   FYE: June 30

	REVENUE ($ mil.)	NET INCOME ($ mil.)	NET PROFIT MARGIN	EMPLOYEES
06/21	709.3	319.8	45.1%	1,897
06/20	598.7	229.6	38.4%	1,710
06/19	598.3	262.7	43.9%	1,600
06/18	499.5	148.6	29.8%	1,466
06/17	482.9	162.2	33.6%	1,419
Annual Growth	**10.1%**	**18.5%**	**—**	**7.5%**

2021 Year-End Financials

Debt ratio: 20.1%
Return on equity: 50.4%
Cash ($ mil.): 379.8
Current ratio: 5.43
Long-term debt ($ mil.): 273.1

No. of shares (mil.): 67.9
Dividends
  Yield: —
  Payout: —
Market value ($ mil.): 9,341.0

	STOCK PRICE ($) FY Close	P/E High/Low		Earnings	PER SHARE ($) Dividends	Book Value
06/21	137.54	34	20	4.67	0.00	11.79
06/20	103.61	42	23	3.34	0.00	6.89
06/19	124.28	33	20	3.71	0.00	5.73
06/18	92.74	48	27	2.04	0.00	(3.99)
06/17	55.26	30	19	2.11	0.00	(3.55)
Annual Growth	**25.6%**			**— — 22.0%**	**—**	**—**

Atkore Inc

Auditors: DELOITTE & TOUCHE LLP

LOCATIONS

HQ: Atkore Inc
  16100 South Lathrop Avenue, Harvey, IL 60426
Phone: 708 339-1610
Web: www.atkore.com

HISTORICAL FINANCIALS

Company Type: Public

Income Statement   FYE: September 30

	REVENUE ($ mil.)	NET INCOME ($ mil.)	NET PROFIT MARGIN	EMPLOYEES
09/21	2,928.0	587.8	20.1%	4,000
09/20	1,765.4	152.3	8.6%	3,700
09/19	1,916.5	139.0	7.3%	3,900
09/18	1,835.1	136.6	7.4%	3,500
09/17	1,503.9	84.6	5.6%	3,500
Annual Growth	**18.1%**	**62.3%**	**—**	**3.4%**

2021 Year-End Financials

Debt ratio: 34.3%
Return on equity: 94.5%
Cash ($ mil.): 576.2
Current ratio: 2.71
Long-term debt ($ mil.): 758.3

No. of shares (mil.): 46.0
Dividends
  Yield: —
  Payout: —
Market value ($ mil.): 3,998.0

	STOCK PRICE ($) FY Close	P/E High/Low		Earnings	PER SHARE ($) Dividends	Book Value
09/21	86.92	8	2	12.19	0.00	18.80
09/20	22.73	14	4	3.10	0.00	7.98
09/19	30.35	11	6	2.83	0.00	4.96
09/18	26.53	11	7	2.48	0.00	2.59
09/17	19.51	20	12	1.27	0.00	5.70
Annual Growth	**45.3%**			**— — 76.0%**	**—**	**34.8%**

Atlantic Union Bankshares Corp

Union Bankshares Corporation is a community bank that provides fill retail commercial municipal banking and asset management. The bank also provides trust services through about 20 banking offices less than 5 loan centers and several ATMs across northern Vermont and northern New Hampshire. The bank serves individuals and commercial banking services to small and medium sized corporations partnerships and sole proprietorships as well as nonprofit organizations local municipalities and school districts.

Operations

Union Bankshares generates income from interest and fees on loan and earning on other investments. The company loan portfolio include Commercial real estate which accounts for about 40% of the company's loan portfolio followed by Residential real estate at about 25%. The bank's loan portfolio also includes Commercial (some 15%) Municipal (nearly 15%) Construction real estate (more than 5%) and Loans held for sale (about 5%). Consumer loans of the bank accounted for the remaining.

Geographic Reach

The company is headquarters in Morrisville Vermont. The bank provides trust services through about 20 banking offices less than 5 loan centers and several ATMs across northern Vermont and northern New Hampshire.

Sales and Marketing

The bank used about $544000 and $555000 in 2020 for advertising and public relations respectively.

Financial Performance

Union Bankshares Corporation's performance have fluctuated for the span of five years but has overall had an upward trend.

The bank's net income increased by$2.1 million to $12.8 million in 2020 as compared to 2019's revenue of $10.6 million.

The bank held $122.7 million at the end of the year. Operating activities provided $5.7 million. Investing activities and financing activities used $33000 and $5.6 million respectively.

EXECUTIVES

Chief Human Resource Officer, Executive Vice President, Loreen Lagatta
President, Chief Executive Officer, Director, John Asbury, $826,667 total compensation
Executive Vice President, Chief Information Officer & Head Of Bank Operations, M. Dean Brown, $368,114 total compensation
Independent Vice Chairman Of The Board, Patrick McCann
Chief Operating Officer, Executive Vice President, President - Atlantic Union Bank, Maria Tedesco, $485,925 total compensation
Executive Vice President And Commercial Banking Group Executive, David Ring, $391,472 total compensation
Independent Chairman Of The Board, Ronald Tillett
Executive Vice President, Consumer Banking Group Executive, Shawn O'brien
Chief Financial Officer, Executive Vice President, Robert Gorman, $422,573 total compensation
Auditors: Ernst & Young LLP

LOCATIONS

HQ: Atlantic Union Bankshares Corp
  1051 East Cary Street, Suite 1200, Richmond, VA 23219
Phone: 804 633-5031
Web: www.bankatunion.com

34   HOOVER'S HANDBOOK OF EMERGING COMPANIES 2022

PRODUCTS/OPERATIONS

2015 Sales

	$ mil.	% of total
Interest		
Loans including fees	247.5	72
Other	29.3	9
Noninterest		
Other service charges commission and fees	15.6	5
Service charges on deposit accounts	18.9	5
others	30.8	9
Adjustments	(0.3)	
Total	**341.8**	**100**

Selected Subsidiaries

Union First Market Bank
Union Insurance Group LLC
Union Investment Services Inc.
Union Mortgage Group Inc.

COMPETITORS

BANCFIRST CORPORATION
BYLINE BANCORP INC.
C&F FINANCIAL CORPORATION
CITIZENS & NORTHERN CORPORATION
CLOVER COMMUNITY BANK
D. L. EVANS BANK
DNB FINANCIAL CORPORATION
FIRST FEDERAL BANK CORPORATION
FIRSTMERIT CORPORATION
FLAGSTAR BANCORP INC.
HANCOCK WHITNEY CORPORATION
LAKELAND FINANCIAL CORPORATION
MIDWESTONE FINANCIAL GROUP INC.
OCEANFIRST FINANCIAL CORP.
PEAPACK-GLADSTONE FINANCIAL CORPORATION
PEOPLE'S UNITED FINANCIAL INC.
TWO RIVER BANCORP
UNITY BANCORP INC.
UNIVEST FINANCIAL CORPORATION
WESTERN ALLIANCE BANCORPORATION

HISTORICAL FINANCIALS

Company Type: Public

Income Statement — FYE: December 31

	ASSETS ($ mil.)	NET INCOME ($ mil.)	INCOME AS % OF ASSETS	EMPLOYEES
12/20	19,628.4	158.2	0.8%	1,879
12/19	17,562.9	193.5	1.1%	1,989
12/18	13,765.6	146.2	1.1%	1,609
12/17	9,315.1	72.9	0.8%	1,149
12/16	8,426.7	77.4	0.9%	1,416
Annual Growth	23.5%	19.5%	—	7.3%

2020 Year-End Financials

Return on assets: 0.8%
Return on equity: 6.0%
Long-term debt ($ mil.): —
No. of shares (mil.): 78.7
Sales ($ mil): 784.9
Dividends
Yield: 3.0%
Payout: 52.3%
Market value ($ mil.): 2,593.0

	STOCK PRICE ($) FY Close	P/E High/Low		PER SHARE ($) Earnings	Dividends	Book Value
12/20	32.94	20	10	1.93	1.00	34.40
12/19	37.55	16	12	2.41	0.96	31.41
12/18	28.23	19	12	2.22	0.88	29.17
12/17	36.17	23	18	1.67	0.81	23.92
12/16	35.74	21	12	1.77	0.77	22.95
Annual Growth	(2.0%)	—	—	2.2%	6.8%	10.6%

Atlanticus Holdings Corp

Suffering from a fiscal near-death experience? Let Atlanticus Holdings help resuscitate you. Subprime is the strategy for this company. Formerly named CompuCredit until November 2012 it traditionally issued unsecured Visa and MasterCard credit cards to customers with low credit scores and charged them more for the risk. The economic downturn compelled the firm to close most of its active credit card accounts. However Atlanticus continues to collect on portfolios of credit card receivables underlying now-closed credit card accounts. The company current portfolio offers Credit and Other Investments; and Auto Finance.

Operations

Within the Credit and Other Investments segment the company offers point-of-sale financing whereby they partner with retailers and service providers to provide credit to their customers for the purchase of goods and services or rental of merchandise to their customers under rent-to-own arrangements.

The operations of Auto Finance segment are principally conducted through CAR platform which purchases and/or services loans secured by automobiles from or for a pre-qualified network of independent automotive dealers and automotive finance companies in the buy-here pay-here used car business.

Geographic Reach

The company has operations across the US and in the UK.

Financial Performance

Atlanticus' revenues have been restated due to the divestiture of Investments in the Previously Charged-Off Receivables segment along with its balance transfer card operations. In 2013 the company's revenues grew by 55% due to credit card account closures and net credit card receivables portfolio liquidations. Also included within their other income category are certain reimbursements it received in respect of one of its portfolios.

In 2013 the company reported a net loss of $17.7 million (compared to a net income of $24.5 million in 2012) thanks to higher other operating expenses as a result of higher card and loan servicing expenses based on new product efforts (which outpaced continuing credit card and auto finance receivables portfolio liquidations); increases in marketing; and solicitation costs associated with new product efforts.

That year Atlanticus posted cash outflow of $26.9 million (compared to cash inflow of $2.98 million in fiscal 2012) primarily due to a net loss increased depreciation of rental merchandise provision for losses on loans and fees receivable and increase in income tax liability.

Strategy

The company is expanding its point-of-sale finance offerings including its own rent-to-own offerings. As with many early stage endeavors these product offerings may experience under-capitalization delays lack of funding and many other problems delays and expenses many of which are beyond the company's control.

Company Background

Atlanticus sold its 300 US microloan retail locations — which provided payday loans under such banners as First American Cash Advance and First Southern Cash Advance — to Advance America for more than $46 million in 2011. Prior to selling off its retail stores the company planned to spin them off as a publicly traded company called Purpose Financial Holdings. The proposed transaction would allow Atlanticus to focus on its core operations. The company chose instead to sell in order to raise capital.

In 2011 Atlanticus also sold its UK payday loan operations. The sales came in the midst of a difficult period for the company. The credit crunch hampered its ability to raise funds to fuel its lending activities and new regulations passed in the US outlawed many of the high-fee products that the company marketed.

The move also followed other restructurings at the company. It has exited several lines of business since 2007 including its stored-value cards and investment in and servicing of loans secured by motorcycles personal watercraft and other "big boy toys." Atlanticus ceased writing new auto loans in 2009 and as with its credit card accounts is focusing on servicing that portfolio. Also that year Atlanticus sold its marketing unit to Las Vegas-based Selling Source shortly after it settled the FDIC lawsuit. The company additionally laid off hundreds of employees and closed a number of office locations.

As a way to diversify its holdings the company has invested in international credit card receivables. Lending abroad might be in the cards if the regulatory environment allows. Subprime lending in the US proved a risky affair though: In 2008 the company agreed to a $116 million settlement with the FDIC and FTC. As part of an broader investigation of the subprime credit industry federal regulators had looked into allegations that Atlanticus provided inadequate policy disclosures to customers. Most of the settlement funds were credited to certain accounts opened between 2001 and 2005.

Chairman David Hanna and his brother Frank a director together own more than half of Atlanticus; each holds an equal stake around 27% apiece.

EXECUTIVES

Independent Director, Denise Harrod
Independent Director, Joann Jones
President, Chief Executive Officer, Director, Jeffrey Howard, $600,000 total compensation
Executive Chairman Of The Board, David Hanna, $600,000 total compensation
Chief Technology Officer, Linda Brooks
Chief Financial Officer, William Mccamey, $550,000 total compensation
Independent Director, Mack Mattingly
Independent Director, Deal Hudson
Auditors: BDO USA, LLP

LOCATIONS

HQ: Atlanticus Holdings Corp
Five Concourse Parkway, Suite 300, Atlanta, GA 30328
Phone: 770 828-2000
Web: www.Atlanticus.com

PRODUCTS/OPERATIONS

Selected Products & Services
Auto Lending
Credit Card Lending
Loan Servicing and Portfolio Acquisitions
Retail Finance

COMPETITORS

AMERICAN EXPRESS COMPANY
CAPITAL ONE FINANCIAL CORPORATION
CONSUMER PORTFOLIO SERVICES INC.
FIRST INVESTORS FINANCIAL SERVICES GROUP
  INC.
GREEN DOT CORPORATION
NICHOLAS FINANCIAL INC.
ONEMAIN HOLDINGS INC.
PREMIUM CREDIT LIMITED

HISTORICAL FINANCIALS

Company Type: Public

Income Statement

FYE: December 31

	REVENUE ($ mil.)	NET INCOME ($ mil.)	NET PROFIT MARGIN	EMPLOYEES
12/20	563.4	94.1	16.7%	327
12/19	458.1	26.4	5.8%	319
12/18	233.5	7.8	3.4%	310
12/17	135.4	(40.7)	—	297
12/16	113.6	(6.3)	—	292
Annual Growth	49.2%	—	—	2.9%

2020 Year-End Financials

Debt ratio: 75.3%
Return on equity: 61.2%
Cash ($ mil.): 258.9
Current ratio: 0.27
Long-term debt ($ mil.): 24.3
No. of shares (mil.): 16.1
Dividends
  Yield: —
  Payout: —
Market value ($ mil.): 397.0

	STOCK PRICE ($) FY Close	P/E High/Low		PER SHARE ($) Earnings	Dividends	Book Value
12/20	24.63	5	1	3.95	0.00	13.44
12/19	9.01	6	2	1.66	0.00	5.66
12/18	3.64	8	3	0.56	0.00	(1.40)
12/17	2.40	—	—	(2.93)	0.00	(2.36)
12/16	2.84	—	—	(0.46)	0.00	0.38
Annual Growth	71.6% 144.4%	—	—	—	—	—

AtriCure Inc

AtriCure Inc. provides innovative technologies for the treatment of Afib and related conditions. Afib affects more than 33 million people worldwide. The medical device maker markets the Synergy Ablation System used in the treatment of atrial fibrillation (AFib) a common type of heart arrhythmia. Cardiothoracic surgeons use the AtriCure Synergy Ablation System in conjunction with elective surgical ablation procedures to treat patients through minimally invasive procedures. AtriCure also sells reusable and disposable cryoablation devices (probes using extreme cold) to ablate cardiac tissue. Additionally the company offers the AtriClip Left Atrial Appendage System or AtriClip system designed to help surgeons exclude the left atrial appendage. Its US markets accounts for about 80% of revenues.

Operations

AtriCure's Isolator Synergy Ablation System is the first medical device to receive FDA approval for the treatment of persistent Afib. AtriCure's AtriClip Left Atrial Appendage Exclusion System products are the most widely sold LAA management devices worldwide. AtriCure's Hybrid AF Therapy is a minimally invasive procedure that provides a lasting solution for long-standing persistent Afib patients. AtriCure's cryoICE cryoSPHERE probe is cleared for temporary ablation of peripheral nerves to block pain providing pain relief in cardiac and thoracic procedures.

Ablation and Appendage accounts for almost all of the company's revenue.

Geographic Reach

Headquartered in Ohio AtriCure also has offices in Minnesota and California as well as in the Netherlands.

US sales account for about 80% of the firm's revenues while Europe Asia and other international countries accounts the rest.

Sales and Marketing

In the US the company sell its products to medical centers through direct sales in about 55 sales territories. It markets and sells its products in other markets through independent distributors and in European and Middle Eastern markets through a European subsidiary which has independent distributors and direct sales staff. AtriCure also sells its products to other international distributors primarily in Asia South America and Canada. Over 10% of sales were generated from the company's top ten customers.

Advertising expense was $655 $635 and $785 in 2020 2019 and 2018 respectively.

Financial Performance

Revenue for fiscal 2020 decreased by 11% to $206.5 million compared from the prior year with $230.8 million.

Net loss for fiscal 2020 increased to $48.2 million compared from the prior year with $35.2 million.

Cash held by the company at the end of fiscal 2020 increased to $41.9 million. Cash provided by financing activities was $189.4 million while cash used for operations and investing activities were $19.9 million $156.2 million respectively.

Strategy

The key elements of AtriCure's strategy include:
New product innovation by developing new and innovative products including those that allow it to enter new market opportunities or expand its growth in existing markets;

Investing in clinical science by investing in landmark clinical trials and making clinical research grants to support its product development efforts and expand the body of clinical evidence;

Building physician and societal relationships to provide insight regarding treatment trends input on future product direction and education for providers involved in treating the disease;

Providing training and education by instituting a program to train providers on the use of the Isolator Synergy System to treat persistent and long-standing persistent Afib in patients undergoing open-heart surgery; and

Evaluating acquisition opportunities on a variety of factors including investment in clinical science product innovation and strategic and financial considerations.

Expanding Adoption of its Minimally Invasive Products. Atricure believes that the catalysts for expanded adoption of its minimally invasive products include completing clinical trials including the CONVERGE aMAZE IDE and DEEP AF IDE clinical trials procedural advancements such as the hybrid or multi-disciplinary procedure continued innovation and product development and the publication of additional scientific evidence supporting the safety and efficacy of hybrid treatments for persistent and long-standing persistent Afib.

Evaluating Acquisition Opportunities. The company expects to continue to be opportunistic with respect to acquisitions.

Company Background

Michael Hooven and his wife Sue Spies co-founded ENABLE Medical Corporation. ENABLE Medical's first product was a pair of radio frequency energized surgical scissors designed to harvest saphenous veins in cardiac bypass procedures IMA harvesting and general surgical applications. In 2000 AtriCure was established as an independent business focused on atrial fibrillation. ENABLE Medical provided contract development and manufacturing services to AtriCure.

EXECUTIVES

Independent Director, Robert White
Independent Director, Karen Prange
Independent Director, Daniel Florin
Chief Financial Officer, Angela Wirick, $327,920
  total compensation
Director, Maggie Yuen
Director, Deborah Telman
Chief Technical Officer, Salvatore Privitera,
  $369,556 total compensation
President, Chief Executive Officer, Director,
  Michael Carrel, $717,898 total compensation
Chief Operating Officer, Douglas Seith, $473,374
  total compensation
Chief Marketing And Strategy Officer, Justin
  Noznesky, $368,790 total compensation
Independent Director, Sven Wehrwein
Independent Chairman Of The Board, B. Kristine
  Johnson
Auditors: DELOITTE & TOUCHE LLP

LOCATIONS

HQ: AtriCure Inc
  7555 Innovation Way, Mason, OH 45040
Phone: 513 755-4100
Web: www.atricure.com

PRODUCTS/OPERATIONS

2014 Sales

	$ mil.	% of total
Open-heart	61.1	57
Minimally invasive	23.9	22
AtriClip	18.9	18
Valve tools	3.6	3
Total	**107.5**	**100**

Selected Products

Cardiac Ablation Devices
Left Atrial Appendage Exclusion Devices
Maze Testing
Soft Tissue Dissection System

COMPETITORS

ACELITY L.P. INC.
ACORDA THERAPEUTICS
  INC.
ANGIODYNAMICS INC.
EDWARDS LIFESCIENCES
  CORPORATION
ESCALON MEDICAL CORP.
GLOBUS MEDICAL INC.

ANIKA THERAPEUTICS INC.
ARTIVION INC.
BOSTON SCIENTIFIC CORPORATION
DELTEX MEDICAL GROUP PLC
DEXCOM INC.
HAEMONETICS CORPORATION
INTERSECT ENT INC.
LIVANOVA PLC
MEDTRONIC PUBLIC LIMITED COMPANY
NUVASIVE INC.
THORATEC LLC

HISTORICAL FINANCIALS

Company Type: Public

Income Statement				FYE: December 31
	REVENUE ($ mil.)	NET INCOME ($ mil.)	NET PROFIT MARGIN	EMPLOYEES
12/21	274.3	50.2	18.3%	875
12/20	206.5	(48.1)	—	750
12/19	230.8	(35.1)	—	730
12/18	201.6	(21.1)	—	620
12/17	174.7	(26.8)	—	570
Annual Growth	11.9%	—	—	11.3%

2021 Year-End Financials

Debt ratio: 11.3%
Return on equity: 11.2%
Cash ($ mil.): 43.6
Current ratio: 3.47
Long-term debt ($ mil.): 69.8

No. of shares (mil.): 46.0
Dividends
 Yield: —
 Payout: —
Market value ($ mil.): 3,199.0

	STOCK PRICE ($) FY Close	P/E High/Low		PER SHARE ($) Earnings	Dividends	Book Value
12/21	69.53	79	48	1.09	0.00	10.51
12/20	55.67	—	—	(1.14)	0.00	9.09
12/19	32.51	—	—	(0.94)	0.00	6.24
12/18	30.60	—	—	(0.62)	0.00	6.46
12/17	18.24	—	—	(0.83)	0.00	4.66
Annual Growth	39.7%	—	—	—	—	22.6%

Aura Minerals Inc (British Virgin Islands)

Aura Minerals digs deep to make a profit. The mid-tier producer of gold and copper owns operating projects in Honduras Mexico and Brazil. The company's diversified portfolio of precious metal assets include the San Andres producing gold mine in Honduras the Sao Francisco producing gold mine in Brazil and the copper-gold-silver Aranzazu mine in Mexico (where operations were temporarily suspended in late 2015 due to disruptions caused by unauthorized persons entering the company mine). Aura Minerals' core development asset is the copper-gold-iron Serrote project in Brazil.In early 2018 the company acquired fellow gold miner Rio Novo.

EXECUTIVES

Non-executive Independent Director, Philip Reade
Chief Operating Officer, Glauber Luvizotto, $193,827 total compensation
Director, Fabio Ribeiro
General Manager - Brazil Operations, Jorge Camargo

Non-executive Chairman Of The Board, Paulo Brito
Director, Richmond Fenn
General Manager - Mexico Operations, Henrique Rodrigues
General Manager - Honduras Operations, Julio Beraun Sanchez
General Manager - Gold Road Mine, Kevin Shiell
Independent Director, Bruno Mauad
Director, Paulo De Brito Filho
Chief Financial Officer, Joao Cardoso, $200,000 total compensation
Non-executive Lead Independent Director, Stephen Keith
Auditors: PricewaterhouseCoopers

LOCATIONS

HQ: Aura Minerals Inc (British Virgin Islands)
78 SW 7th Street, Suite # 7144, Miami, FL 33130
Phone: 305 239-9499
Web: www.auraminerals.com

COMPETITORS

Cosigo Resources Ltd
GOLD RESOURCE CORPORATION

HISTORICAL FINANCIALS

Company Type: Public

Income Statement				FYE: December 31
	REVENUE ($ mil.)	NET INCOME ($ mil.)	NET PROFIT MARGIN	EMPLOYEES
12/20	299.8	68.4	22.8%	1,102
12/19	226.2	24.8	11.0%	863
12/18	157.7	51.9	33.0%	863
12/17	157.7	10.1	6.5%	783
12/16	146.2	19.0	13.0%	1,170
Annual Growth	19.7%	37.7%	—	(1.5%)

2020 Year-End Financials

Debt ratio: 13.1%
Return on equity: 26.8%
Cash ($ mil.): 117.7
Current ratio: 1.80
Long-term debt ($ mil.): 41.9

No. of shares (mil.): 70.7
Dividends
 Yield: —
 Payout: —
Market value ($ mil.): —

Autodesk Inc

Autodesk is a global leader in 3D design engineering and entertainment software and services offering customers productive business solutions through powerful technology products and services. The AutoCAD and Revit software programs are used by architects engineers and structural designers to design draft and make models of products buildings and other objects. The company also provides product and manufacturing software for manufacturers in automotive transportation industrial machinery consumer products and building product industries with comprehensive digital design engineering manufacturing and production solutions. The company's digital media and entertainment products provide tools for digital sculpting modeling animation effects rendering and compositing for design visualization visual effects and

games production. Customers in the US account for nearly 35% sales.

Operations

Autodesk's biggest operating segment is Architecture Engineering and Construction (AEC) which generates more than 40% of revenue. It develops software for designing building and managing buildings civil infrastructure and manufacturing plants. The segment's BIM 360 product helps manage construction projects. BIM stands for building information modeling.

The Manufacturing segment which generates more than 20% of revenue makes prototyping software. The AutoCAD and AutoCAD LT business which accounts for close to 30% of revenue is the home of Autodesk's flagship product and biggest revenue producer AutoCAD. The companion product AutoCAD LT allows sharing of documents.

The Media and Entertainment segment more than 5% of revenue offers computer animation programs such as Autodesk Maya for design visualization visual effects and games production.

Overall subscription revenue generates almost 85% followed by maintenance for over 10% while the rest comes from other.

Geographic Reach

Autodesk's revenue is spread among its major geographic regions. The US is Autodesk's biggest single market accounting for about 35% sales but the Europe Middle East and Africa region generates 40% of sales and the Asia/Pacific region accounts for about 20% of sales. The company's products are translated and localized for users who speak German French Italian Spanish Russian Japanese Korean and simplified and traditional Chinese. Autodesk is based in San Rafael California.

Sales and Marketing

Autodesk relies significantly upon major distributors and resellers in both the US and international regions including Tech Data Corporation and its global affiliates and Ingram Micro Inc. Total sales to Tech Data and Ingram Micro accounted for about 35% and 10% of Autodesk's total revenue respectively.

Autodesk sells directly to enterprise and named account customers as well as those who buy from its online store.

Total advertising expenses incurred were $60.4 million in fiscal 2021 $42.2 million in fiscal 2020 and $37.5 million in fiscal 2019.

Financial Performance

Autodesk's revenue has increased by 86% over the past five years.

Autodesk's net income in 2021 increased to $629.1 million from $343 million in 2020. Sales surged 16% to $3.8 billion in 2021 from about $3.3 billion in 2020. The most evident growth ($272 million) came from architecture engineering and construction.

Autodesk's profit in 2021 increased to $1.2 billion from $215 million in 2020.

The company's cash holdings in 2021 decreased by $2.5 million. Operating activities produced $1.4 billion or an increase of $22 million from 2020 while investing activities used $404 million and financing activities used $1 billion.

Strategy

Autodesk's strategy is to build enduring relationships with customers delivering innovative technology that provides valuable automation and insight into their design and makes the process. To drive the execution of this strategy the company

HOOVER'S HANDBOOK OF EMERGING COMPANIES 2022

is focused on three strategic priorities: delivering on the promise of subscription digitizing the company and reimagining construction manufacturing and production. To support its strategic priority of re-imagining AEC the company is strengthening the foundation of its AEC solutions with both organic and inorganic investments.

As part of the company's strategy in manufacturing it continues to attract both global manufacturing leaders and disruptive startups with its generative design and cloud-based Fusion 360 technology enhancements.

Mergers and Acquisitions
In fiscal 2021 Autodesk acquired Spacemaker a leading provider of cloud-based artificial intelligence (AI) and generative design to help architects urban designers and real estate developers make faster and more informed early-stage design decisions which can help maximize the long-term sustainability and return from property investments. Other acquisitions in fiscal 2021 included solutions that use artificial intelligence and machine learning to extract and process data from project plans and specifications allowing general contractors subcontractors and owners to automate workflows such as submittals and project closeout as well as a leading provider of post-processing and machine simulation solutions in manufacturing.

Company Background
John Walker founded Autodesk in 1982 as a diversified PC software supplier and when he bought the software rights to AutoCAD from inventor Michael Riddle Autodesk took off. While competitors went after more complex computer systems Autodesk focused on PC software. When PC sales boomed in the early 1980s the firm was there to take advantage of a growing market. Autodesk went public in 1985.

HISTORY

John Walker founded Autodesk in 1982 as a diversified PC software supplier and when he bought the software rights to AutoCAD from inventor Michael Riddle Autodesk took off. While competitors went after more complex computer systems Autodesk focused on PC software. When PC sales boomed in the early 1980s the firm was there to take advantage of a growing market. Autodesk went public in 1985.

The company established a multimedia unit and released its first animation tool 3D Studio in 1990. In 1993 Autodesk acquired 3-D graphics specialist Ithaca Software. That year Autodesk lost a trade secret lawsuit to Vermont Microsystems and was ordered to pay $25.5 million; the fine was later lowered to $7.8 million.

In 1996 the company spun off its multimedia unit as Kinetix geared toward 3-D PC and Web applications. Continuing its acquisition drive Autodesk bought interior decorating software developer Creative Imaging Technologies in 1996 and rival CAD software developer Softdesk in 1997.

In an effort to expand its presence in the entertainment software realm the company bought digital video effects and editing tools maker Discreet Logic for $520 million in 1999. Later that year Autodesk bolstered its geographic information systems division by acquiring Canadian mapping software company VISION*Solutions from WorldCom for $26 million. Product delays helped prompt Autodesk that year to reorganize into four divisions and cut 350 jobs — about 10% of its workforce.

EXECUTIVES

Chief Executive Officer, President, And Director, Andrew Anagnost, $975,559 total compensation
Independent Chairman Of The Board, Stacy Smith
Independent Director, Lorrie Norrington
Independent Director, Stephen Milligan
Independent Director, Reid French
Independent Director, Karen Blasing
Independent Director, Blake Irving
Chief Financial Officer, Executive Vice President, Deborah Clifford
Independent Director, Ayanna Howard
Chief People Officer, Rebecca Pearce
Senior Vice President - Corporate Affairs, Chief Legal Officer, Secretary, Pascal Di Fronzo, $513,793 total compensation
Chief Revenue Officer, Steven Blum, $591,187 total compensation
Independent Director, Elizabeth Rafael
Auditors: Ernst & Young LLP

LOCATIONS

HQ: Autodesk Inc
111 McInnis Parkway, San Rafael, CA 94903
Phone: 415 507-5000
Web: www.autodesk.com

PRODUCTS/OPERATIONS

2019 Sales

	$ mil.	% of total
Architecture Engineering and Construction	1,021.6	40
AutoCAD and AutoCAD LT	731.8	28
Manufacturing	616.2	24
Media and Entertainment	182.0	7
Other	18.2	1
Total	**2,569.8**	**100**

2019 Sales

	$ mil.	% of total
Subscription	1,802.3	70
Subscription	635.1	25
Other	132.4	5
Total	**2,569.8**	**100**

COMPETITORS

AMERICAN SOFTWARE INC. CORPORATION	MICROSOFT
AVID TECHNOLOGY INC.	Open Text Corporation
CA INC.	PTC INC.
DATAWATCH CORPORATION	Software AG
INFOR (US) LLC	
MENTOR GRAPHICS CORPORATION	

HISTORICAL FINANCIALS

Company Type: Public

Income Statement

FYE: January 31

	REVENUE ($ mil.)	NET INCOME ($ mil.)	NET PROFIT MARGIN	EMPLOYEES
01/21	3,790.4	1,208.2	31.9%	11,500
01/20	3,274.3	214.5	6.6%	10,100
01/19	2,569.8	(80.8)	—	9,600
01/18	2,056.6	(566.9)	—	8,800
01/17	2,031.0	(582.1)	—	9,000
Annual Growth	**16.9%**	—	—	**6.3%**

2021 Year-End Financials

Debt ratio: 22.4%
Return on equity: 291.6%
Cash ($ mil.): 1,772.2
Current ratio: 0.83
Long-term debt ($ mil.): 1,637.2
No. of shares (mil.): 219.6
Dividends
 Yield: —
 Payout: —
Market value ($ mil.): 60,924.0

	STOCK PRICE ($) FY Close	P/E High/Low	PER SHARE ($)		
			Earnings	Dividends	Book Value
01/21	277.43	58 25	5.44	0.00	4.40
01/20	196.85	204143	0.96	0.00	(0.63)
01/19	147.20	— —	(0.37)	0.00	(0.96)
01/18	115.62	— —	(2.58)	0.00	(1.17)
01/17	81.34	— —	(2.61)	0.00	3.33
Annual Growth	**35.9%**	— —	—	—	**7.2%**

Avid Bioservices Inc

Peregrine Pharmaceuticals is spreading its wings and taking flight to attack and kill its prey: cancer and viral infections. While nearly all its revenue comes from its Avid Bioservices subsidiary which provides contract antibody and protein manufacturing to drug companies Peregrine is focused on shepherding its own candidates through clinical trials. Up first is bavituximab a monoclonal antibody candidate being tested to treat lung pancreatic and liver cancers as well as for other oncology and infectious disease applications. Next is Cotara being tested to treat glioblastoma multiforme a deadly brain cancer. The company also has development programs for potential diagnostic imaging agents.

Operations
The company supports its development activities with revenues earned by Avid Bioservices subsidiary which accounts for nearly all of Peregrine's revenues.

The company also seeks out licensing and development partnerships to bring in additional funding for its research operations. For instance it has licensed some of its development technologies to the likes of Affitech and Merck KGaA. It also had a collaboration with the Department of Defense to develop antibodies to treat viral hemorrhagic fever infections that brought in revenues for several years until 2012 when the contract ended.

Geographic Reach
Peregrine conducts its research programs at facilities in the US which accounts for nearly all revenue. Avid Bioservices serves customers primarily located in North America and Europe.

Financial Performance
As a development-stage drug company Peregrine Pharmaceuticals' revenues fluctuate each year depending on how much the company earns from its licensing development and contract manufacturing agreements. Revenues increased by 42% in 2012 due to increased contract manufacturing activities at the Avid Biosciences unit. Like many pharmaceutical R&D firms Peregrine Pharmaceuticals has yet to turn a profit as its research expenses outweigh earnings. Its net loss for 2013 did decrease by 29% as R&D expense dropped.

Strategy
Peregrine is focused on the development of its two core drug candidates with the ultimate goal of commercializing the drugs in the US and international markets. It als seeks to license the core technologies used in its candidates to additional partners. Bavituximab uses its PS-targeting (phosphatidylserine-targeting) technology which works by turning off natural immune suppression

allowing the body to fight off infections with more vigor. Cotara uses Peregrine's TNT (tumor necrosis therapy) which uses radioisotopes to attack tumor cells without harming healthy tissue.

Once Peregrine's products gain regulatory approval the company plans to market the drugs through collaborative partners or via a direct sales force.

EXECUTIVES

Chief Operations Officer, Richard Richieri, $173,558 total compensation
Vice President, General Counsel, Corporate Secretary, Mark Ziebell, $395,503 total compensation
Non-executive Independent Chairman Of The Board, Joseph Carleone
Independent Director, Catherine Mackey
Investor Relations / Corporate Communications, Stephanie Diaz
Independent Director, Jeanne Thoma
Independent Director, Esther Alegria
Chief Commercial Officer, Matthew Kwietniak
Chief Financial Officer, Daniel Hart, $423,698 total compensation
President, Chief Executive Officer And Director, Nicholas Green, $420,962 total compensation
Auditors: Ernst & Young LLP

LOCATIONS

HQ: Avid Bioservices Inc
2642 Michelle Drive, Suite 200, Tustin, CA 92780
Phone: 714 508-6100
Web: www.avidbio.com

PRODUCTS/OPERATIONS

2015 Sales

	$ mil.	% of total
Contract manufacturing	44.4	99
Licensing	0.3	1
Total	**44.7**	**100**

COMPETITORS

ALNYLAM PHARMACEUTICALS INC.	INNATE PHARMA IONIS PHARMACEUTICALS
AVEO PHARMACEUTICALS INC.	INC.
GLOBEIMMUNE INC.	SELLAS LIFE SCIENCES GROUP INC.
INCYTE CORPORATION	TRANSGENE

HISTORICAL FINANCIALS

Company Type: Public

Income Statement

FYE: April 30

	REVENUE ($ mil.)	NET INCOME ($ mil.)	NET PROFIT MARGIN	EMPLOYEES
04/21	95.8	11.2	11.7%	257
04/20	59.7	(10.4)	—	227
04/19	53.6	(4.2)	—	215
04/18	53.6	(21.8)	—	186
04/17	57.6	(28.1)	—	323
Annual Growth	**13.6%**	**—**	**—**	**(5.6%)**

2021 Year-End Financials

Debt ratio: 36.5%	No. of shares (mil.): 61.0
Return on equity: 18.7%	Dividends
Cash ($ mil.): 169.9	Yield: —
Current ratio: 2.93	Payout: —
Long-term debt ($ mil.): 96.9	Market value ($ mil.): 1,307.0

	STOCK PRICE ($) FY Close	P/E High/Low	Earnings	PER SHARE ($) Dividends	Book Value
04/21	21.41	364 88	0.06	0.00	1.27
04/20	6.10	— —	(0.27)	0.00	0.74
04/19	4.79	— —	(0.16)	0.00	0.95
04/18	3.67	— —	(0.56)	0.00	1.00
04/17	0.62	— —	(0.88)	0.00	1.22
Annual Growth	**142.8%**	**— —**	**—**	**—**	**1.1%**

Avidbank Holdings Inc

EXECUTIVES

Ceo, Mark Mordell
Pres, Robert Holden
Exec V Pres, William Phillips
Evp-Cco, Geoff Butner
Senior Vp, Porter McKay
Vp, Holly Hayes
Svp, Private Banking, An N Tran
Vice President, Tami Benedict
Evp-Venture Lending Group, Sam Bhaumik
Svp, Corporate Banking Divisio, Joe Wilson
Svp, SW Regional Manager, Randy Churchill
Auditors: Crowe LLP

LOCATIONS

HQ: Avidbank Holdings Inc
400 Emerson Street, Palo Alto, CA 94301
Phone: 650 843-2265   **Fax:** 650 289-9192
Web: www.The-Private-Bank.com

HISTORICAL FINANCIALS

Company Type: Public

Income Statement

FYE: December 31

	ASSETS ($ mil.)	NET INCOME ($ mil.)	INCOME AS % OF ASSETS	EMPLOYEES
12/20	1,430.6	9.6	0.7%	0
12/19	1,131.5	12.8	1.1%	0
12/18	916.9	11.1	1.2%	0
12/17	782.9	5.6	0.7%	0
12/16	646.6	7.2	1.1%	0
Annual Growth	**22.0%**	**7.3%**	**—**	**—**

2020 Year-End Financials

Return on assets: 0.7%	Dividends
Return on equity: 7.8%	Yield: —
Long-term debt ($ mil.): —	Payout: —
No. of shares (mil.): 6.1	Market value ($ mil.): 108.0
Sales ($ mil): 53.5	

	STOCK PRICE ($) FY Close	P/E High/Low	Earnings	PER SHARE ($) Dividends	Book Value
12/20	17.50	15 8	1.61	0.00	20.74
12/19	24.75	11 9	2.17	0.00	19.12
12/18	21.00	14 11	1.90	0.00	16.84
12/17	23.95	22 16	1.08	0.00	15.12
12/16	18.10	12 9	1.56	0.00	13.50
Annual Growth	**(0.8%)**	**— —**	**0.8%**	**—**	**11.3%**

Axcelis Technologies Inc

Axcelis Technologies designs manufactures and services ion implantation and other processing equipment used in the fabrication of semiconductor chips. Axcelis Technologies manufactures its ion implantation devices in house at its plant in Beverly Massachusetts. In addition to equipment it offers aftermarket service and support including used tools spare parts equipment upgrades and maintenance services. While the company sells its products around the world the US accounts for some third-quarter of sales. Axcelis' business commenced in 1978.

Operations

The company operates in one business segment which is the manufacture of capital equipment for the semiconductor chip manufacturing industry. Ion implantation systems and services surrounding them account for 95% of Axcelis Technologies' revenue. The other 5% comes from other systems and services. The company works with customers and industry experts to design applications and processes at its Advanced Technology Center in Beverly Massachusetts.

Product revenue which includes new system sales sales of spare parts product upgrades and used system sales was about 95% of revenue in 2020. And the remaining revenue was from Services revenue which includes the labor component of maintenance and service contracts and fees for service hours provided by on-site service personnel.

The company's systems sales account for more than 60% of sales while aftermarket sales account for the rest.

Geographic Reach

Massachusetts-based Axcelis Technologies has about 40 other properties of which around 10 are located in the United States and the remainder are located in Asia and Europe including offices in Taiwan Singapore South Korea China Japan Italy and Germany. The US is its largest market with about 75% of sales while sales to customers in Asia make some 20% of revenues and Europe accounts for around 5%.

The company has field offices serving customers in more than 30 countries. Sales by location where products are shipped includes Asia Pacific with around 80% of sales while North America and Europe accounts for the rest.

Sales and Marketing

Axcelis Technologies sells equipment and services through a direct sales force from offices in the United States China Germany Italy Singapore South Korea and Taiwan.

The company also has a limited customer base; two customers accounted for almost 20% and around 15% of revenue and its top 10 customers accounted for about 75% of revenue.

Its sales and marketing expenses were $38.7 million $34.3 million and $4.5 million in 2020 2019 and 2018 respectively.

Financial Performance

Axcelis Technologies' revenues may fluctuate from year to year and period to period as the semiconductor capital equipment industry is subject to cyclical swings in capital spending by semiconductor chip manufacturers. Despite this 2020 was an exceptional year for the company resulting from the strength of the overall electronics market and the continued growth of the Purion product family.

Revenue for 2020 was $475 million an increase of 39% from the year prior. Product revenue increased 41% that year resulting from an increase in the number of Purion systems sold. Services revenue also increased by 5%.

Net income for the year was $50 million in 2020 from $17 million the year prior. The increase was mainly due to the increase in revenue despite corresponding increases in the company's operating and research and development expenses.

The company had $204.2 million in cash and cash equivalents in 2020 a $57.7 million increase from the year prior. Operating activities provided $69.7 million while investing and financing activities used $7.3 million and $2.4 million respectively. Axcelis' main cash uses in 2020 were capital expenditures repurchase of common stock and net settlement on restricted stock grants.

Strategy

Axcelis Technologies' 2021 strategic directives are achieving a $550 million run rate in 2021 positioning the company to achieve its $550 million model in 2022 and its $650 million model by 2024; executing a capital strategy that funds appropriate investments in the business; and preparing for a post-COVID business environment.

Axcelis continues to invest in research and development to ensure its products meet the needs of its customers. The company takes pride in its scientists and engineers who are adding to its portfolio of patents and unpatented proprietary technology to ensure that its investment in technology leadership translates into unique product advantages. Axcelis strives for operational excellence by focusing on ways to lower its product manufacturing and design costs and to improve its delivery times to its customers. Global Customer Teams and a focused account management structure maintain and strengthen its customer relationships and increase customer satisfaction. Finally Axcelis endeavors to maintain a strong cash balance to ensure sufficient capital to fund business growth.

Company Background

Axcelis' business commenced in 1978 and its current corporate entity was incorporated in Delaware in 1995.

HISTORY

Axcelis Technologies began as part of the Semiconductor Equipment Operations of industrial manufacturer Eaton. In 2000 Eaton spun off the operations as a wholly owned subsidiary and Axcelis completed an IPO that year selling less than 20% of the company's shares to the public. Brian Bachman Eaton SVP and group executive for hydraulics semiconductor equipment and specialty controls was named vice chairman and CEO of the spinoff.

At the end of 2000 Eaton distributed the remaining 82% ownership it held in Axcelis as a stock dividend to its shareholders fully ending its involvement in the semiconductor production equipment market.

Bachman resigned as vice chairman and CEO in 2002. Mary Puma the company's president and COO was elevated to the chief executive's post to succeed him. A former General Electric executive Puma worked at Eaton for four years before the Axcelis spinoff including two years in leadership positions with the Semiconductor Equipment Operations. Puma added the title of chairman of the Axcelis board in 2005.

EXECUTIVES

Pres-Ceo, Mary G Puma
Chb*, Richard J Faubert
Exec V Pres-Cfo, Kevin J Brewer
Exec V Pres-General Counsel-Co, Lynnette C Fallon
Exec V Pres Corp Mkt & Strateg, Douglas A Lawson
Executive Vice President, Russell J Low
Evp Customer Operations, John E Aldeborgh
Evp Product Development, William Bintz
Auditors: Ernst & Young LLP

LOCATIONS

HQ: Axcelis Technologies Inc
108 Cherry Hill Drive, Beverly, MA 01915
Phone: 978 787-4000 **Fax:** 978 787-3000
Web: www.axcelis.com

PRODUCTS/OPERATIONS

2014 Sales

	$ mil.	% of total
Ion implantation systems services & royalties	183.2	90
Other products services & royalties	19.9	10
Total	**203.1**	**100**

2014 Sales

	$mil.
% of total	
Product	88
Services	12
Total	**100**

COMPETITORS

ADVANTEST CORPORATION LLC	FEDERAL-MOGUL
APTIV PLC	FLEX LTD.
COLUMBUS MCKINNON TECHNOLOGIES CORPORATION	TRANSENSE PLC
D rr AG	ULTRATECH INC.
EVOQUA WATER TECHNOLOGIES CORP.	VALHI INC.
	VEECO INSTRUMENTS INC.

HISTORICAL FINANCIALS

Company Type: Public

Income Statement — FYE: December 31

	REVENUE ($ mil.)	NET INCOME ($ mil.)	NET PROFIT MARGIN	EMPLOYEES
12/20	474.5	49.9	10.5%	1,004
12/19	342.9	17.0	5.0%	1,009
12/18	442.5	45.8	10.4%	1,079
12/17	410.5	126.9	30.9%	985
12/16	266.9	11.0	4.1%	845
Annual Growth	**15.5%**	**46.0%**	**—**	**4.4%**

2020 Year-End Financials

Debt ratio: 7.7%
Return on equity: 11.0%
Cash ($ mil.): 203.4
Current ratio: 5.58
Long-term debt ($ mil.): 47.3
No. of shares (mil.): 33.6
Dividends
 Yield: —
 Payout: —
Market value ($ mil.): 979.0

STOCK PRICE ($) FY Close	P/E High/Low		PER SHARE ($) Earnings	Dividends	Book Value
12/20	29.12	21 9	1.46	0.00	14.32
12/19	24.10	48 27	0.50	0.00	12.87
12/18	17.80	22 11	1.35	0.00	12.54
12/17	28.70	9 3	3.80	0.00	11.03
12/16	14.55	38 6	0.36	0.00	6.82
Annual Growth	**18.9%**	**— —**	**41.9%**	**—**	**20.4%**

Axos Financial Inc

Formerly BofI Holding Axos Financial is the holding company for Axos Bank which provides consumers and businesses a variety of deposit and loan products via the internet. It has designed its online banking platform and its workflow processes to handle traditional banking functions with elimination of duplicate and unnecessary paperwork and human intervention. Most of its business originates in its home state of California though its operations attract customers from every US state. Founded in 2000 the company holds over $14 billion in assets and a total portfolio of net loans and leases of about $12 billion.

Operations

Axos Financial operates through two segments: Banking Business (generated approximately all of the company's sales) and Securities Business.

The Banking Business includes a broad range of banking services including online banking concierge banking and mortgage vehicle and unsecured lending through online and telephonic distribution channels to serve the needs of consumers and small businesses nationally. In addition the Banking Business focuses on providing deposit products nationwide to industry verticals (Title and Escrow) cash management products to a variety of businesses and commercial & industrial and commercial real estate lending to clients. The Banking Business also includes a bankruptcy trustee and fiduciary service that provides specialized software and consulting services to Chapter 7 bankruptcy and non-Chapter 7 trustees and fiduciaries.

The Securities Business includes the Clearing Broker-Dealer Registered Investment Advisor and Introducing Broker-Dealer lines of businesses. These lines of business offer products independently to their own customers as well as to Banking Business clients. The products offered by the lines of business in the Securities Business primarily generate net interest and non-banking service fee income.

More than 80% of Axos' revenue is generated by net interest income; non-interest income is derived mostly from banking and service fees. The bank's net loan and lease portfolio is dominated by single-family real estate: nearly 40% of its value is represented by mortgages. Some 20% is secured by multifamily real estate and another roughly 30% is made up of commercial and real estate loans.

Geographic Reach

Las Vegas Nevada-based Axos Financial holds deposits from customers in every US state with large sources of balances in Florida and the Mid-

Atlantic states. Over 70% of its mortgage portfolio is secured by real estate in California. Its next largest geographic segments by loan principal are New York and Florida which comprises about 15% and less than 5% respectively.

Sales and Marketing

The bank creates brand awareness through direct mail email digital marketing personal sales and print advertising. It also garners deposits through financial advisory companies and affinity partnerships.

Its advertising and promotional expenses for the years 2021 and 2020 were $14.2 million and $14.5 million respectively.

Financial Performance

The company's revenue for fiscal 2021 increased to $620.3 million compared from the prior year with $538.4 million.

Net income for the fiscal year ended June 30 2021 was $215.7 million compared to $183.4 million and $155.1 million for the fiscal years ended June 30 2020 and 2019 respectively.

Cash held by the company at the end of fiscal 2021 to $1 billion. Cash provided by operations was $412.6 million while cash used for investing and financing activities were $866.8 million and $458.6 million respectively. Main uses of cash were decrease in deposits and origination of loans held for investment.

Strategy

The company's business strategy is to grow its loan originations and its deposits to achieve increased economies of scale and reduce the cost of products and services to its customers by leveraging its distribution channels and technology. Axos has designed its online banking platform and its workflow processes to handle traditional banking functions with elimination of duplicate and unnecessary paperwork and human intervention.

Axos' long-term business plan includes the following principal objectives: maintain an annualized return on average common stockholders' equity of 17% or better; annually increase average interest-earning assets by 12% or more; and maintain an annualized efficiency ratio at the Bank to a level 40% or lower.

Company Background

Axos Financial launched in 2000 as Bank of Internet USA as a digital bank offering checking accounts. The company went public in 2005 as BofI Holding. In 2018 after launching its Universal Digital Bank Platform BofI changed its name to Axos Financial in tandem with a listing on the NYSE.

EXECUTIVES

Executive Vice President - Finance, Andrew Micheletti, $245,000 total compensation
Independent Director, Edward Ratinoff
Executive Vice President, Chief Credit Officer, Thomas Constantine, $270,000 total compensation
Independent Director, James Court
Independent Director, James Argalas
Executive Vice President - Specialty Finance, Chief Legal Officer, Eshel Bar-Adon, $310,000 total compensation
Executive Vice President, Head - Consumer Bank, Brian Swanson, $285,000 total compensation
Executive Vice President And Chief Financial Officer, Derrick Walsh
Independent Director, Uzair Dada
Executive Vice President, Chief Governance, Risk And Compliance Officer, John Tolla
Independent Director, Tamara Bohlig

Executive Vice President - Commercial Banking And Treasury Management, David Park
President Of Axos Clearing Llc, Jeff Sime
Executive Vice President, Chief Operating Officer, Raymond Matsumoto, $320,000 total compensation
Independent Director, Stefani Carter
Independent Vice Chairman Of The Board, Nicholas Mosich
Independent Chairman Of The Board, Paul Grinberg
President, Chief Executive Officer And Director, Gregory Garrabrants, $700,000 total compensation
Auditors: BDO USA, LLP

LOCATIONS

HQ: Axos Financial Inc
9205 West Russell Road, STE 400, Las Vegas, NV 89148
Phone: 858 649-2218
Web: www.axosfinancial.com

PRODUCTS/OPERATIONS

2018 Sales

	$ mil.	% of total
Interest and dividend income:		
Loans and leases including fees	447.0	79
Investments	28.1	5
Interest expense	(106.6)	-
Non-interest income:		
Banking and service fees	47.8	11
Mortgage banking income	13.7	3
Gain on sale - other	5.7	1
Prepayment penalty fee income	3.9	1
Gain (loss) on sale of securities	(0.2)	-
Total	**455.3**	**100**

COMPETITORS

COLUMBIA BANKING SYSTEM INC.	OCEANFIRST FINANCIAL CORP.
COMMERCE BANCSHARES INC.	PROVIDENT FINANCIAL SERVICES INC.
FLAGSTAR BANCORP INC.	SIGNATURE BANK
LEGACYTEXAS FINANCIAL GROUP INC.	TERRITORIAL BANCORP INC.
M&T BANK CORPORATION	THE SOUTHERN BANC COMPANY INC
META FINANCIAL GROUP INC.	UMPQUA HOLDINGS CORPORATION
MIDWESTONE FINANCIAL GROUP INC.	WSFS FINANCIAL CORPORATION
NATIONAL BANK HOLDINGS CORPORATION	
NEWCASTLE BUILDING SOCIETY	

HISTORICAL FINANCIALS

Company Type: Public

Income Statement				FYE: June 30
	ASSETS ($ mil.)	NET INCOME ($ mil.)	INCOME AS % OF ASSETS	EMPLOYEES
06/21	14,265.5	215.7	1.5%	1,165
06/20	13,851.9	183.4	1.3%	1,099
06/19	11,220.2	155.1	1.4%	1,007
06/18	9,539.5	152.4	1.6%	801
06/17	8,501.6	134.7	1.6%	681
Annual Growth	13.8%	12.5%	—	14.4%

2021 Year-End Financials

Return on assets: 1.5%	Dividends
Return on equity: 16.3%	Yield: —
Long-term debt ($ mil.): —	Payout: —
No. of shares (mil.): 59.3	Market value ($ mil.): 2,752.0
Sales ($ mil): 723.1	

	STOCK PRICE ($)	P/E		PER SHARE ($)		
	FY Close	High/Low	Earnings	Dividends	Book Value
06/21	46.39	14	5	3.56	0.00	23.62
06/20	22.08	10	5	2.98	0.00	20.65
06/19	27.25	17	10	2.48	0.00	17.55
06/18	40.91	19	10	2.37	0.00	15.32
06/17	23.72	16	7	2.07	0.00	13.13
Annual Growth	18.3%	—	—	14.5%	—	15.8%

AZEK Co Inc (The)

When it comes to CPG's building products appearance is key. Through its AZEK Scranton and Vycom operating segments CPG is a leading manufacturer of synthetic building products and other materials used in residential remodeling and construction as well as by commercial and industrial clients in the US and Canada. Its core AZEK unit manufactures PVC-based residential products such as trim deck rail moulding and porch materials made to look like wood and other natural materials. CPG's Scranton unit makes polyurethane bathroom partitions and lockers for commercial and institutional end-users while Vycom makes PVC plastic sheeting for industrial uses. CPG's TimberTech unit makes decking and railings.

Operations

The company operates through three business units: Residential Commercial and Industrial.

CPG International offers high-performance residential building products (including trim decking moulding railing porch lighting).

Subsidiary Scranton Products offers a line of synthetic commercial building products including locker systems bathroom partitions counter tops shower stalls and other products.

Vycom makes and markets PVC and Olefin industrial products for the marine graphic display saferoom food processing playground equipment and semiconductor industries.

Geographic Reach

CPG owns and operates five manufacturing facilities in Scranton Pennsylvania. In addition it manufactures its AZEK deck products at its facility in Foley Alabama and Timbertech products in Wilmington Ohio. The Boise Cascade Building Material Distribution branch in Lathrop California supplies Northern California and the Carson City area of Nevada; the Riverside California branch serves Southern California.

Sales and Marketing

The company sells its products through distributors dealers and retail outlets. CPG's brands include AZEK Trim and Moulding AZEK Deck AZEK Rail TimberTech TuffTec Duralife Lockers Seaboard Hiny Hider and Celtec.

Strategy

CPG is focused on capitalizing on the economic and functional advantages of its products relative to wood metal and other synthetic products. It grows its product offerings partly through acquisitions of (and partnerships with) complementary businesses.

In 2013 the company formed a partnership with Boise Cascade Building Materials Distribution to distribute TimberTech products throughout California and the Carson City area of Nevada.

Mergers and Acquisitions

In 2012 it acquired TimberTech a decking and railing manufacturer and a subsidiary of Ohio-based Crane Group Co. CPG combined TimberTech with its AZEK business to boost its strength as a leading manufacturer in the trim decking and railing market. Both have strong distribution channels in the US and Canada.

Company Background

CPG filed to go public in 2011. The company intended to use a significant portion of the proceeds that it raised in its IPO (up to $150 million) to repay debt and for general corporate purposes. However the IPO never went through and the company was acquired in 2013. Prior to this deal CPG was majority owned by AEA Investors which acquired its stake in 2005.

The company got its start in the mid-1980s as a plastic sheet manufacturer; it subsequently expanded its product offerings during the 1990s to include bathroom partitions and later in the decade residential building products.

EXECUTIVES

Ceo, Jesse Singh
Pres, Joe Ochoa
V Pres, Don Wharton
Sr V Pres, Ken Buck
V Pres, Jim Gross
Cmo, Jeanine Gaffke
Svp-Cfo, Ralph Nicoletti
Svp-Clo-Sec, Robert Perna
Clo, Paul J Kardish
Manager, Ken Vermilion
Marketing, Bethany Sanker

LOCATIONS

HQ: AZEK Co Inc (The)
1330 W. Fulton Street, Suite 350, Chicago, IL 60607
Phone: 877 275-2935
Web: www.azekco.com

PRODUCTS/OPERATIONS

Selected Brands
AZEK
Acacia
Arbor Collection
Celtec
Cobre
Corrtec
Fawn
Flametec
Harvest Collection
Hiny Hiders
Kona
Morado
Playboard
Procell
Redland Rose
Resistall
Sanatec
Scranton Products
Seaboard
Sedona
Silver Oak
Tahoe
TimberTech
TuffTec Lockers
Vycom

COMPETITORS

ALLIED BUILDING PRODUCTS CORP.
MEDPLAST GROUP INC.
MI WINDOWS AND DOORS

BEMIS MANUFACTURING COMPANY LLC
BRENTWOOD INDUSTRIES INC.
INTERMETRO INDUSTRIES CORPORATION LLC
PATRICK INDUSTRIES INC.
REHRIG PACIFIC COMPANY
TENSAR
CORPORATION
TNEMEC COMPANY INC.

HISTORICAL FINANCIALS

Company Type: Public

Income Statement

FYE: September 30

	REVENUE ($ mil.)	NET INCOME ($ mil.)	NET PROFIT MARGIN	EMPLOYEES
09/21	1,178.9	93.1	7.9%	2,072
09/20	899.2	(122.2)	—	1,663
09/19	794.2	(20.2)	—	1,540
09/18	681.8	6.7	1.0%	0
Annual Growth	20.0%	139.9%	—	—

2021 Year-End Financials

Debt ratio: 21.2%
Return on equity: 6.8%
Cash ($ mil.): 250.5
Current ratio: 3.12
Long-term debt ($ mil.): 464.7
No. of shares (mil.): 154.8
Dividends
 Yield: —
 Payout: —
Market value ($ mil.): 5,657.0

	STOCK PRICE ($) FY Close	P/E High/Low		PER SHARE ($) Earnings	Dividends	Book Value
09/21	36.53	83	55	0.59	0.00	9.22
09/20	34.81	—	—	(1.01)	0.00	8.43
09/19	0.00	—	—	(0.19)	0.00	4.53
Annual Growth	—			—	—	42.6%

B Riley Financial Inc

EXECUTIVES

Chairman Of The Board, Co-chief Executive Officer, Bryant Riley, $600,000 total compensation
Co-chief Executive Officer, Director, Thomas Kelleher, $600,000 total compensation
Chief Financial Officer, Chief Operating Officer, Phillip Ahn, $400,000 total compensation
President, Kenneth Young, $550,000 total compensation
Executive Vice President, General Counsel, Secretary, Alan Forman, $375,000 total compensation
Independent Director, Michael Sheldon
Chief Executive Officer Of B. Riley Fbr, Andrew Moore, $500,000 total compensation
Independent Director, Mikel Williams
Independent Director, Robert Antin
Independent Director, Marian Walters
Independent Director, Renee Labran
Independent Director, Tammy Brandt
Senior Vice President, Chief Accounting Officer, Howard Weitzman
Auditors: Marcum LLP

LOCATIONS

HQ: B Riley Financial Inc
11100 Santa Monica Blvd., Suite 800, Los Angeles, CA 90025
Phone: 310 966-1444
Web: www.brileyfin.com

HISTORICAL FINANCIALS

Company Type: Public

Income Statement

FYE: December 31

	REVENUE ($ mil.)	NET INCOME ($ mil.)	NET PROFIT MARGIN	EMPLOYEES
12/20	902.7	205.1	22.7%	996
12/19	652.1	81.6	12.5%	982
12/18	422.9	15.5	3.7%	1,071
12/17	322.1	11.5	3.6%	833
12/16	190.3	21.5	11.3%	388
Annual Growth	47.6%	75.7%	—	26.6%

2020 Year-End Financials

Debt ratio: 66.1%
Return on equity: 46.8%
Cash ($ mil.): 103.6
Current ratio: 1.90
Long-term debt ($ mil.): 962.3
No. of shares (mil.): 25.7
Dividends
 Yield: 3.0%
 Payout: 84.3%
Market value ($ mil.): 1,140.0

	STOCK PRICE ($) FY Close	P/E High/Low		PER SHARE ($) Earnings	Dividends	Book Value
12/20	44.22	6	2	7.56	1.33	19.88
12/19	25.18	10	4	2.95	1.49	13.37
12/18	14.20	38	24	0.58	0.74	9.70
12/17	18.10	43	27	0.48	0.67	10.01
12/16	18.45	16	7	1.17	0.28	7.80
Annual Growth	24.4%			—	59.4%	47.5% 26.3%

B&G Foods Inc

Peter Piper picks more than a peck of peppers from B&G Foods. The company makes markets and distributes a wide variety of shelf-stable foods frozen foods and household goods. Many of B&G's products are regional or national best-sellers including B&M and B&G (beans condiments) Clabber Girl (baking) Green Giant (frozen and canned foods) Spice Islands (seasonings) McCann's (oatmeal) Ortega (Mexican foods) Grandma's and Brer Rabbit (molasses) Snackwell's (snacks) and Underwood (meat spread). They are sold through B&G's subsidiaries to supermarkets mass merchants warehouse clubs and drug store chains as well as institutional and food service operators in the US Canada and Puerto Rico.

Operations

B&G Foods operates in a single industry segment. It offers a diverse portfolio of more than 50 brands that include Green Giant (frozen) which generates more than 20% of the company's total revenue Spices & Seasonings (approximately 15%) Ortega (about 10%) Green Giant ? shelf stable (more than 5%) Maple Grove Farms of Vermont Back to Nature Cream of Wheat Mrs. Dash and Clabber Girl (nearly 5% each) all other brands generate about 30%.

Geographic Reach

Headquartered in Four Gatehall Drive Parsippany B&G Foods operates nearly a dozen of manufacturing facilities including in Ontario Iowa Maryland Mexico Wisconsin and Indiana.

Sales and Marketing

B&G Foods sells markets and distributes its products through a multiple-channel sales marketing and distribution system to all major US food channels including sales and shipments to supermarkets mass merchants warehouse clubs wholesalers foodservice distributors and direct accounts specialty food distributors military commissaries and non-food outlets such as drug dollar store chains and e-tailers. The company primarily sells its products through broker sales networks that handle the sale of B&G Foods' products at the retail level.

Financial Performance

B&G Foods has seen its sales rise during the past five years. Overall sales have increased by 73% since 2015.

In fiscal 2019 the company saw its revenue decreased 2% to $1.7 billion compared to the prior year. The decrease was primarily attributable to the Pirate Brands divestiture offset in part by the McCann's and Clabber Girl acquisitions.

Net income in fiscal 2019 fell 56% to $76.4 million mainly due to lower net sales.

Cash and cash equivalents at the end of the year were $11.3 million. Net cash provided by operating activities was $46.5 million and financing activities provided another $77.7 million. Investing activities used $124.7 million for acquisition of businesses and capital expenditures.

Strategy

The company has been built upon a successful track record of acquisition-driven growth. Its goal is to continue to increase sales profitability and cash flow through strategic acquisitions new product development and organic growth.

It intends to implement its growth strategy through the following initiatives: expanding its brand portfolio with disciplined acquisitions of complementary branded businesses continuing to develop new products and delivering them to market quickly leveraging its multiple channel sales and distribution system and continuing to focus on higher growth customers and distribution channels.

Mergers and Acquisitions

In late 2020 B&G Foods completed the acquisition of the iconic Crisco brand of oils and shortening from The J. M. Smucker Co. for $550 million in cash subject to a customary adjustment based upon inventory at closing. Crisco is the number one brand of shortening the number one brand of vegetable oil and also holds a leadership position in other cooking oils and cooking sprays. As part of the acquisition B&G Foods also acquired a manufacturing facility and warehouse in Cincinnati Ohio.

In early 2020 B&G Foods acquired Farmwise LLC proud creator of Veggie Fries Veggie Tots and Veggie Rings. "We are excited to increase our great tasting plant-based product offerings with the acquisition of Farmwise" stated Jordan Greenberg Executive Vice President and Chief Commercial Officer of B&G Foods. B&G Foods funded the acquisition with cash on hand. Terms of the transaction were not disclosed.

In 2019 B&G Foods acquired the Clabber Girl Corporation a leader in baking products including baking powder baking soda and corn starch from Hulman & Company. In addition to Clabber Girl the number one retail baking powder brand Clabber Girl Corporation's product offerings include the Rumford Davis Hearth Club and Royal brands of retail baking powder baking soda and corn starch and the Royal brand of foodservice dessert mixes.

EXECUTIVES

Independent Director, Charles Marcy
Independent Director, Robert Mills
Executive Vice President And Chief Customer Officer, Ellen Schum
Independent Director, Debra Chase
President, Chief Executive Officer, Kenneth Keller
Chief Compliance Officer, Executive Vice President, General Counsel, Secretary, Scott Lerner, $495,190 total compensation
Chief Financial Officer, Executive Vice President - Finance, Bruce Wacha, $449,788 total compensation
Executive Vice President And Chief Supply Chain Officer, Erich Fritz, $421,275 total compensation
Independent Chairman Of The Board, Stephen Sherrill
Executive Vice President And Chief Commercial Officer, Jordan Greenberg, $385,313 total compensation
Chief Human Resource Officer, Executive Vice President Of Human Resources, Eric Hart
Independent Director, DeAnn Brunts
Independent Director, Dennis Mullen
Independent Director, Alfred Poe
Independent Director, Cheryl Palmer
Auditors: KPMG LLP

LOCATIONS

HQ: B&G Foods Inc
   Four Gatehall Drive, Parsippany, NJ 07054
Phone: 973 401-6500
Web: www.bgfoods.com

PRODUCTS/OPERATIONS

2016 Sales

	$ mil.	% of total
Green Giant	506.7	36
Ortega	142.0	10
Pirate Brands	84.9	6
Maple Grove Farms of Vermont	72.8	5
Cream of Wheat	62.2	4
Mrs. Dash	60.6	4
Bear Creek Country Kitchens	52.9	4
Las Palmas	39.1	3
Mama Mary's	35.8	2
Polaner	34.3	2
New York Style	33.1	2
Spices & Seasonings	28.2	2
All other brands	238.6	17
Total	**1,391.3**	**100**

Selected Products

Bagel chips
Canned meats and beans
Dry soups
Frozen and canned vegetables
Fruit spreads
Hot cereals
Hot sauces
Maple syrup
Mexican-style sauces
Molasses
Nut clusters
Peppers
Pickles
Pizza crusts
Puffed corn
Rice snacks
Salad dressings
Salsas
Seasonings
Spices
Taco shells and kits
Wine vinegar

Selected Brands

Ac'cent
B&G
B&M
Baker's Joy
Brer Rabbit
Cream of Rice
Cream of Wheat
Devonsheer
Don Pepino
Emeril's (licensed)
Grandma's Molasses
JJ Flats
Joan of Arc
Kleen Guard (sells and distributes)
Las Palmas
Maple Grove Farms of Vermont
Molly McButter
Mrs. Dash
New York Style
Old London
Ortega
Polaner
Red Devil
Regina
Sa-son
Sclafani
Static Guard (sells and distributes)
Sugar Twin
Trappey's
TrueNorth
Underwood
Vermont Maid
Wright's

COMPETITORS

FRESH MARK INC.
JOHN B. SANFILIPPO & SON INC.
JOHNSONVILLE LLC
LINDEN FOODS
MONOGRAM FOOD SOLUTIONS LLC
PILGRIM'S PRIDE LTD.
POST HOLDINGS INC.
THE HILLSHIRE BRANDS COMPANY
THE J M SMUCKER COMPANY
TREEHOUSE FOODS INC.

HISTORICAL FINANCIALS

Company Type: Public

Income Statement

FYE: January 2

	REVENUE ($ mil.)	NET INCOME ($ mil.)	NET PROFIT MARGIN	EMPLOYEES
01/21*	1,967.9	131.9	6.7%	3,207
12/19	1,660.4	76.3	4.6%	2,899
12/18	1,700.7	172.4	10.1%	2,675
12/17	1,668.0	217.4	13.0%	2,680
12/16	1,391.2	109.4	7.9%	2,590
Annual Growth	**9.1%**	**4.8%**	**—**	**5.5%**

*Fiscal year change

2021 Year-End Financials

Debt ratio: 61.9%
Return on equity: 15.7%
Cash ($ mil.): 52.1
Current ratio: 3.00
Long-term debt ($ mil.): 2,334.0

No. of shares (mil.): 64.2
Dividends
   Yield: 0.1%
   Payout: 116.4%
Market value ($ mil.): 1,782.0

	STOCK PRICE ($) FY Close	P/E High/Low		PER SHARE ($) Earnings	Dividends	Book Value
01/21*	27.73	15	6	2.04	2.38	12.95
12/19	18.22	26	13	1.17	1.43	12.69
12/18	29.96	14	8	2.60	1.89	13.71
12/17	35.15	15	9	3.26	1.86	13.25
12/16	43.80	30	19	1.73	1.73	11.83
Annual Growth	**(10.8%)**	**—**	**—**	**4.2%**	**8.3%**	**2.3%**

*Fiscal year change

BancFirst Corp. (Oklahoma City, Okla)

This Oklahoma bank wants to be more than OK. It wants to be super . BancFirst Corporation is the holding company for BancFirst a super-community bank that emphasizes decentralized management and centralized support. BancFirst operates more than 100 branches in more than 50 Oklahoma communities. It serves individuals and small to midsized businesses offering traditional deposit products such as checking and savings accounts CDs and IRAs. Commercial real estate lending (including farmland and multifamily residential loans) makes up more than a third of the bank's loan portfolio while one-to-four family residential mortgages represent about 20%. The bank also issues business construction and consumer loans.

Operations

The company operates three core units: metropolitan banks community banks and other financial service. Metropolitan and community banks offer traditional banking products such as commercial and retail lending and a full line of deposit accounts in the metropolitan Oklahoma City and Tulsa areas. Community banks consist of banking locations in communities throughout Oklahoma. Other financial services are specialty product business units including guaranteed small business lending residential mortgage lending trust services securities brokerage electronic banking and insurance.

The company's BancFirst Insurance Services arm sells property/casualty coverage while the bank's trust and investment management division oversees some $1.21 billion of assets on behalf of clients. Bank subsidiaries Council Oak Investment Corporation and Council Oak Real Estate focus on small business and property investments respectively.

Like other retail banks BancFirst makes the bulk of its money from interest income. More than 60% of its total revenue came from loan interest (including fees) during 2015 while another 2% came from interest on taxable securities. The rest of its revenue came from service charges on deposits (19% of revenue) insurance commissions (5%) trust revenue (3%) securities transactions (3%) and loan sales (1%).

Geographic Reach

BancFirst has 95 banking locations serving more than 52 communities across Oklahoma.

Sales and Marketing

The bank customers are generally small to medium-sized businesses engaged in light manufacturing local wholesale and retail trade commercial and residential real estate development and construction services agriculture and the energy industry.

BancFirst spent about $6.9 million for advertising and promotion during 2015 compared to $6.6 million in each of 2014 and 2013.

Financial Performance

BancFirst's annual revenues have risen 20% since 2011 thanks to continued loan asset and deposit growth (partly thanks to branch expansion). The company's annual profits have grown more than 40% over the same period as it's kept a lid on operating expenses and loan loss provisions.

BancFirst's revenue climbed 6% to $306.85 million during 2015 thanks to a combination of loan asset growth and gains on the sales of some of its securities.

Revenue growth in 2015 drove the company's net income up nearly 4% to $66.17 million. The bank's operating cash levels increased by almost 2% to $78.1 million with the rise in cash-based earnings.

Strategy

BancFirst's strategy focuses on providing a full range of commercial banking services to retail customers and small to medium-sized businesses in both the non-metropolitan trade centers and cities in the metropolitan statistical areas of Oklahoma. It operates as a 'super community bank' managing its community banking offices on a decentralized basis which permits them to be responsive to local customer needs. Underwriting funding customer service and pricing decisions are made by presidents in each market within the company's strategic parameters.

Mergers and Acquisitions

In October 2015 BancFirst purchased $196 million-asset CSB Banchsares and its Bank of Commerce branches in Yukon Mustang and El Reno in Oklahoma. The deal also added $148 million in new loan business and $170 million in deposits.

Company Background

The company has been buying smaller banks to expand in Oklahoma. In 2011 it acquired FBC Financial Corporation and its subsidiary bank 1st Bank Oklahoma with about five branches throughout the state. In 2010 BancFirst acquired Union Bank of Chandler Okemah National Bank and Exchange National Bank of Moore adding about another five branches. It acquired First State Bank Jones in 2009 to expand in eastern Oklahoma.

President and CEO David Rainbolt owns some 40% of BancFirst .

EXECUTIVES

Director, President And Chief Executive Officer Of Bancfirst, Darryl Schmidt, $600,000 total compensation
Vice Chairman Of The Board; Chief Executive Officer Of Council Oak Partners, Llc, William Johnstone
Independent Director, Tom McCasland
Vice Chairman, Dennis Brand, $375,000 total compensation
President, Chief Executive Officer, Director, David Harlow, $600,000 total compensation
Independent Director, David Lopez
Independent Director, Michael Wallace
Lead Independent Director, G. Rainey Williams
Independent Director, Natalie Shirley
Independent Director, Gregory Wedel
Chief Financial Officer, Executive Vice President, Treasurer, Kevin Lawrence, $320,000 total compensation
Independent Director, Francis Keating
Independent Director, Joseph Ford
Independent Director, Bill Lance
Independent Director, F. Ford Drummond
Independent Director, Robin Roberson
Director, Mautra Jones
Executive Chairman Of The Board, David Rainbolt, $400,000 total compensation
Vice Chairman Of The Board, James Daniel
Independent Director, C. Craig
Auditors: BKD, LLP

LOCATIONS

HQ: BancFirst Corp. (Oklahoma City, Okla)
101 N. Broadway, Oklahoma City, OK 73102-8405
Phone: 405 270-1086 **Fax:** 405 270-1089
Web: www.bancfirst.com

PRODUCTS/OPERATIONS

2015 Sales

	$ mil.	% of total
Interest		
Loans including fees	190.3	63
Securities	6.5	2
Interest-bearing deposit	4.2	1
Noninterest		
Service charges on deposits	57.7	18
Insurance commissions	14.8	5
Security transactions	9.3	3
Trust revenue	9.1	3
Income from sale of loans	2.0	1
Cash management	7.5	2
Other	5.5	2
Total	**306.9**	**100**

Selected Subsidiaries

BancFirst
  BancFirst Agency Inc. (credit life insurance)
  BancFirst Community Development Corporation
  Council Oak Investment Corporation (small business investments)
  Council Oak Real Estate Inc. (real estate investments)
Council Oak Partners LLC
BancFirst Insurance Services Inc.

COMPETITORS

CITY HOLDING COMPANY
COLUMBIA BANKING SYSTEM INC.
COMMERCE BANCSHARES INC.
COMMUNITY BANK SYSTEM INC.
EAGLE BANCORP INC.
ENTERPRISE FINANCIAL SERVICES CORP
FINANCIAL INSTITUTIONS INC.
FIRSTMERIT CORPORATION
GUARANTY BANCORP
HANCOCK WHITNEY CORPORATION
LEGACYTEXAS FINANCIAL GROUP INC.
M&T BANK CORPORATION
PEOPLE'S UNITED FINANCIAL INC.
SIGNATURE BANK

HISTORICAL FINANCIALS

Company Type: Public

Income Statement

	ASSETS ($ mil.)	NET INCOME ($ mil.)	INCOME AS % OF ASSETS	EMPLOYEES
12/20	9,212.3	99.5	1.1%	2,036
12/19	8,565.7	134.8	1.6%	1,948
12/18	7,574.2	125.8	1.7%	1,906
12/17	7,253.1	86.4	1.2%	1,782
12/16	7,018.9	70.6	1.0%	1,773
Annual Growth	**7.0%**	**9.0%**	**—**	**3.5%**

FYE: December 31

2020 Year-End Financials

Return on assets: 1.1%
Return on equity: 9.5%
Long-term debt ($ mil.): —
No. of shares (mil.): 32.7
Sales ($ mil): 464.3
Dividends
Yield: 2.2%
Payout: 43.8%
Market value ($ mil.): 1,921.0

	STOCK PRICE ($)	P/E		PER SHARE ($)		
	FY Close	High/Low	Earnings	Dividends	Book Value
12/20	58.70	21 9	3.00	1.32	32.64
12/19	62.44	15 12	4.05	1.24	30.74
12/18	49.90	17 13	3.76	1.02	27.69
12/17	51.15	40 18	2.65	0.80	24.32
12/16	93.05	42 23	2.22	0.74	22.49
Annual Growth	(10.9%)	— —	7.8%	15.6%	9.8%

Bank First Corp

EXECUTIVES

Independent Director, Peter Van Sistine
Director, Phillip Maples
Independent Director, Robert Holmes
Director, Stephen Johnson
Independent Director, Judy Heun
Independent Director, Mary-Kay Bourbulas
Chief Financial Officer, Kevin Lemahieu, $268,775 total compensation
President, Director, Michael Dempsey, $346,981 total compensation
Independent Director, Robert Gregorski
Chairman Of The Board, Michael Ansay
Independent Director, David Sachse
Chief Executive Officer, Director, Michael Molepske, $551,250 total compensation
Auditors: Dixon Hughes Goodman LLP

LOCATIONS

HQ: Bank First Corp
402 North 8th Street, Manitowoc, WI 54220
Phone: 920 652-3100 **Fax:** 920 652-3182
Web: www.bankfirstnational.com

HISTORICAL FINANCIALS

Company Type: Public

Income Statement   FYE: December 31

	ASSETS ($ mil.)	NET INCOME ($ mil.)	INCOME AS % OF ASSETS	EMPLOYEES
12/20	2,718.0	38.0	1.4%	314
12/19	2,210.1	26.6	1.2%	284
12/18	1,793.1	25.4	1.4%	253
12/17	1,753.4	15.3	0.9%	249
12/16	1,316.0	14.9	1.1%	173
Annual Growth	19.9%	26.4%	—	16.1%

2020 Year-End Financials

Return on assets: 1.5%
Return on equity: 14.4%
Long-term debt ($ mil.): —
No. of shares (mil.): 7.7
Sales ($ mil): 120.9

Dividends
Yield: 1.2%
Payout: 17.6%
Market value ($ mil.): 500.0

	STOCK PRICE ($)	P/E		PER SHARE ($)		
	FY Close	High/Low	Earnings	Dividends	Book Value
12/20	64.82	14 9	5.07	0.81	38.25
12/19	70.01	19 12	3.87	0.80	32.49
12/18	46.60	15 11	3.81	0.68	26.37
12/17	44.70	18 14	2.44	0.64	23.76
12/16	33.33	14 11	2.40	0.59	20.53
Annual Growth	18.1%	— —	20.6%	8.2%	16.8%

Bank Of Princeton (The)

Auditors: BDO USA, LLP

LOCATIONS

HQ: Bank Of Princeton (The)
183 Bayard Lane, Princeton, NJ 08540
Phone: 609 921-1700
Web: www.thebankofprinceton.com

HISTORICAL FINANCIALS

Company Type: Public

Income Statement   FYE: December 31

	ASSETS ($ mil.)	NET INCOME ($ mil.)	INCOME AS % OF ASSETS	EMPLOYEES
12/20	1,602.8	13.8	0.9%	176
12/19	1,454.8	10.1	0.7%	178
12/18	1,251.5	14.7	1.2%	151
12/17	1,200.5	11.0	0.9%	146
12/16	1,026.0	11.8	1.2%	135
Annual Growth	11.8%	3.9%	—	6.9%

2020 Year-End Financials

Return on assets: 0.9%
Return on equity: 6.8%
Long-term debt ($ mil.): —
No. of shares (mil.): 6.7
Sales ($ mil): 66.4

Dividends
Yield: 1.7%
Payout: 21.0%
Market value ($ mil.): 159.0

	STOCK PRICE ($)	P/E		PER SHARE ($)		
	FY Close	High/Low	Earnings	Dividends	Book Value
12/20	23.41	16 9	2.01	0.40	30.75
12/19	31.49	22 17	1.47	0.19	28.98
12/18	27.90	16 12	2.14	0.03	27.69
12/17	34.34	19 15	1.90	0.00	25.69
12/16	30.00	12 11	2.36	0.00	22.01
Annual Growth	(6.0%)	— —	(3.9%)	—	8.7%

Bank OZK

Bank of the Ozarks is the holding company for the bank of the same name which has about 260 branches in Alabama Arkansas California the Carolinas Florida Georgia New York and Texas. Focusing on individuals and small to midsized businesses the $12-billion bank offers traditional deposit and loan services in addition to personal and commercial trust services retirement and financial planning and investment management. Commercial real estate and construction and land development loans make up the largest portion of Bank of the Ozarks' loan portfolio followed by residential mortgage business and agricultural loans. Bank of the Ozarks grows its loan and deposit business by acquiring smaller banks and opening branches across the US.

Operations

The bank makes three-fourths of its total revenue from interest income while the rest comes from fee-based sources. About 43% of Bank of the Ozark's total revenue came from non-purchased loan interest in 2014 while another 26% came from interest on purchased loans and a further 8% came from interest on its investment securities. The rest of its revenue came from service charges on deposit accounts (8% of revenue) mortgage lending income (1%) trust income (1%) and other non-recurring sources.

Geographic Reach

Bank of the Ozarks had 174 branches in eight states at the end of 2014 with 81 of them in Alabama and another 75 branches split among Georgia North Carolina and Texas. It has two loan offices in Houston and Manhattan that serve as an extension of the bank's Dallas-based Real Estate Specialties Group.

Sales and Marketing

The bank spent $3.03 million on advertising and public relations expenses in 2014 compared to $2.2 million and $4.09 million in 2013 and 2012 respectively.

Financial Performance

Bank of the Ozarks' annual revenues and profits have doubled since 2010 mostly as its loan assets have doubled from recent bank acquisitions spawning higher interest income.

The bank's revenue jumped 31% to $376 million during 2014 mostly thanks to strong purchased and non-purchased loan asset growth during the year from recent bank acquisitions. Its non-interest income grew 12% thanks to a 20% increase in deposit account service charges stemming from newly acquired deposit customers.

Strong revenue growth in 2014 boosted Bank of the Ozarks' net income by 30% to $119 million for the year. Its operating cash levels jumped 22% to $61 million during the year mostly thanks to higher cash earnings.

Strategy

Bank of the Ozarks continues its strategy of loan and deposit volume growth by acquiring smaller banks in new and existing geographic markets. It has also opened new branches and loan offices sparingly. During 2014 for example the bank opened retail branches in Bradenton Florida; Cornelius North Carolina; and Hilton Head Island South Carolina along with a new loan production office in Asheville North Carolina.

Mergers and Acquisitions

In July 2016 Bank of the Ozarks acquired Georgia-based Community & Southern Holdings and its Community & Southern Bank subsidiary. Adding some 45 branch locations in Georgia plus another in Florida it was the company's largest acquisition to-date.

Also in July 2016 the bank purchased C1 Financial along with its 32 CI Bank branches on the west coast of Florida and in Miami-Dade and Orange Counties. The deal added $1.7 billion in total assets $1.4 billion in loans and $1.3 billion in deposits. This transaction was the bank's fifteenth acquisition in the past six years.

In August 2015 the bank purchased Bank of the Carolinas Corporation (BCAR) — and its eight Bank of the Carolinas branches in North Carolina $345 million in total assets $277 million in loans and $296 million in deposits — for a total price of $65.4 million.

In February 2015 Bank of the Ozarks bought Intervest Bancshares Corporation and its seven Intervest National Bank branches in (five in Clearwater Florida and two more in New York City and Pasadena Florida) for $238.5 million. The deal added $1.5 billion in assets including $1.1 billion in loans and $1.2 billion in deposits.

In May 2014 it bought Arkansas-based Summit Bancorp Inc. and its 23 Summit Bank branches across Arkansas for $42.5 million though it closed more than a handful of them later in the year.

In March 2014 the company acquired Houston-based Bancshares Inc. and its subsidiary Omni-bank N.A. for $21.5 million adding three branches in Houston Texas and a branch each in Austin Cedar Park Lockhart and San Antonio.

Company Background

The expansion strategy of Bank of the Ozarks - which had a mere five branches in Arkansas 20 years ago — centered on opening new locations in smaller communities in Arkansas. But with the financial crash the bank was able to expand to more states through a series of FDIC-assisted transactions to take over failed banks. It bought Chestatee State Bank First Choice Community Bank Horizon Bank Oglethorpe Bank Park Avenue Bank Unity National and Woodlands Bank.

Chairman and CEO George Gleason initially bought the bank more than three decades ago at age 25.

Auditors: PricewaterhouseCoopers LLP

LOCATIONS

HQ: Bank OZK
  18000 Cantrell Road, Little Rock, AR 72223
Phone: 501 978-2265   **Fax:** 501 978-2224
Web: www.bankozarks.com

PRODUCTS/OPERATIONS

2014 Sales

	$ mil.	% of total
Interest income		
Non-purchased loans and leases	162.5	43
Purchased loans	98.2	26
Investment securities	30.7	8
Non-interest income		
Service charges on deposit accounts	26.6	8
Other income from purchased loans net	14.8	4
Others	43.5	11
Total	**376.3**	**100**

Selected Services

Personal Banking
Apple PayChecking AccountsCredit CardsFree Bill PayFREE Debit CardsCustom Debit CardsEMV Chip CardsMobile BankingMortgage LoansMy Change KeeperOnline BankingOverdraft ProtectionPersonal LoansReloadable Spending CardsRetirement PlanningReorder ChecksSafe
Business Banking
Business ProductsApple Pay for BusinessDebit CardEMV Chip CardsBusiness Credit CardsChecking & Money MarketCommercial LoansExpress DepositMerchant ProcessingOnline BankingOverdraft ProtectionReorder ChecksTreasury Management Services
Online & Mobile Banking
Online BankingMobile BankingMobile DepositOnline Bill Pay
Wealth Management Services
Investment ProgramsFinancial PlanningCustomer Service

COMPETITORS

IBERIABANK CORPORATION   WILSHIRE
  BANCORP INC.
MIDLAND STATES BANCORP
  INC.

HISTORICAL FINANCIALS
Company Type: Public

Income Statement   FYE: December 31

	ASSETS ($ mil.)	NET INCOME ($ mil.)	INCOME AS % OF ASSETS	EMPLOYEES
12/20	27,162.6	291.9	1.1%	2,652
12/19	23,555.7	425.9	1.8%	2,774
12/18	22,388.0	417.1	1.9%	2,563
12/17	21,275.6	421.8	2.0%	2,400
12/16	18,890.1	269.9	1.4%	2,315
Annual Growth	**9.5%**	**2.0%**		**3.5%**

2020 Year-End Financials

Return on assets: 1.1%	Dividends
Return on equity: 6.9%	Yield: 3.4%
Long-term debt ($ mil.): —	Payout: 47.6%
No. of shares (mil.): 129.3	Market value ($ mil.): 4,045.0
Sales ($ mil): 1,185.3	

	STOCK PRICE ($) FY Close	P/E High/Low		PER SHARE ($) Earnings	Dividends	Book Value
12/20	31.27	14	7	2.26	1.08	33.03
12/19	30.51	10	7	3.30	0.94	32.19
12/18	22.83	16	7	3.24	0.80	29.32
12/17	48.45	17	12	3.35	0.37	26.98
12/16	52.59	21	13	2.58	0.63	23.02
Annual Growth	**(12.2%)**			**(3.3%)**	**14.4%**	**9.4%**

Bank7 Corp

Auditors: BKD, LLP

LOCATIONS

HQ: Bank7 Corp
  1039 N.W., 63rd Street, Oklahoma City, OK 73116-7361
Phone: 405 810-8600
Web: www.bank7.com

HISTORICAL FINANCIALS
Company Type: Public

Income Statement   FYE: December 31

	ASSETS ($ mil.)	NET INCOME ($ mil.)	INCOME AS % OF ASSETS	EMPLOYEES
12/20	1,016.6	19.2	1.9%	0
12/19	866.3	8.2	0.9%	78
12/18	770.5	25.0	3.2%	72
12/17	703.5	23.7	3.4%	74
12/16	613.7	16.8	2.7%	0
Annual Growth	**13.4%**	**3.5%**		

2020 Year-End Financials

Return on assets: 2.0%	Dividends
Return on equity: 18.5%	Yield: 2.8%
Long-term debt ($ mil.): —	Payout: 20.8%
No. of shares (mil.): 9.0	Market value ($ mil.): 128.0
Sales ($ mil): 54.9	

	STOCK PRICE ($) FY Close	P/E High/Low		PER SHARE ($) Earnings	Dividends	Book Value
12/20	14.20	9	3	2.05	0.41	11.87
12/19	18.96	24	16	0.81	0.60	9.96
12/18	13.35	6	4	3.03	7.71	8.68
Annual Growth	**3.1%**			**—**	**(17.7%)**	**(76.9%)**
16.9%						

BankFirst Capital Corp.

Auditors: T. E. Lott & Company

LOCATIONS

HQ: BankFirst Capital Corp.
  900 Main Street, Columbus, MS 39701
Phone: 662 328-2345
Web: www.bankfirstfs.com

HISTORICAL FINANCIALS
Company Type: Public

Income Statement   FYE: December 31

	REVENUE ($ mil.)	NET INCOME ($ mil.)	NET PROFIT MARGIN	EMPLOYEES
12/20	81.5	13.4	16.5%	0
12/19	65.5	11.8	18.0%	0
12/18	48.7	9.8	20.1%	0
12/17	43.6	6.1	14.0%	0
Annual Growth	**23.1%**	**30.0%**	**—**	**—**

2020 Year-End Financials

Debt ratio: 3.1%	No. of shares (mil.): 5.2
Return on equity: 10.2%	Dividends
Cash ($ mil.): 128.9	Yield: 0.0%
Current ratio: 0.09	Payout: 18.1%
Long-term debt ($ mil.): 54.7	Market value ($ mil.): 104.0

	STOCK PRICE ($) FY Close	P/E High/Low		PER SHARE ($) Earnings	Dividends	Book Value
12/20	19.75	9	5	2.76	0.50	27.89
12/19	23.85	10	9	2.72	0.50	25.62
12/18	0.00	—	—	2.51	0.47	23.30
Annual Growth	**—**			**4.9%**	**3.1%**	**9.4%**

Bar Harbor Bankshares

Bar Harbor Bankshares which holds Bar Harbor Bank & Trust is a Maine -stay. Boasting $1.6 billion in assets the bank offers traditional deposit and retirement products trust services and a variety of loans to individuals and businesses through 15 branches in the state's Hancock Knox and Washington counties. Commercial real estate and residential mortgages loans make up nearly 80% of the bank's loan portfolio though it also originates business construction agricultural home equity and other consumer loans. About 10% of its loans are to the tourist industry which is associated with nearby Acadia National Park. Subsidiary Bar Harbor Trust Services offers trust and estate planning services.

Operations

Around 80% of the bank's loan assets are tied to real estate. About 41% of its loan portfolio was made up of residential real estate mortgages at the end of 2015 while another 37% was made up of commercial real estate mortgages. The rest of the portfolio was tied to commercial and industrial loans (8% of loan assets) home equity loans (5%) agricultural and farming loans (3%) commercial construction (3%) and other consumer loans (1%).

More than 80% of Bar Harbor's revenue comes from interest income. About 61% of its total revenue came from loan interest (including fees) during 2015 while another 25% came from interest income on investment securities. The remainder of its revenue came from trust and other financial services (6% of revenue) debit card service charges and fees (3%) deposit account service charges (1%) and other miscellaneous income sources.

Geographic Reach

The Bar Harbor Maine-based group operates 15 branches across the downeast midcoast and central regions of Maine more specifically in Bar Harbor Northeast Harbor Southwest Harbor Somesville Deer Isle Blue Hill Ellsworth Rockland Topsham South China Augusta Winter Harbor Milbridge Machias and Lubec.

Sales and Marketing

Bar Harbor serves individuals and retirees nonprofits municipalities as well as businesses that are vital to Maine's coastal economy including retailers restaurants seasonal lodging bio research laboratories.

Financial Performance

The group's annual revenues have risen more than 10% since 2011 as its loan assets have swelled over 35% to $990 million. Its profits have grown more than 30% over the same period as Bar Harbor has kept a lid on rising operating costs and as it's enjoyed low interest rates.

Bar Harbor's revenue climbed 4% to $64.2 million during 2015 mostly as its loan and other interest earning assets grew by more than 7%.

Revenue growth in 2015 drove the bank's net income up 4% to $15.15 million. Bar Harbor's operating cash levels spiked 31% to $20.33 million for the year mainly thanks to favorable working capital changes related to changes in other assets.

Strategy

Bar Harbor Bankshares looks to grow its loan and deposit business organically and through strategic bank acquisitions targeting the downeast midcoast and central Maine markets. It also continued in 2016 to focus on managing its operating expenses building upon its strong efficient ratio of 56.3% in 2015.

EXECUTIVES

Independent Chairman Of The Board, David Woodside
President, Chief Executive Officer, Director, Curtis Simard, $655,000 total compensation
Independent Director, Matthew Caras
Chief Financial Officer, Executive Vice President, Treasurer, Josephine Iannelli, $420,000 total compensation
Executive Vice President, Chief Lending Officer, John Mercier, $310,000 total compensation
Independent Director, Stephen Theroux
Independent Director, Lauri Fernald

Independent Director, Steven Dimick
Independent Director, David Colter
Independent Director, Daina Belair
Independent Director, Kenneth Smith
Independent Director, Scott Toothaker
Independent Director, Martha Dudman
Independent Director, Brendan O'Halloran
Executive Vice President - Director Of Retail Delivery, Marion Colombo, $310,000 total compensation
President - Bhts And Ctc, Jason Edgar
Chief Human Resource Officer, Senior Vice President, Jennifer Svenson
Auditors: RSM US LLP

LOCATIONS

HQ: Bar Harbor Bankshares
P.O. Box 400, 82 Main Street, Bar Harbor, ME 04609-0400
Phone: 207 288-3314
Web: www.barharbor.bank

PRODUCTS/OPERATIONS

2015 sales

	$ mil.	% of total
Interest and dividend income		
Interest and fees on loans	39.3	61
Interest on securities	15.3	24
Dividends on FHLB stock	0.6	1
Non-interest income		
Trust and other financial services	3.9	6
Debit card service charges and fees	1.7	3
Net services gains	1.3	2
Other operating income	1.2	2
Service charges on deposit accounts	0.9	1
Total	**64.2**	**100**

Selected Services

Retail Products and Services
Retail Brokerage Services
Electronic Banking Services
Commercial Products and Services

COMPETITORS

CITIZENS & NORTHERN CORPORATION
CNB FINANCIAL CORPORATION
STOCK YARDS BANCORP INC.

HISTORICAL FINANCIALS

Company Type: Public

Income Statement

FYE: December 31

	ASSETS ($ mil.)	NET INCOME ($ mil.)	INCOME AS % OF ASSETS	EMPLOYEES
12/20	3,725.7	33.2	0.9%	531
12/19	3,669.1	22.6	0.6%	460
12/18	3,608.4	32.9	0.9%	445
12/17	3,565.1	25.9	0.7%	423
12/16	1,755.3	14.9	0.9%	186
Annual Growth	20.7%	22.1%	—	30.0%

2020 Year-End Financials

Return on assets: 0.9%	Dividends
Return on equity: 8.2%	Yield: 3.9%
Long-term debt ($ mil.): —	Payout: 40.3%
No. of shares (mil.): 14.9	Market value ($ mil.): 337.0
Sales ($ mil): 169.0	

	STOCK PRICE ($) FY Close	P/E High/Low		PER SHARE ($) Earnings	Dividends	Book Value
12/20	22.59	12	6	2.18	0.88	27.58
12/19	25.39	19	15	1.45	0.86	25.48
12/18	22.43	14	10	2.12	0.79	23.87
12/17	27.01	28	15	1.70	0.75	22.96
12/16	47.33	30	18	1.63	0.73	17.19
Annual Growth	(16.9%)	—	—	7.5%	4.9%	12.5%

Barnwell Industries, Inc.

Barnwell Industries has more than a barnful of assets which range from oil and gas production contract well drilling and Hawaiian land and housing investments. Barnwell Industries explores for and produces oil and natural gas primarily in Alberta. In 2009 it reported proved reserves of 1.3 million barrels of oil and 20.6 billion cu. ft. of gas. Subsidiary Water Resources International drills water and geothermal wells and installs and repairs water pump systems in Hawaii. The company also owns a 78% interest in Kaupulehu Developments which owns leasehold rights to more than 1000 acres in Hawaii and is engaged in other real estate activities.

EXECUTIVES

President, Chief Executive Officer, Chief Operating Officer, General Counsel, Director, Alexander Kinzler, $210,000 total compensation
Chief Financial Officer, Executive Vice President, Treasurer, Company Secretary, Russell Gifford, $210,000 total compensation
Independent Chairman Of The Board, Kenneth Grossman
Independent Director, Philip McPherson
Independent Director, Peter O Malley
Independent Director, Bradley Tirpak
Independent Director, Douglas Woodrum
Independent Director, Colin O'Farrell
Auditors: Weaver and Tidwell, L.L.P.

LOCATIONS

HQ: Barnwell Industries, Inc.
1100 Alakea Street, Suite 2900, Honolulu, HI 96813-2840
Phone: 808 531-8400
Web: www.brninc.com

PRODUCTS/OPERATIONS

Subsidiaries

Barnwell of Canada Ltd. (oil and natural gas)
Kaupulehu Developments (78% land investment)
Kaupulehu 2007 LLLP (80% real estate development)
Water Resources International Inc. (contract drilling)

COMPETITORS

HIGHPOINT OPERATING CORPORATION
NOBLE ENERGY INC.
QEP RESOURCES INC.
RILEY EXPLORATION PERMIAN INC.

HOOVER'S HANDBOOK OF EMERGING COMPANIES 2022

HISTORICAL FINANCIALS
Company Type: Public

Income Statement — FYE: September 30

	REVENUE ($ mil.)	NET INCOME ($ mil.)	NET PROFIT MARGIN	EMPLOYEES
09/21	18.1	6.2	34.5%	36
09/20	18.3	(4.7)	—	43
09/19	12.0	(12.4)	—	43
09/18	9.3	(1.7)	—	31
09/17	13.0	1.1	9.0%	29
Annual Growth	8.6%	52.0%	—	5.6%

2021 Year-End Financials
Debt ratio: 0.1%
Return on equity: 167.7%
Cash ($ mil.): 11.2
Current ratio: 3.06
Long-term debt ($ mil.): 0.0

No. of shares (mil.): 9.4
Dividends
  Yield: —
  Payout: —
Market value ($ mil.): 29.0

	STOCK PRICE ($) FY Close	P/E High/Low		Earnings	Dividends	Book Value
09/21	3.03	8	1	0.73	0.00	1.01
09/20	0.85	—	—	(0.57)	0.00	(0.25)
09/19	0.52	—	—	(1.50)	0.00	0.15
09/18	1.78	—	—	(0.21)	0.00	1.94
09/17	1.80	18	11	0.14	0.00	2.08
Annual Growth	13.9% (16.7%)	—	—	51.1%	—	—

BayCom Corp

Auditors: Moss Adams LLP

LOCATIONS

HQ: BayCom Corp
  500 Ygnacio Valley Road, Suite 200, Walnut Creek, CA 94596
Phone: 925 476-1800
Web: www.unitedbusinessbank.com

HISTORICAL FINANCIALS
Company Type: Public

Income Statement — FYE: December 31

	ASSETS ($ mil.)	NET INCOME ($ mil.)	INCOME AS % OF ASSETS	EMPLOYEES
12/20	2,195.6	13.7	0.6%	315
12/19	1,994.1	17.3	0.9%	304
12/18	1,478.4	14.4	1.0%	214
12/17	1,245.7	5.2	0.4%	0
12/16	675.3	5.9	0.9%	0
Annual Growth	34.3%	23.4%	—	—

2020 Year-End Financials
Return on assets: 0.6%
Return on equity: 5.4%
Long-term debt ($ mil.): —
No. of shares (mil.): 11.3
Sales ($ mil.): 95.9

Dividends
  Yield: —
  Payout: —
Market value ($ mil.): 171.0

	STOCK PRICE ($) FY Close	P/E High/Low		Earnings	Dividends	Book Value
12/20	15.17	20	9	1.15	0.00	22.36
12/19	22.74	17	14	1.47	0.00	20.43
12/18	23.09	18	13	1.50	0.00	18.47
12/17	19.45	24	18	0.81	0.00	15.82
12/16	14.86	14	11	1.09	0.00	14.26
Annual Growth	0.5%	—	—	1.3%	—	11.9%

BCB Bancorp Inc

BCB Bancorp be the holding company for BCB Community Bank which opened its doors in late 2000. The independent bank serves Hudson County and the surrounding area from about 15 offices in New Jersey's Bayonne Hoboken Jersey City and Monroe. The bank offers traditional deposit products and services including savings accounts money market accounts CDs and IRAs. Funds from deposits are used to originate mortgages and loans primarily commercial real estate and multi-family property loans (which together account for more than half of the bank's loan portfolio). BCB agreed to acquire IA Bancorp in a $20 million deal in 2017.

EXECUTIVES

Independent Director, James Collins
Independent Director, Joseph Lyga
Independent Director, Spencer Robbins
Chief Compliance Officer, Chief Risk Officer Of Bcb Community Bank, Sandra Sievewright, $169,308 total compensation
Independent Director, August Pellegrini
Senior Vice President, Chief It & Information Security Officer For The Bank, Wing Siu
Independent Director, Vincent DiDomenico
Independent Director, John Pulomena
Senior Vice President, Chief Lending Officer, David Garcia
Chief Operating Officer, Senior Vice President, Ryan Blake
Senior Vice President And Chief Strategy And Risk Officer Of The Bank, Kenneth Emerson
Independent Director, Robert Ballance
Independent Director, Judith Bielan
Executive Vice President And Chief Operating Officer Of The Company And Bcb Community Bank, Michael Lesler, $331,000 total compensation
Independent Chairman Of The Board, Mark Hogan
President, Chief Executive Officer And Director Of The Bcb Bancorp, Inc And Bcb Community Bank, Thomas Coughlin, $585,000 total compensation
Chief Financial Officer Of Bcb Bancorp, Inc And Bcb Community Bank, Thomas Keating, $258,000 total compensation
Auditors: Wolf & Company, P.C.

LOCATIONS

HQ: BCB Bancorp Inc
  104-110 Avenue C, Bayonne, NJ 07002
Phone: 201 823-0700
Web: www.bcb.bank

COMPETITORS

FIRST CENTURY BANKSHARES INC.

FIRSTFED BANCORP INC.

HISTORICAL FINANCIALS
Company Type: Public

Income Statement — FYE: December 31

	ASSETS ($ mil.)	NET INCOME ($ mil.)	INCOME AS % OF ASSETS	EMPLOYEES
12/20	2,821.0	20.8	0.7%	302
12/19	2,907.4	21.0	0.7%	365
12/18	2,674.7	16.7	0.6%	365
12/17	1,942.8	9.9	0.5%	314
12/16	1,708.2	8.0	0.5%	353
Annual Growth	13.4%	27.1%	—	(3.8%)

2020 Year-End Financials
Return on assets: 0.7%
Return on equity: 8.5%
Long-term debt ($ mil.): —
No. of shares (mil.): 17.1
Sales ($ mil): 125.9

Dividends
  Yield: 5.0%
  Payout: 54.9%
Market value ($ mil.): 189.0

	STOCK PRICE ($) FY Close	P/E High/Low		Earnings	Dividends	Book Value
12/20	11.07	12	7	1.14	0.56	14.57
12/19	13.79	12	9	1.20	0.56	13.67
12/18	10.47	16	10	1.01	0.56	12.60
12/17	14.50	22	16	0.75	0.56	11.73
12/16	13.00	21	16	0.63	0.56	11.63
Annual Growth	(3.9%)	—	—	16.0%	(0.0%)	5.8%

BellRing Brands Inc

Auditors: PricewaterhouseCoopers LLP

LOCATIONS

HQ: BellRing Brands Inc
  2503 S. Hanley Road, St. Louis, MO 63144
Phone: 314 644-7600
Web: www.bellringbrands.com

HISTORICAL FINANCIALS
Company Type: Public

Income Statement — FYE: September 30

	REVENUE ($ mil.)	NET INCOME ($ mil.)	NET PROFIT MARGIN	EMPLOYEES
09/21	1,247.1	27.6	2.2%	355
09/20	988.3	23.5	2.4%	390
09/19	854.4	123.1	14.4%	400
09/18	827.5	96.1	11.6%	380
09/17	713.2	35.2	4.9%	0
Annual Growth	15.0%	(5.9%)	—	—

2021 Year-End Financials
Debt ratio: 85.7%
Return on equity: ***,***.*%
Cash ($ mil.): 152.6
Current ratio: 1.54
Long-term debt ($ mil.): 481.2

No. of shares (mil.): 39.5
Dividends
  Yield: —
  Payout: 89.1%
Market value ($ mil.): 1,215.0

48 HOOVER'S HANDBOOK OF EMERGING COMPANIES 2022

	STOCK PRICE ($) FY Close	P/E High/Low	PER SHARE ($) Earnings	Dividends	Book Value
09/21	30.75	49 26	0.70	0.00	(77.52)
09/20	20.74	40 24	0.60	0.00	(55.36)
Annual Growth	48.3%	— —	16.7%	—	

Bio-Techne Corp

Bio-Techne is a biotechnology research specialist. Through subsidiaries including Research and Diagnostic Systems (R&D Systems) Boston Biochem Bionostics and Tocris the company makes and distributes life science reagents instruments and services for the research diagnostics and bioprocessing markets worldwide. Bio-Techne's product lines extend to more than 350000 products most of which the company manufactures itself in multiple locations in North America as well as the UK and China. It also makes hematology controls and calibrators for blood analysis systems and sells them to equipment makers. The US accounts the largest for about 55% of total revenue.

Operations

Bio-Techne operates through two reportable segments: Protein Sciences segment and Diagnostics and Genomics segment.

The Protein Sciences segment is comprised of divisions with complementary product offerings serving many of the same customers ? the Reagent Solutions division and the Analytical Solutions division. Reagent Solutions division consists of specialized proteins such as cytokines and growth factors antibodies small molecules tissue culture sera and cell selection technologies while the Analytical Solutions division includes manual and automated protein analysis instruments and immunoassays that are used in quantifying proteins in a variety of biological fluids. The segment accounts about 75% of total revenue.

The Diagnostics and Genomics segment (about 25%) also includes two divisions focused primarily in the diagnostics market ? the Diagnostics Reagents division and the Genomics division. Diagnostic Reagents division consists of regulated products traditionally used as calibrators and controls in the clinical setting. Also included are instrument and process control products for hematology blood chemistry blood gases coagulation controls and reagents used in various diagnostic applications. Genomics division includes products aimed at nucleic acid (RNA or DNA) analysis that can be used for diagnostic or research applications. Key product brands include Advanced Cell Diagnostics or ACD Asuragen and Exosome Diagnostics.

Altogether Bio-Techne sells more than 350000 products under such brands as Novus Biologicals Tocris Bioscience ProteinSimple and R&D Systems.

Overall consumables accounts nearly 80% of total revenue instruments approximately 10% while services and royalty revenues accounts the remainder.

Geographic Reach

Headquartered in Minneapolis Minnesota The US market accounts for about 55% of Bio-Techne's annual revenues. EMEA (excluding the UK) is the second-largest region accounting for more than 20% of sales; the company also conducts sales in Asia Pacific and other regions.

The company has operations in the US Europe and China.

Sales and Marketing

Bio-Techne's protein sciences segment customers include researchers in academia government and industry (chiefly pharmaceutical and biotech companies) as well as diagnostic/companion diagnostic and therapeutic customers especially customers engaged in the development of cell and gene based therapies. Diagnostic and genomics customers include physicians prescribing such tests for the patients. The company spent approximately $4.7 million $4.2 million and $4.1 million in advertising expenses for fiscal 2021 2020 and 2019 respectively.

Financial Performance

For fiscal 2021 consolidated net sales increased 26% as compared to fiscal 2020. Organic growth was 22% with currency translation and acquisitions having a 3% and 1% impact on revenue respectively. Organic revenue growth was broad based and driven by accelerated momentum of the company's long-term growth strategy as well as customer site closures in the latter half of fiscal 2020 due to the COVID-19 pandemic.

In 2021 the company had a net income of $139.6 million a 39% decrease from the previous year's net income of $229.3 million.

The company's cash for the year ended 2021 was $199.1 million. Operating activities generated $352.2 million while investing activities used $243.5 million mainly for acquisitions. Financing activities used another $62.6 million primarily for contingent consideration payments.

Strategy

Over the last eight years the company has been implementing a disciplined strategy to accelerate growth in part by acquiring businesses and product portfolios that leveraged and diversified its existing product lines filled portfolio gaps with differentiated high growth businesses and expanded its geographic scope. From fiscal years 2013 through 2020 it has acquired sixteen companies that have expanded the product offerings and geographic footprint of both operating segments. Recognizing the importance of an integrated global approach to meeting its mission and accomplishing its strategies It has maintained many of the brands of the companies it has acquired but unified under a single global brand — Bio-Techne.

As part of its business strategy the company acquires businesses makes investments and enters into joint ventures and other strategic relationships in the ordinary course and it also from time to time completes more significant transactions. The company joined with two partners to establish a collaborative marketing venture ScaleReady LLC to address the needs of the rapidly expanding cell and gene therapy market.

Mergers and Acquisitions

In early 2021 Bio-Techne acquired the Texas-based Asuragen a leader in the development manufacturing and commercialization of genetic carrier screening and oncology testing kits. Its products leverage proprietary chemistries which can be used on widely available platforms including PCR qPCR

capillary electrophoresis and next-generation sequencing instruments. The transaction included initial consideration of $215 million in cash plus contingent consideration of up to $105 million upon the achievement of certain future milestones. The Asuragen acquisition adds a leading portfolio of best-in-class molecular diagnostic and research products including genetic screening and oncology testing kits molecular controls a Good Manufacturing Practice (GMP)-compliant 50000 square foot manufacturing facility and a CLIA-certified laboratory plus a team with deep expertise navigating products through the global diagnostic regulatory environment.

HISTORY

David Mundschenk founded biological products maker Research and Diagnostics Systems in 1976. In 1983 Mundschenk made a disastrous move buying heavily indebted French hematology instrument maker Hycel. R&D System's disgruntled board named Thomas Oland (at the time a consultant) CEO.

Enter TECHNE. Founded in 1981 by George Kline and Peter Peterson to pursue profitable acquisitions it went public in 1983 and in 1985 bought R&D Systems (which became an operating subsidiary of TECHNE) a sign of their confidence in Oland. TECHNE formed a biotechnology division in 1986 to produce and market human cytokines. In 1988 Kline resigned following a failed acquisition attempt by medical test kit maker Incstar.

In 1991 TECHNE bought Amgen's research reagent and diagnostic assay kit business and began selling Quantikine cytokine diagnostic kits. In 1993 it acquired what would become the company's R&D Europe unit.

In 1995 the company debuted 10 new Quantikine immunoassay kits. TECHNE restructured its European research operation in 1997 pulling underperforming molecular biology products from the market and refocusing on TECHNE's core cytokine-related products. The next year TECHNE bought Genzyme's research products business (antibodies proteins and research kits) for about $65 million.

As drug and biotechnology research became growth markets in the late 1990s and early 21st century TECHNE expanded through purchases. In 1999 it bought the reagent business and immunoassay patents of partner Cistron. The next year the firm increased its ownership in drug developer ChemoCentryx to almost 50% (reduced in 2001 to about 25% and then again in 2004 to 20%). TECHNE also acquired research and diagnostic market rights to all products developed by the firm. A similar deal was made in 2001 with functional genomics firm Discovery Genomics; that investment was not realized to TECHNE's satisfaction so it wrote off the investment in 2004.

It didn't wait long to fill the gap when it acquired the operations of Fortron Bio Science and Biospacific in 2005. The makers of antibodies and reagents had been partners since 1992 before they were integrated into TECHNE's R&D Systems division.

In 2007 the company set up a sales and distribution subsidiary in Shanghai to capitalize on the growing Chinese market. In 2007 TECHNE acquired minority stakes in two additional companies: diagnostics developer Nephromics and biotechnology firm ACTGen.

EXECUTIVES

Independent Chairman Of The Board, Robert Baumgartner
Independent Director, Alpna Seth
Independent Director, Joseph Keegan
Independent Director, Rupert Vessey
Independent Director, Julie Bushman
President - Protein Sciences, N. David Eansor, $585,000 total compensation
President - Protein Sciences Segment, William Geist
Independent Director, Randolph Steer
Independent Director, John Higgins
Independent Director, Roeland Nusse
Chief Executive Officer, President, And Director, Chuck Kummeth, $1,116,000 total compensation
Chief Financial Officer, Executive Vice President - Finance, James Hippel, $600,500 total compensation
Executive Vice President, General Counsel, Company Secretary, Brenda Furlow, $503,500 total compensation
President - Diagnostics And Genomics, Kim Kelderman, $530,000 total compensation
Auditors: KPMG LLP

LOCATIONS

HQ: Bio-Techne Corp
614 McKinley Place N.E., Minneapolis, MN 55413
Phone: 612 379-8854
Web: www.bio-techne.com

PRODUCTS/OPERATIONS

2015 Sales by Segment

	$ mil.	% of total
Biotechnology	325.9	72
Protein Platforms	66.2	15
Clinical Controls	60.4	13
Adjustments	(0.3)	-
Total	**452.2**	**100**

Selected Products and Services
R&D Systems
  Activity assays and reagents
  Antibodies
  Biomarker testing service
  ELISAs
  ELISpot kits & FluoroSpot kits
  Flow cytometry and cell selection/detection
  General laboratory reagents
  Multiplex assays/arrays
  Proteins
  Stem cell and cell culture products
Tocris
  Caged compounds
  Controlled substances
  Fluorescent probes
  Ligand sets
  Peptides
  Screening libraries
  Small molecules
  Toxins
Boston Biochem
  Affinity matrices/proteins
  Antibodies
  Buffers solutions and standards
  Fractions
  Inhibitors
  Kits
  Proteasome
  Substrate Proteins
  Ubiquitin

COMPETITORS

ABBOTT LABORATORIES	MYRIAD GENETICS INC.
FUJIFILM CELLULAR DYNAMICS INC.	PERKINELMER INC.
	QUIDEL CORPORATION
IMMUNOMEDICS INC.	Qiagen N.V.

LIFE TECHNOLOGIES CORPORATION
LUMINEX CORPORATION
MERIDIAN BIOSCIENCE INC.
ROCHE DIAGNOSTICS CORPORATION
STRATEC SE

HISTORICAL FINANCIALS
Company Type: Public

Income Statement
FYE: June 30

	REVENUE ($ mil.)	NET INCOME ($ mil.)	NET PROFIT MARGIN	EMPLOYEES
06/21	931.0	140.4	15.1%	2,600
06/20	738.6	229.3	31.0%	2,300
06/19	714.0	96.0	13.5%	2,250
06/18	642.9	126.1	19.6%	2,000
06/17	563.0	76.0	13.5%	1,800
Annual Growth	**13.4%**	**16.6%**	**—**	**9.6%**

2021 Year-End Financials

Debt ratio: 15.0%	No. of shares (mil.): 38.9
Return on equity: 9.5%	Dividends
Cash ($ mil.): 199.0	Yield: 0.2%
Current ratio: 3.35	Payout: 27.8%
Long-term debt ($ mil.): 328.8	Market value ($ mil.): 17,540.0

	STOCK PRICE ($) FY Close	P/E High/Low		Earnings	PER SHARE ($) Dividends	Book Value
06/21	450.26	124	64	3.47	1.28	40.12
06/20	264.07	47	27	5.82	1.28	35.92
06/19	208.49	85	52	2.47	1.28	30.73
06/18	147.95	49	34	3.31	1.28	28.69
06/17	117.50	58	48	2.03	1.28	25.42
Annual Growth	**39.9%**	**—**	**—**	**14.3%**	**(0.0%)**	**12.1%**

BioDelivery Sciences International Inc

BioDelivery Sciences International (BDSI) is a specialty pharmaceutical firm that takes already approved drugs to patients living with chronic pain and associated conditions. Drugs delivered via its BEMA (BioErodible MucoAdhesive) systems focus on the areas of pain management and opioid-induced constipation. Its BEMA fentanyl product ONSOLIS is a buccally delivered polymer film used for the treatment of cancer pain. Other FDA-approved product includes BUNAVAIL for the treatment of opioid dependence and BELBUCA for chronic severe pain management.

Operations
The company also include FDA approved product Symproic (naldemedine) for the treatment of OIC in adult patients with chronic non-cancer pain including patients with chronic pain related to prior cancer or its treatment who do not require frequent (weekly) opioid dosage escalation. It licenses its product ONSOLIS to TTY Biopharm which markets the product as PAINKYL in Taiwan and to Mylan which markets the product as BREAKYL in Europe.

The company generates revenue from its product sales that account for more than 95% of total revenues while a small portion comes from product royalties.

Geographic Reach
The company commercializes its products around the world but primarily in North America as well as in Taiwan and South Korea.

Sales and Marketing
The company commercializes its products in the US through its own sales force its about 120 sales representatives and nearly 15 regional sales managers that support its BELBUCA and Symproic products. It works in partnership with third parties to commercialize its products outside the US.

Reflecting the increased activity around product approvals BDSI spent $11 million $10.8 million and $4.5 million on advertising for the FY 2020 2019 and 2018 respectively.

Financial Performance
The company revenue for the last five years has been fluctuating but still registered positive growth with 2020 as its highest performing year.

BDSI's revenue decreased by about $45 million to $156.4 million in 2020 as compared to 2019's revenue of about $111.4 million

In 2020 the company had a net income of $25.7 million compared to the prior year's net loss of $15.3 million.

Cash and cash equivalents at the end of the year were $111.6 million. Net cash flows provided by operating activities was $24.9 million. Investing activities used $13000 primarily for acquisition of equipment. On the other hand financing activities was able to provide $22.7 million to the coffers.

Strategy
The company strategy is evolving with the establishment of its commercial footprint in the management of chronic pain. It seeks to continue to build a well-balanced diversified high-growth specialty pharmaceutical company. Through its industry-leading commercialization infrastructure it is executing the commercialization of its existing products. As part of its corporate growth strategy it has licensed and will continue to explore opportunities to acquire or license additional products that meet the needs of patients living with debilitating chronic conditions and treated primarily by therapeutic specialists. As it gains access to these drugs and technologies it will employ its commercialization experience to bring them to the marketplace. With a strong commitment to patient access and a focused business-development approach for transformative acquisitions or licensing opportunities it will leverage its experience and apply it to developing new partnerships that enable it to commercialize novel products that can change the lives of people suffering from debilitating chronic conditions.

Its commercial strategy for BELBUCA is to further drive continued adoption in the large longacting opioid (LAO) market based on its unique profile coupled with growing physician interest policy tailwinds and expanding payer access. It aims to leverage the specialized commercial infrastructure it established for BELBUCA as a vehicle to enable commercial growth in Symproic which is being increasingly seen as a complementary asset.

Mergers and Acquisitions
In 2021 BDSI has completed the acquisition of U.S. and Canadian rights to ELYXYB (celecoxib oral solution) from Dr. Reddy's Laboratories Limited. ELYXYB is the first and only FDA-approved ready-to-use oral solution for the acute treatment of migraine with or without aura in adults. BDSI

intends to launch ELYXYB in the first quarter of 2022. Additionally BDSI plans to conduct an ELYXYB pediatric study which will have the potential to address the significant unmet needs of pediatric and adolescent patients suffering from migraine attacks. The acquisition of ELYXYB represents a critical step to building its presence in Neurology which is an excellent strategic adjacency to its pain franchise.

EXECUTIVES

Chief Executive Officer, Director, Jeffrey Bailey, $383,497 total compensation
Independent Director, Vanila Singh
President, Chief Commercial Officer, Scott Plesha, $390,313 total compensation
Independent Chairman Of The Board, Peter Greenleaf
Senior Vice President - Operations, Joseph Lockhart
Chief Financial Officer, John Golubieski
Chief Medical Officer, Thomas Smith, $371,823 total compensation
Independent Director, Todd Davis
Chief Compliance Officer, General Counsel, Corporate Secretary, James Vollins, $336,953 total compensation
Senior Vice President - Business Development, Kevin Ostrander
Auditors: Ernst & Young LLP

LOCATIONS

HQ: BioDelivery Sciences International Inc
4131 ParkLake Avenue, Suite 225, Raleigh, NC 27612
Phone: 919 582-9050
Web: www.bdsi.com

PRODUCTS/OPERATIONS

2014 Sales

	$ mil.	% of total
Contract revenue	22.7	58
Research & development reimbursement	12.7	33
Product royalty	3.4	9
Product sales	0.1	-
Total	**38.9**	**100**

Selected Products
BELBUCA
BUNAVAIL
ONSOLIS

COMPETITORS

ADAMAS PHARMACEUTICALS THERAPEUTICS INC.	HERON INC.
ALMIRALL SA	IONIS PHARMACEUTICALS
ARDELYX INC.	INC.
COLLEGIUM PHARMACEUTICAL INC.	IRONWOOD PHARMACEUTICALS INC.
CONCERT PHARMACEUTICALS INC.	PARATEK PHARMACEUTICALS INC.
Clementia Pharmaceuticals Inc	PROGENICS PHARMACEUTICALS INC.
EXELIXIS INC.	TESARO INC.
FLEXION THERAPEUTICS INC.	ULTRAGENYX PHARMACEUTICAL INC.

HISTORICAL FINANCIALS
Company Type: Public

Income Statement
FYE: December 31

	REVENUE ($ mil.)	NET INCOME ($ mil.)	NET PROFIT MARGIN	EMPLOYEES
12/20	156.4	25.7	16.4%	176
12/19	111.3	(15.3)	—	178
12/18	55.6	(33.8)	—	164
12/17	61.9	5.2	8.5%	116
12/16	15.5	(67.1)	—	99
Annual Growth	**78.1%**	—	—	**15.5%**

2020 Year-End Financials

Debt ratio: 32.7%
Return on equity: 28.8%
Cash ($ mil.): 111.5
Current ratio: 3.44
Long-term debt ($ mil.): 78.4
No. of shares (mil.): 101.3
Dividends
  Yield: —
  Payout: —
Market value ($ mil.): 426.0

	STOCK PRICE ($) FY Close	P/E High/Low		Earnings	PER SHARE ($) Dividends	Book Value
12/20	4.20	24	12	0.24	0.00	1.07
12/19	6.32	—	—	(0.18)	0.00	0.73
12/18	3.70	—	—	(0.73)	0.00	0.42
12/17	2.95	35	16	0.09	0.00	0.16
12/16	1.75	—	—	(1.25)	0.00	(0.33)
Annual Growth	**24.5%**					

BioMarin Pharmaceutical Inc

Auditors: KPMG LLP

LOCATIONS

HQ: BioMarin Pharmaceutical Inc
770 Lindaro Street, San Rafael, CA 94901
Phone: 415 506-6700
Web: www.bmrn.com

HISTORICAL FINANCIALS
Company Type: Public

Income Statement
FYE: December 31

	REVENUE ($ mil.)	NET INCOME ($ mil.)	NET PROFIT MARGIN	EMPLOYEES
12/20	1,860.4	859.1	46.2%	3,059
12/19	1,704.0	(23.8)	—	3,001
12/18	1,491.2	(77.2)	—	2,849
12/17	1,313.6	(117.0)	—	2,581
12/16	1,116.8	(630.2)	—	2,293
Annual Growth	**13.6%**	—	—	**7.5%**

2020 Year-End Financials

Debt ratio: 18.3%
Return on equity: 23.7%
Cash ($ mil.): 649.1
Current ratio: 4.76
Long-term debt ($ mil.): 1,075.1
No. of shares (mil.): 181.7
Dividends
  Yield: —
  Payout: —
Market value ($ mil.): 15,937.0

	STOCK PRICE ($) FY Close	P/E High/Low		Earnings	PER SHARE ($) Dividends	Book Value
12/20	87.69	28	15	4.53	0.00	22.59
12/19	84.55	—	—	(0.13)	0.00	17.36
12/18	85.15	—	—	(0.44)	0.00	16.65
12/17	89.17	—	—	(0.67)	0.00	15.97
12/16	82.84	—	—	(3.81)	0.00	16.02
Annual Growth	**1.4%**			—	—	**9.0%**

Bioqual Inc

EXECUTIVES

Director, David Landon
Chief Financial Officer, David Newcomer, $99,092 total compensation
Chairman Of The Board, President, Chief Executive Officer, Mark Lewis
Auditors: Aronson LLC

LOCATIONS

HQ: Bioqual Inc
9600 Medical Center Drive, Suite 101, Rockville, MD 20850
Phone: 240 404-7654
Web: www.bioqual.com

HISTORICAL FINANCIALS
Company Type: Public

Income Statement
FYE: May 31

	REVENUE ($ mil.)	NET INCOME ($ mil.)	NET PROFIT MARGIN	EMPLOYEES
05/21	57.6	6.3	11.0%	0
05/20	46.3	4.2	9.1%	0
05/19	39.4	2.8	7.2%	0
05/18	35.8	3.6	10.2%	0
05/17	36.6	3.9	10.8%	0
Annual Growth	**12.0%**	**12.4%**		

2021 Year-End Financials

Debt ratio: —
Return on equity: 20.5%
Cash ($ mil.): 7.7
Current ratio: 3.44
Long-term debt ($ mil.): —
No. of shares (mil.): 0.8
Dividends
  Yield: 0.0%
  Payout: 15.5%
Market value ($ mil.): 73.0

	STOCK PRICE ($) FY Close	P/E High/Low		Earnings	PER SHARE ($) Dividends	Book Value
05/21	81.10	13	9	7.08	1.10	37.49
05/20	60.00	16	6	4.73	0.70	31.51
05/19	36.00	13	9	3.17	0.60	27.46
05/18	33.45	11	8	4.10	0.60	24.65
05/17	36.50	8	5	4.44	0.45	21.17
Annual Growth	**22.1%**			— —	**12.4% 25.0%**	**15.4%**

Blackhawk Bancorp Inc

This Blackhawk's mission is to increase your bottom line. Blackhawk Bancorp is the holding company for Blackhawk State Bank (aka Blackhawk Bank) which has nearly 10 locations in south-central Wisconsin and north-central Illinois. Serving area consumers and businesses the bank offers standard financial services such as checking savings and money market accounts CDs credit cards and wealth management. It also caters to the Hispanic community by offering bilingual services at some of its branches. Blackhawk Bank maintains a somewhat diverse loan portfolio with residential mortgages commercial and industrial loans and commercial real estate loans accounting for the bulk of its lending activities.

EXECUTIVES

Ceo-Chb, R Richard Bastian
Exec V Pres-Cfo-Sec-treas, Todd J James
Pres, David Adkins
Senior Vice President, Todd L Larson
Executive Vice President Chief, James Todd
Director of Loans, Stephen P Carter
Assistant Vice President Relat, Shelly Kuhl
Vice President, Sharon Burnett
Vice President, Jim Pieschel
Management, Orlando Leyva
Assistant Vp, Shawn Murphy
Auditors: Plante & Moran, PLLC

LOCATIONS

HQ: Blackhawk Bancorp Inc
  400 Broad Street, Beloit, WI 53511
Phone: 608 364 8911   **Fax:** 608 363 6186
Web: www.blackhawkbank.com

COMPETITORS

OXFORD BANK   UNITY BANCORP INC.
PACIFIC FINANCIAL
  CORPORATION

HISTORICAL FINANCIALS
Company Type: Public

Income Statement   FYE: December 31

	ASSETS ($ mil.)	NET INCOME ($ mil.)	INCOME AS % OF ASSETS	EMPLOYEES
12/20	1,141.6	10.8	1.0%	0
12/19	963.8	9.6	1.0%	0
12/18	817.2	8.1	1.0%	0
12/17	720.6	6.2	0.9%	0
12/16	665.7	5.9	0.9%	0
Annual Growth	14.4%	16.1%		

2020 Year-End Financials

Return on assets: 1.0%
Return on equity: 10.3%
Long-term debt ($ mil.): —
No. of shares (mil.): 3.3
Sales ($ mil): 61.1

Dividends
  Yield: 1.5%
  Payout: 14.8%
Market value ($ mil.): 94.0

	STOCK PRICE ($) FY Close	P/E High/Low		PER SHARE ($) Earnings	Dividends	Book Value
12/20	28.00	10	6	3.25	0.44	33.14
12/19	27.85	10	9	2.90	0.40	29.54
12/18	26.60	12	11	2.47	0.38	25.76
12/17	27.05	13	11	2.01	0.28	24.02
12/16	23.00	9	7	2.59	0.16	21.68
Annual Growth	5.0%	—	—	5.8%	28.8%	11.2%

Blackstone Mortgage Trust Inc

Capital Trust thinks investing in commercial mortgages is a capital idea. The self-managed real estate investment trust (REIT) originates underwrites and invests in commercial real estate assets on its own behalf and for other investors. Its portfolio includes first mortgage and bridge loans mezzanine loans and collateralized mortgage-backed securities. Subsidiary CT Investment Management which the company is selling manages five private equity funds and a separate account for third parties. Most Capital Trust's assets are related to US properties but the REIT does make occasional investments in international instruments.

EXECUTIVES

Independent Director, Leonard Cotton
Director, Jonathan Pollack
Chief Legal Officer And Secretary, Leon Volchyok
Independent Director, Lynne Sagalyn
Independent Director, Thomas Dobrowski
Independent Director, Martin Edelman
Senior Managing Director, Head - Investor Relations, Weston Tucker
Managing Director - Head Of Asset Management, Robert Sitman
Head Of Accounting, Paul Kolodziej
Director, Nnenna Lynch
Chief Executive Officer, President, And Director, Katharine Keenan
Executive Vice President, Capital Markets And Treasurer, Douglas Armer
Executive Chairman Of The Board, Michael Nash
Chief Financial Officer, Principal Accounting Officer And Assistant Secretary, Anthony Marone
Auditors: DELOITTE & TOUCHE LLP

LOCATIONS

HQ: Blackstone Mortgage Trust Inc
  345 Park Avenue, 24th Floor, New York, NY 10154
Phone: 212 655-0220
Web: www.blackstonemortgagetrust.com

COMPETITORS

ARBOR REALTY TRUST   MADISON SQUARE
  CAPITAL   CAPITAL
  INC.   INC.
EASTERN LIGHT CAPITAL
  INCORPORATED

HISTORICAL FINANCIALS
Company Type: Public

Income Statement   FYE: December 31

	REVENUE ($ mil.)	NET INCOME ($ mil.)	NET PROFIT MARGIN	EMPLOYEES
12/21	854.6	419.1	49.0%	0
12/20	779.6	137.6	17.7%	0
12/19	882.6	305.5	34.6%	0
12/18	756.1	285.0	37.7%	0
12/17	537.9	217.6	40.5%	0
Annual Growth	12.3%	17.8%		

2021 Year-End Financials

Debt ratio: 76.9%
Return on equity: 9.8%
Cash ($ mil.): 551.1
Current ratio: 3.60
Long-term debt ($ mil.): 17,459.4

No. of shares (mil.): 168.1
Dividends
  Yield: 8.1%
  Payout: 96.5%
Market value ($ mil.): 5,150.0

	STOCK PRICE ($) FY Close	P/E High/Low		PER SHARE ($) Earnings	Dividends	Book Value
12/21	30.62	12	9	2.77	2.48	27.28
12/20	27.53	42	13	0.97	2.48	26.48
12/19	37.22	16	13	2.35	2.48	27.87
12/18	31.86	14	12	2.50	2.48	27.25
12/17	32.18	14	13	2.27	2.48	26.98
Annual Growth	(1.2%)	—	—	5.1%	(0.0%)	0.3%

Blue Ridge Bankshares Inc (Luray, VA)

EXECUTIVES

Ceo, Brian Plum
Pres-Ceo*, Brian K Plum
Evp-Chief Banking Officer*, Don Andree
Pres-Chief Banking Officer*, Gary R Shook
Vice President of Operations, Cynthia D Fravel
Assistang Vp, Dianna C Keeney
Retail Operations Officer, Ann M Mann
Business Officer, Jonathan B Comer
Pres Charlottesville, VA Marke, Kelly Potter
Assistant Vice President Credi, Julie Catron
Svp Busi Dev't, Mike Knotts

LOCATIONS

HQ: Blue Ridge Bankshares Inc (Luray, VA)
  1807 Seminole Trail, Charlottesville, VA 22835
Phone: 540 743-6521   **Fax:** 540 743-5536
Web: www.mybrb.com

HISTORICAL FINANCIALS
Company Type: Public

Income Statement   FYE: December 31

	ASSETS ($ mil.)	NET INCOME ($ mil.)	INCOME AS % OF ASSETS	EMPLOYEES
12/20	1,498.2	17.7	1.2%	386
12/19	960.8	4.5	0.5%	271
12/18	539.5	4.5	0.8%	196
12/17	424.1	3.3	0.8%	0
Annual Growth	52.3%	74.1%		—

2020 Year-End Financials

Return on assets: 1.4%
Return on equity: 17.6%
Long-term debt ($ mil.): —
No. of shares (mil.): 8.5
Sales ($ mil): 111.2

Dividends
  Yield: 4.8%
  Payout: 27.5%
  Market value ($ mil.): 153.0

	STOCK PRICE ($) FY Close	P/E High/Low		PER SHARE ($) Earnings	Dividends	Book Value
12/20	17.81	11	6	2.07	0.57	12.59
12/19	20.95	31	23	0.73	0.57	10.85
12/18	17.25	25	15	1.09	0.54	9.41
12/17	17.00	28	19	0.81	0.21	8.74
/0.00	—	—		(0.00) 0.00	(0.00)	
Annual Growth	—	—		—	—	—

Bluerock Residential Growth REIT Inc

Auditors: Grant Thornton LLP

LOCATIONS

HQ: Bluerock Residential Growth REIT Inc
1345 Avenue of the Americas, 32nd Floor, New York, NY 10105
Phone: 212 843-1601
Web: www.bluerockresidential.com

HISTORICAL FINANCIALS

Company Type: Public

Income Statement   FYE: December 31

	REVENUE ($ mil.)	NET INCOME ($ mil.)	NET PROFIT MARGIN	EMPLOYEES
12/20	219.8	30.6	13.9%	0
12/19	209.9	36.7	17.5%	0
12/18	184.7	(1.1)	—	0
12/17	123.1	(15.6)	—	0
12/16	77.0	(4.3)	—	0
Annual Growth	30.0%	—	—	—

2020 Year-End Financials

Debt ratio: 61.2%
Return on equity: 3.6%
Cash ($ mil.): 83.8
Current ratio: 4.65
Long-term debt ($ mil.): 1,490.9

No. of shares (mil.): 22.1
Dividends
  Yield: 5.1%
  Payout: —
  Market value ($ mil.): 280.0

	STOCK PRICE ($) FY Close	P/E High/Low		PER SHARE ($) Earnings	Dividends	Book Value
12/20	12.67	—	—	(1.91)	0.65	38.88
12/19	12.05	—	—	(0.91)	0.65	34.30
12/18	9.02	—	—	(1.82)	0.65	26.81
12/17	10.11	—	—	(1.79)	1.16	23.86
12/16	13.72	—	—	(0.91)	1.16	23.26
Annual Growth	(2.0%)	—	—		(13.5%)	13.7%

BNCCORP Inc

BNCCORP is the holding company for BNC National Bank which has about 20 branches in Arizona North Dakota and Minnesota. Serving individuals and small and midsized businesses the bank offers deposit accounts credit cards and wealth management services. It also has residential mortgage banking operations in Iowa Kansas and Missouri. Real estate loans account for nearly half of the company's portfolio; commercial industrial construction agricultural and consumer loans make up most of the remainder. BNCCORP sold BNC Insurance Services to Hub International in 2007 for more than $37 million. It arranged to sell some of its operations in Arizona and Minnesota to Alerus Financial in 2010.

EXECUTIVES

President Of Bnc National Bank's Minnesota Market, E. Thomas Welch, $200,000 total compensation
Director, Gaylen Ghylin
Director, Richard Johnsen
Senior Vice President, Chief Information Officer, Mark Peiler, $120,000 total compensation
Director, John Palmer
Director, Bradley Bonga
Director, Jerry Woodcox
Chairman Of The Board, Michael Vekich
Director, Stephen Roman
Chief Operating Officer, Compliance Officer Of Bnc National Bank, Shawn Cleveland Goll, $100,000 total compensation
President Of Bnc National Bank's North Dakota Market, Jerry Renk, $150,000 total compensation
President Of Bnc National Bank's Arizona Market, Jess Roman, $157,500 total compensation
President And Chief Executive Officer Of Bnc Insurance Services, Richard Milne, $304,166 total compensation
Interim Chief Credit Officer, Toby Aeilts
Auditors: CliftonLarsonAllen LLP

LOCATIONS

HQ: BNCCORP Inc
322 East Main Avenue, Bismarck, ND 58501
Phone: 701 250-3040   **Fax:** 701 222-3653
Web: www.bnccorp.com

COMPETITORS

BOK FINANCIAL CORPORATION	PINNACLE FINANCIAL PARTNERS INC.
HANMI FINANCIAL CORPORATION	SIMMONS FIRST NATIONAL CORPORATION
HUNTINGTON BANCSHARES FINANCIAL INCORPORATED	TRUIST CORPORATION
NORTHWEST BANCORPORATION INC.	WOODFOREST FINANCIAL GROUP INC.

HISTORICAL FINANCIALS

Company Type: Public

Income Statement   FYE: December 31

	ASSETS ($ mil.)	NET INCOME ($ mil.)	INCOME AS % OF ASSETS	EMPLOYEES
12/20	1,074.1	44.6	4.2%	0
12/19	966.7	10.2	1.1%	0
12/18	971.0	6.8	0.7%	0
12/17	946.1	4.8	0.5%	0
12/16	910.4	7.1	0.8%	0
Annual Growth	4.2%	58.0%	—	—

2020 Year-End Financials

Return on assets: 4.3%
Return on equity: 41.4%
Long-term debt ($ mil.): —
No. of shares (mil.): 3.5
Sales ($ mil.): 122.5

Dividends
  Yield: 17.6%
  Payout: 84.6%
  Market value ($ mil.): 160.0

	STOCK PRICE ($) FY Close	P/E High/Low		PER SHARE ($) Earnings	Dividends	Book Value
12/20	45.25	4	1	12.52	8.00	33.39
12/19	34.65	12	7	2.88	0.00	27.39
12/18	20.50	16	10	1.93	0.00	22.26
12/17	31.00	22	18	1.38	0.00	22.40
12/16	26.05	13	7	2.03	0.00	21.47
Annual Growth	14.8%	—	—	57.6%	—	11.7%

BOK Financial Corp

BOK Financial began in 1910 as a regional source of capital for the energy industry. It has seven principal banking divisions in eight midwestern and southwestern states. In addition to traditional deposit lending and trust services its banks provide investment management wealth advisory and mineral and real estate management services through a network of branches in Arizona Arkansas Colorado Kansas Missouri New Mexico Oklahoma and Texas. With nearly 120 branches in the US more than half of the bank's deposit franchise are located in Oklahoma and over 30% of its loan portfolio are in Texas.

Operations

BOK Financial operates through three primary segments: Commercial Banking Consumer Banking and Wealth Management.

The Commercial Banking segment brings in nearly 60% of BOK's total revenue with offerings including lending treasury and cash management and risk management products for small midsized and large companies.

The Consumer Banking segment which brings in nearly 20% of total revenue is the retail arm providing lending and deposit services and all mortgage activities.

The Wealth Management segment (more than 20%) provides private bank and investment advisory services across all markets and it has more than $90 billion in assets under management. The segment is also engaged in trading and it underwrites state and municipal securities.

Geographic Reach

Most of Tulsa-based BOK Financial's locations are located in and around Tulsa; Oklahoma City;

Dallas/Fort Worth; Houston; Albuquerque New Mexico; Denver; Phoenix; and Kansas City in Kansas and Missouri. The company's primary operations facilities are in Tulsa; Oklahoma City; Dallas; and Albuquerque New Mexico.

The bank's loans to businesses and individuals with collateral primarily located in Texas totaled $7.2 billion or some 30% of the total loan portfolio. Loans to businesses and individuals with collateral primarily located in Oklahoma totaled $3.8 billion or more than 15% of its total loan portfolio. Loans to businesses and individuals with collateral primarily located in Colorado totaled $2.8 billion or over 10% of its total loan portfolio.

Sales and Marketing

In 2020 BOK Financials spent $14.5 million on promotional costs versus $35.7 million in 2019 and $30.5 million in 2018.

Financial Performance

BOK's revenues and net income have been trending upward for the past years but declined in the most recent fiscal year.

Revenue increased 8% to $1.9 billion in 2020. Net interest revenue totaled $1.1 billion for 2020 consistent with the prior year. Net interest margin was 2.83% for 2020 compared to 3.11% for 2019.

Net income in 2020 totaled $435.0 million or $6.19 per diluted share compared with net income of $500.8 million or $7.03 per diluted share for the year ended December 31 2019.

The company ended 2020 with $1.2 billion in net cash some $78 million less than it had at the end of 2019. Operating activities used $416.3 million and investing activities used 2.5 billion. Financing activities provided $2.8 billion.

Strategy

BOK Financial's overall strategic objective is to emphasize growth in long-term value by building on its leadership position in Oklahoma through expansion into other high- growth markets in contiguous states. Its acquisition strategy targets fairly priced quality organizations with demonstrated solid growth that would supplement its principal lines of business. It provides additional growth opportunities by hiring talent to enhance competitiveness adding locations and broadening product offerings.

The company is also focused on diversifying its revenue stream by growing its mortgage banking brokerage and wealth management operations.

With banking operations in several major oil- and natural gas-producing states about 15% of the group's lending portfolio is in the energy sector. Because the energy industry has been challenged with low commodity prices BOK's energy-related charge-offs have grown significantly. In 2020 net charge-offs reached nearly $70 million primarily related to energy borrowers.

EXECUTIVES

Chief Financial Officer, Executive Vice President And Director, Steven Nell, $548,333 total compensation
Executive Vice President, Chief Auditor, Rebecca Keesling
Independent Director, Douglas Hawthorne
Executive Vice President, Chief Risk Officer, Martin Grunst
Executive Vice President, Chief Information Officer, Joseph Grotton
Independent Director, Kimberley Henry
Independent Director, Jack Finley

Chief Human Resource Officer, Executive Vice President, Kelley Weil
Independent Director, Claudia San Pedro
Director, Rose Washington
Executive Vice President - Consumer Banking Services, Derek Martin
Independent Director, Chester Cadieux
Independent Director, Edward Joullian
Chief Operating Officer, Executive Vice President, Director, Stacy Kymes, $525,000 total compensation
Senior Vice President, Chief Accounting Officer, John Morrow
Independent Director, Joseph Craft
Independent Director, Steven Malcolm
Independent Director, David Griffin
Executive Vice President, Chief Credit Officer, Marc Maun
Chairman And Chief Executive Officer Of Bank Of Texas And Executive Vice President - Regional Banks, Norman Bagwell, $482,500 total compensation
Executive Vice President - Wealth Management, Chief Executive Officer Of Bok Financial Securities, Scott Grauer, $539,889 total compensation
Independent Director, Emmet Richards
Independent Director, John Coffey
Director, Michael Turpen
Director, Alan Armstrong
Independent Chairman Of The Board, George Kaiser
Independent Director, Stanley Lybarger
Director, V. Burns Hargis
Auditors: Ernst & Young LLP

LOCATIONS

HQ: BOK Financial Corp
Bank of Oklahoma Tower, Boston Avenue at Second Street, Tulsa, OK 74172
Phone: 918 588-6000
Web: www.bokf.com

PRODUCTS/OPERATIONS

2017 Sales

	% of total
Commercial Banking	76
Consumer Banking	7
Wealth Management	17
Total	**100**

Selected Banking Subsidiaries

Bank of Albuquerque National Association
Bank of Arizona National Association
Bank of Arkansas National Association
Bank of Oklahoma National Association
Bank of Texas National Association
Colorado State Bank & Trust
Mobank

COMPETITORS

AMERICAN NATIONAL BANKSHARES INC.
BOKF MERGER CORPORATION NUMBER SIXTEEN
FIRST FINANCIAL BANCORP.
FIRST HORIZON CORPORATION
FIRSTMERIT CORPORATION
LAKELAND FINANCIAL CORPORATION
NATIONAL BANK HOLDINGS CORPORATION
PACIFIC CONTINENTAL CORPORATION
PACWEST BANCORP
PINNACLE FINANCIAL PARTNERS INC.
SIMMONS FIRST NATIONAL CORPORATION
TCF FINANCIAL CORPORATION
TEXAS CAPITAL BANCSHARES INC.
VALLEY NATIONAL BANCORP
WASHINGTON FEDERAL INC.
WEBSTER FINANCIAL CORPORATION

HISTORICAL FINANCIALS

Company Type: Public

Income Statement
FYE: December 31

	ASSETS ($ mil.)	NET INCOME ($ mil.)	INCOME AS % OF ASSETS	EMPLOYEES
12/20	46,671.0	435.0	0.9%	4,915
12/19	42,172.0	500.7	1.2%	5,107
12/18	38,020.5	445.6	1.2%	5,313
12/17	32,272.1	334.6	1.0%	4,930
12/16	32,772.2	232.6	0.7%	4,884
Annual Growth	9.2%	16.9%	—	0.2%

2020 Year-End Financials

Return on assets: 0.9%
Return on equity: 8.5%
Long-term debt ($ mil.): —
No. of shares (mil.): 69.6
Sales ($ mil): 2,112.9
Dividends
Yield: 2.9%
Payout: 36.9%
Market value ($ mil.): 4,769.0

	STOCK PRICE ($) FY Close	P/E High/Low		PER SHARE ($) Earnings	Dividends	Book Value
12/20	68.48	14	6	6.19	2.05	75.62
12/19	87.40	13	10	7.03	2.01	68.80
12/18	73.33	16	11	6.63	1.90	61.45
12/17	92.32	18	15	5.11	1.77	53.45
12/16	83.04	24	13	3.53	1.73	50.12
Annual Growth	(4.7%)	—	—	15.1%	4.3%	10.8%

Boomer Holdings Inc

Auditors: Benjamin & Ko

LOCATIONS

HQ: Boomer Holdings Inc
8670 W. Cheyenne Avenue, Las Vegas, NV 89129
Phone: 888 266-6370
Web: www.boomernaturals.com

HISTORICAL FINANCIALS

Company Type: Public

Income Statement
FYE: January 31

	REVENUE ($ mil.)	NET INCOME ($ mil.)	NET PROFIT MARGIN	EMPLOYEES
01/21*	45.1	7.3	16.2%	120
07/20	11.4	(15.5)	—	80
07/19	0.0	(0.0)	—	0
07/18	0.0	(0.0)	—	0
07/17	0.0	(0.0)	—	0
Annual Growth	605.6%			
*Fiscal year change				

2021 Year-End Financials

Debt ratio: 22.2%
Return on equity: ***,***.*%
Cash ($ mil.): 1.1
Current ratio: 0.74
Long-term debt ($ mil.): 0.3
No. of shares (mil.): 155.2
Dividends
Yield: —
Payout: —
Market value ($ mil.): 108.0

	STOCK PRICE ($) FY Close	P/E High/Low		PER SHARE ($) Earnings	Dividends	Book Value
01/21*	0.70	86	12	0.05	0.00	(0.03)
07/20	2.75			(0.12)	0.00	(0.09)
Annual Growth	(74.7%)	—	—	—	—	—
*Fiscal year change						

Boot Barn Holdings Inc

Auditors: DELOITTE & TOUCHE LLP

LOCATIONS

HQ: Boot Barn Holdings Inc
15345 Barranca Pkwy., Irvine, CA 92618
Phone: 949 453-4400
Web: www.bootbarn.com

HISTORICAL FINANCIALS

Company Type: Public

Income Statement — FYE: March 27

	REVENUE ($ mil.)	NET INCOME ($ mil.)	NET PROFIT MARGIN	EMPLOYEES
03/21	893.4	59.3	6.6%	4,900
03/20	845.5	47.9	5.7%	3,200
03/19	776.8	39.0	5.0%	4,000
03/18*	677.9	28.8	4.3%	3,500
04/17	629.8	14.2	2.3%	3,000
Annual Growth	9.1%	43.0%	—	13.0%

*Fiscal year change

2021 Year-End Financials

Debt ratio: 11.7%
Return on equity: 16.6%
Cash ($ mil.): 73.1
Current ratio: 1.69
Long-term debt ($ mil.): 109.7

No. of shares (mil.): 29.2
Dividends
  Yield: —
  Payout: —
Market value ($ mil.): 1,852.0

	STOCK PRICE ($) FY Close	P/E High/Low		PER SHARE ($) Earnings	Dividends	Book Value
03/21	63.30	32	5	2.01	0.00	13.50
03/20	13.37	28	6	1.64	0.00	11.17
03/19	29.44	23	11	1.35	0.00	9.32
03/18*	17.73	18	6	1.05	0.00	7.86
04/17	9.89	31	11	0.53	0.00	6.77
Annual Growth	59.1%	—	—	39.6%	—	18.8%

*Fiscal year change

Boston Beer Co Inc (The)

The Boston Beer Company Inc. is a high-end alcoholic beverage company and one of the largest craft brewers in the United States. In fiscal 2020 Boston Beer sold approximately 7.4 million barrels of its proprietary products. The company's brands include Truly Hard Seltzer Twisted Tea Samuel Adams Angry Orchard Hard Cider and Dogfish Head Craft Brewery as well as other local craft beer brands. Boston Beer produces alcohol beverages including hard seltzer malt beverages (beers) and hard cider at company-owned breweries and its cidery and under contract arrangements at other brewery locations.

Geographic Reach

Headquartered in Boston The Boston Beer Company owns breweries in Cincinnati; Breinigsville Pennsylvania; and Milton Delaware. The company distributes its brews primarily in the US but they are also sold in Canada Europe Israel Australia New Zealand the Caribbean the Pacific Rim Mexico and Central and South America.

Subsidiary A&S Brewing has breweries in LA Miami and Brooklyn.

Sales and Marketing

The company sells its beverages in various packages. Sleek cans standard cans and bottles are sold primarily for off-premise retailers which include grocery stores club stores convenience stores and liquor stores. Kegs are sold primarily for on-premise retailers which include bars restaurants stadiums and other venues.

The company's media campaigns include TV digital and social radio billboards and print. The brewer complements is media buying by sponsoring which currently include such as National Hockey League The Boston Red Sox the Boston Marathon local concert and festivals industry-related trade shows and promotional events at local establishments to the extent permitted under local laws and regulations.

Total advertising and sales promotional expenditures of $477.6 million $355.6 million and $304.9 million were included in advertising promotional and selling expenses in the accompanying consolidated statements of comprehensive income for fiscal years 2020 2019 and 2018 respectively.

Financial Performance

Net revenue increased by $486.6 million or 39% to $1.7 billion in 2020 as compared to $1.2 billion in 2019 due primarily to increased shipments.

Net income for fiscal 2020 increased to $192.0 million compared with $110.0 million in the prior year.

Cash held by the company at the end of fiscal 2021 increased to $163.3 million. Cash provided by operations and financing activities were $253.4 million and $12.3 million respectively. Investing activities used $139.1 million mainly for purchases of property plant and equipment.

Strategy

The company continues to pursue a production strategy that includes production at breweries owned by the company and breweries and packaging facilities owned by others. During 2019 and 2020 the company brewed fermented and packaged approximately 74% and 65% of its volume at breweries owned by the company respectively. The company made capital investments in 2020 of approximately $140.0 million most of which represented investments in the company's breweries. These investments were made to increase production drive efficiencies and cost reductions and support product innovation and future growth. Based on its current estimates of future volumes and mix the company expects to invest between $300 million and $400 million in 2021 to meet those estimates. Because actual capital investments are highly dependent on meeting demand the actual amount spent may well be significantly different from the company's current expectations.

Company Background

Management consultant James Koch started The Boston Beer Company with his former secretary Rhonda Kallman in 1983. With Koch's $100000 in life savings plus $300000 raised from family and friends the company contracted with Pittsburgh Brewing to make beer using Koch's great-great-grandfather's recipe. (Louis Koch had brewed beer in Germany before opening a St. Louis brewery in 1860.)

EXECUTIVES

Senior Vice President - Supply Chain, Quincy Troupe, $449,617 total compensation
Independent Director, Michael Spillane
Independent Director, Meghan Joyce
Independent Director, Julio Nemeth
Head , Brewery And Director, Samuel Calagione
Chief People Officer, Carolyn O'Boyle, $347,308 total compensation
President, Chief Executive Officer, Director, David Burwick, $790,327 total compensation
Chief Marketing Officer, Lesya Lysyj, $319,712 total compensation
Chief Sales Officer, John Geist, $556,215 total compensation
Vice President - Brewing, David Grinnell
Lead Independent Director, Jean-Michel Valette
Chairman, C. James Koch, $424,577 total compensation
Chief Accounting Officer, Matthew Murphy
Vice President - Legal, Deputy General Counsel, Tara Heath
Chief Financial Officer, Treasurer, Frank Smalla, $556,215 total compensation
Auditors: DELOITTE & TOUCHE LLP

LOCATIONS

HQ: Boston Beer Co Inc (The)
One Design Center Place, Suite 850, Boston, MA 02210
Phone: 617 368-5000   **Fax:** 617 368-5500
Web: www.bostonbeer.com

PRODUCTS/OPERATIONS

Selected Brands and Year Introduced
Barrel Room Collection
  Samuel Adams American Kriek 2009
  Samuel Adams New World Tripel 2009
  Samuel Adams Stony Brook Red 2009
  Samuel Adams Thirteenth Hour 2011
Brewmaster's Collection
  Samuel Adams Black Lager 2005
  Samuel Adams Blackberry Witbier 2009
  Samuel Adams Boston Ale 1987
  Samuel Adams Cherry Wheat 1995
  Samuel Adams Coastal Wheat 2009
  Samuel Adams Cranberry Lambic 1990
  Samuel Adams Cream Stout 1993
  Samuel Adams Irish Red 2008
  Samuel Adams Latitude 48 IPA 2010
  Samuel Adams Pale Ale 1999
Core Focus Beers
  Samuel Adams Boston Lager 1984
  Sam Adams Light 2001
Flavored Malt Beverages
  Twisted Tea Backyard Batch Hard Iced Tea 2009
  Twisted Tea Half Hard Iced Tea & Half Hard Lemonade 2003
  Twisted Tea Hard Iced Tea 2001
  Twisted Tea Light Hard Iced Tea 2007
  Twisted Tea Peach Hard Iced Tea 2005
  Twisted Tea Raspberry Hard Iced Tea 2001
  Twisted Tea Blueberry Hard Iced Tea 2011
Hard Cider
  Angry Orchard Crisp Apple 2011
  Angry Orchard Apple Ginger 2011
  HardCore Crisp Hard Cider 1997
Imperial Series
  Samuel Adams Double Bock 1988
  Samuel Adams Imperial Stout 2009
  Samuel Adams Imperial White 2009
  Samuel Adams Wee Heavy 2011
Limited Edition Beers
  Infinium 2010
  Samuel Adams Utopias 2001
Seasonal Beers
  Samuel Adams Octoberfest 1989
  Samuel Adams Summer Ale 1996
  Samuel Adams Winter Lager 1989
  Samuel Adams Alpine Spring 2011

COMPETITORS

ANHEUSER-BUSCH COMPANIES LLC	DIAGEO PLC
Anheuser-Busch InBev	FOSTER'S GROUP PTY LTD
BIG 5 SPORTING GOODS	KEURIG DR PEPPER INC.
BEVERAGE CORPORATION	MOLSON COORS
BROWN-FORMAN CORPORATION	COMPANY USA LLC
CORPORATION LIMITED	SAN MIGUEL
	SHEPHERD NEAME
Companhia de Bebidas das Americas Ambev	THE HERSHEY COMPANY

HISTORICAL FINANCIALS
Company Type: Public

Income Statement
FYE: December 26

	REVENUE ($ mil.)	NET INCOME ($ mil.)	NET PROFIT MARGIN	EMPLOYEES
12/20	1,736.4	191.9	11.1%	2,423
12/19	1,249.8	110.0	8.8%	2,128
12/18	995.6	92.6	9.3%	1,543
12/17	862.9	99.0	11.5%	1,439
12/16	906.4	87.3	9.6%	1,505
Annual Growth	17.6%	21.8%	—	12.6%

2020 Year-End Financials

Debt ratio: —
Return on equity: 22.7%
Cash ($ mil.): 163.2
Current ratio: 1.59
Long-term debt ($ mil.): —

No. of shares (mil.): 12.1
Dividends
 Yield: —
 Payout: —
Market value ($ mil.): 12,365.0

	STOCK PRICE ($) FY Close	P/E High/Low		Earnings	PER SHARE ($) Dividends	Book Value
12/20	1,014.93	69	19	15.53	0.00	78.55
12/19	378.75	48	25	9.16	0.00	61.08
12/18	238.82	41	21	7.82	0.00	40.03
12/17	191.10	24	16	8.09	0.00	36.44
12/16	169.85	29	21	6.79	0.00	36.11
Annual Growth	56.3%	—	—	23.0%	—	21.4%

Bridgewater Bancshares Inc

Auditors: CliftonLarsonAllen LLP

LOCATIONS

HQ: Bridgewater Bancshares Inc
 4450 Excelsior Boulevard, Suite 100, St. Louis Park, Bloomington, MN 55416
Phone: 952 893-6868
Web: www.bridgewaterbankmn.com

HISTORICAL FINANCIALS
Company Type: Public

Income Statement
FYE: December 31

	ASSETS ($ mil.)	NET INCOME ($ mil.)	INCOME AS % OF ASSETS	EMPLOYEES
12/20	2,927.3	27.1	0.9%	185
12/19	2,268.8	31.4	1.4%	160
12/18	1,973.7	26.9	1.4%	140
12/17	1,616.6	16.8	1.0%	114
12/16	1,260.3	13.2	1.0%	0
Annual Growth	23.5%	19.8%	—	—

2020 Year-End Financials

Return on assets: 1.0%
Return on equity: 10.6%
Long-term debt ($ mil.): —
No. of shares (mil.): 28.1
Sales ($ mil.): 120.6

Dividends
 Yield: —
 Payout: —
Market value ($ mil.): 352.0

	STOCK PRICE ($) FY Close	P/E High/Low		Earnings	PER SHARE ($) Dividends	Book Value
12/20	12.49	15	9	0.93	0.00	9.43
12/19	13.78	13	9	1.05	0.00	8.45
12/18	10.55	14	11	0.91	0.00	7.34
Annual Growth	8.8%	—	—	1.1%	—	13.3%

BrightView Holdings Inc

Auditors: DELOITTE & TOUCHE LLP

LOCATIONS

HQ: BrightView Holdings Inc
 980 Jolly Road, Blue Bell, PA 19422
Phone: 484 567-7204
Web: www.brightview.com

HISTORICAL FINANCIALS
Company Type: Public

Income Statement
FYE: September 30

	REVENUE ($ mil.)	NET INCOME ($ mil.)	NET PROFIT MARGIN	EMPLOYEES
09/21	2,553.6	46.3	1.8%	20,500
09/20	2,346.0	(41.6)	—	19,700
09/19	2,404.6	44.4	1.8%	21,500
09/18	2,353.6	(15.0)	—	20,000
09/17	1,713.5	(13.9)	—	19,000
Annual Growth	10.5%	—	—	1.9%

2021 Year-End Financials

Debt ratio: 35.2%
Return on equity: 3.5%
Cash ($ mil.): 123.7
Current ratio: 1.43
Long-term debt ($ mil.): 1,130.6

No. of shares (mil.): 105.2
Dividends
 Yield: —
 Payout: —
Market value ($ mil.): 1,553.0

	STOCK PRICE ($) FY Close	P/E High/Low		Earnings	PER SHARE ($) Dividends	Book Value
09/21	14.76	43	27	0.44	0.00	12.76
09/20	11.40	—	—	(0.40)	0.00	12.12
09/19	17.15	46	22	0.43	0.00	12.29
09/18	16.05	—	—	(0.18)	0.00	11.75
Annual Growth	(2.8%)	—	—	—	—	2.8%

Broadmark Realty Capital Inc

LOCATIONS

HQ: Broadmark Realty Capital Inc
 1420 Fifth Avenue, Suite 2000, Seattle, WA 98101
Phone: 206 971-0800
Web: www.broadmark.com

HISTORICAL FINANCIALS
Company Type: Public

Income Statement
FYE: December 31

	REVENUE ($ mil.)	NET INCOME ($ mil.)	NET PROFIT MARGIN	EMPLOYEES
12/20	122.3	90.2	73.7%	54
12/19*	15.9	5.3	33.3%	41
11/19	115.0	69.9	60.8%	0
12/18	95.8	81.7	85.3%	0
12/17	52.2	45.3	86.9%	0
Annual Growth	23.7%	18.7%	—	—
*Fiscal year change

2020 Year-End Financials

Debt ratio: —
Return on equity: 7.6%
Cash ($ mil.): 223.3
Current ratio: 18.43
Long-term debt ($ mil.): —

No. of shares (mil.): 132.5
Dividends
 Yield: 7.6%
 Payout: 114.7%
Market value ($ mil.): 1,352.0

	STOCK PRICE ($) FY Close	P/E High/Low		Earnings	PER SHARE ($) Dividends	Book Value
12/20	10.20	19	9	0.68	0.78	8.86
12/19*	12.75	318	273	0.04	0.12	8.97
Annual Growth (1.2%)	(20.0%)	—	—	1600.0%	550.0%	—
*Fiscal year change

56   HOOVER'S HANDBOOK OF EMERGING COMPANIES 2022

Broadstone Net Lease Inc

LOCATIONS

HQ: Broadstone Net Lease Inc
800 Clinton Square, Rochester, NY 14604
Phone: 585 287-6500

HISTORICAL FINANCIALS

Company Type: Public

Income Statement   FYE: December 31

	REVENUE ($ mil.)	NET INCOME ($ mil.)	NET PROFIT MARGIN	EMPLOYEES
12/20	321.6	51.1	15.9%	71
12/19	298.8	79.3	26.6%	71
12/18	237.4	69.3	29.2%	0
12/17	181.5	54.8	30.2%	0
Annual Growth	21.0%	(2.3%)	—	—

2020 Year-End Financials

Debt ratio: 36.1%	No. of shares (mil.): 145.6
Return on equity: 2.5%	Dividends
Cash ($ mil.): 100.4	Yield: 0.0%
Current ratio: 2.59	Payout: 187.5%
Long-term debt ($ mil.): 1,541.1	Market value ($ mil.): 2,851.0

	STOCK PRICE ($) FY Close	P/E High/Low	PER SHARE ($) Earnings	Dividends	Book Value
12/20	19.58	45 37	0.44	0.83	15.79
12/19	0.00	— —	0.83	0.21	16.03
Annual Growth (1.5%)	—	— —	(46.8%)	297.6%	

Brown & Brown Inc

Insurance agency Brown & Brown is the sixth largest independent insurance brokerages in the US. The company provides property/casualty life and health insurance plus risk management services through its Retail segment mainly to commercial clients. Its National Programs division designs customized programs for such niche clients as dentists lawyers and optometrists. Brown & Brown's Wholesale Brokerage unit distributes excess and surplus commercial insurance as well as reinsurance to retail agents while the firm's Services segment provides self-insured and third-party administrator services. The company has more than 300 offices in about 45 states and in England the Cayman Islands and Bermuda.

Operations

Brown & Brown's business is divided into four reportable segments: Retail National Programs Wholesale Brokerage and Services.

The company's Retail segment accounts for more than 55% company's annual revenue. The division provides property/casualty and employee benefit offerings to commercial public professional and individual customers. Products include commercial packages property risk general liability workers' compensation and group medical. It also offers ancillary products for groups and individuals including life accident disability health hospitalization and dental.

The National Programs segment about 20% of sales provides managing general agency services in five categories: Professional Programs (profession-specific liability) Personal Lines Programs (personal property auto earthquake and marine coverage via Arrowhead subsidiary) Commercial Programs (industry trade and market niches) Public Entity-Related Programs (insurance trusts for cities counties and other government agencies) and National Flood Programs (Wright Flood policies).

The Wholesale Brokerage segment (nearly 15% of revenue) sells excess and surplus commercial insurance policies to retail insurance agencies (including the Retail segment's offices).

The Services segment (less than 10% of sales) provides third-party claims administration and comprehensive medical utilization management services in both the workers' compensation and all-lines liability arenas as well as Medicare Set-aside services Social Security disability and Medicare benefits advocacy services and claims adjusting services.

Geographic Reach

Based in Florida Brown & Brown operates more than 300 locations in about 45 states. Its largest market is Florida where it operates more than 50 agency locations followed by California Texas New York Massachusetts Washington New Jersey Pennsylvania Georgia and Louisiana. Although the company has expanded its operations to serve the UK Canada Bermuda and Cayman Islands the US still accounts for nearly all of its revenue.

Sales and Marketing

Brown & Brown's network of agency offices sells insurance policies that are underwritten by third-party carriers. The Retail division receives commission fees on policy sales to customers including commercial businesses government agencies professionals and individual consumers. The National Programs division sells niche policies to businesses and professionals through a nationwide network of independent agents and through the Retail segment's offices. The Wholesale Brokerage division sells commercial policies to independent brokers and agents (as well as some Retail segment offices).

Financial Performance

Brown & Brown has achieved year-over-year revenue growth for the past five years increasing by 44% from 2015 to 2019. Meanwhile net income increased from 2015 to 2017 then fell in 2018. 2019 saw net income rise back up but still a little less compared to 2017 net income.

Revenue was $2.4 billion 19% higher compared to $2 billion in the previous year. This resulted from an increase in revenue among its segments.

Net income increased by 16% to $398.5 million from $344.3 million in the previous year.

Cash and cash equivalents at the end of the year were $963.0 million a 24% increase from $777.6 million in 2018. Cash provided by operations was $678.2 million. Investing activities used $413.6 million primarily for payments for businesses acquired while financing activities used $79.2 million primarily for payments on revolving credit facilities.

Strategy

Part of Brown & Brown's business strategy is to attract high-quality insurance intermediaries and service organizations to join its operations. From 1993 through the fourth quarter of 2019 it acquired 536 insurance intermediary operations excluding acquired books of business.

In November 2018 the company completed the acquisition of certain assets and assumption of certain liabilities of Hays. The company may pay additional consideration to Hays in the form of earn-out payments in the aggregate amount of up to $25.0 million in cash over three years which is subject to certain conditions and the successful achievement of average annual EBITDA targets for the acquired business during 2019 2020 and 2021.

Mergers and Acquisitions

In 2020 Brown & Brown agreed to acquire the assets of Loan Protector. Based in Cleveland Ohio Loan Protector Insurance Services has focused on lender placed insurance and insurance tracking services for the mortgage servicing industry. The company believes that adding Loan Protector's capabilities with its solutions will benefit its collective customers.

Company Background

Brown & Brown traces its roots to 1939 when Metropolitan Life insurance agent Adrian Brown partnered with his cousin Charles "Cov" Owen to open their own agency (named Brown & Owen) in Daytona Beach Florida. Adrian's son Hyatt Brown joined in 1959 creating Brown & Brown and still serves as Chairman.

In 1993 the company merged with Poe & Associates (founded in 1958) and operated as Poe & Brown until 1999 when the Brown & Brown name was revived. Throughout its history the company has embarked on a steady growth strategy to buy middle-market insurance brokers across the US.

EXECUTIVES

Executive Vice President, General Counsel, Secretary, Robert Lloyd
Independent Director, Toni Jennings
Chairman Of The Board, J. Hyatt Brown
Independent Director, Theodore Hoepner
Independent Director, Hugh Brown
Independent Director, Chilton Varner
President And Chief Executive Officer, J. Powell Brown, $1,038,462 total compensation
Executive Vice President, President – Retail Segment, P. Barrett Brown
Independent Director, James Hunt
Executive Vice President, President, Wholesale Brokerage Segment, Stephen Boyd
Independent Director, Lawrence Gellerstedt
Executive Vice President, Chief Acquisition Officer, Jerome Penny, $618,461 total compensation
Vice Chairman Of The Board, James Hays
Chief Information Officer, Gray Nester
Independent Director, Timothy Main
Executive Vice President, President – National Programs Segment, Chris Walker, $724,615 total compensation
Chief Financial Officer, Executive Vice President, Treasurer, R. Andrew Watts, $618,461 total compensation
Auditors: Deloitte & Touche LLP

LOCATIONS

HQ: Brown & Brown Inc
300 North Beach Street, Daytona Beach, FL 32114
Phone: 386 252-9601
Web: www.bbinsurance.com

PRODUCTS/OPERATIONS

2015 Sales

	% of total
Core commissions and fees	96
Profit-sharing contingent commissions	3
Guaranteed supplemental commissions	1
Investment income	-
Other income net	-
Total	**100**

2015 Sales

	% of total
Retail	52
National Programs	26
Wholesale Brokerage	13
Services	9
Other	
Total	**100**

Selected Products and Services

Personal Insurance
Business Insurance
Employee Benefits
Wholesale Brokerage
Services Division
Financial Services
Trade Credit
Surety Bonds
Risk Management

COMPETITORS

AMERICAN NATIONAL INSURANCE COMPANY
CRAWFORD & COMPANY
GUARDIA LLC
HALLMARK FINANCIAL SERVICES INC.
NATIONAL GENERAL HOLDINGS CORP.
PRINCIPAL FINANCIAL GROUP INC.
SELECTIVE INSURANCE GROUP INC.
UNIVERSAL INSURANCE HOLDINGS INC.

HISTORICAL FINANCIALS

Company Type: Public

Income Statement				FYE: December 31
	REVENUE ($ mil.)	NET INCOME ($ mil.)	NET PROFIT MARGIN	EMPLOYEES
12/21	3,051.4	587.1	19.2%	12,023
12/20	2,613.3	480.4	18.4%	11,136
12/19	2,392.1	398.5	16.7%	10,083
12/18	2,014.2	344.2	17.1%	1,281
12/17	1,881.3	399.6	21.2%	8,491
Annual Growth	**12.9%**	**10.1%**	**—**	**9.1%**

2021 Year-End Financials

Debt ratio: 20.6%	No. of shares (mil.): 282.5
Return on equity: 14.7%	Dividends
Cash ($ mil.): 887.0	Yield: 0.5%
Current ratio: 1.25	Payout: 18.5%
Long-term debt ($ mil.): 1,980.4	Market value ($ mil.): 19,854.0

	STOCK PRICE ($) FY Close	P/E High/Low		PER SHARE ($) Earnings	Dividends	Book Value
12/21	70.28	34	21	2.07	0.38	14.86
12/20	47.41	29	19	1.69	0.35	13.27
12/19	39.48	28	19	1.40	0.33	11.89
12/18	27.56	43	20	1.22	0.31	10.73
12/17	51.46	36	29	1.45	0.28	9.35
Annual Growth	**8.1%**	**—**	**—**	**9.3%**	**8.2%**	**12.3%**

Business First Bancshares Inc

Auditors: Hannis T. Bourgeois, LLP

LOCATIONS

HQ: Business First Bancshares Inc
500 Laurel Street, Suite 101, Baton Rouge, LA 70801
Phone: 225 248-7600
Web: www.b1bank.com

HISTORICAL FINANCIALS

Company Type: Public

Income Statement				FYE: December 31
	ASSETS ($ mil.)	NET INCOME ($ mil.)	INCOME AS % OF ASSETS	EMPLOYEES
12/20	4,160.3	29.9	0.7%	590
12/19	2,273.8	23.7	1.0%	355
12/18	2,094.9	14.0	0.7%	333
12/17	1,321.2	4.8	0.4%	219
12/16	1,105.8	5.1	0.5%	208
Annual Growth	**39.3%**	**55.6%**	**—**	**29.8%**

2020 Year-End Financials

Return on assets: 0.9%	Dividends
Return on equity: 8.6%	Yield: 1.9%
Long-term debt ($ mil.): —	Payout: 30.0%
No. of shares (mil.): 20.6	Market value ($ mil.): 420.0
Sales ($ mil): 171.3	

	STOCK PRICE ($) FY Close	P/E High/Low		PER SHARE ($) Earnings	Dividends	Book Value
12/20	20.36	16	6	1.64	0.40	19.88
12/19	24.93	14	13	1.74	0.38	21.47
12/18	24.23	23	17	1.22	0.24	19.68
Annual Growth	**(8.3%)**	**—**	**—**	**15.9%**	**29.1%**	**0.5%**

BWX Technologies inc

BWX Technologies is a specialty manufacturer of nuclear components a developer of nuclear technologies and a service provider with an operating history of more than 100 years. Its core businesses focus on the design engineering and manufacture of precision naval nuclear components reactors and nuclear fuel for the US government. It also provides precision manufactured components nuclear fuel and services to the commercial nuclear industry and provides special nuclear materials processing environmental site restoration services and a variety of products and services to customers in the critical medical radioisotopes and radiopharmaceuticals industries. US government agencies are its largest customers. Additionally the US is responsible for about 85% of the sales. The company was founded in 1867.

Operations

BWX operates in three reportable segments: Nuclear Operations Group (accounts for over 75%) Nuclear Power Group (more than 15%) and Nuclear Services Group (more than 5%).

Nuclear Operations Group segment specializes in the design and manufacture of close-tolerance and high-quality equipment for nuclear applications.

The Nuclear Power Group designs and manufactures commercial nuclear steam generators heat exchangers pressure vessels reactor components and other auxiliary equipment including containers for the storage of spent nuclear fuel and other high-level nuclear waste. BWX has supplied the nuclear industry with more than 1300 large heavy components worldwide.

Nuclear Services Group provides special nuclear materials processing environmental site restoration services and management and operating services.

Among its product and service lines are government programs (around 70% of sales) and nuclear manufacturing (over 10%) nuclear services and engineering (around 5%).

Geographic Reach

Headquartered in Virginia BWX owns and operates manufacturing plants in Lynchburg Virginia; Mount Vernon Indiana; Euclid Ohio; Barberton Ohio; and Erwin Tennessee. In addition the company has plants in Canada.

The US accounts for roughly 85% of BWX's revenues while Canda generates some 15%.

Sales and Marketing

The US government is BWX's largest customer accounting for more than 75% of net sales. Additionally it serves the US Department of Energy (DOE)/National Nuclear Security Administration's (NNSA) Naval Nuclear Propulsion Program and perform development and fabrication activities for missile launch tubes for US Navy submarines.

Financial Performance

Consolidated revenues increased 12% or $228.6 million to $2.1 billion 2020 compared to $1.9 billion for the corresponding period of 2019 due to increases in revenues from its Nuclear Operations Group Nuclear Power Group and Nuclear Services Group segments totaling $217.7 million $18.6 million and $5.2 million respectively.

In 2020 the company had a net income of $279.2 million a 14% increase from the previous year.

The company's cash at the end of 2020 was $48.3 million. Operating activities generated $196.4 million while investing activities used $265.3 million mainly for purchases of property plant and equipment. Financing activities used another $271000 mainly for repayments of long-term debt.

Strategy

In 2020 BWX Technologies announced that its Nuclear Operations Group Inc. subsidiary has been awarded a competitively bid contract by the Idaho National Laboratory (INL) to expand and upgrade its TRISO nuclear fuel manufacturing line. This $26 million 20-month contract award will both expand BWXT's TRISO capacity for the manufacture of TRISO fuel compacts as well as upgrade existing systems for delivering production-scale quantities of TRISO fuel.

In September 2020 Ontario Power Generation's (OPG) Centre for Canadian Nuclear Sustainability (CCNS) has announced an innovative collaboration agreement between Laurentis Energy Partners (LEP) and BWXT Canada Ltd. (BWXT) to develop technology that will assist in the recycling of heavy water at OPG's nuclear facilities.

HISTORY

Stephen Wilcox patented the water tube boiler in 1856 and two year later Wilcox and George Babcock established Babcock Wilcox & Company. At the turn of the century B&W boilers powered New York's first subway and President Roosevelt's Great White Fleet. In the mid-1940s the company provided components and materials for the Manhattan Project and designed components for the the world's first nuclear powered submarine the USS Nautilus a decade later.

Babcock & Wilcox became a subsidiary of engineering and construction giant McDermott International in 1978. As a result of mounting asbestos liability costs B&W filed for bankruptcy in 2000. McDermott deconsolidated B&W's operations from its own financial statements at that time. Emergence from Chapter 11 in early 2006 returned B&W to full reporting status.

To further its ambitions in government operations in 2007 the company bought Marine Mechanical Corporation for $71.5 million. MMC manufactures and supplies electro-mechanical equipment for the US Navy. The next year it acquired three companies first paying $20 million for the Intech group of companies (Intech Inc. Ivey-Cooper Services L.L.C. and Intech International Inc.) a provider of nuclear inspection and maintenance services in the US and Canada. Delta Power Services LLC which serves the US power generation industry complements the company's fossil fuel and biomass markets and will help it to expand into the natural gas-fired power generation market. Delta Power was bought for $13.5 million. Specialty nuclear fuels and service provider Nuclear Fuel Services bought for $157 million brought experience in converting highly-enriched uranium into fuel for commercial nuclear reactors. Its fuel production facility is where the US military's submarines and aircraft carriers get their nuclear fill-up.

The company made two acquisitions in late 2009 and early 2010 to boost its international presence. First it bought Instrumentacion y Mantenimiento de Calderas S.A. a boiler manufacturer in Mexico. A few months later it purchased G ¶taverken Milj ¶ a Swedish company specializing in flue gas cleaning and energy recovery giving the company an entr ©e to the international energy market. The acquisition was made a part of B&W's Volund unit which creates thermal energy through byproducts such as household waste and biofuels.

EXECUTIVES

Independent Director, Jan Bertsch
Senior Vice President, Chief Administrative Officer, Richard Loving, $406,000 total compensation
Independent Director, John Richardson
Independent Director, Leland Melvin
Independent Director, Gerhard Burbach
Chief Financial Officer, Robb Lemasters
Chief Accounting Officer, Vice President, Jason Kerr
Independent Director, Robert Nardelli
President Of Government Operations, Robert Smith
Non-executive Chairman Of The Board, John Fees
Senior Vice President, Chief Compliance Officer, General Counsel, Secretary, Thomas McCabe, $532,500 total compensation

President - Bwxt Nuclear Operations Group, Joel Duling, $479,250 total compensation
Lead Independent Director, Kenneth Krieg
Independent Director, James Jaska
Independent Director, Barbara Niland
President, Chief Executive Officer, Director, Rex Geveden, $925,000 total compensation
Auditors: DELOITTE & TOUCHE LLP

LOCATIONS

HQ: BWX Technologies inc
800 Main Street, 4th Floor, Lynchburg, VA 24504
Phone: 980 365-4300

PRODUCTS/OPERATIONS

2016 Sales

	% of total
Nuclear Operations	82
Technical Services	6
Nuclear Energy	12
Adjustments and Eliminations	-
Total	**100**

COMPETITORS

AREVA	REGAL REXNORD
ENERGYSOLUTIONS INC.	CORPORATION
FRANKLIN ELECTRIC CO.	WILLIAMS INDUSTRIAL
INC.	SERVICES GROUP INC.
FUELCELL ENERGY INC.	YASKAWA ELECTRIC
HITACHI LTD.	CORPORATION

HISTORICAL FINANCIALS

Company Type: Public

Income Statement   FYE: December 31

	REVENUE ($ mil.)	NET INCOME ($ mil.)	NET PROFIT MARGIN	EMPLOYEES
12/20	2,123.5	278.6	13.1%	6,700
12/19	1,894.9	244.1	12.9%	6,450
12/18	1,799.8	226.9	12.6%	6,250
12/17	1,687.7	147.8	8.8%	6,100
12/16	1,550.5	183.0	11.8%	5,900
Annual Growth	**8.2%**	**11.1%**	**—**	**3.2%**

2020 Year-End Financials

Debt ratio: 37.6%	No. of shares (mil.): 95.3
Return on equity: 54.3%	Dividends
Cash ($ mil.): 42.6	Yield: 1.2%
Current ratio: 1.46	Payout: 26.5%
Long-term debt ($ mil.): 862.7	Market value ($ mil.): 5,745.0

	STOCK PRICE ($) FY Close	P/E High/Low		PER SHARE ($) Earnings	Dividends	Book Value
12/20	60.28	24	14	2.91	0.76	6.48
12/19	62.08	25	15	2.55	0.68	4.24
12/18	38.23	31	16	2.27	0.64	2.47
12/17	60.49	42	26	1.47	0.42	2.87
12/16	39.70	23	15	1.76	0.36	1.51
Annual Growth	**11.0%**	**—**	**—**	**13.4%**	**20.5%**	**43.9%**

Byline Bancorp Inc

Auditors: Moss Adams LLP

LOCATIONS

HQ: Byline Bancorp Inc
180 North LaSalle Street, Suite 300, Chicago, IL 60601
Phone: 773 244-7000
Web: www.bylinebancorp.com

HISTORICAL FINANCIALS

Company Type: Public

Income Statement   FYE: December 31

	ASSETS ($ mil.)	NET INCOME ($ mil.)	INCOME AS % OF ASSETS	EMPLOYEES
12/20	6,390.6	37.4	0.6%	931
12/19	5,521.8	57.0	1.0%	1,001
12/18	4,942.5	41.1	0.8%	943
12/17	3,366.1	21.7	0.6%	844
12/16	3,295.8	66.7	2.0%	791
Annual Growth	**18.0%**	**(13.4%)**	**—**	**4.2%**

2020 Year-End Financials

Return on assets: 0.6%	Dividends
Return on equity: 4.8%	Yield: 0.7%
Long-term debt ($ mil.): —	Payout: 11.3%
No. of shares (mil.): 38.6	Market value ($ mil.): 597.0
Sales ($ mil): 301.2	

	STOCK PRICE ($) FY Close	P/E High/Low		PER SHARE ($) Earnings	Dividends	Book Value
12/20	15.45	21	9	0.96	0.12	20.86
12/19	19.57	14	11	1.48	0.03	19.61
12/18	16.66	20	13	1.18	0.00	17.90
12/17	22.97	59	50	0.38	0.00	15.64
Annual Growth	**(12.4%)**	**—**	**—**	**36.2%**	**—**	**10.1%**

Cable One Inc

Sparklight (formerly Cable ONE) gives small-town folk CNN and The Cartoon Network. The company provides cable television service primarily to non- metropolitan secondary and tertiary markets. Its core service areas are the Gulf Coast region and Boise Idaho. Approximately 773000 subscribers receive data services from Sparklight some 314000 subscribers to video services and around 139000 subscribers to voice services. The company also offers voice-over-Internet-protocol (VoIP) computer telephony and digital video services. Quarter-fifth of revenue comes from Residential. In 2019 the company rebrand its business as Sparklight.

Operations

Sparklight has its four primary product lines: Residential data Residential video Residential voice and Business services.

Residential data services represent about 50% of the company's total revenues. It offers simplified data plans with lower pricing and higher speeds across its premium tiers. The product line also offer its customers the option to purchase an unlimited data plan and advanced Wi-Fi service.

Residential video services offer a broad variety of residential video services including: basic video service that consists of governmental and public access network and weather shopping and religious channels; and digital video service includes music channels and an interactive electronic programming guide with parental controls. It also offers premium channels such as HBO Showtime Starz and Cinemax. The product line generates nearly 30% of revenue.

Residential voice services account for less than 5% of revenue and offers transmit digital voice signals over its network and are interconnected Voice over Internet Protocol (VoIP) services. It also offers traditional telecommunications services through some of the company's subsidiaries.

Business services (produce more than 15% of revenue) offer services for businesses ranging in size from small to mid-market in addition to enterprise wholesale and carrier customers. The offer for its small businesses are generally provided over the company's coaxial network. It offer delivery of data and voice services over EPON technology primarily for mid-market customers with Piranha Fiber. Furthermore it also offer dedicated bandwidth and Enterprise Wi-Fi in addition to multiple voice services via fiber optic technology for its enterprise and wholesale customers.

Geographic Reach

Sparklight has operations in more than 20 states throughout the midwestern southern and western US.

The company's headquarters is located in Phoenix Arizona. It has customers in Arizona Idaho Illinois Mississippi Missouri Oklahoma and Texas.

Sales and Marketing

Sparklight has about 80% of its customers located in more than five states. In addition its biggest customer concentrations are in the Mississippi Gulf Coast region and in the greater Boise Idaho region.

The total amount of advertising expense recorded was $34.3 million $28.6 million and $25.3 million in 2019 2018 and 2017 respectively.

Financial Performance

Sparklight's revenue growth have been solid for the last five years posting a 45% increase since 2015.

Revenues increased $95.7 million in 2019 to $1.2 billion or 9% due primarily to increases in residential data and business services revenues of $54.4 million and $48.5 million respectively. The increase was the result of organic growth in its higher margin product lines of residential data and business services the acquired Fidelity and Clearwave operations a residential video rate adjustment and the implementation of modem rental charges to certain business customers partially offset by decreases in residential video and other revenues.

Net income for the year increased by 8% to $178.6 million mainly due to higher revenue.

Cash at the end of the year was $125.3 million 53% lower from prior year. Net cash provided by operating activities was $491.7 million and the cash provided by the financing activities was $503.7 million. Investing activities used $1.1 billion for purchase of business and capital expenditures.

Strategy

The company has a multi-faceted strategy that builds upon its long track record of focusing on the right markets the right products and the right customers as well as controlling its operating and capital costs. More specifically its strategy includes the following principal components: Focus on non-metropolitan markets by continuing on offering products primarily in these markets. Because price points for services in non-metropolitan markets are generally lower and customers in non-metropolitan markets tend to subscribe to fewer PSUs its average revenue per customer and its PSUs per customer are lower than they might be in metropolitan markets; Maximize Adjusted EBITDA less capital expenditures and drive profitable growth; Target higher relative value residential customers;

Drive growth in residential data and business services by diversifying its revenue streams away from video; Continue its culture of cost leadership; Balanced capital allocation by committing to a disciplined approach to evaluating acquisitions internal and external investments capital structure optimization and return of capital.

Mergers and Acquisitions

In late 2019 Sparklight acquired Fidelity Communications Co. (Fidelity) for about $525 million. Fidelity's network passes about 190000 homes in Arkansas Illinois Louisiana Missouri Oklahoma and Texas. Fidelity counts some 114000 residential and 20000 business customers. The network fits into Cable ONE's geographic footprint.

In early 2019 the company acquired Delta Communications (Clearwave) for a purchase price of $358.8 million in cash on a debt-free basis. Clearwave is a facilities-based service provider that owns and operates a high-capacity fiber network offering dense regional coverage in Southern Illinois. The acquisition provides the company with a premier fiber network within its existing footprint further enables them to supply its customers with enhanced business services solutions and provides a platform to allow the company to replicate Clearwave's strategy in several of its other markets.

Company Background

In 1986 The Washington Post Company (former corporate parent Graham Holdings Company) acquired 53 cable television systems with approximately 350000 subscribers in 15 Western Midwestern and Southern states. Since then the company completed over 30 acquisitions and dispositions of cable systems both through cash sales and system trades. In the process they substantially reshaped their original geographic footprint and resized their typical system including exiting a number of metropolitan markets and acquiring cable systems in non-metropolitan markets that fit their business model. In mid-2015 they became an independent company traded under the ticker symbol "CABO" on the New York Stock Exchange after completion of its spin-off from GHC.

EXECUTIVES

Chairman Of The Board, President, Chief Executive Officer, Julia Laulis, $752,885 total compensation
Chief Operating Officer, Michael Bowker, $399,808 total compensation
Independent Director, Mary Meduski
Independent Director, Kristine Miller
Senior Vice President , Business Services , Emerging Markets, Christopher Boone
Independent Director, Deborah Kissire
Independent Director, Wallace Weitz
Independent Director, Brad Brian
Independent Director, Katharine Weymouth
Senior Vice President , Operations . Integration, Eric Lardy, $253,000 total compensation
Senior Vice President - Technology Services, Kenneth Johnson
Senior Vice President Of Sales And Marketing, James Obermeyer, $222,730 total compensation
Independent Director, Sherrese Smith
Chief Financial Officer, Steven Cochran, $394,615 total compensation
Auditors: PricewaterhouseCoopers LLP

LOCATIONS

HQ: Cable One Inc
210 E. Earll Drive, Phoenix, AZ 85012
Phone: 602 364-6000
Web: www.cableone.net

PRODUCTS/OPERATIONS

2014 Sales

	$ mil.	% of total
Video	361.0	44
Data	265.7	33
Business Sales	72.7	9
Voice	62.4	8
Advertising sales	35.4	4
Others	17.6	2
Total	**814.8**	**100**

COMPETITORS

AMC NETWORKS INC.
Cogeco Communications Inc
DISH NETWORK CORPORATION
GTT COMMUNICATIONS INC.
LUMEN TECHNOLOGIES INC.
SHENANDOAH TELECOMMUNICATIONS COMPANY
WIDEOPENWEST INC.
WINDSTREAM HOLDINGS INC.

HISTORICAL FINANCIALS

Company Type: Public

Income Statement
FYE: December 31

	REVENUE ($ mil.)	NET INCOME ($ mil.)	NET PROFIT MARGIN	EMPLOYEES
12/20	1,325.2	304.3	23.0%	2,716
12/19	1,168.0	178.5	15.3%	2,751
12/18	1,072.3	164.7	15.4%	2,224
12/17	960.0	234.0	24.4%	2,310
12/16	819.6	98.9	12.1%	1,877
Annual Growth	12.8%	32.4%	—	9.7%

2020 Year-End Financials

Debt ratio: 48.4%	No. of shares (mil.): 6.0
Return on equity: 25.9%	Dividends
Cash ($ mil.): 574.9	Yield: 0.4%
Current ratio: 3.04	Payout: 22.1%
Long-term debt ($ mil.): 2,148.8	Market value ($ mil.): 13,428.0

	STOCK PRICE ($) FY Close	P/E High/Low	PER SHARE ($) Earnings	Dividends	Book Value
12/20	2,227.72	44 22	51.27	9.50	248.07
12/19	1,488.47	49 26	31.12	8.50	147.25
12/18	820.10	32 21	28.77	7.50	135.95
12/17	703.35	19 14	40.72	6.50	117.15
12/16	621.73	36 23	17.14	6.00	79.62
Annual Growth	37.6%	— —	31.5%	12.2%	32.9%

Cactus Inc

Auditors: PricewaterhouseCoopers LLP

LOCATIONS

HQ: Cactus Inc
920 Memorial City Way, Suite 300, Houston, TX 77024
Phone: 713 626-8800
Web: www.CactusWHD.com

HISTORICAL FINANCIALS

Company Type: Public

Income Statement

FYE: December 31

	REVENUE ($ mil.)	NET INCOME ($ mil.)	NET PROFIT MARGIN	EMPLOYEES
12/20	348.5	34.4	9.9%	660
12/19	628.4	85.6	13.6%	1,100
12/18	544.1	51.6	9.5%	1,200
12/17	341.1	66.5	19.5%	880
12/16	155.0	(8.1)	—	880
Annual Growth	22.4%	—	—	(6.9%)

2020 Year-End Financials

Debt ratio: 0.7%
Return on equity: 10.1%
Cash ($ mil.): 288.6
Current ratio: 8.69
Long-term debt ($ mil.): 2.2

No. of shares (mil.): 75.3
Dividends
 Yield: 1.3%
 Payout: 35.2%
Market value ($ mil.): 1,965.0

	STOCK PRICE ($) FY Close	P/E High/Low		PER SHARE ($) Earnings	Dividends	Book Value
12/20	26.07	48	12	0.72	0.36	4.68
12/19	34.32	21	13	1.88	0.09	4.36
12/18	27.41	25	13	1.58	0.00	2.37
Annual Growth	(2.5%)		—	— (32.5%)	—	40.5%

Cadence Bank

Like Elvis Presley BancorpSouth has grown beyond its Tupelo roots. It's the holding company for BancorpSouth Bank which operates some 290 branches in nine southern and midwestern states. Catering to consumers and small and midszed businesses the bank offers checking and savings accounts loans credit cards and commercial banking services. BancorpSouth also sells insurance and provides brokerage investment advisory and asset management services throughout most of its market area. Real estate loans including consumer and commercial mortgages and home equity construction and agricultural loans comprise approximately three-quarters of its loan portfolio. BancorpSouth has assets of $13 billion.

Geographic Reach

Mississippi-based BancorpSouth Bank operates in Alabama Arkansas Florida Illinois Louisiana Mississippi Missouri Tennessee and Texas. BancorpSouth's insurance and financial advisory businesses also operate in Illinois and Florida respectively.

Financial Performance

BancorpSouth reported net income of $94.1 million in 2013 an increase of 12% versus 2012. The decreased provision for credit losses was the primary factor contributing to the rise. Net interest revenue — the bank's primary source of revenue — fell 4% year over year to $$398.9 million the fourth consecutive year of decline. Net interest revenue declined because the decrease in interest expense was more than offset by the decrease in interest revenue as the yield on earning assets declined by a greater amount than that of interest-bearing liabilities. Noninterest income also declined on lower mortgage origination revenue in 2013 versus 2012.

Strategy

The regional bank has grown via the acquisition of other banks and insurance agencies and by opening new branches most recently in Texas and Louisiana. To reduce its reliance on interest-related revenue BancorpSouth hopes to diversify its revenue stream by increasing the amount it generates from mortgage lending insurance brokerage and securities activities. To this end subsidiary BancorpSouth Insurance Services has acquired small insurance agencies in Arkansas Missouri and Texas.

Mergers and Acquisitions

In 2014 BancorpSouth agreed to acquire Central Community Corp. the holding company for First State Bank Central Texas headquartered in Austin Texas. First State Bank operates 31 branches in Austin Round Rock Killeen and several other Central Texas communities. BancorpSouth has also agreed to purchase Ouachita Bancshares Corp. with a dozen branches in Louisiana. Both deals were announced in January 2014 and were expected to close promptly. However they've been delayed because BancorpSouth needs more time to get regulatory approvals and to meet "closing conditions necessary to complete" the mergers.

Auditors: BKD, LLP

LOCATIONS

HQ: Cadence Bank
 One Mississippi Plaza, 201 South Spring Street,
 Tupelo, MS 38804
Phone: 662 680-2000
Web: www.bancorpsouth.com

PRODUCTS/OPERATIONS

2016 Sales

	$ mil.	% of total
Interest		
Loans & leases	440.7	58
Securities	41.5	5
Deposits with other banks	1.1	-
Noninterest		
Insurance commissions	115.9	15
Deposit service charges	43.4	6
Mortgage lending	41.8	5
Credit card debit card and merchant fees	37.0	5
Wealth management	21.1	3
Other	19.7	3
Total	762.2	100

Selected Subsidiaries

BancorpSouth Bank
 BancorpSouth Insurance Services Inc.
 BancorpSouth Investment Services Inc.
 BancorpSouth Municipal Development Corporation
 Century Credit Life Insurance Company
 Personal Finance Corporation

COMPETITORS

CENTRAL BANCOMPANY INC.	EAGLE BANCORP INC.
CVB FINANCIAL CORP.	PROSPERITY BANCSHARES INC.

HISTORICAL FINANCIALS

Company Type: Public

Income Statement

FYE: December 31

	ASSETS ($ mil.)	NET INCOME ($ mil.)	INCOME AS % OF ASSETS	EMPLOYEES
12/20	24,081.1	228.0	0.9%	4,596
12/19	21,052.5	234.2	1.1%	4,693
12/18	18,001.5	221.3	1.2%	4,445
12/17	15,298.5	153.0	1.0%	3,947
12/16	14,724.3	132.7	0.9%	3,998
Annual Growth	13.1%	14.5%	—	3.5%

2020 Year-End Financials

Return on assets: 1.0%
Return on equity: 8.2%
Long-term debt ($ mil.): —
No. of shares (mil.): 102.5
Sales ($ mil.): 1,136.0

Dividends
 Yield: 2.7%
 Payout: 35.1%
Market value ($ mil.): 2,814.0

	STOCK PRICE ($) FY Close	P/E High/Low		PER SHARE ($) Earnings	Dividends	Book Value
12/20	27.44	15	8	2.12	0.75	27.52
12/19	31.41	14	11	2.30	0.71	25.69
12/18	26.14	16	11	2.23	0.62	22.10
12/17	31.45	20	16	1.67	0.14	18.97
12/16	31.05	22	13	1.41	0.45	18.40
Annual Growth	(3.0%)		—	10.7%	13.4%	10.6%

Cadence Design Systems Inc

Cadence Design Systems is a leader in electronic design building upon more than 30 years of computational software expertise. Customers use Cadence products to design integrated circuits (ICs) printed circuit boards (PCBs) smartphones laptop computers gaming systems and more. The company offer software hardware services and reusable IC design blocks which are commonly referred to as intellectual property (IP). The company also provides maintenance and support and design and methodology consulting services. International customers account for nearly 60% of the company's sales.

Operations

Cadence Design Systems has five product areas each making a robust contribution to total revenue.

Digital IC Design and Signoff delivers some 30% of the company's revenue. Digital IC design and Signoff offerings are used to create logical representations of a digital circuit or an IC that can be verified for correctness prior to implementation.

Its logic design offering is comprised of logic synthesis test and equivalence checking capabilities. Functional verification products are used by customers to verify that the circuitry or the software they have designed will perform as intended.

Verification takes place during and after custom and analog design and before manufacturing the circuitry significantly reducing the risk of discovering a costly error in the completed product. Its Verification Suite includes four primary verification engines starting with the JasperGold Formal Verification Platform and Xcelium. This segment generates more than 20% of the company's revenue.

Custom IC design and simulation offerings are used by customers to create schematic and physical representations of circuits down to the transistor level for analog mixed-signal custom digital memory and RF designs. These representations are verified using simulation tools optimized for each type of design including the design capture environment simulation and IC layout within the Virtuoso custom design platform. This segment accounts for some 25% of the company's sales.

Other segment includes System design and analysis (10% of the company's sales) and IP (about 15% of the company's sales).

The company's emulation and prototyping hardware including all individual PCBs custom ICs and Field-Programmable Gate Array (FPGA)-based prototyping components is manufactured assembled and tested by subcontractors before delivery to its customers.

Geographic Reach

With its main headquarters in California Cadence Design Systems has placed regional headquarters near customers in China India UK and Japan. Overall the company operates its business in more than 20 countries.

The US is Cadence's largest single market accounting for more than 40% of sales. Customers in Asia (including Japan and China) account 40% of sales and European customers including Middle East and Africa account for about 20%.

Sales and Marketing

Cadence market its products and provide services to existing and prospective customers through a direct sales force consisting of sales people and applications engineers. The company also promote products and services through advertising marketing automation trade shows public relations and the internet. Internationally the company market its products and services through subsidiaries as well as third-party distributor to license their products and services to certain customers in Japan.

The company's advertising expenses were $7.1 million $8.4 million and $7.6 million during fiscal 2020 2019 and 2018 respectively.

Financial Performance

Cadence Design Systems' revenue has been rising consistently. It has a 48% growth between 2016 and 2020.

In 2020 Cadence's revenue grew by 15% from $2.3 billion to $2.7 billion. This growth was primarily driven by the increase of product and maintenance revenues because of increased investments by its customers in new complex designs for their products that include the design of electronic systems for consumer hyperscale computing 5G communications automotive aerospace and defense industrial and healthcare.

Net income fell by 40% or $590 million in 2020 from $989 million in 2019.

Cash and cash equivalents totaled $928.4 billion. Operating activities generated $904.9 billion while investing and financing activities used $292.2 billion and $415.3 billion respectively.

Strategy

Cadence's strategy which it calls Intelligent System Design provides the technologies necessary for customers to develop and optimize a complete and functional electronic product. The company addresses the challenges posed by the needs and trends of electronic systems companies as well as semiconductor companies delivering greater portions of these systems. The development of electronic products or their sub-components is complex and requires many engineers using its solutions with specialized knowledge and skill.

The second layer of Cadence's strategy centers on system innovation. It includes tools and services used for system design of the packages that encapsulate the ICs and the PCBs system simulation which includes electromagnetic electro-thermal and other multi-physics analysis necessary as part of optimizing the full system's performance Radio

Frequency ("RF") and microwave systems and embedded software.

The third layer of the company's strategy is enabling pervasive intelligence in new electronics. It starts with providing solutions and services to develop AI-enhanced systems and includes machine learning and deep learning capabilities being added to the Cadence technology portfolio to make IP and tools more automated and to produce optimized results faster supported by cloud access to address the growing computation needs of customers.

Mergers and Acquisitions

In early 2021 the company entered into a definitive agreement to acquire all of the outstanding equity of Belgium-based NUMECA a leader in CFD mesh generation multi-physics simulation and optimization. The addition of NUMECA's technologies and talent supports the company's Intelligent System Design strategy.

In 2020 Cadence completed the acquisitions of AWR and Integrand. The aggregate cash consideration for these acquisitions of approximately $196 million was allocated to the assets acquired and liabilities assumed based on their respective estimated fair values on the respective acquisition dates. These acquisitions enhance the company's technology portfolio to address growing radio frequency design activity driven by expanding use of 5G communications.

Company Background

Cadence Design Systems arose from the 1988 merger of software firms ECAD (formed in 1982) and SDA Systems (founded 1983). The stock market crash of 1987 helped propel SDA Systems an EDA company that gave up its planned IPO in the wake of the crash into its merger with ECAD which was publicly held to form Cadence Design. Private venture capital investor and SDA chairman Donald Lucas became chairman of Cadence. Joe Costello the young charismatic and tall (6-foot-7) president and COO of SDA was named president and CEO of Cadence. It became the world's leading electronic design automation (EDA) software supplier by enlarging and improving the range of software it developed in-house and via such acquisitions as Tangent Systems (1989) and Valid Logic Systems (1991).

The company grew through a series of acquisitions. Cadence concluded long-running litigation with Avant! (after Avant! was acquired by Synopsys) with a $265 million payment to Cadence.

HISTORY

Cadence Design Systems arose from the 1988 merger of software firms ECAD (formed in 1982) and SDA Systems (founded 1983). The stock market crash of 1987 helped propel SDA Systems an EDA company that gave up its planned IPO in the wake of the crash into its merger with ECAD which was publicly held to form Cadence Design. Private venture capital investor and SDA chairman Donald Lucas became chairman of Cadence. Joe Costello the young charismatic and tall (6-foot-7) president and COO of SDA was named president and CEO of Cadence. It became the world's leading electronic design automation (EDA) software supplier by enlarging and improving the range of software it developed in-house and via such acquisitions as Tangent Systems (1989) and Valid Logic Systems (1991).

The company grew through a series of acquisitions. Cadence concluded long-running litigation

with Avant! (after Avant! was acquired by Synopsys) with a $265 million payment to Cadence.

EXECUTIVES

Independent Director, Alberto Sangiovanni-Vincentelli

Lead Independent Director, John Shoven

Chief Executive Officer, Director, Lip-Bu Tan, $738,942 total compensation

Chief Revenue Officer, Senior Vice President - World Wide Field Operations, Neil Zaman, $400,000 total compensation

Independent Director, James Plummer

Senior Vice President - Research And Development, Thomas Beckley, $375,000 total compensation

President, Chief Executive Officer, Director, Anirudh Devgan, $561,539 total compensation

Senior Vice President - Research And Development, Surendra Mandava, $375,000 total compensation

Chief Financial Officer, Senior Vice President, John Wall, $448,462 total compensation

Senior Vice President - Research And Development, Chin-Chi Teng, $407,692 total compensation

Independent Director, Ita Brennan

Independent Director, Lewis Chew

Senior Vice President, Chief Legal Officer And Corporate Secretary, Alinka Flaminia, $244,423 total compensation

Independent Director, Julia Liuson

Director, Mary Krakauer

Independent Director, Young Sohn

Auditors: PricewaterhouseCoopers LLP

LOCATIONS

HQ: Cadence Design Systems Inc
2655 Seely Avenue, Building 5, San Jose, CA 95134
Phone: 408 943-1234
Web: www.cadence.com

PRODUCTS/OPERATIONS

Selected Software

Analog simulators (Spectre)
Cycle-based simulators (SpeedSim)
Deep submicron design (Envisia)
Digital IC design (Encounter platform including First Encounter SoC Encounter and Nano Encounter)
Digital simulators (NC-simulator NC-Verilog NC-VHDL)
Editing and synthesis compaction device-level editing (Virtuoso family)
Equivalence checking (Affirma)
Hardware emulators (CoBALT Mercury)
Model checking (Affirma Formalcheck)
Place and routing (Envisia Silicon Ensemble)
Printed circuit board design and packaging (Allegro SPECCTRA)
Synthesis (Envisia Ambit BuildGates)
Verification (Assura line including Diva and Dracula; Incisive platform; Palladium)

Selected Services

Education
IC design services (Cadence Design Foundry)
IC implementation
Intellectual property (IP Gallery)
Methodology
Wireless design

2017 Sales

	% of total
Functional verification & design IP	22
Digital IC design and Signoff	29
Custom IC design	27
System interconnect and Analysis	10
IP	12
Total	100

2017 Sales

		% of total
Product and Maintenance	1814	93
Services	129	7
Total	**1943**	**100**

COMPETITORS

ASPEN TECHNOLOGY INC. SOFTWARE	PROGRESS
COGNEX CORPORATION	CORPORATION
FUJITSU LIMITED	Sangoma Technologies
ORACLE CORPORATION	Corporation
PDF SOLUTIONS INC.	VERSANT CORPORATION
PERASO INC.	VICOR CORPORATION

HISTORICAL FINANCIALS
Company Type: Public

Income Statement   FYE: January 1

	REVENUE ($ mil.)	NET INCOME ($ mil.)	NET PROFIT MARGIN	EMPLOYEES
01/22	2,988.2	695.9	23.3%	9,300
01/21*	2,682.8	590.6	22.0%	8,800
12/19	2,336.3	988.9	42.3%	8,100
12/18	2,138.0	345.7	16.2%	7,500
12/17	1,943.0	204.1	10.5%	7,200
Annual Growth	11.4%	35.9%	—	6.6%

*Fiscal year change

2022 Year-End Financials

Debt ratio: 7.9%	No. of shares (mil.): 276.8
Return on equity: 26.6%	Dividends
Cash ($ mil.): 1,088.9	Yield: —
Current ratio: 1.77	Payout: —
Long-term debt ($ mil.): 347.5	Market value ($ mil.): 51,581.0

	STOCK PRICE ($) FY Close	P/E High/Low	PER SHARE ($) Earnings	Dividends	Book Value
01/22	186.35	75 47	2.50	0.00	9.90
01/21*	136.43	63 25	2.11	0.00	8.94
12/19	70.29	21 11	3.53	0.00	7.51
12/18	43.34	38 28	1.23	0.00	4.60
12/17	41.82	61 34	0.73	0.00	3.51
Annual Growth	45.3%	— —	36.0%	—	29.6%

*Fiscal year change

California First Leasing Corp

California First National Bancorp (CFNB) is a leasing company and a bank. Its California First Leasing (CalFirst Leasing) subsidiary leases equipment for a wide variety of industries including computers and software. Other leases include retail point-of-sale systems office furniture and manufacturing telecommunications and medical equipment. The bank holding company also operates California First National Bank (CalFirst Bank) a branchless FDIC-insured retail bank that conducts business mainly over the Internet but also by mail and phone. About three-quarters of its revenue comes from interest.

Operations

About 68% of CalFirst's revenue comes from finance and loan income. Another major source of revenue 9% comes from the sale of leases loans and leased property.

Geographic Reach

CalFirst is based in Irvine California and does business throughout the US.

Sales and Marketing

CalFirst's 10 largest customers accounted for 19% of the lease and loan portfolio in 2015 compared to 24% in 2014.

Financial Performance

In 2015 sales increased 25% from 2014 driven by higher interest income from finance and lending.

The company's net income rose 28% in 2015 from 2014 on the higher revenue.

Strategy

CalFirst maintains diversification in geography and customers to spreading risk across its portfolio.

HISTORY

Lured by the profit margins of the leasing business Patrick Paddon and Dion Cairns founded Amplicon in California in 1977. The two disagreed over how to run the business and Cairns soon moved on. Paddon had previously been manager of corporate planning and budgets at Business Systems Technologies an IBM-compatible peripherals maker.

Early customers of Amplicon included Borden Campbell Soup SANYO Manufacturing and Wherehouse Entertainment. The company implemented its centralized telemarketing operations in 1981. Amplicon went public in 1987 and by the end of the 1980s its sales had topped $100 million.

Amplicon actually thrived in the recession of the early 1990s as the economy prompted companies to lease rather than buy capital equipment. Sales dipped in 1992 but after an overhaul of the company's recruiting training and sales management processes Amplicon rebounded.

Rapidly changing technology also boosted Amplicon's business because many companies chose to lease rather than buy equipment that would quickly become outdated. Sales increased by 11% in 1994 and by 14% in 1995.

Amplicon introduced a Web site for online sales in 1998. The following year it announced plans to sponsor the creation of a national bank to fund the purchase of equipment to be leased to Amplicon's customers. In 2001 the company changed its name to California First National Bancorp and became a bank holding company after it organized California First National Bank.

EXECUTIVES

Independent Director, Michael Lowry
Independent Director, Robert Kelley
Chairman Of The Board, President, Chief Executive Officer, Patrick Paddon, $180,000 total compensation
Chief Financial Officer, Vice President - Finance, S. Leslie Jewett, $250,000 total compensation
Chief Operating Officer, Secretary, Director, Glen Tsuma, $180,000 total compensation
Independent Director, Harris Ravine
Independent Director, Danilo Cacciamatta
Auditors: Eide Bailly LLP

LOCATIONS

HQ: California First Leasing Corp
5000 Birch Street, Suite 500, Newport Beach, CA 92660
Phone: 949 255-0500   **Fax:** 949 255-0501
Web: www.calfirstlease.com

PRODUCTS/OPERATIONS

2015 sales

	% of total
Interest income	
Finance and loan income	68
Investment interest income	5
Non-interest income	
Operating and sales-type lease income	1
Gain on sale of leases loans and leased property	14
Realized gain on sale of investment securities	2
Recovery realized on TFT-LCD settlement	9
Other fee income	1
Total	**100**

Products & Services

ATM Cards
Certificates of Deposit
Check Orders
Interest Checking
Money Market Checking
Online Bill Paying
Premium Savings

Selected Items for Lease

Accounting systems (hardware software installation training)
Broadcasting equipment
Exercise training equipment
Furniture fixtures and related equipment
Internet-related software hardware
Laboratory equipment
Imaging equipment
Internet-related software hardware
LAN/WAN and telecommunications equipment
Medical equipment
Network cabling/routers
Network servers
Personal and laptop computers
Point-of-sale equipment
Printers/copiers
Printing presses
Security equipment
Sports field improvements and scoreboards
Video recording and editing equipment

COMPETITORS

3I GROUP PLC	PRESIDIO TECHNOLOGY
CIT GROUP INC.	CAPITAL LLC
CSI LEASING INC.	SILVERFLEET CAPITAL
FORD MOTOR CREDIT COMPANY LLC	LIMITED
	STANDARD CHARTERED PLC
FORSYTHE TECHNOLOGY LLC	U.S. BANCORP
	YORKSHIRE BANK PUBLIC
GENERAL ELECTRIC CAPITAL CORPORATION	LIMITED COMPANY
MUFG AMERICAS HOLDINGS CORPORATION	

HISTORICAL FINANCIALS
Company Type: Public

Income Statement   FYE: June 30

	ASSETS ($ mil.)	NET INCOME ($ mil.)	INCOME AS % OF ASSETS	EMPLOYEES
06/21	242.9	36.2	14.9%	0
06/20	267.7	(2.3)	—	0
06/19	304.9	7.3	2.4%	0
06/18	389.2	12.5	3.2%	0
06/17	715.5	11.1	1.6%	98
Annual Growth	(23.7%)	34.3%	—	—

2021 Year-End Financials

Return on assets: —
Return on equity: —
Long-term debt ($ mil.): —
No. of shares (mil.): 10.2
Sales ($ mil): 51.1

Dividends
  Yield: 2.9%
  Payout: 200.0%
  Market value ($ mil.): 188.0

	STOCK PRICE ($) FY Close	P/E High/Low		PER SHARE ($) Earnings	Dividends	Book Value
06/21	18.31	5	4	3.52	0.54	22.39
06/20	15.30	—	—	(0.23)	0.52	19.41
06/19	15.80	25	20	0.71	0.50	20.16
06/18	15.80	15	11	1.22	0.48	19.93
06/17	18.85	18	13	1.08	0.46	19.07
Annual Growth	(0.7%)	—	—	34.4%	4.1%	4.1%

Calloway's Nursery, Inc.

Calloway's Nursery babies its customers with green-thumb know-how — about half of its employees are certified nursery professionals. The company owns and operates about 20 nurseries under the Calloway's name in the Dallas/Fort Worth area and San Antonio and under the Cornelius Nurseries banner in Houston. The company also sells plants online. Offerings include trees shrubs flowers landscaping materials soil fertilizer and Christmas goods. Christmas merchandise includes trees poinsettias wreaths and garlands.

EXECUTIVES

Vice President - Operations, Director, John Peters, $175,000 total compensation
President, Chief Operating Officer, Director, Marce Ward
Director, Timothy McKibben
Vice President, Director, George Wechsler
Vice President - Merchandising, David Weger, $125,000 total compensation
Director, David Alexander
Vice President - Finance, Secretary, Amy Yoon
Director - Marketing, Jennifer Hatalski
Vice President - Marketing, Alicia Hicks
Auditors: Whitley Penn LLP

LOCATIONS

HQ: Calloway's Nursery, Inc.
  9003 Airport Freeway, Suite G350, North Richland Hills, TX 76180
Phone: 817 222-1122
Web: www.calloways.com

PRODUCTS/OPERATIONS

Selected Products
Annuals
Bedding plants
Blooming tropicals
Christmas merchandise
  Garlands
  Poinsettias
  Trees
  Wreaths
Clay pots (Malaysian Chinese Mexican)
Gardening accessories
  Gloves
  Hats
  Kneelers

Gardening tools and equipment
Gifts
Grasses
Ground covers
Natural dog and cat food
Perennials
Potted plants
Seeds and bulbs
Shrubs
Soil amendments and fertilizers including organic
Trees

COMPETITORS

ENGLISH GARDENS & FAIRLANE FLORISTS INC.
MEADOWS FARMS INC.
MOLBAK'S LLC

HISTORICAL FINANCIALS

Company Type: Public

Income Statement				FYE: December 31
	REVENUE ($ mil.)	NET INCOME ($ mil.)	NET PROFIT MARGIN	EMPLOYEES
12/20	73.7	9.7	13.2%	0
12/19	58.7	3.0	5.1%	0
12/18	56.6	4.3	7.7%	0
12/17	55.4	5.0	9.1%	0
12/16	50.8	1.9	3.8%	0
Annual Growth	9.8%	49.6%	—	—

2020 Year-End Financials

Debt ratio: 25.5%
Return on equity: 40.4%
Cash ($ mil.): 11.8
Current ratio: 1.67
Long-term debt ($ mil.): 13.7

No. of shares (mil.): 7.3
Dividends
  Yield: 10.3%
  Payout: 75.1%
  Market value ($ mil.): 71.0

	STOCK PRICE ($) FY Close	P/E High/Low		PER SHARE ($) Earnings	Dividends	Book Value
12/20	9.63	8	3	1.33	1.00	3.44
12/19	6.10	21	14	0.41	0.00	3.11
12/18	8.00	15	12	0.60	0.50	2.70
12/17	8.30	12	5	0.69	0.50	2.57
12/16	3.84	15	10	0.26	0.00	2.76
Annual Growth	25.8%	—	—	50.4%	—	5.6%

Cambium Networks Corp

Auditors: KPMG LLP

LOCATIONS

HQ: Cambium Networks Corp
  3800 Golf Road, Suite 360, Rolling Meadows, IL 60008
Phone: 345 943-3100
Web: www.cambiumnetworks.com

HISTORICAL FINANCIALS

Company Type: Public

Income Statement				FYE: December 31
	REVENUE ($ mil.)	NET INCOME ($ mil.)	NET PROFIT MARGIN	EMPLOYEES
12/20	278.4	18.5	6.7%	512
12/19	267.0	(17.6)	—	533
12/18	241.7	(1.5)	—	516
12/17	216.6	9.1	4.2%	0
12/16	181.4	2.2	1.3%	0
Annual Growth	11.3%	69.0%		

2020 Year-End Financials

Debt ratio: 26.3%
Return on equity: 35.8%
Cash ($ mil.): 62.4
Current ratio: 1.53
Long-term debt ($ mil.): 24.9

No. of shares (mil.): 26.0
Dividends
  Yield: —
  Payout: —
  Market value ($ mil.): —

Cambridge Bancorp

Cambridge Bancorp is the nearly $2 billion-asset holding company for Cambridge Trust Company a community bank serving Cambridge and the Greater Boston area through about a dozen branch locations in Massachusetts. It offers standard retail products and services including checking and savings accounts CDs IRAs and credit cards. Residential mortgages including home equity loans account for about 50% of the company's loan portfolio while commercial real estate loans make up more than 40%. The company also offers commercial industrial and consumer loans. Established in 1892 the bank also offers trust and investment management services.

Operations

The commercial bank operates a traditional retail banking line focused on lending as well as its Wealth Management Group which investment management and trust business. The bank had $1.8 billion in total assets and $2.4 billion in client assets under management at the end of 2015.

As with other retail banks Cambridge Bancorp makes the bulk of its revenue from interest income. About 58% of its total revenue came from loan interest during 2015 while another 10% came from interest on taxable and tax-exempt investment securities. The rest of its revenue came from wealth management income (24% of revenue) deposit account fees (3%) ATM/Debit card income (1%) and other non-interest income sources.

Geographic Reach

Cambridge Bancorp has 12 branches in Massachusetts in Cambridge Boston Belmont Concord Lexington Lincoln and Weston. It also has wealth management offices in Boston as well as in New Hampshire in Concord Manchester and Portsmouth.

Sales and Marketing

The company spent $2.38 million on marketing during 2015 up from $2.12 million in 2014.

Financial Performance

Cambridge's annual revenues and profits have been steadily rising over the past several years thanks to continued commercial real estate mortgage growth and as its Wealth Management business has nearly doubled its managed assets since 2011 spurring higher fee revenue.

The bank's revenue climbed 7% to $80.2 million during 2015 on 10% loan growth mostly driven by commercial real estate loans which spurred higher interest income. The company's wealth management business income grew 7% as its client assets continued to grow with new investor inflows.

Revenue growth in 2015 drove Cambridge Bancorp's net income up 5% to $15.7 million. The bank's operating cash levels rose 24% to $20 million for the year with an increase in cash-based earnings and favorable changes in working capital mostly related to a change in accrued interest receivable deferred taxes and other assets and liabilities.

Strategy

Cambridge Bancorp continued in 2016 to lean on the success of its commercial mortgage business though it plans to pivot more to commercial and industrial lending to diversify its commercial lending portfolio.

To better prepare for rising interest rates Cambridge Bancorp in 2015 and 2016 modified its commercial loan strategy from long-term fixed-rate loans (which are vulnerable to interest rate risk) to a new interest rate derivative product to offer an alternative long-term financing for its customers while helping the bank earn a variable rate of interest on its loans. For its consumer banking unit the bank in 2015 began a plan to sell the majority of its long-term residential mortgage production including secondary loans to the secondary market.

EXECUTIVES

Independent Director, Hambleton Lord
Senior Vice President, Director Of Human Resources, Pilar Pueyo
Independent Director, Cathleen Schmidt
Independent Director, Kathryn Hinderhofer
Independent Director, Simon Gerlin
Executive Vice President, Director, Chief Banking Officer, Thomas Fontaine, $259,615 total compensation
Lead Independent Director, R. Gregg Stone
Chief Financial Officer, Treasurer, Michael Carotenuto, $300,000 total compensation
Senior Vice President - Director Of Consumer Lending, John Sullivan
Senior Vice President, Director Of Private Banking Offices, Kerri Mooney
Executive Vice President - Wealth Management, Jennifer Pline, $437,091 total compensation
Independent Director, Jeanette Clough
Executive Vice President, Chief Lending Officer, Martin Millane, $329,677 total compensation
Chairman Of The Board, President, Chief Executive Officer, Denis Sheahan, $558,000 total compensation
Senior Vice President, Chief Marketing Officer, Jennifer Willis
Director, Ceo New Hampshire Markets, Daniel Morrison
Independent Director, Pamela Hamlin
Independent Director, Christine Fuchs
Independent Director, Laila Partridge
Independent Director, Jody Rose
Senior Vice President, Chief Information Officer, Puneet Nevatia
Independent Director, Edward Jankowski
Independent Director, Thalia Meehan
Auditors: KPMG LLP

LOCATIONS

HQ: Cambridge Bancorp
1336 Massachusetts Avenue, Cambridge, MA 02138
Phone: 617 876-5500
Web: www.cambridgetrust.com

PRODUCTS/OPERATIONS

2015 Sales

	% of total
Interest Income	
Interest on loans	58
Interest on taxable investment securities	7
Interest on tax exempt investment securities	3
Non-Interest Income	
Wealth Management Income	24
Deposits accounts fee	3
ATM/Debit card income	1
Bank Owned life insurance income	1
Gain on disposition on investment securities	1
Gain on loans held of sale	1
Other income	1
Loan related derivative income	-
Total	**100**

Products/Services

Personal Banking
Checking
Savings CDs & IRAs
Online Banking
Mobile Banking
Mortgages
Home Equity
Credit Cards
Personal Loans
More Services
Business Banking
Checking & Savings
Commercial Lending
Commercial Real Estate
Cash Management
Remote Deposit Capture
Online Banking
Mobile Banking
Professional Services Program
More Services
Wealth Management
Investment Process
Investment Management
Fiduciary & Planning Services
Estate Settlement
Wealth Management Personnel
Forums
Online Access

COMPETITORS

ASSOCIATED BANC-CORP	FIRST REPUBLIC BANK
BANGOR SAVINGS BANK	HSBC USA INC.
ENTERPRISE BANCORP CORP. INC.	INDEPENDENT BANK
	OFG BANCORP
FIRST FINANCIAL BANCORP.	

HISTORICAL FINANCIALS

Company Type: Public

Income Statement

FYE: December 31

	ASSETS ($ mil.)	NET INCOME ($ mil.)	INCOME AS % OF ASSETS	EMPLOYEES
12/20	3,949.3	31.9	0.8%	383
12/19	2,855.5	25.2	0.9%	321
12/18	2,101.3	23.8	1.1%	262
12/17	1,949.9	14.8	0.8%	247
12/16	1,849.0	16.9	0.9%	0
Annual Growth	**20.9%**	**17.3%**	**—**	**—**

2020 Year-End Financials

Return on assets: 0.9%	Dividends
Return on equity: 9.2%	Yield: 3.0%
Long-term debt ($ mil.): —	Payout: 48.2%
No. of shares (mil.): 6.9	Market value ($ mil.): 483.0
Sales ($ mil): 168.9	

	STOCK PRICE ($) FY Close	P/E High/Low		PER SHARE ($) Earnings	Dividends	Book Value
12/20	69.75	15	9	5.03	2.12	58.00
12/19	80.15	16	13	5.37	2.04	53.06
12/18	83.25	16	13	5.77	1.96	40.67
12/17	79.80	24	17	3.61	1.86	36.24
12/16	62.29	15	11	4.15	1.84	33.36
Annual Growth	**2.9%**	**—**	**—**	**4.9%**	**3.6%**	**14.8%**

Canandaigua National Corp.

Canandaigua National can undoubtedly stake its claim as the holding company for Canandaigua National Bank and Trust which operates more than two dozen branches in the Finger Lakes region of upstate New York. In addition to traditional deposits and loans the bank also offers online brokerage insurance and wealth management services including corporate retirement plan management and individual financial planning. The company also owns Genesee Valley Trust Company and the recently formed Canandaigua National Trust Company of Florida. Canandaigua National's loan portfolio is composed largely of commercial mortgages other business loans and residential mortgages.

Geographic Reach

The company has also slowly expanded its branch network by opening new locations in Monroe and Ontario counties.

Strategy

Although the tepid economy has impacted community banks with lower yields Canandaigua's presence in the relatively stable Rochester region has helped keep things from looking too grim. The quality of the company's loan portfolio has been improving so it has had to dip in to less of its loan loss reserves.

EXECUTIVES

Independent Director, Caroline Shipley
Independent Vice Chairman Of The Board, Daniel Fuller
Independent Director, Sue Stewart
Director, Robert Sheridan
Director, Michael Goonan
Director, James Watters
Director, Richard Plympton
Executive Vice President, Chief Administrative Officer Of The Canandaigua National Bank And Trust Company, A.Rosamond Zatyko
Executive Vice President, Wealth Management Of The Canandaigua National Bank And Trust, Salvatore Guerrieri
Senior Vice President Fo Commercial Services And Group Manager Of Canandaigua National Bank And Trust Company, Charles Vita
Chairman Of The Board, George Hamlin
Executive Vice President - Retail Banking And Marketing Of Bank And Trust, Karen Serinis

HOOVER'S HANDBOOK OF EMERGING COMPANIES 2022

President, Chief Executive Officer, Director, Frank Hamlin
Director, Lawrence Heilbronner-Kolthoff
Director, Gary Babbitt
Executive Vice President, Information Technology & Project Management Of The Canandaigua National Bank And Trust Company, Annette Joyce
Executive Vice President, Consumer Lending Of The Canandaigua National Bank And Trust Company, Brian Pasley
Chief Financial Officer, Executive Vice President, Vincent Yacuzzo
Director, Thomas Richards
Independent Director, Alan Stone

LOCATIONS

HQ: Canandaigua National Corp.
72 South Main Street, Canandaigua, NY 14424
Phone: 585 394-4260   **Fax:** 585 394-4001
Web: www.cnbank.com

COMPETITORS

ANCHOR BANCORP WISCONSIN INC.
FARMERS CAPITAL BANK CORPORATION
FNBH BANCORP INC.
PLAINSCAPITAL CORPORATION
ZIONS BANCORPORATION

HISTORICAL FINANCIALS

Company Type: Public

Income Statement				FYE: December 31
	ASSETS ($ mil.)	NET INCOME ($ mil.)	INCOME AS % OF ASSETS	EMPLOYEES
12/20	3,635.3	42.2	1.2%	580
12/19	3,015.6	39.1	1.3%	572
12/18	2,862.4	35.9	1.3%	556
12/17	2,661.7	22.0	0.8%	541
12/16	2,476.1	22.4	0.9%	533
Annual Growth	10.1%	17.1%		2.1%

2020 Year-End Financials

Return on assets: 1.2%
Return on equity: 15.0%
Long-term debt ($ mil.): —
No. of shares (mil.): 1.8
Sales ($ mil): 184.9
Dividends
Yield: 0.0%
Payout: 31.2%
Market value ($ mil.): 352.0

	STOCK PRICE ($) FY Close	P/E High/Low		Earnings	Dividends	Book Value
12/20	188.00	10	6	22.43	7.00	158.09
12/19	202.25	10	8	20.77	5.70	142.18
12/18	175.00	10	8	18.97	4.80	124.85
12/17	152.00	15	12	11.58	4.30	111.11
12/16	140.00	15	11	11.84	3.87	103.87
Annual Growth	7.6%	—	—	17.3%	16.0%	11.1%

Capital Bancorp Inc (MD)

Auditors: Elliott Davis, PLLC

LOCATIONS

HQ: Capital Bancorp Inc (MD)
2275 Research Boulevard, Suite 600, Rockville, MD 20850
Phone: 301 468-8848
Web: www.capitalbankmd.com

HISTORICAL FINANCIALS

Company Type: Public

Income Statement				FYE: December 31
	ASSETS ($ mil.)	NET INCOME ($ mil.)	INCOME AS % OF ASSETS	EMPLOYEES
12/20	1,876.5	25.8	1.4%	247
12/19	1,428.5	16.9	1.2%	230
12/18	1,105.0	12.7	1.2%	204
12/17	1,026.0	7.1	0.7%	195
12/16	905.6	9.4	1.0%	0
Annual Growth	20.0%	28.6%		

2020 Year-End Financials

Return on assets: 1.5%
Return on equity: 17.6%
Long-term debt ($ mil.): —
No. of shares (mil.): 13.7
Sales ($ mil): 158.3
Dividends
Yield: —
Payout: —
Market value ($ mil.): 192.0

	STOCK PRICE ($) FY Close	P/E High/Low		Earnings	Dividends	Book Value
12/20	13.93	8	4	1.87	0.00	11.58
12/19	14.89	12	9	1.21	0.00	9.60
12/18	11.41	13	11	1.02	0.00	8.38
Annual Growth	10.5%	—	—	35.4%	—	17.6%

Capital City Bank Group, Inc.

Capital City Bank Group is the holding company for Capital City Bank (CCB). The bank provides traditional deposit and credit services mortgage banking asset management trust merchant services bank cards data processing and securities brokerage services through some 60 banking offices in Florida Georgia and Alabama. Through Capital City Home Loans the company has about 30 additional offices in mortgage banking in the Southeast. In addition to CCB other assets include Capital City Trust Company and Capital City Investments. The bank was founded in 1895.

EXECUTIVES

Independent Director, Robert Antoine
Independent Director, Bonnie Davenport
Independent Director, Ashbel Williams
Independent Director, Kimberly Crowell
Independent Director, William Butler
Independent Director, Stanley Connally
Independent Director, Eric Grant
Chairman Of The Board, President And Chief Executive Officer, William Smith, $430,000 total compensation
Treasurer, President Of Capital City Bank, Director, Thomas Barron, $395,000 total compensation
Independent Director, Cader Cox
Lead Independent Director, J. Everitt Drew
Chief Financial Officer, Executive Vice President, J. Kimbrough Davis, $318,000 total compensation
Independent Director, John Sample
Independent Director, Marshall Criser
Auditors: BKD, LLP

LOCATIONS

HQ: Capital City Bank Group, Inc.
217 North Monroe Street, Tallahassee, FL 32301
Phone: 850 402-7821
Web: www.ccbg.com

PRODUCTS/OPERATIONS

2015 Sales

	$ mil.	% of total
Interest		
Loans including fees	73.2	55
Investment securities	5.9	5
Funds sold	0.6	-
Noninterest income		
Deposit fee	22.6	17
Bank card fees	11.3	8
Wealth management fees	7.5	6
Mortgage Banking fees	4.5	3
Data processing fees	1.5	1
Other	6.6	5
Total	**133.7**	**100**

COMPETITORS

ALDERMORE GROUP PLC
ALLEGHENY VALLEY BANCORP INC.
BGEO GROUP LIMITED
CAPITAL BANK FINANCIAL CORP.
CITY HOLDING COMPANY
COUNTY BANK CORP.
FIRST CITIZENS BANCORPORATION INC.
FIRSTRAND LTD
HARBOR BANKSHARES CORPORATION
NORTHERN STAR FINANCIAL INC
PACIFIC FINANCIAL CORPORATION
SHINSEI BANK LIMITED
SOUTH STATE CORPORATION
SOUTHWEST GEORGIA FINANCIAL CORPORATION
UNION BANK AND TRUST COMPANY
UNITED BANKSHARES INC.
Woori Finance Holdings Co. Ltd.

HISTORICAL FINANCIALS

Company Type: Public

Income Statement				FYE: December 31
	ASSETS ($ mil.)	NET INCOME ($ mil.)	INCOME AS % OF ASSETS	EMPLOYEES
12/20	3,798.0	31.5	0.8%	773
12/19	3,088.9	30.8	1.0%	815
12/18	2,959.1	26.2	0.9%	819
12/17	2,898.7	10.8	0.4%	825
12/16	2,845.2	11.7	0.4%	853
Annual Growth	7.5%	28.0%		(2.4%)

2020 Year-End Financials

Return on assets: 0.9%
Return on equity: 9.4%
Long-term debt ($ mil.): —
No. of shares (mil.): 16.7
Sales ($ mil): 217.3
Dividends
Yield: 2.3%
Payout: 29.5%
Market value ($ mil.): 413.0

	STOCK PRICE ($) FY Close	P/E High/Low		Earnings	Dividends	Book Value
12/20	24.58	16	9	1.88	0.57	20.42
12/19	30.50	17	12	1.83	0.48	19.50
12/18	23.21	17	14	1.54	0.32	18.07
12/17	22.94	41	28	0.64	0.24	16.73
12/16	20.48	32	19	0.69	0.17	16.34
Annual Growth	4.7%	—	—	28.5%	35.3%	5.7%

CapStar Financial Holdings Inc

Auditors: Elliot Davis Decosimo, LLC

LOCATIONS

HQ: CapStar Financial Holdings Inc
1201 Demonbreun Street, Suite 700, Nashville, TN
37203
Phone: 615 732-6400
Web: www.capstarbank.com

HISTORICAL FINANCIALS
Company Type: Public

Income Statement				FYE: December 31
	ASSETS ($ mil.)	NET INCOME ($ mil.)	INCOME AS % OF ASSETS	EMPLOYEES
12/20	2,987.0	24.7	0.8%	380
12/19	2,037.2	22.4	1.1%	289
12/18	1,963.8	9.6	0.5%	295
12/17	1,344.4	1.5	0.1%	175
12/16	1,333.6	9.1	0.7%	170
Annual Growth	22.3%	28.4%	—	22.3%

2020 Year-End Financials

Return on assets: 0.9%
Return on equity: 7.9%
Long-term debt ($ mil.): —
No. of shares (mil.): 21.9
Sales ($ mil): 135.1

Dividends
  Yield: 1.3%
  Payout: 16.3%
Market value ($ mil.): 324.0

	STOCK PRICE ($) FY Close	P/E High/Low		PER SHARE ($) Earnings	Dividends	Book Value
12/20	14.75	14	6	1.22	0.20	15.62
12/19	16.65	14	11	1.20	0.19	14.87
12/18	14.73	30	19	0.67	0.08	14.35
12/17	20.77	169	125	0.12	0.00	12.69
12/16	21.96	22	16	0.81	0.00	12.42
Annual Growth	(9.5%)	—	—	10.8%	—	5.9%

Cara Therapeutics Inc

Cara Therapeutics cares about pain therapy. The clinical-stage biopharmaceutical company focuses on developing and commercializing new chemical products designed to alleviate pain by selectively targeting kappa opioid receptors. Its proprietary class of product candidates targets the body's peripheral nervous system. In a test with patients with moderate-to-severe pain they have demonstrated efficacy without inducing many of the undesirable side effects often associated with pain therapeutics. Cara's most advanced product candidates are KORSUVA (CR845/difelikefalin) injection and Oral KORSUVA (CR845/difelikefalin). Founded in 2004 the company is based in Stamford Connecticut.

Operations

Its product candidate CR845/difelikefalin is a new chemical entity which is designed to selectively stimulate kappa rather than mu and delta opioid receptors. CR845/difelikefalin has been designed with specific chemical characteristics to restrict its entry into the CNS and further limit its mechanism of action to KORs in the peripheral nervous system and on immune cells. Activation of kappa receptors in the CNS is known to result in some undesirable effects including dysphoria. Since CR845/difelikefalin modulates kappa receptor signals peripherally without any significant activation of opioid receptors in the CNS it is generally not expected to produce the CNS-related side effects of mu opioid agonists (such as addiction and respiratory depression) or centrally-active kappa opioid agonists (such as dysphoria and hallucinations).

Sales and Marketing

Cara Therapeutics plan to have its own specialty sales force to launch KORSUVA (CR845/difelikefalin) injection in the hemodialysis setting in the US as well as through collaborations with other pharmaceutical or biotechnology companies or third-party manufacturing and sales organizations. If approved for marketing outside the US the existing or new partners will commercialize KORSUVA (CR845/difelikefalin) injection with its own or its collaborators' sales force.

Financial Performance

In the last five years the company reported increased revenue as a License and milestone fee starts to trickle in.

In 2019 revenue increased by 48% to $19.9 million primarily due to a $6.3 million increase in License and milestone fees.

Net loss for 2019 increased by $32.4 million to $106.4 million mainly due to high operating expenses.

Cash and cash equivalents at the end of the period were $18.7 million. Net cash used in operating activities was $109.2 million and investing activities used another $30.5 million. Financing activities provided $142.6 million to the company coffers.

Strategy

The company strategy is to develop and commercialize a novel and first-in-class portfolio of peripherally-acting kappa opioid receptor agonists with KORSUVA (CR845/difelikefalin) injection and Oral KORSUVA (CR845/difelikefalin) as its lead candidates. It has designed and is developing product candidates that have clearly defined clinical development programs and target significant commercial market opportunities. The key elements of its strategy are as follows:

Advance KORSUVA (CR845/difelikefalin) injection for the treatment of moderate-to-severe CKD-aP in patients undergoing hemodialysis to support regulatory approval;

Build a specialty sales and marketing organization to commercialize KORSUVA (CR845/ difelikefalin) injection for the treatment of CKD-aP in hemodialysis patients in the United States if approved;

Expand the use of Oral KORSUVA (CR845/difelikefalin) in other pruritic indications by establishing proof-of-concept in clinical conditions such as non-dialysis stage III-V CKD-aP CLD-aP and AD; and

Establish partnerships for further development and commercialization of I.V. CR845/difelikefalin for the treatment of moderate-to-severe acute pain and/or PONV in acute care settings in the United States

EXECUTIVES

Senior Vice President, Research And Development, Chief Scientific Officer, Frederique Menzaghi, $451,200 total compensation
Chief Compliance Officer, General Counsel, Secretary, Scott Terrillion, $412,000 total compensation
Independent Director, Harrison Bains
President, Ceo And Director, Christopher Posner
Chief Medical Officer, Joana Goncalves, $451,200 total compensation
Independent Director, Susan Shiff
Chief Financial Officer, Thomas Reilly, $100,000 total compensation
Auditors: Ernst & Young LLP

LOCATIONS

HQ: Cara Therapeutics Inc
4 Stamford Plaza, 107 Elm Street, 9th Floor, Stamford, CT 06902
Phone: 203 406-3700
Web: www.caratherapeutics.com

PRODUCTS/OPERATIONS

2015 Sales

	$ mil.	% of total
Collaborative revenue	2.1	55
License and milestone fee	1.7	45
Total	**3.8**	**100**

COMPETITORS

AGENUS INC.
ALEXION PHARMACEUTICALS INC.
BLUEPRINT MEDICINES CORPORATION
FIBROGEN INC.
INFINITY PHARMACEUTICALS INC.
PACIRA BIOSCIENCES INC.
RIGEL PHARMACEUTICALS INC.
SAGE THERAPEUTICS INC.
TG THERAPEUTICS INC.
XOMA CORPORATION

HISTORICAL FINANCIALS
Company Type: Public

Income Statement				FYE: December 31
	REVENUE ($ mil.)	NET INCOME ($ mil.)	NET PROFIT MARGIN	EMPLOYEES
12/20	135.0	8.4	6.2%	80
12/19	19.8	(106.3)	—	67
12/18	13.4	(74.0)	—	55
12/17	0.9	(58.1)	—	37
12/16	0.0	(57.2)	—	34
Annual Growth	529.5%	—	—	23.9%

2020 Year-End Financials

Debt ratio: —
Return on equity: 3.8%
Cash ($ mil.): 31.6
Current ratio: 10.55
Long-term debt ($ mil.): —

No. of shares (mil.): 49.8
Dividends
  Yield: —
  Payout: —
Market value ($ mil.): 755.0

	STOCK PRICE ($) FY Close	P/E High/Low		PER SHARE ($) Earnings	Dividends	Book Value
12/20	15.13	100	51	0.18	0.00	4.99
12/19	16.11	—	—	(2.49)	0.00	4.00
12/18	13.00	—	—	(2.06)	0.00	3.38
12/17	12.24	—	—	(1.86)	0.00	2.66
12/16	9.29	—	—	(2.10)	0.00	1.86
Annual Growth	13.0%	—	—	—	—	28.0%

Cardinal Ethanol LLC

EXECUTIVES

Independent Director, Danny Huston
Independent Director, Gerald Forsythe
Independent Director, Daniel Sailer
Commodity Manager, Casey Bruns, $118,969 total compensation
Director, J. Phillip Zicht
Plant Manager, Jeremey Herlyn, $159,188 total compensation
Independent Director, Robert Baker
Vice Chairman Of The Board, Thomas Chalfant
Independent Director, Steven Snider
Independent Chairman Of The Board, Robert Davis
Independent Director, Dale Schwieterman
Director, Cyril LeFevre
Independent Director, Lewis Roch
Chief Financial Officer, Treasurer, William Dartt, $153,346 total compensation
President, Chief Executive Officer, Jeffrey Painter, $273,327 total compensation
Secretary, Independent Director, Thomas Chronister
Auditors: Boulay PLLP

LOCATIONS

HQ: Cardinal Ethanol LLC
  1554 N. County Road 600 E., Union City, IN 47390
Phone: 765 964-3137
Web: www.cardinalethanol.com

HISTORICAL FINANCIALS

Company Type: Public

Income Statement				FYE: September 30
	REVENUE ($ mil.)	**NET INCOME** ($ mil.)	**NET PROFIT MARGIN**	**EMPLOYEES**
09/21	404.0	27.1	6.7%	58
09/20	244.7	(1.1)	—	57
09/19	260.6	(6.6)	—	59
09/18	266.8	7.6	2.9%	56
09/17	228.5	13.4	5.9%	55
Annual Growth	15.3%	19.2%	—	1.3%

2021 Year-End Financials

Debt ratio: —
Return on equity: 23.2%
Cash ($ mil.): 33.9
Current ratio: 3.22
Long-term debt ($ mil.): —

No. of shares (mil.): 0.0
Dividends
  Yield: 0.1%
  Payout: 41.7%
Market value ($ mil.): 106.0

	STOCK PRICE ($) FY Close	P/E High/Low		PER SHARE ($) Earnings	Dividends	Book Value
09/21	7,230.00	4		31,856.00	775.00	8,540
09/20	5,000.00	—	—	(78.00)	150.00	7,459
09/19	7,102.00	—		(452.00)	100.00	7,687
09/18	9,985.00	27	18	522.00	950.00	8,238
09/17	15,500.00	17	15	919.00	1,175.00	8,666
Annual Growth	(17.4%)	—	—	19.2%	(9.9%)	(0.4%)

CareTrust REIT Inc

Auditors: DELOITTE & TOUCHE LLP

LOCATIONS

HQ: CareTrust REIT Inc
  905 Calle Amanecer, Suite 300, San Clemente, CA 92673
Phone: 949 542-3130
Web: www.caretrustreit.com

HISTORICAL FINANCIALS

Company Type: Public

Income Statement				FYE: December 31
	REVENUE ($ mil.)	**NET INCOME** ($ mil.)	**NET PROFIT MARGIN**	**EMPLOYEES**
12/21	192.3	71.9	37.4%	16
12/20	178.3	80.8	45.3%	15
12/19	163.4	46.3	28.4%	52
12/18	156.9	57.9	36.9%	57
12/17	132.9	25.8	19.5%	50
Annual Growth	9.7%	29.1%	—	(24.8%)

2021 Year-End Financials

Debt ratio: 41.0%
Return on equity: 7.8%
Cash ($ mil.): 19.9
Current ratio: 0.43
Long-term debt ($ mil.): 673.4

No. of shares (mil.): 96.3
Dividends
  Yield: 4.6%
  Payout: 137.6%
Market value ($ mil.): 2,198.0

	STOCK PRICE ($) FY Close	P/E High/Low		PER SHARE ($) Earnings	Dividends	Book Value
12/21	22.83	34	27	0.74	1.06	9.51
12/20	22.18	28	9	0.85	1.00	9.60
12/19	20.63	52	37	0.49	0.90	9.75
12/18	18.46	28	18	0.72	0.82	8.95
12/17	16.76	56	42	0.35	0.74	7.88
Annual Growth	8.0%	—	—	20.6%	9.4%	4.8%

CarGurus Inc

Auditors: Ernst & Young LLP

LOCATIONS

HQ: CarGurus Inc
  2 Canal Park, 4th Floor, Cambridge, MA 02141
Phone: 617 354-0068
Web: www.cargurus.com

HISTORICAL FINANCIALS

Company Type: Public

Income Statement				FYE: December 31
	REVENUE ($ mil.)	**NET INCOME** ($ mil.)	**NET PROFIT MARGIN**	**EMPLOYEES**
12/20	551.4	77.5	14.1%	827
12/19	588.9	42.1	7.2%	921
12/18	454.0	65.1	14.4%	732
12/17	316.8	13.2	4.2%	549
12/16	198.1	6.5	3.3%	514
Annual Growth	29.2%	85.9%	—	12.6%

2020 Year-End Financials

Debt ratio: —
Return on equity: 24.5%
Cash ($ mil.): 190.3
Current ratio: 4.99
Long-term debt ($ mil.): —

No. of shares (mil.): 113.3
Dividends
  Yield: —
  Payout: —
Market value ($ mil.): 3,598.0

	STOCK PRICE ($) FY Close	P/E High/Low		PER SHARE ($) Earnings	Dividends	Book Value
12/20	31.73	55	23	0.68	0.00	3.29
12/19	35.18	113	75	0.37	0.00	2.29
12/18	33.73	93	49	0.57	0.00	1.76
12/17	29.98	251	212	0.12	0.00	1.20
Annual Growth	1.9%	—	—	78.3%	—	40.1%

Casella Waste Systems, Inc.

The wasteful habits of Americans are big business for Casella Waste Systems which operates regional waste-hauling businesses mainly in the northeastern US. The company serves residential commercial industrial and municipal customers. In 2019 it owned and/or operated about 45 solid waste collection operations about 60 transfer stations about 20 recycling facilities more than five Subtitle D landfills less than landfill gas-to-energy facilities and one landfill permitted to accept construction and demolition materials. With a strategy focused on increasing waste volumes at its landfills Casella Waste Systems added about 1.2 million tons in 2019. The company were founded in 1975.

Operations

Casella Waste System managed their operations through four operating segments including two regional operating segments which were designated as Eastern (accounts for about 30% of revenue) and Western regions (about 45%) Recycling(more than 5%) which comprises of larger-scale recycling operations and the commodity brokerage operations and "Other"(nearly 20%) which comprises organic services ancillary operations along with major accounts and industrial services.

Casella Waste Systems' broad portfolio of waste service assets includes solid waste collection businesses disposal facilities recycling plants transfer stations and gas-to-energy and waste-to-energy facilities.

The company's operations comprise a full range of non-hazardous solid waste services including collections transfer stations Material Recovery Facilities (MRFs) and disposal facilities. In 2019 it generated about 50% of its total revenues from its collection business and about 25% from its disposal activities. The remaining revenue accounts for recycling customer solutions organic and processing.

Geographic Reach

Casella Waste Systems conducts its operation on a geographic basis through two regional operating segments: the Eastern and Western regions; and a third operating segment Recycling which comprises larger-scale recycling operations and commodity brokerage operations.

The company provides integrated solid waste services in six states: Vermont New Hampshire New York Massachusetts Maine and Pennsylvania. Its corporate headquarters is located in Vermont.

Sales and Marketing

The waste services company serves commercial industrial municipal and residential customers. The name and logo or where appropriate that of the divisional operations are displayed on all of containers and trucks. The company attend and make presentations at municipal and state meetings and advertise in a variety of media throughout their service footprint.

Financial Performance

Casella Waste System's revenue grew by 36% since 2015 on the back of the yearly increase in revenue of its commercial industrial and municipal services.

In 2019 the company saw a 13% increase in revenue ending the year with $743.3 million. The increase in revenue were primarily impacted by favorable collection and disposal pricing.

Casella Waste System's net income ballooned to $31.7 million in 2019 almost quadrupling the income from the prior year. The increase was attributable to higher revenue higher operating income and higher income tax benefit.

Cash and cash equivalents at the end of 2019 was $3.5 million. Net cash provided by operating activities was $116.8 million while financing activities added another $60.1 million. Investing activities however used $177.5 million for acquisitions and additions to property plant and equipment.

Strategy

In early August 2017 the company announced an updated long-term strategic plan through its fiscal year ending December 2021 (the "2021 Plan"). The 2021 Plan remains focused on enhancing shareholder returns by improving cash flows and reducing debt leverage through the following strategic initiatives: Increasing landfill returns by driving pricing in excess of inflation in the disposal capacity constrained markets in the Northeast and working to maximize capacity utilization; Driving additional profitability in its collection operations through profitable revenue growth and operating efficiencies; Creating incremental value through its resource solutions offerings in its recycling organics and customer solutions operations; Using technology to drive profitable growth and efficiencies through its efforts to update key systems to drive back office transformation operating efficiencies and sales force effectiveness; and Allocating capital to balance debt delivering with smart growth through continued capital discipline and selective acquisitions of complementary businesses and assets.

To support its efforts the company continue to invest in its employees through leadership development its career paths program that helps to build long-term development for its employees technical training for key roles such as drivers and mechanics and incentive compensation structures that seek to align its employees' incentives with its long-term goal to improve cash flows and returns on invested capital. Over the last three years it has grown its workforce by approximately 32% and believe that continuing to invest in its team and culture are keys to its continued success.

Mergers and Acquisitions

In 2019 Casella Waste Systems announced that it has completed the acquisition of solid waste hauling and transfer assets in Albany NY and Cheshire MA from select subsidiaries of Republic Services Inc. The acquired assets are expected to generate approximately $30 million of annualized revenues.

Also in 2019 Casella Waste Systemshas acquired three solid waste businesses with hauling transfer and recycling operations in Maine Massachusetts and Vermont. All transactions closed in May 2019.The Company acquired the assets of D & E Rubbish Removal Inc. the assets of Bin Dump'n Trash and the stock of TAM Inc. and its wholly owned and related subsidiaries. In total the Company expects to generate approximately $11.5 million of annualized revenues from these acquisitions. Financial terms were not disclosed.

Company Background

The company was founded in 1975 with one truck.

EXECUTIVES

Chairman, Chief Executive Officer & Secretary, John Casella, $610,000 total compensation

Vice Chairman Of The Board, Douglas Casella, $302,610 total compensation

Independent Director, Joseph Doody

Independent Director, Michael Burke

Chief Accounting Officer, Vice President - Finance, Christopher Heald, $237,100 total compensation

President And Chief Operating Officer, Edwin Johnson, $434,000 total compensation

Chief Financial Officer, Senior Vice President, Treasurer, Edmond Coletta, $440,000 total compensation

Independent Director, Michael Battles

Independent Director, Rose Kirk

Independent Director, Gary Sova

Vice President, General Counsel, Shelley Sayward

Auditors: RSM US LLP

LOCATIONS

HQ: Casella Waste Systems, Inc.
25 Greens Hill Lane, Rutland, VT 05701
Phone: 802 775-0325
Web: www.casella.com

PRODUCTS/OPERATIONS

2015 Sales

	$ mil.	% of total
Solid Waste Operations		
Collection	238.3	44
Disposal	156.5	29
Power generation	6.8	1
Processing	6.1	1
Customer Solutions	53.3	10
Recycling	46.3	8
Organics	39.1	7
Total	**546.4**	**100**

COMPETITORS

ADVANCED DISPOSAL SERVICES INC.
BASIC ENERGY SERVICES INC.
CLEAN
CLEAN HARBORS INC.
ENERGYSOLUTIONS INC.
EVOQUA WATER TECHNOLOGIES CORP.
FCC ENVIRONMENT (UK) LIMITED
HARSCO CORPORATION
HERITAGE-CRYSTAL INC.
STERICYCLE INC.
WASTE MANAGEMENT INC.

HISTORICAL FINANCIALS

Company Type: Public

Income Statement

FYE: December 31

	REVENUE ($ mil.)	NET INCOME ($ mil.)	NET PROFIT MARGIN	EMPLOYEES
12/21	889.2	41.1	4.6%	2,900
12/20	774.5	91.1	11.8%	2,500
12/19	743.2	31.6	4.3%	2,500
12/18	660.6	6.4	1.0%	2,300
12/17	599.3	(21.8)	—	2,000
Annual Growth	**10.4%**	**—**	**—**	**9.7%**

2021 Year-End Financials

Debt ratio: 43.0%
Return on equity: 10.4%
Cash ($ mil.): 33.8
Current ratio: 0.96
Long-term debt ($ mil.): 542.5

No. of shares (mil.): 51.4
Dividends
  Yield: —
  Payout: —
Market value ($ mil.): 4,392.0

	STOCK PRICE ($) FY Close	P/E High/Low		PER SHARE ($) Earnings	Dividends	Book Value
12/21	85.42	112	68	0.80	0.00	8.22
12/20	61.95	34	19	1.86	0.00	7.09
12/19	46.03	71	41	0.66	0.00	2.57
12/18	28.49	225	149	0.15	0.00	(0.37)
12/17	23.02	—	—	(0.52)	0.00	(0.90)
Annual Growth	**38.8%**	**—**	**—**	**—**	**—**	**—**

Cashmere Valley Bank Washington (New)

EXECUTIVES

Pres, Greg Oakes
Chief Retail Banking Officer*, Connie Fritz
Prin*, Alex Cruz
Prin*, Jana Flores
Supervisor, Shirley Reyes
Vice President Chief Financial, Aaron Strong
Vice President, Russell Jones
Customer Representativ, Lauren Antonsen
Site Manager, Claudia Robles
Loan Officer, Gary Waunch
Chief Retail Banking Officer, Jenny Pulver
Auditors: BDO USA, LLP

LOCATIONS

HQ: Cashmere Valley Bank Washington (New)
117 Aplets Way, Cashmere, WA 98815
Phone: 509 782-2092   **Fax:** 509 782-1643
Web: www.cashmerevalleybank.com

HISTORICAL FINANCIALS

Company Type: Public

Income Statement
FYE: December 31

	ASSETS ($ mil.)	NET INCOME ($ mil.)	INCOME AS % OF ASSETS	EMPLOYEES
12/20	1,994.2	25.5	1.3%	0
12/19	1,651.5	23.4	1.4%	0
12/18	1,520.7	21.7	1.4%	0
12/17	1,516.0	18.4	1.2%	0
12/16	1,454.2	17.5	1.2%	0
Annual Growth	8.2%	9.9%	—	—

2020 Year-End Financials

Return on assets: 1.4%
Return on equity: 11.4%
Long-term debt ($ mil.): —
No. of shares (mil.): 3.9
Sales ($ mil.): 74.6

Dividends
 Yield: 0.0%
 Payout: 52.9%
Market value ($ mil.): 209.0

	STOCK PRICE ($) FY Close	P/E High/Low		PER SHARE ($) Earnings	Dividends	Book Value
12/20	52.61	10	6	6.42	3.40	60.09
12/19	63.00	11	10	5.69	1.30	51.78
12/18	54.01	14	10	5.27	2.70	45.54
12/17	58.00	13	11	4.47	1.08	43.90
12/16	47.25	11	9	4.27	0.98	40.50
Annual Growth	2.7%		—	— 10.7%	36.5%	10.4%

Catalent Inc

Auditors: Ernst & Young LLP

LOCATIONS

HQ: Catalent Inc
 14 Schoolhouse Road, Somerset, NJ 08873
Phone: 732 537-6200
Web: www.catalent.com

HISTORICAL FINANCIALS

Company Type: Public

Income Statement
FYE: June 30

	REVENUE ($ mil.)	NET INCOME ($ mil.)	NET PROFIT MARGIN	EMPLOYEES
06/21	3,998.0	585.0	14.6%	17,300
06/20	3,094.3	220.7	7.1%	13,900
06/19	2,518.0	137.4	5.5%	12,300
06/18	2,463.4	83.6	3.4%	10,700
06/17	2,075.4	109.8	5.3%	10,800
Annual Growth	17.8%	51.9%	—	12.5%

2021 Year-End Financials

Debt ratio: 35.5%
Return on equity: 15.0%
Cash ($ mil.): 896.0
Current ratio: 2.44
Long-term debt ($ mil.): 3,166.0

No. of shares (mil.): 170.5
Dividends
 Yield: —
 Payout: —
Market value ($ mil.): 18,434.0

	STOCK PRICE ($) FY Close	P/E High/Low		PER SHARE ($) Earnings	Dividends	Book Value
06/21	108.12	40	23	3.11	0.00	25.07
06/20	73.30	68	32	1.14	0.00	21.53
06/19	54.21	59	32	0.90	0.00	15.70
06/18	41.89	74	53	0.63	0.00	8.14
06/17	35.10	43	25	0.87	0.00	5.79
Annual Growth	32.5%		— —	37.5%		— 44.3%

Cathay General Bancorp

Cathay General Bancorp is the holding company for Cathay Bank which mainly serves Chinese and Vietnamese communities from some 30 branches in California and about 20 more in Illinois New Jersey New York Massachusetts Washington and Texas. It also has a branch in Hong Kong and offices in Shanghai and Taipei. Catering to small to medium-sized businesses and individual consumers the bank offers standard deposit services and loans. Commercial mortgage loans account for more than half of the bank's portfolio; business loans comprise nearly 25%. The bank's Cathay Wealth Management unit offers online stock trading mutual funds and other investment products and services through an agreement with PrimeVest.

Geographic Reach
California state-chartered Cathay Bank has branches in California Illinois Massachusetts New Jersey New York Texas and Washington. Overseas it has a branch in Hong Kong and offices in Shanghai and Taipei.

Financial Performance
The bank's revenue is on a downward trend. In 2012 revenue declined more than 5% vs. 2011 after posting a 3% decline in the previous annual comparison. Indeed between 2008 and 2012 revenue dipped by about 17% on lower interest income and dividend income. However the bank's profit picture is improving with net income up in 2012 for the third consecutive year.

Strategy
With 60% of its branches in California — a state hard hit by the downturn in the housing market — Cathay Bank's real estate secured loan portfolio has suffered as the value of the underlying collateral plummeted. In 2010 the company entered into a memorandum of understanding with the FDIC to reduce its concentration of commercial real estate loans improve its capital ratios reduce overall risk and strengthen asset quality. The moves have helped the company to cut its losses. The bank has also been successful growing deposits.

Mergers and Acquisitions
In 2016 Cathay Bank agreed to buy SinoPac Bancorp from Taiwan's Bank SinoPac for $340 million. SinoPac's Far East National Bank operates nine branches including five in Los Angeles. After the deal closes Cathay plans to close a number of branches. The transaction will help boost the company's balance sheet.

EXECUTIVES

Independent Director Of The Company And The Bank, Kelly Chan
Vice Chairman Of The Board Of The Company And The Bank, Anthony Tang
Executive Vice President, Chief Risk Officer Of The Bank, Kim Bingham, $378,158 total compensation
Chief Financial Officer, Executive Vice President, Treasurer Of The Company And Executive Vice President, Chief Financial Officer Of The Bank, Heng Chen, $506,642 total compensation
Independent Director Of The Company And The Bank, Joseph Poon
Independent Director Of The Company And The Bank, Jane Jelenko
Independent Director Of The Company And The Bank, Felix Fernandez
Independent Director Of The Company And The Bank, Richard Sun
Executive Vice President, Chief Credit Officer Of Cathay Bank, Mark Lee, $349,185 total compensation
Independent Director, Maan-Huei Hung
Executive Chairman Of The Board Of The Company And The Bank, Dunson Cheng, $830,339 total compensation
Vice Chairman Of The Board Of The Company And The Bank, Peter Wu
Lead Independent Director, Nelson Chung
Auditors: KPMG LLP

LOCATIONS

HQ: Cathay General Bancorp
 777 North Broadway, Los Angeles, CA 90012
Phone: 213 625-4700
Web: www.cathaybank.com

PRODUCTS/OPERATIONS

2015 sales

	$ mil.	% of total
Interest and Dividend income		
Loan receivable	427.6	88
Investment securities- taxable	21.5	4
Federal Home Loan Bank stock	3.2	1
Deposits with banks	1.4	-
Non-Interest income		
Securities losses net	(3.3)	
Letters of credit commissions	5.6	1
Depository service fees	5.3	1
Other operating income	25.1	5
Total	**486.4**	**100**

Products/Services

Personal
Accounts
Checking Accounts
Savings Accounts
CDs
IRA CD
Debit Cards
Loans
Mortgage Loan
Home Equity Financing
Auto Loan
Credit Cards
Cathay Online Banking
Mobile Banking
Business/Commercial
Business Accounts
Business Checking Account
Business Savings Account
CDs
Cash Management Services
Merchant Deposit Capture
Zero Balance Account
Lockbox Service
Merchant Bankcard Services
Courier Deposit Service

Armored Transport Services
Cash Vault Services
Business Online Banking
Loans
Commercial Financing
Real Estate & Construction Financing
International Banking & Financing
Smart Capital Line
SBA Guaranteed Loan Program
Credit Cards

COMPETITORS

BANK OF HAWAII CORPORATION	REGIONS FINANCIAL CORPORATION
BANNER CORPORATION	TRICO BANCSHARES
F.N.B. CORPORATION	U.S. BANCORP
HSBC HOLDINGS PLC	WILSHIRE BANCORP INC.
MIDLAND FINANCIAL CO.	
PROSPERITY BANCSHARES INC.	

HISTORICAL FINANCIALS

Company Type: Public

Income Statement

FYE: December 31

	ASSETS ($ mil.)	NET INCOME ($ mil.)	INCOME AS % OF ASSETS	EMPLOYEES
12/20	19,043.1	228.8	1.2%	1,205
12/19	18,094.1	279.1	1.5%	1,219
12/18	16,784.7	271.8	1.6%	1,277
12/17	15,640.1	176.0	1.1%	1,271
12/16	14,520.7	175.1	1.2%	1,129
Annual Growth	7.0%	6.9%	—	1.6%

2020 Year-End Financials

Return on assets: 1.2%
Return on equity: 9.6%
Long-term debt ($ mil.): —
No. of shares (mil.): 79.5
Sales ($ mil): 743.3

Dividends
Yield: 3.8%
Payout: 43.9%
Market value ($ mil.): 2,559.0

	STOCK PRICE ($) FY Close	P/E High/Low		PER SHARE ($) Earnings	Dividends	Book Value
12/20	32.19	13	6	2.87	1.24	30.41
12/19	38.05	11	9	3.48	1.24	28.78
12/18	33.53	13	10	3.33	1.03	26.36
12/17	42.17	20	16	2.17	0.87	24.39
12/16	38.03	17	12	2.19	0.75	22.97
Annual Growth	(4.1%)	—	—	7.0%	13.4%	7.3%

Cavco Industries Inc (DE)

Cavco Industries designs makes and sells manufactured homes under brands that include Cavco Palm Harbor Friendship and Fleetwood. Its products include full-sized homes (about 500 sq. ft. to 3300 sq. ft.); park model homes (less than 400 sq. ft.) for use as recreational and retirement units; camping cabins; and commercial structures for use as portable classrooms showrooms and offices. Cavco sold some 14200 factory-built homes through company-owned and independent distribution channels. The company's finance arm offers mortgages and insurance.

Operations

Cavco operates two business segments: factory-built housing which includes wholesale and retail factory-built housing operations and accounts for about 95% of sales and a finance and insurance segment (some 5% of sales) which includes manufactured housing consumer finance and insurance.

Cavco's mortgage subsidiary CountryPlace is an approved Fannie Mae and Freddie Mac seller and servicer and a Ginnie Mae mortgage-backed securities offering mortgages to buyers of the company's homes. Its insurance subsidiary Standard Casualty provides property and casualty insurance to owners of manufactured homes.

Its factory-built houses are marketed under brand names such as Cavco Homes Fleetwood Homes Palm Harbor Homes Fairmont Homes Friendship Homes Chariot Eagle Destiny and most recently acquired Lexington Homes. Its park model RVs vacation cabins and systems-built commercial structures as well as modular homes are marketed primarily under its Nationwide Homes brand.

Geographic ReachBased in Phoenix Arizona Cavco operates about 20 homebuilding facilities located in about a dozen of US states.

Sales and MarketingCavco distributes its homes through about 40 company-owned US retail outlets and a network of independent distributors in some 45 states Canada. Texas is Cavco's biggest market with more than 30 company-owned stores.

Financial Performance

Cavco's has steadily built higher revenue every year this past half-decade while net income followed its growth path.

In 2021 (ended March) sales rose 4% to $1.1 billion. Factory-built housing revenue increased by 4% and financial services segment revenue also increased primarily from higher premium revenue from a greater number of insurance policies in force.

In 2021 net income increased by 2% to $76.6 million.

Cavco closed 2021 (ended March) with $339.3 million in cash compared to $255.6 million at the end of 2020 (ended March). The company generated about $114 million from operations while investing and financing activities used $23.3 million and $7 million respectively. Main cash uses were for acquisitions purchases of property and equipment and payments for exercise of stock options.

Strategy

The company's marketing efforts are focused on providing manufactured homes that are customizable and appeal to a wide range of home buyers on a regional basis in the markets it serves. The primary demographics for its products are entry-level and move-up buyers and persons age 55 and older. The company also markets to special niches such as subdivision developers and vacation home buyers. It focuses on developing and maintaining the resources necessary to meet its customer's desire for varied and unique specifications in an efficient factory production environment. This enables the company to attract distributors and consumers who desire the flexibility the custom home building process provides but who also seek the value and affordability created by building a home on a factory production line.

The company has strategically expanded its factory operations and related business initiatives primarily through the acquisition of other industry participants. This has enabled Cavco to participate in the affordable housing space on a national basis.

Company Background

Alfred Ghelfi and partner Bob Curtis began a part-time business in 1965 making pickup truck camper shells. The business Roadrunner Manufacturing became Cavalier Manufacturing in 1966 incorporated in 1968 and went public in 1969. The Cavalier name was already in use so in 1974 the company's name was changed to Cavco. After the 1970s oil crisis nearly wiped out the firm Ghelfi bought out Curtis' share and began making mobile homes. In time Cavco began leasing movable storage buildings but the only successful part of that business was the security container segment (the rest was sold in 1994). A mid-1980s housing market crash in Arizona spurred Cavco to enter a totally-new field — health care utilization management — in 1987.

In 1995 Cavco partnered with Japan's Auto Berg Enterprises to begin selling modular housing in Japan. The next year Cavco teamed up with Arizona Public Service to develop solar-powered manufactured housing and it also sold its health care business. Centex acquired nearly 80% of Cavco for $75 million in 1997. The next year Cavco moved into Texas (one of the biggest markets for factory-built homes) acquiring Texas retailer Boerne Homes.

HISTORY

Alfred Ghelfi and partner Bob Curtis began a part-time business in 1965 making pickup truck camper shells. The business Roadrunner Manufacturing became Cavalier Manufacturing in 1966 incorporated in 1968 and went public in 1969. The Cavalier name was already in use so in 1974 the company's name was changed to Cavco. After the 1970s oil crisis nearly wiped out the firm Ghelfi bought out Curtis' share and began making mobile homes. In time Cavco began leasing movable storage buildings but the only successful part of that business was the security container segment (the rest was sold in 1994). A mid-1980s housing market crash in Arizona spurred Cavco to enter a totally new field — health care utilization management — in 1987.

In 1995 Cavco partnered with Japan's Auto Berg Enterprises to begin selling modular housing in Japan. The next year Cavco teamed up with Arizona Public Service to develop solar-powered manufactured housing and it also sold its health care business. Centex acquired nearly 80% of Cavco for $75 million in 1997. The next year Cavco moved into Texas (one of the biggest markets for factory-built homes) acquiring Texas retailer Boerne Homes.

With demand shrinking and surplus inventory building up the company closed its Belen New Mexico factory in 2000 and moved its production to plants in Phoenix and Seguin Texas. That fall Centex tapped manufactured housing veteran Joseph Stegmayer as chairman of its manufactured housing segment.

In 2001 the company launched Factory Liquidators a new retail concept focusing on repossessed homes.

Centex's board of directors approved the tax-free distribution to its shareholders of all of Cavco's outstanding common stock in 2003. The spin-off was completed in June of that year. Continued weakness within the industry forced Cavco to close

HOOVER'S HANDBOOK OF EMERGING COMPANIES 2022

eight of its company-owned retail outlets in fiscal 2004 and seven more in 2005.

EXECUTIVES

President, Country Place Acceptance, Corp, Lyle Zeller, $268,269 total compensation
President, Standard Casualty Company, Gavin Ryan
Non-executive Independent Chairman Of The Board, Steven Bunger
President, Chief Executive Officer, Director, William Boor, $825,000 total compensation
Chief Accounting Officer, Paul Bigbee, $155,385 total compensation
Senior Vice President, Steven Like, $145,000 total compensation
Ir Contact Officer, Mark Fusler
Independent Director, Steven Moster
Chief Human Resource Officer, Senior Vice President, Simone Reynolds
President, Retail, Matthew Nino, $200,000 total compensation
Independent Director, David Greenblatt
Executive Vice President, Chief Compliance Officer, General Counsel, Corporate Secretary, Mickey Dragash, $325,000 total compensation
Auditors: RSM US LLP

LOCATIONS

HQ: Cavco Industries Inc (DE)
3636 North Central Ave., Ste. 1200, Phoenix, AZ 85012
Phone: 602 256-6263
Web: www.cavco.com

PRODUCTS/OPERATIONS

2017 Sales

	$ mil.	% of total
Factory-built housing	815.5	94
Financial Services	55.7	6
Total	871.0	100

Selected Products

Manufactured Homes
Modular Homes
Park Model RVs and Cabins
Commercial Structures
Mortgage Lending
Insurance

Selected Brands

Cavco Homes
Chariot Eagle
Fleetwood Homes
Palm Harbor Homes
Fairmont Homes
Friendship Homes
Lexington Homes

COMPETITORS

AMERICAN HOMESTAR CORPORATION
AUTONATION INC.
CHAMPION ENTERPRISES HOLDINGS LLC
CLAYTON HOMES INC.
D.R. HORTON INC.
DELTEC HOMES INC.
FOUR SEASONS HOUSING INC.
GILES INDUSTRIES OF TAZEWELL INCORPORATED
HORTON HOMES INC.
HOVNANIAN ENTERPRISES INC.
KB HOME
MANUFACTURED HOUSING ENTERPRISES INC.
MERITAGE HOMES CORPORATION
NOBILITY HOMES INC.
NVR INC.
PULTEGROUP INC.
SOUTHERN ENERGY HOMES INC.

HISTORICAL FINANCIALS

Company Type: Public

Income Statement

FYE: April 3

	REVENUE ($ mil.)	NET INCOME ($ mil.)	NET PROFIT MARGIN	EMPLOYEES
04/21*	1,108.0	76.6	6.9%	4,700
03/20	1,061.7	75.0	7.1%	5,000
03/19	962.7	68.6	7.1%	4,650
03/18	871.2	61.5	7.1%	4,500
04/17	773.8	37.9	4.9%	4,300
Annual Growth	9.4%	19.2%	—	2.2%

*Fiscal year change

2021 Year-End Financials

Debt ratio: 1.0%
Return on equity: 11.6%
Cash ($ mil.): 322.2
Current ratio: 2.75
Long-term debt ($ mil.): 10.3

No. of shares (mil.): 9.2
Dividends
Yield: —
Payout: —
Market value ($ mil.): 2,146.0

	STOCK PRICE ($) FY Close	P/E High/Low		Earnings	PER SHARE ($) Dividends	Book Value
04/21*	232.41	28	13	8.25	0.00	74.03
03/20	148.47	28	14	8.10	0.00	66.23
03/19	117.53	34	15	7.40	0.00	58.21
03/18	173.75	26	16	6.68	0.00	50.54
04/17	116.40	28	20	4.17	0.00	43.85
Annual Growth	18.9%	—	—	18.6%	—	14.0%

*Fiscal year change

Cboe Global Markets Inc

CBOE or Chicago Board Options Exchange provides cutting-edge trading and investment solutions to market participants around the world. The company is committed to defining markets through product innovation leading edge technology and seamless trading solutions. The company offers trading across a diverse range of products in multiple asset classes and geographies including options futures US Canadian and European equities exchange-traded products (ETPs) global foreign exchange (FX) and volatility products based on the Cboe Volatility Index (VIX Index) recognized as the world's premier gauge of US equity market volatility. In addition the company operates one of the largest stock exchanges by value traded in Europe and owns EuroCCP a leading pan-European equities clearing house. Cboe Global Markets also is a leading market globally for ETP listings and trading.

Operations

Cboe Global Markets operates through five segments: North American Equities Options Futures European Equities and Global FX.

Its North American Equities segment includes trading of listed cash equities and ETP transaction services that occur on BZX BYX EDGX and EDGA and Canadian equities and other transaction services that occur on or through the MATCHNow ATS. It also includes the listing business where

ETPs and the company are listed on BZX. It accounts for about half of total revenue.

The Options segment includes trading of listed market indexes mostly on an exclusive basis as well as on non-exclusive "multiply listed" options such as on the stock of individual corporation and options on other exchange- traded products (ETP options) such as exchange ? traded funds (ETF options) and exchange ? traded notes (ETN options) that occur on Cboe Options C2 BZX and EDGX all US national security exchanges. The options segment accounts for roughly 40% of revenue.

Its European Equities segment includes trading of pan-European listed equities transaction services ETPs exchange-traded commodities and international depository receipts that are hosted on MTFs operated by Cboe Europe Equities. It also includes the ETP listings business on RMs and clearing activities of EuroCCP. Cboe Europe Equities operates lit and dark pools a periodic auctions book and a Large-in-Scale (LIS) trading negotiation facility. Cboe Europe Equities also includes revenue generated from the licensing of proprietary market data and from access and capacity services. It accounts for around 5% of revenue.

The Futures segment includes transaction services provided by the company's fully electronic futures exchange CFE which includes offerings for trading of VIX futures and other futures products the licensing of proprietary market data as well as access and capacity services. The futures segment accounts for about 5% of revenue.

Its Global FX segment includes institutional FX services on the Cboe FX platform as well as non-deliverable forward FX transactions executed on Cboe SEF and Cboe Swiss as well as revenue generated from the licensing of proprietary market data and from access and capacity services. It accounts for less than 5% of revenue.

Overall transaction and clearing fees account for about 70% of revenue while regulatory fees account for some 15% and more than 5% came from market data fees and access and capacity fees.

Geographic Reach

Cboe Global Markets is headquartered in Chicago with a network of domestic and global offices across the Americas Europe and Asia including main hubs in New York London Kansas City and Amsterdam.

Sales and Marketing

Cboe Global Markets advertises through advertising costs for special events sponsorship of industry conferences options education seminars.

Travel and promotional expenses decreased in 2020 compared to the same period in 2019 primarily due to travel restrictions implemented in March 2020 in response to the COVID-19 pandemic coupled with a decline in marketing expenses also driven by lack of sponsored events due to the COVID-19 pandemic. Travel and Promotional Expenses were $6.6 million $68.3 million and 68.3 million in 2020 2019 and 2018 respectively.

Its customers include financial institutions institutional and individual investors and professional traders.

Financial Performance

The company's revenue for fiscal 2020 increased by 37% to $3.4 billion compared from the prior year with $2.5 billion. The increase was primarily due to a $701.8 million or 41% increase in transaction and clearing fees as a result of an increase in market volumes on the U.S. Equities exchanges and in the Options segment coupled with an increase in regulatory fees.

Net income in 2020 was $468.2 million or 37% of revenues less cost of revenues compared to $370.8 million or 33% of revenues less cost of revenues in 2019 an increase of $97.4 million or 26%.

Cash held by the company at the end of fiscal 2020 increased to $1.1 billion. Cash provided by operations was $1.5 billion while cash used for investing and financing activities were $430.5 million and $201.7 million respectively. Main cash uses were purchase of common stock and acquisitions.

Strategy

Cboe Global Markets expects to further grow its business and increase its revenues and profitability by pursuing the following growth strategies: build upon core proprietary products; and leverage leading proprietary trading technology; diversify business mix with growth of non-transactional revenues; broaden geographic reach; and expand product lines across asset classes.

Cboe Global Markets is diversifying its business mix through the growth of its non-transactional revenues which primarily consists of increasing the distribution of proprietary market data and enhanced market data offering insightful information to support our customers' needs and providing tools that draw users to its markets and drive volume. In 2020 the company delivered on this initiative by growing its proprietary market data and access and capacity fees and also increased recurring revenues with its information solutions acquisitions.

Mergers and Acquisitions

In 2021 Cboe Global Markets agreed to acquire Chi-X Asia Pacific Holdings Ltd. (Chi-X Asia Pacific) an alternative market operator and provider of innovative market solutions from J.C. Flowers & Co. LLC. This acquisition will provide Cboe with a single point of entry into two key capital markets ? Australia and Japan ? to help enable it to expand its global equities business into Asia Pacific bring other products and services to the region and further expand access to its unique proprietary product suite in the region. Terms of the deal were not disclosed.

In early 2021 Cboe Global Markets completed its acquisition of BIDS Trading a registered broker-dealer and the operator of the BIDS Alternative Trading System (ATS) the largest block-trading ATS by volume in the US. Through ownership of BIDS Trading Cboe gains a competitive foothold in the off-exchange segment of the US equities market which now accounts for more than 40% of overall US equities trading volume. The acquisition of BIDS Trading also provides Cboe with the opportunity to expand its global footprint and diversify its product and service offerings in markets beyond U.S. equities and options. Terms of the deal were not disclosed.

In mid-2020 Cboe Global Markets completed its acquisition of Toronto-based MATCHNow the largest equities alternative trading system (ATS) in Canada. With this acquisition Cboe gains a foothold in a key global capital market while expanding the company's geographic presence and diversifying the product capabilities of its equities business. Following a proven playbook used to grow its European equities business Cboe plans to leverage its world-class technology product in-

novation and expertise in operating markets to build out a more complete North American equities business. Terms of the deal were not disclosed.

Also in mid-2020 Cboe Global Markets completed its acquisition of Amsterdam-based EuroCCP a leading pan-European equities clearing house. The acquisition paves the way for the planned launch of Cboe Europe Derivatives a new Amsterdam-based futures and options market in the first half of 2021 subject to regulatory approvals. Cboe sees an opportunity to further grow this business by capitalizing on the strength of its pan-European network and by pursuing the development of derivatives trading and clearing capabilities in the region.

In 2020 Cboe Global Markets acquired the business of Trade Alert LLC a real-time alerts and order flow analysis service provider based in New York. Trade Alert will integrate with Cboe Information Solutions' comprehensive suite of data solutions analytics and indices that help market participants understand and access financial markets. With Trade Alert Cboe can deliver real-time trade data market information and alerts and Cboe content including thought leadership directly to customers.

In early 2020 Cboe Global Markets acquired Hanweck Associates LLC a real-time risk analytics company based in New York and the business of FT Providers LLC a portfolio management platform provider based in Chicago commonly referred to as FT Options. Hanweck and FT Options services will integrate with Cboe Information Solutions which offers a comprehensive suite of data solutions analytics and indices to help market participants understand and access Cboe markets. The addition of Hanweck and FT Options to this robust offering is expected to further enhance the customer experience through greater visibility into portfolio and balance sheet risk.

Company Background

In early 2012 the company bought the fully electronic National Stock Exchange. The move boosted the exchange's stock market presence by about half. In 2010 CBOE launched C2 an all-electronic options market capable of trading all of CBOE's products electronically.

CBOE went public in 2010 to better compete in the highly competitive options industry. As a corporation CBOE had better access to capital markets and was able to more easily enter joint ventures or other business combinations. The long-delayed IPO was also part of CBOE's restructuring efforts and a shift from being member-owned to a for-profit corporation.

The company was founded in 1973 by the Chicago Board of Trade (now part of CME Group).

HISTORY

The company was founded in 1973 by the Chicago Board of Trade (now part of CME Group).

CBOE went public in 2010 to better compete in the highly competitive options industry. As a corporation CBOE has better access to capital markets and is able to more easily enter joint ventures or other business combinations. CBOE raised $339 million in a 2010 initial public offering (IPO). The long-delayed IPO was part of CBOE's restructuring efforts and a shift from being member-owned to a for-profit corporation. CBOE allotted funds raised in its IPO for general corporate purposes and for the issuance of common stock shares to existing members.

CBOE launched an all-electronic options market in 2010. Named C2 the new platform was capable of trading all of CBOE's products electronically.

In 2011 the CBOE Stock Exchange moved its trading operations from Chicago to the East Coast to better compete with other stock exchanges and better serve its primarily East Coast-based clientele.

In early 2012 the company bought the fully electronic National Stock Exchange which it continues to run as a separate entity. The move boosted the exchange's stock market presence by about half.

EXECUTIVES

Executive Vice President, President Europe, David Howson, $575,400 total compensation
Executive Vice President, General Counsel And Corporate Secretary, Patrick Sexton
Chief Financial Officer, Executive Vice President, Treasurer, Brian Schell, $525,000 total compensation
Independent Director, Joseph Ratterman
Independent Director, Edward Fitzpatrick
Independent Director, Alexander Matturri
Independent Director, Ivan Fong
Independent Director, Fredric Tomczyk
Independent Director, James Parisi
Senior Vice President, Chief Accounting Officer, Jill Griebenow
Independent Director, William Farrow
Chief Operating Officer, Executive Vice President, Christopher Isaacson, $650,000 total compensation
Executive Vice President, Chief Strategy Officer, John Deters
Independent Director, Jill Goodman
Independent Director, Jennifer McPeek
Chief Executive Officer, President, And Chairman, Edward Tilly, $1,265,000 total compensation
Independent Director, Roderick Palmore
Lead Independent Director, Eugene Sunshine
Independent Director, Janet Froetscher
Auditors: KPMG LLP

LOCATIONS

HQ: Cboe Global Markets Inc
433 West Van Buren Street, Chicago, IL 60607
Phone: 312 786-5600
Web: www.cboe.com

PRODUCTS/OPERATIONS

Sales 2015

	$ mil.	% of total
Transaction fees	456.0	72
Access fees	53.3	8
Exchange services and other fees	42.2	7
Market data fees	30.0	5
Regulatory fees	33.5	5
Other revenue	19.5	3
Total	**634.5**	**100**

COMPETITORS

E TRADE FINANCIAL CORPORATION
FIDESSA GROUP HOLDINGS LIMITED
INTERACTIVE BROKERS GROUP INC.
INTERCONTINENTAL EXCHANGE INC.
LIQUIDNET HOLDINGS INC.
MATSUI SECURITIES CO. LTD.
NEX INTERNATIONAL LIMITED
STONEX GROUP INC.
TMX Group Limited
TRADEWEB MARKETS LLC
VIRTU FINANCIAL INC.

HISTORICAL FINANCIALS

Company Type: Public

Income Statement
FYE: December 31

	REVENUE ($ mil.)	NET INCOME ($ mil.)	NET PROFIT MARGIN	EMPLOYEES
12/21	3,494.8	529.0	15.1%	1,196
12/20	3,427.1	468.2	13.7%	1,010
12/19	2,496.1	374.9	15.0%	823
12/18	2,768.8	426.5	15.4%	842
12/17	2,229.1	401.7	18.0%	889
Annual Growth	11.9%	7.1%	—	7.7%

2021 Year-End Financials

Debt ratio: 19.0%
Return on equity: 15.2%
Cash ($ mil.): 341.9
Current ratio: 1.31
Long-term debt ($ mil.): 1,299.3
No. of shares (mil.): 106.6
Dividends
 Yield: 0.0%
 Payout: 36.5%
Market value ($ mil.): 13,907.0

	STOCK PRICE ($) FY Close	P/E High/Low		PER SHARE ($) Earnings	Dividends	Book Value
12/21	130.40	27	18	4.92	1.80	33.80
12/20	93.12	30	18	4.27	1.56	31.21
12/19	120.00	37	27	3.34	1.34	30.32
12/18	97.83	36	24	3.76	1.16	29.04
12/17	124.59	34	20	3.69	1.04	27.59
Annual Growth	1.1%	—	—	7.5%	14.7%	5.2%

Celsius Holdings Inc

Celsius Holdings wants consumers to enjoy the taste of burning calories. The company develops markets and distributes nutritional drinks that claim to burn calories raise metabolism and boost energy. Its first product Celsius is a canned sparkling beverage that comes in a variety of flavors and is marketed as an alternative to soda coffee and traditional energy drinks. Although it has undergone independent clinical studies results have not been US FDA approved. Its products which also include non-carbonated Celsius green tea drinks and single-serving powder mix packets that can be added to water are manufactured by third-party co-packers. Celsius Holdings was founded in 2004 under the name Elite FX.

EXECUTIVES

Chief Financial Officer, Edwin Negron-Carballo, $270,000 total compensation
Chairman Of The Board, President, Chief Executive Officer, John Fieldly, $464,526 total compensation
Independent Director, Caroline Levy
Independent Director, Alexandre Ruberti
Corporate Secretary, Marcus Sandifer
Director, Joyce Russell
Director, Damon DeSantis
Director, Cheryl Miller
Lead Independent Director, Hal Kravitz
Auditors: Ernst & Young LLP

LOCATIONS

HQ: Celsius Holdings Inc
2424 N. Federal Highway, Suite 208, Boca Raton, FL 33431
Phone: 561 276-2239
Web: www.celsius.com

COMPETITORS

CHARLIE'S HOLDINGS INC
MONSTER BEVERAGE CORPORATION
NUTRASWEET PROPERTY HOLDINGS INC. LLC
ODWALLA INC.
REED'S INC.
SNAPPLE BEVERAGE CORP (DEL)
SWEET GREEN FIELDS

HISTORICAL FINANCIALS

Company Type: Public

Income Statement
FYE: December 31

	REVENUE ($ mil.)	NET INCOME ($ mil.)	NET PROFIT MARGIN	EMPLOYEES
12/20	130.7	8.5	6.5%	154
12/19	75.1	9.9	13.3%	120
12/18	52.6	(11.2)	—	50
12/17	36.1	(8.2)	—	39
12/16	22.7	(3.0)	—	39
Annual Growth	54.8%	—	—	41.0%

2020 Year-End Financials

Debt ratio: 0.2%
Return on equity: 10.1%
Cash ($ mil.): 43.2
Current ratio: 3.53
Long-term debt ($ mil.): 0.0
No. of shares (mil.): 72.2
Dividends
 Yield: —
 Payout: —
Market value ($ mil.): 3,636.0

	STOCK PRICE ($) FY Close	P/E High/Low		PER SHARE ($) Earnings	Dividends	Book Value
12/20	50.31	370	27	0.11	0.00	1.44
12/19	4.83	32	20	0.16	0.00	0.92
12/18	3.47	—	—	(0.23)	0.00	0.21
12/17	5.25	—	—	(0.19)	0.00	0.38
12/16	0.42	—	—	(0.09)	0.00	0.27
Annual Growth	230.8%	—	—	—	—	51.7%

Central Garden & Pet Co

Central Garden & Pet is among the leading US producers and distributors of consumer lawn garden and pet supplies providing its products to retailers home improvement centers nurseries and mass merchandisers. Central Garden & Pet operates about 55 manufacturing plants and nearly 70 sales and distribution centers throughout the US. The company sells private label brands as well as brands from other manufacturers. It offers product lines such as AMDRO fire ant bait Four Paws animal products Kaytee bird seed Nylabone dog chews and TFH pet books. The company was founded by Bill Brown in 1980 as Central Garden Supply.

Operations

Central Garden & Pet operates two primary business lines Pet and Garden.

The Pet segment generates more than 55% of revenue by producing distributing marketing and selling a wide variety of pet related products for the US. This segment includes: products for dogs and cats including edible bones premium healthy edible and non-edible chews rawhide toys pet beds pet carriers grooming supplies and other accessories; products for birds small animals and specialty pets including cages and habitats toys chews and related accessories; animal and household health and insect control products; products for fish reptiles and other aquarium-based pets including aquariums furniture and lighting fixtures pumps filters water conditioners and supplements and information and knowledge resources; and products for horses and livestock.

The Garden segment accounts for about 45% of total revenue. It produces and markets proprietary and non-proprietary grass seed; wild bird feed bird feeders bird houses and other birding accessories; weed grass and other herbicides insecticide and pesticide products; fertilizers; and decorative outdoor lifestyle products including pottery.

While the company relies on its sales and logistics network to promote its proprietary brands to thousands of independent specialty stores other garden products account for over 25% of Central Garden & Pet's total revenue. Other pet products and other manufacturers' products provide about 25% each dog and cat products bring in over 15% and wild bird represent approximately 10%.

Geographic Reach

Central Garden & Pet is headquartered in Walnut Creek California. The company operates nearly 55 manufacturing facilities and about 70 sales and logistics facilities including office and warehouse space. In addition its garden segment leases approximately 150 acres of land in Oregon New Jersey and Virginia used in its grass seed and live plant operations and owns approximately 430 acres of land in Virginia North Carolina Maryland and Ohio for live plant operations. Although most operations are in the US the company operates facilities in the UK Canada and China.

Sales and Marketing

Central Garden & Pet relies heavily on just a few national retail chains for much of its sales. Walmart its largest customer represents about 15% of total sales while Home Depot its second largest accounts for approximately 15%. Lowe's Costco and Petco are also significant customers and together with Walmart and Home Depot generate around half of sales. The company relies on a domestic and international distribution network to deliver its proprietary brands to thousands of independent specialty stores and mass market customers.

Central Garden & Pet advertising costs were approximately $54.6 million $37.0 million and $27.5 million in fiscal 2021 2020 and 2019 respectively.

Financial Performance

Net sales for fiscal 2021 increased $608.2 million or 23% to $3.3 billion with organic net sales increasing $335.3 million and sales from its four recent acquisitions of $272.9 million. The company's Pet segment sales increased 13% and its Garden segment sales increased 39%.

In 2021 the company had a net income of $152.8 million a 26% increase from the previous year's net income of $121.5 million.

The company's cash at the end of 2021 was $439.2 million. Operating activities generated

$250.8 million while investing activities used $899.4 million mainly for businesses acquired. Financing activities provided another $420.5 million.

Strategy

The company's Central to Home strategy reinforces its unique purpose to nurture happy and healthy homes and its ambition to lead the future of the pet and garden industries. The company's objective is to grow net sales operating income and cash flows by developing new products increasing market share acquiring businesses and working in partnership with customers to grow the categories in which it participates. It runs its business with a long-term perspective and we believe the successful delivery of its strategy will enable it to create long-term value for its shareholders. To achieve its objective the company plans to capitalize on strengths and favorable industry trends by executing on five key strategic pillars to drive growth:

Consumer: Build and Grow Brands that Consumers Love; Customer: Win with Winning Customers and Channels; Central: Fortify the Central Portfolio; Cost: Reduce Cost to Improve Margins and Fuel Growth; and Culture: Strengthen Our Entrepreneurial Business-Unit Led Growth Culture.

Mergers and Acquisitions

In mid-2021 Central Garden & Pet acquired D&D Commodities (D&D). Headquartered in Stephen Minnesota D&D is a provider of high-quality premium bird feed. The addition of D&D's brands will expand Central's portfolio in the bird feed category and further deepen the company's relationship with major retailers.

In early 2021 Central Garden & Pet closed the previously announced acquisition of Green Garden Products (Green Garden) formerly known as Plantation Products for approximately $532 million from private equity firm Freeman Spogli & Co and other shareholders. Green Garden headquartered in Norton Massachusetts is a leading provider of vegetable herb and flower seed packets seed starters and plant nutrients in North America shipping over 250 million seed packets annually. Under the terms of the merger agreement the company paid a total of $532 million subject to certain post-closing adjustments.

Company Background

Central Garden & Pet Company's roots go back to 1955 when it was founded as a small California distributor of lawn and garden supplies. After nearly three decades of unremarkable growth it was purchased in 1980 by William Brown a former VP of finance at camera maker Vivitar. The company acquired small distributors but let them operate autonomously. By 1987 Central had sales of $25 million with distribution in California.

The company's first major acquisition was the result of a restructuring of forestry giant Weyerhaeuser which had diversified into insurance home building and diapers among other products but was selling noncore divisions to focus solely on timber. It sold Weyerhaeuser Garden Supply to Central in 1990 for $32 million.

Overnight Central became a national powerhouse with 25 distribution centers serving 38 states. In 1991 sales reached $280 million of which acquired operations accounted for nearly 70%. The purchase also gave Central 10 high-volume retail customers — including Costco Kmart and Wal-Mart — which accounted for half of its busi-

ness. That year the company also acquired a pet distributor its first move into pet supplies.

To pay down debt associated with the Weyerhaeuser acquisition the company (then officially known as Central Garden & Pet Company) went public in 1993 (a 1992 IPO was withdrawn when a warehouse fire damaged inventory). With the capital for growth Central continued to acquire other distributors (from early 1993 to early 1994 it acquired six distributors with about $70 million in sales).

HISTORY

Central Garden & Pet Company's roots go back to 1955 when it was founded as a small California distributor of lawn and garden supplies. After nearly three decades of unremarkable growth it was purchased in 1980 by William Brown a former VP of finance at camera maker Vivitar. The company acquired small distributors but let them operate autonomously. By 1987 Central had sales of $25 million with distribution in California.

The company's first major acquisition was the result of a restructuring of forestry giant Weyerhaeuser which had diversified into insurance home building and diapers but was selling noncore divisions to focus solely on timber. It sold Weyerhaeuser Garden Supply to Central in 1990 for $32 million.

Overnight Central became a national powerhouse with 25 distribution centers serving 38 states. In 1991 sales reached $280 million of which acquired operations accounted for nearly 70%. The purchase also gave Central 10 high-volume retail customers — including Costco Kmart and Wal-Mart — which accounted for half of its business. That year the company also acquired a pet distributor its first move into pet supplies.

To pay down debt associated with the Weyerhaeuser acquisition the company (then officially known as Central Garden & Pet Company) went public in 1993 (a 1992 IPO was withdrawn when a warehouse fire damaged inventory). With the capital for growth Central continued to acquire other distributors (from early 1993 to early 1994 it acquired six distributors with about $70 million in sales).

In 1994 the company's largest supplier Solaris (then a unit of Monsanto and maker of Ortho and Roundup products) decided to bypass Central as its distributor and sell products directly. Solaris products accounted for nearly 40% of the company's sales and revenues dipped in 1995. However that year Solaris decided that self-distribution was too difficult and made Central its exclusive distributor. Total sales increased about 65% in 1996.

Broadening its pet supply distribution network in 1996 Central paid $33 million for Kenlin Pet Supply the East Coast's largest pet distributor and Longhorn Pet Supply in Texas. The following year the company bought Four Paws Products and Sandoz Agro.

In 1997 Central paid $132 million for TFH Publications one of the nation's largest producers of pet books and maker of Nylabone dog snacks and Kaytee Products a maker of bird seed. It added Pennington Seed a maker of grass and bird seed in 1998.

The company broadened its scope in 1999 with the purchase of Norcal Pottery Products. It also tried to buy Solaris but that year Monsanto sold its Solaris unit to grass firm The Scotts Company

(now Scotts Miracle-Gro). In a familiar refrain for Central Scotts then decided to shift partially toward self-distribution costing Central between $200 million and $250 million in annual sales; Scotts would completely sever distribution ties with Central the following year leading to countering lawsuits.

Central said in early 2000 it would spin off its lawn and garden distribution business to shareholders but the company abandoned the plan less than a year later. In March 2000 the company acquired AMDRO fire ant killer and IMAGE a weed herbicide from American Home Products (now Wyeth) for $28 million. Later that year Central purchased All-Glass Aquarium Company a manufacturer and marketer of aquariums and related products.

As a result of no longer being the distributor of Scotts products Central closed 13 of its distribution centers in 2001. Central announced the next year that it would restate its financial results for 1998 through 2002. The company said the changes would improve fiscal 2001 net results by $2 million but decrease net results by $1.7 million in 2000 $0.3 million in 1999 and $0.1 million in 1998. Also that year Mars' Kal Kan Division and Arch Chemicals stopped using Central as a distributor.

In 2003 Central acquired a 49% stake in E. M. Matson a lawn and garden manufacturer in the western US.

In 2004 the company completed a menagerie's worth of acquisitions: Kent Marine an aquarium supplements maker; New England Pottery which sells decorative pottery and Christmas items (from Heritage Partners); Lawrence plc's pet products division Interpet; KRB Seed which does business as Budd Seed (Rebel and Palmer's Pride grass-seed brands); and Energy Savers Unlimited which distributes aquarium lighting systems and related environmental controls and conditioners.

It continued along the same path throughout the rest of the decade acquiring Gulfstream Home & Garden (garden products) Pets International (small animal and specialty pet supplies) Farnam Companies (animal health products) and the assets of family-owned pet food maker Breeder's Choice. The firm also increased its stakes in insect control products supplier Tech Pac (from 20% to 80%) and garden controls manufacturer Matson (from 50% to full ownership).

EXECUTIVES

President - Pet Consumer Products, John Hanson, $501,235 total compensation
Independent Director, Christopher Metz
Independent Director, Michael Griffith
Independent Director, Brendan Dougher
Director, Lisa Coleman
Independent Director, Courtnee Chun
General Counsel, Secretary, George Yuhas, $465,461 total compensation
Chief Executive Officer, Director, Timothy Cofer, $992,404 total compensation
Independent Director, Michael Edwards
President, Garden Branded Business, John Walker, $512,733 total compensation
Lead Independent Director, Mary Springer
Independent Director, John Ranelli
Chief Financial Officer, Nicholas Lahanas, $466,988 total compensation
Chairman Of The Board, William Brown, $246,642 total compensation
Auditors: DELOITTE & TOUCHE LLP

LOCATIONS

HQ: Central Garden & Pet Co
1340 Treat Boulevard, Suite 600, Walnut Creek, CA
94597
Phone: 925 948-4000
Web: www.central.com

PRODUCTS/OPERATIONS

2018 Sales

	$ mil.	% of total
Pet Products		
Dog and cat products	444.4	20
Other pet products	896.5	40
Garden Products		
Garden controls and fertilizer products	345.7	16
Other garden supplies	528.8	24
Total	**2,215.4**	**100**

Selected Products and Brands

Pet products
  Aquatics
  All-Glass Aquarium
  Kent Marine
  Bird and small animal
  Kaytee
  Dog and cat
  Four Paws
  Interpet
  Nylabone
  Pet Select
  TFH
  Insect control and animal health
  Strike
  Zodiac
Garden products
  Garden decor and pottery
  New England Pottery
  Grass seed
  Lofts Seed
  Pennington
  Rebel
  Weed insect and pest control
  AMDRO
  IMAGE
  Lilly Miller
  Over'n Out
  Sevin
  Wild bird
  Kaytee
  Pennington

COMPETITORS

CONCORD RESOURCES LIMITED
MCBRIDE PLC
QUALITY KING DISTRIBUTORS INC.
SOCIETE INTERNATIONALE DE PLANTATIONS
 D'HEVEAS
SPECTRUM BRANDS HOLDINGS INC.
SPECTRUM BRANDS LEGACY INC.
THE SCOTTS MIRACLE-GRO COMPANY
TRAVIS PERKINS PLC
UNITED NATURAL FOODS INC.

HISTORICAL FINANCIALS

Company Type: Public

Income Statement   FYE: September 25

	REVENUE ($ mil.)	NET INCOME ($ mil.)	NET PROFIT MARGIN	EMPLOYEES
09/21	3,303.6	151.7	4.6%	7,000
09/20	2,695.5	120.6	4.5%	6,300
09/19	2,383.0	92.7	3.9%	5,800
09/18	2,215.3	123.5	5.6%	5,400
09/17	2,054.4	78.8	3.8%	4,100
Annual Growth	12.6%	17.8%	—	14.3%

2021 Year-End Financials

Debt ratio: 38.0%
Return on equity: 13.2%
Cash ($ mil.): 439.5
Current ratio: 2.96
Long-term debt ($ mil.): 1,184.6

No. of shares (mil.): 55.2
Dividends
  Yield: —
  Payout: —
Market value ($ mil.): 2,327.0

	STOCK PRICE ($) FY Close	P/E High/Low	Earnings	Dividends	Book Value
09/21	42.14	19 12	2.75	0.00	22.13
09/20	34.23	18 10	2.20	0.00	19.65
09/19	27.95	22 13	1.61	0.00	17.73
09/18	33.14	17 14	2.32	0.00	16.49
09/17	37.19	24 14	1.52	0.00	12.26
Annual Growth	3.2%	— —	16.0%	—	15.9%

Central Valley Community Bancorp

Central Valley Community Bancorp is the holding company for Central Valley Community Bank which offers individuals and businesses traditional banking services through about 25 offices in California's San Joaquin Valley. Deposit products include checking savings and money market accounts; IRAs; and CDs. The bank founded in 1979 offers credit card services and originates a variety of loans including residential and commercial mortgage Small Business Administration and agricultural loans. Through Central Valley Community Insurance Services it markets health property and casualty insurance products primarily to business customers.

EXECUTIVES

Executive Vice President, Chief Credit Officer Of The Company And Bank, Patrick Luis
Executive Vice President, Market Executive Of The Bank, A. Kenneth Ramos, $205,077 total compensation
Independent Vice Chairman Of The Board Of The Company And The Bank, Daniel Cunningham
Independent Chairman Of The Board, Daniel Doyle
Executive Vice President, Chief Banking Officer, Blaine Lauhon, $205,077 total compensation
Executive Vice President, Chief Administrative Officer Of The Bank, Teresa Gilio
Chief Financial Officer, Executive Vice President, David Kinross, $238,308 total compensation
President, Chief Executive Officer, James Kim, $244,346 total compensation
Auditors: Crowe LLP

LOCATIONS

HQ: Central Valley Community Bancorp
7100 N. Financial Dr., Suite 101, Fresno, CA 93720
Phone: 559 298-1775
Web: www.cvcb.com

COMPETITORS

LIBERTY CAPITAL INC.
MBANK
SOUTHERN COMMUNITY FINANCIAL CORPORATION

HISTORICAL FINANCIALS

Company Type: Public

Income Statement   FYE: December 31

	ASSETS ($ mil.)	NET INCOME ($ mil.)	INCOME AS % OF ASSETS	EMPLOYEES
12/20	2,004.1	20.3	1.0%	287
12/19	1,596.7	21.4	1.3%	288
12/18	1,537.8	21.2	1.4%	290
12/17	1,661.6	14.0	0.8%	316
12/16	1,443.3	15.1	1.1%	287
Annual Growth	8.6%	7.6%	—	0.0%

2020 Year-End Financials

Return on assets: 1.1%
Return on equity: 8.5%
Long-term debt ($ mil.): —
No. of shares (mil.): 12.5
Sales ($ mil): 79.8

Dividends
  Yield: 2.9%
  Payout: 27.1%
Market value ($ mil.): 186.0

	STOCK PRICE ($) FY Close	P/E High/Low	Earnings	Dividends	Book Value
12/20	14.89	13 7	1.62	0.44	19.59
12/19	21.67	14 11	1.59	0.43	17.48
12/18	18.87	14 11	1.54	0.31	15.98
12/17	20.18	21 16	1.10	0.24	15.30
12/16	19.96	15 8	1.33	0.24	13.51
Annual Growth	(7.1%)	— —	5.1%	16.4%	9.7%

Cerence Inc

Auditors: BDO USA, LLP

LOCATIONS

HQ: Cerence Inc
1 Burlington Woods Drive, Suite 301A, Burlington, MA 01803
Phone: 857 362-7300
Web: www.cerence.com

HISTORICAL FINANCIALS

Company Type: Public

Income Statement   FYE: September 30

	REVENUE ($ mil.)	NET INCOME ($ mil.)	NET PROFIT MARGIN	EMPLOYEES
09/21	387.1	45.8	11.9%	1,700
09/20	329.6	(20.6)	—	1,500
09/19	303.3	100.2	33.1%	1,400
09/18	276.9	5.8	2.1%	1,300
09/17	244.7	47.2	19.3%	0
Annual Growth	12.2%	(0.7%)	—	—

2021 Year-End Financials

Debt ratio: 15.9%
Return on equity: 4.6%
Cash ($ mil.): 128.4
Current ratio: 1.74
Long-term debt ($ mil.): 265.0

No. of shares (mil.): 38.0
Dividends
  Yield: —
  Payout: —
Market value ($ mil.): 3,655.0

	STOCK PRICE ($) FY Close	P/E High/Low	Earnings	Dividends	Book Value
09/21	96.11	109 40	1.17	0.00	27.14
09/20	48.87	— —	(0.57)	0.00	26.00
Annual Growth	96.7%		—	—	4.4%

CF Bankshares Inc

Central Federal Corporation is the holding company for CFBank. Traditionally a retail-focused savings and loan CFBank has added business banking commercial real estate and business lending to its foundation. It now serves not only local individuals but also businesses through five branches in eastern Ohio and the state capital Columbus. Its deposit products include checking savings NOW and money market accounts as well as CDs. Commercial commercial real estate and multifamily residential mortgages represent nearly 80% of the company's loan portfolio. Single-family mortgages make up about 13% of loans. CFBank traces its roots to 1892.

EXECUTIVES

Independent Director, Thomas Ash
President, Chief Executive Officer Of The Company And Cfbank, Timothy O'Dell, $375,000 total compensation
Independent Chairman Of The Board Of The Company And The Bank, Robert Hoeweler
Independent Director, James Frauenberg
Independent Director, Edward Cochran
Chief Commercial Banking Officer Of Cfbank, Bradley Ringwald
Executive Vice President And Chief Financial Officer, Kevin Beerman, $140,335 total compensation
Auditors: BKD, LLP

LOCATIONS

HQ: CF Bankshares Inc
7000 North High Street, Worthington, OH 43085
Phone: 614 334-7979　　**Fax:** 614 334-7980
Web: www.CFBankonline.com

COMPETITORS

ANCHOR BANCORP WISCONSIN INC.
DNB FINANCIAL CORPORATION
EASTERN VIRGINIA BANKSHARES INC.
FIRST PULASKI NATIONAL CORPORATION
NEFFS BANCORP INC.
PRINCETON NATIONAL BANCORP INC.
THE COMMUNITY FINANCIAL CORPORATION

HISTORICAL FINANCIALS
Company Type: Public

Income Statement				FYE: December 31
	ASSETS ($ mil.)	NET INCOME ($ mil.)	INCOME AS % OF ASSETS	EMPLOYEES
12/20	1,477.0	29.6	2.0%	177
12/19	880.5	9.6	1.1%	125
12/18	665.0	4.2	0.6%	95
12/17	481.4	1.3	0.3%	66
12/16	436.1	1.6	0.4%	64
Annual Growth	35.7%	106.5%	—	29.0%

2020 Year-End Financials

Return on assets: 2.5%
Return on equity: 30.9%
Long-term debt ($ mil.): —
No. of shares (mil.): 6.5
Sales ($ mil): 102.3
Dividends
　Yield: 0.1%
　Payout: 0.7%
Market value ($ mil.): 116.0

	STOCK PRICE ($) FY Close	P/E High/Low		PER SHARE ($) Earnings	Dividends	Book Value
12/20	17.69	4	2	4.47	0.03	16.79
12/19	13.95	7	6	2.03	0.00	15.00
12/18	11.69	16	2	1.00	0.00	10.51
12/17	2.75	14	7	0.22	0.00	9.48
12/16	1.75	7	4	0.28	0.00	13.26
Annual Growth	78.3%	—		—100.8%	—	6.1%

ChampionX Corp

Auditors: PricewaterhouseCoopers LLP

LOCATIONS

HQ: ChampionX Corp
2445 Technology Forest Blvd., Building 4, 12th Floor, The Woodlands, TX 77381
Phone: 281 403-5772
Web: www.apergy.com

HISTORICAL FINANCIALS
Company Type: Public

Income Statement				FYE: December 31
	REVENUE ($ mil.)	NET INCOME ($ mil.)	NET PROFIT MARGIN	EMPLOYEES
12/21	3,074.9	113.3	3.7%	7,000
12/20	1,900.0	(743.9)	—	6,600
12/19	1,131.2	52.1	4.6%	3,000
12/18	1,216.6	94.0	7.7%	3,300
12/17	1,009.5	110.6	11.0%	3,100
Annual Growth	32.1%	0.6%	—	22.6%

2021 Year-End Financials

Debt ratio: 20.5%
Return on equity: 6.6%
Cash ($ mil.): 251.6
Current ratio: 1.82
Long-term debt ($ mil.): 697.6
No. of shares (mil.): 202.9
Dividends
　Yield: —
　Payout: —
Market value ($ mil.): 4,101.0

	STOCK PRICE ($) FY Close	P/E High/Low		PER SHARE ($) Earnings	Dividends	Book Value
12/21	20.21	53	27	0.54	0.00	8.73
12/20	15.30	—	—	(5.01)	0.00	8.11
12/19	33.78	64	36	0.67	0.00	13.33
12/18	27.08	37	22	1.21	0.00	12.65
Annual Growth	(9.3%) (11.6%)	—	—	(23.6%)	—	—

ChannelAdvisor Corp

ChannelAdvisor's proprietary software-as-a-service or SaaS cloud platform helps brands and retailers worldwide improve their online performance by expanding sales channels connecting with consumers around the world optimizing their operations for peak performance and providing actionable analytics to improve competitiveness. The company offers software and support services for brands and retailer worldwide looking for greater product visibility and brand management in marketplaces (such as eBay Amazon and Google) comparison shopping sites (Google Shopping) search engines (Google and Bing) and their own Web stores. Founded in 2001 the company generates around three-quarters of sales domestically.

Operations
ChannelAdvisor offers SaaS solutions that enable clients to integrate manage and optimize the merchandise sales across disparate online channels. In addition the company facilitates improved collaboration between brands and the authorized resellers through solutions that deliver high value leads from brands to the resellers. It generates the majority of revenue from clients' usage of its SaaS solutions which are organized into modules. Each module integrates with a particular type of channel such as third-party marketplaces digital marketing websites and authorized reseller websites.

Overall ChannelAdvisor generates almost 75% of total revenue from Marketplaces some 15% from Digital Marketing and over 10% from other.

Geographic Reach
ChannelAdvisor maintains sales service support and research and development offices in various domestic and international locations. International sales account for about 25% of revenue; the rest is from the US.

The company is headquartered in Morrisville North Carolina.

Sales and Marketing
ChannelAdvisor sells services to brands and retailers as well as advertising agencies that use its solutions on behalf of their clients. The retailers generated some 60% of sales advertising agencies with about 35% while others account for the rest of sales.

ChannelAdvisor's advertising costs for the year 2020 2019 and 2018 were $3.5 million $4.2 million and $5.7 million respectively.

Financial Performance
The company's revenue for the year ended 2020 totaled $145.1 million a 12% increase from the previous year.

In 2020 the company had a net income of $18.8 million.

The company's cash at the end of 2020 was $71.5 million. Operating activities generated $34.3 million while investing activities used $13.2 million. Financing activities used another $1.5 million.

Strategy
ChannelAdvisor's business development team's mission is to expand its sales and market opportunities through strategic partner relationships. The company plans to continue to invest in initiatives to expand its strategic partnership base to further enhance its offerings for brands and retailers and to help support its indirect sales channel efforts. The goal of these strategic partnerships is to further improve the value of the company's platform for its customers and when possible provide ChannelAdvisor opportunities for incremental revenue streams.

Mergers and Acquisitions
In mid-2020 ChannelAdvisor acquired BlueBoard a leading e-commerce analytics company headquartered in Paris France for an undisclosed amount. By acquiring BlueBoard ChannelAdvisor continues to enhance its capabilities for brands seeking to accelerate e-commerce growth. ChannelAdvisor brings BlueBoard's solutions to market as ChannelAdvisor Brand Analytics to help multi-

channel brands manage online distribution improve visibility grow sales and protect the company's reputations by leveraging intelligence related to product assortment pricing brand product content reviews and search performance.

EXECUTIVES

Chief Executive Officer, Director, David Spitz, $411,000 total compensation
Independent Chairman Of The Board, Timothy Buckley
Chief Financial Officer, Treasurer, Richard Cornetta, $288,333 total compensation
Chief Operating Officer, Elizabeth Segovia, $325,000 total compensation
Independent Director, Marshall Heinberg
Vice President - Fp&a And Operations, Jeremy Allen
Vice President, Global Services, Amy Rumford
Director, Linda Crawford
Vice President, General Counsel, Kathryn Twiddy
Director, Himanshu Palsule
Vice President - Global Human Resources, Stephanie Levin
Independent Director, Joseph Cowan
Auditors: Ernst & Young LLP

LOCATIONS

HQ: ChannelAdvisor Corp
3025 Carrington Mill Boulevard, Morrisville, NC 27560
Phone: 919 228-4700
Web: www.channeladvisor.com

PRODUCTS/OPERATIONS

Selected Products & Services
Products
ChannelAdvisor stores (inventory management)
MarketplaceAdvisor (product listing and tracking across marketplace sites)
RichFX (rich media design and management)
SearchAdvisor (keyword and bid management across search engine sites)
ShoppingAdvisor (product performance and reporting across comparison shopping sites for retail marketing managers)
Services
CAGuided (e-commerce campaign training for any-sized retailer)
CAManaged (outsourced e-commerce campaign management for large retailers)
CASelect (outsourced e-commerce campaign management for small to mid-sized retailers)

COMPETITORS

CRITEO	MULESOFT INC.
DEMANDWARE LLC	OKTA INC.
EXACTTARGET LLC	SALESFORCE.COM INC.
FIVE9 INC.	TECHTARGET INC.
HUBSPOT INC.	VERINT SYSTEMS INC.
MICROSTRATEGY INCORPORATED	YEXT INC.

HISTORICAL FINANCIALS

Company Type: Public

Income Statement — FYE: December 31

	REVENUE ($ mil.)	NET INCOME ($ mil.)	NET PROFIT MARGIN	EMPLOYEES
12/21	167.7	47.2	28.1%	846
12/20	145.0	18.8	13.0%	725
12/19	129.9	3.4	2.7%	642
12/18	131.2	(7.6)	—	730
12/17	122.5	(16.5)	—	737
Annual Growth	8.2%	—	—	3.5%

2021 Year-End Financials

Debt ratio: —
Return on equity: 29.6%
Cash ($ mil.): 100.5
Current ratio: 2.97
Long-term debt ($ mil.): —
No. of shares (mil.): 30.1
Dividends
Yield: —
Payout: —
Market value ($ mil.): 745.0

	STOCK PRICE ($) FY Close	P/E High/Low		Earnings	Dividends	Book Value
12/21	24.68	18	10	1.50	0.00	6.23
12/20	15.98	33	7	0.63	0.00	4.48
12/19	9.04	113	70	0.12	0.00	3.55
12/18	11.35	—	—	(0.28)	0.00	3.28
12/17	9.00	—	—	(0.63)	0.00	3.08
Annual Growth	28.7%			—	—	19.3%

Charles & Colvard Ltd

Charles & Colvard hopes that it isn't just some shooting star. The company makes gemstones made from moissanite a diamond substitute created in laboratories. Composed of silicon and carbon moissanite (aka silicon carbide or SiC) is typically found in meteorites. Charles & Colvard makes its gemstones from SiC crystals purchased primarily from Cree Inc. and Swedish company Norstel. Charles & Colvard markets its gemstones through two distributors (Stuller and Rio Grande) and jewelry manufacturers such as K&G Creations Reeves Park and Samuel Aaron International.

EXECUTIVES

President, Chief Executive Officer, Director, Don O'Connell, $335,000 total compensation
Chief Financial Officer, Treasurer, Clint Pete, $254,322 total compensation
Independent Director, Anne Butler
Independent Director, Benedetta Casamento
Independent Chairman Of The Board, Neal Goldman
Auditors: BDO USA, LLP

LOCATIONS

HQ: Charles & Colvard Ltd
170 Southport Drive, Morrisville, NC 27560
Phone: 919 468-0399
Web: www.charlesandcolvard.com

COMPETITORS

AARON GROUP LLC	RICHLINE GROUP INC.
HARRY WINSTON INC.	

HISTORICAL FINANCIALS

Company Type: Public

Income Statement — FYE: June 30

	REVENUE ($ mil.)	NET INCOME ($ mil.)	NET PROFIT MARGIN	EMPLOYEES
06/21	39.2	12.8	32.7%	51
06/20	29.1	(6.1)	—	48
06/19	32.2	2.2	7.1%	63
06/18*	13.1	(1.2)	—	60
12/17	27.0	(0.4)	—	76
Annual Growth	9.8%	—	—	(9.5%)

*Fiscal year change

2021 Year-End Financials

Debt ratio: —
Return on equity: 26.3%
Cash ($ mil.): 21.4
Current ratio: 6.36
Long-term debt ($ mil.): —
No. of shares (mil.): 29.9
Dividends
Yield: —
Payout: —
Market value ($ mil.): 89.0

	STOCK PRICE ($) FY Close	P/E High/Low		Earnings	Dividends	Book Value
06/21	2.98	8	2	0.42	0.00	1.86
06/20	0.73	—	—	(0.22)	0.00	1.43
06/19	1.58	24	8	0.10	0.00	1.63
06/18*	1.07	—	—	(0.06)	0.00	1.56
12/17	1.35	—	—	(0.02)	0.00	1.62
Annual Growth	21.9%			—	—	3.6%

*Fiscal year change

Charles River Laboratories International Inc.

Charles River Laboratories International provides early-stage contract research organization (CRO) services to pharmaceutical firms and other manufacturers and institutions. The company provides contract drug discovery services including target identification and toxicology through its Discovery and Safety Assessment segment. Its Research Models and Services (RMS) segment is a leading global provider of research models (lab rats and mice) bred specifically for use in medical testing. The Manufacturing Support unit offers biologics testing and chicken eggs for vaccines. Charles River has operations in over 20 countries but generates around 55% of sales in the US. Charles River began operating in 1947 and went public in 2000.

Operations

Charles River operates through three reportable segments: Discovery and Safety Assessment (DSA) Research Models and Services (RMS) and Manufacturing Support.

Its DSA reportable segment (nearly 65% of total revenue) includes services required to take a drug through the early development process including discovery services which are non-regulated services to assist clients with the identification screening and selection of a lead compound for drug development and regulated and non-regulated (GLP and non-GLP) safety assessment services.

The RMS reportable segment (some 20%) includes the Research Models Research Model Services and Research Products businesses. Research Models includes the commercial production and sale of small research models as well as the supply of large research models. Research Model Services includes: Genetically Engineered Models and Services (GEMS) which performs contract breeding and other services associated with genetically engineered models; Research Animal Diagnostic Services (RADS) which provides health monitoring and diagnostics services related to research models; and Insourcing Solutions (IS) which provides colony management of its clients' research operations (including recruitment training staffing and management services). Research Products supplies controlled consistent customized primary cells and blood components derived from normal and mobilized peripheral blood bone marrow and cord blood.

Manufacturing reportable segment (more than 15%) includes Microbial Solutions which provides in vitro (non-animal) lot-release testing products microbial detection products and species identification services; Biologics Testing Services (Biologics) which performs specialized testing of biologics; and Avian Vaccine Services (Avian) which supplies specific-pathogen-free chicken eggs and chickens.

Overall its services accounts more than 75% of total revenue while products accounts the remainders.

Geographic Reach
Based in Wilmington Massachusetts Charles River has over 100 locations in over 20 countries. While sales in the US account for around 55% of its annual revenue the company is growing its operations in other key markets including Europe (nearly 30% of sales) Canada (about 10%) and the Asia/Pacific region (around 5%).

Sales and Marketing
Charles River provides its products and services directly to customers around the globe. Clients include small midsized and large pharmaceutical biotechnology agricultural chemical and life science companies as well as educational health care and government institutions. It also supplies research models to other CROs.

The company primarily sells its products and services through a direct sales force and business development professionals in North America Europe and the Asia/Pacific region. In some markets sales are assisted by international distributors and agents. Marketing efforts include organizing scientific conferences publishing scientific papers conducting webinars and presenting at trade shows. It also participates in online and direct mail marketing.

Financial Performance
The company's revenue totaled $2.9 billion in 2020 a 12% increase from the previous year's revenue of $2.6 billion. This was primarily due to a higher sales volume in the company's service revenue.

In 2020 the company had a net income of $365.3 million a 44% increase from the previous year's net income of $254.1 million.

The company's cash at the end of 2020 was $233.1 million. Operating activities generated $546.6 million while investing activities used $601.5 million mainly for acquisition of businesses and assets. Financing activities provided another $47.2 million.

Strategy
The company's strategy is to deliver a comprehensive and integrated portfolio of drug discovery and non-clinical development products services and solutions to support clients' discovery and early-stage drug research process development scale up and manufacturing efforts and enable them to bring new and improved therapies to market faster and more cost effectively. Separately through its various Manufacturing segment businesses the company aims to be the premier provider of products and services that ensure its clients produce and release their products safely.

The company believes that it has certain competitive advantages in executing this strategy because of its continuing focus on the following:

Providing research models and associated services discovery research studies and services and comprehensive safety assessment studies in both regulated and non-regulated environments;

Offering a portfolio of products services and solutions that supports the process development scale up and quality control efforts of the biopharmaceutical industry;

Providing essential capabilities including biomarkers biologics medicinal chemistry in vitro screening in vivo pharmacology immunology pathology biologics process development testing microbial detection and identification and other specialty service areas that have high infrastructure costs or are cost-prohibitive for clients to maintain independently;

Committing to being a worldwide leader in the humane care of laboratory animals and implementation of the "3Rs" initiative (Replacement Reduction and Refinement); as well as

Maintaining scientific rigor and high-quality standards through management of key performance indicators and an intense focus on biosecurity and quality.

Mergers and Acquisitions
In mid-2021 Charles River acquired Vigene Biosciences Inc. for $292.5 million in cash. In addition to the initial purchase price the transaction includes additional payments of up to $57.5 million contingent on future performance. Based in Rockville Maryland Vigene Biosciences is a premier gene therapy contract development and manufacturing organization (CDMO) providing viral vector-based gene delivery solutions. The acquisition complements Charles River's existing cell and gene therapy contract manufacturing capabilities and establishes an end-to-end gene-modified cell therapy solution in the US. In addition the acquisition enables clients to seamlessly conduct analytical testing process development and manufacturing for advanced modalities with the same scientific partner facilitating their goal of driving greater efficiency and accelerating their speed to market.

In 2021 Charles River acquired UK-based Retrogenix Limited an early-stage contract research organization (CRO) providing specialized bioanalytical services utilizing its proprietary cell microarray technology. The acquisition of Retrogenix enhances Charles River's scientific expertise with additional large molecule and cell therapy discovery capabilities. Retrogenix provides the premier platform for off-target screening for preclinical safety assurance in CAR T cell therapies.

Also in 2021 Charles River completed the acquisition of Tennessee-based Cognate BioServices Inc. for approximately $875 million. Cognate BioServices is a premier cell and gene therapy contract development and manufacturing organization (CDMO) offering comprehensive manufacturing solutions for cell therapies as well as for production of plasmid DNA and other inputs in the CDMO value chain. The acquisition establishes Charles River as a premier scientific partner for cell and gene therapy development testing and manufacturing providing clients with an integrated solution from basic research and discovery through CGMP production.

In early 2021 Charles River acquired California-based Distributed Bio a next-generation antibody discovery company. The acquisition marks the culmination of an exclusive partnership between these companies that was initiated in October 2018. The acquisition of Distributed Bio expands Charles River's scientific capabilities with an innovative large-molecule discovery platform. The transaction combines Distributed Bio's antibody libraries and immuno-engineering platform with Charles River's extensive drug discovery and non-clinical development expertise to create an integrated end-to-end platform for therapeutic antibody and cell and gene therapy discovery and development.

In 2020 Charles River acquires Massachusetts-based Cellero (formerly Key Biologics and Astarte Biologics) a premier provider of cellular products for cell therapy developers and manufacturers worldwide. Cellero will complement Charles River's recent acquisition of HemaCare by enhancing the supply of critical biomaterials including a wide range of human-derived primary cell types to support the discovery development and manufacture of cell therapies. The purchase price for Cellero was $37.4 million in cash.

In early 2020 Charles River Laboratories International Inc. California-based acquired HemaCare Corporation a leader in the production of human-derived cellular products for the cell therapy market for approximately $380 million. HemaCare will become part of Charles River's Research Models and Services segment. Acquiring HemaCare expands Charles River's scientific capabilities in the emerging high-growth cell therapy sector creating a comprehensive portfolio of early-stage research and manufacturing support solutions to help cell therapy developers and manufacturers advance their critical programs from basic research and proof-of-concept to regulatory approval and commercialization.

Company Background
The company was founded in 1947 as Charles River Breeding Laboratories in Boston Massachusetts by Dr. Henry Foster. It began commercial pathogen-free rodent production in 1955 at its new headquarters in Wilmington Massachusetts. In 1966 it expanded overseas by opening an animal production facility in France.

The company was acquired by Bausch & Lomb in 1984. In 1997 Jim Foster purchased Charles River back from Bausch & Lomb. The company went public on the NYSE in 2000.

Acquisitions over the years included Argenta BioFocus Agilux Labs and Brains On-Line.

EXECUTIVES

Chairman Of The Board, President, Chief Executive Officer, James Foster, $1,354,971 total compensation

Lead Independent Director, George Milne

Corporate Executive Vice President And Chief Commercial Officer, William Barbo, $515,126 total compensation

Chief Operating Officer, Corporate Executive Vice President, Birgit Girshick, $475,329 total compensation

Independent Director, Richard Wallman

Corporate Executive Vice President, Corporate Development And Strategy, Joseph LaPlume, $489,858 total compensation

Independent Director, Richard Reese

Chief Financial Officer, Corporate Executive Vice President, David Smith, $599,152 total compensation

Independent Director, Virginia Wilson

Independent Director, Nancy Andrews

HOOVER'S HANDBOOK OF EMERGING COMPANIES 2022

Independent Director, George Llado
Independent Director, Deborah Kochevar
Independent Director, Martin Mackay
Auditors: PricewaterhouseCoopers LLP

LOCATIONS

HQ: Charles River Laboratories International Inc.
251 Ballardvale Street, Wilmington, MA 01887
Phone: 781 222-6000
Web: www.criver.com

PRODUCTS/OPERATIONS

2016 Sales

	$ mil.	% of total
Discovery and safety assessment	836.6	50
Research Models & Services	494.0	29
Manufacturing support	350.8	21
Total	**1,681.4**	**100**

Selected Services

Agrochemical & veterinary services
Antibody production services
Avian products & services
Biopharmaceutical services
Clinical trial services
Consulting & staffing services
Discovery & imaging services
Endotoxin & microbial detection
Equipment & instrumentation
Facilities design & management services
Genetic testing services
Genetically engineered models & services
In Vitro services
Pathology associates
Preclinical services
Program management
Regulatory navigator services
Research animal diagnostic services
Research animal models
Surgical model services

COMPETITORS

APTUIT LLC	MEDTOX SCIENTIFIC INC.
ARCADIA BIOSCIENCES INC.	OPKO HEALTH INC.
	PERKINELMER INC.
ARUP LABORATORIES INC	ROBIN A TECHNOLOGY REALISATIONS
BIO-TECHNE CORPORATION PLC	
KBR WYLE SERVICES LLC	SYNEOS HEALTH INC.
LABCORP DRUG DEVELOPMENT INC.	UNDERWRITERS LABORATORIES INC.

HISTORICAL FINANCIALS

Company Type: Public

Income Statement				FYE: December 25
	REVENUE ($ mil.)	**NET INCOME** ($ mil.)	**NET PROFIT MARGIN**	**EMPLOYEES**
12/21	3,540.1	390.9	11.0%	20,000
12/20	2,923.9	364.3	12.5%	18,400
12/19	2,621.2	252.0	9.6%	17,100
12/18	2,266.1	226.3	10.0%	14,700
12/17	1,857.6	123.3	6.6%	11,800
Annual Growth	**17.5%**	**33.4%**	**—**	**14.1%**

2021 Year-End Financials

Debt ratio: 37.9%	No. of shares (mil.): 50.4
Return on equity: 16.8%	Dividends
Cash ($ mil.): 241.2	Yield: —
Current ratio: 1.23	Payout: —
Long-term debt ($ mil.): 2,663.5	Market value ($ mil.): 18,637.0

STOCK PRICE ($) FY Close	P/E High/Low	PER SHARE ($) Earnings	Dividends	Book Value
12/21 369.20	59 32	7.60	0.00	50.21
12/20 251.71	34 13	7.20	0.00	42.49
12/19 151.93	29 20	5.07	0.00	33.40
12/18 111.72	29 21	4.62	0.00	27.33
12/17 109.45	45 29	2.54	0.00	22.05
Annual Growth 35.5%	— — 31.5%		—	22.8%

Chart Industries Inc

Chart Industries is a leading independent global manufacturer of highly engineered equipment servicing multiple applications in the Energy and Industrial Gas markets. Its unique product portfolio is used in every phase of the liquid gas supply chain including upfront engineering service and repair. Being at the forefront of the clean energy transition Chart is a leading provider of technology equipment and services related to liquefied natural gas hydrogen biogas and CO2 Capture amongst other applications. Chart's customers are mainly large multinational producers and distributors of hydrocarbon and industrial gases. The company generates more than half its sales in the US.

Operations

In 2020 Chart Industries changed its reportable segments to Cryo Tank Solutions Heat Transfer Systems Specialty Products and Repair Service & Leasing.

Chart Industries' Cryo Tank Solutions segment accounts for about 35% of total sales it designs and manufactures cryogenic solutions for the storage and delivery of cryogenic liquids used in industrial gas and LNG applications. Products include bulk microbulk and mobile equipment used in the storage distribution vaporization and application of industrial gases and certain hydrocarbons.

Heat Transfer Systems segment supplies mission critical engineered equipment and systems used in the separation liquefaction and purification of hydrocarbon and industrial gases that span gas-to-liquid applications. Products include brazed aluminum heat exchangers Core-in-Kettle heat exchangers cold boxes air cooled heat exchangers shell & tube heat exchangers axial cooling fans high pressure reactors and vessels along with associated process technologies.

Specialty Products segment (some 20%) supplies highly-engineered equipment used in specialty end-market applications including hydrogen LNG biogas CO2 Capture food and beverage aerospace lasers cannabis and water treatment among others.

Its Repair Service & Leasing segment (nearly 15%) provides installation service repair maintenance and refurbishment of cryogenic products globally in addition to providing equipment leasing solutions.

Geographic Reach

Headquartered in Ball Ground GA Chart Industries has over 25 locations from the US to Asia Australia India Europe and South America. Chart Industries sells its products worldwide but the US generates around 50% of sales and China less than 10%.

Sales and Marketing

Chart Industries' primary customers are large multinational producers and distributors of hydrocarbon and industrial gases?the company has more than 2000 customers worldwide. The company developed relationships with leading companies in the gas production gas distribution gas processing liquefied natural gas or LNG petroleum refining chemical industrial gas spaceflight over the road trucking manufacturing and hydrogen CO2 capture and other clean energy industries including Linde Air Liquide IVECO Air Products Shell Chevron ExxonMobil New Fortress Energy Samsung Plug Power SpaceX and Blue Origin.

It generates almost 65% of its sales in the energy application and more than 35% in the industrial gas application. Sales to its top ten customers accounted for more than 40% of total revenue.

Chart Industries markets its products and services through direct sales personnel and independent sales representatives and distributors. The company use independent sales representatives and distributors to market its products and services in certain foreign countries and in certain North American regions. These independent sales representatives supplement its direct sales force in dealing with language and cultural matters. Its domestic and foreign independent sales representatives earn commissions on sales which vary by product type.

The company's advertising costs of $2.7 million $4.0 million and $3.7 million for the years 2020 2019 and 2018 respectively

Financial Performance

Sales in 2020 decreased by $38.4 million from $1.22 billion to $1.18 billion or 3%. Heat Transfer Systems segment sales decreased by $71.9 million during 2020 as compared to 2019 primarily due to an industry-wide softness in demand for midstream and upstream compression equipment.

The company's net income for fiscal 2020 increased to $309.5 million compared from the prior year with $46.8 million.

Cash held by the company at the end of fiscal 2020 increased to $126.1 million. Cash provided by operations and investing activities were $172.7 million and $185.0 million respectively. Cash used for financing activities was $363.4 million mainly for repayments on term loan.

Mergers and Acquisitions

In early 2021 Chart Industries acquired Cryogenic Gas Technologies for $55 million in cash. Cryo Technologies is a global leader in custom engineered process systems to separate purify refrigerate liquefy and distribute high value industrial gases such as hydrogen helium argon and hydrocarbons with design capabilities for cold boxes for hydrogen and helium use. The combination of Chart and Cryo Technologies offers the market a unique one-stop shop for customers who want to liquefy and market the hydrogen molecule regardless of plant capacity but need an experienced and reliable equipment and process supplier for liquefaction and storage.

In late 2020 Chart Industries completed the acquisition of Sustainable Energy Solutions Inc (SES) for $20 million. SES's Cryogenic Carbon Capture (CCC) technology eliminates most emissions from fossil fuels while enabling better use of intermittent renewables through grid-scale energy storage. Coupling SES's CCC technology with its air-cooled heat exchangers brazed aluminum heat exchangers IPSMR refrigeration/liquefaction system and cryogenic storage and transport equipment creates a one-stop full solution option for those looking for integrated technology and equipment.

In the same year Chart Industries completed the acquisition of BlueInGreen LLC (BIG) a leading dissolved-gas expert providing custom-engineered solutions for water treatment and industrial process applications that delivers tangible economic social and environmental value. The stock purchase was completed for a purchase price of $20 million in cash. The combination of Chart equipment and BlueInGreen's technology enables solutions to efficiently deliver dissolved oxygen carbon dioxide and ozone into water results in a full dissolution package for water treatment.

In 2020 Chart Industries completed the acquisition of the Theodore Alabama cryogenic trailer and hydrogen trailer (transport) assets of Worthington Industries. This acquisition includes ownership of the Theodore Alabama manufacturing site all trailer-related intellectual property manufacturing capabilities equipment and repair backlog. This acquisition will produce strong synergies by combining Chart's deep knowledge of cryogenics and liquid hydrogen storage and handling with the Theodore operation's expertise and experience in the packaging and assembly of liquid hydrogen trailers. The addition of the trailer business to Chart's hydrogen equipment and solution offering expands its mobile equipment to larger sized transports and brings another location already certified by significant hydrogen customers.

HISTORY

In 1986 Arthur Holmes teamed up with his brother Charles to purchase ALTEC International a struggling maker of brazed aluminum heat exchangers that dated to 1949. The brothers turned ALTEC around and used it to acquire undervalued companies. From 1986 to 1991 they purchased storage and transportation equipment for liquefied gases and high-pressure cryogenic equipment including Greenville Tube Corporation (stainless steel tubing 1987); Process Engineering Inc. (cryogenic tanks 1990); and Process Systems International (cold boxes 1991). The Holmes brothers finally established a public holding company in 1992 and named it Chart Industries (for CHarles and ARThur).

EXECUTIVES

Independent Chairman Of The Board, Steven Krablin
Vice President - Risk And Treasury, Treasurer, Tom Pittet
Vice President And Chief Financial Officer, Joe Brinkman
President, Chief Executive Officer, Director, Jillian Evanko, $950,000 total compensation
Independent Director, Michael Molinini
Chief Human Resource Officer, Vice President, Gerald Vinci, $386,802 total compensation
Independent Director, David Sagehorn
Independent Director, Singleton Mcallister
Vice President, General Counsel, Secretary, Herbert Hotchkiss, $386,750 total compensation
Independent Director, Roger Strauch
Independent Director, Paula Harris
Auditors: DELOITTE & TOUCHE LLP

LOCATIONS

HQ: Chart Industries Inc
   3055 Torrington Drive, Ball Ground, GA 30107
Phone: 770 721-8800
Web: www.chartindustries.com

PRODUCTS/OPERATIONS

2017 sales

	$ mil.	% of total
Distribution & Storage	540.3	55
Energy & Chemical	225.6	23
BioMedical	222.9	22
Total	**988.8**	**100**

Selected Products

Products for Energy
   Air cooled heat exchangers
   Brazed aluminum heat exchangers
   Nitrogen rejection units
   LNG equipment and systems
Products for Industry
   Bulk storage tanks
   AirSep commercial products
   Bulk CO2 carbonation
   Flow measurement products
   Vacuum insulation pipe (VIP)
   Packaged gases
   Nitrogen dosing
   Vaporizers
Products for Life Sciences
   Aluminum dewars
   Stainless steel cryogenic freezers
Products for Respiratory Health
   CAIRE Inc. (subsidiary)
   SeQual oxygen products
   AirSep oxygen products

COMPETITORS

BHARAT HEAVY	ITT INC.
ELECTRICALS LIMITED	PAUL MUELLER COMPANY
CLARCOR INC.	RPC GROUP LIMITED
ENERFAB INC.	WORTHINGTON CYLINDER
ENTEGRIS INC.	CORPORATION

HISTORICAL FINANCIALS

Company Type: Public

Income Statement   FYE: December 31

	REVENUE ($ mil.)	NET INCOME ($ mil.)	NET PROFIT MARGIN	EMPLOYEES
12/20	1,177.1	308.1	26.2%	4,318
12/19	1,299.1	46.4	3.6%	5,743
12/18	1,084.3	88.0	8.1%	4,605
12/17	988.8	28.0	2.8%	4,424
12/16	859.1	28.2	3.3%	4,050
Annual Growth	8.2%	81.7%	—	1.6%

2020 Year-End Financials

Debt ratio: 17.2%   No. of shares (mil.): 36.1
Return on equity: 21.9%   Dividends
Cash ($ mil.): 125.1   Yield: —
Current ratio: 1.11   Payout: —
Long-term debt ($ mil.): 221.6   Market value ($ mil.): 4,262.0

	STOCK PRICE ($) FY Close	P/E High/Low		PER SHARE ($) Earnings	Dividends	Book Value
12/20	117.79	14	2	8.45	0.00	43.46
12/19	67.49	69	38	1.32	0.00	34.29
12/18	65.03	28	16	2.73	0.00	28.20
12/17	46.86	53	35	0.89	0.00	26.04
12/16	36.02	44	15	0.91	0.00	22.78
Annual Growth	34.5%	—	—	74.6%	—	17.5%

ChoiceOne Financial Services, Inc.

One choice for a place to park your money is ChoiceOne Financial Services. The institution is the holding company for ChoiceOne Bank which has more than a dozen offices in the western part of Michigan's Lower Peninsula. The bank serves consumers and area businesses offering checking and savings accounts CDs investment planning and other services. Real estate loans including residential and commercial mortgages constitute more than two-thirds of the company's loan portfolio. Agricultural consumer and business loans help to round out the bank's lending activities. ChoiceOne Financial Services sells life health and disability coverage through its ChoiceOne Insurance Agencies subsidiaries.

EXECUTIVES

Senior Vice President, Senior Trust Officer, Steven DeVolder
Senior Vice President - Human Resources Of Choiceone Bank, Heather Brolick
Director, Bradley McGinnis
Chairman Of The Board, Jack Hendon
Independent Director, Nels Nyblad
Chief Executive Officer, Director, Kelly Potes, $360,000 total compensation
Senior Vice President, Chief Credit Officer, Lee Braford, $127,250 total compensation
Independent Director, Roxanne Page
Independent Director, Keith Brophy
Director, Greg Armock
Independent Director, Patrick Cronin
Independent Director, Eric Burrough
Independent Director, Gregory McConnell
Director, Bruce Cady
Independent Director, David Bush
Independent Director, Harold Burns
President, Director, Michael Burke, $310,000 total compensation
Senior Vice President, Chief Lending Officer Of Choiceone Bank, Bradley Henion, $169,423 total compensation
Senior Vice President, Chief Information Officer, Shelly Childers
Senior Vice President, Senior Lender, Peter Batistoni
Auditors: Plante & Moran, PLLC

LOCATIONS

HQ: ChoiceOne Financial Services, Inc.
   109 East Division Street, Sparta, MI 49345
Phone: 616 887-7366
Web: www.choiceone.com

COMPETITORS

CITIZENS FINANCIAL	MACKINAC FINANCIAL
SERVICES INC.	CORPORATION
FIRST COMMUNITY	
CORPORATION	

HOOVER'S HANDBOOK OF EMERGING COMPANIES 2022

81

HISTORICAL FINANCIALS

Company Type: Public

Income Statement				FYE: December 31
	ASSETS ($ mil.)	NET INCOME ($ mil.)	INCOME AS % OF ASSETS	EMPLOYEES
12/20	1,919.3	15.6	0.8%	359
12/19	1,386.1	7.1	0.5%	339
12/18	670.5	7.3	1.1%	174
12/17	646.5	6.1	1.0%	173
12/16	607.3	6.0	1.0%	160
Annual Growth	33.3%	26.5%	—	22.4%

2020 Year-End Financials

Return on assets: 0.9%
Return on equity: 7.4%
Long-term debt ($ mil.): —
No. of shares (mil.): 7.8
Sales ($ mil): 78.4

Dividends
Yield: 2.6%
Payout: 39.6%
Market value ($ mil.): 240.0

	STOCK PRICE ($) FY Close	P/E High/Low		PER SHARE ($) Earnings	Dividends	Book Value
12/20	30.81	16	8	2.07	0.82	29.15
12/19	31.96	21	16	1.58	1.40	26.52
12/18	25.00	15	11	2.02	0.71	22.25
12/17	23.80	14	13	1.70	0.64	21.14
12/16	23.75	14	13	1.68	0.62	19.84
Annual Growth	6.7%	—	—	5.4%	7.4%	10.1%

CIB Marine Bancshares Inc

CIB Marine Bancshares is semper fi to its banking strategy. The company owns CIBM Bank which operates in the Indianapolis Milwaukee and Phoenix markets. Through some 20 branches the bank caters to individuals and small-and midsized-business customers offering checking and savings accounts ATM and debit cards CDs and IRAs. The company's loan portfolio mainly consists of commercial mortgages business loans and commercial real estate construction loans. CIB Marine Bancshares emerged from Chapter 11 bankruptcy protection in early 2010.

EXECUTIVES

Chief Credit Officer, Paul Melnick, $154,231 total compensation
Chairman Of The Board, Mark Elste
Independent Director, Charles Baker
Director, JoAnn Cotter
Director, Gina Cocking
Director, Rhonda Hopps
Independent Director, Willard Bunn
Chief Financial Officer, Patrick Straka, $174,481 total compensation
Executive Vice President, General Counsel, Secretary, Daniel Rasmussen, $159,385 total compensation
Director, John Hickey, $134,532 total compensation
Independent Director, Gary Longman
President, Chief Executive Officer, Director, J. Brian Chaffin

Independent Director, Charles Mires
Independent Director, Ronald Rhoades
Auditors: Crowe LLP

LOCATIONS

HQ: CIB Marine Bancshares Inc
19601 West Bluemound Road, Brookfield, WI 53045
Phone: 262 695-6010 **Fax:** 630 735-2841
Web: www.cibmarine.com

COMPETITORS

AKBANK TURK ANONIM BANCORPORATION SIRKETI
CAPITAL BANK CORPORATION
CENTRAL VIRGINIA BANKSHARES INC.
DCB FINANCIAL CORP
FREMONT
KRUNG THAI BANK PUBLIC COMPANY LIMITED
PACIFIC FINANCIAL CORPORATION
SURUGA BANK LTD.

HISTORICAL FINANCIALS

Company Type: Public

Income Statement				FYE: December 31
	ASSETS ($ mil.)	NET INCOME ($ mil.)	INCOME AS % OF ASSETS	EMPLOYEES
12/20	750.9	8.1	1.1%	0
12/19	703.7	2.0	0.3%	0
12/18	721.2	3.3	0.5%	0
12/17	662.3	26.9	4.1%	183
12/16	653.5	4.0	0.6%	171
Annual Growth	3.5%	19.1%	—	—

2020 Year-End Financials

Return on assets: 1.1%
Return on equity: 8.2%
Long-term debt ($ mil.): —
No. of shares (mil.): 1.2
Sales ($ mil): 48.8

Dividends
Yield: —
Payout: —
Market value ($ mil.): 20.0

	STOCK PRICE ($) FY Close	P/E High/Low		PER SHARE ($) Earnings	Dividends	Book Value
12/20	15.80	3	0	3.79	0.00	81.77
12/19	1.39	1	1	1.05	0.00	75.09
12/18	1.54	0	0	2.25	0.00	74.85
12/17	1.42	0	0	11.10	0.00	80.12
12/16	1.08	0	0	1.65	0.00	57.50
Annual Growth	95.6%	—	—	23.1%	—	9.2%

Citizens & Northern Corp

Citizens & Northern Corp. is the holding company for Citizens & Northern (C&N) Bank Citizens & Northern Investment Corp. and Bucktail Life Insurance Company. Its primary business and largest subsidiary is C&N Bank a community bank that serves individuals and commercial customers in Pennsylvania and New York. The bank operates more than 25 branches and offers online and tele-banking services. The firm's other subsidiaries are Citizens & Northern Investment Corp. which provides investment services and Bucktail Life Insurance a provider of credit life and property/casualty

reinsurance. The bank holding company has assets of more than $1.3 billion.

Operations

C&N Bank offers standard deposit and loan products including savings accounts IRAs and mortgages. Its loan portfolio includes residential mortgages (more than half of total loans) commercial loans (more than 40%) and consumer loans (less than 5%).

Citizens & Northern Corporation also has a trust division which provides 401(k) plans retirement and estate planning and asset management services. Another arm offers personal and commercial insurance coverage as well as mutual funds annuities and other investment products.

Geographic Reach

Wellsboro Pennsylvania-based C&N Bank operates in nine counties in Pennsylvania and New York. Full-service branch offices are located in Bradford Cameron Lycoming McKean Potter Sullivan and Tioga counties in Pennsylvania and Steuben and Chemung counties in New York.

Financial Performance

Citizens & Northern revenue has remained relatively flat for the past few years primarily due to ongoing low interest rates and a slowdown of natural gas activities (which had boomed between 2009 and 2011) in the company's service area. Net income has been creeping downward over the same time period.

In 2017 revenue increased 2% to $58.4 million. Net interest income rose 4% that year as total outstanding loans increased while non-interest income rose 4% as assets under management increased by 13%. Debit card processing revenue also rose with a higher volume of transactions. However other revenue sources declined including net gains from sales of loans and interest on long-term borrowings.

Net income fell 15% to $13.4 million in 2017. This decline was largely due to an additional income tax provision of $2.2 million related to the 2017 Tax Act but operating expenses also increased that year further impacting the bottom line.

The company ended 2017 with $37 million in net cash $8.4 million more than it had at the end of 2016. Operating activities provided $19.4 million and financing activities provided $19.9 million. Investing activities used $30.9 million.

Strategy

These days bank customers make fewer (or no) trips to physical branch locations in favor of online and mobile banking and Citizens & Northern is investing in better serving its customers' changing behaviors. As such the company has made improvements to its brick-and-mortar banking locations while also enhancing its technological capabilities. For example in 2017 it upgraded its business banking platform allowing commercial customers to originate same-day Automated Clearing House electronic money transfer credits. The firm also tweaks or introduces new products such as the specialty package for not-for-profit organizations in launched in 2017. These efforts help Citizens & Northern to build its business by attracting new customers while deepening its relationships with existing customers.

The company also has geographic expansion in its sights as evidenced by the pending acquisition of Monument Bank in Bucks County Pennsylvania.

Mergers and Acquisitions

In 2018 Citizens & Northern agreed to buy Monument Bank for $42.7 million. Monument Bank operates two branches and a loan production office in Bucks County Pennsylvania which will bring Citizens & Northern's operations closer to Philadelphia.

Company Background

Citizens & Northern Bank was formed in 1971 following the consolidation of Northern National Bank of Wellsboro and Citizens National Bank of Towanda.

EXECUTIVES

Independent Director, Timothy Schoener
Independent Director, Bobbi Kilmer
Independent Director, Robert Loughery
Executive Vice President And Southeast Region President Of The Bank, Blair Rush
Director, Kate Shattuck
Independent Director, Aaron Singer
Treasurer, Executive Vice President And Chief Financial Officer Of The Bank, Mark Hughes, $290,000 total compensation
Executive Vice President, Chief Human Resources Officer Of The Bank, Tracy Watkins
Executive Vice President, Chief Digital Channels And Payments Officer Of The Bank, Shelley D'Haene
Executive Vice President And Chief Wealth Management Officer Of The Bank, Janice Ward
Executive Vice President, Chief Credit Officer Of Company & Bank, Stan Dunsmore, $187,000 total compensation
President, Chief Executive Officer, Director Of Citizens & Northern Bank And Corporation, J. Scovill, $475,000 total compensation
Executive Vice President, Chief Delivery Officer And Region President Of The Bank, Thomas Rudy, $117,957 total compensation
Executive Vice President And Chief Risk Management Officer Of The Bank, John Reber
Executive Vice President, Chief Revenue Officer Of The Bank, Harold Hoose, $245,000 total compensation
Independent Director, Clark Frame
Auditors: Baker Tilly US, LLP

LOCATIONS

HQ: Citizens & Northern Corp
90-92 Main Street, Wellsboro, PA 16901
Phone: 570 724-3411
Web: www.cnbankpa.com

PRODUCTS/OPERATIONS

2017 Sales

	$ mil.	% of total
Interest		
Interest & fees on loans	37.0	59
Income from available-for-sale securities	8.7	14
Interest on balances with depository institutions	0.2	-
Non-interest		
Trust & financial management	5.4	9
Service charges on deposit accounts	4.5	7
Interchange revenue on debit card transactions	2.2	4
Realized gains on available-for-sale securities net	0.3	1
Other	4.0	6
Adjustments	(3.9)	-
Total	**58.4**	**100**

COMPETITORS

COLUMBIA BANKING SYSTEM INC.
FIRST CITIZENS
MACATAWA BANK CORPORATION
S & T BANCORP INC.
BANCSHARES INC.
HANCOCK WHITNEY CORPORATION
WESTERN ALLIANCE BANCORPORATION

HISTORICAL FINANCIALS
Company Type: Public

Income Statement
FYE: December 31

	ASSETS ($ mil.)	NET INCOME ($ mil.)	INCOME AS % OF ASSETS	EMPLOYEES
12/21	2,327.6	30.5	1.3%	0
12/20	2,239.1	19.2	0.9%	0
12/19	1,654.1	19.5	1.2%	336
12/18	1,290.8	22.0	1.7%	299
12/17	1,276.9	13.4	1.1%	296
Annual Growth	**16.2%**	**22.8%**	—	—

2021 Year-End Financials

Return on assets: 1.3%
Return on equity: 10.1%
Long-term debt ($ mil.): —
No. of shares (mil.): 15.7
Sales ($ mil): 110.3

Dividends
Yield: 4.2%
Payout: 58.4%
Market value ($ mil.): 412.0

	STOCK PRICE ($) FY Close	P/E High/Low		PER SHARE ($) Earnings	Dividends	Book Value
12/21	26.12	14	10	1.92	1.11	19.13
12/20	19.84	22	12	1.30	1.08	18.84
12/19	28.25	20	16	1.46	1.18	17.82
12/18	26.43	16	12	1.79	1.08	16.02
12/17	24.00	24	20	1.10	1.04	15.43
Annual Growth	**2.1%**	—	—	**14.9%**	**1.6%**	**5.5%**

Citizens Community Bancorp Inc (MD)

Citizens Community Bancorp is the holding company for Citizens Community Federal a community bank with about 20 branches in Wisconsin southern Minnesota and northern Michigan. Serving consumers and businesses the bank offers standard deposit services such as savings checking money market and retirement accounts as well as a variety of loan products. The bank focuses its lending activities on one- to four-family mortgages which represent more than half of its loan portfolio. The bank also offers consumer loans such as auto and personal loans; it does not routinely make commercial loans. Founded in 1938 Citizens Community was a state-chartered credit union until 2001.

EXECUTIVES

Lead Independent Director, Richard McHugh
Independent Director, Michael Swenson
Independent Director, James Lang
Independent Director, James Moll
Independent Director, Francis Felber
Independent Director, Timothy Olson
Independent Director, Kristina Bourget
Chairman Of The Board, President, Chief Executive Officer, Stephen Bianchi, $352,425 total compensation
Chief Financial Officer, Principal Accounting Officer, Treasurer, James Broucek, $208,255 total compensation
Auditors: Eide Bailly LLP

LOCATIONS

HQ: Citizens Community Bancorp Inc (MD)
2174 EastRidge Center, Eau Claire, WI 54701
Phone: 715 836-9994
Web: www.ccf.us

COMPETITORS

BCSB BANCORP INC.
COMMUNITY SHORES BANK CORPORATION
FIRST CITIZENS BANCORPORATION INC.
FIRST NILES FINANCIAL INC.
HFB FINANCIAL CORPORATION
INTRUST FINANCIAL CORPORATION
NORTHEAST COMMUNITY BANCORP INC.
SOUTHCOAST FINANCIAL CORPORATION
UNITED COMMUNITY BANCORP
UNITY BANCORP INC.
VOLUNTEER BANCORP INC
YAKIMA FEDERAL SAVINGS & LOAN ASSOCIATION

HISTORICAL FINANCIALS
Company Type: Public

Income Statement
FYE: December 31

	ASSETS ($ mil.)	NET INCOME ($ mil.)	INCOME AS % OF ASSETS	EMPLOYEES
12/20	1,649.1	12.7	0.8%	251
12/19	1,531.2	9.4	0.6%	288
12/18*	1,287.9	1.2	0.1%	265
09/18	975.4	4.2	0.4%	282
09/17	940.6	2.5	0.3%	224
Annual Growth	**15.1%**	**50.2%**	—	**2.9%**

*Fiscal year change

2020 Year-End Financials

Return on assets: 0.8%
Return on equity: 8.1%
Long-term debt ($ mil.): —
No. of shares (mil.): 11.0
Sales ($ mil): 82.9

Dividends
Yield: 1.9%
Payout: 18.4%
Market value ($ mil.): 120.0

	STOCK PRICE ($) FY Close	P/E High/Low		PER SHARE ($) Earnings	Dividends	Book Value
12/20	10.89	11	5	1.14	0.21	14.52
12/19	12.22	15	12	0.85	0.20	13.36
12/18*	10.90	117	88	0.12	0.36	12.62
09/18	14.00	20	18	0.58	0.20	12.45
09/17	13.95	30	23	0.46	0.16	12.48
Annual Growth	**(6.0%)**	—	—	**25.5%**	**7.0%**	**3.9%**

*Fiscal year change

Citizens Financial Services Inc

Citizens Financial Services is an upstanding resident of the financial community. The holding company for First Citizens National Bank serves north-central Pennsylvania's Tioga Potter and Bradford counties and southern New York. Through some 15 branches the bank offers checking savings time and deposit accounts as well as real estate commercial industrial residential and consumer loans. Residential mortgage loans account for more than half of the bank's total loan portfolio. The Trust and Investment division offers investment advice and employee benefits coordination as well as estate and retirement planning services. Insurance is offered through the First Citizen's Insurance Agency subsidiary.

EXECUTIVES

President, Chief Executive Officer, Director, Randall Black, $495,866 total compensation
Independent Chairman Of The Board, R. Lowell Coolidge
Senior Vice President - Information Systems Manager Of The Bank, Gregory Anna
Senior Vice President - Marketing Manager For The Bank, Kathleen Campbell
Senior Vice President - Wealth Management Division Manager Of The Bank, Robert Mosso
Treasurer, Director, Mickey Jones, $339,859 total compensation
Senior Vice President, Senior Lending Officer, Christopher Landis
Senior Vice President, Chief Retail Banking Officer, Jeffrey Carr, $145,000 total compensation
Executive Vice President, Chief Lending Officer, Jeffrey Wilson, $162,000 total compensation
Independent Director, Christopher Kunes
Independent Director, Robert Chappell
Independent Director, Roger Graham
Independent Director, Alletta Schadler
Independent Director, Thomas Freeman
Independent Director, Rinaldo DePaola
Independent Director, R. Joseph Landy
Independent Director, E. Gene Kosa
Executive Vice President, Director, David Richards, $254,400 total compensation
Vice President Of Human Resources / Training Manager, Amy Wood
Executive Vice President, Chief Credit Office, Zerick Cook
Senior Vice President - Southcentral Region Senior Lender For The Bank, Sean McKinney
Chief Financial Officer, Senior Vice President, Stephen Guillaume, $138,249 total compensation
Auditors: S.R. Snodgrass, P.C.

LOCATIONS

HQ: Citizens Financial Services Inc
15 South Main Street, Mansfield, PA 16933
Phone: 570 662-2121
Web: www.firstcitizensbank.com

COMPETITORS

MBT FINANCIAL CORP.   VOLUNTEER BANCORP INC

HISTORICAL FINANCIALS

Company Type: Public

Income Statement				FYE: December 31
	ASSETS ($ mil.)	NET INCOME ($ mil.)	INCOME AS % OF ASSETS	EMPLOYEES
12/20	1,891.6	25.1	1.3%	306
12/19	1,466.3	19.4	1.3%	268
12/18	1,430.7	18.0	1.3%	274
12/17	1,361.8	13.0	1.0%	273
12/16	1,223.0	12.6	1.0%	270
Annual Growth	11.5%	18.7%	—	3.2%

2020 Year-End Financials

Return on assets: 1.4%
Return on equity: 14.3%
Long-term debt ($ mil.): —
No. of shares (mil.): 3.9
Sales ($ mil): 81.7

Dividends
Yield: 3.4%
Payout: 29.4%
Market value ($ mil.): 222.0

	STOCK PRICE ($) FY Close	P/E High/Low		PER SHARE ($) Earnings	Dividends	Book Value
12/20	56.00	10	6	6.52	1.92	49.04
12/19	61.50	12	10	5.42	1.76	43.04
12/18	55.55	13	11	4.99	1.71	38.56
12/17	63.00	18	14	3.59	1.60	35.56
12/16	53.00	15	14	3.46	1.52	33.98
Annual Growth	1.4%			17.2%	6.0%	9.6%

City Holding Co.

City Holding conducts its principal activities through its wholly owned subsidiary City National Bank of West Virginia. City National offers full range of commercial banking services to corporation and other business customers and provides banking services to consumers including checking savings and money market accounts as well as certificates of deposit and individual retirement accounts. It also provides mortgage banking services and offers specialized services and expertise in the areas of wealth management trust investment and custodial services for commercial and individual customers. City Nationals operates more than 90 branches along the I-64 corridor from Lexington Kentucky through Lexington Virginia and along the I-81 corridor through the Shenandoah Valley from Lexington Virginia to Martinsburg West Virginia.

EXECUTIVES

Director, Gregory Burton
Chief Financial Officer, Executive Vice President Of The Company And City National Bank, David Bumgarner, $280,500 total compensation
Independent Director, William File
President, Chief Executive Officer, Director Of The Company And President, Chief Executive Officer Of City National Bank, Charles Hageboeck, $649,740 total compensation
Independent Director, Sharon Rowe
Independent Director, James Rossi
Independent Director, Tracy Hylton
Executive Vice President, Chief Administrative Officer And Chief Information Office, Jeffrey Dale Legge, $270,300 total compensation
Non-executive Independent Chairman Of The Board, C. Dallas Kayser
Senior Vice President Of Branch Banking For The Company And The Bank, Michael Quinlan, $173,409 total compensation
Director, Javier Reyes
Independent Director, Charles Fairchilds
Auditors: Crowe LLP

LOCATIONS

HQ: City Holding Co.
25 Gatewater Road, Charleston, WV 25313
Phone: 304 769-1100
Web: www.bankatcity.com

PRODUCTS/OPERATIONS

2014 Sales

	$ mil.	% of total
Interest		
Loans including fees	116.6	62
Investment securities & other	13.0	7
Noninterest		
Service charges	265.0	14
Bankcard revenue	15.1	8
Other	171.0	9
Total	**188.3**	**100**

COMPETITORS

BAKER BOYER BANCORP
BROADWAY BANCSHARES INC
COMMERCE NATIONAL FINANCIAL SERVICES INC.
CVB FINANCIAL CORP.
EAGLE BANCORP INC.
FIRST HORIZON CORPORATION
FIRSTMERIT CORPORATION
LYONS NATIONAL BANK
MIDSOUTH BANCORP INC.
OLD NATIONAL BANCORP
PARK NATIONAL CORPORATION
PEOPLES FINANCIAL SERVICES CORP.
S & T BANCORP INC.

HISTORICAL FINANCIALS

Company Type: Public

Income Statement				FYE: December 31
	ASSETS ($ mil.)	NET INCOME ($ mil.)	INCOME AS % OF ASSETS	EMPLOYEES
12/20	5,758.6	89.6	1.6%	926
12/19	5,018.7	89.3	1.8%	918
12/18	4,899.0	70.0	1.4%	891
12/17	4,132.2	54.3	1.3%	839
12/16	3,984.4	52.1	1.3%	847
Annual Growth	9.6%	14.5%	—	2.3%

2020 Year-End Financials

Return on assets: 1.6%
Return on equity: 13.1%
Long-term debt ($ mil.): —
No. of shares (mil.): 15.7
Sales ($ mil): 260.9

Dividends
Yield: 3.2%
Payout: 41.2%
Market value ($ mil.): 1,097.0

	STOCK PRICE ($) FY Close	P/E High/Low		PER SHARE ($) Earnings	Dividends	Book Value
12/20	69.55	15	10	5.55	2.28	44.47
12/19	81.95	15	12	5.42	2.16	40.36
12/18	67.59	18	14	4.49	1.91	36.29
12/17	67.47	21	17	3.48	1.75	32.17
12/16	67.60	20	12	3.45	1.71	29.25
Annual Growth	0.7%			12.6%	7.5%	11.0%

Civista Bancshares Inc

First Citizens Banc Corp. is the holding company for The Citizens Banking Company and its Citizens Bank and Champaign Bank divisions which together operate more than 30 branches in northern Ohio. The banks offer such deposit products as checking and savings accounts and CDs in addition to trust services. They concentrate on real estate lending with residential mortgages and commercial mortgages each comprising approximately 40% of the company's loan portfolio. The Citizens Banking Company's Citizens Wealth Management division provides financial planning brokerage insurance and investments through an agreement with third-party provider UVEST (part of LPL Financial).

EXECUTIVES

Senior Vice President, Controller, Todd Michel, $175,282 total compensation
Independent Director, Allen Nickles
Independent Director, Daniel White
Senior Vice President, Richard Dutton, $264,067 total compensation
Senior Vice President, John Betts
President, Chief Executive Officer, Director, Dennis Shaffer, $444,231 total compensation
Senior Vice President, Charles Parcher, $264,067 total compensation
Lead Independent Director, Dennis Murray
Independent Director, Julie Mattlin
Independent Director, William Ritzmann
Senior Vice President, General Counsel, Secretary, Lance Morrison
Independent Director, Harry Singer
Senior Vice President, Donna Waltz-Jaskolski
Independent Director, Thomas Depler
Senior Vice President, Paul Stark, $197,790 total compensation
Independent Director, Mary Oliver
Auditors: BKD, LLP

LOCATIONS

HQ: Civista Bancshares Inc
100 East Water Street, Sandusky, OH 44870
Phone: 419 625-4121

COMPETITORS

CHOICEONE FINANCIAL SERVICES INC.
COMMUNITY SHORES BANK CORPORATION
EMCLAIRE FINANCIAL CORP.
M&T BANK CORPORATION

HISTORICAL FINANCIALS

Company Type: Public

Income Statement
FYE: December 31

	ASSETS ($ mil.)	NET INCOME ($ mil.)	INCOME AS % OF ASSETS	EMPLOYEES
12/20	2,762.9	32.1	1.2%	459
12/19	2,309.5	33.8	1.5%	457
12/18	2,138.9	14.1	0.7%	432
12/17	1,525.8	15.8	1.0%	350
12/16	1,377.2	17.2	1.3%	337
Annual Growth	19.0%	16.9%	—	8.0%

2020 Year-End Financials

Return on assets: 1.2%
Return on equity: 9.4%
Long-term debt ($ mil.): —
No. of shares (mil.): 15.9
Sales ($ mil) 128.0
Dividends
Yield: 2.5%
Payout: 24.0%
Market value ($ mil.): 279.0

	STOCK PRICE ($) FY Close	P/E High/Low		PER SHARE ($) Earnings	Dividends	Book Value
12/20	17.53	12	6	2.00	0.44	22.02
12/19	24.00	11	8	2.01	0.42	19.78
12/18	17.42	23	15	1.02	0.32	19.16
12/17	22.00	16	13	1.28	0.25	18.09
12/16	19.43	10	5	1.57	0.22	16.49
Annual Growth	(2.5%)	—	—	6.2%	18.9%	7.5%

Civitas Resources Inc

Bonanza Creek Energy searches for a treasure of black gold. The independent oil and natural gas company has exploration and production assets in Arkansas California Colorado and Texas. Unlike many in the industry it operates nearly all of its projects and has an 89% working interest in its holdings. The company reported a 32% increase in proved reserves in 2013 to 69.8 million barrels of oil equivalent resulting primarily from the development of the Wattenberg Field in Colorado. Most of the company's proved reserves are in its Rocky Mountains (Niobara oil shale) and Arkansas (Cotton Valley sands) holdings. Bonanza Creek Energy filed for and emerged from Chapter 11 bankruptcy protection in 2017.

Operations
In 2013 the company drilled 134 wells and completed 121 productive operated wells and participated in drilling 12 and completing 4 productive non-operated wells. The resulting production rates achieved by the drilling program boosted sales volumes by 72% over 2012 to 16219 barrels of oil equivalent per day (of which 72% was crude oil and natural gas liquids-NGLs).
In 2013 Bonanza Creek produced about 3.9 million barrels of oil 20 billion cu. ft. of natural gas and 352800 barrels of natural gas liquids.
That year the company reported about 73889 gross (62003 net) leasehold acres and 684 gross (616.2 net) productive wells.

Geographic Reach
The company's assets and operations are focused in the Rocky Mountains in the Wattenberg Field (primarily the Niobrara oil shale) and in Dorcheat Macedonia Field in southern Arkansas (Cotton Valley sands).
The Rocky Mountain region contributed 66% if the company's total production in 2013; the Mid-Continent region 34%.
Bonanza Creek also has field offices in Houston Texas; Bakersfield California; Stamps Arkansas; and Kersey Colorado.

Sales and Marketing
Though Bonanza Creek sells crude oil natural gas and associated NGLs the majority of sales come from oil. The marketing arm of Plains All American Pipeline accounted for 37% of the company's revenues in 2013; petroleum marketer Lion Trading & Transportation 29%; and Sierra Crude Oil & Marketing 15%.

Financial Performance
The company's revenues increased by 82% in 2013 fueled by higher crude oil natural gas and NGL production and higher crude oil and natural gas prices partially offset by lower NGL prices. Oil natural gas and NGL production increased as a direct result of the $447 million expended for drilling and completion during 2013.
Bonanza Creek's net income grew by 49% in 2013 thanks to higher revenues offset by an increase in lease operating expense related to the increased production volumes attributable to the drilling program and the operation of an additional gas plant (constructed during 2012). The increase in depreciation depletion and amortization expenses is due to a 55% rise in depreciable assets and a loss incurred on derivative contracts during 2013.

The company has seen year over year growth in revenues since 2010 primarily due to its continuous investment in drilling activity which triggered the volume growth and as well through the expansion of its properties and by acquisitions.

Strategy
The company is concentrating on increasing production from existing unconventional assets in its core areas while making complementary acquisitions.
Bonanza Creek capital expenditures for 2014 arein the range of $575 million to $625 million. It is focused on the horizontal development of significant resource potential from the Niobrara and Codell formations in the Wattenberg Field expecting to invest approximately 85% of its 2014 capital budget in this project. The remaining 15% of its 2014 budget is allocated primarily to the vertical development of the Dorcheat Macedonia and McKamie Patton Fields in southern Arkansas targeting oil-rich Cotton Valley sands.
It invested 82% of its 2013 capital budget in the horizontal development in the Niobrara and Codell formations in the Wattenberg Field. While it has focused on the Niobrara B bench primarily using 4000 foot laterals it has begun to develop the Niobara C bench and Codell formation as well as to test extended reach lateral drilling in the Wattenberg Field and down-spacing concepts in both of its core areas.
It also intends to pursue bolt-on acquisitions in the Wattenberg Field and in southern Arkansas where it can take advantage of its core operational and engineering competencies.
In 2013 Bonanza Creek increased its 2013 capital budget to drill a "super-section" test of stacked laterals in multiple zones from multi-well pads in the Wattenberg Field and to drill additional wells in southern Arkansas during the fourth quarter. In addition the expanded budget accommodated increasing non-operated activity and infrastructure projects in the Wattenberg Field. It spent about $472 million in 2013.
In order to focus on its core areas in 2012 the company sold most of its non-core properties in California for $9 million.

Mergers and Acquisitions
In 2012 Bonanza Creek bought leases in the Wattenberg Field from the State of Colorado State Board of Land Commissioners for $60 million.

Company Background
The company went public in 2011. It used its $251 million in IPO proceeds to repay debt and to fund the exploration and development of oil producing assets.
Bonanza Creek was formed in 2006.

EXECUTIVES

Independent Director, Jeffery Wojahn
Independent Chairman Of The Board, Interim Chief Executive Officer, Independent Director, Benjamin Dell
Independent Director, Howard Willard
Chief Operating Officer, Matthew Owens
Independent Director, Morris Clark
Chief Financial Officer, Marianella Foschi
Independent Director, James Trimble
Independent Director, Carrie Fox
Chief Sustainability Officer, Brian Cain
Independent Director, Carrie Hudak
Independent Director, Brian Steck
Senior Vice President - Operation, Dean Tinsley, $299,076 total compensation

Chief Accounting Officer, Treasurer, Sandra Garbiso, $270,133 total compensation
General Counsel And Secretary, Cyrus Marter, $298,145 total compensation
Auditors: DELOITTE & TOUCHE LLP

LOCATIONS

HQ: Civitas Resources Inc
410 17th Street, Suite 1400, Denver, CO 80202
Phone: 720 440-6100 **Fax:** 720 305-0804
Web: www.bonanzacrk.com

PRODUCTS/OPERATIONS

2015 Sales

	$ mil.	% of total
Oil	248.9	85
Natural gas	26.5	9
Natural gas liquids	17.3	6
CO2 - -		
Total	**292.7**	**100**

COMPETITORS

Cequence Energy Ltd
EARTHSTONE ENERGY INC.
EXTRACTION OIL & GAS INC.
GULFPORT ENERGY OPERATING CORPORATION
REX ENERGY CORPORATION
SARATOGA RESOURCES INC
TALOS PETROLEUM LLC
Tourmaline Oil Corp
VAALCO ENERGY INC.
WARREN RESOURCES INC.

HISTORICAL FINANCIALS

Company Type: Public

Income Statement				FYE: December 31
	REVENUE ($ mil.)	NET INCOME ($ mil.)	NET PROFIT MARGIN	EMPLOYEES
12/20	218.0	103.5	47.5%	109
12/19	313.2	67.0	21.4%	125
12/18	276.6	168.1	60.8%	144
12/17*	123.5	(5.0)	—	156
04/17	68.5	2.6	3.9%	0
Annual Growth	33.5%	149.8%	—	—

*Fiscal year change

2020 Year-End Financials

Debt ratio: —
Return on equity: 10.4%
Cash ($ mil.): 24.7
Current ratio: 1.24
Long-term debt ($ mil.): —
No. of shares (mil.): 20.8
Dividends
 Yield: —
 Payout: —
Market value ($ mil.): 403.0

	STOCK PRICE ($) FY Close	P/E High/Low		PER SHARE ($) Earnings	Dividends	Book Value
12/20	19.33	5	2	4.95	0.00	50.16
12/19	23.34	8	5	3.24	0.00	45.37
12/18	20.67	5	2	8.16	0.00	42.05
12/17*	27.59	—	—	(0.25)	0.00	33.65
Annual Growth	(11.2%)	—	—	—	—	14.2%

*Fiscal year change

Clearfield Inc

Broadband providers can get all the fiber they need from Clearfield Inc. The company designs manufactures and distributes fiber protection fiber management and fiber delivery solutions to enable rapid and cost-effective fiber-fed deployment throughout the broadband service provider space across North America. Products include a series of panels cabinets wall boxes and other enclosures that house the Clearfield components; optical components integrated for signal coupling splitting termination and multiplexing among others for a seamless integration within their fiber management platform; fiber management and fiber pathway and protection method. More than 95% of Clearfield's revenue comes from customers in the US.

EXECUTIVES

President, Chief Executive Officer, Director, Cheryl Beranek, $361,753 total compensation
Chief Financial Officer, Daniel Herzog, $240,032 total compensation
Non-executive Independent Chairman Of The Board, Ronald Roth
Independent Director, Charles Hayssen
Independent Director, Donald Hayward
Independent Director, Carol Wirsbinski
Independent Director, Walter Jones
Chief Operating Officer, John Hill, $361,753 total compensation
Auditors: Baker Tilly US, LLP

LOCATIONS

HQ: Clearfield Inc
7050 Winnetka Avenue North, Suite 100, Brooklyn Park, MN 55428
Phone: 763 476-6866
Web: www.clearfieldconnection.com

PRODUCTS/OPERATIONS

Selected products
Accessories
Boxes
Cabinets
Cassettes
Copper Assemblies
Fiber Assemblies
Frames
Optical Components
Panels
Patch Cords
Pedestal Inserts
Pedestals
Pushable Fiber and Microduct
Splice-On Connectors
Terminals
Test Access Points
Vaults
Wall Boxes

COMPETITORS

CHARLES INDUSTRIES LLC
CIENA CORPORATION
CORNING OPTICAL
 COMMUNICATIONS LLC
DZS INC.
FINISAR CORPORATION
Fabrinet
INFINERA CORPORATION
NETGEAR INC.
WESTELL TECHNOLOGIES INC.

HISTORICAL FINANCIALS

Company Type: Public

Income Statement				FYE: September 30
	REVENUE ($ mil.)	NET INCOME ($ mil.)	NET PROFIT MARGIN	EMPLOYEES
09/21	140.7	20.3	14.4%	250
09/20	93.0	7.2	7.8%	230
09/19	85.0	4.5	5.4%	240
09/18	77.6	4.2	5.5%	225
09/17	73.9	3.8	5.2%	230
Annual Growth	17.5%	51.6%	—	2.1%

2021 Year-End Financials

Debt ratio: —
Return on equity: 21.7%
Cash ($ mil.): 13.2
Current ratio: 3.49
Long-term debt ($ mil.): —
No. of shares (mil.): 13.7
Dividends
 Yield: —
 Payout: —
Market value ($ mil.): 606.0

	STOCK PRICE ($) FY Close	P/E High/Low		PER SHARE ($) Earnings	Dividends	Book Value
09/21	44.15	31	14	1.47	0.00	7.56
09/20	20.17	42	17	0.53	0.00	6.06
09/19	11.85	47	26	0.34	0.00	5.49
09/18	13.45	46	33	0.32	0.00	5.05
09/17	13.60	77	41	0.28	0.00	4.67
Annual Growth	34.2%	—	—	51.4%	—	12.8%

CNB Bank Shares Inc

Auditors: Anders Minkler Huber & Helm LLP

LOCATIONS

HQ: CNB Bank Shares Inc
450 West Side Square, Carlinville, IL 62626
Phone: 217 854 2674
Web: www.cnbil.com

HISTORICAL FINANCIALS

Company Type: Public

Income Statement				FYE: December 31
	REVENUE ($ mil.)	NET INCOME ($ mil.)	NET PROFIT MARGIN	EMPLOYEES
12/20	70.7	14.7	20.8%	0
12/19	69.6	13.5	19.4%	0
12/18	57.7	9.4	16.3%	0
12/17	44.6	8.1	18.3%	0
12/16	41.2	8.2	20.0%	0
Annual Growth	14.4%	15.5%	—	—

2020 Year-End Financials

Debt ratio: 4.3%
Return on equity: 10.2%
Cash ($ mil.): 116.8
Current ratio: 0.10
Long-term debt ($ mil.): 27.8
No. of shares (mil.): 5.3
Dividends
 Yield: 0.0%
 Payout: 19.3%
Market value ($ mil.): 97.0

	STOCK PRICE ($) FY Close	P/E High/Low		PER SHARE ($) Earnings	Dividends	Book Value
12/20	18.00	—	—	(0.00)	0.45	28.16
12/19	17.89	—	—	(0.00)	0.41	25.42
12/18	18.80	—	—	(0.00)	0.13	22.45
Annual Growth	(2.2%)	—	—	—	86.1%	12.0%

CNB Community Bancorp Inc

Auditors: Rehmann Robson LLC

LOCATIONS

HQ: CNB Community Bancorp Inc
One South Howell Street, Hillsdale, MI 49242
Phone: 517 439-0401　　**Fax:** 517 439-0403
Web: www.countynationalbank.com

HISTORICAL FINANCIALS

Company Type: Public

Income Statement				FYE: December 31
	REVENUE ($ mil.)	NET INCOME ($ mil.)	NET PROFIT MARGIN	EMPLOYEES
12/20	46.3	10.1	21.8%	0
12/19	39.7	9.1	23.1%	0
12/18	34.8	8.4	24.3%	0
12/17	31.1	6.0	19.4%	3
12/16	28.7	4.7	16.5%	0
Annual Growth	12.7%	20.8%	—	—

2020 Year-End Financials

Debt ratio: 2.2%	No. of shares (mil.): 2.1
Return on equity: 14.8%	Dividends
Cash ($ mil.): 100.4	Yield: 3.0%
Current ratio: 0.12	Payout: 26.2%
Long-term debt ($ mil.): 21.2	Market value ($ mil.): 76.0

	STOCK PRICE ($) FY Close	P/E High/Low		PER SHARE ($) Earnings	Dividends	Book Value
12/20	35.00	9	6	4.77	1.25	33.30
12/19	39.15	10	7	4.37	1.22	29.69
12/18	32.00	9	6	4.06	1.11	26.61
12/17	23.60	8	8	2.93	0.40	23.81
12/16	19.50	—	—	2.32	0.90	21.88
Annual Growth	15.7%	—	—	19.7%	8.6%	11.1%

CNB Financial Corp. (Clearfield, PA)

CNB Financial is the holding company for CNB Bank ERIEBANK and FCBank. The banks and subsidiaries provide traditional deposit and loan services as well as wealth management merchant credit card processing and life insurance through nearly 30 CNB Bank- and ERIEBANK-branded branches in Pennsylvania and nine FCBank branches in central Ohio. Commercial industrial and agricultural loans make up more than one-third of the bank's loan portfolio while commercial mortgages make up another one-third. It also makes residential mortgages consumer and credit card loans. The company's non-bank subsidiaries include CNB Securities Corporation Holiday Financial Services Corporation and CNB Insurance Agency.

Operations

Commercial industrial and agricultural loans made up 36% of the bank's $16.74 billion loan portfolio at the end of 2015 while commercial mortgages made up another 33%. The rest of the portfolio was made up of residential mortgages (15% of loan assets) consumer (14%) overdrafts (less than 1%) and credit card loans (less than 1%).

The group makes more than 80% of its revenue from interest income. About 70% of its revenue came from loan interest during 2015 while another 15% came from interest income from taxable and tax-exempt securities. The remainder of its revenue came from deposit account service charges (4% of revenue) wealth and asset management fees (3%) and other miscellaneous income sources.

Geographic Reach

Clearfield Pennsylvania-based CNB Financial serves clients in its home state as well as in Ohio. CNB Financial serves a specific market area such as the Pennsylvania counties of Cambria Cameron Centre Clearfield Crawford Elk Erie Indiana Jefferson McKean and Warren.

Sales and Marketing

The group serves individuals businesses government and institutional customers.

CNB Financial has been increasing its advertising spend in recent years. It spent $1.6 million during 2015 up from $1.5 million and $1 million in 2014 and 2013 respectively.

Financial Performance

CNB Financial's revenues have risen more than 30% since 2011 as its loan assets have nearly doubled to $1.58 billion. The firm's profits have grown nearly 50% over the same period as low-interest rates and declining loan loss provisions have lowered operating costs.

The group's revenue climbed 1% to $102 million during 2015 thanks to a modest rise in interest income stemming mostly from 16% loan asset growth.

Despite revenue growth in 2015 CNB Financial's net income dipped 4% to $22.2 million mostly due to nearly 10% rise in salary and employee benefit costs from new hires and more expensive benefits. The group's operating cash levels jumped 16% to $34 million for the year thanks to favorable working capital changes related to accrued interest payables and other liabilities.

Strategy

CNB Financial has been acquiring other banks and opening branches in new geographic markets in recent years to boost its loan and deposit business. As a sign of success the bank noted that its assets have nearly doubled in size since 2009 from $1.16 billion to $2.29 billion at the end of 2015.

Toward its branch expansion plans the group's ERIEBANK brand entered Ohio by opening a loan production office there in 2014 with plans to open another by the end of 2016. After opening an FCBank branch in Dublin Ohio in 2014 the group in 2016 also continued to push its FCBank brand which has been enjoying double-digit loan and deposit business growth in the Columbus and Lancaster regions in Ohio. It plans to open a new FCBank branch in Worthington Ohio by the end of 2016.

Mergers and Acquisitions

In 2016 CNB looked expanded into Northeast Ohio after buying Mentor Ohio-based Lake National Bank — and its $152 million in assets — for nearly $25 million. Lake National Bank's operations were folded into ERIEBANK's operations when the transaction closed.

In 2013 extending its reach in Ohio CNB Financial acquired FC Banc Corp. for $41.6 million. The deal gave CNB Financial Farmers Citizens Bank which serves the northern Ohio communities of Bucyrus Cardington Fredericktown Mount Hope and Shiloh as well as the greater Columbus Ohio area.

Company Background

In 2012 CNB Financial acquired an Ebensburg Pennsylvania-based consumer discount company which brought with it a loan portfolio valued at about $1 million.

EXECUTIVES

Senior Executive Vice President, Chief Support Officer And Secretary, Cnb Financial Corp.and Cnb Bank Director Of The Company, Richard Greslick, $320,000 total compensation
Executive Vice President - Customer Experience, Leanne Kassab
Senior Executive Vice President And Chief Commercial Banking Officer, Joseph Dell, $297,000 total compensation
Independent Director, Jeffrey Powell
Independent Director, Joel Peterson
Independent Director, Richard Seager
Executive Vice President, Chief Risk Officer, Gregory Dixon
Senior Executive Vice President - Chief Of Community Banking Of The Corporation And The Bank, Martin Griffith, $257,500 total compensation
Chief Financial Officer, Executive Vice President, Treasurer, Tito Lima, $262,000 total compensation
Executive Vice President - Employee Experience, Mary Conaway
Executive Vice President - Private Client Solutions, Steven Shilling
Auditors: Crowe LLP

LOCATIONS

HQ: CNB Financial Corp. (Clearfield, PA)
1 South Second Street, P.O. Box 42, Clearfield, PA 16830
Phone: 814 765-9621
Web: www.cnbbank.bank

PRODUCTS/OPERATIONS

2015 Sales

	% of total
Interest and Dividend Income	
Loans including fees	70
Securities	
Taxable	10
Tax-exempt	4
Dividends	1
Non-Interest Income	
Wealth and asset management fees	3
Service charges on deposit accounts	4
Other service charges and fees	3
Other revenues	5
Total	**100**

Selected Services

Checking
Credit cards
Loans
Savings

COMPETITORS

GREAT SOUTHERN BANCORP	REPUBLIC FIRST
BANCORP INC.	INC.
OLD SECOND BANCORP INC.	

HISTORICAL FINANCIALS

Company Type: Public

Income Statement

FYE: December 31

	ASSETS ($ mil.)	NET INCOME ($ mil.)	INCOME AS % OF ASSETS	EMPLOYEES
12/20	4,729.4	32.7	0.7%	651
12/19	3,763.6	40.0	1.1%	559
12/18	3,221.5	33.7	1.0%	556
12/17	2,768.7	23.8	0.9%	528
12/16	2,573.8	20.5	0.8%	507
Annual Growth	16.4%	12.4%	—	6.4%

2020 Year-End Financials

Return on assets: 0.7%	Dividends
Return on equity: 9.0%	Yield: 3.1%
Long-term debt ($ mil.): —	Payout: 29.9%
No. of shares (mil.): 16.8	Market value ($ mil.): 358.0
Sales ($ mil): 195.2	

	STOCK PRICE ($) FY Close	P/E High/Low		PER SHARE ($) Earnings	Dividends	Book Value
12/20	21.29	17	7	1.97	0.68	24.72
12/19	32.68	13	9	2.63	0.68	20.00
12/18	22.95	15	10	2.21	0.67	17.28
12/17	26.24	19	13	1.57	0.66	15.98
12/16	26.74	20	12	1.42	0.66	14.64
Annual Growth	(5.5%)	—	—	8.5%	0.7%	14.0%

Coastal Financial Corp (WA)

Auditors: Moss Adams LLP

LOCATIONS

HQ: Coastal Financial Corp (WA)
  5415 Evergreen Way, Everett, WA 98203
Phone: 425 257-9000
Web: www.coastalbank.com

HISTORICAL FINANCIALS

Company Type: Public

Income Statement

FYE: December 31

	ASSETS ($ mil.)	NET INCOME ($ mil.)	INCOME AS % OF ASSETS	EMPLOYEES
12/20	1,766.1	15.1	0.9%	250
12/19	1,128.5	13.2	1.2%	195
12/18	952.1	9.7	1.0%	183
12/17	805.7	5.4	0.7%	159
12/16	740.6	5.0	0.7%	0
Annual Growth	24.3%	31.9%	—	—

2020 Year-End Financials

Return on assets: 1.0%	Dividends
Return on equity: 11.4%	Yield: —
Long-term debt ($ mil.): —	Payout: —
No. of shares (mil.): 11.9	Market value ($ mil.): 251.0
Sales ($ mil): 71.2	

	STOCK PRICE ($) FY Close	P/E High/Low		PER SHARE ($) Earnings	Dividends	Book Value
12/20	21.00	18	7	1.24	0.00	11.73
12/19	16.47	16	13	1.08	0.00	10.42
12/18	15.23	19	13	0.91	0.00	9.18
Annual Growth	17.4%	—	—	16.7%	—	13.0%

CoastalSouth Bancshares Inc

Auditors: Elliott Davis, LLC

LOCATIONS

HQ: CoastalSouth Bancshares Inc
  5 Bow Circle, Hilton Head Island, SC 29928
Phone: 843 341-9958
Web: www.coastalstatesbank.com

HISTORICAL FINANCIALS

Company Type: Public

Income Statement

FYE: December 31

	REVENUE ($ mil.)	NET INCOME ($ mil.)	NET PROFIT MARGIN	EMPLOYEES
12/20	44.1	6.3	14.4%	0
12/19	36.7	2.6	7.1%	0
12/18	26.9	(0.1)	—	0
12/17	22.5	(11.8)	—	0
12/16	30.9	1.4	4.6%	0
Annual Growth	9.2%	45.1%	—	—

2020 Year-End Financials

Debt ratio: 12.7%	No. of shares (mil.): 7.9
Return on equity: 6.5%	Dividends
Cash ($ mil.): 157.0	Yield: —
Current ratio: 0.18	Payout: —
Long-term debt ($ mil.): 146.0	Market value ($ mil.): 97.0

	STOCK PRICE ($) FY Close	P/E High/Low		PER SHARE ($) Earnings	Dividends	Book Value
12/20	12.10	16	11	0.80	0.00	12.76
12/19	12.55	39	32	0.36	0.00	11.60
12/18	10.11	—	—	(0.03)	0.00	10.60
12/17	1.85	—	—	(3.59)	0.00	10.02
Annual Growth	87.0%	—	—	—	—	8.4%

Cognex Corp

Cognex is a leading worldwide provider of machine vision products that capture and analyze visual information in order to automate manufacturing and distribution tasks where vision is required. Manufacturers of consumer electronics and vehicles as well as logistics companies use the company's machine vision and industrial identification systems to position and identify products gauge sizes and locate defects. It also offers a full range of machine vision systems and sensors vision software and industrial image-based barcode readers designed to meet customer needs at different performance and price points. Sales to customers based in the US account for about 40% of sales.

Operations

Cognex operates in one segment machine vision technology.

Its Vision software offers customers the flexibility of the Cognex vision tools library to use with the cameras frame grabbers and peripheral equipment of their choice. Cognex VisionPro software offers an extensive suite of patented vision tools for advanced programming while Cognex Designer allows customers to build complete vision applications with the simplicity of a graphical flowchart-based programming environment.

Vision Systems combine smart cameras and software to perform a wide range of inspection tasks including part location identification measurement assembly verification and robotic guidance. Vision Sensors deliver an easy-to-use low-cost reliable solution for simple pass/fail inspections such as checking the presence and size of parts. In-Sight® vision systems and sensors which includes 2D 3D alignment and deep learning models meet various price and performance requirements for factory automation customers.

The company's Industrial Image-Based Barcode Readers which includes the DataMan line offers bar code readers for use in automotive consumer products medical-related and logistics.

Overall nearly 85% of sales were generated from the company's standard products and services while application from specific customer solutions account for the rest.

Geographic Reach

Customers in US account for about 40% of Cognex's sales while Europe customers supply around 25% and customers in China generate some 20% of sales. The company's products are assembled by a contract manufacturer in Indonesia. Testing and shipping is done from its Natick Massachusetts facility for US customers and from its Ireland facility for customers outside the US.

The company is headquartered in Massachusetts.

Sales and Marketing

Cognex sells through a worldwide direct sales force and via a global network of integration and distribution partners.

The company's customers are in the consumer electronics automotive consumer products food and beverage and medical related industries. Approximately 70% of revenue is from consumer electronics logistics and automotive industries.

The company's advertising cost totaled some $1.44 million $1.39 million and $1.66 million for the years 2020 2019 and 2017 respectively.

Financial Performance

Revenue for the year ended December 31 2020 was $811.0 million compared to $725.6 million for the prior year representing an increase of 12%. The increase was due to higher revenue from customers in the consumer electronics and logistics industries which were the company's two largest markets in 2020.

The company's net income for fiscal 2020 decreased to $176.2 million compared from the prior year with $203.9 million.

Cash held by the company at the end of fiscal 2020 increased to $269.1 million. Cash provided by operations and investing activities were $242.4 million and $169.4 million respectively. Cash used for financing activities was $316.9 million mainly for payment of dividends.

Strategy

Cognex's goal is to expand its position as a leading worldwide provider of machine vision products for industrial customers. The company are selective in choosing growth opportunities that it believe will maintain its historically high gross margin percentages which have ranged in the mid 70% range for the past several years and reflect the value its customers place on its innovative products. The company's high gross margins have the potential to provide it with strong operating leverage in its financial model as any incremental revenue at such margins falls through to operating income at a high ratio. Cognex's strong and unique corporate culture reinforces its values of customer first and innovation and enables the company to attract and retain smart highly educated experienced talent who are motivated to solve the most challenging vision tasks.

The company invests heavily in research and development in order to maintain its position as a technology leader in machine vision. Cognex invests in technology that makes vision easier to use and more affordable and therefore available to a broader base of customers such as its vision sensor products that enable customers with a lower budget to use machine vision without the help of sophisticated engineers. The company also invests in technology that addresses the most challenging vision applications such as its 3D vision products that solve applications where a height or volume measurement is required and its deep learning vision software that solves complex applications with unpredictable defects and deviations.

HISTORY

Robert Shillman and two MIT colleagues Marilyn Matz and William Silver started Cognex (short for "cognition experts") in 1981 to create vision replacement machines for factories. Competition and inadequate technology forced the firm to reevaluate its distribution strategy in 1986. Cognex began supplying machine vision technology to original equipment manufacturers. The company introduced the first custom vision chip in 1988 and went public the next year.

Cognex found success where human vision fails — in the high-speed detailed repetitive processes required in making semiconductors. The company expanded by purchasing Acumen a developer of machine vision systems for semiconductor wafer identification (1995); Isys Controls a maker of quality control systems (1996); and Mayan Automation a maker of surface inspection systems (1997).

Low demand for semiconductor and printed circuit board manufacturing equipment in Asia hurt sales in 1998. Nonetheless the company boosted R&D by 10% and acquired some of Rockwell Automation's machine vision operations also becoming the preferred global supplier to Rockwell's plants. Orders picked up in early 1999 and Cognex invested $1 million in upstart Avalon Imaging (machine vision for the plastics industry) its first investment in such a company.

A series of acquisitions and in-house innovations enabled Cognex to expand into factory automation

inspection which accounts for more than 90% of its business.

EXECUTIVES

Senior Vice President, Director, Patrick Alias
Executive Vice President Of Vision And Id Products, Carl Gerst, $284,710 total compensation
Chairman, Anthony Sun
Senior Vice President Of Employee Services, Sheila DiPalma, $277,773 total compensation
Chief Financial Officer, Senior Vice President - Finance, Paul Todgham, $308,804 total compensation
Independent Director, Sachin Lawande
President, Chief Executive Officer, Director, Robert Willett, $173,469 total compensation
Auditors: Grant Thornton LLP

LOCATIONS

HQ: Cognex Corp
One Vision Drive, Natick, MA 01760-2059
Phone: 508 650-3000
Web: www.cognex.com

PRODUCTS/OPERATIONS

Selected ProductsIn-Sight 8000 SeriesIn-Sight 7000 SeriesIn-Sight Laser Profiler3D Vision SystemsVisionProCognex Designer

COMPETITORS

AMETEK INC.
Beijing Hollysys Co. Ltd.
ELECTROCOMPONENTS PUBLIC LIMITED COMPANY
FORTIVE CORPORATION
HURCO COMPANIES INC.
MKS INSTRUMENTS INC.
MPAC GROUP PLC
RUBIX GROUP INTERNATIONAL LIMITED
STRATASYS LTD
VICOR CORPORATION
VOLEX PLC
ZEBRA TECHNOLOGIES CORPORATION
ZYTRONIC PLC

HISTORICAL FINANCIALS

Company Type: Public

Income Statement   FYE: December 31

	REVENUE ($ mil.)	NET INCOME ($ mil.)	NET PROFIT MARGIN	EMPLOYEES
12/21	1,037.1	279.8	27.0%	2,257
12/20	811.0	176.1	21.7%	2,055
12/19	725.6	203.8	28.1%	2,267
12/18	806.3	219.2	27.2%	2,124
12/17	747.9	177.1	23.7%	1,771
Annual Growth	8.5%	12.1%	—	6.2%

2021 Year-End Financials

Debt ratio: —
Return on equity: 20.7%
Cash ($ mil.): 186.1
Current ratio: 3.39
Long-term debt ($ mil.): —
No. of shares (mil.): 175.4
Dividends
 Yield: 2.8%
 Payout: 136.0%
Market value ($ mil.): 13,645.0

STOCK PRICE ($) FY Close	P/E High/Low	PER SHARE ($)		
		Earnings	Dividends	Book Value
12/21 77.76	59 46	1.56	2.25	8.15
12/20 80.29	81 37	1.00	2.23	7.18
12/19 56.04	48 30	1.16	0.21	7.86
12/18 38.67	55 28	1.24	0.19	6.65
12/17 61.16	142 60	0.99	0.17	6.31
Annual Growth 6.2%	— —	12.0%	91.3%	6.6%

Cohen & Company Inc (New)

Institutional Financial Markets Inc. (IFMI) believes in the institution of the markets. Formerly a real estate investment trust named Alesco Financial (and later Cohen & Company) the company now manages and trades financial investments specializing in credit-related fixed income assets. The company serves institutional investors. IFMI's asset management arm offers funds separately managed accounts collateralized debt obligations international hybrid securities and other investment products; it manages some $10 billion in assets. The firm also has a capital markets division which sells trades and issues corporate and securitized products. IFMI has about 10 offices in the US and London.

EXECUTIVES

Vice Chairman Of The Board; President, Chief Executive - European Operations, Daniel Cohen, $600,000 total compensation
Independent Director, Thomas Costello
Director, Christopher Ricciardi, $666,667 total compensation
Chief Financial Officer, Executive Vice President, Treasurer, Joseph Pooler, $420,000 total compensation
Chief Executive Officer, Lester Brafman, $600,000 total compensation
Chairman Of The Board, Jack DiMaio
Independent Director, Neil Subin
Independent Director, Joseph Donovan
Auditors: Grant Thornton LLP

LOCATIONS

HQ: Cohen & Company Inc (New)
Cira Centre, 2929 Arch Street, Suite 1703, Philadelphia, PA 19104
Phone: 215 701-9555
Web: www.cohenandcompany.com

COMPETITORS

COWEN INC.
National Bank Financial & Co Inc

WESTECH CAPITAL CORP

HISTORICAL FINANCIALS

Company Type: Public

Income Statement — FYE: December 31

	REVENUE ($ mil.)	NET INCOME ($ mil.)	NET PROFIT MARGIN	EMPLOYEES
12/20	130.1	14.2	10.9%	87
12/19	49.6	(2.0)	—	94
12/18	49.3	(2.4)	—	88
12/17	47.5	2.0	4.3%	88
12/16	55.3	2.2	4.1%	79
Annual Growth	23.8%	58.2%		2.4%

2020 Year-End Financials

Debt ratio: 0.7%
Return on equity: 36.6%
Cash ($ mil.): 42.0
Current ratio: 0.02
Long-term debt ($ mil.): 47.1

No. of shares (mil.): 1.3
Dividends
 Yield: —
 Payout: 0.1%
Market value ($ mil.): 22.0

	STOCK PRICE ($) FY Close	P/E High/Low		PER SHARE ($) Earnings	Dividends	Book Value
12/20	16.34	2	0	7.66	0.00	33.13
12/19	3.95	—	—	(1.81)	0.80	27.91
12/18	8.43	—	—	(2.14)	0.80	29.71
12/17	8.02	7	1	1.60	0.20	32.87
12/16	1.19	1	0	1.90	0.80	32.08
Annual Growth	92.5%	—	—	41.7%	—	0.8%

Coherus BioSciences Inc

Auditors: Ernst & Young LLP

LOCATIONS

HQ: Coherus BioSciences Inc
 333 Twin Dolphin Drive, Suite 600, Redwood City, CA 94065
Phone: 650 649-3530
Web: www.coherus.com

HISTORICAL FINANCIALS

Company Type: Public

Income Statement — FYE: December 31

	REVENUE ($ mil.)	NET INCOME ($ mil.)	NET PROFIT MARGIN	EMPLOYEES
12/20	475.8	132.2	27.8%	317
12/19	356.0	89.8	25.2%	291
12/18	0.0	(209.3)	—	232
12/17	1.5	(238.1)	—	122
12/16	190.1	(127.3)	—	152
Annual Growth	25.8%	—	—	20.2%

2020 Year-End Financials

Debt ratio: 48.0%
Return on equity: 68.3%
Cash ($ mil.): 541.1
Current ratio: 5.27
Long-term debt ($ mil.): 404.0

No. of shares (mil.): 72.5
Dividends
 Yield: —
 Payout: —
Market value ($ mil.): 1,260.0

	STOCK PRICE ($) FY Close	P/E High/Low		PER SHARE ($) Earnings	Dividends	Book Value
12/20	17.38	12	6	1.62	0.00	3.87
12/19	18.01	18	6	1.23	0.00	1.50
12/18	9.05	—	—	(3.22)	0.00	(0.57)
12/17	8.80	—	—	(4.48)	0.00	0.53
12/16	28.15	—	—	(3.04)	0.00	0.45
Annual Growth	(11.4%)	—	—	—	—	71.5%

Cohu Inc

Cohu is a leading supplier of semiconductor test and inspection handlers micro-electromechanical system (MEMS) test modules test contactors thermal sub-systems semiconductor automated test equipment and bare board PCB test systems used by global semiconductor and electronics manufacturers and semiconductor test subcontractor. Customers include device manufacturers fabless design houses PCB manufacturers and test subcontractors. China is the California-based company's single biggest market. Cohu was founded in 1957.

Operations

The company report in two segments; Semiconductor Test & Inspection (over 90% of sales) and PCB Test (nearly 10%).

The company currently sells Semiconductor Test (Semiconductor ATE (Automated Test Equipment) is used both for wafer level and device package testing) Semiconductor Handlers (used in conjunction with semiconductor ATE to automate the testing of packaged semiconductor devices) Interface Products (comprised of test contactors probe heads and probe pins) Spares and Kits (design and manufacture a wide range of device dedication kits that enable handlers to process different semiconductor packages) Services (performs installations and necessary maintenance of systems sold) and Bare Board PCB Test Systems (used to test pre-assembly printed circuit boards).

Sales by product line includes semiconductor test & inspection systems (including kits) account for some 50% Interface products spares kits (not as part of systems sales) and services approximately 45% and PCB test systems (around 5%).

Geographic Reach

The company's corporate headquarters is located in San Diego California its Asian sales and service headquarters are located in Singapore and Taiwan and the majority of its sales are made to destinations in Asia. In addition it has Asia-based manufacturing plants in Malaysia Philippines and Japan.

About 25% of sales were generated in China the US with over 15% Taiwan with roughly 15% and the Philippines and Malaysia with nearly 10% each. The rest of the sales were generated from other countries.

Sales and Marketing

The company markets its products worldwide through a combination of a direct sales force and independent sales representatives. Its customers include semiconductor integrated device manufacturers fabless design houses PCB manufacturers and test subcontractors.

Financial Performance

Cohu's consolidated net sales increased 9.0% from $583.3 million in 2019 to $636.0 million in 2020. During the first half of 2020 the company's net sales were impacted by disruptions caused by the COVID-19 pandemic and movement control orders which resulted in supply disruptions impacting its ability to ship product and were further impacted by reduced demand in the automotive segment.

Net loss of company at the end of fiscal 2020 decreased to $13.8 million compared from the prior year with $69.7 million.

Cash held by the company at the end of fiscal 2020 decreased to $149.4 million. Cash provided by operations was $49.7 million while cash used for investing and financing activities were $18.4 million and $38.1 million respectively.

Strategy

Subsequent to the acquisition of Xcerra during the fourth quarter of 2018 Cohu began a strategic restructuring program designed to reposition its organization and improve its cost structure as part of the company's targeted integration plan regarding the recently acquired Xcerra (Integration Program).

HISTORY

Kalbfell Laboratories was incorporated in 1947 an outgrowth of a research and development partnership founded in 1945. The company originally made electronic devices for government agencies. It shifted its emphasis to power supply units in 1952 and a year later expanded into closed-circuit television (CCTV) equipment. The company was renamed Kay Lab in 1954 and Cohu Electronics (after chairman La Motte Cohu) in 1957. It became Cohu Inc. in 1972.

During the 1980s CEO James Barnes directed Cohu's entry into semiconductor test handling equipment. The company acquired microwave equipment maker Broadcast Microwave Services in 1984.

Chip handling gear became Cohu's primary business during the chip boom of the early 1990s. The company established its Singapore subsidiary in 1993. The next year it acquired Daymarc a maker of gravity-feed semiconductor handling equipment to complement its Delta Design pick-and-place machines.

EXECUTIVES

Independent Director, Lynne Camp, $59,452 total compensation
Vice President - Corporate Development, General Counsel, Secretary, Thomas Kampfer, $315,673 total compensation
Independent Director, Nina Richardson, $61,654 total compensation
Senior Vice President, General Manager - Semiconductor Test Group, Ian Lawee
President, Chief Executive Officer, Executive Director, Luis Muller, $543,510 total compensation
Non-executive Chairman Of The Board, James Donahue, $83,673 total compensation
Chief Financial Officer, Vice President - Finance, Jeffrey Jones, $358,081 total compensation
Senior Vice President - Global Customer Group, Christopher Bohrson, $329,808 total compensation
Auditors: Ernst & Young LLP

LOCATIONS

HQ: Cohu Inc
12367 Crosthwaite Circle, Poway, CA 92064-6817
Phone: 858 848-8100
Web: www.cohu.com

PRODUCTS/OPERATIONS

2018 Sales

	% of total
Semiconductor Test & Inspection	98
PCB Test	2
Total	**100**

Operations and Selected Products

Semiconductor Equipment
Delta Design (semiconductor test handling equipment and thermal technology)
Automated test handlers
Burn-in board loaders and unloaders
Device kits
Docking interfaces
Environmental chambers
Rasco (semiconductor test handling)
Gravity-feed and test-on-strip systems
Cohu Electronics (closed-circuit television systems)
Cameras and control equipment
Control systems
Design services
Lenses
Software
Broadcast Microwave Services (microwave communications equipment)
Antenna systems
Microwave radio equipment

COMPETITORS

AGILENT TECHNOLOGIES INC.
INTEST CORPORATION
IXIA
KLA CORPORATION
MAXIM INTEGRATED PRODUCTS INC.
MTS SYSTEMS CORPORATION
OCLARO INC.
PULSE ELECTRONICS CORPORATION
RADISYS CORPORATION
TELEDYNE LECROY INC.
TRANSCAT INC.
ZYGO CORPORATION

HISTORICAL FINANCIALS
Company Type: Public

Income Statement				FYE: December 25
	REVENUE ($ mil.)	NET INCOME ($ mil.)	NET PROFIT MARGIN	EMPLOYEES
12/21	887.2	167.3	18.9%	3,240
12/20	636.0	(13.8)	—	3,250
12/19	583.3	(69.7)	—	3,200
12/18	451.7	(32.1)	—	3,500
12/17	352.7	32.8	9.3%	1,800
Annual Growth	25.9%	50.2%	—	15.8%

2021 Year-End Financials

Debt ratio: 9.3%
Return on equity: 24.0%
Cash ($ mil.): 290.2
Current ratio: 3.90
Long-term debt ($ mil.): 103.3
No. of shares (mil.): 48.7
Dividends
  Yield: —
  Payout: —
Market value ($ mil.): 1,853.0

	STOCK PRICE ($) FY Close	P/E High/Low		PER SHARE ($) Earnings	Dividends	Book Value
12/21	38.01	14	8	3.45	0.00	18.10
12/20	38.75	—	—	(0.33)	0.06	12.14
12/19	22.30	—	—	(1.69)	0.24	11.67
12/18	15.81	—	—	(1.01)	0.24	13.40
12/17	21.95	22	11	1.14	0.24	10.15
Annual Growth	14.7%	—	—	31.9%	—	15.6%

Collegium Pharmaceuticals Inc

Auditors: DELOITTE & TOUCHE LLP

LOCATIONS

HQ: Collegium Pharmaceuticals Inc
100 Technology Center Drive, Stoughton, MA 02072
Phone: 781 713-3699
Web: www.collegiumpharma.com

HISTORICAL FINANCIALS
Company Type: Public

Income Statement				FYE: December 31
	REVENUE ($ mil.)	NET INCOME ($ mil.)	NET PROFIT MARGIN	EMPLOYEES
12/20	310.0	26.7	8.6%	234
12/19	296.7	(22.7)	—	255
12/18	280.4	(39.1)	—	266
12/17	28.4	(74.8)	—	250
12/16	1.7	(94.1)	—	234
Annual Growth	266.9%	—	—	0.0%

2020 Year-End Financials

Debt ratio: 39.9%
Return on equity: 19.5%
Cash ($ mil.): 174.1
Current ratio: 1.16
Long-term debt ($ mil.): 209.5
No. of shares (mil.): 34.6
Dividends
  Yield: —
  Payout: —
Market value ($ mil.): 693.0

	STOCK PRICE ($) FY Close	P/E High/Low		PER SHARE ($) Earnings	Dividends	Book Value
12/20	20.03	33	18	0.76	0.00	5.37
12/19	20.58	—	—	(0.68)	0.00	2.60
12/18	17.17	—	—	(1.19)	0.00	2.75
12/17	18.46	—	—	(2.47)	0.00	3.18
12/16	15.57	—	—	(3.88)	0.00	4.59
Annual Growth	6.5%	—	—	—	—	4.0%

Colony Bankcorp, Inc.

Colony Bankcorp seems to be colonizing Georgia. The multibank holding company owns seven financial institutions doing business under variations of the Colony Bank name throughout central and southern portions of the state. The banks operate more than 25 branches in all. They offer traditional fare such as checking and savings accounts NOW and IRA accounts and CDs. Real estate loans including residential and commercial mortgages and construction and farmland loans make up the largest portion of the company's loan portfolio at more than 80%. The banks also issue business and consumer loans.

EXECUTIVES

Independent Chairman Of The Board, Mark Massee
Independent Director, Scott Downing
Executive Vice President And Chief Banking Officer, M. Eddie Hoyle, $174,939 total compensation
Executive Vice President, Chief Risk Officer, General Counsel, Edward Bagwell
President, Chief Executive Officer And Director, T. Heath Fountain, $360,000 total compensation
Independent Director, Matthew Reed
Independent Director, Jonathan Ross
Executive Vice President, Chief Administrative Officer, Kimberly Dockery
Chief Financial Officer, Executive Vice President, Ir Contact Officer, Tracie Youngblood, $210,000 total compensation
Executive Vice President, Chief Credit Officer, Leonard Bateman, $215,000 total compensation
Independent Director, Michael Dwozan
Independent Director, Meagan Mowry
Auditors: Mauldin & Jenkins, LLC

LOCATIONS

HQ: Colony Bankcorp, Inc.
115 South Grant Street, Fitzgerald, GA 31750
Phone: 229 426-6000
Web: www.colonybank.com

COMPETITORS

CENTRAL BANCORP INC.
PEOPLES FINANCIAL CORPORATION
REGIONS FINANCIAL CORPORATION

HISTORICAL FINANCIALS
Company Type: Public

Income Statement				FYE: December 31
	ASSETS ($ mil.)	NET INCOME ($ mil.)	INCOME AS % OF ASSETS	EMPLOYEES
12/20	1,763.9	11.8	0.7%	376
12/19	1,515.3	10.2	0.7%	370
12/18	1,251.8	11.9	1.0%	330
12/17	1,232.7	7.7	0.6%	326
12/16	1,210.4	8.6	0.7%	333
Annual Growth	9.9%	8.0%	—	3.1%

2020 Year-End Financials

Return on assets: 0.7%
Return on equity: 8.5%
Long-term debt ($ mil.): —
No. of shares (mil.): 9.5
Sales ($ mil): 87.3
Dividends
  Yield: 2.7%
  Payout: 39.2%
Market value ($ mil.): 139.0

	STOCK PRICE ($) FY Close	P/E High/Low		PER SHARE ($) Earnings	Dividends	Book Value
12/20	14.65	13	7	1.24	0.40	15.21
12/19	16.50	16	13	1.12	0.30	13.74
12/18	14.60	14	10	1.40	0.23	11.33
12/17	14.60	17	14	0.87	0.10	10.70
12/16	13.20	16	10	0.84	0.00	11.07
Annual Growth	2.6%	—	—	10.2%	—	8.3%

HOOVER'S HANDBOOK OF EMERGING COMPANIES 2022

Columbia Banking System Inc

Columbia Banking System (CBS) is the roughly $16.6 billion-asset holding company for Columbia Bank. The regional community bank has some 145 branches in Washington from Puget Sound to the timber country in the southwestern part of the state as well as in northern Oregon and Idaho. Targeting retail and small to medium-sized business customers the bank offers standard retail services such as checking and savings accounts CDs IRAs credit cards loans and mortgages. Commercial real estate loans make up about 45% of the company's loan portfolio while business loans make up another nearly 40%. Most of its branches were generated in Washington.

Operations

The company's products and services include Personal Banking which offers an assortment of account products including noninterest and interest-bearing checking savings money market and certificate of deposit accounts; Business Banking which includes a variety of checking savings interest-bearing money market and certificate of deposit accounts are offered to business banking customers to satisfy all their banking needs; and Wealth Management which offers tailored solutions to individuals families and professional businesses in the areas of financial services and private banking as well as trust and investment services.

The company segmented our loan portfolio into two portfolio segments: Commercial which includes Commercial real estate (about 45% of sales) Commercial business (about 40%) and Construction (less than 5%); and Consumer which includes One-to-four family residential real estate (over 5%) and other.

The Commercial segment two-factor models utilize a mix of seven macroeconomic factors including the four most commonly used factors: Real GDP National Unemployment Rate Home Price Index and Commercial Real Estate Index. The three additional factors are Nominal GDP Producer Price Index and Core Consumer Price Index. The Consumer segment two-factor models utilize a mix of three macroeconomic factors: National Unemployment Rate Home Price Index and Prime Rate.

Overall about 85% of sales were generated from its net interest income which includes loans (about 70%) taxable securities (nearly 15%) and tax-exempt securities while Non-interest income accounts for the rest.

Geographic Reach

Headquartered in Tacoma Washington the company has two operations facilities in Pierce County Washington one operations facility in Vancouver Washington and one operations facility in Wilsonville Oregon. It also has some 145 branches of which 70 were in Washington some 60 in Oregon and Idaho with some 15.

Sales and Marketing

The company provides a full range of banking services to small and medium-sized businesses professionals and individuals. Advertising and promotion expenses were $4.5 million $4.9 million and $5.6 million for the years 2020 2019 and 2018 respectively.

Financial Performance

The company's revenue for fiscal 2020 increased to $604.6 million compared from the prior year with $590.6 million.

Net income for fiscal 2020 decreased by 21% to $154.2 million compared from the prior year with $194.5 million.

Cash held by the company at the end of fiscal 2020 increased to $653.8 million. Cash provided by operations and financing activities were $192.3 million and $2.1 billion respectively. Cash used for investing activities was $1.9 billion mainly for Debt securities available for sale.

Strategy

CBS' business strategy is to provide its customers with the financial sophistication and product depth of a regional banking company while retaining the appeal and service level of a community bank. The company continually evaluates its existing business processes while focusing on maintaining asset quality and a diversified loan and deposit portfolio. The company continues to build its strong deposit base expanding total revenue and controlling expenses in an effort to gain operational efficiencies and increase its return on average tangible equity. As a result of its strong commitment to highly personalized relationship-oriented customer service its diverse products its strategic branch locations and the long-standing community presence of its managers and staff the company believes CBS are well positioned to attract and retain new customers and to increase its market share of loans deposits investments and other financial services. The company is dedicated to increasing market share in the communities it serves by continuing to leverage its existing branch network and considering business combinations that are consistent with its expansion strategy throughout the Northwest and beyond. The company has grown its franchise over the past decade through a combination of acquisitions and organic growth.

Mergers and Acquisitions

In 2021 Columbia Banking System Inc. the holding company for Columbia State Bank and Bank of Commerce Holdings announced the signing of a definitive agreement to merge Bank of Commerce into Columbia in an all-stock transaction valued at approximately $266.0 million. Bank of Commerce Holdings is a bank holding company headquartered in Sacramento California is an FDIC-insured California banking corporation providing community banking and financial services in northern California along the Interstate 5 corridor from Sacramento to Yreka and in the wine region north of San Francisco. This transaction is expected to be accretive to Columbia's earnings with 3% accretion to earnings per share in 2022 and 4% accretion in 2023.

Company Background

Columbia Banking System took advantage of the rash of bank failures in past years to increase its presence in the Pacific Northwest region. It added more than 30 branches in 2010 when it acquired most of the deposits and assets of failed banks Columbia River Bank and American Marine Bank a week apart. In similar transactions in 2011 it acquired most of the operations of the failed institutions Summit Bank First Heritage Bank and Bank of Whitman. Those deals added more than a dozen branches in Washington.

EXECUTIVES

Executive Vice President, Chief Marketing And Experience Officer, David Devine
Executive Vice President, Chief Risk Officer, Lisa Dow
Independent Director, Randal Lund
Executive Vice President, Director Of Retail Banking, Dave Hansen
Independent Director, Eric Forrest
Independent Director, S. Mae Numata
Independent Director, Janine Terrano
Chief Financial Officer, Executive Vice President, Aaron Deer, $259,135 total compensation
Independent Director, Laura Alvarez Schrag
Independent Director, Tracy Mack-Askew
Executive Vice President, Chief Operating Officer, Christopher Merrywell, $437,115 total compensation
Independent Director, Mark Finkelstein
Executive Vice President, Chief Digital And Technology Officer, Eric Eid, $334,327 total compensation
Executive Vice President, General Counsel, Kumi Baruffi, $332,212 total compensation
Chief Credit Officer, Executive Vice President, Andrew McDonald, $413,369 total compensation
President, Chief Executive Officer & Director, Clint Stein, $817,308 total compensation
Independent Director, Michelle Lantow
Independent Director, Elizabeth Seaton
Independent Director, Ford Elsaesser
Chief Human Resource Officer, Executive Vice President, David Lawson, $298,077 total compensation
Auditors: DELOITTE & TOUCHE LLP

LOCATIONS

HQ: Columbia Banking System Inc
1301 A Street, Tacoma, WA 98402-2156
Phone: 253 305-1900
Web: www.columbiabank.com

PRODUCTS/OPERATIONS

2018 Revenue

	% of total
Net Interest Income	
Loans	73
Taxable securities	10
Tax-exempt securities	2
Non-interest Income	15
Total	**100**

COMPETITORS

AMERIS BANCORP	M&T BANK CORPORATION
BANCFIRST CORPORATION	MUFG AMERICAS
HOLDINGS	
BANKUNITED INC.	CORPORATION
CASCADE BANCORP	NATIONAL BANK
HOLDINGS	
CENTERSTATE BANK	CORPORATION
CORPORATION	OLD LINE BANCSHARES
CITIZENS FINANCIAL	INC.
GROUP INC.	OLD NATIONAL BANCORP
COMMERCE BANCSHARES	PACIFIC CONTINENTAL
INC.	CORPORATION
FIRST CITIZENS	PINNACLE FINANCIAL
BANCSHARES INC.	PARTNERS INC.
HANCOCK WHITNEY	PRIVATEBANCORP INC.
CORPORATION	REPUBLIC BANCORP INC.
HERITAGE FINANCIAL	STATE BANK FINANCIAL
CORPORATION	CORPORATION

HISTORICAL FINANCIALS
Company Type: Public

Income Statement
FYE: December 31

	ASSETS ($ mil.)	NET INCOME ($ mil.)	INCOME AS % OF ASSETS	EMPLOYEES
12/20	16,584.7	154.2	0.9%	2,091
12/19	14,079.5	194.4	1.4%	2,162
12/18	13,095.1	172.8	1.3%	2,137
12/17	12,716.8	112.8	0.9%	2,120
12/16	9,509.6	104.8	1.1%	1,819
Annual Growth	14.9%	10.1%	—	3.5%

2020 Year-End Financials

Return on assets: 1.0%
Return on equity: 6.8%
Long-term debt ($ mil.): —
No. of shares (mil.): 71.6
Sales ($ mil): 622.3

Dividends
Yield: 3.7%
Payout: 61.7%
Market value ($ mil.): 2,570.0

	STOCK PRICE ($) FY Close	P/E High/Low		PER SHARE ($) Earnings	Dividends	Book Value
12/20	35.90	19	9	2.17	1.34	32.79
12/19	40.69	15	12	2.68	1.40	29.95
12/18	36.29	20	14	2.36	1.14	27.76
12/17	43.44	25	19	1.86	0.88	26.70
12/16	44.68	25	15	1.81	1.53	21.55
Annual Growth	(5.3%)	—	—	4.6%	(3.3%)	11.1%

Columbia Financial Inc

Auditors: KPMG LLP

LOCATIONS

HQ: Columbia Financial Inc
19-01 Route 208 North, Fair Lawn, NJ 07410
Phone: 800 522-4167
Web: www.columbiabankonline.com

HISTORICAL FINANCIALS
Company Type: Public

Income Statement
FYE: December 31

	ASSETS ($ mil.)	NET INCOME ($ mil.)	INCOME AS % OF ASSETS	EMPLOYEES
12/20	8,798.5	57.6	0.7%	628
12/19	8,188.6	54.7	0.7%	698
12/18	6,691.6	22.7	0.3%	663
12/17*	5,766.5	3.6	0.1%	0
09/17	5,429.3	31.0	0.6%	679
Annual Growth	12.8%	16.7%	—	(1.9%)

*Fiscal year change

2020 Year-End Financials

Return on assets: 0.6%
Return on equity: 5.7%
Long-term debt ($ mil.): —
No. of shares (mil.): 110.9
Sales ($ mil): 326.9

Dividends
Yield: —
Payout: —
Market value ($ mil.): 1,726.0

	STOCK PRICE ($) FY Close	P/E High/Low		PER SHARE ($) Earnings	Dividends	Book Value
12/20	15.56	33	21	0.52	0.00	9.12
12/19	16.94	35	30	0.49	0.00	8.64
12/18	15.29	88	74	0.20	0.00	8.39
Annual Growth	0.9%	—	—	61.2%	—	4.2%

Comfort Systems USA Inc

Comfort Systems USA sells and services commercial HVAC (heating ventilation and air conditioning) systems in apartments health care facilities office buildings manufacturing plants retail centers and schools. Some company locations also offer fire protection and electrical services. More than 45% of its revenue was attributable to installation services in newly constructed facilities and nearly 55% was attributable to renovation expansion maintenance repair and replacement services in existing buildings. Comfort Substantially all of its revenue is generated in the US. Systems was established in 1997.

Operations

The company operates in two business segments: mechanical and electrical.

In mechanical business segment customers hire the company to ensure HVAC systems deliver specified or generally expected heating cooling conditioning and circulation of air in a facility. This entails installing core system equipment such as packaged heating and air conditioning units or in the case of larger facilities separate core components such as chillers boilers air handlers and cooling towers. It also typically installs connecting and distribution elements such as piping and ducting. The segment accounts for about 85% of company's revenue.

In electrical business segment its principal business activity is electrical construction and engineering in the commercial and industrial field. It also performs electrical logistics services electrical service work and electrical construction and engineering services. The segment accounts for more than 15%.

Geographic Reach

Houston-based Comfort Systems operates through nearly 140 locations spanning more than 25 US states.

Substantially all of its revenue is generated in the US.

Sales and Marketing

Comfort Systems' customers include building owners and developers and property managers as well as general contractors architects and consulting engineers. Major customers come from categories including industrial (nearly 40% of revenue) education (more than 15%) healthcare (about 15%) office buildings (about 10%) government retail & restaurants and entertainment and multi-family and residential.

Financial Performance

Revenue increased $241.4 million or 9% to $2.9 billion in 2020 compared to 2019. The increase included a 12% increase related to the TAS North Carolina electrical contractor and Walker acquisitions and a 2% decrease in revenue related to same-store activity.

In 2020 the company had a net income of $150.1 million a 31% increase from the previous year.

The company's cash at the end of 2020 was $54.9 million. Operating activities generated $286.5 million while investing activities used $207.8 million mainly for acquisitions. Financing activities used another $74.6 million primarily for payments on revolving credit facility.

Strategy

The company focuses on strengthening core operating competencies leading in sustainability efficiency and technological improvement and on increasing profit margins. The key objectives of its strategy are to improve profitability and generate growth in its operations to enable sustainable and efficient building environments to improve the productivity of its workforce and to acquire complementary businesses.

In order to accomplish these objectives it is currently focused on the following elements:

Achieve excellence in core competencies in safety customer service design and build expertise effective pre-construction processes job and cost tracking leadership in energy efficient and sustainable design and best-in-class servicing of existing building systems;

Achieve operating efficiencies through purchasing economies adopting operational "best practices" and focusing on job management to deliver services in a cost-effective and efficient manner;

Develop and adopt leading technologies by the increasing use of innovative techniques in prefabrication project design and planning as well as in coordination and production methods. It has invested in the refinement and adoption of prefabrication practices;

Seek growth through acquisitions by continuing to opportunistically enter new markets or service lines through acquisition. It has dedicated a significant portion of its cash flow on an ongoing basis to seek opportunities to acquire businesses that have strong assembled workforces excellent historical safety performance leading design and energy efficiency capabilities attractive market positions a record of consistent positive cash flow and desirable market locations.

Mergers and Acquisitions

In 2021 Comfort Systems agreed to acquire Tennessee Electric Company Inc. dba T E C Industrial Construction and Maintenance (T E C) headquartered in Kingsport Tennessee. T E C provides multidisciplined construction and industrial services including electrical mechanical and other plant services. The acquisition is expected to make a neutral to slightly accretive contribution to earnings per share in 2021 and 2022.

In 2020 Comfort Systems entered into a definitive agreement to acquire the Starr Electric Company (Starr) headquartered in Greensboro North Carolina. Starr engages in a broad range of electrical contracting projects and services and has offices in Charlotte Raleigh Greensboro and Fayetteville North Carolina and in Columbia South Carolina. This investment will allow the company to further develop its modular construction offering by adding electrical rooms and other assemblies to its off-site construction business in High Point North Carolina.

In early 2020 Comfort Systems announced that it has entered into a definitive agreement to acquire TAS Energy Inc. (TAS) headquartered in Houston Texas. TAS is a leading engineering design and construction provider of modular construction systems serving the Technology Power and Industrial sectors. The acquisition is expected to make a neutral to slightly accretive contribution to earnings per share in 2020 and 2021.

Company Background

Comfort Systems went public in June 1997 with the intention of becoming a nationwide provider of building systems installation and maintenance.

Its growth came from successfully expanding services to existing customers and attracting companies into its network of subsidiary companies. Many of them have been operating for 60 years or more.

EXECUTIVES

Independent Chairman Of The Board, Franklin Myers
Senior Vice President, Chief Accounting Officer, Julie Shaeff, $307,000 total compensation
Chief Financial Officer, Executive Vice President, William George, $483,000 total compensation
President, Chief Executive Officer, Director, Brian Lane, $765,000 total compensation
Independent Director, Pablo Mercado
Independent Director, William Sandbrook
Vice President, General Counsel, Secretary, Laura Howell, $265,000 total compensation
Chief Operating Officer, Senior Vice President, Trent McKenna, $361,500 total compensation
Auditors: DELOITTE & TOUCHE LLP

LOCATIONS

HQ: Comfort Systems USA Inc
675 Bering Drive, Suite 400, Houston, TX 77057
Phone: 713 830-9600   **Fax:** 713 830-9696
Web: www.comfortsystemsusa.com

PRODUCTS/OPERATIONS

2015 Sales

	% of total
HVAC	77
Plumbing	14
Building automation control systems	5
Other	4
Total	**100**

2015 Sales

	% of total customers
Manufacturing	21
Education	15
Health care	11
Office buildings	13
Government	10
Retail & restaurants	7
Multi-family	5
Lodging & entertainment	5
Distribution	2
Technology	7
Religious/non-profit	1
Residential	1
Other	2
Total	**100**

SOLUTIONS & SERVICES
Construction Services
Retrofit & Replacement
Building Automation Systems
Energy Services

COMPETITORS

ABM INDUSTRIES INCORPORATED
ACUITY BRANDS INC.
GIBRALTAR INDUSTRIES INC.
JOHNSON CONTROLS INTERNATIONAL PUBLIC LIMITED COMPANY
JOURNEO PLC
LARSEN AND TOUBRO LIMITED
LORNE STEWART PLC
PRIMORIS SERVICES CORPORATION
Stantec Inc
TCLARKE PLC

UNITED RENTALS INC.

HISTORICAL FINANCIALS

Company Type: Public

Income Statement

FYE: December 31

	REVENUE ($ mil.)	NET INCOME ($ mil.)	NET PROFIT MARGIN	EMPLOYEES
12/20	2,856.6	150.1	5.3%	11,100
12/19	2,615.2	114.3	4.4%	12,000
12/18	2,182.8	112.9	5.2%	9,900
12/17	1,787.9	55.2	3.1%	8,700
12/16	1,634.3	64.9	4.0%	7,700
Annual Growth	**15.0%**	**23.3%**		**9.6%**

2020 Year-End Financials

Debt ratio: 13.4%
Return on equity: 23.3%
Cash ($ mil.): 54.9
Current ratio: 1.17
Long-term debt ($ mil.): 235.7
No. of shares (mil.): 36.1
Dividends
  Yield: 0.8%
  Payout: 10.3%
Market value ($ mil.): 1,906.0

	STOCK PRICE ($) FY Close	P/E High/Low		PER SHARE ($) Earnings	Dividends	Book Value
12/20	52.66	14	7	4.09	0.43	19.24
12/19	49.85	19	12	3.08	0.40	15.97
12/18	43.68	20	13	3.00	0.33	13.50
12/17	43.65	30	22	1.47	0.30	11.24
12/16	33.30	20	14	1.72	0.28	10.12
Annual Growth	**12.1%**			**24.2%**	**11.5%**	**17.4%**

Communities First Financial Corp

Auditors: Crowe LLP

LOCATIONS

HQ: Communities First Financial Corp
7690 N. Palm Avenue, Suite 101, Fresno, CA 93711
Phone: 559 439-0200
Web: www.fresnofirstbank.com

HISTORICAL FINANCIALS

Company Type: Public

Income Statement

FYE: December 31

	ASSETS ($ mil.)	NET INCOME ($ mil.)	INCOME AS % OF ASSETS	EMPLOYEES
12/20	871.9	11.5	1.3%	0
12/19	538.3	9.2	1.7%	0
12/18	467.2	6.2	1.3%	0
12/17	407.4	3.6	0.9%	0
12/16	363.5	3.0	0.8%	0
Annual Growth	**24.4%**	**39.1%**		

2020 Year-End Financials

Return on assets: 1.6%
Return on equity: 19.0%
Long-term debt ($ mil.): —
No. of shares (mil.): 3.0
Sales ($ mil): 35.8
Dividends
  Yield: —
  Payout: —
Market value ($ mil.): 93.0

	STOCK PRICE ($) FY Close	P/E High/Low		PER SHARE ($) Earnings	Dividends	Book Value
12/20	31.01	9	5	3.79	0.00	22.82
12/19	28.75	10	6	3.09	0.00	17.67
12/18	19.80	12	9	2.14	0.00	14.24
12/17	19.55	17	9	1.28	0.00	12.19
12/16	11.50	10	9	1.12	0.00	10.96
Annual Growth	**28.1%**			**35.6%**		**20.1%**

Community Bank System Inc

Community Bank System is right up front about what it is. The holding company owns Community Bank which operates about 195 branches across upstate New York and northeastern Pennsylvania where it operates as First Liberty Bank and Trust. Focusing on small underserved towns and non-urban markets the bank offers standard products and services such as checking and savings accounts certificates of deposit and loans and mortgages to consumer business and government clients. Boasting over $11.0 billion in assets the bank's loan portfolio consists of mostly business loans residential mortgages and consumer loans. Community Bank System's subsidiaries offer employee benefit services wealth management and insurance products and services.

Operations

Community Bank System operates three business segments. The Banking segment which made up 83% of the company's total revenue during 2015 provides lending and deposit services to individuals businesses and municipalities. Employee Benefit Services (12% of revenue) offers trust investment fund retirement plan actuarial healthcare consulting and other administrative services through Benefit Plan Administrative Services (BPAS). The All Other segment (5% of revenue) includes its Wealth Management (operating through Community Investment Services) and Insurance businesses (operating through CBNA Insurance Agency).

Nearly 70% of the company's revenue comes from interest income. About 49% of its revenue came from loan interest during 2015 while another 19% came from interest on taxable and nontaxable investments. The rest of its revenue came from deposit service fees (14% of revenue) employee benefit services (12%) wealth management and insurance services (5%) and other banking revenues (1%).

Geographic Reach

Community Bank System operated 194 branches and six back-office operating facilities in 36 counties in upstate New York and six counties in northeastern Pennsylvania at the end of 2015.

Sales and Marketing

The bank has been ramping up its advertising spend in recent years. It spent $3.6 million on advertising during 2015 up from $3.2 million and $3.0 million in 2014 and 2013 respectively.

Financial Performance

Community Bank System's annual revenues have been slowly trending higher since 2013 despite a decline in loan interest mostly as it's been building its non-interest related business lines. Meanwhile its net income has risen more than 15% as it's had to pay less in interest expenses on deposits amidst the low interest environment.

The bank's revenue grew 2% to $382.92 million during 2015 thanks to a combination of employee benefit services business growth from new customers and expanding business relationships with existing customers as well as from new service offerings; higher interest income from loans and taxable investments as such interest-earning asset balances grew modestly; and a 13% jump in wealth management and insurance services revenue stemming from the acquisition of OneGroup from the Oneida Financial Group acquisition.

Despite revenue growth in 2015 Community's net income dipped less than 1% to $91.23 million for the year due to costs related to the Oneida acquisition. The company's operating cash levels shrank 5% to $116.46 million mostly due to unfavorable working capital changes related to deferred income tax provisions and changes in other assets and liabilities.

Strategy

Community Bank System looks to continue building its loan and deposit business as well as its non-interest service lines organically and through strategic acquisitions of other banks and financial companies. The financial company in 2015 began exploring expansion opportunities into neighboring markets in eastern Ohio upper New England and New Jersey and in 2017 acquired Northeast Retirement Services (NRS) for around $146 million. NRS provides institutional transfer agency master recordkeeping services custom target date fund administration trust product administration and customized reporting services to institutional clients.

Mergers and Acquisitions

Community Bank System acquired Kinderhook Bank in 2019 for $93.4 million. Kinderhook has 11 offices in five New York counties (including in the Capital District of upstate New York) and holds nearly $640 million in assets and about $560 million in deposits. The deal extends Community Bank's reach into the Capital District markets.

In spring 2017 Community Bank acquired Vermont-based Merchants Bancshares. Merchants operates nearly 35 branches and has assets in excess of $1.8 billion; the acquisition will expand Community Bank's operations into Vermont and western Massachusetts.

Company Background

In mid-2012 the bank purchased about 20 branches in upstate New York from HSBC. The deal which was made to satisfy antitrust concerns regarding First Niagara's purchase of 195 branches in New York from HSBC strengthened Community Bank Systems' geographic footprint.

In 2011 the company bought bank holding company The Wilber Corporation adding about 20 locations in the Catskills Mountains region of central New York.

In 2011 expanding its trust and benefits administration business it bought retirement plan administrator CAI Benefits which has offices in New York and Northern New Jersey.

EXECUTIVES

President, Chief Executive Officer, Director, Mark Tryniski, $844,600 total compensation
Independent Director, Brian Ace
Senior Vice President, Chief Investment Officer, Joseph Lemchak, $290,250 total compensation
Executive Vice President And General Counsel, George Getman, $432,800 total compensation
Independent Director, Neil Fesette
Lead Independent Director, John Whipple
Independent Director, Mark Bolus
Executive Vice President, Chief Banking Officer, Joseph Serbun, $400,000 total compensation
Chief Financial Officer, Executive Vice President, Joseph Sutaris, $400,000 total compensation
Independent Director, Eric Stickels
Independent Director, Raymond Pecor
Independent Director, Jeffrey Davis
Independent Director, Susan Skerritt
Independent Director, Jeffery Knauss
Auditors: PricewaterhouseCoopers LLP

LOCATIONS

HQ: Community Bank System Inc
5790 Widewaters Parkway, DeWitt, NY 13214-1883
Phone: 315 445-2282
Web: www.communitybankna.com

PRODUCTS/OPERATIONS

2015 Sales

	$ mil.	% of total
Interest Income:		
Interest and fees on loans	187.7	49
Taxable investments	52.9	14
Nontaxable investments	19.0	5
Noninterest		
Deposit service fees	52.7	14
Employee benefit services	45.4	12
Wealth management	20.2	5
Other	5.0	1
Total	**382.9**	**100**

Selected Subsidiaries & Affiliates

Benefit Plans Administrative Services Inc.
Benefit Plans Administrative Services LLC
Brilie Corporation
CBNA Insurance Agency Inc.
CBNA Preferred Funding Corp.
CBNA Treasury Management Corporation
Community Bank N.A. (also dba First Liberty Bank & Trust)
Community Investment Services Inc.
First of Jermyn Realty Company
First Liberty Service Corporation
Flex Corporation
Hand Benefit & Trust Company
Hand Securities Inc.
Harbridge Consulting Group LLP
Nottingham Advisors Inc.
Town & Country Agency LLC
Western Catskill Realty Inc.

COMPETITORS

ALDERMORE GROUP PLC	FIRSTMERIT CORPORATION
AMERICAN NATIONAL BANKSHARES INC.	FIRSTRAND LTD INVESTEC PLC
ARROW FINANCIAL CORPORATION	PACIFIC CONTINENTAL CORPORATION
BANCFIRST CORPORATION	PEOPLES FINANCIAL
CAPITAL CITY BANK GROUP INC.	SERVICES CORP. RECORD PLC
CITIZENS & NORTHERN CORPORATION	WEBSTER FINANCIAL CORPORATION
ENTERPRISE FINANCIAL SERVICES CORP	WINTRUST FINANCIAL CORPORATION

FINANCIAL INSTITUTIONS INC.
Woori Finance Holdings Co. Ltd.

HISTORICAL FINANCIALS

Company Type: Public

Income Statement

FYE: December 31

	ASSETS ($ mil.)	NET INCOME ($ mil.)	INCOME AS % OF ASSETS	EMPLOYEES
12/20	13,931.0	164.6	1.2%	3,047
12/19	11,410.3	169.0	1.5%	3,038
12/18	10,607.3	168.6	1.6%	2,933
12/17	10,746.2	150.7	1.4%	2,874
12/16	8,666.4	103.8	1.2%	2,499
Annual Growth	**12.6%**	**12.2%**	**—**	**5.1%**

2020 Year-End Financials

Return on assets: 1.3%	Dividends
Return on equity: 8.3%	Yield: 2.6%
Long-term debt ($ mil.): —	Payout: 54.7%
No. of shares (mil.): 53.5	Market value ($ mil.): 3,339.0
Sales ($ mil): 617.7	

	STOCK PRICE ($) FY Close	P/E High/Low		PER SHARE ($) Earnings	Dividends	Book Value
12/20	62.31	23	16	3.08	1.66	39.26
12/19	70.94	22	17	3.23	1.58	35.82
12/18	58.30	20	16	3.24	1.44	33.43
12/17	53.75	20	16	3.03	1.32	32.26
12/16	61.79	27	15	2.32	1.26	26.96
Annual Growth	**0.2%**	**—**	**—**	**7.3%**	**7.1%**	**9.9%**

Community Financial Corp (The)

Tri-County Financial is trying to create some interest in the Old Line State. The financial institution is the holding company for Community Bank of Tri-County which operates about 10 branches in Calvert Charles and St. Mary's counties in southern Maryland. The bank which was first organized as a savings and loan association in 1950 offers standard retail products and services including checking and savings accounts IRAs and CDs. It uses funds from deposits to write a variety of loans including commercial mortgages (about 40% of its loan book) residential mortgages and business loans. Home equity construction equipment and consumer loans round out its loan portfolio.

EXECUTIVES

Executive Vice President, Chief Financial Officer Of The Company And The Bank, Todd Capitani, $320,000 total compensation
Independent Chairman Of The Board, Austin Slater, $75,800 total compensation
Executive Vice President And Chief Banking Officer For The Bank, Patrick Pierce
Independent Director, Mohammad Javaid, $39,625 total compensation
Independent Director, Kathryn Zabriskie, $45,550 total compensation
Independent Director, Kimberly Briscoe-tonic, $37,925 total compensation

HOOVER'S HANDBOOK OF EMERGING COMPANIES 2022

Independent Director, E. Lawrence Sanders, $47,775 total compensation
Executive Vice President And Chief Digital Officer Of The Bank, John Chappelle
Executive Vice President, Chief Administrative Officer Of The Bank, Lacey Pierce
Executive Vice President, Chief Risk Officer Of The Bank, Tala Tay
Executive Vice President, Chief Banking Officer Of The Bank, Brian Ebron
Independent Director, Rebecca Mcdonald, $27,227 total compensation
Independent Director, Mary Peterson, $50,650 total compensation
Chief Executive Officer, William Pasenelli, $535,000 total compensation
President, Executive Vice President, Director And President Of The Bank, James Burke, $382,000 total compensation
Director, James Di Misa, $23,025 total compensation
Director, Gregory Cockerham, $19,900 total compensation
Chief Operating Officer, Executive Vice President Of The Company And The Bank, Christy Lombardi
Independent Director, Joseph Stone, $49,875 total compensation
Auditors: Dixon Hughes Goodman LLP

LOCATIONS

HQ: Community Financial Corp (The)
3035 Leonardtown Road, Waldorf, MD 20601
Phone: 301 645-5601
Web: www.cbtc.com

COMPETITORS

BCSB BANCORP INC.   SB ONE BANCORP
MUTUALFIRST FINANCIAL INC.

HISTORICAL FINANCIALS
Company Type: Public

Income Statement — FYE: December 31

	ASSETS ($ mil.)	NET INCOME ($ mil.)	INCOME AS % OF ASSETS	EMPLOYEES
12/20	2,026.4	16.1	0.8%	191
12/19	1,797.5	15.2	0.8%	194
12/18	1,689.2	11.2	0.7%	189
12/17	1,405.9	7.2	0.5%	165
12/16	1,334.2	7.3	0.5%	162
Annual Growth	11.0%	21.8%	—	4.2%

2020 Year-End Financials

Return on assets: 0.8%
Return on equity: 8.4%
Long-term debt ($ mil.): —
No. of shares (mil.): 5.9
Sales ($ mil) 79.4

Dividends
Yield: 1.8%
Payout: 20.4%
Market value ($ mil.): 156.0

	STOCK PRICE ($) FY Close	P/E High/Low		PER SHARE ($) Earnings	Dividends	Book Value
12/20	26.48	13	7	2.74	0.50	33.54
12/19	35.57	13	10	2.75	0.50	30.76
12/18	29.24	19	13	2.02	0.40	27.70
12/17	38.30	26	18	1.56	0.40	23.65
12/16	29.00	19	12	1.59	0.40	22.54
Annual Growth	(2.2%)	—	—	14.6%	5.7%	10.5%

Community Healthcare Trust Inc

Auditors: BDO USA, LLP

LOCATIONS

HQ: Community Healthcare Trust Inc
3326 Aspen Grove Drive, Suite 150, Franklin, TN 37067
Phone: 615 771-3052
Web: www.chct.reit

HISTORICAL FINANCIALS
Company Type: Public

Income Statement — FYE: December 31

	REVENUE ($ mil.)	NET INCOME ($ mil.)	NET PROFIT MARGIN	EMPLOYEES
12/21	90.5	22.4	24.8%	30
12/20	75.6	19.0	25.2%	28
12/19	60.8	8.3	13.8%	25
12/18	48.6	4.4	9.1%	16
12/17	37.3	3.5	9.4%	16
Annual Growth	24.8%	59.1%		17.0%

2021 Year-End Financials

Debt ratio: 35.6%
Return on equity: 5.0%
Cash ($ mil.): 2.3
Current ratio: 0.37
Long-term debt ($ mil.): 268.6

No. of shares (mil.): 24.9
Dividends
Yield: 3.6%
Payout: 205.3%
Market value ($ mil.): 1,181.0

	STOCK PRICE ($) FY Close	P/E High/Low		PER SHARE ($) Earnings	Dividends	Book Value
12/21	47.27	60	49	0.87	1.73	18.50
12/20	47.11	65	28	0.80	1.69	18.00
12/19	42.86	132	76	0.37	1.65	16.51
12/18	28.83	170	118	0.19	1.61	14.58
12/17	28.10	151	113	0.19	1.57	15.67
Annual Growth	13.9%	—	—	46.3%	2.5%	4.2%

Community West Bancshares

Community West Bancshares is the holding company for Community West Bank which serves individuals and small to midsized businesses through five branches along California's Central Coast. Services include checking and savings accounts and CDs as well as health savings accounts. Approximately 40% of the bank's loan portfolio is secured by manufactured housing loans; real estate mortgages account for more than 30%. A preferred Small Business Administration lender Community West also writes SBA loans through offices in about a dozen other states.

EXECUTIVES

Independent Chairman Of The Board, William Peeples
Independent Director, Kirk Stovesand
Executive Vice President And Chief Operating Officer Of Cwb, Timothy Stronks, $242,740 total compensation
Chief Financial Officer And Executive Vice President, Richard Pimentel
President, Chief Executive Officer, Director, Martin Plourd, $450,000 total compensation
President Of Community West Bank, William Filippin, $285,000 total compensation
Independent Director, Tom Dobyns
Independent Director, Robert Bartlein
Independent Director, John Illgen
Independent Director, Shereef Moharram
Independent Director, Dana Boutain
Independent Director, Christopher Raffo
Director, Celina Zacarias
Independent Director, James Lokey
Auditors: RSM US LLP

LOCATIONS

HQ: Community West Bancshares
445 Pine Avenue, Goleta, CA 93117
Phone: 805 692-5821   **Fax:** 805 692-5835
Web: www.communitywest.com

PRODUCTS/OPERATIONS

2008 Sales

	$ mil.	% of total
Interest		
Loans	43.0	85
Investment securities	2.2	4
Other	0.3	1
Non-interest		
Loan fees	2.1	4
Loan sales	1.0	2
Other fees	1.7	3
Other	0.3	1
Total	**50.6**	**100**

COMPETITORS

FIRST KEYSTONE CORPORATION

FIRST US BANCSHARES INC.

HISTORICAL FINANCIALS
Company Type: Public

Income Statement — FYE: December 31

	ASSETS ($ mil.)	NET INCOME ($ mil.)	INCOME AS % OF ASSETS	EMPLOYEES
12/20	975.4	8.2	0.8%	128
12/19	913.8	7.9	0.9%	133
12/18	877.2	7.4	0.8%	139
12/17	833.3	4.9	0.6%	128
12/16	710.5	5.2	0.7%	120
Annual Growth	8.2%	12.1%	—	1.6%

2020 Year-End Financials

Return on assets: 0.8%
Return on equity: 9.6%
Long-term debt ($ mil.): —
No. of shares (mil.): 8.4
Sales ($ mil): 47.7

Dividends
Yield: 2.1%
Payout: 20.1%
Market value ($ mil.): 77.0

STOCK PRICE ($)		P/E		PER SHARE ($)		
	FY Close	High/Low		Earnings	Dividends	Book Value
12/20	9.08	12	6	0.97	0.20	10.50
12/19	11.10	12	10	0.93	0.22	9.68
12/18	10.03	14	11	0.88	0.19	8.92
12/17	10.65	18	15	0.57	0.16	8.55
12/16	9.24	15	11	0.62	0.14	8.07
Annual Growth	(0.4%)	—	—	11.8%	9.6%	6.8%

Compass Diversified

Compass Diversified Holdings helps niche companies navigate their way toward profitability. The holding company owns controlling stakes in and manages promising middle-market businesses throughout North America. Its strategy is two-fold: help its portfolio firms grow and increase their profits and increase the size of its own portfolio. Compass invests in niche businesses across a variety of industries including furniture maker AFM Holdings (sold in 2015) and home and gun safes maker Liberty Safe and Security Products. Its arsenal includes helping its holdings make strategic acquisitions enter new business arenas or improve operations to increase profitability.

Strategy

When evaluating acquisition candidates Compass looks for established US-based companies with significant market share in a niche industry with a low risk of technological or product obsolescence. Other investment criteria include a proven management team diversified customer and supplier base and a minimum EBITDA (earnings before interest taxes depreciation and amortization) of $8 million.

To that end in late 2014 Compass spent $163 million to acquire the California-based Candle Lamp Company ("SternoCandleLamp") a leading manufacturer and marketer of portable food warming fuel and creative table lighting solutions for the food service industry. Also in 2014 the company purchased Clean Earth which provides environmental services for contaminated soils dredged materials hazardous waste and other contaminated materials. Shortly after that deal Clean Earth acquired AES Environmental allowing it deepen its presence in the Midwest and Mid-Atlantic.

In late 2015 Compass sold AFM Holdings for some $24 million; it had acquired the firm in 2007 for $93 million. The company reported a loss on the sale of approximately $14 million.

EXECUTIVES

Chairman Of The Board, C. Sean Day
Independent Director, James Bottiglieri
Chief Financial Officer, Co-compliance Officer, Ryan Faulkingham, $450,000 total compensation
Independent Director, Harold Edwards
Investor Relations, Leon Berman
Independent Director, Larry Enterline
Director, Alex Bhathal
Chief Executive Officer, Director, Elias Sabo
Auditors: Grant Thornton LLP

LOCATIONS

HQ: Compass Diversified
301 Riverside Avenue, Second Floor, Westport, CT 06880
Phone: 203 221-1703
Web: www.compassdiversifiedholdings.com

COMPETITORS

BERWIND CORPORATION	Investor AB
CBOE GLOBAL MARKETS INC.	MARKETAXESS HOLDINGS INC.
FENWAY PARTNERS LLC	N L INDUSTRIES INC.
FLEX LTD.	VIRTU ITG HOLDINGS LLC
HARSCO CORPORATION	WADDELL & REED FINANCIAL INC.
INNOVATE CORP.	

HISTORICAL FINANCIALS
Company Type: Public

Income Statement — FYE: December 31

	REVENUE ($ mil.)	NET INCOME ($ mil.)	NET PROFIT MARGIN	EMPLOYEES
12/20	1,560.7	22.7	1.5%	4,598
12/19	1,450.2	301.8	20.8%	3,456
12/18	1,691.6	(5.7)	—	2,416
12/17	1,269.7	27.9	2.2%	837
12/16	978.3	54.6	5.6%	655
Annual Growth	12.4%	(19.7%)	—	62.8%

2020 Year-End Financials

Debt ratio: 34.6%
Return on equity: 2.0%
Cash ($ mil.): 70.7
Current ratio: 2.40
Long-term debt ($ mil.): 899.4
No. of shares (mil.): 64.9
Dividends
Yield: 7.4%
Payout: 394.4%
Market value ($ mil.): 1,262.0

STOCK PRICE ($)		P/E		PER SHARE ($)		
	FY Close	High/Low		Earnings	Dividends	Book Value
12/20	19.45	—	—	(0.34)	1.44	16.95
12/19	24.86	7	4	3.64	1.44	18.62
12/18	12.45	—	—	(0.42)	1.44	14.35
12/17	16.95	—	—	(0.44)	1.44	14.58
12/16	17.90	38	28	0.51	1.44	14.30
Annual Growth	2.1%	—	—	—	(0.0%)	4.3%

ConnectOne Bancorp Inc (New)

ConnectOne Bancorp (formerly Center Bancorp) is the holding company for ConnectOne Bank which operates some two dozen branches across New Jersey. Serving individuals and local businesses the bank offers such deposit products as checking savings and money market accounts; CDs; and IRAs. It also performs trust services. Commercial loans account for about 60% of the bank's loan portfolio; residential mortgages account for most of the remainder. It also has a subsidiary that sells annuities and property/casualty life and health coverage. The former Center Bancorp acquired rival community bank ConnectOne Bancorp in 2014 and took that name.

Geographic Reach

ConnectOne has 24 branches in Bergen Essex Hudson Manhattan Mercer Monmouth Morris and Union Counties in New Jersey.

Mergers and Acquisitions

In 2019 ConnectOne Bancorp agreed to acquire online business lending marketplace company BoeFly. BoeFly connects franchisors and small business owners with lenders and loan brokers in the US and has facilitated more than $5 billion in financing transactions. BoeFly's online platform and client network will enhance and expand ConnectOne's Small Business Adminstration (SBA) line of business.

EXECUTIVES

Independent Director, Nicholas Minoia
Chairman And Chief Executive Officer, Frank Sorrentino, $825,000 total compensation
President - Connect One Bank, Elizabeth Magennis, $422,500 total compensation
Independent Director, Frank Huttle
Director, Michael Kempner
Chief Financial Officer, Executive Vice President, William Burns, $430,000 total compensation
Independent Director, Katherin Nukk-Freeman
Independent Director, Daniel Rifkin
Independent Director, Mark Sokolich
Auditors: Crowe LLP

LOCATIONS

HQ: ConnectOne Bancorp Inc (New)
301 Sylvan Avenue, Englewood Cliffs, NJ 07632
Phone: 201 816-8900
Web: www.centerbancorp.com

COMPETITORS

ARVEST BANK GROUP INC.	UNITY BANCORP INC.
FIRST US BANCSHARES INC.	

HISTORICAL FINANCIALS
Company Type: Public

Income Statement — FYE: December 31

	ASSETS ($ mil.)	NET INCOME ($ mil.)	INCOME AS % OF ASSETS	EMPLOYEES
12/20	7,547.3	71.2	0.9%	413
12/19	6,174.0	73.4	1.2%	0
12/18	5,462.0	60.3	1.1%	0
12/17	5,108.4	43.2	0.8%	0
12/16	4,426.3	31.0	0.7%	0
Annual Growth	14.3%	23.1%	—	—

2020 Year-End Financials

Return on assets: 1.0%
Return on equity: 8.6%
Long-term debt ($ mil.): —
No. of shares (mil.): 39.7
Sales ($ mil): 322.6
Dividends
Yield: 1.8%
Payout: 20.1%
Market value ($ mil.): 787.0

STOCK PRICE ($)		P/E		PER SHARE ($)		
	FY Close	High/Low		Earnings	Dividends	Book Value
12/20	19.79	14	5	1.79	0.36	23.01
12/19	25.72	13	9	2.07	0.35	20.85
12/18	18.47	17	9	1.86	0.30	18.99
12/17	25.75	21	16	1.34	0.30	17.63
12/16	25.95	26	15	1.01	0.30	16.62
Annual Growth	(6.6%)	—	—	15.4%	4.7%	8 5%

HOOVER'S HANDBOOK OF EMERGING COMPANIES 2022

Consolidated Communications Holdings Inc

Consolidated Communications is just what its name implies. The rural local exchange carrier operates systems in Illinois Kansas Missouri Pennsylvania Texas and California providing voice and data telecommunications to business and residential customers. It operates RLECs that offer local access and long-distance internet and TV business phone systems and related services through about 270000 local access lines 167000 voice connections and 290000 data and Internet connections. It also offers directory publishing and carrier services. Subsidiaries include Illinois Consolidated Telephone Company Consolidated Communications of Fort Bend Company and Consolidated Communications of Texas Company.

Operations

Video data and Internet services generate 45% of Consolidated's revenue with local calling services and network access services providing 17% each.

Geographic Reach

In its home base of Illinois (the headquarters is in Mattoon) Consolidated operates 35 incumbent local exchanges serving primarily small towns and rural areas mostly in the central part of the state. It also has operations in East Texas western Pennsylvania around Sacramento Calif. and around Kansas City in Missouri and Kansas.

Sales and Marketing

Consolidated markets services individually and in bundles such as the 'triple-play' of voice data and video services. The company boosted its advertising spending to $8.2 million in 2014 from $7.6 million in 2013.

Financial Performance

Consolidated reported revenue of $635.7 million for 2014 up about 7% from $601.5 million in 2013. The acquisition of Enventis a Mlinnesota telecom lifted revenue. However only video data and Internet services posted a year-to-year revenue gain while revenue from other segments fell.

Net income dropped 51% to $15 million in 2014 from $31 million in 2013. Acquisitions were accompanied by higher operating costs which cut into net income as did depreciation and amortization expenses.

Cash from operations rose to $189 million in 2014 from $164 million in 2013 because of a change in working capital items.

Strategy

One way to view Consolidated's strategy is to look at a map. Starting in Illinois the company has expanded to Pennsylvania Texas Missouri and Kansas and California gobbling up similar telecoms that serve small towns and rural areas. It's tweaking that approach with its move to the Kansas City area and into the Dallas-Fort Worth suburbs.

As the company's wireline business decreases (as it has with most telecom companies) Consolidated is moving to add more Internet data and video services to its lineup. The company is expanding its services in a big way in the Dallas-Fort Worth area where it has 30000 miles of fiber ready to light up with Internet access wide area networks and hosted iPBX for commercial customer. The network had been used for wholesale and carrier customers.

Consolidated offers high-speed Internet service through fiber optic lines in Kansas City and Conroe and Katy Texas. The company gained about 4200 miles of fiber lines with its acquisition of Eventis. Consolidate's capital expenditure budgets include money for continued expansion of fiber in its service areas.

Consolidated also is expanding its services to provide carrier hotel space and data center space in its markets and to support fiber backhaul services to cell sites. It is to have nearly 700 cell tower sites completed by the end of 2014.

Mergers and Acquisitions

Acquisitions play a key role in Consolidated Communications growth strategy and the company continued in 2016 with a deal to buy FairPoint Communications for $1.5 billion (including debt). FairPoint Communications operates in the Eastern US and has a strong network in New England. The deal would extend Consolidated's reach to some 24 states from California to North Carolina and other points on the eastern seaboard. FairPoint's assets bring Consolidated route miles of fiber optic cable to 35100. The transaction is expected to close in mid-2017.

In 2014 Consolidated bought Enventis which has service in Iowa Minnesota North Dakota South Dakota and Wisconsin for about $350 million. Enventis brings about 39000 access lines 21000 high-speed Internet customers 12000 digital TV customers and 90 fiber-to-the tower sites as well as $123 million in revenue.

In 2012 Consolidated bought SureWest Communications a provider of residential and commercial communications and broadband services in the Sacramento California and Kansas City markets in a deal valued at $324 million excluding debt.

EXECUTIVES

Non-executive Chairman Of The Board, Robert Currey

President, Chief Executive Officer & Director, Bob Udell, $600,000 total compensation

President - Commercial And Carrier Services, Michael Smith

Independent Director, Maribeth Rahe

Chief Financial Officer, Steven Childers, $350,000 total compensation

Independent Director, Roger Moore

Independent Director, Thomas Gerke

Independent Director, David Fuller

Executive Vice President, President - Company's Consumer-smb Business Unit, Erik Garr

Director, Andrew Frey

Independent Director, Marissa Solis

Auditors: Ernst & Young LLP

LOCATIONS

HQ: Consolidated Communications Holdings Inc
2116 South 17th Street, Mattoon, IL 61938
Phone: 217 235-3311
Web: www.consolidated.com

PRODUCTS/OPERATIONS

2014 Sales

	$ mil.	% of total
Telephone		
Data Internet & video	287.5	45
Local calling 108.3	17	
Network access	106.3	17
Subsidies	53.2	8
Long distance	19.6	3
Other services	60.8	10
Total	**635.7**	**100**

COMPETITORS

ALTICE USA INC.
AT&T INC.
CABLE ONE INC.
CHARTER COMMUNICATIONS INC.
ELECTRIC LIGHTWAVE COMMUNICATIONS INC.
SHENANDOAH TELECOMMUNICATIONS COMPANY
TDS TELECOMMUNICATIONS CORPORATION
TOWERSTREAM CORPORATION
WINDSTREAM HOLDINGS INC.

HISTORICAL FINANCIALS

Company Type: Public

Income Statement

FYE: December 31

	REVENUE ($ mil.)	NET INCOME ($ mil.)	NET PROFIT MARGIN	EMPLOYEES
12/20	1,304.0	36.9	2.8%	3,200
12/19	1,336.5	(20.3)	—	3,400
12/18	1,399.0	(50.8)	—	3,600
12/17	1,059.5	64.9	6.1%	3,930
12/16	743.1	14.9	2.0%	1,676
Annual Growth	**15.1%**	**25.4%**	**—**	**17.5%**

2020 Year-End Financials

Debt ratio: 55.6%
Return on equity: 10.2%
Cash ($ mil.): 155.5
Current ratio: 1.26
Long-term debt ($ mil.): 1,932.6
No. of shares (mil.): 79.2
Dividends
　Yield: —
　Payout: —
Market value ($ mil.): 387.0

	STOCK PRICE ($) FY Close	P/E High/Low		PER SHARE ($) Earnings	Dividends	Book Value
12/20	4.89	18	8	0.47	0.00	4.83
12/19	3.88	—	—	(0.29)	1.55	4.74
12/18	9.88	—	—	(0.73)	1.55	5.76
12/17	12.19	26	11	1.07	1.55	8.03
12/16	26.85	102	64	0.29	1.55	3.38
Annual Growth	**(34.7%)**	**—**	**—**	**12.8%**	**—**	**9.3%**

Construction Partners Inc

Auditors: RSM US LLP

LOCATIONS

HQ: Construction Partners Inc
290 Healthwest Drive, Suite 2, Dothan, AL 36303
Phone: 334 673-9763
Web: www.constructionpartners.net

HISTORICAL FINANCIALS
Company Type: Public

Income Statement
FYE: September 30

	REVENUE ($ mil.)	NET INCOME ($ mil.)	NET PROFIT MARGIN	EMPLOYEES
09/21	910.7	20.1	2.2%	2,960
09/20	785.6	40.3	5.1%	2,289
09/19	783.2	43.1	5.5%	2,289
09/18	680.1	50.7	7.5%	2,154
09/17	568.2	26.0	4.6%	1,856
Annual Growth	12.5%	(6.2%)	—	12.4%

2021 Year-End Financials
Debt ratio: 26.8%
Return on equity: 5.0%
Cash ($ mil.): 57.2
Current ratio: 1.90
Long-term debt ($ mil.): 206.1
No. of shares (mil.): 52.2
Dividends
Yield: —
Payout: —
Market value ($ mil.): 1,745.0

	STOCK PRICE ($) FY Close	P/E High/Low		PER SHARE ($) Earnings	Dividends	Book Value
09/21	33.37	92	47	0.39	0.00	7.82
09/20	18.20	28	16	0.78	0.00	7.44
09/19	15.58	20	10	0.84	0.00	6.63
09/18	12.10	13	10	1.11	0.00	5.82
Annual Growth	40.2%	—	—	(29.4%)	—	10.3%

Consumers Bancorp, Inc. (Minerva, OH)

You don't have to be a consumer to do business with Consumers — it's happy to serve businesses as well. Consumers Bancorp is the holding company for Consumers National Bank which has about 10 branches in eastern Ohio. The bank offers standard services such as savings and checking accounts CDs and NOW accounts. Business loans make up more than half of the bank's loan portfolio; real estate consumer and construction loans round out its lending activities. CNB Investment Services a division of the bank offers insurance brokerage financial planning and wealth management services through a third-party provider UVEST. Chairman Laurie McClellan owns more than 20% of Consumers Bancorp.

EXECUTIVES
Chairman Of The Board Of The Company And Consumers National Bank, Laurie Mcclellan
Independent Vice Chairman Of The Board Of The Company, And Consumers National Bank, John Furey
Independent Director, Harry Schmuck
Independent Director, Bradley Goris
Senior Vice President Of Retail Operations And Sales, Derek Williams
Executive Vice President, Senior Loan Officer, Scott Dodds, $195,457 total compensation
Independent Director, Richard Kiko
Chief Financial Officer, Executive Vice President, Treasurer, Renee Wood, $197,271 total compensation
Independent Director, John Parkinson

Senior Vice President, Chief Credit Officer, Suzanne Mikes
Independent Director, Michael Wheeler
Independent Director, Shawna L'italien
President, Chief Executive Officer, Director Of The Company And Consumers National Bank, Ralph Lober, $301,221 total compensation
Independent Director, Frank Paden
Auditors: Plante & Moran, PLLC

LOCATIONS
HQ: Consumers Bancorp, Inc. (Minerva, OH)
614 East Lincoln Way, P.O. Box 256, Minerva, OH 44657
Phone: 330 868-7701
Web: www.consumers.bank

COMPETITORS
EMCLAIRE FINANCIAL CORP.
LYONS NATIONAL BANK
WOODFOREST FINANCIAL GROUP INC.

HISTORICAL FINANCIALS
Company Type: Public

Income Statement
FYE: June 30

	ASSETS ($ mil.)	NET INCOME ($ mil.)	INCOME AS % OF ASSETS	EMPLOYEES
06/21	833.8	8.9	1.1%	176
06/20	740.8	5.5	0.7%	172
06/19	553.9	5.5	1.0%	144
06/18	502.6	3.5	0.7%	139
06/17	457.8	2.9	0.7%	128
Annual Growth	16.2%	31.6%	—	8.3%

2021 Year-End Financials
Return on assets: 1.1%
Return on equity: 13.5%
Long-term debt ($ mil.): —
No. of shares (mil.): 3.0
Sales ($ mil): 32.9
Dividends
Yield: 2.9%
Payout: 20.1%
Market value ($ mil.): 59.0

	STOCK PRICE ($) FY Close	P/E High/Low		PER SHARE ($) Earnings	Dividends	Book Value
06/21	19.50	7	5	2.98	0.58	23.08
06/20	14.19	10	7	1.92	0.41	20.97
06/19	18.50	12	8	2.04	0.52	18.72
06/18	24.00	19	14	1.31	0.50	16.03
06/17	19.00	18	14	1.10	0.48	15.98
Annual Growth	0.7%	—	—	28.3%	4.6%	9.6%

Cooper Companies, Inc. (The)

The Cooper Companies specializes in eye care and to a lesser extent lady care. The global company makes specialty medical devices in two niche markets: vision care and gynecology. Its CooperVision subsidiary makes specialty contact lenses including toric lenses for astigmatism multifocal lenses for presbyopia and cosmetic lenses. The company also offers spherical lenses for more common vision problems such as nearsightedness and farsightedness. Subsidiary CooperSurgical special-izes in women's health care; its wide range of products that are based on the point of health care delivery used in medical office and surgical procedures primarily by Obstetricians/Gynecologists (OB/GYN) as well as fertility products and genetic testing services used primarily in fertility clinics and laboratories. Cooper's products are sold in more than 100 countries. The company primarily earns about 45% of revenue from its domestic sales.

Operations
The Cooper Companies operates through two business units: CooperVision and CooperSurgical.

CooperVision accounts for some 75% of annual sales is one of the largest contact lens manufacturers in the world. Toric lenses account for about 25% of the company's net sales while single-use sphere lens accounts for more than 20%. The segment also makes multifocal lenses which represent about 10% of sales. The segment's non-single-use sphere & other products accounts for more than 20%.

CooperSurgical accounts for about 25% of total sales. It provides diagnostic and therapeutic products used by obstetricians and gynecologists. Fertility products used in office and surgical procedures account for the rest.

Geographic Reach
California-based Cooper Companies rings about 45% of its sales in the US and nearly 30% in Europe. The company's primary manufacturing and distribution facilities for optical products are in the Australia Japan US Puerto Rico the UK Hungary Denmark Belgium Spain and Costa Rica. Its medical device and surgical instrument products are primarily manufactured and distributed from facilities in Costa Rica Spain the Netherlands the UK and the US.

Sales and Marketing
CooperVision markets its products through its own field sales representative who call on optometrists ophthalmologists opticians optical chains and distributors. CooperVision also sells to distributors and to mass merchandisers who offer care services. The segment also engages in various activities and offers a variety of services. These include clinical training digital marketing for the customer e-commerce telemarketing social media and journal advertisements.

CooperSurgical's products are marketed by a network of dedicated field representatives independent agents and distributors. The segment augments its sales and marketing activities by participating in national and regional industry trade shows professional educational programs and internet promotions including e-commerce social media and collaborative efforts with professional organizations telemarketing direct mail and advertising professional journals. With the addition of PARAGARD CooperSurgical expanded its awareness campaigns to include direct to consumer elements including print internet/social media radio and television.

Financial Performance
The company had net sales of $2.9 billion in 2021 a 20% increase from the previous year's net sales of $2.4 billion. This was primarily due to a higher sales volume in the company's segments throughout the year.

In 2021 the company had a net income of $2.9 billion a $2.7 billion increase from the previous year's net income of $238.4 million.

The company's cash at the end of 2021 was $96.6 million. Operating activities generated $738.6 million while investing activities used $450.3 million primarily for purchases of property plant and equipment as well as acquisitions of businesses and assets. Financing activities used another $311.4 million primarily for repayments of long-term debt.

Strategy

CooperVision believes that its key accounts which include optical chains global retailers certain buying groups and mass merchandisers are growing faster than the overall market. The company is focused on supporting the growth of all its customers by investing in selling promotional and advertising activities. Further it is increasing investment in its distribution and packaging capabilities to support the growth of business and to continue providing quality service with its industry leading SKU range and customized offerings.

CooperVision believes that myopia management opens up an attractive new market for contact lenses. With MiSight CooperVision offers the only FDA approved and first Chinese NMPA approved product to control the progression of myopia in children. CooperVision is investing to create this new market by educating eye care practitioners patients and their families which increases awareness.

Mergers and Acquisitions

Cooper has been building up both of its segments through acquisitions.

In late 2021 CooperCompanies agreed to acquire Generate Life Sciences a leading provider of donor egg and sperm for fertility treatments fertility cryopreservation services and newborn stem cell storage (cord blood & cord tissue) for a purchase price of approximately $1.6 billion. By adding Generate to CooperSurgical the company is able to provide fertility clinics and Ob/Gyns an even stronger offering.

In mid-2021 CooperCompanies has acquired obp Medical Corporation a US based medical device company that develops and markets differentiated products including single-use vaginal speculums with integrated LED illumination for a purchase price of $60 million. The acquisition is a great strategic fit that builds upon CooperSurgical's strong family of OB/GYN medical devices. obp Medical's differentiated products will integrate seamlessly into the company's business and support its mission of advancing women's healthcare.

In 2021 CooperCompanies has acquired Safe Obstetric Systems a privately held manufacturer of the medical device Fetal Pillow for acquisition price of approximately 37.5 million in cash. This FDA approved product is used to elevate the fetal head during a fully dilated cesarean section making the delivery easier and less traumatic for the mother and baby. The acquisition is an excellent strategic fit for CooperSurgical as it aligns perfectly with its mission of advancing women's healthcare.

Also in 2021 EssilorLuxottica and CooperCompanies have entered into an agreement to create a 50/50 joint venture for the acquisition of SightGlass Vision a US based life sciences company focused on developing innovative spectacle lenses to reduce the progression of myopia in children. EssilorLuxottica and CooperCompanies will leverage their shared expertise and global leadership in myopia management to accelerate the commercialization of SightGlass Vision spectacle lenses. Through this partnership they will further strengthen innovation opportunities and go-to-market capabilities to grow the myopia control category. SightGlass Vision's technology will complement both companies' existing solutions including Essilor's Stellest lens and CooperVision's MiSight and Orthokeratology contact lenses.

Company Background

Parker G. Montgomery founded Martin H. Smith Co. in 1958. The company changed its name to Cooper Tinsley Laboratories in 1961 and went public the following year.

HISTORY

Cooper Labs (medical devices founded in 1958 and dissolved 1985) created CooperVision as a subsidiary in 1980. CooperVision diversified into diagnostic equipment and drugs; by 1987 (when it was renamed The Cooper Companies) debt had increased sixfold and creditors came knocking.

Two scandal-tainted families (the Sturmans and the Singers — fraud/organized crime and Medicaid fraud respectively) then bought their way onto the board. Proxy fights cronyism nepotism indictments and lawsuits ensued. Meanwhile cash-strapped Cooper sold most of its international and part of its US contact lens business as well as its ophthalmic surgical products and medical diagnostics businesses. Co-chairman Gary Singer took a leave of absence after being indicted in 1992.

Cooper bought Hospital Group of America and its hospitals that year. Singer resigned shortly before being convicted on 21 counts including racketeering mail and wire fraud and money laundering in 1994. Pharmaceutical industry veteran Thomas Bender joined the board that year and was named CEO in 1995. He was elected chairman in 2002.

Cooper rebuilt its contact business and turned to the women's health field in the early 1990s. In 1996 it bought a line of disposable gynecological products and worked to boost lens-making capacity. The next year it bought a line of colored contact lenses a minimally invasive gynecological surgical and disposable products company and a UK lens maker.

In 1998 The Cooper Companies discontinued its Hospital Group of America operations. It sold the group's hospitals treatment centers and clinics to Universal Health Services in 1999. In 2000 the company made three acquisitions including two makers of gynecological instruments. In 2002 The Cooper Companies bought Biocompatibles Eye Care one of the world's largest contact lens manufacturers.

The company's acquisitions in 2003 included Avalon Medical Corporation (distributor of female sterilization system) and Prism Enterprises (manufacturer of medical devices for the women's health care markets). The Cooper Companies bought gynecology products manufacturer Milex Products in 2004.

It nearly doubled its revenue with the 2005 acquisition of leading contact lens maker Ocular Sciences. The purchase strengthened its presence in the spheric (non-specialty) lens market; it also opened up new geographic markets particularly Germany and Japan. It also purchased NeoSurg Technologies and Inlet Medical in 2005 both of which made devices used in laparoscopic surgeries.

In 2006 it purchased Lone Star Medical Products adding a line of gynecological surgical products. The following year it added medical instrument maker Wallach Surgical Devices.

EXECUTIVES

President, Chief Executive Officer And Director, Albert White, $925,000 total compensation
Chief Operating Officer And Executive Vice President, Daniel McBride, $700,000 total compensation
Chief Financial Officer, Executive Vice President, Treasurer, Brian Andrews, $500,000 total compensation
Senior Vice President - Finance And Tax, Chief Accounting Officer, Agostino Ricupati, $381,754 total compensation
Independent Director, Teresa Madden
Vice President, General Counsel, Secretary, Mark Drury
Independent Director, Maria Rivas
President - Coopersurgical, Inc., Holly Sheffield, $525,000 total compensation
President, Coopervision, Jerry Warner
Auditors: KPMG LLP

LOCATIONS

HQ: Cooper Companies, Inc. (The)
6101 Bollinger Canyon Road, Suite 500, San Ramon, CA 94583
Phone: 925 460-3600   **Fax:** 925 460-3648
Web: www.coopercos.com

PRODUCTS/OPERATIONS

2018 Sales by Segment

	$ mil.	% of total
CooperVision		
Toric lens	591.4	23
Single-use sphere lens	520.1	20
Multifocal lens	196.6	8
Non-single-use sphere & other	573.9	23
CooperSurgical	650.8	26
Total	**2,352.8**	**100**

COMPETITORS

1-800 CONTACTS INC.	COOPERVISION INC.
BAUSCH & LOMB INCORPORATED	DAVIS VISION INC.
Bausch Health Companies Inc	MEDICAL ACTION INDUSTRIES INC.
CONMED CORPORATION	NATIONAL VISION HOLDINGS INC.
COOPERSURGICAL INC.	SIGNET ARMORLITE INC.

HISTORICAL FINANCIALS

Company Type: Public

Income Statement

FYE: October 31

	REVENUE ($ mil.)	NET INCOME ($ mil.)	NET PROFIT MARGIN	EMPLOYEES
10/21	2,922.5	2,944.7	100.8%	12,000
10/20	2,430.9	238.4	9.8%	12,000
10/19	2,653.4	466.7	17.6%	12,000
10/18	2,532.8	139.9	5.5%	12,000
10/17	2,139.0	372.9	17.4%	11,800
Annual Growth	8.1%	67.6%	—	0.4%

2021 Year-End Financials

Debt ratio: 15.4%	No. of shares (mil.): 49.3
Return on equity: 54.7%	Dividends
Cash ($ mil.): 95.9	Yield: 0.0%
Current ratio: 2.00	Payout: 0.1%
Long-term debt ($ mil.): 1,396.1	Market value ($ mil.): 20,554.0

	STOCK PRICE ($) FY Close	P/E High/Low		PER SHARE ($) Earnings	Dividends	Book Value
10/21	416.92	8	5	59.16	0.06	140.81
10/20	319.05	74	50	4.81	0.06	77.89
10/19	291.00	36	25	9.33	0.06	73.90
10/18	258.31	98	76	2.81	0.06	67.23
10/17	240.26	33	21	7.52	0.06	65.08
Annual Growth	14.8%	—	—	67.5%	(0.0%)	21.3%

Copart Inc

Copart is one of the leading provider of online auctions and vehicle remarketing services. It takes those vehicles and auctions them for insurers as well as auto dealers fleet operations charities and banks. The buyers are mostly rebuilders licensed dismantlers and used-car dealers and exporters. The company has replaced live auctions with internet auctions using a platform known as Virtual Bidding Third Generation (VB3 for short). It also provides services such as towing and storage to buyers and other salvage companies. Copart serves customers throughout North America Europe the Middle East and Brazil although the US accounts for about 85% of sales.

Operations
Copart offers vehicle sellers a full range of vehicle services which expedite each stage of the vehicle sales process minimize administrative and processing costs and maximize the ultimate sales price through the online auction process. The company offers online seller access salvage estimation estimating services end-of-life vehicle processing intelliSeller and transportation services among other.

Overall Copart generates about 85% of its revenue from services it offers and the rest of the revenue comes from vehicle sales.

Geographic Reach
Dallas-based Copart has facilities in every state except Vermont. It also has facilities in Canada the UK Brazil Ireland Germany UAE Spain Oman Bahrain and Finland. The US generates about 85% of total revenue and the rest comes from the international market.

Sales and Marketing
The company's advertising expenses were approximately $13.7 million $7.7 million and $7.5 million for the years ended 2021 2020 and 2019 respectively.

Financial Performance
The company had a revenue of $2.7 billion a 22% increase from the previous year's revenue of $2.2 billion. This is primarily due to a higher sales volume across all of the company's segments.

In 2021 the company had a net income of $936.5 million a 34% increase from the previous year's net income of $699.9 million.

The company's cash at the end of 2021 was $1 billion. Operating activities generated $990.9 million while investing activities used $465.5 million mainly for purchases of property and equipment. Financing activities provided another $40.9 million.

Strategy
Copart's growth strategy is to increase revenues and profitability by among other things acquiring and developing additional vehicle storage facilities in key markets including foreign markets; pursuing global national and regional vehicle seller agreements; increasing its service offerings; and expanding the application of VB3 into new markets. In addition the company implement its pricing structure and auction procedures and attempt to introduce cost efficiencies at each of its acquired facilities by implementing its operational procedures integrating its management information systems and redeploying personnel when necessary.

As part of its overall expansion strategy its objective is to increase its revenues operating profits and market share in the vehicle remarketing industry. To implement its growth strategy it intends to continue to: acquire and develop new vehicle storage facilities in key markets including foreign markets; pursue global national and regional vehicle supply agreements; and expand its service offerings to sellers and members.

HISTORY

Copart was co-founded in 1982 by Willis Johnson who had owned and operated an auto dismantling business for more than 10 years. After buying out his partner in 1986 he became CEO and used his own money to expand the company into a network of four California salvage yards by 1991. In the next two years Copart nearly tripled the number of salvage operations it owned by acquiring companies throughout the US. HPB Associates a private investor group came on board in 1993 buying 26% of the firm for $10 million and the company went public the next year.

Copart doubled its total facilities in 1995 with the acquisition of NER Auction Systems the largest privately held salvage auction company in the US. The firm acquired or opened more than 30 facilities between 1995 and 1997. In 1998 the company started an online auction site; expanded through acquisitions into Alabama Iowa Michigan and South Carolina; and opened new locations in California and Minnesota. The next year rival Insurance Auto Auctions spurned its merger overtures.

In 2000 Copart opened three new salvage vehicle auction facilities and acquired eight more. That year the company also signed an agreement to sell Keystone Automotive Industries' parts through its Web site. In 2001 and 2002 the company acquired or opened 13 new locations. Continuing its acquisition strategy the company opened or acquired five more facilities in 2004.

In 2005 the company made two acquisitions for about $4.5 million: Kentucky Auto Salvage Pool a 25-acre salvage facility in Lexington Kentucky; and Insurance Auctions of Missouri. In November Copart acquired the salvage pool assets of Central Penn Sales a vehicle salvage disposal company with four sites in Pennsylvania and Maryland totaling 255 acres. In December the company opened a second salvage facility in Michigan.

In June 2007 Copart acquired Universal Salvage the operator of about 10 salvage yards in the UK and a vehicle remarketer to the insurance and automotive industries for about $120 million. Adding to its UK holdings in August Copart purchased Century Salvage Sales Limited which has three salvage yards and AG Watson which has four salvage yards in England and Scotland.

During 2008 the company launched CopartDirect. The service allows Copart to sell cars to the general public using its VB 2 application so that individuals can avoid the inconvenience of selling a vehicle themselves.

In February 2010 Willis Johnson relinquished the CEO's title to A. Jayson Adair who formerly served as president of Copart. Johnson continued as chairman of the company.

In 2011 Copart acquired the Indiana-based auto auction firm Barodge Auto Pool expanding its presence in Indiana and surrounding states. The company also broadened its existing range of farming equipment in the UK when it acquired Hewitt International an auctioneer of agricultural vehicles and equipment based in central England in 2011.

In 2012 the company made several acquisitions in international markets including Brazil Canada Germany and Dubai UAE. That year Copart expanded into Germany (the world's fourth largest auto market) with the purchase of WOM Wreck Online Marketing a leading European salvage vehicle auction platform there. Earlier in the year it bought Canada's Diamond Auto Bids and Disposals a privately-held automotive auction that gives Copart a foothold in Western Canada specifically Calgary and Edmonton. It also extended the reach of its business into South America through its purchase of Central de Leiloes LTDA based in Sao Paulo Brazil.

EXECUTIVES

Executive Chairman Of The Board, Willis Johnson
Ceo And Director, A. Jayson Adair, $1 total compensation
President, Chief Executive Officer, North America, Jeffrey Liaw, $686,527 total compensation
Independent Director, Stephen Fisher
Chief Financial Officer, John North, $278,653 total compensation
Independent Director, Cherylyn LeBon
Independent Director, Carl Sparks
Independent Director, Matt Blunt
Auditors: Ernst & Young LLP

LOCATIONS

HQ: Copart Inc
14185 Dallas Parkway, Suite 300, Dallas, TX 75254
Phone: 972 391-5000
Web: www.copart.com

PRODUCTS/OPERATIONS

2018 Sales

	$ mil.	% of total
Services	1,578.5	86
Vehicles	227.2	14
Total	**1,805.7**	**100**

Selected Services
Copart Access (online vehicle information retrieval)
Copart Dealer Services (online trade-in vehicle sales)
Copart Direct (online used car sales)
CoPartfinder (online used-parts search engine)
DMV processing (title document processing)
Monthly reporting (summary of all vehicles processed by company for suppliers)
Online bidding (online auctions)
Salvage brokerage network (coordination of vehicle disposal outside areas of current operation)
Salvage Lynk (software providing online information on vehicles being processed)
Transportation services (fleet of transport trucks)
Vehicle inspection stations (central locations for insurance companies to inspect vehicles)
Vehicle preparation and merchandising (cleaning and weather protection direct mailings to buyers)

HOOVER'S HANDBOOK OF EMERGING COMPANIES 2022

COMPETITORS

ADESA CORPORATION LLC
AUTONATION INC.
AVIS BUDGET GROUP INC.
BRP Inc
COLUMBUS FAIR AUTO AUCTION INC.
COX AUTOMOTIVE INC.
D'Ieteren Group
Dongfeng Motor Group Company Limited
GROUP 1 AUTOMOTIVE INC.
HERC HOLDINGS INC.
MERCEDES-BENZ USA LLC
PENNSYLVANIA AUTO DEALERS' EXCHANGE INC.

HISTORICAL FINANCIALS
Company Type: Public

Income Statement				FYE: July 31
	REVENUE ($ mil.)	NET INCOME ($ mil.)	NET PROFIT MARGIN	EMPLOYEES
07/21	2,692.5	936.5	34.8%	8,600
07/20	2,205.5	699.9	31.7%	7,600
07/19	2,041.9	591.6	29.0%	7,327
07/18	1,805.7	417.8	23.1%	6,026
07/17	1,447.9	394.2	27.2%	5,323
Annual Growth	16.8%	24.1%	—	12.7%

2021 Year-End Financials

Debt ratio: —	No. of shares (mil.): 237.0
Return on equity: 31.1%	Dividends
Cash ($ mil.): 1,048.2	Yield: —
Current ratio: 4.04	Payout: —
Long-term debt ($ mil.): —	Market value ($ mil.): 34,841.0

	STOCK PRICE ($) FY Close	P/E High/Low		PER SHARE ($) Earnings	Dividends	Book Value
07/21	147.00	37	24	3.90	0.00	14.89
07/20	93.25	35	20	2.93	0.00	10.58
07/19	77.53	31	17	2.46	0.00	7.74
07/18	57.39	33	17	1.73	0.00	6.76
07/17	31.49	36	17	1.66	0.00	4.76
Annual Growth	47.0%	—	—	23.8%	—	33.0%

Corcept Therapeutics Inc

Corcept Therapeutics is a commercial-stage firm exploring treatments that regulate the presence of cortisol a steroid hormone associated with some psychiatric and metabolic disorders. Its sole commercial product Korlym is a version of the compound mifepristone (commonly known as RU-486 or the "abortion pill") used to regulate release patterns of cortisol. The drug is approved in the US for use in patients with Cushing's Syndrome a metabolic disorder caused by high levels of cortisol in the blood. The company's lead compounds have other potential treatments for weight gain caused by antipsychotic medications.

Operations

Corcept has discovered more than 1000 proprietaries selective cortisol modulators in four structurally distinct series. These novel molecules share Korlym's affinity for the glucocorticoid receptor (GR) but unlike Korlym do not bind to the progesterone receptor (PR) and therefore do not cause effects arising from antagonism of progesterone activity such as termination of pregnancy endometrial thickening and vaginal bleeding. The composition of these compounds and their methods of use in a wide range of indications are covered by the US and foreign patents. Its lead compounds have entered the clinic as potential treatments for a variety of serious disorders - Cushing's syndrome solid tumors (including advanced high-grade serous ovarian cancer metastatic pancreatic cancer and castration-resistant prostate cancer) weight gain caused by antipsychotic medications and non-alcoholic steatohepatitis (NASH).

The company does not manufacture Korlym or its drug candidates but rather relies on contract manufacturer Produits Chimiques Auxiliaires et de Synthese ("PCAS")

Geographic Reach

Based in Menlo Park California Corcept sells Korlym in the US.

Sales and Marketing

Corcept markets Korlym in the US through sales representatives health care providers and via medical science liaisons.

Financial Performance

Corcept's revenues have been rising rapidly over the past five years with 2020 as its highest performing year over the period.

The company's revenue increased by $47.4 million to $353.9 million compared to $306.5 million. The increase in revenue was due to an increase in Korlym's price for the year ended December 31 2020 was due to a relative decrease in the number of patients covered by Medicaid (which reimburses Korlym at a lower rate) a statutorily-mandated increase in the price paid by other government programs.

Net income also increased by $12 million to $106 million compared to the prior year's net income of $94.2 million.

Cash and cash equivalents at the end of the period were $76.2 million. Net cash provided by operating activities was $151.9 million. Investing activities used $119.3 million while financing activities provided $12.2 million. Main cash uses were for purchases of marketable securities and property and equipment.

Strategy

The company is dependent on revenue from the sale of Korlym and its cash reserves to fund its commercial operations and development programs. If Korlym revenue declines it may need to raise funds to support its plans. It may also choose to raise funds for strategic reasons. It cannot be certain funding will be available on acceptable terms or at all. In any event equity financing would cause dilution and debt financing if available may involve restrictive covenants.

If the company obtains funds through collaborations with other companies it may have to relinquish rights to Korlym or its product candidates. If adequate funds are not available it may have to delay reduce the scope of or eliminate one or more of its development programs or even discontinue operations.

EXECUTIVES

President, Chief Executive Officer, Co-founder, Director, Joseph Belanoff, $769,567 total compensation
Independent Director, David Mahoney
Chief Business Officer, Secretary, Gary Robb, $474,380 total compensation
Chief Commercial Officer, Sean Maduck, $474,380 total compensation
Chief Scientific Officer, Hazel Hunt, $431,873 total compensation
Independent Director, Kimberly Park
Independent Director, Gregg Alton
Independent Director, Gillian Cannon
Chief Financial Officer, Treasurer, Atabak Mokari, $474,380 total compensation
Chief Accounting Officer, Joseph Lyon
Director, Joshua Murray
Chief Development Officer, William Guyer
Independent Chairman Of The Board, James Wilson
Auditors: Ernst & Young LLP

LOCATIONS

HQ: Corcept Therapeutics Inc
149 Commonwealth Drive, Menlo Park, CA 94025
Phone: 650 327-3270
Web: www.corcept.com

COMPETITORS

ALEXION PHARMACEUTICALS INC.	IONIS PHARMACEUTICALS INC.
AMICUS THERAPEUTICS INC.	KARYOPHARM THERAPEUTICS INC.
BIOMARIN PHARMACEUTICAL INC.	LEXICON PHARMACEUTICALS INC.
CHIMERIX INC.	MANNKIND CORPORATION
CYTRX CORPORATION	RADIUS HEALTH INC.
Clementia Pharmaceuticals Inc	SEAGEN INC.
IMMUNE DESIGN CORP.	TETRAPHASE PHARMACEUTICALS INC.
INSMED INCORPORATED	ZOGENIX INC.

HISTORICAL FINANCIALS
Company Type: Public

Income Statement				FYE: December 31
	REVENUE ($ mil.)	NET INCOME ($ mil.)	NET PROFIT MARGIN	EMPLOYEES
12/21	365.9	112.5	30.7%	238
12/20	353.8	106.0	30.0%	236
12/19	306.4	94.1	30.7%	206
12/18	251.2	75.4	30.0%	166
12/17	159.2	129.1	81.1%	136
Annual Growth	23.1%	(3.4%)	—	15.0%

2021 Year-End Financials

Debt ratio: —	No. of shares (mil.): 105.9
Return on equity: 25.0%	Dividends
Cash ($ mil.): 77.6	Yield: —
Current ratio: 5.60	Payout: —
Long-term debt ($ mil.): —	Market value ($ mil.): 2,098.0

	STOCK PRICE ($) FY Close	P/E High/Low		PER SHARE ($) Earnings	Dividends	Book Value
12/21	19.80	32	18	0.89	0.00	3.55
12/20	26.16	30	11	0.85	0.00	4.48
12/19	12.10	21	12	0.77	0.00	3.24
12/18	13.36	39	17	0.60	0.00	2.40
12/17	18.06	18	6	1.04	0.00	1.66
Annual Growth	2.3%	—	—	(3.8%)	—	20.8%

CoreCard Corp

Intelligent Software Solutions (ISS) is no dummy when it comes to software development and IT systems analysis. The privately-held company develops and integrates custom software for data visualization and analysis pattern detection and mission planning for the aerospace defense and maritime industries. Its products include a software tool that counters improvised explosive devices (Dfuze) and public safety management software tool (WebTAS). The company provides on-site product and development support and training. Customers include government military intelligence agencies and local law enforcement in the US and abroad.

Operations
With expertise in counter-terrorism homeland security intelligence and special operations the company has about 100 projects under dozens of contracts. In 2013 ISS was selected as the lead contractor on a $250 million project with a US Air Force unit to replace a system for planning and carrying out military missions. ISS products include Combined Information Data Network Exchange (CIDNE) a web-enabled database that enables users such as agencies in different countries to collect manage and share data through a web-browser to support operations and C2Core database software for planning and carrying out missions.

The company's subsidiary ISS Global works with the Dfuze product and works with military public safety and law enforcement agencies in more than 40 countries.

Geographic Reach
ISS has facilities in Colorado Florida Massachusetts Virginia and Washington DC. The company keeps in close contact with key clients by placing offices nearby. Its Tampa Florida facility houses part of the company's combat systems division that supports the US Central Command (CENTCOM).

Sales and Marketing
The company's customers include the US Department of Defense and Department of Homeland Security national intelligence organizations and other US NATO and government customers. Its international public sector customers include the Hong Kong Police Force the Hungarian National Police Mine Disposal Service New Scotland Yard and the Police Service of Northern Ireland. ISS works with technology companies including Adobe Oracle and RedHat.

Strategy
ISS often used open source software and government off-the-shelf (GOTS) products to make it easier for agencies to integrate its products into their networks. It has taken that expertise to start an open source consulting business Springblox to provide open source software integration education and support to private and public sector customers.

Springblox formed a partnership with MuleSoft which develops software integrating systems. Together they will offer customers programs to effectively organize data.

EXECUTIVES

Independent Director, A. Russell Chandler

Chief Financial Officer, Secretary And Vp, Matthew White, $350,000 total compensation
Independent Director, Elizabeth Camp
Chairman Of The Board, President, Chief Executive Officer, James Strange, $350,000 total compensation
Auditors: Nichols, Cauley and Associates, LLC

LOCATIONS

HQ: CoreCard Corp
4355 Shackleford Road, Norcross, GA 30093
Phone: 770 381-2900
Web: www.intelsys.com

PRODUCTS/OPERATIONS

Selected Portfolio Companies
Alliance Technology Ventures
ChemFree Corporation
CoreCard Software Inc.
NKD Enterprises LLC (dba CoreXpand 26%)

COMPETITORS

ACTUATE CORPORATION
ANALYTICAL GRAPHICS INC.
DIMENSIONAL INSIGHT INCORPORATED
FIBERLINK COMMUNICATIONS CORPORATION
ID TECHNOLOGIES LLC
INFORMATICA LLC
INTERGRAPH CORPORATION
KANA SOFTWARE INC.

HISTORICAL FINANCIALS
Company Type: Public

Income Statement — FYE: December 31

	REVENUE ($ mil.)	NET INCOME ($ mil.)	NET PROFIT MARGIN	EMPLOYEES
12/20	35.8	8.1	22.7%	570
12/19	34.3	10.9	32.0%	530
12/18	20.1	6.2	31.1%	430
12/17	9.3	0.4	5.1%	350
12/16	8.1	(1.1)	—	286
Annual Growth	44.7%	—	—	18.8%

2020 Year-End Financials

Debt ratio: —	No. of shares (mil.): 8.8
Return on equity: 19.9%	Dividends
Cash ($ mil.): 37.9	Yield: —
Current ratio: 4.22	Payout: —
Long-term debt ($ mil.): —	Market value ($ mil.): 356.0

	STOCK PRICE ($) FY Close	P/E High/Low		PER SHARE ($) Earnings	Dividends	Book Value
12/20	40.11	49	27	0.91	0.00	4.97
12/19	39.94	45	11	1.22	0.00	4.18
12/18	12.92	21	6	0.70	0.00	2.94
12/17	4.56	95	70	0.05	0.00	2.22
12/16	4.24	—	—	(0.13)	0.35	2.51
Annual Growth	75.4%	—	—	—	—	18.6%

CoStar Group, Inc.

CoStar is the leading provider of information analytics and online marketplace services through its comprehensive proprietary database of commercial real estate information in the US Canada the UK France Spain and Germany. Its hundreds of data points include location ownership and tenant names. Clients include government agencies real estate brokerages real estate investment trusts (REITs) and property owners and managers who stand to benefit from insight on property values market conditions and current availabilities. Most of CoStar's sales come from subscription fees. The company was founded in 1987. Majority of the company's sales were generated from the North America.

Operations
CoStar has eight flagship brands: CoStar LoopNet Apartments.com STR Ten-X BizBuySell LandsofAmerica and HomeSnap.

CoStar Suite is the company's primary service offering. The subscription-based online marketplace enables commercial property owners landlords and real estate agents to list properties for sale or for lease and to submit detailed information about property listings.

Commercial real estate agents buyers and tenants use LoopNet to search for available property listings that meet their criteria. Apartments.com offers renters a searchable database of apartment listings as well as a comprehensive selection of rentals information on rents and in-depth data on neighborhoods including restaurants nightlife history schools and other facts important to renters. Its network of apartment marketing sites also includes ApartmentFinder.com ForRent.com ApartmentHomeLiving.com WestsideRentals.com AFTER55.com CorporateHousing.com ForRentUniversity.com and Apartamentos.com.

BizBuySell which includes BizQuest provides an online marketplace for businesses for sale while LandsofAmerica which includes LandAndFarm and LandWatch provides an online marketplace for rural lands for sale.

Costar Suite accounts approximately 40% of total sales Multifamily about 35% Commercial property and land about 15% and Information services for about 10% of sales.

Geographic Reach
Washington DC-based CoStar Group manages its business geographically in two operating segments with primary areas of measurement and decision-making being North America which includes the US and Canada and International which primarily includes Europe Asia-Pacific and Latin America. While the company continues its international expansion North America still accounts for nearly all revenue.

The company operates its research functions out of leased office spaces in Richmond Virginia; San Diego California; and Atlanta Georgia. Additionally its lease office space in a variety of other metropolitan areas. These locations include among others the following: Hendersonville Tennessee; Irvine California; Boston Massachusetts; San Francisco California; Ontario California; and Los Angeles California.

Sales and Marketing
CoStar's clients come from across the commercial real estate sector and related businesses and include real estate brokers owners developers landlords property managers financial institutions retailers appraisers investment banks government agencies and other parties involved in commercial real estate.

The company's sales teams are primarily located in field sales offices throughout the US and with

HOOVER'S HANDBOOK OF EMERGING COMPANIES 2022

others in Canada the UK Spain France and Germany. Inside sales teams are primarily located in Washington DC. These teams prospect for new clients and perform product and service demonstrations by telephone and online to support the direct sales force.

To generate brand awareness and site traffic CoStar uses a multi-channel marketing campaign including television and radio advertising online/digital advertising social media and out-of-home ads and search engine marketing.

Advertising costs were approximately $270 million $168 million and $125 million for the years ended 2020 2019 and 2018 respectively.

Financial Performance

Revenues increased to $1.7 billion in 2020 from $1.4 billion in 2019. The $259 million increase was primarily attributable to a $108 million or 22% increase in multifamily revenue.

Net income for fiscal 2020 decreased to $227.1 million compared to the prior year with $315.0 million.

Cash held by the company at the end of fiscal 2020 increased to $3.8 billion. Operating and financing activities provided $486.1 million and $2.7 billion respectively. Investing activities used $464.2 million mainly for acquisitions.

Strategy

The company's strategy is to provide real estate industry professionals and consumers with critical knowledge to explore and complete transactions by offering the most comprehensive timely and standardized information on real estate and the right tools to be able to effectively utilize that information. Over time CoStar has expanded and continues to expand its services for real estate information analytics and online marketplaces to continue to meet the needs of the industry as it grows and evolves.

Mergers and Acquisitions

In late 2021 CoStar acquired COMREAL INFO the owner and operator of BureauxLocaux.com. Based in Paris BureauxLocaux is one of the largest specialized property portals for buying and leasing commercial real estate in France with over 60000 for sale and lease listings and over 425000 visits to its website each month.

In 2021 CoStar completed the acquisition of Homes.com for $156 million in cash. Homes.com has one of the largest real estate portal sales forces and CoStar Group intends to leverage that sales force to sell the Homesnap product with the goal of expanding Homesnap's reach to hundreds of thousands of additional real estate agents.

CoStar in late 2020 acquired Houses.com setting the stage for its entry into residential real estate marketplaces.With the acquisition of the Houses.com domain name CoStar Group plans to develop a vibrant national marketplace for agents and owners to successfully sell homes without disenfranchising or disintermediating valuable real estate agents in the process.

Also in late 2020 CoStar acquired Maryland-based Homesnap Inc. an industry-leading provider of technology solutions to the real estate industry. Adding Homesnap to CoStar Group's network provides significant complementary value to its existing arsenal of broker and agent-centric tools directly benefiting the entire industry.

In mid-2020 CoStar completed the previously announced acquisition of Ten-X for $190 million in cash. Ten-X is the clear leading platform for conducting commercial real estate online auctions

and negotiated bids. The company looks forward to getting to work on combining the strengths of Ten-X with the strengths of CoStar Group to make the platform even more valuable for our brokers and the institutions they represent.

Company Background

Andrew C. Florance founded CoStar Group in 1987 as a company that collected and sold data on office buildings. Over the years it has expanded into industrial retail and rental apartments partly through acquisitions. The company filed an IPO in 1998. CoStar grew significantly when it acquired rival service LoopNet in 2012.

EXECUTIVES

President, Chief Executive Officer And Director, Andrew Florance, $800,000 total compensation
Chief Technology Officer, Frank Simuro
Chairman, Michael Klein
Managing Director - Costar Europe, Matthew Green
Senior Vice President, Global Analytics, Research And News, Lisa Ruggles, $441,154 total compensation
President, Marketplaces, Frederick Saint, $481,539 total compensation
Chief Financial Officer, Scott Wheeler, $486,923 total compensation
General Counsel, Secretary, Jaye Campbell
Independent Director, Michael Glosserman
Independent Director, Christopher Nassetta
Independent Director, Robert Musslewhite
Independent Director, Louise Sams
Chief Human Resource Officer, Michael Desmarais
Senior Vice President - Costar Products, Jack Spivey
Auditors: Ernst & Young LLP

LOCATIONS

HQ: CoStar Group, Inc.
1331 L Street, N.W., Washington, DC 20005
Phone: 202 346-6500   **Fax:** 877 739-0486
Web: www.costargroup.com

PRODUCTS/OPERATIONS

Selected Subscription Products
CoStar COMPS Professional (comparable sales information)
CoStar Property Professional (flagship real estate database)
CoStar Tenant (tenant information)
FOCUS (UK real estate information)

Selected Data
Building characteristics
Contact information
Demographic information
For-sale information
Historical trends
Income and expense histories
Lease expirations
Mortgage and deed information
Number of retail stores
Ownership
Retail sales per square foot
Sales and lease comparables
Site and zoning information
Space availability
Tax assessments
Tenant names

COMPETITORS

ACXIOM LLC	REDFIN CORPORATION
BLUCORA INC.	SABRE CORPORATION
BOOKING HOLDINGS INC.	STEWART INFORMATION

CENTURY COMMUNITIES INC.
COSTAR UK LIMITED
ELAVON INC.
RACKSPACE TECHNOLOGY GLOBAL INC.
SERVICES CORPORATION
TECHTARGET INC.
ZAPLABS LLC

HISTORICAL FINANCIALS
Company Type: Public

Income Statement				FYE: December 31
	REVENUE ($ mil.)	NET INCOME ($ mil.)	NET PROFIT MARGIN	EMPLOYEES
12/20	1,659.0	227.1	13.7%	4,753
12/19	1,399.7	314.9	22.5%	4,337
12/18	1,191.8	238.3	20.0%	3,705
12/17	965.2	122.7	12.7%	3,711
12/16	837.6	85.0	10.2%	3,064
Annual Growth	18.6%	27.8%	—	11.6%

2020 Year-End Financials

Debt ratio: 14.2%	No. of shares (mil.): 394.1
Return on equity: 5.1%	Dividends
Cash ($ mil.): 3,755.9	Yield: —
Current ratio: 11.75	Payout: —
Long-term debt ($ mil.): 986.7	Market value ($ mil.): 364,296.0

	STOCK PRICE ($) FY Close	P/E High/Low	PER SHARE ($) Earnings	Dividends	Book Value
12/20	924.28	1574877	0.59	0.00	13.64
12/19	598.30	732377	0.86	0.00	9.29
12/18	337.34	676449	0.65	0.00	8.29
12/17	296.95	838503	0.37	0.00	7.34
12/16	188.49	849564	0.26	0.00	5.07
Annual Growth	48.8%	—	22.7%	—	28.0%

Cousins Properties Inc

Cousins Properties a real estate investment trust (REIT) which buys develops and manages Class-A office properties mainly in high-growth markets in the Sunbelt region of the US. Its portfolio includes 19.7 million sq. ft. of office space and 310000 square feet of mixed-use space in Atlanta Austin Dallas and Charlotte. The company conducts its operations through Cousins Properties LP ("CPLP"). Its other subsidiary Cousins TRS Services LLC ("CTRS") also manages its own real estate portfolio and also provides real estate related services for other parties.

Operations

Cousin Properties' segments are categorized based on both property type and geographical area. The company's segments by property type are Office properties and Mixed-Use properties. The segments by geographical region are Atlanta Austin Charlotte Dallas Phoenix Tampa and Other.

Majority of the company's revenues came from rentals which accounts for more than 95% of sales.

Geographic Reach

The Atlanta-based REIT owns properties in its Atlanta; Austin Texas; Phoenix and Charlotte. More than 35% of the company's net operating income came from its office properties in Atlanta during 2020 while another 20% came from its office properties in Austin. The rest came from its properties in Charlotte (more than 10% of net operating income) Phoenix (nearly 10%) and the remaining accounts for Tampa Dallas and others.

Sales and Marketing

Reflecting a broad tenant base the REIT's top 20 tenants made up of more than 30% of its annualized base rental income during 2020 with no single tenant accounting for more than 5% of its rental income.

Some of the REIT's tenants include the NCR Corporation Amazon Facebook Expedia and Bank of America among others.

Financial Performance

Cousins Properties' performance over the past five years has seen an increase year-over-year with 2020 as its highest performing year.

REIT's revenue increased by 13% or about $82.8 million to $740.3 million in 2020 compared to $657.5 million in the prior year.

The company's net income also increased by $85.4 million to $238.1 million compared to the prior year's net income of $152.6 million.

Cash held by the company at the end of 2020 amounted to $6.1 million. The company's operating activities provided $351 million to the coffers. Investing and financing activities used $132.4 million and $230 million respectively. Main cash uses were for property acquisition development and tenant asset expenditures as well as for repayment of credit facility.

Strategy

The company's strategy is centered on creating value for its stockholders through ownership of the premier office portfolio in the Sun Belt markets of the US. Cousins Properties focuses on Atlanta Austin Charlotte Phoenix Tampa and Dallas. The company leverages its strong local operating platforms in its major markets in order to implement this strategy.

Company Background

Cousins Properties experienced challenges from the depressed economy and the downturn in the real estate markets following the financial crisis. The REIT responded by restructuring reducing headcount selling non-core assets and curtailing new development projects. It sold all of its industrial properties to focus on Class-A office properties. It also continues to wind down its multifamily residential portfolio.

Institutional investors own about a third of Cousins Properties' stock. Morgan Stanley holds the largest stake at more than 10% followed by BlackRock Inc. and The Vanguard Group. Chairman Emeritus Thomas G. Cousins owns about 10% of the firm's shares.

EXECUTIVES

Independent Director, R. Dary Stone
Executive Vice President, John McColl, $394,000 total compensation
Executive Vice President - Operations, Richard Hickson, $412,000 total compensation
Executive Vice President, General Counsel, Corporate Secretary, Pamela Roper, $366,000 total compensation
Chief Financial Officer, Executive Vice President, Gregg Adzema, $475,000 total compensation
Independent Director, Charles Cannada
Independent Director, Lillian Giornelli
Independent Director, Kent Griffin
Senior Vice President, Chief Accounting Officer, Jeffrey Symes
Executive Vice President, Investments & Managing Director, J. Kennedy Hicks
Independent Director, Dionne Nelson
Independent Director, Donna Hyland

Non-executive Chairman Of The Board, Robert Chapman
Auditors: Deloitte & Touche LLP

LOCATIONS

HQ: Cousins Properties Inc
3344 Peachtree Road NE, Suite 1800, Atlanta, GA 30326-4802
Phone: 404 407-1000
Web: www.cousins.com

PRODUCTS/OPERATIONS

2011 Sales

	$ mil.	% of total
Rental property	135.6	76
Third-party management &leasing	19.4	11
Fee income	13.8	8
Multifamily residential unit sales	4.7	3
Residential & outparcel	3.0	2
Other	2.0	-
Total	**178.5**	**100**

COMPETITORS

ALEXANDRIA REAL ESTATE EQUITIES INC.
AMERICAN ASSETS TRUST INC.
ARMADA/HOFFLER PROPERTIES L.L.C.
BOSTON PROPERTIES INC.
CEDAR REALTY TRUST INC.
DOUGLAS EMMETT INC.
EASTGROUP PROPERTIES INC.
H&R Real Estate Investment Trust
HUDSON PACIFIC PROPERTIES INC.
JBG SMITH PROPERTIES
KENNEDY-WILSON HOLDINGS INC.
LXP INDUSTRIAL TRUST
PROLOGIS INC.
REALTY INCOME CORPORATION
UDR INC.
WHITESTONE REIT

HISTORICAL FINANCIALS

Company Type: Public

Income Statement

FYE: December 31

	REVENUE ($ mil.)	NET INCOME ($ mil.)	NET PROFIT MARGIN	EMPLOYEES
12/21	755.0	278.5	36.9%	294
12/20	740.3	237.2	32.0%	316
12/19	657.5	150.4	22.9%	331
12/18	475.2	79.1	16.7%	257
12/17	466.1	216.2	46.4%	261
Annual Growth	**12.8%**	**6.5%**	**—**	**3.0%**

2021 Year-End Financials

Debt ratio: 30.6%
Return on equity: 6.1%
Cash ($ mil.): 8.9
Current ratio: 0.59
Long-term debt ($ mil.): 2,237.5
No. of shares (mil.): 148.6
Dividends
Yield: 3.0%
Payout: 148.1%
Market value ($ mil.): 5,989.0

	STOCK PRICE ($) FY Close	P/E High/Low		PER SHARE ($) Earnings	Dividends	Book Value
12/21	40.28	22	17	1.87	1.23	30.71
12/20	33.50	27	14	1.60	1.20	30.07
12/19	41.20	35	7	1.17	0.58	29.70
12/18	7.90	13	10	0.76	1.04	26.32
12/17	9.25	5	4	2.08	1.20	26.40
Annual Growth	**44.5%**	**—**	**—**	**(2.6%)**	**0.6%**	**3.9%**

Cowen Inc

Cowen along with its subsidiaries offers investment banking research sales and trading prime brokerage global clearing and commission management services and investment management through its business segments the operating company and the asset company. It provides services primarily to companies and institutional investor clients as well as media and telecommunications consumer and industrials sectors in the US and Europe. Some of its subsidiaries includes UK broker-dealer Cowen International Limited Cowen Execution Services Limited and Cowen and Company (Asia) Limited.

Operations

Cowen operates two main business segments: the Operating Company (Op Co) and the Asset Company (Asset Co).

The Op Co segment consists of four divisions: investment banking division markets division and research division (collectively as its investment banking businesses); Cowen Investment Management (CIM) division which offers advisers to investment funds (including private equity structures and privately placed hedge funds); and registered funds. Op Co's investment banking businesses offer advisory and global capital markets origination and domain knowledge-driven research sales and trading platforms for institutional investors global clearing and commission management services and also a comprehensive suite of prime brokerage services. The segment accounted for almost all of total revenue.

The Asset Co segment consists of the company's private investments private real estate investments and other legacy investment strategies. The focus of Asset Co is to drive future monetization of the invested capital of the segment.

Overall Cowen generated more than 45% of its total revenue from its investment banking brokerage services with some 35% of revenue. Interest and dividends for more than 10% while reinsurance premiums management fees incentive income reimbursement consolidated funds and other revenues accounted the remainder.

Geographic Reach

Based in New York Cowen operates globally through US offices in Boston San Francisco Atlanta Chicago Cleveland Dallas Greenwich Houston Lake Mary Stamford and Washington D.C. as well through international offices in London Belfast and Luxembourg. It provides brokerage services to companies and institutional investor clients in Europe through its broker-dealers located in the UK Cowen International Limited and Cowen Execution Services Limited and in Asia Cowen and Company (Asia) Limited or Cowen Asia.

Sales and Marketing

Cowen's investment banking businesses provides services primarily to companies and institutional investor clients. It also includes sectors from healthcare technology media and telecommunications consumer industrials information and technology services and energy. It provides research and brokerage services to over 6000 domestic and international clients. It also offers prime brokerage services targeting emerging private fund managers.

HOOVER'S HANDBOOK OF EMERGING COMPANIES 2022

Financial Performance

The company in 2020 had a total revenue of $1.6 billion a 55% increase from the previous year.

In 2020 the company had a net income of $207.1 million a $151.2 million increase from the previous year's net income of $55.9 million. This was mainly due to a higher sales volume for the year.

The company's cash at the end of 2020 was $645.2 million. Operating activities generated $521.3 million while investing activities used $20.8 million mainly for purchases of investments. Financing activities generated $25.6 million.

Strategy

The company intends to continually evaluate potential acquisitions investments and strategic alliances to expand its business. In the future we may seek additional acquisitions.

Mergers and Acquisitions

In late 2020 Cowen completed its acquisition of substantially all of the assets of MHT Partners LP (MHT Partners) an investment bank focused on representing innovative companies in growing markets based primarily in Dallas and San Francisco. MHT Partners' expertise as advisor to innovative niche market leaders as well as to private equity firms and family offices complements and extends Cowen's already significant offering to the key clients. The aggregate estimated purchase price of the MHT Acquisition was $9.9 million.

EXECUTIVES

Chairman Of The Board, Chief Executive Officer, Jeffrey Solomon, $1,000,000 total compensation

Chief Financial Officer, Stephen Lasota, $700,000 total compensation

Chief Operating Officer, John Holmes, $700,000 total compensation

General Counsel, Secretary, Owen Littman, $700,000 total compensation

Independent Director, Margaret Poster

Independent Director, Gregg Gonsalves

Independent Director, Douglas Rediker

Independent Director, Katherine Dietze

Independent Director, Steven Kotler

Auditors: KPMG LLP

LOCATIONS

HQ: Cowen Inc
599 Lexington Avenue, New York, NY 10022
Phone: 646 562-1010
Web: www.cowen.com

PRODUCTS/OPERATIONS

2014 Sales

	$ mil.	% of total
Investment Banking	170.5	40
Brokerage	140.1	33
Interest and dividend income	48.9	11
Management fees	40.6	9
Reimbursement from affiliates	12.5	3
Incentive income	2.8	1
Other revenues	9.5	2
Consolidated Funds revenues	2.9	1
Total	**427.8**	**100**

Selected Subsidiaries

Cowen Alternative Investments LLC
Cowen Asia Limited (Hong Kong)
Cowen Capital LLC
Cowen Capital Partners II LLC
Cowen and Company LLC
Cowen and Company (Asia) Limited (Hong Kong)
Cowen Financial Technology LLC

Cowen Healthcare Royalty Management LLC
Cowen Holdings Inc.
Cowen International Limited (UK)
Cowen International Trading Limited (UK)
Cowen Latitude Capital Group LLC
Cowen Latitude China Holdings Limited
Cowen Latitude Investment Consulting Co. Ltd. (China)
Cowen Overseas Investment LP
Cowen Services Company LLC
Cowen Structured Holdings Inc.
Cowen Structured Holdings LLC (Hong Kong)
Cowen Structured Products Specialists LLC
October LLC
Ramius Advisors LLC
Ramius Alternative Solutions LLC
Ramius Asia LLC
Raimus Enterprise Master Fund Ltd (Cayman Islands)
Ramius Japan Ltd.
Ramius LLC
Ramius Optimum Investments LLC
Ramius Securities LLC
Ramius Structured Credit Group LLC

COMPETITORS

BRC MERGER SUB LLC	NATIXIS
BROWN BROTHERS HARRIMAN & CO.	OPPENHEIMER HOLDINGS INC.
Canaccord Genuity Group Inc	OPPENHEIMERFUNDS INC.
EVERCORE INC.	PIPER SANDLER COMPANIES
FRANKLIN RESOURCES INC.	SEI INVESTMENTS COMPANY
HOULIHAN LOKEY INC.	STONEX GROUP INC.
MACQUARIE GROUP LIMITED	THE ZIEGLER COMPANIES INC
MESIROW FINANCIAL HOLDINGS INC	

HISTORICAL FINANCIALS

Company Type: Public

Income Statement

FYE: December 31

	REVENUE ($ mil.)	NET INCOME ($ mil.)	NET PROFIT MARGIN	EMPLOYEES
12/20	1,623.3	216.3	13.3%	1,364
12/19	1,049.4	24.6	2.3%	1,325
12/18	966.9	42.8	4.4%	1,212
12/17	658.7	(60.8)	—	1,124
12/16	471.5	(19.2)	—	843
Annual Growth 36.2%		—	—	12.8%

2020 Year-End Financials

Debt ratio: 37.5%	No. of shares (mil.): 26.8
Return on equity: 24.2%	Dividends
Cash ($ mil.): 830.9	Yield: 0.7%
Current ratio: 0.43	Payout: 30.1%
Long-term debt ($ mil.): 80.8	Market value ($ mil.): 698.0

	STOCK PRICE ($) FY Close	P/E High/Low		PER SHARE ($) Earnings	Dividends	Book Value
12/20	25.99	4	1	7.10	0.20	36.11
12/19	15.75	30	23	0.57	1.94	28.31
12/18	13.34	14	10	1.17	0.99	27.93
12/17	13.65	—	—	(2.29)	0.00	25.24
12/16	15.50	—	—	(0.97)	0.00	28.90
Annual Growth 13.8%		—	—	—	—	5.7%

CRA International Inc

CRA International doing business as Charles River Associates employs nearly 780 consultants offering economic financial and management counsel to corporate clients attorneys government agencies and other clients. Practices are organized into two areas. Litigation Regulatory and Financial Consulting advises on topics such as antitrust and competition damages valuation financial accounting and insurance economics. Management Consulting focus areas include auctions and competitive bidding business strategy and enterprise risk management. Charles River Associates has about 20 offices mainly in North America but also in Europe. Most business is conducted in the US. The firm was founded in 1965.

Operations

Charles River Associates' litigation regulatory and financial consulting arm typically works with law firms working for companies involved in antitrust damages or labor disputes. Its consultants help to develop theory and prepare testimony of expert witnesses. They also provide general litigation support such as legal brief reviews and appeals support.

The management consulting arm provides expertise of its own to companies seeking organizational operational and/or strategic changes. Its specialties include transaction advisory services organization and performance improvement enterprise risk management and corporate strategy.

Majority of CRA's consulting service revenues came from Time and materials which accounts for about 75% and followed by Fixed Price which accounts for about 25%.

Geographic Reach

Headquartered in Boston Massachusetts Charles River Associates has some 20 offices throughout North America and Europe including in New York San Francisco Chicago and London. The US accounts for some 80% of revenue UK accounts for about 15% and other countries accounts for the remaining revenues.

Sales and Marketing

Charles River Associates' clients include domestic and foreign corporations; federal state and local domestic government agencies; governments of foreign countries; public and private utilities; accounting firms; and national and international trade associations. Frequently it works with major law firms on behalf of their clients.

The company relies on its employee consultants particularly vice presidents and principals to market its services. Existing clients are an important source of repeat business and referrals. Charles River Associates supplements referrals with direct marketing to new clients through conferences seminars publications presentations and direct solicitations.

Charles River Associates derived approximately 25% of its revenue from fixed-price contracts in fiscal 2019.

Financial Performance

Revenues increased by $33.8 million or 8% to $451.4 million for fiscal 2019 from $417.6 million for fiscal 2018. The increase in net revenue was a result of an increase in gross revenues of $35.7 million as compared to fiscal 2018 coupled with an increase in write-offs and reserves of $1.9 million as compared to fiscal 2018.

Net income attributable to CRA International Inc. decreased by $1.8 million to net income of $20.7 million for fiscal 2019 from net income of $22.5 million for fiscal 2018.

The company ended 2019 with $25.6 million in net cash a decrease of $12.4 million from the prior year. Operating activities provided $27.8 million investing activities used $16.7 million and financing activities used $12.4 million. The main cash uses in 2019 were for purchase of property and equipment dividends paid and common stock repurchases.

Strategy

The company relies to a significant extent on the efforts of its employee consultants particularly its vice presidents and principals to market its services. CRA encourages its employee consultants to generate new business from both existing and new clients and the company rewards its employee consultants with increased compensation and promotions for obtaining new business. In pursuing new business the company's consultants emphasize its institutional reputation experience and client service while also promoting the expertise of the particular employees who will work on the matter. Many of its consultants have published articles in the industry business economic legal or scientific journals and have made speeches and presentations at industry conferences and seminars which serve as a means of attracting new business and enhancing their reputations. On occasion employee consultants work with one or more non-employee experts to market their services. Also CRA relies upon business development professionals to ensure that the value of its litigation consulting service offerings is fully realized in the marketplace. The company is focused on deepening and broadening client relationships with law firms and general counsels ensuring that both existing and potential clients have access to our broad array of services as well as helping to bring the best talent to any given assignment.

Mergers and Acquisitions

In 2017 Charles River Associates acquired the assets of C1 Consulting a strategy consulting firm specializing in serving life sciences clients including pharmaceuticals and biotech firms.

Company Background

Charles River Associates was founded in 1965 and filed an initial public offering in 1998. The company has expanded through organic growth and strategic acquisitions. Its purchase of Marakon Associates in 2009 significantly strengthened the company's management consulting capabilities.

EXECUTIVES

Chief Financial Officer, Executive Vice President, Principal Accounting Officer, Treasurer, Daniel Mahoney, $400,000 total compensation
Independent Director, Richard Booth
Independent Director, Christine Detrick
Vice President - Risk, Investigations And Analytics Practice, Cynthia Catlett
Vice President - Energy Practice, David Walls
Vice President - Forensic Services Practice, Peggy Daley
Vice President - Antitrust & Competition Economics Practice, Oakland, Elizabeth Bailey
Executive Vice President, Chief Corporate Development Officer, Chad Holmes, $425,000 total compensation
Executive Vice President, General Counsel, Jonathan Yellin, $425,000 total compensation

President, Chief Executive Officer, Director, Paul Maleh, $850,000 total compensation
Independent Director, Nancy Hawthorne
Independent Director, Thomas Avery
Auditors: Grant Thornton LLP

LOCATIONS

HQ: CRA International Inc
  200 Clarendon Street, Boston, MA 02116-5092
Phone: 617 425-3000   **Fax:** 617 425-3132
Web: www.crai.com

PRODUCTS/OPERATIONS

Selected Practice Areas
Litigation regulatory and financial consulting
  Antitrust and competition
  Damages and valuation
  Financial accounting and valuation
  Financial economics
  Forensic and cyber investigations
  Insurance economics
  Intellectual property
  International arbitration
  Labor and employment
  Mergers and acquisitions
  Regulatory economics and compliance
  Securities and financial markets
  Transfer pricing
Management consulting
  Auctions and competitive bidding
  Corporate and business strategy
  Enterprise risk management
  Environmental and energy strategy
  Intellectual property and technology management
  Organization and performance improvement
  Transaction advisory services

Selected Industries Served
Agriculture
Banking and capital markets
Chemicals
Communications and media
Consumer products
Energy
Entertainment
Financial services
Health care
Insurance
Life sciences
Manufacturing
Metals mining and materials
Oil and gas
Real estateRetail
Sports
Telecommunications
Transportation
Technology

COMPETITORS

CBIZ INC.	MANNING & NAPIER INC.
CLIFTONLARSONALLEN LLP INC.	NEWMARK GROUP
EDELMAN FINANCIAL ENGINES LLC	NV5 GLOBAL INC. RESOURCES CONNECTION INC.
GP STRATEGIES CORPORATION	SS&C TECHNOLOGIES HOLDINGS INC.
HURON CONSULTING GROUP INC.	THE HACKETT GROUP INC
MACFARLANES LLP	WIPFLI LLP

HISTORICAL FINANCIALS
Company Type: Public

Income Statement

	REVENUE ($ mil.)	NET INCOME ($ mil.)	NET PROFIT MARGIN	EMPLOYEES
01/21*	508.3	24.5	4.8%	831
12/19	451.3	20.7	4.6%	779
12/18	417.6	22.4	5.4%	687
12/17	370.0	7.6	2.1%	631
12/16	324.7	12.8	4.0%	540
Annual Growth	11.9%	17.4%	—	11.4%

FYE: January 2

*Fiscal year change

2021 Year-End Financials

Debt ratio: —	No. of shares (mil.): 7.6
Return on equity: 11.8%	Dividends
Cash ($ mil.): 45.6	Yield: 0.0%
Current ratio: 1.10	Payout: 30.9%
Long-term debt ($ mil.): —	Market value ($ mil.): 392.0

	STOCK PRICE ($) FY Close	P/E High/Low		PER SHARE ($) Earnings	Dividends	Book Value
01/21*	50.93	18	7	3.07	0.95	27.17
12/19	53.57	21	13	2.53	0.83	25.30
12/18	40.92	21	15	2.61	0.71	24.53
12/17	44.95	52	36	0.89	0.59	24.94
12/16	36.60	25	11	1.49	0.14	24.86
Annual Growth	8.6%	—	—	19.8%	61.4%	2.2%

*Fiscal year change

Crawford United Corp

Like "Wild Bill" of Wild West lore Hickok is quite comfortable shooting it out with competitors on its own measured road to success. The company manufactures testing equipment used by automotive technicians to repair cars. Hickok also makes instruments indicators and gauges for manufacturers of aircraft and locomotives. While Ford and General Motors traditionally were the company's largest customers its biggest customer now is Environmental Systems Products (ESP) at 53% of sales. Hickok sells products primarily in the US. In 2019 Hickok bought Data Genomix which develops social media marketing applications for political legal and recruiting campaigns. The companies are based in Cleveland Ohio.

HISTORY

Robert D. Hickok founded Hickok Electrical Instrument in Atlanta in 1910 and moved it to Cleveland in 1913. The company introduced the first AC/DC radio tube tester in 1920 and began making electrical instrumentation for aircraft during the mid-1930s. In 1950 after his father's death Robert D. Hickok Jr. took over the firm; he took it public in 1959. During the 1960s the company acquired a number of firms and Robert Bauman became chief engineer. In 1969 Robert D. Hickok Jr. retired. Hickok began its relationship with Ford Motor in 1981 moving into automotive diagnostic tools. Bauman became president in 1991 and later CEO (1992) and chairman (1993).

HOOVER'S HANDBOOK OF EMERGING COMPANIES 2022

To expand its product line Hickok acquired Allen-Bradley Co. (fastening systems) in 1994. Hickok's name was changed to Hickok Incorporated the next year. Diversification efforts in 1996 included acquiring Maradyne's Beacon Gage Division (railroad and transit car pressure gauges). Sales and earnings suffered in 1997 when Ford and General Motors delayed purchasing automotive diagnostic and fastening systems.

Transitioning to the aftermarket business Hickok bought automotive diagnostic and specialty toolmaker Waekon Industries (renamed Waekon Corp.) in 1998. The acquisition fit into the company's long-term plan to decrease its dependence on a few large occasional orders from carmakers and to increase its presence in the more stable automotive aftermarket. Hickok recorded a loss in fiscal 1999 in part because of its change to a lower-margin product mix.

In 2000 Hickok closed its Kirkwood Pennsylvania plant and moved production to the firm's Greenwood Mississippi factory to reduce costs. The company's line of DIGILOG aircraft instruments was approved by the FAA in fiscal 2002; since that time other models which had potential in the aircraft retrofit market also were certified.

Hickock unsuccessfully attempted to buy out enough of its outstanding shares to enable it to go private in 2004. The company's intention to end its obligations for SEC registration was to eliminate expenses related to compliance with the Sarbanes-Oxley Act and to focus on its operations.

EXECUTIVES

Independent Director, Kirin Smith
Independent Director, Steven Rosen
Chairman Of The Board, President, Chief Executive Officer, Brian Powers, $240,000 total compensation
Independent Director, Matthew Crawford
Independent Director, Luis Jimenez
Chief Financial Officer, Jay Daly, $47,083 total compensation
Director, James Wert
Auditors: Meaden & Moore, Ltd.

LOCATIONS

HQ: Crawford United Corp
  10514 Dupont Avenue, Cleveland, OH 44108
Phone: 216 243-2614
Web: www.crawfordunited.com

PRODUCTS/OPERATIONS

Selected Subsidiaries
Supreme Electronics Corp.
Waekon Corp.

COMPETITORS

AMETEK INC.	THE LEE COMPANY
KEITHLEY INSTRUMENTS LLC	THERMO KING CORPORATION
MKS INSTRUMENTS INC.	

HISTORICAL FINANCIALS
Company Type: Public

Income Statement
FYE: December 31

	REVENUE ($ mil.)	NET INCOME ($ mil.)	NET PROFIT MARGIN	EMPLOYEES
12/20	85.0	5.8	6.9%	260
12/19	89.7	6.9	7.8%	271
12/18	66.3	3.6	5.4%	275
12/17*	11.7	0.5	4.3%	200
09/17	23.8	1.4	5.9%	180
Annual Growth	37.5%	42.7%	—	9.6%

*Fiscal year change

2020 Year-End Financials

Debt ratio: 39.5%	No. of shares (mil.): 3.3
Return on equity: 23.7%	Dividends
Cash ($ mil.): 6.1	Yield: —
Current ratio: 2.00	Payout: —
Long-term debt ($ mil.): 26.9	Market value ($ mil.): 62.0

	STOCK PRICE ($) FY Close	P/E High/Low		PER SHARE ($) Earnings	Dividends	Book Value
12/20	18.74	13	7	1.76	0.00	8.27
12/19	19.75	9	4	2.13	0.00	6.52
12/18	10.50	10	6	1.14	0.00	4.69
12/17*	10.49	62	39	0.16	0.00	3.60
09/17	9.40	19	3	0.46	0.00	3.42
Annual Growth	18.8%	—	—	39.9%	—	24.7%

*Fiscal year change

Credit Acceptance Corp (MI)

Credit Acceptance Corporation (CAC) offers financing programs that enable automobile dealers to sell vehicles to consumers. CAC makes the effort a reality. Working with approximately 60000 independent and franchised automobile dealers in the US CAC provides financing programs through a nationwide network of automobile dealers who benefit from sales of vehicles to consumers who otherwise could not obtain financing; from repeat and referral sales generated by these same customers; and from sales to customers responding to advertisements for the company's financing programs. CAC which concentrates its operations in a handful of US states typically funds about 3.6 million auto loans per year.

Operations

CAC derives its revenues from finance charges (about 95% of sales) which are comprised of interest income earned on loans; administrative fees earned from ancillary products; program fees charged to dealers under the Portfolio Program; Consumer Loan assignment fees charged to dealers; and direct origination costs incurred on Dealer Loans. Premiums earned on the reinsurance of vehicle service contracts and other income generate the remaining. It primarily consists of ancillary product profit sharing remarketing fees dealer enrollment fees interest dealer support products and services.

In addition the company offers two programs: the Portfolio Program and the Purchase Program.

Under the Portfolio Program the company advances money to Dealers (Dealer Loan) in exchange for the right to service the underlying Consumer Loans. Under the Purchase Program the company buys the Consumer Loans from the Dealers (Purchased Loan) and keep all amounts collected from the consumer. Dealer Loans and Purchased Loans are collectively referred to as "Loans". Portfolio Program accounts about 65% of unit volume while Purchase Program accounts the remainder.

Geographic Reach

Michigan-based CAC serves consumers nationwide. In addition to Michigan its largest markets include Ohio New York Texas and Tennessee.

Sales and Marketing

CAC caters to and partners with approximately 60000 independent and franchised automobile dealers throughout the US.

Advertising expenses were approximately $0.1 million $0.3 million and $0.2 million for FY 2020 2019 and 2018 respectively.

Financial Performance

Revenue for fiscal 2020 increased by 12% to $1.7 billion compared with $1.5 billion in the prior year.

For 2020 consolidated net income was $421.0 million compared to $656.1 million in 2019. The decrease in 2020 consolidated net income was primarily due to an increase in its provision for credit losses primarily due to its adoption of CECL on January 1 2020.

Cash held by the company at the end of fiscal 2020 decreased to $396.2 million. Cash provided by operations was $985.2 million while cash used for investing and financing activities were $673.5 million and $433.2 million respectively. Main cash uses were advances to Dealers and repayments under revolving secured line of credit.

Strategy

While the company believes that its existing information systems are sufficient to meet its current demands and continued expansion its future growth may require additional investment in these systems. Its systems and the equipment software and Internet access on which they depend may be subject to cyber-attacks security breaches and other cybersecurity incidents. Although the cybersecurity incidents it has experienced to date have not had a material effect on its business financial condition or results of operations there can be no assurance that cybersecurity incidents will not have a material adverse effect on the company in the future.

HISTORY

Donald Foss was a used-car dealer in Detroit where to make sales he sometimes financed cars out of his own pocket. As Foss' chain of dealerships grew so did his financing business. In 1972 he established it as a separate company and 20 years later took it public.

For most of its history CAC stood alone in the field of subprime auto lending but stagnating salaries made it a competitive growth business in the early 1990s. At mid-decade the company entered Canada and the UK to tap similar markets there. In 1996 CAC acquired Montana Investment Group a credit reporting service.

Even as rising consumer debt and bad credit continued to pump buyers into CAC's loan pipeline the economic boom of the mid-1990s paradoxically made used cars less desirable. The soft used-car market squeezed several of CAC's competitors out of business; a staggering default rate — nearing 40% — also pressured CAC whose auditors insisted it increase reserves to cover losses. The subsequent earnings dive spurred a shareholder lawsuit accusing CAC of hiding its poor fiscal health. Although bad loans had damaged its bottom line the company adopted more stringent lending policies to reduce risk. Consumers filed class-action suits alleging unethical practices in 1998 but many claims were dismissed.

To pay off debt acquired through bad loans CAC sold Montana Investment Group in 1999. In 2000 it launched CAC Leasing to further offset losses from a decrease in subprime lending but in 2002 the company exited that line deciding the lending field was more profitable. CAC stopped originating new loans in the UK and Canada in 2003.

In 2005 the SEC investigated CAC's accounting methods specifically related to its loan portfolio and the company restated portions of its past financial results.

The company found itself in hot water again in 2008 when it agreed to pay some 15000 Missouri customers to settle a class action lawsuit. The lawsuit filed more than a decade prior alleged that CAC overcharged customers for fees and interest on their loans. As part of the settlement CAC said it would write off $39 million in outstanding accounts and distribute another $13 million to customers.

EXECUTIVES

Chief Treasury Officer, Nvestor Relations, Douglas Busk
President, Chief Executive Officer, Kenneth Booth, $572,126 total compensation
Chief Analytics Officer, Arthur Smith, $572,126 total compensation
Chief Sales Officer, Daniel Ulatowski, $572,126 total compensation
Chief Information Officer, Noah Kotch
Chief Operating Officer, Jonathan Lum
Senior Vice President, Assistant General Counsel – Regulatory Compliance, Erin Kerber
Principal Accounting Officer, Jay Martin
Independent Director, Vinayak Hegde
Independent Director, Scott Vassalluzzo
Auditors: Grant Thornton LLP

LOCATIONS

HQ: Credit Acceptance Corp (MI)
25505 West Twelve Mile Road, Southfield, MI 48034-8339
Phone: 248 353-2700

PRODUCTS/OPERATIONS

2016 Sales

	$ mil.	% of total
Finance charges	874.3	90
Premiums earned	43.0	5
Other	51.9	5
Total	**969.2**	**100**

Selected Subsidiaries

Buyers Vehicle Protection Plan Inc.
CAC Leasing Inc.
CAC Reinsurance Ltd.
CAC Warehouse Funding Corp. II III IV
Credit Acceptance Wholesale Buyers Club Inc.
Vehicle Remarketing Services Inc.
VSC Re Company

COMPETITORS

AMBAC FINANCIAL GROUP INC.
AMERICAN EXPRESS COMPANY
COGNITION FINANCIAL CORPORATION
ENOVA INTERNATIONAL INC.
FIRST INVESTORS FINANCIAL SERVICES GROUP INC.
GENERAL MOTORS FINANCIAL COMPANY INC.
MGIC INVESTMENT CORPORATION
NICHOLAS FINANCIAL INC.
ONEMAIN HOLDINGS INC.
PPDAI Group Inc
SLM CORPORATION

HISTORICAL FINANCIALS

Company Type: Public

Income Statement				FYE: December 31
	REVENUE ($ mil.)	NET INCOME ($ mil.)	NET PROFIT MARGIN	EMPLOYEES
12/21	1,856.0	958.3	51.6%	2,073
12/20	1,669.3	421.0	25.2%	2,033
12/19	1,489.0	656.1	44.1%	2,016
12/18	1,285.8	574.0	44.6%	2,040
12/17	1,110.0	470.2	42.4%	1,817
Annual Growth	**13.7%**	**19.5%**	**—**	**3.4%**

2021 Year-End Financials

Debt ratio: 65.4%
Return on equity: 46.4%
Cash ($ mil.): 23.3
Current ratio: 3.46
Long-term debt ($ mil.): 4,616.3

No. of shares (mil.): 14.1
Dividends
  Yield: —
  Payout: —
Market value ($ mil.): 9,728.0

	STOCK PRICE ($) FY Close	P/E High/Low		PER SHARE ($) Earnings	Dividends	Book Value
12/21	687.68	12	5	59.52	0.00	128.96
12/20	346.14	22	9	23.47	0.00	134.71
12/19	442.33	14	11	34.57	0.00	128.33
12/18	381.76	16	10	29.39	0.00	104.94
12/17	323.48	14	8	24.04	0.00	79.53
Annual Growth	**20.7%**	—	—	**25.4%**	—	**12.8%**

Crescent Capital BDC Inc

LOCATIONS

HQ: Crescent Capital BDC Inc
11100 Santa Monica Blvd., Suite 2000, Los Angeles, CA 90025
Phone: 310 235-5900
Web: www.crescentbdc.com

HISTORICAL FINANCIALS

Company Type: Public

Income Statement				FYE: December 31
	REVENUE ($ mil.)	NET INCOME ($ mil.)	NET PROFIT MARGIN	EMPLOYEES
12/20	77.1	49.8	64.7%	0
12/19	53.4	31.6	59.2%	0
12/18	33.3	17.7	53.2%	0
12/17	22.2	9.9	44.4%	0
Annual Growth	**51.2%**	**71.4%**	**—**	**—**

2020 Year-End Financials

Debt ratio: 44.7%
Return on equity: 10.2%
Cash ($ mil.): 14.8
Current ratio: 0.91
Long-term debt ($ mil.): 471.9

No. of shares (mil.): 28.1
Dividends
  Yield: 11.2%
  Payout: 103.1%
Market value ($ mil.): 410.0

	STOCK PRICE ($) FY Close	P/E High/Low		PER SHARE ($) Earnings	Dividends	Book Value
12/20	14.57	9	3	1.98	1.64	19.88
12/19	0.00	—	—	1.69	1.64	19.50
Annual Growth	**—**	—	—	**17.2%**	**(0.0%)**	**1.9%**

Crexendo Inc

Crexendo (formerly iMergent) would like to help increase the volume on your e-commerce business. Catering to home-based small and medium-sized businesses the company's cloud-based software helps merchants create manage and promote their e-commerce website and process orders. Premium services include site and logo design supplier integration and search engine optimization. The company has primarily used training seminars around the country to sell its products to aspiring e-commerce mavens but hopes to open more sales channels. More than 90% of sales come from customers in North America (US and Canada). Chairman and CEO Steven Mihaylo founder and former CEO of Inter-Tel owns more than a third of Crexendo.

EXECUTIVES

Independent Director, Anil Puri
Independent Director, Todd Goergen
President, Chief Operating Officer, Doug Gaylor, $258,847 total compensation
Chief Financial Officer, Ronald Vincent, $201,729 total compensation
Chief Revenue Officer, Jon Brinton, $19,712 total compensation
Independent Director, David Williams
Chairman Of The Board, Chief Executive Officer, Steven Mihaylo, $5,100 total compensation
Independent Director, Jeffrey Bash
Auditors: Urish Popeck & Co., LLC

LOCATIONS

HQ: Crexendo Inc
1615 South 52nd Street, Tempe, AZ 85281
Phone: 602 714-8500
Web: www.crexendo.com

PRODUCTS/OPERATIONS

Selected Software and Services
E-commerce seminars
Search engine optimization
StoresOnline (e-commerce development platform)
Web hosting
Website development and design
Hosted telecommunications

COMPETITORS

ALTERYX INC.
ASPECT SOFTWARE GROUP
HOLDINGS LTD.
ASTADIA INC.
BLUETIE INC.
GEOWEB SERVICES INC

HISTORICAL FINANCIALS
Company Type: Public

Income Statement				FYE: December 31
	REVENUE ($ mil.)	NET INCOME ($ mil.)	NET PROFIT MARGIN	EMPLOYEES
12/20	16.3	7.9	48.5%	58
12/19	14.4	1.1	7.9%	56
12/18	11.9	(0.2)	—	56
12/17	10.3	(1.0)	—	54
12/16	9.1	(2.7)	—	53
Annual Growth	15.8%	—	—	2.3%

2020 Year-End Financials

Debt ratio: 6.6%
Return on equity: 52.5%
Cash ($ mil.): 17.5
Current ratio: 7.72
Long-term debt ($ mil.): 1.9
No. of shares (mil.): 17.9
Dividends
  Yield: —
  Payout: —
Market value ($ mil.): 125.0

	STOCK PRICE ($) FY Close	P/E High/Low	PER SHARE ($) Earnings	Dividends	Book Value
12/20	6.93	23 6	0.46	0.00	1.43
12/19	4.25	58 22	0.07	0.00	0.29
12/18	2.00	— —	(0.02)	0.00	0.14
12/17	2.10	— —	(0.07)	0.00	0.09
12/16	1.45	— —	(0.21)	0.00	0.04
Annual Growth	47.9% 147.9%	— —	—	—	—

Crocs Inc

Crocs is one of the world's largest footwear companies. Its shoe collection has grown by leaps and bounds from its ubiquitous classic slip-on clog to a range of trainers sandals and boots. Branded as Crocs its shoes are made of proprietary closed-cell resin and designed for men women and children. Jibbitz are the company's decorative add-on charms. It reaches customers via nearly 350 owned stores first- and third-party e-commerce sites and third-party retailers. Sold approximately 69.1 million pairs of shoes worldwide the company has customers in more than 80 countries and earns most of its sales outside the US. Every pair of Crocs is manufactured by other companies mostly in Vietnam and China.

Operations

Crocs has three reportable operating segments based on the geographic nature of its operations: the Americas (more than 60%) Asia Pacific (ap-

proximately 20%) and Europe Middle East and Africa (about 20%).

The company offers a broad portfolio of all-season products while remaining true to its core molded footwear heritage. The vast majority of Crocs shoes feature Croslite material a proprietary revolutionary technology that gives each pair of shoes the soft comfortable lightweight non-marking and odor-resistant.

By channel the company's wholesale channel accounts for approximately 50% of sales. It includes domestic and international multi-brand brick-and-mortar retailers e-tailers and distributors in certain countries including partner store operators. Brick-and-mortar customers typically include family footwear retailers national and regional retail chains sporting goods stores and independent footwear retailers. E-commerce channel generates about 25%. It offers products through nearly 15 company-operated e-commerce sites worldwide and also on third-party marketplaces. Retail provides about 25% of sales operates through three platforms: company-operated full-price retail stores outlet stores and store-in-store locations.

Geographic Reach

Headquartered in Broomfield Colorado Crocs has offices and distribution centers worldwide and also leases about 350 retail locations worldwide. Operating in more than 80 countries the company generates about 60% of sales from the US while international sales account for the remaining. It prioritizes five core markets including: US Japan China South Korea and Germany.

Sales and Marketing

Crocs markets its products through media advertising (television radio print social digital) and tactical advertising (signs banners point-of-sale materials).

The company's total marketing expenses inclusive of advertising production promotion and agency expenses including variable marketing expenses were approximately $101.0 million $83.2 million and $68.6 million for the years ended 2020 2019 and 2018 respectively.

Financial Performance

Revenues for the year totaled $1.4 billion a 13% increase from the previous year's net revenue of $1.2 billion.

In 2020 the company had a net income of $312.9 million a 162% increase from the previous year.

The company's cash at the end of 2020 was $139.3 million. Operating activities generated $266.9 million while investing activities used $41.8 million mainly for purchases of property equipment and software. Financing activities used another $198 million mainly for repayment of borrowings.

Strategy

Crocs' strategy is to maintain a flexible globally-diversified cost-efficient third-party manufacturing base. The company sources its inventory production from multiple third-party manufacturers primarily in Vietnam and China.

EXECUTIVES

President, Michelle Poole, $585,769 total compensation
Senior Vice President And Chief Product And Merchandising Officer, Lori Foglia
Independent Director, Tracy Gardner
Svp And General Manager, Emma Minto
Independent Director, Charisse Hughes

Executive Vice President, Chief Operations And Transformations Officer, Elaine Boltz, $466,154 total compensation
Independent Director, Beth Kaplan
Independent Director, Douglas Treff
Chief Financial Officer, Executive Vice President, Anne Mehlman, $543,654 total compensation
Chief Executive Officer, Director, Andrew Rees, $984,231 total compensation
Executive Vice President, Chief Legal And Risk Officer, Daniel Hart, $514,476 total compensation
Independent Chairman Of The Board, Thomas Smach
Independent Director, Ronald Frasch
Auditors: DELOITTE & TOUCHE LLP

LOCATIONS

HQ: Crocs Inc
13601 Via Varra, Broomfield, CO 80020
Phone: 303 848-7000
Web: www.crocs.com

PRODUCTS/OPERATIONS

2018 Sales

	% of total
Wholesale	53
Retail	30
Internet	17
Total	**100**

2018 Stores

	No.
Retail	120
Outlet	195
Kiosk	68
Total	**383**

COMPETITORS

ACCO BRANDS CORPORATION
DECKERS OUTDOOR CORPORATION
GUESS ? INC.
Grendene S/A
Pegasus International Holdings Limited
SIMPLE SHOES INC.
SKECHERS U.S.A. INC.
TILLY'S INC.
V.F. CORPORATION
VANS INC.
ZUMIEZ INC.

HISTORICAL FINANCIALS
Company Type: Public

Income Statement				FYE: December 31
	REVENUE ($ mil.)	NET INCOME ($ mil.)	NET PROFIT MARGIN	EMPLOYEES
12/21	2,313.4	725.6	31.4%	5,770
12/20	1,385.9	312.8	22.6%	4,600
12/19	1,230.5	119.5	9.7%	3,803
12/18	1,088.2	50.4	4.6%	3,901
12/17	1,023.5	10.2	1.0%	4,382
Annual Growth	22.6%	190.2%	—	7.1%

2021 Year-End Financials

Debt ratio: 49.9%
Return on equity: 476.3%
Cash ($ mil.): 213.2
Current ratio: 1.72
Long-term debt ($ mil.): 771.3
No. of shares (mil.): 58.3
Dividends
  Yield: —
  Payout: —
Market value ($ mil.): 7,475.0

	STOCK PRICE ($) FY Close	P/E High/Low		PER SHARE ($) Earnings	Dividends	Book Value
12/21	128.22	16	5	11.39	0.00	0.24
12/20	62.66	14	2	4.56	0.00	4.41
12/19	41.89	24	10	1.66	0.00	1.93
12/18	25.98	—	—	(1.01)	0.00	2.05
12/17	12.64	—	—	(0.07)	0.00	5.35
Annual Growth 78.5% (53.9%)		—	—	—	—	—

CrossFirst Bankshares Inc

Auditors: BKD, LLP

LOCATIONS

HQ: CrossFirst Bankshares Inc
11440 Tomahawk Creek Parkway, Leawood, KS 66211
Phone: 913 312-6822
Web: www.crossfirstbankshares.com

HISTORICAL FINANCIALS
Company Type: Public

Income Statement				FYE: December 31
	ASSETS ($ mil.)	NET INCOME ($ mil.)	INCOME AS % OF ASSETS	EMPLOYEES
12/20	5,659.3	12.6	0.2%	328
12/19	4,931.2	28.4	0.6%	357
12/18	4,107.2	19.5	0.5%	360
12/17	2,961.1	5.8	0.2%	0
Annual Growth 24.1%		29.2%	—	—

2020 Year-End Financials
Return on assets: 0.2%
Return on equity: 2.0%
Long-term debt ($ mil.): —
No. of shares (mil.): 51.6
Sales ($ mil): 215.1
Dividends
Yield: —
Payout: —
Market value ($ mil.): 556.0

	STOCK PRICE ($) FY Close	P/E High/Low		PER SHARE ($) Earnings	Dividends	Book Value
12/20	10.75	60	24	0.24	0.00	12.08
12/19	14.42	25	21	0.58	0.00	11.58
12/18	0.00	—	—	0.47	0.00	10.88
Annual Growth	—	—	—	(28.5%)	—	5.4%

Crossroads Systems Inc (New)

Crossroads Systems sets up shop where business and information intersect. The company provides storage networking equipment and data archiving systems used to manage and protect critical data. Its products include StrongBox (network attached storage appliance that uses linear tape file system technology) RVA (monitoring tape media and the condition of disk drives) and SPHiNX (protecting data by working as a network attached storage device or virtual tape library). Crossroads Systems sells directly to manufacturers such as HP (45% of sales) and EMC and through distributors. The company was founded in 1996.

Geographic Reach

Headquartered in Austin TX Crossroads Systems also has a sales office in Germany. International sales account for less than 10% of revenues.

Sales and Marketing

Crossroads relies on a small number of distributors that offer its products as part of an overall data protection package since many of its tape and disk products are incorporated into larger storage systems such as those sold by Fujifilm. These distributors can also install and support its products on behalf of Crossroads; its internal sales force is only responsible for managing the OEM and strategic partner relationships.

The company counts on a small number of customers; its top three account for more than two-thirds of sales. End users include small businesses large corporations and government agencies.

Financial Performance

Crossroads has also been at a financial crossroads with a history of losses and declining sales. Revenue was down 10% in 2013 to $12.6 million. Sales from its RVA and SPHiNX product lines experienced decreases while its StrongBox product grew $2 million in its first full year of sales.

Products account for about 60% of sales and the other 40% comes from companies that license its intellectual property. Crossroads has a software license and distribution agreement with HP where the computer giant pays Crossroads royalties and support fees; the deal makes up a huge chunk of Crossroads' revenues every year.

Strategy

Crossroads presents itself as a cost-effective storage company compared with the likes of IBM and Hitachi Data Systems. The markets for its products are characterized by significant price competition and it anticipates that its products will continue to face price pressure.

HISTORY

Crossroads delisted its shares from the Nasdaq National Market in 2006. The company cited the increased costs of operating as a publicly held company especially those associated with complying with Section 404 of the federal Sarbanes-Oxley Act as the reason for the listing change. Trading of the company's shares shifted to the Pink Sheets.

In 2007 Crossroads Systems purchased assets of Grau Data Storage namely its hierarchical storage management (HSM) software product called FileMigrator Agent for less than $1 million in cash. That same year the company cut its workforce (primarily in product development) by about 8% in order to reduce expenses.

In September 2011 Crossroads Systems began trading on the Nasdaq Capital Market.

EXECUTIVES

Ceo, Eric Donnelly
Chb*, Robert H Alpert
Cfo, Jennifer Ray Crane
Evp Corp Dev't, Mark Hood
Board Member, Hannah Bible
Officer, Robert Sims
Sales, Shelia Gregg
Executive Director, Richard K Coleman
Supervisor, Luzma Dietz
Auditors: Baker Tilly US, LLP

LOCATIONS

HQ: Crossroads Systems Inc (New)
4514 Cole Avenue, Suite 1600, Dallas, TX 75205
Phone: 214 999-0149
Web: www.crossroads.com

COMPETITORS

ACACIA RESEARCH CORPORATION
APEX GLOBAL BRANDS INC.
PENDRELL CORPORATION
QUADIENT S.A.

HISTORICAL FINANCIALS
Company Type: Public

Income Statement				FYE: October 31
	REVENUE ($ mil.)	NET INCOME ($ mil.)	NET PROFIT MARGIN	EMPLOYEES
10/21	930.6	194.7	20.9%	34
10/20	36.6	3.0	8.2%	27
10/19	37.7	1.7	4.6%	0
10/18	28.4	23.8	83.8%	0
10/17	0.0	(1.6)	—	0
Annual Growth 970.0%		—	—	—

2021 Year-End Financials
Debt ratio: 91.3%
Return on equity: 1,852.7%
Cash ($ mil.): 589.0
Current ratio: 1.70
Long-term debt ($ mil.): 3,176.2
No. of shares (mil.): 5.9
Dividends
Yield: 1.4%
Payout: —
Market value ($ mil.): 111.0

	STOCK PRICE ($) FY Close	P/E High/Low		PER SHARE ($) Earnings	Dividends	Book Value
10/21	18.60	—	—	(0.00)	40.00	(1.91)
10/20	9.00	—	—	(0.00)	0.00	5.43
10/19	8.50	—	—	(0.00)	0.00	8.55
10/18	6.90	—	—	(0.00)	0.00	4.61
10/17	3.30	—	—	(1.51)	0.00	0.85
Annual Growth 54.1%		—	—	—	—	—

CSB Bancorp Inc (OH)

EXECUTIVES

President, Chief Executive Officer, Director Of The Bank And The Company, Eddie Steiner, $275,000 total compensation
Chief Financial Officer, Senior Vice President, Paula Meiler, $164,000 total compensation
Independent Director, Jeffery Robb
Chief Operating Officer, Executive Vice President, Chief Information Officer, Brett Gallion, $153,154 total compensation
Independent Director, Julian Coblentz
Independent Director, Vikki Briggs
Independent Director, Cheryl Kirkbride
Independent Chairman Of The Board, Robert Baker
Auditors: S.R. Snodgrass, P.C.

HOOVER'S HANDBOOK OF EMERGING COMPANIES 2022

LOCATIONS

HQ: CSB Bancorp Inc (OH)
91 North Clay Street, P.O. Box 232, Millersburg, OH
44654
Phone: 330 674-9015
Web: www.csb1.com

HISTORICAL FINANCIALS

Company Type: Public

Income Statement				FYE: December 31
	ASSETS ($ mil.)	NET INCOME ($ mil.)	INCOME AS % OF ASSETS	EMPLOYEES
12/20	1,031.6	10.5	1.0%	187
12/19	818.6	10.4	1.3%	187
12/18	731.7	9.4	1.3%	190
12/17	707.0	7.1	1.0%	187
12/16	669.9	6.7	1.0%	182
Annual Growth	11.4%	11.9%	—	0.7%

2020 Year-End Financials

Return on assets: 1.1%
Return on equity: 11.7%
Long-term debt ($ mil.): —
No. of shares (mil.): 2.7
Sales ($ mil): 38.0
Dividends
Yield: 0.0%
Payout: 29.3%
Market value ($ mil.): 96.0

	STOCK PRICE ($) FY Close	P/E High/Low		PER SHARE ($) Earnings	Dividends	Book Value
12/20	35.00	11	7	3.85	1.13	34.23
12/19	40.97	11	10	3.80	1.08	31.17
12/18	38.50	13	10	3.43	0.98	27.91
12/17	33.11	13	11	2.59	0.84	25.72
12/16	31.00	14	9	2.46	0.78	23.85
Annual Growth	3.1%	—	—	11.8%	9.7%	9.4%

Customers Bancorp Inc

Customers Bancorp makes it pretty clear who they want to serve. Boasting some $8.5 billion in assets the bank holding company operates about 15 branches mostly in southeastern Pennsylvania but also in New York and New Jersey. It offers personal and business checking savings and money market accounts as well as loans certificates of deposit credit cards and concierge or appointment banking (they come to you seven days a week). Around 95% of the bank's loan portfolio is made up of commercial loans while the rest consists of consumer loans. It was formed in 2010 as a holding company for Customers Bank which was created in 1994 as New Century Bank.

Operations

Customers Bancorp operates two main business lines: Commercial Lending and Consumer Lending. Its Commercial Lending business provides commercial and industrial loans small and middle-market business banking and small business administration (SBA) loans multi-family and commercial real estate loans and commercial loans to mortgage originators. Its Consumer Lending division mostly makes local market mortgage loans and home equity loans. More than 95% of the bank's loan portfolio was made up of commercial loans at the end of 2015 while the rest consisted of consumer loans.

Broadly speaking the bank makes roughly 90% of its revenue from interest income. About 66% of its revenue came from loan interest during 2015 while another 19% came from interest loans held for sale and 4% came from interest on investment securities. The remainder of its revenue came from mortgage warehouse transactional fees (4%) and other miscellaneous and non-recurring sources.

Geographic Reach

The bank had 14 branches at the end of 2015 including nine in Philadelphia and Southeastern Pennsylvania; four in Berks County Pennsylvania; one in Westchester County New York; and one in Mercer County New Jersey. It also had a handful of additional offices in Boston; New York City; Portsmouth New Hampshire; Providence Rhode Island; and Suffolk County New York.

Sales and Marketing

Customers Bancorp's customers include private businesses business customers non-profits and consumers. Its commercial lending division typically makes loans to companies with revenues between $1 million to $50 million needing between $0.5 million to $10 million in credit.

The bank has been ramping up its advertising spend in recent years. It spent $1.48 million on advertising in 2015 up from $1.33 million and $1.27 million in 2014 and 2013 respectively.

Financial Performance

The bank's annual revenues have nearly quadrupled since 2011 as its loan assets have more than tripled (its loan assets reached $5.45 billion by of the end of 2015). Meanwhile growing revenues strong cost controls and low interest rates have pushed the bank's annual profits up almost 15-fold over the same period.

Customers Bancorp's revenue jumped 29% to $277.5 million during 2015 mostly as its average balance of interest-earning loan and securities assets rose by 31% to $6.7 billion for the year.

Revenue growth in 2015 drove the bank's net income up 36% to $58.5 million. Customer Bancorp's operating cash levels declined sharply to $356.6 million for the year as the bank originated more loans held for sale than it actually sold.

Strategy

With its eye on becoming the leading regional bank holding company Customers Bancorp continued in 2016 to focus on expanding its market share with its high-touch personalized Concierge Banking services and its "high-tech" BankMobile offerings which include remote account opening remote deposit capture and mobile banking. The BankMobile and online banking channels allow Customers Bancorp to slow expensive branch-expansion plans and cut operating costs significantly while giving customers faster access to banking services.

But even with digital banking the bank occasionally opens new branches (and selectively acquire others) to grow its loan and deposit business. In January 2016 it opened and replaced an existing branch in Hamilton New Jersey onto Route 33 in the same city. In June 2015 Customers opened a new Long Island location in Mellville New York to expand its private and commercial banking services to local clients there.

Mergers and Acquisitions

In December 2015 Customers Bank expanded its deposit business and added 2 million new student customers after buying the One Account Student Checking and Refund Management Disbursement Services business from higher education

refund disbursement provider Higher One Inc for $42 million.

Company Background

In late 2011 Customers purchased Berkshire Bancorp and picked up five branches in Berks County Pennsylvania for about $11.3 million.

EXECUTIVES

Director, Robert Mackay
Chairman And Chief Executive Officer, Jay Sidhu, $764,308 total compensation
Lead Independent Director, Daniel Rothermel
Independent Director, Steven Zuckerman
Chief Financial Officer, Carla Leibold, $415,385 total compensation
Independent Director, Rick Burkey
Independent Director, Andrea Allon
Principal Accounting Officer, Jessie Velasquez
Independent Director, Robert Buford
Head, Corporate Development, Samvir Sidhu, $351,923 total compensation
Executive Vice President, General Counsel, Corporate Secretary, Andrew Sachs
Director, Bernard Banks
Auditors: DELOITTE & TOUCHE LLP

LOCATIONS

HQ: Customers Bancorp Inc
701 Reading Avenue, West Reading, PA 19611
Phone: 610 933-2000
Web: www.customersbank.com

PRODUCTS/OPERATIONS

2015

	% of total
Interest income	
Loans receivable including fees	66
Loans held for sale	19
Investment securities	4
Other	2
Non interest income	
Mortgage warehouse transnational fees	4
Bank-owned life insurance	3
Gains on sales of loans	1
Deposit fees	0
Mortgage loan and banking income	0
Gain (loss) on sale of investment securities	0
Other	1
Total	**100**

Products include

Equipment Loans
Mortgage Warehouse Loans
Multi-Family And Commercial Real Estate Loans
Residential Mortgage Loans
Small Business Loans

COMPETITORS

BYLINE BANCORP INC.
CENTURY BANCORP INC.
CITY HOLDING COMPANY
EAGLE BANCORP INC.
FIRST COMMONWEALTH FINANCIAL CORPORATION
FIRSTMERIT CORPORATION
MIDDLESEX SAVINGS BANK
OLD LINE BANCSHARES INC.
WILSHIRE BANCORP INC.

HISTORICAL FINANCIALS

Company Type: Public

Income Statement

FYE: December 31

	ASSETS ($ mil.)	NET INCOME ($ mil.)	INCOME AS % OF ASSETS	EMPLOYEES
12/20	18,439.2	132.5	0.7%	830
12/19	11,520.7	79.3	0.7%	867
12/18	9,833.4	71.7	0.7%	827
12/17	9,839.5	78.8	0.8%	765
12/16	9,382.7	78.7	0.8%	739
Annual Growth	18.4%	13.9%	—	2.9%

2020 Year-End Financials

Return on assets: 0.8%
Return on equity: 12.1%
Long-term debt ($ mil.): —
No. of shares (mil.): 31.7
Sales ($ mil): 645.0

Dividends
Yield: —
Payout: —
Market value ($ mil.): 576.0

	STOCK PRICE ($) FY Close	P/E High/Low		PER SHARE ($) Earnings	Dividends	Book Value
12/20	18.18	6	2	3.74	0.00	35.23
12/19	23.81	12	8	2.05	0.00	33.60
12/18	18.20	18	9	1.78	0.00	30.86
12/17	25.99	17	12	1.97	0.00	29.35
12/16	35.82	15	9	2.31	0.00	28.26
Annual Growth	(15.6%)	—	—	12.8%	—	5.7%

CVB Financial Corp

CVB Financial is into the California Vibe Baby. The holding company's Citizens Business Bank offers community banking services to primarily small and midsized businesses but also to consumers through nearly 50 branch and office locations across central and southern California. Boasting more than $7 billion in assets the bank offers checking money market CDs and savings accounts trust and investment services and a variety of loans. Commercial real estate loans account for about two-thirds of the bank's loan portfolio which is rounded out by business consumer and construction loans; residential mortgages; dairy and livestock loans; and municipal lease financing.

Operations

In addition to its 40 business financial centers CVB operates seven Commercial Banking Centers (CBCs). The CBCs operate primarily as sales offices and focus on business clients professionals and high-net-worth individuals. The bank also has three trust offices.

Citizens Business Bank provides auto and equipment leasing and brokers mortgage loans through its Citizens Financial Services Division; CitizensTrust offers trust and investment services.

Overall the bank made 63% of its total revenue from interest income on loans and leases in 2014 with another 24% of total revenue coming from interest income on the bank's investment securities. About 5% of total revenue came from service charges on deposit accounts and 3% came from trust and investment services income.

Geographic Reach

CVB Financial has 40 Business Financial Centers located in the Inland Empire Los Angeles County Orange County San Diego County and the Central Valley regions in California.

Sales and Marketing

CVB Financial provides services to companies from a variety of industries including: industrial and manufacturing dairy and livestock agriculture education nonprofit entertainment medical professional services title and escrow government and property management.

Financial Performance

CVB's revenue has been in decline in recent years due to shrinking interest margins on loans amidst the low-interest environment. The firm's profits however have been rising thanks to declining loan loss provisions as its loan portfolio's credit quality has been improving in the strengthening economy.

CVB enjoyed a breakout year in 2014 with revenue rebounding by 12% to $289.32 million mostly thanks to higher interest income as the bank grew its loan and lease assets by 7% during the year and grew its investment security assets by 18%. Most of its loan growth came from commercial real estate loans while SFR mortgage loans consumer loans and construction loans also helped boost the company's top line. The bank's non-interest income also jumped by 44% during the year thanks to a $6 million gain on loans held-for-sale and a net $3.6 million decrease in its FDIC loss sharing asset.

Higher revenue and a $16.1 million loan loss provision recapture in 2014 also drove the bank's net income higher by 9% to $104.02 million.

Despite higher earnings for the year CVB's operating cash levels shrank by 22% to $87.70 million as the bank used more cash toward employee payments and income taxes.

Strategy

CVB Financial continues to seek out acquisitions of smaller banking trust and investment companies to grow its loan and deposit business as well as its geographic reach in key markets in (mostly Southern) California. With its 2014 acquisition of American Security Bank for example CVB boosted its assets by 6% to over $7 billion while adding branches in more than a handful of key markets in Southern California.

Remaining profitable throughout the economic downturn CVB Financial credits its success in part to its strict loan underwriting standards. The bank targets family-owned or other privately held businesses with annual revenues of up to $200 million with the goal of maintaining its client relationships for decades.

Mergers and Acquisitions

In March 2014 CVB Financial through its Citizens Business Bank (CBB) subsidiary purchased Southern California-based American Security Bank (the flagship subsidiary of American Bancshares) for a total of $57 million. The deal would add American Security Bank's $431 million in assets and boost CBB's branch presence across key markets in Newport Beach Corona Laguna Niguel Lancastar Victorville and Apple Valley.

In 2016 CVB Financial agreed to buy the $416 million-asset Valley Commerce Bancorp the holding company for Valley Business Bank. Valley Business has four banking locations in California's Visalia Tulare Fresno and Woodlake.

Company Background

In 2009 CVB Financial healthier than most California banks acquired the failed San Joaquin Bank after the FDIC took it over. The deal added five branches banking centers in the Bakersfield area.

EXECUTIVES

Independent Vice Chairman Of The Board, George Borba

Chief Financial Officer Of The Company And Executive Vice President And Chief Financial Officer Of The Bank, E. Allen Nicholson, $391,923 total compensation

President, Chief Executive Officer, Director, David Brager, $551,539 total compensation

Executive Vice President And Chief Risk Officer, Yamynn DeAngelis

Executive Vice President, Chief Operations Officer Of The Bank, David Harvey, $413,077 total compensation

Independent Chairman Of The Board, Raymond O'Brien

Executive Vice President, General Counsel, Richard Wohl, $291,154 total compensation

Independent Director, Jane Olvera

Executive Vice President And Chief Credit Officer Of The Bank, David Farnsworth, $312,693 total compensation

Auditors: KPMG LLP

LOCATIONS

HQ: CVB Financial Corp
701 North Haven Ave., Suite 350, Ontario, CA 91764
Phone: 909 980-4030
Web: www.cbbank.com

PRODUCTS/OPERATIONS

2014 Sales

	$ mil.	% of total
Interest		
Loans including fees	181.6	62
Investment securities	68.4	24
Other	2.9	1
Noninterest		
Service charges on deposit accounts	15.8	5
Trust & investment services	8.1	3
Bankcard services	3.4	1
BOLI income	2.4	1
Other	10.3	3
Adjustments	(3.6)	-
Total	**289.3**	**100**

COMPETITORS

BANCFIRST CORPORATION
BOKF MERGER CORPORATION NUMBER SIXTEEN
CAPITAL BANK FINANCIAL CORP.
CITY HOLDING COMPANY
EAGLE BANCORP INC.
FIRST MIDWEST BANCORP INC.
GUARANTY BANCORP
PACWEST BANCORP
PROVIDENT FINANCIAL SERVICES INC.
SIGNATURE BANK
STATE BANK FINANCIAL CORPORATION
WSFS FINANCIAL CORPORATION

HISTORICAL FINANCIALS

Company Type: Public

Income Statement
FYE: December 31

	ASSETS ($ mil.)	NET INCOME ($ mil.)	INCOME AS % OF ASSETS	EMPLOYEES
12/20	14,419.3	177.1	1.2%	1,052
12/19	11,282.4	207.8	1.8%	0
12/18	11,529.1	152.0	1.3%	0
12/17	8,270.5	104.4	1.3%	0
12/16	8,073.7	101.4	1.3%	0
Annual Growth	15.6%	15.0%	—	—

2020 Year-End Financials

Return on assets: 1.3%
Return on equity: 8.8%
Long-term debt ($ mil.): —
No. of shares (mil.): 135.6
Sales ($ mil): 480.2

Dividends
  Yield: 3.6%
  Payout: 55.3%
Market value ($ mil.): 2,644.0

	STOCK PRICE ($) FY Close	P/E High/Low		Earnings	PER SHARE ($) Dividends	Book Value
12/20	19.50	17	12	1.30	0.72	14.81
12/19	21.58	16	14	1.48	0.68	14.23
12/18	20.23	20	15	1.24	0.56	13.22
12/17	23.56	26	21	0.95	0.52	9.70
12/16	22.93	25	15	0.94	0.36	9.15
Annual Growth	(4.0%)	—	—	8.4%	18.9%	12.8%

CW Bancorp

LOCATIONS

HQ: CW Bancorp
  2111 Business Center Drive, Irvine, CA 92612
Phone: 949 251-6959   **Fax:** 949 251-6958
Web: www.cwbk.com

HISTORICAL FINANCIALS

Company Type: Public

Income Statement
FYE: December 31

	ASSETS ($ mil.)	NET INCOME ($ mil.)	INCOME AS % OF ASSETS	EMPLOYEES
12/20	1,318.8	9.0	0.7%	0
12/19	883.3	8.2	0.9%	60
12/18	798.1	5.9	0.7%	0
12/17	769.3	5.0	0.7%	0
Annual Growth	19.7%	22.0%	—	—

2020 Year-End Financials

Return on assets: 0.8%
Return on equity: 13.4%
Long-term debt ($ mil.): —
No. of shares (mil.): 3.5
Sales ($ mil): 35.1

Dividends
  Yield: 3.9%
  Payout: 32.2%
Market value ($ mil.): 71.0

	STOCK PRICE ($) FY Close	P/E High/Low		Earnings	PER SHARE ($) Dividends	Book Value
12/20	20.10	9	6	2.48	0.80	19.88
12/19	24.00	11	9	2.14	0.68	17.86
12/18	19.95	17	13	1.47	0.68	16.26
12/17	23.00	18	13	1.22	0.68	16.04
/0.00	—	—	(0.00)	0.00	(0.00)	
Annual Growth		—	—	—	—	—

CyrusOne Inc

EXECUTIVES

Executive Vice President, General Counsel, Secretary, Robert Jackson, $400,269 total compensation
Chief Financial Officer And Executive Vice President, Katherine Motlagh, $78,846 total compensation
Lead Independent Chairman Of The Board, Alex Shumate
Chief Operating Officer And Executive Vice President, John Hatem, $107,308 total compensation
Independent Director, Lynn Wentworth
Independent Director, William Sullivan
Independent Director, John Gamble
Chief Executive Officer And Interim President, David Ferdman
Independent Director, T.Tod Nielsen
Auditors: DELOITTE & TOUCHE LLP

LOCATIONS

HQ: CyrusOne Inc
  2850 N. Harwood Street, Suite 2200, Dallas, TX 75201
Phone: 972 350-0060
Web: www.cyrusone.com

HISTORICAL FINANCIALS

Company Type: Public

Income Statement
FYE: December 31

	REVENUE ($ mil.)	NET INCOME ($ mil.)	NET PROFIT MARGIN	EMPLOYEES
12/21	1,205.7	25.3	2.1%	456
12/20	1,033.5	41.4	4.0%	441
12/19	981.3	41.4	4.2%	452
12/18	821.4	1.2	0.1%	448
12/17	672.0	(83.5)		416
Annual Growth	15.7%	—	—	2.3%

2021 Year-End Financials

Debt ratio: 46.8%
Return on equity: 0.9%
Cash ($ mil.): 346.3
Current ratio: 1.15
Long-term debt ($ mil.): 3,492.9

No. of shares (mil.): 129.5
Dividends
  Yield: 2.3%
  Payout: 490.4%
Market value ($ mil.): 11,624.0

	STOCK PRICE ($) FY Close	P/E High/Low	Earnings	PER SHARE ($) Dividends	Book Value
12/21	89.72	451311	0.20	2.06	22.57
12/20	73.15	247129	0.35	2.02	21.24
12/19	65.43	220138	0.36	1.92	21.21
12/18	52.88	— —	(0.00)	1.84	20.55
12/17	59.53	— —	(0.95)	1.68	17.83
Annual Growth	10.8%	— —	—	5.2%	6.1%

Dart Financial Corp

Auditors: Doeren Mayhew

LOCATIONS

HQ: Dart Financial Corp
  368 S. Park Street, Mason, MI 48854
Phone: 517 676-3661
Web: www.dartbank.com

HISTORICAL FINANCIALS

Company Type: Public

Income Statement
FYE: December 31

	REVENUE ($ mil.)	NET INCOME ($ mil.)	NET PROFIT MARGIN	EMPLOYEES
12/20	59.7	9.8	16.4%	0
12/19	37.1	3.1	8.5%	0
12/18	31.4	3.7	12.0%	0
12/17	28.8	3.5	12.4%	0
12/16	26.4	2.8	10.8%	0
Annual Growth	22.6%	36.1%	—	

2020 Year-End Financials

Debt ratio: 10.8%
Return on equity: 21.5%
Cash ($ mil.): 29.3
Current ratio: 0.07
Long-term debt ($ mil.): 67.4

No. of shares (mil.): 1.1
Dividends
  Yield: —
  Payout: 14.6%
Market value ($ mil.): —

Davey Tree Expert Co. (The)

The company's roots extend back to 1880 when John Davey founded the arboricultural horticultural services environmental and consulting firm which branched into residential commercial utility and other natural resource management services. With offices in the US and Canada Davey's services include treatment preservation maintenance and removal of trees shrubs and other plants; landscaping; grounds maintenance; tree surgery; tree feeding and tree spraying; the application of fertilizers herbicides and insecticides. It also natural resource management and consulting forestry research and development and environmental planning. Davey has been employee-owned since 1979. The US generates some 95% of Davey's total revenue.

Operations

Davey operates through two main segments: Commercial; and Utility Services and Residential. Other services include natural resource management and consulting forestry research and technical support.

The Utility segment accounts about 60% of revenue provide services to its utility customers—investor-owned municipal utilities and rural electric cooperatives—including: the practice of line-clearing and vegetation management around power lines rights-of-way and chemical brush control; and natural resource management and consulting forestry research and development and environmental planning.

The Residential and Commercial segment generates more than 40% of company's total revenue. The segment provides services to residential and commercial customers including: the treatment preservation maintenance removal and planting of trees shrubs and other plant life; the practice of landscaping grounds maintenance tree surgery tree feeding and tree spraying; the application of fertilizer herbicides and insecticides; and natural resource management and consulting forestry research and development and environmental planning.

Geographic Reach

The company corporate headquarters campus is located in Kent Ohio together with The Davey Institute's research technical support and laboratory diagnostic facilities.

Davey has administrative functions in Livermore California (Utility Services). Their Canadian operations' administrative functions are located in the provinces of Ontario and British Columbia. The company has also some 200 properties in more than 30 states and five provinces.

About 95% of Davey's total revenue were generated from US operations.

Sales and Marketing

Davey gets business from residential customers principally through referrals direct mail programs and through the placement of advertisements in national magazines trade journals local newspapers and yellow pages. Davey also employs online marketing and lead generation strategies including email marketing campaigns search engine optimization search engine marketing and social media communication. Business from utility and commercial customers is obtained principally through negotiated contracts and competitive bidding. The company carries out all of its sales and services through its employees.

Pacific Gas and Electric accounts for more than 15% of sales the company's largest customer.

Financial Performance

Revenues of $1.3 million increased $143800 compared with the $1.1 million reported in 2019. Utility increased $131600 or 22% from the prior year. The increase was primarily attributable to additional revenues from increased work year-over-year on existing accounts rate increases and new accounts.

In 2020 the company had a net income of $60.9 million a 48% increase from the previous year.

The company's cash at the end of 2020 was $16.2 million. Operating activities generated $152.1 million while investing activities used $54.9 million mainly for capital expenditures. Financing activities used another $92.1 million primarily for revolving credit facility payments.

Strategy

The company solicits business from residential customers principally through referrals direct mail programs and to a lesser extent through the placement of advertisements in national magazines and trade journals local newspapers and "yellow pages" telephone directories. Davey Tree also employs online marketing and led generation strategies including email marketing campaigns search engine optimization search engine marketing and social media communication. Business from utility and commercial customers is obtained principally through negotiated contracts and competitive bidding. The company carries out all of its sales and services through its employees. Davey Tree generally does not use agents and does not franchise its name or business.

Mergers and Acquisitions

In 2021 Davey has acquired certain assets of AJ's Tree Service Inc. The firm provides residential and commercial tree care services to the region Southeast of Nashville. The team at AJ's has done tremendous work in the Nashville community and earned a reputation for high-quality service. AJ's clients can continue to expect excellent service and

will benefit from additional resources Davey offers.

Also in 2021 Davey announce the addition of Chippers Inc. of Woodstock VT to its family of brands. Chippers will strengthen the Davey brand.

EXECUTIVES

President, Chief Executive Officer, Chief Operating Officer, Director, Patrick Covey, $319,692 total compensation
Chief Financial Officer, Secretary, Joseph Paul, $256,615 total compensation
Executive Vice President And General Manager, Commercial Landscape Services, Dan Joy
Chairman Of The Board, Karl Warnke, $619,385 total compensation
Counsel, Assistant Secretary, Marjorie Conner
Corporate Vice President - Operations Support Services, Fred Johnson
Vice President - Personnel Recruiting And Development, Gordon Ober
Vice President, General Manager - Davey Resource Group, Brent Repenning
Executive Vice President, U.s. Residential Operations, James Stief, $257,923 total compensation
Executive Vice President - U.s. Utility Operations, Steven Marshall, $257,646 total compensation
Vice President, General Manager - Eastern Utility Services, Mark Vaughn
Corporate Vice President, Canadian Operations, Richard Ramsey
Principal Accounting Officer, Controller, Thea Sears
Treasurer, Christopher Bast
Independent Director, William Ginn
Independent Director, Douglas Hall
Independent Director, John Warfel
Director, Donald Brown
Executive Vice President, General Manager, James Doyle
Auditors: DELOITTE & TOUCHE LLP

LOCATIONS

HQ: Davey Tree Expert Co. (The)
1500 North Mantua Street, P.O. Box 5193, Kent, OH 44240
Phone: 330 673-9511
Web: www.davey.com

PRODUCTS/OPERATIONS

2016 Sales

	$ mil.	% of total
Utility Services	433.4	51
Residential & Commercial Services	410.9	49
Other	1.4	0
Total	**845.7**	**100**

Selected Mergers and AcquisitionsSelected Tree Care Services

Cabling and bracing
Hazardous tree assessment
Insect and disease management
Large tree moving
Lightning protection
Root collar excavation
Removals and stump grinding
Shrub pruning
Tree cavity treatment
Tree pruning
Tree and shrub fertilization
Tree and shrub planting

COMPETITORS

ARBOR TREE SURGERY
ARCADIS U.S. INC.
GRAHAM HOLDINGS COMPANY
JACOBS ONE LIMITED
NV5 GLOBAL INC.
R C M TECHNOLOGIES INC.
SITEONE LANDSCAPE SUPPLY INC.
Stantec Inc
TERMINIX GLOBAL HOLDINGS INC.
TYLER TECHNOLOGIES INC.
UNITED RENTALS INC.
US ECOLOGY HOLDINGS INC.

HISTORICAL FINANCIALS

Company Type: Public

Income Statement — FYE: December 31

	REVENUE ($ mil.)	NET INCOME ($ mil.)	NET PROFIT MARGIN	EMPLOYEES
12/20	1,287.5	60.9	4.7%	9,600
12/19	1,143.7	40.8	3.6%	9,700
12/18	1,024.7	27.9	2.7%	8,900
12/17	915.9	22.1	2.4%	8,200
12/16	845.6	22.2	2.6%	8,000
Annual Growth	11.1%	28.6%	—	4.7%

2020 Year-End Financials

Debt ratio: 16.0%
Return on equity: 28.9%
Cash ($ mil.): 16.2
Current ratio: 1.39
Long-term debt ($ mil.): 83.5
No. of shares (mil.): 45.6
Dividends
Yield: —
Payout: 3.7%
Market value ($ mil.): —

Deckers Outdoor Corp.

Deckers Outdoor is a global leader in designing marketing and distributing innovative footwear apparel and accessories developed for both everyday casual lifestyle use and high-performance activities. It designs and markets the iconic UGG brand of luxury sheepskin footwear in addition to Teva sports sandals ? a cross between a hiking boot and a flip-flop used for walking hiking and rafting among other pursuits. Other product lines include Sanuk HOKA One One and Koolaburra. Deckers Outdoor which generates most of its revenue in the US sells its footwear through approximately 140 retail stores worldwide independent distributors and e-commerce sites such as Amazon.com Zappos.com and Zalando.com.

Operations

Deckers Outdoor's six reportable operating segments include the worldwide wholesale operations of the UGG brand HOKA brand Teva brand Sanuk brand and Other brands as well as DTC.

The UGG brand accounts for about 35% of the company's revenue is one of the most iconic and recognized brands in the industry which highlights the company's successful track record of building niche brands into lifestyle and fashion market leaders.

The HOKA brand (brings in about 15% of the company's revenue) is an authentic premium line of year-round performance footwear and apparel that offers enhanced cushioning and inherent stability with minimal weight. Originally designed for ultra-runners the brand now appeals to world champions taste makers and everyday athletes. It

HOOVER'S HANDBOOK OF EMERGING COMPANIES 2022

is quickly becoming a leading brand within run specialty wholesale accounts with strong marketing fueling both domestic and international sales growth.

On the other hand the Teva brand has grown into a multi-category modern outdoor lifestyle brand offering a range of performance casual and trail lifestyle products and has emerged as a leader in footwear sustainability observed through recent growth fueled by young and diverse consumers passionate for the outdoors and the planet. The Sanuk brand originated in Southern California surf culture and has emerged into a lifestyle brand with a presence in the relaxed casual shoe and sandal categories with a focus on innovation in comfort and sustainability. The segments provide approximately 5% of the company's revenue.

In addition Direct-to-Consumer and other brands wholesale represent the remaining sales. Other brands consist primarily of the Koolaburra by UGG brand while the company's DTC business for all its brands is comprised of retail stores and e-commerce websites which in an omni-channel marketplace are intertwined and interdependent.

Geographic Reach

California-based Deckers Outdoor boasts a global presence with operations in the US Canada Australia Vietnam Japan the Netherlands France Switzerland China as well as Europe. However it is a lot more dependent on the US which accounts for about 70% of sales than many of its competitors.

Sales and Marketing

Deckers Outdoor sells its products through a strong network of domestic and international retailers and international distributors as well as directly to consumers worldwide. It also uses about 70 retail concept stores and nearly 70 retail outlet stores to get its products in consumers' hands. The company also has an operated e-commerce business through its company-owned websites and mobile platforms.

The company advertise its business through media advertising such as television radio print social digital as well as tactical advertising which includes signs banners and point-of-sale materials.

Customers have included such big names as Nordstrom Dillard's Zappos.com REI Dick's Sporting Goods Macy's and DSW among others. The company's 10 largest customers account for about 30% of total sales.

The company's wholesale channel accounts for nearly 60% of the company's revenue while direct-to-consumer represents more than 40%.

The company's advertising expenses were approximately $188345 $144948 and $118291 for the years ended 2021 2020 and 2019 respectively.

Financial Performance

The company's net sales for 2021 was $2.5 billion a 19% increase from the previous year. Total net sales increased primarily due to higher DTC sales as well as higher HOKA brand wholesale sales partially offset by lower UGG brand Teva brand and Sanuk brand wholesale sales.

In 2021 the company had a net income of $382.6 million a 39% increase from the previous year's net income of $276.1 million. The increase in net income was due to higher net sales at higher gross margins partially offset by higher SG&A expenses.

The company's cash at the end of 2021 was $1.1 billion. Operating activities generated $596.2 million while investing activities used $32.2 million mainly for purchases of property and equipment. Financing activities used another $129.6 million primarily for repurchases of common stock.

Strategy

As part of Deckers' overall growth strategy it continually seeks out opportunities to enhance the positioning of its brands diversify product offerings extend brands into complementary product categories and markets expand geographically optimize retail presence both in stores and online and improve financial performance and operational efficiency. In addition as part of the company's international growth strategy it may continue to transition from a third-party distribution model to a direct distribution model for certain brands. Conversely it may shift from a direct distribution model to a third-party distribution model for certain other brands. Further the company is exploring relationships with third parties for the expansion of the UGG brand into different product categories including licensee and sourcing agent arrangements.

Company Background

Douglas Otto and his former partner Karl Lopker founded Styled Steers in 1973. But the small obscure maker of leather sandals gained prominence with a line of multicolored rubber sandals. Surfers in Hawaii called them "deckers" and the company soon adopted the name. In 1985 Deckers Outdoor licensed Teva from river guide Mark Thatcher who invented the Teva strapping system for rafters to ensure sandals remained attached in turbulent waters. Teva sport sandals became a popular form of casual footwear largely through word of mouth.

A continuing rise in UGG sales has extended debates over whether the name is generic or a trademark that could possibly be defended over international boundaries. Australian makers of the sheepskin boots traditionally called uggs contend that the name is generic akin to trying to protect the name "sneaker" as a trademark.

EXECUTIVES

President, Performance Lifestyle, Wendy Yang
President - Omni-channel, Stefano Caroti, $650,000 total compensation
Independent Director, Nelson Chan
Independent Director, Juan Figuereo
Independent Director, Victor Luis
Director, Maha Ibrahim
Independent Director, David Burwick
Independent Chairman Of The Board, Michael Devine
Chief Administrative Officer, Thomas Garcia
Chief Financial Officer, Steven Fasching, $600,000 total compensation
Chief Executive Officer, President, And Director, David Powers, $1,100,000 total compensation
Chief Operating Officer, David Lafitte, $700,000 total compensation
Independent Director, Bonita Stewart
Auditors: KPMG LLP

LOCATIONS

HQ: Deckers Outdoor Corp.
250 Coromar Drive, Goleta, CA 93117
Phone: 805 967-7611
Web: www.deckers.com

PRODUCTS/OPERATIONS

2019 Sales

	$ mil.	% of total
Wholesale		
UGG brand	888.3	44
HOKA brand	185.1	9
Teva brand	119.4	6
Sanuk brand	69.8	4
Other brands	42.8	2
Direct-to-Consumer		
UGG brand	644.5	32
HOKA brand	38.1	2
Teva brand	18.0	1
Sanuk brand	12.8	-
Other brands	1.6	-
Total	**2,020.4**	**100**

COMPETITORS

ARKTIS LIMITED	OXFORD INDUSTRIES INC.
COLUMBIA SPORTSWEAR COMPANY	SUPERDRY PLC
	V.F. CORPORATION
CROCS INC.	WYEDEAN WEAVING
CROWN CRAFTS INC.	COMPANY LIMITED(THE)
EMILIO PUCCI SRL	ZUMIEZ INC.

HISTORICAL FINANCIALS

Company Type: Public

Income Statement

FYE: March 31

	REVENUE ($ mil.)	NET INCOME ($ mil.)	NET PROFIT MARGIN	EMPLOYEES
03/21	2,545.6	382.5	15.0%	3,400
03/20	2,132.6	276.1	12.9%	3,600
03/19	2,020.4	264.3	13.1%	3,500
03/18	1,903.3	114.3	6.0%	3,500
03/17	1,790.1	5.7	0.3%	3,300
Annual Growth	9.2%	186.1%	—	0.7%

2021 Year-End Financials

Debt ratio: —	No. of shares (mil.): 27.9
Return on equity: 29.6%	Dividends
Cash ($ mil.): 1,089.3	Yield: —
Current ratio: 3.52	Payout: —
Long-term debt ($ mil.): —	Market value ($ mil.): 9,222.0

	STOCK PRICE ($) FY Close	P/E High/Low		PER SHARE ($) Earnings	Dividends	Book Value
03/21	330.42	25	9	13.47	0.00	51.75
03/20	134.00	21	9	9.62	0.00	40.72
03/19	146.99	17	10	8.84	0.00	35.86
03/18	90.03	27	15	3.58	0.00	30.90
03/17	59.73	381	250	0.18	0.00	29.83
Annual Growth	53.4%	—		—194.1%	—	14.8%

DexCom Inc

DexCom is a medical device company that develops and markets continuous glucose monitoring or CGM systems for the management of diabetes by patients caregivers and clinicians around the world. It develops and manufactures continuous glucose monitoring systems such as its G7 features are 60% reduction in size of the on-body wearable fully disposable and reduced packaging. DexCom launched its latest generation system the Dexcom G6 integrated Continuous Glucose Monitoring System or G6 in 2018. DexCom's products are marketed to physicians endocrinologists and diabetes educators in the US and selected international markets. The company's largest geographic market is the US.

Operations

DexCom is working with partners to develop combined glucose monitoring and insulin delivery systems. Among these partners are Eli Lilly Insulet Novo Nordisk Tandem Diabetes and The Ypsomed Group.

Geographic Reach

Although the majority of Dexcom's revenue has been generated in the US the company expanded its operations to include certain countries in Africa Asia Europe Latin America and the Middle East as well as Australia Canada and New Zealand.

DexCom's corporate headquarters is located in San Diego California.

Sales and Marketing

DexCom has its own sales force that targets endocrinologists doctors and diabetes educators in the US Canada and some parts of Europe. Dexcom also uses third-party distributors.

Broadly speaking revenue by sales channel Distributor accounts for about 75% and Direct accounts for around 25%.

Advertising expenses were approximately $76.5 million $31.8 million and $25.4 million for the years ended in 2020 2019 and 2018 respectively.

Financial Performance

Total revenue increased $450.7 million or 31% in 2020 compared to 2019. The revenue increase was primarily driven by increased sales volume of its disposable sensors due to the continued growth of its worldwide customer base partially offset by pricing pressure due to the evolution of its channel strategy and product mix.

Net income for fiscal 2020 increased to $493.6 million compared from the prior year with $101.1 million.

Cash held by the company at the end of fiscal 2020 increased to $818.2 million. Cash provided by operations and financing activities were $475.6 million and $912.1 million respectively. Cash used for investing activities was $1.0 billion mainly for purchase of marketable securities.

Strategy

DexCom's objective is to remain a leading provider of CGM systems and related products to enable people with diabetes to more effectively and conveniently manage their disease. It is also developing and commercializing products that integrate its CGM technologies into the insulin delivery systems or data platforms of its respective partners. Also it continues to pursue development partnerships with other insulin delivery companies including automated insulin delivery systems.

To achieve these objectives it is focusing on the following business strategies: Establishing and maintaining its technology platform as the leading approach to CGM and leveraging its development expertise to rapidly bring products to market including for expanded indications; Driving the adoption of its ambulatory products through a direct sales and marketing effort as well as key distribution arrangements; Driving additional adoption through technology integration partnerships such as its current partnerships with Eli Lilly Insulet Novo Nordisk Tandem Diabetes and others; Seeking broad coverage policies and reimbursement for its products from private third-party payors and national health systems; Driving increased uti-

lization and adoption of its products through a cloud-based data repository platform that enables people with diabetes to aggregate and analyze data from numerous diabetes devices and share the data with their healthcare providers and other individuals involved in their diabetes management and care; Expanding the use of its products to other patient care settings and patient demographics including use in the hospital setting people with Type 2 diabetes and people who are pregnant; Providing a high level of customer support service and education; and Pursuing the highest safety and quality levels for its products.

Company Background

Dexcom was founded based on the groundbreaking research of Dr. Stuart J. Updike and George P. Hicks in 1967?implantable long-performing glucose sensors that the body would not reject. Dr. Updike joined Dexcom that year to continue CGM innovation. In 2004 Short-term sensor program was created.

EXECUTIVES

Independent Director, Richard Collins
Lead Independent Director, Mark Foletta
Independent Director, Steven Altman
Independent Director, Eric Topol
Executive Vice President - Global Operations, Barry Regan
Independent Director, Kyle Malady
Independent Director, Karen Dahut
Chief Financial Officer, Executive Vice President, Jereme Sylvain
Executive Vice President - Global Revenue, Paul Flynn
Executive Vice President, Global Business Services, It, Quality And Regulatory Affairs, Donald Abbey, $355,300 total compensation
Executive Vice President - Global Marketing, Chad Patterson
Senior Vice President, Chief Risk Officer, Sumi Shrishrimal
Senior Vice President - Information Technology, Shelly Selvaraj
Executive Vice President, Chief Legal Officer, Patrick Murphy
Chief Human Resource Officer, Executive Vice President, Sadie Stern
Executive Vice President, Chief Technology Officer, Jacob Leach, $409,406 total compensation
Independent Director, Jay Skyler
General Manager - Dexcom Ventures, Steven Pacelli, $384,300 total compensation
Chairman Of The Board, President, Chief Executive Officer, Kevin Sayer, $800,000 total compensation
Executive Vice President - Regulatory Strategy, Clinical Affairs, And Strategic Partnership Development, Andrew Balo, $384,300 total compensation
Auditors: Ernst & Young LLP

LOCATIONS

HQ: DexCom Inc
6340 Sequence Drive, San Diego, CA 92121
Phone: 858 200-0200
Web: www.dexcom.com

COMPETITORS

ACORDA THERAPEUTICS INC.	GRIFOLS SA
BOSTON SCIENTIFIC CORPORATION	HAEMONETICS CORPORATION
	IMMUCOR INC.

CARDIOVASCULAR SYSTEMS CORPORATION INC.	INSULET
DELTEX MEDICAL GROUP PLC	MASIMO CORPORATION
GENMARK DIAGNOSTICS INC.	MGC DIAGNOSTICS CORPORATION
GLOBUS MEDICAL INC.	NUVASIVE INC.
	QUIDEL CORPORATION

HISTORICAL FINANCIALS

Company Type: Public

Income Statement · FYE: December 31

	REVENUE ($ mil.)	NET INCOME ($ mil.)	NET PROFIT MARGIN	EMPLOYEES
12/21	2,448.5	154.7	6.3%	7,000
12/20	1,926.7	493.6	25.6%	6,400
12/19	1,476.0	101.1	6.8%	5,200
12/18	1,031.6	(127.1)	—	3,900
12/17	718.5	(50.2)	—	2,990
Annual Growth	35.9%	—	—	23.7%

2021 Year-End Financials

Debt ratio: 36.1%
Return on equity: 7.5%
Cash ($ mil.): 1,052.6
Current ratio: 5.11
Long-term debt ($ mil.): 1,759.7

No. of shares (mil.): 97.0
Dividends
  Yield: —
  Payout: —
Market value ($ mil.): 52,084.0

	STOCK PRICE ($) FY Close	P/E High/Low	Earnings	Dividends	Book Value
12/21	536.95	407 202	1.55	0.00	23.21
12/20	369.72	86 37	5.06	0.00	19.01
12/19	218.74	206 100	1.10	0.00	9.64
12/18	119.80	— —	(1.44)	0.00	7.37
12/17	57.39	— —	(0.58)	0.00	4.82
Annual Growth	74.9%	— —	—	—	48.1%

Digi International Inc

Digi International is a global provider of business and mission-critical Internet of Things (IoT) connectivity products services and solutions. The IoT Products & Services segment provides its customers with a device management platform and other professional services to enable customers to capture and manage data from devices they connect to networks. Digi serves over 81000 customer including industries such as food service retail healthcare (primarily pharmacies) and supply chain. The company sells directly and through resellers and distributors. About 75% of company's total revenue comes from North America

Operations

Digi International operates in two reportable segments: IoT Products & Services segment (about 85%); and IoT Solutions segment (some 15%).

IoT Products & Services segment offers hardware products such as cellular routers and gateways cellular remote management radio frequency embedded and network. Its services include Digi Remote Manager (centralized remote device management solution) Lighthouse Management Software (recurring revenue cloud-based service) and Technical Services (professional services cata plan subscriptions and enhanced technical support offers to customers).

The IoT Solutions segment offers wireless temperature and other condition-based monitoring services as well as employee task management services. These solutions are focused on the following vertical markets: food service retail healthcare (primarily pharmacies) transportation/logistics and education. These solutions are marketed as SmartSense by Digi.

Geographic Reach

Digi International gets nearly 75% of its sales in North America. The Europe Middle East and Africa region accounts for about 15% while other countries accounts for the rest.

Based in Hopkins Minnesota Digi International has locations in Massachusetts Florida Utah New Jersey and Indiana. Internationally it has facilities in Australia and Germany.

Sales and Marketing

The company sells through distributors value-added resellers and systems integrators as well as directly to original equipment manufacturers (OEMs). Digi's marketing strategy has seen it place increasing emphasis on distribution channel sales which account for more than 35% of sales. Large enterprise customers and other end user customers which accounted nearly 55% total revenue. Its largest distributors include Arrow Electronics Avnet Bressner Technology GmbH Digi-Key Express Systems & Peripherals Ingram Micro Mouser Electronics Solid State Supplies Symmetry Electronics Synnex Tech Data Tokyo Electron Device and Venco Electr nica SA. Digi International also has strategic alliances with several corporations including Bell Mobility NXP Orange Rogers Silicon Laboratories and AT&T.

Financial Performance

The company's revenue for fiscal 2021 increased by 11% to $308.6 million compared from the prior year's $279.3 million.

Net income for fiscal 2021 increased to $10.4 million compared from the prior year with $8.4 million.

Cash held by the company at the end of fiscal 2021 increased to $152.4 million. Cash provided by operations and financing activities were $57.7 million and $62.2 million respectively. Cash used for investing activities was $21.4 million mainly for acquisition of businesses.

Strategy

The company remains focused on taking steps that it believes will deliver consistent long-term growth with higher levels of profitability. Over the last six years acquisitions have helped significantly advance its strategy for growth and profitability in both business segments. Over time Digi International expects to continue to be active in making further acquisitions.

Mergers and Acquisitions

In late 2021 Digi International has acquired Connecticut-based Ventus Holdings a leader in Managed Network-as-a-Service (MNaaS) solutions that simplify the complexity of enterprise wide area network (WAN) connectivity. The acquisition will enable the company to provide software and subscription service plans along with its award-winning hardware thereby strengthening its position as a supplier of complete high-value networking solutions. Digi acquired Ventus for $347.4 million in cash.

In 2021 Digi International has acquired Ctek Inc. a company specializing in solutions for remote monitoring and industrial controls. Terms of the transaction were not immediately disclosed. Through the acquisition of Ctek Digi is uniquely-positioned to provide customers with both battery and hardwired options for the control and monitoring of critical infrastructure from complex offshore oil rig locations to localized deployments such as municipal park lighting. In addition Ctek's offering and existing client portfolio is set to further Digi's reach in a rapidly expanding market.

Also in 2021 Digi International has acquired Dallas-based Haxiot an industry leader in end-to-end LoRaWAN-based solutions. Terms of the acquisition were not immediately disclosed. Haxiot is a leading provider of low power wide area (LPWA) wireless technology and has an extensive LoRaWAN product portfolio that includes high performance client modules intelligent industrial devices gateways and the highly scalable X-ON cloud IoT platform. The acquisition of Haxiot significantly enhances Digi's embedded systems portfolio and immediately extends the company's market reach with a complete LoRaWAN offering including embedded modules gateways network server solution and SaaS offering.

HISTORY

John Schinas was working for a computer company that stopped making digital circuit boards in 1985. He quit that year mortgaged his home bought the company's inventory and started selling under the name DigiBoard. The enterprise became Digi International and went public in 1989. Digi's quality engineering and strong network of distributors fostered growth.

Digi began buying companies in 1991 with the purchase of competitor Arnet. It expanded into the LAN market buying connectivity device maker MiLAN in 1993. In 1995 Digi bought LAN Access and began developing network and remote-access products. But the acquisitions resulted in drastically lower earnings and a management shakeup in 1996. The following year CEO Ervin Kamm was replaced by consultant Jerry Dusa. Shareholders filed suit against Digi alleging it misrepresented the financial results of a soured investment in development-stage company AetherWorks.

Losses in 1997 caused the company to take a restructuring charge consolidate operations reduce its workforce by 33% and write off its remaining AetherWorks stake. Digi pursued the growing Internet telephony market with the 1998 purchase of ITK International. Losses resulted that year leading to Dusa's resignation in 1999. Later in 1999 former Lucent executive Joseph Dunsmore was named CEO.

In 2000 the company exited the Internet telephony market when it wrote off its NetBlazer line. That year the company also restructured its European operations moving all product development and manufacturing to its US facilities. The following year Digi cut about 13% of its workforce.

In 2002 the company acquired networking equipment maker NetSilicon for about $55 million. Digi sold its MiLAN subsidiary which made local-area networking devices to Communications Systems for $8.5 million. In 2003 Digi repurchased all shares held in the company by Sorrento Networks. Sorrento received the shares through its equity ownership in NetSilicon.

The company grew its embedded product line when it acquired Rabbit Semiconductor a supplier of microprocessors MPU modules and single-board computers for $49 million in cash in 2005. Such products were used in building security point of sale parking systems telecommunications vehicle and ship systems and container tracking. In addition to acquiring Rabbit Semi Digi also bought FS Forth-Systeme and Sistemas Embebidos from Embedded Solutions AG adding to its portfolio of modules and software for the embedded networking market.

Digi purchased MaxStream a developer of radio-frequency (RF) modules and modems used in wireless networking in 2006.

In 2008 the company acquired Sarian Systems a UK-based developer of IP routers and other networking equipment for about $31 million. Sarian primarily markets to customers in the finance lottery remote access retail and telemetry markets.

Digi purchased wireless development services provider Spectrum Design Solutions in 2008. In 2009 it bought MobiApps an Indian developer of machine-to-machine (M2M) technology including mixed-signal ASICs. The acquisition moved Digi into the satellite communications market and increased its presence in India and Singapore.

The global recession dampened sales and profitability in fiscal 2009. Digi reacted by restructuring operations closing two facilities in California and reducing its workforce by about 13%. The company added more than 60 employees with the acquisition of MobiApps following the restructuring.

Internationally the company discontinued manufacturing at its Breisach Germany facility and consolidated the facility's operations into its Minnesota location.

The company moved into the cloud with the 2009 introduction of iDigi an M2M (machine-to-machine) cloud-based Internet platform for monitoring and controlling electronic devices.

EXECUTIVES

Independent Director, Spiro Lazarakis
Independent Non-executive Chairman Of The Board, Satbir Khanuja
Independent Director, Christopher Heim
Independent Director, Sally Smith
Independent Director, Hatem Naguib
President - Smartsense, Guy Yehiav
President, Chief Executive Officer And Director, Ronald Konezny, $478,523 total compensation
Chief Financial Officer, Senior Vice President, Treasurer, James Loch, $321,162 total compensation
Vice President Of Corporate Development, General Counsel And Corporate Secretary, David Sampsell, $282,798 total compensation
Vice President- Supply Chain Management, Terrence Schneider
Auditors: Grant Thornton LLP

LOCATIONS

HQ: Digi International Inc
9350 Excelsior Blvd., Suite 700, Hopkins, MN 55343
Phone: 952 912-3444
Web: www.digi.com

PRODUCTS/OPERATIONS

2015 Sales

	$ mil.	% of total
Cellular routers and gateways	58.7	50
RF	34.4	16
Embedded	51.1	24
Network	51.3	24
Service	17.4	8
Total	**212.9**	**100**

2015 Sales

	$ mil.	% of total
Growth hardware products and all services	133.6	63
Mature hardware products	79.3	37
Total	**212.9**	**100**

2015 Sales

	$ mil.	% of total
Hardware products	195.5	92
Service	17.4	8
Total	**212.9**	**100**

Selected Products

Non-embedded
  Cameras and sensors
  Cellular routers
  Console servers
  Gateways
  Network management software
  Remote display products
  Serial cards
  Serial servers
  USB connected products
  Wireless communications adapters
Embedded
  Chips
  Modules
  Network interface cards
  Single-board computers
  Software and development tools
  Wireless solutions

COMPETITORS

8X8 INC.
ADTRAN INC.
BANDWIDTH INC.
BT GROUP PLC
CIENA CORPORATION
CONTINENTAL RESOURCES
  COMPANY
  INC.
FLEX LTD.

LEVEL 3 PARENT LLC
SCANSOURCE INC.
Shaw Communications
  Inc
TELEWARE PUBLIC
  LIMITED

TESSCO TECHNOLOGIES
  INCORPORATED

HISTORICAL FINANCIALS

Company Type: Public

Income Statement
FYE: September 30

	REVENUE ($ mil.)	NET INCOME ($ mil.)	NET PROFIT MARGIN	EMPLOYEES
09/21	308.6	10.3	3.4%	659
09/20	279.2	8.4	3.0%	656
09/19	254.2	9.9	3.9%	543
09/18	228.3	1.3	0.6%	516
09/17	181.6	9.3	5.2%	514
Annual Growth	**14.2%**	**2.6%**	**—**	**6.4%**

2021 Year-End Financials

Debt ratio: 7.3%
Return on equity: 2.4%
Cash ($ mil.): 152.4
Current ratio: 4.18
Long-term debt ($ mil.): 45.8

No. of shares (mil.): 34.2
Dividends
  Yield: —
  Payout: —
Market value ($ mil.): 720.0

	STOCK PRICE ($) FY Close	P/E High/Low	PER SHARE ($) Earnings	Dividends	Book Value
09/21	21.02	79 46	0.31	0.00	13.79
09/20	15.63	64 22	0.28	0.00	12.74
09/19	13.62	40 26	0.35	0.00	12.36
09/18	13.45	282 189	0.05	0.00	12.04
09/17	10.60	40 25	0.35	0.00	12.01
Annual Growth	**18.7%**	**— —**	**(3.0%)**	**—**	**3.5%**

Digital Realty Trust Inc

One of the largest publicly traded Real estate investment trust (REIT) Digital Realty Trust owns or leases some 290 data center and technology properties with around 43.6 million sq. ft. of rentable space. Active in around 50 metropolitan areas across some two dozen countries on six continents the company provides data center colocation and interconnection services for tenants in fields such as financial services cloud and IT tech manufacturing energy healthcare and consumer products. It also holds some 45 properties with approximately4.75 million rentable square feet as investments. The company operates through Digital Realty Trust LP. The US operation generates some two-thirds of company's total sales.

Operations

Operating through a single reporting segment Digital Realty Trust owns approximately 43.6 million sq. ft. of rentable space. It also has approximately 5.4 million sq. ft. under active development and some 2.3 million sq. ft. held for future development. The company has more than 4000 tenants across its properties.

The REIT's interconnection services include cross connects campus connect metro connect Interxion Cloud Connect internet exchange IP Bandwidth pathway and service exchange. Its portfolio of high-quality data centers provides secure highly connected and continuously available environments for the exchange processing and storage of critical data. Data centers are used for digital communication disaster recovery purposes transaction processing and housing mission-critical corporate IT applications. Its internet gateway data centers are highly interconnected network-dense facilities that serve as hubs for internet and data communications within and between major metropolitan areas.

Vast majority of the revenue comes from rents and other services.

Geographic Reach

San Francisco-based Digital Realty Trust has regional U.S. offices in Boston Chicago Dallas Los Angeles New York Northern Virginia Phoenix and San Francisco and regional international offices in Amsterdam Dublin London S o Paulo Singapore Sydney Tokyo and Hong Kong.

In the US the REIT has properties in the Atlanta Boston Chicago Dallas Los Angeles New York northern Virginia Phoenix San Francisco Seattle Silicon Valley and Toronto metropolitan areas. In Europe is operates in Amsterdam Athens Brussels Copenhagen Dublin Dusseldorf Frankfurt London Madrid Marseille Stockholm Vienna Zagreb Zurich and Paris; the Fortaleza Quer ©taro Rio de Janeiro Santiago and Sao Paulo metropolitan areas in Latin America; its Asia-Pacific operations are in Tokyo Seoul Singapore Sydney Melbourne Hong Kong and Osaka.

The US and UK generate about 65% and 35% of the company's revenue respectively. Northern Virginia provides roughly 20% of the company's revenue and Chicago brings in around 10%.

Sales and Marketing

Digital Realty Trust's occupancy rate is around 85%. The company's top 20 tenants account for some 50% of sales. It has more than 4000 customers?the largest of which provides roughly 10% of its rental income.

The REIT's tenants come from a wide array of global market sectors including energy financial services consumer products life sciences cloud and IT services gaming and manufacturing. Its largest tenants by rental revenue include Fortune 50 Software IBM Facebook Oracle America Equinix and Fortune 25 Investment Grade-Rated Company.

Financial Performance

The company's revenue for fiscal 2020 increased by 22% to $3.9 billion compared from the prior year with $3.2 billion. The increase was mainly due to higher rental and services revenue.

Net income for 2020 decreased to $356.4 million compared from the prior year $579.8 million.

Cash held by the company at the end of fiscal 2020 increased to $123.7 million. Cash provided by operations and financing activities were $1.7 billion and $935.7 million respectively. Cash used for investing activities was $2.6 billion mainly for improvements to investments in real estate.

Strategy

Through Digital Realty's recent investments and strategic partnerships the company has significantly expanded its capabilities as a leading provider of interconnection and cloud-enablement services globally. The company believes interconnection is an attractive line of business that would be difficult to build organically and enhances the overall value proposition of its data center product offerings. Furthermore through product offerings such as its Service Exchange and Interxion Cloud Connect and partnerships with cloud service providers Digital Realty is able to support its customers' hybrid cloud architecture requirements.

Digital Realty's primary business objectives are to maximize: sustainable long-term growth in earnings and funds from operations per share and unit cash flow and returns to its stockholders and its Operating Partnership's unitholders through the payment of dividends and distributions and return on invested capital. The company expect to accomplish these objectives by achieving superior risk-adjusted returns prudently allocating capital diversifying its product offerings accelerating its global reach and scale and driving revenue growth and operating efficiencies.

Mergers and Acquisitions

In late 2020 Interxion a Digital Realty company acquired Lamda Hellix Southeastern Europe's leading colocation and interconnection provider. The acquisition provides Digital Realty access to one of the region's fastest-growing markets and a gateway to an increasingly important connectivity hub. The acquisition bolsters Interxion's and Digital Realty's global footprint which includes more than 700 connectivity providers in over 280 data centres across 24 countries. The transaction also reflects Digital Realty's continued investment in PlatformDIGITAL.

Also in 2020 Interxion a Digital Realty company acquired Altus IT the leading carrier-neutral data centre provider in Croatia offering a gateway for interconnection and peering with a number of prominent service providers in southeast Europe. The acquisition bolsters Digital Realty's access to a global footprint of more than 700 connectivity providers in over 280 data centres across 22 countries. Digital Realty's ongoing expansion demonstrates its continued investment in PlatformDIGITAL.

In 2020 Digital Realty Trust acquired European data center provider Interxion for $7.0 billion. The deal is expected to help Digital Realty become one of the largest global data center providers and expand its footprint in Europe the Middle East and Asia.

In early 2020 Digital Realty had an agreement with Clise Properties to acquire a 49% ownership interest in the Westin Building Exchange in Seattle Washington. This transaction further strengthens the company's interconnection platform and demonstrates its commitment to accelerating digital business on PlatformDIGITAL.

Company Background

Digital Realty Trust acquired 15 properties in 2010 (the busiest that the company had been since 2007) including some in new markets. The REIT added its first property in Asia when it bought a data center in Singapore. It entered Massachusetts and Connecticut with the acquisition of three data centers there.

Digital Realty Trust purchased more than a dozen properties in 2011 and 2012 including some in new markets such as London and Sydney. The latter deals added to the company's international presence in Dublin Melbourne Paris and Singapore.

EXECUTIVES

Independent Director, VeraLinn Jamieson
Independent Director, Jean F.H.P. Mandeville
Executive Vice President, Strategic Advisor, David Ruberg
Senior Vice President - Investor Relations, John Stewart
Chief Technology Officer, Christopher Sharp, $420,192 total compensation
Chief Human Resource Officer, Cindy Fiedelman
Chief Operating Officer, Erich Sanchack, $465,192 total compensation
Chief Investment Officer, Gregory Wright, $590,385 total compensation
Chief Revenue Officer, Corey Dyer, $384,729 total compensation
Independent Chairman Of The Board, Laurence Chapman
Executive Vice President, General Counsel, Secretary, Joshua Mills, $514,006 total compensation
President, Chief Financial Officer, Andrew Power, $620,192 total compensation
Independent Director, Afshin Mohebbi
Independent Director, Mark Patterson
Senior Vice President - Finance And Accounting, Matthew Mercier
Independent Director, Mary Hogan Preusse
Independent Director, Alexis Bjorlin
Auditors: KPMG LLP

LOCATIONS

HQ: Digital Realty Trust Inc
5707 Southwest Parkway, Building 1, Suite 275, Austin, TX 78735
Phone: 737 281-0101   **Fax:** 415 738-6501
Web: www.digitalrealty.com

PRODUCTS/OPERATIONS

2018 Sales

	$ mil.	% of total
Rental and other services	2,412.1	79
Tenant reimbursements	624.6	21
Fee income and other	9.8	-
Total	**3,046.5**	**100**

COMPETITORS

CENTERPOINT PROPERTIES TRUST	KILROY REALTY CORPORATION
CYRUSONE LLC	PROLOGIS INC.
DUKE REALTY CORPORATION	VORNADO REALTY TRUST
EASTGROUP PROPERTIES INC.	

HISTORICAL FINANCIALS
Company Type: Public

Income Statement
FYE: December 31

	REVENUE ($ mil.)	NET INCOME ($ mil.)	NET PROFIT MARGIN	EMPLOYEES
12/20	3,903.6	356.4	9.1%	2,878
12/19	3,209.2	579.7	18.1%	1,550
12/18	3,046.4	331.2	10.9%	1,530
12/17	2,457.9	248.2	10.1%	1,436
12/16	2,142.2	426.1	19.9%	1,345
Annual Growth	16.2%	(4.4%)	—	20.9%

2020 Year-End Financials

Debt ratio: 36.8%
Return on equity: 2.5%
Cash ($ mil.): 108.5
Current ratio: 0.65
Long-term debt ($ mil.): 13,304.7

No. of shares (mil.): 280.2
Dividends
　Yield: 3.2%
　Payout: 448.0%
Market value ($ mil.): 39,103.0

	STOCK PRICE ($) FY Close	P/E High/Low	PER SHARE ($) Earnings	Dividends	Book Value
12/20	139.51	160 107	1.00	4.48	63.36
12/19	119.74	57 43	2.35	4.32	47.49
12/18	106.55	103 81	1.21	4.04	47.84
12/17	113.90	127 100	0.99	3.72	50.63
12/16	98.26	51 33	2.20	3.52	32.05
Annual Growth	9.2%	—	— (17.9%)	6.2%	18.6%

Digital Turbine Inc

When it comes to mobile digital content Digital Turbine (formerly Mandalay Digital) doesn't play games (but it does make them). Through its Twistbox and AMV subsidiaries the company develops content for 3G mobile phones including games images chat services and other products. Its content is targeted to users aged 18 to 40 and covers a variety of themes including mature entertainment. The company distributes its products in 40 European North American Latin American and Asian countries through agreements with major mobile phone operators including Verizon Virgin Mobile T-Mobile and Vodafone.

EXECUTIVES

Chief Financial Officer, Executive Vice President, Barrett Garrison, $350,000 total compensation
Chief Accounting Officer, Michael Miller
Independent Director, Holly Groos
Independent Director, Roy Chestnutt
Independent Director, Mohanbir Gyani
Chief Technology Officer, Christine Collins, $300,000 total compensation
Independent Director, Jeffrey Karish

Controller, David Wesch, $150,000 total compensation
Chairman, Robert Deutschman
Chief Executive Officer, Director, William Stone, $550,000 total compensation
Auditors: Grant Thornton LLP

LOCATIONS

HQ: Digital Turbine Inc
110 San Antonio Street, Suite 160, Austin, TX 78701
Phone: 512 387-7717
Web: www.digitalturbine.com

COMPETITORS

ATRION INC.	GAMELOFT SE
ATTACHMATE CORPORATION	TIM WE - SGPS S.A.
DADA ENTERTAINMENT INC.	WORLDWIDE TECHSERVICES LLC
ENTERTAINMENT DIGITAL NETWORK	

HISTORICAL FINANCIALS
Company Type: Public

Income Statement
FYE: March 31

	REVENUE ($ mil.)	NET INCOME ($ mil.)	NET PROFIT MARGIN	EMPLOYEES
03/21	313.5	54.8	17.5%	280
03/20	138.7	13.9	10.0%	207
03/19	103.5	(6.0)	—	161
03/18	74.7	(52.8)	—	161
03/17	91.5	(24.2)	—	146
Annual Growth	36.0%	—	—	17.7%

2021 Year-End Financials

Debt ratio: 5.5%
Return on equity: 49.3%
Cash ($ mil.): 30.7
Current ratio: 0.88
Long-term debt ($ mil.): —

No. of shares (mil.): 89.9
Dividends
　Yield: —
　Payout: —
Market value ($ mil.): 7,228.0

	STOCK PRICE ($) FY Close	P/E High/Low	PER SHARE ($) Earnings	Dividends	Book Value
03/21	80.36	153 6	0.57	0.00	1.61
03/20	4.31	52 20	0.16	0.00	0.89
03/19	3.50	— —	(0.08)	0.00	0.45
03/18	2.01	— —	(0.75)	0.00	0.36
03/17	0.94	— —	(0.36)	0.00	0.93
Annual Growth	204.1%	—	—	—	14.7%

Diodes, Inc.

Diodes Incorporated (also known as Diodes) knows how important it is to be discrete in business. The company makes discrete semiconductors — fixed-function devices that are much less complex than integrated circuits. Diodes' products include diodes transistors amplifiers comparators and rectifiers; they are used by computer and consumer electronics manufacturers in products such as notebooks LCD monitors smartphones and game consoles. Other applications include power supplies climate control systems GPS devices and networking gear. The company's products are sold throughout Asia (accounts for some 80% of sales; the largest among its geographic regions) Europe and the Americas.

Operations

Diodes operate in a single segment standard semiconductor products through our various design manufacturing and distribution facilities. Semiconductors are critical components used to manufacture of a broad range of electronic products and systems. The company's product portfolio addresses the design needs of advanced electronic equipment including high-volume consumer electronic devices such as LCD and LED televisions and LCD panels set-top boxes and consumer portables such as smartphones tablets and notebooks.

Most of the company's sales were generated from distribution sales accounting to around 65% of sales while direct sales accounted for nearly 35% of total sales.

Geographic Reach

Asia is the Texas-based company's largest market accounting for about 80% of its annual sales followed by Europe with nearly 15% of sales and Americas with the rest.

Its design marketing and engineering centers are located in Plano; Milpitas; Taipei Taoyuan City Zhubei City Taiwan; Shanghai Yangzhou China; Oldham England; and Neuhaus Germany. Diodes' wafer fabrication facilities are located in Oldham Greenock UK and Shanghai and Wuxi China and Keelung and Hsinchu Taiwan. Diodes has assembly and test facilities located in Shanghai Jinan Chengdu and Wuxi China as well as in Neuhaus Germany and Jhongli and Keelung Taiwan. Additional engineering sales warehouse and logistics offices are located in Taipei Taiwan; Hong Kong; Oldham UK; Shanghai Shenzhen Wuhan and Yangzhou China; Seongnam-si South Korea; and Munich Frankfurt Germany; with support offices throughout the world.

Sales and Marketing

The company markets and sells its products worldwide through direct sales and marketing personnel independent sales representatives and distributors in the US Europe and Asia. Customers include some 335 direct customers as well as major electronic manufacturing service (EMS) providers. Additionally Diodes has about 121 distributor customers through which it indirectly serves tens of thousands of customers worldwide.

The company's direct sales and EMS customers together accounted for roughly 40% of the company's net sales. One customer a broad-based distributor serving thousands of customers accounted for 10% of total sales.

End users for the company's semiconductors include the: industrial (about 25% of sales); consumer electronics (some 25%) communications (around 20% of sales each); computing (some 20% of sales); and automotive industries (around 10% of sales).

Financial Performance

Company revenue for fiscal 2020 decreased by 2% to $1.23 billion compared from the prior year with $1.25 billion. Net sales decreased for the twelve months ended December 31 2020 compared to the same period last year due to the negative effect of COVID-19 on the global economy and the company's business.

In 2020 net income was a $98.1 million compared to $153.3 million in 2019.

Cash held by the company at the end of fiscal 2020 increased to $320.5 million. Cash provided by operations was $187.2 million while cash used for investing and financing activities were $106.8 million and $54.3 million respectively. Main uses of cash were purchases of property plant and equipment; and repayments of long-term debt.

Strategy

Acquisitions remain a key part of Diodes' growth strategy to reach its revenue goal and in November 2020 the company acquired Lite-On Semiconductor Corporation ("LSC") and its subsidiaries. The acquisition of LSC broadens its discrete product offerings including providing the company with a leadership position in glass-passivated bridges and rectifiers that will allow Diodes to further extend its position in the automotive and industrial market spaces consistent with Diodes' overall growth strategy. Further the acquisition expands its wafer fabrication and assembly and test capacity and provides Diodes an opportunity to improve LSC's profitability through operating and manufacturing improvements as well as increased factory utilization.

The principal elements of the company's strategy include the following: continue to rapidly introduce innovative discrete logic and analog and mixed-signal semiconductor products; expand Diodes' available market opportunities; maintain intense customer focus; and pursue selective strategic acquisitions.

Mergers and Acquisitions

In late 2020 Diodes has completed its acquisition of Lite-On Semiconductor (LSC) that was announced on mid-2019. As approved by the Board of Directors of both LSC and Diodes the Outside Date included in the Share Swap Agreement has been updated from mid-2020 to fiscal 2020 and is consistent with the previously communicated anticipated close date of the second half of 2020. The amendment was enacted to accommodate the review schedule of the relevant Chinese authorities and associated operational processes that will need to be completed. As stated previously Diodes remains confident the transaction will close as planned once the final regulatory approvals have been secured.

EXECUTIVES

Independent Director, Warren Chen
Independent Director, Angie Button
Senior Vice President - Worldwide Discrete Products, Francis Tang, $390,500 total compensation
Senior Vice President - Corporate Operations, Julie Holland, $390,500 total compensation
Senior Vice President - Business Groups, Gary Yu
Independent Director, Peter Menard
Independent Director, Christina Sung
Chief Financial Officer, Brett Whitmire, $286,685 total compensation
Independent Director, Michael Giordano
Senior Vice President - Worldwide Analog Products, Jin Zhao
Senior Vice President - Worldwide Power Products, Evan Yu
Senior Vice President - Worldwide Sales And Marketing, Emily Yang, $294,000 total compensation
Auditors: Moss Adams LLP

LOCATIONS

HQ: Diodes, Inc.
4949 Hedgcoxe Road, Suite 200, Plano, TX 75024
Phone: 972 987-3900
Web: www.diodes.com

PRODUCTS/OPERATIONS

2015 Sales by Market

	% of total
Consumer electronics	32
Computing	18
Industrial	21
Communications	24
Automotive	5
Total	**100**

Selected Products

Diodes
  Schottky diodes
  Switching diodes
  Zener diodes
High-density arrays
Metal oxide semiconductor field-effect transistors (MOSFETs)
Rectifiers
  Bridge rectifiers
  Schottky rectifiers
  Standard fast superfast and ultrafast recovery rectifiers
Transient voltage suppressors
  Thyristor surge protection devices
  Zener transient-voltage suppressors
Transistors
  Bipolar transistors
  Darlington transistors
  Prebiased transistors

COMPETITORS

APPLIED MATERIALS INC.	POWER INTEGRATIONS INC.
FORMFACTOR INC.	
INTEVAC INC.	SANMINA CORPORATION
KIMBALL ELECTRONICS INC.	SEMTECH CORPORATION
LINEAR TECHNOLOGY LLC	ULTRA CLEAN HOLDINGS INC.
MAXIM INTEGRATED PRODUCTS INC.	VICOR CORPORATION
ON SEMICONDUCTOR CORPORATION	VOLEX PLC

HISTORICAL FINANCIALS

Company Type: Public

Income Statement   FYE: December 31

	REVENUE ($ mil.)	NET INCOME ($ mil.)	NET PROFIT MARGIN	EMPLOYEES
12/21	1,805.1	228.7	12.7%	8,921
12/20	1,229.2	98.0	8.0%	8,939
12/19	1,249.1	153.2	12.3%	7,271
12/18	1,213.9	104.0	8.6%	7,710
12/17	1,054.2	(1.8)	—	8,586
Annual Growth	**14.4%**	—	—	**1.0%**

2021 Year-End Financials

Debt ratio: 13.7%	No. of shares (mil.): 45.0
Return on equity: 20.7%	Dividends
Cash ($ mil.): 363.6	Yield: —
Current ratio: 2.52	Payout: —
Long-term debt ($ mil.): 265.6	Market value ($ mil.): 4,943.0

	STOCK PRICE ($)	P/E		PER SHARE ($)		
	FY Close	High/Low	Earnings	Dividends	Book Value
12/21	109.81	22 14	5.00	0.00	27.48
12/20	70.50	38 17	1.88	0.00	21.77
12/19	56.37	18 10	2.96	0.00	21.61
12/18	32.26	19 13	2.04	0.00	18.55
12/17	28.67	— —	(0.04)	0.00	16.92
Annual Growth	39.9%	— —	—	—	12.9%

DLH Holdings Corp

Dlh Holdings provides temporary and permanent medical office administration and technical staffing services to US government facilities nationwide. Its services on behalf of government agencies include case management healthcare IT systems and tools physical and behavioral health examinations; health and nutritional support for children and adults biological research disaster and emergency response staffing among others. The company has contracts with the Department of Defense Health and Human Services and Veterans Affairs. It traces its roots back to 1969.

HISTORY

In 1969 Sheldon Kass founded Digital Solutions to provide payroll services to clients in construction. He took the company public in 1989. Kass agreed to resign in 1990 following a lawsuit by board members Raymond Skiptunis and Steven Levine over Kass' employment contract that included a loan for more than $1 million. Skiptunis became CEO.

Skiptunis moved the firm into the professional employer organization (PEO) industry during the 1990s. Digital Solutions expanded through acquisitions of assets from Staff-Rx in 1994 and the employee leasing assets of Texas-based Turnkey Services in 1995. George Eklund became CEO in 1996.

Losses in 1997 prompted Digital Solutions to implement a cost-cutting drive. Later that year Donald Kappauf was appointed CEO. In 1999 the company doubled in size when it acquired 10 human resources services firms operating under the TeamStaff Companies trade name prompting Digital Solutions' name change. In 2000 it bought PEO Synadyne from Outsource International (later Tandem Staffing Solutions).

The following year the company made several acquisitions including the purchase of BrightLane a Georgia-based provider of online payroll and procurement services. In 2002 TeamStaff bought PEO Corporate Staffing Concepts.

HoneyBaked Ham president Kent Smith was named CEO of TeamStaff in 2003 replacing Kappauf. To focus on medical staffing TeamStaff sold two noncore units to Gevity HR: human resource outsourcing (2003) and PEO (2004). The company bought nursing staffing firm Nursing Innovations in 2004 and the next year it acquired Georgia-based RS Staffing a provider of health care and other staffing services to the federal government.

Smith left the company in 2007 amid a management shake-up and CFO Rick Filipelli was named president and CEO. A few years later in early 2010 Filipelli resigned.

In 2008 TeamStaff sold its Nursing Innovations Per Diem unit which offered temporary and permanent nursing placement services to Temps Inc. in order to focus on its core business.

EXECUTIVES

Independent Director, Frances Murphy
President Of Social And Scientific Systems, Inc. And Public Health And Scientific Research Operating Unit, Jeanine Christian, $275,184 total compensation
Chief Growth Officer, Jacqueline Everett, $265,000 total compensation
Independent Director, Stephen Zelkowicz
Chief Scientific Officer, Sandra Halverson
Chief Human Resources Officer, G. Maliek Ferebee
Independent Chairman Of The Board, Frederick Wasserman
President, Chief Executive Officer, Director, Zachary Parker, $478,950 total compensation
Chief Financial Officer, Kathryn JohnBull, $355,000 total compensation
Independent Director, Austin Yerks
Independent Director, Martin Delaney
Independent Director, James Allen
Independent Director, Elder Granger
President Of Danya International Llc And Mission Services And Solutions Operating Unit, Helene Fisher, $275,184 total compensation
Auditors: WithumSmith+Brown, PC

LOCATIONS

HQ: DLH Holdings Corp
3565 Piedmont Road, Building 3, Suite 700, Atlanta, GA 30305
Phone: 770 554-3545
Web: www.dlhcorp.com

COMPETITORS

ASGN INCORPORATED
EXPRESS SERVICES INC.
INSPERITY INC.
ROBERT HALF INTERNATIONAL INC.
TEAM HEALTH HOLDINGS INC.
TRC COMPANIES INC.

HISTORICAL FINANCIALS

Company Type: Public

Income Statement — FYE: September 30

	REVENUE ($ mil.)	NET INCOME ($ mil.)	NET PROFIT MARGIN	EMPLOYEES
09/21	246.0	10.1	4.1%	2,300
09/20	209.1	7.1	3.4%	2,200
09/19	160.3	5.3	3.3%	1,900
09/18	133.2	1.8	1.4%	1,500
09/17	115.6	3.2	2.8%	1,400
Annual Growth	20.8%	32.5%	—	13.2%

2021 Year-End Financials

Debt ratio: 22.6%	No. of shares (mil.): 12.7
Return on equity: 17.0%	Dividends
Cash ($ mil.): 24.0	Yield: —
Current ratio: 0.93	Payout: —
Long-term debt ($ mil.): 44.6	Market value ($ mil.): 156.0

	STOCK PRICE ($)	P/E		PER SHARE ($)		
	FY Close	High/Low	Earnings	Dividends	Book Value
09/21	12.30	17 9	0.75	0.00	5.16
09/20	7.25	19 5	0.54	0.00	4.31
09/19	4.46	15 9	0.41	0.00	3.79
09/18	5.76	45 35	0.14	0.00	3.31
09/17	6.48	25 15	0.27	0.00	3.05
Annual Growth	17.4%	—	29.1%	—	14.1%

Dorian LPG Ltd.

Auditors: Deloitte Certified Public Accountants S.A.

LOCATIONS

HQ: Dorian LPG Ltd.
c/o Dorian LPG (USA) LLC, 27 Signal Road, Stamford, CT 06902
Phone: 203 674-9900
Web: www.dorianlpg.com

HISTORICAL FINANCIALS

Company Type: Public

Income Statement — FYE: March 31

	REVENUE ($ mil.)	NET INCOME ($ mil.)	NET PROFIT MARGIN	EMPLOYEES
03/21	315.9	92.5	29.3%	602
03/20	333.4	111.8	33.5%	585
03/19	158.0	(50.9)	—	564
03/18	159.3	(20.4)	—	69
03/17	167.4	(1.4)	—	69
Annual Growth	17.2%	—		71.9%

2021 Year-End Financials

Debt ratio: 37.4%	No. of shares (mil.): 41.4
Return on equity: 9.6%	Dividends
Cash ($ mil.): 79.3	Yield: —
Current ratio: 1.87	Payout: —
Long-term debt ($ mil.): 539.6	Market value ($ mil.): —

Dorman Products Inc

Markets approximately 81000 unique parts Dorman Products is a leading supplier of automotive replacement parts (including brake parts) fasteners and service line products to the automotive aftermarket. Approximately 75% of the company's products are sold under brands that the company owns. Dorman sells to auto aftermarket retailers and warehouse distributors (such as Advance AutoZone and O'Reilly) as well as to parts manufacturers for resale under private labels. The company services over 3600 active accounts. Dorman distributes its products primarily into Canada and Mexico Europe the Middle East and Australia. About 95% of the company's total sales is generated from the US.

Operations

The company markets its products under the DORMAN brand name and several sub-brands which identify products that address specific segments of the automotive aftermarket industry. In addition across all of its sub-brands customers can find a subset of products that have been branded OE Fix products.

Its OE FIX products solve common problems with the original equipment manufacturer (OEM) repair alternative. The company's DORMAN OE Solutions is a wide variety of replacement parts the company introduced to the automotive aftermarket covering many product categories across all areas of the vehicle including fluid reservoirs variable value timing components complex electronics and integrated door lock actuators. The DORMAN Conduct-Tite is a wide array of electrical components for common repairs as well as for enthusiasts to customize and upgrade their vehicles. In addition DORMAN HELP! is a broad assortment of small automotive replacement parts that are primarily sold in retail store fronts such as door handles keyless remotes and cases and door hinge repair parts. Lastly DORMAN HD Solutions include lighting cooling engine management wheel hardware air tanks and cab products.

The company's major products are grouped into four; powertrain which generates approximately 40% of sales; chassis which generates around 30% of sales; automotive body which accounts roughly 25%; and hardware which accounts some 5% of sales.

Geographic Reach

Pennsylvania-based Dorman Products has about 15 warehouse and office facilities throughout US Canada China Taiwan and India. Dorman purchases more than 75% of its products from international suppliers primarily in China. About 95% of the company's sale come from customers in US.

Sales and Marketing

About half of Dorman's products are primarily sold through automotive aftermarket retails including through its online platforms; national regional and local warehouse distributors (such as Genuine Parts Co. ? NAPA (NAPA)); and specialty markets and salvage yards International customers sales to mass merchants (including Walmart Stores) and salvage yards represent the rest. Advance AutoZone and O'Reilly each accounted for more than 10% of total sales and in the aggregate accounted for about 55% of total sales.

Financial Performance

Net sales increased 10% to $1.1 billion in fiscal 2020 from $991.3 million in fiscal 2019. The increase in net sales was primarily organic and driven by increased volumes particularly in the second half of 2020.

The company's net income for fiscal 2020 increased to $106.9 million compared from the prior year with $83.8 million.

Cash held by the company at the end of fiscal 2020 increased to $155.6 million. Cash provided by operations was $152.0 million while cash used for investing and financing activities were $30.3 million and $34.5 million respectively. Main cash uses were for property plant and equipment additions and payments of revolving credit line.

Strategy

Product development and continuous innovation are central to Dorman's business. The development of a broad range of products many of which are not conveniently or economically avail-able elsewhere has enabled it to grow to its present size and is an important driver for its future growth. Its product strategy has been to design and engineer products many of which it believes are better and easier to install and/or use than the original parts they replace and to commercialize automotive parts for the broadest possible range of uses. New product ideas are reviewed by its product management staff and a cross-functional in-house team.

Mergers and Acquisitions

In early 2020 the company acquired the remaining approximately 60% of the outstanding stock of Power Train Industries (PTI) a privately-held supplier of parts to the automotive aftermarket based in Reno Nevada. The purchase price was $18.2 million subject to working capital adjustments and was accounted for as a business combination. Prior to the acquisition date the company accounted for its approximately 40% interest in PTI which was acquired in 2016 as an equity-method investment.

Company Background

In late 1978 Dorman Products Inc. was incorporated in Pennsylvania.

EXECUTIVES

Executive Chairman Of The Board, Steven Berman
Executive Vice President - Commercial, Michael Kealey, $464,446 total compensation
Senior Vice President, Sales And Marketing, Jeff Darby, $407,895 total compensation
Independent Director, Kelly Romano
Lead Independent Director, Paul Lederer
Independent Director, G. Michael Stakias
Chief Financial Officer, Senior Vice President, Treasurer, David Hession, $435,750 total compensation
Independent Director, Lisa Bachmann
Independent Director, J. Darrell Thomas
Independent Director, Richard Riley
President, Chief Executive Officer, Director, Kevin Olsen, $614,885 total compensation
Independent Director, John Gavin
Senior Vice President, General Counsel, Corporate Secretary, Joseph Braun, $384,303 total compensation
Auditors: KPMG LLP

LOCATIONS

HQ: Dorman Products Inc
3400 East Walnut Street, Colmar, PA 18915
Phone: 215 997-1800
Web: www.dormanproducts.com

PRODUCTS/OPERATIONS

2014 Sales

	% of total
Power-train	37
Automotive body	29
Chassis	26
Hardware	8
Total	**100**

Selected Subsidiaries

Allparts Inc.
RB Distribution Inc.
RB Management Inc.
RB Vest Inc.

COMPETITORS

ADVANCE AUTO PARTS INC.	MOTORCAR PARTS OF AMERICA INC.
AUTOLIV INC.	O'REILLY AUTOMOTIVE INC.
COMMERCIAL VEHICLE GROUP INC.	THE HILLMAN COMPANIES INC
LCI INDUSTRIES	TRIMAS CORPORATION
LKQ CORPORATION	
MERITOR INC.	

HISTORICAL FINANCIALS

Company Type: Public

Income Statement

FYE: December 25

	REVENUE ($ mil.)	NET INCOME ($ mil.)	NET PROFIT MARGIN	EMPLOYEES
12/21	1,345.2	131.5	9.8%	3.360
12/20	1,092.7	106.8	9.8%	2.681
12/19	991.3	83.7	8.4%	2.742
12/18	973.7	133.6	13.7%	2.370
12/17	903.2	106.6	11.8%	2.061
Annual Growth	**10.5%**	**5.4%**	**—**	**13.0%**

2021 Year-End Financials

Debt ratio: 14.3%
Return on equity: 14.7%
Cash ($ mil.): 58.7
Current ratio: 1.62
Long-term debt ($ mil.): —

No. of shares (mil.): 31.6
Dividends
  Yield: —
  Payout: —
Market value ($ mil.): 3,364.0

	STOCK PRICE ($) FY Close	P/E High/Low		PER SHARE ($) Earnings	Dividends	Book Value
12/21	106.42	30	21	4.12	0.00	29.51
12/20	89.56	30	14	3.30	0.00	26.53
12/19	75.11	37	27	2.56	0.00	23.76
12/18	88.35	22	15	4.02	0.00	22.05
12/17	61.14	27	19	3.13	0.00	18.91
Annual Growth	**14.9%**	**—**	**—**	**7.1%**	**—**	**11.8%**

Dropbox Inc

Auditors: Ernst & Young LLP

LOCATIONS

HQ: Dropbox Inc
1800 Ownes Street, San Francisco, CA 94158
Phone: 415 857-6800
Web: www.dropbox.com

HISTORICAL FINANCIALS

Company Type: Public

Income Statement

FYE: December 31

	REVENUE ($ mil.)	NET INCOME ($ mil.)	NET PROFIT MARGIN	EMPLOYEES
12/21	2,157.9	335.8	15.6%	2,667
12/20	1,913.9	(256.3)	—	2,760
12/19	1,661.3	(52.7)	—	2,801
12/18	1,391.7	(484.9)	—	2,323
12/17	1,106.8	(111.7)	—	1,858
Annual Growth	**18.2%**	**—**	**—**	**9.5%**

HOOVER'S HANDBOOK OF EMERGING COMPANIES 2022

2021 Year-End Financials

Debt ratio: 53.6%
Return on equity: 1,683.2%
Cash ($ mil.): 533.0
Current ratio: 1.57
Long-term debt ($ mil.): 1,538.0

No. of shares (mil.): 375.5
Dividends
　Yield: —
　Payout: —
Market value ($ mil.): 9,215.0

	STOCK PRICE ($)	P/E	PER SHARE ($)		
	FY Close	High/Low	Earnings	Dividends	Book Value
12/21	24.54	37 25	0.85	0.00	(0.78)
12/20	22.19	— —	(0.62)	0.00	0.82
12/19	17.91	— —	(0.13)	0.00	1.94
12/18	20.43	— —	(1.35)	0.00	1.65
Annual Growth	6.3%	— —	—	—	—

Duke Realty Corp

Duke Realty is a self-managed and self-administered real estate investment trust (REIT). It owns and develops industrial properties primarily in major cities that are key logistics markets. In addition to about 535 properties totaling more than 159.6 million sq. ft. of rentable space the company owns some 1000 acres of land and control an additional 800 acres through purchase options. The REIT leases its properties to a variety of tenants including e-commerce manufacturing retail wholesale and distribution firms. Duke's service operations include construction and development asset and property management and leasing. The company was founded in 1972.

Operations

The company's business operations primarily consist of two reportable operating segments: rental operations of industrial properties and service operations. Duke Realty makes most of its money from its industrial real estate leases as well as unsold commercial properties. Some 5% of its revenue comes from service operations such as property management asset management development general contracting and construction management. The company owns part of its portfolio outright and another part of its portfolio through unconsolidated joint ventures.

It has about 15 properties with some 6.9 million sq. ft. of space under development and one unconsolidated joint venture property under development with 517000 square feet.

Geographic Reach

Based in Indianapolis Duke Realty has regional offices or significant operations in about 20 states. Its properties in Chicago Indianapolis and Atlanta combined account for nearly 30% of its total gross leasable area. Other primary markets include Southern California South Florida New Jersey and Dallas.

Financial Performance

In 2020 revenue increased 2% to $993.2 million. Rental and related revenue increased by $73.4 million offset by a 46% decrease in general contractor and service fee.

Net income declined 30% to $302.8 million compared to the company's $432.6 million net income from the previous year.

Duke Realty ended 2020 with $67.2 million in net cash on hand. Operating activities provided $566.4 million and financing activities added another $235.6 million. Investing activities used $856.2 million for the development of real estate investments.

Strategy

Duke Realty's overall strategy is to continue to increase its investment in quality industrial properties primarily through development on both a speculative and build-to-suit basis supplemented with acquisitions in higher barrier markets with the highest growth potential.

Its operational focus is to drive profitability by maximizing cash from operations as well as NAREIT FFO through maintaining property occupancy and increasing rental rates while also keeping lease-related capital costs contained by effectively managing its portfolio of existing properties; selectively developing new build-to-suit substantially pre-leased and in select markets speculative development projects; and providing a full line of real estate services to its tenants and to third parties.

Company Background

Duke Realty launched its business in 1972 with the development of an industrial building in Indianapolis. With $40000 in capital and limited knowledge of commercial real estate John Rosebrough Phil Duke and John Wynne embarked on their first industrial development in Park 100 on the northwest side of the city. Over the years Duke Realty transformed Park 100 into one of the country's largest industrial parks eventually encompassing 1500 acres.

EXECUTIVES

Lead Independent Director, David Stockert
Independent Director, John Case
Independent Director, Chris Sultemeier
Independent Director, Warren Thompson
Independent Director, Tamara Fischer
Executive Vice President - Construction, Peter Harrington, $332,308 total compensation
Chief Operating Officer, Executive Vice President, Steven Schnur, $498,846 total compensation
Chairman Of The Board, Chief Executive Officer, James Connor, $926,154 total compensation
Independent Director, Lynn Thurber
Chief Financial Officer, Executive Vice President, Mark Denien, $596,923 total compensation
Executive Vice President, Chief Investment Officer, Nicholas Anthony, $488,846 total compensation
Executive Vice President, General Counsel, Corporate Secretary, Ann Dee, $491,923 total compensation
Independent Director, Melanie Sabelhaus
Independent Director, Norman Jenkins
Independent Director, Michael Szymanczyk
Auditors: KPMG LLP

LOCATIONS

HQ: Duke Realty Corp
　8711 River Crossing Boulevard, Indianapolis, IN 46240
Phone: 317 808-6000
Web: www.dukerealty.com

PRODUCTS/OPERATIONS

2017 Sales

	$ mil.	% of total
Rental Operations		
Industrial	661.2	85
Non-reportable	24.1	3
Service Operations	94.4	12
Other	1.2	-
Total	**780.9**	**100**

COMPETITORS

ACADIA REALTY TRUST
ALEXANDER & BALDWIN INC.
APARTMENT INVESTMENT AND MANAGEMENT COMPANY
ARMADA/HOFFLER PROPERTIES L.L.C.
CAMDEN PROPERTY TRUST
COUSINS PROPERTIES INCORPORATED
CTO REALTY GROWTH INC.
DOUGLAS EMMETT INC.
H&R Real Estate Investment Trust
JBG SMITH PROPERTIES
LIBERTY PROPERTY TRUST
STAG INDUSTRIAL INC.

HISTORICAL FINANCIALS

Company Type: Public

Income Statement
FYE: December 31

	REVENUE ($ mil.)	NET INCOME ($ mil.)	NET PROFIT MARGIN	EMPLOYEES
12/21	1,105.9	852.9	77.1%	340
12/20	993.2	299.9	30.2%	350
12/19	973.7	428.9	44.1%	400
12/18	947.8	383.7	40.5%	400
12/17	780.9	1,634.4	209.3%	400
Annual Growth	9.1%	(15.0%)	—	(4.0%)

2021 Year-End Financials

Debt ratio: 35.3%
Return on equity: 15.2%
Cash ($ mil.): 69.7
Current ratio: 1.15
Long-term debt ($ mil.): 3,689.2

No. of shares (mil.): 382.5
Dividends
　Yield: 1.5%
　Payout: 43.0%
Market value ($ mil.): 25,108.0

	STOCK PRICE ($)	P/E	PER SHARE ($)		
	FY Close	High/Low	Earnings	Dividends	Book Value
12/21	65.64	29 17	2.25	1.05	15.80
12/20	39.97	51 32	0.80	0.96	13.83
12/19	34.67	30 21	1.18	0.88	13.64
12/18	25.90	27 23	1.07	0.82	12.98
12/17	27.21	7 5	4.56	1.62	12.72
Annual Growth	24.6%	— —	(16.2%)	(10.4%)	5.6%

Duluth Holdings Inc

Auditors: KPMG LLP

LOCATIONS

HQ: Duluth Holdings Inc
　201 East Front Street, Mount Horeb, WI 53572
Phone: 608 424-1544
Web: www.duluthtrading.com

HISTORICAL FINANCIALS

Company Type: Public

Income Statement
FYE: January 31

	REVENUE ($ mil.)	NET INCOME ($ mil.)	NET PROFIT MARGIN	EMPLOYEES
01/21*	638.7	13.5	2.1%	2,977
02/20	615.6	18.9	3.1%	3,004
02/19	568.1	23.1	4.1%	2,794
01/18	471.4	23.3	5.0%	2,172
01/17	376.1	21.3	5.7%	1,627
Annual Growth	14.2%	(10.7%)	—	16.3%
*Fiscal year change				

2021 Year-End Financials

Debt ratio: 23.6%
Return on equity: 7.3%
Cash ($ mil.): 47.2
Current ratio: 2.20
Long-term debt ($ mil.): 116.2

No. of shares (mil.): 32.8
Dividends
  Yield: —
  Payout: —
Market value ($ mil.): 410.0

	STOCK PRICE ($) FY Close	P/E High/Low		Earnings	PER SHARE ($) Dividends	Book Value
01/21*	12.47	40	8	0.42	0.00	5.89
02/20	8.45	45	13	0.58	0.00	5.48
02/19	23.48	48	23	0.72	0.00	4.92
01/18	18.68	32	21	0.72	0.00	4.19
01/17	22.97	55	21	0.66	0.00	3.43
Annual Growth	(14.2%)	—	—	(10.7%)	—	14.4%

*Fiscal year change

Dynatrace Inc

Auditors: BDO USA, LLP

LOCATIONS

HQ: Dynatrace Inc
  1601 Trapelo Road, Suite 116, Waltham, MA 02451
Phone: 617 530-1000
Web: www.dynatrace.com

HISTORICAL FINANCIALS

Company Type: Public

Income Statement

FYE: March 31

	REVENUE ($ mil.)	NET INCOME ($ mil.)	NET PROFIT MARGIN	EMPLOYEES
03/21	703.5	75.7	10.8%	2,779
03/20	545.8	(418.0)	—	2,243
03/19	430.9	(116.1)	—	1,981
03/18	398.0	9.2	2.3%	0
03/17	406.3	0.8	0.2%	0
Annual Growth	14.7%	212.3%	—	—

2021 Year-End Financials

Debt ratio: 17.3%
Return on equity: 7.3%
Cash ($ mil.): 324.9
Current ratio: 1.05
Long-term debt ($ mil.): 391.9

No. of shares (mil.): 283.1
Dividends
  Yield: —
  Payout: —
Market value ($ mil.): 13,658.0

	STOCK PRICE ($) FY Close	P/E High/Low		Earnings	PER SHARE ($) Dividends	Book Value
03/21	48.24	208	76	0.26	0.00	3.93
03/20	23.84	—	—	(1.58)	0.00	3.42
Annual Growth	102.3%	—	—	—	—	14.9%

EACO Corp

EACO Corporation lost its appetite for the buffet business. For a half-dozen years after selling its restaurant operations to pursue a new line of business the company generated revenues from a handful of rental properties including restaurant and industrial properties. (Tenant NES Rentals accounts for about half of its rental revenues.) In 2010 the company acquired Bisco Industries which distributes electronics components in the US and Canada. EACO was once the sole franchisee of Ryan's Restaurant Group restaurants in Florida; it also owned a chain of 16 Whistle Junction and Florida Buffet locations. CEO Glen Ceiley owns 98.9% of EACO.

EXECUTIVES

Chairman Of The Board, Chief Executive Officer, Glen Ceiley, $206,200 total compensation
Independent Director, Stephen Catanzaro
Independent Director, William Means
President, Chief Operating Officer Of Bisco, Donald Wagner, $250,535 total compensation
Vice President - Sales And Marketing Of Bisco Industries, Inc, Zachary Ceiley, $174,253 total compensation
Principal Accounting Officer, Controller, Michael Narikawa
Auditors: Haskell & White LLP

LOCATIONS

HQ: EACO Corp
  5065 East Hunter Avenue, Anaheim, CA 92807
Phone: 714 876-2490
Web: www.eacocorp.com

COMPETITORS

AVNET INC.
COBRA ELECTRONICS CORPORATION
FLEX LTD.
HOST HOTELS & RESORTS INC.
JOHNSON CONTROLS INTERNATIONAL PUBLIC LIMITED COMPANY
N. F. SMITH & ASSOCIATES L.P.
OBH INC.
RUTH'S HOSPITALITY GROUP INC.

HISTORICAL FINANCIALS

Company Type: Public

Income Statement

FYE: August 31

	REVENUE ($ mil.)	NET INCOME ($ mil.)	NET PROFIT MARGIN	EMPLOYEES
08/20	225.2	7.7	3.5%	525
08/19	221.2	9.4	4.3%	489
08/18	193.2	6.9	3.6%	464
08/17	156.9	4.0	2.6%	407
08/16	148.5	4.1	2.8%	414
Annual Growth	11.0%	17.5%	—	6.1%

2020 Year-End Financials

Debt ratio: 9.3%
Return on equity: 14.1%
Cash ($ mil.): 6.0
Current ratio: 2.51
Long-term debt ($ mil.): 4.8

No. of shares (mil.): 4.8
Dividends
  Yield: —
  Payout: —
Market value ($ mil.): 84.0

	STOCK PRICE ($) FY Close	P/E High/Low		Earnings	PER SHARE ($) Dividends	Book Value
08/20	17.38	15	8	1.59	0.00	12.10
08/19	19.55	10	6	1.92	0.00	10.53
08/18	14.00	10	4	1.41	0.00	8.62
08/17	6.32	11	7	0.82	0.00	7.16
08/16	5.96	7	6	0.83	0.00	6.34
Annual Growth	30.7%	—	—	17.6%	—	17.5%

Eagle Bancorp Inc (MD)

For those nest eggs that need a little help hatching holding company Eagle Bancorp would recommend its community-oriented EagleBank subsidiary. The bank serves businesses and individuals through more than 20 branches in Maryland Virginia and Washington DC and its suburbs. Deposit products include checking savings and money market accounts; certificates of deposit; and IRAs. Commercial real estate loans represent more than 70% of its loan portfolio while construction loans make up another more than 20%. The bank which has significant expertise as a Small Business Administration lender also writes business consumer and home equity loans. EagleBank offers insurance products through an agreement with The Meltzer Group.

Operations

Like other retail banks Eagle Bancorp makes the bulk of its money from loan interest. About 86% of its total revenue came from loan interest (including fees) during 2015 while another 4% came from interest on investment securities. The rest of its revenue came from deposit account service charges (2% of revenue) and non-recurring income sources.

The bank has two direct subsidiaries: Bethesda Leasing LLC which holds the bank's foreclosed real estate (owned and acquired); and Eagle Insurance Services LLC which provides commercial and retail insurance products through a referral arrangement with insurance broker The Meltzer Group.

Geographic Reach

The Bethesda Maryland-based bank operates 21 branches in Maryland Virginia and Washington DC (as of mid-2016) including nine in Northern Virginia seven in Montgomery County and five in the District of Columbia.

Sales and Marketing

Eagle Bancorp serves local businesses professional clients individuals sole proprietors small and medium-sized businesses non-profits and investors. Other clients are from the healthcare accountant and attorney markets.

The bank spent $2.7 million on marketing and advertising during 2015 up 38% from the $2 million it spent in 2014 mostly due to higher digital and print advertising and sponsorship costs.

Financial Performance

Eagle Bancorp's annual revenue has more than doubled since 2011 mostly thanks to strong loan growth with the addition of new branches. Meanwhile its net income has more than tripled as the bank has kept a lid on credit loss provisions and overhead costs.

The bank's revenue jumped 33% to $279.8 million during 2015 largely thanks to a rise in interest income as its loan assets grew 16%.

Strong revenue growth in 2015 coupled with an absence of merger expenses drove Eagle Bancorp's net income up 55% to $84.1 million. The bank's operating cash levels spiked 66% to $98.5 million for the year thanks to a strong rise in cash-based earnings.

Strategy

The company has been focused on growing within its existing markets. Its strategy for further growth includes continuing to seek opportunities to open or acquire new banking locations while

HOOVER'S HANDBOOK OF EMERGING COMPANIES 2022

waiting out record low interest rates. Eagle's strict loan underwriting standards — it didn't write subprime residential mortgages and didn't buy securities backed by subprime mortgages — has helped it have fewer problem loans the downfall for many banks.

Beyond its core lending and deposit businesses Eagle Bancorp continues to expand its other product offerings as well. In 2015 it introduced a Full Service Equipment Leasing program which provided alternative and convenient financing for all types of business equipment for customers.

Mergers and Acquisitions

In November 2014 Eagle Bancorp significantly expanded its presence in Northern Virginia after it purchased Fairfax County-based Virginia Heritage. The deal added six Virginia Heritage Bank branches (renamed as EagleBank) in northern Virginia along with $917.4 million in assets — including $715 million in loans and $737 million in deposits.

EXECUTIVES

Independent Director, Kathy Raffa
Independent Director, Theresa LaPlaca
Independent Director, Benjamin Soto
Independent Director, Matthew Brockwell
Executive Vice President, Chief Legal Officer, Paul Saltzman
Lead Independent Director, James Soltesz
Independent Director, A. Leslie Ludwig
Independent Director, Ernest Jarvis
Independent Director, Steven Freidkin
Director - Investor Relations, David Danielson
Executive Chairman Of The Board, Norman Pozez
President, Chief Executive Officer, Director, Susan Riel, $800,000 total compensation
Senior Executive Vice President, Chief Credit Officer Of The Bank, Janice Williams, $510,144 total compensation
Executive Vice President, Chief Risk Officer, Jeffery Curry
Senior Executive Vice President, President Of Commercial Banking, Antonio Marquez, $509,834 total compensation
Executive Vice President And Chief Lending Officer – Commercial And Industrial Of The Bank, Lindsey Rheaume, $421,656 total compensation
Chief Financial Officer, Executive Vice President, Charles Levingston, $417,514 total compensation
Auditors: Crowe LLP

LOCATIONS

HQ: Eagle Bancorp Inc (MD)
7830 Old Georgetown Road, Third Floor, Bethesda, MD 20814
Phone: 301 986-1800
Web: www.eaglebankcorp.com

PRODUCTS/OPERATIONS

Selected Subsidiaries
EagleBank
  Bethesda Leasing LLC
  Eagle Insurance Services LLC
  Fidelity Mortgage Inc.
Eagle Commercial Ventures LLC

COMPETITORS

BYLINE BANCORP INC.
CENTERSTATE BANK CORPORATION
CITIZENS & NORTHERN CORPORATION
CITY HOLDING COMPANY
CUSTOMERS BANCORP INC.
F.N.B. CORPORATION
FIRST COMMONWEALTH FINANCIAL CORPORATION
FIRST MIDWEST BANCORP INC.
FIRSTMERIT CORPORATION
HERITAGE FINANCIAL CORPORATION
PEOPLES FINANCIAL SERVICES CORP.
REPUBLIC FIRST BANCORP INC.

HISTORICAL FINANCIALS

Company Type: Public

Income Statement   FYE: December 31

	ASSETS ($ mil.)	NET INCOME ($ mil.)	INCOME AS % OF ASSETS	EMPLOYEES
12/20	11,117.8	132.2	1.2%	515
12/19	8,988.7	142.9	1.6%	492
12/18	8,389.1	152.2	1.8%	470
12/17	7,479.0	100.2	1.3%	466
12/16	6,890.1	97.7	1.4%	469
Annual Growth	12.7%	7.9%	—	2.4%

2020 Year-End Financials

Return on assets: 1.3%
Return on equity: 10.8%
Long-term debt ($ mil.): —
No. of shares (mil.): 31.7
Sales ($ mil): 435.6

Dividends
  Yield: 2.1%
  Payout: 21.5%
Market value ($ mil.): 1,313.0

	STOCK PRICE ($) FY Close	P/E High/Low		Earnings	PER SHARE ($) Dividends	Book Value
12/20	41.30	12	6	4.09	0.88	39.05
12/19	48.63	14	9	4.18	0.44	35.82
12/18	48.71	15	10	4.42	0.00	32.25
12/17	57.90	23	17	2.92	0.00	27.80
12/16	60.95	22	15	2.86	0.00	24.77
Annual Growth	(9.3%)		—	9.4%	—	12.0%

Eagle Bancorp Montana, Inc.

Eagle Bancorp Montana hopes to swoop down on every potential account holder in its home state. The holding company owns American Federal Savings Bank a thrift that serves businesses and residents of southwestern Montana through six branches and seven ATMs. American Federal primarily writes mortgages on one- to four-family residences (these comprise almost half of its loan book); the rest of its portfolio consists of commercial mortgages (25%) home equity (about 20%) and consumer business and construction loans. The bank's deposit products include checking money market and savings accounts; CDs; IRAs; and Visa debit cards. Eagle Bancorp Montana is buying seven branches from Sterling Financial.

EXECUTIVES

Senior Vice President, Chief Operations Officer, Rachel Amdahl
Senior Vice President, Chief Risk Officer, Chantelle Nash

Senior Vice President, Chief Credit Officer, Dale Field
Independent Chairman Of The Board, Rick Hays
Independent Director, Shavon Cape
Independent Director, Tanya Chemodurow
Independent Vice Chairman Of The Board, Thomas McCarvel
Independent Director, Maureen Rude
Independent Director, Corey Jensen
Director, Benjamin Ruddy
Senior Vice President, Chief Lending Officer, Mark O'Neil
Senior Vice President, Chief Information Officer, P. Darryl Rensmon, $161,000 total compensation
Independent Director, Cynthia Utterback
Senior Vice President, Chief Retail Officer, Linda Chilton
President, Chief Executive Officer, Director Of The Company And The Bank, Peter Johnson, $312,000 total compensation
Chief Financial Officer, Chief Operating Officer, Executive Vice President, Laura Clark, $220,000 total compensation
Auditors: Moss Adams LLP

LOCATIONS

HQ: Eagle Bancorp Montana, Inc.
1400 Prospect Avenue, Helena, MT 59601
Phone: 406 442-3080
Web: www.opportunitybank.com

COMPETITORS

CENTRAL BANCORP INC. FIRSTFED BANCORP INC.

HISTORICAL FINANCIALS

Company Type: Public

Income Statement   FYE: December 31

	ASSETS ($ mil.)	NET INCOME ($ mil.)	INCOME AS % OF ASSETS	EMPLOYEES
12/20	1,257.6	21.2	1.7%	354
12/19	1,054.2	10.8	1.0%	298
12/18	853.9	4.9	0.6%	249
12/17	716.7	4.1	0.6%	207
12/16	673.9	5.1	0.8%	200
Annual Growth	16.9%	42.6%	—	15.3%

2020 Year-End Financials

Return on assets: 1.8%
Return on equity: 15.4%
Long-term debt ($ mil.): —
No. of shares (mil.): 6.7
Sales ($ mil): 98.7

Dividends
  Yield: 1.8%
  Payout: 14.1%
Market value ($ mil.): 144.0

	STOCK PRICE ($) FY Close	P/E High/Low		Earnings	PER SHARE ($) Dividends	Book Value
12/20	21.22	7	4	3.11	0.39	22.57
12/19	21.39	13	9	1.69	0.38	18.94
12/18	16.50	24	17	0.91	0.37	17.31
12/17	20.95	22	17	0.99	0.34	16.68
12/16	21.10	16	8	1.32	0.32	15.60
Annual Growth	0.1%		—	23.9%	5.1%	9.7%

Eagle Financial Services, Inc.

EXECUTIVES

Independent Director, Cary Nelson
Director, Edward Hill
Director, Tanya Matthews
President, Chief Executive Officer, Director, Brandon Lorey, $440,000 total compensation
Secretary; Executive Vice President And Chief Human Resources Officer Of The Bank, Kaley Crosen
Independent Chairman Of The Board, Thomas Gilpin
Independent Director, Douglas Rinker
Executive Vice President, Chief Fiduciary Officer Of The Bank, Carl Esterhay
Chief Financial Officer, Executive Vice President, Kathleen Chappell, $243,500 total compensation
Independent Director, Mary Glaize
Independent Director, John Stokely
Independent Director, Scott Hamberger
Independent Director, Robert Smalley
Independent Director, Thomas Byrd
Executive Vice President, Chief Revenue Officer Of The Bank, Joseph Zmitrovich, $299,462 total compensation
Auditors: Yount, Hyde & Barbour, P.C.

LOCATIONS

HQ: Eagle Financial Services, Inc.
2 East Main Street, P.O. Box 391, Berryville, VA 22611
Phone: 540 955-2510
Web: www.bankofclarke.com

HISTORICAL FINANCIALS

Company Type: Public

Income Statement   FYE: December 31

	ASSETS ($ mil.)	NET INCOME ($ mil.)	INCOME AS % OF ASSETS	EMPLOYEES
12/20	1,130.1	11.1	1.0%	204
12/19	877.3	9.7	1.1%	191
12/18	799.6	9.0	1.1%	184
12/17	765.7	7.7	1.0%	181
12/16	700.1	6.3	0.9%	189
Annual Growth	12.7%	15.1%	—	1.9%

2020 Year-End Financials

Return on assets: 1.1%
Return on equity: 11.0%
Long-term debt ($ mil.): —
No. of shares (mil.): 3.4
Sales ($ mil): 47.4
Dividends
Yield: 3.5%
Payout: 30.9%
Market value ($ mil.): 100.0

	STOCK PRICE ($) FY Close	P/E High/Low		PER SHARE ($) Earnings	Dividends	Book Value
12/20	29.50	10	7	3.27	1.04	30.86
12/19	31.05	12	10	2.84	1.00	28.08
12/18	30.99	15	11	2.60	0.94	25.42
12/17	32.00	15	11	2.24	0.88	24.30
12/16	25.75	14	13	1.81	0.82	22.90
Annual Growth	3.5%	—	—	15.9%	6.1%	7.7%

East West Bancorp, Inc

East Wes Bancorp is the holding company for East West Bank which provides standard banking services and loans operating in more than 120 locations in the US and China. Boasting $52 billion in assets East West Bank focuses on making commercial and industrial real estate loans which account for the majority of the company's loan portfolio. Catering to the Asian-American community it also provides international banking and trade financing to importers/exporters doing business in the Asia/Pacific region.

Operations

East West Bancorp operates three business segments. Consumer and Business Banking Commercial Banking and Other operations.

The Consumer and Business Banking segment which provided $187 million in net income for 2020 primarily provides financial products and services to consumer and commercial customers through the company's domestic branch network. The segment offers consumer and commercial deposits mortgage and home equity loans and other products and services.

The Commercial Banking segment which provided $226 million generates the company's commercial loans and deposits. The segment's products include commercial business loans and lines of credit trade finance loans and letters of credit CRE loans construction and land lending affordable housing loans and letters of credit asset-based lending and equipment financing.

The bank's Other segment centralizes functions including the corporate treasury activities of the company and elimination of inter-segment amounts have been aggregated to this segment. The segment also provides broad administrative support to the company's two core segments.

Geographic Reach

East West's bank network in the US is mainly in California Texas New York Washington Georgia Massachusetts and Nevada. Internationally the bank has branches in Hong Kong and Greater China (Shanghai Shantou and Shenzhen) and five representative offices in Beijing Chongqing Guangzhou Xiamen and Taiwan.

Financial Performance

East West Bancorp's performance for the span of five years has fluctuated but increased overall as compared to 2016's performance gradually increasing and fluctuating between the $1.6 billion from 2018 to 2020.

East West Bancorp's revenue decreased by about $78 million to $1.61 billion as compared to 2019's revenue of $1.69 billion. This decrease was primarily due to lower net interest income partially offset by an increase in noninterest income.

The bank's net income also decreased by about $107 million to $567 million in 2020 as compared to the prior year's net income of $674 million. The decrease primarily came from a higher provision for credit losses and lower net interest income partially offset by a decrease in income tax expense.

The bank's cash held amounted to $4 billion which is higher by $756 million to 2019's cash held of $3.2 billion. Operating activities and financing activities provided $693 million and $6.9 billion respectively. While investing activities used another $6.8 billion for 2020.

Strategy

East West Bancorp continues to improve and solidify its banking presence through its overseas branches and representative offices. These offices include four full-service branches in Greater China located in Hong Kong Shanghai Shantou and Shenzhen.

The bank is continuing to explore opportunities that enable the company to establish foreign offices subsidiaries strategic investments and partnerships to expand its international banking capabilities and to capitalize on long-term cross-border business opportunities between the US and Greater China.

Company Background

East West Bancorp was founded in 1998.

In 2009 the company acquired more than 60 branches and most of the banking operations of larger rival United Commercial Bank which had been seized by regulators. The deal gave East West Bank about 40 more California branches plus some 20 additional US locations beyond the state.

EXECUTIVES

Independent Director, Lester Sussman
Chief Financial Officer, Executive Vice President Of The Company And The Bank, Irene Oh, $635,524 total compensation
Chief Operating Officer, Executive Vice President, Parker Shi
Executive Vice President, Head Of Commercial Banking, Nick Huang
Independent Director, Archana Deskus
Senior Vice President, Head Of Human Resources, Gary Teo, $361,685 total compensation
Independent Director, Paul Irving
Independent Director, Iris Chan
Chairman Of The Board, Chief Executive Officer Of The Company And The Bank, Dominic Ng, $1,275,000 total compensation
Auditors: KPMG LLP

LOCATIONS

HQ: East West Bancorp, Inc
135 North Los Robles Ave., 7th Floor, Pasadena, CA 91101
Phone: 626 768-6000
Web: www.eastwestbank.com

PRODUCTS/OPERATIONS

2011 Sales

	$ mil.	% of total
Commercial lending	619.8	57
Retail banking	358.8	33
Other & adjustments	112.8	10
Total	**1,091.4**	**100**

COMPETITORS

AMERIS BANCORP	NEWBRIDGE BANCORP
BANK OF THE WEST	PACIFIC CONTINENTAL
CATHAY GENERAL BANCORP	CORPORATION
CITIZENS & NORTHERN CORPORATION	PEOPLE'S UNITED FINANCIAL INC.
CITIZENS FINANCIAL GROUP INC.	REGIONS FINANCIAL CORPORATION
CITY NATIONAL CORPORATION	S & T BANCORP INC.
COLUMBIA BANKING SYSTEM INC. INC.	SOUTH STATE CORPORATION
	SOUTHWEST BANCORP
FIRST CITIZENS PLC	STANDARD CHARTERED
BANCSHARES INC.	VALLEY NATIONAL

HOOVER'S HANDBOOK OF EMERGING COMPANIES 2022

FIRST MIDWEST BANCORP INC.
HANCOCK WHITNEY CORPORATION
M&T BANK CORPORATION
BANCORP
WESTERN ALLIANCE BANCORPORATION
WILSHIRE BANCORP INC.

HISTORICAL FINANCIALS

Company Type: Public

Income Statement — FYE: December 31

	ASSETS ($ mil.)	NET INCOME ($ mil.)	INCOME AS % OF ASSETS	EMPLOYEES
12/20	52,156.9	567.8	1.1%	3,200
12/19	44,196.1	674.0	1.5%	3,300
12/18	41,042.3	703.7	1.7%	3,200
12/17	37,150.2	505.6	1.4%	3,000
12/16	34,788.8	431.6	1.2%	2,873
Annual Growth	10.7%	7.1%	—	2.7%

2020 Year-End Financials

Return on assets: 1.1%
Return on equity: 11.0%
Long-term debt ($ mil.): —
No. of shares (mil.): 141.5
Sales ($ mil): 1,830.5

Dividends
Yield: 2.1%
Payout: 27.7%
Market value ($ mil.): 7,179.0

	STOCK PRICE ($) FY Close	P/E High/Low		PER SHARE ($) Earnings	Dividends	Book Value
12/20	50.71	13	6	3.97	1.10	37.22
12/19	48.70	12	8	4.61	1.06	34.46
12/18	43.53	15	8	4.81	0.86	30.52
12/17	60.83	18	14	3.47	0.80	26.58
12/16	50.83	17	9	2.97	0.80	23.78
Annual Growth	(0.1%)	—	—	7.5%	8.3%	11.9%

Easterly Government Properties Inc

Auditors: PricewaterhouseCoopers LLP

LOCATIONS

HQ: Easterly Government Properties Inc
2001 K Street NW, Suite 775 North, Washington, DC 20006
Phone: 202 595-9500
Web: www.easterlyreit.com

HISTORICAL FINANCIALS

Company Type: Public

Income Statement — FYE: December 31

	REVENUE ($ mil.)	NET INCOME ($ mil.)	NET PROFIT MARGIN	EMPLOYEES
12/20	245.0	11.9	4.9%	45
12/19	221.7	7.2	3.3%	37
12/18	160.5	5.7	3.6%	32
12/17	130.6	4.4	3.4%	30
12/16	104.6	3.4	3.3%	27
Annual Growth	23.7%	36.8%	—	13.6%

2020 Year-End Financials

Debt ratio: 39.8%
Return on equity: 1.0%
Cash ($ mil.): 8.4
Current ratio: 4.69
Long-term debt ($ mil.): 978.2

No. of shares (mil.): 82.1
Dividends
Yield: 4.5%
Payout: 693.3%
Market value ($ mil.): 1,860.0

	STOCK PRICE ($) FY Close	P/E High/Low	PER SHARE ($) Earnings	Dividends	Book Value
12/20	22.65	195 129	0.15	1.04	14.06
12/19	23.73	235 154	0.10	1.30	14.20
12/18	15.68	238 170	0.08	1.04	14.69
12/17	21.34	201 175	0.10	1.00	14.91
12/16	20.02	187 150	0.10	0.92	15.17
Annual Growth	3.1%	— —	10.7%	3.1%	(1.9%)

EastGroup Properties Inc

EastGroup Properties points its compass all across the Sunbelt. The self-administered real estate investment trust (REIT) invests in develops and manages industrial properties with a particular emphasis on Florida Texas Arizona and California. EastGroup's distribution space properties are typically multitenant buidings. Its distribution space for location sensitive customers ranges from about 15000 to 70000 sq. ft. in size located near major transportation hubs. Its portfolio includes some 360 industrial properties and an office building totaling more than 40 million sq. ft. of leasable space.

Operations
EastGroup has one reportable segment ? industrial properties. All of its revenues came from real estate rentals.

Geographic Reach
Ridgeland Mississippi-based EastGroup Properties has regional offices in Orlando Miami Houston and Phoenix. Although its portfolio is focused on the Sun Belt (Arizona California Florida North Carolina and Texas) the REIT also owns properties in Colorado Louisiana Mississippi and Nevada.

Sales and Marketing
EastGroup's operating portfolio was about 95% leased to approximately 1500 tenants with no single tenant accounting for approximately 1.0% of the company's income from real estate operations.

Financial Performance
The company revenue for the last five years saw a 41% increase since 2015. Net income also reported an increasing trend for the same period.

The REIT reported revenue of $331.4 million in 2019 an increase of 10% from 2018. Real estate revenue increased $31.8 million offset by a $0.8 million decrease in Other revenue.

Net income rose by 37% to $121.7 million in 2019. The increase was due to higher total revenue and a gain of $41 million from sale of real estate investments.

Cash and cash equivalents at the end of the year were $224000. Net cash provided by operations was $195.9 million and financing activities added another $247.3 million. Investing activities used $443.3 million for development and value-add properties and Purchases of real estate.

Strategy

EastGroup's strategy for growth is based on ownership of premier distribution facilities generally clustered near major transportation features in supply-constrained submarkets.

EastGroup's goal is to maximize shareholder value by being a leading provider in its markets of functional flexible and quality business distribution space for location sensitive customers (primarily in the 15000 to 70000 square foot range). The company develops acquires and operates distribution facilities the majority of which are clustered around major transportation features in supply-constrained submarkets in major Sunbelt regions. The company's core markets are in the states of Florida Texas Arizona California and North Carolina.

During 2019 EastGroup increased its holdings in real estate properties through its acquisition and development programs. The company purchased 1774000 square feet of operating and value-add properties and 188 acres of land for a total of $269 million. Also during 2019 the company began construction of 18 development projects containing 2.7 million square feet and transferred 13 projects which contain 1.8 million square feet and had costs of $156.7 million at the date of transfer from its development and value-add program to real estate properties. And also during that time EastGroup completed dispositions including 617000 square feet of operating properties and 0.2 acres of land which generated gross proceeds of $68.7 million.

HISTORY

New York-based Third ICM Realty was founded in 1969 and went public two years later as ICM Realty. The company specialized in sale/leaseback transactions. Mississippi investor Leland Speed became a director of the company in 1978; two years later Speed staged a management coup through his Eastover Corp. and Citizens Growth Properties taking over the company and moving it to Mississippi. The company was renamed EastGroup Properties in 1983.

Speed continued to divide his time among his various companies. Eastover was at first trying to sell then to find a joint venture partner for a golf course development in 1989 and 1990. In the 1990s Speed began consolidating his holdings under EastGroup Properties merging Eastover into it in 1994. The company also bought Copley Properties that year. These transactions left the company in possession of a wide variety of properties including hotels stores and apartments.

EastGroup Properties started to reposition its portfolio by selling off the noncore properties. As it gained capital from these sales it began making more acquisitions both of individual sites and property portfolios. In 1997 EastGroup Properties bought into Meridian Point Realty Trust completing the purchase the next year and with it adding some 2.6 million sq. ft. of property to its portfolio. Also in 1998 the company bought Ensign Properties an industrial developer in the Orlando Florida area.

In 1999 EastGroup Properties announced that it planned to make $50-60 million worth of investments financed through the sale of existing properties. In 2000 the company expanded its industrial portfolio in Tempe Arizona; and in Houston Dallas and El Paso Texas through acquisitions and new developments. The company disposed of its last remaining apartment property a 240-unit site in Atlanta the same year. By 2005 it had one last office property in its portfolio.

EXECUTIVES

Pres-Ceo, Marshall A Loeb
Chb*, David H Hoster II
Sr V Pres-Cfo-Treas, Brent W Wood
Exec V Pres, John C Coleman
Sr V Pres, R Reid Dunbar
Sr V Pres, Ryan M Collins
Sr V Pres-Cao-Sec, Staci Tyler
Property Accountant, Haley Boykin
Property Manager, Jennifer Ryan
Property Manager, Lisa Brown
Auditors: KPMG LLP

LOCATIONS

HQ: EastGroup Properties Inc
   400 W Parkway Place, Suite 100, Ridgeland, MS 39157
Phone: 601 354-3555
Web: www.eastgroup.net

PRODUCTS/OPERATIONS

2016 Sales

	$ mil.	% of total
Income from Real estate operations	252.2	100
Other	0.8	-
Total	**253.0**	**100**

COMPETITORS

COUSINS PROPERTIES INCORPORATED	RETAIL PROPERTIES OF AMERICA INC.
LIBERTY PROPERTY TRUST	THE HOWARD HUGHES
PIEDMONT OFFICE REALTY TRUST INC.	CORPORATION
	WEINGARTEN REALTY
RETAIL OPPORTUNITY INVESTMENTS CORP.	INVESTORS
	WHITESTONE REIT

HISTORICAL FINANCIALS

Company Type: Public

Income Statement				FYE: December 31
	REVENUE ($ mil.)	NET INCOME ($ mil.)	NET PROFIT MARGIN	EMPLOYEES
12/21	409.4	157.5	38.5%	82
12/20	363.0	108.3	29.9%	80
12/19	331.3	121.6	36.7%	77
12/18	300.3	88.5	29.5%	75
12/17	274.1	83.1	30.3%	71
Annual Growth	10.6%	17.3%	—	3.7%

2021 Year-End Financials

Debt ratio: 45.1%
Return on equity: 11.1%
Cash ($ mil.): 4.3
Current ratio: 0.65
Long-term debt ($ mil.): 1,451.7

No. of shares (mil.): 41.2
Dividends
   Yield: 1.5%
   Payout: 116.2%
Market value ($ mil.): 9,403.0

	STOCK PRICE ($) FY Close	P/E High/Low		PER SHARE ($) Earnings	Dividends	Book Value
12/21	227.85	58 34		3.90	3.58	38.04
12/20	138.06	53 32		2.76	3.08	32.00
12/19	132.67	42 27		3.24	2.94	30.84
12/18	91.73	41 31		2.49	2.72	24.74
12/17	88.38	39 28		2.44	2.52	21.56
Annual Growth	26.7%	— —		12.4%	9.2%	15.3%

Ebix Inc

Ebix Inc. supplies on-demand software designed to streamline the way insurance professionals manage distribution marketing sales customer service and accounting activities. Its EbixCash Exchange (EbixCash) is primarily derived from the sales of prepaid gift cards and consideration paid by customers for financial transaction services including services like transferring or exchanging money. It also offers several other services including payment services and ticketing and travel services for which revenue is impacted by varying factors. Ebix also Software-as-a-Service (SaaS) enterprise solutions in the area of customer relationship management (CRM) front-end & back-end systems outsourced administrative and risk compliance. Ebix generated majority of its sales in India.

Operations

Ebix reports as a single segment. Its revenues are derived from three product/service groups: EbixCash Exchanges (over 60% of sales) Insurance Exchanges (about 30%) and Risk Compliance Solutions (nearly 10%).

EbixCash revenues are primarily derived from the sales of prepaid gift cards and consideration paid by customers for financial transaction services including services like transferring or exchanging money. It also offers several other services including payment services and ticketing and travel services.

Insurance Exchanges revenues are primarily derived from consideration paid by customers related to its SaaS platforms related services and the licensing of software. A typical contract for its SaaS platform will also include services for setup customization transaction processing maintenance and/or hosting.

Risk Compliance Services revenues consist of two revenue streams - Certificates of Insurance (COI) and Consulting Services. COI revenues are derived from consideration paid by customers for the creation and tracking of certificates of insurance. These are transactional-based revenues. Consulting Services revenues are driven by distinct consulting service engagements rendered to customers for which revenues are recognized using the output method on a time and material basis as the services are performed.

Geographic Reach

Atlanta-based Ebix's largest market is the India accounting for around 60% of its sales with US and Australia accounting for over 25% and some 5% respectively. It has office space primarily for sales and operations support in Salt Lake City Utah Pittsburgh Pennsylvania Pasadena California Birmingham Alabama and Phoenix Arizona. The company leases office space in New Zealand Australia Singapore Dubai Brazil Canada Indonesia Philippines and London for support operations and sales offices. It also leases approximately 140 facilities across India while owning six facilities in India.

Sales and Marketing

Ebix employs skilled technology and business professionals who provide products services support and consultancy services to thousands of customers. The company's advertising costs were approximately $4.8 million $9.7 million and $7.5 million in 2020 2019 and 2018 respectively.

Financial Performance

The company's revenue for fiscal 2020 increased to $625.6 million compared from the prior year with $580.6 million.

Net income in 2020 decreased by 4% to $92.4 million compared from 2019 with $96.7 million.

Cash held by the company at the end of fiscal 2020 increased to $120.2 million. Cash provided by operations was $100.4 million while cash used for investing and financing activities were $44.8 million and $42.0 million respectively. Main uses of cash were purchases of marketable securities and payment to revolving line of credit.

Strategy

The company seeks to acquire businesses that complement Ebix's existing products and services. Any acquisition made by Ebix typically will fall into one of two different categories: the acquired company has products and/or services that are competitive to its existing products and services; or the acquired company's products and services are either a complement to or an extension of its existing products and services or its core business competencies.

The company's integration strategies are targeted at improving the efficiency of its business centralizing key functions exercising better control over its operations and providing consistent technology and product vision across all functions entities and products. This is a key part of Ebix's business philosophy designed to enable Ebix to operate at a high level of efficiency and facilitate a consistent end-to-end strategic vision for the industries it serve.

Mergers and Acquisitions

In late 2020 EbixCash a fully owned subsidiary of Ebix Inc. has acquired a 70 percent stake in a 1800 strong pan-India based BPO company AssureEdge Global Services. AssureEdge is today recognized as the first independent customer retention and customer response organization in India with a variety of BPO offerings via six contact centers across the country. AssureEdge can serve to handle fulfillment collections and last mile delivery for EbixCash as it converges with EbixCash financial and insurance technology platforms. Terms were not disclosed.

EXECUTIVES

Chairman Of The Board, President, Chief Executive Officer, Robin Raina
Independent Director, Hans Benz
Independent Director, Rolf Herter
Independent Director, Pavan Bhalla
Lead Independent Director, Hans Keller
Senior Vice President - Ebixhealth, James Senge, $225,000 total compensation
Corporate Executive Vice President, Managing Director - Ebix Australia Group, Leon D'apice, $207,197 total compensation
Global Chief Financial Officer, Corporate Executive Vice President, Steven Hamil, $231,250 total compensation
Independent Director, Priyanka Kaul
Independent Director, George Hebard
Auditors: KG Somani & Co.

LOCATIONS

HQ: Ebix Inc
   1 Ebix Way, Johns Creek, GA 30097
Phone: 678 281-2020
Web: www.ebix.com

PRODUCTS/OPERATIONS

2017 Sales

	$ mil.	% of total
Exchanges	259,470.0	71
Risk Compliance Solutions	86,832.0	24
Broker systems	14,672.0	4
Carrier systems	2,995.0	1
Total	**363,971.0**	**100**

COMPETITORS

ATOS SYNTEL INC.
EPAM SYSTEMS INC.
FIDESSA GROUP HOLDINGS LIMITED
FLEETCOR TECHNOLOGIES CORP. INC.
FORESCOUT TECHNOLOGIES INC.
JACK HENRY & ASSOCIATES INC.
MICROSTRATEGY INCORPORATED
NIC INC.
PREMIER INC.
PROOFPOINT INC.
PROS HOLDINGS INC.
SECUREWORKS
Tecsys Inc
The Descartes Systems Group Inc
VIRTUSA CORPORATION
VISA PAYMENTS LIMITED
WEX INC.
WORKDAY INC.

HISTORICAL FINANCIALS

Company Type: Public

Income Statement				FYE: December 31
	REVENUE ($ mil.)	NET INCOME ($ mil.)	NET PROFIT MARGIN	EMPLOYEES
12/20	625.6	92.3	14.8%	9,802
12/19	580.6	96.7	16.7%	7,975
12/18	497.8	93.1	18.7%	9,263
12/17	363.9	100.6	27.6%	4,515
12/16	298.2	93.8	31.5%	2,988
Annual Growth	20.3%	(0.4%)	—	34.6%

2020 Year-End Financials

Debt ratio: 44.3%
Return on equity: 15.8%
Cash ($ mil.): 105.0
Current ratio: 1.89
Long-term debt ($ mil.): 671.5
No. of shares (mil.): 30.5
Dividends
 Yield: 0.7%
 Payout: 9.9%
Market value ($ mil.): 1,159.0

	STOCK PRICE ($) FY Close	P/E High/Low		PER SHARE ($) Earnings	Dividends	Book Value
12/20	37.97	13	3	3.02	0.30	20.09
12/19	33.41	19	10	3.16	0.30	18.04
12/18	42.56	29	14	2.95	0.30	15.64
12/17	79.25	26	17	3.19	0.30	15.62
12/16	57.05	22	10	2.86	0.30	13.30
Annual Growth	(9.7%)	—	—	1.4%	(0.0%)	10.9%

Educational Development Corp.

Educational Development Corporation (EDC) likes being in a bind as long as the cover appeals to youngsters. The company is the exclusive US distributor of a line of about 1500 children's books published by the UK's Usborne Publishing Limited. EDC's Home Business Division markets the books to individuals using independent sales reps who sell through personal websites home parties direct sales and book fairs; this division also distributes books to public and school libraries. EDC's Publishing Division distributes the Usborne line to a network of book toy and other retail stores. EDC bought multi-cultural children's book publisher Kane/Miller in 2008 to complement its product offerings.

EXECUTIVES

Executive Chairman Of The Board, Randall White, $270,000 total compensation
President, Chief Executive Officer, Director, Craig White, $193,400 total compensation
Lead Independent Director, John Clerico
Independent Director, Kara Neal
Chief Sales And Marketing Officer, Heather Cobb
Chief Financial Officer, Corporate Secretary, Dan O'Keefe, $216,900 total compensation
Independent Director, Joshua Peters
Auditors: HoganTaylor LLP

LOCATIONS

HQ: Educational Development Corp.
 5402 South 122nd East Avenue, Tulsa, OK 74146
Phone: 918 622-4522
Web: www.edcpub.com

COMPETITORS

BLACKWELL'S DELAWARE INCORPORATED
GL GROUP INC.
NIPPAN GROUP HOLDINGS INC.

HISTORICAL FINANCIALS

Company Type: Public

Income Statement				FYE: February 28
	REVENUE ($ mil.)	NET INCOME ($ mil.)	NET PROFIT MARGIN	EMPLOYEES
02/21	204.6	12.6	6.2%	214
02/20	113.0	5.6	5.0%	201
02/19	118.8	6.6	5.6%	178
02/18	111.9	5.2	4.7%	193
02/17	106.6	2.8	2.7%	202
Annual Growth	17.7%	44.9%	—	1.5%

2021 Year-End Financials

Debt ratio: 18.2%
Return on equity: 36.2%
Cash ($ mil.): 1.8
Current ratio: 1.53
Long-term debt ($ mil.): 10.4
No. of shares (mil.): 8.3
Dividends
 Yield: 0.0%
 Payout: 21.3%
Market value ($ mil.): 130.0

	STOCK PRICE ($) FY Close	P/E High/Low		PER SHARE ($) Earnings	Dividends	Book Value
02/21	15.61	13	2	1.50	0.32	4.82
02/20	5.16	13	8	0.68	0.20	3.52
02/19	8.05	33	9	0.81	0.20	3.16
02/18	19.35	36	11	0.64	0.05	2.49
02/17	9.55	42	20	0.35	0.18	1.86
Annual Growth	13.1%	—	—	43.9%	15.5%	26.9%

eHealth Inc

eHealth is a leading health insurance marketplace with a technology and service platform that provides consumer engagement education and health insurance enrollment solutions. The company created a marketplace that offers consumers a broad choice of insurance products that includes thousands of Medicare Advantage Medicare Supplement Medicare Part D prescription drug individual and family small business and other ancillary health insurance products. Licensed to sell insurance policies throughout the US the company has partnerships with more than 200 health insurance carriers for which it processes and delivers potential members' applications in return for commission on policy sales. It lets consumers compare products online ? including health dental and vision insurance products from the likes of Aetna Humana and UnitedHealth.

Operations

Through a combination of demand generation strategies the company actively market a large selection of Medicare-related health insurance plans and to a lesser extent ancillary products such as dental and vision insurance to their Medicare-eligible customers. eHealth's technology platform and nationwide presence allow customers to get online rate quotes and side-by-side plan comparisons from a much wider range of providers. The company's online applications are delivered electronically to insurance carriers' information systems reducing the time it takes to process and enroll new members.

The company manages its business into two business segments: Medicare segment (about 90% of sales); and Individual Family and Small Business Segment (nearly 10%).

Most of its revenues came from commissions which accounts for more than 85% and the remaining accounts for others.

Geographic Reach

A portion of technology and content group is located at their wholly-owned subsidiary in China where technology development costs are generally lower than in the US. Its corporate office is located in Santa Clara California. In addition it also has offices in Utah Texas China and Indiana.

Sales and Marketing

eHealth focus on building brand awareness increasing individual family and small business customer visits to its websites increasing Medicare customer visits to its websites and telephonic sales centers and converting these visitors into members. Its three top clients Humana UnitedHealthcare and Aetna represent more than 20% about 20% and approximately 15% of total revenue.

Its online advertising member acquisition channel consists of consumers who access the company's website or call centers through paid keyword search advertising from search engines such as Google Bing and Yahoo! paid social platforms like Facebook as well as various Internet marketing programs such as display advertising and retargeting campaigns. Its online advertising programs are delivered across all internet-enabled devices including desktop computers tablet computers and smart phones.

Marketing and advertising expense were approximately $209.3 million $150.3 million and $82.9

million for the years ended 2020 2019 and 2018 respectively.

Financial Performance

The company's revenue in 2020 was $582.8 million a 15% increase from the previous year's revenue of $506.2 million. The increase in commission revenue from the Medicare segment was driven by a 16% increase in Medicare plan approved members primarily attributable to a 39% growth in Medicare Advantage plan approved members.

In 2020 the company had a net income of $45.5 million a 32% decrease from the previous year's net income of $66.9 million.

The company's cash at the end of 2020 was $47.1 million. Financing activities generated $201.2 million while investing activities used another $73.3 million mainly for purchase of marketable securities. Operating activities used another $107.9 million.

Strategy

The company believes its consumer engagement platform and approach to bringing value to consumers is unique in the health insurance market and creates significant opportunities for growth in its core Medicare business and in other areas of the health insurance market. It intends to pursue the following strategies to further advance its business.

Increase Medicare Membership and Commission Revenue by enrolling additional Medicare Advantage Medicare Supplement and Medicare Part D prescription drug plan members for its commercial carrier partners.

Enhance post-enrollment consumer engagement and increase customer retention by enhancing its consumer experience both online and telephonically to simplify and encourage the use of its platform for future enrollments as consumer needs and plan selection evolves. Its goal is to over time increase the contribution from repeat customers to its total enrollments.

Increase online enrollment to improve margins and enhance operating leverage by scaling growth more rapidly and at an incrementally lower cost basis through its online platform which significantly reduces its reliance on and financial and managerial resources associated with its call center operations.

Expand its strategic relationships through greater data integration co-branding and further investments to improve the customer experience with its platform.

Acquire capabilities that leverage its consumer engagement platform by pursuing strategic relationships or acquisitions that expand its platform provide additional capabilities or enable it to access adjacent markets within the broader health insurance and related customer facing segments of the healthcare industry.

Company Background

eHealth was founded in 1997.

It began actively marketing Medicare policies through its eHealthMedicare and PlanPrescriber websites following the 2010 acquisition of privately held PlanPrescriber for roughly $30 million. PlanPrescriber provides online and pharmacy-based tools to help seniors navigate Medicare health insurance options. The acquisition has helped accelerate eHealth's penetration of the large and steadily growing senior market. eHealth intends to continue to expand its online Medicare enrollment ca-

pabilities as the baby boomer generation continues to shift into the Medicare bracket.

EXECUTIVES

Director, Erin Russell
Director, Aaron Tolson
Chief Financial Officer, Senior Vice President, Principal Accounting Officer, Christine Janofsky
Chief Executive Officer, Director, Francis Soistman
Interim Chief Revenue Officer, Robert Hurley, $325,000 total compensation
Senior Vice President, Investor Relations And Strategy, Kate Sidorovich
Independent Director, Andrea Brimmer
Chairman, Dale Wolf
Chief Digital Officer, Phillip Morelock, $330,346 total compensation
President - Medicare, Gregg Ratkovic, $302,929 total compensation
Independent Director, Cesar Soriano
Auditors: Ernst & Young LLP

LOCATIONS

HQ: eHealth Inc
2625 Augustine Drive, Second Floor, Santa Clara, CA 95054
Phone: 650 584-2700
Web: www.eHealth.com

PRODUCTS/OPERATIONS

2015 Sales

	$ mil.	% of total
Commissions	171.3	90
Other	18.2	10
Total	**189.5**	**10**

Selected Insurance Carriers

Aetna
Altius
Anthem Blue Cross and Blue Shield
Assurant Health
BlueCross BlueShield of Texas
Blue Shield of California
CareFirst BlueCross BlueShield
Celtic Insurance Company
CIGNA
ConnectiCare
Coventry Health Care
Delta Dental
EmblemHealth
HealthNet
Highmark
Humana
IHC Group
Kaiser Permanente
LifeWise Health Plans
Regence BlueCross BlueShield
Scott & White Health Plan
Security Life Insurance Company of America
UniCare
UnitedHealth
WellPath Select
WellPoint

Selected Products

Health Insurance
Medicare
Maternity Coverage
PPO Plans
HMO Plans
Individual and Family
Individual Health Insurance
Family Health Insurance
Medicare
Short-term Health Insurance
Student Health Insurance
Health Savings Accounts
International Health Insurance

Individual Dental Insurance
Discount Cards
Vision Insurance
Life Insurance
Accident Insurance
Critical Illness Insurance
Travel Health Insurance
FSmall Business
Group Health Insurance
Group Dental Insurance
Group Vision Insurance
Medicare
Medicare Insurance Plans
Medicare Supplement
Medicare Advantage
Medicare Part D
Short Term
Short-term Health Insurance
Dental
Individual Dental Insurance
Group Dental Insurance
Vision
Individual Vision Insurance
Group Vision Insurance
Life
Life Insurance
Other
Travel Health Insurance
International Health Insurance
Pet Insurance
Prescription Discount Card
Telemedicine

COMPETITORS

A ACUITY MUTUAL COMPANY
INSURANCE COMPANY
ALLIANZ INSURANCE PLC
COMPUTER PROGRAMS AND SYSTEMS INC.
CORVEL CORPORATION
DONEGAL GROUP INC.
EXTEND HEALTH LLC
FEDNAT HOLDING
HCI GROUP INC.
HEALTHEQUITY INC.
MULTIPLAN INC.
NATIONAL RESEARCH CORPORATION
PREMIER INC.

HISTORICAL FINANCIALS

Company Type: Public

Income Statement

FYE: December 31

	REVENUE ($ mil.)	NET INCOME ($ mil.)	NET PROFIT MARGIN	EMPLOYEES
12/20	582.7	45.4	7.8%	1,960
12/19	506.2	66.8	13.2%	1,500
12/18	251.4	0.2	0.1%	1,079
12/17	172.3	(25.4)	—	1,079
12/16	186.9	(4.8)	—	944
Annual Growth	32.9%	—	—	20.0%

2020 Year-End Financials

Debt ratio: —
Return on equity: 6.6%
Cash ($ mil.): 43.7
Current ratio: 3.92
Long-term debt ($ mil.): —
No. of shares (mil.): 25.9
Dividends
  Yield: —
  Payout: —
Market value ($ mil.): 1,830.0

	STOCK PRICE ($) FY Close	P/E High/Low		PER SHARE ($) Earnings	Dividends	Book Value
12/20	70.61	83	35	1.68	0.00	32.31
12/19	96.08	38	12	2.73	0.00	22.79
12/18	38.42	401	21365	0.01	0.00	15.60
12/17	17.37	—	—	(1.37)	0.00	3.28
12/16	10.65	—	—	(0.27)	0.00	4.23
Annual Growth	60.5%	—	—	—	—	66.3%

HOOVER'S HANDBOOK OF EMERGING COMPANIES 2022

Ellington Residential Mortgaging Real Estate Investment Trust

Ellington Financial LLC is ready to double its money. The investment firm formed Ellington Residential Mortgage REIT a real estate residential trust (REIT) to invest in agency residential mortgage-backed securities (Agency RMBS) or those guaranteed by federally sponsored entities Fannie Mae Freddie Mac and Ginnie Mae. (Agency RMBS carry less risk than privately issued mortgage securities.) The trust's portfolio is balanced out with about 10% non-Agency RMBS such as residential whole mortgage loans mortgage servicing rights (MSRs) and residential real properties. (Non-Agency RMBS carry more risk but might offer better returns.) The trust went public in 2013.

IPO

The trust plans to spend at least 80% of the proceeds from its $129 million IPO to invest in Agency RMBS backed by 15-year and 30-year fixed rate mortgages. The remaining 20% will be used to invest in Agency RMBS backed by hybrid and adjustable rate mortgages and non-Agency RMBS backed by Alt-A prime and subprime mortgages.

Operations

Ellington Residential Mortgage REIT formed in August 2012 by affiliates of Ellington Financial and investment firm The Blackstone Group. As a REIT it is exempt from paying federal income tax as long as it makes a quarterly distribution to shareholders. And as a trust Ellington Residential Mortgage does not have any employees. It is externally managed and advised by Ellington Residential Mortgage Management LLC.

Strategy

The company's investment philosophy revolves around pursuing various types of mortgage-backed securities and related assets without any restriction as to ratings structure or position in the capital structure. Of course there are risks associated with mortgage investments but Ellington believes balancing its portfolio with agency-backed securities somewhat levels its risk.

EXECUTIVES

Co-chief Investment Officer, Mark Tecotzky
President, Chief Executive Officer, Trustee, Laurence Penn
Co-chief Investment Officer, Trustee, Michael Vranos
Independent Trustee, Mary Mcbride
General Counsel, Daniel Margolis
Independent Trustee, David Miller
Independent Trustee, Ronald Simon
Independent Chairman Of The Board Of Trustees, Robert Allardice
Chief Operating Officer, Treasurer, J. R. Herlihy, $50,000 total compensation
Chief Financial Officer, Christopher Smernoff, $44,813 total compensation
Auditors: PricewaterhouseCoopers LLP

LOCATIONS

HQ: Ellington Residential Mortgaging Real Estate Investment Trust
53 Forest Avenue, Old Greenwich, CT 06870
Phone: 203 698-1200
Web: www.earnreit.com

COMPETITORS

ARMOUR RESIDENTIAL REIT INC.
CHERRY HILL MORTGAGE INVESTMENT CORPORATION
RC MERGER SUBSIDIARY LLC
WESTERN ASSET MORTGAGE CAPITAL CORPORATION

HISTORICAL FINANCIALS

Company Type: Public

Income Statement — FYE: December 31

	ASSETS ($ mil.)	NET INCOME ($ mil.)	INCOME AS % OF ASSETS	EMPLOYEES
12/20	1,194.8	20.1	1.7%	150
12/19	1,489.1	22.2	1.5%	0
12/18	1,675.5	(11.3)	—	150
12/17	1,887.0	10.7	0.6%	160
12/16	1,429.1	11.9	0.8%	160
Annual Growth	(4.4%)	14.0%	—	(1.6%)

2020 Year-End Financials

Return on assets: 1.4%
Return on equity: 12.2%
Long-term debt ($ mil.): —
No. of shares (mil.): 12.3
Sales ($ mil): 35.9
Dividends
Yield: 8.5%
Payout: 68.7%
Market value ($ mil.): 161.0

	STOCK PRICE ($) FY Close	P/E High/Low		PER SHARE ($) Earnings	Dividends	Book Value
12/20	13.04	8	2	1.63	1.12	13.48
12/19	10.85	7	5	1.79	1.18	12.91
12/18	10.23	—	—	(0.88)	1.45	12.30
12/17	12.04	17	13	0.93	1.57	14.45
12/16	13.01	11	8	1.31	1.65	15.52
Annual Growth	0.1%		—	5.6%	(9.2%)	(3.5%)

Embassy Bancorp Inc

EXECUTIVES

Senior Executive Vice President, Senior Lending Officer Of The Bank, James Bartholomew, $363,352 total compensation
Director, Frank Banko
Independent Director, Patti Smith
Independent Director, John Pittman
Executive Vice President, Assistant Secretary Of The Company And The Bank, Lynne Neel
Chairman Of The Board, President, Chief Executive Officer Of The Company And The Bank, David Lobach, $690,493 total compensation
Director, Bernard Lesavoy
Executive Vice President Of The Company And The Bank, Diane Cunningham
First Executive Officer, Chief Operating Officer, Chief Financial Officer Of The Company And The Bank, Judith Hunsicker, $478,848 total compensation
Independent Director, John Englesson
Independent Director, Geoffrey Boyer
Auditors: Baker Tilly US, LLP

LOCATIONS

HQ: Embassy Bancorp Inc
One Hundred Gateway Drive, Suite 100, Bethlehem, PA 18017
Phone: 610 882-8800
Web: www.embassybank.com

HISTORICAL FINANCIALS

Company Type: Public

Income Statement — FYE: December 31

	ASSETS ($ mil.)	NET INCOME ($ mil.)	INCOME AS % OF ASSETS	EMPLOYEES
12/20	1,442.0	12.8	0.9%	96
12/19	1,176.1	10.8	0.9%	95
12/18	1,099.3	10.0	0.9%	91
12/17	996.9	7.3	0.7%	84
12/16	924.2	7.1	0.8%	83
Annual Growth	11.8%	15.7%	—	3.7%

2020 Year-End Financials

Return on assets: 0.9%
Return on equity: 12.0%
Long-term debt ($ mil.): —
No. of shares (mil.): 7.5
Sales ($ mil): 46.7
Dividends
Yield: 1.5%
Payout: 12.9%
Market value ($ mil.): 110.0

	STOCK PRICE ($) FY Close	P/E High/Low		PER SHARE ($) Earnings	Dividends	Book Value
12/20	14.60	11	6	1.70	0.22	14.90
12/19	18.50	13	10	1.44	0.20	13.32
12/18	14.95	13	10	1.34	0.17	11.69
12/17	16.00	16	13	0.97	0.14	10.71
12/16	13.00	14	11	0.96	0.13	9.84
Annual Growth	2.9%		—	15.4%	14.1%	10.9%

Emclaire Financial Corp.

Emclaire Financial is the holding company for the Farmers National Bank of Emlenton which operates about a dozen branches in northwestern Pennsylvania. Serving area consumers and businesses the bank offers standard deposit products and services including checking and savings accounts money market accounts and CDs. The bank is mainly a real estate lender with commercial mortgages residential first mortgages and home equity loans and lines of credit making up most of its loan portfolio. Emclaire Financial also owns title insurance and real estate settlement services provider Emclaire Settlement Services.

EXECUTIVES

Independent Vice Chairman Of The Board, David Cox
Independent Director, John Mason
Chairman Of The Board, President, Chief Executive Officer Of The Company And The Bank, William Marsh, $417,857 total compensation
Chief Financial Officer, Treasurer, Senior Vice President, Chief Financial Officer Of The Bank, Amanda Engles

Independent Director, Milissa Bauer
Independent Director, Deanna McCarrier
Independent Director, Mark Freemer
Independent Director, Robert Freeman
Independent Director, Nicholas Varischetti
Independent Director, James Crooks
Independent Director, Henry Deible
Senior Vice President, Chief Credit Officer Of The Bank, Eric Gantz
Secretary, Senior Vice President And Chief Operating Officer Of The Bank, Jennifer Poulsen, $194,151 total compensation
Independent Director, Steven Hunter
Auditors: BKD, LLP

LOCATIONS

HQ: Emclaire Financial Corp.
 612 Main Street, Emlenton, PA 16373
Phone: 844 767-2311
Web: www.emclairefinancial.com

COMPETITORS

FIDELITY D & D BANCORP INC.
 INC.
FIRST KEYSTONE CORPORATION
IDAHO INDEPENDENT BANK
LYONS NATIONAL BANK

NEFFS BANCORP

PINNACLE BANKSHARES CORPORATION
THE COMMERCE BANK OF WASHINGTON

HISTORICAL FINANCIALS

Company Type: Public

Income Statement

FYE: December 31

	ASSETS ($ mil.)	NET INCOME ($ mil.)	INCOME AS % OF ASSETS	EMPLOYEES
12/20	1,032.3	6.7	0.7%	160
12/19	915.3	7.9	0.9%	162
12/18	898.8	4.2	0.5%	164
12/17	750.0	4.2	0.6%	137
12/16	692.1	3.9	0.6%	131
Annual Growth	10.5%	14.1%	—	5.1%

2020 Year-End Financials

Return on assets: 0.6%
Return on equity: 7.5%
Long-term debt ($ mil.): —
No. of shares (mil.): 2.7
Sales ($ mil): 41.5

Dividends
 Yield: 3.9%
 Payout: 49.7%
Market value ($ mil.): 83.0

	STOCK PRICE ($) FY Close	P/E High/Low		PER SHARE ($) Earnings	Dividends	Book Value
12/20	30.63	14	7	2.41	1.20	33.62
12/19	32.53	13	10	2.86	1.16	31.70
12/18	30.34	22	17	1.72	1.12	29.65
12/17	30.35	16	13	1.93	1.08	26.02
12/16	29.25	16	12	1.85	1.04	25.12
Annual Growth	1.2%	—	—	6.8%	3.6%	7.6%

Emergent BioSolutions Inc

Emergent BioSolutions a global life sciences company focused on providing innovative preparedness and response solutions addressing accidental deliberate and naturally occurring public health threats (PHTs). Primary product BioThrax is the only FDA-approved anthrax vaccine. Most BioThrax revenue comes from direct sales to US federal agencies including the Department of Defense (DOD) and the Department of Health and Human Services (HHS). Other offerings include vaccines ACAM2000 (smallpox) Vivotif (typhoid fever) and Vaxchora (cholera); opioid overdose drug Narcan; and inhaled anthrax treatment raxibacumab. Emergent also has contract manufacturing and research operations.

Operations

The company is focused on products and solutions that address the following six distinct PHT categories: Chemical Biological Radiological Nuclear and Explosives (CBRNE); emerging infectious diseases (EID); travel health; emerging health crises; and acute/emergency care.

Its product portfolio comprises ten marketed products (vaccines therapeutics and drug-device combination products) that are sold to government and commercial customers. Its product portfolio also includes two product candidates designated AV7909 (vaccine) and Trobigard Auto-Injector (drug-device combination) that are not approved by the FDA or any other regulatory health authority but which are procured under special circumstances by certain government agencies.

The company's product development pipeline portfolio consists of a diversified mix of both preclinical and clinical-stage product candidates encompassing a mix of vaccines therapeutics and drug-device combination products. In some cases certain candidates are supported by external nondilutive funding sources (government agencies non-governmental organizations pharma/biotech innovators). Certain other candidates are supported solely by internal funding sources.

Emergent's portfolio of CDMO services consists of three distinct but interrelated service pillars: development services (process and analytical development); drug substance manufacturing; and drug product manufacturing (fill/finish) and packaging. These services which refers to as molecule-to-market offerings employ five technology platforms (mammalian microbial viral plasma and gene therapy) across a network of nine geographically distinct development and manufacturing sites operated by the company for its internal products and pipeline and CDMO services for both clinical-stage projects and commercial-stage projects. It directs these CDMO services for a variety of third-party customers including innovative pharmaceutical companies government agencies and non-government organizations.

Emergent's revenues are derived from a combination of the sale and procurement of its product portfolio and the provision of is CDMO services to external customers.

Geographic Reach

Headquartered in Gaithersburg Maryland Emergent has manufacturing laboratories fill/finish facility services offices and warehouse in about 25 locations in North America and Europe. Some of its main location are in Michigan Maryland Massachusetts California and Canada as well as in Switzerland.

Sales and Marketing

The company serves the pharma and biotech industry and government agencies as well as non-government organizations. The US Government is largest customer and also provides the company with substantial funding for the development of a number of product candidates.

The US Government accounts for about 85% of total revenue while US non-government customers' accounts about 15%.

Some of other customers for it specific products are state health departments local law enforcement agencies community-based organizations substance abuse centers federal agencies and consumers through pharmacies fulfilling physician-directed or standing order prescriptions.

Financial Performance

The company's revenue for fiscal 2020 increased to 41% to $1.6 billion compared from the prior year with $1.1 billion.

Net income for fiscal 2020 increased to $305.1 million compared from the prior year with $54.5 million.

Cash held by the company at the end of fiscal 2020 increased to $621.5 million. Cash provided by operations and financing activities were $536.0 million and $69.5 million respectively. Cash used for investing activities was $151.0 million mainly for purchases of property plant and equipment and other.

Strategy

The company's current five-year strategic plan 2020-2024 is focused on leveraging core competencies relationships and operating systems the company have developed over the last 22 years and driving growth across various segments of the PHT market. The strategic plan includes achievement of the following financial goals by the end of 2024: Total revenue of at least $2 billion; and Adjusted EBITDA margin of 27%-30%.

In pursuit of these goals the strategic plan specifies employing five core strategies. They are: Execute Core Business; Grow Through Mergers and Acquisitions (M&A); Strengthen R&D Portfolio; Build Scalable Capabilities; and Evolve the Culture.

Company Background

Emergent BioSolutions was founded in 1998 in Michigan and was reorganized as Delaware corporation in 2004.

In 2014 Emergent acquired Cangene gaining treatments BAT (botulism) Anthrasil (anthrax infection) and VIGIV (adverse vaccine reactions).

In 2016 the firm spun off its biosciences division which worked on therapies for leukemia and lymphoma and vaccines for such infectious diseases as influenza as the new public company Aptevo Therapeutics.

In 2017 Emergent acquired smallpox vaccine ACAM2000 from Sanofi. It also purchased raxibacumab an antibody product for treatment of inhalated anthrax from Human Genome Sciences GlaxoSmithKline.

EXECUTIVES

Executive Chairman, Fuad El-Hibri, $1,192,202 total compensation
Chief Executive Officer, President, And Director, Robert Kramer, $893,860 total compensation
Chief Operating Officer And Executive Vice President, Adam Havey, $546,507 total compensation
Executive Vice President, Human Resources And Chief Human Resources Officer, Katherine Strei
Executive Vice President And Chief Medical Officer, Karen Smith
Director, Marvin White

Chief Financial Officer, Executive Vice President, Treasurer, Richard Lindahl, $549,390 total compensation
Executive Vice President, Corporate Development, External Affairs, And General Counsel, Atul Saran, $528,803 total compensation
Executive Vice President - Manufacturing And Technical Operations, Sean Kirk
Auditors: Ernst & Young LLP

LOCATIONS

HQ: Emergent BioSolutions Inc
400 Professional Drive Suite 400, Gaithersburg, MD 20879
Phone: 240 631-3200
Web: www.emergentbiosolutions.com

PRODUCTS/OPERATIONS

2014 Sales

	$ mil.	% of total
Products	308.3	68
Contracts & grants	110.9	25
Contract manufacturing	30.9	7
Total	**450.1**	**100**

2014 Sales

	% of total
Biodefense	82
Biosciences	18
Total	**100**

Selected Acquisitions and Ventures

COMPETITORS

ACORDA THERAPEUTICS INC.
ASTELLAS PHARMA INC.
BIOMARIN PHARMACEUTICAL INC.
CATALENT INC.
CHARLES RIVER LABORATORIES INTERNATIONAL INC.
GRIFOLS SA
HERON THERAPEUTICS INC.
IONIS PHARMACEUTICALS INC.
NOVAVAX INC.
OPKO HEALTH INC.
ORASURE TECHNOLOGIES INC.
PTC THERAPEUTICS INC.
ULTRAGENYX PHARMACEUTICAL INC.
UNITED THERAPEUTICS CORPORATION

HISTORICAL FINANCIALS

Company Type: Public

Income Statement

FYE: December 31

	REVENUE ($ mil.)	NET INCOME ($ mil.)	NET PROFIT MARGIN	EMPLOYEES
12/20	1,555.4	305.1	19.6%	700
12/19	1,106.0	54.5	4.9%	1,834
12/18	782.4	62.7	8.0%	1,705
12/17	560.8	82.5	14.7%	1,256
12/16	488.7	51.7	10.6%	1,098
Annual Growth	**33.6%**	**55.8%**	**—**	**(10.6%)**

2020 Year-End Financials

Debt ratio: 30.3%
Return on equity: 24.0%
Cash ($ mil.): 621.3
Current ratio: 3.11
Long-term debt ($ mil.): 841.0
No. of shares (mil.): 53.1
Dividends
Yield: —
Payout: —
Market value ($ mil.): 4,758.0

STOCK PRICE ($) FY Close	P/E High/Low		PER SHARE ($) Earnings	Dividends	Book Value
12/20	89.60	23 9	5.67	0.00	27.25
12/19	53.95	62 38	1.04	0.00	21.05
12/18	59.28	59 36	1.22	0.00	19.74
12/17	46.47	24 14	1.71	0.00	18.47
12/16	32.84	34 19	1.13	0.00	14.69
Annual Growth	**28.5%**	**—**	**49.7%**	**—**	**16.7%**

ENB Financial Corp

EXECUTIVES

Independent Director, Joshua Hoffman
Independent Director, Mark Wagner
Independent Director, Willis Lefever
Independent Director, Jay Martin
Chairman Of The Board, President, Chief Executive Officer Of The Company And Ephrata National Bank, Jeffrey Stauffer, $261,322 total compensation
Senior Vice President, Chief Lending Officer, Eric Williams
Chief Operating Officer, Senior Vice President, Matthew Long
Chief Human Resource Officer, Senior Vice President, Cindy Hoffman
Independent Director, Roger Zimmerman
Principal Financial Officer, Treasurer, Rachel Bitner
Executive Vice President And Chief Risk Officer Of Ephrata National Bank, Nicholas Klein
Independent Director, Brian Reed
Independent Director, Susan Nicholas
Director, Aaron Groff
Independent Director, Judith Weaver
Auditors: S.R. Snodgrass, P.C.

LOCATIONS

HQ: ENB Financial Corp
31 E. Main St., Ephrata, PA 17522-0457
Phone: 717 733-4181
Web: www.enbfc.com

HISTORICAL FINANCIALS

Company Type: Public

Income Statement

FYE: December 31

	ASSETS ($ mil.)	NET INCOME ($ mil.)	INCOME AS % OF ASSETS	EMPLOYEES
12/20	1,462.3	12.3	0.8%	276
12/19	1,171.7	11.4	1.0%	280
12/18	1,097.8	9.7	0.9%	294
12/17	1,033.6	6.3	0.6%	285
12/16	984.2	7.5	0.8%	270
Annual Growth	**10.4%**	**13.0%**	**—**	**0.6%**

2020 Year-End Financials

Return on assets: 0.9%
Return on equity: 9.9%
Long-term debt ($ mil.): —
No. of shares (mil.): 5.5
Sales ($ mil): 57.4
Dividends
Yield: 0.0%
Payout: 29.0%
Market value ($ mil.): 104.0

STOCK PRICE ($) FY Close	P/E High/Low		PER SHARE ($) Earnings	Dividends	Book Value
12/20	18.60	11 8	2.20	0.64	23.39
12/19	20.75	20 10	2.01	0.62	20.69
12/18	34.55	22 20	1.71	0.58	18.02
12/17	34.25	32 29	1.12	0.56	17.50
12/16	34.40	26 24	1.33	0.55	16.65
Annual Growth	**(14.2%)**	**—**	**13.5%**	**4.1%**	**8.9%**

Encore Capital Group Inc

Encore Capital Group is an international specialty finance company that provides debt recovery solutions and other related services across a broad range of financial assets. Encore Capital purchase portfolios of defaulted consumer receivables at deep discounts to face value and manage them by working with individuals as they repay their obligations and work toward financial recovery. Defaulted receivables are consumers' unpaid financial commitments to credit originators including banks credit unions consumer finance companies and commercial retailers. Defaulted receivables may also include receivables subject to bankruptcy proceedings. The company also provide debt servicing and other portfolio management services to credit originators for non-performing loans. Around 65% of total revenue comes from domestic operation.

Operations

Encore Capital provides debt recovery solutions and other related services for consumers across a broad range of financial assets. It also provide debt servicing and other portfolio management services to credit originators for non-performing loans. Overall revenues from receivable portfolios accounts about 90% while services and others accounts the remainder of total revenue.

Encore Capital has two primary business units: Midland Credit Management (MCM) and its and domestic affiliates; Cabot Credit Management Limited (CCM) and its subsidiaries and European affiliates Cabot. Through MCM Encore Capital is a market leader in portfolio purchasing and recovery in the US including Puerto Rico. Cabot's primary business of portfolio purchasing and recovery also provides a range of debt servicing offerings such as early stage collections business process outsourcing (BPO) including through Wescot Credit Services Limited (Wescot) a leading U.K. contingency debt collection and BPO services company.

Geographic Reach

The San Diego-headquartered Encore Capital operates in US Europe and Latin America. Encore Capital maintain domestic collection call centers in Phoenix Arizona St. Cloud Minnesota Troy Michigan and Roanoke Virginia and international call centers in Gurgaon India and San Jose Costa Rica.

Its largest market is the US where it generated around 65% of its revenue while Europe accounted for roughly 35% and other countries accounts for the remaining revenue.

Sales and Marketing

Encore Capital maintain relationships with various financial service providers such as banks credit unions consumer finance companies retailers utilities companies and government agencies. It markets services through direct mail call centers legal action third-party collection agencies and digital collections.

Financial Performance

The company's revenue for fiscal 2020 increased to $1.5 billion compared from the prior year with $1.4 billion.

Net income for fiscal 2020 increased to $212.5 million compared from the prior year with $168.9 million.

Cash held by the company at the end of fiscal 2020 decreased to $189.2 million. Cash provided by operations and investing activities were $312.9 million and $82.8 million respectively. Cash used for financing activities were $403.2 million mainly for repayment of credit facilities.

Strategy

The company's long-term growth strategy is focused on continuing to invest in its core portfolio purchasing and recovery business in the United States and United Kingdom and strengthening and developing its business in the rest of Europe. It is striving to enhance its competitive advantages through innovation which it expects will result in collections growth and improved productivity. To continue generating strong risk-adjusted returns the company intends to continue investing in analytics and technology risk management and compliance. It will also continue investing in initiatives that enhance its relationships with consumers expand its digital capabilities and collections improve liquidation rates on own portfolios or reduce costs.

Encore Capital continues to concentrate on its core portfolio purchasing and recovery business in the U.S. and the U.K. markets where scale helps it generate its highest risk-adjusted returns. The company believes these markets have attractive structural characteristics including a large and consistent flow of purchasing opportunities a strong regulatory framework with barriers to entry that support issuers to outsource or sell a high degree of sophistication and data availability and stable long term returns and resilience in the event of macroeconomic disruption.

It is also focusing on strengthening its balance sheet while delivering strong financial and operational results. This includes increasing its cash flow through efficient collection operations and applying excess cash flows to reduce its debt which allows it to grow estimated remaining collections and earnings while at the same time reducing financial leverage.

Company Background

In early 2016 the company sold its San Antonio Texas-based Propel Acquisition LLC subsidiary which acquired and serviced residential and commercial tax liens on property. The firm was the largest tax lien company in Texas.

EXECUTIVES

Executive Vice President, Chief Administrative Officer, General Counsel, Corporate Secretary, Gregory Call, $421,132 total compensation
President - Midland Credit Management, Ryan Bell, $433,644 total compensation
Independent Director, Richard Srednicki
Independent Director, Laura Olle
Independent Director, Wendy Hannam
Independent Director, Ashwini Gupta
Independent Director, Richard Stovsky
Independent Director, Jeffrey Hilzinger
Independent Director, Angela Knight
Chief Executive Officer Of The Cabot Credit Management Group, Craig Buick, $490,118 total compensation
Senior Vice President, Chief Risk, And Compliance Officer, Steve Carmichael
President, Chief Executive Officer, Director, Ashish Masih, $764,260 total compensation
Non-executive Independent Chairman Of The Board, Michael Monaco
Chief Financial Officer, Executive Vice President, Treasurer, Jonathan Clark, $605,377 total compensation
Auditors: BDO USA, LLP

LOCATIONS

HQ: Encore Capital Group Inc
350 Camino De La Reina, Suite 100, San Diego, CA 92108
Phone: 877 445-4581
Web: www.encorecapital.com

PRODUCTS/OPERATIONS

2015 Sales

	$ mil.	% of total
Portfolio purchasing and recovery	1,130.0	97
Tax lien business	31.6	3
Total	**1,161.6**	**100**

Selected Subsidiaries

Ascension Capital Group Inc.
Cabot Financial (UK Ireland)
Grove Financial (UK)
Marlin Financial Group (UK)
MCM Midland Management Costa Rica S.r.l.
Midland Credit Management Inc.
Midland Credit Management India Private Limited
Midland Funding LLC
Midland Funding NCC-2 Corporation
Midland India LLC
Midland International LLC
Midland Portfolio Services Inc.
MRC Receivables Corporation
Propel Financial Services (US)
Refinancia S.A. (Colombia Peru)

COMPETITORS

ABN AMRO COMMERCIAL FINANCE PLC	NATIONAL AUSTRALIA BANK LIMITED
ACCESS CAPITAL INC.	NICHOLAS FINANCIAL INC.
ALLY COMMERCIAL FINANCE LLC	The Bank of Nova Scotia
AMERISOURCE FUNDING INC.	UMPQUA HOLDINGS CORPORATION
Banco Bradesco S/A	WHITE OAK COMMERCIAL FINANCE LLC
Bank of Communications Co. Ltd.	

HISTORICAL FINANCIALS

Company Type: Public

Income Statement

FYE: December 31

	REVENUE ($ mil.)	NET INCOME ($ mil.)	NET PROFIT MARGIN	EMPLOYEES
12/20	1,501.4	211.8	14.1%	7,725
12/19	1,397.6	167.8	12.0%	7,300
12/18	1,362.0	115.8	8.5%	7,900
12/17	1,187.0	83.2	7.0%	8,200
12/16	1,029.2	76.5	7.4%	6,700
Annual Growth	**9.9%**	**29.0%**	**—**	**3.6%**

2020 Year-End Financials

Debt ratio: 67.4%	No. of shares (mil.): 31.3
Return on equity: 18.8%	Dividends
Cash ($ mil.): 189.1	Yield: —
Current ratio: 1.18	Payout: —
Long-term debt ($ mil.): 3,281.6	Market value ($ mil.): 1,221.0

	STOCK PRICE ($) FY Close	P/E High/Low		PER SHARE ($) Earnings	Dividends	Book Value
12/20	38.95	7	2	6.68	0.00	33.85
12/19	35.36	7	5	5.33	0.00	32.87
12/18	23.50	11	5	4.06	0.00	26.49
12/17	42.10	15	9	3.15	0.00	22.55
12/16	28.65	10	6	2.96	0.00	21.85
Annual Growth	**8.0%**	**—**	**—**	**22.6%**	**—**	**15.5%**

Encore Wire Corp.

A low-cost manufacturer of copper electrical building wire and cable Encore Wire produces NM-B cable a sheathed cable used to wire homes apartments and manufactured housing and UF-B cable an underground feeder cable for outside lighting and remote residential building connections. Its inventory of stock-keeping units include THWN-2 cable an insulated feeder circuit and branch wiring for commercial and industrial buildings and other wires like armored cable. The company's principal customers are wholesale electrical distributors that sells its products to electrical contractors. The company was founded in 1989.

Operations

The company conducts its business in one segment ? the manufacture of electric building wire principally NM-B cable for use primarily as interior wiring in homes apartments and manufactured housing and THHN/THWN-2 cable and metal-clad and armored cable for use primarily as wiring in commercial and industrial buildings. It also offers UF-B cable XHHW-2 USE-2 RHH/RHW-2 and other types of wire products including SEU SER Photovoltaic URD tray cable metal-clad and armored cable. All of these products are manufactured with copper or aluminum as the current-carrying component of the conductor.

Geographic Reach

Encore primarily maintains its headquarters and manufacturing plants in McKinney Texas.

Sales and Marketing

Encore mainly provides interior electrical wiring in commercial and industrial buildings homes apartments manufactured housing and data centers. The principal customers for Encore's wire are wholesale electrical distributors who sell building wire and a variety of other products to electrical contractors. It sells its products primarily through independent manufacturers' representatives located throughout US and to a lesser extent through its own direct in-house marketing efforts.

Financial Performance

Net sales for the twelve months ended December 31 2020 were $1.277 billion compared to $1.275 billion during the same period in 2019. Copper unit volume measured in pounds of copper contained in the wire sold decreased 5% in the twelve months ended December 31 2020 versus the twelve months ended December 31 2019.

In 2020 the company had a net income of $76.1 million a 31% increase from the previous year's net income of $58.1 million.

The company's cash at the end of 2020 was $183.1 million. Operating activities generated $57.5 million while investing activities used $86 million primarily for purchases of property plant and equipment. Financing activities used another $19.3 million primarily for purchase of treasury stock.

Strategy

Encore's strategy is to further expand its share of the building wire market primarily by emphasizing a high level of customer service and the addition of new products that complement its current product line while maintaining and enhancing its low-cost production capabilities. Encore's low-cost production capability features an efficient plant design incorporating highly automated manufacturing equipment an integrated production process and a highly-motivated work force. Encore's plants are all located on one large campus. This single-site campus enables and enhances low-cost manufacturing distribution and administration as well as helping to build and maintain a cohesive company culture.

Customer Service: Encore is highly focused on responding to customer needs with an emphasis on building and maintaining strong customer relationships. Encore seeks to establish customer loyalty by achieving an industry-leading order fill rate and rapidly handling customer orders shipments inquiries and returns. The company maintains product inventories sufficient to meet anticipated customer demand and believes that the speed and completeness with which it fills orders are key competitive advantages critical to marketing its products.

Product Innovation: Encore has been a leader in bringing new ideas to a commodity product. Encore pioneered the widespread use of color feeder sizes of commercial wire and colors in residential non-metallic cable. The colors have improved on-the-job safety reduced installation times for contractors and enabled building inspectors to rapidly and accurately inspect construction projects. Encore Wire's patented SmartColor ID system for metal-clad and armor-clad cables allows for quick and accurate identification of gauge number of conductors wire and jacket type.

Low-Cost Production: Encore's low-cost production capability features an efficient plant design and an incentivized work force.

Company Background

Industry veterans Vincent Rego and Donald Spurgin founded Encore Wire in 1989 to make wire for residential use after their previous company Capital Wire was bought out by Penn Central in 1988. Encore rolled through the home-building recession of the early 1990s gathering market share along the way. The company went public in 1992.

EXECUTIVES

Chairman Of The Board, President, Chief Executive Officer, Daniel Jones, $925,000 total compensation
Independent Director, Scott Weaver
Lead Independent Director, John Wilson
Independent Director, William Thomas
Independent Director, Gregory Fisher

Chief Financial Officer, Vice President - Finance, Treasurer, Secretary, Bret Eckert, $400,000 total compensation
Independent Director, Gina Norris
Auditors: Ernst & Young LLP

LOCATIONS

HQ: Encore Wire Corp.
1329 Millwood Road, McKinney, TX 75069
Phone: 972 562-9473   **Fax:** 972 562-4744
Web: www.encorewire.com

PRODUCTS/OPERATIONS

Selected Products

Armored Cable (multiple conductors insulated with PVC and coated with nylon used primarily as feeder circuit and branch wiring in commercial and industrial buildings)
NM-B Cable (non-metallic sheathed cable for interior wiring in homes)
Photovoltaic Cable (used by the solar industry providing connections between PV panels colllector boxes and inverters)
THWN-2 Cable (single conductor insulated with PVC and coated with nylon used primarily as feeder circuit and branch wiring in commercial and industrial buildings)
UF-B Cable (underground feeder cable for conducting power underground to outside lighting and other remote residential applications)
USE-2 Cable (general purpose applications; conduit or installed in underground sites or in recognized raceways for service feeders and branch-circuit wiring)
XHHW-2 Cable (used as feeder circuit and branch wiring in commercial and industrial buildings)

COMPETITORS

ASSOCIATED MATERIALS LLC	KAISER ALUMINUM CORPORATION
CHAMPLAIN CABLE CORPORATION	KALAS MFG. INC.
CORNING OPTICAL COMMUNICATIONS LLC	OLYMPIC STEEL INC.
	OMEGA FLEX INC.
FUJIKURA LTD.	SUPERIOR ESSEX INC.
HOUSTON WIRE & CABLE COMPANY	Taihan Cable & Solution Co. Ltd.
INTERNATIONAL WIRE GROUP INC.	VOLEX PLC
	W. L. GORE & ASSOCIATES INC.

HISTORICAL FINANCIALS

Company Type: Public

Income Statement

FYE: December 31

	REVENUE ($ mil.)	NET INCOME ($ mil.)	NET PROFIT MARGIN	EMPLOYEES
12/21	2,592.7	541.4	20.9%	1,440
12/20	1,276.9	76.0	6.0%	1,289
12/19	1,274.9	58.1	4.6%	1,380
12/18	1,288.6	78.1	6.1%	1,278
12/17	1,164.2	67.0	5.8%	1,235
Annual Growth	22.2%	68.6%	—	3.9%

2021 Year-End Financials

Debt ratio: —	No. of shares (mil.): 20.1
Return on equity: 49.7%	Dividends
Cash ($ mil.): 438.9	Yield: 0.0%
Current ratio: 6.72	Payout: 0.3%
Long-term debt ($ mil.): —	Market value ($ mil.): 2,882.0

	STOCK PRICE ($) FY Close	P/E High/Low		PER SHARE ($) Earnings	Dividends	Book Value
12/21	143.10	6	2	26.22	0.08	66.49
12/20	60.57	16	10	3.68	0.08	40.75
12/19	57.40	22	18	2.77	0.08	37.26
12/18	50.18	15	11	3.74	0.08	34.51
12/17	48.65	15	12	3.21	0.08	30.79
Annual Growth	31.0%	—	—	69.1%	(0.0%)	21.2%

Energizer Holdings Inc (New)

Auditors: PricewaterhouseCoopers LLP

LOCATIONS

HQ: Energizer Holdings Inc (New)
533 Maryville University Drive, St. Louis, MO 63141
Phone: 314 985-2000
Web: www.energizerholdings.com

HISTORICAL FINANCIALS

Company Type: Public

Income Statement

FYE: September 30

	REVENUE ($ mil.)	NET INCOME ($ mil.)	NET PROFIT MARGIN	EMPLOYEES
09/21	3,021.5	160.9	5.3%	6,000
09/20	2,744.8	(93.3)	—	5,900
09/19	2,494.5	51.1	2.0%	7,500
09/18	1,797.7	93.5	5.2%	4,000
09/17	1,755.7	201.5	11.5%	4,400
Annual Growth	14.5%	(5.5%)	—	8.1%

2021 Year-End Financials

Debt ratio: 68.9%	No. of shares (mil.): 66.8
Return on equity: 48.4%	Dividends
Cash ($ mil.): 238.9	Yield: 3.0%
Current ratio: 1.52	Payout: 857.1%
Long-term debt ($ mil.): 3,333.4	Market value ($ mil.): 2,611.0

	STOCK PRICE ($) FY Close	P/E High/Low		PER SHARE ($) Earnings	Dividends	Book Value
09/21	39.05	24	18	2.11	1.20	5.32
09/20	39.14	—	—	(1.58)	1.20	4.51
09/19	43.58	104	57	0.58	1.20	7.89
09/18	58.65	42	27	1.52	1.16	0.41
09/17	46.05	18	13	3.22	1.10	1.40
Annual Growth	(4.0%)	—	—	(10.0%)	2.2%	39.6%

Energy Recovery Inc

Desalination makes seawater potable; Energy Recovery (ERI) makes desalination practical. The company designs develops and manufactures energy recovery devices used in sea water reverse osmosis (SWRO) desalination plants. The SWRO process is energy intensive using high pressure to drive salt water through membranes to produce fresh water. The company's main product the PX Pressure Exchanger helps recapture and recycle up to 98% of the energy available in the high-pressure reject stream a by-product of the SWRO process. The PX can reduce the energy consumption of a desalination plant by up to 60% compared with a plant lacking an energy recovery device. Subsidiary Pump Engineering also makes high pressure pumps.

Geographic Reach

ERI has its headquarters and main manufacturing center located in California. Other offices reside in Shanghai and Dubai.

Sales and Marketing

Primary customers for ERI consist of international engineering procurement and construction firms that build large desalination plants. Energy Recovery also sells its products and services to OEMs of pumps and other water-related equipment for small to mid-size plants used in hotels cruise ships farm operations and power plants. Major customers have included IDE Technologies Ltd Thiess Degremont J.V. Hydrochem Acciona Agua and UTE Mostaganem.

Financial Performance

ERI's revenues decreased 29% from 2013 to 2014. The decrease was primarily due to significantly lower mega-project (MPD) shipments as well as lower OEM shipments. The decreases in MPD and OEM sales were offset by higher aftermarket shipments and revenue attributable to an oil and gas operating lease and lease buy-out.

ERI has suffered five straight years of net losses. Its $19 million net loss in 2014 was fueled by higher sales and marketing expenses coupled with the lower net revenue. Research and development expenses also spiked during 2014.

Strategy

Going forward ERI intends to benefit from a significant presence in Spain and other countries. Energy Recovery's lineup for example supports most of Spain's desalination plants. ERI also plans to enter into the material science and manufacturing of ceramics — a key component of its PX devices. The strategy aims to boost device production cut costs and improve product quality.

EXECUTIVES

Chief Technology Officer, Farshad Ghasripoor, $281,709 total compensation
Chief Financial Officer, Joshua Ballard, $332,813 total compensation
Lead Independent Director, Pamela Tondreau
Director, Lisa Pollina
Director, Joan Chow
Chairman Of The Board, President, Chief Executive Officer, yu Lang Mao, $481,539 total compensation
Independent Director, Olav Fjell
Chief Legal Officer, William Yeung
Independent Director, Alexander Buehler
Senior Vice President Of Water, Rodney Clemente, $315,000 total compensation
Auditors: DELOITTE & TOUCHE LLP

LOCATIONS

HQ: Energy Recovery Inc
1717 Doolittle Drive, San Leandro, CA 94577
Phone: 510 483-7370
Web: www.energyrecovery.com

PRODUCTS/OPERATIONS

2014 Sales

	$ mil.	% of total
PX devices & related products & services	20.9	69
Turbochargers & pumps	8.7	29
Oil and gas product operating lease	0.8	2
Total	**30.4**	**100**

PRODUCTS

VorTeq
IsoBoost
IsoGen
IsoBoost for Syngas & Ammonia
PX Pressure Exchanger
Turbochargers
Pumping Systems

Selected Products

Energy recovery devices
 PX pressure exchanger devices (PX-300 the 65 series the 4S series and brackish PX devices)
 Turbochargers (HTCAT series the HALO line and the LPT series for brackish water desalination)
 High pressure and circulation pumps (AquaBold series the AquaSpire series and a line of small circulation pumps)
Technical support and replacement parts

COMPETITORS

ADVANTEST CORPORATION
AMERICAN SUPERCONDUCTOR CORPORATION
AMTECH SYSTEMS INC.
AXCELIS TECHNOLOGIES INC.
Andritz AG
D rr AG
FEDERAL-MOGUL LLC
INTEVAC INC.
PMFG INC.
SPX FLOW INC.
TRANSENSE TECHNOLOGIES PLC
VEECO INSTRUMENTS INC.

HISTORICAL FINANCIALS

Company Type: Public

Income Statement				FYE: December 31
	REVENUE ($ mil.)	NET INCOME ($ mil.)	NET PROFIT MARGIN	EMPLOYEES
12/20	118.9	26.3	22.2%	216
12/19	86.9	10.9	12.6%	188
12/18	74.5	22.0	29.6%	143
12/17	63.1	12.3	19.6%	133
12/16	54.7	1.0	1.9%	120
Annual Growth	**21.4%**	**124.8%**	**—**	**15.8%**

2020 Year-End Financials

Debt ratio: —	No. of shares (mil.): 56.3
Return on equity: 17.1%	Dividends
Cash ($ mil.): 94.2	Yield: —
Current ratio: 9.10	Payout: —
Long-term debt ($ mil.): —	Market value ($ mil.): 769.0

	STOCK PRICE ($) FY Close	P/E High/Low		PER SHARE ($)		
				Earnings	Dividends	Book Value
12/20	13.64	29	14	0.47	0.00	3.05
12/19	9.79	59	34	0.19	0.00	2.46
12/18	6.73	24	16	0.40	0.00	2.10
12/17	8.75	49	27	0.22	0.00	1.53
12/16	10.35	818268		0.02	0.00	1.23
Annual Growth	**7.1%**	**—**	**—120.2%**		**—**	**25.6%**

Enerkon Solar International Inc

EXECUTIVES

President, Chief Executive Officer, Chief Financial Officer, Director, Benjamin Ballout
Secretary, Treasurer And Director, Michael Studer
Vice President - International Business Development, Ibrahim Nattar
Chairman Of The Board, Daniel Priscu
Auditors: Massella Rubenstein LLP

LOCATIONS

HQ: Enerkon Solar International Inc
477 Madison Avenue, 6th Floor - #6834, New York, NY 10022
Phone: 877 573-7797
Web: www.enerkoninternational.com

HISTORICAL FINANCIALS

Company Type: Public

Income Statement				FYE: September 30
	REVENUE ($ mil.)	NET INCOME ($ mil.)	NET PROFIT MARGIN	EMPLOYEES
09/20	65.1	13.1	20.2%	0
09/19	76.0	14.2	18.8%	0
09/18	18.9	1.8	9.7%	0
09/17	0.0	(0.1)	—	0
09/16	0.0	(0.2)	—	0
Annual Growth	**838.7%**			

2020 Year-End Financials

Debt ratio: 8.5%	No. of shares (mil.): 65.6
Return on equity: 38.7%	Dividends
Cash ($ mil.): 24.0	Yield: —
Current ratio: 1.85	Payout: —
Long-term debt ($ mil.): 8.3	Market value ($ mil.): 3.0

	STOCK PRICE ($) FY Close	P/E High/Low		PER SHARE ($)		
				Earnings	Dividends	Book Value
09/20	0.04	—	—	(0.00)	0.00	0.74
09/19	0.17	—	—	(0.00)	0.00	0.42
09/18	0.10	—	—	(0.00)	0.00	0.11
09/17	0.05	—	—	(0.00)	0.00	0.00
09/16	0.05	—	—	(0.01)	0.00	0.01
Annual Growth	**(2.9%) 247.3%**			**—**	**—**	**—**

Enova International Inc

Auditors: PricewaterhouseCoopers LLP

LOCATIONS

HQ: Enova International Inc
175 West Jackson Blvd., Chicago, IL 60604
Phone: 312 568-4200
Web: www.enova.com

HOOVER'S HANDBOOK OF EMERGING COMPANIES 2022

HISTORICAL FINANCIALS

Company Type: Public

Income Statement
FYE: December 31

	REVENUE ($ mil.)	NET INCOME ($ mil.)	NET PROFIT MARGIN	EMPLOYEES
12/20	1,083.7	377.8	34.9%	1,549
12/19	1,174.7	36.6	3.1%	1,325
12/18	1,114.0	70.1	6.3%	1,218
12/17	843.7	29.2	3.5%	1,109
12/16	745.5	34.6	4.6%	1,099
Annual Growth	9.8%	81.8%	—	9.0%

2020 Year-End Financials

Debt ratio: 44.9%
Return on equity: 58.2%
Cash ($ mil.): 369.2
Current ratio: 3.23
Long-term debt ($ mil.): 946.4

No. of shares (mil.): 35.7
Dividends
  Yield: —
  Payout: —
Market value ($ mil.): 886.0

	STOCK PRICE ($) FY Close	P/E High/Low		PER SHARE ($) Earnings	Dividends	Book Value
12/20	24.77	2	1	11.70	0.00	25.65
12/19	24.06	28	18	1.06	0.00	11.42
12/18	19.46	19	8	1.99	0.00	10.35
12/17	15.20	19	13	0.86	0.00	8.41
12/16	12.55	13	5	1.03	0.00	7.26
Annual Growth	18.5%	—	—	83.6%	—	37.1%

Enphase Energy Inc.

Enphase Energy is ready to usher in a new phase of solar power. The company makes all-in-one solar panel systems for residential and commercial use in the US and Canada. Unlike typical small-scale photovoltaic systems Enphase's solar modules are connected on a microinverter system where each panel has its own inverter that converts the sun's rays into electricity. The company claims its microinverter technology is more energy efficient than having all the panels hooked up to one big inverter. Enphase Energy sells its solar power systems to a network of thousands of distributors.

Operations

Enphase Energy's microinverters convert direct current produced by solar panels to alternating current that's routed to the grid. Solar farms typically connect multiple panels to a single larger inverter while Enphase's smaller products are designed to be wired to a single panel thereby increasing efficiency. Since its founding in 2008 the company has sold approximately 11 million microinverters. The company outsources the manufacturing of its products to two key manufacturing partners Flextronics International Ltd. and Phoenix Contact GmbH & Co. KG.

Geographic Reach

California-based Enphase rings up 85% of its sales in the US. International markets include Canada Mexico the UK the Benelux region France China New Zealand and Australia.

Sales and Marketing

Enphase counts solar distributors Vivint Solar and CED Greentech among its major customers accounting for 12% and 7% of total net revenues

respectively in 2015. The company also sell directly to large installers OEMs and strategic partners.

Financial Performance

The company has experienced significant growth with revenues peaking at a record-setting $357 million in 2015. The company credited the gain to increased in microinverter units shipped as well as a larger mix of microinverter accessories. Despite the historic revenues Enphase reported a loss of nearly $22 million during 2015 mostly due to an uptick in expenses from salaries and stock-based compensation. In addition the company has posted eight straight years of negative operating cash flow.

Strategy

Enphase's goal is to maintain its status as the leading provider of microinverter systems for the solar industry worldwide and to accelerate the shift from traditional center inverters to microinverter technology. It plans to do so by expanding its market share in its core US market entering new geographic markets increasing power and efficiency and reducing cost per watt generated and extending its technological innovation. It also aims to expand its product offering for commercial installations and utility-scale installations.

The company also intends to further increase its market share in Europe the Asia Pacific region and Latin America. In addition it intends to expand into new markets with new and existing products and local go-to-market capabilities.

EXECUTIVES

Lead Independent Director, Steven Gomo
Independent Director, Jamie Haenggi
Chief Operating Officer, Executive Vice President, Jeffrey McNeil, $316,260 total compensation
Independent Director, Joseph Malchow
Chief Marketing Officer, Allison Johnson
President, Chief Executive Officer And Director, Badrinarayanan Kothandaraman, $450,000 total compensation
Executive Vice President And Chief Commercial Officer, David Ranhoff, $400,000 total compensation
Auditors: DELOITTE & TOUCHE LLP

LOCATIONS

HQ: Enphase Energy Inc.
  47281 Bayside Parkway, Fremont, CA 94538
Phone: 877 774-7000
Web: www.enphase.com

COMPETITORS

AMERICAN SUPERCONDUCTOR CORPORATION
BLOOM ENERGY CORPORATION
GENERAC HOLDINGS INC.
LATTICE SEMICONDUCTOR CORPORATION
MONOLITHIC POWER SYSTEMS INC.
POWER INTEGRATIONS INC.
SOLAREDGE TECHNOLOGIES INC.
ULTRA CLEAN HOLDINGS INC.

HISTORICAL FINANCIALS

Company Type: Public

Income Statement
FYE: December 31

	REVENUE ($ mil.)	NET INCOME ($ mil.)	NET PROFIT MARGIN	EMPLOYEES
12/21	1,382.0	145.4	10.5%	2,260
12/20	774.4	134.0	17.3%	850
12/19	624.3	161.1	25.8%	577
12/18	316.1	(11.6)	—	427
12/17	286.1	(45.1)	—	336
Annual Growth	48.2%	—	—	61.0%

2021 Year-End Financials

Debt ratio: 49.9%
Return on equity: 31.8%
Cash ($ mil.): 119.3
Current ratio: 3.33
Long-term debt ($ mil.): 951.5

No. of shares (mil.): 133.8
Dividends
  Yield: —
  Payout: —
Market value ($ mil.): 24,495.0

	STOCK PRICE ($) FY Close	P/E High/Low		PER SHARE ($) Earnings	Dividends	Book Value
12/21	182.94	246	105	1.02	0.00	3.21
12/20	175.47	170	22	0.95	0.00	3.75
12/19	26.13	25	3	1.23	0.00	2.21
12/18	4.73	—	—	(0.12)	0.00	0.07
12/17	2.41	—	—	(0.54)	0.00	(0.11)
Annual Growth	195.2%					

Ensign Group Inc

The Ensign Group offers skilled nursing senior living and rehabilitative care services through nearly 230 senior living facilities as well as other ancillary businesses (including mobile diagnostics and medical transportation) in about a dozen of states. In addition it acquire lease and own healthcare real estate in addition to servicing the post-acute care continuum through accretive acquisition and investment opportunities in healthcare properties. Its transitional and skilled services companies provided skilled nursing care at nearly 220 operations with more than 23170 operational beds. It provides short and long-term nursing care services for patients with chronic conditions prolonged illness and the elderly.

Operations

In the fourth quarter of 2020 Ensign began reporting the results of its real estate portfolio as a new segment due to its expanding real estate investment strategy. The company has now two reportable segments: transitional and skilled services (accounts for nearly 95% of total revenue) which includes the operation of skilled nursing facilities and rehabilitation therapy services; and real estate (less than 5%) which is primarily comprised of properties owned by the company and leased to skilled nursing and senior living operations including its own operating subsidiaries and third-party operators and are subject to triple-net long-term leases.

Other business (about 5% of total revenue) includes operating results from its senior living operations mobile diagnostics transportation and other ancillary operations.

Geographic Reach

California-based Ensign has facilities in more than a dozen states: Arizona California Colorado Idaho Iowa Kansas Nebraska Nevada South Carolina Texas Utah Washington and Wisconsin.

California and Texas are the company's largest markets home to more than half of its nursing home beds.

Sales and Marketing

As part of its business the company relies on reimbursement from government and commercial health insurance plans as well as sales to private pay customers. Ensign generates about 75% of its revenue from Medicaid and Medicare programs. Managed care companies account for more than 15% of sales with private payers and others accounting for the rest of revenue.

Financial Performance

Ensign has seen strong steady growth in recent years with revenue almost doubling between 2016 and 2020. Net income declined in 2017 but recovered and posted increases in the next three years.

Revenue increased by 18% in 2020 to some $2.4 billion. The increase in revenue was primarily driven by strong performance across its transitional and skilled services operations which collectively grew by $353.9 million or about 18% with Medicare and managed care revenue accounting for the majority of the increase.

Net income increased by 54% to $170.5 million in 2020 due largely to higher revenue.

The company ended 2020 with $236.8 million in cash up $177.4 million from 2019. Operating activities contributed $373.4 million while investing and financing activities used $58.7 million and $137.3 million respectively. Ensign's main cash uses in 2020 were payments on revolving credit facility and purchases of property and equipment.

Strategy

The company believes that the following strategies are primarily responsible for its growth to date and will continue to drive the growth of its business:

Grow Talent Base and Develop Future Leaders: The strategy is to expand its talent base and develop future leaders. A key component of its organizational culture is its belief that strong local leadership is a primary key to the success of each operation.

Increase Mix of High Acuity Patients: Ensign believes that it can continue to attract high acuity patients to its operations by maintaining and enhancing its reputation for quality care and continuing its community focused approach.

Focus on Organic Growth and Internal Operating Efficiencies: It plans to continue to grow organically by focusing on increasing patient occupancy within its existing operations. It also believes it can generate organic growth by improving operating efficiencies and the quality of care at the patient level. By focusing on staff development clinical systems and the efficient delivery of quality patient care it believes it will be able to deliver higher quality care at lower costs than many of its competitors.

Add New Facilities and Expand Existing Facilities: It plans to take advantage of the fragmented skilled nursing industry by acquiring operations within select geographic markets and may consider the construction of new facilities. In addition it has targeted facilities that it believed were performing and operations that were underperforming and where it believed it could improve service delivery occupancy rates and cash flow.

Mergers and Acquisitions

Ensign regularly boosts its facility portfolio through purchases of both struggling and well-performing businesses.

In 2021 Ensign acquired the real estate and operations of Windsor Rehabilitation and Healthcare a 108-bed skilled nursing facility located in Terrell TX. This acquisition brings Ensign's growing portfolio to 236 healthcare operations 22 of which also include senior living operations across thirteen states. Ensign owns 95 real estate assets.

Also in 2021 Ensign acquired Boulder Canyon Health and Rehabilitation a 140-bed skilled nursing facility located in Boulder CO; Berthoud Care and Rehabilitation a 76-bed skilled nursing facility located in Berthoud CO; and South Valley Post Acute Rehabilitation a 106-bed skilled nursing facility located in Denver CO.

In early 2021 Ensign acquired Golden Hill Post Acute a skilled nursing facility with 99 skilled nursing beds located in San Diego CA; St. Catherine Healthcare a skilled nursing facility with 99 skilled nursing beds located in Fullerton CA; and Camino Healthcare a skilled nursing facility with 99 skilled nursing beds located in Hawthorne CA.

Ensign acquired the operations of San Pedro Manor a 150-bed skilled nursing facility located in San Antonio Texas in 2021. This acquisition is a perfect fit with its existing facilities in Texas and for the continued growth in the San Antonio area.

Also in 2020 it acquired the real estate and operations of a post-acute care retirement campus located in Tempe AZ. The acquisition includes Tempe Post Acute a 62-bed skilled nursing facility and Desert Marigold Senior Living of Tempe a senior living center with 72 assisted living beds and 90 independent living units.

In 2020 the company acquired the real estate and operations of The Healthcare Center at Patriot Heights a healthcare campus with 59 skilled nursing beds and 158 independent living units located in San Antonio Texas. The acquisition is to strengthen its presence in Texas with the addition of this healthcare campus which greatly enhances its existing operations in the San Antonio market. It also acquired the operations of two skilled nursing facilities located in Commerce City Colorado. The acquisitions include Ridgeview Post Acute a skilled nursing facility with 105 skilled nursing beds and Irondale Post Acute a skilled nursing facility with 83 skilled nursing beds.

Company Background

Ensign Group was founded in 1999. The company spun off some of its assets into CareTrust REIT in 2014.

EXECUTIVES

Independent Director, Swati Abbott

Chief Financial Officer, Executive Vice President, Director, Suzanne Snapper, $391,400 total compensation

Co-founder, Executive Chairman, Chairman Of The Board, Christopher Christensen, $538,579 total compensation

Chief Executive Officer, Director, Barry Port, $473,800 total compensation

Independent Director, Barry Smith

Executive Vice President, Chief Investment Officer, Secretary, Chad Keetch, $355,350 total compensation

President, Chief Operating Officer, Spencer Burton, $301,275 total compensation

Auditors: DELOITTE & TOUCHE LLP

LOCATIONS

HQ: Ensign Group Inc
29222 Rancho Viejo Road, Suite 127, San Juan Capistrano, CA 92675
Phone: 949 487-9500
Web: www.ensigngroup.net

PRODUCTS/OPERATIONS

2016 Sales

	$ mil.	% of total
Medicaid	558.0	34
Medicare	477.0	29
Private & other	266.9	16
Managed care	265.5	16
Medicaid - skilled	87.5	5
Total	**1,654.9**	**100**

2016 Sales

	$ mil.	% of total
Transitional and Skilled Services	1,377.7	83
Assisted and Independent Living Services	123.7	7
Home Health and Hospice Services	115.8	7
All Other	42.8	3
Elimination -5.1 -		
Total	**1,341.8**	**100**

COMPETITORS

ADDUS HOMECARE CORPORATION
ALERISLIFE INC.
BROOKDALE SENIOR LIVING INC.
CONSULATE MANAGEMENT COMPANY LLC
GENESIS HEALTHCARE INC.
HANGER INC.
IASIS HEALTHCARE LLC
NATIONAL HEALTHCARE CORPORATION
ODYSSEY HEALTHCARE INC.
SONIDA SENIOR LIVING INC.

HISTORICAL FINANCIALS

Company Type: Public

Income Statement

FYE: December 31

	REVENUE ($ mil.)	NET INCOME ($ mil.)	NET PROFIT MARGIN	EMPLOYEES
12/21	2,627.4	194.6	7.4%	25,900
12/20	2,402.6	170.4	7.1%	24,400
12/19	2,036.5	110.5	5.4%	24,500
12/18	2,040.6	92.3	4.5%	23,463
12/17	1,849.3	40.4	2.2%	21,301
Annual Growth	**9.2%**	**48.1%**	**—**	**5.0%**

2021 Year-End Financials

Debt ratio: 5.5%
Return on equity: 21.1%
Cash ($ mil.): 262.2
Current ratio: 1.22
Long-term debt ($ mil.): 152.8
No. of shares (mil.): 55.1
Dividends
  Yield: 0.2%
  Payout: 6.2%
Market value ($ mil.): 4,634.0

	STOCK PRICE ($) FY Close	P/E High/Low		PER SHARE ($)		
			Earnings	Dividends	Book Value
12/21	83.96	27 19	3.42	0.21	18.50
12/20	72.92	24 8	3.06	0.20	14.98
12/19	45.37	29 18	1.97	0.19	12.23
12/18	38.79	27 13	1.70	0.18	11.24
12/17	22.20	31 22	0.77	0.17	9.59
Annual Growth	**39.5%**	**— —**	**45.2%**	**5.4%**	**17.9%**

HOOVER'S HANDBOOK OF EMERGING COMPANIES 2022

Entegris Inc

Entegris makes products integral to the manufacture of semiconductors and computer disk drives. The company makes some 21000 standard and custom products used to transport and protect semiconductor and disk drive materials during processing. Its products include filtration wafer carriers storage boxes and chip trays as well as chemical delivery systems such as pipes fittings and valves. Its disk drive offerings include shippers stamper cases and transport trays. Semiconductor manufacturers including Taiwan Semiconductor Manufacturing Co. are among the company's customers. Massachusetts-based Entegris gets about 80% of revenue from international customers.

Operations

Entegris' three operating segments cover the semiconductor manufacturing process and each provide roughly a third of revenue.

The Specialty Chemicals and Engineered Materials (SCEM) segment about a third of revenue provides high-purity process chemistries gases and materials and efficient delivery systems for semiconductor and other advanced manufacturing processes.

The Microcontamination Control segment offers products and processes that filter and purify critical liquid chemistries and gases used in manufacturing processes for semiconductors and other complex products.

The Advanced Materials Handling segment's products monitor protect transport and deliver critical liquid chemistries wafers and other substrates for a broad set of applications in manufacturing.

Entegris operates manufacturing plants that meet critical purity standards and use processes such as 3D printing for production prototypes of products. The company also uses contract manufacturers to make some of its gas purification systems and electronic materials products.

Geographic Reach

Entegris based in Billerica Massachusetts has manufacturing and research and development facilities in France Singapore China Japan Malaysia South Korea Taiwan and the US. It also has sales and service offices throughout Asia and Europe.

The US and Taiwan each account for about 20% of the company's revenue followed by South Korea Japan and China each providing around 15% of Entegris' revenue. Overall customers in Asia account for about 70% of the company's revenue. Taiwan Semiconductor Manufacturing Co. accounts for more than 10% of sales.

Sales and Marketing

Entegris sells its products through a direct sales force and strategic distributors serving a range of markets including semiconductor flat panel display manufacturing compound semiconductor disk data storage aerospace solar/clean energy life sciences emerging technologies and water treatment industries.

While the company sells to more than 3100 customers it relies on its 10 biggest for about 45% of revenue.

Financial Performance

Entegris has posted steadily increasing revenue over the past five years and has been consistently profitable.

In 2018 sales rose 15% to $1.5 billion an increase of $208 million from 2017. Most of the growth came from higher organic sales of fluid handling products liquid chemistry filtration products and specialty materials. Acquisitions and currency effects also added revenue.

Entegris reported $240.8 million in net income in 2018 compared to $85.1 million in 2017 when the company had a higher tax provision due to the US Tax Cuts and Jobs Act.

The company carries a high level of debt about $950 million which could limit its ability to get additional financing for future working capital capital expenditures or acquisitions as well as increase its vulnerability to changes in economic or industry conditions.

Strategy

In order to counter the cycles of the semiconductor industry Entegris has expanded into adjacent and ancillary markets including applications in solar flat-panel displays and high-purity chemicals. Non-semiconductor industries include the aerospace biomedical glass container and electrical discharge machining markets. Its focus includes strategic acquisitions and partnerships and related transactions that enable it to complement its product markets and broaden its technological capabilities and product offerings.

Entegris made several acquisitions in 2018 and 2019 strengthening its process control and purity businesses. Two acquired companies PSS and SAES contributed to higher sales in 2018 and had strong backlogs.

The company has focused on the Microcontamination Control segment answering customers' concerns about the purity of the materials they use. Purification products and systems — liquid filters and purifiers as well as gas filters diffusers and purifiers — posted the strongest sales growth in Entegris' portfolio in 2018. About a third of the company's capital expenditures in 2018 went to the unit.

Entegris agreed to merge with Versum to create a bigger more comprehensive materials handling company. But that deal was scuttled when Versum accepted a higher bid from Merck in 2019. Entegris received a $140 million termination payment.

Mergers and Acquisitions

In 2018 Entegris acquired SAES Pure Gas a provider of high-capacity gas purification systems used in semiconductor manufacturing and adjacent markets for about $350 million in cash. The addition builds out Entegris' gas purification offerings. The SAES business became a part of the Microcontamination Control division.

EXECUTIVES

Independent Chairman Of The Board, Paul Olson
Chief Financial Officer, Executive Vice President, Treasurer, Gregory Graves, $548,077 total compensation
President, Chief Executive Officer And Director, Bertrand Loy, $946,154 total compensation
Independent Director, Michael Bradley
Senior Vice President And General Manager, Advanced Materials Handling, William Shaner, $326,058 total compensation
Chief Accounting Officer, Vice President, Controller, Michael Sauer
Chief Operating Officer, Executive Vice President, Todd Edlund, $525,289 total compensation
Senior Vice President And General Manager, Specialty Chemicals And Engineered Materials, Stuart Tison, $342,788 total compensation
Senior Vice President - Business Development, Corey Rucci
Senior Vice President And General Manager, Microcontamination Control, Clinton Haris, $364,327 total compensation
Senior Vice President - Finance, Bruce Beckman
Independent Director, Azita Saleki - Gerhardt
Independent Director, Yvette Kanouff
Independent Director, Rodney Clark
Independent Director, James Gentilcore
Senior Vice President - Global Human Resources, Susan Rice, $408,173 total compensation
Chief Technology Officer & Senior Vice President, James O'Neill
Auditors: KPMG LLP

LOCATIONS

HQ: Entegris Inc
129 Concord Road, Billerica, MA 01821
Phone: 978 436-6500
Web: www.entegris.com

PRODUCTS/OPERATIONS

2018 Sales

	$ mil.	% of total
Specialty Chemicals and Engineered Materials	530.2	34
Microcontamination Control	552.9	36
Advanced Materials Handling	467.4	30
Total	**1,550.5**	**100**

COMPETITORS

APPLIED MATERIALS INC.	MYERS INDUSTRIES INC.
BERRY GLOBAL GROUP INC.	PHILLIPS-MEDISIZE CORPORATION
CMC MATERIALS INC.	SPX FLOW INC.
ILLINOIS TOOL WORKS INC.	TOYODA GOSEI CO. LTD.
MEDPLAST GROUP INC.	ULTRA CLEAN HOLDINGS INC.
MKS INSTRUMENTS INC.	

HISTORICAL FINANCIALS

Company Type: Public

Income Statement

FYE: December 31

	REVENUE ($ mil.)	NET INCOME ($ mil.)	NET PROFIT MARGIN	EMPLOYEES
12/21	2,298.8	409.1	17.8%	6,850
12/20	1,859.3	294.9	15.9%	5,800
12/19	1,591.0	254.8	16.0%	5,300
12/18	1,550.5	240.7	15.5%	4,900
12/17	1,342.5	85.0	6.3%	3,900
Annual Growth	**14.4%**	**48.1%**	**—**	**15.1%**

2021 Year-End Financials

Debt ratio: 29.3%	No. of shares (mil.): 135.5
Return on equity: 26.4%	Dividends
Cash ($ mil.): 402.5	Yield: 0.2%
Current ratio: 3.47	Payout: 11.5%
Long-term debt ($ mil.): 937.0	Market value ($ mil.): 18,780.0

	STOCK PRICE ($) FY Close	P/E High/Low	PER SHARE ($) Earnings	Dividends	Book Value
12/21	138.58	51 31	3.00	0.32	12.65
12/20	96.10	45 18	2.16	0.32	10.22
12/19	50.09	27 15	1.87	0.30	8.65
12/18	27.90	23 14	1.69	0.28	7.44
12/17	30.45	55 30	0.59	0.07	7.03
Annual Growth	**46.1%**	**— —**	**50.2%**	**46.2%**	**15.8%**

Enterprise Bancorp, Inc. (MA)

Enterprise Bancorp caters to more customers than just entrepreneurs. The holding company owns Enterprise Bank and Trust which operates more than 20 branches in north-central Massachusetts and southern New Hampshire. The $2 billion-asset bank offers traditional deposit and loan products specializing in lending to businesses professionals high-net-worth individuals and not-for-profits. About half of its loan portfolio is tied to commercial real estate while another one-third is tied to commercial and industrial and commercial construction loans. Subsidiaries Enterprise Investment Services and Enterprise Insurance Services provide investments and insurance geared to the bank's target business customers.

Operations

More than 50% of Enterprise Bancorp's $1.86 billion loan portfolio was tied to commercial real estate loans at the end of 2015 while commercial and industrial and commercial construction loans made up another 25% and 11% of the bank's loan assets. The rest of the bank's portfolio was tied to residential mortgages (9% of loan assets) home equity loans and lines of credit (4%) and consumer loans (less than 1%).

Nearly 80% of the bank's total revenue comes from loan interest while investment advisory fees and deposit and interchange fees each make up another 5%.

Geographic Reach

The Lowell Massachusetts-based bank operated 23 branches mostly located in the greater Merrimack Valley and North Central regions of Massachusetts and Southern New Hampshire at the end of 2015.

Sales and Marketing

Enterprise spent $2.7 million on advertising and public relations during 2015 down from $2.9 million in 2014.

Financial Performance

The bank's annual revenues have risen more than 40% since 2011 as its loan assets have swelled by 50% to $1.86 billion. Meanwhile its net income has grown more than 50% as it's kept a lid on loan loss provisions and operating costs.

Enterprise Bancorp's revenue climbed 8% to $98.4 million during 2015 thanks to 11% loan asset growth driven by a "seasoned" lending team a sales and service culture and geographic market expansion. Commercial construction loans grew the fastest rate during the year though all loans grew albeit at a slightly slower rate.

Revenue growth in 2015 drove the bank's net income up 10% to $16.1 million despite higher salary and employee benefit expenses. Enterprise Bancorp's operating cash levels nearly doubled to $25.7 million for the year largely thanks to positive changes in working capital mainly related to prepaid expenses and other assets.

Strategy

Enterprise Bancorp has traditionally expanded its loan and deposit business by opening new branches rather than by acquiring other banks. Enterprise hopes to take advantage of the trend to switch from larger banks to smaller community-oriented institutions. The company has also invested in upgrading its branches and operations systems.

EXECUTIVES

Executive Vice President And Chief Human Resources Officer Of The Bank, Jamie Gabriel
Executive Vice President, Chief Digital And Operations Officer Of The Bank, Brian Collins
Independent Director, Anita Worden
Executive Vice President And Chief Information Officer Of The Bank, Keith Soucie
Executive Vice President And Branch Administration Director Of The Bank, Susan Covey
Executive Vice President And Chief Mortgage And Consumer Lending Officer Of The Bank, Diane Silva
Executive Vice President And Chief Risk Officer Of The Bank, Michael Gallagher
Executive Vice President And Construction Lending Director Of The Bank, Marlene Hoyt
Executive Vice President And Regional Commercial Lending Manager Of The Bank, Ryan Dunn
Executive Vice President And New Hampshire Community Banking And Lending Director Of The Bank, Peter Rayno
Vice Chairman Of The Board, Lead Independent Director, James Conway
Executive Vice President And Chief Commercial Lending Officer Of The Bank, Brian Bullock
Executive Chairman Of The Board, George Duncan, $428,480 total compensation
President, Director, Richard Main, $321,360 total compensation
Chief Executive Officer Of The Company And The Bank, Director, John Clancy, $525,944 total compensation
Executive Vice President, Managing Director Wealth Management And Chief Operating Officer Of The Bank, Stephen Irish, $352,259 total compensation
Independent Director, Nickolas Stavropoulos
Executive Vice President And Chief Sales, Community And Customer Relationship Officer Of The Bank, Chester Szablak
Chief Financial Officer, Executive Vice President, Treasurer, Joseph Lussier, $210,769 total compensation
Executive Vice President And Chief Banking Officer Of The Bank, Steven Larochelle
Auditors: RSM US LLP

LOCATIONS

HQ: Enterprise Bancorp, Inc. (MA)
222 Merrimack Street, Lowell, MA 01852
Phone: 978 459-9000
Web: www.enterprisebanking.com

PRODUCTS/OPERATIONS

2015 Sales

	$ mil.	% of total
Interest and dividend income:		
Loans and loans held for sale	77.9	79
Investment securities	5.3	5
Other interest-earning assets	0.2	-
Non-interest income:		
Investment advisory fees	4.8	5
Deposit and interchange fees	4.9	5
Net gains on sales of investment securities	1.8	2
Income on bank-owned life insurance net	0.5	1
Gains on sales of loans	0.5	1
Other income	2.5	3
Total	**98.4**	**100**

Products and Services

Lending Products:
Residential Loans
Home Equity Loans and Lines of Credit
Consumer Loans
Credit Risk and Allowance for Loan Losses
Deposit Products:
Cash Management Services
Product Delivery Channels
Investment Services
Insurance Services

COMPETITORS

CAMBRIDGE BANCORP	FIRST FINANCIAL
CENTURY BANCORP INC.	CORPORATION
CUSTOMERS BANCORP INC.	TRUSTCO BANK
	CORP N Y

HISTORICAL FINANCIALS

Company Type: Public

Income Statement

FYE: December 31

	ASSETS ($ mil.)	NET INCOME ($ mil.)	INCOME AS % OF ASSETS	EMPLOYEES
12/20	4,014.3	31.4	0.8%	527
12/19	3,235.0	34.2	1.1%	538
12/18	2,964.3	28.8	1.0%	508
12/17	2,817.5	19.3	0.7%	482
12/16	2,526.2	18.7	0.7%	468
Annual Growth	12.3%	13.8%	—	3.0%

2020 Year-End Financials

Return on assets: 0.8%
Return on equity: 9.9%
Long-term debt ($ mil.): —
No. of shares (mil.): 11.9
Sales ($ mil): 162.0
Dividends
Yield: 2.7%
Payout: 26.5%
Market value ($ mil.): 305.0

	STOCK PRICE ($) FY Close	P/E High/Low		PER SHARE ($) Earnings	Dividends	Book Value
12/20	25.55	13	8	2.64	0.70	28.01
12/19	33.87	12	9	2.89	0.64	25.09
12/18	32.16	17	12	2.46	0.58	21.80
12/17	34.05	23	18	1.66	0.54	19.97
12/16	37.56	22	12	1.70	0.52	18.72
Annual Growth	(9.2%)	—	—	11.6%	7.7%	10.6%

Enterprise Financial Services Corp

Enterprise Financial Services wants you to boldly bank where many have banked before. It's the holding company for Enterprise Bank & Trust which mostly targets closely-held businesses and their owners but also serves individuals in the St. Louis Kansas City and Phoenix metropolitan areas. Boasting $3.8 billion in assets and 16 branches Enterprise offers standard products such as checking savings and money market accounts and CDs. Commercial and industrial loans make up over half of the company's lending activities while real estate loans make up another 45%. The bank also writes consumer and residential mortgage loans. Bank subsidiary Enterprise Trust offers wealth management services.

Operations

Enterprise Trust the company's wealth management unit targets business owners wealthy individuals and institutional investors providing financial planning business succession planning and related services. The unit also invests in Missouri state tax credits from funds for affordable housing development which it then sells to clients and others.

About 82% of Enterprise Financial's total revenue came from loan interest (including fees) in 2014 while another 7% came from interest on its taxable and tax-exempt investment securities. The rest of its revenue came from wealth management income (4%) service fees (3%) gains on state tax credits (1%) and other miscellaneous income sources. The bank had a staff of 452 full-time employees at the end of 2014.

Geographic Reach

Enterprise Bank & Trust operates eight banking locations in or around Kansas City six banking locations and a support center in the St. Louis area and two banking locations in the Phoenix metro area.

Financial Performance

The company has struggled to consistently grow its revenues in recent years mostly due to shrinking interest margins on its loans amidst the low-interest environment. Its profits however have mostly trended higher thanks to declining loan loss provisions as its loan portfolio's credit quality has improved with higher property valuations in the strengthened economy.

Enterprise Financials' revenue fell by 9% to $148.4 million in 2014 mostly due to double-digit declines in interest income as its purchased credit-impaired (PCI) loan balances and accelerated payments declined and as interest margins on its loans continued to shrink. The bank's portfolio loan balances increased however helping to offset some of its interest income decline.

Lower revenue and higher loan loss provisions (it received a loan loss benefit of $642 thousand in 2013) in 2014 caused the bank's net income to dive 18% to $27.2 million. Enterprise Financial's operating cash levels rose by 7% to $31.5 million despite lower earnings for the year mostly thanks to favorable changes in its working capital related to a $12-million change in other asset balances.

Strategy

Enterprise Financial Services planned in 2015 to continue its long-term strategy of keeping a "relationship-oriented distribution and sales approach"; growing its fee income and niche businesses; practicing "prudent" credit and interest rate risk management; and using advanced technology and controlled-expense growth. The company added that it planned on "operating branches with larger average deposits and employing experienced staff who are compensated on the basis of performance and customer service."

Though it just had two branches in Phoenix in 2015 the bank believes the fast-growing Phoenix market offers long-term growth opportunities for the company with its underlying demographic and geographic factors. Indeed at the end of 2014 the market had over 90000 privately-held businesses and 80000-plus households each with investable assets of more than $1 million.

Mergers and Acquisitions

In 2017 Enterprise Financial Services completed the acquisition of Jefferson County Bancshares the holding company of Eagle Bank and Trust Company in Missouri. The deal added 13 branches in metropolitan St. Louis and Perry County Missouri.

The acquisition expanded EFS's assets to nearly $5 billion.

Company Background

In a restructuring move Enterprise Financial Services sold life insurance arm Millennium Brokerage in 2010 five years after investing in the company.

EXECUTIVES

Independent Director, Michael DeCola
President Of Enterprise Bank & Trust, Executive Vice President And Director Of Commercial Banking & Wealth Management, Scott Goodman, $366,073 total compensation
President, Chief Executive Officer, Director, James Lally, $619,809 total compensation
Independent Chairman Of The Board, John Eulich
Chief Credit Officer, Douglas Bauche, $310,911 total compensation
Independent Director, Judith Heeter
Independent Director, Sandra Van Trease
Independent Director, James Havel
Executive Vice President, Chief Risk Officer, General Counsel - Eb&t, Corporate Secretary - Efsc, Nicole Iannacone, $295,078 total compensation
Independent Director, Robert Guest
Independent Director, Anthony Scavuzzo
Director, Richard Sanborn
Executive Vice President, Chief Administrative Officer, Mark Ponder, $212,500 total compensation
Chief Financial Officer, Executive Vice President, Keene Turner, $416,443 total compensation
Independent Director, Michael Holmes
Independent Director, Eloise Schmitz
Independent Director, Nevada Kent
Auditors: Deloitte & Touche LLP

LOCATIONS

HQ: Enterprise Financial Services Corp
150 North Meramec, Clayton, MO 63105
Phone: 314 725-5500
Web: www.enterprisebank.com

PRODUCTS/OPERATIONS

2011 Sales

	$ mil.	% of total
Interest		
Loans including fees	130.1	79
Securities	11.8	7
Other	0.9	1
Noninterest		
Wealth management	6.8	4
Service charges on deposit accounts	5.1	3
Gain on state tax credits net	3.7	2
Other service charges and fee income	1.7	1
Other	4.7	3
Adjustments	(3.5)	-
Total	**161.3**	**100**

COMPETITORS

ASSOCIATED BANC-CORP
BOKF MERGER CORPORATION NUMBER SIXTEEN
CENTRAL BANCOMPANY INC.
CITY HOLDING COMPANY
FIRST BUSINESS FINANCIAL SERVICES INC.
FIRST FINANCIAL NORTHWEST INC.
FIRSTMERIT CORPORATION
GUARANTY BANCORP
RESONA HOLDINGS INC.
SIGNATURE BANK
THE SOUTHERN BANC COMPANY INC
WSFS FINANCIAL CORPORATION

HISTORICAL FINANCIALS

Company Type: Public

Income Statement				FYE: December 31
	ASSETS ($ mil.)	NET INCOME ($ mil.)	INCOME AS % OF ASSETS	EMPLOYEES
12/20	9,751.5	74.3	0.8%	0
12/19	7,333.7	92.7	1.3%	805
12/18	5,645.6	89.2	1.6%	650
12/17	5,289.2	48.1	0.9%	635
12/16	4,081.3	48.8	1.2%	479
Annual Growth	24.3%	11.1%	—	—

2020 Year-End Financials

Return on assets: 0.8%
Return on equity: 7.6%
Long-term debt ($ mil.): —
No. of shares (mil.): 31.2
Sales ($ mil): 359.2

Dividends
Yield: 2.0%
Payout: 26.0%
Market value ($ mil.): 1,091.0

	STOCK PRICE ($) FY Close	P/E High/Low		PER SHARE ($) Earnings	Dividends	Book Value
12/20	34.95	18	9	2.76	0.72	34.57
12/19	48.21	14	11	3.55	0.62	32.67
12/18	37.63	15	10	3.83	0.47	26.47
12/17	45.15	22	18	2.07	0.44	23.76
12/16	43.00	18	10	2.41	0.41	19.31
Annual Growth	(5.1%)	—	—	3.4%	15.1%	15.7%

Envela Corp

Attracted to things gold and shiny? If so DGSE is for you. The company buys and sells jewelry bullion rare coins fine watches and collectibles to retail and wholesale customers across the US through its various websites and 30-plus retail stores in California Texas and South Carolina. The company's eight e-commerce sites let customers buy and sell jewelry and bullion interactively and obtain current precious-metal prices. In all more than 7500 items are available for sale on DGSE websites including $2 million in diamonds. DGSE also owns Fairchild Watches a leading vintage watch wholesaler and the rare coin dealer Superior Galleries. The company sold its pair of pawn shops in Dallas in 2009.

EXECUTIVES

Independent Director, Jim Ruth
Independent Director, Alexandra Griffin
Chief Financial Officer, Bret Pedersen, $165,000 total compensation
Chief Information Officer, Joel Friedman
Director, Allison DeStefano
Chairman Of The Board, President And Chief Executive Officer, John Loftus
Auditors: Whitley Penn LLP

LOCATIONS

HQ: Envela Corp
1901 Gateway Drive, Ste 100, Irving, TX 75038
Phone: 972 587-4049 **Fax:** 972 674-2596
Web: www.envela.com

COMPETITORS

BULOVA CORPORATION Pandora A/S

HISTORICAL FINANCIALS

Company Type: Public

Income Statement
FYE: December 31

	REVENUE ($ mil.)	NET INCOME ($ mil.)	NET PROFIT MARGIN	EMPLOYEES
12/20	113.9	6.3	5.6%	152
12/19	82.0	2.7	3.4%	135
12/18	54.0	0.6	1.2%	52
12/17	61.9	1.8	3.0%	54
12/16	48.3	(4.0)	—	77
Annual Growth	23.9%	—	—	18.5%

2020 Year-End Financials

Debt ratio: 37.9%
Return on equity: 44.2%
Cash ($ mil.): 9.2
Current ratio: 3.88
Long-term debt ($ mil.): 13.2

No. of shares (mil.): 26.9
Dividends
 Yield: —
 Payout: —
Market value ($ mil.): 140.0

	STOCK PRICE ($) FY Close	P/E High/Low		PER SHARE ($) Earnings	Dividends	Book Value
12/20	5.20	25	6	0.24	0.00	0.65
12/19	1.35	16	4	0.10	0.00	0.42
12/18	0.46	53	19	0.02	0.00	0.31
12/17	0.93	25	12	0.07	0.00	0.29
12/16	1.24	—	—	(0.30)	0.00	0.22
Annual Growth	43.1%	—	—	—	—	31.3%

Enviva Inc

Auditors: Ernst & Young LLP

LOCATIONS

HQ: Enviva Inc
 7272 Wisconsin Ave., Suite 1800, Bethesda, MD 20814
Phone: 301 657-5560
Web: www.envivabiomass.com

HISTORICAL FINANCIALS

Company Type: Public

Income Statement
FYE: December 31

	REVENUE ($ mil.)	NET INCOME ($ mil.)	NET PROFIT MARGIN	EMPLOYEES
12/20	875.0	17.0	2.0%	0
12/19	684.3	(2.9)	—	0
12/18	573.7	6.9	1.2%	0
12/17	543.2	17.5	3.2%	0
12/16	464.2	21.3	4.6%	0
Annual Growth	17.2%	(5.5%)	—	—

2020 Year-End Financials

Debt ratio: 64.7%
Return on equity: —
Cash ($ mil.): 10.0
Current ratio: 1.21
Long-term debt ($ mil.): 912.7

No. of shares (mil.): 39.8
Dividends
 Yield: 0.0%
 Payout: —
Market value ($ mil.): 1,808.0

	STOCK PRICE ($) FY Close	P/E High/Low		PER SHARE ($) Earnings	Dividends	Book Value
12/20	45.42	—	—	(0.36)	2.90	8.15
12/19	37.31	—	—	(0.54)	2.62	8.39
12/18	27.75	8256	28	0.04	2.51	5.54
12/17	27.65	48	38	0.61	2.28	7.99
12/16	26.80	30	15	0.91	2.03	11.90
Annual Growth	14.1%	—	—	—	9.3%	(9.0%)

Epam Systems, Inc.

EPAM is the world's leading provider of digital platform engineering software development and other IT services to customers primarily in North America Europe Asia and Australia. The company provides software development product engineering services and other business processes. Its key service offerings and solutions include five practice areas such as engineering operations optimization consulting and design. The company has development centers in Russia Belarus Ukraine Hungary Poland India and China that employ more than 36735 professionals. Around 60% of sales come from North America. EPAM was founded in 1993.

Operations

The company's operations consist of three reportable segments: North America (approximately 60% of sales) Europe (about 35%) and Russia (about 5%).

EPAM has operations in five practice areas: engineering operations optimization consulting and design.

Through its engineering services the company builds enterprise technologies that improve business processes offer smarter analytics and result in greater operational excellence through requirements analysis and platform selection deep and complex customization cross-platform migration implementation and integration. It has deep expertise and the ability to offer a comprehensive set of software product development services including product research customer experience design and prototyping program management component design and integration full lifecycle software testing product deployment and end-user customization performance tuning product support and maintenance managed services as well as porting and cross-platform migration.

EPAM also offers proprietary platforms and engineering practices in order to turn customers' operations into intelligent enterprise hubs.

A key optimization service is implementing automation transforming legacy processes to increase customers' revenues and reduce costs.

Consulting and design services include industry expertise and data visualization among others.

The company's professional services account for roughly all of its revenue.

Geographic Reach

EPAM is based in Newtown Pennsylvania. North America is the company's biggest market accounting for approximately 60% of revenue. European customers provide about 35%. The CIS (includes revenues from customers in Belarus Kazakhstan Russia Georgia and Ukraine) and APAC (includes revenues from customers in East Asia Southeast Asia and Australia) accounts for the rest.

The company has the largest concentration of IT professionals in Belarus the majority of which are based in Minsk. EPAM also employs a significant number of professional in Ukraine and Russia. Continuing military activities in Ukraine have combined with the country's weak economic conditions to fuel ongoing economic uncertainty in Ukraine and Russia. The company continues to monitor the situation and has contingency plans that include relocating work and personal as appropriate.

EPAM has additional key operations in the US Hungary Poland India and China.

The company also offers the EPAM E-KIDS program in about 15 countries.

Sales and Marketing

The company markets and sells its services through its senior management sales and business development teams account managers and professional staff.

EPAM maintains industry specialization and markets its services to six industry groups: Business Information & Media Financial Services and Software & Hi-Tech (about 20% each) Travel & Consumer (more than 15%) Life Sciences & Healthcare and Emerging Verticals (about 10% each).

The company has established relationships with many of its customers with nearly 60% and about 25% of revenue comes from customers that had used its services for at least five and ten years respectively. Its top five customers accounted for more than 20% of revenue while its top ten customers accounted for nearly 30%.

Financial Performance

In 2020 EPAM's revenue increased to $2.7 billion compared from the prior year with $2.3 billion. Business Information & Media became the company's largest vertical during 2020 growing 33% as compared to 2019 largely driven by growth in one of its top 5 customers and the expansion of services to a customer which was previously in its top 50 customers and is now in its top 10 customers.

Net income for fiscal 2020 increased to $327.2 million compared from the prior year with $261.1 million.

Cash held by the company at the end of fiscal 2020 increased to $1.3 billion. Cash provided by operations was $544.4 million while cash used for investing and financing activities were $167.2 million and $0.8 million respectively. Main cash uses were for Purchases of short-term investments and Payments of withholding taxes related to net share settlements of restricted stock units.

Strategy

EPAM's service offerings continuously evolve to provide more customized and integrated solutions to its customers where it combines best-in-class software engineering with customer experience design business consulting and technology innovation services. It is continually expanding its service capabilities moving beyond traditional services into business consulting design and physical product development and areas such as artificial intelligence robotics and virtual reality.

Mergers and Acquisitions

In early 2021 EPAM acquired Just-BI to further expand their comprehensive portfolio of data and analytics services. Just-BI is a niche consultancy firm specializing in Data and Analytics. Based in the Netherlands the acquisition brings expanded EU APAC and global advisory capabilities around the full SAP ecosystem as well as extending EPAM's already rich Data BI and Advanced Analytics capabilities.

Also in early 2021 EPAM acquired White-Hat a leading cybersecurity services company to expand its comprehensive cybersecurity expertise portfolio and diversifying their EMEA delivery capabilities. White-Hat headquartered in Tel Aviv Israel safeguards its customers' businesses using innovative methodologies and an in-depth understanding of the attacker's mindset and landscape.

In a separate transaction in 2021 EPAM acquired PolSource an expert Salesforce Consulting Partner with more than 350 experienced Salesforce specialists across the Americas and Europe. PolSource brings a reputation for industry innovation ? delivering successful multi-cloud end-to-end solutions across many key industries including consumer goods retail manufacturing automotive technology healthcare and life sciences.

In late 2020 EPAM acquired Malta-based Ricston Ltd. a leading software integration and connectivity solutions provider for an undisclosed amount. The acquisition will expand EPAM's growing consulting and engineering portfolio of API microservices management and integration services.

Company Background

Arkadily Dobkin and Leo Lozner founded EPAM in Princeton New Jersey and Minsk Belarus respectively in 1993. The company's first significant product development client was SAP. EPAM debuted as the first company with Belarusian engineering roots on the NYSE in 2012.

EXECUTIVES

Senior Vice President, General Counsel, Corporate Secretary, Edward Rockwell
Senior Vice President, Co-head Of Global Business, Boris Shnayder, $257,500 total compensation
Senior Vice President, Chief People Officer, Larry Solomon, $360,000 total compensation
Non-executive Independent Director, Helen Shan
Non-executive Independent Director, Eugene Roman
Non-executive Independent Director, Jill Smart
Chief Financial Officer, Senior Vice President, Treasurer, Jason Peterson, $420,000 total compensation
Chief Accounting Officer, Vice President, Corporate Controller, Gary Abrahams
Senior Vice President, Chief Marketing Officer, Strategy Officer, Elaina Shekhter, $273,400 total compensation
Senior Vice President, Co-head Of Global Business, Sergey Yezhkov
Non-executive Independent Director, Richard Mayoras
Senior Vice President, Head Of Global Delivery, Viktar Dvorkin, $360,000 total compensation
Chairman Of The Board, President, Chief Executive Officer, Arkadiy Dobkin, $625,000 total compensation
President Of Eu , Apac Markets, Balazs Fejes, $448,949 total compensation
Auditors: DELOITTE & TOUCHE LLP

LOCATIONS

HQ: Epam Systems, Inc.
41 University Drive, Suite 202, Newtown, PA 18940
Phone: 267 759-9000
Web: www.epam.com

PRODUCTS/OPERATIONS

2014 Sales

	$ mil.	% of total
Software development	504.6	69
Application testing services	140.4	19
Application maintenance & support	58.8	8
Infrastructure services	14.2	2
Licensing	3.6	1
Reimbursable expenses & other revenues	8.4	1
Total	**730.0**	**100**

2014 Sales by Industry

	$ mil.	% of total
Banking & financial services	215.4	29
Independent software vendors & technology	157.9	22
Travel & hospitality	157.8	22
Business information & media	91.7	13
Other verticals	98.8	13
Reimbursable expenses & other revenues	8.4	1
Total	**730.0**	**100**

Selected Services

Application development
Application maintenance and support
Application testing
Business intelligence
Business process management
Content management
Customer Relationship Management (CRM)
Data warehousing and business intelligence
E-commerce
Enterprise application integration
Enterprise resource planning
Infrastructure and hosting
Knowledge management
Localization
Offshore software development
Quality assurance consulting and testing strategy transformation
Server and network management

COMPETITORS

ASPEN TECHNOLOGY INC.
COGNIZANT TECHNOLOGY SOLUTIONS CORPORATION
CORNERSTONE ONDEMAND INC.
EPLUS INC.
GP STRATEGIES CORPORATION
HCL TECHNOLOGIES LIMITED
LARSEN & TOUBRO INFOTECH LIMITED
NETCALL PLC
PERFICIENT INC.
PROS HOLDINGS INC.
Software AG
TTEC HOLDINGS INC.

HISTORICAL FINANCIALS

Company Type: Public

Income Statement				FYE: December 31
	REVENUE ($ mil.)	NET INCOME ($ mil.)	NET PROFIT MARGIN	EMPLOYEES
12/20	2,659.4	327.1	12.3%	41,168
12/19	2,293.8	261.0	11.4%	36,739
12/18	1,842.9	240.2	13.0%	30,156
12/17	1,450.4	72.7	5.0%	25,962
12/16	1,160.1	99.2	8.6%	22,383
Annual Growth	23.0%	34.7%	—	16.5%

2020 Year-End Financials

Debt ratio: 0.9%
Return on equity: 18.2%
Cash ($ mil.): 1,322.1
Current ratio: 4.11
Long-term debt ($ mil.): 25.0

No. of shares (mil.): 56.1
Dividends
Yield: —
Payout: —
Market value ($ mil.): 20,106.0

	STOCK PRICE ($)	P/E		PER SHARE ($)		
	FY Close	High/Low		Earnings	Dividends	Book Value
12/20	358.35	61	27	5.60	0.00	35.34
12/19	212.16	45	24	4.53	0.00	28.92
12/18	116.01	32	23	4.24	0.00	23.35
12/17	107.43	78	45	1.32	0.00	18.40
12/16	64.31	40	29	1.87	0.00	15.29
Annual Growth	53.6%	—	—	31.5%	—	23.3%

Equitrans Midstream Corp

Auditors: Ernst & Young LLP

LOCATIONS

HQ: Equitrans Midstream Corp
2200 Energy Drive, Canonsburg, PA 15317
Phone: 724 271-7600
Web: www.equitransmidstream.com

HISTORICAL FINANCIALS

Company Type: Public

Income Statement				FYE: December 31
	REVENUE ($ mil.)	NET INCOME ($ mil.)	NET PROFIT MARGIN	EMPLOYEES
12/20	1,510.8	423.1	28.0%	771
12/19	1,630.2	(203.7)	—	800
12/18	1,495.1	218.4	14.6%	0
12/17	895.5	(27.1)	—	0
12/16	732.2	65.1	8.9%	0
Annual Growth	19.8%	59.6%	—	—

2020 Year-End Financials

Debt ratio: 56.8%
Return on equity: 18.4%
Cash ($ mil.): 208.0
Current ratio: 0.94
Long-term debt ($ mil.): 6,928.3

No. of shares (mil.): 432.4
Dividends
Yield: 11.1%
Payout: 84.9%
Market value ($ mil.): 3,477.0

	STOCK PRICE ($)	P/E		PER SHARE ($)		
	FY Close	High/Low		Earnings	Dividends	Book Value
12/20	8.04	13	4	1.06	0.90	9.00
12/19	13.36	—	—	(0.80)	1.76	2.64
12/18	20.02	27	22	0.86	0.41	1.80
Annual Growth	(36.6%)	—	—	11.0%	48.2%	123.6%

Erie Indemnity Co.

Founded in 1925 as an auto insurer Erie Indemnity now provides management services that relate to the sales underwriting and issuance of policies of one customer: Erie Insurance Exchange. The Exchange is a reciprocal insurance exchange that pools the underwriting of several property/casualty insurance firms. The principal personal lines products are private passenger automobile and homeowners. The principal commercial lines products are commercial multi-peril commercial automobile and workers compensation. Historically due to policy renewal and sales patterns the Exchange's direct and affiliated assumed written premiums are greater in the second and third quarters than in the first and fourth quarters of the calendar year. Erie Indemnity charges a management fee of 25% of all premiums written or assumed for the Exchange.

Operations

Management fees (consist of policy issuance and renewal services and administrative services) account for more than 75% of Erie Indemnity's revenue; service agreements and investment income account for the remainder.

The Exchange and its subsidiaries (Erie Insurance Erie Insurance Company of New York Erie Insurance Property and Casualty and Flagship City Insurance) together operate as a property/casualty insurer. The group also owns Erie Family Life Insurance and the Exchange and its wholly owned subsidiaries meet the definition of an insurance holding company system.

Personal lines — primarily private passenger automobile and homeowners products — comprise some 70% of the direct and assumed premiums written; commercial lines — primarily multi-peril workers' compensation and commercial automobile — make up the rest.

Geographic Reach

Headquartered in Erie Pennsylvania Indemnity and the Exchange also operate 25 field offices in 12 states to perform primarily claims-related activities. The Exchange owns seven field offices and the remaining field offices are leased from third parties. Commitments for properties leased from other parties expire periodically through 2027. They expect that most leases will be renewed or replaced upon expiration. Rental costs of shared facilities are allocated based upon usage or square footage occupied.

Sales and Marketing

The Exchange is represented by independent agencies that serve as its sole distribution channel. In addition to their principal role as salespersons the independent agents play a significant role as underwriting and service providers and are an integral part of the Exchange's success.

Financial Performance

The company's revenue for fiscal 2020 increased to $2.54 billion compared to the prior year with $2.48 billion.

Net income for fiscal 2020 decreased by 7% to $293.3 million compared to the prior year with $316.8 million.

Cash held by the company at the end of fiscal 2020 decreased to $161.2 million. Cash provided by operations was $342.6 million while cash used for investing and financing activities were $243.2 million and $274.9 million respectively. Main uses of cash were purchase of investments and dividends paid to shareholders.

Strategy

The Exchange's strategic focus as a reciprocal insurer is to employ a disciplined underwriting philosophy and to leverage its strong surplus position to generate higher risk adjusted investment re-

turns. The goal is to produce acceptable returns on a long-term basis through careful risk selection rational pricing and superior investment returns. This focus allows the Exchange to accomplish its mission of providing as near perfect protection as near perfect service as is humanly possible at the lowest possible costs.

Company Background

Erie Indemnity's structure and relationship to other parts of the larger Erie Insurance Group are complex to say the least. The company operated as a property/casualty insurer through its wholly-owned subsidiaries Erie Insurance Co. Erie New York and Erie Insurance Property and Casualty throughout 2010. At year-end however Erie Indemnity sold all of its outstanding capital stock and voting shares of these subsidiaries to the Exchange. As a result now all of its former property/casualty insurance operations are owned by the Exchange and Erie Indemnity serves as the management company. The sale of the subsidiaries did not affect its pooling agreement. The company also sold its approximate 22% ownership in Erie Family Life to the Exchange which became Erie's' full parent.

EXECUTIVES

President, Chief Executive Officer, Timothy Necastro, $940,385 total compensation
Independent Chairman Of The Board, Thomas Hagen
Independent Director, C. Scott Hartz
Independent Director, George Lucore
Executive Vice President - Claims & Customer Service, Lorianne Feltz, $424,231 total compensation
Independent Director, Thomas Palmer
Independent Director, Elizabeth Vorsheck
Executive Vice President - Sales & Products, Douglas Smith, $424,231 total compensation
Chief Financial Officer, Executive Vice President, Gregory Gutting, $540,385 total compensation
Executive Vice President, Law Division And Internal Audit, General Counsel, Secretary, Brian Bolash
Independent Director, Brian Hudson
Independent Director, LuAnn Datesh
Independent Director, Eugene Connell
Independent Director, Salvatore Correnti
Independent Vice Chairman Of The Board, Jonathan Hagen
Auditors: Ernst & Young LLP

LOCATIONS

HQ: Erie Indemnity Co.
100 Erie Insurance Place, Erie, PA 16530
Phone: 814 870-2000
Web: www.erieinsurance.com

PRODUCTS/OPERATIONS

2017 Sales

	$ mil.	% of total
Operating revenue		
Net management fees	1,662.6	97
Service agreements	29.1	2
Investment income	28.6	1
Total	**1,720.3**	**100**

COMPETITORS

ALLEGHANY CORPORATION
FBL FINANCIAL GROUP INC.
FEDNAT HOLDING COMPANY

HCI GROUP INC.
OLD REPUBLIC INTERNATIONAL CORPORATION
ONEMAIN HOLDINGS INC.
PROTECTIVE INSURANCE CORPORATION
SELECTIVE INSURANCE GROUP INC.
THE HANOVER INSURANCE GROUP INC
THE NAVIGATORS GROUP INC
TRANSATLANTIC HOLDINGS INC.
UNITED FIRE GROUP INC.
UNIVERSAL INSURANCE HOLDINGS INC.

HISTORICAL FINANCIALS

Company Type: Public

Income Statement | | | | FYE: December 31

	ASSETS ($ mil.)	NET INCOME ($ mil.)	INCOME AS % OF ASSETS	EMPLOYEES
12/20	2,117.1	293.3	13.9%	5 914
12/19	2,016.2	316.8	15.7%	5 700
12/18	1,778.3	288.2	16.2%	5 500
12/17	1,665.8	197.0	11.8%	5 300
12/16	1,548.9	210.3	13.6%	5 000
Annual Growth	**8.1%**	**8.7%**	**—**	**4.3%**

2020 Year-End Financials

Return on assets: 14.1%
Return on equity: 25.2%
Long-term debt ($ mil.): —
No. of shares (mil.): 46.1
Sales ($ mil): 2,569.3

Dividends
Yield: 1.9%
Payout: 87.2%
Market value ($ mil.): 11,345.0

	STOCK PRICE ($) FY Close	P/E High/Low	PER SHARE ($) Earnings	Dividends	Book Value
12/20	245.60	40 21	5.61	4.90	25.72
12/19	166.00	40 19	6.06	3.60	24.53
12/18	133.31	22 18	5.51	3.36	21.08
12/17	121.84	30 26	3.76	3.13	18.56
12/16	112.45	25 20	4.01	2.19	17.69
Annual Growth	**21.6%**		**8.8%**	**22.3%**	**9.8%**

Escalade, Inc.

Escalade is the world's largest producer of tables for table tennis residential in-ground basketball goals and archery bows. Its other sporting goods include hockey and soccer tables play systems archery darts and fitness equipment. Products are sold under the STIGA Ping-Pong Goalrilla Silverback USWeight and Woodplay names as well as private labels. The company manufactures imports and distributes widely recognized products through major sporting goods retailers specialty dealers key on-line retailers traditional department stores and mass merchants. Escalade operates through more than five manufacturing and distribution facilities across North America. Almost all of Escalade's revenue comes from the North America.

Operations

Escalade operates in one business segment: the Sporting Goods segment which consists of home entertainment products such as table tennis tables and accessories; basketball goals; pool tables and accessories; outdoor playsets; soccer and hockey tables; archery equipment and accessories; and fitness arcade and darting products.

Geographic Reach

Based in Indiana Escalade operates over five manufacturing and distribution facilities across North America in Indiana Illinois Florida and abroad operations in Mexico and China.

The company manufactures its products in the US Mexico and imports products from Asian contract manufacturers. North America accounts almost all of net revenue.

Sales and Marketing

Escalade sells its products through retailers sporting goods stores specialty dealers key on-line retailers traditional department stores and mass merchants. Amazon.com contributed about 25% of Escalade's total revenues.

The company's sales channels include key on-line retailers or e-commerce (around 35% of sales) mass merchants (nearly 35%) specialty dealers (about 25%) and international (less than 5%). Customers include retailers dealers and wholesalers.

Financial Performance

In 2020 Escalade's revenue increased by 52% to $273.6 million compared to $180.5 million in 2019. The increase was primarily due to factory utilization changes in sales mix and supply chain improvements made throughout the year.

Net income in 2020 increased to $25.9 million compared to $7.3 billion in the prior year.

Cash held by the company at the end of 2020 decreased to $3.5 million. Cash provided by operations and financing activities were $2.6 million and $16.0 million respectively. Cash used for investing activities was $21.0 million mainly for acquisitions.

Strategy

Core components of Escalade's business development and growth strategy have been and continue to be making strategic acquisitions developing strong brand names and investing in product innovation.

Within the sporting goods industry the company has successfully built a robust market presence in several niche markets. This strategy is heavily dependent on expanding the company's customer base barriers to entry strong brands excellent customer service and a commitment to innovation. A key strategic advantage is the company's established relationships with major customers that allow the company to bring new products to market in a cost-effective manner while maintaining a diversified portfolio of products to meet the demands of consumers.

To enhance growth opportunities the company has focused on promoting new product innovation and development and brand marketing. In addition the company has embarked on a strategy of acquiring companies or product lines that complement or expand the company's existing product lines or provide expansion into new or emerging categories in sporting goods.

Mergers and Acquisitions

In late 2020 Escalade Sports a wholly owned subsidiary of Escalade has acquired substantially all of the business and assets of Revel Match dba RAVE Sports a brand known for its innovative and high-quality water recreation products. Adding this business to Escalade's existing portfolio expands its powerful stable of recreational brands and positions the company for continued revenue and profit growth.

Also in late 2020 Escalade Sports a wholly owned subsidiary of Escalade has acquired the assets of the billiard table game room and recre-

ational product lines of American Heritage Billiards including the related intellectual property. Escalade agreed to pay a gross purchase price of $1.55 million which was paid in cash at closing.

EXECUTIVES

Vice President - Corporate Development, Investor Relations, Director, Patrick Griffin, $175,909 total compensation
Chief Financial Officer, Vice President - Finance, Secretary, Stephen Wawrin, $265,735 total compensation
Independent Director, Katherine Franklin
Independent Director, Edward Williams
Independent Director, Richard Baalmann
Chairman Of The Board, President, Chief Executive Officer, Walter Glazer
Auditors: BKD, LLP

LOCATIONS

HQ: Escalade, Inc.
817 Maxwell Ave., Evansville, IN 47711
Phone: 812 467-1358
Web: www.escaladeinc.com

PRODUCTS/OPERATIONS

Selected Brands

Accudart
American Legend
Arachnid
Atomic
Bear Archery
Cajun Bowfishing
Childlife
Goaliath
Goalrilla
Goalsetter
Hoopstar
Lucasi
Minnesota Fats
Mizerak
Nodor
Onix
Pickleball Now
Ping-Pong
Players
Prince
PureX
Rage
Redline
Silverback
STIGA
The STEP
Trophy Ridge
Unicorn
USWeight
Viva Sol
Whisker Biscuit
Winmau
Woodplay
Zume Games

COMPETITORS

ACUSHNET HOLDINGS CORP.	LIFE FITNESS INC.
ARIAL SOFTWARE LLC	MIZUNO USA INC.
BIG 5 SPORTING GOODS CORPORATION	NAUTILUS INC.
	QUADIENT INC.
CALLAWAY GOLF COMPANY	SPORTSMAN'S WAREHOUSE HOLDINGS INC.
CYBEX INTERNATIONAL INC.	SUPERIOR GROUP OF COMPANIES INC.
DICK'S SPORTING GOODS INC.	TELLERMATE LIMITED
ENTRUST CORPORATION	THE INTERTECH GROUP INC.
Francotyp-Postalia GmbH	TSI INCORPORATED
JOHNSON OUTDOORS INC.	UNDER ARMOUR INC.
LANE INDUSTRIES INC	VISTA OUTDOOR INC.

HISTORICAL FINANCIALS

Company Type: Public

Income Statement

FYE: December 25

	REVENUE ($ mil.)	NET INCOME ($ mil.)	NET PROFIT MARGIN	EMPLOYEES
12/21	313.6	24.4	7.8%	676
12/20	273.6	25.9	9.5%	704
12/19	180.5	7.2	4.0%	468
12/18	175.7	20.4	11.6%	531
12/17	177.3	14.0	7.9%	501
Annual Growth	15.3%	14.8%	—	7.8%

2021 Year-End Financials

Debt ratio: 22.8%
Return on equity: 17.1%
Cash ($ mil.): 4.3
Current ratio: 3.55
Long-term debt ($ mil.): 50.4
No. of shares (mil.): 13.4
Dividends
  Yield: 0.0%
  Payout: 31.8%
Market value ($ mil.): 212.0

	STOCK PRICE ($) FY Close	P/E High/Low		PER SHARE ($) Earnings	Dividends	Book Value
12/21	15.69	14	9	1.76	0.56	10.87
12/20	21.69	12	3	1.82	0.53	10.00
12/19	9.79	26	19	0.50	0.50	8.88
12/18	11.44	11	8	1.41	0.50	8.89
12/17	12.30	14	12	0.98	0.46	7.77
Annual Growth	6.3%	—	—	15.8%	5.0%	8.7%

Esquire Financial Holdings Inc

Auditors: Crowe LLP

LOCATIONS

HQ: Esquire Financial Holdings Inc
100 Jericho Quadrangle, Suite 100, Jericho, NY 11753
Phone: 516 535-2002
Web: www.esquirebank.com

HISTORICAL FINANCIALS

Company Type: Public

Income Statement

FYE: December 31

	ASSETS ($ mil.)	NET INCOME ($ mil.)	INCOME AS % OF ASSETS	EMPLOYEES
12/20	936.7	12.6	1.3%	99
12/19	798.0	14.1	1.8%	86
12/18	663.9	8.7	1.3%	74
12/17	533.6	3.6	0.7%	61
12/16	424.8	2.8	0.7%	52
Annual Growth	21.9%	45.4%	—	17.5%

2020 Year-End Financials

Return on assets: 1.4%
Return on equity: 10.6%
Long-term debt ($ mil.): —
No. of shares (mil.): 7.7
Sales ($ mil): 53.2
Dividends
  Yield: —
  Payout: —
Market value ($ mil.): 150.0

STOCK PRICE ($)		P/E		PER SHARE ($)		
	FY Close	High/Low		Earnings	Dividends	Book Value
12/20	19.19	15	7	1.65	0.00	16.18
12/19	26.07	14	11	1.82	0.00	14.51
12/18	21.70	23	16	1.13	0.00	12.32
12/17	19.74	36	25	0.58	0.00	11.38
Annual Growth	(0.9%)	—	—	41.7%	—	12.4%

Essential Properties Realty Trust Inc

Auditors: Grant Thornton LLP

LOCATIONS

HQ: Essential Properties Realty Trust Inc
902 Carniege Center Blvd., Suite 520, Princeton, NJ 08540
Phone: 609 436-0619
Web: www.essentialproperties.com

HISTORICAL FINANCIALS

Company Type: Public

Income Statement — FYE: December 31

	REVENUE ($ mil.)	NET INCOME ($ mil.)	NET PROFIT MARGIN	EMPLOYEES
12/21	230.2	95.7	41.6%	37
12/20	164.0	42.2	25.8%	33
12/19	139.3	41.8	30.0%	27
12/18	96.2	15.6	16.2%	18
12/17	54.5	6.3	11.6%	19
Annual Growth	43.4%	97.5%	—	18.1%

2021 Year-End Financials

Debt ratio: 35.3%
Return on equity: 5.3%
Cash ($ mil.): 59.7
Current ratio: 1.82
Long-term debt ($ mil.): 1,165.7
No. of shares (mil.): 124.6
Dividends
Yield: 3.4%
Payout: 161.2%
Market value ($ mil.): 3,594.0

STOCK PRICE ($)		P/E		PER SHARE ($)		
	FY Close	High/Low		Earnings	Dividends	Book Value
12/21	28.83	40	25	0.82	1.00	16.34
12/20	21.20	66	17	0.44	0.93	14.81
12/19	24.81	41	21	0.63	0.88	14.26
12/18	13.84	56	51	0.26	0.43	12.85
Annual Growth	27.7%	—	—	46.6%	32.1%	8.3%

Essential Utilities Inc

Essential Utilities (Essential) formerly Aqua America provides water or wastewater services to some 3 million customers in Pennsylvania Ohio Texas Illinois North Carolina New Jersey Indiana and Virginia. It is the holding company for several regulated utilities the largest being Aqua Pennsylvania. Additionally the company provides non-utility water supply services for the natural gas drilling industry manages a water system operating and maintenance contracts as well as sewer line protection solutions and repair service to households. The company was formed in 1968. Some 55% of Essential's total sales comes from Pennsylvania.

Operations

Essential have identified ten operating segments and have one reportable segment based on the following: eight segments are composed of their water and wastewater regulated utility operations in the eight states where they provide these services and aggregated into one reportable segment named the "Regulated water segment"; and two segments are composed of Aqua Resources and Aqua Infrastructure which are included as a component of "Other".

Regulated water segment consists of residential water (accounting for about 60% of total revenue) commercial water (over 15%) wastewater (more than 10%) fire protection industrial water other water (generates for nearly 5% each) and other utility (two percent).

Geographic Reach

Primarily serving Pennsylvania (headquarters) Essential provides services in Ohio Texas Illinois North Carolina New Jersey Indiana and Virginia. Almost 55% of company revenue comes from over 25 counties in Pennsylvania and major areas around Philadelphia.

Sales and Marketing

Essential's customers are mostly residential and commercial customers. It also serves fire protection departments industries wastewater clients and other utility customers. Residential water and commercial customers bring in about 75% of annual revenue and wastewater customers bring in more than 10% more.

Financial Performance

Operating revenues totaled $889.7 million in 2019 a 6% growth from $838.1 million in 2018. The increase was primarily due to higher sales in the company's wastewater residential water and commercial water segments.

Essential's net income grew 17% from $192 million in 2018 to $224.5 million in 2019. The higher expenses were offset by even higher revenue.

Cash at the end of 2019 was $1.9 billion. Operating activities generated $338.5 million while investing activities used $604.6 million mainly for capital expenditures. Financing activities generated another $2.1 billion.

Strategy

Despite maintaining a program to monitor condemnation interests and activities that may affect it over time one of Essential's primary strategies continues to be to acquire additional water and wastewater systems to maintain its existing systems where there is a business or a strategic benefit and to actively oppose unilateral efforts by municipal governments to acquire any of its operations particularly for less than the fair market value of the company's operations or where the municipal government seeks to acquire more than it is entitled to under the applicable law or agreement. On occasion Essential may voluntarily agree to sell systems or portions of systems in order to help focus its efforts in areas where we have more critical mass and economies of scale or for other strategic reasons.

Mergers and Acquisitions

In mid-2020 Essential Utilities' Aqua Texas water utility has signed an agreement with The Commons Water Supply Inc. to purchase the company's water treatment and distribution system in The Commons of Lake Houston in Huffman Texas. The system serves more than 1000 homes in the development. The transaction is a milestone for Essential as it will be the first acquisition to use a new Texas law that allows regulated water companies to pay a fair market value for the purchase of water and wastewater systems. Financial terms were not disclosed.

In early 2020 the company has successfully completed the acquisition of Peoples a Pittsburgh-based natural gas distribution company in an all-cash transaction that reflects an enterprise value of $4.275 billion including the assumption of approximately $1.1 billion of debt. As previously disclosed the transaction was financed through an appropriate mix of equity and debt which supports a strong balance sheet and continued investment-grade credit ratings for the combined business. Essential which changed its name from Aqua America in early 2020 began trading under the NYSE ticker symbol (WTRG) the same day.

Also in early 2020 Aqua America's (Essential Utilities at present) Ohio subsidiary has completed the purchase of the City of Campbell's water treatment plant and distribution system which serves about 3200 connections in Mahoning County for $7.5 million. This is the first acquisition by an Aqua America subsidiary in 2020. Financial terms were not disclosed.

EXECUTIVES

Chief Financial Officer, Executive Vice President, Daniel Schuller, $442,515 total compensation
Independent Director, Christopher Womack
Independent Director, Ellen Ruff
Senior Vice President, Chief Accounting Officer, Controller, Robert Rubin
Chairman Of The Board, President, Chief Executive Officer, Christopher Franklin, $858,846 total compensation
Executive Vice President - Strategy And Corporate Development, Matthew Rhodes. $424,415 total compensation
Independent Director, Elizabeth Amato
Independent Director, Francis Idehen
Independent Director, David Ciesinski
Executive Vice President, General Counsel, Secretary, Christopher Luning, $379,860 total compensation
Chief Operating Officer, Executive Vice President, Richard Fox, $425,454 total compensation
Auditors: PricewaterhouseCoopers LLP

LOCATIONS

HQ: Essential Utilities Inc
762 W Lancaster Avenue, Bryn Mawr, PA 19010-3489
Phone: 610 527-8000
Web: www.essential.co

PRODUCTS/OPERATIONS

2015 Sales

	$ mil.	% of total
Regulated		
Residential water	477.8	59
Commercial water	126.8	16
Fire protection	29.7	4
Industrial water	28.0	3
Other water	27.2	3
Wastewater	79.4	10
Other utility	10.7	1
Other and eliminations	34.6	4
Total	**814.2**	**100**

HOOVER'S HANDBOOK OF EMERGING COMPANIES 2022

Selected Subsidiaries

Aqua Illinois Inc.
Aqua Indiana Inc.
Aqua New Jersey Inc.
Aqua North Carolina Inc.
Aqua Ohio Inc.
Aqua Pennsylvania Inc.
Aqua Resources Inc.
Aqua Services Inc.
Aqua Texas Inc.
Aqua Utilities Inc.
Aqua Virginia Inc.

COMPETITORS

COVANTA HOLDING CORPORATION	SAN ANTONIO WATER SYSTEM
DENVER BOARD OF WATER COMMISSIONERS	SJW GROUP
EVOQUA WATER TECHNOLOGIES LLC	TUCSON ELECTRIC POWER COMPANY
NORTHWESTERN CORPORATION	UNITED UTILITIES GROUP PLC
ORLANDO UTILITIES COMMISSION (INC)	WATER PLUS GROUP LIMITED

HISTORICAL FINANCIALS

Company Type: Public

Income Statement | | | | FYE: December 31

	REVENUE ($ mil.)	NET INCOME ($ mil.)	NET PROFIT MARGIN	EMPLOYEES
12/20	1,462.7	284.8	19.5%	3,180
12/19	889.6	224.5	25.2%	1,583
12/18	838.0	191.9	22.9%	1,570
12/17	809.5	239.7	29.6%	1,530
12/16	819.8	234.1	28.6%	1,551
Annual Growth	15.6%	5.0%	—	19.7%

2020 Year-End Financials

Debt ratio: 41.3%
Return on equity: 6.6%
Cash ($ mil.): 4.8
Current ratio: 0.63
Long-term debt ($ mil.): 5,507.7
No. of shares (mil.): 245.3
Dividends
  Yield: 2.0%
  Payout: 97.9%
Market value ($ mil.): 11,605.0

	STOCK PRICE ($) FY Close	P/E High/Low		Earnings	PER SHARE ($) Dividends	Book Value
12/20	47.29	47	29	1.12	0.97	19.09
12/19	46.94	45	32	1.04	0.91	17.58
12/18	34.19	36	30	1.08	0.85	11.28
12/17	39.23	29	22	1.35	0.79	11.02
12/16	30.04	27	22	1.32	0.74	10.43
Annual Growth	12.0%			—	(4.0%) 7.1%	16.3%

Etsy Inc

Auditors: PricewaterhouseCoopers LLP

LOCATIONS

HQ: Etsy Inc
  117 Adams Street, Brooklyn, NY 11201
Phone: 718 880-3660
Web: www.etsy.com

HISTORICAL FINANCIALS

Company Type: Public

Income Statement | | | FYE: December 31

	REVENUE ($ mil.)	NET INCOME ($ mil.)	NET PROFIT MARGIN	EMPLOYEES
12/20	1,725.6	349.2	20.2%	1,414
12/19	818.3	95.8	11.7%	1,240
12/18	603.6	77.4	12.8%	874
12/17	441.2	81.8	18.5%	744
12/16	364.9	(29.9)	—	1,043
Annual Growth	47.5%	—		7.9%

2020 Year-End Financials

Debt ratio: 46.4%
Return on equity: 60.6%
Cash ($ mil.): 1,244.1
Current ratio: 4.17
Long-term debt ($ mil.): 1,107.2
No. of shares (mil.): 125.8
Dividends
  Yield: —
  Payout: —
Market value ($ mil.): 22,387.0

	STOCK PRICE ($) FY Close	P/E High/Low		Earnings	PER SHARE ($) Dividends	Book Value
12/20	177.91	69	11	2.69	0.00	5.90
12/19	44.30	91	51	0.76	0.00	3.44
12/18	47.57	90	28	0.61	0.00	3.35
12/17	20.45	32	14	0.68	0.00	3.26
12/16	11.78	—	—	(0.26)	0.00	2.97
Annual Growth	97.1%			—	—	18.7%

Evans Bancorp, Inc.

Evans National Bank wants to take care of Buffalo's bills. The subsidiary of Evans Bancorp operates about a dozen branches in western New York (including Buffalo). The bank primarily uses funds gathered from deposits to originate commercial and residential real estate loans (more than 70% of its loan portfolio) and to invest in securities. Subsidiaries include ENB Insurance Agency which sells property/casualty insurance; ENB Associates offering mutual funds and annuities to bank customers; and Evans National Leasing which provides financing for business equipment throughout the US. In 2009 Evans Bancorp acquired the assets and single branch of the failed Waterford Village Bank in Clarence New York.

EXECUTIVES

Independent Director, David Pfalzgraf
Treasurer Of The Company, Chief Financial Officer Of Evans Bank, N.a., John Connerton, $252,693 total compensation
President And Chief Executive Officer Of The Company And The Bank, Director, David Nasca, $545,192 total compensation
President Of The Evans Agency, Llc, Aaron Whitehouse, $202,616 total compensation
Independent Director, Kevin Maroney
Independent Director, Kimberley Minkel
Independent Director, Christina Orsi
Investor Relations, Jessica Brosius
Independent Director, Jody Lomeo
Independent Director, James Biddle
Independent Director, Nora Sullivan
Independent Director, Michael Battle
Independent Director, Michael Rogers

Independent Chairman Of The Board, Lee Wortham
Independent Director, Thomas Waring
Auditors: Crowe LLP

LOCATIONS

HQ: Evans Bancorp, Inc.
  6460 Main St, Williamsville, NY 14221
Phone: 716 926-2000
Web: www.evansbancorp.com

COMPETITORS

KISH BANCORP INC.	VALLEY NATIONAL
LCNB CORP.	BANCORP

HISTORICAL FINANCIALS

Company Type: Public

Income Statement | | | FYE: December 31

	ASSETS ($ mil.)	NET INCOME ($ mil.)	INCOME AS % OF ASSETS	EMPLOYEES
12/20	2,044.1	11.2	0.6%	309
12/19	1,460.2	17.0	1.2%	250
12/18	1,388.2	16.3	1.2%	237
12/17	1,295.6	10.4	0.8%	271
12/16	1,100.7	8.2	0.8%	254
Annual Growth	16.7%	8.0%	—	5.0%

2020 Year-End Financials

Return on assets: 0.6%
Return on equity: 7.0%
Long-term debt ($ mil.): —
No. of shares (mil.): 5.4
Sales ($ mil): 86.4
Dividends
  Yield: 4.2%
  Payout: 54.4%
Market value ($ mil.): 149.0

	STOCK PRICE ($) FY Close	P/E High/Low		Earnings	PER SHARE ($) Dividends	Book Value
12/20	27.54	19	10	2.13	1.16	31.21
12/19	40.10	12	9	3.42	1.04	30.12
12/18	32.51	14	9	3.32	0.92	27.13
12/17	41.90	20	15	2.16	0.80	24.74
12/16	31.55	19	12	1.90	0.76	22.50
Annual Growth	(3.3%)			—	2.9% 11.2%	8.5%

Evercore Inc

Evercore is the leading independent investment banking advisory firm in the world based on the dollar volume of announced worldwide merger and acquisition (M&A) transactions. The company provides advisory services on mergers and mergers and acquisitions strategic shareholder advisory restructurings and capital structure to corporate clients. Boasting some $10.2 billion in assets under management the company's investment management business principally manages and invests capital for clients including institutional investors and private equity businesses. Evercore also makes private equity investments. Beyond the US the company operates globally through subsidiaries such as Evercore Partners in the UK. About 75% of the company's revenue comes from its domestic operations. Evercore was founded in 1995.

HOOVER'S HANDBOOK OF EMERGING COMPANIES 2022

Operations

Evercore operates through two business segments: Investment Banking and Investment Management.

The Investment Banking segment is further divided into four categories. The first is the strategic corporate advisory business which offers strategic and financial consulting for public and private companies across a range of industries and geographies. The second is the capital markets advisory business in which Evercore acts as an independent advisor capital placement agent or underwriter based on each client's needs. The institution equities business is known as Evercore ISI and comprises about 40 senior trading professionals that support customers' money management needs. The fourth category ? Other ? under Investment Banking represents the company's interest in Luminis Partners an independent corporate advisory firm based in Australia.

The Investment Management segment includes wealth management and trust services through Evercore Wealth Management as well as private equity through investments in entities that manage private equity funds.

Geographic Reach

While Evercore operates globally the US accounts for more than 75% of the firm's revenue. Europe and other countries make up around 20% and Latin America represents less than 5%. Evercore operates from its offices in 30 cities around the globe and through its affiliates worldwide. Its principal offices are in New York and London.

Sales and Marketing

Evercore serves companies in financial transition creditors shareholders and potential acquirers.

Financial Performance

Net revenues were $2.3 billion in 2020 an increase of $255.2 million or 13% versus net revenues of $2.0 billion in 2019.

Net Income Attributable to Evercore Inc. was $350.6 million in 2020 an increase of $53.1 million or 18% compared to $297.4 million in 2019.

Cash held by the company at the end of 2020 increased to $838.2 million. Cash provided by operations was $978.4 million while cash used for investing and financing activities were $438.9 million and $307.8 million respectively. Main uses for cash were purchases of investment securities and futures contracts activity and purchase of treasury stock and noncontrolling interests.

Strategy

The company expects to deploy the majority of its capital to continue to grow its Investment Banking businesses. Evercore intends to continue to grow and diversify its businesses and to further enhance its profile and competitive position through the following strategies:

Add and Promote Highly Qualified Investment Banking Professionals. The company hired three new Senior Managing Directors in 2020 expanding the company's capabilities in its Capital Markets Advisory practice by strengthening its coverage of the Technology sector as well as enhancing its advisory capabilities on complex and large cap corporate realignments and expanding the company's capital raising and distribution capabilities with convertible debt. Of equal importance following Evercore's long-term strategy of developing internal talent it also promoted seven internal candidates to Senior Managing Director in its Advisory business in 2020 and intend to continue to promote its most talented professionals in the future.

Evercore intend to continue to recruit and promote high-caliber strategic corporate strategic and capital markets advisory as well as equity research professionals to add depth in industry sectors and products and services in areas that the company believe it already have strength and to extend its reach to sectors or new business lines and geographies that the company have identified as particularly attractive. On occasion these additions may result from the acquisition of boutique independent advisory firms with leading professionals in a market or sector.

Achieve Organic Growth and Improved Profitability in Investment Management. Evercore are focused on managing its current Investment Management business effectively. The company also continue to selectively evaluate opportunities to expand Wealth Management.

Company Background

Some of Evercore's past high-profile transactions include the 2012 breakup of Kraft Foods (now Mondelez International) the recapitalizations of GM and CIT Group and the acquisition of Lubrizol by Berkshire Hathaway.

Evercore was launched in 1996 (it went public 10 years later) by Roger Altman who formerly led investment banking and merger advisory practices at Lehman Brothers and The Blackstone Group.

EXECUTIVES

Senior Chairman, Roger Altman, $500,000 total compensation
Lead Independent Director, Gail Harris
Independent Director, Richard Beattie
Independent Director, Robert Millard
General Counsel, Corporate Secretary, Jason Klurfeld, $500,000 total compensation
Independent Director, William Wheeler
Independent Director, Simon Robertson
Independent Director, Willard Overlock
Independent Director, Sarah Williamson
Independent Director, Ellen Futter
Senior Managing Director, Juan Pedro Perez Cozar
Chief Financial Officer, Senior Managing Director, Celeste Mellet Brown
Senior Managing Director, David Lischer
Co-chairman Of The Board, Co-chief Executive Officer, Ralph Schlosstein, $500,000 total compensation
Co-chairman Of The Board, Co-chief Executive Officer, John Weinberg, $500,000 total compensation
Vice Chairman, Chairman Of Evercore Isi, Edward Hyman, $400,000 total compensation
Auditors: DELOITTE & TOUCHE LLP

LOCATIONS

HQ: Evercore Inc
55 East 52nd Street, New York, NY 10055
Phone: 212 857-3100 **Fax:** 212 857-3101
Web: www.evercore.com

PRODUCTS/OPERATIONS

2018 Sales

	$ mil.	% of total
Investment banking		
Advisory fees	1,743.5	84
Commissions and related fees	200.0	10
Underwriting fees	71.7	3
Asset management and administration fees	48.2	2
Other	19.1	1
Interest Expense	(17.8)	-
Total	**2,064.7**	**100**

COMPETITORS

AFFILIATED MANAGERS GROUP INC.	PRINCIPAL GLOBAL INVESTORS LLC
COWEN INC.	Power Corporation of Canada
Canaccord Genuity Group Inc	ROCKWOOD REALISATION PLC
JEFFERIES FINANCIAL GROUP INC.	SEI INVESTMENTS COMPANY
LPL FINANCIAL HOLDINGS INC.	THE ZIEGLER COMPANIES INC
OPPENHEIMER HOLDINGS INC.	

HISTORICAL FINANCIALS

Company Type: Public

Income Statement — FYE: December 31

	REVENUE ($ mil.)	NET INCOME ($ mil.)	NET PROFIT MARGIN	EMPLOYEES
12/20	2,263.9	350.5	15.5%	1 800
12/19	2,008.7	297.4	14.8%	1 900
12/18	2,064.7	377.2	18.3%	1 700
12/17	1,704.3	125.4	7.4%	1 600
12/16	1,440.0	107.5	7.5%	1 475
Annual Growth	12.0%	34.4%	—	5.1%

2020 Year-End Financials

Debt ratio: 11.1%	No. of shares (mil.): 40.7
Return on equity: 33.2%	Dividends
Cash ($ mil.): 829.6	Yield: 2.1%
Current ratio: 2.23	Payout: 28.5%
Long-term debt ($ mil.): 338.5	Market value ($ mil.): 4,468.0

	STOCK PRICE ($) FY Close	P/E High/Low		PER SHARE ($) Earnings	Dividends	Book Value
12/20	109.64	13	4	8.22	2.35	30.21
12/19	74.76	13	10	6.89	2.24	22.20
12/18	71.56	12	7	8.33	1.90	19.07
12/17	90.00	29	21	2.80	1.42	13.91
12/16	68.70	26	15	2.43	1.27	13.45
Annual Growth	12.4%	—	—	35.6%	16.6%	22.4%

EVI Industries Inc

EnviroStar (formerly DRYCLEAN USA) is anything but hard pressed. The firm franchises and licenses more than 400 retail dry cleaners in three US states the Caribbean and Latin America through its DRYCLEAN USA unit. However most of its sales are generated by subsidiary Steiner-Atlantic which sells coin-operated laundry machines steam boilers and other laundry equipment; most are sold under the Aero-Tech Green-Jet and Multi-Jet names to some 750 customers and include independent dry cleaners hotels cruise lines and hospitals. The company was founded in 1963 under the name Metro-Tel Corp. It changed its name to DRYCLEAN USA in 1999.

EXECUTIVES

Independent Director, David Blyer
Chief Financial Officer, Chief Accounting Officer, Robert Lazar, $205,000 total compensation
Chairman Of The Board, President, Chief Executive Officer, Henry Nahmad, $550,000 total compensation

Independent Director, Hal Lucas
Executive Vice President - Corporate Strategy, Director, Dennis Mack, $300,000 total compensation
Executive Vice President - Business Development And President - West Region, Thomas Marks, $300,000 total compensation
Independent Director, Timothy Lamacchia
Independent Director, Glen Kruger
Auditors: BDO USA, LLP

LOCATIONS

HQ: EVI Industries Inc
 4500 Biscayne Blvd., Suite 340, Miami, FL 33137
Phone: 305 402-9300
Web: www.evi-ind.com

COMPETITORS

AERUS LLC
BERENDSEN LIMITED
DS SERVICES OF AMERICA INC.
MARIETTA CORPORATION
NORTHERN TOOL & EQUIPMENT COMPANY INC.
RED DOT CORPORATION
TACONY CORPORATION
TRITON SYSTEMS OF DELAWARE LLC

HISTORICAL FINANCIALS

Company Type: Public

Income Statement				FYE: June 30
	REVENUE ($ mil.)	**NET INCOME** ($ mil.)	**NET PROFIT MARGIN**	**EMPLOYEES**
06/21	242.0	8.3	3.5%	526
06/20	235.8	0.7	0.3%	493
06/19	228.3	3.7	1.6%	475
06/18	150.0	3.9	2.6%	264
06/17	93.9	3.1	3.4%	138
Annual Growth	26.7%	27.6%	—	39.7%

2021 Year-End Financials

Debt ratio: 6.6%
Return on equity: 8.6%
Cash ($ mil.): 6.0
Current ratio: 1.32
Long-term debt ($ mil.): 11.8

No. of shares (mil.): 12.2
Dividends
 Yield: —
 Payout: —
Market value ($ mil.): 349.0

	STOCK PRICE ($) FY Close	**P/E** High/Low		**PER SHARE ($)** Earnings	Dividends	Book Value
06/21	28.40	70	32	0.61	0.00	8.69
06/20	21.71	625	234	0.06	0.00	7.36
06/19	38.27	158	91	0.29	0.13	6.93
06/18	40.30	126	65	0.33	0.12	5.10
06/17	27.05	101	12	0.31	0.10	3.08
Annual Growth	1.2%	—	—	18.4%	—	29.6%

Exelixis Inc

Exelixis is an oncology-focused biotechnology company that strives to accelerate the discovery development and commercialization of new medicines for difficult-to-treat cancers. Its flagship molecule cabozantinib is the origin of two commercial products Cabometyx a tablets approved for advanced renal cell carcinoma and Cometriq capsules approved for progressive metastatic medullary thy-

roid cancer. It also include Cotellic (cobimetinib) a treatment for advanced melanoma and marketed under a collaboration with Genentech. It also has other drug development candidates against multiple target classes for oncology inflammation and metabolic diseases. The US accounts for about 80% of total revenue.

Operations

Exelixis offers four product from its clinical development and established a commercial presence in various location worldwide. Its first FDA approved products include Cabometyx a tablets approved for advanced renal cell carcinoma (RCC) and previously treated hepatocellular carcinoma (HCC); and Cometriq capsules approved for progressive metastatic medullary thyroid cancer (MTC). Outside the US and Japan Cabometyx and Cometriq are marketed by its collaboration partner Ipsen. Should Cabometyx be approved in Japan it will be marketed by collaboration partner Takeda Pharmaceutical.

The other two products: Cotellic (cobimetinib) an inhibitor of MEK approved as part of a combination regimen to treat advanced melanoma and marketed under a collaboration with Genentech (a member of the Roche Group); and Minnebro (esaxerenone) an oral non-steroidal selective blocker of the mineralocorticoid receptor (MR) approved for the treatment of hypertension in Japan and licensed to Daiichi Sankyo.

Overall its net product accounts about 80% of total revenue while collaboration accounts around 20%.

Geographic Reach

The company is headquartered in Alameda California. The US accounts for about 80% of total revenue Europe for about 15% while Japan accounts the remainder.

Sales and Marketing

Its customers include Ipsen and CVS Health that accounts about 15% each of revenues and around 10% each from affiliates of McKesson and affiliates of AmerisourceBergen. It has contracts with a third-party logistics provider with multiple distribution locations to provide shipping and warehousing services for its commercial supply of both CABOMETYX and COMETRIQ in the US.

Exelixis contracts with third parties to manufacture clinical and commercial supplies of its products.

Financial Performance

As a development-stage company Exelixis has struggled to turn a profit. It did manage to grow its revenues each year for several years by entering new partnerships and licensing agreements and by achieving milestone payouts on existing contracts. From 2015 to 2019 the company posted a staggering more than 2500% increase in revenue.

In 2019 revenue increased by 13% to $967.8 million. Net product revenues increased by 23% partially offset by an 11% decrease in Collaboration revenues.

Net income decreased by 53% in 2019 to $321 million. The decrease in income was due to an increase of $183.3 million in operating expenses and $77.1 million in income tax provision.

Cash and cash equivalents at the end of the period were $268.1 million. Net cash provided by operating activities was $527.0 million and financing activities provided another $12.6 million. Investing activities used $587.2 million for purchases of investments.

Strategy

The growth that the company has experienced in recent years is largely attributable to cabozantinib's clinical and commercial success; consistent with its values and legal obligations it is committed to ensuring that all patients who are prescribed cabozantinib are able to access this essential medicine.

Over the course of 2019 revenues from CABOMETYX and COMETRIQ sales and from the royalties and milestone payments it has received pursuant to collaboration agreements with its partners coupled with disciplined expense management have fueled the growth of its organization. The company believes in its long-term growth prospects which are supported by a healthy cash position and profitability over the past three fiscal years. It is utilizing its cash and investments to enable potential future success by expanding the development program for cabozantinib and by building a pipeline of new drug candidates through internal drug discovery efforts and the execution of strategic transactions that align with its oncology drug development and commercialization expertise.

EXECUTIVES

Independent Chairman Of The Board, Co-founder, Stelios Papadopoulos
President, Chief Executive Officer, Director, Michael Morrissey, $1,058,216 total compensation
Executive Vice President - Scientific Strategy, Chief Scientific Officer, Peter Lamb, $517,617 total compensation
Independent Director, Lance Willsey
Independent Director, Jack Wyszomierski
Independent Director, George Poste
Executive Vice President - Product Development And Medical Affairs, Chief Medical Officer, Vicki Goodman
Executive Vice President, General Counsel, Jeffrey Hessekiel, $576,091 total compensation
Independent Director, Julie Smith
Executive Vice President - Commercial, Patrick Haley, $500,953 total compensation
Independent Director, Charles Cohen
Independent Director, Maria Freire
Chief Financial Officer, Executive Vice President, Christopher Senner, $648,358 total compensation
Independent Director, Carl Feldbaum
Director, Jacqueline Wright
Auditors: Ernst & Young LLP

LOCATIONS

HQ: Exelixis Inc
 1851 Harbor Bay Parkway, Alameda, CA 94502
Phone: 650 837-7000
Web: www.exelixis.com

COMPETITORS

ACORDA THERAPEUTICS INC.
BIOCRYST PHARMACEUTICALS INC.
CYTRX CORPORATION
DURECT CORPORATION
DYNAVAX TECHNOLOGIES CORPORATION
INOVIO PHARMACEUTICALS INC.
PDL BIOPHARMA INC.
PTC THERAPEUTICS INC.

150 HOOVER'S HANDBOOK OF EMERGING COMPANIES 2022

HISTORICAL FINANCIALS

Company Type: Public

Income Statement

FYE: December 31

	REVENUE ($ mil.)	NET INCOME ($ mil.)	NET PROFIT MARGIN	EMPLOYEES
12/21*	1,434.9	231.0	16.1%	954
01/21	987.5	111.7	11.3%	773
01/20	967.7	321.0	33.2%	617
12/18	853.8	690.0	80.8%	484
12/17	452.4	154.2	34.1%	372
Annual Growth	33.4%	10.6%	—	26.5%

*Fiscal year change

2021 Year-End Financials

Debt ratio: —
Return on equity: 11.3%
Cash ($ mil.): 647.1
Current ratio: 5.43
Long-term debt ($ mil.): —

No. of shares (mil.): 318.8
Dividends
 Yield: —
 Payout: —
Market value ($ mil.): 5,828.0

	STOCK PRICE ($) FY Close	P/E High/Low		PER SHARE ($) Earnings	Dividends	Book Value
12/21*	18.28	35	22	0.72	0.00	6.93
01/21	20.07	76	40	0.35	0.00	6.03
01/20	17.01	23	14	1.02	0.00	5.53
12/18	19.44	14	6	2.21	0.00	4.29
12/17	30.40	59	28	0.49	0.00	0.96
Annual Growth	(11.9%)	—	—	10.1%	—	63.8%

*Fiscal year change

ExlService Holdings Inc

ExlService Holdings known as EXL offers business process management (BPM) research and analytics and consulting services through its operating segments. EXL's BPM offerings which generate most of its sales include claims processing clinical operations and finance and accounting services. Customers come mainly from the banking financial services and insurance industries as well as from the utilities and telecommunications sectors. EXL operates around the world but generates nearly 85% of revenue from the US. The company was established in 1999.

Operations

EXL's reportable segments are Analytics Insurance Finance and Accounting (F&A) Healthcare and Travel Transportation and Logistics (TT&L). All Other consists of the remaining business including banking and financial services utilities and consulting operations.

The Analytics operating segment uses a range of advanced analytical tools and techniques including in-house machine learning and artificial intelligence (AI) capabilities. The segment accounts for more than 35% of sales.

Insurance accounts for close to 30% of sales and serves property and casualty insurance life insurance disability insurance annuity and retirement services companies. It provides BPM services such as claims processing subrogation premium benefits administration policy research premium audit surveys and billing and collection.

Finance and accounting (about 10% of sales) provides finance and accounting BPM and digital transformation services across an array of F&A processes including procure-to-pay order-to-cash hire-to-retire record-to-report and treasury and tax processes.

The Healthcare segment (around 10%) primarily serves US-based healthcare payers providers and life sciences organizations. It provides services related to care management utilization management disease management payment integrity revenue optimization and customer engagement.

The Travel Transportation and Logistics business (nearly 10%) comprises services to clients in the travel and leisure and transportation industries (less-than-truckload intermodal logistics and truckload sectors). This segment provides services like reservations customer service fulfillment finance and accounting. The remaining came from other business.

Geographic Reach

Headquartered in New York City EXL operates through multiple offices in the US more than 25 offices in India about five in the Philippines and an operations center in each of Australia the UK South Africa Colombia Bulgaria Romania and the Czech Republic.

US generates more than 80% of company's revenue followed by UK (about 10%).

Sales and Marketing

The company provides services through its sales and client management teams. Sales teams which operate out of the US Europe Australia and South Africa are aligned by industry verticals including finance and accounting and consulting.

EXL has about 470 clients with its top three clients generating about 15% of its revenue (Its top ten customers represent more than 35% of revenue).

Financial Performance

EXL's revenue growth for the past five years have been on an upward trend and has increased by 58% since 2015.

Sales in 2019 reached $991.3 million a 12% increase over $883.1 million in 2018. Growth was driven by the Analytics division Insurance Healthcare and Finance offset by decrease in revenue of Travel and Logistics.

Net income posted a 12% increase to $67.6 million in 2019 as a result of increase in income from operations ($26.6 million) and increase in other income ($3.5 million) partially offset by higher income tax expense ($11.8 million) higher interest expense of $6.4 million and lower foreign exchange gain ($1.0 million).

Cash at the end of fiscal 2019 was $127 million an increase of $22.9 million from the prior year. Cash from operations contributed to the coffers was $168.4million while investing activities used $51.4 million mainly for purchases of investments. Financing activities used another $93.1 million repayment of borrowings and acquisition of stocks.

Strategy

In line with EXL's strategy of vertical integration and focus on domain expertise it has integrated its Finance & Accounting and Consulting operating segments within each of the Insurance and Healthcare operating segments based on the respective industry-specific clients. Finance & Accounting and Consulting Services to clients outside of those industries will now be part of the newly formed business unit and reportable segment 'Emerging Business'. In addition it has integrated its former Travel Transportation and Logistics Banking and Financial Services and Utilities operating segments under "Emerging Business" to further leverage and optimize the operating scale in providing operations management services.

EXL is a business process management company providing operations management and analytics services and is a "Strategic Digital Transformation Partner" for its clients by deploying its Digital Intelligence framework. The company helps its clients become digitally intelligent by leveraging capabilities across data advanced analytics digital operations and domain expertise to deliver business outcomes across customer experience efficiency and revenue.

This can be summarized best by the following strategies: Expanding its services in large addressable markets; Integrating its capabilities by integrating solutions and services under one brand; Recruiting training and retaining the most talented professionals; Cultivating long-term relationships and expanding its client base; Expanding its global delivery footprint and operational infrastructure; and Pursuing strategic relationships and acquisitions.

EXECUTIVES

Independent Director, Kristy Pipes
Chief Marketing Officer, Jennifer Lemming
Executive Vice President And Business Head, Insurance, Vikas Bhalla, $229,016 total compensation
Independent Director, Anne Minto
Vice Chairman And Chief Executive Officer, Rohit Kapoor, $599,016 total compensation
Senior Vice President, General Counsel And Corporate Secretary, Ajay Ayyappan
Chief Human Resource Officer, Executive Vice President, Nalin Miglani, $404,631 total compensation
Independent Director, Clyde Ostler
Independent Director, Som Mittal
Independent Director, Nitin Sahney
Independent Director, Jaynie Studenmund
Chairman Of The Board, Vikram Pandit
Executive Vice President And Business Head, Healthcare, Samuel Meckey, $382,152 total compensation
Executive Vice President And Business Head, Analytics, Vivek Jetley
Chief Financial Officer, Executive Vice President, Maurizio Nicolelli, $384,283 total compensation
Executive Vice President And Chief Growth Officer, Anita Mahon
Auditors: DELOITTE & TOUCHE LLP

LOCATIONS

HQ: ExlService Holdings Inc
 320 Park Avenue, 29th Floor, New York, NY 10022
Phone: 212 277-7100
Web: www.exlservice.com

PRODUCTS/OPERATIONS

2018 Sales

	$ mil.	% of total
Analytics	285.3	32
BPM and related services		
Insurance	258.2	29
F&A	97.9	11
Healthcare	84.4	10
TT&L	70.2	8
All Other	87.1	10
Total	**883.1**	**100**

COMPETITORS

CAPITA PLC	ICF INTERNATIONAL INC.
CBIZ INC.	MASTEC INC.
CHARTERHOUSE GROUP	MSCI INC.
INC.	NV5 GLOBAL INC.
CONDUENT INCORPORATED	R1 RCM INC.
CORVEL CORPORATION	RECALL CORPORATION
ENVESTNET INC.	TTEC HOLDINGS INC.
EPLUS INC.	VIRTUSA CORPORATION
EVERTEC INC	WEX INC.

HISTORICAL FINANCIALS
Company Type: Public

Income Statement   FYE: December 31

	REVENUE ($ mil.)	NET INCOME ($ mil.)	NET PROFIT MARGIN	EMPLOYEES
12/20	958.4	89.4	9.3%	31,900
12/19	991.3	67.6	6.8%	31,700
12/18	883.1	56.7	6.4%	29,100
12/17	762.3	48.8	6.4%	27,800
12/16	685.9	61.7	9.0%	26,000
Annual Growth	8.7%	9.7%	—	5.2%

2020 Year-End Financials

Debt ratio: 18.2%	No. of shares (mil.): 33.5
Return on equity: 12.8%	Dividends
Cash ($ mil.): 402.8	Yield: —
Current ratio: 2.76	Payout: —
Long-term debt ($ mil.): 202.2	Market value ($ mil.): 2,857.0

	STOCK PRICE ($) FY Close	P/E High/Low		Earnings	PER SHARE ($) Dividends	Book Value
12/20	85.13	33	16	2.59	0.00	21.43
12/19	69.46	36	26	1.95	0.00	19.60
12/18	52.62	40	30	1.62	0.00	18.06
12/17	60.35	43	31	1.39	0.00	17.70
12/16	50.44	29	23	1.79	0.00	15.82
Annual Growth	14.0%	—	—	9.7%	—	7.9%

eXp World Holdings Inc

EXECUTIVES

Chb-Ceo, Glenn Sanford
V Chb*, Randall Miles
Cfo-Cco, Jeff Whiteside
CIO, John Tobison
Cmo, Courtney Chakarun
Chief Legal Counsel-General Co, James Bramble
Affiliate Broker, Realtor, Angie Griffith
Realtor, Anna Fuentes
Licensed Real Estate Salespers, Anu Narwal-Shukla
Real Estate Agent, Barbara Harris
Realtor, Bobby Lester
Auditors: DELOITTE & TOUCHE LLP

LOCATIONS

HQ: eXp World Holdings Inc
2219 Rimland Drive, Suite 301, Bellingham, WA 98226
Phone: 360 685-4206
Web: www.exprealty.com

HISTORICAL FINANCIALS
Company Type: Public

Income Statement   FYE: December 31

	REVENUE ($ mil.)	NET INCOME ($ mil.)	NET PROFIT MARGIN	EMPLOYEES
12/20	1,798.2	31.1	1.7%	900
12/19	979.9	(9.5)	—	634
12/18	500.1	(22.4)	—	15,854
12/17	156.1	(22.1)	—	6,695
12/16	54.1	(26.0)	—	94
Annual Growth	140.0%			75.9%

2020 Year-End Financials

Debt ratio: 1.7%	No. of shares (mil.): 144.1
Return on equity: 32.0%	Dividends
Cash ($ mil.): 100.1	Yield: —
Current ratio: 2.20	Payout: —
Long-term debt ($ mil.): 2.8	Market value ($ mil.): 9,098.0

	STOCK PRICE ($) FY Close	P/E High/Low		Earnings	PER SHARE ($) Dividends	Book Value
12/20	63.12	371	32	0.21	0.00	0.98
12/19	11.33	—	—	(0.08)	0.00	0.40
12/18	7.08	—	—	(0.20)	0.00	0.25
12/17	7.60	—	—	(0.21)	0.00	0.04
12/16	4.05	—	—	(0.26)	0.00	0.02
Annual Growth	98.7% 152.5%	—	—	—	—	—

Extra Space Storage Inc

Extra Space Storage is a self-administered and self-managed real estate investment trust (REIT) that owns some 1700 self-storage properties which comprise approximately 1.4 million units and approximately 153.4 million square feet of rentable storage space offering customers conveniently located and secure storage units across the country including boat storage RV storage and business storage. Extra Space is the second largest owner and/or operator of self-storage properties in the United States and is the largest self-storage management company in the US. Founded in 1977 Extra Space Storage went public in 2004.

Operations

Extra Space Storage operates through two segments: storage operations; and tenant reinsurance.

The storage operations segment which accounts for about 85% of sales focuses on activities include rental operations of wholly-owned stores. Tenant reinsurance (around 10%) covers the reinsurance of risks relating to the loss of goods stored by tenants in the company's self-storage facilities.

Geographic Reach

Utah-based Extra Space Storage operates its business throughout the US in about 40 states Puerto Rico and Washington DC.

Sales and Marketing

Approximately 1.1 million tenants were leasing storage units at the operating stores that the company owns and/or manages primarily on a month-to-month basis providing the flexibility to increase

rental rates over time as market conditions permit.

Extra Space Storage's advertising costs were $28336 $25106 and $16153 for the years 2020 2019 and 2018 respectively.

Financial Performance

Extra Space Storage's total revenues have consistently risen year after year in the last five years. Revenues rose 37% between 2016 and 2020.

Revenue increased 4% to $1.4 million in 2020 from $1.3 million in 2019. Property rental revenue tenant reinsurance revenue and management fees and other income all increased that year contributing to the rise in the company's total revenues.

Net income increased 15% to $481.8 million in 2020 from $420 million the year prior. The relatively higher total revenue and increase in gain on real estate transactions led to the rise in net income.

Cash and cash equivalents at the end of the year were $120 million $57.3 million higher from the year prior. Operating activities generated $771.2 million in 2020 while financing activities provided another $241.5 million to the company. Investing activities used $955.4 million for acquisition of real estate assets and issuance and purchases of notes receivables.

Strategy

Extra Space Storage continues to evaluate a range of growth initiatives and opportunities.

Its primary strategies include maximizing the performance of its stores through strategic efficient and proactive management; acquiring self-storage stores; growing its management business; expansion of its bridge loan program; and investing in other self-storage business selectively.

Extra Space Storage pursues revenue-generating and expense-minimizing opportunities in its operations. It continually analyzes its portfolio to look for long-term value-enhancing opportunities. It proactively redevelops properties to add units or modify existing unit mix to better meet the demand in a given market and to maximize revenue. Extra Space Storage also redevelops properties to reduce their effective useful age increase visual appeal enhance security and to improve brand consistency across the portfolio.

The company's acquisitions team continues to pursue the acquisition of multi-store portfolios and single stores that it believes can provide stockholder value. In addition to the pursuit of stabilized stores from time to time it develops stores from the ground up and provides the construction capital. It also purchases stores at the completion of construction from third-party developers who build to the company's specifications.

Extra Space Storage pursues strategic relationships with owners whose stores would enhance its portfolio in the event an opportunity arises to acquire such stores. To broaden the opportunities available it has recently implemented a bridge lending program under which it provides financing to operating properties that it manages. The company anticipates that this program will help it increase its management business create additional future acquisition opportunities and strengthen its relationships with partners all while providing interest income.

The company has also made investments in preferred stock of other self-storage companies. These investments benefit the company by not only providing dividend income but also have increased its management business creating additional future acquisition opportunities through creating and strengthening relationships with the companies in which it invests.

EXECUTIVES

Independent Director, Dennis Letham
Independent Director, Gary Crittenden
Independent Director, Joseph Bonner
Independent Director, Julia Ploeg
Executive Chairman Of The Board, Kenneth Woolley
Chief Executive Officer, Director, Joseph Margolis, $850,000 total compensation
Lead Independent Director, Roger Porter
Executive Vice President, Chief Legal Officer, Gwyn McNeal, $400,000 total compensation
Executive Vice President, Chief Marketing Officer, Samrat Sondhi, $410,000 total compensation
Executive Vice President And Chief Investment Officer, Zachary Dickens
Independent Director, Diane Olmstead
Chief Operating Officer, Executive Vice President, Matthew Herrington, $299,700 total compensation
Executive Vice President And Chief Strategy And Partnership Officer, Noah Springer
Chief Financial Officer, Executive Vice President, Peter Stubbs, $475,000 total compensation
Auditors: Ernst & Young LLP

LOCATIONS

HQ: Extra Space Storage Inc
2795 East Cottonwood Parkway, Suite 300, Salt Lake City, UT 84121
Phone: 801 365-4600
Web: www.extraspace.com

PRODUCTS/OPERATIONS

2015 Sales

	$ mil.	% of total
Property rental	676.1	87
Tenant reinsurance	72.0	9
Management & franchise fees	34.2	4
Total	782.3	100

COMPETITORS

99 CENTS ONLY STORES LLC
AGILITY PUBLIC WAREHOUSING CO. KSCP
AMERICOLD REALTY TRUST
ASSOCIATED WHOLESALE GROCERS INC.
CASESTACK LLC
Canadian Apartment Properties Real Estate Investment Tru
MOBILE MINI INC.
NATIONAL STORAGE AFFILIATES TRUST
NORISH LIMITED
PUBLIC STORAGE
SP PLUS CORPORATION
URBAN EDGE PROPERTIES
URM STORES INC.

HISTORICAL FINANCIALS
Company Type: Public

Income Statement				FYE: December 31
	REVENUE ($ mil.)	NET INCOME ($ mil.)	NET PROFIT MARGIN	EMPLOYEES
12/20	1,356.2	481.7	35.5%	4,013
12/19	1,308.4	419.9	32.1%	4,048
12/18	1,196.6	415.2	34.7%	3,624
12/17	1,105.0	479.0	43.3%	3,380
12/16	991.8	366.1	36.9%	3,287
Annual Growth	8.1%	7.1%	—	5.1%

2020 Year-End Financials

Debt ratio: 61.1%	No. of shares (mil.): 131.3
Return on equity: 18.8%	Dividends
Cash ($ mil.): 109.1	Yield: 3.1%
Current ratio: 0.12	Payout: 97.0%
Long-term debt ($ mil.): 4,797.3	Market value ($ mil.): 15,219.0

	STOCK PRICE ($) FY Close	P/E High/Low	Earnings	PER SHARE ($) Dividends	Book Value
12/20	115.86	32 20	3.71	3.60	19.40
12/19	105.62	38 27	3.24	3.56	19.61
12/18	90.48	31 24	3.27	3.36	18.99
12/17	87.45	23 19	3.76	3.12	18.66
12/16	77.24	32 24	2.91	2.93	17.83
Annual Growth	10.7%	— —	6.3%	5.3%	2.1%

Exxe Group Inc

LOCATIONS

HQ: Exxe Group Inc
1345 Avenue of The Americas, 2nd Floor, New York, NY 10105
Phone: 855 285-2285
Web: www.exxegroup.com

HISTORICAL FINANCIALS
Company Type: Public

Income Statement				FYE: March 31
	REVENUE ($ mil.)	NET INCOME ($ mil.)	NET PROFIT MARGIN	EMPLOYEES
03/21	33.9	6.6	19.6%	0
03/20	15.3	3.5	23.2%	0
03/19	2.1	1.6	80.2%	0
03/18	0.0	0.1	221.1%	0
Annual Growth	654.8%	236.6%	—	—

2021 Year-End Financials

Debt ratio: 31.4%	No. of shares (mil.): 526.9
Return on equity: 18.4%	Dividends
Cash ($ mil.): 0.2	Yield: —
Current ratio: 0.98	Payout: —
Long-term debt ($ mil.): 66.2	Market value ($ mil.): 38.0

	STOCK PRICE ($) FY Close	P/E High/Low	Earnings	PER SHARE ($) Dividends	Book Value
03/21	0.07	10 0	0.01	0.00	0.08
03/20	0.01	3 1	0.01	0.00	0.07
03/19	0.01	33 0	0.01	0.00	0.10
03/18	0.00	— —	(0.00)	0.00	(0.00)
/0.00	—	—(0.00)	0.00	(0.00)	
Annual Growth	—	— —	—	—	—

F & M Bank Corp.

F & M Bank has deep roots in Virginia's Shenandoah Valley. Founded in 1908 the holding company operates about 10 Farmers & Merchants Bank branches in the northern Virginia counties of Rockingham and Shenandoah. Farmers & Merchants caters to individuals and businesses. It provides typical deposit products including checking and savings accounts CDs and IRAs. Some 40% of its loans are mortgages; it also writes agricultural business construction and consumer loans. The company offers insurance brokerage and financial services through TEB Life Insurance and Farmers & Merchants Financial Services.

EXECUTIVES

Chief Financial Officer, Executive Vice President, Carrie Comer
Independent Director, Daniel Harshman
Independent Chairman Of The Board Of The Bank & Company, Michael Pugh
Vice Chairman Of The Board, Dean Withers
Director, Larry Caplinger
Executive Vice President, Chief Banking Officer, Stephanie Shillingburg, $186,067 total compensation
President, Chief Executive Officer Of The Company And Bank, Mark Hanna, $389,384 total compensation
Chief Operating Officer, Executive Vice President And Chief Strategy And Risk Officer Of The Company And The Bank, Barton Black, $259,452 total compensation
Independent Director, Edward Burkholder
Executive Vice President, Chief Strategy And Risk Officer, Edward Strunk, $177,013 total compensation
Independent Director, Peter Wray
Independent Director, Christopher Runion
Director, Anne Keeler
Auditors: Yount, Hyde & Barbour, P.C.

LOCATIONS

HQ: F & M Bank Corp.
P.O. Box 1111, Timberville, VA 22853
Phone: 540 896-8941
Web: www.FMBankVA.com

COMPETITORS

MBANK   VOLUNTEER BANCORP INC

HISTORICAL FINANCIALS
Company Type: Public

Income Statement				FYE: December 31
	ASSETS ($ mil.)	NET INCOME ($ mil.)	INCOME AS % OF ASSETS	EMPLOYEES
12/20	966.9	8.7	0.9%	151
12/19	814.0	4.5	0.6%	173
12/18	780.2	9.0	1.2%	172
12/17	753.2	9.0	1.2%	178
12/16	744.8	9.5	1.3%	173
Annual Growth	6.7%	(2.1%)	—	(3.3%)

2020 Year-End Financials

Return on assets: 0.9%	Dividends
Return on equity: 9.3%	Yield: 4.5%
Long-term debt ($ mil.): —	Payout: 45.4%
No. of shares (mil.): 3.2	Market value ($ mil.): 74.0
Sales ($ mil.): 49.0	

	STOCK PRICE ($)	P/E		PER SHARE ($)		
	FY Close	High/Low		Earnings	Dividends	Book Value
12/20	23.01	11	6	2.56	1.04	29.85
12/19	29.00	27	19	1.30	1.01	28.34
12/18	30.00	15	11	2.53	1.20	28.43
12/17	33.10	13	10	2.48	0.91	27.86
12/16	26.05	10	8	2.57	0.80	26.29
Annual Growth	(3.1%)	—	—	(0.1%)	6.8%	3.2%

Fair Isaac Corp

Fair Isaac also known as FICO is a company that provides credit scores and risk management tools for businesses worldwide including banks credit card issuers mortgage and auto lenders retailers insurance firms and health care providers. It also serve consumers through online services that enable people to access and understand their FICO Scores the standard measure in the US of consumer credit risk empowering them to manage their financial health. While the US accounts for more than 70% of its revenue the company operates globally in more than 120 countries.

Operations

FICO operates in three operating segments: Applications Scores and Decision Management Software.

FICO's Applications segment generates more than 45%of the company's revenue and includes pre-configured decision management applications designed for a specific type of business problem or process ? such as marketing account origination customer management fraud financial crimes compliance collections and insurance claims management ? as well as associated professional services. These applications are available to its customers as on-premises software and many are available as hosted software-as-a-service (SaaS) applications through the FICO Analytic Cloud or Amazon Web Services (AWS). The company's Scores segment about 40% of revenue includes its business-to-business scoring products its business-to-consumer scoring products and services including the myFICO product for consumers and associated professional services.

FICO Decision Management Software nearly 15% of revenue composed of analytic and decision management software tools that clients can use to create their own custom decision management applications its FICO Decision Management Suite as well as associated professional services.

Overall transactional and maintenance generates some 75% of revenue professional services with some 15% and license generates around 10% of revenue.

Geographic Reach

San Jose-based FICO operates in some 45 locations in the US Canada Latin America the Caribbean Europe the Middle East and Africa and the Asia Pacific region.

More than 70% of revenue comes from the US while some 15% of revenue comes from the Europe Middle East and Africa. The remaining revenue comes from Asia Pacific and Latin America

Sales and Marketing

FICO's client base includes more than 600 insurers 300 retailers and general merchandisers more than 200 government or public sector agencies and more than 200 health and pharmaceutical companies. End users of its products include 96 of the 100 largest financial institutions in the US and two-thirds of the largest 100 banks in the world.

About one ? third of FICO's revenue is concentrated in Experian TransUnion and Equifax.

The company markets its products and services through their own direct sales division that is organized around its vertical markets. Outside of the US FICO markets through subsidiary sales organizations that promote FICO products in their local countries not reached by its direct marketing. FICO also markets through indirect channels that include alliance partners and other resellers.

Advertising and promotion costs totaled $8.7 million $3.6 million and $4.1 million in fiscal 2020 2019 and 2018 respectively.

Financial Performance

The company in 2020 had a total revenue of $1.29 billion a 12% increase from the previous year. FICO continues to drive growth in its Scores segment.

Net income increased 23% to $236.4 million in fiscal 2020 from $192.1 million in fiscal 2019 primarily due to an increase in operating income.

The company's cash at the end of 2020 was $157.4 million. Operating activities generated $364.9 million while financing activities used $289.4 million mainly as payments on credit lines. Investing activities provided another $24.6 million for capital expenditures.

Strategy

FICO continues to expand the pursuit of its business objective to become a leader in helping businesses automate and improve decisions across their enterprises an approach that it commonly refers to as Decision Management or DM. Its DM strategy is designed to enable it to increase its business by selling multiple connectable and extensible DM products to clients as well as to enable the development of custom client solutions and to allow its clients to more easily expand their usage and the use cases they enable over time.

Company Background

Mathematician William Fair and electrical engineer Earl Isaac founded Fair Isaac as a management consulting firm in 1956. They sought a means for analyzing consumer behavior patterns to help in decision-making and came up with the credit scorecard.

The company flourished over the next three decades. It enjoyed a symbiotic relationship with the evolving credit industry which could not have grown as it did without Fair Isaac's tools. The firm began selling overseas in the 1970s. Earl Isaac died in 1983. Fair Isaac went public in 1987. William Fair retired in 1992 and died in 1996.

In 1992 Fair Isaac bought consumer database management company DynaMark. Three years later the company introduced the Small Business Scoring Service an automated system for small-business loan approval. Fair Isaac in 1995 co-developed a marketing relational database with credit card processor Total System Services.

The company acquired Risk Management Technologies in 1997. It began CreditFYI an Internet business credit-report provider in 1998 with Web business adviser Net Earnings and credit bureau

Experian Information Solutions. In 1999 the firm merged DynaMark into its own operations to hasten its move into online services.

In 2000 the company launched several products and services over the Internet in order to position itself as an application service provider (ASP). Fair Isaac also continued to strengthen its customer relationship management (CRM) offerings through the acquisition of smaller CRM businesses. Fair Isaac teamed up with Experian in 2001 on a product to sell consumers their FICO scores. The next year it began offering more consumer-targeted services including tips on improving one's score.

Fair Isaac acquired HNC Software in 2002. The Fair Isaac executive suite was revamped to include leaders from HNC which was absorbed into its new parent. The acquisition was part of a growth strategy that had Fair Isaac looking outside its traditional top market (the financial services industry) and beyond the borders of the US.

The company dropped the comma from its name in 2003 to become Fair Isaac Corporation.

In 2004 the company acquired UK-based London Bridge Software Holdings thereby adding clients and financial services software that focuses on customer credit and mortgage management. Later in the year Fair Isaac acquired Braun Consulting a marketing strategy and technology consulting firm.

Fair Isaac rebranded itself as FICO in 2009 underscoring the importance of its flagship FICO Score. Though it retained its legal name it added "FICO" to the names of most of its products and changed its website and brand logo to follow suit. The company also streamlined operations to cut costs by discontinuing some businesses selling others closing some facilities and cutting staff. It sold its noncore LiquidCredit for Telecom and RoamEx units and exited its Fast Panel and Cortonics product lines.

HISTORY

Mathematician William Fair and electrical engineer Earl Isaac founded Fair Isaac as a management consulting firm in 1956. They sought a means for analyzing consumer behavior patterns to help in decision-making and came up with the credit scorecard.

The company flourished over the next three decades. It enjoyed a symbiotic relationship with the evolving credit industry which could not have grown as it did without Fair Isaac's tools. The firm began selling overseas in the 1970s. Earl Isaac died in 1983. Fair Isaac went public in 1987. William Fair retired in 1992 and died in 1996.

In 1992 Fair Isaac bought consumer database management company DynaMark. Three years later the company introduced the Small Business Scoring Service an automated system for small-business loan approval. Fair Isaac in 1995 co-developed a marketing relational database with credit card processor Total System Services.

The company acquired Risk Management Technologies in 1997. It began CreditFYI an Internet business credit-report provider in 1998 with Web business adviser Net Earnings and credit bureau Experian Information Solutions. In 1999 the firm merged DynaMark into its own operations to hasten its move into online services.

In 2000 the company launched several products and services over the Internet in order to position itself as an application service provider (ASP). Fair Isaac also continued to strengthen its customer relationship management (CRM) offerings through the acquisition of smaller CRM businesses. Fair Isaac teamed up with Experian in 2001 on a product to sell consumers their FICO scores. The next year it began offering more consumer-targeted services including tips on improving one's score.

Fair Isaac acquired HNC Software in 2002. The Fair Isaac executive suite was revamped to include leaders from HNC which was absorbed into its new parent. The acquisition was part of a growth strategy that had Fair Isaac looking outside its traditional top market (the financial services industry) and beyond the borders of the US.

The company dropped the comma from its name in 2003 to become Fair Isaac Corporation.

In 2004 the company acquired UK-based London Bridge Software Holdings thereby adding clients and financial services software that focuses on customer credit and mortgage management. Later in the year Fair Isaac acquired Braun Consulting a marketing strategy and technology consulting firm.

Fair Isaac rebranded itself as FICO in 2009 underscoring the importance of its flagship FICO Score. Though it retained its legal name it added "FICO" to the names of most of its products and changed its website and brand logo to follow suit. The company also streamlined operations to cut costs by discontinuing some businesses selling others closing some facilities and cutting staff. It sold its noncore LiquidCredit for Telecom and RoamEx units and exited its Fast Panel and Cortonics product lines.

EXECUTIVES

Ceo, William J Lansing
Chb*, Braden R Kelly
Exec V Pres-Cfo, Michael I McLaughlin
Exec V Pres-Cto, Claus Moldt
V Pres-Cao, Michael S Leonard
Exec V Pres-Chief Hr Officer, Richard S Deal
Exec V Pres-General Counsel-Co, Mark R Scadina
Evp Corporate Strategy, Thomas A Bowers
Evp Sales & Marketing, Stephanie Covert
Evp Scores, James M Wehmann
Auditors: Deloitte & Touche LLP

LOCATIONS

HQ: Fair Isaac Corp
 5 West Mendenhall, Suite 105, Bozema, MT 59715
Phone: 406 982-7276
Web: www.fico.com

PRODUCTS/OPERATIONS

2017 Sales

	$ mil.	% of total
Transactional & maintenance	652.7	70
Professional services	179.6	19
License	99.9	11
Total	**932.2**	**100**

2017 Sales by Segment

	$ mil.	% of total
Applications	553.2	59
Scores	266.4	29
Decision Management Software	112.6	12
Total	**932.2**	**100**

Selected Products and Services

FICO Xpress Optimization
FICO Decision Management Suite
FICO Score
FICO Score Open Access
FICO Payment Integrity Platform

FICO TONBELLER Siroon AML
FICO TONBELLER Siron KYC
FICO Debt Manager Solution
FICO Falcon Fraud Manager
FICO Originator Manager
FICO TRIAD Customer Manager
FICO Blaze Advisor Decision Rules Manager
FICO Blaze Strategy Directory for Deposit Manager

COMPETITORS

ACXIOM LLC	DELUXE CORPORATION
AEGIS COMMUNICATIONS GROUP LLC	EQUIFAX INC.
	EUROVESTECH PLC
CAPITA PLC	FIRST DATA CORPORATION
COMPUTACENTER PLC	RELX GROUP PLC

HISTORICAL FINANCIALS

Company Type: Public

Income Statement   FYE: September 30

	REVENUE ($ mil.)	NET INCOME ($ mil.)	NET PROFIT MARGIN	EMPLOYEES
09/21	1,316.5	392.0	29.8%	3,662
09/20	1,294.5	236.4	18.3%	4,003
09/19	1,160.0	192.1	16.6%	4,009
09/18	1,032.4	142.4	13.8%	3,668
09/17	932.1	128.2	13.8%	3,299
Annual Growth	**9.0%**	**32.2%**	**—**	**2.6%**

2021 Year-End Financials

Debt ratio: 80.3%
Return on equity: 356.2%
Cash ($ mil.): 195.3
Current ratio: 0.99
Long-term debt ($ mil.): 1,009.0

No. of shares (mil.): 27.5
Dividends
 Yield: —
 Payout: —
Market value ($ mil.): 10,970.0

	STOCK PRICE ($) FY Close	P/E High/Low	PER SHARE ($) Earnings	Dividends	Book Value
09/21	397.93	41 29	13.40	0.00	(4.02)
09/20	425.38	55 26	7.90	0.00	11.38
09/19	303.52	56 26	6.34	0.00	10.01
09/18	228.55	50 30	4.57	0.00	9.09
09/17	140.50	35 27	3.98	0.04	14.10
Annual Growth	**29.7%**	**— —**	**35.5%**	**—**	**—**

Farmers & Merchants Bancorp (Lodi, CA)

EXECUTIVES

Chairman Of The Board, President, Chief Executive Officer Of The Company & Bank, Kent Steinwert, $915,653 total compensation
Independent Director, Edward Corum
Independent Director, Calvin Suess
Executive Vice President, Retail Banking Division Of The Bank, Ryan Misasi, $309,554 total compensation
Independent Director, Kevin Sanguinetti
Independent Director, Terrence Young
Executive Vice President, Wholesale Banking Division Of The Bank, David Zitterow, $318,923 total compensation
Independent Director, Steven Green

Executive Vice President, Wholesale Banking Division Of The Bank, Chief Credit Officer, Jay Colombini, $337,083 total compensation
Executive Vice President, Chief Administrative Officer Of The Bank., Deborah Skinner, $368,307 total compensation
Independent Director, Gary Long
Chief Financial Officer, Executive Vice President, Mark Olson
Auditors: Moss Adams LLP

LOCATIONS

HQ: Farmers & Merchants Bancorp (Lodi, CA)
 111 W. Pine Street, Lodi, CA 95240
Phone: 209 367-2300
Web: www.fmbonline.com

HISTORICAL FINANCIALS

Company Type: Public

Income Statement   FYE: December 31

	ASSETS ($ mil.)	NET INCOME ($ mil.)	INCOME AS % OF ASSETS	EMPLOYEES
12/20	4,550.4	58.7	1.3%	366
12/19	3,721.8	56.0	1.5%	365
12/18	3,434.2	45.5	1.3%	376
12/17	3,075.4	28.3	0.9%	330
12/16	2,922.1	29.7	1.0%	339
Annual Growth	**11.7%**	**18.6%**	**—**	**1.9%**

2020 Year-End Financials

Return on assets: 1.4%
Return on equity: 14.7%
Long-term debt ($ mil.): —
No. of shares (mil.): 0.7
Sales ($ mil): 174.3

Dividends
 Yield: 1.9%
 Payout: 19.9%
Market value ($ mil.): 600.0

	STOCK PRICE ($) FY Close	P/E High/Low	PER SHARE ($) Earnings	Dividends	Book Value
12/20	760.00	11 9	74.03	14.75	536.53
12/19	768.10	13 10	71.18	14.20	465.68
12/18	700.00	13 11	56.82	13.90	397.10
12/17	676.00	20 17	35.03	13.55	363.90
12/16	640.00	17 13	37.44	13.10	346.80
Annual Growth	**4.4%**	**— —**	**18.6%**	**3.0%**	**11.5%**

Farmers & Merchants Bancorp Inc (OH)

EXECUTIVES

President, Chief Executive Officer, Director, Lars Eller, $387,962 total compensation
Independent Chairman Of The Board, Jack Johnson
Executive Vice President Chief Lending Officer Of The Bank, Rex Rice, $209,192 total compensation
Independent Vice Chairman Of The Board, Kevin Sauder
Independent Director, K. Brad Stamm
Chief Financial Officer, Executive Vice President And Chief Retail Banking Officer Of The Bank, Barbara Britenriker, $237,148 total compensation
Independent Director, Jo Hornish

Independent Director, Eugene Burkholder
Independent Director, Steven Planson
Independent Director, Marcia Latta
Independent Director, Lori Johnston
Independent Director, Frank Simon
Auditors: BKD, LLP

LOCATIONS

HQ: Farmers & Merchants Bancorp Inc (OH)
307 North Defiance Street, Archbold, OH 43502
Phone: 419 446-2501
Web: www.fm-bank.com

HISTORICAL FINANCIALS
Company Type: Public

Income Statement — FYE: December 31

	ASSETS ($ mil.)	NET INCOME ($ mil.)	INCOME AS % OF ASSETS	EMPLOYEES
12/20	1,909.5	20.1	1.1%	367
12/19	1,607.3	18.4	1.1%	357
12/18	1,116.1	14.9	1.3%	288
12/17	1,107.0	12.7	1.1%	275
12/16	1,055.9	11.6	1.1%	273
Annual Growth	16.0%	14.6%	—	7.7%

2020 Year-End Financials

Return on assets: 1.1%
Return on equity: 8.3%
Long-term debt ($ mil.): —
No. of shares (mil.): 11.2
Sales ($ mil): 86.9

Dividends
Yield: 2.8%
Payout: 36.6%
Market value ($ mil.): 258.0

	STOCK PRICE ($) FY Close	P/E High/Low		Earnings	PER SHARE ($) Dividends	Book Value
12/20	23.00	17	10	1.80	0.66	22.25
12/19	30.15	24	15	1.66	0.61	20.68
12/18	38.49	30	22	1.61	0.56	15.43
12/17	40.80	63	25	1.38	0.50	14.48
12/16	35.00	32	21	1.27	0.46	13.59
Annual Growth	(10.0%)	—	—	9.2%	9.7%	13.1%

Farmers National Banc Corp. (Canfield,OH)

Farmers National Banc is willing to help even nonfarmers grow their seed income into thriving bounties of wealth. The bank provides commercial and personal banking from nearly 20 branches in Ohio. Founded in 1887 Farmers National Banc offers checking and savings accounts credit cards and loans and mortgages. Farmers' lending portfolio is composed of real estate mortgages consumer loans and commercial loans. The company also includes Farmers National Insurance and Farmers Trust Company a non-depository trust bank that offers wealth management and trust services.

Geographic Reach

Farmers National Banc operates 19 branches located throughout Mahoning Trumbull Columbiana Stark and Cuyahoga Counties. Farmers Trust Company operates two offices located in Boardman and Howland Ohio.

Financial Performance

The company's revenues have ranged from $40 million to $60 million in the past decade. In 2013 overall sales fell 1% to $54 million; the slight dip was due to lessened interest income on loans and taxable securities. (Financial institutions make their money on interest income from loans and non-interest income from fees.) Its non-interest income experienced growth from service charges insurance agency commissions and consulting fees for retirement planning.

Profits decreased by 22% to $8 million in 2013 due to increase in a provision for loan losses and non-interest expenses such as salary and employee benefits.

Mergers and Acquisitions

In 2013 the bank added retirement planning services to their portfolio with the acquisition of Cleveland-based National Associates Inc. for $4.4 million. The acquisition was part of its plan to boost noninterest income and complement its existing retirement services.

EXECUTIVES

Independent Director, Ralph Macali
President, Chief Executive Officer, Director Of The Company And Farmers Bank, Kevin Helmick, $454,308 total compensation
Senior Vice President And Chief Information Officer Of Farmers Bank, Brian Jackson, $130,300 total compensation
Independent Chairman Of The Board, Lance Ciroli
Senior Vice President And Chief Human Resources Officer Of Farmers Bank, Mark Nicastro
Chief Accounting Officer, Vice President, Joseph Sabat
Executive Vice President Of The Company And Chief Credit Officer Of The Farmers National Bank Of Canfield, Timothy Shaffer, $180,873 total compensation
Chairman, James Smail
Independent Director, Anne Crawford
Independent Director, Terry Moore
Executive Vice President And Chief Retail/marketing Officer Of Farmers Bank, Amber Wallace Soukenik, $184,523 total compensation
Senior Vice President And Chief Wealth Management Officer Of Farmers Bank, Mark Wenick, $233,071 total compensation
Senior Vice President And Chief Risk Officer Of Farmers Bank, Michael Oberhaus
Chief Financial Officer, Executive Vice President, Troy Adair
Director, Richard Thompson
Director, Neil Kaback
Independent Director, David Paull
Auditors: CliftonLarsonAllen LLP

LOCATIONS

HQ: Farmers National Banc Corp. (Canfield,OH)
20 South Broad Street, Canfield, OH 44406
Phone: 330 533-3341
Web: www.farmersbankgroup.com

PRODUCTS/OPERATIONS

Selected Products

Personal

Certificate of DepositChecking AccountsChildren's AccountsConsumer LoansHome Equity Loans & LinesMortgage LoansOnline BankingPersonal Credit CardPersonal Debit CardPhone BankingRetirementSavings Accounts

Business

Business Credit CardBusiness Debit CardBusiness DepositsBusiness LoansCash ManagementRemote Deposit Capture

Wealth Management and Insurance

Farmers Trust CompanyFarmers National InvestmentsFarmers National Insurance

On-line banking

COMPETITORS

INDEPENDENT BANK CORP.
THE SOUTHERN BANC
PEOPLES FINANCIAL SERVICES CORP.
COMPANY INC
STATE BANK FINANCIAL CORPORATION

HISTORICAL FINANCIALS
Company Type: Public

Income Statement — FYE: December 31

	ASSETS ($ mil.)	NET INCOME ($ mil.)	INCOME AS % OF ASSETS	EMPLOYEES
12/20	3,071.1	41.8	1.4%	444
12/19	2,449.1	35.7	1.5%	450
12/18	2,328.8	32.5	1.4%	453
12/17	2,159.0	22.7	1.1%	445
12/16	1,966.1	20.5	1.0%	441
Annual Growth	11.8%	19.5%	—	0.2%

2020 Year-End Financials

Return on assets: 1.5%
Return on equity: 12.8%
Long-term debt ($ mil.): —
No. of shares (mil.): 28.1
Sales ($ mil): 149.4

Dividends
Yield: 3.3%
Payout: 29.9%
Market value ($ mil.): 374.0

	STOCK PRICE ($) FY Close	P/E High/Low		Earnings	PER SHARE ($) Dividends	Book Value
12/20	13.27	11	7	1.47	0.44	12.42
12/19	16.32	13	10	1.28	0.38	10.82
12/18	12.74	14	10	1.16	0.30	9.44
12/17	14.75	19	15	0.82	0.22	8.79
12/16	14.20	20	11	0.76	0.16	7.88
Annual Growth	(1.7%)	—	—	17.9%	28.8%	12.0%

Farmland Partners Inc

Auditors: Plante & Moran, PLLC

LOCATIONS

HQ: Farmland Partners Inc
4600 South Syracuse Street, Suite 1450, Denver, CO 80237-2766
Phone: 720 452-3100
Web: www.farmlandpartners.com

HISTORICAL FINANCIALS
Company Type: Public

Income Statement
FYE: December 31

	REVENUE ($ mil.)	NET INCOME ($ mil.)	NET PROFIT MARGIN	EMPLOYEES
12/20	50.6	7.1	14.0%	14
12/19	53.5	13.8	25.9%	13
12/18	56.0	12.2	21.9%	13
12/17	46.2	7.9	17.1%	16
12/16	31.0	4.3	13.9%	18
Annual Growth	13.1%	13.4%	—	(6.1%)

2020 Year-End Financials
Debt ratio: 46.4%
Return on equity: 1.6%
Cash ($ mil.): 27.2
Current ratio: 1.79
Long-term debt ($ mil.): 506.6
No. of shares (mil.): 30.5
Dividends
  Yield: 2.3%
  Payout: —
Market value ($ mil.): 266.0

	STOCK PRICE ($) FY Close	P/E High/Low		PER SHARE ($) Earnings	Dividends	Book Value
12/20	8.70	—	—	(0.18)	0.20	14.06
12/19	6.78	176	127	0.04	0.20	14.60
12/18	4.54	—	—	(0.01)	0.36	14.33
12/17	8.68	381	274	0.03	0.51	14.06
12/16	11.16	133	111	0.09	0.51	9.33
Annual Growth	(6.0%)	—	—	—	(20.9%)	10.8%

FB Financial Corp

Auditors: Crowe LLP

LOCATIONS
HQ: FB Financial Corp
  211 Commerce Street, Suite 300, Nashville, TN 37201
Phone: 615 564-1212
Web: www.firstbankonline.com

HISTORICAL FINANCIALS
Company Type: Public

Income Statement
FYE: December 31

	ASSETS ($ mil.)	NET INCOME ($ mil.)	INCOME AS % OF ASSETS	EMPLOYEES
12/20	11,207.3	63.6	0.6%	1,852
12/19	6,124.9	83.8	1.4%	1,399
12/18	5,136.7	80.2	1.6%	1,356
12/17	4,727.7	52.4	1.1%	1,386
12/16	3,276.8	40.5	1.2%	1,108
Annual Growth	36.0%	11.9%	—	13.7%

2020 Year-End Financials
Return on assets: 0.7%
Return on equity: 6.1%
Long-term debt ($ mil.): —
No. of shares (mil.): 47.2
Sales ($ mil): 616.5
Dividends
  Yield: 1.0%
  Payout: 21.5%
Market value ($ mil.): 1,640.0

	STOCK PRICE ($) FY Close	P/E High/Low		PER SHARE ($) Earnings	Dividends	Book Value
12/20	34.73	23	9	1.67	0.36	27.35
12/19	39.59	15	11	2.65	0.32	24.56
12/18	35.02	17	13	2.55	0.20	21.87
12/17	41.99	23	13	1.86	0.00	19.54
12/16	25.95	12	9	2.10	4.03	13.71
Annual Growth 18.8%	7.6%	—	—	(5.6%)	(45.3%)	

FCN Banc Corp

EXECUTIVES
Director, Donald Smith
Chb, Donald R Smith
Pres-Ceo, Edwin D Roberts
Vp, Randall W Listerman
Secretary, Arthur K Hildebrand
Treasurer, Matthew Branstetter
Chief Retail Officer, Jacob Linkel
Commercial Lender, Martin Eisele

LOCATIONS
HQ: FCN Banc Corp
  501 Main Street, Brookville, IN 47012
Phone: 765 647-4116   **Fax:** 765 647-2680
Web: www.fcnbank.com

HISTORICAL FINANCIALS
Company Type: Public

Income Statement
FYE: December 31

	ASSETS ($ mil.)	NET INCOME ($ mil.)	INCOME AS % OF ASSETS	EMPLOYEES
12/20	683.2	6.9	1.0%	0
12/19	474.0	5.7	1.2%	110
12/18	443.5	5.7	1.3%	0
12/17	442.3	4.0	0.9%	0
12/16	432.3	3.9	0.9%	0
Annual Growth	12.1%	15.1%	—	—

2020 Year-End Financials
Return on assets: 1.2%
Return on equity: 10.7%
Long-term debt ($ mil.): —
No. of shares (mil.): 1.7
Sales ($ mil): 27.9
Dividends
  Yield: 0.0%
  Payout: 33.3%
Market value ($ mil.): 69.0

	STOCK PRICE ($) FY Close	P/E High/Low		PER SHARE ($) Earnings	Dividends	Book Value
12/20	39.66	20	9	4.08	1.36	41.91
12/19	40.20	10	8	3.83	1.35	37.68
12/18	30.50	9	7	3.84	1.22	33.08
12/17	29.50	11	10	2.66	1.12	31.07
12/16	29.50	11	10	2.63	1.08	29.34
Annual Growth	7.7%	—	—	11.6%	5.9%	9.3%

Federal Agricultural Mortgage Corp

Farmer Mac (Federal Agricultural Mortgage Corporation) is stockholder-owned federally chartered corporation that combines private capital and public sponsorship to serve a public purpose. The company provides a secondary market for a variety of loans made to borrowers in rural America. The company's market activities include purchasing eligible loans directly from lenders and more. Farmer Mac is an institution of the Farm Credit System (FCS) which is composed of the banks associations and related entities including Farmer Mac and its subsidiaries. Farmer Mac was chartered by Congress in 1987 and established under federal legislation first enacted in 1988.

EXECUTIVES
Independent Vice Chairman Of The Board, Lowell Junkins
Independent Director, Mitchell Johnson
Independent Director, Dennis Brack
Executive Vice President, General Counsel, Secretary, Stephen Mullery, $435,000 total compensation
Independent Director, Sara Faivre
Independent Director, Richard Davidson
Independent Director, Lajuana Wilcher
Independent Director, Amy Gales
Senior Vice President – Enterprise Risk Officer, Brian Brinch, $285,000 total compensation
President, Chief Executive Officer, Bradford Nordholm, $750,000 total compensation
Senior Vice President – Operations, Robert Maines
Chief Financial Officer, Executive Vice President, Treasurer, Aparna Ramesh, $500,000 total compensation
Independent Director, Todd Ware
Executive Vice President, Chief Business Officer, Zachary Carpenter, $410,000 total compensation
Independent Director, Everett Dobrinski
Independent Director, Charles Stones
Independent Director, Eric Mckissack
Senior Vice President – Chief Credit Officer, Marc Crady
Independent Director, Roy Tiarks
Independent Director, Myles Watts
Auditors: PricewaterhouseCoopers LLP

LOCATIONS
HQ: Federal Agricultural Mortgage Corp
  1999 K Street, N.W., 4th Floor, Washington, DC 20006
Phone: 202 872-7700

PRODUCTS/OPERATIONS

2015 Sales

	% of total
Interest income	
Farmer Mac Guaranteed Securities and USDA Securities	47
Loans	41
Investments and cash equivalents	5
Noninterest income	
Guarantee and commitment fees	5
Gains on financial derivatives and hedging activities	1
Other	1
Total	**100**

2015 Sales

	% of total
Farm & Ranch	39
USDA Guarantees	28
Rural Utilities	18
Institutional Credit	10
Corporate	4
Reconciling Adjustments	1
Total	**100**

Selected Operations

Farm & Ranch (Farmer Mac I)
USDA Guarantees (Farmer Mac II)
Rural Utilities

COMPETITORS

ASSOCIATED BANC-CORP
BOKF MERGER CORPORATION NUMBER SIXTEEN
CAMBRIDGE BANCORP
COBANK ACB
FEDERAL HOME LOAN BANK OF CHICAGO
FEDERAL HOME LOAN BANK OF DES MOINES
FEDERAL HOME LOAN BANK OF INDIANAPOLIS
FEDERAL HOME LOAN BANK OF NEW YORK
FEDERAL HOME LOAN BANK OF PITTSBURGH
FEDERAL NATIONAL MORTGAGE ASSOCIATION
NORINCHUKIN BANK THE

HISTORICAL FINANCIALS

Company Type: Public

Income Statement				FYE: December 31
	ASSETS ($ mil.)	NET INCOME ($ mil.)	INCOME AS % OF ASSETS	EMPLOYEES
12/20	24,355.5	108.6	0.4%	121
12/19	21,709.3	109.5	0.5%	103
12/18	18,694.3	108.0	0.6%	103
12/17	17,792.2	84.4	0.5%	88
12/16	15,606.0	77.3	0.5%	81
Annual Growth	11.8%	8.9%	—	10.6%

2020 Year-End Financials

Return on assets: 0.4%
Return on equity: 12.0%
Long-term debt ($ mil.): —
No. of shares (mil.): 10.7
Sales ($ mil): 519.5
Dividends
Yield: 4.3%
Payout: 38.6%
Market value ($ mil.): 797.0

	STOCK PRICE ($) FY Close	P/E High/Low		PER SHARE ($) Earnings	Dividends	Book Value
12/20	74.25	10	5	8.27	3.20	92.44
12/19	83.50	10	7	8.69	2.80	74.62
12/18	60.44	11	6	8.83	2.32	70.54
12/17	78.24	12	8	6.60	1.44	66.69
12/16	57.27	10	4	5.97	1.04	61.05
Annual Growth	6.7%	—	—	8.5%	32.4%	10.9%

Federal Home Loan Bank New York

Federal Home Loan Bank of New York (FHLBNY) provides funds for residential mortgages and community development to more than 330 member banks savings and loans credit unions and life insurance companies in New York New Jersey Puerto Rico and the US Virgin Islands. One of a dozen Federal Home Loan Banks in the US it is cooperatively owned by its member institutions and supervised by the Federal Housing Finance Agency. FHLBNY like others in the system is privately capitalized; it receives no taxpayer funding. The bank instead raises funds mainly by issuing debt instruments in the capital markets.

Operations

FHLBNY is a secured lender that requires collateral for its advances which are typically used by members to underwrite residential mortgages or to invest in US Treasury and agency securities mortgage-backed securities and other real estate-related assets.

A large part of FHLBNY's business is in making collateralized loans or advances to members. It serves the public through its mortgage programs. Three members — Citibank (25%) Met Life (14%) and New York Community Bank (11%) — accounted for half of total advances.

Geographic Reach

Based in New York FHLBNY serves not only New York but New Jersey Puerto Rico and the US Virgin Islands.

Sales and Marketing

FHLBNY caters to more than 330 member banks credit unions life insurance companies and savings and loans.

Financial Performance

Revenue dropped by 14% to $801 million in fiscal 2013 from 2012's $934.9 million. FHLBNY attributes the decline to a decrease in interest income and other income. Net income also dropped some 16% in 2013 to $304.6 million vs. $360.7 million in 2012. It attributes net income decreases to declining revenue and rising other expenses. Operating cash flow decreased in fiscal 2013 to $525.6 million compared to 2012's $678.9 million.

Strategy

Credit unions are a possible area of growth for FHLBNY. The bank has identified more than 50 credit unions and banks that are not members but are eligible. To be under consideration an institution must have more than $50 million in assets ($100 million for banks) be an established wholesale lender maintain a high deposit-to-loan ratio and have management that has done business with an FHLB in the past.

Beginning in 2014 it's also funding — with the help of $35.5 million in subsidies — 48 affordable housing initiatives throughout New Jersey New York Puerto Rico the US Virgin Islands Florida Maryland and Pennsylvania. The effort involves the creation or rehabilitation of more than 3000 affordable housing units.

EXECUTIVES

President, Chief Executive Officer, Jose Gonzalez, $700,000 total compensation
Senior Vice President And Chief Business Officer, Adam Goldstein
Chief Financial Officer, Senior Vice President, Kevin Neylan, $405,995 total compensation
Director, Thomas Hoy
Senior Vice President, Chief Risk Officer, Melody Feinberg
Director, Kevin Cummings
Director, David Nasca
Director, Christopher Martin
Director, Gerald Lipkin
Independent Director, Richard Mroz
Chairman Of The Board, John Buran
Director, Carlos Vazquez
Vice Chairman Of Board, Larry Thompson
Independent Director, DeForest Soaries
Senior Vice President - Head Of Corporate Services And Director Of Diversity And Inclusion, Edwin Artuz
Auditors: PricewaterhouseCoopers LLP

LOCATIONS

HQ: Federal Home Loan Bank New York
101 Park Avenue, New York, NY 10178
Phone: 212 681-6000
Web: www.fhlbny.com

PRODUCTS/OPERATIONS

2013 Sales

	$ mil.	% of total
Interest		
Advances	444.5	55
Long-term securities	244.0	30
Mortgage loans held for portfolio	68.3	9
Available-for-sale securities	16.6	2
Other	14.3	2
Non-interest	13.3	2
Total	**801.0**	**100**

COMPETITORS

EAGLE BANCORP INC.
EXPORT-IMPORT BANK OF THE UNITED STATES
FARM CREDIT EAST ACA
FEDERAL AGRICULTURAL MORTGAGE CORPORATION
FEDERAL HOME LOAN BANK OF ATLANTA
FEDERAL HOME LOAN BANK OF DES MOINES
FEDERAL HOME LOAN BANK OF PITTSBURGH
FEDERAL HOME LOAN MORTGAGE CORPORATION
REPUBLIC FIRST BANCORP INC.
TEXAS GUARANTEED STUDENT LOAN CORPORATION

HISTORICAL FINANCIALS

Company Type: Public

Income Statement				FYE: December 31
	ASSETS ($ mil.)	NET INCOME ($ mil.)	INCOME AS % OF ASSETS	EMPLOYEES
12/20	136,996.3	442.3	0.3%	354
12/19	162,062.0	472.5	0.3%	342
12/18	144,381.3	560.4	0.4%	314
12/17	158,918.3	479.4	0.3%	308
12/16	143,606.2	401.1	0.3%	280
Annual Growth	(1.2%)	2.5%	—	6.0%

2020 Year-End Financials

Return on assets: 0.3%
Return on equity: 5.9%
Long-term debt ($ mil.): —
No. of shares (mil.): 53.6
Sales ($ mil): 1,883.0
Dividends
Yield: —
Payout: 79.5%
Market value ($ mil.): —

Federal Home Loan Bank Of Dallas

Auditors: PricewaterhouseCoopers LLP

LOCATIONS

HQ: Federal Home Loan Bank Of Dallas
8500 Freeport Parkway South, Suite 600, Irving, TX
75063-2547
Phone: 214 441-8500
Web: www.fhlb.com

HISTORICAL FINANCIALS

Company Type: Public

Income Statement — FYE: December 31

	ASSETS ($ mil.)	NET INCOME ($ mil.)	INCOME AS % OF ASSETS	EMPLOYEES
12/20	64,912.5	198.7	0.3%	203
12/19	75,381.6	227.2	0.3%	203
12/18	72,773.2	198.7	0.3%	197
12/17	68,524.3	150.2	0.2%	205
12/16	58,212.0	79.4	0.1%	218
Annual Growth	2.8%	25.8%	—	(1.8%)

2020 Year-End Financials

Return on assets: 0.2%
Return on equity: 5.3%
Long-term debt ($ mil.): —
No. of shares (mil.): 21.0
Sales ($ mil): 823.4

Dividends
Yield: —
Payout: 19.4%
Market value ($ mil.): —

Federal Signal Corp.

Federal Signal designs manufactures and supplies a suite of products and integrated solutions for municipal governmental industrial and commercial customers. Offerings include street sweepers vacuum- and hydro-excavation trucks and water blasters for general alarm/public address systems; industrial communications and public warning systems for public safety. In addition the company engages in the sale of parts service and repair equipment rentals and training as part of a comprehensive aftermarket offering to its customers. Federal Signal generates majority of sales from the US market.

Operations

Federal Signal divides its operations across two segments. Environmental solutions accounts for around 80% of revenue. It is a leading manufacturer and supplier of a full range of street sweepers sewer cleaners industrial vacuum loaders safe-digging trucks high-performance waterblasting equipment road-marking and line-removal equipment dump truck bodies and trailers. It manufactures vehicles and equipment that are sold under the Elgin Vactor Guzzler TRUVAC Westech Jetstream Mark Rite Lines Ox Bodies Crysteel J-Craft Duraclass Rugby and Travis brand names.

The safety & security systems segment nearly 20% of revenue is a leading manufacturer and supplier of comprehensive systems and products that law enforcement fire rescue emergency medical services campuses military facilities and industrial sites use to protect people and property. Offerings include systems for community alerting emergency vehicles first responder interoperable communications and industrial communications. Products are sold under the Federal Signal Federal Signal VAMA and Victor brand names.

Geographic Reach

The majority of the company's sales (more than 75%) are made in the US about 15% in Europe and nearly 10% in Canada.

Headquartered at Oak Brook Illinois the company utilized about a dozen principal manufacturing plants located throughout the US as well as two in Europe one in Canada and one in South Africa.

Sales and Marketing

The Environmental Solutions Group uses either a dealer network or direct sales to serve customers. Its direct sales channel concentrates primarily on the industrial utility and construction market segments. It also engages in the sale of parts service and repair equipment rentals and training through its service centers located across North America. The Safety and Security Systems Group sells to industrial customers through wholesalers and distributors who are supported by company sales personnel or independent manufacturer representatives. Products are also sold to municipal and governmental customers through active independent distributors as well as through original equipment manufacturers and the direct sales force.

Financial Performance

The company's revenue decreased by 7% to $1.1 billion in 2020 compared to $1.2 billion in 2019. Within the Environmental Solutions Group net sales decreased by $77.1 million or 8% largely due to decreases in shipments of safe-digging trucks industrial vacuum loaders sweepers dump bodies waterblasting equipment sewer cleaners trailers and snow removal equipment of $26.4 million $22.0 million $20.7 million $7.8 million $7.5 million $6.7 million $4.7 million and $3.2 million respectively.

Net income decreased by $12.3 million to $96.2 million in 2020 compared to $108.5 million in 2019.

Cash held by the company at the end of fiscal 2020 increased to $81.7 million. Operating activities provided $136.2 million while investing and financing activities used $34.4 million and $53.4 million respectively. Main cash uses were purchases of properties and equipment and cash dividends paid to stockholders.

Mergers and Acquisitions

In early 2021 Federal Signal Corporation announced the completion of the acquisition of OSW Equipment and Repair LLC (OSW) for cash consideration of $52.5 million. OSW is a leading manufacturer of dump truck bodies and custom upfitter of truck equipment and trailers and is headquartered in Snohomish Washington with an upfitting location in Tempe Arizona. The acquisition of OSW represents a highly strategic transaction adding three premier brands that serve attractive infrastructure construction and other industrial end-markets on the West Coast in Arizona and in parts of Canada.

In early 2020 Federal Signal Corporation announced the acquisition of certain assets and operations of Public Works Equipment and Supply Inc. (PWE) a distributor of maintenance and infrastructure equipment covering North Carolina South Carolina and parts of Tennessee. The acquisition included a purchase price of $2.5 million plus an additional payment to acquire certain fixed assets and inventory. The acquisition will add a third location to its current footprint in this population-dense region which will allow it to better

serve its customers and accelerate the growth of its aftermarket business.

EXECUTIVES

President, Chief Executive Officer And Director, Jennifer Sherman, $783,158 total compensation
Independent Chairman Of The Board, Dennis Martin
Chief Operating Officer, Senior Vice President, Mark Weber, $464,892 total compensation
Vice President, General Counsel, Secretary, Daniel Dupre, $326,581 total compensation
Vice President, Corporate Controller, Lauren Elting
Independent Director, William Owens
Vice President, General Manager Of Tbei, Robert Fines, $392,808 total compensation
Independent Director, Eugene Lowe
Director, Shashank Patel
Lead Independent Director, Brenda Reichelderfer
Chief Financial Officer, Principal Financial Officer, Senior Vice President, Ian Hudson, $394,523 total compensation
Auditors: DELOITTE & TOUCHE LLP

LOCATIONS

HQ: Federal Signal Corp.
1415 West 22nd Street, Oak Brook, IL 60523
Phone: 630 954-2000   **Fax:** 630 954-2030
Web: www.federalsignal.com

PRODUCTS/OPERATIONS

2015 Sales

	$ mil.	% of total
Environmental Solutions	534.1	70
Safety and Security Systems	233.9	30
Total	**768.0**	**100**

Selected Products

Alerting systems
Hydro-excavators
Industrial vacuum loaders
Mining systems
Parking systems
Sewer cleaners
Sirens
Street sweepers
Truck-mounted aerial platforms
Water blasters

COMPETITORS

CAPSTONE GREEN ENERGY SPA
CORPORATION
CARVANA CO.
H&E EQUIPMENT SERVICES INC
INC.
ICHIKOH INDUSTRIESLTD.
KOITO MANUFACTURING CO. LTD.
MARELLI EUROPE
MYR GROUP INC.
REV GROUP INC.
STREET GLOW
TITAN MACHINERY INC.
WATSCO INC.
Wajax Corporation

HISTORICAL FINANCIALS

Company Type: Public

Income Statement				FYE: December 31
	REVENUE ($ mil.)	NET INCOME ($ mil.)	NET PROFIT MARGIN	EMPLOYEES
12/20	1,130.8	96.2	8.5%	3,500
12/19	1,221.3	108.5	8.9%	3,600
12/18	1,089.5	94.0	8.6%	3,300
12/17	898.5	61.6	6.9%	3,100
12/16	707.9	43.8	6.2%	2,200
Annual Growth	12.4%	21.7%	—	12.3%

2020 Year-End Financials

Debt ratio: 17.3%
Return on equity: 14.2%
Cash ($ mil.): 81.7
Current ratio: 2.73
Long-term debt ($ mil.): 209.8

No. of shares (mil.): 60.5
Dividends
 Yield: 0.9%
 Payout: 20.5%
Market value ($ mil.): 2,007.0

	STOCK PRICE ($) FY Close	P/E High/Low		PER SHARE ($)		
			Earnings	Dividends	Book Value	
12/20	33.17	22 15	1.56	0.32	11.60	
12/19	32.25	19 11	1.76	0.32	10.60	
12/18	19.90	18 12	1.54	0.31	8.81	
12/17	20.09	22 13	1.02	0.28	7.62	
12/16	15.61	23 16	0.71	0.28	6.61	
Annual Growth	20.7%	— —	21.7%	3.4%	15.1%	

Fentura Financial Inc

It just makes cents to say that Fentura Financial has its hands full. Fentura Financial is the holding company for Michigan community banks The State Bank Davison State Bank West Michigan Community Bank and Community Bancorp. From about 20 branch locations the banks provide commercial and consumer banking services and products including checking and savings accounts and loans. Commercial loans account for some two-thirds of the bank's combined loan portfolio. The State Bank Fentura's first subsidiary traces its origins to 1898. Fentura acquired St. Charles-based Community Bancorp in late 2016.

EXECUTIVES

President, Chief Executive Officer Of The Company And The Bank, Ronald Justice, $137,695 total compensation
Chairman Of The Board, Brian Petty
Director, Thomas Mckenney
Senior Vice President Of The Company And The State Bank, Holly Pingatore, $104,181 total compensation
Senior Vice President Of The Company And The State Bank, Dennis Leyder, $145,000 total compensation
Independent Director, William Dery
Independent Director, JoAnne Shaw
Vice Chairman Of The Board, Ronald Rybar
Chief Financial Officer, James Distelrath
Independent Director, Randy Hicks
Independent Director, Frederick Dillingham
Auditors: Rehmann Robson LLC

LOCATIONS

HQ: Fentura Financial Inc
 P.O. Box 725, Fenton, MI 48430-0725
Phone: 810 629-2263
Web: www.fentura.com

COMPETITORS

COMMUNITY TRUST BANCORP INC.
FB CORPORATION

UNITED BANCSHARES INC.
VOLUNTEER BANCORP INC

HISTORICAL FINANCIALS

Company Type: Public

Income Statement				FYE: December 31
	ASSETS ($ mil.)	NET INCOME ($ mil.)	INCOME AS % OF ASSETS	EMPLOYEES
12/20	1,251.4	15.4	1.2%	0
12/19	1,034.7	11.5	1.1%	0
12/18	926.4	10.1	1.1%	0
12/17	781.4	8.6	1.1%	0
12/16	703.3	4.4	0.6%	0
Annual Growth	15.5%	36.6%	—	—

2020 Year-End Financials

Return on assets: 1.3%
Return on equity: 14.1%
Long-term debt ($ mil.): —
No. of shares (mil.): 4.6
Sales ($ mil): 65.6

Dividends
 Yield: 1.3%
 Payout: 10.4%
Market value ($ mil.): 103.0

	STOCK PRICE ($) FY Close	P/E High/Low		PER SHARE ($)		
			Earnings	Dividends	Book Value	
12/20	22.00	8 4	3.31	0.30	24.68	
12/19	25.23	10 8	2.49	0.28	21.75	
12/18	21.00	8 7	2.65	0.24	19.31	
12/17	18.88	8 6	2.39	0.20	16.37	
12/16	16.00	9 8	1.70	0.40	14.00	
Annual Growth	8.3%	— —	18.1%	(6.9%)	15.2%	

FFD Financial Corp

FFD Financial is the holding company for First Federal Community Bank which serves Tuscarawas County and contiguous portions of eastern Ohio through about five branches. Founded in 1898 the bank offers a full range of retail products including checking and savings accounts CDs IRAs and credit cards. The bank mainly uses these funds to originate one- to four-family residential mortgages nonresidential real estate loans and land loans. First Federal Community Bank also originates business consumer and multifamily residential real estate loans. In 2012 First Federal Community Bank converted its charter from a savings bank to a national commercial bank.

EXECUTIVES

Independent Chairman Of The Board, Enos Loader
Chief Financial Officer, Senior Vice President, Treasurer, Robert Gerber, $77,000 total compensation
Independent Director, Stephen Clinton

Executive Vice President, Scott Finnell, $118,450 total compensation
Secretary, Sally O'Donnell, $88,500 total compensation
Independent Director, Robert Sensel
Independent Director, Richard Brinkman
President, Chief Executive Officer, Trent Troyer, $130,000 total compensation
Independent Director, David Kaufman
Independent Director, Leonard Gundy
Auditors: Clark, Schaefer, Hackett & Co.

LOCATIONS

HQ: FFD Financial Corp
 321 North Wooster Avenue, Dover, OH 44622
Phone: 330 364-7777
Web: www.firstfed.com

COMPETITORS

PIEDMONT FEDERAL SAVINGS BANK

PVF CAPITAL CORP.

HISTORICAL FINANCIALS

Company Type: Public

Income Statement				FYE: June 30
	ASSETS ($ mil.)	NET INCOME ($ mil.)	INCOME AS % OF ASSETS	EMPLOYEES
06/21	591.5	8.8	1.5%	0
06/20	522.2	6.9	1.3%	0
06/19	413.9	6.3	1.5%	0
06/18	382.1	4.8	1.3%	72
06/17	341.4	4.1	1.2%	0
Annual Growth	14.7%	20.6%	—	—

2021 Year-End Financials

Return on assets: 1.5%
Return on equity: 18.5%
Long-term debt ($ mil.): —
No. of shares (mil.): 2.9
Sales ($ mil): 23.8

Dividends
 Yield: 0.0%
 Payout: 68.0%
Market value ($ mil.): 214.0

	STOCK PRICE ($) FY Close	P/E High/Low		PER SHARE ($)		
			Earnings	Dividends	Book Value	
06/21	72.60	26 21	2.99	2.04	17.36	
06/20	62.05	32 22	2.33	0.95	14.89	
06/19	52.70	25 22	2.12	1.52	13.08	
06/18	47.06	29 24	1.63	1.25	11.26	
06/17	39.15	28 21	1.40	1.12	10.13	
Annual Growth	16.7%	— —	20.9%	16.2%	14.4%	

Fidelity D&D Bancorp Inc

Fidelity D & D Bancorp has loyal banking customers. The institution is the holding company for The Fidelity Deposit and Discount Bank serving Lackawanna and Luzerne counties in northeastern Pennsylvania through about a dozen locations and about the same number of ATM locations. The bank attracts local individuals and business customers by offering such products and services as checking and savings accounts certificates of de-

160   HOOVER'S HANDBOOK OF EMERGING COMPANIES 2022

posit investments and trust services. Commercial real estate loans account for the bulk of the company's loan portfolio followed by consumer loans business and industrial loans and residential mortgages. The bank also writes construction loans and direct financing leases.

EXECUTIVES

Independent Director, William Joyce
Independent Director, Richard Hotchkiss
Independent Director, HelenBeth Vilcek
Independent Director, Alan Silverman
Senior Executive Vice President And Chief Business Development Officer, Timothy O'Brien, $207,000 total compensation
Independent Director, Richard Lettieri
Executive Vice President And Chief Lending Officer, Michael Pacyna, $193,000 total compensation
President, Chief Executive Officer, Director Of The Company And The Bank, Daniel Santaniello, $345,000 total compensation
Chairman, Brian Cali
Vice President And Chief Operating Officer Of The Company, Executive Vice President And Chief Operating Officer Of The Bank, Eugene Walsh, $220,000 total compensation
Independent Director, Kristin O'Donnell
Treasurer And Chief Financial Officer Of The Company, Executive Vice President And Chief Financial Officer Of The Bank, Salvatore DeFrancesco, $226,000 total compensation
Secretary, Independent Director, John Cognetti
Auditors: RSM US LLP

LOCATIONS

HQ: Fidelity D&D Bancorp Inc
Blakely & Drinker Streets, Dunmore, PA 18512
Phone: 570 342-8281
Web: www.bankatfidelity.com

COMPETITORS

EMCLAIRE FINANCIAL CORP.
KISH BANCORP INC.
LYONS NATIONAL BANK
NEFFS BANCORP INC.

HISTORICAL FINANCIALS

Company Type: Public

Income Statement — FYE: December 31

	ASSETS ($ mil.)	NET INCOME ($ mil.)	INCOME AS % OF ASSETS	EMPLOYEES
12/20	1,699.5	13.0	0.8%	265
12/19	1,009.9	11.5	1.1%	189
12/18	981.1	11.0	1.1%	181
12/17	863.6	8.7	1.0%	175
12/16	792.9	7.6	1.0%	167
Annual Growth	21.0%	14.1%	—	12.2%

2020 Year-End Financials

Return on assets: 0.9%
Return on equity: 9.5%
Long-term debt ($ mil.): —
No. of shares (mil.): 4.9
Sales ($ mil): 64.1
Dividends
Yield: 1.7%
Payout: 40.4%
Market value ($ mil.): 320.0

	STOCK PRICE ($) FY Close	P/E High/Low		PER SHARE ($) Earnings	Dividends	Book Value
12/20	64.36	24	11	2.82	1.14	33.48
12/19	62.21	22	18	3.03	1.06	28.25
12/18	64.18	25	15	2.90	0.98	24.89
12/17	41.30	25	14	2.33	0.88	23.40
12/16	36.10	18	15	2.09	0.83	21.91
Annual Growth	15.6%	—	—	7.8%	8.4%	11.2%

Finance of America Companies Inc

LOCATIONS

HQ: Finance of America Companies Inc
909 Lake Carolyn Parkway, Suite 1550, Irving, TX 75039
Phone: 972 999-1833
Web: www.financeofamerica.com

HISTORICAL FINANCIALS

Company Type: Public

Income Statement — FYE: December 31

	REVENUE ($ mil.)	NET INCOME ($ mil.)	NET PROFIT MARGIN	EMPLOYEES
12/20	1,797.0	518.3	28.8%	5,900
12/19	894.0	54.4	6.1%	5,600
12/18	789.2	32.0	4.1%	0
12/17	778.4	52.6	6.8%	0
Annual Growth	32.2%	114.3%	—	—

2020 Year-End Financials

Debt ratio: 43.8%
Return on equity: 93.0%
Cash ($ mil.): 233.1
Current ratio: 0.05
Long-term debt ($ mil.): 8,568.0
No. of shares (mil.): —
Dividends
Yield: —
Payout: —
Market value ($ mil.): —

	STOCK PRICE ($) FY Close	P/E High/Low		PER SHARE ($) Earnings	Dividends	Book Value
12/20	0.00	—	—	(0.00)	0.00	(0.00)
Annual Growth	—	—	—	—	—	—

Finemark Holdings Inc

Auditors: Hacker, Johnson & Smith P.A.

LOCATIONS

HQ: Finemark Holdings Inc
12681 Creekside Lane, Fort Myers, FL 33919
Phone: 239 461-3850
Web: www.finemarkbank.com

HISTORICAL FINANCIALS

Company Type: Public

Income Statement — FYE: December 31

	REVENUE ($ mil.)	NET INCOME ($ mil.)	NET PROFIT MARGIN	EMPLOYEES
12/20	104.3	21.9	21.0%	0
12/19	95.5	15.2	15.9%	0
12/18	81.4	15.1	18.6%	0
12/17	65.4	9.6	14.7%	178
12/16	54.5	7.9	14.6%	0
Annual Growth	17.6%	28.8%	—	—

2020 Year-End Financials

Debt ratio: 13.7%
Return on equity: 11.2%
Cash ($ mil.): 227.9
Current ratio: 0.11
Long-term debt ($ mil.): 384.9
No. of shares (mil.): 8.9
Dividends
Yield: —
Payout: —
Market value ($ mil.): 210.0

	STOCK PRICE ($) FY Close	P/E High/Low		PER SHARE ($) Earnings	Dividends	Book Value
12/20	23.41	10	8	2.42	0.00	23.57
12/19	25.10	17	14	1.69	0.00	20.15
Annual Growth	(6.7%)	—	—	43.2%	—	17.0%

Finward Bancorp

NorthWest Indiana Bancorp is the holding company for Peoples Bank which serves individuals and businesses customers through about 10 branches in northwest Indiana's Lake County. The savings bank offers traditional deposit services such as checking and savings accounts money market accounts and CDs. It primarily uses the funds collected to originate loans secured by single-family residences and commercial real estate; it also makes construction consumer and business loans. The bank's Wealth Management Group provides retirement and estate planning investment accounts land trusts and profit-sharing and 401(k) plans.

EXECUTIVES

Executive Chairman Of The Bancorp And Bank, David Bochnowski, $279,576 total compensation
Independent Director, Joel Gorelick
Independent Director, Kenneth Krupinski
Independent Director, James Wieser
Independent Director, Donald Fesko
Independent Director, Amy Han
Chief Operating Officer, Executive Vice President Of The Bancorp And The Bank, Robert Lowry, $227,920 total compensation
Executive Vice President, Chief Banking Officer Of The Bancorp And The Bank, Todd Scheub, $230,130 total compensation
Executive Vice President, Chief Risk Officer, General Counsel, Corporate Secretary Of The Bancorp And The Bank, Leane Cerven, $214,868 total compensation
Independent Director, Robert Johnson
Independent Director, Anthony Puntillo
Independent Director, Edward Furticella

Executive Vice President, Chief Information And Technology Officer Of The Bancorp And The Bank, Tanya Leetz
Chief Financial Officer, Executive Vice President, Treasurer Of The Bancorp And The Bank, Peymon Torabi
Director, Robert Youman
Independent Director, Danette Garza
President, Chief Executive Officer, Director, Benjamin Bochnowski, $355,350 total compensation
Auditors: Plante & Moran, PLLC

LOCATIONS

HQ: Finward Bancorp
9204 Columbia Avenue, Munster, IN 46321
Phone: 219 836-4400
Web: www.ibankpeoples.com

COMPETITORS

AMB FINANCIAL CORP.
ASB FINANCIAL CORP
DCB FINANCIAL CORP
FIRST FEDERAL BANK CORPORATION
LAFAYETTE COMMUNITY BANCORP
LIBERTY CAPITAL INC.
PEOPLES BANCORP
PEOPLES-SIDNEY FINANCIAL CORPORATION
VOLUNTEER BANCORP INC

HISTORICAL FINANCIALS

Company Type: Public

Income Statement — FYE: December 31

	ASSETS ($ mil.)	NET INCOME ($ mil.)	INCOME AS % OF ASSETS	EMPLOYEES
12/20	1,497.5	16.6	1.1%	263
12/19	1,328.7	12.1	0.9%	290
12/18	1,096.1	9.3	0.9%	276
12/17	927.2	8.9	1.0%	217
12/16	913.6	9.1	1.0%	216
Annual Growth	13.1%	16.1%	—	5.0%

2020 Year-End Financials

Return on assets: 1.1%
Return on equity: 11.5%
Long-term debt ($ mil.): —
No. of shares (mil.): 3.4
Sales ($ mil): 69.7
Dividends
Yield: 0.0%
Payout: 25.8%
Market value ($ mil.): 125.0

	STOCK PRICE ($) FY Close	P/E High/Low		PER SHARE ($) Earnings	Dividends	Book Value
12/20	36.10	10	6	4.80	1.24	44.16
12/19	45.90	13	12	3.53	1.23	38.85
12/18	43.00	15	13	3.17	1.19	33.50
12/17	44.50	14	12	3.13	1.15	32.14
12/16	38.85	12	9	3.20	1.11	29.41
Annual Growth	(1.8%)	—	—	10.7%	2.8%	10.7%

First Bancorp (NC)

Don't confuse this First Bancorp with Virginia's First Bancorp or First BanCorp in Puerto Rico. This one is the holding company for First Bank which operates about 100 branch locations in east-central North Carolina east South Carolina and western Virginia (where it operates under the name First Bank of Virginia). In addition to offering standard commercial banking services such as deposit accounts and lending the bank offers investment products and discount brokerage services. Another subsidiary First Bank Insurance Services offers property/casualty products. First Bank focuses its lending on mortgages which account for more than half of its loan portfolio.

EXECUTIVES

Independent Director, Dennis Wicker
Independent Director, Virginia Thomasson
Independent Director, Frederick Taylor
Chief Executive Officer, Director, Richard Moore, $408,654 total compensation
Independent Director, Daniel Blue
President, President And Chief Executive Officer Of First Bank, Director, Michael Mayer, $558,654 total compensation
Independent Director, Abby Donnelly
Independent Director, John Gould
Director, Suzanne DeFerie
Independent Director, O. Temple Sloan
Lead Independent Director, James Crawford
General Counsel And Cfo, Elizabeth Bostian
Auditors: BDO USA, LLP

LOCATIONS

HQ: First Bancorp (NC)
300 S.W. Broad St., Southern Pines, NC 28387
Phone: 910 246-2500
Web: www.localFirstbank.com

PRODUCTS/OPERATIONS

2016 Sales

	$ mil.	% of total
Interest Income	130.9	84
Non-interest Income	25.6	16
Total	**156.5**	**100**

COMPETITORS

AMERICAN BANK INCORPORATED
COMMUNITY FIRST BANCORPORATION
FIRST HAWAIIAN BANK
FIRST PLACE BANK
FIRST SOUTH BANK
FIRST US BANCSHARES INC.
SOUTHEASTERN BANK FINANCIAL CORPORATION
SURREY BANCORP

HISTORICAL FINANCIALS

Company Type: Public

Income Statement — FYE: December 31

	ASSETS ($ mil.)	NET INCOME ($ mil.)	INCOME AS % OF ASSETS	EMPLOYEES
12/20	7,289.7	81.4	1.1%	1,118
12/19	6,143.6	92.0	1.5%	1,111
12/18	5,864.1	89.2	1.5%	1,098
12/17	5,547.0	45.9	0.8%	1,166
12/16	3,614.8	27.5	0.8%	861
Annual Growth	19.2%	31.2%	—	6.7%

2020 Year-End Financials

Return on assets: 1.2%
Return on equity: 9.3%
Long-term debt ($ mil.): —
No. of shares (mil.): 28.5
Sales ($ mil): 318.4
Dividends
Yield: 2.1%
Payout: 25.6%
Market value ($ mil.): 967.0

	STOCK PRICE ($) FY Close	P/E High/Low		PER SHARE ($) Earnings	Dividends	Book Value
12/20	33.83	14	7	2.81	0.72	31.26
12/19	39.91	13	10	3.10	0.54	28.80
12/18	32.66	14	10	3.01	0.40	25.71
12/17	35.31	21	15	1.82	0.32	23.38
12/16	27.14	21	13	1.33	0.32	17.66
Annual Growth	5.7%	—	—	20.6%	22.5%	15.3%

First Bancorp Inc (ME)

It may not actually be the first bank but The First Bancorp (formerly First National Lincoln) was founded over 150 years ago. It is the holding company for The First a regional bank serving coastal Maine from more than 15 branches. The bank offers traditional retail products and services including checking and savings accounts CDs IRAs and loans. Residential mortgages make up about 40% of the company's loan portfolio; business loans account for another 40%; and home equity and consumer loans comprise the rest. Bank subsidiary First Advisors offers private banking and investment management services. Founded in 1864 the bank now boasts more than $1.4 billion in assets.

Operations

Subsidiary First Advisors acts as the bank's Trust and Investment services division which managed some $740 million in investor assets as of late 2014.

The First Bancorp generated 57% of its total revenue from interest income on loans (including fees) while another 25% came from interest and dividends on its investments. Service charges on deposit accounts (4%) Fiduciary and investment management income (3%) mortgage origination (2%) and net securities gains (2%) made up most of the rest of its total revenue.

Geographic Reach

The Damariscotta-based bank boasts more than 15 branches in Mid-Coast Eastern and Down East regions of Maine in Lincoln Knox Hancock Washington and Penobscot counties.

Sales and Marketing

The community-oriented bank concentrates on marketing to small businesses and individuals within its local markets.

Financial Performance

The First Bancorp's revenues have slowly declined over the past few years mostly with as its loan business has stagnated and as its interest margins on loans and investments have been shrinking in the low-interest rate environment. Its profits however have been steadily rising thanks to declining loan loss provisions as its loan portfolio's credit quality has improved with the strengthened economy.

The company's revenue inched up by less than one-tenth of a percent to $62.07 million in 2014 mostly as the bank carried more interest-earning investment assets during the year. The bank's non-interest income however declined by 9% as it collected less from the origination and sale of refinanced mortgage loans into the secondary market.

The First Bancorp's net income jumped by 13% to $14.7 million in 2014 thanks primarily to a continued decline in loan loss provisions as its portfolio's credit quality improved. Slightly higher revenue and lower interest expenses on deposits also helped pad the company's bottom line. The bank's operating cash levels fell by 18% to $20.5 million after adjusting its earnings for non-cash items related to its loan loss provisions and its net proceeds from the sale of its mortgage loans held for sale.

Strategy

As management reiterated in early 2015 remaining well capitalized "remains a top priority for The First Bancorp" and has been key to its profit growth over the past several years. Indeed its de-risking initiatives for its loan portfolio assets have taken the bank's risk-based capital ratio from 11.13% in 2008 to 16.27% at the end of 2014 well above the FDIC's suggested threshold of 10%. As a result the bank's loan loss provisions have declined over the period and its profits have blossomed despite a lack of revenue growth.

Company Background

First National Lincoln acquired competitor FNB Bankshares and its First National Bank of Bar Harbor subsidiary in 2005. It merged that bank into its own subsidiary The First National Bank of Damariscotta which was renamed The First.

EXECUTIVES

Independent Director, Robert Gregory
Director Of The Company And The Bank, F. Stephen Ward
Treasurer, Executive Vice President, Chief Financial Officer, Richard Elder, $225,000 total compensation
Independent Director, Bruce Tindal
President, Chief Executive Officer, Director Of The Company And The First Bank, Tony McKim, $575,000 total compensation
Executive Vice President And Clerk Of The Company, Executive Vice President And Senior Loan Officer Of The Bank, Susan Norton, $250,000 total compensation
Independent Chairman Of The Board, Mark Rosborough
Independent Director, Cornelius Russell
Independent Director, Renee Kelly
Executive Vice President, Chief Banking Officer, Sarah Tolman, $223,000 total compensation
Executive Vice President, Chief Information Officer Of The Bank, Tammy Plummer
Auditors: Berry Dunn McNeil & Parker, LLC

LOCATIONS

HQ: First Bancorp Inc (ME)
223 Main Street, Damariscotta, ME 04543
Phone: 207 563-3195
Web: www.thefirstbancorp.com

PRODUCTS/OPERATIONS

2007 Sales

	$ mil.	% of total
Interest		
Loans including fees	60.6	74
Investments & other	11.1	14
Noninterest		
Service charges on deposit accounts	2.7	3
Fiduciary & investment management income	1.1	1
Other	6.4	8
Total	**81.9**	**100**

COMPETITORS

FIRST COMMONWEALTH FINANCIAL CORPORATION
FIRST HORIZON CORPORATION
FIRSTMERIT CORPORATION
MIDSOUTH BANCORP INC.
SUN BANCORP INC.
TCF FINANCIAL CORPORATION
WESTAMERICA BANCORPORATION

HISTORICAL FINANCIALS

Company Type: Public

Income Statement
FYE: December 31

	ASSETS ($ mil.)	NET INCOME ($ mil.)	INCOME AS % OF ASSETS	EMPLOYEES
12/20	2,361.2	27.1	1.1%	255
12/19	2,068.8	25.5	1.2%	245
12/18	1,944.5	23.5	1.2%	239
12/17	1,842.9	19.5	1.1%	235
12/16	1,712.8	18.0	1.1%	235
Annual Growth	**8.4%**	**10.8%**	**—**	**2.1%**

2020 Year-End Financials

Return on assets: 1.2%
Return on equity: 12.4%
Long-term debt ($ mil.): —
No. of shares (mil.): 10.9
Sales ($ mil): 95.2

Dividends
Yield: 4.8%
Payout: 49.1%
Market value ($ mil.): 278.0

	STOCK PRICE ($) FY Close	P/E High/Low		PER SHARE ($) Earnings	Dividends	Book Value
12/20	25.40	12	7	2.48	1.22	20.43
12/19	30.23	13	10	2.34	1.18	19.50
12/18	26.30	14	11	2.17	1.06	17.63
12/17	27.23	18	14	1.81	1.06	16.74
12/16	33.10	20	11	1.66	0.90	15.98
Annual Growth	**(6.4%)**	**—**	**—**	**10.6%**	**7.9%**	**6.3%**

First Bancshares Inc (MS)

Hoping to be first in the hearts of its customers The First Bancshares is the holding company for The First a community bank with some two dozen branch locations in southern Mississippi's Hattiesburg Alabama and Louisiana. The company provides such standard deposit products as checking and savings accounts NOW and money market accounts and IRAs. Real estate loans account for about 80% of the bank's lending portfolio including about equal portions of residential mortgages commercial mortgages and construction loans. The bank also writes business loans and consumer loans. The bank which has expanded beyond Mississippi through several acquisitions has approximately $970 million in assets.

Mergers and Acquisitions

In April 2013 The First Bancshares acquired First National Bank (FNB) of Baldwin Country a community bank in Alabama with five branches along the Gulf Coast. The purchase of FNB marked The First's entry into the Alabama market. In 2011 The First expanded into Louisiana and strengthened its hold on southern Mississippi with the ac-

quisition of seven branch banks from Whitney National Bank and one branch from Hancock Bank of Louisiana for an undisclosed amount.

EXECUTIVES

Independent Director, Andrew Stetelman
Independent Director, Thomas Mitchell
Chief Financial Officer, Executive Vice President, Donna Lowery, $297,978 total compensation
Independent Director, Ted Parker
Independent Director, David Bomboy
Independent Director, J. Seidenburg
Independent Director, Charles Lightsey
Independent Director, Fred McMurry
Independent Director, Renee Moore
Independent Director, Rodney Bennett
President, Chief Executive Officer, Vice Chairman Of The Board, M. Ray Cole, $522,566 total compensation
Independent Chairman Of The Board, E. Gibson
Auditors: Crowe LLP

LOCATIONS

HQ: First Bancshares Inc (MS)
6480 U.S. Highway 98 West, Suite A, Hattiesburg, MS 39402
Phone: 601 268-8998
Web: www.thefirstbank.com

COMPETITORS

AMARILLO NATIONAL BANCORP INC
COMMUNITYONE BANCORP
FIRST NATIONAL BANK OF FINANCIAL ALASKA
NEFFS BANCORP INC.
SIMMONS FIRST NATIONAL CORPORATION
TRUIST CORPORATION

HISTORICAL FINANCIALS

Company Type: Public

Income Statement
FYE: December 31

	ASSETS ($ mil.)	NET INCOME ($ mil.)	INCOME AS % OF ASSETS	EMPLOYEES
12/20	5,152.7	52.5	1.0%	744
12/19	3,941.8	43.7	1.1%	697
12/18	3,003.9	21.2	0.7%	641
12/17	1,813.2	10.6	0.6%	487
12/16	1,277.3	10.1	0.8%	315
Annual Growth	**41.7%**	**50.9%**	**—**	**24.0%**

2020 Year-End Financials

Return on assets: 1.1%
Return on equity: 8.8%
Long-term debt ($ mil.): —
No. of shares (mil.): 21.1
Sales ($ mil): 221.2

Dividends
Yield: 1.3%
Payout: 16.6%
Market value ($ mil.): 652.0

	STOCK PRICE ($) FY Close	P/E High/Low		PER SHARE ($) Earnings	Dividends	Book Value
12/20	30.88	14	6	2.52	0.42	30.54
12/19	35.52	14	11	2.55	0.31	28.91
12/18	30.25	25	17	1.62	0.20	24.49
12/17	34.20	31	24	1.11	0.15	19.92
12/16	27.50	15	8	1.64	0.15	17.19
Annual Growth	**2.9%**	**—**	**—**	**11.3%**	**29.4%**	**15.5%**

HOOVER'S HANDBOOK OF EMERGING COMPANIES 2022

First Bank (Williamstown, NJ)

EXECUTIVES

Executive Vice President And Chief Deposits Officer, Emilio Cooper, $222,500 total compensation
Chief Operating Officer, Executive Vice President, John Shepardson
Executive Vice President, Chief Risk Officer, Maria Mayshura
President, Chief Executive Officer, Director, Patrick Ryan, $477,800 total compensation
Executive Vice President And Chief Lending Officer, Peter Cahill, $245,500 total compensation
Director, Gary Hofing
Independent Director, Glenn Josephs
Independent Director, Peter Pantages
Independent Director, Scott Gamble
Independent Director, Michael Salz
Independent Director, Deborah Hanson
Independent Director, Douglas Borden
Lead Independent Vice Chairman Of The Board, Leslie Goodman
Independent Director, John Strydesky
Independent Director, Elbert Basolis
Independent Director, Patricia Costante
Chairman Of The Board, Patrick Ryan
Independent Director, Christopher Chandor
Auditors: RSM US LLP

LOCATIONS

HQ: First Bank (Williamstown, NJ)
2465 Kuser Road, Hamilton, NJ 08690
Phone: 877 821-2265
Web: www.firstbanknj.com

HISTORICAL FINANCIALS

Company Type: Public

Income Statement

	ASSETS ($ mil.)	NET INCOME ($ mil.)	INCOME AS % OF ASSETS	EMPLOYEES
12/20	2,346.2	19.4	0.8%	207
12/19	2,011.5	13.4	0.7%	221
12/18	1,711.1	17.5	1.0%	188
12/17	1,452.3	6.9	0.5%	153
12/16	1,073.2	6.4	0.6%	110
Annual Growth	21.6%	32.0%	—	17.1%

FYE: December 31

2020 Year-End Financials

Return on assets: 0.8%
Return on equity: 8.3%
Long-term debt ($ mil.): —
No. of shares (mil.): 19.7
Sales ($ mil): 95.5
Dividends
Yield: 1.2%
Payout: 12.3%
Market value ($ mil.): 185.0

	STOCK PRICE ($) FY Close	P/E High/Low		PER SHARE ($) Earnings	Dividends	Book Value
12/20	9.38	11	6	0.97	0.12	12.08
12/19	11.05	17	15	0.69	0.12	11.07
12/18	12.12	15	12	0.95	0.12	10.43
12/17	13.85	30	23	0.48	0.08	9.36
12/16	11.60	20	10	0.61	0.00	7.78
Annual Growth	(5.2%)	—	—	12.3%	—	11.6%

First Busey Corp

First Busey conducts banking related banking services asset management brokerage and fiduciary services through its wholly-owned bank subsidiary Busey Bank which boasts approximately $10.2 billion in assets and about 70 branches across Illinois Florida Missouri and Indiana. The bank offers a range of diversified financial products and services for consumers and businesses including online and mobile banking capabilities. Its primary sources of income are interest and fees on loans and investments wealth management fees and service fees. Subsidiary FirsTech provides retail payment processing services. Most of Busey Bank's branches are located in downstate Illinois.

Operations

First Busey manages its operations through three operating segments consisting of Banking Remittance Processing and Wealth Management. The Banking operating segment (about 95%) provides a full range of banking services to individual and corporate customers through its banking center network in Illinois; the St. Louis Missouri metropolitan area; southwest Florida; and through its banking center in Indianapolis Indiana. The Remittance Processing operating segment (nearly 5%) provides solutions for online bill payments lockbox and walk-in payments. The Wealth Management operating segment (about 5%) provides a full range of asset management investment and fiduciary services to individuals businesses and foundations tax preparation philanthropic advisory services and farm and brokerage services.

The company's lending can be summarized into five primary areas: commercial loans commercial real estate loans real estate construction loans retail real estate loans and retail other loans. Commercial loans typically comprise working capital loans or business expansion loans including loans for asset purchases and other business loans. Commercial real estate loans are subject to underwriting standards and guidelines similar to commercial loans. Real estate construction loans are primarily commercial in nature. Retail real estate loans are comprised of direct consumer loans that include residential real estate home equity lines of credit and home equity loans. Retail other loans consist of installment loans to individuals including automotive loans.

Busey Bank's commercial services include commercial commercial real estate real estate construction and agricultural loans as well as commercial depository services such as cash management. Retail banking services include residential real estate home equity lines of credit and consumer loans customary types of demand and savings deposits money transfers safe deposit services and IRA and other fiduciary services through our banking center ATM and technology-based networks. Brokerage-related services are offered by Busey Investment Services a division of Busey Bank through a third-party arrangement with Raymond James Financial Services. In addition Busey Bank provides professional farm management and brokerage services to the agricultural industry.

About 70% of First Busey's total revenue came from net interest income. The rest of its revenue came from non-interest income (nearly 30%).

Geographic Reach

Busey Bank has nearly 55 branches in Illinois four locations in southwest Florida 10 in Missouri and another office in Indianapolis. Its FirsTech subsidiary accepts payments from its approximately 5800 agent locations across the US.

Sales and Marketing

First Busey serves individuals businesses and foundations.

Financial Performance

The company's net interest income for the year 2020 was $282.9 million a 1% decrease from the previous year's net interest income of $287.2 million.

In 2020 the company had a net income of $100.3 million a 3% decline from the previous year's net income of $103 million. Decline in net income were due to lower performances from the Banking and Wealth Management segments.

The company's cash at the end of 2020 was $529.3 million. Operating activities generated $169.3 million while investing activities used $735.7 million primarily for purchases of debt securities available for sale. Financing activities provided another $725.6 million.

Mergers and Acquisitions

In mid-2021 First Busey acquired Cummins-American the holding company for Glenview State Bank. This partnership benefits the company's clients through enhanced capabilities and products while a growing dynamic organization presents more professional growth opportunities for associates. It enhances Busey's existing deposit commercial banking and wealth management presence in the Chicago-Naperville-Elgin IL-IN-WI Metropolitan Statistical Area (MSA). Each share of CAC common stock was converted into the right to receive 444.4783 First Busey common stock shares and $14173.96 in cash. The transaction carried an aggregate value of nearly $187 million.

EXECUTIVES

Vice Chairman Of The Board, Gregory Lykins
President And Chief Executive Officer Of Busey Bank, Robin Elliott, $450,000 total compensation
Chief Risk Officer, Monica Bowe
Independent Director, Thomas Sloan
General Counsel, John Powers, $350,000 total compensation
Independent Director, Stephen King
Independent Director, George Barr
Chief Of Staff, Amy Randolph, $375,000 total compensation
Independent Director, Frederic Kenney
Chief Financial Officer, Jeffrey Jones, $400,000 total compensation
Independent Director, Karen Jensen
Independent Director, Samuel Banks
Chairman Of The Board, President, Chief Executive Officer, Van Dukeman, $675,000 total compensation
Lead Independent Director, Stanley Bradshaw
Auditors: RSM US LLP

LOCATIONS

HQ: First Busey Corp
100 W. University Avenue, Champaign, IL 61820
Phone: 217 365-4544

PRODUCTS/OPERATIONS

2014 Sales

	$ mil.	% of total
Interest		
Loans including fees	92.4	55
Interest & dividends on securities	15.7	10
Noninterest		
Trust fees	19.6	11
Service charges on deposit accounts	12.0	7
Remittance processing	9.4	6
Gain on sales of loans	4.7	3
Commissions and broker's fees net	2.7	2
Other	10.5	6
Total	**167.0**	**100**

COMPETITORS

ASSOCIATED BANC-CORP
BANKFINANCIAL CORPORATION
BANKUNITED INC.
BBVA USA
BOKF MERGER CORPORATION NUMBER SIXTEEN
CENTRAL PACIFIC FINANCIAL CORP.
COMMERCE BANCSHARES INC.
ENTERPRISE FINANCIAL SERVICES CORP
F.N.B. CORPORATION
FIRSTMERIT CORPORATION
GREAT WESTERN BANCORP INC.
M&T BANK CORPORATION
MECHANICS BANK
PACWEST BANCORP
PEAPACK-GLADSTONE FINANCIAL CORPORATION
SIMMONS FIRST NATIONAL CORPORATION
THE SOUTHERN BANC COMPANY INC
UMB FINANCIAL CORPORATION
UNIVEST FINANCIAL CORPORATION
WINTRUST FINANCIAL CORPORATION

HISTORICAL FINANCIALS

Company Type: Public

Income Statement

FYE: December 31

	ASSETS ($ mil.)	NET INCOME ($ mil.)	INCOME AS % OF ASSETS	EMPLOYEES
12/20	10,544.0	100.3	1.0%	1,346
12/19	9,695.7	102.9	1.1%	1,531
12/18	7,702.3	98.9	1.3%	1,270
12/17	7,860.6	62.7	0.8%	1,347
12/16	5,425.1	49.6	0.9%	1,295
Annual Growth	18.1%	19.2%	—	1.0%

2020 Year-End Financials

Return on assets: 0.9%
Return on equity: 8.0%
Long-term debt ($ mil.): —
No. of shares (mil.): 54.4
Sales ($ mil): 444.8

Dividends
Yield: 4.0%
Payout: 48.0%
Market value ($ mil.): 1,172.0

	STOCK PRICE ($) FY Close	P/E High/Low		PER SHARE ($) Earnings	Dividends	Book Value
12/20	21.55	15	8	1.83	0.88	23.34
12/19	27.50	15	13	1.87	0.84	22.28
12/18	24.54	16	12	2.01	0.80	20.36
12/17	29.94	22	19	1.45	0.72	19.21
12/16	30.78	22	13	1.40	0.68	15.54
Annual Growth	(8.5%)	—	—	6.9%	6.7%	10.7%

First Commonwealth Financial Corp (Indiana, PA)

First Commonwealth Financial is the holding company for First Commonwealth Bank which provides consumer and commercial banking services about120 bank offices throughout central and western Pennsylvania counties as well as in Columbus Ohio. The bank's loan portfolio mostly consists of commercial and industrial loans including real estate operating agricultural and construction loans. It also issues consumer loans such as automobile and home equity loans and offers wealth management insurance financial planning retail brokerage and trust services. The company has total assets of some $9.1 billion with deposits of roughly $7.4 billion.

EXECUTIVES

President, Chief Executive Officer, Director, Thomas Price, $488,000 total compensation
Independent Director, Julie Caponi
Independent Director, Johnston Glass
Non-executive Lead Independent Chairman Of The Board, David Dahlmann
Independent Director, Ray Charley
Executive Vice President, Chief Audit Executive, Leonard Lombardi
Independent Director, Robert Ventura
Executive Vice President, Business Integration Of First Commonwealth Bank, Norman Montgomery, $287,334 total compensation
Executive Vice President, Chief Risk Officer, General Counsel, Matthew Tomb, $346,667 total compensation
Executive Vice President - Human Resources, Carrie Riggle
Independent Director, David Greenfield
Independent Director, Gary Claus
Independent Director, Luke Latimer
Independent Director, Jon Gorney
Chief Financial Officer, Executive Vice President, Treasurer, James Reske, $412,000 total compensation
Independent Director, Aradhna Oliphant
Executive Vice President, Chief Revenue Officer, Director; President Of First Commonwealth Bank, Jane Grebenc, $464,667 total compensation
Executive Vice President, Chief Credit Officer Of First Commonwealth Bank, Brian Karrip, $388,167 total compensation
Independent Director, Bart Johnson
Independent Director, Stephen Wolfe
Auditors: Ernst & Young LLP

LOCATIONS

HQ: First Commonwealth Financial Corp (Indiana, PA)
601 Philadelphia Street, Indiana, PA 15701
Phone: 724 349-7220
Web: www.fcbanking.com

PRODUCTS/OPERATIONS

2014 Sales

	$ mil.	% of total
Interest		
Loans including fees	171.2	65
Taxable investments	31.0	12
Noninterest		
Service charges on deposit accounts	15.7	7
Insurance & retail brokerage commissions	6.5	2
Trust income	6.0	2
Others	32.6	12
Total	**263.0**	**100**

Selected Subsidiaries

First Commonwealth Bank
First Commonwealth Insurance Agency
First Commonwealth Home Mortgage LLC (49.9%)
First Commonwealth Financial Advisors Incorporated

COMPETITORS

BOK FINANCIAL CORPORATION
CAMDEN NATIONAL CORPORATION
CAPITAL BANK FINANCIAL CORP.
DNB FINANCIAL CORPORATION
EAGLE BANCORP INC.
EMCLAIRE FINANCIAL CORP.
FIRST FEDERAL OF NORTHERN MICHIGAN BANCORP INC.
FIRST FINANCIAL BANCORP.
FIRSTMERIT CORPORATION
PEOPLES FINANCIAL SERVICES CORP.
QNB CORP.
S & T BANCORP INC.
SIMMONS FIRST NATIONAL CORPORATION
TALMER BANCORP INC.
TCF FINANCIAL CORPORATION
UMB FINANCIAL CORPORATION

HISTORICAL FINANCIALS

Company Type: Public

Income Statement

FYE: December 31

	ASSETS ($ mil.)	NET INCOME ($ mil.)	INCOME AS % OF ASSETS	EMPLOYEES
12/20	9,068.1	73.4	0.8%	1,393
12/19	8,308.7	105.3	1.3%	1,571
12/18	7,828.2	107.5	1.4%	1,512
12/17	7,308.5	55.1	0.8%	1,476
12/16	6,684.0	59.5	0.9%	1,376
Annual Growth	7.9%	5.4%	—	0.3%

2020 Year-End Financials

Return on assets: 0.8%
Return on equity: 6.9%
Long-term debt ($ mil.): —
No. of shares (mil.): 96.1
Sales ($ mil): 395.6

Dividends
Yield: 4.0%
Payout: 58.6%
Market value ($ mil.): 1,052.0

	STOCK PRICE ($) FY Close	P/E High/Low		PER SHARE ($) Earnings	Dividends	Book Value
12/20	10.94	19	9	0.75	0.44	11.12
12/19	14.51	14	11	1.07	0.40	10.74
12/18	12.08	16	10	1.08	0.35	9.90
12/17	14.32	26	21	0.58	0.32	9.11
12/16	14.18	21	12	0.67	0.28	8.43
Annual Growth	(6.3%)	—	—	2.9%	12.0%	7.2%

First Community Corp (SC)

Putting first things first First Community is the holding company for First Community Bank which serves individuals and smaller businesses in central South Carolina. Through about a dozen offices the bank which was founded in 1995 offers such products and services as checking and savings accounts money market accounts CDs IRAs credit cards insurance and investment services. Commercial mortgages make up about 60% of First Community Bank's loan portfolio which also includes residential mortgages and business consumer and construction loans. The company's First Community Financial Consultants division offers asset management and estate planning.First Community is merging with Cornerstone Bancorp expanding its presence in upstate SC.

EXECUTIVES

President, Chief Executive Officer, Director, Michael Crapps, $447,848 total compensation
Independent Director, Roderick Todd
Independent Director, Thomas Brown
Independent Vice Chairman Of The Board, W. James Kitchens
Independent Director, Alexander Snipe
Chief Banking Officer And President, Chief Banking Officer Of Bank, John Nissen, $260,000 total compensation
Chief Human Resource Officer, Chief Marketing Officer, Robin Brown, $192,400 total compensation
Independent Director, Jane Sosebee
Chief Credit Officer, John Walker
Independent Chairman Of The Board, C. Jimmy Chao
Chief Financial Officer, Executive Vice President, Donald Jordan
Independent Director, Ray Jones
Independent Director, E. Leland Reynolds
Chief Operating Officer, Chief Risk Officer, Tanya Butts, $220,000 total compensation
Independent Director, Edward Tarver
Auditors: Elliott Davis, LLC

LOCATIONS

HQ: First Community Corp (SC)
5455 Sunset Boulevard, Lexington, SC 29072
Phone: 803 951-2265
Web: www.firstcommunitysc.com

COMPETITORS

CHOICEONE FINANCIAL SERVICES INC.
FIRST NATIONAL CORPORATION
SOUTHCOAST FINANCIAL CORPORATION

HISTORICAL FINANCIALS

Company Type: Public

Income Statement — FYE: December 31

	ASSETS ($ mil.)	NET INCOME ($ mil.)	INCOME AS % OF ASSETS	EMPLOYEES
12/20	1,395.3	10.1	0.7%	244
12/19	1,170.2	10.9	0.9%	242
12/18	1,091.6	11.2	1.0%	226
12/17	1,050.7	5.8	0.6%	224
12/16	914.7	6.6	0.7%	202
Annual Growth	11.1%	10.9%	—	4.8%

2020 Year-End Financials

Return on assets: 0.7%
Return on equity: 7.8%
Long-term debt ($ mil.): —
No. of shares (mil.): 7.5
Sales ($ mil): 57.5
Dividends
Yield: 2.8%
Payout: 35.5%
Market value ($ mil.): 127.0

	STOCK PRICE ($) FY Close	P/E High/Low		Earnings	PER SHARE ($) Dividends	Book Value
12/20	16.99	16	9	1.35	0.48	18.18
12/19	21.61	15	12	1.45	0.44	16.16
12/18	19.43	18	13	1.45	0.40	14.73
12/17	22.60	29	21	0.83	0.36	13.93
12/16	18.05	19	13	0.98	0.32	12.20
Annual Growth	(1.5%)		—	8.3%	10.7%	10.5%

First Farmers Financial Corp

Auditors: BKD, LLP

LOCATIONS

HQ: First Farmers Financial Corp
123 North Jefferson Street, Converse, IN 46919
Phone: 765 395-3316
Web: www.ffbt.com

HISTORICAL FINANCIALS

Company Type: Public

Income Statement — FYE: December 31

	REVENUE ($ mil.)	NET INCOME ($ mil.)	NET PROFIT MARGIN	EMPLOYEES
12/20	108.0	30.4	28.2%	0
12/19	103.6	29.5	28.5%	0
12/18	94.5	27.7	29.3%	0
12/17	82.3	21.7	26.4%	0
12/16	74.9	17.0	22.7%	0
Annual Growth	9.6%	15.6%	—	—

2020 Year-End Financials

Debt ratio: 9.4%
Return on equity: 14.4%
Cash ($ mil.): 191.3
Current ratio: 0.11
Long-term debt ($ mil.): 208.5
No. of shares (mil.): 7.0
Dividends
Yield: 2.9%
Payout: 31.6%
Market value ($ mil.): 309.0

	STOCK PRICE ($) FY Close	P/E High/Low		Earnings	PER SHARE ($) Dividends	Book Value
12/20	43.71	11	10	4.29	1.29	31.30
12/19	47.01	11	10	4.13	1.22	27.78
12/18	42.00	22	11	3.87	1.02	24.03
12/17	71.50	26	20	3.04	0.69	21.44
12/16	65.00	27	27	2.38	0.65	18.94
Annual Growth	(9.4%)		—	15.9%	18.9%	13.4%

First Financial Bancorp (OH)

The holding company's flagship subsidiary First Financial Bank operates more than 140 banking centers in Ohio Indiana Kentucky and Illinois. Founded in 1863 the bank offers checking and savings accounts money market accounts CDs credit cards private banking and wealth management services through its First Financial Wealth Management subsidiary. Commercial loans including real estate and construction loans make up more than 50% of First Financial's total loan portfolio; the bank also offers residential mortgage and consumer loans. First Financial Bancorp boasts nearly $16 billion in assets including nearly $10 billion in loans.

Operations

The company's private banking business First Financial Wealth Management had $16 billion in assets under management in early 2020.

First Financial provides banking and financial services products to business and retail clients through its six lines of business: Commercial Retail Banking Mortgage Banking Wealth Management Investment Commercial Real Estate and Commercial Finance. Commercial Finance provides equipment and leasehold improvement financing for franchisees in the quick service and casual dining restaurant sector and commission-based financing primarily to insurance agents and brokers throughout the United States. Wealth Management had $3.0 billion in assets under management as of December 31 2020 and provides the following services: financial planning investment management trust administration estate settlement brokerage services and retirement planning.

Overall net interest income generate some 75% of company's total revenue.

Geographic Reach

The company operates some 145 full service banking centers. Its core banking operating markets are located within the four state region of Ohio Indiana Kentucky and Illinois. First Financial's executive office is a leased facility located in Cincinnati Ohio and it operates roughly 65 banking centers in Ohio three banking centers in Illinois about 65 banking centers in Indiana and around 15 banking centers in Kentucky.

In addition the company operates its Commercial Finance division responsible for its insurance lending business and franchise lending business from a non-banking center location in Indiana.

Sales and Marketing

First Financial spent $6.4 million on marketing in 2020 compared to $6.9 million and $7.6 million in 2019 and 2018 respectively.

Financial Performance

First Financial's revenue and net income have both consistently grown in the last five years.

Net interest income in 2020 decreased $27.7 million or 5.7% from 2019 to $456.5 million primarily driven by lower yields earned on the loan and investment portfolios resulting from a lower interest rate environment. The net interest margin on a fully tax equivalent basis was 3.51% for 2020 compared to 4.00% in 2019.

First Financial's net income decreased $42.3 million or 21.3% to $155.8 million in 2020 compared to net income of $198.1 million in 2019. The decrease was primarily related to a $27.7 million or 5.7% decrease in net interest income as well as a $40.1 million or 131.9% increase in provision expense and a $48.3 million or 14.1% increase in noninterest expenses which was partially offset by a $57.8 million or 44.0% increase in noninterest income and a $16.2 million or 36.1% decrease in income tax expense during 2020.

The company's cash at the end of the 2020 was $231 million. Operating activities provided $109.9 million while investing activities used $1.2 billion mainly for purchases of securities available-for-sale. Financing activities generated $1.1 billion in 2020.

Strategy

First Financial aims to develop a competitive advantage by utilizing a local market focus to provide superior service and build long-term relationships with clients while helping them achieve greater financial success. First Financial serves a combination of metropolitan and community markets in Ohio Indiana Kentucky and Illinois through its full-service banking centers and provides financing to franchise owners and clients within the financial services industry throughout the United States. First Financial's market selection process includes a number of factors but markets are primarily chosen for their potential for long-term profitability and growth.

First Financial intends to concentrate plans for future growth and capital investment within its current metropolitan markets and will continue to evaluate additional growth opportunities in metropolitan markets located within or in close proximity to the company's current geographic footprint. Additionally First Financial may assess strategic acquisitions that provide product line extensions or additional industry verticals that complement its existing business and diversify its product suite and revenue streams. First Financial's investment in community markets is an important part of the Bank's core funding base and has historically provided stable low-cost funding sources.

Company Background

In the past the bank acquired 16 branches in western Ohio from Liberty Savings Bank and bought 22 Indianapolis-area branches from Flagstar Bank in 2011. Together the two acquisitions furthered the bank's growth strategy for the key markets of Dayton and Indianapolis.

EXECUTIVES

Independent Director, Cynthia Booth
Independent Director, Maribeth Rahe
Chairman, Claude Davis
Independent Director, Corinne Finnerty

Independent Director, Susan Knust
Independent Director, William Kramer
Executive Vice President, Chief Strategy Officer, Amanda Neeley
Chief Operating Officer, Executive Vice President, John Gavigan, $362,693 total compensation
Independent Director, John Neighbours
Chief Corporate Banking Officer, President Of First Commercial Finance, Richard Dennen, $399,900 total compensation
President, Chief Executive Officer And Director, Archie Brown, $800,207 total compensation
Chief Financial Officer, Executive Vice President, James Anderson, $407,693 total compensation
Independent Director, William Barron
Executive Vice President, Chief Credit Officer, William Harrod, $272,586 total compensation
Executive Vice President, Chief Risk Officer, General Counsel, Karen Woods, $377,692 total compensation
Executive Vice President - Consumer Banking, Catherine Myers
Executive Vice President - Commercial Banking, Chief Commercial Banking Officer, Andrew Hauck, $393,462 total compensation
Auditors: Crowe LLP

LOCATIONS

HQ: First Financial Bancorp (OH)
255 East Fifth Street, Suite 800, Cincinnati, OH 45202
Phone: 877 322-9530
Web: www.bankatfirst.com

PRODUCTS/OPERATIONS

2014 Sales

	$ mil.	% of total
Interest		
Loans including fees	208.8	66
Investment securities	44.5	14
(Adjustment)	(5.5)	-
Noninterest		
Service charges on deposit accounts	20.3	7
Trust and wealth management fees	13.6	5
Bankcard income	10.7	3
Net gains from sales on loans	4.4	1
Accelerated discount on covered/formerly covered loans	4.2	1
Others	10.8	3
Total	**311.8**	**100**

COMPETITORS

ACCESS NATIONAL CORPORATION
AMERIS BANCORP
ASSOCIATED BANC-CORP
BOK FINANCIAL CORPORATION
CAPITAL BANK FINANCIAL CORP.
CENTERSTATE BANK CORPORATION
CITIZENS FINANCIAL GROUP INC.
COMMERCE BANCSHARES INC.
FIRST COMMONWEALTH FINANCIAL CORPORATION
FIRST EAGLE PRIVATE CREDIT LLC
FIRST MIDWEST BANCORP INC.
M&T BANK CORPORATION
MIDWESTONE FINANCIAL GROUP INC.
OLD LINE BANCSHARES INC.
PROVIDENT FINANCIAL SERVICES INC.
S & T BANCORP INC.
SIGNATURE BANK
TCF FINANCIAL CORPORATION
TEXAS CAPITAL BANCSHARES INC.
TRISTATE CAPITAL HOLDINGS INC.
UMB FINANCIAL CORPORATION
WASHINGTON TRUST BANCORP INC.
WEBSTER FINANCIAL CORPORATION
WINTRUST FINANCIAL CORPORATION

HISTORICAL FINANCIALS

Company Type: Public

Income Statement

FYE: December 31

	ASSETS ($ mil.)	NET INCOME ($ mil.)	INCOME AS % OF ASSETS	EMPLOYEES
12/21	16,329.1	205.1	1.3%	2,010
12/20	15,973.1	155.8	1.0%	2,107
12/19	14,511.6	198.0	1.4%	2,123
12/18	13,986.6	172.6	1.2%	2,131
12/17	8,896.9	96.7	1.1%	1,366
Annual Growth	16.4%	20.7%	—	10.1%

2021 Year-End Financials

Return on assets: 1.2%
Return on equity: 9.0%
Long-term debt ($ mil.): —
No. of shares (mil.): 94.1
Sales ($ mil): 654.7

Dividends
 Yield: 3.7%
 Payout: 43.4%
Market value ($ mil.): 2,295.0

	STOCK PRICE ($) FY Close	P/E High/Low		PER SHARE ($) Earnings	Dividends	Book Value
12/21	24.38	12	8	2.14	0.92	23.99
12/20	17.53	16	7	1.59	0.92	23.28
12/19	25.44	14	11	2.00	0.90	22.82
12/18	23.72	17	11	1.93	0.78	21.23
12/17	26.35	19	15	1.56	0.68	14.99
Annual Growth	(1.9%)	—	—	8.2%	7.8%	12.5%

First Financial Bankshares, Inc.

Texas hold 'em? Well sort of. First Financial Bankshares is the holding company for eleven banks consolidated under the First Financial brand all of which are located in small and midsized markets in Texas. Together they have about 50 locations. The company maintains a decentralized management structure with each of the subsidiary banks having their own local leadership and decision-making authority. Its First Financial Trust & Asset Management subsidiary administers retirement and employee benefit plans in addition to providing trust services. First Financial Bankshares also owns an insurance agency.

EXECUTIVES

Chairman, President And Chief Executive Officer, F. Scott Dueser, $1,056,667 total compensation
Independent Director, Ivan Lancaster
Executive Vice President, Chief Administrative Officer, Ronald Butler, $541,667 total compensation
Executive Vice President, Chief Lending Officer, T. Luke Longhofer
Executive Vice President - Commercial Banking, David Bailey
Independent Director, Kade Matthews
Independent Director, David Copeland
Independent Director, Robert Nickles
Independent Director, Vianei Braun
Chief Financial Officer, Executive Vice President, James Gordon, $375,000 total compensation

Executive Vice President Of Marketing, Chris Cook
Director, Eli Jones
Auditors: Ernst & Young LLP

LOCATIONS

HQ: First Financial Bankshares, Inc.
400 Pine Street, Abilene, TX 79601
Phone: 325 627-7155
Web: www.ffin.com

PRODUCTS/OPERATIONS

2015 sales

	$ mil.	% of total
Interest Income		
Interest and fees on loans	151.7	51
Interest on investment securities	69.7	24
Interest on federal funds sold and interest-bearing deposits in banks	0.2	-
Non-Interest Income		
ATM interchange and credit card fees	21.9	7
Trust fees	19.2	6
Service charges on deposit accounts	17.2	6
Real estate mortgage operations	10.4	4
Net gain on sale of available-for-sale securities	0.5	-
Net gain on sale of foreclosed assets	0.5	-
Net loss on sale of assets	(0.8)	-
Other	4.6	2
Total	**295.1**	**100**

Products/ServicesPersonal
Learn
Online Banking
Mobile Banking
Consumer Education
FAQS
Privacy & Security Information
Resources
Testimonials
Tools
Bank
Checking
Savings
Invest
CDS & IRAS
Broker Services
Borrow
Mortgage Loans
Mortgage Lenders
Auto Loans
Recreational Loans
Home Equity Loans
Personal Line of Credit
CD Secured Loans
Banking with First Financial
Mobile Banking
Online Banking
Pay Bills
Get Cash
Make Deposit
Move Money
Keep Track
Business
Learn
Online Banking
Mobile Banking
Business Education
Starting your Business
Growing your Business
Tools
Business Banking Services
Manage Cash
Send Payments
Receive Payments
Manage Fraud and Risk
Other Services
Trust & Wealth Management
Investment Management
Trust Management
Estate Management
Oil & Gas Management
Real Estate and Property Management
Company Retirement Plans

Selected Subsidiaries

First Financial Bank National Association Abilene Texas.
First Technology Services Inc. Abilene Texas (wholly owned subsidiary of First Financial Bank National Association Abilene Texas).
First Financial Trust & Asset Management Company National Association Abilene Texas.
First Financial Insurance Agency Inc. Abilene Texas.
First Financial Investments Inc. Abilene Texas.

COMPETITORS

AIG RETIREMENT SERVICES
B loise Holding AG
CIVISTA BANCSHARES INC.
FB FINANCIAL CORPORATION
FIFTH THIRD BANCORP
KEYCORP
LEGAL & GENERAL GROUP PLC
NORTHERN TRUST CORPORATION
SB FINANCIAL GROUP INC.
THE BANK OF NEW YORK MELLON CORPORATION
TRUIST FINANCIAL CORPORATION

HISTORICAL FINANCIALS

Company Type: Public

Income Statement

FYE: December 31

	ASSETS ($ mil.)	NET INCOME ($ mil.)	INCOME AS % OF ASSETS	EMPLOYEES
12/21	13,102.4	227.5	1.7%	1,500
12/20	10,904.5	202.0	1.9%	1,500
12/19	8,262.2	164.8	2.0%	1,345
12/18	7,731.8	150.6	1.9%	1,350
12/17	7,254.7	120.3	1.7%	1,300
Annual Growth	**15.9%**	**17.3%**	**—**	**3.6%**

2021 Year-End Financials

Return on assets: 1.9%	Dividends
Return on equity: 13.2%	Yield: 1.1%
Long-term debt ($ mil.): —	Payout: 36.0%
No. of shares (mil.): 141.6	Market value ($ mil.): 7,199.0
Sales ($ mil): 518.5	

	STOCK PRICE ($) FY Close	P/E High/Low	Earnings	Dividends	Book Value
12/21	50.84	34 22	1.59	0.58	12.42
12/20	36.18	25 17	1.42	0.51	11.88
12/19	35.10	53 24	1.21	0.47	9.09
12/18	57.69	60 40	1.11	0.41	7.83
12/17	45.05	53 41	0.91	0.38	7.02
Annual Growth	**3.1%**	**— —**	**15.1%**	**11.5%**	**15.4%**

First Financial Northwest Inc

Searching for green in The Evergreen State First Financial Northwest is the holding company for First Financial Northwest Bank (formerly First Savings Bank Northwest). The small community bank offers deposit services like checking and savings accounts and a variety of lending services to customers in western Washington. Almost 40% of First Savings Bank's loan portfolio consists of one-to four-family residential loans while commercial real estate loans made up another 35%. Because the bank focuses almost exclusively on real estate loans it writes very few unsecured consumer and commercial loans.

Operations

About 17% of First Financial Northwest Bank's loan portfolio was comprised of multi-family mortgage loans while construction/land development loans made up 7%. Less than 2% of the bank's portfolio was made up of business and consumer loans.

The bank generated 93% of its total revenue from loan interest (including fees) in 2014 and another 6% came from interest on its investments available-for-sale.

Geographic Reach

Renton-based First Financial Northwest Bank's one branch office primarily serves King county as well as Pierce Snohomish and Kitsap counties (to a lesser extent) in the western part of Washington State.

Financial Performance

First Financial Northwest's revenues have been in decline in recent years due to shrinking interest margins on loans amidst the low-interest environment. The firm's profits however have trended thanks to declining loan loss provisions as its loan portfolio's credit quality has improved with the strengthened housing market and overall economy.

The company's revenue remained mostly flat around $39.2 million in 2014 with slightly higher interest income as it grew its loan business but with slightly lower non-interest income as it had sold an investment property for a $325000 gain in 2013.

First Financial's net income plummeted by 56% to $10.7 million despite stable revenue in 2014 mostly because it had collected a (non-recurring) $13.5 million tax benefit in 2013 (compared to a tax expense of $5.9 million in 2014) after a reversal of its deferred tax asset valuation allowance. Not counting this event the company's before-tax profit grew by more than 50% as its operational expenses fell and its loan loss provisions continued to decline. First Financial's operating levels rose by 22% to $18.6 million thanks to higher cash earnings.

Strategy

First Financial Northwest's long-term business strategy is to grow First Financial Northwest Bank "as a well-capitalized and profitable community bank" with continued focus on one-to-four family residential loans and commercial real estate loans. It also planned in 2015 to promote its "diversified array" of deposit loan and other products and services to individuals and businesses highlighting its locality in its target Puget Sound regional market.

To ensure low-cost funding sources the bank in 2015 planned to continue using wholesale funding sources from Federal Home Loan Bank advances and acquired deposits in the national brokered certificate of deposit market. To minimize risk it would continue to diversify its loan types and manage its loss-invoking credit risk and diminish interest rate risk to keep its interest margins up.

The bank in 2015 also expected to improve profitability through "disciplined pricing expense control and balance sheet management while continuing to provide excellent customer service."

Company Background

First Financial Northwest changed the name of its subsidiary bank to First Financial Northwest Bank from First Savings Bank Northwest in July

2015 to reflect that it was "more than just a savings bank" according to the company's CEO.

EXECUTIVES

Independent Director, Joann Lee
Chief Risk Officer, Senior Vice President, Ronnie Clariza, $207,500 total compensation
Principal Accounting Officer, Vice President, Controller, Christine Huestis
Chief Banking Officer, Dalen Harrison, $230,962 total compensation
Independent Director, Diane Davis
Director, Cindy Runger
Senior Vice President And Chief Credit Officer, Simon Soh, $257,500 total compensation
President, Chief Executive Officer, Director, Joseph Kiley, $478,350 total compensation
Chief Financial Officer, Chief Operating Officer, Executive Vice President, Director, Richard Jacobson, $320,000 total compensation
Independent Director, Roger Molvar
Auditors: Moss Adams LLP

LOCATIONS

HQ: First Financial Northwest Inc
201 Wells Avenue South, Renton, WA 98057
Phone: 425 255-4400

PRODUCTS/OPERATIONS

2014 Sales

	% of total
Interest income	
Loans(including fees)	93
Investments available-for-sale	6
Interest-earning deposits with banks	-
Non-interest income	1
Total	**100**

COMPETITORS

BANK MUTUAL CORPORATION
FIRST CONNECTICUT INC.
BANCORP INC.
FIRST FINANCIAL CORPORATION
HOMESTREET INC.

LEGACYTEXAS FINANCIAL GROUP INC.
NORTHWEST BANCORP
THE SOUTHERN BANC COMPANY INC
UNITED COMMUNITY FINANCIAL CORP.

HISTORICAL FINANCIALS

Company Type: Public

Income Statement
FYE: December 31

	ASSETS ($ mil.)	NET INCOME ($ mil.)	INCOME AS % OF ASSETS	EMPLOYEES
12/20	1,387.6	8.5	0.6%	151
12/19	1,341.8	10.3	0.8%	158
12/18	1,252.4	14.9	1.2%	156
12/17	1,210.2	8.4	0.7%	145
12/16	1,037.5	8.8	0.9%	121
Annual Growth	**7.5%**	**(1.0%)**	**—**	**5.7%**

2020 Year-End Financials

Return on assets: 0.6%	Dividends
Return on equity: 5.4%	Yield: 3.5%
Long-term debt ($ mil.): —	Payout: 45.4%
No. of shares (mil.): 9.7	Market value ($ mil.): 111.0
Sales ($ mil): 60.5	

	STOCK PRICE ($) FY Close	P/E High/Low		PER SHARE ($) Earnings	Dividends	Book Value
12/20	11.40	17	9	0.88	0.40	16.05
12/19	14.94	16	13	1.03	0.35	15.25
12/18	15.47	14	10	1.43	0.31	14.35
12/17	15.51	26	18	0.81	0.27	13.27
12/16	19.74	27	17	0.74	0.24	12.63
Annual Growth	**(12.8%)**	**—**	**—**	**4.4%**	**13.6%**	**6.2%**

First Foundation Inc

Auditors: Eide Bailly LLP

LOCATIONS

HQ: First Foundation Inc
200 Crescent Court, Suite 1400, Dallas, TX 75201
Phone: 469 638-9636
Web: www.ff-inc.com

HISTORICAL FINANCIALS

Company Type: Public

Income Statement
FYE: December 31

	ASSETS ($ mil.)	NET INCOME ($ mil.)	INCOME AS % OF ASSETS	EMPLOYEES
12/20	6,957.1	84.3	1.2%	502
12/19	6,314.4	56.2	0.9%	485
12/18	5,840.4	42.9	0.7%	482
12/17	4,541.1	27.5	0.6%	394
12/16	3,975.4	23.3	0.6%	335
Annual Growth	**15.0%**	**37.9%**	**—**	**10.6%**

2020 Year-End Financials

Return on assets: 1.2%	Dividends
Return on equity: 12.8%	Yield: 1.6%
Long-term debt ($ mil.): —	Payout: 17.5%
No. of shares (mil.): 44.6	Market value ($ mil.): 893.0
Sales ($ mil): 298.5	

	STOCK PRICE ($) FY Close	P/E High/Low		PER SHARE ($) Earnings	Dividends	Book Value
12/20	20.00	11	4	1.88	0.33	15.58
12/19	17.40	14	10	1.25	0.20	13.74
12/18	12.86	20	12	1.01	0.00	12.57
12/17	18.54	36	17	0.78	0.00	10.34
12/16	28.50	41	28	0.70	0.00	8.69
Annual Growth	**(8.5%)**	**—**	**—**	**28.0%**	**—**	**15.7%**

First Guaranty Bancshares, Inc.

EXECUTIVES

Vice Chairman Of The Board, President And Chief Executive Officer, Alton Lewis, $371,250 total compensation

Independent Chairman Of The Board, Marshall Reynolds
Independent Director, William Hood
Independent Director, Jack Rossi
Chief Financial Officer, Treasurer, Secretary, Eric Dosch, $159,115 total compensation
Auditors: Castaing, Hussey & Lolan, LLC

LOCATIONS

HQ: First Guaranty Bancshares, Inc.
400 East Thomas Street, Hammond, LA 70401
Phone: 985 345-7685
Web: www.eguaranty.com

HISTORICAL FINANCIALS

Company Type: Public

Income Statement
FYE: December 31

	ASSETS ($ mil.)	NET INCOME ($ mil.)	INCOME AS % OF ASSETS	EMPLOYEES
12/20	2,473.0	20.3	0.8%	453
12/19	2,117.2	14.2	0.7%	457
12/18	1,817.2	14.2	0.8%	373
12/17	1,750.4	11.7	0.7%	349
12/16	1,500.9	14.0	0.9%	304
Annual Growth	**13.3%**	**9.6%**	**—**	**10.5%**

2020 Year-End Financials

Return on assets: 0.8%	Dividends
Return on equity: 11.7%	Yield: 3.9%
Long-term debt ($ mil.): —	Payout: 33.6%
No. of shares (mil.): 10.7	Market value ($ mil.): 190.0
Sales ($ mil): 124.4	

	STOCK PRICE ($) FY Close	P/E High/Low		PER SHARE ($) Earnings	Dividends	Book Value
12/20	17.77	12	6	1.90	0.64	16.67
12/19	21.77	18	14	1.34	0.60	15.50
12/18	23.21	21	15	1.33	0.58	13.82
12/17	25.00	26	20	1.13	0.54	13.51
12/16	23.93	17	11	1.39	0.53	12.28
Annual Growth	**(7.2%)**	**—**	**—**	**8.1%**	**4.9%**	**7.9%**

First Horizon Corp

The bank holding company provide diversified financial services primarily through their principal subsidiary. Boasting more than $80 billion in total assets it offers traditional banking services like loans deposit accounts and credit cards as well as trust asset management financial advisory and investment services. In 2020 the company shortened its company name from First Horizon National Corporation to First Horizon Bank.

Operations

First Horizon operates three core business segments: Regional Banking Specialty banking and Corporate.

Regional Banking provides traditional banking products and services to retail and commercial customers mostly in Southern US banking. The division also provides investments financial planning trust services and asset management as well as correspondent banking services such as credit depository and other banking related services for financial institutions.

Specialty banking consists of businesses that deliver product offerings and services with specialized industry knowledge. The segment offers asset-based ending mortgage warehouse lending commercial real estate franchise finance correspondent banking equipment finance mortgage and title insurance. In addition the segment also has a business line that focuses on fixed income securities sales trading underwriting and strategies for institutional clients in the US.

The corporate segment provide risk management audit accounting finance executive office and corporate communications. The segment also includes centralized management of capital and funding to support the business activities of the company including management of wholesale funding liquidity and capital management and allocation.

Geographic Reach

First Horizon Bank operates about 500 First Tennessee Bank and Capital Bank Branches in twelve states. More than 30% of the branches are in Tennessee while the remaining are in the states of Georgia (northwestern area) Mississippi (northwestern area) North Carolina Virginia South Carolina Texas and Florida.

Sales and Marketing

The company spent $18.68 million on advertising and public relations in 2014 up from $18.24 million and $17.44 million in 2013 and 2012 respectively.

Financial Performance

First Horizon Bank's performance for the span of five years have been fluctuating but ended with a significant rise in 2020.

First Horizon's revenue increased by more than 40% or $1.3 billion to $3.1 billion as compared to 2019's revenue of $1.8 billion.

Net income was $845 million in 2020 an increase of $441 million as compared to the prior year's net income $435 million.

The company's cash held at the end of 2020 amounted to $827 million. Operating activities provided $167 million for 2020. Investing activities and financing activities generated $96 million and $195 million respectively.

Mergers and Acquisitions

First Horizon Bank completed a merger of equals transaction with IBERIABANK corporation and acquired 30 branches from Truist Bank.

Company Background

Frank S. Davis submitted a national charter to establish First National Bank of Memphis in 1864. The bank continued to grow over the years and in 1977 First National changed its name to First Tennessee to reflect the bank's expansion beyond Memphis.

In 2004 the company changed its name to First Horizon National Corporation. In 2020 as a result of a merger of equals with IBERIABANK Corporation the company changed its name from First Horizon National Corporation to First Horizon Bank.

EXECUTIVES

Lead Independent Director, Colin Reed
Independent Director, Vicki Palmer
President - Specialty Banking Of First Horizon And The Bank, David Popwell, $550,000 total compensation
Executive Vice President, Chief Accounting Officer, Corporate Controller Of First Horizon And The Bank, Jeff Fleming

Independent Director, Rajesh Subramaniam
Independent Director, Cecelia Stewart
Director, R. Eugene Taylor
Independent Director, Kenneth Burdick
Independent Director, Wendy Davidson
Chief Operating Officer, Tammy LoCascio
President, Regional Banking And Interim Chief Financial Officer, Anthony Restel, $326,000 total compensation
Independent Director, John Casbon
Independent Director, William Fenstermaker
Independent Director, Harry Barton
Independent Director, Rosa Sugranes
Senior Executive Vice President, Chief Risk Officer Of First Horizon And The Bank, Terry Akins
Independent Director, J. Michael Kemp
Senior Executive Vice President, Chief Communications Officer Of First Horizon And The Bank, Elizabeth Ardoin
Executive Chairman Of The Board Of First Horizon And The Bank, Daryl Byrd, $552,885 total compensation
Independent Director, E. Stewart Shea
Chief Human Resources Officer, Tanya Hart
Independent Director, Ricky Maples
President - Dallas/fort Worth Market, Key Coker
President, Chief Executive Officer, Director Of First Horizon And The Bank, David Jordan, $1,037,538 total compensation
Independent Director, John Compton
Senior Executive Vice President, Chief Credit Officer Of First Horizon And The Bank, Susan Springfield, $400,000 total compensation
Senior Executive Vice President And Chief Financial Officer, Hope Dmuchowski
Auditors: KPMG LLP

LOCATIONS

HQ: First Horizon Corp
165 Madison Avenue, Memphis, TN 38103
Phone: 901 523-4444
Web: www.firsthorizon.com

PRODUCTS/OPERATIONS

2014 Sales

	$ mil.	% of total
Interest		
Loans including fees	571.8	45
Investment securities	93.2	7
Trading securities	32.0	3
Loans held for sale	11.2	1
Other	1.1	-
Noninterest		
Capital markets	200.5	16
Deposit transactions & cash management	112.0	9
Mortgage banking	71.3	6
Brokerage management fees & commissions	49.1	4
Trust services and investment management	27.7	2
Bankcard income	23.7	2
Bank owned life insurance	16.4	1
Other	49.3	4
Total	**1,259.3**	**100**

COMPETITORS

AMERIS BANCORP HOLDINGS	MUFG AMERICAS
BANK OF THE WEST	CORPORATION
Banco Bradesco S/A	National Bank of Canada
CITIZENS FINANCIAL GROUP INC.	OLD NATIONAL BANCORP
COLUMBIA BANKING SYSTEM INC.	PINNACLE FINANCIAL PARTNERS INC.
COMERICA INCORPORATED	REGIONS FINANCIAL
COMMUNITY BANK SYSTEM INC.	CORPORATION
	SUNTRUST BANKS INC.

FB CORPORATION	TCF FINANCIAL
FIFTH THIRD BANCORP	CORPORATION
FINANCIAL INSTITUTIONS INC.	THE PNC FINANCIAL SERVICES GROUP INC
FIRST CITIZENS BANCSHARES INC.	WEBSTER FINANCIAL CORPORATION
FIRST MIDWEST BANCORP	WELLS FARGO & COMPANY INC.

HISTORICAL FINANCIALS

Company Type: Public

Income Statement
FYE: December 31

	ASSETS ($ mil.)	NET INCOME ($ mil.)	INCOME AS % OF ASSETS	EMPLOYEES
12/20	84,209.0	845.0	1.0%	6,802
12/19	43,310.9	440.9	1.0%	5,017
12/18	40,832.2	545.0	1.3%	5,577
12/17	41,423.3	165.5	0.4%	5,984
12/16	28,555.2	227.0	0.8%	4,288
Annual Growth	31.0%	38.9%	—	12.2%

2020 Year-End Financials

Return on assets: 1.3%
Return on equity: 13.1%
Long-term debt ($ mil.): —
No. of shares (mil.): 555.0
Sales ($ mil): 3,390.0

Dividends
Yield: 4.7%
Payout: 31.7%
Market value ($ mil.): 7,082.0

	STOCK PRICE ($) FY Close	P/E High/Low		PER SHARE ($) Earnings	Dividends	Book Value
12/20	12.76	9	4	1.89	0.60	14.44
12/19	16.56	12	10	1.38	0.56	15.35
12/18	13.16	12	7	1.65	0.48	14.09
12/17	19.99	31	24	0.65	0.36	13.11
12/16	20.01	22	12	0.94	0.28	10.31
Annual Growth	(10.6%)	—	—	19.1%	21.0%	8.8%

First Internet Bancorp

First Internet Bancorp was formed in 2006 to be the holding company for First Internet Bank of Indiana (First IB). Launched in 1999 the bank was the first state-chartered FDIC-insured institution to operate solely via the Internet. It now operates two locations in Indianapolis after adding one via its 2007 purchase of Landmark Financial (the parent of Landmark Savings Bank) a deal that also brought aboard residential mortgage brokerage Landmark Mortgage. First IB offers traditional checking and savings accounts in addition to CDs IRAs credit and check cards consumer installment and residential mortgage loans and lines of credit. It serves customers in all 50 states.

EXECUTIVES

Chairman And Chief Executive Officer, First Internet Bancorp And First Internet Bank, David Becker, $800,000 total compensation
Independent Vice Chairman Of The Board, David Lovejoy
President And Chief Operating Officer, First Internet Bancorp And First Internet Bank, Nicole Lorch, $330,000 total compensation

Executive Vice President, Secretary, C. Charles
 Perfetti, $255,000 total compensation
Chief Financial Officer, Executive Vice President,
 Kenneth Lovik, $320,000 total compensation
Independent Director, Ana Dutra
Director, Ann Dee
Director, Justin Christian
Auditors: BKD, LLP

LOCATIONS

HQ: First Internet Bancorp
 11201 USA Parkway, Fishers, IN 46037
Phone: 317 532-7900
Web: www.firstinternetbancorp.com

COMPETITORS

FIRST SAVINGS	THE FIRST BANK AND
FINANCIAL GROUP INC.	TRUST COMPANY
HOPFED BANCORP INC.	UNITED BANCSHARES INC.

HISTORICAL FINANCIALS

Company Type: Public

Income Statement				FYE: December 31
	ASSETS ($ mil.)	NET INCOME ($ mil.)	INCOME AS % OF ASSETS	EMPLOYEES
12/20	4,246.1	29.4	0.7%	257
12/19	4,100.0	25.2	0.6%	231
12/18	3,541.6	21.9	0.6%	201
12/17	2,767.6	15.2	0.6%	206
12/16	1,854.3	12.0	0.7%	192
Annual Growth	23.0%	25.0%	—	7.6%

2020 Year-End Financials

Return on assets: 0.7%	Dividends
Return on equity: 9.2%	Yield: 0.8%
Long-term debt ($ mil.): —	Payout: 9.2%
No. of shares (mil.): 9.8	Market value ($ mil.): 282.0
Sales ($ mil): 173.2	

	STOCK PRICE ($) FY Close	P/E High/Low		PER SHARE ($) Earnings	Dividends	Book Value
12/20	28.74	10	4	2.99	0.24	33.77
12/19	23.71	10	7	2.51	0.24	31.30
12/18	20.44	18	8	2.30	0.24	28.39
12/17	38.15	19	12	2.13	0.24	26.65
12/16	32.00	14	10	2.30	0.24	23.76
Annual Growth	(2.7%)	—	—	6.8%	(0.0%)	9.2%

First Interstate BancSystem Inc

First Interstate BancSystem (FIB) is a financial
and bank holding company focused on community
banking that operates 150 banking offices including detached drive-up facilities in communities
across six states?Idaho Montana Oregon South
Dakota Washington and Wyoming. Through the
company's bank subsidiary First Interstate Bank
they deliver a comprehensive range of banking
products and services?including online and mobile
banking?to individuals businesses municipalities
and others throughout their market areas. The
company's principal business activity is lending to
accepting deposits from and conducting financial
transactions with and for individuals businesses
municipalities and other entities.

Operations

FIB operates through one segment: community
banking. The segment encompasses commercial
and consumer banking services provided through
its bank are primarily the acceptance of deposits
extensions of credit mortgage loan origination and
servicing and trust employee benefit investment
and insurance services.

Through lending activities the company offers
offer real estate consumer commercial agricultural
and other loans to individuals and businesses in
their market areas. Its deposit products include
checking savings and time deposits. The company
also offers repurchase agreements primarily to
commercial and municipal depositors. Under repurchase agreements FIB sells investment securities held by the bank to their clients under an
agreement to repurchase the investment securities
at a specified time or on demand.

Through their wealth management services FIB
provides a wide range of trust employee benefit
investment management insurance agency and
custodial services to individuals businesses and
nonprofit organizations. These services include the
administration of estates and personal trusts management of investment accounts for individuals
employee benefit plans and charitable foundations
and insurance planning.

FIB's centralized operational activities generally
support their banking offices in the delivery of
products and services to clients and include marketing credit review loan servicing credit card issuance and servicing mortgage loan sales and servicing loan collections among others.

The Real estate loans (commercial construction
residential and agricultural) account for 65% of
the company's loan portfolio followed by commercial loans (more than 20%) consumer loans (some
10%) and agricultural loans (less than 5%).

Geographic Reach

Montana-based FIB provides banking services
at 150 locations in Idaho Montana Oregon South
Dakota Washington and Wyoming of which some
40 properties are leased from independent third
parties and about 110 properties are owned by
the company. With more than 45 branches Montana accounts for the largest percentage of market
deposits (almost 18%) followed by Wyoming (almost 15%) with 15 branches.

Sales and Marketing

FIB delivers a comprehensive range of banking
products and services?including online and mobile
banking?to individuals businesses municipalities
and others. It provides lending opportunities to
clients that participate in a wide variety of industries including agriculture construction education
energy governmental services healthcare hospitality housing mining real estate development and
retail among others.

Advertising expense was $2.8 million $4.2 million and $3.2 million in 2020 2019 and 2018 re-
spectively.

Financial Performance

FIB's revenue increased by about 3% or $653.7
million in 2020 compared to the prior year. The
company's non-interest income increased $14.1
million or 9.9% to $156.7 million in 2020 as com-
pared to $142.6 million in 2019. Mortgage banking
revenues increased to $47.3 million in 2020 driven
by increased mortgage loan production due to
higher levels of refinance activity as a result of the
favorable interest rate environment. Service
charges decreased $3.5 million or 16.6% to $17.6
million in 2020 due to changes in client behavior
in addition to the company waiving continuous
overdraft fees and regular overdraft fees for clients
receiving U.S. government stimulus checks during
the second quarter of 2020.

The company's net income decreased by almost
$20 million or $161.2 in 2020.

The company ended 2020 with cash and cash
equivalents of around $2.3 billion an increase of
$1.2 billion from the prior year. Operating activities
provided $268.3 million while investing activities
used $1.9 billion primarily for purchases of invest-
ment securities and financing activities generated
$2.8 billion.

Strategy

FIB's business model is strategically aligned
around four key pillars which help them align organize and prioritize business strategies. These pillars guide the company's actions related to their
employees clients and operations ultimately leading to their financial success and creating value
for their shareholders.

Through the first pillar "Our People Our Priority" the company is building a diverse company attracting the right people retaining them in the right
jobs and developing them to meet our long-term
needs. The second pillar "Relentless Client Focus"
enables the company to connect their clients' goals
and dreams to the right products and services by
listening to them and learning their needs. The
third pillar is "Future Ready Today" in which the
company is focused on adapting its products and
processes to be scalable and sustainable. The
fourth pillar is "Financial Vitality" in which the
company strategically focuses on balance sheet
management and goal-oriented financial rigor the
keep the company a top-performing bank.

The company's long-term perspective emphasizes providing high-quality financial products and
services delivering exceptional client service influ-
encing business leadership within their communities through professional and dedicated bankers
supporting their communities through financial
contributions and socially responsible leadership
and cultivating a strong corporate culture. FIB
plans to continue its business in a disciplined and
prudent manner fueled by organic growth in their
existing market areas and expansion into new and
complementary markets when appropriate acquisition and other opportunities arise.

EXECUTIVES

**Executive Vice President, General Counsel And
 Corporate Secretary,** Kirk Jensen, $327,098 total
 compensation
Executive Vice President And Chief Risk Officer,
 Philip Gaglia, $280,907 total compensation
**Chief Financial Officer And Executive Vice
 President,** Marcy Mutch, $440,385 total
 compensation
**Executive Vice President And Chief Information
 Officer,** Kade Peterson
**Executive Vice President And Chief Banking
 Officer,** Russell Lee, $358,462 total compensation
Independent Director, Joyce Phillips
Independent Director, Stephen Bowman
Independent Director, Alice Cho
Chairman, David Jahnke

President, Chief Executive Officer, Director, Kevin Riley, $823,423 total compensation
Chief Operating Officer And Executive Vice President, Jodi Hubbell, $418,933 total compensation
Auditors: RSM US LLP

LOCATIONS

HQ: First Interstate BancSystem Inc
401 North 31st Street, Billings, MT 59116-0918
Phone: 406 255-5390
Web: www.fibk.com

PRODUCTS/OPERATIONS

Selected ServicesBanking
Checking Accounts
Credit Cards
Debit Cards
Escrow Services
Foreign Currency
Overdraft Protection
Personal Resources
Prepaid Cards
Savings Accounts
Borrowing
AdvanceLine
Auto & Recreation
Debt Consolidation
Home Equity
Home Mortgage
Personal Loans
Create & Build Wealth
Long-Term Planning
Planning for the Unexpected
Saving for College
Saving for Retirement
Wealth Resources
Protect & Preserve Wealth
Asset Management
Employee Exit Strategies
Health Concerns
Investment Services
Retirement Plan Services

Sales 2015

	$ mil.	% of total
Interest income	282.4	70
Non-interest income	121.0	30
Total	**403.4**	**100**

COMPETITORS

ASSOCIATED BANC-CORP
Banco Bradesco S/A
CARDINAL FINANCIAL CORPORATION
CASCADE BANCORP
CITIZENS FINANCIAL GROUP INC.
COMMERCE BANCSHARES INC.
CORELOGIC INC.
China Construction Bank Corporation
F.N.B. CORPORATION
M&T BANK CORPORATION
MACATAWA BANK CORPORATION
NASB FINANCIAL INC.
NATIONAL BANK HOLDINGS CORPORATION
NEWMARK GROUP INC.
PRIVATEBANCORP INC.
RENASANT CORPORATION
SEACOAST BANKING CORPORATION OF FLORIDA
SIGNATURE BANK
SUFFOLK BANCORP.
TRUSTCO BANK CORP N Y
UMB FINANCIAL CORPORATION
UMPQUA HOLDINGS CORPORATION
VIRGINIA COMMERCE BANCORP INC.
WESBANCO INC.
WINTRUST FINANCIAL CORPORATION

HISTORICAL FINANCIALS
Company Type: Public

Income Statement
FYE: December 31

	ASSETS ($ mil.)	NET INCOME ($ mil.)	INCOME AS % OF ASSETS	EMPLOYEES
12/20	17,648.7	161.2	0.9%	2,462
12/19	14,644.2	181.0	1.2%	2,473
12/18	13,300.2	160.2	1.2%	2,330
12/17	12,213.2	106.5	0.9%	2,207
12/16	9,063.9	95.6	1.1%	1,721
Annual Growth	18.1%	13.9%	—	9.4%

2020 Year-End Financials

Return on assets: 1.0%
Return on equity: 8.0%
Long-term debt ($ mil.): —
No. of shares (mil.): 62.1
Sales ($ mil): 680.3

Dividends
Yield: 4.9%
Payout: 79.0%
Market value ($ mil.): 2,532.0

	STOCK PRICE ($) FY Close	P/E High/Low	PER SHARE ($) Earnings	Dividends	Book Value
12/20	40.77	16 10	2.53	2.00	31.56
12/19	41.92	15 13	2.83	1.24	30.87
12/18	36.56	17 13	2.75	1.12	27.94
12/17	40.05	22 16	2.05	0.96	25.28
12/16	42.55	20 12	2.13	0.88	21.87
Annual Growth	(1.1%)	— —	4.4%	22.8%	9.6%

First Merchants Corp

First Merchants is the holding company that owns First Merchants Bank which operates some 120 branches in Indiana Illinois and western Ohio. Through its Lafayette Bank & Trust and First Merchants Private Wealth Advisors divisions the bank provides standard consumer and commercial banking services including checking and savings accounts CDs check cards and consumer commercial agricultural and real estate mortgage loans. First Merchants also provides trust and asset management services. Founded in 1982 First Merchants has nearly $9.4 billion worth of consolidated assets.

Operations
Real estate loans made up about 70% of First Merchants's loan portfolio while commercial and industrial agricultural and consumer loans account for the remainder of the bank's lending activity.

Geographic Reach
Muncie Indiana-based First Merchants's 120-plus bank branches are located across Indiana and in two counties each in Illinois and Ohio.

Sales and Marketing
First Merchants's marketing expense was $3.73 million in 2017 $3 million (2016) and $3.5 million (2015).

Financial Performance
Revenue jumped by 19% to $348.2 million in 2017 driven by higher interest income from more organic and inorganic loan business and more investment security income following the bank's recent acquisitions. The bank also collected significantly more non-interest income from deposit account service charges electronic card fees and insurance-related gains as it grew its customer base through acquisitions. Higher revenue drove the bank's net income up 18% to $96 million.

Total cash on hand at the end of fiscal 2017 stood at $154.9 million which was $27 million higher than cash at the start of the year. Cash from operations contributed $126 million and cash generated through financing activities added $535.8 while investments in securities and other uses used $635.3 million.

Strategy
A key part of the First Merchants's growth strategy is to expand geographically through acquisitions of small community banks operating in its key Indiana Illinois and western Ohio markets.

In 2017 and 2018 First Merchants added more nearly 3 dozen branches to its banking network after acquiring Michigan-based Monroe Bank & Trust Ohio-based Arlington Bank and Independent Alliance Banks located in Indiana. The bank has in recent years acquired 1-2 community banks operating in these states each year often adding a handful of branches as well as loans and other assets through each transaction.

Mergers and Acquisitions
In 2018 First Merchants acquired MBT Financial Corporation the holding company for Monroe Bank & Trust and its 20 branches serving Monroe Michigan and the southeastern Michigan area.

In 2017 First Merchants bought Columbus Ohio-based Arlington Bank. for $82.6 million. The same year it spent $238.8 million to acquire a majority stake in Independent Alliance Banks and IAB's 16 banking centers located in and around Fort Wayne Indiana.

EXECUTIVES

Chief Executive Officer, Director, Mark Hardwick, $398,858 total compensation
Executive Vice President, Chief Credit Officer, John Martin, $285,349 total compensation
Independent Director, Jean Wojtowicz
Independent Director, Patrick Sherman
Independent Chairman Of The Board, Charles Schalliol
Chief Risk Officer, Senior Vice President, Jeffrey Lorentson
President, Michael Stewart, $358,772 total compensation
Senior Vice President, Chief Information Officer, Stephan Fluhler, $281,515 total compensation
Independent Director, Gary Lehman
Chief Financial Officer, Executive Vice President, Michele Kawiecki
Senior Vice President, Director Of Human Resources, Steven Harris
Independent Director, Michael Fisher
Independent Director, Clark Kellogg
Independent Director, Susan Brooks
Independent Director, F. Howard Halderman
Auditors: BKD, LLP

LOCATIONS

HQ: First Merchants Corp
200 East Jackson Street, Muncie, IN 47305-2814
Phone: 765 747-1500
Web: www.firstmerchants.com

PRODUCTS/OPERATIONS

2017 Sales

	$ mil.	% of total
Interest		
Loans	274.4	71
Investment Securities	38.9	10
Federal Reserve and Federal Home Loan Bank stock .9 -		
Interest Expense/Other	(36.9)	-
Non-interest		
Service charges on deposits	18.7	5
Fiduciary activities	11.6	3
Other customer fees	20.9	5
Earnings on cash surrender value of life insurance	3.9	1
Net gains and fees on sales of loans	7.6	2
Net realized gains on sales of available for sale securities	2.6	1
Others	5.7	2
Total	**348.3**	**100**

COMPETITORS

ALLEGHANY CORPORATION	LOEWS CORPORATION
AMERICAN FINANCIAL GROUP INC.	MAINSOURCE FINANCIAL GROUP INC.
BERKSHIRE HATHAWAY INC. GROUP	OLD NATIONAL BANCORP SAFETY INSURANCE
F.N.B. CORPORATION	INC.
HEARTLAND FINANCIAL USA INC.	W. R. BERKLEY CORPORATION
KINSALE CAPITAL GROUP INC.	

HISTORICAL FINANCIALS

Company Type: Public

Income Statement

FYE: December 31

	ASSETS ($ mil.)	NET INCOME ($ mil.)	INCOME AS % OF ASSETS	EMPLOYEES
12/20	14,067.2	148.6	1.1%	1,907
12/19	12,457.2	164.4	1.3%	1,891
12/18	9,884.7	159.1	1.6%	1,702
12/17	9,367.4	96.0	1.0%	1,684
12/16	7,211.6	81.0	1.1%	1,449
Annual Growth	18.2%	16.4%	—	7.1%

2020 Year-End Financials

Return on assets: 1.1%	Dividends
Return on equity: 8.0%	Yield: 2.7%
Long-term debt ($ mil.): —	Payout: 37.9%
No. of shares (mil.): 53.9	Market value ($ mil.): 2,017.0
Sales ($ mil): 558.4	

	STOCK PRICE ($) FY Close	P/E High/Low		PER SHARE ($) Earnings	Dividends	Book Value
12/20	37.41	15	8	2.74	1.04	34.78
12/19	41.59	13	10	3.19	1.00	32.26
12/18	34.27	15	10	3.22	0.84	28.54
12/17	42.06	21	17	2.12	0.69	26.52
12/16	37.65	19	11	1.98	0.54	22.04
Annual Growth	(0.2%)	—	—	8.5%	17.8%	12.1%

First Mid Bancshares Inc

Money doesn't grow on trees so when farmers in Illinois need a little cash they turn to First Mid-Illinois Bank & Trust. The primary subsidiary of First Mid-Illinois Bancshares is a major supplier of farm credit (including real estate machinery and production loans; inventory financing; and lines of credit) in its market area. In addition to agricultural loans the bank offers commercial consumer and real estate lending. It also provides deposit products such as savings and checking accounts plus trust and investment services through a partnership with Raymond James. First Mid-Illinois Bank & Trust has about 40 branches.Other subsidiaries provide data processing services and insurance products and services.

EXECUTIVES

Executive Vice President, Amanda Lewis
Chief Operating Officer, Senior Executive Vice President, Michael Taylor, $323,008 total compensation
Executive Vice President & Executive Vice President, Chief Operations Officer Of First Mid Bank, Laurel Allenbaugh, $177,440 total compensation
Independent Director, Steven Grissom
Senior Vice President, Senior Vice President, Chief Risk Officer Of First Mid Bank, Christopher Slabach
Chairman Of The Board, President, Chief Executive Officer, Joseph Dively, $490,537 total compensation
Executive Vice President, Chief Trust And Wealth Management Officer Of First Mid Bank, Bradley Beesley, $192,224 total compensation
Senior Vice President, Director Of Human Resources, Rhonda Gatons
Senior Vice President, Chief Information Officer, David Hiden
Executive Vice President, Clay Dean
Independent Director, James Zimmer
Independent Director, Mary Westerhold
Chief Financial Officer, Executive Vice President, Matthew Smith, $253,088 total compensation
Lead Independent Director, Holly Bailey
Independent Director, Robert Cook
Independent Director, Zachary Horn
Senior Vice President, General Counsel, Jason Crowder
Director, J. Kyle Mccurry
Director, Gisele Marcus
Auditors: BKD, LLP

LOCATIONS

HQ: First Mid Bancshares Inc
1421 Charleston Avenue, Mattoon, IL 61938
Phone: 217 234-7454   **Fax:** 217 258-0485
Web: www.firstmid.com

PRODUCTS/OPERATIONS

Selected Subsidiaries

The Checkley Agency Inc. (dba First Mid Insurance Group)
First Mid-Illinois Bank & Trust N.A.
First Mid-Illinois Statutory Trust I II
Mid-Illinois Data Services Inc.

COMPETITORS

GREAT FLORIDA BANK   SB ONE BANCORP

HISTORICAL FINANCIALS

Company Type: Public

Income Statement

FYE: December 31

	ASSETS ($ mil.)	NET INCOME ($ mil.)	INCOME AS % OF ASSETS	EMPLOYEES
12/20	4,726.3	45.2	1.0%	824
12/19	3,839.4	47.9	1.2%	827
12/18	3,839.7	36.6	1.0%	818
12/17	2,841.5	26.6	0.9%	592
12/16	2,884.5	21.8	0.8%	598
Annual Growth	13.1%	20.0%	—	8.3%

2020 Year-End Financials

Return on assets: 1.0%	Dividends
Return on equity: 8.2%	Yield: 2.4%
Long-term debt ($ mil.): —	Payout: 30.0%
No. of shares (mil.): 16.7	Market value ($ mil.): 564.0
Sales ($ mil): 203.6	

	STOCK PRICE ($) FY Close	P/E High/Low		PER SHARE ($) Earnings	Dividends	Book Value
12/20	33.66	13	7	2.70	0.81	33.94
12/19	35.25	13	11	2.87	0.76	31.58
12/18	31.92	17	12	2.52	1.04	28.59
12/17	38.54	20	14	2.13	0.66	24.32
12/16	34.00	17	11	2.05	0.62	22.51
Annual Growth	(0.3%)	—	—	7.1%	6.9%	10.8%

First Northwest Bancorp

Auditors: Moss Adams LLP

LOCATIONS

HQ: First Northwest Bancorp
105 West 8th Street, Port Angeles, WA 98362
Phone: 360 457-0461
Web: www.ourfirstfed.com

HISTORICAL FINANCIALS

Company Type: Public

Income Statement

FYE: December 31

	ASSETS ($ mil.)	NET INCOME ($ mil.)	INCOME AS % OF ASSETS	EMPLOYEES
12/20	1,654.3	10.3	0.6%	230
12/19	1,307.3	9.0	0.7%	197
12/18	1,258.7	7.1	0.6%	210
12/17*	1,215.6	1.6	0.1%	204
06/17	1,087.6	5.1	0.5%	204
Annual Growth	11.1%	19.2%	—	3.0%

*Fiscal year change

2020 Year-End Financials

Return on assets: 0.7%	Dividends
Return on equity: 5.6%	Yield: 1.3%
Long-term debt ($ mil.): —	Payout: 19.0%
No. of shares (mil.): 10.2	Market value ($ mil.): 160.0
Sales ($ mil): 67.5	

STOCK PRICE ($)	P/E	PER SHARE ($)		
FY Close	High/Low	Earnings	Dividends	Book Value
12/20	15.60	16 8	1.10	0.21	18.19
12/19	18.13	20 16	0.91	0.13	16.48
12/18	14.83	26 20	0.68	0.03	15.42
12/17*	16.30	114 95	0.16	0.00	15.02
06/17	15.77	37 28	0.46	0.00	14.93
Annual Growth	(0.3%)	—	24.4%	—	5.1%

*Fiscal year change

First Reliance Bancshares Inc

EXECUTIVES

Executive Vice President And Chief Credit Officer, Jesse Nance
Independent Chairman Of The Board, Leonard Hoogenboom
Senior Vice President, Chief Banking Officer, Thomas Ewart, $161,500 total compensation
Senior Vice President, Assistant Secretary, Director, Paul Saunders
Independent Director, J. Scott
Director, A.Dale Porter
Independent Director, James Lingle
Chief Financial Officer, Executive Vice President, Director, Ir Contact Officer, Jeffrey Paolucci, $186,000 total compensation
Independent Director, C. Dale Lusk
Independent Director, Julius Parris
President, Chief Executive Officer, Director, F. Saunders, $282,000 total compensation
Independent Director, John Jebaily
Auditors: Elliott Davis, LLC

LOCATIONS

HQ: First Reliance Bancshares Inc
2170 West Palmetto Street, Florence, SC 29501
Phone: 843 656-5000
Web: www.firstreliance.com

HISTORICAL FINANCIALS

Company Type: Public

Income Statement   FYE: December 31

	ASSETS ($ mil.)	NET INCOME ($ mil.)	INCOME AS % OF ASSETS	EMPLOYEES
12/20	710.1	10.6	1.5%	0
12/19	661.6	4.0	0.6%	0
12/18	584.9	2.4	0.4%	0
12/17	458.6	(0.6)	—	0
12/16	408.1	3.5	0.9%	0
Annual Growth	14.9%	31.8%	—	—

2020 Year-End Financials

Return on assets: 1.5%
Return on equity: 16.8%
Long-term debt ($ mil.): —
No. of shares (mil.): 8.5
Sales ($ mil): 50.3

Dividends
Yield: —
Payout: —
Market value ($ mil.): —

STOCK PRICE ($)	P/E	PER SHARE ($)		
FY Close	High/Low	Earnings	Dividends	Book Value
12/20	0.00	— —	1.32	0.00	8.03
12/19	0.00	— —	0.51	0.00	6.76
Annual Growth	—	—	−158.8%	—	18.7%

First Savings Financial Group Inc

First Savings Financial Group was formed in 2008 to be the holding company for First Savings Bank a community bank serving consumers and small businesses in southern Indiana. Through more than a dozen branches the bank offers standard deposit services like savings checking and retirement accounts as well as a variety of lending services. One- to four- family residential loans make up about 60% of First Savings Bank's loan portfolio; other loans in the bank's portfolio include commercial real estate construction consumer and commercial business. In 2012 First Savings Financial expanded its footprint by acquiring the four Indiana branches of First Financial Service Corporation.

EXECUTIVES

Independent Director, Steven Stemler
Independent Director, L.Chris Fordyce
Independent Director, Troy Hanke
Independent Chairman Of The Board And Board Of Directors Of The Bank, John Colin
Independent Director, Pamela Bennett-Martin
Independent Director, Frank Czeschin
Chief Financial Officer, Anthony Schoen, $210,107 total compensation
President, Chief Executive Officer, Director, Larry Myers, $337,616 total compensation
Independent Director, Samuel Eckart
Director, John Lawson
Independent Director, Martin Padgett
Chief Operating Officer, Jacqueline Journell, $201,631 total compensation
Auditors: Monroe Shine & Co., Inc.

LOCATIONS

HQ: First Savings Financial Group Inc
702 North Shore Drive, Suite 300, Jeffersonville, IN 47130
Phone: 812 283-0724
Web: www.fsbbank.net

COMPETITORS

CHOICEONE FINANCIAL SERVICES INC.
COLONIAL FINANCIAL SERVICES INC.
COMMUNITY SHORES BANK CORPORATION
EMCLAIRE FINANCIAL CORP.
FB CORPORATION
OCEANFIRST FINANCIAL CORP.

HISTORICAL FINANCIALS

Company Type: Public

Income Statement   FYE: September 30

	ASSETS ($ mil.)	NET INCOME ($ mil.)	INCOME AS % OF ASSETS	EMPLOYEES
09/21	1,720.5	29.5	1.7%	590
09/20	1,764.6	33.3	1.9%	696
09/19	1,222.5	16.1	1.3%	473
09/18	1,034.4	10.9	1.1%	364
09/17	891.1	9.3	1.0%	201
Annual Growth	17.9%	33.5%	—	30.9%

2021 Year-End Financials

Return on assets: 1.7%
Return on equity: 17.5%
Long-term debt ($ mil.): —
No. of shares (mil.): 7.1
Sales ($ mil): 185.7

Dividends
Yield: 1.0%
Payout: 5.2%
Market value ($ mil.): 199.0

STOCK PRICE ($)	P/E	PER SHARE ($)		
FY Close	High/Low	Earnings	Dividends	Book Value
09/21	27.96	21 7	4.12	0.29	25.31
09/20	54.34	14 6	4.68	0.22	22.07
09/19	63.22	29 19	2.27	0.21	17.17
09/18	68.28	46 33	1.53	0.20	14.37
09/17	53.40	39 25	1.32	0.18	13.84
Annual Growth	(14.9%)	—	32.8%	12.5%	16.3%

First Western Financial Inc

Auditors: Crowe LLP

LOCATIONS

HQ: First Western Financial Inc
1900 16th Street, Suite 1200, Denver, CO 80202
Phone: 303 531-8100
Web: www.myfw.com

HISTORICAL FINANCIALS

Company Type: Public

Income Statement   FYE: December 31

	ASSETS ($ mil.)	NET INCOME ($ mil.)	INCOME AS % OF ASSETS	EMPLOYEES
12/20	1,973.6	24.5	1.2%	305
12/19	1,251.6	8.0	0.6%	255
12/18	1,084.3	5.6	0.5%	245
12/17	969.6	2.0	0.2%	263
12/16	916.0	2.3	0.3%	0
Annual Growth	21.2%	80.7%	—	—

2020 Year-End Financials

Return on assets: 1.5%
Return on equity: 17.3%
Long-term debt ($ mil.): —
No. of shares (mil.): 7.9
Sales ($ mil): 104.5

Dividends
Yield: —
Payout: —
Market value ($ mil.): 156.0

	STOCK PRICE ($) FY Close	P/E High/Low		PER SHARE ($) Earnings	Dividends	Book Value
12/20	19.57	6	4	3.08	0.00	19.49
12/19	16.47	17	11	1.01	0.00	16.08
12/18	11.71	31	17	0.63	0.00	14.67
Annual Growth	29.3%	—	—121.1%		—	15.3%

FirstCash Holdings Inc

Formed in 1988 FirstCash operates almost 2750 pawnshops and cash advance stores in the US Colombia Mexico El Salvador and Guatemala. The company lends money secured by such personal property as jewelry electronics tools sporting goods and musical equipment. The company also melts certain quantities of non-retailable scrap jewelry and sells the gold silver and diamonds in the commodity markets. Pawn stores provide a quick and convenient source of small secured consumer loans also known as pawn loans to unbanked under-banked and credit-challenged customers. Pawn loans are safe and affordable non-recourse loans for which the customer has no legal obligation to repay. The US operations generate about 65% of total revenue.

Operations

FirstCash made most of its money from merchandise sales. About 65% of its total revenue came from retail merchandise sales of collateral forfeitures and over-the-counter store purchases from customers while another some 30% of revenue came from pawn loan fees. The rest of its income came from wholesale scrap jewelry revenue (around 5% of revenue) and consumer loan and credit services fees.

Geographic Reach

Texas-based FirstCash operated more than 1600 stores in some 30 states in Mexico while more than 1000 stores in about 25 US states (with its largest markets being in Texas Florida Ohio Tennessee and North Carolina) and some 60 stores in Guatemala. FirstCash also operated more than 25 combine stores in Colombia and El Salvador. The company generated more than 65% of its revenue from its shops in the US and some 35% generated from Latin America with most of that coming from Mexico.

Sales and Marketing

Advertising expenses in 2020 2019 and 2018 was $1.1 million $1.2 million and $1.4 million respectively.

Financial Performance

The company in 2020 had a total revenue of $466.5 million a 13% increase from the previous year.

In 2020 the company had a net income of $106.6 million a 35% decrease from the previous year.

The company's cash at the end of 2020 was $65.9 million. Operating activities generated $222.3 million while investing activities used $20.4 million mainly for purchases of store real property acquisitions of pawn stores and purchases of furniture fixtures equipment and improvements. Financing activities used another $186.5 million primarily for repayments of unsecured credit facilities.

Strategy

The company's long-term business plan is to grow revenues and income by opening new ("de novo") retail pawn locations acquiring existing pawn stores in strategic markets and increasing revenue and operating profits in existing stores. In pursuing its business strategy the company seeks to establish clusters of several stores in specific geographic areas with favorable regulations and customer demographics and to achieve certain economies of scale relative to management and supervision pricing and purchasing information and accounting systems and security/loss prevention.

Company Background

The company first expanded its presence into Mexico in 2008 with the acquisition of Presta Max a chain of 16 pawn shops in southern Mexico.

HISTORY

First Cash grew from a single pawnshop in Dallas. John Payne traded some land in Colorado for the store after selling his Dallas bank in 1979. He and his wife ran the shop until 1985 when they sold it and built a new shop in the suburbs aiming to achieve the ambience of a video store.

It was an opportune moment: The Texas economy particularly the banking industry was just beginning its slide. Payne (who later left the company) incorporated First Cash in 1988 and brought in professional management under former banker Rick Powell in 1990.

Eight-store First Cash went public in 1991. Acquisitions and expansions included the 1994 purchase of a Baltimore/Washington DC area chain. The next year First Cash upgraded its computers to improve inventory control and loan valuations and became the first major pawn chain to stop selling or making loans on handguns.

In 1996 and 1997 First Cash added stores in Maryland and Texas. The next year it bought 10-store chain JB Pawn (from a brother of First Cash director Richard Burke) and about 20 individual shops. First Cash also moved into check-cashing buying 11-store Miraglia.

To reflect the diversification the company changed its name to First Cash Financial Services in early 1999. That year First Cash joined other pawnbrokers and short-term lenders in moving into Mexico. In 2000 First Cash partnered with Pawnbroker.com to provide online financial and support services to pawn shops.

First Cash discontinued its auto loan operations in 2008 two years after purchasing dealer and lender Auto Master. In the midst of a worldwide credit crunch First Cash sold Auto Master to Minneapolis-based Interstate Auto Group (dba CarHop).

The company first expanded its presence into Mexico in 2008 with the acquisition of Presta Max a chain of 16 pawn shops in southern Mexico.

EXECUTIVES

Independent Director, James Graves
President, Chief Operating Officer, T. Brent Stuart, $746,750 total compensation
Independent Director, Paula Garrett
Lead Independent Director, Mikel Faulkner
Independent Director, Randel Owen
Chief Executive Officer, Vice Chairman Of The Board, Rick Wessel, $1,210,250 total compensation

Chief Financial Officer, Executive Vice President, Treasurer, Company Secretary, R. Douglas Orr, $695,250 total compensation
Senior Vice President - Latin American Operations, Raul Ramos, $454,230 total compensation
Chairman Of The Board, Daniel Feehan
Independent Director, Daniel Berce
Auditors: RSM US LLP

LOCATIONS

HQ: FirstCash Holdings Inc
1600 West 7th Street, Fort Worth, TX 76102
Phone: 817 335-1100
Web: www.firstcash.com

PRODUCTS/OPERATIONS

2015 Sales

	$ mil.	% of total
Retail merchandise	449.3	63
Pawn loan fees	195.4	28
Wholesale Scrap jewelry	32.0	5
Consumer loan and credit services fees	27.9	4
Total	704.6	100

Selected Subsidiaries

All Access Special Events LLC
American Loan Employee Services S.A. de C.V. (Mexico)
Cardplus Inc.
College Park Jewelers Inc.
Famous Pawn Inc.
FCFS MO Inc.
FCFS OK Inc.
FCFS SC Inc.
First Cash Corp.
First Cash Credit Ltd.
First Cash Inc.
First Cash Credit Management LLC
First Cash Ltd.
First Cash Management LLC
First Cash S.A. de C.V. (Mexico)
King Pawn Inc.
King Pawn II Inc.
Maryland Precious Metals Inc.
SHAC LLC
T.J. Unlimited LLC

COMPETITORS

399 STRAND LIMITED	DOVER STREET LIMITED
AMERICA'S CAR-MART INC.	MARKET VELOCITY INC.
COSTCO WHOLESALE CORPORATION	PRICESMART INC.
	SAVERS INC.
DOLLAR GENERAL CORPORATION	STEIN MART INC.
	TARGET CORPORATION
	XPONENTIAL INC.

HISTORICAL FINANCIALS

Company Type: Public

Income Statement				FYE: December 31
	REVENUE ($ mil.)	NET INCOME ($ mil.)	NET PROFIT MARGIN	EMPLOYEES
12/20	1,631.2	106.5	6.5%	17.000
12/19	1,864.4	164.6	8.8%	21.000
12/18	1,780.8	153.2	8.6%	19.000
12/17	1,779.8	143.8	8.1%	17.000
12/16	1,088.3	60.1	5.5%	16.200
Annual Growth	10.6%	15.4%	—	1.2%

2020 Year-End Financials

Debt ratio: 25.9%	No. of shares (mil.): 41.0
Return on equity: 8.0%	Dividends
Cash ($ mil.): 65.8	Yield: 0.0%
Current ratio: 3.03	Payout: 42.1%
Long-term debt ($ mil.): 615.9	Market value ($ mil.): 2,874.0

	STOCK PRICE ($) FY Close	P/E High/Low	PER SHARE ($) Earnings	Dividends	Book Value
12/20	70.04	34 20	2.56	1.08	31.28
12/19	80.63	28 18	3.81	1.02	31.89
12/18	72.35	28 20	3.41	0.91	30.23
12/17	67.45	23 14	3.00	0.77	31.45
12/16	47.00	31 18	1.72	0.57	29.89
Annual Growth	10.5%	— —	10.5%	17.6%	1.1%

Five Below Inc

Five Below may be growing as quickly as its youthful clientele. Operating a fast-growing chain of specialty retail stores it sells a broad range of trend-right products all priced under $5. The company which targets teen and pre-teen girls and boys operates approximately 900 stores in shopping centers in some three dozen US states; it also operates an e-commerce site. Core merchandise includes fun but inexpensive items meant to entice teens such as jewelry and accessories novelty T-shirts novelty socks sports gear decor and crafts and mobile phone accessories. Five Below was founded in 2002.

Operations

Five Below has three categories of youth-oriented merchandise: leisure fashion and home and party and snack.

Leisure is the largest segment accounting for about 50% of revenue and includes games tech books electronics accessories and sporting goods among other products. Fashion and home (about 30%) includes "attitude" T-shirts personal accessories home goods and beauty offerings while party and snack (nearly 20%) includes candy beverages greeting cards and party goods.

Working with a large number of vendors (about 800) allows the chain to switch products quickly as it tries to capitalize on the popular items of the moment. Its stores measure about 8500 sq. ft.

Geographic Reach

From its base in the Northeast (the company is headquartered in Philadelphia) Five Below has aggressively expanded into the South and Midwest. With additional moves into Texas and California the company has stores in about 35 states across all regions of the country. Texas Pennsylvania and Florida are its largest markets.

The company has distribution centers in Pedricktown New Jersey and Olive Branch Mississippi. It is building a new distribution center in Forsyth Georgia (just south of Atlanta).

Sales and Marketing

Five Below's markets through traditional advertising in newspapers and on television as well as digital advertising commercial and a growing social media presence. New store openings which are grouped by market to leverage the company's efforts generally include contests giveaways and signature events such as "Five Cent" hot dogs. Its stores are often located in community and lifestyle shopping centers in urban suburban and semi-rural markets.

As its geography and store count has increased so has Five Below's spending on advertising. It spent $48.1 million $42.2 million and $30.8 million in fiscal 2019 fiscal 2018 and fiscal 2017 respectively.

Financial Performance

Amid a rapidly expanding network of stores Five Below has seen strong growth over the past five years. Revenue has more than doubled since fiscal 2015 (ended January 2016) and net income has more than tripled. Over the past five years the company has invested a significant amount of capital in infrastructure and systems necessary to support its future growth and it expects to incur additional capital expenditures related to expansion of its infrastructure and system in future periods.

In fiscal 2019 (ended January 2019) the company reported revenue of $1.8 billion up 18% from the prior year. The results were the result of a non-comparable sales increase of $278.2 million and a comparable sales increase of $8.9 million. The increase in non-comparable sales was primarily driven by new stores that opened in the fiscal year.

Primarily as a result of the strong revenue growth net income was also up in fiscal 2019. It increased 17% to $175.1 million from $149.6 million the year prior.

Cash at the end of fiscal 2019 was $202.5 million a decrease of $49.3 million from the prior year. Cash from operations contributed $187 million to the coffers while investing activities used $193.6 million mainly for capital expenditures. Financing activities used another $42.7 million for common shares withheld for taxes and repurchases and retirement of common stock.

Strategy

Five Below believes it can grow its net sales and earnings by executing on its strategies. The company aims to grow its store base; drive comparable sales; increase brand awareness; and enhance operating margins.

Five Below believes there is significant opportunity to expand its store base throughout the US from 900 locations as of February 2020 to more than 2500 locations within the US over time. The company opened 150 new stores in fiscal 2019 and it planned to open new stores in fiscal 2020. The company's new store model assumes approximately 8500 square feet and is primarily in-line locations within power community and lifestyle shopping centers across a variety of urban suburban and semi-rural markets.

The company expects to continue generating positive comparable sales growth by continuing to hone and refine its dynamic merchandising offering and differentiated in-store shopping experience. It intends to increase its brand awareness through cost-effective marketing efforts and enthusiastic customer engagement. In executing these strategies the company will increase the frequency of purchases by its existing customers and attract new customers to its stores.

Five Below has a cost-effective marketing strategy designed to promote brand awareness and drive store and website traffic. Its strategy for increasing brand awareness includes the use of digital marketing streaming video television print media philanthropic and local community marketing to support existing and new market entries. The company leverages its growing e-mail database mobile website and social media presence to drive brand engagement and increased store visits within existing and new markets.

Lastly Five Below believes that it has further opportunities to drive margin improvement over time. A primary driver of its expected margin expansion will come from leveraging its cost structure as it continues to increase its store base and drive its average net sales per store. The company intends to capitalize on opportunities across its supply chain as it grows its business and achieve further economies of scale.

Company Background

Five Below was founded in 2002 as Cheap Holdings by former CEO Thomas Vellios and David Schlessinger. The company changed its name to Five Below later in 2002 and went public in 2012.

EXECUTIVES

Chief Financial Officer, Treasurer, Kenneth Bull, $572,332 total compensation
Non-executive Chairman Of The Board, Thomas Vellios
Independent Director, Thomas Ryan
President, Chief Executive Officer And Director, Joel Anderson, $901,923 total compensation
Chief Administrative Officer, Eric Specter, $525,759 total compensation
Independent Director, Kathleen Barclay
Independent Director, Ronald Sargent
Independent Director, Dinesh Lathi
Independent Director, Michael Devine
Chief Merchandising Officer, Michael Romanko, $574,639 total compensation
Independent Director, Richard Markee
Executive Vice President - Operations, George Hill, $481,154 total compensation
Chief Experience Officer, Judith Werthauser, $518,846 total compensation
Auditors: KPMG LLP

LOCATIONS

HQ: Five Below Inc
701 Market Street, Suite 300, Philadelphia, PA 19106
Phone: 215 546-7909
Web: www.fivebelow.com

PRODUCTS/OPERATIONS

2018 Sales

	% of total
Leisure	51
Fashion & home	31
Party & snack	18
Total	**100**

COMPETITORS

ESSELUNGA SPA	PRICESMART INC.
EXPRESS INC.	THE CHILDREN'S PLACE
FHC COLLECTIONS INC.	INC
FRED'S INC.	TUESDAY MORNING
HIBBETT INC.	CORPORATION
OLLIE'S BARGAIN OUTLET HOLDINGS INC.	

HISTORICAL FINANCIALS

Company Type: Public

Income Statement — FYE: January 30

	REVENUE ($ mil.)	NET INCOME ($ mil.)	NET PROFIT MARGIN	EMPLOYEES
01/21*	1,962.1	123.3	6.3%	19,000
02/20	1,846.7	175.0	9.5%	16,600
02/19	1,559.5	149.6	9.6%	13,900
02/18	1,278.2	102.4	8.0%	12,100
01/17	1,000.4	71.8	7.2%	9,500
Annual Growth	**18.3%**	**14.5%**	**—**	**18.9%**

*Fiscal year change

2021 Year-End Financials

Debt ratio: —
Return on equity: 15.0%
Cash ($ mil.): 268.7
Current ratio: 1.73
Long-term debt ($ mil.): —

No. of shares (mil.): 55.9
Dividends
Yield: —
Payout: —
Market value ($ mil.): 9,829.0

	STOCK PRICE ($) FY Close	P/E High/Low	PER SHARE ($) Earnings	Dividends	Book Value
01/21*	175.73	88 24	2.20	0.00	15.77
02/20	113.22	47 33	3.12	0.00	13.64
02/19	124.73	50 23	2.66	0.00	11.03
02/18	62.94	39 20	1.84	0.00	8.27
01/17	37.60	40 25	1.30	0.00	6.04
Annual Growth	47.0%	— —	14.1%	—	27.1%

*Fiscal year change

Flagstar Bancorp, Inc.

Flagstar Bancorp is the holding company for Flagstar Bank which operates around 160 branches mostly in Michigan. Beyond offering traditional deposit and loan products Flagstar's mortgages originations specializes in originating purchasing and servicing one-to-four family residential mortgage loans across roughly 30 states through a network of brokers and correspondents. Around 80% of the Flagstar's revenue is linked to mortgage origination and servicing while another some 10% comes from its community banking business. Boasting $31.0 billion in assets Flagstar is 6th largest bank mortgage originator in the nation and the 6th largest sub-servicer of mortgage loans nationwide.

Operations

Flagstar Bancorp operates three business segments: Mortgage Originations Mortgage Servicing and Community Banking.

Mortgage Originations which made up some 60% of its total revenue and acquires and sells one-to-four family residential mortgage loans; Mortgage Servicing (around 30% of revenue) which charges a fee to service and sub-service mortgage loans for others through scalable servicing platform; and Community Banking (more than 10%) which provides originates loans deposit and fee based services to businesses individuals government entities and mortgage customers.

About 40% of its revenue came from interest income (mostly from loans) while most of the rest came from gains on loan sales (about 45% of revenue) loan fees and charges (less than 10%) deposit fees and charges and loan administration income for less than 5% each and other non-interest income for about 5%.

Geographic Reach

The Troy Michigan-based company has nearly 160 branches in Michigan Indiana California Wisconsin and Ohio. It also has some 140 retail mortgage locations four wholesale lending offices and ten commercial lending offices. These locations are primarily leased and located in about 30 states.

Sales and Marketing

The company offers full set of banking products to consumer commercial and government customers.

Flagstar's advertising expenses totaled $22 million $25 million and $26 million for the years ended December 31 2020 2019 and 2018 respectively.

Financial Performance

In 2020 the company had a net interest income of $685 million a 22% growth from the previous year.

Net income for the year 2020 was $538 million a 147% increase from the previous year.

The company's cash for the end of 2020 was $654 million. Operating activities used $8 billion while investing activities provided $3 billion. Financing activities generated another $5.2 billion.

Strategy

As a part of the company's risk management strategy it uses derivative financial instruments to minimize fluctuation in earnings caused by market risk. The company uses forward sales commitments to hedge its unclosed mortgage closing pipeline and funded mortgage LHFS. All of the company's derivatives and mortgage loan production originated for sale are accounted for at fair market value.

Company Background

In 2011 to raise capital after suffering the effects of the housing bust the company sold 27 bank branches in the suburbs north of Atlanta along with their deposits to PNC. The company also sold its 22 Indiana branches to First Financial Bancorp later that year. In addition to bringing in some cash the divestitures help Flagstar focus on its Michigan operations.

MP Thrift an affiliate of private equity firm MatlinPatterson Global Advisors assumed a controlling stake of Flagstar in 2009. Today it owns 64% of the company.

EXECUTIVES

Executive Vice President, Interim General Counsel, Paul Borja, $334,750 total compensation
President, Chief Executive Officer, Director, Alessandro DiNello, $1,000,000 total compensation
Executive Vice President, President Of Banking, Reginald Davis
Director, Peter Schoels
Independent Chairman Of The Board, John Lewis
Executive Vice President, Chief Risk Officer, Stephen Figliuolo, $425,000 total compensation
Independent Director, Bruce Nyberg
Director, Toan Huynh
Director, Lori Jordan
Executive Vice President, Director Of Operations, Karen Buck
Independent Director, James Ovenden
Executive Vice President, President Of Mortgage, Lee Smith, $750,000 total compensation
Chief Financial Officer, Executive Vice President, James Ciroli, $500,000 total compensation
Independent Director, Jennifer Whip
Auditors: PricewaterhouseCoopers LLP

LOCATIONS

HQ: Flagstar Bancorp, Inc.
5151 Corporate Drive, Troy, MI 48098-2639
Phone: 248 312-2000
Web: www.flagstar.com

PRODUCTS/OPERATIONS

2015 Sales

	$ mil.	% of total
Interest income		
Loans	295.0	36
Investment securities	59.0	7
Interest-earning deposits and other	1.0	-
Non interest income		
Net gain on loan sales	288.0	36
Loan fees & charges	67.0	8
Deposit fees and charges	25.0	3
Loan administration income	26.0	3
Net return on mortgage serving assets	28.0	3
Net (loss) gain on sale of assets	(1)	-
Representation and warranty benefit (provision)	19.0	2
Other non-interest income	18.0	2
Total	**825.0**	**100**

2015 Sales

	% of total
Mortgage origination	58
Community Banking	24
Mortgage Servicing	12
Others	6
Total	**100**

Selected Products/Services

Personal Banking
Banking
Checking Accounts
Checking
Savings Accounts
Savings Accounts: Personal
Banking Goals
View All Rates
Online Banking Login: Personal Accounts
Mobile Banking
Detroit Red Wings Partnership
Foreign Currency
Loans
Home Loans
Refinance
Home Equity Solutions
Credit Cards
Money Market
Investment Accounts: Personal

COMPETITORS

ASSOCIATED BANC-CORP
FIRSTMERIT CORPORATION
KEARNY FINANCIAL CORP.
BANCORP INC.
MERIDIAN INTERSTATE
BANCORP INC.
PEOPLE'S UNITED
FINANCIAL INC.
PROVIDENT FINANCIAL
SERVICES INC.
REPUBLIC
TIAA FSB HOLDINGS INC.
UNIVEST FINANCIAL
CORPORATION

HISTORICAL FINANCIALS

Company Type: Public

Income Statement — FYE: December 31

	ASSETS ($ mil.)	NET INCOME ($ mil.)	INCOME AS % OF ASSETS	EMPLOYEES
12/20	31,038.0	538.0	1.7%	5.214
12/19	23,266.0	218.0	0.9%	4.453
12/18	18,531.0	187.0	1.0%	3.938
12/17	16,912.0	63.0	0.4%	3.525
12/16	14,053.0	171.0	1.2%	2.886
Annual Growth	21.9%	33.2%	—	15.9%

2020 Year-End Financials

Return on assets: 1.9%
Return on equity: 26.9%
Long-term debt ($ mil.): —
No. of shares (mil.): 52.6
Sales ($ mil): 2,144.0

Dividends
Yield: 0.4%
Payout: 2.1%
Market value ($ mil.): 2,146.0

	STOCK PRICE ($) FY Close	P/E High/Low		PER SHARE ($) Earnings	Dividends	Book Value
12/20	40.76	4	2	9.52	0.20	41.80
12/19	38.25	10	7	3.80	0.16	31.57
12/18	26.40	12	8	3.21	0.00	27.19
12/17	37.42	35	23	1.09	0.00	24.41
12/16	26.94	11	6	2.66	0.00	23.51
Annual Growth	10.9%	—	—	37.5%	—	15.5%

Floor & Decor Holdings Inc

Auditors: Ernst & Young LLP

LOCATIONS

HQ: Floor & Decor Holdings Inc
2500 Windy Ridge Parkway SE, Atlanta, GA 30339
Phone: 404 471-1634
Web: www.FloorandDecor.com

HISTORICAL FINANCIALS

Company Type: Public

Income Statement				FYE: December 31
	REVENUE ($ mil.)	NET INCOME ($ mil.)	NET PROFIT MARGIN	EMPLOYEES
12/20	2,425.7	194.9	8.0%	8,790
12/19	2,045.4	150.6	7.4%	7,317
12/18	1,709.8	116.1	6.8%	6,566
12/17	1,384.7	102.7	7.4%	5,534
12/16	1,050.7	43.0	4.1%	4,391
Annual Growth	23.3%	45.9%		18.9%

2020 Year-End Financials

Debt ratio: 7.2%
Return on equity: 21.7%
Cash ($ mil.): 307.7
Current ratio: 1.49
Long-term debt ($ mil.): 207.1

No. of shares (mil.): 104.3
Dividends
  Yield: —
  Payout: —
Market value ($ mil.): 9,691.0

	STOCK PRICE ($) FY Close	P/E High/Low		PER SHARE ($) Earnings	Dividends	Book Value
12/20	92.85	53	14	1.84	0.00	9.56
12/19	50.30	34	17	1.44	0.00	7.53
12/18	26.01	48	20	1.11	0.00	5.99
12/17	49.59	43	28	1.03	0.00	4.64
Annual Growth	23.3%	—	—	21.3%	—	27.3%

FNB Corp

F.N.B. Corporation is a bank holding company and a financial holding company. Through the company's largest subsidiary it provides a full range of financial services principally to consumers corporations governments and small- to medium-sized businesses in its market areas through its subsidiary network. The company has nearly 360 banking offices throughout Pennsylvania Ohio Maryland West Virginia North Carolina and South Carolina. In addition to community banking and consumer finance FNB also has segments devoted to insurance and wealth management. It also offers leasing and merchant banking services.

Operations

F.N.B operates in three business segments with the largest being the Community Banking segment consisting of a regional community bank. The Wealth Management segment consists of a trust company a registered investment advisor and a subsidiary that offers broker-dealer services through a third-party networking arrangement with a non-affiliated licensed broker-dealer entity. The Insurance segment consists of an insurance agency and a reinsurer.

Community Banking segment consists of FNBPA which offers commercial and consumer banking services. Commercial banking solutions include corporate banking small business banking investment real estate financing business credit capital markets and lease financing. Consumer banking products and services include deposit products mortgage lending consumer lending and a complete suite of mobile and online banking services. Additionally Bank Capital Services LLC a subsidiary of FNBPA offers commercial loans and leases to customers in need of new or used equipment.

Wealth Management segment delivers wealth management services to individuals corporations and retirement funds as well as existing customers of the Community Banking segment located primarily within the company's geographic markets.

Insurance segment operates principally through FNIA which is a subsidiary of FNB. FNIA is a full-service insurance brokerage agency offering numerous lines of commercial and personal insurance through major carriers to businesses and individuals primarily within FNB's geographic markets. This segment also includes a reinsurance subsidiary Penn-Ohio.

The majority of the company's revenue comes from loans and leases.

Geographic Reach

F.N.B. headquartered in Pittsburgh Pennsylvania is a diversified financial services company operating in seven states and the District of Columbia. The company's market coverage spans several major metropolitan areas including: Pittsburgh Pennsylvania; Baltimore Maryland; Cleveland Ohio; and Charlotte Raleigh Durham and the Piedmont Triad (Winston-Salem Greensboro and High Point) in North Carolina.

Sales and Marketing

Marketing expense totaled $12.6 million $13.1 million and $12.8 million for 2020 2019 and 2018 respectively.

Financial Performance

F.N.B. Corportation's annual revenues have risen about 51% since 2016. The company's 2020 revenue increased by almost 1% or $922 million compared to the prior year.

However the company's net income decreased by 26% or $286 million in 2020. The results for 2020 included the impact of $45.6 million of significant items including loss on debt extinguishment and related hedge termination of $25.6 million related to the prepayment of higher-rate FHLB borrowings given continued strong deposit growth; branch consolidation costs of $18.7 mil-

lion resulting from their branch optimization efforts and continued customer migration to digital channels; COVID-19 related expenses of $11.3 million including $2.5 million in contributions to its FNB Foundation to continue to support their communities as they deal with the ongoing pandemic; and service charge refunds of $3.8 million partially offset by a $13.8 million gain on the sale of all of the FNBPA's holdings of Visa Class B shares.

F.N.B. ended 2020 with total cash and cash equivalents of $1.4 billion. Operating activities provided $113 million while investing activities used $1.8 billion and financing activities generated $2.5 billion.

Strategy

F.N.B. Corporations's business strategy focuses primarily on providing quality consumer- and commercial-based financial services adapted to the needs of each of the markets it serves. F.N.B. seeks to maintain its community orientation by providing local management with certain autonomy in decision making enabling them to respond to customer requests more quickly and to concentrate on transactions within their market areas. The company seeks to preserve some decision making at a local level however it has centralized legal loan review credit underwriting accounting investment audit loan operations deposit operations and data processing functions. The centralization of these processes enables FNB to maintain consistent quality of these functions and to achieve certain economies of scale.

Company Background

Founded in 1864 F.N.B. provides a full range of commercial banking consumer banking and wealth management solutions through its subsidiary network which is led by its largest affiliate First National Bank of Pennsylvania The company trades on the New York Stock Exchange under the ticker symbol "FNB."

EXECUTIVES

Chief Financial Officer, Vincent Calabrese, $524,480 total compensation
Chief Legal Officer, Corporate Secretary, James Orie, $165,000 total compensation
Independent Director, William Strimbu
Chief Audit Executive, Christine Tvaroch
Independent Director, David Malone
Chief Risk Officer, Thomas Whitesel
Director - Corporate Communications, Jennifer Reel
Chief Credit Officer, Gary Guerrieri, $481,434 total compensation
Independent Director, John Stanik
Independent Director, David Motley
Independent Director, Robert Hormell
Independent Director, Heidi Nicholas
Independent Director, Pamela Bena
Chief Consumer Banking Officer, Barry Robinson, $405,160 total compensation
Independent Director, Mary Dively
Independent Director, Frank Mencini
Chief Wholesale Banking Officer, David Mitchell
Compliance Director, Barbara Cottrell
Auditors: Ernst & Young LLP

LOCATIONS

HQ: FNB Corp
One North Shore Center, 12 Federal Street, Pittsburgh, PA 15212
Phone: 800 555-5455
Web: www.fnb-online.com

PRODUCTS/OPERATIONS

2015 Sales by Segment

	$ mil.	% of total
Community banking	616.2	87
Consumer finance	42.8	6
Wealth management	35.2	5
Insurance	13.1	2
parent & other	1.8	-
Total	**709.1**	**100**

2015 Sales

	$ mil.	% of total
Interest		
Loans including fees	482.1	68
Securities including dividends	64.6	9
Other	0.1	-
Non-interest		
Service charges	70.7	10
Trust Services	20.8	3
Insurance commissions & fees	16.3	2
Securities commissions & fees	13.6	2
Other	40.9	6
Total	**709.1**	**100**

Selected Subsidiaries

F.N.B. Capital Corporation (merchant banking)
First National Bank of Pennsylvania
   Bank Capital Services LLC (also dba F.N.B.
   Commercial Leasing)
   First National Trust Company
   F.N.B. Investment Advisors
   First National Investment Services Company
First National Insurance Agency LLC
Regency Finance Company
   Citizens Financial Services Inc.
   F.N.B. Consumer Discount Company
   Finance and Mortgage Acceptance Corporation

COMPETITORS

ACCESS NATIONAL CORPORATION	HILLTOP HOLDINGS INC.
ALLY FINANCIAL INC.	M&T BANK CORPORATION
BANKUNITED INC.	MAINSOURCE FINANCIAL GROUP INC.
BBVA USA BANCORP	MIDLAND STATES
CITIZENS FINANCIAL GROUP INC. INC.	INC.
	NORTHWEST BANCORP
CITY HOLDING COMPANY	OLD NATIONAL BANCORP
COLUMBIA BANKING SYSTEM INC.	SIGNATURE BANK
COMMERCE BANCSHARES INC.	SIMMONS FIRST NATIONAL CORPORATION
EAGLE BANCORP INC.	UMB FINANCIAL CORPORATION
FIRST CITIZENS BANCSHARES INC.	UNITED BANKSHARES INC.
FIRST COMMUNITY BANKSHARES INC.	WEBSTER FINANCIAL CORPORATION
FULTON FINANCIAL CORPORATION	

HISTORICAL FINANCIALS

Company Type: Public

Income Statement				FYE: December 31
	ASSETS ($ mil.)	NET INCOME ($ mil.)	INCOME AS % OF ASSETS	EMPLOYEES
12/20	37,354.0	286.0	0.8%	4,197
12/19	34,615.0	387.0	1.1%	4,223
12/18	33,102.0	373.0	1.1%	4,420
12/17	31,417.6	199.2	0.6%	4,748
12/16	21,844.8	170.8	0.8%	3,821
Annual Growth	**14.4%**	**13.7%**	**—**	**2.4%**

2020 Year-End Financials

Return on assets: 0.7%	Dividends
Return on equity: 5.8%	Yield: 5.0%
Long-term debt ($ mil.): —	Payout: 56.4%
No. of shares (mil.): 321.6	Market value ($ mil.): 3,055.0
Sales ($ mil): 1,424.0	

	STOCK PRICE ($) FY Close	P/E High/Low		PER SHARE ($) Earnings	Dividends	Book Value
12/20	9.50	15	7	0.85	0.48	15.42
12/19	12.70	11	8	1.16	0.48	15.02
12/18	9.84	13	8	1.12	0.48	14.21
12/17	13.82	26	19	0.63	0.48	13.63
12/16	16.03	21	14	0.78	0.48	12.18
Annual Growth	**(12.3%)**	**—**	**—**	**2.2%**	**(0.0%)**	**6.1%**

Focus Financial Partners Inc

Auditors: DELOITTE & TOUCHE LLP

LOCATIONS

HQ: Focus Financial Partners Inc
875 Third Avenue, 28th Floor, New York, NY 10022
Phone: 646 519-2456
Web: www.focusfinancialpartners.com

HISTORICAL FINANCIALS

Company Type: Public

Income Statement				FYE: December 31
	REVENUE ($ mil.)	NET INCOME ($ mil.)	NET PROFIT MARGIN	EMPLOYEES
12/21	1,797.9	10.4	0.6%	4,400
12/20	1,361.3	28.0	2.1%	3,600
12/19	1,218.3	(12.8)	—	3,400
12/18	910.8	(0.5)	—	2,600
12/17	662.8	(48.3)	—	2,000
Annual Growth	**28.3%**	**—**		**21.8%**

2021 Year-End Financials

Debt ratio: 50.8%	No. of shares (mil.): 76.7
Return on equity: 1.4%	Dividends
Cash ($ mil.): 310.6	Yield: —
Current ratio: 2.54	Payout: —
Long-term debt ($ mil.): 2,393.6	Market value ($ mil.): 4,584.0

	STOCK PRICE ($) FY Close	P/E High/Low		PER SHARE ($) Earnings	Dividends	Book Value
12/21	59.72	379	230	0.18	0.00	11.34
12/20	43.50	80	24	0.57	0.00	7.52
12/19	29.47	—	—	(0.28)	0.00	6.97
12/18	26.33	—	—	(0.01)	0.00	6.80
Annual Growth	**31.4%**	**—**	**—**	**—**	**—**	**18.6%**

Forestar Group Inc (New)

A majority-owned subsidiary of D.R. Horton?which is one of the largest homebuilders in the US?residential lot development company Forestar Group owns or controls over 38300 residential lots. Most of those are under contract are either under contract to sell to D.R. Horton or are assigned to D.R. Horton for right of first offer. The company owns approximately 4400 developed lots. Forestar operates in about 50 markets across about 20 states and while it sometimes develops land for commercial properties?including apartments retail centers and offices?Forestar primarily sells lots to homebuilders and developers for single-family homes.

Operations

Forestar Group manage their operations through one real estate reporting segment.

The real estate segment primarily acquires land and develops infrastructure for single-family residential communities. The company's real estate segment generates its revenues principally from sales of residential single-family finished lots to local regional and national homebuilders. Forestar generates most of its revenue?more than 80%—from sales of residential lots. Approximately 12800 lots it owns or controls are under contract to sell to D.R. Horton. D.R. Horton also has the right of first offer on almost another 10600 of the majority-owned subsidiaries lots. Additionally Forestar makes short-term investments in finished lots and undeveloped land which it then sells to D.R. Horton. Forestar owns around 4400 developed lots.

Geographic Reach

Arlington Texas-based Forestar Group operates in about 50 markets across about 20 US states. The company leases office space in Atlanta Georgia; Dallas Texas; and Houston Texas.

Sales and Marketing

Beyond its relationship with D.R. Horton Forestar group targets its lot sales to local regional and national homebuilders.

Financial Performance

In 2019 the company's revenue increased by about $314 million to $428.3 million from the prior year. Residential lots sold and residential lot sales revenues have increased as they have grown their business primarily through their strategic relationship with D.R. Horton. In fiscal 2019 the company sold 3728 residential lots to D.R. Horton for $311.7 million. In the nine months ended September 30 2018 Forestar sold 642 residential lots to D.R. Horton for $43.6 million.

Net income in 2019 decreased by 52% to $33 million from $68.8 million in 2018. The decrease was due to the great increase on their cost of sales by about $313.2 million even though with the increase of revenue for about $350 million.

Forestar's cash increased by $47.8 million in 2019. Operations used $391.2 million mostly for net expenditures on real estate development and acquisitions. Due to the loss of their proceeds from sales of assets the company's investing activities used $0.9 million. Additions to debt drove gains from financing activities to $439.8 million.

Strategy

The company's strategy is focused on making investments in land acquisition and development to expand their residential lot development business across a geographically diversified national platform. They are primarily investing in short duration phased development projects that generate returns similar to production-oriented homebuilders. This strategy is a unique lower-risk business model that they expect will produce more consistent returns than other public and private land developers.

Forestar's business strategy has changed substantially over the last few years. They divested their non-core assets in the oil and gas lodging multifamily and timberland sectors and began to refocus on residential single-family lot development.

Mergers and Acquisitions

Company Background

In 2017 US homebuilding giant D.R. Horton acquired a 75% stake in Forestar Group for more than $550 million.

EXECUTIVES

Executive Chairman Of The Board, Donald Tomnitz, $350,000 total compensation
Independent Director, Donald Spitzer
Independent Director, Samuel Fuller
Chief Financial Officer, James Allen, $300,000 total compensation
Chief Executive Officer, Daniel Bartok, $350,000 total compensation
Auditors: Ernst & Young LLP

LOCATIONS

HQ: Forestar Group Inc (New)
2221 E. Lamar Blvd., Suite 790, Arlington, TX 76006
Phone: 817 769-1860
Web: www.forestargroup.com

PRODUCTS/OPERATIONS

2018 Sales

	$ mil.	% of total
Real estate	75.6	96
Commercial real estate	2.0	3
Other	0.7	1
Total	**78.3**	**100**

COMPETITORS

D.R. HORTON INC.	THE NEW HOME COMPANY
DAITO TRUST	INC
CONSTRUCTION CO.LTD.	THE ST JOE COMPANY
HOME GROUP LIMITED	TRI POINTE HOMES INC.
INVITATION HOMES INC.	UDR INC.
MID-AMERICA APARTMENT	WEINGARTEN REALTY
COMMUNITIES INC.	INVESTORS

HISTORICAL FINANCIALS

Company Type: Public

Income Statement — FYE: September 30

	REVENUE ($ mil.)	NET INCOME ($ mil.)	NET PROFIT MARGIN	EMPLOYEES
09/21	1,325.8	110.2	8.3%	250
09/20	931.8	60.8	6.5%	143
09/19	428.3	33.0	7.7%	78
09/18*	78.3	68.8	87.9%	41
12/17	114.3	50.2	44.0%	34
Annual Growth	**84.5%**	**21.7%**	**—**	**64.7%**

*Fiscal year change

2021 Year-End Financials

Debt ratio: 33.5%
Return on equity: 11.6%
Cash ($ mil.): 153.6
Current ratio: 0.52
Long-term debt ($ mil.): 704.5

No. of shares (mil.): 49.5
Dividends
  Yield: —
  Payout: —
Market value ($ mil.): 924.0

	STOCK PRICE ($) FY Close	P/E High/Low		PER SHARE ($) Earnings	Dividends	Book Value
09/21	18.63	11	7	2.25	0.00	20.47
09/20	17.70	18	8	1.26	0.00	18.12
09/19	18.28	27	16	0.79	0.00	16.84
09/18*	21.20	16	12	1.64	0.00	16.06
12/17	22.00	19	11	1.19	0.00	14.41
Annual Growth	**(4.1%)**	**—**	**—**	**17.3%**	**—**	**9.2%**

*Fiscal year change

FormFactor Inc

FormFactor is a leading provider of test and measurement technologies. It provides a broad range of high-performance probe cards analytical probes probe stations metrology systems thermal systems and cryogenic systems to both semiconductor companies and scientific institutions. FormFactor designs probe cards to provide for a precise match with the thermal expansion characteristics of the wafer under test across the range of test operating temperatures. Its customers can use the same probe card for both low and high temperature testing. The majority of sales are to customers in China its largest single market. FormFactor began life in 1993 when former IBM researcher Igor Khandros began developing products for the semiconductor industry in a tiny New York lab.

Operations

FormFactor operates in two reportable segments consisting of the Probe Cards Segment (generates about 85% of company's total revenue) and the Systems Segment (more than 15% of revenue). Sales of the company's probe cards and analytical probes are included in the Probe Cards Segment while sales of their probe stations metrology systems and thermal sub-systems are included in the Systems Segment.

Geographic Reach

FormFactor primarily manufactures its products in Livermore San Jose Carlsbad and Baldwin Park California; Beaverton Oregon; Boulder Colorado in the US; and in Thiendorf Germany but it also has smaller manufacturing facilities in Gladbach Germany; Suzhou China; and Yokohama Japan. It also has sales offices in China Germany Japan Singapore South Korea and Taiwan. Outside US China is the biggest market for FormFactor products accounting for some 25% of revenue followed by Taiwan with more than 20% and about 15% from South Korea. Nearly 20% of sales come from customers in the US.

Sales and Marketing

FormFactor sell their products worldwide through a global direct sales force and a combination of manufacturers' representatives and distributors.

The company's customers include companies universities and institutions that design or make semiconductor and semiconductor related products in the Foundry & Logic (about 65% of sales) DRAM (around 15%) Flash (some 5%) Display and Sensor markets. Sales to its largest customer Intel accounted for about 30% of 2020 sales. Another top customer Samsung Electronics accounted for nearly 15% of sales.

Financial Performance

Revenue jumped 18% higher in 2020 to $693.6 million boosted by a 18% increase in the Probe cards market and a 14% increase in the Systems market.

FormFactor's net income for 2020 was $78.5 million doubled from 2019. The huge increase in net income in fiscal 2020 was primarily due to higher revenue and lower provision for income taxes.

Cash and cash equivalents at the end of fiscal 2020 were $191.1 million. Net cash provided by operating activities was $169.3 million while cash used in investing and financing activities were $98.9 million and $30.9 million respectively. Main cash uses for the year were for capital expenditures acquisition of businesses purchases of securities and payment of loans.

Strategy

FormFactor must continue to innovate and to invest in research and development to improve its competitive position and to meet the test and measurement requirements of its customers. The company's future growth depends in significant part upon its ability to work effectively with and anticipate the future technical and operational needs of its customers and to develop and support new products and product enhancements to meet these needs on a timely and cost-effective basis. Its customers' needs are becoming more challenging as the semiconductor industry continues to experience rapid technological change driven by the demand for complex circuits that are shrinking in size are increasing in speed and functionality and are produced on shorter cycle times and at reduced unit cost.

Company Background

FormFactor was incorporated in 1993 and introduced its first product in 1995. In late-2012 the company acquired Astria Semiconductor Holdings Inc. including its subsidiary Micro-Probe Incorporated (MicroProbe) in mid- 2016 they acquired Cascade Microtech Inc. (CMI) and in late-2019 they acquired FRT GmbH.

EXECUTIVES

President, Chief Executive Officer And Director, Michael Slessor, $519,231 total compensation
Independent Director, Raymond Link
Independent Director, Jorge Titinger, $165,123 total compensation
Independent Chairman Of The Board, Thomas St. Dennis
Chief Financial Officer, Shai Shahar, $311,850 total compensation
Auditors: KPMG LLP

LOCATIONS

HQ: FormFactor Inc
7005 Southfront Road, Livermore, CA 94551
Phone: 925 290-4000
Web: www.formfactor.com

PRODUCTS/OPERATIONS

2014 Sales by Market

	$ mil.	% of total
System-on-a-Chip (SoC)	142.3	53
DRAM	110.8	41
Flash memory devices	15.4	6
Total	**268.5**	**100**

Selected Products

DRAM
  Harmony eXP
  PH150XP and PH Series
Flash
  Harmony OneTouch
Known good die (KGD)
  HFTAP (K1 K3 K5)
Logic/SoC
  BladeRunner 175
  TrueScale PP40
MicroSpring interconnect technology
Probe cards
Probe heads (PH50 PH75 PH100 PH150 models)
Special Products
  Parametric
  Takumi Pico
  Takumi Femto
TRE test technology

COMPETITORS

APPLIED MATERIALS INC.
CTS CORPORATION
ELECTRO SCIENTIFIC INDUSTRIES INC.
INPHI CORPORATION
KLA CORPORATION
LAM RESEARCH CORPORATION
LINEAR TECHNOLOGY LLC
MACOM TECHNOLOGY SOLUTIONS HOLDINGS INC.
MAXIM INTEGRATED PRODUCTS INC.
OCLARO INC.
ONTO INNOVATION INC.
SEMTECH CORPORATION
TERADYNE INC.
ULTRA CLEAN HOLDINGS INC.
VEECO INSTRUMENTS INC.

HISTORICAL FINANCIALS

Company Type: Public

Income Statement

FYE: December 25

	REVENUE ($ mil.)	NET INCOME ($ mil.)	NET PROFIT MARGIN	EMPLOYEES
12/21	769.6	83.9	10.9%	2,293
12/20	693.6	78.5	11.3%	2,166
12/19	589.4	39.3	6.7%	1,836
12/18	529.6	104.0	19.6%	1,676
12/17	548.4	40.9	7.5%	1,685
Annual Growth	**8.8%**	**19.7%**	**—**	**8.0%**

2021 Year-End Financials

Debt ratio: 2.3%
Return on equity: 10.7%
Cash ($ mil.): 151.0
Current ratio: 3.52
Long-term debt ($ mil.): 15.4

No. of shares (mil.): 78.2
Dividends
  Yield: —
  Payout: —
Market value ($ mil.): 3,482.0

	STOCK PRICE ($) FY Close	P/E High/Low		PER SHARE ($) Earnings	Dividends	Book Value
12/21	44.51	47	31	1.06	0.00	10.43
12/20	42.58	44	16	0.99	0.00	9.61
12/19	26.04	50	25	0.51	0.00	8.46
12/18	14.01	12	8	1.38	0.00	7.83
12/17	15.65	32	19	0.55	0.00	6.32
Annual Growth	**29.9%**	—	—	**17.8%**	—	**13.3%**

Forrester Research Inc.

Forrester is one of the leading research and advisory firms in the world. The firm works closely with business and technology leaders to develop strategies for driving growth. Forrester gains powerful insights through its annual surveys of more than 675000 consumers and business leaders worldwide. The firm's reports and briefs provide insight into market forces industry trends and consumer behavior. Through proprietary research data and analytics custom consulting exclusive executive peer groups certification and events Forrester is revolutionizing how businesses grow in an era of powerful customers. The US is its largest market generating some 80% of total sales.

Operations

In 2019 Forrester realigned its management structure into Research (around 65% of sales) Consulting (more than 30%) and Events (less than 5%).

The Research segment includes revenues from Research products and the cost of the organizations responsible for developing and delivering the research products (excluding SiriusDecisions). In addition the segment includes consulting revenues primarily from the delivery of advisory services (such as workshops speeches and advisory days) delivered by the research analysts.

Forrester's Consulting products include consulting projects and advisory services and leverage its Research Technographics and CX Index data as well as its proprietary consulting frameworks to deliver focused insights and recommendations that assist clients with their challenges in developing and executing technology and business strategy including customer experience digital strategy marketing informing critical decisions and reducing business risk.

The company host multiple events in various locations in North America Europe and the Asia-Pacific region throughout the year. Events bring together executives and other participants serving or interested in the particular subject matter or professional role(s) on which an event focuses.

Geographic Reach

Headquartered in Cambridge Massachusetts Forrester has offices in San Francisco New York City Dallas McLean Virginia Nashville Austin Amsterdam Frankfurt London Paris New Delhi Singapore Lausanne Switzerland and Sydney. The firm's products are present in various locations including North America Europe and Asia Pacific.

The US is its largest market generating some 80% of total sales.

Sales and Marketing

Forrester sells its products and services through its direct sales force. The firm's products and services were delivered to more than 2600 client companies in 2020.

Advertising expenses for the years 2020 2019 and 2018 were $0.7 million $1.3 million and $0.6 million respectively.

Financial Performance

Company's revenue for fiscal 2020 decreased by 3% to $449.0 million compared from the prior year with $461.7 million. The decrease in revenues attributable to customers outside of the U.S. was primarily due to a decrease in revenues in Canada and the United Kingdom.

Net income for fiscal 2020 was $10.0 million compared from the prior year with a net loss was $9.6 million.

Cash held by the company at the end of fiscal 2020 increased to $90.7 million. Cash provided by operations was $47.8 million while cash used for investing and financing activities were $4.6 million and $23.7 million respectively. Main uses of cash were purchases of property and equipment and payments on borrowings.

Strategy

The company believe that market dynamics ? from empowered customers to the COVID-19 pandemic ? have fundamentally changed business and technology. Executives and the companies they lead need to adapt to new challenges such as accelerating digital transformation or even pivoting to entirely new business models.

In furtherance of its strategy Forrester: help its clients understand what is changing in their markets and how their customers and technology are changing; provide guidance on how clients should build their strategies to achieve competitive advantage; gather real-time data to enable our clients to immediately improve their customer experience; and provide specific actionable guidance for how to execute on those strategies quickly and decisively. The company's broad set of products services and engagement opportunities are designed to help its clients shorten the distance between a bold vision and superior execution.

HISTORY

George Forrester Colony started Forrester Research (named after his grandmother) in 1983 initially offering a research service called Computing Strategy. New services followed at regular intervals including advisories on networks (1986) software (1990) people and technology (1994) interactive technology (1996 the year it went public) and entertainment and technology (1997).

The company staked its claim in Europe in 1998 opening Amsterdam's Forrester European Research Center which conducts research on the European market for high technology. The next year Forrester launched initiatives to deliver more of its products online cut costs and increase margins. Forrester furthered its reputation for candor with a 1999 report asserting that HDTV (high definition television) will fail to get off the ground as a viable commercial technology. That year it extended its reach into the UK when it bought Fletcher Research.

In 2000 Forrester Research formed Netquity a joint venture with Information Resources to deliver Internet-branding research. The following year the company partnered with firms such as NetRatings and Experian to launch new products and services. It also cut about 15% of its workforce (around 110 jobs) and sold online ad product InternetAd-Watch in response to the poor economy. The company cut more jobs in 2002.

The following year Forrester acquired rival market research firm Giga Information Group for about $62 million. Giga provided answers on day-to-day information technology issues a complementary feature to Forrester's core industry-focused information.

Forrester has also taken advantage of cost-cutting and redundancy measures. It sold off its Ultimate Consumer Panel operations (credit card financial statements and transaction data analysis)

HOOVER'S HANDBOOK OF EMERGING COMPANIES 2022

to research panelist Lightspeed Online in October 2006.

Forrester purchased New Strategic Oxygen a company that sold tools to marketing professionals back in 2009. In 2011 the company acquired Springboard Research a research and advisory firm with expertise in the Asia/Pacific markets. The acquisition laid the groundwork for Forrester to market its products and services in China.

EXECUTIVES

Chairman Of The Board, President, Chief Executive Officer, George Colony, $425,000 total compensation
Lead Independent Director, Robert Galford
Chief Accounting Officer, Treasurer, Scott Chouinard
Chief Information Officer, Mike Kasparian
Chief Sales Officer, Kelley Hippler, $340,112 total compensation
Chief People Officer, Sherri Kottmann
Chief Legal Officer And Secretary, Ryan Darrah
Chief Business Technology Officer, Steven Peltzman, $357,485 total compensation
Independent Director, Anthony Friscia
Independent Director, David Boyce
Independent Director, Yvonne Wassenaar
Independent Director, Jean Birch
Chief Research Officer, Carrie Johnson, $371,354 total compensation
Chief Marketing Officer, Shirley Macbeth
Chief Financial Officer, Chris Finn
Auditors: PricewaterhouseCoopers LLP

LOCATIONS

HQ: Forrester Research Inc.
60 Acorn Park Drive, Cambridge, MA 02140
Phone: 617 613-6000
Web: www.forrester.com

COMPETITORS

FACTSET RESEARCH SYSTEMS INC.
INFORMATION RESOURCES INC.
IPSOS MORI UK LIMITED
IQVIA HOLDINGS INC.
LGC (HOLDINGS) LIMITED
NETCALL PLC
NIELSEN CONSUMER INSIGHTS INC.
THE ADVISORY BOARD COMPANY
TTEC HOLDINGS INC.

HISTORICAL FINANCIALS

Company Type: Public

Income Statement — FYE: December 31

	REVENUE ($ mil.)	NET INCOME ($ mil.)	NET PROFIT MARGIN	EMPLOYEES
12/20	448.9	9.9	2.2%	1,798
12/19	461.7	(9.5)	—	1,795
12/18	357.5	15.3	4.3%	1,432
12/17	337.6	15.1	4.5%	1,392
12/16	326.1	17.6	5.4%	1,378
Annual Growth	8.3%	(13.3%)	—	6.9%

2020 Year-End Financials

Debt ratio: 16.7%
Return on equity: 5.7%
Cash ($ mil.): 90.2
Current ratio: 0.81
Long-term debt ($ mil.): 95.3
No. of shares (mil.): 19.0
Dividends
　Yield: —
　Payout: —
Market value ($ mil.): 797.0

STOCK PRICE ($) FY Close	P/E High/Low	PER SHARE ($) Earnings	Dividends	Book Value
12/20	41.90	87 43	0.53	0.00	9.77
12/19	41.70	— —	(0.52)	0.00	8.48
12/18	44.70	58 44	0.84	0.80	8.28
12/17	44.20	56 42	0.83	0.76	7.83
12/16	42.95	45 28	0.97	0.72	8.17
Annual Growth	(0.6%)	— —	(14.0%)	—	4.6%

Fortinet Inc

Fortinet is a global leader in cybersecurity solutions provided to a wide variety of organizations including enterprises communication service providers government organizations and small businesses. The company makes network security appliances (sold under its FortiGate line) and software that integrate antivirus firewall content filtering intrusion prevention systems (IPS) and anti-spam functions to protect against computer viruses worms and inappropriate web content. The company also offers complementary products that include its FortiManager security management and FortiAnalyzer event analysis systems. To support its broadly dispersed global channel and end-customer base it has sales professionals in over 80 countries around the world. Over 40% of the revenue comes from the Americas.

Operations

Fortinet's five area of businesses are Security-Driven Networking which sells the FortiGate line of network security appliances; the Infrastructure Security Fabric platform automated and integrated security platform that extends beyond the network to cover other attack vectors; Dynamic Cloud Security which helps customers connect securely to cloud environments; the Endpoint Protection Internet of Things and Operational Technology which tracks the flow of data across multiple devices; and the AI-Driven Security Operations which develop and provide Artificial Intelligence (AI) driven security operations solutions including FortiGuard and other security subscription services endpoint detection and response and its security orchestration automation and response capabilities and solutions that can be applied across the entire Fortinet Security Fabric platform.

The company's services account for almost 65% of sales of which some 35% comes from security subscriptions and technical support and other with about 30% while its products supply about 35% of sales.

The company's Fortinet outsources the manufacturing of its appliance products to contract manufacturers and original design manufacturers. The company's manufacturers include Micro-Star International Co. Ltd. IBASE Technology Adlink Technology Inc. Wistron and several Taiwan-based manufacturers.

Geographic Reach

California-based Fortinet's sales are well spread geographically. The Americas accounts for over 40% of revenue followed by the Europe Middle East and Africa region about 40% and the Asia/Pacific region about 20%.

Sales and Marketing

Fortinet typically sells its security solutions to distributors that sell to resellers service providers and managed security service providers (MSSPs) who in turn sell to end-customers that range from small businesses to large enterprises and industries that include government telecommunications technology government financial services education retail manufacturing and health care. Customers may also access its products via the cloud through certain cloud providers such as Amazon Web Services Microsoft Azure Google Cloud Oracle Cloud Alibaba Cloud and IBM Cloud. The company gets 40% of revenue from just two customers Exclusive Networks Group some 30% of revenue and Ingram Micro Inc. approximately 10%.

Financial Performance

For the last five years Fortinet's revenue increased by 103%.

Total revenue was $2.6 billion in 2020 an increase of 20% compared to $2.2 billion in 2019. Product revenue was $916.5 million in 2020 an increase of 16% compared to $788.5 million in 2019. Service revenue was $1.68 billion in 2020 an increase of 22% compared to $1.37 billion in 2019.

The company had a net income of $488.5 million in 2020 an increase of 47% compared to the net income of $331.7 million from the previous year. The jump in income was primarily due to higher revenue for that year.

The company's cash and cash equivalents for 2020 were $1.1 billion 13% lower from the $1.2 billion in 2019. Operating activities provided $1.1 billion while investing activities used $72.8 million mainly for purchases of investments. Financing activities used another $1.17 billion mainly for repurchases and retirements of common stock.

Strategy

Fortinet's marketing strategy is focused on building its brand and driving end-customer demand for security solutions. The company uses a combination of internal marketing professionals and a network of regional and global channel partners. The company also focuses its resources on campaigns programs and activities that can be leveraged by partners worldwide to extend its marketing reaches such as sales tools and collateral product awards and technical certifications media engagement training regional seminars and conferences webinars and various other demand-generation activities.

Another important part of its growth strategy is to increase sales of its products to large and medium-sized businesses service providers and government organizations.

Mergers and Acquisitions

In late 2020 Fortinet has acquired Illinois-based Panopta the SaaS platform innovator that provides full stack visibility and automated management of the health of an enterprise network including servers network devices containers applications databases virtual appliances and cloud infrastructure. With the Panopta acquisition Fortinet will deliver the industry's most comprehensive Security-driven Networking platform by adding new capabilities in network monitoring detection and incident response. Terms were not disclosed.

In mid-2020 Fortinet has acquired OPAQ Networks a Secure Access Service Edge (SASE) cloud provider based in Herndon Virginia. OPAQ's Zero Trust Network Access (ZTNA) cloud solution protects organizations' distributed networks ? from

182　　　HOOVER'S HANDBOOK OF EMERGING COMPANIES 2022

data centers to branch offices to remote users and Internet of Things (IoT) devices. Given remote workforce trends with exponentially more users devices applications services and data outside of a traditional enterprise edge than inside the integration of Fortinet's broad Security Fabric with OPAQ's cloud platform will offer customers and partners even more choices in how they can consume best-of-breed security and is yet another unique and differentiated way Fortinet is empowering customers with the best integrated security and networking innovation in real-time. Terms were not disclosed.

EXECUTIVES

Chairman And Ceo, Ken Xie, $797,000 total compensation
President, Chief Technology Officer And Director, Michael Xie, $445,000 total compensation
Lead Independent Director, William Neukom
Chief Financial Officer, Chief Accounting Officer, Keith Jensen, $490,000 total compensation
Independent Director, Ming Hsieh
Independent Director, Jean Hu
Independent Director, Kenneth Goldman
Executive Vice President, Corporate Development, General Counsel And Corporate Secretary, John Whittle, $429,000 total compensation
Independent Director, Judith Sim
Auditors: DELOITTE & TOUCHE LLP

LOCATIONS

HQ: Fortinet Inc
899 Kifer Road, Sunnyvale, CA 94086
Phone: 408 235-7700   **Fax:** 408 235-7737
Web: www.fortinet.com

PRODUCTS/OPERATIONS

2018 Sales

	$ mil.	% of total
Security Subscription	606.1	34
Technical Support and Other	520.7	29
Products	674.4	37
Total	**1801.2**	**100**

Selected Products

Database security appliance (FortiDB)
E-mail antispam (FortiMail)
Endpoint security software (FortiClient)
Endpoint vulnerability management appliance (FortiScan)
Network event correlation and content archiving (FortiAnalyzer)
Network security appliances (FortiGate)
Secure wireless access product (FortiAP)
Security management (FortiManager)
Spam and virus control subscription (FortiGuard)
Support (FortiCare)
Web application firewall appliance (FortiWeb)

COMPETITORS

ARISTA NETWORKS INC.
TECHNOLOGIES
ASTRONOVA INC.
EXTREME NETWORKS INC.
GRAPHICS
F5 INC.
MANDIANT INC.
MCAFEE LLC
NETSCOUT SYSTEMS INC.
PALO ALTO NETWORKS
INC.
SAILPOINT

HOLDINGS INC.
SILICON

INTERNATIONAL CORP.
Silicom Ltd.
ZEBRA TECHNOLOGIES
CORPORATION

HISTORICAL FINANCIALS
Company Type: Public

Income Statement
FYE: December 31

	REVENUE ($ mil.)	NET INCOME ($ mil.)	NET PROFIT MARGIN	EMPLOYEES
12/20	2,594.4	488.5	18.8%	8,238
12/19	2,156.2	326.5	15.1%	7,082
12/18	1,801.2	332.2	18.4%	5,845
12/17	1,494.9	31.4	2.1%	5,066
12/16	1,275.4	32.1	2.5%	4,665
Annual Growth	**19.4%**	**97.4%**	**—**	**15.3%**

2020 Year-End Financials

Debt ratio: —
Return on equity: 44.7%
Cash ($ mil.): 1,061.8
Current ratio: 1.50
Long-term debt ($ mil.): —
No. of shares (mil.): 162.5
Dividends
  Yield: —
  Payout: —
Market value ($ mil.): 24,136.0

	STOCK PRICE ($) FY Close	P/E High/Low		Earnings	PER SHARE ($) Dividends	Book Value
12/20	148.53	51	25	2.91	0.00	5.27
12/19	106.76	57	35	1.87	0.00	7.70
12/18	70.43	47	22	1.91	0.00	5.95
12/17	43.69	251	167	0.18	0.00	3.51
12/16	30.12	196	125	0.18	0.00	4.84
Annual Growth	**49.0%**		**—**	**—100.5%**	**—**	**2.1%**

Founders Bay Holdings

Auditors: S.R. Chourasiya & Co.

LOCATIONS

HQ: Founders Bay Holdings
913 Market Street, Suite 200, Wilmington, DE 19801
Phone: 302 416-4816
Web: www.fbaytech.com

HISTORICAL FINANCIALS
Company Type: Public

Income Statement
FYE: December 31

	REVENUE ($ mil.)	NET INCOME ($ mil.)	NET PROFIT MARGIN	EMPLOYEES
12/20	15.6	7.1	45.4%	0
12/19	12.5	3.7	30.1%	0
12/18	10.1	3.2	32.3%	0
12/17	8.7	3.0	34.8%	0
12/16	7.0	1.7	25.1%	0
Annual Growth	**22.3%**	**41.7%**	**—**	**—**

2020 Year-End Financials

Debt ratio: —
Return on equity: 32.3%
Cash ($ mil.): 0.6
Current ratio: 230.83
Long-term debt ($ mil.): —
No. of shares (mil.): 49.9
Dividends
  Yield: —
  Payout: —
Market value ($ mil.): 487.0

	STOCK PRICE ($) FY Close	P/E High/Low		Earnings	PER SHARE ($) Dividends	Book Value
12/20	9.75	—	—	(0.00)	0.00	0.51
12/19	9.28	160	61	0.07	0.00	0.37
12/18	8.47	—	—	(0.00)	0.00	0.29
12/17	6.25	—	—	(0.00)	0.00	0.23
12/16	0.01	—	—	(0.00)	0.00	(0.00)
Annual Growth	**416.5%**					

Four Corners Property Trust Inc

Auditors: KPMG LLP

LOCATIONS

HQ: Four Corners Property Trust Inc
591 Redwood Highway, Suite 3215, Mill Valley, CA 94941
Phone: 415 965-8030
Web: www.fcpt.com

HISTORICAL FINANCIALS
Company Type: Public

Income Statement
FYE: December 31

	REVENUE ($ mil.)	NET INCOME ($ mil.)	NET PROFIT MARGIN	EMPLOYEES
12/20	170.9	77.3	45.2%	349
12/19	160.2	72.6	45.3%	361
12/18	143.6	82.4	57.4%	361
12/17	133.2	71.3	53.6%	342
12/16	124.0	156.8	126.4%	324
Annual Growth	**8.4%**	**(16.2%)**	**—**	**1.9%**

2020 Year-End Financials

Debt ratio: 45.1%
Return on equity: 9.8%
Cash ($ mil.): 11.0
Current ratio: 0.75
Long-term debt ($ mil.): 753.8
No. of shares (mil.): 75.8
Dividends
  Yield: 4.1%
  Payout: 114.1%
Market value ($ mil.): 2,259.0

	STOCK PRICE ($) FY Close	P/E High/Low		Earnings	PER SHARE ($) Dividends	Book Value
12/20	29.77	30	13	1.08	1.23	11.09
12/19	28.19	28	24	1.06	1.15	10.30
12/18	26.20	22	17	1.28	1.10	10.13
12/17	25.70	23	17	1.18	1.00	8.39
12/16	20.52	9	5	2.63	9.29	7.76
Annual Growth	**9.7%**		**—**	**—(19.9%)**	**(39.6%)**	**9.3%**

Fox Factory Holding Corp

Fox Factory Holding Corp. designs engineers manufactures and markets performance-defining products and systems for customers worldwide.

The company's premium brand performance-defining products and systems are used primarily on bicycles side-by-side vehicles on-road vehicles with and without off-road capabilities off-road vehicles and trucks all-terrain vehicles (ATVs) snowmobiles specialty vehicles and applications motorcycles and commercial trucks. Fox generates most of its sales from North America region.

Operations

Fox operates in one reportable segments: manufacturing sale and service of performance-defining products. The company's products fall into two product categories: powered vehicles (around 60% of totals sales) which include Side-by-Sides certain on-road vehicles with off-road capabilities off-road vehicles and trucks ATVs snowmobiles specialty vehicles and applications motorcycles and commercial trucks; and specialty sports products (some 40%) which consist primarily of bike suspension and component products.

Geographic Reach

Headquartered in Braselton Georgia Fox generates more than 65% of total revenue from North America followed by Asia and Europe with over 15% each. The remainder is from the rest of the world. Some of the company's administrative research and development and manufacturing operations are located in California. It also manufactures in the US States of Georgia Michigan Alabama and Indiana and internationally in Taiwan and Canada and maintain sales and service offices in the US and Europe.

Sales and Marketing

Fox sells its suspension products to approximately 150 OEMs and distributes its products to more than 5000 retail dealers and distributors worldwide. Some 55% of total sales were to OEM customers and approximately 45% were to dealers and distributors for resale in the aftermarket channel. Some of the company's OEM customers are Giant Pivot Santa Cruz Bicycles Specialized Scott Trek Yeti Cycles and YT in Specialty Sports; and BRP Ford Honda Jeep Kawasaki Polaris Toyota Triumph and Yamaha in Powered Vehicles.

Fox's advertising costs were $2188 $1413 and $902 for the years ended January 2021 2020 and December 2018 respectively.

Financial Performance

The company's revenue for fiscal year 2021 increased to $890.6 million compared to $751.0 million in the prior year. Sales for the year 2021 (ended January) increased approximately $139.6 million or 19% compared to year 2020 (ended January). The sales increase reflects a 22% increase in Specialty Sports products as well as a 16% growth in Powered Vehicle products for the year 2021 compared to the prior year.

Net income decreased $2.8 million or 3 % to $91.7 million in the fiscal year 2021 (ended January) from $94.5 million for the same period in 2019.

Cash held by the company at the end of fiscal 2020 increased to $245.8 million. Cash provided by operations and financing activities was $82.7 million and $506.7 million respectively. Cash used for investing activities was $388.5 million mainly for acquisition of businesses.

Strategy

Fox's goal is to expand its leadership position as a designer manufacturer and marketer of performance-defining products designed to enhance ride dynamics and performance. The company intends to focus on the following key strategies in pursuit of this goal: continue to develop new and innovative products in current end-markets; leverage technology and brand to expand into new categories and end-markets; opportunistically expand the company's business platform through acquisitions; increase the company's aftermarket penetration; accelerate international growth; and improve operating and supply chain efficiencies.

Mergers and Acquisitions

In early 2020 Fox through its subsidiary Fox Factory Inc. has signed a definitive agreement to acquire 100% of the issued and outstanding capital stock of SCA Performance Holdings Inc. (SCA) from Southern Rocky Holdings LLC a portfolio company of Kinderhook Industries for $328 million. SCA is a leading OEM authorized specialty vehicle manufacturer (SVM) for light duty trucks and SUVs with headquarters in Trussville Alabama. The acquisition is complementary to Fox's Tuscany business expanding its North American geographic manufacturing footprint and broadening its product offering in a growing segment of the automotive industry.

Company Background

Fox Factory was founded in 1974 by Robert Fox who built a racing suspension shock in his friend's garage. The company was bought by Compass Diversified Holdings in 2008. In 2013 Fox Factory went public and Compass held onto a majority share; Compass subsequently divested shares in Fox Factory but still maintains a minority ownership stake.

EXECUTIVES

Chief Purpose & Inclusion Officer, Jackie Martin
Chief Executive Officer & Director, Michael Dennison, $667,539 total compensation
Independent Director, Jean Hlay
Senior Vice President - Finance, John Blocher, $260,000 total compensation
Chief Financial Officer, Treasurer, Scott Humphrey, $210,000 total compensation
Independent Director, Sidney Johnson
Chief Legal Officer, Company Secretary, Toby Merchant
President - Pvg Business & Corporate Strategy, Thomas Fletcher
President, Specialty Sports Group, Christopher Tutton, $336,231 total compensation
President, Powered Vehicles Group, Richard Winters, $357,212 total compensation
Auditors: Grant Thornton LLP

LOCATIONS

HQ: Fox Factory Holding Corp
2055 Sugarloaf Circle, Suite 300, Duluth, GA 30097
Phone: 831 274-6500
Web: www.ridefox.com

PRODUCTS/OPERATIONS

2015 Sales

	$ mil.	% of total
Bikes	211.7	58
Power vehicles	155.1	42
Total	**366.8**	**100**

COMPETITORS

ALLISON TRANSMISSION HOLDINGS INC.
BAJAJ AUTO LIMITED
BRG SPORTS INC.
EDELBROCK LLC
Giant Manufacturing Co.Ltd.

HERO MOTOCORP LIMITED
LCI INDUSTRIES
LEHMAN TRIKES U.S.A. INC.
MERITOR INC.
POLARIS INC.
Shanghai Automotive Industry Corporation (Group)

HISTORICAL FINANCIALS

Company Type: Public

Income Statement

FYE: January 1

	REVENUE ($ mil.)	NET INCOME ($ mil.)	NET PROFIT MARGIN	EMPLOYEES
01/21	890.5	90.6	10.2%	3,000
01/20*	751.0	93.0	12.4%	2,600
12/18	619.2	84.0	13.6%	2,240
12/17	475.6	43.1	9.1%	1,800
12/16	403.0	35.6	8.9%	1,700
Annual Growth	21.9%	26.3%	—	15.3%

*Fiscal year change

2021 Year-End Financials

Debt ratio: 30.2%
Return on equity: 15.9%
Cash ($ mil.): 245.7
Current ratio: 3.52
Long-term debt ($ mil.): 377.0

No. of shares (mil.): 41.8
Dividends
Yield: —
Payout: —
Market value ($ mil.): 4,419.0

	STOCK PRICE ($) FY Close	P/E High/Low	Earnings	Dividends	Book Value
01/21	105.71	49 16	2.22	0.00	17.20
01/20*	69.78	36 23	2.38	0.00	10.95
12/18	59.93	34 15	2.16	0.00	8.45
12/17	38.85	38 22	1.11	0.00	6.24
12/16	27.75	29 15	0.94	0.00	5.01
Annual Growth	39.7%	— —	24.0%	—	36.1%

*Fiscal year change

Franchise Group Inc

Franchise Group Inc. formerly known as Liberty Tax is an owner and operator of franchised and franchisable businesses that continually looks to grow its portfolio of brands while utilizing its operating and capital allocation philosophies to generate strong cash flows. Its business lines include American Freight The Vitamin Shoppe Liberty Tax Service Buddy's Home Furnishings and Pet Supplies Plus which was acquired in 2021 for $700 million. Franchise Group operates more than 4000 locations predominantly located in the US and Canada consisting of some 2750 franchised locations and 1280 company run locations.

Financial Performance

Liberty Tax's fiscal 2012 (ends April) sales increased 14% vs. the prior year while net income grew 10% over the same period. Sales were buoyed by double-digit increases in financial products revenue tax preparation fees and to a lesser extent increases in royalties and advertising fees. The increase in financial products revenue which accounted for 21% of fiscal 2012 sales was driven by the continuing growth of JTH Financial. The increase in net income was due to the increase in revenue partially offset by higher operating expenses and a decrease in other income. Fiscal 2012 marked the third consecutive year of increasing sales and profits as the company adds tax preparation offices and financial products.

EXECUTIVES

Independent Director, Lisa Fairfax
Independent Director, Megan Starr
Chief Franchising Officer, Todd Evans, $161,539 total compensation
Independent Director, Cynthia Dubin
Independent Director, Thomas Herskovits
Executive Vice President, Chief Administrative Officer, Andrew Kaminsky, $463,846 total compensation
Chief Financial Officer, Eric Seeton, $382,153 total compensation
Executive Vice President, Director, Andrew Laurence, $463,846 total compensation
Independent Chairman Of The Board, Matthew Avril
Independent Director, Lawrence Miller
President, Chief Executive Officer And Director, Brian Kahn, $810,000 total compensation
Independent Director, Patrick Cozza
Auditors: DELOITTE & TOUCHE LLP

LOCATIONS

HQ: Franchise Group Inc
109 Innovation Court, Suite J, Delaware, OH 43015
Phone: 740 363-2222
Web: www.franchisegrp.com

PRODUCTS/OPERATIONS

2016 sales

	$ mil.	% of total
Royalties & advertising fees	80.3	46
Financial products	45.3	26
Interest income	13.6	8
Tax preparation fees net of discounts	19.3	11
Franchise Fee	5.0	3
AD fees	6.0	4
Other	3.9	2
Total	**173.4**	**100**

COMPETITORS

AMSCOT FINANCIAL INC.
EDWARD D. JONES & CO. HOLDINGS L.P.
EXACTAX INC.
NICHOLAS FINANCIAL INC.
RUBINBROWN LLP
SKODA MINOTTI LLC
WORLD ACCEPTANCE CORPORATION

HISTORICAL FINANCIALS

Company Type: Public

Income Statement

	REVENUE ($ mil.)	NET INCOME ($ mil.)	NET PROFIT MARGIN	EMPLOYEES
				FYE: December 26
12/20	2,152.5	25.0	1.2%	8,083
12/19*	149.5	(68.4)	—	8,038
04/19	132.5	(2.1)	—	795
04/18	174.8	0.1	0.1%	1,514
04/17	173.9	13.0	7.5%	1,498
Annual Growth	**87.5%**	**17.8%**	**—**	**52.4%**

*Fiscal year change

2020 Year-End Financials

Debt ratio: 31.2%
Return on equity: 9.7%
Cash ($ mil.): 151.5
Current ratio: 1.05
Long-term debt ($ mil.): 468.6
No. of shares (mil.): 40.0
Dividends
  Yield: 0.0%
  Payout: 160.7%
Market value ($ mil.): 1,148.0

	STOCK PRICE ($) FY Close	P/E High/Low		PER SHARE ($) Earnings	Dividends	Book Value
12/20	28.64	42	9	0.70	1.13	9.61
12/19*	24.13	—	—	(4.11)	0.25	6.87
04/19	9.00	—	—	(0.16)	0.16	7.38
04/18	10.30	1490	780	0.01	0.64	8.56
04/17	14.05	17	11	0.94	0.64	9.04
Annual Growth	**19.5%**			**(7.1%)**	**15.1%**	**1.5%**

*Fiscal year change

Franklin Wireless Corp

Franklin Wireless hopes lightning strikes with its wireless data products. The company makes high speed connectivity products for wireless devices. Its products include USB embedded and standalone modems as well as modules PC cards and Wi-Fi hotspot routers. Customers use its products to connect their mobile computers to wireless broadband networks. Franklin Wireless primarily sells directly to wireless operators but also through partners and distributors. The US is its largest market but the Caribbean and South America have collectively grown to nearly 25% of sales. The company uses contract manufacturers such as South Korea-based shareholder (about 13%) C-Motech and Samsung Electro-Mechanics.

EXECUTIVES

President, Secretary, Director, O. Kim, $286,667 total compensation
Independent Chairman Of The Board, Gary Nelson
Director, Johnathan Chee
Chief Operating Officer, Yun Lee, $286,667 total compensation
Independent Director, Heidy Chow
Independent Director, Kristina Kim
Acting Chief Financial Officer, David Brown, $40,032 total compensation
Auditors: Benjamin & Ko

LOCATIONS

HQ: Franklin Wireless Corp
9707 Waples Street, Suite 150, San Diego, CA 92121
Phone: 858 623-0000   **Fax:** 858 623-0050
Web: www.franklinwireless.com

COMPETITORS

FINISAR CORPORATION
INFINERA CORPORATION
MINIM INC.
MULTI-TECH SYSTEMS INC.
NETGEAR INC.
SLING MEDIA L.L.C.
STARHUB LTD.
VODAFONE IRELAND LIMITED

HISTORICAL FINANCIALS

Company Type: Public

Income Statement

	REVENUE ($ mil.)	NET INCOME ($ mil.)	NET PROFIT MARGIN	EMPLOYEES
				FYE: June 30
06/21	184.1	17.7	9.6%	74
06/20	75.0	5.5	7.4%	71
06/19	36.4	(1.2)	—	71
06/18	30.0	(2.0)	—	67
06/17	48.5	0.8	1.8%	76
Annual Growth	**39.5%**	**112.1%**	**—**	**(0.7%)**

2021 Year-End Financials

Debt ratio: —
Return on equity: 54.4%
Cash ($ mil.): 51.1
Current ratio: 4.92
Long-term debt ($ mil.): —
No. of shares (mil.): 11.5
Dividends
  Yield: —
  Payout: —
Market value ($ mil.): 106.0

	STOCK PRICE ($) FY Close	P/E High/Low		PER SHARE ($) Earnings	Dividends	Book Value
06/21	9.17	16	3	1.53	0.00	3.86
06/20	5.52	11	4	0.52	0.00	1.92
06/19	2.45	—	—	(0.12)	0.00	1.40
06/18	1.85	—	—	(0.20)	0.00	1.52
06/17	2.25	38	24	0.08	0.00	1.72
Annual Growth	**42.1%**			**(109.1%)**	**—**	**22.3%**

Friedman Industries, Inc.

Steel processor Friedman Industries operates in two business segments: coil products and tubular products. The company's Texas Tubular Products unit the larger of Friedman Industries' segments buys pipe and coil material and processes it for use in pipelines oil and gas drilling and piling and structural applications. Friedman Industries' coil products unit purchases hot-rolled steel coils and processes them into sheet and plate products. The company's XSCP unit sells surplus prime secondary and transition steel coils. Friedman Industries' processing facilities are located near mills operated by U.S. Steel and Nucor Corp. and work closely with both facilities.

Operations

Friedman Industries operates two business segments: coil and tubular. The coil business segment engages in the processing and distribution of hot-rolled steel coils at its locations in Hickman Arkansas and Decatur Alabama. Its XSCP division markets surplus prime and secondary hot-rolled steel coils.

The tubular business segment of Friedman Industries operates as Texas Tubular Products (TTP) division. TTP is located in Lone Star Texas and engages in the manufacturing processing and distribution of steel pipe.

Geographic Reach

The company has locations in Humble Lone Star and Longview (all in Texas); Decatur Alabama; and Hickman Arkansas.

Sales and Marketing

U.S. Steel (USS)'s Tubular Products subsidiary is both a supplier to and a customer of Friedman Industries.

The company sells coil products and processing services to 150 customers primarily in the midwestern southwestern and southeastern areas of the US. Its principal customers include steel distributors and customers fabricating steel products such as storage tanks steel buildings farm machinery and equipment construction equipment transportation equipment conveyors and other similar products. It sells most of its coil products through its own sales force.

Tubular products are sold across the US to 170 customers (steel and pipe distributors piling contractors and USS. Sales of pipe to USS accounted for 14% of company's total sales in 2013 and 24% in 2012. Tubular products are sold through Friedman Industries' own sales team.

Financial Performance

The company's revenues declined by 16% in 2013. Tubular sales dropped by 25% as the result of lower volumes sold (111500 tons in 2012 compared to 92000 tons in 2013) and lower prices ($828 per ton in 2012 compared to $754 per ton in 2013).

Coil sales decreased by 3% due to lower prices (from $807 per ton in 2012 compared to $727 in 2013) partially offset by higher coil tons sold.

Friedman Industries' net income decreased by 25% in 2013 due to a decrease in revenues.

Strategy

The company's financial health is heavily affected by steel commodity and product pricing in the market as well as its dependency on one of two major suppliers.

HISTORY

In 1939 Mendel Friedman founded a steel business in El Dorado Arkansas. His sons Jack and Harold joined him and in 1965 the family consolidated its businesses to form Friedman Industries. The company had a steel service center in Houston and a steel service center and a structural pipe manufacturing plant in Fort Worth Texas.

Faced with strong competition the firm diversified in 1969 by building a steel coil-processing plant near the Lone Star Steel plant in Lone Star Texas. In 1970 Friedman closed its Fort Worth facilities and sold its pipe manufacturing equipment. The company went public in 1972 and used the proceeds to expand the Lone Star plant.

Friedman performed well in the mid-1980s and returned to the pipe business. In the early 1990s steel producer Nucor asked the company to set up shop near its Hickman Arkansas minimill. Friedman agreed and construction was completed in early 1994.

Rising oil prices in 2000 led to sales increases in Friedman's tubular products but softness in steel coil sales more than offset the gains and the company saw its profits decline about 7%. Again in 2001 Friedman prospered in its tubular sector with the increase in domestic oil drilling; however the coil-processing sector took a hit with the influx of cheap imported steel.

In late 2002 the company announced that it would boost its higher-producing operations by closing its marginally productive coil-processing unit in Houston. In 2004 Friedman Industries opened a second pipe mill at its Lone Star facility.

In past years it has generally purchased enough pipe from USS to account for about 30% of Friedman Industries' overall sales. In 2009 when its orders dried up USS idled its Texas plant adjacent to the Friedman facility significantly affecting sales. In response Friedman cut its workforce and lowered its output. A weak economy also affected Friedman Industries' other operations.

By early 2010 the USS plant was operating again but only at about half-capacity. By then the financial damage was done: Friedman Industries' revenues for 2010 dropped almost 70% to $65 million from $208 million the previous year; net income dropped even further (some 95%) to about $650000 down from almost $14 million in 2009.

EXECUTIVES

Chairman Of The Board, President, Chief Executive Officer, Michael Taylor, $279,996 total compensation
Independent Director, Durga Agrawal
Independent Director, Joel Spira
Independent Director, Joe Williams
Independent Director, Max Reichenthal
Director, Tim Stevenson
Chief Financial Officer, Treasurer, Secretary, Alex Larue, $165,000 total compensation
Auditors: Moss Adams LLP

LOCATIONS

HQ: Friedman Industries, Inc.
1121 Judson Road, Suite 124, Longview, TX 75601
Phone: 903 758-3431

PRODUCTS/OPERATIONS

2015 Segment Sales

	% of total
Coil	67
Tubular	33
Total	**100**

COMPETITORS

ACINDAR INDUSTRIA ARGENTINA DE ACEROS S.A.
CLEVELAND-CLIFFS STEEL HOLDING CORPORATION
GREER INDUSTRIES INC.
KG Dongbu Steel Co. Ltd.
NUCOR CORPORATION
SCHNITZER STEEL INDUSTRIES INC.
ThyssenKrupp Electrical Steel GmbH
ULBRICH STAINLESS STEELS & SPECIAL METALS INC.
UNITED STATES STEEL CORPORATION

HISTORICAL FINANCIALS

Company Type: Public

Income Statement				FYE: March 31
	REVENUE ($ mil.)	NET INCOME ($ mil.)	NET PROFIT MARGIN	EMPLOYEES
03/21	126.1	11.4	9.1%	94
03/20	142.1	(5.2)	—	103
03/19	187.1	5.1	2.7%	104
03/18	121.1	2.7	2.3%	91
03/17	77.7	(2.6)	—	82
Annual Growth	**12.8%**	**—**	**—**	**3.5%**

2021 Year-End Financials

Debt ratio: 1.7%
Return on equity: 17.2%
Cash ($ mil.): 8.1
Current ratio: 2.67
Long-term debt ($ mil.): 0.1
No. of shares (mil.): 6.9
Dividends
  Yield: 0.9%
  Payout: 4.9%
Market value ($ mil.): 56.0

	STOCK PRICE ($) FY Close	P/E High/Low		PER SHARE ($)		
				Earnings	Dividends	Book Value
03/21	8.09	6	3	1.63	0.08	9.47
03/20	4.41	—	—	(0.75)	0.12	9.46
03/19	7.67	15	8	0.73	0.17	10.39
03/18	5.87	17	13	0.39	0.04	9.00
03/17	6.45	—	—	(0.39)	0.04	8.61
Annual Growth	**5.8%**			**—**	**18.9%**	**2.4%**

FRMO Corp.

EXECUTIVES

Chairman Of The Board, Chief Executive Officer, Murray Stahl
President, Chief Financial Officer, Chief Operating Officer, Treasurer, Director, Steven Bregman
Vice President, Secretary, Director, Peter Doyle
Independent Director, Dov Glickman
Independent Director, Herbert Chain
Independent Director, Alice Brennan
Auditors: Baker Tilly US, LLP

LOCATIONS

HQ: FRMO Corp.
1 North Lexington Avenue, Suite 12C, White Plains, NY 10601
Phone: 914 632-6730
Web: www.frmocorp.com

HISTORICAL FINANCIALS

Company Type: Public

Income Statement				FYE: May 31
	REVENUE ($ mil.)	NET INCOME ($ mil.)	NET PROFIT MARGIN	EMPLOYEES
05/21	150.5	60.1	40.0%	0
05/20	22.1	(14.5)	65.8%	5
05/19	19.5	4.7	24.1%	0
05/18	16.4	14.0	85.6%	0
05/17	7.6	3.4	45.9%	0
Annual Growth	**110.8%**	**103.7%**	**—**	**—**

2021 Year-End Financials

Debt ratio: 0.2%
Return on equity: 41.0%
Cash ($ mil.): 34.9
Current ratio: 24.96
Long-term debt ($ mil.): 0.7
No. of shares (mil.): 44.0
Dividends
  Yield: —
  Payout: —
Market value ($ mil.): 513.0

	STOCK PRICE ($) FY Close	P/E High/Low		PER SHARE ($)		
				Earnings	Dividends	Book Value
05/21	11.65	11	3	1.37	0.00	4.04
05/20	4.80	—	—	(0.33)	0.00	2.61
05/19	7.25	75	45	0.11	0.00	2.87
05/18	8.25	41	13	0.32	0.00	2.72
05/17	4.40	71	49	0.08	0.00	2.35
Annual Growth	**27.6%**			**—103.4%**	**—**	**14.5%**

Frontdoor Inc

Auditors: DELOITTE & TOUCHE LLP

LOCATIONS

HQ: Frontdoor Inc
150 Peabody Place, Memphis, TN 38103
Phone: 901 701-5000
Web: www.frontdoorhome.com

HISTORICAL FINANCIALS

Company Type: Public

Income Statement				FYE: December 31
	REVENUE ($ mil.)	NET INCOME ($ mil.)	NET PROFIT MARGIN	EMPLOYEES
12/20	1,474.0	112.0	7.6%	2,190
12/19	1,365.0	153.0	11.2%	2,300
12/18	1,258.0	125.0	9.9%	2,200
12/17	1,157.0	160.0	13.8%	2,700
12/16	1,020.0	124.0	12.2%	0
Annual Growth	9.6%	(2.5%)	—	—

2020 Year-End Financials

Debt ratio: 69.4%
Return on equity: ***,***.*%
Cash ($ mil.): 597.0
Current ratio: 1.55
Long-term debt ($ mil.): 968.0
No. of shares (mil.): 85.4
Dividends
Yield: —
Payout: —
Market value ($ mil.): 4,292.0

	STOCK PRICE ($) FY Close	P/E High/Low		Earnings	PER SHARE ($) Dividends	Book Value
12/20	50.21	39	23	1.31	0.00	(0.73)
12/19	47.42	29	14	1.80	0.00	(2.10)
12/18	26.61	33	14	1.47	0.00	(4.07)
Annual Growth	37.4%			— —	(5.6%)	— —

FRP Holdings Inc

Patriot Transportation Holding has plenty of tanks but hasn't fired a shot. The company's Transportation segment comprising Florida Rock & Tank Lines subsidiary transports liquid and dry bulk commodities mainly petroleum (including ethanol) and chemicals in tank trucks. Patriot Transportation's combined fleet of about 435 trucks and 530 trailers operates primarily in the southeastern and mid-Atlantic US. The company's Real Estate unit comprising Florida Rock Properties and FRP Development owns office and warehouse properties as well as sand and gravel deposits on the East Coast that are leased to Vulcan Materials Company.

Operations

The company operates in three segments: transportation (67% of net sales) mining royalty (4%) and land and developed property rentals (16%). In addition fuel surcharges account for 13% of the remaining revenue.

Geographic Reach

Florida Rock & Tank Lines has 20 terminal locations spanning Florida Georgia North Carolina South Carolina Alabama and Tennessee. In addition the company has 13 locations used by its min-

ing operations. Out of these seven locations are being mined in Grandin Keuka and Newberry Florida; Columbus Macon and Tyrone Georgia; and Manassas Virginia.

Sales and Marketing

Patriot's 10 largest customers accounted for 54% of its total transportation segment revenue for 2013. Murphy Oil alone accounts for roughly 20% of this segment's revenues each year. The loss of one of these customers could have a detrimental effect on its revenue and income.

Financial Performance

Patriot has enjoyed significant revenue growth over the years. Revenues jumped 10% from $128 million in 2012 to roughly $140 million in 2013. Profits skyrocketed by 97% from $7.8 million to $15 million. (Both represented the company's highest totals since the Great Recession.)

The growth for 2013 was fueled by a 18% spike in mining royalty revenues due to new royalties from property purchased in mid-2012. Patriot experienced a 14% jump in land property rentals due to higher occupancy rates and the purchase of a park it made in 2013. The transportation segment's revenue climbed due to increased revenue miles as a result of a slightly longer average haul length and increased revenue per mile due to rate increases throughout 2013. Fuel surcharge revenue also jumped in 2013 due to higher fuel costs.

The profit surge for 2013 was driven by the higher revenue coupled with a sizable gain on investment lands and properties it sold in 2013.

Strategy

Patriot's strategy for growth involves acquiring related businesses and increasing it fleet size so it can carry more loads and attract additional customers. In 2013 it purchased 96 new tractors and 33 trailers; for 2014 its capital budget includes 90 new tractors. and 30 new trailers.

It is also focused on growing its mining and property segments. In late 2013 its transportation subsidiary Florida Rock and Tank Lines acquired the assets of Florida-based Pipeline Transportation. Also that year Patriot snatched up Transit Business Park in Baltimore Maryland which consists of 5 buildings on 14.5 acres totaling 232318 sq. ft.

Auditors: Hancock Askew & Co., LLP

LOCATIONS

HQ: FRP Holdings Inc
200 West Forsyth Street, 7th Floor, Jacksonville, FL 32202
Phone: 904 396-5733
Web: www.frpholdings.com

PRODUCTS/OPERATIONS

2013 Sales

	$ mil.	% of total
Transportation	93.2	67
Property rentals	22.4	16
Fuel surcharges	18.9	13
Mining royalty land	5.3	4
Total	**139.8**	**100**

COMPETITORS

OLD DOMINION FREIGHT LINE INC.
SEACO GLOBAL LIMITED
USA TRUCK INC.

HISTORICAL FINANCIALS

Company Type: Public

Income Statement				FYE: December 31
	REVENUE ($ mil.)	NET INCOME ($ mil.)	NET PROFIT MARGIN	EMPLOYEES
12/20	23.5	12.7	53.9%	13
12/19	23.7	16.1	68.1%	12
12/18	22.0	124.4	565.2%	10
12/17	43.1	41.7	96.7%	19
12/16	9.5	1.6	17.7%	0
Annual Growth	25.5%	65.8%		

2020 Year-End Financials

Debt ratio: 16.7%
Return on equity: 3.4%
Cash ($ mil.): 73.9
Current ratio: 39.14
Long-term debt ($ mil.): 89.9
No. of shares (mil.): 9.3
Dividends
Yield: —
Payout: —
Market value ($ mil.): 427.0

	STOCK PRICE ($) FY Close	P/E High/Low		Earnings	PER SHARE ($) Dividends	Book Value
12/20	45.55	39	23	1.32	0.00	39.26
12/19	49.81	34	28	1.63	0.00	38.19
12/18	46.01	5	3	12.32	0.00	36.57
12/17	44.25	11	9	4.16	0.00	24.32
12/16	37.70	235	183	0.17	0.00	20.05
Annual Growth	4.8%			— — 66.9%	—	18.3%

FS Bancorp (Indiana)

EXECUTIVES

Ceo, Joseph Pierce
Secretary*, C Lynn Tracey
Vice President of Marketing, Melissa Abraham
Senior Marketing Executive, Nic Engle
Auditors: Crowe LLP

LOCATIONS

HQ: FS Bancorp (Indiana)
220 South Detroit Street, La Grange, IN 46761
Phone: 260 463-7111   **Fax:** 260 463-7341
Web: www.farmersstatebank.com

HISTORICAL FINANCIALS

Company Type: Public

Income Statement				FYE: December 31
	ASSETS ($ mil.)	NET INCOME ($ mil.)	INCOME AS % OF ASSETS	EMPLOYEES
12/20	993.5	14.3	1.4%	0
12/19	837.9	13.2	1.6%	0
12/18	760.5	9.3	1.2%	0
12/17	734.0	7.5	1.0%	0
12/16	680.4	7.4	1.1%	0
Annual Growth	9.9%	17.6%	—	—

2020 Year-End Financials

Return on assets: 1.5%
Return on equity: 16.1%
Long-term debt ($ mil.): —
No. of shares (mil.): 4.3
Sales ($ mil): 41.0
Dividends
Yield: 0.0%
Payout: 51.9%
Market value ($ mil.): 217.0

HOOVER'S HANDBOOK OF EMERGING COMPANIES 2022

	STOCK PRICE ($) FY Close	P/E High/Low		PER SHARE ($) Earnings	Dividends	Book Value
12/20	50.00	19	14	3.26	1.69	21.77
12/19	61.00	23	19	2.99	1.59	18.88
12/18	79.90	56	26	2.11	1.44	16.27
12/17	92.00	54	40	1.68	1.23	15.05
12/16	68.25	48	36	1.67	1.17	14.04
Annual Growth	(7.5%)	—	—	18.2%	9.6%	11.6%

FS Bancorp Inc (Washington)

FS Bancorp is the holding company for 1st Security Bank of Washington which operates six branches in the Puget Sound region. The bank provides standard deposit products such as checking and savings accounts CDs and IRAs to area businesses and consumers. Its lending activities are focused on consumer loans (more than half of its portfolio) including home improvement boat and automobile loans. The bank also writes business and construction loans and commercial and residential mortgages. FS Bancorp went public via in initial public offering in 2012.

EXECUTIVES

Executive Vice President , Chief Operating Officer, Lisa Cleary
Independent Chairman Of The Board, Ted Leech
Chief Executive Officer, Director, Joseph Adams, $475,000 total compensation
Chief Financial Officer, Treasurer, Secretary, Matthew Mullet, $330,000 total compensation
Executive Vice President , Chief Risk Officer And Cra Officer Of The Bank, Erin Burr
Chief Credit Officer, Robert Fuller
Executive Vice President , Chief Human Resources Officer/wow! Officer Of The Bank, Vickie Jarman
Executive Vice President , Retail Banking And Marketing Of The Bank, Kelli Nielsen
Independent Director, Michael Mansfield
Independent Director, Marina Cofer-Wildsmith
Executive Vice President, Home Lending Production Of The Bank, Donn Costa, $330,000 total compensation
Executive Vice President , Chief Lending Officer Of The Bank, Dennis O Leary, $300,000 total compensation
Independent Director, Joseph Zavaglia
Independent Director, Pamela Andrews
Auditors: Moss Adams LLP

LOCATIONS

HQ: FS Bancorp Inc (Washington)
6920 220th Street SW, Mountlake Terrace, WA 98043
Phone: 425 771-5299
Web: www.fsbwa.com

COMPETITORS

EASTERN BANK CORPORATION
FIRST BANCTRUST
HOME CITY FINANCIAL CORPORATION

CORPORATION

HISTORICAL FINANCIALS

Company Type: Public

Income Statement FYE: December 31

	ASSETS ($ mil.)	NET INCOME ($ mil.)	INCOME AS % OF ASSETS	EMPLOYEES
12/20	2,113.2	39.2	1.9%	506
12/19	1,713.0	22.7	1.3%	452
12/18	1,621.6	24.3	1.5%	424
12/17	981.7	14.0	1.4%	326
12/16	827.9	10.5	1.3%	306
Annual Growth	26.4%	39.1%		13.4%

2020 Year-End Financials

Return on assets: 2.0%
Return on equity: 18.2%
Long-term debt ($ mil.): —
No. of shares (mil.): 8.4
Sales ($ mil): 144.2
Dividends
Yield: 3.0%
Payout: 18.7%
Market value ($ mil.): 464.0

	STOCK PRICE ($) FY Close	P/E High/Low		PER SHARE ($) Earnings	Dividends	Book Value
12/20	54.80	14	6	4.49	0.84	27.14
12/19	63.79	25	17	2.51	0.65	22.45
12/18	42.88	20	13	3.15	0.53	20.04
12/17	54.57	25	15	2.14	0.22	16.58
12/16	35.95	21	13	1.76	0.19	13.24
Annual Growth	11.1%	—	—	26.4%	46.0%	19.6%

Fulgent Genetics Inc

Auditors: DELOITTE & TOUCHE LLP

LOCATIONS

HQ: Fulgent Genetics Inc
4978 Santa Anita Avenue, Temple City, CA 91780
Phone: 626 350-0537
Web: www.fulgentgenetics.com

HISTORICAL FINANCIALS

Company Type: Public

Income Statement FYE: December 31

	REVENUE ($ mil.)	NET INCOME ($ mil.)	NET PROFIT MARGIN	EMPLOYEES
12/20	421.7	214.3	50.8%	429
12/19	32.5	(0.4)	—	139
12/18	21.3	(5.6)	—	123
12/17	18.7	(2.5)	—	98
12/16	18.2	(5.3)	—	70
Annual Growth	119.2%	—	—	57.3%

2020 Year-End Financials

Debt ratio: 2.1%
Return on equity: 65.5%
Cash ($ mil.): 87.4
Current ratio: 4.02
Long-term debt ($ mil.): —
No. of shares (mil.): 28.1
Dividends
Yield: —
Payout: —
Market value ($ mil.): 1,468.0

	STOCK PRICE ($) FY Close	P/E High/Low		PER SHARE ($) Earnings	Dividends	Book Value
12/20	52.10	5	1	8.91	0.00	20.21
12/19	12.90	—	—	(0.02)	0.00	3.85
12/18	3.17	—	—	(0.31)	0.00	2.81
12/17	4.38	—	—	(0.14)	0.00	3.04
12/16	11.57	—	—	(1.00)	0.00	3.08
Annual Growth	45.7%	—	—	—	—	60.0%

Fuller (HB) Company

H.B. Fuller is one of the world's top adhesive sealant and specialty chemical manufacturers with sales in about 35 countries across the world. The company's core product industrial adhesives is used in the manufacturing process of a wide range of consumer and industrial goods like food and beverage containers doors and windows electronic appliances textiles marine products and automobiles among others. With some 20 independently operating regional sales offices and manufacturing plants outside of the US H.B. Fuller enjoys a wide market reach matched by only a few other global firms. The company's brands include Advantra Clarity Rakoll Silaprene and Eternabond among others. H.B. Fuller generates about 45% of sales from US.

HISTORY

In 1887 armed with a wood stove and an iron kettle Harvey Benjamin Fuller Sr. began making wet paste to sell to paperhangers in St. Paul Minnesota. The company became incorporated as the Fuller Manufacturing Company with $600 in capital from three Minneapolis lawyers. It began marketing glue to shoe companies bookbinders and other customers and producing ink for the city's schools. In 1888 Fuller's son Albert joined his father instantly doubling the firm's workforce.

After the 1892 acquisition of competitor Minnesota Paste Company Fuller grew largely through sales spurred by a series of inventions. Fuller's two cold-water products a dry wall cleaner and dry paste proved wildly successful. In 1905 the company was shipping to Australia Germany and the UK. Fuller's son Harvey Jr. joined the company in 1909.

In 1915 Fuller reincorporated as the H.B. Fuller Company. During WWI it supplied adhesives for canned goods shipped to the troops but business fell off after the war. Harvey Sr. died in 1921. Despite facing possible bankruptcy Harvey Jr. made a fateful decision to hire a full-time chemist. With Ray Burgess' inventions the company achieved record sales by the end of the 1920s.

After the stock market crashed Fuller acquired the Selvasize Company makers of a combination wallpaper- and plaster-adhesive. Fuller rode out the Depression with the success of new products such as Ice Proof (a glue resistant to cold water) and Nu-Type Hot Pick-Up (used in automated labeling). However in 1937 the company learned that three salespeople had been undercutting orders through a phantom firm which they then claimed to represent. Fuller's sales dropped almost

$50000 the following year. In 1939 Harvey Jr. suffered a stroke.

In 1941 competitor Paisley Products of Chicago offered to buy the company for $50000. Instead Elmer Andersen (a business whiz who had joined the company as a salesman in the mid-1930s) persuaded Harvey to turn the reins over to him and give him a majority stake. WWII began bringing numerous government contracts to the company. During and after the war H.B. Fuller decentralized operations by opening branch plants beginning with Kansas City in 1943. By 1950 H.B. Fuller was the fourth-largest adhesives company in the US.

Andersen went on to become a state senator and eventually governor of Minnesota. Under the leadership of Al Vigard in the 1950s and 1960s the company expanded into Canada Costa Rica Panama and other countries. H.B. Fuller went public in 1968. In 1971 Tony Andersen (Elmer's son) took over and further pushed international sales. From 1971 to 1980 the company made some two dozen acquisitions — about half in foreign countries — and increased sales fivefold. In 1980 Andersen began revamping the company which had become inefficient because of its geographic expansion. By 1985 earnings were solid again.

In 1991 the company suffered adverse publicity after social activists accused it of marketing its Resistol glue in Latin America while knowing that street kids were sniffing the glue. In 1997 H.B. Fuller entered a joint venture with Switzerland's EMS-Chemie Holding AG to combine their automotive coatings sealants and adhesives businesses. CEO Walter Kissing whose efforts to reduce costs in the 1990s failed to improve margins retired in 1998.

The next year Andersen retired as chairman and Al Stroucken a former Bayer executive took the helm. Stroucken quickly announced a restructuring that would reduce the company's plant operations and lay off 10% of its workforce. From 2001-2003 the company eliminated 20% of its manufacturing plants and cut more than 550 employees. It restructured its adhesives business which was run through four geographic regions into one global unit. The company also reduced its product offerings by half allowing it to deliver products on time more consistently.

While H.B. Fuller did increase sales in 2003 over the previous year that improvement was due mainly to the weakened dollar (against the Euro and other foreign currencies) and the resulting exchange differences. Sales volume decreased as did prices. Revenues increased again in 2004 partly due to the same trend; however the company also benefited from the increased sales volume of global adhesives and specialty products and from its February 2004 acquisition of the adhesives business of Portugese chemical firm Probos.

Due to accounting irregularities during 1999 through 2004 H.B. Fuller conducted an internal investigation into the finances of its Chilean operations in 2005. As a result the company made minor adjustments in its 2004 financial statements.

Also in 2005 the firm combined its Chinese and Japanese adhesives businesses with those of Sekisui Chemical through joint ventures. Three years later H.B. Fuller acquired a business in Egypt called Egymelt to establish a presence in North Africa.

The company reorganized its business segments in 2007. H.B. Fuller rearranged its operations along geographic lines merging the former Global Adhesives and Full Valu/Specialty segments into regional operations. The new segments are Asia/Pacific Europe Latin America and North America. The move followed a gradual coming-together of the company's product groups. Fuller had worked to make its adhesive products more specialized and less of a commodity.

Jim Owens was named president and CEO of H.B. Fuller in 2010. He replaced Michele Volpi who resigned from the company. Owens was previously SVP of H.B. Fullers' Americas operations.

In 2011 the company bought a 20% stake that Sekisui Chemical had held in its Chinese operations for $8.6 million.

The company acquired the global industrial adhesives business of Forbo in 2012. The $394 million cash deal expanded H.B. Fuller's position in the international adhesives industry increasing H.B. Fuller's business in China by as much as 50% and strengthening its position in such markets as packaging and durable assembly.

In 2012 the firm bought Engent Inc. a provider of manufacturing research and development services to the electronics industry based in Norcross Georgia. The deal added development capabilities testing resources and technical support infrastructure increasing H.B. Fuller's capabilities in a wide range of microelectronic assembly technologies.

In 2012 the company sold its Central American paints business to Colombia-based paints company Compania Global de Pinturas (Pintuco) part of Grupo Mundial for $120 million. Pintuco has a strong market position in Central America and H.B. Fuller wanted to focus on its core adhesives operations.

Solidifying its position in the South American adhesives industry in 2013 the company bought Plexbond Qu mica S/A a provider of chemical polyurethane specialties and polyester resins based in Curitiba Brazil.

EXECUTIVES

Pres-Ceo, James J Owens
Chb*, Lee R Mitau
V Chb*, R William Van Sant
Exec V Pres-Coo, Theodore M Clark
Exec V Pres-Cfo, John J Corkrean
V Pres-General Counsel-Corp SE, Timothy J Keenan
Vp Global Bus Prcss Imprvemnt, Traci L Jensen
Svp Global Cnstrction Adhsves, M Shahbaz Malik
Evp Hygiene/Health/Cnsmble Adh, Andrew E Tometich
Vp Human Resources, Nathanial D Weaver
Employee, Barbara Pereta
Auditors: Ernst & Young LLP

LOCATIONS

HQ: Fuller (HB) Company
1200 Willow Lake Boulevard, St. Paul, MN 55110-5101
Phone: 651 236-5900   **Fax:** 651 236-5161
Web: www.hbfuller.com

PRODUCTS/OPERATIONS

2018 Sales

	% of total
Americas Adhesives	36
EIMEA	24
Asia Pacific	9
Construction Products	15
Engineering Adhesives	16
Total	**100**

Selected Brands

Adecol
Advantra
Bacon
CILBOND
Chapco
Childers
Clarity
Clean Melt
Close Sesame
Conforma
Cyberbond
Flexel
Flextra
Full-Care
Prospec
ODOGard
Open Sesame
Rakoll
Rapidex
Royal
Sesame
Swiftbond
Swiftlock
Swiftmelt
Swifttak
Swifttherm
TEC
Tile Perfect
Thermonex
TONSAN
Weld Mount
Wisdom

COMPETITORS

Akzo Nobel N.V.
BEARDOW AND ADAMS (ADHESIVES) LIMITED
FIRST ATLANTIC CAPITAL LTD.
ILLINOIS TOOL WORKS INC.
LYONDELLBASELL ADVANCED POLYMERS INC.
PRC - DESOTO INTERNATIONAL INC.
SAINT-GOBAIN CORPORATION
SIKA CORPORATION

HISTORICAL FINANCIALS

Company Type: Public

Income Statement

FYE: November 27

	REVENUE ($ mil.)	NET INCOME ($ mil.)	NET PROFIT MARGIN	EMPLOYEES
11/21	3,278.0	161.3	4.9%	6,500
11/20	2,790.2	123.7	4.4%	6,428
11/19*	2,897.0	130.8	4.5%	6,400
12/18	3,041.0	171.2	5.6%	6,500
12/17	2,306.0	58.2	2.5%	6,000
Annual Growth	9.2%	29.0%	—	2.0%

*Fiscal year change

2021 Year-End Financials

Debt ratio: 37.8%
Return on equity: 10.8%
Cash ($ mil.): 61.7
Current ratio: 1.66
Long-term debt ($ mil.): 1,591.4

No. of shares (mil.): 52.7
Dividends
  Yield: 0.0%
  Payout: 22.3%
Market value ($ mil.): 3,900.0

	STOCK PRICE ($) FY Close	P/E High/Low		PER SHARE ($) Earnings	Dividends	Book Value
11/21	73.90	26	17	2.97	0.67	30.25
11/20	53.73	23	11	2.36	0.65	26.61
11/19*	49.88	20	15	2.52	0.64	23.85
12/18	48.24	17	12	3.29	0.62	22.70
12/17	55.65	51	41	1.13	0.59	20.71
Annual Growth	7.3%	—	—	27.3%	3.0%	9.9%

*Fiscal year change

FVCBankcorp Inc

Auditors: Yount, Hyde & Barbour, P.C.

LOCATIONS

HQ: FVCBankcorp Inc
11325 Random Hills Road, Suite 240, Fairfax, VA
22030
Phone: 703 436-3800
Web: www.fvcbank.com

HISTORICAL FINANCIALS
Company Type: Public

Income Statement				FYE: December 31
	ASSETS ($ mil.)	NET INCOME ($ mil.)	INCOME AS % OF ASSETS	EMPLOYEES
12/20	1,821.4	15.5	0.9%	121
12/19	1,537.3	15.8	1.0%	124
12/18	1,351.5	10.8	0.8%	128
12/17	1,053.2	7.6	0.7%	0
12/16	909.3	6.9	0.8%	0
Annual Growth	19.0%	22.3%	—	—

2020 Year-End Financials

Return on assets: 0.9%
Return on equity: 8.3%
Long-term debt ($ mil.): —
No. of shares (mil.): 13.5
Sales ($ mil): 69.9

Dividends
Yield: —
Payout: —
Market value ($ mil.): 199.0

	STOCK PRICE ($) FY Close	P/E High/Low		PER SHARE ($) Earnings	Dividends	Book Value
12/20	14.70	15	8	1.10	0.00	14.03
12/19	17.47	17	14	1.07	0.00	12.88
12/18	17.61	22	17	0.85	0.00	11.55
12/17	17.52	28	23	0.67	0.00	9.04
12/16	16.80	29	23	0.63	0.00	7.84
Annual Growth	(3.3%)		—	14.9%	—	15.6%

Gaming & Leisure Properties, Inc

EXECUTIVES

Senior Vice President, Chief Development Officer,
Steven Ladany
Independent Director, Carol Lynton
Independent Director, JoAnne Epps
Independent Director, James Perry
Independent Director, Barry Schwartz
Senior Vice President, Chief Investment Officer,
Matthew Demchyk, $360,000 total compensation
Chairman, President And Chief Executive Officer,
Peter Carlino, $1,808,468 total compensation
Executive Vice President, General Counsel,
Secretary, Brandon Moore, $425,000 total
compensation
Senior Vice President, Chief Accounting Officer,
Treasurer, Desiree Burke, $400,000 total
compensation
Lead Independent Director, Joseph Marshall
Auditors: Deloitte & Touche

LOCATIONS

HQ: Gaming & Leisure Properties, Inc
845 Berkshire Blvd., Suite 200, Wyomissing, PA 19610
Phone: 610 401-2900
Web: www.glpropinc.com

HISTORICAL FINANCIALS
Company Type: Public

Income Statement				FYE: December 31
	REVENUE ($ mil.)	NET INCOME ($ mil.)	NET PROFIT MARGIN	EMPLOYEES
12/20	1,153.1	505.7	43.9%	560
12/19	1,153.4	390.8	33.9%	648
12/18	1,055.7	339.5	32.2%	644
12/17	971.3	380.6	39.2%	714
12/16	828.2	289.3	34.9%	751
Annual Growth	8.6%	15.0%	—	(7.1%)

2020 Year-End Financials

Debt ratio: 63.7%
Return on equity: 21.2%
Cash ($ mil.): 486.4
Current ratio: 6.18
Long-term debt ($ mil.): 5,754.6

No. of shares (mil.): 232.4
Dividends
Yield: 7.5%
Payout: 154.5%
Market value ($ mil.): 9,856.0

	STOCK PRICE ($) FY Close	P/E High/Low		PER SHARE ($) Earnings	Dividends	Book Value
12/20	42.40	22	7	2.30	3.20	11.51
12/19	43.05	24	18	1.81	2.74	9.66
12/18	32.31	23	20	1.58	2.57	10.58
12/17	37.00	22	17	1.79	2.50	11.56
12/16	30.62	22	15	1.60	2.32	11.72
Annual Growth	8.5%		—	9.5%	8.4%	(0.5%)

Generac Holdings Inc

Generac Holdings is a leading global designer and manufacturer of a wide range of energy technology solutions. The company provides power generation equipment energy storage systems grid service solutions and other power products serving the residential light commercial and industrial markets. Generac's residential generator products provide emergency standby power for homes. The company's commercial and industrial backup generators provide standby power for everything from restaurants and gas stations to hospitals and manufacturing facilities. Other products include light towers mobile generators and heaters used in construction mining energy and other industries. Generac sells its products through retailers and wholesale distributors. The US accounts for about 85% of the company's sales.

Operations

Generac's key focus is in power generation and offers one of the widest ranges of products in the market place. The company recently starts providing energy storage systems as a clean energy solution for residential use that capture and store electricity from solar panels or other power sources and help reduce home energy costs while also protecting homes from brief power outages. It designs manufactures sources and modifies engines alternators transfer switches and other components necessary for power products which are fueled by natural gas liquid propane gasoline and Bi-Fuel. Generac also designs sources modifies and integrates batteries inverters power electronics controls energy monitoring devices and other components into its energy storage systems.

Overall the company generates about 65% of total sales from residential products followed by nearly 30% from commercial & industrial products.

Geographic Reach

Generac is headquartered in Waukesha Wisconsin and has other operations manufacturing and sales offices in Mexico Italy Spain China Brazil Australia India the United Arab Emirates France Canada and the Dominican Republic as well as several other countries throughout Europe.

The company provides access to numerous independent distributors in over 150 countries.

Generac's Domestic segment generates nearly 85% of total sales and includes the legacy Generac business (excluding its traditional Latin American export operations) and the acquisitions that are based in the US and Canada.

The International segment which accounts for around 15% of total sales includes the Latin American export operations and the acquisitions from outside the US and Canada.

Sales and Marketing

Generac's power products and solutions are available globally through a broad network of independent dealers distributors retailers e-commerce partners wholesalers and equipment rental companies as well as sold direct to certain end user customers. The company's advertising expenses were $53678 in 2020; $44153 in 2019; and $34792 in 2018.

Financial Performance

The company in 2020 had a total revenue of $2.5 billion a 13% increase from the previous year. This was due to the increase in the company's domestic sales which was caused by strong growth in shipments of home standby generators and portable generators as elevated outage activity and nationwide stay-at-home orders heightened consumer awareness of power reliability concerns.

In 2020 the company had a net income of $347.2 million a 38% increase from the previous year's net income of $252.3 million.

The company's cash at the end of 2020 was $655.1 million. Operating activities generated $486.5 million while investing activities used $124.1 million mainly for the acquisition of business and expenditures for property and equipment. Financing activities used another $30.4 million primarily for repayments of short-term borrowings.

Strategy

The company has been executing its strategic plan called "Power Our Future" which serves as the framework for the significant investments it has made to capitalize on the long-term growth prospects of Generac. Generac's strategic plan centers around a number of key mega-trends that it believes will drive significant secular growth opportunities for its business. "Grid 2.0" climate change the abundance of natural gas globally an aging infrastructure and 5G telecommunications are all major themes that Generac believes will drive future long-term growth. The onset of the COVID-19 pandemic in early 2020 has led to a new and emerging trend that it refers to as "Home as a Sanctuary" where millions of people are working learning shopping entertaining and in general spending more time at home which has resulted

190   HOOVER'S HANDBOOK OF EMERGING COMPANIES 2022

in a significantly increased awareness for backup power security and willingness to invest more in home improvement projects.

Mergers and Acquisitions

In mid-2021 Generac Holdings Inc. announced the acquisition of Deep Sea Electronics Limited an advanced controls designer and manufacturer based in the UK. With the addition of Deep Sea Electronics Generac has bolstered its engineering and control capabilities which will advance and support innovation of its products to meet the dynamic needs of the evolving energy technology market and its customers. Terms were not disclosed.

In late 2020 Generac acquired Enbala Power Networks Inc. (Enbala) a leading distributed energy resources technology company based in Denver. The deal solidifies Generac's position as a market leader in Smart Grid 2.0 technologies and opens opportunities for the company as a grid services provider. Terms were not disclosed.

EXECUTIVES

Independent Director, John Bowlin
Executive Chairman, President And Chief Executive Officer, Aaron Jagdfeld, $944,151 total compensation
Chief Financial Officer, York Ragen, $447,911 total compensation
Chief Marketing Officer, Russell Minick, $462,075 total compensation
Executive Vice President, Industrial, Americas, Erik Wilde, $379,995 total compensation
Independent Director, William Jenkins
Independent Director, Andrew Lampereur
Independent Director, Dominick Zarcone
Lead Independent Director, Bennett Morgan
Independent Director, Kathryn Roedel
Independent Director, Marcia Avedon
Chief Operations Officer, Thomas Pettit
Executive Vice President, General Counsel, Company Secretary, Raj Kanuru
Chief Technology Officer, Patrick Forsythe, $402,493 total compensation
Auditors: DELOITTE & TOUCHE LLP

LOCATIONS

HQ: Generac Holdings Inc
 S45 W29290 Hwy 59, Waukesha, WI 53189
Phone: 262 544-4811
Web: www.generac.com

PRODUCTS/OPERATIONS

2015 Sales

	$ mil.	% of total
Residential power products	673.8	51
Commercial & Industrial products	548.4	42
Other	95.1	7
Total	**1,317.3**	**100**

Selected Products and Brands

Generators
 Commercial (QuietSource)
 Industrial (gaseous diesel bi-fuel modular power systems (MPS) Gemini)
 Portable (GP XG XP iX)
 Recreational vehicle (gasoline propane diesel)
 Residential (QuietSource Guardian)

Selected Markets

Agricultural/mining
Business office
Commercial/retail
Data center
Education

Healthcare
Manufacturing
Municipal
Research
Residential
Telecom

COMPETITORS

ALLIED MOTION TECHNOLOGIES INC.
ELECTROCOMPONENTS PUBLIC LIMITED COMPANY
EMERSON ELECTRIC CO.
FRANKLIN ELECTRIC CO. INC.
GIBRALTAR INDUSTRIES INC.
HITACHI LTD.
Nordex SE
P10 HOLDINGS INC.
YASKAWA ELECTRIC CORPORATION

HISTORICAL FINANCIALS

Company Type: Public

Income Statement

FYE: December 31

	REVENUE ($ mil.)	NET INCOME ($ mil.)	NET PROFIT MARGIN	EMPLOYEES
12/21	3,737.1	550.4	14.7%	9,540
12/20	2,485.2	350.5	14.1%	6,797
12/19	2,204.3	252.0	11.4%	5,689
12/18	2,023.4	238.2	11.8%	5,664
12/17	1,672.4	159.3	9.5%	4,556
Annual Growth	**22.3%**	**36.3%**	**—**	**20.3%**

2021 Year-End Financials

Debt ratio: 20.0%
Return on equity: 30.5%
Cash ($ mil.): 147.3
Current ratio: 1.60
Long-term debt ($ mil.): 902.0

No. of shares (mil.): 63.7
Dividends
 Yield: —
 Payout: —
Market value ($ mil.): 22,424.0

	STOCK PRICE ($) FY Close	P/E High/Low	Earnings	Dividends	Book Value
12/21	351.92	59 26	8.30	0.00	34.74
12/20	227.41	42 14	5.48	0.00	22.12
12/19	100.59	25 12	4.03	0.00	16.50
12/18	49.70	17 12	3.54	0.00	12.24
12/17	49.52	20 13	2.56	0.00	8.97
Annual Growth	**63.3%**		**34.2%**	**—**	**40.3%**

Genie Energy Ltd

Genie Energy is a global provider of residential and commercial energy services. The company operates through three subsidiaries ? Genie Retail Energy (GRE) Genie Solar Energy and Genie Retail Energy International (GREI). GRE resells electricity and natural gas bought from the wholesale commodities markets reselling those commodities to residential and small to large commercial customers throughout the US. Genie Solar Energy offers a variety of products and configurations to meet efficiency and ROI goals while GREI holds interests in a portfolio of innovative growing companies that supply energy to retail customers in deregulated markets outside of the US. Headquartered in Newark New Jersey Genie Energy is controlled by CEO Michael Stein.

EXECUTIVES

Chief Financial Officer, Avraham Goldin, $350,000 total compensation
Lead Independent Director, W. Wesley Perry
Independent Director, Allan Sass
Chief Executive Officer, Michael Stein, $365,384 total compensation
Company Secretary, Joyce Mason
Non-executive Independent Chairman Of The Board, Howard Jonas, $248,846 total compensation
Auditors: BDO USA, LLP

LOCATIONS

HQ: Genie Energy Ltd
 520 Broad Street, Newark, NJ 07102
Phone: 973 438-3500
Web: www.genie.com

PRODUCTS/OPERATIONS

2015 sales

	% of total
Electricity	80
Natural gas	19
Other	1
Total	**100**

COMPETITORS

CENTERPOINT ENERGY INC.
CMS ENERGY CORPORATION
NEW JERSEY RESOURCES CORPORATION
ONEOK INC.
SOUTHERN COMPANY GAS
VECTREN CORPORATION
VIA RENEWABLES INC.

HISTORICAL FINANCIALS

Company Type: Public

Income Statement

FYE: December 31

	REVENUE ($ mil.)	NET INCOME ($ mil.)	NET PROFIT MARGIN	EMPLOYEES
12/20	379.3	13.1	3.5%	125
12/19	315.2	4.1	1.3%	163
12/18	280.3	22.7	8.1%	183
12/17	264.2	(6.9)	—	178
12/16	212.1	(24.5)	—	180
Annual Growth	**15.6%**	**—**	**—**	**(8.7%)**

2020 Year-End Financials

Debt ratio: 0.7%
Return on equity: 13.6%
Cash ($ mil.): 36.9
Current ratio: 1.37
Long-term debt ($ mil.): —

No. of shares (mil.): 26.2
Dividends
 Yield: 4.5%
 Payout: 75.0%
Market value ($ mil.): 189.0

	STOCK PRICE ($) FY Close	P/E High/Low	Earnings	Dividends	Book Value
12/20	7.21	21 12	0.44	0.33	3.74
12/19	7.73	119 64	0.10	0.30	3.60
12/18	6.03	9 5	0.83	0.30	3.86
12/17	4.36	— —	(0.36)	0.30	3.38
12/16	5.75	— —	(1.14)	0.24	3.92
Annual Growth	**5.8%**		**—**	**8.3%**	**(1.1%)**

HOOVER'S HANDBOOK OF EMERGING COMPANIES 2022

German American Bancorp Inc

German American Bancorp is the holding company for German American Bank which operates some 65 branches in southern Indiana and Kentucky. Founded in 1910 the bank offers such standard retail products as checking and savings accounts certificates of deposit and IRAs. It also provides trust services while sister company German American Investment Services provides trust investment advisory and brokerage services. German American Bancorp also owns German American Insurance which offers corporate and personal insurance products. The group's core banking operations provide more than 90% of its total sales.

Geographic Reach

German American is headquartered in Jasper Indiana. Its subsidiaries operate from more than 60 locations in southern Indiana and Kentucky.

Sales and Marketing

German American Bancorp spent $3.5 million on advertising in 2017. Advertising expenses totaled $2.7 million in 2016 and $3.7 million in 2015.

Financial Performance

German American's revenue has been climbing steadily for the past five years thanks to the company's acquisitions of other area banks. Similarly net income has also been on the rise. In 2017 the company marked its eighth consecutive year of record earnings.

In 2017 revenue increased 4% to $131.8 million. That increase was partially due to the addition of River Valley Financial Bank which German American acquired in 2016. Growth in the company's loan portfolio also boosted net interest income. This was slightly offset by a 1% decline in non-interest income. Although trust and insurance operations rose other operating income declined $1.1 million (29%).

Net income rose 16% to $35.2 million in 2017; in addition to having higher revenue the company recognized a benefit related to the reduced corporate tax rate that year.

German American ended 2017 with $70.4 million in net cash $5.5 million more than it had at the end of 2016. Operating activities provided $54.9 million in cash and financing activities provided $139.9 million. Investing activities used $189.3 million.

Strategy

German American Bancorp has grown recently through a number of acquisitions including bank branches an insurance office and other bank holding companies. These acquisitions have also helped the company grow into new geographic markets including locations in Kentucky.

Growth by acquisition can be somewhat risky though. The company could unknowingly acquire problem assets or have difficulties integrating other banks it purchases. These issues could bring down its financial performance.

German American operates in a relatively small region which leaves it vulnerable to economic downturns in that area. If economic conditions in its market decline German American faces the risk of increased delinquencies and charge-offs. The company's larger more widespread competitors would be less impacted in such a case.

Mergers and Acquisitions

German American Bancorp agreed to acquire Citizens First in early 2019 in a cash-and-stock transaction valued at about $70 million. German American will gain Citizens' branch offices in the Barren Hart Simpson and Warren counties of Kentucky. Citizens has about $475 million in assets loans of some $375 million and deposits of around $390 million.

In October 2018 German American Bancorp acquired Kentucky's First Security Bank for $101 million. With that deal the company expanded into Kentucky's Owensboro Bowling Green and Lexington markets.

EXECUTIVES

Director, Sue Ellspermann
Independent Director, Tyson Wagler
Independent Director, Christina Ryan
Independent Director, Jack Sheidler
Independent Director, Zachary Bawel
Independent Director, Jason Kelly
Chief Financial Officer, Chief Operating Officer, Senior Executive Vice President, Bradley Rust, $339,500 total compensation
Independent Director, M. Darren Root
President, Chief Executive Officer, Secretary, Director, D. Dauby, $310,375 total compensation
Executive Vice President And Chief Credit Officer, Keith Leinenbach, $295,000 total compensation
Independent Director, Marc Fine
Independent Director, J. David Lett
Executive Chairman Of The Board, Mark Schroeder, $600,000 total compensation
Auditors: Crowe LLP

LOCATIONS

HQ: German American Bancorp Inc
711 Main Street, Jasper, IN 47546
Phone: 812 482-1314
Web: www.germanamerican.com

PRODUCTS/OPERATIONS

2017 Sales

	$ mil.	% of total
Interest		
Loans including fees	91.7	64
Securities including dividends	19.2	13
Short-term investments	0.1	-
Non-interest		
Insurance	8.0	6
Service charges on deposit accounts	6.2	4
Trust & investment product fees	5.3	4
Other	12.4	9
Adjustments	(11.1)	-
Total	**131.8**	**100**

COMPETITORS

AMERICAN NATIONAL BANKSHARES INC.
BANKUNITED INC.
BYLINE BANCORP INC.
CENTERSTATE BANK CORPORATION
CITIZENS & NORTHERN CORPORATION
CNB FINANCIAL CORPORATION
F.N.B. CORPORATION
FIRST MIDWEST BANCORP INC.
GLACIER BANCORP INC.
HANCOCK WHITNEY CORPORATION
HEARTLAND FINANCIAL USA INC.
NATIONAL BANK HOLDINGS CORPORATION
OLD LINE BANCSHARES INC.
OLD NATIONAL BANCORP
SEACOAST BANKING CORPORATION OF FLORIDA

HISTORICAL FINANCIALS

Company Type: Public

Income Statement

FYE: December 31

	ASSETS ($ mil.)	NET INCOME ($ mil.)	INCOME AS % OF ASSETS	EMPLOYEES
12/20	4,977.5	62.2	1.2%	770
12/19	4,397.6	59.2	1.3%	817
12/18	3,929.0	46.5	1.2%	738
12/17	3,144.3	40.6	1.3%	614
12/16	2,955.9	35.1	1.2%	597
Annual Growth	13.9%	15.3%	—	6.6%

2020 Year-End Financials

Return on assets: 1.3%
Return on equity: 10.3%
Long-term debt ($ mil.): —
No. of shares (mil.): 26.5
Sales ($ mil): 228.8
Dividends
  Yield: 2.3%
  Payout: 35.3%
Market value ($ mil.): 877.0

	STOCK PRICE ($) FY Close	P/E High/Low		PER SHARE ($) Earnings	Dividends	Book Value
12/20	33.09	15	10	2.34	0.76	23.57
12/19	35.62	16	12	2.29	0.68	21.51
12/18	27.77	19	13	1.99	0.60	18.37
12/17	35.33	30	17	1.77	0.52	15.90
12/16	52.61	34	19	1.57	0.48	14.43
Annual Growth	(10.9%)	—	—	10.4%	12.2%	13.1%

Glacier Bancorp, Inc.

Glacier Bancorp provide a full range of banking services to both individuals and businesses to about 200 locations in Montana Idaho Utah Washington Arizona Colorado and Wyoming. The bank offers retail banking business banking real estate commercial agriculture and consumer loans as well as mortgage originating and loan servicing.

Geographic Reach

The bank operates in roughly 200 locations including more than 170 branches and more than 20 loan or administrative offices in about 70 counties within Montana Idaho Utah Washington Wyoming Colorado Arizona and Nevada. The state of Montana accounts for the largest percent of deposits of the bank to more than 20%.

Financial Performance

Glacier's financial performance is seeing growth year-by-year for the span of five years with net income being the highest for 2020 and assets seeing an increase as well.

For 2020 the company generated an interest income and non-interest income of $627 million and $172 million respectively. Net income for the year increased $55.8 million to $266 million or 24% higher as compared to the prior year's net income of about $211 million.

Glacier Bancorp ended 2020 with $633 million in cash an increase of more than $300 million over the previous year. Operating activities provided about $190 million. Financing activities provided $633 million while investing activities used $3.6 billion.

Strategy

Glacier Bancorp focuses its growth as a business through internal growth and selective acquisitions.

The company continues to look for profitable expansion opportunities in existing and new markets in the Rocky Mountain and Western states.

Mergers and Acquisitions

On February 2020 Glacier Bancorp Inc. completed its acquisition of State Bank Corp. which is the bank holding company for the State Bank of Arizona. The company acquired the State Bank of Arizona for $125.8 million.

EXECUTIVES

Independent Director, James English
Independent Chairman Of The Board, Craig Langel
Independent Director, Annie Goodwin
President, Chief Executive Officer, Director, Randall Chesler, $799,335 total compensation
Independent Director, Kristen Heck
Independent Director, Robert Cashell
Independent Director, Michael Hormaechea
Independent Director, Douglas McBride
Chief Financial Officer, Executive Vice President, Secretary, Ronald Copher, $432,289 total compensation
Chief Administrative Officer, Executive Vice President, Don Chery, $377,657 total compensation
Independent Director, George Sutton
Auditors: BKD, LLP

LOCATIONS

HQ: Glacier Bancorp, Inc.
49 Commons Loop, Kalispell, MT 59901
Phone: 406 756-4200
Web: www.glacierbank.com

PRODUCTS/OPERATIONS

2016 Sales

	% of total
Interest income	
Commercial loans	47
Investment securities	17
Residential real estate loans	7
Consumer and other loans	7
Non-interest income	
Service charges and other fees	14
Gain on sale of loans	6
Miscellaneous loan fees and charges	1
(Loss) gain on sale of investments	-
Other income	2
Total	**100**

Selected Services

Commercial loan
Consumer loan
Deposits
Mortgage origination services
Real estate loan
Retail brokerage services
Transaction and savings

Selected Bank Divisions

1st Bank (Wyoming)
Bank of the San Juans (Colorado)
Big Sky Western Bank (Montana)
Citizens Community Bank (Idaho)
Collegiate Peaks Bank
First Bank of Montana
First Bank of Wyoming
First Security Bank (Montana)
First State Bank (Wyoming)
Foothills Bank
Glacier Bank (Montana)
Mountain West Bank (Idaho)
North Cascades Bank (Washington)
Valley Bank of Helena (Montana)
Western Security Bank (Montana)

COMPETITORS

ATLANTIC UNION BANKSHARES CORPORATION
BOK FINANCIAL CORPORATION
BYLINE BANCORP INC.
COLUMBIA BANKING SYSTEM INC.
FIRST MIDWEST BANCORP INC.
GERMAN AMERICAN BANCORP INC.
HANCOCK WHITNEY CORPORATION
HEARTLAND FINANCIAL USA INC.
IBERIABANK CORPORATION
INDEPENDENT BANK GROUP INC.
MAINSOURCE FINANCIAL GROUP INC.
NATIONAL BANK HOLDINGS CORPORATION
REPUBLIC BANCORP INC.
UNITED COMMUNITY BANKS INC.
WASHINGTON FEDERAL INC.

HISTORICAL FINANCIALS

Company Type: Public

Income Statement

	ASSETS ($ mil.)	NET INCOME ($ mil.)	INCOME AS % OF ASSETS	EMPLOYEES
12/20	18,504.2	266.4	1.4%	3,032
12/19	13,684.0	210.5	1.5%	3,046
12/18	12,115.4	181.8	1.5%	2,723
12/17	9,706.3	116.3	1.2%	2,354
12/16	9,450.6	121.1	1.3%	2,291
Annual Growth	18.3%	21.8%	—	7.3%

FYE: December 31

2020 Year-End Financials

Return on assets: 1.6%
Return on equity: 12.4%
Long-term debt ($ mil.): —
No. of shares (mil.): 95.4
Sales ($ mil): 799.9
Dividends
Yield: 3.0%
Payout: 49.1%
Market value ($ mil.): 4,391.0

	STOCK PRICE ($) FY Close	P/E High/Low		PER SHARE ($) Earnings	Dividends	Book Value
12/20	46.01	17	10	2.81	1.38	24.18
12/19	45.99	19	16	2.38	1.41	21.25
12/18	39.62	22	17	2.17	1.01	17.93
12/17	39.39	27	21	1.50	1.44	15.37
12/16	36.23	24	14	1.59	1.10	14.59
Annual Growth	6.2%	—	—	15.3%	5.8%	13.4%

Gladstone Commercial Corp

Gladstone Commercial a real estate investment trust (REIT) invests in and owns office and industrial real estate properties. The company owns more than 120 properties in more than 25 states with assets that include office buildings medical office buildings warehouses retail stores and manufacturing facilities. Gladstone generally provides net leases with terms between seven and 15 years for small to very large private and public companies. The business is managed by its external adviser Gladstone Management which is also headed by chairman and CEO David Gladstone. The company's largest revenue generating states are Texas and Florida.

Operations

Gladstone Commercial owns about 120 properties totaling nearly 15 million sq. ft. — including office buildings medical office buildings warehouses retail stores and manufacturing facilities ? across the US states. Virtually all of the REIT's revenue comes from rental income from tenants most of whom sign net leases which require them to pay most or all of a property's operating maintenance repair and insurance costs and real estate taxes.

Geographic Reach

Headquartered in McLean Virginia Gladstone Commercial owns properties in more than 25 states . Texas and Florida account for the most rental revenue with about 15% each followed by Pennsylvania (more than 10%) and Ohio (about 10%). Other large markets include Utah North Carolina Georgia and South Carolina.

Sales and Marketing

Gladstone's largest industry served is telecommunications with more than 15% of the company's total revenue. It also derives at least 10% of its rental revenue from tenants in each of the automobile healthcare and diversified/conglomerate services industries. Its five largest tenants account for approximately 15% of rental revenue.

Financial Performance

Since 2015 Gladstone Commercial's revenue reported yearly increases. Overall revenue growth for that five-year period was 37%.

In 2019 the company reported a revenue of $114.4 million up by 7% from the prior year as lease revenues increased by 7%.

The company net income decreased by 23% to $9.5 million in 2019 owing to increased operating expenses and higher interest expense.

Cash at the end of fiscal 2019 was $11.5 million an increase of 26% from the prior year. Cash contributed from operations was $60.2 million and financing activities added another $74.2 million. Investing activities used $132 million mainly for acquisition of real estate.

Strategy

The company strategy is to invest in and own a diversified portfolio of leased properties (primarily office and industrial) that it believes will produce stable cash flow and increase in value. It may sell some of its real estate assets when its adviser determines that doing so would be advantageous to the company and its stockholders. It also expects to occasionally make mortgage loans secured by the income-producing office or industrial real estate which loans may have some form of equity participation. In addition to cash on hand and cash from operations it uses funds from various other sources to finance its acquisitions and operations including equity Credit Facility mortgage financing and other sources that may become available from time to time. It believes that moderate leverage is prudent and it aspires to become an investment grade borrower over time. It also intends to primarily use non-recourse mortgage financing that will allow it to limit its loss exposure on any property to the amount of equity invested in such property.

On the other hand the company has formed relationships with nationally recognized strategic partners to assist it with the management of its properties in each of its markets. These relationships provide local expertise to ensure that its properties are properly maintained and that its tenants have local points of contact to address prop-

HOOVER'S HANDBOOK OF EMERGING COMPANIES 2022

erty issues. This strategy improves its operating efficiencies increases local market intelligence for the adviser and generally does not increase costs as the local property managers are reimbursed by the tenants in accordance with the lease agreements.

Mergers and Acquisitions

In late 2020 Gladstone Commercial announced that it acquired a 153600 square foot distribution building in Terre Haute Indiana for $10.6 million. The initial capitalization rate for the acquisition was 7.3% with an average capitalization rate of 8.0%. The property is 100% leased by Clabber Girl Corporation with a full guaranty from Clabber Girl's publicly traded parent company B&G Foods. The acquisition of the industrial property is consistent with Gladstone Commercial's strategy of acquiring high-quality industrial assets with creditworthy tenants located in its targeted growth markets.

In early 2020 Gladstone Commercial announced that it acquired a 504400 square foot industrial distribution center in Crandall GA for $30.3 million. The property is 100% leased to Haier US Appliance Solutions Inc. a wholly-owned subsidiary of worldwide appliance leader Haier Smart Home. The acquisition of the Haier facility continues Gladstone Commercial's strategic expansion into its targeted growth locations and a great addition to the company's portfolio.

Company Background

The REIT Gladstone Commercial is part of the Gladstone Companies which include the three affiliated public entities Gladstone Capital Gladstone Investment and Gladstone Land. Gladstone Capital and Gladstone Investment invest in small and medium sized private businesses while Gladstone Land invests in farmland.

EXECUTIVES

Independent Director, Michela English
Independent Director, Walter Wilkinson
Independent Director, Anthony Parker
Lead Independent Director, Paul Adelgren
Vice Chairman Of The Board, Chief Operating Officer, Director, Terry Brubaker
Chairman Of The Board, Chief Executive Officer, Director, David Gladstone
Senior Vice President,southeast Investments, EJ Wislar
Senior Vice President, Asset Management, Perry Finney
Senior Vice President,asset Management, Karen Priesman
Co-president, Arthur Cooper
Chief Financial Officer, Gary Gerson
Co-president, Robert Cutlip
Treasurer, Jay Beckhorn
Independent Director, John Outland
Auditors: PricewaterhouseCoopers LLP

LOCATIONS

HQ: Gladstone Commercial Corp
1521 Westbranch Drive, Suite 100, McLean, VA 22102
Phone: 703 287-5800 **Fax:** 703 287-5801
Web: www.GladstoneCommercial.com

PRODUCTS/OPERATIONS

2017 Sales

	$ mil.	% of total
Rental	92.8	98
Tenant recovery	2.0	2
Total	**94.8**	**100**

COMPETITORS

ACADIA REALTY TRUST
AGREE REALTY CORPORATION
COUSINS PROPERTIES INCORPORATED
DOUGLAS EMMETT INC.
EQUITY ONE INC.
FIRST INDUSTRIAL REALTY TRUST INC.
GETTY REALTY CORP.
JBG SMITH PROPERTIES
KITE REALTY GROUP TRUST
LIBERTY PROPERTY TRUST
REALTY INCOME CORPORATION
WEINGARTEN REALTY INVESTORS

HISTORICAL FINANCIALS

Company Type: Public

Income Statement

FYE: December 31

	REVENUE ($ mil.)	NET INCOME ($ mil.)	NET PROFIT MARGIN	EMPLOYEES
12/21	137.6	9.7	7.1%	0
12/20	133.1	14.9	11.2%	0
12/19	114.3	9.6	8.4%	0
12/18	106.8	12.3	11.5%	0
12/17	94.8	5.9	6.3%	0
Annual Growth	**9.8%**	**13.3%**	**—**	**—**

2021 Year-End Financials

Debt ratio: 61.8%
Return on equity: 2.6%
Cash ($ mil.): 7.9
Current ratio: 2.01
Long-term debt ($ mil.): 707.5
No. of shares (mil.): 38.0
Dividends
Yield: 5.8%
Payout: 3,004.3%
Market value ($ mil.): 981.0

	STOCK PRICE ($) FY Close	P/E High/Low		PER SHARE ($) Earnings	Dividends	Book Value
12/21	25.77	—	—	(0.12)	1.50	9.76
12/20	18.00	251	87	0.09	1.50	10.32
12/19	21.86	—	—	(0.16)	1.50	10.79
12/18	17.92	694	561	0.03	1.50	11.13
12/17	21.06	—	—	(0.19)	1.50	11.96
Annual Growth	**5.2%**	—	—	—	**0.0%**	**(5.0%)**

Global Net Lease Inc

Auditors: PricewaterhouseCoopers LLP

LOCATIONS

HQ: Global Net Lease Inc
650 Fifth Ave., 30th Floor, New York, NY 10019
Phone: 212 415-6500
Web: www.globalnetlease.com

HISTORICAL FINANCIALS

Company Type: Public

Income Statement

FYE: December 31

	REVENUE ($ mil.)	NET INCOME ($ mil.)	NET PROFIT MARGIN	EMPLOYEES
12/20	330.1	10.7	3.3%	1
12/19	306.2	46.4	15.2%	1
12/18	282.2	10.9	3.9%	1
12/17	259.3	23.5	9.1%	1
12/16	214.1	47.1	22.0%	1
Annual Growth	**11.4%**	**(30.9%)**	**—**	**0.0%**

2020 Year-End Financials

Debt ratio: 57.1%
Return on equity: 0.6%
Cash ($ mil.): 124.2
Current ratio: 0.36
Long-term debt ($ mil.): 1,774.9
No. of shares (mil.): 89.6
Dividends
Yield: 10.1%
Payout: —
Market value ($ mil.): 1,536.0

	STOCK PRICE ($) FY Close	P/E High/Low		PER SHARE ($) Earnings	Dividends	Book Value
12/20	17.14	—	—	(0.09)	1.73	17.10
12/19	20.28	51	44	0.39	2.13	18.98
12/18	17.62	2222	1564	0.01	2.13	18.74
12/17	20.58	83	25	0.30	1.78	21.00
12/16	7.83	11	8	0.81	0.00	20.34
Annual Growth	**21.6%**	—	—	—	**—**	**(4.2%)**

Globus Medical Inc

Globus Medical makes procedural and therapeutic medical devices used during spinal surgery. Offerings range from screws and plates to disc replacement systems and bone void fillers. The company has two product segments: Musculoskeletal Solutions (implantable devices biologics surgical instruments and accessories) and Enabling Technologies (imaging navigation and robotic-assisted surgery systems). Globus Medical has more than 220 spinal devices on the market in the US where it earns most of its revenue; its products are also sold in more than 50 countries worldwide.

Operations

The company manages two product categories: Musculoskeletal Solutions and Enabling Technologies.

Musculoskeletal Solutions (about 95% of total revenue) consist primarily of implantable devices biologics accessories and unique surgical instruments used in an expansive range of spinal orthopedic and neurosurgical procedures. Its broad spectrum of spine products addresses the vast majority of conditions affecting the spine including degenerative conditions deformity tumors and trauma. It includes traditional fusion implants such as pedicle screw and rod systems plating systems intervertebral spacers and corpectomy devices.

Enabling Technologies (about 5%) are comprised of imaging navigation and robotics (INR) solutions for assisted surgery which are advanced computer-assisted intelligent systems designed to enhance a surgeon's capabilities and ultimately improve patient care and reduce radiation exposure for all involved by streamlining surgical procedures to be safer less invasive and more accurate. It includes the ExcelsiusGPS platform a robotic guidance and navigation system that supports minimally invasive and open procedures by improving visualization of patient anatomy using patient images and by guiding instruments and implants to the specified trajectory using a robotic arm to ultimately enhance the surgeon's decision making process.

Geographic Reach

Headquartered in Audubon Pennsylvania Globus Medical has research and manufacturing facilities in Massachusetts Pennsylvania and Texas and distribution center in Heerlen Netherlands for its international operations. The US is the largest single market accounting for about 85% of total revenue.

Sales and Marketing
Globus Medical serves hospitals ambulatory surgery centers and physicians as wells as patients with musculoskeletal disorders. It sell products through a combination of direct sales representatives and distributor sales representatives by exclusive independent distributors who distribute products for a commission that is generally based on a percentage of sales.

The company's advertising expense was $0.6 million $1.1 million and $1.9 million for the years ended December 31 2020 2019 and 2018 respectively.

Financial Performance
The company's revenue for fiscal 2020 increased by 1% to $789.0 million compared from the prior year with $785.4 million.

Net income for fiscal 2020 decreased to $102.3 million compared from the prior year with $155.2 million.

Cash held by the company at the end of fiscal 2020 increased to $239.4 million. Cash provided by operations was $198.8 million while cash used for investing and financing activities were $117.3 million and $38.7 million respectively. Main uses for cash were purchases of marketable securities and repurchase of common stock.

Strategy
The company's goal is to become the market leader in providing innovative Musculoskeletal Solutions and Enabling Technologies to promote healing in patients with musculoskeletal disorders. To achieve this goal it employs the following business strategies:

Leverage its integrated product development engine by developing new Musculoskeletal Solutions products and Enabling Technologies products using its product development engine. The company believes its team-oriented approach active surgeon input and demonstrated capabilities position it to maintain a rapid rate of new product launches. It launched 10 new products in 20 have potential new products in various stages of development and expect to regularly launch new products;

Increase the size scope and productivity of its exclusive US sales force by increasing the number of its direct and distributor sales representatives in the United States to expand into new geographic territories and to deepen its penetration in existing territories. It will also continue to provide its sales representatives with specialized development programs designed to improve their productivity;

Continue to expand into international markets by increasing its international presence through the commercialization of additional Musculoskeletal Solutions and Enabling Technologies products and the expansion of its international sales force; and

Pursue strategic acquisitions and alliances that complement its strategic plan and provide innovative technologies personnel with significant relevant experience or increased market penetration. It is currently evaluating possible acquisitions and strategic relationships and believes that its resources and experience make it an attractive acquirer or partner.

Company Background
Globus Medical was founded in 2003 by CEO David Paul a former product development director at medical device maker Synthes. Globus Medical relied on venture capital funding prior to its 2012 IPO.

In 2016 Globus Medical acquired the international business of medical device firm Alphatec for $80 million. The deal included international distribution operations in Japan Brazil the UK Italy and other nations.

In 2017 Globus Medical acquired KB Medical a Swiss robotics developer. That transaction underscored the firm's commitment to producing robotic technology for surgeries.

EXECUTIVES

President, Chief Executive Officer, Director, David Demski, $483,972 total compensation
Executive Chairman Of The Board, David Paul, $403,309 total compensation
Senior Vice President, General Counsel, Corporate Secretary, Kelly Huller, $315,000 total compensation
Independent Director, Ann Rhoads
Executive Vice President, Chief Commercial Officer And President - Trauma, Daniel Scavilla, $384,080 total compensation
Chief Financial Officer, Senior Vice President, Keith Pfeil, $339,900 total compensation
Independent Director, Daniel Lemaitre
Auditors: DELOITTE & TOUCHE LLP

LOCATIONS

HQ: Globus Medical Inc
2560 General Armistead Avenue, Audubon, PA 19403
Phone: 610 930-1800 **Fax:** 302 636-5454
Web: www.globusmedical.com

PRODUCTS/OPERATIONS

2015 Sales

	$ mil.	% of total
Innovative fusion	288.1	53
Disruptive technologies	256.7	47
Total	**544.8**	**100**

Selected Products
Innovative Fusion Products:
Cervical
ASSURE (anterior cervical plate system)
ELLIPSE (posterior occipital cervical thoracic stabilization system)
PROVIDENCE (anterior cervical plate system)
VIP (anterior cervical plate system)
XTEND (anterior cervical plate system)
Thoracolumbar:
BEACON Posted Screw (posted pedicle screw system)
REVERE Degen (comprehensive pedicle screw and rod system)
SI-LOK (sacroiliac joint fixation system)
Interbody/Corpectomy
COALITION (anterior cervical stand-alone fusion device)
COLONIAL (anterior cervical interbody fusion device)
FORTIFY (self-locking expandable corpectomy device)
INDEPENDENCE (anterior lumbar stand-alone fusion device)
SUSTAIN (spacers for partial or complete vertebrectomy)
XPAND (expandable corpectomy spacer)
Deformity Tumor and Trauma
REVERE Anterior (pedicle screw and rod deformity system)
REVERE Deformity (comprehensive pedicle screw hook and rod deformity system)
TRUSS (lateral compressible thoracolumbar plate system)
Minimally Invasive Surgery Products:
CALIBER (expandable posterior lumbar interbody fusion device)
CALIBER-L (expandable lateral lumbar fusion device)
INTERCONTINENTAL (lateral lumbar interbody fusion device)
MARS 3V (three-blade retractor system)
REVOLVE (minimally invasive pedicle screw and rod system)
SIGNATURE (articulating transforaminal interbody fusion device)
TRANSCONTINENTAL (lateral lumbar interbody fusion device)
Motion Preservation:
FLEXUS (minimally invasive unilateral PEEK interspinous process spacer)
ORBIT-R (anterior lumbar disc replacement)
SECURE-CR (articulating cervical disc replacement device)
SP-FIX (interspinous process fusion device)
TRANSITION (stabilization system)
TRIUMPH (transforaminal lumbar disc replacement device)
ZYFLEX (stabilization system)

COMPETITORS

ANGIODYNAMICS INC.	HOLOGIC INC.
ANIKA THERAPEUTICS INC.	MERIT MEDICAL SYSTEMS INC.
BOSTON SCIENTIFIC CORPORATION	QUIDEL CORPORATION SURGALIGN SPINE
CARDIOVASCULAR SYSTEMS INC.	TECHNOLOGIES
INC.	SURGICAL INNOVATIONS
CONMED CORPORATION	LIMITED
DEXCOM INC. SYSTEMS	VARIAN MEDICAL
ENDOLOGIX INC.	INC.

HISTORICAL FINANCIALS
Company Type: Public

Income Statement
FYE: December 31

	REVENUE ($ mil.)	NET INCOME ($ mil.)	NET PROFIT MARGIN	EMPLOYEES
12/21	958.1	149.1	15.6%	2,400
12/20	789.0	102.2	13.0%	2,200
12/19	785.3	155.2	19.8%	2,000
12/18	712.9	156.4	21.9%	1,800
12/17	635.9	107.3	16.9%	1,500
Annual Growth	**10.8%**	**8.6%**	—	**12.5%**

2021 Year-End Financials

Debt ratio: —	No. of shares (mil.): 101.5
Return on equity: 9.1%	Dividends
Cash ($ mil.): 193.0	Yield: —
Current ratio: 6.17	Payout: —
Long-term debt ($ mil.): —	Market value ($ mil.): 7,331.0

	STOCK PRICE ($) FY Close	P/E High/Low	Earnings	PER SHARE ($) Dividends	Book Value
12/21	72.20	57 41	1.44	0.00	17.15
12/20	65.22	63 34	1.01	0.00	15.11
12/19	58.88	38 24	1.52	0.00	14.05
12/18	43.28	36 26	1.54	0.00	12.03
12/17	41.10	37 22	1.10	0.00	10.01
Annual Growth	**15.1%**	— —	**7.0%**	—	**14.4%**

GMS Inc

Auditors: Ernst & Young LLP

LOCATIONS

HQ: GMS Inc
100 Crescent Centre Parkway, Suite 800, Tucker, GA 30084
Phone: 800 392-4619
Web: www.gms.com

HISTORICAL FINANCIALS

Company Type: Public

Income Statement				FYE: April 30
	REVENUE ($ mil.)	NET INCOME ($ mil.)	NET PROFIT MARGIN	EMPLOYEES
04/21	3,298.8	105.5	3.2%	5,843
04/20	3,241.3	23.3	0.7%	5,308
04/19	3,116.0	56.0	1.8%	5,800
04/18	2,511.4	62.9	2.5%	4,600
04/17	2,319.1	48.8	2.1%	4,400
Annual Growth	9.2%	21.2%	—	7.3%

2021 Year-End Financials

Debt ratio: 39.3%
Return on equity: 14.5%
Cash ($ mil.): 167.0
Current ratio: 1.96
Long-term debt ($ mil.): 932.4

No. of shares (mil.): 43.0
Dividends
  Yield: —
  Payout: —
Market value ($ mil.): 1,883.0

	STOCK PRICE ($) FY Close	P/E High/Low		PER SHARE ($) Earnings	Dividends	Book Value
04/21	43.71	19	7	2.44	0.00	19.09
04/20	18.38	57	19	0.55	0.00	14.90
04/19	17.62	24	10	1.31	0.00	15.58
04/18	31.16	25	18	1.49	0.00	14.11
04/17	36.16	30	17	1.19	0.00	12.56
Annual Growth	4.9%	—	—	19.7%	—	11.0%

GoDaddy Inc

Auditors: Ernst & Young LLP

LOCATIONS

HQ: GoDaddy Inc
  2155 E. GoDaddy Way, Tempe, AZ 85284
Phone: 480 505-8800
Web: www.godaddy.com

HISTORICAL FINANCIALS

Company Type: Public

Income Statement				FYE: December 31
	REVENUE ($ mil.)	NET INCOME ($ mil.)	NET PROFIT MARGIN	EMPLOYEES
12/21	3,815.7	242.3	6.4%	6,611
12/20	3,316.7	(495.1)	—	6,621
12/19	2,988.1	137.0	4.6%	7,024
12/18	2,660.1	77.1	2.9%	6,821
12/17	2,231.9	136.4	6.1%	5,990
Annual Growth	14.3%	15.4%	—	2.5%

2021 Year-End Financials

Debt ratio: 52.3%
Return on equity: 704.3%
Cash ($ mil.): 1,255.7
Current ratio: 0.78
Long-term debt ($ mil.): 3,858.2

No. of shares (mil.): 167.2
Dividends
  Yield: —
  Payout: —
Market value ($ mil.): 14,190.0

	STOCK PRICE ($) FY Close	P/E High/Low		PER SHARE ($) Earnings	Dividends	Book Value
12/21	84.86	64	46	1.42	0.00	0.49
12/20	82.95	—	—	(2.94)	0.00	(0.08)
12/19	67.92	103	76	0.76	0.00	4.43
12/18	65.62	168	98	0.45	0.00	4.53
12/17	50.28	41	28	0.79	0.00	2.90
Annual Growth	14.0% (35.9%)	—	—	15.8%	—	—

Goldman Sachs BDC Inc

Auditors: PricewaterhouseCoopers LLP

LOCATIONS

HQ: Goldman Sachs BDC Inc
  200 West Street, New York, NY 10282
Phone: 212 902-0300
Web: www.goldmansachsbdc.com

HISTORICAL FINANCIALS

Company Type: Public

Income Statement				FYE: December 31
	REVENUE ($ mil.)	NET INCOME ($ mil.)	NET PROFIT MARGIN	EMPLOYEES
12/20	172.9	109.9	63.5%	0
12/19	147.2	79.7	54.1%	0
12/18	146.7	82.8	56.5%	0
12/17	136.7	79.9	58.5%	0
12/16	125.1	76.2	60.9%	0
Annual Growth	8.4%	9.6%	—	—

2020 Year-End Financials

Debt ratio: 49.1%
Return on equity: 9.5%
Cash ($ mil.): 32.1
Current ratio: 0.87
Long-term debt ($ mil.): 1,627.0

No. of shares (mil.): 101.5
Dividends
  Yield: 9.4%
  Payout: 88.2%
Market value ($ mil.): 1,941.0

	STOCK PRICE ($) FY Close	P/E High/Low		PER SHARE ($) Earnings	Dividends	Book Value
12/20	19.12	11	4	2.04	1.80	15.91
12/19	21.28	11	9	1.98	1.80	16.75
12/18	18.38	11	9	2.06	1.80	17.65
12/17	22.18	20	17	1.28	1.80	18.09
12/16	23.52	21	16	1.12	1.80	18.31
Annual Growth	(5.0%)	—	—	16.2%	(0.0%)	(3.5%)

Good Times Restaurants Inc.

Good Times Restaurants operates and franchises more than 50 Good Times Drive Thru fast-food eateries located primarily in the Denver area. The hamburger chain is made up mostly of double drive-through and walk-up eateries that feature a menu of burgers fries and frozen custard. A limited number of Good Times outlets also offer dine-in seating. More than 20 of the locations are operated by franchisees while the rest are co-owned and co-operated under joint venture agreements. The family of director Geoffrey Bailey owns almost 30% of the company.

EXECUTIVES

Act Ceo, Ryan Zink
Chb*, Robert J Stetson
Cfo, James K Zielke
V Pres Oprs, Scott G Lefever
Controller, Susan M Knutson
Independent Director, Jason Maceda
Auditors: Moss Adams LLP

LOCATIONS

HQ: Good Times Restaurants Inc.
  651 Corporate Circle, Golden, CO 80401
Phone: 303 384-1400
Web: www.goodtimesburgers.com

COMPETITORS

CHECKERS DRIVE-IN	MCDONALD'S
RESTAURANTS	
RESTAURANTS INC.	LIMITED
KFC CORPORATION	

HISTORICAL FINANCIALS

Company Type: Public

Income Statement				FYE: September 28
	REVENUE ($ mil.)	NET INCOME ($ mil.)	NET PROFIT MARGIN	EMPLOYEES
09/21	123.9	16.7	13.5%	2,230
09/20	109.8	(13.9)	—	2,318
09/19	110.7	(5.1)	—	2,535
09/18	99.2	(1.0)	—	2,368
09/17	79.0	(2.2)	—	1,970
Annual Growth	11.9%	—	—	3.1%

2021 Year-End Financials

Debt ratio: —
Return on equity: 77.5%
Cash ($ mil.): 8.8
Current ratio: 0.89
Long-term debt ($ mil.): —

No. of shares (mil.): 12.1
Dividends
  Yield: —
  Payout: —
Market value ($ mil.): 62.0

	STOCK PRICE ($) FY Close	P/E High/Low		PER SHARE ($) Earnings	Dividends	Book Value
09/21	5.15	4	1	1.31	0.00	2.45
09/20	1.42	—	—	(1.10)	0.00	1.09
09/19	1.68	—	—	(0.41)	0.00	2.18
09/18	4.88	—	—	(0.08)	0.00	2.72
09/17	2.85	—	—	(0.18)	0.00	2.78
Annual Growth	15.9%	—	—	—	—	(3.1%)

Goosehead Insurance Inc

Auditors: DELOITTE & TOUCHE LLP

LOCATIONS

HQ: Goosehead Insurance Inc
1500 Solana Blvd., Building 4, Suite 4500, Westlake, TX 76262
Phone: 469 480-3669
Web: www.goosehead.com

HISTORICAL FINANCIALS
Company Type: Public

Income Statement				FYE: December 31
	ASSETS ($ mil.)	NET INCOME ($ mil.)	INCOME AS % OF ASSETS	EMPLOYEES
12/20	185.8	9.2	5.0%	949
12/19	64.6	3.5	5.5%	595
12/18	34.8	(8.9)	—	403
12/17	16.7	8.6	51.9%	282
12/16	8.6	4.7	54.3%	0
Annual Growth	115.0%	18.4%	—	—

2020 Year-End Financials

Return on assets: 7.4%
Return on equity: ***,***.*%
Long-term debt ($ mil.): —
No. of shares (mil.): 36.7
Sales ($ mil): 117.0

Dividends
Yield: 0.9%
Payout: 383.1%
Market value ($ mil.): 4,585.0

	STOCK PRICE ($) FY Close	P/E High/Low	Earnings	Dividends	Book Value
12/20	124.76	238 71	0.51	1.15	(0.13)
12/19	42.40	213 103	0.22	0.41	(0.25)
12/18	26.29	— —	(0.66)	0.00	(0.00)
Annual Growth	117.8%	— —	—	—	—

GrafTech International Ltd

GrafTech International is a leading maker in the US of graphite electrodes which are essential to the production of electric arc furnaces steel and various other ferrous and nonferrous metals. GrafTech has the most competitive portfolio of low-cost ultra-high power (UHP) graphite electrode manufacturing facilities in the industry including three of the highest capacity facilities in the world. It is the only large scale graphite electrode producer that is substantially vertically integrated into petroleum needle coke a key raw material for graphite electrode manufacturing. Customers have included major steel producers and other ferrous and non-ferrous metal producers which sell their products into the automotive construction appliance machinery equipment and transportation industries. Majority of its sales were generated outside US. The company traces its roots back to 1886.

Operations
GrafTech's only reportable segment Industrial Materials is comprised of its two major product categories: graphite electrodes and needle coke products. Needle coke is the key raw material to producing graphite electrodes. The Industrial Materials segment manufactures high-quality graphite

electrodes essential to the production of EAF steel and other ferrous and non-ferrous metals.

Overall its graphite electrodes generated more than 95% of sales of which over 85% comes from long-term agreements. The remaining less than 5% comes from by-products and other.

Geographic Reach
Headquartered in Ohio the company has sales offices and manufacturing facilities in Mexico Pennsylvania Texas Brazil France Spain and Switzerland. It currently has the capacity to manufacture approximately 202000 metric tons of graphite electrodes annually. GrafTech gets about 80% of its total sales from outside the US with the EMEA region accounting to about 55%.

Sales and Marketing
The company sells its products primarily through a direct sales force independent sales representatives and distributors. Its customers include major steel producers and other ferrous and nonferrous metal producers in Europe Russia and other Commonwealth of Independent States countries the Middle East and Africa (collectively EMEA) the Americas and Asia-Pacific (APAC) which sell their products into the automotive construction appliance machinery equipment and transportation industries.

Financial Performance
Net sales decreased by $566.4 million or 32% from $1.8 billion in 2019 to $1.2 billion in 2020. This decrease was primarily driven by a 21% decrease in sales volume of GrafTech manufactured electrodes and decreased pricing for its products both driven by lower customer demand as a result of the COVID-19 pandemic and prolonged customer destocking taking place for the majority of 2020.

In 2020 the company had a net income of $434.4 million a 42% decrease from the previous year.

The company's cash at the end of 2020 was $145.4 million. Operating activities generated $563.6 million while financing activities used $463.7 million primarily for principal payments on long-term debt. Investing activities used another $35.7 million mainly for capital expenditures.

Strategy
In 2017 the company reoriented its commercial strategy around a long-term take-or-pay contract framework and restructured its sales force incentives. As graphite electrodes are an essential consumable in the EAF steel production process and require a long lead time to manufacture the company believes its strategic customers are highly focused on securing certainty of supply of reliable high-quality graphite electrodes. Prior to the company's long-term take-or-pay contract initiative its sales of graphite electrodes were generally negotiated annually through purchase orders on an uncontracted nonbinding basis. The majority of its customers sought to secure orders for a supply of their anticipated volume requirements each upcoming year. The remaining small balance of the company's graphite electrode customers purchased their electrodes as needed throughout the year at industry spot prices.

EXECUTIVES

Director, David Gregory
Senior Vice President, Quinn Coburn, $393,383 total compensation
Chairman Of The Board, Dennis Turcotte
Independent Director, Catherine Clegg

Presiding Independent Director, Michel Dumas
Independent Director, Brian Acton
Chief Legal Officer, Corporate Secretary, Gina Gunning, $355,366 total compensation
Independent Director, Leslie Dunn
Senior Vice President - Commercial, Inigo Perez Ortiz, $370,269 total compensation
Independent Director, Henry Keizer
Independent Director, Debra Fine
Independent Director, Jean-Marc Germain
Chief Financial Officer, Vice President - Finance, Treasurer, Timothy Flanagan
President, Chief Executive Officer, Director, David Rintoul, $691,875 total compensation
Chief Operating Officer, Executive Vice President, Jeremy Halford, $461,250 total compensation
Auditors: DELOITTE & TOUCHE LLP

LOCATIONS

HQ: GrafTech International Ltd
982 Keynote Circle, Brooklyn Heights, OH 44131
Phone: 216 676-2000
Web: www.graftech.com

PRODUCTS/OPERATIONS

Selected Products
Carbon and graphite cathodes (conductors of electricity in aluminum smelters)
Carbon electrodes (used to produce silicon metal ferronickel and thermal phosphorus)
Flexible graphite (used in gaskets and other sealing applications)
Graphite electrodes (used to generate heat for melting steel in steel minimills)
Refractory products (carbon and graphite used to protect walls of blast furnaces)

COMPETITORS

3M TECHNICAL CERAMICS CO.LTD.	NIPPON CARBON
INC.	NLMK PAO
CABOT CORPORATION	Raymor Industries Inc
HAYNES INTERNATIONAL INC.	SCHUNK CARBON TECHNOLOGY LLC
JAPAN STEEL WORKS LTD.	SGL COMPOSITES
INC. THE	SPECIAL METALS
LUXFER HOLDINGS PLC	CORPORATION
MECHEL PAO	TIMKENSTEEL
MINTEQ INTERNATIONAL INC.	CORPORATION
	TOKAI CARBON CO. LTD.

HISTORICAL FINANCIALS
Company Type: Public

Income Statement				FYE: December 31
	REVENUE ($ mil.)	NET INCOME ($ mil.)	NET PROFIT MARGIN	EMPLOYEES
12/20	1,224.3	434.3	35.5%	1,285
12/19	1,790.7	744.6	41.6%	1,346
12/18	1,895.9	854.2	45.1%	1,387
12/17	550.7	7.9	1.4%	1,310
12/16	437.9	(235.8)	—	1,244
Annual Growth	29.3%	—	—	0.8%

2020 Year-End Financials

Debt ratio: 99.1%
Return on equity: ***,***.*%
Cash ($ mil.): 145.4
Current ratio: 3.18
Long-term debt ($ mil.): 1,420.0

No. of shares (mil.): 267.1
Dividends
Yield: 1.0%
Payout: 7.1%
Market value ($ mil.): 2,848.0

STOCK PRICE ($)	P/E	PER SHARE ($)		
FY Close	High/Low	Earnings	Dividends	Book Value
12/20 10.66	8 4	1.62	0.12	(1.23)
12/19 11.62	6 4	2.58	0.34	(2.55)
12/18 11.44	8 4	2.87	0.93	(3.71)
Annual Growth (3.5%)	— —	(24.9%)	(64.9%)	—

Granite Falls Energy LLC

EXECUTIVES

Independent Vice Chairman Of The Board Of Governor, Rodney Wilkison
Chairman Of The Board Of Governors, Paul Enstad
Independent Governor, Robin Spaude
Chief Financial Officer, Stacie Schuler, $219,158 total compensation
Secretary, Governor, Dean Buesing
Plant Manager, Cory Heinrich
Independent Governor, Sherry Larson
Independent Governor, Leslie Bergquist
Independent Governor, Bruce Lavigne
Independent Governor, Kenton Johnson
Independent Governor, Marten Goulet
Risk Manager, Eric Baukol, $96,363 total compensation
Auditors: Boulay PLLP

LOCATIONS

HQ: Granite Falls Energy LLC
15045 Highway 23 S.E., Granite Falls, MN 56241-0216
Phone: 320 564-3100
Web: www.granitefallsenergy.com

HISTORICAL FINANCIALS

Company Type: Public

Income Statement   FYE: October 31

	REVENUE ($ mil.)	NET INCOME ($ mil.)	NET PROFIT MARGIN	EMPLOYEES
10/21	309.6	23.6	7.6%	82
10/20	164.9	(13.2)	—	82
10/19	208.7	(8.3)	—	82
10/18	210.3	2.8	1.4%	82
10/17	215.7	11.4	5.3%	82
Annual Growth	9.4%	19.8%	—	0.0%

2021 Year-End Financials

Debt ratio: 22.5%
Return on equity: 37.5%
Cash ($ mil.): 29.3
Current ratio: 2.16
Long-term debt ($ mil.): 27.6
No. of shares (mil.): 0.0
Dividends
  Yield: —
  Payout: —
Market value ($ mil.): —

STOCK PRICE ($)	P/E	PER SHARE ($)		
FY Close	High/Low	Earnings	Dividends	Book Value
10/21 0.00 2,415.27	— —	772.96	0.00	
10/20 1,800.00 1,702.66	— —	(433.85)	0.00	
10/19 2,000.00 2,139.08	— —	(274.16)	40.00	
10/18 3,200.00 2,453.24	37 33	93.58	385.00	
Annual Growth —	— —	102.1%	—	(0.5%)

Gray Television Inc

Gray Television is one of the largest independent operators of TV stations in the US. It owns and operates local TV stations in nearly 95 markets including some 150 affiliates of ABC NBC CBS and FOX. Its station portfolio reaches about 25% of total US TV households. The company also owns video production marketing and digital businesses including Raycom Sports Tupelo-Raycom and RTM Studios. Revenue comes primarily from broadcast and internet ads and from retransmission consent fees. Gray Television's roots begin in January 1891 with the creation of the Albany Herald in Albany Georgia.

Operations

The company operates in two business segments: Broadcasting and Production companies.

The broadcasting segment operates television stations in local markets in the United States. It generates for more than 95% of company's revenue.

The production companies segment which accounts for less than 5% of revenue includes the production of television and event content.

Among the company's type of revenues retransmission consent generates most of the sales accounting to over 35%.

Geographic Reach

The company principal executive offices are located in Atlanta Georgia. The company's largest market by revenue were Charlotte North Carolina and Cleveland-Akron Ohio which each contributed approximately 5% of total revenue.

Sales and Marketing

Gray Television is diversified across its markets and network affiliations. Its CBS-affiliated channels accounted for about 36% of the company's revenue; NBC-affiliated channels accounted for more than 30%; ABC-affiliated channels accounted for nearly 15%; and FOX-affiliated channels accounted for about 10%.

The company refer to CBS NBC ABC and FOX collectively as the "Big Four". Its top 10 markets by revenue contributed nearly 25% of sales.

The company's advertising expense $1 million $2 million and $1 million for 2020 2019 and 2018 respectively.

Financial Performance

Total revenue increased by 12% to $2.4 billion for 2020 compared to 2019 primarily as a result of increased political advertising revenue due to 2020 being the "on-year" of the two-year election cycle and increases in retransmission consent revenue. Political advertising revenue increased approximately $362 million or 532% to $430 million. Retransmission consent revenue increased by approximately $71 million or 9% to $867 million primarily due to higher retransmission consent rates.

The company's net income increased by $231 million or $358 million in 2020 compared to $127 million from 2019.

Cash at the end of 2020 was $773 million. Cash from operations was $652 million while investing activities used $211 million. Financing activities contributed $120 million. Main cash uses in 2020 were for acquisition of television businesses and licenses purchases of property and equipment and long-term debt repayment.

Strategy

The company's success is based on the following strategies: Grow by leveraging its diverse national footprint; Maintain and grow its market leadership position; Continue to monetize digital spectrum; Continue to maintain prudent cost management; Further strengthen its balance sheet; and Continue to pursue strategic growth and accretive acquisition opportunities.

Gray Television intends to maintain its market leadership position through continued prudent investment in its news and syndicated programs as well as continued technological advances and workflow improvements. Gray Television expect to continue to invest in technological upgrades in the future. The company believes the foregoing will help it maintain and grow its market leadership; thereby enhancing its ability to grow and further diversify its revenues and cash flows.

In addition to each of Gray Television stations' primary channel the company also broadcast a number of secondary channels. Certain of its secondary channels are affiliated with more than one network simultaneously. The company's strategy includes expanding upon its digital offerings and sales. Gay Television also evaluate opportunities to use spectrum for future delivery of data to mobile devices using a new transmission standard.

Mergers and Acquisitions

In May 2021 Gray Television announced a deal with Meredith Corp. to acquire 17 TV stations for about 2.7 billion. Gray's acquisition of Meredith's television stations will transform Gray into the nation's second largest television broadcaster. Gray's portfolio of television stations including all announced transactions and less divestitures will serve 113 local markets reaching approximately 36 percent of US television households. Meredith plans to focus on magazine publishing and digital assets and to spin off its National Media Group unit to existing shareholders involved in the transaction with the company.

In early 2021 Gray Television agreed to acquire all of the outstanding shares of capital stock of Illinois-based Quincy for $925 million in cash. Upon closing the transaction Gray will own television stations serving 102 television markets that collectively reach 25.4 percent of US television households including the number-one ranked television station in 77 markets and the first and/or second highest ranked television station in 93 markets according to Comscore's average all-day ratings for calendar year 2020. With the addition of these professionals and their stations Gray will become a stronger company with an even larger platform of high quality television stations to better serve the public interest first.

The company ended the year with the acquisition of television Station KLCW-TV (CW) and certain low power television stations in the Lubbock Texas market (DMA 142) as well as certain non-license assets of KJTV-TV (FOX) and two additional low power stations and certain real estate for a combined purchase price of $23 million using cash on hand.

In late 2020 the company entered into a new network affiliation agreement with the FOX Broadcasting Network for one of its television stations in the Sioux Falls South Dakota television market (DMA 115) that utilize certain non-license assets that Gray acquired at the same time from Independent Communications Inc. for $22 million using cash on hand for the former FOX affiliate for the market.

In 2020 the company acquired certain non-license assets of WLTZ-TV (NBC) in the Columbus Georgia market (DMA129) and entered into shared services and other related agreements with SagamoreHill of Columbus GA LLC to provide news and back-office services to WLTZ-TV. The transaction totaled to $22 million to SagamoreHill using cash on hand.

In mid-2020 Gray Television completed the acquisition of television station operations in the Anchorage and Juneau Alaska television market (DMA 148 and 207 respectively) for $19 million using cash on hand.

In early 2020 Gray Television announced a strategic partnership with TEGNA in which Gray will acquire a minority ownership interest in Premion TEGNA's leading Connected TV (CTV)/overthe-top (OTT) advertising business. As part of this new partnership Gray will serve as a reseller of Premion's services across all of Gray's 93 television markets. Under the terms of the agreement Gray will resell Premion in its local television markets and TEGNA and Gray will each have the right to independently sell Premion in markets where they both operate a local television station.

EXECUTIVES

Executive Vice President, Chief Operating Officer, Local Media, Robert Smith, $715,000 total compensation
President, Co-chief Executive Officer, Director, Donald Laplatney, $1,040,000 total compensation
Executive Vice President, Chief Legal And Development Officer, Secretary, Kevin Latek, $794,351 total compensation
Director, Robin Howell
Independent Director, T. L. Elder
Independent Director, Luis Garcia
Independent Director, Paul Mctear
Independent Director, Sterling Spainhour
Executive Chairman Of The Board, Chief Executive Officer, Hilton Howell, $1,227,633 total compensation
Chief Financial Officer, Executive Vice President, James Ryan, $754,961 total compensation
Independent Director, Richard Hare
Independent Director, Richard Boger
Lead Independent Director, Howell Newton
Auditors: RSM US LLP

LOCATIONS

HQ: Gray Television Inc
4370 Peachtree Road N.E., Atlanta, GA 30319
Phone: 404 504-9828
Web: www.gray.tv

PRODUCTS/OPERATIONS

2016 sales

	% of total
Local	50
National	12
Political	11
Retransmission consent	25
Other	2
Total	**100**

Selected Television Stations

KAKE (ABC; Wichita-Hutchinson KS)
KBTX (CBS; Bryan TX)
KCRG (ABC MY ANT; Cedar Rapids IA)
KCWY (NBC; Casper WY)
KGIN (CBS; Grand Island NE)
KGWN (CBS NBC CW; Cheyenne WY)
KKCO (NBC; Grand Junction CO)
KKTV (CBS; Colorado Springs CO)
KLBY (ABC; Colby KS)
KMVT (CBS CWTwin Falls ID)
KNOE (CBS CW ABC; Monroe-El Dorado LA)
KOLN (CBS; Lincoln-Hastings-Kearney NE)
KOLO (ABC; Reno NV)
KOSA(CBS MY; Odessa - Midland TX)
KSNB (NBC MY; Lincoln - Hastings - Kearney NE)
KSTB (CBS CW; Scottsbluff NE)
KSVT (FOX MY; Twin Falls ID)
KUPK (ABC; Garden City KS)
KWTX (CBS; Waco-Temple-Bryan TX)
KXII (CBS; ShermanTX)
WAGM (FOX CBS; Presque Isle ME)
WAHU (FOX; Charlottesville VA)
WBKO (ABC; Bowling Green KY)
WCAV (CBS; Charlottesville VA)
WCTV (CBS; Tallahassee FL)
WEAU (NBC La Crosse-Eau Claire WI)
WHSV (ABC; Harrisonburg VA)
WIBW (CBS; Topeka KS)
WIFR (CBS; Rockford IL)
WILX (NBC; Lansing MI)
WITN (NBC; Greenville NC)
WJHG (NBC; Panama City FL)
WKYT (CBS; Lexington KY)
WMTV (NBC; Madison WI)
WNDU (NBC; South Bend IN)
WOWT (NBC; Omaha NE)
WRDW (CBS; Augusta GA)
WSAW (CBS; Wausau-Rhinelander WI)
WSAZ (NBC; Charleston WV)
WSWG (CBS; Albany GA)
WTAP (NBC; Parkersburg WV)
WTOK (ABC; Meridian MS)
WTVY (CBS; Dothan AL)
WVAW (ABC; Charlottesville VA)
WVLT (CBS; Knoxville TN)
WYMT (CBS; Hazard KY)

COMPETITORS

CM WIND DOWN TOPCO INC.
Central European Media Enterprises Ltd
ENTRAVISION COMMUNICATIONS CORPORATION
LIN MEDIA LLC
SAGA COMMUNICATIONS INC.
SCRIPPS NETWORKS INTERACTIVE INC.
SINCLAIR BROADCAST GROUP INC.
TOWNSQUARE MEDIA INC.
VIACOMCBS INC.
YOUNG BROADCASTING LLC

HISTORICAL FINANCIALS

Company Type: Public

Income Statement

FYE: December 31

	REVENUE ($ mil.)	NET INCOME ($ mil.)	NET PROFIT MARGIN	EMPLOYEES
12/20	2,381.0	410.0	17.2%	7,262
12/19	2,122.0	179.0	8.4%	8,018
12/18	1,084.1	210.8	19.4%	8,523
12/17	882.7	261.9	29.7%	3,938
12/16	812.4	62.2	7.7%	3,996
Annual Growth	**30.8%**	**60.2%**	—	**16.1%**

2020 Year-End Financials

Debt ratio: 52.0%
Return on equity: 18.1%
Cash ($ mil.): 773.0
Current ratio: 5.11
Long-term debt ($ mil.): 3,974.0
No. of shares (mil.): 95.1
Dividends
  Yield: —
  Payout: —
Market value ($ mil.): 1,703.0

	STOCK PRICE ($) FY Close	P/E High/Low		PER SHARE ($) Earnings	Dividends	Book Value
12/20	17.89	6	2	3.69	0.00	25.24
12/19	21.44	19	11	1.27	0.00	21.24
12/18	14.74	8	4	2.37	0.00	13.38
12/17	16.75	5	3	3.55	0.00	11.05
12/16	10.85	19	8	0.86	0.00	6.80
Annual Growth	**13.3%**	—	—	**43.9%**	—	**38.8%**

Green Brick Partners Inc

Green Brick Partners acquires and develops land and provides land and construction financing to its wholly owned and controlled builders. Also known as Green Brick it is engaged in all aspects of the homebuilding process including land acquisition and development entitlements design construction title and mortgage services marketing and sales and the creation of brand images at its residential neighborhoods and master planned communities. Based in Dallas the company owns or controls over 12000 prime home sites in high-growth sub-markets throughout the Dallas and Atlanta metropolitan areas and the Vero Beach Florida market.

EXECUTIVES

Chairman Of The Board, David Einhorn
Chief Operating Officer, Jed Dolson, $559,103 total compensation
Chief Executive Officer, Director, James Brickman, $1,500,000 total compensation
Independent Director, Elizabeth Blake
Chief Financial Officer, Richard Costello, $400,000 total compensation
Auditors: RSM US LLP

LOCATIONS

HQ: Green Brick Partners Inc
2805 Dallas Parkway, Suite 400, Plano, TX 75093
Phone: 469 573-6755
Web: www.greenbrickpartners.com

COMPETITORS

CENTURY COMMUNITIES INC.
HOVNANIAN ENTERPRISES INC.
KB HOME
LENNAR CORPORATION
M/I HOMES INC.
MID-AMERICA APARTMENT PROPERTIES COMMUNITIES INC.
PULTEGROUP INC.
REYAL URBIS SA (EN LIQUIDACION)
RIOFISA SA
SACYR SA.
TDINDUSTRIES INC.
TOLL BROTHERS INC.
URBAN EDGE

HISTORICAL FINANCIALS

Company Type: Public

Income Statement
FYE: December 31

	REVENUE ($ mil.)	NET INCOME ($ mil.)	NET PROFIT MARGIN	EMPLOYEES
12/20	976.0	113.6	11.6%	440
12/19	791.6	58.6	7.4%	460
12/18	623.6	51.6	8.3%	390
12/17	454.3	14.9	3.3%	260
12/16	380.3	23.7	6.2%	220
Annual Growth	26.6%	47.9%	—	18.9%

2020 Year-End Financials

Debt ratio: 22.2%
Return on equity: 19.0%
Cash ($ mil.): 19.4
Current ratio: 8.36
Long-term debt ($ mil.): 219.8

No. of shares (mil.): 50.6
Dividends
Yield: —
Payout: —
Market value ($ mil.): 1,163.0

	STOCK PRICE ($) FY Close	P/E High/Low		PER SHARE ($) Earnings	Dividends	Book Value
12/20	22.96	11	3	2.24	0.00	12.90
12/19	11.48	10	6	1.16	0.00	10.63
12/18	7.24	12	7	1.02	0.00	9.43
12/17	11.30	40	30	0.30	0.00	8.23
12/16	10.05	21	10	0.49	0.00	7.86
Annual Growth	22.9%		—	46.2%	—	13.2%

Green Dot Corp

Bank holding company Green Dot offers prepaid debit cards through more than 90000 retail locations in the US under brand names including Green Dot GoBank MoneyPak and TPG. Through its retail and direct bank Green Dot offers a broad set of financial products to consumers and businesses including debit prepaid checking credit and payroll cards as well as robust money processing services tax refunds cash deposits and disbursements. Founded in 1999 Green Dot has served more than 33 million customers directly.

Operations

Green Dot divide its operations into two reportable segments: Account Services and Processing and Settlement Services.

The Account Services segment consists of revenues and expenses derived from deposit account programs such as prepaid cards debit cards consumer and small business checking accounts secured credit cards payroll debit cards and gift cards. These deposit account programs are marketed under several leading consumer brand names and under the brand names of Banking as

a Service or "BaaS" partners. The segment accounts for more than 75% of revenue.

The Processing and Settlement Services segment consists of revenues and expenses derived from products and services that specialize in facilitating the movement of cash on behalf of consumers and businesses such as consumer cash processing services wage disbursements and tax refund processing services. This segment accounts for about 25% of revenue.

The company also generates its revenue from cards and other fees (more than 45% of revenue) interchange revenues (approximately 30%) processing and settlement service (around 25%) and interest income (less than 5%).

Geographic Reach

Its headquarters is located in Pasadena California.

Sales and Marketing

Green Dot offers their branded card programs and the Walmart MoneyCard to a broad group of consumers ranging from never-banked to fully-banked consumers. It focuses its sales and marketing efforts on acquisition of long-term users of its products enhancing brands and image building market adoption and awareness of products improving customer retention and increasing card usage.

The company's advertising and marketing expenses were $37.5 million $51.1 million and $23.2 million for the years 2020 2019 and 2018 respectively.

Financial Performance

The company's revenue for fiscal 2020 increased to $1.3 billion compared from the prior year with $1.1 billion. Card revenues and other fees totaled $593.9 million for the year ended December 31 2020 an increase of $134.5 million or 29% from the comparable prior year period.

Net income for fiscal 2020 decreased to $23.1 million compared from the prior year with $99.9 million.

Cash held by the company at the end of fiscal 2020 increased to $1.5 billion. Cash provided by operations and financing activities were $209.2 million and $1.0 billion respectively. Cash used for investing activities was $785.8 million mainly to purchases of available-for-sale investment securities.

Mergers and Acquisitions

In 2021 Green Dot and Republic Bank a subsidiary of Republic Bancorp announced they have entered into a definitive agreement pursuant to which Green Dot will purchase the assets and operations of Republic Bank's Tax Refund Solutions (TRS) business segment for $165 million in cash. The acquisition of TRS presents unique opportunities for near- and long-term growth of its tax processing business as it works to deliver more accessible and beneficial tax products and services to customers nationwide.

Company Background

The company's July 2010 initial public offering exceeded its own expectations raising nearly $165 million. Although the IPO of secondary shares raised a significant amount Green Dot did not keep any of the money for itself. Instead the money was distributed to existing shareholders the most prominent being Wal-Mart. Prior to the IPO the retail giant took a minority stake in Green Dot — a move that cemented the pair's partnership.

EXECUTIVES

Executive Vice President & Chief Product, Strategy And Development Officer, Daniel Eckert, $346,881 total compensation
Independent Director, J. Chris Brewster
Independent Chairman Of The Board, William Jacobs, $416,250 total compensation
Independent Director, Glinda Hodges
General Counsel, Kristina Lockwood, $390,009 total compensation
Chief Financial Officer, Chief Operating Officer, Director, George Gresham
Independent Director, Saturnino Fanlo
President, Chief Executive Officer, Director, Daniel Henry, $650,750 total compensation
Independent Director, George Shaheen
Chief Human Resource Officer, Jason Bibelheimer, $518,270 total compensation
Independent Director, Ellen Richey
Executive Vice President - Retail, Tax And Paycard, Brandon Thompson
Chief Technology Officer, Gyorgy Tomso
Executive Vice President, Banking As A Service, Amit Parikh
Independent Director, Raj Date
Auditors: Ernst & Young LLP

LOCATIONS

HQ: Green Dot Corp
3465 E. Foothill Blvd., Pasadena, CA 91107
Phone: 626 765-2000
Web: www.greendot.com

PRODUCTS/OPERATIONS

2018 Revenue

	$ mil.	% of total
Card revenues and other fees	482.9	46
Processing and settlement service revenues	248.0	24
Interchange revenues	310.9	30
Total	**1,041.8**	**100**

COMPETITORS

ALLIANCE DATA SYSTEMS CORPORATION
CLAYTON DUBILIER & RICE INC.
COGNITION FINANCIAL CORPORATION
CREDIT ACCEPTANCE CORPORATION
ENOVA INTERNATIONAL INC.
FLEETCOR TECHNOLOGIES INC.
GENERAL MOTORS FINANCIAL COMPANY INC.
MONEYGRAM INTERNATIONAL INC.
NELNET INC.
PAYPAL HOLDINGS INC.
SYNCHRONY FINANCIAL
TOYOTA MOTOR CREDIT CORPORATION

HISTORICAL FINANCIALS

Company Type: Public

Income Statement
FYE: December 31

	REVENUE ($ mil.)	NET INCOME ($ mil.)	NET PROFIT MARGIN	EMPLOYEES
12/20	1,253.7	23.1	1.8%	1,200
12/19	1,108.6	99.9	9.0%	1,200
12/18	1,041.7	118.7	11.4%	1,100
12/17	890.1	85.8	9.6%	1,152
12/16	718.7	41.6	5.8%	974
Annual Growth	14.9%	(13.6%)	—	5.4%

2020 Year-End Financials

Debt ratio: —
Return on equity: 2.3%
Cash ($ mil.): 1,491.8
Current ratio: 0.78
Long-term debt ($ mil.): —

No. of shares (mil.): 54.0
Dividends
  Yield: —
  Payout: —
Market value ($ mil.): 3,015.0

	STOCK PRICE ($) FY Close	P/E High/Low		PER SHARE ($) Earnings	Dividends	Book Value
12/20	55.80	150	39	0.42	0.00	18.69
12/19	23.30	44	12	1.88	0.00	17.90
12/18	79.52	41	25	2.18	0.00	17.19
12/17	60.26	38	14	1.61	0.00	14.95
12/16	23.55	31	19	0.80	0.00	13.54
Annual Growth	24.1%	—		— (14.9%)	—	8.4%

Green Thumb Industries Inc

Auditors: Macias Gini & O'Connell LLP

LOCATIONS

HQ: Green Thumb Industries Inc
325 West Huron Street, Suite 700, Chicago, IL 60654
Phone: 312 471-6720
Web: www.gtigrows.com

HISTORICAL FINANCIALS

Company Type: Public

Income Statement   FYE: December 31

	REVENUE ($ mil.)	NET INCOME ($ mil.)	NET PROFIT MARGIN	EMPLOYEES
12/20	556.5	14.9	2.7%	2,200
12/19	216.4	(59.1)	—	1,700
12/18	62.4	(5.2)	—	0
12/17	16.5	(4.2)	—	0
Annual Growth	222.9%	—	—	—

2020 Year-End Financials

Debt ratio: 7.2%
Return on equity: 1.7%
Cash ($ mil.): 83.7
Current ratio: 1.54
Long-term debt ($ mil.): 98.7

No. of shares (mil.): 178.4
Dividends
  Yield: —
  Payout: —
Market value ($ mil.): 4,372.0

	STOCK PRICE ($) FY Close	P/E High/Low		PER SHARE ($) Earnings	Dividends	Book Value
12/20	24.50	361	58	0.07	0.00	5.10
12/19	9.75	—	—	(0.31)	0.00	6.48
12/18	8.03	—	—	(0.04)	0.00	7.52
12/17	0.02	—	—	(0.07)	0.00	(0.00)
/0.00	—	—	(0.00)	0.00	(0.00)	
Annual Growth	—	—		—	—	—

Greene County Bancorp Inc

This company helps put the "green" in upstate New York. Greene County Bancorp is the holding company for The Bank of Greene County serving New York's Catskill Mountains region from about a dozen branches. Founded in 1889 as a building and loan association the bank offers traditional retail products such as savings NOW checking and money market accounts; IRAs; and CDs. Real estate loans make up about 85% of the bank's lending activities; it also writes business and consumer loans. Through affiliations with Fenimore Asset Management and Essex Corp. Greene County Bancorp offers investment products. Subsidiary Greene County Commercial Bank is a state-chartered limited purpose commercial bank.

EXECUTIVES

Independent Chairman Of The Board, Paul Slutzky
Independent Director, David Jenkins
President, Chief Executive Officer, Director, Donald Gibson, $531,000 total compensation
Independent Director, Peter Hogan
Independent Director, Jay Cahalan
Independent Director, Charles Schaefer
Chief Financial Officer, Chief Operating Officer, Senior Executive Vice President, Director, Michelle Plummer, $312,000 total compensation
Director, Stephen Nelson, $145,300 total compensation
Auditors: Bonadio & Co., LLP

LOCATIONS

HQ: Greene County Bancorp Inc
302 Main Street, Catskill, NY 12414
Phone: 518 943-2600
Web: www.tbogc.com

COMPETITORS

CHICOPEE BANCORP INC.
PRUDENTIAL BANCORP
INC. OF PENNSYLVANIA

HISTORICAL FINANCIALS

Company Type: Public

Income Statement   FYE: June 30

	ASSETS ($ mil.)	NET INCOME ($ mil.)	INCOME AS % OF ASSETS	EMPLOYEES
06/21	2,200.3	23.9	1.1%	193
06/20	1,676.8	18.7	1.1%	186
06/19	1,269.4	17.4	1.4%	172
06/18	1,151.4	14.4	1.3%	164
06/17	982.2	11.1	1.1%	146
Annual Growth	22.3%	21.0%	—	7.2%

2021 Year-End Financials

Return on assets: 1.2%
Return on equity: 17.2%
Long-term debt ($ mil.): —
No. of shares (mil.): 8.5
Sales ($ mil): 68.0

Dividends
  Yield: 1.7%
  Payout: 19.3%
Market value ($ mil.): 239.0

	STOCK PRICE ($) FY Close	P/E High/Low		PER SHARE ($) Earnings	Dividends	Book Value
06/21	28.12	11	7	2.81	0.48	17.57
06/20	22.30	13	8	2.20	0.44	15.13
06/19	29.42	17	14	2.05	0.40	13.16
06/18	33.90	22	13	1.69	0.39	11.27
06/17	27.20	21	12	1.31	0.38	9.82
Annual Growth	0.8%	—		— 21.0%	6.0%	15.6%

GreenSky Inc

Auditors: PricewaterhouseCoopers LLP

LOCATIONS

HQ: GreenSky Inc
5565 Glenridge Connector, Suite 700, Atlanta, GA 30342
Phone: 678 264-6105
Web: www.greensky.com

HISTORICAL FINANCIALS

Company Type: Public

Income Statement   FYE: December 31

	REVENUE ($ mil.)	NET INCOME ($ mil.)	NET PROFIT MARGIN	EMPLOYEES
12/20	525.6	9.9	1.9%	1,164
12/19	529.6	31.9	6.0%	1,174
12/18	414.6	24.2	5.8%	1,088
12/17	325.8	103.2	31.7%	949
12/16	263.8	99.2	37.6%	0
Annual Growth	18.8%	(43.7%)	—	—

2020 Year-End Financials

Debt ratio: 62.7%
Return on equity: 100.2%
Cash ($ mil.): 147.7
Current ratio: 4.84
Long-term debt ($ mil.): 955.6

No. of shares (mil.): 182.9
Dividends
  Yield: —
  Payout: —
Market value ($ mil.): 847.0

	STOCK PRICE ($) FY Close	P/E High/Low		PER SHARE ($) Earnings	Dividends	Book Value
12/20	4.63	64	21	0.14	0.00	(0.03)
12/19	8.90	31	12	0.49	0.00	0.14
12/18	9.57	62	20	0.41	0.00	0.14
Annual Growth	(30.4%)	—		— (41.6%)	—	—

Griffon Corp.

Griffon Corporation is a diversified management and holding company that conducts business through wholly-owned subsidiaries. The company operates in two segments ? consumer and professional products and home and building products. AMES and ClosetMaid Griffon's consumer and professional products subsidiaries make wood and wire closet organizations yard tools cleaning and storage products. The home and building segment operates through Clopay which has become the largest manufacturer and marketer of garage doors and rolling steel doors in North America. The US accounts for about 75% of Griffon's total revenue.

Operations

Griffon has two reportable segments: Consumer and Professional Products (CPP) and Home & Building Products (HBP).

CPP segment operates through AMES a manufacturer of home storage and organizations landscaping and outdoor lifestyle. CCP sells its product globally through its brands including True Temper AMES and ClosetMaid. The segment account for about 55% of total revenue.

HBP segment conducts its operation through Clopay the largest manufacturer and marketer of garage doors and rolling steel doors in North America. Residential and commercial sectional garage doors are sold under the brands Clopay Ideal and Holmes. Rolling steel door and grille products designed are sold under the CornellCookson brand. The segment brings in about 45% of Griffon's total revenue.

Geographic Reach

Headquartered in New York Griffon's various businesses sell products primarily in North America (the US accounts for about 75% of sales) but also in Canada Australia New Zealand and Europe. The company has facilities (offices factories and warehouses) throughout the US Canada Mexico Australia the UK and China.

Sales and Marketing

AMES and ClosetMaid sell products through small retailers hardware stores garden centers and mass merchandisers. Major customers include The Home Depot Lowe's Walmart Bunnings and Menards.

Telephonics sells to the US Department of Defense and other defense industry businesses like Lockheed Martin Boeing Northrop Grumman Corporation Oshkosh Airbus Helicopters Leonardo Helicopters SAAB and Airbus Military.

The Home Depot accounts for about 20% of company's revenue.

Financial Performance

Revenue for the year ended September 30 2021 was $2.3 million compared to $2.1 million in the year ended September 30 2020 an increase of 10% resulting from increased revenue at HBP and CPP of 12% and 8% respectively.

In 2021 the company had a net income of $79.2 million a 48% increase from the previous year's net income of $53.4 million. This was mainly due to a higher sales volume coupled with a lower interest expense for the year.

The company's cash at the end of 2021 was $248.7 million. Operating activities generated $71 million while investing activities used $56.2 million primarily for acquisition of property plant and equipment. Financing activities used another $28.2 million mainly for payments of long-term debt.

Strategy

Griffon plans to seek and acquire businesses in multiple industries and geographic markets. The objective is to maintain leading positions in the markets it serves by providing innovative branded products with superior quality and industry-leading service. It emphasizes its iconic and well-respected brands which helps to differentiate the company's offerings from its competitors and strengthens the relationship with customers and those who ultimately use its products.

Through operating a diverse portfolio of businesses the company expects to reduce variability caused by external factors such as market cyclicality seasonality and weather. It achieves diversity by providing various product offerings and brands through multiple sales and distribution channels and conducting business across multiple countries.

Griffon oversees the operations of its subsidiaries allocates resources among them and manages its capital structures. Griffon provides direction and assistance to its subsidiaries in connection with acquisition and growth opportunities as well as in connection with divestitures. As long-term investors having substantial experience in a variety of industries the intent of the company is to continue the growth and strengthening of its existing businesses and to diversify further through investments in its businesses and through acquisitions.

Mergers and Acquisitions

In late 2021 Griffon through its subsidiary The AMES Companies Inc. has entered into a definitive agreement to acquire Hunter Fan Company a market leader in residential ceiling commercial and industrial fans from MidOcean Partners for $845 million. The acquisition of Hunter along with the expected sale of Griffon's Defense Electronics business marks a repositioning and strengthening of the Griffon portfolio which will further accelerate Griffon's growth increase shareholder value and is an effective use of its capital.

In 2021 Griffon announced that its subsidiary The AMES Companies Inc. acquired Quatro Design Pty Ltd a leading Australian manufacturer and supplier of glass fiber reinforced concrete landscaping products for residential commercial and public sector projects. This acquisition further expands AMES's product portfolio and sales channels in the Australian market. Quatro is expected to contribute approximately $5 million in annualized revenue and be accretive to Griffon's earnings in the fiscal year ending September 30 2021. Financial terms of the transaction were not disclosed.

Company Background

Griffon was founded in 1959 by Helmuth W. Waldorf as Waldorf Controls Corporation but soon assumed the name Instrument System Corporation (ISC). In 1986 the company went public. ISC became Griffon in 1995 after the mythical creature that is part lion part eagle. In 2010 Griffon relocates its headquarters from Jericho NY to New York City.

HISTORY

Founded in 1959 as Waldorf Controls the company changed its name to Instrument Systems that year. Under chairman Edward Garrett the business acquired 80 companies in the 1960s and 1970s including Telephonics (1962) and Concord Electronics (1971). In 1983 Harvey Blau assumed management replacing Garrett his father-in-law as CEO. The company bought Clopay for $40 million in 1986.

Telephonics expanded Instrument Systems' market focus in the 1990s to include commercial and nondefense governmental clients. The company built its Clopay unit adding garage door makers Ideal Door (1992) and Atlas Roll-lite (1995). The name Griffon Corporation was adapted in 1995.

In 1997 Telephonics won its largest contract ever — a $114 million contract to supply British Aerospace (now BAE SYSTEMS) with communications systems. That year Griffon bought garage-door maker and installer Holmes-Hally Industries ($80 million in annual sales). The next year it picked up Bohme Verpackungsfolien (plastic packaging and specialty films Germany).

Griffon faced restructuring charges and capacity restraints in 1999. To boost profits it exited the self-storage warehouse-door business and closed or consolidated other operations.

Griffon bought the search and weather radar products business of Honeywell International for $16 million in 2000. In late 2001 Telephonics Corporation received a $13.5 million contract from the US Air Force to upgrade its Airborne Warning and Control System (AWACS) aircraft with new "friend or foe" identification technology.

In fiscal 2002 the company citing unprofitability of the unit adopted a plan to divest its peripheral operation selling slatted steel coiling doors for commercial users. That year through its Clopay subsidiary Griffon acquired majority ownership in Isofilme (plastic hygienic and specialty films Brazil) and renamed the company Clopay do Brasil. Also that year its Telephonics subsidiary was awarded a $15 million contract from Boeing Defense Space & Security (BDS; formerly Boeing Integrated Defense Systems) for the first production of Telephonics' Communications Open Systems Architecture (COSA) Integrated Radio Management System (IRMS) for use by the US Air Force on its C-17A Globemaster III transport aircraft.

In 2004 Telephonics was awarded a multi-year contract valued at more than $40 million from Lockheed Martin Systems Integration-Owego to produce cockpit communications management systems for the US Navy's MH-60R and MH-60S helicopters. The next year Telephonics purchased The Systems Engineering Group (SEG) based in Columbia Maryland to operate as a subsidiary. SEG provides electronic systems and subsystems analysis simulation and support.

Also in 2005 Telephonics was awarded a $20 million contract by the US Navy for a digital audio intercommunication system for its P-C3 Orion aircraft.

In 2013 its Telephonics subsidiary and Mahindra & Mahindra one of India's leading business houses formed a joint venture that provides the Indian Ministry of Defence and the Indian Civil sector with radar and surveillance systems identification devices and communication systems. In addition it will provide systems for air traffic management services homeland security and other emerging surveillance requirements.

As its profits fell in 2013 the company is also keeping a close lid on costs. It announced in 2013 it was closing manufacturing facilities in two Pennsylvania locations in order to improve its production efficiencies. Clopay Building Products also in 2013 closed an Auburn Washington facility and consolidated it into its Russia Ohio location in order to streamline its manufacturing processes.

EXECUTIVES

Independent Director, James Sight
Independent Director, Cheryl Turnbull
Independent Director, Jerome Coben
Independent Director, Robert Harrison
Chairman Of The Board, Chief Executive Officer,
Ronald Kramer, $1,143,005 total compensation
Independent Director, Henry Alpert
Independent Director, William Waldorf

Senior Vice President, General Counsel, Secretary, Seth Kaplan, $441,237 total compensation
Chief Financial Officer, Senior Vice President, Brian Harris, $474,961 total compensation
President, Chief Operating Officer, Director, Robert Mehmel, $1,014,586 total compensation
Independent Director, Victor Renuart
Independent Director, Thomas Brosig
Independent Director, Samanta Stewart
Independent Director, Lacy Johnson
Auditors: Grant Thornton LLP

LOCATIONS

HQ: Griffon Corp.
712 Fifth Avenue, 18th Floor, New York, NY 10019
Phone: 212 957-5000
Web: www.griffon.com

PRODUCTS/OPERATIONS

2018 Sales

	$ mil.	% of total
Home & Building Products		
CBP	698.0	35
AMES	953.6	48
Telephonics	326.3	17
Total	**1,977.9**	**100**

Selected Products

Home and building products
　Ames True Temper (non-powered lawn and garden tools)
　Garden hoses and hose reels
　Long-handle tools
　Planters and lawn accessories
　Pruning
　Snow tools
　Striking tools
　Wheelbarrows
　Clopay Building Products (residential commercial and industrial garage doors)
　ClosetMaid
　Containers
　Shelving
　Storage cabinets
Telephonics (high-technology integrated information communication and sensor systems)
　Airborne maritime surveillance radar
　Aircraft intercommunication management systems
　Air traffic management
　Identification friend or foe equipment
　Integrated circuits
　Integrated homeland security systems
　Logistical support for aircraft intercommunication systems
　Radar

COMPETITORS

Celestica Inc
FLEX LTD.
HORMANN LLC
JOHNSON CONTROLS INTERNATIONAL PUBLIC LIMITED COMPANY
LIXIL CORPORATION
OVERHEAD DOOR CORPORATION
PERMASTEELISA SPA
RYTEC CORPORATION
SYPRIS SOLUTIONS INC.

HISTORICAL FINANCIALS

Company Type: Public

Income Statement

FYE: September 30

	REVENUE ($ mil.)	NET INCOME ($ mil.)	NET PROFIT MARGIN	EMPLOYEES
09/21	2,270.6	79.2	3.5%	6,700
09/20	2,407.5	53.4	2.2%	7,400
09/19	2,209.2	37.2	1.7%	7,300
09/18	1,977.9	125.6	6.4%	7,200
09/17	1,525.0	14.9	1.0%	4,700
Annual Growth	**10.5%**	**51.8%**	**—**	**9.3%**

2021 Year-End Financials

Debt ratio: 40.1%
Return on equity: 10.5%
Cash ($ mil.): 248.6
Current ratio: 2.57
Long-term debt ($ mil.): 1,033.2

No. of shares (mil.): 56.6
Dividends
　Yield: 1.3%
　Payout: 21.6%
Market value ($ mil.): 1,393.0

	STOCK PRICE ($) FY Close	P/E High/Low		PER SHARE ($) Earnings	Dividends	Book Value
09/21	24.60	18	12	1.48	0.32	14.26
09/20	19.54	20	8	1.19	0.30	12.47
09/19	20.97	23	11	0.87	0.29	10.21
09/18	16.15	8	5	2.96	1.28	10.39
09/17	22.20	75	45	0.35	0.24	8.47
Annual Growth	**2.6%**	**—**	**—**	**43.4%**	**7.5%**	**13.9%**

Grocery Outlet Holding Corp

Auditors: DELOITTE & TOUCHE LLP

LOCATIONS

HQ: Grocery Outlet Holding Corp
5650 Hollis Street, Emeryville, CA 94608
Phone: 510 845-1999
Web: www.groceryoutlet.com

HISTORICAL FINANCIALS

Company Type: Public

Income Statement

FYE: January 2

	REVENUE ($ mil.)	NET INCOME ($ mil.)	NET PROFIT MARGIN	EMPLOYEES
01/21*	3,134.6	106.7	3.4%	946
12/19	2,559.6	15.4	0.6%	847
12/18	2,287.6	15.8	0.7%	906
12/17	2,075.4	20.6	1.0%	0
12/16	1,831.5	10.2	0.6%	0
Annual Growth	**14.4%**	**79.9%**	**—**	**—**

*Fiscal year change

2021 Year-End Financials

Debt ratio: 55.4%
Return on equity: 12.5%
Cash ($ mil.): 105.3
Current ratio: 1.64
Long-term debt ($ mil.): 1,330.6

No. of shares (mil.): 94.8
Dividends
　Yield: —
　Payout: —
Market value ($ mil.): 3,723.0

	STOCK PRICE ($) FY Close	P/E High/Low		PER SHARE ($) Earnings	Dividends	Book Value
01/21*	39.25	40	25	1.08	0.00	9.72
12/19	33.47	233	143	0.19	0.00	8.37
Annual Growth	**17.3%**	**—**	**—**	**468.4%**	**—**	**16.1%**

*Fiscal year change

Guaranty Bancshares Inc

Guaranty Bancshares is the holding company for Guaranty Bond Bank which operates about a dozen branches in northeast Texas and another in West Texas. Guaranty Bond Bank's deposit products and services include CDs and savings checking NOW and money market accounts. Its lending activities include one- to four-family residential mortgages (more than a third of the company's loan portfolio) in addition to commercial mortgage construction business agriculture and personal loans. The company's GB Financial division provides wealth management retirement planning and trust services.

EXECUTIVES

Chairman Of The Board, Chief Executive Officer, Director, Tyson Abston, $423,500 total compensation
President, Director, Kirk Lee, $307,500 total compensation
Chief Financial Officer, Senior Executive Vice President, Director, Clifton Payne, $280,500 total compensation
Executive Vice President, General Counsel, Randall Kucera
Independent Director, William Priefert
Lead Independent Director, Christopher Elliott
Independent Director, Bradley Drake
Independent Director, Carl Johnson
Independent Director, Jeffrey Brown
Independent Director, James Nolan
Independent Director, Molly Curl
Auditors: Whitley Penn LLP

LOCATIONS

HQ: Guaranty Bancshares Inc
16475 Dallas Parkway, Suite 600, Addison, TX 75001
Phone: 888 572-9881
Web: www.gnty.com

PRODUCTS/OPERATIONS

2008 Sales

	$ mil.	% of total
Interest		
Loans including fees	31.2	70
Securities	6.3	13
Other	1.1	2
Noninterest		
Service charges	4.2	8
Other	3.3	7
Total	**46.1**	**100**

HOOVER'S HANDBOOK OF EMERGING COMPANIES 2022

COMPETITORS

CHOICEONE FINANCIAL SERVICES INC.
EASTERN VIRGINIA BANKSHARES INC.
EMCLAIRE FINANCIAL CORP.
LIBERTY CAPITAL INC.

HISTORICAL FINANCIALS

Company Type: Public

Income Statement

FYE: December 31

	ASSETS ($ mil.)	NET INCOME ($ mil.)	INCOME AS % OF ASSETS	EMPLOYEES
12/20	2,740.8	27.4	1.0%	467
12/19	2,318.4	26.2	1.1%	467
12/18	2,266.9	20.6	0.9%	454
12/17	1,962.6	14.4	0.7%	407
12/16	1,828.3	12.1	0.7%	397
Annual Growth	10.7%	22.6%	—	4.1%

2020 Year-End Financials

Return on assets: 1.0%
Return on equity: 10.2%
Long-term debt ($ mil.): —
No. of shares (mil.): 10.9
Sales ($ mil) 119.2

Dividends
Yield: 2.6%
Payout: 35.4%
Market value ($ mil.): 328.0

	STOCK PRICE ($) FY Close	P/E High/Low		PER SHARE ($) Earnings	Dividends	Book Value
12/20	29.95	13	8	2.46	0.71	24.93
12/19	32.88	17	13	2.05	0.64	20.59
12/18	29.82	22	18	1.61	0.55	18.80
12/17	30.65	27	22	1.27	0.36	17.04
12/16	26.50	—	—	1.23	0.47	14.74
Annual Growth	3.1%		— —	19.0%	10.7%	14.0%

Guaranty Federal Bancshares Inc (Springfield, MO)

EXECUTIVES

Exec V Pres, William B Williams
Oo-Cfo-Ev Pres, Carter Peters
Evp-Coo, Robin E Robeson
Evp-Chief Lending Officer, H Charles Puls
Evp-Chief Comml Banking Office, Craig Dunn
Evp-Cao, Stephanie Rutledge
Branch Mgr, Theresa Mann
Coordinator, Devon Angus
Financial Analyst, Zachary Towe
Vice President Residential Len, Brad Farris
Purchasing Coordinator, Mary Harmon
Auditors: BKD, LLP

LOCATIONS

HQ: Guaranty Federal Bancshares Inc (Springfield, MO)
2144 E. Republic Rd., Suite F200, Springfield, MO 65804
Phone: 833 875-2492
Web: www.gbankmo.com

HISTORICAL FINANCIALS

Company Type: Public

Income Statement

FYE: December 31

	ASSETS ($ mil.)	NET INCOME ($ mil.)	INCOME AS % OF ASSETS	EMPLOYEES
12/20	1,146.2	6.8	0.6%	234
12/19	1,012.0	9.4	0.9%	229
12/18	965.1	7.3	0.8%	226
12/17	794.4	5.1	0.6%	173
12/16	687.9	5.5	0.8%	172
Annual Growth	13.6%	5.1%	—	8.0%

2020 Year-End Financials

Return on assets: 0.6%
Return on equity: 7.8%
Long-term debt ($ mil.): —
No. of shares (mil.): 4.3
Sales ($ mil): 50.9

Dividends
Yield: 3.4%
Payout: 31.7%
Market value ($ mil.): 76.0

	STOCK PRICE ($) FY Close	P/E High/Low		PER SHARE ($) Earnings	Dividends	Book Value
12/20	17.46	16	8	1.57	0.60	20.38
12/19	25.20	12	10	2.11	0.52	19.51
12/18	21.84	15	12	1.64	0.48	18.05
12/17	22.45	19	16	1.16	0.30	16.93
12/16	21.18	17	12	1.27	0.34	15.87
Annual Growth	(4.7%)		— —	5.4%	15.3%	6.5%

Halozyme Therapeutics Inc

Halozyme Therapeutics is a biopharma technology platform company. Its Hylenex recombinant is used as an adjuvant for drug and fluid infusions. Most of Halozyme's products and candidates (including Hylenex) are based on rHuPH20 its patented recombinant human hyaluronidase enzyme while its lead cancer program is PEGPH20 which targets solid tumors. Halozyme partners with such pharmaceuticals as Roche Pfizer Janssen Baxalta and AbbVie for its ENHANZE drug delivery platform which enables biologics and small molecule compounds to be delivered subcutaneously. US generates the majority of revenue which accounts for about 40%.

Operations

Halozyme operates its business in one segment which includes all activities related to the research development and commercialization of proprietary enzymes. This segment also includes revenues and expenses related to royalties (nearly 35% of sales) research and development and bulk rHuPH20 manufacturing activities conducted under collaborative agreements (about 45%) with third parties and product sales (about 20%) of Hylenex recombinant.

Geographic Reach

Halozyme is headquartered in and has research facilities in San Diego California.

The US accounts for about 40% of the company's revenue while Switzerland accounts for around 35% and Ireland some 10%.

Sales and Marketing

Integrated Commercial Solutions a division of AmerisourceBergen is the exclusive distributor for Hylenex recombinant in the US.

The company employs outside vendors such as advertising agencies market research firms and marketing firms to help support its commercial activities.

Financial Performance

Company's revenue for fiscal 2020 increased to $267.6 million compared from the prior year with $196.0 million.

Net income for fiscal 2020 was $129.1 million compared from the prior year with a net loss of $72.2 million.

Cash held by the company at the end of fiscal 2020 increased to $148.2 million. Cash provided by operations and investing activities were $55.5 million and $78.4 million respectively. Cash used for financing activities were $106.3 million mainly for repurchase of common stock.

Strategy

Halozyme collaborate with leading pharmaceutical and biotechnology companies to help them develop products that combine its ENHANZE technology with their proprietary compounds. The company target large attractive markets where EN-HANZE-enabled subcutaneous delivery has the potential to deliver competitive differentiation and other important benefits to its partners such as larger injection volumes administered rapidly extended dosing intervals and reduced treatment burden and healthcare costs. In addition EN-HANZE has been demonstrated to enable the combination of two therapeutic antibodies in a single injection as well as the development of new co-formulation intellectual property. We leverage its strategic technical regulatory and alliance management skills in support of its partners' efforts to develop new subcutaneously delivered products. Halozyme currently have ten collaborations with five current product approvals and additional product candidates in development using its ENHANZE technology. The company intend to work with its existing collaborators to expand its collaborations to add new targets and develop targets and product candidates under the terms of the operative collaboration agreements. The company will also continue its efforts to enter into new collaborations to further derive additional value from its proprietary technology.

EXECUTIVES

Independent Director, James Daly
Independent Director, Jeffrey Henderson
President, Chief Executive Officer And Director, Helen Torley, $791,440 total compensation
Independent Director, Matthew Posard
Senior Vice President, Chief Compliance Officer, General Counsel, Company Secretary, Mark Snyder
Senior Vice President, Chief Financial Officer, Nicole LaBrosse
Independent Director, Bernadette Connaughton
Senior Vice President, Chief Technical Officer, Michael LaBarre, $475,000 total compensation
Independent Chairman Of The Board, Connie Matsui
Auditors: Ernst & Young LLP

LOCATIONS

HQ: Halozyme Therapeutics Inc
11388 Sorrento Valley Road, San Diego, CA 92121
Phone: 858 794-8889
Web: www.halozyme.com

PRODUCTS/OPERATIONS

2014 Revenues

	$ mil.	% of total
Product sales	37.8	50
Collaborative agreements	28.1	37
Royalties	9.4	13
Total	**75.3**	**100**

COMPETITORS

ACCELERON PHARMA INC.
ACORDA THERAPEUTICS INC.
CYTRX CORPORATION
DYNAVAX TECHNOLOGIES CORPORATION
INOVIO PHARMACEUTICALS INC.
LUMINEX CORPORATION
NANOSTRING TECHNOLOGIES INC.
NEKTAR THERAPEUTICS
PFENEX INC.
PROGENICS PHARMACEUTICALS INC.
REGENERON PHARMACEUTICALS INC.
SEAGEN INC.

HISTORICAL FINANCIALS

Company Type: Public

Income Statement — FYE: December 31

	REVENUE ($ mil.)	NET INCOME ($ mil.)	NET PROFIT MARGIN	EMPLOYEES
12/20	267.5	129.0	48.2%	136
12/19	195.9	(72.2)	—	132
12/18	151.8	(80.3)	—	281
12/17	316.6	62.9	19.9%	255
12/16	146.6	(103.0)	—	259
Annual Growth	16.2%	—	—	(14.9%)

2020 Year-End Financials

Debt ratio: 68.5%	No. of shares (mil.): 135.0
Return on equity: 106.0%	Dividends
Cash ($ mil.): 147.7	Yield: —
Current ratio: 1.32	Payout: —
Long-term debt ($ mil.): —	Market value ($ mil.): 5,767.0

	STOCK PRICE ($) FY Close	P/E High/Low	Earnings	Dividends	Book Value
12/20	42.71	46 15	0.91	0.00	1.12
12/19	17.73	— —	(0.50)	0.00	0.67
12/18	14.63	— —	(0.56)	0.00	1.72
12/17	20.26	45 22	0.45	0.00	1.46
12/16	9.88	— —	(0.81)	0.00	(0.25)
Annual Growth	44.2%	— —	—	—	—

Hamilton Lane Inc

Auditors: Ernst & Young LLP

LOCATIONS

HQ: Hamilton Lane Inc
110 Washington Street, Suite 1300, Consholocken, PA 19428
Phone: 610 934-2222
Web: www.hamiltonlane.com

HISTORICAL FINANCIALS

Company Type: Public

Income Statement — FYE: March 31

	REVENUE ($ mil.)	NET INCOME ($ mil.)	NET PROFIT MARGIN	EMPLOYEES
03/21	341.6	98.0	28.7%	450
03/20	274.0	60.8	22.2%	400
03/19	252.1	33.5	13.3%	370
03/18	244.0	17.3	7.1%	340
03/17	179.8	0.6	0.3%	290
Annual Growth	17.4%	255.7%	—	11.6%

2021 Year-End Financials

Debt ratio: 14.3%	No. of shares (mil.): 53.0
Return on equity: 49.8%	Dividends
Cash ($ mil.): 87.3	Yield: 1.4%
Current ratio: 0.50	Payout: 51.2%
Long-term debt ($ mil.): 163.1	Market value ($ mil.): 4,696.0

	STOCK PRICE ($) FY Close	P/E High/Low	Earnings	Dividends	Book Value
03/21	88.56	34 17	2.81	1.25	4.49
03/20	55.31	34 19	2.15	1.10	2.98
03/19	43.58	37 23	1.40	0.85	2.17
03/18	37.23	42 19	0.93	0.70	1.61
03/17	18.67	642601	0.03	0.00	1.28
Annual Growth	47.6%	—	—211.1%	—	36.9%

Hannon Armstrong Sustainable Infrastructure Capital Inc

Hannon Armstrong Sustainable Infrastructure Capital has its hands in both kinds of green. The REIT provides securitized funding for environmentally friendly infrastructure projects. It is a key provider of financing for the US government's energy efficiency projects. Hannon Armstrong focuses on energy efficiency renewable energy and other sustainable projects including water and communications that improve energy consumption and the use of natural resources. The company manages approximately $6.2 billion in assets and operates mostly in the US.

IPO

Operations

Hannon Armstrong manages about $6.2 billion in assets across more than 200 investments in projects to improve energy efficiency and develop renewable energy sources and sustainable infrastructure. About 80% of the REIT's projects are focused on solar energy; wind or BTM; energy efficiency some 10%; and sustainable infrastructure (which includes water and seismic retrofit projects) about 10%.

Nearly 55% of the company's revenue is derived from interest income on receivables. Almost 20%

each comes from rental income and gain on sale of receivables and investments.

When making investment decisions Hannon Armstrong calculates the estimated metric tons of carbon emissions or equivalent avoided a calculation it calls CarbonCount. The company's 2019 CarbonCount calculation estimates its investments will reduce carbon emissions by about 385000 metric tons.

Geographic Reach

Based in Annapolis Maryland Hannon Armstrong operates primarily in the US.

Sales and Marketing

Hannon Armstrong provides securitized funding for environmentally friendly infrastructure projects by US federal state and local governments and high credit quality institutions.

Financial Performance

Thanks to growing popularity and falling costs of efficient and renewable energy Hannon Armstrong has seen more than a 141% expansion of revenue in the last five years accompanying a jump in net income to more than $30 million in 2017 compared with $8 million in 2015.

In 2019 the REIT reported revenue of $142 million up 1% from the prior year. Hannon Armstrong's fee income accounted for the majority of the slight increase as fee income increased by 167%.

Hannon Armstrong's net income in 2019 ballooned 95% to $82 million as a result of a $2 million increase in total revenue a $2 million decrease in total expenses a $42 million increase in income from equity and method investments and a $6 million increase in income tax expense.

Cash at the end of fiscal 2019 was $106.6 million double that of the prior year. Cash from operations provided $29.5 million while investing activities used $201.1 million due mostly to equity method investments and purchases of and investments in receivables. Financing activities added another $218.9 million primarily from proceeds from credit facilities.

Strategy

Hannon Armstrong intends to continue investing in clean energy technologies that it believes benefit society and that generally are tied to long-term utility contracts.

The company's investments are focused on three areas: Behind-the-Meter; Grid-Connected; and Sustainable Infrastructure. Hannon Armstrong prefers investments where the assets have a long-term investment-grade rated off-taker or counterparties. As of 2019 the company's portfolio consisted of over 180 investments and Hannon Armstrong seeks to manage the diversity of its portfolio by among other factors project type project operator type of investment type of technology transaction size geography obligor and maturity.

In mid-2020 Hannon Armstrong formed a partnership with a subsidiary of ENGIE S.A. that owned a 2.3 gigawatt portfolio of wind and utility-scale solar assets. The partnership combined Hannon Armstrong's extensive experience in providing long-term investment for climate solutions with the best-in-class development and operations experience of ENGIE.

In 2019 Hannon Armstrong and Empower Energies to jointly invest in renewable energy products in the commercial & industrial (C&I) and municipal university school and hospital (MUSH) markets across the United States. Hannon Armstrong also partnered with Summit Ridge Energy in 2019 to jointly invest in community solar projects across several US markets including Maryland where the initial solar power plants will come on-line in Prince George's and Baltimore counties that summer.

Mergers and Acquisitions

In 2019 Hannon Armstrong and Morgan Properties announced a new joint venture that will acquire the B-Piece from Virginia-based Freddie Mac's previously settled KG series focused on environmental and social impact and part of Freddie Mac's flagship K-Deal program. The issuance K-G02 is exclusively comprised of securitized workforce housing loans made through Freddie Mac's Green Advantage® program which requires borrowers to make energy and/or water efficiency improvements to their properties. Expansion into this new asset class will further diversify the company's portfolio and bolster its efforts to decarbonize buildings including multi-family properties. Terms were not disclosed.

Company Background

Formed in 2012 to be a REIT the company went public in 2013 though it traces its roots to the 1980s and Hannon Armstrong Capital LLC.

EXECUTIVES

Executive Vice President, Co-chief Investment Officer, Nathaniel Rose, $386,667 total compensation
Executive Vice President, Joseph Herron, $400,000 total compensation
Executive Vice President, Portfolio Management, Daniel McMahon, $361,667 total compensation
Executive Vice President, General Counsel, Secretary, Chief Legal Officer, Steven Chuslo, $366,667 total compensation
Chairman And Chief Executive Officer, Jeffrey Eckel, $639,500 total compensation
Executive Vice President, Co-chief Investment Officer, Marc Pangburn
Chief Human Resource Officer, Senior Vice President, Katherine Dent
Senior Vice President, Chief Accounting Officer, Charles Melko
Independent Director, Richard Osborne
Lead Independent Director, Teresa Brenner
Independent Director, Charles O'Neil
Independent Director, Steven Osgood
Chief Financial Officer, Chief Operating Officer, Executive Vice President, Treasurer, Jeffrey Lipson, $383,333 total compensation
Executive Vice President And Chief Client Officer, Susan Nickey
Independent Director, Michael Eckhart
Independent Director, Simone Lagomarsino
Executive Vice President And Chief Analytics Officer, Richard Santoroski
Independent Director, Clarence Armbrister
Independent Director, Nancy Floyd
Auditors: Ernst & Young LLP

LOCATIONS

HQ: Hannon Armstrong Sustainable Infrastructure Capital Inc
1906 Towne Centre Blvd., Suite 370, Annapolis, MD 21401
Phone: 410 571-9860
Web: www.hannonarmstrong.com

PRODUCTS/OPERATIONS

2017 Sales

	$ mil.	% of total
Interest income financing receivables	56.7	53
Rental income	19.8	19
Gain on sale of receivables and investments	21.0	20
Interest income investments	5.1	5
Fee income	3.0	3
Total	**105.6**	**100**

Selected Project Types

Clean Energy
Energy Efficiency
Other Sustainable Infrastructure

COMPETITORS

ACADIA REALTY TRUST
ACRES COMMERCIAL REALTY CORP.
BLUEROCK RESIDENTIAL GROWTH REIT INC.
Brookfield Asset Management Inc
CLEARWAY ENERGY INC.
Innergex Inc
JBG SMITH PROPERTIES

MID-AMERICA APARTMENT COMMUNITIES INC.
NATIONAL STORAGE AFFILIATES TRUST
PATTERN ENERGY GROUP INC.
PROLOGIS INC.
SEMBCORP INDUSTRIES LTD
UDR INC.

HISTORICAL FINANCIALS

Company Type: Public

Income Statement

FYE: December 31

	REVENUE ($ mil.)	NET INCOME ($ mil.)	NET PROFIT MARGIN	EMPLOYEES
12/20	186.9	82.4	44.1%	73
12/19	141.5	81.5	57.6%	60
12/18	137.8	41.5	30.2%	49
12/17	105.5	30.8	29.2%	47
12/16	81.2	14.6	18.0%	40
Annual Growth	23.2%	54.0%	—	16.2%

2020 Year-End Financials

Debt ratio: 63.2%
Return on equity: 7.6%
Cash ($ mil.): 286.2
Current ratio: 20.17
Long-term debt ($ mil.): 2,166.3
No. of shares (mil.): 76.4
Dividends
 Yield: 2.1%
 Payout: 123.6%
Market value ($ mil.): 4,850.0

	STOCK PRICE ($) FY Close	P/E High/Low		PER SHARE ($) Earnings	Dividends	Book Value
12/20	63.43	58	15	1.10	1.36	15.74
12/19	32.18	26	16	1.24	1.34	14.12
12/18	19.05	32	23	0.75	1.32	13.24
12/17	24.06	44	32	0.57	1.32	12.37
12/16	18.99	78	52	0.32	1.23	12.27
Annual Growth	35.2%	—	—	36.2%	2.5%	6.4%

HarborOne Bancorp Inc (New)

Auditors: Crowe LLP

LOCATIONS

HQ: HarborOne Bancorp Inc (New)
770 Oak Street, Brockton, MA 02301
Phone: 508 895-1000
Web: www.harborone.com

HISTORICAL FINANCIALS

Company Type: Public

Income Statement

FYE: December 31

	ASSETS ($ mil.)	NET INCOME ($ mil.)	INCOME AS % OF ASSETS	EMPLOYEES
12/20	4,483.6	44.7	1.0%	633
12/19	4,058.9	18.2	0.5%	675
12/18	3,653.1	11.3	0.3%	658
12/17	2,684.9	10.3	0.4%	581
12/16	2,448.3	5.9	0.2%	614
Annual Growth	16.3%	65.8%	—	0.8%

2020 Year-End Financials

Return on assets: 1.0%
Return on equity: 6.5%
Long-term debt ($ mil.): —
No. of shares (mil.): 57.2
Sales ($ mil): 287.7
Dividends
 Yield: 0.8%
 Payout: 15.5%
Market value ($ mil.): 621.0

	STOCK PRICE ($) FY Close	P/E High/Low		PER SHARE ($) Earnings	Dividends	Book Value
12/20	10.86	14	8	0.82	0.09	12.17
12/19	10.99	60	30	0.33	0.00	11.40
12/18	15.89	56	42	0.36	0.00	10.98
12/17	19.16	67	49	0.33	0.00	10.52
12/16	19.34	—	—	(0.00)	0.00	10.25
Annual Growth	(13.4%)			—	—	4.4%

Hawthorn Bancshares Inc

EXECUTIVES

Ceo, James E Smith
Sr V Pres, Gene Henry
Sr V Pres, Ernie Spaashelm
Exec Dir, David Garnett
Chief Operations, Kathleen Bruegenhemke
Human Resources Coordinator, Jennifer Lamb
Senior Vice-President, Chris Schrimpf
Regional President, Keith Asel
Loan Officer, Dan Lewis
Vice-President, Lynn McClure
Human Resources, Jill Smith
Auditors: KPMG LLP

LOCATIONS

HQ: Hawthorn Bancshares Inc
132 East High Street, Box 688, Jefferson City, MO 65102
Phone: 573 761-6100
Web: www.hawthornbancshares.com

HISTORICAL FINANCIALS

Company Type: Public

Income Statement

FYE: December 31

	ASSETS ($ mil.)	NET INCOME ($ mil.)	INCOME AS % OF ASSETS	EMPLOYEES
12/20	1,733.7	14.2	0.8%	306
12/19	1,492.9	16.1	1.1%	294
12/18	1,481.6	10.7	0.7%	301
12/17	1,429.2	3.4	0.2%	349
12/16	1,287.0	7.2	0.6%	343
Annual Growth	7.7%	18.4%	—	(2.8%)

2020 Year-End Financials

Return on assets: 0.8%	Dividends
Return on equity: 11.6%	Yield: 2.2%
Long-term debt ($ mil.): —	Payout: 22.7%
No. of shares (mil.): 6.7	Market value ($ mil.): 148.0
Sales ($ mil): 77.7	

	STOCK PRICE ($) FY Close	P/E High/Low		PER SHARE ($) Earnings	Dividends	Book Value
12/20	21.90	12	6	2.12	0.48	19.38
12/19	25.50	12	9	2.38	0.43	16.95
12/18	21.03	15	13	1.58	0.34	14.64
12/17	20.75	46	34	0.50	0.23	13.47
12/16	17.70	17	13	1.06	0.17	13.32
Annual Growth	5.5%			— — 18.8%	29.8%	9.8%

Healthcare Trust Of America Inc

EXECUTIVES

Independent Director, Jay Leupp
Independent Director, H. Lee Cooper
Chairman, W. Bradley Blair
President, Ceo & Independent Director, Peter Foss
Chief Financial Officer, Treasurer, Company Secretary, Robert Milligan, $600,000 total compensation
Executive Vice President - Asset Management, Amanda Houghton, $450,000 total compensation
Auditors: Deloitte & Touche LLP

LOCATIONS

HQ: Healthcare Trust Of America Inc
16435 N. Scottsdale Road, Suite 320, Scottsdale, AZ 85254
Phone: 480 998-3478   **Fax:** 480 991-0755
Web: www.htareit.com

HISTORICAL FINANCIALS
Company Type: Public

Income Statement				FYE: December 31
	REVENUE ($ mil.)	NET INCOME ($ mil.)	NET PROFIT MARGIN	EMPLOYEES
12/20	738.9	52.6	7.1%	333
12/19	692.0	30.1	4.4%	303
12/18	696.4	213.4	30.7%	282
12/17	613.9	63.9	10.4%	270
12/16	460.9	45.9	10.0%	214
Annual Growth	12.5%	3.5%	—	11.7%

2020 Year-End Financials

Debt ratio: 44.5%	No. of shares (mil.): 218.5
Return on equity: 1.6%	Dividends
Cash ($ mil.): 118.7	Yield: 4.5%
Current ratio: 0.59	Payout: 527.0%
Long-term debt ($ mil.): 3,027.0	Market value ($ mil.): 6,020.0

	STOCK PRICE ($) FY Close	P/E High/Low		PER SHARE ($) Earnings	Dividends	Book Value
12/20	27.54	142	87	0.24	1.27	14.52
12/19	30.28	208	165	0.14	1.25	15.51
12/18	25.31	29	23	1.02	1.23	15.86
12/17	30.04	94	82	0.34	1.21	16.00
12/16	29.11	102	77	0.33	1.19	11.91
Annual Growth	(1.4%)			— — (7.7%)	1.5%	5.1%

HealthEquity Inc

Auditors: PricewaterhouseCoopers LLP

LOCATIONS

HQ: HealthEquity Inc
15 West Scenic Pointe Drive, Suite 100, Draper, UT 84020
Phone: 801 727-1000
Web: www.healthequity.com

HISTORICAL FINANCIALS
Company Type: Public

Income Statement				FYE: January 31
	REVENUE ($ mil.)	NET INCOME ($ mil.)	NET PROFIT MARGIN	EMPLOYEES
01/21	733.5	8.8	1.2%	3,039
01/20	531.9	39.6	7.5%	2,931
01/19	287.2	73.9	25.7%	1,141
01/18	229.5	47.3	20.6%	1,027
01/17	178.3	26.3	14.8%	875
Annual Growth	42.4%	(23.9%)	—	36.5%

2021 Year-End Financials

Debt ratio: 36.4%	No. of shares (mil.): 77.1
Return on equity: 0.7%	Dividends
Cash ($ mil.): 328.8	Yield: —
Current ratio: 2.25	Payout: —
Long-term debt ($ mil.): 924.2	Market value ($ mil.): 6,447.0

	STOCK PRICE ($) FY Close	P/E High/Low		PER SHARE ($) Earnings	Dividends	Book Value
01/21	83.55	758	338	0.12	0.00	17.87
01/20	66.06	143	88	0.58	0.00	14.50
01/19	62.34	84	42	1.17	0.00	7.64
01/18	50.62	69	50	0.77	0.00	5.69
01/17	46.25	108	35	0.44	0.00	4.40
Annual Growth	15.9%			— — (27.7%)	—	42.0%

Heartland BancCorp

EXECUTIVES

Chb-Ceo, Scott G McComb
Vice Chb, Jay Eggspuehle
Evp-Cfo, Carrie Almendinger
Coo, Benjamin Babcanec
Director, Beverly Donaldson
Svp, Molly Z Brown
Chief Credit Officer, Paula A Hughes
Commercial Lending Assistant, Donna Baskerville
Ao, Market Leader, Daniel Miller
Market Pres, Cincinnati Region, Brian Brockhoff
Auditors: BKD, LLP

LOCATIONS

HQ: Heartland BancCorp
430 North Hamilton Road, Whitehall, OH 43213
Phone: 614 337-4600
Web: www.heartlandbank.com

HISTORICAL FINANCIALS
Company Type: Public

Income Statement				FYE: December 31
	ASSETS ($ mil.)	NET INCOME ($ mil.)	INCOME AS % OF ASSETS	EMPLOYEES
12/20	1,547.0	14.7	1.0%	279
12/19	1,114.8	13.2	1.2%	0
12/18	1,047.0	11.4	1.1%	0
12/17	900.9	8.8	1.0%	0
12/16	781.3	7.9	1.0%	0
Annual Growth	18.6%	16.6%	—	—

2020 Year-End Financials

Return on assets: 1.1%	Dividends
Return on equity: 10.9%	Yield: 0.0%
Long-term debt ($ mil.): —	Payout: 31.1%
No. of shares (mil.): 1.9	Market value ($ mil.): 165.0
Sales ($ mil): 70.1	

	STOCK PRICE ($) FY Close	P/E High/Low		PER SHARE ($) Earnings	Dividends	Book Value
12/20	82.99	13	7	7.33	2.28	70.70
12/19	95.15	15	12	6.45	2.08	63.55
12/18	81.00	15	12	6.68	1.89	57.08
12/17	82.60	15	12	5.40	1.72	48.77
12/16	64.01	14	9	4.97	1.55	45.10
Annual Growth	6.7%			— — 10.2%	10.2%	11.9%

Heartland Financial USA, Inc. (Dubuque, IA)

Founded in 1981 Heartland Financial USA is an $18 billion multi-bank holding company that owns flagship subsidiary Dubuque Bank and Trust (Iowa) and ten other banks that together operate more than 125 branches in about a dozen states primarily in the West and Midwest. In addition to standard deposit loan and mortgage services the banks also offer retirement wealth management trust insurance and investment services. Heartland also owns consumer lender Citizens Finance which has about a dozen offices in Illinois Iowa and Wisconsin.

Operations

Heartland Financial USA is engaged in the business of community banking and operate as a single business segment. Its Banks provide a wide range of commercial small business and consumer banking services to businesses including public sector and non-profit entities and to individuals. It has a broad customer base and are not dependent upon a single or a few customers. It provides a contemporary menu of traditional and non-traditional service channels including online banking mobile banking and telephone banking. Its Banks provide a comprehensive suite of banking services comprised of competitively priced deposit and credit offerings along with treasury management and retirement plan services.

Heartland's subsidiaries include: Citywide Banks (approximately $2.2 billion total deposits) New Mexico Bank & Trust ($1.7 billion) Dubuque Bank and Trust Company ($1.5 billion) Wisconsin Bank & Trust ($1.1 billion) First Bank & Trust ($2.6 billion) Premier Valley Bank ($837 million) Illinois Bank & Trust ($1.3 billion) Arizona Bank & Trust ($1.4 billion) Rocky Mountain Bank ($538 million) Bank of Blue Valley ($1.1 billion) and Minnesota Bank & Trust ($789.6 million.

Geographic Reach

Dubuque Iowa-based Heartland Financial USA operates through about 145 locations (including branches and loan production offices) in local communities in Iowa Illinois Wisconsin New Mexico Arizona Montana Colorado Minnesota Kansas Missouri Texas and California. The company's three largest bank subsidiaries by number of locations are First Bank & Trust with over 30 Colorado's Citywide Banks with about 25 and New Mexico Bank & Trust with about 20 locations.

Sales and Marketing

Heartland Financial USA offers its banking services to businesses public sector and non-profit entities and individuals.

The company provides a contemporary menu of traditional and non-traditional service channels including online banking mobile banking and telephone banking. Its Banks provide a comprehensive suite of banking services comprised of competitively priced deposit and credit offerings along with treasury management and retirement plan services.

Financial Performance

Heartland Financial USA has recorded nearly 20% asset growth rate over the last five years amounting to nearly $18 billion in 2020.

Total interest income increased $22.3 million or 4% to $536.6 million from $514.3 million due to an increase in average earning assets which was partially offset by a decrease in the average rate on earning assets.

Net income available to common stockholders was $133.5 million in 2020 compared to $149.1 million from the prior year. Return on average common equity was 8.06% and return on average assets was 0.90% for 2020 compared to 10.12% and 1.24% respectively for 2019.

Heartland lost $40.8 million from its cash stores in 2020 to end the year with $337.9 million. Operations brought in $190.4 million while investments used $2.3 billion. Financing activities used up $2.1 billion.

Strategy

Heartland Financial USA's primary objectives are to increase profitability and diversify its market area and asset base by expanding through acquisitions and to grow organically by increasing its customer base in the markets it serves. In the current environment it is continuing to seek opportunities for growth through acquisitions. Although it is focused on opportunities in its existing and adjacent markets it would consider acquisitions in new growth markets if they fit its business model support its customer-centric culture provide a sufficient return on investment and would be accretive to earnings within the first year of combined operations. It typically considers acquisitions of established financial institutions primarily commercial banks or thrifts.

In recent years it has focused on markets with growth potential in the Midwestern Southwestern and Western regions of the US. Its strategy is to balance the growth in its Southwestern and Western markets with the stability of its Midwestern markets.

Mergers and Acquisitions

In 2020 Heartland completed the acquisition of AimBank headquartered in Levelland Texas for $264.5 million. AimBank was merged with and into Heartland's wholly-owned Texas subsidiary First Bank and Trust and the combined entity operates as First Bank and Trust. As of the closing date AimBank had at fair value total assets of $1.97 billion which included gross loans of $1.09 billion and deposits of $1.67 billion.

In late 2020 Arizona Bank & Trust (AB&T) a wholly-owned subsidiary of Heartland headquartered in Phoenix Arizona completed its acquisition of certain assets and assumed substantially all of the deposits and certain other liabilities of Johnson Bank's Arizona operations which includes four banking centers. Johnson Bank is a wholly-owned subsidiary of Johnson Financial Group Inc. headquartered in Racine Wisconsin. As of the closing date AB&T acquired at fair value total assets of $419.7 million which included gross loans of $150.7 million and deposits of $415.5 million.

Company Background

Heartland Financial USA was founded in 1981 although it traces its roots back to the 1935 establishment of Dubuque Bank and Trust. It made its first bank acquisition in in 1989 – Key City Bank – and has continued acquiring community banks since.

EXECUTIVES

Executive Chairman Of The Board, Lynn Fuller, $536,250 total compensation
Lead Independent Vice Chairman Of The Board, Thomas Flynn
Executive Vice President, Deputy Chief Financial Officer, Principal Accounting Officer, Janet Quick
Independent Director, Duane White
Chief Financial Officer, Executive Vice President, Bryan McKeag, $405,000 total compensation
Executive Vice President - Commercial Banking, David Prince, $367,500 total compensation
Independent Director, Susan Murphy
Independent Director, Jennifer Hopkins
Executive Vice President, Chief Risk Officer, Tamina O'Neill
Chief Operating Officer, Executive Vice President, Daniel Stevens, $350,000 total compensation
Executive Vice President, Senior General Counsel, Corporate Secretary, Jay Kim
Executive Vice President, Chief Credit Officer, Nathan Jones
Independent Director, Chris Hylen
President, Chief Executive Officer, Director, Bruce Lee, $731,250 total compensation
Chief Human Resource Officer, Executive Vice President, Deborah Deters
Executive Vice President, Chief Banking Officer, Kevin Quinn
Auditors: KPMG LLP

LOCATIONS

HQ: Heartland Financial USA, Inc. (Dubuque, IA)
1398 Central Avenue, Dubuque, IA 52001
Phone: 563 589-2100　　**Fax:** 563 589-2011
Web: www.htlf.com

PRODUCTS/OPERATIONS

2017 Sales

	$ mil.	% of total
Interest		
Loans & leases including fees	304.0	65
Securities	58.1	13
Other	1.6	-
Interest expense	(33.3)	-
Noninterest		
Gains on sales of loans	22.2	5
Service charges and fees	39.2	8
Trust fees	15.8	3
Loan serving income	5.6	1
Brokerage & insurance commissions	4.0	1
Security gains	7.0	2
Other	8.1	2
Total	**432.3**	**100**

Selected Subsidiaries

Arizona Bank & Trust
Citywide Banks (Colorado)
Dubuque Bank and Trust Company (Iowa)
　DB&T Community Development Corp.
　DB&T Insurance
Illinois Bank & Trust
Minnesota Bank & Trust
Morrill & Janes Bank and Trust Company (Kansas)
New Mexico Bank & Trust
Premier Valley Bank (California)
Rocky Mountain Bank (Montana)
Wisconsin Bank & Trust

COMPETITORS

BANCFIRST CORPORATION	GLACIER BANCORP INC.
BANK OF THE OZARKS CORPORATION INC.	IBERIABANK
BYLINE BANCORP INC.	MACATAWA BANK CORPORATION
CITIZENS & NORTHERN CORPORATION	MAINSOURCE FINANCIAL GROUP INC.
CITIZENS FINANCIAL GROUP INC. HOLDINGS	MB FINANCIAL INC. NATIONAL BANK
COLUMBIA BANKING SYSTEM INC.	CORPORATION
F.N.B. CORPORATION	OLD NATIONAL BANCORP
FIRST CITIZENS BANCSHARES INC.	PACWEST BANCORP PEOPLE'S UNITED FINANCIAL INC.
FIRST MERCHANTS CORPORATION	REPUBLIC BANCORP INC. TCF FINANCIAL
FIRST MIDWEST BANCORP INC.	CORPORATION WINTRUST FINANCIAL
FIRSTMERIT CORPORATION	CORPORATION

HISTORICAL FINANCIALS

Company Type: Public

Income Statement				FYE: December 31
	ASSETS ($ mil.)	NET INCOME ($ mil.)	INCOME AS % OF ASSETS	EMPLOYEES
12/20	17,908.3	137.9	0.8%	2,013
12/19	13,209.6	149.1	1.1%	1,908
12/18	11,408.0	117.0	1.0%	2,045
12/17	9,810.7	75.2	0.8%	2,008
12/16	8,247.0	80.3	1.0%	1,864
Annual Growth	21.4%	14.5%	—	1.9%

2020 Year-End Financials

Return on assets: 0.8%
Return on equity: 7.5%
Long-term debt ($ mil.): —
No. of shares (mil.): 42.0
Sales ($ mil): 656.9

Dividends
Yield: 1.9%
Payout: 22.1%
Market value ($ mil.): 1,699.0

	STOCK PRICE ($) FY Close	P/E High/Low		PER SHARE ($) Earnings	Dividends	Book Value
12/20	40.37	14	7	3.57	0.80	49.40
12/19	49.74	12	10	4.14	0.73	43.00
12/18	43.95	17	12	3.52	0.59	38.44
12/17	53.65	20	16	2.65	0.51	33.10
12/16	48.00	15	8	3.22	0.50	28.37
Annual Growth	(4.2%)	—	—	2.6%	12.5%	14.9%

Helios Technologies Inc

Helios Technologies Inc. (formerly known as Sun Hydraulics) develops and manufactures solutions for both the hydraulics and electronics markets. The Hydraulics segment includes products sold under the Sun Hydraulics Faster and Custom Fluidpower brands. The Electronics segment includes products sold under the Enovation Controls Balboa and Murphy brands. Products are sold through value-add distributors and directly to OEMs. The Americas represents almost 45% of its sales. It was originally founded in 1970 as Sun Hydraulics Corporation which designed and manufactured cartridge valves for hydraulics systems.

Operations

Helios operates in two business segments Hydraulics (nearly 80% of the total sales) and Electronics (over 20%).

The Hydraulics segment markets and sells products globally under the brands of Sun Hydraulics for its cartridge valve technology Custom Fluid Power for its hydraulic system design and Faster which provides quick release coupling solutions.

Global Electronics brands include Enovation Controls and Murphy for fully-tailored solutions with a broad range of rugged and reliable instruments such as displays controls and instrumentation products.

Geographic Reach

Headquartered in Sarasota Florida about 45% of Helios' sales are from the Americas followed by APAC with some 30% and EMEA accounts for over 25%. In addition Helios leases office spaces that are used for sales engineering and administrative activities in Argentina Australia Brazil China Germany India and Vietnam.

Sales and Marketing

Helios' products are sold globally through a combination independent and authorized distributors. In addition to distributors the company sells directly to other companies within the hydraulics industry it markets and sells hydraulic products through value-add distributors and directly to OEMs. Globally approximately 60% of sales are attributed to its channel partners who generally combine its products with other hydraulic components to design a complete hydraulic system.

Furthermore Helios provides end users with technical information through the websites of its operating companies and catalogs in multiple languages including all information necessary to specify and obtain its products.

Financial Performance

Consolidated net sales for the 2020 year totaled $523.0 million down 6% compared with 2019. The Company's acquisition of Balboa on November 6 2020 added $26.1 million in sales for the year.

Net income for fiscal 2020 decreased by 77% to $14.2 million compared from the prior year with $60.3 million.

Cash held by the company at the end of fiscal 2020 increased to $25.3 million. Cash provided by operations and financing activities were $108.6 million and $137.7 million respectively. Cash used for investing activities was $235.9 million mainly for acquisitions of a business.

Strategy

Helios' strategy is underpinned by the execution of acquisitions which the company expect to include bolt-on flywheel type acquisitions (up to $100 million in enterprise value) and the evaluation of more transformative type acquisitions ($100 million to $1 billion in enterprise value). The objective of its acquisition strategy is to enhance Helios by: growing its current product portfolio or adding new technologies and capabilities that complement our current offerings; expanding geographic presence; and bringing new customers or markets.

A primary focus of its strategic thinking is the identification of megatrends that will impact the future capital equipment and industrial goods markets. The company have identified three megatrends: globalization growing sophistication of safe machinery and equipment and increased computing power.

Mergers and Acquisitions

In 2021 Helios Technologies Inc. has entered into a definitive agreement to acquire assets related to the electronic control systems and parts business of Shenzhen Joyonway Electronics & Technology Co. Ltd and its related entities. A fast-growing developer of control panels software systems and accessories for the health and wellness industry Joyonway operates in two cities Shenzhen and Dongguan which are in the hub of electronics and software development in China. With the addition of Joyonway the company cost effectively expands its electronic controls platform with more capabilities strengthen its supply chain through broader geographic reach and increase its manufacturing capacity to meet growing global demand with the opportunity to improve its margins over time. Terms were not disclosed.

In early 2021 Helios Technologies has acquired substantially all of the assets of Texas-based BJN Technologies LLC an innovative engineering solutions provider. With the acquisition Helios has formed its Center of Engineering Excellence (HCEE) to augment and coordinate Helios's technology advancements and new product development and better leverage existing talents with the acquired capabilities of BJN. Financial terms were not disclosed.

In late 2020 Helios Technologies has completed the acquisition of BWG Holdings I Corp. (operating as Balboa Water Group hereinafter "Balboa") for $218.5 million from investment funds affiliated with AEA Investors LP. Headquartered in Costa Mesa Balboa is an innovative market leader of electronic controls for the health and wellness industry with proprietary and patented technology that enables end-to-end electronic control systems for therapy bath and spas. With the acquisition Helios is further advancing its Vision 2025 strategy by executing on the value streams focused on product and technology expansion and market diversification.

EXECUTIVES

Chief Financial Officer, Tricia Fulton, $405,662 total compensation
Independent Chairman Of The Board, Philippe Lemaitre
President - Cartridge Valve Technology, Jason Morgan
Independent Director, Douglas Britt
Chief Legal And Compliance Officer, Secretary, Melanie Nealis, $332,800 total compensation
President Of Quick Release Couplings, Matteo Arduini, $271,419 total compensation
Independent Director, Laura Brown
Independent Director, Cariappa Chenanda
Chief Commercial Officer, John Shea
President, Chief Executive Officer, Director, Josef Matosevic, $406,154 total compensation
Auditors: Grant Thornton LLP

LOCATIONS

HQ: Helios Technologies Inc
7456 16th St. E., Sarasota, FL 34243
Phone: 941 362-1200
Web: www.sunhydraulics.com

PRODUCTS/OPERATIONS

Selected Products
Integrated packages (using custom designed manifolds)
Screw-in hydraulic cartridge valves (electrically actuated and non-electrically actuated)
Standard manifolds

COMPETITORS

APPLIED INDUSTRIAL TECHNOLOGIES INC.
APTARGROUP INC.
BARNES GROUP INC.
CROSS TECHNOLOGIES INC.
DIXON VALVE & COUPLING COMPANY LLC
ELECTROCOMPONENTS PUBLIC LIMITED COMPANY
EMERSON ELECTRIC CO.
EVOQUA WATER TECHNOLOGIES CORP.
JET RESEARCH DEVELOPMENT INC.
REPLIGEN CORPORATION
STRATASYS LTD
TRIMAS CORPORATION
VOLEX PLC

HISTORICAL FINANCIALS

Company Type: Public

Income Statement   FYE: January 2

	REVENUE ($ mil.)	NET INCOME ($ mil.)	NET PROFIT MARGIN	EMPLOYEES
01/21*	523.0	14.2	2.7%	2,000
12/19	554.6	60.2	10.9%	1,960
12/18	508.0	46.7	9.2%	2,065
12/17	342.8	31.5	9.2%	1,150
12/16	196.9	23.3	11.8%	1,100
Annual Growth	27.7%	(11.6%)	—	16.1%

*Fiscal year change

2021 Year-End Financials

Debt ratio: 35.6%
Return on equity: 2.3%
Cash ($ mil.): 25.2
Current ratio: 1.98
Long-term debt ($ mil.): 445.8

No. of shares (mil.): 32.1
Dividends
Yield: 0.0%
Payout: 81.8%
Market value ($ mil.): 1,712.0

	STOCK PRICE ($)	P/E	PER SHARE ($)		
	FY Close	High/Low	Earnings	Dividends	Book Value
01/21*	53.29	122 68	0.44	0.36	18.92
12/19	45.50	28 17	1.88	0.36	18.02
12/18	33.36	47 21	1.49	0.36	16.60
12/17	64.69	56 29	1.17	0.29	10.07
12/16	39.97	48 28	0.87	0.40	8.78
Annual Growth	7.5%	—	—(15.7%)	(2.6%)	21.2%

*Fiscal year change

Helix Energy Solutions Group Inc

Helix Energy Solutions (Helix) is in the energy services mix as a top marine deepwater contractor. Its well intervention unit primarily works in water depths ranging from 200 to 10000 feet using dynamically positioned and remotely operated vehicles (ROVs) that offer a range of engineering repair maintenance and pipe and cable burial services in global offshore markets. Former subsidiary Energy Resource Technology (ERT) bought and operated mature fields primarily in the Gulf of Mexico but in 2013 Helix Energy Solutions sold this business in order to focus on its offshore contracting operations. About 40% of the company's total sales comes the US. Helix was incorporated in 1979 and re-incorporated in 1983.

Operations
The company operates in three major segments: Well Intervention (generates more than 70% of total revenue) Robotics (over 20% of revenue) and Production Facilities (beyond 5%).

Well Intervention includes vessels and related equipment that are used to perform both heavy and light well intervention services primarily in the Gulf of Mexico Brazil the North Sea and West Africa.

The Robotics segment operates five chartered vessels and also includes ROVs trenchers and ROVDrills designed to complement offshore construction and well intervention services.

The Production Facilities segment includes the HP I and the HFRS as well as their ownership interest in Independence Hub and oil and gas properties.

Geographic Reach
Texas-based Helix operates in the Gulf of Mexico Brazil North Sea Asia Pacific and West Africa.

The US is the largest market in terms of revenue which generates for about 40% followed by Brazil accounting for almost 30% and over 25% of revenue were produced from the UK.

Sales and Marketing
The company's more than 50 customers include major and independent oil and gas producers and suppliers pipeline transmission companies alternative (renewable) energy companies and offshore engineering and construction firms. In 2019 Petrobras BP and Shell (Helix Energy Solutions' major customers) accounted for about 30% some 15% and nearly 15% of the company's total revenues respectively.

Customers from long-term contract generates almost 60% of company's total sales while the remaining comes from short-term contract.

Financial Performance
The revenue growth of the company for the last five years was on an upward trend despite a decline in 2016. The company posted net income after losses in 2015 and 2016.In 2019 Helix Energy Solutions' revenues increased by 2% to $751.9 million reflecting a mix of higher revenues from its Well Intervention and Robotics business segments lower revenues from its Production Facilities business segment and higher intercompany eliminations.

The company's net income increased by 103% to $57.9 million primarily due to higher revenues reduced cost of sales and a decrease in interest expense.

Cash at the end of fiscal 2019 was $262.6 million 6% lower from the previous year. Net cash provided by operating activities was $169.7 million while cash used in investing activities was $142.4 million. Financing activities used another $45.8 million. Main cash uses for the year were for capital expenditures and repayment of loans.

Strategy
Helix Energy Solutions Group is an international offshore energy services company that provides specialty services to the offshore energy industry with a focus on well intervention and robotics operations. The company believes that focusing on these services should deliver favorable long-term financial returns. From time to time it may make strategic investments that expand its service capabilities and/or the regions in which it operates or adds capacity to existing services in its key operating regions. Its well intervention fleet expanded with the delivery in November 2019 of the Q7000 a newbuild semi-submersible vessel. The Q7000 commenced operations in Nigeria in January 2020. Chartering vessels with additional capabilities such as the Grand Canyon vessels should enable its robotics business to better serve the needs of its customers. It expects to benefit from longer-term contracts that offer firm utilization for its vessels and equipment and it seeks to improve utilization of its well intervention fleet in the Gulf of Mexico as it acquires oil and gas properties and perform the plug and abandonment ("P&A") of the acquired assets as its schedule permits subject to regulatory timelines.

In January 2015 Helix OneSubsea LLC OneSubsea B.V. Schlumberger Technology Corporation Schlumberger B.V. and Schlumberger Oilfield Holdings Ltd. entered into a Strategic Alliance Agreement and related agreements for the parties to design develop manufacture promote market and sell on a global basis integrated equipment and services for subsea well intervention. The alliance leverages the parties' capabilities to provide a unique fully integrated offering to clients combining marine support with well access and control technologies.

Mergers and Acquisitions
In mid-2019 the company acquired a 70% controlling interest in Subsea Technologies Group Limited (STL) a subsea engineering firm based in Aberdeen Scotland for $5.1 million including $4.1 million in cash and $1.0 million that they loaned to STL in late 2018. The acquisition is expected to strengthen the company's supply of subsea intervention systems.

In early 2019 Helix has acquired from Marathon Oil Corporation (Marathon Oil) certain operating depths associated with the Droshky Prospect on Green Canyon Block 244 along with related infrastructure. As part of the transaction Helix will perform the required plug and abandonment operations for which Marathon Oil will pay certain agreed upon amounts. Financial terms were not disclosed.

Company Background
Helix Energy Solutions Group Inc. was incorporated in 1979 and in 1983 was re-incorporated in the state of Minnesota.

EXECUTIVES

President, Chief Executive Officer, Director, Owen Kratz, $597,917 total compensation
Independent Director, John Lovoi
Independent Chairman Of The Board, William Transier
Senior Vice President, General Counsel, Secretary, Kenneth Neikirk, $339,000 total compensation
Independent Director, Jan Rask
Chief Operating Officer, Executive Vice President, Scott Sparks, $433,167 total compensation
Chief Financial Officer, Executive Vice President, Erik Staffeldt, $414,333 total compensation
Independent Director, Amerino Gatti
Independent Director, Amy Nelson
Director, T. Mitchell Little
Chief Accounting Officer, Controller, Brent Arriaga
Auditors: KPMG LLP

LOCATIONS

HQ: Helix Energy Solutions Group Inc
3505 West Sam Houston Parkway North, Suite 400, Houston, TX 77043
Phone: 281 618-0400   **Fax:** 281 618-0500
Web: www.HelixESG.com

PRODUCTS/OPERATIONS

2013 Sales

	% of total
Well Intervention	48
Robotics	35
Production Facility	9
Subsea Construction	8
Adjustments	-
Total	**100**

COMPETITORS

C&J ENERGY SERVICES INC.
CHIYODA CORPORATION
China Railway Engineering Group Co. Ltd.
China Railway Group Limited
FLUOR CORPORATION
HOCHTIEF AG
LARSEN AND TOUBRO LIMITED
SAIPEM SPA
SESI HOLDINGS INC.
VolkerWessels Nederland B.V.

HISTORICAL FINANCIALS

Company Type: Public

Income Statement
FYE: December 31

	REVENUE ($ mil.)	NET INCOME ($ mil.)	NET PROFIT MARGIN	EMPLOYEES
12/20	733.5	22.1	3.0%	1,536
12/19	751.9	57.9	7.7%	1,650
12/18	739.8	28.6	3.9%	1,546
12/17	581.3	30.0	5.2%	1,600
12/16	487.5	(81.4)	—	1,474
Annual Growth	10.8%	—	—	1.0%

2020 Year-End Financials

Debt ratio: 13.9%
Return on equity: 1.2%
Cash ($ mil.): 291.3
Current ratio: 1.88
Long-term debt ($ mil.): 258.9

No. of shares (mil.): 150.3
Dividends
  Yield: —
  Payout: —
Market value ($ mil.): 631.0

	STOCK PRICE ($) FY Close	P/E High/Low		PER SHARE ($) Earnings	Dividends	Book Value
12/20	4.20	74	8	0.13	0.00	11.58
12/19	9.63	25	15	0.38	0.00	11.42
12/18	5.41	57	27	0.19	0.00	10.92
12/17	7.54	48	25	0.20	0.00	10.61
12/16	8.82	—	—	(0.73)	0.00	10.63
Annual Growth	(16.9%)	—	—	—		2.2%

Heritage Commerce Corp

Heritage Commerce is the holding company for Heritage Bank of Commerce which operates about 15 branches in the southern and eastern regions of the San Francisco Bay area. Serving consumers and small to midsized businesses and their owners and managers the bank offers savings and checking accounts money market accounts and CDs as well as cash management services and loans. Commercial and commercial real estate loans make up most of the company's loan portfolio which is rounded out by land construction and home equity loans.

Operations

Heritage Commerce's two operating segments are banking and factoring (buying accounts receivables from clients at a discount); the divisions account for about 90% and 10% of the holding company's revenue respectively.

Heritage offers savings and checking accounts money market accounts and CDs as well as cash management services and loans to small to midsized businesses and their owners and managers. Loans account for about 75% of total revenue with commercial real estate accounting for about half of its loan portfolio; commercial loans account for about a third. Home equity loans and land and construction loans each comprise about five percent of the portfolio.

The company's Bay View Funding subsidiary provides working capital factoring financing to industrial clients across the US.

Geographic Reach

San Jose-based Heritage Commerce serves banking customers in the Santa Clara Alameda Contra Costa San Benito and San Mateo counties of California through about 15 Heritage Bank of Commerce branches. The company's Santa Clara-based Bay View Funding subsidiary provides industry clients with working capital factoring financing across the US.

Sales and Marketing

Despite a focus on personalized banking with in-branch officers and staff Heritage Commerce offers its customers internet banking services that do not include origination of deposit accounts or loan applications.

Financial Performance

Heritage Commerce has seen strong growth since 2013 doubling revenue and income and nearly tripling its cash as the company grew its loan portfolio through acquisitions. The company had about $40 million in long-term debt at the end of 2017 all of which it accrued that year.

Heritage's ? revenue trended up 8% to $111.1 million owing to increased interest income from loans including fees taxable securities and other investments and interest-bearing deposits in other financial institutions.

Heritage's net income decreased 13% to $23.8 million due to increased income tax expense associated with the passage of the Tax Cuts and Jobs Act.

The company grew its cash stores by 19% to $316.2 million. Operations contributed $41.4 million and financing activities provided $246.1 million primarily because of a net change in deposits. Investments used $237.3 million related to purchases of securities.

Strategy

Heritage Commerce's strategy is to grow through expanding its geographic footprint primarily through acquisitions in the San Francisco Bay Area. The company also seeks to use acquisitions to inhibit competitors from expanding into local markets. The company is third in deposit market share among Bay Area independent community banks.

Mergers and Acquisitions

Heritage Commerce acquired Presidio Bank in 2019 for $200.3 million. The deal gave Heritage $4 billion in additional assets and 17 new branches in the San Francisco Bay Area.

In April 2018 Heritage purchased Tri-Valley Bank for $33.2 million. The bank had $150.3 million in assets $134.1 million in deposits and $125.2 million in net loans.

Heritage acquired United American Bank in May 2018 for $46.9 million. United had $319.7 million in assets $286.6 million in deposits and $218.3 million in net loans.

United American had three branches in San Mateo Redwood City and Half Moon Bay. Tri-Valley had two branches in San Ramon and Livermore. Heritage closed the Half Moon Bay and San Ramon branches following the acquisitions.

Company Background

Heritage Commerce was founded in 1984.

EXECUTIVES

Executive Vice President Of Business Banking Manager Of Heritage Bank Of Commerce, Michael Benito, $302,660 total compensation
Chairman Of The Board, Jack Conner
President, Chief Executive Officer Of Heritage Commerce Corp And Heritage Bank Of Commerce, Director, Walter Kaczmarek
Executive Vice President, Corporate Secretary, Debbie Reuter
Executive Vice President/president Of Community Business Banking Group For Heritage Bank Of Commerce, Robertson Jones, $322,088 total compensation
Independent Director, Laura Roden
Independent Director, Julianne Biagini-Komas
Independent Director, Ranson Webster
Executive Vice President, Chief Credit Officer Of Heritage Bank Of Commerce, Margo Butsch, $296,525 total compensation
Independent Director, Marina Sutton
Independent Director, Bruce Cabral
Director, Kamran Husain
Auditors: Crowe LLP

LOCATIONS

HQ: Heritage Commerce Corp
224 Airport Parkway, San Jose, CA 95110
Phone: 408 947-6900
Web: www.heritagecommercecorp.com

PRODUCTS/OPERATIONS

2017 Sales

	$ mil.	% of total
Interest		
Loans including fees	86.4	74
Taxable securities	13.7	12
Other	6.8	6
Interest expense	(5.4)	-
Noninterest		
Service charges & fees on deposit accounts	3.2	3
Increase in cash surrender value of life insurance	1.7	1
Gain on sales of SBA loans	1.1	1
Servicing income	1.0	1
Other	2.6	2
Total	**111.1**	**100**

COMPETITORS

AMERICAN NATIONAL BANKSHARES INC.	FULTON FINANCIAL CORPORATION
CENTERSTATE BANK CORPORATION	HOMESTREET INC.
CENTRAL PACIFIC FINANCIAL CORP.	PACIFIC CONTINENTAL CORPORATION
CITY HOLDING COMPANY	PACWEST BANCORP
COLUMBIA BANKING SYSTEM INC.	SOUTHSIDE BANCSHARES INC.
	WILSHIRE BANCORP INC.

HISTORICAL FINANCIALS

Company Type: Public

Income Statement
FYE: December 31

	ASSETS ($ mil.)	NET INCOME ($ mil.)	INCOME AS % OF ASSETS	EMPLOYEES
12/20	4,634.1	35.3	0.8%	335
12/19	4,109.4	40.4	1.0%	357
12/18	3,096.5	35.3	1.1%	302
12/17	2,843.4	23.8	0.8%	278
12/16	2,570.8	27.3	1.1%	263
Annual Growth	15.9%	6.6%	—	6.2%

2020 Year-End Financials

Return on assets: 0.8%
Return on equity: 6.1%
Long-term debt ($ mil.): —
No. of shares (mil.): 59.9
Sales ($ mil): 160.3

Dividends
  Yield: 5.8%
  Payout: 118.1%
Market value ($ mil.): 531.0

	STOCK PRICE ($) FY Close	P/E High/Low	PER SHARE ($) Earnings	Dividends	Book Value
12/20	8.87	22 11	0.59	0.52	9.64
12/19	12.83	17 13	0.84	0.48	9.71
12/18	11.34	21 13	0.84	0.44	8.49
12/17	15.32	26 21	0.62	0.40	7.10
12/16	14.43	20 13	0.72	0.36	6.85
Annual Growth	(11.5%)	— —	(4.9%)	9.6%	8.9%

Heritage Financial Corp (WA)

Heritage Financial is ready to answer the call of Pacific Northwesterners seeking to preserve their heritage. Heritage Financial is the holding company for Heritage Bank which operates more than 65 branches throughout Washington and Oregon. Boasting nearly $4 billion in assets the bank offers a range of deposit products to consumers and businesses such as CDs IRAs and checking savings NOW and money market accounts. Commercial and industrial loans account for over 50% of Heritage Financial's loan portfolio while mortgages secured by multi-family real estate comprise about 5%. The bank also originates single-family mortgages land development construction loans and consumer loans.

Operations

The bank also does business under the Central Valley Bank name in the Yakima and Kittitas counties of Washington and under the Whidbey Island Bank name on Whidbey Island.

About 79% of Heritage Financial's total revenue came from loan interest (including fees) in 2014 while another 7% came from interest on its investment securities. The rest of its revenue came from service charges and other fees (8%) Merchant Visa income (1%) and other miscellaneous fees. The company had a staff of 748 employees at the end of that year.

Geographic Reach

The Olympia-based bank operates more than 65 branches across Washington and the greater Portland area. It has additional offices in eastern Washington mostly in Yakima county.

Sales and Marketing

Heritage targets small and medium-sized businesses along with their owners as well as individuals.

Financial Performance

Fueled by loan and deposit growth from a series of bank acquisitions Heritage Financial's revenues and profits have been on the rise in recent years.

The company's revenue jumped 70% to a record $137.6 million in 2014 mostly thanks to new loan business stemming from its acquisition of Washington Banking Company. Deposit service charge income also increased thanks to new deposit business from the acquisition.

Higher revenue in 2014 allowed Heritage Financial's net income to more than double to a record $21 million while its operating cash levels rose 66% to $51.3 million on higher cash earnings and net proceeds from the sale of its loans.

Strategy

The bank reiterated in 2015 that it would continue to pursue strategic acquisitions of community banks to grow market share across the Pacific Northwest (its region of expertise) expand its business lines and grow its loan and deposit business.

With its focus on business and commercial lending the bank also in 2015 emphasized the importance of seeking high asset quality loans lending to familiar markets that have a historical record of success. Recruiting and retaining "highly competent personnel" to execute its strategies was also key to its long-term agenda.

Mergers and Acquisitions

In May 2014 Heritage acquired Washington Banking Company and its Whidbey Island Bank subsidiary for $265 million which "significantly expanded and enhanced" its product offerings across its core geographic market.

In July 2013 the bank acquired Puyallup Washington-based Valley Community Bancshares and its eight Valley Bank branches for $44 million.

In January 2013 the company purchased Lakewood Washington-based Northwest Commercial Bank along with its two branch locations in Washington state for $5 million.

EXECUTIVES

President, Chief Executive Officer, Director, Jeffrey Deuel, $575,000 total compensation
Executive Vice President And Chief Credit Officer Of Heritage And Heritage Bank, Tony Chalfant, $266,225 total compensation
Chairman Of The Board, Brian Vance
Executive Vice President And Chief Banking Officer Of Heritage Bank, Cindy Huntley, $263,040 total compensation
Executive Vice President And President, Chief Operating Officer Of Heritage Bank, Bryan McDonald, $385,020 total compensation
Independent Director, Frederick Rivera
Director, Trevor Dryer
Director, Gail Giacobbe
Executive Vice President And Chief Financial Officer Of Heritage And Heritage Bank, Donald Hinson, $339,694 total compensation
Auditors: Crowe LLP

LOCATIONS

HQ: Heritage Financial Corp (WA)
201 Fifth Avenue SW, Olympia, WA 98501
Phone: 360 943-1500
Web: www.HF-WA.com

PRODUCTS/OPERATIONS

2014 Sales

	$ mil.	% of total
Interest income		
Interest and fees on loans	110.4	79
Investment securities	10.2	7
Others	0.5	-
Non-interest income		
Service charges and others	11.1	8
Merchant Visa income	1.1	1
Others	4.3	5
Total	**137.6**	**100**

COMPETITORS

BANCFIRST CORPORATION
BANCORP
CITY HOLDING COMPANY
COLUMBIA BANKING SYSTEM INC.
OLD NATIONAL BANCORP
PEOPLES FINANCIAL SERVICES CORP.
WASHINGTON TRUST

F.N.B. CORPORATION
NORTHWEST BANCORP INC.
BANCORP INC.
OLD LINE BANCSHARES INC.
BANCORP INC.
WILSHIRE

HISTORICAL FINANCIALS

Company Type: Public

Income Statement				FYE: December 31
	ASSETS ($ mil.)	NET INCOME ($ mil.)	INCOME AS % OF ASSETS	EMPLOYEES
12/20	6,615.3	46.5	0.7%	856
12/19	5,552.9	67.5	1.2%	884
12/18	5,316.9	53.0	1.0%	859
12/17	4,113.2	41.7	1.0%	735
12/16	3,878.9	38.9	1.0%	760
Annual Growth	14.3%	4.6%	—	3.0%

2020 Year-End Financials

Return on assets: 0.7%
Return on equity: 5.7%
Long-term debt ($ mil.): —
No. of shares (mil.): 35.9
Sales ($ mil): 251.5
Dividends
  Yield: 3.4%
  Payout: 73.3%
Market value ($ mil.): 840.0

	STOCK PRICE ($) FY Close	P/E High/Low	PER SHARE ($) Earnings	Dividends	Book Value
12/20	23.39	22 12	1.29	0.80	22.85
12/19	28.30	18 14	1.83	0.84	22.10
12/18	29.72	25 19	1.49	0.72	20.63
12/17	30.80	23 16	1.39	0.61	16.98
12/16	25.75	20 13	1.30	0.72	16.08
Annual Growth	(2.4%)	— —	(0.2%)	2.7%	9.2%

Hess Midstream LP

Auditors: Ernst & Young LLP

LOCATIONS

HQ: Hess Midstream LP
1501 McKinney Street, Houston, TX 77010
Phone: 713 496-4200
Web: www.hessmidstream.com

HISTORICAL FINANCIALS

Company Type: Public

Income Statement				FYE: December 31
	REVENUE ($ mil.)	NET INCOME ($ mil.)	NET PROFIT MARGIN	EMPLOYEES
12/20	1,091.9	24.0	2.2%	196
12/19	848.3	15.1	1.8%	176
12/18	662.4	70.8	10.7%	0
12/17	565.8	41.2	7.3%	176
12/16	509.8	206.3	40.5%	0
Annual Growth	21.0%	(41.6%)	—	—

2020 Year-End Financials

Debt ratio: 56.6%
Return on equity: 18.6%
Cash ($ mil.): 2.6
Current ratio: 0.81
Long-term debt ($ mil.): 1,900.1
No. of shares (mil.): 284.4
Dividends
  Yield: 8.8%
  Payout: 132.4%
Market value ($ mil.): 5,567.0

	STOCK PRICE ($) FY Close	P/E High/Low		PER SHARE ($) Earnings	Dividends	Book Value
12/20	19.57	19	5	1.31	1.73	0.44
12/19	22.68	19	15	1.20	1.62	0.46
12/18	16.98	19	13	1.27	1.41	61.13
12/17	19.81	35	25	0.75	0.90	57.84
Annual Growth (80.3%)	(0.4%)			— —	20.4%	24.3%

Hibbett Inc

Small-town sports fans are the bread and butter for Hibbett Sports. The company sells brand-name sports equipment athletic apparel and footwear in small to midsized markets in about 35 states mainly in the South and Midwest. Its flagship Hibbett Sports chain boasts more than 1080 locations; stores are primarily found in malls and strip centers anchored by a Wal-Mart. Hibbett also operates nearly 150 of City Gear stores which stock urban streewear and about 20 mall-based Sports Additions shoe shops most of which are situated near Hibbett Sports stores. The company also trades online. The company was founded in 1945.

Operations
Hibbett offers personalized customer service and access to coveted footwear (about 65% of the total sales) apparel (more than 25%) and equipment (nearly 10%) from top brands like Nike Jordan Brand Adidas and Under Armour. In addition Hibbett Sports through its subsidiaries operates under the Hibbett Sporting Goods and City Gear brands and an omni-channel platform.

Geographic Reach
Hibbett headquartered in Birmingham Alabama most of its stores are located in Georgia Texas Alabama and Mississippi. It has presence in 35 states and has about 1100 stores in total. About 250 are in enclosed malls more than 30 are free-standing and some 800 are in strip-shopping centers which are frequently near a major chain retailer.

Sales and Marketing
In terms of sales its mobile apps buy online pickup in store (BOPIS) and reserve online pickup in store (ROPIS) complements its e-commerce site and provides its customers with customized advanced features and shopping experiences.

Financial Performance
Hibbett has recorded steady growth over the last five years.

Net sales increased $235.4 million or 20% to $1.42 billion for Fiscal 2021 from $1.18 billion for Fiscal 2020. Comparable store net sales for Fiscal 2021 increased 22% compared to Fiscal 2020 primarily driven by strength in men's women's and kids' footwear coupled with increased volume in sneaker-connected apparel and accessories. These strengths were partially offset by softer sales in team sports. For Fiscal 2021 1015 stores were included in the comparable store sales comparison.

Net income increased by $46.9 million to $74.3 million mainly due to higher net sales.

Hibbett's cash on hand rose to $209.3 million in 2021 from $66.1 million in 2020. The company's operations generated $197.7 million while investing and financing activities used $33.0 mil-lion and $21.6 million respectively. Main cash uses for the year were for capital expenditures and for repayments and repurchases.

Strategy
Hibbett targets underserved markets with branded products and provide a high level of customer service. This market strategy enables the company to achieve significant cost benefits including lower corporate expenses reduced logistics costs and increased economies of scale from marketing activities.

Hibbett uses information systems to maintain tight controls over inventory and operating costs and continually search for ways to improve efficiencies and the customer experience through information system upgrades. In addition it establishes greater customer vendor and landlord recognition as a leading specialty retailer in these communities. The company believe its ability to align its merchandising mix to local preferences and trends differentiates it from its national competitors.

Hibbett identifies markets for its stores under a clustered expansion program. This approach primarily focuses on opening new stores within close proximity of existing locations allowing it to take advantage of efficiencies in logistics marketing and regional management. It also aids the company in building a better understanding of appropriate merchandise selection for the local market. In addition to proximity to existing stores it also considers population economic conditions local competitive dynamics availability of suitable real estate and potential for return on investment when evaluating potential markets.

HISTORY
Rufus Hibbett a high school coach and educator in Florence Alabama founded single-store Dixie Supply which sold athletic marine and small aircraft equipment in 1945. Rufus' boys Ike and George got involved in the business and in 1952 the company took the name Hibbett & Sons and began to focus on team sports sales. It changed its name and emphasis again in the mid-1960s when as Hibbett Sporting Goods it became primarily a retailer.

The Anderson family owners of the Alabama-based retailer now known as Books-A-Million bought Hibbett in 1980 and continued its gradual expansion. With just over 10 stores Hibbett promoted company veteran Mickey Newsome to president two years later.

Starting in 1993 the chain began opening about 10 new stores each year. Hibbett opened its first Sports & Co. store in 1995. That year the Anderson family sold control of the company to Saunders Karp & Megrue Partners which took it public in 1996. Also in 1996 the chain doubled its store-opening pace.

Hibbett opened 33 stores in fiscal 1998 and 53 stores in fiscal 1999. Newsome was appointed CEO in 1999. By 2000 the company had weathered a shake-out of sporting goods retailers and expanded its store base more than 270% over five years opening 50 stores in fiscal 2000. The company opened more than 60 stores the following year.

In March 2004 chairman John Megrue Jr. retired and Newsome was given the position. Overall the company added 53 Hibbett Sports stores and a single Sports Additions store in 2004.

In August 2005 Brian Priddy joined Hibbett from Bombay Company as president. Newsome retained the titles of chairman and CEO.

In early 2007 the company created its holding company Hibbett Sports to separate itself from its existing operating entity. Priddy resigned in 2007 to pursue other interests. That fiscal year the company opened 64 stores.

In fiscal 2008 it opened 75 retail stores bringing its total count to 688. The following year it added 60 retail stores which boosted its network to 748 locations.

In fiscal 2009 the company opened about 20 stores.

EXECUTIVES
Senior Vice President And Chief Merchant, Jared Briskin, $380,000 total compensation
Independent Director, Alton Yother
Senior Vice President And General Counsel, David Benck
Independent Director, James Hilt
Independent Director, Karen Etzkorn
Independent Director, Dorlisa Flur
President, Chief Executive Officer, And Director, Michael Longo, $500,000 total compensation
Senior Vice President, Operations, Benjamin Knighten
Chief Financial Officer, Robert Volke, $335,000 total compensation
Director, Linda Hubbard
Senior Vice President, Digital Commerce, William Quinn, $345,000 total compensation
Senior Vice President And Chief Information Officer, Ronald Blahnik, $340,000 total compensation
Auditors: Ernst & Young LLP

LOCATIONS
HQ: Hibbett Inc
2700 Milan Court, Birmingham, AL 35211
Phone: 205 942-4292
Web: www.hibbett.com

PRODUCTS/OPERATIONS

2019 Stores
	No.
Hibbett Sports Stores	1,007
City Gear	138
Sports Additions	18
Total	**1,163**

2019 Sales
	% of total
Footwear	49
Apparel	29
Equipment	22
Total	**100**

COMPETITORS
ALLEN EDMONDS LLC
CALERES INC.
DESTINATION XL GROUP INC.
FIVE BELOW INC.
LOWE'S COMPANIES INC.
MAHWAH BERGEN RETAIL GROUP INC.
SCHUH LIMITED
SHOE CARNIVAL INC.
SPARTANNASH COMPANY
TARGET CORPORATION
WEYCO GROUP INC.

HISTORICAL FINANCIALS

Company Type: Public

Income Statement

FYE: January 30

	REVENUE ($ mil.)	NET INCOME ($ mil.)	NET PROFIT MARGIN	EMPLOYEES
01/21*	1,419.6	74.2	5.2%	10,700
02/20	1,184.2	27.3	2.3%	10,200
02/19	1,008.6	28.4	2.8%	10,600
02/18	968.2	35.0	3.6%	9,200
01/17	972.9	61.0	6.3%	9,300
Annual Growth	9.9%	5.0%	—	3.6%

*Fiscal year change

2021 Year-End Financials

Debt ratio: 0.4%
Return on equity: 20.6%
Cash ($ mil.): 209.2
Current ratio: 1.95
Long-term debt ($ mil.): 2.6

No. of shares (mil.): 16.4
Dividends
Yield: —
Payout: —
Market value ($ mil.): 930.0

	STOCK PRICE ($) FY Close	P/E High/Low		PER SHARE ($) Earnings	Dividends	Book Value
01/21*	56.45	13	2	4.36	0.00	23.73
02/20	24.78	19	10	1.52	0.00	19.51
02/19	16.31	19	9	1.51	0.00	18.37
02/18	22.15	20	6	1.71	0.00	16.86
01/17	32.70	17	11	2.72	0.00	15.41
Annual Growth	14.6%	—	—	12.5%	—	11.4%

*Fiscal year change

Hillenbrand Inc

Hillenbrand is a global diversified industrial company with multiple leading brands that serve a wide variety of industries worldwide. It has three very distinct businesses: Advanced Process Solutions designs develops manufactures and services highly engineered industrial equipment throughout the world; Molding Technology Solutions a global leader in highly engineered and customized systems and service in plastic technology and processing; and Batesville a recognized leader in the death care industry in North America. Founded by John A. Hillenbrand in 1906 Hillenbrand generates just more than 50% of its sales in the US.

Operations

Hillenbrand's Advanced Process Solutions generates about 45% of the overall revenue. The segment is a leading global provider of compounding extrusion and material handling; screening and separating; flow control; and size reduction products and services for a wide variety of manufacturing and other industrial processes. Its products include material handling equipment (under the Coperion and K-Tron names) and screening and separating equipment (Rotex and BM&M). Aftermarket parts and service account for about 30% of Advanced Process Solutions's revenue.

Molding Technology Solutions accounts for approximately 35% of the company's total revenue. The segment has a full-line product portfolio that includes injection molding and extrusion equipment hot runner systems process control systems mold bases and components and maintenance repair and operating (MRO) supplies. Aftermarket parts and services represents about 25% of Molding Technology Solutions' total net revenue.

Hillenbrand's Advanced Process Solutions generates about 45% of the overall revenue. The segment is a leading global provider of compounding extrusion and material handling; screening and separating; flow control; and size reduction products and services for a wide variety of manufacturing and other industrial processes. Its products include material handling equipment (under the Coperion and K-Tron names) and screening and separating equipment (Rotex and BM&M). Aftermarket parts and service account for about 30% of Advanced Process Solutions's revenue.

Molding Technology Solutions accounts for approximately 35% of the company's total revenue. The segment has a full-line product portfolio that includes injection molding and extrusion equipment hot runner systems process control systems mold bases and components and maintenance repair and operating (MRO) supplies. Aftermarket parts and services represents about 25% of Molding Technology Solutions' total net revenue.

By products and services equipment provides about 55% of the company's total sales parts and services account for nearly 25% death care brings in more than 20% of total sales while others generate the remaining. By timing of transfer point in time provides about 80% of the company's total sales. Over time generates the remaining more than 20%.

Geographic Reach

Indiana-based Hillenbrand operates worldwide but generates more than 50% of its revenue from the US. Geographically about 25% of Advanced Process Solutions' net revenue came from the Americas nearly 45% from Asia and about 30% from EMEA (Europe the Middle East and Africa). In addition about 55% of Molding Technology Solutions' net revenue came from the Americas some 30% from Asia and more than 15% from EMEA (Europe the Middle East and Africa). The Batesville segment operates primarily in North America.

Advanced Process Solutions has about 15 significant manufacturing facilities in the US (New Jersey Kansas Ohio Illinois North Carolina and Virginia) Germany Switzerland China India and the UK. It also has sales office in the US Europe Asia Canada and South America.

Molding Technology Solutions operates more than 10 significant manufacturing facilities located in the US (in Ohio Kansas Georgia and Michigan) Germany China India Canada and the US as well as warehouse distribution centers service centers and sales offices located in the US Mexico Canada Europe Asia and South America.

Batesville has manufacturing facilities in Indiana Tennessee Mississippi and Mexico as well as warehouse distribution centers and other facilities in the US Mexico Canada and Australia.

Sales and Marketing

Hillenbrand employs a direct sales team to market both its industrial equipment and funeral products. The company also uses a network of independent sales reps who work on commission for its industrial equipment.

Customers include local regional national and global businesses in a variety of industries (plastics pharmaceuticals chemicals fertilizers wastewater treatment) for its industrial equipment automotive consumer goods packaging construction and electronics for Molding Technology Solutions and funeral directors and funeral homes for its funeral products.

By end market plastics provide approximately 30% of the company's revenue. Automotive chemicals consumer goods food and pharmaceuticals custom molders packaging construction minerals and mining electronics medical death care and other industrial markets account for the rest.

Financial Performance

The company's revenue for fiscal 2021 increased by 14% to $2.9 billion compared with $2.5 billion.

Net income for fiscal 2021 was $249.9 million compared with a net loss of $60.1 million.

Cash held by the company at the end of fiscal 2021 increased to $450.9 million. Cash provided by operations and investing activities were $528.4 million and $126.0 million respectively. Cash used for financing activities was $523.3 million mainly for repayments of long-term debt.

Strategy

Hillenbrand's strategy is to leverage its historically strong financial foundation and the implementation of the HOM to deliver sustainable profit growth revenue expansion and substantial free cash flow and then reinvest available cash in new growth initiatives focused on building platforms with leadership positions in its core markets and near adjacencies both organically and inorganically in order to create shareholder value.

In fiscal 2021 the company began aligning sustainability with the HOM. Hillenbrand believes sustainability to be a source of value creation that must be aligned with the core strategy of the company. The company expects to continue developing this part of its strategy as it grows in its sustainability practice. Among other things the company believes climate change will require meaningful action on a global scale and Hillenbrand expects that further developing its understanding of its energy consumption and emissions will be an important part of examining the challenges posed by climate change as well as continuing to develop its sustainability strategy. To date the company's costs relating to addressing climate change have not been material.

Company Background

Batesville Coffin Company was founded in 1884. In 1906 it was purchased by John A. Hillenbrand and renamed Batesville Casket Company. It became part of the larger family-owned Hillenbrand Industries which went public in 1971.

In 2008 Hillenbrand Industries spun off its funeral business with Hillenbrand Inc. created as the parent company for Batesville Casket.

From 2010 to 2016 Hillenbrand Inc. made multiple strategic acquisitions to add a second line of business industrial equipment. It purchased diversified industrial manufacturer K-Tron in 2010 screening machine developer Rotex in 2011 bulk materials handling equipment seller Coperion in 2012 displacement pumps business ABEL Pumps in 2015 and flow control firm Red Valve in 2016.

EXECUTIVES

Senior Vice President - Strategy And Corporate Development, J. Michael Whitted, $435,963 total compensation
Chief Accounting Officer, Vice President, Controller, Andrew Kitzmiller
Senior Vice President, President - Mold-masters, Ling An-Heid, $433,805 total compensation
Chief Information Officer, Vice President, Bhavik Soni

Independent Director, Jennifer Rumsey
Chief Human Resource Officer, Senior Vice President, Peter Dyke
Vice President - Global Supply Management, Michael Prado
Senior Vice President - Operations Center Of Excellence, Leo Kulmaczewski
Independent Director, Dennis Pullin
Independent Director, Inderpreet Sawhney
Senior Vice President, Ulrich Bartel
Independent Director, Neil Novich
Independent Director, Stuart Taylor
Independent Chairman Of The Board, F. Joseph Loughrey
President, Chief Executive Officer, Director, Kimberly Ryan-Dennis, $566,913 total compensation
Vice Chairperson, Helen Cornell
Senior Vice President, President - Milacron Injection Molding And Extrusion, Michael Jones
Senior Vice President, President - Batesville Casket Company, Christopher Trainor, $474,792 total compensation
Independent Director, Joy Greenway
Chief Financial Officer, Senior Vice President, Kristina Cerniglia, $561,806 total compensation
Senior Vice President, Chief Compliance Officer, General Counsel, Secretary, Nicholas Farrell
Independent Director, Daniel Hillenbrand
Auditors: Ernst & Young LLP

LOCATIONS

HQ: Hillenbrand Inc
One Batesville Boulevard, Batesville, IN 47006
Phone: 812 934-7500
Web: www.hillenbrand.com

PRODUCTS/OPERATIONS

2018 Sales

	$ mil.	% of total
Process Equipment Group	1,219.5	69
Batesville	550.6	31
Total	**1,770.1**	**100**

COMPETITORS

Andritz AG	KIMBALL ELECTRONICS INC.
BARNES GROUP INC.	
ENERPAC TOOL GROUP CORP.	L. B. FOSTER COMPANY
EVOQUA WATER TECHNOLOGIES LLC	N L INDUSTRIES INC.
	NORDSON CORPORATION
FLEX LTD.	PLEXUS CORP.
ITT INC.	SUPERIOR GROUP OF COMPANIES INC.

HISTORICAL FINANCIALS

Company Type: Public

Income Statement

FYE: September 30

	REVENUE ($ mil.)	NET INCOME ($ mil.)	NET PROFIT MARGIN	EMPLOYEES
09/21	2,864.8	249.9	8.7%	10,500
09/20	2,517.0	(60.1)	—	11,000
09/19	1,807.3	121.4	6.7%	6,500
09/18	1,770.1	76.6	4.3%	6,500
09/17	1,590.2	126.2	7.9%	6,000
Annual Growth	15.9%	18.6%	—	15.0%

2021 Year-End Financials

Debt ratio: 30.2%	No. of shares (mil.): 72.7
Return on equity: 22.0%	Dividends
Cash ($ mil.): 446.1	Yield: 2.0%
Current ratio: 1.39	Payout: 34.6%
Long-term debt ($ mil.): 1,212.9	Market value ($ mil.): 3,101.0

	STOCK PRICE ($) FY Close	P/E High/Low		PER SHARE ($) Earnings	Dividends	Book Value
09/21	42.65	15	9	3.31	0.86	16.64
09/20	28.36	—	—	(0.82)	0.85	14.16
09/19	30.88	27	14	1.92	0.84	12.03
09/18	52.30	44	32	1.20	0.83	11.74
09/17	38.85	20	15	1.97	0.82	11.91
Annual Growth	2.4%	—	—	13.9%	1.2%	8.7%

Hingham Institution for Savings

The Hingham Institution for Savings serves businesses and retail customers in Boston's south shore communities operating more than 10 branches in Massachusetts in Boston Cohasset Hingham Hull Norwell Scituate South Hingham and South Weymouth. Founded in 1834 the bank offers traditional deposit products such as checking and savings accounts IRAs and certificates of deposit. More than 90% of its loan portfolio is split between commercial mortgages and residential mortgages (including home equity loans) though the bank also originates construction business and consumer loans. More than 95% of the company's revenue comes from loan interest.

Operations

The Hingham Institution for Savings made 96% of its total revenue from loan interest during 2015 while about 2% came from interest in equities CODs and other investments. The rest of its revenue mostly came from service fees on deposit accounts.

Of its $1.4 billion loan portfolio (at the end of 2015) about 48% was made up of commercial real estate mortgages (including multi-family housing) while 45% was tied to residential mortgages (including home equity). The remainder of the portfolio was made up of residential and commercial construction loans (7% of loan assets) and commercial business loans and consumer loans (1%).

Subsidiary Hingham Unpledged Securities Corporation holds title to certain securities available for sale.

Geographic Reach

The company mostly serves clients in Boston the South Shore and the island of Nantucket. Its branches are in Boston Cohasset Hingham Hull Nantucket Norwell Scituate South Hingham and South Weymouth Massachusetts.

Sales and Marketing

The Hingham Institution for Savings serves both individuals and small businesses in its three target markets in Massachusetts. Some of its clients (as of mid-2016) include Lyons Associates The Hub TCR Development SYA+FH Steven Young Architect + Fine Home Builder and Park Drive Inc.

The bank spent $489000 on marketing expenses during 2015 down from $557000 in each of 2014 and 2013.

Financial Performance

The bank's annual revenues have slowly trended higher over the past several years as the promising Boston real estate market has fueled its commercial real estate and residential loan business growth.

Hingham's revenue dipped 1% to $64.34 million during 2015 despite 13% mortgage loan growth mostly because in 2014 it earned a gains on life insurance distributions. The bank also continued to lose fee income as it has eliminated many fees on its deposit products to simplify offerings and attract customer deposits.

Revenue declines and higher income tax provisions in 2015 (in 2014 it earned non-taxed death benefit proceeds) caused the bank's net income to fall 13% to $19.34 million. Hingham's operating cash levels rose 11% to $20.2 million for the year thanks to a jump in cash-based earnings.

Strategy

The Hingham Institution for Savings continued in 2016 to focus on originating commercial multi-family and single-family mortgage loans in its target markets of Boston the South Shore and the island of Nantucket in Massachusetts especially as the healthy real estate market in and around Boston has provided a tailwind for its lending business.

EXECUTIVES

President, Chief Operating Officer, Director, Patrick Gaughen, $841,208 total compensation
Vice President - Commercial Lending, Shawn Sullivan, $390,312 total compensation
Director, Kara Smith
Independent Director, Robert Sheridan
Independent Director, Michael Desmond
Vice President - Specialized Deposit Group, Holly Cirignano, $188,462 total compensation
Chairman Of The Board, Chief Executive Officer, Robert Gaughen, $2,041,988 total compensation
Independent Director, Stacey Page
Director, Kevin Gaughen
Independent Director, Geoffrey Wilkinson
Independent Director, Jacqueline Youngworth
Independent Director, Scott Moser
Chief Financial Officer, Vice President, Cristian Melej, $483,917 total compensation
Director, Julio Hernando
Independent Director, Brian Kenner
Independent Director, Howard Berger
Independent Director, Ronald Falcione
Director, Robert Lane
Auditors: Wolf & Company, P.C.

LOCATIONS

HQ: Hingham Institution for Savings
55 Main Street, Hingham, MA 02043
Phone: 781 749-2200 **Fax:** 781 740-4839
Web: www.hinghamsavings.com

COMPETITORS

BANK MUTUAL CORPORATION INC.	HOMESTREET INC.
	NORTHWEST BANCORP
FIRSTRUST SAVINGS BANK	

HOOVER'S HANDBOOK OF EMERGING COMPANIES 2022

HISTORICAL FINANCIALS
Company Type: Public

Income Statement
FYE: December 31

	ASSETS ($ mil.)	NET INCOME ($ mil.)	INCOME AS % OF ASSETS	EMPLOYEES
12/20	2,857.0	50.7	1.8%	87
12/19	2,590.3	38.9	1.5%	90
12/18	2,408.5	30.4	1.3%	96
12/17	2,284.6	25.7	1.1%	101
12/16	2,014.6	23.4	1.2%	103
Annual Growth	9.1%	21.3%	—	(4.1%)

2020 Year-End Financials
Return on assets: 1.8%
Return on equity: 18.7%
Long-term debt ($ mil.): —
No. of shares (mil.): 2.1
Sales ($ mil): 115.5

Dividends
  Yield: 1.1%
  Payout: 11.9%
  Market value ($ mil.): 462.0

	STOCK PRICE ($) FY Close	P/E High/Low		PER SHARE ($) Earnings	Dividends	Book Value
12/20	216.00	10	5	23.25	2.47	137.02
12/19	210.20	12	9	17.83	2.04	115.75
12/18	197.74	16	14	13.90	1.73	99.67
12/17	207.00	19	14	11.81	1.62	87.29
12/16	196.78	18	11	10.89	1.52	75.50
Annual Growth	2.4%	—	—	20.9%	12.9%	16.1%

Home Bancorp Inc

Making its home in Cajun Country Home Bancorp is the holding company for Home Bank a community bank which offers deposit and loan services to consumers and small to midsized businesses in southern Louisiana. Through about two dozen branches the bank offers standard savings and checking accounts as well as lending services such as mortgages consumer loans and credit cards. Its loan portfolio includes commercial real estate commercial and industrial loans as well as construction and land loans. Home Bancorp also operates about half a dozen bank branches in west Mississippi which were formerly part of Britton & Koontz Bank.

Geographic Reach
Home Bancorp serves the Louisiana areas of Greater Lafayette Baton Rouge Greater New Orleans and Northshore (of Lake Pontchartrain). Its markets in Mississippi include Vicksburg and Natchez.

Financial Performance
Although the company saw assets and loans grow in 2013 net income fell 20% that year to $7.3 million on lower operating income.

Mergers and Acquisitions
In early 2014 Home Bancorp spent about $35 million on Britton & Koontz Capital Corporation the holding company of Britton & Koontz Bank; the deal added five branches in west Mississippi to Home Bancorp's operations.

EXECUTIVES

Chairman Of The Board, President, Chief Executive Officer, John Bordelon, $400,500 total compensation
Independent Director, John Hendry
Independent Director, Paul Blanchet
Executive Vice President And Chief Credit Officer Of The Company And The Bank, Darren Guidry, $189,960 total compensation
Executive Vice President, Chief Operations Officer Of The Company And Bank, Jason Freyou, $223,253 total compensation
Chief Financial Officer, Executive Vice President, David Kirkley, $119,615 total compensation
Director, J. Scott Ballard
Director, Donald Washington
Auditors: Wipfli LLP

LOCATIONS

HQ: Home Bancorp Inc
  503 Kaliste Saloom Road, Lafayette, LA 70508
Phone: 337 237-1960   **Fax:** 337 264-9280
Web: www.home24bank.com

COMPETITORS

BNCCORP INC.	SOUTHWEST BANCORP INC.
PRUDENTIAL BANCORP INC. OF PENNSYLVANIA	THE FIRST BANCSHARES INC
RIDGEWOOD SAVINGS BANK BANCORPORATION	ZIONS
SOUTHERN CONNECTICUT ASSOCIATION BANCORP INC.	NATIONAL

HISTORICAL FINANCIALS
Company Type: Public

Income Statement
FYE: December 31

	ASSETS ($ mil.)	NET INCOME ($ mil.)	INCOME AS % OF ASSETS	EMPLOYEES
12/20	2,591.8	24.7	1.0%	0
12/19	2,200.4	27.9	1.3%	0
12/18	2,153.6	31.5	1.5%	0
12/17	2,228.1	16.8	0.8%	0
12/16	1,556.7	16.0	1.0%	0
Annual Growth	13.6%	11.5%	—	—

2020 Year-End Financials
Return on assets: 1.0%
Return on equity: 7.7%
Long-term debt ($ mil.): —
No. of shares (mil.): 8.7
Sales ($ mil): 118.4

Dividends
  Yield: 3.1%
  Payout: 39.2%
  Market value ($ mil.): 245.0

	STOCK PRICE ($) FY Close	P/E High/Low		PER SHARE ($) Earnings	Dividends	Book Value
12/20	27.99	14	7	2.85	0.88	36.82
12/19	39.19	13	11	3.05	0.84	34.19
12/18	35.40	14	10	3.40	0.71	32.14
12/17	43.22	19	14	2.28	0.55	29.57
12/16	38.61	17	10	2.25	0.41	24.47
Annual Growth	(7.7%)	—	—	6.1%	21.0%	10.8%

Home BancShares Inc

Home BancShares is the holding company for Centennial Bank which operates some 160 branches in Arkansas Florida and Alabama with an additional branch in each of New York City and Los Angeles (through which the company is building out a national lending platform). With $14.9 billion in assets the bank offers traditional services such as checking savings and money market accounts and CDs. About 60% of its lending portfolio is focused on commercial real estate loans — including non-farm and non-residential and construction and land development. The bank also writes residential mortgages and business and consumer loans. Through a subsidiary Home BancShares offers insurance services.

Operations
About 80% of Home Bancshares' $10.8 billion loan portfolio comprises real estate loans including non-farm and non-residential commercial loans which make up more than 40% of the total. Residential one-to-four-family loans and commercial construction and land development loans contribute about 20% and 15% respectively. Commercial and industrial loans make up around 10%.

The holding company has built a $6.3 billion portfolio of non-farm and non-residential commercial real estate loans primarily secured by commercial real estate. Around 50% 30% and 15% of the company's commercial real estate loan portfolio is in Florida Arkansas and with its Centennial Finance Group (CFG). Home Bancshares established the group in 2015 to manage loans acquired in the company's acquisition of the Florida Panhandle business of Banco Popular and to originate new loans (with a focus on commercial real estate and commercial and industrial loans) via a national lending platform.

About 30% and 60% of the company's $2.6 billion residential real estate loan portfolio are for one-to-four-family properties and non-owner occupied one-to-four family properties respectively.

The company's commercial and industrial loans account for about $1.3 billion of the portfolio; Arkansas Florida and Centennial CFG house about 40% 35% and 25% of that segment respectively.

Geographic Reach
Conway Arkansas-based Home Bancshares' holding company's Centennial Bank operates about 90 branches in Florida more than 75 in Arkansas around five in Southern Alabama and one in each of New York City and Los Angeles.

Sales and Marketing
Home Bancshares' non-farm and non-residential lending (comprising about 40% of the total) is made up of loans for shopping and retail centers hotels and motels offices industrial warehouses churches marinas and nursing homes.

Residential one-to-four-family residential mortgages for individuals make up some 20% of the company's portfolio. About 30% and 60% of its residential mortgage loans are for one-to-four-family owner-occupied and non-owner-occupied properties respectively.

The holding company also lends heavily to residential and commercial developers to construct commercial properties and develop land. Construction and land development loans make up about 15% of its portfolio.

216   HOOVER'S HANDBOOK OF EMERGING COMPANIES 2022

Around 10% of the value of Home Bancshares' loans go to commercial and industrial clients.

Financial Performance

Home Bancshares reported revenue of $555.5 million in 2017 up 174% from 2013 and net income of $135.1 million up 103% over the same period. The company's cash stores and long-term debt both about tripled during that time to $635.9 million and $1.7 billion respectively.

The holding company's revenue increased 13% in 2017 compared with 2016 owing to increased interest income from loans.

Home Bancshares' net income fell 24% due mostly to an increase in income tax expense related to the passage of the Tax Cuts and Jobs Act.

The company's $419.3 million to its cash in 2017. Operating activities provided $176.9 million down from the previous year based on decreased net income and increased charges from indemnification and other assets and accrued interest payable on other liabilities. Investments used $355.5 million while financings added $597.8 million driven mostly by proceeds from issuance of subordinated debentures.

Strategy

Home Bancshares' strategy is focused on expanding in its core Florida market through the purchase of local managed community banks including four in 2017 and 2018.

In addition to growing its geographic footprint Home Bancshares is also diversifying its product offerings through acquisitions. In 2018 the company bought the Shore Premier Finance division of Union Bankshares. Shore originated direct consumer loans for high-end sail and power boats in southeast Florida.

Mergers and Acquisitions

Home Bancshares acquired Giant Holdings The Bank of Commerce and Stonegate Bank in 2017 as well as former Union Bankshares subsidiary Shore Premier Finance in 2018.

The holding company purchased Giant Holdings for $96 million. Giant operated six branches in the Ft. Lauderdale Florida area and had $398.1 million in total assets $327.8 million in loans and $304 million in deposits.

Home Bancshares acquired The Bank of Commerce from Bank of Commerce Holdings as part of that company's bankruptcy for $4.2 million. Bank of Commerce – which had $182.5 million in assets $127.5 million in loans and $141.7 million in deposits – operated three branches in the Sarasota Florida area.

Home Bancshares bought Stonegate Bank for $820 million adding the company's $3.1 billion in total assets $2.4 billion in loans and $2.6 billion in deposits to its books. Stonegate had 24 offices in Florida markets including Broward and Sarasota counties.

In 2018 the company acquired the Shore Premier Finance division of Union Bankshares for $374.5 million in cash and 1.3 million shares. Shore originates direct consumer loans for high-end sail and power boats at 16 locations in southeast Florida. At the deal's close Shore had $384.2 million in assets including $383.4 million in total loans.

Company Background

Home Bancshares formed in 1998 as First State Bank.

EXECUTIVES

Executive Chairman Of The Board, President, Chief Executive Officer, John Allison, $461,506 total compensation

Chief Financial Officer, Treasurer, Director, Brian Davis, $353,184 total compensation

Executive Officer, Russell Carter

Chief Accounting Officer, Jennifer Floyd

Independent Director, Karen Garrett

Independent Director, Milburn Adams

Vice Chairman Of The Board, Jack Engelkes

Independent Director, James Hinkle

Chief Lending Officer, Kevin Hester, $408,183 total compensation

Senior Executive Vice President And Director Of Investor Relations, Director, Donna Townsell

Chief Operating Officer, John Tipton, $388,196 total compensation

Independent Director, Mike Beebe

Executive Officer, Director, Tracy French, $580,615 total compensation

Independent Director, Robert Adcock

Auditors: BKD, LLP

LOCATIONS

HQ: Home BancShares Inc
719 Harkrider, Suite 100, Conway, AR 72032
Phone: 501 339-2929
Web: www.homebancshares.com

COMPETITORS

BEAR STATE FINANCIAL GROUP INC.

BSB BANCORP INC.

FLAGSTAR BANCORP INC.

HANCOCK WHITNEY CORPORATION

HERITAGE FINANCIAL GROUP INC.

INDEPENDENT BANK INC.

LAKELAND BANCORP INC.

REPUBLIC BANCORP INC.

SOUTHSIDE BANCSHARES INC.

HISTORICAL FINANCIALS

Company Type: Public

Income Statement				FYE: December 31
	ASSETS ($ mil.)	NET INCOME ($ mil.)	INCOME AS % OF ASSETS	EMPLOYEES
12/20	16,398.8	214.4	1.3%	2,018
12/19	15,032.0	289.5	1.9%	1,920
12/18	15,302.4	300.4	2.0%	1,815
12/17	14,449.7	135.0	0.9%	1,744
12/16	9,808.4	177.1	1.8%	1,503
Annual Growth	13.7%	4.9%	—	7.6%

2020 Year-End Financials

Return on assets: 1.3%
Return on equity: 8.3%
Long-term debt ($ mil.): —
No. of shares (mil.): 165.1
Sales ($ mil): 787.7

Dividends
Yield: 2.7%
Payout: 40.7%
Market value ($ mil.): 3,216.0

	STOCK PRICE ($) FY Close	P/E High/Low		PER SHARE ($)		
				Earnings	Dividends	Book Value
12/20	19.48	16	8	1.30	0.53	15.78
12/19	19.66	12	10	1.73	0.51	15.10
12/18	16.34	15	9	1.73	0.46	13.76
12/17	23.25	33	24	0.89	0.40	12.70
12/16	27.77	35	15	1.26	0.34	9.45
Annual Growth	(8.5%)	—	—	0.8%	11.5%	13.7%

HomeTrust Bancshares Inc.

EXECUTIVES

Chief Executive Officer, President, And Chairman, Dana Stonestreet, $542,207 total compensation

Chief Financial Officer, Executive Vice President, Treasurer, Corporate Secretary, Tony VunCannon, $263,889 total compensation

Coo, C. Hunter Westbrook, $394,029 total compensation

Executive Vice President, Chief Information Officer, Marty Caywood, $246,298 total compensation

Executive Vice President, Chief Risk Officer, R. Parrish Little

Independent Director, John Switzer

Independent Director, Rebekah Lowe

Chief Human Resource Officer, Executive Vice President, Anna Smith

Executive Vice President, Chief Credit Officer, Keith Houghton, $245,390 total compensation

Independent Director, Robert James

Auditors: Dixon Hughes Goodman LLP

LOCATIONS

HQ: HomeTrust Bancshares Inc.
10 Woodfin Street, Asheville, NC 28801
Phone: 828 259-3939
Web: www.htb.com

HISTORICAL FINANCIALS

Company Type: Public

Income Statement				FYE: June 30
	ASSETS ($ mil.)	NET INCOME ($ mil.)	INCOME AS % OF ASSETS	EMPLOYEES
06/21	3,524.7	15.6	0.4%	575
06/20	3,722.8	22.7	0.6%	590
06/19	3,476.1	27.1	0.8%	582
06/18	3,304.1	8.2	0.2%	520
06/17	3,206.5	11.8	0.4%	486
Annual Growth	2.4%	7.3%	—	4.3%

2021 Year-End Financials

Return on assets: 0.4%
Return on equity: 3.9%
Long-term debt ($ mil.): —
No. of shares (mil.): 16.6
Sales ($ mil): 158.5

Dividends
Yield: 1.1%
Payout: 19.1%
Market value ($ mil.): 464.0

	STOCK PRICE ($) FY Close	P/E High/Low		PER SHARE ($)		
				Earnings	Dividends	Book Value
06/21	27.90	31	14	0.94	0.31	23.83
06/20	16.00	20	9	1.30	0.27	23.99
06/19	25.14	20	16	1.46	0.18	22.74
06/18	28.15	65	50	0.44	0.00	21.49
06/17	24.40	41	27	0.65	0.00	20.96
Annual Growth	3.4%	—	—	9.7%	—	3.3%

HOOVER'S HANDBOOK OF EMERGING COMPANIES 2022

Hope Bancorp Inc

EXECUTIVES

Director, Mary Thigpen
Independent Director, William Lewis
Chief Financial Officer, Chief Operating Officer, Senior Executive Vice President, Alex Ko, $389,491 total compensation
Senior Executive Vice President, Regional President - Eastern Region, Kyu Kim, $403,051 total compensation
Senior Executive Vice President And Chief Operating Officer, Peter Koh
Director, Lisa Pai
Chief Executive Officer, President, And Chairman, Kevin Kim, $999,838 total compensation
Senior Executive Vice President, Western Regional President Of Bank Of Hope, Jason Kim, $231,577 total compensation
Honorary Chairman Of The Board Of Directors, Steven Koh
Independent Director, Dale Zuehls
Independent Director, Donald Byun
Independent Director, Daisy Ha
Independent Director, Jinho Doo
Independent Director, Joon Kyung Kim
Executive Vice President, Chief Risk Officer Of Bank Of Hope, Thomas Stenger, $423,169 total compensation
Auditors: Crowe LLP

LOCATIONS

HQ: Hope Bancorp Inc
3200 Wilshire Boulevard, Suite 1400, Los Angeles, CA 90010
Phone: 213 639-1700   **Fax:** 213 235-3033
Web: www.bankofhope.com

HISTORICAL FINANCIALS

Company Type: Public

Income Statement

	ASSETS ($ mil.)	NET INCOME ($ mil.)	INCOME AS % OF ASSETS	EMPLOYEES
12/20	17,106.6	111.5	0.7%	1,408
12/19	15,667.4	171.0	1.1%	1,441
12/18	15,305.9	189.5	1.2%	1,494
12/17	14,206.7	139.4	1.0%	1,470
12/16	13,441.4	113.7	0.8%	1,372
Annual Growth	6.2%	(0.5%)	—	0.6%

FYE: December 31

2020 Year-End Financials

Return on assets: 0.6%
Return on equity: 5.4%
Long-term debt ($ mil.): —
No. of shares (mil.): 123.2
Sales ($ mil): 652.3

Dividends
Yield: 5.1%
Payout: 54.9%
Market value ($ mil.): 1,345.0

	STOCK PRICE ($) FY Close	P/E High/Low		PER SHARE ($) Earnings	Dividends	Book Value
12/20	10.91	17	8	0.90	0.56	16.66
12/19	14.86	11	9	1.35	0.56	16.19
12/18	11.86	13	8	1.44	0.54	15.03
12/17	18.25	22	15	1.03	0.50	14.23
12/16	21.89	20	13	1.10	0.45	13.72
Annual Growth	(16.0%)	—	—	(4.9%)	5.6%	5.0%

Horizon Bancorp Inc

For those in Indiana and Michigan Horizon Bancorp stretches as far as the eye can see. The company is the holding company for Horizon Bank (and its Heartland Community Bank division) which provides checking and savings accounts IRAs CDs and credit cards to customers through more than 50 branches in north and central Indiana and southwest and central Michigan. Commercial financial and agricultural loans make up the largest segment of its loan portfolio which also includes mortgage warehouse loans (loans earmarked for sale into the secondary market) consumer loans and residential mortgages. Through subsidiaries the bank offers trust and investment management services; life health and property/casualty insurance; and annuities.

Operations

Horizon boasted more than $2.08 billion in total assets and $1.48 billion in deposits in 2014. Commercial loans made up 49% of the bank's total loan portfolio. The bank employed nearly 450 full and part time employees that year.

Horizon's subsidiaries include: Horizon Investments which manages the bank's investment portfolio; Horizon Properties which manages the real estate investment trust; Horizon Insurance Services which sells through the company's Wealth Management; and Horizon Grantor Trust which holds title to certain company-owned life insurance policies.

The bank generated 61% of its revenue from interest income on loans in 2014 while another 13% came from interest on its taxable and tax-exempt investments. About 8% of revenues came from gains on its mortgage sales while the remainder of revenues were mostly generated by a mix of service charges on deposit accounts interchange fees and fiduciary activities fees.

Geographic Reach

The bank's more than 30 branches serve customers in north and central Indiana and southwest and central Michigan. Its mortgage-banking services are offered across the Midwest.

Financial Performance

Horizon Bancorp's revenues and profits have been trending higher over the past few years mostly as it's continued to grow its loan business and deposit customer base through acquisitions.

The bank's revenue rose by 2% to $102.5 million in 2014 mostly as the bank increased its interest-earning assets during the year. Its non-interest income also increased thanks to higher service charges on deposits and interchange fee income resulting from the growth in transactional deposit accounts and volume.

Despite higher revenue in 2014 the company's net income fell by 9% to $18.1 million for the year on higher provisions for loan losses due to loan growth and a write off of a commercial account coupled with an increase in transaction costs related to its Summit acquisition and an increase in salaries and employee benefits due to growth. Horizon's operating cash levels fell by 62% to $17.7 million after adjusting its earnings for non-cash items related to its net proceeds on the sale of its held-for-sale loans.

Strategy

Horizon Bancorp continues to expand its geographic reach and loan business through acquisi-

tions and new branches. It acquired several banks and opened new branches throughout 2016 and 2017.

Mergers and Acquisitions

In 2017 Horizon Bancorp agreed to buy Wolverine Bancorp for $92 million and Lafayette Community Bancorp for $32 million

In 2016 Horizon Bancorp bought LaPorte Bancorp for $98.9 million boosting its total assets by 20% to more than $3.24 billion while expanding its branch reach into the LaPorte area of Indiana. It also agreed to buy CNB Bancorp which operates Central National Bank & Trust in Attica Indiana.

In 2015 Horizon Bancorp agreed to buy Peoples Bancorp and subsidiary Peoples Federal Savings Bank of DeKalb County.

In April 2014 the company purchased SCP Bancorp including subsidiary Summit Community Bank and its two branches.

EXECUTIVES

Chairman Of The Board, Chief Executive Officer, Craig Dwight, $585,000 total compensation
Chief Financial Officer, Executive Vice President Of The Company And The Bank, Mark Secor, $303,021 total compensation
President Of The Company And The Bank, James Neff, $401,709 total compensation
Independent Director, Spero Valavanis
Independent Director, Susan Aaron
Independent Director, Peter Pairitz
Independent Director, James Dworkin
Independent Director, Lawrence Burnell
Lead Independent Director, Daniel Hopp
Executive Vice President And Executive Vice President, Senior Operations Officer, Bank, Kathie DeRuiter, $270,400 total compensation
Independent Director, Steven Reed
Independent Director, Eric Blackhurst
Independent Director, Michele Magnuson
Executive Vice President, General Counsel, Corporate Secretary, Todd Etzler
Independent Director, Julie Scheck Freigang
Executive Vice President, Senior Commercial Credit Officer, Lynn Kerber
Executive Vice President Of The Company And Executive Vice President, Chief Commercial Banking Officer Of The Bank, Dennis Kuhn, $267,800 total compensation
Auditors: BKD, LLP

LOCATIONS

HQ: Horizon Bancorp Inc
515 Franklin Street, Michigan City, IN 46360
Phone: 219 879-0211
Web: www.horizonbank.com

PRODUCTS/OPERATIONS

Selected Subsidiaries
Horizon Bank National Association
Horizon Insurance Services Inc.
Horizon Investments Inc.
Horizon Trust & Investment Management N.A.

COMPETITORS

CASCADE BANCORP
FIRST FINANCIAL BANCORP.

STATE BANK FINANCIAL CORPORATION

HISTORICAL FINANCIALS
Company Type: Public

Income Statement
FYE: December 31

	ASSETS ($ mil.)	NET INCOME ($ mil.)	INCOME AS % OF ASSETS	EMPLOYEES
12/20	5,886.6	68.5	1.2%	815
12/19	5,246.8	66.5	1.3%	839
12/18	4,246.6	53.1	1.3%	716
12/17	3,964.3	33.1	0.8%	701
12/16	3,141.1	23.9	0.8%	665
Annual Growth	17.0%	30.1%	—	5.2%

2020 Year-End Financials
Return on assets: 1.2%
Return on equity: 10.1%
Long-term debt ($ mil.): —
No. of shares (mil.): 43.8
Sales ($ mil.): 265.0
Dividends
  Yield: 3.0%
  Payout: 32.6%
Market value ($ mil.): 696.0

	STOCK PRICE ($) FY Close	P/E High/Low		PER SHARE ($) Earnings	Dividends	Book Value
12/20	15.86	12	5	1.55	0.48	15.78
12/19	19.00	13	10	1.53	0.44	14.59
12/18	15.78	24	11	1.38	0.39	12.82
12/17	27.80	30	26	0.95	0.32	11.94
12/16	28.00	40	26	0.79	0.27	10.25
Annual Growth	(13.2%)		—	18.2%	15.8%	11.4%

Hostess Brands Inc

Auditors: KPMG LLP

LOCATIONS
HQ: Hostess Brands Inc
  7905 Quivira Road, Lenexa, KS 66215
Phone: 816 701-4600
Web: www.hostessbrands.com

HISTORICAL FINANCIALS
Company Type: Public

Income Statement
FYE: December 31

	REVENUE ($ mil.)	NET INCOME ($ mil.)	NET PROFIT MARGIN	EMPLOYEES
12/20	1,016.6	64.7	6.4%	3,000
12/19	907.6	63.1	7.0%	2,000
12/18	850.3	62.9	7.4%	2,000
12/17	776.1	223.9	28.8%	1,340
12/16	112.0	(4.4)		1,350
Annual Growth	73.6%	—	—	22.1%

2020 Year-End Financials
Debt ratio: 33.4%
Return on equity: 4.1%
Cash ($ mil.): 173.0
Current ratio: 1.95
Long-term debt ($ mil.): 1,113.0
No. of shares (mil.): 130.3
Dividends
  Yield: —
  Payout: —
Market value ($ mil.): 1,908.0

	STOCK PRICE ($) FY Close	P/E High/Low		PER SHARE ($) Earnings	Dividends	Book Value
12/20	14.64	28	18	0.51	0.00	12.44
12/19	14.54	26	19	0.55	0.00	11.38
12/18	10.94	24	16	0.61	0.00	9.21
12/17	14.81	8	5	2.13	0.00	8.69
12/16	13.00	—	—	(0.05)	0.00	6.90
Annual Growth	3.0%		—	—	—	15.9%

Houlihan Lokey Inc

Auditors: KPMG LLP

LOCATIONS
HQ: Houlihan Lokey Inc
  10250 Constellation Blvd., 5th Floor, Los Angeles, CA 90067
Phone: 310 788-5200
Web: www.hl.com

HISTORICAL FINANCIALS
Company Type: Public

Income Statement
FYE: March 31

	REVENUE ($ mil.)	NET INCOME ($ mil.)	NET PROFIT MARGIN	EMPLOYEES
03/21	1,525.4	312.7	20.5%	1,574
03/20	1,159.3	183.7	15.9%	1,491
03/19	1,084.3	159.1	14.7%	1,354
03/18	963.3	172.2	17.9%	1,228
03/17	872.0	108.3	12.4%	1,171
Annual Growth	15.0%	30.3%	—	7.7%

2021 Year-End Financials
Debt ratio: 0.0%
Return on equity: 26.4%
Cash ($ mil.): 1,055.4
Current ratio: 1.61
Long-term debt ($ mil.): 0.8
No. of shares (mil.): 68.2
Dividends
  Yield: 1.9%
  Payout: 32.5%
Market value ($ mil.): 4,536.0

	STOCK PRICE ($) FY Close	P/E High/Low		PER SHARE ($) Earnings	Dividends	Book Value
03/21	66.51	15	11	4.55	1.30	20.29
03/20	52.12	20	14	2.80	1.24	15.02
03/19	45.85	21	14	2.42	1.08	13.63
03/18	44.60	19	12	2.60	0.80	12.96
03/17	34.45	19	12	1.63	0.71	11.01
Annual Growth	17.9%		—	—	29.3%	16.3%	16.5%

HV Bancorp Inc

Auditors: S.R. Snodgrass, P.C.

LOCATIONS
HQ: HV Bancorp Inc
  2005 South Easton Road, Suite 304, Doylestown, PA 18901
Phone: 267 280-4000
Web: www.myhvb.com

HISTORICAL FINANCIALS
Company Type: Public

Income Statement
FYE: December 31

	ASSETS ($ mil.)	NET INCOME ($ mil.)	INCOME AS % OF ASSETS	EMPLOYEES
12/20	861.6	5.7	0.7%	126
12/19*	354.5	0.5	0.2%	97
06/19	344.2	0.8	0.3%	92
06/18	297.7	0.7	0.3%	71
06/17	216.7	0.5	0.3%	74
Annual Growth	41.2%	78.4%	—	14.2%

*Fiscal year change

2020 Year-End Financials
Return on assets: 0.9%
Return on equity: 15.8%
Long-term debt ($ mil.): —
No. of shares (mil.): 2.1
Sales ($ mil): 30.6
Dividends
  Yield: —
  Payout: —
Market value ($ mil.): 38.0

	STOCK PRICE ($) FY Close	P/E High/Low		PER SHARE ($) Earnings	Dividends	Book Value
12/20	17.17	6	3	2.84	0.00	17.78
12/19*	17.00	65	55	0.26	0.00	14.81
06/19	15.08	41	34	0.43	0.00	14.40
06/18	14.82	43	36	0.38	0.50	13.60
06/17	14.48	26	24	0.56	0.00	14.41
Annual Growth	4.4%		—	—	50.1%	—	5.4%

*Fiscal year change

IAC/InterActiveCorp (New)

EXECUTIVES
Independent Director, Edward Gelfand
President, Ittella Italy, Giuseppe Bardari, $431,532 total compensation
Independent Director, Bryan Rosenberg
Independent Director, Marie Quintero-Johnson
Independent Director, Jennifer Fellner
Chief Financial Officer, Company Secretary, Stephanie Dieckmann, $163,846 total compensation
Creative Director, Sarah Galletti
Independent Director, Paula Ciaramitaro
Chairman Of The Board, President, Chief Executive Officer, Salvatore Galletti, $272,095 total compensation
Independent Director, Ryan Olohan
Independent Director, Daniel Williamson
Chief Operating Officer, Gaspare Guarrasi
Independent Director, David Boris

LOCATIONS
HQ: IAC/InterActiveCorp (New)
  555 West 18th Street, New York, NY 10011
Phone: 212 314-7300
Web: www.iac.com

HOOVER'S HANDBOOK OF EMERGING COMPANIES 2022

HISTORICAL FINANCIALS
Company Type: Public

Income Statement — FYE: December 31

	REVENUE ($ mil.)	NET INCOME ($ mil.)	NET PROFIT MARGIN	EMPLOYEES
12/20	3,047.6	269.7	8.9%	8,200
12/19	2,705.8	22.9	0.8%	6,400
12/18	2,533.0	246.7	9.7%	0
12/17	1,952.6	37.0	1.9%	0
Annual Growth	16.0%	93.9%	—	—

2020 Year-End Financials

Debt ratio: 7.8%
Return on equity: 5.8%
Cash ($ mil.): 3,701.1
Current ratio: 5.49
Long-term debt ($ mil.): 712.2

No. of shares (mil.): 88.7
Dividends
  Yield: —
  Payout: —
Market value ($ mil.): 16,808.0

	STOCK PRICE ($) FY Close	P/E High/Low	PER SHARE ($) Earnings	Dividends	Book Value
12/20	189.35	102 34	2.97	0.00	74.33
12/19	249.11	— —	(0.00)	0.00	29.78
12/18	183.04	— —	(0.00)	0.00	(0.00)
12/17	122.28	— —	(0.00)	0.00	(0.00)
/0.00	—		(0.00)	0.00	(0.00)
Annual Growth	—		—	—	—

Ichor Holdings Ltd

Auditors: KPMG LLP

LOCATIONS

HQ: Ichor Holdings Ltd
  3185 Laurelview Ct., Fremont, CA 94538
Phone: 510 897-5200
Web: www.ichorsystems.com

HISTORICAL FINANCIALS
Company Type: Public

Income Statement — FYE: December 25

	REVENUE ($ mil.)	NET INCOME ($ mil.)	NET PROFIT MARGIN	EMPLOYEES
12/20	914.2	33.2	3.6%	2,030
12/19	620.8	10.7	1.7%	1,715
12/18	823.6	57.8	7.0%	1,490
12/17	655.8	56.4	8.6%	1,760
12/16	405.7	16.6	4.1%	787
Annual Growth	22.5%	18.9%	—	26.7%

2020 Year-End Financials

Debt ratio: 25.8%
Return on equity: 10.5%
Cash ($ mil.): 252.9
Current ratio: 3.06
Long-term debt ($ mil.): 191.5

No. of shares (mil.): 27.9
Dividends
  Yield: —
  Payout: —
Market value ($ mil.): —

ICU Medical Inc

ICU is one of the world's leading pure-play infusion therapy companies with global operations and a wide-ranging product portfolio that includes IV solutions IV smart pumps with pain management and safety software technology dedicated and non-dedicated IV sets and needle-free connectors designed to help meet clinical safety and workflow goals. In addition ICU manufactures automated pharmacy IV compounding systems with workflow technology closed system transfer devices for preparing and administering hazardous IV drugs and cardiac monitoring systems for critically ill patients. ICU Medical which sells its products to other equipment makers and distributors gets most of its revenue from US customers.

Operations
ICU Medical operates in four product lines: Infusion Consumables IV Solutions Infusion Systems and Critical Care.

Infusion Consumables more than 35% of revenue provides infusion therapy sets used in hospitals and ambulatory clinics consist of a tube running from a bottle or plastic bag containing a solution to a catheter inserted in a patient's vein that may or may not be used with an IV pump.

The IV Solutions segment about 30% of revenue provides intravenous systems irrigation and nutritionals to help provide safe and effective patient care.

The Infusion Systems segment about 30% of revenue offers infusion pumps dedicated IV sets and software IV mediation safety software and professional services.

Critical Care products segment about 5% of revenue offers a portfolio of monitoring systems and advanced sensors and catheters that help clinicians get access to patients' hemodynamic and cardiac status.

Geographic Reach
ICU Medical based in San Clemente California sells its products in more than 90 countries around the world.

The company maintains manufacturing facilities in Salt Lake City Utah; Austin Texas; Baja California Mexico; and La Aurora Costa Rica. ICU Medical has distribution warehouses in Texas Pennsylvania and California. It has device service center in Sligo Ireland.

ICU relies on the US for more than 70% of its revenue while the Europe the Middle East and Africa region and other countries combining for about 30% of sales.

Sales and Marketing
ICU Medical sells to acute care hospitals wholesalers ambulatory clinics and alternate site facilities such as clinics home health care providers and long-term care facilities. It reaches customers through direct sales and distributors.

Advertising expenses were $0.2 million in 2020 $0.1 million in 2019 and $0.6 million in 2018.

Financial Performance
Company's revenue for fiscal 2020 increased to $1.271 billion compared from the prior year with $1.266 billion.

Net income for fiscal 2020 decreased to $86.9 million compared from the prior year with $101.0 million.

Cash held by the company at the end of fiscal 2020 increased to $396.1 million. Cash provided by operations was $222.8 million while cash used for investing was $98.1 million mainly for purchases of property plant and equipment. Cash used for financing activities was below $1 million.

Strategy
Restructuring strategic transaction and integration expenses were $28.4 million $80.6 million and $105.4 million for the years ended December 31 2020 2019 and 2018 respectively.

In 2020 restructuring charges were primarily related to severance and costs related to office and other facility closures.

ICU Medical's have and may continue to seek to supplement its internal growth through acquisitions of complementary businesses technologies services or products as well as investments and strategic alliances.

Company Background
ICU released is signature product the Clave needlefree intravenous connection device in 1993. Subsequent products include the MicroClave Clear connector the Tego needlefree connector for use in hemodialysis and products for handling hazardous drugs including the ChemoClave and ChemoLock CSTDs (closed-system transfer devices) and the Diana hazardous drug compounding system.

EXECUTIVES

Independent Director, Laurie Hernandez
Independent Director, Kolleen Kennedy
Chairman And Chief Executive Officer, Vivek Jain, $650,000 total compensation
Chief Operating Officer, Christian Voigtlander, $420,000 total compensation
Chief Financial Officer, Treasurer, Brian Bonnell, $395,000 total compensation
Independent Director, Donald Abbey
Corporate Vice President, General Manager - Infusion Systems, Daniel Woolson, $300,000 total compensation
Lead Independent Director, David Greenberg
Independent Director, David Hoffmeister
Corporate Vice President, General Counsel And Secretary, Virginia Sanzone, $300,000 total compensation
Auditors: DELOITTE & TOUCHE LLP

LOCATIONS

HQ: ICU Medical Inc
  951 Calle Amanecer, San Clemente, CA 92673
Phone: 949 366-2183
Web: www.icumed.com

PRODUCTS/OPERATIONS

2018 Sales

	% of total
IV Solutions	36
Infusion Consumables	35
Infusion Systems	25
Critical Care	4
Total	**100**

COMPETITORS

ANGIODYNAMICS INC.
ATRION CORPORATION
AVANOS MEDICAL INC.
B. Braun Melsungen AG
BECTON DICKINSON AND CORPORATION COMPANY

HANGER INC.
INTEGER HOLDINGS CORPORATION
INTEGRA LIFESCIENCES HOLDINGS

MESA LABORATORIES INC.

CAREFUSION CORPORATION	ORASURE
TECHNOLOGIES	INC.
DEXCOM INC.	
FRESENIUS MEDICAL CARE	STERIS LIMITED
HOLDINGS INC.	TERUMO CORPORATION
HAEMONETICS	UTAH MEDICAL PRODUCTS
CORPORATION	INC.

HISTORICAL FINANCIALS

Company Type: Public

Income Statement

FYE: December 31

	REVENUE ($ mil.)	NET INCOME ($ mil.)	NET PROFIT MARGIN	EMPLOYEES
12/20	1,271.0	86.8	6.8%	7,900
12/19	1,266.2	101.0	8.0%	8,000
12/18	1,400.0	28.7	2.1%	8,100
12/17	1,292.6	68.6	5.3%	6,802
12/16	379.3	63.0	16.6%	2,803
Annual Growth	35.3%	8.3%	—	29.6%

2020 Year-End Financials

Debt ratio: —	No. of shares (mil.): 21.0
Return on equity: 6.0%	Dividends
Cash ($ mil.): 410.7	Yield: —
Current ratio: 4.71	Payout: —
Long-term debt ($ mil.): —	Market value ($ mil.): 4,517.0

	STOCK PRICE ($) FY Close	P/E High/Low		PER SHARE ($) Earnings	Dividends	Book Value
12/20	214.49	56	38	4.02	0.00	71.34
12/19	187.12	53	31	4.69	0.00	66.40
12/18	229.63	220	151	1.33	0.00	61.67
12/17	216.00	63	38	3.29	0.00	59.29
12/16	147.35	39	22	3.66	0.00	40.41
Annual Growth	9.8%	—	—	2.4%	—	15.3%

Idexx Laboratories, Inc.

A leading animal health care company IDEXX develops manufactures and distributes products for pets livestock dairy and poultry markets. Veterinarians use the company's VetTest analyzers for blood and urine chemistry and its SNAP in-office test kits to detect heartworms feline leukemia and other diseases. The company also provides lab testing services and practice management software. In addition IDEXX makes products to test for contaminants in water. The company sells its products worldwide but the Americas account for nearly 70% of its total revenue.

Operations

IDEXX operates through three primary segments: Companion Animal Group (CAG) Water Quality Products (Water) and Livestock Poultry and Dairy (LPD).

CAG segment account for about 90% of IDEXX's sales. Most of that revenue comes from diagnostic products and services including chemistry analyzers rapid test kits and laboratory services. The company operates a network of laboratories to which vets can send patient samples for analysis.

The LPD segment (horses cows pigs and chickens) is the second-largest business bringing in about 5% of total revenue. The segment sells di-

agnostic tests services and related instrumentation. Its products can test for Bovine Viral Diarrhea Virus (BVDV) as well as porcine illnesses and poultry diseases.

The Water segment (about 5% of sales) makes tests which detect coliforms and E. coli in water. Water utilities and government laboratories are the primary customers for these products.

The company also makes and distributes diagnostics for the human market but those are not a substantial part of its business.

Majority of sales is are generated form its products which accounts for about 60% of company' sales and service revenue accounts for the remaining.

Geographic Reach

Approximately 70% of IDEXX's sales are made in the US but it also maintains sales offices outside the US in Africa the Asia/Pacific region Europe the Middle East North America and Latin America.

Many of its products and materials are manufactured by third parties but the company also maintains manufacturing and assembly facilities in Georgia and Maine and in Bern Switzerland and Montpellier France. Its headquarters is located in Westbrook Maine.

Sales and Marketing

IDEXX distributes its products through its own marketing customer service sales and technical service groups as well as through independent distributors and other resellers.

Advertising costs were $1.4 million $1.5 million and $1.8 million for 2020 2019 and 2018 respectively.

Financial Performance

IDEXX' revenue grew 12% from $2.4 billion in 2019 to $2.7 billion in 2020. The increase was primarily due to higher sales in all of the company's segments.

Net income attributable to IDEXX Laboratories Inc. in 2020 was $581.8 million a 36% increase from the previous year.

IDEXX' cash at the end of 2020 was $383.9 million. Operating activities provided $648.1 million while investing activities used $109.4 million mainly for capital expenditures. Financing activities used another $248.4 million mainly for repurchases of common stocks and repayment on revolving credit facilities.

Strategy

A few of the elements of the company's strategy are:

Developing manufacturing and marketing innovative new or improved and cost competitive inclinic laboratory analyzers that drive sales of IDEXX VetLab instruments grow its installed base of instruments and increase demand for related recurring sales of consumable products services and accessories;

Developing and introducing new proprietary diagnostic tests and services for both its reference laboratories and in-clinic applications that provide valuable medical information to customers and effectively differentiate products and services from those of the company's competitors;

Increasing the value to its customers of its companion animal products and services by enhancing the integration of the information and transactions of these products and the management of diagnostic information derived from the company's products;

As well as maintaining premium pricing including by effectively implementing price increases for the company's differentiated products and services through among other things effective communication and promotion of the value of its products and services in an environment where many of the company's competitors promote market and sell lesser offerings at prices lower than the company's.

Mergers and Acquisitions

In 2021 IDEXX acquired New Zealand-based ezyVet a fast-growing innovative practice information management system (PIMS). With the acquisition IDEXX further expands its world-class cloud software offerings that support customers with technology solutions that raise the standard of care for patients improve practice efficiency and enable more effective communication with pet owners.

HISTORY

David Shaw founded IDEXX in 1984 as AgriTech Systems. An MBA who had specialized in agribusiness consulting Shaw wanted to cut the costs and time involved in lab testing for diseases by producing kits that could be used on-site; an initial line of poultry disease tests proved successful. The company changed its name to IDEXX in 1988 and went public in 1991.

In 1994 IDEXX acquired AMIS International a leading Japanese test lab for veterinarians. The next year the company opened offices in Spain and the Netherlands and introduced the SNAP test which detects allergies in dogs.

In 1997 IDEXX acquired two software companies Advanced Veterinary Systems and Professionals Software and merged them to create IDEXX Informatics. That year the firm also bought Acumedia Manufacturers a producer of more than 300 varieties of dehydrated culture media. Looking to expand into animal drug development the company bought animal health firm Blue Ridge Pharmaceuticals in 1998. In 2000 IDEXX sold Acumedia as well as its food microbiology operations. It also launched VetConnect.com which provides veterinary information and support and product sales.

In 2008 the company sold its veterinary pharmaceutical operations which were miniscule to focus on its core test kit and consumable business.

EXECUTIVES

Pres-Ceo, Jonathan J Mazelsky
Non Exec Chb*, Lawrence D Kingsley
Exec V Pres-Cfo-Treas, Brian P McKeon
Exec V Pres-Cco, James F Polewaczyk
Corp V Pres-Cmo, Kathy V Turner
Corp V Pres-Chief Hr Officer, Giovani Twigge
Corp V Pres-General Counsel-Co, Sharon E Underberg
Evp-Gen Mgr, Tina Hunt
Evp-Gen Mgr, Michael J Lane
Information Technology Analyst, Mark K Ramos
Manager, Anneliese Lemmo
Auditors: PricewaterhouseCoopers LLP

LOCATIONS

HQ: Idexx Laboratories, Inc.
One IDEXX Drive, Westbrook, ME 04092
Phone: 207 556-0300   **Fax:** 207 856-0346
Web: www.idexx.com

PRODUCTS/OPERATIONS

2016 Sales

	$ mil.	% of total
CAG	1,522.7	86
Water	133.6	6
LPD	126.5	7
Other	22.6	1
Total	**1,775.4**	**100**

2016 Sales

	$ mil.	% of total
Product	1,071.0	60
Service	704.4	40
Total	**1,775.4**	**100**

COMPETITORS

AMERICAN VANGUARD
  CORPORATION
APTARGROUP INC.
GRIFOLS SA
HESKA CORPORATION
MEDICAL ACTION
  INDUSTRIES INC.

MOCON INC.
ORASURE TECHNOLOGIES
  INC.
QUIDEL CORPORATION
Qiagen N.V.
STERIS LIMITED
STRATEC SE

HISTORICAL FINANCIALS
Company Type: Public

Income Statement				FYE: December 31
	REVENUE ($ mil.)	NET INCOME ($ mil.)	NET PROFIT MARGIN	EMPLOYEES
12/21	3,215.3	744.8	23.2%	10,350
12/20	2,706.6	581.7	21.5%	9,300
12/19	2,406.9	427.7	17.8%	9,200
12/18	2,213.2	377.0	17.0%	8,377
12/17	1,969.0	263.1	13.4%	7,600
Annual Growth	13.0%	29.7%	—	8.0%

2021 Year-End Financials

Debt ratio: 37.9%
Return on equity: 112.6%
Cash ($ mil.): 144.4
Current ratio: 1.25
Long-term debt ($ mil.): 775.2

No. of shares (mil.): 84.5
Dividends
  Yield: —
  Payout: —
Market value ($ mil.): 55,681.0

	STOCK PRICE ($) FY Close	P/E High/Low	PER SHARE ($) Earnings	Dividends	Book Value
12/21	658.46	81 53	8.60	0.00	8.16
12/20	499.87	73 27	6.71	0.00	7.40
12/19	261.13	58 36	4.89	0.00	2.08
12/18	186.02	59 36	4.26	0.00	(0.11)
12/17	156.38	57 39	2.94	0.00	(0.62)
Annual Growth	43.2%	— —	30.8%	—	—

IES Holdings Inc

IES installs and maintains electrical and communications systems for residential commercial and industrial customers. Work on commercial buildings and homes includes custom design construction and maintenance on electrical and mechanical systems such as intrusion and fire alarms audio/video and data network systems. IES performs electrical and mechanical systems construction and installation for industrial properties including office buildings manufacturing facilities data centers chemical plants municipal infrastruc-

ture and health care facilities. Banking investor Jeffrey Gendell through Tontine Capital Partners owns 56% of IES.

Operations

IES operates its business through four segments — Residential Communications Commercial and Industrial and Infrastructure Solutions.

The residential segment provides electrical installation services to single-family housing and multi-family apartment complexes as well as HVAC and plumbing installation services in certain markets and cable television installations for residential and light commercial applications. The segment accounts for about 45% of total sales.

Its communications segment provides infrastructure for corporate data centers as well as design building and maintenance of data network systems for audio/visual telephone fire and alarm systems. The segment accounts for nearly 30% of total sales.

IES's commercial and industrial segment provides electrical and mechanical design construction and maintenance services for projects including power plants data centers chemical plants wind farms solar facilities and office buildings. The segment accounts for more than 15% of total sales.

The company's infrastructure solutions segment provides electro-mechanical solutions for industrial operations to domestic and international customers. Its Custom Power Solutions business includes the manufacture of custom commercial and industrial generator enclosures and the manufacture of custom-engineered power distribution equipment including metal enclosed bus duct solutions used in power distribution. Its Industrial Services business includes the maintenance and repair of alternating current (AC) and direct current (DC) electric motors and generators as well as power generating and distribution equipment; the manufacture re-manufacture and repair of industrial lifting magnets; and maintenance and repair of railroad main and auxiliary generators main alternators and traction motors. The segment accounts for some 10% of total sales.

Geographic Reach

Houston Texas-based IES maintains about 100 locations in the US. The company has about 50 locations that house its residential business activities (Texas Sunbelt Western Northeastern and Mid-Atlantic regions) about 20 locations for its commercial and industrial unit (in Texas Nebraska Oregon Wisconsin and the Southeast and Mid-Atlantic regions) about 15 locations for its Tempe Arizona-based communications division and ten locations for its infrastructure operations (covering Alabama Georgia Illinois Indiana Ohio West Virginia and is headquartered in Massillon Ohio).

Sales and Marketing

IES' commercial and industrial and communications segments rely significantly on long-term repeat business which the company continues to cultivate. The majority of its customers for infrastructure services are located within a 200-mile radius of its facilities allowing the company to quickly respond to repair requests. For the company's residential services most of its single-family sales come from Texas while most of its multifamily sales come from the Mid-Atlantic and Western states.

Financial Performance

IES' revenue has been rising in the last few years with a 90% overall increase between 2017 and 2021. The company's net income follows a similar

trend with the exception of the drop in 2018. Still it has an overall growth of 398% between 2017 and 2021.

Consolidated revenues for the year ended September 30 2021 were $345.6 million higher at $1.5 billion compared to the year ended September 30 2020 an increase of 29% with increases across all segments driven by strong demand and the contribution of acquired businesses.

In 2021 the company had a net income of $68.7 million a 69% increase from the previous year's net income of $40.1 million. This was mainly due to the higher sales volume in 2021.

The company's cash at the end of 2021 was $23.1 million. Operating activities generated $37.9 million while investing activities used $100 million primarily for cash paid in conjunction with business combinations or dispositions. Financing activities provided another $31.2 million.

Strategy

IES seeks to create shareholder value through improving operating margins and generating free cash flow by investing in its existing businesses and completing acquisitions. The company seeks to acquire businesses that strategically complement its existing business segments or to acquire or invest in stand-alone platform companies based in North America.

Company Background

Between its 1997 IPO and its 2011 transition to a holding company model IES comprised a group of electrical contractors. Member companies included South Texas-based Bexar Electric (which became a founding subsidiary of IES) South Carolina-based Davis Electrical Constructors Virginia-based ARC Electric Texas-based Houston-Stafford Electric Nebraska-based Kayton Electric and Arizona-based Federal Communication Group.

EXECUTIVES

Independent Director, Jennifer Baldock
Director, David Gendell
Chief Financial Officer, Senior Vice President, Treasurer, Tracy McLauchlin, $409,000 total compensation
Independent Director, Elizabeth Leykum
Chief Operating Officer, Matthew Simmes
Chairman Of The Board, Chief Executive Officer, Jeffrey Gendell, $750,000 total compensation
Auditors: Ernst & Young LLP

LOCATIONS

HQ: IES Holdings Inc
  5433 Westheimer Road, Suite 500, Houston, TX 77056
Phone: 713 860-1500
Web: www.ies-corporate.com

PRODUCTS/OPERATIONS

2018 Sales

	$ mil.	% of total
Residential	285.7	33
Commercial & Industrial	274.3	31
Communications	219.6	25
Infrastructure Solutions	97.2	11
Total	**876.8**	**100**

Selected Services
Alarm & safety systems
Construction services
Design/build
Engineering services
Home standby generators
Solar installation

Structured cabling
Support services
Training resources

COMPETITORS

ABM INDUSTRIES INCORPORATED
GUARANTEE ELECTRICAL COMPANY
JOHNSON CONTROLS INTERNATIONAL PUBLIC
 LIMITED COMPANY
LARSEN AND TOUBRO LIMITED
PRIMORIS SERVICES CORPORATION
ROSENDIN ELECTRIC INC.
TCLARKE PLC
UNITED RENTALS INC.

HISTORICAL FINANCIALS
Company Type: Public

Income Statement   FYE: September 30

	REVENUE ($ mil.)	NET INCOME ($ mil.)	NET PROFIT MARGIN	EMPLOYEES
09/21	1,536.4	66.6	4.3%	6,845
09/20	1,190.8	41.6	3.5%	5,243
09/19	1,077.0	33.2	3.1%	5,389
09/18	876.8	(14.1)	—	4,564
09/17	810.7	13.4	1.7%	3,532
Annual Growth	17.3%	49.3%	—	18.0%

2021 Year-End Financials

Debt ratio: 5.1%
Return on equity: 21.1%
Cash ($ mil.): 23.1
Current ratio: 1.55
Long-term debt ($ mil.): 39.7

No. of shares (mil.): 20.7
Dividends
Yield: —
Payout: —
Market value ($ mil.): 947.0

	STOCK PRICE ($) FY Close	P/E High/Low		PER SHARE ($) Earnings	Dividends	Book Value
09/21	45.69	17	10	3.15	0.00	16.69
09/20	31.77	18	7	1.94	0.00	13.65
09/19	20.59	13	10	1.55	0.00	11.63
09/18	19.50	—	—	(0.67)	0.00	10.39
09/17	17.30	36	23	0.62	0.00	11.09
Annual Growth	27.5%	—	—	50.1%	—	10.7%

II-VI Inc

II-VI develops manufactures and markets engineered materials optoelectronic components and devices for use in optical communications industrial aerospace and defense consumer electronics semiconductor capital equipment life sciences and automotive applications and markets. The company products are deployed in a variety of applications including optical data and wireless communications products; laser cutting welding and marking operations; 3D sensing consumer applications; aerospace and defense applications including intelligence surveillance and reconnaissance; semiconductor processing tools; and thermoelectric cooling and power-generation solutions. The company has manufacturing operations throughout the US as well as in Asia and Germany. Customers have included Coherent Inc. Nikon Corporation Aurubis AG and Apple Inc. among others. The US is its largest single market accounting for some 65% of sales.

Operations

The company operates two reporting segments: Photonic Solutions (around 65% of sales) and Compound Semiconductors (nearly 35%).

The Photonic Solutions Segment leverages II-VI's compound semiconductor technology platforms and deep knowledge of end-user applications for its key end markets to deliver differentiated components and subsystems. Its business unit includes ROADM transceivers and advanced optics.

The Compound Semiconductors Segment is a market leader in engineered materials and optoelectronic devices such as those based on GaAs InP GaN and SiC. Its business units include engineered materials and laser optics laser devices and systems new ventures & wide-bandgap electronics and optoelectronic & RF devices.

Geographic Reach

Headquartered in Saxonburg Pennsylvania the US is II-VI's largest market accounting for some 65% of its sales. China is next representing around 10% of annual sales while Hong Kong represents over 10% and Germany some 5%. The company has RD&E manufacturing and sales facilities located in Arizona California Colorado Connecticut Delaware Florida Illinois Massachusetts Michigan Mississippi New Jersey New York Ohio Oregon Pennsylvania and Texas and its non-US production and RD&E operations are based in Australia China Germany Malaysia the Philippines Singapore Sweden Switzerland Thailand the United Kingdom and Vietnam. In addition to sales offices co-located at most of its manufacturing sites it has sales and marketing subsidiaries in Belgium Canada China Germany Hong Kong Italy Japan South Korea Switzerland Taiwan and the United Kingdom.

Sales and Marketing

The company market its products through a direct sales force and through representatives and distributors around the world. Its customers in communications industry account for approximately two-thirds of its sales while the industrial consumer aerospace and defense and other industries account for the rest. Its photonic solutions customers include Ciena Corp. Alibaba Group and Coherent Inc. among others while compound semiconductor customers include Bystronic Laser AG ASML Holding NV Aurubis AG Lockheed Martin Corporation and more.

Financial Performance

The company's revenue in 2021 was $3.1 billion a 30% increase from the previous year. Revenue for 2021 was a record with growth across all end markets compared to the same period last fiscal year.

In 2021 the company had a net income of $297.6 million a massive improvement of $364.6 million from the previous year's net loss of $67 million.

The company's cash at the end of 2021 was $1.6 billion. Operating activities generated $574.3 million while investing activities used $173 million mainly for additions to property plant & equipment. Financing activities provided another $675.7 million.

Strategy

II-VI's strategy is to grow businesses with world-class engineered materials capabilities to advance its current customers' strategies reach new markets through innovative technologies and platforms and enable new applications in large and growing markets. A key strategy of the company

is to develop and manufacture high-performance materials and in certain cases components incorporating those materials that are differentiated from those produced by its competitors. II-VI's focus on providing components that are critical to the heart of customers' products that serve the applications mentioned above.

The company continues to grow the number and size of its key accounts. A significant portion of its business is based on sales orders with market leaders which enables its forward planning and production efficiencies. The company intends to continue capitalizing and executing on this proven model participating effectively in the growth of the markets discussed above and continuing its focus on operational excellence as the company executes its primary business strategies.

Mergers and Acquisitions

In 2020 II-VI Incorporated it has entered into a definitive agreement to acquire all the outstanding shares of Sweden-based Ascatron AB a leader in silicon carbide (SiC) epitaxial wafers and devices for power electronics. II-VI also announced that it will acquire all the outstanding interests of the owners of the parent of Colorado-based INNOViON Corporation a leader in ion implantation technology for silicon and compound semiconductor devices. Ascatron produces state-of-the-art SiC epitaxial wafers and devices that enable a wide range of high-voltage power electronics applications. INNOViON is the largest provider of ion implantation services in the world with 30 implanters across a global footprint that support unique capabilities in semiconductor materials processing for up to 300 mm wafers. The technology platforms of Ascatron and INNOViON are best in class and a perfect complement to its market-leading SiC substrates. This builds upon its deep expertise in SiC substrates and adds advanced SiC epitaxy device fabrication and module design to meet the rapidly growing demand for SiC power electronics. Terms were not disclosed.

Company Background

Electrical engineer Carl Johnson who had worked at Bell Labs (now part of Alcatel-Lucent) among other companies founded II-VI in 1971 to produce infrared optical materials for the emerging laser market. These materials — including cadmium zinc telluride zinc selenide and zinc sulfide — gave the company its name; they are from the "two-six" family of materials. (Cadmium and zinc are from column two on the periodic table; tellurium and selenium are from column six.)

By the 1980s II-VI was the leading maker of optical components for carbon dioxide lasers. The company went public in 1987 and the next year added a factory in Singapore.

HISTORY

Electrical engineer Carl Johnson who had worked at Bell Labs (now part of Alcatel-Lucent) among other companies founded II-VI in 1971 to produce infrared optical materials for the emerging laser market. These materials — including cadmium zinc telluride zinc selenide and zinc sulfide — gave the company its name; they are from the "two-six" family of materials. (Cadmium and zinc are from column two on the periodic table; tellurium and selenium are from column six.)

By the 1980s II-VI was the leading maker of optical components for carbon dioxide lasers. The company went public in 1987 and the next year added a factory in Singapore.

EXECUTIVES

Chairman Of The Board And Chief Executive Officer, Vincent Mattera, $950,833 total compensation
Independent Director, Stephen Pagliuca
Independent Director, Howard Xia
Chief Strategy Officer, President - Compound Semiconductors, Giovanni Barbarossa, $515,000 total compensation
President, Walter Bashaw, $472,760 total compensation
Independent Director, Shaker Sadasivam
Lead Independent Director, Enrico Digirolamo
Independent Director, Patricia Hatter
Independent Director, Michael Dreyer
Independent Director, David Motley
Independent Director, Lisa Neal-graves
Chief Financial Officer, Treasurer, Mary Raymond, $465,340 total compensation
Chief Technology Officer, Christopher Koeppen
Chairman Of Emeritus, Francis Kramer
Independent Director, Joseph Corasanti
Auditors: Ernst & Young LLP

LOCATIONS

HQ: II-VI Inc
375 Saxonburg Boulevard, Saxonburg, PA 16056
Phone: 724 352-4455
Web: www.ii-vi.com

PRODUCTS/OPERATIONS

2015 Sales Chart

	% of total
II-VI Laser Solutions	39
II-VI Photonics	35
II-VI Performance Products	26
Total	**100**

Selected Business Segments

dvanced Materials Development Center (AMDC)
AOFR
Aegis Lightwave
HIGHYAG Lasertechnologie
LightWorks Optical Systems
M Cubed
Marlow Industries
Max Levy Autograph
Photop Technologies
Pacific Rare Specialty Metals & Chemicals (PRM)
Wide Bandgap Materials Group

Selected Products

Beam expanders
Beam splitters
Detectors
Etalons
Infrared and near-infrared optics
Laser crystals
    Clear yttrium aluminum garnet (YAG) laser crystals
    Custom crystals and fluorides
    Machined and polished laser rods
    Monolithic crystal assemblies (MCA)
    Neodymium doped YAG
    Non-linear crystals
    Oxide laser crystal products
    Ruby laser crystals
Laser gain materials
Lenses
Military infrared optics
Mirrors
Modulators
One micron laser
Optical assemblies
Optical coatings
Output windows
Partial reflectors
Phase retarders
Polarization devices
Prisms

Rhombs
Selenium metal (material processing and refinement)
Silicon carbide substrates (SiC)
Solid-state laser optics and optical cavities
Substrates
Tellurium metal (material processing and refinement)
Thermo-electric coolers
Wave plates

COMPETITORS

APPLIED MATERIALS INC.
COHERENT INC.
Carl Zeiss AG
DATACOLOR INC.
HOYA CORPORATION
HUNTER ASSOCIATES LABORATORY INCORPORATED
IPG PHOTONICS CORPORATION
LIGHTPATH TECHNOLOGIES INC.
LUMIBIRD
TOPCON CORPORATION
U.S. VISION INC.
VEECO INSTRUMENTS INC.
WOLFSPEED INC.

HISTORICAL FINANCIALS

Company Type: Public

Income Statement

FYE: June 30

	REVENUE ($ mil.)	NET INCOME ($ mil.)	NET PROFIT MARGIN	EMPLOYEES
06/21	3,105.8	297.5	9.6%	23,000
06/20	2,380.0	(67.0)	—	22,969
06/19	1,362.5	107.5	7.9%	12,487
06/18	1,158.7	88.0	7.6%	11,443
06/17	972.0	95.2	9.8%	10,349
Annual Growth	33.7%	32.9%		22.1%

2021 Year-End Financials

Debt ratio: 21.1%
Return on equity: 9.5%
Cash ($ mil.): 1,591.8
Current ratio: 4.15
Long-term debt ($ mil.): 1,313.0

No. of shares (mil.): 105.4
Dividends
  Yield: —
  Payout: —
Market value ($ mil.): 7,657.0

	STOCK PRICE ($) FY Close	P/E High/Low		PER SHARE ($) Earnings	Dividends	Book Value
06/21	72.59	40	15	2.37	0.00	39.17
06/20	47.22	—	—	(0.79)	0.00	22.44
06/19	36.56	30	18	1.63	0.00	17.79
06/18	43.45	38	24	1.35	0.00	16.18
06/17	34.30	26	12	1.48	0.00	14.26
Annual Growth	20.6%			12.5%	—	28.7%

Incyte Corporation

Incyte is a biopharmaceutical company focused on the discovery development and commercialization of proprietary therapeutics. It is focused on developing and selling drugs that inhibit specific enzymes associated with cancer and other diseases. The company's lead program is its JAK (Janus associated kinase) inhibitor program. Its first commercial product Jakafi is approved for treatment of polycythemia vera and myelofibrosis (two rare blood cancers) and graft-versus-host-disease in the US; partner Novartis markets the drug internationally. Another inhibitor drug Iclusig is

marketed for certain forms of leukemia in Europe. Incyte has a number of product candidates in research and clinical development stages partially through partnerships with other drugmakers for various cancers inflammatory ailments and other conditions.

Operations

The JAK family is composed of four tyrosine kinases?JAK1 JAK2 JAK3 and Tyk2?that are involved in the signaling of a number of cytokines and growth factors. JAKs are central to a number of biologic processes including the formation and development of blood cells and the regulation of immune functions. Dysregulation of the JAK-STAT signaling pathway has been associated with a number of diseases including myeloproliferative neoplasms other hematological malignancies rheumatoid arthritis and other chronic inflammatory diseases. It has discovered multiple potent selective and orally bioavailable JAK inhibitors that are selective for JAK1 or JAK1 and JAK2. JAKAFI is the most advanced compound in JAK program. It is an oral JAK1 and JAK2 inhibitor.

Other clinical program outside oncology include (Phase II trial) JAK1 selective inhibitor treatment for patient with hidradenitis suppurativa an inflammatory skin disease and a Phase II trial of parsaclisib in patients with autoimmune hemolytic anemia a rare red blood cell disorder. It also has product under clinical development for disorder of muscle tissue and connective tissue ulcerative colitis and patients with Sj¶gren's syndrome.

Its products accounts for more than 80% of total revenue royalties for about 15% and milestone and contract revenue accounts for the remainder.

Geographic Reach

Incyte's global headquarters is in Wilmington Delaware. Other locations are in Pennsylvania and it also conducst development and commercial operations from offices in (Geneva and Lausanne) Switzerland and Tokyo Japan.

Sales and Marketing

JAKAFI is marketed in the US through its own specialty sales force and commercial team. It distributed primarily through a network of specialty pharmacy providers and wholesalers which allows to deliver the medication by mail directly to patients or directly deliver to the patient's pharmacy. The distribution process uses a model that is well-established and familiar to physicians who practice within the oncology field.

Financial Performance

Incyte has reported steadily increasing revenue over the past five years with sales almost tripling between 2015 and 2019. Net income reported a loss in 2017 but generally following an upward trend.

The company reported a 15% revenue increase in 2019 to some $2.2 billion due to increased revenue from sales of Jakafi and Iclusig as well as from higher product royalty from partners.

Net income rose to $446.9 million in 2019 a vast improvement from $109.5 million in 2018 as the company reported stronger sales higher Other income and an unrealized gain on long-term investment of $39.9 million.

The company ended 2019 with $1.8 billion in cash up $668.7 million from 2018. Operating activities contributed $710.7 million and financing activities added $45.7 million while investing activities used $87.5 million for purchases of marketable securities and capital expenditures.

Strategy

Incyte's commercial strategy is to develop and commercialize its compounds on its own in selected markets where it believes a company of its size can successfully compete such as in myelofibrosis polycythemia vera GVHD and other oncology indications. In May 2019 JAKAFI was approved for the treatment of steroid-refractory acute GVHD in adult and pediatric patients 12 years and older. It has expanded the marketing medical sales and operational infrastructure to support continued commercialization of JAKAFI in its three indications and to prepare for potential future indications of JAKAFI in the United States. It is expanding marketing medical and operational infrastructure outside of the United States and within the United States to prepare for potential approval of other products.

Its manufacturing strategy is to contract with third parties to manufacture the raw materials its active pharmaceutical ingredients or API and finished dosage form for clinical and commercial uses. It currently do not operate manufacturing facilities for clinical or commercial production of JAKAFI ICLUSIG or its drug candidates. In addition it expects for the foreseeable future to continue to rely on third parties for the manufacture of commercial supplies of the raw materials API and finished drug product for any drugs that it successfully develops and are approved for commercial sale. In this manner it continues to build and maintain its supply chain and quality assurance resources.

HISTORY

British entrepreneur Roy Whitfield and researcher Randal Scott met in 1989 while working for Invitron a biotech company that soon went under. They founded Incyte Pharmaceuticals in 1991 to design develop and market genomic database products software tools and related services.

The company went public in 1993 and in 1994 Pfizer became its first gene expression database subscriber. Two years later Incyte bought gene-mapping firms Genome Systems and Combion. The firm opened an office in Cambridge UK and formed joint venture diaDexus with SmithKline Beecham (now GlaxoSmithKline) to create and market diagnostic tests that use genetic data to develop effective drug reagents and services.

In 1998 the firm bought microarray maker Synteni. It made its own attempt to map the human genome using LifeSeq buying British firm Hexagen for the mapping unit. Two years later diaDexus filed an IPO and the company changed its name to Incyte Genomics to reflect its focus. The name change however seemed shortsighted when in 2001 the firm announced plans to become a drug developer. It even teamed with one-time rival Agilent to share DNA microarray technologies.

In 2003 the company made another name change — this time simply to "Incyte Corporation" — to represent its growing focus on drug development. As part of that focus that year Incyte acquired the rights to Reverset in 2003 through a licensing agreement with Pharmasset. It launched its janus associated kinase (JAK) research program that year.

In 2004 the company transitioned away from its former business — providing access to its genomic database and set of patents. In that year Incyte closed its Palo Alto California research facilities and headquarters. It also terminated further

development of its information products including LifeSeq — a library of information and expressed sequences that links biological information analysis with proprietary genetic information to aid drug discovery. In addition to closing the Palo Alto office the company reduced its workforce by more than 50%.

Following the transition a leading product candidate for the company was dexelvucitabine (also known as Reverset) to treat patients with HIV but clinical trials were discontinued in 2006. In 2008 it also halted development on a CCR5 antagonist designed to prevent the entry of HIV into target cells.

Incyte gained FDA approval to market Jakafi for several types of myelofibrosis in the US market in November 2011 and the company launched the drug shortly after. The drug also gained approval for myelofibrosis treatment in the European Union in 2012 (through a partnership with Novartis). Jakafi gained approval in December 2014 for the treatment of certain forms of polycythemia vera.

EXECUTIVES

Executive Vice President, Global Strategy And Corporate Development, Vijay Iyengar, $552,278 total compensation
Independent Director, Jacqualyn Fouse
Executive Vice President, General Counsel, Maria Pasquale, $365,753 total compensation
Executive Vice President And Head Of Global Technical Operations, Michael Morrissey
Executive Vice President, General Manager - Europe, Jonathan Dickinson
Independent Director, Edmund Harrigan
Independent Director, Katherine High
Director, Otis Brawley
Chairman, President, Chief Executive Officer, Herve Hoppenot, $1,094,731 total compensation
Independent Director, Jean-Jacques Bienaime
Executive Vice President, Chief Medical Officer, Steven Stein, $576,321 total compensation
Executive Vice President, Chief Scientific Officer, Dashyant Dhanak
Chief Financial Officer, Executive Vice President, Christiana Stamoulis, $585,468 total compensation
Executive Vice President - Human Resources, Paula Swain, $354,029 total compensation
Lead Independent Director, Julian Baker
Independent Director, Paul Clancy
Executive Vice President And General Manager - Us, Barry Flannelly, $480,542 total compensation
Auditors: Ernst & Young LLP

LOCATIONS

HQ: Incyte Corporation
1801 Augustine Cut-Off, Wilmington, DE 19803
Phone: 302 498-6700
Web: www.incyte.com

PRODUCTS/OPERATIONS

2016 Sales

	$ mil.	% of total
Product revenues net	882.4	80
Product royalty revenues	110.7	10
Contract revenues	112.6	10
Other revenues	0.0	-
Total	**1,105.7**	**100**

COMPETITORS

ALEXION	HUMANIGEN INC.
PHARMACEUTICALS INC.	Sierra Oncology Canada
AUTOGENOMICS INC.	ULC
CELLDEX THERAPEUTICS	TRANSGENE
INC.	VERTEX
PHARMACEUTICALS	
HUMAN GENOME SCIENCES	INCORPORATED
INC.	

HISTORICAL FINANCIALS
Company Type: Public

Income Statement				FYE: December 31
	REVENUE ($ mil.)	NET INCOME ($ mil.)	NET PROFIT MARGIN	EMPLOYEES
12/21	2,986.2	948.5	31.8%	2,094
12/20	2,666.7	(295.7)	—	1,773
12/19	2,158.7	446.9	20.7%	1,456
12/18	1,881.8	109.4	5.8%	1,367
12/17	1,536.2	(313.1)	—	1,208
Annual Growth	**18.1%**	**—**	**—**	**14.7%**

2021 Year-End Financials

Debt ratio: 0.6%	No. of shares (mil.): 221.0
Return on equity: 29.7%	Dividends
Cash ($ mil.): 2,057.4	Yield: —
Current ratio: 3.65	Payout: —
Long-term debt ($ mil.): 31.6	Market value ($ mil.): 16,228.0

	STOCK PRICE ($) FY Close	P/E High/Low		PER SHARE ($)		
				Earnings	Dividends	Book Value
12/21	73.40	23	15	4.27	0.00	17.05
12/20	86.98	—	—	(1.36)	0.00	11.90
12/19	87.32	46	31	2.05	0.00	12.02
12/18	63.59	194	113	0.51	0.00	9.03
12/17	94.71	—	—	(1.53)	0.00	7.72
Annual Growth	**(6.2%)**	**—**	**—**	**—**	**—**	**21.9%**

Independence Realty Trust Inc

Auditors: KPMG LLP

LOCATIONS

HQ: Independence Realty Trust Inc
1835 Market Street, Suite 2601, Philadelphia, PA 19103
Phone: 267 270-4800
Web: www.irtliving.com

HISTORICAL FINANCIALS
Company Type: Public

Income Statement				FYE: December 31
	REVENUE ($ mil.)	NET INCOME ($ mil.)	NET PROFIT MARGIN	EMPLOYEES
12/20	211.9	14.7	7.0%	444
12/19	203.2	45.9	22.6%	444
12/18	191.2	26.2	13.7%	455
12/17	161.2	30.2	18.7%	421
12/16	153.3	(9.8)	—	395
Annual Growth	**8.4%**	**—**	**—**	**3.0%**

2020 Year-End Financials

Debt ratio: 54.5%
Return on equity: 2.2%
Cash ($ mil.): 8.7
Current ratio: 0.34
Long-term debt ($ mil.): 945.6
No. of shares (mil.): 101.8
Dividends
  Yield: 4.0%
  Payout: 192.8%
Market value ($ mil.): 1,367.0

	STOCK PRICE ($) FY Close	P/E High/Low	PER SHARE ($) Earnings	Dividends	Book Value
12/20	13.43	103 44	0.16	0.54	6.96
12/19	14.08	30 18	0.51	0.72	6.73
12/18	9.18	35 28	0.30	0.72	6.99
12/17	10.09	26 21	0.41	0.72	7.37
12/16	8.92	— —	(0.19)	0.72	7.35
Annual Growth	10.8%	— —	—	(5.9%)	(1.4%)

Independent Bank Corp (MA)

Independent Bank is a state chartered federally registered bank holding company. The company is the sole stockholder of Rockland Trust Company ("Rockland Trust"or the "Bank"). Its banking subsidiary Rockland Trust operates almost 95 retail branches as well two limited service branches located in Barnstable Bristol Dukes and more in Eastern Massachusetts.Serving area consumers and small to midsized businesses the bank offers standard services such as checking and savings accounts CDs and credit cards in addition to insurance products financial planning trust services. Commercial loans including industrial construction and small business loans. Incorporated in 1985 the bank boasts total assets of some $13.2 billion.

EXECUTIVES

Executive Vice President, Chief Technology And Operations Officer Of The Company And Of Rockland Trust, Barry Jensen, $304,538 total compensation
Independent Director, Daniel O'Brien
Independent Director, Mary Lentz
Executive Vice President, Chief Risk Officer Of The Company And General Counsel Of Rockland Trust, Edward Seksay, $383,654 total compensation
Independent Director, John Morrissey
Independent Director, Donna Abelli
Independent Director, Kevin Jones
Senior Vice President And Director Of Human Resources For Rockland Trust, Maria Harris
Independent Director, James Morton
Independent Director, Warren Fields
Independent Director, Susan O'day
Director, President Of Rockland Trust, Gerard Nadeau, $447,852 total compensation
Independent Director, Frederick Taw
Independent Director, Michael Hogan
President, Chief Executive Officer, Director And Chief Executive Officer, Rockland Trust, Christopher Oddleifson, $792,885 total compensation
Executive Vice President, Chief Operating Officer Of The Company And Of Rockland Trust, Robert Cozzone, $447,596 total compensation

Chief Financial Officer And Accounting Officer, Mark Ruggiero, $311,539 total compensation
Auditors: Ernst & Young LLP

LOCATIONS

HQ: Independent Bank Corp (MA)
  2036 Washington Street, Hanover, MA 02339
Phone: 781 878-6100
Web: www.RocklandTrust.com

PRODUCTS/OPERATIONS

2012 Sales

	$ mil.	% of total
Interest		
Loans	178.3	69
Taxable securities including dividends	16.7	6
Other	1.0	-
Noninterest		
Service charges on deposit accounts	16.0	6
Wealth management	14.8	6
Interchange & ATM fees	9.8	4
Other	21.7	9
Adjustments	(0.1)	-
Total	**258.2**	**100**

COMPETITORS

BANCFIRST CORPORATION
BOKF MERGER CORPORATION NUMBER SIXTEEN
CAMBRIDGE BANCORP
CENTRAL PACIFIC FINANCIAL CORP.
CENTURY BANCORP INC.
CITY HOLDING COMPANY
EASTERN VIRGINIA BANKSHARES INC.
FIRSTMERIT CORPORATION
MBT FINANCIAL CORP.
PACIFIC FINANCIAL CORPORATION
STOCK YARDS BANCORP INC.
UNION BANKSHARES INC.
UNITED BANKSHARES INC.

HISTORICAL FINANCIALS

Company Type: Public

Income Statement — FYE: December 31

	ASSETS ($ mil.)	NET INCOME ($ mil.)	INCOME AS % OF ASSETS	EMPLOYEES
12/20	13,204.3	121.1	0.9%	1,375
12/19	11,395.1	165.1	1.4%	1,348
12/18	8,851.5	121.6	1.4%	1,188
12/17	8,082.0	87.2	1.1%	1,108
12/16	7,709.3	76.6	1.0%	1,103
Annual Growth	14.4%	12.1%	—	5.7%

2020 Year-End Financials

Return on assets: 0.9%
Return on equity: 7.0%
Long-term debt ($ mil.): —
No. of shares (mil.): 32.9
Sales ($ mil.): 512.8
Dividends
  Yield: 2.5%
  Payout: 50.5%
Market value ($ mil.): 2,408.0

	STOCK PRICE ($) FY Close	P/E High/Low	PER SHARE ($) Earnings	Dividends	Book Value
12/20	73.04	23 14	3.64	1.84	51.65
12/19	83.25	17 13	5.03	1.76	49.69
12/18	70.31	21 15	4.40	1.52	38.23
12/17	69.85	24 19	3.19	1.28	34.38
12/16	70.45	24 14	2.90	1.16	32.02
Annual Growth	0.9%	— —	5.8%	12.2%	12.7%

Independent Bank Corporation (Ionia, MI)

Independent Bank Corporation is the holding company for Independent Bank which serves rural and suburban communities of Michigan's Lower Peninsula from more than 100 branches. The bank offers traditional deposit products including checking and savings accounts and CDs. Loans to businesses account for about 40% of the bank's portfolio; real estate mortgages are more than a third. Independent Bank also offers additional products and services like title insurance through subsidiary Independent Title Services and investments through agreement with third-party provider PrimeVest.
Operations
The company also owns Mepco Finance which acquires and services payment plans for extended automobile warranties.
Financial Performance
The company's revenue has been trending down year-over-year. However its net income and cash on hand have both been spiking up across recent fiscal years.
Strategy
As Michigan's economy has exhibited signs of stabilizing and the company's results have relatively improved as well. Independent Bank has reduced its number of high-risk loans non-performing loans and delinquency rates.

EXECUTIVES

Executive Vice President, Chief Risk Officer, Stefanie Kimball, $274,000 total compensation
Senior Vice President, Controller, James Twarozynski
President, Chief Executive Officer, Director, William Kessel, $510,000 total compensation
Independent Director, Stephen Gulis
Independent Chairman Of The Board, Michael Magee
Executive Vice President, Chief Lending Officer, Joel Rahn
Lead Independent Director, William Boer
Independent Director, Christina Keller
Independent Director, Joan Budden
Independent Director, Terrance Beia
Executive Vice President - Operations And Digital Banking, Larry Daniel
Independent Director, Ronia Kruse
Chief Financial Officer, Executive Vice President, Corporate Secretary, Gavin Mohr, $86,154 total compensation
Independent Director, Dennis Archer
Executive Vice President - Mortgage Banking, Patrick Ervin, $256,500 total compensation
Independent Director, Michael Cok
Auditors: Crowe LLP

LOCATIONS

HQ: Independent Bank Corporation (Ionia, MI)
  4200 East Beltline, Grand Rapids, MI 49525
Phone: 616 527-5820
Web: www.independentbank.com

COMPETITORS

BANCFIRST CORPORATION
BANKUNITED INC.
MACATAWA BANK CORPORATION

CENTRAL BANCOMPANY INC.
COLUMBIA BANKING SYSTEM INC.
M&T BANK CORPORATION
REGIONS FINANCIAL CORPORATION
WASHINGTON FEDERAL INC.

HISTORICAL FINANCIALS
Company Type: Public

Income Statement				FYE: December 31
	ASSETS ($ mil.)	NET INCOME ($ mil.)	INCOME AS % OF ASSETS	EMPLOYEES
12/20	4,204.0	56.1	1.3%	983
12/19	3,564.6	46.4	1.3%	994
12/18	3,353.2	39.8	1.2%	976
12/17	2,789.3	20.4	0.7%	911
12/16	2,548.9	22.7	0.9%	885
Annual Growth	13.3%	25.3%	—	2.7%

2020 Year-End Financials
Return on assets: 1.4%
Return on equity: 15.1%
Long-term debt ($ mil.): —
No. of shares (mil.): 21.8
Sales ($ mil): 220.5
Dividends
Yield: 4.3%
Payout: 33.7%
Market value ($ mil.): 404.0

	STOCK PRICE ($) FY Close	P/E High/Low		PER SHARE ($) Earnings	Dividends	Book Value
12/20	18.47	9	4	2.53	0.80	17.82
12/19	22.65	12	9	2.00	0.72	15.58
12/18	21.02	16	12	1.68	0.60	14.38
12/17	22.35	24	20	0.95	0.42	12.42
12/16	21.70	21	13	1.05	0.34	11.71
Annual Growth	(3.9%)	—	—	24.6%	23.9%	11.1%

Independent Bank Group Inc.

The bank holding company Independent Bank Group does business through subsidiary Independent Bank which operates more than 90 full-services branches which more than 70 of these branches are company-owned. The company operates in the Dallas/North Texas area Austin/Central Texas Area and the Houston Texas metropolitan area. The banks offer standard personal and business accounts and services including some focused on small business owners. IBG has total assets of more than $17 billion and loans of about $13 billion. The company traces its roots back 100 years but took its current shape in 2002.
IPO
Operations
The company's portfolio is segmented into categories which includes: commercial loans (30% of company's loan portfolio) consumer loans commercial real estate loans (more than 40%) residential real estate loans (10%) and agricultural loans.
Geographic Reach
Based in McKinney Texas Independent Bank has branches in the Dallas/North Texas area including McKinney Dallas Fort Worth and Sherman/Denison the Austin/Central Texas area including Austin and Waco the Houston Texas metropolitan area and along the Colorado Front Range area including Denver Colorado Springs and Fort Collins.
Financial Performance
Independent Bank Group's financial performance for the span of five years have experienced growth annually with 2020 as its highest performing year.

The bank's net income increased by $8.47 million to $201.2 million in 2020 as compared to the previous year's net income of $192.7 million.

The bank held a total of $1.8 billion cash at the end of 2020. Operating activities provided $154.3 million. Investing activities used $1.4 billion while financing activities provided $2.5 billion.
Strategy
Independent Bank Group's strategy is all about growth. It seeks organic growth in loans and deposits in existing locations by developing customer relationships while maintaining the quality of its loan portfolio. It also makes acquisitions: since 2010 it has made 12 acquisitions most recently of Guaranty Bancorp in 2019.

EXECUTIVES

Independent Director, Michael Viola
Independent Director, Donald Poarch
Independent Director, William Fair
Independent Director, Alicia Harrison
President And Chief Operating Officer, Michael Hobbs, $415,942 total compensation
Independent Director, Paul Washington
Vice Chairman, Daniel Brooks, $464,375 total compensation
Executive Vice President And Chief Operations Officer, James White, $310,000 total compensation
Executive Vice President And General Counsel, Mark Haynie, $347,917 total compensation
Chairman And Chief Executive Officer, David Brooks, $798,542 total compensation
Chief Financial Officer And Executive Vice President, Michelle Hickox, $408,542 total compensation
Executive Vice President And Head, Corporate Responsibility, James Tippit, $250,000 total compensation
Auditors: RSM US LLP

LOCATIONS

HQ: Independent Bank Group Inc.
7777 Henneman Way, McKinney, TX 75070-1711
Phone: 972 562-9004
Web: www.ibtx.com

PRODUCTS/OPERATIONS

2012 Loan Portfolio

	% of total
Real estate	
Commercial	47
Residential	23
Construction land & land development	7
Single-family interim construction	5
Commercial	12
Agricultural	3
Consumer	3
Total	**100**

Selected Acquisition
Town Center Bank (2010 North Texas)
Farmersville Bancshares Inc. (2010 North Texas)
I Bank Holding Company Inc. (2012 Austin/Central Texas)
The Community Group Inc. (2012 Dallas/North Texas)

COMPETITORS

BANCFIRST CORPORATION
BANK OF THE WEST
FIRST MIDWEST BANCORP INC.
HEARTLAND FINANCIAL USA INC.
IBERIABANK CORPORATION
MUFG AMERICAS HOLDINGS CORPORATION
NEWBRIDGE BANCORP
NORTHWEST BANCORP INC.
OLD LINE BANCSHARES INC.
OLD NATIONAL BANCORP
PEOPLE'S UNITED FINANCIAL INC.
PROSPERITY BANCSHARES INC.
SEACOAST BANKING CORPORATION OF FLORIDA
SUNTRUST BANKS INC.
TEXAS CAPITAL BANCSHARES INC.
UNITED COMMUNITY BANKS INC.
WILSHIRE BANCORP INC.

HISTORICAL FINANCIALS
Company Type: Public

Income Statement				FYE: December 31
	ASSETS ($ mil.)	NET INCOME ($ mil.)	INCOME AS % OF ASSETS	EMPLOYEES
12/20	17,753.4	201.2	1.1%	1,513
12/19	14,958.2	192.7	1.3%	1,469
12/18	9,849.9	128.2	1.3%	1,087
12/17	8,684.4	76.5	0.9%	924
12/16	5,852.8	53.5	0.9%	577
Annual Growth	32.0%	39.2%	—	27.3%

2020 Year-End Financials
Return on assets: 1.2%
Return on equity: 8.2%
Long-term debt ($ mil.): —
No. of shares (mil.): 43.1
Sales ($ mil): 696.5
Dividends
Yield: 1.6%
Payout: 23.3%
Market value ($ mil.): 2,697.0

	STOCK PRICE ($) FY Close	P/E High/Low		PER SHARE ($) Earnings	Dividends	Book Value
12/20	62.52	13	4	4.67	1.05	58.31
12/19	55.44	14	11	4.46	1.00	54.48
12/18	45.77	18	10	4.33	0.54	52.50
12/17	67.60	24	18	2.97	0.40	47.28
12/16	62.40	22	9	2.88	0.34	35.63
Annual Growth	0.0%	—	—	12.8%	32.6%	13.1%

Industrial Logistics Properties Trust

Auditors: DELOITTE & TOUCHE LLP

LOCATIONS

HQ: Industrial Logistics Properties Trust
Two Newton Place, 255 Washington Street, Suite 300, Newton, MA 02458-1634
Phone: 617 219-1460

HISTORICAL FINANCIALS

Company Type: Public

Income Statement

FYE: December 31

	REVENUE ($ mil.)	NET INCOME ($ mil.)	NET PROFIT MARGIN	EMPLOYEES
12/21	219.8	119.6	54.4%	0
12/20	254.5	82.0	32.2%	0
12/19	229.2	52.5	22.9%	0
12/18	162.5	74.3	45.8%	0
12/17	156.5	80.1	51.2%	0
Annual Growth	8.9%	10.6%	—	—

2021 Year-End Financials

Debt ratio: 43.3%
Return on equity: 11.7%
Cash ($ mil.): 29.4
Current ratio: 3.51
Long-term debt ($ mil.): 828.1

No. of shares (mil.): 65.4
Dividends
  Yield: 5.2%
  Payout: 88.5%
Market value ($ mil.): 1,638.0

	STOCK PRICE ($) FY Close	P/E High/Low		Earnings	PER SHARE ($) Dividends	Book Value
12/21	25.05	16	12	1.83	1.32	15.87
12/20	23.29	19	11	1.26	1.32	15.36
12/19	22.42	28	23	0.81	1.32	15.28
12/18	19.67	21	16	1.16	0.93	15.80
Annual Growth	8.4%		—	16.4%	12.4%	0.1%

InfuSystem Holdings Inc

EXECUTIVES

Executive Vice President, Chief Administrative Officer, Jeannine Sheehan
Chief Financial Officer, Executive Vice President, Barry Steele, $220,000 total compensation
Independent Director, Paul Gendron
Vice Chairman Of The Board, Gregg Lehman
Independent Chairman Of The Board, Scott Shuda
Chief Executive Officer, Director, Richard Diiorio, $449,601 total compensation
Independent Director, Christopher Sansone
Independent Director, Darrell Montgomery
President, Chief Operating Officer, Director, Carrie Lachance, $268,291 total compensation
Executive Vice President, Chief Commercial Officer, Thomas Ruiz, $220,850 total compensation
Auditors: BDO USA, LLP

LOCATIONS

HQ: InfuSystem Holdings Inc
  3851 West Hamlin Road, Rochester Hills, MI 48309
Phone: 248 291-1210
Web: www.infusystem.com

HISTORICAL FINANCIALS

Company Type: Public

Income Statement

FYE: December 31

	REVENUE ($ mil.)	NET INCOME ($ mil.)	NET PROFIT MARGIN	EMPLOYEES
12/20	97.3	17.3	17.8%	292
12/19	81.1	1.3	1.7%	269
12/18	67.1	(1.1)	—	251
12/17	71.0	(20.7)	—	245
12/16	70.5	(0.2)	—	250
Annual Growth	8.4%	—		4.0%

2020 Year-End Financials

Debt ratio: 40.0%
Return on equity: 54.8%
Cash ($ mil.): 9.6
Current ratio: 1.29
Long-term debt ($ mil.): 29.3

No. of shares (mil.): 20.3
Dividends
  Yield: —
  Payout: —
Market value ($ mil.): 381.0

	STOCK PRICE ($) FY Close	P/E High/Low		Earnings	PER SHARE ($) Dividends	Book Value
12/20	18.78	23	7	0.80	0.00	2.01
12/19	8.53	123	49	0.07	0.00	1.12
12/18	3.44	—	—	(0.05)	0.00	1.04
12/17	2.30	—	—	(0.91)	0.00	1.36
12/16	2.55	—	—	(0.01)	0.00	2.24
Annual Growth	64.7%	—		—	—	(2.7%)

Innovative Industrial Properties Inc

Auditors: BDO USA, LLP

LOCATIONS

HQ: Innovative Industrial Properties Inc
  1389 Center Drive, Suite 200, Park City, UT 84098
Phone: 858 997-3332
Web: www.innovativeindustrialproperties.com

HISTORICAL FINANCIALS

Company Type: Public

Income Statement

FYE: December 31

	REVENUE ($ mil.)	NET INCOME ($ mil.)	NET PROFIT MARGIN	EMPLOYEES
12/20	116.9	65.7	56.2%	15
12/19	44.6	23.4	52.6%	13
12/18	14.7	6.9	47.2%	6
12/17	6.4	(0.0)	—	6
12/16	0.3	(4.3)	—	5
Annual Growth	336.8%	—		31.6%

2020 Year-End Financials

Debt ratio: 7.7%
Return on equity: 6.3%
Cash ($ mil.): 126.0
Current ratio: 1.77
Long-term debt ($ mil.): 136.6

No. of shares (mil.): 23.9
Dividends
  Yield: 2.4%
  Payout: 136.7%
Market value ($ mil.): 4,384.0

	STOCK PRICE ($) FY Close	P/E High/Low		Earnings	PER SHARE ($) Dividends	Book Value
12/20	183.13	60	14	3.27	4.47	63.71
12/19	75.87	67	22	2.03	2.83	43.37
12/18	45.39	72	32	0.75	1.20	27.04
12/17	32.31	—	—	(0.13)	0.55	21.01
12/16	18.19	—	—	(4.56)	0.00	17.69
Annual Growth	78.1%	—		—	—	37.8%

Innoviva Inc

Innoviva (formerly Theravance) is a company with a portfolio of royalties that include respiratory assets partnered with Glaxo Group Limited (GSK). The company collaborates with GSK to develop and commercialize once-daily products for the treatment of chronic obstructive pulmonary disease (COPD) and asthma. The collaboration has developed three combination products Relvar once-daily combination medicine consisting of a LABA vilanterol and an inhaled corticosteroid fluticasone furoate; Anoro Ellipta once-daily medicine combining a long-acting muscarinic antagonist; and Trelegy Ellipta once-daily combination medicine consisting of an inhaled corticosteroid long-acting muscarinic antagonist and LABA. Founded in 1996.

Operations

The company has LABA collaboration agreement with GSK to develop and commercialize once-daily products for the treatment of chronic obstructive pulmonary disease (COPD) and asthma. The collaboration has developed three combination products: Relvar/Breo that accounts for around 70% of total revenue Trelegy and Anoro for about 15% each.

Geographic Reach

Headquartered in Burlingame California Innoviva sells its products in the US Japan and Canada Germany and Europe among others.

Sales and Marketing

The company entered into a collaboration agreement with GSK to develop and commercialize its product.

Financial Performance

The company's revenues grew by a whopping 384% to $261 million from 2015 to 2019. Over that span net income had increased after a loss in 2015.

Total net revenue increased slightly in 2019 to $261 million. Royalties for RELVAR/BREO ELLIPTA decreased primarily due to increased pricing pressure in the US offset by volume growth in both the US and non-US markets. The decrease was offset by continued growth in prescriptions and market share for TRELEGY ELLIPTA. Royalties for ANORO ELLIPTA increased slightly year over year.

Innoviva has reported a net income of $157.3 million lower by $237.8 million from 2018. An interest expense of $18.7 million income tax expense of $41.9 million and $33.7 million income from non-controlling interest contributed to the decrease in net income.

Cash and cash equivalents at the end of the period were $278.1 million. Net cash provided by operating activities was $257.5 million while investing and financing activities each used $18 million and $23.8 million respectively. Main cash uses for the year were for purchases of marketable securities and payments of loans.

Strategy

The company strategy is currently focused on the goal of maximizing stockholder value by among other things maximizing the potential value of its respiratory assets partnered with GSK and optimizing its operations and capital allocation.

Company Background

Innoviva began operating in 1997 under the name Advanced Medicine.

EXECUTIVES

Independent Chairman Of The Board, Odysseas Kostas
Chief Accounting Officer, Marianne Zhen, $284,625 total compensation
Independent Director, Sarah Schlesinger
Independent Director, Jules Haimovitz
Independent Director, Mark Dipaolo
Chief Executive Officer, Pavel Raifeld, $222,000 total compensation
Independent Director, Deborah Birx
Auditors: Grant Thornton LLP

LOCATIONS

HQ: Innoviva Inc
1350 Old Bayshore Highway Suite 400, Burlingame, CA 94010
Phone: 650 238-9600
Web: www.inva.com

PRODUCTS/OPERATIONS

2014 Sales

	% of total
Royalty revenue	87
MABA program license	13
Total	**100**

Selected Development Products

Bacterial Infections
 TD-1792 (antibiotic for staph infections)
 VIBATIV (telavancin for complicated skin and skin structure infections or cSSSI including staph infections)
Central Nervous System/Pain
 TD-1211 (opioid-induced constipation)
 TD-9855 (chronic pain)
Cognitive Disorders
 TD-5108 (Alzheimer's disease)
Gastrointestinal
 TD-5108 (for severe constipation and irritable bowel syndrome)
 TD-8954 (motility)
Respiratory
 LAMA/LABA (or GSK573719/Vilanterol for chronic obstructive pulmonary disease or COPD with GlaxoSmithKline)
 MABA (or GSK961081 for COPD with GlaxoSmithKline)
 RELOVAIR (for asthma with GlaxoSmithKline)

COMPETITORS

CELLECTIS	REGENERON
COLLEGIUM	PHARMACEUTICALS INC.
PHARMACEUTICAL INC.	SUPERNUS
EXELIXIS INC.	PHARMACEUTICALS INC.
HALOZYME THERAPEUTICS	ULTRAGENYX
INC.	PHARMACEUTICAL INC.
INDIVIOR PLC	UNITED THERAPEUTICS
LIGAND PHARMACEUTICALS	CORPORATION
INCORPORATED	VANDA PHARMACEUTICALS
OMEROS CORPORATION	INC.
PDL BIOPHARMA INC.	

HISTORICAL FINANCIALS

Company Type: Public

Income Statement

FYE: December 31

	REVENUE ($ mil.)	NET INCOME ($ mil.)	NET PROFIT MARGIN	EMPLOYEES
12/20	336.7	224.4	66.6%	5
12/19	261.0	157.2	60.3%	6
12/18	261.0	395.0	151.4%	6
12/17	217.2	134.1	61.8%	12
12/16	133.5	59.5	44.6%	14
Annual Growth	26.0%	39.3%	—	(22.7%)

2020 Year-End Financials

Debt ratio: 38.5%
Return on equity: 52.4%
Cash ($ mil.): 246.4
Current ratio: 55.98
Long-term debt ($ mil.): 385.5
No. of shares (mil.): 101.3
Dividends
 Yield: —
 Payout: —
Market value ($ mil.): 1,256.0

	STOCK PRICE ($) FY Close	P/E High/Low		PER SHARE ($) Earnings	Dividends	Book Value
12/20	12.39	7	4	2.02	0.00	5.33
12/19	14.16	13	6	1.43	0.00	3.10
12/18	17.45	5	3	3.53	0.00	1.52
12/17	14.19	12	8	1.17	0.00	(2.38)
12/16	10.70	26	15	0.53	0.00	(3.26)
Annual Growth	3.7%	—	—	39.7%		

Inotiv Inc

Bioanalytical Systems Inc. (BASi) now operating under the trade name "Inotiv" provides contract research and development services for the pharmaceutical chemical and medical device industries. The company also sells analytical instruments to these customers which include pharmaceutical biotechnology biomedical device academic and government organizations. Some of its services include analytical method development and validation stability testing archiving services among others. Vast majority of its total revenue accounted in the US. The company has been providing services involving the research of products and treatment of diseases through products since 1974.

Operations

The company operates in two primary segments — contract research services and research products. Contract research services offers screening and formulation development as well as testing for quality control regulatory compliance and preclinical safety. Research products design develop manufacture in vivo sampling systems and accessories (including disposables training and systems qualification) physiology monitoring tools and liquid chromatography and electrochemistry instruments platforms. Services' revenue accounts for more than 90% of total revenue while products account the remainder.

BASi's blood sampling instrument lines are marketed under the Culex brand.

Geographic Reach

Headquarters in West Lafayette the company has a network of about 20 distributors from Japan South Korea China India Central America South America South Africa the Middle East and Europe.

Majority of the company's revenue is from its operations in the US.

Sales and Marketing

BASi's customers include pharmaceutical firms biotechnology companies biomedical device academic institutions and government organizations.

To promote its offerings the company communicates directly with scientists and carries out centralized corporate marketing initiatives concentrated business development efforts. In addition the company uses social media to pharmaceutical and medical device companies as well as academic and government research institutions.

Financial Performance

The company's performance for the span of five years have seen an upward trend with 2020 as its highest performing year.

BASi's 2020 revenue increased by 39% or $16.8 million to $60.4 million compared to $43.6 million. Internal growth from existing operations contributed approximately 33% or $5.6 million of the increase in revenue. While approximately $11.3 million or 67% of the growth was attributable to additional revenues from the Smithers Avanza Acquisition and the PCRS Acquisition of $6.5 million and $4.8 million respectively.

Net loss in 2020 increased to about $4.7 million compared to net loss of about $790000 in 2019.

Cash and cash equivalents at the end of the year were $1.4 million. Cash provided by operating activities was $1.3 million. Investing activities used $10.1 million while financing activities provided $9.6 million. Main cash uses were for capital expenditures and cash paid in acquisitions.

Strategy

The company's strategy is to provide services that generates high-quality and timely data supporting new drug and product approval or expansion of their use.

EXECUTIVES

Independent Director, Nigel Brown
Independent Director, Scott Cragg
Chief Commercial Officer, Michael Garrett
General Counsel, Secretary, Mark Bibi
Executive Vice President, Adrian Hardy
Chief Operating Officer - Research Models And Services, James Harkness
President, Chief Executive Officer, Director, Robert Leasure, $450,751 total compensation
Chief Financial Officer, Vice President - Finance, Beth Taylor, $273,635 total compensation
Senior Vice President- Preclinical Services, Philip Downing, $201,250 total compensation
Independent Director, Richard Johnson
Independent Chairman Of The Board, Gregory Davis
Chief Strategy Officer, Director, John Sagartz, $322,674 total compensation
Independent Director, R. Matthew Neff
Chief Human Resource Officer, William Pitchford
Chief Operating Officer, John Beattie
Auditors: RSM US LLP

LOCATIONS

HQ: Inotiv Inc
2701 Kent Avenue, West Lafayette, IN 47906
Phone: 765 463-4527
Web: www.inotivco.com

HOOVER'S HANDBOOK OF EMERGING COMPANIES 2022

229

PRODUCTS/OPERATIONS

2015 Sales

	% of total
Services	78
Product	22
Total	**100**

COMPETITORS

AGILENT TECHNOLOGIES INC.
BIO-RAD LABORATORIES INC.
CHARLES RIVER LABORATORIES INTERNATIONAL INC.
EXACT SCIENCES CORPORATION
INVENTIV HEALTH INC.
IQVIA HOLDINGS INC.
NANOSTRING TECHNOLOGIES INC.
ORASURE TECHNOLOGIES INC.
PRA HEALTH SCIENCES INC.
Qiagen N.V.
SEQUENOM INC.
SYNEOS HEALTH LLC
TRANSCAT INC.

HISTORICAL FINANCIALS

Company Type: Public

Income Statement				FYE: September 30
	REVENUE ($ mil.)	NET INCOME ($ mil.)	NET PROFIT MARGIN	EMPLOYEES
09/21	89.6	10.9	12.2%	567
09/20	60.4	(4.6)	—	421
09/19	43.6	(0.7)	—	322
09/18	26.3	(0.1)	—	235
09/17	24.2	0.8	3.6%	155
Annual Growth	38.7%	87.4%		38.3%

2021 Year-End Financials

Debt ratio: 51.4%
Return on equity: 19.3%
Cash ($ mil.): 156.9
Current ratio: 3.43
Long-term debt ($ mil.): 154.2

No. of shares (mil.): 15.9
Dividends
  Yield: —
  Payout: —
Market value ($ mil.): 466.0

	STOCK PRICE ($) FY Close	P/E High/Low		PER SHARE ($) Earnings	Dividends	Book Value
09/21	29.24	60	6	0.19	0.00	6.60
09/20	4.78	—	—	(0.43)	0.00	0.69
09/19	3.59	—	—	(0.08)	0.00	1.02
09/18	1.61	—	—	(0.02)	0.00	1.06
09/17	1.76	17	6	0.10	0.00	1.03
Annual Growth	101.9%	—	—	17.4%	—	59.2%

Installed Building Products Inc

Installed Building Products (IBP) is a leading new residential insulation installer with more than 190 branches in almost all 50 continental US states and the District of Columbia. IBP manages all aspects of the installation process for its customers including direct purchases of materials from national manufacturers delivery and installation. In addition to insulation IBP waterproofs and fire-proofs homes and installs garage doors rain gutters shower doors shelving and mirrors. Founded in 1977 as Edwards Insulation.

IPO

Operations

IBP operates through a single reporting segment. Residential new construction comprises about 75% of its revenues while commercial construction accounts for about 20% and repair and remodel accounts for about 5%.

About 65% of its sales are for insulation of which fiberglass and cellulose insulation accounts for about 85% and spray foam insulation generates the remaining 15% of insulation revenue. Waterproofing; shower doors shelving and mirrors; garage doors; rain gutters; and other building products each contribute anywhere from about 5% of revenue.

Geographic Reach

Columbus Ohio-based IBP has more than 190 branches serving almost all 50 continental US states the District of Columbia.

It also has warehouse and office space in more than 35 states with Ohio Texas and Indiana representing the squarest footage. In addition IBP also owns its cellulose manufacturing facility in Bucyrus Ohio.

Sales and Marketing

IBP sales force is made up of about 650 employees who on average have been with the company for about nine years. The company focuses on cross-selling services to existing customers and identifying customers who may need multiple services. In addition to the efforts of its sales staff IBP markets its product and service offerings on the internet in the local yellow pages on the radio and through advertisements in trade journals. It primarily conducts its marketing using local trademarks and trade names.

Its customers include homebuilders construction firms contractors and individuals. The top 10 customers which includes both national and regional builders accounted for about 15% of revenue.

IBP's advertising expense was approximately $3.9 million $3.9 million and $3.8 million for the years ended December 31 2020 2019 and 2018 respectively.

Financial Performance

Company's revenue for fiscal 2020 increased by 9% to $1.7 billion compared from the prior year with $1.5 billion. The increase was primarily driven by acquisitions increased sales volume of complimentary products and increased selling prices.

Net income for fiscal 2020 increased to $97.2 million compared from the prior year with $68.2 million.

Cash held by the company at the end of fiscal 2020 increased to $231.5 million. Cash provided by operations was $180.8 million while cash used for investing and financing activities were $77.8 million and $49.4 million respectively. Main uses of cash were acquisitions of businesses and repurchase of common stock.

Strategy

IBP believe its geographic footprint long-standing relationships with national insulation manufacturers streamlined value chain and proven track record of successful acquisitions provides the company with opportunities for continued growth in its existing markets and expansion into new markets. IBP believe its continued emphasis on expanding its product offering further expansion into the commercial construction market and targeting geographies where IBP look to grow market share will reduce potential future cyclicality of its operations.

IBP's current strategic objectives include: capitalize on the new residential and large commercial construction markets; continue to strengthen its market share position by working with the best customers. IBP seek to work with the most profitable and efficient builders and commercial general contractors in its markets; recruit develop and retain an exceptional workforce by investing in its employees and its communities and promoting a family-oriented culture; capitalize on its ability to cross-sell products through existing markets as well as new markets entered as a result of organic expansion and acquisitions; enhance profitability from the company's operating leverage and national scale; continue expansion in the multibillion-dollar commercial end market; pursue value enhancing acquisitions by continuing its disciplined approach to valuations and pricing; and the company integrate new acquisitions quickly and seamlessly into its corporate infrastructure including our accounting and employee systems.

Mergers and Acquisitions

In mid-2021 IBP announced the acquisition of General Ceiling & Partitions Inc. (GCP). Founded in 1986 GCP is headquartered in Colorado Springs Colorado and primarily installs drywall framing ceiling tiles and fire-stopping/insulation for commercial customers. IBP also announced the acquisition of Reliable Glass & Mirror LLC a Louisiana based provider of glass and mirror installation services to residential and commercial customers. GCP and Reliable Glass & Mirror further expands its commercial installation services to the compelling Colorado Springs market and increases its presence within Louisiana.

In 2021 IBP announced the acquisition of Alpine Construction Services LLC (Alpine). Founded in 2015 Alpine is headquartered in Colorado Springs and primarily provides fiberglass and spray foam insulation installation services to residential and multifamily customers. Alpine is a fast-growing installer that expands its residential and multifamily insulation installation services to the compelling Colorado Springs market.

Also in 2021 IBP announced the acquisition of Alert Insulation. Founded in 1992 Alert Insulation is headquartered in La Puente California and primarily provides fiberglass insulation installation fireproofing services and acoustical ceiling system installation to commercial customers. Alert Insulation significantly expands its commercial insulation installation services throughout California.

In early 2021 IBP announced today the acquisition of I.W. International Insulation Inc. doing business as Intermountain West Insulation (Intermountain). Founded in 1981 Intermountain has six locations throughout Washington state and is headquartered in Kennewick. The company primarily provides insulation installation services to residential customers throughout Washington Oregon and Idaho. Intermountain significantly expands our single-family residential insulation installation services in the Pacific Northwest.

In late 2020 IBP announced the acquisition of Custom Glass & Doors Inc. (CGD). Founded in 1986 CGD is headquartered in Norcross Georgia and primarily provides glass shower shelving and mirror installation services to residential and multifamily customers. CGD expands its complemen-

230   HOOVER'S HANDBOOK OF EMERGING COMPANIES 2022

tary installation services in the greater Atlanta market.

Also in 2020 IBP announced today the acquisition of Storm Master Gutters ("Storm Master"). Founded in 1977 Storm Master is headquartered in Cherry Hill New Jersey and primarily provides gutter installation services to residential and multi-family customers throughout New Jersey Pennsylvania Delaware Maryland Massachusetts Virginia New York West Virginia and Tennessee. Storm Master significantly expands its presence across several compelling markets in the Northeast Mid-Atlantic and Southeastern US. In addition Storm Master's mix of both residential and multi-family customers aligns well with the current growth the company experiencing in multi-family markets across the country.

In 2020 IBP has acquired the North Charleston SC and Pooler GA branches from Energy One America LLC. The acquired branches will operate under the names Charleston Insulation and Foam and Savannah Insulation and Foam respectively. Both branches offer spray foam fiberglass and air barrier installation services to residential multi-family and commercial customers. The acquisition add approximately $22.0 million of combined revenue.

Company Background

Installed Building Products (IBP) was founded as Edwards Insulation in 1977. It had one location in Columbus Ohio. In the late 1990s it established a national presence with an aggressive acquisition strategy.

EXECUTIVES

Senior Vice President - Finance And Investor Relations, Jason Niswonger, $313,423 total compensation

Presiding Independent Director, Margot Carter

Independent Director, Lawrence Hilsheimer

President - Commercial Development, Director, Vikas Verma

Chief Financial Officer, Executive Vice President, Director, Michael Miller, $353,731 total compensation

Independent Director, David Meuse

Chief Accounting Officer, Treasurer, Todd Fry, $241,346 total compensation

Chief Operating Officer, Jay Elliott, $423,846 total compensation

Chairman, President And Chief Executive Officer, Jeffrey Edwards, $720,539 total compensation

President - External Affairs, W. Jeffrey Hire, $335,038 total compensation

Auditors: Deloitte & Touche LLP

LOCATIONS

HQ: Installed Building Products Inc
495 South High Street, Suite 50, Columbus, OH 43215
Phone: 614 221-3399
Web: www.installedbuildingproducts.com

PRODUCTS/OPERATIONS

2017 Sales

	% of total
Residential new construction and repair and remodel	83
Commercial construction	17
Total	**100**

2017 Sales

	% of total
Insulation	67
Waterproofing	8
Shower doors shelving & mirrors	7
Garage doors	5
Rain gutters	4
Other	9
Total	**100**

COMPETITORS

ALLENBUILD LIMITED
BEACON ROOFING SUPPLY INC.
BUILDERS FIRSTSOURCE INC.
GMS INC.
JELD-WEN HOLDING INC.
KAJIMA CORPORATION
KINGFISHER PLC
LENDLEASE CORPORATION LIMITED
LLANMOOR DEVELOPMENT CO. LIMITED
SAFEGUARD PROPERTIES MANAGEMENT LLC
TAISEI CORPORATION
TAKENAKA CORPORATION
TOPBUILD CORP.
WESTON HOMES PLC

HISTORICAL FINANCIALS

Company Type: Public

Income Statement

FYE: December 31

	REVENUE ($ mil.)	NET INCOME ($ mil.)	NET PROFIT MARGIN	EMPLOYEES
12/20	1,653.2	97.2	5.9%	8,950
12/19	1,511.6	68.1	4.5%	8,500
12/18	1,336.4	54.7	4.1%	7,700
12/17	1,132.9	41.1	3.6%	6,900
12/16	862.9	38.4	4.5%	5,292
Annual Growth	17.6%	26.1%	—	14.0%

2020 Year-End Financials

Debt ratio: 47.6%
Return on equity: 34.0%
Cash ($ mil.): 231.5
Current ratio: 2.64
Long-term debt ($ mil.): 541.9
No. of shares (mil.): 29.6
Dividends
Yield: —
Payout: —
Market value ($ mil.): 3,020.0

	STOCK PRICE ($) FY Close	P/E High/Low		PER SHARE ($) Earnings	Dividends	Book Value
12/20	101.93	36	9	3.27	0.00	10.77
12/19	68.87	33	15	2.28	0.00	8.33
12/18	33.69	44	17	1.75	0.00	6.10
12/17	75.95	60	31	1.30	0.00	6.61
12/16	41.30	36	15	1.23	0.00	4.89
Annual Growth	25.3%	—	—	27.7%	—	21.8%

Insteel Industries, Inc.

Insteel Industries manufactures steel welded wire reinforcement (WWR) which is used primarily in concrete construction materials; pre-stressed concrete strand (PC strand); engineered structural mesh (ESM); concrete pipe reinforcement (CPR); and standard welded wire reinforcement (SWWR). Its PC strand products are the spine for concrete structures from bridges to parking garages. Insteel's customers include manufacturers of concrete products distributors and rebar fabricators and contractors. A majority of its sales come from manufacturers of non-residential concrete con-

struction products. The US is responsible for almost all of its total sales. The company was founded in 1953 by Howard O. Woltz Jr.

Operations

Insteel's major products consist of WWR and PC strand. WWR product sales accounted for more than 60% of the company's total sales while PC strand accounted for some 40%.

WWR is produced as either a standard or a specially engineered reinforcing product. It also produces a full range of WWR products including ESM CPR and SWWR. ESM is an engineered made-to-order product that is used as the primary reinforcement for concrete elements or structures. PC strand is a high strength seven-wire strand that is used to impart compression forces into precast concrete elements and structures.

Geographic Reach

Headquartered in North Carolina Insteel operates ten manufacturing facilities located in Dayton Texas; Gallatin Tennessee; Hazleton Pennsylvania; Hickman Kentucky; Houston Texas; Jacksonville Florida; Kingman Arizona; Mount Airy North Carolina; Sanderson Florida; and St. Joseph Missouri. Additionally it is currently pursuing the sale of an idle facility located in Summerville South Carolina.

The US operation accounts for the vast majority of the company's total revenue.

Sales and Marketing

Insteel sells its products nationwide as well as into Canada Mexico and Central and South America delivering its products primarily by truck using common or contract carriers. Products are sold primarily to manufacturers of concrete products that are used in nonresidential construction; and to a lesser extent distributors rebar fabricators and contractors.

About 85% of the company's net sales were to manufacturers of concrete products and 15% were to residential construction.

Financial Performance

Net sales increased 25% to $590.6 million in 2021 from $472.6 million in 2020 reflecting a 26% increase in selling prices partially offset by a 1% decrease in shipments. The increase in average selling prices was driven by price increases implemented in the current year primarily to recover the escalation in raw material costs together with strong demand for its products.

The company had net earnings of $66.6 million in 2020 a 250% increase from the previous year. The increase is primarily due to a higher sales volume for the year.

The company's cash for the year ended 2021 was $89.9 million. Operating activities generated $69.9 million while investing activities used $17.8 million mainly for capital expenditures. Financing activities used another $30.9 million mainly for payment for dividends.

Strategy

The company's business strategy is focused on: Achieving leadership positions in its markets; Operating as the lowest cost producer in its industry; and pursuing growth opportunities within its core businesses that further the company's penetration of the markets it currently serves or expands its footprint.

Its growth strategy is focused on organic opportunities as well as strategic acquisitions in existing or related markets that leverage the company's infrastructure and core competencies in the manufacture and marketing of concrete reinforcing products.

Mergers and Acquisitions

In early 2020 Insteel Industries announced that its wholly-owned subsidiary Insteel Wire Products Company has acquired substantially all of the assets of Strand-Tech Manufacturing Inc. (STM) for $19.4 million. STM is a leading manufacturer of PC strand for concrete construction applications based in South Carolina. The STM acquisition represents a significant milestone for the company's PC strand business and strengthens its competitive position by leveraging its operating costs and optimizing its manufacturing footprint.

Company Background

Howard Woltz Sr. bought a premixed concrete and concrete-block plant and formed Exposaic Industries Inc. in 1953. Son Howard Woltz Jr. took over as chairman and president in 1958 adding welded-wire production equipment to the plant in 1975 during a shortage of wire reinforcing for its precast-concrete operations. Exposaic diversified again into industrial wire products in 1981 and went public in 1985. The company sold its precast concrete unit in 1988.

EXECUTIVES

Independent Director, Jon Ruth
Independent Director, Anne Lloyd
Independent Director, Abney Boxley
Senior Vice President - Sourcing And Logistics, James York, $245,385 total compensation
Independent Director, Joseph Rutkowski
Chief Financial Officer, Senior Vice President, Treasurer, Mark Carano, $345,000 total compensation
Vice President - Administration, Secretary, Chief Legal Officer, James Petelle, $244,231 total compensation
Independent Director, G. Kennedy Thompson
Chairman Of The Board, President, Chief Executive Officer, H. Woltz, $665,769 total compensation
Chief Operating Officer, Senior Vice President, Richard Wagner, $345,385 total compensation
Auditors: Grant Thornton LLP

LOCATIONS

HQ: Insteel Industries, Inc.
1373 Boggs Drive, Mount Airy, NC 27030
Phone: 336 786-2141
Web: www.insteel.com

PRODUCTS/OPERATIONS

2015 Sales

	$ mil.	% of total
Welded wire reinforcement	225.2	57
Prestressed concrete strand	192.3	43
Total	**447.5**	**100**

Selected Products:

Drawn wire:Continuous length (ASTM A1064) smooth or deformedStraightened and cut (ASTM A1064) smooth or deformedPrestressing single wirePC strand:Welded wire reinforcementEngineered structural meshStandard welded wire reinforcementConcr
Insteel Wire Products Company
Intercontinental Metals Corporation (an inactive subsidiary)

COMPETITORS

BEKAERT CORPORATION
CORNERSTONE BUILDING BRANDS INC.
GMS INC.
HEADWATERS INCORPORATED

HITACHI METALS LTD.
MASTER-HALCO INC.
MITSUBISHI STEEL MFG. CO. LTD.
TOKYO STEEL MANUFACTURING CO.LTD.
TOPY INDUSTRIESLIMITED
UFP INDUSTRIES INC.
voestalpine Wire Rod Austria GmbH

HISTORICAL FINANCIALS

Company Type: Public

Income Statement

FYE: October 2

	REVENUE ($ mil.)	NET INCOME ($ mil.)	NET PROFIT MARGIN	EMPLOYEES
10/21	590.6	66.6	11.3%	913
10/20*	472.6	19.0	4.0%	881
09/19	455.7	5.6	1.2%	834
09/18	453.2	36.2	8.0%	810
09/17	388.8	22.5	5.8%	803
Annual Growth	**11.0%**	**31.1%**	—	**3.3%**

*Fiscal year change

2021 Year-End Financials

Debt ratio: —
Return on equity: 23.5%
Cash ($ mil.): 89.8
Current ratio: 3.59
Long-term debt ($ mil.): —

No. of shares (mil.): 19.4
Dividends
Yield: 0.0%
Payout: 47.5%
Market value ($ mil.): 757.0

	STOCK PRICE ($) FY Close	P/E High/Low		PER SHARE ($) Earnings	Dividends	Book Value
10/21	39.00	13	6	3.41	1.62	15.56
10/20*	18.95	26	11	0.98	0.12	13.72
09/19	20.71	122	61	0.29	0.12	12.77
09/18	35.88	23	13	1.88	1.12	12.57
09/17	26.11	36	20	1.17	1.37	11.73
Annual Growth	**10.6%**	—	—	**30.7%**	**4.3%**	**7.3%**

*Fiscal year change

Insulet Corp

Insulet wants to isolate an insolent disease. The medical device company manufactures an insulin pump for people with insulin-dependent diabetes. Its disposable waterproof product called the OmniPod Insulin Management System a small lightweight and adheres directly to the patient's skin making it more discrete than most insulin infusion systems that typically clip to a belt or fit in a pocket. It also includes a handheld device to wirelessly program the OmniPod with insulin delivery instructions. The company have partnered with pharmaceutical and biotechnology companies to tailor the Omnipod System technology platform and sells it to customers both directly and through its distribution partners. The US is the company's largest market which accounts for about 65% of total revenue.

Operations

The Omnipod System consists of the following: Omnipod Insulin Management System (Omnipod) and the Omnipod DASHTM Insulin Management System (DASH) and its next generation digital mobile Omnipod platform.

The Omnipod System features two discreet devices: self-adhesive disposable tubeless Omnipod

device (Pod) that is worn on the body for up to three days at a time and its wireless companion the handheld Personal Diabetes Manager (PDM). The Pod can be worn in multiple locations including the abdomen hip back of upper arm upper thigh or lower back. The Omnipod System communicates wirelessly provides for virtually pain-free automated cannula insertion and eliminates the need for traditional MDI therapy or the use of traditional pump and tubing. Omnipod DASH features a secure Bluetooth enabled Pod and PDM with a color touch screen user interface supported by smartphone connectivity.

Overall sales of Omnipod in the US accounts more than 55% of total revenue while about 35% for international and about 10% for drug delivery.

Geographic Reach

The company sells its products in the US Canada Europe and the Middle East. Headquartered in Massachusetts the US accounts about 65% of Insulent's total revenue while 35% comes from other market.

Sales and Marketing

The company markets its products directly to wholesalers private healthcare organizations healthcare facilities mail order pharmacies and independent retailers. The Omnipod System is also marketed and sold through distributors as well as marketed to physicians and consumers (generally have commercial insurance Medicare or Medicaid coverage that pays for the product). It also sells directly to consumers through distribution partners and most recently in the US through the pharmacy channel.

In addition sales and marketing efforts are focused on customer retention and growing user clinician and payor demand for the Omnipod System. It has a uniform sales and marketing approach aligned across users physicians and providers to capitalize on the benefits of Omnipod System technology. Customer Cardinal Health and affiliates accounts for more than 10% of total revenue.

Financial Performance

Insulet saw consistent rising revenue in the last five years rising 180% between 2015 and 2019. While the company's revenue maintained steady growth its net income has only seen improvement in recent years. After three consecutive years of net losses Insulet finally managed to post profits in 2018 and 2019.

Revenue increased 31% to $738.2 million in 2019 compared with $563.8 million in 2018 due to strong growth in its U.S. and International Omnipod revenue. U.S. Omnipod revenue increased $96.9 million and International Omnipod revenue increased $81.1 million. However Drug Delivery revenue decreased by $3.6 million.

Net income increased considerably by $8.3 million to $11.6 million in 2019 from $3.3 million in 2018. The increase was mainly due to a significant increase in revenue as the company's operating expenses increased as well.

Insulet's cash position strengthened by $99.8 million in 2019 ending the year with $213.7 million in cash holdings. Operating activities generated $98.4 million and financing activities provided another $73.5 million from issuance of convertible debt. Investing activities used $73.6 million mainly for capital expenditures and purchases of investments.

Strategy

Insulet aims to improve the lives of people with diabetes. To assist in achieving this mission the company is focused on the following strategic objectives: delivering consumer-focused innovation; ensuring the best customer experience globally; expanding its global footprint; and driving operational excellence.

In 2019 Insulet began production at its new highly automated manufacturing facility in Acton Massachusetts which also serves as its new global headquarters. Insulet expects that the new facility will allow it to lower its manufacturing costs increase supply redundancy add capacity closer to its largest customer base and support growth.

Additionally Insulet completed a full market launch of Omnipod DASH in the United States in early 2019 and by the end of the year the company introduced DASH to select European markets. It also completed its pre-pivotal trial for Omnipod Horizon a closed loop control system that utilizes the DASH mobile platform to allow the Pod to communicate with a continuous glucose monitor and help control insulin delivery utilizing an algorithm located on the Pod. Insulet is set to launch Omnipod Horizon in the second half of 2020.

Insulet's long-term financial objective is to sustain profitable growth thus it is primarily focused on the launch of Omnipod Horizon in the US Insulet also plans to focus on the startup of its second manufacturing line in its Acton facility and the installation of a third US manufacturing line which it expects to begin production on in 2021. The company also looks to enter five new countries in Western Europe and the Middle East and further roll out DASH in Europe and Canada to expand the commercial sale of Omnipod and its global footprint.

Company Background
Insulet was founded in 2000 and went public through an IPO in 2007.

EXECUTIVES

President, Chief Executive Officer And Director, Shacey Petrovic, $708,846 total compensation
Senior Vice President, Innovation And Strategy, Eric Benjamin
Senior Vice President - Regulatory Affairs And Compliance, Michael Spears, $137,500 total compensation
Independent Director, David Lemoine
Independent Director, James Hollingshead
Senior Vice President, General Counsel, Secretary, John Kapples, $315,385 total compensation
Independent Director, Wayne Frederick
Chief Human Resource Officer, Senior Vice President, Dan Manea, $261,539 total compensation
Director, Luciana Borio
Independent Chairman Of The Board, Timothy Scannell
Independent Director, Jessica Hopfield
Chief Operating Officer, Executive Vice President, Charles Alpuche, $481,860 total compensation
Executive Vice President , Chief Commercial Officer, Bret Christensen, $446,105 total compensation
Independent Director, Michael Minogue
Chief Financial Officer, Executive Vice President, Treasurer, Wayde McMillan, $465,231 total compensation
Auditors: Grant Thornton LLP

LOCATIONS

HQ: Insulet Corp
100 Nagog Park, Acton, MA 01720
Phone: 978 600-7000
Web: www.insulet.com

COMPETITORS

ACCURAY INCORPORATED
ASENSUS SURGICAL INC.
ATRICURE INC.
CUTERA INC.
GENMARK DIAGNOSTICS INC.
HAEMONETICS CORPORATION
HEARTWARE INTERNATIONAL INC.
INOGEN INC.
ITRON INC.
MASIMO CORPORATION
MGC DIAGNOSTICS CORPORATION
PHILIPS IMAGE GUIDED THERAPY CORPORATION
VIVEVE MEDICAL INC.

HISTORICAL FINANCIALS
Company Type: Public

Income Statement				FYE: December 31
	REVENUE ($ mil.)	NET INCOME ($ mil.)	NET PROFIT MARGIN	EMPLOYEES
12/20	904.4	6.8	0.8%	1,900
12/19	738.2	11.6	1.6%	1,350
12/18	563.8	3.2	0.6%	1,169
12/17	463.7	(26.8)	—	857
12/16	366.9	(28.8)	—	640
Annual Growth	25.3%	—		31.3%

2020 Year-End Financials

Debt ratio: 56.5%
Return on equity: 2.0%
Cash ($ mil.): 907.2
Current ratio: 6.01
Long-term debt ($ mil.): 1,043.7

No. of shares (mil.): 66.0
Dividends
 Yield: —
 Payout: —
Market value ($ mil.): 16,876.0

	STOCK PRICE ($) FY Close	P/E High/Low		PER SHARE ($) Earnings	Dividends	Book Value
12/20	255.63	241	71	182 0.10	0.00	9.14
12/19	171.20	979	381	0.19	0.00	1.21
12/18	79.32	1802	1142	0.05	0.00	3.58
12/17	69.00	—	—	(0.46)	0.00	2.72
12/16	37.68	—	—	(0.51)	0.00	1.10
Annual Growth	61.4%	—	—	—	—	69.8%

Integra LifeSciences Holdings Corp

Integra LifeSciences makes surgical equipment and instruments for neurological orthopedic and other medical procedures. The company develops medical equipment used in cranial procedures small bone and joint reconstruction and the repair and reconstruction of soft tissue nerves and tendons. Integra's products include tissue ablation equipment drainage catheters bone fixation devices regenerative technologies and basic surgical instruments. Its offerings are marketed worldwide through direct sales and distributors. The US market accounts for a majority of sales. Integra was founded in 1989 by Richard Caruso and the company acquired collagen technology.

Operations
Integra operates in two segments: Codman Specialty Surgical and Orthopedics and Tissue Technologies.

The Codman Specialty Surgical segment bringing in 65% of revenue includes the Neurosurgery business which sells a full line of products for neurosurgery and neuro critical care such as tissue ablation equipment dural repair products cerebral spinal fluid management devices intracranial monitoring equipment and cranial stabilization equipment and the Instruments business which sells more than 40000 instrument patterns and surgical and lighting products to hospitals surgery centers dental podiatry and veterinary offices.

The Orthopedics and Tissue Technologies segment (35% of sales) includes such offerings as skin and wound repair bone and joint fixation implants in the upper and lower extremities bone grafts and nerve and tendon repair products.

Geographic Reach
Headquartered in Princeton New Jersey Integra's main manufacturing and research centers are located in the US (Massachusetts New Jersey Tennessee California and Ohio) Canada Switzerland France Germany Ireland and Puerto Rico. Its distribution centers are in the US (Nevada Ohio and Kentucky) Australia Belgium Canada Japan and France. Integra also has repair centers in the US (California Massachusetts and Ohio) Australia Japan and Germany.

In addition Integra owns facilities in Biot France Saint Aubin Le Monial France Rietheim-Weilheim Germany and Ohio while its third parties own and operate the facilities in US (Nevada and Kentucky) Japan and Belgium.

The US accounts for more than 70% of total revenue while Europe accounts for nearly 15% and Asia brings in about 10%.

Sales and Marketing
Integra sells its products worldwide through an internal sales force and via distributors wholesalers and strategic partnerships. Customers include health networks hospitals surgery centers physicians and group purchasing organizations.

Financial Performance
For the year ended December 31 2020 total revenues decreased by $145.7 million or 10% to $1.4 billion from $1.5 million during the prior year. The net decrease of $145.7 million was a result of decline in both segments due to disruption from the COVID-19 pandemic $22.7 million due to discontinued and divested products and $4.7 million due to favorable impact of foreign exchange.

In 2020 the company had a net income of $133.9 million an $83.7 million increase from the previous year's net income of $50.2 million.

The company's cash at the end of 2020 was $470.2 million. Operating activities generated $203.8 million while investing activities used $68.1 million primarily for capital expenditures. Financing activities provided another $121.6 million.

Strategy
Integra is committed to delivering high quality products that positively impact the lives of millions of patients and their families. The company focus on four key pillars of its strategy: building an execution-focused culture achieving relevant scale improving agility and innovation and leading in customer experience. Integra believes that by sharpening its focus on these areas through improved planning and communication optimization of its infrastructure and strategically aligned tuck-

HOOVER'S HANDBOOK OF EMERGING COMPANIES 2022

233

in acquisitions the company can build scale increase competitiveness and achieve its long-term goals.

To this end the executive leadership team has established the following key priorities aligned to the following areas of focus: strategic acquisitions; portfolio optimization and new product introductions; commercial channel investments; and customer experience.

Mergers and Acquisitions

In 2021 Integra completed the previously-disclosed acquisition of ACell Inc. for an upfront cash payment of $300 million. ACell is an innovative regenerative medicine company with a product portfolio based on a proprietary porcine urinary bladder matrix platform technology MatriStem UBM. The acquisition of ACell is the next step in the expansion of Integra's Orthopedics and Tissue Technologies (OTT) segment. The porcine UBM technology is a strong strategic fit with its human amniotic tissue and bovine-derived engineered collagen and acellular dermal matrices. The acquisition also supports Integra's long-term growth and profitability strategy with a financial profile similar to Integra's tissue products.

Company Background

Integra LifeSciences was founded by Richard Caruso in 1989 to explore an acquired collagen technology. It developed a dermal regeneration template in 1995; the template was approved for use on third-degree burns in 1996. The Integra DuraGen graft matrix was approved by the FDA in 1999.

Acquisitions have included Jarit Surgical (2003) Mayfield (2004) Miltex (2006) Ascension Orthopedics (2011) DuraSeal (2014) TEI (2015) Derma Sciences (2017) and Codman NeuroSurgery (2017).

To focus on core offerings Integra separated its orthobiologics and spinal fusion hardware business into SeaSpine Holdings which became a public company in 2015.

EXECUTIVES

Chairman, Stuart Essig
Independent Director, Keith Bradley
Independent Presiding Director, Barbara Hill
Executive Vice President, Chief Human Resources Officer, Lisa Evoli
Executive Vice President, Chief Legal Officer, Secretary, Eric Schwartz, $425,000 total compensation
Independent Director, Rhonda Ballintyn
Independent Director, Shaundra Clay
President, Chief Executive Officer, Director, Jan De Witte
Independent Director, Christian Schade
Independent Director, Raymond Murphy
Executive Vice President, President - Tissue Technologies, Robert Davis, $449,600 total compensation
Independent Director, Donald Morel
Chief Operating Officer, Executive Vice President, Glenn Coleman, $559,615 total compensation
Senior Vice President, Principal Accounting Officer, Jeffrey Mosebrook
Chief Financial Officer, Executive Vice President, Carrie Anderson, $466,346 total compensation
Executive Vice President And President - Codman Specialty Surgical, Michael Mcbreen, $385,308 total compensation
Auditors: PricewaterhouseCoopers LLP

LOCATIONS

HQ: Integra LifeSciences Holdings Corp
1100 Campus Road, Princeton, NJ 08540
Phone: 609 275-0500
Web: www.integralife.com

PRODUCTS/OPERATIONS

2015 Sales

	$ mil.	% of total
Specialty Surgical Solutions	586.9	66
Orthopedics and Tissue Technologies	295.8	34
Total	**882.7**	**100**

Selected Acquisitions

COMPETITORS

ANGIODYNAMICS INC.
ANIKA THERAPEUTICS INC.
BECTON DICKINSON AND COMPANY
CANTEL MEDICAL LLC
CONMED CORPORATION HOLDINGS
GLOBUS MEDICAL INC.
HOLOGIC INC.
INTEGER HOLDINGS CORPORATION
LEMAITRE VASCULAR INC.
NUVASIVE INC.
TERUMO CORPORATION
ZIMMER BIOMET INC.

HISTORICAL FINANCIALS

Company Type: Public

Income Statement				FYE: December 31
	REVENUE ($ mil.)	NET INCOME ($ mil.)	NET PROFIT MARGIN	EMPLOYEES
12/20	1,371.8	133.8	9.8%	3,700
12/19	1,517.5	50.2	3.3%	4,000
12/18	1,472.4	60.8	4.1%	4,500
12/17	1,188.2	64.7	5.4%	4,400
12/16	992.0	74.5	7.5%	3,700
Annual Growth	8.4%	15.8%	—	0.0%

2020 Year-End Financials

Debt ratio: 43.0%
Return on equity: 9.1%
Cash ($ mil.): 470.1
Current ratio: 3.09
Long-term debt ($ mil.): 1,408.2

No. of shares (mil.): 84.3
Dividends
Yield: —
Payout: —
Market value ($ mil.): 5,475.0

	STOCK PRICE ($) FY Close	P/E High/Low		PER SHARE ($) Earnings	Dividends	Book Value
12/20	64.92	42	23	1.57	0.00	17.96
12/19	58.28	109	73	0.58	0.00	16.50
12/18	45.10	92	58	0.72	0.00	16.15
12/17	47.86	101	49	0.82	0.00	12.28
12/16	85.79	87	55	0.94	0.00	11.24
Annual Growth	(6.7%)	—	—	13.7%	—	12.4%

Interactive Brokers Group Inc

Global electronic broker Interactive Brokers Group performs low-cost trade order management execution and portfolio management services through its Interactive Brokers subsidiaries. Catering to institutional and experienced individual investors the company offers access to more than 135 electronic exchanges and trading centers worldwide processing trades in stocks options futures foreign exchange instruments bonds and mutual funds. The company also licenses its trading interface to large banks and brokerages through white branding agreements. Interactive Brokers operates worldwide but generates about 70% of its revenue in the US.

Operations

Interactive Brokers offers IBKR Pro IBKR Lite and IBKR Integrated Investment Account.

IBKR Pro is the traditional IBKR service designed for sophisticated investors. IBKR Pro offers the lowest cost access to stocks options futures forex bonds mutual funds and ETFs on over 135 electronic exchanges and market centers in about 35 countries.

IBKR Lite provides unlimited commission-free trades on US exchange-listed stocks and ETFs as well as low cost access to global markets without required account minimums or inactivity fees to participating US customers.

IBKR Lite was designed to meet the needs of investors who are seeking a simple commission-free way to trade US exchange-listed stocks and ETFs and do not wish to consider its efforts to obtain greater price improvement through its IB SmartRouting system.

BKR Integrated Investment Account include Interactive Brokers Debit Mastercard Bill Pay Direct Deposit and Mobile Check Deposit Insured Bank Deposit Sweep Program Investors' Marketplace Mutual Fund Marketplace Bonds Marketplace Fractional Trading.

Interactive Brokers garners more than 45% of its revenue from net interest income while about 45% comes from commissions.

Geographic Reach

Greenwich Connecticut-based Interactive Brokers' customers span in more than 200 countries and territories. It has US offices in cities including Chicago Illinois and other nine locations. The company's overseas offices are in Canada the United Kingdom Ireland Luxembourg Switzerland Hungary India China (Hong Kong and Shanghai) Japan Singapore and Australia. The US generates about 70% the company's revenue while international countries generates for about 30%.

Sales and Marketing

Interactive Brokers categorizes its clients into the two groups of cleared customers and non-cleared customers (or trade execution customers). Cleared customers include small group and individual market makers institutional and individual traders introducing brokers financial advisors and hedge funds. Non-cleared customers who clear with another prime broker or custodian bank encompass online brokers and commercial bank customer trading units.

Financial Performance

Total net revenues for the current year increased $281 million or 15% compared to the prior year to $2.2 billion. The increase in net revenues was primarily due to higher commissions other fees and services and other income partially offset by lower net interest income.

Net income for 2020 was $1.2 billion an 8% increase from the previous year's net income of $1.1 billion.

The company's cash at the end of 2020 was $20.2 billion. Operating activities generated $8.1 billion while investing activities used $50 million mainly for capital expenditures. Financing activities used another $229 million primarily for distributions from IBG LLC to non-controlling interests.

Strategy

As an electronic broker the company executes clear and settle trades globally for both institutional and individual customers. Capitalizing on its proprietary technology the company's systems provide its customers with the capability to monitor multiple markets around the world simultaneously and to execute trades electronically in these markets at a low cost in multiple products and currencies from a single trading account. The company offers its customers access to all classes of tradable primarily exchange-listed products including stocks options futures forex bonds mutual funds and ETFs.

Company Background

Founder chairman and CEO Thomas Peterffy controls Interactive Brokers Group. Peterffy started the company in 1978 as T.P. & Co. It was the first market making firm to use daily-printed computer-generated fair value sheets.

EXECUTIVES

Chairman, Thomas Peterffy, $640,000 total compensation
Independent Vice Chairman Of The Board, Earl Nemser, $540,000 total compensation
Chief Financial Officer, Treasurer, Secretary, Director, Paul Brody, $480,000 total compensation
Executive Vice President, Chief Information Officer, Thomas Frank, $480,000 total compensation
President, Chief Executive Officer, Director, Milan Galik, $480,000 total compensation
Independent Director, Gary Katz
Independent Director, John Damgard
Independent Director, Nicole Yuen
Independent Director, William Peterffy
Executive Director, Cecelia Zhong
Lead Independent Director, Lawrence Harris
Auditors: DELOITTE & TOUCHE LLP

LOCATIONS

HQ: Interactive Brokers Group Inc
One Pickwick Plaza, Greenwich, CT 06830
Phone: 203 618-5800
Web: www.interactivebrokers.com

PRODUCTS/OPERATIONS

Trading Services
Account Management
Employee Track Management
Funding Reference
Investors' Marketplace
IRA Information
New Features Poll
Securities Financing

2018 Revenue

	$ mil.	% of total
Commissions	777.0	32
Interest income	1,392.0	59
Trading gains	39.0	2
Other	158.0	7
Interest expense	(463)	-
Total	**1,903.0**	**100**

2018 Revenue

	$ mil.	% of total
Electronic brokerage	1,842.0	96
Market making	76.0	4
Corporate	(15)	-
Total	**1,903.0**	**100**

COMPETITORS

CBOE GLOBAL MARKETS INC.
CME GROUP INC.
E TRADE FINANCIAL CORPORATION
FIDESSA GROUP HOLDINGS MARKETS LLC LIMITED
INTERCONTINENTAL EXCHANGE INC.
MARKETAXESS HOLDINGS INC.
OPPENHEIMER HOLDINGS INC.
STONEX GROUP INC.
TRADEWEB
VIRTU ITG HOLDINGS LLC

HISTORICAL FINANCIALS

Company Type: Public

Income Statement FYE: December 31

	REVENUE ($ mil.)	NET INCOME ($ mil.)	NET PROFIT MARGIN	EMPLOYEES
12/20	2,218.0	195.0	8.8%	2,033
12/19	1,937.0	161.0	8.3%	1,643
12/18	1,903.0	169.0	8.9%	1,413
12/17	1,702.0	76.0	4.5%	1,228
12/16	1,396.0	84.0	6.0%	1,204
Annual Growth	**12.3%**	**23.4%**	**—**	**14.0%**

2020 Year-End Financials

Debt ratio: 10.4%
Return on equity: 11.4%
Cash ($ mil.): 20,987.0
Current ratio: 1.04
Long-term debt ($ mil.): —
No. of shares (mil.): 90.7
Dividends
Yield: 0.6%
Payout: 18.5%
Market value ($ mil.): 5,530.0

	STOCK PRICE ($) FY Close	P/E High/Low		Earnings	PER SHARE ($) Dividends	Book Value
12/20	60.92	26	14	2.42	0.40	21.49
12/19	46.62	23	21	2.10	0.40	18.92
12/18	55.78	35	24	2.28	0.40	17.07
12/17	59.21	57	31	1.07	0.40	15.25
12/16	36.51	34	24	1.25	0.40	14.33
Annual Growth	**13.7%**		**—**	**—** **18.0%**	**(0.0%)**	**10.7%**

Investar Holding Corp

Auditors: HORNE LLP

LOCATIONS

HQ: Investar Holding Corp
10500 Coursey Boulevard, Baton Rouge, LA 70816
Phone: 225 227-2222

HISTORICAL FINANCIALS

Company Type: Public

Income Statement FYE: December 31

	ASSETS ($ mil.)	NET INCOME ($ mil.)	INCOME AS % OF ASSETS	EMPLOYEES
12/20	2,321.1	13.8	0.6%	326
12/19	2,148.9	16.8	0.8%	324
12/18	1,786.4	13.6	0.8%	255
12/17	1,622.7	8.2	0.5%	258
12/16	1,158.9	7.8	0.7%	152
Annual Growth	**19.0%**	**15.2%**	**—**	**21.0%**

2020 Year-End Financials

Return on assets: 0.6%
Return on equity: 5.7%
Long-term debt ($ mil.): —
No. of shares (mil.): 10.6
Sales ($ mil): 105.8
Dividends
Yield: 1.5%
Payout: 21.3%
Market value ($ mil.): 175.0

	STOCK PRICE ($) FY Close	P/E High/Low		Earnings	PER SHARE ($) Dividends	Book Value
12/20	16.54	19	7	1.27	0.25	22.93
12/19	24.00	15	13	1.66	0.23	21.55
12/18	24.80	21	15	1.39	0.17	19.22
12/17	24.10	26	20	0.96	0.07	18.15
12/16	18.65	18	12	1.10	0.04	15.88
Annual Growth	**(3.0%)**		**—** **—**	**3.7%**	**56.1%**	**9.6%**

Investors Title Co.

Investors Title insures you in case your land is well not completely yours. It's the holding company for Investors Title Insurance and Northeast Investors Title Insurance which underwrite land title insurance and sell reinsurance to other title companies. (Title insurance protects those who invest in real property against loss resulting from defective titles.) Investors Title Insurance serves customers from about 30 offices in North Carolina South Carolina Michigan and Nebraska and through branches or agents in 20 additional states. Northeast Investors Title operates through an agency office in New York. Founder and CEO J. Allen Fine and his family own more than 20% of Investors Title.

EXECUTIVES

Executive Vice President, Secretary, Director, W. Morris Fine, $385,833 total compensation
Independent Director, James Morton
Independent Director, David Francis
Founder, Chairman And Chief Executive Officer, James Fine, $385,833 total compensation
Independent Director, James Speed
Lead Independent Director, Richard Hutson
Independent Director, Elton Parker
Independent Director, Tammy Coley
Auditors: Dixon Hughes Goodman LLP

LOCATIONS

HQ: Investors Title Co.
121 North Columbia Street, Chapel Hill, NC 27514
Phone: 919 968-2200
Web: www.invtitle.com

PRODUCTS/OPERATIONS

Selected Subsidiaries
Investors Title Accommodation Corporation
Investors Title Exchange Corporation
Investors Title Insurance Company
Investors Title Management Services Inc.
Northeast Investors Title Insurance Company

COMPETITORS

AMERICAN COAST TITLE COMPANY INC.
CALIFORNIA COUNTIES TITLE COMPANY
STEWART TITLE COMPANY

HISTORICAL FINANCIALS

Company Type: Public

Income Statement
FYE: December 31

	ASSETS ($ mil.)	NET INCOME ($ mil.)	INCOME AS % OF ASSETS	EMPLOYEES
12/20	282.9	39.4	13.9%	456
12/19	263.8	31.4	11.9%	402
12/18	244.2	21.8	9.0%	385
12/17	248.9	25.7	10.3%	383
12/16	228.9	19.5	8.5%	320
Annual Growth	5.4%	19.2%		9.3%

2020 Year-End Financials

Return on assets: 14.3%	Dividends
Return on equity: 20.0%	Yield: 10.9%
Long-term debt ($ mil.): —	Payout: 93.0%
No. of shares (mil.): 1.8	Market value ($ mil.): 289.0
Sales ($ mil): 236.4	

	STOCK PRICE ($) FY Close	P/E High/Low		PER SHARE ($) Earnings	Dividends	Book Value
12/20	153.00	9	5	20.80	16.76	105.93
12/19	159.20	11	8	16.59	9.60	101.30
12/18	176.68	18	14	11.54	12.20	93.08
12/17	198.35	15	9	13.56	3.75	94.29
12/16	158.18	17	8	10.19	0.72	82.28
Annual Growth	(0.8%)		—	19.5%	119.7%	6.5%

Invitation Homes Inc

Auditors: DELOITTE & TOUCHE LLP

LOCATIONS

HQ: Invitation Homes Inc
  1717 Main Street, Suite 2000, Dallas, TX 75201
Phone: 972 421-3600
Web: www.invitationhomes.com

HISTORICAL FINANCIALS

Company Type: Public

Income Statement
FYE: December 31

	REVENUE ($ mil.)	NET INCOME ($ mil.)	NET PROFIT MARGIN	EMPLOYEES
12/21	1,996.6	261.4	13.1%	1,240
12/20	1,822.8	196.2	10.8%	1,149
12/19	1,764.6	145.4	8.2%	1,140
12/18	1,722.9	(4.9)	—	1,231
12/17	1,054.4	(105.3)	—	1,445
Annual Growth	17.3%	—	—	(3.8%)

2021 Year-End Financials

Debt ratio: 43.1%	No. of shares (mil.): 601.0
Return on equity: 2.8%	Dividends
Cash ($ mil.): 610.1	Yield: 1.5%
Current ratio: 2.28	Payout: 151.1%
Long-term debt ($ mil.): 7,998.6	Market value ($ mil.): 27,251.0

	STOCK PRICE ($) FY Close	P/E High/Low		PER SHARE ($) Earnings	Dividends	Book Value
12/21	45.34	100	63	0.45	0.68	16.30
12/20	29.70	93	46	0.35	0.60	15.00
12/19	29.97	115	73	0.27	0.52	15.17
12/18	20.08	—	—	(0.01)	0.44	15.81
12/17	23.57	—	—	(0.26)	0.22	16.37
Annual Growth	17.8%		—	—	32.6%	(0.1%)

iRobot Corp

iRobot is a leading consumer robot company that designs and builds robots that empower people to do more around the globe. Models range from basic sweepers to higher-end devices that can be programed for specific houses. iRobot has also introduced robotic mops and is developing a robotic lawn mower. The company sells its home products worldwide through retailers and distributors. It operates worldwide but generates just more than half its revenue in the US. Since its founding iRobot has sold more than 30 million robots.

Operations
iRobot sells consumer products that are designed for both indoor and outdoor cleaning applications. It offers Roomba floor vacuuming robots at prices ranging from $250 to $1099. The company also offers the Braava family of mopping robots at price points ranging from $199 to $450. It also offers robots designed to help children learn how to code. The Root coding robots priced at $129 and $199 are designed to make coding easy and natural to learn.

The company holds about 540 US patents more than 1000 foreign patents additional design registrations and has more than 1500 patent applications pending worldwide.

Geographic Reach
Bedford Massachusetts-based iRobot has offices and subsidiaries in the US the UK China Austria Belgium France Germany Netherlands Portugal Spain Japan and Hong Kong. Its research and development facilities are in Bedford and Pasadena California. Sales to customers outside the US account for nearly half of the company's revenue.

The company contracts manufacturing to third parties in China. Strained trade relations between the US and China that involve higher tariffs could have a negative impact on iRobot's sales.

Sales and Marketing
Robot sells through distributors and retailers as well as online.

The company markets its products through national advertising consumer and industry trade shows and direct marketing.

During the years ended 2021 2019 and 2018 advertising expense totaled $145.2 million $125.0 million and $114.0 million respectively.

Financial Performance
The company's total revenue for 2020 was $1.4 billion which represents an 18% increase from revenue of $1.2 billion for 2019. Domestic revenue grew $141.0 million or 23% and international revenue increased by $75.4 million or 12% primarily as a result of higher sales of its premium robots.

In 2020 the company had a net income of $147.1 million a 72% increase from the previous year's net income of $61.8 million.

The company's cash at the end of 2020 was $432.6 million. Operating activities generated $232 million while investing activities used $22.2 million mainly for $capital expenditures. Financing activities used another $21.3 million primarily for stock repurchases.

Strategy
The company's long-term strategy to drive sustainable profitable growth is focused on: Designing and marketing a portfolio of floor cleaning robots with differentiated value propositions that appeal to an expanding range of consumers around the world enabling the company to continue increasing category penetration globally; Advancing innovation through the introduction of new models of floor cleaning robots and new features and enhanced functionality of existing models of floor cleaning robots that will address the needs of new and existing customers; Forging enduring relationships with millions of consumers worldwide in ways that will ultimately increase their spending with them over the lifetime of those relationships; Continuing to diversify its product portfolio beyond RVCs; and Balancing investments in key technology product development sales and marketing manufacturing and other initiatives with an ongoing focus on controlling costs increasing productivity and driving efficiency.

The three key elements in its strategy are Differentiating the cleaning experience; Building long-term enduring customer relationships; and Nurturing the lifetime value of customer relationships. By executing on each element of its strategy the company believes it can better position iRobot to build and defend its category leadership participate meaningfully in continued category growth build a stronger direct-to-consumer sales channel to complement its extensive retail partnerships and convert its top-line growth into even faster operating profit and earnings per share expansion.

Mergers and Acquisitions
In 2017 iRobot acquired Robopolis SAS a French company to expand its enhance distribution network provide consistent branding and improved service for European customers.

Also in 2017 iRobot bought Sales On Demand Corp. (SODC) in Japan for the same reasons it acquired Robopolis.

Company Background
iRobot Corporation was founded in 1990 by engineers from the Massachusetts Institute of Technology.

EXECUTIVES

Chief Financial Officer, Executive Vice President, Julie Zeiler, $382,123 total compensation
Executive Vice President, Chief Product Officer, Keith Hartsfield, $400,000 total compensation
Independent Director, Karen Golz
Executive Vice President - Human Resources, Corporate Communications, Russell Campanello, $392,308 total compensation
Chairman Of The Board, Chief Executive Officer, Colin Angle, $825,000 total compensation
Chief Legal Officer, Executive Vice President, Glen Weinstein, $410,000 total compensation
Independent Director, Deborah Ellinger
Independent Director, Ruey-Bin Kao
Independent Director, Eva Manolis
Auditors: PricewaterhouseCoopers LLP

LOCATIONS

HQ: iRobot Corp
  8 Crosby Drive, Bedford, MA 01730
Phone: 781 430-3000
Web: www.irobot.com

COMPETITORS

AXCELIS TECHNOLOGIES INC.
BUILD-A-BEAR WORKSHOP INC.
CARVANA CO.
COLUMBUS MCKINNON CORPORATION
EVOQUA WATER TECHNOLOGIES CORP.
FLEX LTD.
GLOBANT S.A.
O'REILLY AUTOMOTIVE INC.
PHOTRONICS INC.
SONIM TECHNOLOGIES INC.
UKG INC.
WAYFAIR INC.
YETI HOLDINGS INC.
YETI HOLDINGS LLC

HISTORICAL FINANCIALS

Company Type: Public

Income Statement

FYE: January 1

	REVENUE ($ mil.)	NET INCOME ($ mil.)	NET PROFIT MARGIN	EMPLOYEES
01/22	1,564.9	30.3	1.9%	1,372
01/21*	1,430.3	147.0	10.3%	1,209
12/19	1,214.0	85.3	7.0%	1,128
12/18	1,092.5	87.9	8.1%	1,032
12/17	883.9	50.9	5.8%	920
Annual Growth	15.4%	(12.1%)	—	10.5%

*Fiscal year change

2022 Year-End Financials

Debt ratio: —
Return on equity: 4.0%
Cash ($ mil.): 201.4
Current ratio: 2.00
Long-term debt ($ mil.): —
No. of shares (mil.): 27.0
Dividends
  Yield: —
  Payout: —
Market value ($ mil.): 1,779.0

	STOCK PRICE ($) FY Close	P/E High/Low		PER SHARE ($) Earnings	Dividends	Book Value
01/22	65.88	147	58	1.08	0.00	26.54
01/21*	80.29	18	6	5.14	0.00	28.54
12/19	52.20	43	14	2.97	0.00	23.00
12/18	81.32	37	18	3.07	0.00	19.26
12/17	76.70	58	29	1.77	0.00	16.83
Annual Growth	(3.7%)	—	—	(11.6%)	—	12.1%

*Fiscal year change

Ironwood Pharmaceuticals Inc

Ironwood Pharmaceuticals takes a stand against gastrointestinal ailments and other medical conditions. The firm develops internally discovered gastrointestinal drugs; its first commercial product Linzess (or linaclotide) a treatment for irritable bowel syndrome (IBS) and chronic constipation is sold in the US and in Canada under the brand name Constella. To support the development and commercialization of linaclotide worldwide it partnered with pharmaceutical companies including with Allergan in the US AstraZeneca in China and Astellas in Japan. The company is also advancing its MD-7246 a delayed release formulation of linaclotide as an oral intestinal non-opioid pain-relieving agent for patients with abdominal pain associated with certain GI diseases. MD-7246 is designed to have the pain-relieving effect of linaclotide with minimal impact on bowel function.

Operations

Ironwood Pharmaceuticals is focused on creating first-in-class medicines primarily for the treatment of gastrointestinal disorders. Manufacturing of its candidates is conducted through third parties and partners.

Ironwood Pharmaceuticals' first FDA-approved drug Linzess a treatment for adult patients suffering from irritable bowel syndrome with constipation or chronic idiopathic constipation. The company is also advancing another GI development program IW-3718 a gastric retentive formulation of a bile acid sequestrant for the potential treatment of refractory gastroesophageal reflux disease or refractory GERD. It is also leveraging its leading capabilities in GI to bring additional treatment options to GI patients. This includes the US disease education and promotional agreement with Alnylam Pharmaceuticals for Alnylam's GIVLAARI (givosiran) an RNAi therapeutic targeting aminolevulinic acid synthase 1 for the treatment of acute hepatic porphyria or AHP.

Its collaborative agreements accounts about 90% of total revenue while sale of active pharmaceutical ingredients accounts the remainder.

Geographic Reach

Ironwood's headquarters and operations are located in Boston Massachusetts. It products are sold through its partnership in North America and Europe as well as in Mexico Canada Japan and China (including Hong Kong and Macau).

Sales and Marketing

The company's partnership with Allergan execute its commercialization plan that includes an agreed upon marketing campaign that targets the physicians who see patients who could benefit from LINZESS treatment. Its marketing campaign also targets the adult men and women who suffer from IBS-C or CIC.

Financial Performance

The company revenue in the last five years had a year-over-year increase since 2015 posting 155% revenue growth over that span.

In 2019 revenue increased by 24% to $428.4 million. Collaborative revenue increased by $106.8 million while product and pharmaceutical ingredient sales all decreased.

Net income in 2019 was $21.5 million compared to a loss of $282.4 million in 2018. Higher revenue and lower operating expenses helped the company get out of the red.

Cash and cash equivalents at the end of the period were $179.2 million. Net cash provided by operating activities was $10.7 million while investing and financing activities each used $11.1 million and $1.2 million respectively. Main cash uses were for purchases of property and equipment and payments on notes.

Strategy

Ironwood Pharmaceuticals' vision is to become the leading US GI-focused healthcare company. To achieve this vision it is dedicated to leveraging its development and commercial expertise to advance the treatment of GI diseases and redefine the standard of care for millions of patients in the US suffering from GI diseases. Its strategy is focused on three core priorities: drive LINZESS growth advance our GI development portfolio and strengthen our financial profile. Key elements of its strategy include:

Key elements of its strategy include: assembling a team with a singular passion and documented success in creating developing and commercializing GI medicines that can make a significant difference in patients' lives; successfully and profitably commercializing LINZESS in collaboration with Allergan in the US; exploring development opportunities to enhance the clinical profile of LINZESS by studying linaclotide in additional indications populations and formulations to assess its potential to treat various conditions; leveraging its US.-focused commercial capabilities in marketing reimbursement patient engagement and sales to expand the commercial potential of LINZESS and its other product candidates in the US and collaborating with global partners who share its vision values culture and processes to develop and commercialize linaclotide outside of the US; investing in its pipeline of novel product candidates IW-3718 and MD-7246; evaluating external candidates for in-licensing or acquisition opportunities; and executing its strategy with its stockholders' long-term interests in mind by delivering sustainable profits and long-term per share cash flows.

Company Background

Ironwood Pharmaceuticals conducted an IPO in 2010. The company's decision to go public helped it generate additional funds to push the development and commercialization of Linzess forward.

Founded in 1998 by CEO Peter Hecht and director Gina Borino Miller the company changed its name from Microbia to Ironwood Pharmaceuticals in 2008 to reflect its focus on the development of human therapeutics. To further focus on its core operations in 2010 Ironwood Pharmaceuticals sold its Microbia subsidiary which was involved in the development of fermentation technologies used to produce specialty ingredients and biomaterials to Royal DSM.

EXECUTIVES

President, Chief Executive Officer, Director, Thomas McCourt, $576,120 total compensation
Principal Accounting Officer, Corporate Controller, Ronald Silver
Executive Chairman Of The Board, Julie Mchugh
Chief Operating Officer, Senior Vice President, Jason Rickard, $473,314 total compensation
Independent Director, Catherine Moukheibir
Independent Director, Marla Kessler
Independent Director, Jon Duane
Chief Medical Officer & Senior Vice President, Michael Shetzline, $464,681 total compensation
Independent Director, Jay Shepard
Senior Vice President, Chief Legal Officer, John Minardo
Senior Vice President And Chief Financial Officer, Sravan Emany
Auditors: Ernst & Young LLP

LOCATIONS

HQ: Ironwood Pharmaceuticals Inc
  100 Summer Street, Suite 2300, Boston, MA 02110
Phone: 617 621-7722
Web: www.ironwoodpharma.com

PRODUCTS/OPERATIONS

2014 Sales

	% of total
Actavis plc	63
Astellas Pharma Inc.	23
Almirall S.A	10
AstraZeneca AB	4
Total	**100**

COMPETITORS

ACCELERON PHARMA INC. INC.	CHEMOCENTRYX INC.
ACORDA THERAPEUTICS INC.	INCYTE CORPORATION
ALMIRALL SA	INSMED INCORPORATED
ARDELYX INC.	LEXICON PHARMACEUTICALS INC.
ARENA PHARMACEUTICALS INC.	PARATEK PHARMACEUTICALS INC.
BIODELIVERY SCIENCES INTERNATIONAL INC.	

HISTORICAL FINANCIALS

Company Type: Public

Income Statement				FYE: December 31
	REVENUE ($ mil.)	NET INCOME ($ mil.)	NET PROFIT MARGIN	EMPLOYEES
12/21	413.7	528.4	127.7%	219
12/20	389.5	106.1	27.3%	232
12/19	428.4	21.5	5.0%	317
12/18	346.6	(282.3)	—	515
12/17	298.2	(116.9)	—	730
Annual Growth	8.5%	—	—	(26.0%)

2021 Year-End Financials

Debt ratio: 40.3%
Return on equity: 158.0%
Cash ($ mil.): 620.1
Current ratio: 4.61
Long-term debt ($ mil.): 337.3
No. of shares (mil.): 162.0
Dividends
  Yield: —
  Payout: —
Market value ($ mil.): 1,889.0

	STOCK PRICE ($) FY Close	P/E High/Low		Earnings	Dividends	PER SHARE ($) Book Value
12/21	11.66	4	3	3.21	0.00	3.74
12/20	11.39	21	13	0.66	0.00	0.39
12/19	13.31	109	59	0.14	0.00	(0.59)
12/18	10.36	—	—	(1.85)	0.00	(1.27)
12/17	14.99	—	—	(0.78)	0.00	0.07
Annual Growth	(6.1%) 174.9%	—	—	—	—	—

Janus International Group Inc

LOCATIONS

HQ: Janus International Group Inc
135 Janus International Blvd., , GA, Temple, GA 30179
Phone: 866 562-2580
Web: www.janusintl.com

HISTORICAL FINANCIALS

Company Type: Public

Income Statement				FYE: December 26
	REVENUE ($ mil.)	NET INCOME ($ mil.)	NET PROFIT MARGIN	EMPLOYEES
12/20	548.9	56.8	10.4%	1,603
12/19	565.2	39.4	7.0%	0
12/18*	438.9	5.5	1.3%	0
02/18	45.7	6.7	14.7%	0
Annual Growth	128.9%	103.8%	—	—

*Fiscal year change

2020 Year-End Financials

Debt ratio: 71.4%
Return on equity: 41.9%
Cash ($ mil.): 45.2
Current ratio: 1.77
Long-term debt ($ mil.): 617.6
No. of shares (mil.): 0.0
Dividends
  Yield: —
  Payout: —
Market value ($ mil.): —

	STOCK PRICE ($) FY Close	P/E High/Low	Earnings	Dividends	PER SHARE ($) Book Value
12/20	0.00 31,458.87	— —	35.30	0.00	
Annual Growth	—	— —	—	—	—

John Marshall Bancorp Inc

Auditors: Yount, Hyde & Barbour, P.C.

LOCATIONS

HQ: John Marshall Bancorp Inc
1943 Isaac Newton Square E., Suite 100, Reston, VA 20190
Phone: 703 584-0840   **Fax:** 703 584-0859

HISTORICAL FINANCIALS

Company Type: Public

Income Statement				FYE: December 31
	REVENUE ($ mil.)	NET INCOME ($ mil.)	NET PROFIT MARGIN	EMPLOYEES
12/20	74.0	18.5	25.0%	0
12/19	70.3	15.9	22.6%	0
12/18	59.1	12.1	20.6%	0
12/17	50.5	8.9	17.8%	0
12/16	43.3	8.3	19.1%	0
Annual Growth	14.3%	22.2%	—	—

2020 Year-End Financials

Debt ratio: 2.4%
Return on equity: 10.6%
Cash ($ mil.): 138.4
Current ratio: 0.18
Long-term debt ($ mil.): 46.6
No. of shares (mil.): 13.5
Dividends
  Yield: —
  Payout: —
Market value ($ mil.): 194.0

	STOCK PRICE ($) FY Close	P/E High/Low	Earnings	Dividends	PER SHARE ($) Book Value
12/20	14.30	13 7	1.35	0.00	13.75
12/19	16.50	14 12	1.17	0.00	12.39
12/18	14.95	20 16	0.89	0.00	11.08
12/17	17.80	33 25	0.66	0.00	10.12
12/16	20.75	32 24	0.63	0.00	9.38
Annual Growth	(8.9%)	— —	20.9%	—	10.0%

Johnson Outdoors Inc

Founded in 1987 Johnson Outdoors keeps sports buffs from staying indoors. The company makes markets and sells camping and outdoor equipment (such as Jetboil cooking systems and Eureka! tents and backpacks). It also focuses on supplying equipment for water activities with its diving gear (Scubapro and Uwatec masks fins snorkels and tanks) trolling motors (Minn Kota) fish finders (Humminbird) and watercraft (Old Town canoes). With GPS technologies and electric boat motors The Johnson family including CEO Helen Johnson-Leipold controls the company. Most of the company's sales come from the US.

Operations

Johnson Outdoors operates under four reportable business segments; Fishing Diving Camping and Watercraft recreation.

The fishing segment generate about 75% of net sales. It offers electric motors marine battery chargers shallow water anchors sonar and GPS equipment. Through its key brands Minn Kota Humminbird and Cannon.

The Diving segment generate about 10% of net sales. It manufactures and markets underwater diving products for recreational divers which it sells and distributes under the SCUBAPRO brand name.

Camping segment (more than 5% of net sales) offers portable outdoor cooking systems tent camping furniture camping stoves and other recreational camping products.

Watercraft recreation gives in nearly 10% of net sales. designs and markets canoes and kayaks under the Ocean Kayaks and Old Town brand names for family recreation touring angling and tripping.

Geographic Reach

Wisconsin-based Johnson Outdoors has domestic manufacturing facilities in Georgia New York Alabama California Minnesota New Hampshire and Maine. Some of its international manufacturing facilities are located in Spain Indonesia France Belgium Canada Australia and Mexico. The US is Johnson Outdoors' largest market representing more than 85% of its sales. Other markets include Canada Europe and the Pacific Basin.

Sales and Marketing

Johnson Outdoors sells its products to major retailers outdoor specialty stores (Cabela's Bass Pro Shops) and catalog and online merchants. It also provides boat motors and other products for original equipment manufacturers of boat brands such as Tracker Skeeter and Ranger.

The company's consumer marketing and promotion activities include: product placements on fishing-related TV shows; print advertising and editorial coverage in outdoor general interest and sport magazines; professional angler and tournament sponsorships; packaging and point-of-purchase materials and offers to increase consumer appeal and sales; branded websites; social media networks; and online promotions.

Advertising and promotions expense in fiscal year 2021 2020 and 2019 totaled $30882 $26727 and $28397 respectively.

Financial Performance

Johnson Outdoors has reported steady revenue growth over the past five years with sales increasing by about 53% between 2017 and 2021. Net income followed the same growth trend for the same period.

Net sales in fiscal 2021 increased by 26% to $751.7 million compared to $594.2 million in 2020 driven primarily by strong performance in the Fishing Camping and Watercraft Recreation segments where the company saw strong demand for its outdoor recreation products as a result of consumers recreating outdoors in light of COVID-19.

The company reported net income of $83.4 million in fiscal 2021 an increase of 34% from $55.2 million in fiscal 2020.

Cash at the end of fiscal 2021 was $240.4 million. Cash provided by operating activities was $53.3 million while cash used for investing activities was $21.4 million. Financing activities used $9.0 million for dividends paid.

Strategy

Through a combination of innovative products strong marketing a talented and passionate workforce and efficient distribution the company seeks to set itself apart from the competition in its markets. Its subsidiaries operate as a network that promotes innovation and leverages best practices and synergies following the strategic vision set by executive management.

Because the company expects that the same supply chain disruptions will continue into fiscal 2022 the company remains focused on evaluating and pursuing additional options (beyond building inventory) to manage its supply chain to meet the continued strong consumer demand for its products. Nonetheless these supply chain disruptions remain fluid and will likely impact the cost of goods sold for future sales of product or the company's ability to fill all customer demand for its products especially given the volatility and changing circumstances brought on by the COVID-19 pandemic.

HISTORY

Cleaning products maker S.C. Johnson & Son (Johnson Wax) set up subsidiary Johnson Diversified in 1970 which then began acquiring and developing a number of leisure products companies worldwide. Renamed Johnson Worldwide Associates (JWA) the unit was taken public in 1987. By decade's end JWA had emerged as the #1 maker of electric fishing-boat motors. The company went on a 19-company buying spree between 1989 and 1991 a growth strategy that led to declining earnings.

As sporting goods retailers consolidated in the mid-1990s with fewer companies accumulating more buying power manufacturers were forced to keep prices competitive. Ronald Whitaker became president and CEO in 1996 and reorganized the company expanding product classifications from three (fishing/marine camping and diving) to five and assigning a manager to each. JWA also re-

duced inventory taking an $11 million charge. It bought small manufacturers to expand its product offerings.

JWA dumped Plastimo its unprofitable European marine division in 1997. It also expanded its watercraft division buying Ocean Kayak (1997) Plastiques (1997 Dimension kayaks) Leisure Life Limited (1998 recreational boats) and Necky Kayaks and Escape Sailboat (1999). Whitaker resigned in 1999 and Samuel Johnson's daughter Helen Johnson-Leipold a former JWA executive rejoined the company from S.C. Johnson as chairman and CEO.

In 2000 JWA changed its name to Johnson Outdoors to better reflect its core business. Johnson Outdoors also sold its fishing business to Berkley (Pure Fishing) for $34.5 million that year.

In 2001 the company acquired Fibrekraft Manufacturers a New Zealand-based maker of paddles and other watercraft accessories to accelerate growth in international markets. Also that year Johnson Outdoors won a hefty government contract to make extreme weather tents. Samuel Johnson was named the 2001 National Ernst & Young Master Entrepreneur Of The Year.

In September 2002 Johnson Outdoors sold its Jack Wolfskin subsidiary for $62.9 million to Bain Capital a global private investment firm.

The company acquired sonar and video viewing equipment maker Techsonic Industries from Teleflex in May 2004. The purchase added the Humminbird brand to Johnson's marine electronics line. A significant decline in military tent sales in early 2005 led the company to eliminate more than 70 positions (5% of Johnson Outdoors' workforce) at its plant in Binghamton New York.

Refocused on growth Johnson Outdoors in late 2006 added Scotland-based Lendal Paddles to its paddle sports portfolio. In April 2007 the company acquired the German diving equipment company Seemann Sub from owners Robert and Ella Stoss for about $9 million. Also that year Johnson Outdoors purchased Italy's Geonav which makes chart plotters marine autopilots VHF radios and fish finders for nearly $6 million.

EXECUTIVES

Independent Director, Edward Lang
Chairman Of The Board, Chief Executive Officer, Helen Johnson-Leipold, $804,473 total compensation
Chief Financial Officer, Vice President, David Johnson, $422,289 total compensation
Vice Chairman Of The Board, Thomas Pyle
Independent Director, Katherine Bell
Independent Director, Richard Sheahan
Independent Director, William Perez
Independent Director, Paul Alexander
Independent Director, Liliann Zipfel
Independent Director, Edward Stevens
Auditors: RSM US LLP

LOCATIONS

HQ: Johnson Outdoors Inc
  555 Main Street, Racine, WI 53403
Phone: 262 631-6600
Web: www.johnsonoutdoors.com

PRODUCTS/OPERATIONS

2016 Sales

	$ mil.	% of total
Marine electronics	274.9	63
Diving	69.1	16
Watercraft	50.4	12
Outdoor equipment	40.0	9
Adjustments	(0.7)	-
Total	**433.7**	**100**

Selected Brands

Diving
  SCUBAPRO
  Seemann
  UWATEC
Marine Electronics
  Cannon
  Humminbird
  Minn Kota
  Navicontrol
Outdoor Equipment
  Eureka!
  Jetboil
  Silva
  Tech40
Watercraft
  Carlisle
  Extrasport
  Lendal
  Necky
  Ocean Kayak
  Old Town

COMPETITORS

AMF BOWLING WORLDWIDE INCORPORATED INC.	ESCALADE INC.
BIG 5 SPORTING GOODS CORPORATION	POLARIS INC.
BRUNSWICK CORPORATION	SPECTRUM BRANDS HOLDINGS INC.
CAMELBAK PRODUCTS LLC	THE INTERTECH GROUP
CYBEX INTERNATIONAL INC.	INC
	THOR INDUSTRIES INC.
	VISTA OUTDOOR INC.

HISTORICAL FINANCIALS

Company Type: Public

Income Statement

FYE: October 1

	REVENUE ($ mil.)	NET INCOME ($ mil.)	NET PROFIT MARGIN	EMPLOYEES
10/21	751.6	83.3	11.1%	1,400
10/20*	594.2	55.2	9.3%	1,200
09/19	562.4	51.4	9.1%	1,200
09/18	544.2	40.6	7.5%	1,200
09/17	490.5	35.1	7.2%	1,100
Annual Growth	11.3%	24.1%	—	6.2%

*Fiscal year change

2021 Year-End Financials

Debt ratio: —	No. of shares (mil.): 10.1
Return on equity: 19.9%	Dividends
Cash ($ mil.): 240.4	Yield: 0.7%
Current ratio: 3.57	Payout: 9.2%
Long-term debt ($ mil.): —	Market value ($ mil.): 1,111.0

	STOCK PRICE ($) FY Close	P/E High/Low		PER SHARE ($) Earnings	Dividends	Book Value
10/21	109.67	18	10	16.42	0.84	45.27
10/20*	86.18	17	9	5.47	0.68	37.49
09/19	58.63	18	11	5.11	0.56	32.31
09/18	92.99	26	15	4.05	0.44	27.92
09/17	73.28	19	9	3.51	0.36	24.31
Annual Growth	10.6%	—	—	47.1%	23.6%	16.8%

*Fiscal year change

Joint Corp (New)

Auditors: BDO USA, LLP

LOCATIONS

HQ: Joint Corp (New)
16767 North Perimeter Drive, Suite 110. Scottsdale,
AZ 85260
Phone: 480 245-5960
Web: www.thejoint.com

HISTORICAL FINANCIALS

Company Type: Public

Income Statement				FYE: December 31
	REVENUE ($ mil.)	NET INCOME ($ mil.)	NET PROFIT MARGIN	EMPLOYEES
12/20	58.6	13.1	22.4%	425
12/19	48.4	3.3	6.9%	150
12/18	31.7	0.2	0.8%	138
12/17	25.1	(3.2)	—	148
12/16	20.5	(15.1)	—	94
Annual Growth 30.0%		—	—	45.8%

2020 Year-End Financials

Debt ratio: 7.5%
Return on equity: 99.2%
Cash ($ mil.): 20.5
Current ratio: 1.35
Long-term debt ($ mil.): 2.1

No. of shares (mil.): 14.1
Dividends
  Yield: —
  Payout: —
Market value ($ mil.): 372.0

	STOCK PRICE ($) FY Close	P/E High/Low	PER SHARE ($) Earnings	Dividends	Book Value
12/20	26.26	29 9	0.90	0.00	1.47
12/19	16.14	87 33	0.23	0.00	0.41
12/18	8.32	460 235	0.02	0.00	0.17
12/17	4.96	— —	(0.25)	0.00	0.36
12/16	2.65	— —	(1.20)	0.00	0.53
Annual Growth 77.4%		— —		—	28.8%

Kadant Inc

Kadant is a global supplier of high-value critical components and engineered systems used in process industries. It develops and manufactures a range of products and equipment used in process industries such as paper packaging and tissue; wood products; mining; metals; food processing; and recycling and waste management among others. Kadant's diverse customer base includes global and regional industrial manufacturers and distributors who participate in the broader resource transformation sector. Its major product brands many of which are sold under the Kadant name through its subsidiaries include well-known industry names such as AES Black Clawson (stock preparation) Carmanah Goslin Johnson Lamort Link-Belt Lodding Nicholson Manufacturing Noss PAAL Syntron Unaflex Valon Kone and Vickery. Most of Kadant's revenues are generated outside the US.

Operations

In 2020 Kadant changed its reportable segment to better align with its strategic initiatives to grow both organically and through acquisitions. Its three new reportable operating segments: Flow Control Industrial Processing and Material Handling.

Its Industrial Processing segment (about 35%) provides equipment machinery and technologies used to recycle paper and paperboard and process timber for use in the packaging tissue wood products and alternative fuel industries among others. In addition we provide industrial automation and digitization solutions to process industries. The Industrial Processing segment consists of its wood processing and stock-preparation product lines.

Kadant's Flow Control segment (more than 35% of revenue) provides custom-engineered products systems and technologies that control the flow of fluids used in industrial and commercial applications to keep critical processes running efficiently in the packaging tissue food metals and other industrial sectors. The Flow Control segment consists of its fluid-handling and doctoring cleaning & filtration product lines.

The Material Handling segment (some 25%) provides products and engineered systems used to handle bulk and discrete materials for secondary processing or transport in the aggregates mining food and waste management industries among others. In addition it manufactures and sells biodegradable absorbent granules used as carriers in agricultural applications and for oil and grease absorption. The Material Handling segment consists of our conveying and screening baling and fiber-based product lines.

Geographic Reach

Based in Westford Massachusetts Kadant sell its products globally including sales to customers in China South America Russia and India and operate multiple manufacturing operations worldwide including operations in Canada China Europe Mexico and Brazil.

Approximately 55% of its sales are to customers outside the US principally in Canada Europe and China.

Sales and Marketing

Kadant sells its products services and systems using a combination of direct sales independent sales agents and distributors. Technical service personnel product specialists and independent sales agents and distributors are utilized in certain markets and for certain product lines.

Financial Performance

Company revenue decreased by 10% to $635.0 million due to lower capital equipment revenue at the company's Industrial Processing and Flow Control segments and lower parts and consumables revenue at its segments.

Net income increased $3.2 million to $55.7 million in 2020 primarily due a $6.2 million decrease in other expense net and a $5.3 million decrease in interest expense offset in part by a $6.7 million decrease in operating income and a $1.6 million increase in provision for income taxes.

Cash held by the company at the end of fiscal 2020 decreased to $66.6 million. Cash provided by operations was $92.9 million while cash used for investing and financing activities were $14.5 million and $84.6 million respectively. Main uses of cash were purchases of property plant and equipment; and repayment of short- and long-term obligations.

Strategy

The company develops a broad range of products for all facets of the markets it serve. Kadant operate research and development facilities in the United States Europe and Canada and focuses its product innovations on process industry challenges and the need for improved fiber processing heat transfer roll and fabric cleaning fluid handling timber harvesting wood processing and secondary material handling. In addition to internal product development activities its research centers allow customers to simulate their own operating conditions and applications to identify and quantify opportunities for improvement.

The company's research and development expenses were $11.3 million in 2020 $10.9 million in 2019 and $10.6 million in 2018.

EXECUTIVES

Executive Chairman Of The Board, Jonathan Painter
Chief Operating Officer, Executive Vice President, Eric Langevin, $466,000 total compensation
President, Chief Executive Officer And Director, Jeffrey Powell, $810,000 total compensation
Executive Vice President, Chief Financial Officer, Michael Mckenney, $466,000 total compensation
Independent Director, John Albertine
Independent Director, Erin Russell
Vice President, General Counsel, Secretary, Stacy Krause, $376,000 total compensation
Vice President, Fredrik Westerhout
Vice President, Thomas Blanchard
Senior Vice President, Chief Accounting Officer, Deborah Selwood
Vice President, Peter Flynn, $360,000 total compensation
Vice President, Michael Colwell
Auditors: KPMG LLP

LOCATIONS

HQ: Kadant Inc
One Technology Park Drive, Westford, MA 01886
Phone: 978 776-2000
Web: www.kadant.com

PRODUCTS/OPERATIONS

2017 Sales

	$ mil.	% of total
Papermaking Systems		
Stock Preparation	193.8	38
Doctoring Cleaning & Filtration	109.6	21
Fluid Handling	104.1	20
Wood Processing Systems	95.1	19
Fiber-based Products	12.4	2
Total	**515.0**	**100**

Selected Products

Doctoring Cleaning and Filtration
  Doctoring
  Cleaning
  Filtration
  Forming
Fluid Handling
  Rotary joints and unions
  Expansion joints and flexible connectors
  Jet devices
  Condensate pumps
  Steam systems
  Accessories
Fiber Processing
  OCC recycled stock and pulp preparation
  Chemical pulping
Recycling Machinery
  Balers for recyclable materials
  Balers for waste RDF alfalfa
  Conveyors
Wood Processing
  Engineered wood (OSB)
  Chipping/screening
  Debarking
  Granules

COMPETITORS

CRANE CO.
ENTEGRIS INC.
FLOWSERVE CORPORATION
ITT INC.
ITT LLC
KIMBALL ELECTRONICS
  INC.

Le Groupe Intertape
Polymer Inc
QUIPP INC.
SPX FLOW INC.

HISTORICAL FINANCIALS

Company Type: Public

Income Statement   FYE: January 2

	REVENUE ($ mil.)	NET INCOME ($ mil.)	NET PROFIT MARGIN	EMPLOYEES
01/21*	635.0	55.2	8.7%	2,600
12/19	704.6	52.0	7.4%	2,800
12/18	633.7	60.4	9.5%	2,500
12/17	515.0	31.0	6.0%	2,400
12/16	414.1	32.0	7.7%	2,000
Annual Growth	11.3%	14.5%	—	6.8%

*Fiscal year change

2021 Year-End Financials

Debt ratio: 25.1%   No. of shares (mil.): 11.5
Return on equity: 11.7%   Dividends
Cash ($ mil.): 65.6   Yield: 0.0%
Current ratio: 2.15   Payout: 19.9%
Long-term debt ($ mil.): 232.0   Market value ($ mil.): 1,627.0

	STOCK PRICE ($) FY Close	P/E High/Low		PER SHARE ($) Earnings	Dividends	Book Value
01/21*	140.98	29	11	4.77	0.95	42.92
12/19	105.76	23	17	4.54	0.91	37.31
12/18	81.12	20	14	5.30	0.87	33.57
12/17	100.40	40	20	2.75	0.82	30.06
12/16	61.20	22	12	2.88	0.74	25.84
Annual Growth	23.2%			13.4%	6.4%	13.5%

*Fiscal year change

Kearny Financial Corp (MD)

Auditors: Crowe LLP

LOCATIONS

HQ: Kearny Financial Corp (MD)
  120 Passaic Avenue, Fairfield, NJ 07004
Phone: 973 244-4500
Web: www.kearnybank.com

HISTORICAL FINANCIALS

Company Type: Public

Income Statement   FYE: June 30

	ASSETS ($ mil.)	NET INCOME ($ mil.)	INCOME AS % OF ASSETS	EMPLOYEES
06/21	7,283.7	63.2	0.9%	584
06/20	6,758.1	44.9	0.7%	552
06/19	6,634.8	42.1	0.6%	565
06/18	6,579.8	19.6	0.3%	565
06/17	4,818.1	18.6	0.4%	466
Annual Growth	10.9%	35.8%	—	5.8%

2021 Year-End Financials

Return on assets: 0.9%   Dividends
Return on equity: 5.9%   Yield: 2.9%
Long-term debt ($ mil.): —   Payout: 50.0%
No. of shares (mil.): 78.9   Market value ($ mil.): 944.0
Sales ($ mil): 259.1

	STOCK PRICE ($) FY Close	P/E High/Low		PER SHARE ($) Earnings	Dividends	Book Value
06/21	11.95	18	9	0.77	0.35	13.21
06/20	8.18	26	14	0.55	0.29	12.96
06/19	13.29	31	26	0.46	0.37	12.65
06/18	13.45	65	54	0.24	0.25	12.74
06/17	14.85	73	57	0.22	0.10	12.53
Annual Growth	(5.3%)			36.8%	36.8%	1.3%

Kilroy Realty L.P.

Auditors: DELOITTE & TOUCHE LLP

LOCATIONS

HQ: Kilroy Realty L.P.
  12200 W. Olympic Boulevard, Suite 200, Los Angeles, CA 90064
Phone: 310 481-8400
Web: www.kilroyrealty.com

HISTORICAL FINANCIALS

Company Type: Public

Income Statement   FYE: December 31

	REVENUE ($ mil.)	NET INCOME ($ mil.)	NET PROFIT MARGIN	EMPLOYEES
12/20	898.4	189.6	21.1%	252
12/19	837.4	198.7	23.7%	267
12/18	747.3	263.2	35.2%	276
12/17	719.0	167.4	23.3%	251
12/16	642.5	300.0	46.7%	245
Annual Growth	8.7%	(10.8%)	—	0.7%

2020 Year-End Financials

Debt ratio: 39.2%   No. of shares (mil.): 117.1
Return on equity: —   Dividends
Cash ($ mil.): 731.9   Yield: —
Current ratio: 1.50   Payout: 121.6%
Long-term debt ($ mil.): 3,923.6   Market value ($ mil.): —

Kimball Electronics Inc

Auditors: DELOITTE & TOUCHE LLP

LOCATIONS

HQ: Kimball Electronics Inc
  1205 Kimball Boulevard, Jasper, IN 47546
Phone: 812 634-4000
Web: www.kimballelectronics.com

HISTORICAL FINANCIALS

Company Type: Public

Income Statement   FYE: June 30

	REVENUE ($ mil.)	NET INCOME ($ mil.)	NET PROFIT MARGIN	EMPLOYEES
06/21	1,291.8	56.7	4.4%	6,400
06/20	1,200.5	18.2	1.5%	6,400
06/19	1,181.8	31.5	2.7%	6,300
06/18	1,072.0	16.7	1.6%	5,700
06/17	930.9	34.1	3.7%	5,400
Annual Growth	8.5%	13.5%	—	4.3%

2021 Year-End Financials

Debt ratio: 8.1%   No. of shares (mil.): 24.9
Return on equity: 13.8%   Dividends
Cash ($ mil.): 106.4   Yield: —
Current ratio: 1.94   Payout: —
Long-term debt ($ mil.): 40.0   Market value ($ mil.): 543.0

	STOCK PRICE ($) FY Close	P/E High/Low		PER SHARE ($) Earnings	Dividends	Book Value
06/21	21.74	13	5	2.24	0.00	17.71
06/20	13.54	25	14	0.71	0.00	15.18
06/19	16.24	17	12	1.21	0.00	14.55
06/18	18.30	35	25	0.62	0.00	13.40
06/17	18.05	15	10	1.24	0.00	12.75
Annual Growth	4.8%			15.9%	—	8.6%

Kinsale Capital Group Inc

Auditors: KPMG LLP

LOCATIONS

HQ: Kinsale Capital Group Inc
  2035 Maywill Street, Suite 100, Richmond, VA 23230
Phone: 804 289-1300   **Fax:** 804 673-5697
Web: www.kinsalecapitalgroup.com

HISTORICAL FINANCIALS

Company Type: Public

Income Statement   FYE: December 31

	ASSETS ($ mil.)	NET INCOME ($ mil.)	INCOME AS % OF ASSETS	EMPLOYEES
12/20	1,546.9	88.4	5.7%	335
12/19	1,090.5	63.3	5.8%	275
12/18	773.0	33.7	4.4%	190
12/17	667.8	24.9	3.7%	164
12/16	614.3	26.1	4.3%	145
Annual Growth	26.0%	35.6%	—	23.3%

2020 Year-End Financials

Return on assets: 6.6%   Dividends
Return on equity: 17.9%   Yield: 0.0%
Long-term debt ($ mil.): —   Payout: 9.3%
No. of shares (mil.): 22.7   Market value ($ mil.): 4,554.0
Sales ($ mil): 459.8

HOOVER'S HANDBOOK OF EMERGING COMPANIES 2022

	STOCK PRICE ($)	P/E	PER SHARE ($)		
	FY Close	High/Low	Earnings	Dividends	Book Value
12/20	200.13	63 21	3.87	0.36	25.32
12/19	101.66	37 19	2.86	0.32	18.28
12/18	55.56	40 27	1.56	0.28	12.43
12/17	45.00	38 24	1.16	0.24	11.32
12/16	34.01	61 32	0.56	0.10	10.03
Annual Growth	55.7%		62.1%	37.7%	26.1%

Kish Bancorp Inc.

Get your banking needs sealed with a Kish. Kish Bancorp is the holding company for Kishacoquillas Valley National Bank commonly referred to as Kish Bank. The bank serves individual and business customers through about 10 offices in Centre Huntingdon and Mifflin counties in central Pennsylvania. It offers checking and savings accounts IRAs CDs and other retail products and uses funds from deposits to write primarily real estate loans (commercial and residential mortgages each account for about one-third of its loan portfolio). Other subsidiaries of Kish Bancorp provide insurance investment management financial planning and travel services.

EXECUTIVES

Chb-Pres-Ceo, William P Hayes
V Chb*, James L Lakso
Sr Exec V Pres-Cfo-Sr Risk Off, Sangeeta Kishore
Exec V Pres-Gen Counsel, Robert S McMinn
SEC*, William L Dancy
Vice President, Alta Wolf
Business, Terry Horner
Executive Vice President, John Arrington
Vp Commercial, Larry Burger
Business, Jackie Confer
Assistant Vice President, Lana Walker
Auditors: S.R. Snodgrass, P.C.

LOCATIONS

HQ: Kish Bancorp Inc.
4255 East Main Street, Belleville, PA 17004
Phone: 844 554-4748
Web: www.KishBank.com

COMPETITORS

COMMERCE NATIONAL FINANCIAL SERVICES INC.
EMCLAIRE FINANCIAL CORP.
LANDMARK BANCORP INC.
NEFFS BANCORP INC.
WCF FINANCIAL BANK

HISTORICAL FINANCIALS
Company Type: Public

Income Statement — FYE: December 31

	ASSETS ($ mil.)	NET INCOME ($ mil.)	INCOME AS % OF ASSETS	EMPLOYEES
12/20	1,106.6	8.0	0.7%	0
12/19	918.3	7.0	0.8%	0
12/18	850.5	6.0	0.7%	0
12/17	811.1	4.1	0.5%	0
12/16	725.0	4.6	0.6%	0
Annual Growth	11.1%	14.9%		

2020 Year-End Financials

Return on assets: 0.7%
Return on equity: 11.9%
Long-term debt ($ mil.): —
No. of shares (mil.): 2.6
Sales ($ mil): 49.5
Dividends
Yield: 2.8%
Payout: 25.9%
Market value ($ mil.): 74.0

	STOCK PRICE ($)	P/E	PER SHARE ($)		
	FY Close	High/Low	Earnings	Dividends	Book Value
12/20	28.50	10 8	3.12	0.81	26.88
12/19	30.75	12 10	2.70	1.00	24.91
12/18	32.00	28 13	2.37	1.63	23.27
12/17	58.00	17 14	3.33	0.92	45.08
12/16	46.00	12 11	3.77	0.86	43.14
Annual Growth	(11.3%) (11.2%)			(4.6%)	(1.5%)

KKR Real Estate Finance Trust Inc

Auditors: DELOITTE & TOUCHE LLP

LOCATIONS

HQ: KKR Real Estate Finance Trust Inc
30 Hudson Yards, Suite 7500, New York, NY 10001
Phone: 212 750-8300
Web: www.kkrreit.com

HISTORICAL FINANCIALS
Company Type: Public

Income Statement — FYE: December 31

	REVENUE ($ mil.)	NET INCOME ($ mil.)	NET PROFIT MARGIN	EMPLOYEES
12/21	292.1	137.1	47.0%	0
12/20	270.4	54.4	20.1%	0
12/19	280.3	89.9	32.1%	0
12/18	203.6	89.7	44.1%	0
12/17	100.8	59.0	58.6%	0
Annual Growth	30.5%	23.5%		

2021 Year-End Financials

Debt ratio: 79.1%
Return on equity: 11.4%
Cash ($ mil.): 271.4
Current ratio: 7.32
Long-term debt ($ mil.): 5,302.4
No. of shares (mil.): 61.3
Dividends
Yield: 8.2%
Payout: 80.7%
Market value ($ mil.): 1,278.0

	STOCK PRICE ($)	P/E	PER SHARE ($)		
	FY Close	High/Low	Earnings	Dividends	Book Value
12/21	20.83	10 8	2.21	1.72	22.18
12/20	17.92	23 10	0.96	1.72	18.80
12/19	20.42	13 12	1.57	1.72	19.55
12/18	19.15	13 12	1.58	1.69	19.71
12/17	20.01	18 15	1.30	0.99	19.75
Annual Growth	1.0%		14.2%	14.8%	3.0%

Lakeland Bancorp, Inc.

Lakeland Bancorp is the holding company for Lakeland Bank which serves northern and central New Jersey from around 50 branch offices. Targeting individuals and small to midsized businesses the bank offers standard retail products such as checking and savings accounts money market and NOW accounts and CDs. It also offers financial planning and advisory services for consumers. The bank's lending activities primarily consist of commercial loans and mortgages (around three-quarters of the company's loan portfolio) and residential mortgages. Lakeland also offers commercial lease financing for commercial equipment.

Operations

Lakeland Bancorp operates through a single business segment. Around 70% of its $4.3 billion loan portfolio is made up of commercial mortgages. Industrial commercial loans residential mortgages real estate construction loans and home equity and consumer loans each represent between 5%-10% of the company's lending activity. The company holds $5.5 billion in assets and $4.4 billion in deposits.

Geographic Reach

Headquartered in Oak Ridge New Jersey Lakeland Bancorp boasts about 50 banking offices across the New Jersey counties of Bergen Essex Morris Ocean Passaic Somerset Sussex Union and Warren. The company also has a branch in Highland Mills New York; six New Jersey regional commercial lending centers in Bernardsville Jackson Montville Newton Teaneck and Waldwick; and two commercial loan production offices serving Middlesex and Monmouth counties in New Jersey and the Hudson Valley region of New York.

Sales and Marketing

Lakeland Bancorp serves a variety of customers from individuals to businesses to municipalities.

One-fifth of Lakeland's commercial loan segment – the largest in its portfolio – is made up of owner-occupied real estate loans. Multifamily and retail loans make up about 15% each and industrial and office loans each comprise around 10%.

Financial Performance

Lakeland Bancorp has seen major five-year growth expanding revenue by 53% to $190.7 million net income by 111% to $52.6 million and cash by 39% to $142.9 million between 2013 and 2017. However the company's debt has risen 85% to $296.9 million in that time.

The holding company's revenue increased 14% in 2017 owing primarily to increased net interest income from growing average earning assets. Net income added 27% on the strength of those gains.

Lakeland's cash dipped $32.9 million in 2017. Operations and financings contributed $67.5 million and investments used $355.1 million. Financings provided $254.8 million down nearly $200 million from the previous year following an increase in net deposits federal funds purchased and securities sold under repurchase agreements.

Strategy

Lakeland Bancorp is focused on growth through acquisitions. The company has acquired at least eight community banks since its inception including Highlands Bancorp. which operates in northern New Jersey. The company also offers internet banking mobile banking and cash management services.

Mergers and Acquisitions

In January 2019 Lakeland Bancorp acquired Vernon New Jersey-based Highlands Bancorp in a deal valued at $56.7 million. The holding company – which operated branches in the New Jersey municipalities of Sparta Totowa and Denville – had consolidated total assets of $5.53 billion.

Company Background

Lakeland Bancorp was founded in 1969. It organized into a bank holding company in 1989.

EXECUTIVES

Independent Director, Robert Nicholson
President, Chief Executive Officer, Director, Thomas Shara, $903,798 total compensation
Independent Director, Mark Fredericks
Executive Vice President, Chief Administrative Officer, General Counsel, Corporate Secretary Of Lakeland And Lakeland Bank, Timothy Matteson, $341,172 total compensation
Independent Chairman Of The Board, Mary Deacon
Executive Vice President, Chief Banking Officer Of The Company And The Bank, Ellen Lalwani
Executive Vice President, Chief Risk Officer Of Lakeland And Lakeland Bank, James Nigro, $341,172 total compensation
Independent Director, Janeth Hendershot
Executive Vice President And Chief Lending Officer Of The Company And The Bank, John Rath, $284,616 total compensation
Independent Director, Brian Flynn
Independent Director, Lawrence Inserra
Executive Vice President And Chief Financial Officer Of Lakeland And Lakeland Bank, Thomas Splaine, $383,301 total compensation
Independent Director, James Hanson
Independent Director, Bruce Bohuny
Independent Director, Brian Gragnolati
Executive Vice President, Chief Information Officer, Paul Ho Sing Loy
Chief Operating Officer, Senior Executive Vice President Of The Company And The Bank, Ronald Schwarz, $419,474 total compensation
Auditors: KPMG LLP

LOCATIONS

HQ: Lakeland Bancorp, Inc.
250 Oak Ridge Road, Oak Ridge, NJ 07438
Phone: 973 697-2000
Web: www.lakelandbank.com

PRODUCTS/OPERATIONS

2017 Sales

	$ mil.	% of total
Interest		
Loans & fees	172.3	80
Investment securities and other	17.9	8
Interest expense	(25.0)	-
Non-interest		
Service charges on deposit accounts	10.7	5
Commissions & fees	4.9	2
Income on bank owned life insurance	2.4	1
Other	7.5	4
Total	**190.7**	**100**

Selected Services

401K and IRA Rollovers
Certificates of deposit & individual retirement accounts
Checking accounts
Consumer loans
Home loans
Insurance
Investment management
Online services
Retirement income planning
Savings and money market accounts

COMPETITORS

CUSTOMERS BANCORP INC.	HERITAGE COMMERCE CORP
F.N.B. CORPORATION	HOME BANCSHARES INC.
FIRST MERCHANTS CORPORATION	MERIDIAN INTERSTATE BANCORP INC.
FIRST MIDWEST BANCORP BANCORP INC.	NORTHFIELD BANCORP INC.
FULTON FINANCIAL CORPORATION	S & T BANCORP INC.
HANCOCK WHITNEY BANKS CORPORATION	UNITED BANKSHARES INC. UNITED COMMUNITY INC.

HISTORICAL FINANCIALS

Company Type: Public

Income Statement   FYE: December 31

	ASSETS ($ mil.)	NET INCOME ($ mil.)	INCOME AS % OF ASSETS	EMPLOYEES
12/20	7,664.3	57.5	0.8%	711
12/19	6,711.2	70.6	1.1%	692
12/18	5,806.0	63.4	1.1%	652
12/17	5,405.6	52.5	1.0%	621
12/16	5,093.1	41.5	0.8%	592
Annual Growth	**10.8%**	**8.5%**	**—**	**4.7%**

2020 Year-End Financials

Return on assets: 0.8%	Dividends
Return on equity: 7.7%	Yield: 3.9%
Long-term debt ($ mil.): —	Payout: 44.2%
No. of shares (mil.): 50.4	Market value ($ mil.): 641.0
Sales ($ mil): 275.9	

	STOCK PRICE ($) FY Close	P/E High/Low		PER SHARE ($) Earnings	Dividends	Book Value
12/20	12.70	15	8	1.13	0.50	15.13
12/19	17.38	13	10	1.38	0.49	14.36
12/18	14.81	16	11	1.32	0.45	13.14
12/17	19.25	20	16	1.09	0.40	12.31
12/16	19.50	21	10	0.95	0.37	11.65
Annual Growth	**(10.2%)**	**—**	**—**	**4.4%**	**7.8%**	**6.8%**

Lakeland Financial Corp

Lakeland Financial is the holding company for Lake City Bank which serves area business customers and individuals through around 50 branches scattered across about 15 northern and central Indiana counties. With $4.8 billion in assets the community bank offers such standard retail services as checking and savings accounts money market accounts and CDs. Commercial loans including agricultural loans and mortgages make up about 90% of the bank's loan portfolio. Lake City Bank also offers investment products and services such as corporate and personal trust brokerage and estate planning.

Operations

Lakeland Financial operates through a single business segment. About 80% of the holding company's revenue is derived from net interest income mostly from interest and fees on loans.

Commercial and industrial loans comprise about 40% of its loan portfolio as does commercial real estate and multifamily residential loans. Consumer family mortgages make up about 10% and agribusiness and agricultural loans represent more than 5%.

Lakeland holds around $4 billion in deposits; retail public funds and commercial deposits make up about 40% 30% and 25% of that total respectively.

Geographic Reach

Warsaw Indiana-based Lakeland Financial serves customers at about 50 bank branches in around 15 northern and central Indiana counties including some half a dozen in and around Indianapolis.

Sales and Marketing

Lakeland Financial targets larger Indiana cities it believes have better-than-average growth potential.

The company is focused on commercial banking and has a team of more than 40 commercial bankers. Lakeland offers internet business banking and online treasury management services to its commercial customers.

Financial Performance

Lakeland Financial has undergone moderate five-year revenue and net income growth of 42% and 48% respectively in conjunction with a 216% ballooning in its in cash. The company's long-term debt has remained flat in that time.

The holding company's revenue trended up 14% to $171.9 million in 2017 owing to improved net interest income driven by increased average earning assets and its average commercial loan portfolio. That growth also spurred the company's 10% rise in net income to $57.3 million.

Lakeland had cash of $176.2 million at the end of 2017 up $8.9 million from the previous year. Financings provided $327.7 million while operations provided $19.9 million. Investments used $396 million down $46.4 million from 2016 thanks mostly to a net increase in total loans with increased proceeds from sale of securities available for sale also contributing.

Lakeland had $40 million in long-term debt at the end of 2017.

HOOVER'S HANDBOOK OF EMERGING COMPANIES 2022

Strategy

Lakeland Financial is focused on increasing the percentage of its portfolio made up of commercial loans and steadily growing its branch locations without making acquisitions.

In 2017 Lakeland's commercial loans comprised about 90% of its portfolio with an average increase of 12.5% that year compared to the year prior.

The company opened five branches from 2013-2017.

Company Background

Lakeland Financial was founded in 1872.

EXECUTIVES

Independent Director, Ronald Truex
Independent Chairman Of The Board, Michael Kubacki
President, Chief Executive Officer, Director, David Findlay, $637,281 total compensation
Independent Director, M. Scott Welch
Independent Director, Steven Ross
Independent Director, Emily Pichon
Executive Vice President, Head Of Commercial Banking Department, Eric Ottinger, $329,897 total compensation
Executive Vice President, Chief Administrative Officer, Kristin Pruitt, $313,846 total compensation
Independent Director, Blake Augsburger
Independent Director, Bradley Toothaker
Chief Financial Officer, Executive Vice President, Lisa O'Neill, $276,769 total compensation
Independent Director, Brian Smith
Independent Director, Darrianne Christian
Independent Director, Daniel Evans
Director, Faraz Abbasi
Auditors: Crowe LLP

LOCATIONS

HQ: Lakeland Financial Corp
202 East Center Street, Warsaw, IN 46580
Phone: 574 267-6144
Web: www.lakecitybank.com

PRODUCTS/OPERATIONS

2017 Sales

	$ mil.	% of total
Interest		
Loans	151.0	75
Securities	14.3	7
Other	0.3	-
Interest expense	(29.8)	-
Noninteresst		
Service charges on deposit accounts	13.7	7
Loan and service fees	7.9	4
Wealth advisory fees	5.5	3
Investment brokerage fees	1.3	-
Other	7.7	4
Total	**171.9**	**100**

COMPETITORS

AMERICAN NATIONAL BANKSHARES INC. CORP.	HOME BANCSHARES INC. INDEPENDENT BANK
BOK FINANCIAL CORPORATION	LEGACYTEXAS FINANCIAL GROUP INC.
BSB BANCORP INC.	UNIVEST FINANCIAL CORPORATION
CLIFTON BANCORP INC.	WESTAMERICA BANCORPORATION
FLAGSTAR BANCORP INC.	
HANCOCK WHITNEY CORPORATION	

HISTORICAL FINANCIALS

Company Type: Public

Income Statement

FYE: December 31

	ASSETS ($ mil.)	NET INCOME ($ mil.)	INCOME AS % OF ASSETS	EMPLOYEES
12/20	5,830.4	84.3	1.4%	585
12/19	4,946.7	87.0	1.8%	568
12/18	4,875.2	80.4	1.6%	553
12/17	4,682.9	57.3	1.2%	539
12/16	4,290.0	52.0	1.2%	524
Annual Growth	**8.0%**	**12.8%**	—	**2.8%**

2020 Year-End Financials

Return on assets: 1.5%
Return on equity: 13.4%
Long-term debt ($ mil.): —
No. of shares (mil.): 25.2
Sales ($ mil): 239.9

Dividends
Yield: 2.2%
Payout: 37.6%
Market value ($ mil.): 1,352.0

	STOCK PRICE ($) FY Close	P/E High/Low	PER SHARE ($) Earnings	Dividends	Book Value
12/20	53.58	17 10	3.30	1.20	26.03
12/19	48.93	15 12	3.38	1.16	23.50
12/18	40.16	16 12	3.13	1.00	20.76
12/17	48.49	23 18	2.23	0.63	18.72
12/16	47.36	26 16	2.05	0.73	17.12
Annual Growth	**3.1%**	— —	**12.6%**	**13.4%**	**11.0%**

Lakeland Industries, Inc.

The wrong clothing can be hazardous to your health — not based on style but by OSHA and EPA standards. Lakeland makes protective clothing for on-the-job hazards. It uses DuPont specialty fabrics such as Kevlar TyChem and Tyvek as well as its own fabrics to make industrial disposable garments toxic-waste cleanup suits fire- and heat-resistant apparel (including Fyrepel gear for firefighters) industrial work gloves high-visibility garments and industrial/medical garments. Lakeland manufactures its products in Brazil China India Mexico and the US. Customers — nearly 65% are outside of the US — include high tech electronics manufacturers construction companies hospitals and laboratories.

Operations

The company also supplies federal state and local government agencies such as the Department of Defense the Department of Homeland Security and the Centers for Disease Control. All total Lakeland distributes to a network of more than 1200 North American safety and mill supply distributors and end users as well as to international clients. It has also developed a number of patented production machinery and fabrics including Micromax ChemMax Despro and Thermbar.

The company's business is fueled by crises. Its products are useful in situations involving fire and chemical/biological threats such as the anthrax scare SARs epidemic ricin letters and Avian flu — all of which have occurred in the last decade. Many Asian and South American countries have since adopted legislation akin to the US Occupational Safety and Health Act in order to be a part of the World Trade Organization. To meet the stricter WTO standards these countries need to use appropriate gear causing orders for protective clothing and equipment to increase.

Geographic Reach

Lakeland sells its products to more than 40 countries primarily in Argentina Australia Brazil Canada Chile China Europe and Southeast Asia. The US accounts for roughly 35% of total sales; China 30%.

Sales and Marketing

Lakeland products are sold by an in-house customer service group regional sales managers and independent sales representatives selling to a network of over 1200 North American safety and mill supply distributors.

The company spent $263 million on advertising in 2013 and $310 million in 2012. The Department for Homeland Security is one of its biggest clients.

Financial Performance

Lakeland's balance sheet is heading in the wrong direction; it has suffered revenue declines and net losses over the last two years. Revenues fell 2% from $96.3 million in 2012 to $95.1 million in 2013 as it posted a net loss of $26 million for 2013.

The decrease was driven by a 19% drop in US disposables sales resulting from the loss of its Tyvek license from DuPont. This offset international gains in Brazil Chile and Argentina. China sales also jumped 26% from 2012 to 2013.

Its net loss for 2013 increased primarily due to an arbitration settlement and goodwill impairment charge from its operations in Brazil.

Strategy

To be closer to customers and to take advantage of the lower production and workforce costs the company has moved some of its manufacturing to international facilities in Brazil China India and Mexico. It is also sourcing more raw materials from China than from the US or Europe. In 2011 it opened new sales offices in India Kazakhstan and Russia.

Lakeland has altered its product mix in an attempt to combat competition. Domestic sales of Tyvek once a major staple in the company's line of products have fallen off in recent years. Increased sales in the company's line of Hi-Visibility products have partially offset the decline in Tyvek's sales.

Lakeland's expansion strategy takes advantage of smaller companies that are experiencing their own crises — economically. The protective gear industry is fragmented and made up of many smaller companies unlike mega-competitors Kimberly Clark and DuPont which along with Lakeland have jumped at the chance to pick up smaller companies that have hit on hard times. Lakeland has made acquisitions to build on its product portfolio increase its ability to cross-sell and give it a geographic foothold in emerging markets.

EXECUTIVES

President, Chief Executive Officer, Secretary, Director, Charles Roberson, $324,038 total compensation
Executive Chairman Of The Board, Christopher Ryan, $415,385 total compensation
Vice President - Corporate Development, Joshua Sletten

Lead Independent Director, Alfred Kreft
Independent Director, Thomas McAteer
Independent Director, James Jenkins
Executive Vice President Of Sales And Marketing,
  Steven Harvey, $13,846 total compensation
Independent Director, Nikki Hamblin
Independent Director, Jeffrey Schlarbaum
Chief Operating And Financial Officer, Allen
  Dillard, $240,000 total compensation
Auditors: Friedman LLP

LOCATIONS

HQ: Lakeland Industries, Inc.
  1525 Perimeter Parkway, Suite 325, Huntsville, AL
  35806
Phone: 256 350-3873   **Fax:** 256 350-0773
Web: www.lakeland.com

PRODUCTS/OPERATIONS

Selected Products
Fire fighting and heat protective apparel
Gloves and arm guards
High-end chemical protective suits
High visibility clothing
Limited use/disposable protective clothing
Raingear
Reflective vests and other high visibility clothing
Reusable woven garments

COMPETITORS

ALLIANCE LAUNDRY	MSA SAFETY
HOLDINGS LLC	INCORPORATED
AVANOS MEDICAL INC.	TS03 Inc
GRAHAM PACKAGING	Tembec Inc
COMPANY L.P.	VCP MOBILITY INC.
K2M GROUP HOLDINGS	ZIMMER BIOMET
HOLDINGS	
INC.	INC.

HISTORICAL FINANCIALS

Company Type: Public

Income Statement				FYE: January 31
	REVENUE ($ mil.)	**NET INCOME** ($ mil.)	**NET PROFIT MARGIN**	**EMPLOYEES**
01/21	159.0	35.1	22.1%	2,000
01/20	107.8	3.2	3.0%	1,829
01/19	99.0	1.4	1.5%	1,632
01/18	95.9	0.4	0.5%	1,072
01/17	86.1	3.8	4.5%	993
Annual Growth	16.5%	73.3%	—	19.1%

2021 Year-End Financials

Debt ratio: —	No. of shares (mil.): 7.9
Return on equity: 33.6%	Dividends
Cash ($ mil.): 52.6	Yield: —
Current ratio: 8.03	Payout: —
Long-term debt ($ mil.): —	Market value ($ mil.): 222.0

	STOCK PRICE ($) FY Close	P/E High/Low		PER SHARE ($) Earnings	Dividends	Book Value
01/21	27.80	7	3	4.31	0.00	15.39
01/20	13.94	39	24	0.41	0.00	10.67
01/19	11.12	89	56	0.18	0.00	10.39
01/18	14.10	274	166	0.06	0.00	10.21
01/17	10.85	25	15	0.53	0.00	9.84
Annual Growth	26.5%		—	— 68.9%	—	11.8%

Landmark Bancorp Inc

Landmark Bancorp is a tourist attraction for Kansas money. It is the holding company for Landmark National Bank which has about 15 branches in communities in central eastern and southwestern Kansas. The bank provides standard commercial banking products including checking savings and money market accounts as well as CDs and credit and debit cards. It primarily uses funds from deposits to write residential and commercial mortgages and business loans. Landmark National Bank offers non-deposit investment services through its affiliation with Investment Planners.

EXECUTIVES

Chairman And Director Of Landmark Bancorp And Landmark National Bank, Patrick Alexander
Vice President, Secretary, Chief Financial Officer, Treasurer, Executive Vice President And Chief Financial Officer - Bank, Mark Herpich, $244,000 total compensation
Independent Director, Jim Lewis
Independent Director, Richard Ball
Lead Independent Director, Brent Bowman
Director, David Snapp
President, Chief Executive Officer Of The Company And The Bank, Michael Scheopner, $385,000 total compensation
Independent Director, Wayne Sloan
Independent Director, Sarah Hill-Nelson
Executive Vice President - Market President-central Region, Mark Oliphant, $191,500 total compensation
Independent Director, Sandra Moll
Auditors: Crowe LLP

LOCATIONS

HQ: Landmark Bancorp Inc
  701 Poyntz Avenue, Manhattan, KS 66502
Phone: 785 565-2000
Web: www.landmarkbancorpinc.com

COMPETITORS

COMMERCE NATIONAL FINANCIAL SERVICES INC.
EMCLAIRE FINANCIAL CORP.
LYONS NATIONAL BANK
PRINCETON NATIONAL BANCORP INC.
WCF FINANCIAL BANK

HISTORICAL FINANCIALS

Company Type: Public

Income Statement				FYE: December 31
	ASSETS ($ mil.)	**NET INCOME** ($ mil.)	**INCOME AS % OF ASSETS**	**EMPLOYEES**
12/20	1,188.0	19.4	1.6%	292
12/19	998.4	10.6	1.1%	289
12/18	985.7	10.4	1.1%	291
12/17	929.4	4.3	0.5%	286
12/16	911.3	8.9	1.0%	292
Annual Growth	6.9%	21.4%	—	0.0%

2020 Year-End Financials

Return on assets: 1.7%	Dividends
Return on equity: 16.5%	Yield: 3.5%
Long-term debt ($ mil.): —	Payout: 19.5%
No. of shares (mil.): 4.9	Market value ($ mil.): 114.0
Sales ($ mil) 64.1	

	STOCK PRICE ($) FY Close	P/E High/Low		PER SHARE ($) Earnings	Dividends	Book Value
12/20	22.85	7	5	3.90	0.76	25.39
12/19	25.05	12	10	2.10	0.73	21.43
12/18	23.20	14	11	2.06	0.69	18.16
12/17	28.99	36	31	0.87	0.66	17.66
12/16	28.03	15	13	1.81	0.63	17.21
Annual Growth	(5.0%)		—	— 21.2%	5.0%	10.2%

LCI Industries

LCI Industries makes components for recreational vehicle (RVs) and other original equipment manufacturers. Through its primary operating subsidiary Lippert Components the company makes windows and doors chassis furniture and slide-out walls for travel trailers and fifth-wheel RVs. The company also serves adjacent markets including manufactured home buses trailers used to haul boats livestock equipment and other cargo trucks modular housing and trains. LCI's aftermarket segment sells to RV and trailer dealers distributors and service centers. Over 90% of the company's sales came from its customers from its US customers.

Operations

LCI Industries operates through two segments: the original equipment manufacturers (OEM) segment and the aftermarket segment.

The OEM segment (nearly 80% of total sales) manufactures recreational vehicle components including windows and doors slide-out mechanisms axles chassis furniture and awnings for travel trailers and fifth wheels (more than 45% of segment sales) and motorhomes (more than 5% of segment revenue). Customers in adjacent OEM markets account for some 25% of segment sales.

The company's aftermarket segment (more than 20% of total sales) sells RV parts and accessories to RV dealers and service centers warehouse distributors and direct to consumers.

When it comes to its products' sales chassis chassis parts and slide-out mechanism accounts for about 20% of sales followed by the aftermarket products with about 25% and windows and doors with over 20%. Other products include furniture and mattresses (about 15%) axles and suspensions (some 5%) and other (accounts for the rest).

Geographic Reach

Based in Indiana LCI Industries has more than over 100 manufacturing and warehousing locations in the North America and Europe.

Over 90% of its total sales comes from domestic operations.

Sales and Marketing

LCI Industries' OEM products are sold primarily to major manufacturers of RVs such as Thor Industries Forest River and Winnebago as well as to manufacturers in other adjacent industries including buses; trailers used to haul boats livestock equipment and other cargo; trucks; boats; trains; manufactured homes; and modular housing. The company's aftermarket products are sold to wholesale distributors dealerships service centers and direct to customers. Aftermarket customers are supported by multiple call centers staffed by mar-

HOOVER'S HANDBOOK OF EMERGING COMPANIES 2022   245

keting and product training teams that provide quick response for product orders and technical support to limit customer downtime.

The company's marketing and advertising expenditures were $10.4 million $6.4 million and $4.1 million in 2020 2019 and 2018 respectivel

Financial Performance

Consolidated net sales in 2020 were $2.8 billion an increase of 18 percent from the consolidated net sales in 2019 of $2.4 billion. The increase in year-over-year net sales was primarily driven by the impact of acquisitions organic growth in the Aftermarket Segment and a significant increase in RV retail demand following COVID-19 shutdowns in the first half of the year.

In 2020 the company had a net income of $158.4 million an 8% increase from the previous year's net income of $146.5 million.

The company's cash at the end of 2020 was $51.8 million. Operating activities generated $231.4 million while investing activities used $232.3 million mainly for acquisitions of businesses. Financing activities generated another $14 million.

Strategy

The company is executing a strategic initiative to diversify the markets it serves away from the historical concentration within the North American RV OEM industry. The company's goal is to have 60 percent of net sales be generated outside of the North American RV OEM industry by the end of 2022.

Mergers and Acquisitions

In the 2nd quarter of 2021 LCI Industries through its wholly-owned subsidiary Lippert Components Inc. announced that its new wholly-owned German subsidiary LCI Industries GmbH acquired 100% of the shares of Schaudt GmbH Elektrotechnik & Apparatebau (Schaudt) a leading supplier of electronic controls and energy management systems for the European Caravan Industry located in Markdorf Germany. The formation of LCI Industries GmbH and the subsequent acquisition of Schaudt is part of Lippert's larger European strategy to be closer to its key German customers and to have local contacts within the country. Terms were not disclosed.

Also in 2021 LCI Industries through its wholly-owned subsidiary Lippert Components Inc. announced the acquisition of Kaspar Ranch Hand Equipment LLC (Ranch Hand) a South Texas based manufacturer of custom bumpers grill guards and steps for the automotive aftermarket. Ranch Hand is synonymous with front-end protection and has enjoyed a leadership position in the automotive accessory aftermarket industry for years. The company believes that its design manufacturing and distribution expertise will help the brand to continue to expand its reach and pursue long-term success. Terms were not disclosed.

In early 2021 Lippert Components Inc. announces today that it has acquired the assets of Wolfpack Chassis LLC (Wolfpack) a chassis manufacturer in Kendallville Indiana to add to its ongoing expansion of chassis production capacity for an undisclosed amount. The acquisition of Wolfpack is set to help immediately accommodate customer demands with the expansive resources the company will contribute.

Company Background

In 1956 Larry Lippert and Don Baldwin founded B&L Industries in Indiana to manufacture galvanized roofing for mobile homes. Two years later the company expanded into mobile home chassis and other components with the purchase of Riverdale Steel Works.

Throughout the 1960s the company expanded to additional locations in Indiana Michigan North Carolina Texas and Alabama. The company was incorporated in 1964 and became Drew National Corporation. The company's primary operating subsidiary was Lippert Components.

Demand for manufactured housing took off in the early 1970s and the company's North Carolina facility served the growing needs of Clayton Homes and Oxford Homes. Drew National managed to stay afloat when tighter monetary policy reversed the fortunes of the mobile home industry in the early 1980s. The company changed its name to Drew Industries in 1984.

In 1992 disaster brought opportunity for the company when Hurricane Andrew devastated Florida and Drew Industries received an order for 10000 FEMA trailer chassis. The company expanded into travel trailer chassis in 1997. In 2000 the company opened a facility in Ontario Canada.

Over the next dozen years the company continued to expand its product offerings and manufacturing footprint in the US. By the end of 2012 Drew Industries operated 30 manufacturing facilities in 11 states. In 2014 the company changed its name to LCI Industries.

EXECUTIVES

Director, James Gero
President, Chief Executive Officer, Director, Chief Executive Officer Of Lippert Components, Jason Lippert, $1,013,462 total compensation
Cfo, Brian Hall, $465,231 total compensation
Independent Director, Kieran O Sullivan
Chairman Of The Board, Tracy Graham
Chief Human Resource Officer, Executive Vice President, Nick Fletcher, $400,000 total compensation
Group President - Aftermarket, Jamie Schnur, $492,308 total compensation
Independent Director, Frank Crespo
Director, Ronald Fenech
Corporate Controller, Principal Accounting Officer, Vice President - Finance, Kip Emenhiser
Executive Vice President, Chief Legal Officer And Corporate Secretary, Andrew Namenye, $425,945 total compensation
Independent Director, John Sirpilla
Independent Director, Stephanie Mains
Group President - North America, Ryan Smith, $576,923 total compensation
Auditors: KPMG LLP

LOCATIONS

HQ: LCI Industries
3501 County Road 6 East, Elkhart, IN 46514
Phone: 574 535-1125
Web: www.lci1.com

PRODUCTS/OPERATIONS

2013 Sales

	$ mil.	% of total
Recreational vehicles	893.7	88
Manufactured housing	121.9	12
Total	**1,015.6**	**100**

Selected Products

Manufactured housing (MH) products
Aluminum and vinyl patio doors
Axles
Entry doors
Steel and fiberglass entry doors
Steel chassis
Steel chassis parts
Replacement windows doors thermoformed bath products
Thermoformed bath and kitchen products
Vinyl and aluminum windows and screens
Recreational vehicle (RV) products (travel trailers and fifth-wheel RVs)
Aluminum windows and screens
Chassis components
Entry and baggage doors
Entry steps
Furniture and mattresses
Manual electric and hydraulic stabilizer and lifting systems
Patio doors
Slide-out mechanisms
Specialty trailers for hauling boats personal watercraft snowmobiles and equipment
Thermoformed bath kitchen and other products
Towable axles and suspensions
Towable steel chassis
Toy hauler ramp doors

COMPETITORS

DORMAN PRODUCTS INC.
FEDERAL-MOGUL LLC
FOX FACTORY HOLDING CORP.
LEAR CORPORATION
MANN+HUMMEL FILTRATION TECHNOLOGY INTERMEDIATE HOLDINGS
MILLER INDUSTRIES INC.
NAVISTAR INTERNATIONAL CORPORATION
STRATTEC SECURITY CORPORATION
TENNECO INC.
TWIN DISC INCORPORATED

HISTORICAL FINANCIALS

Company Type: Public

Income Statement				FYE: December 31
	REVENUE ($ mil.)	NET INCOME ($ mil.)	NET PROFIT MARGIN	EMPLOYEES
12/20	2,796.1	158.4	5.7%	12,400
12/19	2,371.4	146.5	6.2%	10,500
12/18	2,475.8	148.5	6.0%	10,260
12/17	2,147.7	132.8	6.2%	9,852
12/16	1,678.9	129.6	7.7%	7,654
Annual Growth	**13.6%**	**5.1%**	**—**	**12.8%**

2020 Year-End Financials

Debt ratio: 32.1%
Return on equity: 18.4%
Cash ($ mil.): 51.8
Current ratio: 2.09
Long-term debt ($ mil.): 720.4

No. of shares (mil.): 25.1
Dividends
Yield: 2.1%
Payout: 51.0%
Market value ($ mil.): 3,262.0

	STOCK PRICE ($) FY Close	P/E High/Low		PER SHARE ($)		
			Earnings	Dividends	Book Value
12/20	129.68	21 9	6.27	2.80	36.11
12/19	107.13	19 11	5.84	2.55	31.97
12/18	66.80	22 10	5.83	2.35	28.41
12/17	130.00	25 17	5.24	2.05	26.12
12/16	107.75	21 10	5.20	1.40	22.23
Annual Growth	**4.7%**	**— —**	**4.8%**	**18.9%**	**12.9%**

LCNB Corp

It just makes cents that LCNB counts bucks in the Buckeye State. The firm is the holding company for LCNB National Bank which operates some 36 offices across southwestern Ohio. The bank serves about 10 Ohio counties offering personal and commercial banking services. such as checking and savings accounts money markets IRAs and CDs. Residential mortgages account for nearly half of the company's loan book. Other offerings include commercial mortgages consumer loans including credit cards and business loans. It also provides trust services. LCNB's subsidiary Dakin Insurance Agency sells commercial and personal property/casualty insurance.

Geographic Reach
Headquartered in Ohio LCNB Corp. serves several of the state's counties including Butler Clermont Clinton Fayette Hamilton Montgomery Preble Ross and Warren.

Strategy
The financial institution has been growing through acquisitions.

The company expanded into Preble County in 2014 when it acquired Eaton National Bank & Trust Co. from Colonial Banc Corp. Eaton was folded into the company's LCNB National Bank network.

LCNB also bought First Capital Bancshares (FCB) a bank holding company in a stock-and-cash deal valued at about $19.6 million. FCB is the parent of six-branch Citizens National Bank of Chillicothe. The purchase of FCB allowed LCNB to expand into the Ross and Fayette Country markets.

EXECUTIVES

Independent Director, Stephen Wilson
President, Chief Executive Officer, Director, Eric Meilstrup, $315,000 total compensation
Chief Financial Officer, Executive Vice President, Robert Haines, $211,000 total compensation
Independent Chairman Of The Board, Spencer Cropper
Secretary, Independent Director, Anne Krehbiel
Executive Vice President, Chief Investment Officer, Trust Officer, Bradley Ruppert, $193,000 total compensation
Director, William Kaufman
Independent Director, Michael Johrendt
Independent Director, William Huddle
Chief Operating Officer, Executive Vice President, Lawrence Mulligan
Independent Director, Craig Johnson
Independent Director, Takeitha Lawson
Auditors: BKD, LLP

LOCATIONS

HQ: LCNB Corp
2 North Broadway, Lebanon, OH 45036
Phone: 513 932-1414
Web: www.lcnb.com

COMPETITORS

BNCCORP INC.
CNB CORPORATION
HUNTINGTON BANCSHARES INCORPORATED
PENDLETON COMMUNITY BANK INC.
TRUIST FINANCIAL CORPORATION

HISTORICAL FINANCIALS
Company Type: Public

Income Statement
FYE: December 31

	ASSETS ($ mil.)	NET INCOME ($ mil.)	INCOME AS % OF ASSETS	EMPLOYEES
12/20	1,745.8	20.0	1.1%	331
12/19	1,639.3	18.9	1.2%	332
12/18	1,636.9	14.8	0.9%	325
12/17	1,295.6	12.9	1.0%	310
12/16	1,306.8	12.4	1.0%	282
Annual Growth	7.5%	12.6%	—	4.1%

2020 Year-End Financials
Return on assets: 1.1%
Return on equity: 8.5%
Long-term debt ($ mil.): —
No. of shares (mil.): 12.8
Sales ($ mil): 79.5

Dividends
Yield: 4.9%
Payout: 49.3%
Market value ($ mil.): 189.0

	STOCK PRICE ($) FY Close	P/E High/Low		PER SHARE ($) Earnings	Dividends	Book Value
12/20	14.69	12	7	1.55	0.73	18.73
12/19	19.30	14	11	1.44	0.69	17.63
12/18	15.15	17	12	1.24	0.65	16.47
12/17	20.45	19	14	1.29	0.64	14.99
12/16	23.25	20	12	1.25	0.64	14.30
Annual Growth	(10.8%)	—	—	5.5%	3.3%	7.0%

Ledyard Financial Group Inc

Auditors: Berry Dunn McNeil & Parker, LLC

LOCATIONS

HQ: Ledyard Financial Group Inc
38 South Main Street, P.O. Box 799, Hanover, NH 03755
Phone: 603 643-2244   **Fax:** 603 643-7464
Web: www.ledyardbank.com

HISTORICAL FINANCIALS
Company Type: Public

Income Statement
FYE: December 31

	ASSETS ($ mil.)	NET INCOME ($ mil.)	INCOME AS % OF ASSETS	EMPLOYEES
12/20	684.7	6.7	1.0%	0
12/19	500.3	5.8	1.2%	0
12/18	488.0	5.1	1.1%	0
12/17	476.6	3.8	0.8%	0
12/16	476.3	4.1	0.9%	0
Annual Growth	9.5%	13.0%	—	—

2020 Year-End Financials
Return on assets: 1.1%
Return on equity: 10.9%
Long-term debt ($ mil.): —
No. of shares (mil.): 3.3
Sales ($ mil): 33.4

Dividends
Yield: 0.0%
Payout: 36.0%
Market value ($ mil.): 63.0

	STOCK PRICE ($) FY Close	P/E High/Low		PER SHARE ($) Earnings	Dividends	Book Value
12/20	18.99	12	7	2.11	0.76	20.13
12/19	24.90	14	11	1.83	0.74	17.19
12/18	22.25	14	13	1.64	0.70	15.02
12/17	21.60	56	16	1.23	0.65	14.05
12/16	54.20	41	35	1.29	0.64	14.03
Annual Growth	(23.1%)	—	—	13.1%	4.4%	9.4%

Lee Enterprises, Inc.

Lee Enterprises is a trusted local news provider and an innovative digitally focused marketing solutions company operating in more than 75 mid-sized markets across some 25 states. Its local media operations range from large daily newspapers and the associated digital products such as the St. Louis Post-Dispatch and The Buffalo News to non-daily newspapers with news websites and digital platforms serving smaller communities. Lee also offers services including a full service digital marketing agency in Amplified Digital Agency as well as one of the largest web-hosting and content management services providers in North America through their majority-owned subsidiary Town-News. The company's printed newspapers reach almost 1.2 million households daily.

Operations
The company's local media operations generate revenue through advertising (print and digital) digital marketing services subscriptions and digital services primarily through TownNews.

Advertising and Marketing Services accounts nearly 50% of revenue that was derived from advertising and marketing services: Local retail (top local accounts and Small to Medium Businesses); Classified (major categories of employment real estate automotive obituaries and legal notices); National (print or digital display advertising space preprinted advertising and national accounts); Niche publications (specialty publications such as lifestyle business health orhome improvement); and Marketing services (events contests and digital promotions).

Subscription Revenue produces over 40% of total sales that was derived from full access subscription model whereby subscribers receive complete access to its content in all platforms including print and digital and from digital-only subscriptions. Lee also generates revenue from the sale of single copy editions.

Digital Services generates less than 5% of the company's revenue most of which is revenue from TownNews that operates through owned subsidiary (INN Partners).

Lee operations also provide commercial printing distribution of third party publications and management services to other local media operations.

Geographic Reach
Iowa-based Lee has a property leased for Madison Wisconsin (which is owned by MNI) and Tucson Arizona (which is jointly owned by Star Publishing and Citizen).

Sales and Marketing
The company's sales force uses a multi-platform sales approach that maximizes audience reach for

HOOVER'S HANDBOOK OF EMERGING COMPANIES 2022

their advertisers by tailoring advertising and marketing services packages based on the size and scale of the advertiser. Through Amplified Lee creates sophisticated digital campaigns on their owned and operated sites and on third party inventory that give advertisers the ability to target their message. The company partners with Google to provide key metrics and analytics to measure campaign effectiveness.

Financial Performance

Total operating revenue totaled $618 million in 2020 or 21% compared to 2019. Total operating revenue increased primarily due to acquired revenue of $203 million.

Net loss was $1.3 million in 2020 compared to net income of $15.9 million in 2019. The decrease in net income is predominately due to a reduction in operating income.

Cash held by the company at the end of 2020 was $33.7 million higher by $25.1 million compared to the prior year. Cash provided by operations was $49.9 million while investing activities used $118.2 million primarily for acquisitions. Cash generated by financing activities was $93.4 million.

Strategy

Lee's focus is on the local market - including local news and information local advertising and marketing services to top local accounts and SMBs and digital services to local content curators. To align with the core strength of their company their post-pandemic operating strategy is locally focused around three pillars.

To align with customer expectations the company will transform the way they present local news and information and provide perspective both in digital and print. The company seeks to maintain its position as the leading provider of news and information by providing best-in-class digital experiences to improve consumer engagement and grow its audiences. Lee aims to achieve this by delivering relevant useful and engaging content to the consumer using a multi-media approach with heavy emphases on video and audio.

Lee Enterprises will transform their print-centric audience model into a robust digital subscription model. In 2021 the company expects to use data and analytics combined with metering technology to drive its acquisition and retention tactics. This allows them to maximize meter stop rates and paid subscription conversion rates in order to drive consumers down the conversion funnel. Their primary acquisition tactics include sophisticated data-mining techniques leveraging both online and offline consumer behaviors to target full access and digital-only subscription offers.

The company will diversify and transform the services and products they offer advertisers especially for top local accounts and SMB's.

Mergers and Acquisitions

In 2020 Lee Enterprises completed the acquisition of BH Media Group Inc. (BH Media) and The Buffalo News Inc. (Buffalo News) The acquisition nearly doubled Lee's audience size and added 30 daily newspapers more than 49 paid weekly publications with digital sites and 32 other print products from BHMG as well as The Buffalo News to Lee's portfolio of high-quality local publications. Lee's portfolio is now comprised of 77 publications in 77 communities.

Company Background

Lee was founded in 1890 in Iowa by A.W. Lee. Most of thier papers trace their beginnings to the mid-1800s. Among thier alumni teenage Sam Clemens wrote for the Muscatine Journal in Iowa before becoming world-renowned as Mark Twain. A reporter from the company's newspaper in Bismarck North Dakota died with George Custer at the Battle of the Little Big Horn. In 1973 their newspaper in Davenport Iowa became the first in the world to be produced totally by computer.

HISTORY

Alfred Lee began buying up newspapers in the Midwest in 1890 beginning with the Ottumwa Daily Courier (Iowa). His strategy was simple: Find a newspaper with potential and let a good manager run it without interference. Lee died in 1907 leaving one of those managers E. P. Adler to run the company. Adler continued building the company and in 1937 bought a radio station in Iowa (later sold). The company formed Madison Newspapers a jointly owned venture with The Capital Times Co. in 1948. Adler died in 1949 and Lee Loomis a nephew of Alfred Lee took over.

Loomis expanded the company into TV broadcasting in 1953 and bought six Montana newspapers in 1960. That year the company was consolidated as Lee Enterprises Incorporated. Loomis later retired and Philip Adler (son of E. P.) took charge. He brought Lee public in 1969 raising money for acquisitions. When Adler retired the next year David Gottlieb (a distant relative) took control. The company had newspapers and radio and TV stations in 10 states.

In 1972 Lee began to produce advanced printing plates through a joint venture NAPP Systems. (It bought out its partner in 1990 and sold the business in 1997.) Gottlieb died of a heart attack in 1973 and Lloyd Schermer (related to Gottlieb by marriage) became president. Under his leadership the company acquired TV stations in western states during the 1980s. Schermer was elevated to chairman in 1986. By 1990 Lee had 19 newspapers and six stations in 13 states. Schermer stepped down as CEO in 1991 and was replaced by Richard Gottlieb son of David Gottlieb. (Richard Gottlieb took the chairman title in 2000.)

In 1997 Lee acquired Pacific Northwest Publishing Group from Walt Disney which gave it 24 publications mainly in the Northwest. In 1999 the company bought the Ravalli Republic a daily in Montana. It also traded the Daily Sun in Nebraska and some cash for two dailies and two weeklies.

In 2000 it bought three more dailies — Columbus Telegram and Fremont Tribune in Nebraska and Chippewa Herald in Wisconsin — as well as 15 other publications. To focus on its core operations the company sold its TV stations to Emmis Communications for about $560 million. Gottlieb stepped down as CEO in 2001 and was replaced by Mary Junck. She added chairman to her title in 2002 when Gottlieb retired. Also in 2002 the company sold off five specialty publications in the western US.

Lee purchased 16 daily newspaper titles from Howard Publications for $694 million in 2002. Its 50%-owned Madison Newspapers unit bought several publications in 2002 including a daily newspaper in Beaver Dam Wisconsin. The company picked up Iowa's Sioux City Journal daily newspaper later that year. It also sold two publications to Ottaway Newspapers (later Dow Jones Local Media Group) a subsidiary of Dow Jones & Company.

In 2004 the company exchanged its daily newspapers in Freeport Illinois and Corning New York and about $2 million in cash for Liberty Group Publishing's two daily newspapers in Burley Idaho and Elko Nevada and eight weekly and specialty publications.

Lee took a major step to expand its business the following year when it acquired newspaper rival Pulitzer for about $1.4 billion. The deal included such papers as the St. Louis Post Dispatch and boosted the company's overall circulation by more than 50%.

Lee agreed to sell its Wisconsin daily The Daily News in Rhinelander as well as jointly-owned paper Shawano Leader to BlueLine Media Holdings for $2.2 million in 2006. That same year it inked a pact with Yahoo! to sell job listings on the online giant's HotJobs employment portal. (HotJobs was eventually sold to industry leader Monster.com in 2010.)

As readership and advertising revenue continued to decline the company began reducing staff at many of its papers in an effort to cut costs. It also shuttered the print edition of The Capital Times owned by Madison Newspapers during 2008 due to increasing losses.

Lee also worked to boost revenue through new technologies and investments in its online operations. The company launched a system of targeting online ads based on audience behavior during 2009 in an effort to attract new advertisers to its Internet properties.

The company filed for bankruptcy in 2011.

EXECUTIVES

Independent Director, Richard Cole
Chairman, Mary Junck
President, Chief Executive Officer And Director, Kevin Mowbray, $837,692 total compensation
Independent Director, Gregory Schermer
Independent Director, William Mayer
Lead Independent Director, Herbert Moloney
Vice President, Audience Development, Suzanna Frank
Vice President, Information Technology And Chief Information Officer, Michele White, $325,000 total compensation
Vice President - Production Operations, Douglas Ranes
Operating Vice President And Vice President, Advertising, Ray Farris, $456,077 total compensation
Vice President, News And Chief Content Officer, John Humenik, $335,000 total compensation
Operating Vice President And Vice President, Consumer Sales And Marketing, Nathan Bekke, $385,000 total compensation
Vice President, Chief Financial Officer And Treasurer, Timothy Millage, $390,000 total compensation
Independent Director, Margaret Liberman
Vice President, Local Advertising, Joseph Battistoni
Independent Director, Steven Fletcher
Independent Director, David Pearson
Vice President - Brand, Alexa Wilson
Independent Director, Brent Magid
Vice President, Digital, James Green, $340,000 total compensation
Vice President, Human Resources And Legal, Astrid Garcia
Auditors: BDO USA LLP

LOCATIONS

HQ: Lee Enterprises, Inc.
4600 E. 53rd Street, Davenport, IA 52807
Phone: 563 383-2100

PRODUCTS/OPERATIONS

2016 Sales

	$ mil.	% of total
Advertising and marketing services revenue		
Retail	239.1	39
Classified	100.6	16
National	22.1	4
Niche publications and other	11.6	2
Subscription	194.0	32
Digital services	14.2	2
Commercial printing	12.3	2
Other	20.4	3
Total	**614.3**	**100**

Selected Operations

Daily newspapers
 Arizona Daily Star (Tucson)
 Billings Gazette (Montana)
 The Bismarck Tribune (North Dakota)
 Casper Star-Tribune (Wyoming)
 The Courier (Waterloo IA)
 The Daily Herald (Provo UT)
 Herald & Review (Decatur IL)
 The Journal Times (Racine WI)
 La Crosse Tribune (Wisconsin)
 Lincoln Journal Star (Nebraska)
 Missoulian (Missoula MT)
 The Pantagraph (Bloomington IL)
 The Post-Star (Glens Falls NY)
 Quad-City Times (Davenport IA)
 Rapid City Journal (South Dakota)
 Sioux City Journal (Iowa)
 St. Louis Post Dispatch
 The Times (Munster IN)
 Wisconsin State Journal (50% Madison)
Commercial printing
 Farcountry Press (Helena MT)
 Hawkeye Printing and Trico Communications
 (Davenport IA)
 Journal Star Commercial Printing (Lincoln NE)
 Plaindealer Publishing (Tekamah NE)
 Platen Press (Butte MT)
 Selma Enterprises (Selma CA)
 William Street Press (Decatur IL)
 Wingra Printing (50%; Madison WI)

COMPETITORS

DOW JONES & COMPANY INC.
GANNETT CO. INC.
GANNETT MEDIA CORP.
HAWKEYE ACQUISITION INC.
JOURNAL REGISTER COMPANY
RENTPATH LLC
THE INTERPUBLIC GROUP OF COMPANIES INC.
TRIBUNE PUBLISHING COMPANY
VALASSIS COMMUNICATIONS INC.

HISTORICAL FINANCIALS

Company Type: Public

Income Statement				FYE: September 26
	REVENUE ($ mil.)	NET INCOME ($ mil.)	NET PROFIT MARGIN	EMPLOYEES
09/21	794.6	22.7	2.9%	5,130
09/20	618.0	(3.1)	—	5,613
09/19	509.8	14.2	2.8%	2,954
09/18	543.9	45.7	8.4%	3,241
09/17	566.9	27.4	4.8%	3,555
Annual Growth	**8.8%**	**(4.6%)**	**—**	**9.6%**

2021 Year-End Financials

Debt ratio: 57.2%	No. of shares (mil.): 5.8
Return on equity: 198.6%	Dividends
Cash ($ mil.): 26.1	Yield: —
Current ratio: 0.77	Payout: —
Long-term debt ($ mil.): 476.5	Market value ($ mil.): 140.0

	STOCK PRICE ($) FY Close	P/E High/Low		PER SHARE ($) Earnings	Dividends	Book Value
09/21	23.74	9	0	3.91	0.00	9.27
09/20	0.82	—	—	(0.50)	0.00	(5.41)
09/19	2.01	1	1	2.50	0.00	(6.68)
09/18	2.65	0	0	8.20	0.00	(6.54)
09/17	2.10	1	0	5.00	0.00	(16.26)
Annual Growth	**83.4%**	—	—	**(6.0%)**		

Legacy Housing Corp

Auditors: Weaver and Tidwell, LLP

LOCATIONS

HQ: Legacy Housing Corp
1600 Airport Freeway, #100, Bedford, TX 76022
Phone: 817 799-4900
Web: www.legacyhousingcorp.com

HISTORICAL FINANCIALS

Company Type: Public

Income Statement				FYE: December 31
	REVENUE ($ mil.)	NET INCOME ($ mil.)	NET PROFIT MARGIN	EMPLOYEES
12/20	176.7	38.0	21.5%	870
12/19	168.9	28.8	17.1%	800
12/18	161.8	21.5	13.3%	800
12/17	128.7	26.3	20.5%	800
12/16	110.5	17.3	15.7%	0
Annual Growth	**12.4%**	**21.7%**	**—**	**—**

2020 Year-End Financials

Debt ratio: 10.6%	No. of shares (mil.): 24.1
Return on equity: 15.7%	Dividends
Cash ($ mil.): 0.7	Yield: —
Current ratio: 1.51	Payout: —
Long-term debt ($ mil.): 36.1	Market value ($ mil.): 366.0

	STOCK PRICE ($) FY Close	P/E High/Low		PER SHARE ($) Earnings	Dividends	Book Value
12/20	15.11	11	5	1.57	0.00	10.71
12/19	16.64	15	8	1.18	0.00	9.14
12/18	11.93	11	10	1.07	0.00	7.89
Annual Growth	**12.5%**	—	—	**21.1%**	**—**	**16.5%**

LeMaitre Vascular Inc

LeMaitre Vascular makes both disposable and implanted surgical vascular devices including catheters and stents under such brands as AnastoClip and Pruitt-Inahara. Originally founded by a vascular surgeon to develop a valvulotome to prepare veins for arterial bypass surgery the company has since expanded its offerings to include a device to create dialysis access sites and another to treat aortic aneurysms. Le Maitre sells about 15 product lines most of which are used in open vascular surgery and some of which are used in endovascular procedures. Its US operation accounts for the highest geographic market.

Operations

LeMaitre has about 15 product offerings include seven that are biologic implants and one that is a service of processing and cryopreserving human tissue for implantation. These offerings include the XenoSure patch (bovine pericardium) CardioCel and VascuCel patches (bovine pericardium) ProCol graft (bovine mesenteric vein) Artegraft (bovine carotid artery) Omniflow II biosynthetic graft (ovine tissue and synthetic mesh) surgical glue (porcine gelatin) and the RestoreFlow Allograft cryopreserved graft (human cadaver tissue). These biologic product lines represented some 45% of its sales.

Geographic Reach

LeMaitre's worldwide headquarters is located in Burlington Massachusetts and it also has North American sales offices in Chandler Arizona and Vaughan Canada. It European headquarters is located in Sulzbach Germany with additional European sales offices in Milan Italy; Madrid Spain; and Hereford England. The Asia/Pacific Rim headquarters is located in Singapore with additional Asia/Pacific Rim sales offices in Tokyo Japan; Shanghai China; and Kensington Australia.

Americas region accounts for nearly 65% of sales followed by EMEA region which accounts for about 30% and the remaining accounts for Asia and Pacific region.

Sales and Marketing

LeMaitre sells its products and services through a direct sales force comprising of about 80 sales representatives in North America and Europe/Asia Pacific including two export managers. Outside its direct markets it generally sells its products through country-specific distributors such as South Korea Russia and Brazil.

In addition the company engage in direct marketing efforts including direct mail and exhibitions at medical congresses which were believe are important to its brand development.

Approximately 95% of its net sales were generated through its direct-to-hospital sales force.

The company advertising cost for the years ended 2020 2019 and 2018 were approximately $0.2 million $0.3 million and 0.3 million respectively.

Financial Performance

Net sales increased 10% or $12.1 million to $129.4 million for the year ended December 31 2020 compared to $117.2 million for the year ended December 31 2019. The increase was largely from recently acquired products including Artegraft bovine grafts of $10.8 million and CardioCel bovine cardiac patches of $5.3 million.

Net income for fiscal 2020 increased to $21.2 million compared from the prior year with $17.9 million.

Cash held by the company at the end of fiscal 2020 increased to $26.8 million. Cash provided by operations and financing activities were $34.8 million and $32.2 million respectively. Cash used for investing was $52.9 million mainly for payments related to acquisitions.

Strategy

LeMaitre has grown its business by using a three-pronged strategy: focusing on the vascular surgeon call point competing for sales in low rivalry niche markets and expanding its growth platform through its worldwide direct sales force as well as acquiring and developing complementary vascular devices.

Focused call point. The company have historically directed its product offering and selling efforts towards the vascular surgeon and estimate that in 2020 approximately 80% of the company's sales were to hospitals for use by vascular surgeons. As vascular surgeons are typically positioned to perform both open vascular surgeries and endovascular procedures the company sells devices in both the open and endovascular markets to the same end user. More recently LeMaitre have begun to explore adjacent market customers or non-vascular surgeon customers who can be served by its vascular device technologies such as cardiac surgeons and neurosurgeons.

Low rivalry niche segments. The company seeks to build and maintain leading positions in niche product and services segments which LeMaitre defines as under $200 million in annual worldwide revenue. The company believes that the relative lack of competitive focus on these segments by larger competitors as well as the differentiated features and consistent quality of its products enable higher selling prices and market share gains.

Direct sales force expansion and the addition of complementary products through acquisitions and to a lesser extent research and development. The company sells its products primarily through a direct sales force in North America Europe and Asia/Pacific Rim. Since 1998 the company has built its sales force from zero to 80 direct sales representatives including two export managers.

Mergers and Acquisitions

In 2020 LeMaitre has acquired the business and assets of Artegraft Inc. for approximately $90.0 million as well as potential earnout payments of $17.5 million payable based upon future sales of the acquired business. Under the terms of the deal LeMaitre will continue to operate Artegraft's manufacturing facility in North Brunswick NJ for at least three and a half years and will retain most of Artegraft's employees including seven sales & marketing personnel.

Company Background

LeMaitre was founded in 1983 by vascular surgeon George D. LeMaitre to develop a valvulotome to prepare veins for arterial bypass surgery.

In 2006 LeMaitre Vascular raised more than $30 million from its initial public offering. The company spent part of the proceeds to pay off debt; it also used proceeds toward its goals of increasing research and development efforts hiring new sales representatives and acquiring complementary products or businesses.

EXECUTIVES

Vice President - Research And Development, Ryan Connelly

Director - Human Resources, Daniel Mumford

Director - Sales, Central Europe, Ina Leininger

President, Director, David Roberts, $303,357 total compensation

Senior Vice President - Operations, Trent Kamke, $210,048 total compensation

Vice President - Information Technology, Jonathan Ngau

Vice President - Marketing, Kimberly Cieslak

Independent Director, John O'Connor

Vice President - Quality Affairs, Roli Kumar-Choudhury

Senior Vice President - Clinical, Regulatory, Quality Affairs, Andrew Hodgkinson

Vice President - Sales, The Americas, Chance Kriesel

Vice President - Asia-pac, Jacob Petersen

Senior Vice President - Emea Operations, Stephane Maier

Vice President - Sales, Southern Europe, Giovannella Deiure

Chief Financial Officer, Director, Joseph Pellegrino, $270,403 total compensation

Independent Director, John Roush

Senior Vice President, General Counsel, Laurie Churchill

Vice President - Production And Supply Chain, James Russell

Vice President - Regulatory Affairs, Xiang Zhang

Country Manager - Canada, Christopher Minnett

Independent Director, Bridget Ross

Director - Sales, Northern Europe, Helen Goulding

Auditors: Grant Thornton LLP

LOCATIONS

HQ: LeMaitre Vascular Inc
63 Second Avenue, Burlington, MA 01803
Phone: 781 221-2266
Web: www.lemaitre.com

PRODUCTS/OPERATIONS

Selected Products

Vascular
  Balloon catheters (for removing blood clots; occlusion and facilitation of blood flow)
  Carotid shunts (facilitation of blood flow to brain during carotid plaque removal)
  Remote endarterectomy devices (for removing blockages in major arteries in the leg)
  Valvulotomes (destroys vein valves to create vein bypass grafts)
  Vascular grafts (synthetic vessels used in bypass and replacement procedures)
  Vascular patches (synthetic and biological patches used in closing incisions in a blood vessel)
  Vein strippers (single-incision removal of varicose veins)
  Vessel closure systems (attachment of blood vessels mainly for dialysis access)

Endovascular
  Aortic stent grafts (endovascular repair of abdominal and thoracic aortic aneurysms and thoracic dissections; in clinical studies)
  Manual contrast injectors (contrast media injection into blood vessels)
  Modeling catheters (for improved sealing of aortic stent grafts; application submitted)
  Radiopaque tape (for improved precision of vascular and endovascular procedures)

General surgery
  Laparoscopic cholecystectomy devices (for introducing dye into the cystic duct and related uses)

COMPETITORS

ARTIVION INC.	NANOSTRING
ATRICURE INC.	TECHNOLOGIES INC.
BOSTON SCIENTIFIC	NUVASIVE INC.
CORPORATION	PHILIPS IMAGE GUIDED
CARDIOVASCULAR SYSTEMS	THERAPY
CORPORATION	
INC.	SPECTRANETICS LLC
ESCALON MEDICAL CORP.	STAAR SURGICAL
COMPANY	
HAEMONETICS	TRIVASCULAR
CORPORATION	TECHNOLOGIES INC.

HOLOGIC INC.	UNITED THERAPEUTICS
MASIMO CORPORATION	CORPORATION
MERIT MEDICAL SYSTEMS	ZIMMER BIOMET
HOLDINGS	
INC.	INC.

HISTORICAL FINANCIALS
Company Type: Public

Income Statement
FYE: December 31

	REVENUE ($ mil.)	NET INCOME ($ mil.)	NET PROFIT MARGIN	EMPLOYEES
12/20	129.3	21.2	16.4%	403
12/19	117.2	17.9	15.3%	479
12/18	105.5	22.9	21.7%	483
12/17	100.8	17.1	17.0%	423
12/16	89.1	10.5	11.9%	397
Annual Growth	9.8%	19.0%	—	0.4%

2020 Year-End Financials

Debt ratio: 15.0%
Return on equity: 13.2%
Cash ($ mil.): 26.7
Current ratio: 3.75
Long-term debt ($ mil.): 35.5

No. of shares (mil.): 20.5
Dividends
  Yield: 0.9%
  Payout: 41.3%
Market value ($ mil.): 831.0

	STOCK PRICE ($) FY Close	P/E High/Low	PER SHARE ($) Earnings	Dividends	Book Value
12/20	40.50	39 20	1.04	0.38	8.41
12/19	35.95	40 25	0.88	0.34	7.35
12/18	23.64	35 19	1.13	0.28	6.64
12/17	31.84	43 24	0.86	0.22	5.70
12/16	25.34	45 22	0.55	0.18	4.71
Annual Growth	12.4%	— —	17.3%	20.5%	15.6%

Leslie's Inc

LOCATIONS

HQ: Leslie's Inc
2005 East Indian School Road, Phoenix, AZ 85016
Phone: 602 366-3999
Web: www.lesliespool.com

HISTORICAL FINANCIALS
Company Type: Public

Income Statement
FYE: October 2

	REVENUE ($ mil.)	NET INCOME ($ mil.)	NET PROFIT MARGIN	EMPLOYEES
10/21	1,342.9	126.6	9.4%	3,700
10/20*	1,112.2	58.5	5.3%	3,700
09/19	928.2	0.7	0.1%	5,081
09/18	892.6	17.1	1.9%	0
Annual Growth	14.6%	94.8%	—	—

*Fiscal year change

2021 Year-End Financials

Debt ratio: 76.0%
Return on equity: ***,***.*%
Cash ($ mil.): 345.0
Current ratio: 1.94
Long-term debt ($ mil.): 786.1

No. of shares (mil.): 189.8
Dividends
  Yield: —
  Payout: —
Market value ($ mil.): 3,908.0

STOCK PRICE ($)		P/E	PER SHARE ($)		
	FY Close	High/Low	Earnings	Dividends	Book Value
10/21	20.59	46 29	0.67	0.00	(1.15)
10/20*	0.00	— —	0.37	0.00	(5.28)
Annual Growth	—	— —	81.1%	—	—

*Fiscal year change

Level One Bancorp Inc

Auditors: Plante & Moran, PLLC

LOCATIONS

HQ: Level One Bancorp Inc
32991 Hamilton Court, Farmington Hills, MI 48334
Phone: 248 737-0300
Web: www.levelonebank.com

HISTORICAL FINANCIALS

Company Type: Public

Income Statement   FYE: December 31

	ASSETS ($ mil.)	NET INCOME ($ mil.)	INCOME AS % OF ASSETS	EMPLOYEES
12/20	2,442.9	20.4	0.8%	282
12/19	1,584.9	16.1	1.0%	253
12/18	1,416.2	14.3	1.0%	251
12/17	1,301.2	9.8	0.8%	235
12/16	1,127.5	11.0	1.0%	0
Annual Growth	21.3%	16.6%	—	—

2020 Year-End Financials

Return on assets: 1.0%
Return on equity: 10.5%
Long-term debt ($ mil.): —
No. of shares (mil.): 7.6
Sales ($ mil): 112.3
Dividends
  Yield: 0.9%
  Payout: 9.3%
Market value ($ mil.): 154.0

STOCK PRICE ($)		P/E	PER SHARE ($)		
	FY Close	High/Low	Earnings	Dividends	Book Value
12/20	20.23	10 6	2.57	0.20	28.21
12/19	25.16	13 11	2.05	0.16	22.12
12/18	22.43	15 11	1.91	0.09	19.58
Annual Growth	(5.0%)	— —	16.0%	49.1%	20.0%

LGI Homes, Inc.

LGI Homes is engaged in the design construction and sale of new homes in markets in West Northwest Central Midwest Florida Southeast and Mid-Atlantic. Its product offerings include entry-level homes including both detached and attached homes and move-up homes which are sold under its LGI Homes brand and its luxury series homes which are sold under its Terrata Homes brand. Its homes were priced between $140000 and $700000 and ranged from 1000 to 4500 sq. ft. The builder's higher-quality Terrata Homes started at average sales price of $418000 home. LGI

Homes has constructed and closed over 45000 homes since its founding in 2003.

EXECUTIVES

Chief Marketing Officer, Rachel Eaton, $355,000 total compensation
Lead Independent Director, Bryan Sansbury
Executive Vice President - Acquisitions, Jack Lipar, $335,000 total compensation
Independent Director, Ryan Edone
Independent Director, Robert Vahradian
General Counsel And Corporate Secretary, Scott Garber
Independent Director, Shailee Parikh
Independent Director, Maria Sharpe
Chief Financial Officer, Treasurer, Charles Merdian, $515,000 total compensation
Chairman Of The Board, Chief Executive Officer, Eric Lipar, $850,000 total compensation
President, Chief Operating Officer, Michael Snider, $625,000 total compensation
Auditors: Ernst & Young LLP

LOCATIONS

HQ: LGI Homes, Inc.
1450 Lake Robbins Drive, Suite 430, The Woodlands, TX 77380
Phone: 281 362-8998
Web: www.lgihomes.com

COMPETITORS

CALATLANTIC GROUP INC. CORPORATION	LENDLEASE
D.R. HORTON INC.	LIMITED
DAIWA HOUSE INDUSTRY DEVELOPMENT CO. LTD.	LLANMOOR CO. LIMITED
GALLIERS HOMES LIMITED LTD.	SEKISUI HOUSE
HUNT BUILDING COMPANY HOMES LTD	WILLIAM LYON
INSTALLED BUILDING PRODUCTS INC.	

HISTORICAL FINANCIALS

Company Type: Public

Income Statement   FYE: December 31

	REVENUE ($ mil.)	NET INCOME ($ mil.)	NET PROFIT MARGIN	EMPLOYEES
12/21	3,050.1	429.6	14.1%	952
12/20	2,367.9	323.9	13.7%	938
12/19	1,838.1	178.6	9.7%	953
12/18	1,504.4	155.2	10.3%	857
12/17	1,257.9	113.3	9.0%	726
Annual Growth	24.8%	39.5%	—	7.0%

2021 Year-End Financials

Debt ratio: 34.2%
Return on equity: 33.9%
Cash ($ mil.): 50.5
Current ratio: 15.37
Long-term debt ($ mil.): 805.2
No. of shares (mil.): 23.9
Dividends
  Yield: —
  Payout: —
Market value ($ mil.): 3,695.0

STOCK PRICE ($)		P/E	PER SHARE ($)		
	FY Close	High/Low	Earnings	Dividends	Book Value
12/21	154.48	11 6	17.25	0.00	58.36
12/20	105.85	10 3	12.76	0.00	45.59
12/19	70.65	11 6	7.02	0.00	33.33
12/18	45.22	11 5	6.24	0.00	28.89
12/17	75.03	15 5	4.73	0.00	22.42
Annual Growth	19.8%	— —	38.2%	—	27.0%

LHC Group Inc

LHC Group administers post-acute health care services through more than 825 home nursing agencies hospices and long-term acute care hospitals (LTACH) in about 35 US states and the District of Columbia ? reaching 60% of the US population aged 65 and older. LHC's home health nursing agencies provide care to Medicare beneficiaries offering such services as private duty nursing physical therapy and medically-oriented social services. Its hospices provide palliative care for terminal patients while its LTACHs serve patients who no longer need intensive care but still require complex care in a hospital setting.

Operations

LHC Group services are classified into five segments: home health services hospice services home and community-based services (HCBS) facility-based services primarily offered through its long-term acute care hospitals (LTACHs) and healthcare innovations (HCI).

Home health service (more than 70% of revenue) offers a wide range of services including skilled nursing medically-oriented social services and physical occupational and speech therapy.

Hospices (more than 10%) provide end-of-life care to patients with terminal illnesses through interdisciplinary teams of physicians nurses home health aides counselors and volunteers. It offers a wide range of services including pain and symptom management emotional and spiritual support in-patient and respite care homemaker services and counseling.

HCBS (about 10%) offer assistance with activities of daily living to elderly chronically ill and disabled patients performed by skilled nursing and paraprofessional personnel.

LTACH (about 5%) provide services primarily to patients with complex medical conditions who have transitioned out of a hospital intensive care unit but whose conditions remain too severe for treatment in a non-acute setting.

HCI segment reports on developmental activities outside its other business segments. The HCI segment includes Imperium Health Management LLC an Accountable Care Organization (ACO) enablement and management company; Long Term Solutions Inc. an in-home assessment company serving the long-term care insurance industry and certain assets operated by Advance Care House Calls which provides primary medical care for patients with chronic and acute illnesses who have difficulty traveling to a doctor's office.

HOOVER'S HANDBOOK OF EMERGING COMPANIES 2022

251

Geographic Reach

Louisiana-based LHC Group has more than 825 service provider locations in about 35 states in the US.

Financial Performance

The company's revenue for fiscal 2020 decreased to $2.06 billion compared to the prior year with $2.08 billion.

Net income for fiscal 2020 increased by 21% to $137.9 million compared from 2019 with $113.9 million.

Cash held by the company at the end of fiscal 2020 increased to $286.6 million. Cash provided by operations was $529.2 million while cash used for investing and financing activities were $82.5 million and $191.9 million respectively. Main uses of cash were purchases of property building and equipment; and payments on line of credit.

Strategy

LHC Group's objective is to become the leading provider of in-home healthcare services in the United States while also providing a complementary suite of other post-acute healthcare service offerings through its facility-based and HCI segments. To achieve this objective the company intends to: drive internal growth in existing markets; achieve margin improvement through the active management of costs; expand into new markets; and pursue strategic acquisitions and develop joint ventures.

The company intends to drive internal growth in its current markets by increasing the number of (health care) providers from whom it receives referrals and by expanding the breadth of its services in each market. LHC intends to achieve this growth by continuing to educate health care providers about the benefits of its services reinforcing the position of the company's agencies and facilities as community assets maintaining its emphasis on high-quality medical care for its patients identifying related products and services needed by its patients and their communities and providing a superior work environment for the company's employees.

Mergers and Acquisitions

In 2020 LHC Group acquired the majority-ownership of thirteen home health agencies six hospice agencies four home and community-based agencies and one physician practice. The total aggregate purchase price for these transactions was $42.1 million. The purchase prices were determined based on the Company's analysis of comparable acquisitions and the target market's potential future cash flows.

Company Background

LHC Group was founded in 1994 as a single home health agency in small-town America with a mission to serve the neediest and most vulnerable members of the community.

EXECUTIVES

Chairman, Chief Executive Officer And Director, Keith Myers, $996,000 total compensation
Independent Director, John Indest
Independent Director, Monica Azare
President, Joshua Proffitt, $663,000 total compensation
Independent Director, W. Earl Reed
Independent Director, Jonathan Goldberg
Lead Independent Director, Clifford Holtz
Executive Vice President, Chief Strategy And Innovation Officer, Bruce Greenstein, $540,750 total compensation
Independent Director, W. Brent Turner

Independent Director, Teri Fontenot
Executive Vice President, General Counsel, Nicholas Gachassin, $400,000 total compensation
Chief Financial Officer, Executive Vice President, Treasurer, Dale Mackel, $83,333 total compensation
Auditors: KPMG LLP

LOCATIONS

HQ: LHC Group Inc
   901 Hugh Wallis Road South, Lafayette, LA 70508
Phone: 337 233-1307   **Fax:** 337 235-8037
Web: www.lhcgroup.com

PRODUCTS/OPERATIONS

2018 Sales

	$ mil.	% of total
Home health	1,291.5	71
Hospice	199.1	11
Home and community-based	172.5	10
Facility-based	113.8	6
Healthcare innovations	33.1	2
Total	**1,810.0**	**100**

COMPETITORS

ALMOST FAMILY INC.	GENTIVA HEALTH
APRIA HEALTHCARE GROUP	SERVICES INC.
LLC	PHARMERICA
CORPORATION	
ENCOMPASS HEALTH	TIVITY HEALTH INC.
CORPORATION	VISITING NURSE SERVICE
GENESIS HEALTHCARE	OF NEW YORK
INC.	

HISTORICAL FINANCIALS

Company Type: Public

Income Statement
FYE: December 31

	REVENUE ($ mil.)	NET INCOME ($ mil.)	NET PROFIT MARGIN	EMPLOYEES
12/20	2,063.2	111.6	5.4%	27,959
12/19	2,080.2	95.7	4.6%	30,399
12/18	1,809.9	63.5	3.5%	30,985
12/17	1,072.0	50.1	4.7%	14,554
12/16	914.8	36.5	4.0%	11,598
Annual Growth	**22.5%**	**32.2%**	**—**	**24.6%**

2020 Year-End Financials

Debt ratio: 4.5%	No. of shares (mil.): 31.1
Return on equity: 7.5%	Dividends
Cash ($ mil.): 286.5	Yield: —
Current ratio: 0.95	Payout: —
Long-term debt ($ mil.): 20.0	Market value ($ mil.): 6,643.0

	STOCK PRICE ($) FY Close	P/E High/Low	Earnings	PER SHARE ($) Dividends	Book Value
12/20	213.32	64 29	3.56	0.00	49.09
12/19	137.76	44 29	3.07	0.00	45.60
12/18	93.88	45 26	2.29	0.00	42.93
12/17	61.25	25 16	2.79	0.00	25.29
12/16	45.70	22 16	2.07	0.00	22.45
Annual Growth	**47.0%**	**— —**	**14.5%**	**—**	**21.6%**

Liberty Broadband Corp

Auditors: KPMG LLP

LOCATIONS

HQ: Liberty Broadband Corp
   12300 Liberty Boulevard, Englewood, CO 80112
Phone: 720 875-5700
Web: www.libertybroadband.com

HISTORICAL FINANCIALS

Company Type: Public

Income Statement
FYE: December 31

	REVENUE ($ mil.)	NET INCOME ($ mil.)	NET PROFIT MARGIN	EMPLOYEES
12/20	50.7	397.6	784.2%	0
12/19	14.8	117.2	788.9%	0
12/18	22.2	69.9	314.3%	0
12/17	13.0	2,033.6	15533.7%	0
12/16	30.5	917.3	2999.1%	0
Annual Growth	**13.5%**	**(18.9%)**	**—**	**—**

2020 Year-End Financials

Debt ratio: 22.9%	No. of shares (mil.): 196.5
Return on equity: 3.2%	Dividends
Cash ($ mil.): 1,417.8	Yield: —
Current ratio: 3.02	Payout: —
Long-term debt ($ mil.): 4,878.0	Market value ($ mil.): 31,124.0

	STOCK PRICE ($) FY Close	P/E High/Low	Earnings	PER SHARE ($) Dividends	Book Value
12/20	158.37	76 42	2.17	0.00	68.71
12/19	125.75	193 112	0.64	0.00	58.65
12/18	72.03	248 176	0.38	0.00	58.44
12/17	85.16	9 7	11.10	0.00	57.84
12/16	74.07	12 7	6.00	0.00	46.62
Annual Growth	**20.9%**	**— —**	**(22.5%)**	**—**	**10.2%**

LICT Corp

LICT (formerly Lynch Interactive) is a holding company that operates through 12 small (mostly rural) local-exchange phone companies located primarily in the Midwestern and Western US; it also has a limited presence in the Northeast. The company provides local telephone service over nearly 60000 access lines while dial-up and broadband Internet service lines number about 50000. Subsidiaries include JBN Telephone Haviland Telephone and Giant Communications in Kansas; CentraCom Interactive in Utah; and Bretton Woods Telephone in New Hampshire. Chairman Mario Gabelli owns 24% of LICT.

EXECUTIVES

Director, Robert Dolan, $213,350 total compensation
Senior Vice President - Regulatory Dynamics, Evelyn Jerden, $244,467 total compensation

Independent Director, Salvatore Muoio
Chairman Of The Board, Chief Executive Officer,
 Mario Gabelli, $150,000 total compensation
Vice President - Finance, Stephen Moore
Independent Director, Avrum Gray
Corporate Controller, John Aoki
Independent Director, Salvatore Salibello
Chief Administrator, Secretary, Christina McEntee
Senior Vice President - Broadband Of Lict,
 Matthew Favre
Chief Operating Officer, Kevin Errity
Auditors: BDO USA, LLP

LOCATIONS

HQ: LICT Corp
 401 Theodore Fremd Avenue, Rye, NY 10580-1430
Phone: 914 921-8821 **Fax:** 914 921-6410
Web: www.lictcorp.com

COMPETITORS

BREDA TELEPHONE CORP.
E.N.M.R. TELEPHONE COOPERATIVE
FARMERS TELECOMMUNICATIONS COOPERATIVE
 INC.
HARGRAY TELEPHONE COMPANY INC.
HECTOR COMMUNICATIONS CORP
OTELCO INC.
PIONEER TELEPHONE COOPERATIVE INC.
TDS METROCOM INC.

HISTORICAL FINANCIALS
Company Type: Public

Income Statement FYE: December 31

	REVENUE ($ mil.)	NET INCOME ($ mil.)	NET PROFIT MARGIN	EMPLOYEES
12/20	124.1	37.2	30.0%	343
12/19	117.9	26.2	22.2%	338
12/18	115.8	25.7	22.3%	315
12/17	106.7	22.3	21.0%	206
12/16	90.7	7.2	8.0%	293
Annual Growth	8.2%	50.5%	—	4.0%

2020 Year-End Financials
Debt ratio: 22.2%
Return on equity: 22.1%
Cash ($ mil.): 67.3
Current ratio: 1.89
Long-term debt ($ mil.): 20.8
No. of shares (mil.): 0.0
Dividends
 Yield: —
 Payout: —
Market value ($ mil.): 330.0

	STOCK PRICE ($) FY Close	P/E High/Low		Earnings	PER SHARE ($) Dividends	Book Value
12/20	17,800.00 9,744.51	9		61,982.00	0.00	
12/19	18,000.00 8,043.83	15		111,342.00	0.00	
12/18	14,450.00 7,042.67	12		91,271.97	0.00	
12/17	11,650.00 5,960.15	12		51,063.80	0.00	
12/16	5,950.00 5,096.99	17	14	338.32	0.00	
Annual Growth	31.5%	—	—	55.6%	—	17.6%

Limbach Holdings Inc

Auditors: Crowe LLP

LOCATIONS

HQ: Limbach Holdings Inc
 1251 Waterfront Place, Suite 201, Pittsburgh, PA
 15222
Phone: 412 359-2100
Web: www.limbachinc.com

HISTORICAL FINANCIALS
Company Type: Public

Income Statement FYE: December 31

	REVENUE ($ mil.)	NET INCOME ($ mil.)	NET PROFIT MARGIN	EMPLOYEES
12/20	568.2	5.8	1.0%	1,700
12/19	553.3	(1.7)	—	1,900
12/18	546.5	(1.8)	—	1,700
12/17	485.7	0.7	0.1%	1,580
12/16	225.6	(0.7)	—	1,420
Annual Growth	26.0%	—	—	4.6%

2020 Year-End Financials
Debt ratio: 16.4%
Return on equity: 11.5%
Cash ($ mil.): 42.1
Current ratio: 1.33
Long-term debt ($ mil.): 36.5
No. of shares (mil.): 7.9
Dividends
 Yield: —
 Payout: —
Market value ($ mil.): 98.0

	STOCK PRICE ($) FY Close	P/E High/Low		Earnings	PER SHARE ($) Dividends	Book Value
12/20	12.33	18	3	0.72	0.00	6.78
12/19	3.78	—	—	(0.23)	0.00	6.10
12/18	3.68	—	—	(0.52)	0.00	6.11
12/17	13.83	—	—	(0.13)	0.00	7.48
12/16	14.10	—	—	(0.19)	0.00	7.76
Annual Growth	(3.3%)			—	—	(3.3%)

Limestone Bancorp Inc

Porter Bancorp could be a stout evaluator of what "ales" your finances. It is the holding company for PBI Bank which serves local residents and businesses through about 20 offices in Louisville and other portions of central Kentucky. The company also operates Ascencia a nationwide online banking platform. PBI Bank offers standard financial services such as checking savings and money market accounts certificates of deposit and trust services. Loans collateralized by real estate such as commercial mortgages (more than 35% of the company's loan portfolio) residential mortgages (more than 25%) and construction loans (approximately 20%) comprise the lion's share of the company's loan portfolio.

EXECUTIVES

Independent Director, Bradford Ray
Independent Director, Michael Levy
Chief Credit Officer Of Limestone Bank, John
 Davis, $258,542 total compensation
Executive Vice President Of Limestone Bank,
 Joseph Seiler, $248,483 total compensation
Independent Chairman Of The Board, W. Glenn
 Hogan
Independent Director, Celia Catlett
Independent Director, Kevin Kooman

**President, Chief Executive Officer And Director
Of Limestone Bancorp President, Chief
Executive Officer And Chairman Of The Board
Of Directors Of Limestone Bank,** John Taylor,
$431,021 total compensation
Independent Director, Edmond Seifried
**Chief Financial Officer Limestone Bancorp And
Limestone Bank,** Phillip Barnhouse, $248,483
total compensation
Auditors: Crowe LLP

LOCATIONS

HQ: Limestone Bancorp Inc
 2500 Eastpoint Parkway, Louisville, KY 40223
Phone: 502 499-4800
Web: www.limestonebank.com

COMPETITORS

ANNAPOLIS BANCORP INC.
CITIZENS HOLDING
 COMPANY
CLOVER COMMUNITY BANK
DNB FINANCIAL
 CORPORATION
FIRST UNITED
 CORPORATION
NATIONAL BANK OF
 ARIZONA
NB&T FINANCIAL GROUP
 INC.

HISTORICAL FINANCIALS
Company Type: Public

Income Statement FYE: December 31

	ASSETS ($ mil.)	NET INCOME ($ mil.)	INCOME AS % OF ASSETS	EMPLOYEES
12/20	1,312.3	9.0	0.7%	226
12/19	1,245.7	10.5	0.8%	251
12/18	1,069.6	8.7	0.8%	214
12/17	970.8	38.4	4.0%	217
12/16	945.1	(2.7)	—	238
Annual Growth	8.6%	—	—	(1.3%)

2020 Year-End Financials
Return on assets: 0.7%
Return on equity: 8.1%
Long-term debt ($ mil.): —
No. of shares (mil.): 7.5
Sales ($ mil): 57.6
Dividends
 Yield: —
 Payout: —
Market value ($ mil.): 94.0

	STOCK PRICE ($) FY Close	P/E High/Low		Earnings	PER SHARE ($) Dividends	Book Value
12/20	12.56	15	6	1.20	0.00	15.47
12/19	18.00	13	10	1.41	0.00	14.15
12/18	13.76	14	10	1.23	0.00	12.34
12/17	14.32	3	1	6.15	0.00	12.03
12/16	12.32	—	—	(0.46)	0.00	7.07
Annual Growth	0.5%			—	—	21.6%

Lincoln Educational Services Corp

Lincoln hopes its graduates are better " Abe -l" to get a career. Lincoln Educational Services provides vocational programs from schools including Lincoln Technical Institute and Nashville Auto-Diesel College. It offers programs in automotive technology and skilled trades (including HVAC and electronics). Some 14000 students are en-

HOOVER'S HANDBOOK OF EMERGING COMPANIES 2022 253

rolled at more than 30 campuses and five training sites more than 15 states throughout the US. Lincoln tends to grow by buying smaller schools and by opening campuses in new markets. It also expands its campus facilities to accommodate higher enrollment numbers. The company announced plans to divest its health care and other professions business in 2015.

Operations

All of Lincoln Educational Services schools offer diploma and certificate programs 22 of its schools are approved to offer associate's degree programs and three schools are approved to offer bachelor's degrees. The majority of its students pay for their educations with financial aid provided by the federal government. Indeed in 2011 Title IV loans represented 84% of the company's revenue.

Geographic Reach

Lincoln Educational Services operates 31 campuses in 15 states. Of those schools 16 are located in New Jersey Connecticut and Pennsylvania.

Financial Performance

Changes to regulations affecting for-profit schools like Lincoln have lead to declining enrollment in the last couple of years. In 2013 the company's revenue fell 14% as a result even though some fees were higher. Net loss also increased by $14 million to $51 million due to declining revenue and higher taxes. Cash from operations also decreased with $13 million going out leaving Lincoln with about $3 million in cash from operations.

Strategy

Expanding areas of study its facilities (including online options) and geographic presence are all part of Lincoln's growth strategy. For example in 2014 the company introduced a new Advanced Manufacturing diploma at campuses in Texas and Indiana with support from local manufacturing businesses. It also began partnering with high schools in New Jersey to offer introductory automotive technologies courses in conjunction with Chrysler and BMW.

Lincoln Educational Services' most popular areas of study are health sciences automotive and the skilled trades which combined account for more than 80% of total enrollment. Business and information technology and hospitality services also see their fair share of student interest. Keeping student interest up (and with it enrollment) is germane to Lincoln Educational Services' financial success. If enrollment drops income drops and the company suffers. In order to keep its curriculum fresh the company assesses future job trends and adds degrees and classes accordingly. But the company missed in its forecasting and stricter government rules about transparency around financial aid - both factors lead to sagging enrollment. Between 2011 and 2014 the number of Lincoln campuses fell from 46 to 31 after the company decided to close four locations in Ohio and one in Kentucky; overall enrollment went from 20000 to 13700.

EXECUTIVES

Independent Director, Michael Plater
Company Secretary, Alexandra Luster
Independent Director, Felecia Pryor
President, Chief Executive Officer And Director, Scott Shaw, $500,000 total compensation
Independent Chairman Of The Board, J. Barry Morrow
Independent Director, Celia Currin

Executive Vice President- Campus Operations, Stephen Buchenot, $304,387 total compensation
Chief Financial Officer, Executive Vice President, Treasurer, Brian Meyers, $358,955 total compensation
Independent Director, Ronald Harbour
Independent Director, James Burke
Independent Director, Kevin Carney
Independent Director, John Bartholdson
Independent Director, Carlton Rose
Auditors: DELOITTE & TOUCHE LLP

LOCATIONS

HQ: Lincoln Educational Services Corp
14 Sylvan Way, Suite A, Parsippany, NJ 07054
Phone: 973 736-9340
Web: www.lincolnedu.com

COMPETITORS

MIAMI DADE COLLEGE
MT SAN ANTONIO COMMUNITY COLLEGE DISTRICT
SALT LAKE COMMUNITY COLLEGE

HISTORICAL FINANCIALS

Company Type: Public

Income Statement

FYE: December 31

	REVENUE ($ mil.)	NET INCOME ($ mil.)	NET PROFIT MARGIN	EMPLOYEES
12/20	293.1	48.5	16.6%	1,933
12/19	273.3	2.0	0.7%	1,922
12/18	263.2	(6.5)	—	1,884
12/17	261.8	(11.4)	—	1,980
12/16	196.9	(28.3)	—	2,197
Annual Growth	10.5%	—	—	(3.1%)

2020 Year-End Financials

Debt ratio: 7.0%
Return on equity: 61.2%
Cash ($ mil.): 38.0
Current ratio: 1.11
Long-term debt ($ mil.): 15.2
No. of shares (mil.): 26.4
Dividends
Yield: —
Payout: —
Market value ($ mil.): 172.0

	STOCK PRICE ($) FY Close	P/E High/Low		Earnings	Dividends	Book Value
12/20	6.50	5	1	1.49	0.00	3.89
12/19	2.70	41	21	0.08	0.00	2.18
12/18	3.20	—	—	(0.27)	0.00	1.62
12/17	2.02	—	—	(0.48)	0.00	1.85
12/16	1.92	—	—	(1.21)	0.00	2.22
Annual Growth	35.6%	—	—	—	—	15.1%

Littelfuse Inc

Littelfuse is big on circuit protection. The company is one of the world's largest fuse makers. In addition to its fuses Littelfuse's other circuit protection devices include positive temperature coefficient devices that limit current when too much is being supplied and electrostatic discharge suppressors that redirect transient high voltage. The company's thyristors protect telecommunications circuits from transient voltage caused by lightning strikes. It also supplies fuses for HVAC systems elevators and machine tools. Littelfuse's 7000 cus-

tomers include distributors electronics manufacturers automakers and the automotive aftermarket.

Operations

Littelfuse operates through three business segments: Electronics Automotive and Industrial.

The Electronics segment offers fuses and fuse accessories semiconductor and power semiconductor products and insulated gate bipolar transistors technologies. It covers a broad range of end markets including industrial and automotive electronics electric vehicle infrastructure data and telecommunications medical devices LED lighting consumer electronics and appliances. Electronics account for two-thirds of sales.

The Automotive segment produces circuit protection power control and sensing products for Tier 1 auto manufacturers suppliers and parts distributors. Products include fuses and fuse accessories for combustion and electric engines such as blade fuses battery cable protectors resettable fuses and high current- and high-voltage fuses. Automotive sales account for nearly 30% of total revenue

The Industrial segment makes power fuses protection relays and controls and other circuit protection products for use in various industrial applications such as oil gas mining solar and wind energy electric vehicle infrastructure construction HVAC systems elevator and other industrial equipment. The segment accounts for 5% of sales.

Geographic Reach

Illinois-based Littelfuse operates in three geographic territories — the Americas Europe and Asia/Pacific — and has 65 manufacturing and distribution facilities in China Germany Italy Japan Lithuania Mexico the Netherlands Philippines South Korea Taiwan the UK and the US.

The Asia/Pacific region accounts for around 45% of sales (of which 25% comes from China) the Americas represents a third of sales and Europe the remainder.

Sales and Marketing

Littelfuse's customer base comprises 7000 manufacturers and distributors worldwide. Sales to Arrow Electronics Inc. an electronics distributor account for around 10% of the Littelfuse's revenue.

Products from the Electronics segment are mainly sold through distribution partners including Arrow as well as Future Electronics and TTI Inc and regional and high service distributors. The Automotive segment sells directly to all the major automotive and commercial vehicle OEMs (original equipment manufacturers) system suppliers and Tier One automotive and aftermarket customers globally.

Financial Performance

Littelfuse's sales have grown strongly over the past five years up by nearly $1 billion. Net income has likewise followed an upward trend.

In 2018 Littelfuse's sales grew 41% to $1.7 billion thanks to the acquisition of IXYS and broad-based demand for Electronics products.

Net income jumped 38% to $164.6 million thanks to rising operating income in the Electronics and Automotive segments. A reduced income tax expense also contributed to higher profits a result of an exceptional charge recorded in 2017 relating to the US Tax Cuts and Jobs Act.

Littelfuse's cash on hand grew $60.1 million during 2018 ending the year at $489.7 million. The company's operations generated $331.8 million and its financing yielded $121.9 million partially offset by the $382.2 million used in its investing activities. Littelfuse's main cash uses in 2018 were acquisitions capital expenditures share repurchases and dividends.

Strategy

Littelfuse aims to achieve organic growth by developing new and improved product lines identifying new market opportunities and reaching underrepresented geographies. But the bulk of Littelfuse's recent surging growth was inorganic with the company making notable acquisitions in 2015 and 2017. As well as diversified products geographies and customers the acquisitions provided Littelfuse with a fourth key ingredient: scale. With increased buying power the company has been able to lower its cost base in relative terms driving bottom-line growth.

Mergers and Acquisitions

In 2018 Littelfuse acquired IXYS a maker of power semiconductors and integrated circuits for about $750 million in cash and stock. IXYS focuses on medium to high voltage power control chips for industrial communications consumer and medical markets. Littelfuse was to use IXYS technologies to expand in the industrial and automotive markets. The deal was Littelfuse's biggest to date.

Later in 2018 Littelfuse acquired Monolith Semiconductor a Round Rock-based startup specializing in silicon carbide power device technology. Littelfuse initially partnered with Monolith in 2015 and has steadily increased its ownership stake.

Company Background

Littelfuse was formed in 1927 to make the first small fast-acting fuse able to protect test meters. In 1968 military electronics firm Tracor (later part of the UK's General Electric Company now telent) bought the company. Littelfuse entered the power (industrial) fuse market in 1983. Tracor ran into financial troubles with the end of the Cold War and filed for bankruptcy protection in 1991. As a result of Tracor's reorganization Littelfuse became an independent company in 1992.

EXECUTIVES

President, Chief Executive Officer And Director, David Heinzmann, $845,250 total compensation
Chief Financial Officer, Executive Vice President, Meenal Sethna, $444,087 total compensation
Senior Vice President - Passenger Vehicle Business, General Manager, Alexander Conrad
Senior Vice President, General Manager - Electronics Business, Deepak Nayar, $402,926 total compensation
Independent Director, Maria Green
Senior Vice President And Chief Human Resources Officer, Maggie Chu
Executive Vice President, Chief Legal And Human Resources Officer And Corporate Secretary, Ryan Stafford, $489,994 total compensation
Senior Vice President, Business Development And Strategy, Matthew Cole, $331,449 total compensation
Auditors: Grant Thornton LLP

LOCATIONS

HQ: Littelfuse Inc
8755 West Higgins Road, Suite 500, Chicago, IL 60631
Phone: 773 628-1000
Web: www.littelfuse.com

PRODUCTS/OPERATIONS

2018 Sales

	$ mil.	% of total
Electronics		
Semiconductor	649.0	38
Passive Products and Sensors	475.3	28
Automotive		
Passenger Car	240.5	14
Commercial Vehicle	121.6	7
Automotive Sensor	117.7	7
Industrial	114.4	6
Total	**1,718.5**	**100**

Selected Brands
ATO
JCASE Fuse
MAXI
MEGA
MIDI
MINI
NANO2
OMNI-BLOK
PICO II
POWR-GARD
PulseGuard

Selected Products
Automotive Sensors
Battery Management
Custom-Engineered Electrical Equipment
DC Power Distribution Modules
DC Solenoids and Relays
Fuse Blocks Fuse Holders and Fuse Accessories
Fuses
Fusible Switches and Panels
Gas Discharge Tubes
Magnetic Sensors and Reed Switches
Other Products and Accessories
Power Semiconductors
Protection Relays and Controls
Polymer ESD Suppressors
Resettable PTC Fuses
Semiconductors
Shock-Block GFCI
Surge Protection Module
Switches
Varistors

Selected Services
Custom Circuit Protection Solutions
Custom Power Centers and Electrical Equipment
Electrical Safety Services
MROplus Industrial Fuse Consolidation
Testing Services

COMPETITORS

BARNES GROUP INC.
EATON CORPORATION PUBLIC LIMITED COMPANY
ENCORP INC.
ITT LLC
KYOCERA AVX COMPONENTS CORPORATION
MARWELL CORPORATION
OMRON CORPORATION
ON SEMICONDUCTOR CORPORATION
REGAL REXNORD CORPORATION
SWITCHCRAFT INC.
TECHNOLOGY RESEARCH LLC

HISTORICAL FINANCIALS

Company Type: Public

Income Statement

FYE: January 1

	REVENUE ($ mil.)	NET INCOME ($ mil.)	NET PROFIT MARGIN	EMPLOYEES
01/22*	2,079.9	283.8	13.6%	17,000
12/20	1,445.7	129.9	9.0%	12,200
12/19	1,503.8	139.0	9.2%	11,300
12/18	1,718.4	164.5	9.6%	12,300
12/17	1,221.5	119.5	9.8%	10,700
Annual Growth 14.2%		24.1%	—	12.3%

*Fiscal year change

2022 Year-End Financials

Debt ratio: 20.2%
Return on equity: 15.9%
Cash ($ mil.): 478.4
Current ratio: 2.92
Long-term debt ($ mil.): 611.9
No. of shares (mil.): 24.6
Dividends
Yield: 0.0%
Payout: 17.7%
Market value ($ mil.): 7,768.0

	STOCK PRICE ($) FY Close	P/E High/Low		PER SHARE ($) Earnings	Dividends	Book Value
01/22*	314.68	29	21	11.38	2.02	76.70
12/20	251.66	47	20	5.29	1.92	65.69
12/19	192.02	36	27	5.60	1.82	61.35
12/18	168.03	35	23	6.52	1.60	59.67
12/17	197.82	40	28	5.21	1.40	41.64
Annual Growth 12.3%		—		21.6%	9.6%	16.5%

*Fiscal year change

Live Oak Bancshares Inc

Auditors: Dixon Hughes Goodman LLP

LOCATIONS

HQ: Live Oak Bancshares Inc
1741 Tiburon Drive, Wilmington, NC 28403
Phone: 910 790-5867
Web: www.liveoakbank.com

HISTORICAL FINANCIALS

Company Type: Public

Income Statement

FYE: December 31

	ASSETS ($ mil.)	NET INCOME ($ mil.)	INCOME AS % OF ASSETS	EMPLOYEES
12/20	7,872.3	59.5	0.8%	647
12/19	4,814.9	18.0	0.4%	635
12/18	3,670.4	51.4	1.4%	506
12/17	2,758.4	100.5	3.6%	528
12/16	1,755.2	13.7	0.8%	425
Annual Growth 45.5%		44.2%	—	11.1%

2020 Year-End Financials

Return on assets: 0.9%
Return on equity: 10.7%
Long-term debt ($ mil.): —
No. of shares (mil.): 42.4
Sales ($ mil): 374.4
Dividends
Yield: 0.2%
Payout: 13.6%
Market value ($ mil.): 2,015.0

	STOCK PRICE ($) FY Close	P/E High/Low		PER SHARE ($) Earnings	Dividends	Book Value
12/20	47.46	34	6	1.43	0.12	13.38
12/19	19.01	45	29	0.44	0.12	13.21
12/18	14.81	25	11	1.24	0.12	12.29
12/17	23.85	9	7	2.65	0.10	10.95
12/16	18.50	50	30	0.39	0.07	6.51
Annual Growth	26.6%	—		38.4%	14.4%	19.7%

Live Ventures Inc

LiveDeal (formerly YP Corp.) is an Internet yellow pages and local online classifieds provider. The company offers goods and services listed for sale through its online classified marketplace at classifieds.livedeal.com; LiveDeal also publishes about 17 million business listings via its business directory at yellowpages.livedeal.com. Sources of revenue include advertising sales a pay-per-lead program with major auto dealers and optional listing upgrade and e-commerce/fraud prevention fees. The company changed its name from YP Corp. after its 2007 purchase of online local classifieds marketplace LiveDeal.

EXECUTIVES

President, Chief Executive Officer, Director, Jon Isaac, $350,000 total compensation
Financial Planning And Strategist/economist, Director, Antonios Isaac
President And Chief Executive Officer Of Vintage Stock, Inc., Rodney Spriggs, $270,000 total compensation
Chief Executive Officer Of Marquis Industries, Inc., Weston Godfrey, $307,344 total compensation
Chief Executive Officer Of Precision Industries, Inc., Thomas Sedlak
Chief Operating Officer, Eric Althofer, $126,923 total compensation
Chief Accounting Officer, David Verret
Auditors: Frazier & Deeter LLC

LOCATIONS

HQ: Live Ventures Inc
325 E. Warm Springs Road, Suite 102, Las Vegas, NV 89119
Phone: 702 997-5968
Web: www.liveventures.com

COMPETITORS

BURST MEDIA CORPORATION
MARCHEX INC.
VERIZON MEDIA INC.
YAHOO-UK LIMITED

HISTORICAL FINANCIALS
Company Type: Public

Income Statement				FYE: September 30
	REVENUE ($ mil.)	NET INCOME ($ mil.)	NET PROFIT MARGIN	EMPLOYEES
09/21	272.9	31.2	11.4%	1,253
09/20	191.7	10.9	5.7%	1,150
09/19	193.2	(4.0)	—	1,000
09/18	199.6	5.9	3.0%	1,155
09/17	152.0	6.5	4.3%	1,211
Annual Growth	15.8%	48.0%	—	0.9%

2021 Year-End Financials
Debt ratio: 26.2%
Return on equity: 52.2%
Cash ($ mil.): 4.6
Current ratio: 1.52
Long-term debt ($ mil.): 39.5
No. of shares (mil.): 1.5
Dividends
  Yield: —
  Payout: —
Market value ($ mil.): 59.0

	STOCK PRICE ($) FY Close	P/E High/Low		PER SHARE ($) Earnings	Dividends	Book Value
09/21	37.00	4	0	9.80	0.00	47.73
09/20	8.94	2	1	3.09	0.00	27.65
09/19	8.57	—	—	(2.11)	0.00	18.69
09/18	9.00	7	3	1.58	0.00	20.28
09/17	12.40	9	1	1.61	0.00	16.86
Annual Growth	31.4%	—	—	57.1%	—	29.7%

Lovesac Co

Auditors: Marcum LLP

LOCATIONS

HQ: Lovesac Co
Two Landmark Square, Suite 300, Stamford, CT 06901
Phone: 888 636-1223
Web: www.lovesac.com

HISTORICAL FINANCIALS
Company Type: Public

Income Statement				FYE: January 31
	REVENUE ($ mil.)	NET INCOME ($ mil.)	NET PROFIT MARGIN	EMPLOYEES
01/21*	320.7	14.7	4.6%	778
02/20	233.3	(15.2)	—	781
02/19	165.8	(6.7)	—	590
02/18	101.8	(5.5)	—	441
01/17	76.3	(6.8)	—	0
Annual Growth	43.2%	—	—	—

*Fiscal year change

2021 Year-End Financials
Debt ratio: —
Return on equity: 14.9%
Cash ($ mil.): 78.3
Current ratio: 2.55
Long-term debt ($ mil.): —
No. of shares (mil.): 15.0
Dividends
  Yield: —
  Payout: —
Market value ($ mil.): 849.0

	STOCK PRICE ($) FY Close	P/E High/Low		PER SHARE ($) Earnings	Dividends	Book Value
01/21*	56.54	57	4	0.96	0.00	7.19
02/20	11.35	—	—	(1.07)	0.00	6.23
02/19	23.74	—	—	(3.28)	0.00	5.80
Annual Growth	54.3%	—	—	—	—	11.4%

*Fiscal year change

Lumentum Holdings Inc

Auditors: DELOITTE & TOUCHE LLP

LOCATIONS

HQ: Lumentum Holdings Inc
1001 Ridder Park Drive, San Jose, CA 95131
Phone: 408 546-5483
Web: www.lumentum.com

HISTORICAL FINANCIALS
Company Type: Public

Income Statement				FYE: July 3
	REVENUE ($ mil.)	NET INCOME ($ mil.)	NET PROFIT MARGIN	EMPLOYEES
07/21*	1,742.8	397.3	22.8%	5,618
06/20	1,678.6	135.5	8.1%	5,473
06/19	1,565.3	(36.4)	—	5,161
06/18	1,247.7	248.1	19.9%	2,930
07/17	1,001.6	(102.5)	—	2,057
Annual Growth	14.9%	—	—	28.6%

*Fiscal year change

2021 Year-End Financials
Debt ratio: 33.2%
Return on equity: 21.0%
Cash ($ mil.): 774.3
Current ratio: 3.67
Long-term debt ($ mil.): 789.8
No. of shares (mil.): 73.0
Dividends
  Yield: —
  Payout: —
Market value ($ mil.): 6,093.0

	STOCK PRICE ($) FY Close	P/E High/Low		PER SHARE ($) Earnings	Dividends	Book Value
07/21*	83.47	21	13	5.07	0.00	27.02
06/20	76.13	52	27	1.75	0.00	23.29
06/19	53.41	—	—	(0.54)	0.00	19.53
06/18	57.90	19	11	3.82	0.00	14.75
07/17	57.05	—	—	(1.71)	0.00	10.07
Annual Growth	10.0%	—	—	—	—	28.0%

*Fiscal year change

Luther Burbank Corp

Auditors: Crowe LLP

LOCATIONS

HQ: Luther Burbank Corp
520 Third Street, Fourth Floor, Santa Rosa, CA 95401
Phone: 844 446-8201
Web: www.lutherburbanksavings.com

HISTORICAL FINANCIALS
Company Type: Public

Income Statement
FYE: December 31

	ASSETS ($ mil.)	NET INCOME ($ mil.)	INCOME AS % OF ASSETS	EMPLOYEES
12/20	6,906.1	39.9	0.6%	277
12/19	7,045.8	48.8	0.7%	277
12/18	6,937.2	45.0	0.6%	278
12/17	5,704.3	69.3	1.2%	266
12/16	5,064.5	52.1	1.0%	274
Annual Growth	8.1%	(6.5%)	—	0.3%

2020 Year-End Financials

Return on assets: 0.5%
Return on equity: 6.4%
Long-term debt ($ mil.): —
No. of shares (mil.): 52.2
Sales ($ mil): 243.9
Dividends
Yield: 2.3%
Payout: 28.4%
Market value ($ mil.): 512.0

	STOCK PRICE ($) FY Close	P/E High/Low		PER SHARE ($) Earnings	Dividends	Book Value
12/20	9.80	16	10	0.75	0.23	11.75
12/19	11.53	14	11	0.87	0.23	10.97
12/18	9.02	17	10	0.79	0.19	10.31
12/17	12.04	8	7	1.62	1.58	9.74
Annual Growth	(6.6%)	—		(22.6%)	(47.4%)	6.4%

Lyons Bancorp Inc.

EXECUTIVES

Director, James Homburger
Executive Vice President, Chief Commercial Lending Officer Of The Lyons National Bank Of The Company, Clair Britt
Director, Carol Snook
Director, Dale Hemminger
Director, David Breen
Director, Bradley Person
Director Of Lyons Bancorp, Inc And The Lyons National Bank, Joseph Bartolotta
Director, Joseph Fragnoli
Director Of Lyons Bancorp, Inc. And The Lyons National Bank, Teresa Jackson
Director Of Lyons Bancorp, Inc. And The Lyons National Bank, John Colaruotolo
Director, Kaye Stone- Gansz
Director, Case Marshall
Auditors: Bonadio & Co., LLP

LOCATIONS

HQ: Lyons Bancorp Inc.
399 Exchange Street, Geneva, NY 14456
Phone: 315 946-4871
Web: www.bankwithlnb.com

HISTORICAL FINANCIALS
Company Type: Public

Income Statement
FYE: December 31

	ASSETS ($ mil.)	NET INCOME ($ mil.)	INCOME AS % OF ASSETS	EMPLOYEES
12/20	1,423.1	10.2	0.7%	0
12/19	1,163.6	11.0	0.9%	0
12/18	1,081.7	9.9	0.9%	0
12/17	1,031.8	8.0	0.8%	0
Annual Growth	11.3%	8.6%	—	—

2020 Year-End Financials

Return on assets: 0.7%
Return on equity: 11.2%
Long-term debt ($ mil.): —
No. of shares (mil.): 3.1
Sales ($ mil): 62.9
Dividends
Yield: 0.0%
Payout: 39.7%
Market value ($ mil.): 127.0

	STOCK PRICE ($) FY Close	P/E High/Low		PER SHARE ($) Earnings	Dividends	Book Value
12/20	40.00	13	10	3.12	1.24	30.06
12/19	39.75	14	11	3.33	1.22	27.36
12/18	41.10	15	11	3.03	1.14	24.48
12/17	35.50	19	13	2.42	1.05	23.13
/0.00	—		—	(0.00)	0.00	(0.00)
Annual Growth	—	—		—	—	—

M/I Homes Inc

M/I Homes is one of the nation's leading builders of single-family homes having sold over 127650 homes since commencing homebuilding activities in 1976. The company's homes are marketed and sold primarily under the M/I Homes brand. It delivers homes to first-time move-up empty-nest and luxury buyers at prices ranging from about $200000 to $1.1 million (averaging $381000) and sizes ranging from 1100 to 5500 sq. ft. M/I Homes also builds attached townhomes in select markets. It caters to about 15 markets located in ten states. Its M/I Financial mortgage banking subsidiary provides title and mortgage services.

Operations

M/I Homes' homebuilding operations comprise the Northern and Southern regions generating some 95% of total revenue.

Its Showcase collection is an exclusive brand of M/I Homes. Other plans include Smart Series (entry-level and move-down buyers) and City Collection (upscale urban lifestyle). The company also currently develops new floor plans and communities specifically for the growing empty-nester market. It currently offers over 600 different floor plans across all of its divisions.

Complementing its homebuilding activities the company provides mortgage banking and title services through its wholly owned subsidiary M/I Financial Corp. It accounts for less than 5% of total revenue.

Geographic Reach

M/I Homes is based in Columbus Ohio. The Northern region includes Ohio Indiana Illinois Minnesota and Michigan. M/I Homes' Southern region includes Florida North Carolina and Texas.

Sales and Marketing

The company markets its homes using traditional media such as newspapers direct mail billboards radio and television. It also uses enhanced search engine optimization search engine marketing and display advertising to increase the reach of its website. It maintains a presence on referral sites such as Zillow.com and NewHomeSource.com to drive sales leads to online sales associates.

M/I Homes also uses email marketing to maintain communication with existing prospects and customers. It uses its social media presence to communicate to potential homebuyers the experiences of customers who have purchased its homes and to provide content about its homes and design features.

Financial Performance

In 2020 the company recorded a total revenue of $3.05 billion of which $2.94 billion was from homes delivered $19.2 million was from land sales and $87.0 million was from its financial services operations.

On the same year the company achieved a net income of $239.9 million which includes the after-tax impact of both the asset impairment charges and stucco-related charges compared to net income of $127.6 million in 2019.

Cash at the end of fiscal 2020 was $260.8 million an increase of $254.7 million over the previous year. Operating and financing activities each provided $168.3 million and $120.3 million to the company coffers respectively. Investing activities used $33.9 million for purchases of property and equipment and Investment in and advances to joint venture arrangements.

Strategy

The company remains focused on increasing its profitability by generating additional revenue continuing to expand its market share shifting its product mix to include more affordable designs and investing in attractive land opportunities to increase its number of active communities.

Consistent with its focus on improving long-term financial results it expects to emphasize the following strategic business objectives in 2021: managing our land spend and inventory levels; accelerating the opening of new communities wherever possible; maintaining a strong balance sheet and liquidity levels; expanding the availability of our more affordable Smart Series homes; and emphasizing customer service product quality and design and premier locations.

Company Background

M/I Homes was founded in 1976 in Ohio by Melvin and Irving Schottenstein. The company expanded into new markets in the 1980s including Florida Indiana and North Carolina. The company established M/I Financial in 1983.

EXECUTIVES

Chairman Of The Board, President, Chief Executive Officer, Robert Schottenstein, $1,000,000 total compensation
Chief Financial Officer, Executive Vice President, Director, Phillip Creek, $650,000 total compensation
Independent Director, Norman Traeger
Lead Independent Director, Friedrich Bohm
Independent Director, William Carter
Independent Director, Michael Glimcher
Independent Director, Nancy Kramer
Independent Director, Elizabeth Ingram
Independent Director, Kumi Walker

Senior Vice President, Chief Legal Officer And Secretary, Susan Krohne
Auditors: Deloitte & Touche LLP

LOCATIONS

HQ: M/I Homes Inc
4131 Worth Avenue, Suite 500, Columbus, OH 43219
Phone: 614 418-8000 **Fax:** 614 418-8080
Web: www.mihomes.com

PRODUCTS/OPERATIONS

2015 Sales

	$ mil.	% of total
Southern Homebuilding	514.7	36
Midwest homebuilding	500.9	35
Mid-Atlantic homebuilding	366.8	26
Financial services	36.0	3
Total	**1,418.4**	**100**

Selected Markets

Charlotte NC
Chicago IL
Cincinnati OH
Columbus OH
Dayton OH
Houston TX
Indianapolis IN
Maryland
Orlando FL
Raleigh NC
San Antonio TX
Tampa FL
Virginia

COMPETITORS

AV HOMES INC.	NVR INC.
CENTURY COMMUNITIES INC.	PROLOGIS INC.
D.R. HORTON INC.	TAYLOR MORRISON HOME II CORPORATION
GREEN BRICK PARTNERS INC.	TRI POINTE HOMES INC.
HOMESERVE PLC	URBAN EDGE PROPERTIES
HOVNANIAN ENTERPRISES INC.	

HISTORICAL FINANCIALS
Company Type: Public

Income Statement
FYE: December 31

	REVENUE ($ mil.)	NET INCOME ($ mil.)	NET PROFIT MARGIN	EMPLOYEES
12/21	3,745.8	396.8	10.6%	1,657
12/20	3,046.1	239.8	7.9%	1,515
12/19	2,500.2	127.5	5.1%	1,401
12/18	2,286.2	107.6	4.7%	1,359
12/17	1,961.9	72.0	3.7%	1,238
Annual Growth	17.5%	53.2%	—	7.6%

2021 Year-End Financials

Debt ratio: 29.6%
Return on equity: 27.5%
Cash ($ mil.): 236.3
Current ratio: 7.63
Long-term debt ($ mil.): 961.9
No. of shares (mil.): 28.5
Dividends
  Yield: —
  Payout: —
Market value ($ mil.): 1,772.0

	STOCK PRICE ($) FY Close	P/E High/Low		PER SHARE ($) Earnings	Dividends	Book Value
12/21	62.18	5	3	13.28	0.00	56.99
12/20	44.29	6	1	8.23	0.00	43.68
12/19	39.35	10	5	4.48	0.00	35.35
12/18	21.02	10	5	3.70	0.00	31.08
12/17	34.40	14	9	2.26	0.00	26.83
Annual Growth	16.0%			— 55.7%	—	20.7%

Magnolia Oil & Gas Corp

Auditors: KPMG LLP

LOCATIONS

HQ: Magnolia Oil & Gas Corp
Nine Greenway Plaza, Suite 1300, Houston, TX 77046
Phone: 713 842-9050
Web: www.magnoliaoilgas.com

HISTORICAL FINANCIALS
Company Type: Public

Income Statement
FYE: December 31

	REVENUE ($ mil.)	NET INCOME ($ mil.)	NET PROFIT MARGIN	EMPLOYEES
12/21	1,078.3	417.2	38.7%	192
12/20	534.5	(1,208.3)		136
12/19	936.1	50.2	5.4%	45
12/18*	433.2	39.1	9.0%	27
07/18	449.1	218.5	48.7%	0
Annual Growth	24.5%	17.5%		

*Fiscal year change

2021 Year-End Financials

Debt ratio: 22.2%
Return on equity: 61.1%
Cash ($ mil.): 366.9
Current ratio: 2.37
Long-term debt ($ mil.): 388.0
No. of shares (mil.): 228.5
Dividends
  Yield: 0.4%
  Payout: 4.8%
Market value ($ mil.): 4,313.0

	STOCK PRICE ($) FY Close	P/E High/Low		PER SHARE ($) Earnings	Dividends	Book Value
12/21	18.87	9	3	2.36	0.08	3.57
12/20	7.06	—	—	(7.27)	0.00	2.20
12/19	12.58	48	34	0.28	0.00	7.02
12/18*	11.21	61	40	0.25	0.00	6.72
07/18	12.26	—	—	(0.00)	0.00	(0.00)
Annual Growth	11.4%			—	—	—

*Fiscal year change

MainStreet Bancshares Inc

Auditors: Yount, Hyde & Barbour, P.C.

LOCATIONS

HQ: MainStreet Bancshares Inc
10089 Fairfax Boulevard, Fairfax, VA 22030
Phone: 703 481-4567
Web: www.mstreetbank.com

HISTORICAL FINANCIALS
Company Type: Public

Income Statement
FYE: December 31

	ASSETS ($ mil.)	NET INCOME ($ mil.)	INCOME AS % OF ASSETS	EMPLOYEES
12/20	1,643.1	15.7	1.0%	126
12/19	1,277.3	13.9	1.1%	126
12/18	1,100.6	9.2	0.8%	110
12/17	807.9	3.8	0.5%	0
12/16	575.7	3.8	0.7%	0
Annual Growth	30.0%	41.9%	—	—

2020 Year-End Financials

Return on assets: 1.0%
Return on equity: 10.2%
Long-term debt ($ mil.): —
No. of shares (mil.): 7.4
Sales ($ mil.): 69.5
Dividends
  Yield: —
  Payout: —
Market value ($ mil.): 126.0

	STOCK PRICE ($) FY Close	P/E High/Low		PER SHARE ($) Earnings	Dividends	Book Value
12/20	16.91	13	6	1.85	0.00	22.52
12/19	23.00	15	10	1.69	0.00	16.59
12/18	17.06	17	13	1.38	0.00	14.83
12/17	17.52	21	17	0.85	0.00	12.57
12/16	14.20	16	13	0.87	0.00	10.34
Annual Growth	4.5%			— 20.9%	—	21.5%

Malibu Boats Inc

EXECUTIVES

Independent Director, Joan Lewis
Independent Chairman Of The Board, Michael Hooks
Independent Director, Michael Connolly
Chief Operating Officer, Ritchie Anderson, $385,000 total compensation
Chief Financial Officer, Wayne Wilson, $394,808 total compensation
Independent Director, James Buch
Independent Director, Ivar Chhina
Chief Executive Officer, Director, Jack Springer, $754,615 total compensation
Independent Director, John Stokely
Auditors: KPMG LLP

LOCATIONS

HQ: Malibu Boats Inc
5075 Kimberly Way, Loudon, TN 37774
Phone: 865 458-5478
Web: www.malibuboats.com

HISTORICAL FINANCIALS
Company Type: Public

Income Statement
FYE: June 30

	REVENUE ($ mil.)	NET INCOME ($ mil.)	NET PROFIT MARGIN	EMPLOYEES
06/21	926.5	109.8	11.9%	2,645
06/20	653.1	61.5	9.4%	1,795
06/19	684.0	66.0	9.7%	1,835
06/18	497.0	27.6	5.6%	1,345
06/17	281.9	28.3	10.1%	586
Annual Growth	34.6%	40.3%	—	45.8%

2021 Year-End Financials

Debt ratio: 19.2%	No. of shares (mil.): 20.8
Return on equity: 34.9%	Dividends
Cash ($ mil.): 41.4	Yield: —
Current ratio: 1.58	Payout: —
Long-term debt ($ mil.): 139.0	Market value ($ mil.): 1,529.0

	STOCK PRICE ($) FY Close	P/E High/Low		PER SHARE ($) Earnings	Dividends	Book Value
06/21	73.33	17	9	5.23	0.00	17.91
06/20	51.95	18	6	2.95	0.00	12.36
06/19	38.85	18	10	3.15	0.00	9.79
06/18	41.94	33	18	1.36	0.00	6.54
06/17	25.87	16	8	1.58	0.00	2.74
Annual Growth	29.8%	—	—	34.9%	—	59.9%

ManTech International Corp

ManTech International is more than willing to lend a little high-tech staffing to ensure its country's security. ManTech provides security-focused IT services to agencies primarily US government intelligence entities such as the Department of Defense (DoD) Homeland Security and the military. Its national security offerings include intelligence communications computer forensics and security systems development and support. The contractor also offers security design and engineering and system testing and evaluation. ManTech is active in other countries but makes essentially all of its sales to US customers.

Operations

ManTech provides services in cyber security; enterprise information technology (IT); software application and systems development; multi-disciplined intelligence; intelligence command control communications computers combat systems intelligence surveillance and reconnaissance (C5ISR); program protection and mission assurance; systems engineering; training; and supply chain management and logistics.

The company provides its services and solutions under three types of contracts: cost-reimbursable (approximately 70% of the total revenue); fixed-price (some 20%); and time-and-materials (approximately 10%).

Geographic Reach

Based in Virginia the company has nearly 15 operations in the US including Alabama Arizona California Texas Washington and Texas among others.

Sales and Marketing

ManTech customers include intelligence community the Department of Defense (DoD) and federal civilian agencies including the diplomatic homeland security healthcare and space communities.. ManTech derives vast majority of its revenues from US government customers.

Financial Performance

The company's revenue increased by 14% to $2.2 billion in 2019 compared from the prior year with $2.0 billion. The primary driver of its increase in revenues relates to revenues from new contract awards growth on existing contracts and the acquisitions the company completed during the year.

Net income for 2019 increased by 5% to $113.9 million while in the prior year with $82.1 million.

Cash held by the company at the end of 2019 increased by $3.6 million to $8.9 million. Cash provided by operations was $221.4 million while cash used for investing and financing activities were $214.9 million and $2.9 million respectively. Main uses of cash were acquisition of businesses-net of cash acquired and repayments under revolving credit facility.

Mergers and Acquisitions

The company has added to its expertise through acquisitions.

In 2020 ManTech acquired Tapestry Technologies a leading provider of advanced cyber solutions. Headquartered in Chambersburg Pennsylvania Tapestry Technologies offers a full range of cyber defense solutions and expertise including cyber architecture and policy development DevSecOps-based systems and software engineering and cyber training. This acquisition enhances and extends ManTech's cyber defense capabilities within the Department of Defense adding customers new past performance qualifications as well as mission-critical contracts.

Also in 2020 ManTech acquired Minerva Engineering a leading provider of advanced cyber solutions. Headquartered in Hanover Maryland Minerva Engineering offers a range of advanced cyber services that support the intelligence community (IC) including risk and vulnerability assessment incident response and cyber intrusion detection and wireless signal discovery. This acquisition enhances and expands ManTech's cyber defense capabilities within the IC adding new customers new past performance qualifications as well as mission-critical contracts.

In 2019 ManTech acquired H2M Group a provider of intelligence analysis services to the National Geospatial-Intelligence Agency. This acquisition was made to enable ManTech help government agencies implement automation so analysts can more effectively navigate large amounts of data.

In 2019 ManTech acquired Kforce Government Solutions the federal government business of Kforce and its 500 employees for $115 million. The deal expands ManTech's footprint at the US Department of Veterans Affairs and allows it to become part of the VA's Transformation Twenty-One Total Technology Next Generation program a 10-year project.

Company Background

ManTech was founded in 1968 to provide advanced technological services to the US government. Co-founder George J. Pedersen controls about 85% of the company's voting power.

EXECUTIVES

Independent Director, Peter LaMontagne
Chief Growth Officer, Joseph Cubba
Director, George Pedersen, $1,960,003 total compensation
Chairman, Ceo And President, Kevin Phillips, $820,833 total compensation
Executive Vice President, Business Services, Bonnie Cook, $461,083 total compensation
Chief Human Resource Officer, Julie Barker
Chief Financial Officer, Executive Vice President, Judith Bjornaas, $664,167 total compensation
Chief Operating Officer, Matthew Tait, $936,250 total compensation
Auditors: DELOITTE & TOUCHE LLP

LOCATIONS

HQ: ManTech International Corp
 2251 Corporate Park Drive, Herndon, VA 20171
Phone: 703 218-6000
Web: www.mantech.com

PRODUCTS/OPERATIONS

2018 Sales

	% of total
Department of Defense and intelligence agencies	74
Federal civilian agencies	24
State agencies international agencies and commercial entities	2
Total	**100**

2018 Sales

	$ in mil.
% of total	
Cost-reimbursable	68
Fixed-price	22
Time-and-material	10
Total	**100**

Selected Services

C4ISR
 Ground airborne and space systems
 New technology development testing and infusion
 Telecommunications systems and elevated sensors
Cyber Security
 Computer forensics and exploitation
 Counter-intrusion support
 Insider threat protection
 Program protection and security
Health Care
 Behavioral health
 Health care research
 Imaging
 Informatics
Information Technology Services
 Biometrics and identity management
 Embedded software engineering
 Network and database administration
 Real-time software applications
 Social media and collaboration environments
Systems Engineering Services
 Border security
 Enterprise architecture
 Risk management
 Tactical systems development and integration

COMPETITORS

AEROVIRONMENT INC.
CSRA INC.
F5 INC.
MANDIANT INC.
MAXAR TECHNOLOGIES INC.
NETSCOUT SYSTEMS INC.
QINETIQ GROUP PLC
SCIENCE APPLICATIONS INTERNATIONAL CORPORATION
TELECOMMUNICATION SYSTEMS INC.
TELOS CORPORATION
VALINAR LLC

HISTORICAL FINANCIALS

Company Type: Public

Income Statement

FYE: December 31

	REVENUE ($ mil.)	NET INCOME ($ mil.)	NET PROFIT MARGIN	EMPLOYEES
12/20	2,518.3	120.5	4.8%	9,400
12/19	2,222.5	113.8	5.1%	8,900
12/18	1,958.5	82.1	4.2%	7,800
12/17	1,717.0	114.1	6.6%	7,600
12/16	1,601.6	56.3	3.5%	7,000
Annual Growth	12.0%	20.9%	—	7.6%

2020 Year-End Financials

Debt ratio: 0.6%
Return on equity: 7.8%
Cash ($ mil.): 41.1
Current ratio: 1.42
Long-term debt ($ mil.): 15.0

No. of shares (mil.): 40.4
Dividends
Yield: 1.4%
Payout: 43.1%
Market value ($ mil.): 3,599.0

	STOCK PRICE ($) FY Close	P/E High/Low		PER SHARE ($) Earnings	Dividends	Book Value
12/20	88.94	29	19	2.97	1.28	39.03
12/19	79.88	28	18	2.83	1.08	37.10
12/18	52.30	32	23	2.06	1.00	35.24
12/17	50.19	18	11	2.91	0.84	34.23
12/16	42.25	31	18	1.47	0.84	32.05
Annual Growth	20.5%	—	—	19.2%	11.1%	5.0%

MarineMax Inc

MarineMax is the largest recreational boat and yacht retailer and superyacht services company in the world. It has nearly 80 locations in around 20 states. The company sells new and used recreational boats and related marine products including engines trailers parts and accessories. The company also arranges related boat financing insurance and extended service contracts; provides boat repair and maintenance services; offers yacht and boat brokerage sales; and where available offers slip and storage accommodations. MarineMax is the largest retailer of Sea Ray and Boston Whaler.

Operations

In 2021 MarineMax changed its reportable segments as a result of its acquisition of Cruisers Yachts. The company now operates through two new reportable segments: Retail Operations and Product Manufacturing.

Retail Operations segment accounting for nearly 100% of the total revenue includes the sale of new and used recreational boats including pleasure and fishing boats with a focus on premium brands in each segment. The segment also includes selling related marine products including engines trailers parts and accessories. In addition they provide repair maintenance and slip and storage services; arrange related boat financing insurance and extended service contracts; offer boat and yacht brokerage sales; yacht charter services.

Product Manufacturing segment includes activity of Cruisers Yachts a wholly-owned MarineMax subsidiary manufacturing sport yacht and yachts with sales through the company's select retail dealership locations and through independent dealers.

Geographic Reach

MarineMax is based in Florida (Clearwater) and the state accounts for more than half of its sales. The other 20 states in which it has retail locations are Alabama California Connecticut Florida Georgia Illinois Maryland Massachusetts Michigan Minnesota Missouri New Jersey New York North Carolina Ohio Oklahoma Rhode Island South Carolina Texas Washington and Wisconsin. The company is also in the British Virgin Islands.

Sales and Marketing

MarineMax sells used boats at their retail locations online and at various third-party marinas and other offsite locations; Marine engines and propellers are sold primarily to its retail customers as replacements for its existing engines and propellers; a broad variety of parts and accessories are sold at its retail locations and at various offsite locations and through its print catalog; the company offers maintenance repair and slip and storage services at most of its retail locations; finance and insurance products are offered at most of their retail locations and at various offsite locations and to its customers and independent boat dealers and brokers; MarineMax offers boat and yacht brokerage sales at most of its retail locations and at various offsite locations; and it conducts a charter business which is based in the British Virgin Islands in which the company offer customers the opportunity to charter third-party and company owned power catamarans.

MarineMax's advertising and promotional expenses approximated $18.8 million $14.0 million and $14.8 million for 2019 2020 and 2021 respectively.

Financial Performance

In fiscal 2021 MarineMax reported a revenue of $2 billion or an increase of $554 million from the prior year. Of the revenue increase $202.9 million was attributable to a 13.4% increase in comparable-store sales and an approximate $350.6 million net increase was related to stores opened including acquired or closed that were not eligible for inclusion in the comparable-store base. The increase in their comparable-store sales was primarily due to demand driven increases in new and used boat revenue and their higher margin finance and insurance products brokerage parts service and storage services.

In fiscal 2021 net income was $154.9 million an increase of $80.3 million from $74.6 million in the prior year.

The company had about $222.2 million in cash in 2021 up from about $155.5 million in 2020. Cash provided by operating activities was $373.9 million. Cash used in investing activities was $56.3 million primarily for acquisitions. Cash used in financing activities was approximately $45.71 million primarily for net payments on short-term borrowings.

Strategy

MarineMax's primary goal remains to enhance its position as the nation's leading recreational boat and yacht retailer. In addition it has broadened its strategy including through recent acquisitions of Fraser Yachts Group Northrop & Johnson and SkipperBud's to increase the business' superyacht brokerage and luxury yacht services and marina/storage services. Expansion of strategy is aimed to potentially increase margins.

The company also continues to broaden and strengthen its digital initiatives which are always available and offer full selection of boats yachts

and charters as well as expert team to answer customers' questions and help them find a boat virtually. Additionally its Boatyard digital platform allows marine businesses effective and customized digital solutions delivering great customer experiences by enabling customers to interact through a personalized experience tailored to their needs.

Apart from acquisitions the company opened 35 new retail locations in existing territories excluding those opened on a temporary basis for a specific purpose.

Mergers and Acquisitions

In late 2021 MarineMax acquired Intrepid Powerboats a premier manufacturer of powerboats and Texas MasterCraft a premier watersports dealer in Northern Texas. Intrepid is recognized as a world class producer of customized boats carefully reflecting the unique desires of each individual owner. Texas Mastercraft specializes in ski and wakeboard boats. The activity of Intrepid will be included in their Product Manufacturing segment. The activity of Texas MasterCraft will be included in their Retail Operations segment.

In 2021 MarineMax acquired KCS International Inc. better known as Cruisers Yachts headquartered in Oconto Wisconsin. Cruisers Yachts (Cruisers) is recognized as one of the world's premier manufacturers of premium yachts producing models from 33' to 60' feet. The strategic acquisition of Cruisers Yachts benefits MarineMax's customers by filling a meaningful void in its product portfolio which was created in 2018 by the loss of Sea Ray sport yacht and yacht models. The acquisition also aligns with MarineMax's long-term strategy of expanding its gross margins by adding a higher margin business. Cruisers has a seasoned passionate and successful team.

EXECUTIVES

Independent Director, Rebecca White
Independent Director, Joseph Watters
Independent Director, Charles Oglesby
Chief Financial Officer, Executive Vice President, Secretary, Director, Michael McLamb, $470,000 total compensation
President, Chief Executive Officer, Director, William McGill, $740,000 total compensation
Independent Director, Hilliard Eure
Chief Revenue Officer, Executive Vice President, Charles Cashman, $395,000 total compensation
Chief Accounting Officer, Vice President, Anthony Cassella, $250,000 total compensation
Lead Independent Director, Clint Moore
Independent Director, George Borst
Auditors: KPMG LLP

LOCATIONS

HQ: MarineMax Inc
2600 McCormick Drive, Suite 200, Clearwater, FL 33759
Phone: 727 531-1700
Web: www.MarineMax.com

PRODUCTS/OPERATIONS

2017 Sales

	$ mil.	% of total
New boat sales	747.0	70
Used boat sales	157.0	15
Maintenance repair & storage services	60.0	6
Marine Engines Related Marine Equipment and Boating Parts and Accessories	38.0	2
F&I Products	25.0	4
Brokerage Sales	20.0	2
Total	**1,052.0**	**100**

Selected Products & Trade Names

Motor Yachts
- Azimut
- Hatteras Motor Yachts

Convertibles
- Cabo
- Hatteras Convertibles

Pleasure Boats
- Meridian
- Sea Ray

Fishing Boats
- Boston Whaler
- Grady White

Ski Boats
- Axis
- Malibu

COMPETITORS

BRUNSWICK CORPORATION INC.	HERC HOLDINGS
CAMPING WORLD HOLDINGS SERVICES INC.	KAR AUCTION INC.
CARVANA CO.	MALIBU BOATS LLC
CENTURY COMMUNITIES INC.	SILVER MERGER SUB 1 LLC
COPART INC.	SPORTSMAN'S WAREHOUSE
DOUGLAS DYNAMICS INC.	HOLDINGS INC.
ESCALADE INCORPORATED OF	SUPERIOR GROUP
H&E EQUIPMENT SERVICES INC.	COMPANIES INC. VIAD CORP

HISTORICAL FINANCIALS

Company Type: Public

Income Statement — FYE: September 30

	REVENUE ($ mil.)	NET INCOME ($ mil.)	NET PROFIT MARGIN	EMPLOYEES
09/21	2,063.2	154.9	7.5%	2,666
09/20	1,509.7	74.6	4.9%	1,736
09/19	1,237.1	35.9	2.9%	1,754
09/18	1,177.3	39.3	3.3%	1,573
09/17	1,052.3	23.5	2.2%	1,516
Annual Growth	18.3%	60.2%	—	15.2%

2021 Year-End Financials

Debt ratio: 7.4%
Return on equity: 29.5%
Cash ($ mil.): 222.1
Current ratio: 2.06
Long-term debt ($ mil.): 47.5

No. of shares (mil.): 21.8
Dividends
  Yield: —
  Payout: —
Market value ($ mil.): 1,059.0

	STOCK PRICE ($) FY Close	P/E High/Low		PER SHARE ($) Earnings	Dividends	Book Value
09/21	48.52	9	4	6.78	0.00	27.26
09/20	25.67	10	2	3.37	0.00	20.83
09/19	15.48	16	9	1.57	0.00	17.30
09/18	21.25	14	9	1.71	0.00	15.57
09/17	16.55	24	14	0.95	0.00	13.81
Annual Growth	30.9%		—	63.4%	—	18.5%

MarketAxess Holdings Inc.

A little creative spelling never got in the way of a good bond trade. MarketAxess offers an electronic multi-dealer platform for institutional traders buying and selling US corporate high-yield and emerging market bonds as well as Eurobonds. Over 1700 institutional investor and broker-dealer firms are active users of the company patent trading technology. The company also provides real-time the ability to view indicative prices from its broker-dealer clients' inventory available on its platform access to real-time pricing information and analytical tools available through its Corporate BondTicker service. Majority of its revenue accounts in United States. The company was incorporated in the year 2000.

Operations

Nearly 90% of the company's revenue comes from commissions for transactions executed on its platform between institutional investor and broker-dealer clients. About 5% of its revenue comes from its information products and services. Less than 5% of its revenue comes from its post-trade services from its Trax division which provides trade matching regulatory transaction reporting and market and reference data across a range of fixed income products. MarketAxess had a staff of more than 525 employees with about 325 of them based in the US and the others mostly in the UK.

Geographic Reach

New York based MarketAxess generates nearly 85% of its revenue from the US while nearly all of the remainder comes from the UK. The company has office locations in the US UK Brazil Netherlands Hong Kong and Singapore.

Sales and Marketing

To boost awareness of its brand and electronic trading platform MarketAxess uses advertising direct marketing digital and social media promotional mailings and participates in industry conferences and media engagement. As an example it worked with The Wall Street Journal to make its Corporate BondTicker service the source of WSJ's information for its daily corporate bond and high-yield tables.

In the US high-grade corporate bond market more than 200 active institutional investors and over 90 broker-dealers used MarketAxess' platform including all of the top 20 broker-dealers as ranked by 2019 US corporate bond new-issue underwriting volume. The company's broker-dealer clients made up of more than 95% of all underwriting activity for newly-issued corporate bonds.

Overall the firm spent about $11500 on advertising in 2019 from more than $12100 million spent in 2018.

Financial Performance

MarketAxess' revenues and profits have risen at a healthy clip over the past five years largely as the bond market has become more attractive to investors which has led to growth in both MarketAxess' commission income and information and post-trade services income. It posted growth of 69% over that period.

The firm's revenue rose by 17% to $511.4 million in 2019 mostly thanks to commission income

growth and revenue from Information services segments.

Net income for 2019 was $204.9 million higher by $32 million than in 2018. The increase in income was mainly due to increase in total revenues.

Cash and cash equivalents at the end of the period were $274.3 million. Net cash provided by operating activities was $265.9 million while cash used in investing and financing activities were $122.1 million and $118.1 million. Main cash uses were for purchases of investments acquisitions of businesses and cash dividends on common stock.

Strategy

MarketAxess objective is to provide the leading global electronic trading platforms for fixed-income securities connecting broker-dealers and institutional investors more easily and efficiently while offering a broad array of information trading and technology services to market participants across the trading cycle. The key elements of its strategy are:

Broadening its client base in its existing markets and increase penetration with existing clients by increasing its international presence by increasing the number of firms located outside the US that access its platforms through its venues in Europe Asia and Latin America increasing the number of local currencies available for trading on its platforms; and subject to regulatory requirements increasing the number of countries in which it can offer its platforms;

Enhance the liquidity of securities traded on its platforms by leveraging its client network and open trading protocols and by deploying innovative technology solutions designed to increase the number of potential trading counterparties on its platforms and to address different trade sizes bond liquidity characteristics and trading preferences;

Continue to develop innovative next-generation technologies that will allow its clients to further automate and improve the performance of their trading desks by launching a number of innovative technologies that rely on machine-learning automation and algorithms that are designed to improve the trading decisions and workflows of its clients while reducing trading inefficiencies and human errors;

Expand and strengthen its trade-related service data and analytical offerings throughout the trading cycle so that MarketAxess is more fully integrated into the workflow of its broker-dealer and institutional investor clients; and

Pursue select acquisitions and strategic alliances that will enable it to enter new markets provide new products or services or otherwise enhance the value of its platform and existing trade-related services to its clients.

Mergers and Acquisitions

In 2020 MarketAxess has completed its previously announced acquisition of Regulatory Reporting Hub the regulatory reporting business of Deutsche B ¶rse Group. MarketAxess acquired the business through Trax NL B.V. its wholly owned subsidiary in the Netherlands. The Regulatory Reporting Hub is a pan-European reporting and compliance platform that enables buy- and sell-side clients to meet their regulatory obligations and transparency requirements across multiple regulations such as MiFID II and EMIR. Services include transaction and trade reporting best execution reporting and SI services as well as APA and ARM services. Terms were not disclosed.

In 2019 MarketAxess has completed its previously announced acquisition of LiquidityEdge a leading provider of an electronic U.S. Treasuries marketplace. The acquisition was completed on November 1 2019 following approval from the necessary regulatory authorities. The purchase price is approximately $150 million including $100 million in cash and 146450 shares of MarketAxess common stock subject to customary purchase price adjustments.

EXECUTIVES

Global Head - Sales, Kevin Mcpherson, $300,000 total compensation
Independent Director, Steven Begleiter
Independent Director, William Cruger
Independent Director, Jane Chwick
General Counsel, Scott Pintoff
Independent Director, Richard Ketchum
Independent Director, Emily Portney
Head Of Emea And Apac, Christophe Roupie, $399,000 total compensation
Independent Director, Justin Gmelich
Independent Director, Kourtney Gibson
Independent Director, Xiaojia Li
President, Chief Financial Officer, Chief Operating Officer, Director, Christopher Concannon, $500,000 total compensation
Ceo, Richard Mcvey, $500,000 total compensation
Chief Information Officer, Nicholas Themelis, $300,000 total compensation
Auditors: PricewaterhouseCoopers LLP

LOCATIONS

HQ: MarketAxess Holdings Inc.
55 Hudson Yards, 15th Floor, New York, NY 10001
Phone: 212 813-6000 **Fax:** 212 813-6390
Web: www.marketaxess.com

PRODUCTS/OPERATIONS

2014 Sales

	$ mil.	% of total
Commissions	221.1	84
Information and post-trade services	31.5	12
Technology products and services	6.9	3
Investment income	0.5	-
Others	2.8	1
Total	**262.8**	**100**

Selected Mergers and Acquisitions

FY2012
Xtrakter Limited (undisclosed price; London UK; provider of regulatory transaction reporting)

COMPETITORS

E TRADE FINANCIAL CORPORATION
EDWARD D. JONES & CO. L.P.
EUROMONEY INSTITUTIONAL INVESTOR PLC
FIDESSA GROUP HOLDINGS LIMITED
INTERACTIVE BROKERS GROUP INC.
INTERCONTINENTAL EXCHANGE INC.
SAILPOINT TECHNOLOGIES HOLDINGS INC.
STIFEL FINANCIAL CORP.
STONEX GROUP INC.
VIRTU ITG HOLDINGS LLC
WADDELL & REED FINANCIAL INC.

HISTORICAL FINANCIALS

Company Type: Public

Income Statement — FYE: December 31

	REVENUE ($ mil.)	NET INCOME ($ mil.)	NET PROFIT MARGIN	EMPLOYEES
12/21	698.9	257.8	36.9%	676
12/20	689.1	299.3	43.4%	606
12/19	511.3	204.9	40.1%	527
12/18	435.5	172.8	39.7%	454
12/17	397.4	148.0	37.3%	429
Annual Growth	**15.2%**	**14.9%**	**—**	**12.0%**

2021 Year-End Financials

Debt ratio: —
Return on equity: 25.8%
Cash ($ mil.): 506.7
Current ratio: 2.66
Long-term debt ($ mil.): —

No. of shares (mil.): 37.9
Dividends
Yield: 0.6%
Payout: 36.1%
Market value ($ mil.): 15,595.0

	STOCK PRICE ($) FY Close	P/E High/Low	Earnings	Dividends	Book Value
12/21	411.27	84 50	6.77	2.64	27.46
12/20	570.56	74 35	7.85	2.40	25.13
12/19	379.11	76 38	5.40	2.04	20.30
12/18	211.31	49 37	4.57	1.68	16.15
12/17	201.75	52 37	3.89	1.32	13.68
Annual Growth	**19.5%**	**—**	**14.9%**	**18.9%**	**19.0%**

Masimo Corp.

Masimo is a global medical technology company that develops manufactures and markets a variety of noninvasive monitoring technologies and hospital automation solutions. The company's product range which is based on Signal Extraction Technology (SET) offers pulse oximeters in both handheld and stand-alone (bedside) form. Product benefits include the provision of real-time information and elimination of signal interference such as patient movements. Its US market generates the majority of sales. Joe Kiani founded Masimo in 1989 as a private "garage start-up" company.

Operations
Masimo's primary products include patient monitoring solutions sensor products and other devices and accessories such as adapter cables.

All of the company's revenue came from product sales.

Geographic Reach
While the US accounts for more than 65% of its sales Masimo is working to grow its operations in Africa Asia Australia Europe and the Middle East and accounting for the remaining sales.

Based in Irvine California Masimo has locations in Switzerland and two manufacturing facilities in Mexico.

Sales and Marketing
Masimo provide its products to hospitals emergency medical service (EMS) providers home care providers long-term care facilities physician offices veterinarians and consumers through its direct sales force distributors and original equipment manufacturers (OEM) partners. Two distributors Medline Industries and Cardinal Health each account for more than 10% of sales.

Advertising costs for the years 2021 (ended January) 2019 (ended December) and 2018 (ended December) were $30.8 million $14.0 million and $17.9 million respectively.

Financial Performance
Total revenue increased $205.9 million or 22.% to $1.1 billion for the year ended January 2 2021 from $937.8 million for the year ended December 28 2019. This increase was primarily due to higher revenue from monitors consumables boards and services a portion of which the company believes is related to a continued overall demand for its products due to the global COVID-19 pandemic.

In 2020 the company had a net income of $240.3 million a 22% increase from the previous year.

The company's cash in 2020 was $645 million. Operating activities generated $211 million while investing activities used $82.8 million mainly for business combinations. Financing activities used another $54.3 million primarily for repurchases of common stock.

Strategy
The company intends to continue to grow its business and improve its market position by pursuing the following strategies: Continuing to expand its market share in Pulse Oximetry; Expanding the Pulse Oximetry market to other patient care setting; Expanding the use of rainbow technology in hospital settings; Expanding the use of rainbow technology in non-hospital settings; Expanding the use of Root in hospital settings; Expanding hospital automation and connectivity in hospital settings; Utilizing its customer base and OEM relationships to market Masimo rainbow SET O3 SedLine and Capnography products incorporating licensed rainbow technology; and Continuing to innovate and maintain its technology leadership position.

Its future growth strategy is also closely tied to its focus on international expansion opportunities. Since 2007 it has continued to expand its sales and marketing presence in Europe Asia Asia Pacific Middle East Canada and Latin America. The company accomplished this by both additional staffing and adding or expanding sales offices in many of these territories. By centralizing a portion of its international operations including sales management marketing customer support planning logistics and administrative functions in Neuch tel Switzerland it has developed a more efficient and scalable international organization that is capable of being even more responsive to the business needs of its international customers under this centralized management structure.

Mergers and Acquisitions
In 2021 Masimo completed the acquisition of the LiDCO Group Plc a leading provider of advanced hemodynamic monitoring solutions (LiDCO).

In early 2020 Masimo agreed to acquire TNI medical AG (TNI) an innovative ventilation company headquartered in W rzburg Germany. Masimo believes this technology will provide clinicians with important additional tools to address the growing number of people affected by pulmonary diseases and respiratory-related illnesses including those suffering from COVID-19.

In 2020 Masimo agreed to acquire the Connected Care assets from NantHealth Inc. for approximately $47.25 million. NantHealth's Connected Care solutions provide medical device interoperability to hospitals and health systems.

The portfolio includes DCX device connectivity (formerly known as DeviceConX) VCX patient vitals software (formerly known as VitalsConX) HBox connectivity hub and Shuttle interface cable. The acquisition supports Masimo's goal to help hospitals improve the continuum of great care through hospital automation connectivity and innovative noninvasive monitoring technologies.

EXECUTIVES

Chairman And Chief Executive Officer, Joseph Kiani, $1,142,392 total compensation
Executive Vice President, General Counsel, Corporate Secretary, Tom McClenahan, $434,109 total compensation
Chief Operating Officer, Bilal Muhsin, $558,249 total compensation
Executive Vice President - Business Development, Tao Levy, $344,826 total compensation
Independent Director, Julie Shimer
Chief Financial Officer, Executive Vice President, Micah Young, $436,049 total compensation
Auditors: Grant Thornton LLP

LOCATIONS

HQ: Masimo Corp.
52 Discovery, Irvine, CA 92618
Phone: 949 297-7000
Web: www.masimo.com

PRODUCTS/OPERATIONS

2017 Sales

	$ mil.	% of total
Products	741.3	93
Royalties	56.8	7
Total	**798.1**	**100**

COMPETITORS

FORESCOUT TECHNOLOGIES GUIDED INC.	PHILIPS IMAGE
HOLOGIC INC.	THERAPY CORPORATION
ITRON INC.	PREMIER INC.
LUMENIS LTD.	STERIS LIMITED
NATUS MEDICAL SYSTEMS INCORPORATED	Tecsys Inc
	VARIAN MEDICAL INC.
OLYMPUS CORPORATION	VOCERA
COMMUNICATIONS	
PERKINELMER INC.	INC.

HISTORICAL FINANCIALS

Company Type: Public

Income Statement — FYE: January 1

	REVENUE ($ mil.)	NET INCOME ($ mil.)	NET PROFIT MARGIN	EMPLOYEES
01/22	1,239.1	229.6	18.5%	6,200
01/21*	1,143.7	240.3	21.0%	6,200
12/19	937.8	196.2	20.9%	5,300
12/18	858.2	193.5	22.5%	4,500
12/17	798.1	131.6	16.5%	4,600
Annual Growth	**11.6%**	**14.9%**	**—**	**7.7%**

*Fiscal year change

2022 Year-End Financials

Debt ratio: —	No. of shares (mil.): 55.3
Return on equity: 15.5%	Dividends
Cash ($ mil.): 745.2	Yield: —
Current ratio: 4.63	Payout: —
Long-term debt ($ mil.): —	Market value ($ mil.): 16,201.0

	STOCK PRICE ($) FY Close	P/E High/Low		PER SHARE ($) Earnings	Dividends	Book Value
01/22	292.78	73	50	3.98	0.00	28.02
01/21*	268.38	62	34	4.14	0.00	25.48
12/19	159.49	44	28	3.44	0.00	21.75
12/18	105.56	34	22	3.45	0.00	18.25
12/17	84.80	41	26	2.36	0.00	13.69
Annual Growth	**36.3%**	—	—	**14.0%**	—	**19.6%**

*Fiscal year change

Mastech Digital Inc

Mastech provides outsourced staffing services primarily for businesses in need of contract information technology (IT) personnel. The company provides systems integrators and other IT staffing companies with temporary technical staff on a wholesale basis. It also serves companies in other industries directly. The company mainly serves customers in the US but it has international recruiting operations in India. Apart from finance clients come from such industries as consumer products health care retail technology and telecom. Formerly a subsidiary of IGATE Corporation Mastech was spun off to its parent company's shareholders in 2008.

EXECUTIVES

Independent Director, Gerhard Watzinger
Chief Financial Officer, Corporate Secretary, John Cronin, $335,000 total compensation
Co-chairman Of The Board, Sunil Wadhwani
Independent Director, John Ausura
Co-chairman, Ashok Trivedi
Independent Director, Brenda Galilee
President And Chief Executive Officer, Vivek Gupta, $456,667 total compensation
Auditors: UHY LLP

LOCATIONS

HQ: Mastech Digital Inc
1305 Cherrington Parkway, Building 210, Suite 400, Moon Township, PA 15108
Phone: 412 787-2100
Web: www.mastechdigital.com

COMPETITORS

Cobragon Limited	IMPELLAM GROUP PLC
DATEC (PNG) LIMITED CAPITAL	MANAGEMENT AND
GENESIS HR SOLUTIONS INC.	PARTNERS LLC
	Neusoft Corporation
HINDUJA GLOBAL SOLUTIONS LIMITED	OASIS OUTSOURCING HOLDINGS INC.

HISTORICAL FINANCIALS

Company Type: Public

Income Statement — FYE: December 31

	REVENUE ($ mil.)	NET INCOME ($ mil.)	NET PROFIT MARGIN	EMPLOYEES
12/20	194.1	9.8	5.1%	1,671
12/19	193.5	11.1	5.8%	1,745
12/18	177.1	6.6	3.8%	1,680
12/17	147.8	1.6	1.1%	1,530
12/16	132.0	2.5	1.9%	1,125
Annual Growth	**10.1%**	**40.6%**	**—**	**10.4%**

2020 Year-End Financials

Debt ratio: 16.9%	No. of shares (mil.): 11.3
Return on equity: 18.5%	Dividends
Cash ($ mil.): 7.6	Yield: —
Current ratio: 1.87	Payout: —
Long-term debt ($ mil.): 12.8	Market value ($ mil.): 181.0

	STOCK PRICE ($) FY Close	P/E High/Low		PER SHARE ($) Earnings	Dividends	Book Value
12/20	15.90	33	9	0.83	0.00	5.23
12/19	11.07	11	5	0.99	0.00	4.19
12/18	6.30	35	10	0.60	0.00	3.12
12/17	10.06	80	37	0.17	0.00	2.49
12/16	6.81	29	22	0.28	0.00	2.12
Annual Growth	**23.6%**	—	—	**31.2%**	—	**25.3%**

MasterCraft Boat Holdings Inc

Auditors: DELOITTE & TOUCHE LLP

LOCATIONS

HQ: MasterCraft Boat Holdings Inc
100 Cherokee Cove Drive, Vonore, TN 37885
Phone: 423 884-2221
Web: www.mastercraft.com

HISTORICAL FINANCIALS

Company Type: Public

Income Statement — FYE: June 30

	REVENUE ($ mil.)	NET INCOME ($ mil.)	NET PROFIT MARGIN	EMPLOYEES
06/21	525.8	56.1	10.7%	1,500
06/20	363.0	(24.0)	—	884
06/19	466.3	21.3	4.6%	1,195
06/18	332.7	39.6	11.9%	882
06/17	228.6	19.5	8.6%	490
Annual Growth	**23.1%**	**30.2%**	**—**	**32.3%**

2021 Year-End Financials

Debt ratio: 33.6%	No. of shares (mil.): 18.9
Return on equity: 71.7%	Dividends
Cash ($ mil.): 39.2	Yield: —
Current ratio: 1.48	Payout: —
Long-term debt ($ mil.): 90.2	Market value ($ mil.): 498.0

	STOCK PRICE ($) FY Close	P/E High/Low		PER SHARE ($) Earnings	Dividends	Book Value
06/21	26.29	11	5	2.96	0.00	5.69
06/20	19.05	—	—	(1.28)	0.00	2.59
06/19	19.59	33	16	1.14	0.00	3.85
06/18	28.95	15	8	2.12	0.00	2.81
06/17	19.55	19	10	1.05	0.00	0.63
Annual Growth	7.7%	—	—	29.6%	—	73.3%

MaxLinear Inc

MaxLinear is a provider of communications systems-on-chip (SoC) solutions used in broadband mobile and wireline infrastructure data center and industrial and multi-market applications. It is a fabless integrated circuit design company whose products integrate all or substantial portions of a high-speed communication system including integrated radio-frequency (RF) high-performance analog mixed-signal digital signal processing security engines data compression and networking layers and power management. Its products are used in cable TV set-top boxes cable modems automobiles and personal computers. The company sells to module makers OEMs distributors and original design manufacturers (ODMs). Majority of its sales were generated from Asian customers.

Operations

MaxLinear operates in one segment as it has developed marketed and sold primarily only one class of similar products radio-frequency high-performance analog and mixed-signal communications system-on-chip solutions for the connected home wired and wireless infrastructure markets and industrial and multi-market applications. It provides communications systems-on-chip (SoC) solutions used in broadband mobile and wireline infrastructure data center and industrial and multi-market applications.

The development of broadband (around 50% of sales) low power integrated communication systems-on-chip solutions is at the heart of competitiveness across a range of different businesses spanning broadband wireline access mobile data services hyperscale cloud data centers and cloud computation and storage markets.

In the Industrial & Multi-Market (about 20%) manufacturing equipment and appliances are connected to each other and to the cloud to better optimize utilization improve power consumption and plant management. Legacy equipment and new installations need to communicate with each other via newer and older connectivity protocol standards. Other end markets such as infrastructure and connected some accounts for around 15% each.

Geographic Reach

Based in Carlsbad California MaxLinear has operations in Irvine California; San Jose California; Boston Massachusetts; Burnaby Canada; Bangalore India; Singapore; Taipei and Hsinchu Taiwan; Shenzhen Shanghai and Hong Kong China; Seoul South Korea; Tokyo Japan; Paterna Spain; Villach Austria; Munich Germany; and in Petah Tikva Israel.

MaxLinear has heavy customer concentration in Asia where it generates over 80% of revenue. US customers supply less than 5% of sales with the rest split among other markets.

Sales and Marketing

MaxLinear uses a direct sales force in the US and certain markets in Asia and Europe. In other areas it uses third-party sales representatives and a network of distributors. Distributors account for about 50% of sales. The company sells its roducts directly and indirectly to original equipment manufacturers or OEMs module makers and original design manufacturers or ODMs.

The top ten customers account for about 70% of MaxLinear's sales with two of its direct customers represented about 30% of net revenue.

Financial Performance

Net revenue increased $161.4 million to $478.6 million for the year ended December 31 2020 as compared to $317.2 million for the year ended December 31 2019. The increase in broadband net revenue of $125.1 million primarily was the result of a partial-year contribution of gateway revenues attributable to our acquisition of the Wi-Fi and Broadband assets business on July 31 2020 and to a lesser extent improvements in cable product shipments partially offset by reductions in satellite product shipments.

Net loss for fiscal 2020 increased to $98.6 million compared from the prior year with $19.9 million.

Cash held by the company at the end of fiscal 2020 increased to $150.0 million. Cash provided by operations and financing activities were $73.6 million and $159.6 million respectively. Cash used for investing activities was $175.3 million mainly for acquisitions.

Strategy

MaxLinear's objective is to be the leading provider of communications SoCs for the connected home wired and wireless infrastructure and industrial and multi-market applications. The company aim to continue to leverage its core analog and digital signal co-processing competencies to expand into other communications markets with similar performance requirements. The key elements of the company's strategy are: extend technology leadership in RF transceivers and RF transceiver + digital signal processing + embedded processor SoCs; leverage and expand the company's existing customer base; target additional high-growth markets; expand global presence; and attract and retain top talent.

Mergers and Acquisitions

In 2020 MaxLinear entered into a definitive agreement with Intel Corporation to acquire Intel's Home Gateway Platform Division assets in an all-cash asset transaction valued at $150 million. The Home Gateway Platform Division comprises Wi-Fi Access Points Ethernet and Home Gateway SoC products deployed across operator and retail markets. The acquisition will enable MaxLinear to complement its existing portfolio bringing together a complete and scalable platform of connectivity and access solutions for its customers across target end-markets as well as creating potential new revenue opportunities in adjacent target end-markets.

EXECUTIVES

Vice President - Worldwide Operations, W. Kelly Jones, $74,055 total compensation
Chief Financial Officer, Chief Corporate Strategy Officer, Steven Litchfield, $379,729 total compensation
Chairman Of The Board, President, Chief Executive Officer, Kishore Seendripu, $589,152 total compensation
Lead Independent Director, Thomas Pardun
Chief Technical Officer, Curtis Ling, $285,649 total compensation
Vice President, Marketing Infrastructure, Brendan Walsh, $260,378 total compensation
Vice President - Central Engineering, Madhukar Reddy, $334,729 total compensation
Vice President, General Manager, Broadband Group, William Torgerson, $327,805 total compensation
Vice President - Sales, Michael Bollesen, $109,795 total compensation
Independent Director, Theodore Tewksbury
Corporate Controller, Principal Accounting Officer, Connie Kwong
Independent Director, Albert Moyer
Independent Director, Donald Schrock
Vice President - Marketing, High Performance Analog, James Lougheed, $169,027 total compensation
Independent Director, Daniel Artusi
Independent Director, Carolyn Beaver
Independent Director, Gregory Dougherty
Independent Director, Tsu- Jae King Liu
Auditors: Grant Thornton LLP

LOCATIONS

HQ: MaxLinear Inc
5966 La Place Court, Suite 100, Carlsbad, CA 92008
Phone: 760 692-0711
Web: www.maxlinear.com

PRODUCTS/OPERATIONS

2017 Sales by Product

	$ mil.	% of total
Connected Home	288.6	69
Infrastructure	71.8	17
Industrial and multi-market	59.9	14
Total	**420.3**	**100**

COMPETITORS

APPLIED OPTOELECTRONICS INC.
AVAGO TECHNOLOGIES LIMITED
CAVIUM LLC
CLEARONE INC.
COMMSCOPE HOLDING COMPANY INC.
DSP GROUP INC.
KEYSIGHT TECHNOLOGIES INC.
MACOM TECHNOLOGY SOLUTIONS HOLDINGS INC.
MONOLITHIC POWER SYSTEMS INC.
NXP Semiconductors N.V.
ON SEMICONDUCTOR CORPORATION
PERASO INC.
QORVO INC.
SEMTECH CORPORATION
SILICON LABORATORIES INC.
SKYWORKS SOLUTIONS INC.
Sierra Wireless Inc
TE Connectivity Ltd.

HISTORICAL FINANCIALS
Company Type: Public

Income Statement				FYE: December 31
	REVENUE ($ mil.)	NET INCOME ($ mil.)	NET PROFIT MARGIN	EMPLOYEES
12/21	892.4	41.9	4.7%	1,503
12/20	478.6	(98.5)	—	1,420
12/19	317.1	(19.9)	—	697
12/18	385.0	(26.2)	—	739
12/17	420.3	(9.1)	—	753
Annual Growth	20.7%	—	—	18.9%

2021 Year-End Financials
Debt ratio: 29.1%
Return on equity: 9.5%
Cash ($ mil.): 130.6
Current ratio: 1.95
Long-term debt ($ mil.): 306.1

No. of shares (mil.): 76.7
Dividends
  Yield: —
  Payout: —
Market value ($ mil.): 5,788.0

	STOCK PRICE ($) FY Close	P/E High/Low		PER SHARE ($) Earnings	Dividends	Book Value
12/21	75.39	140	56	0.53	0.00	6.37
12/20	38.19	—	—	(1.35)	0.00	5.25
12/19	21.22	—	—	(0.28)	0.00	5.77
12/18	17.60	—	—	(0.38)	0.00	5.75
12/17	26.42	—	—	(0.14)	0.00	5.75
Annual Growth	30.0%			—	—	2.6%

Maxus Realty Trust Inc

Maxus Realty Trust believes in the value of maximizing housing space. The real estate investment trust (REIT) invests in income-producing properties primarily multifamily residential properties. It owns a portfolio of approximately 10 apartment communities in the Midwest US. Maxus Realty Trust was originally established to invest in office and light industrial facilities but switched gears and began focusing on residential real estate in 2000. The REIT de-registered with the SEC and stopped trading on the NASDAQ in 2008.

EXECUTIVES

Principal Financial Officer, Treasurer, John Alvey
Trustee, Christopher Garlich
Trustee, W. Robert Kohorst
Trustee, Jose Evans
Chairman Of The Board Of Trustee, President, Chief Executive Officer, David Johnson
Vice President, Michael McRobert
Trustee, Kevan Acord
Principal Accounting Officer, Corporate Secretary, DeAnn Totta
Trustee, Danley Sheldon
Trustee, Monte McDowell
Auditors: Mayer Hoffman McCann P.C.

LOCATIONS

HQ: Maxus Realty Trust Inc
104 Armour Road, P.O. Box 34729, North Kansas City, MO 64116
Phone: 816 303-4500   **Fax:** 816 221-1829
Web: www.mrti.com

COMPETITORS

SILVER BAY REALTY TRUST CORP.

STEADFAST INCOME REIT INC.

HISTORICAL FINANCIALS
Company Type: Public

Income Statement				FYE: December 31
	REVENUE ($ mil.)	NET INCOME ($ mil.)	NET PROFIT MARGIN	EMPLOYEES
12/19	118.7	13.1	11.1%	0
12/18	113.7	6.4	5.6%	0
12/17	89.1	13.9	15.7%	0
12/16	74.3	14.6	19.7%	0
12/15	60.5	4.5	7.5%	0
Annual Growth	18.3%	30.5%	—	—

2019 Year-End Financials
Debt ratio: 75.4%
Return on equity: 29.7%
Cash ($ mil.): 12.0
Current ratio: 0.61
Long-term debt ($ mil.): 690.5

No. of shares (mil.): 1.1
Dividends
  Yield: 5.9%
  Payout: 84.3%
Market value ($ mil.): 142.0

	STOCK PRICE ($) FY Close	P/E High/Low		PER SHARE ($) Earnings	Dividends	Book Value
12/19	120.90	13	10	7.83	7.20	39.23
12/18	112.00	26	17	4.63	6.70	35.88
12/17	100.00	10	5	10.44	5.00	38.31
12/16	75.00	7	4	11.34	3.55	30.51
12/15	49.00	15	7	3.33	1.50	20.83
Annual Growth	25.3%			23.8%	48.0%	17.1%

Medical Properties Trust Inc

Hospitals trust Medical Properties is a self-advised real estate investment trust (REIT) formed in 2003 to acquire and develop net-leased healthcare facilities. It has investments in approximately 430 facilities and approximately 43000 licensed beds in about 35 states in the US in six countries in Europe across Australia and in Colombia in South America. Its facilities consist of more than 200 general acute care hospitals 110 inpatient rehabilitation hospitals (IRFs) 20 long-term acute care hospitals (LTACHs) some 50 freestanding ER/urgent care facilities (FSERs) and 45 behavioral health facilities.

EXECUTIVES

Chairman Of The Board, President, Chief Executive Officer, Edward Aldag, $1,000,000 total compensation
Lead Independent Director, Michael Stewart
Independent Director, G. Steven Dawson
Chief Financial Officer, Executive Vice President, Director, R. Steven Hamner, $675,000 total compensation
Chief Operating Officer, Executive Vice President, Secretary, Emmett McLean, $550,000 total compensation
Independent Director, Elizabeth Pitman

Independent Director, Caterina Mozingo
Independent Director, Daniel Sparks
Independent Director, C. Reynolds Thompson
Auditors: PricewaterhouseCoopers LLP

LOCATIONS

HQ: Medical Properties Trust Inc
1000 Urban Center Drive, Suite 501, Birmingham, AL 35242
Phone: 205 969-3755   **Fax:** 205 969-3756
Web: www.medicalpropertiestrust.com

PRODUCTS/OPERATIONS

2015 Sales by Property Type

	% of total
General acute care hospitals	58
Rehabilitation hospitals	30
Long-term acute care hospitals	12
Wellness centers	—
Total	**100**

COMPETITORS

CARE CAPITAL PROPERTIES INC.
CARETRUST REIT INC.
DIVERSIFIED HEALTHCARE TRUST
MEDEQUITIES REALTY TRUST INC.
NATIONAL HEALTH INVESTORS INC.

UNITED FIRE GROUP INC.
UNITED INSURANCE HOLDINGS CORP.
UNIVERSAL
REALTY INCOME TRUST
VENTAS INC.
WELLTOWER INC.

HISTORICAL FINANCIALS
Company Type: Public

Income Statement				FYE: December 31
	REVENUE ($ mil.)	NET INCOME ($ mil.)	NET PROFIT MARGIN	EMPLOYEES
12/20	1,249.2	431.4	34.5%	106
12/19	854.2	374.6	43.9%	86
12/18	784.5	1,016.6	129.6%	77
12/17	704.7	289.7	41.1%	66
12/16	541.1	225.0	41.6%	54
Annual Growth	23.3%	17.7%	—	18.4%

2020 Year-End Financials
Debt ratio: 52.6%
Return on equity: 5.9%
Cash ($ mil.): 549.8
Current ratio: 2.29
Long-term debt ($ mil.): 8,865.4

No. of shares (mil.): 541.4
Dividends
  Yield: 4.9%
  Payout: 133.3%
Market value ($ mil.): 11,798.0

	STOCK PRICE ($) FY Close	P/E High/Low		PER SHARE ($) Earnings	Dividends	Book Value
12/20	21.79	30	16	0.81	1.08	13.55
12/19	21.11	25	18	0.87	1.02	13.58
12/18	16.08	6	4	2.76	1.00	12.27
12/17	13.78	17	15	0.82	0.96	10.48
12/16	12.30	18	11	0.86	0.91	10.13
Annual Growth	15.4%			(1.5%)	4.4%	7.5%

Medifast Inc

Medifast is the global company behind one of the fastest-growing health and wellness communities called OPTAVIA which offers Lifelong Transformation One Healthy Habit at a Time. Medifast help clients to achieve their health goals through a network of more than 44000 independent OPTAVIA Coaches approximately 90% of whom were clients first and have impacted almost 2.0 million lives to date. OPTAVIA Coaches introduce clients to a set of healthy habits in most cases starting with the habit of healthy eating and offer exclusive OPTAVIA-branded nutritional products or Fuelings. Fuelings are nutrient-dense portion-controlled nutritionally interchangeable and simple to use.

Operations

Medifast's OPTAVIA covers almost 100% of company's total sales. OPTAVIA brand offers a highly competitive and effective lifestyle solution centered on developing new healthy habits through smaller foundational changes called micro-habits. The program is built around four key components: Independent OPTAVIA Coaches the OPTAVIA Community the Habits of Health Transformational System and Scientifically Developed Products and Clinically Proven Plans.

Medifast also has products under the Medifast brand name. Its Medifast meal replacement line includes more than 30 options including but not limited to bars bites pretzels puffs cereal crunch drinks hearty choices oatmeal pancakes pudding shakes and soft bakes. It also offers a variety of weight loss weight management and healthy living products under the Medifast Optimal Health and Flavors of Home brands.

Subsidiary Jason Pharmaceuticals makes some of the company's products.

Geographic Reach

Medifast operates a manufacturing plant in Owings Mills Maryland and in Baltimore Maryland which serves as the company headquarters. It has distribution facilities in Ridgley Maryland and outsources a domestic distribution center in Reno Nevada and an international distribution center in Hong Kong. The firm has a raw materials warehouse in Arbutus Maryland.

Sales and Marketing

Medifast uses multiple marketing strategies to reach its target audiences. It uses word-of-mouth communications digital marketing public relations events direct mail and social media channels. Advertising costs totaled $4.4 million $5.3 million and $6.0 million in 2020 2019 and 2018 respectively.

Financial Performance

Revenue increased $221.1 million or 31% to $934.8 million in 2020 from $713.7 million in 2019. The average revenue per active earning OPTAVIA Coach increased 13% for the three months ended December 31 2020 compared to the three months ended December 31 2019.

In 2020 the company had a net income of $102.9 million a 32% increase compared to the previous year.

The company's cash at the end of 2020 was $163.7 million. Operating activities generated $145.2 million while investing activities used $1.3 million mainly for purchase of property and equipment. Financing activities used another $56.1 million mainly for cash dividends paid to stockholders.

Strategy

Global expansion is an important component of Medfast's long-term growth strategy. In July 2019 it commenced its international operations entering into the Asia Pacific markets of Hong Kong and Singapore. Its decision to enter these markets was based on industry market research that reflects a dynamic shift in how health care is being prioritized and consumed in those countries.

Company Background

Medifast's promotion and distribution model has changed over time. When it was founded in 1993 the company primarily sold its products through doctor's offices. Customers received supervision from their family physician who in turn received commissions on any products sold. However as physicians had increasingly less time to spend with patients the method grew less effective. At the beginning of 2018 the company discontinued the sales of products through physicians thus reducing the complexity of its product distribution.

The company also exited the corporate support center model in 2014. It sold 41 centers to franchise partners and closed its remaining 34 corporate centers.

EXECUTIVES

Executive Vice President, General Counsel, And Corporate Secretary, Jason Groves, $200,000 total compensation
Independent Director, Constance Hallquist
Chief Marketing Officer, Anthony Tyree, $373,961 total compensation
Executive Vice President, Information Technology, William Baker, $363,277 total compensation
Independent Director, Michael Hoer
Executive Vice President, Coach Success And President, Market, Nicholas Johnson, $339,231 total compensation
Independent Director, Ming Xian
Executive Vice President , Human Resources, Claudia Greninger
Independent Director, Andrea Thomas
Executive Vice President, Supply Chain Operations, Lauren Walker
Chief Accounting Officer, Jonathan Mackenzie
Chairman And Chief Executive Officer, Daniel Chard, $909,173 total compensation
Chief Financial Officer, James Maloney, $187,981 total compensation
Auditors: RSM US LLP

LOCATIONS

HQ: Medifast Inc
100 International Drive, Baltimore, MD 21202
Phone: 410 581-8042
Web: www.medifastnow.com

PRODUCTS/OPERATIONS

2017 Sales

	$ mil.	% of total
OPTAVIA	256.6	85
Medifast Direct	31.9	11
MWCC	12.2	4
Medifast Wholesale	1.0	
Total	**301.7**	**100**

Selected Subsidiaries

Jason Enterprises Inc.
Jason Pharmaceuticals Inc.
Jason Properties LLC
Medifast Franchise Systems Inc.
Medifast Nutrition Inc.
OPTAVIA LLC
Seven Crondall Associates LLC

COMPETITORS

AJINOMOTO CO. INC.	MCCORMICK & COMPANY
COLUMBUS MCKINNON	INCORPORATED
CORPORATION	NATURE'S SUNSHINE
CRANSWICK PLC	PRODUCTS INC.
EBRO FOODS SA	Ontex Group
GENERAL MILLS INC.	Premium Brands
MANNATECH INCORPORATED	Holdings
Corporation	
MASIMO CORPORATION	

HISTORICAL FINANCIALS

Company Type: Public

Income Statement

FYE: December 31

	REVENUE ($ mil.)	NET INCOME ($ mil.)	NET PROFIT MARGIN	EMPLOYEES
12/20	934.8	102.8	11.0%	713
12/19	713.6	77.9	10.9%	550
12/18	501.0	55.7	11.1%	420
12/17	301.5	27.7	9.2%	399
12/16	274.5	17.8	6.5%	422
Annual Growth	35.8%	55.0%	—	14.0%

2020 Year-End Financials

Debt ratio: —	No. of shares (mil.): 11.7
Return on equity: 78.2%	Dividends
Cash ($ mil.): 163.7	Yield: 2.3%
Current ratio: 2.10	Payout: 56.5%
Long-term debt ($ mil.): —	Market value ($ mil.): 2,311.0

	STOCK PRICE ($) FY Close	P/E High/Low		PER SHARE ($) Earnings	Dividends	Book Value
12/20	196.34	24	6	8.68	4.52	13.36
12/19	109.58	24	11	6.43	3.38	8.91
12/18	125.02	55	14	4.62	2.19	9.19
12/17	69.81	32	17	2.29	1.44	9.07
12/16	41.63	28	18	1.49	1.07	8.09
Annual Growth	47.4%		—	55.4%	43.4%	13.4%

Medpace Holdings Inc

Auditors: DELOITTE & TOUCHE LLP

LOCATIONS

HQ: Medpace Holdings Inc
5375 Medpace Way, Cincinnati, OH 45227
Phone: 513 579-9911
Web: www.medpace.com

HISTORICAL FINANCIALS

Company Type: Public

Income Statement

FYE: December 31

	REVENUE ($ mil.)	NET INCOME ($ mil.)	NET PROFIT MARGIN	EMPLOYEES
12/21	1,142.3	181.8	15.9%	4,500
12/20	925.9	145.3	15.7%	3,600
12/19	860.9	100.4	11.7%	3,500
12/18	704.5	73.1	10.4%	2,900
12/17	436.1	39.1	9.0%	2,500
Annual Growth	27.2%	46.8%	—	15.8%

2021 Year-End Financials

Debt ratio: —
Return on equity: 20.6%
Cash ($ mil.): 461.3
Current ratio: 1.24
Long-term debt ($ mil.): —

No. of shares (mil.): 36.0
Dividends
Yield: —
Payout: —
Market value ($ mil.): 7,837.0

	STOCK PRICE ($) FY Close	P/E High/Low		PER SHARE ($) Earnings	Dividends	Book Value
12/21	217.64	45	26	4.81	0.00	26.47
12/20	139.20	37	15	3.84	0.00	22.69
12/19	84.06	31	18	2.67	0.00	20.14
12/18	52.93	31	16	1.97	0.00	16.53
12/17	36.26	38	22	0.98	0.00	14.20
Annual Growth	**56.5%**	—	—	**48.8%**	—	**16.8%**

Mercantile Bank Corp.

Mercantile Bank Corporation is the holding company for Mercantile Bank of Michigan (formerly Mercantile Bank of West Michigan) which boasts assets of nearly $3 billion and operates more than 50 branches in central and western Michigan around Grand Rapids Holland and Lansing. The bank targets local consumers and businesses offering standard deposit services such as checking and savings accounts CDs IRAs and health savings accounts. Commercial loans make up more than three-fourths of the bank's loan portfolio. Outside of banking subsidiary Mercantile Insurance Center sells insurance products.

Operations

Mercantile Bank Corp. generated 82% of its total revenue from loan interest (including fees) in 2014 with securities interest contributing another 8% to total revenue. Service charges on deposit and sweep accounts and credit and debit card fees made up another 5% of Mercantile's total revenue while its mortgage banking income generated another 2%.

Sales and Marketing

Mercantile provides its banking services to businesses individuals and government organizations. Its commercial banking services mostly cater to small- to medium-sized businesses.

The company spent $1.315 million on advertising in 2014 compared to $1.113 million and $1.167 million in 2013 and 2012 respectively.

Financial Performance

Mercantile Bank Corp's revenues had been declining for a number of years as its loan business withered while profits have remained mostly flat.

The company had a breakout year in 2014 however after its historic acquisition of FirstBank Corp. The bank's revenue skyrocketed by 53% to $99.15 million (the highest level since 2009) mostly as the acquisition nearly doubled its loan assets and boosted its interest income on loans and securities by significant amounts. The bank's non-interest income also grew by 46% thanks to higher fee income across the board also resulting from the recent acquisition.

Higher revenue and a $3.2 million reduction in loan loss provisions with a stronger credit portfolio in 2014 also pushed the company's net income up by 2% to $17.33 million for the year. Mercantile's operating cash declined by 50% to $14.41 million due to changes in accrued interest and other liabilities during the year.

Strategy

Mercantile Bank Corporation has been growing its loan business and branch network reach through strategic acquisitions of smaller banks and bank branches. Its mid-2014 acquisition of Firstbank Corporation was perhaps the most effective to date as the purchase doubled its assets and boosted the size of its branch network nearly seven-fold from seven branches to a whopping 53.

Mergers and Acquisitions

In June 2014 Mercantile Bank Corp. purchased Firstbank Corp of Alma Michigan for a total purchase price of $173 million adding 46 branches and $1.3 billion in assets. The deal which made Mercantile the third-largest bank based in the state also expanded the bank's service offerings diversified its loan portfolio boosted its loan origination capacity and significantly extended its geographic footprint into Michigan's lower peninsula.

EXECUTIVES

Executive Vice President, Chief Financial Officer, Treasurer Of The Company And Executive Vice President And Chief Financial Officer Of The Bank, Charles Christmas, $389,341 total compensation
Chairman Of The Board Of The Mercantile And Bank, Michael Price
President, Chief Executive Officer, Director Of The Company And Chief Executive Officer Of The Bank, Robert Kaminski, $538,962 total compensation
Executive Vice President Of Mercantile, President And Director Of The Bank, Raymond Reitsma, $400,621 total compensation
Chief Operating Officer, Senior Vice President, General Counsel, Secretary Of The Company And Bank, Robert Worthington, $270,000 total compensation
Independent Director, Michelle Eldridge
Independent Director, David Cassard
Independent Director, Jeff Gardner
Senior Vice President, Human Resource Director Of Mercantile And The Bank, Lonna Wiersma, $281,197 total compensation
Independent Director, David Ramaker
Independent Director, Michael Davenport
Auditors: BDO USA, LLP

LOCATIONS

HQ: Mercantile Bank Corp.
310 Leonard Street N.W., Grand Rapids, MI 49504
Phone: 616 406-3000
Web: www.mercbank.com

PRODUCTS/OPERATIONS

2014 Sales

	$ mil.	% of total
Interest income		
Loans and leases including fees	80.8	82
Securities taxable	6.4	6
Securities tax-exempt	1.6	2
Other	0.2	-
Noninterest income		
Service charges on accounts	2.6	3
Credit and debit card fees	2.5	2
Mortgage banking activities	1.7	2
Other	3.3	3
Total	**99.1**	**100**

COMPETITORS

CASCADE BANCORP
CENTERSTATE BANK CORPORATION
COLUMBIA BANKING SYSTEM INC.
FIRST COMMONWEALTH FINANCIAL CORPORATION
FIRSTMERIT CORPORATION
LEGACYTEXAS FINANCIAL GROUP INC.
NATIONAL BANK HOLDINGS CORPORATION
OFG BANCORP
STATE BANK FINANCIAL CORPORATION
TCF FINANCIAL CORPORATION
WSFS FINANCIAL CORPORATION

HISTORICAL FINANCIALS
Company Type: Public

Income Statement
FYE: December 31

	ASSETS ($ mil.)	NET INCOME ($ mil.)	INCOME AS % OF ASSETS	EMPLOYEES
12/20	4,437.3	44.1	1.0%	665
12/19	3,632.9	49.4	1.4%	683
12/18	3,363.9	42.0	1.2%	693
12/17	3,286.7	31.2	1.0%	701
12/16	3,082.5	31.9	1.0%	682
Annual Growth	**9.5%**	**8.4%**	—	**(0.6%)**

2020 Year-End Financials

Return on assets: 1.0%
Return on equity: 10.2%
Long-term debt ($ mil.): —
No. of shares (mil.): 16.3
Sales ($ mil): 193.4

Dividends
Yield: 4.1%
Payout: 42.1%
Market value ($ mil.): 444.0

	STOCK PRICE ($) FY Close	P/E High/Low		PER SHARE ($) Earnings	Dividends	Book Value
12/20	27.17	13	6	2.71	1.12	27.04
12/19	36.47	12	10	3.01	1.06	25.36
12/18	28.26	15	11	2.53	1.68	22.70
12/17	35.37	20	15	1.90	0.74	22.05
12/16	37.70	19	11	1.96	1.16	20.76
Annual Growth	**(7.9%)**	—	—	**8.4%**	**(0.9%)**	**6.8%**

Merchants Bancorp (Indiana)

Auditors: BKD, LLP

LOCATIONS

HQ: Merchants Bancorp (Indiana)
410 Monon Blvd., Carmel, IN 46032
Phone: 317 569-7420
Web: www.merchantsbankofindiana.com

HISTORICAL FINANCIALS
Company Type: Public

Income Statement
FYE: December 31

	ASSETS ($ mil.)	NET INCOME ($ mil.)	INCOME AS % OF ASSETS	EMPLOYEES
12/20	9,645.3	180.5	1.9%	404
12/19	6,371.9	77.3	1.2%	329
12/18	3,884.1	62.8	1.6%	259
12/17	3,393.1	54.6	1.6%	194
12/16	2,718.5	33.1	1.2%	157
Annual Growth	**37.2%**	**52.8%**	—	**26.7%**

2020 Year-End Financials

Return on assets: 2.2%
Return on equity: 24.5%
Long-term debt ($ mil.): —
No. of shares (mil.): 43.1
Sales ($ mil): 410.2

Dividends
Yield: 1.7%
Payout: 8.3%
Market value ($ mil.): 1,191.0

	STOCK PRICE ($) FY Close	P/E High/Low		PER SHARE ($) Earnings	Dividends	Book Value
12/20	27.63	8	3	3.85	0.32	18.80
12/19	19.71	16	10	1.58	0.28	15.18
12/18	19.96	21	14	1.38	0.24	9.79
12/17	19.68	14	11	1.52	0.05	8.54
Annual Growth	12.0%	—	—	36.3%	85.7%	30.1%

Mercury Systems Inc

Mercury Systems (formerly Mercury Computer Systems) delivers digital signals faster than a wing-footed messenger. The company delivers innovative technology solutions for the homeland security military and aerospace and telecommunications markets. In addition it manufactures essential components modules and subsystem. It provides customers process radar electronic warfare weapons and missile defense . It also makes specialized electronics used in semiconductor wafer inspection and airport baggage screeners. Mercury Systems acts as a subcontractor to prime contractors such as Northrop Grumman and Raytheon. The company was founded in 1981. In late 2019 the company acquired American Panel Corporation.

Operations

Company manages its business on the basis of one reportable segment. In general the company manufactures essential components modules and subsystems.

Components include technology elements typically performing a single discrete technological function which when physically combined with other components may be used to create a module or subassembly. Modules and subassemblies include combinations of multiple functional technology elements and/or components that work together to perform multiple functions but are typically resident on or within a single board or housing. Integrated subsystems include multiple modules and/or subassemblies combined with a backplane or similar functional element and software to enable a solution. In addition the company pioneered or contributed to the development of many of the defense industry's current and emerging open standards including standards such as RACEway RapidIO VXS VPX REDI and notably OpenVPX.

In terms of end application Radar (30% of the total sales) includes end-use applications where radio frequency signals are utilized to detect track and identify objects. Electronic Warfare (20%) includes end-use applications comprising the offensive and defensive use of the electromagnetic spectrum. Other Sensor and Effector products (less than 15%) include all Sensor and Effector end markets other than Radar and Electronic Warfare. C4I (more than 25%) includes rugged secure rack-mount servers that are designed to drive the most powerful military processing applications. Other

(more than 10%) products include all component and other sales where the end use is not specified.

When it comes to platforms Airborne platform (more than 50% of the total sales) includes products that relate to personnel equipment or pieces of equipment designed for airborne applications. Land platform (less than 15%) includes products that relate to fixed or mobile equipment or pieces of equipment for personnel weapon systems vehicles and support elements operating on land. Naval platform (nearly 20%) includes products that relate to personnel equipment or pieces of equipment designed for naval operations.

Geographic Reach

Headquartered in Andover Massachusetts Mercury Systems has research and development centers and other facilities in the US (Arizona California Massachusetts New Hampshire Virginia and Georgia) Switzerland Japan Spain Canada UK and France. It generates more than 90% of sales from the US; Europe accounts for more than five percent and the Asia-Pacific region accounts for less than five percent.

Sales and Marketing

The company sells to defense prime contractors the U.S. government and original equipment manufacturers ("OEM") commercial aerospace companies.

Its top two customers are Raytheon Technologies and Lockheed Martin Corporation. These two accounted for more than 30% of the total sales. Other customers are customers include Airbus BAE Systems Boeing General Atomics General Dynamics L3Harris Technologies Leonardo and Northrop Grumman.

Financial Performance

Since 2016 the revenue performance of the company is encouraging as it posted a 195% jump in the last five years. Net income followed the same trend and posted a 334% increase for the same period.

Revenue jumped 22% in 2020 to $796.6 million. The increase in total revenue was primarily due to $91.4 million and $50.5 million of organic revenues and acquired revenues respectively. These increases were driven by higher demand throughout all product groupings especially integrated subsystems across all end applications and in particular radar within the airborne naval and land platforms.

Mercury posted a net income of $85.7 million in 2020 $38.9 million higher than in 2019. The increase was brought about by higher revenues higher interest income and lower income tax provision.

Cash and cash equivalents at the end of the year were $226.8 million. Net cash provided by operating activities was $115.2 million while investing and financing activities each used $135.5 million and $10.9 million respectively for acquisitions and payments under credit facility.

Strategy

The company strategies for growth are: Investing to grow organically; Expanding capabilities market access and penetration through mergers & acquisitions; Investing in trusted secure Innovation that Matters; Continuously improve operational capability and scalability; and Attracting and retaining the right talent.

These strategies are built around its key strengths as a leading technology company serving the aerospace and defense industry. These strategies include innovation and investment in scaling

existing capabilities as well as augmenting its capabilities through an acquisition strategy designed to focus on adjacent technologies. The company believes its investment in R&D is more than double that of its competitors on a percentage basis. Its consistent strategies allow it to assist its customers mostly defense prime contractors to reduce program cost minimize technical risk stay on schedule and budget and ensure trust and security in the supply chain. As a result it has successfully penetrated strategic programs including Aegis Patriot Surface Electronic Warfare Improvement Program (SEWIP) Gorgon Stare Predator F-35 Reaper F-16 SABR E2-D Hawkeye Paveway Filthy Buzzard PGK P-8 Advanced Integrated Defensive Electronic Warfare Suite (AIDEWS) Common Display System (CDS) and WIN-T.

Mercury Systems announced in June 2020 the availability of miniaturization packaging services that complement the U.S. Government's global positioning system (GPS) modernization efforts advancing the development of smaller more agile missiles and guided munitions to support mission success. Mercury's innovative three-dimensional (3D) packaging manufacturing and test services optimize the size weight and power (SWaP) of new secure military code (M-Code) GPS receivers. Leveraging Mercury's expertise in trusted 3D packaging and selective availability anti-spoofing modules (SAASM) assembly and testing defense prime contractors can reduce their current electronics design footprint and deliver the greater payload and standoff capability the warfighter requires.

Mergers and Acquisitions

Mercury Systems uses acquisitions to add products services and technical capabilities.

In late 2019 Mercury agreed to acquire American Panel Corp. which develops large area display technology for about $100 million. The company's capabilities are used in the US Army's Apache attack helicopter and M1A2 Abrams battle tank as well as the F-35 F-15 F-16 and F-18 fighter jets.

In early 2019 the Athena Group Inc and Syntonic Microwave LLC were acquired. Both cost for $46000. Athena was a privately-held company based in Gainesville Florida and a leading provider of cryptographic and countermeasure IP vital to securing defense computing systems. Syntonic was a privately held company based in Campbell California and a leading provider of advanced synthesizers wideband phase coherent tuners and microwave.

In early 2019 Mercury Systems Inc. has acquired GECO Avionics LLC (GECO) for a total purchase price of $36500. Based in Mesa Arizona GECO has over twenty years of experience designing and manufacturing affordable safety-critical avionics and mission computing solutions.

Company Background

The company was founded in 1981. In 2011 Mercury acquired LNX Corporation of Salem N.H.

EXECUTIVES

Independent Director, Mary Krakauer
Independent Chairman Of The Board, William O'Brien
President, Chief Executive Officer And Director, Mark Aslett, $722,692 total compensation
Executive Vice President; President - Processing Division, Brian Perry
Independent Director, James Bass
Independent Director, Michael Daniels

Chief Financial Officer, Executive Vice President, Treasurer, Michael Ruppert, $413,879 total compensation
Independent Director, Barry Nearhos
Independent Director, Orlando Carvalho
Evp And Chief Transformation Officer, Thomas Huber
Executive Vice President, General Counsel, Secretary, Christopher Cambria, $385,265 total compensation
Independent Director, Lisa Disbrow
Auditors: KPMG LLP

LOCATIONS

HQ: Mercury Systems Inc
  50 Minuteman Road, Andover, MA 01810
Phone: 978 256-1300
Web: www.mrcy.com

PRODUCTS/OPERATIONS

2015 Sales

	$ mil.	% of total
Mercury Commercial Electronics	207.1	88
Mercury Defense Systems	27.4	12
Eliminations	0.3	-
Total	**234.8**	**100**

COMPETITORS

ASTRONICS CORPORATION	JABIL INC.
BENCHMARK ELECTRONICS INC.	MEGGITT PLC
CTS CORPORATION	MOOG INC.
EXELIS INC.	SYPRIS SOLUTIONS INC.
HEICO CORPORATION	TTM TECHNOLOGIES INC.
HON HAI PRECISION INDUSTRY CO. LTD.	

HISTORICAL FINANCIALS

Company Type: Public

Income Statement

FYE: July 2

	REVENUE ($ mil.)	NET INCOME ($ mil.)	NET PROFIT MARGIN	EMPLOYEES
07/21	924.0	62.0	6.7%	2,384
07/20*	796.6	85.7	10.8%	1,947
06/19	654.7	46.7	7.1%	1,661
06/18	493.1	40.8	8.3%	1,320
06/17	408.5	24.8	6.1%	1,159
Annual Growth 22.6%	25.7%		—	19.8%

*Fiscal year change

2021 Year-End Financials

Debt ratio: 10.2%	No. of shares (mil.): 55.2
Return on equity: 4.3%	Dividends
Cash ($ mil.): 113.8	Yield: —
Current ratio: 4.26	Payout: —
Long-term debt ($ mil.): 200.0	Market value ($ mil.): 3,646.0

	STOCK PRICE ($) FY Close	P/E High/Low		PER SHARE ($) Earnings	Dividends	Book Value
07/21	66.00	78	51	1.12	0.00	26.87
07/20*	80.27	59	36	1.56	0.00	25.31
06/19	70.35	77	39	0.96	0.00	23.68
06/18	38.06	61	36	0.86	0.00	16.45
06/17	42.09	71	37	0.58	0.00	15.67
Annual Growth 11.9%		—	— 17.9%		—	14.4%

*Fiscal year change

Meridian Bioscience Inc.

Meridian is a fully-integrated life science company with principal businesses in the development manufacture sale and distribution of diagnostic testing systems and kits primarily for certain gastrointestinal and respiratory infectious diseases and elevated blood lead levels; and the manufacture and distribution of bulk antigens antibodies immunoassay blocking reagents specialized Polymerase Chain Reaction (PCR) master mixes and bioresearch reagents used by other diagnostic test manufacturers and researchers in immunological and molecular tests for human animal plant and environmental applications. Founded in 1977 majority of its sales were generated in Americas.

Operations

The company's reportable segments are Life Science (about 60% of revenue) and Diagnostics (about 40%).

The Life Science segment develops manufactures sells and distributes bulk antigens antibodies immunoassay blocking reagents specialized PCR master mixes isothermal reagents enzymes nucleotides and bioresearch reagents used predominantly by in vitro device (IVD) manufacturing companies and to a lesser degree by researchers and non-human clinical customers such as veterinary food and environmental.

The Diagnostic segment product portfolio includes approximately 200 diagnostic tests and transport media. Its testing platforms include: Real-time PCR Amplification (Revogene brand); Isothermal DNA Amplification (Alethia brand); Lateral Flow Immunoassay using fluorescent chemistry (Curian brand); Rapid Immunoassay (Immuno-Card and ImmunoCard STAT! brands); Enzyme-linked Immunoassay (PREMIER brand); Anodic Stripping Voltammetry (LeadCare and Pediastat brands); and urea breath testing for H. pylori (BreathID and BreathTek brand).

Non-molecular assay accounts for about 55% of revenue and Molecular assays at more than 45%.

Geographic Reach

Headquartered in Cincinnati Ohio Meridian Bioscience sells its products and services into approximately 70 countries. The Life Science segment has manufacturing operations in Memphis Tennessee; Boca Raton Florida; London England; and Luckenwalde Germany while Diagnostic segment has sales and distribution center near Milan Italy and rents office space in Paris France and Braine-l'Alleud Belgium for sales and administrative functions and space in Manasquan New Jersey and Changzhou China to house BreathID technical service and repair functions.

About 45% of sales were generated in the Americas EMEA with over 35% and the rest of the world with some 15%.

Sales and Marketing

Its Diagnostics Segment relies on a direct sales force in four countries and distribuiin networks. It also uses independent distributors either in a complementary manner with its direct sales force or solely to supply its products to end-users. It has two independent distribution customers and a reference laboratory customer that together com-

prised roughly 35% of Diagnostics segment net revenues in fiscal 2021 with each contributing 10% or greater of the Diagnostics segment's net revenues.

Financial Performance

Consolidated revenues for fiscal 2021 totaled $317.9 million an increase of 25% compared to fiscal 2020 (22% increase on a constant-currency basis). With a 66% increase in revenues from molecular reagents products and a 10% increase in revenues from immunological reagents products revenues for the company's Life Science segment increased 43% to $190.1 million during fiscal 2021 compared to fiscal 2020.

In 2021 the company had a net income of $71.4 million a 55% increase from the previous year's net income of $46.2 million.

The company's cash at the end of 2021 was $49.8 million. Operating activities generated $66.9 million while investing activities used $40.4 million primarily for acquisitions and purchase of property plant and equipment. Financing activities used another $31.1 million mainly for payment of acquisition consideration.

Strategy

Meridian Bioscience Inc. announced in December 2020 that it has launched an Air-Dryable RT-qPCR Mix driving innovation in the development of molecular tests with ambient temperature stability. This specialized master mix is designed for air-drying a cost-effective and easier alternative to lyophilization. With this new product addition Meridian has the most comprehensive offering of master mixes for developing both DNA and RNA based molecular diagnostic assays at ambient temperature removing the need for cold chain shipping and storage.

Meridian's Air-Dryable RT-qPCR Mix has been designed to simplify development manufacturing and storage of molecular assays while delivering fast detection of RNA targets an ideal solution for COVID-19 assay development. Its one-tube format chemistry containing all reagents necessary for a RT-qPCR including magnesium dNTP and reverse transcriptase not only shortens assay optimization but is also compatible with air-drying protocols. This new mix shows exceptionally high performance in both singleplex and multiplex reactions following rehydration making it ideally suited for a wide range of instruments from automated high-throughput platforms to point-of-care devices.

Mergers and Acquisitions

In 2021 Meridian Bioscience has completed previously announced acquisition of the North American BreathTek business from Otsuka America Pharmaceutical Inc for $20 million in cash. With this acquisition Meridian will assume the customer relationships in North America to supply BreathTek a urea breath test for the detection of Helicobacter pylori. The acquisition is expected to add more than $20 million of annual revenue strengthening Meridian's position as a leading provider of gastrointestinal diagnostic solutions and is expected to be accretive to earnings and cash immediately.

In early 2020 Meridian Bioscience has completed its previously announced acquisition of Exalenz Bioscience Ltd. the Modiin Israel based provider of the BreathID Breath Test Systems a urea breath test platform for the detection of Helicobacter pylori. The combination of Meridian's leading stool antigen tests with the Exalenz BreathID urea breath test positions Meridian as the only company in the U.S. with a complete offering of non-invasive diagnostic assays for a H. pylori active infection. The purchase price of the acquisition amounted to approximately $56.3 million.

HISTORY

Microbiology and diagnostics specialists William Motto and Jerry Ruyan launched Meridian Diagnostics in 1977 naming it for their desire to reach the highest point in diagnostic technology. The company began as a research and development lab but soon developed a variety of commercial products including test kits for pneumocystis carinii pneumonia (a leading cause of death in AIDS patients) and mycoplasmal (or "walking") pneumonia.

In the 1990s Meridian made key acquisitions to further its offerings including the ImmunoCard rapid-response systems from Disease Detection International and the MonoSpot and Monolert mononucleosis diagnostics technologies from Johnson & Johnson. Other acquisitions include tests for Lyme disease and the viruses that cause pediatric diarrhea.

As a result of its entry into the life sciences market (spurred by its acquisitions of antibody reagent maker BIODESIGN in 1999 and antigens and test kits maker Viral Antigens in 2000) Meridian Diagnostics changed its name to Meridian Bioscience in 2001.

In 2005 the company expanded its life sciences division once again by purchasing OEM Concepts a manufacturer of antibody products. The following year Meridian Bioscience combined BIODESIGN Viral Antigens Meridian Biologics and OEM Concepts into a new Life Sciences business segment with the former businesses becoming four distinct brands within that unit.

The Life Sciences division expanded its operations in 2007 when it won a five-year contract with the National Institute for Allergies and Infectious Diseases (part of the NIH) to manufacture experimental vaccines; the contract was worth up to $12.2 million.

In 2008 the company broadened the Life Science division by acquiring technologies and products including proteins and antigens for applications in infectious disease and cardiac research from private life sciences firm Vybion.

EXECUTIVES

Chief Executive Officer, Director, John Kenny, $690,000 total compensation
Executive Vice President - Diagnostics, Tony Serafini-Lamanna, $367,891 total compensation
Chairman Of The Board, John McIlwraith
Independent Director, Catherine Sazdanoff
Executive Vice President - Life Science, Lourdes Weltzien, $383,847 total compensation
Independent Director, Felicia Williams
Independent Director, John Rice
Julie Smith To The Position Of Senior Vice President, Controller And Principal Accounting Officer, Julie Smith
Auditors: Ernst & Young LLP

LOCATIONS

HQ: Meridian Bioscience Inc.
3471 River Hills Drive, Cincinnati, OH 45244
Phone: 513 271-3700
Web: www.meridianbioscience.com

PRODUCTS/OPERATIONS

2016 Sales

	$ mil.	% of total
Diagnostics	1,451.0	74
Life Science	50.9	26
Total	**196.0**	**100**

Selected Products and Brands

Diagnostics
Enzyme Immunoassay (EIA)/Rapid tests
ImmunoCard
MONOLERT
Premier
Immunofluorescence
MERIFLUOR
Molecular Amplification
illumigene
Particle Agglutination
Meritec
MonoSpot
Other
Macro-CON
Para-Pak
SpinCon
Life Science
BIODESIGN (monoclonal and polyclongal antibodies and assay reagents)
Bioline (biological reagents)
Biologics (contract biologics development and manufacturing)
OEM Concepts (custom antibody production)
Viral Antigens (custom infectious disease antigens)

COMPETITORS

ABBOTT LABORATORIES
CHARLES RIVER LABORATORIES INTERNATIONAL INC.
FLUIDIGM CORPORATION
LGC CLINICAL DIAGNOSTICS INC.
LIFE TECHNOLOGIES CORPORATION
LUMINEX CORPORATION
MYMD PHARMACEUTICALS INC.
MYRIAD GENETICS INC.
ORASURE TECHNOLOGIES INC.
PRECIPIO INC.
ROCHE DIAGNOSTICS CORPORATION
STRECK INC.

HISTORICAL FINANCIALS

Company Type: Public

Income Statement — FYE: September 30

	REVENUE ($ mil.)	NET INCOME ($ mil.)	NET PROFIT MARGIN	EMPLOYEES
09/21	317.9	71.4	22.5%	560
09/20	253.6	46.1	18.2%	750
09/19	201.0	24.3	12.1%	660
09/18	213.5	23.8	11.2%	585
09/17	200.7	21.5	10.7%	640
Annual Growth	**12.2%**	**34.9%**		**(3.3%)**

2021 Year-End Financials

Debt ratio: 13.3%
Return on equity: 24.8%
Cash ($ mil.): 49.7
Current ratio: 4.09
Long-term debt ($ mil.): 60.0
No. of shares (mil.): 43.3
Dividends
  Yield: —
  Payout: —
Market value ($ mil.): 834.0

	STOCK PRICE ($) FY Close	P/E High/Low		Earnings	Dividends	Book Value
09/21	19.24	18	10	1.62	0.00	7.57
09/20	16.98	24	5	1.07	0.00	5.75
09/19	9.49	35	16	0.57	0.38	4.47
09/18	14.90	30	24	0.56	0.50	4.14
09/17	14.30	38	24	0.51	0.58	4.02
Annual Growth	**7.7%**		—	**33.5%**	—	**17.2%**

Meridian Corp

Auditors: Crowe LLP

LOCATIONS

HQ: Meridian Corp
9 Old Lincoln Highway, Malvern, PA 19355
Phone: 484 568-5000
Web: www.meridianbanker.com

HISTORICAL FINANCIALS

Company Type: Public

Income Statement — FYE: December 31

	ASSETS ($ mil.)	NET INCOME ($ mil.)	INCOME AS % OF ASSETS	EMPLOYEES
12/20	1,720.2	26.4	1.5%	381
12/19	1,150.0	10.4	0.9%	0
12/18	997.3	8.1	0.8%	0
12/17	856.0	3.0	0.4%	0
12/16	733.6	4.9	0.7%	0
Annual Growth	**23.7%**	**52.2%**	—	—

2020 Year-End Financials

Return on assets: 1.8%
Return on equity: 20.1%
Long-term debt ($ mil.): —
No. of shares (mil.): 6.1
Sales ($ mil): 149.5
Dividends
  Yield: 1.2%
  Payout: 7.5%
Market value ($ mil.): 128.0

	STOCK PRICE ($) FY Close	P/E High/Low		Earnings	Dividends	Book Value
12/20	20.80	6	3	4.27	0.25	23.08
12/19	20.19	12	10	1.63	0.00	18.84
12/18	17.17	16	13	1.27	0.00	17.15
12/17	19.98	42	35	0.49	0.00	15.86
Annual Growth	**1.3%**		—	**105.8%**	—	**13.3%**

Meritage Hospitality Group Inc

This company is really big on the beef in Michigan. Meritage Hospitality Group is a leading franchisee of Wendy's fast food hamburger restaurants with about 70 locations operating mostly in western and southern Michigan. The units franchised from Wendy's/Arby's Group offer a menu of burgers and other sandwiches fries and other items. In addition to its quick-service operations Meritage runs four franchised O'Charley's casual dining restaurants in Michigan near Grand Rapids and Detroit. The company was founded in 1986 as Thomas Edison Inns. The family of chairman Robert Schermer Sr. including CEO Robert Schermer Jr. controls Meritage.

EXECUTIVES

Director, Duane Kluting
Executive Vice President Of Wendys Operations, Greg Corr

Chief Executive Officer, Director, Robert Schermer, $261,000 total compensation
General Counsel, Robert Potts, $121,518 total compensation
Director, Joseph Maggini
Chief Financial Officer, Vice President, Treasurer, Company Secretary, Tracey Smith, $182,000 total compensation
Vice President Of Real Estate, Douglas Poland
Vice President Of Human Resources, Jeff Vanhaitsma
Director, Dirk Pruis
Director, Peter Wierenga
Director, Chris Armbruster
President, Chief Operating Officer, Director, Gary Rose, $231,000 total compensation
Auditors: BDO USA LLP

LOCATIONS

HQ: Meritage Hospitality Group Inc
45 Ottawa Ave. S.W., Suite 600, Grand Rapids, MI 49503
Phone: 616 776-2600　　**Fax:** 616 776-2776
Web: www.meritagehospitality.com

COMPETITORS

BRIAD CORP.
FILI ENTERPRISES INC.
GREEN MILL RESTAURANTS LLC
KITCHEN INVESTMENT GROUP INC.
LEGAL SEA FOODS LLC
MARY'S LONG BEACH INC
SERVUS!

HISTORICAL FINANCIALS

Company Type: Public

Income Statement　　　　　　　　　　FYE: January 3

	REVENUE ($ mil.)	NET INCOME ($ mil.)	NET PROFIT MARGIN	EMPLOYEES
01/21*	516.1	14.9	2.9%	11,000
12/19	467.5	12.0	2.6%	11,000
12/18	435.3	13.0	3.0%	10,000
12/17	312.5	8.9	2.9%	6,800
01/17	235.7	6.4	2.7%	5,700
Annual Growth	21.6%	23.3%	—	17.9%

*Fiscal year change

2021 Year-End Financials

Debt ratio: 25.9%
Return on equity: 16.1%
Cash ($ mil.): 32.3
Current ratio: 0.49
Long-term debt ($ mil.): 148.8
No. of shares (mil.): 6.6
Dividends
Yield: 0.0%
Payout: 8.8%
Market value ($ mil.): 128.0

	STOCK PRICE ($) FY Close	P/E High/Low		PER SHARE ($) Earnings	Dividends	Book Value
01/21*	19.20	10	5	1.58	0.14	14.81
12/19	19.80	12	10	1.27	0.24	13.09
12/18	17.50	—	—	(0.00)	0.15	9.17
12/17	20.00	—	—	(0.00)	0.10	6.25
01/17	11.15	—	—	(0.00)	0.07	4.37
Annual Growth	14.6%		— —		— 18.9%	35.7%

*Fiscal year change

Mesabi Trust

In the Iron Range of Mesabi the stockholders trust. Mesabi Trust collects royalties and bonuses from the sale of minerals that are shipped from Northshore Mining's Silver Bay Minnesota facility. The mining company is a wholly owned subsidiary of Cliffs a supplier of iron ore products to the steel industry. Northshore Mining pays royalties to Mesabi Trust based on production and sales of crude ore pulled from the trust's property; it has curtailed its extraction efforts citing lack of demand. Independent consultants track production and sales for Mesabi Trust. Deutsche Bank Trust Company Americas is the corporate trustee of Mesabi Trust.

EXECUTIVES

Trustee, Michael Mlinar
Trustee, James Ehrenberg
Trustee, Robin Radke
Trustee, Robert Berglund
Auditors: Baker Tilly US, LLP

LOCATIONS

HQ: Mesabi Trust
c/o Deutsche Bank Trust Company Americas, Trust & Agency Services, 60 Wall Street, 24th Floor, New York, NY 10005
Phone: 904 271-2520
Web: www.mesabi-trust.com

COMPETITORS

Antarchile S.A.
CANDOVER INVESTMENTS HOLDINGS INC.
PLC
Clairvest Group Inc.
ENEOS HOLDINGS INC.
NOMURA
Riverstone Energy Limited

HISTORICAL FINANCIALS

Company Type: Public

Income Statement　　　　　　　　　　FYE: January 31

	REVENUE ($ mil.)	NET INCOME ($ mil.)	NET PROFIT MARGIN	EMPLOYEES
01/21	25.9	23.4	90.2%	0
01/20	31.9	30.0	94.0%	0
01/19	47.2	45.5	96.3%	0
01/18	34.5	33.5	96.9%	0
01/17	10.7	9.6	89.5%	0
Annual Growth	24.7%	24.9%	—	—

2021 Year-End Financials

Debt ratio: —
Return on equity: 164.9%
Cash ($ mil.): 12.5
Current ratio: 3.55
Long-term debt ($ mil.): —
No. of shares (mil.): 13.1
Dividends
Yield: 0.0%
Payout: 80.1%
Market value ($ mil.): 327.0

	STOCK PRICE ($) FY Close	P/E High/Low		PER SHARE ($) Earnings	Dividends	Book Value
01/21	24.89	17	5	1.78	1.43	1.26
01/20	20.41	14	9	2.29	2.67	0.90
01/19	27.44	9	6	3.47	3.00	1.28
01/18	24.80	12	5	2.55	2.53	0.80
01/17	13.70	19	5	0.73	0.64	0.78
Annual Growth	16.1%		— —	24.9%	22.3%	12.7%

Meta Financial Group Inc

Delivering financial products and services to Iowa and South Dakota is the calling of Meta Financial Group. The company's full-services banking subsidiary MetaBank primarily consists of attracting deposits and investing those funds in its loan and lease portfolios along with providing prepaid cards and other financial products and solutions to business and consumer customers. In addition to originating loans and leases the MetaBank also occasionally contracts to sell loans such as tax refund advance loans consumer credit product loans and government guaranteed loans to third party buyers. It holds $3.3 billion in loan portfolio and $4.98 billion deposit portfolio.

Operations

Meta Financial operates through three reportable segments Consumer (nearly 55% of total sales) Commercial (more than 40%) and Corporate Services/Other (less than 5% of sales).

The consumer segment includes Meta Payment Systems consumer credit products Tax Services and Warehouse finance while commercial segment includes Crestmark division and AFS/IBEX division and corporate services/other includes certain shared services retained community bank portfolio treasury and student loan lending portfolio.

Overall net interest income accounts for about 55% of total sales.

Geographic Reach

Sioux Falls SD-based Meta Financial has about 15 non-branch facilities from which its divisions of payments commercial finance tax services and consumer lending operate.

The payments division operates out of the company's home office along with one additional office in Sioux Falls. The commercial finance division operates out of offices in Troy Michigan; Dallas Texas; Newport Beach California; Boynton Beach Florida; Baton Rouge Louisiana; Franklin Tennessee; and Toronto Ontario Canada.

The tax services division has offices located in Louisville Kentucky and Easton Pennsylvania. The company has corporate and shared services offices located in Scottsdale Arizona and Washington D.C. The company also has an office located in Hurst Texas.

Financial Performance

Total revenue for the fiscal year 2020 (ended September) was $498.8 million an increase of 2% from the fiscal year 2019.

The company recorded net income of $104.7 million for the fiscal year 2020 compared to $97.0 million for the fiscal year ended 2019 an increase of $7.7 million. Total revenue for fiscal 2020 was $498.8 million compared to $486.8 million for fiscal 2019 an increase of 2%. The increase in net income and revenue was primarily due to an increase in noninterest income and a decrease in noninterest expense partially offset by a slight decrease in net interest income.

Cash held by the company at the end of fiscal 2020 decreased to $4.8 million compared to $8.1 million in the prior year. Cash provided by operations was $119.8 million while cash used for investing and financing activities were $0.8 million and $122.4 million respectively. Main uses of cash

HOOVER'S HANDBOOK OF EMERGING COMPANIES 2022

were alternative Investments and shares repurchased for tax withholdings on stock compensation.

EXECUTIVES

Director, Bradley Hanson, $866,745 total compensation
Executive Vice President, Chief Technology And Product Officer, Charles Ingram, $383,100 total compensation
Executive Vice President, Chief People And Inclusion Officer, Kia Tang, $216,346 total compensation
Executive Vice President, Chief Governance, Risk, And Compliance Officer, Sonja Theisen
Independent Director, Elizabeth Hoople
Co-president And Chief Operating Officer, Metabank, Brett Pharr, $420,000 total compensation
Independent Director, Lizabeth Zlatkus
Independent Director, Ronald McCray
Executive Vice President, Chief Legal Officer, Nadia Dombrowski
Chief Financial Officer, Executive Vice President, Glen Herrick, $488,520 total compensation
Independent Chairman Of The Board And Meta Bank, Douglas Hajek
Independent Vice Chairman Of The Board, Becky Shulman
President, Anthony Sharett, $395,187 total compensation
Auditors: Crowe LLP

LOCATIONS

HQ: Meta Financial Group Inc
   5501 South Broadband Lane, Sioux Falls, SD 57108
Phone: 877 497-7497
Web: www.metabank.com

COMPETITORS

AMERICAN NATIONAL BANKSHARES INC.	NBT BANCORP INC.
BOK FINANCIAL CORPORATION	PACIFIC CONTINENTAL CORPORATION
CAMDEN NATIONAL CORPORATION	TCF FINANCIAL CORPORATION
FIRST MIDWEST BANCORP INC.	UNIVEST FINANCIAL CORPORATION
FLAGSTAR BANCORP INC.	WEBSTER FINANCIAL CORPORATION
KEARNY FINANCIAL CORP.	WESBANCO INC.

HISTORICAL FINANCIALS

Company Type: Public

Income Statement — FYE: September 30

	ASSETS ($ mil.)	NET INCOME ($ mil.)	INCOME AS % OF ASSETS	EMPLOYEES
09/21	6,690.6	141.7	2.1%	1,134
09/20	6,092.0	104.7	1.7%	1,015
09/19	6,182.8	97.0	1.6%	1,186
09/18	5,835.0	51.6	0.9%	1,219
09/17	5,228.3	44.9	0.9%	827
Annual Growth	6.4%	33.3%	—	8.2%

2021 Year-End Financials

Return on assets: 2.2%
Return on equity: 16.5%
Long-term debt ($ mil.): —
No. of shares (mil.): 31.6
Sales ($ mil): 556.7
Dividends
   Yield: 0.3%
   Payout: 4.6%
Market value ($ mil.): 1,662.0

	STOCK PRICE ($) FY Close	P/E High/Low		PER SHARE ($) Earnings	Dividends	Book Value
09/21	52.48	12	5	4.38	0.20	27.49
09/20	19.22	14	5	2.94	0.20	24.55
09/19	32.61	33	7	2.49	0.20	22.22
09/18	82.65	70	46	1.67	0.18	19.00
09/17	78.40	66	39	1.61	0.17	15.05
Annual Growth	(9.5%)	—	—	28.4%	3.6%	16.3%

MetroCity Bankshares Inc

Auditors: Crowe LLP

LOCATIONS

HQ: MetroCity Bankshares Inc
   5114 Buford Highway, Doraville, GA 30340
Phone: 770 455-4989
Web: www.metrocitybank.bank

HISTORICAL FINANCIALS

Company Type: Public

Income Statement — FYE: December 31

	ASSETS ($ mil.)	NET INCOME ($ mil.)	INCOME AS % OF ASSETS	EMPLOYEES
12/20	1,897.4	36.3	1.9%	211
12/19	1,631.8	44.7	2.7%	208
12/18	1,432.6	41.3	2.9%	0
12/17	1,288.9	31.9	2.5%	0
12/16	1,100.0	20.2	1.8%	0
Annual Growth	14.6%	15.8%	—	—

2020 Year-End Financials

Return on assets: 2.0%
Return on equity: 15.7%
Long-term debt ($ mil.): —
No. of shares (mil.): 25.6
Sales ($ mil): 104.8
Dividends
   Yield: 2.7%
   Payout: 27.4%
Market value ($ mil.): 370.0

	STOCK PRICE ($) FY Close	P/E High/Low		PER SHARE ($) Earnings	Dividends	Book Value
12/20	14.42	13	6	1.41	0.40	9.54
12/19	17.51	16	7	1.81	0.42	8.49
12/18	33.00	19	11	1.69	0.38	6.95
12/17	19.90	—	—	(0.00)	0.23	5.61
Annual Growth	(10.2%)	—	—	—	21.1%	19.3%

Metropolitan Bank Holding Corp

Auditors: Crowe LLP

LOCATIONS

HQ: Metropolitan Bank Holding Corp
   99 Park Avenue, New York, NY 10016
Phone: 212 659-0600
Web: www.mcbankny.com

HISTORICAL FINANCIALS

Company Type: Public

Income Statement — FYE: December 31

	ASSETS ($ mil.)	NET INCOME ($ mil.)	INCOME AS % OF ASSETS	EMPLOYEES
12/20	4,330.8	39.4	0.9%	189
12/19	3,357.5	30.1	0.9%	167
12/18	2,182.6	25.5	1.2%	153
12/17	1,759.8	12.3	0.7%	129
12/16	1,220.3	5.0	0.4%	118
Annual Growth	37.3%	67.5%	—	12.5%

2020 Year-End Financials

Return on assets: 1.0%
Return on equity: 12.3%
Long-term debt ($ mil.): —
No. of shares (mil.): 8.3
Sales ($ mil): 160.1
Dividends
   Yield: —
   Payout: —
Market value ($ mil.): 301.0

	STOCK PRICE ($) FY Close	P/E High/Low		PER SHARE ($) Earnings	Dividends	Book Value
12/20	36.27	11	4	4.66	0.00	41.08
12/19	48.23	13	8	3.56	0.00	35.98
12/18	30.85	18	10	3.06	0.00	32.19
12/17	42.10	21	15	2.34	0.00	28.90
Annual Growth	(4.8%)	—	—	25.8%	—	12.4%

Mettler-Toledo International, Inc.

Mettler-Toledo International measures up as one of the top suppliers of precision instruments and services in the world. The company is recognized as an innovation leader and its solutions are critical in research and development quality control and manufacturing processes for its customers. The company makes a range of bench and floor scales that precisely weigh materials as little as one ten-millionth of a gram to more than 60 kilograms. The company's main markets are laboratory industrial and food retail among others. Mettler-Toledo also makes analytical instruments and software for life science engineering and drug and chemical compound development. The US accounts for about a third of the company's revenue.

Operations

Mettler-Toledo has five reportable segments: U.S. Operations (about 35% of revenue) Chinese Operations (more than 20%) Western European Operations (more than 20%) Swiss Operations (some 5%) and Other.

Sales of Mettler-Toledo's laboratory products account for more than half of the company's revenue. Its lab product categories are laboratory balances pipettes analytical instruments laboratory software (called LabX) automated chemistry tools and process analytics.

Industrial products bring in nearly 40% of the company's revenue. Industrial product categories are weighing instruments industrial terminals transportation and logistics equipment vehicle scale systems industrial software and product inspection (includes metal detectors and x-ray and camera-based systems).

Retail systems account for the remaining revenue. For retailers the company offers networked scales and software which can integrate information collected from throughout the store into an inventory management system. It also offers standalone scales for counter weighing and pricing price finding and label printing. In North America and select other markets it offers automated packaging and labeling equipment for the meat backroom.

Mettler-Toledo also offers services such as calibration certification repairs and spare parts supply. The company makes proprietary components in its own plants and it contracts with other manufacturers to produce some non-proprietary components.

Geographic Reach

Mettler-Toledo's products are sold in more than 140 countries and has a direct presence in approximately 40 countries. The Americas accounts for about 40% of revenue and Europe and Asia (and other countries) each for about 30% each.

Mettler-Toledo makes components in plants in China Switzerland the UK Germany the UK and Mexico. The company maintains executive offices in Columbus Ohio and Greifensee Switzerland.

Sales and Marketing

Mettler-Toledo sells through a variety of channels. Its direct sales force focuses on technically sophisticated products while less complicated products are handled by the company's indirect sales group. In the Americas a significant portion of sales including Ohaus-branded products is made through indirect channels. Ohaus products target markets such as education in which customers pay less and get fewer features and less support and service.

Mettler-Toledo's customers are spread across the electronics food retailing laboratory pharmaceutical precious metals and transportation markets among others.

Financial Performance

Mettler-Toledo's performance for the past five years has continued to increase with 2021 as its highest performing year.

In 2021 net sales increased by $632 million or 18% to $3.7 billion in 2021 compared to $3.1 billion in 2020. The PendoTECH acquisition contributed 1% to its net sales in 2021. In 2021 Mettler-Toledo experienced broad-based growth with robust customer demand in most businesses and regions with particularly strong growth in China.

The company's net income in 2021 increased by $167.2 million to $769 million compared to the prior year's $603 million due to higher revenue in 2021.

Mettler-Toledo had cash and equivalents of $98.5 million at the end of the year. The company's operations generated $908.8 million in 2021. Investing activities and financing activities used $314.1 million and $590.5 million respectively. Main cash uses were for acquisitions and repayments of borrowings.

Strategy

In 2022 Mettler-Toledo expects to continue to pursue the overall business growth strategies which they have followed in recent years:

Gaining Market Share - The company's global sales and marketing initiative "Spinnaker" continues to be an important growth strategy. It aims to gain market share by implementing sophisticated sales and marketing programs leveraging its ex-

tensive customer databases and leveraging its product offering to larger customers through key account management.

Expanding Emerging Markets - Emerging markets comprising Asia (excluding Japan) Eastern Europe Latin America Middle East and Africa account for approximately 35% of its total net sales. The company has a two-pronged strategy in emerging markets: first to capitalize on long-term growth opportunities in these markets and second to leverage its low-cost manufacturing operations in China.

Extending Its Technology Lead - Mettler-Toledo continues to focus on product innovation. In the last three years the company spent approximately 5% of net sales on research and development. It seeks to accelerate product replacement cycles as well as improve its product offerings and its capabilities with additional integrated technologies and software which also support its pricing differentiation. In addition it aims to create value for its customers by having an intimate knowledge of its processes via the company's significant installed product base.

Expanding Its Margins - Mettler-Toledo continues to strive to improve its margins by more effectively pricing its products and services and optimizing its cost structure.

Pursuing Strategic Acquisitions - The company seeks to pursue "bolt-on" acquisitions that may leverage its global sales and service network respected brand extensive distribution channels and technological leadership. It has identified life sciences product inspection and process analytics as three key areas for acquisitions.

Mergers and Acquisitions

In early 2021 Mettler-Toledo International acquired PendoTECH for an initial $185 million initial payment with a contingent consideration of up to $20 million and other post-closing amounts. PendoTECH is a manufacturer of single-use sensors transmitters control systems and software for measuring monitoring and data collection primarily in bioprocess applications. The acquisition enables the company to expand its offering to include various sensors including pressure which is an important and common control parameter in downstream and upstream bioprocess applications.

HISTORY

Engineer Erhard Mettler weighed in to the precision scale industry in 1945 when he started Mettler Instrumente AG in Kusnacht Switzerland. Mettler invented a single-pan analytical balance that proved to be more accurate than the then-standard two-pan weighing equipment. By the mid-1950s the company expanded into the US and its equipment's popularity had the industry using "Mettler balance" to refer to nearly any high-precision laboratory scale.

In the early 1960s the company made its first acquisition and began expanding into analytical measuring instruments. Mettler moved its headquarters to Greifensee Switzerland near the decade's end. During the 1970s the company diversified into food retailing products and converted its product offerings from mechanical to electronic systems.

Swiss conglomerate Ciba-Geigy (now part of Novartis) bought Mettler in 1980; Erhard Mettler retired. In 1989 Ciba bought US industrial scale manufacturer Toledo Scale Corporation (founded

1901) and merged it with Mettler renaming the unit Mettler-Toledo.

EXECUTIVES

President, Director, Oliver Filliol, $749,266 total compensation

Head Of European And North American Market Organizations, Marc de la Gueronniere, $257,575 total compensation

Head, Human Resources, Christian Magloth

Independent Chairman Of The Board, Robert Spoerry

Chief Financial Officer, Shawn Vadala, $367,883 total compensation

Head Of Process Analytics, Gerhard Keller, $303,937 total compensation

Independent Director, Richard Francis

Head Of Divisions And Operations, Peter Aggersbjerg, $420,480 total compensation

Independent Director, Domitille Doat-Le Bigot

Chief Executive Officer Designate, Patrick Kaltenbach

Independent Director, Michael Kelly

Independent Director, Elisha Finney

Auditors: PricewaterhouseCoopers LLP

LOCATIONS

HQ: Mettler-Toledo International, Inc.
1900 Polaris Parkway, Columbus, OH 43240
Phone: 614 438-4511   **Fax:** 614 438-4646
Web: www.mt.com

PRODUCTS/OPERATIONS

2018 Sales by Sector

	% of total
Laboratory	51
Industrial	41
Retail	8
Total	**100**

2018 Sales

	$ mil.	% of total
Products	2,300.1	78
Service	635.5	22
Total	**2,935.6**	**100**

2018 Sales

	$ in mil.
% of total	
U.S. Operations	27
Swiss Operations	22
Chinese Operations	19
Western European Operations	19
Other	13
Eliminations and Corporate	-
Total	**100**

Selected Products:

Laboratory Instruments:
Laboratory balances
Liquid pipetting solutions
Titrators
Physical value analyzers
Thermal analysis systems
Other analytical instruments Moisture analyzers Density refractometers
Food Retail Industrial Instruments:Indust

COMPETITORS

AGILENT TECHNOLOGIES INC.
BARNES GROUP INC.
BIO-RAD LABORATORIES INC.
ELECTROCOMPONENTS PUBLIC LIMITED COMPANY
KIMBALL ELECTRONICS INC.
MSA SAFETY INCORPORATED
NORDSON CORPORATION

PACIFIC BIOSCIENCES OF CALIFORNIA INC.
STANDEX INTERNATIONAL CORPORATION
THERMO FISHER SCIENTIFIC INC.
VIAVI SOLUTIONS INC.

HISTORICAL FINANCIALS
Company Type: Public

Income Statement | | | | FYE: December 31

	REVENUE ($ mil.)	NET INCOME ($ mil.)	NET PROFIT MARGIN	EMPLOYEES
12/21	3,717.9	768.9	20.7%	17,800
12/20	3,085.1	602.7	19.5%	16,500
12/19	3,008.6	561.1	18.6%	16,200
12/18	2,935.5	512.6	17.5%	16,000
12/17	2,725.0	375.9	13.8%	15,400
Annual Growth	8.1%	19.6%	—	3.7%

2021 Year-End Financials

Debt ratio: 50.5%
Return on equity: 338.6%
Cash ($ mil.): 98.5
Current ratio: 1.11
Long-term debt ($ mil.): 1,580.8

No. of shares (mil.): 22.8
Dividends
  Yield: —
  Payout: —
Market value ($ mil.): 38,770.0

	STOCK PRICE ($) FY Close	P/E High/Low		PER SHARE ($) Earnings	Dividends	Book Value
12/21	1,697.21	51	31	32.78	0.00	7.50
12/20	1,139.68	47	23	24.91	0.00	12.04
12/19	793.28	38	22	22.47	0.00	17.44
12/18	565.58	34	26	19.88	0.00	23.68
12/17	619.52	47	28	14.24	0.00	21.43
Annual Growth	28.7% (23.1%)	—	—	23.2%	—	—

Mid Penn Bancorp Inc

Mid Penn Bancorp is the holding company for Mid Penn Bank which operates more than a dozen branches in central Pennsylvania's Cumberland Dauphin Northumberland and Schuylkill counties. The bank offers full-service commercial banking insurance and trust services. Its deposit products include checking savings money market and NOW accounts. Commercial real estate construction and land development loans account for nearly 80% of the company's loan portfolio; the bank also writes residential mortgages and business agricultural and consumer loans. Mid Penn is a descendant of Millersburg Bank founded in 1868. Trust company CEDE & Co. owns about a third of Mid Penn Bancorp.

EXECUTIVES

Independent Vice Chairman Of The Board, William Specht
Non-executive Independent Chairman Of The Board, Robert Grubic
Independent Director, Kimberly Brumbaugh
Director, William Poole
Independent Director, Robert Abel
Senior Executive Vice President And Chief Revenue Officer Of The Bank, Scott Micklewright, $271,728 total compensation
Independent Director, John Noone

Senior Executive Vice President, Chief Operating Officer Of The Bank, Justin Webb, $271,728 total compensation
Executive Vice President, Chief Of Staff Of The Bank, Joan Dickinson, $234,848 total compensation
Chairman, President And Chief Executive Officer, Rory Ritrievi, $500,000 total compensation
Executive Vice President, Director Of Trust And Wealth Management Of The Bank, Joseph Paese, $194,092 total compensation
Independent Director, Gregory Kerwin
Independent Director, Donald Kiefer
Director, David Sparks
Independent Director, Brian Hudson
Interim Chief Financial Officer, Donald Holt
Independent Director, Howard Greenawalt
Independent Director, Maureen Gathagan
Auditors: RSM US LLP

LOCATIONS

HQ: Mid Penn Bancorp Inc
  349 Union Street, Millersburg, PA 17061
Phone: 866 642-7736
Web: www.midpennbank.com

COMPETITORS

COUNTY BANK CORP.
FIDELITY BANCORP INC.
KS BANCORP INC.

HISTORICAL FINANCIALS
Company Type: Public

Income Statement | | | | FYE: December 31

	ASSETS ($ mil.)	NET INCOME ($ mil.)	INCOME AS % OF ASSETS	EMPLOYEES
12/20	2,998.9	26.2	0.9%	466
12/19	2,231.1	17.7	0.8%	444
12/18	2,077.9	10.6	0.5%	406
12/17	1,170.3	7.0	0.6%	277
12/16	1,032.6	7.8	0.8%	257
Annual Growth	30.5%	35.4%	—	16.0%

2020 Year-End Financials

Return on assets: 1.0%
Return on equity: 10.5%
Long-term debt ($ mil.): —
No. of shares (mil.): 8.4
Sales ($ mil): 125.8

Dividends
  Yield: 3.5%
  Payout: 24.8%
Market value ($ mil.): 184.0

	STOCK PRICE ($) FY Close	P/E High/Low		PER SHARE ($) Earnings	Dividends	Book Value
12/20	21.90	9	5	3.10	0.77	30.37
12/19	28.80	14	10	2.09	0.79	28.05
12/18	23.02	25	15	1.48	0.70	26.38
12/17	33.10	21	14	1.67	0.77	17.85
12/16	23.83	13	8	1.85	0.68	16.65
Annual Growth	(2.1%)	—	—	13.8%	3.2%	16.2%

Middlefield Banc Corp.

Here's your cash stuck in the Middlefield Banc with you. The firm is the holding company for Middlefield Bank which has about 10 offices in northeast and central Ohio. The community bank offers standard deposit services such as checking and savings accounts CDs and IRAs. Investments insurance and brokerage services are offered through an agreement with UVEST a division of LPL Financial. Residential mortgage loans comprise more than 60% of the company's loan portfolio; commercial and industrial loans make up about 20%. The bank also offers commercial mortgages construction loans and consumer installment loans. Middlefield Banc is buying Liberty Bank which operates three branches in northeast Ohio.

EXECUTIVES

Chief Financial Officer, Senior Vice President, Treasurer Of Company, Executive Vice President And Treasurer Of Middlefield Bank, Donald Stacy, $216,685 total compensation
Independent Director, James McCaskey
President, Chief Executive Officer Of Company And Middlefield Bank, Director, Thomas Caldwell, $381,600 total compensation
Independent Chairman Of The Board, William Skidmore
Chief Operating Officer, Executive Vice President Of Company And Middlefield Bank, Director, James Heslop, $252,800 total compensation
Chief Financial Officer Of Middlefield Bank, Michael Ranttila
Senior Vice President - Risk Officer Of Middlefield Bank, Courtney Erminio
President – Central Ohio Region, Charles Moore
Director, Kevin Digeronimo
Executive Vice President, Chief Banking Officer Of Middlefield Bank, Michael Allen
Executive Vice President, Chief Credit And Risk Officer Of Middlefield Bank, John Lane
Auditors: S.R. Snodgrass, P.C.

LOCATIONS

HQ: Middlefield Banc Corp.
  15985 East High Street, Middlefield, OH 44062-0035
Phone: 440 632-1666

COMPETITORS

GUARANTY BANCSHARES INC.
PARKE BANCORP INC.
QNB CORP.

HISTORICAL FINANCIALS
Company Type: Public

Income Statement | | | | FYE: December 31

	ASSETS ($ mil.)	NET INCOME ($ mil.)	INCOME AS % OF ASSETS	EMPLOYEES
12/20	1,391.9	8.3	0.6%	0
12/19	1,182.4	12.7	1.1%	194
12/18	1,248.4	12.4	1.0%	200
12/17	1,106.3	9.4	0.9%	190
12/16	787.8	6.4	0.8%	139
Annual Growth	15.3%	6.8%	—	—

2020 Year-End Financials

Return on assets: 0.6%
Return on equity: 5.9%
Long-term debt ($ mil.): —
No. of shares (mil.): 6.3
Sales ($ mil): 58.6

Dividends
  Yield: 2.6%
  Payout: 43.1%
Market value ($ mil.): 144.0

274

HOOVER'S HANDBOOK OF EMERGING COMPANIES 2022

	STOCK PRICE ($) FY Close	P/E High/Low	PER SHARE ($) Earnings	Dividends	Book Value
12/20	22.50	20 10	1.30	0.60	22.54
12/19	26.09	25 12	1.95	0.57	21.45
12/18	42.43	28 21	1.92	0.59	19.77
12/17	48.20	35 25	1.55	0.54	18.63
12/16	38.70	26 21	1.52	0.54	17.00
Annual Growth	(12.7%)	— —	(3.8%)	2.7%	7.3%

Midland States Bancorp Inc

Born in rural Illinois Midland States Bancorp is now discovering banking life in new states. It is the $3 billion-asset holding company for Midland States Bank a community bank that operates more than 35 branches in central and northern Illinois and around 15 branches in the St. Louis metropolitan area. The bank offers traditional consumer and commercial banking products and services as well as merchant card services insurance and financial planning. Subsidiary Midland Wealth Management which boasts $1.2 billion-plus in assets under administration provides wealth management services while Heartland Business Credit offers commercial equipment leasing services. Midland States Bancorp went public in 2016.

IPO

The bank holding company raised $80.1 million in its initial public offering. It plans to contribute some $25 million to Midland States Bank and use the rest for general corporate purposes including possible acquisitions.

Operations

About 57% of Midland States Bancorp's total revenue came from loan interest during 2014 while another 17% came from interest income from investment securities. The rest came from wealth management fees (8% of revenue) deposit account service charges (3%) ATM and interchange revenue (3%) mortgage banking revenue (3%) merchant services revenue (1%) and nonrecurring gains on the sales of assets (around 8%).

Subsidiary Love Funding provides multifamily and healthcare facility FHA financing.

Geographic Reach

Midland has more than 80 branches and offices across the US with around 50 in Illinois and around the St. Louis metro area and the rest in California Colorado Florida Massachusetts North Carolina Ohio Tennessee and Texas.

Financial Performance

Midland States Bancorp's revenue climbed 3% to $93 million despite a decline in loan interest income during 2014 mostly thanks to profitable asset sales and other income.

Despite modest revenue growth in 2014 the bank's net income dove 67% to $3.2 billion as acquisition and integration expenses stemming from its late 2014 acquisition of Heartland ate up any revenue gains it had made. Excluding these nonrecurring items the bank's net income grew modestly.

Strategy

Midland States Bancorp has been pursuing an acquisition and branch expansion growth strategy since 2007 after it replaced its executive management and laid out a plan to expand Midland States Bank's presence in Illinois. Midland States Bank continues to focus on moving into suburban areas and other markets in Illinois and Missouri that have growing populations. During 2015 it opened a new branches in the St. Louis region (in Jennings) downtown Joliet and downtown Effingham areas as well as a wealth management office in downtown Decatur.

The company also planned in 2016 to continue building its fast-growing wealth management business which now makes up nearly 10% of its total revenue. Thanks to Midland's efforts the business' wealth management assets under administration have skyrocketed twelve-fold since 2008 growing from $95 million then to $1.19 billion at the end of 2014.

Mergers and Acquisitions

Midland States Bancorp agreed to acquire HomeStar Financial Group in 2019 in a transaction valued at about $10 million. HomeStar's Manteno Illinois-based HomeStar Bank and Financial Services has about $375 million in assets $220 million in loans and $330 million in deposits. HomeStar has five locations in northern Illinois. The deal expands Midland's presence in the Kankakee Illinois metropolitan area.

In 2017 CEO Leon Holschbach signed a $175 million deal with rival Centrue Bank to merge. The two banks had been treading on each others' toes in Princeton Illinois.

Company Background

Between 2008 and 2010 the bank's branch locations grew from just a half-dozen in central Illinois and St. Louis to nearly 30 around the state and in the St. Louis metropolitan area. During that time the bank acquired the assets of Waterloo Bancshares and WestBridge in St. Louis AMCORE in northern Illinois and Strategic Capital in central Illinois. It also opened new locations in some of its faster-growing markets. As a result of its efforts Midland States Bancorp has watched its revenue and profits trend upward significantly from 2007 levels.

EXECUTIVES

President, Chief Executive Officer And Chief Executive Officer Of The Bank, Director, Jeffrey Ludwig, $572,000 total compensation
Independent Director, Jerry Mcdaniel
Independent Director, Dwight Miller
Senior Vice President, Corporate Counsel And Director Of Investor Relations, Douglas Tucker, $354,320 total compensation
President Of The Bank And Executive Vice President, Jeffrey Mefford, $400,000 total compensation
Chief Risk Officer Of The Bank, James Stewart, $324,450 total compensation
Independent Chairman Of The Board, Jeffrey Smith
Independent Director, Deborah Golden
Senior Vice President, Chief Credit Officer Of The Bank, Jeffrey Brunoehler, $123,750 total compensation
Independent Director, Jennifer Dimotta
Principal Accounting Officer, Donald Spring, $218,373 total compensation
Chief Financial Officer, Eric Lemke, $305,000 total compensation

Independent Director, R. Dean Bingham
Auditors: Crowe LLP

LOCATIONS

HQ: Midland States Bancorp Inc
  1201 Network Centre Drive, Effingham, IL 62401
Phone: 217 342-7321
Web: www.midlandsb.com

PRODUCTS/OPERATIONS

2014 Sales

	% of total
Interest income	
Loans	57
Investment Securities & others	17
Noninterest income	
Wealth management revenue	8
Service charges on deposit accounts	3
Mortgage banking revenue	3
Gain on sale of other assets	3
ATM and interchange revenue	3
Impairments	-
Other	6
Total	**100**

Selected Services

Bank By Phone
Bill Paying
Checking
Debit Card
Online Banking
Savings & CDs

COMPETITORS

AMERICAN NATIONAL BANKSHARES INC.	PARK STERLING CORPORATION
BANK OF THE OZARKS INC.	PROSPERITY BANCSHARES INC.
COLUMBIA BANKING SYSTEM INC.	S & T BANCORP INC.
FIRST CITIZENS BANKS BANCSHARES INC.	UNITED BANKSHARES INC. UNITED COMMUNITY INC.
IBERIABANK CORPORATION BANCORP INC.	WILSHIRE
OLD NATIONAL BANCORP	

HISTORICAL FINANCIALS

Company Type: Public

Income Statement				FYE: December 31
	ASSETS ($ mil.)	NET INCOME ($ mil.)	INCOME AS % OF ASSETS	EMPLOYEES
12/20	6,868.5	22.5	0.3%	904
12/19	6,087.0	55.7	0.9%	1,100
12/18	5,637.6	39.4	0.7%	1,100
12/17	4,412.7	16.0	0.4%	840
12/16	3,233.7	31.5	1.0%	715
Annual Growth	**20.7%**	**(8.1%)**	**—**	**6.0%**

2020 Year-End Financials

Return on assets: 0.3%	Dividends
Return on equity: 3.5%	Yield: 5.9%
Long-term debt ($ mil.): —	Payout: 97.2%
No. of shares (mil.): 22.3	Market value ($ mil.): 399.0
Sales ($ mil): 306.1	

	STOCK PRICE ($)	P/E		PER SHARE ($)		
	FY Close	High/Low	Earnings	Dividends	Book Value	
12/20	17.87	30 13	0.95	1.07	27.83	
12/19	28.96	13 10	2.26	0.97	27.10	
12/18	22.34	21 12	1.66	0.88	25.62	
12/17	32.48	40 33	0.87	0.80	23.51	
12/16	36.18	17 9	2.17	0.36	20.78	
Annual Growth	(16.2%)	—	—(18.7%)	31.3%	7.6%	

MidWestOne Financial Group, Inc.

MidWestOne Financial Group is the holding company for MidWestOne Bank which operates about 35 branches throughout central and east-central Iowa. The bank offers standard deposit products such as checking and savings accounts CDs and IRAs in addition to trust services private banking home loans and investment services. More than two-thirds of MidWestOne Financial's loan portfolio consists of commercial real estate loans and commercial mortgages and industrial loans. Founded in 1983 MidWestOne has total assets of $4.65 billion.

Operations
MidWestOne Financial Group provides a wide range of commercial and retail lending services to businesses individuals and government agencies. The company's credit activities include commercial and residential real estate loans (approximately 70% of total loan portfolio) commercial and industrial loans (almost 25%) agricultural loans (nearly 5%) and consumer loans (less than 5%).

Overall MidWestOne Financial Group generates roughly 85% of its revenue from interest income more than 75% comes from interest and fees on loans the remaining 10% comes from investment securities the rest of its revenue comes from non-interest income.

Geographic Reach
Headquartered in Iowa City MidWestOne Financial Group's MidWestOne Bank has branch offices and operating facilities in Minnesota Wisconsin Florida and Colorado.

Sales and Marketing
MidWestOne Financial Group market its services to qualified lending customers. Lending officers actively solicit the business of new companies entering their market areas as well as long-standing members of the business communities in which the company operate.

Financial Performance
The company's revenue in 2019 increased by 36% to $174.9 million compared to $128.5 million in the prior year.

MidWestOne's consolidated net income for 2019 was $43.6 million an increase of $13.3 million or 44% compared to $30.4 million for 2018. The increase in net income was due primarily to an increase in net interest income of $38.4 million which was primarily attributable to the increased volume of interest-earning assets as a consequence of the ATBancorp merger.

Cash held by the company at the end of 2019 increased to $73.5 million. Cash provided by operations and investing activities were $47.3 million and $72.7 million respectively. Cash used for financing activities was $92.1 million mainly for short-term borrowings.

Strategy
MidWestOne's operating strategy is based upon a community banking model of delivering a comprehensive suite of financial products and services while following five operating principles: take care of its customers; hire and retain excellent employees; conduct business with the utmost integrity; work as one team; and learn constantly so the company can continually improve. Management believes the depth and breadth of the Company's products and services coupled with the personal and professional delivery of the same provides an appealing alternative to competitors.

Mergers and Acquisitions
In early 2019 MidWestOne Financial Group acquired ATBancorp a bank holding company whose wholly-owned banking subsidiaries were ATSB and ABTW for paid cash in the amount of $34.8 million. The acquisition helps to expand the company's business into new markets and grow the size of the company's business.

EXECUTIVES

Chief Executive Officer And Director, Charles Funk, $500,000 total compensation
Independent Chairman Of The Board, Kevin Monson
Senior Executive Vice President, Chief Investment Officer, Treasurer, James Cantrell, $236,506 total compensation
Chief Financial Officer, Executive Vice President, Barry Ray, $294,405 total compensation
Executive Vice President, Chief Credit Officer, Gary Sims, $242,785 total compensation
Independent Director, Matthew Hayek
Independent Director, Janet Godwin
Executive Vice President, Retail Banking Of The Bank, David Lindstrom, $235,600 total compensation
President, Chief Operating Officer, Len Devaisher, $167,820 total compensation
Auditors: RSM US LLP

LOCATIONS

HQ: MidWestOne Financial Group, Inc.
102 South Clinton Street, Iowa City, IA 52240
Phone: 319 356-5800
Web: www.midwestone.com

PRODUCTS/OPERATIONS

2015 Sales

	$ mil.	% of total
Interest Income		
Interest and fees on loans	86.5	71
Interest on investment securities	13.3	11
Other	0.9	1
Non-Interest Income		
Trust investment and insurance fees	6.0	5
Other service charges commissions and fees	5.7	5
Service charges and fees on deposit accounts	4.4	3
Mortgage origination and loan servicing fees	2.8	2
Other	2.3	2
Total	**121.9**	**100**

Selected Subsidiaries
MidWestOne Bank
MidWestOne Insurance Services Inc.
MidWestOne Statutory Trust II

COMPETITORS

ASSOCIATED BANC-CORP
CNB FINANCIAL CORP.
COLUMBIA BANKING SYSTEM INC.
COMMERCE BANCSHARES INC.
ENTERPRISE FINANCIAL SERVICES CORP
FIRST FINANCIAL BANCORP.
HILLTOP HOLDINGS INC.
INDEPENDENT BANK CORPORATION
SIGNATURE BANK
UNIVEST FINANCIAL CORPORATION
WESTERN BANCORPORATION
WINTRUST FINANCIAL CORPORATION

HISTORICAL FINANCIALS
Company Type: Public

Income Statement				FYE: December 31
	ASSETS ($ mil.)	NET INCOME ($ mil.)	INCOME AS % OF ASSETS	EMPLOYEES
12/20	5,556.6	6.6	0.1%	780
12/19	4,653.5	43.6	0.9%	771
12/18	3,291.4	30.3	0.9%	597
12/17	3,212.2	18.7	0.6%	610
12/16	3,079.5	20.3	0.7%	587
Annual Growth	15.9%	(24.5%)	—	7.4%

2020 Year-End Financials

Return on assets: 0.1%
Return on equity: 1.2%
Long-term debt ($ mil.): —
No. of shares (mil.): 16.0
Sales ($ mil): 223.4
Dividends
Yield: 3.5%
Payout: 400.0%
Market value ($ mil.): 392.0

	STOCK PRICE ($)	P/E		PER SHARE ($)		
	FY Close	High/Low	Earnings	Dividends	Book Value	
12/20	24.50	88 40	0.41	0.88	32.17	
12/19	36.23	13 9	2.93	0.81	31.49	
12/18	24.83	14 10	2.48	0.78	29.32	
12/17	33.53	25 21	1.55	0.67	27.85	
12/16	37.60	22 14	1.78	0.64	26.71	
Annual Growth	(10.2%)	—	(30.7%)	8.3%	4.8%	

Mitek Systems, Inc.

Mitek Systems is a company with character A software development company with expertise in computer vision artificial intelligence and machine learning. Serving more than 6500 financial services organizations and leading marketplace and financial technology brands across the globe its solutions are used by more than 80 million consumers. Using camera-equipped smartphone or tablet Mobile Deposit allows its individuals and businesses to deposit checks remotely. Mobile Verify is an identity verification solution designed for the world's leading marketplace and sharing platforms and financial services organizations. In addition the company's other services include Mobile Fill and Mobile Docs.

EXECUTIVES

Independent Chairman Of The Board, Bruce Hansen

Senior Vice President, General Manager - Digital Banking, Michael Diamond, $302,750 total compensation
Independent Director, James Hale
Secretary, Chief Legal, And Compliance Officer, Jason Gray, $317,500 total compensation
Chief Executive Officer And Director, Scipio Carnecchia, $450,000 total compensation
Independent Director, Kimberly Stevenson
Independent Director, Susan Repo
Independent Director, Alex Hart
Chief Technology Officer, Stephen Ritter, $298,119 total compensation
Cfo And Svp, Frank Teruel, $73,636 total compensation
Auditors: Mayer Hoffman McCann P.C.

LOCATIONS

HQ: Mitek Systems, Inc.
600 B Street, Suite 100, San Diego, CA 92101
Phone: 619 269-6800
Web: www.miteksystems.com

PRODUCTS/OPERATIONS

Selected Products and Services
ImageNet (financial document processing payment processing photo & video processing)
FraudProtect (image-based fraud detection signature comparison)

COMPETITORS

F5 INC.	RNA Productions Inc
FORTINET INC.	SECURITY FIRST CORP.
HEROIX LLC	Wistron Corporation
INQUISITE INC.	ZEBRA TECHNOLOGIES
LANTRONIX INC.	CORPORATION
LATTICE TECHNOLOGY USA INC	

HISTORICAL FINANCIALS

Company Type: Public

Income Statement				FYE: September 30
	REVENUE ($ mil.)	NET INCOME ($ mil.)	NET PROFIT MARGIN	EMPLOYEES
09/21	119.8	7.9	6.7%	448
09/20	101.3	7.8	7.7%	360
09/19	84.5	(0.7)	—	284
09/18	63.5	(11.8)	—	308
09/17	45.3	14.0	31.0%	141
Annual Growth	27.5%	(13.3%)	—	33.5%

2021 Year-End Financials

Debt ratio: 28.8%
Return on equity: 4.9%
Cash ($ mil.): 30.3
Current ratio: 5.20
Long-term debt ($ mil.): 120.9

No. of shares (mil.): 44.1
Dividends
Yield: —
Payout: —
Market value ($ mil.): 817.0

	STOCK PRICE ($) FY Close	P/E High/Low		PER SHARE ($) Earnings	Dividends	Book Value
09/21	18.50	128	63	0.18	0.00	4.37
09/20	12.74	69	29	0.18	0.00	3.17
09/19	9.65	—	—	(0.02)	0.00	2.66
09/18	7.05	—	—	(0.33)	0.00	2.51
09/17	9.50	25	13	0.40	0.00	1.82
Annual Growth	18.1%	—	—	(18.1%)	—	24.4%

MKS Instruments Inc

MKS Instruments makes systems that analyze and control gases during semiconductor manufacturing and other thin film industrial processes such as those used to make flat panel displays LEDs solar cells and data storage media. Top customers include chip equipment heavyweights Applied Materials and Lam Research. Other applications include flexible and rigid printed circuit board (PCB) processing/fabrication glass coating laser marking measurement and scribing natural gas and oil production electronic thin films and environmental monitoring. MKS Instruments generates some 45% of its revenue from customers in the US.

Operations
The company groups its product offering by three segments: Vacuum & Analysis (some 60% of sales) Light & Motion (approximately 30%) and Equipment & Solutions (around 10%).

The Vacuum & Analysis segment provides a broad range of instruments components and subsystems which are derived from our core competencies in pressure measurement and control flow measurement and control gas and vapor delivery gas composition analysis electronic control technology reactive gas generation and delivery power generation and delivery and vacuum technology.

The Light & Motion segment provides a broad range of instruments components and subsystems which are derived from its core competencies in lasers photonics optics precision motion control and vibration control.

The Equipment & Solutions segment provides a range of laser-based system and test products.

Overall its products account for around 85% of sales while its services account for the rest.

Geographic Reach
Headquartered in Andover Massachusetts the company has offices manufacturing facilities sales research and development and warehouses in Beaverton and Portland (Oregon) Broomfield (Colorado) Irvine Milpitas and Santa Clara (California) Rochester (New York) and Wilmington (Massachusetts). It also has international operations in China France Israel Mexico and Singapore.

The US market accounts for some 45% of sales followed by South Korea and China with over 10% of sales each. Sales Europe accounts for nearly 10% and the rest were generated from other Asian countries.

Sales and Marketing
The company markets and sells its products and services through its global direct sales organization an international network of independent distributors and sales representatives its websites and product catalogs. It primary serves markets including semiconductor industrial technologies life and health sciences research and defense.

Its top ten customers accounted for approximately 45% of sales in 2020. Its two largest customers Lam Research Corporation and Applied Materials Inc. accounted for about 25% of sales combined.

Financial Performance
In 2020 the company's revenue 2020 increased to $2.3 billion compared from the prior year with $1.9 billion. Higher revenues was due to a great increase on the company's product revenue and a slight increase on service revenue.

Net income for fiscal 2020 increased to $350.1 million compared from the previous year with $140.4 million.

Cash held by the company at the end of fiscal 2020 increased to $608.3 million. Cash provided by operations was $513.2 million while cash used for investing and financing activities were $202.4 million and $121.5 million respectively.

Strategy
MKS' products incorporate sophisticated technologies to measure monitor deliver analyze power control and improve complex semiconductor and advanced manufacturing processes thereby enhancing uptime yield and throughput for its customers. The company's products have continuously advanced as it strive to meet its customers' evolving needs.

The company involves its marketing engineering manufacturing and sales personnel in the development of new products in order to reduce the time to market for new products. The company's employees also work closely with its customers' development personnel helping MKS to identify and define future technical needs on which to focus research and development efforts. The company supports research at academic institutions targeted at advances in materials science semiconductor process development and photonics.

Mergers and Acquisitions
In 2021 MKS Instruments Inc. has entered into a definitive agreement to acquire Photon Control Inc. in an all-cash transaction valued at approximately CAD$387 million with an estimated enterprise value of CAD$343 million. Photon Control is headquartered in Richmond British Columbia Canada. Photon Control acquisition will help the company to deliver on one of its long-term strategic objectives which is to broaden its portfolio of key technologies to better serve its customers. The acquisition will also further advance the MKS strategy to enhance its Surround the Chamber offering by adding optical sensors for temperature control for critical etch and deposition applications in semiconductor wafer fabrication.

EXECUTIVES

Chief Financial Officer, Senior Vice President, Treasurer, Seth Bagshaw, $555,736 total compensation
Chairman Of The Board, Gerald Colella, $4,000 total compensation
Senior Vice President, General Counsel, Secretary, Kathleen Burke, $440,394 total compensation
President, Chief Executive Officer, and Director, John Lee, $850,000 total compensation
Senior Vice President And General Manager, Vacuum And Analysis Division, Eric Taranto
Senior Vice President - Corporate Marketing, Project Management Office & Global Service, David Henry
Independent Director, Rajeev Batra
Chief Operating Officer, Senior Vice President, James Schreiner, $407,769 total compensation
Independent Director, Michelle Warner
Independent Director, Joseph Donahue
Director, Peter Cannone
Senior Vice President And General Manager, Light And Motion Division, Mark Gitin
Auditors: PricewaterhouseCoopers LLP

LOCATIONS

HQ: MKS Instruments Inc
2 Tech Drive, Suite 201, Andover, MA 01810
Phone: 978 645-5500
Web: www.mksinst.com

PRODUCTS/OPERATIONS

2018 Sales by Products

	% of total
Vacuum Solutions Products	26
Power Plasma and Reactive Gas Solutions Products	29
Analytical and Control Solutions Products	6
Laser Products	13
Optics Products	11
Photonics Products	15
Total	**100**

2018 Sales

	$ mil
% of total	
Vacuum and Analysis	61
Light and Motion	39
Total	**100**

Selected Products

Instruments and Control Systems
  Pressure Measurement and Control Products
  Baratron®; Pressure Measurement Products
  Automatic Pressure and Vacuum Control Products
  Materials Delivery Products
  Flow Measurement and Control Products
  Gas Composition Analysis Products
  Mass Spectrometry-Based Gas Composition Analysis Instruments
  Fourier Transform Infra-Red (FTIR) Based Gas Composition Analysis Products
  Control and Information Technology Products
  Control Products
  Information Technology Products
Power and Reactive Gas Products
  Power Delivery Products
  Reactive Gas Generation Products
  Processing Thin Films
  Equipment Cleaning
Vacuum Products
  Vacuum Gauging Products
  Vacuum Valves Stainless Steel Components Process Solutions and Custom Stainless Steel Hardware
  Custom Manufactured Components

COMPETITORS

AXCELIS TECHNOLOGIES INC.
Beijing Hollysys Co. Ltd.
FORTIVE CORPORATION
HURCO COMPANIES INC.
KEITHLEY INSTRUMENTS LLC
NANOSTRING TECHNOLOGIES INC.
NOVANTA INC.
OMRON CORPORATION
ONTO INNOVATION INC.
RUBIX GROUP INTERNATIONAL LIMITED
Siemens AG
ULTRA CLEAN HOLDINGS INC.
VEECO INSTRUMENTS INC.
WATERS CORPORATION

HISTORICAL FINANCIALS

Company Type: Public

Income Statement   FYE: December 31

	REVENUE ($ mil.)	NET INCOME ($ mil.)	NET PROFIT MARGIN	EMPLOYEES
12/20	2,330.0	350.1	15.0%	5,800
12/19	1,899.7	140.3	7.4%	5,500
12/18	2,075.1	392.9	18.9%	4,851
12/17	1,915.9	339.1	17.7%	4,923
12/16	1,295.3	104.8	8.1%	4,667
Annual Growth	**15.8%**	**35.2%**	**—**	**5.6%**

2020 Year-End Financials

Debt ratio: 21.2%
Return on equity: 15.9%
Cash ($ mil.): 608.3
Current ratio: 4.83
Long-term debt ($ mil.): 815.0
No. of shares (mil.): 55.2
Dividends
  Yield: 0.5%
  Payout: 12.6%
Market value ($ mil.): 8,304.0

	STOCK PRICE ($) FY Close	P/E High/Low		PER SHARE ($) Earnings	Dividends	Book Value
12/20	150.45	25	11	6.33	0.80	42.77
12/19	110.01	45	25	2.55	0.80	37.06
12/18	64.61	17	8	7.14	0.78	34.66
12/17	94.50	17	10	6.16	0.71	29.23
12/16	59.40	31	16	1.94	0.68	23.14
Annual Growth	**26.2%**	**—**		**34.4%**	**4.1%**	**16.6%**

Moelis & Co

Auditors: DELOITTE & TOUCHE LLP

LOCATIONS

HQ: Moelis & Co
399 Park Avenue, 5th Floor, New York, NY 10022
Phone: 212 883-3800
Web: www.moelis.com

HISTORICAL FINANCIALS

Company Type: Public

Income Statement   FYE: December 31

	REVENUE ($ mil.)	NET INCOME ($ mil.)	NET PROFIT MARGIN	EMPLOYEES
12/20	943.2	178.8	19.0%	903
12/19	746.5	105.1	14.1%	879
12/18	885.8	140.6	15.9%	845
12/17	684.6	29.4	4.3%	749
12/16	613.3	38.3	6.3%	645
Annual Growth	**11.4%**	**46.9%**	**—**	**8.8%**

2020 Year-End Financials

Debt ratio: —
Return on equity: 38.6%
Cash ($ mil.): 202.4
Current ratio: 0.58
Long-term debt ($ mil.): —
No. of shares (mil.): 63.9
Dividends
  Yield: 8.8%
  Payout: 332.2%
Market value ($ mil.): 2,992.0

	STOCK PRICE ($) FY Close	P/E High/Low		PER SHARE ($) Earnings	Dividends	Book Value
12/20	46.76	15	8	2.95	4.15	7.50
12/19	31.92	23	14	1.89	3.25	7.33
12/18	34.38	21	10	2.78	4.88	7.21
12/17	48.50	52	35	0.78	2.48	6.09
12/16	33.90	19	12	1.58	3.29	4.10
Annual Growth	**8.4%**	**—**		**16.9%**	**6.0%**	**16.3%**

Monolithic Power Systems Inc

Monolithic Power Systems (MPS) is a leading semiconductor company that designs develops and markets high-performance power solutions. The fabless semiconductor company offers mixed-signal and analog microchips ? especially DC-to-DC converters for powering networking and telecommunication infrastructure wireless access points notebook computers set-top boxes and other consumer electronic devices. Its core strengths include deep system-level and applications knowledge strong analog design expertise and innovative proprietary process technologies. The company was founded in 1997. It generates majority of sales outside its home country the US.

Operations

MPS operates in one reportable segment that includes the design development marketing and sale of high-performance analog solutions. The company divides its revenue into two major product families. Its DC-to-DC products convert and control voltages within a broad range of electronic systems such as portable electronic devices wireless LAN access points computers and notebooks monitors infotainment applications and medical equipment. The DC-to-DC chips are monolithic in which it accounts for some 95% of the company's total sales. MPS's lighting control products are used to backlight LCD screens. The segment generates approximately 5% of total sales.

Geographic Reach

MPS is headquartered in Kirkland Washington but generates most of its revenue are in Asia. Its semiconductor products are assembled and packaged by independent subcontractors in China and Malaysia after its wafers are manufactured in foundries located in China Taiwan and Korea. The finished products don't have far to go since over 60% of sales are in China; followed by about 15% from Taiwan. MPS has sales offices in the US Europe Singapore India China Korea and Japan.

Sales and Marketing

MPS sells through distributors value-added resellers and directly to original equipment manufacturers (OEMs) original design manufacturers (ODMs) and electronic manufacturing service (EMS) companies. Sales to its largest distributor accounted for about 25% of revenue in 2020. In addition MPS generates around 30% of total sales from Computing and Storage end market followed by Consumers with about 25%. The remaining sales are from Industrial Communications and Automotive which brings in about 45% of total sales combined.

Financial Performance

Revenue in 2020 was $844.5 million an increase of $216.6 million or 35% from $627.9 million in 2019. This increase was driven by higher sales in all of its end markets. Overall unit shipments increased by 7% and average sales prices increased by approximately 24% compared to the same period in 2019.

In 2020 the company had a net income of $164.4 million a 51% increase from the previous year.

The company's cash at the end of 2020 was $335.1 million. Operating activities generated $267.8 million while investing activities used $39.2 million mainly for purchases of short-term investments. Financing activities used another $71.6 million primarily for dividends and dividend equivalents paid.

Strategy

MPS has entered into a distribution agreement with Farnell Electronics a global online distributor specializing in high-service distribution of technology products services and solutions for electronic systems design. This partnership will give customers access to MPS extensive portfolio of high-performance highly integrated power solutions in industrial applications telecom infrastructures and cloud computing automotive and consumer applications. MPS patented technologies integrate the maximum number of components into a single package providing an entire power system in one device and accelerating customers' time to market.

This distribution agreement will allow MPS to leverage Farnell's experience and global presence to provide extensive power product offerings to customers of all sizes. The company is confident that with Farnell's two million-plus customer contacts and their excellent engineering community they will expand MPS growth in EMEA and APAC.

In early 2020 the company has assembled an emergency ventilator inspired by the open-source MIT design to aid in the fight against COVID-19. MPS is applying its expertise in power management and motor controls toward a solution that can safely and easily automate a manual resuscitator when a full ICU ventilator may not be available.

EXECUTIVES

Vice President - Strategic Corporate Development, General Counsel, Corporate Secretary, Saria Tseng, $340,000 total compensation
Director, Carintia Martinez
Lead Independent Director, Herbert Chang
Independent Director, Victor Lee
Chief Financial Officer, Vice President, Bernie Blegen, $320,000 total compensation
Independent Director, Eugen Elmiger
President - Asia Operations, Deming Xiao, $340,000 total compensation
Senior Vice President - Worldwide Sales And Marketing, Maurice Sciammas, $340,000 total compensation
Chairman Of The Board, President, Chief Executive Officer, Michael Hsing, $650,000 total compensation
Auditors: Ernst & Young LLP

LOCATIONS

HQ: Monolithic Power Systems Inc
  5808 Lake Washington Blvd. NE, Kirkland, WA 98033
Phone: 425 296-9956
Web: www.monolithicpower.com

PRODUCTS/OPERATIONS

2011 Sales

	$ mil.	% of total
DC-to-DC converters	165.6	85
LCD backlight inverters	26.5	13
Audio amplifiers	4.4	2
Total	**196.5**	**100**

Selected Products

AC/DC Offline
  Bridge rectifier
  Controllers and regulators
  Synchronous rectifiers
Audio amplifiers
Backlighting solutions
  EL drivers
  White LED drivers (inductors and charge pumps)
Automotive
Battery chargers
  Cradle chargers
  Linear chargers
  Protection
  Switching chargers
Full-bridge and half-bridge power drivers
Isolated and transformer-based power supplies
Lighting and illumination
Low dropout (LDO) linear regulators
Motor drivers
  Brushless DC motor drivers
  Stepper DC motor drivers
Photo-flash chargers and drivers
Power Over Ethernet powered device (PD) solutions
  PD controllers
  PD identity
Precision analog
  Analog switches
  High-side current sense amplifiers
  Operational amplifiers
  Voltage reference
Supervisory circuits and voltage supervisors
Switching power supply regulators
  DC-DC (step-down)
  Controller
  Intelli-Phase (monolithic driver + MOSFET)
  Non-synchronous switcher
  Synchronous switcher
  DC-DC (step-up)
  Controller
  Energy storage and release management
  LNB power supply
  Non-synchronous switcher
  Synchronous switcher
USB and current-limit load switches

COMPETITORS

DSP GROUP INC.
KEYSIGHT TECHNOLOGIES INC.
MACOM TECHNOLOGY SOLUTIONS HOLDINGS INC.
MAXIM INTEGRATED PRODUCTS INC.
MAXLINEAR INC.
NXP Semiconductors N.V.
ON SEMICONDUCTOR CORPORATION
ONTO INNOVATION INC.
PERASO INC.
SILICON LABORATORIES INC.
SKYWORKS SOLUTIONS INC.
VICOR CORPORATION
VOLEX PLC

HISTORICAL FINANCIALS

Company Type: Public

Income Statement   FYE: December 31

	REVENUE ($ mil.)	NET INCOME ($ mil.)	NET PROFIT MARGIN	EMPLOYEES
12/20	844.4	164.3	19.5%	2,209
12/19	627.9	108.8	17.3%	2,002
12/18	582.3	105.2	18.1%	1,737
12/17	470.9	65.2	13.8%	1,534
12/16	388.6	52.7	13.6%	1,417
Annual Growth	21.4%	32.9%	—	11.7%

2020 Year-End Financials

Debt ratio: —
Return on equity: 18.8%
Cash ($ mil.): 334.9
Current ratio: 5.73
Long-term debt ($ mil.): —
No. of shares (mil.): 45.2
Dividends
  Yield: 0.5%
  Payout: 60.7%
Market value ($ mil.): 16,578.0

	STOCK PRICE ($) FY Close	P/E High/Low		PER SHARE ($) Earnings	Dividends	Book Value
12/20	366.23	98	37	3.50	2.00	21.35
12/19	178.02	73	43	2.38	1.60	17.73
12/18	116.25	61	42	2.36	1.20	15.06
12/17	112.36	80	52	1.50	0.80	12.54
12/16	81.93	66	43	1.26	0.80	10.57
Annual Growth	45.4%	—	—	29.1%	25.7%	19.2%

Morningstar Inc

Morningstar offers investment management services and research to individuals financial advisors asset managers retirement-plan providers and sponsors and institutional investors in the private capital markets. The company supports asset managers individual and institutional investors and financial advisors with an extensive product line of web-based tools investment data and research. The company also provides investment-management services investment analysis platforms and portfolio management and accounting software tools to advisors and financial institutions. The United States is the company's largest market; it provides around 70% of its revenue.

Operations

Morningstar operates through a single reporting segment and categorizes its revenue streams as license- asset- and transaction-based. License-based revenue derives from subscription services grant access to the company's technology and data on either a per-user or enterprise basis for a specified period of time. Its products include Morningstar Data Morningstar Direct Morningstar Advisor Workstation Morningstar Office Cloud PitchBook Premium Memberships on Morningstar.com and other similar products. License sales represent almost two-thirds of the company's revenue.

Morningstar garners asset-based revenue from fees for assets that it manages or on which it advises. Products in the category include Morningstar Investment Management Workplace Solutions and Morningstar Indexes. Ad sales on the company's website and credit rating products make up the company's transaction-based revenue. Asset-based and transaction-based sales account for around 15% of Morningstar's revenue each.

Geographic Reach
Chicago-based Morningstar has operations in over 25 countries including Australia Brazil Switzerland Taiwan Thailand the United Kingdom the US India Japan China South Africa the United Arab Emirates and Singapore.

About 70% of its sales come from the US. The UK and Continent Europe provide nearly 10% each while Canada accounts for about 5% of revenue.

Sales and Marketing
Its largest customer accounts for less than 2% of its revenue. The company focuses on six primary customer groups: advisor; asset management; fixed-income security issuers and arrangers; private market/venture capital investors; workplace/retirement; and individual investors.

Morningstar's sales and marketing expenses were $206.4 million $177.9 million and $1487.8 million for the years 2020 2019 and 2018 respectively.

Financial Performance
The company's revenue decreased by 18% to $1.4 billion from $1.2 billion in 2019. The company experienced strong revenue growth across all revenue types during 2020.

Net income increased to $223.6 million in 2020 from $152.0 million in 2019.

Cash held by the company at the end of 2020 increased to $422.5 million. Operating activities provided $384.3 million while investing and financing activities used $123.8 million and $182.2 million respectively. Main cash uses were capital expenditures and repayment of term facility.

Strategy
Morningstar's strategy is to deliver insights and experiences essential to investing. Proprietary data sets meaningful analytics independent research and effective investment strategies are at the core of the powerful digital solutions that investors across its client segments rely on. The company has a keen focus on innovation across data research product and delivery so that it can effectively cater to the evolving needs and expectations of investors globally.

The company focused on these four strategic priorities: Deliver differentiated insights across asset classes to public and private market investors; Establish leading ESG position across each business;

Drive operational excellence and scalability to support growth targets and Build an inclusive culture that drives exceptional talent engagement and development.

Company Background
In 1984 Joe Mansueto establishes Morningstar in his Chicago apartment. In 1999 Morningstar establishes presence in Australia and New Zealand and expands operations into Canada and launches online retirement advice service in 2000.

HISTORY
Joseph Mansueto founded Morningstar in 1984 using a line borrowed from Thoreau's Walden ("The sun is but a morning star"). Armed with an MBA and experience culled from a stint as a securities analyst for Harris Associates Mansueto published Mutual Fund Sourcebook a tome outlining performance histories and other information on 400 stock mutual funds. The boom in mutual funds during the early 1980s spurred interest in

Morningstar's product and prompted the company to add a second publication Morningstar Mutual Funds two years later.

The company's 1994 acquisition of MarketBase helped the firm add stock information to its coverage. A 5% staff cut in 1996 and the cessation of some of its publications helped reverse Morningstar's sagging fortunes. It took to cyberspace the following year when it launched Morningstar.net (now Morningstar.com). That year the company partnered with Japanese digital dynamo SOFTBANK to create Morningstar Japan and present financial information to investors in that country.

Don Phillips who had joined Morningstar as its first analyst in 1986 was appointed CEO in 1998. The company began offering a subscription-based premium service feature for its website to provide users with expanded financial coverage. In 1999 Morningstar extended its reach partnering with FPG Research to offer financial information to residents of Australia and New Zealand. Later that year SOFTBANK invested $91 million in Morningstar.

In 2000 Morningstar established website MorningstarAdvisor.com relaunched its flagship site with additional information and tools and opened offices in Hong Kong South Korea and the UK. Founder and chairman Joe Mansueto also assumed the role of CEO in 2000 and made Phillips a managing director of the company.

The following year the company launched its website in Germany Italy the Netherlands Spain and the UK. Morningstar added Australian financial publisher Aspect Huntley to its stable in 2006. It paid nearly $23 million for the provider of equity information research and financial trade publishing in order to expand outside the US. In 2007 Morningstar paid some $58 million for the mutual fund data business from Standard & Poor's.

A significant acquisition for Morningstar was the 2008 purchase of 10-K Wizard an electronic provider of SEC filing documents for $12.5 million. The purchase bolstered Morningstar's research capabilities and aids in the company's goal of providing greater transparency to equity investments.

Other 2008 purchases included London market data firm Tenfore Systems for 13.5 million ($20.9 million). Tenfore provides information on stocks commodities derivatives and other investments and the deal allows Morningstar to bundle real-time data such as stock prices with its research. The company purchased Fundamental Data Limited a provider of data on closed-end funds in the UK for some 11 million (approximately $19 million) as well as the Hemscott data media and investor relations website businesses from Ipreo for about $52 million.

The acquisitive Morningstar entered a new distribution channel in 2009 with the nearly $52 million buy of Logical Information Machines a provider of market pricing data and data management services to the agricultural energy and financial sectors. The Logical Information Machines acquisition complements and expands many of the services already provided by Morningstar including data and software management.

Also in 2009 the company grew its investment management business with the acquisition of Intech Pty Ltd. Now doing business as Ibbotson Associates the subsidiary provides multi-manager and investment portfolio solutions in Sydney Australia.

In 2010 Morningstar acquired Realpoint a statistical ratings organization that specializes in structured finance for some $52 million in cash and stock. Morningstar made the deal to build on its recent entry into corporate credit ratings. (In 2011 it rebranded Realpoint under the Morningstar name.)

International acquisitions in 2010 included Old Broad Street Research a provider of fund research ratings and investment consulting services in the UK for about 12 million (or approximately $18 million). Also in 2010 it purchased Seeds Group a provider of investment consulting services and fund research in France. The company launched local language versions of Morningstar Direct in Spain France and Germany in 2010 adding to existing versions in China and Italy.

EXECUTIVES
Executive Chairman Of The Board, Joe Mansueto, $100,000 total compensation
Independent Director, William Lyons
Head Of Talent And Culture, Bevin Desmond, $270,000 total compensation
Independent Director, Cheryl Francis
Director, Stephen Joynt
Chief Executive Officer, Director, Kunal Kapoor, $400,000 total compensation
Independent Director, Gail Landis
Independent Director, Robin Diamonte
Chief Revenue Officer, Danny Dunn, $300,000 total compensation
General Counsel, Corporate Secretary, Patrick Maloney
Chief Financial Officer, Jason Dubinsky, $400,000 total compensation
Auditors: KPMG LLP

LOCATIONS
HQ: Morningstar Inc
22 West Washington Street, Chicago, IL 60602
Phone: 312 696-6000
Web: www.morningstar.com

PRODUCTS/OPERATIONS

Selected Products and Services
Morningstar Advisor Workstation (Web-based investment planning software)
Morningstar FundInvestor (monthly mutual fund newsletter)
Morningstar Licensed Data (electronic investment data feeds)
Morningstar Mutual Funds (semimonthly information on 1600 mutual funds)
Morningstar Principia (CD-ROM-based investment planning software)
Morningstar StockInvestor (monthly stock newsletter)
MorningstarAdvisor.com (market analysis stock and fund information portfolio tools and investment research for advisors)
Morningstar.com (market analysis stock and fund information portfolio tools and investment research for individuals)

COMPETITORS
ALLIANCEBERNSTEIN HOLDING L.P.	KKR & CO. INC.
APOLLO ASSET MANAGEMENT INC.	SEI INVESTMENTS COMPANY
E TRADE FINANCIAL CORPORATION	SS&C TECHNOLOGIES HOLDINGS INC.
FACTSET RESEARCH SYSTEMS INC.	T. ROWE PRICE GROUP INC.
GAMCO INVESTORS INC.	THOMSON REUTERS CORPORATION
INVESCO LTD.	

HISTORICAL FINANCIALS
Company Type: Public

Income Statement
FYE: December 31

	REVENUE ($ mil.)	NET INCOME ($ mil.)	NET PROFIT MARGIN	EMPLOYEES
12/20	1,389.5	223.6	16.1%	7,979
12/19	1,179.0	152.0	12.9%	6,737
12/18	1,019.9	183.0	17.9%	5,416
12/17	911.7	136.9	15.0%	4,920
12/16	798.6	161.0	20.2%	4,595
Annual Growth	14.9%	8.6%	—	14.8%

2020 Year-End Financials

Debt ratio: 16.6%	No. of shares (mil.): 42.9
Return on equity: 18.9%	Dividends
Cash ($ mil.): 422.5	Yield: 0.5%
Current ratio: 1.17	Payout: 29.9%
Long-term debt ($ mil.): 449.1	Market value ($ mil.): 9,934.0

	STOCK PRICE ($) FY Close	P/E High/Low		Earnings	PER SHARE ($) Dividends	Book Value
12/20	231.57	44	21	5.18	1.22	29.64
12/19	151.31	46	30	3.52	1.12	25.29
12/18	109.84	33	21	4.25	1.00	21.93
12/17	96.97	30	23	3.18	0.92	18.92
12/16	73.56	24	18	3.72	0.88	16.22
Annual Growth	33.2%	—	—	8.6%	8.4%	16.3%

Morris St Bancshares Inc

LOCATIONS
HQ: Morris St Bancshares Inc
301 Bellevue Avenue, Dublin, GA 31021
Phone: 478 272-5202
Web: www.morris.bank

HISTORICAL FINANCIALS
Company Type: Public

Income Statement
FYE: December 31

	REVENUE ($ mil.)	NET INCOME ($ mil.)	NET PROFIT MARGIN	EMPLOYEES
12/20	59.1	17.4	29.4%	0
12/19	51.6	13.6	26.4%	0
12/18	41.1	15.2	37.0%	0
12/17	35.9	13.3	37.2%	0
12/16	32.1	11.0	34.5%	0
Annual Growth	16.5%	11.9%	—	—

2020 Year-End Financials

Debt ratio: 2.2%	No. of shares (mil.): 2.0
Return on equity: 14.4%	Dividends
Cash ($ mil.): 149.8	Yield: 0.0%
Current ratio: 0.34	Payout: 21.0%
Long-term debt ($ mil.): 28.6	Market value ($ mil.): 127.0

	STOCK PRICE ($) FY Close	P/E High/Low		Earnings	PER SHARE ($) Dividends	Book Value
12/20	60.50	8	6	8.31	1.75	61.81
12/19	65.00	11	9	6.87	0.00	53.10
Annual Growth	(6.9%)	—	—	21.0%	—	16.4%

Mountain Commerce Bancorp Inc

Auditors: Dixon Hughes Goodman LLP

LOCATIONS
HQ: Mountain Commerce Bancorp Inc
6101 Kingston Pike, P.O. Box 52942, Knoxville, TN 37919
Phone:
Web: www.mcb.com

HISTORICAL FINANCIALS
Company Type: Public

Income Statement
FYE: December 31

	REVENUE ($ mil.)	NET INCOME ($ mil.)	NET PROFIT MARGIN	EMPLOYEES
12/20	46.1	10.1	22.0%	0
12/19	43.8	12.3	28.2%	0
12/18	37.5	10.1	27.1%	0
12/17	30.2	5.4	18.1%	0
12/16	25.1	4.2	16.8%	0
Annual Growth	16.3%	24.5%	—	—

2020 Year-End Financials

Debt ratio: 6.6%	No. of shares (mil.): 6.2
Return on equity: 10.4%	Dividends
Cash ($ mil.): 72.3	Yield: —
Current ratio: 0.17	Payout: —
Long-term debt ($ mil.): 63.9	Market value ($ mil.): 129.0

	STOCK PRICE ($) FY Close	P/E High/Low		Earnings	PER SHARE ($) Dividends	Book Value
12/20	20.50	14	8	1.62	0.00	16.52
12/19	22.10	—	—	(0.00)	0.00	14.57
12/18	17.72	13	11	1.63	0.00	12.45
12/17	17.50	21	14	0.89	0.00	11.04
Annual Growth	5.4%	—	—	22.1%	—	14.4%

Mr Cooper Group Inc

EXECUTIVES
Independent Director, Busy Burr
Independent Director, Steven Scheiwe
Independent Director, Christopher Harrington
Independent Director, Tagar Olson
President, Vice Chairman Of The Board, Chief Financial Officer, Christopher Marshall, $738,462 total compensation
Lead Independent Director, Michael Malone
Independent Director, Roy Guthrie
Chief Executive Officer - Xome Holdings Llc, Michael Rawls, $448,077 total compensation
Independent Director, Shveta Mujumdar
Executive Vice President, Chief Legal Officer, Eldridge Burns, $182,692 total compensation
Executive Vice President, Chief Revenue Officer, Shawn Stone
Executive Vice President, Jay Jones
Chairman And Chief Executive Officer, Jesse Bray, $1,000,000 total compensation
Auditors: Ernst & Young LLP

LOCATIONS
HQ: Mr Cooper Group Inc
8950 Cypress Waters Blvd., Coppell, TX 75019
Phone: 469 549-2000
Web: www.mrcoopergroup.com

HISTORICAL FINANCIALS
Company Type: Public

Income Statement
FYE: December 31

	ASSETS ($ mil.)	NET INCOME ($ mil.)	INCOME AS % OF ASSETS	EMPLOYEES
12/21	14,204.0	1,454.0	10.2%	8,200
12/20	24,165.0	305.0	1.3%	9,800
12/19	18,305.0	274.0	1.5%	9,100
12/18*	16,973.0	884.0	5.2%	8,500
07/18	0.0	154.0	***************%	0
Annual Growth	—	75.3%	—	—

*Fiscal year change

2021 Year-End Financials

Return on assets: 7.5%	Dividends
Return on equity: 49.5%	Yield: —
Long-term debt ($ mil.): —	Payout: —
No. of shares (mil.): 73.7	Market value ($ mil.): 3,070.0
Sales ($ mil): 3,318.0	

	STOCK PRICE ($) FY Close	P/E High/Low		Earnings	PER SHARE ($) Dividends	Book Value
12/21	41.61	3	2	16.53	0.00	45.62
12/20	31.03	9	2	3.20	0.00	27.98
12/19	12.51	5	2	2.95	0.00	24.50
12/18*	11.67	2	0	9.54	0.00	21.39
07/18	1.36	1	0	1.55	0.00	(0.00)
Annual Growth	135.2%	—	—	80.7%	—	—

*Fiscal year change

MSCI Inc

MSCI formerly Morgan Stanley Capital International manages more than 246000 daily equity fixed income and hedge fund indices use by large asset management firms. Its leading research-enhanced products and services include indexes; portfolio construction and risk management analytics; environmental social and governance (ESG) and climate solutions; and real estate benchmarks return analytics and market insights. Through its integrated franchise MSCI provides solutions across its products and services to support its clients' dynamic and complex needs. MSCI has over 4400 clients across more than 95 countries. The Americas accounts for about half of the company's total sales.

Operations

The company operates through five operating segments - Index Analytics ESG Real Estate and Burgiss.

Clients use its indexes in many areas of the investment process including for indexed product creation (e.g. ETFs mutual funds annuities futures options structured products over-the-counter derivatives) performance benchmarking portfolio construction and rebalancing and asset allocation.

The company's Analytics segment offers risk management performance attribution and portfolio management content applications and services that provide clients with an integrated view of risk and return and tools for analyzing market credit liquidity and counterparty risk across all major asset classes spanning short- medium- and long-term time horizons.

MSCI ESG Research analyzes over 8500 entities worldwide to help institutional investors understand how ESG and climate considerations can impact the long-term risks and opportunities in financial markets.

The company's Real Estate segment includes research reporting market data and benchmarking offerings that provide real estate performance analytics for funds investors and managers.

Geographic Reach

MSCI has more than 30 offices in over 10 countries worldwide including headquarters in New York and offices in Chicago Illinois; Geneva Switzerland; San Francisco California; Beijing China; Frankfurt Germany; Shanghai China; Hong Kong China; Paris France; Tokyo Japan; Portland Maine; Sydney Australia; Toronto Canada; and Singapore. As part of its global expansion efforts in the last few years MSCI has opened international offices in Budapest Monterrey and Mumbai.

Around half of the company's revenues come from outside the Americas.

Sales and Marketing

Clients receive index data directly from the company or from third-party vendors worldwide while clients access the Analytics content through its proprietary applications and APIs (application programming interfaces) third-party applications or directly through the own platforms.

MSCI served over 4400 clients which include Asset owners Asset managers Financial intermediaries and Wealth managers. The company's largest client organization BlackRock accounted for over 10% of the company's total sales.

Financial Performance

Total operating revenues grew 9% to $1.7 billion in 2020 from $1.6 billion in 2019.

Net income in 2020 increased 6.8% to $601.8 million compared to $563.6 million in 2019.

Cash held by the company at the end of fiscal 2020 decreased to $1.3 billion. Operating activities provided $811.1 million while investing and financing activities used $241.8 million and $779.0 million respectively. Main cash uses were acquisitions of equity method investment and repayment of borrowings.

Strategy

The company provides critical tools and solutions that enable investors to manage the transformations taking place in the investment industry better understand performance and risk and build portfolios more effectively and efficiently to achieve their investment objectives. The company is focused on the following key initiatives to deliver actionable and integrated client solutions: Extend leadership in research-enhanced content across asset classes; Enhance distribution and content-enabling technology; Expand solutions that empower client customization; Growth through strengthening existing client relationships and developing new ones; and Execute strategic relationships and acquisitions with complementary content and technology companies.

EXECUTIVES

Chief Human Resources Officer, Scott Crum, $550,000 total compensation
Independent Director, Jacques Perold
Independent Director, Catherine Kinney
Independent Director, Linda Riefler
Chairman And Chief Executive Officer, Henry Fernandez, $1,000,000 total compensation
General Counsel, Robert Gutowski, $450,000 total compensation
Lead Independent Director, Robert Ashe
Chief Financial Officer, Andrew Wiechmann, $500,000 total compensation
Independent Director, Marcus Smith
Independent Director, Wayne Edmunds
Independent Director, Paula Volent
Independent Director, Sandy Rattray
President And Chief Operating Officer, Baer Pettit, $802,253 total compensation
Independent Director, Rajat Taneja
Auditors: PricewaterhouseCoopers LLP

LOCATIONS

HQ: MSCI Inc
7 World Trade Center, 250 Greenwich Street, 49th Floor, New York, NY 10007
Phone: 212 804-3900
Web: www.msci.com

PRODUCTS/OPERATIONS

2014 Sales

	$ mil.	% of total
Index real estate and ESG	582.6	59
Risk management analytics	309.7	31
Portfolio management analytics	104.4	10
Total	**996.7**	**100**

Selected Offerings

Barra (equity and multi-asset class portfolio analytics product)
CFRA (forensic accounting risk research legal/regulatory risk assessment due-diligence and educational services)
FEA (entergy and commodity asset valuation analytics)
ISS (governance research and outsourced proxy voting and reporting services)
MSCI Indices (flagship global equity indices)
RiskMetrics (risk and wealth management products)

COMPETITORS

APTITUDE SOFTWARE GROUP PLC
BROADRIDGE FINANCIAL SOLUTIONS INC.
CAPITA PLC
CORELOGIC INC.
EXPERIAN PLC
FACTSET RESEARCH SYSTEMS INC.
INNERWORKINGS INC.
INTERNATIONAL FINANCE CORPORATION
LIQUIDITY SERVICES INC.
LIQUIDNET HOLDINGS INC.
NASDAQ INC.
NATIONAL RESEARCH CORPORATION
NV5 GLOBAL INC.
QUINSTREET INC.
STONEX GROUP INC.
TRADEWEB MARKETS LLC

HISTORICAL FINANCIALS

Company Type: Public

Income Statement

FYE: December 31

	REVENUE ($ mil.)	NET INCOME ($ mil.)	NET PROFIT MARGIN	EMPLOYEES
12/21	2,043.5	725.9	35.5%	4,303
12/20	1,695.3	601.8	35.5%	3,633
12/19	1,557.8	563.6	36.2%	3,396
12/18	1,433.9	507.8	35.4%	3,112
12/17	1,274.1	303.9	23.9%	3,038
Annual Growth	12.5%	24.3%	—	9.1%

2021 Year-End Financials

Debt ratio: 75.5%
Return on equity: ***,***.*%
Cash ($ mil.): 1,421.4
Current ratio: 1.71
Long-term debt ($ mil.): 4,161.4
No. of shares (mil.): 82.4
Dividends
Yield: 0.5%
Payout: 44.1%
Market value ($ mil.): 50,510.0

	STOCK PRICE ($) FY Close	P/E High/Low		PER SHARE ($) Earnings	Dividends	Book Value
12/21	612.69	77	45	8.70	3.64	(1.98)
12/20	446.53	62	31	7.12	2.92	(5.37)
12/19	258.18	40	21	6.59	2.52	(0.90)
12/18	147.43	31	22	5.66	1.92	(1.98)
12/17	126.54	38	23	3.31	1.32	4.45
Annual Growth	48.3%			—	27.3%	28.9%

Muncy Bank Financial, Inc. (Muncy, PA)

EXECUTIVES

Pres, Darren Berninger
Sr V Pres*, David Mayer
Sr V Pres*, Craig W Kremser
V Pres*, Charles Shaffer
Cashier*, Helen M Smith
Asst V Pres*, Ester A Houseknecht
SEC*, Beth Benson
Human Resources Executive, Karen Brandis
Human Resources, Michelle Rohrbach
Administrative Assistant, Susan Tollackson
Vice President Chief Credit, Jason A Fischer
Auditors: S.R. Snodgrass, P.C.

LOCATIONS

HQ: Muncy Bank Financial, Inc. (Muncy, PA)
2 North Main Street, Muncy, PA 17756
Phone: 570 546-2211
Web: www.muncybank.com

HISTORICAL FINANCIALS

Company Type: Public

Income Statement

FYE: December 31

	ASSETS ($ mil.)	NET INCOME ($ mil.)	INCOME AS % OF ASSETS	EMPLOYEES
12/20	531.5	5.7	1.1%	0
12/19	489.4	5.2	1.1%	0
12/18	459.6	4.6	1.0%	0
12/17	427.4	2.8	0.7%	0
12/16	393.3	3.9	1.0%	62
Annual Growth	7.8%	10.0%	—	—

2020 Year-End Financials

Return on assets: 1.1%
Return on equity: 10.9%
Long-term debt ($ mil.): —
No. of shares (mil.): 1.5
Sales ($ mil): 24.4

Dividends
Yield: 4.0%
Payout: 35.8%
Market value ($ mil.): 57.0

	STOCK PRICE ($) FY Close	P/E High/Low		PER SHARE ($) Earnings	Dividends	Book Value
12/20	37.00	11	7	3.75	1.41	35.55
12/19	41.00	13	10	3.26	1.32	31.03
12/18	34.75	12	11	2.89	1.24	28.28
12/17	34.55	22	20	1.72	1.11	26.83
12/16	34.90	17	12	2.39	1.03	26.05
Annual Growth	1.5%	—	—	12.0%	8.1%	8.1%

MVB Financial Corp

EXECUTIVES

Independent Chairman Of The Board, David Alvarez

President, Chief Executive Officer, Director, Larry Mazza, $778,355 total compensation

Executive Vice President, Chief Financial Officer And Corporate Development Officer, Donald Robinson, $411,035 total compensation

Independent Director, Gary LeDonne

Chief People And Culture Officer, Executive Vice President, Craig Greathouse, $274,588 total compensation

Independent Director, John Ebert

Independent Director, Anna Sainsbury

Independent Director, W. Marston Becker

Chief Operating Officer, John Marion, $150,350 total compensation

Auditors: Dixon Hughes Goodman LLP

LOCATIONS

HQ: MVB Financial Corp
301 Virginia Avenue, Fairmont, WV 26554
Phone: 304 363-4800
Web: www.mvbbanking.com

HISTORICAL FINANCIALS

Company Type: Public

Income Statement

FYE: December 31

	ASSETS ($ mil.)	NET INCOME ($ mil.)	INCOME AS % OF ASSETS	EMPLOYEES
12/20	2,331.4	37.4	1.6%	344
12/19	1,944.1	26.9	1.4%	443
12/18	1,750.9	12.0	0.7%	0
12/17	1,534.3	7.5	0.5%	0
12/16	1,418.8	12.9	0.9%	382
Annual Growth	13.2%	30.5%	—	(2.6%)

2020 Year-End Financials

Return on assets: 1.7%
Return on equity: 16.5%
Long-term debt ($ mil.): —
No. of shares (mil.): 11.5
Sales ($ mil): 172.2

Dividends
Yield: 1.5%
Payout: 14.8%
Market value ($ mil.): 261.0

	STOCK PRICE ($) FY Close	P/E High/Low		PER SHARE ($) Earnings	Dividends	Book Value
12/20	22.68	8	3	3.06	0.36	20.78
12/19	24.92	11	7	2.20	0.20	17.74
12/18	18.04	19	16	1.00	0.11	15.23
12/17	20.10	29	18	0.68	0.10	14.38
12/16	12.80	10	7	1.31	0.08	14.57
Annual Growth	15.4%	—	—	23.6%	45.6%	9.3%

MYR Group Inc

MYR Group is a holding company of specialty contractor builds and maintains electric delivery infrastructure systems for utilities and commercial clients. MYR Group constructs transmission and distribution lines for the electric utility infrastructure commercial and industrial construction markets. The Group also installs and maintains electrical wiring in commercial and industrial facilities and traffic and rail systems. The Group operates nationwide through subsidiaries including The L.E. Myers Co. Harlan Electric Sturgeon Electric MYR Transmission Services and Great Southwestern Construction.

Operations

The Group's Transmission & Distribution (T&D) segment generated about 50% of revenue while Commercial & Industrial (C&I) segment brought in some 50%.

The T&D segment provides a broad range of services on electric networks and substation facilities which include design engineering procurement construction upgrade and maintenance and repair services with a focus on construction maintenance and repair. T&D services also include the construction and maintenance of high voltage transmission lines substations lower voltage underground and overhead distribution systems renewable power facilities and limited gas construction services. It also provides emergency restoration services in response to hurricane ice or other storm-related damage.

Its C&I segment provides services such as the design installation maintenance and repair of commercial and industrial wiring the installation of

traffic networks and the installation of bridge roadway and tunnel lighting.

MYR Group's completed projects include the Cabot Station Generating Plant Harry Allen-El Dorado Transmission Line Sloan Canyon Switchyard & Transmission Line Behr Paint Headquarters Cinnaminson Landfill Solar Farm Nansemond River Crossing and Southern Reinforcement Project.

The Group provides services to customers through contracts. Its fixed price contracts accounted for roughly 65% of total revenue. The remaining sales are from unit price T&E and others.

Geographic Reach

The Group is based in Henderson Colorado with additional offices in Thornton Colorado and Rolling Meadows Illinois. It owns some 15 operating facilities. It serves markets in the US and western Canada.

Sales and Marketing

T&D customers include investor-owned utilities cooperatives private developers government-funded utilities independent power producers independent transmission companies industrial facility owners and other contractors. Its C&I segment provides electrical contracting services to property owners and general contractors commercial and industrial facility owners governmental agencies and developers. Overall its market from electric construction accounted about 50% of total revenue followed by transmission for roughly 35% and distribution for nearly 20%.

Its top 10 customers accounted for about 30% of revenues with no single customer accounted for more than 10% of revenue.

MYR Group's advertising costs were $0.7 million $0.8 million and $0.7 million in 2020 2019 and 2018 respectively.

Financial Performance

Revenues increased $176.2 million or 9% to $2.3 billion for the year ended December 31 2020 from $2.1 billion for the year ended December 31 2019. The increase was primarily due to incremental revenues from the CSI acquisition partially offset by impacts related to the COVID-19 pandemic primarily associated with its C&I segment.

Net income attributable to MYR Group Inc. increased to $58.8 million for the year ended December 31 2020 from $37.7 million for the year ended December 31 2019.

Cash held by the company at the end of fiscal 2020 increased to $22.7 million. Cash provided by operations was $175.2 million while cash used for investing and financing activities were $40.9 million and $124.3 million respectively. Main uses of cash were purchases of property and equipment; and net repayments under revolving lines of credit.

Strategy

MYR Group strives to maintain its status as a preferred provider to its T&D and C&I customers. In an effort to support its growth strategy and maximize stockholder returns the company seeks to efficiently manage its capital. Through 2020 MYR Group continued to implement strategies that further expanded its capabilities and allowed opportunities to provide prudent capital returns. On July 15 2019 the company completed the acquisition of substantially all the assets of CSI Electrical Contractors Inc. ("CSI") which expanded its C&I operations in California. Additionally MYR Group ended 2020 with $364.6 million available under its credit facility.

HOOVER'S HANDBOOK OF EMERGING COMPANIES 2022

Company Background

MYR was founded in 1891 by Lewis Edward Myers who briefly worked as a salesman with Thomas Edison.

EXECUTIVES

Senior Vice President, Chief Operating Officer - Transmission & Distribution, Tod Cooper, $447,923 total compensation
President, Chief Executive Officer, Director, Richard Swartz, $716,539 total compensation
Chief Financial Officer, Senior Vice President, Betty Johnson, $436,058 total compensation
Independent Director, Maurice Moore
Senior Vice President, Chief Operating Officer - Commercial & Industrial, Jeffrey Waneka, $403,846 total compensation
Independent Chairman Of The Board, Kenneth Hartwick
Independent Director, Jennifer Lowry
Vice President, Chief Legal Officer, Secretary, William Fry, $349,327 total compensation
Independent Director, Shirin O'connor
Independent Director, Donald Lucky
Auditors: Crowe LLP

LOCATIONS

HQ: MYR Group Inc
12150 East 112th Avenue, Henderson, CO 80640
Phone: 303 286-8000
Web: www.myrgroup.com

PRODUCTS/OPERATIONS

2014 Sales by Segment

	% of total
Transmission & Distribution	74
Commercial & Industrial	26
Total	**100**

Selected Services

Electrical
  Commercial/Industrial
  Construction
  Design-build services
  Directional boring
  Emergency storm response
  Fiber optics
  Foundations & caissons
  Gas distribution
  Highway lighting
  Overhead distribution
  PCS/Cellular towers
  Preconstruction services
  Substation
  Telecommunications
  Traffic signals
  Transmission
  Underground distribution
Mechanical
  Boiler construction and maintenance
  Erection of piping systems
  General contracting
  In-house fabrication
  Instrumentation
  Maintenance
  Preconstruction services
  Retrofit to existing systems

Selected Subsidiaries

ComTel Technology Inc.
Great Southwestern Construction Inc.
Harlan Electric Company
Hawkeye Construction Inc.
Meyers International Inc.
MYR Transmission Services Inc.
MYRpower Inc.
The L.E. Myers Co.
Sturgeon Electric Company Inc.

COMPETITORS

ARB INC.	MUNICIPAL ELECTRIC
BASIC ENERGY SERVICES INC.	AUTHORITY OF GEORGIA
FEDERAL SIGNAL CORPORATION COMPANY	POWELL INDUSTRIES INC.
	RPC INC.
	TAMPA ELECTRIC
JGC HOLDINGS CORPORATION HOLDINGS	TEAM INC.
	THERMON GROUP
LAYNE CHRISTENSEN COMPANY	INC.
	Wajax Corporation
MAMMOTH ENERGY SERVICES INC.	

HISTORICAL FINANCIALS

Company Type: Public

Income Statement
FYE: December 31

	REVENUE ($ mil.)	NET INCOME ($ mil.)	NET PROFIT MARGIN	EMPLOYEES
12/20	2,247.3	58.7	2.6%	7,200
12/19	2,071.1	37.6	1.8%	7,100
12/18	1,531.1	31.0	2.0%	5,500
12/17	1,403.3	21.1	1.5%	5,275
12/16	1,142.4	21.4	1.9%	4,600
Annual Growth	18.4%	28.7%	—	11.9%

2020 Year-End Financials

Debt ratio: 2.9%	No. of shares (mil.): 16.7
Return on equity: 14.7%	Dividends
Cash ($ mil.): 22.6	Yield: —
Current ratio: 1.44	Payout: —
Long-term debt ($ mil.): 25.0	Market value ($ mil.): 1,006.0

	STOCK PRICE ($) FY Close	P/E High/Low		PER SHARE ($) Earnings	Dividends	Book Value
12/20	60.10	17	5	3.48	0.00	25.65
12/19	32.59	17	12	2.26	0.00	21.89
12/18	28.17	21	14	1.87	0.00	19.50
12/17	35.73	33	18	1.28	0.00	17.43
12/16	37.68	32	15	1.23	0.00	16.11
Annual Growth	12.4%	—	—	29.7%	—	12.3%

NASB Financial Inc

NASB Financial is the holding company for North American Savings Bank which operates about 15 branches and loan offices in the Kansas City and Springfield Missouri areas. Established in 1927 the bank offers standard deposit products to retail and commercial customers including checking and savings accounts and CDs. Mortgages secured by residential or commercial properties make up most of the bank's lending activities; it also originates business consumer and construction loans. Subsidiary Nor-Am sells annuities mutual funds and credit life and disability insurance. Chairman David Hancock and his wife Linda who is also a member of the company's board of directors own about 45% of NASB Financial.

Operations

In 2012 North American Savings Bank entered into a consent order with the Office of the Comptroller of the Currency to improve its asset quality and maintain adequate provisions for loan losses among other measures. The order is a continuance of a similar one agreed to with the bank's former regulator the Office of Thrift Supervision.

Financial Performance

The company's revenue decreased slightly in fiscal 2013 compared to the previous fiscal period. It reported revenue of $113.3 million in fiscal 2013 after bringing in $114.9 million in revenue for fiscal 2012.

However even with the slight decline in annual revenue the company's net income increased in fiscal 2013 compared to fiscal 2012. It cleared more than $27 million in net profit for fiscal 2013 after netting about $18 million in fiscal 2012.

Cash flow increased from negative levels during fiscal 2012 up to a positive $124 million in fiscal 2013.

EXECUTIVES

Chairman Of The Board, David Hancock, $323,958 total compensation
Vice President, Dena Sanders
Vice President, Treasurer, Rhonda Nyhus, $195,042 total compensation
Independent Director, Barrett Brady
Director, Linda Hancock
Chief Executive Officer, Director, Paul Thomas, $336,458 total compensation
Vice President, Director, Thomas Wagers
Independent Director, W. Russell Welsh
Vice President, Burke Walker
Vice President, J. Enrique Venegas
Independent Director, Rich Agar
Independent Director, Laura Brady
Auditors: BKD, LLP

LOCATIONS

HQ: NASB Financial Inc
12498 South 71 Highway, Grandview, MO 64030
Phone: 816 765-2200
Web: www.nasb.com

COMPETITORS

ASTORIA FINANCIAL CORPORATION
BENEFICIAL MUTUAL BANCORP INC.
FIRST FEDERAL SAVINGS AND LOAN ASSOCIATION OF LAKEWOOD
FIRST FINANCIAL NORTHWEST INC.
HUDSON VALLEY HOLDING CORP.
THE SOUTHERN BANC COMPANY INC
TIAA FSB HOLDINGS INC.
TRUSTCO BANK CORP N Y
VIRGINIA COMMERCE BANCORP INC.

HISTORICAL FINANCIALS

Company Type: Public

Income Statement
FYE: September 30

	ASSETS ($ mil.)	NET INCOME ($ mil.)	INCOME AS % OF ASSETS	EMPLOYEES
09/21	2,359.3	73.7	3.1%	0
09/20	2,552.2	103.5	4.1%	0
09/19	2,605.2	43.1	1.7%	0
09/18	2,060.3	29.1	1.4%	0
09/17	2,062.3	29.4	1.4%	0
Annual Growth	3.4%	25.8%	—	—

2021 Year-End Financials

Return on assets: 3.0%	Dividends
Return on equity: 19.8%	Yield: 6.4%
Long-term debt ($ mil.): —	Payout: 40.7%
No. of shares (mil.): 7.4	Market value ($ mil.): 466.0
Sales ($ mil): 259.0	

STOCK PRICE ($) FY Close	P/E High/Low		PER SHARE ($) Earnings	Dividends	Book Value
09/21	63.00	8	6	9.94	4.05	53.13
09/20	60.00	4	2	14.01	2.15	47.42
09/19	44.20	8	6	5.85	2.00	35.56
09/18	40.60	11	9	3.94	3.82	31.37
09/17	36.11	10	8	3.98	1.22	31.55
Annual Growth	14.9%	—	—	25.7%	35.0%	13.9%

National Bank Holdings Corp

National Bank Holdings is the holding company for NBH Bank which operates some 90 branches in four south and central US states under various brands including: Bank Midwest in Kansas and Missouri Community Banks of Colorado in Colorado and Hillcrest Bank in Texas. Targeting small to medium-sized businesses and consumers the banks offer traditional checking and savings accounts as well as commercial and residential mortgages agricultural loans and commercial loans. The bank boasted $6.7 billion in assets at the end of 2020 including $4.4 billion in loans and $5.7 billion in deposits. Around 60% of its total revenue is made up of interest income.

Operations

Through the bank the company's primary business is to offer a full range of traditional banking products and financial services to its commercial business and consumer clients. It conducts its banking business through 90 banking centers and offers a high level of personalized service to our clients through our relationship managers and banking center associates.

Around 55% of the bank's total revenue came from loan interest (including fees) during 2020 while some 5% came from interest on its investment securities. The rest of its revenue came from mortgage banking (nearly 30%) service charges (roughly 5%) bank card fees (nearly 5%) and other miscellaneous income sources.

In addition its loan portfolio comprises commercial loans with approximately 65% commercial real estate non-owner occupied and residential real estate with nearly 15% each and PPP loans which generates the rest of sales.

Geographic Reach

Denver Colorado-based National Bank Holdings had a network of some 90 banking centers with some half of those in Colorado over 35 in Missouri and Kansas two branches in Texas one in Utah and five in new Mexico.

Sales and Marketing

The bank serves small- to medium-sized businesses and consumers via its network of banking locations and through online and mobile banking products.

Financial Performance

The company had a net interest income of $192.9 million a 6% decrease from the previous year's net interest income of $205.8 million.

In 2020 the company had a net income of $88.6 million a 10% increase from the previous year's net income of $80.4 million.

The company's cash at the end of 2020 was $615.6 million. Financing activities provided $615.6 million while operating activities used $9.9 million. Investing activities used another $148.9 million mainly for purchase of investment securities available-for-sale as well as purchase of investment securities held-to-maturity.

Strategy

As part of the company's goal of becoming a leading regional community bank holding company it seeks to continue to generate strong organic growth as well as pursue selective acquisitions of financial institutions and other complementary businesses. Its focus is on building organic growth through strong banking relationships with small- and medium-sized businesses and consumers in its primary markets while maintaining a low-risk profile designed to generate reliable income streams and attractive returns.

While the company remains focused on executing on its business strategies in 2020 the COVID-19 pandemic necessitated a shift to focus its immediate attention on the following three priorities: 1) protecting the health of associates and clients 2) ensuring the safety and soundness of its bank and 3) acting on every opportunity to prudently support its clients and the communities where it does business. The company continues to leverage its digital banking platform with its clients and have been working diligently to support clients who are experiencing financial hardship through participation in the Small Business Administration's ("SBA") Paycheck Protection Program ("PPP") created under the Coronavirus Aid Relief and Economic Security Act ("CARES Act") including assistance with PPP loan forgiveness applications for the first draw loans PPP loan applications for the second draw and loan modifications as needed.

The key components of its strategic plan are:

Focus on client-centered relationship-driven banking strategy. The company's business and commercial bankers focus on small- and medium-sized businesses with an advisory approach that emphasizes understanding the client's business and offering a complete array of loan deposit and treasury management products and services;

Expansion of commercial banking business banking and specialty businesses. It has made significant investments in its commercial relationship managers as well as developed significant capabilities across its business banking and several specialty commercial banking offerings; as well as

Expansion through organic growth and competitive product offerings. The company believes that its focus on serving consumers and small- to medium-sized businesses coupled with competitive product offerings will provide an expanded revenue base and new sources of fee income.

Company Background

Formed in 2009 National Bank Holdings went public in 2012. Prior to its filing National Bank Holdings was minority-owned by a number of private shareholders and corporate entities including Taconic Capital Advisors Wellington Management and Paulson & Co.

EXECUTIVES

Independent Lead Director, Ralph Clermont
Independent Director, Micho Spring
Independent Director, Robert Dean
Chief Risk Management Officer, Richard Newfield, $375,000 total compensation
Independent Director, Arthur Zeile
Chief Financial Officer, Aldis Birkans, $338,269 total compensation
Executive Vice President - Personal, Private And Residential Banking Of The Bank, Brendan Zahl, $275,000 total compensation
Chief Client Executive And Deposit Operations Executive Of The Bank, Ruth Stevenson
Chief Administrative Officer, General Counsel, Angela Petrucci
Director, Alka Gupta
Independent Director, Fred Joseph
Executive Vice President - Commercial, Specialty And Business Banking Of The Bank, Christopher Randall, $275,000 total compensation
Director, Patrick Sobers, $260,673 total compensation
Chairman Of The Board, President, Chief Executive Officer, G. Timothy Laney, $750,000 total compensation
Independent Director, Burney Warren
Auditors: KPMG LLP

LOCATIONS

HQ: National Bank Holdings Corp
7800 East Orchard Road, Suite 300, Greenwood Village, CO 80111
Phone: 303 892-8715
Web: www.nationalbankholdings.com

PRODUCTS/OPERATIONS

2015 Sales

	% of total
Interest and dividend income:	
Interest and fees on loans	63
Interest and dividends on investment securities	18
Dividends on non-marketable securities	1
Interest on interest-bearing bank deposits	-
Total	**82**
Non-interest income:	
Service charges	7
Bank card fees	5
Gain on sales of mortgages net	1
Bank-owned life insurance income	1
Other non-interest income	2
Bargain purchase gain	1
Gain on previously charged-off acquired loans	
OREO related write-ups and other income	1
FDIC indemnification asset amortization net of gain on termination	-
FDIC loss sharing income (expense)	-
Total Non-Interest Income	18
Total	**100**

COMPETITORS

AMERIS BANCORP
BEAR STATE FINANCIAL INC.
Banco Bradesco S/A
CAPITAL BANK FINANCIAL CORP.
CENTERSTATE BANK CORPORATION
CITIZENS FINANCIAL GROUP INC.
CITY HOLDING COMPANY
COLUMBIA BANKING SYSTEM INC.
FINANCIAL INSTITUTIONS INC.
FIRST COMMONWEALTH FINANCIAL CORPORATION
FIRST FINANCIAL CORPORATION
FIRST HORIZON CORPORATION
IBW FINANCIAL CORPORATION
KEYCORP
MIDSOUTH BANCORP INC.
MUFG AMERICAS HOLDINGS CORPORATION
OLD NATIONAL BANCORP
PACWEST BANCORP
PEOPLES FINANCIAL SERVICES CORP.
PINNACLE FINANCIAL PARTNERS INC.
SIGNATURE BANK
THE CO-OPERATIVE BANK P.L.C.

HISTORICAL FINANCIALS

Company Type: Public

Income Statement
FYE: December 31

	ASSETS ($ mil.)	NET INCOME ($ mil.)	INCOME AS % OF ASSETS	EMPLOYEES
12/20	6,659.9	88.5	1.3%	1,224
12/19	5,895.5	80.3	1.4%	1,298
12/18	5,676.6	61.4	1.1%	1,332
12/17	4,843.4	14.5	0.3%	926
12/16	4,573.0	23.0	0.5%	1,004
Annual Growth	9.9%	40.0%	—	5.1%

2020 Year-End Financials

Return on assets: 1.4%
Return on equity: 11.1%
Long-term debt ($ mil.): —
No. of shares (mil.): 30.6
Sales ($ mil): 358.2

Dividends
  Yield: 2.4%
  Payout: 30.8%
Market value ($ mil.): 1,004.0

	STOCK PRICE ($) FY Close	P/E High/Low		PER SHARE ($) Earnings	Dividends	Book Value
12/20	32.76	13	7	2.85	0.80	26.79
12/19	35.22	15	12	2.55	0.75	24.60
12/18	30.87	21	15	1.95	0.54	22.59
12/17	32.43	68	56	0.53	0.34	19.81
12/16	31.89	40	23	0.79	0.22	20.32
Annual Growth	0.7%		—	—	37.8% 38.1%	7.2%

National Rural Utilities Cooperative Finance Corp

Cooperation may work wonders on Sesame Street but in the real world it takes money to pay the power bill. The National Rural Utilities Cooperative Finance Corporation provides financing and investment services for rural electrical and telephone projects throughout the US. The group is owned by some 1500 member electric utility and telecommunications systems. National Rural supplements the government loans that traditionally have fueled rural electric utilities by selling commercial paper medium-term notes and collateral trust bonds to fund its loan programs. National Rural was formed in 1969 by the National Rural Electric Cooperative Association a lobby representing the nation's electric co-ops.

EXECUTIVES

Chief Executive Officer, J. Andrew Don, $422,500 total compensation
Senior Vice President, Loan Operations, Robin Reed
Senior Vice President - Credit Risk Management, John Borak, $260,049 total compensation
Vice President - Capital Market Relations, Ling Wang
Senior Vice President, General Counsel, Roberta Aronson, $320,804 total compensation
Senior Vice President - Corporate Relations, Brad Captain

Senior Vice President - Member Services, Joel Allen
Senior Vice President - Business And Industry Development, Gregory Starheim, $371,364 total compensation
Senior Manager, Corporate Administration, Mary Harden
President, Alan Wattles
Independent Director, Doyle Hanson
Independent Director, Robert Brockman
Independent Director, Bradley Schardin
Director, Marsha Thompson
Independent Director, Jimmy LaFoy
Director, Todd Ware
Vice President, Director, Bruce Vitosh
Director, Jeffrey Rehder
Chief Financial Officer, Senior Vice President, Yu Ling Wang
Auditors: KPMG LLP

LOCATIONS

HQ: National Rural Utilities Cooperative Finance Corp
20701 Cooperative Way, Dulles, VA 20166
Phone: 703 467-1800   **Fax:** 703 709-6779
Web: www.nrucfc.coop

PRODUCTS/OPERATIONS

Selected Subsidiaries and Affiliates
National Cooperative Services Corporation (financing for members and affiliated not-for-profit entities)
Rural Telephone Finance Cooperative (rural telecommunications lending)

COMPETITORS

AMERICAN EXPRESS COMPANY	TOYOTA MOTOR CREDIT CORPORATION
CLAYTON DUBILIER & RICE INC.	WORLD ACCEPTANCE CORPORATION
INTERNATIONAL PERSONAL FINANCE PLC	

HISTORICAL FINANCIALS

Company Type: Public

Income Statement
FYE: May 31

	REVENUE ($ mil.)	NET INCOME ($ mil.)	NET PROFIT MARGIN	EMPLOYEES
05/21	1,641.8	811.6	49.4%	248
05/20	384.1	(585.2)	—	253
05/19	787.6	(149.2)	—	257
05/18	1,326.6	455.1	34.3%	254
05/17	1,149.5	309.9	27.0%	248
Annual Growth	9.3%	27.2%	—	0.0%

2021 Year-End Financials

Debt ratio: 92.5%
Return on equity: 81.1%
Cash ($ mil.): 295.0
Current ratio: 0.10
Long-term debt ($ mil.): 22,844.1

No. of shares (mil.): —
Dividends
  Yield: —
  Payout: —
Market value ($ mil.): —

National Storage Affiliates Trust

Auditors: KPMG LLP

LOCATIONS

HQ: National Storage Affiliates Trust
8400 East Prentice Avenue, 9th Floor, Greenwood Village, CO 80111
Phone: 720 630-2600
Web: www.nationalstorageaffiliates.com

HISTORICAL FINANCIALS

Company Type: Public

Income Statement
FYE: December 31

	REVENUE ($ mil.)	NET INCOME ($ mil.)	NET PROFIT MARGIN	EMPLOYEES
12/20	432.2	48.6	11.2%	1,684
12/19	387.9	3.9	1.0%	1,559
12/18	330.9	14.1	4.3%	1,561
12/17	268.1	2.9	1.1%	1,211
12/16	199.0	17.9	9.0%	995
Annual Growth	21.4%	28.3%	—	14.1%

2020 Year-End Financials

Debt ratio: 54.5%
Return on equity: 5.1%
Cash ($ mil.): 18.7
Current ratio: 0.88
Long-term debt ($ mil.): 1,916.9

No. of shares (mil.): 71.2
Dividends
  Yield: 3.7%
  Payout: 281.2%
Market value ($ mil.): 2,569.0

	STOCK PRICE ($) FY Close	P/E High/Low		PER SHARE ($) Earnings	Dividends	Book Value
12/20	36.03	72	43	0.53	1.35	13.59
12/19	33.62	—	—	(0.15)	1.27	15.41
12/18	26.46	457331		0.07	1.16	16.18
12/17	27.26	27592124		0.01	1.04	16.73
12/16	22.07	38	27	0.31	0.88	13.39
Annual Growth	13.0%		—	—	14.3% 11.3%	0.4%

National Vision Holdings Inc

Auditors: DELOITTE & TOUCHE LLP

LOCATIONS

HQ: National Vision Holdings Inc
2435 Commerce Avenue, Building 2200, Duluth, GA 30096
Phone: 770 822-3600
Web: www.nationalvision.com

HISTORICAL FINANCIALS

Company Type: Public

Income Statement
FYE: January 2

	REVENUE ($ mil.)	NET INCOME ($ mil.)	NET PROFIT MARGIN	EMPLOYEES
01/21*	1,711.7	36.2	2.1%	12,792
12/19	1,724.3	32.8	1.9%	11,781
12/18	1,536.8	23.6	1.5%	10,668
12/17	1,375.3	45.8	3.3%	10,902
12/16	1,196.2	14.7	1.2%	10,360
Annual Growth	9.4%	25.2%	—	5.4%

*Fiscal year change

2021 Year-End Financials

Debt ratio: 28.0%
Return on equity: 4.2%
Cash ($ mil.): 373.9
Current ratio: 1.72
Long-term debt ($ mil.): 651.7

No. of shares (mil.): 81.2
Dividends
  Yield: —
  Payout: —
Market value ($ mil.): 3,679.0

	STOCK PRICE ($) FY Close	P/E High/Low		PER SHARE ($) Earnings	Dividends	Book Value
01/21*	45.29	107	30	0.44	0.00	11.16
12/19	33.10	84	54	0.40	0.00	9.74
12/18	28.98	147	85	0.30	0.00	9.51
12/17	40.61	53	36	0.74	0.00	8.84
Annual Growth	3.7%	—	—	(15.9%)	—	8.1%

*Fiscal year change

Natural Alternatives International, Inc.

Natural Alternatives International (NAI) is a natural alternative for nutritional supplement marketers who want to outsource manufacturing. The company provides private-label manufacturing of vitamins minerals herbs and other customized nutritional supplements. Its main customers are direct sellers such as Mannatech and NSA International for whom it makes JuicePlus+ chewables capsules and powdered products. NAI also makes some branded products for sale in the US: the Pathway to Healing brand of nutritional supplements promoted by doctor and evangelist Reginald B. Cherry.

Operations

Natural Alternatives International (NAI) operates through three business segments. Private-label contract manufacturing is by far the largest representing more than 85% of sales. Its Branded Products business (just 2% of sales) markets and distributes branded nutritional supplements through direct-to-consumer marketing programs. NAI's Patent and Trademark licensing business segment is engaged in the sale and licensing of beta-alanine (an amino acid used by bodybuilders) under the CarnoSyn trade name.

NSA International and Mannatech are the company's biggest clients accounting for about 45% and 20% respectively of the company's sales. In addition to manufacturing products for its private-label clients NAI offers a range of complementary services such as regulatory assistance and packaging design.

Geographic Reach

The company has manufacturing and distribution facilities in California and in Switzerland. It also has sales support operations in Japan in order to assist clients operating in the Pacific Rim. The US accounts for 60% of NAI's sales. Outside the US NAI's primary market is Europe.

Financial Performance

The company's net sales grew a robust 30% in fiscal 2012 (ends June) vs. the prior year while net income fell by about 18% over the same period. Revenue from NAI's patent and trademark licensing business surged more than 350% in fiscal 2012 vs. 2011 driven by the increase in popularity of CarnoSyn as a sports nutrition supplement and expanded distribution of the product. The Private-label contract manufacturing segment saw its sales rise more than 20% due to increased sales to its two largest customers NSA International and Mannatech. Branded products was the laggard posting a 14% drop off in sales for the year which NAI blamed on soft sales of the Pathway to Healing product line.

Strategy

A key element of NAI's growth strategy is the commercialization of its beta-alanine patent through contract manufacturing royalty and licensing agreements and the protection of its proprietary rights (by legal means where necessary). Indeed the 350% surge in fiscal 2012 sales in the company's licensing business was credited to the CarnoSyn brand. To that end NAI in 2011 expanded its beta-alanine licensing programs through a supply agreement with Nestle Nutrition and a license and supply agreement with Abbott Laboratories. While the Nestle agreement expired in mid-2012 and was not renewed the agreement granting Abbott exclusive license for the use of beta-alanine in certain medical foods and medical nutritionals continues. Also NAI is looking to growth the CarnoSyn beta-alanine business through accretive acquisitions.

The company is also focusing on developing and growing its own line of branded products primarily through direct-to-consumer sales and distribution channels. To bolster is faltering Pathway to Healing line of branded products NAI relaunched the product line and increased its marketing and advertising activities to support future sales.

HISTORY

Marie Le Doux and her son Mark founded Natural Alternatives International (NAI) with $25000 in 1980. Mark a lawyer and former premed student had previously worked for a small California-based vitamin company and was a firm believer in the virtues of vitamins. He studied the beneficial properties of nutrients and began making vitamins for health food retailers and drugstores.

Finding the retail market too competitive for a small company the Le Doux duo refocused on specialty direct markets. Mark ramped up their production facility bringing in automated equipment from Italy. The company went public in 1986 and created private-label lines for several new customers.

Trouble struck in 1989 when NAI was forced to recall its products containing L-tryptophan (an amino acid often marketed as a sleep aid) after the FDA linked it to the potentially fatal eosinophilia-myalgia syndrome.

To help boost overseas sales NAI in 1997 bought a tablet and chewables manufacturing plant doubling its manufacturing capacity. In 1998 the firm acquired the rights to manufacture Glucotrol a fat- and cholesterol-binding diet supplement used in Japan. The next year it established subsidiary Natural Alternatives International Europe in Switzerland and began manufacturing operations there.

Faced with increased competition and decreased demand in 2000 (the company lost the business of Nu Skin Enterprises which had accounted for some 20% of its revenues) NAI cut jobs to reduce operating costs.

NAI expanded its branded products segment considerably with its 2005 Real Health Laboratories. The purchase brought in a line of products sold via mass retail outlets as well as a mail-order catalog business (As We Change) that sold proprietary and third-party nutritional and personal care products aimed at women over 40. However the lines did not meet the company's expectations and NAI first sold the catalog business to Miles Kimball Company in 2008 and then sold the remaining assets to PharmaCare in 2009.

EXECUTIVES

Chairman Of The Board Of Directors, Chief Executive Officer, Mark Ledoux, $425,000 total compensation
Independent Director, Alan Dunn
Chief Financial Officer, Michael Fortin, $250,000 total compensation
Independent Director, Laura Matherly
Independent Director, Guru Ramanathan
President, Chief Operating Officer, Secretary, Kenneth Wolf, $400,000 total compensation
Auditors: Haskell & White LLP

LOCATIONS

HQ: Natural Alternatives International, Inc.
1535 Faraday Ave, Carlsbad, CA 92008
Phone: 760 736-7700
Web: www.nai-online.com

COMPETITORS

4LIFE RESEARCH USA LLC
BLENDS INC.
Atrium Innovations Inc
FAES FARMA SA
Herbalife Nutrition Ltd.
NATURE'S SUNSHINE PRODUCTS INC.
RESONATE
TEVA PHARMACEUTICAL INDUSTRIES LIMITED
THE NATURE'S BOUNTY CO

HISTORICAL FINANCIALS

Company Type: Public

Income Statement

FYE: June 30

	REVENUE ($ mil.)	NET INCOME ($ mil.)	NET PROFIT MARGIN	EMPLOYEES
06/21	178.5	10.7	6.0%	342
06/20	118.8	(1.6)	—	316
06/19	138.2	6.5	4.7%	312
06/18	132.4	5.0	3.8%	266
06/17	121.9	7.2	5.9%	227
Annual Growth	10.0%	10.5%	—	10.8%

2021 Year-End Financials

Debt ratio: —
Return on equity: 14.2%
Cash ($ mil.): 32.1
Current ratio: 3.64
Long-term debt ($ mil.): —

No. of shares (mil.): 6.4
Dividends
  Yield: —
  Payout: —
Market value ($ mil.): 108.0

	STOCK PRICE ($) FY Close	P/E High/Low		PER SHARE ($) Earnings	Dividends	Book Value
06/21	16.83	11	4	1.69	0.00	12.44
06/20	6.84	—	—	(0.25)	0.00	10.57
06/19	11.66	15	10	0.92	0.00	10.53
06/18	10.15	16	12	0.73	0.00	9.03
06/17	9.95	13	8	1.09	0.00	8.81
Annual Growth	14.0%	—	—	11.6%	—	9.0%

Natural Grocers By Vitamin Cottage Inc

Natural Grocers by Vitamin Cottage (Natural Grocer) is an expanding specialty retailer of natural and organic groceries and dietary supplements. The fast-growing company (both in sales and store count) operates more than 160 stores in some 20 US states that sell natural and organic food including fresh produce meat frozen food and nonperishable bulk food; vitamins and dietary supplements; personal care products; pet care products; and books. The company sources from approximately 1100 suppliers and offer approximately 3200 brands that range from small independent businesses to multi-national conglomerates. Founded by Margaret and Philip Isely in 1958 Natural Grocers is run by members of the Isely family.

IPO

Operations

The company's stores range in size from 5000 sq. ft. to 16000 sq. ft. (A typical new store averages 11000 sq. ft.) Each store offers about 21000 different natural and organic products and 6900 different dietary supplements.

Natural Grocers generates about 70% of its revenue from groceries with dietary supplements accounting for around 20% and the remainder coming from body care pet care books and general merchandise.

Geographic Reach

Colorado is the company's home state and also its largest market with about a quarter of its stores. Other major markets for the company include Texas (home to about 15% of stores) as well as Oregon Arizona Utah and Kansas. It operates a bulk food repackaging facility and distribution center in Colorado.

Sales and Marketing

The company seeks to attract new customers by enhancing their nutrition knowledge through the distribution of printed and digital versions of its broad range of educational resources including the Health Hotline magazine. The chain devotes considerable marketing resources to educating customers on the benefits of natural and organic grocery products and dietary supplements. The company maintains www.naturalgrocers.com as its official company website to host store information sale and discount offers educational materials product and standards information policies and contact forms advocacy and news items and e-commerce capabilities. Its website is interlinked with other online and social media outlets including Facebook Instagram Twitter Pinterest and YouTube.

Natural Grocers reported total advertising and marketing expenses for years ended 2021 2020 and 2019 were $6.3 million $6.6 million and $8.2 million respectively.

Financial Performance

Net sales increased $18.7 million to $1.1 billion in fiscal 2021 (ended September) compared to $1 billion in fiscal 2020 primarily due to a $4.2 million increase in comparable store sales and a $14.5 million increase in new store sales.

Net income in fiscal 2021 (ended September) was $20.6 million compared to $20 million fiscal 2020.

Cash held by the company at the end of 2021 decreased to $23.7 million compared to 2020 with $28.5 million. Cash provided by operations was $53.9 million while cash used for investing and financing activities were $27.7 million and $30.9 million respectively. Main uses of cash were acquisition of property and equipment; and repayments under credit facility.

Strategy

Natural Grocers is pursuing several strategies to continue its profitable growth including expanding its store base; increasing sales from an existing customer; growing its customer base; and improving operating margins.

In order to increase its average ticket and the number of customer transactions the company plan to continue offering an engaging customer experience by providing science-based nutrition education and a differentiated merchandising strategy that delivers affordable high-quality natural and organic grocery products and dietary supplements. The company also plan to continue to utilize targeted marketing efforts to reach its existing customers including through the {N}power customer loyalty program ({N}power) which it anticipates will drive customer transactions increase the average ticket and convert occasional single-category customers into a core multi-category customers.

EXECUTIVES

Chairman Of The Board, Co-president, Kemper Isely, $607,800 total compensation
Co-president, Director, Zephyr Isely, $576,000 total compensation
Executive Vice President, Director, Elizabeth Isely, $528,000 total compensation
Independent Director, Richard Halle
Chief Financial Officer, Todd Dissinger, $479,160 total compensation
Independent Director, David Rooney
Independent Director, Edward Cerkovnik
Executive Vice President, Corporate Secretary, Director, Heather Isely, $528,000 total compensation
Auditors: KPMG LLP

LOCATIONS

HQ: Natural Grocers By Vitamin Cottage Inc
12612 West Alameda Parkway, Lakewood, CO 80228
Phone: 303 986-4600
Web: www.naturalgrocers.com

PRODUCTS/OPERATIONS

2017 Sales

	% of total
Grocery	67
Dietary supplements	22
Body care pet care and other	11
Total	**100**

COMPETITORS

A.F.BLAKEMORE AND SON LIMITED
CORE-MARK HOLDING COMPANY INC.
MARKET FRESH DIRECT HOLDINGS INC.
GNC HOLDINGS INC.
GNC HOLDINGS LLC
GROCERY OUTLET INC.
PETMED EXPRESS INC.
SPROUTS FARMERS INC.
TEAVANA CORPORATION
VITAMIN WORLD INC.

HISTORICAL FINANCIALS

Company Type: Public

Income Statement

FYE: September 30

	REVENUE ($ mil.)	NET INCOME ($ mil.)	NET PROFIT MARGIN	EMPLOYEES
09/21	1,055.5	20.5	1.9%	4,192
09/20	1,036.8	20.0	1.9%	4,272
09/19	903.5	9.4	1.0%	3,681
09/18	849.0	12.6	1.5%	3,598
09/17	769.0	6.8	0.9%	3,270
Annual Growth	8.2%	31.5%	—	6.4%

2021 Year-End Financials

Debt ratio: 10.1%
Return on equity: 13.0%
Cash ($ mil.): 23.6
Current ratio: 1.01
Long-term debt ($ mil.): 61.3
No. of shares (mil.): 22.6
Dividends
  Yield: 20.3%
  Payout: 300.0%
Market value ($ mil.): 254.0

	STOCK PRICE ($) FY Close	P/E High/Low		PER SHARE ($) Earnings	Dividends	Book Value
09/21	11.22	20	11	0.91	2.28	6.31
09/20	9.86	19	7	0.89	0.28	7.68
09/19	9.99	54	20	0.42	0.00	6.99
09/18	16.89	34	8	0.56	0.00	6.56
09/17	5.58	44	18	0.31	0.00	5.96
Annual Growth	19.1%		—	30.9%	—	1.4%

Nautilus Inc

Nautilus makes and markets cardio and strength-building fitness equipment for home use. Its products include home gyms free weights and benches treadmills exercise bikes and elliptical machines that are sold under the popular brand names Bowflex Nautilus Schwinn and JRNY. Nautilus sells its fitness equipment directly to consumers through its variety of brand websites and catalogs as well as through TV commercials. The company also markets its gear through specialty retailers in the US Europe and Canada. The company generates majority of sales in the US. Nautilus was founded in 1986 and went public in 1999.

Operations

The company operates its fitness equipment business through a pair of reportable segments. As part of its Retail segment (about 55%) Nautilus sells products through a network of third-party retailers that operate websites and stores located in the US and internationally. Its Direct segment (almost 45% of revenue) sells products directly to consumers through TV advertising the Internet and catalogs.

Nautilus also derives a portion of its revenue from the licensing of its brands and intellectual property.

Geographic Reach

Washington-based Nautilus operates in the US Europe Asia and Canada with warehouse and distribution facilities located in Oregon and Ohio in the US. Its quality assurance and software engineering office is located in China.

The US accounts for about 85% of revenue. The remaining revenues are from Canada EMEA and other countries.

Sales and Marketing

Nautilus sells its products to fitness enthusiasts and to those who want to work out regularly. It sells through two sales channels: direct and retail. The company utilize its websites social media digital advertising capital inquiry-response mailings catalogs and inbound/outbound call centers.

Advertising and promotion costs totaled $36.3 million $46.8 million and $65.7 million in 2020 2019 and 2018 respectively.

Financial Performance

Net sales for 2020 were $552.6 million reflecting a 79% increase as compared to net sales of $309.3 million for 2019.

In 2020 the company had a net income of $59.8 million a $152.6 million improvement compared to the previous year's net loss of $92.8 million.

The company's cash at the end of 2020 was $57.9 million. Operating activities generated $71.7 million while investing activities used $24.5 million mainly for purchases of available-for-sale-securities. Financing activities used another $3.1 million primarily for payments on long-term debt.

Strategy

Nautilus empowers healthier living through individualized connected fitness experiences. The company develops and markets home fitness equipment and related products to meet the needs of a broad range of consumers. It has diversified its business by expanding its portfolio of high quality fitness equipment into multiple product lines utilizing the company's well-recognized brand names. The company views the continual innovation of its product offerings as a key aspect of its business strategy. The company regularly refreshes its existing product lines with new technologies and finishes and focuses significant effort and resources on the development or acquisition of innovative new fitness products and technologies for introduction to the marketplace at periodic intervals.

The company's long-term strategy involves: enhancing its product lines by designing personalized connected-fitness equipment that meets or exceeds the high expectations of its existing and new customers; continuing its investment in innovation with a particular focus on expanding the reach of its digital platform JRNY; creatively marketing its equipment both directly to consumers and through its retail customers while leveraging its well-known brand names; increasing its international retail sales and distribution; and maximizing available royalty revenues from the licensing of the company's brands and intellectual property.

Company Background

Nautilus Inc. was founded in 1986 and incorporated in the State of Washington in 1993. Their headquarters are located in Vancouver Washington.

EXECUTIVES

Vice President, General Manager, North American Retail, Jay Mcgregor
Vice President, General Manager, International And Commercial Specialty, Jeffrey Collins, $255,385 total compensation
Senior Vice President - Innovation, Christopher Quatrochi, $286,731 total compensation
Principal Financial, Accounting Officer And Corporate Controller, Sarah Jones
Chief Financial Officer, Aina Konold, $370,192 total compensation

Chief Marketing Officer, Becky Alseth, $221,400 total compensation
Independent Director, Patricia Ross
Senior Vice President, Chief Digital Officer, Garry Wiseman
Chief People Officer, Ellen Raim
Chief Legal Officer, Alan Chan
Director, Shailesh Prakash
Director, Kelley Hall
Independent Chairman Of The Board, M. Johnson
Chief Executive Officer And Director, James Barr, $571,154 total compensation
Chief Supply Chain Officer, John Goelz
Auditors: Grant Thornton LLP

LOCATIONS

HQ: Nautilus Inc
17750 S.E. 6th Way, Vancouver, WA 98683
Phone: 360 859-2900
Web: www.nautilusinc.com

PRODUCTS/OPERATIONS

2014 Sales

	% of total
Direct	64
Retail	34
Royalty income	2
Total	**100**

Selected Brands

Bowflex
Nautilus
Schwinn Fitness
Universal

COMPETITORS

ACUSHNET HOLDINGS CORP.
BUILD-A-BEAR WORKSHOP INC.
INC.
DICK'S SPORTING GOODS INC.
ESCALADE INCORPORATED
FRASERS GROUP PLC
GLOBAL INDUSTRIAL COMPANY
IFIT INC.
IMEDIA BRANDS INC.
LIFE FITNESS INC
THE INTERTECH GROUP
TRUECAR INC.
USANA HEALTH SCIENCES INC.

HISTORICAL FINANCIALS

Company Type: Public

Income Statement — FYE: December 31

	REVENUE ($ mil.)	NET INCOME ($ mil.)	NET PROFIT MARGIN	EMPLOYEES
12/20	552.5	59.8	10.8%	412
12/19	309.2	(92.8)	—	434
12/18	396.7	14.6	3.7%	460
12/17	406.1	26.2	6.5%	491
12/16	406.0	34.1	8.4%	469
Annual Growth	**8.0%**	**15.0%**	**—**	**(3.2%)**

2020 Year-End Financials

Debt ratio: 4.2%	No. of shares (mil.): 30.3
Return on equity: 48.9%	Dividends
Cash ($ mil.): 92.7	Yield: —
Current ratio: 2.00	Payout: —
Long-term debt ($ mil.): 10.7	Market value ($ mil.): 550.0

STOCK PRICE ($) FY Close	P/E High/Low		PER SHARE ($) Earnings	Dividends	Book Value
12/20	18.14	14 1	1.86	0.00	5.05
12/19	1.75	— —	(3.13)	0.00	3.04
12/18	10.90	34 21	0.48	0.00	6.18
12/17	13.35	23 14	0.85	0.00	5.91
12/16	18.50	23 14	1.09	0.00	5.22
Annual Growth	(0.5%)	— —	14.3%	—	(0.8%)

Nelnet Inc

Nelnet is a diverse company with a purpose to serve others and a vision to make customers' dreams possible by delivering customer focused products and services. Nelnet is mostly known for servicing federal student loans. Nelnet helps students and families plan and pay for their education and makes the administrative processes for schools more efficient with student loan servicing tuition payment processing school administration software and college planning resources. Nelnet also offers fiber-optic services directly to homes and businesses for ultra-fast fiber internet television and telephone services. The company also makes investments in real estate developments and new ventures.

Operations

The company reportable operating segments include Loan Servicing and Systems (LSS) Education Technology Services and Payment Processing (ETS&PP) Communications Asset Generation and Management (AGM) and Nelnet Bank.

LSS focuses on student and consumer loan origination services and servicing loan origination and servicing-related technology solutions and outsourcing business services. Brands include Nelnet Diversified Solutions Nelnet Loan Servicing Nelnet Servicing Great Lakes Educational Loan Services Inc. (Great Lakes) Firstmark Services GreatNet and Nelnet Renewable Energy.

ETS&PP provide services such as tuition payment plans and billing financial needs assessment services online payment and refund processing school information system software payment technologies and professional development and educational instruction services. Brands include FACTS Nelnet Campus Commerce PaymentSpring FACTS Education Solutions Aware3 Higher-School Instructional Services Catholic Faith Technologies CD2 Learning and Nelnet International.

Communications focuses on providing fiber optic service directly to homes and businesses for internet telephone and television services. Includes the operations of ALLO prior to the deconsolidation of ALLO in late 2020.

AGM includes the acquisition and management of student and other loan assets. AGM also referred to as Nelnet Financial Services.

Nelnet Bank is an internet Utah-chartered industrial bank focused on the private education loan marketplace.

Geographic Reach

Headquartered in Lincoln Nebraska Nelnet has facilities in Colorado Idaho Texas New York Minnesota Connecticut Rhode Island Utah Nebraska

South Dakota and Wisconsin. Substantially all of its revenue comes from US customers.

ETS&PP provides services and technology in Australia New Zealand and Southeast Asia.

Sales and Marketing
The company's customers include students and families colleges and universities specifically financial aid business and admissions offices K-12 schools lenders state agencies and government entities.

Financial Performance
The company had an interest income of $289.6 million a 16% growth compared to the previous year.

In 2020 the company had a net income of $352.4 million a 149% increase from the previous year's $141.8 million.

The company's cash for the year ended 2020 totaled $163 million. Operating activities provided $212.8 million while investing activities provided another $621.2 million. Financing activities used $1.1 billion primarily for purchases of available-for-sale securities.

Strategy
The company's talent strategy is focused on attracting the best talent from a diverse range of sources recognizing and rewarding their performance and continually developing engaging and retaining them.

The company is committed to the continued development of its people. Strategic talent reviews and succession planning occur on a planned cadence annually across all business areas. The executive team convenes meetings with senior leadership and the board of directors to review top enterprise talent. The company continues to provide opportunities for associates to grow their careers internally with over half of open management positions filled internally during 2020.

Mergers and Acquisitions
In 2021 Nelnet Business Services a division of Nelnet Inc. is expanding its church technology offerings with the recent acquisition of Catholic Faith Technologies (CFT) an online learning and formation platform company located in Overland Park KS. This acquisition will enable the company to expand services to its faith community partners as well as enter into and support new markets.

Company Background
Nelnet has been through a turbulent few years as student loan reform and the financial crisis disrupted business and sent revenues down. The company's ability to adapt to the economic pressures and policy changes have helped it land face-up following the recession. Measures taken including laying off staff and tightening lending practices helped boost profits despite lower revenues. Although non-FFELP servicing income and payment processing revenues grew in 2011 FFELP servicing revenues declined as the portfolio further shrunk and school marketing sales decreased as schools cut back on spending. As a result revenues fell that year by 8% to $979 million. Net income increased 8% (to $204 million) in 2011 compared to 2010 when the company had expenses related to restructuring. Also in 2010 Nelnet paid the US government $55 million to settle a lawsuit claiming it had made false statements to receive extra subsidies.

In a blow to the student lending industry President Barack Obama eliminated the FFELP and prohibited private lenders from making federal student loans in 2010. All new federal student loans began going directly through the Department of Education's Direct Loan Program. As a result Nelnet no longer originates new FFELP loans.

But the change didn't put an end to Nelnet. The company was awarded a five-year servicing contract for federally owned student loans including existing FFELP loans. Nelnet also began servicing new loans generated directly under the Federal Direct Loan Program. The contract was a major win for the company. Nelnet expects that its fee-based revenue will increase as the servicing volume for these loans increases (while the FFELP portfolio declines). The company is also focusing on improving its customer service to increase the allotted percentage of new government loans it services.

CEO Michael Dunlap controls the company holding 68% of the voting power for Nelnet. Dunlap and his family also own Farmers & Merchants Investment.

EXECUTIVES

Executive Chairman Of The Board, Michael Dunlap, $562,754 total compensation
Chief Operating Officer, Terry Heimes, $759,718 total compensation
Independent Director, James Abel
Lead Independent Director, Thomas Henning
Chief Executive Officer, Jeffrey Noordhoek, $759,718 total compensation
President, Timothy Tewes, $700,000 total compensation
Corporate Secretary,general Counsel,chief Governance Officer, William Munn, $245,850 total compensation
Independent Director, Kathleen Farrell
Independent Director, Kimberly Rath
Independent Director, William Cintani
Chief Financial Officer, James Kruger, $700,000 total compensation
Independent Director, David Graff
Independent Director, Preeta Bansal
Auditors: KPMG LLP

LOCATIONS

HQ: Nelnet Inc
121 South 13th Street, Suite 100, Lincoln, NE 68508
Phone: 402 458-2370
Web: www.nelnetinvestors.com

PRODUCTS/OPERATIONS

2015 Sales

	$ mil.	% of total
Interest		
Loans	726.3	60
Investments	7.8	1
Noninterest		
Loan & guaranty servicing	239.9	20
Enrollment services	70.7	6
Tuition payment processing & campus commerce revenue	120.4	10
Gains on sale of loans & debt repurchases net	5.1	1
Other	32.0	2
Total	**1,202.2**	**100**

COMPETITORS

ATLANTICUS HOLDINGS CORPORATION
CLAYTON DUBILIER & RICE INC.
CREDIT ACCEPTANCE CORPORATION
FIRST INTERSTATE BANCSYSTEM INC.
HIGHER ONE HOLDINGS INC.
PERFORMANT FINANCIAL CORPORATION
TYLER TECHNOLOGIES INC.
WORLD ACCEPTANCE CORPORATION

HISTORICAL FINANCIALS
Company Type: Public

Income Statement				FYE: December 31
	ASSETS ($ mil.)	NET INCOME ($ mil.)	INCOME AS % OF ASSETS	EMPLOYEES
12/20	22,646.1	352.4	1.6%	6,199
12/19	23,708.9	141.8	0.6%	6,600
12/18	25,220.9	227.9	0.9%	6,200
12/17	23,964.4	173.1	0.7%	4,300
12/16	27,180.1	256.7	0.9%	3,700
Annual Growth	(4.5%)	8.2%	—	13.8%

2020 Year-End Financials

Return on assets: 1.5%
Return on equity: 14.0%
Long-term debt ($ mil.): —
No. of shares (mil.): 38.3
Sales ($ mil): 1,730.0

Dividends
Yield: 1.1%
Payout: 19.9%
Market value ($ mil.): 2,732.0

	STOCK PRICE ($) FY Close	P/E High/Low		PER SHARE ($) Earnings	Dividends	Book Value
12/20	71.24	8	4	9.02	0.82	68.63
12/19	58.24	20	15	3.54	0.74	60.07
12/18	52.34	11	9	5.57	0.66	57.24
12/17	54.78	14	9	4.14	0.58	52.67
12/16	50.75	9	5	6.02	0.50	48.96
Annual Growth	8.8%	—	—	10.6%	13.2%	8.8%

Neurocrine Biosciences, Inc.

For Neurocrine Biosciences drug development is all about body chemistry. The development-stage biotech develops treatments for neurological and endocrine hormone-related diseases such as insomnia depression and menstrual pain. Lead drug candidate Elagolix is designed to treat endometriosis which causes pain and irregular menstrual bleeding in women. Second in line is NBI-98854 a treatment for movement disorders. Neurocrine Biosciences works in additional therapeutic areas including anxiety cancer epilepsy and diabetes. The company has about a dozen drug candidates in various stages of research and clinical development through both internal programs and collaborative agreements with partners.

EXECUTIVES

Chief Business Development And Strategy Officer, Kyle Gano, $487,700 total compensation
Chief Commercial Officer, Eric Benevich, $499,900 total compensation
Independent Director, George Morrow
Independent Director, Leslie Norwalk
Chief Corporate Affairs Officer, David Boyer
Independent Director, Shalini Sharp
Director, Johanna Mercier
Chief Scientific Officer, Jude Onyia
Chief Legal Officer, Corporate Secretary, Darin Lippoldt
Chief Human Resource Officer, Julie Cooke
Chief Financial Officer, Matthew Abernethy, $545,200 total compensation

Chief Medical Officer, Eiry Roberts, $575,900 total compensation
Chief Executive Officer, Director, Kevin Gorman, $775,000 total compensation
Chief Research Officer, Dimitri Grigoriadis, $331,100 total compensation
Independent Director, Richard Pops
Chairman, William Rastetter
Chief Regulatory Officer, Malcolm Lloyd-Smith
Auditors: Ernst & Young LLP

LOCATIONS

HQ: Neurocrine Biosciences, Inc.
12780 El Camino Real, San Diego, CA 92130
Phone: 858 617-7600
Web: www.neurocrine.com

PRODUCTS/OPERATIONS

Selected Drug Candidates

Aptiepileptic drug (epileptic seizures)
CRF 1 Antagonist (stree-related disorder)
Elagolix (endometriosis)
Elagolix (uterine fibroids with AbbVie)
GPR 119 (type II diabetes with Boehringer Ingelheim)
GnRH Antagonist (oncology and men and women's health with AbbVie)
Indiplon (insomnia with Dainippon Sumitomo Pharma)
VMAT2 Inhibitor (movement disorders central nervous system)
VMAT2 (NBI-98854) (movement disorder with AbbVie)

COMPETITORS

BLUEBIRD BIO INC.	SEELOS THERAPEUTICS
CSL BEHRING L.L.C.	INC.
EMD SERONO INC.	TITAN PHARMACEUTICALS
GENE BIOTHERAPEUTICS	INC.
INC.	UCB Pharma GmbH
IDERA PHARMACEUTICALS	WINDTREE
THERAPEUTICS	THERAPEUTICS
INC.	INC.
SANGAMO THERAPEUTICS	
INC.	

HISTORICAL FINANCIALS

Company Type: Public

Income Statement				FYE: December 31
	REVENUE ($ mil.)	**NET INCOME** ($ mil.)	**NET PROFIT MARGIN**	**EMPLOYEES**
12/21	1,133.5	89.6	7.9%	900
12/20	1,045.9	407.3	38.9%	845
12/19	788.0	37.0	4.7%	700
12/18	451.2	21.1	4.7%	585
12/17	161.6	(142.5)	—	400
Annual Growth	62.7%	—	—	22.5%

2021 Year-End Financials

Debt ratio: 16.1%	No. of shares (mil.): 94.9
Return on equity: 7.1%	Dividends
Cash ($ mil.): 340.8	Yield: —
Current ratio: 3.96	Payout: —
Long-term debt ($ mil.): 335.1	Market value ($ mil.): 8,083.0

	STOCK PRICE ($) FY Close	P/E High/Low	PER SHARE ($) Earnings	Dividends	Book Value
12/21	85.17	126 84	0.92	0.00	14.48
12/20	95.85	31 17	4.16	0.00	12.04
12/19	107.49	296173	0.39	0.00	6.90
12/18	71.41	547297	0.22	0.00	5.29
12/17	77.59	— —	(1.62)	0.00	4.19
Annual Growth	2.4%	— —	—	—	36.3%

New Residential Investment Corp

New Residential Investment Corp. also known as New Residential is an investment manager with a vertically integrated mortgage platform. It is structured as a real estate investment trust (REIT) for US federal income tax purposes. Its diversified portfolio includes mortgage origination subsidiary NewRez; entities that provide mortgage servicing rights (MSRs) a leading mortgage origination and servicing company related ancillary mortgage services businesses residential mortgage-backed securities and loans consumer loans and other opportunistic investments. Other subsidiaries and affiliates include Shellpoint (mortgage services) Avenue 365 (title insurance) eStreet (appraisal management) Covius (diversified mortgage services) and Guardian Asset Management (field services and property management). New Residential Investment has nearly $33.3 billion in total assets.

Operations

New Residential conducts its business through five segments: Originations Residential Securities and Loans Consumer Loans and MSR Related Investments.

Servicing and originations which accounts for about 75% of total net interest income includes originations servicing and MSR related investments segments.

The residential securities and loans includes real estate securities or RMBS and residential mortgage loans; it accounts for more than 20% of total net interest income.The remainder of the company's revenue is generated from consumer loans.

Gain on originated mortgage loans held-for-sale accounts for around 55% of sales while interest income accounts for the rest.

Geographic Reach

New Residential is headquartered in New York US.

Sales and Marketing

As a lender New Residential provides refinance opportunities to eligible existing servicing customers primarily through its direct-to-consumer channel and also originates or purchases loans from brokers or originators through retail wholesale and correspondent channels.

Financial Performance

New Residential in 2020 had a revenue of $1.9 billion a 25% decrease from the previous year. This was mainly due to a lower volume in the company's interest income.

In 2020 the company suffered a $1.4 billion compared to a net income of $505.0 million in 2019.

The company's cash for the year ended 2020 was $1.1 billion. Operating activities provided $1.9 billion while investing activities provided another $8.6 billion. Financing activities used $10.1 billion mainly for repayments of secured financing agreements.

Strategy

New Residential seeks to generate long-term value for its investors by using its investment expertise to identify manage and invest in mortgage related assets including operating companies that offer attractive risk-adjusted returns.

New Residential's investment strategy also involves opportunistically pursuing acquisitions and seeking to establish strategic partnerships that it believes enables it to maximize the value of the mortgage loans it originates and/or service by offering products and services to customers servicers and other parties through the lifecycle of transactions that affect each mortgage loan and underlying residential property.

New Residential's general investment guidelines prohibit any investment that would cause it to fail to qualify as a REIT and any investment that would cause it to be regulated as an investment company. Its financing strategy's objective is to generate attractive risk-adjusted returns for its stockholders which at times incorporates the use of leverage. It also employs a hedging strategy in order to maintain its qualification as a REIT and exclusion from registration under the 1940 Act which utilizes derivative financial instruments to hedge the interest rate risk associated with its borrowings.

It has also made strategic investments and acquisitions in Covius Guardian Asset Management and Ditech Holding Corporation and Ditech Financial. These investments and acquisitions will further New Residential's growth and opportunities.

Mergers and Acquisitions

In early 2021 New Residential Investment Corp. has entered into a definitive agreement with an affiliate of Lone Star Funds to acquire Caliber Home Loans Inc. a proven leader in the US mortgage market with a diversified customer-centric purchase-focused platform with headquarters in Coppell Texas. With this acquisition New Residential intends to bring together the platforms of Caliber and NewRez LLC New Residential's wholly owned mortgage originator and servicer. Terms were not disclosed.

Company Background

New Residential was spun off from real estate investment firm Newcastle Investment Corp. in mid-2013.

EXECUTIVES

Chairman Of The Board, President, Chief Executive Officer, Michael Nierenberg
Independent Director, Kevin Finnerty
Independent Director, David Saltzman
Independent Director, Andrew Sloves
Independent Director, Pamela Lenehan
Independent Director, Patrice Le Melle
Chief Financial Officer, Chief Accounting Officer, Treasurer, Nicola Santoro
Auditors: Ernst & Young LLP

LOCATIONS

HQ: New Residential Investment Corp
1345 Avenue of the Americas, New York, NY 10105
Phone: 212 798-3150
Web: www.newresi.com

COMPETITORS

ARES COMMERCIAL REAL	PNMAC HOLDINGS INC.
ESTATE CORPORATION	RAIT FINANCIAL TRUST
IMPAC MORTGAGE	RC MERGER SUBSIDIARY
HOLDINGS INC.	LLC
NATIONSTAR MORTGAGE	READY CAPITAL
HOLDINGS INC.	CORPORATION
OCWEN FINANCIAL	REDWOOD TRUST INC.
CORPORATION	WALKER & DUNLOP INC.
ORCHID ISLAND CAPITAL	
INC.	

HISTORICAL FINANCIALS

Company Type: Public

Income Statement
FYE: December 31

	REVENUE ($ mil.)	NET INCOME ($ mil.)	NET PROFIT MARGIN	EMPLOYEES
12/21	3,521.4	772.2	21.9%	12,296
12/20	1,013.6	(1,410.3)	—	5,471
12/19	2,585.6	563.3	21.8%	3,387
12/18	2,237.5	963.9	43.1%	0
12/17	2,151.8	957.5	44.5%	0
Annual Growth	13.1%	(5.2%)	—	—

2021 Year-End Financials

Debt ratio: 74.9%
Return on equity: 12.9%
Cash ($ mil.): 1,332.5
Current ratio: 1.40
Long-term debt ($ mil.): 29,780.9

No. of shares (mil.): 466.7
Dividends
Yield: 8.4%
Payout: 65.2%
Market value ($ mil.): 4,999.0

	STOCK PRICE ($) FY Close	P/E High/Low		PER SHARE ($) Earnings	Dividends	Book Value
12/21	10.71	7	6	1.51	0.90	14.15
12/20	9.94	—	—	(3.52)	0.50	12.83
12/19	16.11	13	10	1.34	2.00	17.23
12/18	14.21	7	5	2.81	2.00	16.25
12/17	17.88	6	5	3.15	1.98	15.26
Annual Growth	(12.0%) (1.9%)			—	(16.8%)	(17.9%)

Newmark Group Inc

Auditors: Ernst & Young LLP

LOCATIONS

HQ: Newmark Group Inc
125 Park Avenue, New York, NY 10017
Phone: 212 372-2000
Web: www.ngkf.com

HISTORICAL FINANCIALS

Company Type: Public

Income Statement
FYE: December 31

	REVENUE ($ mil.)	NET INCOME ($ mil.)	NET PROFIT MARGIN	EMPLOYEES
12/20	1,905.0	80.0	4.2%	5,800
12/19	2,218.1	117.3	5.3%	5,600
12/18	2,047.5	106.7	5.2%	5,200
12/17	1,596.4	144.4	9.1%	4,800
12/16	1,349.9	168.4	12.5%	4,600
Annual Growth	9.0%	(17.0%)	—	6.0%

2020 Year-End Financials

Debt ratio: 44.5%
Return on equity: 12.3%
Cash ($ mil.): 191.4
Current ratio: 1.07
Long-term debt ($ mil.): 680.3

No. of shares (mil.): 182.4
Dividends
Yield: 1.7%
Payout: 39.3%
Market value ($ mil.): 1,330.0

	STOCK PRICE ($) FY Close	P/E High/Low		PER SHARE ($) Earnings	Dividends	Book Value
12/20	7.29	33	6	0.39	0.13	3.70
12/19	13.46	23	13	0.59	0.39	3.50
12/18	8.02	26	12	0.65	0.27	3.33
12/17	15.90	15	13	1.08	0.00	1.82
Annual Growth	(22.9%)			— (28.8%)	—	26.6%

Newtek Business Services Corp

Newtek Business Services provides a suite of business and financial services to small to midsized businesses including electronic merchant payment processing website hosting Small Business Administration (SBA) loans data storage insurance accounts receivable financing and payroll management. The company serves more than 100000 business accounts throughout the US. Newtek also has investments in certified capital companies (Capcos) which are authorized in eight states and Washington DC. It has stakes in about a dozen Capcos that traditionally have issued debt and equity securities to insurance firms then used the funds to mainly invest in small and midsized financial and business services firms.

Operations

The company's largest business segment is electronic payment processing which brings in about two-thirds of all sales. Web hosting services is comprised of its CrystalTech Web Hosting subsidiary and accounts for about 15% of revenues. Another segment Small Business Finance provides loans so small businesses.

Geographic Reach

Stationed in New York Newtek has additional sales and support offices in Milwaukee and Brownsville Texas. Although the majority of its revenue is generated from the US the company provides pre-paid website hosting services to customers in 120 countries.

Sales and Marketing

Newtek markets its array of services under agreements with alliance partners which are principally financial institutions including banks credit unions and other related businesses that are able to refer potential customers through Newtek's NewTracker referral system. In addition the company enters into agreements with independent sales agents throughout the country.

The company targets select markets such as restaurants financial institutions medical practices law firms accountants retail and technology service providers for channel business and reselling.

Financial Performance

Newtek's revenues have been growing slowly but steadily for years. Revenues were up 5% from $125 million in 2011 to $131 million in 2012 a historic milestone for the company. Profits also skyrocketed by 62% from $3.5 million in 2011 to nearly $5.6 million in 2012. (This marks the continuation of a major turnaround as the company lost money every year between 2006 and 2009.)

The revenue growth for 2012 was led by a 4% bump in electronic payment processing a 30% surge in interest income and a jump in servicing fee income. It also attributes the growth to its efforts to attract more business customers — the company has been on a bit of a marketing blitz — and increase its small business lending.

Newtek has been focused on cutting expenses and has even cut some staff positions that no longer fit in with its long-term growth strategy. Its rise in profits for 2012 was attributed to lower technology expenses driven by a decline in deprecation and amortization costs.

Strategy

Newtek plans to concentrate on organically growing its business services activities which also includes bookkeeping and website design and development. It also grows through selective merchant portfolio acquisitions.

EXECUTIVES

Independent Director, Salvatore Mulia
Director, Halli Razon - Feingold
Independent Director, Gregory Zink
Chief Operating Officer, David Simon
Chief Risk Officer, Nicolas Young
Director, Fernando Perez-Hickman
Chief Compliance Officer, Secretary And Chief Legal Officer, Michael Schwartz, $360,000 total compensation
Independent Director, Richard Salute
Chief Accounting Officer, Nicholas Leger
Auditors: RSM US LLP

LOCATIONS

HQ: Newtek Business Services Corp
4800 T Rex Avenue, Suite 120, Boca Raton, FL 33431
Phone: 212 356-9500
Web: www.newtekone.com

PRODUCTS/OPERATIONS

Selected Subsidiaries

Automated Merchant Services Inc.
Business Connect LLC
CCC Real Estate Holdings Co. LLC
CDS Business Services Inc. (dba Newtek Business Credit)
CrystalTech Web Hosting Inc. (dba Newtek Technology Services)
Exponential Business Development Co. Inc.
First Bankcard Alliance of Alabama LLC
Fortress Data Management LLC
Newtek Insurance Agency LLC
Newtek Small Business Finance Inc.
Small Business Lending Inc.
Solar Processing Solutions LLC
Summit Systems and Design LLC
The Texas Whitestone Group LLC
Universal Processing Services of Wisconsin LLC
The Whitestone Group LLC
Wilshire Alabama Partners LLC
Wilshire Colorado Partners LLC
Wilshire DC Partners LLC
Wilshire Holdings I Inc.
Wilshire Holdings II Inc.
Wilshire Louisiana Bidco LLC
Wilshire Louisiana Capital Management Fund LLC
Wilshire Louisiana Partners II LLC
Wilshire Louisiana Partners III LLC
Wilshire Louisiana Partners IV LLC
Wilshire New York Advisers II LLC
Wilshire New York Partners III LLC
Wilshire New York Partners IV LLC
Wilshire New York Partners V LLC
Wilshire Partners LLC
Wilshire Texas Partners I LLC

COMPETITORS

CAPITAL ON DECK INC
HITACHI CAPITAL (UK)
PLC

NATIONAL FUNDING INC.
PURPOSE FINANCIAL INC.

HISTORICAL FINANCIALS

Company Type: Public

Income Statement
FYE: December 31

	REVENUE ($ mil.)	NET INCOME ($ mil.)	NET PROFIT MARGIN	EMPLOYEES
12/20	92.2	31.9	34.7%	110
12/19	59.3	(5.6)	—	109
12/18	49.5	(7.4)	—	175
12/17	38.9	(7.8)	—	162
12/16	30.9	(9.2)	—	137
Annual Growth	31.4%	—	—	(5.3%)

2020 Year-End Financials

Debt ratio: 53.7%
Return on equity: 9.6%
Cash ($ mil.): 2.0
Current ratio: 0.92
Long-term debt ($ mil.): 365.4

No. of shares (mil.): 21.9
Dividends
 Yield: 10.4%
 Payout: 152.9%
Market value ($ mil.): 433.0

	STOCK PRICE ($) FY Close	P/E High/Low		PER SHARE ($) Earnings	Dividends	Book Value
12/20	19.69	15	6	1.51	2.05	15.45
12/19	22.65	—	—	(0.29)	2.15	15.70
12/18	17.44	—	—	(0.40)	1.80	15.19
12/17	18.49	—	—	(0.45)	3.39	15.08
12/16	15.90	—	—	(0.64)	3.14	14.30
Annual Growth	5.5%	—	—	—	(10.1%)	1.9%

NexPoint Residential Trust Inc

Auditors: KPMG LLP

LOCATIONS

HQ: NexPoint Residential Trust Inc
 300 Crescent Court, Suite 700, Dallas, TX 75201
Phone: 214 276-6300
Web: www.nexpointliving.com

HISTORICAL FINANCIALS

Company Type: Public

Income Statement
FYE: December 31

	REVENUE ($ mil.)	NET INCOME ($ mil.)	NET PROFIT MARGIN	EMPLOYEES
12/21	219.2	23.0	10.5%	3
12/20	204.8	44.0	21.5%	3
12/19	181.0	99.1	54.8%	3
12/18	146.6	(1.6)	—	2
12/17	144.2	53.3	37.0%	2
Annual Growth	11.0%	(18.9%)	—	10.7%

2021 Year-End Financials

Debt ratio: 75.3%
Return on equity: 5.2%
Cash ($ mil.): 49.4
Current ratio: 3.00
Long-term debt ($ mil.): 1,554.5

No. of shares (mil.): 25.5
Dividends
 Yield: 1.6%
 Payout: 157.7%
Market value ($ mil.): 2,138.0

	STOCK PRICE ($) FY Close	P/E High/Low		PER SHARE ($) Earnings	Dividends	Book Value
12/21	83.83	90	43	0.89	1.40	18.42
12/20	42.31	29	12	1.74	1.28	16.31
12/19	45.00	12	8	4.03	1.14	16.88
12/18	35.05	—	—	(0.08)	1.03	12.60
12/17	27.94	12	9	2.49	0.91	11.38
Annual Growth	31.6%	—	—	(22.7%)	11.4%	12.8%

NI Holdings Inc

Auditors: Mazars USA LLP

LOCATIONS

HQ: NI Holdings Inc
 1101 First Avenue North, Fargo, ND 58102
Phone: 701 298-4200
Web: www.niholdingsinc.com

HISTORICAL FINANCIALS

Company Type: Public

Income Statement
FYE: December 31

	ASSETS ($ mil.)	NET INCOME ($ mil.)	INCOME AS % OF ASSETS	EMPLOYEES
12/20	617.6	40.3	6.5%	205
12/19	508.1	26.4	5.2%	186
12/18	458.4	31.0	6.8%	178
12/17	376.9	15.9	4.2%	136
12/16	278.7	4.5	1.6%	129
Annual Growth	22.0%	72.6%	—	12.3%

2020 Year-End Financials

Return on assets: 7.1%
Return on equity: 12.3%
Long-term debt ($ mil.): —
No. of shares (mil.): 21.3
Sales ($ mil): 306.3

Dividends
 Yield: —
 Payout: —
Market value ($ mil.): 350.0

	STOCK PRICE ($) FY Close	P/E High/Low		PER SHARE ($) Earnings	Dividends	Book Value
12/20	16.42	10	6	1.84	0.00	16.15
12/19	17.20	16	12	1.19	0.00	13.85
12/18	15.73	13	11	1.39	0.00	12.28
12/17	16.98	26	20	0.71	0.00	11.30
Annual Growth	(1.1%)	—	—	37.4%	—	12.6%

Nicolet Bankshares Inc

EXECUTIVES

Senior Vice President – Wealth Management Of Nicolet Bank, Patrick Madson, $267,692 total compensation
Independent Director, Dustin McClone
Independent Director, Terrence Fulwiler
Independent Director, Donald Long
Independent Director, Oliver Smith
Independent Director, Susan Merkatoris
Independent Director, Rachel Campos-Duffy
Chief Financial Officer, H. Phillip Moore
President, Chief Executive Officer, Michael Daniels, $521,419 total compensation
Executive Chairman Of The Board, Robert Atwell, $521,419 total compensation
Independent Director, Christopher Ghidorzi
Independent Director, Andrew Hetzel
Independent Director, John Dykema
Executive Vice President Of Nicolet Bank, Eric Witczak, $316,750 total compensation
Auditors: BKD, LLP

LOCATIONS

HQ: Nicolet Bankshares Inc
 111 North Washington Street, Green Bay, WI 54301
Phone: 920 430-1400
Web: www.nicoletbank.com

HISTORICAL FINANCIALS

Company Type: Public

Income Statement
FYE: December 31

	ASSETS ($ mil.)	NET INCOME ($ mil.)	INCOME AS % OF ASSETS	EMPLOYEES
12/20	4,551.7	60.1	1.3%	573
12/19	3,577.2	54.6	1.5%	575
12/18	3,096.5	41.0	1.3%	550
12/17	2,932.4	33.1	1.1%	535
12/16	2,300.8	18.4	0.8%	480
Annual Growth	18.6%	34.3%	—	4.5%

2020 Year-End Financials

Return on assets: 1.4%
Return on equity: 11.3%
Long-term debt ($ mil.): —
No. of shares (mil.): 10.0
Sales ($ mil): 211.8

Dividends
 Yield: —
 Payout: —
Market value ($ mil.): 664.0

	STOCK PRICE ($) FY Close	P/E High/Low		PER SHARE ($) Earnings	Dividends	Book Value
12/20	66.35	13	8	5.70	0.00	53.86
12/19	73.85	13	9	5.52	0.00	48.76
12/18	48.80	14	11	4.12	0.00	40.72
12/17	54.74	17	13	3.33	0.00	37.09
12/16	47.69	19	12	2.37	0.00	32.26
Annual Growth	8.6%	—	—	24.5%	—	13.7%

NMI Holdings Inc

NMI Holdings provides mortgage insurance through two primary subsids ? National Mortgage Insurance Corp (NMIC) and National Mortgage Reinsurance Inc. One (Re One). NMIC is its primary insurance subsidiary approved to write coverage in all 50 states and Washington DC. Re One provides reinsurance to NMIC on insured loans with coverage levels in excess of about 25%. The company also provides outsourced loan review services to mortgage loan originators through NMI Services. Mortgage insurance protects lenders and investors from default-related losses.

Operations

NMI Holdings offers primary mortgage insurance which provides protection on individual mortgage loans. Mortgages are insured on a loan-by-loan basis at the time of origination. The company previously offered pool insurance which covers the excess of loss on defaulted mortgages not covered under primary mortgage insurance.

Net Premiums accounts for more than 90% of revenues and the net investment income and net realized investment gains account for the rest.

Geographic Reach

NMI Holdings gets all of its revenue in the US. Ten states account for more than half of its total risk-in-force (RIF) or the total dollar amount of claims it expects to receive during the year. California Texas and Virginia account for more than 10% nearly 10% and less than 5% of RIF respectively.

Its corporate office is located in Emeryville California.

Sales and Marketing

NMI structure its sales force into National Accounts that focus on relationships with national or large regional lenders and Regional Accounts that focus on relationships with small or regional lenders such as community banks credit unions mortgage bankers and branches of National Accounts. It also maintains a dedicated customer service team which is refer to as the Solution Center and which offers support in loan submission and underwriting service risk management and technology to support our sales efforts. The company has Master Policies in around 1475 customers.

Financial Performance

NIH's revenues have been climbing rapidly over the past five years but net income has only been rising after a dip in 2017.

Revenue increased 38% to $378.8 million in 2019. Net premiums earned increased $93.8 million in 2019 primarily due to the growth of its IIF.

Net income rose 59% to $172 million in 2019 which were driven by growth in total revenues partially offset by increases in total expenses.

The company ended 2019 with $41.1 million in cash and cash equivalents 62% more than it had at the beginning of the year. Although operating cash flow provided $208.2 million and financing activities another $2 million cash used for investments was $194.4 million mainly for purchases of investments and software and equipment.

Strategy

The company strategy is to continue to build on its position in the private MI market expand its customer base and grow its insured portfolio of high-quality residential loans by focusing on long-term customer relationships disciplined and proactive risk selection and pricing fair and transparent claims payment practices responsive customer service financial strength and profitability.

National Mortgage Insurance Corporation (National MI) a subsidiary of NMI Holdings Inc. announced in September 2020 that it is fully integrated with Lender Price a leading cloud-based product pricing and eligibility (PPE) engine provider for the mortgage finance industry. Loan officers now have instant access to National MI's risk-based Rate GPS through the Lender Price PPE platform. According to the company this integration reinforces its commitment to streamlining and automating the process of ordering private mortgage insurance while mitigating the chance for errors. It also reduces the time from application to closing for loan originators and consumers.

EXECUTIVES

President And Ceo, Adam Pollitzer, $550,000 total compensation
Executive Vice President And Chief Financial Officer, Ravi Mallela
Independent Director, Regina Muehlhauser
Executive Chairman, Bradley Shuster, $650,000 total compensation
Independent Director, James Jones
Executive Vice President - Operationa And It, Patrick Mathis, $465,000 total compensation
Executive Vice President, Chief Legal Officer General Counsel, Secretary, William Leatherberry, $485,000 total compensation
Chief Risk Officer, Robert Smith
Independent Director, Michael Embler
Independent Director, Michael Montgomery
Independent Director, Lynn McCreary
Independent Director, Priya Huskins
Auditors: BDO USA, LLP

LOCATIONS

HQ: NMI Holdings Inc
   2100 Powell Street, Emeryville, CA 94608
Phone: 855 530-6642
Web: www.nationalmi.com

PRODUCTS/OPERATIONS

2017 Sales

	% of total
Net premiums earned	91
Net investment income	9
Net realized investment gains	-
Other	-
Total	**100**

COMPETITORS

ASSOCIATED BANC-CORP
BOKF MERGER CORPORATION NUMBER SIXTEEN
EMC INSURANCE GROUP INC.
ONEMAIN HOLDINGS INC.
PNMAC HOLDINGS INC.
PROASSURANCE CORPORATION
PROSIGHT SPECIALTY INSURANCE GROUP INC.
REPUBLIC MORTGAGE INSURANCE COMPANY

HISTORICAL FINANCIALS

Company Type: Public

Income Statement				FYE: December 31
	ASSETS ($ mil.)	NET INCOME ($ mil.)	INCOME AS % OF ASSETS	EMPLOYEES
12/21	2,450.5	231.1	9.4%	247
12/20	2,166.6	171.5	7.9%	262
12/19	1,364.8	171.9	12.6%	321
12/18	1,092.0	107.9	9.9%	304
12/17	894.8	22.0	2.5%	299
Annual Growth	28.6%	79.9%	—	(4.7%)

2021 Year-End Financials

Return on assets: 10.0%
Return on equity: 15.7%
Long-term debt ($ mil.): —
No. of shares (mil.): 85.7
Sales ($ mil): 485.0
Dividends
Yield: —
Payout: —
Market value ($ mil.): 1,875.0

	STOCK PRICE ($) FY Close	P/E High/Low		PER SHARE ($) Earnings	Dividends	Book Value
12/21	21.85	10	7	2.65	0.00	18.25
12/20	22.65	16	4	2.13	0.00	16.08
12/19	33.18	14	7	2.47	0.00	13.61
12/18	17.85	14	8	1.60	0.00	10.58
12/17	17.00	48	27	0.35	0.00	8.41
Annual Growth	6.5%	—	—	65.9%	—	21.4%

Northeast Bank (ME)

Northeast Bancorp is the holding company for Northeast Bank which operates about a dozen branches in western and southern Maine. Founded in 1872 the bank offers standard retail services such as checking and savings accounts NOW and money market accounts CDs and trust services as well as financial planning and brokerage. Residential mortgages account for about a third of all loans; commercial mortgages and consumer loans each make up about 25%. The bank also writes business and construction loans. Newly created investment entity FHB Formation acquired a 60% stake in Northeast Bancorp in 2010. The deal brought in $16 million in capital. The 2011 sale of insurance agency Varney added another $8.4 million.

Auditors: RSM US LLP

LOCATIONS

HQ: Northeast Bank (ME)
   27 Pearl Street, Portland, ME 04101
Phone: 207 786-3245
Web: www.northeastbank.com

COMPETITORS

COMMUNITY TRUST INC.
BANCORP INC.
CUSTOMERS BANCORP
EAGLE BANCORP INC.

HISTORICAL FINANCIALS

Company Type: Public

Income Statement				FYE: June 30
	ASSETS ($ mil.)	NET INCOME ($ mil.)	INCOME AS % OF ASSETS	EMPLOYEES
06/21	2,174.4	71.5	3.3%	178
06/20	1,257.6	22.7	1.8%	182
06/19	1,153.8	13.8	1.2%	183
06/18	1,157.7	16.1	1.4%	185
06/17	1,076.8	12.3	1.1%	195
Annual Growth	19.2%	55.2%	—	(2.3%)

2021 Year-End Financials

Return on assets: 4.1%
Return on equity: 36.0%
Long-term debt ($ mil.): —
No. of shares (mil.): 8.1
Sales ($ mil): 150.1
Dividends
Yield: 0.1%
Payout: 0.5%
Market value ($ mil.): 243.0

	STOCK PRICE ($)	P/E	PER SHARE ($)		
	FY Close	High/Low	Earnings	Dividends	Book Value
06/21	29.87	4 2	8.55	0.04	28.51
06/20	17.55	9 3	2.53	0.04	20.09
06/19	27.58	18 10	1.52	0.04	16.98
06/18	21.80	16 11	1.77	0.04	15.49
06/17	20.35	15 8	1.38	0.04	13.90
Annual Growth	10.1%	— —	57.8%	(0.0%)	19.7%

NorthEast Community Bancorp Inc (MD)

Northeast Community Bancorp is the holding company for Northeast Community Bank which serves consumers and businesses in the New York metropolitan area and Massachusetts. Through about a half-dozen branches the thrift offers traditional deposit services like checking and savings accounts as well as a variety of lending products such as commercial and multi-family real estate loans home equity construction and secured loans. While its deposit services are confined to New York and Massachusetts it markets its loan products throughout the northeastern US. The bank offers investment and financial planning services through Hayden Wealth Management. Northeast Community Bank's roots date back to 1934.

EXECUTIVES

Chairman Of The Board, Chief Executive Officer, Kenneth Martinek, $400,400 total compensation
President, Chief Operating Officer, Director, Jose Collazo, $312,000 total compensation
Independent Director, John Mckenzie
Independent Director, Diane Cavanaugh
Independent Director, Kenneth Thomas
Chief Financial Officer, Executive Vice President, Donald Hom, $245,000 total compensation
Independent Director, Eugene Magier
Senior Vice President, Chief Compliance Officer, Director, Charles Martinek
Independent Director, Kevin O'Malley
Independent Director, Charles Cirillo
Auditors: S.R. Snodgrass, P.C.

LOCATIONS

HQ: NorthEast Community Bancorp Inc (MD)
325 Hamilton Avenue, White Plains, NY 10601
Phone: 914 684-2500
Web: www.necommunitybank.com

COMPETITORS

1ST COLONIAL BANCORP	FEDFIRST FINANCIAL
ASB FINANCIAL CORP	CORPORATION
BANK OF THE JAMES	FINWARD BANCORP
FINANCIAL GROUP INC.	PEOPLES BANCORP
CITIZENS COMMUNITY	SURUGA BANK LTD.
BANCORP INC	

HISTORICAL FINANCIALS

Company Type: Public

Income Statement
FYE: December 31

	ASSETS ($ mil.)	NET INCOME ($ mil.)	INCOME AS % OF ASSETS	EMPLOYEES
12/20	968.2	12.3	1.3%	125
12/19	955.1	12.9	1.4%	0
12/18	870.3	13.0	1.5%	0
12/17	814.8	8.0	1.0%	0
12/16	734.5	5.0	0.7%	0
Annual Growth	7.2%	25.1%	—	—

2020 Year-End Financials

Return on assets: 1.2%
Return on equity: 8.3%
Long-term debt ($ mil.): —
No. of shares (mil.): 12.1
Sales ($ mil): 51.4
Dividends
Yield: 0.0%
Payout: 11.7%
Market value ($ mil.): 168.0

	STOCK PRICE ($)	P/E	PER SHARE ($)		
	FY Close	High/Low	Earnings	Dividends	Book Value
12/20	13.80	14 7	1.02	0.12	12.61
12/19	12.05	11 10	1.08	0.12	11.65
12/18	11.10	12 9	1.09	0.12	10.63
12/17	10.10	15 11	0.67	0.12	9.59
12/16	7.90	19 15	0.42	0.12	8.96
Annual Growth	15.0%	— —	24.8%	(0.0%)	8.9%

Northern Technologies International Corp.

Northern Technologies International (NTIC) keeps rust away with its proprietary corrosion-inhibiting packaging. Its ZERUST product line features special packaging that emits corrosion-inhibiting molecules and compounds; the packaging comes in films and bags liquids and coatings rust removers and cleaners vapor capsules and pipe strips for residue-free protection of pipes thermal spray coatings and cathodic protection technologies. NTIC's customers include automotive electronics power generation and metal processing firms. The company makes approximately 45% of its sales in United States.

Operations
Most of the company's sales come from ZERUST but the company has expanded its product mix. Its new product development focus is on biodegradable polymer resins which it sells under its Natur-Tec brand. The company is hoping to tap into a growing market emerging as a result of lower petroleum prices and increased interest in environmentally friendly alternatives to traditional plastics.

Its Natur-Tec resins are manufactured out of combination of biodegradable polymers and organic materials. Specific products include compost and trash bags agricultural films and various consumer goods packaging.

Geographic Reach
Based in Minnesota the company sells its products in over about countries including countries in North America South America Europe Asia and the Middle East. It generates approximately 45% of sales from United States followed by around 5% from Brazil and about 35% each from India and China.

NTIC also maintains a manufacturing laboratory and warehouse space located in Beachwood Ohio. It also has warehousing agreements in place in California and Indiana.

Sales and Marketing
NTIC's marketing activities include advertising and direct mail campaigns and also trade shows and technical forums. Customers include universities and school districts and film extruders and injection molders that produce bio-based and compostable end products such as film bags and cutlery.

Financial Performance
NTIC's consolidated net sales increased 8% to $55.8 million during fiscal 2019 compared to $51.4 million during fiscal 2018. NTIC's consolidated net sales to unaffiliated customers excluding NTIC's joint ventures increased 10% to $53.1 million during fiscal 2019 compared to $48.5 million during fiscal 2018. These increases were primarily a result of an increase in sales of Natur-Tec products.

Net income attributable to NTIC decreased to $5.2 million for fiscal 2019 compared to $6.7 for fiscal 2018 a decrease of $1.5 million. This decrease was primarily the result of the increase in operating expenses and decrease in joint venture operations during fiscal 2019 compared to fiscal 2018 partially offset by the increase in gross profit.

Cash held by the company at the end of 2019 increased by $1.7 million to $5.9 million compared from the prior year with $4.2 million. Cash provided by operations was $5.5 million while cash provided by investing and financing activities were $1.3 million and $2.4 million respectively. Main use for cash was proceeds from the sale of available for sale securities and dividends paid on NTIC common stock.

Strategy
One of NTIC's strategic initiatives is to expand into and penetrate other markets for its ZERUST corrosion prevention technologies. Accordingly for the past several years NTIC has focused significant sales and marketing efforts on the oil and gas industry as the infrastructure that supports the industry is typically constructed using metals that are highly susceptible to corrosion.

NTIC's strategy of expanding its corrosion prevention solutions into the oil and gas industry and continuing the expansion of its Natur-Tec bioplastics resin compounds and finished products either directly or indirectly through joint ventures and independent distributors and agents.

EXECUTIVES

President, Chief Executive Officer, Director, G. Patrick Lynch, $435,392 total compensation
Chief Financial Officer, Corporate Secretary, Matthew Wolsfeld, $321,812 total compensation
Vice President And Director – Global Market Development – Oil & Gas, Gautam Ramdas
Vice President And Director – Global Market Development – Natur-tec®, Vineet Dalal
Director, Ramani Narayan
Independent Director, Sunggyu Lee
Non-executive Independent Chairman Of The Board, Richard Nigon
Independent Director, Konstantin Von Falkenhausen

Independent Director, Nancy Calderon
Vice President Of Operations – North America,
  Brian Haglund
Auditors: Baker Tilly US, LLP

LOCATIONS

HQ: Northern Technologies International Corp.
  4201 Woodland Road, P.O. Box 69, Circle Pines, MN
  55014
Phone: 763 225-6600
Web: www.ntic.com

PRODUCTS/OPERATIONS

2015 Sales

	$ mil.	% of total
ZERUST	26.0	86
Natur-Tec	4.3	14
Total	**30.3**	**100**

Selected Products
Corrosion Products Division (ZERUST products)
  Bags
  Bubble cushioning
  Can Liners
  Corrugated plastic and profile board
  Corrugated solid fiber and chipboard
  Cutlery
  Dunnage trays and bins
  Foam sheeting
  Lawn and leaf bags
  Pet waste collection bags
Pipe strips
  Shrink film
  Tube strips
  Vapor capsules

Selected Solutions
Diffusers
Liquids and Coatings
Plastic and Paper Packaging
Rust Removers and Cleaners
Z-CIS Technical Services
ZERUST Corrosion Prevention Solutions
ZERUST Corrosion Prevention Solutions
ZERUST Flange Savers
ZERUST ReCAST-R VCI Dispensers
ZERUST ReCAST-SSB Solutions
ZERUST Zerion

COMPETITORS

CABOT CORPORATION	INTERSTATE RESOURCES
ECOVYST INC.	INC.
FUTUREFUEL CORP.	KOPPERS HOLDINGS INC.
GRAPHIC PACKAGING	TRINSEO PLC
HOLDING COMPANY	VENATOR MATERIALS PLC
GREEN BAY PACKAGING	WESTROCK COMPANY
INC.	

HISTORICAL FINANCIALS
Company Type: Public

Income Statement
FYE: August 31

	REVENUE ($ mil.)	NET INCOME ($ mil.)	NET PROFIT MARGIN	EMPLOYEES
08/21	56.4	6.2	11.1%	171
08/20	47.6	(1.3)	—	142
08/19	55.7	5.2	9.3%	137
08/18	51.4	6.7	13.0%	136
08/17	39.5	3.4	8.6%	71
Annual Growth	9.3%	16.4%	—	24.6%

2021 Year-End Financials

Debt ratio: —	No. of shares (mil.): 9.1
Return on equity: 10.5%	Dividends
Cash ($ mil.): 7.6	Yield: 1.1%
Current ratio: 3.96	Payout: 72.2%
Long-term debt ($ mil.): —	Market value ($ mil.): 153.0

	STOCK PRICE ($) FY Close	P/E High/Low		Earnings	PER SHARE ($) Dividends	Book Value
08/21	16.67	30	12	0.64	0.20	6.79
08/20	8.31	—	—	(0.15)	0.19	6.23
08/19	10.95	64	18	0.55	0.24	6.23
08/18	36.40	54	22	0.72	0.20	5.84
08/17	17.60	51	33	0.38	0.00	5.39
Annual Growth	(1.3%)	—	—	14.3%	—	6.0%

Northrim BanCorp Inc

Can you get banking services at the north rim of the world? Of course! Northrim BanCorp formed in 2001 to be the holding company for Northrim Bank provides a full range of commercial and retail banking services and products through some 10 banking offices in Alaska's Anchorage Fairbanks North Star and Matanuska Susitna counties. Division offices that provide short-term capital to customers also are located in Washington and Oregon. The bank offers standard deposit products including checking savings and money market accounts; CDs; and IRAs. It uses funds from deposits to write commercial loans (40% of loan portfolio) and real estate term loans (nearly 35%) as well as construction and consumer loans.

EXECUTIVES

Independent Director, Larry Cash
Independent Director, Karl Hanneman
Executive Vice President, Chief Lending Officer,
  Michael Huston, $281,254 total compensation
Independent Director, Joseph Marushack
Independent Director, Linda Thomas
**Chief Financial Officer, Executive Vice President
  Of The Company And The Bank,** Jed Ballard,
  $275,641 total compensation
**Chairman Of The Board, President, Chief
  Executive Officer, Chief Operating Officer,**
  Joseph Schierhorn, $434,692 total compensation
Independent Director, Anthony Drabek
**Executive Vice President, Chief Information
  Officer,** Benjamin Craig, $240,238 total
  compensation
**Executive Vice President, General Counsel,
  Corporate Secretary,** Michael Martin, $317,043
  total compensation
Lead Independent Director, John Swalling
Independent Director, David McCambridge
Auditors: Moss Adams LLP

LOCATIONS

HQ: Northrim BanCorp Inc
  3111 C Street, Anchorage, AK 99503
Phone: 907 562-0062
Web: www.northrim.com

PRODUCTS/OPERATIONS

2007 Sales

	$ mil.	% of total
Interest		
Loans including fees	66.5	80
Securities	4.6	6
Other	2.0	2
Noninterest		
Service charges on deposit accounts	3.1	4
Purchased receivable income	2.5	3
Other	4.2	5
Total	**82.9**	**100**

COMPETITORS

APOLLO ASSET	JAMES BREARLEY & SONS
MANAGEMENT INC.	LIMITED
CENTRAL COMMUNITY	OPPENHEIMERFUNDS INC.
CORPORATION	PINNACLE SUMMER
COAST BANCORP	INVESTMENTS INC.
COMMUNITY CAPITAL	SOUTHERN CUSTOM BUILT
BANCSHARES INC.	HOMES L.L.C.
Fiera Capital	WESTERN LIBERTY
Corporation	BANCORP

HISTORICAL FINANCIALS
Company Type: Public

Income Statement
FYE: December 31

	ASSETS ($ mil.)	NET INCOME ($ mil.)	INCOME AS % OF ASSETS	EMPLOYEES
12/20	2,121.8	32.8	1.6%	438
12/19	1,644.0	20.6	1.3%	431
12/18	1,502.9	20.0	1.3%	430
12/17	1,519.1	13.1	0.9%	429
12/16	1,526.5	14.4	0.9%	451
Annual Growth	8.6%	22.9%	—	(0.7%)

2020 Year-End Financials

Return on assets: 1.7%	Dividends
Return on equity: 15.3%	Yield: 4.0%
Long-term debt ($ mil.): —	Payout: 32.7%
No. of shares (mil.): 6.2	Market value ($ mil.): 212.0
Sales ($ mil): 140.2	

	STOCK PRICE ($) FY Close	P/E High/Low		Earnings	PER SHARE ($) Dividends	Book Value
12/20	33.95	8	4	5.11	1.38	35.45
12/19	38.30	14	11	3.04	1.26	31.58
12/18	32.87	16	11	2.86	1.02	29.92
12/17	33.85	20	14	1.88	0.86	28.06
12/16	31.60	16	10	2.06	0.78	27.05
Annual Growth	1.8%	—	—	25.5%	15.3%	7.0%

Northwest Pipe Co.

Northwest Pipe is the largest manufacturer of engineered steel water pipeline systems in North America. Its solution-based products serve a wide range of markets including water transmission and infrastructure water and wastewater plant piping structural stormwater and sewer systems trenchless technology and pipeline rehabilitation. As the leader in manufacturing large-diameter high-pressure engineered welded steel pipeline systems its sales have historically been driven by the need for new water infrastructure. In addition to fabricating pipes for water transmission primarily related to drinking water systems the company also makes products for wastewater systems industrial plant piping systems and certain structural applications. The US generates roughly 90% of the company's total sales.

Operations
Northwest Pipe operates through one segment Water Infrastructure which produces engineered pipeline systems including steel pipe reinforced concrete pipe Permalok steel casing pipe bar-wrapped concrete cylinder pipe as well as linings coatings joints fittings and specialized components.

The company's water transmission pipe is manufactured generally from steel concrete ductile iron PVC or HDPE. Each pipe material has advantages and disadvantages. Steel and concrete are more common materials for larger-diameter water transmission pipelines because ductile iron pipe generally is limited in diameter due to the manufacturing process.

Geographic Reach

Headquartered in Vancouver Washington the company has approximately 10 manufacturing facilities strategically positioned in the US (located in Portland Oregon; Adelanto California; Saginaw Texas; Tracy California; Parkersburg West Virginia; Salt Lake City Utah; Orem Utah; St. George Utah; St. Louis Missouri; and San Luis R o Colorado Mexico). Approximately 90% of sales is generated from the US while Canada accounts the remaining sales.

Sales and Marketing

Northwest Pipe markets its water infrastructure and tubular products through an in-house sales force (comprised of sales representatives engineers and support personnel who work closely with public water agencies contractors and engineering firms often years in advance of projects being bid).

One customer accounts for nearly 15% and no customer accounts for approximately 10% or more of total sales.

Financial Performance

Net sales increased 2% to $285.9 million in 2020 compared to $279.3 million in 2019 as the $44.2 million contribution from its acquired Geneva operations was nearly entirely offset by the decrease in net sales at its legacy steel pipe facilities.

Net income for fiscal 2020 decreased to $19.1 million compared from the prior year with $27.9 million.

Cash held by the company at the end of fiscal 2020 increased to $37.9 million. Cash provided by operations and financing activities were $56.1 million and $12.3 million respectively. Cash used for investing was $61.4 million mainly for acquisition of business.

Strategy

Northwest Pipe's marketing strategy emphasizes early identification of potential water projects promotion of specifications consistent with its capabilities and products and close contact with the project designers and owners throughout the design phase.

In January 2020 the company completed the 100% acquisition of Geneva Pipe Company Inc. for approximately $49.4 million. Geneva is a concrete pipe and precast concrete products manufacturer based in Utah. This acquisition expands Northwest Pipe's water infrastructure product capabilities by adding additional reinforced concrete pipe capacity and a full line of precast concrete products including storm drains and manholes catch basins vaults and curb inlets as well as innovative products that extend the life of concrete pipe and manholes for sewer applications.

Mergers and Acquisitions

In early 2020 Northwest Pipe completed the acquisition of 100% of Geneva Pipe Company Inc. for a purchase price of approximately $49.4 million. Geneva is a concrete pipe and precast concrete products manufacturer based in Utah. This acquisition expands the company's water infrastructure product capabilities by adding additional reinforced concrete pipe capacity and a full line of

precast concrete products including storm drains and manholes catch basins vaults and curb inlets as well as innovative products that extend the life of concrete pipe and manholes for sewer applications. Operations will continue with Geneva's current management and workforce at the three Utah manufacturing facilities located in Salt Lake City Orem and St. George.

Company Background

In 2012 Northwest Pipe announced plans to expand its Saginaw Texas manufacturing facility. The expansion enables the company to better serve the needs of anticipated large water projects in the area. Completion of the Saginaw expansion will allow the company to leverage its proximity to Tarrant Regional Water District's planned Integrated Pipeline Project and give it expanded capabilities to serve additional water projects in the region. Northwest Pipe was founded in 1966.

EXECUTIVES

Independent Director, Amanda Kulesa
Chairman Of The Board, Richard Roman
Senior Vice President Of Sales And Marketing, Water Transmission, Eric Stokes, $266,250 total compensation
President, Chief Executive Officer, Director, Scott Montross, $577,368 total compensation
Executive Vice President Of Water Transmission Engineered Systems, William Smith, $326,820 total compensation
Vice President Of Human Resources, Megan Kendrick
Chief Financial Officer, Vice President Of Finance, Corporate Controller, And Corporate Secretary, Aaron Wilkins, $305,000 total compensation
Executive Vice President, Miles Brittain, $297,709 total compensation
Independent Director, John Paschal
Independent Director, William Yearsley
Auditors: Moss Adams LLP

LOCATIONS

HQ: Northwest Pipe Co.
201 NE Park Plaza Drive, Suite 100, Vancouver, WA 98684
Phone: 360 397-6250   **Fax:** 360 397-6257
Web: www.nwpipe.com

COMPETITORS

AEGION CORPORATION	INSTEEL INDUSTRIES INC.
AMTROL INC.	
CHART INDUSTRIES INC.	MCDERMOTT INTERNATIONAL INC
Chicago Bridge & Iron Company N.V. PRODUCTS	MUELLER WATER INC.
ENERFAB INC.	
HANCOR INC.	OLYMPIC STEEL INC.
HEADWATERS INCORPORATED	RPC GROUP LIMITED STEEL DYNAMICS INC.

HISTORICAL FINANCIALS

Company Type: Public

Income Statement

FYE: December 31

	REVENUE ($ mil.)	NET INCOME ($ mil.)	NET PROFIT MARGIN	EMPLOYEES
12/20	285.9	19.0	6.7%	956
12/19	279.3	27.9	10.0%	765
12/18	172.1	20.3	11.8%	691
12/17	132.7	(10.1)	—	0
12/16	156.2	(9.2)	—	583
Annual Growth	16.3%	—	—	13.2%

2020 Year-End Financials

Debt ratio: 3.6%	No. of shares (mil.): 9.8
Return on equity: 7.3%	Dividends
Cash ($ mil.): 37.9	Yield: —
Current ratio: 4.18	Payout: —
Long-term debt ($ mil.): 5.8	Market value ($ mil.): 277.0

	STOCK PRICE ($) FY Close	P/E High/Low		Earnings	PER SHARE ($) Dividends	Book Value
12/20	28.30	19	10	1.93	0.00	27.50
12/19	33.31	12	8	2.85	0.00	25.46
12/18	23.29	12	8	2.09	0.00	22.45
12/17	19.14	—	—	(1.06)	0.00	20.82
12/16	17.22	—	—	(0.97)	0.00	21.79
Annual Growth	13.2%			—	—	6.0%

Norwood Financial Corp.

Norwood Financial not Batman owns Wayne Bank. The bank serves individuals and local businesses through about 30 branches in northeastern Pennsylvania. It offers standard deposit products and services including checking and savings accounts money market savings accounts CDs and IRAs. Mortgages account for about 80% of Wayne Bank's loan portfolio. The bank also runs a trust and wealth management division; subsidiary Norwood Investment provides annuities and mutual funds; Norwood Settlement (70%-owned) offers title and settlement services. Norwood Financial bought Delaware Bancshares and its National Bank of Delaware County subsidiary in mid-2016; the purchase nearly doubled its branch network.

EXECUTIVES

Executive Vice President And Chief Credit Officer, John Carmody, $139,000 total compensation
Chief Financial Officer, Executive Vice President, Secretary, William Lance, $225,000 total compensation
Executive Vice President And Chief Operating Officer Of The Bank And Company, Robert Mancuso, $144,000 total compensation
Independent Director, Susan Campfield
Independent Director, Kevin Lamont
Independent Director, Jeffrey Gifford
Independent Director, Alexandra Nolan
Independent Vice Chairman Of The Board, Andrew Forte
Independent Director, Joseph Adams
Independent Director, Meg Hungerford
Independent Chairman Of The Board, William Davis
President, Chief Executive Officer, Director, Lewis Critelli, $390,000 total compensation
Senior Vice President – Retail Lending Manager For The Bank, John Sanders, $111,227 total compensation
Independent Director, Ralph Matergia
Auditors: S.R. Snodgrass, P.C.

LOCATIONS

HQ: Norwood Financial Corp.
717 Main Street, Honesdale, PA 18431
Phone: 570 253-1455
Web: www.waynebank.com

COMPETITORS

BAY BANCORP INC.
FIRST KEYSTONE
CORPORATION

QNB CORP.

HISTORICAL FINANCIALS

Company Type: Public

Income Statement				FYE: December 31
	ASSETS ($ mil.)	NET INCOME ($ mil.)	INCOME AS % OF ASSETS	EMPLOYEES
12/20	1,851.8	15.0	0.8%	265
12/19	1,230.6	14.2	1.2%	220
12/18	1,184.5	13.6	1.2%	210
12/17	1,132.9	8.2	0.7%	214
12/16	1,111.1	6.7	0.6%	215
Annual Growth	13.6%	22.4%	—	5.4%

2020 Year-End Financials

Return on assets: 0.9%
Return on equity: 9.0%
Long-term debt ($ mil.): —
No. of shares (mil.): 8.2
Sales ($ mil): 66.2

Dividends
Yield: 3.8%
Payout: 52.0%
Market value ($ mil.): 215.0

	STOCK PRICE ($) FY Close	P/E High/Low		PER SHARE ($) Earnings	Dividends	Book Value
12/20	26.17	19	10	2.09	1.00	23.68
12/19	38.90	17	12	2.25	0.96	21.72
12/18	33.00	18	13	2.17	0.88	19.43
12/17	33.00	34	21	1.31	0.86	18.51
12/16	33.14	30	23	1.15	0.83	17.80
Annual Growth	(5.7%)	—	—	16.0%	4.9%	7.4%

Novanta Inc

Novanta is a leading supplier of core technology solutions that uses its expertise in laser and motion control technologies to design and manufacture sets of products that are geared to the medical and healthcare and advanced industrial markets. Sealed CO2 lasers ultrafast lasers and optical light engines are sold primarily to the industrial and scientific markets. Novanta supplies lasers optics encoders and air bearing spindles to the healthcare and medical markets as well as OEM customers for high-precision cutting drilling marking and measuring. The company changed its name to Novanta from GSI Group in 2016. International customers account for more than 60% of sales.

Operations

Novanta conducts business through three primary segments: Vision (about 45%) Photonics (nearly 35% of net sales) and Precision Motion (more than 20%).

The Vision segment makes and sells a range of medical technologies including medical insufflators (tools for pumping powder or gas into a body cavity) pumps and related disposables; surgical displays and operating room integration technologies; optical data collection and machine vision technologies; radio frequency identification (RFID) technologies; thermal printers; spectrometry technologies; and embedded touch screens.

Photonics designs makes and sells photonics-based tools that include laser scanning and laser beam delivery instruments CO2 lasers continuous wave and ultrafast lasers and optical light engine products.

The Precision Motion segment's products include optical encoders precision motor and motion control technology air bearing spindles and precision machines components.

Novanta operates through several trade names that include Cambridge Technology Lincoln Laser Synrad Laser Quantum WOM Reach Technology JADAK ThingMagic Photo Research Celera Motion Applimotion and Westwind.

Geographic Reach

Novanta based in Bedford Massachusetts operates manufacturing and administration facilities in the US Germany and China. The US generates Novanta's largest amount of sales (about 40%) followed by Europe (approximately 35%) and China and other countries in the Asia/Pacific region (more than 25%).

Additional manufacturing research and development sales service and logistics sites are located in California Florida New York Arizona and Oregon within the US and in Germany UK Czech Republic Japan China Spain and Italy.

Sales and Marketing

Novanta sells its products worldwide through a direct sales force and through resellers or distributors who in turn sell to OEMs. Novanta primarily customers are in the medical and advanced industrial markets.

Financial Performance

The company's revenue for fiscal 2020 $590.6 million compared to $620.1 million in the prior.

Net income for fiscal 2020 increased to $44.5 million compared to $40.8 million in the prior year.

Cash held by the company at the end of fiscal 2020 increased to $125.1 million. Cash provided by operations was $140.2 million while cash used for investing and financing activities were $13.2 million and $84.4 million respectively. Main uses of cash were purchases of property plant and equipment; and borrowings under revolving credit facilities.

Strategy

The company strategy is to drive sustainable profitable growth through short-term and long-term initiatives including: disciplined focus on its diversified business model of providing components and sub-systems to long life-cycle OEM customer platforms in attractive medical and advanced industrial niche markets; improving its business mix to increase medical sales as a percentage of total revenue; increasing its penetration of high growth advanced industrial applications such as laser materials processing robotics laser additive manufacturing automation and metrology by working closely with OEM customers to launch application specific products that closely match the requirements of each application; broadening its portfolio of enabling proprietary technologies and capabilities through increased investment in new product development and investments in application development to further penetrate existing customers while expanding the applicability of its solutions to new markets; broadening its product and service offerings through the acquisition of innovative and complementary technologies and solutions in medical and advanced industrial technology applications including increasing its recurring revenue streams such as services spare parts and consumables; expanding sales and marketing channels to reach new target customers; improving its existing operations to expand profit margins and improve customer satisfaction by implementing lean manufacturing principles strategic sourcing across its major production sites and optimizing and limiting the growth of its fixed cost base; and attracting retaining and developing world-class talented and motivated employees.

Company Background

The Company was founded and in Massachusetts in 1968 as General Scanning Inc. In 1999 General Scanning merged with Lumonics Inc. The post-merger entity GSI Lumonics Inc. continued its operation in Canada. In 2005 the Company changed its name to GSI Group Inc. Through a series of strategic divestitures and acquisitions the Company transformed from one that was more focused on the semiconductor industry to one that primarily sells components and sub-systems to OEMs in the medical and advanced industrial markets. The Company changed its name to Novanta Inc. in May 2016.

EXECUTIVES

Chief Financial Officer, Robert Buckley, $417,937 total compensation
Independent Director, Maxine Mauricio
Independent Director, Katherine Owen
Independent Director, Lonny Carpenter
Independent Director, Brian King
Chief Executive Officer And Chairman, Matthijs Glastra, $625,004 total compensation
Independent Director, Thomas Secor
Independent Director, Ira Lamel
Independent Director, Deborah Eldracher
Chief Human Resource Officer, Brian Young, $280,381 total compensation
Auditors: PricewaterhouseCoopers LLP

LOCATIONS

HQ: Novanta Inc
125 Middlesex Turnpike, Bedford, MA 01730
Phone: 781 266-5700   **Fax:** 781 266-5114
Web: www.gsig.com

PRODUCTS/OPERATIONS

2017 sales

	$ mil.	% of total
Photonics	232.4	45
Vision	183.0	35
Precision Motion	105.8	20
Total	**521.2**	**100**

Selected Products and Brands

Laser products
  Lasers and laser-based systems (Synrad)
  Light and color measurement systems (Photo Research Inc.)
  Optics (The Optical Corporation)
  Scanners (Cambridge Technology)
Precision motion
  Encoders (MicroE Systems)
  Lasers (eCO2 Lasers Spectron Lasers)
  Optics (ExoTec Precision)
  Printed circuit board spindles (Westwind Air Bearings)
Medical technologies
Visualizations solutions
Imaging Informatics

298   HOOVER'S HANDBOOK OF EMERGING COMPANIES 2022

COMPETITORS

APPLIED INDUSTRIAL TECHNOLOGIES INC.	FORTIVE CORPORATION
AZZ INC.	ISC8 INC.
CHECKPOINT SYSTEMS INC.	MKS INSTRUMENTS INC.
COHERENT INC.	OLYMPUS CORPORATION
COMPX INTERNATIONAL INC.	ROGERS CORPORATION
CYMER INC.	SMA Solar Technology AG
DOVER CORPORATION	ULTRA CLEAN HOLDINGS INC.

HISTORICAL FINANCIALS

Company Type: Public

Income Statement				FYE: December 31
	REVENUE ($ mil.)	NET INCOME ($ mil.)	NET PROFIT MARGIN	EMPLOYEES
12/20	590.6	44.5	7.5%	2,200
12/19	626.1	40.7	6.5%	2,290
12/18	614.3	49.1	8.0%	2,133
12/17	521.2	60.0	11.5%	2,034
12/16	384.7	22.0	5.7%	1,269
Annual Growth	11.3%	19.3%	—	14.7%

2020 Year-End Financials

Debt ratio: 24.9%
Return on equity: 9.9%
Cash ($ mil.): 125.0
Current ratio: 2.66
Long-term debt ($ mil.): 200.8

No. of shares (mil.): 35.1
Dividends
  Yield: —
  Payout: —
Market value ($ mil.): 4,157.0

	STOCK PRICE ($) FY Close	P/E High/Low		PER SHARE ($) Earnings	Dividends	Book Value
12/20	118.22	100	53	1.25	0.00	13.56
12/19	88.44	81	52	1.15	0.00	11.90
12/18	63.00	54	33	1.43	0.00	10.56
12/17	50.00	48	18	1.13	0.00	9.01
12/16	21.00	34	19	0.63	0.00	7.51
Annual Growth	54.0%		—	— 18.7%	—	15.9%

Nuvera Communications Inc

New Ulm Telecom operates three incumbent local-exchange carriers (ILECs) serving southern Minnesota and northern Iowa: an ILEC serving New Ulm Minnesota and surrounding communities; subsidiary Western Telephone operating in the Springfield Minnesota area; and Peoples Telephone serving portions of Cherokee and Buena Vista counties in Iowa. Operating under the common NU-Telecom brand they make up New Ulm's Telecom Segment and provide traditional phone services such as local exchange access and long-distance as well as cable TV and Internet access. The company's Phonery division provides customer premise equipment (CPE) offers transport services and resells long distance toll services.

EXECUTIVES

Chief Operating Officer, Vice President, Corporate Secretary, Barbara Bornhoft, $213,585 total compensation
Independent Director, Perry Meyer
Director, Bill Otis
Independent Director, Dennis Miller
Independent Director, Wesley Schultz
Independent Director, Suzanne Spellacy
Independent Director, Colleen Skillings
Independent Director, James Seifert
President, Chief Executive Officer, Glenn Zerbe, $255,000 total compensation
Auditors: Olsen Thielen & Co., Ltd.

LOCATIONS

HQ: Nuvera Communications Inc
27 North Minnesota Street, New Ulm, MN 56073
Phone: 507 354-4111
Web: www.nuvera.net

COMPETITORS

COMPORIUM INC.	TRUCONNECT COMMUNICATIONS INC.
SRT COMMUNICATIONS INC.	

HISTORICAL FINANCIALS

Company Type: Public

Income Statement				FYE: December 31
	REVENUE ($ mil.)	NET INCOME ($ mil.)	NET PROFIT MARGIN	EMPLOYEES
12/20	64.9	9.8	15.2%	204
12/19	64.9	8.3	12.8%	187
12/18	56.6	7.7	13.7%	172
12/17	46.8	9.9	21.2%	134
12/16	42.3	2.8	6.7%	145
Annual Growth	11.3%	36.2%	—	8.9%

2020 Year-End Financials

Debt ratio: 32.0%
Return on equity: 11.6%
Cash ($ mil.): 8.6
Current ratio: 1.25
Long-term debt ($ mil.): 47.1

No. of shares (mil.): 5.2
Dividends
  Yield: 1.3%
  Payout: 15.1%
Market value ($ mil.): 100.0

	STOCK PRICE ($) FY Close	P/E High/Low		PER SHARE ($) Earnings	Dividends	Book Value
12/20	19.30	10	7	1.89	0.26	16.85
12/19	19.00	13	11	1.60	0.51	15.56
12/18	18.29	13	11	1.50	0.44	14.41
12/17	17.72	9	5	1.93	0.40	13.27
12/16	9.69	17	12	0.56	0.36	11.72
Annual Growth	18.8%		—	— 35.5%	(7.7%)	9.5%

NV5 Global Inc

NV5 Global is a provider of professional and technical engineering and consulting solutions to public and private sector clients in the infrastructure utility services construction real estate and environmental markets operating nationwide and abroad. The company's clients include the US federal state and local governments and the private sector. NV5's enviable projects have included Air-

port Public Institutions hospitals and clinic Wynn Resorts NV & Macau and a water conservation board in Colorado. NV5 originally operated as Nolte Associates Inc. in California prior to its acquisition in 2010. NV5 went public in 2013. Its US operations generates the majority of gross sales of the company.

Operations

Effective the beginning of fiscal year 2020 NV5 re-evaluated the structure of its internal organization structure as a result of the 2019 acquisition of QSI. To reflect management's revised perspective it is now organized into three operating and reportable segments:

Infrastructure (INF) includes its engineering civil program management utility services and construction quality assurance testing and inspection practices; Building Technology & Sciences (BTS) includes its environmental health sciences buildings and program management and MEP & technology engineering practices; and Geospatial Solutions (GEO) includes its geospatial technology services practice.

INF accounts for about 55% of gross revenue while BTS for around 25% and GEO for more than 20% of gross revenue.

Geographic Reach

Headquartered in Hollywood Florida NV5 operates its business from more than 105 locations in the US. and abroad. All of the company's offices utilize its shared services platform which consists of human resources marketing finance information technology legal corporate development and other resources.

Majority of the revenues came from US. The state of California has historically been and is considered to be a key geographic region for the business as roughly 30% of gross revenues.

Sales and Marketing

NV5 primary clients include US federal state municipal and local government agencies and military and defense clients. It also serves quasi-public (nearly 70% of gross revenue) and private sector (more than 30%) clients from the education healthcare energy and public utility industries including schools universities hospitals health care providers insurance providers large utility service providers and large to small energy producers. Some 90% of gross revenue were generated from the cost-reimbursable contracts while the rest were generated from fixed-unit contracts.

The company's advertising costs were $940 $939 and $1019 during fiscal years 2020 2019 and 2018 respectively.

Financial Performance

Nv5 consolidated gross revenues increased by $150.4 million or 30% in 2020 compared to 2019. The increase in gross revenue was primarily due to incremental gross revenues from QSI of $145.0 million incremental gross revenues from other acquisitions completed since the beginning of 2019 of $33.3 million and an increase in its infrastructure support services of $2.5 million.

Net income for fiscal 2020 increased to 21.0 million compared from the prior year with $23.8 million.

Cash held by the company at the end of fiscal 2020 increased to $64.9 million. Cash provided by operations was $96.0 million while cash used for investing and financing activities were $9.1 million and $53.9 million respectively. Main uses of cash were purchase of property and equipment; and payments of borrowings from Senior Credit Facility.

Strategy

NV5 intends to pursue the following growth strategies as it seeks to expand its market share and position itself as a preferred single-source provider of professional engineering and technical consulting services to clients:

Seeking strategic acquisitions to enhance or expand the company's services offerings. NV5 seeks acquisitions that allow it to expand or enhance its capabilities in existing service offerings or to supplement existing service offerings with new closely related service offerings.

Continuing to focus on public sector clients while building private sector client capabilities. The company has historically derived the majority of its revenue from public and quasi-public sector clients. NV5 is also positioned to address the challenges presented by the aging infrastructure system of the United States and the need to provide solutions for transportation energy water and wastewater requirements.

Strengthening and supporting its human capital. The company's experienced employees and management team are its most valuable resources. Attracting training and retaining key personnel has been and will remain critical to the company's success. To achieve its human capital goals NV5 intends to remain focused on providing its personnel with entrepreneurial opportunities to expand its business within their areas of expertise. The company will also continue to provide its personnel with personal and professional growth opportunities including additional training performance-based incentives such as opportunities for stock ownership and other competitive benefits.

Mergers and AcquisitionsIn 2021 NV5 acquired PES Environmental an environmental engineering and consulting company providing environmental site assessment water resources and stormwater management permitting and compliance industrial hygiene and litigation support services. PES Environmental's strong management team regulatory expertise and robust client portfolio make it a good fit for the continued expansion of NV5's environmental platform. The acquisition was made with a combination of cash and stock and will be immediately accretive to NV5's earnings. In the same year NV5 acquired North Carolina-based Geodynamics LLC (Geodynamics) a provider of sonar-based deep-water geospatial solutions. Geodynamics will operate within NV5's Geospatial vertical adding full-ocean depth hydrographic and geophysical surveying to NV5's topographic and nearshore geospatial capabilities. The $42 million acquisition which includes an earn out provision was made with a combination of cash and stock and will be immediately accretive to NV5's earnings. In early 2021 NV5 acquired TerraTech Engineers Inc. (TerraTech) a geotechnical engineering environmental consulting and materials testing company headquartered in North Carolina. The addition of TerraTech strengthens NV5's environmental geotechnical and testing capabilities in the growing Southeast market and will support its infrastructure operations throughout the region. Also in early 2021 NV5 agreed to acquire Industrial Design Associates International (IDA) an international engineering services consulting company. The addition of IDA will expand its international MEP design building commissioning and subscription-based energy services revenue.

In mid-2020 NV5 agreed to acquire Mediatech Design Group (Mediatech) a technology company providing security enterprise IT and building technology solutions in the Middle East and North Africa (MENA) region and South East Asia. Mediatech is headquartered in Dubai and is a leader in technology design services for the hospitality industrial healthcare commercial retail and convention center markets. The addition of Mediatech strengthens NV5's technology services and expands NV5's Dubai office to 40 full-time equivalent employees.

EXECUTIVES

Executive Vice President, General Counsel, Richard Tong, $313,331 total compensation
Executive Vice President, Donald Alford, $328,000 total compensation
President, Chief Operating Officer, Director, Alexander Hockman, $421,831 total compensation
Executive Vice President, Chief Administrative Officer, Secretary, Director, MaryJo O'Brien
Independent Director, Francois Tardan
Chief Financial Officer, Edward Codispoti, $326,539 total compensation
Independent Director, Denise Dickins
Chairman Of The Board, Chief Executive Officer, Dickerson Wright, $632,308 total compensation
Auditors: DELOITTE & TOUCHE LLP

LOCATIONS

HQ: NV5 Global Inc
200 South Park Road, Suite 350, Hollywood, FL 33021
Phone: 954 495-2112
Web: www.nv5.com

COMPETITORS

BANCTEC INC.
CONDUENT INCORPORATED
ENVESTNET INC.
EXLSERVICE HOLDINGS INC.
FIDELITY NATIONAL INFORMATION SERVICES INC.
ICF INTERNATIONAL INC.
KBC ADVANCED TECHNOLOGIES LIMITED
KBR INC.
MSCI INC.
PIPEHAWK PLC
QUINSTREET INC.
R C M TECHNOLOGIES INC.
WILLDAN GROUP INC.

HISTORICAL FINANCIALS

Company Type: Public

Income Statement — FYE: January 2

	REVENUE ($ mil.)	NET INCOME ($ mil.)	NET PROFIT MARGIN	EMPLOYEES
01/21*	659.3	21.0	3.2%	3,197
12/19	508.9	23.7	4.7%	3,362
12/18	418.0	26.8	6.4%	2,384
12/17	333.0	24.0	7.2%	2,023
12/16	223.9	11.6	5.2%	1,532
Annual Growth	31.0%	16.0%	—	20.2%

*Fiscal year change

2021 Year-End Financials

Debt ratio: 34.9%
Return on equity: 5.5%
Cash ($ mil.): 64.9
Current ratio: 2.12
Long-term debt ($ mil.): 283.3

No. of shares (mil.): 13.2
Dividends
 Yield: —
 Payout: —
Market value ($ mil.): 1,045.0

	STOCK PRICE ($) FY Close	P/E High/Low	PER SHARE ($) Earnings	Dividends	Book Value
01/21*	78.78	47 17	1.65	0.00	29.70
12/19	48.31	44 23	1.90	0.00	27.70
12/18	58.24	37 17	2.33	0.00	25.30
12/17	54.15	25 14	2.23	0.00	16.62
12/16	33.40	29 12	1.22	0.00	14.02
Annual Growth	23.9%	— —	7.8%	—	20.6%

*Fiscal year change

Oak Valley Bancorp (Oakdale, CA)

Oak Valley Bancorp was formed in 2008 to be the holding company for Oak Valley Community Bank which serves individuals and local businesses through about 10 branches in California's Central Valley. Eastern Sierra Community Bank a division of Oak Valley has three locations. The banks provide standard deposit products such as savings checking and retirement accounts and CDs. Their lending activities consist of commercial real estate loans (more than half of their combined loan portfolio) and business real estate construction agricultural residential mortgage and consumer loans. Investment products and services are offered through an agreement with PrimeVest Financial Services.

EXECUTIVES

President, Chief Operating Officer, Richard McCarty, $256,550 total compensation
Executive Vice President, Chief Credit Officer, Michael Rodrigues, $219,261 total compensation
Executive Vice President, Chief Information Officer, Russell Stahl
Chief Financial Officer, Senior Vice President, Jeffrey Gall, $185,606 total compensation
Independent Director, Ronald Martin
President, Chief Executive Officer And Director, Christopher Courtney, $369,910 total compensation
Independent Director, H. Randolph Holder
Independent Director, Allison Lafferty
Executive Vice President - Commercial Banking Group, Gary Stephens, $188,257 total compensation
Executive Vice President - Risk Management, Janis Powers
Independent Director, Gary Strong
Independent Chairman Of The Board, Terrance Withrow
Independent Director, Danny Titus
Independent Director, James Gilbert
Independent Director, Donald Barton
Director, Thomas Haidlen
Auditors: RSM US LLP

LOCATIONS

HQ: Oak Valley Bancorp (Oakdale, CA)
125 N. Third Ave., Oakdale, CA 95361
Phone: 209 848-2265
Web: www.ovcb.com

COMPETITORS

COMMUNITY SHORES BANK CORPORATION
SOUTHERN COMMUNITY FINANCIAL CORPORATION

HISTORICAL FINANCIALS

Company Type: Public

Income Statement

FYE: December 31

	ASSETS ($ mil.)	NET INCOME ($ mil.)	INCOME AS % OF ASSETS	EMPLOYEES
12/20	1,511.4	13.6	0.9%	191
12/19	1,147.7	12.4	1.1%	192
12/18	1,094.8	11.5	1.1%	186
12/17	1,034.8	9.0	0.9%	175
12/16	1,002.1	7.6	0.8%	169
Annual Growth	10.8%	15.6%	—	3.1%

2020 Year-End Financials

Return on assets: 1.0%
Return on equity: 11.2%
Long-term debt ($ mil.): —
No. of shares (mil.): 8.2
Sales ($ mil): 50.9

Dividends
Yield: 1.6%
Payout: 18.6%
Market value ($ mil.): 137.0

	STOCK PRICE ($) FY Close	P/E High/Low		PER SHARE ($) Earnings	Dividends	Book Value
12/20	16.62	11	7	1.68	0.28	15.78
12/19	19.46	13	10	1.54	0.27	13.71
12/18	18.30	17	12	1.42	0.26	12.09
12/17	19.54	18	11	1.13	0.25	11.21
12/16	12.55	13	10	0.95	0.24	10.19
Annual Growth	7.3%	—	—	15.3%	3.9%	11.5%

Ocean Bio-Chem, Inc.

Ocean Bio-Chem provides everything but the elbow grease to scrub down boats planes RVs and automobiles. The company makes and distributes Star Brite and StarTron brand maintenance and appearance products. Its marine and automotive lines include waxes lubricants and coolants and its recreational vehicle and power sports equipment offerings primarily consist of polishes and cleaners. Ocean Bio-Chem's products are sold by both national retailers and specialty stores including Wal-Mart West Marine and Bass Pro Shops. The company handles its manufacturing in-house through its Alabama-based Kinpak subsidiary which also provides contract services. President and CEO Peter Dornau owns about 70% of the company.

EXECUTIVES

Chairman Of The Board, President, Chief Executive Officer, Peter Dornau, $208,053 total compensation
Director, James Kolisch
Independent Director, John Turner
Vice President – Chief Operating Officer, Secretary, Director, William Dudman, $213,877 total compensation
Executive Vice President - Sales And Marketing, Director, Gregor Dornau, $261,834 total compensation
Independent Director, Diana Conard

Independent Director, Kimberly Krause
Chief Financial Officer, Vice President - Finance, Director, Jeffrey Barocas, $216,394 total compensation
Auditors: Accell Audit & Compliance, PA

LOCATIONS

HQ: Ocean Bio-Chem, Inc.
  4041 SW 47 Avenue, Fort Lauderdale, FL 33314
Phone: 954 587-6280
Web: www.oceanbiochem.com

COMPETITORS

Cantol Corp   GOJO INDUSTRIES INC.

HISTORICAL FINANCIALS

Company Type: Public

Income Statement

FYE: December 31

	REVENUE ($ mil.)	NET INCOME ($ mil.)	NET PROFIT MARGIN	EMPLOYEES
12/20	55.5	9.6	17.3%	200
12/19	42.2	3.5	8.3%	154
12/18	41.8	2.8	6.7%	152
12/17	38.9	2.6	6.7%	142
12/16	36.2	2.1	5.8%	128
Annual Growth	11.3%	46.4%	—	11.8%

2020 Year-End Financials

Debt ratio: 8.8%
Return on equity: 27.1%
Cash ($ mil.): 11.1
Current ratio: 9.70
Long-term debt ($ mil.): 3.7

No. of shares (mil.): 9.4
Dividends
  Yield: 0.6%
  Payout: 8.0%
Market value ($ mil.): 127.0

	STOCK PRICE ($) FY Close	P/E High/Low		PER SHARE ($) Earnings	Dividends	Book Value
12/20	13.36	19	3	1.02	0.08	4.21
12/19	3.31	11	8	0.37	0.05	3.25
12/18	3.28	15	10	0.30	0.12	2.94
12/17	4.34	19	13	0.28	0.06	2.69
12/16	3.76	19	8	0.23	0.06	2.46
Annual Growth	37.3%	—	—	45.1%	7.5%	14.4%

OceanFirst Financial Corp

Ask the folks at OceanFirst Bank for a home loan and they might say "shore." The subsidiary of holding company OceanFirst Financial operates 25 branches in the coastal New Jersey counties of Middlesex Monmouth and Ocean. The community-oriented bank caters to individuals and small to midsized businesses in the Jersey Shore area offering standard products such as checking and savings accounts CDs and IRAs. It uses funds from deposits mainly to invest in mortgages loans and securities. One- to four-family residential mortgages make up more than half of OceanFirst Financial's loan portfolio which also includes commercial real estate (about 30%) business construction and consumer loans.

Operations

The Bank's principal business is attracting deposits from the general public in the communities surrounding its branch offices and investing those deposits primarily in single-family owner-occupied residential mortgage loans and commercial real estate loans. It active subsidiaries include Ocean-First Services LLC OceanFirst REIT Holdings Inc. and 975 Holdings LLC.

Geographic Reach
OceanFirst has operations in the New Jersey counties of Middlesex Monmouth and Ocean.

Financial Performance
OceanFirst's revenues dropped by 4% in 2012 due to decrease in loans and mortgage-backed securities partially offset by higher revenues from investment securities and other.

Net income declined by 3% in 2012 due to an increase in provision for loan losses and non-interest expenses (higher professional fees).

Strategy
OceanFirst seeks to grow commercial loans receivable by offering commercial lending services to local businesses; grow core deposits through broader product offerings andbranch expansion; and increase non-interest income by expanding its fee-based products and services.

Part of the company's strategy for growth includes expanding its fee-based offerings. The bank for example offers trust and asset management services. Company subsidiary OceanFirst Services sells mutual funds annuities and insurance products from third-party vendors. OceanFirst is also seeking opportunities to grow by opening new branch locations within its existing markets.

In 2013 the Bank opened a full service Financial Solutions Center in Red Bank New Jersey offering deposit lending and asset management services. It also opened an additional branch office in Jackson New Jersey.

Since 1995 OceanFirst has opened sixteen branch offices (twelve in Ocean County and four in Monmouth County).

Mergers and Acquisitions
In January 2016 OceanFirst Financial agreed to buy Cape Bancorp— along with its 22 branches in central and southern New Jersey counties $1.1 billion in loans and $1.3 billion in deposits — for $208.1 million. The deal would grow OceanFirst's total total assets by over 60% and nearly double the size of its branch network.

Company Background
OceanFirst Bank's employee stock option plan owns more than 10% of OceanFirst Financial's shares. The company's charitable foundation OceanFirst Foundation owns 7%.

The Bank was founded as a state-chartered building and loan association in 1902. It converted to a Federal savings and loan association in 1945 and became a Federally-chartered mutual savings bank in 1989.

EXECUTIVES

Chief Financial Officer, Executive Vice President Of The Company And The Bank, Michael Fitzpatrick, $349,423 total compensation
Executive Vice President, Chief Retail Banking Officer Of The Bank, Anthony Giordano
Executive Vice President, Chief Administrative Officer Of The Bank, Michele Estep
Executive Vice President, Chief Risk Officer, Director Of The Company And The Bank, Grace Vallacchi, $324,423 total compensation

HOOVER'S HANDBOOK OF EMERGING COMPANIES 2022

Independent Director, Anthony Coscia
Independent Director, Steven Scopellite
Chief Information Officer Of The Bank, Karthik Sridharan
Independent Director, Joseph Murphy
Independent Director, Patricia Turner
Chief Operating Officer, Executive Vice President And President Of The Bank, Joseph Lebel, $398,846 total compensation
Executive Vice President, General Counsel, Corporate Secretary Of The Company And The Bank, Steven Tsimbinos, $324,423 total compensation
Chairman Of The Board, President, Chief Executive Officer Of The Company; Chairman And Chief Executive Officer Of The Bank, Christopher Maher, $946,154 total compensation
Chief Accounting Officer, Angela Ho
Auditors: DELOITTE & TOUCHE LLP

LOCATIONS

HQ: OceanFirst Financial Corp
110 West Front Street, Red Bank, NJ 07701
Phone: 732 240-4500
Web: www.oceanfirst.com

PRODUCTS/OPERATIONS

2016 sales

	% of total
Interest Income	
Loans	80
Mortgage-backed securities	4
Investment securities & other	2
Non-interest	
Bankcard services revenue	3
Wealth management revenue	2
Fees & service charges	7
Loan Servicing income	-
Net gains on sales of loans	1
Net loss from other real estate operations	-
Income from Bank owned Life Insurance	1
Other	-
Total	**100**

COMPETITORS

AXOS FINANCIAL INC.	GUARANTY BANCORP
BANCFIRST CORPORATION	Hanley Economic Building Society
BANKUNITED INC.	
CHARTER FINANCIAL CORPORATION	MIDLAND FINANCIAL CO.
	NORTHFIELD BANCORP INC.
DOLLAR BANK FEDERAL SAVINGS BANK	PRIVATEBANCORP INC.
FLAGSTAR BANCORP INC.	SIGNATURE BANK

HISTORICAL FINANCIALS

Company Type: Public

Income Statement
FYE: December 31

	ASSETS ($ mil.)	NET INCOME ($ mil.)	INCOME AS % OF ASSETS	EMPLOYEES
12/20	11,448.3	63.3	0.6%	1,008
12/19	8,246.1	88.5	1.1%	924
12/18	7,516.1	71.9	1.0%	892
12/17	5,416.0	42.4	0.8%	684
12/16	5,167.0	23.0	0.4%	797
Annual Growth	22.0%	28.7%	—	6.0%

2020 Year-End Financials

Return on assets: 0.6%
Return on equity: 4.7%
Long-term debt ($ mil.): —
No. of shares (mil.): 60.3
Sales ($ mil.): 445.4
Dividends
Yield: 3.6%
Payout: 71.5%
Market value ($ mil.): 1,125.0

	STOCK PRICE ($) FY Close	P/E High/Low	PER SHARE ($)		
			Earnings	Dividends	Book Value
12/20	18.63	25 12	1.02	0.68	24.57
12/19	25.54	15 12	1.75	0.68	22.88
12/18	22.51	20 14	1.51	0.62	21.68
12/17	26.25	23 18	1.28	0.60	18.47
12/16	30.03	30 16	0.98	0.54	17.80
Annual Growth	(11.3%)	— —	1.0%	5.9%	8.4%

Old Second Bancorp., Inc. (Aurora, Ill.)

Old Second won't settle for a silver finish when it comes to community banking around Chicago. Old Second Bancorp is the holding company for Old Second National Bank which serves the Chicago metropolitan area through 25 branches in Kane Kendall DeKalb DuPage LaSalle Will and Cook counties. The bank provides standard services such as checking and savings accounts credit and debit cards CDs mortgages loans and trust services to consumers and business clients. Subsidiary River Street Advisors offers investment management and advisory services. Another unit Old Second Affordable Housing Fund provides home-buying assistance to lower-income customers.

Operations

Commercial real estate loans accounted for 53% of Old Second's loan portfolio at the end of 2015 while residential mortgages made up another 31%. The rest was made up of general commercial loans (12% of loan assets) and construction lending (2%).

Roughly 70% of the bank's revenue comes from interest income. About 54% of its revenue came from loan interest (including fees) during 2015 with another 15% coming from interest on investment securities. The remainder of Old Second's revenue came from deposit account service charges (7%) trust income (6%) mortgage loan sale gains (6%) secondary mortgage fees (1%) and other sources.

Geographic Reach

The bank mostly serves customers in Aurora Illinois (which is 40 miles west of Chicago) and surrounding communities. Its 24 branches are located in the Kane Kendall DeKalb DuPage LaSalle Will and Cook counties of Illinois.

Sales and Marketing

Old Second has been ramping up its advertising spend in recent years. It spent $1.34 million on advertising in 2015 up from $1.28 million and $1.23 million in 2014 and 2013 respectively.

Financial Performance

Old Second's annual revenues have fallen 20% since 2011 as it's had to sell of many of its nonperforming loan assets to de-risk its loan portfolio. The company's profits however have been on the mend as its de-risking measures have led to declining loan loss provisions.

The bank's revenue rebounded by less than 1% to $97.46 million during 2015 as its average loans including loans held for sale grew by 2% for the year.

Revenue growth in 2015 combined with lower interest and amortization costs on deposits drove Old Second Bancorp's net income up by over 50% to $15.39 million. The bank's operating cash levels jumped sharply to $21.14 million (operations had used $6.3 million in 2014) partially thanks to earnings growth but mostly thanks to positive working capital changes related to sales proceeds from loans held for sale and changes in accrued interest payable and other liabilities.

Strategy

Old Second Bancorp continued in 2016 to focus on shedding riskier loan assets that led it to deep losses in 2011 while focusing on securing high-quality loans with more creditworthiness. Its efforts began to pay off in 2015 as its average loan balances and revenues began to grow again after years of being in decline.

EXECUTIVES

Chairman Of The Board, William Skoglund
Independent Director, Edward Bonifas
Independent Director, William Kane
President, Chief Executive Officer And Director, James Eccher, $566,582 total compensation
Lead Independent Director, Barry Finn
Independent Director, John Ladowicz
Executive Vice President And Chief Lending Officer, Donald Pilmer, $284,688 total compensation
Vice Chairman Of The Board, Gary Collins, $324,645 total compensation
Independent Director, James Tapscott
Independent Director, Duane Suits
Independent Director, Patti Rocks
Executive Vice President, Wealth Management, Richard Gartelmann, $223,238 total compensation
Independent Director, Jill York
Independent Director, Billy Lyons
Independent Director, Dennis Klaeser
Chief Financial Officer, Executive Vice President, Bradley Adams, $329,933 total compensation
Auditors: Plante & Moran PLLC

LOCATIONS

HQ: Old Second Bancorp., Inc. (Aurora, Ill.)
37 South River Street, Aurora, IL 60507
Phone: 630 892-0202
Web: www.oldsecond.com

PRODUCTS/OPERATIONS

2015 sales

	% of total
Interest and dividend income	
Loans including fees	54
Taxable	14
Tax exempt	1
Non-interest income	
Service charges on deposits	7
Trust income	6
Net gain on sales of mortgage loans	6
Debit card interchange income	4
Secondary mortgage fees	1
Increase in cash surrender value of bank-owned life insurance	1
Other income	6
Total	**100**

Products/Services

Personal Banking
Card Services
Checking
Loans
Money Services
Online and Mobile Banking
Prime Time Club
Retirement Services

Savings
Loans
Auto and Personal Loans
Home Equity Loans
Home Loans
Mortgage Lenders
Required Documents
SAFE Act
Business Banking
Commercial Banking
Online and Mobile Banking
Small Business Banking
Wealth Management
Business Plan Options
Real Estate Services
Retirement Services

COMPETITORS

AMERIS BANCORP	CASCADE BANCORP
ASTORIA FINANCIAL	FIRST FINANCIAL
CORPORATION	CORPORATION
BANKFINANCIAL	GREAT SOUTHERN
BANCORP	
CORPORATION	INC.
BEAR STATE FINANCIAL	TRUSTCO BANK CORP N Y
INC.	

HISTORICAL FINANCIALS

Company Type: Public

Income Statement

FYE: December 31

	ASSETS ($ mil.)	NET INCOME ($ mil.)	INCOME AS % OF ASSETS	EMPLOYEES
12/20	3,040.8	27.8	0.9%	533
12/19	2,635.5	39.4	1.5%	535
12/18	2,676.0	34.0	1.3%	518
12/17	2,383.4	15.1	0.6%	450
12/16	2,251.1	15.6	0.7%	467
Annual Growth	7.8%	15.4%	—	3.4%

2020 Year-End Financials

Return on assets: 0.9%
Return on equity: 9.4%
Long-term debt ($ mil.): —
No. of shares (mil.): 29.3
Sales ($ mil): 141.7

Dividends
Yield: 0.4%
Payout: 4.0%
Market value ($ mil.): 296.0

	STOCK PRICE ($) FY Close	P/E High/Low		PER SHARE ($) Earnings	Dividends	Book Value
12/20	10.10	14	7	0.92	0.04	10.47
12/19	13.47	11	9	1.30	0.04	9.28
12/18	13.00	14	11	1.12	0.04	7.70
12/17	13.65	28	20	0.50	0.04	6.76
12/16	11.05	22	12	0.53	0.03	5.93
Annual Growth	(2.2%)	—	—	14.8%	7.5%	15.3%

Ollie's Bargain Outlet Holdings Inc

Auditors: KPMG LLP

LOCATIONS

HQ: Ollie's Bargain Outlet Holdings Inc
6295 Allentown Boulevard, Suite 1, Harrisburg, PA 17112
Phone: 717 657-2300
Web: www.ollies.us

HISTORICAL FINANCIALS

Company Type: Public

Income Statement

FYE: January 30

	REVENUE ($ mil.)	NET INCOME ($ mil.)	NET PROFIT MARGIN	EMPLOYEES
01/21*	1,808.8	242.7	13.4%	9,800
02/20	1,408.2	141.1	10.0%	8,300
02/19	1,241.3	135.0	10.9%	7,700
02/18	1,077.0	127.5	11.8%	6,700
01/17	890.3	59.7	6.7%	5,500
Annual Growth	19.4%	42.0%	—	15.5%

*Fiscal year change

2021 Year-End Financials

Debt ratio: 0.0%
Return on equity: 20.3%
Cash ($ mil.): 447.1
Current ratio: 2.85
Long-term debt ($ mil.): 0.6

No. of shares (mil.): 65.4
Dividends
Yield: —
Payout: —
Market value ($ mil.): 6,201.0

	STOCK PRICE ($) FY Close	P/E High/Low		PER SHARE ($) Earnings	Dividends	Book Value
01/21*	94.73	30	9	3.68	0.00	20.39
02/20	53.04	45	24	2.14	0.00	16.80
02/19	79.35	45	24	2.05	0.00	14.96
02/18	53.75	28	14	1.96	0.00	12.85
01/17	29.35	33	19	0.96	0.00	10.72
Annual Growth	34.0%	—	—	39.9%	—	17.4%

*Fiscal year change

OneMain Finance Corp

EXECUTIVES

Executive Vice President - Branch Operations, Bradford Borchers, $300,000 total compensation
Chairman Of The Board, Chief Executive Officer, Douglas Shulman
Chief Financial Officer, Executive Vice President, Micah Conrad
Chief Operating Officer, Executive Vice President, Rajive Chadha
Chief Human Resource Officer, Executive Vice President, Heather McHale

LOCATIONS

HQ: OneMain Finance Corp
601 Northwest Second Street, Evansville, IN 47708
Phone: 812 424-8031
Web: www.omf.com

HISTORICAL FINANCIALS

Company Type: Public

Income Statement

FYE: December 31

	REVENUE ($ mil.)	NET INCOME ($ mil.)	NET PROFIT MARGIN	EMPLOYEES
12/21	3,958.0	1,314.0	33.2%	8,800
12/20	3,867.0	730.0	18.9%	8,300
12/19	3,777.0	858.0	22.7%	9,700
12/18	3,314.0	461.0	13.9%	10,200
12/17	876.0	94.0	10.7%	2,500
Annual Growth	45.8%	93.4%	—	37.0%

2021 Year-End Financials

Debt ratio: 80.5%
Return on equity: 40.4%
Cash ($ mil.): 510.0
Current ratio: 986.00
Long-term debt ($ mil.): 17,750.0

No. of shares (mil.): 10.1
Dividends
Yield: —
Payout: 127.7%
Market value ($ mil.): —

OneWater Marine Inc

LOCATIONS

HQ: OneWater Marine Inc
6275 Lanier Islands Parkway, Buford, GA 30518
Phone: 678 541-6300
Web: www.onewatermarine.com

HISTORICAL FINANCIALS

Company Type: Public

Income Statement

FYE: September 30

	REVENUE ($ mil.)	NET INCOME ($ mil.)	NET PROFIT MARGIN	EMPLOYEES
09/21	1,228.2	79.0	6.4%	1,785
09/20	1,022.9	17.4	1.7%	1,169
09/19	767.6	35.6	4.6%	1,102
09/18	602.8	1.1	0.2%	0
09/17	391.4	(4.2)	—	0
Annual Growth	33.1%			

2021 Year-End Financials

Debt ratio: 31.7%
Return on equity: 45.3%
Cash ($ mil.): 62.6
Current ratio: 1.23
Long-term debt ($ mil.): 103.0

No. of shares (mil.): 15.1
Dividends
Yield: 4.4%
Payout: 25.8%
Market value ($ mil.): 607.0

	STOCK PRICE ($) FY Close	P/E High/Low		PER SHARE ($) Earnings	Dividends	Book Value
09/21	40.21	8	3	6.96	1.80	14.97
09/20	20.49	11	1	2.77	0.00	8.20
Annual Growth	96.2%	—	—	151.3%	—	82.4%

Onto Innovation Inc

Onto Innovation (formerly Nanometrics) is a worldwide leader in the design development manufacture and support of process control tools that perform macro defect inspection and metrology lithography systems and process control analytical software used by semiconductor wafer and advanced packaging device manufacturers. Its products are also used in a number of other high technology industries including: silicon wafer; light emitting diode (LED); vertical-cavity surface-emitting laser (VCSEL); micro-electromechanical system (MEMS); CMOS image sensor (CIS); power device; RF filter; data storage; and certain industrial and scientific applications. Top customers include Samsung Electronics Taiwan Semiconductor Manufacturing Company and SK Hynix. Onto in-

HOOVER'S HANDBOOK OF EMERGING COMPANIES 2022

303

novation generates most of its sales in Asia. The company Nanometrics was founded in 1975.

Operations

Onto Innovation engaged in the design development manufacture and support of high-performance control metrology defect inspection lithography and data analysis systems used by microelectronics device manufacturers. It gets some 80% of sales from its systems and software over 10% from parts and the rest were generated from its services.

Its products have included the Automated Metrology Systems which are primarily consist of fully automated metrology systems that are employed in semiconductor production environments. The Atlas family of products represent our line of high-performance metrology systems providing OCD and thin film metrology and wafer stress metrology for transistor and interconnect metrology applications. It also offers Integrated Metrology Systems (installed directly onto wafer processing equipment to provide near real-time measurements for improved process control and maximum throughput); Silicon Wafer All-surface Inspection/Characterization (refers to inspection of the wafer frontside edge and backside as well as wafer's locator notch); and Macro Defect Inspection (deploy advanced macro defect inspection throughout the production line to monitor key process steps gather process-enhancing information and ultimately lower manufacturing costs). Other products include Automated Defect Classification and Pattern Analysis; Yield Analysis; Opaque Film Metrology; Probe Card Test and Analysis; Industrial Scientific and Research Markets ? 4D Technology; and Advanced Packaging Lithography.

Geographic Reach

Onto Innovation is based in Wilmington Massachusetts. It owns its facilities in Milpitas and Richardson and lease facilities for corporate engineering manufacturing sales and service-related purposes in the United States and seven other countries- China France Germany Japan South Korea Singapore and Taiwan.

The company's sales are concentrated in Asia with China and Taiwan with over 20% each followed by Korea with around 15% and Japan with some 10%. The US accounts for some 15% of the company's revenue while Europe and Southeast Asia accounts for the rest.

It has a manufacturing operations in Milpitas California Tucson Arizona Wilmington Massachusetts Bloomington Minnesota and at various contract manufacturers around the world.

Sales and Marketing

The company provides local direct sales service and application support through its worldwide offices and work with selected dealers and sales representatives. Its top three customers include Samsung Electronics Taiwan Semiconductor Manufacturing Co. and SK Hynix.

Financial Performance

Onto Innovation's revenue is derived from the sale of its systems and software sparer parts and services. Its revenue was $556.5 million for 2020 representing an increase of 82% from 2019. Total systems and software revenue increased primarily due to the inclusion of revenue from legacy Nanometrics for the period.

Net income increased to $31 million in 2020 from $1.9 million the year prior. The increase is

mainly due to the significant increase in revenue for the fiscal year.

Cash at the end of the period was $136.7 million a $6 million increase from the year prior. Operating activities provided $106 million to the coffers while investing and financing activities used $48.6 million and $53.7 million respectively. Onto's main cash uses in 2020 were purchases of marketable securities and purchases of common stock.

Strategy

Onto Innovation combines the scale of a global leader with an expanded portfolio of leading-edge technologies that include: unpatterned wafer quality; 3D metrology spanning the chip from nanometer-scale transistors to micron-level die-interconnects; macro defect inspection of wafers and packages; metal interconnect composition; factory analytics; and lithography for advanced semiconductor packaging. The breadth of this portfolio allows Onto to collaborate with customers about their process yields and process variations from bare silicon wafers through the wafer fab to the final back-end packaging. Onto's software brings an understanding of how individual processes affect the overall product enabling customers to improve product quality and reliability.

Onto released new products in recent years further improving its product portfolio. In early 2021 the company launched a new Dragonfly G3 inspection platform designed to meet the most advanced 2D and 3D sensitivity requirements for advanced packaging and specialty device manufacturers. This latest inspection advances have resulted in multiple orders from a top 3 OSAT and a top 3 image sensor manufacturer. In 2020 Onto launched the Element material analysis platform which enables customers to monitor and control layers of dielectric thin films measuring dopants as well as monitoring process by-products such as hydrogen. It also launched a suite of process control metrology solutions for advanced device manufacturing: the new Atlas V IMPULSE V and revolutionary Aspect optical systems.

Mergers and Acquisitions

In early 2021 Onto Innovation Inc. acquired Inspectrology LLC. Headquartered in Sudbury Massachusetts USA Inspectrology is a leading supplier of overlay metrology for controlling lithography and etch processes in the compound semiconductor market. The acquisition expands the company's position in the high growth compound semiconductor market driven by higher content in 5G RF and electric vehicles and its Onto Innovation's Advanced Process Control (APC) software and Dragonfly System are expected to provide revenue synergies when combined with Inspectrology products. Terms were not disclosed.

HISTORY

Nanometrics was incorporated in 1975 and has been publicly traded since 1984. In 2006 the company acquired Accent Optical Technologies a supplier of semiconductor process control and metrology equipment for around $81 million in stock and assumed debt. Following the merger previous Nanometrics shareholders owned approximately 73% of the combined company and Accent Optical shareholders owned about 27%. Also that year the company acquired Soluris a supplier of overlay and critical-dimension measurement equipment for $7 million in cash.

Expanding its portfolio of metrology products in 2008 the company acquired the assets of Tevet

Process Control Technologies a supplier of integrated metrology systems for manufacturing semiconductors and solar cells for about $3.5 million.

In 2011 Nanometrics bought Germany-based Nanda Technologies a maker of fully automated wafer inspection systems for $23 million in cash. With the acquisition Nanometrics added a differentiated macro defect inspection technology to its portfolio of metrology products.

EXECUTIVES

Chief Operating Officer, James Harlow
Global Vice President Human Resources, Barry Hartunian
Vice President, General Manager - Wafer Business Unit, Robert Fiordalice
Independent Director, Christine Tsingos
Independent Director, Edward Brown
Senior Vice President, General Manager - Metrology Business Unit, Rodney Smedt, $321,083 total compensation
Chief Executive Officer, Director, Michael Plisinski, $592,089 total compensation
Independent Director, Leo Berlinghieri
Senior Vice President - Finance And Administration, Chief Financial Officer, Steven Roth, $400,975 total compensation
Vice President, General Manager, Lithography Business Unit, Elvino da Silveira
Senior Vice President, General Manager, Inspection Business Unit, Ju Jin
Senior Vice President - Manufacturing Operations, Dean Iacopetti
Vice President, General Manager, Enterprise Business Unit, Danielle Baptiste
Independent Director, Karen Rogge
Independent Chairman Of The Board, Christopher Seams
Auditors: Ernst & Young LLP

LOCATIONS

HQ: Onto Innovation Inc
16 Jonspin Road, Wilmington, MA 01887
Phone: 978 253-6200
Web: www.ontoinnovation.com

PRODUCTS/OPERATIONS

2017 Sales

	$ mil.	% of total
Products		
Automated systems	151.4	59
Integrated System	42.2	16
Material characterization systems	21.3	17
Service	43.7	17
Total	**258.6**	**100**

COMPETITORS

APPLIED MATERIALS INC.
DANAHER CORPORATION
ELECTRO SCIENTIFIC INDUSTRIES INC.
ENTEGRIS INC.
FARO TECHNOLOGIES INC.
FORMFACTOR INC.
GEOSPACE TECHNOLOGIES CORPORATION
KLA CORPORATION
MKS INSTRUMENTS INC.
MOCON INC.
OCLARO INC.
OXFORD INSTRUMENTS PLC
TRIMBLE INC.
VEECO INSTRUMENTS INC.

HISTORICAL FINANCIALS
Company Type: Public

Income Statement
FYE: December 26

	REVENUE ($ mil.)	NET INCOME ($ mil.)	NET PROFIT MARGIN	EMPLOYEES
12/20	556.5	31.0	5.6%	1,247
12/19	305.9	1.9	0.6%	1,340
12/18	324.5	57.6	17.8%	701
12/17	258.6	30.2	11.7%	592
12/16	221.1	44.0	19.9%	532
Annual Growth	26.0%	(8.4%)	—	23.7%

2020 Year-End Financials

Debt ratio: —
Return on equity: 2.4%
Cash ($ mil.): 373.7
Current ratio: 6.09
Long-term debt ($ mil.): —

No. of shares (mil.): 48.7
Dividends
Yield: —
Payout: —
Market value ($ mil.): 2,341.0

	STOCK PRICE ($) FY Close	P/E High/Low		PER SHARE ($) Earnings	Dividends	Book Value
12/20	48.02	76	33	0.63	0.00	25.94
12/19	36.54	613442		0.06	0.00	25.19
12/18	27.65	19	10	2.34	0.00	12.84
12/17	24.92	27	20	1.17	0.00	10.65
12/16	25.06	14	7	1.75	0.00	9.72
Annual Growth	17.7%	—	—	(22.5%)	—	27.8%

OP Bancorp

Auditors: Crowe LLP

LOCATIONS

HQ: OP Bancorp
1000 Wilshire Blvd., Suite 500, Los Angeles, CA 90017
Phone: 213 892-9999
Web: www.myopenbank.com

HISTORICAL FINANCIALS
Company Type: Public

Income Statement
FYE: December 31

	ASSETS ($ mil.)	NET INCOME ($ mil.)	INCOME AS % OF ASSETS	EMPLOYEES
12/20	1,366.8	13.1	1.0%	173
12/19	1,179.5	16.7	1.4%	138
12/18	1,044.1	14.2	1.4%	154
12/17	901.0	9.2	1.0%	129
12/16	761.2	7.4	1.0%	0
Annual Growth	15.8%	15.3%	—	—

2020 Year-End Financials

Return on assets: 1.0%
Return on equity: 9.2%
Long-term debt ($ mil.): —
No. of shares (mil.): 15.0
Sales ($ mil) 64.4

Dividends
Yield: 3.6%
Payout: 32.5%
Market value ($ mil.): 116.0

	STOCK PRICE ($) FY Close	P/E High/Low		PER SHARE ($) Earnings	Dividends	Book Value
12/20	7.70	12	7	0.85	0.28	9.55
12/19	10.37	11	8	1.03	0.20	8.95
12/18	8.87	15	9	0.89	0.00	8.18
12/17	9.80	15	10	0.66	0.00	6.94
12/16	7.70	14	10	0.53	0.00	6.30
Annual Growth	(0.0%)	—	—	12.5%	—	10.9%

Oppenheimer Holdings Inc

Oppenheimer Holdings is a leading middle-market investment bank and full service broker-dealer. Through its subsidiaries Oppenheimer & Co. Oppenheimer Asset Management and Oppenheimer Trust it provides a range of financial services including brokerage investment banking asset management lending and research. The company's Private Client segment which offers service brokerage wealth planning and margin lending to affluent and business clients in the Americas makes up the bulk of sales. It held client assets under administration of approximately $104.8 billion. Oppenheimer employs more than 125 investment banking professionals in the US the UK Germany and Israel. The Americas accounts for about 95% of the company's revenues.

Operations

Oppenheimer operates three main business segments. Its Private Client segment which brought in about 55% of its total revenue has more than 1000 financial advisors at more than 90 offices throughout the US. The segment which held some $104.8 billion in client assets under administration.

Oppenheimer's Capital Markets segment (approximately 35% of revenue) includes investment banking institutional equities sales trading research taxable fixed income sales public finance and municipal trading. The Asset Management segment (nearly 10% of revenue) responsible for the company advisory programs and alternative investment business. It has approximately $38.8 billion of client assets under management in fee-based programs.

Broadly speaking the company generates nearly 40% of its revenue from advisory fees while commissions investment banking bank deposit sweep income and interest income made up about 35% about 20% nearly 5% and about 5% of revenue respectively and principal transaction and others for the remainder.

Geographic Reach

The New York-based the company generates about 95% of its revenue from customers in the Americas while the rest came from Europe/Middle East (about 5%) and Asia. Oppenheimer has satellite US offices in Troy Michigan; and Edison New Jersey. Its international offices are in London England St. Helier Isle of Jersey Geneva Switzerland Frankfurt Germany Tel Aviv Israel and Hong Kong China.

Sales and Marketing

Oppenheimer serves high-net-worth individuals and families corporate executives and public and private businesses operating in a variety of sectors including: consumer and retail energy financial institutions healthcare rental services technology and transportation and logistics.

Financial Performance

Oppenheimer's revenue from 2016 to 2020 saw a trend of yearly progression with $857.8 million in 2016 to $1.2 billion in 2020.

In 2020 the company revenue amounted approximately to $1.2 billion with the bulk coming from Commissions Advisor fees and Investment banking.

Net income for the year was $123 million an increase of 132% compared to the net income from 2019. The increase was mostly due to higher revenue generated for this year.

Oppenheimer's cash and cash equivalents decreased 55% to $35.4 million. Financing activities provided $13.9 million while operating and investing activities used $54.1 million and $3.9 million respectively. Main cash uses were for payables to brokers and dealers and purchases of furniture and leasehold improvements.

Strategy

Oppenheimer takes a pragmatic approach to human capital strategy and continuously makes investments in its people processes and technology. This approach allows the company to adapt quickly to evolving business needs and maintain a competitive position with the ability to readily implement change and employ best practices to meet or exceed industry standards. Its methods have proven to motivate and empower its employees to cultivate an entrepreneurial mindset while fostering a culture of compliance.

The company continuously invests in and improves its technology platform to support client service and to remain competitive while continuously managing expenses. The company's long-term growth plan is to continue to expand existing offices by hiring experienced professionals as well as expand through the purchase of operating branch offices from other broker-dealers or the opening of new branch offices in attractive locations and to continue to grow and develop the existing trading investment banking investment advisory and other divisions.

EXECUTIVES

Chb-Ceo, Albert G Lowenthal
Cfo, Jeffrey J Alfano
Employee, Aaron Golub
Executive Director, Albert Murad
Director, Alexandra Heller
Director, Allison Taylor
Sales Assistant, Angela Catalano
Client Associate, Anthony Conte
Vice President, Bernard Reis
Director Investments, Bill Pomeroy
Investment Director, Brian Kutsmeda
Auditors: DELOITTE & TOUCHE LLP

LOCATIONS

HQ: Oppenheimer Holdings Inc
85 Broad Street, New York, NY 10004
Phone: 212 668-8000
Web: www.oppenheimer.com

HOOVER'S HANDBOOK OF EMERGING COMPANIES 2022

PRODUCTS/OPERATIONS

2014 Sales

	$ mil.	% of total
Commissions	469.8	47
Advisory fees	281.7	28
Investment banking	125.6	12
Interest	49.2	5
Principal transactions net	29.7	3
Other	48.4	5
Total	**1,004.5**	**100**

2014 Sales by Segment

	$ mil.	% of total
Private Client	582.4	58
Capital Markets	298.6	30
Asset Management	100.0	10
Commercial Mortgage banking	23.3	2
Others	0.2	-
Total	**1,004.5**	**100**

COMPETITORS

AFFILIATED MANAGERS GROUP INC.
BGC PARTNERS INC.
BRC MERGER SUB LLC
Bank of Communications Co. Ltd.
COMMERCE BANCSHARES COMPANIES INC.
Canaccord Genuity Group Inc
FRANKLIN RESOURCES INC.
JEFFERIES FINANCIAL GROUP INC.
NATIONAL AUSTRALIA BANK LIMITED
OPPENHEIMERFUNDS INC.
STIFEL FINANCIAL CORP.
THE CHARLES SCHWAB CORPORATION
THE ZIEGLER INC
VIRTU FINANCIAL INC.
WESTWOOD HOLDINGS GROUP INC.

HISTORICAL FINANCIALS

Company Type: Public

Income Statement				FYE: December 31
	REVENUE ($ mil.)	NET INCOME ($ mil.)	NET PROFIT MARGIN	EMPLOYEES
12/20	1,198.6	122.9	10.3%	2,908
12/19	1,033.3	52.9	5.1%	2,971
12/18	958.1	28.8	3.0%	2,976
12/17	920.3	22.8	2.5%	2,992
12/16	857.7	(1.1)	—	3,098
Annual Growth	**8.7%**	**—**		**(1.6%)**

2020 Year-End Financials

Debt ratio: 7.5%
Return on equity: 19.1%
Cash ($ mil.): 35.4
Current ratio: 1.25
Long-term debt ($ mil.): 123.8
No. of shares (mil.): 12.4
Dividends
  Yield: 4.7%
  Payout: 29.9%
Market value ($ mil.): 392.0

	STOCK PRICE ($) FY Close	P/E High/Low		Earnings	PER SHARE ($) Dividends	Book Value
12/20	31.43	3	2	9.30	1.48	54.93
12/19	27.48	8	6	3.82	0.46	46.31
12/18	25.55	16	11	2.05	0.44	41.81
12/17	26.80	17	9	1.67	0.44	39.55
12/16	18.60	—	—	(0.09)	0.44	38.22
Annual Growth	**14.0%**	—	—	**—**	**35.4%**	**9.5%**

Orange County Bancorp Inc

Auditors: Crowe LLP

LOCATIONS

HQ: Orange County Bancorp Inc
212 Dolson Ave, Middletown, NY 10940
Phone: 845 341-5000
Web: www.orangebanktrust.com

HISTORICAL FINANCIALS

Company Type: Public

Income Statement				FYE: December 31
	ASSETS ($ mil.)	NET INCOME ($ mil.)	INCOME AS % OF ASSETS	EMPLOYEES
12/20	1,664.9	11.6	0.7%	0
12/19	1,228.4	11.1	0.9%	0
12/18	1,064.8	7.5	0.7%	0
12/17	960.7	2.3	0.2%	150
12/16	909.7	3.6	0.4%	0
Annual Growth	**16.3%**	**33.9%**		

2020 Year-End Financials

Return on assets: 0.8%
Return on equity: 9.0%
Long-term debt ($ mil.): —
No. of shares (mil.): 4.4
Sales ($ mil): 64.8
Dividends
  Yield: 2.9%
  Payout: 32.1%
Market value ($ mil.): 122.0

	STOCK PRICE ($) FY Close	P/E High/Low		Earnings	PER SHARE ($) Dividends	Book Value
12/20	27.25	12	8	2.59	0.80	30.21
12/19	29.40	12	11	2.47	0.80	26.85
12/18	27.00	30	13	1.87	0.80	24.11
12/17	56.05	93	77	0.60	0.82	23.32
12/16	46.52	52	49	0.93	0.82	23.61
Annual Growth	**(12.5%)**	—	—	**29.2%**	**(0.6%)**	**6.4%**

Origin Bancorp Inc

Auditors: BKD, LLP

LOCATIONS

HQ: Origin Bancorp Inc
500 South Service Road East, Ruston, LA 71270
Phone: 318 255-2222
Web: www.origin.bank

HISTORICAL FINANCIALS

Company Type: Public

Income Statement				FYE: December 31
	ASSETS ($ mil.)	NET INCOME ($ mil.)	INCOME AS % OF ASSETS	EMPLOYEES
12/20	7,628.2	36.3	0.5%	749
12/19	5,324.6	53.8	1.0%	751
12/18	4,821.5	51.6	1.1%	761
12/17	4,154.0	14.6	0.4%	686
12/16	4,071.4	12.8	0.3%	0
Annual Growth	**17.0%**	**29.7%**	**—**	**—**

2020 Year-End Financials

Return on assets: 0.5%
Return on equity: 5.8%
Long-term debt ($ mil.): —
No. of shares (mil.): 23.5
Sales ($ mil): 293.3
Dividends
  Yield: 1.3%
  Payout: 27.9%
Market value ($ mil.): 653.0

	STOCK PRICE ($) FY Close	P/E High/Low		Earnings	PER SHARE ($) Dividends	Book Value
12/20	27.77	24	11	1.55	0.38	27.53
12/19	37.84	17	14	2.28	0.28	25.52
12/18	34.08	19	15	2.20	0.10	23.17
Annual Growth	**(9.7%)**	—	—	**(16.1%)**	**96.8%**	**9.0%**

Orion Energy Systems Inc

Orion Energy Systems wants customers to see the light ... high intensity fluorescent (HIF) lighting systems that is. Orion designs manufactures and installs energy management systems that include HIF lighting and intelligent lighting controls. Its Apollo Light Pipe product collects and focuses daylight without consuming electricity. The firm estimates its HIF lineup can help cut customers' lighting-related electricity costs by up to 50% boost quantity and quality of light and reduce related carbon-dioxide emissions. In addition its engineered systems division makes solar photovoltaic products that allow customers to convert sunlight into electricity.

Operations

Orion divides its operations across several segments. Energy management (almost 75% of total sales) supplies its HIF lighting systems while the engineered systems division makes solar and wind alternative renewable energy systems (primarily solar photovoltaic systems). In mid-2014 the company restructured its business and added a new division — US markets — which includes the US operations of its Orion engineered systems and Orion distribution services.

Geographic Reach

Operating majorly in North America the company has its manufacturing unit and a technology center located in Manitowoc Wisconsin and office properties in Green Cove Springs Florida; and Jacksonville Florida.

Sales and Marketing

The company sells its products and services indirectly to customers through electrical contractors or distributors. Orion also sells its products on a wholesale basis to electrical contractors and value-added resellers. (About 60% of its total lighting revenue comes from its reseller network.) As such its sales strategy involves building upon these customer relationships with these electrical contractors and value-added resellers to widen the geographic scope of its sales reach.

Financial Performance

In fiscal 2014 Orion's revenues climbed by 3% to $89 million. The growth was due to an increase in service revenues fueled by high installations from a previous acquisition and a single landfill solar project installed during the year.

Orion has posted two straight years of net losses mostly due to a bump in expenses related to acquisitions. In 2014 the company's operating cash flow increased to $10 million due to an increase in accounts receivable attributed to decreased inventories and increased cash collections.

Strategy

Orion largely targets commercial and industrial customers who are kept awake at night trying to choose the right technology to reduce their business expenses. These customers call Orion for an energy "retrofit" or replacement of high-intensity discharge products with the company's HIF lighting system. The company is specifically targeting utilities and electrical grid operators for this type of need. It has been growing its LED offerings to customers to capitalize on the fast-growing LED trend in the lighting manufacturing industry. While still predominantly a HIF and solar lighting company Orion has joined Cree Revolution Lighting and several other lighting manufacturers offering LED lighting and systems to customers.

Orion capitalizes on its customers' existing electrical contractor to deliver installation and monitoring services as well as sells its products wholesale to electrical contractors and resellers. Wholesale channels are a promising route to market and have grown to about 60% of the company's revenue.

Mergers and Acquisitions

Expanding its product portfolio in 2013 Orion acquired Florida-based Harris Manufacturing Inc. and Harris LED LLC. for $10 million. Harris engineers designs sources and makes energy-efficient lighting systems including fluorescent and LED lighting and day-lighting products.

EXECUTIVES

Independent Director, Mark Williamson
Chairman Of The Board, Chief Executive Officer, Michael Altschaefl, $402,500 total compensation
Executive Vice President, President Of Orion Services Group, Scott Green, $333,250 total compensation
Lead Independent Director, Anthony Otten
Chief Operating Officer, Executive Vice President, Michael Jenkins
Independent Director, Ellen Richstone
Chief Financial Officer, Executive Vice President, Chief Accounting Officer, Treasurer, J. Per Brodin, $159,316 total compensation
Auditors: BDO USA, LLP

LOCATIONS

HQ: Orion Energy Systems Inc
2210 Woodland Drive, Manitowoc, WI 54220
Phone: 920 892-9340
Web: www.orionlighting.com

PRODUCTS/OPERATIONS

2014 Sales

	$ mil.	% of total
Energy management	66.8	75
Engineered systems	21.8	22
Total	**88.6**	**100**

Selected Products

Apollo Solar Light Pipe (lens-based device that collects & focuses renewable daylight)
Compact Modular product line (high intensity fluorescent (HIF) lighting systems)
Agribusiness fixtures
LED freezer applications
Outdoor application fixtures
Parking lot fixtures
Private label resale
Roadway fixtures
InteLite Wireless Controls (remote control of fixtures via web-based software)
Renewable Energy Projects (test solar photovoltaic electricity generating projects)

COMPETITORS

ADB SAFEGATE AMERICAS LLC
AMERICAN SUPERCONDUCTOR CORPORATION
COOPER LIGHTING LLC
Carmanah Technologies Corporation
DEXTRA LIGHTING LIMITED
GENERAC HOLDINGS INC.
LIME ENERGY CO.
LSI INDUSTRIES INC.
PELICAN PRODUCTS INC.
SOLAREDGE TECHNOLOGIES INC.
STREAMLIGHT INC.
Signify Netherlands B.V.
XENONICS HOLDINGS INC.

HISTORICAL FINANCIALS

Company Type: Public

Income Statement				FYE: March 31
	REVENUE ($ mil.)	NET INCOME ($ mil.)	NET PROFIT MARGIN	EMPLOYEES
03/21	116.8	26.1	22.4%	213
03/20	150.8	12.4	8.3%	181
03/19	65.7	(6.6)	—	321
03/18	60.3	(13.1)	—	214
03/17	70.2	(12.2)	—	264
Annual Growth	13.6%	—		(5.2%)

2021 Year-End Financials

Debt ratio: 0.0%
Return on equity: 58.6%
Cash ($ mil.): 19.3
Current ratio: 1.86
Long-term debt ($ mil.): 0.0

No. of shares (mil.): 30.8
Dividends
  Yield: —
  Payout: —
Market value ($ mil.): 214.0

	STOCK PRICE ($) FY Close	P/E High/Low		PER SHARE ($) Earnings	Dividends	Book Value
03/21	6.96	14	4	0.83	0.00	1.89
03/20	3.70	15	2	0.40	0.00	1.03
03/19	0.89	—	—	(0.23)	0.00	0.61
03/18	0.85	—	—	(0.46)	0.00	0.81
03/17	1.98	—	—	(0.44)	0.00	1.25
Annual Growth	36.9%	—	—	—	—	10.8%

Orrstown Financial Services, Inc.

Orrstown Financial Services keeps both paddles in the money pool. The institution is the holding company for Orrstown Bank which operates some 20 branches in Pennsylvania's Cumberland Perry and Franklin counties as well as in Maryland's Washington County. In addition to traditional retail deposit offerings Orrstown also provides investment management services including retirement planning and investment analysis. Real estate mortgages account for about 40% of the bank's lending portfolio followed by commercial construction and consumer loans. Orrstown is growing its mortgage lending capabilities. It launched an online application system in order to increase mortgage origination sales.

EXECUTIVES

Independent Chairman Of The Board, Joel Zullinger
Independent Director, Glenn Snoke
Independent Director, Andrea Pugh
Executive Vice President And Chief Trust Officer, Philip Fague, $242,857 total compensation
Chief Human Resource Officer, Executive Vice President, Barbara Brobst, $154,274 total compensation
Executive Vice President And Market President, Jeffrey Gayman, $180,281 total compensation
Independent Director, Mark Keller
Executive Vice President And Chief Revenue Officer, Adam Metz, $275,940 total compensation
Executive Vice President, Chief Risk Officer, Company Secretary, Robert Coradi, $255,003 total compensation
Executive Vice President, Market President, Maryland Region, Christopher Holt, $325,000 total compensation
Executive Vice President, Market President, Eastern Region, David Hornberger
Senior Vice President, Executive Vice President And Chief Retail Officer, Marketing And Corporate Communications, Luke Bernstein
Independent Director, Michael Rice
Chief Operating Officer And Logistics Officer, Executive Vice President And Market President, Robert Fignar
Executive Vice President, Market President, Central Region, Zachary Khuri
Chief Financial Officer, Executive Vice President, Neelesh Kalani
Chief Accounting Officer, Sean Mulcahy
President, Chief Executive Officer, Director, Thomas Quinn, $534,959 total compensation
Independent Director, Eric Segal
Independent Director, Cindy Joiner
Independent Director, Thomas Longenecker
Auditors: Crowe LLP

LOCATIONS

HQ: Orrstown Financial Services, Inc.
77 East King Street, P.O. Box 250, Shippensburg, PA 17257
Phone: 717 532-6114
Web: www.orrstown.com

COMPETITORS

BANKUNITED INC.
EMCLAIRE FINANCIAL CORP.
FIRST BUSEY CORPORATION
LIBERTY BANCORP INC.
OCEANFIRST FINANCIAL CORP.

HISTORICAL FINANCIALS

Company Type: Public

Income Statement
FYE: December 31

	ASSETS ($ mil.)	NET INCOME ($ mil.)	INCOME AS % OF ASSETS	EMPLOYEES
12/20	2,750.5	26.4	1.0%	418
12/19	2,383.2	16.9	0.7%	460
12/18	1,934.3	12.8	0.7%	386
12/17	1,558.8	8.0	0.5%	338
12/16	1,414.5	6.6	0.5%	327
Annual Growth	18.1%	41.4%	—	6.3%

2020 Year-End Financials

Return on assets: 1.0%
Return on equity: 11.2%
Long-term debt ($ mil.): —
No. of shares (mil.): 11.2
Sales ($ mil): 127.9

Dividends
  Yield: 4.1%
  Payout: 36.3%
Market value ($ mil.): 185.0

	STOCK PRICE ($) FY Close	P/E High/Low		PER SHARE ($) Earnings	Dividends	Book Value
12/20	16.55	9	5	2.40	0.68	21.98
12/19	22.62	14	11	1.61	0.60	19.93
12/18	18.21	18	12	1.50	0.51	18.39
12/17	25.25	27	20	0.98	0.42	17.34
12/16	22.40	29	20	0.81	0.35	16.28
Annual Growth	(7.3%)	—	—	31.2%	18.1%	7.8%

OTC Markets Group Inc

EXECUTIVES

Director, Louisa Schneider
Chief Financial Officer, Beatrice Ordonez, $305,000 total compensation
Executive Vice President, Issuer And Information Services, Lisabeth Heese, $290,000 total compensation
President, Chief Executive Officer, And Director, R. Cromwell Coulson, $564,940 total compensation
Executive Vice President, Corporate Services, Director, Otc Markets Group International Ltd, Jason Paltrowitz, $335,000 total compensation
Executive Vice President, Market Data, Matthew Fuchs, $292,000 total compensation
Chief Technology Officer, Bruce Ostrover, $260,000 total compensation
General Counsel And Chief Of Staff, Daniel Zinn, $305,000 total compensation
Director, Andrew Wimpfheimer
Chief Marketing Officer, Kristie Harkins
Director, Gary Baddeley
Chief Financial Officer, Antonia Georgieva
President, Otc Link Llc, Michael Modeski, $446,000 total compensation
Chairman, Neal Wolkoff
Auditors: DELOITTE & TOUCHE LLP

LOCATIONS

HQ: OTC Markets Group Inc
  300 Vesey Street, 12th Floor, New York, NY 10282
Phone: 212 896-4400   **Fax:** 212 868-3848
Web: www.otcmarkets.com

HISTORICAL FINANCIALS

Company Type: Public

Income Statement
FYE: December 31

	REVENUE ($ mil.)	NET INCOME ($ mil.)	NET PROFIT MARGIN	EMPLOYEES
12/20	71.2	18.2	25.7%	102
12/19	62.8	14.9	23.8%	99
12/18	59.2	16.2	27.4%	93
12/17	54.6	12.5	23.0%	90
12/16	50.8	10.5	20.7%	88
Annual Growth	8.8%	14.8%	—	3.8%

2020 Year-End Financials

Debt ratio: —
Return on equity: 97.9%
Cash ($ mil.): 33.7
Current ratio: 1.40
Long-term debt ($ mil.): —

No. of shares (mil.): 11.7
Dividends
  Yield: 3.6%
  Payout: 91.2%
Market value ($ mil.): 398.0

	STOCK PRICE ($) FY Close	P/E High/Low		PER SHARE ($) Earnings	Dividends	Book Value
12/20	34.00	23	15	1.53	1.25	1.67
12/19	35.00	31	23	1.25	1.25	1.52
12/18	29.04	23	17	1.36	1.23	1.42
12/17	29.05	29	17	1.06	1.16	1.21
12/16	23.00	25	16	0.90	1.16	1.36
Annual Growth	10.3%	—	—	14.2%	1.9%	5.2%

Otter Tail Corp.

Like the broad end of its furry namesake Otter Tail covers a swath of businesses from electric services and construction to manufacturing equipment and plastics. The electric utility (Otter Tail Power Corporation; OTP) is the company's core business; it keeps the lights on for some 130000 customers in Minnesota and the Dakotas. The company also makes PVC pipes (Northern Pipe Products and Vinyltech Corporation) and manufactures parts and trays (BTD Manufacturing and T.O. Plastics).

Operations

The Otter Tail's businesses are divided into three major segments: Electric Manufacturing and Plastics. Electric accounted for some 50% of the company's revenues; Manufacturing accounts for around 30% and Plastics for approximately 20%.

The Electric segment includes the production transmission distribution and sale of electric energy in Minnesota North Dakota and South Dakota by OTP. In addition OTP is a participant in the Midcontinent Independent System Operator Inc. (MISO) markets.

Manufacturing segment consists of businesses in the following manufacturing activities: contract machining metal parts stamping fabrication and painting and production of plastic thermoformed horticultural containers life science and industrial packaging and material handling components.

The Plastics segment consists of businesses producing polyvinyl chloride (PVC) pipe at plants in North Dakota and Arizona.

Geographic Reach

Headquartered in Minnesota Otter Tail has manufacturing facilities in Georgia Illinois and Min-

nesota. The OTP owns more than 25 wind turbines at the Langdon North Dakota Wind Energy Center; over 30 wind turbines in Barnes County North Dakota; and nearly 35 wind turbines in Counties North Dakota. The Minnesota has the largest retail electric revenue with over 50%.

Sales and Marketing

The OTP provides electricity to more than 130000 customers. The principal method for distribution of the manufacturing companies' products is by direct shipment to the customer by common carrier ground transportation. The manufacturing segment's top two customers combined accounted for some 35% and the top five customers combined accounted for some 55% of sales.

PVC pipe products are marketed through a combination of independent sales representatives company salespersons and customer service representatives to serve wholesalers and distributors. Its top two customers combined accounted for some 45% of sales.

Financial Performance

For the past five years the company revenue growth was on increasing trend. Net income was pretty much the same in terms of growth.

Otter Tail's revenue increased by $3.1 million to $919.5 million in 2019 as the Electric and Manufacturing segments have 2% and 3% increase in sales respectively offset by 7% decrease in revenue by the Plastic segment.

Net income rose 5% to $86.9 million in 2019 due to $4.6 million increase in Electric segment $0.1 million increase in Manufacturing segment and $3.2 million decrease in Plastics segment net income resulted from reduced sales and lower margins.

Cash at the end of fiscal 2019 was $21.2 million. Net cash provided by operating activities was $185 million and financing activities added another $44.8 million. Investing activities used $209.5 million for capital expenditures and investments.

Strategy

The main strategy of the company is to continue to grow its largest business the regulated electric utility which will lower the company overall risk create a more predictable earnings stream improve its credit quality and preserve its ability to fund the dividend. Over time Otter tail expects the electric utility business will provide approximately 75% to 85% of its overall earnings.

As part of the company business strategy it intends to increase capital expenditures in its existing businesses and to continually assess its mix of businesses and potential strategic acquisitions or dispositions. It has a substantial capital investment program planned for the next five years including investments in renewables a natural gas-fired plant transmission assets and potential technology and infrastructure projects.

Major growth strategies and initiatives in the future include planned capital budget expenditures of approximately $984 million for the years 2020 through 2024 of which $897 million is for capital projects at Otter Tail Power Company (OTP).

Company Background

Otter Tail was founded in 1907.

EXECUTIVES

Chief Financial Officer And Senior Vice President, Kevin Moug, $471,000 total compensation

President, Chief Executive Officer, And Director, Charles Macfarlane, $679,688 total compensation
Independent Chairman Of The Board, Nathan Partain
Independent Director, Karen Bohn
Vice President, General Counsel, And Corporate Secretary, Jennifer Smestad, $360,000 total compensation
Independent Director, Kathryn Johnson
Senior Vice President, Electric Platform And President, Otter Tail Power, Timothy Rogelstad, $378,263 total compensation
Senior Vice President, Manufacturing Platform And President, Varistar, John Abbott, $370,674 total compensation
Independent Director, Thomas Webb
Director, Michael Lebeau
Independent Director, James Stake
Independent Director, Steven Fritze
Auditors: DELOITTE & TOUCHE LLP

LOCATIONS

HQ: Otter Tail Corp.
   215 South Cascade Street, P.O. Box 496, Fergus Falls, MN 56538-0496
Phone: 866 410-8780
Web: www.ottertail.com

COMPETITORS

AVISTA CORPORATION	PEPCO HOLDINGS LLC
GREAT PLAINS ENERGY INCORPORATED	SOUTH JERSEY INDUSTRIES INC.
KENNAMETAL INC.	THE EMPIRE DISTRICT ELECTRIC COMPANY
NORTHWESTERN CORPORATION	TIMKENSTEEL CORPORATION
NOVELIS ALR ALUMINUM HOLDINGS CORPORATION	TUCSON ELECTRIC POWER
PATTERN ENERGY GROUP INC.	COMPANY VISTRA CORP.

HISTORICAL FINANCIALS

Company Type: Public

Income Statement				FYE: December 31
	REVENUE ($ mil.)	NET INCOME ($ mil.)	NET PROFIT MARGIN	EMPLOYEES
12/21	1,196.8	176.7	14.8%	2,487
12/20	890.1	95.8	10.8%	2,074
12/19	919.5	86.8	9.4%	2,208
12/18	916.4	82.3	9.0%	2,321
12/17	849.3	72.4	8.5%	2,097
Annual Growth	9.0%	25.0%	—	4.4%

2021 Year-End Financials

Debt ratio: 31.0%	No. of shares (mil.): 41.5
Return on equity: 18.9%	Dividends
Cash ($ mil.): 1.5	Yield: 2.1%
Current ratio: 0.95	Payout: 45.2%
Long-term debt ($ mil.): 734.0	Market value ($ mil.): 2,968.0

	STOCK PRICE ($) FY Close	P/E High/Low		PER SHARE ($) Earnings	Dividends	Book Value
12/21	71.42	17	9	4.23	1.56	23.84
12/20	42.61	24	14	2.34	1.48	21.00
12/19	51.29	26	21	2.17	1.40	19.46
12/18	49.64	25	19	2.06	1.34	18.38
12/17	44.45	26	20	1.82	1.28	17.62
Annual Growth	12.6%	—	—	23.5%	5.1%	7.9%

Overstock.com Inc (DE)

Overstock.com allows you to shop an online bazaar of clothes housewares music books and more. It is an online retailer and advancer of blockchain technology. Through its online retail business it offer a broad range of price-competitive products including furniture home decor bedding and bath and housewares among other products. It offered millions of which majority were n-line products (products in active production). Entirely separate from Overstock's retail business Medici Ventures and its main subsid tZERO work to develop blockchain technologies. Started in 1999 Dr. Patrick M. Byrne acquired the company Discounts Direct and rebranded it as Overstock.com.

Operations

Overstock operates in four reportable segments ? Retail which generates nearly of company's revenue. Retail includes furniture home d ©cor including rugs bedding and bath home improvement and kitchen items. All its retail sales are through its websites were from transaction in which the company fulfilled orders through its network of approximately 3000 partners selling on its website.

Other segments have included tZERO MVI and Other. tZERO segment primarily consists of amounts earned through securities transaction through its broker-dealers and costs incurred to execute its tZERO business initiatives excluding intercompany transactions eliminated in consolidation. MVI segment primarily consists of costs incurred to create or foster a set of products and solutions that leverage blockchain technology to generate efficiencies and increase security and control through its Medici Ventures initiatives excluding intercompany transactions eliminated in consolidation. Other consists of unallocated corporate support costs Bitt and Medici Land Governance.

Geographic Reach

Based in Salt Lake City Utah Overstock.com has over 1320 facilities mostly in US used for corporate office space data centers warehouse fulfillment and customer service space.

Sales and Marketing

Overstock targets the Millennial consumer a demographic comfortable purchasing online and who are now at family-starting age. The company uses a variety of methods to target its retail consumer audience including online campaigns such as advertising through keywords product listing ads display ads search engines affiliate marketing social coupon websites portals banners email direct mail viral and social media. It also advertises on TV video on demand radio print and event sponsorship.

Overstock's advertising expense totaled $245.3 million and $124.3 million during the years ended 2020 and 2019 respectively.

Financial Performance

Revenue has been fluctuating for Overstock.com in the last five years. Still it has an overall growth of 42% between 2016 and 2020.

The company's net revenue totaled $2.5 billion in 2020 a 75% increase compared to the previous year. Both segments of the company had higher sales volume for the year.

Net income attributable to the company totaled $56 million a 146% improvement compared to the previous year's net loss of $121.8 million.

The company's cash for the year ended 2020 was $519.2 million. Operating activities generated $196.5 million while investing activities used $23.6 million mainly for capital expenditures. Financing activities provided another $231.4 million.

Strategy

Retail business initiatives enable its long-term focus on its three brand pillars - Product Findability Smart Value and Easy Delivery and Support. Overstock is focusing on ensuring its mobile experience is fast frictionless and meets the unique needs of the mobile shopping journey. It's also improving its ability to address site assortment and pricing issues more quickly by enhancing its real-time visibility into site category and marketing channel performance. In addition Overstock is accelerating the "Overstock Sponsored Product" program a platform for its drop ship partners to promote their products to shoppers through a cost-per-click auction platform.

Medici Ventures' strategy is to create or foster a set of products and solutions that leverage blockchain technology to generate efficiencies and increase security and control in six areas: identity management property rights and management central banking and currencies capital markets supply chains and commerce and voting systems.

Company Background

EXECUTIVES

Chief Technology Officer, Joel Weight, $300,981 total compensation
Chief Merchandising And Operations Officer, Ronald Hilton
Chief Administrative Officer, Acting Chief Marketing Officer, Carter Lee, $322,116 total compensation
Chief Customer Officer, Krista Mathews
Independent Director, William Nettles, $37,500 total compensation
Independent Director, Barbara Messing, $18,750 total compensation
Chief Legal Officer, E. Glen Nickle
Chief Financial Officer, Adrianne Lee, $304,616 total compensation
Ceo And Director, Jonathan Johnson, $629,808 total compensation
Chairman, Allison Abraham, $150,000 total compensation
Chief People Officer, Meghan Tuohig
President, David Nielsen, $449,039 total compensation
Chief Product Officer, Mark Baker
Auditors: KPMG LLP

LOCATIONS

HQ: Overstock.com Inc (DE)
   799 West Coliseum Way, Midvale, UT 84047
Phone: 801 947-3100
Web: www.overstock.com

PRODUCTS/OPERATIONS

Selected Product Categories
Bed & Bath
Dé;cor
Furniture
Home Improvement
Jewelry
Kids & Baby
Kitchen
Men
Outdoor
Rugs
Watches
Women

COMPETITORS

CHANNELADVISOR CORPORATION
EMERALD HOLDING INC.
FLEETCOR TECHNOLOGIES INC.
GLOBAL INDUSTRIAL COMPANY
GRUBHUB INC.
LIMELIGHT NETWORKS INC.
LIQUIDITY SERVICES INC.
PCM INC.
QVC INC.
TRUECAR INC.
WAYFAIR INC.
ZULILY INC.
Zalando SE

HISTORICAL FINANCIALS
Company Type: Public

Income Statement — FYE: December 31

	REVENUE ($ mil.)	NET INCOME ($ mil.)	NET PROFIT MARGIN	EMPLOYEES
12/20	2,549.7	56.0	2.2%	1,750
12/19	1,459.4	(121.8)	—	1,613
12/18	1,821.5	(206.0)	—	2,060
12/17	1,744.7	(109.8)	—	1,800
12/16	1,799.9	12.5	0.7%	1,800
Annual Growth	9.1%	45.4%	—	(0.7%)

2020 Year-End Financials

Debt ratio: 4.9%
Return on equity: 22.8%
Cash ($ mil.): 519.1
Current ratio: 1.78
Long-term debt ($ mil.): 41.3
No. of shares (mil.): 42.7
Dividends
  Yield: —
  Payout: —
Market value ($ mil.): 2,052.0

	STOCK PRICE ($) FY Close	P/E High/Low		Earnings	PER SHARE ($) Dividends	Book Value
12/20	47.97	98	2	1.24	0.00	8.74
12/19	7.05	—	—	(3.46)	0.00	2.92
12/18	13.58	—	—	(6.83)	0.00	4.10
12/17	63.90	—	—	(4.28)	0.00	6.39
12/16	17.50	39	21	0.49	0.00	6.89
Annual Growth	28.7%		—	— 26.1%		6.1%

Pacific Premier Bancorp Inc

EXECUTIVES

Pres-Ceo, Steven R Gardner
Chb*, Jeff C Jones
Sr V Pres-Cfo*, Kent Smith
Sr Exec Vpres-Cfo*, Ronald J Nicolas Jr
Cro*, Michael Karr
Evp-Cco*, Donn Jakosky
Evp-Chief Acctg Officer*, Lori Wright
Senior Vice President Director, Thomas Galindo
Desk Manager, Robert Prater
Vp Information Technology, Dinorah Roggero
Credit Analyst, Carol Hiegl
Auditors: Crowe LLP

LOCATIONS

HQ: Pacific Premier Bancorp Inc
  17901 Von Karman Avenue, Suite 1200, Irvine, CA 92614
Phone: 949 864-8000
Web: www.ppbi.com

HISTORICAL FINANCIALS
Company Type: Public

Income Statement — FYE: December 31

	ASSETS ($ mil.)	NET INCOME ($ mil.)	INCOME AS % OF ASSETS	EMPLOYEES
12/20	19,736.5	60.3	0.3%	1,478
12/19	11,776.0	159.7	1.4%	1,006
12/18	11,487.3	123.3	1.1%	1,030
12/17	8,024.5	60.1	0.7%	846
12/16	4,036.3	40.1	1.0%	448
Annual Growth	48.7%	10.8%	—	34.8%

2020 Year-End Financials

Return on assets: 0.3%
Return on equity: 2.5%
Long-term debt ($ mil.): —
No. of shares (mil.): 94.4
Sales ($ mil): 702.0
Dividends
  Yield: 3.2%
  Payout: 257.5%
Market value ($ mil.): 2,960.0

	STOCK PRICE ($) FY Close	P/E High/Low		Earnings	PER SHARE ($) Dividends	Book Value
12/20	31.33	44	20	0.75	1.03	29.07
12/19	32.61	13	10	2.60	0.88	33.82
12/18	25.52	20	10	2.26	0.00	31.52
12/17	40.00	26	20	1.56	0.00	26.86
12/16	35.35	24	13	1.46	0.00	16.54
Annual Growth	(3.0%)		—	— (15.3%)		15.1%

Pacira BioSciences Inc

Pacira BioSciences (formerly Pacira Pharmaceuticals) develops pain management products that don't involve opioids. The company develops sustained-release therapies based on DepoFoam an injectable drug delivery technology that allows both immediate and sustained release. Pacira's primary drug EXPAREL is an injectable local anesthetic. The company is conducting development and licensing programs on other DepoFoam candidates as well. Through the acquisition of MyoScience (now Pacira CryoTech) Pacira gained another commercial product the iovera pain management system. The iovera system is a handheld device that delivers precise doses of cold temperature to targeted nerves.

Operations

The company's EXPAREL provides continuous and extended postsurgical analgesia and reduces the consumption of opioid medications. EXPAREL simplifies postsurgical pain management minimizes breakthrough episodes of pain and has the potential to result in improved patient care and outcomes as well as enhanced hospital economics. EXPAREL accounts almost all of its revenue while the remainder comes from other products and royalties. The iovera system is highly complementary to EXPAREL as a non-opioid therapy that delivers cryoanalgesia via a handheld device to alleviate pain by disrupting pain signals being transmitted to the brain from the site of injury or surgery. The system is 510(k) cleared in the US for the blocking of pain pain relief and symptoms associated with osteoarthritis of the knee as well as general surgical use.

DepoFoam platform for acute sub-acute and chronic pain applications has several DepoFoam-based products in preclinical development. It prioritized two programs for clinical development: the intrathecal delivery of a DepoFoam-based analgesic for acute and chronic pain and DepoDexmedetomidine a sedative-analgesic for end-of-life pain and painful conditions in the elderly.

Geographic Reach

Pacira has manufacturing and research facilities in Fremont and San Diego California. It also has administration and commercialization offices in Parsippany New Jersey.

Sales and Marketing

Pacira has marketing and sales organization to commercialize its products. Its primary target markets are healthcare practitioners who influence pain management decisions including anesthesiologists surgeons pharmacists and nurses.

Financial Performance

The company's revenue increased by 25% to $421.0 million compared to $337.3 million in the prior year. EXPAREL revenue grew 23% in 2019 compared to 2018 primarily due to an increase in net product sales of EXPAREL units of 27% and a 3% increase in gross selling price per unit partially offset by the mix of EXPAREL product sizes.

The net loss of the company at the end of 2019 increased by $10.5 million to $11.0 million compared from the prior year with $0.5 million.

Cash held by the company at the end of 2019 decreased by $54.3 million to $78.2 million. Cash provided by operations and financing activities were $70.5 million and $3.7 million respectively. Cash used by investing activities was $128.5 million mainly for purchases of investments.

Strategy

Pacira continues to advance its goal to be a global leader in delivering innovative non-opioid pain management and regenerative health solutions. To achieve this the company is advancing a three-pronged strategy: expanding the use of EXPAREL and iovera° for opioid-sparing pain management; pursuing innovative acquisition targets that align with its strategy; and advancing a pipeline of new clinical candidates.

Pacira is expanding the clinical evidence for EXPAREL through Phase 4 clinical trials across several surgical specialties. The company has published positive results from a Phase 4 multicenter randomized controlled trial or RCT in TKA in the Journal of Arthroplasty. Positive findings from a multicenter RCT in C-section were presented at the most recent annual meeting of the Society for Obstetric Anesthesia and Perinatology (SOAP) and it recently reported positive topline results from a follow-on Phase 4 study in C-section procedures that compared an opioid-free EXPAREL arm to an opioid-based standard of care arm.

Mergers and Acquisitions

In 2019 Pacira acquired Myoscience a medical device company specializing in pain relief in a deal valued at up to $220 million. That deal added MyoScience's FDA-approved iovera pain management system a non-opioid treatment using cold therapy.

Company Background

Once the injectables subsidiary of drug-delivery company SkyePharma PLC Pacira Pharmaceuticals was bought out in 2007 by an investor group led by MPM Capital OrbiMed HBM Bioventures and Sanderling Ventures. Pacira went public in early 2011 through an IPO valued at about $42 million.

In 2019 the company acquired MyoScience and its iovera pain management system. Upon the closing of that transaction Pacira Pharmaceuticals changed its name to Pacira BioSciences.

EXECUTIVES

Chairman Of The Board, Chief Executive Officer, David Stack, $889,935 total compensation
Chief Administrative Officer, Secretary, Kristen Williams, $518,462 total compensation
Chief Financial Officer, Charles Reinhart, $463,692 total compensation
Chief Customer Officer, Dennis McLoughlin, $319,231 total compensation
Chief Technical Officer, Charles Laranjeira
Chief Clinical Officer, Interim Chief Medical Officer, Roy Winston, $408,654 total compensation
Director, Christopher Christie
President, Rest Of World, Max Reinhardt, $555,000 total compensation
Auditors: KPMG LLP

LOCATIONS

HQ: Pacira BioSciences Inc
5401 West Kennedy Boulevard, Suite 890, Tampa, FL 33609
Phone: 813 553-6680
Web: www.pacira.com

PRODUCTS/OPERATIONS

2015 Sales

	$ mil.	% of total
Exparel	239.9	96
DepoCyt	4.6	2
Royalties	3.1	1
Collaborative licensing & development	1.4	1
Total	**249.0**	**100**

COMPETITORS

ACORDA THERAPEUTICS INC.
ADAMAS PHARMACEUTICALS CORPORATION INC.
ARENA PHARMACEUTICALS INC.
BIODELIVERY SCIENCES INTERNATIONAL INC.
DURECT CORPORATION
INTERSECT ENT INC.
SAGE THERAPEUTICS INC.
THORATEC LLC

HISTORICAL FINANCIALS
Company Type: Public

Income Statement
FYE: December 31

	REVENUE ($ mil.)	NET INCOME ($ mil.)	NET PROFIT MARGIN	EMPLOYEES
12/20	429.6	145.5	33.9%	624
12/19	421.0	(11.0)	—	606
12/18	337.2	(0.4)	—	518
12/17	286.6	(42.6)	—	489
12/16	276.3	(37.9)	—	503
Annual Growth	**11.7%**	**—**		**5.5%**

2020 Year-End Financials
Debt ratio: 38.5%
Return on equity: 29.7%
Cash ($ mil.): 99.9
Current ratio: 2.57
Long-term debt ($ mil.): 326.6
No. of shares (mil.): 43.6
Dividends
  Yield: —
  Payout: —
Market value ($ mil.): 2,611.0

	STOCK PRICE ($) FY Close	P/E High/Low		PER SHARE ($) Earnings	Dividends	Book Value
12/20	59.84	19	8	3.33	0.00	14.20
12/19	45.30	—	—	(0.27)	0.00	8.47
12/18	43.02	—	—	(0.01)	0.00	7.79
12/17	45.65	—	—	(1.07)	0.00	6.87
12/16	32.30	—	—	(1.02)	0.00	5.84
Annual Growth	**16.7%**	**—**	**—**	**—**	**—**	**24.9%**

Palomar Holdings Inc

Auditors: Ernst & Young LLP

LOCATIONS

HQ: Palomar Holdings Inc
7979 Ivanhoe Avenue, Suite 500, La Jolla, CA 92037
Phone: 619 567-5290
Web: www.PalomarSpecialty.com

HISTORICAL FINANCIALS
Company Type: Public

Income Statement
FYE: December 31

	ASSETS ($ mil.)	NET INCOME ($ mil.)	INCOME AS % OF ASSETS	EMPLOYEES
12/20	729.0	6.2	0.9%	122
12/19	395.4	10.6	2.7%	77
12/18	231.1	18.2	7.9%	63
12/17	188.3	3.7	2.0%	0
12/16	0.0	6.6	***************%	0
Annual Growth	**—**	**(1.4%)**	**—**	**—**

2020 Year-End Financials
Return on assets: 1.1%
Return on equity: 2.1%
Long-term debt ($ mil.): —
No. of shares (mil.): 25.5
Sales ($ mil): 168.4
Dividends
  Yield: —
  Payout: —
Market value ($ mil.): 2,268.0

	STOCK PRICE ($) FY Close	P/E High/Low		PER SHARE ($) Earnings	Dividends	Book Value
12/20	88.84	477	168	0.24	0.00	14.25
12/19	50.49	113	38	0.49	0.00	9.31
Annual Growth	**76.0%**	**—**	**—**	**(51.0%)**	**—**	**53.0%**

Pangaea Logistics Solutions Ltd.

Auditors: Grant Thornton LLP

LOCATIONS

HQ: Pangaea Logistics Solutions Ltd.
c/o Phoenix Bulk Carriers (US) LLC, 109 Long Wharf, Newport, RI 02840
Phone: 401 846-7790
Web: www.pangaeals.com

HISTORICAL FINANCIALS
Company Type: Public

Income Statement
FYE: December 31

	REVENUE ($ mil.)	NET INCOME ($ mil.)	NET PROFIT MARGIN	EMPLOYEES
12/20	382.9	11.3	3.0%	445
12/19	412.2	11.6	2.8%	500
12/18	372.9	17.7	4.8%	504
12/17	385.0	7.8	2.0%	504
12/16	238.0	7.4	3.1%	446
Annual Growth	**12.6%**	**11.1%**	**—**	**(0.1%)**

2020 Year-End Financials
Debt ratio: 35.9%
Return on equity: 6.4%
Cash ($ mil.): 46.9
Current ratio: 1.02
Long-term debt ($ mil.): 95.0
No. of shares (mil.): 45.4
Dividends
  Yield: 3.7%
  Payout: 7.6%
Market value ($ mil.): —

Parade Technologies Ltd.

EXECUTIVES

Chief Financial Officer, Judy Wang
Senior Deputy General Manager-worldwide Sales, Peter Oaklander
Independent Director, Dennis Segers
Deputy General Manager-operation, KP Yang
Senior Deputy General Manager-truetouch Business, Joseph Montalbo
Director, Hao Chen
Senior Deputy General Manager-operations, Randy Baker
Director, Ta-Lun Huang
Vice Chairman Of The Board, General Manager, Ming Qu
Executive Deputy General Manager-product Development, Ding Lu
Director, Ying-Chun Tsui
Chairman Of The Board, Chief Executive Officer, Ji Zhao
Independent Director, Xiaoli Huang
Director, Jackie Yang
General Counsel, Senior Deputy General Manager-legal Affairs, Yun Hwa Chou
Executive Deputy General Manager-marketing, Jingwu Chiu
Independent Director, Jen-Lin Shen
Auditors: PricewaterhouseCoopers, Taiwan

LOCATIONS

HQ: Parade Technologies Ltd.
2720 Orchard Parkway, San Jose, CA 95134
Phone: 408 329-5540   **Fax:** 408 329-5541
Web: www.paradetech.com

HOOVER'S HANDBOOK OF EMERGING COMPANIES 2022

HISTORICAL FINANCIALS
Company Type: Public

Income Statement
FYE: December 31

	REVENUE ($ mil.)	NET INCOME ($ mil.)	NET PROFIT MARGIN	EMPLOYEES
12/20	543.7	124.7	22.9%	0
12/19	394.4	81.2	20.6%	0
12/18	338.8	64.3	19.0%	0
12/17	349.1	65.1	18.7%	0
12/16	281.4	41.9	14.9%	0
Annual Growth	17.9%	31.3%	—	—

2020 Year-End Financials

Debt ratio: —	No. of shares (mil.): 80.6
Return on equity: 29.2%	Dividends
Cash ($ mil.): 303.1	Yield: —
Current ratio: 3.29	Payout: 49.8%
Long-term debt ($ mil.): —	Market value ($ mil): —

Park National Corp (Newark, OH)

Park National Bank is a financial holding company with the principal business of owning and supervising its subsidiaries. The holding company owns Park National Bank which operates more than 100 branches in Ohio and northern Kentucky and Carolina. The bank engages in commercial banking and trust business in small and medium population areas such Ohio North Carolina and South Carolina. Park National Bank delivers financial services through more than 95 financial services offices and a network of more than 115 automated teller machines. Park National's nonbank units include consumer finance outfit Guardian Finance SE Property Holdings Scope Leasing and Vision Bancshares Trust.

EXECUTIVES

Independent Director, Frederic Bertley
Independent Director, D. Byrd Miller
Chief Financial Officer, Treasurer, Secretary, Brady Burt, $375,000 total compensation
Independent Director, Alicia Hupp
Director, C. Daniel Delawder, $287,500 total compensation
Independent Director, Mark Ramser
Independent Director, Jason Judd
Independent Director, Robert O'Neill
Independent Director, Donna Alvarado
President, Director, Matthew Miller, $575,000 total compensation
Independent Director, Stephen Kambeitz
Independent Director, Timothy McLain
Independent Director, F. William Englefield
Lead Independent Director, Leon Zazworsky
Chairman Of The Board, Chief Executive Officer, David Trautman, $785,000 total compensation
Auditors: Crowe LLP

LOCATIONS

HQ: Park National Corp (Newark, OH)
50 North Third Street, P.O. Box 3500, Newark, OH 43058-3500
Phone: 740-349-8451
Web: www.parknationalcorp.com

PRODUCTS/OPERATIONS

2015 Sales

	$ mil.	% of total
Interest and fees on loans	228.0	66
Interest and dividends	37.1	10
Income from fiduciary activities	20.2	7
Service charges on deposit accounts	14.7	4
Checkcard fee income	14.6	4
Other service income	11.4	3
Other	16.6	6
Total	**342.6**	**100**

Selected Affiliates
Century National Bank
Fairfield National Bank
Farmers Bank
First-Knox National Bank
Guardian Finance Company
Park National Bank
Richland Bank
Scope Aircraft Finance
Second National Bank
Security National Bank
United bank
Unity National Bank

COMPETITORS

BROADWAY BANCSHARES INC
CITY HOLDING COMPANY
COLUMBIA BANKING SYSTEM INC.
EVANS BANCORP INC.
FIRST COMMONWEALTH FINANCIAL CORPORATION
HEARTLAND FINANCIAL USA INC.
LCNB CORP.
NATIONAL BANK HOLDINGS CORPORATION
NATIONAL BANKSHARES INC.
STATE BANK FINANCIAL CORPORATION
ZIONS BANCORPORATION NATIONAL ASSOCIATION

HISTORICAL FINANCIALS
Company Type: Public

Income Statement
FYE: December 31

	ASSETS ($ mil.)	NET INCOME ($ mil.)	INCOME AS % OF ASSETS	EMPLOYEES
12/20	9,279.0	127.9	1.4%	1,778
12/19	8,558.3	102.7	1.2%	1,907
12/18	7,804.3	110.3	1.4%	1,782
12/17	7,537.6	84.2	1.1%	1,746
12/16	7,467.5	86.1	1.2%	1,726
Annual Growth	5.6%	10.4%	—	0.7%

2020 Year-End Financials

Return on assets: 1.4%	Dividends
Return on equity: 12.7%	Yield: 4.0%
Long-term debt ($ mil.): —	Payout: 54.8%
No. of shares (mil.): 16.3	Market value ($ mil.): 1,713.0
Sales ($ mil): 483.3	

	STOCK PRICE ($) FY Close	P/E High/Low		PER SHARE ($) Earnings	Dividends	Book Value
12/20	105.01	14	8	7.80	4.28	63.76
12/19	102.38	17	14	6.29	4.24	59.28
12/18	84.95	17	11	7.07	4.07	53.03
12/17	104.00	22	17	5.47	3.76	49.46
12/16	119.66	22	14	5.59	3.76	48.38
Annual Growth	(3.2%)	—	—	8.7%	3.3%	7.1%

Parke Bancorp Inc

Community banking is a walk in the park for Parke Bancorp holding company for Parke Bank which has three branches in the New Jersey communities of Sewell and Northfield as well as two loan production offices in the Philadelphia area. The bank provides such traditional products as checking and savings accounts money market and individual retirement accounts and certificates of deposit. Parke Bank has a strong focus on business lending — including operating loans commercial mortgages and construction loans — which accounts for about 90% of the company's loan portfolio. The bank also writes residential real estate and consumer loans.

EXECUTIVES

Chairman, Celestino Pennoni
Independent Director, Edward Infantolino
Independent Director, Jack Sheppard
Independent Director, Daniel Dalton
Independent Director, Fred Choate
Independent Director, Anthony Jannetti
Director, Elizabeth Milavsky
Investor Relations, John Hawkins, $285,387 total compensation
Independent Director, Arret Dobson
Chief Operating Officer, Executive Vice President, Ralph Gallo, $238,407 total compensation
Chief Credit Officer And Senior Vice President, Paul Palmieri, $125,000 total compensation
President, Chief Executive Officer, Director, Vito Pantilione, $955,336 total compensation
Senior Vice President And Chief Lending Officer, Nicholas Pantilione
Chief Financial Officer, Senior Vice President, John Kaufman
Auditors: RSM US LLP

LOCATIONS

HQ: Parke Bancorp Inc
601 Delsea Drive, Washington Township, NJ 08080
Phone: 856 256-2500
Web: www.parkebank.com

COMPETITORS

FIDELITY BANCORP INC. SVB & T CORPORATION
FIRSTFED BANCORP INC.

HISTORICAL FINANCIALS
Company Type: Public

Income Statement
FYE: December 31

	ASSETS ($ mil.)	NET INCOME ($ mil.)	INCOME AS % OF ASSETS	EMPLOYEES
12/20	2,078.3	28.4	1.4%	97
12/19	1,681.1	29.8	1.8%	101
12/18	1,467.4	24.8	1.7%	98
12/17	1,137.4	11.8	1.0%	91
12/16	1,016.1	18.5	1.8%	86
Annual Growth	19.6%	11.3%	—	3.1%

2020 Year-End Financials

Return on assets: 1.5%	Dividends
Return on equity: 14.9%	Yield: 4.0%
Long-term debt ($ mil.): —	Payout: 26.9%
No. of shares (mil.): 11.8	Market value ($ mil.): 185.0
Sales ($ mil): 88.7	

	STOCK PRICE ($)		P/E		PER SHARE ($)		
	FY Close		High/Low		Earnings	Dividends	Book Value
12/20	15.60		10	4	2.37	0.63	16.95
12/19	25.39		10	7	2.48	0.60	14.99
12/18	18.72		11	7	2.07	0.50	13.08
12/17	20.55		21	16	1.02	0.35	13.89
12/16	20.15		11	6	1.55	0.22	13.92
Annual Growth	(6.2%)		—	—	11.2%	29.5%	5.1%

Parkway Acquisition Corp

Auditors: Elliott Davis, PLLC

LOCATIONS

HQ: Parkway Acquisition Corp
101 Jacksonville Circle, Floyd, VA 24091
Phone: 540 745-4191

HISTORICAL FINANCIALS
Company Type: Public

Income Statement				FYE: December 31
	ASSETS ($ mil.)	NET INCOME ($ mil.)	INCOME AS % OF ASSETS	EMPLOYEES
12/20	855.3	5.8	0.7%	230
12/19	706.2	7.1	1.0%	216
12/18	680.2	4.5	0.7%	211
12/17	547.9	2.4	0.4%	177
12/16	558.8	2.4	0.4%	176
Annual Growth	11.2%	24.8%	—	6.9%

2020 Year-End Financials

Return on assets: 0.7%
Return on equity: 7.0%
Long-term debt ($ mil.): —
No. of shares (mil.): 6.0
Sales ($ mil): 37.0

Dividends
Yield: 2.6%
Payout: 27.0%
Market value ($ mil.): 59.0

	STOCK PRICE ($)		P/E		PER SHARE ($)		
	FY Close		High/Low		Earnings	Dividends	Book Value
12/20	9.80		13	8	0.97	0.26	14.08
12/19	12.65		11	9	1.16	0.24	13.27
12/18	10.90		16	14	0.81	0.20	12.17
12/17	12.25		27	18	0.48	0.16	11.39
12/16	8.65		15	13	0.60	0.06	11.05
Annual Growth	3.2%		—	—	12.8%	44.3%	6.2%

Pathfinder Bancorp Inc. (MD)

Auditors: Bonadio & Co., LLP

LOCATIONS

HQ: Pathfinder Bancorp Inc. (MD)
214 West First Street, Oswego, NY 13126
Phone: 315 343-0057
Web: www.pathfinderbank.com

HISTORICAL FINANCIALS
Company Type: Public

Income Statement				FYE: December 31
	ASSETS ($ mil.)	NET INCOME ($ mil.)	INCOME AS % OF ASSETS	EMPLOYEES
12/20	1,227.4	6.9	0.6%	183
12/19	1,093.8	4.2	0.4%	163
12/18	933.1	4.0	0.4%	163
12/17	881.2	3.4	0.4%	144
12/16	749.0	3.2	0.4%	139
Annual Growth	13.1%	20.7%	—	7.1%

2020 Year-End Financials

Return on assets: 0.6%
Return on equity: 7.3%
Long-term debt ($ mil.): —
No. of shares (mil.): 4.5
Sales ($ mil): 48.9

Dividends
Yield: 2.0%
Payout: 20.3%
Market value ($ mil.): 52.0

	STOCK PRICE ($)		P/E		PER SHARE ($)		
	FY Close		High/Low		Earnings	Dividends	Book Value
12/20	11.48		12	8	1.17	0.24	21.51
12/19	13.90		20	16	0.80	0.24	19.20
12/18	15.66		17	14	0.94	0.24	14.72
12/17	15.40		19	15	0.83	0.21	14.44
12/16	13.49		17	14	0.78	0.20	13.67
Annual Growth	(4.0%)		—	—	10.7%	4.7%	12.0%

Patrick Industries Inc

Patrick Industries is a leading manufacturer and distributor of building materials and prefinished products primarily for the manufactured home (MH) recreational vehicle (RV) and marine industries. Patrick Industries manufactures decorative paper and vinyl panels moldings countertops doors and cabinet and slotwall components. In addition to these the firm distributes roofing siding flooring drywall ceiling and wall panels household electronics electrical and plumbing supplies and adhesives. Founded in 1959 the company operates roughly 140 manufacturing plants and about 60 distribution centers and warehouses in about two dozen US states China Canada and the Netherlands.

Operations

Patrick Industries operates roughly 140 manufacturing plants where it makes furniture shelving wall counter and cabinet products mouldings interior passage doors and slotwall panels and components among other products. Its manufacturing segment contributes approximately 70% of annual revenue.

The company also distributes prefinished wall and ceiling panels drywall and drywall finishing products electronics wiring electrical and plumbing products shower doors fireplaces and other miscellaneous products from about 60 warehouse and distribution facilities. Distribution accounts for the remaining revenue (30%).

Geographic Reach

Patrick Industries is based in Elkhart Indiana where a number of RV makers are clustered. The company operates facilities in nearly two dozen states as well as internationally in Canada China and the Netherlands.

Sales and Marketing

Patrick Industries counts most of the major manufactured housing (MH) and recreational vehicle (RV) manufacturers among its clientele but it also serves customers in the kitchen cabinet office and household furniture fixtures and commercial furnishings markets. The company has over 3300 active customers of which two (Forest River and Thor) account for roughly 40% of its sales.

The RV industry represents roughly 55% of the company's sales while the manufactured housing generates more than 15% and marine and industrial generate about 15% each of sales.

Financial Performance

Net sales in 2020 increased approximately $149.5 million or 6% to $2.5 billion from $2.3 billion in 2019. The increase was attributable to an 8% increase in sales from the RV industry a 14% increase in the company's sales from the industrial markets and a 3% increase in sales from the marine industry.

Net income for fiscal 2020 increased to $97.1 million compared from the prior year with $89.6 million.

Cash held by the company at the end of fiscal 2020 increased to $44.8 million. Cash provided by operations and financing activities were $160.2 million and $83.1 million respectively. Cash used for financing activities was $337.9 million mainly for business acquisitions.

Strategy

The company's strategic and capital allocation strategy is to optimally manage and utilize its resources and leverage its platform of operating brands to continue to grow and reinvest in its business. Through strategic acquisitions geographic expansion expansion into new product lines and investment in infrastructure and capital expenditures Patrick seek to ensure that its operating network contains capacity technology and innovative thought processes to support anticipated growth needs effectively respond to changes in market conditions inventory and sales levels and successfully integrate manufacturing distribution and administrative functions.

Over the last three years we have executed several new product initiatives and invested approximately $705 million in acquisitions that directly complement the company's core competencies and existing product lines as well as expand its presence in our primary end markets.

Mergers and Acquisitions

In early 2021 Patrick Industries acquired Elkhart Indiana-based Alpha Systems (Alpha) a leading manufacturer and distributor of component products and accessories primarily serving the recreational vehicle (RV) industry in addition to the manufactured housing commercial building and marine markets. Alpha's major product categories include adhesives and sealants roofing membranes for RVs roto/blow and injection molded products butyl tape shutters and various other parts and accessories.

Also in early 2021 Patrick Industries acquired Hyperform a leading manufacturer of high-quality non-slip foam flooring operating under the SeaDek brand name for the marine OEM market and aftermarket. Hyperform also serves the pool and spa powersports and utility markets under the highly complementary brands of SwimDek and EndeavorDek (collectively SeaDek). SeaDek operates out of two manufacturing facilities located in Rockledge Florida and in Cocoa Florida which possess

HOOVER'S HANDBOOK OF EMERGING COMPANIES 2022   313

full marketing laboratory prototyping and research and development capabilities.

In a separate transaction in 2021 Patrick Industries acquired Everett Washington-based Sea-Dog Corporation a leading distributor of a comprehensive suite of marine and powersports hardware and accessories to distributors wholesalers retailers on-line providers and manufacturers and its sister company Sea-Lect Plastics which provides plastic injection molding design product development and expert tooling to companies and government entities (collectively Sea-Dog).

In late 2020 Patrick Industries acquired Taco Metals (Taco) a leading manufacturer of boating products including rub rail systems canvas and tower components sport fishing and outrigger systems helm chairs and pedestals and specialty hardware for leading OEMs in the recreational boating industry and the related aftermarket. Taco is head-quartered in Miami Florida with manufacturing facilities in Tennessee and Florida and distribution centers in Tennessee Florida South Carolina and Massachusetts.

Also in late 2020 Patrick Industries acquired Lake Zurich Illinois-based Geremarie Corporation (Geremarie) a leading designer manufacturer and fabricator of a full suite of high-precision aluminum components serving the marine industry in addition to the medical aerospace defense commercial and industrial markets.

In mid-2020 Patrick Industries acquired Michigan-based Inland Plywood Company a premier supplier laminator and wholesale distributor of treated untreated and laminated plywood medium density overlay panels and other specialty products primarily serving the marine market as well as the recreational vehicle (RV) and industrial markets for an undisclosed amount. The acquisition of Inland includes the acquisition of working capital machinery and equipment and real estate. Patrick will continue to operate Inland on a stand-alone basis under its brand name in its existing facilities.

Company Background

Patrick Industries Inc. was founded in 1959 and is a major manufacturer and distributor of component and building products for the Recreational Vehicle Marine Manufactured Housing and industries.

EXECUTIVES

Chief Executive Officer And Director, Andy Nemeth, $589,423 total compensation
Executive Chairman Of The Board, Todd Cleveland, $568,846 total compensation
Chief Human Resource Officer, Executive Vice President - Human Resources, Courtney Blosser, $223,731 total compensation
President, Jeffrey Rodino, $399,664 total compensation
Independent Director, John Forbes, $209,135 total compensation
Executive Vice President - Operations, Chief Operating Officer, Kip Ellis, $424,904 total compensation
Independent Director, Denis Suggs
Chief Financial Officer, Executive Vice President - Finance, Treasurer, Jacob Petkovich, $31,058 total compensation
Independent Director, Joseph Cerulli
Auditors: DELOITTE & TOUCHE LLP

LOCATIONS

HQ: Patrick Industries Inc
107 West Franklin Street, P.O. Box 638, Elkhart, IN 46515
Phone: 574 294-7511
Web: www.patrickind.com

PRODUCTS/OPERATIONS

Selected Products:

AdornAIA CountertopsBetter Way Products
Carrera Custom Painting
Charleston
Creative Wood Designs
Custom Vinyls
Dé;cor Manufacturing
Foremost Fabricator
sFrontline Manufacturing
Gravure Ink Praxis Group
Gustafson Lighting
Infinity GraphicsInte

	$ mil.	% of total
Manufacturing	720.4	78
Distribution	199.9	22
Total	**920.3**	**100**

2015 Sales by Customer Type

	% of total
RV industry	75
Manufactured housing	14
Industrial market	11
Total	**100**

COMPETITORS

AMERICAN GYPSUM COMPANY
ARMSTRONG WORLD INDUSTRIES INC.
BMC STOCK HOLDINGS INC.
BUILDERS FIRSTSOURCE INC.
CRANE CO.
GRACO INC.
MUELLER INDUSTRIES INC.
MYERS INDUSTRIES INC.
PARK-OHIO HOLDINGS CORP.
RPM INTERNATIONAL INC.
THE DYSON-KISSNER-MORAN CORPORATION
UFP INDUSTRIES INC.
ZURN WATER SOLUTIONS CORPORATION

HISTORICAL FINANCIALS

Company Type: Public

Income Statement				FYE: December 31
	REVENUE ($ mil.)	NET INCOME ($ mil.)	NET PROFIT MARGIN	EMPLOYEES
12/20	2,486.6	97.0	3.9%	8,700
12/19	2,337.0	89.5	3.8%	7,500
12/18	2,263.0	119.8	5.3%	8,113
12/17	1,635.6	85.7	5.2%	6,721
12/16	1,221.8	55.5	4.5%	4,497
Annual Growth	**19.4%**	**15.0%**	**—**	**17.9%**

2020 Year-End Financials

Debt ratio: 46.6%	No. of shares (mil.): 23.3
Return on equity: 18.3%	Dividends
Cash ($ mil.): 44.7	Yield: 1.5%
Current ratio: 2.32	Payout: 30.1%
Long-term debt ($ mil.): 810.9	Market value ($ mil.): 1,597.0

	STOCK PRICE ($) FY Close	P/E High/Low		PER SHARE ($) Earnings	Dividends	Book Value
12/20	68.35	17	5	4.20	1.03	23.95
12/19	52.43	14	8	3.85	0.25	20.94
12/18	29.61	14	6	4.93	0.00	17.37
12/17	69.45	29	17	3.48	0.00	14.63
12/16	76.30	32	12	2.43	0.00	8.07
Annual Growth	**(2.7%)**	**—**	**—**	**14.7%**	**—**	**31.3%**

Paycom Software Inc

Auditors: Grant Thornton LLP

LOCATIONS

HQ: Paycom Software Inc
7501 W. Memorial Road, Oklahoma City, OK 73142
Phone: 405 722-6900
Web: www.paycom.com

HISTORICAL FINANCIALS

Company Type: Public

Income Statement				FYE: December 31
	REVENUE ($ mil.)	NET INCOME ($ mil.)	NET PROFIT MARGIN	EMPLOYEES
12/21	1,055.5	195.9	18.6%	5,385
12/20	841.4	143.4	17.0%	4,218
12/19	737.6	180.5	24.5%	3,765
12/18	566.3	137.0	24.2%	3,050
12/17	433.0	66.8	15.4%	2,548
Annual Growth	**24.9%**	**30.9%**	**—**	**20.6%**

2021 Year-End Financials

Debt ratio: 0.9%	No. of shares (mil.): 58.0
Return on equity: 25.3%	Dividends
Cash ($ mil.): 277.9	Yield: —
Current ratio: 1.13	Payout: —
Long-term debt ($ mil.): 27.3	Market value ($ mil.): 24,086.0

	STOCK PRICE ($) FY Close	P/E High/Low		PER SHARE ($) Earnings	Dividends	Book Value
12/21	415.19	163	90	3.37	0.00	15.41
12/20	452.25	187	66	2.46	0.00	11.36
12/19	264.76	89	37	3.09	0.00	9.13
12/18	122.45	69	34	2.34	0.00	5.84
12/17	80.33	74	38	1.13	0.00	2.34
Annual Growth	**50.8%**	**—**	**—**	**31.4%**	**—**	**60.1%**

Paylocity Holding Corp

Auditors: KPMG LLP

LOCATIONS

HQ: Paylocity Holding Corp
1400 American Lane, Schaumburg, IL 60173
Phone: 847 463-3200
Web: www.paylocity.com

HISTORICAL FINANCIALS

Company Type: Public

Income Statement
FYE: June 30

	REVENUE ($ mil.)	NET INCOME ($ mil.)	NET PROFIT MARGIN	EMPLOYEES
06/21	635.6	70.8	11.1%	4,150
06/20	561.3	64.4	11.5%	3,600
06/19	467.6	53.8	11.5%	3,050
06/18	377.5	38.6	10.2%	2,600
06/17	300.0	6.7	2.2%	2,115
Annual Growth	20.6%	80.2%	—	18.4%

2021 Year-End Financials

Debt ratio: —
Return on equity: 16.2%
Cash ($ mil.): 202.2
Current ratio: 1.09
Long-term debt ($ mil.): —

No. of shares (mil.): 54.5
Dividends
  Yield: —
  Payout: —
Market value ($ mil.): 10,417.0

	STOCK PRICE ($) FY Close	P/E High/Low		PER SHARE ($) Earnings	Dividends	Book Value
06/21	190.80	165	98	1.26	0.00	8.74
06/20	145.89	125	62	1.15	0.00	7.30
06/19	93.82	101	53	0.97	0.00	5.80
06/18	58.86	86	58	0.70	0.00	4.03
06/17	45.18	378	230	0.12	0.00	2.85
Annual Growth	43.4%			— —	80.0%	— 32.3%

PBF Logistics LP

Auditors: Deloitte & Touche LLP

LOCATIONS

HQ: PBF Logistics LP
One Sylvan Way, Second Floor, Parsippany, NJ 07054
Phone: 973 455-7500
Web: www.pbflogistics.com

HISTORICAL FINANCIALS

Company Type: Public

Income Statement
FYE: December 31

	REVENUE ($ mil.)	NET INCOME ($ mil.)	NET PROFIT MARGIN	EMPLOYEES
12/21	355.5	153.2	43.1%	89
12/20	360.2	147.4	40.9%	91
12/19	340.2	100.2	29.5%	92
12/18	283.4	85.4	30.2%	82
12/17	254.8	100.2	39.4%	39
Annual Growth	8.7%	11.2%	—	22.9%

2021 Year-End Financials

Debt ratio: 69.0%
Return on equity: 73.7%
Cash ($ mil.): 33.9
Current ratio: 3.65
Long-term debt ($ mil.): 622.5

No. of shares (mil.): 62.5
Dividends
  Yield: 10.6%
  Payout: 53.3%
Market value ($ mil.): 707.0

	STOCK PRICE ($) FY Close	P/E High/Low		PER SHARE ($) Earnings	Dividends	Book Value
12/21	11.30	7	4	2.44	1.20	3.97
12/20	9.15	9	1	2.36	1.42	2.68
12/19	20.25	14	11	1.71	2.05	1.69
12/18	20.10	13	11	1.73	1.97	0.52
12/17	20.95	10	9	2.17	1.86	(0.35)
Annual Growth	(14.3%)			— —	3.0% (10.4%)	—

PCB Bancorp

EXECUTIVES

Independent Director, Haeyoung Cho
Director, Janice Chung
President, Chief Executive Officer And Director, Henry Kim, $350,000 total compensation
Executive Vice President, Chief Risk Officer, Corporate Secretary, Andrew Chung, $211,150 total compensation
Independent Director, Hong Kyun Park
Independent Director, Don Rhee
Independent Director, Sarah Jun
Chief Financial Officer, Executive Vice President, Timothy Chang, $229,860 total compensation
Senior Vice President, Chief Credit Officer Of The Bank, Brian Bang, $160,008 total compensation
Chairman Of The Board, Sang Young Lee
Independent Director, Kijun Ahn
Auditors: Crowe LLP

LOCATIONS

HQ: PCB Bancorp
3701 Wilshire Boulevard, Suite 900, Los Angeles, CA 90010
Phone: 213 210-2000
Web: www.paccitybank.com

HISTORICAL FINANCIALS

Company Type: Public

Income Statement
FYE: December 31

	ASSETS ($ mil.)	NET INCOME ($ mil.)	INCOME AS % OF ASSETS	EMPLOYEES
12/20	1,922.8	16.1	0.8%	248
12/19	1,746.3	24.1	1.4%	256
12/18	1,697.0	24.3	1.4%	248
12/17	1,442.0	16.4	1.1%	228
12/16	1,226.6	14.0	1.1%	0
Annual Growth	11.9%	3.7%	—	—

2020 Year-End Financials

Return on assets: 0.8%
Return on equity: 7.0%
Long-term debt ($ mil.): —
No. of shares (mil.): 15.3
Sales ($ mil): 91.5

Dividends
  Yield: 4.7%
  Payout: 51.6%
Market value ($ mil.): 156.0

	STOCK PRICE ($) FY Close	P/E High/Low		PER SHARE ($) Earnings	Dividends	Book Value
12/20	10.11	16	8	1.04	0.48	15.19
12/19	17.28	12	9	1.49	0.25	14.44
12/18	15.65	12	8	1.65	0.12	13.16
12/17	15.50	13	10	1.21	0.12	10.60
12/16	13.00	12	9	1.11	0.11	9.48
Annual Growth	(6.1%)			— —	(1.6%) 44.8%	12.5%

Peapack-Gladstone Financial Corp.

Peapack-Gladstone Financial is the $3.4 billion-asset holding company for the near-century-old Peapack-Gladstone Bank which operates more than 20 branches in New Jersey's Hunterdon Morris Somerset Middlesex and Union counties. Founded in 1921 the bank provides traditional deposit accounts credit cards and loans to individuals and small businesses as well as trust and investment management services through its PGB Trust and Investments unit. Multifamily residential mortgages represent nearly 50% of the company's loan portfolio while commercial mortgages make up around 15%. The bank also originates construction consumer and business loans.

Operations

Peapack-Gladstone Financial operates two main divisions: Banking which offers traditional deposit and loan services merchant card services; and Wealth Management which boasts more than $3.3 billion in assets under administration (as of early 2016) and operates through PGB Trust and Investments which offers asset management services for individuals and institutions as well as personal trust services. More than 80% of the bank's total revenue came from interest income (mostly on its loans) during 2015 while 14% came from its wealth management fee income and 3% came from service charges and fees.

Multifamily residential mortgages represented nearly 50% of the company's loan portfolio at the end of 2015 while commercial mortgages made up another 15%. The rest of its portfolio was made up of construction consumer and business loans.

Geographic Reach

The bank's branches are located across New Jersey in Somerset Morris Hunterdon Middlesex and Union counties Its private banking and wealth management locations are located in Bedminster Morristown Princeton and Teaneck.

Sales and Marketing

The bank's commercial banking business serves business owners professionals retailers contractors and real estate investors. Its wealth management division serves individuals families foundations endowments trusts and estates.

Peapack-Gladstone has been ramping up its advertising spend in recent years. It spent $637000 on advertising during 2015 up from $594000 and $519000 in 2014 and 2013 respectively.

HOOVER'S HANDBOOK OF EMERGING COMPANIES 2022

Financial Performance

Peapack-Gladstone's annual revenues and profits have swelled more than 60% since 2011 as its nearly tripled its loan assets to over $2.9 billion.

The bank's revenue jumped 27% to $122.86 million during 2015 mostly thanks to higher interest income as its loan assets grew by 30% with exceptional increases in its multifamily mortgage and commercial loan volumes. Peapack-Gladstone's wealth management division income grew 20% with increases in securities gains service charges and other non-interest income.

Strong revenue growth in 2015 drove Peapack-Gladstone's net income up 34% to $19.97 million. The bank's operating cash levels climbed 11% to $30.31 million thanks to a rise in cash-based earnings.

Strategy

Peapack-Gladstone Financial continued in 2016 to focus on: enhancing its risk management to keep its loan provisions at a minimum and its profits up; expanding its multi-family loans as well as its commercial real estate loans (to a lesser extent); growing its commercial and industrial (C&I) lending business through its private banking divisions; and expanding its wealth management business which now accounts for 15% of its annual revenue.

Mergers and Acquisitions

In May 2015 Peapack-Gladstone bolstered its wealth management division after buying Morristown-based Wealth Management Consultants LLC for $2.8 million. The deal boosted the bank's assets under advisement and administration to $3.5 billion.

EXECUTIVES

Independent Director, Anthony Consi
Independent Chairman Of The Board, F. Duffield Meyercord
Senior Executive Vice President And President, Commercial Banking, Gregory Smith, $320,000 total compensation
President, Chief Executive Officer And Director, Douglas Kennedy, $695,000 total compensation
Independent Director, Beth Welsh
Independent Director, Edward Gramigna
Senior Executive Vice President, President - Private Wealth Management, John Babcock, $545,000 total compensation
Independent Director, Philip Smith
Independent Director, Susan Cole
Independent Director, Patrick Mullen
Independent Director, Steven Kass
Chief Financial Officer, Jeffrey Carfora, $376,000 total compensation
Independent Director, Richard Daingerfield
Chief Operating Officer, Robert Plante, $365,000 total compensation
Independent Director, Anthony Spinelli
Independent Director, Carmen Bowser
Auditors: Crowe LLP

LOCATIONS

HQ: Peapack-Gladstone Financial Corp.
500 Hills Drive, Suite 300, Bedminster, NJ 07921-0700
Phone: 908 234-0700
Web: www.pgbank.com

PRODUCTS/OPERATIONS

2015 Sales

	$ mil.	% of total
Interest Income		
Loans including fees	94.3	77
Securities available for sale	4.6	4
Other	0.3	-
Other Income		
Wealth management fee income	17.0	14
Service charges and fees	3.3	3
Bank owned life insurance	1.3	1
Other Income	1.0	1
Other	1.1	-
Total	**122.9**	**100**

COMPETITORS

BANCFIRST CORPORATION
BOKF MERGER CORPORATION NUMBER SIXTEEN
COMMERCE BANCSHARES INC.
CVB FINANCIAL CORP.
FIRST BUSEY CORPORATION
FIRST EAGLE PRIVATE CREDIT LLC
FIRSTMERIT CORPORATION
MACATAWA BANK CORPORATION
MB FINANCIAL INC.
OFG BANCORP
PROVIDENT FINANCIAL SERVICES INC.
SIGNATURE BANK
WINTRUST FINANCIAL CORPORATION

HISTORICAL FINANCIALS

Company Type: Public

Income Statement

FYE: December 31

	ASSETS ($ mil.)	NET INCOME ($ mil.)	INCOME AS % OF ASSETS	EMPLOYEES
12/20	5,890.4	26.1	0.4%	501
12/19	5,182.8	47.4	0.9%	446
12/18	4,617.8	44.1	1.0%	409
12/17	4,260.5	36.5	0.9%	384
12/16	3,878.6	26.4	0.7%	338
Annual Growth	11.0%	(0.3%)	—	10.3%

2020 Year-End Financials

Return on assets: 0.4%	Dividends
Return on equity: 5.0%	Yield: 0.8%
Long-term debt ($ mil.): —	Payout: 10.8%
No. of shares (mil.): 18.9	Market value ($ mil.): 432.0
Sales ($ mil): 227.5	

	STOCK PRICE ($) FY Close	P/E High/Low		PER SHARE ($) Earnings	Dividends	Book Value
12/20	22.76	23	9	1.37	0.20	27.78
12/19	30.90	13	10	2.44	0.20	26.61
12/18	25.18	16	10	2.31	0.20	24.25
12/17	35.02	18	14	2.03	0.20	21.68
12/16	30.88	20	10	1.60	0.20	18.79
Annual Growth	(7.3%)	—	—	(3.8%)	(0.0%)	10.3%

Pennant Group Inc

Auditors: DELOITTE & TOUCHE LLP

LOCATIONS

HQ: Pennant Group Inc
1675 East Riverside Drive, Suite 150, Eagle, ID 83616
Phone: 208 506-6100
Web: www.pennantgroup.com

HISTORICAL FINANCIALS

Company Type: Public

Income Statement

FYE: December 31

	REVENUE ($ mil.)	NET INCOME ($ mil.)	NET PROFIT MARGIN	EMPLOYEES
12/20	390.9	15.7	4.0%	5,223
12/19	338.5	2.5	0.8%	4,700
12/18	286.0	15.6	5.5%	0
12/17	250.9	9.8	3.9%	0
12/16	217.2	7.8	3.6%	0
Annual Growth	15.8%	18.8%	—	—

2020 Year-End Financials

Debt ratio: 1.6%	No. of shares (mil.): 28.2
Return on equity: 18.7%	Dividends
Cash ($ mil.): 0.0	Yield: —
Current ratio: 0.67	Payout: —
Long-term debt ($ mil.): 8.2	Market value ($ mil.): 1,640.0

	STOCK PRICE ($) FY Close	P/E High/Low	PER SHARE ($) Earnings	Dividends	Book Value
12/20	58.06	112 18	0.52	0.00	3.42
12/19	33.07	317 137	0.11	0.00	2.55
Annual Growth	75.6%	—	—372.7%	—	33.9%

PennyMac Financial Services Inc (New)

The parent of investment management loan services and investment trust companies PennyMac Financial Services (PennyMac) focuses on the US residential mortgage market offering loans and investment management services. Through its Private National Mortgage Acceptance Company the company's PennyMac Loan Services (PLS) originates service loans in all 50 states the District of Columbia Guam and the US Virgin Island and loans in 49 states and District of Columbia. The PennyMac Correspondent Group (PCG) also known as PennyMac Corp. specializes in the acquisition of newly originated US residential home loans from small and mid-sized banks credit unions and other mortgage lenders. PennyMac went public in 2013.

Operations

PennyMac conducts its business in three segments: production servicing (together production and servicing comprise its mortgage banking activities) and investment management.

The production segment performs loan sources new prime credit quality first-lien residential conventional and government-insured or guaranteed mortgage loans through three channels: correspondent production consumer direct lending and broker direct lending. The segment accounts for about three-fourths of total revenue.

The servicing segment (some 25%) performs loan administration collection and default management activities including the collection and remittance of loan payments; response to customer inquiries; accounting for principal and interest; holding custodial (impounded) funds for the payment of property taxes and insurance premiums;

counseling delinquent borrowers; and supervising foreclosures and property dispositions.

The investment management segment represents its investment management activities which include the activities associated with investment asset acquisitions and dispositions such as sourcing due diligence negotiation and settlement. It operates as an investment manager through PNMAC Capital Management (PCM). PCM manages PennyMac Mortgage Investment Trust (PMT) a mortgage real estate investment trust.

Geographic Reach

While PennyMac serves nearly the entire US its portfolio is heavily weighted toward California Florida Texas Virginia and Maryland.

Based in California PennyMac has three loan production centers location in Roseville CA Honolulu HI Edina MN and one collocated in its Summerlin NV office. Its loan servicing operations are primarily housed in Moorpark CA Fort Worth TX and Summerlin NV. The consumer direct lending business occupies a 36000 square foot leased facility in Pasadena CA. Additionally it has facilities in Plano TX Tampa FL Phoenix AZ and St. Louis MO primarily for its correspondent production activities.

Financial Performance

Revenue for fiscal 2020 increased to $2.7 billion compared to $1.5 billion from the prior year.

The company's net income for fiscal 2020 increased to $1.6 billion compared to $393.0 million from the prior year.

Cash held by the company at the end of fiscal 2020 increased to $532.8 million. Cash provided by investing and financing activities were $783.0 million and $5.8 billion respectively. Operating activities used $6.2 billion mainly for the purchase of loans from Ginnie Mae securities and early buyout investors for modification and subsequent sale.

Strategy

The company's growth strategies include: Growing consumer direct lending through portfolio recapture and non-portfolio originations; Growing broker direct lending; Growing correspondent production through expanding seller relationships and adding products and services; Growing its mortgage loan servicing portfolio; and Expansion into new markets and products.

PennyMac expects to grow its correspondent production business by expanding the number and types of sellers from which it purchases loans and increasing the volume of loans that it purchases from its sellers as it continues to expand to the loan products and services it offers. Over the past several years a number of large banks have exited or reduced the size of their correspondent production businesses creating an opportunity for non-bank entities to gain market share.

EXECUTIVES

Chairman And Chief Executive Officer, David Spector, $1,000,000 total compensation
Chief Investment Officer, Senior Managing Director, Vandad Fartaj, $400,000 total compensation
President, Chief Mortgage Banking Officer, Douglas Jones, $600,000 total compensation
Chief Financial Officer, Senior Managing Director, Daniel Perotti
Senior Managing Director, Chief Legal Officer And Secretary, Derek Stark
Independent Director, Emily Youssouf
Independent Director, James Hunt

Lead Independent Director, Jeffrey Perlowitz
Fvp - Investor Relations, Isaac Garden
Independent Director, Lisa Shalett
Independent Director, Jonathon Jacobson
Chief Human Resource Officer, Managing Director, Jenny Rhodes
Independent Director, Theodore Tozer
Auditors: DELOITTE & TOUCHE LLP

LOCATIONS

HQ: PennyMac Financial Services Inc (New)
3043 Townsgate Road, Westlake Village, CA 91361
Phone: 818 224-7442
Web: www.pennymacfinancial.com

COMPETITORS

ACCESS NATIONAL CORPORATION
FIRST BUSEY CORPORATION
FIRST BUSINESS FINANCIAL SERVICES INC.
FIRST EAGLE PRIVATE CREDIT LLC
M&T BANK CORPORATION
NEW RESIDENTIAL INVESTMENT CORP.
NMI HOLDINGS INC.
OCWEN FINANCIAL CORPORATION
PENNYMAC MORTGAGE INVESTMENT TRUST
READY CAPITAL CORPORATION
SIMMONS FIRST NATIONAL CORPORATION
THE SOUTHERN BANC COMPANY INC
WINTRUST FINANCIAL CORPORATION

HISTORICAL FINANCIALS

Company Type: Public

Income Statement — FYE: December 31

	ASSETS ($ mil.)	NET INCOME ($ mil.)	INCOME AS % OF ASSETS	EMPLOYEES
12/20	31,597.8	1,646.8	5.2%	6,000
12/19	10,204.0	392.9	3.9%	4,215
12/18	7,478.5	87.6	1.2%	3,460
12/17	7,368.0	100.7	1.4%	3,189
12/16	5,133.9	66.0	1.3%	3,038
Annual Growth	57.5%	123.4%	—	18.5%

2020 Year-End Financials

Return on assets: 7.8%	Dividends
Return on equity: 60.2%	Yield: 0.8%
Long-term debt ($ mil.): —	Payout: 3.1%
No. of shares (mil.): 70.9	Market value ($ mil.): 4,653.0
Sales ($ mil): 3,977.1	

	STOCK PRICE ($) FY Close	P/E High/Low		PER SHARE ($) Earnings	Dividends	Book Value
12/20	65.62	3	1	20.92	0.54	47.80
12/19	34.04	7	4	4.89	0.12	26.26
12/18	21.26	9	7	2.59	0.40	21.34
12/17	22.35	5	4	4.03	0.00	19.95
12/16	16.65	6	4	2.94	0.00	15.49
Annual Growth	40.9%	—	—	63.3%	—	32.5%

Pennymac Mortgage Investment Trust

PennyMac Mortgage Investment Trust trusts in its ability to acquire distressed US residential mortgage loans. The company seeks to acquire prima-

rily troubled home mortgage loans and mortgage-backed securities mortgage servicing right and credit risk transfer including CRT agreements and CRT securities. PennyMac is managed by investment adviser PNMAC Capital Management and offers primary and special loan servicing through PennyMac Loan Services. The company is held by Private National Mortgage Acceptance Company (PNMAC).

Operations

The Company operates in four segments: credit sensitive strategies interest rate sensitive strategies correspondent production and corporate.

The credit sensitive strategies segment represents the Company's investments in credit risk transfer (CRT) arrangements including CRT Agreements and CRT strips (together CRT arrangements) distressed loans real estate and non-Agency subordinated bonds. The segment accounts for about 40% of revenues.

The correspondent production segment (about 50%) represents the Company's operations aimed at serving as an intermediary between lenders and the capital markets by purchasing pooling and re-selling newly originated prime credit quality loans either directly or in the form of MBS.

The interest rate sensitive strategies segment (about 10%) represents the Company's investments in mortgage servicing rights (MSRs) excess servicing spread (ESS) purchased from PennyMac Financial Services Inc. (PFSI) Agency and senior non-Agency mortgage-backed securities (MBS) and the related interest rate hedging activities.

The corporate segment includes management fees corporate expense amounts and certain interest income.

Geographic Reach

Its corporate headquarters is located in Westlake Village California.

Financial Performance

The company had a net investment income of $488.8 million in 2019 a 39% growth from the previous year. This was primarily due to net gain on investments more than tripling in the year.

Net income for 2019 totaled $226.4 million a 48% growth from the previous year.

The company's cash at the end of 2019 was $104.1 million a 74% growth from the previous year. Operating activities used $3.0 billion mainly for purchase of loans acquired for sale at fair value from non-affiliates. Investing activities used another $704.7 million mainly for purchases of mortgage-backed securities at fair value. Financing activities generated $3.7 billion.

Strategy

The company's investment focus is on residential mortgage-backed securities (MBS) and mortgage-related assets that it creates through its correspondent production activities including mortgage servicing rights (MSRs) and credit risk transfer (CRT) investments including CRT agreements (CRT Agreements) and CRT securities (together CRT arrangements).

EXECUTIVES

Chb-Ceo, David A Spector
Coo, Steve Bailey
Cfo, Anne D McCallion
Chief ADM & Legal Officer-Sec, Jeffrey P Grogin
Chief Correspondent Lending, Douglas Jones
Chief Operations Offi, Steve R Bailey
Senior Managing Director, Andrew S Chang
Trustee, David Spector

HOOVER'S HANDBOOK OF EMERGING COMPANIES 2022

317

Senior Managing Director, Doug Jones
Senior Managing Director, Vandad Fartaj
Independent Trustee, Frank Willey
Auditors: DELOITTE & TOUCHE LLP

LOCATIONS

HQ: Pennymac Mortgage Investment Trust
3043 Townsgate Road, Westlake Village, CA 91361
Phone: 818 224-7442
Web: www.pennymacmortgageinvestmenttrust.com

PRODUCTS/OPERATIONS

2015 Sales

	$ mil.	% of total
Interest income	201.3	51
Net gain on investments	54.0	14
Net gain on mortgage loans acquired for sale	51.0	13
Net mortgage loan servicing fee	49.3	13
Mortgage Loan origination fees	28.7	7
Other	8.3	2
Results of real estate acquired in settlement of loans	(9.2)	-
Total	**373.4**	**100**

COMPETITORS

BANK OF THE WEST
DITECH HOLDING
   CORPORATION
IMPAC MORTGAGE
   HOLDINGS INC.
INVESCO MORTGAGE
   CAPITAL INC.
KKR REAL ESTATE
   FINANCE TRUST INC.

NATIONSTAR MORTGAGE
   HOLDINGS INC.
NEW RESIDENTIAL
   INVESTMENT CORP.
NEW YORK MORTGAGE
   TRUST INC.
READY CAPITAL
   CORPORATION

HISTORICAL FINANCIALS

Company Type: Public

Income Statement   FYE: December 31

	REVENUE ($ mil.)	NET INCOME ($ mil.)	NET PROFIT MARGIN	EMPLOYEES
12/20	740.1	52.3	7.1%	1
12/19	786.2	226.3	28.8%	1
12/18	526.2	152.8	29.0%	3
12/17	469.3	117.7	25.1%	3
12/16	421.8	75.8	18.0%	3
Annual Growth	15.1%	(8.8%)	—	(24.0%)

2020 Year-End Financials

Debt ratio: 19.7%
Return on equity: 2.2%
Cash ($ mil.): 57.7
Current ratio: 0.02
Long-term debt ($ mil.): 331.5

No. of shares (mil.) 97.8
Dividends
Yield: 8.6%
Payout: 562.9%
Market value ($ mil.): 1,721.0

	STOCK PRICE ($) FY Close	P/E High/Low		PER SHARE ($) Earnings	Dividends	Book Value
12/20	17.59	87	21	0.27	1.52	23.47
12/19	22.29	9	7	2.42	1.88	24.46
12/18	18.62	10	7	1.99	1.88	25.69
12/17	16.07	12	10	1.48	1.88	25.18
12/16	16.37	16	10	1.08	1.88	20.26
Annual Growth	1.8%		—	(29.3%)	(5.2%)	3.7%

People's United Financial Inc

People's United Financial is the holding company for People's United Bank (formerly People's Bank) which boasts more than 415 traditional branches supermarket branches commercial banking offices investment and brokerage offices and equipment leasing offices across New England and eastern New York. In addition to retail and commercial banking services the bank offers trust wealth management brokerage and insurance services. Its lending activities consist mainly of commercial mortgages (more than a third of its loan portfolio) commercial and industrial loans (more than a quarter) residential mortgages equipment financing and home equity loans. Founded in 1842 the bank has $63 billion in assets.

Operations

People's United operates two core business segments Retail Banking and Commercial Banking which both share duties of the bank's now-defunct Wealth Management division. The bank also has a non-core Treasury division that manages the company's securities portfolio and other investments.

Commercial Banking provides business loans equipment financing (through People's Capital and Leasing Corp. or PCLC and People's United Equipment Finance Corp or PUEFC) and municipal banking as well as trust services for corporations and institutions and private banking services for wealthy individuals.

Retail Banking provides deposit services residential mortgages and home equity loans financial advisory and investment management services.

Overall the bank generated some 70% of its total revenue from loan interest and less than 10% from interest on securities. About 5% of total revenues came from bank service charges while investment management fees commercial banking lending fees and insurance revenue each made up less than 5% of overall revenue.

Geographic Reach

Connecticut is its largest lending market with 25% of the bank's loan portfolio being extended to consumers and businesses in the region in 2020. Massachusetts and New York are the bank's next largest markets with about 20% each share of its loan portfolio.

People's United's corporate headquarters is located in Bridgeport Connecticut. The headquarters building had a net book value of $42 million and People's United occupies about 90% of the building. People's United delivers its financial services through a network of more than 415 branches located throughout Connecticut southeastern New York Massachusetts Vermont New Hampshire and Maine. People's United's branch network is primarily concentrated in Connecticut where it has more than 170 offices (including 84 located in Stop & Shop supermarkets). People's United also has about 100 branches in southeastern New York (including 56 located in Stop & Shop supermarkets) some 65 branches in Massachusetts nearly 40 branches in Vermont 25 branches in New Hampshire and more than 15 branches in Maine. People's United owns roughly 145 of its branches

which had an aggregate net book value of $124 million.

Sales and Marketing

The bank sells its products and services through investment and brokerage offices commercial branches online banking and investment trading and through its 24-hour telephone banking service. The company's PCLC PUEFC and LEAF affiliates have a sales presence in more than 15 states to support equipment financing operations throughout the US. The Bank maintains a mortgage warehouse lending group located in Kentucky and a national credits group that has participations in commercial loans and commercial real estate loans to borrowers in various industries on a national scale.

People's United spent $13.3 million on advertising in 2020 compared to $16.4 million and $15.8 million in 2019 and 2018 respectively.

Financial Performance

Total revenue of People's United has consistently grown over the last five years as well as its net income which fell in 2020.

FTE net interest income totaled $1.6 billion in 2020 a $163.9 million increase from the year-ago period and the net interest margin decreased 15 basis points from 2019 to 3%. The decrease in the net interest margin primarily reflects lower yields on the loan portfolio partially offset by lower rates on deposits and borrowings.

People's United reported net income of $219.6 million in 2020 compared to $520.4 million in 2019. Included in the 2020 results are: a goodwill impairment charge (non-tax-deductible) totaling $353.0 million or $(0.83) per common share; merger-related expenses totaling $45.9 million ($36.5 million after-tax) or $(0.09) per common share; and a $75.9 million ($60.4 million after-tax) or $0.14 per common share net gain recognized on the sale of PUIA.

Cash at the end of fiscal year 2020 was $4.2 billion $3.4 billion higher compared to $801 million of the prior year. Operations generated $842.9 million while investing activities used $1.3 billion primarily for purchases of debt securities available-for-sale. Financing activities provided $3.9 billion.

Strategy

People's United's strategy is to focus on increasing deposits by providing a wide range of convenient services to commercial retail business and wealth management customers. The expansion of People's United's branch network and its commitment to developing full-service relationships with its customers are integral components of People's United's strategy to expand market share and continue growing deposits.

One element of the Bank's strategy is to focus on increasing deposits by providing a wide range of convenient services to its customers. An integral component of this strategy is the Bank's supermarket banking initiative pursuant to which as of December 31 2020 the Bank has established 140 full-service Stop & Shop branches throughout Connecticut and southeastern New York most of which are in close proximity to its traditional branches which provide customers with the convenience of seven-days-a-week banking in most locations. In late 2020 34% of the Bank's branches were located in Stop & Shop supermarkets and 11% of its total deposits at that date were held in Stop & Shop branches.

Company Background

One of the main goals of People's United has been to build its presence in the two largest metropolitan areas in its market New York City and Boston. One of the largest in the Boston area Danvers Bancorp added some 30 branches and carried a price tag of approximately $493 million. People's United also acquired LSB Corporation and Butler Bank the latter in an FDIC-assisted transaction that included a loss-sharing agreement with the regulator covering all acquired loans and foreclosed real estate of the failed bank bringing in another 10 branches in the Boston area. In 2010 People's United bought Bank of Smithtown which had about 30 branches primarily on Long Island in New York.

People's United Financial acquired commercial lender Financial Federal Corporation in 2010 (now People's United Equipment Finance) which provides financing and leasing to small and midsized business nationwide.

People's United Financial underwent significant transformation in past years. The company demutualized and converted to a stock holding company in 2007 and early the following year acquired multibank holding company Chittenden Corporation. The deal added some 140 branches doubling People's United Bank's branch network and expanding its reach beyond Connecticut and New York and into the rest of New England.

EXECUTIVES

Independent Director, Collin Baron
Lead Independent Director, George Carter
Independent Director, Jerry Franklin
Senior Executive Vice President, Chief Administrative Officer, Lee Powlus, $516,074 total compensation
Independent Director, Mark Richards
Independent Director, John Dwight
Independent Director, Janet Hansen
Senior Executive Vice President - Retail Banking, Sara Longobardi
Chief Financial Officer, Senior Executive Vice President, R. David Rosato, $511,846 total compensation
President, Jeffrey Tengel, $612,404 total compensation
Independent Director, Nancy McAllister
Executive Vice President, Chief Risk Officer, Daniel Roberts
Executive Vice President, General Counsel And Corporate Secretary, Kristy Berner
Executive Vice President, Head Of Wealth Management, Michael Boardman
Executive Vice President, Chief Credit Officer, Richard Barry
Senior Executive Vice President, Chief Human Resources Officer, David Norton, $411,231 compensation
Chairman Of The Board, Chief Executive Officer, John Barnes, $1,126,878 total compensation
Evp, Kirk Walters, $524,092 total compensation
Independent Director, William Cruger
Executive Vice President, Chief Marketing Officer, Mark Herron
Independent Director, Jane Chwick
Auditors: KPMG LLP

LOCATIONS

HQ: People's United Financial Inc
850 Main Street, Bridgeport, CT 06604
Phone: 203 338-7171   **Fax:** 203 338-2545
Web: www.peoples.com

PRODUCTS/OPERATIONS

2014 Sales

	$ mil.	% of total
Interest & dividends		
Loans		
Commercial real estate	354.2	26
Commercial	351.0	26
Residential mortgage	153.5	12
Consumer	73.9	5
Securities	96.8	7
Other	1.2	-
Noninterest		
Bank service charges	128.6	10
Investment management fees	41.6	3
Operating lease income	41.6	3
Commercial banking lending fees	33.4	2
Insurance revenue	29.9	2
Other	76.6	4
Adjustment	(0.9)	-
Total	**1,381.4**	**100**

COMPETITORS

AXOS FINANCIAL INC.
BANCFIRST CORPORATION
BANKUNITED INC.
BEAR STATE FINANCIAL INC.
CITIZENS & NORTHERN CORPORATION
COLUMBIA BANKING SYSTEM INC.
F.N.B. CORPORATION
FIRST FEDERAL SAVINGS AND LOAN ASSOCIATION OF LAKEWOOD
FLAGSTAR BANCORP INC.
KEARNY FINANCIAL CORP.
MERIDIAN INTERSTATE BANCORP INC.
MIDLAND FINANCIAL CO.
MUFG AMERICAS HOLDINGS CORPORATION
NEWCASTLE BUILDING SOCIETY
OLD NATIONAL BANCORP

HISTORICAL FINANCIALS
Company Type: Public

Income Statement				FYE: December 31
	ASSETS ($ mil.)	NET INCOME ($ mil.)	INCOME AS % OF ASSETS	EMPLOYEES
12/20	63,091.8	219.6	0.3%	5,987
12/19	58,589.8	520.4	0.9%	6,499
12/18	47,877.3	468.1	1.0%	5,920
12/17	44,453.4	337.2	0.8%	5,584
12/16	40,609.8	281.0	0.7%	5,173
Annual Growth	**11.6%**	**(6.0%)**	**—**	**3.7%**

2020 Year-End Financials

Return on assets: 0.3%
Return on equity: 2.8%
Long-term debt ($ mil.): —
No. of shares (mil.): 424.6
Sales ($ mil): 2,256.8

Dividends
Yield: 5.5%
Payout: 61.8%
Market value ($ mil.): 5,491.0

	STOCK PRICE ($) FY Close	P/E High/Low		PER SHARE ($) Earnings	Dividends	Book Value
12/20	12.93	34	19	0.49	0.72	17.90
12/19	16.90	14	11	1.27	0.71	17.91
12/18	14.43	16	11	1.29	0.70	17.32
12/17	18.70	20	16	0.97	0.69	16.79
12/16	19.36	22	15	0.92	0.68	16.28
Annual Growth	**(9.6%)**	**—**	**—**	**(14.6%)**	**1.4%**	**2.4%**

PerkinElmer, Inc.

PerkinElmer develops and sells equipment such as instruments tests and software used by scientists researchers and clinicians to address the most critical challenges across science and healthcare. More than 2 million scientists are using PerkinElmer's laboratory software to store and analyze research data and collaborate on experiments. PerkinElmer technologies have contributed to the development of more than 20 novel therapeutic drugs. The company which distributes its offerings in more than 190 countries generates most of its sales from US. Richard Perkin and Charles Elmer came together to form the PerkinElmer brand in 1937.

Operations

PerkinElmer sells its products in two segments: Discovery & Analytical Solutions and Diagnostics.

Diagnostics about 55% of revenue sells tools and applications for clinical customers in the reproductive health emerging market diagnostics and applied genomics markets. Among its brands are Vanadis (prenatal and maternal health screening) NeoBase (detection of metabolic disorders in newborns) and Viacord (stem cell banking).

Discovery & Analytical Solutions which offers products and services for the environmental industrial food life sciences research and laboratory services markets generates about 45% of sales. The unit's brands include Radiometric (detection instruments) Opera Phenix (high content screening systems) Clarus (gas chromatography and mass spectrometery equipment) and Flexar (liquid chromatography systems).

Diagnostics about 40% of revenue sells tools and applications for clinical customers in the reproductive health emerging market diagnostics and applied genomics markets.

Among its brands are Vanadis (prenatal and maternal health screening) NeoBase (detection of metabolic disorders in newborns) and Viacord (stem cell banking).

Geographic Reach

Based in Waltham Massachusetts PerkinElmer market its products and services in more than 190 countries. About a third of PerkinElmer's sales are to customers in the US. China is the next biggest market with about 15% of sales. Customers in the UK France Germany and Italy combine for about 25% of the company's revenue.

Sales and Marketing

PerkinElmer's customers include academic and research organizations biotechnology and pharmaceutical companies doctors government agencies laboratories private health care organizations and public health authorities.

PerkinElmer tries to reach many of those customers through its direct sales unit of some 5500 sales and service reps operating in about 40 countries. The company operates through distributors in areas where it doesn't have staff on the ground.

The diagnostics generated the largest share with some 55% of the company's total sales. The life sciences products accounted for more than 25% and nearly 20% came from applied markets products.

Financial Performance

The company's overall revenue in fiscal year 2020 increased $899.1 million or 31% as compared to fiscal year 2019 reflecting an increase of

$929.4 million or 82% in its Diagnostics segment revenue partially offset by a decrease of $30.4 million or 2% in its Discovery & Analytical Solutions segment revenue.

In 2020 the company had a net income of $727.9 million a 220% or $500.1 million increase from the previous year.

The company's cash at the end of 2020 was $402.6 million. Operating activities generated $892.2 million while investing activities used $504.5 million mainly for capital expenditures. Financing activities used another $202.9 million primarily for payments on borrowings.

Strategy

The company's strategy is to develop and deliver innovative products services and solutions in high-growth markets that utilizes its knowledge and expertise to address customers' critical needs and drive scientific breakthroughs. To execute on this strategy and accelerate revenue growth it focuses on broadening its offerings through both the acquisition of innovative technology and investment in research and development and the acquisition of innovative technology.

The strategy includes: Strengthening its position within key markets by expanding its global product and service offerings maintaining superior product quality and driving an enhanced customer experience; Attracting retaining and developing talented and engaged employees; Accelerating transformational innovation through both internal research and development and third-party collaborations and alliances; Augmenting growth in both of the company's core business segments Discovery & Analytical Solutions and Diagnostics through strategic acquisitions and licensing; Engraining focused operational excellence to improve organizational efficiency and agility; and Opportunistically utilizing its share repurchase programs to help drive shareholder value.

As part of its strategy to grow its core businesses it has completed the acquisition of four businesses for aggregate consideration of $438.7 million and restructuring activities.

Mergers and Acquisitions

In 2021 PerkinElmer completed the acquisition of UK-based Oxford Immunotec Global PLC a global leader of proprietary test kits for latent tuberculosis. Through this Acquisition PerkinElmer will grow its portfolio of advanced infectious disease testing solutions to include tuberculosis detection to better serve customers around the world. Moreover the deal will enable PerkinElmer to combine its channel expertise and leading workflow and testing capabilities with Oxford Immunotec's leading proficiencies in T cell immunology with its proprietary test kits for latent tuberculosis.

In late 2020 PerkinElmer agreed to acquire UK-based cell engineering company Horizon Discovery for $383 million (296 million). With this investment PerkinElmer will expand its portfolio of leading automated life sciences discovery and applied genomics solutions to include gene editing and gene modulation tools. The acquisition will enable PerkinElmer to better partner with academic and pharma/biopharma scientists to help meet today's research challenges. It will also provide an opportunity to provide important tools for exploring next generation cell engineering and customized cell lines for relevant biological models ? important for the future of precision medicine.

Company Background

PerkinElmer traces its roots back to the invention of the strobe light in 1931. MIT professor Harold Edgerton who invented the strobe light while doing research on electric motors formed a consulting business with former student Kenneth Germeshausen that used strobe lights and high-speed photography to solve manufacturing problems.

PerkinElmer was founded by Richard Perkin and Charles Elmer in 1937 to design optical products. The company moved into the analytical instruments business in the 1940s.

The companies merged in 1999 and took the PerkinElmer name.

HISTORY

PerkinElmer traces its roots back to the invention of the strobe light in 1931. MIT professor Harold Edgerton who invented the strobe light while doing research on electric motors formed a consulting business with former student Kenneth Germeshausen that used strobe lights and high-speed photography to solve manufacturing problems. As business picked up they brought in another former student Herbert Grier and in 1947 formed Edgerton Germeshausen and Grier. Their first contract job was to photograph nuclear weapons tests for the US government. The company went public in 1959 and changed its name to EG&G in 1966.

Over the next 30 years EG&G bought scores of companies involved in electronic instruments and components biomedical services energy and nuclear weapons R&D seal and gasket manufacturing automotive testing and the aerospace industry. Key acquisitions included Reynolds Electrical & Engineering (1967) which provided support services for the Department of Defense (including the nuclear weapons testing program); Sealol (1968) a maker of seals for industrial applications; and Automotive Research Associates (1973).

EXECUTIVES

Senior Vice President, Administration, General Counsel And Secretary, Joel Goldberg, $532,713 total compensation

Chief Financial Officer, Senior Vice President, James Mock, $569,602 total compensation

Vice President And Chief Accounting Officer, Andrew Okun

Independent Director, Peter Barrett

Senior Vice President, Strategy And Business Develoment, Daniel Tereau, $485,192 total compensation

Independent Director, Pascale Witz

Independent Director, Samuel Chapin

Director, Frank Witney

Independent Non-executive Chairman Of The Board, Alexandros Michas

Independent Director, Michel Vounatsos

Senior Vice President And Chief Commercial Officer, Miriame Victor

President, Chief Executive Officer And Director, Prahlad Singh, $900,000 total compensation

Senior Vice President, Global Operations, Tajinder Vohra, $426,185 total compensation

Auditors: DELOITTE & TOUCHE LLP

LOCATIONS

HQ: PerkinElmer, Inc.
940 Winter Street, Waltham, MA 02451
Phone: 781 663-6900   **Fax:** 781 663-6052
Web: www.perkinelmer.com

PRODUCTS/OPERATIONS

2018 Sales

	$ mil.	% of total
Discovery & Analytical Solutions		
Product	1,010.9	36
Service	682.3	25
Diagnostics		
Product	924.6	33
Service	160.2	6
Total	**2,778.0**	**100**

Selected Products

Human health
  Diagnostics
    BACs-on-Beads (chromosomal abnormality detection)
    DELFIA Xpress (prenatal screening)
    GSP Neonatal (congenital screening from a drop of blood)
    NeoGram (metabolic disorder detection)
  Research
    AlphaLISA (research assays)
    Columbus (image data storage and analysis)
    EnVision (label reader)
    JANUS Automated Workstation (liquid handling)
    Opera/Operetta (cell-based assay high content screening/imaging)
    TSA Plus (biotin kits for increasing sensitivity of histochemistry and cytochemistry)
    Volocity (3D image analysis software)
  Environmental health
    Atomax (cathode lamps)
    Clarus (gas sample handling)
    Flexar (liquid chromatography)
    NexION (mass spectrometer)
    Spectrum (infrared analysis)

COMPETITORS

AGILENT TECHNOLOGIES INC.
BIO-TECHNE CORPORATION
CONMED CORPORATION
CUTERA INC.
FUJIFILM SONOSITE INC.
LUMENIS LTD.
LUMINEX CORPORATION
NATUS MEDICAL INCORPORATED
OLYMPUS CORPORATION
STRATEC SE
THERMO FISHER SCIENTIFIC INC.
VARIAN MEDICAL SYSTEMS
INC.
VIVEVE MEDICAL INC.

HISTORICAL FINANCIALS

Company Type: Public

Income Statement   FYE: January 3

	REVENUE ($ mil.)	NET INCOME ($ mil.)	NET PROFIT MARGIN	EMPLOYEES
01/21*	3,782.7	727.8	19.2%	14,000
12/19	2,883.6	227.5	7.9%	13,000
12/18	2,778.0	237.9	8.6%	12,500
12/17	2,256.9	292.6	13.0%	11,000
01/17	2,115.5	234.3	11.1%	8,000
Annual Growth	15.6%	32.8%	—	15.0%

*Fiscal year change

2021 Year-End Financials

Debt ratio: 25.0%
Return on equity: 21.8%
Cash ($ mil.): 402.0
Current ratio: 1.36
Long-term debt ($ mil.): 1,609.7
No. of shares (mil.): 112.0
Dividends
Yield: 0.0%
Payout: 4.3%
Market value ($ mil.): 16,085.0

	STOCK PRICE ($)	P/E	PER SHARE ($)		
	FY Close	High/Low	Earnings	Dividends	Book Value
01/21*	143.50	23 10	6.49	0.28	33.33
12/19	97.05	49 35	2.04	0.28	25.32
12/18	77.29	45 33	2.13	0.28	23.37
12/17	73.12	28 19	2.64	0.28	22.68
01/17	52.15	27 19	2.12	0.28	19.65
Annual Growth 28.8%		— —	32.3%	(0.0%)	14.1%

*Fiscal year change

PGT Innovations Inc

PGT makes and sells WinGuard impact-resistant doors and windows for the residential market. The energy-efficient customizable doors and windows are made of aluminum or vinyl with laminated glass and are designed to withstand hurricane-strength winds. PGT also makes Eze-Breeze porch enclosure panels and garage door screens New-South Window replacement windows and doors and Estate Collection windows and doors for high-end homes resorts hotels and in schools and office buildings. The company has various manufacturing facilities in Florida and Arizona. PGT sells its products through some 2000 window distributors dealers and contractors in the Southeastern US Canada Central America and the Caribbean.

Operations

PGT's capabilities include in-house glass cutting tempering laminating and insulating. The company generates around 70% of total sales from impact-resistant window and door products and over 30% from non-impact window & door products. It operates its two segments based on geography: the Southeast segment (generates some 85% of sales) and the Western segment (approximately 15%). Products have included PGT Custom Window and Doors CGI and CGI Commercial WinDoor Western Window Systems NEW South and ECO Window Systems.

Geographic Reach

Florida-based PGT currently conducts business in the Southeastern US Western US Gulf Coast Coastal mid-Atlantic the Caribbean Central America and Canada.

Sales and Marketing

The home repair and remodeling end markets represented about 55% each of PGT's sales while new construction markets account for the rest. The company's advertising expenses were $11.6 million $5.2 million and $3.2 million for the years 2020 2019 and 2018 respectively.

PGT markets its products through print and web-based advertising consumer dealer and builder promotions and selling and collateral materials. It markets its products based on quality building code compliance outstanding service shorter lead times and on-time delivery utilizing its fleet of trucks and trailers. Its top ten customers account for approximately 20% of sales.

Financial Performance

The company's sales grew to $882.6 million in the 2020 fiscal year an increase of $137.7 million or 18% compared to $745.0 million in 2019. The increase in net sales in 2020 of $137.6 million was primarily driven by the inclusion of the net sales of its NewSouth Acquisition from its February 1 2020 acquisition date but also by organic sales growth in its Southeast segment.

In 2020 the company had a net income of $45.1 million a 3% growth from the previous year.

The company's cash at the end of 2020 was $100.3 million. Operating activities generated $75.5 million while investing activities used $114.4 million mainly for acquisitions. Financing activities provided another $42 million.

Strategy

With the company's acquisition of NewSouth Window Solutions in February 2020 its sales strategy also focuses on direct-to-consumer sales for the types of jobs and customers that its dealers historically have not targeted or serviced.

PGT's marketing strategy is designed to reinforce the quality of its products and focuses on both coastal and inland markets. The company supports customers through print and web-based advertising consumer dealer and builder promotions and selling and collateral materials. It also works with dealers and distributors to educate architects building officials consumers and homebuilders on the advantages of using impact-resistant and energy-efficient products. PGT markets products based on expectations of quality building code compliance outstanding service shorter lead times and on-time delivery using its fleet of trucks and trailers.

Mergers and Acquisitions

In early 2021 PGT Innovations Inc. has completed its acquisition of a 75% ownership stake in Eco Window Systems and its related companies (collectively Eco). Eco is a leading manufacturer and installer of aluminum impact-resistant windows and doors serving the South Florida region. This acquisition further advances its strategy of expanding and diversifying its product lines with strong brands. Terms were not disclosed.

In early 2020 PGT completed the acquisition of Florida-based window and door maker NewSouth Window Solutions for $92 million. NewSouth sells factory-direct windows and doors that are energy efficient and offers impact-resistant and non-impact residential products. With the completion of the acquisition PGT Innovations has taken an important step in enhancing its go-to-market strategy and has done so with a strong brand that leads in the direct-to-consumer channel. In addition it implemented its geographic expansion plans for New-South Window Solutions and expanding the presence of PGT Innovations in areas outside of its core markets.

EXECUTIVES

Independent Director, Sheree Bargabos
Senior Vice President Of Corporate Sales And Innovation, Brent Boydston, $313,562 total compensation
Chairman Of The Board, Rodney Hershberger
Independent Director, Alexander Castaldi
Independent Director, Brett Milgrim
Independent Director, Floyd Sherman
Independent Director, Richard Feintuch
President, Western Business Unit, Mike Wothe, $359,423 total compensation
Svp, Customer Strategy And Innovation, Southeast Division, Robert Keller, $365,822 total compensation
Independent Director, Frances Hawes
Independent Director, Xavier Boza

Chief Financial Officer, Senior Vice President, John Kunz
Interim Chief Financial Officer, Svp, Corporate Development And Treasurer, Bradley West, $285,000 total compensation
Auditors: Ernst & Young LLP

LOCATIONS

HQ: PGT Innovations Inc
  1070 Technology Drive, North Venice, FL 34275
Phone: 941 480-1600
Web: www.pgtinnovations.com

PRODUCTS/OPERATIONS

2013 Sales

	$ mil.	% of total
Impact window and door products	183.4	77
Other window & door products	56.9	23
Total	**239.3**	**100**

COMPETITORS

BUILDERS FIRSTSOURCE INC.
INSTALLED BUILDING PRODUCTS INC.
JELD-WEN HOLDING INC.
JELD-WEN INC.
LIXIL CORPORATION
OVERHEAD DOOR CORPORATION
PERMASTEELISA SPA
RYTEC CORPORATION
TOPBUILD CORP.

HISTORICAL FINANCIALS

Company Type: Public

Income Statement
FYE: January 2

	REVENUE ($ mil.)	NET INCOME ($ mil.)	NET PROFIT MARGIN	EMPLOYEES
01/21*	882.6	45.1	5.1%	3,500
12/19	744.9	43.6	5.9%	3,000
12/18	698.4	53.9	7.7%	3,000
12/17	511.0	39.8	7.8%	2,700
12/16	458.5	23.7	5.2%	2,600
Annual Growth 17.8%		17.4%	—	7.7%

*Fiscal year change

2021 Year-End Financials

Debt ratio: 38.7%	No. of shares (mil.): 59.0
Return on equity: 9.6%	Dividends
Cash ($ mil.): 100.3	Yield: —
Current ratio: 3.33	Payout: —
Long-term debt ($ mil.): 412.1	Market value ($ mil.): 1,200.0

	STOCK PRICE ($)	P/E	PER SHARE ($)		
	FY Close	High/Low	Earnings	Dividends	Book Value
01/21*	20.34	27 9	0.76	0.00	8.22
12/19	14.80	24 18	0.74	0.00	7.38
12/18	15.72	25 14	1.00	0.00	6.64
12/17	16.85	21 13	0.77	0.00	3.52
12/16	11.45	25 18	0.47	0.00	2.69
Annual Growth 15.4%		— —	12.8%	—	32.2%

*Fiscal year change

Phillips 66 Partners LP

How many ways can you break up an oil and gas company? The ConocoPhillips and Phillips 66 family of companies may be trying to find out.

Phillips 66 Partners is the mid-stream component owning and acquiring crude oil refined petroleum and natural gas liquids pipelines terminals and storage facilities in the US. The company has capacity for about 650 million barrels a day and its assets include 135 miles of pipeline connected to Phillips 66 refineries in Texas Louisiana and Illinois. Phillips 66 Partners earns revenue from fees it charges for transportation and storage of petroleum. In 2017 it bought mid-stream assets from its general partner Phillips 66 for a total transaction value of $2.4 billion.

IPO

The company plans to use its $378 million in IPO proceeds to repay debt and for general corporate purposes including possible future acquisitions.

Strategy

Going forward Phillips 66 Partners plans to provide its transportation and storage services to Phillips 66 and third parties. It also intends to pursue acquisitions through a right-of-first-refusal deal with Phillips 66 and through third parties.

EXECUTIVES

Independent Director Of General Partner, P. Bairrington
Independent Director Of The General Partner, Charles Johnson
Vice President, Controller, J. Scott Pruitt
President, Chief Operating Officer, Mark Lashier
Lead Independent Director Of General Partner, M.A. Haney
Chairman Of The Board Of Directors, Chief Executive Officer Of General Partner, Gregory Garland
Independent Director Of General Partner, Joseph O'Toole
Vice President, Director Of General Partner, Robert Herman
Chief Financial Officer, Vice President, Director Of The General Partner, Kevin Mitchell
Vice President - Operations, Director Of General Partner, Timothy Roberts
Auditors: Ernst & Young LLP

LOCATIONS

HQ: Phillips 66 Partners LP
2331 CityWest Blvd., Houston, TX 77042
Phone: 855 283-9237
Web: www.phillips66partners.com

COMPETITORS

ANADARKO PETROLEUM CORPORATION	DEVON ENERGY CORPORATION
AltaGas Ltd	PHILLIPS 66
CHESAPEAKE ENERGY CORPORATION	RANGE RESOURCES CORPORATION

HISTORICAL FINANCIALS
Company Type: Public

Income Statement				FYE: December 31
	REVENUE ($ mil.)	NET INCOME ($ mil.)	NET PROFIT MARGIN	EMPLOYEES
12/20	1,618.0	791.0	48.9%	0
12/19	1,667.0	923.0	55.4%	0
12/18	1,486.0	796.0	53.6%	0
12/17	1,169.0	524.0	44.8%	0
12/16	873.0	408.0	46.7%	0
Annual Growth	16.7%	18.0%	—	—

2020 Year-End Financials

Debt ratio: 53.8%
Return on equity: —
Cash ($ mil.): 7.0
Current ratio: 0.22
Long-term debt ($ mil.): 3,444.0
No. of shares (mil.): 228.3
Dividends
Yield: 13.2%
Payout: 107.0%
Market value ($ mil.): 6,030.0

	STOCK PRICE ($) FY Close	P/E High/Low		PER SHARE ($) Earnings	Dividends	Book Value
12/20	26.41	20	7	3.27	3.50	12.25
12/19	61.64	14	10	4.29	3.40	12.41
12/18	42.11	13	10	4.00	2.94	19.82
12/17	52.35	22	17	2.59	2.41	17.42
12/16	48.64	29	20	2.20	1.98	14.32
Annual Growth	(14.2%)	—	—	10.4%	15.4%	(3.8%)

Phillips Edison & Co Inc

Auditors: DELOITTE & TOUCHE LLP

LOCATIONS

HQ: Phillips Edison & Co Inc
11501 Northlake Drive, Cincinnati, OH 45249
Phone: 513 554-1110
Web: www.phillipsedison.com

HISTORICAL FINANCIALS
Company Type: Public

Income Statement				FYE: December 31
	REVENUE ($ mil.)	NET INCOME ($ mil.)	NET PROFIT MARGIN	EMPLOYEES
12/21	532.8	15.1	2.8%	290
12/20	498.0	4.7	1.0%	300
12/19	536.7	(63.5)	—	300
12/18	430.3	39.1	9.1%	300
12/17	311.5	(38.3)	—	304
Annual Growth	14.4%	—	—	(1.2%)

2021 Year-End Financials

Debt ratio: 40.5%
Return on equity: 0.7%
Cash ($ mil.): 92.5
Current ratio: 0.74
Long-term debt ($ mil.): 1,891.7
No. of shares (mil.): 113.2
Dividends
Yield: 1.3%
Payout: 293.3%
Market value ($ mil.): 3,741.0

	STOCK PRICE ($) FY Close	P/E High/Low	PER SHARE ($) Earnings	Dividends	Book Value
12/21	33.04	228 181	0.15	0.44	18.99
Annual Growth	—	—	—	—	—

Photronics, Inc.

Photronics is the world's leading manufacturer of photomasks which are high precision photographic quartz or glass plates containing microscopic images of electronic circuits. Photomasks is a key tool in the process for manufacturing integrated circuits (ICs) and flat-panel displays (FPDs) and are used as masters to transfer circuit patterns onto semiconductor wafers and FPD substrates during the fabrication of ICs a variety of FPDs and to a lesser extent other types of electrical and optical components. About 80% of the company's sales are from customers in Asia. The company was founded in 1969.

Operations

Photronics operates as a single operating segment as a manufacturer of photomasks which are high precision quartz or glass plates containing microscopic images of electronic circuits for use in the fabrication of IC's and FPDs.

It gets about 70% of its revenue from making photomasks for integrated circuits and the rest from photomasks for flat panel displays.

Geographic Reach

Photronics' products are made at some 10 manufacturing plants - one in South Korea two in China two in Europe (Germany and Wales) three in Taiwan and three in the US (Connecticut Idaho and Texas). It primarily conducts research and development activities for IC photomasks at Boise Idaho facility as well as at Photronics Cheonan Ltd. (formerly PK Ltd.) its subsidiary in Korea and Photronics DNP Mask Corporation (PDMC) one of its joint venture subsidiaries in Taiwan. Research and development for FPD photomasks is primarily conducted at Photronics Cheonan Ltd.

Over 35% of Photronics' revenue comes from customers in Taiwan and about 25% from Korean manufacturers. China customers generate over 15% of sales. The company gets around 15% of sales from US while Europe generated some 5%.

Sales and Marketing

The market for photomasks primarily consists of domestic and non-US semiconductor and FPD manufacturers and designers. Photronics conducts its sales and marketing activities primarily through a staff of full-time sales personnel and customer service representatives who work closely with the company's management and technical personnel.

Photronics has about 530 customers with its five biggest customers accounting for about 45% of its company's sales. The company's sales might become even more concentrated because of consolidation in the semiconductor manufacturing business. Customers include United Microelectronics Corp. Co. Ltd. (more than 15% of sales) and Samsung Electronics (over 10% of sales).

Financial Performance

Revenue increased 9% in 2021 compared with 2020 to $663.8 million. IC revenue increased 10% due to both improved pricing for mainstream photomasks and improved pricing and increased demand for high-end masks at the largest node levels.

In the fiscal year 2021 net income has increased about 95% to $78.8 million from the prior year.

Photronics had cash and cash equivalents of $276.7 million at the end of 2021 compared with $278.6 million at the end of fiscal 2020. Net cash provided by operating activities was $150.8 million. Net cash used in investing activities was $103.5 million mostly for purchases of property plant and equipment. Net cash used in financing activities was $53.9 million for purchases of treasury stock.

Strategy

As part of Photronics' business growth strategy it has acquired businesses and entered into joint ventures in the past and it may pursue acquisitions and joint venture opportunities in the future. Future efforts to grow the company may include expanding into new or related markets or industries.

HISTORY

Constantine (Deno) Macricostas who came to the US from Greece in 1954 as an exchange student and four partners started Photronic Labs in a garage in 1969. Weary of infighting Macricostas left the firm in 1972 but bought it two years later with the help of banker (and later long-time board member) Michael Yomazzo and a loan from the Small Business Administration. The company went public in 1987 and changed its name to Photronics in 1990.

A string of acquisitions starting with Beta Squared in 1990 increased the company's customer base. In 1993 it became the #1 independent photomask maker in the US with the purchase of Toppan Printronics the US operations of Toppan Printing. The deal gave Toppan Printing a stake in Photronics which Photronics bought back five years later.

EXECUTIVES

Chairman Of The Board, Constantine Macricostas
Chief Executive Officer, Director, Peter Kirlin, $628,318 total compensation
Executive Vice President, Chief Technology Officer And Strategic Planning, Christopher Progler, $400,004 total compensation
Independent Director, Mary Paladino
Independent Director, Daniel Liao
Executive Vice President, Chief Administrative Officer, General Counsel, Secretary, Richelle Burr, $365,003 total compensation
Chief Financial Officer, Executive Vice President, John Jordan, $366,011 total compensation
President Of Asia Ic Photomask, Frank Lee, $446,146 total compensation
Auditors: Deloitte & Touche LLP

LOCATIONS

HQ: Photronics, Inc.
   15 Secor Road, Brookfield, CT 06804
Phone: 203 775-9000
Web: www.photronics.com

PRODUCTS/OPERATIONS

2016 Sales

	$ mil.	% of total
Integrated Circuits	364.6	75
Flat Panel Displays	118.9	25
Total	**483.5**	**100**

COMPETITORS

CYBEROPTICS CORPORATION
FLEX LTD.
FORMFACTOR INC.
INTEGRATED SILICON SOLUTION INC.
LAM RESEARCH CORPORATION
LATTICE SEMICONDUCTOR CORPORATION
MATTSON TECHNOLOGY INC.
ONTO INNOVATION INC.
TRIFAST PLC
ULTRATECH INC.
ZYTRONIC PLC

HISTORICAL FINANCIALS
Company Type: Public

Income Statement

	REVENUE ($ mil.)	NET INCOME ($ mil.)	NET PROFIT MARGIN	EMPLOYEES
10/21	663.7	55.4	8.4%	1,728
10/20	609.6	33.8	5.5%	1,728
10/19	550.6	29.7	5.4%	1,775
10/18	535.2	42.0	7.9%	1,575
10/17	450.6	13.1	2.9%	1,475
Annual Growth	**10.2%**	**43.4%**		**4.0%**

FYE: October 31

2021 Year-End Financials

Debt ratio: 8.6%	No. of shares (mil.): 60.0
Return on equity: 6.8%	Dividends
Cash ($ mil.): 276.6	Yield: —
Current ratio: 3.13	Payout: —
Long-term debt ($ mil.): 89.4	Market value ($ mil.): 780.0

	STOCK PRICE ($) FY Close	P/E High/Low		Earnings	PER SHARE ($) Dividends	Book Value
10/21	12.99	17	11	0.89	0.00	13.72
10/20	9.75	31	16	0.52	0.00	12.75
10/19	11.80	28	18	0.44	0.00	11.74
10/18	9.74	18	12	0.59	0.00	11.31
10/17	9.55	62	40	0.19	0.00	10.84
Annual Growth	**8.0%**	—	—	**47.1%**	—	**6.1%**

Physicians Realty Trust

Physicians Realty Trust doesn't make house calls. The real estate investment trust (REIT) owns and manages healthcare properties that are leased to physicians hospitals and healthcare delivery systems. A self-managed REIT its portfolio consists of more than 250 medical office buildings in about 30 states. Tenants include Hackley Hospital and Valley West Hospital. Physicians Realty Trust was formed in 2013. As a REIT it is exempt from paying federal income tax as long as it distributes about 90% of profits back to shareholders. Physicians Realty Trust went public in 2013 raising $120 million.

Operations

The company receive a cash rental stream from healthcare providers under our leases. Approximately 95% of the annualized base rent payments from properties as of 2019 are from absolute and triple-net leases pursuant to which the tenants are responsible for all operating expenses relating to the property including but not limited to real estate taxes utilities property insurance routine maintenance and repairs and property management.

The company's rental revenues account for nearly 75% of sales while expense recoveries and interest income on real estate loans and other accounts for the rest.

Geographic Reach

Based in Milwaukee Physicians Realty Trust has properties in about 30 states including Georgia Texas and Michigan.

Sales and Marketing

The company's five largest tenants based upon rental revenue represents approximately $57.6 million or about 20% of the annualized base rent from its consolidated properties. No single tenant accounted for more than 5% of total annualized base rent or about 5% of total base revenue as of December 31 2019; however more than 15% of total annualized base rent as of December 31 2019 were from tenants affiliated with CommonSpirit.

Financial Performance

The revenue of the company is on an upward trend in the last five years despite a slight dip in 2019. Net income is also going on the same path over the same period.

In 2019 the revenue of the company had a slight drop of 2% to $415.3 million. Rental revenue had a 3% drop Interest income on real estate loans and others had a 6% decrease offset by a 3% increase in expense recoveries.

Net income for 2019 was $74.5 million up 32% from the prior year. The increase was due to lower operating expenses and a gain of $31.3 million from sale of investment properties.

Cash at the end of the year for the company was $2.4 million. Net cash provided by operating activities was $201.2 million and cash provided by financing activities was $37.3 million. Investing activities used $255.3 million for acquisitions and issuance of real estate loans receivables.

Strategy

The company intends to grow its portfolio of high-quality healthcare properties leased to physicians hospitals healthcare delivery systems and other healthcare providers primarily through acquisitions of existing healthcare facilities that provide stable revenue growth and predictable long-term cash flows. It may also selectively finance the development of new healthcare facilities through a joint venture or fee arrangements with premier healthcare real estate developers. Generally it expects to make investments in new development properties when approximately 80% or more of the development property has been pre-leased before construction commences.

The company also seeks to invest in properties where it can develop strategic alliances with financially sound healthcare providers and healthcare delivery systems that offer need-based healthcare services in sustainable healthcare markets. It focuses its investment activity on the following types of healthcare properties: medical office buildings; outpatient treatment and diagnostic facilities; physician group practice clinics; ambulatory surgery centers; and specialty hospitals and treatment centers.

EXECUTIVES

Independent Trustee, Richard Weiss
President, Chief Executive Officer & Trustee, John Thomas, $908,938 total compensation
Executive Vice President, Asset And Investment Management, Mark Theine, $428,000 total compensation
Independent Trustee, Mark Baumgartner
Senior Vice President And Controller, Laurie Becker
Independent Trustee, William Ebinger
Chief Accounting Officer, John Lucey, $287,115 total compensation
Independent Trustee, Pamela Kessler
Senior Vice President, Leasing And Physician Strategy, Amy Hall
Non-executive Independent Chairman Of The Board Of Trustees, Thomas Thompson
Chief Financial Officer, Executive Vice President, Jeff Theiler, $541,055 total compensation

Senior Vice President, General Counsel, Bradley Page, $382,628 total compensation
Deputy Chief Investment Officer, Daniel Klein, $293,615 total compensation
Auditors: Ernst & Young LLP

LOCATIONS

HQ: Physicians Realty Trust
309 N. Water Street, Suite 500, Milwaukee, WI 53202
Phone: 414 367-5600
Web: www.docreit.com

COMPETITORS

DIVERSIFIED HEALTHCARE HEALTH TRUST
HEALTHCARE REALTY TRUST INCORPORATED
HEALTHPEAK PROPERTIES INC.
NATIONAL INVESTORS INC.
OMEGA HEALTHCARE INVESTORS INC.
VENTAS INC.

HISTORICAL FINANCIALS

Company Type: Public

Income Statement				FYE: December 31
	REVENUE ($ mil.)	NET INCOME ($ mil.)	NET PROFIT MARGIN	EMPLOYEES
12/20	437.5	66.1	15.1%	81
12/19	415.2	74.4	17.9%	77
12/18	422.5	56.2	13.3%	70
12/17	343.5	38.1	11.1%	63
12/16	241.0	29.9	12.4%	41
Annual Growth	16.1%	21.9%	—	18.6%

2020 Year-End Financials

Debt ratio: 32.6%	No. of shares (mil.): 209.5
Return on equity: 2.6%	Dividends
Cash ($ mil.): 2.5	Yield: 5.1%
Current ratio: 0.12	Payout: 287.5%
Long-term debt ($ mil.): 1,438.8	Market value ($ mil): 3,730.0

	STOCK PRICE ($) FY Close	P/E High/Low		PER SHARE ($)	
			Earnings	Dividends	Book Value
12/20	17.80	65 36	0.32	0.92	12.60
12/19	18.94	49 40	0.39	0.92	12.68
12/18	16.03	60 48	0.30	0.92	13.04
12/17	17.99	95 75	0.23	0.91	13.63
12/16	18.96	100 72	0.22	0.90	12.79
Annual Growth	(1.6%)	— —	9.8%	0.6%	(0.4%)

Pinnacle Financial Partners Inc

Pinnacle Financial Partners is the holding company for Tennessee-based Pinnacle Bank which has grown to some 115 offices in Tennessee North Carolina South Carolina Virginia and Georgia since its founding in 2000. Serving consumers and small- to mid-sized business the $35 billion financial institution provides standard services such as checking and savings accounts CDs credit cards and loans and mortgages. The company also offers investment and trust services through Pinnacle Asset Management while its insurance brokerage subsidiary Miller Loughry Beach specializes in property/casualty policies.

Operations

Pinnacle Financial Partners' commercial and industrial loans and commercial real estate loans account for 35% each of its total portfolio of loans.

As part of its primary services to both individual and commercial clients Tennessee-based subsidiary Pinnacle Bank provides core deposits including savings checking interest-bearing checking money market and certificate of deposit accounts.

The bank's lending products include commercial real estate and consumer loans to individuals and small- to medium-sized businesses and professional entities. Additionally it offers Pinnacle-branded consumer credit cards to select clients.

Pinnacle Bank contracts with Raymond James Financial Services Inc. (RJFS) a registered broker-dealer and investment adviser to offer and sell various securities and other financial products to the public through associates who are employed by both Pinnacle Bank and RJFS. RJFS is a subsidiary of Raymond James Financial Inc.

Geographic Reach

Based in Tennessee Pinnacle Financial Partners has about 115 offices including nearly 50 offices in Tennessee about 35 in North Carolina 20 in South Carolina nine offices in Virginia and one in Georgia. It boasts locations in Nashville Knoxville Davidson Murfreesboro Chattanooga Memphis Greensboro Highpoint Charlotte Concord Gastonia Roanoke Winston and Salem.

Sales and Marketing

Pinnacle Bank traditionally has obtained its deposits through personal solicitation by its officers and directors although it has used media advertising more in recent years due to its advertising and banking sponsorship with the Tennessee Titans NFL Football team. While it would prefer its customers to bank in person the institution allows customers to bank remotely.

Its convenience-centered products and services include 24-hour telephone and Internet banking debit and credit cards direct deposit and cash management services.

Its marketing and other business development costs have risen in recent years: $10.7 million $13.3 million and $311.7 million in 2020 2019 and 2018 respectively.

Financial Performance

Pinnacle Financial Partners has enjoyed steady revenue and profit growth for the past several years except net income fell in 2020.

Pinnacle's net interest income increased to $821.8 million for 2020 compared to $766.1 million for 2019. The increase was largely the result of lower cost of funds the impact of both interest and fees related to PPP its building of additional liquidity in response to the economic uncertainty resulting from the COVID-19 pandemic and organic loan growth during the comparable periods.

Net income for 2020 fell 22% to $312.3 million compared to $400.9 million in net income in 2019.

Cash at the end of the fiscal year 2020 was $4 billion compared to $526.7 million in the prior year. Operating activities generated $427.8 million while investing activities used $3.6 billion mostly for activities in securities available-for-sale and increase in loans. Financing activities provided $6.6 billion in 2020.

Strategy

A substantial focus of Pinnacle's marketing and business strategy is to serve small to medium-sized businesses in its market areas. As a result a relatively high percentage of its loan portfolio consists of commercial loans primarily to small to medium-sized businesses. The bank expects to seek to expand the amount of commercial and industrial loans and commercial real-estate loans in its portfolio during 2021. During periods of lower economic growth or challenging economic periods like those resulting from the COVID-19 pandemic small to medium-sized businesses may be impacted more severely and more quickly than larger businesses.

Much of Pinnacle's organic loan growth that it experienced in recent years (and a key part of its loan growth strategy in 2021 and beyond) was the result not of strong loan demand but rather of its ability to attract experienced financial services professionals who have been able to attract customers from other financial institutions. Pinnacle's growth strategy necessarily entails growth in overhead expenses as it adds new offices and staff.

EXECUTIVES

Chairman Of The Board, Robert McCabe, $1,007,000 total compensation
Chief Financial Officer, Executive Vice President, Principal Financial Officer, Principal Accounting Officer, Harold Carpenter, $548,880 total compensation
Chief Administrative Officer, Hugh Queener, $548,880 total compensation
Independent Director, Reese Smith
President, Chief Executive Officer, Director, M. Terry Turner, $1,060,000 total compensation
Independent Director, Renda Burkhart
Independent Director, Charles Brock
Lead Independent Director, Marty Dickens
Independent Director, Joseph Galante
Independent Director, Thomas Farnsworth
Vice Chairman Of The Board, Ronald Samuel
Chief Credit Officer, Timothy Huestis
Director, Decosta Jenkins
Independent Director, Glenda Glover
Executive Director, Richard Callicutt, $701,000 total compensation
Independent Director, Abney Boxley
Auditors: Crowe LLP

LOCATIONS

HQ: Pinnacle Financial Partners Inc
150 Third Avenue South, Suite 900, Nashville, TN 37201
Phone: 615 744-3700
Web: www.pnfp.com

PRODUCTS/OPERATIONS

2014 Revenue

	% of total
Interest Income	80
Non-interest Income	20
Total	100

Selected Subsidiaries

Pinnacle Advisory Services Inc.
Pinnacle Credit Enhancement Holdings Inc.
Pinnacle National Bank
  Miller & Loughry Inc. (dba Miller Loughry Beach)
  PFP Title Company
  Pinnacle Community Development Corporation
  Pinnacle Nashville Real Estate Inc.
  Pinnacle Rutherford Real Estate Inc.
  Pinnacle Rutherford Towers Inc.
  Pinnacle Service Company Inc.
PNFP Insurance Inc.

COMPETITORS

BOK FINANCIAL CORPORATION
BOKF MERGER CORPORATION NUMBER SIXTEEN
COLUMBIA BANKING SYSTEM INC.
F.N.B. CORPORATION
FINANCIAL INSTITUTIONS INC.
FIRST COMMONWEALTH FINANCIAL CORPORATION
FIRST HORIZON CORPORATION
FIRST MIDWEST BANCORP INC.
HERITAGE FINANCIAL CORPORATION
KEYCORP
M&T BANK CORPORATION
MIDSOUTH BANCORP INC.
NATIONAL BANK HOLDINGS CORPORATION
PACIFIC CONTINENTAL CORPORATION
PACWEST BANCORP
PRIVATEBANCORP INC.
SIMMONS FIRST NATIONAL CORPORATION
SUNTRUST BANKS INC.
U.S. BANCORP
UMB FINANCIAL CORPORATION
VALLEY NATIONAL BANCORP
WEBSTER FINANCIAL CORPORATION
WINTRUST FINANCIAL CORPORATION

HISTORICAL FINANCIALS

Company Type: Public

Income Statement

FYE: December 31

	ASSETS ($ mil.)	NET INCOME ($ mil.)	INCOME AS % OF ASSETS	EMPLOYEES
12/20	34,932.8	312.3	0.9%	2,634
12/19	27,805.5	400.8	1.4%	2,487
12/18	25,031.0	359.4	1.4%	2,297
12/17	22,205.7	173.9	0.8%	2,132
12/16	11,194.6	127.2	1.1%	1,180
Annual Growth 32.9%		25.2%	—	22.2%

2020 Year-End Financials

Return on assets: 0.9%
Return on equity: 6.7%
Long-term debt ($ mil.): —
No. of shares (mil.): 75.8
Sales ($ mil): 1,338.8

Dividends
Yield: 0.9%
Payout: 16.5%
Market value ($ mil.): 4,885.0

	STOCK PRICE ($) FY Close	P/E High/Low		Earnings	PER SHARE ($) Dividends	Book Value
12/20	64.40	16	8	4.03	0.64	64.66
12/19	64.00	12	9	5.22	0.64	56.89
12/18	46.10	15	9	4.64	0.58	51.18
12/17	66.30	26	21	2.70	0.56	47.70
12/16	69.30	24	15	2.91	0.56	32.28
Annual Growth (1.8%)		—	—	8.5%	3.4%	19.0%

Pinterest Inc

Auditors: Ernst & Young LLP

LOCATIONS

HQ: Pinterest Inc
  505 Brannan Street, San Francisco, CA 94107
Phone: 415 762-7100
Web: www.pinterest.com

HISTORICAL FINANCIALS

Company Type: Public

Income Statement

FYE: December 31

	REVENUE ($ mil.)	NET INCOME ($ mil.)	NET PROFIT MARGIN	EMPLOYEES
12/21	2,578.0	316.4	12.3%	3,225
12/20	1,692.6	(128.3)	—	2,545
12/19	1,142.7	(1,361.3)	—	2,217
12/18	755.9	(62.9)	—	1,797
12/17	472.8	(130.0)	—	0
Annual Growth 52.8%		—	—	—

2021 Year-End Financials

Debt ratio: —
Return on equity: 11.9%
Cash ($ mil.): 1,419.6
Current ratio: 12.25
Long-term debt ($ mil.): —

No. of shares (mil.): 656.8
Dividends
  Yield: —
  Payout: —
Market value ($ mil.): 23,877.0

	STOCK PRICE ($) FY Close	P/E High/Low		Earnings	PER SHARE ($) Dividends	Book Value
12/21	36.35	182	71	0.46	0.00	4.63
12/20	65.90	—	—	(0.22)	0.00	3.58
12/19	18.64	—	—	(3.24)	0.00	3.55
Annual Growth 39.6%		—	—	—	—	14.1%

Piper Sandler Companies

Investment bank Piper Sandler Companies specializes in supplying clients with mergers and acquisitions advice financing and industry research. Founded in 1895 Piper Sandler provides a broad set of products and services including financial advisory services; equity and debt capital markets products; public finance services; equity research and institutional brokerage; fixed income services; and private equity strategies. Piper Sandler targets a variety of clients including corporations government entities not-for-profits and middle-market companies across the consumer financial services healthcare technology and industrial sectors. Majority of its revenue comes from US customers.

Operations

Piper Sandler operates in one reportable segment providing investment banking and institutional sales trading and research services for various equity and fixed income products.

Investment Banking provides advisory services which includes mergers and acquisitions; equity and debt private placements; and debt and restructuring advisory for its corporate clients. For its government and non-profit clients it underwrite municipal issuances provide municipal financial advisory and loan placement services and offer various over-the-counter derivative products. Its public finance investment banking capabilities focus on state and local governments cultural and social service non-profit entities special districts project financings and the education healthcare hospitality senior living and transportation sectors.

Through Equity and Fixed Income Institutional Brokerage Piper Sandler offers equity and fixed income advisory and trade execution services for institutional investors and government and non-profit entities. Fixed income services provides advice on balance sheet management investment strategy and customized portfolio solutions.

Alternative Asset Management Funds involve equity investments in late stage private companies and in the energy sector whose principal activity is to invest in oil and gas services companies headquartered in Europe.

Overall its investment banking accounts for nearly 70% total sales and some 30% accounts for institutional brokerage.

Geographic Reach

Headquartered in Minneapolis Minnesota and has 60-plus offices across the US London Aberdeen and Hong Kong.

The majority of its revenue comes from US.

Sales and Marketing

Piper Sandler serves corporations private equity groups public entities non-profit entities and institutional investors.

Financial Performance

Net revenues from continuing operations for 2020 increased 48% to $1.2 billion compared with $834.6 million in the year-ago period driven by record corporate financing revenues.

In 2020 the company recorded net income from continuing operations applicable to Piper Sandler Companies of $40.5 million.

Cash held for fiscal 2020 increased to $507.9 million. Cash provided by operations was $779.8 million while cash used for investing and financing activities were $435.0 million and $87.6 million respectively. Main uses of cash were business acquisitions and decrease in short-term financing.

Strategy

The company's long-term strategic objectives are to drive revenue growth build a stronger and more durable platform continue to gain market share and maximize shareholder value. In order to meet these objectives we are focused on the following: continuing to transform its business through strategic investments and selectively adding partners who share its client-centric culture and who can leverage the company's platform to better serve clients; growing its investment banking platform through market share gains accretive combinations developing internal talent and continued sector and geographic expansion. The company also believes there is an opportunity to capitalize on the strength of its US franchises by expanding in Europe; leveraging the scale within the equity brokerage and fixed income services platforms driven by its recently expanded client base and product offerings to grow market share; and prudently managing capital to maintain its balance sheet strength with ample liquidity and flexibility through all market conditions.

Mergers and Acquisitions

In late 2020 Piper Sandler completed the acquisition of TRS Advisors an independent advisory firm focused on advising and executing restructurings reorganizations and other complex financial transactions for public private and governmental clients. TRS Advisors will operate as Piper Sandler's restructuring group. The acquisition strengthen its strong investment banking relationships across multiple industry sectors with their expertise advising in complex matters.

Piper Sandler acquired Valence Group in early 2020. The Valence Group is an innovative entrepreneur-led global investment bank that offers

M&A advisory services to companies and financial sponsors with deep expertise in chemicals materials and related sectors. The Valence Group will form Piper Sandler's new chemicals group adding yet another industry-leading advisory practice to the Piper Sandler platform.

In 2020 Piper Jaffray Companies and Sandler O'Neill + Partners L.P. announced the completion of their merger to become Piper Sandler Companies. The resulting company represents one of the broadest and most capable full-service investment banking platforms on Wall Street complemented by one of the largest securities distribution and trading franchises with market-leading research aligned to serve the middle-market. The purchase price was $485.0 million.

HISTORY

In 1913 Harry Piper and Palmer Jaffray founded a commercial paper brokerage that helped finance companies like Pillsbury and Archer-Daniels-Midland. It soon moved into public finance and underwriting. It gained a seat on the NYSE with its purchase of Hopwood & Co. which was hard hit by the 1929 crash. Piper Jaffray & Hopwood grew over the next 40 years going public in 1971. Three years later it became Piper Jaffray.

During the 1980s boom Piper Jaffray still managed by the Piper family expanded into asset management and mutual funds. It was relatively unscathed by the 1987 crash.

Real trouble hit in 1994 when a derivatives-heavy bond mutual fund foundered. Investors claiming they were uninformed of the risk brought a class-action suit against the firm which paid out more than $100 million in settlements beginning in 1995.

In 1997 Piper Jaffray began offering new classes of shares of its mutual funds to provide more fee options for investors. The SEC sued the company for fraud related to the 1994 mutual fund debacle in 1998.

That year U. S. Bancorp looking to expand its securities business bought the company and bundled its own investment operations into U. S. Bancorp Piper Jaffray. In 1999 the unit expanded with the purchase of investment banker Libra Investments. The firm also entered an alliance with Tel Aviv-based investment bank Nessuah Zannex to back technology and health care ventures in Israel.

Piper Jaffray traditionally has taken pride in its investment research yet it was one of several investment banks scrutinized for alleged conflicts-of-interest between research and I-banking operations. In 2003 the firm was fined $25 million and required to pay an additional $7.5 million to provide independent research for investors. As part of the settlement the company combined its research functions into a single group and implemented firewalls between its analysts and investment bankers. Losing money Piper Jaffray was spun off from U.S. Bancorp and returned to the publicly traded arena that same year.

Piper Jaffray sold its Private Client business which offered mutual funds securities and annuities to individual investors to UBS Financial Services in 2006. Piper Jaffray used proceeds from the sale of the unit which included some 90 branches mainly west of the Mississippi to expand its industry focus. It built its asset management business with the 2007 purchases of St. Louis-based Fiduciary Asset Management (FAMCO) which brought

in some $6 billion of assets under management and Hong Kong-based Goldbond Capital.

EXECUTIVES

Chb-Ceo, Chad R Abraham
V Chm, James J Dunne III
V Chm, Jonathan J Doyle
Pres, Debbra L Schoneman
Cfo, Timothy L Carter
Gen Counsel-Sec, John W Geelan
Managing Dir, Richard Singh
Managing Dir, Austin Harbour
Managing Director, Mark Cieciura
Senior Research Analyst, Matthew Clark
Associate Investment Banking, Melissa French
Auditors: Ernst & Young LLP

LOCATIONS

HQ: Piper Sandler Companies
800 Nicollet Mall, Suite 900, Minneapolis, MN 55402
Phone: 612 303-6000
Web: www.piperjaffray.com

PRODUCTS/OPERATIONS

2018 Revenue

	$ mil.	% of total
Investment banking	589.0	74
Institutional brokerage	124.5	15
Asset management	49.8	6
Interest	32.7	4
Other	4.9	1
Adjustments	(16.5)	-
Total	**784.4**	**100**

Selected Services

Investment Banking
  Services
    Mergers & Acquisitions
    Capital Markets
    Private Placements
    Restructuring
    Debt Advisory
    Corporate & Venture Services
Public Finance
    Government Expertise
    Local Municipalities
    States & State Agencies

COMPETITORS

BRC MERGER SUB LLC
E TRADE FINANCIAL CORPORATION
FRANKLIN RESOURCES INC.
HOULIHAN LOKEY INC.
JEFFERIES FINANCIAL GROUP INC.
LPL FINANCIAL HOLDINGS INC.
PRINCIPAL GLOBAL INVESTORS LLC
SCHRODERS PLC
SEI INVESTMENTS COMPANY
STIFEL FINANCIAL CORP.
WADDELL & REED FINANCIAL INC.

HISTORICAL FINANCIALS
Company Type: Public

Income Statement				FYE: December 31
	REVENUE ($ mil.)	NET INCOME ($ mil.)	NET PROFIT MARGIN	EMPLOYEES
12/20	1,252.6	40.5	3.2%	1,511
12/19	846.3	111.7	13.2%	1,565
12/18	800.9	57.0	7.1%	1,262
12/17	895.1	(61.9)	—	1,301
12/16	769.8	(21.9)	—	1,315
Annual Growth	12.9%	—		3.5%

2020 Year-End Financials

Debt ratio: 17.3%
Return on equity: 5.1%
Cash ($ mil.): 507.9
Current ratio: 1.29
Long-term debt ($ mil.): 195.0
No. of shares (mil.): 13.7
Dividends
  Yield: 1.9%
  Payout: 73.5%
Market value ($ mil.): 1,390.0

	STOCK PRICE ($) FY Close	P/E High/Low		PER SHARE ($) Earnings	Dividends	Book Value
12/20	100.90	36	12	2.72	2.00	60.21
12/19	79.94	10	8	7.39	2.51	53.31
12/18	65.84	26	16	3.72	3.12	52.13
12/17	86.25	—	—	(5.07)	1.25	53.70
12/16	72.50	—	—	(1.73)	0.00	61.27
Annual Growth	8.6%			—	—	(0.4%)

PJT Partners Inc

Auditors: DELOITTE & TOUCHE LLP

LOCATIONS

HQ: PJT Partners Inc
280 Park Avenue, New York, NY 10017
Phone: 212 364-7800
Web: www.pjtpartners.com

HISTORICAL FINANCIALS
Company Type: Public

Income Statement				FYE: December 31
	REVENUE ($ mil.)	NET INCOME ($ mil.)	NET PROFIT MARGIN	EMPLOYEES
12/20	1,052.3	117.5	11.2%	749
12/19	717.6	29.5	4.1%	678
12/18	580.2	27.1	4.7%	590
12/17	499.2	(32.5)	—	473
12/16	499.4	(3.0)	—	419
Annual Growth	20.5%	—	—	15.6%

2020 Year-End Financials

Debt ratio: —
Return on equity: 126.2%
Cash ($ mil.): 299.5
Current ratio: 2.22
Long-term debt ($ mil.): —
No. of shares (mil.): 23.8
Dividends
  Yield: 0.2%
  Payout: 4.5%
Market value ($ mil.): 1,792.0

	STOCK PRICE ($) FY Close	P/E High/Low		PER SHARE ($) Earnings	Dividends	Book Value
12/20	75.25	16	5	4.40	0.20	6.48
12/19	45.13	38	29	1.21	0.20	1.36
12/18	38.76	49	29	1.16	0.20	(3.83)
12/17	45.60	—	—	(1.73)	0.20	(8.48)
12/16	30.88	—	—	(0.17)	0.20	(0.48)
Annual Growth	24.9%			—	— (0.0%)	—

Plumas Bancorp Inc

Plumas Bancorp is the holding company for Plumas Bank which serves individuals and businesses in the northeastern corner of California from Lake Tahoe to the Oregon border. Through more than a dozen branches the bank offers deposit products such as checking savings and retirement accounts and certificates of deposit. Loans secured by real estate account for more than half of Plumas Bank's loan portfolio; combined commercial and agricultural loans make up about a quarter. The bank writes consumer loans as well. It also provides access to investment products and services such as financial planning mutual funds and annuities.

EXECUTIVES

Executive Vice President And Chief Credit Officer Of The Bank, Jeffery Moore
Independent Director, Richard Kenny
Independent Director, Steven Coldani
Independent Vice Chairman Of The Board, Robert Mcclintock
Ir Contact Officer, Jamie Huynh
Executive Vice President And Chief Information Officer Of The Bank, Aaron Boigon
Independent Director, Gerald Fletcher
Chief Financial Officer, Executive Vice President Of The Company And The Bank, Richard Belstock, $212,000 total compensation
President, Chief Executive Officer, Director, Andrew Ryback, $347,000 total compensation
Executive Vice President And Chief Banking Officer Of Plumas Bank, B. North, $205,000 total compensation
Independent Director, Secretary Of The Board, Terrance Reeson
Independent Chairman Of The Board, Daniel West
Auditors: Eide Bailly LLP

LOCATIONS

HQ: Plumas Bancorp Inc
 5525 Kietzke Lane, Suite 100, Reno, NV 89511
Phone: 775 786-0907
Web: www.plumasbank.com

COMPETITORS

CITIZENS BANK INC	FIRST NORTHERN
EMCLAIRE FINANCIAL	COMMUNITY BANCORP
CORP.	SVB & T CORPORATION

HISTORICAL FINANCIALS
Company Type: Public

Income Statement				FYE: December 31
	ASSETS ($ mil.)	**NET INCOME** ($ mil.)	**INCOME AS % OF ASSETS**	**EMPLOYEES**
12/20	1,111.5	14.4	1.3%	177
12/19	865.1	15.5	1.8%	183
12/18	824.4	13.9	1.7%	174
12/17	745.4	8.1	1.1%	161
12/16	657.9	7.4	1.1%	155
Annual Growth	14.0%	18.0%	—	3.4%

2020 Year-End Financials

Return on assets: 1.4%	Dividends
Return on equity: 15.6%	Yield: 1.5%
Long-term debt ($ mil.): —	Payout: 13.3%
No. of shares (mil.): 5.1	Market value ($ mil.): 122.0
Sales ($ mil): 48.0	

	STOCK PRICE ($) FY Close	P/E High/Low		PER SHARE ($) Earnings	Dividends	Book Value
12/20	23.50	10	5	2.77	0.36	19.33
12/19	26.38	9	7	2.97	0.46	16.36
12/18	22.71	11	8	2.68	0.36	13.03
12/17	23.20	14	10	1.58	0.28	11.00
12/16	19.00	12	5	1.47	0.10	9.80
Annual Growth	5.5%	—	—	17.2%	37.7%	18.5%

Pool Corp

Pool Corporation swims laps around its competitors as the world's largest wholesale distributor of swimming pool supplies equipment and related leisure products and is one of the leading distributors of irrigation and landscape products in the United States. It operates about 400 service centers throughout the North America Europe and Australia serving some 120000 wholesale customers such as pool builders and remodelers retail pool stores and pool repair and service companies. Pool Corporation's more than 200000 products include private-label and name-brand pool maintenance items (chemicals cleaners) equipment (pumps filters) accessories (heaters lights) and packaged pool kits. Founded in 1993 as SCP Holding Pool Corporation generates most of its sales in the US.

Operations

Pool Corporation operates through four distribution networks: SCP Distributors Superior Pool Products Horizon Distributors and National Pool Tile.

The SCP Distribution and Superior Pool Products networks offer pool supplies equipment and related leisure products. Horizon Distributors locations sell supply irrigation and landscape products and National Pool Tile stores feature tile decking materials and interior pool finishes as well as hardscape and natural stone products pool supplies and equipment.

Pool Corporation has some 600 product lines and more than 50 product categories. Its largest product category is pool and hot tub chemicals which account for some 10% of total sales.

The company's largest suppliers include Pentair plc (approximately 20%) Hayward Pool Products (some 10%) and Zodiac Pool Systems (about 10%).

Geographic Reach

The US accounts for some 90% of Pool Corporation's sales. The company's largest markets — with the highest concentration of swimming pools — are California Florida Texas and Arizona representing about 55% of total sales.

Beyond the US Covington Louisiana-based Pool Corporation has operations in Australia Canada Mexico and more than half a dozen countries in Europe (Belgium Croatia France Germany Italy Portugal Spain and the UK).

The company's network of about 400 sales centers spans the Americas Europe and Australia.

Sales and Marketing

Pool Corporation sells its products primarily to swimming pool remodelers and builders; specialty retailers that sell swimming pool supplies; swimming pool repair and service businesses; irrigation construction and landscape maintenance contractors; and commercial customers who service large commercial installations such as hotels universities and community recreational facilities. Most customers are small family-owned businesses with relatively limited capital resources.

Pool Corporation sells its products through sales centers and maintains its own trucks as well as partnering with third party carrier services to provide doorstep delivery.

The company's advertising costs were $6.8 million $7.8 million and $7.4 for the years 2020 2019 and 2018 respectively.

Financial Performance

Net sales increased 23% to $3.9 billion for the year ended December 31 2020 compared to $3.2 billion in 2019. The company realized broad sales gains across nearly all product categories. Pool Corpration's sales benefited from greater swimming pool usage and high demand for residential pool products which was driven by home-centric trends influenced by the COVID-19 pandemic and aided by warmer weather conditions during the year.

Net income increased 40% to $366.7 million in 2020 compared to $261.6 million in 2019.

Cash held by the company at the end of fiscal 2020 increased to $34.1 million. Cash provided by operations was $397.6 million while cash used for investing and financing activities were $146.3 million and $244.4 million respectively. Main uses of cash were acquisition of businesses; and payments on revolving line of credit.

Strategy

The company's mission is to provide exceptional value to its customers and suppliers creating exceptional return to its shareholders while providing exceptional opportunities to our employees. Pool Corporation's core strategies are as follows: to promote the growth of its industry; to promote the growth of its customers' businesses; and to continuously strive to operate more effectively.

Company Background

Pool Corporation traces its history to Frank St. Romain who began his career in the pool distribution industry as a warehouse manager. Romain and partner Richard Smith established their own company South Central Pool Supply in 1981. It grew opening sales centers across the southeastern US.

Industry veteran Wilson B. "Rusty" Sexton joined the company as a consultant in 1990 and became CEO of the entity created when the company partnered with investment firm Code Hennessy & Simmons in 1993 — SCP Pool Corporation.

SCP Pool went public in 1995. It took the Pool Corporation name in 2006.

EXECUTIVES

Treasurer, Chief Financial & Accounting Officer, Melanie Housey Hart
Independent Director, Debra Oler
President Of Horizon Distributors, Inc., Jeffrey Clay
Vice President - Operations And Supply Chain, David Collier
Director, Martha Gervasi
Corporate Controller, Walker Saik
President, Chief Executive Officer, Director, Peter Arvan, $500,000 total compensation
Group Vice President, Kenneth St. Romain, $325,000 total compensation

Lead Independent Chairman Of The Board, John Stokely
Vice President, Corporate Secretary, Chief Legal Officer, Jennifer Neil, $250,000 total compensation
Auditors: Ernst & Young LLP

LOCATIONS

HQ: Pool Corp
109 Northpark Boulevard, Covington, LA 70433-5001
Phone: 985 892-5521 **Fax:** 985 892-2438
Web: www.poolcorp.com

PRODUCTS/OPERATIONS

Selected Products
ASME heaters
Building materials
Chemicals
Cleaners
Commercial pumps
Decking materials
Electrical supplies
Filters
Grills
Hardscapes
Heaters
irrigation and landscape products
Lights
Liners
Natural stone
Packaged pools
Parts and supplies
Pumps
Recreational products
Replacement parts
Repair parts
Spas and spa accessories
Swimming pool equipment and accessories
Tiles
Walls

COMPETITORS

AMAZON.COM INC.
ATLANTIC DIVING SUPPLY INC.
DAIWA CORPORATION
KING PAR LLC
MAURICE SPORTING GOODS OF DELAWARE INC.
PURE FISHING INC.
TARGET CORPORATION

HISTORICAL FINANCIALS

Company Type: Public

Income Statement   FYE: December 31

	REVENUE ($ mil.)	NET INCOME ($ mil.)	NET PROFIT MARGIN	EMPLOYEES
12/20	3,936.6	366.7	9.3%	4,500
12/19	3,199.5	261.5	8.2%	4,500
12/18	2,998.1	234.4	7.8%	4,000
12/17	2,788.1	191.6	6.9%	4,000
12/16	2,570.8	148.9	5.8%	3,900
Annual Growth	11.2%	25.3%	—	3.6%

2020 Year-End Financials

Debt ratio: 23.9%	No. of shares (mil.): 40.2
Return on equity: 69.6%	Dividends
Cash ($ mil.): 34.1	Yield: 0.6%
Current ratio: 2.32	Payout: 28.7%
Long-term debt ($ mil.): 404.1	Market value ($ mil.): 14,986.0

STOCK PRICE ($) FY Close	P/E High/Low	PER SHARE ($) Earnings	Dividends	Book Value
12/20	372.50	42 18	8.97	2.29	15.89
12/19	212.38	33 22	6.40	2.10	10.24
12/18	148.65	30 22	5.62	1.72	5.66
12/17	129.65	28 21	4.51	1.42	5.55
12/16	104.34	30 21	3.47	1.19	4.99
Annual Growth	37.5%	—	26.8%	17.8%	33.6%

PotlatchDeltic Corp

PotlatchDeltic Corporation (formerly Potlatch Corporation) is a real estate investment trust (REIT) harvests timber from some 1.8 million acres of hardwood and softwood forestland in Alabama Arkansas Idaho Mississippi Louisiana and Minnesota; it claims to be the largest private landowner in Idaho. Potlatch operates six sawmills and an industrial grade plywood mill a residential and commercial real estate development business and a rural timberland sales program. Beyond wood product sales the company generates revenue by leasing its land for hunting recreation mineral rights biomass production and carbon sequestration. It also sells real estate through PotlatchDeltic TRS.

Operations
PotlatchDeltic operates three main business segments: Wood Products Timberlands Real Estates.

Its Wood Products segment which made up of nearly 60% of its sales makes and sells lumber plywood and residual products. Its Timberlands segment (more than 30% of sales) manages timberland leases it for hunting recreation mineral rights biomass production and carbon sequestration. The real estate segment (about 10% of sales) sells non-strategic or low-revenue generating land holdings through PotlatchDeltic TRS.

Geographic Reach
Washington-based PotlatchDeltic harvested almost all of its revenue from sales in the US. The REIT has sawmills in Alabama Arkansas Idaho Louisiana Mississippi and Minnesota.

Sales and Marketing
The company sells its products directly through its sales offices to end users retailers or national wholesalers. Its products are mostly used in home building industrial products or other construction. Timberlands' customers range in size from small operators to multinational corporations.

Financial Performance
Revenues were approximately $1.0 billion an increase of $213.8 million compared to 2019. The increase in 2020 was a result of historically high lumber prices during the second half of the year along with increased lumber shipments increased harvest volumes higher sawlog prices in the Northern region and the 72440 acre conservation land sale to TCF.

Net income for fiscal 2020 increased to $166.8 million compared from the prior year with $55.7 million.

Cash held by the company at the end of fiscal 2020 increased to $252.3 million. Cash provided by operations was $335.3 million while cash used for investing and financing activities were $42.2 million and $125.0 million respectively. Main cash uses were for capital expenditures and distributions to common stockholders.

Strategy
The company's business strategy encompasses the following key elements: timberlands provide stability; leverage to lumber prices; integrated timberlands and wood products operating model; efficient and productive wood products facilities; capturing incremental value of its real estate holdings; pursuing attractive acquisitions; committed to responsible environmental social and governance values.

Internal log sales to the company's mills comprised 37% of its Timberlands revenues in 2020. This represented 51% of its mill needs on a volume basis. This strategy enables the company to maximize the value of its assets and because Potlatchdeltic are a net log buyer in the South its integrated model provides a natural hedge against southern sawlog prices that remain below long-term levels.

Company Background
Founded in 1903 by Frederick Weyerhaeuser Potlatch have a rich history in timberland management and forest products. The Potlatch Lumber Company was founded along the banks of the Palouse River in North Central Idaho. The rugged and colorful lumberjacks and lumber mill workers from its early founding years transitioned into modern day forestry professionals and wood products experts. Both were and continue to be admirers of the trees and of the forests where they grow.

HISTORY

Lumber magnate Frederick Weyerhaeuser led a swarm of midwestern lumber companies into virgin northern Idaho forests at the turn of the 20th century. Two primary rivals — William Deary of Northland Pine Company (a firm helped by Weyerhaeuser) and Henry Turrish of Wisconsin Log & Lumber — bought thousands of acres of white pine around the state's Palouse Potlatch and Elk river basins. They kept land prices down by purchasing it together. In 1903 they merged more than 100000 acres and created Potlatch Lumber. Weyerhaeuser's son Charles served as president.

Potlatch struggled for three decades in the high-risk lumber business. Maintaining a mill and a company town (Potlatch Idaho) was expensive and the company's policy of harvesting all tree varieties instead of those in demand didn't help. With the opening of the Panama Canal in 1914 Pacific Coast companies were able to undercut Potlatch in eastern markets by using the cheap transportation alternative. Before his death in 1914 Weyerhaeuser reportedly referred to Potlatch as an appropriate name for a company that spent piles of money with miniscule returns. To survive the Depression the company merged with two major competitors Clearwater and Edward Rutledge in 1931. The new company Potlatch Forests was headed by Weyerhaeuser's descendants.

The WWII boom helped Potlatch raise badly needed profits from lumber orders. Afterwards the company introduced new products including paperboard used in milk cartons plywood and laminated decking. It expanded its timber reserves through acquisitions in Arkansas and Minnesota. In the 1960s Potlatch bought Clearwater Tissue Mills. The company moved its headquarters to San Francisco in 1965 and changed its name in 1973 to Potlatch Corporation.

Richard Madden became chairman and CEO in 1971 and reduced operations from 20 product lines to four — wood printed papers pulp and paperboard and tissue. The company emphasized capital expenditures such as its 1981 construction of the first US plant to make plywood-alternative oriented strand board.

In 1994 Madden retired and COO Pendleton Siegel succeeded him. In 1997 the company moved its headquarters to Spokane Washington; the following year it announced plans to spend more than $200 million to modernize and expand its Cloquet Minnesota pulp mill.

Potlatch and Anderson-Tully Company hatched a plan in 1998 to combine their Arkansas timber holdings into the Timberland Growth Corporation the first public real estate investment trust (REIT) to focus on timber ownership. The plan fell apart in 1999 however because of a weak timber market in Asia and weakened confidence in US markets after declines in the autumn of 1998.

The company's upgrade of its Cloquet pulp mill (including a new pulp machine) was completed in late 1999. Poor performance by the company's Minnesota pulp and paper division in 2000 led the company to trim about 300 jobs. It eliminated an additional 124 positions early in 2001.

In 2002 Potlatch sold its Cloquet Minnesota coated fine pulp and printing papers facilities to a subsidiary of Sappi Limited for $480 million in cash. Early the next year the company sold its Brainerd Minnesota paper mill and related assets to Missota Paper Company for $4.44 million in cash.

The company reorganized itself as a REIT in 2006. Under this arrangement Potlatch was able to derive tax benefits from its timberland holdings without having to divest its non-real estate operations. It handled those operations through taxable subsidiary Potlatch Forest Products. As a result much of the company's activities became geared toward shifting around its forestland holdings.

Pendleton Siegel stepped down as chairman and CEO in 2006. He was succeeded by Michael Covey a 23-year veteran of competitor Plum Creek Timber.

In 2007 Potlatch acquired more than 75000 acres of Wisconsin forestland in a deal worth about $65 million. It picked up more forestland the following year when it acquired about 180000 acres in central Idaho from Western Pacific Timber.

Soon after the 2008 financial crisis softened demand in the US brought on by the weak housing market compelled the company to curtail some of its plywood and lumber production operations. It cut or halted production at many of its facilities in 2009 (but did not do so in 2010). It closed down an Arkansas lumber mill in 2008 and sold the property two years later. The company also sold its particleboard plant and a railroad in Idaho in 2010.

In 2012 the REIT completed two timberland purchases — totaling 9285 acres — in and around land it owns in Arkansas for a total consideration of $11.8 million.

EXECUTIVES

Vice President, General Counsel, Corporate Secretary, Michele Tyler, $358,885 total compensation
Vice President - Wood Products, Ashlee Cribb
Director, Anne Alonzo

Vice President - Real Estate, William DeReu, $215,129 total compensation
Chief Financial Officer, Vice President, Jerald Richards, $410,154 total compensation
Independent Director, William Driscoll
Independent Director, Lawrence Peiros
Executive Chairman Of The Board, Michael Covey, $924,615 total compensation
President, Chief Executive Officer, Director, Eric Cremers, $614,231 total compensation
Vice President - Timberlands, Darin Ball, $283,615 total compensation
Independent Director, Linda Breard
Principal Accounting Officer, Controller, Wayne Wasechek
Independent Director, D. Mark Leland
Independent Director, Lenore Sullivan
Independent Director, R. Hunter Pierson
Auditors: KPMG LLP

LOCATIONS

HQ: PotlatchDeltic Corp
601 West First Avenue, Suite 1600, Spokane, WA 99201
Phone: 509 835-1500
Web: www.potlatch.com

PRODUCTS/OPERATIONS

2015 Sales

	$ mil.	% of total
Wood Products	336.3	53
Resource	263.9	42
Real estate	29.0	5
Intersegment eliminations	(53.7)	-
Total	**575.3**	**100**

COMPETITORS

BOISE CASCADE COMPANY	RAYONIER INC.
Canfor Corporation	Resolute Forest
DELTIC TIMBER	Products Inc
CORPORATION	THE ST JOE COMPANY
GEORGIA-PACIFIC LLC	WEYERHAEUSER
COMPANY	
LOEWS CORPORATION	West Fraser Timber Co.
PHX MINERALS INC.	Ltd

HISTORICAL FINANCIALS

Company Type: Public

Income Statement

FYE: December 31

	REVENUE ($ mil.)	NET INCOME ($ mil.)	NET PROFIT MARGIN	EMPLOYEES
12/21	1,337.4	423.8	31.7%	1,299
12/20	1,040.9	166.8	16.0%	1,316
12/19	827.1	55.6	6.7%	1,307
12/18	974.5	122.8	12.6%	1,471
12/17	678.6	86.4	12.7%	963
Annual Growth	18.5%	48.8%	—	7.8%

2021 Year-End Financials

Debt ratio: 29.9%	No. of shares (mil.): 69.0
Return on equity: 29.9%	Dividends
Cash ($ mil.): 296.1	Yield: 9.4%
Current ratio: 3.34	Payout: 79.1%
Long-term debt ($ mil.): 715.2	Market value ($ mil.): 4,159.0

STOCK PRICE ($) FY Close	P/E High/Low		PER SHARE ($) Earnings	Dividends	Book Value
12/21	60.22	10	8	6.26	5.67	22.10
12/20	50.02	21	9	2.47	1.61	19.51
12/19	43.27	54	38	0.82	1.60	18.25
12/18	31.64	27	14	1.99	5.14	19.46
12/17	49.90	25	19	2.10	1.53	4.94
Annual Growth	4.8%		— —	31.4%	38.9%	45.4%

Power Integrations Inc.

Power Integrations designs develops and markets analog and mixed-signal integrated circuits (ICs) and other electronic components and circuitry used in high-voltage power conversion. A large percentage of its products are ICs used in AC-DC power supplies which convert the high-voltage AC from a wall outlet to the low-voltage DC required by most electronic devices. It also offers high-voltage gate drivers?either standalone ICs or circuit boards containing ICs electrical isolation components and other circuitry?used to operate high-voltage switches such as insulated-gate bipolar transistors (IGBTs) and silicon-carbide (SiC) MOSFETs. Power Integrations sells its chips to electronics manufacturers and distributors such Avnet. The company makes nearly all of its sales overseas.

Operations

The company is organized and operates as one reportable segment the design development manufacture and marketing of integrated circuits and related components for use primarily in the high-voltage power conversion markets.

The fabless manufacturing model allows Power Integrations to focus on engineering and design and still have access to high-volume manufacturing capacity. Power Integrations relies on manufacturers to fabricate its chips: Lapis Semiconductor Seiko Epson and X-FAB. These contractors manufacture wafers using its proprietary high-voltage process technologies at fabrication facilities located in Japan Germany and the United States.

The company categorize their sales into the four major end-market groupings: consumer (about 35% of company's total revenue) industrial (some 30% of revenue) communications (some 30% of revenue) and computer (over 5% of revenue). Consumer market consist of primary applications such as appliances air conditioners TV set-top boxes digital cameras TVs and video-game consoles. Industrial market has controls LED lighting utility meters motor controls uninterruptible power supplies tools networked thermostats power strips and other "smart home" devices industrial motor drives renewable energy systems electric locomotives electric buses and other electric vehicles high-voltage DC transmission systems. Communications market's primary applications are mobile-phone chargers routers cordless phones broadband modems voice-over-IP phones other network and telecom gear. Computer market has desktop PCs and monitors servers adapters for tablets and notebook computers other computer peripherals.

Geographic Reach

Asia is Power Integrations' largest market representing about 80% of sales (China and Hong Kong the company's fastest-growing market contribute nearly 65% of overall revenue). Europe and Americas account for over 10% and less than 5% of sales respectively. The company has sales offices in China Germany India Italy Japan the Philippines Singapore South Korea Taiwan the UK and the US.

Power Integrations has principal executive administrative manufacturing and technical offices located in San Jose California (headquarters). The company has Research and development (R&D) facility in New Jersey and a test facility in Biel Switzerland. They also have administrative office space in Singapore and Switzerland R&D facilities in Canada United Kingdom.

Sales and Marketing

The company sell their products to original equipment manufacturers (OEMs) and merchant power-supply manufacturers through its direct sales staff and a worldwide network of independent sales representatives and distributors. Some 75% of the company's sales are made to distributors such as Avnet (which accounted for about 20% of revenue) and Honestar Technologies (around 10%) while the rest come from original equipment manufacturers and merchant power supply manufacturers.

In 2020 advertising costs amounted to $1.2 million and $1.4 million and $1.2 million in 2019 and 2018 respectively.

Financial Performance

In 2020 revenues increased by $67.6 million or 16% to $488.3 million due to growth across all end markets reflecting increased adoption of higher-power chargers for mobile phones and tablets increased sales for desktop computers and monitors as well as a broad range of industrial and consumer-appliance applications.

In 2020 the company had a net income of $71.2 million a 63% decrease from the previous year's net income of $193.5 million.

The company's cash at the end of 2020 was $258.9 million. Operating activities generated $125.6 million while investing activities used $28.3 million mainly for purchases of marketable securities. Financing activities used another $17.2 million primarily for payments of dividends to stockholders.

Strategy

Power Integration's strategy includes two elements: increase penetration of the markets it serves and increase the size of its addressable market.

The company currently addresses AC-DC applications with power outputs up to approximately 500 watts gate-driver applications of approximately ten kilowatts and higher and motor-drive applications up to approximately 300 watts. Through its research and development efforts it seeks to introduce more advanced products for these markets to offer higher levels of integration and performance compared to earlier products. The company also continues to expand its sales and application-engineering staff and its network of distributors as well as its offerings of technical documentation and design-support tools and services to help customers use its products. These tools and services include its PI Expert design software which is offered free of charge and its transformer-sample service.

The company's market-penetration strategy also includes capitalizing on the importance of energy efficiency and renewable energy in the power conversion market.

Prior to 2010 the company's addressable market consisted of AC-DC applications with up to about 50 watts of output a served available market (SAM) opportunity of approximately $1.5 billion. Since that time it expanded its SAM to more than $4 billion through a variety of means.

Company Background

In 1988 Power Integrations founded by Klas Eklund Art Fury and Steve Sharp. TOPSwitch family debuted as company's first commercial product in 1994. In 1997 Initial public offering on NASDAQ at $4/share (split-adjusted).

HISTORY

At the end of 2007 Power Integrations acquired Potentia Semiconductor a Canadian developer of controller chips for high-power AC-DC power supplies. The company paid about $5.5 million in cash for Potentia.

In another example of the widening corporate scandals on options backdating where executives and board members have skirted US regulations on the timing and purchasing of stock-option grants Power Integrations reported in 2006 that its board of directors formed a special committee of independent directors to investigate company practices related to stock-option grants to executives and board members. Chairman Howard Earhart a former CEO of Power Integrations and CFO John Cobb resigned. The board soon after named Steven Sharp as non-executive chairman to succeed Earhart. Power Integrations later restated financial results for 2001 through 2004 and for the first three quarters of 2005.

The SEC's staff notified the company in 2007 that the commission's investigation into its past practices in granting stock options ended without any enforcement action recommended against Power Integrations. The company still faces a probe by the US Department of Justice regarding stock options. In addition Power Integrations is being audited by the Internal Revenue Service.

EXECUTIVES

Vice President - Corporate Development, Clifford Walker, $325,077 total compensation
Vice President, Marketing, Douglas Bailey, $288,692 total compensation
Independent Director, Steven Sharp
Independent Director, Nicholas Brathwaite
Chief Financial Officer, Vice President - Finance, Sandeep Nayyar, $393,577 total compensation
Vice President - Technology, Radu Barsan, $368,384 total compensation
Independent Director, Anita Ganti
Independent Director, Jennifer Lloyd
Vice President - Operations, Sunil Gupta
Vice President Of Sales, Yang Chiah Yee
Independent Director, Wendy Arienzo
Ceo, Balu Balakrishnan, $638,231 total compensation
Vice President - Product Development, David Matthews, $334,231 total compensation
Independent Chairman Of The Board, William George
Auditors: DELOITTE & TOUCHE LLP

LOCATIONS

HQ: Power Integrations Inc.
5245 Hellyer Avenue, San Jose, CA 95138
Phone: 408 414-9200　　　**Fax:** 408 414-9201
Web: www.power.com

PRODUCTS/OPERATIONS

2014 Sales by Market

	% of total
Consumer	37
Industrial electronics	35
Communications	18
Computer	10
Total	**100**

Selected Products

AC-to-DC power conversion products (LinkSwitch)
DC-to-DC power conversion products (DPA-Switch)
Capacitor discharge ICs (CAPZero)
High-voltage analog ICs for power conversion
　(TOPSwitch TinySwitch Hiper SENZero)
Off-line switcher ICs (PeakSwitch)

COMPETITORS

ANALOG DEVICES INC.
Celestica Inc
DSP GROUP INC.
EXAR CORPORATION
LINEAR TECHNOLOGY LLC
MACOM TECHNOLOGY SOLUTIONS HOLDINGS INC.
MAXLINEAR INC.
ON SEMICONDUCTOR CORPORATION
PERASO INC.
SANMINA CORPORATION
SEMTECH CORPORATION
SILICON LABORATORIES INC.
TERADYNE INC.
VICOR CORPORATION
VOLEX PLC

HISTORICAL FINANCIALS

Company Type: Public

Income Statement				FYE: December 31
	REVENUE ($ mil.)	NET INCOME ($ mil.)	NET PROFIT MARGIN	EMPLOYEES
12/21	703.2	164.4	23.4%	773
12/20	488.3	71.1	14.6%	725
12/19	420.6	193.4	46.0%	699
12/18	415.9	69.9	16.8%	662
12/17	431.7	27.6	6.4%	646
Annual Growth	13.0%	56.2%	—	4.6%

2021 Year-End Financials

Debt ratio: —	No. of shares (mil.): 59.9
Return on equity: 19.0%	Dividends
Cash ($ mil.): 158.1	Yield: 0.5%
Current ratio: 9.50	Payout: 21.8%
Long-term debt ($ mil.): —	Market value ($ mil.): 5,565.0

	STOCK PRICE ($) FY Close	P/E High/Low		PER SHARE ($) Earnings	Dividends	Book Value
12/21	92.89	40	27	2.67	0.54	—
12/20	81.86	106	43	1.17	0.42	13.53
12/19	98.91	30	17	3.25	0.70	12.31
12/18	60.98	67	42	1.16	0.64	9.12
12/17	73.55	181	134	0.45	0.28	9.19
Annual Growth	6.0%	—	—	56.1%	17.8%	13.4%

Preferred Bank (Los Angeles, CA)

Preferred Bank wants to be the bank of choice of Chinese-Americans in Southern California. Employing a multilingual staff the bank provides international banking services to companies doing business in the Asia/Pacific region. It targets middle-market businesses typically manufacturing service distribution and real estate firms as well as entrepreneurs professionals and high-net-worth individuals through about a dozen branches in Los Angeles Orange and San Francisco Counties. Preferred Bank offers standard deposit products such as checking accounts savings money market and NOW accounts. Specialized services include private banking and international trade finance.

Geographic Reach
Preferred Bank markets its services in half a dozen Southern Californian counties: Los Angeles Orange Riverside San Bernardino San Francisco and Ventura.

Financial Performance
In 2013 Preferred Bank reported about $72 million in revenue up just more than 10% from the prior year. The increase was solely from interest income as non-interest income (a very small part of overall revenue anyway) fell more than 40%. The company saw growth in its loan portfolio that year as well as overall deposit growth. Net income fell 20% to $19 million; the decline was primarily related to a boost in net income for 2012 because of a $20 million income tax benefit (compared to income tax expense of $12 million in 2013).

Strategy
Historically the company was focused on the Chinese-American market and although it continues to cater to that clientele most of its current customer base is from the diversified mainstream market.

EXECUTIVES

Independent Director, Wayne Wu
Independent Director, Chih-Wei Wu
Independent Director, Gary Nunnelly
Independent Director, Shirley Wang
Independent Director, Kathleen Shane
Chief Financial Officer And Executive Vice President, Edward Czajka, $366,667 total compensation
Chairman And Chief Executive Officer, Li Yu, $950,000 total compensation
Vice Chairman, Clark Hsu
Executive Vice President, Chief Credit Officer, Nick Pi, $245,436 total compensation
Executive Vice President And Deputy Chief Operating Officer, Johnny Hsu, $244,000 total compensation
President And Chief Operating Officer, Wellington Chen, $536,667 total compensation
Auditors: Crowe LLP

LOCATIONS

HQ: Preferred Bank (Los Angeles, CA)
601 S. Figueroa Street, 48th Floor, Los Angeles, CA 90017
Phone: 213 891-1188
Web: www.preferredbank.com

PRODUCTS/OPERATIONS

2015 Sales

	% of total
Interest income	
Loans and leases	90
Investment securities available for sale	6
Federal funds sold	-
Non-interest income	
Fees and service charges on deposit accounts	1
Trade finance income	2
BOLI income	-
Other income	1
Total	**100**

COMPETITORS

BANCFIRST CORPORATION
BANKUNITED INC.
CITIZENS & NORTHERN CORPORATION
COLUMBIA BANKING SYSTEM INC.
FIRST REPUBLIC BANK
HSBC USA INC.
METROPOLITAN BANK HOLDING CORP.
SEACOAST BANKING CORPORATION OF FLORIDA
TEXAS CAPITAL BANCSHARES INC.
TURKIYE GARANTI BANKASI ANONIM SIRKETI
WILSHIRE BANCORP INC.

HISTORICAL FINANCIALS
Company Type: Public

Income Statement
FYE: December 31

	ASSETS ($ mil.)	NET INCOME ($ mil.)	INCOME AS % OF ASSETS	EMPLOYEES
12/20	5,143.6	69.4	1.4%	266
12/19	4,628.4	78.3	1.7%	279
12/18	4,216.4	70.9	1.7%	263
12/17	3,769.8	43.3	1.2%	238
12/16	3,221.6	36.3	1.1%	218
Annual Growth	**12.4%**	**17.6%**	**—**	**5.1%**

2020 Year-End Financials

Return on assets: 1.4%	Dividends
Return on equity: 13.9%	Yield: 2.3%
Long-term debt ($ mil.): —	Payout: 26.2%
No. of shares (mil.): 14.9	Market value ($ mil.): 754.0
Sales ($ mil): 220.3	

	STOCK PRICE ($) FY Close	P/E High/Low		PER SHARE ($) Earnings	Dividends	Book Value
12/20	50.47	14	6	4.65	1.20	35.19
12/19	60.09	12	8	5.16	1.20	31.47
12/18	43.35	15	9	4.64	0.94	27.22
12/17	58.78	22	16	2.96	0.76	23.48
12/16	52.42	20	10	2.56	0.60	20.94
Annual Growth	**(0.9%)**	**—**	**—**	**16.1%**	**18.9%**	**13.9%**

Preformed Line Products Co.

Preformed Line Products (PLP) is an international designer and manufacturer of products and systems employed in the construction and maintenance of overhead ground-mounted and underground networks for the energy telecommunication cable operators information (data communication) and other similar industries. It provides formed wire products (for maintenance and repair of aging plant infrastructures) protective fiber-optic closures and splice cases solar hardware systems and mounting hardware for a variety of solar power applications and data communication cabinets for data communications networks. PLP-USA is responsible for about 45% of the total sales. The company was founded in 1947.

Operations
PLP's operations are divided into four operating segments along geographic lines: PLP-USA (about 45% of total sales) The Americas (around 15%) EMEA (around 20%; Europe Middle East & Africa) and Asia/Pacific (roughly 20%). US operations adhere specifically to domestic energy and telecommunications products while the other three segments work across geographic regions.

The company's products include energy (around 65% of sales) communications (nearly 25%) and special industries (some 10%) products.

Energy Products are used to support protect terminate and secure both power conductor and fiber communication cables and to control cable dynamics (such as vibration). Formed wire products are based on the principle of forming a variety of stiff wire materials into a helical (spiral) shape.

Communications Products including splice cases are used to protect fixed line communication networks such as copper cable or fiber optic cable from moisture environmental hazards and other potential contaminants.

Special Industries Products include data communication cabinets hardware assemblies pole line hardware resale products underground connectors solar hardware systems guy markers tree guards fiber optic cable markers pedestal markers and urethane products.

Geographic Reach
Headquartered in Mayfield Village Ohio PLP serves worldwide markets through international operations in Argentina Australia Austria Brazil Czech Republic Canada China Indonesia Malaysia Mexico New Zealand Poland South Africa Spain Great Britain and Thailand.

Sales and Marketing
Domestically and internationally the company markets its products through a direct sales force and manufacturing representatives. The direct sales force is employed by the company and works with manufacturers' representatives as well as key direct accounts and distributors who also buy and resell the company's products. The manufacturer's representatives are independent organizations that represent the company as well as other complimentary product lines. These organizations are paid a commission based on the sales amount they generate. Additionally the company markets its products to the energy telecommunication cable data communication and special industries.

Advertising costs are expensed as incurred and totaled $3 million in 2020 and $1.9 million in both 2019 and 2018.

Financial Performance
In 2020 net sales were $466.4 million an increase of $21.6 million or 5% compared to 2019. The increase in PLP-USA net sales of $23.0 million or 13% was primarily due to a volume increase in energy and communication product sales. International net sales 2020 were unfavorably affected by $16.9 million when local currencies were converted to US dollars.

In 2020 the company had a net income of $29.8 million a 28% increase from the previous year's net income of $23.3 million.

The company's cash in 2020 was $45.2 million. Operating activities generated $41.6 million while investing activities used $14 million. Financing activities used another $23.2 million.

Strategy

Despite the continuous changes in the current global economy the company believes its business fundamentals and its financial position are sound and strategically well-positioned. It remained focused on assessing its global market opportunities and overall manufacturing capacity in conjunction with the requirements of local manufacturing in the markets that it serves.

If necessary it will utilize its global manufacturing network to manage costs while driving sales and delivering value to its customers. It has continued to invest in the business to expand into new markets for it to improve efficiency develop new products increase its capacity and become an even stronger supplier to its current and new customers.

EXECUTIVES

Director Emeritus, Barbara Ruhlman
Vice President - Asia Pacific Region, William Haag, $320,004 total compensation
Director, David Sunkle, $360,000 total compensation
Executive Vice President - U.s. Operations, John Hofstetter
Independent Director, Glenn Corlett
Chief Operating Officer, Dennis Mckenna, $470,004 total compensation
Independent Director, Richard Gascoigne
General Counsel, Corporate Secretary, Caroline Vaccariello
Vice President - Research And Engineering, John Olenik
Vice President - Human Resources, Timothy O'Shaughnessy
Independent Director, Matthew Frymier
Director, Maegan Cross
Director, Vice President - Marketing & Business Development, J. Ryan Ruhlman
Independent Director, R. Steven Kestner
Independent Director, Michael Gibbons
Chief Financial Officer, Andrew Klaus, $266,595 total compensation
Chairman Of The Board, President, Chief Executive Officer, Robert Ruhlman, $925,008 total compensation
Auditors: Ernst & Young LLP

LOCATIONS

HQ: Preformed Line Products Co.
660 Beta Drive, Mayfield Village, OH 44143
Phone: 440 461-5200   **Fax:** 440 442-8816
Web: www.preformed.com

PRODUCTS/OPERATIONS

2015 sales

	% of total
Formed wire	61
Protective closures	17
Plastic products	4
Other products	18
Total	**100**

Selected Products

Copper splice closures
Data communication cabinets
Fiber optic products (COYOTE brand)
Formed wire and related hardware products
High-speed cross-connect devices
Plastic products
Power transmission products (THERMOLIGN)
Protective closures (ARMADILLO stainless vault closures)
RAPTOR PROTECTOR (protects birds from power lines)

Selected Markets

Communication and cable
Data communication
Electric utilities and distribution
Electric utilities and transmission
Energy
Solar

COMPETITORS

ANIXTER INTERNATIONAL INC.
ASTEC INDUSTRIES INC.
BELDEN INC.
GATES INDUSTRIAL CORPORATION PLC
HALMA PUBLIC LIMITED COMPANY
ITT LLC
MACOM TECHNOLOGY SOLUTIONS HOLDINGS INC.
N L INDUSTRIES INC.
POWELL INDUSTRIES INC.
REXEL
SANMINA CORPORATION
STRATTEC SECURITY CORPORATION
TD SYNNEX CORPORATION
THE DURHAM CO
THERMON GROUP HOLDINGS INC.
VOLEX PLC
ZURN WATER SOLUTIONS CORPORATION

HISTORICAL FINANCIALS

Company Type: Public

Income Statement

FYE: December 31

	REVENUE ($ mil.)	NET INCOME ($ mil.)	NET PROFIT MARGIN	EMPLOYEES
12/20	466.4	29.8	6.4%	2,969
12/19	444.8	23.3	5.2%	2,983
12/18	420.8	26.5	6.3%	2,650
12/17	378.2	12.6	3.3%	2,762
12/16	336.6	15.2	4.5%	2,579
Annual Growth	8.5%	18.2%	—	3.6%

2020 Year-End Financials

Debt ratio: 12.1%
Return on equity: 10.6%
Cash ($ mil.): 45.1
Current ratio: 2.47
Long-term debt ($ mil.): 33.3
No. of shares (mil.): 4.9
Dividends
Yield: 1.1%
Payout: 12.2%
Market value ($ mil.): 336.0

	STOCK PRICE ($) FY Close	P/E High/Low		PER SHARE ($) Earnings	Dividends	Book Value
12/20	68.44	11	6	5.98	0.80	59.58
12/19	60.35	16	10	4.58	0.80	53.78
12/18	54.25	17	9	5.21	0.80	49.67
12/17	71.05	34	18	2.47	0.80	47.35
12/16	58.12	20	11	2.95	0.80	43.68
Annual Growth	4.2%	—	—	19.3%	(0.0%)	8.1%

Premier Financial Corp

Named for its hometown not its attitude First Defiance Financial is the holding company for First Federal Bank of the Midwest which operates more than 30 branches serving northwestern Ohio western Indiana and southern Michigan. The thrift offers standard deposit products including checking savings and money market accounts and CDs. Commercial real estate loans account for more than half of the bank's loan portfolio; commercial loans make up another quarter of all loans. The company's insurance agency subsidiary First Insurance Group of the Midwest which accounts for some 7% of the company's revenues provides life insurance property/casualty coverage and investments. In 2019 First Defiance Financial agreed to merge with Ohio-based United Community Financial (the holding company for Home Savings Bank and HSB Insurance) in a deal valued at $473 million.

Strategy

First Defiance Financial has boosted its non-banking product lines via acquisitions. It bought the employee benefits insurance business of another local agency Andres O'Neil & Lowe in 2010; and property/casualty agency Payak-Dubbs Insurance Agency in 2011. Both additions became part of First Insurance Group of the Midwest (formerly named First Insurance & Investments).

In 2016 the company agreed to buy another bank serving northwest Ohio Commercial Bancshares. The deal is valued at some $63 million and adds seven branches and $342 million in assets.

Mergers and Acquisitions

In 2019 First Defiance Financial agreed to merge with Ohio-based United Community Financial (the holding company for Home Savings Bank and HSB Insurance) in a deal valued at $473 million. United Community's Home Savings Bank subsidiary will merge into First Federal to create a bank with more than $6 billion in assets. First Defiance shareholders will have a 52.5% stake in the new company.

EXECUTIVES

Independent Director, Jean Hubbard
Executive Vice President And Chief Operations Officer, Dennis Rose, $178,869 total compensation
Chief Human Resource Officer, Executive Vice President, Sharon Davis, $176,057 total compensation
Independent Director, Charles Niehaus
Independent Director, Terri Bettinger
Executive Chairman Of The Board, Donald Hileman, $534,135 total compensation
Independent Director, Mark Robison
Chief Financial Officer, Executive Vice President, Paul Nungester, $310,742 total compensation
Independent Director, Lee Burdman
Executive Vice President, Chief Lending Officer, Matthew Garrity, $287,500 total compensation
Independent Director, Zahid Afzal
Independent Director, Marty Adams
Independent Director, Louis Altman
Executive Vice President, Chief Legal Officer, Shannon Kuhl
Executive Vice President, Chief Risk Officer, Tina Shaver
Director, Nikki Lanier
Independent Director, John Bookmyer

President, Chief Executive Officer, Director, Gary Small, $442,308 total compensation
Independent Vice Chairman Of The Board, Richard Schiraldi
Auditors: Crowe LLP

LOCATIONS

HQ: Premier Financial Corp
601 Clinton Street, Defiance, OH 43512
Phone: 419 782-5015
Web: www.fdef.com

PRODUCTS/OPERATIONS

2016 Sales

	$ mil.	% of total
Interest		
Loans	80.2	66
Investment securities		
Taxable	3.2	3
Tax-exempt	3.0	2
Interest-bearing deposits	0.4	-
FHLB stock dividends	0.6	1
Non-interest		
Service fees & other charges	10.9	9
Insurance commissions	10.4	9
Mortgage banking income	7.3	6
Trust income	1.7	1
Gain on sale of non-mortgage loans	0.8	1
Income from bank owned life insurance	0.9	1
Gain on sale or call of securities	0.5	-
Other	1.5	1
Total	**121.4**	**100**

COMPETITORS

FIRST FEDERAL SAVINGS AND LOAN ASSOCIATION
OF LAKEWOOD
MIDLAND FINANCIAL CO.
NORTHWEST BANCORP INC.
OLD NATIONAL BANCORP
UNITED COMMUNITY FINANCIAL CORP.
UNITED FINANCIAL BANCORP INC.
WATERSTONE FINANCIAL INC.

HISTORICAL FINANCIALS
Company Type: Public

Income Statement				FYE: December 31
	ASSETS ($ mil.)	NET INCOME ($ mil.)	INCOME AS % OF ASSETS	EMPLOYEES
12/20	7,211.7	63.0	0.9%	1,195
12/19	3,468.9	49.3	1.4%	699
12/18	3,181.7	46.2	1.5%	696
12/17	2,993.4	32.2	1.1%	674
12/16	2,477.6	28.8	1.2%	581
Annual Growth	**30.6%**	**21.6%**	**—**	**19.8%**

2020 Year-End Financials

Return on assets: 1.1%
Return on equity: 8.9%
Long-term debt ($ mil.): —
No. of shares (mil.): 37.2
Sales ($ mil): 318.6

Dividends
Yield: 3.8%
Payout: 63.3%
Market value ($ mil.): 858.0

	STOCK PRICE ($) FY Close	P/E High/Low		PER SHARE ($)		
				Earnings	Dividends	Book Value
12/20	23.00	18	7	1.75	0.88	26.34
12/19	31.49	13	10	2.48	0.79	21.60
12/18	24.51	30	10	2.26	0.64	19.81
12/17	51.97	35	29	1.61	0.50	18.38
12/16	50.74	32	22	1.60	0.44	16.31
Annual Growth	**(17.9%)**	**—**	**—**	**2.3%**	**18.9%**	**12.7%**

Primerica Inc

EXECUTIVES

Chb, Rick Williams
Co Chb*, John Addison
Pres*, David T Chadwick
Dir*, Michael K Wells
Coo*, Douglas G Elliott
SEC*, Stacey K Geer
Cfo*, Allison Rand
Vice President, Ron Kennett
Office Manager, Vanessa N Hill
Employee, Donald-Colema Felecia
Employee, Melchiore Abel
Auditors: KPMG LLP

LOCATIONS

HQ: Primerica Inc
1 Primerica Parkway, Duluth, GA 30099
Phone: 770 381-1000
Web: www.primerica.com

HISTORICAL FINANCIALS
Company Type: Public

Income Statement				FYE: December 31
	ASSETS ($ mil.)	NET INCOME ($ mil.)	INCOME AS % OF ASSETS	EMPLOYEES
12/20	14,905.2	386.1	2.6%	2,824
12/19	13,688.5	366.3	2.7%	2,803
12/18	12,595.0	324.0	2.6%	2,699
12/17	12,460.7	350.2	2.8%	2,718
12/16	11,438.9	219.4	1.9%	2,662
Annual Growth	**6.8%**	**15.2%**	**—**	**1.5%**

2020 Year-End Financials

Return on assets: 2.6%
Return on equity: 22.0%
Long-term debt ($ mil.): —
No. of shares (mil.): 39.3
Sales ($ mil): 2,217.5

Dividends
Yield: 1.1%
Payout: 16.7%
Market value ($ mil.): 5,264.0

	STOCK PRICE ($) FY Close	P/E High/Low		PER SHARE ($)		
				Earnings	Dividends	Book Value
12/20	133.93	15	6	9.57	1.60	46.71
12/19	130.56	16	11	8.62	1.36	40.10
12/18	97.71	17	12	7.33	1.00	34.23
12/17	101.55	14	9	7.61	0.78	32.07
12/16	69.15	16	9	4.59	0.70	26.71
Annual Growth	**18.0%**	**—**	**—**	**20.2%**	**23.0%**	**15.0%**

Primis Financial Corp

Southern National Bancorp of Virginia is the holding company for Sonabank which has some 20 locations in central and northern Virginia and southern Maryland. Founded in 2005 the bank serves small and midsized businesses their owners and retail consumers. It offers standard deposit products including checking savings and money market accounts and CDs. The bank's lending is focused on commercial real estate single-family residential construction and single-family homes

as well as other types of consumer and commercial loans. In 2009 Southern National Bancorp acquired the failed Greater Atlantic Bank in an FDIC-assisted transaction; in 2012 it acquired the loans and deposits of HarVest Bank of Maryland.

EXECUTIVES

Independent Director Of The Company And The Bank, Robert Clagett
Independent Director Of The Company And The Bank, F. Garrett
Independent Director Of The Company And The Bank, Eric Johnson
Independent Director Of The Company And The Bank, John Biagas
Non-executive Chairman Of The Board, W. Rand Cook
Executive Vice President And Chief Sba Lending Officer Of Each Of The Company And The Bank, Marie Leibson, $222,120 total compensation
President, Chief Executive Officer, Director Of The Company And Bank, Dennis Zember, $520,000 total compensation
Chief Financial Officer, Executive Vice President, Matthew Switzer
Executive Vice President And Chief Strategy Officer Of Each Of The Company And The Bank, Stephen Weber, $192,159 total compensation
Independent Director Of The Company And Bank, John Eggemeyer
Independent Director Of The Company And Bank, Allen Jones
Executive Vice President, Chief Accounting Officer, Jeffrey Karafa, $273,042 total compensation
Chief Operating Officer, Executive Vice President, Chief Information Officer, George Sheflett, $221,427 total compensation
Auditors: Dixon Hughes Goodman LLP

LOCATIONS

HQ: Primis Financial Corp
6830 Old Dominion Drive, McLean, VA 22101
Phone: 703 893-7400
Web: www.sonabank.com

COMPETITORS

BCSB BANCORP INC.
PACIFIC FINANCIAL CORPORATION

HISTORICAL FINANCIALS
Company Type: Public

Income Statement				FYE: December 31
	ASSETS ($ mil.)	NET INCOME ($ mil.)	INCOME AS % OF ASSETS	EMPLOYEES
12/20	3,088.6	23.2	0.8%	382
12/19	2,722.1	33.1	1.2%	350
12/18	2,701.3	33.6	1.2%	348
12/17	2,614.2	2.4	0.1%	393
12/16	1,142.4	10.3	0.9%	162
Annual Growth	**28.2%**	**22.6%**	**—**	**23.9%**

2020 Year-End Financials

Return on assets: 0.8%
Return on equity: 6.0%
Long-term debt ($ mil.): —
No. of shares (mil.): 24.3
Sales ($ mil): 143.2

Dividends
Yield: 3.3%
Payout: 41.6%
Market value ($ mil.): 295.0

	STOCK PRICE ($)	P/E		PER SHARE ($)		
	FY Close	High/Low	Earnings	Dividends	Book Value
12/20	12.11	17 8	0.96	0.40	16.03
12/19	16.35	12 10	1.36	0.36	15.60
12/18	13.22	13 9	1.39	0.32	14.48
12/17	16.03	142118	0.13	0.32	13.48
12/16	16.34	20 14	0.83	0.32	10.30
Annual Growth	(7.2%)	— —	3.7%	5.7%	11.7%

Primoris Services Corp

Primoris Services provides construction engineering and maintenance services including underground pipeline replacement and repair industrial plant upgrades and maintenance concrete structures design and buildings and water and wastewater facility construction. It also engineers industrial machinery used in oil refineries petrochemical plants and other facilities. Founded as ARB in 1960 the firm primarily operates in the US. Primoris' largest clients are public and private gas and electric utilities state Departments of Transportation pipeline operators and chemical and energy producers as well as Chevron Sempra and Kinder Morgan.

Operations

Primoris Services is well diversified across five primary segments: Utilities and Distribution (Utilities); Pipeline and Underground (Pipeline); Power Industrial and Engineering (Power); Transmission and Distribution (Transmission); and Civil.

Operating mostly in California the Midwest and the Southeast the Utilities segment maintains and installs utility lines and fiber optic cables distributes gas and electricity and builds streetlights. The segment accounts for about 25% of Primoris' revenue.

Through its Pipeline division Primoris constructs and maintains pipelines and compressor and pump stations for petrochemical companies as well as gas water and sewer utilities in the US. The segment accounts for around 25% of total revenue.

The Power segment spans the US and Canada and markets its services to the petroleum traditional and renewable power generators and petrochemical industries. In addition to engineering procurement and construction of power facilities the segment conducts retrofits upgrades repairs and maintenance. The segment accounts for nearly 25% of Primoris' revenue.

Transmission also operates in the Southeast Midwest Atlantic Coast and the Gulf Coast and accounts for around 15% of sales. Its services include encompass installation and maintenance of new and existing electric utility transmission substation and distribution systems for entities in the electric utility market.

The Civil segment builds highways bridges and airport runways and conducts projects for mass excavation flood control drainage and soil stabilization. It does business mainly in the Southeast and along the Gulf Coast and represents more than 10% of the company's revenue.

By contract type Primoris generate some 45% of revenue from unit-price while about 30% from fixed-price and more than 25% from cost reimbursable.

Geographic Reach

Dallas Texas-based Primoris garners almost all its revenue in the US although its operations extend to Canada. The firm has regional offices in Louisiana California Colorado Texas Florida Minnesota and Canada.

Sales and Marketing

Primoris customer include major public utilities petrochemical firms energy companies and municipalities. The company's top ten customers generate some 50% of its total revenue. Its customers have included the Texas and Louisiana Departments of Transportation Chevron Sempra Kinder Morgan and among others.

Financial Performance

Revenue for the year ended 2020 was $3.5 billion a 12% increase from the previous year's. All of the company's segments increased throughout the year except the Utilities segment.

The company's net income for the year ended 2020 totaled $105 million a 28% increase from the previous year.

The company's cash for the year ended 2020 was $326.7 million. Operating activities generated $311.9 million while investing activities used $42.5 million mainly for capital expenditures. Financing activities used another $62.8 million primarily for repayment of long-term debt.

Strategy

The company's strategy has remained consistent from year to year and continues to emphasize the following key elements:

Diversification Through Controlled Expansion - Primoris continues to emphasize the expansion of its scope of services beyond its current focus by increasing the scope of services offered to current customers and by adding new customers.

Emphasis on MSA Revenue Growth and Retention of Existing Customers - In order to fully leverage relationships with existing customer base the company believes it is important to maintain strong customer relationships. The company is also focused on expanding its base of services provided under MSAs which are generally multi-year agreements that provide visible recurring revenue.

Ownership of Equipment. Many of its services are equipment intensive - The company believes that its ownership of a large and varied construction fleet and maintenance facilities enhances its access to reliable equipment at a favorable cost.

Stable Work Force - Primoris' business model emphasizes self-performance of a significant portion of its work. In each of its segments the company maintains a stable work force of skilled experienced craft professionals many of whom are cross-trained on projects such as pipeline and facility construction refinery maintenance gas and electrical distribution and piping systems.

Selective Bidding - The company selectively bids on projects that it believes offer an opportunity to meet profitability objectives or that offer the opportunity to enter promising new markets.

Maintain a strong balance sheet and a conservative capital structure - The company has maintained a capital structure that provides access to debt financing as needed while relying on strong operating cash flows to provide the primary support for its operations.

Mergers and Acquisitions

In 2021 Primoris acquired Future Infrastructure in an all-cash transaction valued at $620 million.

The transaction directly aligns with Primoris' strategy to grow in large higher growth higher margin markets and expands the company's utility services capabilities. Future Infrastructure is a provider of non-discretionary maintenance repair upgrade and installation services to the telecommunication regulated gas utility and infrastructure markets. As a result of the acquisition Future Infrastructure will be integrated into the company's Utilities Segment furthering Primoris' strategic plan to expand its service lines enter new markets and grow the company's MSA revenue base.

Company Background

Traces its roots to 1960 with the founding of ARB Inc. of Bakersfield CA a pipeline construction company. ARB met the growing demand for energy infrastructure that accompanied the mid-century oil boom in the west and quickly established the reputation for great quality and reliability. ARB's work and reputation fueled significant growth and laid the foundation for Primoris which is today one of the largest specialty contractors in the country.

Primoris was formed in 2004 as the parent company and is traded on NASDAQ under the symbol PRIM.

EXECUTIVES

Chief Operating Officer, Executive Vice President, John Moreno, $514,519 total compensation
Chief Financial Officer, Executive Vice President, Kenneth Dodgen, $421,956 total compensation
Non-executive Independent Chairman Of The Board, David King
Independent Director, Terry McCallister
Independent Director, Patricia Wagner
President, Chief Executive Officer, Director, Thomas McCormick, $653,365 total compensation
Independent Director, Robert Tintsman
Executive Vice President, Chief Legal Officer, Secretary, John Perisich, $481,749 total compensation
Auditors: Moss Adams LLP

LOCATIONS

HQ: Primoris Services Corp
2300 N. Field Street, Suite 1900, Dallas, TX 75201
Phone: 214 740-5600
Web: www.prim.com

PRODUCTS/OPERATIONS

2018 Sales

	$ mil.	% of total
Utilities	902.8	31
Power	694.1	23
Pipeline	590.9	20
Civil	465.0	16
Transmission	286.7	10
Total	**2,939.5**	**100**

2018 Sales

	$ mil.	% of total
MSA	1,128.6	38
Non-MSA	1,810.9	62
Total	**2,939.5**	**100**

2018 Sales

	$ mil.	% of total
Unit-Price	1,139.7	39
Cost Reimbursable	996.0	34
Fixed-Price	803.8	37
Total	**2,939.5**	**100**

Selected Subsidiaries

ARB Inc.
Stellaris LLC
ARB Structures Inc.
BW Primoris LLC
Cardinal Contractors Inc.
James Construction Group LLC
JCG Heavy Civil DivisionJCG Industrial DivisionJCG
  Infrastructure and Maintenance Division
OnQuest Canada ULC
OnQuest Inc.
Primoris Energy Services Corporation
Q3 Contracting Inc.
Rockford Corporation
Silva Group

COMPETITORS

ARB INC.
INSITUFORM
  TECHNOLOGIES LLC
JGC HOLDINGS
  CORPORATION
LAYNE CHRISTENSEN
  COMPANY

MASTEC INC.
MUNICIPAL ELECTRIC
  AUTHORITY OF GEORGIA
SNC-Lavalin Group Inc
WILLBROS GROUP INC.

HISTORICAL FINANCIALS

Company Type: Public

Income Statement — FYE: December 31

	REVENUE ($ mil.)	NET INCOME ($ mil.)	NET PROFIT MARGIN	EMPLOYEES
12/20	3,491.5	104.9	3.0%	10,414
12/19	3,106.3	82.3	2.7%	9,700
12/18	2,939.4	77.4	2.6%	10,600
12/17	2,380.0	72.3	3.0%	7,102
12/16	1,996.9	26.7	1.3%	7,926
Annual Growth	15.0%	40.8%	—	7.1%

2020 Year-End Financials

Debt ratio: 16.0%
Return on equity: 15.5%
Cash ($ mil.): 326.7
Current ratio: 1.46
Long-term debt ($ mil.): 268.8

No. of shares (mil.): 48.1
Dividends
  Yield: 0.8%
  Payout: 11.8%
Market value ($ mil.): 1,328.0

	STOCK PRICE ($) FY Close	P/E High/Low		Earnings	PER SHARE ($) Dividends	Book Value
12/20	27.61	13	5	2.16	0.24	14.86
12/19	22.24	15	11	1.61	0.24	12.91
12/18	19.13	19	12	1.50	0.24	11.91
12/17	27.19	21	16	1.40	0.23	10.82
12/16	22.78	48	33	0.51	0.22	9.64
Annual Growth	4.9%	—	—	43.5%	2.2%	11.4%

Private Bancorp Of America Inc

Auditors: Eide Bailly LLP

LOCATIONS

HQ: Private Bancorp Of America Inc
  9404 Genesee Avenue, Suite 100, La Jolla, CA 90237
Phone: 858 875-6900
Web: www.calprivate.bank

HISTORICAL FINANCIALS

Company Type: Public

Income Statement — FYE: December 31

	REVENUE ($ mil.)	NET INCOME ($ mil.)	NET PROFIT MARGIN	EMPLOYEES
12/20	55.3	10.8	19.7%	0
12/19	44.5	(0.4)		0
12/18	31.6	4.1	13.1%	0
12/17	23.4	3.4	14.6%	0
12/16	20.1	4.3	21.4%	0
Annual Growth	28.7%	26.0%	—	—

2020 Year-End Financials

Debt ratio: 6.9%
Return on equity: 10.6%
Cash ($ mil.): 276.2
Current ratio: 0.25
Long-term debt ($ mil.): 92.9

No. of shares (mil.): 5.6
Dividends
  Yield: —
  Payout: —
Market value ($ mil.): 104.0

	STOCK PRICE ($) FY Close	P/E High/Low		Earnings	PER SHARE ($) Dividends	Book Value
12/20	18.50	12	6	1.94	0.00	19.24
12/19	22.25	—	—	(0.08)	0.00	17.15
12/18	22.95	33	28	0.80	0.00	16.41
12/17	25.45	35	27	0.71	0.00	15.88
12/16	19.38	18	14	1.06	0.00	14.20
Annual Growth	(1.2%)	—	— 16.3%		—	7.9%

Professional Holding Corp

LOCATIONS

HQ: Professional Holding Corp
  396 Alhambra Circle, Suite 255, Coral Gables, FL 33134
Phone: 786 483-1757
Web: www.proholdco.com

HISTORICAL FINANCIALS

Company Type: Public

Income Statement — FYE: December 31

	ASSETS ($ mil.)	NET INCOME ($ mil.)	INCOME AS % OF ASSETS	EMPLOYEES
12/20	2,057.2	8.3	0.4%	0
12/19	1,053.1	2.3	0.2%	0
12/18	662.3	6.8	1.0%	135
12/17	539.1	3.9	0.7%	0
Annual Growth	56.3%	28.0%	—	—

2020 Year-End Financials

Return on assets: 0.5%
Return on equity: 5.6%
Long-term debt ($ mil.): —
No. of shares (mil.): 13.5
Sales ($ mil): 73.4

Dividends
  Yield: —
  Payout: —
Market value ($ mil.): 209.0

	STOCK PRICE ($) FY Close	P/E High/Low		Earnings	PER SHARE ($) Dividends	Book Value
12/20	15.43	29	15	0.67	0.00	15.93
12/19	19.00	48	38	0.40	0.00	13.52
12/18	15.20	9	8	1.91	0.00	14.89
12/17	15.51	13	11	1.14	0.00	12.71
/0.00	—	—	(0.00)	0.00	(0.00)	
Annual Growth	—	—	—	—	—	—

Progyny Inc

Auditors: Ernst & Young LLP

LOCATIONS

HQ: Progyny Inc
  1359 Broadway, New York, NY 10018
Phone: 212 888-3124
Web: www.progyny.com

HISTORICAL FINANCIALS

Company Type: Public

Income Statement — FYE: December 31

	REVENUE ($ mil.)	NET INCOME ($ mil.)	NET PROFIT MARGIN	EMPLOYEES
12/20	344.8	46.4	13.5%	210
12/19	229.6	(8.5)	—	167
12/18	105.4	0.6	0.6%	163
12/17	48.5	(12.4)	—	0
Annual Growth	92.2%	—	—	—

2020 Year-End Financials

Debt ratio: —
Return on equity: 32.9%
Cash ($ mil.): 70.3
Current ratio: 2.45
Long-term debt ($ mil.): —

No. of shares (mil.): 87.0
Dividends
  Yield: —
  Payout: —
Market value ($ mil.): 3,690.0

	STOCK PRICE ($) FY Close	P/E High/Low		Earnings	PER SHARE ($) Dividends	Book Value
12/20	42.39	80	31	0.47	0.00	1.92
12/19	27.45	—	—	(0.41)	0.00	1.36
12/18	0.00	—	—	0.04	0.00	2.16
Annual Growth	—	—	—242.8%		—	(5.7%)

Prosperity Bancshares Inc.

Prosperity Bancshares reaches banking customers across the Lone Star State. The holding company for Prosperity Bank operates about 230 branches across Texas and about 15 more in Oklahoma. Serving consumers and small to midsized businesses the bank offers traditional deposit and loan services in addition to wealth management retail brokerage and mortgage banking investment services. Prosperity Bank focuses on real estate lending: Commercial mortgages make up the largest segment of the company's loan portfolio (33%) followed by residential mortgages (24%). Credit cards business auto consumer home equity loans round out its lending activities.

Operations

About 63% of Prosperity's total revenue came from loan interest (including fees) in 2014 while another 22% came from interest on its investment securities. The rest of its revenue came from non-sufficient fund fees (4%) credit and debit card income (3%) deposit account service charges (2%) trust income (1%) mortgage income (1%) and brokerage income (1%).

Geographic Reach

Prosperity Bancshares operates 230 Texas banking locations across Houston South Texas the Dallas/Fort Worth metroplex East Texas Bryan/College Station Central Texas and West Texas. It also has 15 branch locations in Oklahoma (including Tulsa).

Sales and Marketing

The bank mainly targets consumers and small and medium-sized businesses and tailors its products to the specific needs of a given market.

Financial Performance

Prosperity's revenues and profits have been prospering thanks to loan and deposit business growth from acquisitions and declining loan loss provisions as its loan portfolio's credit quality has improved with higher property valuations in a strengthened economy.

The company's revenue jumped by 32% to $837.7 million in 2014 mostly as its loan interest income swelled by 40% on loan asset growth from its F&M acquisition. The bank's non-interest income rose by 29% as well from new deposit account service fees from the acquisition and additional income from its newly added brokerage and trust business.

Higher revenue and strong operating cost controls in 2014 drove Prosperity's net income higher by 34% to $297.4 million while its operating cash levels rose by 13% to $348.3 million on higher cash earnings.

Strategy

Prosperity Bancshares bases its growth strategy on three key elements: Internal loan and deposit business growth through "individualized customer service" and service line expansion opportunities; cost controls to maximize profitability; and acquisitions.

Toward its internal business growth initiatives Prosperity spent 2012 and 2013 launching its new trust brokerage mortgage lending and credit card products and services to customers for the first time.

With cost-controls in mind the bank tracks its branches "as separate profit centers" noting each branch's interest income efficiency ratio deposit growth loan growth and overall profitability. That way it can reward individual branch managers and presidents accordingly by merit rather than giving higher compensation across the board.

The acquisitive Prosperity Bancshares has been buying up small banks in Texas — and now Oklahoma — as it hopes to hit a sweet spot in the market between the national giants that dominate the Texas banking scene and smaller community banks.

Mergers and Acquisitions

In January 2016 furthering its presence in the Houston market Prosperity Bancshares purchased Tradition Bancshares along with its seven branches in the Houston Area (Bellaire Katy and the Woodlands) $540 million in assets $239 million in loans and $483.8 million in deposits.

In April 2014 toward expansion in the Oklahoma and Dallas markets Prosperity purchased Tulsa-based F&M Bancorporation and its subsidiary The F&M Bank & Trust Company. The deal added 13 branches including nine in Tulsa and surrounding areas three in Dallas and a loan production office in Oklahoma City.

In April 2013 it acquired Coppermark Bank one of Oklahoma City's largest banks with six branches in Oklahoma City and three locations in North Dallas for $194 million. The deal also added the credit card and agent bank merchant processing business from its subsidiary Bankers Credit Card Services.

In January 2013 the company boosted its market share in East Texas after buying East Texas Financial Services and its four First Federal Bank Texas branch locations including three branches in Tyler and one in Gilmer.

Company Background

In early 2012 Prosperity acquired Texas Bankers a three-branch Austin bank with some $72 million in assets. The merger increased Prosperity's number of Central Texas branches to 34 banking locations. It followed that deal with the purchase of The Bank Arlington a single-branch bank operating in the Dallas/Ft. Worth area. It acquired single-branch Community National Bank of Bellaire Texas in late 2012.

Also in 2012 Prosperity expanded into West Texas after it merged American State Financial Corporation and its American State Bank subsidiary into its operations. The deal added $3 billion in assets and 37 West Texas banking offices in Lubbock Midland/Odessa and Abilene.

EXECUTIVES

Independent Director, Ned Holmes
Chairman Of The Board And Chief Operating Officer Of The Bank, H. Timanus, $537,346 total compensation
Senior Chairman Of The Board, Chief Executive Officer Of The Company And Bank, David Zalman, $1,020,807 total compensation
Executive Vice President Of The Company, Senior Executive Vice President, Chief Lending Officer Of The Bank, Randy Hester, $366,579 total compensation
Advisory Director, Vice Chairman, Director And Vice Chairman Of Bank, Edward Safady, $537,067 total compensation
Executive Vice President, General Counsel, Senior Executive Vice President And General Counsel Of The Bank, Charlotte Rasche, $366,579 total compensation
Executive Vice President Of The Company And Senior Executive Vice President Of The Bank, Robert Dowdell
President, Chief Operating Officer, Director, Kevin Hanigan, $1,020,807 total compensation
Independent Director, Bruce Hunt
Executive Vice President And Director Of Corporate Strategy Of The Company And Senior Executive Vice President And Director Of Corporate Strategy Of The Bank, J. Mays Davenport

Chief Financial Officer, Asylbek Osmonov, $315,000 total compensation
Auditors: DELOITTE & TOUCHE LLP

LOCATIONS

HQ: Prosperity Bancshares Inc.
Prosperity Bank Plaza, 4295 San Felipe, Houston, TX 77027
Phone: 281 269-7199
Web: www.prosperitybankusa.com

PRODUCTS/OPERATIONS

2014 Sales

	$ mil.	% of total
Interest		
Loans including fees	525.7	63
Securities	188.7	22
Federal funds sold	0.3	-
Noninterest		
Non-sufficient funds fees	37.0	4
Debit card and ATM card income	22.9	3
Service charges on deposit accounts	16.5	2
Trust income	8.1	1
Brokerage income	5.9	1
Mortgage income	4.4	1
Other	28.2	3
Total	**837.7**	**100**

COMPETITORS

BANCFIRST CORPORATION	OLD NATIONAL BANCORP
CAPITAL BANK FINANCIAL CORP.	PACWEST
CITY HOLDING COMPANY	SOUTHWEST BANCORP INC.
CVB FINANCIAL CORP.	WASHINGTON TRUST BANCORP INC.
EAGLE BANCORP INC.	WESTERN ALLIANCE
FIRST COMMUNITY BANKSHARES INC.	BANCORPORATION
	WILSHIRE BANCORP INC.

HISTORICAL FINANCIALS

Company Type: Public

Income Statement				FYE: December 31
	ASSETS ($ mil.)	NET INCOME ($ mil.)	INCOME AS % OF ASSETS	EMPLOYEES
12/20	34,059.2	528.9	1.6%	3,756
12/19	32,185.7	332.5	1.0%	3,901
12/18	22,693.4	321.8	1.4%	3,036
12/17	22,587.2	272.1	1.2%	3,035
12/16	22,331.0	274.4	1.2%	3,035
Annual Growth	11.1%	17.8%	—	5.5%

2020 Year-End Financials

Return on assets: 1.5%	Dividends
Return on equity: 8.7%	Yield: 2.7%
Long-term debt ($ mil.): —	Payout: 36.1%
No. of shares (mil.): 92.5	Market value ($ mil.): 6,421.0
Sales ($ mil): 1,275.4	

	STOCK PRICE ($) FY Close	P/E High/Low		PER SHARE ($) Earnings	Dividends	Book Value
12/20	69.36	13	8	5.68	1.87	66.23
12/19	71.89	17	14	4.52	1.69	63.02
12/18	62.30	17	12	4.61	1.49	58.02
12/17	70.07	20	14	3.92	1.38	55.03
12/16	71.78	19	9	3.94	1.24	52.41
Annual Growth	(0.9%)	—	—	9.6%	10.8%	6.0%

Proto Labs Inc

Proto Labs is the world's largest and fastest digital manufacturer of custom prototypes and on-demand production parts. The company targets its products to the millions of product developers and engineers who use three-dimensional computer-aided design (3D CAD) software to design products across a diverse range of end-markets. It manufactures prototype and low volume production parts for companies worldwide who are under increasing pressure to bring their finished products to market faster than their competition. It utilizes injection molding computer numerical control (CNC) machining 3D printing and sheet metal fabrication to manufacture custom parts for its customers. The US accounts for around 80% of Proto Labs' sales. The company was founded in 1999 by Larry Lukis.

Operations
The company derived its revenue from its Injection Molding CNC Machining 3D Printing and Sheet Metal product lines.

The Injection Molded division (approximately half of sales) product line uses its 3D CAD-to-CNC machining technology for the automated design and manufacture of molds which are then used to produce custom plastic and liquid silicone rubber injection-molded parts and over-molded and insert-molded injection-molded parts on commercially available equipment.

Proto Labs' CNC Machining segment (some 30% of sales) uses commercially available CNC machines to offer milling and turning. CNC milling is a manufacturing process that cuts plastic and metal blocks into one or more custom parts based on the 3D CAD model uploaded by the product developer or engineer.

The 3D Printing division (approximately 15% of sales) product line includes SL SLS DMLS MJF PolyJet and Carbon DLS processes which offers customers a wide-variety of high-quality precision rapid prototyping and low volume production.

The company's Sheet Metal segment (approximately 5% of sales) product line includes quick-turn and e-commerce-enabled custom sheet metal parts providing customers with prototype and low-volume production parts.

Geographic Reach
Proto Labs' headquarters are located in Maple Plain Minnesota. Its operations are comprised of three geographic operating segments in the United States (some 80% of sales) Europe (over 15%) and Japan (nearly 5%). It also manufacture all of its products in over 10 manufacturing facilities located in Maple Plain Minnesota; Rosemount Minnesota; Plymouth Minnesota; Brooklyn Park Minnesota; Cary North Carolina; Nashua New Hampshire (3 facilities); Telford United Kingdom; Feldkirchen Germany; Eschenlohe Germany; and Zama Kanagawa Japan.

Sales and Marketing
The company maintains an internal sales team trained in the basics of part design and the capabilities of its manufacturing product lines as well as the key advantages of its processes over alternate methods of custom parts manufacturing.

Proto Labs' advertising expenses were approximately $11.5 million $13.0 million and $11.8 million for the years ended in 2020 2019 and 2018 respectively.

Financial Performance
The company's revenue for fiscal 2020 decreased by 5% to $434.4 million compared from the prior year with $458.7 million. Proto Lab's revenue decline in 2020 was the result of a decrease in the volume of product developers and engineers we served.

Net income for fiscal 2020 decreased by 20% to $50.9 million compared from the prior year with $63.7 million.

Cash held by the company at the end of fiscal 2020 increased to $127.6 million. Cash provided by operations was $107.0 million while cash used for investing and financing activities were $95.5 million and $10.7 million respectively. Main uses of cash were purchases of marketable securities and repurchases of common stock.

Strategy
The company's growth strategy consists of: Expanding the Customer Base; Launching New Manufacturing Technology; Enhancing Customer Experience; and Broadening the Parts Envelope.

The company's business strategy is to continue to be a leading online and technology-enabled manufacturer of quick-turn on-demand injection-molded CNC-machined CNC-turned 3D-printed and sheet metal custom parts for prototyping and low-volume production. In order to achieve its goals the company anticipates continued substantial investments in technology and personnel resulting in increased operating expenses.

Mergers and Acquisitions
In early 2021 Proto Labs Inc. has completed its acquisition of 3D Hubs Inc. a leading online manufacturing platform that provides customers with on-demand access to a global network of approximately 240 premium manufacturing partners based in Amsterdam. The completion of this transaction creates the world's most comprehensive digital manufacturing offer for custom parts. It also brings two great benefits to Protolabs' customers: a complementary network of manufacturing partners to fulfill a breadth of capabilities outside of its current envelope and a broader selection of pricing and lead time options. Protolabs acquired 3D Hubs for aggregate closing consideration of $280 million consisting of $130 million in cash and $150 million in Protolabs stock.

Company Background
Proto Labs began as The Protomold Company (molded plastic parts) but added CNC metal part machining its Firstcut business in 2007. In 2009 both branches began operating under the Proto Labs banner. It all started when founder and computer geek Lawrence Lukis started a desktop printer design business and was astounded at the long turnaround (weeks) and cost (thousands) for prototype parts. He turned his computer skills to solving the problem and found a way to completely automate the entire process and produce a part in a day for prices starting at $1500.

EXECUTIVES

Independent Director, Donald Krantz
Vice President, Investor Relations And Fp&a, Dan Schumacher
Director, Stacy Greiner
President, Chief Executive Officer, Director, Robert Bodor, $338,658 total compensation
Vice President, General Manager And Managing Director - Europe, Middle East And Africa, Bjoern Klaas, $324,274 total compensation
Independent Director, Sven Wehrwein
Chief Technology Officer, Arthur Baker, $317,044 total compensation
Independent Chairman Of The Board, Archie Black
Independent Director, Sujeet Chand
Independent Director, Moonhie Chin
Auditors: Ernst & Young LLP

LOCATIONS

HQ: Proto Labs Inc
5540 Pioneer Creek Drive, Maple Plain, MN 55359
Phone: 763 479-3680
Web: www.protolabs.com

PRODUCTS/OPERATIONS

2013 Sales

	$ mil.	% of total
Protomold	115.1	71
Firstcut	48.0	29
Total	**163.1**	**100**

COMPETITORS

ARC GROUP WORLDWIDE INC.	HARDINGE INC.
COLFAX CORPORATION	KAISER ALUMINUM CORPORATION
DBM GLOBAL INC.	MTS SYSTEMS CORPORATION
ELECTRO SCIENTIFIC INDUSTRIES INC.	NN INC.
FRAZIER INDUSTRIAL COMPANY	NORDSON CORPORATION
GULF ISLAND FABRICATION INC.	SABRE INDUSTRIES INC.

HISTORICAL FINANCIALS
Company Type: Public

Income Statement				FYE: December 31
	REVENUE ($ mil.)	NET INCOME ($ mil.)	NET PROFIT MARGIN	EMPLOYEES
12/21	488.1	33.3	6.8%	2,663
12/20	434.4	50.8	11.7%	2,408
12/19	458.7	63.6	13.9%	2,535
12/18	445.6	76.5	17.2%	2,487
12/17	344.4	51.7	15.0%	2,266
Annual Growth	9.1%	(10.4%)	—	4.1%

2021 Year-End Financials

Debt ratio: 0.2%	No. of shares (mil.): 27.4
Return on equity: 4.5%	Dividends
Cash ($ mil.): 65.9	Yield: —
Current ratio: 3.34	Payout: —
Long-term debt ($ mil.): 1.3	Market value ($ mil.): 1,410.0

	STOCK PRICE ($) FY Close	P/E High/Low		PER SHARE ($) Earnings	Dividends	Book Value
12/21	51.35	208	40	1.21	0.00	30.16
12/20	153.40	99	34	1.89	0.00	24.06
12/19	101.55	55	38	2.35	0.00	21.87
12/18	112.79	58	36	2.81	0.00	20.07
12/17	103.00	55	25	1.93	0.00	17.19
Annual Growth	(16.0%)	—	—	(11.0%)	—	15.1%

Provident Bancorp Inc (MD)

Auditors: Crowe LLP

LOCATIONS

HQ: Provident Bancorp Inc (MD)
5 Market Street, Amesbury, MA 01913
Phone: 978 834-8555
Web: www.theprovidentbank.com

HISTORICAL FINANCIALS

Company Type: Public

Income Statement — FYE: December 31

	ASSETS ($ mil.)	NET INCOME ($ mil.)	INCOME AS % OF ASSETS	EMPLOYEES
12/20	1,505.7	11.9	0.8%	158
12/19	1,121.7	10.8	1.0%	144
12/18	974.0	9.3	1.0%	132
12/17	902.2	7.9	0.9%	135
12/16	795.5	6.3	0.8%	128
Annual Growth	17.3%	17.3%	—	5.4%

2020 Year-End Financials

Return on assets: 0.9%
Return on equity: 5.1%
Long-term debt ($ mil.): —
No. of shares (mil.): 19.0
Sales ($ mil): 63.9

Dividends
Yield: 0.7%
Payout: 60.0%
Market value ($ mil): 229.0

	STOCK PRICE ($) FY Close	P/E High/Low	Earnings	PER SHARE ($) Dividends	Book Value
12/20	12.00	19 11	0.66	0.09	12.38
12/19	12.45	47 18	0.60	0.00	11.86
12/18	21.68	30 20	1.00	0.00	13.05
12/17	26.45	31 20	0.86	0.00	12.02
12/16	17.90	28 19	0.69	0.00	11.31
Annual Growth	(9.5%)	— —	(1.1%)	—	2.3%

Prudential Bancorp Inc (New)

Auditors: S.R. Snodgrass, P.C.

LOCATIONS

HQ: Prudential Bancorp Inc (New)
1834 West Oregon Avenue, Philadelphia, PA 19145
Phone: 215 755-1500
Web: www.prudentialsavingsbank.com

HISTORICAL FINANCIALS

Company Type: Public

Income Statement — FYE: September 30

	ASSETS ($ mil.)	NET INCOME ($ mil.)	INCOME AS % OF ASSETS	EMPLOYEES
09/21	1,100.4	7.7	0.7%	90
09/20	1,223.3	9.5	0.8%	93
09/19	1,289.4	9.5	0.7%	88
09/18	1,081.1	7.0	0.7%	83
09/17	899.5	2.7	0.3%	87
Annual Growth	5.2%	29.4%	—	0.9%

2021 Year-End Financials

Return on assets: 0.6%
Return on equity: 5.9%
Long-term debt ($ mil.): —
No. of shares (mil.): 7.7
Sales ($ mil): 41.6

Dividends
Yield: 1.8%
Payout: 34.5%
Market value ($ mil.): 119.0

	STOCK PRICE ($) FY Close	P/E High/Low	Earnings	PER SHARE ($) Dividends	Book Value
09/21	15.26	16 11	0.98	0.28	16.79
09/20	10.54	17 9	1.12	0.71	15.86
09/19	17.01	17 14	1.07	0.65	15.71
09/18	17.31	25 21	0.78	0.70	14.29
09/17	18.53	57 44	0.32	0.12	15.12
Annual Growth	(4.7%)	— —	32.3%	23.6%	2.7%

PTC Inc

PTC is a global software and services company that serves industrial companies through its offerings in CAD PLM the IoT and AR that help customers digitize operations and collaborate. In computer aided design (CAD) its Creo offering is used to create 3D computer models for products ranging from engines to phones. PTC's Windchill software suite for product lifecycle management (PLM) enables collaborative content and process management over the internet. With ThingWorx PTC provides a platform for developing applications for the Internet of Things (IoT). The augmented reality (AR) product Vuforia Studio overlays digital information such as repair instructions onto the view of physical objects and processes. The Americas account for more than 40% of PTC's revenue.

Operations

PTC has two operating and reportable segments: Software Products (90% of sales) and Professional Services (about 10% of sales).

Software Products which includes license subscription and related support revenue (including updates and technical support) for all its products; and Professional Services which includes consulting implementation and training services.

Geographic Reach

Boston-based PTC has nearly 90 office locations used in operations in the United States and internationally predominately as sales and/or support offices and for research and development work. Most of its research and development activities are conducted in India. Operations in Americas accounts for more than 40% of PTC's revenue.

Sales and Marketing

PTC devices most of its sales from products and services sold directly by its sales force to end-user customers. Approximately 30% to 35% of its sales of products and services are through third-party resellers. Its sales force focuses on large accounts while its reseller channel provides a cost-effective means of covering the small-and-medium-size business market.

Total advertising expenses incurred were $7.1 million $3.8 million and $3.6 million in 2021 2020 and 2019 respectively.

Financial Performance

PTC's revenue has consistently increased in the last five years ending it with 2021 as its highest performing year.

The company's revenue for fiscal 2021 increased by $346 million to $1.8 billion compared to $1.5 billion in the prior year. Professional services revenue grew in fiscal 2021 by 10%; where fiscal 2020 revenue was negatively impacted by the COVID-19 pandemic fiscal 2021 benefited from increased delivery activity associated with PLM deployments.

PTC's net income also increased by $345 thousand to $476.9 million as compared to the prior year's net income of about $130.7 million.

The company held about $327 million by the end of the year. Operations of the company provided about $368.8 million. Investing activities used about $688 million while financing activities used about $370.3 million. Main cash uses were for acquisition of businesses additions to property and equipment and repayments of borrowings under credit facility.

Strategy

The three key elements to the company's strategy to deliver long-term shareholder value include aligning with market demand to build a strong pipeline; optimizing new and renewal sales and customer success to power top line ARR growth; and creating an efficient business model and operation that enables the company to drive free cash flow growth. Further the company aims to shift the company's organizational structure to align better with a traditional SaaS model and create an improved customer experience.

Mergers and Acquisitions

In 2021 PTC completed the acquisition of Arena Solutions the industry's leading software as a services (SaaS) product lifecycle management (PLM) solution for $715 million. The combination of Arena Solutions and Onshape which PTC acquired in 2019 establishes PTC as the leading provider of pure SaaS solutions for the product development market and broadly extends PTC's presence in the attractive mid-market where SaaS solutions are becoming the standards.

HISTORY

Geometry professor Samuel Geisberg fled the USSR in 1974 and worked for computer-aided design (CAD) software development firms Computervision and Applicon. At the urging of his brother Vladimir (who had emigrated in 1980 and started his own software firm) he founded Parametric Technology in 1985 to remedy flaws in mechanical design software.

With financial backing from Charles River Ventures and other investors Geisberg developed his CAD/CAM (computer-aided manufacturing) product. Charles River also brought in Steven Walske as CEO in 1986. The first Pro/ENGINEER product was shipped in 1988 and Parametric went public the next year building market strength by marketing to engineers and keeping prices at half those of competitors' products.

In 1994 Walske became chairman when Geisberg retired and took up the position of senior scientist. The next year Parametric purchased Evans & Sutherland Computer's conceptual design and rendering software business and model simulation firm Rasna which offered tools that let users simulate the operation of products in real-life settings. In 1996 Parametric acquired project modeling and management software from Greenshire License Company.

EXECUTIVES

Independent Chairman Of The Board, Robert Schechter
Executive Vice President, General Counsel, Secretary, Aaron Von Staats, $399,231 total compensation
President, Chief Executive Officer, Director, James Heppelmann, $800,000 total compensation
Independent Director, Paul Lacy
President Of Velocity Business, Michael Ditullio, $424,231 total compensation
Independent Director, Blake Moret
President - Digital Thread Solutions, Troy Richardson, $528,846 total compensation
Independent Director, Mark Benjamin
Chief Financial Officer, Executive Vice President, Kristian Talvitie, $500,000 total compensation
Auditors: PricewaterhouseCoopers LLP

LOCATIONS

HQ: PTC Inc
121 Seaport Boulevard, Boston, MA 02210
Phone: 781 370-5000
Web: www.ptc.com

PRODUCTS/OPERATIONS

2018 Sales

	$ mil.	% of total
Software	1,088.5	88
Services	153.5	12
Total	**1,241.8**	**100**

2018 Sales by Product

	$ mil.	% of total
CAD	499.8	40
PLM	483.3	39
IoT	139.3	11
IoT	119.4	10
Total	**1,241.8**	**100**

Selected Software

2-D and 3-D visualization and virtual reality mockup (Division)
Collaborative product development (Windchill)
Entry-level product development (Pro/DESKTOP)
Product design automation and management (Pro/ENGINEER)
Simulation (Pro/MECHANICA)

COMPETITORS

ACTUA CORPORATION
AEROHIVE NETWORKS INC.
AMERICAN SOFTWARE INC. INC.
CMTSU LIQUIDATION INC
ELECO PUBLIC LIMITED COMPANY
GODADDY INC.
INFOR (US) LLC
ITRON INC.
JACK HENRY & ASSOCIATES
NANTHEALTH INC.
ONESPAN INC.
SA ESKER
UNISYS CORPORATION

HISTORICAL FINANCIALS

Company Type: Public

Income Statement

FYE: September 30

	REVENUE ($ mil.)	NET INCOME ($ mil.)	NET PROFIT MARGIN	EMPLOYEES
09/21	1,807.1	476.9	26.4%	6,709
09/20	1,458.4	130.7	9.0%	6,243
09/19	1,255.6	(27.4)	—	6,055
09/18	1,241.8	51.9	4.2%	6,110
09/17	1,164.0	6.2	0.5%	6,041
Annual Growth	**11.6%**	**195.7%**	**—**	**2.7%**

2021 Year-End Financials

Debt ratio: 31.9%
Return on equity: 27.4%
Cash ($ mil.): 326.5
Current ratio: 1.38
Long-term debt ($ mil.): 1,439.4
No. of shares (mil.): 117.1
Dividends
  Yield: —
  Payout: —
Market value ($ mil.): 14,035.0

	STOCK PRICE ($) FY Close	P/E High/Low		PER SHARE ($) Earnings	Dividends	Book Value
09/21	119.79	37	20	4.03	0.00	17.40
09/20	82.72	86	43	1.12	0.00	12.39
09/19	68.18	—	—	(0.23)	0.00	10.46
09/18	106.19	236	125	0.44	0.00	7.41
09/17	56.28	1194	865	0.05	0.00	7.68
Annual Growth	**20.8%**		**—**	**-199.6%**	**—**	**22.7%**

Pure Cycle Corp.

Struggling to survive in the barren waste without a trace of water is no longer the fate of inhabitants of the Lowry Range thanks to Pure Cycle. The water utility has the exclusive right to provide water and wastewater services to about 24000 acres of the Lowry Range near Denver. Pure Cycle generates revenues from three sources: water and wastewater fees; construction fees; and monthly service fees. In 2009 it served 247 single-family water connections and 157 wastewater connections in the southeastern Denver area. It also has 60000 acre-feet of water rights in the Arkansas River basin in Southern Colorado. In 2010 Pure Cycle acquired the 931-acre Sky Ranch Property near Denver for $7 million.

EXECUTIVES

Independent Director, Wanda Abel
Independent Director, Frederick Fendel
Independent Director, Daniel Kozlowski
Chief Financial Officer, Vice President, Kevin McNeill, $225,000 total compensation
Independent Director, Jeffrey Sheets
Independent Chairman Of The Board, Patrick Beirne
President, Chief Executive Officer, Director, Mark Harding, $500,000 total compensation
Independent Director, Peter Howell
Auditors: Plante & Moran PLLC

LOCATIONS

HQ: Pure Cycle Corp.
34501 E. Quincy Avenue, Building 34, Watkins, CO 80137
Phone: 303 292-3456
Web: www.purecyclewater.com

COMPETITORS

SAN ANTONIO WATER SYSTEM
SJW GROUP
SOUTHERN WATER SERVICES LIMITED

HISTORICAL FINANCIALS

Company Type: Public

Income Statement

FYE: August 31

	REVENUE ($ mil.)	NET INCOME ($ mil.)	NET PROFIT MARGIN	EMPLOYEES
08/21	17.1	20.1	117.4%	31
08/20	25.8	6.7	26.1%	31
08/19	20.3	4.8	23.6%	29
08/18	6.9	0.4	6.0%	19
08/17	1.2	(1.7)	—	11
Annual Growth	**93.3%**			**29.6%**

2021 Year-End Financials

Debt ratio: —
Return on equity: 21.7%
Cash ($ mil.): 20.1
Current ratio: 3.11
Long-term debt ($ mil.): —
No. of shares (mil.): 23.9
Dividends
  Yield: —
  Payout: —
Market value ($ mil.): 358.0

	STOCK PRICE ($) FY Close	P/E High/Low		PER SHARE ($) Earnings	Dividends	Book Value
08/21	14.95	20	10	0.83	0.00	4.30
08/20	9.76	49	28	0.28	0.00	3.44
08/19	10.85	59	46	0.20	0.00	3.14
08/18	11.25	560	333	0.02	0.00	2.92
08/17	7.25	—	—	(0.07)	0.00	2.84
Annual Growth	**19.8%**		**—**	**—**	**—**	**10.9%**

QCR Holdings Inc

Quad City is muscling in on the community banking scene in the Midwest. QCR Holdings is the holding company for Quad City Bank & Trust Cedar Rapids Bank & Trust Rockford Bank & Trust and Community State Bank. Together the banks have about 20 offices serving the Quad City area of Illinois and Iowa as well as the communities of Cedar Rapids Iowa; Rockford Illinois; and Milwaukee. The banks offer traditional deposit products and services and concentrate their lending activities on local businesses: Commercial real estate loans make up about half of the loan portfolio; commercial loans and leases make up another third.

Operations

QCR Holdings' Bancard subsidiary provides credit card processing services; its majority-owned M2 Lease Funds leases machinery and equipment to commercial and industrial businesses.

Strategy

QCR Holdings has grown by launching operations in new geographic markets and then building upon them. It also expands through acquisitions. In mid-2016 the company acquired Iowa-based Community State Bank which operates some 10 branches in the Des Moines area.

EXECUTIVES

Executive Vice President, Chief Lending Officer, Dana Nichols, $216,300 total compensation
Independent Director, James Field
President Of Cedar Rapids Bank And Trust, James Klein
Independent Director, Brent Cobb
Independent Director, Elizabeth Jacobs
President And Chief Executive Officer Of Community State Bank, Kurt Gibson
Independent Director, Mark Kilmer
President, Chief Financial Officer, Chief Operating Officer, Director, Todd Gipple, $334,000 total compensation
Independent Director, Donna Sorensen
Senior Vice President, Director Of Human Resources, Anne Howard
Independent Director, John-Paul Besong
Independent Chairman Of The Board, Marie Ziegler
Chief Executive Officer, Director, Larry Helling, $359,700 total compensation
Independent Director, Mary Bates
Auditors: RSM US LLP

LOCATIONS

HQ: QCR Holdings Inc
 3551 7th Street, Moline, IL 61265
Phone: 309 736-3580
Web: www.qcrh.com

PRODUCTS/OPERATIONS

2015 Sales

	$ mil.	% of total
Quad City Bank & Trust	52.8	46
Cedar Rapids Bank & Trust	37.5	32
Rockford Bank & Trust	14.8	13
Wealth Management	9.1	8
All other	0.7	1
Inter-company Eliminations	(0.4)	-
Total	**114.5**	**100**

COMPETITORS

AMERICAN RIVER BANKSHARES	NORTHEAST COMMUNITY BANCORP INC.
COMMUNITY SHORES BANK	OAK VALLEY
BANCORP.	
CORPORATION	SOUTH STATE
FARMERS CAPITAL BANK	CORPORATION
CORPORATION	UNION BANK AND TRUST
FIRSTBANK CORPORATION	COMPANY
MIDLAND FINANCIAL CO.	

HISTORICAL FINANCIALS
Company Type: Public

Income Statement				FYE: December 31
	ASSETS ($ mil.)	NET INCOME ($ mil.)	INCOME AS % OF ASSETS	EMPLOYEES
12/20	5,682.8	60.5	1.1%	739
12/19	4,909.0	57.4	1.2%	697
12/18	4,949.7	43.1	0.9%	755
12/17	3,982.6	35.7	0.9%	641
12/16	3,301.9	27.6	0.8%	572
Annual Growth	14.5%	21.6%	—	6.6%

2020 Year-End Financials

Return on assets: 1.1%
Return on equity: 10.7%
Long-term debt ($ mil.): —
No. of shares (mil.): 15.8
Sales ($ mil): 312.1

Dividends
 Yield: 0.6%
 Payout: 6.5%
Market value ($ mil.): 626.0

	STOCK PRICE ($) FY Close	P/E High/Low		Earnings	PER SHARE ($) Dividends	Book Value
12/20	39.59	11	6	3.80	0.24	37.57
12/19	43.86	12	9	3.60	0.24	33.82
12/18	32.09	17	10	2.86	0.24	30.10
12/17	42.85	18	15	2.61	0.20	25.38
12/16	43.30	20	10	2.17	0.16	21.82
Annual Growth	(2.2%)	—		15.0%	10.7%	14.5%

Quaker Houghton

EXECUTIVES

Prin, Ronald J Naples
Global Business Manager Mining, Kevin Dickey
Manager, Brad Wellensiek
Senior Financial Reporting Ana, Joseph Geller
Chemical Technician, Ryan McGrath
Senior Tax Analyst, Yinong Xing
Manager, Tax, Bob Katch
Manager, Manufacturing, Dan Ramsay
Assistant Controller, David Will
Director, Learning and Organiz, Janice Johnson
Business Manager, Jeffrey Wetzel
Auditors: PricewaterhouseCoopers LLP

LOCATIONS

HQ: Quaker Houghton
 901 E. Hector Street, Conshohocken, PA 19428-2380
Phone: 610 832-4000   **Fax:** 610 832-8682
Web: www.quakerchem.com

HISTORICAL FINANCIALS
Company Type: Public

Income Statement				FYE: December 31
	REVENUE ($ mil.)	NET INCOME ($ mil.)	NET PROFIT MARGIN	EMPLOYEES
12/20	1,417.6	39.6	2.8%	4,200
12/19	1,133.5	31.6	2.8%	4,500
12/18	867.5	59.4	6.9%	2,160
12/17	820.0	20.2	2.5%	2,110
12/16	746.6	61.4	8.2%	2,020
Annual Growth	17.4%	(10.4%)	—	20.1%

2020 Year-End Financials

Debt ratio: 30.7%
Return on equity: 3.0%
Cash ($ mil.): 181.8
Current ratio: 2.07
Long-term debt ($ mil.): 849.0

No. of shares (mil.): 17.8
Dividends
 Yield: 0.6%
 Payout: 69.8%
Market value ($ mil.): 4,523.0

	STOCK PRICE ($) FY Close	P/E High/Low		Earnings	PER SHARE ($) Dividends	Book Value
12/20	253.39	116	50	2.22	1.55	73.97
12/19	164.52	108	69	2.08	1.51	69.96
12/18	177.71	47	32	4.45	1.45	32.62
12/17	150.79	108	82	1.52	1.40	30.63
12/16	127.94	29	15	4.63	1.33	30.33
Annual Growth	18.6%	—		(16.8%)	3.9%	25.0%

Qualys, Inc.

Qualys is a pioneer and leading provider of a cloud-based platform delivering information technology (IT) security and compliance solutions. The Qualys Cloud Platform is a cloud security and compliance management software suite and container security solutions which refers to the Qualys Cloud Apps that leverage its shared and extensible core services and its highly scalable multi-tenant cloud infrastructure. Its biggest product Vulnerability Management includes continuous monitoring threat protection and IT asset tracking through a cloud agent. The company counts more than 19000 customers in some 130 countries. Qualys reaches many customers through partnerships with managed service providers consultants and resellers including IBM Fujitsu Optiv and Verizon Communications.

Operations

Qualys designed its qualys cloud platform to transform the way organizations secure and protect their IT infrastructures and applications. The company cloud platform offers an integrated suite of solutions that automates the lifecycle of asset discovery and management security assessments and compliance management for an organization's IT infrastructure and assets whether such infrastructure and assets reside inside the organization on their network perimeter on endpoints or in the cloud. In addition the cloud platform providing the customers with advantages such as no hardware to buy or manage real time visibility in one place anytime and anywhere easy global scanning seamless scaling up to date resources and data stored securely.

Geographic Reach

Qualys is based in Foster California and has US offices in Bellevue Washington and Raleigh North Carolina and international offices in Courbevoie France; Moscow Russia; Munich Germany; Frankfurt Germany; Nuremberg Germany; Milan Italy; Almere the Netherlands Dubai United Arab Emirates; Reading United Kingdom; and Tokyo Japan.

It operates principal data centers at third-party facilities in Santa Clara California; Las Vegas Nevada; Ashburn Virginia; Ontario Canada; Geneva Switzerland; Pune India; Dubai United Arab Emirates; and Amsterdam the Netherlands.

About 65% of its revenue comes from US operations.

Sales and Marketing

Qualys markets its products through customers directly through the company sales teams as well in indirectly through network channel partners. In additions the company markets and sell through enterprise government entities small and medium sized businesses across a broad range of industries including education financial services government healthcare insurance manufacturing media retail technology and utilities.

Advertising costs were $207 thousand $74 thousand and $87 thousand for 2020 2019 and 2018 respectively.

Financial Performance

Revenue for the year 2020 totaled $363 million a 13% increase from the previous year's $321.6 million.

In 2020 the company had a net income of $91.6 million a 32% increase from the previous year.

The company's cash at the end of 2020 was $75.3 million. Operating activities provided $180.1 million while investing activities used $80.9 million mainly for purchases of marketable securities. Financing activities used another $112.6 million mainly for repurchases of common stock.

Strategy

Qualys intends to strengthen its leadership position as a trusted provider of cloud-based IT security and compliance solutions. The key elements of its growth strategy are:

Continuing to innovate and enhance its cloud platform and suite of solutions. Qualys intends to continue to make significant investments in research and development to extend its cloud platform's functionality by developing new security solutions and capabilities and further enhancing the company's existing suite of solutions;

Expanding the use of the company's suite of solutions by its large and diverse customer base. With more than 19000 customers including active subscribers of the company's free services across many industries and geographies Qualys believes it has a significant opportunity to sell additional solutions to customers and expand their use of its suite of solutions;

Driving new customer growth and broadening its global reach. The company is pursuing new customers by targeting key accounts releasing free IT security and compliance services and expanding both sales and marketing organization and network of channel partners; and

Selectively pursuing technology acquisitions to bolster its capabilities and leadership position. Qualys may explore acquisitions that are complementary to and can expand the functionality of its cloud platform. The company may also seek to acquire development teams to supplement its own personnel and acquire technology to increase the breadth of the company's cloud-based IT security and compliance solutions.

Mergers and Acquisitions

Qualys bought Layered Insight in 2018 to add more security to its offerings. Layered Insight provides security to applications running on virtual container systems. Pairing the two companies products is to provide their customers with greater visibility and security. Qualys expects to integrate Layered Insight's offerings into its systems by the second half of 2018.

EXECUTIVES

Vice President, General Counsel, Corporate Secretary, Bruce Posey, $315,833 total compensation
Chief Financial Officer, Joo Mi Kim, $169,167 total compensation
Chief Executive Officer, Sumedh Thakar, $382,500 total compensation
Independent Director, Kristi Rogers

Independent Director, Wendy Pfeiffer
Independent Director, John Zangardi
Principal Accounting Officer, Saikat Paul
Chief Revenue Officer, Allan Peters
Director, William Berutti
Independent Director, Peter Pace
Independent Director, Jeffrey Hank
Auditors: Grant Thornton LLP

LOCATIONS

HQ: Qualys, Inc.
919 E. Hillsdale Boulevard, 4th Floor, Foster City, CA 94404
Phone: 650 801-6100
Web: www.qualys.com

PRODUCTS/OPERATIONS

2018 Sales

	% of total
Direct	59
Partner	41
Total	**100**

COMPETITORS

COGNIZANT TECHNOLOGY SOLUTIONS CORPORATION
EPAM SYSTEMS INC.
JUNIPER NETWORKS INC.
MICROSTRATEGY INCORPORATED
PEGASYSTEMS INC.
PERFICIENT INC.
RACKSPACE TECHNOLOGY GLOBAL INC.
SERENA SOFTWARE INC.
SERVICENOW INC.
SERVICESOURCE INTERNATIONAL INC.
TENABLE INC.
TRIPWIRE INC.
WORKDAY INC.

HISTORICAL FINANCIALS

Company Type: Public

Income Statement   FYE: December 31

	REVENUE ($ mil.)	NET INCOME ($ mil.)	NET PROFIT MARGIN	EMPLOYEES
12/20	362.9	91.5	25.2%	1,498
12/19	321.6	69.3	21.6%	1,289
12/18	278.8	57.3	20.5%	1,194
12/17	230.8	40.4	17.5%	869
12/16	197.9	19.2	9.7%	684
Annual Growth	**16.4%**	**47.7%**	**—**	**21.7%**

2020 Year-End Financials

Debt ratio: —	No. of shares (mil.): 39.2
Return on equity: 23.0%	Dividends
Cash ($ mil.): 74.1	Yield: —
Current ratio: 1.86	Payout: —
Long-term debt ($ mil.): —	Market value ($ mil.): 4,784.0

	STOCK PRICE ($) FY Close	P/E High/Low		PER SHARE ($) Earnings	Dividends	Book Value
12/20	121.87	54	29	2.24	0.00	10.30
12/19	83.37	54	39	1.68	0.00	9.88
12/18	74.74	66	40	1.37	0.00	9.18
12/17	59.35	57	30	1.01	0.00	8.90
12/16	31.65	71	32	0.50	0.00	7.21
Annual Growth	**40.1%**		**—**	**45.5%**	**—**	**9.3%**

Quidel Corp.

Quidel Corporation makes rapid diagnostic in vitro test products used at the point-of-care (POC) usually at a doctor's office or other outpatient setting. The diagnostic solutions aid in the detection and diagnosis of many critical diseases and other medical conditions including infectious diseases cardiovascular diseases and conditions women's health gastrointestinal diseases autoimmune diseases bone health and thyroid diseases. Its cardiac immunoassay tests are used in physician offices hospital laboratories and emergency departments and other urgent care or alternative site settings. Majority of its revenue comes from its domestic operation.

Operations

The company's diagnostic testing solutions are divided in four product categories: rapid immunoassay cardiac immunoassay specialized diagnostic solutions and molecular diagnostic solutions.

Rapid Immunoassay offers the easy-to-use Sofia and Sofia 2 analyzers combined with unique software and Sofia FIA tests to yield an automatic objective result that is readily available on the instrument's screen in a hard-copy printout and in a transmissible electronic form that can network via a lab information system to hospital and medical center databases. QuickVue is the brand name for its rapid visually-read lateral flow immunoassay products and InflammaDry and AdenoPlus products for lateral-flow based. It accounted for around 70% of total revenue.

Cardiac Immunoassay offers Triage MeterPro a portable testing platform that runs a comprehensive menu of tests that enable physicians to promote improved health outcomes through the rapid diagnosis of critical diseases and health conditions as well as the detection of certain drugs of abuse. It also offers a version of the Triage BNP Test for use on Beckman Coulter lab analyzers. It accounted for about 15% of total revenue.

Specialized Diagnostic Solutions (nearly 15%) provide a wide variety of traditional cell lines specimen collection devices media and controls for use in laboratories and also provide a variety of biomarkers for bone health and produce both clinical and research products for the assessment of osteoporosis.

Molecular Diagnostic Solutions (less than 5%) offers Solana an easy to run amplification and detection system that has the ability to concurrently run up to 12 assays at a time Lyra (open system molecular assays run on several thermocyclers) and developing the Savanna system as a low-cost fully-integrated system with sample in/result out simplicity.

Geographic Reach

Headquartered in San Diego California Quidel has three primary manufacturing sites two are in San Diego California and one is located in Athens Ohio. In addition the company is building out an additional manufacturing site in Carlsbad California. It also has operations in China and Ireland.

Domestic sales accounted for more than 85% while International sales account for nearly 15% of revenue.

Sales and Marketing

Quidel sells its products directly to end users and distributors for professional use in physician offices hospitals clinical laboratories reference laboratories urgent care clinics leading universities retail clinics pharmacies and wellness screening centers. It markets its products through a network of distributors and through a direct sales force.

The company's advertising costs were $1.1 million $1.3 million and $0.9 million for the 2020 2019 and 2018 respectively.

Products are sold internationally with the majority of international sales to customers are in Europe and Asia-Pacific. To help penetrate foreign markets which have been less receptive to POC diagnostics than the US Quidel enters into agreements with international distributors.

Financial Performance
The company's revenue for the last five years was increasing with overall increase of 700% since 2016.

In 2020 total revenue increased 211% to $1.7 billion as compared to revenue in 2019. Its revenues can be highly concentrated over a small number of products. For the year ended December 31 2020 sales of its COVID-19 products accounted for 70% of total revenue.

Quidel reported a $737.4 million increase in net income in 2020 ending the year at $810.3 million. The increase was mainly due to a $1.1 billion increase in sales.

Cash at the end of 2020 was $489.9 million. Net cash provided by operating activities was $629.8 million while investing activities used $63.3 million. Financing activities used another $130.3 million. Main cash uses were for acquisitions of property and equipment and other payments.

Strategy
The company's primary strategy is to target market segments that represent significant total market opportunities and in which it can be successful by applying its expertise and know-how to develop differentiated technologies and products.

In order to achieve this strategy the company must focus on innovative products and markets and leverage our core competency in new product development for our QuickVue Sofia and Triage immunoassay brands and next-generation products; leverage our manufacturing expertise to address increasing demand for our products including through expanded manufacturing capacity; utilize our molecular assay development competencies to further develop our molecular diagnostics franchise that includes distinct testing platforms such as Lyra Solana and Savanna; and strengthen our position with distribution partners and our end-user customers to gain more emphasis on our products and enter new markets.

The company is also focusing its research and development efforts on three areas: new proprietary product platform development the creation of new and improved products for use on its established platforms to address unmet clinical needs and pursuit of collaborations with or acquisitions of other companies for new and existing products and markets that advance its differentiated strategy.

Company Background
Originally incorporated as Monoclonal Antibodies Inc. in California in 1979 and re-incorporated as Quidel Corporation in the State of Delaware in 1987.

EXECUTIVES

Independent Director, Kenneth Widder

President, Chief Executive Officer, Director, Douglas Bryant, $777,738 total compensation
Senior Vice President, General Counsel, Michelle Hodges
Independent Director, Joseph Wilkins
Independent Director, Ann Rhoads
Independent Director, Edward Michael
Senior Vice President - Cardiometabolic Business Unit, William Ferenczy
Senior Vice President - Business Development, Edward Russell, $372,708 total compensation
Senior Vice President, R&d, Werner Kroll, $421,856 total compensation
Senior Vice President - Molecular Business, Tamara Ranalli
Chief Financial Officer, Randall Steward, $494,495 total compensation
Senior Vice President - Digital Health Business Unit, Karen Gibson
Chief Operating Officer, Robert Bujarski, $512,402 total compensation
Independent Chairman Of The Board, Kenneth Buechler
Auditors: Ernst & Young LLP

LOCATIONS

HQ: Quidel Corp.
9975 Summers Ridge Road, San Diego, CA 92121
Phone: 858 552-1100
Web: www.quidel.com

PRODUCTS/OPERATIONS

2015 Sales

	$ mil.	% of total
Infectious disease products	141.8	72
Women's health products	37.2	19
Gastrointestinal disease products	7.2	4
Royalty license fees and grants	6.2	3
Other products	3.7	2
Total	**196.1**	**100**

Selected Subsidiaries
BioHelix Corporation
Diagnostic Hybrids Inc.
Litmus Concepts Inc.
Metra Biosystems Inc.
Osteo Sciences Corporation
Pacific Biotech Inc.
Quidel China Ltd.
Quidel Germany GmbH
Quidel International LLC

Selected Brands
AmpliVue
Copan
D3 Direct Detection
ELVIS
Lyra brands
QuickVue
Sofia
Thyretain

COMPETITORS

ABBOTT LABORATORIES
ACCELERATE DIAGNOSTICS INC.
BIO-TECHNE CORPORATION
DEXCOM INC.
IDEXX LABORATORIES INC.
IMMUNOMEDICS INC.
LIFE TECHNOLOGIES CORPORATION
LUMINEX CORPORATION
MERIDIAN BIOSCIENCE INC.
GENETICS INC.
MYRIAD
OPKO HEALTH INC.
ROCHE DIAGNOSTICS CORPORATION
STRECK INC.

HISTORICAL FINANCIALS
Company Type: Public

Income Statement
FYE: December 31

	REVENUE ($ mil.)	NET INCOME ($ mil.)	NET PROFIT MARGIN	EMPLOYEES
12/21	1,698.5	704.2	41.5%	1,600
12/20	1,661.6	810.2	48.8%	1,370
12/19	534.8	72.9	13.6%	1,250
12/18	522.2	74.1	14.2%	1,224
12/17	277.7	(8.1)	—	1,193
Annual Growth	**57.3%**	—		**7.6%**

2021 Year-End Financials

Debt ratio: —	No. of shares (mil.): 41.6
Return on equity: 43.1%	Dividends
Cash ($ mil.): 802.7	Yield: —
Current ratio: 4.45	Payout: —
Long-term debt ($ mil.): —	Market value ($ mil.): 5,627.0

	STOCK PRICE ($) FY Close	P/E High/Low		PER SHARE ($) Earnings	Dividends	Book Value
12/21	134.99	15	6	16.43	0.00	46.28
12/20	179.65	16	4	18.60	0.00	31.51
12/19	75.03	42	27	1.73	0.00	13.37
12/18	48.82	39	21	1.86	0.00	10.81
12/17	43.35	—	—	(0.24)	0.00	6.58
Annual Growth	**32.8%**				—	**62.9%**

QuinStreet, Inc.

QuinStreet is a pioneer in delivering online marketplace solutions to match searchers with brands in digital media and is committed to providing consumers with the information and tools they need to research find and select the products and brands that meet their needs. The company specializes in customer acquisition for clients in high value information-intensive markets or "verticals" including financial services and home services. Its clients include some of the world's largest companies and brands in those markets. The company was founded in 1999 and generates vast majority of sales domestically.

Operations
QuinStreet's two largest client verticals are financial services and home services. Its financial services segment represented roughly 75% of revenue. QuinStreet's home services client vertical represented about 25% of revenue.

Geographic Reach
QuinStreet's corporate headquarters is located in Foster City California with additional offices in the US and India. Nearly all of the company's revenues come from the US.

Sales and Marketing
QuinStreet generates revenue from fees earned through the delivery of qualified leads clicks inquiries calls customers and display advertisements.

QuinStreet's sales and marketing expenses were $11.0 million in 2021 $8.9 million in 2020 and $8.8 million in 2019.

Financial Performance
Net revenue increased by $88.1 million or 18% to $578.5 million in fiscal year 2021 compared to fiscal year 2020. Revenue from home services

client vertical increased by $84.6 million or 169% primarily as a result of inorganic and organic (synergy) revenue effects from the acquisition of Modernize completed in fiscal year 2021.

In 2021 the company had a net income of $23.6 million a 30% increase from the previous year's net income of $18.1 million.

QuinStreet's cash at the end of fiscal 2021 was $110.3 million. Operations generated $50.6 million in cash while investing activities used $36.5 million mainly for business acquisitions. Financing activities used another $11.3 million for payment of withholding taxes and contingent considerations related to acquisitions.

Strategy

QuinStreet's goal is to continue to be one of the largest and most successful performance marketing companies on the Internet and eventually in other digitized media forms. It believes that it is in the early stages of a very large and long-term market opportunity. The strategy for pursuing this opportunity includes the following key components: focus on generating sustainable revenues by providing measurable value to its clients; build QuinStreet and its industry sustainably by behaving ethically in all it does and by providing quality content and website experiences to Internet visitors; remain vertically focused choosing to grow through depth expertise and coverage in its current client verticals; enter new client verticals selectively over time organically and through acquisitions; build a world class organization with best-in-class capabilities for delivering measurable marketing results to clients and high yields or returns on media costs; develop and evolve the best products technologies and platform for managing successful performance marketing campaigns on the Internet; focus on technologies that enhance media yield improve client results and achieve scale efficiencies; build and apply unique data advantages from running some of the largest campaigns over long periods of time in its client verticals including the steep learning curves of what campaigns work best to optimize each media type and each client's results; build and partner with vertical content websites that attract high intent visitors in the client and media verticals it serves; and be a client-driven organization and develop a broad set of media sources and capabilities to reliably meet client needs.

Mergers and Acquisitions

In mid-2020 QuinStreet acquired Texas-based Modernize a leader in home improvement performance marketing services. Modernize Home Services will serve as QuinStreet's flagship brand in home services going forward advancing its mission to set the standard for transparency and trust in the home improvement and home services selection process enabling millions of homeowners to make good and confident decisions. The consideration paid for the acquisition totaled $67.5 million in cash.

EXECUTIVES

Independent Director, Asmau Ahmed
Senior Vice President, Curtis Godfrey, $300,000 total compensation
Independent Director, Andrew Sheehan
Independent Director, Matthew Glickman
Chief Technology Officer, President - Product And Technology, Nina Bhanap, $404,790 total compensation
Lead Independent Director, James Simons

Executive Vice President, Timothy Stevens, $365,000 total compensation
Chief Financial Officer, Gregory Wong, $385,000 total compensation
Executive Vice President, Andreja Stevanovic, $324,450 total compensation
Independent Director, David Pauldine
Chief Legal And Privacy Officer, Martin Collins, $331,660 total compensation
Independent Director, Stuart Huizinga
Independent Director, Anna Fieler
Independent Director, Hillary Smith
Chairman And Chief Executive Officer, Douglas Valenti, $540,750 total compensation
Auditors: PricewaterhouseCoopers LLP

LOCATIONS

HQ: QuinStreet, Inc.
  950 Tower Lane, 6th Floor, Foster City, CA 94404
Phone: 650 578-7700
Web: www.quinstreet.com

PRODUCTS/OPERATIONS

Selected Industries Served
Financial services
Education
Business-to-business technology
Home services
Medical

COMPETITORS

APTITUDE SOFTWARE GROUP PLC	MSCI INC.
CRITEO	NATIONAL RESEARCH CORPORATION
EGAIN CORPORATION	NETCALL PLC
EMERALD HOLDING INC.	PFSWEB INC.
EUROVESTECH PLC	STARTEK INC.
EXPERIAN PLC	TECHTARGET INC.
LIQUIDITY SERVICES INC.	VERINT SYSTEMS INC.
	WEX INC.
LIVEPERSON INC.	ZOOM INFORMATION LLC

HISTORICAL FINANCIALS

Company Type: Public

Income Statement				FYE: June 30
	REVENUE ($ mil.)	NET INCOME ($ mil.)	NET PROFIT MARGIN	EMPLOYEES
06/21	578.4	23.5	4.1%	614
06/20	490.3	18.1	3.7%	592
06/19	455.1	62.4	13.7%	637
06/18	404.3	15.9	3.9%	506
06/17	299.7	(12.2)	—	469
Annual Growth	17.9%	—		7.0%

2021 Year-End Financials

Debt ratio: —	No. of shares (mil.): 53.7
Return on equity: 8.5%	Dividends
Cash ($ mil.): 110.3	Yield: —
Current ratio: 1.78	Payout: —
Long-term debt ($ mil.): —	Market value ($ mil.): 999.0

	STOCK PRICE ($) FY Close	P/E High/Low	PER SHARE ($) Earnings	Dividends	Book Value
06/21	18.58	56 23	0.43	0.00	5.49
06/20	10.46	48 17	0.34	0.00	4.90
06/19	15.85	16 10	1.18	0.00	4.41
06/18	12.70	43 10	0.32	0.00	3.08
06/17	4.17	— —	(0.27)	0.00	2.60
Annual Growth	45.3%		—	—	20.5%

R1 RCM Inc

R1 RCM (formerly Accretive Health) provides revenue cycle management (RCM) services to health care providers. It handles patient registration benefits verification medical treatment documentation and coding billing and other tasks for clients. The company specializes in enhancing efficiencies and quality while reducing costs. It provides technology solutions and process workflows. Typical customers are not-for-profit and for-profit hospital systems such as Ascension Health and Intermountain Health as well as independent medical centers physician groups and EMS organizations. The company operates more than 25 offices in the US and seven offices overseas.

Operations
R1 RCM's significant operations are organized around the single business of providing revenue cycle operations for healthcare providers. The company views its operations and manages its business as one operating and reporting segment. All of the net services revenue and trade accounts receivable are derived from healthcare providers.

Most of the company's sale were generated from net operating fees accounting to nearly 85% of total sales while incentive fees and other services account for the rest.

Geographic Reach
R1 RCM's headquarters is located in Chicago Illinois. The company has over 25 offices domestically and approximately 390000 square feet of office space throughout seven offices internationally.

Sales and Marketing
R1 RCM has more than 900 clients nationwide. New business opportunities are generated by the company's sales and marketing team and other members of its senior management team. The company's customer acquisition process utilizes traditional and non-traditional techniques to inform the marketplace of R1's solutions.

The company's customers typically are healthcare providers including health systems and hospitals physician groups and municipal and private EMS providers. Hospital systems affiliated with Ascension have accounted for about 65% of the company's net services revenue.

Financial Performance
Net services revenue increased by $84.7 million or 7.1% from $1.2 billion in 2019 to $1.3 billion in 2020. The increase was primarily driven by a $56.6 million increase in net operating fees largely as a result of new customers onboarded since the beginning of 2019 a $14.4 million increase in incentive fees driven by better operational execution and an $11.1 million increase driven by the acquisitions of SCI and RevWorks partially offset by the EMS Disposition in the third quarter of 2020.

In 2020 the company had a net income of $117.1 million a $105.1 million increase from the previous year.

The company's cash at the end of 2020 was $174.8 million. Operating activities generated $61.8 million while investing activities used $117 million mainly for $the acquisition of SCI. Financing activities provided $137.9 million.

Strategy
R1 RCM continues to invest capital to achieve its strategic initiatives. In addition the company plans to continue to enhance customer service by

continuing its investment in technology to enable its systems to more effectively integrate with customers' existing technologies in connection with its strategic initiatives. The company plans to continue to deploy resources to strengthen its information technology infrastructure including automation to drive additional value for customers. R1 RCM also expects to continue to invest in its global business services infrastructure and capabilities and selectively pursue acquisitions and/or strategic relationships that will enable it to broaden or further enhance its offerings.

Mergers and Acquisitions

In mid-2021 R1 RCM completed the acquisition of VisitPay the leading digital payment solution provider for approximately $300 million in cash. The acquisition will combine VisitPay's best-in-class consumer payments platform with R1's leading patient access technology to enable providers to deliver a seamless financial journey for their patients.

In mid-2020 R1 RCM completed the acquisition of the Kansas-based Cerner RevWorks services business and commercial non-federal client relationships. Through the commercial partnership R1 is offering a powerful RCM solution that combines the company's collective revenue cycle expertise to produce both operational and patient-centric results. As such the company look forward to delivering scalable innovations and successful client outcomes to Cerner's customers as well as other healthcare organizations. R1 will pay a reported $30 million for the revenue cycle management-outsourcing division.

In early 2020 R1 RCM completed the acquisition of SCI Solutions (SCI) a leading provider of SaaS-based scheduling and patient access solutions headquartered in Seattle. The combination of R1 and SCI is expected to deliver enhanced value for healthcare providers by enabling them to expand digital front door strategies for their patients improve operating efficiency and increase capacity utilization among other benefits. The acquisition price is $190M.

Company Background

The company was formed in 2003 as Healthcare Services. It changed its name to Accretive Health in 2009 and went public in 2010. Accretive Health changed its name to R1 RCM in 2017.

R1 has had a relationship with Ascension Health since its founding; the companies expanded their agreement to encompass a larger number of Ascension-affiliated hospitals in 2016.

EXECUTIVES

President, Chief Executive Officer And Director, Joseph Flanagan, $895,000 total compensation
Chief Financial Officer, Executive Vice President, Treasurer, Rachel Wilson, $271,250 total compensation
Independent Director, Ian Sacks
Executive Vice President, Chief Commercial Officer, Gary Long, $460,000 total compensation
Independent Director, Neal Moszkowski
Director, Albert Zimmerli
Director, Anthony Speranzo
Independent Director, Jill Smith
Chief Operating Officer, Executive Vice President - Operations And Delivery, John Sparby
Director, Anthony Tersigni
Executive Vice President - Strategy And Corporate Development, Chief Solutions Officer, Vijay Kotte

Director, David Dill
Chief Technology And Digital Officer, Jay Sreedharan
Independent Director, Agnes Scanlan
Auditors: Ernst & Young LLP

LOCATIONS

HQ: R1 RCM Inc
434 W. Ascension Way, 6th Floor, Murray, UT 84123
Phone: 312 324-7820
Web: www.r1rcm.com

PRODUCTS/OPERATIONS

2013 Sales

	$ mil.	% of total
RCM services net operating fee	225.0	44
RCM services incentive fees	210.3	42
Other services	69.5	14
Total	**504.8**	**100**

Selected Customers

Ascension Health
Catholic Health East
Fairview Health Services
Intermountain Healthcare

COMPETITORS

CARECLOUD INC.
CITY OF HOPE
EXLSERVICE HOLDINGS INC.
FRC FOUNDERS CORPORATION
MASTEC INC.
MEDASSETS INC.
MULTIPLAN INC.
NETCALL PLC
OAK MANAGEMENT CORPORATION
PREMIER INC.
RECALL CORPORATION
STERICYCLE INC.

HISTORICAL FINANCIALS

Company Type: Public

Income Statement				FYE: December 31
	REVENUE ($ mil.)	NET INCOME ($ mil.)	NET PROFIT MARGIN	EMPLOYEES
12/21	1,474.6	97.2	6.6%	22,000
12/20	1,270.8	117.1	9.2%	20,200
12/19	1,186.1	12.0	1.0%	22,500
12/18	868.5	(45.3)	—	18,600
12/17	449.8	(58.8)	—	9,965
Annual Growth	34.6%	—	—	21.9%

2021 Year-End Financials

Debt ratio: 53.2%
Return on equity: 28.3%
Cash ($ mil.): 130.1
Current ratio: 1.43
Long-term debt ($ mil.): 754.9
No. of shares (mil.): 278.2
Dividends
  Yield: —
  Payout: —
Market value ($ mil.): 7,092.0

	STOCK PRICE ($) FY Close	P/E High/Low		Earnings	PER SHARE ($) Dividends	Book Value
12/21	25.49	—	—	(1.86)	0.00	1.25
12/20	24.02	59	18	0.33	0.00	2.80
12/19	12.98	—	—	(0.08)	0.00	2.17
12/18	7.95	—	—	(0.60)	0.00	1.94
12/17	4.41	—	—	(0.75)	0.00	2.13
Annual Growth	55.1% (12.6%)			—	—	—

Rand Worldwide Inc.

EXECUTIVES

Director, Philip Livingston
Director, David Schneider
President, Chief Executive Officer, Director, Lawrence Rychlak, $281,000 total compensation
Chief Financial Officer, Vice President, Treasurer, Secretary, John Kuta, $164,333 total compensation
Independent Director, Peter Kamin
Auditors: Dixon Hughes Goodman LLP

LOCATIONS

HQ: Rand Worldwide Inc.
11201 Dolfield Boulevard, Suite 112, Owings Mills, MD 21117
Phone: 410 581-8080
Web: www.rand.com

HISTORICAL FINANCIALS

Company Type: Public

Income Statement				FYE: June 30
	REVENUE ($ mil.)	NET INCOME ($ mil.)	NET PROFIT MARGIN	EMPLOYEES
06/21	257.3	20.8	8.1%	0
06/20	281.0	23.3	8.3%	0
06/19	222.4	12.0	5.4%	0
06/18	116.4	2.6	2.2%	0
06/17	81.0	3.6	4.5%	0
Annual Growth	33.5%	54.2%	—	—

2021 Year-End Financials

Debt ratio: 44.7%
Return on equity: 71.8%
Cash ($ mil.): 1.6
Current ratio: 0.75
Long-term debt ($ mil.): 30.2
No. of shares (mil.): 33.5
Dividends
  Yield: 11.5%
  Payout: 282.2%
Market value ($ mil.): 507.0

	STOCK PRICE ($) FY Close	P/E High/Low		Earnings	PER SHARE ($) Dividends	Book Value
06/21	15.10	27	18	0.62	1.75	0.18
06/20	11.50	16	9	0.71	0.25	1.61
06/19	6.70	—	—	(0.00)	0.00	1.17
06/18	3.14	—	—	(0.00)	0.00	0.79
06/17	2.70	—	—	(0.00)	0.00	0.71
Annual Growth	53.8% (28.8%)			—	—	—

Randolph Bancorp Inc

Auditors: Crowe LLP

LOCATIONS

HQ: Randolph Bancorp Inc
2 Batterymarch Park, Suite 301, Quincy, MA 02169
Phone: 781 963-2100
Web: www.randolphsavings.com

HOOVER'S HANDBOOK OF EMERGING COMPANIES 2022

HISTORICAL FINANCIALS
Company Type: Public

Income Statement
FYE: December 31

	ASSETS ($ mil.)	NET INCOME ($ mil.)	INCOME AS % OF ASSETS	EMPLOYEES
12/20	721.0	19.9	2.8%	208
12/19	631.0	3.4	0.5%	217
12/18	614.3	(2.0)	—	199
12/17	531.8	(2.1)	—	187
12/16	481.2	0.4	0.1%	220
Annual Growth	10.6%	156.1%	—	(1.4%)

2020 Year-End Financials
Return on assets: 2.9%
Return on equity: 22.3%
Long-term debt ($ mil.): —
No. of shares (mil.): 5.5
Sales ($ mil): 79.0

Dividends
  Yield: —
  Payout: —
Market value ($ mil.): 121.0

	STOCK PRICE ($) FY Close	P/E High/Low		PER SHARE ($) Earnings	Dividends	Book Value
12/20	22.06	6	2	3.86	0.00	18.16
12/19	17.65	27	21	0.64	0.00	14.07
12/18	14.15	—	—	(0.37)	0.00	13.21
12/17	15.35	—	—	(0.39)	0.00	13.50
12/16	16.12	—	—	(0.00)	0.00	14.19
Annual Growth	8.2%			—	—	6.4%

Rattler Midstream LP

Auditors: Grant Thornton LLP

LOCATIONS
HQ: Rattler Midstream LP
  500 West Texas, Suite 1200, Midland, TX 79701
Phone: 432 221-7400
Web: www.rattlermidstream.com

HISTORICAL FINANCIALS
Company Type: Public

Income Statement
FYE: December 31

	REVENUE ($ mil.)	NET INCOME ($ mil.)	NET PROFIT MARGIN	EMPLOYEES
12/20	423.9	34.6	8.2%	0
12/19	447.6	185.7	41.5%	0
12/18	184.4	62.9	34.1%	0
12/17	39.3	20.6	52.6%	0
Annual Growth	121.0%	18.8%	—	—

2020 Year-End Financials
Debt ratio: 31.5%
Return on equity: —
Cash ($ mil.): 23.9
Current ratio: 2.26
Long-term debt ($ mil.): 569.9

No. of shares (mil.): 150.1
Dividends
  Yield: 11.2%
  Payout: 133.7%
Market value ($ mil.): 1,424.0

	STOCK PRICE ($) FY Close	P/E High/Low		PER SHARE ($) Earnings	Dividends	Book Value
12/20	9.48	24	4	0.74	1.07	2.58
12/19	17.79	31	22	0.64	0.34	4.88
12/18	0.00	—	—	(0.00)	0.00	(0.00)
Annual Growth	—			—	—	—

RBB Bancorp

Auditors: Eide Bailly LLP

LOCATIONS
HQ: RBB Bancorp
  1055 Wilshire Blvd., Suite 1200, Los Angeles, CA 90017
Phone: 213 627-9888
Web: www.royalbusinessbankusa.com

HISTORICAL FINANCIALS
Company Type: Public

Income Statement
FYE: December 31

	ASSETS ($ mil.)	NET INCOME ($ mil.)	INCOME AS % OF ASSETS	EMPLOYEES
12/20	3,350.0	32.9	1.0%	371
12/19	2,788.5	39.2	1.4%	355
12/18	2,974.0	36.1	1.2%	365
12/17	1,691.0	25.5	1.5%	203
12/16	1,395.5	19.0	1.4%	177
Annual Growth	24.5%	14.6%	—	20.3%

2020 Year-End Financials
Return on assets: 1.0%
Return on equity: 7.8%
Long-term debt ($ mil.): —
No. of shares (mil.): 19.5
Sales ($ mil): 153.1

Dividends
  Yield: 2.1%
  Payout: 20.5%
Market value ($ mil.): 301.0

	STOCK PRICE ($) FY Close	P/E High/Low		PER SHARE ($) Earnings	Dividends	Book Value
12/20	15.38	13	6	1.65	0.33	21.90
12/19	21.17	11	9	1.92	0.40	20.35
12/18	17.57	16	8	2.01	0.43	18.73
12/17	27.37	15	12	1.68	0.08	16.67
Annual Growth	(17.5%)			— (0.6%)60.4%		9.5%

Re/Max Holdings Inc

EXECUTIVES
Lead Independent Director, Roger Dow
Vice Chairman Of The Board, Co-founder, Gail Liniger
Chief Financial Officer, Karri Callahan, $358,333 total compensation
Chief Executive Officer, Director, Adam Contos, $700,000 total compensation
Independent Director, Joseph DeSplinter
President Of Motto Franchising, Ward Morrison, $270,833 total compensation
Chief Of Staff And Chief Operating Officer, Serene Smith, $338,333 total compensation
Independent Director, Christine Riordan
Independent Director, Teresa Van De Bogart
Independent Director, Kathleen Cunningham
Independent Director, Ronald Harrison
President Of The Company And Re/max, Llc, Nicholas Bailey, $358,333 total compensation
Independent Director, Stephen Joyce
Independent Director, Laura Kelly
Chairman, David Liniger, $1,583,076 total compensation
Auditors: KPMG LLP

LOCATIONS
HQ: Re/Max Holdings Inc
  5075 South Syracuse Street, Denver, CO 80237
Phone: 303 770-5531   **Fax:** 303 796-3599
Web: www.remax.com

HISTORICAL FINANCIALS
Company Type: Public

Income Statement
FYE: December 31

	REVENUE ($ mil.)	NET INCOME ($ mil.)	NET PROFIT MARGIN	EMPLOYEES
12/20	266.0	10.9	4.1%	545
12/19	282.2	25.0	8.9%	500
12/18	212.6	27.0	12.7%	500
12/17	195.9	12.8	6.5%	350
12/16	176.3	22.7	12.9%	344
Annual Growth	10.8%	(16.7%)	—	12.2%

2020 Year-End Financials
Debt ratio: 40.1%
Return on equity: 2.1%
Cash ($ mil.): 101.3
Current ratio: 1.42
Long-term debt ($ mil.): 221.1

No. of shares (mil.): 18.3
Dividends
  Yield: 2.4%
  Payout: 146.6%
Market value ($ mil.): 668.0

	STOCK PRICE ($) FY Close	P/E High/Low		PER SHARE ($) Earnings	Dividends	Book Value
12/20	36.33	68	24	0.60	0.88	28.12
12/19	38.49	31	18	1.40	0.84	27.91
12/18	30.75	40	19	1.52	0.80	(0.00)
12/17	48.50	93	64	0.72	0.72	(0.00)
12/16	56.00	44	24	1.29	0.60	(0.00)
Annual Growth	(10.3%)			— —(17.4%)10.0%		—

Ready Capital Corp

Ready Capital is a multi-strategy real estate finance company that originates acquires finances and services SBC loans SBA loans residential mortgage loans and to a lesser extent MBS collateralized primarily by SBC loans or other real estate-related investments. Its loans range in original principal amounts generally up to approximately $35 million and are used by businesses to purchase real estate used in their operations or by investors seeking to acquire small multi-family office retail mixed use or warehouse properties. In addition to its loan portfolio which concentrates across California Texas New York Florida and Illinois the company also invests in countries outside the US.

Operations

Ready Capital's origination and acquisition platforms consist of four operating segments: SBC Originations Acquisitions SBA Originations Acquisitions and Servicing and Residential Mortgage Banking.

Under the Residential Mortgage Banking segment (generates more than 40% of total revenue) the company operates its residential mortgage loan origination segment through its wholly-owned subsidiary GMFS. GMFS originates residential mortgage loans eligible to be purchased guaranteed or insured by the Federal National Mortgage Association (Fannie Mae) Freddie Mac Federal Housing Administration (FHA) U.S. Department of Agriculture (USDA) and U.S. Department of Veterans Affairs (VA) through retail correspondent and broker channels. These originated loans are then sold to third parties primarily agency lending programs.

SBC Originations segment generates about 30% of the company's total revenue originates SBC loans secured by stabilized or transitional investor properties using multiple loan origination channels through its wholly-owned subsidiary ReadyCap Commercial (ReadyCap Commercial). These originated loans are generally held-for-investment or placed into securitization structures. Additionally as part of this segment the company originates and services multi-family loan products under the Federal Home Loan Mortgage Corporation's Small Balance Loan Program (Freddie Mac and the Freddie Mac program). These originated loans are held for sale then sold to Freddie Mac.

SBA Originations Acquisitions and Servicing segment represents approximately 15% of the company's total revenue. It acquires originates and services owner-occupied loans guaranteed by the SBA under its Section 7(a) loan program (the SBA Section 7(a) Program) through its wholly-owned subsidiary ReadyCap Lending. It holds an SBA license as one of only 14 non-bank Small Business Lending Companies (SBLCs) and has been granted preferred lender status by the SBA. These originated loans are either held-for-investment placed into securitization structures or sold.

Accounts for nearly 15% of the company's total revenue Acquisitions segment holds performing SBC loans to term and it seeks to maximize the value of the non-performing SBC loans acquired by the company through borrower-based resolution strategies. It typically acquires non-performing loans at a discount to their unpaid principal balance (UPB). Ready Capital also acquires purchased future receivables through Knight Capital LLC (Knight Capital) platfor

Geographic Reach

New York-based Ready Capital has office locations in New Jersey Texas Florida and Louisiana among other.

Sales and Marketing

The company has extensive relationships with commercial real estate brokers bank loan officers and mortgage brokers.

Financial Performance

The company's revenue in 2020 increased by 65% to $417.9 million compared with $252.7 million in the prior year.

Consolidated net income of $46.1 million for 2020 represented a decrease of $29.0 million from the prior year primarily due to an increase of reserves on loans due to the uncertainty of loan performance and recovery related to COVID-19 as well as an increase in unrealized losses on residential mortgage servicing rights partially offset by net income on PPP activities.

Cash held by the company at the end of fiscal 2020 increased to $200.5 million. Cash provided by operations and financing activities were $68.9 million and $63.1 million respectively. Investing activities used $59.4 million mainly for origination of loans.

Strategy

The company's investment strategy is to opportunistically expand its market presence in its acquisition and origination segments and to further grow its SBC securitization capabilities which serve as a source of attractively priced match-term financing. Capitalizing on its experience in under-

writing and managing commercial real estate loans Ready Capital has grown its SBC and SBA origination and acquisition capabilities and selectively complimented its SBC strategy with residential agency mortgage originations.

The company acquisition strategy complements its origination strategy by increasing its market intelligence in potential origination geographies providing additional data to support its underwriting criteria and offering securitization market insight for various product offerings.

Mergers and Acquisitions

In late 2021 Ready Capital entered into a definitive merger agreement pursuant to which Ready Capital has agreed to acquire a series of privately held real estate structured finance opportunities funds with a focus on construction lending managed by MREC Management (the Mosaic Manager). The acquisition is expected to further expand Ready Capital's investment portfolio to include a diverse portfolio of construction assets with attractive portfolio yields resulting in expected earnings accretion and a reduced leverage profile. Under the terms of the merger agreement Ready Capital will acquire all of the outstanding equity interests in Mosaic Real Estate Credit (MREC Onshore) Mosaic Real Estate Credit TE (MREC TE) and MREC International Incentive Split (MREC IIS and together with MREC Onshore and MREC TE the Mosaic Merger Entities). Expected value of deal at closing is approximately $471 million and could surpass $550 million with earn-out provisions.

EXECUTIVES

Chief Investment Officer, Thomas Buttacavoli
Chairman Of The Board And Chief Executive Officer, Thomas Capasse
President, Director, Jack Ross
Independent Director, Frank Filipps
Independent Director, J. Mitchell Reese
Chief Credit Officer, Adam Zausmer
Independent Director, Dominique Mielle
Chief Financial Officer, Andrew Ahlborn, $345,833 total compensation
Chief Operating Officer, Gary Taylor, $354,167 total compensation
Auditors: Deloitte & Touche LLP

LOCATIONS

HQ: Ready Capital Corp
1251 Avenue of the Americas, 50th Floor, New York, NY 10020
Phone: 212 257-4600
Web: www.readycapital.com

COMPETITORS

ARLINGTON ASSET INVESTMENT CORP.
ECC CAPITAL CORPORATION
FIRST EAGLE PRIVATE CREDIT LLC

IMPAC MORTGAGE HOLDINGS INC.
OCWEN FINANCIAL CORPORATION
PENNYMAC MORTGAGE INVESTMENT TRUST

HISTORICAL FINANCIALS

Company Type: Public

Income Statement				FYE: December 31
	REVENUE ($ mil.)	NET INCOME ($ mil.)	NET PROFIT MARGIN	EMPLOYEES
12/20	478.8	44.8	9.4%	0
12/19	352.7	72.9	20.7%	0
12/18	295.1	59.2	20.1%	4
12/17	211.4	43.2	20.5%	0
12/16	171.4	49.1	28.7%	0
Annual Growth	29.3%	(2.3%)	—	—

2020 Year-End Financials

Debt ratio: 76.7%
Return on equity: 5.4%
Cash ($ mil.): 138.9
Current ratio: 2.24
Long-term debt ($ mil.): 4,120.7

No. of shares (mil.): 54.3
Dividends
  Yield: 10.4%
  Payout: 160.4%
Market value ($ mil.): 677.0

	STOCK PRICE ($) FY Close	P/E High/Low		PER SHARE ($)		
				Earnings	Dividends	Book Value
12/20	12.45	21	5	0.81	1.30	15.00
12/19	15.42	10	8	1.72	1.60	16.14
12/18	13.83	9	7	1.84	1.57	16.97
12/17	15.15	12	9	1.38	1.48	16.75
12/16	13.45	8	7	1.85	1.55	16.80
Annual Growth	(1.9%)	—	—	(18.7%)	(4.3%)	(2.8%)

Realty Income Corp

Realty Income Corporation is an S&P 500 company and member of the S&P 500 Dividend Aristocrats index. The self-administered real estate investment trust (REIT) acquires owns and manages primarily free-standing highly-occupied single-tenant properties which it leases to regional and national consumer retail and service chains. Realty Income owns more than 6590 (mostly retail) properties spanning approximately 110.8 million sq. ft. of leasable space across every US state except Hawaii though about 40% of the REIT's rental revenue comes from its properties in Texas Florida Ohio Georgia Illinois and Tennessee. Realty Income's top five tenants include Walgreens FedEx 7 Eleven Dollar General FedEx and Dollar Tree / Family Dollar.

Operations

Realty Income owns more than 6590 properties during 2020 more than 95% of which were retail and the rest being industrial office and agriculture.

About 95% of its revenues came from rentals and about 5% came from reimbursements.

Geographic Reach

California-based Realty Income's largest markets include Texas Florida Ohio Georgia Illinois and Tennessee. Nearly 15% of its rental revenue came from properties in Texas in 2020 while properties in Florida contributed another more than 5%.

Sales and Marketing

Realty Income's occupancy rate has been more than 95% every year since its 1969 founding; with an average remaining lease term of approximately 9.0 years.

Its tenants have included owners of restaurants convenience stores theaters child care providers

346   HOOVER'S HANDBOOK OF EMERGING COMPANIES 2022

automotive care centers health and fitness facilities grocery stores and drug stores. Realty Income's top five tenants ? Walgreens 7 Eleven Dollar General FedEx and Dollar Tree / Family Dollar ? combined generated more than 20% of its total revenue in 2020. More than 10% of its client types were owners of convenience stores.

Financial Performance

The company's total revenue for 2020 was $1.7 billion an 11% increase from the previous year's revenue of $1.5 billion. This was mainly due to a higher sales volume in the company's rental business.

In 2020 the company had a net income of $396.5 million a 9% decrease from the previous year's net income of $437.5 million.

The company's cash at the end of 2020 was $850.7 million. Operating activities generated $1.1 billion while investing activities used $2 billion mainly for investment in real estate. Financing activities provided another $1.7 billion.

Strategy

Its investment strategy focuses on acquiring high-quality real estate that tenants consider important to the successful operation of their business. The company generally seek to acquire real estate that has the following characteristics: Properties that are freestanding commercially-zoned with a single tenant; Properties that are in significant markets or strategic locations critical to generating revenue for its tenants; Properties that it deemed to be profitable for the tenants; and Properties with real estate valuations that approximate replacement costs among others.

The company also seeks to invest in properties owned or leased by clients that are already or could become leaders in their respective businesses supported by mechanisms including (but not limited to) occupancy of prime real estate locations pricing merchandise assortment service quality economies of scale consumer branding e-commerce and advertising. In addition it frequently acquires large portfolios of single-client properties net leased to different clients operating in a variety of industries.

Mergers and Acquisitions

In late 2021 Realty Income The Monthly Dividend Company and VEREIT announced the completion of their previously announced merger. The common stock of the combined company will trade under the symbol "O" on the NYSE. The closing follows the satisfaction of all conditions to the closing of the merger including receipt of approval of the transaction by Realty Income and VEREIT stockholders which stockholder approvals were obtained in mid-2021. Realty Income acquired VEREIT in an all-stock transaction creating a combined company with an enterprise value of approximately $50 billion. Under the terms of the agreement VEREIT shareholders will receive 0.705 shares of Realty Income stock for every share of VEREIT stock they own. "We are pleased to announce the completion of our merger with VEREIT strengthening our position as the leading net lease REIT and global consolidator of the net lease space" said Sumit Roy Realty Income's President and Chief Executive Officer.

EXECUTIVES

Non-executive Independent Chairman Of The Board, Lead Independent Director, Michael Mckee
Executive Vice President - Asset Management And Real Estate Operations, Benjamin Fox

President, Chief Executive Officer, Director, Sumit Roy, $900,000 total compensation
Independent Director, Gerardo Lopez
Chief Financial Officer, Executive Vice President, Treasurer, Christie Kelly
Executive Vice President, Chief Strategy Officer, Neil Abraham, $475,000 total compensation
Executive Vice President, Chief Investment Officer, Mark Hagan, $430,000 total compensation
Evp, Chief Legal Officer, General Counsel And Secretary, Michelle Bushore
Auditors: KPMG LLP

LOCATIONS

HQ: Realty Income Corp
  11995 El Camino Real, San Diego, CA 92130
Phone: 858 284-5000
Web: www.realtyincome.com

PRODUCTS/OPERATIONS

2014 Properties

	No.	% of rental
Retail	4.1	79
Industrial and distribution	82.0	10
Office	44.0	7
Manufacturing	14.0	2
Agriculture	15.0	2
Total	**4,327.0**	**100**

2014 Sales

	% of total
Rental	96
Tenant reimbursement	4
Others	-
Total	**100**

COMPETITORS

ACADIA REALTY TRUST
COUSINS PROPERTIES INCORPORATED
CTO REALTY GROWTH INC.
FEDERAL REALTY INVESTMENT TRUST
GETTY REALTY CORP.
GLADSTONE COMMERCIAL CORPORATION
H&R Real Estate Investment Trust
LXP INDUSTRIAL TRUST
NATIONAL RETAIL PROPERTIES INC.
RPT REALTY
WASHINGTON PRIME GROUP L.P.
WASHINGTON REAL ESTATE INVESTMENT
WEINGARTEN REALTY INVESTORS

HISTORICAL FINANCIALS

Company Type: Public

Income Statement

FYE: December 31

	REVENUE ($ mil.)	NET INCOME ($ mil.)	NET PROFIT MARGIN	EMPLOYEES
12/21	2,080.4	359.4	17.3%	371
12/20	1,651.6	395.4	23.9%	210
12/19	1,491.5	436.4	29.3%	194
12/18	1,327.8	363.6	27.4%	165
12/17	1,215.7	318.8	26.2%	152
Annual Growth	**14.4%**	**3.0%**	**—**	**25.0%**

2021 Year-End Financials

Debt ratio: 35.8%
Return on equity: 1.9%
Cash ($ mil.): 258.5
Current ratio: 0.66
Long-term debt ($ mil.): 15,442.6
No. of shares (mil.): 591.2
Dividends
  Yield: 3.9%
  Payout: 233.2%
Market value ($ mil.): 42,328.0

	STOCK PRICE ($) FY Close	P/E High/Low		PER SHARE ($) Earnings	Dividends	Book Value
12/21	71.59	85	66	0.87	2.85	42.37
12/20	62.17	72	37	1.14	2.80	30.41
12/19	73.63	59	45	1.38	2.72	29.30
12/18	63.04	53	38	1.26	2.64	26.63
12/17	57.02	57	48	1.10	2.54	25.94
Annual Growth	**5.9%**	**—**	**—**	**(5.7%)**	**2.9%**	**13.1%**

Red River Bancshares Inc

Auditors: Postlethwaite & Netterville

LOCATIONS

HQ: Red River Bancshares Inc
  1412 Centre Court Drive, Suite 501, Alexandria, LA 71301
Phone: 318 561-5028
Web: www.redriverbank.net

HISTORICAL FINANCIALS

Company Type: Public

Income Statement

FYE: December 31

	ASSETS ($ mil.)	NET INCOME ($ mil.)	INCOME AS % OF ASSETS	EMPLOYEES
12/20	2,642.6	28.1	1.1%	336
12/19	1,988.2	24.8	1.2%	325
12/18	1,860.5	23.0	1.2%	321
12/17	1,724.2	13.9	0.8%	309
Annual Growth	**15.3%**	**26.3%**	**—**	**2.8%**

2020 Year-End Financials

Return on assets: 1.2%
Return on equity: 10.4%
Long-term debt ($ mil.): —
No. of shares (mil.): 7.3
Sales ($ mil): 100.5
Dividends
  Yield: 0.4%
  Payout: 6.3%
Market value ($ mil.): 363.0

	STOCK PRICE ($) FY Close	P/E High/Low		PER SHARE ($) Earnings	Dividends	Book Value
12/20	49.55	15	8	3.83	0.24	38.97
12/19	56.06	16	12	3.49	0.00	34.48
12/18	0.00	—	—	3.41	0.00	29.23
Annual Growth	**—**	**—**	**—**	**6.0%**	**—**	**15.5%**

Regional Management Corp

Regional Management Corp. is a diversified consumer finance company that provides attractive easy-to-understand installment loan products primarily to customers with limited access to consumer credit from banks thrifts credit card companies and other lenders. Regional Management operates under the name "Regional Finance" in about 365 branch locations across a dozen states in the Southeastern Southwestern Mid-Atlantic and Midwestern US. Regional Management sources loans through its multiple channel platform which includes branches centrally-managed direct mail campaigns digital partners retailers and its consumer website. The company offers loan products that are structured on a fixed rate fixed term basis with fully amortizing equal monthly installment payments repayable at any time without penalty.

EXECUTIVES

Vice President - Financial Planning And Analysis, Michael Dymski, $256,672 total compensation
Independent Director, Roel Campos
Independent Director, Jonathan Brown
Executive Vice President, Chief Credit Risk Officer, Manish Parmar, $330,423 total compensation
Independent Director, Sandra Johnson
Principal Accounting Officer, Vice President, Corporate Controller, Steven Barnette
Chief Data And Analytics Officer, Chris Peterson
Independent Director, Philip Bancroft
Executive Vice President, Chief Strategy And Development Officer, Brian Fisher, $370,164 total compensation
Director, Michael Dunn
Chief Operating Officer, Executive Vice President, John Schachtel, $415,000 total compensation
President, Chief Executive Officer, Director, Robert Beck, $557,036 total compensation
Chief Financial Officer, Executive Vice President, Harpreet Rana, $42,623 total compensation
Senior Vice President, General Counsel, Secretary, Catherine Atwood
Auditors: RSM US LLP

LOCATIONS

HQ: Regional Management Corp
979 Batesville Road, Suite B, Greer, SC 29651
Phone: 864 448-7000
Web: www.regionalmanagement.com

PRODUCTS/OPERATIONS

2015 Sales

	% of total
Interest and fee income	90
Insurance income net	5
Other	5
Total	**100**

COMPETITORS

CASS INFORMATION SYSTEMS INC.
EQUIFAX INC.
Hanley Economic Building Society
MARLIN BUSINESS SERVICES CORP.

PSCU INCORPORATED
UPS CAPITAL CORPORATION
WALKER & DUNLOP INC.
WORLDPAY INC.

HISTORICAL FINANCIALS

Company Type: Public

Income Statement

FYE: December 31

	ASSETS ($ mil.)	NET INCOME ($ mil.)	INCOME AS % OF ASSETS	EMPLOYEES
12/20	1,103.8	26.7	2.4%	1,542
12/19	1,158.5	44.7	3.9%	1,638
12/18	956.4	35.3	3.7%	1,535
12/17	829.4	29.9	3.6%	1,448
12/16	712.2	24.0	3.4%	1,363
Annual Growth	11.6%	2.7%	—	3.1%

2020 Year-End Financials

Return on assets: 2.3%
Return on equity: 9.2%
Long-term debt ($ mil.): —
No. of shares (mil.): 10.9
Sales ($ mil): 373.9

Dividends
Yield: 0.6%
Payout: 8.3%
Market value ($ mil.): 326.0

	STOCK PRICE ($) FY Close	P/E High/Low		PER SHARE ($) Earnings	Dividends	Book Value
12/20	29.86	12	4	2.40	0.20	24.89
12/19	30.03	9	6	3.80	0.00	27.49
12/18	24.05	12	8	2.93	0.00	23.70
12/17	26.31	10	7	2.54	0.00	20.53
12/16	26.28	13	6	1.99	0.00	18.12
Annual Growth	3.2%	—		4.8%	—	8.3%

Renasant Corp

Those who are cognizant of their finances may want to do business with Renasant Corporation. The holding company owns Renasant Bank which serves consumers and local business through about 80 locations in Alabama Georgia Mississippi and Tennessee. The bank offers standard products such as checking and savings accounts CDs credit cards and loans and mortgages as well as trust retail brokerage and retirement plan services. Its loan portfolio is dominated by residential and commercial real estate loans. The bank also offers agricultural business construction and consumer loans and lease financing. Subsidiary Renasant Insurance sells personal and business coverage.Shareholders approved a merger with Metropolitan Bank in mid-2017.

Financial Performance
The company's revenue increased in fiscal 2013 compared to the prior year. It reported revenue of $252.6 million for fiscal 2013 up from $228 million in revenue for fiscal 2012.

Renasant's net income also went up in fiscal 2013 compared to the previous fiscal period. It reported net income of about $33.5 million for fiscal 2013 up from net income of $26.6 million in fiscal 2012.

The company's cash on hand decreased by about $24 million in fiscal 2013 compared to fiscal 2012 levels.

Strategy
Renasant has looked to diversify its loan portfolio. The bank has reduced its amount of loans for construction and land development — a sector that has been hit particularly hard — by tightening its underwriting standards.

It's also been growing through acquistions. In late 2014 for example Renasant purchased Heritage Financial Group in an all stock merger deal that amounted to $258 million. The move added $1.9 billion in assets $1.2 billion in loan assets and $1.3 billion in deposit assets to Renasant's collection. In addition the move significantly expanded the bank's geographic reach adding 48 banking mortgage and investment offices in Alabama Florida and Georgia. All told the deal made Renasant one of the largest community banks in the Southeast region of the United States.

Mergers and Acquisitions
In 2017 Renasant agreed to a $190 million merger with Metropolitan Bank.

EXECUTIVES

Executive Vice President, Tracey Adams
Independent Director, Connie Engel
Executive Vice President, General Counsel, Mark Jeanfreau
Independent Director, Sean Suggs
Independent Director, Donald Clark
Executive Vice President, Curtis Perry, $435,625 total compensation
Executive Vice President, David Meredith
Chief Accounting Officer, Kelly Hutcheson
Independent Director, Gary Butler
Independent Director, Michael Shmerling
Independent Director, Albert Dale
Independent Director, Jill Deer
Chief Financial Officer, Executive Vice President, James Mabry, $212,019 total compensation
Executive Vice President, William Williams
Chief Operating Officer, Executive Vice President, Kevin Chapman, $563,750 total compensation
Executive Vice President, Mary Witt
President, Chief Executive Officer, Director, C. Mitchell Waycaster, $717,500 total compensation
Independent Director, Neal Holland
Executive Vice President, Chief Community And Business Banking Officer, President - Western Region Of The Bank, James Cochran, $461,250 total compensation
Lead Independent Director, John Creekmore
Executive Chairman Of The Board, Edward McGraw, $563,750 total compensation
Auditors: HORNE LLP

LOCATIONS

HQ: Renasant Corp
209 Troy Street, Tupelo, MS 38804-4827
Phone: 662 680-1001
Web: www.renasant.com

PRODUCTS/OPERATIONS

2015 Sales

	$ mil.	% of total
Interest income		
Loans	236.3	64
Securities	26.5	7
Other	0.2	-
Non-interest income		
Mortgage banking income	35.8	10
Service charges on deposit accounts	29.3	8
Fees and commissions	16.1	4
Wealth management	9.8	3
Other	17.3	4
Total	**371.3**	**100**

COMPETITORS

AMERIS BANCORP
CARDINAL FINANCIAL

SHINSEI BANK LIMITED
SUFFOLK BANCORP.

CORPORATION
COMMUNITY BANK OF THE
BANCORPORATION
BAY
FIRST INTERSTATE
BANCSYSTEM INC.
PT. BANK MANDIRI
(PERSERO) TBK

WESBANCO INC.
WEST
INC.
YAPI VE KREDI BANKASI
ANONIM SIRKETI

HISTORICAL FINANCIALS

Company Type: Public

Income Statement

FYE: December 31

	ASSETS ($ mil.)	NET INCOME ($ mil.)	INCOME AS % OF ASSETS	EMPLOYEES
12/20	14,929.6	83.6	0.6%	2,524
12/19	13,400.6	167.6	1.3%	2,527
12/18	12,934.8	146.9	1.1%	2,359
12/17	9,829.9	92.1	0.9%	2,102
12/16	8,699.8	90.9	1.0%	1,965
Annual Growth	14.5%	(2.1%)	—	6.5%

2020 Year-End Financials

Return on assets: 0.5%
Return on equity: 3.9%
Long-term debt ($ mil.): —
No. of shares (mil.): 56.2
Sales ($ mil): 733.6

Dividends
Yield: 2.6%
Payout: 59.4%
Market value ($ mil.): 1,893.0

	STOCK PRICE ($) FY Close	P/E High/Low		PER SHARE ($) Earnings	Dividends	Book Value
12/20	33.68	24	13	1.48	0.88	37.95
12/19	35.42	13	11	2.88	0.87	37.39
12/18	30.18	18	10	2.79	0.80	34.91
12/17	40.89	23	19	1.96	0.73	30.72
12/16	42.22	20	14	2.17	0.71	27.81
Annual Growth	(5.5%)	—	—	(9.1%)	5.5%	8.1%

Repligen Corp.

Repligen supplies bio-engineered drug ingredients to the pharmaceutical industry. The company's bioprocessing business develops and commercializes proteins and other agents used in the production of biopharmaceuticals. Repligen is a major supplier of Protein A a recombinant protein used in the production of monoclonal antibodies and other biopharmaceutical manufacturing applications. Its product portfolio also includes filtration products and chromatography devices. Repligen's two largest customer is Cytiva (formerly GE Healthcare) and MilliporeSigma with which it has a multi-year supply agreement. North America accounts for about half of the company's total revenue.

Operations

Revenue from its filtration products (about 50%) includes the sale of its XCell ATF systems and consumables KrosFlo filtration products and SIUS filtration products. Revenue from chromatography products (around 20%) includes the sale of its OPUS chromatography columns chromatography resins and ELISA test kits. Revenue from protein products (more than 20%) includes the sale of its Protein A ligands and cell culture growth factors. Revenue from its Process Analytics products (less

than 5%) includes the sale of its SoloVPE and FlowVPE systems and consumables. Other revenue primarily consists of revenue from the sale of its operating room products to hospitals as well as freight revenue.

Geographic Reach

Headquartered in Massachusetts Repligen has manufacturing facilities in the US (Massachusetts California New York and New Jersey) Australia Canada China France Germany India Japan Korea Sweden UK.

The company's two largest single markets are the North America which accounts for about 50% of revenue and Europe which brings in another roughly 40%.

Sales and Marketing

Customers for its bioprocessing products include major life sciences companies contract manufacturing organizations biopharmaceutical companies diagnostics companies and laboratory researchers. The company's largest customers MilliporeSigma and Cytiva (formerly GE Healthcare) account for more than 10% each of revenue.

Advertising expense for the years ended 2020 2019 and 2018 was approximately $ 0.3 million $0.1 million and $0.2 million respectively

Financial Performance

In 2020 Repligen's revenue increased by 36% to $366.3 million compared to $270.2 million in the prior year. For 2020 product revenue increased by $96.0 million or 35.6% as compared to 2019. The increase is due to the continued adoption of its products by key bioprocessing customers across all its key product lines.

Net income for fiscal 2020 increased to $59.9 million compared from 2019 with a net income of $21.4 million.

Cash held by the company at the end of fiscal 2020 increased to $717.3 million. Cash provided by operations and financing activities were $62.6 million and $305.9 million respectively. Cash used for investing activities was $201.4 million mainly for acquisitions.

Strategy

Repligen is focused on the development production and commercialization of differentiated technology-leading solutions or products that address specific pressure points in the biologics manufacturing process and delivers substantial value to its customers. The company's products are designed to increase customers' product yield and Repligen is committed to supporting its customers with strong customer service and applications expertise.

The company intends to build on its recent history of developing market-leading solutions and delivering strong financial performance through the following strategies:

Continued innovation. The company plans to capitalize on its internal technological expertise to develop products that address unmet needs in upstream and downstream bioprocessing. Repligen intends to invest further in its Proteins franchise while developing platform and derivative products to support its Filtration Chromatography and Process Analytics franchises.

Platforming its products. A key strategy for accelerating market adoption of its products is delivery of enabling technologies that become the standard or "platform" technology in markets where it compete. Repligen focuses its efforts on winning early-stage technology evaluations through direct

interaction with the key biomanufacturing decision makers in process development labs.

Targeted acquisitions. The company intends to continue to selectively pursue acquisitions of innovative technologies and products. Repligen intends to leverage its balance sheet to acquire technologies and products that improve its overall financial performance by improving its competitiveness in filtration chromatography or process analytics or by moving the company into adjacent markets with common commercial call points.

Geographical expansion. The company intends to expand its global commercial presence by continuing to selectively build out its global sales marketing field applications and services infrastructure.

Operational efficiency. Repligen seeks to expand operating margins through capacity utilization and process optimization strategies designed to increase its manufacturing yields. The company plans to invest in systems to support its global operations optimizing resources across its global footprint to maximize productivity.

Mergers and Acquisitions

In mid-2021 Repligen agreed to acquire privately-held ARTeSYN Biosolutions (ARTeSYN) an Irish company for approximately $200 million comprised of approximately $130 million in cash and approximately $70 million in Repligen common stock. The addition of ARTeSYN Biosolutions and Non-Metallic Solutions further strengthens Repligen's Systems offering. The ARTeSYN portfolio expands on the market success of its hollow fiber systems and complements its market leading chromatography and TFF filtration product lines.

In 2020 Repligen announced that it has entered into an agreement to acquire Albany New York based Engineered Molding Technology ("EMT") an innovator and manufacturer of single-use silicone assemblies and components used in the manufacturing of biologic drugs. EMT's standard and custom molded and over-molded connectors and silicone tubing products are key components in single-use filtration and chromatography systems. The acquisition of EMT expands the company's line of single-use ProConnex flow paths streamlines its supply chain for ATF and gives the company more flexibility as it scale and expand its single-use and systems portfolios. Terms were not disclosed.

Company Background

Repligen was founded in 1981 by two distinguished scientists who pioneered breakthrough advances in science and technology.

EXECUTIVES

Chairman, Karen Dawes
Independent Director, Nicolas Barthelemy
Senior Vice President Of Filtration And Chromatography, Christine Gebski
Independent Director, Rohin Mhatre
Chief Operating Officer, James Bylund
Independent Director, Carrie Manner
President, Chief Executive Officer And Director, Anthony Hunt, $725,000 total compensation
Chief Financial Officer, Jon Snodgres, $393,594 total compensation
Independent Director, Glenn Muir
Senior Vice President - Research And Development, Ralf Kuriyel, $346,080 total compensation
Auditors: Ernst & Young LLP

LOCATIONS

HQ: Repligen Corp.
41 Seyon Street, Bldg. 1, Suite 100, Waltham, MA
02453
Phone: 781 250-0111 **Fax:** 781 250-0115
Web: www.repligen.com

PRODUCTS/OPERATIONS

2017 Sales

	$ mil.	% of total
Product revenue		
Protein products	54.0	38
Filtration products	49.0	35
Chromatography products	36.3	26
Other	1.8	1
Royalties & other	0.1	-
Total	**141.2**	**100**

COMPETITORS

ACCELERON PHARMA INC.
  PHARMACEUTICALS
ACORDA THERAPEUTICS
  INC.
APTARGROUP INC.
CERUS CORPORATION
DYNAVAX TECHNOLOGIES
  BIOSCIENCES OF
  CORPORATION
ELEMENT SOLUTIONS INC
EVOQUA WATER
  TECHNOLOGIES CORP.
HELIOS TECHNOLOGIES
  INC.

INOVIO

INC.
LUMINEX CORPORATION
NANOSTRING
  TECHNOLOGIES INC.
PACIFIC

CALIFORNIA INC.
  SEAGEN INC.
STRATASYS LTD

HISTORICAL FINANCIALS

Company Type: Public

Income Statement   FYE: December 31

	REVENUE ($ mil.)	NET INCOME ($ mil.)	NET PROFIT MARGIN	EMPLOYEES
12/21	670.5	128.2	19.1%	309
12/20	366.2	59.9	16.4%	1,100
12/19	270.2	21.4	7.9%	761
12/18	194.0	16.6	8.6%	548
12/17	141.2	28.3	20.1%	476
Annual Growth	47.6%	45.8%	—	(10.2%)

2021 Year-End Financials

Debt ratio: 10.8%	No. of shares (mil.): 55.3
Return on equity: 7.8%	Dividends
Cash ($ mil.): 603.8	Yield: —
Current ratio: 2.48	Payout: —
Long-term debt ($ mil.): —	Market value ($ mil.): 14,651.0

	STOCK PRICE ($) FY Close	P/E High/Low	PER SHARE ($) Earnings	Dividends	Book Value
12/21	264.84	139 71	2.24	0.00	31.63
12/20	191.63	181 75	1.11	0.00	27.92
12/19	92.50	217 112	0.44	0.00	20.35
12/18	52.74	181 81	0.37	0.00	14.02
12/17	36.28	62 39	0.72	0.00	13.57
Annual Growth	64.4%	— —	32.8%	—	23.6%

Republic Bancorp, Inc. (KY)

As one of the top five bank holding companies based in Kentucky $4 billion-asset Republic Bancorp is the parent of Republic Bank & Trust (formerly First Commercial Bank) which offers deposit accounts loans and mortgages credit cards private banking and trust services through more than 30 branches in across Kentucky and around 10 more in southern Indiana Nashville Tampa and Cincinnati Ohio. About one-third of the bank's $3 billion-loan portfolio is tied to residential real estate while another 25% is made up of commercial real estate loans. Warehouse lines of credit home equity loans and commercial and industrial loans make up most of the rest. The company also offers short-term consumer loans and tax refund loans.

Operations

Republic Bancorp operates three "core banking" segments: Traditional Banking which generated more than 80% of the company's total profit during 2015; Warehouse (almost 20% of profit) and Mortgage Banking (less than 1%). Its Warehouse lending business offers short-term credit facilities secured by single-family residences to mortgage bankers nationwide. Its Republic Processing Group segment offers short-term consumer loans prepaid debit cards and tax refund loans.

The bank made 75% of its total revenue from interest income almost entirely from loans during 2015 though a small percentage came from taxed investments and Federal Home Loan Bank stock. The rest of its revenue came from net refund transfer fees from its Republic Processing Group segment (9% of revenue) deposit account service charges (7%) interchange fee income (4%) mortgage banking income (2%) and other miscellaneous income sources.

Subsidiary Republic Insurance Services (also known as the Captive) provides property and casualty insurance coverage to the company and eight other third-party insurance captives for which insurance may not be available or cost effective.

Geographic Reach

The company had 40 RB&T branches at the end of 2015 including 32 in Kentucky mostly in the Louisville Metro area and others in the Central Western and Northern parts of the state. It had 3 branches in southern Indiana (in Floyds Knobs Jeffersonville and New Albany); two branches in the Tampa Florida metro area; two branches in the Nashville Tennessee metro area; and one more in the Cincinnati Ohio metro area.

Sales and Marketing

Republic spent $3.16 million on marketing and development expenses during 2015 compared to $3.26 million and $3.11 million in 2014 and 2013 respectively.

Financial Performance

Republic Bancorp's revenues and profits have been trending higher since 2013 as its loan assets have risen more than 30% over the period.

The company's revenue climbed 9% to $190 million during 2015 mostly thanks to higher interest income as its loan assets grew by 9% to $3.33 billion with commercial loans (real estate and business loans) and residential mortgage loans and lines of credit driving most of the growth.

Strong revenue growth in 2015 drove Republic's net income up 22% to $35 million for the year. The company's operating cash levels nearly doubled to $50 million after adjusting its earnings for non-cash items related to mortgage loan sales and thanks to favorable working capital changes related to changes in other liabilities.

Strategy

Republic Bancorp is moving toward building its commercial loans business launching a Corporate Banking division in 2015 to originate commercial loans with amounts ranging from $2.5 million to $25 million to borrowers with the highest credit ratings in its existing geographic markets. It also acquires smaller community banks to expand into new geographic markets while building its loan and deposit business.

Additionally Republic Bancorp has been moving into other revolving credit lines while also looking to take advantage of the rapidly growing prepaid card market. During 2015 for example it partnered with netSpend to become a pilot issuer of netSpend-branded prepaid cards; and partnered with ClearBalance to originate revolving lines of credit nationally for hospital receivables.

Mergers and Acquisitions

In October 2015 Republic Bancorp expanded its presence in Florida and grew its loan business after agreeing to buy $250 million-asset Cornerstone Bancorp along its four Cornerstone Community Bank branches in the Tampa Florida metro area $190 million in loans and $200 million in deposits. The deal was expected to be completed in the first half of 2016.

Company Background

In 2012 Republic Bancorp entered the Nashville and Minneapolis market through the FDIC-assisted acquisitions of the failed Tennessee Commerce Bank and First Commercial Bank respectively.

EXECUTIVES

Executive Chairman Of The Board, Chief Executive Officer, Steven Trager, $425,000 total compensation
Chief Financial Officer, Executive Vice President, Chief Accounting Officer, Kevin Sipes, $354,055 total compensation
Independent Director, Michael Rust
President Of Republic Processing Group, William Nelson, $382,538 total compensation
Executive Vice President Of Republic Bank And Trust, Margaret Wendler
Executive Vice President Of Republic Bank And Trust, John Rippy, $275,922 total compensation
Independent Director, Craig Greenberg
Independent Director, Susan Tamme
Executive Vice President Of Republic Bank And Trust, Steven DeWeese, $239,978 total compensation
Director, Senior Vice President Of Republic Bank And Trust Company, Andrew Trager-Kusman
Executive Vice President Of Republic Bank And Trust, Anthony Powell
President, Vice Chairman Of The Board, A. Scott Trager, $372,000 total compensation
Executive Vice President Of Republic Bank And Trust, Juan Montano, $326,863 total compensation
Director, David Feaster
Independent Director, W. Patrick Mulloy
Independent Director, Ernest Marshall
Independent Director, Ronald Barnes
Independent Director, Laura Douglas
Independent Director, W. Kenneth Oyler

Independent Director, Heather Howell
Director, President And Chief Executive Officer Of Republic Bank & Trust And Company, Logan Pichel, $350,000 total compensation
Executive Vice President Of Republic Bank And Trust, Pedro Bryant
Auditors: Crowe LLP

LOCATIONS

HQ: Republic Bancorp, Inc. (KY)
   601 West Market Street, Louisville, KY 40202
Phone: 502 584-3600
Web: www.republicbank.com

PRODUCTS/OPERATIONS

2015 Sales

	$ mil.	% of total
Interest		
Loans including fees	134.0	70
Taxable investment securities	7.0	4
Other	1.4	1
Noninterest		
Net refund transfer fees	17.4	9
Service charges on deposit accounts	13.0	7
Interchange fee income	8.4	4
Mortgage banking	4.4	2
Other	5.1	3
Adjustments	(0.3)	-
Total	**190.4**	**100**

Selected Services

Checking
Credit & Debit Cards
Internet & Mobile Banking
Lending
Private Banking & Wealth Management
Savings & Investing

COMPETITORS

BEAR STATE FINANCIAL INC.
CENTURY BANCORP INC.
CITY HOLDING COMPANY INC.
FIRST FINANCIAL CORPORATION
GREAT SOUTHERN BANCORP INC.
OLD LINE BANCSHARES INC.
REPUBLIC FIRST BANCORP INC.
STATE BANK FINANCIAL CORPORATION
UNITED COMMUNITY BANKS INC.

HISTORICAL FINANCIALS

Company Type: Public

Income Statement   FYE: December 31

	ASSETS ($ mil.)	NET INCOME ($ mil.)	INCOME AS % OF ASSETS	EMPLOYEES
12/20	6,168.3	83.2	1.3%	1,104
12/19	5,620.3	91.7	1.6%	1,092
12/18	5,240.4	77.8	1.5%	1,064
12/17	5,085.3	45.6	0.9%	1,009
12/16	4,816.3	45.9	1.0%	954
Annual Growth	6.4%	16.0%	—	3.7%

2020 Year-End Financials

Return on assets: 1.4%
Return on equity: 10.4%
Long-term debt ($ mil.): —
No. of shares (mil.): 20.9
Sales ($ mil): 339.3

Dividends
Yield: 3.1%
Payout: 12.5%
Market value ($ mil.): 754.0

	STOCK PRICE ($) FY Close	P/E High/Low		PER SHARE ($) Earnings	Dividends	Book Value
12/20	36.07	6	4	7.62	1.14	39.40
12/19	46.80	6	5	8.38	1.06	36.49
12/18	38.72	7	5	7.14	0.97	33.03
12/17	38.02	19	15	2.20	0.87	30.33
12/16	39.54	18	11	2.22	0.83	28.97
Annual Growth	(2.3%)	—	—	36.1%	8.5%	8.0%

ResMed Inc.

ResMed develops makes and distributes medical equipment used to diagnose and treat respiratory disorders that occur during sleep such as sleep apnea. Most of its products treat obstructive sleep apnea (OSA) a condition in which a patient's air flow is periodically obstructed causing multiple disruptions during sleep that can lead to daytime sleepiness and other conditions such as high blood pressure. Its products include air-flow generators face masks diagnostic products and accessories. ResMed sells directly and through distributors worldwide to home health equipment dealers sleep clinics and hospitals. ResMed was founded in Australia in 1989 by Dr. Peter Farrell who remains chairman. US generates about 60% of total sales.

Operations

ResMed operates in two operating segments: Sleep and Respiratory Care and Software as a Service (SaaS).

Sleep and Respiratory Care generates about 90% of total sales supports clinical trials in many countries to develop new clinical applications for our technology. SaaS accounts roughly 10% of total sales relates primarily to the provision of software access with maintenance and support over an agreed term and material rights associated with future discounts upon renewal of some SaaS contracts.

The company also produces CPAP VPAP and AutoSet systems for the titration and treatment of SDB which deliver positive airway pressure through a patient interface either a small nasal mask nasal pillows system full-face mask or cannula. Its VPAP units deliver ultra-quiet comfortable bilevel therapy while AutoSet systems are based on a proprietary technology to monitor breathing and can also be used in the diagnosis treatment and management of OSA.

Additionally ResMed's products and solutions are designed to improve patient quality of life reduce the impact of chronic disease and lower healthcare costs as global healthcare systems continue to drive a shift in care from hospitals to the home and lower cost settings. Its cloud-based software digital health applications to diagnose treat and manage respiratory disorders including sleep disordered breathing (SDB) chronic obstructive pulmonary disease (COPD) neuromuscular disease and other chronic diseases. SDB includes obstructive sleep apnea or OSA and other respiratory disorders that occur during sleep.

Geographic Reach

Headquartered in San Diego California ResMed manufactures its products primarily at its Australian facility though it has additional production plants in China Singapore Malaysia France and the US. The company also has R&D and office facilities in Australia China Germany Singapore and the US. It leases warehousing and distribution facilities in the US (2) the UK Germany France Switzerland Sweden Norway Japan and China.

The company's systems are sold in about 120 countries. The US accounts for nearly 60% of annual revenues.

Sales and Marketing

ResMed's products are sold through its own subsidiaries (mainly in the US Europe and the Asia Pacific region) and through its direct sales forces and independent distributors. Marketing efforts target consumers and health care professionals sleep clinics hospitals home health care systems and third-party payors.

The company do not sell its SaaS products in combined Europe Asia and other markets.

Financial Performance

ResMed's revenue has been trending upward in recent years as demand for its products has grown. In fact the number of people with sleep apnea worldwide is nearing 1 billion. Net income has been declining slowly though as the company spends money to produce and launch new products.

Net revenue in fiscal year 2019 increased to $2606.6 million an increase of 11% compared to fiscal year 2018.

Net income for the year ended June 30 2019 was $404.6 million or $2.80 per diluted share compared to net income of $315.6 million or $2.19 per diluted share for the year ended June 30 2018.

The company ended 2019 with $147.1 million in cash and cash equivalents a decline from the $188.7 million it had at the end of 2018. Operating activities provided $459.1 million and investing activities used $1.1 billion. Financing activities generated $147.1 million.

Strategy

ResMed is benefiting from the growing awareness in the medical community and among the general population of the dangers of sleep disordered breathing (SDB). These include chronic daytime fatigue (and the resulting loss of productivity) heart disease stroke type 2 diabetes depression and other conditions. With the number of people with sleep apnea nearing 1 billion around the world ResMed has strong motivation to get the word out. It targets special interest groups such as the American Heart Association and it has partnered with other organizations to conduct medical research.

The company is investing in R&D activities to facilitate the development of new diagnostic and treatment products. During 2017 it launched the AirFit N20 nasal and F20 full face masks as well as the AirMini the smallest CPAP device on the market. The following year it introduced the Mobi portable oxygen concentrator the QuietAir diffuser vent elbow for its CPAP full face masks and the AirFit F30 its first minimal-contact CPAP full face mask. Recent acquisitions have helped expand the company's product portfolio.

ResMed is also investing in sales and marketing activities to promote itself around the world. The company has its sights set on the growing market potential for SDB COPD and respiratory care products in China.

The company continuously develop and innovate its SDB Respiratory Care Products and expand SaaS solutions in Out-of-Hospital Care set-

HOOVER'S HANDBOOK OF EMERGING COMPANIES 2022

tings by introducing a number of new software solutions including its ResMed Resupply GoScripts and new features and enhancements within its cloud-based software offerings. The company acquired Propeller Health and its digital health platform for inhalers rounding out our portfolio to treat COPD patients through all stages of their disease and by offer software solutions across multiple out-of-hospital healthcare settings from home medical equipment to home health and hospice skilled nursing and private duty.

In early 2019 the company launched its automated ResMed ReSupply solution for all US home medical equipment (HME) providers to increase sleep apnea patients' long-term therapy adherence and improve patient satisfaction.

Mergers and Acquisitions

In 2019 Resmed bought digital therapeutics firm Propeller Health for $225 million. Propeller specializes in helping patients manage chronic obstructive pulmonary disease and asthma. It continues to operate as a standalone business. Also that year the company acquired South Korea's HB Healthcare which specializes in sleep and respiratory care devices to help treat sleep apnea.

HISTORY

ResMed was founded as ResCare in 1989 after Peter Farrell led a management buyout of Baxter Healthcare's respiratory technology unit. ResCare initially developed the SULLIVAN nasal CPAP systems (named after inventor Colin Sullivan) in Australia. In 1991 it introduced the Bubble Mask and the APD2 portable CPAP device. Three years later ResCare began marketing its first VPAP which applied different air pressures for inhalation and exhalation in the US.

In 1995 the company went public changing its name to ResMed (its former name was already taken by another medical company). Over the next two years ResMed expended a lot of oxygen in court suing rival Respironics for patent infringements; judgments in 1997 and 1998 found in favor of Respironics but ResMed made plans to appeal. In 1998 the firm received FDA approval to market its VPAP device as a critical-care treatment for lung diseases.

The firm's listing was switched from Nasdaq to the NYSE in 1999 to stabilize stock prices after court losses against Respironics; it also listed on the Australian Stock Exchange.

EXECUTIVES

Chief Administrative Officer, Global General Counsel, Secretary, David Pendarvis, $533,710 total compensation
Chief Executive Officer, Director, Michael Farrell, $1,050,000 total compensation
President - Sleep And Respiratory Care Business, Jim Hollingshead, $707,000 total compensation
President - Saas Business, Bobby Ghoshal
President, Asia And Latin America, Justin Leong
Independent Director, Harjit Gill
Independent Director, Karen Drexler
Chief Technology Officer, Urvashi Tyagi
Independent Director, Richard Sulpizio
Non-executive Chairman Of The Board, Peter Farrell
Chief Financial Officer, Brett Sandercock, $494,225 total compensation
Auditors: KPMG LLP

LOCATIONS

HQ: ResMed Inc.
9001 Spectrum Center Blvd., San Diego, CA 92123
Phone: 858 836-5000
Web: www.resmed.com

PRODUCTS/OPERATIONS

Selected Products
Accessories
  Astral external battery
  Chin restraint
  ClimateLineAir heated tube
  Gecko nasal pad
  SlimLine tubing
  Standard Trolley
Devices
  AirMini
  AirStart 10 CPAP
  Astral 100
  Astral 150
  Lumis 100 VPAP S
  Stellar 100
  Stellar 150
Humidifiers
  H4i
Masks
  AirFit N20 Classic
  AirFit P10
  AirTouch F20
  Mirage FX
  Pixi
  Quattro Air
  Swift FX

COMPETITORS

ACCURAY INCORPORATED
ATRICURE INC.
BOSTON SCIENTIFIC CORPORATION
DELTEX MEDICAL GROUP PLC
LIVANOVA PLC
LIVANOVA USA INC.
MEDTRONIC PUBLIC LIMITED COMPANY
MGC DIAGNOSTICS CORPORATION
NATUS MEDICAL INCORPORATED
UTAH MEDICAL PRODUCTS INC.

HISTORICAL FINANCIALS

Company Type: Public

Income Statement — FYE: June 30

	REVENUE ($ mil.)	NET INCOME ($ mil.)	NET PROFIT MARGIN	EMPLOYEES
06/21	3,196.8	474.5	14.8%	7,970
06/20	2,957.0	621.6	21.0%	7,770
06/19	2,606.5	404.5	15.5%	740
06/18	2,340.2	315.5	13.5%	5,940
06/17	2,066.7	342.2	16.6%	6,030
Annual Growth	11.5%	8.5%	—	7.0%

2021 Year-End Financials

Debt ratio: 13.8%
Return on equity: 17.6%
Cash ($ mil.): 295.2
Current ratio: 1.73
Long-term debt ($ mil.): 643.3
No. of shares (mil.): 145.6
Dividends
  Yield: 0.6%
  Payout: 49.8%
Market value ($ mil.): 35,905.0

	STOCK PRICE ($) FY Close	P/E High/Low		PER SHARE ($) Earnings	Dividends	Book Value
06/21	246.52	76	51	3.24	1.56	19.81
06/20	192.00	44	27	4.27	1.56	17.23
06/19	122.03	44	32	2.80	1.48	14.42
06/18	103.58	49	33	2.19	1.40	14.43
06/17	77.87	33	24	2.40	1.32	13.79
Annual Growth	33.4%		—	7.8%	4.3%	9.5%

Retractable Technologies Inc

Retractable Technologies knows you can't be too safe when you work around needles all day. The company develops makes and markets safety syringes and other injection technologies for the health care industry. Its flagship VanishPoint syringe retracts after injection reducing the risk of both syringe reuse and accidental needlesticks (both are means of transmitting HIV and other infectious diseases). Retractable also makes blood collection needles and IV catheters using the VanishPoint technology which was invented by Thomas Shaw the company's founder CEO and majority owner. The firm sells to hospitals and other care providers in the US and abroad both directly and through distributors.

EXECUTIVES

Chairman Of The Board, President, Chief Executive Officer, Thomas Shaw, $490,247 total compensation
Independent Director, Amy Mack
Vice President, General Counsel, Secretary, Michele Larios, $350,000 total compensation
Vice President, Sales Development, Russell Kuhlman, $148,728 total compensation
Vice President, Chief Financial Officer, Treasurer, Director, John Fort, $200,000 total compensation
Independent Director, Marco Laterza
Independent Director, Walter Bigby
Independent Director, Darren Findley
Auditors: Moss Adams LLP

LOCATIONS

HQ: Retractable Technologies Inc
511 Lobo Lane, Little Elm, TX 75068-5295
Phone: 972 294-1010
Web: www.retractable.com

PRODUCTS/OPERATIONS

Selected Products and Brands
Syringes
  Patient Safe®; syringes
Tuberculin
  VanishPoint®; syringes (2mL 3mL 5mL and 10mL)
Other
  Patient Safe®; Luer Caps
  Small-diameter tube adapters
  VanishPoint®; blood collection tube holders
  VanishPoint®; IV safety catheters

COMPETITORS

Beijing Dehaier Medical Technology Co. Ltd.
DEROYAL INDUSTRIES INC.
SAFETY SYRINGES INC.
SPACELABS HEALTHCARE INC.
Technologies M ©dicales Internationales (MIT
UTAH MEDICAL PRODUCTS INC.

HISTORICAL FINANCIALS
Company Type: Public

Income Statement
FYE: December 31

	REVENUE ($ mil.)	NET INCOME ($ mil.)	NET PROFIT MARGIN	EMPLOYEES
12/20	81.8	24.2	29.6%	182
12/19	41.8	3.1	7.5%	140
12/18	33.2	(1.3)	—	125
12/17	34.4	(3.7)	—	150
12/16	29.8	(3.6)	—	135
Annual Growth	28.7%	—	—	7.8%

2020 Year-End Financials

Debt ratio: 3.5%	No. of shares (mil.): 33.9
Return on equity: 61.6%	Dividends
Cash ($ mil.): 17.5	Yield: —
Current ratio: 2.49	Payout: —
Long-term debt ($ mil.): 2.7	Market value ($ mil.): 365.0

	STOCK PRICE ($) FY Close	P/E High/Low		PER SHARE ($) Earnings	Dividends	Book Value
12/20	10.74	19	1	0.80	0.00	1.47
12/19	1.50	22	8	0.07	0.00	0.87
12/18	0.60	—	—	(0.06)	0.00	0.78
12/17	0.68	—	—	(0.14)	0.00	0.83
12/16	0.93	—	—	(0.15)	0.00	0.95
Annual Growth	84.3%	—	—	—	—	11.6%

Revolve Group Inc

Auditors: KPMG LLP

LOCATIONS

HQ: Revolve Group Inc
 12889 Moore Street, Cerritos, CA 90703
Phone: 562 677-9480
Web: www.revolve.com

HISTORICAL FINANCIALS
Company Type: Public

Income Statement
FYE: December 31

	REVENUE ($ mil.)	NET INCOME ($ mil.)	NET PROFIT MARGIN	EMPLOYEES
12/20	580.6	56.7	9.8%	843
12/19	600.9	35.6	5.9%	1,008
12/18	498.7	30.6	6.2%	1,055
12/17	399.6	5.3	1.3%	0
Annual Growth	13.3%	119.8%	—	—

2020 Year-End Financials

Debt ratio: —	No. of shares (mil.): 71.4
Return on equity: 34.2%	Dividends
Cash ($ mil.): 146.0	Yield: —
Current ratio: 2.62	Payout: —
Long-term debt ($ mil.): —	Market value ($ mil.): 2,225.0

	STOCK PRICE ($) FY Close	P/E High/Low		PER SHARE ($) Earnings	Dividends	Book Value
12/20	31.17	40	9	0.79	0.00	2.80
12/19	18.36	—	—	(0.09)	0.00	1.89
12/18	0.00	—	—	0.44	0.00	1.90
Annual Growth	—	—	—	34.0%	—	21.3%

Rexford Industrial Realty Inc

Rexford Industrial Realty knows that there's more to business in Southern California than moviemaking and fashion. A real estate investment trust or REIT Rexford Industrial owns and manages a portfolio of nearly 215 industrial properties in Southern California and surrounding areas. Its portfolio comprises about 26.6 million sq. ft. of warehouse distribution and light manufacturing space that's leased to small and midsized businesses. It manages about 20 more properties — altogether comprising about 1.0 million sq. ft. of rentable space. A self-administered and self-managed REIT Rexford Industrial was formed in 2013 from the assets of its predecessor.

Operations
Rexford Industrial's portfolio spans several California counties including Los Angeles Orange Ventura San Bernardino and San Diego.

Geographic Reach
The company portfolio is geographically diversified within the Southern California market across the following submarkets: Los Angeles (53%); San Bernardino (14%); Orange County (13%); San Diego (11%); and Ventura (9%).

Its corporate headquarters is located in Los Angeles California.

Sales and Marketing
No single tenant accounts for more than 5% of total annualized base rent. By industry Rexford Industrial top tenants hail from the wholesale trade; warehousing; manufacturing; retail; and transportation.

Financial Performance
Revenue rose for Rexford Industrial by 185% in the last five years buoyed by rising rental rates.

In 2019 revenue increased by 26% to $267.2 million. The increase in revenue was due to a 26% increase in rental income and an 85% increase in interest income offset by a 14% decrease in management leasing and development services.

Net income increased by 36% to $64 million in 2019 which was mostly due to higher revenue for that year.

Cash and cash equivalents at the end of the period were $78.9 million. Net cash provided by operating activities was $139.5 million and another $731.5 million was added by financing activities. Investing activities used $972.7 million for acquisitions of investments and capital expenditures.

Strategy
The company's primary business objective is to generate attractive risk-adjusted returns for its stockholders through dividends and capital appreciation. Rexford believes that pursuing the following strategies will enable the company to achieve this objective.

Internal growth through intensive value-add asset management through a proactive renewal of existing tenants re-tenanting to achieve higher rents and repositioning industrial property by renovating modernizing or increasing functionality to increase cash flow and value.

External growth through disciplined acquisitions in prime Southern California infill markets. The company seeks to acquire assets with value-add opportunities to increase its cash flow and asset values often targeting off-market or lightly marketed transactions where its execution abilities and market credibility encourage owners to sell assets to Rexford at what it considers pricing that is more favorable than heavily marketed transactions. It also seeks to source transactions from owners with generational ownership shift fund divestment sale-leaseback/corporate surplus maturing loans some facing liquidity needs or financial stress including loans that lack economical refinancing options. The company believes its deep market presence and relationships may enable it to selectively acquire assets in marketed transactions that may be difficult to access for less focused buyers.

Mergers and Acquisitions
In 2020 Rexford Industrial Realty announced the acquisition of five industrial properties for about $73.2 million. The acquisitions were funded using cash on hand. The Company acquired a three-property industrial portfolio located in Sun Valley within the LA ? San Fernando Valley submarket for $35.1 million or $169 per square foot. It also acquired 15650-15700 S. Avalon Boulevard located in Los Angeles within the LA ? South Bay submarket for $28.1 million or $169 per square foot and acquired 15850 Slover Avenue located in Fontana within the Inland Empire ? West submarket for $10.0 million or $166 per square foot.

EXECUTIVES

Chief Financial Officer, Laura Clark, $121,667 total compensation
General Counsel, Secretary, David Lanzer, $375,000 total compensation
Independent Director, Angela Kleiman
Independent Director, Debra Morris
Independent Director, Robert Antin
Independent Director, Peter Schwab
Chairman Of The Board, Richard Ziman
Co-chief Executive Officer, Director, Michael Frankel, $675,000 total compensation
Co-chief Executive Officer, Director, Howard Schwimmer, $675,000 total compensation
Auditors: Ernst & Young LLP

LOCATIONS

HQ: Rexford Industrial Realty Inc
 11620 Wilshire Boulevard, Suite 1000, Los Angeles, CA 90025
Phone: 310 966-1680
Web: www.rexfordindustrial.com

PRODUCTS/OPERATIONS

2015 Revenue

	$ mil.	% of total
Rental		
Rental Revenues	81.1	86
Tenant Reimbursements	10.5	11
Management Leasing & Development Services	0.6	1
Other Income	1.0	1
Interest Income	0.7	1
Total	**93.9**	**100**

Selected Property Categories
Core
Core Plus
First Mortgages Tied to Target Industrial Property
Value Add

COMPETITORS

DCT INDUSTRIAL TRUST INC.	Granite REIT Inc
EQUITY ONE INC.	LIBERTY PROPERTY TRUST
	PROLOGIS INC.

FIRST INDUSTRIAL REALTY TRUST INC. TERRENO REALTY CORPORATION

HISTORICAL FINANCIALS
Company Type: Public

Income Statement				FYE: December 31
	REVENUE ($ mil.)	NET INCOME ($ mil.)	NET PROFIT MARGIN	EMPLOYEES
12/21	452.2	128.2	28.4%	186
12/20	330.1	76.4	23.1%	147
12/19	267.2	61.9	23.2%	123
12/18	212.4	46.2	21.7%	108
12/17	161.3	40.7	25.2%	98
Annual Growth	29.4%	33.2%	—	17.4%

2021 Year-End Financials
Debt ratio: 20.6%
Return on equity: 3.1%
Cash ($ mil.): 43.9
Current ratio: 0.18
Long-term debt ($ mil.): 1,399.5

No. of shares (mil.): 160.5
Dividends
  Yield: 1.1%
  Payout: 141.1%
Market value ($ mil.): 13,019.0

	STOCK PRICE ($) FY Close	P/E High/Low		PER SHARE ($) Earnings	Dividends	Book Value
12/21	81.11	101	58	0.80	0.96	29.81
12/20	49.11	105	67	0.51	0.86	24.69
12/19	45.67	103	61	0.47	0.74	22.46
12/18	29.47	79	63	0.41	0.64	19.38
12/17	29.16	66	45	0.48	0.58	17.07
Annual Growth	29.1%			— 13.6%	13.4%	15.0%

RF Industries Ltd.

RF Industries (RFI) helps keep the world connected. The company's core business is conducted by its RF Connector division which makes coaxial connectors used in radio-frequency (RF) communications and computer networking equipment. Its Neulink Division makes wireless digital transmission devices such as modems and antennas used to link wide-area computer networks and global positioning systems. Through its Bioconnect division RF Industries also makes cable assemblies including electric cabling and interconnect products used in medical monitoring applications. Customers in the US account for more than 80% of sales. In 2019 RF Industries bought C Enterprises a maker of connectivity tools sold to telecommunications and data communications distributors.

EXECUTIVES

President, Chief Executive Officer And Director, Robert Dawson, $400,000 total compensation
Independent Director, Marvin Fink
Chief Revenue Officer, Ray Bibisi, $161,538 total compensation
Chief Financial Officer, Company Secretary, Peter Yin, $181,827 total compensation
Independent Director Chairman Of The Board, Mark Holdsworth
Investor Relations, Todd Kehrli
Auditors: CohnReznick LLP

LOCATIONS

HQ: RF Industries Ltd.
7610 Miramar Road, Building 6000, San Diego, CA 92126-4202
Phone: 858 549-6340
Web: www.rfindustries.com

PRODUCTS/OPERATIONS

Selected Products
Adapters
Antennas
Coaxial cable assemblies
Coaxial connectors
Disposable ECG cables
Electromechanical wiring harnesses
Hand tools
Radio-frequency (RF) data links
Receivers
Safety and snap leads
Wireless modems

COMPETITORS

HOSIDEN CORPORATION
MAC LEAN-FOGG COMPANY
METHODE ELECTRONICS INC.
WOODHEAD INDUSTRIES LLC

HISTORICAL FINANCIALS
Company Type: Public

Income Statement				FYE: October 31
	REVENUE ($ mil.)	NET INCOME ($ mil.)	NET PROFIT MARGIN	EMPLOYEES
10/21	57.4	6.1	10.8%	300
10/20	43.0	(0.0)	—	271
10/19	55.3	3.5	6.4%	281
10/18	50.2	5.8	11.6%	186
10/17	30.9	0.3	1.2%	195
Annual Growth	16.7%	100.6%	—	11.4%

2021 Year-End Financials
Debt ratio: —
Return on equity: 17.2%
Cash ($ mil.): 13.0
Current ratio: 4.34
Long-term debt ($ mil.): —

No. of shares (mil.): 10.0
Dividends
  Yield: —
  Payout: —
Market value ($ mil.): 77.0

	STOCK PRICE ($) FY Close	P/E High/Low		PER SHARE ($) Earnings	Dividends	Book Value
10/21	7.61	15	7	0.61	0.00	3.94
10/20	4.28	—	—	(0.01)	0.04	3.27
10/19	5.94	23	16	0.36	0.08	3.33
10/18	7.76	19	4	0.61	0.08	2.99
10/17	2.45	68	35	0.04	0.08	2.41
Annual Growth	32.8%			— 97.6%	—	13.1%

Rhinebeck Bancorp Inc

Auditors: Wolf & Company, P.C.

LOCATIONS

HQ: Rhinebeck Bancorp Inc
2 Jefferson Plaza, Poughkeepsie, NY 12601
Phone: 845 454-8555
Web: www.rhinebeckbank.com

HISTORICAL FINANCIALS
Company Type: Public

Income Statement				FYE: December 31
	ASSETS ($ mil.)	NET INCOME ($ mil.)	INCOME AS % OF ASSETS	EMPLOYEES
12/20	1,128.8	5.9	0.5%	176
12/19	973.9	5.9	0.6%	173
12/18	882.4	4.3	0.5%	166
12/17	742.1	3.0	0.4%	153
12/16	722.5	2.6	0.4%	152
Annual Growth	11.8%	21.8%	—	3.7%

2020 Year-End Financials
Return on assets: 0.5%
Return on equity: 5.2%
Long-term debt ($ mil.): —
No. of shares (mil.): 11.1
Sales ($ mil.): 52.7

Dividends
  Yield: —
  Payout: —
Market value ($ mil.): 95.0

	STOCK PRICE ($) FY Close	P/E High/Low		PER SHARE ($) Earnings	Dividends	Book Value
12/20	8.55	21	11	0.55	0.00	10.46
12/19	11.31	22	18	0.56	0.00	9.87
Annual Growth	(24.4%)			— (1.8%)	—	6.0%

Ribbon Communications Inc

Auditors: DELOITTE & TOUCHE LLP

LOCATIONS

HQ: Ribbon Communications Inc
6500 Chase Oaks Boulevard, Suite 100, Plano, TX 75023
Phone: 978 614-8100
Web: www.ribboncommunications.com

HISTORICAL FINANCIALS
Company Type: Public

Income Statement				FYE: December 31
	REVENUE ($ mil.)	NET INCOME ($ mil.)	NET PROFIT MARGIN	EMPLOYEES
12/20	843.8	88.5	10.5%	3,784
12/19	563.1	(130.0)	—	2,209
12/18	577.9	(76.8)	—	2,245
12/17	329.9	(35.2)	—	2,457
12/16	252.5	(13.9)	—	0
Annual Growth	35.2%	—	—	—

2020 Year-End Financials
Debt ratio: 24.9%
Return on equity: 15.1%
Cash ($ mil.): 128.4
Current ratio: 1.37
Long-term debt ($ mil.): 370.5

No. of shares (mil.): 145.4
Dividends
  Yield: —
  Payout: —
Market value ($ mil.): 954.0

	STOCK PRICE ($)		P/E		PER SHARE ($)		
	FY Close		High/Low	Earnings	Dividends		Book Value
12/20	6.56		12 3	0.61	0.00		4.72
12/19	3.10		— —	(1.19)	0.00		4.37
12/18	4.82		— —	(0.74)	0.00		5.53
12/17	7.73		— —	(0.60)	0.00		6.05
Annual Growth	(5.3%)		— —	—			(7.9%)

Richmond Mutual Bancorporation Inc

Auditors: BKD, LLP

LOCATIONS

HQ: Richmond Mutual Bancorporation Inc
31 North 9th Street, Richmond, IN 47374
Phone: 765 962-2581
Web: www.mutualbancorp.com

HISTORICAL FINANCIALS
Company Type: Public

Income Statement				FYE: December 31
	REVENUE ($ mil.)	NET INCOME ($ mil.)	NET PROFIT MARGIN	EMPLOYEES
12/20	49.6	10.0	20.2%	170
12/19	45.4	(14.0)	—	166
12/18	39.4	5.6	14.4%	172
12/17	33.6	2.7	8.1%	174
Annual Growth	13.9%	54.5%	—	(0.8%)

2020 Year-End Financials
Debt ratio: 15.6%
Return on equity: 5.2%
Cash ($ mil.): 48.7
Current ratio: 0.08
Long-term debt ($ mil.): 170.0

No. of shares (mil.): 13.1
Dividends
  Yield: 1.1%
  Payout: 18.2%
Market value ($ mil.): 180.0

	STOCK PRICE ($)		P/E		PER SHARE ($)		
	FY Close		High/Low	Earnings	Dividends		Book Value
12/20	13.66		19 11	0.82	0.15		14.61
12/19	15.96		— —	(0.00)	0.00		13.88
12/18	0.00		— —	(0.00)	0.00		
	858,530.32						
Annual Growth (99.6%)			—	— —	—		—

Risk George Industries Inc

George Risk Industries (GRI) wants customers to be able to manage risks. The company makes burglar alarm components and systems including panic buttons (for direct access to alarm monitoring centers). In addition to security products GRI manufactures pool alarms which are designed to sound alerts when a pool or spa area has been entered. The company also makes thermostats specialty computer keyboards and keypads custom-engraved key caps and push-button switches. Chairman President and CEO Stephanie Risk-McElroy granddaughter of founder George Risk and daughter of former CEO Ken Risk controls the company.

EXECUTIVES

Chairman Of The Board, Chief Executive Officer, Chief Financial Officer, Stephanie Risk-McElroy, $105,000 total compensation
Treasurer. Corporate Secretary, Sharon Westby
Director, Stock Transfer Agent At Gri, Bonita Risk, $41,000 total compensation
Director, Retired Gri Plant Manager, Donna Debowey
Director, Firstier Banks, Joel Wiens
Director, Retired Business Owner, Jerry Knutsen
Auditors: Haynie & Company

LOCATIONS

HQ: Risk George Industries Inc
802 South Elm St., Kimball, NE 69145
Phone: 308 235-4645
Web: www.grisk.com

COMPETITORS

ECONOLITE CONTROL PRODUCTS INC.
NAPCO SECURITY TECHNOLOGIES INC.
SEPURA LIMITED

HISTORICAL FINANCIALS
Company Type: Public

Income Statement				FYE: April 30
	REVENUE ($ mil.)	NET INCOME ($ mil.)	NET PROFIT MARGIN	EMPLOYEES
04/21	18.5	10.8	58.5%	195
04/20	14.8	2.1	14.2%	175
04/19	14.1	3.2	23.2%	175
04/18	11.9	2.5	21.3%	175
04/17	10.9	2.4	22.0%	130
Annual Growth	14.1%	45.7%	—	10.7%

2021 Year-End Financials
Debt ratio: —
Return on equity: 24.6%
Cash ($ mil.): 7.3
Current ratio: 16.86
Long-term debt ($ mil.): —

No. of shares (mil.): 4.9
Dividends
  Yield: 3.3%
  Payout: 31.8%
Market value ($ mil.): 62.0

	STOCK PRICE ($)		P/E		PER SHARE ($)		
	FY Close		High/Low	Earnings	Dividends		Book Value
04/21	12.52		6 3	2.18	0.42		9.79
04/20	8.40		25 17	0.42	0.40		8.00
04/19	8.25		13 12	0.66	0.38		7.98
04/18	8.55		17 15	0.51	0.36		7.59
04/17	8.49		18 15	0.48	0.35		7.23
Annual Growth	10.2%		—	46.0%	4.7%		7.9%

River Financial Corp

Auditors: Mauldin & Jenkins, LLC

LOCATIONS

HQ: River Financial Corp
2611 Legends Drive, Prattville, AL 36066
Phone: 334 290-1012
Web: www.riverbankandtrust.com

HISTORICAL FINANCIALS
Company Type: Public

Income Statement				FYE: December 31
	REVENUE ($ mil.)	NET INCOME ($ mil.)	NET PROFIT MARGIN	EMPLOYEES
12/20	75.2	17.0	22.7%	231
12/19	58.8	11.1	18.9%	232
12/18	43.5	8.5	19.5%	195
12/17	38.4	8.3	21.6%	151
12/16	35.2	7.9	22.5%	134
Annual Growth	20.9%	21.3%	—	14.6%

2020 Year-End Financials
Debt ratio: 1.0%
Return on equity: 10.8%
Cash ($ mil.): 60.2
Current ratio: 0.35
Long-term debt ($ mil.): 20.3

No. of shares (mil.): 6.5
Dividends
  Yield: 0.0%
  Payout: 13.8%
Market value ($ mil.): 137.0

	STOCK PRICE ($)		P/E		PER SHARE ($)		
	FY Close		High/Low	Earnings	Dividends		Book Value
12/20	21.00		11 6	2.60	0.36		25.87
12/19	28.00		15 15	1.88	0.33		22.66
12/18	30.00		18 13	1.60	0.27		19.60
Annual Growth (16.3%)			— —	27.5%	15.5%		14.9%

RLI Corp

You might wonder what folks in Illinois know about earthquake insurance but as a specialty property/casualty insurer Peoria-based RLI knows how to write such policies. Through its subsidiaries the company mainly offers coverage for US niche markets — risks that are hard to place in the standard market and are otherwise underserved. It focuses on public and private companies as well as non-profit organizations. RLI's commercial property/casualty lines include products liability property damage marine cargo directors and officers liability medical malpractice and general liability. It also writes commercial surety bonds and a smattering of specialty personal insurance.

Operations

RLI operates into three segments; Casualty Property and Surety. Casualty segment accounts for about 55% of revenue followed by property (more than 15%) and surety (about 10%).

RLI's specialty commercial property/casualty operations are conducted through its RLI Insurance Mt. Hawley Insurance Contractors Bonding and Insurance Company and RLI Indemnity subsidiaries. Personal offerings account for small portion of RLI's revenues and include homeowners

HOOVER'S HANDBOOK OF EMERGING COMPANIES 2022

insurance in Hawaii home business coverage and personal umbrella (supplemental property/casualty) policies.

The company's net premium earns generated nearly 85% of sales while net investment income and net realized gains account for the rest.

Geographic Reach

While the company operates in all 50 US states the District of Columbia the Virgin Islands Guam and Puerto Rico California is RLI's largest market accounting for more than 15% of the company's premiums.

Its corporate headquarters is located in Peoria Illinois.

Sales and Marketing

RLI markets its products to brokers and independent agents through branch offices scattered across the US.

Financial Performance

The company posted revenue growth for the last five years despite a slight drop in 2017. Net income continued its drop from 2015 to 2018 until the company arrested its decline.

Consolidated revenue totaled $1.0 billion in 2019 compared to $0.8 billion in 2018. Increased levels of earned premium and net investment income as well as unrealized gains on equity securities led to increased consolidated revenue in 2019.

Net earnings for 2019 totaled $191.6 million up from $64.2 million in 2018. Improved underwriting income net investment income and equity in earnings of unconsolidated investees contributed to the overall increase. Additionally 2019 experienced a larger benefit from increased gains on equity securities.

Cash at the end of the year was $46.2 million. Net cash provided by operating activities was $276.9 million while cash used by investing and financing activities were $184.8 million and $76.1 million respectively.

Strategy

RLI's investment portfolio serves as the primary resource for loss payments and secondly as a source of income to support operations. Its investment strategy is based on the preservation of capital as the priority with a secondary focus on growing book value through total return. Investments of the highest quality and marketability are critical for preserving its claims-paying ability.

Its portfolio contains no derivatives or off-balance sheet structured investments. In addition it has a diversified investment portfolio that distributes credit risk across many issuers and a policy that limits aggregate credit exposure. Despite periodic fluctuations in market value its equity portfolio is part of a long-term asset allocation strategy and has contributed significantly to its growth in book value.

Company Background

Gerald Stephens founded the company in 1961 and served as its chairman from 2001 until his retirement in 2011.

EXECUTIVES

Vice President, Controller, Seth Davis
President, Chief Executive Officer, Director, Craig Kliethermes, $525,000 total compensation
Chief Financial Officer, Vice President, Todd Bryant, $330,000 total compensation
Chairman Of The Board, Jonathan Michael, $775,000 total compensation

Senior Vice President, Chief Legal Officer & Corporate Secretary, Jeffrey Fick, $336,269 total compensation
Lead Independent Director, John Baily
Independent Director, Jordan Graham
Chief Operating Officer, Jennifer Klobnak, $370,000 total compensation
Vice President, Chief Investment Officer And Treasurer, Aaron Diefenthaler, $315,000 total compensation
Independent Director, Robert Restrepo
Independent Director, David Duclos
Independent Director, Debbie Roberts
Independent Director, Susan Fleming
Independent Director, Kaj Ahlmann
Independent Director, Michael Angelina
Independent Director, Calvin Butler
Auditors: DELOITTE & TOUCHE LLP

LOCATIONS

HQ: RLI Corp
9025 North Lindbergh Drive, Peoria, IL 61615
Phone: 309 692-1000   **Fax:** 309 692-1068
Web: www.rlicorp.com

PRODUCTS/OPERATIONS

2016 Revenues

	$ mil.	% of total
Net premiums earned		
Casualty	454.8	56
Property	152.2	19
Surety	121.6	15
Net investment income	53.1	6
Net realized gains	34.6	4
Total	**816.3**	**100**

Selected Products

Commercial
  Casualty
  Contractors bonding and insurance
  Executive products liability
  Marine
  Professional services
  Property
  Reinsurance
  Specialty programs
  Transportation
Personal
  Homeowners (Hawaii)
  Home business owners
  Personal umbrella
Surety Bonds

COMPETITORS

ARTHUR J. GALLAGHER & CO.
DONEGAL GROUP INC.
EQUITABLE FINANCIAL LIFE INSURANCE COMPANY
HALLMARK FINANCIAL SERVICES INC.
HCI GROUP INC.
MERCURY GENERAL CORPORATION
Manulife Financial Corporation
STATE AUTO FINANCIAL CORPORATION
UNIVERSAL INSURANCE HOLDINGS INC.

HISTORICAL FINANCIALS

Company Type: Public

Income Statement

FYE: December 31

	ASSETS ($ mil.)	NET INCOME ($ mil.)	INCOME AS % OF ASSETS	EMPLOYEES
12/21	4,508.3	279.3	6.2%	913
12/20	3,938.4	157.0	4.0%	875
12/19	3,545.7	191.6	5.4%	905
12/18	3,105.0	64.1	2.1%	912
12/17	2,947.2	105.0	3.6%	902
Annual Growth	**11.2%**	**27.7%**	**—**	**0.3%**

2021 Year-End Financials

Return on assets: 6.6%
Return on equity: 23.6%
Long-term debt ($ mil.): —
No. of shares (mil.): 45.2
Sales ($ mil): 1,179.2
Dividends
  Yield: 2.6%
  Payout: 50.9%
Market value ($ mil.): 5,077.0

	STOCK PRICE ($) FY Close	P/E High/Low		PER SHARE ($) Earnings	Dividends	Book Value
12/21	112.10	19	16	6.11	2.99	27.14
12/20	104.15	31	20	3.46	1.95	25.16
12/19	90.02	23	15	4.23	1.91	22.18
12/18	68.99	55	40	1.43	1.87	18.13
12/17	60.66	26	21	2.36	2.58	19.33
Annual Growth	**16.6%**	**—**	**—**	**26.8%**	**3.8%**	**8.9%**

RMR Group Inc (The)

Auditors: Deloitte & Touche LLP

LOCATIONS

HQ: RMR Group Inc (The)
Two Newton Place, 255 Washington Street, Suite 300, Newton, MA 02458-1634
Phone: 617 796-8230
Web: www.rmrgroup.com

HISTORICAL FINANCIALS

Company Type: Public

Income Statement

FYE: September 30

	REVENUE ($ mil.)	NET INCOME ($ mil.)	NET PROFIT MARGIN	EMPLOYEES
09/21	607.2	35.7	5.9%	600
09/20	589.5	28.7	4.9%	600
09/19	713.3	74.5	10.5%	50,600
09/18	404.9	96.0	23.7%	52,600
09/17	271.7	42.2	15.6%	53,475
Annual Growth	**22.3%**	**(4.2%)**	**—**	**(67.5%)**

2021 Year-End Financials

Debt ratio: —
Return on equity: 14.5%
Cash ($ mil.): 159.8
Current ratio: 3.14
Long-term debt ($ mil.): —
No. of shares (mil.): 31.4
Dividends
  Yield: 25.4%
  Payout: 504.1%
Market value ($ mil.): 1,053.0

	STOCK PRICE ($)	P/E	PER SHARE ($)		
	FY Close	High/Low	Earnings	Dividends	Book Value
09/21	33.45	21 12	2.15	8.52	6.20
09/20	27.47	28 13	1.75	1.52	9.43
09/19	45.48	20 9	4.59	1.40	9.22
09/18	92.80	16 9	5.92	1.00	7.45
09/17	51.35	21 13	2.63	1.00	4.80
Annual Growth (10.2%)		— —	(4.9%)	70.8%	6.6%

Roku Inc

Auditors: DELOITTE & TOUCHE LLP

LOCATIONS

HQ: Roku Inc
1155 Coleman Avenue, San Jose, CA 95110
Phone: 408 556-9040
Web: www.roku.com

HISTORICAL FINANCIALS

Company Type: Public

Income Statement				FYE: December 31
	REVENUE ($ mil.)	NET INCOME ($ mil.)	NET PROFIT MARGIN	EMPLOYEES
12/21	2,764.5	242.3	8.8%	3,000
12/20	1,778.3	(17.5)	—	1,925
12/19	1,128.9	(59.9)	—	1,650
12/18	742.5	(8.8)	—	1,111
12/17	512.7	(63.5)	—	817
Annual Growth	52.4%	—	—	38.4%

2021 Year-End Financials

Debt ratio: 2.2%
Return on equity: 11.8%
Cash ($ mil.): 2,146.0
Current ratio: 4.19
Long-term debt ($ mil.): 79.9

No. of shares (mil.): 135.1
Dividends
  Yield: —
  Payout: —
Market value ($ mil.): 30,838.0

	STOCK PRICE ($)	P/E	PER SHARE ($)		
	FY Close	High/Low	Earnings	Dividends	Book Value
12/21	228.20	262 111	1.71	0.00	20.47
12/20	332.02	— —	(0.14)	0.00	10.37
12/19	133.90	— —	(0.52)	0.00	5.83
12/18	30.64	— —	(0.08)	0.00	2.23
12/17	51.78	— —	(2.24)	0.00	1.54
Annual Growth 44.9%		— —	—	—	91.1%

Rollins, Inc.

If Rollins has anything to do with it you'll sleep tight and the bed bugs won't bite. Rollins is a solid leader in the pest control industry offering an array of residential and commercial pest control and termite control services. Rollins also provides recurring maintenance monitoring or inspection services to help protect consumer's property for any future sign of termite activities after the original treatment. The company serves around 2.4 million customers in some 65 countries globally. The US operations account for more than 90% of revenues. Other Rollins brands include and HomeTeam Pest Defense and IFC.

Operations

The company has only one reportable segment its pest and termite control business.

Rollins provides pest control services to protect residential and commercial properties from common pests including rodents and insects. Pest control generally consists of assessing a customer's property for conditions that invite pests tackling current infestations and stopping the life cycle to prevent future invaders. It also provides both traditional and baiting termite protection services. Traditional termite protection uses "Termidor" liquid treatment and/or dry foam and Orkin foam to treat voids and spaces around the property while baiting termite protection uses baits to disrupt the molting process termites require for growth and offers ongoing protection.

In connection with the initial service offerings Rollins may offer other miscellaneous services such as cleaning and equipment rentals.

Geographic Reach

Atlanta Georgia-based Rollins owns or leases over 550 branch offices and operating facilities used in its business as well as the Rollins Training Center located in Atlanta Georgia; the Rollins Customer Service Center located in Covington Georgia; and the Pacific Division Administration and Training Center in Riverside California. The company has operations in the United States Canada Australia Europe and Asia with international franchises in Mexico Canada Central and South America the Caribbean Europe the Middle East Asia Africa and Australia.

The US accounts for more than 90% of the company's total sale.

Sales and Marketing

The company serves around 2.4 million customers. The residential customers generate nearly 45% of sales while the commercial customers bring in roughly 40%

The advertising cost for the years 2019 2018 and 2017 were $81.1 million $69.9 million and $66.1 million respectively.

Financial Performance

Revenues in 2019 were $2.0 billion an increase of $194 million or 11% from 2018 revenues of $1.8 billion. Growth occurred across all service lines with its Canadian and Australian companies being hindered by unfavorable foreign currency exchange rates.

Net income decreased 12% to $203.3 million in 2019 primarily due to the presence of pension settlement loss.

Cash at the end of 2019 was $94.3 million. Cash from operations was $309.2 million while investing activities used $455.1 million. Financing activities provided $127.7 million. The main cash uses for the year were for capital expenditures and dividends paid.

Strategy

The company has relationships with a national pest control product distributor and other suppliers for pest and termite control treatment products. The company maintains a sufficient level of chemicals materials and other supplies to fulfill its immediate servicing needs and to alleviate any potential short-term shortage in availability from its national network of suppliers.

Expenditures by the company on research activities relating to the development of new products or services are not significant. Some of the new and improved service methods and products are researched developed and produced by unaffiliated universities and companies. Also a portion of these methods and products are produced to the specifications provided by the company.

Rollins maintains a close relationship with several universities for research and validation of treatment procedures and material selection.

The company conducts tests of new products with the specific manufacturers of such products. The company also works closely with leading scientists educators industry consultants and suppliers to improve service protocols and materials.

Mergers and Acquisitions

Rollinss subsidiary Rollins UK Holdings Ltd. (Rollins UK) acquired two environmentally friendly companies in the first quarter of 2020. Rollins UK expanded its holdings with Albany Environmental Services Ltd. based in central London and Van Vynck Environmental Services based in Essex. Albany Environmental utilizes footmen primarily for walking routes within London yielding a minimal carbon footprint and Van Vynck Environmental is widely known for their bird management program utilizing falconry. With these latest acquisitions the company now covers all of southern and central England including central London and from Cornwall to Essex. Terms not disclosed.

Rollins in early 2020 announced that its subsidiary Clark Pest Control of Stockton Inc. has completed the acquisition of Clark Pest Control Inc. based in Bakersfield CA. This transaction will optimally positioned to serve markets in California and Nevada with the finest pest management and associated services. Terms were not disclosed.

In early 2019 Rollins has completed the purchase of Clark Pest Control of Stockton Inc. located in Lodi CA. Clark Pest Control is a leading pest management company in California. Geotech Supply is included in the acquisition and will continue to expand its current operations maintaining a commitment to quality service delivery. Terms of this transaction were not disclosed.

Company Background

Rollins has taken on several education initiatives. The company partners with the Centers for Disease Control in efforts to teach the public about pest-related illnesses and its O. Orkin Insect Zoo at the Smithsonian Museum of Natural History in Washington DC remains a popular exhibit. The Orkin name for the pest control business came from Atlanta businessman Otto Orkin who founded the company in 1901.

HISTORY

Brothers O. Wayne and John Rollins founded the company in 1948 as Rollins Broadcasting. John's auto leasing company which later became Rollins Truck Leasing was an early advertiser on Wayne's radio station. The company went public in 1961 and soon extended its reach to include cosmetics and citrus-fruit growing.

Rollins engineered one of the first leveraged buyouts in history when it purchased the much larger Orkin in 1964. (Orkin was founded in 1901 by Otto Orkin who launched his extermination empire by selling rat killer door-to-door; his efforts earned him the nickname "Orkin the Rat Catcher.") Adopting the Rollins Inc. name in 1965 the company diversified further in the 1970s and 1980s

HOOVER'S HANDBOOK OF EMERGING COMPANIES 2022

making purchases that included oil and gas textiles and burglar alarms systems. In 1984 Rollins spun off Rollins Communications and RPC Energy Services and retained its consumer services which included pest control lawn care (Orkin Lawncare) and security services (Rollins Protective Services).

The company was forced to modify its termite services when the Environmental Protection Agency banned the use of Chlordane in 1988 (the insecticide had caused cancer in laboratory animals). Chlordane had been the most widely used termite insecticide prior to the ban; its prohibition prompted confusion among consumers which translated into a downturn in consumer demand for termite services. In 1998 a jury found Orkin liable for treating a Florida family's home with Chlordane in 1993. The family was awarded a $2 million judgment.

Wayne Rollins died in 1991 leaving his sons Randall and Gary in charge. Recognizing heightened demand for commercial services the company formed a commercial division in 1996. The following year Rollins sold its security and lawn care businesses allowing the company to focus exclusively on pest control.

Orkin expanded its pest control empire that year with acquisitions of 10 pest control businesses in the US and Canada. In 1999 Orkin bought the pest control business of S.C. Johnson Professional (a division of S.C. Johnson & Son). The two companies also teamed to market pest elimination services to retailers. In 2001 the company launched Acurid a customized approach to pest control that helps businesses meet industry regulations.

In 2003 the company began limited offerings of mosquito control programs in response to fears of West Nile virus which is carried by the insect. The company strengthened its presence in the northeastern US through the 2004 acquisition of New Jersey-based Western Pest Services the pest control operation of Western Industries.

Rollins obtained pest management business Crane Pest Control in 2009 after buying the assets of rival HomeTeam Pest Defense from homebuilder Centex for about $137 million in 2008. In 2010 Rollins acquired pest control firm Waltham Services and the company also expanded its international presence opening several foreign locations.

EXECUTIVES

Chairman & Chief Executive Officer, Gary Rollins, $1,152,308 total compensation
Independent Director, Thomas Lawley
President, Chief Operating Officer, Director, Jerry Gahlhoff, $412,654 total compensation
Senior Vice President - Sustainability, Paul Northen, $564,923 total compensation
Director, Pamela Rollins
Vice President, General Counsel, Corporate Secretary, Elizabeth Chandler, $421,000 total compensation
Lead Independent Director, Jerry Nix
Independent Director, Patrick Gunning
Independent Director, Susan Bell
Director, Gregory Morrison
Vice Chairman Of The Board And Assistant To The Chairman, John Wilson, $853,846 total compensation
Chief Financial Officer, Treasurer, Julie Bimmerman
Auditors: Grant Thornton LLP

LOCATIONS

HQ: Rollins, Inc.
2170 Piedmont Road, N.E., Atlanta, GA 30324
Phone: 404 888-2000
Web: www.rollins.com

PRODUCTS/OPERATIONS

Selected Subsidiaries
Crane Acquisitions Inc.
  PCO Holdings Inc.
  Orkin Canada Limited Partnership
HomeTeam Pest Defense Inc.
IFC Company Holdings Inc.
  IFC Properties LLC
  The Industrial Fumigant Company
International Food Consultants LLC
Orkin
  Orkin International Inc.
  Orkin Systems Inc
Orkin-IFC Properties LLC
Rollins Continental Inc.
  Rollins;Western Real Estate Holding LLC
Trutech LLC
Waltham Services LLC
Western Industries North Inc.
Western Industries South Inc

Selected Pest Control Products and Services
Baits
Crack and crevice treatment
Direct contact services
Dusting treatment
Inspections
Mosquito control
Perimeter defense system
Traps
Void treatment

COMPETITORS

ABM INDUSTRIES INCORPORATED	CARTER & ASSOCIATES ENTERPRISES INC.
AIRE-MASTER OF AMERICA SERVICES INC. INC.	COPESAN
AMERISOURCEBERGEN CORPORATION	EMCOR GROUP INC. NCH CORPORATION ORKIN LLC

HISTORICAL FINANCIALS
Company Type: Public

Income Statement
FYE: December 31

	REVENUE ($ mil.)	NET INCOME ($ mil.)	NET PROFIT MARGIN	EMPLOYEES
12/20	2,161.2	260.8	12.1%	15,616
12/19	2,015.4	203.3	10.1%	14,952
12/18	1,821.5	231.6	12.7%	13,734
12/17	1,673.9	179.1	10.7%	13,126
12/16	1,573.4	167.3	10.6%	12,153
Annual Growth	8.3%	11.7%	—	6.5%

2020 Year-End Financials
Debt ratio: 11.0%
Return on equity: 29.6%
Cash ($ mil.): 98.4
Current ratio: 0.67
Long-term debt ($ mil.): 185.8
No. of shares (mil.): 491.6
Dividends
  Yield: 0.6%
  Payout: 61.6%
Market value ($ mil.): 19,207.0

	STOCK PRICE ($) FY Close	P/E High/Low		PER SHARE ($) Earnings	Dividends	Book Value
12/20	39.07	119	60	0.53	0.33	1.91
12/19	33.16	106	76	0.41	0.31	1.66
12/18	36.10	136	71	0.47	0.31	1.45
12/17	46.53	131	90	0.36	0.25	1.33
12/16	33.78	100	70	0.34	0.22	1.16
Annual Growth	3.7%	—	—	11.6%	10.1%	13.3%

Royalty Pharma plc

EXECUTIVES

Chb-Ceo, Pablo Legorreta
Exec V Pres-V Chm, Christopher Hite
Exec V Pres-Cfo, Terrance Coyne
Exec V Pres Research & Investm, James Reddoch
Exec V Pres Investments-Gen Co, George Lloyd
Exec V Pres Research & Investm, Marshall Urist

LOCATIONS

HQ: Royalty Pharma plc
110 East 59th Street, New York, NY 10022
Phone: 212 883-0200
Web: www.royaltypharma.com

HISTORICAL FINANCIALS
Company Type: Public

Income Statement
FYE: December 31

	REVENUE ($ mil.)	NET INCOME ($ mil.)	NET PROFIT MARGIN	EMPLOYEES
12/21	2,289.4	619.7	27.1%	66
12/20	2,122.3	975.0	45.9%	51
12/19	1,814.2	2,348.5	129.4%	35
12/18	1,794.8	1,377.7	76.8%	0
12/17	1,597.9	1,210.0	75.7%	0
Annual Growth	9.4%	(15.4%)	—	—

2021 Year-End Financials
Debt ratio: 40.5%
Return on equity: 11.7%
Cash ($ mil.): 1,541.0
Current ratio: 16.81
Long-term debt ($ mil.): 7,096.0
No. of shares (mil.): 968.4
Dividends
  Yield: 1.7%
  Payout: 35.0%
Market value ($ mil.): —

Sachem Capital Corp

Auditors: Hoberman & Lesser, CPA's, LLP

LOCATIONS

HQ: Sachem Capital Corp
698 Main Street, Branford, CT 06405
Phone: 203 433-4736
Web: www.sachemcapitalcorp.com

HISTORICAL FINANCIALS
Company Type: Public

Income Statement
FYE: December 31

	REVENUE ($ mil.)	NET INCOME ($ mil.)	NET PROFIT MARGIN	EMPLOYEES
12/20	18.6	8.9	48.3%	17
12/19	12.6	6.2	48.9%	10
12/18	11.7	7.7	66.3%	11
12/17	7.0	4.8	69.5%	7
12/16	4.1	3.0	73.8%	0
Annual Growth	45.7%	31.0%	—	—

2020 Year-End Financials
Debt ratio: 61.2%
Return on equity: 10.9%
Cash ($ mil.): 19.4
Current ratio: 29.68
Long-term debt ($ mil.): 138.4
No. of shares (mil.): 22.1
Dividends
  Yield: 8.6%
  Payout: 87.8%
Market value ($ mil.): 92.0

	STOCK PRICE ($)		P/E		PER SHARE ($)		
	FY Close		High/Low	Earnings	Dividends		Book Value
12/20	4.16		11 3	0.41	0.36		3.66
12/19	4.34		18 12	0.32	0.53		3.73
12/18	3.91		9 7	0.50	0.61		3.42
12/17	3.94		14 10	0.38	0.26		3.54
Annual Growth	1.8%		— —	2.6%	11.5%		1.1%

Safehold Inc

Auditors: Deloitte & Touche LLP

LOCATIONS

HQ: Safehold Inc
1114 Avenue of the Americas, 39th Floor, New York, NY 10036
Phone: 212 930-9400
Web: www.safeholdinc.com

HISTORICAL FINANCIALS

Company Type: Public

Income Statement   FYE: December 31

	REVENUE ($ mil.)	NET INCOME ($ mil.)	NET PROFIT MARGIN	EMPLOYEES
12/21	187.0	73.1	39.1%	0
12/20	155.4	59.2	38.1%	0
12/19	93.4	27.6	29.7%	0
12/18	49.7	11.7	23.6%	0
12/17	17.2	(3.6)	—	0
Annual Growth	81.6%	—	—	0

2021 Year-End Financials

Debt ratio: 59.7%	No. of shares (mil.): 56.6
Return on equity: 4.7%	Dividends
Cash ($ mil.): 29.6	Yield: 0.8%
Current ratio: 3.32	Payout: 52.9%
Long-term debt ($ mil.): 2,697.5	Market value ($ mil.): 4,521.0

	STOCK PRICE ($)		P/E		PER SHARE ($)		
	FY Close		High/Low	Earnings	Dividends		Book Value
12/21	79.85		70 50	1.35	0.67		29.71
12/20	72.49		63 34	1.17	0.64		25.92
12/19	40.30		48 19	0.89	0.61		22.85
12/18	18.81		31 24	0.64	0.60		19.44
12/17	17.60		— —	(0.25)	0.31		19.57
Annual Growth	45.9%		— —	—	21.7%		11.0%

Saia Inc

Saia is a holding company for less-than-truckload (LTL) carrier Saia Motor Freight Line a leading LTL carrier that serves about 45 states and provides LTL services to Canada and Mexico through relationships with third-party interline carriers. Saia Motor Freight specializes in offering its customers a range of LTL services including time-definite and expedited options. The carrier operates a fleet of some 5700 tractors and approximately 17400 trailers from a network of about 175 terminals. Saia's service territory spans throughout the South Southwest Midwest as well as Pacific Northwest West and portions of the Northeast US. The company was founded in 1924.

Operations

Saia provides less-than-truckload (LTL) services through a single integrated organization. While more than 95% of its revenue is derived from transporting LTL shipments it also offers customers a wide range of other value-added services including non-asset truckload expedited and logistics services across North America through its wholly-owned subsidiaries: Saia Motor Freight Line. The trucking industry consists of three segments: private fleets and two "for-hire" carrier groups. The private carrier segment consists of fleets owned and operated by shippers who move their own goods. The two "for-hire" carrier groups truckload and LTL are defined by the typical shipment sizes handled by the transportation service companies.

Saia Motor Freight provides its customers with solutions for shipments between 100 and 10000 pounds.

Geographic Reach

The company operates through about 175 terminals in nearly 45 US states in the South Southwest Midwest Pacific Northwest West and portions of Northeast. It also provides LTL services to Canada and Mexico through relationships with third-party interline carriers.

Sales and Marketing

Saia's advertising costs were $4.6 million $6.1 million and $3.9 million in 2020 2019 and 2018 respectively.

Financial Performance

In fiscal 2020 consolidated revenue increased 2% percent to $1.8 billion primarily as a result of pricing actions and terminal expansion partially offset by a decrease in fuel surcharge revenue as a result of lower fuel prices.

Net income for fiscal 2020 increased to $138.3 million compared from the prior year with $113.7 million.

Cash held by the company at the end of fiscal 2020 increased to $25.3 million. Cash provided by operations was $309.1 million while cash used for investing and financing activities were $218.8 million and $65.3 million respectively. Main uses of cash were acquisition of property and equipment; and repayment of revolving credit agreement.

Strategy

Saia has grown historically through a combination of organic growth and geographic integration or "tuck-in" acquisitions of smaller trucking and logistics companies. More recently Saia has grown largely through organic growth.

Key elements of its business strategy include: Continue to focus on operating safely; Manage yields and business mix; Increase density in existing geographies; Continue to focus on delivering best-in-class service; Continue to focus on improving operating efficiencies; and the organization for growth and expand geographic footprint.

EXECUTIVES

Independent Director, Jeffrey Ward
Vice President, Stephanie Maschmeier
Vice President, Human Resources, Karla Staver, $335,016 total compensation
Chief Financial Officer, Executive Vice President, Douglas Col, $368,445 total compensation
President, Chief Executive Officer, Director, Frederick Holzgrefe, $664,320 total compensation
Independent Director, Donna Epps
Independent Director, Susan Ward
Independent Director, John Gainor
Director, Kevin Henry
Director, Donald James
Chief Accounting Officer, Vice President, Controller, Kelly Benton
Executive Vice President, Chief Customer Officer, Raymond Ramu, $463,512 total compensation
Lead Independent Director, Randolph Melville
Chairman, Richard O'Dell, $328,320 total compensation
Auditors: KPMG LLP

LOCATIONS

HQ: Saia Inc
11465 Johns Creek Parkway, Suite 400, Johns Creek, GA 30097
Phone: 770 232-5067
Web: www.saia.com

PRODUCTS/OPERATIONS

Selected Coverage Area
Alabama
Arizona
Arkansas
California
Colorado
Florida
Georgia
Idaho
Illinois
Indiana
Iowa
Kansas
Kentucky
Louisiana
Michigan
Minnesota
Mississippi
Missouri
Nebraska
Nevada
New Mexico
North Carolina
North Dakota
Ohio
Oklahoma
Oregon
South Carolina
South Dakota
Tennessee
Texas
Utah
Virginia
Washington
Wisconsin

COMPETITORS

EXPEDITORS INTERNATIONAL OF WASHINGTON INC.
FORWARD AIR CORPORATION
HEARTLAND EXPRESS INC.
LANDSTAR SYSTEM INC.
MARTEN TRANSPORT LTD.
OLD DOMINION FREIGHT LINE INC.
ROADRUNNER TRANSPORTATION SYSTEMS INC.
SCHNEIDER NATIONAL INC.
U.S. XPRESS ENTERPRISES INC.
USA TRUCK INC.
WERNER ENTERPRISES INC.

HISTORICAL FINANCIALS

Company Type: Public

Income Statement
FYE: December 31

	REVENUE ($ mil.)	NET INCOME ($ mil.)	NET PROFIT MARGIN	EMPLOYEES
12/20	1,822.3	138.3	7.6%	10,600
12/19	1,786.7	113.7	6.4%	10,400
12/18	1,653.8	104.9	6.3%	10,300
12/17	1,378.5	91.1	6.6%	9,800
12/16	1,218.4	48.0	3.9%	8,900
Annual Growth	10.6%	30.3%	—	4.5%

2020 Year-End Financials

Debt ratio: 4.5%
Return on equity: 15.5%
Cash ($ mil.): 25.3
Current ratio: 0.99
Long-term debt ($ mil.): 50.3

No. of shares (mil.): 26.2
Dividends
  Yield: —
  Payout: —
Market value ($ mil.): 4,744.0

	STOCK PRICE ($) FY Close	P/E High/Low		PER SHARE ($) Earnings	Dividends	Book Value
12/20	180.80	36	12	5.20	0.00	36.64
12/19	93.12	24	12	4.30	0.00	31.43
12/18	55.82	21	13	3.99	0.00	27.08
12/17	70.75	20	12	3.49	0.00	22.80
12/16	44.15	25	10	1.87	0.00	19.08
Annual Growth	42.3%	—		29.1%	—	17.7%

Sandy Spring Bancorp Inc

Sandy Spring Bancorp is the holding company for Sandy Spring Bank which operates around 50 branches in the Baltimore and Washington DC metropolitan areas. Founded in 1868 the bank is one of the largest and oldest headquartered in Maryland. It provides standard deposit services including checking and savings accounts money market accounts and CDs. Commercial and residential real estate loans account for nearly three-quarters of the company's loan portfolio; the remainder is a mix of consumer loans business loans and equipment leases. The company also offers personal investing services wealth management trust services insurance and retirement planning.

Operations

Sandy Spring Bancorp's nonbank subsidiaries include money manager West Financial Services and Sandy Spring Insurance which sells annuities and operates insurance agencies Chesapeake Insurance Group and Neff & Associates.

Financial Performance

The company's revenue increased in fiscal 2013 compared to the previous year. It reported $196.9 million in revenue for fiscal 2013 after bringing in revenue of $190.8 million in fiscal 2012.

The company's net income also went up in fiscal 2013 compared to the prior period. It claimed a profit of about $44 million in fiscal 2013 after netting a little more than $36 million in fiscal 2012.

Sandy Spring Bancorp's cash on hand increased by about $43 million in fiscal 2013 compared to fiscal 2012 levels.

Mergers and Acquisitions

In 2012 Sandy Spring Bancorp acquired CommerceFirst Bancorp a small Maryland bank with a strong Small Business Administration lending practice. The $25.4 million transaction added five branches to Sandy Spring Bank's network.

EXECUTIVES

Chief Financial Officer & Executive Vice President, Philip Mantua, $419,885 total compensation
Independent Chairman Of The Board, Robert Orndorff
Independent Director, Craig Ruppert
Vice Chairman, President & Chief Executive Officer, Daniel Schrider, $804,808 total compensation
Independent Director, Mark Friis
Executive Vice President, Chief Information Officer, John Sadowski
Executive Vice President Of The Bank, R. Louis Caceres, $412,462 total compensation
Independent Director, Gary Nakamoto
Independent Director, Ralph Boyd
Executive Vice President, Chief Risk Officer, Kevin Slane, $362,283 total compensation
Executive Vice President, Kenneth Cook
Independent Director, Brian Lemek
Independent Director, Christina O'meara
Independent Director, Walter Martz
Executive Vice President, General Counsel, Secretary, Aaron Kaslow, $141,346 total compensation
Independent Director, Mona Stephenson
Executive Vice President And Chief Banking Officer, Joseph O'brien, $487,885 total compensation
Executive Vice President, Chief Credit Officer Of The Bank, Ronda Mcdowell
Auditors: Ernst & Young

LOCATIONS

HQ: Sandy Spring Bancorp Inc
17801 Georgia Avenue, Olney, MD 20832
Phone: 301 774-6400
Web: www.sandyspringbank.com

PRODUCTS/OPERATIONS

2015 Sales

	$ mil.	% of total
Interest Income:		
Interest and fees on loans and leases	135.2	65
Interest and dividends on investment securities	22.5	11
Other	0.6	-
Non-interest Income:		
Wealth management income	19.9	10
Service charges on deposit accounts	7.6	4
Insurance agency commissions	5.2	2
Bank card fees	4.7	2
Mortgage banking activities	3.1	2
Other Income	9.4	4
Total	208.2	100

COMPETITORS

BERKSHIRE HILLS BANCORP INC.
BNC BANCORP
CAMDEN NATIONAL CORPORATION
CITY HOLDING COMPANY
FIRST COMMONWEALTH FINANCIAL CORPORATION
FIRST MIDWEST BANCORP INC.
MAINSOURCE FINANCIAL GROUP INC.
PACIFIC CONTINENTAL CORPORATION
S & T BANCORP INC.
SUN BANCORP INC.
WESBANCO INC.
WEST BANCORPORATION INC.

HISTORICAL FINANCIALS

Company Type: Public

Income Statement
FYE: December 31

	ASSETS ($ mil.)	NET INCOME ($ mil.)	INCOME AS % OF ASSETS	EMPLOYEES
12/21	12,590.7	235.1	1.9%	1,116
12/20	12,798.4	96.9	0.8%	1,152
12/19	8,629.0	116.4	1.3%	932
12/18	8,243.2	100.8	1.2%	932
12/17	5,446.6	53.2	1.0%	754
Annual Growth	23.3%	45.0%	—	10.3%

2021 Year-End Financials

Return on assets: 1.8%
Return on equity: 15.7%
Long-term debt ($ mil.): —
No. of shares (mil.): 45.1
Sales ($ mil): 552.3

Dividends
  Yield: 2.6%
  Payout: 24.5%
Market value ($ mil.): 2,169.0

	STOCK PRICE ($) FY Close	P/E High/Low		PER SHARE ($) Earnings	Dividends	Book Value
12/21	48.08	10	6	4.98	1.28	33.68
12/20	32.19	17	9	2.18	1.20	31.24
12/19	37.88	12	9	3.25	1.18	32.40
12/18	31.34	15	11	2.82	1.10	30.06
12/17	39.02	21	17	2.20	1.04	23.50
Annual Growth	5.4%	—		22.7%	5.3%	9.4%

Santa Cruz County Bank (CA)

Auditors: Crowe LLP

LOCATIONS

HQ: Santa Cruz County Bank (CA)
740 Front Street Ste 220, Santa Cruz, CA 95060
Phone: 831 457-5003
Web: www.sccountybank.com

HISTORICAL FINANCIALS

Company Type: Public

Income Statement
FYE: December 31

	ASSETS ($ mil.)	NET INCOME ($ mil.)	INCOME AS % OF ASSETS	EMPLOYEES
12/20	1,422.8	17.5	1.2%	0
12/19	1,070.9	12.2	1.1%	0
12/18	662.4	11.3	1.7%	0
12/17	629.9	6.7	1.1%	0
12/16	588.2	6.4	1.1%	0
Annual Growth	24.7%	28.2%	—	

2020 Year-End Financials

Return on assets: 1.4%
Return on equity: 10.9%
Long-term debt ($ mil.): —
No. of shares (mil.): 4.2
Sales ($ mil): 55.9

Dividends
  Yield: 0.8%
  Payout: 7.8%
Market value ($ mil.): 172.0

	STOCK PRICE ($) FY Close	P/E High/Low		PER SHARE ($) Earnings	Dividends	Book Value
12/20	40.51	14	7	4.13	0.30	39.76
12/19	52.50	13	11	4.06	0.27	35.68
12/18	45.60	13	11	4.19	0.28	25.44
12/17	48.95	20	15	2.51	0.17	21.49
12/16	39.50	16	11	2.43	0.17	19.13
Annual Growth	0.6%	—	—	14.2%	16.1%	20.1%

SB Financial Group Inc

SB Financial Group (formerly Rurban Financial) is the holding company The State Bank and Trust Company (dba State Bank) which has more than 20 branches in northwestern Ohio and another in northeastern Indiana. The banks offer products including checking and savings accounts money market accounts credit cards IRAs and CDs. Commercial and agricultural loans account for approximately two-thirds of the company's loan portfolio; the bank also writes mortgage and consumer loans. State Bank Wealth Management (formerly Reliance Financial Services) a unit of State Bank offers trust and investment management services as well as brokerage services through an alliance with Raymond James.

Strategy

The company changed its name to SB Financial Group in April 2013. Concurrently it changed the name of its bank to State Bank to more closely identify the holding company with its primary revenue generator State Bank. The firm also changed its trading symbol from RBNF to SBFG.

The company spun off its technology subsidiary RDSI Banking Systems as a separate entity in 2010.

EXECUTIVES

Chairman Of The Board, President, Chief Executive Officer, Mark Klein, $411,623 total compensation
Independent Director, Robert Fawcett
Independent Director, Rita Kissner
Lead Independent Director, Richard Hardgrove
Executive Vice President, Chief Risk Officer, Secretary, Keeta Diller, $135,000 total compensation
Independent Director, Gaylyn Finn
Independent Director, George Carter
Executive Vice President And Chief Technology Innovation And Operations Officer, Ernesto Gaytan, $217,039 total compensation
Independent Director, Tom Helberg
Independent Director, Timothy Claxton
Chief Financial Officer, Executive Vice President Of The Company And State Bank, Anthony Cosentino, $227,793 total compensation
Independent Director, Timothy Stolly
Independent Director, William Martin
Auditors: BKD, LLP

LOCATIONS

HQ: SB Financial Group Inc
401 Clinton Street, Defiance, OH 43512
Phone: 419 783-8950
Web: www.yourSBFinancial.com

PRODUCTS/OPERATIONS

Selected Subsidiaries and Divisions
The State Bank and Trust Company
Reliance Financial Services
RDSI Banking Systems

COMPETITORS

CITIZENS HOLDING COMPANY
CIVISTA BANCSHARES INC.
FB FINANCIAL CORPORATION
FIFTH THIRD BANCORP
SYNOVUS FINANCIAL CORP.

HISTORICAL FINANCIALS
Company Type: Public

Income Statement
FYE: December 31

	ASSETS ($ mil.)	NET INCOME ($ mil.)	INCOME AS % OF ASSETS	EMPLOYEES
12/20	1,257.8	14.9	1.2%	244
12/19	1,038.5	11.9	1.2%	252
12/18	986.8	11.6	1.2%	250
12/17	876.6	11.0	1.3%	234
12/16	816.0	8.7	1.1%	227
Annual Growth	11.4%	14.2%	—	1.8%

2020 Year-End Financials
Return on assets: 1.3%
Return on equity: 10.6%
Long-term debt ($ mil.): —
No. of shares (mil.): 7.7
Sales ($ mil): 72.7
Dividends
Yield: 2.3%
Payout: 21.4%
Market value ($ mil.): 142.0

	STOCK PRICE ($) FY Close	P/E High/Low		PER SHARE ($) Earnings	Dividends	Book Value
12/20	18.28	11	5	1.87	0.40	18.46
12/19	19.69	12	10	1.44	0.36	16.70
12/18	16.45	13	10	1.44	0.32	19.10
12/17	18.49	9	7	1.66	0.27	18.68
12/16	16.05	11	7	1.31	0.23	17.02
Annual Growth	3.3%	—	—	9.2%	15.0%	2.1%

Schnitzer Steel Industries Inc

Schnitzer Steel Industries is one of North America's largest recyclers of ferrous and nonferrous metal including end-of-life vehicles and a manufacturer of finished steel products. The company scrap to steelmakers primarily in the Western US and Western Canada. Schnitzer offers a range of products and services to meet global demand through its network that includes approximately 50 retail self-service auto parts stores more than 50 metals recycling facilities and an electric arc furnace (EAF) steel mill. Its Pick-n-Pull unit procures the significant majority of the company's salvaged vehicles and sell serviceable used auto parts from these vehicles. The US accounts for more than 40% of the total sales.

Operations

Schnitzer acquires processes and recycles end-of-life (salvaged) vehicles rail cars home appliances industrial machinery manufacturing scrap and construction and demolition scrap through its facilities.

The company invests in nonferrous metal extraction and separation technologies in order to maximize the recoverability of valuable nonferrous metal and to meet the metal purity requirements of customers. In addition to the sale of recycled metal processed at the company's facilities it also provides a variety of recycling and related services including brokering the sale of ferrous and nonferrous scrap metal generated by industrial entities and demolition projects to customers in the domestic market among other services.

Its steel mill melt shop includes an EAF a ladle refining furnace with enhanced steel chemistry refining capabilities and a five-strand continuous billet caster. The rolling mill has an effective annual production capacity under current conditions of approximately 580 thousand tons of finished steel products.

Recycled ferrous metal is a key feedstock used in the production of finished steel and is largely categorized into heavy melting steel (HMS) plate and structural (bonus) and shredded scrap (shred). Selling catalytic converters to specialty processors that extract the nonferrous precious metals including platinum palladium and rhodium nonferrous products include mixed metal joint products recovered from the shredding process as well as aluminum copper stainless steel nickel brass titanium lead and high temperature alloys.

Overall ferrous products account for about 55% nonferrous provides approximately 25% steel products generates nearly 15% and retail and other represent the remaining sales.

Geographic Reach

Headquartered in Portland Oregon Schnitzer has about 45 operating facilities and administrative offices in some two dozen US states Puerto Rico and Western Canada. It has seven deep water export facilities located on both the East and West Coasts of the US and in Hawaii and Puerto Rico. The company's auto parts business sells used auto parts through its nearly 50 self-service facilities located in North America. Schnitzer serves customers in nearly 25 countries. About more than 40% of the company's revenue is generated from the US.

Sales and Marketing

The company sells steel directly from its minimill in McMinnville Oregon and its owned distribution center in California (near Los Angeles).

Specialty steelmakers foundries refineries smelters wholesalers and other recycled metal processors globally are the primary end markets for its recycled nonferrous metal products. It delivers recycled ferrous and nonferrous scrap metal to customers outside of the US by ship and to US-based customers by barge rail and truck.

The company spends $6 million annually on advertising.

Financial Performance

The company's revenue for 2021 was $2.8 billion a 61% growth compared to the previous year's revenue of $1.7 billion. The increase is primarily due to a higher sales volume in the company's ferrous and nonferrous business.

HOOVER'S HANDBOOK OF EMERGING COMPANIES 2022

In 2021 the company had a net income of $170 million a $172.2 million increase from the previous year's net loss of $2.2 million.

The company's cash at the end of 2021 was $27.8 million. Operating activities generated $190.1 million while investing activities used $117.6 million mainly for capital expenditures. Financing activities used another $62.8 million primarily for repayments of long-term debt.

Strategy

Schnitzer invests in nonferrous metal extraction and separation technologies in order to maximize the recoverability of valuable nonferrous metal and to meet the metal purity requirements of customers. It has a major strategic initiative currently underway and partially complete to replace upgrade and add to its existing nonferrous metal recovery technologies that is expected to increase metal recovery yields provide for additional product optionality create higher quality furnace-ready products and reduce the metallic portion of shredder residue disposed in landfills. The rollout of these new technologies is anticipated to be completed in fiscal 2022 with total capital expenditures estimated to be $115 million of which $77 million has been incurred including $36 million during fiscal 2021.

Mergers and Acquisitions

In mid-2021 Schnitzer entered into a definitive agreement with the US-based Columbus Recycling a leading provider of ferrous and non-ferrous metal recycling products and services to acquire eight operating facilities across several states in the Southeast including Mississippi Tennessee and Kentucky.

HISTORY

Sam Schnitzer a draftee into the Russian army found his way to Austria then to the US in 1904. The next year he moved to Portland where he and partner Henry Wolf formed Alaska Junk in 1908. The enterprise grew buying sawmills logging camps and shipyards. Sam's son Morris formed Schnitzer Steel Products on his own in 1936. After WWII the patriarch turned Alaska Junk over to sons Gilbert Leonard Manuel and Morris.

The brothers changed the company's name to Alaska Steel and acquired Woodbury a local steel distributor in 1956. The Schnitzers formed Lasco Shipping in 1963. Morris' Schnitzer Steel Products returned to family control and in 1978 Alaska Steel and Woodbury combined to make Metra Steel. The company boosted its vertical integration by acquiring the Cascade Steel minimill in 1984.

Leonard Schnitzer's son-in-law Robert Philip became president in 1991. Two years later the family's steel businesses went public as Schnitzer Steel Industries. In 1994 the company launched a $42 million expansion program. It bought Manufacturing Management (then Washington's #1 scrap processor 1995) and Proler International (scrap-related environmental services 1996) adding 17 scrap-collecting and -processing facilities primarily on the East Coast.

Schnitzer Steel Industries began producing wire rod and coiled rebar at its Oregon facility in 1997.The next year Schnitzer Steel Industries and joint venture partner Hugo Neu added facilities in Maine Massachusetts and New Hampshire.

In 2002 the company's Portland Oregon metals recycling facility went through a $4.4 million renovation to increase efficiency in loading recycled metal cargoes. The next year Schnitzer Steel In-

dustries purchased Pick-N-Pull a major operator of auto salvage yards for about $71 million.

Schnitzer Steel Industries unwound its joint ventures with Hugo Neu in 2005.

In 2009 the company divested its full-service auto parts operations selling the business to LKQ Corporation in exchange for that company's self-service auto parts business. Schnitzer then rebranded the former LKQ businesses with the Pick-N-Pull name.

In fiscal 2013 the company spent $26 million to buy four used auto parts facilities in Richmond and Surrey British Columbia; two used auto parts facilities in Kansas and Missouri; two used auto parts facilities in Massachusetts; and one used auto parts facility in Rhode Island.

In 2013 Schnitzer acquired all of the equity interests of Pick A Part Inc. a used auto parts business with one store in the Olympia metropolitan area in Washington which expanded its presence in the Pacific Northwest.

EXECUTIVES

Chairman Of The Board, President, Chief Executive Officer, Tamara Lundgren, $1,193,530 total compensation

Independent Director, Judith Johansen

Senior Vice President, President, Operations, Michael Henderson, $637,322 total compensation

Independent Director, David Jahnke

Senior Vice President, President - Recycling Products And Services, Steven Heiskell, $558,602 total compensation

Independent Director, Rhonda Hunter

Senior Vice President, General Counsel, Corporate Secretary, Peter Saba, $526,712 total compensation

Chief Human Resource Officer, Senior Vice President, Chief - Corporate Operations, Erich Wilson

Independent Director, Glenda Minor

Chief Financial Officer, Executive Vice President, Chief Strategy Officer, Richard Peach, $737,766 total compensation

Deputy Chief Financial Officer, Chief Accounting Officer, Vice President, Stefano Gaggini

Independent Director, Michael Sutherlin

Auditors: PricewaterhouseCoopers LLP

LOCATIONS

HQ: Schnitzer Steel Industries Inc
299 SW Clay Street, Suite 350, Portland, OR 97201
Phone: 503 224-9900
Web: www.schnitzersteel.com

PRODUCTS/OPERATIONS

2016 sales

	$ mil.	% of total
Ferrous scrap metal	619.1	46
Nonferrous scrap metal	340.0	25
Finished steel products	269.4	20
Retail & Other	123.5	9
Semi-finished steel products	0.5	-
Total	**1,352.5**	**100**

2016 sales

	$ mil.	% of total
Auto & Metal Recycling Business	1,173.0	87
Steel Manufacturing Business	269.9	20
Eliminations (90.2) (7)		
Total	**1,352.5**	**100**

COMPETITORS

CARAUSTAR RECOVERED FIBER GROUP INC.
CLEVELAND-CLIFFS STEEL HOLDING
HOLDING CORPORATION
COMMERCIAL METALS COMPANY
DERICHEBOURG EUROPEAN METAL INDUSTRIES RECYCLING LIMITED
METALS USA HOLDINGS CORP.
OMNISOURCE LLC
RECYLEX SA
RYERSON CORPORATION
SGK VENTURES LLC
UNITED STATES STEEL CORPORATION
WORTHINGTON INC.

HISTORICAL FINANCIALS

Company Type: Public

Income Statement

FYE: August 31

	REVENUE ($ mil.)	NET INCOME ($ mil.)	NET PROFIT MARGIN	EMPLOYEES
08/21	2,758.5	165.1	6.0%	3,167
08/20	1,712.3	(4.1)	—	3,032
08/19	2,132.7	56.3	2.6%	3,363
08/18	2,364.7	156.4	6.6%	3,575
08/17	1,687.5	44.5	2.6%	3,183
Annual Growth	**13.1%**	**38.8%**	**—**	**(0.1%)**

2021 Year-End Financials

Debt ratio: 5.0%
Return on equity: 21.8%
Cash ($ mil.): 27.8
Current ratio: 1.54
Long-term debt ($ mil.): 71.3
No. of shares (mil.): 27.5
Dividends
Yield: 1.9%
Payout: 21.6%
Market value ($ mil.): 1,303.0

	STOCK PRICE ($) FY Close	P/E High/Low		PER SHARE ($) Earnings	Dividends	Book Value
08/21	47.31	10	3	5.66	0.94	30.36
08/20	19.74	—	—	(0.15)	0.75	24.97
08/19	22.14	14	10	2.00	0.75	26.14
08/18	26.35	7	4	5.47	0.75	24.94
08/17	26.90	19	11	1.58	0.75	19.72
Annual Growth	**15.2%**			**37.6%**	**5.7%**	**11.4%**

SciPlay Corp

Auditors: DELOITTE & TOUCHE LLP

LOCATIONS

HQ: SciPlay Corp
6601 Bermuda Road, Las Vegas, NV 89119
Phone: 702 897-7150
Web: www.sciplay.com

HISTORICAL FINANCIALS

Company Type: Public

Income Statement

FYE: December 31

	REVENUE ($ mil.)	NET INCOME ($ mil.)	NET PROFIT MARGIN	EMPLOYEES
12/20	582.2	20.9	3.6%	602
12/19	465.8	32.4	7.0%	501
12/18	416.2	39.0	9.4%	390
12/17	361.4	23.1	6.4%	0
Annual Growth	**17.2%**	**(3.3%)**	**—**	**—**

2020 Year-End Financials

Debt ratio: —	No. of shares (mil.): 126.3
Return on equity: 31.0%	Dividends
Cash ($ mil.): 268.9	Yield: —
Current ratio: 6.03	Payout: —
Long-term debt ($ mil.): —	Market value ($ mil.): 1,749.0

	STOCK PRICE ($) FY Close	P/E High/Low		PER SHARE ($) Earnings	Dividends	Book Value
12/20	13.85	20	7	0.86	0.00	0.63
12/19	12.29	11	6	1.43	0.00	0.43
12/18	0.00	—	—	(0.00)	0.00	(0.00)
Annual Growth	—			—	—	—

Scripps (EW) Company (The)

The E. W. Scripps Company (Scripps) is a diverse media enterprise serving audiences and businesses through a portfolio of local and national media brands including next-generation national news network Newsy; five national multicast networks ? Bounce Grit Laff Court TV and Court TV Mystery ? that make up the Katz Networks; and Triton a global leader in digital audio technology and measurement services. Scripps also owns about 60 local TV stations in nearly 40 markets that reach about 25% of US television households. The company has affiliations with all of the "Big Four" television networks as well as the CW and MyNetworkTV networks. The Scripps family controls the company through various trusts. In early 2021 Scripps acquired the Florida-based ION Media from Black Diamond for approximately $2.65 billion.

Operations

The company operates in two business segments: Local Media (about 80% of sales) and National Media (nearly 20%).

The Local Media segment includes some 60 local broadcast stations and its related digital operations. It is comprised of roughly 20 ABC affiliates some 10 NBC affiliates nine CBS affiliates and four FOX affiliates. It also has more than 10 CW affiliates ? four on full power stations and eight on multicast; two MyNetwork TV affiliates; three independent stations and ten additional low power stations. It primarily earns revenue from the sale of advertising to local national and political advertisers and retransmission fees received from cable operators telecommunication companies and satellite carriers. It receives retransmission fees from over-the-top virtual MVPDs such as Hulu YouTubeTV and AT&T Now.

The National Media segment includes the company's collection of national brands such as Katz Newsy Triton and other national brands. These operations earn revenue primarily through the sale of advertising.

Scripps' portfolio of content holdings includes Newsy a next-generation national news network; Katz operates five national multicast networks ? Bounce Grit Laff Court TV and Court TV Mystery; and Triton provides innovative technology that enables broadcasters podcasters and online music services to build their audience maximize their revenue and streamline their operations.

The company also runs an investigative reporting newsroom in Washington DC and is the steward of the Scripps National Spelling Bee.

Overall some 65% of the company's revenue came from advertising while retransmission and carriage and other account for the rest.

Geographic Reach

The Cincinnati Ohio-based Scripps has some 60 stations in about 40 markets.

Sales and Marketing

The company's core advertising is comprised of sales to local and national customers. The advertising includes a combination of broadcast spots as well as digital and OTT advertising. Its core advertising revenues accounted for about 40% of Local Media segment's revenues in 2020. National advertising time is generally sold through national sales representative firms that call upon advertising agencies whose clients typically include automobile manufacturers and dealer groups telecommunications companies and insurance providers. Through its sales offices in Washington DC Political advertising is sold to presidential gubernatorial Senate and House of Representative candidates as well as for state races and local issues. It is also sold to political action groups (PACs) or other advocacy groups. Political advertising revenues were about 20% of its Local Media segment's revenues in 2020.

The company also has consent agreements with multi-channel video programming distributors (MVPD). The MVPDs are cable operators telecommunication companies and satellite carriers who pays the company to offer its programming to the customers.

Financial Performance

The company's revenue for fiscal 2020 increased by 37% to $1.9 billion compared to the prior year's $1.4 billion. The increase was driven by an increase in political advertising revenue during this presidential election year as well as an increase in retransmission revenue and growth in its National Media businesses.

Net income for fiscal 2020 was $269.3 million compared to a net loss of $18.4 million.

Cash held by the company at the end of fiscal 2020 increased to $1.6 billion. Operating investing and financing activities provided $277.4 million $317.4 million and $998.2 million respectively.

Strategy

In addition to news programming the company's television stations run network programming syndicated programming and original programming. Scripps' strategy is to balance syndicated programming with original programming that we control. The company believes this strategy improves its Local Media division's financial performance. Original shows it produces itself or in partnership with others.

Mergers and Acquisitions

In early 2021 Scripps acquired the Florida-based ION Media from Black Diamond a national broadcast television network that delivers popular crime and justice procedural programming to more than 100 million US homes through its over-the-air broadcast and pay TV platforms for approximately $2.65 billion. The acquisition strengthens the Scripps' leadership position in broadcasting and accelerates its multiplatform strategy to serve diverse audiences everywhere they seek to be informed and entertained.

Company Background

Founded in 1878 by entrepreneurial journalist E.W. Scripps the company has a long and proud legacy of innovation and an unwavering commitment to journalism.

HISTORY

Edward Willis "E. W." Scripps launched a newspaper empire in 1878 with his creation of The Penny Press in Cleveland. While adding to his string of inexpensive newspapers Scripps demonstrated his fondness for economy by shunning "extras" such as toilet paper and pencils for his employees.

In 1907 Scripps gave the Associated Press a new rival combining three wire services to form United Press. E. W. Scripps' health began deteriorating in the 1920s and Roy Howard was named chairman. Howard's contribution to the burgeoning media enterprise soon was acknowledged when the company's name was changed to the Scripps Howard League. E. W. Scripps died in 1926 leaving a newspaper chain second in size only to Hearst.

In the 1930s Scripps made a foray into radio buying WCPO (Cincinnati) and KNOX (Knoxville Tennessee). Roy Howard placed his son Jack in charge of Scripps' radio holdings; under Jack's leadership Scripps branched into TV. Its first TV station Cleveland's WEWS began broadcasting in 1947. Scripps also made Charlie Brown a household name when it launched the Peanuts comic strip in 1950. By the time Charles Scripps (E. W.'s grandson) became chairman and Jack Howard was appointed president in 1953 the company had amassed 19 newspapers and a handful of radio and TV stations.

United Press merged with Hearst's International News Service in 1958 to become United Press International (UPI). In 1963 Scripps took its broadcasting holdings public as Scripps Howard Broadcasting Company (Scripps retained controlling interest). Scripps Howard Broadcasting expanded its TV station portfolio in the 1970s and 1980s buying KJRH (Tulsa Oklahoma; 1971) KSHB (Kansas City; 1977) KNXV (Phoenix; 1985) WFTS (Tampa; 1986) and WXYZ (Detroit; 1986).

With UPI facing mounting losses Scripps sold the news service in 1982. Under leadership of chief executive Lawrence Leser Scripps began streamlining jettisoning extraneous investments and refocusing on its core business lines. In 1988 after decades of family ownership the company went public as The E. W. Scripps Company (the Scripps family retained a controlling interest).

In 1994 Scripps Howard Broadcasting merged back into E. W. Scripps Company. That year Scripps branched into cable TV when its Home & Garden Television network went on the air. Former newspaper editor William Burleigh became CEO in 1996. Scripps' 1997 purchase of the newspaper and broadcast operations of Harte-Hanks marked the largest acquisition in its history. Scripps promptly traded Harte-Hanks' broadcasting operations for a controlling interest in the Food Network.

Scripps sold television production unit Scripps Howard Productions in 1998. The company sold its Dallas Community Newspaper Group in 1999 and launched the Do It Yourself cable network and affiliated Web site later that year. In 2000 Scripps' financially struggling Rocky Mountain News entered into a joint operating agreement with rival The Denver Post (owned by MediaNews). The Justice Department approved the agreement in 2001. Scripps launched cable channel Fine Living in 2002 aimed at affluent households. (Fine Living was rebranded as the Cooking Channel in 2010.) That year the company shuttered its Scripps Ventures fund which invested in Internet and online commerce businesses.

In late 2002 the company bought a 70% stake in home shopping network company Summit America Television (owner of the Shop At Home cable network) for $49 million. It bought the remaining 30% of the company in 2004.

The Shop At Home network came to an end in 2006 when Scripps shut down the network after several years of nothing but losses at the channel. Scripps later sold its five Shop At Home affiliate television stations to Multicultural Television Broadcasting for $170 million.

Former chairman Charles Scripps died in 2007. At the end of that year the company shuttered the Cincinnati Post and the following year it ceased publication of The Albuquerque Tribune . E. W. Scripps spun off its cable TV operations as Scripps Networks Interactive later in 2008. It shuttered the Rocky Mountain News early in 2009 after attempts to sell the money-losing paper failed.

EXECUTIVES

Executive Vice President, Chief Administrative Officer, Laura Tomlin, $333,443 total compensation
Vice President And General Manager,kmtv, Dave German
Chief Financial Officer, Executive Vice President, Jason Combs
Independent Director, Lauren Fine, $63,939 total compensation
Vice President And General Manager For Wtkr, Scripps, Adam Chase
Independent Director, Wonya Lucas, $61,939 total compensation
Independent Director, R. Michael Scagliotti, $61,939 total compensation
Independent Director, Marcellus Alexander, $61,939 total compensation
Vice President And General Manager For Kxxv And Krhd, Andres Chaparro
Vice President - Emerging Products, Joseph Naylor
President, Chief Executive Officer, Director, Adam Symson, $926,503 total compensation
President - Local Media, Brian Lawlor, $630,960 total compensation
Independent Director, John Hayden, $77,939 total compensation
Executive Vice President, General Counsel, William Appleton, $460,344 total compensation
Executive Vice President, National Networks, Lisa Knutson, $565,027 total compensation
Independent Director, Anne La Dow, $61,939 total compensation
Independent Director, Kelly Conlin, $70,939 total compensation
Independent Director, Charles Barmonde, $60,939 total compensation
Vice President, Controller, Daniel Perschke
Auditors: Deloitte & Touche LLP

LOCATIONS

HQ: Scripps (EW) Company (The)
312 Walnut Street, Cincinnati, OH 45202
Phone: 513 977-3000
Web: www.scripps.com

PRODUCTS/OPERATIONS

Selected Operations
Newspapers
Abilene Reporter-News (Texas)
Anderson Independent-Mail (South Carolina)
Corpus Christi Caller-Times (Texas)
Evansville Courier & Press (Indiana)
Ft. Pierce Tribune (Florida)
Henderson Gleaner (Kentucky)
Kitsap Sun (Washington)
Knoxville News Sentinel (Tennessee)
Memphis Commercial Appeal (Tennessee)
Naples Daily News (Florida)
Redding Record-Searchlight (California)
San Angelo Standard-Times (Texas)
Stuart News (Florida)
Ventura County Star (California)
Wichita Falls Times Record News (Texas)
Television stations
KJRH (NBC; Tulsa OK)
KMCI (Ind; Lawrence KS)
KNXV (ABC Phoenix)
KSHB (NBC Kansas City)
WCPO (ABC Cincinnati)
WEWS (ABC Cleveland)
WFTS (ABC Tampa)
WMAR (ABC Baltimore)
WPTV (NBC; West Palm Beach FL)
WXYZ (ABC Detroit)

COMPETITORS

COX COMMUNICATIONS INC.
CROWN MEDIA HOLDINGS INC.
FORMER CHARTER COMMUNICATIONS PARENT INC.
HAWKEYE ACQUISITION INC.
IHEARTCOMMUNICATIONS INC.
LEE ENTERPRISES INCORPORATED
LIBERTY MEDIA CORPORATION
LIN MEDIA LLC
NBCUNIVERSAL MEDIA LLC
SINCLAIR BROADCAST GROUP INC.

HISTORICAL FINANCIALS

Company Type: Public

Income Statement

FYE: December 31

	REVENUE ($ mil.)	NET INCOME ($ mil.)	NET PROFIT MARGIN	EMPLOYEES
12/20	1,857.4	269.3	14.5%	5,400
12/19	1,423.8	(18.3)	—	5,900
12/18	1,208.4	20.3	1.7%	3,950
12/17	864.8	(13.1)	—	4,100
12/16	943.0	67.2	7.1%	4,100
Annual Growth	18.5%	41.5%		7.1%

2020 Year-End Financials

Debt ratio: 60.3%
Return on equity: 26.0%
Cash ($ mil.): 576.0
Current ratio: 5.84
Long-term debt ($ mil.): 2,923.3
No. of shares (mil.): 81.7
Dividends
Yield: 1.3%
Payout: 50.0%
Market value ($ mil.): 1,250.0

	STOCK PRICE ($) FY Close	P/E High/Low		PER SHARE ($) Earnings	Dividends	Book Value
12/20	15.29	5	2	3.21	0.20	14.23
12/19	15.71	—	—	(0.23)	0.20	11.09
12/18	15.73	71	43	0.24	0.20	11.48
12/17	15.63	—	—	(0.16)	0.00	11.48
12/16	19.33	24	16	0.79	0.00	11.54
Annual Growth	(5.7%)	—	—	42.0%	—	5.4%

Seacoast Banking Corp. of Florida

Seacoast Banking Corporation is the holding company for Seacoast National Bank. It operates some 50 branches in Florida with a concentration in four large city markets. Serving individuals and businesses the bank offers a range of financial products and services including deposit accounts credit cards trust services and private banking. Commercial and residential real estate loans make up most of the bank's lending activities; to a lesser extent it also originates business and consumer loans.

Operations
Seacoast Bank offers traditional banking products such as deposit accounts checking & savings accounts CDs business loans home mortgages and the like. It also makes available to its customers brokerage and annuity services along with insurance products. A division of the bank Seacoast Marine Finance specializes in boat loans which it typically originates itself and then sells into the secondary market.

Geographic Reach
Seacoast National Bank has some 50 branches in 14 counties across Florida stretching from Broward County north through the Treasure Coast and into Orlando and west to Okeechobee and surrounding counties. Its primary markets are Tampa Orlando Port St. Lucie and West Palm Beach/Ft. Lauderdale.

Financial Performance
Seacoast Banking Corporation has done well in recent years steadily growing interest income to nearly $200 million in 2017 up from a low of $70 million just four years prior. The bank registered positive earnings from 2013 forward albeit the results fluctuated wildly.

In 2017 interest income grew 30% to $192 million and non-interest income improved by 25% to $170 million. Its loan portfolio grew ? through organic means as well as via acquisitions ? by almost 30% against which it earned additional interest income. The bank's average net interest margin rose 10 basis points to 3.73%.

Net income also lodged an excellent year increasing 48% from the prior year to $43 million. Although the company incurred an $8.6 million impairment of its deferred tax assets due to the change in US Federal tax law the increase in revenue along with a $15 million gain on the sale an investment it made in Visa company stock pushed up yearly earnings.

Cash at the end of the year was $109 million unchanged from 2016. Financing activities contributed $196 million mostly from an increase in deposits from acquisitions. Investing activities used $246 million in the process of buying and selling securities and originating new loans. Operating activities added $49 million.

Strategy
Seacoast Bank has grown mostly through acquisitions in recent years. Since 2014 it opened one new office and acquired 49 branches (19 of which were subsequently shuttered). Orlando has been a hot destination for it as it transformed its presence there just a few branches to the largest Florida-based bank in the market by 2017. The

bank anticipates continued geographic growth in Florida through organic means but also through acquisition if the right opportunity arises as with the 2017 purchases of NorthStar Banking and Palm Beach Community Bank.

Although it caters to personal customers as well as business clients the focus on businesses has sparked significant growth in the associated loan portfolio. The company tends to commercial clients with revenues exceeding $5 million in specific industry verticals. It takes a comprehensive relationship approach by providing business treasury lending and wealth management services. The commercial loan portfolio grew nearly 300% between year-end 2013 and year-end 2017 from $632 million to $2.5 billion.

The bank significantly expanded its banking technology platform by introducing digital deposit capture on smartphones updating its mobile platforms for consumer and business customers and enhancing its ATM capabilities. Customers have taken to the online functionality and in 2017 the bank processed more digital transactions than it did through its physical branch network.

Mergers and Acquisitions

In 2017 Seacoast purchased NorthStar Banking Corporation adding more than $200 million in assets $170 million in deposits and nearly $140 million in loans to Seacoast's balance sheet. In the same year it acquired Palm Beach Community Bank for some $70 million adding $270 million in loans and four bank branches to Seacoast's operations.

EXECUTIVES

Executive Vice President, Chief Risk Officer, Joseph Forlenza, $325,000 total compensation
Independent Director, Julie Daum
Independent Director, Dennis Arczynski
Chief Financial Officer, Executive Vice President, Tracey Dexter, $289,949 total compensation
President, Chief Executive Officer, And Chairman, Charles Shaffer, $475,000 total compensation
Executive Vice President, Chief Banking Officer, Juliette Kleffel, $375,000 total compensation
Independent Director, Hugh Culbreth
Independent Director, Jacqueline Bradley
Independent Director, Alvaro Monserrat
Independent Director, Maryann Goebel
Auditors: Crowe LLP

LOCATIONS

HQ: Seacoast Banking Corp. of Florida
815 Colorado Avenue, Stuart, FL 34994
Phone: 772 287-4000
Web: www.seacoastbanking.com

PRODUCTS/OPERATIONS

Selected Services
Commercial and retail banking
Mortgage services
Wealth management

COMPETITORS

BANKUNITED INC.	M&T BANK CORPORATION
BYLINE BANCORP INC.	OLD LINE BANCSHARES
CLIFTON BANCORP INC.	INC.
CUSTOMERS BANCORP INC.	SOUTHSIDE BANCSHARES
FIRSTMERIT CORPORATION	INC.
LEGACYTEXAS FINANCIAL GROUP INC.	THE FIRST OF LONG ISLAND CORPORATION

HISTORICAL FINANCIALS

Company Type: Public

Income Statement

FYE: December 31

	ASSETS ($ mil.)	NET INCOME ($ mil.)	INCOME AS % OF ASSETS	EMPLOYEES
12/20	8,342.3	77.7	0.9%	965
12/19	7,108.5	98.7	1.4%	867
12/18	6,747.6	67.2	1.0%	902
12/17	5,810.1	42.8	0.7%	805
12/16	4,680.9	29.2	0.6%	725
Annual Growth	15.5%	27.7%	—	7.4%

2020 Year-End Financials

Return on assets: 1.0%
Return on equity: 7.3%
Long-term debt ($ mil.): —
No. of shares (mil.): 55.2
Sales ($ mil): 348.6

Dividends
Yield: —
Payout: —
Market value ($ mil.): 1,627.0

	STOCK PRICE ($) FY Close	P/E High/Low		PER SHARE ($) Earnings	Dividends	Book Value
12/20	29.45	21	10	1.44	0.00	20.46
12/19	30.57	16	12	1.90	0.00	19.13
12/18	26.02	24	17	1.38	0.00	16.83
12/17	25.21	26	21	0.99	0.00	14.70
12/16	22.06	29	17	0.78	0.00	11.45
Annual Growth	7.5%	—	—	16.6%	—	15.6%

Security Federal Corp (SC)

Security Federal is the holding company for Security Federal Bank which has about a dozen offices in southwestern South Carolina's Aiken and Lexington counties. It expanded into Columbia South Carolina and eastern Georgia in 2007. The bank offers checking and savings accounts credit cards CDs IRAs and other retail products and services. Commercial business and mortgage loans make up more than 60% of the company's lending portfolio which also includes residential mortgages (about 25%) and consumer loans. Security Federal also offers trust services investments and life home and auto insurance.

EXECUTIVES

Independent Director, William Clyburn
Independent Director, Thomas Moore
Independent Chairman Of The Board, Timothy Simmons
Chief Executive Officer And Director, Chairman Of The Board And Chief Executive Officer Of The Bank, J. Chris Verenes, $363,462 total compensation
President, Director Of Security Federal And The Bank, Roy Lindburg, $278,519 total compensation
Independent Director, Harry Weeks
Director, Richard Harmon
President Of Security Federal Bank, Philip Wahl, $202,800 total compensation
Independent Director, Frampton Toole
Independent Director, Frank Thomas
Chief Financial Officer, Darrell Rains
Secretary, Independent Director, Robert Alexander
Auditors: Elliott Davis, LLC

LOCATIONS

HQ: Security Federal Corp (SC)
238 Richland Avenue Northwest, Aiken, SC 29801
Phone: 803 641-3000
Web: www.securityfederalbank.com

PRODUCTS/OPERATIONS

Selected Subsidiaries
Federal Trust
Security Federal Bank
Security Federal Insurance Inc.
Security Federal Investments Inc.
Security Federal Services Corporation
Security Federal Trust Inc.

COMPETITORS

FIRST UNITED CORPORATION	SB ONE BANCORP

HISTORICAL FINANCIALS

Company Type: Public

Income Statement

FYE: December 31

	ASSETS ($ mil.)	NET INCOME ($ mil.)	INCOME AS % OF ASSETS	EMPLOYEES
12/20	1,171.7	7.0	0.6%	0
12/19	963.2	7.7	0.8%	250
12/18	912.6	7.2	0.8%	233
12/17	868.8	5.9	0.7%	223
12/16	812.6	5.9	0.7%	219
Annual Growth	9.6%	4.4%	—	—

2020 Year-End Financials

Return on assets: 0.6%
Return on equity: 6.9%
Long-term debt ($ mil.): —
No. of shares (mil.): 3.2
Sales ($ mil): 48.5

Dividends
Yield: 0.0%
Payout: 18.2%
Market value ($ mil.): 84.0

	STOCK PRICE ($) FY Close	P/E High/Low		PER SHARE ($) Earnings	Dividends	Book Value
12/20	25.75	16	10	2.19	0.40	34.40
12/19	35.00	13	11	2.50	0.38	31.03
12/18	28.30	13	12	2.32	0.36	27.26
12/17	31.30	16	12	1.91	0.36	26.39
12/16	35.00	17	10	1.99	0.32	22.60
Annual Growth	(7.4%)	—	—	2.4%	5.7%	11.1%

Security National Financial Corp

There are three certainties — life death and mortgage payments — and Security National Financial has you covered on all fronts. Its largest unit SecurityNational Mortgage makes residential and commercial mortgage loans through some 70 offices in more than a dozen states. Its Security National Life Memorial Insurance Company and Southern Security Life subsidiaries sell life and diving or related sports accident insurance annuities and funeral plans in about 40 states. Security National Financial also owns about 15 mortuaries and cemeteries in Utah Arizona and California. The family of chairman and CEO George Quist controls more than half of Security National Financial.

EXECUTIVES

Chairman Of The Board, President, Chief Executive Officer, Scott Quist, $558,950 total compensation
Independent Director, H. Craig Moody
Independent Director, Robert Hunter
Vice President, National Marketing Director Of Life Insurance, Director, Jason Overbaugh
Vice President - Memorial Services, Assistant Secretary, General Counsel, Adam Quist
Vice President, General Counsel, Director, S. Andrew Quist, $365,667 total compensation
Senior General Counsel, Secretary, Jeffrey Stephens, $205,167 total compensation
Chief Financial Officer, Treasurer, Garrett Sill, $239,333 total compensation
Vice President - Mortgage Operations, President Of Security National Mortgage, Stephen Johnson, $360,000 total compensation
Independent Director, Gilbert Fuller
Independent Director, John Cook
Auditors: DELOITTE & TOUCHE LLP

LOCATIONS

HQ: Security National Financial Corp
433 West Ascension Way, Salt Lake City, UT 84123
Phone: 801 264-1060   **Fax:** 801 265-9882
Web: www.securitynational.com

PRODUCTS/OPERATIONS

Selected Subsidiaries
California Memorial Estates Inc.
Cottonwood Mortuary Inc.
Crystal Rose Funeral Home Inc.
Deseret Memorial Inc.
Greer-Wilson Funeral Home Inc.
Holladay Memorial Park Inc.
Insuradyne Corporation
Memorial Estates Inc.
Memorial Insurance Company of America
Memorial Mortuary
Paradise Chapel Funeral Home Inc.
Security National Capital Inc.
Security National Life Insurance Company

COMPETITORS

CINCINNATI FINANCIAL CORPORATION
DIRECT GENERAL CORPORATION
Industrial Alliance Insurance and Financial Services In
STANCORP FINANCIAL GROUP INC.
WEST COAST LIFE INSURANCE COMPANY

HISTORICAL FINANCIALS

Company Type: Public

Income Statement   FYE: December 31

	ASSETS ($ mil.)	NET INCOME ($ mil.)	INCOME AS % OF ASSETS	EMPLOYEES
12/20	1,548.9	55.6	3.6%	1,708
12/19	1,334.4	10.8	0.8%	1,293
12/18	1,050.8	21.6	2.1%	1,433
12/17	982.1	14.1	1.4%	1,453
12/16	854.0	14.2	1.7%	1,657
Annual Growth	16.0%	40.5%	—	0.8%

2020 Year-End Financials

Return on assets: 3.8%
Return on equity: 24.0%
Long-term debt ($ mil.): —
No. of shares (mil.): 19.9
Sales ($ mil): 481.4

Dividends
Yield: —
Payout: 5.6%
Market value ($ mil.): 167.0

	STOCK PRICE ($) FY Close	P/E High/Low		PER SHARE ($) Earnings	Dividends	Book Value
12/20	8.35	3	1	2.74	0.00	13.21
12/19	5.85	11	8	0.56	0.00	10.09
12/18	5.16	5	4	1.11	0.00	8.84
12/17	5.25	10	7	0.73	0.00	7.78
12/16	6.50	10	6	0.75	0.00	6.85
Annual Growth	6.5%	—	—	38.1%	—	17.8%

Selective Insurance Group Inc

Property/casualty insurance holding company Selective Insurance Group's reach primarily covers the entire eastern US seaboard and much of the Midwest. Commercial policies include workers' compensation and commercial automobile property and liability insurance. Personal lines include homeowners and automobile insurance. The company also offers federal flood insurance administration services throughout the US and some excess and surplus (E&S nonstandard) insurance. Selective Insurance Group operates through four reportable segments: Standard Commercial Lines Standard Personal Lines E&S Lines and Investments.

Operations

Selective operates in four segments: Standard Commercial Lines; Standard Personal Lines; E&S Lines; and Investments.

Selective's Standard Commercial Lines segment is comprised of property and casualty insurance products and services provided in the standard marketplace to commercial enterprises; typically businesses non-profit organizations and local government agencies and accounts for about three-fourths of Selective's total revenue.

Standard Personal Lines is comprised of property and casualty insurance products and services provided primarily to individuals acquiring coverage in the standard marketplace. It generates more than 10% of total revenue.

The E&S Lines segment is comprised of property and casualty insurance products and services provided to customers who are unable to obtain coverage in the standard marketplace. The company is currently only write commercial lines E&S coverages. The segment accounts for nearly 10% of total revenue.

Investments (less than 10% of total revenue) which invests the premiums collected by its insurance operations and amounts generated through its capital management strategies which include the issuance of debt and equity securities.

The company's flood insurance is sold to businesses and individuals through the National Flood Insurance Program.

Geographic Reach

Selective primarily writes commercial policies in more than 25 Eastern Midwestern and Southwestern states and the Washington DC. Personal policies are primarily sold in about 15 states in the Eastern Southwestern and Midwest. The company also offers flood and E&S insurance policies in all 50 states and the Washington DC.

It maintains its headquarters in New Jersey and regional branch offices in New Jersey Indiana Maryland North Carolina Pennsylvania and Arizona.

Sales and Marketing

Some 1400 independent retail agents sell Selective's Standard Commercial Lines products and the 850 of these distribution partners also sells its Standard Personal Lines business with a focus on providing policies to small and mid-sized businesses and government entities. The company's nationwide flood protection products are sold by a network of some 6000 retail agents while E&S policies are sold through about 90 wholesale agencies and brokers.

Target clients include manufacturing and wholesale contractor community and public services and mercantile and services customers.

Financial Performance

The company in 2020 had a total revenue of $2.9 billion a 3% increase from the previous year's total revenue of $2.8 billion. The company had higher net premiums earned as well as net investment income earned for the year.

In 2020 the company had a net income of $246.4 million a 9% decrease from the previous year's net income of $271.6 million.

The company's cash at the end of the year was $394000. Operating activities generated $90.9 million while investing activities used $231.2 million mainly for purchase of short-term investments. Financing activities provided another $140.4 million.

Strategy

Selective's three primary areas of interest are improving its overall customer experience refining its underwriting tools and enhancing its technological capabilities.

As part of its digital strategy Selective provides customers with a mobile application and a web-based portal that provides its customers with on-demand self-service access to account information and the ability to electrically pay the bills and report claims. It also provides value-added services such as proactive messaging about vehicle and product recalls adverse weather activity and claim status updates.

In mid-2020 Selective announced the launch of Smart Secure an all-in-one smart home and security program that gives Selective's customers new levels of control over their home protection. The new Smart Secure incorporates years of customer insights into a unique offering centered on giving customers the power of choice to design a system to meet their needs. This development enhances Selective's technological capabilities even further.

Company Background

In the 1920s Daniel L.B. Smith was a general store operator in Sussex County New Jersey. Almost by accident he began selling insurance out of one of his store locations and he decided that the area needed a local insurance company. With an initial investment of $20000 Smith and several partners opened Selected Risks Insurance Company. The company expanded beyond its New Jersey origins over the next several decades.

EXECUTIVES

Chairman, Gregory Murphy, $807,692 total compensation
Independent Director, John Burville

Executive Vice President, Chief Compliance Officer, General Counsel, Michael Lanza, $579,615 total compensation
President, Chief Executive Officer, Director, John Marchioni, $951,923 total compensation
Non-independent Director, William Rue
Lead Independent Director, J. Brian Thebault
Independent Director, Philip Urban
Chief Financial Officer, Executive Vice President, Mark Wilcox, $661,733 total compensation
Independent Director, John Scheid
Independent Director, H. Elizabeth Mitchell
Independent Director, Thomas McCarthy
Independent Director, Robert Doherty
Auditors: KPMG LLP

LOCATIONS

HQ: Selective Insurance Group Inc
40 Wantage Avenue, Branchville, NJ 07890
Phone: 973 948-3000   **Fax:** 973 948-0282
Web: www.selective.com

PRODUCTS/OPERATIONS

2017 Sales by Segment

	$ mil.	% of total
Standard Commercial Lines	1,798.0	73
Standard Personal Lines	290.9	12
E&S Lines	212.8	8
Investments	168.2	7
Total	**2,470.0**	**100**

2017 Sales

	$ mil.	% of total
Net premiums earned	2,291.0	93
Net investment income earned	161.8	7
Other	10.7	-
Net realized gains	6.4	-
Total	**2,470.0**	**100**

COMPETITORS

ALLIANZ INSURANCE PLC
AMERITRUST GROUP INC.
ARTHUR J. GALLAGHER & CO.
DONEGAL GROUP INC.
HALLMARK FINANCIAL SERVICES INC.
HCI GROUP INC.
INFINITY PROPERTY AND CASUALTY CORPORATION
PROTECTIVE INSURANCE CORPORATION
SAFETY INSURANCE GROUP INC.
STATE AUTO FINANCIAL CORPORATION
THE HANOVER INSURANCE GROUP INC

HISTORICAL FINANCIALS

Company Type: Public

Income Statement   FYE: December 31

	ASSETS ($ mil.)	NET INCOME ($ mil.)	INCOME AS % OF ASSETS	EMPLOYEES
12/21	10,461.3	403.8	3.9%	2,440
12/20	9,687.9	246.3	2.5%	2,400
12/19	8,797.1	271.6	3.1%	2,400
12/18	7,952.7	178.9	2.3%	2,290
12/17	7,686.4	168.8	2.2%	2,260
Annual Growth	8.0%	24.4%		1.9%

	STOCK PRICE ($) FY Close	P/E High/Low		Earnings	PER SHARE ($) Dividends	Book Value
12/21	81.94	13	10	6.50	1.03	49.56
12/20	66.98	17	10	4.09	0.94	45.72
12/19	65.19	18	13	4.53	0.83	36.91
12/18	60.94	22	18	3.00	0.74	30.40
12/17	58.70	21	14	2.84	0.66	29.28
Annual Growth	8.7%	—	—	23.0%	11.8%	14.1%

SelectQuote Inc

LOCATIONS

HQ: SelectQuote Inc
6800 West 115th Street, Suite 2511, Overland Park, KS 66211
Phone: 913 599-9225
Web: www.selectquote.com

HISTORICAL FINANCIALS

Company Type: Public

Income Statement   FYE: June 30

	REVENUE ($ mil.)	NET INCOME ($ mil.)	NET PROFIT MARGIN	EMPLOYEES
06/21	937.8	131.0	14.0%	1,944
06/20	531.5	81.1	15.3%	1,900
06/19	337.4	72.5	21.5%	1,800
06/18	233.6	34.9	14.9%	0
Annual Growth	58.9%	55.4%	—	—

2021 Year-End Financials

Debt ratio: 32.1%	No. of shares (mil.): 163.5
Return on equity: 21.4%	Dividends
Cash ($ mil.): 286.4	Yield: —
Current ratio: 4.53	Payout: —
Long-term debt ($ mil.): 459.0	Market value ($ mil.): 3,149.0

	STOCK PRICE ($) FY Close	P/E High/Low		Earnings	PER SHARE ($) Dividends	Book Value
06/21	19.26	40	21	0.79	0.00	4.13
06/20	25.33	—	—	(0.16)	0.00	3.36
06/19	0.00	—	—	0.55	0.00	3.02
Annual Growth	—	—	—	19.8%	—	16.9%

Semler Scientific Inc

Semler Scientific is an emerging medical device maker with a single product. The company markets the FloChec a medical device that measures arterial blood flow to the extremities (fingers and toes) quickly and easily in the doctor's office to diagnose peripheral artery disease. FloChec received FDA clearance in early 2010 and the company began commercially leasing the product in 2011. Founded in 2007 by Dr. Herbert Semler who invented the technology used in FloChec the Portland-based company went public in 2014 with an offering valued at $10 million.

IPO
Semler Scientific went public in February 2014 with an offering of 1.4 million shares of stock priced at $7 each. The IPO raised about $10 million well below the initial expectations of nearly $16 million.

Financial Performance
In 2012 Semler reported total revenue of $1.2 million and a net loss of $2.7 million compared with revenue of $316000 and a loss of nearly $1.9 million in 2011.

EXECUTIVES

Vice President - Finance, Daniel Conger, $210,000 total compensation
Chief Executive Officer, Director, Douglas Murphy-Chutorian, $400,000 total compensation
Independent Director, Wayne Pan
Senior Vice President - Finance And Accounting, Andrew Weinstein, $294,792 total compensation
Independent Director, Arthur Leibowitz
Independent Director, Daniel Messina
Independent Director, Cindy Moon
Auditors: BDO USA, LLP

LOCATIONS

HQ: Semler Scientific Inc
2340-2348 Walsh Avenue, Suite 2344, Santa Clara, CA 95051
Phone: 877 774-4211
Web: www.semlerscientific.com

COMPETITORS

GENMARK DIAGNOSTICS INC.
HAEMONETICS CORPORATION
INOGEN INC.
INTERSECT ENT INC.
LEMAITRE VASCULAR INC.
STRYKER CORPORATION
SURMODICS INC.
UNILIFE CORPORATION

HISTORICAL FINANCIALS

Company Type: Public

Income Statement   FYE: December 31

	REVENUE ($ mil.)	NET INCOME ($ mil.)	NET PROFIT MARGIN	EMPLOYEES
12/20	38.6	14.0	36.3%	86
12/19	32.7	15.0	46.0%	67
12/18	21.4	5.0	23.3%	46
12/17	12.4	(1.5)	—	37
12/16	7.4	(2.5)	—	29
Annual Growth	51.0%	—	—	31.2%

2020 Year-End Financials

Debt ratio: —	No. of shares (mil.): 6.7
Return on equity: 65.1%	Dividends
Cash ($ mil.): 22.0	Yield: —
Current ratio: 5.82	Payout: —
Long-term debt ($ mil.): —	Market value ($ mil.): 630.0

	STOCK PRICE ($) FY Close	P/E High/Low		Earnings	PER SHARE ($) Dividends	Book Value
12/20	94.00	43	14	1.74	0.00	4.45
12/19	48.00	22	15	1.88	0.00	2.00
12/18	34.40	48	9	0.66	0.00	0.66
12/17	8.00	—	—	(0.28)	0.00	(0.44)
12/16	1.45	—	—	(0.50)	0.00	(0.57)
Annual Growth	183.8%	—	—	—	—	—

ServisFirst Bancshares Inc

ServisFirst Bancshares is a bank holding company for ServisFirst Bank a regional commercial bank with about a dozen branches located in Alabama and the Florida panhandle. The bank also

HOOVER'S HANDBOOK OF EMERGING COMPANIES 2022   367

has a loan office in Nashville. ServisFirst Bank targets privately-held businesses with $2 million to $250 million in annual sales as well as professionals and affluent customers. The bank focuses on traditional commercial banking services including loan origination deposits and electronic banking services such as online and mobile banking. Founded in 2005 by its chairman and CEO Thomas Broughton III the bank went public in 2014 with an offering valued at nearly $57 million.

IPO

ServisFirst Bancshares sold 625000 shares priced at $91 per share. Proceeds from the May 2014 IPO will be used to support the bank's growth plans both in Alabama and in other states.

Geographic Reach

Birmingham-based ServisFirst Bank has branches in Birmingham Huntsville Montgomery Mobile Dothan Pensacola and Nashville.

Financial Performance

The bank reported net income of $41.2 million in 2013 compared with $34 million in 2012. The increase was primarily due to an increase in net interest income which rose nearly 20% to $112.5 million. Noninterest income increased 4% to $10 million in 2013.

As of March 2014 the bank had total assets of approximately $3.6 billion total loans of $2.9 billion and total deposits of about $3.0 billion.

EXECUTIVES

Chief Operating Officer, Executive Vice President, Rodney Rushing, $327,000 total compensation
Executive Vice President And Tampa Bay Area President And Chief Executive Officer Of The Bank, Gregory Bryant
Executive Vice President And Pensacola President And Chief Executive Officer Of The Bank, Rex McKinney
Chief Financial Officer, Executive Vice President, Treasurer, Secretary, William Foshee, $300,000 total compensation
Chairman Of The Board, President, Chief Executive Officer, Thomas Broughton, $525,000 total compensation
Executive Vice President, Huntsville President And Chief Executive Officer Of The Bank, Andrew Kattos, $190,000 total compensation
Executive Vice President And Charleston President And Chief Executive Officer Of The Bank, Thomas Trouche
Executive Vice President , Montgomery President And Chief Executive Officer Of The Bank, G. Carlton Barker, $205,000 total compensation
Chief Executive Officer Of Dothan Regional, B. Harrison Morris
Independent Director, Irma Tuder
Lead Independent Director, James Filler
Executive Vice President And Nashville President And Chief Executive Officer Of The Bank, Bradford Vieira
Chief Executive Officer, William Lamar
Independent Director, Michael Fuller
Executive Vice President, Atlanta President And Chief Executive Officer Of The Bank, J. Harold Clemmer
Senior Vice President, Chief Credit Officer, Henry Abbott, $195,000 total compensation
Independent Director, Christopher Mettler
Auditors: Dixon Hughes Goodman LLP

LOCATIONS

HQ: ServisFirst Bancshares Inc
2500 Woodcrest Place, Birmingham, AL 35209
Phone: 205 949-0302
Web: www.servisfirstbank.com

COMPETITORS

AMERIS BANCORP
CLIFTON BANCORP INC.
CNB FINANCIAL CORPORATION
HERITAGE FINANCIAL HOLDINGS GROUP INC.
HOME BANCSHARES INC.
LAKELAND FINANCIAL CORPORATION
MAINSOURCE FINANCIAL GROUP INC.
MERCHANTS BANCSHARES INC.
NATIONAL BANK CORPORATION
SQUARE 1 FINANCIAL INC.

HISTORICAL FINANCIALS

Company Type: Public

Income Statement				FYE: December 31
	ASSETS ($ mil.)	NET INCOME ($ mil.)	INCOME AS % OF ASSETS	EMPLOYEES
12/20	11,932.6	169.5	1.4%	493
12/19	8,947.6	149.2	1.7%	505
12/18	8,007.3	136.9	1.7%	473
12/17	7,082.3	93.0	1.3%	434
12/16	6,370.4	81.4	1.3%	420
Annual Growth	17.0%	20.1%	—	4.1%

2020 Year-End Financials

Return on assets: 1.6%
Return on equity: 18.4%
Long-term debt ($ mil.): —
No. of shares (mil.): 53.9
Sales ($ mil): 419.1
Dividends
Yield: 1.8%
Payout: 23.1%
Market value ($ mil.): 2,173.0

	STOCK PRICE ($) FY Close	P/E High/Low		PER SHARE ($) Earnings	Dividends	Book Value
12/20	40.29	13	8	3.13	0.73	18.40
12/19	37.68	14	10	2.76	0.63	15.71
12/18	31.87	17	12	2.53	0.48	13.39
12/17	41.50	25	19	1.72	0.20	11.46
12/16	37.44	48	23	1.52	0.19	9.93
Annual Growth	1.9%			— 19.8%	39.8%	16.7%

Sharps Compliance Corp.

Sharps Compliance is on the cutting edge of the medical waste disposal business — and wants to make sure people don't get hurt. The company offers services to health care providers to make the disposal of medical waste safer and more efficient. It also serves customers in the pharmaceutical agricultural hospitality industrial and retail industries. Products include medical sharps (needles and other sharp objects) disposal systems disposable IV poles waste and equipment return boxes linen recovery systems and biohazardous spill clean-up kits. Sharps Compliance also provides regulatory compliant waste tracking incineration and disposal verification services as well as consulting services.

EXECUTIVES

Vice President - Operations, Gregory Davis, $206,219 total compensation
President, Chief Executive Officer, Director, David Tusa, $361,507 total compensation
Independent Director, Gary Enzor
Independent Director, William Mulloy
Independent Director, Susan Vogt
Non-executive Independent Chairman Of The Board, Sharon Gabrielson
Vice President - Sales And Marketing, Dennis Halligan, $131,654 total compensation
Chief Financial Officer, Executive Vice President, Diana Diaz, $255,753 total compensation
Auditors: BDO USA, LLP

LOCATIONS

HQ: Sharps Compliance Corp.
9220 Kirby Drive, Suite 500, Houston, TX 77054
Phone: 713 432-0300
Web: www.sharpsinc.com

COMPETITORS

ADVANCED DISPOSAL SERVICES INC.
CAPRIUS INC.
CLEAN HARBORS INC.
Promotora Ambiental S.A.B. de C.V.
US ECOLOGY HOLDINGS INC.

HISTORICAL FINANCIALS

Company Type: Public

Income Statement				FYE: June 30
	REVENUE ($ mil.)	NET INCOME ($ mil.)	NET PROFIT MARGIN	EMPLOYEES
06/21	76.4	12.8	16.8%	192
06/20	51.1	2.2	4.4%	184
06/19	44.3	0.2	0.5%	164
06/18	40.1	(0.6)	—	152
06/17	38.1	(1.2)	—	130
Annual Growth	18.9%	—	—	10.2%

2021 Year-End Financials

Debt ratio: 6.5%
Return on equity: 33.7%
Cash ($ mil.): 27.7
Current ratio: 2.63
Long-term debt ($ mil.): 4.0
No. of shares (mil.): 17.1
Dividends
Yield: —
Payout: —
Market value ($ mil.): 177.0

	STOCK PRICE ($) FY Close	P/E High/Low		PER SHARE ($) Earnings	Dividends	Book Value
06/21	10.30	24	7	0.76	0.00	2.71
06/20	7.03	57	25	0.14	0.00	1.81
06/19	3.56	402	307	0.01	0.00	1.62
06/18	3.69	—	—	(0.04)	0.00	1.57
06/17	4.23	—	—	(0.08)	0.00	1.58
Annual Growth	24.9%			—	—	14.5%

Shell Midstream Partners LP

Auditors: Ernst & Young LLP

LOCATIONS

HQ: Shell Midstream Partners LP
150 N. Dairy Ashford, Houston, TX 77079
Phone: 832 337-2034
Web: www.shellmidstreampartners.com

HISTORICAL FINANCIALS
Company Type: Public

Income Statement · FYE: December 31

	REVENUE ($ mil.)	NET INCOME ($ mil.)	NET PROFIT MARGIN	EMPLOYEES
12/20	481.0	543.0	112.9%	0
12/19	503.0	528.0	105.0%	0
12/18	524.7	464.1	88.5%	0
12/17	470.1	295.3	62.8%	0
12/16	291.3	244.9	84.1%	0
Annual Growth	13.4%	22.0%	—	—

2020 Year-End Financials

Debt ratio: 115.7%	No. of shares (mil.): 393.2
Return on equity: —	Dividends
Cash ($ mil.): 320.0	Yield: 18.2%
Current ratio: 4.80	Payout: 147.2%
Long-term debt ($ mil.): 2,716.0	Market value ($ mil.): 3,964.0

	STOCK PRICE ($) FY Close	P/E High/Low		PER SHARE ($) Earnings	Dividends	Book Value
12/20	10.08	18	6	1.25	1.84	(1.22)
12/19	20.21	13	10	1.66	1.69	(3.26)
12/18	16.41	20	11	1.50	1.43	(1.24)
12/17	29.82	27	20	1.28	1.19	(3.07)
12/16	29.09	32	20	1.32	0.97	0.54
Annual Growth	(23.3%)	—	—	(1.4%)	17.4%	—

Shutterstock Inc

Shutterstock brings the online marketplace mentality to the world of digital images illustrations and videos. It is a global technology company offering a creative platform which provides high-quality content tools and services to creative professionals. The company's primary customers include marketing professionals and organization media and broadcast companies and small and medium-sizes businesses. Shutterstock's marketplace is available in over 20 languages and some 150 countries where its images are used for corporate communications websites ads books and other published materials. The company was formed in 2003.

Operations

The company's high-quality products and services and the experience it provides to the customers combined with its focus on continuous innovation have allowed Shutterstock to establish premium brands including: Shutterstock Bigstock Offset Shutterstock Select Shutterstock Custom Shutterstock Editorial and Shutterstock Music and PremiumBeat.

The Shutterstock is the company's flagship brand and the majority of its revenue is generated through shutterstock.com. The Bigstock maintains a separate extensive library of images vectors illustrations and footage that is specifically curated to meet the needs of independent creators and others seeking to incorporate cost-effective imagery into their projects. The Offset brand provides authentic and exceptional content featuring work from top assignment photographers and illustrators from around the world.

Geographic Reach

Headquartered in New York Shutterstock has office facilities in the United States and abroad. The North America generates some 35% of the company's total revenues Europe with nearly 35% of sales and the rest of the world accounts for the remaining.

Sales and Marketing

Customer sales are made through E-commerce (around 60% of sales) and Enterprise (some 40% of sales).

Marketing and communications professionals incorporate licensed content in the work they produce for their organizational or clients' business communications. Whether providing graphic design web design interactive design advertising public relations communications or marketing materials these professional users and teams support organizations of various sizes including the largest global agencies large not-for-profit organizations and Fortune 500 companies.

Media organizations and professionals incorporate licensed content into their work which includes digital publications newspapers books magazines television and film as well as to market their products effectively.

Organizations of all sizes utilize creative content for a wide range of internal- and external-use communications such as websites print and digital advertisements merchandise brochures employee communications newsletters social media email marketing campaigns and other presentations.

The company's advertising costs totaled $81.2 million $102.3 million and $91.5 million for the years 2020 2019 and 2018 respectively.

Financial Performance

Revenue increased by $16.2 million or 2% to $666.7 million in 2020 as compared to 2019. The company's revenue growth in 2020 is primarily driven by its subscription business.

Net income for fiscal 2020 increased to $71.8 million compared from the prior year with $20.1 million.

Cash held by the company at the end of fiscal 2020 increased to $428.6 million. Cash provided by operations was $165.1 million while cash used for investing and financing activities were $35.3 million and $4.6 million respectively. Main uses of cash were capital expenditures and payment of cash dividends.

Company Background

Shutterstock launched its platform in 2003 and in 2012 it reorganized as Shutterstock Inc. a Delaware corporation from Shutterstock Images LLC a New York limited liability company and completed its initial public offering. Its common stock is listed on the New York Stock Exchange under the symbol "SSTK".

EXECUTIVES

Independent Director, Paul Hennessy
Independent Director, Deirdre Bigley
Chief Executive Officer, Director, Stan Pavlovsky, $610,385 total compensation
Executive Chairman Of The Board, Founder, Jonathan Oringer, $1 total compensation
Independent Director, Rachna Bhasin
Chief Financial Officer, Jarrod Yahes, $539,423 total compensation
Chief Technology Officer, Peter Silvio, $392,308 total compensation
General Counsel, John Lapham
Auditors: PricewaterhouseCoopers LLP

LOCATIONS

HQ: Shutterstock Inc
350 Fifth Avenue, 21st Floor, New York, NY 10118
Phone: 646 710-3417
Web: www.shutterstock.com

COMPETITORS

ASCENTIAL GROUP LIMITED	KEYNOTE LLC
AUDACY INC.	MAGNITE INC.
BRIGHTCOVE INC.	PROOFPOINT INC.
CASTLIGHT HEALTH INC.	SPOTIFY TECHNOLOGY S.A.
COVISINT CORPORATION	STARTEK INC.
CSG SYSTEMS INTERNATIONAL INC.	TRUECAR INC.
INNODATA INC.	VERISK ANALYTICS INC.
	YEXT INC.

HISTORICAL FINANCIALS
Company Type: Public

Income Statement · FYE: December 31

	REVENUE ($ mil.)	NET INCOME ($ mil.)	NET PROFIT MARGIN	EMPLOYEES
12/21	773.4	91.8	11.9%	1,148
12/20	666.6	71.7	10.8%	967
12/19	650.5	20.1	3.1%	1,116
12/18	623.2	54.6	8.8%	1,029
12/17	557.1	16.7	3.0%	1,130
Annual Growth	8.5%	53.1%	—	0.4%

2021 Year-End Financials

Debt ratio: —	No. of shares (mil.): 36.4
Return on equity: 20.6%	Dividends
Cash ($ mil.): 314.0	Yield: 0.7%
Current ratio: 1.16	Payout: 31.0%
Long-term debt ($ mil.): —	Market value ($ mil.): 4,038.0

	STOCK PRICE ($) FY Close	P/E High/Low		PER SHARE ($) Earnings	Dividends	Book Value
12/21	110.88	50	26	2.46	0.84	12.86
12/20	71.70	37	15	1.97	0.68	11.64
12/19	42.88	85	59	0.57	0.00	9.24
12/18	36.01	35	21	1.54	3.00	8.18
12/17	43.03	114	66	0.47	0.00	9.06
Annual Growth	26.7%	—	—	51.3%	—	9.2%

Sierra Bancorp

Sierra Bancorp is the holding company for the nearly $2 billion-asset Bank of the Sierra which operates approximately 30 branches in Central California's San Joaquin Valley between (and including) Bakersfield and Fresno. The bank offers traditional deposit products and loans to individuals and small and mid-size businesses. About 70% of its loan portfolio is made up of real estate loans while another 15% is made up of mortgage warehouse loans and a further 10% is tied to commercial and industrial loans (including SBA loans and direct finance leases). The bank also issues agricultural loans and consumer loans.

Operations

Bank of the Sierra makes almost 80% of its revenue from interest income. About 64% of its total revenue came from interest income on loans and leases (including fees) during 2015 while another

HOOVER'S HANDBOOK OF EMERGING COMPANIES 2022 · 369

14% came from interest income on taxed and tax-exempt securities. The rest of its revenue came from deposit account service charges (12% of revenue) checkcard fees (5%) and other non-interest income sources.

Geographic Reach
The Porterville California-based bank operates branches and offices mostly in the San Joaquin Valley in Porterville Arroyo Grande Atascadero Bakersfield California City Clovis Delano Dinuba Exeter Farmersville Fillmore Fresno Hanford Lindsay Oxnard Paso Robles Reedley San Luis Obispo Santa Clarita Santa Paula Selma Tehachapi Three Rivers Visalia and Tulare.

Sales and Marketing
Bank of the Sierra has been gradually increasing its advertising spend in recent years. It spent $2.3 million on advertising and promotion in 2015 up from $2.2 million and $1.9 million in 2014 and 2013 respectively.

Financial Performance
The bank's revenue has been steadily rising over the past few years mostly as bank acquisitions and organic loan business growth has spurred higher interest income. Meanwhile its profits have more than doubled since 2011 thanks to declining loan loss provisions as its loan portfolio's credit quality has improved with higher property valuations in the strengthened economy.

Sierra Bancorp's revenue jumped 13% to $80.4 million during 2015 thanks to higher interest income from continued double-digit loan asset growth led by a jump in mortgage warehouse lines from increased line utilization a first-quarter purchase of residential mortgage loans and strong organic growth in non-farm real estate and agricultural production loans. Deposit account service fees also grew thanks to organic deposit client growth.

Strong revenue growth and lower acquisition costs in 2015 drove the bank's net income up 19% to $18 million. Sierra's operating cash levels rose 4% to $29.78 million during the year as its cash-based earnings increased.

Strategy
While the Bank of Sierra has traditionally grown organically by opening around one new branch per year in the Central Valley it has more recently acquired small area banks and individual branches to bolster its deposit and loan business while expanding into untapped markets such as further south into the Santa Clara Valley.

Mergers and Acquisitions
In July 2016 the bank bought $145 million-asset Coast Bancorp and its Coast National Bank branches in San Luis Obispo Paso Robles Arroyo Grande and Atascadero California.

In November 2014 Sierra Bancorp bought $129 million-asset Santa Clara Valley Bank N.A. and its branches in Santa Paula Santa Clarita and Fillmore in California for $15 million. the deal expanded Sierra's reach outside of its traditional market for the first time more south into the Santa Clara Valley of California.

EXECUTIVES

Independent Chairman Of The Board, Morris Tharp
Independent Vice Chairman Of Board, James Holly
Independent Director, Gordon Woods
Independent Director, Albert Berra

President, Chief Executive Officer, Director Of Company, Kevin Mcphaill, $575,000 total compensation
Independent Director, Lynda Scearcy
Executive Vice President, Chief Banking Officer Of The Company & Bank, Michael Olague, $380,000 total compensation
Independent Director, Vonn Christenson
Independent Director, Laurence Dutto
Senior Vice President, Chief Accounting Officer, Cindy Dabney
Chief Financial Officer, Executive Vice President, Christopher Treece, $380,000 total compensation
Executive Vice President, Chief Administrative Officer, Jennifer Johnson, $322,667 total compensation
Independent Director, Susan Abundis
Auditors: Eide Bailly LLP

LOCATIONS

HQ: Sierra Bancorp
86 North Main Street, Porterville, CA 93257
Phone: 559 782-4900
Web: www.bankofthesierra.com

COMPETITORS

BANK OF THE OZARKS INC.
GLACIER BANCORP INC.
INTERNATIONAL BANCSHARES CORPORATION
PARK STERLING CORPORATION
UNITED COMMUNITY BANKS INC.

HISTORICAL FINANCIALS
Company Type: Public

Income Statement				FYE: December 31
	ASSETS ($ mil.)	NET INCOME ($ mil.)	INCOME AS % OF ASSETS	EMPLOYEES
12/20	3,220.7	35.4	1.1%	512
12/19	2,593.8	35.9	1.4%	513
12/18	2,522.5	29.6	1.2%	556
12/17	2,340.3	19.5	0.8%	576
12/16	2,032.8	17.5	0.9%	497
Annual Growth	12.2%	19.2%	—	0.7%

2020 Year-End Financials

Return on assets: 1.2%	Dividends
Return on equity: 10.8%	Yield: 3.3%
Long-term debt ($ mil.): —	Payout: 34.3%
No. of shares (mil.): 15.3	Market value ($ mil.): 368.0
Sales ($ mil): 136.3	

	STOCK PRICE ($) FY Close	P/E High/Low		PER SHARE ($) Earnings	Dividends	Book Value
12/20	23.92	13	6	2.32	0.80	22.35
12/19	29.12	13	10	2.33	0.74	20.24
12/18	24.03	16	12	1.92	0.64	17.84
12/17	26.56	21	17	1.36	0.56	16.81
12/16	26.59	20	12	1.29	0.48	14.94
Annual Growth	(2.6%)	—	—	15.8%	13.6%	10.6%

SIGA Technologies Inc

SIGA Technologies is trying to put itself on the front lines of US biodefense efforts. The drug company has a number of development programs for vaccines antivirals and antibiotics for drug resistant infections; however its main focus is on vaccines for bio-defense. Its lead product TPOXX (aka tecovirimat) was the first treatment to be approved for the treatment of smallpox in case of a bioterrorist attack; it was given approval in mid-2018. SIGA is also developing vaccines for use against hemorrhagic fevers and other infectious diseases and biothreats. Much of its work is done through funding from the NIH and the HHS. SIGA emerged from a short stint under Chapter 11 bankruptcy protection in 2016.

Bankruptcy

The company filed for bankruptcy protection after it was given a court ruling to pay $232 million in damages to competitor PharmAthene. SIGA plans to continue operating as usual as well as pursuing a lowering of the penalty. Because of its status as the country's only maker of smallpox treatment the company enjoys a certain level of government protection.

PharmAthene sued SIGA in 2006 claiming it should share in the potential $5 billion in sales primarily from the manufacture of Arestvyr (the development of which it helped fund).

Operations
SIGA's lead candidate is Arestvyr which is still going through trials despite being fast-tracked by the FDA. Other candidates in testing include treatments and preventions for dengue fever Lassa fever Junin Ebola Marburg and bunyaviruses. All told the company has about $420 million in grant money available if it can deliver on various projects.

Geographic Reach
SIGA has its headquarters in New York and R&D facilities in Oregon. Its treatments have the potential to be used worldwide.

Sales and Marketing
The company uses a small force of its own personnel to sell Arestvyr to the US government. As it expands its products and customer base it may expand its sales force or use third-parties.

Financial Performance
SIGA reported a 30% drop in revenue as some contracts concluded and others got restructured. It also saw related net loss and drop in cash flow as it used operating cash for the manufacture and marketing of Arestvyr.

Strategy
The company's key strategy is to expand its customer base beyond the US government.

EXECUTIVES

Vice President And Chief Scientific Officer, Dennis Hruby, $633,386 total compensation
Chief Administrative Officer, General Counsel, Robin Abrams, $551,499 total compensation
Lead Independent Director, Michael Plansky
Independent Director, Julie Kane
Independent Director, Julian Nemirovsky
Independent Director, Jaymie Durnan
Chief Financial Officer, Executive Vice President, Secretary, Daniel Luckshire, $636,540 total compensation
Chief Executive Officer, Director, Phillip Gomez, $819,545 total compensation
Auditors: PricewaterhouseCoopers LLP

LOCATIONS

HQ: SIGA Technologies Inc
  31 East 62nd Street, New York, NY 10065
Phone: 212 672-9100
Web: www.siga.com

COMPETITORS

ADAMAS PHARMACEUTICALS
  CORPORATION
  INC.
AFFYMAX INC.
GLOBEIMMUNE INC.

MANNKIND

PARATEK
  PHARMACEUTICALS INC.

HISTORICAL FINANCIALS

Company Type: Public

Income Statement — FYE: December 31

	REVENUE ($ mil.)	NET INCOME ($ mil.)	NET PROFIT MARGIN	EMPLOYEES
12/20	124.9	56.3	45.1%	42
12/19	26.7	(7.2)	—	41
12/18	477.0	421.8	88.4%	41
12/17	12.2	(36.2)	—	37
12/16	14.9	(39.7)	—	36
Annual Growth	69.9%	—		3.9%

2020 Year-End Financials

Debt ratio: —	No. of shares (mil.): 77.2
Return on equity: 49.3%	Dividends
Cash ($ mil.): 117.8	Yield: —
Current ratio: 13.70	Payout: —
Long-term debt ($ mil.): —	Market value ($ mil.): 561.0

	STOCK PRICE ($) FY Close	P/E High/Low		PER SHARE ($) Earnings	Dividends	Book Value
12/20	7.27	11	6	0.71	0.00	1.68
12/19	4.77	—	—	(0.15)	0.00	1.20
12/18	7.90	2	1	5.18	0.00	1.27
12/17	4.85	—	—	(0.46)	0.00	(4.09)
12/16	2.88	—	—	(0.69)	0.00	(3.65)
Annual Growth	26.0%	—	—	—	—	—

Signature Bank (New York, NY)

Signature Bank provides customized banking and financial services to smaller private businesses their owners and their top executives through some 35 branches across the New York metropolitan area including those in Connecticut as well as in California and North Carolina. The bank's lending activities mainly entail real estate and business loans. Subsidiary Signature Securities offers wealth management brokerage services asset management and insurance while its Signature Financial subsidiary offers equipment financing and leasing. Founded in 2001 the bank now boasts assets of roughly $73 billion.

Operations

Signature Bank's operations are organized into two reportable segments representing its core businesses ? Commercial Banking and Specialty Finance.

Commercial Banking accounts for more than 90% of revenue and principally consists of commercial real estate lending fund banking venture banking and other commercial and industrial lending and commercial deposit gathering activities while Specialty Finance (nearly 10%) principally consists of financing and leasing products including equipment transportation taxi medallion commercial marine municipal and national franchise financing or leasing.

Mortgage loans including commercial real estate loans multifamily residential mortgages home loans and lines of credit and construction and land loans comprise the bulk of Signature Bank's loan portfolio (and much of its asset base as well).

The bank generated over 80% of its revenue from interest on loans and leases that year while nearly 10% came from interest on its securities available-for-sale and less than 5% came from securities held-to-maturity.

Geographic Reach

Based in New York Signature Bank operates more than 35 private client offices throughout New York metropolitan area including those in Connecticut as well as in California and North Carolina.

Sales and Marketing

Signature Bank mostly serves privately-owned businesses their owners and senior managers (typically with a net worth between $500000 and $20 million).

Financial Performance

The company's revenues and profits have risen in recent years thanks to strong organic loan business growth and declining loan loss provisions as its loan portfolio's credit quality has improved with higher property valuations in the strengthened economy.

Net interest income in 2020 was $1.52 billion an increase of $207.5 million or 15.8% over the year 2019. The increase in net interest income for 2020 was largely driven by a $11.30 billion increase in average interest-earning assets partially offset by a 71 basis point decrease in yield on interest-earning assets to 3.25% when compared to the same period last year.

Net income in 2020 was $528.4 million compared to $586.5 million in 2019. The decrease was primarily due to an increase of $225.5 million in the provision for credit losses predominantly attributable to the impact of COVID-19 on the US economy.

Cash at the end of 2020 was $12.3 billion $11.6 billion higher to $789.8 million in 2019. Operating activities generated $904.4 million while investing activities used $11.9 million mostly due to net increase in loans and leases. Financing activities $22.5 billion in 2020.

Strategy

Signature Bank has long targeted privately-held businesses that have fewer than 1000 employees and revenues of less than $200 million. Some of its target clients include real estate owners/companies law firms accounting firms entertainment business managers medical professionals retail establishments money management firms and nonprofit foundations.

The bank intends to increase its presence as a premier relationship-based financial services organization serving the needs of privately owned business clients their owners and their senior managers in major metropolitan areas by continuing to focus on a niche market of privately owned

businesses their owners and their senior managers; provide clients a wide array of high-quality banking brokerage and insurance products and services through private client group structure and a seamless financial services solution; and offer incentive-based compensation that rewards private client banking teams for developing their business and retaining their clients.

Additionally it also focuses on strategies that is committed to a sound risk management process while focusing on profitability; maintains a flat organization structure for business development purposes that provides clients and group directors with direct access to senior management; develops and maintains operations support that is client-centric and service oriented; and maintain an appropriate balance between cost control incentive compensation and business expansion initiatives.

Company Background

The bank's emphasis on personal service helped it to grow its deposit base and loan portfolio in 2011. During a time when many other banks struggled under the weight of bad loans in a bad economy Signature Bank achieved record earnings for the fourth consecutive year.

Founded in 2001 as an alternative to megabanks Signature Bank was spun off from Bank Hapoalim in 2004.

EXECUTIVES

Executive Chairman Of The Board, Scott Shay, $659,200 total compensation
President, Chief Executive Officer, Director, Joseph DePaolo, $927,000 total compensation
Executive Vice Chairman Of The Board, John Tamberlane, $500,000 total compensation
Chief Operations Officer And Business Development, Eric Howell, $500,000 total compensation
Independent Director, Kathryn Byrne
Chief Human Resource Officer, Senior Vice President, Ana Harris
Executive Vice President, Chief Administrative Officer, Vito Susca, $450,000 total compensation
Senior Vice President, Chief Credit Officer, Brian Twomey
Lead Independent Director, Judith Huntington
Chief Financial Officer, Senior Vice President, Stephen Wyremski
Independent Director, Derrick Cephas
Executive Vice President And Chief Lending Officer, Thomas Kasulka
Senior Vice President And Deputy Chief Lending Officer, Dawn Juliano
Senior Vice President, Chief Investment Officer, Treasurer, Kevin Hickey
Senior Vice President, Chief Corporate Social Impact Officer, Lisa Bond
Senior Vice President, Chief Risk Officer, Keisha Hutchinson
Independent Director, Barney Frank
Auditors: KPMG LLP

LOCATIONS

HQ: Signature Bank (New York, NY)
  565 Fifth Avenue, New York, NY 10017
Phone: 646 822-1500
Web: www.signatureny.com

HOOVER'S HANDBOOK OF EMERGING COMPANIES 2022

PRODUCTS/OPERATIONS

2014 Sales

	$ mil.	% of total
Interest		
Loans net	655.6	68
Securities available for sale	193.6	20
Securities held to maturity	69.8	7
Other	5.3	1
Noninterest		
Fees & service charges	19.3	2
Commissions	10.6	1
Net gains on sales of loans	5.4	1
Net gains on sales of securities	5.3	-
Other	2.2	-
Adjustments	(7.8)	-
Total	**959.3**	**100**

COMPETITORS

ACCESS NATIONAL CORPORATION
ASSOCIATED BANC-CORP
BOKF MERGER CORPORATION NUMBER SIXTEEN
CITIZENS FINANCIAL GROUP INC.
CITY HOLDING COMPANY
COLUMBIA BANKING SYSTEM INC.
COMMERCE BANCSHARES INC.
CVB FINANCIAL CORP.
EAGLE BANCORP INC.
ENTERPRISE FINANCIAL SERVICES CORP
FIRST EAGLE PRIVATE CREDIT LLC
GUARANTY BANCORP
M&T BANK CORPORATION
MACATAWA BANK CORPORATION
MIDWESTONE FINANCIAL GROUP INC.
NATIONAL BANK HOLDINGS CORPORATION
OCEANFIRST FINANCIAL CORP.
PACWEST BANCORP
PEOPLES FINANCIAL SERVICES CORP.
WINTRUST FINANCIAL CORPORATION

HISTORICAL FINANCIALS

Company Type: Public

Income Statement

FYE: December 31

	ASSETS ($ mil.)	NET INCOME ($ mil.)	INCOME AS % OF ASSETS	EMPLOYEES
12/20	73,888.3	528.3	0.7%	1,652
12/19	50,616.4	588.9	1.2%	1,472
12/18	47,364.8	505.3	1.1%	1,393
12/17	43,117.7	387.2	0.9%	1,305
12/16	39,047.6	396.3	1.0%	1,218
Annual Growth	17.3%	7.5%	—	7.9%

2020 Year-End Financials

Return on assets: 0.8%
Return on equity: 9.9%
Long-term debt ($ mil.): —
No. of shares (mil.): 53.5
Sales ($ mil): 2,006.8
Dividends
Yield: 1.6%
Payout: 23.6%
Market value ($ mil.): 7,247.0

	STOCK PRICE ($) FY Close	P/E High/Low		Earnings	PER SHARE ($) Dividends	Book Value
12/20	135.29	15	7	9.96	2.24	108.78
12/19	136.61	13	10	10.87	2.24	89.12
12/18	102.81	17	11	9.23	1.12	80.07
12/17	137.26	23	17	7.12	0.00	73.33
12/16	150.20	21	15	7.37	0.00	66.15
Annual Growth	(2.6%)	—	—	7.8%	—	13.2%

Sila Realty Trust Inc

LOCATIONS

HQ: Sila Realty Trust Inc
4890 West Kennedy Blvd., Suite 650, Tampa, FL 33609
Phone: 813 287-0101
Web: www.silarealtytrust.com

HISTORICAL FINANCIALS

Company Type: Public

Income Statement

FYE: December 31

	REVENUE ($ mil.)	NET INCOME ($ mil.)	NET PROFIT MARGIN	EMPLOYEES
12/20	276.5	36.7	13.3%	74
12/19	210.9	2.7	1.3%	0
12/18	177.3	28.8	16.3%	0
12/17	125.0	21.2	17.0%	0
Annual Growth	30.3%	20.0%	—	—

2020 Year-End Financials

Debt ratio: 43.2%
Return on equity: 2.1%
Cash ($ mil.): 53.1
Current ratio: 0.66
Long-term debt ($ mil.): 1,386.5
No. of shares (mil.): 222.0
Dividends
Yield: —
Payout: 282.3%
Market value ($ mil.): —

	STOCK PRICE ($) FY Close	P/E High/Low	Earnings	PER SHARE ($) Dividends	Book Value
12/20	0.00	— —	0.17	0.48	7.45
Annual Growth	—	— —	—	—	—

Silvergate Capital Corp

Auditors: Crowe LLP

LOCATIONS

HQ: Silvergate Capital Corp
4250 Executive Square, Suite 300, La Jolla, CA 92037
Phone: 858 362-6300
Web: www.silvergatebank.com

HISTORICAL FINANCIALS

Company Type: Public

Income Statement

FYE: December 31

	ASSETS ($ mil.)	NET INCOME ($ mil.)	INCOME AS % OF ASSETS	EMPLOYEES
12/20	5,586.2	26.0	0.5%	218
12/19	2,128.1	24.8	1.2%	215
12/18	2,004.3	22.3	1.1%	209
12/17	1,891.9	7.6	0.4%	0
Annual Growth	43.5%	50.5%	—	—

2020 Year-End Financials

Return on assets: 0.6%
Return on equity: 9.8%
Long-term debt ($ mil.): —
No. of shares (mil.): 18.8
Sales ($ mil): 98.7
Dividends
Yield: —
Payout: —
Market value ($ mil.): 1,400.0

	STOCK PRICE ($) FY Close	P/E High/Low		Earnings	PER SHARE ($) Dividends	Book Value
12/20	74.31	53	5	1.36	0.00	15.63
12/19	15.91	12	9	1.35	0.00	12.38
12/18	0.00	—	—	1.31	0.00	10.73
Annual Growth	—	—	—	1.9%	—	20.7%

Simmons First National Corp

Simmons First National is a financial holding company of Simmons Bank an Arkansas state-chartered bank that has been operating since 1903. Simmons Bank provides banking and other financial products and services to individuals and businesses using a network of more than 200 financial centers in Arkansas Illinois Kansas Missouri Oklahoma Tennessee and Texas. The company offers commercial banking products and services to business and other corporate customers; it extends loans for a broad range of corporate purposes including financing commercial real estate construction of particular properties commercial and industrial uses acquisition and equipment financings and other general corporate needs.

Operations

Aside from banking products and services offered to corporate customers as well as loans and financing Simmons Bank also engages in small business administration (SBA) and agricultural finance lending and it offers corporate credit card products as well as corporate deposit products and treasury management services. The bank also offers a variety of consumer banking products and services including savings time and checking deposit products; ATM services; internet and mobile banking platforms; overdraft facilities; real estate home equity and other consumer loans and lines of credit; consumer credit card products; and safe deposit boxes.

Like other retail banks Simmons makes the bulk of its money from interest income. The majority of the company's revenue comes from loans and investment securities. Its loan portfolio averaged $14.3 billion wherein the most significant components of the loan portfolio were loans to businesses (commercial loans commercial real estate loans and agricultural loans) and individuals (consumer loans credit card loans and single-family residential real estate loans).

Simmons First Insurance Services Inc. and Simmons First Insurance Services of TN LLC are wholly-owned subsidiaries of Simmons Bank and are insurance agencies that offer various lines of personal and corporate insurance coverage to individual and commercial customers.

Geographic Reach

Simmons First Financial and its subsidiaries own or lease additional offices in the states of Arkansas Illinois Kansas Missouri Oklahoma Tennessee and Texas. They conduct financial operations from more than 200 financial centers located in communities throughout Arkansas Illinois Kansas Missouri Oklahoma Tennessee and Texas.

Sales and Marketing

Simmons Bank also maintains a networking arrangement with a third-party broker-dealer that offers brokerage services to Simmons Bank customers as well as a trust department that provides a variety of trust investment agency and custodial services for individual and corporate clients (including among other things administration of estates and personal trusts and management of investment accounts).

The company's marketing expenses were $19.4 million $16.5 million and $8.4 million in 2020 2019 and 2018 respectively.

Financial Performance

Simmons First National Bank's net interest income over the past three years has grown 17% since 2018.

In 2020 the company reported net interest income of around $639.7 million. Non-interest income grew 21% or $248.5 million in 2020 compared to the prior year. The increase in net interest income was primarily the result of a $61.4 million decrease in interest expense partially offset by a reduction in interest income of $19.7 million.

The bank's total cash and cash equivalents reached $996.6 million at the end of 2020. Operating activities provided $202.5 million while investing activities generated another $1.2 billion. Financing activities provided another $1.1 billion.

Strategy

The bank has established a presence in a greater number of metro markets which often have different characteristics from the community markets Simmons Bank has traditionally served. As a result in 2021 Simmons Bank expects to make additional organizational changes to provide for a community bank and metro bank divisions as a way to further enhance its ability to both effectively compete in and service the needs of the different types of markets that are now included in its footprint.

Merger and acquisition activities are an important part of the company's growth strategy. Simmons intends to focus its near-term merger and acquisition strategy on traditional mergers and acquisitions. It expects that its target areas for mergers and acquisitions will continue to be primarily banks operating in growth markets within its existing footprint of Arkansas Kansas Missouri Oklahoma Tennessee and Texas. In addition Simmons will pursue opportunities with financial service companies with specialty lines of business within the existing markets as and when it arises.

EXECUTIVES

Independent Director, Robert Shoptaw
Independent Director, William Clark
Independent Director, Eugene Hunt
Independent Director, W. Scott McGeorge
Independent Director, Edward Drilling
Executive Vice President, Executive Director Of Finance & Accounting, Chief Accounting Officer, David Garner
Executive Vice President, Chief Banking Officer, Simmons Bank, Matthew Reddin, $400,000 total compensation
Executive Vice President, Chief Administrative Officer, Stephen Massanelli, $330,001 total compensation
Independent Director, Jay Burchfield

Executive Vice President, Chief Information Officer, Paul Kanneman, $255,000 total compensation
Independent Director, Tom Purvis
Independent Director, Susan Lanigan
Independent Director, Russell Teubner
Executive Vice President, Chief People, Corporate Strategy Officer, Jennifer Compton, $330,001 total compensation
Independent Director, Julie Stackhouse
Chief Financial Officer, Executive Vice President, Treasurer, James Brogdon
Executive Vice President, Chief Credit Officer, Simmons Bank, Johnathan Barber
President, Chief Operating Officer, Robert Fehlman, $550,000 total compensation
Independent Director, Mark Doramus
Independent Director, Jerry Hunter
Independent Director, Mindy West
Executive Vice President, General Counsel, Company Secretary, George Makris
Auditors: BKD, LLP

LOCATIONS

HQ: Simmons First National Corp
501 Main Street, Pine Bluff, AR 71601
Phone: 870 541-1000
Web: www.simmonsbank.com

PRODUCTS/OPERATIONS

2015 Sales

	$ mil.	% of total
Interest Income		
Loans	268.4	65
Investment securities	30.6	8
Others	2.0	-
Non-interest income		
Service charges on deposit accounts	31.0	8
Debit and credit card fees	26.7	6
Mortgage lending income	11.4	3
Trust income	9.2	2
Other service charges and fees	9.9	2
others	22.4	6
Net (loss) gain on assets covered by FDIC loss share agreements	(14.8)	-
Total	**396.8**	**100**

COMPETITORS

AMERICAN NATIONAL BANKSHARES INC.
BANC OF CALIFORNIA INC.
BOK FINANCIAL CORPORATION
CAMDEN NATIONAL CORPORATION
CAPITAL BANK FINANCIAL CORP.
DIME COMMUNITY BANCSHARES INC.
F.N.B. CORPORATION
FINANCIAL INSTITUTIONS INC.
FIRST BUSEY CORPORATION
FIRST COMMONWEALTH FINANCIAL CORPORATION
FIRST MERCHANTS CORPORATION
GREAT WESTERN BANCORP INC.
M&T BANK CORPORATION
NATIONAL BANK HOLDINGS CORPORATION
OLD NATIONAL BANCORP
PACWEST BANCORP
PINNACLE FINANCIAL PARTNERS INC.
PROSPERITY BANCSHARES INC.
SOUTHWEST BANCORP INC.
THE BANCORP INC
UMB FINANCIAL CORPORATION
WEBSTER FINANCIAL CORPORATION
WINTRUST FINANCIAL CORPORATION

HISTORICAL FINANCIALS

Company Type: Public

Income Statement

FYE: December 31

	ASSETS ($ mil.)	NET INCOME ($ mil.)	INCOME AS % OF ASSETS	EMPLOYEES
12/20	22,359.7	254.9	1.1%	2,923
12/19	21,259.1	238.1	1.1%	3,270
12/18	16,543.3	215.7	1.3%	2,654
12/17	15,055.8	92.9	0.6%	2,640
12/16	8,400.0	96.8	1.2%	1,875
Annual Growth	**27.7%**	**27.4%**	**—**	**11.7%**

2020 Year-End Financials

Return on assets: 1.1%
Return on equity: 8.5%
Long-term debt ($ mil.): —
No. of shares (mil.): 108.0
Sales ($ mil): 1,008.2
Dividends
  Yield: 3.1%
  Payout: 29.6%
Market value ($ mil.): 2,333.0

	STOCK PRICE ($) FY Close	P/E High/Low		PER SHARE ($) Earnings	Dividends	Book Value
12/20	21.59	12	6	2.31	0.68	27.54
12/19	26.79	11	9	2.41	0.64	26.30
12/18	24.13	26	10	2.32	0.60	24.33
12/17	57.10	47	37	1.33	0.50	22.65
12/16	62.15	42	25	1.57	0.48	18.40
Annual Growth	**(23.2%)**	**—**	**—**	**10.2%**	**9.1%**	**10.6%**

Simply Good Foods Company (The)

Auditors: DELOITTE & TOUCHE LLP

LOCATIONS

HQ: Simply Good Foods Company (The)
1225 17th Street, Suite 1000, Denver, CO 80202
Phone: 303 633-2840
Web: www.thesimplygoodfoodscompany.com

HISTORICAL FINANCIALS

Company Type: Public

Income Statement

FYE: August 28

	REVENUE ($ mil.)	NET INCOME ($ mil.)	NET PROFIT MARGIN	EMPLOYEES
08/21	1,005.6	40.8	4.1%	263
08/20	816.6	34.7	4.2%	300
08/19	523.3	47.5	9.1%	150
08/18	431.4	70.4	16.3%	141
08/17	56.3	0.4	0.8%	145
Annual Growth	**105.5%**	**208.7%**	**—**	**16.1%**

2021 Year-End Financials

Debt ratio: 21.9%
Return on equity: 3.3%
Cash ($ mil.): 75.3
Current ratio: 2.63
Long-term debt ($ mil.): 450.5
No. of shares (mil.): 95.7
Dividends
  Yield: —
  Payout: —
Market value ($ mil.): 3,386.0

	STOCK PRICE ($) FY Close	P/E High/Low	PER SHARE ($) Earnings	Dividends	Book Value
08/21	35.35	88 44	0.42	0.00	12.41
08/20	25.39	82 40	0.35	0.00	12.89
08/19	29.63	51 29	0.56	0.00	10.23
08/18	17.98	18 11	0.96	0.00	9.53
08/17	11.88	1223 1175	0.01	0.00	8.48
Annual Growth	31.3%	—	−154.6%	—	10.0%

Simpson Manufacturing Co., Inc. (DE)

Through its subsidiaries Simpson Manufacturing designs engineers and is a leading manufacturer of high quality wood and concrete building construction products designed to make structures safer and more secure and that perform at high levels. Subsidiary Simpson Strong-Tie (SST) makes more than 15000 types of standard and custom products that are used to connect and reinforce joints between wood concrete and masonry building components which the company markets globally and distributes through home centers and a network of contractor and dealer distributors. The company's products are sold primarily in Canada Europe Asia the US and the Pacific. About 85% of sales were generated from the US.

Operations

The company is organized into three reporting segments: North America (over 85% of sales) Europe (over 10%) and the Asia/Pacific.

The North America segment is comprised primarily of the company's operations in the US and Canada the Europe segment and the Asia/Pacific segment is comprised of the company's operations in Asia the South Pacific and the Middle East.

Simpson divides its product lines across two main categories: wood construction (around 85% of net sales) and concrete construction (about 15%).

Geographic Reach

Headquartered in Pleasanton California the company has manufacturing facilities in Stockton and San Bernardino County California McKinney Texas West Chicago Illinois Columbus Ohio and Gallatin Tennessee. The principal manufacturing facilities located outside the US. are in France Denmark Germany Poland Switzerland Sweden Portugal and China. It also owns and leases smaller manufacturing facilities warehouses research and development facilities and sales offices in the U. Canada the United Kingdom Europe Asia Australia New Zealand and Chile. The US accounted for about 85% of its revenue the company's largest market.

Sales and Marketing

Simpson sells its products through multiple channels including contractor distributors home centers and co-ops lumber dealers and OEMs. SST markets its products to the residential construction light industrial and commercial construction remodeling and do-it-yourself (DIY) markets.

Advertising costs were $8.2 million $7.9 million and $7.6 million in 2020 2019 and 2018 respectively.

Financial Performance

Net Sales increased 12% to $1.3 billion from $1.1 billion. Net sales to home centers lumber dealers and dealer distributors increased due to higher sales volumes while net sales to contractor distributors decreased due to lower sales volumes.

In 2020 the company had a net income of $187 million a 40% increase compared to the previous year's net income of $134 million.

The company's cash at the end of 2020 was $274.6 million. Operating activities generated $207.6 million while investing activities used $39.9 million mainly for capital expenditures. Financing activities used another $126.8 million primarily for repayments of line of credit and capital leases.

Strategy

The company attracts and retains customers by designing manufacturing and selling high quality products that perform well are easy to use and cost-effective for customers. The company manufactures and warehouses its products in geographic proximity to its markets to provide availability and rapid delivery of products to customers and prompt response to customer requests for specially designed products and services. The company maintains levels of inventory intended to operate with a little backlog and fill most customer orders within a few days. High levels of manufacturing automation and flexibility allow the company to maintain its quality standards while continuing to provide prompt delivery.

The company intends to continue efforts to increase market share in both the wood construction and concrete construction product groups by: maintaining frequent customer contacts and service levels; continuing to sponsor seminars to inform architects engineers contractors and building officials on appropriate use proper installation and identification of the company's products; continuing to invest in mobile web and software applications for customers to help them do their jobs more efficiently and connect with customers utilizing social media blog posts and videos; continuing to invest in Building Information Modeling (BIM) software services and solutions for home builders and lumber-building material suppliers; and continuing to innovate and diversify its product offerings.

The company's strategy is to ensure that the home center retail stores are fully stocked with adequate supplies of the company's products carried by those stores. The company has further developed extensive bar coding and merchandising aids and has devoted a portion of its research and development efforts to DIY products.

EXECUTIVES

Chief Operating Officer, Michael Olosky
Independent Non-executive Chairman Of The Board, James Andrasick, $165,500 total compensation
Independent Director, Kenneth Knight
Senior Vice President - Finance, Kevin Swartzendruber, $300,500 total compensation
President, North American Sales, Simpson Strong-tie Company Inc., Roger Dankel, $470,000 total compensation
Chief Financial Officer And Treasurer, Brian Magstadt, $515,000 total compensation

President, Chief Executive Officer, And Director, Karen Colonias, $800,000 total compensation
Auditors: Grant Thornton LLP

LOCATIONS

HQ: Simpson Manufacturing Co., Inc. (DE)
5956 W. Las Positas Blvd., Pleasanton, CA 94588
Phone: 925 560-9000 **Fax:** 925 833-1496
Web: www.simpsonmfg.com

PRODUCTS/OPERATIONS

2015 Sales

	% of total
Wood construction	85
Concrete construction	15
Other	-
Total	**100**

Selected Products

Simpson Strong-Tie
  Adhesives
  Mechanical anchors
  Powder-actuated tools
  Screw fastening systems
  Shearwalls
  Wood-to-concrete connectors
  Wood-to-masonry connectors
  Wood-to-wood connectors

Selected Subsidiaries

Simpson Strong-Tie Australia Inc.
Simpson Strong-Tie Canada Limited
Simpson Strong-Tie Company Inc.
Simpson Strong-Tie Europe EURL
Simpson Strong-Tie International Inc.
Simpson Strong-Tie Japan Inc.

COMPETITORS

ASTEC INDUSTRIES INC.
BEACON ROOFING SUPPLY INC.
BUILDERS FIRSTSOURCE INC.
GOULD ELECTRONICS INC.
HUTTIG BUILDING PRODUCTS INC.
LAWSON PRODUCTS INC.
MITSUI MINING AND SMELTING COMPANY LIMITED
MSC INDUSTRIAL DIRECT CO. INC.
NANOPHASE TECHNOLOGIES CORPORATION
RMI TITANIUM COMPANY LLC
Rio Tinto Fer et Titane Inc
SITEONE LANDSCAPE SUPPLY INC.
TITON HOLDINGS PLC

HISTORICAL FINANCIALS

Company Type: Public

Income Statement				FYE: December 31
	REVENUE ($ mil.)	NET INCOME ($ mil.)	NET PROFIT MARGIN	EMPLOYEES
12/20	1,267.9	187.0	14.7%	3,562
12/19	1,136.5	133.9	11.8%	3,337
12/18	1,078.8	126.6	11.7%	3,135
12/17	977.0	92.6	9.5%	2,902
12/16	860.6	89.7	10.4%	2,647
Annual Growth	10.2%	20.1%	—	7.7%

2020 Year-End Financials

Debt ratio: —
Return on equity: 19.9%
Cash ($ mil.): 274.6
Current ratio: 3.88
Long-term debt ($ mil.): —
No. of shares (mil.): 43.3
Dividends
  Yield: 0.9%
  Payout: 21.5%
Market value ($ mil.): 4,049.0

	STOCK PRICE ($)	P/E	PER SHARE ($)		
	FY Close	High/Low	Earnings	Dividends	Book Value
12/20	93.45	24 11	4.27	0.92	22.64
12/19	80.23	28 18	2.98	0.91	20.18
12/18	54.13	28 18	2.72	0.86	19.01
12/17	57.41	31 21	1.94	0.78	18.93
12/16	43.75	26 16	1.86	0.68	18.25
Annual Growth 20.9%		— —	23.1%	7.8%	5.5%

Simulations Plus Inc

Molecular modeling software plus applications to help individuals with disabilities equals Simulations Plus. The company is a leading provider of applications used by pharmaceutical researchers to model absorption rates for orally dosed drug compounds. Its Words+ subsidiary provides augmentative communication software and input devices that help people with disabilities use computers. Simulations Plus also provides educational software targeted to high school and college students through its FutureLab unit. Pharmaceutical giants GlaxoSmithKline and Roche are among its clients. CEO Walter Woltosz and his wife Virginia (a director) together own about 40% of the company.

EXECUTIVES

Chairman, Walter Woltosz
President - Simulations Plus Division, John DiBella, $257,453 total compensation
President - Cognigen Division, Jill Fiedler-kelly, $220,565 total compensation
Chief Executive Officer, Shawn O'Connor, $444,231 total compensation
Independent Director, Lisa LaVange
Chief Financial Officer, Secretary, William Frederick, $196,096 total compensation
Independent Director, Sharlene Evans
President - Dilisym Division, Brett Howell, $218,136 total compensation
Auditors: Rose, Snyder & Jacobs LLP

LOCATIONS

HQ: Simulations Plus Inc
42505 10th Street West, Lancaster, CA 93534-7059
Phone: 661 723-7723 **Fax:** 661 723-5524
Web: www.simulations-plus.com

PRODUCTS/OPERATIONS

Selected Products
Augmentative Communication Products
  Cyberlink
  E Z Keys for Windows
  Freedom 2000
  HeadMouse
  MessageMate
  SoftSwitch
  Talking Screen for Windows
  Tracker One
  TuffTalker
Educational Software
  Circuits for Physical Science
  Gravity for Physical Science
  Ideal Gas for Chemistry
  Optics for Physical Science

Universal Gravitation for Physical Science
Pharmaceutical Applications
  GastroPlus
  QMPRchitect
  QMPRPlus

COMPETITORS

COMPUTER PROGRAMS AND SYSTEMS INC.
INFORMATION BUILDERS INC.
SOFT COMPUTER CONSULTANTS INC.
SUNQUEST INFORMATION SYSTEMS INC.

HISTORICAL FINANCIALS
Company Type: Public

Income Statement				FYE: August 31
	REVENUE ($ mil.)	NET INCOME ($ mil.)	NET PROFIT MARGIN	EMPLOYEES
08/21	46.4	9.7	21.1%	146
08/20	41.5	9.3	22.4%	137
08/19	33.9	8.5	25.3%	111
08/18	29.6	8.9	30.1%	95
08/17	24.1	5.7	24.0%	86
Annual Growth 17.8%		14.0%	—	14.1%

2021 Year-End Financials
Debt ratio: —
Return on equity: 6.0%
Cash ($ mil.): 36.9
Current ratio: 12.04
Long-term debt ($ mil.): —
No. of shares (mil.): 20.1
Dividends
  Yield: 0.5%
  Payout: 42.8%
Market value ($ mil.): 892.0

	STOCK PRICE ($)	P/E	PER SHARE ($)		
	FY Close	High/Low	Earnings	Dividends	Book Value
08/21	44.30	183 86	0.47	0.24	8.23
08/20	59.58	139 52	0.50	0.24	7.83
08/19	36.11	85 36	0.48	0.24	2.14
08/18	20.85	46 28	0.50	0.24	1.83
08/17	14.50	47 25	0.33	0.20	1.49
Annual Growth 32.2%		— —	9.2%	4.7%	53.2%

SiteOne Landscape Supply Inc

Auditors: DELOITTE & TOUCHE LLP

LOCATIONS

HQ: SiteOne Landscape Supply Inc
300 Colonial Center Parkway, Suite 600, Roswell, GA 30076
Phone: 470 277-7000
Web: www.siteone.com

HISTORICAL FINANCIALS
Company Type: Public

Income Statement				FYE: January 3
	REVENUE ($ mil.)	NET INCOME ($ mil.)	NET PROFIT MARGIN	EMPLOYEES
01/21*	2,704.5	121.3	4.5%	4,900
12/19	2,357.5	77.7	3.3%	4,600
12/18	2,112.3	73.9	3.5%	4,300
12/17	1,861.7	54.6	2.9%	3,800
01/17	1,648.2	30.6	1.9%	3,300
Annual Growth 13.2%		41.1%	—	10.4%

*Fiscal year change

2021 Year-End Financials
Debt ratio: 17.9%
Return on equity: 20.0%
Cash ($ mil.): 55.2
Current ratio: 2.31
Long-term debt ($ mil.): 293.1
No. of shares (mil.): 44.2
Dividends
  Yield: —
  Payout: —
Market value ($ mil.): 7,024.0

	STOCK PRICE ($)	P/E	PER SHARE ($)		
	FY Close	High/Low	Earnings	Dividends	Book Value
01/21*	158.63	56 20	2.75	0.00	17.95
12/19	90.46	49 25	1.82	0.00	9.46
12/18	55.59	52 28	1.73	0.00	7.38
12/17	76.70	56 26	1.29	0.00	5.33
01/17	34.73	— —	(3.01)	0.00	3.76
Annual Growth 46.2%		— —	—	—	47.8%

*Fiscal year change

SJW Group

It is hard to water down SJW Group's contribution in quenching America's thirst. A holding company it owns public utility services that engage in the production storage purification distribution and retail sale of water. Its two main subsidiaries the San Jose Water Company and Canyon Lake Water Service Company (CLWSC) serves nearly 1.5 million residents in California and Texas through nearly 250000 water connections. The SJW Land Company is a holder of some undeveloped land in Tennessee. In October 2019 the SJW Group announced the close of their merger with the public utility Connecticut Water Service.

Operations
SJW Group owns four subsidiaries.

Public utility San Jose Water serves about one million Californians through approximately 231000 connections in the San Jose county. It also provides non-tariffed services (water system operations maintenance antenna site leases) under agreements with municipalities and other utilities. The utility's water supply comprises groundwater from wells surface water from watershed run-off and diversion reclaimed water and water purchased from third parties.

CLWSC the second subsidiary supplies water to 54000 Texans through 18000 connections in the growing region between the cities of San Antonio and Austin. Its water supply consists of groundwater from wells and purchased treated and raw water from a third party.

SJWNE LLC is a special purpose entity established to hold SJW Group's investment in Connecticut Water Service Inc. The business provides water service to approximately 137000 connections that serve a population of approximately 480000 people in 80 municipalities throughout Connecticut and Maine and more than 3000 wastewater connections in Southbury Connecticut.

SJW Land Company owns undeveloped real estate property commercial and warehouse properties in Tennessee.

Overall SJW Group generates its revenue from Water Utility Services.

HOOVER'S HANDBOOK OF EMERGING COMPANIES 2022

Geographic Reach

San Jose Water Company's water production system is in Santa Clara California. It owns 7000 acres of land a storage capacity of 2.3 billion-gallon reservoirs and 248 million gallons of distribution as well as about 2500 miles of transmission and distribution mains.

The CLWSC subsidiary has more than 245 sq. mile service area located in the southern region of the Texas hill country in Comal and Blanco counties with 8200 surface acre reservoir (Canyon Lake). It also holds a contract for 2 billion gallons of untreated surface water and 235 million gallons of treated surface water from annually. Additionally the subsidiary owns and operates three surface water treatment plants (9 million gallons/d) about 645 miles of transmission and distribution mains and maintains 63 storage tanks.

SJW Land Company owns approximately 55 acres of property in the state of Tennessee.

Sales and Marketing

SJW Group serves residential business Industrial and Public customers.

Financial Performance

SJW Group revenue has shown an upward trajectory in the last five years. Net income peaked in 2017 but declined the next two years.

Revenue increased 6% to $420.5 million in 2019 primarily due to revenue increase of $22.9 million in Water Utility Services offset by a decrease of $0.08 million from Real Estate Services.

SJW Group's consolidated net income in 2019 was $23403 compared to $38767 for the same period in 2018. The decrease in net income was primarily due to costs incurred related to integration with the new operations in CTWS an increase in production expenses due to higher usage and higher per unit costs for purchased water ground water extraction and energy charges and higher depreciation expenses due to assets placed in service in 2018 partially offset by an increase in operating revenue and decrease in costs due to the increased use of surface water.

SJW Group had only around $18 million in cash holdings at the end of 2019. Operations provided $130 million and financing activities added another $485 million. Investment activities used $1 billion for business payments and acquisitions.

Strategy

The company's business strategy focuses on Regional regulated water utility operations Regional non-tariffed water utility - related services provided following the guidelines established by the Regulators and Out-of-region water and utility - related services. As part of our pursuit of the above three strategic areas we consider from time to time opportunities to acquire businesses and assets for example the merger with CTWS.

SJW Group plans and applies a diligent and disciplined approach to maintaining and improving its water system infrastructures and also seeks to acquire regulated water systems adjacent to or near its existing service territory. CTWS also provides regulated wastewater services through HVWC. It also seeks appropriate non-tariffed business opportunities that complement its existing operations or that allow it to extend its core competencies beyond existing operations.

Mergers and Acquisitions

In late 2019 SJW Group and Connecticut Water Service Inc. closed their merger. "As a leading national water and wastewater utility we are well positioned to deliver significant benefits to all of our stakeholders including shareholders customers employees and the local communities we serve" said Eric W. Thornburg Chairman President and Chief Executive Officer of SJW Group.

Company Background

The company has geographically diversified its regulated water operations moving into Central Texas (through the acquisition of Canyon Lake Water Service) in 2006. SJW acquired four water systems in Comal County (Texas) in 2011.

EXECUTIVES

Independent Director, Heather Hunt

Chief Administrative Officer, Kristen Johnson

Ctws—president, Maureen Westbrook, $75,958 total compensation

Independent Director, Rebecca Klein

Chief Accounting Officer, James Lynch, $480,000 total compensation

Chairman Of The Board, President, Chief Executive Officer, Eric Thornburg, $780,000 total compensation

Independent Director, Carol Wallace

Independent Director, Mary Hanley

Independent Director, Daniel More

Independent Director, Gregory Landis

Chief Financial Officer, Treasurer, Andrew Walters, $415,000 total compensation

Independent Director, Walter Bishop

Independent Director, Carl Guardino

Vice President - Finance, Controller, Assistant Treasurer, Wendy Avila-walker

Chief Corporate Development Officer And Integration Executive, Andrew Gere, $475,000 total compensation

Auditors: Deloitte & Touche LLP

LOCATIONS

HQ: SJW Group
110 West Taylor Street, San Jose, CA 95110
Phone: 408 279-7800
Web: www.sjwater.com

PRODUCTS/OPERATIONS

2016 Sales

	$ mil.	% of total
Water utility services		
Regulated	326.6	96
Non-regulated	6.4	2
Real estate services	6.7	2
Total	**339.7**	**100**

Selected Subsidiaries and Affiliates

California Water Service Group (minority stake water utility)
San Jose Water Company (water utility)
SJW Land Company (parking facilities and commercial real estate)
SJWTX Inc. (Canyon Lake Water Service Company — water utility)
Texas Water Alliance Limited (water supply development)

COMPETITORS

AMERICAN WATER WORKS COMPANY INC.
CALIFORNIA WATER SERVICE GROUP
COLORADO SPRINGS UTILITIES
Consolidated Water Co. Ltd.
DENVER BOARD OF WATER COMMISSIONERS

ESSENTIAL UTILITIES INC.
MIDDLESEX WATER COMPANY
NORTHWESTERN CORPORATION
ORLANDO UTILITIES COMMISSION (INC)
VIDLER WATER RESOURCES INC.

HISTORICAL FINANCIALS

Company Type: Public

Income Statement				FYE: December 31
	REVENUE ($ mil.)	NET INCOME ($ mil.)	NET PROFIT MARGIN	EMPLOYEES
12/20	564.5	61.5	10.9%	748
12/19	420.4	23.4	5.6%	732
12/18	397.7	38.7	9.7%	416
12/17	389.2	59.2	15.2%	411
12/16	339.7	52.8	15.6%	406
Annual Growth	13.5%	3.9%	—	16.5%

2020 Year-End Financials

Debt ratio: 46.4%
Return on equity: 6.7%
Cash ($ mil.): 5.2
Current ratio: 0.36
Long-term debt ($ mil.): 1,287.5

No. of shares (mil.): 28.5
Dividends
  Yield: 1.8%
  Payout: 59.8%
Market value ($ mil.): 1,981.0

	STOCK PRICE ($) FY Close	P/E High/Low		PER SHARE ($) Earnings	Dividends	Book Value
12/20	69.36	35	23	2.14	1.28	32.12
12/19	71.06	91	67	0.82	1.20	31.28
12/18	55.62	37	28	1.82	1.29	31.31
12/17	63.83	24	16	2.86	1.04	22.57
12/16	55.98	22	11	2.57	0.81	20.61
Annual Growth	5.5%	—	—	(4.5%)	12.1%	11.7%

Skyline Champion Corp

Skyline's idea of a beautiful skyline would probably include several rows of double-wides. The company and its subsidiaries design and make manufactured homes. It distributes them to independent dealers and manufactured housing communities throughout the US and Canada. About half of Skyline's revenues come from selling HUD-code manufactured homes (products built according to US Housing and Urban Development standards); the rest of its typically two- to four-bedroom homes are modular in design.

HISTORY

Julius Decio started Skyline Coach in 1951 in a friend's welding garage. At first the company made mobile homes but by 1959 it was also producing travel trailers and recreational vehicles (RVs). Skyline went public in 1960. Two years later it acquired Homette and Layton Homes and in 1963 it bought Buddy Mobile Homes. The company changed its name to Skyline Corporation and acquired Academy Mobile Homes in 1966. It purchased Country Vans Conversion in 1978.

Skyline's manufactured home sales increased during the 1990s but they failed to keep pace with industrywide growth. The company's market share faded. Blaming the loss of market share on a lack of dealers in high-growth regions in 1995 Skyline made plans to increase production expand its product line and boost market penetration. Product lines in 1997 stressed luxury features such as solid-oak cabinets and cedar-lined wardrobes. Harsh winter weather lowered sales that year. A long-reaching industrywide recession which continued into 2004 began during that time.

Although RV sales — especially fifth-wheel and truck camper sales — dropped in fiscal 1998 sales of higher-priced multi-section homes increased. By 2000 rising interest rates and inventories were contributing to industrywide declines: That year Skyline's RV sales fell nearly 25% and its manufactured homes sales were off by more than 15%. Sales of manufactured homes dropped again in fiscal 2001 by 20%. The company's sales continued to drop in 2002 although its operating income increased by about 10% due in part to increased RV sales and containment of operating costs. The next year saw more declines for Skyline. By 2004 the manufactured housing industry hit its lowest level in more than a dozen years. Restrictive retail financing global tensions and uncertain economic conditions were primary factors that contributed to the recession.

In 2004 Skyline moved to expand its product offerings by gaining approval to produce modular homes at 12 of its manufactured housing facilities. The company also began to reposition its RV segment to accommodate a shift in consumer demand for towable RVs.

EXECUTIVES

Independent Director, John Firth
Independent Director, Gary Robinette
Vice President And Controller, Timothy Burkhardt
Chairman, Timothy Bernlohr
Independent Director, Michael Kaufman
Chief Financial Officer, Executive Vice President, Treasurer, Laurie Hough, $425,000 total compensation
President, Chief Executive Officer, Director, Mark Yost, $600,000 total compensation
Independent Director, Michael Berman
Senior Vice President, General Counsel, Secretary, Robert Spence, $325,000 total compensation
Independent Director, Eddie Capel
Independent Director, Erin Nelson
Chief Growth Officer, Timothy Larson
First Vice President Of Marketing, Roland Menassa
Executive Vice President, Operations, Joseph Kimmell, $350,000 total compensation
Executive Vice President, Sales And Business Development, Wade Lyall, $350,000 total compensation
Auditors: Ernst & Young LLP

LOCATIONS

HQ: Skyline Champion Corp
755 West Big Beaver Road, Suite 1000, Troy, MI 48084
Phone: 248 614-8211
Web: www.skylinechampion.com

COMPETITORS

APEX HOMES INC.
ATRM HOLDINGS INC.
CAVCO INDUSTRIES INC.
CHAMPION ENTERPRISES HOLDINGS LLC
DANDI SYSTEMS INC
GLOBAL DIVERSIFIED INDUSTRIES INC.
NOBILITY HOMES INC.
NORTHEASTERN LOG HOMES INC.

HISTORICAL FINANCIALS

Company Type: Public

Income Statement | | | | FYE: April 3

	REVENUE ($ mil.)	NET INCOME ($ mil.)	NET PROFIT MARGIN	EMPLOYEES
04/21*	1,420.8	84.9	6.0%	7,700
03/20	1,369.7	58.1	4.2%	6,600
03/19	1,360.0	(58.2)	—	7,000
03/18	1,064.7	15.8	1.5%	0
05/17	236.5	0.0	0.0%	1,300
Annual Growth	56.6%	1041.5%	—	56.0%

*Fiscal year change

2021 Year-End Financials

Debt ratio: 4.2%	No. of shares (mil.): 56.6
Return on equity: 16.0%	Dividends
Cash ($ mil.): 262.5	Yield: —
Current ratio: 1.90	Payout: —
Long-term debt ($ mil.): 39.3	Market value ($ mil.): 2,686.0

	STOCK PRICE ($) FY Close	P/E High/Low		PER SHARE ($) Earnings	Dividends	Book Value
04/21*	47.42	32	8	1.49	0.00	10.04
03/20	15.42	35	13	1.02	0.00	8.37
03/19	19.00	—	—	(1.09)	0.62	7.27
03/18	22.00	74	16	0.33	0.00	(0.00)
05/17	5.26	—	—	(0.00)	0.00	3.01
Annual Growth	73.3%	—	—	—	—	35.1%

*Fiscal year change

Sleep Number Corp

Sleep Number Corporation (formerly Select Comfort) is at the forefront of delivering this life-changing benefit with its revolutionary Sleep Number 360 smart beds and SleepIQ technology which improved approximately 13 million lives. A leading bedding retailer in the US the company operates more than 600 company-owned stores in the US. The air-bed maker also sells through a company-operated call center its own website phone and chat. Sleep Number was founded in 1987 has grown to become one of the nation's leading bed makers and retailers.

Operations

Sleep Number's vertically integrated business model and role as the exclusive designer manufacturer marketer retailer and servicer of Sleep Number beds offers high-quality individualized sleep solutions and services.

Sleep Number 360 smart beds effortlessly deliver proven quality sleep by allowing each sleeper to set their ideal firmness support and pressure-relieving comfort ? their Sleep Number setting. SleepIQ technology optimizes the smart benefits of the bed continually improving a sleeper's restful time asleep ? their SleepIQ score ? to deliver a life-changing difference to their overall health and wellness.

The company unveils the next generation of 360 smart beds with technology to advance its health and wellness platform and made several new sleep innovations available through SleepIQ technology platform that include Nighttime Heart Rate Variability (HRV) (measures the variation of time between each heartbeat) Sleep Circadian Insights (automatically tracks sleep and wake times for each sleeper in the SleepIQ platform application) and Monthly Sleep Wellness Reports (provides an overview of personalized insights highlighting sleep health circadian stability and respiratory and cardiovascular health via HRV).

In addition to its forthcoming Sleep Number Climate360 smart bed Sleep Number also offers a full line of exclusive FlexFit SleepIQ Kids k2 bed and also a variety of temperature-balancing products including the DualTemp layer.

The company's retail accounts for approximately 85% of the revenue while online phone and chat sales generate some 15%.

Geographic Reach

Headquartered in Minneapolis Minnesota Sleep Number has more than 600 retail stores in about 50 US states. The company leases two manufacturing assembly and distribution centers in Irmo South Carolina and Salt Lake City Utah.

Sales and Marketing

Sleep Number markets and sells its products through customer service staff brochures videos websites customer mailings and in-store signage. Virtually all of the company's net sales are generated by its direct-to-consumer business through a cohesive experience across its Sleep Number stores online at SleepNumber.com and via phone.

The company's advertising expenses were $253 million $242 million and $210 million in 2020 2019 and 2018 respectively.

Financial Performance

Net sales for 2020 increased 9% to $1.9 billion compared with $1.7 billion in 2019. Total Retail comparable sales increased 6% and sales from net opened/closed stores in the past 12 months added 1.5 percentage points (ppt.) of growth in 2020.

Net income in 2020 increased 70% to $139 million compared with net income of $82 million in 2019.

Cash held by the company at the end of fiscal 2020 increased to $4.2 million. Cash provided by operations was $279.7 million while cash used for investing and financing activities were $39.0 million and $238.0 million respectively. Main uses of cash were purchases of property and equipment; and repurchases of common stock.

Mergers and Acquisitions

In 2015 Select Comfort acquired BAM Labs Inc. a provider of biometric sensor and sleep monitoring for data-driven health and wellness. The acquisition broadens and deepens Select Comfort's electrical biomedical software and backend capabilities in providing sleep-related information to mattress customers.

Company Background

Sleep Number was incorporated in 1987 and became publicly traded in 1998 listed on the Nasdaq Stock Market LLC (Nasdaq Global Select Market) under the symbol "SNBR".

EXECUTIVES

Independent Director, Michael Harrison
President, Chief Executive Officer, Director, Shelly Ibach, $746,200 total compensation
Independent Director, Stephen Gulis
Independent Director, Phillip Eyler
Independent Director, Angel Mendez
Chief Financial Officer, Executive Vice President, David Callen, $439,632 total compensation
Executive Vice President, Chief Marketing Officer, Kevin Brown, $433,823 total compensation

HOOVER'S HANDBOOK OF EMERGING COMPANIES 2022

377

Non-executive Independent Chairman Of The Board, Jean-Michel Valette
Independent Director, Brenda Lauderback
Executive Vice President And Chief Supply Chain Officer, Hunter Saklad
Independent Director, Kathleen Nedorostek
Executive Vice President And Chief Innovation Officer, Andrea Bloomquist, $467,106 total compensation
Executive Vice President And Chief Sales And Services Officer, Melissa Barra, $316,133 total compensation
Senior Vice President And Chief Legal And Risk Officer And Secretary, Samuel Hellfeld
Independent Director, Barbara Matas
Independent Director, Deborah Kilpatrick
Chief Human Resource Officer, Senior Vice President, Christopher Krusmark
Independent Director, Julie Howard
Auditors: DELOITTE & TOUCHE LLP

LOCATIONS

HQ: Sleep Number Corp
1001 Third Avenue South, Minneapolis, MN 55404
Phone: 763 551-7000
Web: www.SleepNumber.com

PRODUCTS/OPERATIONS

2015 Sales

	% of total
Retail	92
Online and call center	6
Wholesale	2
Total	**100**

Selected Products

Bed frames
Foundations
Mattress pads
Mattresses
Pillows
Pillowtops
Sleep Number SofaBed

COMPETITORS

DOMESTIC & GENERAL GROUP LIMITED
HAVERTY FURNITURE COMPANIES INC.
HYPNOS LIMITED
MANNATECH INCORPORATED
MASIMO CORPORATION
NATURE'S SUNSHINE PRODUCTS INC.
O'REILLY AUTOMOTIVE INC.
SEALY CORPORATION
SSB MANUFACTURING COMPANY
TEMPUR SEALY INTERNATIONAL INC.
WELLINGTON REALISATIONS LIMITED
ZYTRONIC PLC

HISTORICAL FINANCIALS

Company Type: Public

Income Statement				FYE: January 2
	REVENUE ($ mil.)	NET INCOME ($ mil.)	NET PROFIT MARGIN	EMPLOYEES
01/21*	1,856.5	139.1	7.5%	4,679
12/19	1,698.3	81.8	4.8%	4,476
12/18	1,531.5	69.5	4.5%	4,220
12/17	1,444.5	65.0	4.5%	4,099
12/16	1,311.2	51.4	3.9%	3,768
Annual Growth	**9.1%**	**28.3%**	—	**5.6%**

*Fiscal year change

2021 Year-End Financials

Debt ratio: 30.5%
Return on equity: ***,***.*%
Cash ($ mil.): 4.2
Current ratio: 0.28
Long-term debt ($ mil.): —
No. of shares (mil.): 25.3
Dividends
Yield: —
Payout: —
Market value ($ mil.): 2,078.0

	STOCK PRICE ($) FY Close	P/E High/Low		PER SHARE ($) Earnings	Dividends	Book Value
01/21*	81.86	18	3	4.90	0.00	(8.82)
12/19	49.59	19	11	2.70	0.00	(5.70)
12/18	32.13	20	14	1.92	0.00	(3.55)
12/17	37.59	24	12	1.55	0.00	2.30
12/16	22.62	25	14	1.10	0.00	3.68
Annual Growth	**37.9%**			— — 45.3%	—	—

*Fiscal year change

SLM Corp.

SLM Corporation more commonly known as Sallie Mae holds some $18.4 billion in private education loans and originates some $5.3 billion of loans. Its Private Education Loans include important protections for the family including loan forgiveness in case of death or permanent disability of the student borrower a free quarterly FICO score benefit to students and cosigners and for borrowers with a Smart Option Student Loan on-line tutoring services to help students succeed in school. SLM's main subsidiary Sallie Mae Bank is one of the nation's largest education loan providers and specializes in originating acquiring financing and servicing private student loans which are not guaranteed by the government.

HISTORY

The Student Loan Marketing Association was chartered in 1972 as a response to problems in the Guaranteed Student Loan Program of 1965. For years the GSL program had tinkered with rates to induce banks to make loans but servicing the small loans was expensive and troublesome. Sallie Mae began operations in 1973 buying loans from their originators; its size provided economies of scale in loan servicing.

Originally only institutions making educational or student loans were allowed to own stock in Sallie Mae. This was later changed so that anyone could buy nonvoting stock. In 1993 voting stock was listed on the NYSE.

Sallie Mae was always a political football altered again and again to reflect the education policies of the party in power. When it was founded during the Nixon administration its loans were restricted by a needs test which was repealed during the Carter years. The Reagan administration reimposed the needs test and at the same time sped up the schedule under which the company was to become self-supporting which it did by late 1981.

Forced to rely on its own resources Sallie Mae turned to creative financing. One of its traditional advantages was that its loan interest rates were linked to Treasury bills traditionally about 3% above the T-bill rate. The company became a master at riding the spread between its cost of funds and the interest rates it charged.

Between 1983 and 1992 Sallie Mae's assets swelled by more than 400% and its income rose by almost 500%. As the firm grew management became more visible with high pay and extravagant perks. Although salaries were not inconsistent with those of executives at comparable private corporations the remuneration level and perks irked Congress. But Sallie Mae kept growing — in 1992 it expanded its facilities and added 900 new staff members.

The 1993 Omnibus Budget Reconciliation Act with its transfer of the student loan program directly to the government and its surcharge on Sallie Mae began to adversely affect earnings in 1994. While awaiting permission to alter its charter the company stepped up its marketing efforts especially to school loan officers who advised students on loan options.

In 1995 then-COO Albert Lord led a group of stockholders in a push to cut operating expenses and repackage student loans as securities la Freddie Mac and Fannie Mae. Lord and some of his supporters won seats on the board (as well as the enmity of Lawrence Hough who resigned as CEO in the midst of the melee). That year Sallie Mae bought HICA Holding one of two private insurers of education loans. In 1996 Congress passed legislation forcing Sallie Mae's privatization.

Despite SLM's rising stock shareholders were unhappy with chairman William Arceneaux's status quo business plan. Lord gained control in 1997.

In 1998 the organization became SLM Holding. Assets and earnings were muted that year when unfavorable market conditions prevented Sallie Mae from securitizing its loans.

The firm the next year expanded its lending operations by buying Nellie Mae. Also in 1999 Sallie Mae teamed with Answer Financial to sell insurance. Growth continued in 2000 when the company bought loan servicer Student Loan Funding Resources as well as the marketing student loan servicing and administrative operations of USA Group; the company changed its name to USA Education following the acquisition. The company also cut some 1700 jobs approximately 25% of its workforce.

The following year Sallie Mae teamed with Intuit allowing the financial software company access to Sallie Mae's 7 million customers. It also launched online recruiting service TrueCareers that year.

In 2002 it bought Pioneer Credit Recovery and General Revenue Corporation two of the nation's largest student loan collection agencies. It also reverted to the SLM moniker to reconnect with the name by which it has so long been known.

The privatization plan put into place in the mid-'90s (orchestrated in large part by then-CEO Lord) came to fruition nearly four years ahead of schedule when SLM transitioned to a private organization in December 2004.

In 2007 SLM saw its stock values plummet to their lowest levels in about a decade. A number of industry-wide factors figured into the losses not the least of which was the downturn in the credit market. Also affecting the company was the signing into law of the College Cost Reduction and Access Act (CCRAA). Intended to reform student lending and cut costs for borrowers the act slashed subsidies for lenders participating in the Federal Family Education Loan Program (FFELP). The reform cut into the company's interest-earning operations. As a result SLM increased its focus on higher-yielding private education loans which carry a lower risk.

Additionally SLM that year became ensnared in a student-lending industry probe led by New York attorney general Andrew Cuomo. The company agreed to a $2 million settlement and to abide by a code of conduct regarding its dealings with college employees.

One of the most dramatic results of the troubles was the collapse of a planned acquisition by a consortium of investment firms. The planned $8.8 billion deal included buyers J.C. Flowers (which was to own about a half of SLM) Bank of America and JPMorgan Chase. In the midst of the industry probe J.C. Flowers sought a change in SLM's leadership in an effort to secure regulatory approval for the acquisition; Thomas J. (Tim) Fitzpatrick was ousted as CEO. Ultimately the buyers canceled the deal citing the reduced potential value of SLM. The student lender filed a lawsuit to challenge the termination but eventually dropped the suit. It later cut more than 10% of its workforce.

EXECUTIVES

Chief Financial Officer, Executive Vice President, Steven McGarry, $519,231 total compensation
Independent Director, Frank Puleo
Senior Vice President, Chief Legal, Government Affairs & Communications Officer, Nicolas Jafarieh, $425,000 total compensation
Lead Independent Director, Paul Child
Senior Vice President, Controller, Jonathan Boyles
Chief Operating Officer, Executive Vice President, Daniel Kennedy
Independent Director, Marianne Keler
Independent Director, Robert Strong
Independent Director, Kirsten Wolberg
Independent Director, Mark Lavelle
Chief Executive Officer, Jonathan Witter, $657,692 total compensation
Executive Vice President, Chief Risk And Compliance Officer, Kerri Palmer
Independent Director, Vivian Schneck-Last
Independent Director, Jim Matheson
Executive Vice President, Chief Commercial Officer, Donna Vieira, $467,308 total compensation
Independent Director, Ted Manvitz
Independent Chairman Of The Board, Mary Carter Franke
Independent Director, Samuel Ramsey
Auditors: KPMG LLP

LOCATIONS

HQ: SLM Corp.
300 Continental Drive, Newark, DE 19713
Phone: 302 451-0200
Web: www.salliemakessense.com

PRODUCTS/OPERATIONS

2016 Sales

	$ mil.	% of total
Interest		
Lons	1,060.5	79
Investments	9.2	1
Cash & cash equivalents	7.6	1
Non-Interest income		
Gain on sale of loans	0.2	14
(Losses) gains on derivatives and hedging activities net	(0.9)	5
Other income	69.5	-
Total	**1,146.1**	**100**

Selected Subsidiaries

HICA Holding
Sallie Mae Bank
Sallie Mae Inc.
SLM Education Credit Finance Corporation
Bull Run I LLC
SLM Education Credit Funding LLC
SLM Investment Corporation
Southwest Student Services Corporation

COMPETITORS

AGFIRST FARM CREDIT BANK
BANCO DE SABADELL SA
CAIXABANK SA
CREDIT ACCEPTANCE CORPORATION
FEDERAL HOME LOAN BANK OF BOSTON
FEDERAL HOME LOAN BANK OF NEW YORK
FEDERAL HOME LOAN BANK OF PITTSBURGH
MGIC INVESTMENT CORPORATION
NORINCHUKIN BANK THE
PERFORMANT FINANCIAL CORPORATION
STATE EMPLOYEES' CREDIT UNION
WORLD ACCEPTANCE CORPORATION

HISTORICAL FINANCIALS

Company Type: Public

Income Statement

FYE: December 31

	ASSETS ($ mil.)	NET INCOME ($ mil.)	INCOME AS % OF ASSETS	EMPLOYEES
12/20	30,770.4	880.6	2.9%	1,600
12/19	32,686.4	578.2	1.8%	1,900
12/18	26,638.1	487.4	1.8%	1,700
12/17	21,779.5	288.9	1.3%	1,500
12/16	18,533.0	250.3	1.4%	1,300
Annual Growth	13.5%	37.0%	—	5.3%

2020 Year-End Financials

Return on assets: 2.7%
Return on equity: 29.9%
Long-term debt ($ mil.):—
No. of shares (mil.): 375.2
Sales ($ mil): 2,353.1

Dividends
Yield: 0.9%
Payout: 8.5%
Market value ($ mil.): 4,650.0

	STOCK PRICE ($) FY Close	P/E High/Low		PER SHARE ($) Earnings	Dividends	Book Value
12/20	12.39	5	3	2.25	0.12	6.83
12/19	8.91	9	6	1.30	0.12	7.86
12/18	8.31	11	8	1.07	0.00	6.82
12/17	11.30	20	16	0.62	0.00	5.72
12/16	11.02	21	10	0.53	0.00	5.47
Annual Growth	3.0%			— 43.5%	—	5.7%

Smart Sand Inc

Auditors: Grant Thornton LLP

LOCATIONS

HQ: Smart Sand Inc
1725 Hughes Landing Blvd., Suite 800, The Woodlands, TX 77380
Phone: 281 231-2660
Web: www.smartsand.com

HISTORICAL FINANCIALS

Company Type: Public

Income Statement

FYE: December 31

	REVENUE ($ mil.)	NET INCOME ($ mil.)	NET PROFIT MARGIN	EMPLOYEES
12/20	122.3	37.9	31.0%	228
12/19	233.0	31.6	13.6%	285
12/18	212.4	18.6	8.8%	323
12/17	137.2	21.5	15.7%	198
12/16	59.2	10.3	17.5%	103
Annual Growth	19.9%	38.3%	—	22.0%

2020 Year-End Financials

Debt ratio: 6.8%
Return on equity: 14.2%
Cash ($ mil.): 11.7
Current ratio: 3.01
Long-term debt ($ mil.): 22.4

No. of shares (mil.): 41.5
Dividends
Yield: —
Payout: —
Market value ($ mil.): 72.0

	STOCK PRICE ($) FY Close	P/E High/Low		PER SHARE ($) Earnings	Dividends	Book Value
12/20	1.72	3	1	0.94	0.00	6.95
12/19	2.52	6	3	0.78	0.00	6.07
12/18	2.22	24	4	0.46	0.00	5.24
12/17	8.66	39	9	0.53	0.00	4.70
12/16	16.55	38	25	0.42	0.00	3.67
Annual Growth	(43.2%)			— 22.3%	—	17.3%

SmartFinancial Inc

Cornerstone Bancshares is the holding company for Cornerstone Community Bank which operates about five locations in Chattanooga Tennessee and surrounding communities in addition to two loan production offices in Knoxville Tennessee and Dalton Georgia. The bank offers standard retail and commercial services including checking and savings accounts money market accounts and CDs. Its lending activities primarily consist of commercial real estate loans residential mortgages real estate construction loans and business and agricultural loans. Another subsidiary of Cornerstone Bancshares Eagle Financial purchases accounts receivable and acts as a conduit lender.

EXECUTIVES

Director, John Presley
Independent Director, Monique Berke
Chief Financial Officer, Executive Vice President, Ronald Gorczynski, $267,628 total compensation
Independent Chairman Of The Board, Wesley Welborn, $303,596 total compensation
Executive Vice President, Chief Information Officer Of Smartbank, Daniel Hereford
Executive Vice President, Chief Risk Officer, Gary Petty, $132,500 total compensation
President, Chief Executive Officer And Director, William Carroll, $475,539 total compensation
Independent Director, Keith Whaley
Lead Independent Director, David Ogle
Independent Director, Geoffrey Wolpert
Executive Vice President, Chief Lending Officer Of Smartbank, Gregory Davis

HOOVER'S HANDBOOK OF EMERGING COMPANIES 2022

Executive Vice President, Chief Credit Officer Of Smartbank, Rhett Jordan, $188,522 total compensation
Independent Director, Steven Tucker
Independent Director, Victor Barrett
Independent Director, Ottis Phillips
Executive Vice President , Director Of Financial Planning And Analysis Of Smartbank, Cynthia Cain
Executive Vice President , Chief People Officer Of Smartbank, Rebecca Boyd
Auditors: Dixon Hughes Goodman LLP

LOCATIONS

HQ: SmartFinancial Inc
5401 Kingston Pike, Suite 600, Knoxville, TN 37919
Phone: 855 437-5700
Web: www.smartfinancialinc.com

COMPETITORS

FIRST CHEROKEE BANCSHARES INC
FIRST COMMONWEALTH FINANCIAL CORPORATION
NEFFS BANCORP INC.

HISTORICAL FINANCIALS

Company Type: Public

Income Statement — FYE: December 31

	ASSETS ($ mil.)	NET INCOME ($ mil.)	INCOME AS % OF ASSETS	EMPLOYEES
12/20	3,304.9	24.3	0.7%	475
12/19	2,449.1	26.5	1.1%	399
12/18	2,274.4	18.1	0.8%	387
12/17	1,720.7	5.0	0.3%	343
12/16	1,062.4	5.8	0.5%	222
Annual Growth 32.8%		43.1%	—	20.9%

2020 Year-End Financials

Return on assets: 0.8%
Return on equity: 7.2%
Long-term debt ($ mil.): —
No. of shares (mil.): 15.1
Sales ($ mil.): 133.0

Dividends
Yield: 1.1%
Payout: 13.3%
Market value ($ mil.): 274.0

	STOCK PRICE ($) FY Close	P/E High/Low		PER SHARE ($) Earnings	Dividends	Book Value
12/20	18.14	14	7	1.62	0.20	23.64
12/19	23.65	13	9	1.89	0.05	22.33
12/18	18.27	19	12	1.45	0.00	20.31
12/17	21.70	47	33	0.55	0.00	18.46
12/16	18.56	24	18	0.78	0.00	17.85
Annual Growth (0.6%)		—	—	20.0%	—	7.3%

SolarWinds Corp

Auditors: PricewaterhouseCoopers LLP

LOCATIONS

HQ: SolarWinds Corp
7171 Southwest Parkway, Building 400, Austin, TX 78735
Phone: 512 682-9300
Web: www.solarwinds.com

HISTORICAL FINANCIALS

Company Type: Public

Income Statement — FYE: December 31

	REVENUE ($ mil.)	NET INCOME ($ mil.)	NET PROFIT MARGIN	EMPLOYEES
12/20	1,019.2	158.4	15.5%	3,340
12/19	932.5	18.6	2.0%	3,251
12/18	833.0	(102.0)	—	2,738
12/17	728.0	(83.8)	—	2,540
12/16	422.0	(262.5)	—	0
Annual Growth 24.7%		—	—	—

2020 Year-End Financials

Debt ratio: 33.3%
Return on equity: 5.5%
Cash ($ mil.): 370.5
Current ratio: 1.04
Long-term debt ($ mil.): 1,882.6

No. of shares (mil.): 156.5
Dividends
Yield: —
Payout: —
Market value ($ mil.): 2,340.0

	STOCK PRICE ($) FY Close	P/E High/Low		PER SHARE ($) Earnings	Dividends	Book Value
12/20	14.95	23	12	1.00	0.00	19.24
12/19	18.55	171	109	0.12	0.00	17.19
12/18	13.83	4	2	5.12	0.00	17.16
Annual Growth 4.0%		—	—	(55.8%)	—	5.9%

Solera National Bancorp Inc

EXECUTIVES

Chief Financial Officer, Senior Vice President, Secretary, Melissa Larkin
Director, Michael Quagliano
Director, Jackson Lounsberry
Director, Carlyle Griffin
Director, Rene Morin
President, Chief Executive Officer, Kreighton Reed
Auditors: Eide Bailly, LLP

LOCATIONS

HQ: Solera National Bancorp Inc
319 S. Sheridan Blvd, Lakewood, CO 80226
Phone: 303 209-8600
Web: www.solerabank.com

HISTORICAL FINANCIALS

Company Type: Public

Income Statement — FYE: December 31

	ASSETS ($ mil.)	NET INCOME ($ mil.)	INCOME AS % OF ASSETS	EMPLOYEES
12/20	435.7	5.9	1.4%	0
12/19	282.1	3.5	1.3%	0
12/18	220.6	2.2	1.0%	0
12/17	173.9	0.5	0.3%	0
12/16	156.0	3.1	2.0%	0
Annual Growth 29.3%		17.4%	—	—

2020 Year-End Financials

Return on assets: 1.6%
Return on equity: 13.3%
Long-term debt ($ mil.): —
No. of shares (mil.): 4.2
Sales ($ mil.): 16.6

Dividends
Yield: —
Payout: —
Market value ($ mil.): 47.0

	STOCK PRICE ($) FY Close	P/E High/Low		PER SHARE ($) Earnings	Dividends	Book Value
12/20	11.00	8	6	1.41	0.00	11.23
12/19	11.55	14	10	0.86	0.00	9.78
12/18	8.90	17	13	0.62	0.00	8.68
12/17	8.25	45	38	0.19	0.00	8.64
12/16	7.40	7	4	1.15	0.00	8.38
Annual Growth 10.4%		—	—	5.2%	—	7.6%

Sonos Inc

Auditors: PricewaterhouseCoopers LLP

LOCATIONS

HQ: Sonos Inc
614 Chapala Street, Santa Barbara, CA 93101
Phone: 805 965-3001
Web: www.sonos.com

HISTORICAL FINANCIALS

Company Type: Public

Income Statement — FYE: October 2

	REVENUE ($ mil.)	NET INCOME ($ mil.)	NET PROFIT MARGIN	EMPLOYEES
10/21	1,716.7	158.6	9.2%	1,525
10/20*	1,326.3	(20.1)	—	1,427
09/19	1,260.8	(4.7)	—	1,446
09/18	1,137.0	(15.6)	—	1,352
09/17	992.5	(14.2)	—	1,478
Annual Growth 14.7%		—	—	0.8%

*Fiscal year change

2021 Year-End Financials

Debt ratio: —
Return on equity: 36.6%
Cash ($ mil.): 640.1
Current ratio: 2.01
Long-term debt ($ mil.): —

No. of shares (mil.): 126.9
Dividends
Yield: —
Payout: —
Market value ($ mil.): 4,097.0

	STOCK PRICE ($) FY Close	P/E High/Low		PER SHARE ($) Earnings	Dividends	Book Value
10/21	32.26	34	11	1.13	0.00	4.48
10/20*	15.50	—	—	(0.18)	0.00	2.65
09/19	13.51	—	—	(0.05)	0.00	2.59
09/18	16.04	—	—	(0.24)	0.00	2.08
Annual Growth 26.2%		—	—	—	—	29.1%

*Fiscal year change

Sound Financial Bancorp Inc

Auditors: Moss Adams LLP

LOCATIONS

HQ: Sound Financial Bancorp Inc
2400 3rd Avenue, Suite 150, Seattle, WA 98121
Phone: 206 448-0884
Web: www.soundcb.com

HISTORICAL FINANCIALS

Company Type: Public

Income Statement				FYE: December 31
	ASSETS ($ mil.)	NET INCOME ($ mil.)	INCOME AS % OF ASSETS	EMPLOYEES
12/20	861.4	8.9	1.0%	120
12/19	719.8	6.6	0.9%	132
12/18	716.7	7.0	1.0%	119
12/17	645.2	5.1	0.8%	121
12/16	588.3	5.3	0.9%	106
Annual Growth	10.0%	13.5%	—	3.1%

2020 Year-End Financials

Return on assets: 1.1%
Return on equity: 10.9%
Long-term debt ($ mil.): —
No. of shares (mil.): 2.5
Sales ($ mil): 42.3

Dividends
Yield: 2.5%
Payout: 28.5%
Market value ($ mil.): 82.0

	STOCK PRICE ($) FY Close	P/E High/Low		PER SHARE ($) Earnings	Dividends	Book Value
12/20	31.75	11	5	3.42	0.80	32.97
12/19	36.00	14	13	2.57	0.56	30.27
12/18	32.55	14	12	2.74	0.54	28.15
12/17	34.02	17	13	2.00	0.60	25.95
12/16	28.00	14	10	2.09	0.30	24.12
Annual Growth	3.2%	—	—	13.1%	27.8%	8.1%

South Atlantic Bancshares Inc

Auditors: Elliot Davis LLC

LOCATIONS

HQ: South Atlantic Bancshares Inc
630 29th Avenue North, Myrtle Beach, SC 29577
Phone: 843 839-4412
Web: www.southatlantic.bank

HISTORICAL FINANCIALS

Company Type: Public

Income Statement				FYE: December 31
	ASSETS ($ mil.)	NET INCOME ($ mil.)	INCOME AS % OF ASSETS	EMPLOYEES
12/20	946.5	7.2	0.8%	146
12/19	718.4	6.0	0.8%	0
12/18	630.2	3.4	0.5%	0
12/17	519.1	3.4	0.7%	97
12/16	444.5	2.6	0.6%	0
Annual Growth	20.8%	28.9%	—	—

2020 Year-End Financials

Return on assets: 0.8%
Return on equity: 7.7%
Long-term debt ($ mil.): —
No. of shares (mil.): 7.5
Sales ($ mil): 41.5

Dividends
Yield: —
Payout: —
Market value ($ mil.): 92.0

	STOCK PRICE ($) FY Close	P/E High/Low		PER SHARE ($) Earnings	Dividends	Book Value
12/20	12.25	13	8	0.96	0.00	13.03
12/19	12.60	16	13	0.80	0.00	11.78
12/18	11.03	34	23	0.47	0.00	10.57
12/17	16.35	31	22	0.57	0.00	9.44
12/16	16.00	26	16	0.60	0.00	8.88
Annual Growth	(6.5%)	—	—	12.5%	—	10.0%

South Jersey Industries Inc

South Jersey Industries (SJI) is Atlantic City's answer to cold casino nights. Its main subsidiary South Jersey Gas (SJG) provided natural gas to nearly 404886 residential commercial and industrial customers in southern New Jersey including Atlantic City. The utility has more than 6900 miles of transmission and distribution mains; it also sells and transports wholesale gas. The company was founded in 1969.

Operations

SJI operates in several different reportable operating segments. These segments are as follows:

SJG utility operations account for about 35% of revenue and consist primarily of natural gas distribution to residential commercial and industrial customers in southern New Jersey.

ETG utility operations (more than 20% of revenue) consist primarily of natural gas distribution to residential commercial and industrial customers in northern and central New Jersey.

Prior to its divestiture ELK utility operations consist of natural gas distribution to residential commercial and industrial customers in Maryland.

Wholesale energy operations (more than 35%) include the activities of SJRG and SJEX.

Retail electric operations (less than 4%) at SJE consist of electricity acquisition and transportation to commercial industrial and residential customers.

Appliance service operations includes SJESP which receives commissions on appliance service contracts from a third party.

Midstream was formed to invest in infrastructure and other midstream projects including an investment in PennEast.

Corporate & Services segment includes costs related to acquisitions and divestitures along with other unallocated costs.

Geographic Reach

Headquartered in Folsom New Jersey SJI's South Jersey Gas service territory covers approximately 2500 square miles in southern New Jersey including about 115 towns and cities in Atlantic Cape May Cumberland and Salem counties and portions of Burlington Camden and Gloucester counties. SJI also markets natural gas storage commodity and transportation assets on a wholesale basis in the mid-Atlantic Appalachia and the southern US.

Sales and Marketing

SJG served approximately 404900 residential commercial and industrial customers in southern New Jersey. SJG served around 378100 residential customers 26365 commercial customers and 415 industrial customers.

Financial Performance

In 2021 the company's decreased to $1.5 billion from $1.6 billion.

SJI's net income for 2020 increased $80.1 million to $157.0 million compared to 2019.

Cash held by the company at the end of fiscal 2020 increased to $41.8 million. Cash provided by operations and financing activities were $311.6 million and $209.6 million respectively. Investing activities were $507.8 million mainly for capital expenditures.

Strategy

In developing SJI's current business model SJI's focus has been on its core Utilities and natural extensions of those businesses as well as strategic opportunities in our nonutility business that align with the goals of the EMP. That focus enables the company to concentrate on business activities that match its core competencies. Going forward the company expects to pursue business opportunities that fit and complement this model.

EXECUTIVES

Independent Director, Sunita Holzer
Independent Director, Kevin O'Dowd
Independent Director, Christopher Paladino
Independent Director, Victor Fortkiewicz
Independent Director, Sarah Barpoulis
Independent Director, Frank Sims
Independent Non-executive Chairman Of The Board, Joseph Rigby
Senior Vice President, President - Sji Utilities, Melissa Orsen, $368,654 total compensation
Independent Director, G. Edison Holland
President, Chief Executive Officer, Director, Michael Renna, $794,423 total compensation
Chief Financial Officer, Senior Vice President, Steven Cocchi, $344,354 total compensation
Auditors: DELOITTE & TOUCHE LLP

LOCATIONS

HQ: South Jersey Industries Inc
1 South Jersey Plaza, Folsom, NJ 08037
Phone: 609 561-9000
Web: www.sjiindustries.com

PRODUCTS/OPERATIONS

2014 Sales

	$ mil.	% of total
Gas utility	501.9	57
Energy Group:		
Retail Gas and other operations	127.0	14
Retail electricity operation	123.8	14
Wholesale energy operation	77.0	9
Energy Services:		
On-Site energy production	56.1	6
Corporate & services	30.2	3
Appliance service operations	10.5	1
Adjustment (intersegment sales) (39.5) (4)		
Total	**887.0**	**100**

Selected Subsidiaries

Marina Energy LLC (energy project development)
South Jersey Energy Company (retail energy marketer energy management services)
South Jersey Energy Service Plus LLC (HVAC systems installation and appliance servicing)
South Jersey Exploration LLC (oil and gas assets)
South Jersey Gas Company (natural gas utility)
South Jersey Resources Group LLC (wholesale natural gas marketing trading transportation and management services)

COMPETITORS

ALABAMA POWER COMPANY	NORTHWESTERN CORPORATION
ATCO Ltd	
CHESAPEAKE UTILITIES CORPORATION	OGE ENERGY CORP.
CONSUMERS ENERGY COMPANY HOLDINGS	ORIGIN ENERGY LIMITED
	OTTER TAIL CORPORATION
	SOUTHWEST GAS
DTE ENERGY COMPANY	INC.
EXELON CORPORATION	TAMPA ELECTRIC COMPANY
Emera Incorporated	TUCSON ELECTRIC POWER
GEORGIA POWER COMPANY	COMPANY
MDU RESOURCES GROUP INC.	VECTREN CORPORATION
NEW JERSEY RESOURCES CORPORATION	

HISTORICAL FINANCIALS

Company Type: Public

Income Statement				FYE: December 31
	REVENUE ($ mil.)	NET INCOME ($ mil.)	NET PROFIT MARGIN	EMPLOYEES
12/20	1,541.3	157.0	10.2%	1,130
12/19	1,628.6	76.9	4.7%	1,100
12/18	1,641.3	17.6	1.1%	1,100
12/17	1,243.0	(3.4)	—	760
12/16	1,036.5	118.8	11.5%	750
Annual Growth	10.4%	7.2%		10.8%

2020 Year-End Financials

Debt ratio: 43.6%
Return on equity: 10.1%
Cash ($ mil.): 34.0
Current ratio: 0.44
Long-term debt ($ mil.): 2,776.4
No. of shares (mil.): 100.5
Dividends
  Yield: 5.5%
  Payout: 73.3%
Market value ($ mil.): 2,168.0

	STOCK PRICE ($) FY Close	P/E High/Low		Earnings	PER SHARE ($) Dividends	Book Value
12/20	21.55	21	11	1.62	1.19	16.51
12/19	32.98	41	32	0.84	1.16	15.41
12/18	27.80	172	124	0.21	1.13	14.82
12/17	31.23	—	—	(0.04)	1.10	14.99
12/16	33.69	22	15	1.56	1.06	16.22
Annual Growth	(10.6%)	—	—	0.9%	2.8%	0.4%

South Plains Financial Inc

Auditors: Weaver and Tidwell, LLP

LOCATIONS

HQ: South Plains Financial Inc
  5219 City Bank Parkway, Lubbock, TX 79407
Phone: 806 792-7101
Web: www.spfi.bank

HISTORICAL FINANCIALS

Company Type: Public

Income Statement				FYE: December 31
	ASSETS ($ mil.)	NET INCOME ($ mil.)	INCOME AS % OF ASSETS	EMPLOYEES
12/20	3,599.1	45.3	1.3%	682
12/19	3,237.1	29.2	0.9%	679
12/18	2,712.7	29.2	1.1%	684
12/17	2,573.3	23.6	0.9%	0
Annual Growth	11.8%	24.3%	—	—

2020 Year-End Financials

Return on assets: 1.3%
Return on equity: 13.3%
Long-term debt ($ mil.): —
No. of shares (mil.): 18.0
Sales ($ mil): 239.8
Dividends
  Yield: 0.7%
  Payout: 5.6%
Market value ($ mil.): 343.0

	STOCK PRICE ($) FY Close	P/E High/Low		Earnings	PER SHARE ($) Dividends	Book Value
12/20	18.95	9	5	2.47	0.14	20.47
12/19	20.87	12	9	1.71	0.06	16.98
12/18	0.00	—	—	1.98	2.03	14.40
Annual Growth	—	—	—	11.7%	(73.7%)	19.2%

Southern First Bancshares, Inc.

Southern First Bancshares operates in two markets: Greenville South Carolina where it operates under the Greenville First Bank moniker and in Columbia South Carolina as Southern First Bank. Selling itself as a local alternative to larger institutions the company which has more than five bank branches targets individuals and small to midsized businesses. It offers traditional deposit services and products including checking accounts savings accounts and CDs. The banks use funds from deposits mainly to write commercial mortgages residential mortgages and commercial business loans.

EXECUTIVES

Independent Chairman Of The Board, James Orders
Chief Executive Officer, Head, Media Relations, And Director, R. Arthur Seaver, $495,000 total compensation
Independent Director, Andrew Cajka

Chief Human Resource Officer, Silvia King, $175,000 total compensation
Director, Ray Lattimore
Chief Financial Officer, Chief Operating Officer, Executive Vice President, Michael Dowling, $340,000 total compensation
Director, Mark Cothran
Independent Director, Tecumseh Hooper
Independent Director, Anna Locke
Chief Banking Officer, Calvin Hurst, $223,500 total compensation
Director, William Maner
Director, Terry Grayson-Caprio
Auditors: Elliott Davis, LLC

LOCATIONS

HQ: Southern First Bancshares, Inc.
  100 Verdae Boulevard, Suite 100, Greenville, SC 29607
Phone: 864 679-9000
Web: www.southernfirst.com

COMPETITORS

FIRST CAPITAL INC.	PACIFIC FINANCIAL
FREMONT BANCORPORATION	CORPORATION

HISTORICAL FINANCIALS

Company Type: Public

Income Statement				FYE: December 31
	ASSETS ($ mil.)	NET INCOME ($ mil.)	INCOME AS % OF ASSETS	EMPLOYEES
12/20	2,482.5	18.3	0.7%	254
12/19	2,267.2	27.8	1.2%	242
12/18	1,900.6	22.2	1.2%	229
12/17	1,624.6	13.0	0.8%	198
12/16	1,340.9	13.0	1.0%	179
Annual Growth	16.6%	8.9%	—	9.1%

2020 Year-End Financials

Return on assets: 0.7%
Return on equity: 8.4%
Long-term debt ($ mil.): —
No. of shares (mil.): 7.7
Sales ($ mil): 122.1
Dividends
  Yield: —
  Payout: —
Market value ($ mil.): 275.0

	STOCK PRICE ($) FY Close	P/E High/Low		Earnings	PER SHARE ($) Dividends	Book Value
12/20	35.35	18	9	2.34	0.00	29.37
12/19	42.49	12	9	3.58	0.00	26.83
12/18	32.07	16	10	2.88	0.00	23.29
12/17	41.25	23	17	1.76	0.00	20.37
12/16	36.00	18	11	1.94	0.00	17.00
Annual Growth	(0.5%)	—	—	4.8%	—	14.7%

Southern Michigan Bancorp Inc (United States)

Southern Michigan Bancorp is the holding company for Southern Michigan Bank & Trust which operates about 20 branches in a primarily rural area near Michigan's border with Indiana and

Ohio. The bank provides standard deposit services such as checking and savings accounts money market and heath savings accounts CDs and IRAs. It originates commercial financial agricultural consumer and mortgage loans. The banks also offers trust and investment services. Southern Michigan Bank & Trust got its start in the room of a hotel named Southern Michigan Hotel in 1872.

EXECUTIVES

Director, Melissa Bauer
Chairman Of The Board, Chief Executive Officer, John Castle, $232,188 total compensation
President, Director, Kurt Miller, $185,961 total compensation
Independent Director, Nolan Hooker
Independent Director, Gregory Hull
Independent Director, John Carton
Director, Patrick Flannery
Chief Financial Officer, Senior Vice President, Treasurer, Secretary, Danice Chartrand, $127,152 total compensation
Director, Charles Clark
Independent Director, H. Kenneth Cole
Independent Director, Freeman Riddle
Independent Director, Thomas Kolassa
Independent Director, Dean Calhoun
Independent Director, Donald Labrecque
Independent Director, Gary Haberl
Independent Director, Brian McConnell
Director, Stacey Hamlin
Auditors: CliftonLarsonAllen LLP

LOCATIONS

HQ: Southern Michigan Bancorp Inc (United States)
51 West Pearl Street, Coldwater, MI 49036
Phone: 517 279-5500   **Fax:** 517 279-5578
Web: www.smb-t.com

COMPETITORS

COUNTY BANK CORP.
SOUTHEASTERN BANK FINANCIAL CORPORATION

HISTORICAL FINANCIALS

Company Type: Public

Income Statement — FYE: December 31

	ASSETS ($ mil.)	NET INCOME ($ mil.)	INCOME AS % OF ASSETS	EMPLOYEES
12/20	997.5	7.3	0.7%	0
12/19	809.7	8.6	1.1%	208
12/18	738.8	8.1	1.1%	0
12/17	712.3	5.4	0.8%	0
12/16	641.5	6.1	1.0%	0
Annual Growth	11.7%	4.9%	—	—

2020 Year-End Financials

Return on assets: 0.8%	Dividends
Return on equity: 8.3%	Yield: 0.0%
Long-term debt ($ mil.): —	Payout: 14.3%
No. of shares (mil.): 2.3	Market value ($ mil.): 78.0
Sales ($ mil): 40.2	

	STOCK PRICE ($) FY Close	P/E High/Low		PER SHARE ($) Earnings	Dividends	Book Value
12/20	34.00	12	8	3.21	0.46	40.40
12/19	37.60	11	10	3.74	0.45	36.00
12/18	38.10	13	10	3.51	0.43	32.62
12/17	37.10	17	13	2.30	0.41	30.23
12/16	29.90	12	10	2.54	0.36	29.14
Annual Growth	3.3%	—	—	6.0%	6.3%	8.5%

Southern Missouri Bancorp, Inc.

Southern Missouri Bancorp is the holding company for Southern Bank (formerly Southern Missouri Bank and Trust) which serves local residents and businesses in southeastern Missouri and northeastern Arkansas through more than 10 branches. Residential mortgages account for the largest percentage of the bank's loan portfolio followed by commercial mortgages and business loans. Construction and consumer loans round out its lending activities. Deposit products include checking savings and money market accounts CDs and IRAs. The bank also offers financial planning and investment services. Originally chartered in 1887 Southern Bank acquired Arkansas-based Southern Bank of Commerce in 2009.

EXECUTIVES

President, Chief Executive Officer, Director, Greg Steffens, $400,724 total compensation
Independent Chairman Of The Board, L. Douglas Bagby
Independent Director, Sammy Schalk
Chief Operations Officer, Kimberly Capps, $166,769 total compensation
Independent Director, Rebecca Brooks
Chief Risk Officer, Lora Daves, $136,892 total compensation
Chief Strategies Officer, Brett Dorton
Independent Director, Todd Hensley
Chief Lending Officer, Richard Windes, $245,177 total compensation
Chief Credit Officer, Mark Hecker, $249,547 total compensation
Chief Financial Officer, Matthew Funke, $236,911 total compensation
Independent Director, David Tooley
Regional President, West Region, Justin Cox, $231,946 total compensation
Chief Legal Officer, Martin Weishaar
Auditors: BKD, LLP

LOCATIONS

HQ: Southern Missouri Bancorp, Inc.
2991 Oak Grove Road, Poplar Bluff, MO 63901
Phone: 573 778-1800
Web: www.bankwithsouthern.com

COMPETITORS

CHICOPEE BANCORP INC. TIMBERLAND BANCORP
EASTERN BANK   INC.
  CORPORATION   W V S FINANCIAL CORP.
JACKSONVILLE BANCORP
  INC.

HISTORICAL FINANCIALS

Company Type: Public

Income Statement — FYE: June 30

	ASSETS ($ mil.)	NET INCOME ($ mil.)	INCOME AS % OF ASSETS	EMPLOYEES
06/21	2,700.5	47.1	1.7%	488
06/20	2,542.1	27.5	1.1%	492
06/19	2,214.4	28.9	1.3%	470
06/18	1,886.1	20.9	1.1%	415
06/17	1,707.7	15.5	0.9%	390
Annual Growth	12.1%	32.0%	—	5.8%

2021 Year-End Financials

Return on assets: 1.8%	Dividends
Return on equity: 17.4%	Yield: 1.3%
Long-term debt ($ mil.): —	Payout: 14.0%
No. of shares (mil.): 8.9	Market value ($ mil.): 400.0
Sales ($ mil): 129.5	

	STOCK PRICE ($) FY Close	P/E High/Low		PER SHARE ($) Earnings	Dividends	Book Value
06/21	44.96	9	4	5.22	0.62	31.83
06/20	24.30	13	7	2.99	0.60	28.30
06/19	34.83	13	10	3.14	0.52	25.66
06/18	39.02	17	13	2.39	0.44	22.31
06/17	32.26	18	11	2.07	0.40	20.15
Annual Growth	8.7%	—	—	26.0%	11.6%	12.1%

SouthState Corp

South State Corporation (formerly First Financial Holdings) is the holding company for South State Bank. The bank operates through correspondent banking and capital markets service division for over 700 small and medium sized community banks through United States. The bank has 285 network branches located in Florida South Carolina Alabama Georgia and more. The company provides commercial real estate residential real estate loans commercial and industrial loans and consumer loans. the banks provide deposit accounts loans and mortgages as well as trust and investment planning services. .In 2020 the company acquired all the outstanding common stock of CFSL of Winter Haven. CFSL merged with the company and South State Bank.

EXECUTIVES

Director, Robert Horger
Executive Chairman, Robert Hill, $695,417 total compensation
Senior Executive Vice President, Director, John Pollok, $614,806 total compensation
Chief Operating Officer, Renee Brooks, $462,083 total compensation
Independent Director, Cynthia Hartley
Chief Banking Officer, Greg Lapointe, $473,407 total compensation
Independent Director, Martin Davis
Independent Director, Jean Davis
Director, John Holcomb
Chief Executive Officer And Director, John Corbett, $565,000 total compensation
Lead Independent Director, Charles McPherson
Independent Director, William Pou

Independent Director, G. Ruffner Page
Independent Director, Joshua Snively
General Counsel, Corporate Secretary, Beth DeSimone
Chief Financial Officer, William Matthews V, $306,250 total compensation
Independent Director, Kevin Walker
President - Central Banking Group, John Goettee, $408,967 total compensation
Auditors: Dixon Hughes Goodman LLP

LOCATIONS
HQ: SouthState Corp
1101 First Street South, Suite 202, Winter Haven, FL 33880
Phone: 863 293-4710
Web: www.southstatebank.com

PRODUCTS/OPERATIONS

2011 Sales

	$ mil.	% of total
Interest		
Loans including fees	319.9	70
Investment securities	20.3	4
Other	1.8	-
Noninterest		
Service charges on deposit accounts	36.2	10
Bankcard services income	29.6	6
Trust and investment services income	18.3	4
Mortgage banking	16.2	4
Securities gains net -	0	
Amortization of FDIC indemnification asset	(21.9)	0
Other	16.2	4
Total	**436.7**	**100**

COMPETITORS

ALDERMORE GROUP PLC
ALLEGHENY VALLEY BANCORP INC.
BGEO GROUP LIMITED
CENTRAL COMMUNITY CORPORATION
COAST BANCORP INC.
COMMUNITY CAPITAL BANCSHARES INC.
F.N.B. CORPORATION
FIRST CITIZENS BANCORPORATION INC.
FIRST CITIZENS BANCSHARES INC.
LLOYDS BANKING GROUP PLC
METROPOLITAN BANK HOLDING CORP.
NORTHWEST BANCORP
Shinhan Financial Group Co. Ltd.
Woori Finance Holdings Co. Ltd.

HISTORICAL FINANCIALS
Company Type: Public

Income Statement — FYE: December 31

	ASSETS ($ mil.)	NET INCOME ($ mil.)	INCOME AS % OF ASSETS	EMPLOYEES
12/20	37,789.8	120.6	0.3%	5,311
12/19	15,921.0	186.4	1.2%	2,547
12/18	14,676.3	178.8	1.2%	2,602
12/17	14,466.5	87.5	0.6%	2,719
12/16	8,900.5	101.2	1.1%	2,055
Annual Growth	43.5%	4.5%	—	26.8%

2020 Year-End Financials
Return on assets: 0.4%
Return on equity: 3.4%
Long-term debt ($ mil.): —
No. of shares (mil.): 70.9
Sales ($ mil): 1,221.1
Dividends
  Yield: 2.6%
  Payout: 122.8%
Market value ($ mil.): 5,131.0

	STOCK PRICE ($) FY Close	P/E High/Low	PER SHARE ($) Earnings	Dividends	Book Value
12/20	72.30	40 20	2.19	1.88	65.49
12/19	86.75	16 11	5.36	1.67	70.32
12/18	59.95	19 12	4.86	1.38	66.04
12/17	87.15	32 27	2.93	1.32	62.81
12/16	87.40	22 14	4.18	1.21	46.83
Annual Growth	(4.6%)	—	(14.9%)	11.6%	8.7%

Spirit of Texas Bancshares Inc

Auditors: BDO USA, LLP

LOCATIONS
HQ: Spirit of Texas Bancshares Inc
1836 Spirit of Texas Way, Conroe, TX 77301
Phone: 936 521-1836
Web: www.sotb.com

HISTORICAL FINANCIALS
Company Type: Public

Income Statement — FYE: December 31

	ASSETS ($ mil.)	NET INCOME ($ mil.)	INCOME AS % OF ASSETS	EMPLOYEES
12/20	3,084.7	31.3	1.0%	383
12/19	2,384.6	21.1	0.9%	409
12/18	1,466.7	9.9	0.7%	289
12/17	1,030.3	4.7	0.5%	195
12/16	980.4	3.7	0.4%	0
Annual Growth	33.2%	70.4%	—	—

2020 Year-End Financials
Return on assets: 1.1%
Return on equity: 8.8%
Long-term debt ($ mil.): —
No. of shares (mil.): 17.0
Sales ($ mil): 142.4
Dividends
  Yield: 0.4%
  Payout: 4.9%
Market value ($ mil.): 287.0

	STOCK PRICE ($) FY Close	P/E High/Low	PER SHARE ($) Earnings	Dividends	Book Value
12/20	16.80	13 5	1.77	0.07	21.12
12/19	23.00	16 14	1.40	0.00	18.93
12/18	22.78	21 17	1.03	0.00	16.42
Annual Growth	(14.1%)	—	31.1%	—	13.4%

Sportsman's Warehouse Holdings Inc

Auditors: Grant Thornton LLP

LOCATIONS
HQ: Sportsman's Warehouse Holdings Inc
1475 West 9000 South Suite A, West Jordan, UT 84088
Phone: 801 566-6681   **Fax:** 801 304-4388
Web: www.sportsmans.com

HISTORICAL FINANCIALS
Company Type: Public

Income Statement — FYE: January 30

	REVENUE ($ mil.)	NET INCOME ($ mil.)	NET PROFIT MARGIN	EMPLOYEES
01/21*	1,451.7	91.3	6.3%	7,000
02/20	886.4	20.2	2.3%	5,400
02/19	849.1	23.7	2.8%	5,100
02/18	809.6	17.7	2.2%	5,000
01/17	779.9	29.6	3.8%	4,800
Annual Growth	16.8%	32.5%	—	9.9%

*Fiscal year change

2021 Year-End Financials
Debt ratio: —
Return on equity: 58.1%
Cash ($ mil.): 65.5
Current ratio: 1.43
Long-term debt ($ mil.): —
No. of shares (mil.): 43.6
Dividends
  Yield: —
  Payout: —
Market value ($ mil.): 764.0

	STOCK PRICE ($) FY Close	P/E High/Low	PER SHARE ($) Earnings	Dividends	Book Value
01/21*	17.52	9 2	2.06	0.00	4.69
02/20	6.48	18 7	0.46	0.00	2.55
02/19	5.12	11 7	0.55	0.00	1.83
02/18	4.91	18 8	0.42	0.00	1.17
01/17	7.89	20 11	0.70	0.00	0.71
Annual Growth	22.1%	—	31.0%	—	60.3%

*Fiscal year change

SPS Commerce, Inc.

Founded in 1987 as St. Paul Software SPS Commerce is a leading provider of cloud-based supply chain management services that make it easier for suppliers retailers distributors and logistics companies to orchestrate the management of item data order fulfillment inventory control and sales analytics across all channels. The services offered by SPS Commerce eliminate the need for on-premise software and support staff by taking on that capability on the customer's behalf. The services SPS Commerce provides enable its customers to increase their supply cycle agility optimize their inventory levels and sell-through reduce operational costs and gain increased visibility into customer orders. Its business model fundamentally changes how organizations use electronic communication to manage their omnichannel supply chain and other business requirements by replacing the collection of traditional custom-built point-to-point integrations with a model that facilitates a single automated connection to the entire SPS Commerce network of trading partners.

Operations
SPS has only one segment which is Supply chain management solutions.
Supply chain management solutions for critical business processes any defect in its solutions any

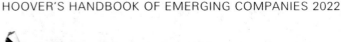

disruption to its solutions or any error in execution could cause recurring revenue customers to cancel their contracts with them cause potential customers to not join its network and harm its reputation.

The company's recurring revenues consist of recurring subscriptions from customers that utilize our Fulfillment (some 80% of sles) Analytics (over 10%) and Other cloud-based supply chain management solutions. The one-time revenues which account for the remaining sales consist of set-up fees from customers and miscellaneous one-time fees.

Geographic Reach

Headquartered in Minnesota the company operates in New Jersey and internationally in China India Australia and the UK. It has sales offices in North America as well as in China Hong Kong and Australia.

Sales and Marketing

SPS boasts approximately 95000 customers many of which are small-to mid-sized suppliers. It also generated revenues from other members of the supply chain ecosystem including retailers distributors third-party logistics providers and other trading partners.

Financial Performance

The company in 2020 had a revenue of $312.6 million a 12% increase from the previous year's revenue of $279.1 million. The increase in revenues resulted from two primary factors: the increase in recurring revenue customers which is driven by continued business growth and by business acquisitions and the increase in average recurring revenues per recurring revenue customer which the company also refers to as wallet share.

In 2020 the company had a net income of $45.6 million a 35% increase from the previous year's net income of $33.7 million.

The company's cash at the end of 2020 was $149.7 million. Operating activities generated $88.6 million while investing activities used $120.5 million mainly for acquisition of business and intangible assets and purchases of investments. Financing activities provided another $2.3 million.

Strategy

The company's objective is to be the leading global provider of supply chain management solutions. Key elements of its strategy include:

Further penetrate its current market by continue leveraging its relationships with customers and their trading partners to obtain new sales leads;

Increase revenues from its customer base by introducing new solutions to sell to its customers;

Expand its distribution channels to gain new customers. The company believes there are valuable opportunities to promote and sell its solutions through collaboration with other providers;

Expand its international presence by increasing its global sales efforts to obtain new customers around the world. It intends to leverage its current global presence to increase the number of integrations it has with retailers in foreign markets to make its solutions more valuable to its trading partners based overseas;

Enhance and expand its services by improving and developing the functionality and features of its cloud-based Platform including from time to time developing new solutions and applications; and

Selectively pursue strategic acquisitions by evaluating potential acquisitions based on the number of new customers revenue functionality or geo-

graphic reach the acquisition would provide relative to the purchase price and its ability to integrate and operate the acquired business.

Mergers and Acquisitions

In late 2020 SPS Commerce Inc. announced the acquisition of Florida-based Data Masons a provider of EDI solutions to hundreds of consumer goods industrial and distribution businesses and resellers. Together SPS Commerce and Data Masons offer unmatched trading partner and system expertise for customers using Microsoft solutions. Under the terms of the acquisition agreement SPS Commerce acquired all equity interests of Data Masons for approximately $100 million in cash.

EXECUTIVES

Chief Financial Officer, Executive Vice President, Kimberly Nelson, $374,000 total compensation
Independent Director, Marty Reaume
Independent Chairman Of The Board, Tami Reller
Independent Director, Anne Ward
Independent Director, James Ramsey
President, Chief Operating Officer, Executive Vice President, James Frome, $374,000 total compensation
Chief Executive Officer, Director, Archie Black, $523,000 total compensation
Auditors: KPMG LLP

LOCATIONS

HQ: SPS Commerce, Inc.
333 South Seventh Street, Suite 1000, Minneapolis, MN 55402
Phone: 612 435-9400
Web: www.spscommerce.com

COMPETITORS

BROADRIDGE FINANCIAL SOLUTIONS INC.	FISERV INC.
CSG SYSTEMS INTERNATIONAL INC.	GB GROUP PLC
	HUBSPOT INC.
DONNELLEY FINANCIAL SOLUTIONS INC. TECHNOLOGIES	NETSCOUT SYSTEMS INC.
	PROOFPOINT INC.
	SAILPOINT
DXC TECHNOLOGY COMPANY	HOLDINGS INC.
EGAIN CORPORATION	SALESFORCE.COM INC.
FACTSET RESEARCH SYSTEMS INC.	TD SYNNEX CORPORATION
	VERISK ANALYTICS INC.

HISTORICAL FINANCIALS

Company Type: Public

Income Statement

FYE: December 31

	REVENUE ($ mil.)	NET INCOME ($ mil.)	NET PROFIT MARGIN	EMPLOYEES
12/20	312.6	45.5	14.6%	1,572
12/19	279.1	33.7	12.1%	1,363
12/18	248.2	23.8	9.6%	1,231
12/17	220.5	(2.4)	—	1,336
12/16	193.3	5.7	3.0%	1,217
Annual Growth	12.8%	68.1%	—	6.6%

2020 Year-End Financials

Debt ratio: —	No. of shares (mil.): 35.4
Return on equity: 11.7%	Dividends
Cash ($ mil.): 149.6	Yield: —
Current ratio: 3.39	Payout: —
Long-term debt ($ mil.): —	Market value ($ mil.): 3,854.0

	STOCK PRICE ($) FY Close	P/E High/Low		PER SHARE ($) Earnings	Dividends	Book Value
12/20	108.59	86	25	1.26	0.00	11.86
12/19	55.42	118	48	0.94	0.00	10.18
12/18	82.38	144	70	0.68	0.00	9.19
12/17	48.59	—	—	(0.07)	0.00	8.08
12/16	69.89	436	231	0.17	0.00	7.30
Annual Growth	11.6%	—	—	66.2%	—	12.9%

SStarTrade Tech Inc

Auditors: Robert L. White & Associates, Inc.

LOCATIONS

HQ: SStarTrade Tech Inc
3773 Howard Hughes Parkway, South Tower, Suite 500, Las Vegas, NV 89169
Phone: 212 371-7799
Web: www.sstartradetech.com

HISTORICAL FINANCIALS

Company Type: Public

Income Statement

FYE: December 31

	REVENUE ($ mil.)	NET INCOME ($ mil.)	NET PROFIT MARGIN	EMPLOYEES
12/20	298.4	45.3	15.2%	0
12/19	195.6	9.7	5.0%	0
12/18	188.4	1.7	0.9%	0
12/17	142.2	5.2	3.7%	0
12/16	0.2	(0.0)	—	0
Annual Growth	522.2%	—	—	—

2020 Year-End Financials

Debt ratio: 12.0%	No. of shares (mil.): 99.6
Return on equity: 86.4%	Dividends
Cash ($ mil.): 56.2	Yield: —
Current ratio: 0.84	Payout: —
Long-term debt ($ mil.): 9.6	Market value ($ mil.): 4.0

	STOCK PRICE ($) FY Close	P/E High/Low		PER SHARE ($) Earnings	Dividends	Book Value
12/20	0.04	—	—	(0.00)	0.00	0.63
12/19	0.05	—	—	(0.00)	0.00	0.42
12/18	0.02	—	—	(0.00)	0.00	(0.00)
12/17	0.06	—	—	(0.00)	0.00	(0.00)
12/16	0.00	—	—	(0.00)	0.00	0.25
Annual Growth	99.5%	—	—	—	—	25.3%

St. Joe Co. (The)

Wanna buy some swampland in Florida? Perhaps something a bit more upscale? St. Joe has it along with timberland and beaches. Formerly operating in paper sugar timber telephone systems and railroads St. Joe is a Florida real estate developer and one of the state's largest private landowners. It holds some 175000 acres of land entitled for future development located mostly in northwest

HOOVER'S HANDBOOK OF EMERGING COMPANIES 2022

Florida. Approximately 90% of its land holdings are within 15 miles of the Gulf of Mexico including beach frontage and other waterfront properties. The company is primarily engaged in developing residential resorts and towns commerce parks and rural property sales. St. Joe also operates a forestry segment which grows harvests and sells timber and wood fiber.

Operations

The company operates its business in four reportable operating segments: hospitality residential real estate commercial leasing and sales and forestry.

The hospitality segment (accounts more than 35% of total revenue) features a private membership club (The Clubs by JOE) hotel operations food and beverage operations golf courses beach clubs retail outlets gulf-front vacation rentals management services marinas and other entertainment assets.

The residential real estate segment (nearly 35% of total revenue) typically plans and develops residential communities of various sizes across a wide range of price points and sells homesites to builders or retail consumers. Residential real estate segment also evaluates opportunities to enter into JV agreements for specific communities such as Latitude Margaritaville Watersound. Some of its major residential development communities includes the WaterColor Camp Creek Watersound Origins and Breakfast Point community.

The commercial leasing and sales segment (more than 15%) includes construction and leasing of multi-family retail office and commercial property cell towers and other assets an assisted living community as well as planning development entitlement management and sale of the company's commercial land holdings for a variety of uses.

Forestry segment (nearly 15%) which holds approximately 113000 acres of lands focuses on the timber holdings in Northwest Florida and generates revenue primarily from open market sales of timber on site. It grow and sell pulpwood sawtimber and other forest products.

Geographic Reach

St. Joe is based in Watersound Florida and owns approximately 175000 acres of land located in Northwest Florida.

Sales and Marketing

The company's customers includes builders and to consumers in communities. In addition one of its joint ventures has initiated more than 55 active adult community in Bay County Florida.

Financial Performance

After a slight dip in 2016 the company posted consecutive years of increase in revenue. Overall revenue growth since 2015 was 21%.

Revenue in 2019 was $127.1 million an increase of 15% from the prior year. Real estate Hospitality and Leasing segments all have increased revenue partially offset by a $1.7 million decrease in the Timber segment.

Net income attributable to the company in 2019 was $26.8 million. Higher revenue and a $5.3 million increase from Other income contributed to the increase in net income.

Cash and cash equivalents at the end of the period were $188.7 million. Net cash provided by operating activities was $30.4 million while investing and financing activities each used $29.3 million and $10.5 million respectively. Main cash uses were for capital expenditures and repurchases of common shares.

Strategy

The company believes that its present liquidity position and its land holdings can provide it with numerous opportunities to continue to increase recurring revenue and create long-term value for its shareholders by allowing it to focus on its core business activity of real estate development and asset management near the Gulf of Mexico Gulf Intracoastal Waterway Northwest Florida Beaches International Airport the Pier Park area and the Scenic Highway 30A corridor.

In 2018 it began the development or construction of 9 new residential hospitality multi-family or commercial projects or phases. By contrast in 2019 it began the development or construction of 27 new residential hospitality multi-family or commercial projects or phases. Several of these projects were completed as of December 31 2019. In addition it continued to develop residential homesites in several communities to deliver on the 930 homesites it has under contract to builders or retail consumers.

As of the end of 2019 it has a total of 468 apartment or assisted living units 597 hotel rooms and 130785 square feet of commercial and hospitality space under development or construction. It anticipates the completion of the construction and placement of these new assets into operations at various times in 2020 and 2021.

In addition to the projects the company began in 2018 and 2019 it also began planning designing and permitting other projects that are expected to move into construction or development in 2020 and beyond. Some of the projects will be constructed through third party joint venture partners. While it expects to commence development and construction of a number of projects in 2020 and beyond timing of some projects may be delayed due to factors beyond its control.

It presently owns and/or operates a wide range of hospitality assets which already generate significant recurring revenue for them. It is expanding the scope and scale of its hospitality assets and services to enable it to enhance the value and revenue those assets provide. It presently owns a wide range of income producing commercial assets. It intends to explore opportunities to increase the size and scope of its assets in ways that can increase recurring revenue while supporting the growth of its residential and hospitality assets.

The company plan to continue to maintain a high degree of liquidity while seeking opportunities to invest its cash in ways that it believes can increase shareholder value including share repurchases real estate and other strategic investments.

Company Background

Formerly engaged in the residential construction and related industries the company saw its sales plummet when Florida was among the hardest-hit markets of the housing bust and economic downturn. The 2010 explosion of the Deepwater Horizon drilling platform off the coast of Louisiana also impacted St. Joe as a result of widespread environmental damage. To combat the economic challenges the company exited several lines of business in order to focus on real estate development and managing its timberland holdings.

HISTORY

After Alfred I. du Pont scandalized society by divorcing his first wife to marry his cousin in 1907 he began investing in Florida land.

Du Pont who lived in Florida for nine years wanted to help revitalize Florida's Depression-era economy. Du Pont died in 1935 and the family's legendary success was passed in part to the Alfred I. du Pont Testamentary Trust formed the year after du Pont's death to unify his holdings and to benefit a charitable foundation.

Edward Ball du Pont's brother-in-law and executor of his estate opened St. Joe Paper in 1936. With his shrewd business sense Ball also invested in transportation infrastructure and banks. St. Joe Paper made scattershot investments over the next several decades including telephone companies railroad and highway improvements and real estate development. Ball made a point of keeping good relations with his employees.

When Ball died in 1981 chairmanship of Alfred du Pont's trust passed to Ball's friend and St. Joe Paper chairman Jacob Belin.

St. Joe Paper sold a 17% stake in itself to the public in 1990. Galvanized by stockholder complaints the company sold its paper mills and telecommunications operations and changed its name to St. Joe Corp. (1996). Income spiked that year with the $98 million condemnation sale of land to the State of Florida for Everglades restoration.

In 1997 St. Joe tapped Disney veteran Peter Rummell as chairman and CEO; he refocused the company on real estate buying into planned-community company Arvida.

St. Joe Corp. changed its name to The St. Joe Company in 1998 and bought Prudential Florida Realty the state's largest residential real estate company.

St. Joe announced in 1999 that it would sell off most of its raw land. In 2000 regulators approved the company's spinoff to investors of its 54% stake in Florida East Coast Industries a member of the company's transportation segment. The company also formed an alliance with a London-based real estate brokerage to promote real estate business between the UK and Florida that year.

The following year St. Joe sold 26 acres of land to the Port Authority of Port St. Joe a city on the Gulf Coast in northwestern Florida for the renovation of a deepwater port. In 2002 the company sold Arvida Realty (the former Prudential Florida Realty) to Cendant now Avis Budget Group Inc. Cendant spun off its real estate operations in 2006 as Realogy.

In 2003 the company opened the first of its RiverCamps series of homesites within rustic developments in northwestern Florida (as part of its New Ruralism product portfolio which also includes farm and ranch developments).

The company sold its property management subsidiary Advantis/GVA in 2005 to that company's management although Advantis/GVA retained management responsibilities for much of its portfolio. The sale was described as a step in strengthening St. Joe's core geographic focus (Advantis/GVA is active in a broader geographic area).

The company undertook a significant restructuring in 2007 at which time it exited the homebuilding market cut its workforce and sold its office holdings in Florida Tennessee and Virginia to Eola Capital. St. Joe's decision to shut down its homebuilding operations didn't mean the company quit the residential market. Instead it concentrated on the land development side actively seeking business partners interested in purchasing entitled land and investing capital into projects. The restructuring also meant giving up the property management side of business. St. Joe began outsourcing property management of its resorts golf courses and marinas.

St. Joe saw its sales plummet when Florida was among the hardest-hit markets of the housing bust and economic downturn. To free up some liquidity St. Joe in 2009 sold property developments including communities and golf courses in central Florida and homes in North and South Carolina. It also renegotiated its credit terms and utilized a tax strategy to help its earnings but the books ultimately reflected a loss of $130 million that year.

EXECUTIVES

President, Chief Executive Officer, Director, Jorge Gonzalez, $380,769 total compensation
Independent Director, Thomas Murphy
Independent Director, Cesar Alvarez
Senior Vice President, General Counsel, Corporate Secretary, Elizabeth Walters, $301,154 total compensation
Senior Vice President, Chief Administrative Officer, Rhea Goff, $153,885 total compensation
Independent Director, Howard Frank
Independent Chairman Of The Board, Bruce Berkowitz
Chief Financial Officer, Executive Vice President, Chief Accounting Officer, Marek Bakun, $351,346 total compensation
Auditors: Grant Thornton LLP

LOCATIONS

HQ: St. Joe Co. (The)
130 Richard Jackson Boulevard, Suite 200, Panama City Beach, FL 32407
Phone: 850 231-6400
Web: www.joe.com

PRODUCTS/OPERATIONS

2015 Sales

	$ mil.	% of total
Resorts and leisure revenues	54.5	53
Real estate sales	33.7	32
Leasing revenues	9.0	9
Timber sales	6.7	6
Total	**103.9**	**100**

2015 sales

	% of total
Resorts and leisure	52
Residential real estate	20
Forestry	12
Leasing operations	9
Commercial real estate	7
Total	**100**

Selected Subsidiaries

Artisan Park L.L.C.
Crooked Creek Utility Company
East San Marco LLC
Florida Timber Finance I LLC
Georgia Timber Finance I LLC
Panama City Beach Venture LLC
Paradise Pointe L.L.C.
Park Point Land LLC
Paseos LLC
Plume Street LLC
Plume Street Manager LLC
Residential Community Title Company
Rivercrest LLC
St. James Island Utility Company
SweetTea Publishing L.L.C.
Talisman Sugar Corporation

COMPETITORS

COUNTRYWIDE GROUP LIMITED
HOVNANIAN ENTERPRISES INC.
KENNEDY-WILSON HOLDINGS INC.
LENDLEASE CORPORATION LIMITED
MIRVAC LIMITED
SEGRO PUBLIC LIMITED COMPANY
THE MACERICH COMPANY
TRANSWESTERN COMMERCIAL SERVICES L.L.C.

HISTORICAL FINANCIALS

Company Type: Public

Income Statement				FYE: December 31
	REVENUE ($ mil.)	NET INCOME ($ mil.)	NET PROFIT MARGIN	EMPLOYEES
12/20	160.5	45.2	28.2%	48
12/19	127.0	26.7	21.1%	55
12/18	110.2	32.3	29.4%	53
12/17	98.8	59.5	60.3%	47
12/16	95.7	15.9	16.6%	47
Annual Growth	13.8%	29.9%	—	0.5%

2020 Year-End Financials

Debt ratio: 32.4%
Return on equity: 8.4%
Cash ($ mil.): 106.7
Current ratio: 1.48
Long-term debt ($ mil.): 336.2
No. of shares (mil.): 58.8
Dividends
Yield: 0.1%
Payout: 9.0%
Market value ($ mil.): 2,500.0

	STOCK PRICE ($) FY Close	P/E High/Low	PER SHARE ($) Earnings	Dividends	Book Value
12/20	42.45	64 21	0.77	0.07	9.35
12/19	19.83	45 29	0.45	0.00	8.74
12/18	13.17	38 25	0.52	0.00	8.54
12/17	18.05	23 19	0.84	0.00	8.76
12/16	19.00	102 69	0.21	0.00	9.00
Annual Growth	22.3%	— —	38.4%	—	1.0%

Staar Surgical Co.

STAAR Surgical Company designs develops manufactures and sells implantable lenses for the eye and delivery systems used to deliver the lenses into the eye. STAAR is the leading manufacturer of lenses used worldwide in corrective or "refractive" surgery. The company also makes lenses for use in surgery that treats cataracts. Its primary products include Visian-branded implantable lenses (ICLs) for correcting such refractive conditions as near- and far-sightedness and astigmatism. The company sells its products in about 75 countries. China is STAAR's largest single market.

Operations
STAAR manufactures the proprietary collagen-containing raw material used in its ICLs internally. The company's principal products are ICLs (accounting for nearly 90% of total sales) used in refractive surgery and IOLs used in cataract surgery (more than 10% of total sales).

The company had about 80 domestic and foreign patents and some 25 patent applications pending.

Geographic Reach
California-based STAAR operates from leased facilities around the world. It has corporate offices

manufacturing operations and warehousing and distribution operations in Monrovia California and in Nidau and Brugg Switzerland. The company also has additional R&D facilities and a raw material production facility in California. In Japan the company has corporate offices and an inspection packaging and distribution site.

China brings in about 45% of STAAR's revenue followed by Japan which gives in more than 20% of revenue. The US generate roughly 5% and the rest comes from other countries combined.

Sales and Marketing
STARR sells its products in more than 75 countries around the world. It has direct distribution channels in the US Canada Singapore Japan Spain Germany and the UK; it sells through independent distributors elsewhere.

Products are marketed to a variety of health care providers including hospitals ophthalmic surgeons surgical centers vision centers and government agencies.

The company spent $9.2 million $11 million and $9 million for advertising in fiscal years 2020 2019 and 2018 respectively.

Financial Performance
STAAR has seen rising revenue in the past five years especially due to higher sales of ICL products and in 2019 the company started to post profits after several years of losses.

Revenue increased by 9% to $163.5 million in 2020. The increase in net sales was due to an increase in ICL sales of $12.1 million.

Net income decreased by 58% to $5.9 million in 2020.

The company ended 2020 with $150 million in net cash $32 million more than it had at the end of 2019. Operating activities provided $20.9 million and financing activities provided $19.6 million. Investing activities used $8.4 million in cash for the acquisition of property and equipment.

Strategy
The strategic priority of the company for 2021 is to continue achieving and strengthening its 2020 strategic priorities which are to position EVO implantable lenses as a special and transformational pathway to Visual Freedom; execute a go-to-market strategy to significantly expand market share globally; innovate and develop a pipeline of next generation premium Collamer-based intraocular lenses; support the transformation of the refractive surgery paradigm to lens-based through clinical validation and medical affairs excellence; continue our focus on and commitment to STAAR's Culture of Quality; and deliver shareholder value.

To realize these priorities it is planning to continue to invest in manufacturing and facilities expansion that includes among other things: (i) increasing manufacturing capacity at the Monrovia California facility for its myopia ICLs; (ii) reopening and expanding its manufacturing and distribution facilities in Switzerland; (iii) preparing for the validation of its Lake Forest California facility for the manufacturing of its ICL with EDOF for presbyopia lenses which it expects to be approved for sale initially in CE Mark countries; Continue market share gains in all global markets including China; Continue to increase investment in Direct-to-Consumer marketing and patient education in targeted markets; and Continue to strengthen existing and finalize new strategic agreements and alliances with global partners.

HOOVER'S HANDBOOK OF EMERGING COMPANIES 2022

387

EXECUTIVES

Senior Vice President - Commercial Operations, Direct Markets Europe And China, Hans-Martin Blickensdoerfer, $411,643 total compensation
Chief Legal Officer, Corporate Secretary, Samuel Gesten, $357,590 total compensation
Senior Vice President - Commercial Operations, North America And Apac, James Francese, $274,185 total compensation
President, Chief Executive Officer, Director, Caren Mason, $667,235 total compensation
Independent Chairman Of The Board, Louis Silverman
Chief Manufacturing Officer, Senior Vice President - Global Operations, Graydon Hansen
Chief Medical Officer, Scott Barnes, $458,390 total compensation
Independent Director, Stephen Farrell
Independent Director, Gilbert Kliman
Independent Director, Thomas Frinzi
Chief Financial Officer, Patrick Williams, $182,308 total compensation
Independent Director, K. Peony Yu
Independent Director, Elizabeth Yeu
Vice President - Global Clinical And Medical Affairs, Jon Hayashida
Chief Technology Officer, Keith Holliday, $385,710 total compensation
Auditors: BDO USA, LLP

LOCATIONS

HQ: Staar Surgical Co.
25651 Atlantic Ocean Drive, Lake Forest, CA 92630
Phone: 626 303-7902
Web: www.staar.com

PRODUCTS/OPERATIONS

2017 Sales

	$ mil.	% of total
ICL	68.3	75
IOL	17.3	19
Other	5.0	6
Total	**90.6**	**100**

Selected Products

ICL
  EVO Visian ICL
  EVO+ Visian ICL
  Visian ICL
IOL
  Collamer IOL
  Pre-loaded IOL

COMPETITORS

1-800 CONTACTS INC.
APTARGROUP INC.
ASENSUS SURGICAL INC.
AXCELIS TECHNOLOGIES INC.
BAUSCH & LOMB INCORPORATED
CANTEL MEDICAL LLC
COOPERVISION INC.
DAVIS VISION INC.
ESSILOR OF AMERICA INC.
HIKMA PHARMACEUTICALS PUBLIC LIMITED COMPANY
LEMAITRE VASCULAR INC.
MASIMO CORPORATION
WATERS CORPORATION

HISTORICAL FINANCIALS

Company Type: Public

Income Statement

FYE: January 1

	REVENUE ($ mil.)	NET INCOME ($ mil.)	NET PROFIT MARGIN	EMPLOYEES
01/21	163.4	5.9	3.6%	575
01/20*	150.1	14.0	9.4%	550
12/18	123.9	4.9	4.0%	475
12/17	90.6	(2.1)	—	353
12/16	82.4	(12.1)	—	336
Annual Growth	**18.7%**	**—**	**—**	**14.4%**

*Fiscal year change

2021 Year-End Financials

Debt ratio: 0.6%
Return on equity: 3.3%
Cash ($ mil.): 152.4
Current ratio: 5.25
Long-term debt ($ mil.): 0.0
No. of shares (mil.): 46.4
Dividends
  Yield: —
  Payout: —
Market value ($ mil.): 3,680.0

	STOCK PRICE ($) FY Close	P/E High/Low	PER SHARE ($) Earnings	Dividends	Book Value
01/21	79.22	637 192	0.12	0.00	4.25
01/20*	34.38	127 72	0.30	0.00	3.57
12/18	31.26	422 116	0.11	0.00	3.00
12/17	15.50	— —	(0.05)	0.00	1.04
12/16	10.85	— —	(0.30)	0.00	0.93
Annual Growth	**64.4%**	**—**	**—**	**—**	**46.2%**

*Fiscal year change

STAG Industrial Inc

If STAG Industrial were to show up alone at a party it would likely be on the hunt for single tenants looking to lease industrial space. The self-managed and self-administered real estate investment trust (REIT) has built a business acquiring and managing single-tenant industrial properties located across more than 35 states. The company's portfolio consists primarily of about 91.4 million sq. ft. of leasable warehouse distribution manufacturing and office space located in secondary markets. STAG conducts most of its business through its operating partner STAG Industrial Operating Partnership. Pennsylvania accounts for the highest annual base rental revenue.

Operations

STAG's property portfolio consists of 450 buildings spanning about 91.4 million sq. ft. across more than 35 states. Approximately 75% of its rental income comes from its fixed lease payments while about 20% comes from its variable lease payments. The rest of its rental revenue comes from its straight-line rental. Its properties are about 95% leased to a collective nearly 415 tenants.

Key subsidiaries include STAG Industrial Operating Partnership STAG Industrial GP STAG Industrial Management STAG Industrial TRS and STAG Investments Holdings III among others.

Geographic Reach

Based in Massachusetts STAG owns and manages single-tenant industrial properties across 35-plus states. More than 35% of its rental income came from its properties in the states of North Carolina Ohio Illinois Pennsylvania and Texas.

Sales and Marketing

STAG made about 40% of its rental income from tenants out of five industries including: Automotive; Commercial Services & Supplies; Containers & Packaging; Air Freight and Logistics; and Machinery. While none of its tenants accounted for more than 2% of its total rental income its top five customers in 2019 included Amazon General Service Administration XPO Logistics Inc. DHL Supply Chain and Solo Cup.

Financial Performance

STAG Industrial's revenues have nearly doubled since 2015 as it has expanded its property portfolio through acquisitions and has charged higher rental rates as the economy has strengthened. The REIT has also experienced a fluctuation in recent years mostly as its interest expenses on its long-term debt have been higher than its operating profits.

The REIT's revenue jumped 16% to a new record of $406 million in 2019 thanks to a $55.7 million increase in rental income.

Net income in 2019 decreased by $45.6 million to $49.3 million. The decrease in net income was due to a $30 million increase in operating expenses and higher Other expenses.

Cash at the end of the period was $11.9 million. Net cash provided by operating activities was $233.4 million and cash provided by financing activities was $978.5 million. Investing activities used $1.2 billion for acquisition and building improvements.

Strategy

The company's primary business objectives are to own and operate a balanced and diversified portfolio of binary risk investments (individual single-tenant industrial properties) that maximize cash flows available for distribution to its stockholders and to enhance stockholder value over time by achieving sustainable long-term growth in distributable cash flow from operations.

Stag Industrial believes that its focus on owning and operating a portfolio of individually-acquired single-tenant industrial properties throughout the United States will when compared to other real estate portfolios generate returns for its stockholders that are attractive to them.

It seeks to identify properties for acquisition that offer relative value across all locations industrial property types and tenants through the principled application of its proprietary risk assessment model; operate its properties in an efficient cost-effective manner; and capitalize its business appropriately given the characteristics of its assets.

Company Background

The company's CEO and founder Benjamin S. Butcher founded STAG Industrial's predecessor companies in 2003. Butcher and other investors formed STAG Industrial to consolidate the companies' assets under a REIT umbrella for tax purposes and to raise public funds.

EXECUTIVES

Senior Vice President, Chief Accounting Officer, Principal Accounting Officer, Jaclyn Paul
Lead Independent Director, Larry Guillemette
Independent Director, Virgis Colbert
Independent Director, Michelle Dilley
Independent Director, Jit Chin
Independent Director, Francis Jacoby
Independent Director, Hans Weger
Independent Director, Jeffrey Furber
Chief Operating Officer, Executive Vice President, Stephen Mecke, $450,000 total compensation

Independent Director, Christopher Marr
President, Chief Financial Officer, Treasurer,
William Crooker, $400,000 total compensation
Executive Vice President, General Counsel,
Secretary, Jeffrey Sullivan, $300,000 total
compensation
Chairman Of The Board, President And Chief
Executive Officer, Benjamin Butcher, $650,000
total compensation
Auditors: PricewaterhouseCoopers LLP

LOCATIONS

HQ: STAG Industrial Inc
One Federal Street, 23rd Floor, Boston, MA 02110
Phone: 617 574-4777   **Fax:** 617 574-0052
Web: www.stagindustrial.com

PRODUCTS/OPERATIONS

2014 Sales

	$ mil.	% of total
Rental income	149.5	86
Tenant recoveries	23.6	14
Others	0.7	-
Total	**173.8**	**100**

COMPETITORS

ACADIA REALTY TRUST PROPERTY	LONDONMETRIC PLC
AGREE REALTY CORPORATION	MID-AMERICA APARTMENT COMMUNITIES INC.
COUSINS PROPERTIES INCORPORATED	PROLOGIS INC.
CUBESMART L.P.	SITE CENTERS CORP.
DUKE REALTY GROUP CORPORATION	WASHINGTON PRIME L.P.
JBG SMITH PROPERTIES	
KITE REALTY GROUP TRUST	

HISTORICAL FINANCIALS

Company Type: Public

Income Statement   FYE: December 31

	REVENUE ($ mil.)	NET INCOME ($ mil.)	NET PROFIT MARGIN	EMPLOYEES
12/21	562.1	192.3	34.2%	86
12/20	483.4	202.1	41.8%	78
12/19	405.9	49.2	12.1%	72
12/18	350.9	92.9	26.5%	73
12/17	301.0	31.2	10.4%	72
Annual Growth	16.9%	57.5%	—	4.5%

2021 Year-End Financials

Debt ratio: 38.0%
Return on equity: 6.3%
Cash ($ mil.): 18.9
Current ratio: 0.77
Long-term debt ($ mil.): 2,218.2

No. of shares (mil.): 177.7
Dividends
  Yield: 3.0%
  Payout: 115.0%
Market value ($ mil.): 8,526.0

	STOCK PRICE ($) FY Close	P/E High/Low		Earnings	PER SHARE ($) Dividends	Book Value
12/21	47.96	42	26	1.15	1.45	18.72
12/20	31.32	26	14	1.32	1.44	17.17
12/19	31.57	90	69	0.35	1.43	16.14
12/18	24.88	36	28	0.79	1.42	14.39
12/17	27.33	120	95	0.23	1.41	14.01
Annual Growth	15.1%	—	—	49.5%	0.8%	7.5%

Starwood Property Trust Inc.

Starwood Property Trust hopes to shine brightly in the world of mortgages. A real estate investment trust (REIT) the company originates finances and manages US commercial and residential mortgage loans commercial mortgage-backed securities and other commercial real estate debt investments. It acquires discounted loans from failed banks and financial institutions some through the FDIC which typically auctions off large pools of loan portfolios. Starwood Property Trust is externally managed by SPT Management LLC an affiliate of Starwood Capital Group. As a REIT the trust is exempt from paying federal income tax so long as it distributes quarterly dividends to shareholders.

Financial Performance

Overall revenues grew 63% in 2012 to $327 million up from $201 million in 2011. The trust primarily earns money on interest income from mortgage-backed securities and loans.

Mergers and Acquisitions

In 2013 Starwood Property Trust bought LNR Property LLC a real estate investment finance management and development firm. The trust paid $862 million for LNR's US special servicer the US investment securities portfolio Archetype Mortgage Capital (now Starwood Mortgage Capital) Archetype Financial Institution Services LNR Europe and 50% of LNR's interest in Auction.com.

Later that year it moved to spin off its single-family residential business as a new REIT named Starwood Waypoint Residential Trust. The trust which will be affiliated with Waypoint Homes will invest own and operate single-family rental homes and non-performing residential mortgage loans in the US.

EXECUTIVES

Chb-Ceo, Barry S Sternlicht
Pres, Jeffrey F Dimodica
Exec V Pres-Gen Counsel-Coo-Cc, Andrew J Sossen
Treas-Cfo-Pfo-cao, Rina Paniry
Senior Vice President, Ali Amirali
Director, Loan Servicing, Ir, Derek Olson
Vice President, Eddie Moreno
Vice President, Rachel Naylor
Auditors: DELOITTE & TOUCHE LLP

LOCATIONS

HQ: Starwood Property Trust Inc.
591 West Putnam Avenue, Greenwich, CT 06830
Phone: 203 422-7700
Web: www.starwoodpropertytrust.com

COMPETITORS

ELLINGTON RESIDENTIAL ESTATE	PETRA REAL
MORTGAGE REIT	OPPORTUNITY TRUST
INVESCO MORTGAGE CAPITAL INC.	RAIT FINANCIAL TRUST
	TPG RE FINANCE TRUST INC.
LNR PROPERTY LLC	
NEW RESIDENTIAL INVESTMENT CORP.	

HISTORICAL FINANCIALS

Company Type: Public

Income Statement   FYE: December 31

	ASSETS ($ mil.)	NET INCOME ($ mil.)	INCOME AS % OF ASSETS	EMPLOYEES
12/20	80,873.5	331.6	0.4%	282
12/19	78,042.3	509.6	0.7%	296
12/18	68,262.4	385.8	0.6%	290
12/17	62,941.2	400.7	0.6%	312
12/16	77,256.2	365.1	0.5%	340
Annual Growth	1.2%	(2.4%)	—	(4.6%)

2020 Year-End Financials

Return on assets: 0.4%
Return on equity: 7.2%
Long-term debt ($ mil.): —
No. of shares (mil.): 284.6
Sales ($ mil): 1,136.1

Dividends
  Yield: 9.9%
  Payout: 165.5%
Market value ($ mil.): 5,494.0

	STOCK PRICE ($) FY Close	P/E High/Low		Earnings	PER SHARE ($) Dividends	Book Value
12/20	19.30	23	8	1.16	1.92	15.77
12/19	24.86	14	11	1.79	1.92	16.66
12/18	19.71	16	13	1.42	1.92	16.70
12/17	21.35	15	14	1.52	1.92	17.13
12/16	21.95	15	11	1.50	1.92	17.44
Annual Growth	(3.2%)	—	—	(6.2%)	(0.0%)	(2.5%)

StepStone Group Inc

LOCATIONS

HQ: StepStone Group Inc
450 Lexington Avenue, 31st Floor, New York, NY 10017
Phone: 212 351-6100
Web: www.stepstonegroup.com

HISTORICAL FINANCIALS

Company Type: Public

Income Statement   FYE: March 31

	REVENUE ($ mil.)	NET INCOME ($ mil.)	NET PROFIT MARGIN	EMPLOYEES
03/21	787.7	62.6	8.0%	570
03/20	446.6	131.9	29.5%	526
03/19	256.2	54.2	21.1%	0
03/18	264.2	81.4	30.8%	0
Annual Growth	43.9%	(8.4%)	—	—

2021 Year-End Financials

Debt ratio: —
Return on equity: 26.9%
Cash ($ mil.): 179.8
Current ratio: 0.33
Long-term debt ($ mil.): —

No. of shares (mil.): 94.8
Dividends
  Yield: 0.2%
  Payout: 3.4%
Market value ($ mil.): 3,344.0

	STOCK PRICE ($) FY Close	P/E High/Low		Earnings	PER SHARE ($) Dividends	Book Value
03/21	35.27	19	12	2.06	0.07	2.63
03/20	0.00	—	—	(0.00)	0.00	(0.00)
Annual Growth	—	—	—	—	—	—

Sterling Construction Co Inc

Sterling Construction company specializes in the building reconstruction and repair of transportation and water infrastructure. It also works on specialty projects such as excavation shoring and drilling. The heavy civil construction company and its subsidiaries (Texas Sterling Construction Ralph L. Wadsworth Contractors RDI Foundation Drilling Myers and Sons Banicki Construction and Road and Highway Builders) primarily serve public sector clients throughout the Southwest and West. Transportation projects include excavation and asphalt paving as well as construction of bridges and rail systems. Water projects include work on sewers and storm drainage systems.

Geographic Reach

Houston-based Sterling Construction and its subsidiaries operate from offices in Texas California Arizona Utah and Nevada. The firm's major markets include Texas Utah and Nevada.

Financial Performance

The economic recession and prolonged recovery has taken its toll on Sterling Construction. The company reported a net loss of $297 million in 2012 following a loss of $36 million in 2011. The company attributed the losses which continued in 2013 primarily to additional write-downs on three large projects booked prior to 2012 in Texas that continue to have a negative impact on profitability. Sterling says it expects the projects to be substantially complete by mid-2014.

Revenue is improving however. In 2012 sales increased 26% compared with 2011 to $630.5 million driven by projects in in Arizona and California. Indeed 2012 marked the third consecutive year of rising sales for the firm. While the revenue picture is brighter profits are still expected to suffer as Sterling faces increased competitive pressure to bid low for construction projects.

Strategy

Sterling Construction and other companies that rely heavily on government highway work have been hurt buy Congress' inability to pass the Federal Highway Bill. Without new legislation new projects and funding for the work is uncertain. In response to the uncertain outlook Sterling refocused on project execution and conservative bidding. The company also sold some equipment in order to raise cash to upgrade its fleet.

Sterling Construction's long-term strategy is to expand its geographic footprint to attractive markets. The company also seeks to add to its construction capabilities. It has mostly used acquisitions to achieve those goals.

Increased competition has sent Sterling looking for work in new markets. As a result it has landed contracts in places such as Hawaii Montana Idaho and Louisiana. Sterling also expanded its operations in Texas to include El Paso and Corpus Christi. The company continues to seek opportunities in new markets in western southwestern and southeastern states. Sterling also is seeking to work on larger higher-margin design/build projects by entering joint ventures. One example is Ralph L. Wadsworth Contractors' joint venture with Fluor and two other companies to build a $1.2 billion project on I-15 in Utah.

Mergers and Acquisitions

In January 2013 the firm acquired the remaining 20% interest in Ralph L. Wadsworth Construction Co. from its management for $23.1 million. In 2011 Sterling expanded into Arizona and California with the acquisition of J. Banicki Construction. Also that year Sterling bought a 50% stake in California-based Myer & Sons Construction.

EXECUTIVES

Chief Executive Officer, Director, Joseph Cutillo, $740,000 total compensation
Chief Financial Officer, Executive Vice President, Chief Accounting Officer, Ronald Ballschmiede, $506,400 total compensation
Independent Director, Charles Patton
Independent Director, Julie Dill
Independent Director, Dwayne Wilson
Chief Compliance Officer, General Counsel, Corporate Secretary, Mark Wolf, $119,346 total compensation
Independent Chairman Of The Board, Thomas White
Independent Director, Dana O'Brien
Auditors: Grant Thornton LLP

LOCATIONS

HQ: Sterling Construction Co Inc
1800 Hughes Landing Blvd., The Woodlands, TX 77380
Phone: 281 214-0777
Web: www.strlco.com

PRODUCTS/OPERATIONS

Selected Subsidiaries
J. Banicki Construction Inc. (Banicki)
Myers and Sons Construction
Ralph L. Wadsworth Contractors LLC (RLW)
RDI Foundation Drilling (RDI)
Road and Highway Builders LLC (RHB)
Road and Highway Builders of California (RHBCa)
Texas Sterling Construction Co. (TSC)

COMPETITORS

BALFOUR BEATTY INFRASTRUCTURE INC.
BAM NUTTALL LIMITED
COLAS SA
FERROVIAL SA
GMS INC.
HASEKO CORPORATION
HILL & SMITH INFRASTRUCTURE PRODUCTS GROUP LIMITE
LOEWS CORPORATION
MORO CORPORATION
NEW ENTERPRISE STONE & LIME CO. INC.
S. R. DRAPER PAVING COMPANY
TAKENAKA CORPORATION
THE SUNDT COMPANIES INC

HISTORICAL FINANCIALS

Company Type: Public

Income Statement — FYE: December 31

	REVENUE ($ mil.)	NET INCOME ($ mil.)	NET PROFIT MARGIN	EMPLOYEES
12/20	1,427.4	42.3	3.0%	2,600
12/19	1,126.2	39.9	3.5%	2,800
12/18	1,037.6	25.1	2.4%	1,935
12/17	957.9	11.6	1.2%	1,740
12/16	690.1	(9.2)	—	1,684
Annual Growth	19.9%	—		11.5%

2020 Year-End Financials

Debt ratio: 38.7%
Return on equity: 17.3%
Cash ($ mil.): 66.1
Current ratio: 1.12
Long-term debt ($ mil.): 291.2
No. of shares (mil.): 28.1
Dividends
 Yield: —
 Payout: —
Market value ($ mil.): 525.0

	STOCK PRICE ($) FY Close	P/E High/Low		PER SHARE ($) Earnings	Dividends	Book Value
12/20	18.61	13	5	1.50	0.00	9.48
12/19	14.08	11	7	1.47	0.00	7.92
12/18	10.89	17	11	0.93	0.00	6.18
12/17	16.28	41	18	0.43	0.00	5.22
12/16	8.46	—	—	(0.40)	0.00	4.30
Annual Growth	21.8%			—	—	21.9%

Stock Yards Bancorp Inc

Stock Yards Bancorp is the holding company of Stock Yards Bank & Trust which operates about 35 branches mostly in Louisville Kentucky but also in Indianapolis and Cincinnati. Founded in 1904 the $3 billion-asset bank targets individuals and regional business customers offering standard retail services such as checking and savings accounts credit cards certificates of deposit and IRAs. It also provides trust services while brokerage and credit card services are offered through agreements with other banks. Commercial real estate mortgages make up 40% of the bank's loan portfolio which also includes commercial and industrial loans (30%) residential mortgages (15%) construction loans and consumer loans.

Operations

Stock Yards Bank & Trust operates two main business lines: Commercial Banking which provides loans and deposits to individual consumers and businesses as well as mortgage origination and company brokerage activity; and Investment Management and Trust which provides wealth management services such as investment management trust estate administration and retirement plan services.

About 63% of the company's total revenue came from loan interest during 2015 while another 7% came from interest income on its securities. The rest came from its investment management and trust services (13% of revenue) deposit account service charges (7%) bankcard transaction revenue (4%) mortgage banking revenue (3%) brokerage commissions and fees (1%) and other non-interest sources.

Geographic Reach

Kentucky-based Stock Yards Bancorp had 37 branches at the end of 2015 including 28 branches in the Louisville Kentucky metro area and the rest in the Indianapolis Indiana and Cincinnati Ohio metro areas.

Financial Performance

Stock Yards' annual revenues have risen 11% since 2011 thanks to a combination of mostly organic loan growth and investment management and trust services fee growth. Meanwhile its annual profits have grown more than 55% on declining loan loss provisions as its loan portfolio's credit quality has improved with higher property valuations in the strengthened economy.

The bank's revenue climbed 4% to a record $133.12 million during 2015 on higher interest income mostly as its loan assets grew 9% to $2 billion with record loan production.

Revenue growth and a decline in interest expense on deposits in 2015 drove Stock Yard's net income up 7% to a record $34.82 million. The bank's operating cash levels jumped 8% to $43.17 million mostly thanks to the increase in cash-based earnings.

Strategy

Stock Yards outlined its plans for 2016 and beyond to maintain stable net interest margins achieve near-double digit loan growth manage credit quality to keep loan loss provisions down and increasing its regulatory readiness.

Mergers and Acquisitions

In 2013 the bank extended the reach of its operations into Oldham County through its purchase of $146 million-asset The BANcorp Inc. and its five THE BANK branches in the region for $19.9 million.

EXECUTIVES

Senior Executive Vice President, Director Of Bancorp And The Bank, Kathy Thompson, $364,000 total compensation
Executive Vice President And Chief Risk Officer Of The Bank, William Dishman, $289,000 total compensation
President, Bancorp And The Bank, Philip Poindexter, $396,000 total compensation
Chief Financial Officer, Executive Vice President, Treasurer Of Bancorp And The Bank, T. Stinnett, $317,000 total compensation
Chairman And Chief Executive Officer, James Hillebrand, $560,000 total compensation
Independent Director, Carl Herde
Executive Vice President And Chief Lending Officer Of The Bank, Michael Rehm
Independent Director, Stephen Priebe
Executive Vice President And Director Of Retail Banking Of The Bank, Michael Croce
Independent Director, John Schutte
Director, Shannon Arvin
Director, Edwin Saunier
Independent Director, J. McCauley Brown
Auditors: BKD, LLP

LOCATIONS

HQ: Stock Yards Bancorp Inc
1040 East Main Street, Louisville, KY 40206
Phone: 502 582-2571
Web: www.syb.com

PRODUCTS/OPERATIONS

2015 Revenues by Category

	$ mil.	% of total
Interest income	93.1	70
Non-interest income	40.0	30
Total	**133.1**	**100**

Selected Products & Services

Personal Banking
  Banking
  Personal Lending
  Personal Investing & Wealth Management Services
Business Banking
  Credit Loans & Leasing
  Deposit Services
  Treasury Management

Business Retirement Plans
Wealth Management Services
  Investment Management
  Financial Planning
  Trust & Estate Services
  Brokerage Service

COMPETITORS

ASSOCIATED BANC-CORP
CAMBRIDGE BANCORP
CASCADE BANCORP
MACATAWA BANK CORPORATION
MB FINANCIAL INC.
PEAPACK-GLADSTONE FINANCIAL CORPORATION

HISTORICAL FINANCIALS

Company Type: Public

Income Statement

FYE: December 31

	ASSETS ($ mil.)	NET INCOME ($ mil.)	INCOME AS % OF ASSETS	EMPLOYEES
12/20	4,608.6	58.8	1.3%	641
12/19	3,724.2	66.0	1.8%	615
12/18	3,302.9	55.5	1.7%	591
12/17	3,239.6	38.0	1.2%	580
12/16	3,039.4	41.0	1.3%	578
Annual Growth	11.0%	9.4%	—	2.6%

2020 Year-End Financials

Return on assets: 1.4%	Dividends
Return on equity: 13.8%	Yield: 2.6%
Long-term debt ($ mil.): —	Payout: 42.5%
No. of shares (mil.): 22.6	Market value ($ mil.): 919.0
Sales ($ mil) 199.7	

	STOCK PRICE ($) FY Close	P/E High/Low		Earnings	PER SHARE ($) Dividends	Book Value
12/20	40.48	17	9	2.59	1.08	19.42
12/19	41.06	15	11	2.89	1.04	17.97
12/18	32.80	17	12	2.42	0.96	16.11
12/17	37.70	28	19	1.66	0.80	14.71
12/16	46.95	26	15	1.80	0.72	13.88
Annual Growth	(3.6%)	—	—	9.5%	10.8%	8.8%

STORE Capital Corp

EXECUTIVES

Executive Vice President, Chief Compliance Officer, General Counsel, Secretary, Chad Freed, $375,000 total compensation
Chief Financial Officer, Executive Vice President, Treasurer, Secretary, Sherry Rexroad
Chairman, Tawn Kelley
Independent Director, William Hipp
Independent Director, Einar Seadler
Executive Vice President - Underwriting, Portfolio Management, Craig Barnett
Independent Director, Quentin Smith
Executive Vice President Of Acquisitions, Tyler Maertz, $596,545 total compensation
President, Chief Executive Officer, Director, Mary Fedewa, $612,500 total compensation
Auditors: Ernst & Young LLP

LOCATIONS

HQ: STORE Capital Corp
8377 East Hartford Drive, Suite 100, Scottsdale, AZ 85255
Phone: 480 256-1100
Web: www.storecapital.com

HISTORICAL FINANCIALS

Company Type: Public

Income Statement

FYE: December 31

	REVENUE ($ mil.)	NET INCOME ($ mil.)	NET PROFIT MARGIN	EMPLOYEES
12/20	694.2	212.6	30.6%	106
12/19	665.7	284.9	42.8%	97
12/18	540.7	216.9	40.1%	90
12/17	452.8	162.0	35.8%	80
12/16	376.3	123.3	32.8%	68
Annual Growth	16.5%	14.6%	—	11.7%

2020 Year-End Financials

Debt ratio: 41.3%	No. of shares (mil.): 266.1
Return on equity: 4.4%	Dividends
Cash ($ mil.): 166.3	Yield: 4.1%
Current ratio: 1.74	Payout: 169.0%
Long-term debt ($ mil.): 3,722.2	Market value ($ mil.): 9,043.0

	STOCK PRICE ($) FY Close	P/E High/Low		Earnings	PER SHARE ($) Dividends	Book Value
12/20	33.98	48	17	0.84	1.42	18.85
12/19	37.24	33	22	1.24	1.36	18.70
12/18	28.31	29	21	1.06	1.28	17.48
12/17	26.04	29	22	0.90	1.20	16.36
12/16	24.71	38	27	0.82	1.12	15.58
Annual Growth	8.3%	—	—	0.6% 6.1%	4.9%

Strategic Education Inc

Students who wander from traditional learning paths can turn to Strategic Education (formerly Strayer Education). The company's Strayer University offers more than 100 different degree diploma and certificate programs from more than 75 campuses in more than 15 US states and Washington DC. Strategic Education's online Capella University offers nearly 55 degrees to some 41200 students throughout the US. The company also offers an executive MBA online through Jack Welch Management Institute. Strayer Education merged with Capella Education to create Strategic Education.

Operations

Strategic Education has three segments: Strayer University Capella University and non-degree programs segment.

Strayer University offers undergraduate and graduate degree programs in business administration accounting information technology education health services administration public administration and criminal justice. Strayer University offers an executive MBA online through the Jack Welch Management Institute (JWMI). It also offers programs both online and in physical classrooms to cater working adult students. This segment accounts nearly 55% of total revenue.

Capella University is an online post-secondary education company that offers a variety of bachelor's master's and doctoral degree programs primarily delivered to working adults. Capella University's program offerings span six primary disciplines: public service leadership; nursing and health sciences; psychology; business and technology; counseling and human services; and education. The university focuses on master's and doctoral degrees with 68% of its learners enrolled in a master's or doctoral degree program. This segment accounts around 45% of total revenue.

Non-degree programs offers DevMountain a software development school offering web development iOS development and UX design programs in person at DevMountain's classrooms. Also Hackbright Academy a software engineering school for women offering accelerated software development programs and its Sophia Learning an innovative company which leverages technology and high quality academic content to provide self-paced online courses eligible for transfer credit into over 2000 colleges and universities. This accounts a small portion of revenue.

Geographic Reach
Virginia-based Strategic Education operates more than 75 physical campuses predominantly located in the eastern US. Other primary locations are in Minneapolis also the headquarters for Capella University and Washington DC serves as the headquarters and main campus of Strayer University. Some of its non-degree programs are located in Lehi Utah Dallas Texas and Phoenix Arizona.

Sales and Marketing
Strayer University engages in a broad range of activities to identify its potential students as well as to inform working adults and their employers about the programs offered. These activities include direct digital and social media marketing marketing to existing students and graduates print and broadcast advertising student referrals and corporate and government outreach activities. All information relevant to prospective students is published on the website www.strayer.edu. Strayer University maintains booths and information tables at appropriate conferences and expos as well as at transfer days at community colleges.

For Capella University it engages in a range of relationship-based marketing activities to build the Capella brand differentiate it from other educational providers increase awareness and consideration with prospective learners generate inquiries for enrollment and stimulate referrals from current learners and graduates. These include Internet television print radio email social media and direct mail advertising campaigns. Other marketing activities include supportive outreach to current learners participation in seminars and trade shows and development of key marketing relationships with corporate healthcare armed forces government and educational organizations. Online advertising (display social mobile search and through aggregators) currently generates the largest volume of inquiries from prospective learners.

Advertising costs were $66.8 million $102.6 million and $149.8 million for the FY 2017 2018 and 2019 respectively.

Financial Performance
Strategic Education had its revenues gradually rise in the last five years. Revenues rose by about 130% between 2015 and 2019. Despite the exceptional rise in revenue the company's net income

has been a little more sporadic rising and falling in the same five-year period and falling once into a loss in 2018.

Revenue rose 57% to $997.1 million in 2019 from $634.2 million in 2018. The increase was primarily related to the inclusion of CEC revenue for the full year. In the Strayer University segment enrollment grew 11% which resulted in a 12% revenue growth. Capella University segment revenue also rose that year reflecting activity after the completion of the CEC merger. Non-Degree Programs segment revenues also increased due to incremental revenues generated from the operations of Hackbright DevMountain and Sophia Learning which were acquired in the CEC merger.

From a loss of $15.7 million in 2019 Strategic Education managed to post a profit of $81.1 million in 2019. Income from operations was $110.5 million in 2019 compared to a loss from operations of $22.7 million in 2018 principally due to higher revenues due to enrollment growth and lower merger and integration costs and impairment charges than in 2018.

Cash and equivalents at the end of 2019 were $420.5 million a $108.3 million increase from the year prior. Cash from operations were $202.1 million while investing and financing activities used $38.1 million and $55.8 million respectively. Strategic Education's main cash uses in 2019 were purchases of marketable securities dividends paid and net payments for stock awards.

Strategy
Strategic Education's goal is to be the leading innovator and provider of career-relevant and meaningful education programs that prepare students for advancement in their careers and professional lives and promote economic mobility. Its strategic priorities are as follows: improve student success; enhance the student experience; address affordability; establish new platforms for growth; and build a high performing culture.

As the company's success depends on the success of its students it continues to hire outstanding faculty produce high quality academic content and employ cutting edge technology that enables it to deploy faculty and content in increasingly efficient and effective ways.

The company's Strayer University and Capella University have also instituted various other tuition reductions and scholarships. It continues to monitor and assess the impact of its affordability initiatives and explore other ways to make its offerings as affordable as possible. Strategic Education has also begun to deploy more aggressive technology innovations including artificial intelligence and automation which enables it to lower its operating costs and thus improve its ability to support lower tuition.

Company Background
Then-named Strayer Education moved to add "name brand" education to its offerings through its 2011 acquisition of the Jack Welch Management Institute. Its online executive MBA program and certification programs are based on the management lessons of the former General Electric chairman and CEO and are geared for both individual students and corporations seeking continuing education for their executives.

EXECUTIVES

Chairman, Robert Silberman, $754,000 total compensation

Chief Executive Officer, Director, Raymond McDonnell, $880,000 total compensation
Independent Director, G. Thomas Waite
Chief Financial Officer, Executive Vice President, Daniel Jackson, $525,000 total compensation
Independent Director, Nathaniel Fick
Independent Director, H. James Dallas
Independent Director, Rita Brogley
Vice Chairman Of The Board, J. Kevin Gilligan
Chief Human Resource Officer, Senior Vice President, Christa Hokenson
Senior Vice President, General Counsel, Lizette Herraiz, $445,000 total compensation
President, U.s. Higher Education, Andrew Watt, $515,000 total compensation
Independent Director, Jerry Johnson
Independent Director, William Slocum
Director, Michael McRobbie
Auditors: PricewaterhouseCoopers LLP

LOCATIONS

HQ: Strategic Education Inc
2303 Dulles Station Boulevard, Herndon, VA 20171
Phone: 703 247-2500
Web: www.strategiceducation.com

PRODUCTS/OPERATIONS

2016 Students by Program Level

	% of total
Bachelor's degree	67
Master's degree	27
Associate degree	5
Non-degree	1
Total	**100**

Selected Degrees and Programs
Master of Business Administration (M.B.A.) Degree
Master of Education (M.Ed.) Degree
Master of Health Services Administration (M.H.S.A.) Degree
Master of Public Administration (M.P.A.) Degree
Master of Science (M.S.) Degree
    Information Systems (with multiple concentrations)
    Professional Accounting
Executive Graduate Certificate Programs
    Business Administration
    Information Systems
    Professional Accounting
Bachelor of Science (B.S.) Degree
    Accounting
    Information Systems
    Economics
    International Business
    Criminal Justice
Bachelor of Business Administration (B.B.A.) Degree
Associate in Arts (A.A.) Degree
    Accounting
    Acquisition and Contract Management
    Business Administration
    Criminal Justice
    Information Systems
    Economics
    General Studies
    Marketing
Diploma Programs
    Accounting
    Acquisition and Contract Management
    Information Systems
Undergraduate Certificate Programs
    Accounting
    Business Administration
    Information Systems

COMPETITORS

2U INC.	UNIVERSITY OF
ADTALEM GLOBAL	GREENWICH
EDUCATION INC.	UNIVERSITY OF
ARIZONA STATE	NOTTINGHAM (THE)
UNIVERSITY	ZOVIO INC
GRAND CANYON EDUCATION	
INC.	

HISTORICAL FINANCIALS

Company Type: Public

Income Statement

FYE: December 31

	REVENUE ($ mil.)	NET INCOME ($ mil.)	NET PROFIT MARGIN	EMPLOYEES
12/20	1,027.6	86.2	8.4%	3,679
12/19	997.1	81.1	8.1%	3,229
12/18	634.1	(15.6)	—	3,158
12/17	454.8	20.6	4.5%	1,544
12/16	441.0	34.8	7.9%	1,869
Annual Growth	23.5%	25.5%		18.4%

2020 Year-End Financials

Debt ratio: 7.6%	No. of shares (mil.): 24.4
Return on equity: 5.3%	Dividends
Cash ($ mil.): 187.5	Yield: 2.5%
Current ratio: 1.43	Payout: 48.8%
Long-term debt ($ mil.): 141.8	Market value ($ mil.): 2,328.0

	STOCK PRICE ($) FY Close	P/E High/Low		PER SHARE ($) Earnings	Dividends	Book Value
12/20	95.33	48	22	3.77	2.40	71.60
12/19	158.90	50	29	3.67	2.10	66.59
12/18	113.42	—	—	(1.03)	1.50	65.55
12/17	89.58	52	39	1.84	1.00	18.73
12/16	80.63	25	13	3.21	0.00	16.98
Annual Growth	4.3%	—	—	4.1%	—	43.3%

Stride Inc

K12 isn't a missing element from the periodic table but it could help kids learn about the periodic table. The company offers online educational programs to students in kindergarten through 12th grade through "virtual schools." It also offers online curriculum to public and private schools. It provides course material and product sales directly to parents and individualized supplemental programs offered through schools. K12 also manages and sells its products and services to blended schools (public schools that combine online and face-to-face instruction) and provides services to US school districts and to international partners. K12 was founded in 2000.

Operations

K12 operates in three lines of business: Managed Public Schools (virtual and blended); Institutional Business (school district partnerships focused on curriculum development and teacher training); and International and Private Pay Business (three online schools and international distribution partnerships).

The company's Managed Public-School segment (its largest revenue generator bringing in about 90% of sales) develops online programs that adhere to the policies of public entities such as public-school districts; independent not-for-profit charter school boards; and state education agencies. Students who attend virtual public schools receive assignments complete lessons and obtain instruction from certified teachers with whom they interact online telephonically in virtual classroom environments and at times face-to-face.

Institutional Business services provided to districts include teacher training programs adminis-

trator support and a student account management system. This segment accounts for about 5% of revenue.

The firm's online private schools are K12 Private Academy (high school) George Washington University Online High School (college prep) and Keystone School (home schooling for middle and high school). This segment accounts for the remaining revenues.

Geographic Reach

K12 serves students in more than 100 countries around the world. K12 operates overseas through the K12 Private Academy a private school that enables K12 to deliver its learning system to students in other countries. The company serves districts or schools in about 50 states and the District of Columbia. Its headquarters is located in Herndon Virginia.

Sales and Marketing

K12's customers include US public private and public charter schools; school districts; regional education agencies; and commercial firms that serve students. Additionally the company sells online courses and supplemental educational materials directly to families.

The company's advertising costs totaled about $32.7 million $38.0 million and $37.5 million for the years ended 2020 2019 and 2018 respectively.

Financial Performance

The company's revenues for 2020 (ended June) were $1.04 billion representing an increase of $25.0 million or 3% from $1.01 billion for 2019 (ended June). Managed Public School Program revenues increased $29.8 million or 3% year over year. The increase in Managed Public School Program revenues was primarily due to the 3% increase in enrollments and increases in the per pupil achieved funding school mix (distribution of enrollments by school) and other factors.

Net income was $24.5 million for the year ended June 30 2020 compared to $37.2 million for the year ended June 30 2019 representing a decrease of $12.7 million. The decrease was due to Galvanize's net loss of $18.1 million.

Cash held by the company at the end of 2020 decreased by $71.3 million to $213.3 million compared to $284.6 million in 2019. Cash provided by operations was $80.4 million while investing activities was $217.4 million primarily for the acquisition of Galvanize Inc. Cash provided by financing activities was $65.6 million primarily from borrowing from credit facility.

Strategy

K12 is committed to maximizing every child's potential by personalizing their educational experience delivering quality education to schools and their students and supporting its customers in their quest to improve academic outcomes and prepare them for college and career readiness. In furtherance of those objectives the company plan to continue investing in our curriculum and learning systems. These investments include initiatives to create and deploy a next generation curriculum and learning platform improve the effectiveness of our school workforce develop new instructional approaches to increase student and parental engagement and improve the company's systems and security architecture. This strategy consists of the following key elements: affect better student outcomes; improve student retention in the company's virtual schools; grow DCA enrollments and expand career training market; introduce new and improved products and services; increase enrollments

at existing virtual and blended public schools; expand virtual and blended public school presence into additional states and cities; grow the company's institutional business; add enrollments in its private schools; pursue international opportunities to offer its learning systems; develop additional channels through which to deliver the company's learning systems; and pursue strategic partnerships and acquisitions.

Mergers and Acquisitions

In 2020 the company acquired 100% of Denver-based Galvanize in exchange for approximately $165.0 million plus working capital of about $12.2 million. Galvanize provides talent development for individuals and enterprises in information technology fields. The acquisition of Galvanize expands the company's offerings to include post-secondary skills training in data science and software engineering technology staffing and developing talent and capabilities for companies. The company also plans to use Galvanize's curriculum to create appropriate content to offer high school students.

EXECUTIVES

Chief Financial Officer, Timothy Medina, $475,000 total compensation
Chief Executive Officer, Director, James Rhyu, $628,404 total compensation
Independent Director, Steven Fink
Independent Director, Guillermo Bron
Independent Director, John Engler
Independent Director, Eliza McFadden
Independent Director, Robert Knowling
Independent Director, Robert Cohen
President - Career Learning Solutions, Shaun McAlmont, $518,462 total compensation
Independent Director, Victoria Harker
Executive Chairman Of The Board, Nathaniel Davis, $769,365 total compensation
Lead Independent Director, Craig Barrett
President - Academic Policy And External Affairs, Kevin Chavous, $519,687 total compensation
Independent Director, Aida Alvarez
Executive Vice President, General Counsel And Secretary, Vincent Mathis, $443,846 total compensation
Auditors: BDO USA, LLP

LOCATIONS

HQ: Stride Inc
2300 Corporate Park Drive, Herndon, VA 20171
Phone: 703 483-7000
Web: www.k12.com

PRODUCTS/OPERATIONS

2016 Sales

	$ mil.	% of total
Managed Public School Programs	717.1	82
Institutional		
Non-managed Public School Programs	55.6	6
Institutional Software & Services	53.0	6
Private Pay Schools and Other	47.0	6
Total	**872.7**	**100**

Selected Schools and Programs

Early Learning Programs
High School Program
K-8 Program
Online Privatre Schools
Online Public Schools

Selected Students Served/Services

Advanced and Enrichable Learners
Athletes and Performers
Credit Recovery (for missed classes make-up credits)

Expat Foreign Service Overseas
Homebound
Homeschoolers
Military Families
Reading Program
Struggling Students
Summer School
Supplemental Education
World Languages

COMPETITORS

AMERICAN PUBLIC EDUCATION INC.
IMAGINE SCHOOLS INC.
PERDOCEO EDUCATION CORPORATION
ROYAL MENCAP SOCIETY
STRATEGIC EDUCATION INC.
THE GIRLS' DAY SCHOOL TRUST
UNIVERSITY OF OREGON
VALLEY VIEW COMMUNITY UNIT SCHOOL DISTRICT 365U

HISTORICAL FINANCIALS

Company Type: Public

Income Statement				FYE: June 30
	REVENUE ($ mil.)	NET INCOME ($ mil.)	NET PROFIT MARGIN	EMPLOYEES
06/21	1,536.7	71.4	4.6%	7,100
06/20	1,040.7	24.5	2.4%	4,950
06/19	1,015.7	37.2	3.7%	4,550
06/18	917.7	27.6	3.0%	4,700
06/17	888.5	0.4	0.1%	4,750
Annual Growth	14.7%	254.8%	—	10.6%

2021 Year-End Financials

Debt ratio: 23.3%
Return on equity: 9.6%
Cash ($ mil.): 386.0
Current ratio: 2.80
Long-term debt ($ mil.): 340.8

No. of shares (mil.): 41.5
Dividends
  Yield: —
  Payout: —
Market value ($ mil.): 1,336.0

	STOCK PRICE ($) FY Close	P/E High/Low		PER SHARE ($) Earnings	Dividends	Book Value
06/21	32.13	29	12	1.71	0.00	19.35
06/20	27.24	51	26	0.60	0.00	16.47
06/19	30.41	39	17	0.91	0.00	15.74
06/18	16.37	26	19	0.68	0.00	14.84
06/17	17.92	2091	1060	0.01	0.00	14.07
Annual Growth	15.7%	—		—261.6%	—	8.3%

Sturgis Bancorp Inc

Sturgis Bancorp is the holding company for Sturgis Bank & Trust which has about 10 branches in south-central Michigan. Founded in 1905 the bank offers checking and savings accounts CDs trust services and other standard banking fare. Real estate loans comprise the bulk of its lending activities: one- to four-family residential mortgages make up more than half of the company's loan portfolio. Subsidiary Oak Leaf Financial Services provides insurance and investment products and services from third-party provider Linsco/Private Ledger.

EXECUTIVES

Vice President, Ronald Scheske, $105,988 total compensation
Vice Chairman Of The Board, James Goethals
Chairman Of The Board, Leonard Eishen, $37,886 total compensation
President, Chief Executive Officer, Director, Eric Eishen, $175,983 total compensation
Chairman Of The Board, Donald Frost
Director, Philip Ward
Director, Raymond Dresser
Director, Kimberlee Bontrager
Chief Financial Officer, Corporate Secretary, Treasurer Of The Company And The Bank, Brian Hoggatt, $117,292 total compensation
Director, Jeffrey Mohney
Director, Jason Halling
Auditors: Crowe LLP

LOCATIONS

HQ: Sturgis Bancorp Inc
  113-125 East Chicago Road, Sturgis, MI 49091
Phone: 269 651-9345
Web: www.sturgisbank.com

COMPETITORS

FIRST FEDERAL BANK CORPORATION
NORTHEAST COMMUNITY BANCORP INC.
SIMPLICITY BANCORP INC.

HISTORICAL FINANCIALS

Company Type: Public

Income Statement				FYE: December 31
	ASSETS ($ mil.)	NET INCOME ($ mil.)	INCOME AS % OF ASSETS	EMPLOYEES
12/20	643.6	6.0	0.9%	0
12/19	473.3	4.9	1.0%	0
12/18	431.5	4.3	1.0%	0
12/17	414.4	3.1	0.8%	0
12/16	398.6	2.6	0.7%	0
Annual Growth	12.7%	22.6%	—	—

2020 Year-End Financials

Return on assets: 1.0%
Return on equity: 13.2%
Long-term debt ($ mil.): —
No. of shares (mil.): 2.1
Sales ($ mil): 30.7

Dividends
  Yield: 3.4%
  Payout: 24.8%
Market value ($ mil.): 39.0

	STOCK PRICE ($) FY Close	P/E High/Low		PER SHARE ($) Earnings	Dividends	Book Value
12/20	18.45	8	5	2.84	0.64	22.19
12/19	21.50	14	9	2.34	0.60	20.61
12/18	19.80	11	9	2.08	0.57	19.11
12/17	18.80	13	9	1.52	0.48	17.78
12/16	13.75	11	8	1.28	0.42	16.65
Annual Growth	7.6%	—		— 22.0%	11.1%	7.4%

Summit Financial Group Inc

Summit Financial Group is at the peak of community banking in West Virginia and northern Virginia. The company owns Summit Community Bank which operates about 20 branches that offer standard retail banking fare such as deposit accounts loans and cash management services. Commercial real estate loans including land development and construction loans account for about 40% of Summit Financial Group's loan portfolio which also includes residential mortgages and a smaller percentage of business and consumer loans. The bank's Summit Insurance Services unit sells both commercial and personal coverage.

EXECUTIVES

Independent Chairman Of The Board, Oscar Bean
Executive Vice President, Chief Of Credit Administration, Patrick Frye, $272,250 total compensation
Independent Director, Charles Piccirillo
Independent Director, James Cookman
Investor Relations, Teresa Ely
Executive Vice President, President Of Summit Community Bank, Bradford Ritchie, $311,250 total compensation
Independent Director, John Gianola
Independent Director, James Geary
Independent Director, John Shott
Independent Director, John Crites
Independent Director, Georgette George
President, Chief Executive Officer, Director, H. Charles Maddy, $507,500 total compensation
Independent Director, J. Scott Bridgeforth
Independent Director, Jason Kitzmiller
Director, Ronald Bowling
Independent Director, Ronald Spencer
Independent Director, Jill Upson
Auditors: Yount, Hyde & Barbour, P.C.

LOCATIONS

HQ: Summit Financial Group Inc
  300 North Main Street, Moorefield, WV 26836
Phone: 304 530-1000
Web: www.summitfgi.com

COMPETITORS

CODORUS VALLEY BANCORP INC.
COMMUNITY SHORES BANK CORPORATION
FIRST BUSEY CORPORATION

HISTORICAL FINANCIALS

Company Type: Public

Income Statement				FYE: December 31
	ASSETS ($ mil.)	NET INCOME ($ mil.)	INCOME AS % OF ASSETS	EMPLOYEES
12/20	3,106.3	31.3	1.0%	415
12/19	2,403.4	31.8	1.3%	383
12/18	2,200.5	28.0	1.3%	371
12/17	2,134.2	11.9	0.6%	349
12/16	1,758.6	17.3	1.0%	251
Annual Growth	15.3%	16.0%	—	13.4%

2020 Year-End Financials

Return on assets: 1.1%
Return on equity: 11.8%
Long-term debt ($ mil.): —
No. of shares (mil.): 12.9
Sales ($ mil): 135.0

Dividends
Yield: 3.0%
Payout: 29.8%
Market value ($ mil.): 286.0

	STOCK PRICE ($)	P/E		PER SHARE ($)		
	FY Close	High/Low		Earnings	Dividends	Book Value
12/20	22.08	11	6	2.41	0.68	21.76
12/19	27.09	11	8	2.53	0.59	19.97
12/18	19.31	12	8	2.26	0.53	17.85
12/17	26.32	28	19	1.00	0.44	16.30
12/16	27.53	18	7	1.61	0.40	14.47
Annual Growth	(5.4%)	—	—	10.6%	14.2%	10.7%

Summit Materials Inc

Auditors: KPMG LLP

LOCATIONS

HQ: Summit Materials Inc
1550 Wynkoop Street, 3rd Floor, Denver, CO 80202
Phone: 303 893-0012
Web: www.summit-materials.com

HISTORICAL FINANCIALS

Company Type: Public

Income Statement
FYE: January 2

	REVENUE ($ mil.)	NET INCOME ($ mil.)	NET PROFIT MARGIN	EMPLOYEES
01/21*	2,332.4	137.9	5.9%	6,000
12/19	2,222.1	61.1	2.8%	6,000
12/18	2,101.0	36.3	1.7%	6,000
12/17	1,932.5	125.8	6.5%	6,000
12/16	1,626.0	46.1	2.8%	5,000
Annual Growth	9.4%	31.5%	—	4.7%

*Fiscal year change

2021 Year-End Financials

Debt ratio: 44.0%
Return on equity: 8.9%
Cash ($ mil.): 418.1
Current ratio: 2.77
Long-term debt ($ mil.): 1,892.3

No. of shares (mil.): 114.3
Dividends
Yield: —
Payout: —
Market value ($ mil.): 2,297.0

	STOCK PRICE ($)	P/E		PER SHARE ($)		
	FY Close	High/Low		Earnings	Dividends	Book Value
01/21*	20.08	20	7	1.20	0.00	13.97
12/19	23.84	47	23	0.52	0.00	12.60
12/18	12.30	112	38	0.30	0.00	11.89
12/17	31.44	29	21	1.11	0.00	11.40
12/16	23.79	47	26	0.52	0.00	8.65
Annual Growth	(4.2%)	—	—	23.1%	—	12.7%

*Fiscal year change

Summit State Bank (Santa Rosa, CA)

Contrary to its name Summit State Bank does business in both the hills and the valleys of Sonoma County in western California. Serving consumers and small to midsized businesses the bank offers standard deposit services like checking savings and retirement accounts as well as lending services such as real estate and commercial loans. Commercial real estate loans account for about 40% of the bank's loan portfolio while commercial and agriculture loans make up about 20%. Its other lending products include single-family and multifamily mortgages construction loans and consumer loans. Summit State Bank operates about half a dozen branches in Petaluma Rohnert Park Santa Rosa and Windsor.

EXECUTIVES

Independent Director, Marshall Reynolds
Independent Director, Sharon Wright
Director, Belinda Guadarrama
Chief Operating Officer, Executive Vice President, Genie Del Secco, $234,775 total compensation
President, Chief Executive Officer, Director, Brian Reed, $316,575 total compensation
Chairman Of The Board, James Brush, $101,146 total compensation
Independent Director, Josh Cox
Independent Director, Nicholas Rado
Independent Director, Richard Pope
Independent Director, John Wright
Independent Director, Todd Fry
Independent Director, Jeffrey Allen
Executive Vice President, Chief Credit Officer, Michael Castlio
Chief Financial Officer, Executive Vice President, Camille Kazarian, $12,171 total compensation
Executive Vice President, Chief Lending Officer, Brandy Seppi, $249,913 total compensation
Auditors: Moss Adams LLP

LOCATIONS

HQ: Summit State Bank (Santa Rosa, CA)
500 Bicentennial Way, Santa Rosa, CA 95403
Phone: 707 568-6000
Web: www.summitstatebank.com

COMPETITORS

ASB FINANCIAL CORP
FIRST CAPITAL INC.
GREAT FLORIDA BANK
HERITAGE SOUTHEAST BANCORPORATION INC.

HIGH COUNTRY BANCORP INC.
KS BANCORP INC.
PEOPLES BANCORP

HISTORICAL FINANCIALS

Company Type: Public

Income Statement
FYE: December 31

	ASSETS ($ mil.)	NET INCOME ($ mil.)	INCOME AS % OF ASSETS	EMPLOYEES
12/20	865.8	10.5	1.2%	99
12/19	695.9	6.4	0.9%	93
12/18	622.1	5.8	0.9%	89
12/17	610.8	3.2	0.5%	78
12/16	513.7	4.9	1.0%	74
Annual Growth	13.9%	20.6%	—	7.5%

2020 Year-End Financials

Return on assets: 1.3%
Return on equity: 14.6%
Long-term debt ($ mil.): —
No. of shares (mil.): 5.5
Sales ($ mil): 40.8

Dividends
Yield: 3.5%
Payout: 27.7%
Market value ($ mil.): 74.0

	STOCK PRICE ($)	P/E		PER SHARE ($)		
	FY Close	High/Low		Earnings	Dividends	Book Value
12/20	13.48	7	3	1.90	0.44	13.71
12/19	12.97	11	9	1.18	0.44	12.20
12/18	11.77	15	10	1.06	0.44	11.16
12/17	12.60	30	20	0.59	0.41	10.87
12/16	15.00	16	14	0.90	0.35	10.71
Annual Growth	(2.6%)	—	—	20.5%	5.7%	6.4%

Sun Communities Inc

Sun Communities helps residents in the Sunshine State and around the US. The self-managed real estate investment trust (REIT) owns develops and operates manufactured housing communities (trailer and recreation vehicle parks) in nearly 30 states. Its portfolio includes more than 200 properties with nearly 80000 developed manufactured home and RV sites. Its Sun Home Services unit sells new and used homes for placement on its properties the majority of which are in Michigan Florida Indiana Texas and Ohio. Sun Communities also acquires at a discount and resells mobile homes that have been repossessed by lenders in its communities.

Operations

Sun Communities operates two lines of business: Real property and homes sales and rentals.

The Real Property business which generates roughly 75% of the company's total revenue owns operates and develops manufactured home (MH) and RV communities and is in the business of acquiring and expanding those communities to grow revenue.

The Home Sales and Rentals segment which operates under the company's Sun Home Services subsidiary sells manufactured homes and provides leasing services to consumers looking to live in their communities.

The company's properties have trained on-site property managers and maintenance personnel as well as such amenities as clubhouses laundry facilities and swimming pools. At the end of 2014 the company owned and operated 217 properties in 29 states including 183 manufactured housing communities 25 RV communities and 9 properties containing both manufactured housing and RV sites. That year Sun Homes Services had 10973 occupied leased homes in its portfolio and boasted an average renewal rate for residents in Sun Communities' rental program of 59%.

Geographic Reach

Sun Communities has nearly 220 properties across 29 states. Around 30% of these properties were in Michigan in 2014 while 17% were in Florida. Texas Indiana and Ohio each held 5% or more of the company's properties. About 20% of properties were in other states in the Northeast and the Southwest.

Sales and Marketing

Sun Communities spent $3.2 million on advertising in 2014 compared to $2.9 million and $2.5 million in 2013 and 2012 respectively.

Financial Performance

Sun Communities has enjoyed years of healthy revenue and profit growth thanks to aggressively property acquisitions and expansions with revenue nearly doubling over the past five years.

The company's revenue grew by 14% to $471.68 million in 2014 mostly thanks to a 14% increase in income from its Real Property segment as the REIT raised its rental rates by 3% during the year and continued to grow its occupied home sites. Rental home revenue also swelled by 20% as more residents took to the company's Rental Program and thanks to higher monthly rental rates. Home sales fell slightly for the company despite higher new home sales mostly as the company sold its pre-owned homes at lower prices during the year.

Higher revenue coupled with a $17.7 million gain on the sale of 10 MH properties in 2014 drove the REIT's net income up by 71% to a record $28.51 million while its operating cash rose by 16% to $133.32 million thanks to higher cash earnings.

Strategy

Sun Communities' main strategy toward growth has been to acquire highly-occupied and high-quality MH and RV communities with attractive amenities that support more potential occupancy and rent growth. Typically these are family or retirement communities with at least 200 home sites located near cities with populations exceeding 100000. In 2015 for example the REIT made two acquisitions totaling more than $1.5 billion (one was its largest acquisition ever) which spread its property portfolio business further into the fast-growing markets of Florida and Arizona.

Sun Communities' solid performance is in part due to increased demand from retiring adults a growing demographic. The company also points to its rental program as key to its success during the recession. Home rentals have become a popular and affordable alternative to customers.

Mergers and Acquisitions

In 2019 Sun Communities acquired the Jensen portfolio which included 31 manufactured housing communities located in eight states and more than 460 additional expansion sites available for development for about $343 million.

In April 2015 the REIT completed its largest acquisition to date with the $1.3 billion-plus purchase of the Green Courte properties which spanned 59 MH communities across 19000 sites in the fast-growing markets of Florida and Arizona.

Additionally in early 2015 Sun Communities purchased seven large manufactured housing communities in the Orlando Florida area for $257 million which spanned 3150 manufactured housing sites (approximately 60% of these were in age-restricted communities) and were 96% occupied. Management believed that the purchase further strengthened its portfolio of high-quality communities particularly in age-restricted communities which it said were essential toward the REIT's sustained growth.

In early 2013 the company acquired ten RV communities (Gwynns Island RV Resort LLC Indian Creek RV Resort LLC Lake Laurie RV Resort LLC Newpoint RV Resort LLC Peters Pond RV Resort Inc. Seaport LLC Virginia Tent LLC Wagon Wheel Maine LLC Westward Ho RV Resort LLC and Wild Acres LLC) with 3700 sites in Connecticut Maine Massachusetts New Jersey Ohio Virginia and Wisconsin for $112.8 million.

In 2012 Sun Communities made seven acquisitions (which included 14 properties in total seven manufactured housing communities five RV communities and two communities containing both manufactured housing and RV communities. The acquisitions included Three Lakes RV Resort Blueberry Hill RV Resort and Grand Lake Estates located in Florida; Blazing Star RV Resort (260 sites located in San Antonio Texas); Northville Crossing Manufactured Home Community (756 sites in Northville Michigan); Rainbow RV Resort (500 sites in Frostproof Florida); four manufactured home communities (the Rudgate Acquisition Properties) in southeast Michigan and Palm Creek Golf & RV Resort (283 manufactured home sites 1580 RV sites and the expansion potential of 550 manufactured housing or 990 RV sites) in Casa Grande Arizona.

EXECUTIVES

Lead Independent Director, Clunet Lewis
Chairman And Chief Executive Officer, Gary Shiffman, $521,027 total compensation
Chief Financial Officer, Executive Vice President, Treasurer, Secretary, Karen Dearing, $323,641 total compensation
President And Chief Operating Officer, John Bandini McLaren, $397,614 total compensation
Independent Director, Meghan Baivier
Independent Director, Ronald Klein
Executive Vice President, Operations And Sales, Bruce Thelen, $376,640 total compensation
Chief Executive Officer, Safe Harbor, Baxter Underwood, $57,500 total compensation
Independent Director, Tonya Allen
Executive Vice President Of Corporate Strategy And Business Development, Aaron Weiss
Auditors: Grant Thornton LLP

LOCATIONS

HQ: Sun Communities Inc
27777 Franklin Rd., Suite 200, Southfield, MI 48034
Phone: 248 208-2500
Web: www.suncommunities.com

PRODUCTS/OPERATIONS

2014 Sales

	$ mil.	% of total
Real property income	357.7	77
Home sales 11		**54.0**
Home rentals	39.2	8
Interest and other	19.8	4
Brokerage commission and other income	1.0	-
Total	**471.7**	**100**

COMPETITORS

AV HOMES INC.
CAMDEN PROPERTY TRUST
EASTGROUP PROPERTIES INC.
EDUCATION REALTY TRUST INC.
GOV NEW OPPTY REIT
LSREF4 LIGHTHOUSE CORPORATE ACQUISITIONS LLC
POST PROPERTIES INC.
TOLL BROTHERS INC.
WCI COMMUNITIES INC.

HISTORICAL FINANCIALS

Company Type: Public

Income Statement

FYE: December 31

	REVENUE ($ mil.)	NET INCOME ($ mil.)	NET PROFIT MARGIN	EMPLOYEES
12/21	2,272.6	392.2	17.3%	5,961
12/20	1,398.3	138.5	9.9%	4,872
12/19	1,264.0	167.6	13.3%	3,146
12/18	1,126.8	111.7	9.9%	2,784
12/17	982.5	76.7	7.8%	2,727
Annual Growth	**23.3%**	**50.3%**	**—**	**21.6%**

2021 Year-End Financials

Debt ratio: 42.0%	No. of shares (mil.): 115.9
Return on equity: 6.1%	Dividends
Cash ($ mil.): 78.2	Yield: 1.5%
Current ratio: 1.12	Payout: 101.8%
Long-term debt ($ mil.): 5,671.8	Market value ($ mil.): 24,351.0

	STOCK PRICE ($) FY Close	P/E High/Low		PER SHARE ($) Earnings	Dividends	Book Value
12/21	209.97	63 41		3.36	3.32	59.61
12/20	151.95	129 76		1.34	3.16	53.79
12/19	150.10	92 54		1.80	3.00	41.83
12/18	101.71	84 65		1.29	2.84	36.71
12/17	92.78	112 90		0.85	2.68	33.15
Annual Growth	**22.7%**	**—**	**—**	**41.0%**	**5.5%**	**15.8%**

Sun Country Airlines Holdings Inc

LOCATIONS

HQ: Sun Country Airlines Holdings Inc
2005 Cargo Road, Minneapolis, MN 55450
Phone: 651 681-3900
Web: www.suncountry.com

HISTORICAL FINANCIALS

Company Type: Public

Income Statement

FYE: December 31

	REVENUE ($ mil.)	NET INCOME ($ mil.)	NET PROFIT MARGIN	EMPLOYEES
12/21	623.0	77.4	12.4%	2,181
12/20	401.4	(3.9)	—	1,699
12/19	701.3	46.0	6.6%	0
12/18*	384.9	(0.3)	—	0
04/18	197.4	25.9	13.1%	0
Annual Growth	**33.3%**	**31.5%**	**—**	**—**

*Fiscal year change

2021 Year-End Financials

Debt ratio: 34.1%
Return on equity: 20.1%
Cash ($ mil.): 309.3
Current ratio: 1.33
Long-term debt ($ mil.): 428.4

No. of shares (mil.): 57.8
Dividends
  Yield: —
  Payout: —
Market value ($ mil.): 1,577.0

	STOCK PRICE ($) FY Close	P/E High/Low	PER SHARE ($) Earnings	Dividends	Book Value
12/21	27.25	31 17	1.31	0.00	8.41
Annual Growth	—	— —	—	··	—

Super Micro Computer Inc

Super Micro Computer manufactures high-performance and high-efficiency server and storage systems based on open standard components (including Intel AMD and NVIDIA processors). In addition to its complete server and storage systems business the company offers a large array of modular server subsystems and accessories such as server boards chassis power supplies and other accessories. The company also sells a host of subsystems and accessories. Super Micro markets its products sold directly and through distributors and resellers to customers in over 110 countries; less than 60% of its sales are generated in the US.

Operations

Super Micro offer a broad range of application-optimized server solutions including storage rackmount and blade server and storage systems and subsystems and accessories. The company's server systems account for about 80% of the total revenue.

The company's server subsystems and accessories products over 20% of revenue range from the entry-level single and dual processor server segment to the high-end multiprocessor market.

Geographic Reach

Super Micro is based in San Jose California and has an office in Jersey City New Jersey. Its European operations are centered in the Netherlands while it maintains a research and development operation in Taiwan with sales and service facilities in China.

The company generates nearly 60% of its sales from the US with Europe and Asia contributing about 20% each.

Sales and Marketing

Super Micro Computer sells to indirect sales channels (about 55% of sales) directly to OEMs and end-users which account for about over 45%% of sales and through distributors resellers and systems integrators. In 2020 the company sold to over 820 direct customers in over 100 countries.

The company's total advertising and promotional expenses were $3.0 million $2.4 million and $3.5 million for the fiscal years 2020 2019 and 2018 respectively.

Financial Performance

Net sales declined by 5% to $3.3 billion in the fiscal year 2020 as compared to the fiscal year 2019 with $3.5 billion.

The company's net income for fiscal 2020 increased to $84.3 million mainly due to lower cost of sales and a higher share of income from equity investee.

Cash held by the company at the end of 2020 decreased by $49.8 million to $212.4 million. Cash provided by financing activities was $23.8 million while cash used for operations and investing activities were $30.3 million and $43.6 million respectively. Main use of cash was purchases of property plant and equipment.

Strategy

Super Micro's objective is to be the world's leading provider of application-optimized high-performance server storage and networking solutions. Achieving this objective requires continuous development and innovation of its solutions with better price-performance and architectural advantages compared with its prior generation of solutions and with solutions offered by its competitors. Through its strategy the company seeks to maintain or improve its relative competitive position in many product areas and pursue markets that provide the company with additional long-term growth opportunities.

Key elements of Super Micro's strategy include executing upon the following: a strong internal research and development and internal manufacturing capability; introducing more innovative products faster; capitalizing on new applications and technologies; driving software and services sales to the company's global enterprise customers; and leveraging its global operating structure.

EXECUTIVES

Independent Director, Shiu Leung Chan
Independent Director, Tally Liu
Independent Director, Saria Tseng
Senior Vice President, Chief Financial Officer, Chief Compliance Officer, David Weigand, $367,709 total compensation
Senior Vice President - Operations, George Kao, $333,858 total compensation
Senior Chief Executive - Strategic Business, Alex Hsu, $305,333 total compensation
Senior Vice President - Worldwide Sales, Don Clegg, $362,140 total compensation
Chairman Of The Board, President And Chief Executive Officer, Charles Liang, $421,785 total compensation
Auditors: DELOITTE & TOUCHE LLP

LOCATIONS

HQ: Super Micro Computer Inc
  980 Rock Avenue, San Jose, CA 95131
Phone: 408 503-8000
Web: www.supermicro.com

PRODUCTS/OPERATIONS

2016 Sales

	$ mil.	% of total
Server systems	1,525.6	69
Subsystems & accessories	690.0	31
Total	**2,215.6**	**100**

Selected Products

Chassis enclosures (pedestal rack-mount tower)
Motherboards (desktop server workstation)
Power supplies
Serverboards
Servers (rack-mount tower)

COMPETITORS

AVIAT NETWORKS INC. TECHNOLOGIES
CRAY INC.
DELL CORPORATION LIMITED
Diebold Nixdorf AG
HP INC.
INTERNATIONAL BUSINESS MACHINES CORPORATION
KEYSIGHT INC.
PERASO INC.
SAP SE
Silicom Ltd.

HISTORICAL FINANCIALS

Company Type: Public

Income Statement   FYE: June 30

	REVENUE ($ mil.)	NET INCOME ($ mil.)	NET PROFIT MARGIN	EMPLOYEES
06/21	3,557.4	111.8	3.1%	4,155
06/20	3,339.2	84.3	2.5%	3,987
06/19	3,500.3	71.9	2.1%	3,670
06/18	3,360.4	46.1	1.4%	3,266
06/17	2,484.9	66.8	2.7%	2,996
Annual Growth	9.4%	13.7%	—	8.5%

2021 Year-End Financials

Debt ratio: 4.3%
Return on equity: 10.3%
Cash ($ mil.): 232.2
Current ratio: 1.93
Long-term debt ($ mil.): 34.7

No. of shares (mil.): 50.5
Dividends
  Yield: —
  Payout: —
Market value ($ mil.): 1,779.0

	STOCK PRICE ($) FY Close	P/E High/Low	PER SHARE ($) Earnings	Dividends	Book Value
06/21	35.18	18 10	2.09	0.00	21.67
06/20	28.39	20 10	1.60	0.00	20.33
06/19	19.35	17 8	1.39	0.00	18.84
06/18	23.65	29 17	0.89	0.00	17.01
06/17	24.65	21 14	1.29	0.00	15.81
Annual Growth	9.3%	— —	12.8%	—	8.2%

Superior Group of Companies Inc

Superior Group of Companies (formerly Superior Uniform Group) makes work clothing and accessories for US employees in several industries. The apparel firm designs makes and markets uniforms for employees in the medical and health fields as well as those who work in hotels fast food joints and other restaurants and public safety industrial and commercial markets. The company also makes and distributes specialty labels such as BAMKO Tangerine and PublicIdentity. Chairman Gerald Benstock and his son CEO Michael run the company which began as Superior Surgical Mfg. Co. in 1920.

Operations

The company operates its business through three reportable segments: Uniforms and Related Products (about 55% of sales) Promotional Products (about 40% of sales) and Remote Staffing Solutions (more than 5%).

Uniforms and Related Products segment its signature marketing brands Fashion Seal Healthcare

HOOVER'S HANDBOOK OF EMERGING COMPANIES 2022

HPI and WonderWink manufactures and sells a wide range of uniforms corporate identity apparel career apparel and accessories for the hospital and healthcare fields; hotels; fast food and other restaurants; transportation; and the private security industrial and commercial markets.

The Promotional Products segment sells wide range of apparel through its brands BAMKO Tangerine and PublicIdentity.

Remote Staffing Solutions segment services the Office Gurus entities including its subsidiaries in El Salvador Belize Jamaica and the US. TOG is a near-shore premium provider of cost effective multilingual telemarketing and business process outsourced solutions.

Geographic Reach

From its headquarters in Florida Superior Uniform serves to outfit companies and customers nationwide boasting manufacturing operations overseas. It operates in El Salvador Belize Jamaica and the US through its The Office Gurus businesses. It has domestic facilities in Georgia Arkansas Mississippi Arkansas Louisiana and California international facilities are located in El Salvador Haiti Jamaica and BeliZe.

Sales and Marketing

The Uniform and Related Products segment has a substantial number of customers but none of its customers accounted for more than 10% of net sales. The Remote Staffing Solutions segment's largest customer represented about 15% of net sales. No customer accounted for more than 10% of the Promotional Products segment's net sales.

Financial Performance

Net sales for the company increased 40% from $376.7 million in 2019 to $526.7 million in 2020. The principal components of this aggregate increase in net sales were an increase in the net sales of its Uniforms and Related Products segment an increase in the net sales for its Promotional Products segment and an increase in net sales for our Remote Staffing Solutions segment after intersegment eliminations.

In 2020 the company had a net income of $41 million a 240% increase from the previous year.

The company's cash and cash equivalents for the year ended 2020 was $5.2 million. Operating activities generated $41.4 million while investing activities used $6.6 million mainly for additions to property plant and equipment. Financing activities used another $38.4 million mainly for repayment of debt.

Strategy

From a long-term perspective Superior Uniform expects to continue its ongoing capital expenditure program designed to improve the effectiveness and capabilities of its facilities and technology. In the near term the company may continue to delay certain capital expenditures relating to non-essential projects until economic conditions begin to stabilize.

Company Background

Superior Group of Companies was founded in 1920 began as Superior Surgical Manufacturing Co. Inc. In 1968 the company went public and issued it initial public offering in AMEX.

EXECUTIVES

Chief Financial Officer, Chief Operating Officer, Treasurer, Director, Andrew Demott, $379,592 total compensation

Chief Executive Officer, Director, Michael Benstock, $483,735 total compensation

Independent Chairman Of The Board, Sidney Kirschner

Senior Vice President, General Counsel, Secretary, Jordan Alpert, $191,218 total compensation

President Of The Office Gurus, Dominic Leide, $224,694 total compensation

Chief Strategy Officer, Philip Koosed, $128,077 total compensation

Independent Director, Venita Fields

Independent Director, Todd Siegel

Auditors: Mayer Hoffman McCann P.C.

LOCATIONS

HQ: Superior Group of Companies Inc
10055 Seminole Boulevard, Seminole, FL 33772-2539
Phone: 727 397-9611
Web: www.superiorgroupofcompanies.com

PRODUCTS/OPERATIONS

2016 sales

	$ mil.	% of total
Uniforms and related products	210.4	82
Promotional Products	27.8	11
Remote staffing solutions	17.9	7
Inter-segment elimination	(3.5)	-
Total	**252.6**	**100**

Selected Brands

Blade
Fashion Seal
Fashion Seal Healthcare
Martin's
Worklon
UniVogue

COMPETITORS

ARKTIS LIMITED	UNIFIRST CORPORATION
AXCELIS TECHNOLOGIES INC.	VALHI INC.
CROWN CRAFTS INC.	VERITIV CORPORATION
EMILIO PUCCI SRL	WYEDEAN WEAVING COMPANY LIMITED(THE)
HILLENBRAND INC.	
MSC INDUSTRIAL DIRECT CO. INC.	

HISTORICAL FINANCIALS

Company Type: Public

Income Statement — FYE: December 31

	REVENUE ($ mil.)	NET INCOME ($ mil.)	NET PROFIT MARGIN	EMPLOYEES
12/20	526.7	41.0	7.8%	4,600
12/19	376.7	12.0	3.2%	3,400
12/18	346.3	16.9	4.9%	2,906
12/17	266.8	15.0	5.6%	2,280
12/16	252.6	14.6	5.8%	1,632
Annual Growth	**20.2%**	**29.4%**	—	**29.6%**

2020 Year-End Financials

Debt ratio: 22.2%	No. of shares (mil.): 15.3
Return on equity: 23.4%	Dividends
Cash ($ mil.): 5.1	Yield: 1.7%
Current ratio: 2.37	Payout: 19.5%
Long-term debt ($ mil.): 72.3	Market value ($ mil.): 358.0

	STOCK PRICE ($) FY Close	P/E High/Low		PER SHARE ($) Earnings	Dividends	Book Value
12/20	23.24	10	2	2.65	0.40	12.45
12/19	13.54	23	16	0.79	0.40	10.35
12/18	17.65	25	14	1.10	0.39	9.93
12/17	26.71	27	16	0.99	0.37	8.29
12/16	19.62	20	14	0.98	0.34	7.62
Annual Growth	**4.3%**	—		**28.2%**	**4.1%**	**13.1%**

Supernus Pharmaceuticals Inc

Supernus Pharmaceuticals wouldn't mind being a drug-maker superhero of sorts to epileptics. As a specialty pharmaceutical company Supernus develops treatments for epilepsy and other central nervous system disorders. It has two marketed products for treating epilepsy: Oxtellar XR and Trokendi XR. In addition it is developing a number of candidates to treat such ailments as attention deficit hyperactivity disorder (ADHD) impulsive aggression in patients with ADHD bipolar disorder and depression. The company utilizes third-party commercial manufacturing organizations (CMOs) for all of its manufacturing. Its products are sold through pharmacies hospitals as well as federal and state entities.

Operations

The company's two products are Trokendi XR (accounts for about 75% of total revenue) and Oxtellar XR (nearly 25%). These two products are the first once-daily extended release oxcarbazepine and topiramate products indicated for the treatment of epilepsy in the US market. Trokendi XR is for the prophylaxis of migraine headaches in adults and adolescents while Oxtellar XR for monotherapy treatment of partial onset epilepsy seizures in adults and children 6 to 17 years of age.

Other product candidates include SPN-812 (viloxazine hydrochloride) as a novel non-stimulant product candidate to treat children 6 to 17 years of age who have ADHD; SPN-604 (extended release oxcarbazepine) for the treatment of bipolar disorder; and its developing SPN-817 for the treatment of severe pediatric epilepsy disorders through its acquisition with Biscayne Neurotherapeutics.

Its key proprietary technology platforms include Microtrol Solutrol and EnSoTrol. These technologies create novel customized product profiles designed to enhance efficacy reduce the frequency of dosing so as to improve patient compliance and improve tolerability. It has employed the technologies in the development of a total of ten products that are currently on the market including its products Trokendi XR and Oxtellar XR along with eight products being marketed by the company's partners.

Geographic Reach

Supernus Pharmaceuticals has its corporate office and laboratory space in Maryland. It markets its product throughout the US.

Sales and Marketing

Supernus markets its products through over 200 sales representatives and distributes them through wholesalers and pharmaceutical distributors. Supernus primarily targets neurologists to grow sales of its epilepsy and migraine franchise. Its three customers AmerisourceBergen Cardinal Health and McKesson accounted for more than 30% of total product revenue.

The company spent approximately $40.8 million $43.3 million and $33.8 million in advertising costs for FY 2019 2018 and 2017 respectively.

Financial Performance

Supernus has recorded increasing revenue from 2015 to 2018 until it dipped in 2019. Overall revenue increased by 166% for the last five years. Meanwhile net income has been fluctuating for the last five years but recorded a 711% increase from 2015 to 2019.

Revenue was $392.8 million a 4% decrease from the previous year. This resulted from a decrease in net product sales and zero licensing revenue offset by an increase in royalty revenue.

Net income increased 2% to $113.1 million compared to $111 million in 2018.

Cash and cash equivalents at the end of the year were $181.4 million $10.9 million less than the previous year. Cash provided by operating activities was $143.1 million. Investing activities used $157.9 million mostly for sales and maturities of marketable securities while financing activities provided $3.9 million from proceeds from issuance of common stock.

Strategy

Supernus aims to drive the prescription growth of Trokendi XR and Oxtellar XR by continuing to dedicate sales and marketing resources in the US.

The company is also actively exploring a broad range of strategic opportunities that fit well with its strong presence in CNS while also exploring other disease areas that are driven by specialty physicians including orphan or rare diseases. These strategic options include in-licensing products and/or entering into development collaborations leading to commercialization rights; opportunities that leverage and/or expand its sales force call points for its marketed products and product candidates; co-development partnerships outside the US for the company's pipeline products; and growth opportunities through value-creating and transformative merger and acquisition transactions including both commercial stage and development stage products.

Through the company's internal research and development efforts it plans to continue to evaluate and develop additional CNS product candidates that are believed have significant commercial potential.

Mergers and Acquisitions

In 2020 Supernus Pharmaceuticals acquired the CNS portfolio of US WorldMeds a privately-held biopharmaceutical company. This transaction builds on Supernus' experience in CNS diseases and expands its marketing and development efforts into Parkinson's disease. "This acquisition significantly expands our business in CNS and increases and diversifies our revenue and earnings streams while continuing to maintain a strong balance sheet" said Jack Khattar President and CEO of Supernus.

EXECUTIVES

Independent Chairman Of The Board, Charles Newhall
Senior Vice President - Regulatory Affairs, Tami Martin, $326,401 total compensation
Senior Vice President, Quality, Gmp Operations And Information Technology, Frank Mottola
Senior Vice President, Chief Medical Officer, Jonathan Rubin
Independent Director, Frederick Hudson
Independent Director, Carrolee Barlow
Chief Financial Officer, Senior Vice President, Timothy Dec
President, Chief Executive Officer, Secretary, Director, Jack Khattar, $836,400 total compensation
Senior Vice President - Intellectual Property, Chief Scientific Officer, Padmanabh Bhatt, $391,401 total compensation
Auditors: KPMG LLP

LOCATIONS

HQ: Supernus Pharmaceuticals Inc
9715 Key West Avenue, Rockville, MD 20850
Phone: 301 838-2500
Web: www.supernus.com

PRODUCTS/OPERATIONS

2015 Sales

	$ mil.	% of total
Net product sales	143.5	99
Revenue from royalty agreement - -		
Licensing revenue	0.9	1
Total	**144.4**	**100**

Selected Products

Oxtellar XR (marketed)
SPN-809(under trail)
SPN-810 (under trail)
SPN-812(under trail)
Trokendi XR (marketed)

COMPETITORS

ACORDA THERAPEUTICS INC.
ADAMAS PHARMACEUTICALS INC.
DURECT CORPORATION
EXELIXIS INC.
IONIS PHARMACEUTICALS INC.
PTC THERAPEUTICS INC.
SUCAMPO
ULTRAGENYX PHARMACEUTICAL INC.
UNITED THERAPEUTICS CORPORATION

HISTORICAL FINANCIALS

Company Type: Public

Income Statement — FYE: December 31

	REVENUE ($ mil.)	NET INCOME ($ mil.)	NET PROFIT MARGIN	EMPLOYEES
12/20	520.4	126.9	24.4%	563
12/19	392.7	113.0	28.8%	464
12/18	408.9	110.9	27.1%	448
12/17	302.2	57.2	19.0%	422
12/16	215.0	91.2	42.4%	363
Annual Growth	24.7%	8.6%	—	11.6%

2020 Year-End Financials

Debt ratio: 24.0%
Return on equity: 18.8%
Cash ($ mil.): 288.6
Current ratio: 2.57
Long-term debt ($ mil.): 361.7
No. of shares (mil.): 52.8
Dividends
  Yield: —
  Payout: —
Market value ($ mil.): 1,330.0

	STOCK PRICE ($) FY Close	P/E High/Low		Earnings	PER SHARE ($) Dividends	Book Value
12/20	25.16	11	6	2.36	0.00	14.09
12/19	23.72	19	9	2.10	0.00	11.33
12/18	33.22	28	14	2.05	0.00	8.66
12/17	39.85	44	21	1.08	0.00	5.21
12/16	25.25	15	6	1.76	0.00	3.84
Annual Growth	(0.1%)	—	—	7.6%	—	38.4%

Surface Oncology Inc

Auditors: PricewaterhouseCoopers LLP

LOCATIONS

HQ: Surface Oncology Inc
50 Hampshire Street, 8th Floor, Cambridge, MA 02139
Phone: 617 714-4096
Web: www.surfaceoncology.com

HISTORICAL FINANCIALS

Company Type: Public

Income Statement — FYE: December 31

	REVENUE ($ mil.)	NET INCOME ($ mil.)	NET PROFIT MARGIN	EMPLOYEES
12/20	126.1	59.3	47.0%	51
12/19	15.3	(54.7)	—	49
12/18	59.4	(6.6)	—	76
12/17	12.8	(45.3)	—	56
12/16	6.6	(17.4)	—	0
Annual Growth	108.8%			

2020 Year-End Financials

Debt ratio: 6.8%
Return on equity: 55.7%
Cash ($ mil.): 175.1
Current ratio: 10.23
Long-term debt ($ mil.): 14.7
No. of shares (mil.): 40.7
Dividends
  Yield: —
  Payout: —
Market value ($ mil.): 376.0

	STOCK PRICE ($) FY Close	P/E High/Low		Earnings	PER SHARE ($) Dividends	Book Value
12/20	9.24	6	1	1.57	0.00	3.83
12/19	1.88	—	—	(1.97)	0.00	2.03
12/18	4.24	—	—	(0.33)	0.00	3.70
Annual Growth	47.6%	—	—	—	—	1.6%

Switch Inc

Auditors: PricewaterhouseCoopers LLP

LOCATIONS

HQ: Switch Inc
7135 S. Decatur Boulevard, Las Vegas, NV 89118
Phone: 702 444-4111
Web: www.switch.com

HISTORICAL FINANCIALS

Company Type: Public

Income Statement
FYE: December 31

	REVENUE ($ mil.)	NET INCOME ($ mil.)	NET PROFIT MARGIN	EMPLOYEES
12/20	511.5	15.5	3.0%	759
12/19	462.3	8.9	1.9%	789
12/18	405.8	4.0	1.0%	731
12/17	378.2	(15.2)	—	723
12/16	318.3	31.3	9.9%	689
Annual Growth	12.6%	(16.1%)	—	2.4%

2020 Year-End Financials

Debt ratio: 49.6%
Return on equity: 6.5%
Cash ($ mil.): 90.7
Current ratio: 1.19
Long-term debt ($ mil.): 1,048.7

No. of shares (mil.): 240.6
Dividends
  Yield: 0.9%
  Payout: 113.4%
Market value ($ mil.): 3,939.0

	STOCK PRICE ($) FY Close	P/E High/Low		PER SHARE ($) Earnings	Dividends	Book Value
12/20	16.37	127	75	0.14	0.16	1.11
12/19	14.82	140	57	0.11	0.12	0.86
12/18	7.00	200	71	0.09	0.07	0.58
12/17	18.19	—	—	(1.88)	0.01	0.43
Annual Growth	(3.5%)	—	—	—	124.7%	36.9%

Synovus Financial Corp

Synovus Financial Corp. is a financial services company and a registered bank holding company headquartered in Columbus Georgia. The company provides commercial and retail banking as well as private banking treasury management wealth management mortgage services premium finance and international banking through Synovus Bank. The bank operates nearly 290 branches and 390 ATMS throughout Alabama Florida Georgia South Carolina and Tennessee. The company also provides other financial services through direct and indirect wholly-owned non-bank subsidiaries such as Synovus Securities and Synovus Trust.

Operations

Synovus has three major reportable business segments: Community Banking Wholesale Banking and Financial Management Services (FMS) with functional activities such as treasury technology operations marketing finance enterprise risk legal human resources corporate communications executive management among others included in Treasury and Corporate Other.

The Community Banking business segment (accounts for more than 55% of total revenue) serves customers using a relationship-based approach through its branch ATM commercial and private wealth network in addition to mobile Internet and telephone banking.

The Wholesale Banking business segment (some 35% of total sales) provides commercial lending and deposit services through specialty teams including middle market CRE senior housing national accounts premium finance structured lending healthcare asset-based lending and community investment capital.

The Financial Management Services (FMS) business segment (some 5% of total sales) serves its customers by providing mortgage and trust services and also specializing in professional portfolio management for fixed-income securities investment banking the execution of securities transactions as a broker/dealer asset management financial planning and family office services as well as the provision of individual investment advice on equity and other securities.

The company's non-bank subsidiaries such as Synovus Securities and Synovus Trust offer other financial services including professional portfolio management for fixed-income securities investment banking the execution of securities transactions as a broker/dealer asset management and financial planning services among others.

Geographic Reach

Georgia-based Synovus Financial has about 290 branches and 390 ATMS in Alabama Florida Georgia South Carolina and Tennessee.

Sales and Marketing

Synovus serves individual small business and corporate customers with an array of comprehensive banking products and services including commercial home equity and other consumer loans credit and debit cards and deposit accounts through its Community Banking segment. The company's Wholesale Banking segment serves larger corporate customers.

Financial Performance

Synovus' revenue fluctuated over the past three years with about 32% revenue growth from 2018 to 2020.

The company reported a total revenue of $1.5 billion in 2020 a 5% decline from the prior year. The decrease in revenue was due to declines of $87.3 million in PAA associated with the FCB acquisition and declines in market interest rates which were somewhat offset by higher average earning assets including the impact of PPP with recognition of $46.0 million in processing fees.

Net income available to common shareholders for 2020 was $340.5 million a decrease of 37% compared to $540.9 million for 2019.

Synovus ended the year with cash and cash equivalents of $4.3 billion. Operating activities provided $17 million while investing activities used $2.4 billion primarily for purchases of investment securities available for sale. Financing activities provided $5.4 billion.

Strategy

Synovus' strategic focus includes expanding and diversifying its franchise in terms of revenues profitability and asset size while maintaining a community banking relationship-based approach to banking. This strategy has encompassed both organic growth as well as acquisitions of complementary banks and financial services businesses.

In the first quarter of 2020 the company announced its transformational Synovus Forward initiative involving cost savings and revenue-generating initiatives that they expect to achieve by the end of 2021 and 2022. These initiatives include cost reductions around Synovus' third party spend program branch optimization back-office staff optimization and early retirement and revenue-based initiatives around market-based repricing of certain product offerings deposit repricing commercial analytics and digital enhancements.

The company's financial performance and strategy rely heavily on their value proposition of relationship-banking delivered through experts committed to delivering an exceptional customer experience and to provide value-added advice and financial solutions. In 2020 its human capital strategy focused on responding to the COVID-19 pandemic and the unique circumstances of its employees.

In January 2020 Synovus announced efficiency initiatives as part of its Synovus Forward plan and recorded restructuring charges of $27.0 million consisting largely of severance charges of $15.6 million.

Company Background

Synovus history can be traced back in 1888 when G. Gunby Jordan established two banks namely Third National Bank and The Columbus Savings Bank. In 1930 the two banks merged and became Columbus Bank and Trust. In 1972 CB&T Bancshares Inc. was created and became the holding company for Columbus Bank and Trust. Two years later the holding company started offering third-party credit card transaction processing to banks in Georgia and other states through The Total System its bankcard processing software. CB&T expanded into other states through acquisitions in Florida and Alabama in the late 80s. In 1989 CB&T Bancshares Inc. became Synovus Financial Corp. and started trading under the symbol SNV on the New York Stock Exchange.

HISTORY

In 1885 W. C. Bradley founded his eponymous company (today a manufacturing and development concern). Three years later he invested in a new bank that would eventually bear the name of its Georgia hometown: Columbus Bank and Trust. (Bradley's investment in Atlanta-based Coca-Cola today accounts for the lion's share of his family's wealth.) When Bradley died his son-in-law Abbott Turner joined the bank's board of directors followed by Turner's son William.

In 1958 the bank hired James Blanchard as president. The next year Columbus Bank and Trust became one of the first banks to issue credit cards. The company's credit processing business grew leading it to computerize the process in 1966 and train its own employees to operate the equipment. (It decided to go it alone after a failed joint-venture attempt with corporate cousin W.C. Bradley Co.)

In a little more than a decade Blanchard led the bank to triple its assets. When he died in 1969 the search for a new leader took the bank's directors in a surprising direction: They offered the position to Blanchard's son Jimmy a young attorney with no banking experience. The board pressed him to take the job which he did in 1971 after a brief apprenticeship.

From the start the younger Blanchard emphasized the company's financial services operations such as credit card processing. Taking advantage of new laws opening up the banking and financial services industry in the early 1970s the bank reorganized in 1972 incorporating CB&T Bancshares to serve as a holding company for Columbus Bank and Trust. In 1973 CB&T's financial services division finished a new software product called the Total System which allowed electronic access to account information. CB&T used the groundbreaking software to start processing other banks' paperwork including an ever-growing number of credit card accounts. In 1983 CB&T spun off financial services division Total System Services

(TSYS) but retained a majority stake in the company.

Blanchard helped win passage of Georgia's multibank holding law and further deregulation in the early 1980s allowed the company to operate across state lines. It bought four banks in Florida and Georgia in 1983 and 1984 and snapped up six more (including an Alabama bank) in 1985. Meanwhile TSYS benefited from the trend to outsource credit card processing.

In 1989 CB&T changed its name to Synovus a combination of the words "synergy" and "novus" the latter word meaning (according to the company) "of superior quality and different from the others listed in the same category."

During the early 1990s Synovus swept up 20 banks in its market area after the bank bust. After 1993 acquisitions dropped off until 1998 when Synovus announced three acquisitions in two weeks. That year it also said it was planning to move further into Internet and investment banking as well as auto and life insurance. In 1999 the company bought banks in Georgia and Florida; it also moved into debt collection with its purchase of Wallace & de Mayo which was renamed Total System Services (TSYS). In 2007 Synovus spun off TSYS.

The company grew its retail investment operations with the acquisitions of Atlanta-area asset managers Creative Financial Group in 2001 and GLOBALT in 2002. Jimmy Blanchard who had ultimately become Synovus Financial's chairman retired as an executive in 2005 but remained on the board. The long-time executive stepped down from the board in 2012.

Fred Green abruptly stepped down as president of Synovus in 2009. CEO Richard Anthony assumed his responsibilities until early 2010 when Kessel Stelling was named president and COO of the company. Stelling was named CEO later that year after Anthony who remained chairman took a medical leave of absence. Anthony retired from the board in 2012. Stelling then took on the additional roll of chairman.

In May 2013 the bank acquired three branches of a failed Valdosta-based bank.

EXECUTIVES

Executive Vice President, Chief Risk Officer, Mark Holladay, $409,902 total compensation
Independent Director, Elizabeth Camp
Executive Chairman Of The Board, Kessel Stelling, $1,125,000 total compensation
Independent Director, Barry Storey
Independent Director, Tim Bentsen
Executive Vice President And Chief Credit Officer, Robert Derrick, $368,015 total compensation
Independent Director, Joseph Prochaska
Independent Director, Diana Murphy
Chief Accounting Officer, Controller, Jill Hurley
Independent Director, Teresa White
Independent Director, Pedro Cherry
Executive Vice President, Chief Audit Executive, Meredith Forrester
Independent Director, Harris Pastides
President, Chief Executive Officer, Chief Operating Officer, Director, Kevin Blair, $695,250 total compensation
Independent Director, F. Dixon Brooke
Chief Financial Officer, Executive Vice President, Andre Gregory, $475,000 total compensation

Executive Vice President And Chief Human Resources Officer, Sharon Goodwine
Auditors: KPMG LLP

LOCATIONS

HQ: Synovus Financial Corp
1111 Bay Avenue, Suite 500, Columbus, GA 31901
Phone: 706 641-6500
Web: www.synovus.com

PRODUCTS/OPERATIONS

2016 Sales

	$ mil.	% of total
Interest income:		
Loans including fees	944.2	73
Investment securities available for sale	67.5	5
Trading account assets	0.1	-
Mortgage loans held for sale	2.6	-
Federal Reserve Bank balances	4.4	-
Other earning assets	4.0	-
Non-interest income:		
Service charges on deposit accounts	81.4	6
Fiduciary and asset management fees	46.6	4
Bankcard fees	33.3	3
Other non-interest income	34.3	3
Brokerage revenue	27.0	2
Mortgage banking income	24.3	2
Other fee income	20.2	2
Investment securities gains net	6.0	-
Total	**1,296.0**	**100**

COMPETITORS

CATTLES LIMITED	STATE STREET
CITIZENS FINANCIAL	CORPORATION
GROUP INC.	SUNTRUST BANKS INC.
FB CORPORATION	THE BANK OF NEW YORK
HUNTINGTON BANCSHARES	MELLON
CORPORATION	
INCORPORATED	THE JONES FINANCIAL
INVESTAR HOLDING	COMPANIES L L L P
CORPORATION	TRUIST FINANCIAL
KEYCORP	CORPORATION
NORTHERN TRUST	U.S. BANCORP
CORPORATION	UniCredit Bank AG
PRIVATEBANCORP INC.	

HISTORICAL FINANCIALS

Company Type: Public

Income Statement — FYE: December 31

	ASSETS ($ mil.)	NET INCOME ($ mil.)	INCOME AS % OF ASSETS	EMPLOYEES
12/20	54,394.1	373.7	0.7%	5,247
12/19	48,203.2	563.7	1.2%	5,389
12/18	32,669.1	428.4	1.3%	4,651
12/17	31,221.8	275.4	0.9%	4,541
12/16	30,104.0	246.7	0.8%	4,436
Annual Growth	**15.9%**	**10.9%**	**—**	**4.3%**

2020 Year-End Financials

Return on assets: 0.7%	Dividends
Return on equity: 7.3%	Yield: 4.0%
Long-term debt ($ mil.): —	Payout: 57.3%
No. of shares (mil.): 148.0	Market value ($ mil.): 4,792.0
Sales ($ mil): 2,311.0	

	STOCK PRICE ($) FY Close	P/E High/Low		PER SHARE ($) Earnings	Dividends	Book Value
12/20	32.37	17	6	2.30	1.32	34.86
12/19	39.20	11	9	3.47	1.20	33.58
12/18	31.99	16	9	3.47	1.00	27.05
12/17	47.94	23	18	2.17	0.60	24.91
12/16	41.08	22	14	1.89	0.48	23.95
Annual Growth	**(5.8%)**	**—**	**—**	**5.0%**	**28.8%**	**9.8%**

Take-Two Interactive Software, Inc.

Crime might not pay in the real world but in the gaming universe it means big money for Take-Two. The company's popular mature-rated Grand Theft Auto series and other games are developed by subsidiary Rockstar Games. Its 2K Games subsidiary publishes franchises such as BioShock Borderlands and Sid Meier's Civilization; the 2K Sports unit carries titles such as Major League Baseball 2K and NBA 2K. Take-Two's games are played on Microsoft Sony and Nintendo game consoles but also on PCs and handheld devices. Its products are sold through outlets including retail chains such as GameStop and Steam and as digital downloads. Nearly 60% of its sales comes from the US.

Operations

Take-Two's Rockstar Games subsidiary is aptly named having racked up sales game-of-the-year awards and controversy to back up the moniker. Focused on hardcore action games its other titles alongside golden child GTA include open-world racing game Midnight Club the Wild West-themed Red Dead series 1940s-era action-detective game L.A. Noire and gritty action shooter Max Payne.

Although sister company 2K Games doesn't have as unruly a reputation it still maintains the action focus of the group. The NBA 2K series is one of the company's top sellers. While intense titles geared toward adults and seasoned gamers have been Take-Two's bread and butter it hedges its bets by also pursuing projects that appeal to children and casual gamers. As part of that push Take-Two established the 2K Play label for its casual gaming and family-oriented efforts offering titles such as BioShock Mafia and Sid Meier's Civilization.

About 75% of the company's revenue comes from console games. Games for PCs and other devices account for the remaining revenue.

Geographic Reach

Take-Two is based in New York City and gets more than 55% of its sales from customers in the US with international customers supplying the rest. The company's subsidiaries Rockstar North in located in Edinburgh while 2K's corporate office is in Novato California.

The company operates development studios and sales operations around the world.

Sales and Marketing

The company sells software titles both physically and digitally through direct relationships with large retail customers including digital storefronts and platform partners and third-party distributors. The company's top customers include Sony Microsoft Steam GameStop and Epic globally. Sales to its five largest customers accounted for more than 70% with Sony and Microsoft each accounting for more than 10%.

The company's products delivered through digital online services (digital download online platforms and cloud streaming) accounts for nearly 80% of sales and physical retail and other account for more than 20%.

Advertising marketing and other promotional expenses for the fiscal years ended March 31 2020

2019 and 2018 amounted to $285607 $249315 and $140618 respectively.

Financial Performance
Take-Two's revenue has been rising in the last five years with an overall growth of $1.7 billion or 119% between 2016 and 2020.

For the fiscal year ended March 31 2020 Take-Two's net revenue increased by $420.6 million to $3.1 billion as compared to the prior year. The increase was due primarily to $371.8 million in net revenue from Borderlands 3 which released in September 2019.

For the year ended 2020 the company had a net income of $404.5 million a 21% increase compared to the previous year. The growth is primarily due to a higher sales volume for the year.

The company's cash for the year ended 2020 amounted to $2 billion. Operating activities generated $685.7 million while financing activities used $77.5 million mainly for tax payment related to net share settlements. Investing activities generated another $4 million.

Strategy
Take-Two's core strategy is to capitalize on the popularity of video games by developing and publishing high-quality interactive entertainment experiences across a range of genres. The company focuses on building compelling entertainment franchises by publishing a select number of titles for which we can create sequels and incremental revenue opportunities through virtual currency add-on content and in-game purchases. The company has established a portfolio of proprietary software content for the major hardware platforms in a wide range of genres including action adventure family/casual racing role-playing shooter sports and strategy which it distributes worldwide.

Mergers and Acquisitions
In November 2020 Take-Two Interactive Software agreed to acquire Codemasters the UK-based game publisher and developer for approximately 759 million ($994 million). The acquisition is anticipated to be completed in the first quarter of calendar 2021. Take-Two believes that the combination of Take-Two and Codemasters would bring together two world-class interactive entertainment portfolios.

Company Background
Take-Two exited the third-party distribution business in 2010.

EXECUTIVES

President, Karl Slatoff, $1 total compensation
Executive Vice President, General Counsel, Chief Legal Officer, Daniel Emerson, $625,000 total compensation
Independent Director, Roland Hernandez
Executive Chairman Of The Board, Chief Executive Officer, Strauss Zelnick, $1 total compensation
Lead Independent Director, Michael Dornemann
Independent Director, Jon Moses
Chief Financial Officer, Lainie Goldstein, $850,000 total compensation
Independent Director, LaVerne Srinivasan
Auditors: Ernst & Young LLP

LOCATIONS

HQ: Take-Two Interactive Software, Inc.
110 West 44th Street, New York, NY 10036
Phone: 646 536-2842
Web: www.take2games.com

PRODUCTS/OPERATIONS

2019 Sales

	% of total
Consoles	84
PCs and other	16
Total	**100**

2019 Sales

	$ mil.	% of total
Product	1,349.4	51
Physical retail and other	1,319.0	49
Total	**2,668.4**	**100**

2017 Sales

	$ mil.	% of total
Full game and other	1,597.5	60
Recurrent consumer spending	1,070.9	40
Total	**2,668.4**	**100**

Selected Titles
Rockstar Games
  Beaterator
  Bully
  Grand Theft Auto
  L.A. Noire
  Manhunt
  Max Payne
  Midnight Club
  Red Dead Redemption
2K Games
  The Bigs
  Bioshock
  Borderlands
  The Darkness
  Duke Nukem Forever
  Mafia
  Sid Meier's Civilization
  Sid Meier's Pirates!
2K Play
  Carnival Games
  Deal or No Deal
  Dora the Explorer
  Family Feud
  Go Diego Go!
2K Sports
  Major League Baseball 2K
  NBA 2K
  NHL 2K
  Top Spin

Selected Customers
GameStop
Wal-Mart
Best Buy
Microsoft
Sony
Steam

COMPETITORS

3517667 Canada Inc
ACTIVISION BLIZZARD INC.
ALPHABET INC.
ELECTRONIC ARTS INC.
FORESCOUT TECHNOLOGIES ENTERTAINMENT INC.
GLU MOBILE INC.
PLAYTECH PLC
SECUREWORKS CORP.
SOFTCAT PLC
TRUECAR INC.
UBISOFT

HISTORICAL FINANCIALS
Company Type: Public

Income Statement
FYE: March 31

	REVENUE ($ mil.)	NET INCOME ($ mil.)	NET PROFIT MARGIN	EMPLOYEES
03/21	3,372.7	588.8	17.5%	6,495
03/20	3,088.9	404.4	13.1%	5,800
03/19	2,668.3	333.8	12.5%	4,896
03/18	1,792.8	173.5	9.7%	4,492
03/17	1,779.7	67.3	3.8%	3,707
Annual Growth	**17.3%**	**72.0%**	**—**	**15.1%**

2021 Year-End Financials

Debt ratio: —
Return on equity: 20.0%
Cash ($ mil.): 1,422.8
Current ratio: 1.89
Long-term debt ($ mil.): —
No. of shares (mil.): 115.1
Dividends
  Yield: —
  Payout: —
Market value ($ mil.): 20,349.0

	STOCK PRICE ($) FY Close	P/E High/Low		PER SHARE ($) Earnings	Dividends	Book Value
03/21	176.70	42	23	5.09	0.00	28.93
03/20	118.61	37	25	3.54	0.00	22.37
03/19	94.37	47	29	2.90	0.00	18.19
03/18	97.78	81	37	1.54	0.00	13.06
03/17	59.27	82	46	0.72	0.00	9.78
Annual Growth	**31.4%**			**—**	**63.1%**	**31.1%**

Teb Bancorp Inc

Auditors: Baker Tilly US, LLP

LOCATIONS

HQ: Teb Bancorp Inc
2290 North Mayfair Road, Wauwatosa, WI 53226
Phone: 414 476-6434
Web: www.tebbancorp.com

HISTORICAL FINANCIALS
Company Type: Public

Income Statement
FYE: June 30

	REVENUE ($ mil.)	NET INCOME ($ mil.)	NET PROFIT MARGIN	EMPLOYEES
06/21	23.7	6.3	26.9%	115
06/20	18.1	1.0	6.0%	116
06/19	15.1	(0.4)	—	116
06/18	10.7	(0.6)	—	0
Annual Growth	**30.3%**	**—**		**—**

2021 Year-End Financials

Debt ratio: 1.5%
Return on equity: 22.5%
Cash ($ mil.): 49.7
Current ratio: 0.31
Long-term debt ($ mil.): 5.0
No. of shares (mil.): 2.6
Dividends
  Yield: —
  Payout: —
Market value ($ mil.): 24.0

	STOCK PRICE ($) FY Close	P/E High/Low		PER SHARE ($) Earnings	Dividends	Book Value
06/21	9.31	4	2	2.43	0.00	12.62
06/20	6.61	23	14	0.42	0.00	8.96
06/19	8.95	—	—	(0.15)	0.00	9.30
06/18	0.00	—	—	(0.00)	0.00	(0.00)
Annual Growth						

TechTarget Inc

TechTarget can help you hit the IT professional's bull's-eye. The company operates a network of over 140 websites that focus on information technology topics such as storage security and networking. TechTarget offers original vendor-generated and user-generated content to approximately 20 million registered members many of whom are technology buyers. Websites include Whatis.com Computerweekly.de SearchCIO.com and LemagIT.fr. TechTarget additionally produces digital media offerings (e-mail newsletters online white papers webcasts and podcasts) aimed at IT professionals. The company generates most of its revenue through lead-generation advertising campaigns. Roughly two-thirds of revenue comes from North America.

Operations

Techtarget offers different products and services to B2B technology companies.

IT Deal Alert. IT Deal Alert is a suite of products and services for B2B technology companies that leverages the detailed purchase intent data that Techtarget collected to end-user enterprise technology organizations.

Demand Solutions. Enable its customers to reach and influence prospective buyers through content marketing programs designed to generate demand for their solutions and through display advertising and other brand programs that influence consideration by prospective buyers.

Brand Solutions. Its suite of brand solutions provides B2B Technology Companies exposure to targeted audiences of enterprise technology and business professionals actively researching information related to their products and services.

Geographic Reach

Headquartered in Massachusetts TechTarget operates through offices in the U.S. U.K. France Germany Australia and Singapore. Two-thirds of the company's revenue comes from North America.

Sales and Marketing

The company maintains an internal direct sales department that works closely with existing and potential customers to develop customized marketing programs. TechTarget's sales and marketing staff consists of approximately 330 people. The majority of the company's sales staff is located at its Newton Massachusetts headquarters and its office in San Francisco.

Financial Performance

Revenues in 2019 increased 10% to $134.0 million over the year 2018. The increase in revenues was due to its successful efforts in obtaining new Priority Engine customers and existing customers increasing its spending on data - driven marketing products.

The company's net income in 2019 increased by 12% to $16.9 million compared to $13.0 million in the prior year. The change was primarily due to higher revenue and provision for income taxes while having almost the same operating expense in the prior year.

Cash held by the company at the end of 2019 increased by $17.8 million to $52.5 million compared to $34.7 million in the prior year. Cash provided by operations was $39.4 million and cash used for investing activities was $10.8 million mainly for purchases of investments. Cash used for financing activities was $10.7 million.

Strategy

The company's goal is to deliver superior performance by continuously enhancing its position as a global leader in purchase intent-driven marketing and sales services that deliver business impact for B2B technology companies by strengthening Techtarget's offerings in its three core capability areas ? its specialized content that connects enterprise technology and business professionals with B2B technology companies in the sectors and sub-sectors that it serves the purchasing intent insight analytics and data services its content and member traffic enables and the marketing services it provides to clients to help meet their business growth objectives.

In order to achieve this goal the company intends to continue to innovate in the area of data-enabled marketing services; expand long-term contractual relationships with customers; expand into complementary sectors; continue to expand the company's international presence; and selectively acquire or partner with complementary businesses.

Mergers and Acquisitions

In early 2020 TechTarget Acquired California-based Data Science Central an independent digital publishing and media company focused on data science and business analytics for an undisclosed amount. "The data science function is a true catalyst for driving data transformation and competitive edge for modern organizations and we are committed to serving these organizations by further enhancing our extensive coverage in this market" said Eileen Corrigan VP and Publisher Information Management Markets TechTarget.

EXECUTIVES

Executive Director, Product Innovation, Donald Hawk, $480,000 total compensation
Executive Chairman Of The Board, Gregory Strakosch, $600,000 total compensation
Lead Independent Director, Bruce Levenson
Independent Director, Robert Burke
Independent Director, Christina Van Houten
Independent Director, Perfecto Sanchez
Chief Executive Officer, Director, Michael Cotoia, $600,000 total compensation
Chief Financial Officer, Daniel Noreck, $225,000 total compensation
Auditors: Stowe & Degon, LLC

LOCATIONS

HQ: TechTarget Inc
275 Grove Street, Newton, MA 02466
Phone: 617 431-9200
Web: www.techtarget.com

PRODUCTS/OPERATIONS

2015 Sales

	$ mil.	% of total
Online	105.6	94
Events	6.2	6
Total	**111.8**	**100**

Selected Products and Operations

Conferences
　The CIO Decisions Conference
　IT Knowledge Exchange
　The ServerSide Java Symposium
Websites
　UK
　SearchSecurity.co.uk
　SearchStorage.co.uk
　US
　Ajaxian.com

Bitpipe.com
Brighthand.com
DigitalCameraReview.com
KnowledgeStorm.com
NotebookReview.com
SearchCIO.com
SearchCRM.com
SearchDataCenter.com
SearchDomino.com
SearchEnterpriseLinux.com
SearchExchange.com
SearchMobileComputing.com
SearchNetworking.com
SearchOracle.com
SearchSAP.com
SearchSecurity.com
SearchSMB.com
SearchSQLServer.com
SearchStorage.com
SearchVMware.com
SearchWindowsServer.com
TheServerSide.com
TheServerSide.NET
Whatis.com
Online Offerings:
IT Deal Alert: Qualified Sales Opportunities
IT Deal Alert: Priority Engine
IT Deal Alert: Deal Data
IT Deal Alert: TechTarget Research
White Papers
Webcasts Podcasts Videocasts and Virtual Trade Shows
Content Sponsorships
On-Network Branding
Off-Network Branding
Microsites

COMPETITORS

ALTERYX INC.	NETSCOUT SYSTEMS INC.
BLUCORA INC.	NEUSTAR INC.
CONVERSANT LLC	QUINSTREET INC.
CRITEO	RACKSPACE TECHNOLOGY
EGAIN CORPORATION	GLOBAL INC.
HUBSPOT INC.	YELP INC.
LINKEDIN CORPORATION	

HISTORICAL FINANCIALS

Company Type: Public

Income Statement

FYE: December 31

	REVENUE ($ mil.)	NET INCOME ($ mil.)	NET PROFIT MARGIN	EMPLOYEES
12/20	148.3	17.0	11.5%	940
12/19	133.9	16.8	12.6%	649
12/18	121.3	12.9	10.7%	647
12/17	108.5	6.8	6.3%	622
12/16	106.6	2.4	2.3%	659
Annual Growth	8.6%	63.0%	—	9.3%

2020 Year-End Financials

Debt ratio: 33.7%　　　　　No. of shares (mil.): 28.1
Return on equity: 9.5%　　　Dividends
Cash ($ mil.): 82.6　　　　　Yield: —
Current ratio: 2.75　　　　　Payout: —
Long-term debt ($ mil.): 153.8　Market value ($ mil.): 1,662.0

	STOCK PRICE ($) FY Close	P/E High/Low	PER SHARE ($) Earnings	Dividends	Book Value
12/20	59.11	101 28	0.61	0.00	7.20
12/19	26.10	48 19	0.60	0.00	5.43
12/18	12.21	72 24	0.45	0.00	4.77
12/17	13.92	56 34	0.24	0.00	4.39
12/16	8.53	115 75	0.08	0.00	4.28
Annual Growth	62.2%	— —	66.2%	—	13.9%

Teledyne Technologies Inc

Offerings of Teledyne Technologies are enabling technologies for industrial growth markets that require advanced technology and high reliability. The company's products include digital imaging sensors cameras and systems within the visible infrared and X-ray spectra monitoring and control instrumentation for marine and environmental applications harsh environment interconnects electronic test and measurement equipment aircraft information management systems and defense electronics and satellite communication subsystems. It also supply engineered systems for defense space environmental and energy applications. Teledyne gets most of its sales from customers in the US.

Operations
Teledyne's four operational segments provide balanced streams of revenue with the biggest Instrumentation accounting for some 35% of revenue and smallest Engineered Systems about 15%. In the middle are Digital Imaging over 30% and Aerospace and Defense Electronics about 20% of revenue.

Instrumentation provides monitoring and control instruments for marine environmental industrial and other applications as well as electronic test and measurement equipment. Its main product lines are Environmental Instrumentation Marine Instrumentation and Test and Measurement Instrumentation.

Digital Imaging provides high-performance sensors cameras and systems within the visible infrared ultraviolet and X-ray spectra for use in industrial scientific government defense & security and medical applications as well as micro electromechanical systems (MEMS) and high-performance high-reliability semiconductors including analog-to-digital and digital-to-analog converters.

The Aerospace and Defense Electronics segment makes electronic components and subsystems data acquisition and communications components and equipment harsh environment interconnects general aviation batteries and other components for a variety of commercial and defense applications that require high performance and high reliability.

Engineered Systems offers systems engineering and integration and advanced technology development as well as complex manufacturing equipment for defense space environmental and energy applications.

Geographic Reach
California-based Teledyne operates through some 70 principal facilities across over 15 states and international locations in Canada France the UK The Netherlands and Denmark.

Teledyne relies on the US for over 65% of its revenue while Canada supplies around 10% and the UK nearly 10%.

Sales and Marketing
A significant portion of Teledyne's sales are to the US government directly or through prime contractors. The biggest customer is the US Department of Defense which accounts for about 25% of the company's revenue.

Other customers include aerospace and defense factory automation air and water quality environmental monitoring medical imaging equipment makers pharmaceutical firms electronics design and development oceanographic research and deepwater oil and gas exploration and production companies. The company sells its products through an internal sales force third-party distributors and third-party representatives and distributors.

Financial Performance
The company's net sales for fiscal 2020 decreased by 2% to $3.1 billion compared from the prior year with $3.2 billion. The decrease in net sales in 2020 compared with 2019 reflected lower net sales in each segment except the Engineered Systems segment.

Net sales in 2020 included $68.9 million in incremental net sales from recent acquisitions. Net income for fiscal 2020 decreased to $401.9 million compared from the prior year with $402.3 million.

Cash held by the company at the end of fiscal 2020 increased to $673.1 million. Cash provided by operations was $618.9 million while cash used for investing and financing activities were $99.4 million and $61.8 million respectively. Main cash uses were purchases of property plant and equipment; and payments on other debt.

Strategy
Teledyne's strategy continues to emphasize growth in its core markets of instrumentation digital imaging aerospace and defense electronics and engineered systems. The company's core markets are characterized by high barriers to entry and include specialized products and services not likely to be commoditized. Teledyne intends to strengthen and expand its core businesses with targeted acquisitions and through product development. It continues to focus on balanced and disciplined capital deployment among capital expenditures product development acquisitions and share repurchases. Teledyne also aggressively pursues operational excellence to continually improve its margins and earnings by emphasizing cost containment and cost reductions in all aspects of its business. At Teledyne operational excellence includes the rapid integration of the businesses it acquires. Using complementary technology across its businesses and internal research and development the company seeks to create new products to grow the company and expand its addressable markets. Teledyne continues to evaluate its businesses to ensure that these are aligned with the company's strategy.

Mergers and Acquisitions
In 2021 Teledyne Technologies announced the successful completion of the acquisition of US-based FLIR Systems Inc. a world-leading industrial technology company focused on intelligent sensing solutions for defense and industrial applications. The aggregate consideration for the transaction was approximately $8.2 billion. FLIR will now be included in Teledyne's Digital Imaging segment and operate under the name Teledyne FLIR. Teledyne expects the acquisition to be immediately accretive to earnings excluding transaction costs and purchase price accounting and accretive to GAAP earnings in the first full calendar year following the acquisition.

In 2020 Teledyne Technologies and its subsidiary Teledyne LeCroy Inc. has acquired OakGate Technology Inc. Based in Loomis California OakGate provides software and hardware designed to test electronic data storage devices from development through manufacturing and end-use applications. Terms of the transaction were not disclosed.

EXECUTIVES

Independent Director, Wesley von Schack
Chief Financial Officer, Senior Vice President, Susan Main, $488,212 total compensation
Chairman, Robert Mehrabian, $917,307 total compensation
Senior Vice President, Chief Compliance Officer, General Counsel, Secretary, Melanie Cibik, $445,710 total compensation
Vice Chairman Of The Board, Jason VanWees, $457,431 total compensation
Senior Vice President - Strategic Sourcing, Tax, Treasurer, Stephen Blackwood
Vice President, Controller, Cynthia Belak
Senior Vice President - Aerospace And Defense Electronics Segment, George Bobb
Vice President - Teledyne, Group President - Teledyne Digital Imaging - Teledyne Dalsa And Teledyne E2v, Edwin Roks, $433,108 total compensation
Executive Vice President - Flir Defense, Jihfen Lei
Independent Director, Denise Cade
Independent Director, Michelle Kumbier
Director, Vincent Morales
Vice President, General Manager, David Cullin
Independent Director, Jane Sherburne
Independent Director, Robert Malone
Auditors: DELOITTE & TOUCHE LLP

LOCATIONS

HQ: Teledyne Technologies Inc
1049 Camino Dos Rios, Thousand Oaks, CA 91360-2362
Phone: 805 373-4545

PRODUCTS/OPERATIONS

2018 Sales

	$ mil.	% of total
Instrumentation	1,021.2	35
Aerospace and Defense Electronics	885.2	31
Digital Imaging	696.5	24
Engineered Systems	298.0	10
Total	**2,901.8**	**100**

COMPETITORS

AGILENT TECHNOLOGIES INC.	PACIFIC AEROSPACE & ELECTRONICS LLC
AMETEK INC.	TECHSHOT INC.
BROADLEY-JAMES CORPORATION	TEKTRONIX INC.
OAKRIDGE GLOBAL ENERGY SOLUTIONS INC.	

HISTORICAL FINANCIALS
Company Type: Public

Income Statement				FYE: January 3
	REVENUE ($ mil.)	NET INCOME ($ mil.)	NET PROFIT MARGIN	EMPLOYEES
01/21*	3,086.2	401.9	13.0%	10,670
12/19	3,163.6	402.3	12.7%	11,790
12/18	2,901.8	333.8	11.5%	10,850
12/17	2,603.8	227.2	8.7%	10,340
01/17	2,149.9	190.9	8.9%	8,970
Annual Growth	9.5%	20.5%	—	4.4%

*Fiscal year change

2021 Year-End Financials

Debt ratio: 15.3%	No. of shares (mil.): 36.9
Return on equity: 13.3%	Dividends
Cash ($ mil.): 673.1	Yield: —
Current ratio: 2.26	Payout: —
Long-term debt ($ mil.): 680.9	Market value ($ mil.): 14,484.0

	STOCK PRICE ($) FY Close	P/E High/Low	PER SHARE ($) Earnings	Dividends	Book Value
01/21*	391.98	36 18	10.62	0.00	87.37
12/19	347.82	32 18	10.73	0.00	74.28
12/18	202.77	27 19	9.01	0.00	61.79
12/17	181.15	29 19	6.26	0.00	54.79
01/17	123.00	23 14	5.37	0.00	44.27
Annual Growth	33.6%	— —	18.6%	—	18.5%

*Fiscal year change

Teradyne, Inc.

Teradyne designs develops manufactures and sells automated test equipment systems for testing semiconductors wireless products data storage and complex electronics systems in many industries including consumer electronics wireless automotive industrial computing communications and aerospace and defense industries. Teradyne's customers are integrated device manufacturers fables foundries and semiconductor assembly and test providers (OSAT). Teradyne developed its industrial robot business mainly through acquisitions. The Massachusetts-based company has operations in Asia Europe and the Americas but it generates most of its sales from customers in Asia.

Operations

Teradyne operates through four reportable segments: the Semiconductor Test Systems Test Industrial Automation segments and Wireless Test.

The Semiconductor Test group which accounts for more than 70% of sales includes the design manufacturing and marketing of semiconductor test products and services used both for wafer level and device package testing.

The Systems Test group about 15% of revenue makes testing products and services for military and aerospace instruments hard disk drive storage and circuit boards.

The Industrial Automation segment about 10% of revenue is composed of Universal Robots Mobile Industrial Robots (MIR) and Energid. The unit produces collaborative robotic arms autonomous mobile robots and advanced robotic control software.

The Wireless segment (around 5%) provides testing tools used in developing and manufacturing wireless devices.

The company relies on subcontractors and outsourced contract manufacturers to make its FLEX and J750 products.

Geographic Reach

Headquartered in Massachusetts Teradyne has operations in Costa Rica Denmark China Japan the Philippines South Korea Singapore Taiwan and the US.

Its two biggest markets are Taiwan about 40% of sales and China some 15% with other Asian countries accounting for another nearly 30% of revenue. US customers account for some 10% of sales.

Sales and Marketing

Teradyne primarily uses a direct sales force to sell most of its products but its robotics are sold through distributors. The company relies on its five largest customers for around 35% of revenue.

The company's advertising costs were $12.8 million $16.6 million and $15.4 million in 2020 2019 and 2018 respectively.

Financial Performance

The company's revenue for fiscal 2020 increased to $3.1 billion compared to the prior year with $2.3 billion. The increase was due to higher revenues in the semiconductor test segment.

Net income for fiscal 2020 increased to $784.1 million compared from the prior year with $467.5 million.

Cash held by the company at the end of fiscal 2020 increased to $914.1 million. Cash provided by operations was $868.9 million while cash used for investing and financing activities were $569.8 million and $158.3 million respectively. Main cash uses were purchases of marketable securities and repurchase of common stock.

Strategy

The company's strategy is to focus on profitably growing market share in its test businesses through the introduction of differentiated products that target growth segments and accelerating growth through continued investment in its Industrial Automation businesses. Teradyne plans to execute on its strategy while balancing capital allocations between returning capital to its shareholders through dividends and stock repurchases and using capital for opportunistic acquisitions.

HISTORY

College pals Nicholas DeWolf and Alexander d'Arbeloff (who met in an alphabetical ROTC lineup at MIT) founded Teradyne in 1960 to develop industrial-grade electronic test equipment. The name combines "tera" (10 to the 12 th power) and "dyne" (a unit of force); to the founding duo it meant "rolling a 15000-ton boulder uphill." The company's first headquarters was a loft over Joe & Nemo's hot dog stand in downtown Boston. In 1961 the company sold its first product — an automatic tester for semiconductor diodes called a go/no-go diode tester — to Raytheon for $5000.

Teradyne grew rapidly during the 1960s as it introduced new products including testers for integrated circuits resistors transistors and diodes. In the latter part of the decade the company began using computers to speed up the testing process helping create the automatic test equipment (ATE) industry. It formed Teradyne Components (later Teradyne Connection Systems) in 1968 to produce electronics connection assemblies.

Teradyne went public in 1970. That year with the first slump in the semiconductor industry the company laid off 15% of its workforce and began diversifying its customer base. DeWolf departed Teradyne in 1971 leaving d'Arbeloff to run operations. The market quickly recovered and the company grew and prospered again. In 1972 it began working on a telephone system testing device the 4Tel. However the market slumped again and in 1975 Teradyne cut its staff by 15% a second time.

EXECUTIVES

President, Chief Executive Officer, Director, Mark Jagiela, $955,000 total compensation
Chairman, Paul Tufano
Vice President, General Counsel, Secretary, Charles Gray, $390,000 total compensation
President - Industrial Automation, Gregory Smith, $400,000 total compensation
President - Wireless Test, Bradford Robbins, $340,000 total compensation
Executive Vice President, Business Development, Walter Vahey, $319,300 total compensation
Independent Director, Mercedes Johnson
President - Semiconductor Test, Richard Burns, $293,624 total compensation
Independent Director, Peter Herweck
Director, Ford Tamer
Chief Financial Officer, Vice President, Treasurer, Sanjay Mehta, $500,000 total compensation
Auditors: PricewaterhouseCoopers LLP

LOCATIONS

HQ: Teradyne, Inc.
600 Riverpark Drive, North Reading, MA 01864
Phone: 978 370-2700
Web: www.teradyne.com

PRODUCTS/OPERATIONS

2018 Sales

	$ mil.	% of total
Semiconductor Test	1,492.4	71
Industrial Automation	261.5	13
System Test	216.1	10
Wireless Test	132.0	6
Corporate and Other	(1.2)	-
Total	**2,100.8**	**100**

2018 Sales

	$ mil.	% of total
Product	1,729.6	82
Service	371.2	18
Total	**2,100.8**	**100**

Selected Products

Semiconductor test systems
  Memory test
  Microcontroller test
  Mixed-signal test (A5 line)
  System-on-a-chip test
  Very large scale integration (VLSI) chip test
Circuit board test and inspection systems
  Automated optical inspection
  In-circuit and functional board test
  Software
Military and aerospace
  Spectrum CTS (avionics systems)
  VICTORY (boundary scan and fault diagnostic software)
Wireless test
  IQfact (chipset)
  IQflex (WLAN)
  IQxstream (multi-device tester for devices)

COMPETITORS

AGILENT TECHNOLOGIES INC.	MTS SYSTEMS CORPORATION
ANALOGIC CORPORATION	OCLARO INC.
COGNEX CORPORATION	ONTO INNOVATION INC.
FLEX LTD.	SANMINA CORPORATION
IXIA	SEMTECH CORPORATION
MAXIM INTEGRATED PRODUCTS INC.	TELEDYNE LECROY INC.
	TRANSCAT INC.

HISTORICAL FINANCIALS

Company Type: Public

Income Statement

FYE: December 31

	REVENUE ($ mil.)	NET INCOME ($ mil.)	NET PROFIT MARGIN	EMPLOYEES
12/21	3,702.8	1,014.5	27.4%	5,900
12/20	3,121.4	784.1	25.1%	5,500
12/19	2,294.9	467.4	20.4%	5,400
12/18	2,100.8	451.7	21.5%	4,900
12/17	2,136.6	257.6	12.1%	4,500
Annual Growth	14.7%	40.9%	—	7.0%

2021 Year-End Financials

Debt ratio: 2.8%
Return on equity: 42.5%
Cash ($ mil.): 1,122.2
Current ratio: 3.20
Long-term debt ($ mil.): 89.2

No. of shares (mil.): 162.2
Dividends
  Yield: 0.2%
  Payout: 7.5%
Market value ($ mil.): 26,533.0

	STOCK PRICE ($) FY Close	P/E High/Low		PER SHARE ($) Earnings	Dividends	Book Value
12/21	163.53	27	17	5.53	0.40	15.80
12/20	119.89	26	9	4.28	0.40	13.31
12/19	68.19	25	11	2.60	0.36	8.89
12/18	31.38	21	12	2.35	0.36	8.67
12/17	41.87	34	20	1.28	0.28	9.99
Annual Growth	40.6%	—		44.2%	9.3%	12.1%

Terreno Realty Corp

Terreno Realty has its eyes set on acquiring industrial real estate. The real estate investment trust (REIT) invests in and operates industrial properties in major US coastal markets including Los Angeles San Francisco Bay Area Seattle Miami Northern New Jersey/New York City and Washington DC. The REIT typically invests in warehouse and distribution facilities flex buildings for light manufacturing and research and development and transshipment and improved land. The company owns about 220 buildings spanning about 13.3 million square feet and about 20 improved land parcels totaling about 77.6 acres.

Operations

About 80% of Terreno Realty's property portfolio consisted of warehouse/distribution properties while flex buildings (including light industrial and R&D facilities) made up another nearly 10%. Trans-shipment properties and improved land made up the rest.

Geographic Reach

San Francisco California- based Terreno Realty operates in six major US markets; Los Angeles Northern New Jersey/New York City San Francisco Bay Area Seattle Miami and Washington D.C.

Sales and Marketing

Some of Terreno Realty's tenants include FedEx Amazon Northrop Grumman Danaher AmerisourceBergen and the US government. No tenant accounts for more than 5% of annual base rent.

Financial Performance

Total revenues increased approximately $19.4 million for 2019 compared to the prior year primarily due to property acquisitions during 2018

and 2019 and increased revenue on new and renewed leases.

Net income for the year 2019 decreased by 12% to $55.5 million compared to the prior year with $63.3 million.

Cash held by the company at the end of 2019 increased by $78.3 million to $112.7 million. Cash provided by operations and financing activities were $94.7 million and $235.1 million respectively. Cash used for investing activities was $251.5 million mainly for proceeds from sales of real estate investments.

Strategy

The primary objective of Terreno Realty's financing strategy is to maintain financial flexibility with a conservative capital structure using retained cash flows proceeds from dispositions of properties long-term debt and the issuance of common and perpetual preferred stock to finance its growth. Over the long term the company intends to: limit the sum of the outstanding principal amount of its consolidated indebtedness and the liquidation preference of any outstanding perpetual preferred stock to less than 35% of the company's total enterprise value; maintain a fixed charge coverage ratio in excess of 2.0x; have staggered debt maturities that are aligned to its expected average lease term (5-7 years) positioning the company to reprice parts of its capital structure as its rental rates change with market conditions.

Mergers and Acquisitions

In 2020 Terreno Realty acquired an industrial property located in South San Francisco California for a purchase price of approximately $6.3 million. The property consists of one industrial building containing approximately 22000 square feet on 0.7 acres. The property is at 179 Starlite Street adjacent to Highway 101 between San Francisco International.

Also in 2020 Terreno Realty acquired an industrial property located in Seattle Washington for a purchase price of approximately $5.6 million. The property consists of one industrial building containing approximately 13000 square feet on 1.1 acres.

In 2019 Terreno Realty acquired an industrial property located in Puyallup Washington for a purchase price of approximately $6.7 million. The property consists of one industrial distribution building containing approximately 41000 square feet on approximately 2.3 acres less than four miles from the Port of Tacoma. The property at 917 Valley Avenue NW provides ten dock-high and four grade-level loading positions parking for 50 cars and is 100% leased to two tenants.

Company Background

The company took itself public in February 2010 in an effort to capitalize on a distressed market ripe with foreclosures and troubled loans. Portions of the net proceeds from its public offering were used to invest in interest-bearing short-term securities to help it gain REIT status.

EXECUTIVES

Independent Director, Linda Assante
President And Director, Michael Coke, $800,000 total compensation
Chairman Of The Board And Chief Executive Officer, W. Blake Baird, $800,000 total compensation
Independent Director, LeRoy Carlson
Independent Director, Dennis Polk

Executive Vice President, Andrew Burke, $333,000 total compensation
Executive Vice President, John Meyer, $333,000 total compensation
Lead Independent Director, Douglas Pasquale
Independent Director, David Lee
Independent Director, Gabriela Parcella
Chief Financial Officer, Executive Vice President, Company Secretary, Jaime Cannon, $333,000 total compensation
Auditors: Ernst & Young LLP

LOCATIONS

HQ: Terreno Realty Corp
  10500 NE 8th Street, Suite 301, Bellevue, WA 98004
Phone: 415 655-4580
Web: www.terreno.com

PRODUCTS/OPERATIONS

2012 Sales

	$ mil.	% of total
Rental	24.5	78
Tenant expense reimbursements	6.7	22
Total	**31.2**	**100**

COMPETITORS

DCT INDUSTRIAL TRUST INC.
EQUITY ONE INC.
FEDERAL REALTY INVESTMENT TRUST
FRANKLIN STREET PROPERTIES CORP.

GOV NEW OPPTY REIT
LXP INDUSTRIAL TRUST
ONE LIBERTY PROPERTIES INC.

HISTORICAL FINANCIALS

Company Type: Public

Income Statement

FYE: December 31

	REVENUE ($ mil.)	NET INCOME ($ mil.)	NET PROFIT MARGIN	EMPLOYEES
12/21	221.9	87.2	39.3%	34
12/20	186.8	79.8	42.7%	26
12/19	171.0	55.5	32.5%	24
12/18	151.6	63.2	41.7%	23
12/17	132.4	53.1	40.1%	22
Annual Growth	13.8%	13.2%	—	11.5%

2021 Year-End Financials

Debt ratio: 24.6%
Return on equity: 4.7%
Cash ($ mil.): 204.4
Current ratio: 2.17
Long-term debt ($ mil.): 720.6

No. of shares (mil.): 75.0
Dividends
  Yield: 1.4%
  Payout: 28.5%
Market value ($ mil.): 6,403.0

	STOCK PRICE ($) FY Close	P/E High/Low		PER SHARE ($) Earnings	Dividends	Book Value
12/21	85.29	69	44	1.23	1.26	27.41
12/20	58.51	53	37	1.16	1.12	23.23
12/19	54.14	67	40	0.85	1.02	22.56
12/18	35.17	36	29	1.09	0.92	20.45
12/17	35.06	40	28	0.95	0.84	18.56
Annual Growth	24.9%	—		6.7%	10.7%	10.2%

Texas Pacific Land Corp

Texas Pacific Land Trust was created to sell the Texas & Pacific Railway's land after its 1888 bankruptcy and yup they're still workin' on it. The trust began with the railroad of about 3.5 million acres; today it is one of the largest private landowners in Texas with more than 901000 acres in about 20 counties. Texas Pacific Land Trust's sales come from oil and gas royalties (about 85% of sales) easements and land sales. It has a perpetual oil and gas royalty interest under some 900000 acres in West Texas.

Operations

The company has two segments: Land and Resource Management and Water Services and Operations.The Land and Resource Management segment encompasses the business of managing approximately 900000 acres of land and related resources in West Texas owned by the Trust. The revenue streams of this segment consist primarily of royalties from oil and gas revenues from easements and commercial leases and land and material sales. The segment accounts for about 75% of revenues.The Water Services and Operations segment encompasses the business of providing full-service water offerings to operators in the Permian Basin. The revenue streams of this segment consist of revenue generated from sales of sourced and treated water as well as revenue from royalties on water service-related activity and accounts for about 25% of total revenues.

Geographic Reach

Texas Pacific owned the surface estate in more than 901000 acres of land comprised of numerous separate tracts located in about 20 counties in the western part of Texas. The trust lease office space in Dallas Texas for its corporate headquarters.

Sales and Marketing

Its top customers include WPX Energy Permian LLC and Anadarko E&P Onshore LLC which accounts for approximately 25% of total revenue.

Financial Performance

In the last five years the revenue performance of the company was outstanding. In such a short span revenue grew by 529%.

Revenues increased $190.3 million or 63% to $490.5 million in 2019 compared to $300.2 million in 2018. Land and Resource Management segment revenues increased $151.9 million and Water Services and Operations segment revenues increased $38.4 million.

Net income increased $109.0 million or 52.0% to $318.7 million in 2019 compared to $209.7 million in 2018. The increase in net income was mainly due to higher revenue.

Cash and cash equivalents at the end of the period were $303.6 million. Cash provided by operating activities was $342.8 million while investing and financing activities was $111.7 million and $50.9 million respectively. Main cash uses were for acquisition of real estate and payments of dividends.

Strategy

In early 2020 the Trust acquired approximately 671 surface acres of land and approximately 755 net royalty acres in Culberson County for a combined purchase price of approximately $14.9 million.

EXECUTIVES

Independent Co-chairman Of The Board Of Trustees, John Norris
Chief Executive Officer, President, And Director, Tyler Glover, $850,000 total compensation
Independent Co-chairman Of The Board Of Trustees, David Barry
Executive Vice President, Chief Commercial Officer, Sameer Parasnis, $378,767 total compensation
Chief Financial Officer, Chris Steddum
Chief Accounting Officer, Stephanie Buffington
Executive Vice President Of Tpwr, Robert A. Crain
Senior Vice President, General Counsel, Company Secretary, Micheal Dobbs, $166,667 total compensation
Independent Director, Murray Stahl
Independent Director, Barbara Duganier
Independent Director, Donald General Cook
Independent Director, Dana McGinnis
Independent Director, Donna Epps
Independent Director, Eric Oliver
Auditors: DELOITTE & TOUCHE LLP

LOCATIONS

HQ: Texas Pacific Land Corp
1700 Pacific Avenue, Suite 2900, Dallas, TX 75201
Phone: 214 969-5530   **Fax:** 214 871-7139
Web: www.TexasPacific.com

PRODUCTS/OPERATIONS

2015 sales

	% of total	
Easements and sundry income	40	
Oil and gas royalties	31	
Land sales	22.6	28
Grazing lease rentals	0.5	1
Interest income from notes receivable	0.0	-
Total	**79.4**	**100**

COMPETITORS

GETTY REALTY CORP.	WASHINGTON REAL ESTATE
HIGHWOODS PROPERTIES	INVESTMENT TRUST
INC.	WEINGARTEN REALTY
RAYONIER INC.	INVESTORS
SELECT INCOME REIT	
THE HOWARD HUGHES	
CORPORATION	

HISTORICAL FINANCIALS

Company Type: Public

Income Statement				FYE: December 31
	REVENUE ($ mil.)	NET INCOME ($ mil.)	NET PROFIT MARGIN	EMPLOYEES
12/20	302.5	176.0	58.2%	102
12/19	490.5	318.7	65.0%	94
12/18	300.2	209.7	69.9%	71
12/17	132.3	76.3	57.7%	32
12/16	59.9	37.2	62.2%	10
Annual Growth	49.9%	47.5%	—	78.7%

2020 Year-End Financials

Debt ratio: —	No. of shares (mil.): 7.7
Return on equity: 35.2%	Dividends
Cash ($ mil.): 281.0	Yield: 0.0%
Current ratio: 6.90	Payout: 114.5%
Long-term debt ($ mil.): —	Market value ($ mil.): 5,639.0

	STOCK PRICE ($) FY Close	P/E High/Low		PER SHARE ($) Earnings	Dividends	Book Value
12/20	727.00	36	14	22.70	26.00	62.55
12/19	781.22	22	14	41.09	6.00	66.03
12/18	541.63	32	16	26.93	4.05	31.52
12/17	446.63	46	27	9.72	1.35	10.12
12/16	296.77	65	24	4.66	0.31	6.01
Annual Growth	25.1%	—	—	48.6%	202.6%	79.6%

The Bancorp Inc

The Bancorp Inc. is a financial holding company of The Bancorp Bank its primary subsidiary. They have four primary lines of specialty lending: securities-backed lines of credit (SBLOC) and insurance policy cash value-backed lines of credit (IBLOC) vehicle fleet and other equipment leasing (direct lease financing) small business loans (SBL) and loans which prior to 2020 were generated for sale into capital markets through commercial loan securitizations and other sales (CMBS). The company offers deposit products and services through its payments business line lending activities through specialty finance as well as affinity group banking products and services.

Operations

The Bancorp operates in three business segments: Specialty Finance (about 60% of the company's revenue) which consists of SBLOC IBLOC and advisor financing; lease financing for commercial and government vehicle fleets; SBL loans for small businesses; and commercial real estate loans. Payments (around 40%) which include checking accounts savings accounts money market accounts commercial accounts and various types of prepaid and debit cards as well as ACH bill payment and other bill payment services. Corporate includes the company's investment portfolio corporate overhead and non-allocated expenses.

Over 55% of its total revenue came from loan interest (including fees) while nearly 15% came from interest income on investment securities. The rest of its revenue came from fees from prepaid and debit cards (about 25%) and service fees on deposit accounts among others.

Geographic Reach

Wilmington Delaware-based The Bancorp maintains business development and administrative offices for SBL in Morrisville North Carolina and Westmont Illinois (suburban Chicago) primarily for SBA lending. Leasing offices are located in Charlotte North Carolina Crofton Maryland Kent Washington Logan Utah Orlando Florida Raritan New Jersey and Norristown and Warminster Pennsylvania. The company also maintains a loan operations office in New York New York. Prepaid and debit card offices and other executive offices are located in Sioux Falls South Dakota.

Sales and Marketing

The company offers deposit products and services to their affinity group clients and their customer bases through direct or private label banking strategies. Specialty Finance services such as SBLOC IBLOC and advisor financing services are offered to individuals trusts and entities which are secured by a pledge of marketable securities maintained in one or more accounts with respect to which it obtain a securities account control agreement.

The Bancorp's card issuing services are offered to end users through their relationships with benefits administrators third-party administrators insurers corporate incentive companies rebate fulfillment organizations payroll administrators large retail chains consumer service organizations and FinTech disruptors. The majority of fees it earns result from contractual fees paid by third-party sponsors computed on a per transaction basis and monthly service fees. The company also acts as the bank sponsor and depository institution for independent service organizations that process such payments and for other companies such as bill payment companies for which they process ACH payments.

The company has a national scope for its affinity group banking operations and it uses a personal sales/targeted media advertising approach to market to existing and potential commercial affinity group organizations. The affinity group organizations with which it has relationships perform marketing functions to the ultimate individual customers. Its marketing program to affinity group organizations consists of print advertising attending and making presentations at trade shows and other events for targeted affinity organizations; and direct contact with potential affinity organizations by their marketing staff with relationship managers focusing on particular regional markets.

Advertising and marketing costs amounted to $1.3 million $0.8 million and $0.4 million for 2020 2019 and 2018 respectively.

Financial Performance

The company's net earnings grew by 117% over the past five years.

In 2020 the Bancorp reported a net interest income of $194.9 million compared to $141.3 million from the prior year. The increase in net interest income resulted primarily from an increase in average loans and leases to $3.94 billion from $2.42 billion in 2019.

The company's net income increased by 55% or $80.1 million in 2020. The increases resulted primarily from net interest income which increased $53.6 million between those periods.

The company's cash and cash equivalents at the end of 2020 was $345.5 million. Operations used $512.2 million while investing activities used another $595.8 million. Financing activities provided $509 million in 2020.

Strategy

The company's principal strategies are to fund their loan and investment portfolio growth with stable deposits and generate non-interest income from prepaid and debit card accounts and other payment processing; develop relationships with Affinity Groups to gain sponsored access to their membership client or customer bases to market their services; and use their existing infrastructure as a platform for growth.

Company Background

The Bancorp was founded by Betsy Z. Cohen in 1999. The company has gained industry recognition as the top issuer of prepaid cards in the US leading merchant servicer and a top ACH originator.

EXECUTIVES

Chairman Of The Board, James McEntee

Executive Vice President, General Counsel, Thomas Pareigat, $400,000 total compensation
Chief Executive Officer, Director And President, Damian Kozlowski, $750,000 total compensation
Chief Financial Officer, Executive Vice President - Strategy, Principal Accounting Officer, Paul Frenkiel, $400,000 total compensation
Executive Vice President, Head Of Credit Markets And Chief Credit Officer, Mark Connolly, $350,000 total compensation
Chief Operating Officer, Executive Vice President, Gregor Garry, $400,000 total compensation
Independent Director, Stephanie Mudick
Independent Director, Daniela Mielke
Director, Cheryl Creuzot
Auditors: Grant Thornton LLP

LOCATIONS

HQ: The Bancorp Inc
409 Silverside Road, Wilmington, DE 19809
Phone: 302 385-5000
Web: www.thebancorp.com

PRODUCTS/OPERATIONS

2015 sales

	$ mil.	% of total
Payments	98.0	45
Specialty finance	67.6	31
Corporate	51.0	24
Total	**216.6**	**100**

2015 Sales

	$ mil.	% of total
Interest income		
Loans including fees	49.9	23
Interest on investment securities:	30.7	14
Federal funds sold/securities purchased under agreements to resell	0.6	-
Interest earning deposits	2.3	1
Non-interest income		
Prepaid card fees	47.5	22
Gain on sale of health savings portfolio	33.6	15
Gain on sale of investment securities	14.4	7
Gain on sale of loans	10.1	5
Service fees on deposit accounts	7.5	3
Card payment and ACH processing fees	5.7	3
Affinity fees	3.4	2
Other	5.3	2
Change in value of investment in unconsolidated entity	1.7	1
Leasing income	2.3	1
Debit card income	1.6	1
Total	**216.6**	**100**

COMPETITORS

BOKF MERGER CORPORATION NUMBER SIXTEEN
Banco Bradesco S/A
CAPITAL BANK FINANCIAL CORP.
CITY HOLDING COMPANY
DISCOVER FINANCIAL SERVICES
F.N.B. CORPORATION
FINANCIAL INSTITUTIONS INC.
FIRST FINANCIAL CORPORATION
M&T BANK CORPORATION
NATIONAL BANK HOLDINGS CORPORATION
PACWEST BANCORP
PINNACLE FINANCIAL PARTNERS INC.
REPUBLIC BANCORP INC.
SIMMONS FIRST NATIONAL CORPORATION
STOCK YARDS BANCORP INC.
SYNCHRONY FINANCIAL
UMB FINANCIAL CORPORATION
UNIVEST FINANCIAL CORPORATION
WEBSTER FINANCIAL CORPORATION

HISTORICAL FINANCIALS

Company Type: Public

Income Statement   FYE: December 31

	ASSETS ($ mil.)	NET INCOME ($ mil.)	INCOME AS % OF ASSETS	EMPLOYEES
12/20	6,276.8	80.0	1.3%	635
12/19	5,656.9	51.5	0.9%	612
12/18	4,437.9	88.6	2.0%	589
12/17	4,708.1	21.6	0.5%	538
12/16	4,858.1	(96.4)	—	589
Annual Growth	6.6%	—		1.9%

2020 Year-End Financials

Return on assets: 1.3%
Return on equity: 14.9%
Long-term debt ($ mil.): —
No. of shares (mil.): 57.6
Sales ($ mil): 295.4

Dividends
Yield: —
Payout: —
Market value ($ mil.): 787.0

	STOCK PRICE ($) FY Close	P/E High/Low		PER SHARE ($) Earnings	Dividends	Book Value
12/20	13.65	10	3	1.37	0.00	10.08
12/19	12.97	15	9	0.90	0.00	8.51
12/18	7.96	7	5	1.55	0.00	7.22
12/17	9.88	26	12	0.39	0.00	5.81
12/16	7.86	—	—	(2.17)	0.00	5.40
Annual Growth	14.8%			—		16.9%

The Trade Desk Inc

Auditors: PricewaterhouseCoopers LLP

LOCATIONS

HQ: The Trade Desk Inc
42 N. Chestnut Street, Ventura, CA 93001
Phone: 805 585-3434
Web: www.thetradedesk.com

HISTORICAL FINANCIALS

Company Type: Public

Income Statement   FYE: December 31

	REVENUE ($ mil.)	NET INCOME ($ mil.)	NET PROFIT MARGIN	EMPLOYEES
12/21	1,196.4	137.7	11.5%	1,967
12/20	836.0	242.3	29.0%	1,545
12/19	661.0	108.3	16.4%	1,310
12/18	477.2	176.2	36.9%	944
12/17	308.2	101.6	33.0%	713
Annual Growth	40.4%	7.9%	—	28.9%

2021 Year-End Financials

Debt ratio: —
Return on equity: 10.8%
Cash ($ mil.): 754.1
Current ratio: 1.71
Long-term debt ($ mil.): —

No. of shares (mil.): 483.4
Dividends
Yield: —
Payout: —
Market value ($ mil.): 44,303.0

	STOCK PRICE ($)		P/E	PER SHARE ($)		
	FY Close		High/Low	Earnings	Dividends	Book Value
12/21	91.64		31 15 2 10	0.28	0.00	3.16
12/20	801.00		18 53 2 76	0.50	0.00	2.14
12/19	259.78		11 46 4 51	0.23	0.00	1.35
12/18	116.06		74 92 06	0.19	0.00	0.90
12/17	45.73		52 82 14	0.12	0.00	0.59
Annual Growth	19.0%		— —	24.9%	—	52.1%

Thomasville Bancshares, Inc.

This Thomasville is more about the money under your bed than the bed itself. Thomasville Bancshares is the holding company for Thomasville National Bank which serves area consumers and businesses from two offices in Thomasville Georgia. Established in 1995 the bank offers standard services such as deposit accounts and credit cards. Real estate mortgages comprise most of the company's loan portfolio followed by commercial financial and agricultural loans. The company provides trust asset management and brokerage services through its TNB Financial Services unit. Executive officers and directors of Thomasville Bancshares collectively own more than a quarter of the company.

EXECUTIVES

President, Chief Executive Officer, Director, Stephen Cheney
Executive Vice President, Charles Hodges
Director, Cochran Scott
Director, Charles Hancock
Director, Richard Singletary
Director, Diane Parker
Director, Charles Balfour
Director, Randall Moore
Director, David Cone
Director, Joel Barrett
Director, Harold Jackson
Auditors: Mauldin & Jenkins, LLC

LOCATIONS

HQ: Thomasville Bancshares, Inc.
301 North Broad Street, Thomasville, GA 31792
Phone: 229 226-3300
Web: www.tnbank.com

COMPETITORS

EXTRACO CORPORATION
HUNTINGTON BANCSHARES INCORPORATED
OLD POINT FINANCIAL CORPORATION
SIMMONS FIRST NATIONAL CORPORATION

HISTORICAL FINANCIALS
Company Type: Public

Income Statement
FYE: December 31

	ASSETS ($ mil.)	NET INCOME ($ mil.)	INCOME AS % OF ASSETS	EMPLOYEES
12/20	1,227.5	19.3	1.6%	0
12/19	956.6	18.7	2.0%	0
12/18	880.5	16.8	1.9%	0
12/17	806.4	12.0	1.5%	0
12/16	780.2	11.8	1.5%	0
Annual Growth	12.0%	13.0%	—	—

2020 Year-End Financials

Return on assets: 1.7%
Return on equity: 19.8%
Long-term debt ($ mil.): —
No. of shares (mil.): 6.0
Sales ($ mil): 60.3
Dividends
Yield: 2.9%
Payout: 51.3%
Market value ($ mil.): 307.0

	STOCK PRICE ($)		P/E		PER SHARE ($)		
	FY Close		High/Low		Earnings	Dividends	Book Value
12/20	51.00		17	13	2.92	1.50	17.06
12/19	46.00		15	13	2.84	1.40	15.31
12/18	40.99		15	14	2.56	1.30	13.60
12/17	40.00		20	17	1.83	1.00	12.05
12/16	35.00		18	14	1.81	0.85	11.10
Annual Growth	9.9%		—	—	12.7%	15.3%	11.3%

Timberland Bancorp, Inc.

Located among the tall trees of the Pacific Northwest Timberland Bancorp is the holding company for Timberland Savings Bank which operates more than 20 branches in western Washington. The bank targets individuals and regional businesses offering checking savings and money market accounts and CDs. Timberland Savings Bank concentrates on real estate lending including commercial and residential mortgages multifamily residential loans and land develoment loans; it also writes business loans and other types of loans. Timberland Savings Bank was founded in 1915 as a savings and loan.

EXECUTIVES

President, Chief Executive Officer, Director Of The Company And Bank, Michael Sand, $451,000 total compensation
Executive Vice President Of Lending Of The Company And Bank, Robert Drugge, $234,000 total compensation
Independent Chairman Of The Board, Jon Parker
Independent Director, David Smith
Senior Vice President, Treasurer Of The Company And Bank, Marci Basich
Executive Vice President And Chief Credit Administrator Of The Company And Bank, Edward Foster, $165,310 total compensation
Chief Operating Officer, Executive Vice President Of The Company And Bank, Jonathan Fischer, $176,904 total compensation
Chief Financial Officer, Executive Vice President, Secretary Of The Company And The Timberland Savings Bank, Ssb, Dean Brydon, $234,000 total compensation
Independent Director, Kelly Suter
Independent Director, Parul Bhandari
Independent Director, Michael Stoney
Independent Director, Kathy Leodler
Auditors: Delap LLP

LOCATIONS

HQ: Timberland Bancorp, Inc.
624 Simpson Avenue, Hoquiam, WA 98550
Phone: 360 533-4747
Web: www.timberlandbank.com

COMPETITORS

CAMBRIDGE FINANCIAL GROUP INC
COMMUNITY BANK
EMIGRANT SAVINGS BANK
PRUDENTIAL BANCORP INC. OF PENNSYLVANIA
SOUTHERN MISSOURI BANCORP INC.
SUMMIT STATE BANK
W V S FINANCIAL CORP.

HISTORICAL FINANCIALS
Company Type: Public

Income Statement
FYE: September 30

	ASSETS ($ mil.)	NET INCOME ($ mil.)	INCOME AS % OF ASSETS	EMPLOYEES
09/21	1,792.1	27.5	1.5%	288
09/20	1,565.9	24.2	1.5%	286
09/19	1,247.1	24.0	1.9%	293
09/18	1,018.2	16.7	1.6%	263
09/17	952.0	14.1	1.5%	274
Annual Growth	17.1%	18.1%	—	1.3%

2021 Year-End Financials

Return on assets: 1.6%
Return on equity: 13.9%
Long-term debt ($ mil.): —
No. of shares (mil.): 8.3
Sales ($ mil): 72.1
Dividends
Yield: 3.5%
Payout: 31.0%
Market value ($ mil.): 241.0

	STOCK PRICE ($)		P/E		PER SHARE ($)		
	FY Close		High/Low		Earnings	Dividends	Book Value
09/21	28.90		9	5	3.27	1.03	24.76
09/20	18.00		11	5	2.88	0.85	22.58
09/19	27.50		11	8	2.84	0.78	20.54
09/18	31.24		17	12	2.22	0.60	16.84
09/17	31.34		16	8	1.92	0.50	15.08
Annual Growth	(2.0%)		—	—	14.2%	19.8%	13.2%

TopBuild Corp

Auditors: PricewaterhouseCoopers LLP

LOCATIONS

HQ: TopBuild Corp
475 North Williamson Boulevard, Daytona Beach, FL 32114
Phone: 386 304-2200
Web: www.topbuild.com

HISTORICAL FINANCIALS

Company Type: Public

Income Statement
FYE: December 31

	REVENUE ($ mil.)	NET INCOME ($ mil.)	NET PROFIT MARGIN	EMPLOYEES
12/20	2,718.0	247.0	9.1%	10,540
12/19	2,624.1	191.0	7.3%	10,400
12/18	2,384.2	134.7	5.7%	10,300
12/17	1,906.2	158.1	8.3%	8,400
12/16	1,742.8	72.6	4.2%	7,900
Annual Growth	11.8%	35.8%	—	7.5%

2020 Year-End Financials

Debt ratio: 25.1%
Return on equity: 19.6%
Cash ($ mil.): 330.0
Current ratio: 1.89
Long-term debt ($ mil.): 683.4

No. of shares (mil.): 33.0
Dividends
  Yield: —
  Payout: —
Market value ($ mil.): 6,078.0

	STOCK PRICE ($) FY Close	P/E High/Low		PER SHARE ($) Earnings	Dividends	Book Value
12/20	184.08	27	8	7.42	0.00	40.85
12/19	103.08	20	8	5.56	0.00	34.43
12/18	45.00	23	11	3.78	0.00	31.01
12/17	75.74	17	8	4.32	0.00	28.00
12/16	35.60	20	12	1.92	0.00	25.72
Annual Growth	50.8%	—	—	40.2%	—	12.3%

Toro Company (The)

The Toro Company is a worldwide provider of turf maintenance equipment and precision irrigation systems. It manufactures lawn mowers snow throwers and other such tools for professional and residential landscaping. Its lineup of products helps create illuminate and irrigate lawns and landscapes; install repair and replace underground utilities; and manage ice and snow. Toro's products are typically used in golf courses sports fields municipal residential and commercial properties. About 80% of its revenue derives from US customers. Toro traces its roots back to 1914 as The Toro Motor Company.

Operations

Toro has two primary business segments: Professional and Residential.

The Professional segment (about 75% of total sales) designs turf landscape construction and agricultural products and markets them worldwide. It also includes professional snow and ice removal equipment. This segment serves the landscape contractor equipment market through the Toro Ventrac and Exmark brands with products such as zero-turn radius mowers heavy- and mid-duty mowers and tree care equipment. Products for the golf course include specialty mowers sprayers and sprinklers and controls and sensors that measure soil moisture and salinity. Snow and ice management products are sold under the BOSS brand and include snow plows salt and sand spreaders and ATVs. The Professional segment also includes rental and specialty products as well as underground construction products such as directional drills and riding trenchers.

Toro's Residential segment (approximately 25% of sales) offers products similar to those of the Professional segment but for use on a smaller scale. Brands include Toro Lawn-Boy and Pope ? and Hayter in the UK. Yard tools include walking and riding mowers trimmers and blowers and snow throwers.

Overall sales to its equipment accounts for nearly 80% of sales and the rest comes from irrigation.

Geographic Reach

Bloomington Minnesota-based Toro rings up about 80% of its sales in the US. The remainder comes from more than 125 other countries including Australia Canada and several in Europe. The company manufactures its products at in the US as well as sites in Mexico Australia and China and five facilities in Europe. It also maintain sales offices in Belgium UK Australia Japan China Italy Poland Germany Spain France and the US.

Sales and Marketing

Toro markets and sells the majority of its products through more than 150 distributors worldwide as well as a large number of equipment dealers irrigation dealers and distributors mass retailers hardware retailers equipment rental centers home centers and online (direct to end-users).

The company's Professional segment sells to clients who manage facilities such as golf courses and sports fields as well as municipal properties and private landscapes. It also sells directly to property owners such as governmental entities and retailers. Its BOSS snow and ice management products are sold through distributors and dealers.

Residential segment products such as walk power mowers zero-turn riding mowers and snow throwers are generally sold to home centers mass retailers dealers hardware retailers as well as online (direct to end-users). In certain markets these same products are sold to distributors for resale to hardware retailers and dealers. Home solutions products are primarily sold to home centers mass retailers and hardware retailers.

Marketing channels include television radio print direct mail email and online channels like social media. Toro's spends approximately $50.5 million $50.3 million and $43.5 million for the fiscal years ended 2021 2020 and 2019 respectively.

Financial Performance

Consolidated net sales in fiscal 2021 were $4.0 billion compared to $3.4 billion in fiscal 2020 an increase of 17%. The increase was primarily driven by increased sales of Professional landscape contractor zero-turn riding mowers due to strong retail demand and low field inventory levels; price increases across its Professional and Residential segment product lines; and strong demand for rental and specialty construction equipment due to favorable construction industry trends.

Net earnings for fiscal 2021 increased to $409.9 million compared from $329.7 million in the prior year. The net earnings increase for fiscal 2021 was primarily driven by the higher sales volumes which were further benefited from improved net price realization as a result of price increases across its Professional and Residential segment product line and favorable product mix; productivity improvements; and acquisition-related costs for its acquisitions of Venture Products and CMW recorded in fiscal 2020 that did not repeat in fiscal 2021.

Cash held by the company at the end of fiscal 2021 decreased to $405.6 million. Cash provided by operations was $555.5 billion while cash used

for investing and financing activities were $128.5 million and $503.7 million respectively. Main uses of cash were purchases of property plant and equipment; and repayments under debt arrangements

Strategy

Toro has continued to complement its brands enhance its product portfolios and improve its technologies through innovation and strategic acquisitions over the more than 100 years it has been in business. The company plan to continue to leverage a strategic and disciplined approach to pursue targeted acquisitions that add value to TTC by complementing its existing brands enhancing its product portfolio and/or improving its technologies.

Toro believes that its longstanding commitment to quality and innovation in its products has been a key driver of its history of market success. The company is committed to an ongoing engineering program dedicated to developing innovative new products and improvements in the quality and performance of existing products and when applicable it may pursue targeted and strategic acquisitions to acquire innovative technologies that the company believe uphold and bolster its longstanding commitment to quality and innovation in its products. For example during the first quarter of fiscal 2021 Toro completed the asset acquisition of Turflynx Lda a developer of innovative autonomous solutions for turf management and during the second quarter of fiscal 2021 the company completed the asset acquisition of Left Hand Robotics Inc. a developer of innovative autonomous solutions for turf and snow management. These strategic asset acquisitions complement and support the development of alternative power smart-connected and autonomous products within its Professional and Residential segments.

Mergers and Acquisitions

In early 2021 Toro acquired Colorado-based Left Hand Robotics a recognized for developing innovative autonomous solutions for turf and snow management. Its patent-pending software and advanced technologies for autonomous navigation are designed to provide professional contractors and grounds managers with future solutions to improve their operational efficiency and tackle outdoor tasks with precision. The acquisition supports the company's strategy of leadership in next generation technologies including alternative power smart connected and autonomous products. Terms of the transaction were not disclosed.

Company Background

Toro Spanish for "bull" was founded in 1914 as The Toro Motor Company to make engines for The Bull Tractor Company. In 1921 Toro provided a tractor fitted with 30-inch lawn mower blades to replace a horse-drawn grass-cutting machine at a Minneapolis country club and the modern power mower industry was born. By 1925 Toro turf maintenance machines were used on many of the US's major golf courses and parks and by 1928 its products were used in Europe.

The company went public in 1935. Toro introduced its first walk-behind power mower for consumers four years later. In 1948 the company entered the rotary mower market when it bought Whirlwind. Toro started making snow removal equipment in 1951. With its 1962 purchase of Moist O' Matic the company's offerings included automatic irrigation for golf courses.

It was renamed The Toro Company in 1971.

HISTORY

Toro — Spanish for "bull" — was founded in 1914 as The Toro Motor Company to make engines for The Bull Tractor Company. In 1921 Toro provided a tractor fitted with 30-inch lawn mower blades to replace a horse-drawn grass-cutting machine at a Minneapolis country club and the modern power mower industry was born. By 1925 Toro turf maintenance machines were used on many of the US's major golf courses and parks and by 1928 its products were used in Europe.

The company went public in 1935. Toro introduced its first walk-behind power mower for consumers four years later. In 1948 the company entered the rotary mower market when it bought Whirlwind. Toro started making snow removal equipment in 1951. With its 1962 purchase of Moist O' Matic the company's offerings included automatic irrigation for golf courses.

It was renamed The Toro Company in 1971.

EXECUTIVES

Vice President - Strategy, Corporate And Channel Development, Kurt Svendsen
Lead Independent Director, Gary Ellis
Independent Director, Katherine Harless
Vice President - Sustainability, Business Analytics And Process Improvement, Blake Grams
Group Vice President - Construction, Contractor And Residential Businesses, Richard Rodier, $515,545 total compensation
Vice President - Strategic Technologies, Darren Redetzke
Vice President, Residential And Landscape Contractor Businesses, Gregory Janey
Vice President - International, Peter Moeller
Chairman Of The Board, President, Chief Executive Officer, Richard Olson, $1,045,930 total compensation
Vice President - Human Resources, General Counsel, Corporate Secretary, Amy Dahl, $480,635 total compensation
Independent Director, Jeffrey Ettinger
Vice President - Boss, Jody Christy
Independent Director, Jeffrey Harmening
Vice President - Construction, Angie Drake
Vice President - Global Operations And Integrated Supply Chain, Kevin Carpenter
Chief Financial Officer, Vice President, Renee Peterson, $566,066 total compensation
Auditors: KPMG LLP

LOCATIONS

HQ: Toro Company (The)
8111 Lyndale Avenue South, Bloomington, MN 55420-1196
Phone: 952 888-8801
Web: www.thetorocompany.com

PRODUCTS/OPERATIONS

2018 Sales

	$ mil.	% of total
Equipment	2,210.0	84
Irrigation & lighting	408.6	16
Total	**2,618.6**	**100**

2018 Sales

	$ mil.	% of total
Professional	1,947.0	74
Residential	654.4	25
Other	17.2	1
Total	**2,618.6**	**100**

BRANDS

Boss
Exmark
Hayter
Irritrol
Lawn-Boy
Pope
Toro
Unique Lighting Systems

Selected Products

Professional
Agricultural irrigation
Aqua-TraXX PBX drip tape
Blue Stripe polyethylene tubing
BlueLine drip line
NGE emittters
Evolution Ag controller
Golf course
Bunker maintenance equipment
Greens rollers
Turf sprayers
Walking and riding mowers
Landscape contractor
Heavy-duty walk-behind mowers
Mid-sized walk-behind mowers
Stand-on movers
Turf renovation and tree care equipment
Zero-turning-radius riding mowers
Sports fields and grounds
Aerators
Blowers
Multipurpose vehicles
Sweepers
Vacuums
Residential
Home solutions
Electric blower-vacuums
Grass trimmers
Lighting
Riding products
Garden tractor models
Lawn tractor models
Zero-turning-radius mowers
Snow removal
Single-stage snow throwers
Two-stage snow throwers
Walk power mowers
Bagging mowers
Mulching mowers
Side discharging mowers
Snow and Ice Management
Snowplows
Salt and sand spreaders
Rental and specialty construction
Compact utility loaders
Walk-behind trenchers
Stump grinders

COMPETITORS

ARIENS COMPANY
DEERE & COMPANY
DOUGLAS DYNAMICS INC.
ELECTROCOMPONENTS PUBLIC LIMITED COMPANY
ENERPAC TOOL GROUP CORP.
FASTENAL COMPANY
FINN CORPORATION
SITEONE LANDSCAPE SUPPLY INC.
SPECTRUM BRANDS HOLDINGS INC.
UNITED RENTALS INC.

HISTORICAL FINANCIALS

Company Type: Public

Income Statement — FYE: October 31

	REVENUE ($ mil.)	NET INCOME ($ mil.)	NET PROFIT MARGIN	EMPLOYEES
10/21	3,959.5	409.8	10.4%	10,982
10/20	3,378.8	329.7	9.8%	10,385
10/19	3,138.0	273.9	8.7%	9,329
10/18	2,618.6	271.9	10.4%	6,715
10/17	2,505.1	267.7	10.7%	6,779
Annual Growth	12.1%	11.2%	—	12.8%

2021 Year-End Financials

Debt ratio: 23.5%
Return on equity: 36.1%
Cash ($ mil.): 405.6
Current ratio: 1.59
Long-term debt ($ mil.): 691.2
No. of shares (mil.): 105.2
Dividends
Yield: 0.0%
Payout: 27.7%
Market value ($ mil.): 10,044.0

	STOCK PRICE ($) FY Close	P/E High/Low	Earnings	PER SHARE ($) Dividends	Book Value
10/21	95.47	31 22	3.78	1.05	10.94
10/20	82.10	29 18	3.03	1.00	10.36
10/19	77.13	30 21	2.53	0.90	8.05
10/18	56.33	26 21	2.50	0.80	6.33
10/17	62.85	30 19	2.41	0.70	5.77
Annual Growth	11.0%	— —	11.9%	10.7%	17.3%

TowneBank

EXECUTIVES

BR Mgr, Becky Zambas
Executive Officer, Anne Conner
Board Member, Douglas Ellis
Board Member, Thomas Broyles
Branch Manager, Caitlyn Holloway
Senior Vice-President, Christina Fender
Vice President, Dawn Provost
Member Representative, Deborah Beddingfield
Computer Operator, Ethan Davidhizar
Senior Vice-President, Jawn Hendrix
Sales Staff, Jessie Denny
Auditors: Dixon Hughes Goodman LLP

LOCATIONS

HQ: TowneBank
5716 High Street, Portsmouth, VA 23703
Phone: 757 638-7500
Web: www.townebank.com

HISTORICAL FINANCIALS

Company Type: Public

Income Statement — FYE: December 31

	ASSETS ($ mil.)	NET INCOME ($ mil.)	INCOME AS % OF ASSETS	EMPLOYEES
12/20	14,626.4	145.5	1.0%	2,897
12/19	11,947.6	138.7	1.2%	2,853
12/18	11,163.0	133.7	1.2%	2,897
12/17	8,522.1	87.6	1.0%	2,727
12/16	7,973.9	67.2	0.8%	2,529
Annual Growth	16.4%	21.3%	—	3.5%

2020 Year-End Financials

Return on assets: 1.0%
Return on equity: 8.5%
Long-term debt ($ mil.): —
No. of shares (mil.): 72.6
Sales ($ mil): 744.3

Dividends
Yield: 3.0%
Payout: 40.0%
Market value ($ mil.): 1,706.0

	STOCK PRICE ($) FY Close	P/E High/Low		PER SHARE ($) Earnings	Dividends	Book Value
12/20	23.48	14	8	2.01	0.72	24.31
12/19	27.82	15	12	1.92	0.70	22.58
12/18	23.95	18	12	1.88	0.62	21.05
12/17	30.75	25	21	1.41	0.55	18.06
12/16	33.25	29	14	1.18	0.51	17.20
Annual Growth	(8.3%)	—		—	14.2%	9.0%	9.0%

Tradeweb Markets Inc

Auditors: DELOITTE & TOUCHE LLP

LOCATIONS

HQ: Tradeweb Markets Inc
1177 Avenue of the Americas, New York, NY 10036
Phone: 646 430-6000
Web: www.tradeweb.com

HISTORICAL FINANCIALS
Company Type: Public

Income Statement

FYE: December 31

	REVENUE ($ mil.)	NET INCOME ($ mil.)	NET PROFIT MARGIN	EMPLOYEES
12/20	892.6	166.3	18.6%	961
12/19	775.5	83.7	10.8%	919
12/18*	178.6	29.3	16.4%	919
09/18	478.9	130.1	27.2%	0
12/17	504.4	83.6	16.6%	0
Annual Growth	15.3%	18.7%	—	—

*Fiscal year change

2020 Year-End Financials

Debt ratio: —
Return on equity: 4.3%
Cash ($ mil.): 791.2
Current ratio: 4.49
Long-term debt ($ mil.): —

No. of shares (mil.): 229.0
Dividends
Yield: 0.5%
Payout: 36.3%
Market value ($ mi.): 14,302.0

	STOCK PRICE ($) FY Close	P/E High/Low		PER SHARE ($) Earnings	Dividends	Book Value
12/20	62.45	74	39	0.88	0.32	18.79
12/19	46.35	88	63	0.54	0.24	15.18
Annual Growth	34.7%	—		—	63.0%	33.3%	23.8%

TransUnion

Auditors: PricewaterhouseCoopers LLP

LOCATIONS

HQ: TransUnion
555 West Adams, Chicago, IL 60661
Phone: 312 985-2000
Web: www.transunion.com

HISTORICAL FINANCIALS
Company Type: Public

Income Statement

FYE: December 31

	REVENUE ($ mil.)	NET INCOME ($ mil.)	NET PROFIT MARGIN	EMPLOYEES
12/21	2,960.2	1,387.1	46.9%	10,200
12/20	2,716.6	343.2	12.6%	8,200
12/19	2,656.1	346.9	13.1%	8,000
12/18	2,317.2	276.6	11.9%	7,100
12/17	1,933.8	441.2	22.8%	5,100
Annual Growth	11.2%	33.2%	—	18.9%

2021 Year-End Financials

Debt ratio: 50.3%
Return on equity: 43.0%
Cash ($ mil.): 1,842.4
Current ratio: 1.94
Long-term debt ($ mil.): 6,251.3

No. of shares (mil.): 191.8
Dividends
Yield: 0.3%
Payout: 14.7%
Market value ($ mil.): 22,744.0

	STOCK PRICE ($) FY Close	P/E High/Low		PER SHARE ($) Earnings	Dividends	Book Value
12/21	118.58	17	12	7.19	0.36	20.38
12/20	99.22	56	30	1.79	0.30	13.33
12/19	85.61	47	29	1.81	0.30	11.90
12/18	56.80	51	35	1.45	0.23	10.18
12/17	54.96	23	13	2.32	0.00	9.44
Annual Growth	21.2%	—		—	32.7%	—	21.2%

Trex Co Inc

Trex Company is one of the world's largest maker of wood-alternative decking and railing products which are used in the construction of residential and commercial decks and rails. Marketed under the Trex name products resemble wood and have the workability of wood but require less long-term maintenance. The Trex Residential composite is made of waste wood fibers and reclaimed plastic. Trex serves professional installation contractors and do-it-yourselfers through the company's more than 50 distributors and merchandisers which in turn sell to retailers including Home Depot and Lowe's. Trex products are available in more than 40 countries worldwide.

Operations

Trex operates in two reportable segments: Trex Residential Products (Trex Residential) and Trex Commercial Products (Trex Commercial).

Trex Residential which generates about 95% of the company's total sales offers a comprehensive set of aesthetically appealing and durable low-maintenance product offerings in the decking railing fencing steel deck framing and outdoor lighting categories.

Trex Commercial (more than 5% of total sales) is a leading national provider of custom-engineered railing and staging systems. The segment designs and engineers' custom railing solutions which target commercial and high-rise applications and portable staging equipment for the performing arts sports and event production and rental market.

Trex produces three principal decking products: Trex Transcend Trex Enhance and Trex Select. Its railing products include Trex Transcend Railing Trex Select Railing Trex Enhance Railing and Trex

Signature aluminum railing. The company's collection also includes Trex Seclusions (a fencing product) Trex DeckLighting (a deck lighting system) and Trex Hideaway (a hidden fastening system for specially grooved boards). The company also has polyethylene pellets made from recycled plastic that it sells to plastic bag and film makers.

Geographic Reach

Based in Virginia Trex has its Trex Residential manufacturing facilities in Virginia and Nevada while its Trex Commercial has a manufacturing facility in Minnesota. It operates globally through international dealers and retailers.

Sales and Marketing

The company's Trex Residential products are sold to distributors and home centers for final resale primarily to the residential market while its Trex Commercial products are marketed to architects specifiers contractors and building owners. Its wood is also the only composite lumber to be code-listed by the nation's building code agencies.

For the years ended in 2020 2019 and 2018 the company's branding expenses including advertising expenses were $31.7 million $35.7 million and $35.0 million respectively.

Financial Performance

The company in 2020 had an increase in net sales of 18% or $135.5 million to $880.8 million in the twelve months ended December 31 2020 compared to $745.3 million in the twelve months ended December 31 2019.

In 2020 the company had a net income of $175.6 million.

The company's cash at the end of 2020 was $121.7 million. Operating activities generated $187.3 million while investing activities used $170.7 million mainly for capital expenditures. Financing activities used another $43.8 million primarily for principal payments under line of credit.

Strategy

Trex' long-term goals are to continue leading the category with beautiful high-performance low-maintenance Trex products including outdoor living products such as composite decking and railing for the residential market and custom-engineered railing systems for the commercial market. To do this the company will increase market share and expand into new product categories and geographic markets through the design creation and marketing of outdoor living products that offer superior aesthetics and quality and by expanding sales to the commercial market. Trex Residential will expand its offering of eco-friendly decking and railing products for a breadth of audiences whether by converting wood buyers who have not previously considered composite decking or appealing to the most discriminating high-end homeowners seeking superior aesthetics and quality. Trex Commercial will extend its position as a leading national provider of custom-engineered railing for the commercial and multi-family market including sports stadiums. Additionally Trex will continue to explore opportunities that leverage its manufacturing and extrusion expertise and recycling heritage.

It intends to employ long-term strategies to achieve its goals through innovation brand channels quality cost and customer service.

Company Background

Trex was formed in 1996 through a buyout of a division of Mobil Corporation. It went public in 1999.

412   HOOVER'S HANDBOOK OF EMERGING COMPANIES 2022

EXECUTIVES

President, Chief Executive Officer, Director, Bryan Fairbanks, $496,500 total compensation
President - Trex Residential Products, Adam Zambanini, $393,750 total compensation
Senior Vice President, General Counsel, Secretary, William Gupp, $372,600 total compensation
Independent Director, Kristine Juster
Independent Director, Gena Lovett
Vice Chairman Of The Board, Ronald Kaplan
Chairman Of The Board, James Cline, $195,082 total compensation
Independent Director, Gerald Volas
Chief Financial Officer, Senior Vice President, Dennis Schemm, $242,964 total compensation
Auditors: Ernst & Young LLP

LOCATIONS

HQ: Trex Co Inc
160 Exeter Drive, Winchester, VA 22603-8605
Phone: 540 542-6300
Web: www.trex.com

PRODUCTS/OPERATIONS

Selected Brands
Decking
  Trex Accents
  Trex Enhance
  Trex Escapes
  Trex Select
  Trex Transcend
Deck Lighting System
  Trex DeckLighting
Fencing
  Trex Seclusions
Hidden Fastening System
  Trex Hideaway
Porch
  Trex Transcend Porch Flooring & Railing System
PVC Outdoor Trim
  TrexTrim
Railing
  Trex Designer Series
  Trex Transcend
Steel Deck Framing System
  Trex Elevations

Selected Products
Decking
Fencing
Railing
Trim

COMPETITORS

ARMSTRONG WORLD INDUSTRIES INC.
ASSOCIATED MATERIALS LLC
CORNERSTONE BUILDING BRANDS INC.
Canfor Corporation
ENVIVA INC.
HUTTIG BUILDING PRODUCTS INC.
Interfor Corporation
J. D. Irving Limited
Q.E.P. CO. INC.
SIERRA PACIFIC INDUSTRIES
TOPBUILD CORP.

HISTORICAL FINANCIALS
Company Type: Public

Income Statement
FYE: December 31

	REVENUE ($ mil.)	NET INCOME ($ mil.)	NET PROFIT MARGIN	EMPLOYEES
12/20	880.8	175.6	19.9%	1,719
12/19	745.3	144.7	19.4%	1,173
12/18	684.2	134.5	19.7%	1,214
12/17	565.1	95.1	16.8%	815
12/16	479.6	67.8	14.1%	830
Annual Growth	16.4%	26.8%	—	20.0%

2020 Year-End Financials

Debt ratio: —
Return on equity: 33.7%
Cash ($ mil.): 121.7
Current ratio: 3.03
Long-term debt ($ mil.): —
No. of shares (mil.): 115.8
Dividends
  Yield: —
  Payout: —
Market value ($ mil.): 9,695.0

	STOCK PRICE ($) FY Close	P/E High/Low		PER SHARE ($) Earnings	Dividends	Book Value
12/20	83.72	102	41	1.51	0.00	5.08
12/19	89.88	74	47	1.24	0.00	3.86
12/18	59.36	113	47	1.14	0.00	2.93
12/17	108.39	145	77	0.81	0.00	1.96
12/16	64.40	123	56	0.57	0.00	1.14
Annual Growth	6.8%		—	—	27.4%	— 45.3%

Tri Pointe Homes Inc

EXECUTIVES

Ceo, Douglas Bauer
Chb*, Barry S Sternlicht
Ceo*, Douglas F Bauer
Pres-Coo, Thomas J Mitchell
Cfo-Treas, Michael D Grubbs
V Pres-Cao-Contrl, Glenn Keeler
V Pres-General Counsel-Sec, Bradley W Blank
Vice President Finance, Scott Pasternak
Customer Representativ, Horacio Gutierrez
Customer Representativ, Ron Babot
Pres-Home Bldg Colorado Div, Darren Dupree
Auditors: Ernst & Young LLP

LOCATIONS

HQ: Tri Pointe Homes Inc
940 Southwood Blvd., Suite 200, Incline Village, NV 89451
Phone: 775 413-1030
Web: www.tripointehomes.com

HISTORICAL FINANCIALS
Company Type: Public

Income Statement
FYE: December 31

	REVENUE ($ mil.)	NET INCOME ($ mil.)	NET PROFIT MARGIN	EMPLOYEES
12/21	3,970.7	469.2	11.8%	1,390
12/20	3,251.3	282.2	8.7%	1,163
12/19	3,079.0	207.1	6.7%	1,386
12/18	3,261.0	269.9	8.3%	1,435
12/17	2,808.9	187.1	6.7%	1,251
Annual Growth	9.0%	25.8%	—	2.7%

2021 Year-End Financials

Debt ratio: 30.8%
Return on equity: 20.0%
Cash ($ mil.): 681.5
Current ratio: 21.07
Long-term debt ($ mil.): 1,337.7
No. of shares (mil.): 109.6
Dividends
  Yield: —
  Payout: —
Market value ($ mil.): 3,058.0

	STOCK PRICE ($) FY Close	P/E High/Low		PER SHARE ($) Earnings	Dividends	Book Value
12/21	27.89	7	4	4.12	0.00	22.32
12/20	17.25	9	3	2.17	0.00	18.32
12/19	15.58	11	8	1.47	0.00	16.06
12/18	10.93	11	6	1.81	0.00	14.52
12/17	17.92	15	9	1.21	0.00	12.77
Annual Growth	11.7%		—	— 35.8%	—	15.0%

TriCo Bancshares (Chico, CA)

People looking for a community bank in California's Sacramento Valley can try TriCo. TriCo Bancshares is the holding company for Tri Counties Bank which serves customers through some 65 traditional and in-store branches in 23 counties in Northern and Central California. Founded in 1974 Tri Counties Bank provides a variety of deposit services including checking and savings accounts money market accounts and CDs. Most patrons are retail customers and small to midsized businesses. The bank primarily originates real estate mortgages which account for about 65% of its loan portfolio; consumer loans contribute about 25%. TriCo has agreed to acquire rival North Valley Bancorp.

Operations

In addition to its retail banking products and services the company provides wholesale banking and investment services; TriCo offers brokerage services through an arrangement with Raymond James Financial. The company does not provide trust or international banking services.

Geographic Reach

Based in Chico California Tri Counties Bank operates 66 branches (41 traditional branches and 25 in-store branches) in 23 counties in Northern and central California including Fresno Kern Mendocino Napa Sacramento and Yuba counties.

Financial Performance

In 2013 net interest income the company's primary source of revenue rose 0.6% compared with 2012 to $102.2 million. The slight increase in net interest income was mainly due to a decrease in average balance of other borrowings a shift in deposit balances from relatively high interest rate earning time deposits to noninterest-earning demand and savings deposits an increase in the average balance of investments securities and an increase in the average balance of loans; all of which were substantially offset by a decrease in the average yield on loans.

Strategy

The bank's growth has been fueled by acquisitions and the opening of new branches; it frequently opens branches within grocery stores or other retailers including Wal-Mart. TriCo in 2010 acquired the three branches of Granite Community Bank which had been seized by regulators. The transaction which also included most of the failed bank's assets and deposits was facilitated by the FDIC and includes a loss-sharing agreement with the agency. The following year TriCo acquired Citizens Bank of Northern California. The FDIC-assisted deal included seven branches. The acquisitions are part of TriCo's strategy of adding new customers.

Mergers and Acquisitions

TriCo in January 2014 announced plans to buy its rival in Northern California North Valley Bancorp (NVB) for about $178.4 million. NVB is the parent company of North Valley Bank which had about $918 million in assets and 22 commercial banking offices across eight Northern California counties at the end of 2013. At closing which is expected in the second or third quarter of 2014 NVB will be merged into Tri Counties Bank. The combined bank would have about $3.6 billion in assets.

EXECUTIVES

Chairman Of The Board, President, Chief Executive Officer, Richard Smith, $825,000 total compensation
Independent Director, John Hasbrook
Independent Director, Donald Amaral
Executive Vice President, Chief Credit Officer Of Bank, Craig Carney, $400,000 total compensation
Independent Director, Michael Koehnen
Lead Independent Director, Cory Giese
Chief Financial Officer, Executive Vice President Of Trico And Tri Counties Bank, Peter Wiese, $480,000 total compensation
Independent Director, Martin Mariani
Independent Director, L. Gage Chrysler
Senior Vice President, General Counsel, Gregory Gehlmann
Independent Director, Thomas McGraw
Independent Director, Margaret Kane
Independent Director, Kirsten Garen
Independent Director, Kimberley Vogel
Chief Human Resource Officer, Senior Vice President, Judi Giem
Executive Vice President And Chief Retail Banking Officer, Daniel Bailey, $400,000 total compensation
Chief Operating Officer, Executive Vice President, John Fleshood, $428,480 total compensation
Auditors: Moss Adams LLP

LOCATIONS

HQ: TriCo Bancshares (Chico, CA)
63 Constitution Drive, Chico, CA 95973
Phone: 530 898-0300
Web: www.tcbk.com

PRODUCTS/OPERATIONS

2015 Sales

	$ mil.	% of total
Interest		
Loans including fees	131.8	64
Debt securities	26.8	13
Dividends	2.1	1
Other	0.7	-
Noninterest		
Service charges & fees	31.8	16
Commissions	3.4	2
Gain on sale of loans	3.1	1
Other	7.1	3
Total	**206.8**	**100**

Selected Services

Business debit cards
Business online banking
Business workshops
Cash management
Education savings and CDs
Loans and credits
Merchant services
Order checks
Overdraft services
Pension and retirement
Personal certificates of deposit
Personal checking
Personal savings and money market
Retirement savings and CDs

COMPETITORS

BANK OF BARODA	HSBC USA INC.
COMMONWEALTH BANK OF FINANCIAL AUSTRALIA	MAINSOURCE FINANCIAL GROUP INC.
COMMUNITY BANK OF THE BAY	NEVADA STATE BANK
BAY INC.	NORTHWEST BANCORP INC.
F.N.B. CORPORATION	OLD NATIONAL BANCORP
FB CORPORATION	S & T BANCORP INC.
FIRST COMMUNITY BANKSHARES INC.	SHINSEI BANK LIMITED SOUTHWEST BANCORP
INC.	
HERITAGE FINANCIAL CORPORATION	UniCredit Bank AG WILSHIRE BANCORP INC.

HISTORICAL FINANCIALS

Company Type: Public

Income Statement

FYE: December 31

	ASSETS ($ mil.)	NET INCOME ($ mil.)	INCOME AS % OF ASSETS	EMPLOYEES
12/20	7,639.5	64.8	0.8%	1,068
12/19	6,471.1	92.0	1.4%	1,184
12/18	6,352.4	68.3	1.1%	1,174
12/17	4,761.3	40.5	0.9%	1,023
12/16	4,517.9	44.8	1.0%	1,063
Annual Growth	14.0%	9.7%	—	0.1%

2020 Year-End Financials

Return on assets: 0.9%
Return on equity: 7.0%
Long-term debt ($ mil.): —
No. of shares (mil.): 29.7
Sales ($ mil): 322.3

Dividends
Yield: 2.4%
Payout: 41.5%
Market value ($ mil.): 1,049.0

	STOCK PRICE ($) FY Close	P/E High/Low	PER SHARE ($) Earnings	Dividends	Book Value
12/20	35.28	19 11	2.16	0.88	31.12
12/19	40.81	14 11	3.00	0.82	29.70
12/18	33.79	16 12	2.54	0.70	27.20
12/17	37.86	25 19	1.74	0.66	22.03
12/16	34.18	18 12	1.94	0.60	20.87
Annual Growth	0.8%	— —	2.7%	10.0%	10.5%

Trimble Inc

Trimble Inc. is a leading provider of technology solutions that enable professionals and field mobile workers to improve or transform their work processes. The company makes GPS Global Navigation Satellite System laser and optical technologies inertial or other technologies to establish real-time position. The company's products target areas such as agriculture architecture civil engineering survey construction geospatial government natural resources transportation and utilities. Trimble sells to end users such as government entities farmers engineering and construction firms as well as equipment manufacturers. More than half of the company's sales were generated in the North America.

HISTORY

Charles Trimble founded Trimble Navigation in 1978 to design navigation products for recreational boating. In 1982 the company began developing devices using the Global Positioning System (GPS) satellite network; in 1984 Trimble introduced its first GPS product. The company went public in 1990 10 days before Saddam Hussein invaded Kuwait. Trimble gained worldwide recognition when allied troops used its GPS devices during the Persian Gulf War.

The war left Trimble expanding too quickly and overproducing. In 1992 Trimble rebounded after reorganizing to focus on nonmilitary products. Two years later it introduced a low-cost handheld unit that helped with utilities fieldwork. In 1998 Trimble ceased manufacturing products for general aviation and allied with Siemens to develop GPS products. That year Charles Trimble was named vice chairman after he stepped down as the company's CEO. The company in 1998 also launched a cost reduction plan that cut its workforce by 8%.

The next year Trimble sold its Sunnyvale California manufacturing operations to contract manufacturer Solectron which agreed to make Trimble's GPS and radio-frequency products for three years. Also in 1999 Steven Berglund a former president of a Spectra-Physics subsidiary was named CEO of Trimble.

In 2000 Trimble acquired the Spectra Precision businesses of Thermo Electron (which later became Thermo Fisher Scientific) for about $294 million. That year the US government stopped scrambling GPS signals opening the door for more precise devices. In 2001 the company formed a subsidiary Trimble Information Services to expand the company's wireless location-based services including fleet management.

The next year Trimble and Caterpillar formed a joint venture Caterpillar Trimble Control Technologies to develop advanced electronic guidance and control technologies for earth-moving construction and mining machines.

The company acquired Eleven Technology a mobile application software developer focused on the consumer packaged goods market in 2006. The company also expanded its laser scanning business by acquiring the assets — including software for engineering and construction plant design — of BitWyse Solutions. Later in 2006 it purchased Visual Statement a developer of crime and collision incident investigation software and XYZ Solutions a 3-D intelligence software provider. It also acquired Meridian Systems a provider of enterprise project management and lifecycle software. Still later in 2006 Trimble bought Spacient Technologies a privately held provider of field service management and mobile mapping software used by municipalities and utilities.

414 HOOVER'S HANDBOOK OF EMERGING COMPANIES 2022

Trimble's buying spree continued in 2007 when it purchased @Road a developer of mobile resource management systems for about $493 million.

The company expanded its ability to serve the farming industry when it acquired NTech Industries in 2009. NTech developed optical crop-sensing technology that helps farmers reduce costs by managing the application of nitrogen herbicides and other crop inputs. Also that year Trimble purchased Accutest Engineering Solutions a UK-based maker of mobile resource management applications for trucking fleets.

In 2010 Trimble acquired Punch Telematix from majority shareholder Punch International for nearly ?14 million ($18 million) in cash and rebranded it as Trimble Transport and Logistics. Punch Telematix made onboard computers for trucks. That year the company also bought ThingMagic a developer of radio frequency identification (RFID) products and RFID integration services for commercial clients in the construction and transportation industries and Cengea a provider of operations and supply chain management software for the forestry agriculture and natural resource industries.

Additionally Trimble bought Mumbai-based Tata AutoComp Mobility Telematics (TMT) in a move to expand its mobile resource management services business in India. TMT provided vehicle tracking and other telematics services to such customers as Bharat Petroleum and Tata Motors. Also that year expanding its engineering and construction portfolio for electrical and mechanical contractors Trimble bought the assets of Accubid a provider of estimating project management and service management software.

Trimble bought 3D modeling software maker Tekla in 2011 in a deal valued at nearly ?340 million ($485 million) to better equip building contractors and engineers to manage construction projects. The follow-up investment came in 2012 when Trimble completed the acquisition of the StruCad and StruEngineer business from AceCad Software. StruCad offers 3D structural detailing while StruEngineer provides engineering companies with 3D steelwork modeling and construction management.

The company acquired a line of software products in 2011 from Norway-based Mesta Entrepren ,r a subsidiary of road and highway construction contractor Mesta Konsern. The deal added office and field data collection applications and improved the company's ability to provide customized systems to construction clients particularly in the area of managing local application requirements compliance. Also in 2011 Trimble strengthened its portfolio and Asia presence with the purchase of China-based Yamei Electronics a manufacturer of electronic automotive products including anti-theft GPS monitoring and tracking systems RFID smart keys and diagnostics systems.

Also that year Trimble acquired the OmniSTAR satellite system assets of Dutch geological engineering company Fugro. The company was interested in OmniSTAR's GPS signal correction technology (used to improve the accuracy of satellite navigation devices) which it is using to expand the functionality of its mapping systems for agricultural and construction purposes among others. It also acquired France-based Ashtech to expand Garmin's selection of survey products including the flagship application Spectra Precision for con-

struction clients. Ashtech became part of Trimble's engineering and construction division.

EXECUTIVES

Director, Thomas Sweet
Senior Vice President - Natural Resources Businesses, Darryl Matthews, $456,106 total compensation
Senior Vice President - Trimble Transportation Businesses, James Langley, $425,769 total compensation
Chief Financial Officer, David Barnes, $519,231 total compensation
Executive Chairman, Board Of Directors, Steven Berglund, $839,808 total compensation
Senior Vice President - Construction Businesses, Bryn Fosburgh, $459,586 total compensation
Vice President, Finance And Chief Accounting Officer, Julie Shepard, $256,058 total compensation
Senior Vice President, General Counsel, Secretary, James Kirkland, $413,000 total compensation
Senior Vice President - Trimble's Surveying And Geospatial Businesses, Ronald Bisio
President, Chief Executive Officer And Director, Robert Painter, $870,950 total compensation
Independent Director, Johan Wibergh
Independent Director, Sandra Macquillan
Independent Director, E. Boerje Ekholm
Director, Ann Fandozzi
Chief Technology Officer, Poppy Crum
Chief Platform Officer, Jennifer Lin
Auditors: Ernst & Young LLP

LOCATIONS

HQ: Trimble Inc
935 Stewart Drive, Sunnyvale, CA 94085
Phone: 408 481-8000
Web: www.trimble.com

PRODUCTS/OPERATIONS

2018 Sales

	% of total
Buildings and Infrastructure	35
Geospatial	23
Resources and Utilities	18
Transportation	24
Total	**100**

COMPETITORS

AGCO CORPORATION	MITAC INTERNATIONAL
DEERE & COMPANY	CORPORATION
Garmin Ltd.	QUALCOMM
INCORPORATED	
Leica Geosystems AG	
MAXAR TECHNOLOGIES	
INC.	

HISTORICAL FINANCIALS

Company Type: Public

Income Statement — FYE: December 31

	REVENUE ($ mil.)	NET INCOME ($ mil.)	NET PROFIT MARGIN	EMPLOYEES
12/21*	3,659.1	492.7	13.5%	11,931
01/21	3,147.7	389.9	12.4%	11,402
01/20	3,264.3	514.3	15.8%	11,484
12/18	3,108.4	282.8	9.1%	11,287
12/17	2,654.2	121.1	4.6%	9,523
Annual Growth	**8.4%**	**42.0%**	**—**	**5.8%**

*Fiscal year change

2021 Year-End Financials

Debt ratio: 18.2%	No. of shares (mil.): 250.9
Return on equity: 13.1%	Dividends
Cash ($ mil.): 325.7	Yield: —
Current ratio: 1.22	Payout: —
Long-term debt ($ mil.): 1,293.2	Market value ($ mil.): 21,876.0

	STOCK PRICE ($) FY Close	P/E High/Low	PER SHARE ($) Earnings	Dividends	Book Value
12/21*	87.19	49 34	1.94	0.00	15.72
01/21	66.77	43 14	1.55	0.00	14.34
01/20	41.51	22 15	2.03	0.00	12.48
12/18	31.94	40 27	1.12	0.00	10.66
12/17	40.64	89 61	0.47	0.00	9.51
Annual Growth	**21.0%**	**— —**	**42.5%**	**—**	**13.4%**

*Fiscal year change

TriState Capital Holdings Inc

TriState Capital Holdings has found its niche right in the middle of the banking industry. The holding company owns TriState Capital Bank a regional business bank that caters to middle-market businesses executives and high-net-worth individuals. TriState Capital has three wholly owned subsidiaries: TriState Capital Bank Chartwell Investment Partners LLC and Chartwell TSC Securities Corp. Its loan portfolio consists of less than 50% for middle-market banking loans less than 30% commercial real estate loans and more than 50% for private banking loans. The bank serves clients from branches in Cleveland; New Jersey; New York City Philadelphia and Pittsburgh. Altogether it has $7.6 billion in assets.

Operations

The company operates two reportable segments: Bank and Investment Management.

The Bank segment provides commercial banking products and services to middle-market businesses and private banking products and services to high-net-worth individuals through the Bank. The Investment Management segment provides investment management services primarily to institutional investors mutual funds and individual investors through Chartwell and also supports marketing efforts for Chartwell's proprietary investment products through CTSC Securities.

Geographic Reach

Headquartered in Pittsburgh Pennsylvania the company also leases office space for each of the four representative bank offices in the metropolitan areas of Philadelphia Pennsylvania; Cleveland Ohio; Edison New Jersey; and New York New York; and it leases office space for Chartwell Investment Partners LLC in Berwyn Pennsylvania.

Sales and Marketing

The company caters to middle-market businesses. Its primary markets and private banking business also serve high-net-worth individuals on a national basis. It primarily sources this business through referral relationships with independent broker/dealers wealth managers family offices

HOOVER'S HANDBOOK OF EMERGING COMPANIES 2022

415

trust companies and other financial intermediaries. In addition its distribution channels pursue and create deposit relationships including treasury management relationships with customers in its primary markets and throughout the US.

Financial Performance

In 2019 total revenue increased $18.0 million or 11% to $179.4 million from $161.4 million in 2018 driven largely by higher net interest income and swap fees for the Bank.

In 2019 the company's net was $54.4 million compared to $52.3 million in 2018 an increase of $2.1 million or 4%. This increase was primarily due to the net impact of a $13.7 million or 12% increase in its net interest income; an increase in the credit to provision for loan and lease losses of $0.8 million; an increase of $4.9 million or 10% in non-interest income; offset by an increase of $11.0 million or 11% in our non-interest expense; a $2.5 million increase in income taxes; and an increase in preferred stock dividends of $3.6 million.

Cash held by the company at the end of 2019 increased to $403.9 million compared to the prior year with $213.9 million. Cash provided by operations and financing activities were $68.2 million and $1.6 billion respectively. Cash used for investing activities was $1.5 billion mainly for net increase in loans and leases.

Strategy

Tristate Capital's success has been built upon the vision and focus of its executive management team to combine the sophisticated products services and risk management efforts of a large financial institution with the personalized service of a community bank. The company believe that a results-based culture combined with a well-managed middle-market and private banking business and its targeted investment management business will continue to grow and generate attractive returns for shareholders. The following are the key components of the company's business strategies: Sales and Distribution Culture; Disciplined Risk Management; Experienced Professionals; Lending Strategy; Deposit Funding Strategy; and Investment Management Strategy.

Company Background

TriState Capital was founded in 2007 by two banking industry executives — chairman and CEO James Getz who spent 20 years at Federated Investors and vice chairman William Schenck the former secretary of banking for Pennsylvania.

EXECUTIVES

Vice Chairman Of The Board, A. William Schenck
Independent Director, Eugene Dewhurst
Independent Director, Helen Casey
Independent Director, Anthony Buzzelli
Executive Officer, Timothy Riddle, $400,000 total compensation
Independent Director, Michael Harris
Independent Director, Audrey Dunning
Independent Director, Christopher Doody
Independent Director, Kim Ruth
President, Chief Executive Officer, Director, Brian Fetterolf, $595,833 total compensation
Chief Financial Officer, David Demas, $450,000 total compensation
Independent Director, John Yasinsky
Executive Chairman Of The Board, James Getz, $945,000 total compensation
Auditors: KPMG LLP

LOCATIONS

HQ: TriState Capital Holdings Inc
One Oxford Centre, 301 Grant Street, Suite 2700, Pittsburgh, PA 15219
Phone: 412 304-0304   **Fax:** 412 304-0391
Web: www.tristatecapitalbank.com

PRODUCTS/OPERATIONS

2015 Sales

	% of total
Interest income	
Loans	67
Investments	3
Interest-earning deposits	-
Noninterest income	
Investment management fees	25
Commitment and other fees	2
Other income	3
Total	**100**

COMPETITORS

BANCFIRST CORPORATION
BOSTON PRIVATE FINANCIAL HOLDINGS INC.
COMMERCE BANCSHARES INC.
FIRST EAGLE PRIVATE CREDIT LLC
FIRST FINANCIAL BANCORP.
LADENBURG THALMANN FINANCIAL SERVICES INC.
M&T BANK CORPORATION
OPPENHEIMER HOLDINGS INC.
PEAPACK-GLADSTONE FINANCIAL CORPORATION
SIGNATURE BANK
WEBSTER FINANCIAL CORPORATION
WINTRUST FINANCIAL CORPORATION

HISTORICAL FINANCIALS
Company Type: Public

Income Statement
FYE: December 31

	ASSETS ($ mil.)	NET INCOME ($ mil.)	INCOME AS % OF ASSETS	EMPLOYEES
12/20	9,896.8	45.2	0.5%	308
12/19	7,765.8	60.1	0.8%	276
12/18	6,035.6	54.4	0.9%	257
12/17	4,777.9	37.9	0.8%	230
12/16	3,930.4	28.6	0.7%	224
Annual Growth	**26.0%**	**12.1%**	**—**	**8.3%**

2020 Year-End Financials

Return on assets: 0.5%
Return on equity: 6.5%
Long-term debt ($ mil.): —
No. of shares (mil.): 32.6
Sales ($ mil): 274.3
Dividends
Yield: —
Payout: —
Market value ($ mil.): 568.0

	STOCK PRICE ($) FY Close	P/E High/Low		Earnings	PER SHARE ($) Dividends	Book Value
12/20	17.40	20	6	1.30	0.00	23.21
12/19	26.12	13	10	1.89	0.00	21.16
12/18	19.46	16	10	1.81	0.00	16.60
12/17	23.00	18	15	1.32	0.00	13.61
12/16	22.10	22	11	1.01	0.00	12.38
Annual Growth	**(5.8%)**	**—**	**—**	**6.5%**	**—**	**17.0%**

Triumph Bancorp Inc

Auditors: Crowe LLP

LOCATIONS

HQ: Triumph Bancorp Inc
12700 Park Central Drive, Suite 1700, Dallas, TX 75251
Phone: 214 365-6900
Web: www.triumphbancorp.com

HISTORICAL FINANCIALS
Company Type: Public

Income Statement
FYE: December 31

	ASSETS ($ mil.)	NET INCOME ($ mil.)	INCOME AS % OF ASSETS	EMPLOYEES
12/21	5,956.2	112.9	1.9%	1,250
12/20	5,935.7	64.0	1.1%	1,125
12/19	5,060.3	58.5	1.2%	1,107
12/18	4,559.7	51.7	1.1%	1,121
12/17	3,499.0	36.2	1.0%	820
Annual Growth	**14.2%**	**32.9%**	**—**	**11.1%**

2021 Year-End Financials

Return on assets: 1.9%
Return on equity: 14.2%
Long-term debt ($ mil.): —
No. of shares (mil.): 25.1
Sales ($ mil): 442.0
Dividends
Yield: —
Payout: —
Market value ($ mil.): 2,996.0

	STOCK PRICE ($) FY Close	P/E High/Low		Earnings	PER SHARE ($) Dividends	Book Value
12/21	119.08	30	11	4.35	0.00	34.14
12/20	48.55	20	8	2.53	0.00	29.23
12/19	38.02	17	12	2.25	0.00	25.50
12/18	29.70	22	13	2.03	0.00	23.62
12/17	31.50	19	11	1.81	0.00	18.81
Annual Growth	**39.4%**	**—**	**—**	**24.5%**	**—**	**16.1%**

TTEC Holdings Inc

TTEC Holdings (formerly TeleTech Holdings) is leading global call center operator. The company provides a range of business process outsourcing (BPO) services in five areas: customer acquisition customer care fraud prevention technology services and professional services. The company serves more than 300 global clients and maintains a network of some 90 facilities in about two dozen countries around the world. Customers mainly major global enterprises come from sectors such as automotive communications financial services government health care logistics media and entertainment retail technology and travel and transportation industries. TTEC also offers management consulting services. Most of the company's sales are generated in the US accounting to around 60% of total sales.

Operations

Effective mid-2019 the segment information was reported consistent with these updated reportable segments comprised of TTEC Engage and TTEC Digital.

TTEC Engage segment accounts for more than 80% of revenue and provides the essential technologies human resources infrastructure and processes to operate customer care acquisition and fraud detection and prevention services. It operated under three services: Customer Acquisition; Customer Care and Fraud Prevention.

TTEC Digital segment (generates about 20% of company's total revenue) designs builds and delivers tech-enabled insight-based and outcome-driven customer experience solutions through our professional services and suite of technology offerings. It also provides Technology Services and Professional Services.

Geographic Reach

Headquartered in Englewood Colorado TTEC has almost 90 delivery centers across North America (US Mexico Canada) Europe (Bulgaria the UK Ireland Germany Poland Greece) and Asia (Thailand India) and the Pacific Rim (China the Philippines Australia). The company also has centers in South Africa and Brazil.

The US accounts for around 60% of the company's revenue. Other major markets include the Philippines (nearly 25%) and Latin America (some 5%).

Sales and Marketing

TTEC has expertise in several major industries including automotive communications government healthcare logistics financial services media and entertainment retail technology travel and transportation industries. It targets Global 1000 clients and serves about 300 clients around the world.

In 2019 the company's top five and ten clients represented more than 35% and 50% of total revenue respectively. Certain of their communications clients provide them with telecommunication services through arm's length negotiated transactions. These clients currently represent over 10% of the total annual revenue.

Financial Performance

In 2019 the company's revenue increased 9% to $1.6 billion over 2018 including an increase of less than 1% or $0.8 million due to foreign currency fluctuations and a decrease of $17.9 million or 1% due to the initial adoption of ASC 606 for revenue in the first quarter of 2018. The increase in revenue was comprised of a $66.5 million or 28% increase for TTEC Digital and a $68.0 million or 5% increase for TTEC Engage.

Profits rose to $77.2 million from $35.8 million in 2018 due to lower other expenses including interest expense.

Cash on hand at the end of 2019 sat at $105.6 million an increase of $27.4 million in cash from the prior year. Cash from operating activities provided $238.0 million while investing activities used $162.9 million partially on property plant and equipment purchases. Financing activities used $47.4 million mostly for debt repayment and dividends paid to shareholders.

Strategy

TTEC Holdings aim to grow its revenue and profitability by focusing on its core customer engagement operational capabilities linking them to higher - margin insights and technology-enabled platforms and managed services to drive a superior experience for their clients' customers. To that end the company continually strive to build deeper more strategic relationships with existing global clients to drive enduring transformational change within its organizations; Pursue new clients who lead its respective industries and who are committed to customer engagement as a differentiator; Invest in its sales leadership team at both the segment level to improve collaboration and speed-to-market and consultative sales level to deliver more integrated strategic and transformational solutions;

Execute strategic acquisitions that further complement and expands its integrated solutions; Invest in technology-enabled platforms and innovation through technology advancements broader and globally protected intellectual property and process optimization; and Work within the company's technology partner ecosystem to deliver best in class solutions with expanding intellectual property through value-add applications integrations services and solutions.

Mergers and Acquisitions

In mid-2020 TTEC Holdings announced that it agreed to acquire VoiceFoundry a global partner of Amazon Web Services creating an end-to-end CX delivery solution for Amazon Connect. The US and European parts of the acquisition has now closed with the Australian and ASEAN acquisition expected to close pending regulatory approvals. By leveraging Amazon Connect CX leaders can increase the ease and speed with which businesses improve customer service. Terms were not disclosed.

In early 2020 the company announced that it has acquired a majority interest in Serendebyte - Headquartered in Dallas Texas an intelligent automation CX solutions provider. Serendebyte strengthens TTEC's ability to deliver intelligent automation solutions globally. The acquisition also expands TTEC's network of engineers and developers to provide a combination of robotics-powered case management AI and analytics. Financial terms were not disclosed.

In 2019 TTEC Holdings Inc. acquired FCR a US-based digitally enabled customer experience provider focused on the direct to consumer e-commerce and hypergrowth markets. The acquisition is anticipated to be immediately accretive and is aligned to TTEC's continued focus on driving organic growth through the omnichannel enablement of the most innovative and disruptive brands in the digital economy. Terms not disclosed.

Company Background

While still in his teens Kenneth Tuchman and his California surfing buddies got stoked on importing Philippine seashells to satisfy the 1970s craze for puka shell necklaces. In 1982 Tuchman founded TeleTech using the money he had earned from selling Christmas trees and luxury cars. He set up his first call center in an abandoned nursery school. The company moved to Denver in 1993 and went public in 1996. The company shortened its name to TTEC in 2018.

EXECUTIVES

Chairman And Chief Executive Officer, Kenneth Tuchman, $1 total compensation
Senior Vice President, Treasurer, Investor Relations Officer, Paul Miller
Executive Vice President, Chief Revenue Officer, Judi Hand, $400,000 total compensation
Global Chief Operating Officer, Regina Paolillo, $425,000 total compensation
Independent Director, Gregory Conley
Independent Director, Robert Frerichs
Independent Director, Marc Holtzman
Independent Director, Ekta Singh-bushell
Independent Director, Steven Anenen
President - Ttec Digital Business, George Demou
Senior Vice President, Global Head Of Ttec Engage Business Segment, Richard Erickson, $99,615 total compensation
Chief Financial Officer, Dustin Semach

Senior Vice President, Chief Risk Officer, General Counsel, Margaret McLean, $375,000 total compensation
Auditors: PricewaterhouseCoopers LLP

LOCATIONS

HQ: TTEC Holdings Inc
9197 South Peoria Street, Englewood, CO 80112
Phone: 303 397-8100
Web: www.ttec.com

PRODUCTS/OPERATIONS

2018 Sales

	$ mil.	% of total
Customer Management Services	1,129.1	75
Customer Technology Services	170.2	11
Customer Growth Services	141.3	9
Customer Strategy Services	68.6	5
Total	**1,509.2**	**100**

Selected Operations & Services

Account collections
Benefits and claims administration
Complex customer management
Customer acquisition
Customer retention
Customer support
Data collection
Direct sales and marketing
Loan processing
Outbound calling
Payroll administration
Recruiting staffing and workforce management
Service provisioning
Training development and delivery
Vendor management
Consulting
Technology
Care services
Growth services

COMPETITORS

ASGN INCORPORATED	MANPOWERGROUP INC.
CSG SYSTEMS INTERNATIONAL INC.	PROS HOLDINGS INC.
EPAM SYSTEMS INC.	ROBERT HALF INTERNATIONAL INC.
EPLUS INC.	SYNERGIE
GP STRATEGIES CORPORATION	TD SYNNEX CORPORATION
KELLY SERVICES INC.	TRUEBLUE INC.

HISTORICAL FINANCIALS

Company Type: Public

Income Statement

FYE: December 31

	REVENUE ($ mil.)	NET INCOME ($ mil.)	NET PROFIT MARGIN	EMPLOYEES
12/20	1,949.2	118.6	6.1%	61,000
12/19	1,643.7	77.1	4.7%	49,500
12/18	1,509.1	35.8	2.4%	52,400
12/17	1,477.3	7.2	0.5%	56,000
12/16	1,275.2	33.6	2.6%	48,000
Annual Growth	11.2%	37.0%	—	6.2%

2020 Year-End Financials

Debt ratio: 25.3%	No. of shares (mil.): 46.7
Return on equity: 27.4%	Dividends
Cash ($ mil.): 132.9	Yield: 3.9%
Current ratio: 1.66	Payout: 132.1%
Long-term debt ($ mil.): 385.0	Market value ($ mil.): 3,409.0

	STOCK PRICE ($)		P/E		PER SHARE ($)		
	FY Close		High/Low	Earnings	Dividends		Book Value
12/20	72.93		31 11	2.52	2.88		9.51
12/19	39.62		30 17	1.65	0.62		9.00
12/18	28.57		54 31	0.77	0.55		7.47
12/17	40.25		271180	0.16	0.47		7.76
12/16	30.50		45 34	0.71	0.39		7.70
Annual Growth	24.4%		—	— 37.3%	65.4%		5.4%

Turning Point Brands Inc

Auditors: RSM US LLP

LOCATIONS

HQ: Turning Point Brands Inc
5201 Interchange Way, Louisville, KY 40229
Phone: 502 778-4421
Web: www.turningpointbrands.com

HISTORICAL FINANCIALS
Company Type: Public

Income Statement				FYE: December 31
	REVENUE ($ mil.)	NET INCOME ($ mil.)	NET PROFIT MARGIN	EMPLOYEES
12/20	405.1	33.0	8.2%	408
12/19	361.9	13.7	3.8%	466
12/18	332.6	25.2	7.6%	520
12/17	285.7	20.2	7.1%	289
12/16	206.2	26.9	13.1%	286
Annual Growth	18.4%	5.3%	—	9.3%

2020 Year-End Financials

Debt ratio: 62.5%	No. of shares (mil.): 19.1
Return on equity: 28.2%	Dividends
Cash ($ mil.): 41.7	Yield: 0.4%
Current ratio: 2.78	Payout: 11.9%
Long-term debt ($ mil.): 294.0	Market value ($ mil.): 853.0

	STOCK PRICE ($)		P/E		PER SHARE ($)		
	FY Close		High/Low	Earnings	Dividends		Book Value
12/20	44.56		28 9	1.67	0.20		6.63
12/19	28.60		78 29	0.69	0.18		5.42
12/18	27.22		34 15	1.28	0.17		4.23
12/17	21.13		20 12	1.04	0.04		2.78
12/16	12.25		10 4	1.49	0.00		1.85
Annual Growth	38.1%		—	— 2.9%			— 37.6%

Turtle Beach Corp

Using proprietary technology Turtle Beach (formerly Parametric Sound) makes speakers that offer focused and directional sound for an immersive experience. Its current product is the HS-3000 line of speakers for the commercial market including digital kiosks and slot machines. The company is developing its Hypersonic line for the consumer market where it hopes its thin two-speaker system will rival traditional multi-speaker setups used for surround sound and be used in computers video games and mobile devices. Turtle Beach sells its products in North America Asia and Europe to OEMs for inclusion in new and existing products.

EXECUTIVES

Chairman Of The Board, President, Chief Executive Officer, Juergen Stark, $550,000 total compensation
Independent Director, Andrew Wolfe
Lead Independent Director, William Keitel
Independent Director, Kelly Thompson
Independent Director, Yie-hsin Hung
Independent Director, L. Gregory Ballard
Chief Financial Officer, Treasurer, Secretary, John Hanson, $365,000 total compensation
Auditors: BDO USA, LLP

LOCATIONS

HQ: Turtle Beach Corp
44 South Broadway, 4th Floor, White Plains, NY 10601
Phone: 888 496-8001
Web: www.parametricsound.com

COMPETITORS

A&R CAMBRIDGE LIMITED INC.
ALPS ALPINE CO. LTD.
CONTROL4 CORPORATION
FKA DISTRIBUTING CO. LLC
Grass Valley Canada
HIWAVE TECHNOLOGIES PLC
MICROVISION INC.
NEONODE INC.
RUBICON TECHNOLOGY INC.
YAMAHA GUITAR GROUP INC.

HISTORICAL FINANCIALS
Company Type: Public

Income Statement				FYE: December 31
	REVENUE ($ mil.)	NET INCOME ($ mil.)	NET PROFIT MARGIN	EMPLOYEES
12/20	360.0	38.7	10.8%	300
12/19	234.6	17.9	7.6%	245
12/18	287.4	39.1	13.6%	154
12/17	149.1	(3.2)	—	135
12/16	173.9	(87.1)	—	172
Annual Growth	19.9%	—	—	14.9%

2020 Year-End Financials

Debt ratio: —	No. of shares (mil.): 15.4
Return on equity: 42.9%	Dividends
Cash ($ mil.): 46.6	Yield: —
Current ratio: 2.16	Payout: —
Long-term debt ($ mil.): —	Market value ($ mil.): 333.0

	STOCK PRICE ($)		P/E		PER SHARE ($)		
	FY Close		High/Low	Earnings	Dividends		Book Value
12/20	21.55		10 2	2.37	0.00		7.52
12/19	9.45		14 7	1.04	0.00		4.38
12/18	14.27		11 0	2.74	0.00		2.63
12/17	0.45		— —	(0.28)	0.00		(1.79)
12/16	1.31		— —	(7.16)	0.00		(1.68)
Annual Growth	101.4%		—	— —			—

Tyler Technologies, Inc.

Tyler Technologies is a major provider of integrated information management solutions and services for the public sector with a focus on local governments. Tyler's products include software for accounting and financial management filing court documents electronically tracking and managing court cases and automating appraisals and assessments. Other products include applications that allow citizens to access utility accounts or pay transactions online. The company counts approximately 3000 counties some 36000 cities and towns and around 12900 school districts customers in all 50 states Canada the Caribbean Australia and the UK.

Operations

The company divides its operations into two segments — enterprise software and appraisal and tax software.

Enterprise software which accounts for some 90% of sales provides public sector entities with software and services for back-office functions such as financial management and courts and justice processes. Appraisal and tax software which makes up the other some 10% of sales provides systems and software that automate the appraisal and assessment of real and personal property land and vital records management as well as property appraisal outsourcing services for local governments and taxing authorities.

Property appraisal outsourcing services include: the physical inspection of commercial and residential properties; data collection and processing; computer analysis for property valuation; preparation of tax rolls; community education; and arbitration between taxpayers and the assessing jurisdiction.

Overall maintenance accounts for over 40% of sales around 30% comes from subscription software services account for over 15% and software licenses and royalties with around 5%. Appraisal services and hardware & other accounts for the rest.

Geographic Reach

Headquartered in Texas Tyler Technologies own or lease offices for its major operations in the states of Arizona Arkansas California Colorado Connecticut Georgia Illinois Iowa Maine Massachusetts Michigan Missouri Montana New Hampshire New York North Carolina Ohio Tennessee Texas Virginia Washington Washington D.C. Wisconsin Ontario and British Columbia Canada Bahamas and the Philippines.

Sales and Marketing

The company uses a direct sales force and marketing personnel. It participates in government associations and attends annual meetings trade shows and educational events to attract new customers. Its customers are primarily county and municipal agencies school districts and other local government offices.

Financial Performance

The company's revenue in fiscal 2020 increased by 3% to $1.12 billion compared to 2019 with $1.09 billion. The increase was due to higher software services and maintenance revenues.

Net income for fiscal 2020 increased to $194.8 million compared from the prior year with $146.5 million.

Cash held by the company at the end of fiscal 2020 increased to $603.6 million. Cash provided by operations and financing activities were $355.1 million and $114.2 million respectively. Cash used for investing activities was $98.3 million mainly for the purchase of marketable security investments.

Strategy

The company's objective is to grow its revenue and earnings organically supplemented by focused strategic acquisitions.

The key components of its business strategy are to: Provide high quality value?added products and services to its clients; Continue to expand its product and service offerings; Expand its client base; Expand its existing client relationships; Grow recurring revenues; Maximize economies of scale and take advantage of financial leverage in its business; Attract and retain highly qualified employees; Pursue selected strategic acquisitions; and Establish strategic alliances.

Mergers and Acquisitions

In 2021 Tyler Technologies has completed the previously announced acquisition of Kansas-based NIC a leading digital government solutions and payments company that serves more than 7100 federal state and local government agencies across the nation for approximately $2.3 billion. With the addition of NIC's highly complementary industry-leading digital government solutions and payment services to Tyler's broad client base and multiple sales channels the combined company will be well equipped to address the tremendous demand at the federal state and local levels for innovative platform solutions.

Also in 2021 Tyler Technologies Inc. has acquired ReadySub a cloud-based platform based in Washington which assists school districts with absence tracking filling substitute teacher assignments and automating essential payroll processes. The acquisition of ReadySub strengthens Tyler's school portfolio and brings more comprehensive solutions to the school districts that it serves. Additionally ReadySub can integrate with districts' payroll processes eliminating duplicate work and streamlining related payroll tasks. Terms were not disclosed.

In early 2021 Tyler Technologies Inc. has acquired DataSpec a market leader dedicated to providing better electronic management of veterans' claims based in Michigan. DataSpec was developed by sisters Tina Roff and Ann Graham. The acquisition offers existing DataSpec clients the strength and stability of Tyler as well as a simple path forward to a next generation of technology. This acquisition will position Tyler as the new market leader in veterans' benefits management solutions. Tyler also has the opportunity to expand its veteran-focused software offerings to VA departments in additional states. Terms were not disclosed.

Company Background

Formerly an auto parts and supplies company established in 1966 Tyler sold its chain of auto parts stores in 1999 and used acquisitions to transform itself into a provider of software for the local government and education markets

EXECUTIVES

Chairman, John Marr, $300,000 total compensation
Chief Financial Officer, Executive Vice President, Treasurer, Brian Miller, $400,000 total compensation

President, Chief Executive Officer And Director, H. Lynn Moore, $525,000 total compensation
Independent Director, Mary Landrieu
Independent Director, Brenda Cline
Independent Director, Daniel Pope
Chief Information Officer, Kevin Iwersen
Auditors: Ernst & Young LLP

LOCATIONS

HQ: Tyler Technologies, Inc.
5101 Tennyson Parkway, Plano, TX 75024
Phone: 972 713-3700
Web: www.tylertech.com

PRODUCTS/OPERATIONS

2014 Sales

	% of total
Enterprise software	89
Appraisal & tax software	11
Corporate	-
Total	**100**

2014 Sales

	% of total
Maintenance	43
Software services	23
Subscriptions	18
Software licenses and royalties	10
Appraisal services	4
Hardware & other	2
Total	**100**

Selected Products

Appraisal and assessment software (property appraisal and assessment)
Criminal justice software (court case tracking and management)
Document management and recording software (image storage and retrieval)
Education software
Finance and accounting software
Law enforcement and corrections software (police dispatch records and jail management)
Municipal court software (case management)
Odyssey (case and court management)
Public Records and content management
Tax collections software (tax collections office operations)
Utility billing software (billing and collections)

Selected Services

Information technology and professional services
Maintenance
Outsourced property appraisals for tax jurisdictions

COMPETITORS

AMERICAN SOFTWARE INC.	LIMELIGHT NETWORKS
APPIAN CORPORATION	INC.
BENTLEY SYSTEMS	LINEDATA SERVICES
INCORPORATED	Open Text Corporation
BLACK KNIGHT INC.	PAYLOCITY HOLDING
CAPITA PLC	CORPORATION
CASS INFORMATION	PREMIER INC.
SYSTEMS INC.	R C M TECHNOLOGIES
CORELOGIC INC.	INC.
CORNERSTONE ONDEMAND	SS&C
TECHNOLOGIES	
INC.	HOLDINGS INC.
GUIDEWIRE SOFTWARE	STEWART INFORMATION
INC.	SERVICES CORPORATION

HISTORICAL FINANCIALS
Company Type: Public

Income Statement
FYE: December 31

	REVENUE ($ mil.)	NET INCOME ($ mil.)	NET PROFIT MARGIN	EMPLOYEES
12/21	1,592.2	161.4	10.1%	6,800
12/20	1,116.6	194.8	17.4%	5,536
12/19	1,086.4	146.5	13.5%	5,368
12/18	935.2	147.4	15.8%	4,525
12/17	840.6	163.9	19.5%	4,069
Annual Growth	17.3%	(0.4%)	—	13.7%

2021 Year-End Financials

Debt ratio: 28.3%	No. of shares (mil.): 41.3
Return on equity: 7.4%	Dividends
Cash ($ mil.): 309.1	Yield: —
Current ratio: 1.16	Payout: —
Long-term debt ($ mil.): 1,311.2	Market value ($ mil.): 22,226.0

	STOCK PRICE ($) FY Close	P/E High/Low	PER SHARE ($) Earnings	Dividends	Book Value
12/21	537.95	140 96	3.82	0.00	56.25
12/20	436.52	95 54	4.69	0.00	48.99
12/19	300.02	79 47	3.65	0.00	41.14
12/18	185.82	65 45	3.68	0.00	34.61
12/17	177.05	42 33	4.18	0.00	30.81
Annual Growth	32.0%	— —	(2.2%)	—	16.2%

U&I Financial Corp

Auditors: Moss Adams LLP

LOCATIONS

HQ: U&I Financial Corp
19315 Highway 99, Lynnwood, WA 98036
Phone: 425 275-9700
Web: www.unibankusa.com

HISTORICAL FINANCIALS
Company Type: Public

Income Statement
FYE: December 31

	REVENUE ($ mil.)	NET INCOME ($ mil.)	NET PROFIT MARGIN	EMPLOYEES
12/20	21.3	6.2	29.1%	0
12/19	20.1	5.6	27.9%	0
12/18	16.0	4.5	28.1%	0
12/17	12.6	3.2	25.3%	0
12/16	14.1	3.5	25.2%	0
Annual Growth	10.8%	14.8%	—	—

2020 Year-End Financials

Debt ratio: 1.2%	No. of shares (mil.): 5.5
Return on equity: 11.3%	Dividends
Cash ($ mil.): 24.9	Yield: —
Current ratio: 0.08	Payout: —
Long-term debt ($ mil.): 5.0	Market value ($ mil.): 50.0

	STOCK PRICE ($)		P/E		PER SHARE ($)		
	FY Close		High/Low	Earnings	Dividends	Book Value
12/20	8.90		9 6	1.12	0.00	10.59
12/19	9.25		9 8	1.02	0.00	9.05
12/18	9.00		12 10	0.82	0.34	7.72
12/17	9.00		16 14	0.58	0.24	7.23
12/16	8.50		13 10	0.71	0.00	7.41
Annual Growth	1.2%		— —	12.1%	—	9.4%

Ubiquiti Inc

EXECUTIVES

Chairman Of The Board, Chief Executive Officer, Founder, Robert Pera
Chief Accounting And Finance Officer, Kevin Radigan, $420,000 total compensation
Independent Director, Brandon Arrindell
Independent Director, Rafael Torres
Auditors: KPMG LLP

LOCATIONS

HQ: Ubiquiti Inc
685 Third Avenue, 27th Floor, New York, NY 10017
Phone: 646 780-7958
Web: www.ubnt.com

HISTORICAL FINANCIALS

Company Type: Public

Income Statement   FYE: June 30

	REVENUE ($ mil.)	NET INCOME ($ mil.)	NET PROFIT MARGIN	EMPLOYEES
06/21	1,898.0	616.5	32.5%	1,223
06/20	1,284.5	380.3	29.6%	1,021
06/19	1,161.7	322.6	27.8%	955
06/18	1,016.8	196.2	19.3%	843
06/17	865.2	257.5	29.8%	725
Annual Growth	21.7%	24.4%	—	14.0%

2021 Year-End Financials

Debt ratio: 55.1%
Return on equity: ***,***.*%
Cash ($ mil.): 249.4
Current ratio: 2.51
Long-term debt ($ mil.): 467.0

No. of shares (mil.): 62.5
Dividends
Yield: 0.5%
Payout: 18.2%
Market value ($ mil.): 19,538.0

	STOCK PRICE ($)		P/E		PER SHARE ($)		
	FY Close		High/Low	Earnings	Dividends	Book Value
06/21	312.19		40 16	9.78	1.60	0.04
06/20	174.56		34 19	5.80	1.20	(4.64)
06/19	131.50		38 18	4.51	1.00	1.43
06/18	84.72		35 20	2.51	0.00	4.26
06/17	51.97		20 12	3.09	0.00	7.50
Annual Growth 56.6% (72.5%)			— —	33.4%	—	

Ultra Clean Holdings Inc

Ultra Clean Holdings is a leading developer and supplier of critical subsystems ultra-high purity cleaning and analytical services primarily for the semiconductor industry. The company which does business as Ultra Clean Technology (UCT) designs engineers and manufactures production tools modules and subsystems for the semiconductor and display capital equipment markets. UCT has extended its know-how in the semiconductor industry to move into display consumer medical industrial research and energy markets. Majority of the company's sales were generated from the US. UCT was founded as a unit of Mitsubishi Metals in 1991.

Operations

The company operates and reports results for two operating segments: Products (around 80% of sales) and Services (nearly 20%).

Its Products business primarily designs engineers and manufactures production tools modules and subsystems for the semiconductor and display capital equipment markets. Products include chemical delivery modules frame assemblies gas delivery systems fluid delivery systems precision robotics process modules as well as other high-level assemblies.

Its Services business provides ultra-high purity parts cleaning process tool part recoating surface encapsulation and high sensitivity micro contamination analysis primarily for the semiconductor device makers and wafer fabrication equipment (WFE) markets.

Geographic Reach

Headquartered in Hayward California Ultra Clean Technology manufacturing and engineering facilities in California Texas Arizona China Singapore Philippines and Czech Republic. The Company has parts cleaning analytics and engineering facilities in Colorado Arizona California Oregon Maine Texas Israel Taiwan South Korea Singapore and China. It also owns buildings and land that are located in South Korea China and the United Kingdom.

Approximately 45% of sales were generated in the US followed by Singapore with nearly 35% while Korea Taiwan China and Austria generated around 5% each.

Sales and Marketing

Ultra Clean Technology sells its products and services primarily to customers in the semiconductor capital equipment and semiconductor integrated device manufacturing industries and it also sells to the display consumer medical energy industrial and research equipment industries. The majority of its total revenues comes from the semiconductor capital equipment industry (OEM customers) which is highly concentrated After several round of consolidation in the semiconductor industry just two customers account for over 65% of UCT's revenue. They are LAM Research and Applied Materials which accounted for more than 10% each.

Financial Performance

Ultra Clean Holdings has seen its revenues rise in the last five years despite a slight fall in 2019. Revenues grew about 150% between 2016 and 2020 while net income increased by over 600% in the same period despite a loss in 2019.

Revenues for 2020 were $1.4 billion a 31% from the year prior. Total Products revenues increased that year primarily due to an increase in customer demand in the semiconductor industry while total Services revenue also increased due to increases in demand across its customer base. On a geographic basis the US and foreign revenue both increased due to an overall increase in demand in the semiconductor industry.

From a loss of $9.4 million in 2019 Ultra Clean posted a net income of $77.6 million in 2020. The recovery was mainly due to the increase in revenue despite the increase in costs and expenses.

Ultra Clean held $200.3 million in cash and equivalents at the end of the period an increase of $37.8 million from the year prior. Operating activities contributed $97.3 million to the coffers while investing and financing activities used $29.8 million and $31.1 million respectively. The company's main cash uses in 2020 were capital expenditures and principal payments on bank borrowings and finance leases.

Strategy

Ultra Clean Holdings' strategy is to grow its position and enhance its value to its customers as a leading solution and service provider in the semiconductor markets it serves while supporting other technologically similar markets in the display consumer medical energy industrial and research industries.

The company's strategy is comprised of the following key elements: expanding its solutions and service market share with semiconductor OEMs and IDMs; developing or acquiring solutions that allow its customers to succeed at the leading edge of the semiconductor processing nodes; leveraging its geographic presence in lower cost manufacturing regions; providing production flexibility to respond rapidly to demand changes; driving profitable growth with its flexible cost structure; continuing to selectively pursue strategic acquisitions; and strengthening vertical integration.

Mergers and Acquisitions

In early 2021 Ultra Clean has completed the acquisition of Ham-Let (Israel-Canada) Ltd. (Ham-Let) for approximately $351 million. Ham-Let Group is one of the world's leading companies in development manufacturing and distribution of industrial flow control systems ? connectors fittings and valves for high pressure and high temperatures transmission systems (gases and liquids). The acquisition expands UCT's addressable market in semiconductors and increases UCT's vertical capabilities and adds high value high gross margin product offerings.

EXECUTIVES

Chairman, Clarence Granger
Independent Director, David Ibnale
Chief Executive Officer And Director, James Scholhamer, $590,031 total compensation
Senior Vice President, Global Human Resources, Joan Sterling, $265,245 total compensation
Independent Director, Barbara Scherer
Chief Financial Officer, Sheri Savage, $424,462 total compensation
Senior Vice President, Chief Accounting Officer, Chris Siu
President , Products Business, W. Joseph Williams, $417,231 total compensation
General Counsel, Corporate Secretary, Paul Cho

President - Fluid Solutions, Amir Widmann
Chief Operating Officer, Vijayan Chinnasami, $497,242 total compensation
President, Services Division, Bill Bentinck, $406,677 total compensation
Auditors: Moss Adams LLP

LOCATIONS

HQ: Ultra Clean Holdings Inc
26462 Corporate Avenue, Hayward, CA 94545
Phone: 510 576-4400
Web: www.uct.com

COMPETITORS

ALLEGRO MICROSYSTEMS LLC
APPLIED MATERIALS INC.
BARNES GROUP INC.
Ballard Power Systems Inc
DIODES INCORPORATED
ENTEGRIS INC.
EXAR CORPORATION
FORMFACTOR INC.
JABIL INC.
LAM RESEARCH CORPORATION
MACOM TECHNOLOGY SOLUTIONS HOLDINGS INC.
MATTSON TECHNOLOGY INC.
MKS INSTRUMENTS INC.
NORDSON CORPORATION
ON SEMICONDUCTOR CORPORATION
ONTO INNOVATION INC.
PHOTRONICS INC.
ULTRATECH INC.

HISTORICAL FINANCIALS

Company Type: Public

Income Statement
FYE: December 25

	REVENUE ($ mil.)	NET INCOME ($ mil.)	NET PROFIT MARGIN	EMPLOYEES
12/20	1,398.6	77.6	5.5%	4,996
12/19	1,066.2	(9.4)	—	4,400
12/18	1,096.5	36.6	3.3%	4,280
12/17	924.3	75.0	8.1%	2,747
12/16	562.7	10.0	1.8%	2,183
Annual Growth	25.6%	66.7%	—	23.0%

2020 Year-End Financials

Debt ratio: 24.4%	No. of shares (mil.): 40.6
Return on equity: 16.0%	Dividends
Cash ($ mil.): 200.3	Yield: —
Current ratio: 2.71	Payout: —
Long-term debt ($ mil.): 261.6	Market value ($ mil.): 1,285.0

	STOCK PRICE ($) FY Close	P/E High/Low		PER SHARE ($) Earnings	Dividends	Book Value
12/20	31.65	19	6	1.89	0.00	13.12
12/19	23.40	—	—	(0.24)	0.00	10.94
12/18	8.21	28	8	0.94	0.00	11.17
12/17	23.09	15	4	2.19	0.00	8.92
12/16	9.70	34	15	0.30	0.00	6.56
Annual Growth	34.4%			— — 58.4%	—	18.9%

UMB Financial Corp

UMB Financial Is a financial holding company that provides banking services and asset servicing to its customer in the US and around the globe.

The company's national bank UMB Bank offers a full complement of banking products and other services to commercial retail government and correspondent-bank customers including a wide range of asset-management trust bankcard and cash-management services. The bank operates more than 90 banking centers. Loans represent the company's largest source of interest income with commercial loans having the largest percent of total loans. Beyond its banking business it offers insurance brokerage services leasing treasury management health savings accounts and proprietary mutual funds.

Operations

The company's products and services are grouped into three segments: Commercial Banking Institutional Banking and Personal Banking. In early 2020 the company merged the Healthcare Services segment into the Institutional Banking segment to better reflect how the core businesses products and services are currently being evaluated by management.

Commercial Banking serves the commercial banking and treasury management needs of the company's small to mid-market businesses through a variety of products and services. Such services include commercial loans commercial real estate financing commercial credit cards letters of credit loan syndication services consultative services. Its specialty lending group offers solutions such as asset-based lending accounts receivable financing mezzanine debt and minority equity investments. It also offers treasury management services including depository services account reconciliation and cash management tools. The segment accounts for about half of total revenue.

Institutional Banking is a combination of banking services fund services asset management services and healthcare services provided to institutional clients. This segment also provides fixed income sales trading and underwriting corporate trust and escrow services as well as institutional custody. The segment accounts for nearly 30% of total revenue.

Personal Banking combines consumer banking and wealth management services offered to clients and delivered through personal relationships and the company's bank branches ATM network and internet banking. Products offered include deposit accounts retail credit cards private banking installment loans home equity lines of credit residential mortgages and small business loans. The segment accounts for about 20% of total revenue.

Overall net interest income generates about 60% of total revenue.

Geographic Reach

UMB Financial is headquartered in Kansas City Missouri and has branches in Arizona Colorado Illinois Kansas Nebraska Oklahoma and Texas.

Sales and Marketing

UMB Financial serves small to mid-market businesses institutional clients insurance carriers third-party administrators employers and financial institutions among others through its branches ATM network and internet banking.

The company's marketing and business development expenses were $14.7 million $26.3 million and $24.4 million in 2020 2019 and 2018 respectively.

Financial Performance

UMB Financial recorded consolidated income from continuing operations of $286.5 million for 2020 an increase of nearly 18% from 2019. The company's net interest income increased to $731.2 million in 2020 compared to $670.9 million in 2019. The favorable volume variance on earning assets was predominantly driven by the increase in average loan balances of $2.4 billion or 18.5% for 2020 compared to the same period in 2019.

The company ended 2020 with cash and cash equivalents of $3.5 billion. Operating activities generated $373.6 million; investing activities used $4.5 billion mainly for purchases of securities available for sale and due to net increase in loans; financing activities provided $5.9 billion.

The company's loan assets grew by 20% to $16.1 billion in 2020 from $13.4 billion in 2019.

Strategy

UMB Financial is dedicated to creating the Unparalleled Customer Experience and its associates are critical to achieving this mission. As part of its efforts to recruit and retain top talent the company strives to offer competitive compensation and benefits programs while fostering a culture rooted in the inclusion of a diverse mix of associates who are empowered to be part of something more.

Company Background

To grow its fee-based business and diversify its business model UMB has made several acquisitions in its past. The company built up its investment advisory and corporate trust business through several 2009 purchases. In 2010 UMB made 10 acquisitions including Prairie Capital Management and Indiana-based Reams Asset Management. The deals more than doubled UMB's Scout Investment Advisors' assets under management to more than $27 billion.

EXECUTIVES

President Of Consumer Banking Of Umb Bank, N.a., Abigail Wendel
Executive Vice President, Chief Credit Officer, Thomas Terry, $360,962 total compensation
Chairman Of The Board, President, Chief Executive Officer, J. Mariner Kemper, $940,032 total compensation
Executive Vice President, General Counsel, Corporate Secretary Of The Company And The Bank, John Pauls
Executive Vice President And Director Of Operations Of Umb Bank, N.a., Kevin Macke, $324,077 total compensation
Executive Vice President, Chief Administrative Officer, Shannon Johnson, $379,038 total compensation
President Of Institutional Banking Of Umb Bank, N.a., James Cornelius, $405,385 total compensation
Chief Financial Officer, Executive Vice President, Ram Shankar, $403,077 total compensation
Executive Vice President, Chief Risk Officer, Stacy King
Vice Chairman Of The Company And President, Chief Executive Officer Of Umb Bank, N.a., James Rine, $542,115 total compensation
Senior Vice President, Chief Accounting Officer, Controller, David Odgers
President Of Private Wealth Management Of Umb Bank, N.a., Nikki Newton
Chief Human Resource Officer, Executive Vice President, Robert Beaird
Independent Director, Janine Davidson
Auditors: KPMG LLP

LOCATIONS

HQ: UMB Financial Corp
1010 Grand Boulevard, Kansas City, MO 64106
Phone: 816 860-7000   **Fax:** 816 860-7143
Web: www.umb.com

PRODUCTS/OPERATIONS

2016 Sales

	$ mil.	% of total
Interest income		
Loans	386.3	29
Securities	131.0	13
Federal funds and resell agreements	2.7	-
Interest-bearing due from banks	2.4	
Trading securities	0.6	
Non-interest income		
Trust and securities processing	239.9	24
Trading and investment banking	21.5	2
Service charges on deposit accounts	86.7	9
Insurance fees and commissions	4.1	-
Brokerage fees	17.8	2
Bankcard fees	68.8	7
Gains on sales of securities available for sale net	8.5	1
Equity earnings (losses) on alternative investments	2.7	-
Other	26.1	3
Total	**999.1**	**100**

Selected Subsidiaries & Affiliates

Grand Distribution Services LLC
J.D. Clark & Company
Kansas City Financial Corporation
Kansas City Realty Company
Prairie Capital Management LLC
Scout Distributors LLC
Scout Investment Advisors Inc.
UMB Banc Leasing Corp.
UMB Bank and Trust n.a.
UMB Bank Arizona n.a.
UMB Bank Colorado n.a.
UMB Capital Corporation
UMB Community Development Corporation
UMB Distribution Services LLC
UMB Financial Services Inc.
UMB Fund Services Inc.
UMB Insurance Inc.
UMB National Bank of America
UMB Realty Company LLC
UMB Redevelopment Corporation
UMB Trust Company of South Dakota
United Missouri Insurance Company

COMPETITORS

BOK FINANCIAL CORPORATION
BOKF MERGER CORPORATION NUMBER SIXTEEN
Banco Bradesco S/A
COMMERCE BANCSHARES INC.
F.N.B. CORPORATION
FIRST BUSINESS FINANCIAL SERVICES INC.
FIRST HORIZON CORPORATION
FIRST MIDWEST BANCORP INC.
FIRSTMERIT CORPORATION
HSBC Bank Canada
M&T BANK CORPORATION
MUFG AMERICAS HOLDINGS CORPORATION
NATIONAL BANK HOLDINGS CORPORATION
PACWEST BANCORP
PRIVATEBANCORP INC.
SIMMONS FIRST NATIONAL CORPORATION
TCF FINANCIAL CORPORATION
THE BANCORP INC
THE PNC FINANCIAL SERVICES GROUP INC
WEBSTER FINANCIAL CORPORATION
WINTRUST FINANCIAL CORPORATION
WSFS FINANCIAL CORPORATION

HISTORICAL FINANCIALS

Company Type: Public

Income Statement

FYE: December 31

	ASSETS ($ mil.)	NET INCOME ($ mil.)	INCOME AS % OF ASSETS	EMPLOYEES
12/20	33,127.5	286.5	0.9%	3,591
12/19	26,561.3	243.6	0.9%	3,670
12/18	23,351.1	195.5	0.8%	3,573
12/17	21,771.5	247.1	1.1%	3,570
12/16	20,682.5	158.8	0.8%	3,688
Annual Growth	12.5%	15.9%		(0.7%)

2020 Year-End Financials

Return on assets: 0.9%
Return on equity: 10.1%
Long-term debt ($ mil.): —
No. of shares (mil.): 48.0
Sales ($ mil): 1,368.6

Dividends
Yield: 1.8%
Payout: 30.7%
Market value ($ mil.): 3,312.0

	STOCK PRICE ($) FY Close	P/E High/Low		PER SHARE ($) Earnings	Dividends	Book Value
12/20	68.99	12	7	5.93	1.25	62.84
12/19	68.64	14	12	4.96	1.21	53.09
12/18	60.97	20	15	3.93	1.17	45.37
12/17	71.92	16	13	4.96	1.04	43.72
12/16	77.12	25	13	3.22	0.99	39.51
Annual Growth	(2.7%)	—	—	16.5%	6.0%	12.3%

Union Bankshares, Inc. (Morrisville, VT)

Union Bankshares is the holding company for Union Bank which serves individuals and small to mid-sized businesses in northern Vermont and Northwestern New Hampshire through 17 branches; it opened its first office in New Hampshire in 2006. Founded in 1891 the bank offers standard deposit products such as savings checking money market and NOW accounts as well as certificates of deposit retirement savings programs investment management and trust services. It uses fund from deposits primarily to originate commercial real estate loans and residential real estate loans. Other loan products include business consumer construction and municipal loans.

EXECUTIVES

President, Chief Executive Officer Of The Company And Bank, Director, David Silverman, $415,385 total compensation
Vice President, Jeffrey Coslett, $165,842 total compensation
Independent Chairman Of The Board, Cornelius Van Dyke
Chief Financial Officer, Vice President, Treasurer, Karyn Hale, $217,046 total compensation
Independent Director, Nancy Putnam
Independent Director, Joel Bourassa
Independent Director, Gregory Sargent
Auditors: Berry Dunn McNeil & Parker, LLC

LOCATIONS

HQ: Union Bankshares, Inc. (Morrisville, VT)
20 Lower Main Street, P.O. Box 667, Morrisville, VT 05661
Phone: 802 888-6600
Web: www.ublocal.com

COMPETITORS

COMMERCIAL NATIONAL FINANCIAL CORPORATION
LIBERTY BANCORP INC.

HISTORICAL FINANCIALS

Company Type: Public

Income Statement

FYE: December 31

	ASSETS ($ mil.)	NET INCOME ($ mil.)	INCOME AS % OF ASSETS	EMPLOYEES
12/20	1,093.5	12.8	1.2%	193
12/19	872.9	10.6	1.2%	201
12/18	805.3	7.0	0.9%	195
12/17	745.8	8.4	1.1%	194
12/16	691.3	8.5	1.2%	191
Annual Growth	12.1%	10.8%		0.3%

2020 Year-End Financials

Return on assets: 1.3%
Return on equity: 16.7%
Long-term debt ($ mil.): —
No. of shares (mil.): 4.4
Sales ($ mil): 52.7

Dividends
Yield: 4.9%
Payout: 48.8%
Market value ($ mil.): 115.0

	STOCK PRICE ($) FY Close	P/E High/Low		PER SHARE ($) Earnings	Dividends	Book Value
12/20	25.71	13	6	2.85	1.28	18.05
12/19	36.26	21	11	2.38	1.24	16.07
12/18	47.75	34	28	1.58	1.20	14.44
12/17	52.95	29	21	1.89	1.16	13.14
12/16	45.45	26	14	1.91	1.11	12.61
Annual Growth	(13.3%)	—	—	10.5%	3.6%	9.4%

United Bancorp, Inc. (Martins Ferry, OH)

United Bancorp is the holding company of Ohio's Citizens Savings Bank which operates as Citizens Savings Bank and The Community Bank. The bank divisions together operate some 20 branches offering deposit and lending products including savings and checking accounts commercial and residential mortgages and consumer installment loans. Commercial loans and mortgages combined account for about 60% of the company's loan portfolio. In 2008 Citizens Savings Bank acquired the deposits of three failed banking offices from the FDIC.

EXECUTIVES

President, Chief Executive Officer, Director, Scott Everson, $356,853 total compensation
Independent Chairman Of The Board, Richard Riesbeck
Chief Operating Officer, Senior Vice President, Matthew Branstetter, $197,118 total compensation
Independent Director, John Hoopingarner
Independent Director, Gary Glessner
Auditors: BKD, LLP

LOCATIONS

HQ: United Bancorp, Inc. (Martins Ferry, OH)
201 South Fourth Street, Martins Ferry, OH 43935-0010
Phone: 740 633-0445   **Fax:** 740 633-1448
Web: www.unitedbancorp.com

COMPETITORS

EMCLAIRE FINANCIAL CORP.

UNITED BANCSHARES INC.
VOLUNTEER BANCORP INC

HISTORICAL FINANCIALS

Company Type: Public

Income Statement — FYE: December 31

	ASSETS ($ mil.)	NET INCOME ($ mil.)	INCOME AS % OF ASSETS	EMPLOYEES
12/20	693.4	7.9	1.1%	132
12/19	685.7	6.8	1.0%	132
12/18	593.2	4.2	0.7%	132
12/17	459.3	3.5	0.8%	126
12/16	438.0	3.5	0.8%	138
Annual Growth	12.2%	22.1%	—	(1.1%)

2020 Year-End Financials

Return on assets: 1.1%
Return on equity: 12.3%
Long-term debt ($ mil.): —
No. of shares (mil.): 5.7
Sales ($ mil): 34.5

Dividends
Yield: 4.3%
Payout: 45.9%
Market value ($ mil.): 76.0

	STOCK PRICE ($) FY Close	P/E High/Low		PER SHARE ($) Earnings	Dividends	Book Value
12/20	13.18	11	7	1.39	0.57	11.80
12/19	14.30	13	9	1.19	0.55	10.86
12/18	11.43	17	13	0.82	0.57	8.82
12/17	13.25	19	16	0.71	0.51	8.37
12/16	13.50	19	12	0.71	0.47	8.19
Annual Growth	(0.6%)	—	—	18.3%	4.9%	9.6%

United Bancshares Inc. (OH)

United Bancshares is a blend of checks and (account) balances. The institution is the holding company for The Union Bank Company a community bank serving northwestern Ohio through about a dozen branches. The commercial bank offers such retail services and products as checking and savings accounts NOW and money market accounts IRAs and CDs. It uses funds from deposits to write commercial loans (about half of its lending portfolio) residential mortgages agriculture loans and consumer loans. The Union Bank Company was originally established in 1904.

EXECUTIVES

President, Chief Executive Officer, Interim Chief Financial Officer, Director, Brian Young, $355,183 total compensation
Independent Director, David Roach, $24,900 total compensation

Independent Director, Steven Unverferth, $25,500 total compensation
Independent Director, Robert Benroth, $29,000 total compensation
Chairman Of The Board, Daniel Schutt, $31,900 total compensation
Secretary, Heather Oatman, $138,192 total compensation
Independent Director, H. Edward Rigel, $26,100 total compensation
Independent Director, Herbert Huffman, $24,900 total compensation
Auditors: Clifton Gunderson LLP

LOCATIONS

HQ: United Bancshares Inc. (OH)
105 Progressive Drive, Columbus Grove, OH 45830
Phone: 419 659-2141
Web: www.theubank.com

COMPETITORS

CITIZENS BANK INC
COMMERCIAL BANCSHARES INC.

FIRST US BANCSHARES INC.

HISTORICAL FINANCIALS

Company Type: Public

Income Statement — FYE: December 31

	ASSETS ($ mil.)	NET INCOME ($ mil.)	INCOME AS % OF ASSETS	EMPLOYEES
12/20	978.5	13.7	1.4%	222
12/19	880.0	10.6	1.2%	217
12/18	830.3	8.2	1.0%	179
12/17	780.4	3.8	0.5%	177
12/16	633.1	5.5	0.9%	155
Annual Growth	11.5%	25.6%	—	9.4%

2020 Year-End Financials

Return on assets: 1.4%
Return on equity: 13.2%
Long-term debt ($ mil.): —
No. of shares (mil.): 3.2
Sales ($ mil): 67.0

Dividends
Yield: 2.0%
Payout: 10.3%
Market value ($ mil.): 83.0

	STOCK PRICE ($) FY Close	P/E High/Low		PER SHARE ($) Earnings	Dividends	Book Value
12/20	25.44	6	3	4.16	0.51	34.11
12/19	22.71	7	6	3.25	0.52	29.00
12/18	20.02	9	7	2.51	0.48	24.76
12/17	22.20	20	17	1.18	0.48	23.17
12/16	21.42	13	10	1.68	0.44	22.21
Annual Growth	4.4%	—	—	25.4%	3.8%	11.3%

United Bankshares Inc

United Bankshares offers a full range commercial and retail banking services and products. The bank owns non-subsidiaries which engage in other community banking services such asset management real property title insurance financial planning mortgage banking and brokerage services The bank operate with 210 branches that serve West Virginia Virginia and Washington DC as well as nearby portions of Maryland Pennsylvania and Ohio. The branches offer traditional deposit trust

and lending services with a focus on residential mortgages and commercial loans. In 2020 the bank completed the acquisition of Carolina Financial Corporation—the parent company of Cress-Com Bank with $5.0 billion assets. The company was founded in 1839.

EXECUTIVES

Independent Director, Theodore Georgelas
Lead Independent Director, P. Clinton Winter
Executive Vice President, Chief Credit Officer, Douglas Ernest
Independent Director, Albert Small
Independent Director, Peter Converse
Chief Information And Risk Officer, Executive Vice President, Darren Williams, $363,731 total compensation
Director, Michael Fitzgerald
Chief Financial Officer, Executive Vice President, Treasurer, W. Mark Tatterson, $464,462 total compensation
Executive Vice President, Director, Jerold Rexroad
Independent Director, Patrice Harris
Independent Director, Mary Weddle
Independent Director, J. Paul McNamara
President, Richard Adams, $595,000 total compensation
Chief Operating Officer, Executive Vice President, James Consagra, $595,000 total compensation
Auditors: Ernst & Young LLP

LOCATIONS

HQ: United Bankshares Inc
300 United Center, 500 Virginia Street, East, Charleston, WV 25301
Phone: 304 424-8716
Web: www.ubsi-inc.com

PRODUCTS/OPERATIONS

2014 Sales

	$ mil.	% of total
Interest		
Loans including fees	383.7	75
Interest and dividends on securities	33.9	7
Other	0.9	-
Noninterest		
Fees from deposit services	42.4	9
Fees from trust & brokerage services	18.1	4
Other	28.9	5
Adjustment (losses)	(8.4)	
Total	**499.5**	**100**

COMPETITORS

AMERICAN NATIONAL BANKSHARES INC.
COMMERCIAL NATIONAL FINANCIAL CORPORATION
DCB FINANCIAL CORP
HERITAGE BANKSHARES INC.
IBERIABANK CORPORATION
LIBERTY CAPITAL INC.
OLD NATIONAL BANCORP
PACIFIC CONTINENTAL CORPORATION
PACIFIC FINANCIAL CORPORATION
SALISBURY BANCORP INC.
UNITED COMMUNITY BANKS INC.
WASHINGTON TRUST BANCORP INC.
WESTERN ALLIANCE BANCORPORATION
WINTRUST FINANCIAL CORPORATION

HISTORICAL FINANCIALS

Company Type: Public

Income Statement

FYE: December 31

	ASSETS ($ mil.)	NET INCOME ($ mil.)	INCOME AS % OF ASSETS	EMPLOYEES
12/20	26,184.2	289.0	1.1%	3,051
12/19	19,662.3	260.1	1.3%	2,204
12/18	19,250.5	256.3	1.3%	2,230
12/17	19,058.9	150.5	0.8%	2,381
12/16	14,508.8	147.0	1.0%	1,701
Annual Growth	15 9%	18.4%	—	15.7%

2020 Year-End Financials

Return on assets: 1 2%	Dividends
Return on equity: 7.5%	Yield: 4.3%
Long-term debt ($ mil.): —	Payout: 58.3%
No. of shares (mil.): 129.1	Market value ($ mil.): 4,186.0
Sales ($ mil): 1,153.1	

	STOCK PRICE ($) FY Close	P/E High/Low		PER SHARE ($) Earnings	Dividends	Book Value
12/20	32.40	16	9	2.40	1.40	33.27
12/19	38.66	16	12	2.55	1.37	33.12
12/18	31.11	16	12	2.45	1.36	31.78
12/17	34.75	30	21	1.54	1.33	30.85
12/16	46.25	25	16	1.99	1.32	27.59
Annual Growth	(8.5%)	—	—	4.8%	1.5%	4.8%

United Community Banks Inc (Blairsville, GA)

United Community Banks is the holding company for United Community Bank (UCB). UCB provides consumer and business banking products and services through nearly 150 branches across Georgia North Carolina Tennessee and South Carolina. Commercial loans including construction loans and mortgages account for the largest portion of UCB's loan portfolio (more than 50%); residential mortgages make up 30%. The company which boasts roughly $10 billion in assets also has a mortgage lending division and provides insurance through its United Community Insurance Services subsidiary (aka United Community Advisory Services).

Operations

The bank's retail mortgage lending division United Community Mortgage Services (UCMS) sells and services mortgages for Fannie Mae and Freddie Mac and provides fixed and adjustable-rate home mortgages. It also offers retail brokerage services through an affiliation with a third-party broker/dealer.

About 65% of UCB's total revenue came from loan interest (including fees) in 2014 while another 16% came from taxable investments. The rest of its revenue came from service charges and fees (10%) mortgage loan fees (2%) and brokerage fees (2%) among other sources.

Geographic Reach

UCB's nearly 105 branches are located in Georgia (in the north the Atlanta-Sandy Springs-Roswell metro area Gainsville metro area and coastal areas); western North Carolina; eastern and central Tennessee; and South Carolina (in the Greenville-Anderson-Mauldin metro area).

Sales and Marketing

The bank provides community banking services for individuals small businesses and corporations.

Financial Performance

UCB has struggled to consistently grow its revenues in recent years due to shrinking interest margins on loans amidst the low-interest environment. Its profits however have been rising thanks to declining loan loss provisions as its loan portfolio's credit quality has improved with higher property valuations in the strengthened economy.

The bank's revenue inched higher by 1% to $304 million in 2014 thanks to an increase in interest income stemming from strategic business growth initiatives designed to add new business lines and expand into new markets as well as balance sheet management and restructuring actions taken in the second quarter of the year.

Despite higher revenue in 2014 UCB's net income dove 75% to $67.6 million mostly because in 2013 it had received a non-recurring income tax benefit of $238 million stemming from reversal of a deferred tax valuation allowance. Not counting this item however the bank's profit before taxes nearly tripled during the year. UCB's operating cash levels dropped by 47% to $101.9 million in 2014 due to lower cash earnings.

Strategy

UCB has been concentrating on growing its small business lending business in recent years. In 2014 it made "significant investments" in its SBA business after acquiring Business Carolina which specialized in SBA and USDA lending.

It also continues to pursue bank acquisitions to expand its reach in its existing core markets and boost its loan and deposit business. Its acquisitions in 2015 and 2014 alone have added over $1 billion in new loan business and $1.3 billion in new deposits.

Mergers and Acquisitions

In 2016 United Community Banks expanded into key markets in coastal South Carolina after buying Mt. Pleasant-based Tidelands and its seven Tidelands Bank branches in the Charleston Myrtle Beach and Hilton Head areas.

In 2015 UCB bought Tennessee-based MoneyTree Corporation and its 10 First National Bank branches in east Tennessee. The deal added $425 million in assets $354 million in deposits and $253 million in new loan business to UCB's books.

In 2014 the company purchased Palmetto Bancshares and its Palmetto Bank branches expanding its footprint into "major" southeastern metro markets in Greenville and the Upstate South Carolina area. The deal also added $1.2 billion in assets $832 million in loans and $967 million in deposits.

Also in 2014 UCB purchased Columbia-based Business Carolina a commercial lender that specialized in SBA and USDA loans for $31.3 million in cash. The deal included $25 million in loans $6 million in other assets and substantially all of the company's employees.

EXECUTIVES

Independent Director, Robert Blalock

Independent Director, Tim Wallis

Lead Independent Director, Thomas Richlovsky

Chief Financial Officer, Executive Vice President, Jefferson Harralson, $420,000 total compensation

Independent Director, Jennifer Mann

Chief Banking Officer, Richard Bradshaw, $385,000 total compensation

Independent Director, Lance Drummond

Chief Information Officer, Mark Terry

Independent Director, James Clements

Executive Vice President, General Counsel, Corporate Secretary, Melinda Lux, $272,083 total compensation

Independent Director, Jennifer Bazante

Chairman And Ceo, Lynn Harton, $775,000 total compensation

Executive Vice President, Chief Risk Officer, Robert Edwards, $385,000 total compensation

Independent Director, David Shaver

Independent Director, David Wilkins

Auditors: PricewaterhouseCoopers LLP

LOCATIONS

HQ: United Community Banks Inc (Blairsville, GA)
125 Highway 515 East, Blairsville, GA 30512
Phone: 706 781-2265
Web: www.ucbi.com

PRODUCTS/OPERATIONS

2011 Sales

	$ mil.	% of total
Interest		
Loans including fees	239.1	69
Taxable investment securities	55.2	16
Other	3.3	1
Noninterest		
Service charges & fees	29.1	8
Mortgage loans & related fees	5.4	2
Brokerage fees	3.0	1
Net securities gains	0.8	-
Other	12.3	3
Adjustment	(0.7)	-
Total	**347.5**	**100**

COMPETITORS

AMERICAN NATIONAL BANKSHARES INC.	PACIFIC CONTINENTAL CORPORATION
CAPITAL BANK FINANCIAL BANCORP CORP.	PACWEST
CENTERSTATE BANK CORPORATION	SOUTHSIDE BANCSHARES INC. STATE BANK FINANCIAL
CITY HOLDING COMPANY	CORPORATION
CVB FINANCIAL CORP.	WILSHIRE BANCORP INC.
F.N.B. CORPORATION	
HEARTLAND FINANCIAL USA INC.	

HISTORICAL FINANCIALS

Company Type: Public

Income Statement

FYE: December 31

	ASSETS ($ mil.)	NET INCOME ($ mil.)	INCOME AS % OF ASSETS	EMPLOYEES
12/20	17,794.3	164.0	0.9%	2,406
12/19	12,916.0	185.7	1.4%	2,309
12/18	12,573.1	166.1	1.3%	2,312
12/17	11,915.4	67.8	0.6%	2,137
12/16	10,708.6	100.6	0.9%	1,916
Annual Growth	13.5%	13.0%	—	5.9%

2020 Year-End Financials

Return on assets: 1.0%
Return on equity: 8.9%
Long-term debt ($ mil.): —
No. of shares (mil.): 86.6
Sales ($ mil): 714.1

Dividends
Yield: 2.5%
Payout: 38.9%
Market value ($ mil.): 2,465.0

	STOCK PRICE ($) FY Close	P/E High/Low		Earnings	PER SHARE ($) Dividends	Book Value
12/20	28.44	16	8	1.91	0.72	23.16
12/19	30.88	14	9	2.31	0.68	20.70
12/18	21.46	16	10	2.07	0.58	18.40
12/17	28.14	33	27	0.92	0.38	16.80
12/16	29.62	21	11	1.40	0.30	15.17
Annual Growth	(1.0%)	—	—	8.1%	24.5%	11.2%

United States 12 Month Oil Fund LP

Auditors: Spicer Jeffries LLP

LOCATIONS

HQ: United States 12 Month Oil Fund LP
1850 Mt. Diablo Boulevard, Suite 640, Walnut Creek, CA 94596
Phone: 510 522-9600
Web: www.uscfinvestments.com

HISTORICAL FINANCIALS

Company Type: Public

Income Statement — FYE: December 31

	REVENUE ($ mil.)	NET INCOME ($ mil.)	NET PROFIT MARGIN	EMPLOYEES
12/20	110.3	108.7	98.6%	0
12/19	14.9	14.4	96.7%	0
12/18	4.8	(5.5)	113.4%	0
12/17	2.6	1.7	64.9%	0
12/16	30.1	29.3	97.3%	0
Annual Growth	38.3%	38.7%	—	—

2020 Year-End Financials

Debt ratio: —
Return on equity: —
Cash ($ mil.): 181.5
Current ratio: 7.88
Long-term debt ($ mil.): —

No. of shares (mil.): 11.4
Dividends
Yield: —
Payout: —
Market value ($ mil.): 196.0

	STOCK PRICE ($) FY Close	P/E High/Low		Earnings	PER SHARE ($) Dividends	Book Value
12/20	17.19	—	—	(5.72)	0.00	17.23
12/19	22.99	4	3	5.52	0.00	22.95
12/18	17.96	—	—	(1.62)	0.00	17.82
12/17	20.92	72	54	0.29	0.00	21.05
12/16	20.40	4	3	4.69	0.00	20.39
Annual Growth	(4.2%)	—	—	—	—	(4.1%)

United States Brent Oil Fund L.P.

Auditors: Spicer Jeffries LLP

LOCATIONS

HQ: United States Brent Oil Fund L.P.
1850 Mt. Diablo Boulevard, Suite 640, Walnut Creek, CA 94596
Phone: 510 522-9600
Web: www.uscfinvestments.com

HISTORICAL FINANCIALS

Company Type: Public

Income Statement — FYE: December 31

	REVENUE ($ mil.)	NET INCOME ($ mil.)	NET PROFIT MARGIN	EMPLOYEES
12/20	121.6	119.0	97.9%	0
12/19	27.5	26.7	97.1%	0
12/18	14.3	(15.1)	106.0%	0
12/17	16.3	15.4	94.5%	0
12/16	38.0	37.0	97.4%	0
Annual Growth	33.8%	33.9%	—	—

2020 Year-End Financials

Debt ratio: —
Return on equity: —
Cash ($ mil.): 311.5
Current ratio: 857.31
Long-term debt ($ mil.): —

No. of shares (mil.): 27.1
Dividends
Yield: —
Payout: —
Market value ($ mil.): 349.0

	STOCK PRICE ($) FY Close	P/E High/Low		Earnings	PER SHARE ($) Dividends	Book Value
12/20	12.88	5	1	4.45	0.00	12.91
12/19	20.85	4	3	5.76	0.00	20.91
12/18	15.33	—	—	(3.14)	0.00	15.18
12/17	18.10	8	5	2.24	0.00	18.18
12/16	15.68	4	2	4.49	0.00	15.70
Annual Growth	(4.8%)	—	—	(0.2%)	—	(4.8%)

United States Gasoline Fund LP

EXECUTIVES

Partner, John Hyland
Auditors: Spicer Jeffries LLP

LOCATIONS

HQ: United States Gasoline Fund LP
1850 Mt. Diablo Boulevard, Suite 640, Walnut Creek, CA 94596
Phone: 510 522-9600
Web: www.uscfinvestments.com

HISTORICAL FINANCIALS

Company Type: Public

Income Statement — FYE: December 31

	REVENUE ($ mil.)	NET INCOME ($ mil.)	NET PROFIT MARGIN	EMPLOYEES
12/20	43.0	42.5	98.7%	0
12/19	13.6	13.3	98.0%	0
12/18	11.1	(11.4)	102.9%	0
12/17	0.6	0.2	34.1%	0
12/16	5.6	5.1	90.3%	0
Annual Growth	66.0%	69.7%	—	—

2020 Year-End Financials

Debt ratio: —
Return on equity: —
Cash ($ mil.): 72.5
Current ratio: 59.20
Long-term debt ($ mil.): —

No. of shares (mil.): 3.3
Dividends
Yield: —
Payout: —
Market value ($ mil.): 80.0

	STOCK PRICE ($) FY Close	P/E High/Low		Earnings	PER SHARE ($) Dividends	Book Value
12/20	24.31	3	1	11.14	0.00	24.29
12/19	32.36	3	2	10.69	0.00	32.31
12/18	22.91	—	—	(8.43)	0.00	22.74
12/17	31.85	299	204	0.11	0.00	32.03
12/16	31.32	17	11	1.81	0.00	31.37
Annual Growth	(6.1%)	—	—	57.5%	—	(6.2%)

Unity Bancorp, Inc.

Unity Bancorp wants to keep you and your money united. The institution is the holding company for Unity Bank a commercial bank that serves small and midsized businesses as well as individual consumers through nearly 20 offices in north-central New Jersey and eastern Pennsylvania. Unity Bank's deposit products include checking savings money market and NOW accounts and CDs. Lending to businesses is the company's life blood: Commercial loans including Small Business Administration (SBA) and real estate loans account for about 60% of its loan portfolio which is rounded out by residential mortgage and consumer loans.

EXECUTIVES

Independent Chairman Of The Board Of The Company And Bank, David Dallas
President, Chief Executive Officer, Director Of The Company And The Bank, James Hughes, $567,194 total compensation
Independent Vice Chairman Of The Board Of The Company And The Bank, Allen Tucker
Chief Operating Officer And Executive Vice President Of The Company And The Bank, John Kauchak, $217,000 total compensation
Independent Director Of The Company And The Bank, Mark Brody
Independent Director Of The Company And The Bank, Raj Patel
Independent Director Of The Company And The Bank, Wayne Courtright
Chief Administrative Officer And Executive Vice President Of The Company And Bank, Janice Bolomey, $220,000 total compensation

HOOVER'S HANDBOOK OF EMERGING COMPANIES 2022

425

Independent Director Of The Company And The Bank, Aaron Tucker
Independent Director Of The Company And The Bank, Peter Maricondo
Independent Director Of The Company And The Bank, Donald Souders
Independent Director Of The Company And The Bank, Robert Dallas
Senior Vice President, Chief Accounting Officer, Laureen Cook, $171,000 total compensation
Chief Financial Officer, Executive Vice President, Ir Contact Officer, George Boyan
Auditors: RSM US LLP

LOCATIONS

HQ: Unity Bancorp, Inc.
64 Old Highway 22, Clinton, NJ 08809
Phone: 908 730-7630
Web: www.unitybank.com

PRODUCTS/OPERATIONS

Selected Subsidiaries
Unity Bank
Unity Financial Services Inc.
Unity Investment Company Inc.

COMPETITORS

BCSB BANCORP INC.	FIRST US BANCSHARES
CF BANKSHARES INC.	INC.

HISTORICAL FINANCIALS
Company Type: Public

Income Statement				FYE: December 31
	ASSETS ($ mil.)	NET INCOME ($ mil.)	INCOME AS % OF ASSETS	EMPLOYEES
12/20	1,958.9	23.6	1.2%	210
12/19	1,718.9	23.6	1.4%	209
12/18	1,579.1	21.9	1.4%	207
12/17	1,455.5	12.8	0.9%	208
12/16	1,189.9	13.2	1.1%	194
Annual Growth	13.3%	15.7%	—	2.0%

2020 Year-End Financials

Return on assets: 1.2%
Return on equity: 14.0%
Long-term debt ($ mil.): —
No. of shares (mil.): 10.4
Sales ($ mil): 91.8
Dividends
Yield: 1.8%
Payout: 15.6%
Market value ($ mil.): 184.0

	STOCK PRICE ($) FY Close	P/E High/Low		PER SHARE ($) Earnings	Dividends	Book Value
12/20	17.55	10	4	2.19	0.32	16.63
12/19	22.57	11	8	2.14	0.31	14.77
12/18	20.76	12	9	2.01	0.27	12.85
12/17	19.75	17	13	1.20	0.23	11.13
12/16	15.70	12	7	1.38	0.17	10.15
Annual Growth	2.8%	—	—	12.2%	17.4%	13.2%

Universal Display Corp

Universal Display thinks the world should be flat and lit with its organic light-emitting diode (OLED) technologies and materials. With its own research and through sponsored research agree-ments with PPG Industries and several universities the company develops OLED technologies and materials which use less energy than other lighting technologies including new and next-generation red green yellow and blue emitters and hosts for screens from cell phones to large flat panel displays and solid-state lighting. Based in the US it has facilities in Europe and the Asia/Pacific region. Universal Display was founded by Sherwin Seligsohn in 1994.

EXECUTIVES

Chairman Of The Board, Founder, Sherwin Seligsohn
President, Chief Executive Officer, Director, Steven Abramson, $781,054 total compensation
Chief Financial Officer, Executive Vice President, Treasurer, Secretary, Director, Sidney Rosenblatt, $781,054 total compensation
Senior Vice President, Chief Technical Officer, Julia Brown, $556,323 total compensation
Lead Independent Director, Elizabeth Gemmill
Independent Director, C. Keith Hartley
Vice President - Legal, General Manager - Patents And Licensing, Mauro Premutico, $470,234 total compensation
Independent Director, Richard Elias
Independent Director, Celia Joseph
Vice President - Technology Commercialization, General Manager - Pholed Material Sales Business, Janice Mohan, $387,203 total compensation
Auditors: KPMG LLP

LOCATIONS

HQ: Universal Display Corp
375 Phillips Boulevard, Ewing, NJ 08618
Phone: 609 671-0980
Web: www.oled.com

PRODUCTS/OPERATIONS

2017 Sales

	$ mil.	% of total
Material sales	200.3	60
Royalty and license fees	126.5	38
Contract research services	8.8	2
Total	**335.6**	**100**

COMPETITORS

ALLEGRO MICROSYSTEMS TECHNOLOGY LLC	RUBICON INC.
Angstrom Engineering Inc	SIGMA DESIGNS INC.
KOPIN CORPORATION	Samsung Electronics Co. Ltd.
OCLARO INC.	TRONY Solar
PHOTRONICS INC.	Corporation.

HISTORICAL FINANCIALS
Company Type: Public

Income Statement				FYE: December 31
	REVENUE ($ mil.)	NET INCOME ($ mil.)	NET PROFIT MARGIN	EMPLOYEES
12/20	428.8	133.3	31.1%	350
12/19	405.1	138.3	34.1%	311
12/18	247.4	58.8	23.8%	267
12/17	335.6	103.8	31.0%	224
12/16	198.8	48.0	24.2%	203
Annual Growth	21.2%	29.1%	—	14.6%

2020 Year-End Financials

Debt ratio: —
Return on equity: 15.4%
Cash ($ mil.): 630.0
Current ratio: 5.61
Long-term debt ($ mil.): —
No. of shares (mil.): 47.6
Dividends
Yield: 0.2%
Payout: 26.9%
Market va ue ($ mil.): 10,949.0

	STOCK PRICE ($) FY Close	P/E High/Low		PER SHARE ($) Earnings	Dividends	Book Value
12/20	229.80	86	38	2.80	0.60	19.16
12/19	206.07	77	27	2.92	0.40	17.09
12/18	93.57	166	65	1.24	0.24	14.59
12/17	172.65	87	19	2.18	0.12	13.99
12/16	56.30	72	41	1.02	0.00	11.26
Annual Growth	42.1%	—	—	28.7%	—	14.2%

Universal Insurance Holdings Inc

While some companies shy away from insuring homes in hurricane-prone Florida Universal Insurance Holdings is right at home there. Operating through its Universal Property & Casualty Insurance Company (UPCIC) and American Platinum Property and Casualty Insurance Company (APPCIC) subsidiaries the company underwrites distributes and administers homeowners property and personal liability insurance. The company's additional subsidiaries process claims perform claims adjustments and property inspections provide administrative duties and negotiate reinsurance. All together the group services some 888000 insurance policies.

Operations

Universal Insurance is Florida's largest private residential homeowners' insurance provider by direct written premiums in-force with some 80% of the market share.

In addition to UPCIC and APPCIC the company owns Evolution Risk Advisors Inc. (managing general agent) Universal Inspection Corporation (underwriting inspections) Universal Adjusting Corporation (claims processing) and Blue Atlantic Reinsurance (reinsurance intermediary).

Through Universal Insurance's Universal Direct platform consumers in all states the group operates in are able to directly purchase home owners policies online without meeting an intermediary face-to-face.

About 90% of sales were generated from net premiums earned.

Geographic Reach

The company is headquartered in Fort Lauderdale Florida. While Florida remains its largest market it also operates in nearly 20 other states: Alabama Delaware Florida Georgia Hawaii Indiana Maryland Massachusetts Michigan Minnesota New Hampshire New Jersey New York North Carolina Pennsylvania South Carolina and Virginia. Although not yet active in Illinois Iowa New Hampshire or West Virginia the company is licensed in those states.

APPCIC writes homeowners multi-peril insurance for homes worth more than $1 million in Florida.

Sales and Marketing

Universal Insurance distributes its products through a network of some 9800 independent agents. It also sells its policies through its online platform Universal Direct.

Financial Performance

Universal Insurance has shown continuous growth in revenue for the past five years and showed a 72% increase from 2015 to 2019. Meanwhile net income has been fluctuating has been unsteady for the past five years and recently recorded its lowest value for the five-year range.

Revenue in 2019 amounted to $939.4 million 16% higher than the previous year thanks to an increase in most of its premiums.

Net income was $46.5 million 60% less than the previous year.

Cash and cash equivalents at the end of the year were $184.7 million $15.7 million more than in 2018. Cash provided by operating activities was $84.6 million. Investing activities used $28.3 million primarily for Purchases of available-for-sale debt securities while financing activities used $97.2 million primarily for purchase of treasury stock.

Strategy

Universal Insurance's strategic focus is on creating a best-in-class experience for its customers. It has more than 20 years of experience providing protection solutions. In 2019 the company rebranded certain of its subsidiaries to better serve its Insurance Entities distinctly identify its capabilities and position the company for continued growth in the future. It has made substantial efforts in recent years to improve and enhance its claims operation including reductions in its claim resolution times and an intensified effort to collect subrogation for the benefit of the Insurance Entities and their policyholders. The company's differentiated capabilities support the Insurance Entities across all aspects of the insurance value chain to provide its customers with a streamlined experience and it continues to evaluate ways in which it can improve the customer experience.

The company's business strategy also aims to provide disciplined underwriting maintain a strong balance sheet backed by its reinsurance programs and geographic diversification and maximize earnings stability through inversely correlated or complementary high-quality earnings streams.

EXECUTIVES

Independent Director, Marlene Gordon
Chief Administrative Officer, Chief Information Officer, Director, Kimberly Campos, $300,000 total compensation
Chief Financial Officer, Principal Accounting Officer, Frank Wilcox, $462,500 total compensation
Chief Executive Officer, Director, Stephen Donaghy, $1,000,000 total compensation
Director, Jon Springer, $1,338,202 total compensation
Executive Chairman Of The Board, Sean Downes, $1,567,813 total compensation
Auditors: Plante & Moran, PLLC

LOCATIONS

HQ: Universal Insurance Holdings Inc
1110 West Commercial Blvd., Fort Lauderdale, FL 33309
Phone: 954 958-1200
Web: www.universalinsuranceholdings.com

PRODUCTS/OPERATIONS

2017 Sales

	$ mil.	% of total
Net premiums earned	688.8	92
Commissions	21.2	3
Policy fees	18.8	2
Net investment income	13.5	2
Net realized gains on investments	2.6	-
Other	7.0	1
Total	**751.9**	**100**

Selected Products and Services

Condominium policy
Dwelling coverage
Dwelling fire policy
Homeowners policy
Other structures coverage
Personal liability coverage
Personal property coverage
Renter's policy

COMPETITORS

AMERICAN NATIONAL INSURANCE COMPANY
ARBELLA SERVICE COMPANY INC.
BROWN & BROWN INC.
CENTRAL MUTUAL INSURANCE COMPANY
DONEGAL GROUP INC.

GUARDIA LLC
MERCURY GENERAL CORPORATION
NATIONAL GENERAL HOLDINGS CORP.
UNITED FIRE GROUP INC.
ZENITH NATIONAL INSURANCE CORP.

HISTORICAL FINANCIALS

Company Type: Public

Income Statement

FYE: December 31

	ASSETS ($ mil.)	NET INCOME ($ mil.)	INCOME AS % OF ASSETS	EMPLOYEES
12/20	1,758.7	19.1	1.1%	909
12/19	1,719.8	46.5	2.7%	805
12/18	1,858.3	117.0	6.3%	734
12/17	1,455.0	106.9	7.3%	558
12/16	1,060.0	99.4	9.4%	483
Annual Growth	13.5%	(33.8%)	—	17.1%

2020 Year-End Financials

Return on assets: 1.1%	Dividends
Return on equity: 4.0%	Yield: 4.2%
Long-term debt ($ mil.): —	Payout: 128.3%
No. of shares (mil.): 31.1	Market value ($ mil.): 470.0
Sales ($ mil): 1,072.7	

	STOCK PRICE ($) FY Close	P/E High/Low		PER SHARE ($) Earnings	Dividends	Book Value
12/20	15.11	46	18	0.60	0.77	14.43
12/19	27.99	30	18	1.36	0.77	15.13
12/18	37.92	15	8	3.27	0.73	14.42
12/17	27.35	9	5	2.99	0.69	12.67
12/16	28.40	10	6	2.79	0.69	10.59
Annual Growth	(14.6%)	—	—	(31.9%)	2.8%	8.0%

University Bancorp Inc. (MI)

University Bancorp is the holding company for University Bank. From one branch in Ann Arbor (the home of The University of Michigan) the bank offers standard services such as deposit accounts and loans. It mainly originates residential mortgages with commercial mortgages business loans and consumer loans rounding out its lending activities. Shariah-compliant banking services (banking consistent with Islamic law) are offered through University Islamic Financial which operates within University Bank's office. University Bancorp also owns University Insurance and Investments Services and a majority of Midwest Loan Services which provides mortgage origination and subservicing to credit unions.

EXECUTIVES

Director, Gary Baker
Executive Vice President - Residential Loans, John Sickler, $97,391 total compensation
President, Chief Executive Officer, Director, Stephen Ranzini, $100,000 total compensation
Director, Michael Talley
Director, Robert Kauffman
Director, Michael Concannon
President And Director Of Midwest Loan Services, Edward Burger, $130,000 total compensation
Director, Paul Ranzini
Director, Joseph Ranzini
Chairman Of The Board, Charles McDowell
Auditors: UHY LLP

LOCATIONS

HQ: University Bancorp Inc. (MI)
959 Maiden Lane, Ann Arbor, MI 48105
Phone: 734 741-5858   **Fax:** 734 741-5859
Web: www.university-bank.com

COMPETITORS

CCFNB BANCORP INC.
CENTRAL VIRGINIA BANKSHARES INC.

QNB CORP.
UNITED BANCSHARES INC.

HISTORICAL FINANCIALS

Company Type: Public

Income Statement

FYE: December 31

	ASSETS ($ mil.)	NET INCOME ($ mil.)	INCOME AS % OF ASSETS	EMPLOYEES
12/20	557.6	28.0	5.0%	0
12/19	361.9	3.6	1.0%	0
12/18	247.0	2.2	0.9%	0
12/17	245.9	5.1	2.1%	0
12/16	190.9	3.8	2.0%	0
Annual Growth	30.7%	64.7%	—	—

2020 Year-End Financials

Return on assets: 6.0%	Dividends
Return on equity: 61.9%	Yield: 1.1%
Long-term debt ($ mil.): —	Payout: 2.8%
No. of shares (mil.): 5.2	Market value ($ mil.): 65.0
Sales ($ mil): 136.9	

	STOCK PRICE ($) FY Close	P/E High/Low		PER SHARE ($) Earnings	Dividends	Book Value
12/20	12.56	2	1	5.31	0.15	10.87
12/19	8.06	15	12	0.63	0.00	6.45
12/18	9.00	28	19	0.42	0.00	5.80
12/17	9.10	—	—	(0.00)	0.00	4.49
12/16	7.20	—	—	(0.00)	0.11	3.54
Annual Growth	14.9%	—	—	—	8.8%	32.3%

Univest Financial Corp

Univest Corporation of Pennsylvania will keep your money close to its vest. The holding company owns $3 billion-asset Univest Bank and Trust which serves the southeastern part of the Keystone State and the broader Mid-Atlantic region online and though 30 branches and provides standard retail and commercial banking services such as checking and savings accounts CDs IRAs and credit cards. Subsidiary Univest Capital provides small-ticket commercial financing while Univest Insurance offers personal and commercial coverage. Univest Investments which boasts some $3 billion in assets under management offers brokerage and investment advisory services.

Operations

Univest operates three main business segments: Banking which accounted for 79% of the company's total revenue during 2015 and provides traditional banking services to consumers businesses and government entities through Univest Bank and Trust; Wealth Management (12% of revenue) which offers investment advisory retirement plan trust municipal pension and broker/dealer services through Univest Investments; and Insurance (9% of revenue) which offers commercial and personal insurance lines as well as benefits and human resources consulting through Univest Insurance.

Broadly speaking Univest Corporation gets more than 60% of its revenue from interest income. About 61% of its total revenue came from loan interest (including fees on loans and leases) during 2015 while another 5% came from interest on its investment securities. The rest of its revenue came from insurance commissions and fees (8% of revenue) investment advisory commission and fee income (7%) trust fee income (5%) deposit account service charges (3%) mortgage banking sales (3%) and other miscellaneous income sources.

More than 40% of the company's loan portfolio was made up of commercial real estate loans at the end of 2015 while another 23% of loan assets were made up of commercial loans that were financial or agricultural-related. The remainder of the portfolio was made up of loans tied to residential properties secured for business purposes (10% of loan assets) residential properties for personal purposes (8%) lease financings (7%) construction real estate loans (4%) and loans to individuals (less than 2%).

Geographic Reach

Souderton Pennsylvania-based Univest Corporation and its subsidiaries serve clients across the Mid-Atlantic region. The company has around 30 bank branches and nearly 20 offices in the Montgomery Bucks Philadelphia Chester Berks Lehigh and Delaware counties of Pennsylvania as well as in Calvert County in Maryland Camden County in New Jersey and Lee County in Florida.

Sales and Marketing

Univest Corporation serves individuals businesses municipalities and non-profit organizations. It spent $2.25 million on marketing and advertising during 2015 to reach these clients up from $1.88 million and $1.95 million in 2014 and 2013 respectively.

Financial Performance

The bank's revenues and profits have been trending higher over the past several years thanks to 50% loan asset growth and 50% non-interest

revenue growth since 2011 along with a continued reduction in loan loss provisions as its loan portfolio's credit quality has improved with higher property valuations in the strengthened economy.

Univest Corporation's revenue jumped 24% to a record $154.41 million during 2015 mostly as 35% loan asset growth (loan balances swelled to $2.16 billion) stemming from its Valley Green Bank acquisition helped boost interest income. The company's non-interest income also rose 9% as its mortgage banking gains doubled during the year on higher volumes and as its insurance commissions and fee income rose 20% after acquiring Sterner Insurance in mid-2014.

Strong revenue growth in 2015 drove the company's net income up 23% to $27.27 million for the year. Univest Corporation's operating cash levels climbed 12% to $35.63 thanks to the rise in earnings.

Strategy

Univest Corporation has been expanding its service lines and building its loan and deposit businesses by strategically acquiring other banks and investment or insurance-related financial firms.

Mergers and Acquisitions

In December 2015 Univest Corporation agreed to buy Fox Chase Bancorp along with its $1.1 billion in assets $768 million in loans $765 million in deposits and several Fox Chase Bank branches in Pennsylvania and New Jersey for a price exceeding $240 million. The deal would also expand Univest's presence in Bucks Chester Philadelphia and Montgomery counties in Pennsylvania as well as into Atlantic and Cape May counties in New Jersey.

In January 2015 the company purchased Valley Green Bank as well as its three branches and two loan production offices in the greater Philadelphia market for $77 million.

In July 2014 Univest bolstered its Univest Insurance subsidiary after acquiring Sterner Insurance Associates a full-service insurance and consultative risk management firm that served individuals and businesses across the Lehigh Valley Berks Bucks and Montgomery counties.

In January 2014 flagship subsidiary Univest Bank and Trust Co. bought registered investment advisory firm Girard Partners Ltd. as well as its $500 million in assets under management. The deal boosted Univest's assets under management by 20% to a total of $3 billion after the acquisition.

EXECUTIVES

Independent Chairman Of The Board Of The Corporation And The Bank, William Aichele
Senior Executive Vice President Of The Corporation And The Bank, Chief Credit Officer Of The Bank, Duane Brobst, $266,500 total compensation
Chief Operating Officer, Senior Executive Vice President Of The Corporation, President And Director Of The Bank, Michael Keim, $445,000 total compensation
Independent Director, Thomas Petro
Executive Vice President, Chief Risk Officer, General Counsel Of The Corporation And The Bank, Megan Santana, $310,000 total compensation
Independent Director, Roger Ballou
Independent Director, Todd Benning
Independent Director, Charles Zimmerman
Independent Director, Robert Wonderling
Independent Director, Suzanne Keenan

President, Chief Executive Officer, Director, Chief Executive Officer Of Univest Bank And Trust Co., Jeffrey Schweitzer, $665,000 total compensation
Chief Financial Officer, Executive Vice President Of Company And Bank, Brian Richardson, $335,000 total compensation
Auditors: KPMG LLP

LOCATIONS

HQ: Univest Financial Corp
14 North Main Street, Souderton, PA 18964
Phone: 215 721-2400
Web: www.univest.net

PRODUCTS/OPERATIONS

2015 sales

	$ mil.	% of total
Banking	120.9	79
Wealth Management	18.9	12
Insurance	14.4	9
Other	0.3	-
Total	**154.5**	**100**

COMPETITORS

AMERICAN NATIONAL BANKSHARES INC.
ASSOCIATED BANC-CORP
BANCFIRST CORPORATION
CITIZENS & NORTHERN CORPORATION
EAGLE BANCORP INC.
FIRST BUSEY CORPORATION
FIRSTMERIT CORPORATION
FLAGSTAR BANCORP INC.
HANCOCK WHITNEY CORPORATION
MB FINANCIAL INC.
PEAPACK-GLADSTONE FINANCIAL CORPORATION
WESTERN ALLIANCE BANCORPORATION
WINTRUST FINANCIAL CORPORATION

HISTORICAL FINANCIALS

Company Type: Public

Income Statement				FYE: December 31
	ASSETS ($ mil.)	NET INCOME ($ mil.)	INCOME AS % OF ASSETS	EMPLOYEES
12/20	6,336.5	46.9	0.7%	896
12/19	5,380.9	65.7	1.2%	873
12/18	4,984.3	50.5	1.0%	841
12/17	4,554.8	44.0	1.0%	855
12/16	4,230.5	19.5	0.5%	840
Annual Growth	**10.6%**	**24.5%**	**—**	**1.6%**

2020 Year-End Financials

Return on assets: 0.8%	Dividends
Return on equity: 6.8%	Yield: 3.8%
Long-term debt ($ mil.): —	Payout: 54.0%
No. of shares (mil.): 29.3	Market value ($ mil.): 603.0
Sales ($ mil): 282.2	

	STOCK PRICE ($) FY Close	P/E High/Low		PER SHARE ($) Earnings	Dividends	Book Value
12/20	20.58	17	9	1.60	0.80	23.64
12/19	26.78	12	10	2.24	0.80	23.01
12/18	21.57	17	12	1.72	0.80	21.32
12/17	28.05	20	16	1.64	0.80	20.57
12/16	30.90	37	22	0.84	0.80	19.00
Annual Growth	**(9.7%)**	**—**	**—**	**17.5%**	**(0.0%)**	**5.6%**

Upstart Holdings Inc

LOCATIONS

HQ: Upstart Holdings Inc
2950 S. Delaware Street, Suite 300, San Mateo, CA 94403
Phone: 650 204-1000
Web: www.Upstart.com

HISTORICAL FINANCIALS

Company Type: Public

Income Statement — FYE: December 31

	REVENUE ($ mil.)	NET INCOME ($ mil.)	NET PROFIT MARGIN	EMPLOYEES
12/21	848.5	135.4	16.0%	1,497
12/20	233.4	5.9	2.6%	554
12/19	164.1	(0.4)	—	429
12/18	99.3	(12.3)	—	0
12/17	57.2	(7.7)	—	0
Annual Growth	96.2%	—	—	—

2021 Year-End Financials

Debt ratio: 38.2%
Return on equity: 24.4%
Cash ($ mil.): 1,191.2
Current ratio: 6.39
Long-term debt ($ mil.): 695.4
No. of shares (mil.): 83.6
Dividends
  Yield: —
  Payout: —
Market value ($ mil.): 12,658.0

	STOCK PRICE ($) FY Close	P/E High/Low	Earnings	Dividends	Book Value
12/21	151.30	225 25	1.43	0.00	9.65
12/20	40.75	— —	(0.00)	0.00	4.10
Annual Growth	271.3%	— —	—	—	135.6%

US Global Investors Inc

While it may be a small world financial investment company U.S. Global Investors wants to make it a little greener after all. Primarily serving the U.S. Global Investors Funds and the U.S. Global Accolade Funds the company is a mutual fund manager providing investment advisory transfer agency broker-dealer and mailing services. It offers a family of no-load mutual funds generally geared toward long-term investing. The company also engages in corporate investment activities. U.S. Global Investors had about $724 million in assets under management in 2015.

EXECUTIVES

CIO-Ceo, Frank E Holmes
Chb, Jerold H Rubinstein
V Chb, Roy D Terracina
Cfo, Lisa C Callicotte
Auditors: BDO USA, LLP

LOCATIONS

HQ: US Global Investors Inc
7900 Callaghan Road, San Antonio, TX 78229
Phone: 210 308-1234
Web: www.usfunds.com

COMPETITORS

EPOCH HOLDING CORPORATION
FRANKLIN RESOURCES INC.
OPPENHEIMERFUNDS INC.
TURNER INVESTMENTS L.P.

HISTORICAL FINANCIALS

Company Type: Public

Income Statement — FYE: June 30

	REVENUE ($ mil.)	NET INCOME ($ mil.)	NET PROFIT MARGIN	EMPLOYEES
06/21	21.6	31.9	147.6%	23
06/20	4.4	(4.6)	—	23
06/19	4.9	(3.3)	—	24
06/18	6.2	0.6	10.3%	25
06/17	6.7	(0.5)	—	26
Annual Growth	33.8%	—	—	(3.0%)

2021 Year-End Financials

Debt ratio: —
Return on equity: 89.9%
Cash ($ mil.): 15.4
Current ratio: 5.20
Long-term debt ($ mil.): —
No. of shares (mil.): 15.0
Dividends
  Yield: 0.6%
  Payout: 1.8%
Market value ($ mil.): 93.0

	STOCK PRICE ($) FY Close	P/E High/Low	Earnings	Dividends	Book Value
06/21	6.19	6 1	2.12	0.04	3.61
06/20	1.90	— —	(0.31)	0.03	1.11
06/19	1.81	— —	(0.22)	0.03	1.43
06/18	1.61	171 32	0.04	0.03	1.69
06/17	1.52	— —	(0.03)	0.03	1.57
Annual Growth	42.1%	— —	—	9.1%	23.1%

USA Compression Partners LP

EXECUTIVES

President, Chief Executive Officer, Director Of General Partner Of Usa Compression Gp, Llc, Eric Long, $688,846 total compensation
Vice President, Human Resources, Sean Kimble, $328,733 total compensation
Independent Director, Glenn Joyce
Director, Christopher Curia
Vice President, General Counsel, Secretary, Christopher Porter, $326,154 total compensation
Independent Director, William Waldheim
Director, Thomas Mason
Director, Thomas Long
Director Of Usa Compression Gp, Llc, Matthew Ramsey
Director, Bradford Whitehurst
Chief Operating Officer, Vice President, Eric Scheller, $314,384 total compensation
Independent Director, Matthew Hartman
Chief Financial Officer, Vice President, Treasurer, Matthew Liuzzi, $427,385 total compensation
Auditors: Grant Thornton LLP

LOCATIONS

HQ: USA Compression Partners LP
111 Congress Avenue, Suite 2400, Austin, TX 78701
Phone: 512 473-2662
Web: www.usacompression.com

HISTORICAL FINANCIALS

Company Type: Public

Income Statement — FYE: December 31

	REVENUE ($ mil.)	NET INCOME ($ mil.)	NET PROFIT MARGIN	EMPLOYEES
12/21	632.6	10.2	1.6%	697
12/20	667.6	(594.7)	—	742
12/19	698.3	39.1	5.6%	879
12/18	584.3	(10.5)	—	864
12/17	280.2	11.4	4.1%	426
Annual Growth	22.6%	(2.6%)	—	13.1%

2021 Year-End Financials

Debt ratio: 71.2%
Return on equity: 2.1%
Cash ($ mil.): —
Current ratio: 1.09
Long-term debt ($ mil.): 1,973.2
No. of shares (mil.): 97.3
Dividends
  Yield: 12.0%
  Payout: —
Market value ($ mil.): 1,699.0

	STOCK PRICE ($) FY Close	P/E High/Low	Earnings	Dividends	Book Value
12/21	17.45	— —	(0.40)	2.10	5.94
12/20	13.60	— —	(6.65)	2.10	8.40
12/19	18.14	— —	(0.02)	2.10	17.16
12/18	12.98	— —	(0.43)	2.10	19.26
12/17	16.54	123 92	0.16	2.10	10.19
Annual Growth	1.3%	— —	—	(0.0%)	(12.6%)

USA Truck, Inc.

Truckload carrier USA Truck moves freight not only in the US but also in Canada and through partners into Mexico. It does most of its business east of the Rocky Mountains. USA Truck has a fleet of about 2000 tractors and 6200 trailers. The company provides both medium-haul and regional truckload services along with dedicated contract carriage in which drivers and equipment are assigned to a customer long-term. USA Truck team members have cultivated a thorough understanding of the needs of shippers in key industries which the company believes helps with the development of long-term service-oriented relationships with its customers.

Operations

The Company has two reportable segments: Trucking consisting of the company's truckload and dedicated freight service offerings and USAT Logistics consisting of the company's freight brokerage and rail intermodal service offerings.

The company's trucking segment transports customer freight over irregular routes utilizing equipment owned or leased by either the company or independent contractors as a medium-haul common carrier. The segment accounts for about 70% of revenue.

USAT Logistics (about 30% of sales) provides freight brokerage logistics and intermodal rail serv-

---

HOOVER'S HANDBOOK OF EMERGING COMPANIES 2022

ice to its customers by utilizing third party capacity.

Geographic Reach

USA Truck offers its services throughout the continental US and in portions of Mexico and Canada.

The company's network consists of about 20 facilities including USAT Logistics offices. USAT's facilities were located in or near the following cities: Arkansas Florida Georgia Illinois Ohio Pennsylvania Texas and Washington.

Sales and Marketing

One customer accounted for more than 10% of the company's consolidated operating revenues. USAT Logistics was also dependent upon a single customer for more than 10% of its operating revenue. The company's largest 10 customers comprised approximately 45% of the company's consolidated operating revenue. The company provided services to more than 800 customers across all USA Truck service offerings.

Financial Performance

Revenue for fiscal 2019 decreased by 2% to $522.6 million compared to $534.1 million in 2018.

The company's net income decreased by $16.9 million resulting to net loss of $4.7 million compared to the prior year with an income of $12.2 million.

Cash held by the company at the end of 2019 decreased to $0.1 million. Cash provided by operations was $43.5 while cash used for investing and financing activities were $24.8 million and $19.6 million respectively. Main uses for cash were capital expenditures and payments on long-term debt.

Company Background

The company got its start in 1983 as Crawford Produce Inc. (with fewer than 10 tractors in operation). It was incorporated under the name USA Truck in 1986 and was purchased by its management in 1989. USA Truck's IPO was completed in 1992.

EXECUTIVES

Senior Vice President - Usat Logistics, George Henry, $240,000 total compensation
Chief Financial Officer, Senior Vice President, Zachary King, $228,389 total compensation
Independent Director, Barbara Faulkenberry
Independent Chairman Of The Board, Alexander Greene
Executive Vice President, Chief Commercial Officer, Timothy Guin, $310,000 total compensation
Independent Director, M. Susan Chambers
Independent Director, Rajan Penkar
Independent Director, Gary Enzor
President, Chief Executive Officer, Director, James Reed, $500,000 total compensation
Senior Vice President- Customer Experience And Chief Information Officer, Kimberly Littlejohn, $240,000 total compensation
Auditors: Grant Thornton LLP

LOCATIONS

HQ: USA Truck, Inc.
3200 Industrial Park Road, Van Buren, AR 72956
Phone: 479 471-2500
Web: www.usa-truck.com

PRODUCTS/OPERATIONS

2014 Sales

	$ mil.	% of total
Trucking	423.5	70
Strategic capacity Solutions	179.0	30
Total	**602.5**	**100**

COMPETITORS

CAI INTERNATIONAL INC.
FORWARD AIR CORPORATION
HEARTLAND EXPRESS INC.
KNIGHT TRANSPORTATION INC.
KNIGHT-SWIFT TRANSPORTATION HOLDINGS INC.
LANDSTAR SYSTEM INC.
MARTEN TRANSPORT LTD.
OLD DOMINION FREIGHT LINE INC.
ROADRUNNER TRANSPORTATION SYSTEMS INC.
SAIA INC.
SCHNEIDER NATIONAL INC.
TOUAX SCA - SGTR - CITE - SGT - CMTE - TAF - SLM TOUAGE INVE

HISTORICAL FINANCIALS

Company Type: Public

Income Statement
FYE: December 31

	REVENUE ($ mil.)	NET INCOME ($ mil.)	NET PROFIT MARGIN	EMPLOYEES
12/21	710.3	24.7	3.5%	2,100
12/20	551.1	4.7	0.9%	2,000
12/19	522.6	(4.7)	—	2,050
12/18	534.0	12.2	2.3%	2,500
12/17	446.5	7.5	1.7%	2,000
Annual Growth	12.3%	34.8%		1.2%

2021 Year-End Financials

Debt ratio: 39.7%
Return on equity: 25.2%
Cash ($ mil.): 1.3
Current ratio: 1.30
Long-term debt ($ mil.): 119.6
No. of shares (mil.): 8.9
Dividends
Yield: —
Payout: —
Market value ($ mil.): 177.0

	STOCK PRICE ($) FY Close	P/E High/Low		Earnings	PER SHARE ($) Dividends	Book Value
12/21	19.88	8	3	2.76	0.00	12.53
12/20	8.93	23	5	0.53	0.00	9.69
12/19	7.45	—	—	(0.55)	0.00	9.14
12/18	14.97	19	10	1.49	0.00	9.62
12/17	18.13	20	6	0.93	0.00	8.02
Annual Growth	2.3%	—	—	31.3%	—	11.8%

Uwharrie Capital Corp.

Uwharrie Capital is the multibank holding company for Anson Bank & Trust Bank of Stanly and Cabarrus Bank & Trust which operate a total of about ten branches in west-central North Carolina. Serving consumers and local business customers the banks offer a variety of deposit accounts and credit cards as well as investments insurance asset management and brokerage services offered by other Uwharrie subsidiaries such as insurance agency BOS Agency securities broker-dealer Strategic Alliance mortgage brokerage Gateway Mortgage and Strategic Investment Ad-

visors. The banks mainly write residential and commercial mortgages but also construction business and consumer loans.

EXECUTIVES

President And Chief Executive Officer, Roger Dick, $248,455 total compensation
Chief Risk Officer, Roy Beaver, $130,000 total compensation
Independent Director, W. Chester Lowder
Director, James Nance
Independent Director, Cynthia Mynatt
Independent Director, Ronald Burleson
Independent Director, Bill Burnside
Independent Chairman Of The Board, Joe Brooks
Independent Director, Thomas Hearne
Executive Vice President - Marketing; Chief Executive Officer Of Strategic Investment Advisors, Inc, Christy Stoner, $153,493 total compensation
Independent Director, W. Stephen Aldridge
Independent Director, Charles Horne
President Of Strategic Investment Advisors, Inc., Jeffrey Talley, $83,784 total compensation
Chief Financial Officer, Uwharrie Capital Corp. And Uwharrie Bank, Heather Almond
Auditors: Dixon Hughes Goodman LLP

LOCATIONS

HQ: Uwharrie Capital Corp.
132 North First Street, Albemarle, NC 28001
Phone: 704 983-6181
Web: www.uwharrie.com

COMPETITORS

COMMERCIAL NATIONAL FINANCIAL CORPORATION
SOUTHWEST GEORGIA FINANCIAL CORPORATION
UNITED BANKSHARES INC.

HISTORICAL FINANCIALS

Company Type: Public

Income Statement
FYE: December 31

	ASSETS ($ mil.)	NET INCOME ($ mil.)	INCOME AS % OF ASSETS	EMPLOYEES
12/20	827.7	7.5	0.9%	315
12/19	656.7	2.5	0.4%	191
12/18	632.3	1.9	0.3%	189
12/17	576.3	1.0	0.2%	184
12/16	548.2	1.6	0.3%	181
Annual Growth	10.9%	46.9%	—	14.9%

2020 Year-End Financials

Return on assets: 1.0%
Return on equity: 17.3%
Long-term debt ($ mil.): —
No. of shares (mil.): 7.2
Sales ($ mil): 44.9
Dividends
Yield: —
Payout: 10.0%
Market value ($ mil.): 38.0

	STOCK PRICE ($) FY Close	P/E High/Low		Earnings	PER SHARE ($) Dividends	Book Value
12/20	5.25	6	4	1.03	0.00	6.69
12/19	5.74	18	14	0.33	0.00	5.12
12/18	5.25	24	18	0.25	0.00	4.52
12/17	5.68	45	41	0.13	0.00	4.36
12/16	5.45	29	19	0.21	0.00	4.19
Annual Growth	(0.9%)	—	—	49.4%	—	12.4%

Valley National Bancorp (NJ)

Valley National Bancorp owns Valley National Bank which serves commercial and retail clients through more than 225 branches in northern and central New Jersey and in the New York City boroughs of Manhattan Brooklyn and Queens as well as on Long Island. The bank provides standard services like checking and savings accounts loans and mortgages credit cards and trust services. Subsidiaries offer asset management mortgage and auto loan servicing title insurance asset-based lending and property/casualty life and health insurance.

Operations

In addition to its commercial and retail banking operations Valley National Bancorp through its subsidiaries operates: an all-line insurance agency that offers property and casualty life and health insurance; a wealth management advisory business; title insurance agencies in New York and New Jersey. It also specializes in commercial equipment leasing and custom financing for health care professionals and law firms.

Geographic Reach

Based in New York Valley National Bancorp conducts business at some 225 retail banking centers locations in northern and central New Jersey the New York City boroughs of Manhattan Brooklyn and Queens Long Island Florida and Alabama.

Financial Performance

Net income totaled $390.6 million or $0.93 per diluted common share for the year ended December 31 2020 compared to $309.8 million in 2019 or $0.87 per diluted common share. The increase in net income compared to 2019 was largely due to a $220.9 million or 25% increase in its net interest income driven primarily by a $5.6 billion increase in average loan balances and a sharp reduction in interest rates of 85 basis points on the cost of total interest bearing liabilities resulting from the low interest environment partially offset by loan yields that were 53 basis points lower and interest expense related to a $3.9 billion increase in average interest bearing liabilities.

Cash and cash equivalent at the end of fiscal year 2020 was $1.3 billion compared to $434.7 million in 2019. Operations generated $151.5 million while investing activities used $2.0 billion primarily for net loan originations and purchases. Financing activities provided $2.8 billion in 2020.

Strategy

Valley National Bancorp's primary focus is to build and develop profitable customer relationships across all lines of business and create a convenient and innovative omni-channel customer experience beyond its traditional branch footprint including through the use and promotion of its mobile and online service offerings such as the ValleyDirect on-line savings account.

For Valley's branch transformation it has embarked on a strategy to continuously overhaul its retail network. Approximately two years ago it established the foundation of what the transformation of its branch network would look like in coming years. It implemented tailored action plans focused on improving profitability and deposit levels as well as upgrades in staffing and training

within a defined timeline. For the overall branch network it continues to monitor the operating performance of each branch and implement tailored action plans focused on improving profitability and deposit levels for those branches that underperform.

EXECUTIVES

Senior Executive Vice President Of Valley National Bancorp And Chief Banking Officer Of Valley National Bank, Thomas Iadanza, $600,000 total compensation

Executive Vice President Of Valley And Chief Risk Officer Of Valley National Bank, Melissa Scofield

Senior Executive Vice President Of Valley And Chief Operating Officer Of Valley National Bank, Robert Bardusch, $475,000 total compensation

Independent Director, Jeffery Wilks

Senior Executive Vice President Of Valley And Chief People Officer Of Valley National Bank, Yvonne Surowiec

Independent Director, Melissa Schultz

Independent Director, Sidney Williams

Senior Executive Vice President, General Counsel, And Corporate Secretary Of Valley And Valley National Bank, Ronald Janis, $515,000 total compensation

Chief Financial Officer, Senior Executive Vice President, Michael Hagedorn, $590,000 total compensation

Lead Independent Director, Andrew Abramson

Independent Director, Marc Lenner

Independent Director, Suresh Sani

Executive Vice President, Joseph Chillura

Chairman Of The Board, President, Chief Executive Officer Of Valley National Bank, Ira Robbins, $1,000,000 total compensation

Independent Director, Peter Baum

Auditors: KPMG LLP

LOCATIONS

HQ: Valley National Bancorp (NJ)
One Penn Plaza, New York, NY 10119
Phone: 973 305-8800
Web: www.valleynationalbank.com

PRODUCTS/OPERATIONS

2016 Sales

	$ mil.	% of total
Interest Income		
Interest and fees on loans	685.9	79
Interest and dividends on investment securities	79.9	9
Interest on federal funds sold and other short-term investments	1.1	0
Non-Interest Income		
Gains on sales of loans net	22.0	3
Service charges on deposit accounts	20.9	2
Insurance commissions	19.1	2
Trust and investment services	10.3	1
Bank owned life insurance	6.7	1
Fees from loan servicing	6.4	1
Gains on sales of assets net	1.4	0
Gains on securities transactions net	0.8	0
Change in FDIC loss-share receivable	(1.3)	0
Other	16.9	2
Total	**870.1**	**100**

COMPETITORS

ASSOCIATED BANC-CORP
BYLINE BANCORP INC.
Banco Bradesco S/A
CITY HOLDING COMPANY
COLUMBIA BANKING SYSTEM INC.
COMMERCE BANCSHARES INC.
COMMUNITY BANK SYSTEM INC.
FIRST COMMONWEALTH FINANCIAL CORPORATION

FIRST MIDWEST BANCORP INC.
FIRSTMERIT CORPORATION
MIDLAND FINANCIAL CO.
MUFG AMERICAS HOLDINGS CORPORATION
NATIONAL BANK HOLDINGS CORPORATION
NEW YORK COMMUNITY BANCORP INC.
OCEANFIRST FINANCIAL CORP.
PACIFIC CONTINENTAL CORPORATION
PEOPLE'S UNITED FINANCIAL INC.
PINNACLE FINANCIAL PARTNERS INC.
SOUTHWEST BANCORP INC.
WEBSTER FINANCIAL CORPORATION

HISTORICAL FINANCIALS

Company Type: Public

Income Statement

FYE: December 31

	ASSETS ($ mil.)	NET INCOME ($ mil.)	INCOME AS % OF ASSETS	EMPLOYEES
12/20	40,686.0	390.6	1.0%	3,155
12/19	37,436.0	309.7	0.8%	3,174
12/18	31,863.0	261.4	0.8%	3,192
12/17	24,002.3	161.9	0.7%	2,842
12/16	22,864.4	168.1	0.7%	2,828
Annual Growth	**15.5%**	**23.5%**	**—**	**2.8%**

2020 Year-End Financials

Return on assets: 1.0%	Dividends
Return on equity: 8.6%	Yield: 4.5%
Long-term debt ($ mil.): —	Payout: 57.1%
No. of shares (mil.): 403.8	Market value ($ mil.): 3,938.0
Sales ($ mil): 1,566.7	

	STOCK PRICE ($) FY Close	P/E High/Low		PER SHARE ($) Earnings	Dividends	Book Value
12/20	9.75	12	7	0.93	0.44	11.37
12/19	11.45	14	10	0.87	0.44	10.87
12/18	8.88	18	11	0.75	0.44	10.11
12/17	11.22	22	18	0.58	0.44	9.58
12/16	11.64	19	13	0.63	0.44	9.02
Annual Growth	**(4.3%)**	**—**	**—**	**10.2%**	**(0.0%)**	**6.0%**

Valley Republic Bancorp

Auditors: Eide Bailly, LLP

LOCATIONS

HQ: Valley Republic Bancorp
5000 California Avenue, Suite 110, Bakersfield, CA 93309
Phone: 661 371-2000　　**Fax:** 661 371-2010
Web: www.valleyrepublicbank.com

HISTORICAL FINANCIALS

Company Type: Public

Income Statement

FYE: December 31

	REVENUE ($ mil.)	NET INCOME ($ mil.)	NET PROFIT MARGIN	EMPLOYEES
12/20	40.4	12.5	31.0%	0
12/19	36.5	9.7	26.6%	0
12/18	28.7	8.9	31.1%	0
12/17	23.2	5.2	22.6%	0
12/16	18.7	4.4	23.8%	0
Annual Growth	**21.2%**	**29.4%**	**—**	**—**

2020 Year-End Financials

Debt ratio: 3.5%
Return on equity: 14.4%
Cash ($ mil.): 140.7
Current ratio: 0.13
Long-term debt ($ mil.): 39.3

No. of shares (mil.): 4.2
Dividends
　Yield: —
　Payout: —
Market value ($ mil.): 92.0

	STOCK PRICE ($) FY Close	P/E High/Low		PER SHARE ($) Earnings	Dividends	Book Value
12/20	21.75	9	5	2.97	0.00	22.55
12/19	26.01	14	11	2.33	0.00	18.59
12/18	31.50	15	12	2.14	0.00	16.87
12/17	29.00	21	12	1.29	0.00	14.94
12/16	16.80	14	11	1.16	0.00	13.60
Annual Growth	6.7%	—	—	26.4%	—	13.5%

Valvoline Inc

Auditors: Ernst & Young LLP

LOCATIONS

HQ: Valvoline Inc
　100 Valvoline Way, Lexington, KY 40509
Phone: 859 357-7777
Web: www.valvoline.com

HISTORICAL FINANCIALS

Company Type: Public

Income Statement　　　　　　　　　FYE: September 30

	REVENUE ($ mil.)	NET INCOME ($ mil.)	NET PROFIT MARGIN	EMPLOYEES
09/21	2,981.0	420.0	14.1%	9,800
09/20	2,353.0	317.0	13.5%	8,800
09/19	2,390.0	208.0	8.7%	7,900
09/18	2,285.0	166.0	7.3%	6,700
09/17	2,084.0	304.0	14.6%	5,600
Annual Growth	9.4%	8.4%	—	15.0%

2021 Year-End Financials

Debt ratio: 53.0%
Return on equity: 1,423.7%
Cash ($ mil.): 230.0
Current ratio: 1.82
Long-term debt ($ mil.): 1,677.0

No. of shares (mil.): 180.0
Dividends
　Yield: 1.6%
　Payout: 24.7%
Market value ($ mil.): 5,612.0

	STOCK PRICE ($) FY Close	P/E High/Low		PER SHARE ($) Earnings	Dividends	Book Value
09/21	31.18	15	8	2.29	0.50	0.75
09/20	19.04	14	5	1.69	0.45	(0.41)
09/19	22.03	21	16	1.10	0.42	(1.37)
09/18	21.51	30	24	0.84	0.30	(1.90)
09/17	23.45	17	13	1.49	0.20	(0.58)
Annual Growth	7.4%	—	—	11.3%	26.4%	—

Vanda Pharmaceuticals Inc

Vanda Pharmaceuticals is a biopharmaceutical company that is developing several drugs for disorders of the central nervous system. The company's first commercial drug was schizophrenia treatment Fanapt (iloperidone). It continues to commercialize another drug Hetlioz (tasimelteon) for the treatment of non-24-hour sleep-wake disorder. Other drug candidates are for the treatments of atopic dermatitis gastroparesis and motion sickness as well as a portfolio of Cystic Fibrosis Transmembrane Conductance Regulator (CFTR) activators and inhibitors for the treatment of dry eye and ocular inflammation. Vanda typically licenses development and commercialization rights for its compounds from (and to) companies including Bristol-Myers Squibb Eli Lilly and Novartis.

Operations

Vanda's product pipeline includes Tradipitant a small molecule neurokinin-1 receptor (NK-1R) antagonist for the treatment of gastroparesis motion sickness atopic dermatitis and COVID-19 pneumonia; VTR-297 a small molecule histone deacetylase (HDAC) inhibitor for the treatment of hematologic malignancies and with potential use as a treatment for several oncology indications; VQW-765 a small molecule nicotinic acetylcholine receptor partial agonist with potential use for the treatment of psychiatric disorders; and a portfolio of Cystic Fibrosis Transmembrane Conductance Regulator (CFTR) activators and inhibitors for the treatment of dry eye and ocular inflammation and for the treatment of secretory diarrhea disorders including cholera.

Fanapt accounts for nearly 65% of the company's revenue while Hetlioz brings in about 35%.

Geographic Reach

Headquartered in Washington DC Vanda commercializes its products in the US and Canada. Its distribution partners launched Fanapt in Israel and Mexico. Vanda began rolling out Hetlioz in some countries in Europe.

Sales and Marketing

Headquartered in Washington DC Vanda commercializes its products in the US and Canada. Its distribution partners launched Fanapt in Israel and Mexico. Vanda began rolling out Hetlioz in some countries in Europe.

Financial Performance

Total revenues increased by $21.0 million or 9% to $248.2 million for the year ended December 31 2020 compared to $227.2 million for the year ended December 31 2019.

Net income for fiscal 2020 decreased to $23.3 million compared from the prior year with $115.6 million.

Cash held by the company at the end of fiscal 2020 increased to $61.6 million. Cash provided by operations and financing activities were $51.8 million and $16.0 million respectively. Cash used for investing activities was $41.5 million mainly for Purchases of property and equipment.

Strategy

Vanda's goal is to further solidify its position as a leading global biopharmaceutical company focused on developing and commercializing innovative therapies addressing high unmet medical needs through the application of its drug development expertise and its pharmacogenetics and pharmacogenomics expertise. The key elements of Vanda's strategy to accomplish this goal are to: Maximize the commercial success of HETLIOZ and Fanapt; Enter into strategic partnerships to supplement our capabilities and to extend its commercial reach; Pursue the clinical development and regulatory approval of its products including tradipitant; Apply its pharmacogenetics and pharmacogenomics expertise to differentiate its products; Expand its product portfolio through the identification and acquisition of additional products; and Utilize novel and innovative approaches in pursuit of each of these strategies.

Company Background

The company was established in 2003 by Dr. Mihael Polymeropoulos Vanda's CEO and a former researcher for Novartis.

EXECUTIVES

Senior Vice President, Chief Marketing Officer, Joakim Wijkstrom, $506,422 total compensation
Chief Financial Officer, Senior Vice President, Treasurer, Kevin Moran, $324,693 total compensation
Independent Director, Phaedra Chrousos
Senior Vice President, General Counsel, Secretary, Timothy Williams, $400,000 total compensation
Senior Vice President - Business Development, Gunther Birznieks, $386,250 total compensation
Independent Director, Richard Dugan
President, Chief Executive Officer And Director, Mihael Polymeropoulos, $746,235 total compensation
Independent Chairman Of The Board, H. Thomas Watkins
Independent Director, Anne Ward
Auditors: PricewaterhouseCoopers LLP

LOCATIONS

HQ: Vanda Pharmaceuticals Inc
　2200 Pennsylvania Avenue N.W., Suite 300 E,
　Washington, DC 20037
Phone: 202 734-3400
Web: www.vandapharma.com

PRODUCTS/OPERATIONS

2015 Sales

	% of total
Fanapt	60
Hetlioz	40
Total	**100**

COMPETITORS

ARENA PHARMACEUTICALS THERAPEUTICS INC.
CHEMOCENTRYX INC.
EXELIXIS INC.
INCYTE CORPORATION
INSMED INCORPORATED
IONIS PHARMACEUTICALS THERAPEUTICS INC.
IRONWOOD PHARMACEUTICALS PHARMACEUTICALS INC.

PTC

SEAGEN INC.
SUCAMPO PHARMACEUTICALS INC.
SUPERNUS PHARMACEUTICALS INC.
UNITED THERAPEUTICS CORPORATION
VERTEX PHARMACEUTICALS INCORPORATED

HISTORICAL FINANCIALS
Company Type: Public

Income Statement
FYE: December 31

	REVENUE ($ mil.)	NET INCOME ($ mil.)	NET PROFIT MARGIN	EMPLOYEES
12/20	248.1	23.3	9.4%	292
12/19	227.1	115.5	50.9%	284
12/18	193.1	25.2	13.1%	270
12/17	165.0	(15.5)	—	273
12/16	146.0	(18.0)	—	142
Annual Growth	14.2%	—		19.7%

2020 Year-End Financials

Debt ratio: —	No. of shares (mil.): 54.8
Return on equity: 5.3%	Dividends
Cash ($ mil.): 61.0	Yield: —
Current ratio: 6.21	Payout: —
Long-term debt ($ mil.): —	Market value ($ mil.): 721.0

	STOCK PRICE ($) FY Close	P/E High/Low		PER SHARE ($) Earnings	Dividends	Book Value
12/20	13.14	39	17	0.42	0.00	8.26
12/19	16.41	14	6	2.11	0.00	7.67
12/18	26.13	63	28	0.48	0.00	5.25
12/17	15.20	—	—	(0.35)	0.00	2.92
12/16	15.95	—	—	(0.41)	0.00	2.98
Annual Growth	(4.7%)	—	—	—	—	29.0%

Veeva Systems Inc

Veeva Systems is breathing new life into software for the health care industry. Its cloud-based software and mobile apps are used by pharmaceutical and biotechnology companies to manage critical business functions. Veeva Systems' customer relationship management software uses Salesforce's platform to manage sales and marketing functions. Its Veeva Vault provides content management and collaboration software for quality management in clinical trials and regulatory compliance for new drug submissions. Its software is used in 75 countries and available in more than 25 languages but North America is its largest market. Founded in 2007 Veeva Systems went public in 2013.

Operations
Veeva sells its products through subscriptions and they account for about three-quarters of its business. The rest comes from professional services it provides for installing and training on its software.

Geographic Reach
Veeva Systems operates from three offices in the US and one in Canada. It also has locations in China Japan and Spain. North America is its largest market accounting for 55% of sales. Europe makes up another 26% while customers in Asia account for about 20% of sales. Sales outside North American increased about 64% in 2015 (ended January).

The company runs its software on data centers in California Illinois and Virginia and Germany Japan and the UK.

Sales and Marketing
The company uses a direct sales force with representatives in more than a dozen countries. Veeva Systems counts about 275 customers including global pharmaceutical companies such as Bayer Boehringer Ingelheim Eli Lilly Gilead Sciences Merck and Novartis.

Financial Performance
Veeva Systems has posted big gains in revenue since 2011. Sales zoomed from $30 million in fiscal 2011 (year-end January) to $313 million in 2015. In addition it has been consistently profitable which is uncommon for a relatively new and growing company. Profit increased almost 50% in 2015. While the company has increased spending on research and development and sales and marketing revenue growth covered the higher spending and then some.

Strategy
The company makes 95% of sales from its Veeva CRM customer relationship management software but new products are also being developed. Its latest software offering is Veeva Network a customer master solution that creates and maintains healthcare provider and organization master data. Veeva Network also contains a proprietary database of people and companies in China and the US using data gathered from state federal and industry sources.

While Veeva Systems currently focuses on the life sciences industry specifically pharmaceutical and biotechnology companies it would like to expand to other specialized companies such as contract research organizations (CROs) and contract manufacturing organizations (CMOs).

Mergers and Acquisitions
In 2015 Veeva acquired Qforma CrowdLink a developer of key opinion leader (KOL) data and services for life sciences' brand medical and market access teams. Veeva introduced a product based on Qforma technology to help its customers get more sophisticated information for introducing products.

EXECUTIVES

Chief Financial Officer, Brent Bowman, $226,827 total compensation
Chief Executive Officer, Peter Gassner, $345,833 total compensation
Director, Timothy Cabral, $219,429 total compensation
Independent Chairman Of The Board, Gordon Ritter
Senior Vice President, General Counsel, Corporate Secretary, Jonathan Faddis, $322,917 total compensation
Senior Vice President - Global Customer Services, Frederic Lequient, $345,833 total compensation
Director, Priscilla Hung
Director, Tina Hunt
Executive Vice President - Global Sales, Alan Mateo, $345,833 total compensation
President, Chief Operating Officer, Thomas Schwenger, $101,042 total compensation
Auditors: KPMG LLP

LOCATIONS

HQ: Veeva Systems Inc
4280 Hacienda Drive, Pleasanton, CA 94588
Phone: 925 452-6500   **Fax:** 925 452-6504
Web: www.veeva.com

PRODUCTS/OPERATIONS

2015 Sales

	% of total
Subscription fees	74
Professional services	26
Total	**100**

Selected Products
Veeva CRM (customer relationship management)
 Veeva CLM (closed-loop marketing)
 Veeva iRep (mobile app for Apple products)
 Veeva CRM Approved Email (tracks regulatory compliant emails between sales reps and physicians)
Veeva Vault (content management and collaboration software)
 Veeva Vault eTMF (document management for clinical trials)
 Veeva Vault Investigator Portal (secure file exchange for clinical trials)
 Veeva Vault MedComms (medical content management)
 Veeva Vault PromoMats (promotional materials management)
 Veeva Vault QualityDocs (quality management)
 Veeva Vault Submissions (document management for regulatory submissions)
Veeva Network (master software and data stewardship)
 Veeva Network Provider Database (proprietary database of people and companies in China and the US)
 Veeva Network Customer Master (cleanse and match people and company data)
 Veeva Network Data Stewardship Services (data management)

COMPETITORS

AMERICAN SOFTWARE INC.	INFOR (US) LLC
CA INC.	PROS HOLDINGS INC.
CALLIDUS SOFTWARE INC.	RAPID7 INC.
DATAWATCH CORPORATION	Software AG
EPAM SYSTEMS INC.	

HISTORICAL FINANCIALS
Company Type: Public

Income Statement
FYE: January 31

	REVENUE ($ mil.)	NET INCOME ($ mil.)	NET PROFIT MARGIN	EMPLOYEES
01/21	1,465.0	380.0	25.9%	4,506
01/20	1,104.0	301.1	27.3%	3,501
01/19	862.2	229.8	26.7%	2,553
01/18	685.5	141.9	20.7%	2,171
01/17	544.0	68.8	12.6%	1,794
Annual Growth	28.1%	53.3%	—	25.9%

2021 Year-End Financials

Debt ratio: —	No. of shares (mil.): 152.0
Return on equity: 19.2%	Dividends
Cash ($ mil.): 730.5	Yield: —
Current ratio: 3.23	Payout: —
Long-term debt ($ mil.): —	Market value ($ mil.): 42,035.0

	STOCK PRICE ($) FY Close	P/E High/Low		PER SHARE ($) Earnings	Dividends	Book Value
01/21	276.44	122	48	2.36	0.00	14.90
01/20	146.61	86	55	1.90	0.00	11.17
01/19	109.06	69	34	1.47	0.00	8.47
01/18	62.86	66	42	0.92	0.00	6.13
01/17	42.33	93	40	0.47	0.00	4.74
Annual Growth	59.9%	—	—	49.7%	—	33.2%

Verisk Analytics Inc

Insurance is a risky business and Verisk Analytics is in the business of helping to manage that risk. The company is a leading data analytics provider serving customers in insurance energy and specialized markets and financial services. Verisk's customers include the top property/casualty insurers in the US; leading credit card issuers in North America the UK and Australia; and the world's largest energy companies as well as chemicals metals and mining power utilities and renewables companies; financial institutions; and governments among others. Verisk was created by subsidiary Insurance Services Office (ISO) as a means of going public. More than 75% of the company's revenue is generated from the US.

Operations

Verisk operates through three segments: Insurance Energy and Specialized Markets and Financial Services.

The Insurance business which brings in more than 70% of revenue primarily serves its P&C insurance customers and focuses on the prediction of loss the selection and pricing of risk and compliance with their reporting requirements in each US state in which they operate. It also develops and utilize machine learned and artificially intelligent models to forecast scenarios and produce both standard and customized analytics that help its customers better manage their businesses including detecting fraud before and after a loss event and quantifying losses.

Energy and Specialized Markets account about 25% of revenue provide analytics for customers in the global energy chemicals power renewables and mining and metals industries.

Financial Services generate more than 5% of revenue provide financial institutions regulators payment processors lenders and merchants with competitive benchmarking decision-making algorithms business intelligence and customized analytics.

Geographic Reach

Based in New Jersey Verisk has offices in over 20 US states and international operations in Argentina Australia Bahrain Belgium Brazil Bulgaria Canada China Czech Republic Denmark France Germany India Indonesia Ireland Israel Italy Japan Malaysia Mexico Nepal Netherlands New Zealand Nigeria Poland Russia Singapore South Africa South Korea Spain Thailand the United Arab Emirates and the UK.

The company's revenue is concentrated in the US which provides more than 75% of sales. The UK supplies over 5% and other countries account for more than 15%.

Sales and Marketing

A majority of Verisk's revenue is generated through annual subscriptions and long-term agreements. The company sells its products and services through salespeople sales support and technical consultants. Verisk also serves clients in the insurance energy financial services and risk management industries.

The company's advertising costs were $8.5 million $10.7 million and $9.0 million for the years 2020 2019 and 2018 respectively.

Financial Performance

Revenues were $2.8 billion for 2020 compared to $2.6 billion for 2019 an increase of $177.5 million or 7%.

The company's net income for fiscal 2020 increased to $712.7 million compared from the prior year with $449.9 million.

Cash held by the company at the end of fiscal 2020 increased to $218.8 million. Cash provided by operations was $1.1 billion while cash used for investing and financing activities were $595.8 million and $445.2 million. Main uses of cash were acquisitions and repayment of short-term debt.

Strategy

Over the past five years Verisk has grown its revenues at a CAGR of 9% through the successful execution of its business plan. Those results reflect strong organic revenue growth new product development and acquisitions. The company has made and continues to make investments in people data sets analytic solutions technology and complementary businesses. The key components of its strategy include the following: increase solution penetration with customers; develop new proprietary data sets and predictive analytics; leverage the company's intellectual capital to expand into adjacent markets and new customer sectors; and pursue strategic acquisitions that complement its leadership positions.

Mergers and Acquisitions

In early 2021 FAST a Verisk business is a leading software provider in individual life insurance is acquiring assets and capabilities of Norway-based 4C Solutions a software advisory firm in group life insurance to help insurers meet the rapidly changing coverage needs of companies and their employees. 4C's experienced staff proven methodology and proprietary data architecture will help FAST serve the unmet needs of group life insurers and institutional annuity providers. Terms were not disclosed.

In late 2020 Verisk has entered into an agreement to acquire Jornaya a leading provider of consumer behavioral data and intelligence based in Pennsylvania. The acquisition will add Jornaya's proprietary view of consumer buying journeys to Verisk's growing set of marketing solutions for the insurance and financial services markets. Terms were not disclosed.

Also in 2020 Verisk has acquired Florida-based Franco Signor a highly-regarded Medicare Secondary Payer (MSP) service provider for an undisclosed amount. Franco Signor will become part of Verisk's Claims Partners business a leading provider of MSP compliance and other analytic claim services. Claims Partners and Franco Signor will be combining forces to provide the single best resource for Medicare compliance.

Vexcel Imaging a leader in aerial imagery data large-format aerial cameras and photogrammetry software in early 2020 hassigned a definitive agreement to acquire the imagery sourcing group from Verisk's Geomni business. The acquisition will combine Geomni's imagery surveying and content-related teams and assets into Vexcel. Verisk will be a minority owner in Vexcel with full access to all aerial imagery libraries. Terms were not disclosed.

Company Background

Verisk traces its roots back to 1971 when ISO was created by an association of insurance companies. Verisk went public in 2009 in one of the largest offerings of the year raising almost $2 billion.

EXECUTIVES

Group President, Chief Financial Officer, Lee Shavel, $656,500 total compensation
Independent Director, Kathleen Hogenson
Independent Director, Annell Bay
Executive Vice President And Chief Human Resources Officer, Sunita Holzer
Independent Director, Vincent Brooks
Independent Director, Laura Ipsen
Independent Director, Therese Vaughan
Executive Vice President, Chief Information Officer, Nick Daffan, $505,000 total compensation
Independent Director, Bruce Hansen
Co-president, Chief Operating Officer, Mark Anquillare, $656,500 total compensation
Independent Director, Constantine Iordanou
Chairman Of The Board, President, Chief Executive Officer, Scott Stephenson, $1,000,000 total compensation
Auditors: DELOITTE & TOUCHE LLP

LOCATIONS

HQ: Verisk Analytics Inc
545 Washington Boulevard, Jersey City, NJ 07310-1686
Phone: 201 469-3000
Web: www.verisk.com

PRODUCTS/OPERATIONS

2018 Sales by Segment

	$ mil.	% of total
Insurance	1,705.9	71
Energy & Specialized Markets	513.3	22
Financial Services	175.9	7
Total	**2,395.1**	**100**

Selected Markets:

P/C Insurance
Energy Metals and Mining
Financial Services
Supply Chain
HR Departments
Retail
Commercial Real Estate
Community Hazard Mitigation

COMPETITORS

AMADEUS IT GROUP SA COMPANY	DXC TECHNOLOGY
BLACKLINE INC.	FACTSET RESEARCH
CAPITA PLC	SYSTEMS INC.
CORELOGIC INC.	GUIDEWIRE SOFTWARE
CORESITE REALTY	INC.
CORPORATION	INNODATA INC.
CSG SYSTEMS	PROOFPOINT INC.
INTERNATIONAL INC.	STARTEK INC.
DONNELLEY FINANCIAL	TTEC HOLDINGS INC.
SOLUTIONS INC.	

HISTORICAL FINANCIALS

Company Type: Public

Income Statement				FYE: December 31
	REVENUE ($ mil.)	NET INCOME ($ mil.)	NET PROFIT MARGIN	EMPLOYEES
12/21	2,998.6	666.2	22.2%	9,367
12/20	2,784.6	712.7	25.6%	8,960
12/19	2,607.1	449.9	17.3%	9,300
12/18	2,395.1	598.7	25.0%	8,184
12/17	2,145.2	555.1	25.9%	7,304
Annual Growth	8.7%	4.7%	—	6.4%

2021 Year-End Financials

Debt ratio: 42.4%
Return on equity: 24.1%
Cash ($ mil.): 280.3
Current ratio: 0.49
Long-term debt ($ mil.): 2,342.8

No. of shares (mil.): 161.6
Dividends
  Yield: 0.5%
  Payout: 27.1%
Market value ($ mil.): 36,975.0

	STOCK PRICE ($) FY Close	P/E High/Low	PER SHARE ($) Earnings	Dividends	Book Value
12/21	228.73	56 39	4.08	1.16	17.42
12/20	207.59	47 28	4.31	1.08	16.57
12/19	149.34	60 38	2.70	1.00	13.86
12/18	109.04	34 25	3.56	0.00	12.63
12/17	96.00	29 23	3.29	0.00	11.68
Annual Growth	24.2%	— —	5.5%	—	10.5%

Veritex Holdings Inc

Auditors: Grant Thornton LLP

LOCATIONS

HQ: Veritex Holdings Inc
  8214 Westchester Drive, Suite 800, Dallas, TX 75225
Phone: 972 349-6200
Web: www.veritexbank.com

HISTORICAL FINANCIALS
Company Type: Public

Income Statement   FYE: December 31

	ASSETS ($ mil.)	NET INCOME ($ mil.)	INCOME AS % OF ASSETS	EMPLOYEES
12/20	8,820.8	73.8	0.8%	643
12/19	7,954.9	90.7	1.1%	679
12/18	3,208.5	39.3	1.2%	330
12/17	2,945.5	15.1	0.5%	324
12/16	1,408.5	12.5	0.9%	171
Annual Growth	58.2%	55.8%	—	39.3%

2020 Year-End Financials

Return on assets: 0.8%
Return on equity: 6.1%
Long-term debt ($ mil.): —
No. of shares (mil.): 49.3
Sales ($ mil): 369.1

Dividends
  Yield: 2.6%
  Payout: 43.3%
Market value ($ mil.): 1,266.0

	STOCK PRICE ($) FY Close	P/E High/Low	PER SHARE ($) Earnings	Dividends	Book Value
12/20	25.66	20 7	1.48	0.68	24.39
12/19	29.13	17 13	1.68	0.50	23.32
12/18	21.38	20 13	1.60	0.00	21.88
12/17	27.59	36 30	0.80	0.00	20.28
12/16	26.71	23 11	1.13	0.00	15.73
Annual Growth	(1.0%)	— —	7.0%	—	11.6%

Veru Inc

Move over Trojan Man! Business at The Female Health Company (FHC) maker of condoms for women is gaining momentum. The female condom is the only female contraceptive that is FDA-approved for preventing both pregnancy and sexually transmitted diseases including HIV/AIDS. The firm's condoms are sold in 140-plus countries worldwide (under the FC2 name) mostly in South Africa Brazil and Uganda. Outside the US many of its products bear the Femidom name among others. FHC also provides low-cost female condoms in Africa through an agreement with the Joint United Nations Programme on HIV/AIDS (UN-AIDS). It sponsors the Female Health Foundation which provides women with health education.

Operations

Focused on developing manufacturing and marketing consumer health care products FHC operates its business in one industry segment. The company's FC2 Female Condom which is available in the US and in more than 140 countries offers women dual protection against sexually transmitted diseases such as HIV/AIDS as well as unintended pregnancy.

It owns certain worldwide rights to the FC2 Female Condom including patents that have been issued in several countries. Patents cover the key aspects of FC2 such as its overall design and manufacturing process.

Geographic Reach

Headquartered in Chicago FHC generated a third of its fiscal 2013 revenue from South Africa and Brazil. The balance of its customers is located in Uganda Nigeria the US Congo Zimbabwe India the UK and Malaysia.

The company boasts manufacturing locations in the UK Malaysia and India.

Sales and Marketing

The FC2 Female Condom is the only currently available female-controlled product that's approved by the FDA. Additionally the World Health Organization (WHO) has cleared FC2 for purchase in United Nations agencies.

Among the company's relatively small customer base are large global agencies such as its three largest customers: the United Nations Population Fund (62% of unit sales) the United States Agency for International Development (less than 10% of unit sales) and South Africa's distributor Sekunjalo Investments Corporation (PTY) Ltd. (less than 10% of unit sales). Other customers include ministries of health or other governmental agencies which either purchase directly from FHC or through in-country distributors or non-governmental organizations (NGOs).

The personal health care products company significantly boosted advertising costs in fiscal 2013. It spent $221718 in 2013 up from $52949 in 1012 and $32858 in 2011.

Financial Performance

Thanks to its increased advertising expenses paired with revenue losses FHC's profits decreased some 6% in fiscal 2013 vs. 2012. The company's revenue dropped by 10% during the reporting period. Unit sales dropped 11% as compared to 2012 due to the Brazil and South Africa shipping large orders. To its benefit the average FC2 sales price rose 1% in 2013.

Strategy

FHC has pledged to significantly boost its global education and training investment through 2018.

The company has built a strong foundation for its current FC2 Female Condom from its first generation product FC1. It's further supported by representatives in global locales who provide technical support and assist with customers' prevention and family planning programs.

FHC generates most of its revenue from the sale of its FC2 Female Condom recognized upon shipment of the product to customers. The company also earns revenue by licensing its intellectual property to Hindustan Lifecare Limited an exclusive distributor that makes and sells the FC2 Female Condom in India.

The FC2 Female Condom is made of a nitrile polymer which allows for a faster cheaper manufacturing process. The primary difference between the first-generation FC1 condom and the FC2 condom is that the FC1 condom can be cleaned and reused several times (a benefit the company doesn't necessarily recommend).

EXECUTIVES

Chief Scientific Officer, K. Barnette, $397,500 total compensation
Independent Director, Michael Rankowitz
Independent Director, Grace Hyun
Chief Financial Officer, Chief Administrative Officer, Michele Greco, $382,500 total compensation
Chairman Of The Board, President, Chief Executive Officer, Mitchell Steiner, $618,000 total compensation
Independent Director, Mario Eisenberger
Vice Chairman And Chief Corporate Officer, Harry Fisch
Auditors: RSM US LLP

LOCATIONS

HQ: Veru Inc
  48 N.W. 25th Street, Suite 102, Miami, FL 33127
Phone: 305 509-6897
Web: www.veruhealthcare.com

COMPETITORS

BIOVERATIV INC.
Bausch Health Companies Inc
Bayer AG
CIPLA LIMITED
DYAX CORP.
HIKMA PHARMACEUTICALS PUBLIC LIMITED COMPANY
NATURAL ALTERNATIVES INTERNATIONAL INC.
NATURE'S SUNSHINE PRODUCTS INC.

HISTORICAL FINANCIALS
Company Type: Public

Income Statement   FYE: September 30

	REVENUE ($ mil.)	NET INCOME ($ mil.)	NET PROFIT MARGIN	EMPLOYEES
09/21	61.2	7.3	12.1%	252
09/20	42.5	(18.9)	—	339
09/19	31.8	(12.0)	—	386
09/18	15.8	(23.9)	—	171
09/17	13.6	(6.6)	—	175
Annual Growth	45.5%	—	—	9.5%

2021 Year-End Financials

Debt ratio: —
Return on equity: 8.1%
Cash ($ mil.): 122.3
Current ratio: 9.62
Long-term debt ($ mil.): —

No. of shares (mil.): 79.9
Dividends
  Yield: —
  Payout: —
Market value ($ mil.): 682.0

	STOCK PRICE ($)		P/E	PER SHARE ($)		
	FY Close		High/Low	Earnings	Dividends	Book Value
09/21	8.53		208 24	0.09	0.00	1.90
09/20	2.62		— —	(0.28)	0.00	0.43
09/19	2.16		— —	(0.19)	0.00	0.50
09/18	1.42		— —	(0.44)	0.00	0.53
09/17	2.65		— —	(0.25)	0.00	0.91
Annual Growth	33.9%		— —	—	—	20.3%

Viavi Solutions Inc

Viavi Solutions facilitates better communication. The company is a leading provider of test and measurement instruments and test tools that are used to build and improve communications equipment and broadband networks. Viavi offers instruments and software and product support that help customers build and maintain communication equipment and broadband networks. It also provides test products and services for private enterprise networks. Another Viavi offering is optical technology which includes tools for detecting counterfeit currency as well as optical filters for sensor applications. About a third of Viavi's sales are to customers in the US. Viavi was created in 2015 when JDS Uniphase split into two companies.

Operations

Viavi operates in three segments: Network Enablement (NE) Service Enablement (SE) and Optical Security and Performance products (OSP).

The NE segment about 65% of revenue provides testing tools for network build-out and maintenance tasks. The tools include instruments software and services to design build activate certify troubleshoot and optimize networks.

The SE segment about 10% of revenue provides embedded systems and enterprise performance management that provide information about network service and application data. The segment's instruments microprobes and software monitor collect and analyze network data to show customer experience and identify revenue and network optimization opportunities.

The OSP segment about a quarter of revenue offers optics for anti-counterfeit efforts guidance systems laser-eye protection smartphone security and night vision systems.

Viavi operates its own manufacturing facilities and uses contract manufacturers as well.

Geographic Reach

Viavi's sales are spread among major geographic regions. The US accounts for about 30% of revenue China supplies about 20% of revenue and the Europe the Middle East and Africa region provides about 30% of revenue.

The company has manufacturing facilities in China France Germany the UK and the US while its most significant contract manufacturers are in China and Mexico.

Sales and Marketing

Viavi's customers include major telecommunications providers government agencies and corporations. Among its customers are Am ©rica M vil AT&T Inc. CenturyLink Inc. Cisco Systems Comcast Nokia and Verizon Communications as well as Lockheed Martin and Seiko Epson Inc.

Financial Performance

Viavi's revenue has fluctuated since the spin off from JDS Uniphase but it took a turn higher in 2019. The company has had net losses for three of the past five years.

Sales jumped 29% to $1.1 billion in 2019 (ended June) an increase of about $254 million from 2017's revenue of about $875.7 million. The NE segment posted a 37% year-over-year increase driven by the AvComm and Wireless (AW) acquisition and growth in the 5G wireless and fiber businesses. The OSP segment's sales advanced about a third due to demand for anti-counterfeiting products and 3D sensing for facial recognition applications in smartphones. SE segment revenue fell about 13% in 2019 from 2018 due to a decline in data center demand.

Higher sales propelled Viavi to $5.4 million in net income compared to a loss of $48.6 million in 2017.

Viavi's net cash was $530.4 million in 2019 compared to $624.3 million the year before. In 2019 operations generated $138.8 million and investing activities provided $80.6 million while financing activities used $330.4 million.

The company issued a total of $685 million in debt in 2017 and 2018 which substantially increased its principal payment obligations. Those payments could draw funds from operations and make it harder to obtain further financing.

Strategy

Since it was created in the split of JDS Uniphase in 2015 Viavi has invested in internal operations to build and diversify its operations and it has made acquisitions to further bolster its offerings.

The company is positioned to take advantage of growth in 5G networking and expansion of fiber capacity throughout the world. Its optical capabilities are poised to reap revenue from increasing use of technologies such as facial recognition in unlocking smartphones.

Viavi has invested some $700 million in internal research and development in 5G fiber and cable instrumentation platforms as well as 3D sensing and anti-counterfeit technologies. Added to that was another $630 million for acquisitions that strengthened those areas as well.

The company has expanded sales in the Asia/Pacific region and Europe reducing its reliance on the US market.

Mergers and Acquisitions

In 2019 Viavi acquired 3Z a provider of antenna alignment installation and monitoring technologies.

In 2018 Viavi Solutions acquired RPC to expand its 3D sensing offerings.

The 2018 deal for the AvComm and Wireless assets of Cobham strengthened Viavi's position in 5G deployment and diversified its offerings into military public safety and avionics test markets.

HISTORY

Engineer Dale Crane was already making helium neon lasers in his garage when he left laser developer Spectra-Physics in 1979 to start Uniphase. Initially the company developed and marketed gas laser subsystems to manufacturers of biomedical industrial process control and printing equipment. In 1992 Demax Software executive Kevin Kalkhoven became CEO and Uniphase formed Ultrapointe introducing the Ultrapointe laser imaging system for semiconductor production the following year. Expenses related to a gas laser subsystem patent-infringement suit filed by Spectra-Physics caused losses in 1993 the year Uniphase went public.

In the mid-1990s Uniphase began to use acquisitions to expand its market share and consolidate product lines. In 1995 the company bought optical components supplier United Technologies Photonics from United Technologies entering the telecom market.

In 1997 it bought IBM's laser business and Australia-based Indx a maker of reflection filters used to increase the carrying capacity of a fiber-optic strand. Uniphase's 1998 acquisitions included Philips Optoelectronics (semiconductor lasers) and Broadband Communications Products (fiber-optic transmitters and receivers). The company sold its Ultrapointe unit to chip equipment maker KLA-Tencor late that year. The acquisition spree contributed to losses for fiscal 1997 and 1998.

In 1999 Uniphase merged with JDS FITEL a Canada-based maker of fiber-optic communications gear in a $7 billion deal. JDS FITEL founded in 1981 by four Nortel engineers focused on making so-called "passive" fiber-optic components that route and manipulate optical signals. It was a complementary fit to Uniphase's "active" gear that generates and transmits signals. The combined company named itself JDS Uniphase. Both JDS FITEL and Uniphase aggressively pursued acquisitions prior to the merger and JDS Uniphase continued shopping.

In fiscal 2000 following a huge run-up in its share price JDS Uniphase made 10 acquisitions including EPITAXX (optical detectors and receivers) and Optical Coating Laboratory. Its largest acquisition was of rival E-Tek Dynamics (for $20.4 billion) which JDSU used to further increase its capacity to produce passive components such as amplifiers and better equip itself to offer customers complete optical systems. That year Kalkhoven retired and co-chairman Jozef Straus (former CEO of JDS FITEL) was named as his replacement.

After making a series of acquisitions in the early 2000s JDSU announced that it would split into two companies.

EXECUTIVES

Chairman, Richard Belluzzo
Independent Director, Masood Jabbar
Independent Director, Keith Barnes
Senior Vice President, General Manager, Optical Security & Performance Products, Luke Scrivanich, $372,000 total compensation
Independent Director, Timothy Campos
Senior Vice President, General Counsel, Secretary, Kevin Siebert
Senior Vice President - Global Operations And Services, Network And Service Enablement, Ralph Rondinone, $352,000 total compensation
President, Chief Executive Officer, Director, Oleg Khaykin, $800,000 total compensation
Senior Vice President - Global Sales, Network And Service Enablement, Gary Staley, $375,000 total compensation
Independent Director, Donald Colvin
Independent Director, Tor Braham
Independent Director, Laura Black
Chief Financial Officer, Executive Vice President, Henk Derksen, $137,308 total compensation

Executive Vice President, Chief Marketing And Strategy Officer, Paul McNab, $435,000 total compensation
Auditors: PricewaterhouseCoopers LLP

LOCATIONS

HQ: Viavi Solutions Inc
7047 E Greenway Pkwy Suite 250, Scottsdale, AZ 85254
Phone: 408 404-3600
Web: www.viavisolutions.com

PRODUCTS/OPERATIONS

2019 Sales

	$ mil.	% of total
Network Enablement	737.8	65
Service Enablement	103.4	9
Optical Security & Performance Products	289.1	26
Total	**1,130.3**	**100**

Selected Products

Communications test & measurement (CommTest)
  Service Assurance Systems
  Services
  Software
  Test instruments
Communications & commercial optical products (CCOP)
  Lasers
  Optical Communications
  Amplifiers
  Couplers/Splitters
  Lasers
  Optical communications
  Detectors/receivers
  Lasers
  Modulators
  Multiplexers
  Switches
  Transceivers
  Transmitter modules
  Transponders
  Photovoltaics
Advanced optical technologies (AOT)
  Custom colors for product finishes and decorative packaging
  Optical thin-film coatings

Selected Customers

Communications test & measurement
  AT&T
  Bell Canada
  Bharti Airtel
  British Telecom
  Brocade
  China Mobile
  China Telecom
  Comcast
  Deutsche Telecom
  EMC
  France Telecom
  Hewlett-Packard
  IBM
  TalkTalk
  Telefónica
  TimeWarner Cable
  Verizon
Communications and commercial optical
  Optical communications equipment manufacturers
  Alcatel-Lucent
  Cisco Systems
  Ericsson
  Fujitsu
  Huawei
  Nokia Siemens Networks
  Tellabs
  Commercial lasers
  ASML
  Beckman Coulter
  Becton Dickinson
  Electro Scientific
  KLA-Tencor
  Solar cell
  Amplifier Research

Beijing Bosin Industrial Technology
ETS-Lindgren
Siemens
Advanced Optical Technologies
  3M
  American Express
  DuPont
  Kingston
  Lockheed Martin
  MasterCard
  Northrop Grumman
  Seiko Epson

COMPETITORS

AGILENT TECHNOLOGIES INC.
BRUKER CORPORATION
EXAR CORPORATION
FEI COMPANY
MACOM TECHNOLOGY SOLUTIONS HOLDINGS INC.
METTLER-TOLEDO INTERNATIONAL INC.
OCLARO INC.
PACIFIC BIOSCIENCES OF CALIFORNIA INC.
SEMTECH CORPORATION
TELEDYNE FLIR LLC
WATERS CORPORATION

HISTORICAL FINANCIALS

Company Type: Public

Income Statement   FYE: July 3

	REVENUE ($ mil.)	NET INCOME ($ mil.)	NET PROFIT MARGIN	EMPLOYEES
07/21*	1,198.9	46.1	3.8%	3,600
06/20	1,136.3	28.7	2.5%	3,600
06/19	1,130.3	5.4	0.5%	3,600
06/18	880.4	(46.0)	—	3,500
07/17	811.4	166.9	20.6%	2,700
Annual Growth	10.3%	(27.5%)	—	7.5%

*Fiscal year change

2021 Year-End Financials

Debt ratio: 31.8%
Return on equity: 6.1%
Cash ($ mil.): 697.8
Current ratio: 1.58
Long-term debt ($ mil.): 209.8
No. of shares (mil.): 228.3
Dividends
  Yield: —
  Payout: —
Market value ($ mil.): 3,988.0

	STOCK PRICE ($) FY Close	P/E High/Low		Earnings	PER SHARE ($) Dividends	Book Value
07/21*	17.47	90	57	0.20	0.00	3.39
06/20	12.50	124	69	0.12	0.00	3.12
06/19	13.29	688	468	0.02	0.00	3.17
06/18	10.24	—	—	(0.20)	0.00	3.17
07/17	10.53	16	9	0.71	0.00	3.45
Annual Growth	13.5%		—	(27.1%)	—	(0.4%)

*Fiscal year change

VICI Properties Inc

Auditors: Deloitte & Touche LLP

LOCATIONS

HQ: VICI Properties Inc
535 Madison Avenue, 20th Floor, New York, NY 10022
Phone: 646 949-4631
Web: www.viciproperties.com

HISTORICAL FINANCIALS

Company Type: Public

Income Statement   FYE: December 31

	REVENUE ($ mil.)	NET INCOME ($ mil.)	NET PROFIT MARGIN	EMPLOYEES
12/20	1,225.5	891.6	72.8%	147
12/19	894.8	545.9	61.0%	140
12/18	897.9	523.6	58.3%	140
12/17	187.6	42.6	22.7%	140
12/16	18.7	0.0	—	140
Annual Growth	184.2%	—	—	1.2%

2020 Year-End Financials

Debt ratio: 39.6%
Return on equity: 10.2%
Cash ($ mil.): 315.9
Current ratio: 1.03
Long-term debt ($ mil.): 6,765.5
No. of shares (mil.): 536.6
Dividends
  Yield: 4.9%
  Payout: 71.7%
Market value ($ mil.): 13,685.0

	STOCK PRICE ($) FY Close	P/E High/Low		Earnings	PER SHARE ($) Dividends	Book Value
12/20	25.50	16	6	1.75	1.26	17.50
12/19	25.55	20	15	1.24	1.17	17.28
12/18	18.78	16	12	1.43	1.00	16.84
12/17	20.50	111	95	0.19	0.00	15.62
Annual Growth	7.5%	—	—109.6%		—	3.9%

Vicor Corp

Vicor makes converters that tame and transfer raw electricity into the stable DC voltages needed to power electronic circuits. The company's zero current and zero voltage switching technologies which allow its converters to operate at high frequencies with relatively little noise are designed to be mounted on a printed circuit board. Customers — including global OEMs and small manufacturers of specialized electronics devices — incorporate the converters into all sorts of electronic equipment ranging from fiber-optic systems to military radar. Vicor power component design methodology offers a comprehensive range of modular building blocks enabling rapid design of a power system. The company also sell a range of electrical and mechanical accessories for use with their products. Vicor derives more than 45% of its sales from customers in the US.

Operations

The company categorize their product portfolios as Brick Products and Advanced Products.

The Brick Products generates more than 70% of company's total revenue it provides integrated transformation rectification isolation regulation filtering and/or input protection necessary to power and protect loads across a range of conventional power architectures. This product also offer a wide range of brick-format DC-DC converters as well as complementary components providing AC line rectification input filtering power factor correction and transient protection.

The Advanced Products consist of the remaining revenue. This portfolio consists of the company's most innovative products which are used to implement its proprietary distribution architecture Factorized Power Architecture (FPA) a highly dif-

HOOVER'S HANDBOOK OF EMERGING COMPANIES 2022   437

ferentiated approach to power distribution that enables flexible rapid power system design using individual components optimized to perform a specific function.

Overall the company's brick products bring in around 70& of the company's total sales while advance products account for the rest.

Geographic Reach

Massachusetts-based Vicor has domestic locations in California Illinois Oregon Rhode Island Texas and Massachusetts. International locations reside in China Germany India Italy Korea Japan Taiwan and the UK. International sales in 2019 accounted for about 55% of revenue while revenues from customers in China accounted for more than 20%.

Sales and Marketing

The company's products are sold worldwide to customers ranging from smaller independent manufacturers of highly specialized electronic devices to larger original equipment manufacturers (OEMs) and their contract manufacturers.

Vicor reach and serve customers through several channels: a direct sales force; a network of independent sales representative organizations in North America and South America; independent authorized non-stocking distributors in Europe and Asia; and three authorized stocking distributors world-wide Digi-Key Corporation Future Electronics Incorporated and Mouser Electronics Inc. In fiscal 2019 direct customers contract manufacturers and non-stocking distributors generates some 85% of company's total sales. Followed by stocking distributors that produces about 15% of revenue and the remaining is from non-recurring engineering.

The company incurred approximately $2.7 million $2.6 million and $2.2 million in advertising costs during 2019 2018 and 2017 respectively.

Financial Performance

Revenue for the company has been fluctuating and it cannot maintain growth for two consecutive years. Net income generally followed that trend for the same period.

Revenue in 2019 decreased by 10% to $263 million. Factors contributing to the decline in bookings and revenue were customer delays in the launch of new Advanced Products programs for use in Artificial Intelligence ("AI") and supercomputing.

Net income for 2019 decreased by 56% to $14.1 million due to lower net revenues and higher operating expenses.

Net cash at the end of fiscal 2019 was $84.7 million. Net cash provided by operating activities was $22.2 million while net cash used for investing activities was $12.5 million. Financing activities added another $4.4 million to the coffers. Main cash uses were for purchases of property plant and equipment.

Strategy

Vicor's strategy emphasizes demonstrable product differentiation and a value proposition based on competitively superior solution performance advantageous design flexibility and a compelling total cost of ownership ("TCO"). Since the company was founded its competitive position has been maintained by continuous innovations in product design and achievements in product performance largely enabled by its focus on the research and development of advanced technologies and processes often implemented in proprietary semiconductor circuitry materials and packaging. Many of its products incorporate patented or proprietary implementations of high-frequency switching topologies which enable the design of power system solutions more efficient and much smaller than conventional alternatives. This efficiency and small size is enabled by its proprietary switching circuitry and magnetic structures as well as its use of highly differentiated packaging.

Given the growth profiles and performance requirements of the market segments served with Advanced Products and Brick Products its strategy involves a transition in organizational focus emphasizing investment in Advanced Products design and manufacturing targeting high growth market segments with a low-mix high-volume operational model while maintaining a profitable business in mature market segments it serves with Brick Products with a high-mix low-volume operational model.

HISTORY

Inspired by an incident in the 1970s — his hi-fi system blew up — Italian physicist Patrizio Vinciarelli left his Princeton fellowship in 1980 to experiment with power-supply technology. Borrowing $500000 from friends and their families he founded Vicor in 1981. By 1982 he developed the basic technology that the company's products are based on. Vicor shipped its first product in 1985 and was profitable by 1987. Early customers included Xcerra and Telco Systems. Vicor went public in 1990.

EXECUTIVES

Corporate Vice President, Chief Accounting Officer, Richard Nagel, $188,073 total compensation
Chairman, President And Chief Executive Officer, Patrizio Vinciarelli, $123,077 total compensation
Corporate Vice President, General Manager, Operations, Director, Michael McNamara, $340,230 total compensation
Corporate Vice President, Director, President Of Picor Corporation, Claudio Tuozzolo, $411,550 total compensation
Corporate Vice President - Engineering, Power Components, Alex Gusinov
Corporate Vice President - Product Marketing And Technical Resources, Robert Gendron, $304,280 total compensation
Corporate Vice President - Engineering, Power Systems, Sean Crilly
Corporate Vice President - Human Resources, Nancy Grava
Director, Andrew D'Amico
Corporate Vice President, Chief Information Officer, Alvaro Doyle
Chief Financial Officer, Corporate Vice President, Treasurer, Company Secretary, Director, James Schmidt
Independent Director, M. Michael Ansour
Corporate Vice President - Global Sales And Marketing, Director, Philip Davies, $373,441 total compensation
Auditors: KPMG LLP

LOCATIONS

HQ: Vicor Corp
25 Frontage Road, Andover, MA 01810
Phone: 978 470-2900
Web: www.vicorpower.com

PRODUCTS/OPERATIONS

2016 Sales

	$ mil.	% of total
Brick Business Unit	151.4	76
VI Chip	38.4	19
Picor	10.5	5
Total	**200.3**	**100**

Selected Products

AC-DC power systems
AC-DC filters
Accessory power-system components
Bus converters
DC-DC filters
DC-DC modular power converters (for mounting on printed circuit boards)
DC-DC power systems
Configurable products
Customer-specific power converters and supplies
EMI filters
Regulators

COMPETITORS

BEL FUSE INC.
CML MICROSYSTEMS PLC
COGNEX CORPORATION
DELTA ELECTRONICS INC.
DIODES INCORPORATED
MONOLITHIC POWER SYSTEMS INC.
NIDEC CORPORATION
NITTO DENKO CORPORATION
Silicom Ltd.
TRANSDIGM GROUP INCORPORATED
ULTRALIFE CORPORATION
VOLEX PLC

HISTORICAL FINANCIALS

Company Type: Public

Income Statement

FYE: December 31

	REVENUE ($ mil.)	NET INCOME ($ mil.)	NET PROFIT MARGIN	EMPLOYEES
12/20	296.5	17.9	6.0%	1,049
12/19	262.9	14.1	5.4%	1,014
12/18	291.2	31.7	10.9%	1,007
12/17	227.8	0.1	0.1%	980
12/16	200.2	(6.2)	—	971
Annual Growth	**10.3%**	**—**		**2.0%**

2020 Year-End Financials

Debt ratio: —
Return on equity: 6.4%
Cash ($ mil.): 161.7
Current ratio: 7.82
Long-term debt ($ mil.): —
No. of shares (mil.): 43.3
Dividends
  Yield: —
  Payout: —
Market value ($ mil.): 3,996.0

	STOCK PRICE ($) FY Close	P/E High/Low		PER SHARE ($) Earnings	Dividends	Book Value
12/20	92.22	227	78	0.41	0.00	8.10
12/19	46.72	137	77	0.34	0.00	5.07
12/18	37.79	80	21	0.78	0.00	4.57
12/17	20.90	—	—	(0.00)	0.00	3.45
12/16	15.10	—	—	(0.16)	0.00	3.35
Annual Growth	**57.2%**	**—**	**—**	**—**		**24.7%**

Victory Capital Holdings Inc (DE)

Auditors: Ernst & Young LLP

LOCATIONS

HQ: Victory Capital Holdings Inc (DE)
15935 La Cantera Parkway, San Antonio, TX 78256
Phone: 216 898-2400

HISTORICAL FINANCIALS

Company Type: Public

Income Statement

FYE: December 31

	REVENUE ($ mil.)	NET INCOME ($ mil.)	NET PROFIT MARGIN	EMPLOYEES
12/20	775.3	212.5	27.4%	429
12/19	612.3	92.4	15.1%	358
12/18	413.4	63.7	15.4%	263
12/17	409.6	25.8	6.3%	267
12/16	297.8	(6.0)	—	276
Annual Growth	27.0%	—	—	11.7%

2020 Year-End Financials

Debt ratio: 44.4%
Return on equity: 34.0%
Cash ($ mil.): 22.7
Current ratio: 0.64
Long-term debt ($ mil.): 769.0
No. of shares (mil.): 67.5
Dividends
Yield: 0.9%
Payout: 8.6%
Market value ($ mil.): 1,676.0

	STOCK PRICE ($) FY Close	P/E High/Low		PER SHARE ($) Earnings	Dividends	Book Value
12/20	24.81	8	4	2.88	0.23	10.48
12/19	20.97	16	8	1.26	0.10	7.95
12/18	10.22	14	8	0.90	0.00	6.74
Annual Growth	55.8%		—	— 78.9%		— 24.6%

Viemed Healthcare Inc

Auditors: Ernst & Young LLP

LOCATIONS

HQ: Viemed Healthcare Inc
625 E. Kaliste Saloom Rd., Lafayette, LA 70508
Phone: 337 504-3802
Web: www.viemed.com

HISTORICAL FINANCIALS

Company Type: Public

Income Statement

FYE: December 31

	REVENUE ($ mil.)	NET INCOME ($ mil.)	NET PROFIT MARGIN	EMPLOYEES
12/20	131.3	31.5	24.0%	511
12/19	80.2	8.5	10.6%	418
12/18	64.4	9.5	14.7%	293
12/17	46.9	8.1	17.4%	0
Annual Growth	40.9%	56.8%	—	—

2020 Year-End Financials

Debt ratio: 6.7%
Return on equity: 50.1%
Cash ($ mil.): 30.9
Current ratio: 2.05
Long-term debt ($ mil.): 5.8
No. of shares (mil.): 39.1
Dividends
Yield: —
Payout: —
Market value ($ mil.): 304.0

	STOCK PRICE ($) FY Close	P/E High/Low		PER SHARE ($) Earnings	Dividends	Book Value
12/20	7.76	14	3	0.78	0.00	2.08
12/19	6.20	37	14	0.21	0.00	1.15
12/18	3.80	25	7	0.24	0.00	0.87
12/17	0.00	—	—	0.22	0.00	0.63
Annual Growth	—		— —	52.5%		— 49.3%

Village Bank & Trust Financial Corp

Does it take a village to raise a bank? Village Bank & Trust is the holding company for Village Bank which has about a dozen branches in the suburbs of Richmond Virginia. It offers standard services including deposit accounts loans and credit cards. Deposit funds are used to write loans for consumers and businesses in the area; commercial real estate loans mainly secured by owner-occupied businesses account for about half of the bank's lending portfolio which also includes business construction residential mortgage and consumer loans. In 2008 Village Bank & Trust acquired the three-branch River City Bank in a transaction worth more than $20 million.

EXECUTIVES

Executive Vice President- Commercial Banking, Max Morehead, $198,536 total compensation
Independent Chairman Of The Board, Craig Bell
Independent Director, George Whittemore
Independent Director, Michael Katzen
Executive Vice President, Chief Credit Officer Of The Bank, Roy Barzel
Executive Vice President - Retail Of The Bank, Rebecca Kline
Independent Director, Raymond Avery
President, Chief Executive Officer, Director, James Hendricks, $256,923 total compensation
Chief Financial Officer, Executive Vice President, Chief Risk Officer, Donald Kaloski
Independent Director, Frank Jenkins
Independent Director, Michael Toalson
Executive Vice President Of Operations Of The Bank, Christy Quesenbery
Independent Director, Mary Kastelberg
President, Chief Executive Officer Of Village Bank Mortgage Corporation, James Winn, $157,114 total compensation
Auditors: Yount, Hyde & Barbour, P.C.

LOCATIONS

HQ: Village Bank & Trust Financial Corp
13319 Midlothian Turnpike, Midlothian, VA 23113
Phone: 804 897-3900
Web: www.villagebank.com

COMPETITORS

BANK OF THE JAMES FINANCIAL GROUP INC.
FIRST TRUST BANK
FULTON FINANCIAL CORPORATION
MECHANICS BANK
MUTUALFIRST FINANCIAL INC.
STONEBRIDGE FINANCIAL CORP
SURUGA BANK LTD.

HISTORICAL FINANCIALS

Company Type: Public

Income Statement

FYE: December 31

	ASSETS ($ mil.)	NET INCOME ($ mil.)	INCOME AS % OF ASSETS	EMPLOYEES
12/20	706.2	8.5	1.2%	152
12/19	540.3	4.4	0.8%	146
12/18	514.8	3.0	0.6%	150
12/17	476.9	(3.1)	—	161
12/16	444.8	13.5	3.0%	178
Annual Growth	12.3%	(10.8%)	—	(3.9%)

2020 Year-End Financials

Return on assets: 1.3%
Return on equity: 17.9%
Long-term debt ($ mil.): —
No. of shares (mil.): 1.4
Sales ($ mil): 38.0
Dividends
Yield: —
Payout: —
Market value ($ mil.): 50.0

	STOCK PRICE ($) FY Close	P/E High/Low		PER SHARE ($) Earnings	Dividends	Book Value
12/20	34.39	8	4	5.86	0.00	35.46
12/19	37.11	12	10	3.10	0.00	29.53
12/18	30.45	17	14	2.04	0.00	25.87
12/17	30.65	—	—	(2.55)	0.00	27.49
12/16	26.70	3	2	8.99	0.00	30.54
Annual Growth	6.5%		— —	(10.1%)	—	3.8%

Virginia National Bankshares Corp

EXECUTIVES

Chb, John B Adams Jr
Pres-Ceo, Marc J Bogan
Exec V Pres-Cco, Gina R Bayes
Exec V Pres-Cfo, Tara Y Harrison
Exec V Pres, Donna G Shewmake
Private Banking and Treasury M, Scott W Waskey
Evp, Jennifer Matheny
Customer Representativ, Amie Eppard
Commercial Lender, Amanda Hallstead
Head of Trading, Tim Starsia
Market President, Arthur Bryant
Auditors: Yount, Hyde & Barbour, P.C.

LOCATIONS

HQ: Virginia National Bankshares Corp
404 People Place, Charlottesville, VA 22911
Phone: 434 817-8621
Web: www.vnbcorp.com

HOOVER'S HANDBOOK OF EMERGING COMPANIES 2022

HISTORICAL FINANCIALS
Company Type: Public

Income Statement				FYE: December 31
	ASSETS ($ mil.)	NET INCOME ($ mil.)	INCOME AS % OF ASSETS	EMPLOYEES
12/20	848.4	7.9	0.9%	86
12/19	702.6	6.6	1.0%	97
12/18	644.8	8.4	1.3%	86
12/17	643.8	6.5	1.0%	81
12/16	605.0	5.7	1.0%	85
Annual Growth	8.8%	8.5%	—	0.3%

2020 Year-End Financials
Return on assets: 1.0%
Return on equity: 10.0%
Long-term debt ($ mil.): —
No. of shares (mil.): 2.7
Sales ($ mil): 33.8

Dividends
  Yield: 0.0%
  Payout: 40.8%
Market value ($ mil.): 74.0

	STOCK PRICE ($) FY Close	P/E High/Low		PER SHARE ($)		
				Earnings	Dividends	Book Value
12/20	27.15	13	8	2.94	1.20	30.43
12/19	37.70	16	14	2.49	1.20	28.27
12/18	34.51	17	11	3.15	1.09	26.49
12/17	39.00	16	11	2.46	0.61	24.50
12/16	28.50	13	10	2.19	0.47	22.61
Annual Growth	(1 2%)	—	—	7.7%	26.6%	7.7%

VirnetX Holding Corp

VirnetX is involved in a net of legal battles. The company owns more than 70 US technology patents for establishing secure mobile internet communications over the 4G LTE network but it claims several major tech firms including Apple and Cisco Systems are giving away its patented internet security software for free. VirnetX bought the core patents from federal IT contractor Leidos in 2006 and has been working to commercialize its mobile communications software branded as GABRIEL Connection Technology as well as a secure domain name registry service. Before the company can convince customers to license its software it must resolve about 10 patent infringement lawsuits against Apple and Cisco.

Operations
VirnetX owns some 185 patents and pending applications. About 40% are in the US and the rest have been granted or filed overseas. The company's patents focus on securing real-time communications over the internet as well as related services such as establishing and maintaining a secure domain name registry.

The company's Gabriel Security Platform allows application developers to automatically perform user authentication cryptographic peer device authentication domain and user policy enforcement and zero click VPN access.

The Gabriel Collaboration Suite includes applications that allow businesses and individuals to communicate and collaborate in a secure end-to-end encrypted invisible network. These applications include Secure Mail Secure Messaging Secure Voice Call Secure Share & Sync and Secure Gateway Service.

Sales and Marketing
VirnetX works with partners to sell its technology has agreements with resellers and managed service providers that target specific markets. They include Asgard MSP (healthcare) Above PAR Advisors (financial) and Max Cybersecurity (government). The company sells its Gabriel line directly to small and medium-sized businesses using online marketing programs and tools.

Financial Performance
VirnetX's revenue of about $1.5 million a year since 2014 comes from a lawsuit settled in 2013. For the record its 2017 revenue was $1.5 million compared to $1.6 million in 2016.

The company's net loss dropped to about $17 million in 2017 from about $28 million in 2016. Its selling general and administrative expenses were $10000 lower in 2017 than 2016 because of a decrease in legal costs.

VirnetX had about $3 million in cash on hand at the end of 2017 compared to about $6.6 million in 2016.

Strategy
VirnetX planned to develop sales and marketing promotions in the US and Japan to recruit more resellers and partners to increase international sales. It also plans to develop direct sales programs. Along those lines the company planned direct marketing of its Gabriel Secure Communication Platform and Gabriel Collaboration Suite products and domain name registry services to service providers and system integrators.

In 2017 the company ended two revenue-sharing marketing programs to develop sales in Japan because of what it termed lack of results.

EXECUTIVES

Independent Director, Michael Angelo
Independent Director, Thomas O'brien
Chief Technical Officer, Victor Larson
Independent Director, Gary Feiner
Chief Financial Officer, Katherine Allanson
Chairman Of The Board, President, Chief Executive Officer, Kendall Larsen, $702,189 total compensation
Auditors: Farber Hass Hurley LLP

LOCATIONS

HQ: VirnetX Holding Corp
  308 Dorla Court, Suite 206, Zephyr Cove, NV 89448
Phone: 775 548-1785
Web: www.virnetx.com

PRODUCTS/OPERATIONS

Selected Services
Connection server software
GABRIEL Connection Technology Software Development Kit
Registrar server software
Relay server software
Secure domain name master registry and connection service
Secure domain name registrar service
Technical support service
VirnetX technology licensing

COMPETITORS

ACACIA RESEARCH CORPORATION
CEVA INC.
MEMBA S. r.l.
QUADIENT S.A.
RPX CORPORATION

HISTORICAL FINANCIALS
Company Type: Public

Income Statement				FYE: December 31
	REVENUE ($ mil.)	NET INCOME ($ mil.)	NET PROFIT MARGIN	EMPLOYEES
12/20	302.6	280.4	92.7%	21
12/19	0.0	(19.1)	—	20
12/18	0.0	(25.4)	—	21
12/17	1.5	(17.2)	—	21
12/16	1.5	(28.5)	—	20
Annual Growth	273.8%	—		1.2%

2020 Year-End Financials
Debt ratio: —
Return on equity: 243.1%
Cash ($ mil.): 192.9
Current ratio: 21.67
Long-term debt ($ mil.): —

No. of shares (mil.): 71.0
Dividends
  Yield: 19.8%
  Payout: 25.5%
Market value ($ mil.): 358.0

	STOCK PRICE ($) FY Close	P/E High/Low		PER SHARE ($)		
				Earnings	Dividends	Book Value
12/20	5.04	2	1	3.92	1.00	3.16
12/19	3.80	—	—	(0.28)	0.00	0.08
12/18	2.40	—	—	(0.40)	0.00	0.15
12/17	3.70	—	—	(0.30)	0.00	0.03
12/16	2.20	—	—	(0.51)	0.00	0.19
Annual Growth	23.0% 101.5%					

Virtu Financial Inc

Auditors: PricewaterhouseCoopers LLP

LOCATIONS

HQ: Virtu Financial Inc
  1633 Broadway, New York, NY 10019
Phone: 212 418-0100
Web: www.virtu.com

HISTORICAL FINANCIALS
Company Type: Public

Income Statement				FYE: December 31
	REVENUE ($ mil.)	NET INCOME ($ mil.)	NET PROFIT MARGIN	EMPLOYEES
12/21	2,811.4	476.8	17.0%	973
12/20	3,239.3	649.2	20.0%	976
12/19	1,530.0	(58.6)	—	1,012
12/18	1,878.7	289.4	15.4%	483
12/17	1,027.9	2.9	0.3%	560
Annual Growth	28.6%	256.9%	—	14.8%

2021 Year-End Financials
Debt ratio: 27.2%
Return on equity: 31.6%
Cash ($ mil.): 1,071.4
Current ratio: 0.57
Long-term debt ($ mil.): 1,605.1

No. of shares (mil.): 182.6
Dividends
  Yield: 3.3%
  Payout: 24.9%
Market value ($ mil.): 5,265.0

	STOCK PRICE ($) FY Close	P/E High/Low		PER SHARE ($) Earnings	Dividends	Book Value
12/21	28.83	8	6	3.91	0.96	8.48
12/20	25.17	5	3	5.16	0.96	7.64
12/19	15.99	—	—	(0.53)	0.96	4.87
12/18	25.76	13	7	2.78	0.96	5.55
12/17	18.30	630	445	0.03	0.96	4.43
Annual Growth	12.0%	—	—	237.9%	(0.0%)	17.6%

Virtus Investment Partners Inc

Virtus Investment Partners provides investment management services to wealthy individuals corporations pension funds endowments and foundations and insurance companies. Boasting more than $108.9 billion in assets under management it operates through affiliated advisors including Duff & Phelps Kayne Anderson Rudnick and Newfleet Asset Management as well as outside subadvisors. Virtus markets diverse investment products such as open- and closed-end funds and managed account services to high-net-worth individuals. It also manages institutional accounts for corporations and other investors. The firm was formed in 1995 through a reverse merger with Duff & Phelps.

Operations

The asset manager operates through several boutique investment firms including: Duff & Phelps Investment Management Ceredex Value Advisors Kayne Anderson Rudnick Investment Management Newfleet Asset Management Rampart Investment Management Seix Investment Advisors Silvant Capital Management and Sustainable Growth Advisers. Virtus offers investors a menu of investment products and services through its affiliates.

Virtus generates more than 80% of its revenue from investment management fees. About 60% of its total revenue came from investment management fees from funds during while such management fees from retail separate accounts and institutional accounts each made up around 20%. The rest of its revenue came from distribution and service fees (about 10% of revenue) and administration and transfer agent fees (more than 5% of revenue).

Of the firm's $108.9 billion in assets under management about 40% of the assets were invested in open-end mutual funds while investments in closed-end funds about 20% of the assets and retail separate managed accounts made up another nearly 30% of the portfolio. The rest of the portfolio was invested in institutional assets and exchange traded funds (ETFs).

Geographic Reach

Hartford Connecticut-based Virtus has offices in California Connecticut Florida Georgia Illinois Massachusetts New Jersey and New York.

Sales and Marketing

Like other mutual fund asset managers Virtus distributes its open-end funds and ETFs through financial intermediaries such as national and regional broker-dealers and registered investment advisers banks and insurance companies. Its retail separate accounts are distributed through financial intermediaries and directly to private clients by teams at an affiliated manager. Its institutional services are marketed through relationships with consultants as well as directly to clients. Its target key market segments including foundations and endowments corporate public and private pension plans and subadvisory relationships.

Its sales efforts are supported by regional sales professionals a national account relationship group and separate teams for ETFs and the retirement and insurance channels.

Financial Performance

Despite a $59.4 million revenue decrease in 2016 overall revenue growth from 2015 to 2019 was still remarkable at 47%.

In 2019 revenue increased 2% to $563.2 million which was primarily due to higher revenues from an increase in average assets primarily as a result of the SGA Acquisition and positive market performance.

Net income for the year increased by 39% to $105.5 million. Higher revenue and higher total Other income contributed to the increase in net income.

Cash and cash equivalents at the end of the year were $321.9 million. Net cash used in operating activities was $36.7 million. Net cash provided by investing activities was $4.4 million and financing activities provided another $99.6 million to the company coffers. Main cash uses were for purchases of investments.

Strategy

The company offers investment strategies for individual and institutional investors in different product structures and through multiple distribution channels. Its investment strategies are available in a diverse range of styles and disciplines managed by a collection of differentiated investment managers. It has offerings in various asset classes (equity fixed income and alternative) geographies (domestic international and emerging) market capitalizations (large mid and small) styles (growth core and value) and investment approaches (fundamental quantitative and thematic). Its retail products include open-end funds and exchange traded funds (ETFs) as well as closed-end funds and retail separate accounts. Its institutional products are offered through separate accounts and pooled or commingled structures to a variety of institutional clients. It also provides sub-advisory services to other investment advisers and serves as the collateral manager for structured products.

It distributes its open-end funds and ETFs principally through financial intermediaries. It has broad distribution access in the retail market with distribution partners that include national and regional broker-dealers independent broker-dealers and registered investment advisers banks and insurance companies. In many of these firms it has a number of products that are on preferred "recommended" lists and on fee-based advisory programs. Its sales efforts are supported by regional sales professionals a national account relationship group and separate teams for ETFs and the retirement and insurance channels. It leverages third-party distributors for off-shore products and in certain international jurisdictions. Its retail separate accounts are distributed through financial intermediaries and directly to private clients by teams at an affiliated manager.

Its institutional services are marketed through relationships with consultants as well as directly to clients. It targets key market segments including foundations and endowments corporate public and private pension plans and sub-advisory relationships.

It uses capital to seed new investment strategies and make investments to introduce new products or enhance distribution access of existing products.

Company Background

Virtus in October 2012 acquired the business and assets of Boston-based Rampart Investment Management Co. a registered investment adviser specializing in customized options strategies for institutional and high-net-worth individuals for $700000 in cash. The Rampart purchase added $1.3 billion in assets under management and added another investment partner to Virtus' group of boutique investment managers.

EXECUTIVES

Chief Operating Officer, Executive Vice President, Richard Smirl
Executive Vice President - Head Of Distribution, Barry Mandinach, $415,000 total compensation
President, Chief Executive Officer, Director, George Aylward, $591,667 total compensation
Chief Financial Officer, Executive Vice President, Treasurer, Michael Angerthal, $375,000 total compensation
Independent Chairman Of The Board, Timothy Holt
Independent Director, Melody Jones
Independent Director, Susan Fleming
Independent Director, Peter Bain
Chief Human Resource Officer, Executive Vice President, Mardelle Pena, $275,000 total compensation
Executive Vice President, Chief Legal Officer, General Counsel, Corporate Secretary, Wendy Hills, $350,000 total compensation
Independent Director, Walter Morris
Auditors: DELOITTE & TOUCHE LLP

LOCATIONS

HQ: Virtus Investment Partners Inc
One Financial Plaza, Hartford, CT 06103
Phone: 800 248-7971
Web: www.virtus.com

PRODUCTS/OPERATIONS

2015 Sales

	% of total
Investment management fees	69
Distribution & service fees	18
Administration & transfer agent fees	13
Other	-
Total	**100**

Selected Subsidiaries & Affiliates

Duff & Phelps Investment Management (Chicago)
Kayne Anderson Rudnick Investment Management (Los Angeles)
Newfleet Asset Management (Hartford Connecticut)
Rampart Investment Management Company LLC (Boston)
Virtus Investment Advisers Inc. (Massachusetts)
Zweig/Euclid Advisors LLC (New York)

COMPETITORS

AMERIPRISE FINANCIAL INC.	PRINCIPAL GLOBAL INVESTORS LLC
BLACKROCK INC.	PZENA INVESTMENT

EATON VANCE CORP.
FRANKLIN RESOURCES INC.
MANNING & NAPIER INC. INVESTMENTS
OAKTREE CAPITAL GROUP LLC
MANAGEMENT INC.
WESTWOOD HOLDINGS GROUP INC.
WISDOMTREE INC.

HISTORICAL FINANCIALS
Company Type: Public

Income Statement
FYE: December 31

	REVENUE ($ mil.)	NET INCOME ($ mil.)	NET PROFIT MARGIN	EMPLOYEES
12/20	603.9	79.9	13.2%	581
12/19	563.2	95.6	17.0%	578
12/18	552.2	75.5	13.7%	577
12/17	425.6	37.0	8.7%	543
12/16	322.5	48.5	15.0%	406
Annual Growth	17.0%	13.3%	—	9.4%

2020 Year-End Financials
Debt ratio: 68.9%
Return on equity: 11.5%
Cash ($ mil.): 339.8
Current ratio: 17.58
Long-term debt ($ mil.): 2,391.6
No. of shares (mil.): 7.5
Dividends
 Yield: 1.3%
 Payout: 38.0%
Market value ($ mil.): 1,646.0

	STOCK PRICE ($) FY Close	P/E High/Low		PER SHARE ($) Earnings	Dividends	Book Value
12/20	217.00	21	5	10.02	2.83	93.78
12/19	121.72	10	6	11.74	2.32	99.23
12/18	79.43	15	8	8.86	1.90	90.02
12/17	115.05	31	24	3.96	1.80	82.20
12/16	118.05	20	11	6.20	1.80	54.62
Annual Growth	16.4%	—	—	12.8%	12.0%	14.5%

Vital Farms Inc

EXECUTIVES
Pres-Ceo, Russell Diez-Canseco
Exec Chb*, Matthew O'Hayer
Coo-Cfo, Jason Dale
Cmo, Scott Marcus
Cso, Peter Pappas
Grower Support Coordinator, Jamie Yarak
Accounts Receivable Specialist, Andreanna Moya
Compliance Coordinator, Cheri Barenberg
Vice President Sales, Jonathan Skaare
Quality Assurance Compliance M, Rhyan Holzer
Contractor, Todd Sternberg

LOCATIONS
HQ: Vital Farms Inc
 3601 South Congress Avenue, Suite C100, Austin, TX 78704
Phone: 877 455-3063
Web: www.vitalfarms.com

HISTORICAL FINANCIALS
Company Type: Public

Income Statement
FYE: December 27

	REVENUE ($ mil.)	NET INCOME ($ mil.)	NET PROFIT MARGIN	EMPLOYEES
12/20	214.2	8.8	4.1%	215
12/19	140.7	2.3	1.7%	161
12/18	106.7	5.8	5.4%	0
12/17	74.0	(1.9)	—	0
Annual Growth	42.5%	—	—	—

2020 Year-End Financials
Debt ratio: —
Return on equity: 10.1%
Cash ($ mil.): 29.5
Current ratio: 5.30
Long-term debt ($ mil.): —
No. of shares (mil.): 39.4
Dividends
 Yield: —
 Payout: —
Market value ($ mil.): 1,052.0

	STOCK PRICE ($) FY Close	P/E High/Low		PER SHARE ($) Earnings	Dividends	Book Value
12/20	26.66	134	80	0.27	0.00	3.60
12/19	0.00	—	—	0.07	0.00	1.22
Annual Growth	195.6%	—		−285.7%	—	—

Voyager Therapeutics Inc

Auditors: Ernst & Young LLP

LOCATIONS
HQ: Voyager Therapeutics Inc
 75 Sidney Street, Cambridge, MA 02139
Phone: 857 259-5340
Web: www.voyagertherapeutics.com

HISTORICAL FINANCIALS
Company Type: Public

Income Statement
FYE: December 31

	REVENUE ($ mil.)	NET INCOME ($ mil.)	NET PROFIT MARGIN	EMPLOYEES
12/20	171.1	36.7	21.5%	179
12/19	104.3	(43.6)	—	186
12/18	7.6	(88.2)	—	124
12/17	10.1	(70.7)	—	89
12/16	14.2	(40.1)	—	78
Annual Growth	86.3%	—	—	23.1%

2020 Year-End Financials
Debt ratio: —
Return on equity: 28.8%
Cash ($ mil.): 104.4
Current ratio: 7.39
Long-term debt ($ mil.): —
No. of shares (mil.): 37.3
Dividends
 Yield: —
 Payout: —
Market value ($ mil.): 267.0

	STOCK PRICE ($) FY Close	P/E High/Low		PER SHARE ($) Earnings	Dividends	Book Value
12/20	7.15	15	7	0.98	0.00	4.13
12/19	13.95	—	—	(1.21)	0.00	2.70
12/18	9.40	—	—	(2.75)	0.00	1.44
12/17	16.60	—	—	(2.64)	0.00	4.25
12/16	12.74	—	—	(1.59)	0.00	5.31
Annual Growth	(13.4%)	—	—	—	—	(6.1%)

W.P. Carey Inc

Need help managing your property portfolio? Keep calm and Carey on. W. P. Carey invests in and manages commercial real estate including office distribution retail and industrial facilities. The company owns more than 1000 properties mainly in the US and Europe and manages properties for several non-traded real estate investment trusts (REITs). Its management portfolio totals some $15 billion. W. P. Carey typically acquires properties and then leases them back to the sellers/occupants on a long-term basis. It also provides build-to-suit financing for investors worldwide. W. P. Carey is converting to a REIT a corporate structure that comes with tax benefits and more flexibilty in investing in real estate.

Geographic Reach

New York-based W. P. Carey owns some 1020 properties in 21 countries. The firm has offices in Dallas London Amsterdam Hong Kong and Shanghai. International investments account for about 31% of the REIT's annual revenue.

Financial Performance

Carey's revenue increased 31% in 2013 versus 2012 to $489.9 million. Revenue growth was spurred by additions to the firm's real estate portfolio made in 2012 including 19 self-storage properties. Net income rose 59% over the same period to $98.9 million due primarily to higher revenue and income from discontinued operations.

Strategy

Since 1979 the REIT has sponsored a series of 18 income-generating investment programs that invest primarily in commercial properties net leased to single tenants under the Corporate Property Associates or CPA brand name. In 2013 the firm managed four global active funds: CPA 16 CPA 17 and CPA 18. W.P. Carey looks to diversify its managed funds and make investments in properties that provide consistent long-term sources of income. Property diversity helps shield W.P. from being reliant on any single industry. A few of its recent investments include a hypermarket in Germany operated by Metro AG a newly-constructed office in Wales the new Siemens AS headquarters in Oslo Norway and a 302-room Hampton Inn & Suites/Homewood Suites by Hilton hotel in Denver's central business district.

In addition to making property investments the firm is focused on diversifying its asset management capabilities. W.P. Carey has launched a lodging-focused fund (Carey Watermark Investors). The new investment program is dedicated to investing in the lodging sector and made its first investments in 2011.

In late 2014 the firm made its first investment in Australia via a 20-year net-lease transaction with Inghams Enterprises Pty. Ltd. The $138 million deal included industrial and agricultural properties.

EXECUTIVES

Chief Executive Officer, Director, Jason Fox, $799,615 total compensation
Independent Director, Jean Hoysradt
President, John Park, $525,000 total compensation
Managing Director, Head - Investments, Gino Sabatini, $500,000 total compensation
Managing Director, Head - Asset Management, Brooks Gordon, $399,385 total compensation
Independent Director, Axel Hansing
Chief Financial Officer, ToniAnn Sanzone, $524,615 total compensation
Independent Non-executive Chairman Of The Board, Christopher Niehaus
Independent Director, Peter Farrell
Independent Director, Mark Alexander
Independent Director, Nicolaas van Ommen
Independent Director, Robert Flanagan
Independent Director, Margaret Lewis
Independent Director, Tonit Calaway
Auditors: PricewaterhouseCoopers LLP

LOCATIONS

HQ: W.P. Carey Inc
One Manhattan West, 395 9th Avenue, 58th Floor, New York, NY 10001
Phone: 212 492-1100
Web: www.wpcarey.com

PRODUCTS/OPERATIONS

2015 sales

	% of total
Real estate ownership	78
Investment management	22
Total	**100**

COMPETITORS

CAPLEASE INC.	HUDSON PACIFIC
CARTER & ASSOCIATES	PROPERTIES INC.
ENTERPRISES INC.	KENNEDY-WILSON
CBRE GROUP INC.	HOLDINGS INC.
COUSINS PROPERTIES	LAND SECURITIES GROUP
INCORPORATED	PLC
DOUGLAS EMMETT INC.	PROLOGIS INC.
DUKE REALTY	
CORPORATION	

HISTORICAL FINANCIALS

Company Type: Public

Income Statement

FYE: December 31

	REVENUE ($ mil.)	NET INCOME ($ mil.)	NET PROFIT MARGIN	EMPLOYEES
12/21	1,331.5	409.9	30.8%	183
12/20	1,209.3	455.3	37.7%	188
12/19	1,232.7	305.2	24.8%	204
12/18	885.7	411.5	46.5%	206
12/17	848.3	277.2	32.7%	207
Annual Growth	**11.9%**	**10.3%**	**—**	**(3.0%)**

2021 Year-End Financials

Debt ratio: 43.8%	No. of shares (mil.): 190.0
Return on equity: 5.6%	Dividends
Cash ($ mil.): 165.4	Yield: 5.1%
Current ratio: 0.22	Payout: 170.9%
Long-term debt ($ mil.): 6,791.6	Market value ($ mil.): 15,591.0

STOCK PRICE ($) FY Close	P/E High/Low	PER SHARE ($) Earnings	Dividends	Book Value
12/21	82.05	37 29	2.24	4.21	39.90
12/20	70.58	34 17	2.60	4.17	39.21
12/19	80.04	53 36	1.78	4.14	40.29
12/18	65.34	20 17	3.49	4.09	41.29
12/17	68.90	28 23	2.56	4.01	29.86
Annual Growth	**4.5%**	**— —**	**(3.3%)**	**1.2%**	**7.5%**

Walker & Dunlop Inc

Walker & Dunlop is one of the leading commercial real estate services and finance companies. The company provides commercial real estate financial services — mainly multifamily loans for apartments health care properties and student housing — to real estate owners and developers across the US. It originates and sells its products (e.g. mortgages supplemental financing construction loans and mezzanine loans) primarily through government-sponsored enterprises (GSEs) like Fannie Mae and Freddie Mac as well as through HUD. To a lesser extent the company originates loans for insurance companies banks and institutional investors.

Operations

The company offers a range of multifamily and other commercial real estate financing products including Agency Lending Debt Brokerage Principal Lending and Investing and Property Sales. It also offers a broad range of commercial real estate finance products to its customers including first mortgage second trust supplemental construction mezzanine preferred equity small-balance and bridge/interim loans. The company provide property sales services to owners and developers of multifamily properties and commercial real estate investment management services for various investors. Through a joint venture it also provide multifamily property appraisals.

Geographic Reach

Walker & Dunlop is headquartered at Bethesda Maryland.

Sales and Marketing

Walker & Dunlop originates and sells loans through the programs of the Federal National Mortgage Association the Federal Home Loan Mortgage Corporation the Government National Mortgage Association and the Federal Housing Administration a division of the US Department of Housing and Urban Development.

Financial Performance

The company's revenue for fiscal 2020 increased by 33% to $1.1 billion compared to $817.2 million in the prior year. The increase in revenues was mainly driven by increases in origination fees MSR Income servicing fees net warehouse interest income and property sales broker fees.

Net income for fiscal 2020 increased to $246.0 million compared from the prior with $173.2 million.

Cash held by the company at the end of fiscal 2020 increased to $358.0 million. Cash used for operations was $1.4 billion while cash provided by investing and financing activities were $115.2 million and $1.5 billion respectively.

Strategy

Walker & Dunlop believe its success in achieving its 2020 goal of $1 billion in revenues positions the company to continue growing and diversifying its business by leveraging its people brand and technology. In the fourth quarter of 2020 the company set new long-term goals to accomplish by the end of 2025 that include:

Grow debt financing volume to $65 billion annually including $5 billion of annual small balance multifamily lending with a servicing portfolio of $160 billion by continuing to hire and acquire the best mortgage bankers in the industry leveraging its brand to continue growing its client base and leveraging proprietary technology to be more insightful and relevant to its clients. Walker & Dunlop continues to increase its market share in the multifamily financing market with a 9% share in 2020.

Grow property sales volume to $25 billion annually by leveraging the strengths of its current team growing volumes within its current markets and continuing to build out its brand and footprint nationally by hiring brokers in new geographic markets and brokers who specialize in different multifamily product types.

Establish investment banking capabilities with a goal to reach $10 billion in assets under management by building on its existing capabilities and developing new capabilities to meet more of its client's needs. The company has routinely been asked by its clients to help them in providing market insights raising more complex capital solutions and undertaking platform valuations. Walker & Dunlop's market-leading position in debt financing and its national reach in its property sales platform gives the company access to substantial amounts of local and macro environmental data.

Remain a leader in environmental social and governance ("ESG") efforts by increasing the percentage of women and minorities within the ranks of its top earners and senior management remaining carbon neutral while reducing its carbon emissions and donating 1% of its annual income from operations to charitable organizations.

Company Background

Walker & Dunlop's relationship with government-related housing finance companies began in the late 1980s after it started originating underwriting and selling loans through Fannie Mae. In 2008 it began working with Freddie Mac and HUD after acquiring a loan servicing portfolio worth $5 billion from Column Guaranteed LLC. The acquisition served to widen Walker & Dunlop's revenue base and increase its sales volume.

EXECUTIVES

Chief Financial Officer, Executive Vice President, Stephen Theobald, $500,000 total compensation
Chairman Of The Board, Chief Executive Officer, William Walker, $900,000 total compensation
President, Director, Howard Smith, $625,000 total compensation
Chief Human Resource Officer, Executive Vice President, Paula Pryor, $361,280 total compensation
Executive Vice President, General Counsel, Secretary, Richard Lucas, $500,000 total compensation
Independent Director, Michael Malone
Independent Director, Ellen Levy
Chief Production Officer, Dana Wade
Independent Director, Donna Wells
Affordable Chief Production Officer, John Ducey
Auditors: KPMG LLP

LOCATIONS

HQ: Walker & Dunlop Inc
7501 Wisconsin Avenue, Suite 1200E, Bethesda, MD 20814
Phone: 301 215-5500
Web: www.walkerdunlop.com

PRODUCTS/OPERATIONS

2014 Sales

	% of total
Gains from mortgage banking activities	62
Servicing fees	27
Net warehouse interest income	5
Escrow earnings & other interest income	1
Other	5
Total	**100**

Selected Products and Services

Capital Markets and Investment Services
Construction loans
Equity investments
FHA Finance
First mortgage loans
Healthcare Finance
Mezzanine loans
Multifamily Finance
Second trust loans
Supplemental financings
Underwriting

COMPETITORS

AMERIPRISE FINANCIAL INC.
AMERIS BANCORP
CARDTRONICS INC.
CELTIC INVESTMENT INC.
CHRISTIE GROUP PLC
CITY OF LONDON GROUP PLC.
EAGLE BANCORP INC.
ENVESTNET INC.
EURAZEO
FIDELITY NATIONAL INFORMATION SERVICES INC.
FIRST CONNECTICUT BANCORP INC.
FIRST EAGLE PRIVATE CREDIT LLC
LIQUIDITY SERVICES INC.
LONDON ASIA CAPITAL PLC
NATIONSTAR MORTGAGE HOLDINGS INC.
SIGNATURE BANK
STATE STREET CORPORATION
VIAD CORP

HISTORICAL FINANCIALS

Company Type: Public

Income Statement

FYE: December 31

	REVENUE ($ mil.)	NET INCOME ($ mil.)	NET PROFIT MARGIN	EMPLOYEES
12/20	1,033.7	246.1	22.7%	988
12/19	817.2	173.3	21.2%	823
12/18	725.2	161.4	22.3%	723
12/17	711.8	211.1	29.7%	623
12/16	575.2	113.9	19.8%	550
Annual Growth	**17.2%**	**21.3%**	**—**	**15.8%**

2020 Year-End Financials

Debt ratio: 60.3%	No. of shares (mil.): 30.6
Return on equity: 22.0%	Dividends
Cash ($ mil.): 321.1	Yield: 1.5%
Current ratio: 23.54	Payout: 18.7%
Long-term debt ($ mil.): 2,808.7	Market value ($ mil.): 2,823.0

	STOCK PRICE ($) FY Close	P/E High/Low		Earnings	PER SHARE ($) Dividends	Book Value
12/20	92.02	12	3	7.69	1.44	38.99
12/19	64.68	12	8	5.45	1.20	34.48
12/18	43.25	12	7	4.96	1.00	30.58
12/17	47.50	8	4	6.56	0.00	26.97
12/16	31.20	8	5	3.65	0.00	20.65
Annual Growth	**31.0%**	**—**		**—**	**20.5%**	**17.2%**

Waterstone Financial Inc (MD)

Auditors: CliftonLarsonAllen LLP

LOCATIONS

HQ: Waterstone Financial Inc (MD)
11200 W. Plank Court, Wauwatosa, WI 53226
Phone: 414 761-1000
Web: www.wsbonline.com

HISTORICAL FINANCIALS

Company Type: Public

Income Statement

FYE: December 31

	ASSETS ($ mil.)	NET INCOME ($ mil.)	INCOME AS % OF ASSETS	EMPLOYEES
12/20	2,184.5	81.1	3.7%	812
12/19	1,996.3	35.9	1.8%	824
12/18	1,915.3	30.7	1.6%	888
12/17	1,806.4	25.9	1.4%	927
12/16	1,790.6	25.5	1.4%	895
Annual Growth	**5.1%**	**33.5%**		**(2.4%)**

2020 Year-End Financials

Return on assets: 3.8%	Dividends
Return on equity: 20.0%	Yield: 6.8%
Long-term debt ($ mil.): —	Payout: 51.0%
No. of shares (mil.): 25.0	Market value ($ mil.): 472.0
Sales ($ mil): 322.5	

	STOCK PRICE ($) FY Close	P/E High/Low		Earnings	PER SHARE ($) Dividends	Book Value
12/20	18.82	6	4	3.30	1.28	16.47
12/19	19.03	14	11	1.37	0.98	14.50
12/18	16.76	16	14	1.11	0.98	14.04
12/17	17.05	21	18	0.93	0.98	13.97
12/16	18.40	20	14	0.93	0.26	13.95
Annual Growth	**0.6%**	**—**		**— 37.2%**	**49.0%**	**4.2%**

Weber Inc

LOCATIONS

HQ: Weber Inc
1415 S. Roselle Road, Palatine, IL 60067
Phone: 847 934-5700
Web: www.weber.com

HISTORICAL FINANCIALS

Company Type: Public

Income Statement

FYE: September 30

	REVENUE ($ mil.)	NET INCOME ($ mil.)	NET PROFIT MARGIN	EMPLOYEES
09/21	1,982.4	47.7	2.4%	2,534
09/20	1,525.2	88.8	5.8%	2,156
09/19	1,296.2	50.1	3.9%	0
09/18	1,340.0	113.3	8.5%	0
Annual Growth	**13.9%**	**(25.0%)**	**—**	**—**

2021 Year-End Financials

Debt ratio: 66.8%	No. of shares (mil.): 286.1
Return on equity: ***,***.*%	Dividends
Cash ($ mil.): 107.5	Yield: —
Current ratio: 1.30	Payout: —
Long-term debt ($ mil.): 1,023.2	Market value ($ mil.): 5,033.0

	STOCK PRICE ($) FY Close	P/E High/Low	Earnings	PER SHARE ($) Dividends	Book Value
09/21	17.59	—	(0.13)	0.00	(0.04)
09/20	0.00	—	160.23	0.00	(78.92)
Annual Growth	**—**	**—**	**—**	**—**	**—**

WesBanco Inc

WesBanco offers a full range of financial services including retail banking corporate trust services personal and corporate trust services brokerage services mortgage banking and insurance. WesBanco operates one commercial bank: WesBanco Bank which has more than 200 branches and ATM machines located in Indiana Kentucky Ohio Pennsylvania and West Virginia. WesBanco offers its services through its community banking and trust and investment services segments. WesBanco's non-banking operations include brokerage firm WesBanco Securities and multi-line insurance provider WesBanco Insurance Services. The company was founded in 1968.

Financial Performance

The company's revenue increased in fiscal 2013 compared to the prior fiscal period. WesBanco reported $287.2 million in revenue for fiscal 2013 up from $276.5 in fiscal 2012.

The company's net income also increased in fiscal 2013 compared to the previous year. It reported net income of $63.9 million in fiscal 2013 up from net income of $49.5 million for fiscal 2012.

As another sign of the company's health WesBanco's cash on hand spiked by about $65 million during fiscal 2013 compared to fiscal 2012 levels.

EXECUTIVES

Senior Executive Vice President, Chief Risk And Administrative Officer, Michael Perkins
Senior Vice President And Chief Accounting Officer, Daniel Weiss
Executive Vice President - Treasury And Strategic Planning, Brent Richmond
Independent Director, Abigail Feinknopf
Independent Chairman Of The Board, Christopher Criss
Independent Director, Reed Tanner

Independent Director, Jay McCamic
Executive Vice President, Chief Internal Auditor, Stephen Lawrence
Independent Director, D. Bruce Knox
Executive Vice President - Wealth Management, Jonathan Dargusch, $302,298 total compensation
Senior Executive Vice President And Group Head - Human Resources & Facilities, Anthony Pietranton, $297,103 total compensation
Executive Vice President, Chief Credit Officer, Ivan Burdine
Director, Denise Knouse-Snyder
Independent Director, Lisa Knutson
Independent Director, Gary Libs
Independent Director, Robert Fitzsimmons
Independent Director, Gregory Proctor
Independent Director, Joseph Robinson
President, Chief Executive Officer, Director, Todd Clossin, $928,743 total compensation
Auditors: Ernst & Young LLP

LOCATIONS

HQ: WesBanco Inc
1 Bank Plaza, Wheeling, WV 26003
Phone: 304 234-9000
Web: www.wesbanco.com

PRODUCTS/OPERATIONS

2016 Sales

	$ mil.	% of total
Interest and Dividend Income		
Loans including fees	227.0	61
Interest and dividends on securities	56.9	15
Other interest income	2.2	1
Non-Interest Income		
Trust fees	21.6	6
Service charges on deposits	18.3	5
Electronic banking fees	15.6	4
Net securities brokerage	6.4	2
Bank-owned life insurance	4.1	1
Net gains on sales of mortgage loans	2.5	1
Net securities gains	2.4	1
Net gain / (loss) on other real estate owned and other assets	0.8	-
others	9.8	3
Total	**367.6**	**100**

Selected Products and Services

Personal Banking
Internet Banking
Checking
Savings
Time Deposits
Debit Cards
Credit Cards
Loans
Mortgage Lending
Other Services
Business
Internet Banking
Checking
Savings
Time Deposits
Credit Cards
Loans
Treasury Management
Insurance Services
Wealth Management

COMPETITORS

CITY HOLDING COMPANY OLD LINE BANCSHARES
FIRST MIDWEST BANCORP INC.
INC. RENASANT CORPORATION
FIRSTMERIT CORPORATION SANDY SPRING
BANCORP
LEGACYTEXAS FINANCIAL INC.
GROUP INC. TCF FINANCIAL
META FINANCIAL GROUP CORPORATION
INC.
NATIONAL BANK HOLDINGS
CORPORATION

HISTORICAL FINANCIALS

Company Type: Public

Income Statement

FYE: December 31

	ASSETS ($ mil.)	NET INCOME ($ mil.)	INCOME AS % OF ASSETS	EMPLOYEES
12/20	16,425.6	122.0	0.7%	2,612
12/19	15,720.1	158.8	1.0%	2,705
12/18	12,458.6	143.1	1.1%	2,383
12/17	9,816.1	94.4	1.0%	1,940
12/16	9,790.8	86.6	0.9%	1,928
Annual Growth	13.8%	8.9%	—	7.9%

2020 Year-End Financials

Return on assets: 0.7%	Dividends
Return on equity: 4.5%	Yield: 4.2%
Long-term debt ($ mil.): —	Payout: 79.0%
No. of shares (mil.): 67.2	Market value ($ mil.): 2,015.0
Sales ($ mil): 669.4	

	STOCK PRICE ($) FY Close	P/E High/Low	PER SHARE ($) Earnings	Dividends	Book Value
12/20	29.96	21 10	1.77	1.28	40.99
12/19	37.79	15 12	2.83	1.24	38.24
12/18	36.69	17 12	2.92	1.16	36.24
12/17	40.65	20 16	2.14	1.04	31.68
12/16	43.06	20 13	2.16	0.96	30.53
Annual Growth	(8.7%)	— —	(4.9%)	7.5%	7.6%

West Bancorporation, Inc.

West Bancorporation is the holding company for West Bank which serves individuals and small to midsized businesses through about a dozen branches mainly in the Des Moines and Iowa City Iowa areas. Founded in 1893 the bank offers checking savings and money market accounts CDs Visa credit cards and trust services. The bank's lending activities primarily consist of commercial mortgages; construction land and land development loans; and business loans such as revolving lines of credit inventory and accounts receivable financing equipment financing and capital expenditure loans to borrowers in Iowa.

Sales and Marketing

West Bank focuses on small to medium-sized businesses in its local markets. The thinking is that smaller local firms want to develop an exclusive relationship with a single bank.

Financial Performance

The company's revenue has been remarkably consistent year-over-year. It reported $61.2 million in annual revenue for fiscal 2013 after claiming $61.7 million in fiscal 2012 and $64.1 million in fiscal 2011.

Net income has also remained very consistent in recent years. The bank reported net income of $16.8 million for fiscal 2013 after clearing $16 million in fiscal 2012 and $15.27 million in fiscal 2011.

The company's net cash on hand has decreased dramatically in recent fiscal years however mostly as a result of property investments.

Strategy

West Bank has slowly but surely been expanding its territory. The company is working on building a new headquarters building and expanding into Minnesota.

EXECUTIVES

Cfo, Douglas Gulling, $318,000 total compensation
Executive Vice President And Chief Financial Officer, Jane Funk
Executive Vice President, Chief Risk Officer And Director, Executive Vice President, Chief Risk Officer Of West Bank, Harlee Olafson, $318,000 total compensation
Executive Vice President And President, Director Of West Bank, Brad Winterbottom, $318,000 total compensation
Non-executive Chairman Of The Board, Independent Director, James Noyce
Independent Director, Therese Vaughan
President, Chief Executive Officer, Director And Chairman, Chief Executive Officer, Director Of West Bank, David Nelson, $462,160 total compensation
Independent Director, Sean Mcmurray
Independent Director, Philip Worth
Independent Director, Steven Gaer
Auditors: RSM US LLP

LOCATIONS

HQ: West Bancorporation, Inc.
1601 22nd Street, West Des Moines, IA 50266
Phone: 515 222-2300
Web: www.westbankstrong.com

PRODUCTS/OPERATIONS

2015 Sales

	$ mil.	% of total
Interest		
Loans including fees	52.5	77
Taxable investment Securities	4.4	6
Tax-exempt investment Securities	3.2	5
Federal funds sold	0.0	-
Noninterest		
Service charges on deposit accounts	2.6	4
Debit card usage fees	1.8	3
Trust services	1.3	2
Revenue from residential mortgage banking	0.1	-
Increase in cash value of bank-owned life insurance	0.7	1
Realized investment securities gains net	0.0	-
Other income	1.6	2
Total	**68.4**	**100**

COMPETITORS

BANK OF THE WEST NEWBRIDGE BANCORP
GREAT SOUTHERN BANCORP NORTH VALLEY
BANCORP
INC. TRUSTCO BANK CORP N Y

HISTORICAL FINANCIALS

Company Type: Public

Income Statement

FYE: December 31

	ASSETS ($ mil.)	NET INCOME ($ mil.)	INCOME AS % OF ASSETS	EMPLOYEES
12/20	3,185.7	32.7	1.0%	350
12/19	2,473.6	28.6	1.2%	171
12/18	2,296.5	28.5	1.2%	163
12/17	2,114.3	23.0	1.1%	162
12/16	1,854.2	23.0	1.2%	165
Annual Growth	14.5%	9.2%	—	20.7%

2020 Year-End Financials

Return on assets: 1.1%
Return on equity: 14.9%
Long-term debt ($ mil.): —
No. of shares (mil.): 16.4
Sales ($ mil): 109.8

Dividends
Yield: 4.3%
Payout: 43.7%
Market value ($ mil.): 318.0

	STOCK PRICE ($) FY Close	P/E High/Low		PER SHARE ($) Earnings	Dividends	Book Value
12/20	19.30	13	8	1.98	0.84	13.58
12/19	25.63	15	11	1.74	0.83	12.93
12/18	19.09	15	10	1.74	0.78	11.72
12/17	25.15	20	15	1.41	0.71	10.98
12/16	24.70	17	11	1.42	0.67	10.25
Annual Growth	(6.0%)	—	—	8.7%	5.8%	7.3%

West Pharmaceutical Services, Inc.

West Pharmaceutical Services is a leading global manufacturer in the design and production of technologically advanced high-quality integrated containment and delivery components for pharmaceutical and health care products. The company's proprietary drug and biologic packaging products include seals and stoppers for injectable medicine syringe components and injection systems. It also provides contract manufacturing services including product design and commercialization injection molding and complex assemblies for pharmaceutical diagnostic and medical device customers. The US is West's largest single market accounting for about 45% of total revenue.

Operations

West operates through two reportable segments: Proprietary Products and Contract-Manufactured Products.

The Proprietary Products segment accounting for about 75% of total revenue makes containment packaging and drug delivery devices for injectable pharmaceuticals and biologic therapies. It also provides analytical lab services to its customers in the biologic and pharmaceutical sectors along with other product development support services. Products include syringe and cartridge components seals and stoppers administration systems films and coatings polymer vials and self-injection devices. This segment's product portfolio also includes drug containment solutions including Crystal Zenith a cyclic olefin polymer in the form of vials syringes and cartridges.

The Contract-Manufactured Products segment bringing in some 25% of total revenue serves as a fully integrated business focused on the design manufacture and automated assembly of complex devices primarily for pharmaceutical diagnostic and medical device customers. These products include a variety of custom contract-manufacturing and assembly solutions which use such technologies as multi-component molding in-mold labeling ultrasonic welding clean room molding and device assembly. It manufacture customer-owned components and devices used in surgical diagnostic ophthalmic injectable and other drug delivery systems as well as consumer products.

Geographic Reach

Headquartered in Exton Pennsylvania West has manufacturing facilities throughout the world including locations in Arizona Florida Michigan Nebraska North Carolina and Pennsylvania in the US and in Brazil China Germany Denmark France India Ireland Puerto Rico Serbia Singapore and the UK abroad. It also has affiliates in Mexico and Japan.

Sales in the US make up about 45% of revenue followed by Germany (nearly 15%) Ireland (about 10%) France (less than 5%) and other European countries (about 15%). Countries in other regions account for more than 10% of revenue.

Sales and Marketing

West's products are distributed through its direct sales force and distribution facilities as well as through select contracted sales agents and regional distributors.

The Proprietary Products segment's customers include major biologic pharma and generic drug companies. The Contract-Manufactured Products segment's customers include pharma medical device and diagnostic companies.

The company's ten largest customers account for more than 40% of revenue.

Financial Performance

The company's revenue and net income have been climbing in the last five years with an overall growth of 42% and 141% respectively between 2016 and 2020.

Consolidated net sales increased by $307 million or 17% to $2.1 billion in 2020. Proprietary Products net sales increased by $250.0 million or 18% in 2020 including a favorable foreign currency translation impact of $2.2 million.

Net income totaled $346.2 million a 43% growth from the previous year. This was due to a higher sales volume for the year which outweighed the expenses.

The company's cash at the end of 2020 was $615.5 million. Operating activities generated $472.5 million while investing activities used $179.5 million mainly for capital expenditures. Financing activities used another $137.1 million.

Strategy

The company employs a supply chain management strategy in its business segments which involves purchasing from integrated suppliers that control their own sources of supply. Due to regulatory control over the company's production processes sole source availability and the cost and time involved in qualifying suppliers the company relies on single-source suppliers for many critical raw materials. It generally purchases certain raw materials in the open market.

The company also continues to pursue innovative strategic platforms in pre-fillable syringes injectable containers and advanced injection and safety and administration systems.

Company Background

West Pharmaceutical was founded in Pennsylvania in 1923.

EXECUTIVES

Senior Vice President, General Counsel And Corporate Secretary, Kimberly MacKay
Independent Director, Thomas Hofmann
Independent Chairman Of The Board, Patrick Zenner
Independent Director, Mark Buthman
Independent Director, Douglas Michels
Independent Director, William Feehery

Independent Director, Myla Lai-Goldman
President, Chief Executive Officer, Director, Eric Green, $989,423 total compensation
Vice President, Corporate Development, Strategy And Investor Relations, Quintin Lai
Independent Director, Paolo Pucci
Senior Vice President, Chief Technology Officer, Silji Abraham, $440,769 total compensation
Independent Director, Deborah Keller Tanner
Independent Director, Robert Friel
Chief Accounting Officer, Principal Accounting Officer, Vice President, Corporate Controller, Chad Winters
Director, Molly Joseph
Chief Human Resource Officer, Senior Vice President, Annette Favorite, $300,000 total compensation
Senior Vice President, Chief Operating And Supply Chain Officer, David Montecalvo, $445,192 total compensation
Chief Financial Officer, Senior Vice President, Bernard Birkett, $593,654 total compensation
Auditors: PricewaterhouseCoopers LLP

LOCATIONS

HQ: West Pharmaceutical Services, Inc.
530 Herman O. West Drive, Exton, PA 19341-0645
Phone: 610 594-2900
Web: www.westpharma.com

PRODUCTS/OPERATIONS

2017 Sales by Segment

	$ mil.	% of total
Proprietary Products	1,236.9	77
Contract-Manufactured Products	362.5	23
Adjustments	(0.3)	-
Total	1,599.1	100

Product Categories
Vial containment solutions
Prefillable systems
Self-injection platforms
Cartridge systems and components
Reconstitution and transfer systems
Intradermal delivery solutions
Specialty components

COMPETITORS

CANTEL MEDICAL LLC
COOPER-STANDARD INDUSTRIAL AND SPECIALTY GROUP LLC
HILLENBRAND INC.
ICON AEROSPACE TECHNOLOGY LTD
KADANT INC.
NORDSON CORPORATION
TELEFLEX INCORPORATED
TOYODA GOSEI NORTH AMERICA CORPORATION
UFP TECHNOLOGIES INC.
VYSTAR CORPORATION

HISTORICAL FINANCIALS

Company Type: Public

Income Statement				FYE: December 31
	REVENUE ($ mil.)	NET INCOME ($ mil.)	NET PROFIT MARGIN	EMPLOYEES
12/21	2,831.6	661.8	23.4%	10,065
12/20	2,146.9	346.2	16.1%	9,200
12/19	1,839.9	241.7	13.1%	8,200
12/18	1,717.4	206.9	12.0%	7,700
12/17	1,599.1	150.7	9.4%	7,500
Annual Growth	15.4%	44.8%	—	7.6%

2021 Year-End Financials

Debt ratio: 7.6%	No. of shares (mil.): 74.2	
Return on equity: 31.5%	Dividends	
Cash ($ mil.): 762.6	Yield: 0.1%	
Current ratio: 2.93	Payout: 8.5%	
Long-term debt ($ mil.): 208.8	Market value ($ mil.): 34,801.0	

	STOCK PRICE ($) FY Close	P/E High/Low		PER SHARE ($) Earnings	Dividends	Book Value
12/21	469.01	53	29	8.67	0.69	31.47
12/20	283.31	64	28	4.57	0.65	25.06
12/19	150.33	46	29	3.21	0.61	21.23
12/18	98.03	44	30	2.74	0.57	18.84
12/17	98.67	50	39	1.99	0.53	17.32
Annual Growth	47.7%	—	—	44.5%	6.8%	16.1%

Western Alliance Bancorporation

Western Alliance Bancorporation and its flagship Western Alliance Bank (WAB) have an alliance with several bank brands in the West operating as the Alliance Bank of Arizona; Bank of Nevada; as well as Bridge Bank and Torrey Pines Bank. The bank provide standard consumer and business deposit and loan products. More than of the Western Alliance's loan portfolio is made up of commercial and industrial loans while about 30% is made up of commercial real estate loans. It also makes land development loans and consumer residential mortgages and other lines of credit.

Operations

Western Alliance focuses on commercial lending. More than 50% of the bank's loan portfolio consisted of commercial and industrial loans at the end of 2020 while about 30% was made up of commercial real estate loans (non-owner and owner occupied). The bank also had construction and land development loans (10% of loan assets) residential mortgages (3%) and consumer loans (less than 1%).

Geographic Reach

Phoenix-based Western Alliance has about 40 branches which includes more than 5 executive and administrative offices.

Sales and Marketing

The bank serves local businesses real estate developers and investors not-for-profit organizations and consumers. It specializes in lending to such customers operating in the healthcare professional services manufacturing and distribution resorts and timeshares technology and startups municipalities and local governments non-profit and renewable energy markets.

Western Alliance spent $4.1 million and $4.2 million for marketing in 2020 and 2019 respectively.

Financial Performance

Western Alliance's performance for the span of five years have seen growth year by year with 2020 as its highest performing year.

The company's net revenue increased by about $132 million to $1.2 billion as compared to 2019's net revenue of $1.2 billion.

Net income increased by $7 million to $506 million as compared to prior year's net income of $499 million.

The company held cash of $55.5 million at the end of the year. The company's operating activities provided $150 million. Investing activities provided $2 million while financing activities used $172 million.

Strategy

Western Alliance Bancorporation looks to expand its branch network and selectively acquire other banks to boost its loan and deposit business and extend its geographic reach. The bank may also buy other financial services businesses to bolster its line of service offerings.

Mergers and Acquisitions

In 2021 Western Alliance Bancorporation acquired Aris Mortgage Holding Company LLC (parent company of AmeriHome Mortgage Company LLC) for a total consideration of approximately $1.22 billion. AmeriHome Mortgage offers a B2B approach to the mortgage ecosystem through relationships with more than 700 independent correspondent mortgage clients. The acquisition of AmeriHome enable the company to extend its national commercial business with a complementary low-risk national mortgage franchise.

EXECUTIVES

Executive Chairman Of The Board, Robert Sarver, $934,616 total compensation
General Counsel, Corporate Secretary, Randall Theisen, $455,539 total compensation
Vice Chairman, Chief Financial Officer, Dale Gibbons, $754,079 total compensation
Lead Independent Director, Bruce Beach
Independent Director, Marianne Johnson
Independent Director, Sung Won Sohn
President, Chief Executive Officer And Director, Kenneth Vecchione, $1,243,846 total compensation
Independent Director, Michael Patriarca
Independent Director, Howard Gould
Independent Director, Adriane Mcfetridge
Chief Operating Officer, Timothy Boothe, $405,000 total compensation
Chief Credit Officer, Tim Bruckner
Independent Director, Juan Figuereo
Chief Human Resource Officer, Barbara Kennedy, $364,421 total compensation
Auditors: RSM US LLP

LOCATIONS

HQ: Western Alliance Bancorporation
One E. Washington Street, Suite 1400, Phoenix, AZ 85004
Phone: 602 389-3500
Web: www.westernalliancebancorporation.com

PRODUCTS/OPERATIONS

2015 Sales

	% of total
Interest income	
Loans including fees	86
Investment securities	7
Dividends	2
Other	-
Non-interest income	
Service charges and fees	2
Income from bank owned life insurance	1
Card income	1
Other	1
Total	**100**

Selected Services

Business Checking & Savings
Business Loans & Credit
Card Services
International Banking
Personal Banking
Treasury Management

COMPETITORS

AMERICAN NATIONAL BANKSHARES INC.
ATLANTIC UNION BANKSHARES CORPORATION
BANCFIRST CORPORATION
BANK OF THE WEST
BYLINE BANCORP INC.
CAPITAL BANK FINANCIAL CORP.
CITIZENS & NORTHERN CORPORATION
CITY HOLDING COMPANY
CVB FINANCIAL CORP.
ENTERPRISE BANCORP INC.
FIRST CITIZENS BANCSHARES INC.
FIRST EAGLE PRIVATE CREDIT LLC
FLAGSTAR BANCORP INC.
HERITAGE FINANCIAL CORPORATION
HSBC USA INC.
LEGACYTEXAS FINANCIAL GROUP INC.
MERCHANTS BANCORP
MIDWESTONE FINANCIAL GROUP INC.
PACWEST BANCORP
PEOPLE'S UNITED FINANCIAL INC.
REPUBLIC FIRST BANCORP INC.
WINTRUST FINANCIAL CORPORATION

HISTORICAL FINANCIALS

Company Type: Public

Income Statement

FYE: December 31

	ASSETS ($ mil.)	NET INCOME ($ mil.)	INCOME AS % OF ASSETS	EMPLOYEES
12/20	36,461.0	506.6	1.4%	1,915
12/19	26,821.9	499.1	1.9%	1,835
12/18	23,109.4	435.7	1.9%	1,787
12/17	20,329.0	325.4	1.6%	1,725
12/16	17,200.8	259.8	1.5%	1,557
Annual Growth	20.7%	18.2%	—	5.3%

2020 Year-End Financials

Return on assets: 1.6%	Dividends	
Return on equity: 15.7%	Yield: 1.6%	
Long-term debt ($ mil.): —	Payout: 22.8%	
No. of shares (mil.): 100.8	Market value ($ mil.): 6,046.0	
Sales ($ mil): 1,332.6		

	STOCK PRICE ($) FY Close	P/E High/Low		PER SHARE ($) Earnings	Dividends	Book Value
12/20	59.95	12	4	5.04	1.00	33.85
12/19	57.00	12	8	4.84	0.50	29.42
12/18	39.49	15	9	4.14	0.00	24.90
12/17	56.62	19	14	3.10	0.00	21.14
12/16	48.71	20	11	2.50	0.00	18.00
Annual Growth	5.3%	—	—	19.2%	—	17.1%

Western Midstream Partners LP

Western Gas Equity Partners LP (WGEP) is taking stock of a fellow energy concern. The entity formed in September 2012 as an investment vehicle for Western Gas Partners LP (WGP). WGEP's sole purpose is to buy a stake in WGP specifically a limited partner interest of almost 45% and a general partner interest of about 2%. As a shareholder of WGP the entity will receive cash distributions at the end of every fiscal quarter from WGP and as a limited partnership WGEP will distribute its profits back to its own shareholders. It will also be exempt from paying federal income taxes. WGEP filed an IPO seeking up to $362.25 million in November 2012 and plans to use the proceeds raised to begin buying shares in WGP.

EXECUTIVES

President, Chief Executive Officer, Chief Financial Officer, Director Of The General Partner, Michael Ure, $641,346 total compensation
Senior Vice President, Chief Commercial Officer Of The General Partner, Robert Bourne, $417,692 total compensation
Chief Accounting Officer, Vice President Of The General Partner, Catherine Green
Senior Vice President, General Counsel, Corporate Secretary Of The General Partner, Christopher Dial
Independent Director Of The General Partner, Lisa Stewart
Independent Director Of The General Partner, Kenneth Owen
Independent Director Of The General Partner, David Schulte
Director Of The General Partner, Nicole Clark
Chief Operating Officer, Senior Vice President Of The General Partner, Craig Collins, $461,923 total compensation
Director Of The General Partner, Oscar Brown
Chairman Of The Board, Peter Bennett
Auditors: KPMG LLP

LOCATIONS

HQ: Western Midstream Partners LP
9950 Woodloch Forest Drive, Suite 2800, The Woodlands, TX 77380
Phone: 346 786-5000
Web: www.westerngas.com

PRODUCTS/OPERATIONS

2011 Sales

	$ mil.	% of total
Natural gas NGLs and condensate sales	502.4	61
Gathering processing & transporation of natural gas & NGLs	301.3	36
Equity income & other	19.6	3
Total	**823.3**	**100**

COMPETITORS

AMERISUR RESOURCES LIMITED
ANADARKO PETROLEUM CORPORATION
BRAZOS VALLEY LONGHORN L.L.C.
CHESAPEAKE ENERGY CORPORATION
EP ENERGY CORPORATION
NK ROSNEFT PAO
ULTRA PETROLEUM CORP.

HISTORICAL FINANCIALS

Company Type: Public

Income Statement — FYE: December 31

	REVENUE ($ mil.)	NET INCOME ($ mil.)	NET PROFIT MARGIN	EMPLOYEES
12/20	2,772.5	527.0	19.0%	1,045
12/19	2,746.1	697.2	25.4%	19
12/18	1,990.2	369.4	18.6%	0
12/17	2,248.3	376.6	16.8%	0
12/16	1,804.2	345.7	19.2%	0
Annual Growth	11.3%	11.1%	—	—

2020 Year-End Financials

Debt ratio: 66.4%
Return on equity: —
Cash ($ mil.): 444.9
Current ratio: 0.98
Long-term debt ($ mil.): 7,415.8
No. of shares (mil.): 422.9
Dividends
Yield: 11.2%
Payout: 126.4%
Market value ($ mil.): 5,844.0

	STOCK PRICE ($) FY Close	P/E High/Low		Earnings	PER SHARE ($) Dividends	Book Value
12/20	13.82	18	3	1.18	1.56	6.53
12/19	19.69	22	11	1.59	2.45	7.05
12/18	27.73	25	16	1.69	2.30	4.35
12/17	37.16	28	20	1.72	2.02	4.85
12/16	42.35	30	13	1.53	1.71	4.79
Annual Growth	(24.4%)	—	—	(6.3%)	(2.3%)	8.1%

Western New England Bancorp Inc

Westfield Financial is the holding company for Westfield Bank which serves western Massachusetts' Hampden County and surrounding areas from more than 20 branch locations. Founded in 1853 the bank has traditionally been a community-oriented provider of retail deposit accounts and loans but it is placing more emphasis on serving commercial and industrial clients. Commercial real estate loans account for approximately 45% of the company's loan portfolio and business loans are more than 25%. The bank also makes a smaller number of consumer and home equity loans. In 2016 Westfield Financial merged with Chicopee Bancorp the holding company of Chicopee Savings Bank (another bank serving Hampden County).

EXECUTIVES

Executive Vice President, Allen Miles, $300,771 total compensation
President, Chief Executive Officer, Director, James Hagan, $545,084 total compensation
Senior Vice President, Deborah McCarthy, $119,990 total compensation
Executive Vice President, Chief Banking Officer, Kevin O'Connor
Senior Vice President - Credit Administration, Chief Credit Officer, Louis Gorman, $167,033 total compensation
Senior Vice President, Chief Information Officer, Darlene Libiszewski
Independent Director, William Masse

Independent Director, Gary Fitzgerald
Independent Director, Paul Picknelly
Independent Director, Gregg Orlen
Independent Director, Laura Benoit
Independent Chairperson Of The Board, Lisa McMahon
Independent Director, Philip Smith
Independent Director, Donna Damon
Senior Vice President Of Retail Banking, Cidalia Inacio
Senior Vice President And Associate General Counsel, John Bonini
Senior Vice President Of Human Resources, Christine Phillips
Chief Financial Officer, Treasurer, Guida Sajdak, $266,161 total compensation
Senior Vice President, Chief Risk Officer, Leo Sagan, $197,123 total compensation
Auditors: Wolf & Company, P.C.

LOCATIONS

HQ: Western New England Bancorp Inc
141 Elm Street, Westfield, MA 01086
Phone: 413 568-1911
Web: www.westfieldbank.com

COMPETITORS

FIRST PLACE BANK   MIDLAND FINANCIAL CO.

HISTORICAL FINANCIALS

Company Type: Public

Income Statement — FYE: December 31

	ASSETS ($ mil.)	NET INCOME ($ mil.)	INCOME AS % OF ASSETS	EMPLOYEES
12/20	2,365.8	11.2	0.5%	358
12/19	2,181.4	13.3	0.6%	340
12/18	2,118.8	16.4	0.8%	320
12/17	2,083.0	12.3	0.6%	317
12/16	2,076.0	4.8	0.2%	310
Annual Growth	3.3%	23.4%	—	3.7%

2020 Year-End Financials

Return on assets: 0.4%
Return on equity: 4.8%
Long-term debt ($ mil.): —
No. of shares (mil.): 25.2
Sales ($ mil): 92.1
Dividends
Yield: 2.9%
Payout: 54.0%
Market value ($ mil.): 174.0

	STOCK PRICE ($) FY Close	P/E High/Low		Earnings	PER SHARE ($) Dividends	Book Value
12/20	6.89	21	10	0.45	0.20	8.97
12/19	9.63	20	17	0.51	0.20	8.74
12/18	10.04	20	16	0.57	0.16	8.35
12/17	10.90	27	22	0.41	0.12	8.11
12/16	9.35	38	30	0.24	0.03	7.85
Annual Growth	(7.3%)	—	—	17.0%	60.7%	3.4%

WidePoint Corp

WidePoint stretches to provide a variety of IT services to government and enterprise customers. The company provides wireless telecom management and business process outsourcing (BPO) services. Its cybersecurity segment provides identity management services including identity proofing credential issuing and public key infrastructure. The company also provides more traditional IT services such as architecture and planning integration services and vulnerability testing. WidePoint focuses its operations toward US federal government clients including the Department of Homeland Security (more than a quarter of sales) the TSA (nearly a quarter) the FBI Customs and Border Protection and the Justice department.

EXECUTIVES

President, Chief Executive Officer, Director, Jin Kang, $350,000 total compensation
Independent Director, Julia Bowen
Chief Financial Officer, Executive Vice President, Kellie Kim, $250,000 total compensation
Independent Director, Phillip Garfinkle
Executive Vice President, Chief Sales And Marketing Officer, President Of Widepoint Cybersecurity Solutions Corporation, Jason Holloway, $265,000 total compensation
Auditors: Moss Adams LLP

LOCATIONS

HQ: WidePoint Corp
11250 Waples Mill Road, South Tower 210, Fairfax, VA 22030
Phone: 703 349-2577
Web: www.widepoint.com

PRODUCTS/OPERATIONS

Selected Services
Consulting
 Application development integration and management
 Business intelligence
 IT architecture and strategic planning
 infrastructure management
 Project management
 Software selection
Forensic Informatics
Identity Management
Wireless Telecommunications Expense Management

COMPETITORS

AMERICAN SYSTEMS
 CORPORATION
CSRA INC.
PRESIDIO INC.

SMARTRONIX LLC
TELOS CORPORATION
VISTRONIX LLC

HISTORICAL FINANCIALS

Company Type: Public

Income Statement — FYE: December 31

	REVENUE ($ mil.)	NET INCOME ($ mil.)	NET PROFIT MARGIN	EMPLOYEES
12/20	180.3	10.3	5.7%	238
12/19	101.7	0.2	0.2%	249
12/18	83.6	(1.4)	—	227
12/17	75.8	(3.5)	—	247
12/16	78.4	(4.1)	—	279
Annual Growth	23.1%	—	—	(3.9%)

2020 Year-End Financials

Debt ratio: —
Return on equity: 31.4%
Cash ($ mil.): 16.0
Current ratio: 1.24
Long-term debt ($ mil.): —
No. of shares (mil.): 9.0
Dividends
 Yield: —
 Payout: —
Market value ($ mil.): 91.0

STOCK PRICE ($) FY Close	P/E High/Low	PER SHARE ($)		
		Earnings	Dividends	Book Value
12/20	10.11	9 0	1.20	0.00	4.48
12/19	0.40	— —	(0.00)	0.00	2.97
12/18	0.42	— —	(0.20)	0.00	2.90
12/17	0.65	— —	(0.40)	0.00	3.04
12/16	0.81	— —	(0.50)	0.00	3.42
Annual Growth 88.0%	— —	—	—	7.0%

Willis Lease Finance Corp.

Hey buddy got any spare Pratt & Whitneys? Willis Lease Finance buys and sells aircraft engines that it leases to commercial airlines air cargo carriers and maintenance/repair/overhaul organizations in some 30 countries. Its portfolio includes about 180 aircraft engines and related equipment made by Pratt & Whitney Rolls-Royce CFMI GE Aviation and International Aero. The engine models in the company's portfolio are used on popular Airbus and Boeing aircraft. The Willis Lease portfolio also includes four de Havilland DHC-8 commuter aircraft. Customers include Island Air Alaska Airlines American Airlines and Southwest Airlines. Almost 80% of the company's engines are leased and operated outside the US.

Operations

The company divides its revenue streams across three segments. Lease rent accounted for 64% of its total sales in 2012 while maintenance reserve generated 28%. The gain of sale on leased equipment and other operations contribute the remainder of revenue.

Geographic Reach

Willis Lease has operations in Africa Asia Canada Europe Mexico the Middle East and the US. The majority of lease revenue comes from Europe (37% of total lease revenue in 2012) Asia (20%) the US (12%) and South America (10%).

Financial Performance

After experiencing revenue and profit increases in 2011 Willis Lease suffered a 6% drop in net revenue and a massive 90% nosedive in profits during 2012. From 2011 to 2012 its revenues dipped from $157 million to $148 million while its profits slipped from $14.5 million to $1.5 million.

The decrease in revenues was attributed a 10% decline in lease rent revenues. This slump reflected lower portfolio utilization in 2012 and a decrease in the average size of the lease portfolio (which translated into a lower amount of equipment on lease). In addition the lower revenue translated to a decrease on the sale of leased equipment which was $5 million in 2012 compared with $11 million in 2011.

The plunge in profits was mainly due to a $15 million loss stemming from the extinguish of debt and derivative instruments.

Strategy

Growth in the spare engine leasing industry is contingent on the number of commercial aircraft in the market and the proportion of leased versus owned engines. Willis Lease is on the flip-side of most companies during economic downturns because it offers cash-strapped businesses a more affordable route — to lease engines rather than buying or repairing them. The company explains that engine repairs can cost as much as $3 million while leasing an engine may cost only $80000.

With fluctuating fuel costs an airline can spend the difference between maintenance and leasing on the cost of fuel. Additionally industry experts estimate that approximately 36000 aircraft will be in flight in less than 20 years. Growth is expected in both established markets as well as emerging markets especially Asia which is showing extraordinary growth in both passenger and cargo traffic.

EXECUTIVES

Chairman Of The Board, Chief Executive Officer, Charles Willis, $971,250 total compensation
Senior Vice President, Corporate Development, Director, Austin Willis, $330,000 total compensation
Senior Vice President, General Counsel, Corporate Secretary, Dean Poulakidas, $391,125 total compensation
Independent Director, Robert Keady
President, Brian Hole, $348,600 total compensation
Chief Financial Officer, Senior Vice President, Scott Flaherty, $312,900 total compensation
Independent Director, Rae McKeating
Auditors: Grant Thornton LLP

LOCATIONS

HQ: Willis Lease Finance Corp.
4700 Lyons Technology Parkway, Coconut Creek, FL 33073
Phone: 561 349-9989
Web: www.willislease.com

COMPETITORS

AQUADRILL CAPRICORN
 LTD.
FLYBE GROUP LIMITED
GoEasy Ltd
HERC HOLDINGS INC.

INTELSAT INFLIGHT LLC
PATRIOT TRANSPORTATION
 INC.
Total Energy Services
 Ltd

HISTORICAL FINANCIALS

Company Type: Public

Income Statement — FYE: December 31

	REVENUE ($ mil.)	NET INCOME ($ mil.)	NET PROFIT MARGIN	EMPLOYEES
12/20	288.6	9.7	3.4%	232
12/19	409.1	66.9	16.4%	232
12/18	348.3	43.2	12.4%	175
12/17	274.8	62.1	22.6%	155
12/16	207.2	14.0	6.8%	147
Annual Growth	8.6%	(8.8%)	—	12.1%

2020 Year-End Financials

Debt ratio: 71.6%
Return on equity: 2.3%
Cash ($ mil.): 42.5
Current ratio: 1.02
Long-term debt ($ mil.): 1,693.7
No. of shares (mil.): 6.5
Dividends
 Yield: —
 Payout: —
Market value ($ mil.): 200.0

HOOVER'S HANDBOOK OF EMERGING COMPANIES 2022

	STOCK PRICE ($) FY Close	P/E High/Low		PER SHARE ($) Earnings	Dividends	Book Value
12/20	30.46	58	14	1.05	0.00	62.97
12/19	58.91	7	3	10.50	0.00	62.93
12/18	34.60	6	4	6.60	0.00	54.46
12/17	24.97	3	2	9.69	0.00	48.04
12/16	25.58	13	8	2.05	0.00	33.74
Annual Growth	4.5%			(15.4%)	—	16.9%

Wilson Bank Holding Co.

EXECUTIVES

Chief Operating Officer, Executive Vice President Of The Company And Wilson Bank And Trust, Clark Oakley, $257,942 total compensation

Executive Vice President Of Wilson Bank And Trust, Gary Whitaker, $295,000 total compensation

Independent Director, William Jordan

Chief Financial Officer, Executive Vice President, Principal Financial And Accounting Officer, Chief Financial Officer Of Wilson Bank And Trust, Lisa Pominski, $280,000 total compensation

President, Chief Executive Officer, Director; Chief Executive Officer Of Wilson Bank And Trust, John McDearman, $500,000 total compensation

Independent Director, James Comer
Independent Director, Michael Maynard
Independent Director, Clinton Swain

Executive Vice President, President Of Wilson Bank And Trust, John Foster, $325,000 total compensation

Independent Director, Deborah Varallo
Director, Jack Bell
Independent Chairman Of The Board, James Patton
Director, James Clemons
Auditors: Maggart & Associates, P.C.

LOCATIONS

HQ: Wilson Bank Holding Co.
623 West Main Street, Lebanon, TN 37087
Phone: 615 444-2265
Web: www.wilsonbank.com

HISTORICAL FINANCIALS
Company Type: Public

Income Statement				FYE: December 31
	ASSETS ($ mil.)	NET INCOME ($ mil.)	INCOME AS % OF ASSETS	EMPLOYEES
12/20	3,369.6	38.4	1.1%	522
12/19	2,794.2	36.0	1.3%	530
12/18	2,543.6	32.5	1.3%	487
12/17	2,317.0	23.5	1.0%	471
12/16	2,198.0	25.6	1.2%	444
Annual Growth	11.3%	10.7%	—	4.1%

Wingstop Inc

Auditors: KPMG LLP

LOCATIONS

HQ: Wingstop Inc
15505 Wright Brothers Drive, Addison, TX 75001
Phone: 972 686-6500
Web: www.wingstop.com

HISTORICAL FINANCIALS
Company Type: Public

Income Statement				FYE: December 25
	REVENUE ($ mil.)	NET INCOME ($ mil.)	NET PROFIT MARGIN	EMPLOYEES
12/21	282.5	42.6	15.1%	890
12/20	248.8	23.3	9.4%	819
12/19	199.6	20.4	10.3%	784
12/18	153.1	21.7	14.2%	661
12/17	105.5	27.3	25.9%	530
Annual Growth	27.9%	11.8%	—	13.8%

2021 Year-End Financials

Debt ratio: 188.3%
Return on equity: ***,***.*%
Cash ($ mil.): 48.5
Current ratio: 1.77
Long-term debt ($ mil.): 469.3

No. of shares (mil.): 29.8
Dividends
  Yield: 0.0%
  Payout: 43.6%
Market value ($ mil.): 5,161.0

	STOCK PRICE ($) FY Close	P/E High/Low		PER SHARE ($) Earnings	Dividends	Book Value
12/21	172.97	129	81	1.42	0.62	(10.37)
12/20	140.76	214	63	0.78	5.50	(11.50)
12/19	86.21	152	87	0.69	0.40	(7.11)
12/18	64.64	100	53	0.73	6.54	(7.67)
12/17	38.98	45	27	0.93	0.14	(1.66)
Annual Growth	45.1%			11.2%	45.1%	—

Winnebago Industries, Inc.

A pioneer in the world of recreational vehicles Winnebago Industries makes products intended to encourage exploration. Almost all the company's sales come from its motor homes and towables which are sold via independent dealers throughout the US and Canada under brands including Winnebago Adventurer Sightseer Grand Design and Minnie Winnie. Winnebago Industries also sells RV parts and provides related services. The company also builds custom specialty vehicles for uses including mobile law enforcement command centers and mobile medical units. In 2018 Winnebago purchased Chris-Craft a manufacturer of recreational power boats. More than 90% of the company's sales are in the US. Winnebago traces its roots back to the 1950s.

Operations
Winnebago's towable offerings (56% of sales) are comprised of travel trailers (which hook up to a hitch on the vehicle's frame) and fifth wheels (which attach to the vehicle with a special fifth wheel hitch). The company's motor homes portfolio (43% of sales) includes three main product lines: Class A (conventional motor homes) Class B (panel-type vans) and Class C (motor homes built on van-type chassis). Specialty vehicles and Chris-Craft boats account for about 1% of sales.

Geographic Reach
Winnebago is based in Forest City Iowa. It owns facilities in Middlebury Forest City Lake Mills Charles City and Waverly Iowa; Junction City Oregon; Middlebury Indiana; and Sarasota Florida.

Sales and Marketing
The company markets its RVs on a wholesale basis to a diversified independent dealer network located throughout the US and to a limited extent in Canada Africa Asia Europe Australia and South America. The RV dealer network in the US and Canada includes about 550 motorized and towable physical dealer locations with some 75 of these locations carrying both Winnebago motorized and towable products. La Mesa RV Center with 11 dealer locations accounted for 10% of Winnebago's total revenue in fiscal 2018.

Financial Performance
Excepting fiscal 2016 when Winnebago's revenue growth was flat the company has seen steady growth over the last five years. Between 2014 and 2018 revenue more than doubled. Growth has been driven by increased demand for towable products and the acquisition of Grand Design.

Sales increased more than 30% to $2.0 billion in fiscal 2018 compared to $1.5 billion the prior year. Revenues for the towable segment saw the strongest growth with a rise of nearly 65% in fiscal 2018. Towable growth was spurred by organic demand as well as the addition of the Grand Design brand. Motorhome sales growth was subdued growing just under 1% in fiscal 2018.

Winnebago's net income rose 44% to 102.4 million in fiscal 2018 mainly due to higher sales in the towable segment and reduced tax liability.

The company's cash and equivalents stood at $2.3 million at the end of fiscal 2018 compared to $35.9 million the year before. Cash from operations contributed $83.3 million to the coffers while investing activities used $111.8 million mainly for the Chris-Craft acquisition and for capital expenditures to expand manufacturing capacity in the towable segment. Financing activities used $5.2 million primarily for payments on the credit agreement used to finance the Grand Design acquisition stock repurchases and shareholder dividends.

Strategy
Winnebago is focused on expanding the company's product offerings particularly in the fast-growing towable product segment. To that end late in 2016 the company bought Grand Design a manufacturer of towable RVs for about $500 million in cash and Winnebago shares. In 2018 the company acquired Chris-Craft which expanded Winnebago's offerings to include recreational power boats.

2020 Year-End Financials

Return on assets: 1.2%
Return on equity: 10.7%
Long-term debt ($ mil.): —
No. of shares (mil.): 10.9
Sales ($ mil): 156.1

Dividends
  Yield: —
  Payout: 34.1%
  Market value ($ mil.): —

450   HOOVER'S HANDBOOK OF EMERGING COMPANIES 2022

The company is also working to build more technology into its products. In 2019 Winnebago formed a new Advanced Technology Group which will work with each of the company's business segments to identify develop and commercialize emerging technologies. Initial efforts of the Advanced Technology Group will be to increase electrification and connectivity of Winnebago's products and use data gathered from products to enhance customer experience.

Mergers and Acquisitions

In 2019 Winnebago acquired fellow RV manufacturer Newmar Corporation in a deal valued at about $270 million. The addition of Newmar will increase Winnebago's offerings in the Class A and Super C motorized RV categories and supports Winnebago's efforts to grow its line-up of motorized RV products.

Company Background

During a mid-1950s economic downturn furniture store owner John Hanson convinced Forest City officials to welcome a local subsidiary of California trailer maker Modernistic Industries. The company's first trailer rolled off the line in 1958. Hanson later bought the plant and in 1960 named the business Winnebago Industries after Forest City's home county. Winnebago Industries went public in 1966. Sales took off when the company offered less-expensive RVs than its competitors.

EXECUTIVES

Senior Vice President, General Counsel, Secretary, Corporate Responsibility, President - Winnebago Industries Foundation, Stacy Bogart, $408,295 total compensation

Senior Vice President - Human Resources And Corporate Relations, Bret Woodson

President, Chief Executive Officer, Director, Michael Happe, $900,000 total compensation

Independent Chairman Of The Board, David Miles

President Of Grand Design Rv, Donald Clark, $400,000 total compensation

Independent Director, Maria Blase

Independent Director, Sara Armbruster

Independent Director, Kevin Bryant

Independent Director, Jacqueline Woods

Senior Vice President - Business Development, Advanced Technology And Enterprise Marketing, Ashis Bhattacharya

Senior Vice President - Enterprise Operations, Christopher West

Independent Director, Richard Moss

Independent Director, John Murabito

Chief Financial Officer, Senior Vice President - Finance, It And Strategic Planning, Bryan Hughes, $525,000 total compensation

President, Winnebago Outdoors, Huw Bower, $486,539 total compensation

Auditors: DELOITTE & TOUCHE LLP

LOCATIONS

HQ: Winnebago Industries, Inc.
13200 Pioneer Trail, Eden Prairie, MN 55347
Phone: 952 829-8600   **Fax:** 641 585-6966
Web: www.winnebagoind.com

PRODUCTS/OPERATIONS

2016 Sales

	$ mil.	% of total
Motorhomes parts and service	875.0	90
Towables and parts	89.4	9
Other manufactured products	10.8	1
Total	**975.2**	**100**

Selected Products

ERA
  ERA
Itasca
  Cambria
  Ellipse
  Impulse
  Impulse Silver
  Meridian
  Meridian V Class
  Navion
  Navion IQ
  Reyo
  Suncruiser
  Sunova
  Sunstar
Winnebago
  Access
  Access Premier
  Adventurer
  Aspect
  Journey
  Journey Express
  Sightseer
  Tour
  Via
  View
  View Profile
  Vista

COMPETITORS

ALL AMERICAN GROUP INC.	LCI INDUSTRIES
	MARINEMAX INC.
CAVCO INDUSTRIES INC.	MILLER INDUSTRIES INC.
COPART INC.	NEWMAR CORPORATION
FOX FACTORY HOLDING CORP.	REXHALL INDUSTRIES INC.
HERC HOLDINGS INC.	

HISTORICAL FINANCIALS

Company Type: Public

Income Statement

FYE: August 28

	REVENUE ($ mil.)	NET INCOME ($ mil.)	NET PROFIT MARGIN	EMPLOYEES
08/21	3,629.8	281.8	7.8%	6,532
08/20	2,355.5	61.4	2.6%	5,505
08/19	1,985.6	111.8	5.6%	4,500
08/18	2,016.8	102.3	5.1%	4,700
08/17	1,547.1	71.3	4.6%	4,060
Annual Growth	**23.8%**	**41.0%**	**—**	**12.6%**

2021 Year-End Financials

Debt ratio: 25.6%
Return on equity: 30.0%
Cash ($ mil.): 434.5
Current ratio: 2.60
Long-term debt ($ mil.): 528.5

No. of shares (mil.): 33.0
Dividends
  Yield: 0.0%
  Payout: 5.8%
Market value ($ mil.): 2,417.0

	STOCK PRICE ($) FY Close	P/E High/Low		PER SHARE ($) Earnings	Dividends	Book Value
08/21	73.11	10	5	8.28	0.48	31.97
08/20	58.41	38	11	1.84	0.44	24.60
08/19	32.02	11	6	3.52	0.43	20.06
08/18	37.30	18	11	3.22	0.40	16.95
08/17	34.55	16	9	2.32	0.40	13.98
Annual Growth	**20.6%**	**—**	**—**	**37.4%**	**4.7%**	**23.0%**

Wintrust Financial Corp (IL)

Wintrust Financial is a holding company for 15 subsidiary banks (mostly named after the individual communities it serves) with more than 180 branches primarily in metropolitan Chicago southern Wisconsin and northwest Indiana. Boasting assets of more than $45 billion the banks offer personal and commercial banking wealth management and specialty finance services with real estate accounting for over 35% of the company's loan portfolio the majority of which is commercial real estate. Wintrust's banks target individuals small to mid-sized businesses local governmental units and institutional clients among others.

Operations

Wintrust operates three business segments: community banking specialty finance and wealth management.

Through its Community Banking its banks provide community-oriented personal and commercial banking services to customers located in its market area. It also engage in the retail origination and purchase of residential mortgages through Wintrust Mortgage as well as consumer direct lending primarily to veterans through its Veterans First brand.

The Specialty Finance provides financing of insurance premiums for businesses and individuals; accounts receivable financing value-added outsourced administrative services; and other specialty finance businesses. FIRST Insurance Funding and Wintrust Life Finance engage in the premium finance receivables business their most significant specialized lending niche including commercial insurance premium finance and life insurance premium finance. The company also engages in commercial insurance premium finance in Canada through our wholly-owned subsidiary FIFC Canada.

Wealth Management offers trust and investment services tax-deferred like-kind exchange services asset management securities brokerage services and 401(k) and retirement plan services through The Chicago Trust Company N.A. Wintrust Investments LLC and Great Lakes Advisors LLC.

Wintrust makes almost 70% of its revenue from interest income.

Geographic Reach

Wintrust Financial's banks operate more than 180 branches and nearly 230 automatic teller machines mostly located in communities throughout the Chicago metropolitan area southern Wisconsin and northwest Indiana as well as one banking location in Florida. Its wealth management offices are in Chicago; Appleton Wisconsin; and Tampa Florida. Its Wintrust Mortgage is headquartered in their corporate headquarters in Rosemont Illinois and has some 40 locations in ten states.

Wintrust Financial is based in Rosemont Illinois.

Sales and Marketing

The bank's customers include individuals small to mid-sized businesses local governmental units and institutional clients residing primarily in the banks' local service areas.

Advertising and marketing expenses in 2020 2019 and 2018 were $36.6 million $48.6 million and $41.1 million respectively.

HOOVER'S HANDBOOK OF EMERGING COMPANIES 2022

451

Financial Performance

Wintrust Financial's annual revenues have risen 57% since 2016 as its loan assets have swelled by 76%.

The banking group's revenue jumped 12% to $1.6 billion during 2020. Net interest income decreased in 2020 compared to 2019 primarily as a result of the reduction in the net interest margin primarily due to the low rate environment driven by monetary policy in response to disruption from the pandemic. This decrease was partially offset by significant growth in earning assets primarily driven by the company's participation in PPP a part of the CARES Act which was enacted in response to COVID-19.

While net income decreased to $292.9 million in 2020 compared to net income of S355.7 million in 2019. Net income in 2020 was significantly impacted by disruption from COVID-19.

The company ended 2020 with cash and cash equivalents of $344.5 million. Operating activities used $518.5 million primarily for originations and purchases of mortgage loans held-for-sale. Investing activities used another $7.2 billion while financing activities provided $7.7 billion.

Strategy

For their Community Banking segment Wintrust continues to add lenders throughout the community banking organization many of whom have joined them because of their ability to offer a range of products and level of services which compete effectively with both larger and smaller market participants. The company has continued to expand its product delivery systems including a wide variety of electronic banking options for their retail and commercial customers which allow them to provide a level of service typically associated with much larger banking institutions.

Company Background

In 2012 Wintrust expanded its premium funding business into Canada with the acquisition of Macquarie Premium Funding Inc which was a subsidiary of Macquarie Group. The deal marked Wintrust's first international venture.

EXECUTIVES

Independent Director, Peter Crist
Independent Director, Scott Heitmann
Independent Director, William Doyle
Executive Vice President - Regional Market Head, Guy Eisenhuth
Independent Director, Marla Glabe
Independent Director, Karin Teglia
Independent Director, Deborah Hall Lefevre
Executive Vice President And Senior Market Head - Wealth Management Services, Thomas Zidar
Executive Vice President, General Counsel, Corporate Secretary, Kathleen Boege
Chief Executive Officer, Founder, Director, Edward Wehmer, $1,150,000 total compensation
Chief Financial Officer, Executive Vice President, David Stoehr, $494,519 total compensation
Vice Chairman Of The Board, Chief Operating Officer, David Dykstra, $810,000 total compensation
Vice Chairman, Chief Lending Officer, Richard Murphy, $609,038 total compensation
Independent Director, Bruce Crowther
Non-executive Independent Chairman Of The Board, H. Patrick Hackett
President, Timothy Crane, $544,231 total compensation
Auditors: Ernst & Young LLP

LOCATIONS

HQ: Wintrust Financial Corp (IL)
9700 W. Higgins Road, Suite 800, Rosemont, IL 60018
Phone: 847 939-9000
Web: www.wintrust.com

PRODUCTS/OPERATIONS

2015 Sales

	$ mil.	% of total
Interest		
Loans including fees	651.8	66
Securities	61.0	6
Other	5.6	-
Non-interest		
Mortgage banking	115.0	12
Wealth management	73.5	7
Service charges on deposit accounts	27.4	3
Fees from covered call options	15.4	2
Other	40.6	4
Trading (losses) gains net	(0.2)	-
Total	**990.1**	**100**

Selected Subsidiaries and Affiliates

Banking
  Barrington Bank & Trust Company N.A.
  Beverly Bank & Trust Company N.A.
  Crystal Lake Bank & Trust Company N.A.
  Hinsdale Bank & Trust Company
  Lake Forest Bank & Trust Company
  Libertyville Bank & Trust Company
  North Shore Community Bank & Trust Company
  Northbrook Bank & Trust Company
  Old Plank Trail Community Bank N.A.
  Schaumburg Bank & Trust Company N.A.
  St. Charles Bank & Trust
  State Bank of The Lakes
  Town Bank
  Village Bank & Trust
  Wheaton Bank and Trust Company
Non-banking
  Chicago Trust Company N.A.
  First Insurance Funding Corporation
  Great Lakes Advisors LLC
  Tricom Inc. of Milwaukee
  Wayne Hummer Asset Management Company
  Wayne Hummer Investments LLC
  Wayne Hummer Trust Company N.A.
  Wintrust Information Technology Services Company
  Wintrust Mortgage Corporation (formerly WestAmerica Mortgage Company)

COMPETITORS

ACCESS NATIONAL CORPORATION	FIRSTMERIT CORPORATION
AMERIS BANCORP	HILLTOP HOLDINGS INC.
ASSOCIATED BANC-CORP	M&T BANK CORPORATION
CITIZENS FINANCIAL GROUP INC.	OLD NATIONAL BANCORP
COLUMBIA BANKING SYSTEM INC.	PACWEST BANCORP
	PINNACLE FINANCIAL PARTNERS INC.
COMMERCE BANCSHARES INC.	PRIVATEBANCORP INC.
COMMUNITY BANK SYSTEM INC.	S & T BANCORP INC.
	SIGNATURE BANK
EAGLE BANCORP INC.	SOUTHSIDE BANCSHARES INC.
FIRST FINANCIAL BANCORP.	WESTERN ALLIANCE BANCORPORATION

HISTORICAL FINANCIALS

Company Type: Public

Income Statement

FYE: December 31

	ASSETS ($ mil.)	NET INCOME ($ mil.)	INCOME AS % OF ASSETS	EMPLOYEES
12/20	45,080.7	292.9	0.6%	5,364
12/19	36,620.5	355.7	1.0%	5,057
12/18	31,244.8	343.1	1.1%	4,727
12/17	27,915.9	257.6	0.9%	4,075
12/16	25,668.5	206.8	0.8%	3,878
Annual Growth	15.1%	9.1%	—	8.4%

2020 Year-End Financials

Return on assets: 0.7%
Return on equity: 7.4%
Long-term debt ($ mil.): —
No. of shares (mil.): 56.7
Sales ($ mil): 1,897.2

Dividends
  Yield: 1.8%
  Payout: 25.0%
Market value ($ mil.): 3,468.0

	STOCK PRICE ($) FY Close	P/E High/Low		PER SHARE ($) Earnings	Dividends	Book Value
12/20	61.09	15	5	4.68	1.12	72.50
12/19	70.90	13	10	6.03	1.00	63.84
12/18	66.49	16	11	5.86	0.76	57.93
12/17	82.37	19	14	4.40	0.56	53.19
12/16	72.57	19	10	3.66	0.48	51.96
Annual Growth	(4.2%)	—		6.3%	23.6%	8.7%

World Wrestling Entertainment Inc

The action might be fake but the business of World Wrestling Entertainment (WWE) is very real. The company is a leading producer and promoter of wrestling matches for TV and live audiences exhibiting approximately 310 live events each year across the globe. Its WWE Network available on a variety of digital streaming and mobile devices has more than 1.3 million paying subscribers. Its most famous live pay-per-view event is its flagship program WrestleMania. Other core content includes RAW and SmackDown Live. WWE also licenses characters for merchandise and sells videos toys and apparel. Two-time WWE world champion Vince McMahon has 83% voting control of the company. WWE's largest market is North America accounting for almost 70% of revenues.

Operations

The company operates three segments: Media Live Events and Consumer Products.

Media the largest segment which accounts for more than three-quarters of total revenue reflects the production and monetization of long-form and short-form video content across various platforms including WWE Network broadcast and pay television digital and social media as well as filmed entertainment.

Live Events (nearly 15%) provide ongoing content for the media platforms. The segment's revenues primarily consist of ticket sales including primary and secondary distribution revenues from events for which WWE receive a fixed fee as well as the sale of travel packages associated with the company's global live events.

Lastly its Consumer Products segment which merchandise the WWE branded products such as video games toys and apparel through licensing arrangements and direct-to-consumer sales accounts for about 10% of total revenue. The segment's revenues principally consist of royalties and licensee fees related to WWE branded products and sales of merchandise distributed at the live events and through eCommerce platforms. WWE produces around 260 live events throughout North America while about 50 for International events.

Geographic Reach

Based in Stamford Connecticut ? WWE has performance centers located in Orlando Florida and the UK which are also used for development and training activities

WWE produces events throughout North America which is also the company's largest market accounting for nearly 70% of total revenue. Europe/Middle East/Africa produce nearly 25% while Asia Pacific and Latin America account for the remaining revenue.

Sales and Marketing

WWE Network is available on select gaming consoles computers mobile devices internet connected TVs and popular digital media players and has around more than 1.3 million paying subscribers.

WWEShop is the direct-to-consumer e-commerce storefront. WWE merchandise is also distributed on other domestic and international e-commerce platforms including Amazon. It also offers venue merchandise business which consists of the design sourcing marketing and distribution of numerous WWE-branded products such as t-shirts belts caps and other novelty items all of which feature Superstars and/or logos.

Its customers include content distributors of WWE media content through its networks and platforms fans who purchase tickets to live events purchase merchandise at venues or online through eCommerce platforms and subscribers to WWE Network advertisers and sponsors consumer product licensees and film distributors/buyers.

The company spent about $21.2 million $21.6 million and $23.6 million on advertising for FY 2019 2018 and 2017 respectively.

Financial Performance

Throughout the five-year period ending in 2019 WWE reported year-over-year revenue growth. During that same period profits also rose except for a slight dip in 2017. While WWE has recently reported strong growth in media the firm has admitted that its live events aren't drawing people as they once did.

The company reported $960.4 million in revenue for 2019 a 3% increase from $930.2 million in 2018. This increase was primarily driven by increased Media revenues of $59.7 million which includes $78.8 million in incremental revenues associated with the October 2019 renewal of its key domestic distribution agreements of its flagship programs Raw and SmackDown as well as the contractual escalations associated with its prior distribution agreements partially offset by a decrease of $14.7 million resulting from a 6% decline in average paid subscribers on WWE Network.

Net income was $77.1 million in 2019 down from $99.6 million the prior year mainly due to increase in provision for income tax.

Cash at the end of 2019 was $90 million. Cash from operations was $121.7 million while investing activities used $35.8 million. Financing activities used another $162.9 million. WWE's main cash uses in 2019 were primarily for dividends paid purchases of short-term investments and purchases of property and equipment.

Strategy

WWE's strategy of creating compelling original content for broadcast on WWE Network has contributed to the popularity of WWE Network which premiered over 340 hours of original content during 2019. This subscription-based network is currently available in all international markets other than embargoed countries including the United Kingdom Canada the Middle East China and Australia among others. Subscribers can access all of WWE's live pay-per-view events exclusive original programming and nearly 11000 hours of our video-on-demand library.

The company is consistently negotiating and entering into new agreements and renewals and extensions of existing agreements for its products and services in international markets. In 2018 WWE embarked on an important long-term partnership with the General Entertainment Authority of the Kingdom of Saudi Arabia for among other things a series of live events in that region. It also holds talent tryouts overseas to discover regional superstars.

WWE have entered into new or complementary businesses and made equity and debt investments in other companies in the past and plan to continue to do so in the future. The company may also enter into business combination transactions make acquisitions or enter into strategic partnerships joint ventures or alliances.

Mergers and Acquisitions

In mid-2020 the company acquired WWN Live's EVOLVE Wrestling. Also known as EVOLVE it was launched in 2010 and was largely ran by Gabe Sapolsky who also works for WWE. The acquisition gives WWE the complete rights to the EVOLVE brand name and producing EVOLVE events moving forward whether they are as regular EVOLVE live events or WWE Network programming. Terms of the transaction were not disclosed.

HISTORY

Jesse McMahon made a name for himself as a boxing promoter in the 1940s before switching to wrestling. His son Vincent joined him in the business and they founded the World Wide Wrestling Federation in 1963. The company operated in Northeastern cities such as New York Philadelphia and Washington DC remaining a regional operation until the early 1980s (it dropped Wide from its name in 1979).

Vince McMahon Jr. inherited control of the WWF from his sick father in 1982 changed its name to Titan Sports and focused on gaining national exposure. McMahon made wrestling hugely popular but angered promoters as well as some fans with his nontraditional ideas. He embraced the idea of wrestling as show business instead of sport involving celebrities such as Cyndi Lauper and Mr. T and pursued a presence on cable TV. McMahon also purchased or put out of business many regional promoters as he spread the business across the US.

In the mid-1980s McMahon hit the jackpot with a former bodybuilder named Terry Gene Bollea. Christened Hulk Hogan he quickly became lord of

the ring making the cover of Sports Illustrated and performing for sellout crowds across the US. His likeness spawned toys clothing and a Saturday morning cartoon. Titan set a record for attracting the largest indoor crowd (more than 93000 fans packed Detroit's Pontiac Silverdome for Wrestlemania III) in 1987 and by the following year was selling $80 million in tickets annually.

Titan was body slammed in 1993 when competitor World Championship Wrestling (WCW formed in 1988 by Ted Turner to broadcast on his TBS network) lured away several major stars including Hogan. Also that year the US government charged Titan with illegal distribution of steroids. The company was acquitted in 1994 but the bad press along with the star defections allowed WCW to take the ratings lead by 1996.

Titan's refashioning of the WWF with more violence and sexual innuendo unleashed a hailstorm of criticism but returned it to the top spot by mid-1998; meanwhile former WWF star Jesse "The Body" Ventura was elected governor of Minnesota. Titan was named a defendant in a wrongful death suit in 1999 filed by the family of wrestler Owen Hart who fell to his death during a pay-per-view event (the case was settled in 2000). The company also changed its name to World Wrestling Federation Entertainment (WWFE) and went public that year. The company later licensed the WWF name for a theme restaurant in New York City.

WWFE continued its bone-crunching ways in 2000 by launching XFL a professional football league that played in the winter following the NFL season. Still smarting from the loss of the NFL broadcast rights to CBS NBC bought half of the new league and broadcast the games on its network. The deal also gave NBC a 3% stake in WWF. The league was a disaster during its first season and it quickly folded. (The company repurchased NBC's shares in 2002.)

Later that year the firm bought the WWF New York Times Square Entertainment Complex from its licensee for $24.5 million. (It closed the location in 2003.) It also abandoned its broadcasting contract with USA Networks (now IAC/InterActiveCorp) in favor of a more lucrative deal with Viacom which also took a 3% stake in the company. (Viacom sold the stake back to the company in 2003.) In 2001 WWFE put a headlock on the wrestling world when it bought the WCW from Turner Broadcasting.

In 2002 WWE received the smackdown in a court battle with the World Wildlife Fund which claimed the company (formerly WWF) lifted the animal preservation group's initials. The company had to change its name from World Wrestling Federation Entertainment to World Wrestling Entertainment as part of a settlement.

After ending its partnership with Viacom's Spike TV in 2005 the WWE cut a deal with NBCUniversal to air Monday Night Raw on the USA Network and on Spanish-language network Telemundo. The following year after The WB and the UPN merged to form The CW Network WWE inked a deal with the upstart broadcaster to air Friday Night SmackDown . (The show moved to MyNetworkTV owned by News Corporation in 2008.) It also created a new show ECW: Extreme Championship Wrestling for NBCUniversal's SCI FI Channel (now Syfy).

The company inked a lucrative toy licensing partnership with Mattel in 2010.

HOOVER'S HANDBOOK OF EMERGING COMPANIES 2022

EXECUTIVES

Chairman Of The Board, Chief Executive Officer, Co-founder, Vincent McMahon, $1,394,615 total compensation
Chief Brand Officer, Director, Stephanie Mcmahon, $724,115 total compensation
Executive Producer & Chief Global Television Production, Kevin Dunn, $922,625 total compensation
Independent Director, Erika Nardini
Executive Vice President, Global Talent Strategy And Development, Paul Levesque, $724,115 total compensation
Independent Director, Jeffrey Speed
Chief Financial Officer And Chief Administrative Officer, Frank Riddick, $782,667 total compensation
Executive Vice President, Operations And Chief Of Staff, Bradley Blum
Independent Director, Man Jit Singh
Independent Director, Alan Wexler
President, Chief Revenue Officer, Director, Nick Khan, $498,462 total compensation
Independent Director, Steve Pamon
Independent Director, Laureen Ong
Auditors: DELOITTE & TOUCHE LLP

LOCATIONS

HQ: World Wrestling Entertainment Inc
1241 East Main Street, Stamford, CT 06902
Phone: 203 352-8600
Web: www.wwe.com

PRODUCTS/OPERATIONS

Selected Operations
Live and televised entertainment
  Live wrestling events
  Pay-per-view programming
  Television programming
  A.M. RAW (USA Network)
  Friday Night SmackDown (Syfy)
  Monday Night Raw (USA Network)
  WWE NXT (WWE.com)
  WWE Superstars (WGN America)
  WWE Classics On Demand (video on demand service)
Consumer products
  Home video
  Magazines
  Product licensing
Digital media
  WWE.com
  WWEShop
WWE Studios (film production)

COMPETITORS

Bertelsmann SE & Co. KGaA	RELATIVITY MEDIA LLC
DCD MEDIA PLC	RICOCHET LIMITED
FRIENDFINDER NETWORKS INC.	SESAME WORKSHOP
ITV PLC	SONY PICTURES ENTERTAINMENT INC.
NEW FRONTIER MEDIA INC.	

HISTORICAL FINANCIALS

Company Type: Public

Income Statement

FYE: December 31

	REVENUE ($ mil.)	NET INCOME ($ mil.)	NET PROFIT MARGIN	EMPLOYEES
12/21	1,095.1	180.4	16.5%	870
12/20	974.2	131.7	13.5%	900
12/19	960.4	77.0	8.0%	960
12/18	930.1	99.5	10.7%	915
12/17	800.9	32.6	4.1%	850
Annual Growth	8.1%	53.3%	—	0.6%

2021 Year-End Financials

Debt ratio: 50.6%
Return on equity: 46.8%
Cash ($ mil.): 134.8
Current ratio: 1.52
Long-term debt ($ mil.): 395.9

No. of shares (mil.): 74.8
Dividends
  Yield: 0.9%
  Payout: 31.3%
Market value ($ mil.): 3,692.0

	STOCK PRICE ($) FY Close	P/E High/Low		PER SHARE ($) Earnings	Dividends	Book Value
12/21	49.34	27	20	2.12	0.48	5.09
12/20	48.05	39	18	1.56	0.48	5.00
12/19	64.87	100	54	0.85	0.48	3.56
12/18	74.72	76	24	1.12	0.48	4.05
12/17	30.58	77	42	0.42	0.48	3.28
Annual Growth	12.7%	—	—	49.9%	(0.0%)	11.6%

WSFS Financial Corp

WSFS isn't a radio station but it is tuned to the banking needs of Delaware. WSFS Financial is the holding company for Wilmington Savings Fund Society (WSFS Bank) a thrift with nearly $5 billion in assets and more than 75 branches mostly in Delaware and Pennsylvania. Founded in 1832 WSFS Bank attracts deposits from individuals and local businesses by offering standard products like checking and savings accounts CDs and IRAs. The bank uses funds primarily to lend to businesses: Commercial loans and mortgages account for about 85% of its loan portfolio. Bank subsidiaries Christiana Trust Cypress Capital Management and WSFS Wealth Investment provide trust and investment advisory services to wealthy clients and institutional investors.

Operations

Its Christiana Trust division boasts nearly $9 billion in assets under administration and provides investment fiduciary agency bankruptcy and commercial domicile services from offices in Delaware and Nevada.

The company's Cash Connect division operates more than 450 ATMs for WSFS Bank which boasts the largest branded ATM network in Delaware. The division also manages some $490 million of vault cash in approximately 15000 ATMs nationwide and provides online reporting and ATM cash management predictive cash ordering armored carrier management and ATM processing and equipment sales.

Overall the bank generated roughly 57% of its total revenue from interest and fees on loans in 2014 plus an additional 10% from interest on its mortgage-back and other investment securities.

About 7% of its total revenue came from wealth management income while mortgage banking income contributed another 2%. The majority of the remaining revenue came from credit/debit card and ATM income and deposit service charges.

Geographic Reach

WSFS Bank has 45 branches throughout Delaware nearly 10 branches in Pennsylvania one branch in Nevada and one in Virginia.

Financial Performance

WSFS Financial's revenues and profits have been trending higher in recent years thanks to sustained growth in its lending business organically and through acquisitions and thanks to declining loan loss provisions as its loan portfolio's credit quality has improved with the strengthened economy.

The company's revenue rose by 5% to $238.62 million in 2014 thanks to interest income growth mostly driven by increased loan business and higher securities interest; which stemmed from a combination of the bank's First Wyoming Financial Corporation acquisition improvements in its balance sheet mix and additional income from its reverse mortgage-related assets.

Higher revenue and a continued decline in loan loss provisions in 2014 pushed WSFS Financial's net income up by 15% to $53.73 million during the year while the company's operating cash levels jumped by 17% to $67.06 million thanks to higher cash earnings.

Strategy

WSFS Financial reiterated its long-term growth strategy in 2015 which included growing the bank's lending business boosting its Trust and Wealth Management group's assets under administration and expanding Cash Connect's ATM customer base and customer cross-sell.

Beyond utilizing its community-oriented and local commercial lending teams the company has been growing its loan business and its branch reach through strategic acquisitions of banks and bank branches in target markets with preference toward markets in southeastern Pennsylvania. Its 2014 acquisition of First Wyoming Financial Corp for example bolstered WSFS' presence in Kent county while strengthening its position as the one of Delaware's top independent community banks.

Mergers and Acquisitions

In mid-2018 WSFS Financial agreed to purchase Philadelphia-based Beneficial Bancorp in a deal worth $1.5 billion. The transaction will create the largest locally headquartered community bank in the Greater Delaware Valley region with about $13 billion in assets.

EXECUTIVES

Independent Director, Karen Buchholz
Executive Vice President, Chief Risk Officer, Michael Reed, $276,667 total compensation
Independent Director, Nancy Foster
Chairman, President And Ceo, Rodger Levenson, $767,667 total compensation
Executive Vice President And Chief Customer Officer, Peggy Eddens, $415,000 total compensation
Independent Director, Jennifer Davis
Independent Director, Francis Brake
Chief Financial Officer, Executive Vice President, Dominic Canuso, $422,475 total compensation
Executive Vice President, Pennsylvania Market President Of Wsfs Bank, Patrick Ward, $322,917 total compensation

Executive Vice President, Chief Wealth Officer, Arthur Bacci

Executive Vice President, Chief Information Officer, Lisa Brubaker

Executive Vice President And Chief Retail Banking Officer, Wsfs Bank, Richard Wright, $379,150 total compensation

Independent Director, Anat Bird

Chief Human Resource Officer, Executive Vice President, Michael Conklin

Executive Vice President - Enterprise Risk Management, Paul Greenplate

Executive Vice President, Chief Commercial Banking Officer, Steve Clark, $401,667 total compensation

Independent Director, Christopher Gheysens

Independent Director, Michael Donahue

Auditors: KPMG LLP

LOCATIONS

HQ: WSFS Financial Corp
500 Delaware Avenue, Wilmington, DE 19801
Phone: 302 792-6000
Web: www.wsfsbank.com

PRODUCTS/OPERATIONS

2014 Sales

	$ mil.	% of total
Interest		
Loans including fees	137.0	57
Mortgage-backed securities	13.5	6
Investment securities	9.8	4
Noninterest		
Credit/debit card & ATM income	24.1	11
Deposit service charges	17.1	7
Wealth management income	17.4	7
Mortgage baning activities	4.0	2
Other	15.7	6
Total	**238.6**	**100**

COMPETITORS

CITY HOLDING COMPANY
CVB FINANCIAL CORP.
ENTERPRISE FINANCIAL SERVICES CORP
FIRST BUSINESS FINANCIAL SERVICES INC.
GUARANTY BANCORP
M&T BANK CORPORATION
NEWBRIDGE BANCORP
NORTHWEST BANCORP INC.
OFG BANCORP
PRIVATEBANCORP INC.
PROVIDENT FINANCIAL SERVICES INC.
STATE BANK FINANCIAL CORPORATION
TCF FINANCIAL CORPORATION
UMB FINANCIAL CORPORATION

HISTORICAL FINANCIALS

Company Type: Public

Income Statement — FYE: December 31

	ASSETS ($ mil.)	NET INCOME ($ mil.)	INCOME AS % OF ASSETS	EMPLOYEES
12/20	14,333.9	114.7	0.8%	1,838
12/19	12,256.3	148.8	1.2%	1,782
12/18	7,248.8	134.7	1.9%	1,177
12/17	6,999.5	50.2	0.7%	1,159
12/16	6,765.2	64.0	0.9%	1,116
Annual Growth	20.6%	15.7%	—	13.3%

2020 Year-End Financials

Return on assets: 0.8%
Return on equity: 6.2%
Long-term debt ($ mil.): —
No. of shares (mil.): 47.7
Sales ($ mil) 713.1

Dividends
Yield: 1.0%
Payout: 21.1%
Market value ($ mil.): 2,143.0

STOCK PRICE ($) FY Close	P/E High/Low		PER SHARE ($) Earnings	Dividends	Book Value
12/20	44.88	20 9	2.27	0.48	37.52
12/19	43.99	15 12	3.00	0.47	35.88
12/18	37.91	13 9	4.19	0.42	26.17
12/17	47.85	33 27	1.56	0.30	23.05
12/16	46.35	22 13	2.06	0.25	21.90
Annual Growth	(0.8%)	— —	2.5%	17.7%	14.4%

XOMA Corp

XOMA Corporation doesn't want to toil in anonymity. Instead the company pairs with larger drug firms to develop and market its products primarily monoclonal antibodies (biotech drugs based on cloned proteins). It's developing lead candidate gevokizumab with Novartis. The firm partners on therapeutics for various clinical development stages targeting the adenosine pathway with potential applications in solid tumors non-Hodgkin's lymphoma asthma/chronic obstructive pulmonary disease inflammatory bowel disease idiopathic pulmonary fibrosis lung cancer psoriasis and nonalcoholic steatohepatitis and other indications. XOMA has collaborative agreements with pharma companies Takeda Pharmaceutical and Merck; it also has metabolic and oncology candidates. The US generates about 95% of the company's revenue.

Operations

Xoma has a pipeline of unique monoclonal antibodies and technologies available to license to pharmaceutical and biotechnology companies to further their clinical development. Some of its proprietary product candidates include IL-2 program. Interleukin 2 has long been recognized as an effective therapy for metastatic melanoma and renal cell carcinoma; PTH1R program generated an antiparathyroid receptor pipeline that includes several functional antibody antagonists targeting PTH1R a G-protein-coupled receptor involved in the regulation of calcium metabolism; XMetA is an insulin receptor-activating antibody designed to provide long-acting reduction of hyperglycemia in Type 2 diabetic patients potentially reducing the advancement to a number of insulin injections needed to control their blood glucose levels; and X213 (formerly LFA 102) is an allosteric inhibitor of prolactin action. It is a humanized IgG1-Kappa monoclonal antibody that binds to the extracellular domain of the human prolactin receptor with high affinity at an allosteric site.

Geographic Reach

Based in Emeryville California the US market accounts the largest for about 95% of total sales while Europe and other countries account the remainder.

Financial Performance

Over the last five years the revenue of the company reported a fluctuation. It's either increasing very high or going down very low. And only in 2017 that the company reported a net income.

In 2019 revenue increased by 247% to $18.4 million. The primary components of revenue from contracts with customers in 2019 was $14.0 million recognized under the license agreement and common stock purchase agreement with Rezolute and $2.5 million in revenue earned from a one-time payment under its license agreement with Janssen.

The company incurred a net loss of $2 million in 2019 $11.5 million lower from 2018. The decrease in net loss was due to higher revenue and $3.8 million from Other income.

Cash at the end of the period was $56.7 million. Operations and Investing activities each used $0.3 million and $19.3 million respectively while financing activities provided $30.5 million to the company.

Strategy

The company strategy is to expand its pipeline by acquiring additional potential milestone and royalty revenue streams on drug product candidates from third parties. Expanding its pipeline through these acquisitions can allow for further diversification across therapeutic areas and development stages. Its ideal target acquisitions are in pre-commercial stages of development have an expected long duration of market exclusivity high revenue potential and are partnered with a large pharmaceutical or biopharmaceutical enterprise.

As part of its royalty aggregator strategy it will purchase future milestone and royalty streams associated with drug products that are in clinical development and have not yet been commercialized. To the extent that any such drug products are not successfully developed and subsequently commercialized the value of its acquired potential milestone and royalty streams will be negatively affected. The ultimate success of its royalty aggregator strategy will depend on its ability to properly identify and acquire high quality products and the ability of the applicable counterparty to innovate develop and commercialize its products in increasingly competitive and highly regulated markets. Its inability to do so would negatively affect its ability to receive royalty and/or milestone payments. In addition the company is dependent to a large extent on third parties to enforce certain rights for its benefit such as protection of a patent estate adequate reporting and other protections and its failure to do so would presumably negatively impact its financial condition and results of operations.

EXECUTIVES

Independent Director, Barbara Kosacz

Independent Director, Natasha Hernday

Independent Director, Heather Franklin

Chairman Of The Board, Chief Executive Officer, James Neal, $533,527 total compensation

Independent Director, Jack Wyszomierski

Lead Independent Director, W. Denman Van Ness

Chief Financial Officer, Senior Vice President - Finance, Thomas Burns, $386,168 total compensation

Independent Director, Joseph Limber

Auditors: DELOITTE & TOUCHE LLP

LOCATIONS

HQ: XOMA Corp
2200 Powell Street, Suite 310, Emeryville, CA 94608
Phone: 510 204-7200
Web: www.xoma.com

PRODUCTS/OPERATIONS

2016 Sales

	$ mil.	% of total
License & collaborative fees & royalties	3.3	59
Contract and other	2.3	41
Total	**5.6**	**100**

2016 Contract & Other Revenue

	$ mil.	% of total
The National Institute of Allergy and Infectious Diseases (NIAID)	1.1	48
Servier	0.6	26
Other	0.6	26
Total	**2.3**	**100**

Selected Pipeline Products

XOMA 358 - Congenital hyperinsulinism & Post-bariatric surgery hyperinsulinism

XOMA 129 - Short-acting reversal of drug-induced hypoglycemia

XOMA 213 - Various hyperprolactinemias

Anti-PTH1R - Hyperparathyroidism Malignancy induced hypercalcemia

Anti-IL-2 - Oncology anti-tumor immunity

COMPETITORS

ALAUNOS THERAPEUTICS INC.

CELLDEX THERAPEUTICS INC.

CHEMOCENTRYX INC.

CONCERT PHARMACEUTICALS INC.

DYNAVAX TECHNOLOGIES CORPORATION

EDITAS MEDICINE INC.

FIBROGEN INC.

FIVE PRIME THERAPEUTICS INC.

IMMUNOGEN INC.

IONIS PHARMACEUTICALS INC.

LEXICON PHARMACEUTICALS INC.

OMEROS CORPORATION

HISTORICAL FINANCIALS

Company Type: Public

Income Statement				FYE: December 31
	REVENUE ($ mil.)	NET INCOME ($ mil.)	NET PROFIT MARGIN	EMPLOYEES
12/20	29.3	13.3	45.3%	10
12/19	18.3	(1.9)	—	10
12/18	5.3	(13.3)	—	11
12/17	52.6	14.6	27.7%	12
12/16	5.5	(53.5)	—	18
Annual Growth	**51.6%**	**—**		**(13.7%)**

2020 Year-End Financials

Debt ratio: 16.6%
Return on equity: 20.3%
Cash ($ mil.): 84.2
Current ratio: 7.16
Long-term debt ($ mil.): 12.7

No. of shares (mil.): 11.2
Dividends
  Yield: —
  Payout: —
Market value ($ mil.): 496.0

	STOCK PRICE ($) FY Close	P/E High/Low		PER SHARE ($) Earnings	Dividends	Book Value
12/20	44.13	56	18	0.78	0.00	7.70
12/19	27.30	—	—	(0.23)	0.00	4.51
12/18	12.65	—	—	(1.59)	0.00	2.16
12/17	35.60	49	5	0.73	0.00	0.70
12/16	4.22	—	—	(8.89)	0.00	(7.72)
Annual Growth	**79.8%**			**—**	**—**	**—**

XPEL Inc

Auditors: DELOITTE & TOUCHE LLP

LOCATIONS

HQ: XPEL Inc
618 W. Sunset Road, San Antonio, TX 78216
Phone: 210 678-3700   **Fax:** 210 678-3701
Web: www.xpel.com

HISTORICAL FINANCIALS

Company Type: Public

Income Statement				FYE: December 31
	REVENUE ($ mil.)	NET INCOME ($ mil.)	NET PROFIT MARGIN	EMPLOYEES
12/20	158.9	18.2	11.5%	330
12/19	129.9	13.9	10.8%	230
12/18	109.9	8.7	7.9%	0
12/17	67.7	1.1	1.8%	0
12/16	51.7	2.2	4.3%	0
Annual Growth	**32.4%**	**69.5%**	**—**	**—**

2020 Year-End Financials

Debt ratio: 7.3%
Return on equity: 41.2%
Cash ($ mil.): 29.0
Current ratio: 2.96
Long-term debt ($ mil.): 3.5

No. of shares (mil.): 27.6
Dividends
  Yield: —
  Payout: —
Market value ($ mil.): 1,424.0

	STOCK PRICE ($) FY Close	P/E High/Low		PER SHARE ($) Earnings	Dividends	Book Value
12/20	51.56	81	13	0.66	0.00	1.93
12/19	14.65	31	9	0.51	0.00	1.27
12/18	6.10	22	4	0.32	0.00	0.75
12/17	1.40	57	32	0.04	0.00	0.51
12/16	1.40	17	8	0.08	0.00	0.40
Annual Growth	**146.3%**			**67.4%**	**—**	**48.1%**

Xperi Holding Corp

Tessera Technologies licenses its portfolio of patented technologies for semiconductor packaging interconnects and imaging in exchange for royalty payments. More than 100 companies such as Intel Sony LG Electronics and Samsung use its designs to produce high-performance packages for mobile computing and communications memory and data storage and 3D integrated circuit technologies. Tessera has more than 4000 US and foreign patents and patents applications. The US is Tessera's biggest geographic market.

Operations

Tessera licenses technologies through subsidiaries. The Invensas subsidiary handles semiconductor related technologies; The FotoNation unit licenses software and technologies for mobile imaging; and the Ziptronix licenses wafer bonding technologies.

While it typically heavily on R&D $32 million in 2015) Tessera also supports a sizable budget for litigation expenses which cost around $14 million in 2015 down from $25 million in 2014. The re-duced litigation spending was due to settlements reached in 2014 and early 2015.

Geographic Reach

Tessera has R&D and marketing support offices in Ireland Japan Romania and the US. Its manufacturing plants are located in China and Taiwan. About 35% of the company's revenue comes from customers in the US followed followed by 32% from South Korea and 21% from Taiwan.

Sales and Marketing

The company is focused on developing direct product design relationships at the technical level with companies that manufacture camera modules and smartphones. Top customers in 2015 were Samsung (19% of sales) Micron Technology (15%) Amkor Technology (14%) and SK Hynix (13%)

Financial Performance

Overall sales fell 2% in 2015 to $273 million from a decline in episodic revenue. Tessera's profit fell 31% to $117 million in 2015 from $170 million in 2014. The main year-to-year difference was a lower tax benefit in 2015. Cash flow was $146 million in 2015 compared to $134 million in 2014.

Strategy

Tessera has gotten its business on a more stable footing with the settlement of several lawsuits which should produce regularly recurring revenue and the signing of new licensing deals.

In January 2015 Tessera reached a settlement with Amkor in which Amkor agreed to pay a total of $155 million of 16 quarterly payments through the fourth quarter of 2018. The company signed new license agreements with Samsung and Micron that resulted in significant revenue.

In 2015 the company closed the last manufacturing operation of its DigitalOptics business. More than 300 workers were let go and facilities in California New York Taiwan and Japan were closed.

Mergers and Acquisitions

The company's acquisition strategy is focused on buy companies that strengthen its position in various markets largely focused on imaging. In 2015 Tessera bought Ziptronix. The $39 million deal expanded Tessera's advanced packaging capabilities by adding a low-temperature wafer bonding technology platform that help it get newer technologies to its semiconductor industry customers.

In 2014 the FotoNation subsidiary bought Smart Sensors Limited which develops iris recognition biometric technology.

EXECUTIVES

Ceo, Tom Lacey
Pres*, Jon E Kirchner
Cfo*, Robert Andersen
Gen Counsel-Sec*, Paul E Davis
Chief Human Resources Officer*, Kris M Graves
Chief Products and Services of*, Geir Skaaden
Cto*, Steve Teig
Cmo*, Peter Van Deventer
Chief Branding Officer*, Kevin Doohan
Engineering & Gen Mgr, Petronel Bigioi
Senior Director Dram Market, David Fisch
Auditors: PricewaterhouseCoopers LLP

LOCATIONS

HQ: Xperi Holding Corp
3025 Orchard Parkway, San Jose, CA 95134
Phone: 408 321-6000
Web: www.xperi.com

COMPETITORS

AXCELIS TECHNOLOGIES INC.
DSP GROUP INC.
FORMFACTOR INC.
GT ADVANCED TECHNOLOGIES INC.
INPHI CORPORATION
ITRON INC.
LAM RESEARCH CORPORATION
MAXIM INTEGRATED PRODUCTS INC.
MKS INSTRUMENTS INC.
NXP Semiconductors N.V.
ONTO INNOVATION INC.
SANMINA CORPORATION
SEQUANS COMMUNICATIONS
TE Connectivity Ltd.

HISTORICAL FINANCIALS

Company Type: Public

Income Statement — FYE: December 31

	REVENUE ($ mil.)	NET INCOME ($ mil.)	NET PROFIT MARGIN	EMPLOYEES
12/20	892.0	146.7	16.5%	1,850
12/19	280.0	(62.5)	—	700
12/18	406.1	(0.2)	—	700
12/17	373.7	(56.5)	—	700
12/16	259.5	56.0	21.6%	700
Annual Growth	36.2%	27.2%	—	27.5%

2020 Year-End Financials

Debt ratio: 31.0%
Return on equity: 14.6%
Cash ($ mil.): 170.1
Current ratio: 2.43
Long-term debt ($ mil.): 795.6
No. of shares (mil.): 104.7
Dividends
 Yield: 0.4%
 Payout: 5.7%
Market value ($ mil.): 2,190.0

	STOCK PRICE ($) FY Close	P/E High/Low		PER SHARE ($) Earnings	Dividends	Book Value
12/20	20.90	12	6	1.75	0.10	13.90
12/19	18.50	—	—	(1.27)	0.00	11.04
12/18	18.39	—	—	(0.01)	0.80	12.80
12/17	24.40	—	—	(1.15)	0.80	8.87
12/16	44.20	40	23	1.12	0.80	10.39
Annual Growth	(17.1%)	—	—	11.8%	(40.5%)	7.5%

Zedge Inc

Auditors: Friedman LLP

LOCATIONS

HQ: Zedge Inc
 1178 Broadway, 3rd Floor, #1450, New York, NY 10001
Phone: 330 577-3424
Web: www.zedge.com

HISTORICAL FINANCIALS

Company Type: Public

Income Statement — FYE: July 31

	REVENUE ($ mil.)	NET INCOME ($ mil.)	NET PROFIT MARGIN	EMPLOYEES
07/21	19.5	8.2	42.1%	53
07/20	9.4	(0.5)	—	39
07/19	8.8	(3.3)	—	53
07/18	10.8	(1.5)	—	57
07/17	10.0	(0.6)	—	64
Annual Growth	18.2%	—	—	(4.6%)

2021 Year-End Financials

Debt ratio: —
Return on equity: 39.2%
Cash ($ mil.): 24.9
Current ratio: 6.61
Long-term debt ($ mil.): —
No. of shares (mil.): 14.3
Dividends
 Yield: —
 Payout: —
Market value ($ mil.): 221.0

	STOCK PRICE ($) FY Close	P/E High/Low		PER SHARE ($) Earnings	Dividends	Book Value
07/21	15.36	31	2	0.59	0.00	2.30
07/20	1.39	—	—	(0.05)	0.00	0.72
07/19	1.61	—	—	(0.33)	0.00	0.67
07/18	2.97	—	—	(0.16)	0.00	0.97
07/17	2.07	—	—	(0.06)	0.00	1.10
Annual Growth	65.0%	—	—	—	—	20.3%

Ziff Davis Inc

EXECUTIVES

Ceo, Nehemia Zucker
Pres*, R Scott Turicchi
Cfo*, Kathleen M Griggs
V Pres-Gen Counsel-Sec*, Jeffrey D Adelman
Senior Business MA, Tim Anderson
Vice-President Corporate Commu, Laura Hinson
Vice-President Corporate Devel, Ken Truesdale
Vice-President Engineering, Vince Niedzielski
Svp&gen Mngr-Voice Business, Ron Burr
Svp-Gen Mgr Backup Business, Timothy Smith
Infrastructure Archi, Quang Than
Auditors: BDO USA, LLP

LOCATIONS

HQ: Ziff Davis Inc
 114 5th Avenue, New York, NY 10011
Phone: 212 503-3500
Web: www.j2.com

COMPETITORS

CommTouch Software
Deltathree
EasyLink
FuzeBox
Notify Technology
Open Text
Satellink

HISTORICAL FINANCIALS

Company Type: Public

Income Statement — FYE: December 31

	REVENUE ($ mil.)	NET INCOME ($ mil.)	NET PROFIT MARGIN	EMPLOYEES
12/20	1,489.5	150.6	10.1%	4,700
12/19	1,372.0	218.8	15.9%	3,090
12/18	1,207.3	128.6	10.7%	2,587
12/17	1,117.8	139.4	12.5%	2,487
12/16	874.2	152.4	17.4%	2,426
Annual Growth	14.3%	(0.3%)	—	18.0%

2020 Year-End Financials

Debt ratio: 43.0%
Return on equity: 11.9%
Cash ($ mil.): 242.6
Current ratio: 0.71
Long-term debt ($ mil.): 1,182.2
No. of shares (mil.): 44.3
Dividends
 Yield: —
 Payout: —
Market value ($ mil.): 4,332.0

	STOCK PRICE ($) FY Close	P/E High/Low		PER SHARE ($) Earnings	Dividends	Book Value
12/20	97.69	32	17	3.18	0.00	27.31
12/19	93.71	22	15	4.39	1.34	27.51
12/18	69.38	34	25	2.59	1.68	21.81
12/17	75.03	32	25	2.83	1.52	21.32
12/16	81.80	26	18	3.13	1.36	19.28
Annual Growth	4.5%			0.4%	—	9.1%

Zoom Video Communications Inc

Auditors: KPMG LLP

LOCATIONS

HQ: Zoom Video Communications Inc
 55 Almaden Boulevard, 6th Floor, San Jose, CA 95113
Phone: 888 799-9666
Web: www.zoom.com

HISTORICAL FINANCIALS

Company Type: Public

Income Statement — FYE: January 31

	REVENUE ($ mil.)	NET INCOME ($ mil.)	NET PROFIT MARGIN	EMPLOYEES
01/21	2,651.3	672.3	25.4%	4,422
01/20	622.6	25.3	4.1%	2,532
01/19	330.5	7.5	2.3%	1,702
01/18	151.4	(3.8)	—	0
01/17	60.8	(0.0)	—	0
Annual Growth	157.0%	—	—	—

2021 Year-End Financials

Debt ratio: —
Return on equity: 28.5%
Cash ($ mil.): 2,240.3
Current ratio: 3.80
Long-term debt ($ mil.): —
No. of shares (mil.): 293.5
Dividends
 Yield: —
 Payout: —
Market value ($ mil.): 109,221.0

	STOCK PRICE ($) FY Close	P/E High/Low		PER SHARE ($) Earnings	Dividends	Book Value
01/21	372.07	240	36	2.25	0.00	13.15
01/20	76.30	1142	689	0.09	0.00	2.99
Annual Growth	387.6%			—	—	—
339.6%			2400.0%		

Zynex Inc

EXECUTIVES

Chairman, President And Chief Executive Officer, Thomas Sandgaard, $480,000 total compensation
Independent Director, Joshua Disbrow
Chief Operating Officer, Anna Lucsok, $110,000 total compensation
Vice President Of Sales, Donald Gregg

Chief Financial Officer, Daniel Moorhead,
  $243,750 total compensation
Auditors: Plante & Moran, PLLC

LOCATIONS

HQ: Zynex Inc
  9655 Maroon Circle, Englewood, CO 80112
Phone: 303 703-4906
Web: www.zynex.com

HISTORICAL FINANCIALS

Company Type: Public

Income Statement

FYE: December 31

	REVENUE ($ mil.)	NET INCOME ($ mil.)	NET PROFIT MARGIN	EMPLOYEES
12/20	80.1	9.0	11.3%	768
12/19	45.4	9.4	20.9%	283
12/18	31.9	9.5	29.9%	182
12/17	23.4	7.3	31.4%	109
12/16	13.3	0.0	0.5%	106
Annual Growth	56.6%	238.6%	—	64.1%

2020 Year-End Financials

Debt ratio: 0.5%
Return on equity: 23.6%
Cash ($ mil.): 39.1
Current ratio: 6.23
Long-term debt ($ mil.): 0.2

No. of shares (mil.): 38.2
Dividends
  Yield: —
  Payout: —
Market value ($ mil.): 515.0

	STOCK PRICE ($) FY Close	P/E High/Low		PER SHARE ($) Earnings	Dividends	Book Value
12/20	13.46	116	32	0.24	0.00	1.49
12/19	7.87	47	11	0.25	0.00	0.55
12/18	2.94	20	9	0.25	0.07	0.26
12/17	3.18	15	1	0.21	0.00	0.14
12/16	0.30	—	—	(0.00)	0.00	(0.11)
Annual Growth	158.8%	—	—	—	—	—

Hoover's Handbook of

Emerging Companies

2022
Indexes

Index by Headquarters

ARE

Abu Dhabi
First Abu Dhabi Bank PJSC W196
Abu Dhabi Commercial Bank W6
Abu Dhabi Islamic Bank W7

Dubai
Dubai Islamic Bank Ltd W168
Mashreqbank W313

AUS

Alexandria
Ampol Ltd W29

Brisbane
Suncorp Group Ltd. W466

Docklands
Australia & New Zealand Banking
  Group Ltd W50
ANZ Bank W33

East Perth
Fortescue Metals Group Ltd W199
Gold Corp Holdings W211

Hawthorn East
Coles Group Ltd (New) W133

Melbourne
Rio Tinto Ltd W404
Telstra Corp., Ltd. W484
National Australia Bank Ltd. W339

Newstead
Bank of Queensland Ltd W70

Perth
Wesfarmers Ltd. W525

Sydney
Woolworths Group Ltd W530
Commonwealth Bank of Australia
  W134
Westpac Banking Corp W527
QBE Insurance Group Ltd. W396
Macquarie Group Ltd W303

AUT

Linz
voestalpine AG W520
Oberbank AG (Austria) W367

Vienna
OMV AG (Austria) W370
Vienna Insurance Group AG W515
Erste Group Bank AG W186
UNIQA Insurance Group AG W511
BAWAG Group AG W77

Villach
Strabag SE-BR W458

BEL

Brussels
Umicore SA W507
Ageas NV W15
Solvay SA W450
KBC Group NV W271
Dexia SA W163

Leuven
Anheuser-Busch InBev SA/NV W32

BHR

Manama
Ahli United Bank W15
Arab Banking Corporation (B.S.C.)
  (Bahrain) W37

BMU

Hamilton
Brookfield Business Partners LP W94
Everest Re Group Ltd W188

Pembroke
Arch Capital Group Ltd W40
RenaissanceRe Holdings Ltd. W399

BRA

Rio de Janeiro
Petroleo Brasileiro SA W379
Vale SA W512

Sao Paulo
Banco Bradesco SA W55
JBS SA W262
Itau Unibanco Holding S.A. W256
Ultrapar Participacoes SA W506
Banco Santander Brasil SA W58
Marfrig Global Foods SA W309
Banco BTG Pactual S.A. W56

CAN

Aurora
Magna International Inc W305

Brampton
Loblaw Companies Ltd W300

Calgary
Enbridge Inc W177
Cenovus Energy Inc W110
Suncor Energy Inc W465
Imperial Oil Ltd W241
Canadian Natural Resources Ltd
  W100

Edmonton
Canadian Western Bank W102

Halifax
Bank of Nova Scotia Halifax W68

Laval
Alimentation Couche-Tard Inc W24

Levis
Desjardins Group W158

Montreal
Power Corp. of Canada W389
Bank of Montreal (Quebec) W68
Metro Inc W322
National Bank of Canada W340
Laurentian Bank of Canada W289

Ottawa
Bank of Canada (Ottawa) W65

Quebec City
IA Financial Corp Inc W239

Saskatoon
Nutrien Ltd W366

Stellarton
Empire Co Ltd W176

Toronto
Brookfield Asset Management Inc
  W93
Manulife Financial Corp W308
Royal Bank of Canada (Montreal,
  Quebec) W411
Weston (George) Ltd W526
Toronto Dominion Bank W497
Sun Life Financial Inc W464
Fairfax Financial Holdings Ltd W190
Canadian Imperial Bank Of Commerce
  (Toronto, Ontario) W98
Intact Financial Corp W249
Canadian Tire Corp Ltd W101

Vancouver
TELUS Corp W485
HSBC Bank Canada W232

Verdun
BCE Inc W81

Winnipeg
Great-West Lifeco Inc W212

CHE

Baar
Glencore PLC W211

Basel
Roche Holding Ltd W407
Novartis AG Basel W364
Baloise Holding AG W54
Bank Sarasin & Co W71

Emmen
Also Holding AG W27

Geneva
Compagnie Financiere Richemont SA
  W136

Hergiswil
Schindler Holding AG W425

Lausanne
Banque Cantonale Vaudoise W72

Liestal
Basellandschaftliche Kantonalbank
  (Switzerland) W75

Lucerne
Valiant Holding Bern (Switzerland)
  W514

Rapperswil-Jona
Holcim Ltd (New) W228

Schaffhausen
TE Connectivity Ltd W480

Schindellegi
Kuehne & Nagel International AG
  W286

Vevey
Nestle SA W347

Worblaufen
SwissCom AG W472

Zurich
Swiss Life Holding AG W471
Adecco Group AG W10
Zurich Insurance Group AG W542
Swiss Re Ltd W472
UBS Group AG W505
Chubb Ltd W125
ABB Ltd W4
Credit Suisse Group AG W143
Swiss Life (UK) plc (United Kingdom)
  W471
DKSH Holding Ltd W165
Vontobel Holding AG W524

CHL

Santiago
AntarChile S.A. (Chile) W33
Empresas COPEC SA W177
Corporacion Nacional del Cobre de
  Chile W141
Cencosud SA W109
Enel Americas SA W179
Banco Santander Chile W58
Banco de Chile W56
Itau CorpBanca W255

HOOVER'S HANDBOOK OF EMERGING COMPANIES 2022

INDEX BY HEADQUARTERS LOCATION

A = AMERICAN BUSINESS
E = EMERGING COMPANIES
P = PRIVATE COMPANIES
W = WORLD BUSINESS

CHN

FIH Mobile Ltd W195
China Hongqiao Group Ltd W116

Anshan City
Angang Steel Co Ltd W30

Baoding
Great Wall Motor Co Ltd W212

Beijing
China Petroleum & Chemical Corp W120
PetroChina Co Ltd W378
Industrial and Commercial Bank of China Ltd W244
China Construction Bank Corp W114
China Railway Group Ltd W120
China Railway Construction Corp Ltd W120
JD.com, Inc. W263
China Communications Constructions Group Ltd W114
Metallurgical Corp China Ltd W321
China Telecom Corp Ltd W124
China Shenhua Energy Co., Ltd. W122
CRRC Corp Ltd W146
China Life Insurance Co Ltd W116
New China Life Insurance Co Ltd W349
Xiaomi Corp W535
Aluminum Corp of China Ltd. W28
Huaneng Power International Inc W236
Longfor Group Holdings Ltd W300
DiDi Global Inc W165
China Coal Energy Co Ltd W114
BOE Technology Group Co Ltd W88
GD Power Development Co, Ltd. W208
BBMG Corp W81
Baidu Inc W54
Huadian Power International Corp., Ltd. W235
Datang International Power Generation Co Ltd W154
Meituan W318
Beijing Shougang Co Ltd W83

Changchun
FAW Car Co., Ltd. W194

Changsha
Hunan Valin Steel Co Ltd W236
Zhejiang Materials Development Co., Ltd. W541
Sany Heavy Industry Co Ltd W418

Changzhou
Changlin Co Ltd W112

Chengdu
New Hope Liuhe Co Ltd W349

Chongqing
Jinke Property Group Co., Ltd. W263
Chong Qing Changan Automobile Co Ltd W125

Dalian
China Grand Automotive Services Co Ltd W116
Hengli Petrochemical Co Ltd W223
Zhongsheng Group Holdings Ltd. W541

Jiangsu Zhongnan Construction Group Co., Ltd. W264

Fuzhou
Sunshine City Group Co., Ltd. W467

Guangzhou
Poly Developments and Holdings Group Co Ltd W387
Vipshop Holdings Ltd W518
China Southern Airlines Co Ltd W123

Hangzhou
Zhejiang Material Industrial Zhongda Yuantong Group Co., Ltd. W541

Hohhot
Inner Mongolia Yili Industrial Group Co., Ltd. W249

Jinan
Shandong Iron & Steel Co Ltd W431

Kunming
Yunnan Copper Co., Ltd. W541

Longyan
Zijin Mining Group Co Ltd W541

Luoyang City
China Molybdenum Co Ltd W118

Maanshan City
Maanshan Iron & Steel Co., Ltd. W303

Mianyang
Sichuan Chang Hong Electric Co Ltd W442

Nanchang
Jiangxi Copper Co., Ltd. W264

Nanjing
Suning.com Co Ltd W467

Qingdao
Haier Smart Home Co Ltd W217

Renhuai
Kweichow Moutai Co., Ltd. W287

Shanghai
SAIC Motor Corp Ltd W415
Shanghai Jinfeng Investment Co Ltd W431
China Pacific Insurance (Group) Co., Ltd. W119
China United Network Communications Ltd W124
Baoshan Iron & Steel Co Ltd W72
Shanghai Construction Group Co., Ltd. W431
Shanghai Pharmaceuticals Holding Co Ltd W431
Future Land Development Holdings Ltd W206
Shanghai Electric Group Co Ltd W431
Huayu Automotive Systems Company Ltd W236

Shangyu
China Fortune Land Development Co Ltd W115

Shenzhen
Tencent Holdings Ltd. W485
China Evergrande Group W115
China Vanke Co Ltd W125
China Merchants Shekou Industrial Zone Holdings Co Ltd W117
Ping An Insurance (Group) Co of China Ltd. W382
Zte Corp. W542
China International Marine Containers Group Ltd. W116

Shenzhen Shenxin Taifeng Group Co Ltd W435
Gemdale Corp W209
Shenzhen Overseas Chinese Town Co Ltd W434

Shijiazhuang
Hebei Iron & Steel Co Ltd W220

Tianjin
Sunac China Holdings Ltd W465
Tianjin Tianhai Investment Co Ltd W490
COSCO Shipping Holdings Co Ltd W141

Tongling
Tongling Nonferrous Metal Group Co Ltd W495

Urumqi
Xinjiang Zhongtai Chemical Co Ltd W535

Weifang
Weichai Power Co Ltd W525

Wuhan
China Gezhouba Group Co., Ltd. W116

Wuhu City
Anhui Conch Cement Co Ltd W33

Xiamen
Xiamen C & D Inc W535
Xiamen Xiangyu Co Ltd W535
Xiamen International Trade Group Corp Ltd W535

Xian
Shaanxi Yanchang Petroleum Chemical Engineering Co., Ltd. W430

Zhengzhou
Hengyi Petrochemical Co Ltd W223

Zhuhai
Gree Electric Appliances Inc Of Zhuhai W213

Zoucheng
Yankuang Energy Group Co Ltd W538

COL

Bogota
Ecopetrol SA W170

Medellin
BanColombia SA W61

CSK

Prague 1
Komercni Banka AS (Czech Republic) W281

DEU

Bad Homburg
Fresenius SE & Co KGaA W203
Fresenius Medical Care AG & Co KGaA W202

Bonn
Deutsche Telekom AG W162
Deutsche Post AG W161

Darmstadt
Merck KGaA (Germany) W320

Duesseldorf
Ceconomy AG W107
Henkel AG & Co KGAA W223
Metro AG (New) W322

Erlangen
Siemens Healthineers AG W444

Essen
E.ON SE W168
innogy SE W249
ThyssenKrupp AG W489
Hochtief AG W226
Evonik Industries AG W189
RWE AG W414
Brenntag SE W91

Frankfurt
Deutsche Lufthansa AG (Germany, Fed. Rep.) W160
Dekabank Deutsche Girozentrale W157

Frankfurt am Main
Deutsche Bank AG W158
Commerzbank AG W134

Hamburg
Hapag-Lloyd Aktiengesellschaft W219
Aurubis AG W49

Hannover
Talanx AG W476
Hannover Rueckversicherung SE W217

Hanover
Continental AG (Germany, Fed. Rep.) W140

Heidelberg
HeidelbergCement AG W220

Herzogenaurach
Adidas AG W11
Schaeffler AG W424

Ingolstadt
AUDI AG W49

Leverkusen
Bayer AG W77
Covestro AG W142

Ludwigshafen
BASF SE W75

Munich
Allianz SE W25
Bayerische Motoren Werke AG W79
Muenchener Rueckversicherungs-Gesellschaft AG (Germany) W336
Siemens AG (Germany) W442
Siemens Energy AG W443
Traton SE W503
BAYWA Bayerische Warenvermittlung Landwirtschaftlicher Genossenschaften AG W80

Neubiberg
Infineon Technologies AG W245

Stuttgart
Mercedes-Benz AG W318
McKesson Europe AG W314

Walldorf
SAP SE W419

Wiesbaden
Aareal Bank AG W2

Wolfsburg
Volkswagen AG W521

462   HOOVER'S HANDBOOK OF EMERGING COMPANIES 2022

INDEX BY HEADQUARTERS LOCATION

DNK

Aarhus N.
Vestas Wind Systems A/S W514

Bagsvaerd
Novo-Nordisk AS W364

Copenhagen K
A.P. Moller - Maersk A/S W1
Danske Bank A/S W153
KommuneKredit (Denmark) W282

Hedehusene
DSV AS W168

Silkeborg
Jyske Bank A/S W267

ESP

Alicante
Banco De Sabadell SA W56

Bilbao
Banco Bilbao Vizcaya Argentaria SA (BBVA) W55
Iberdrola SA W239

La Coruna
Industria De Diseno Textil (Inditex) SA W243

Madrid
Banco Santander SA (Spain) W59
Telefonica SA W482
ACS Actividades de Construccion y Servicios, S.A. W8
Repsol S.A. W400
Mapfre SA W309
Endesa S.A. W178
Naturgy Energy Group SA W343
Compania de Distribucion Integral Logista Holdings SA W139
Bankinter, S.A. W71

Vizcaya
Siemens Gamesa Renewable Energy SA W444

FIN

Espoo
Fortum OYJ W200
Nokia Corp W358
Neste Oyj W346
Kone OYJ W282

Kesko
Kesko OYJ W274

FRA

Bezons
Atos Origin W49

Boulogne-Billancourt
Carrefour S.A. W103
Renault S.A. (France) W400

Clermont-Ferrand
Compagnie Generale des Etablissements Michelin SCA W138

Courbevoie
TotalEnergies SE W498
Engie SA W182
Compagnie de Saint-Gobain W136
Thales W487

Ergue-Gaberic
Compagnie De L Odet W136

Issy-les-Moulineaux
Sodexo W447

Montrouge
Credit Agricole SA W143

Nanterre
Faurecia SE (France) W193

Paris
AXA SA W52
BNP Paribas (France) W85
Electricite de France W174
Societe Generale W447
LVMH Moet Hennessy Louis Vuitton W300
Orange W371
Sanofi W418
Bouygues S.A. W89
L'Oreal S.A. (France) W289
Veolia Environnement SA W514
Danone W151
L'Air Liquide S.A. (France) W289
Schlumberger Ltd W426
SCOR S.E. (France) W428
Safran SA W415
Valeo SE W513
Vivendi SE W518
Kering SA W272
Capgemini SE W102
Rexel SA W402
Colas SA Boulogne W133
Air France-KLM W17
Publicis Groupe S.A. W394
RCI Banque S.A. W398

Paris La Defense
SUEZ SA W459

Rueil-Malmaison
Vinci SA W516
Schneider Electric SE W426
ALD SA W22

Saint-Etienne
Casino Guichard Perrachon S.A. W105

Velizy-Villacoublay
Eiffage SA W173

GBR

Bradford
Yorkshire Building Society W540

Brentford
GlaxoSmithKline Plc W209

Bristol
Imperial Brands PLC W241

Cambridge
AstraZeneca Plc W45

Chertsey
Compass Group PLC (United Kingdom) W139

Dublin 1
Aon plc (Ireland) W34

Edinburgh
NatWest Group PLC W344

Glasgow
Clydesdale Bank PLC (United Kingdom) W129

Guildford
Linde plc W297

Kent
OSB Group plc W375

London
BP PLC W90

HSBC Holdings Plc W233
Legal & General Group PLC (United Kingdom) W290
Lloyds Bank plc W300
Aviva Plc (United Kingdom) W51
Unilever Plc (United Kingdom) W509
BHP Group Ltd W83
Lloyds Banking Group Plc W300
Rio Tinto Plc W405
J Sainsbury PLC W257
Phoenix Group Holdings PLC W382
Barclays PLC W73
British American Tobacco Plc (United Kingdom) W92
Anglo American Plc (United Kingdom) W31
BT Group Plc W95
Barclays Bank Plc W72
LyondellBasell Industries NV W302
BAE Systems Plc W53
CNH Industrial NV W130
Swire (John) & Sons Ltd. (United Kingdom) W471
Johnson Matthey Plc (United Kingdom) W265
M&G plc W302
National Grid plc W341
Lewis (John) Plc (United Kingdom) W295
Lewis (John) Partnership Plc (United Kingdom) W294
HSBC Bank Plc (United Kingdom) W233
Associated British Foods Plc W44
Diageo Plc W163
Royal Mail Plc W413
Kingfisher PLC W275
Bupa Finance plc W97
WPP Plc (New) W532
Rolls-Royce Holdings Plc W409
Currys plc W146
National Westminster Bank Plc W343
Bunzl Plc W96
Marks & Spencer Group PLC W310
Investec plc W252
TSB Banking Group Plc W503

Manchester
Co-Operative Group (CWS) Ltd. W131
Co-operative Bank plc W131

Newbury
Vodafone Group Plc W519

Newcastle Upon Tyne
TechnipFMC plc W481

Slough
Reckitt Benckiser Group Plc W398

Uxbridge
Coca-Cola Europacific Partners plc W133

Welwyn Garden City
Tesco PLC (United Kingdom) W485

Windsor
Centrica Plc W111

Wokingham
Ferguson PLC (New) W194

GRC

Athens
Alpha Services & Holdings SA W27
Eurobank Ergasias Services & Holdings SA W188
Piraeus Financial Holdings SA W383

HKG

China Mobile Limited W117
Alibaba Group Holding Ltd W24
CITIC Ltd W128
Prudential Plc W390
Country Garden Holdings Co Ltd W142
BYD Co Ltd W97
CNOOC Ltd W130
Lenovo Group Ltd W291
AIA Group Ltd. W15
China Unicom (Hong Kong) Ltd W124
Hongkong & Shanghai Banking Corp Ltd W232
CK Hutchison Holdings Ltd W129
Jardine Matheson Holdings Ltd. W261
China Taiping Insurance Holding Co., Ltd. W123
China Resources Land Ltd W121
China Resources Pharmaceutical Group Ltd W122
WH Group Ltd W528
China Overseas Land & Investment Ltd W119
Standard Chartered Plc W455
Fosun International Ltd W202
Kunlun Energy Co., Ltd. W287
Shimao Group Holdings Ltd W435
Geely Automobile Holdings Ltd W208
Cathay Pacific Airways Ltd. W107
Boc Hong Kong Holdings Ltd W87
Hang Seng Bank Ltd. W217
Far East Horizon Ltd. W192
Bank of East Asia Ltd. W66
Dah Sing Financial Holdings Ltd. W146
Dah Sing Banking Group Ltd W146

HUN

Budapest
MOL Magyar Olaj es Gazipari Reszvenytar W333

IDN

Jakarta
P.T. Astra International TBK W376
PT Bank Negara (Indonesia) W392

IND

Bangalore
Infosys Ltd. W246

Fort Mumbai
Tata Steel Ltd W478

Mumbai
Reliance Industries Ltd W399
State Bank of India W457
Tata Motors Ltd W477
ICICI Bank Ltd (India) W239
HDFC Bank Ltd W219
Larsen & Toubro Ltd W289
Union Bank Of India W510

IRL

Cork
Johnson Controls International plc W265

Dublin
Accenture plc W7

HOOVER'S HANDBOOK OF EMERGING COMPANIES 2022

INDEX BY HEADQUARTERS LOCATION

A = AMERICAN BUSINESS
E = EMERGING COMPANIES
P = PRIVATE COMPANIES
W = WORLD BUSINESS

Medtronic PLC W317
CRH Plc W145
DCC Plc W156
Aptiv PLC W36
Bank of Ireland Group plc W66
AIB Group PLC W16

Dublin 1
Adient Plc W12

Dublin 4
Eaton Corp plc W170

Swords
Trane Technologies plc W502

ISR

Ramat Gan
Mizrahi Tefahot Bank Ltd W332

Tel Aviv
Teva Pharmaceutical Industries Ltd W486

Tel-Aviv
Bank Leumi Le-Israel B.M. W63
Bank Hapoalim B.M. (Israel) W63
Israel Discount Bank Ltd. W253

ITA

Bologna
Unipol Gruppo SpA W511
UnipolSai Assicurazioni SpA W511

Milan
Telecom Italia SpA W481
Prysmian SpA W391
Mediobanca Banca Di Credito Finanziario SpA W315

Milano
Unicredito SpA W508

Reggio Emilia
Credito Emiliano Spa Credem Reggio Emilia W144

Rome
Enel Societa Per Azioni W180
ENI S.p.A. W184
Leonardo SpA W293
Poste Italiane SpA W388

Torino
Intesa Sanpaolo S.P.A. W251

Trieste
Assicurazioni Generali S.p.A. W43

JPN

Aki-gun
Mazda Motor Corp. (Japan) W313

Akita
Akita Bank Ltd (The) (Japan) W22

Aomori
Aomori Bank, Ltd. (The) (Japan) W34

Chiba
Aeon Co Ltd W14
Chiba Bank, Ltd W113
Keiyo Bank, Ltd. (The) (Japan) W272

Fukui
Fukui Bank Ltd. W206

Fukuoka
Kyushu Electric Power Co Inc W288

Fukushima
Toho Bank, Ltd. (The) W491

Gifu
Juroku Financial Group Inc W267

Hamamatsu
Suzuki Motor Corp. (Japan) W469

Hino
Hino Motors, Ltd. W225

Hiroshima
Hirogin Holdings Inc W225

Iwata
Yamaha Motor Co Ltd W536

Kadoma
Panasonic Corp W377

Kanazawa
Hokkoku Financial Holdings Inc W227

Kariya
Denso Corp W157
Aisin Corporation W20
Toyota Industries Corporation (Japan) W499

Kobe
Kobe Steel Ltd W279
Kawasaki Heavy Industries Ltd W271

Kochi
Shikoku Bank, Ltd. (Japan) W435

Kofu
Yamanashi Chuo Bank, Ltd. (Japan) W537

Kyoto
Nintendo Co., Ltd. W351
Nidec Corp W349
Kyocera Corp W288
Bank of Kyoto Ltd (Japan) W67

Maebashi
Gunma Bank Ltd (The) W216

Matsue
San-In Godo Bank, Ltd. (The) (Japan) W418

Matsuyama
Iyo Bank, Ltd. (Japan) W257

Miyazaki
Miyazaki Bank, Ltd. (The) W332

Morioka
Bank of Iwate, Ltd. (The) (Japan) W66

Musashino
Iida Group Holdings Co., Ltd. W241

Nagano
Hachijuni Bank, Ltd. (Japan) W216

Nagaokakyo
Murata Manufacturing Co Ltd W337

Nagoya
Toyota Tsusho Corp W502
Chubu Electric Power Co Inc W126
Suzuken Co Ltd W468
Bank of Nagoya, Ltd. W68
Aichi Bank, Ltd. W17

Nara
Nanto Bank, Ltd. W339

Numazu
Suruga Bank, Ltd. W468

Ogaki
Ogaki Kyoritsu Bank, Ltd. W368

Oita
Oita Bank Ltd (Japan) W368

Okayama
Chugoku Bank, Ltd. (The) W127

Osaka
ITOCHU Corp (Japan) W256
Nippon Life Insurance Co. (Japan) W352
Daiwa House Industry Co Ltd W150
Sumitomo Life Insurance Co. (Japan) W462
Kansai Electric Power Co., Inc. (Kansai Denryoku K. K.) (Japan) W268
Sumitomo Electric Industries, Ltd. (Japan) W461
Sekisui House, Ltd. (Japan) W429
Daikin Industries Ltd W148
Kubota Corp. (Japan) W285
Osaka Gas Co Ltd (Japan) W374

Otsu
Shiga Bank, Ltd. W435

Saitama
Musashino Bank, Ltd. W338

Sakai
Sharp Corp (Japan) W432

Sapporo
North Pacific Bank Ltd W364

Sendai
Tohoku Electric Power Co., Inc. (Japan) W491
77 Bank, Ltd. (The) (Japan) W1

Shizuoka
Shizuoka Bank Ltd (Japan) W440

Takamatsu
Hyakujushi Bank, Ltd. W237

Takasaki
Yamada Holdings Co Ltd W536

Tokushima
Awa Bank, Ltd. W52

Tokyo
Honda Motor Co Ltd W230
Mitsubishi Corp W324
Nippon Telegraph & Telephone Corp (Japan) W356
Japan Post Holdings Co Ltd W259
Sony Group Corp W452
Hitachi, Ltd. W226
Mitsui & Co., Ltd. W331
Eneos Holdings Inc W181
Dai-ichi Life Holdings Inc W148
Japan Post Insurance Co Ltd W259
Marubeni Corp. W311
Seven & i Holdings Co. Ltd. W429
Tokyo Electric Power Company Holdings Inc W493
Tokio Marine Holdings Inc W492
KDDI Corp W271
SoftBank Corp (New) W448
Nippon Steel Corp (New) W353
MS&AD Insurance Group Holdings W334
Sumitomo Corp. (Japan) W460
Idemitsu Kosan Co Ltd W240
Mitsubishi UFJ Financial Group Inc W329
Mitsubishi Electric Corp W326
Meiji Yasuda Life Insurance Co. W318
Sumitomo Mitsui Financial Group Inc Tokyo W463
Sompo Holdings Inc W451

Mitsubishi Heavy Industries Ltd W326
Fujitsu Ltd W205
Canon Inc W102
Mitsubishi Chemical Holdings Corp W323
JFE Holdings Inc W264
Bridgestone Corp (Japan) W92
Medipal Holdings Corp W317
Takeda Pharmaceutical Co Ltd W475
Toshiba Corp W498
NEC Corp W345
Subaru Corporation W458
Alfresa Holdings Corp Tokyo W23
Mitsubishi Shokuhin Co., Ltd. W328
NTT Data Corp W365
T&D Holdings Inc W472
Sumitomo Chemical Co., Ltd. W460
Bank of Japan W67
Orix Corp W373
Recruit Holdings Co Ltd W398
Japan Tobacco Inc. W259
Cosmo Energy Holdings Co Ltd W142
FUJIFILM Holdings Corp W205
Komatsu Ltd W281
Asahi Group Holdings Ltd. W41
Fast Retailing Co., Ltd. W192
Asahi Kasei Corp W41
Nippon Express Holdings Inc W352
Nippon Steel Trading Corp W355
Mitsui Fudosan Co Ltd W331
Kirin Holdings Co Ltd W276
Japan Post Bank Co Ltd W259
Isuzu Motors, Ltd. (Japan) W254
Kajima Corp. (Japan) W267
Toray Industries, Inc. W496
Obayashi Corp W366
Tokyo Gas Co Ltd W495
East Japan Railway Co. W169
Hanwa Co Ltd (Japan) W218
Pan Pacific International Holdings Corp W377
Yamato Holdings Co., Ltd. W538
Ricoh Co Ltd W403
Taisei Corp W473
Nippon Yusen Kabushiki Kaisha W356
Sojitz Corp W449
Rakuten Group Inc W396
Otsuka Holdings Co., Ltd. W375
AGC Inc W15
Shin-Etsu Chemical Co., Ltd. W437
Daito Trust Construction Co., Ltd. W149
Mitsubishi Materials Corp. W327
Kao Corp W269
TDK Corp W479
Toppan Inc W495
Shimizu Corp W436
Mitsubishi Motors Corp. (Japan) W328
Sumitomo Mitsui Trust Holdings Inc W464
Tokyo Electron, Ltd. W494
LIXIL Corp W299
Oji Holdings Corp W368
Dai Nippon Printing Co Ltd W147
Resona Holdings Inc Osaka W401
Nomura Holdings Inc W359
Shinsei Bank Ltd W439
Shoko Chukin Bank (The) (Japan) W440
Aozora Bank Ltd W35

Toyama
Hokuhoku Financial Group Inc W228

Toyota
Toyota Motor Corp W500

Tsu
Hyakugo Bank Ltd. (Japan) W237

INDEX BY HEADQUARTERS LOCATION

Yokohama
Nissan Motor Co., Ltd. W357

KOR

Changwon-si
Doosan Heavy Industries & Construction Co Ltd W167

Naju-si
Korea Electric Power Corp W284

Seol
KT Corp (Korea) W285

Seoul
Hyundai Motor Co., Ltd. W237
Shinhan Financial Group Co. Ltd. W438
LG Electronics Inc W296
POSCO (South Korea) W387
KB Financial Group, Inc. W271
Samsung C&T Corp (New) W416
LG Display Co Ltd W295
SK Telecom Co Ltd (South Korea) W444
Woori Financial Group Inc W532

Suwon-si
Samsung Electronics Co Ltd W416

LBN

Beirut
Bank Audi SAL W63
Blom Bank SAL W85

LUX

Luxembourg
ArcelorMittal SA W38

MEX

Mexico City
America Movil SAB de CV W28
Petroleos Mexicanos (Pemex) (Mexico) W380
Wal-Mart de Mexico S.A.B. de C.V. W524
Grupo Bimbo SAB de CV (Mexico) W214
Grupo Financiero Banorte S.A. BDE C V W215
Grupo Financiero Citibanamex SA de CV W216
Banco Santander Mexico SA, Institucion de Banca Multiple, Grupo Financiero Santander Mexico W59

Monterrey
Fomento Economico Mexicano, S.A.B. de C.V. W198

San Pedro Garza Garcia
ALFA SAB de CV W22
Cemex S.A.B. de C.V. W108

MYS

Kuala Lumpur
Malayan Banking Berhad W306
CIMB Group Holdings Bhd W128
Public Bank Berhad (Malaysia) W393
RHB Bank Berhad W402
Hong Leong Bank Berhad W232
AMMB Holdings BHD W29

NLD

Amstelveen
KLM Royal Dutch Airlines W278

Amsterdam
Exor NV W190
Heineken Holding NV (Netherlands) W222
Heineken NV (Netherlands) W222
Koninklijke Philips NV W284
ING Groep NV W247
X5 Retail Group NV W534

Diemen
Randstad NV W397

Leiden
Airbus SE W18

Lijnden
Stellantis NV W457

The Hague
Shell plc W433
AEGON NV W12

The Hauge
NN Group NV (Netherlands) W358

Veldhoven
ASML Holding NV W42

Zaandam
Koninklijke Ahold Delhaize NV W282

NOR

Fornebu
Telenor ASA W483

Lysaker
Storebrand ASA W457

Oslo
Norsk Hydro ASA W362
DNB BANK ASA W166
Kommunalbanken A/S (Norway) W282

Stavanger
Equinor ASA W186
SpareBank 1 SR Bank ASA W454

NZL

Auckland
Fonterra Co-Operative Group Ltd W199

OMN

Seeb
Bank Muscat S.A.O.G W64

PER

Lima
CrediCorp Ltd. W143

PHL

Makati City
BDO Unibank Inc. W82
Metropolitan Bank & Trust Co. (Philippines) W323
Bank of the Philippine Islands W70

Mandaluyong City
San Miguel Corp W417

POL

Warsaw
Bank Polska Kasa Opieki SA W70
mBank SA W314

PRT

Lisboa
Jeronimo Martins S.G.P.S. SA W263

Lisbon
EDP Energias de Portugal S.A. W171
Galp Energia, SGPS, SA W206

Porto
Banco Comercial Portugues SA W56

QAT

Doha
Qatar National Bank W395
Commercial Bank of Qatar W134
Qatar Islamic Bank W395

RUS

Krasnodar
Magnit PJSC W306

Moscow
PJSC Gazprom W384
Rosneft Oil Co OJSC (Moscow) W410
PJSC Lukoil W385
Sberbank Of Russia W423
Transneft W502
Inter RAO UES PJSC W250
MMC Norilsk Nickel PJSC W332
PJSC Rosseti W387

Saint-Petersburg
JSC VTB Bank W266

St. Petersburg
Gazprom Neft PJSC W207

Tyumenskaya Oblast
Surgutneftegas PJSC W467

SAU

Riyadh
Saudi Basic Industries Corp - SABIC (Saudi Arabia) W421
Saudi Electricity Co W422
Saudi Telecom Co W423
Riyad Bank (Saudi Arabia) W407
Saudi British Bank (The) W422
Samba Financial Group W416
Arab National Bank W38

SGP

Flex Ltd W196
Wilmar International Ltd W529
Olam International Ltd. W369
Oversea-Chinese Banking Corp. Ltd. (Singapore) W375
Great Eastern Holdings Ltd (Singapore) W212
DBS Group Holdings Ltd. W154
Jardine Cycle & Carriage Ltd W261
United Overseas Bank Ltd. (Singapore) W511

SWE

Goeteborg
Volvo AB W522

Stockholm
Ericsson W186
Hennes & Mauritz AB W225
Skanska AB W447
Essity Aktiebolag (Publ) W187
AB Electrolux (Sweden) W2
Nordea Bank ABp W361
Atlas Copco AB (Sweden) W47
Skandinaviska Enskilda Banken W445
Svenska Handelsbanken W470

Sundbyberg
Swedbank AB W471

THA

Bangkok
PTT Public Co Ltd W392
Charoen Pokphand Foods Public Co., Ltd. (Thailand) W112
C.P. All Public Co Ltd W98
Siam Cement Public Co. Ltd. W440
Kasikornbank Public Co Ltd W270
Siam Commercial Bank Public Co Ltd (The) W441
Bangkok Bank Public Co., Ltd. (Thailand) W62
Krung Thai Bank Public Co. Ltd. W284
Bank of Ayudhya Public Co Ltd W65
TMBThanachart Bank Public Co Ltd W490

TUR

Istanbul
Koc Holdings AS W280
Turkiye Is Bankasi AS W504
Haci Omer Sabanci Holding AS W216
Turkiye Garanti Bankasi AS W503
Yapi Ve Kredi Bankasi AS W539
AKBANK W21

Korfez
Turkiye Petrol Rafinerileri AS W505

TWN

Hsinchu
Taiwan Semiconductor Manufacturing Co., Ltd. W473
Wistron Corp W530

Kaohsiung
ASE Technology Holding Co Ltd W41

New Taipei
Hon Hai Precision Industry Co Ltd W229

Taipei
Compal Electronics Inc W138
Cathay Financial Holding Co W106

ZAF

Gauteng
MTN Group Ltd (South Africa) W335

Johannesburg
Standard Bank Group Ltd W455
Absa Group Ltd (New) W6

Pretoria
South African Reserve Bank W454

HOOVER'S HANDBOOK OF EMERGING COMPANIES 2022

INDEX BY HEADQUARTERS LOCATION

A = AMERICAN BUSINESS
E = EMERGING COMPANIES
P = PRIVATE COMPANIES
W = WORLD BUSINESS

Sandton
Bid Corp Ltd W85
Sasol Ltd. W420
Nedbank Group Ltd W345
Investec Ltd W252

Stellenbosch
Steinhoff International Holdings NV W457

USA

ALABAMA

ALEXANDER CITY
Medco, L.l.c. P323

ANDALUSIA
Powersouth Energy Cooperative P423

BESSEMER
Piggly Wiggly Alabama Distributing Co., Inc. P416

BIRMINGHAM
Regions Financial Corp (new) A670
Alabama Power Co A24
Protective Life Insurance Co A646
Proassurance Corp A642
Servisfirst Bancshares Inc A707 E367
Brasfield & Gorrie, L.l.c. P85
Mayer Electric Supply Company, Inc. P320
Consolidated Pipe & Supply Company, Inc. P151
B.l. Harbert Holdings, L.l.c. P54
University Of Alabama Health Services Foundation, P.c. P615
The Children's Hospital Of Alabama P549
The Southeastern Conference P580
Childrens Hospital Inc P117
Navigate Affordable Housing Partners, Inc P365
Hibbett Inc E213
Medical Properties Trust Inc E265
Servisfirst Bancshares Inc A707 E367

DOTHAN
Aaa Cooper Transportation P1
Construction Partners Inc E98

HOOVER
Southern Nuclear Operating Company, Inc. P492

HUNTSVILLE
The Health Care Authority Of The City Of Huntsville P561
Huntsville Hospital Health System P257
Huntsville Utilities P257
Lakeland Industries, Inc. E244

MOBILE
Infirmary Health System, Inc. P262
University Of South Alabama P628

MONTGOMERY
State Of Alabama A734 P510

PRATTVILLE
River Financial Corp E355

TUSCALOOSA
University Of Alabama P615

ALASKA

ANCHORAGE
First National Bank Alaska A321
Alaska Housing Finance Corp A27
Arctic Slope Regional Corporation P40
Nana Development Corporation P361
Petro Star Inc. P413
Anchorage, Municipality Of (inc) P36
Chenega Corporation P112
Chugach Alaska Corporation P119
Anchorage School District P36
Gci, Llc P225
Alaska Native Tribal Health Consortium P14
Northrim Bancorp Inc E296

JUNEAU
State Of Alaska A734 P510
Alaska Permanent Fund Corporation A27 P14
State Of Alaska A734 P510
Alaska Permanent Fund Corporation A27 P14
Sealaska Corporation P470

KOTZEBUE
Nana Regional Corporation, Inc., P361

ARIZONA

CHANDLER
Microchip Technology Inc A525

GLENDALE
Don Ford Sanderson Inc P193

MESA
Empire Southwest, Llc P205
City Of Mesa P128
Mesa Unified School District 4 P335

PEORIA
R. Directional Drilling & Underground Technology, Inc. A661 P432

PHOENIX
Freeport-mcmoran Inc A338
Avnet Inc A87
Republic Services Inc A676
Southern Copper Corp A723
On Semiconductor Corp A590
Sprouts Farmers Market Inc A728
Western Alliance Bancorporation A856 E447
State Of Arizona A734 P510
Shamrock Foods Company P475
Mercy Care P329
City Of Phoenix P131
County Of Maricopa P162
Blue Cross And Blue Shield Of Arizona, Inc. P78
Arizona State Lottery P41
Phoenix Children's Hospital, Inc. P415
Shell Medical Plan P480
John C. Lincoln Health Network P273
Maricopa County Special Health Care District P311
Leslie's Inc E250
Western Alliance Bancorporation A856 E447
Cable One Inc E59
Cavco Industries Inc (de) E71

SCOTTSDALE
Taylor Morrison Home Corp (holding Co) A761
Resideo Technologies Inc A678
Meritage Homes Corp A518
Honorhealth P254

Viavi Solutions Inc E436
Healthcare Trust Of America Inc E207
Store Capital Corp E391
Joint Corp (new) E240

SUN CITY
Banner Health A102 P56

TEMPE
Insight Enterprises Inc. A419
Amkor Technology Inc. A58
Carvana Co A155
Salt River Project Agricultural Improvement And Power District P460
Drivetime Automotive Group, Inc. P194
Arizona State University P41
Sundt Construction, Inc. P525
United Dairymen Of Arizona P610
Godaddy Inc E196
Align Technology Inc E14
Crexendo Inc E109

TUCSON
The Sundt Companies Inc P581
City Of Tucson P135
Pima County P418
Tucson Medical Center P604
Banner-university Medical Center Tucson Campus Llc P56

YUMA
Yuma Regional Medical Center Inc P662

ARKANSAS

BENTONVILLE
Walmart Inc A843
Walton Family Foundation Inc P646

CONWAY
Home Bancshares Inc A393 E216

EL DORADO
Murphy Usa Inc A542

LITTLE ROCK
Bank Ozk A100 E45
State Of Arkansas A734 P510
University Of Arkansas System P615
Baptist Health P56
Windstream Eagle Holdings, Llc P658
Arkansas Electric Cooperative Corporation P42
Vcc, Llc P640
Arkansas Electric Cooperatives, Inc. P43
Arkansas Children's Hospital P42
Bank Ozk A100 E45

LOWELL
Hunt (j.b.) Transport Services, Inc. A407

NORTH LITTLE ROCK
Comfort Systems Usa (arkansas), Inc. P144
Bruce Oakley, Inc. P90

PINE BLUFF
Simmons First National Corp A711 E372

ROGERS
America's Car-mart Inc E19

SPRINGDALE
Tyson Foods Inc A802

STUTTGART
Riceland Foods, Inc. P444

VAN BUREN
Usa Truck, Inc. E429

CALIFORNIA

ALAMEDA
Exelixis Inc E150

ALHAMBRA
Apollo Medical Holdings Inc E29

ANAHEIM
City Of Anaheim P123
Eaco Corp E125

AUBURN
County Of Placer P167

BAKERSFIELD
County Of Kern P161
Kern High School Dst P283
Jaco Oil Company P270
Bakersfield Memorial Hospital P54
Valley Republic Bancorp E431

BEVERLY HILLS
Live Nation Entertainment Inc A482
Pacwest Bancorp A605
Cedars-sinai Medical Care Foundation P105

BREA
Sun Mar Management Services P525

BRISBANE
Brisbane School District A134 P87

BURBANK
Disney (walt) Co. (the) A250

BURLINGAME
Mills-peninsula Health Services P344
Innoviva Inc E228

CARLSBAD
Maxlinear Inc E264
Natural Alternatives International, Inc. E287

CARMICHAEL
San Juan Unified School District P463

CERRITOS
Revolve Group Inc E353

CHICO
Trico Bancshares (chico, Ca) A793 E413

CHINO HILLS
Victory International Group, Llc P641

CHULA VISTA
Chg Foundation P114
Sweetwater Union High School District P530

CITY OF INDUSTRY
America Chung Nam (group) Holdings Llc P28

CONCORD
Swinerton Builders, Inc. P530
Ufcw & Employers Trust Llc P608

CORONA
Monster Beverage 1990 Corporation P351

CUPERTINO
Apple Inc A64

DAVIS
University Of California, Davis P616

INDEX BY HEADQUARTERS LOCATION

DOWNEY
Los Angeles County Office Of Education P302

DUARTE
City Of Hope National Medical Center P126

DUBLIN
Ross Stores Inc A686

EL SEGUNDO
A-mark Precious Metals, Inc A3
The Aerospace Corporation P543

ELK GROVE
Grove Elk Unified School District P236

EMERYVILLE
Grocery Outlet Holding Corp E203
Nmi Holdings Inc E293
Xoma Corp E455

FONTANA
Fontana Unified School District P217
California Steel Industries, Inc. P94

FOSTER CITY
Gilead Sciences Inc A354
Quinstreet, Inc E342
Qualys, Inc. E340

FOUNTAIN VALLEY
Memorial Health Services P326
Memorial Health Services Group Return P326

FREMONT
Td Synnex Corp A762
Lam Research Corp A467
Concentrix Corp A215
Asi Computer Technologies Inc P44
Enphase Energy Inc. E138
Ichor Holdings Ltd E220
Acm Research Inc E3

FRESNO
Community Hospitals Of Central California P148
County Of Fresno P159
Fresno Community Hospital And Medical Center P222
Community Hospitals Of Central California P148
Dairyamerica, Inc. P179
California's Valued Trust P95
Central Valley Community Bancorp E76
Communities First Financial Corp E94

FULLERTON
St. Jude Hospital P506

GARDEN GROVE
Garden Grove Unified School District P224

GLENDALE
Avery Dennison Corp A85

GOLETA
Deckers Outdoor Corp. E115
Community West Bancshares E96

HAYWARD
Ultra Clean Holdings Inc E420

HUNTINGTON BEACH
Boardriders, Inc. P82

IMPERIAL
Imperial Irrigation District P260

IRVINE
Edwards Lifesciences Corp A269
Skyworks Solutions Inc A715

Pacific Premier Bancorp Inc A603 E310
Pacific Premier Bank A603 P404
St. Joseph Health System P502
Vizio, Inc. P643
Irvine Unified School Distict P267
Newport Corporation P376
Pacific Premier Bank A603 P404
Masimo Corp. E262
Boot Barn Holdings Inc E55
Pacific Premier Bancorp Inc A603 E310
Cw Bancorp E114

IRWINDALE
Superior Communications, Inc. P527

LA CANADA FLINTRIDGE
Allen Lund Company, Llc P22

LA JOLLA
Silvergate Capital Corp A711 E372
Palomar Holdings Inc E311
Silvergate Capital Corp A711 E372
Private Bancorp Of America Inc E335

LA MESA
Grossmont Hospital Foundation P235

LAKE FOREST
Staar Surgical Co. E387

LANCASTER
Simulations Plus Inc E375

LIVERMORE
Formfactor Inc E180

LODI
Farmers & Merchants Bancorp (lodi, Ca) A294 E155
Pacific Coast Producers P403
Farmers & Merchants Bancorp (lodi, Ca) A294 E155

LOMA LINDA
Loma Linda University Medical Center P301

LONG BEACH
Molina Healthcare Inc A533
Farmers & Merchants Bank Of Long Beach (ca) A294
Ta Chen International, Inc. P532
City Of Long Beach P127
Long Beach Medical Center P301

LOS ALTOS
The David And Lucile Packard Foundation P554

LOS ANGELES
Reliance Steel & Aluminum Co. A673
Kb Home A446
Mercury General Corp. A516
Cathay General Bancorp A157 E70
Hope Bancorp Inc A398 E218
Hanmi Financial Corp. A374
Preferred Bank (los Angeles, Ca) A639 E331
Rbb Bancorp A665 E345
American Business Bank (los Angeles, Ca) A43 E21
County Of Los Angeles A223 P162
Los Angeles Unified School District A486 P303
City Of Los Angeles A186 P127
American Mutual Fund A49 P33
American High Income Trust A48 P31
Amcap Fund Inc A39 P28
The Ucla Foundation A782 P583
County Of Los Angeles A223 P162
Los Angeles Unified School District A486 P303
City Of Los Angeles A186 P127
Capital Income Builder P98

American Mutual Fund A49 P33
Aids Healthcare Foundation P11
The Childrens Hospital Los Angeles P550
The Bond Fund Of America Inc P546
Los Angeles Department Of Water And Power P302
American High Income Trust A48 P31
Amcap Fund Inc A39 P28
American Funds Portfolio Series P30
The Ucla Foundation A782 P583
New World Fund P368
Los Angeles Lomod Corporation P303
Air Lease Corp E9
Ares Management Corp E30
Houlihan Lokey Inc E219
B Riley Financial Inc E42
Kilroy Realty L.p. E241
Cathay General Bancorp A157 E70
Hope Bancorp Inc A398 E218
Rexford Industrial Realty Inc E353
Preferred Bank (los Angeles, Ca) A639 E331
Rbb Bancorp A665 E345
American Business Bank (los Angeles, Ca) A43 E21
Pcb Bancorp E315
Crescent Capital Bdc Inc E109
Op Bancorp E305

LOS GATOS
Netflix Inc A550

MADERA
Valley Children's Healthcare Foundation P638
Valley Children's Hospital P638

MARTINEZ
County Of Contra Costa P157

MENLO PARK
Meta Platforms Inc A519
Robert Half International Inc. A681
Novo Construction, Inc. P392
Corcept Therapeutics Inc E102

MERCED
County Of Merced P163

MILL VALLEY
Redwood Trust Inc A667
Four Corners Property Trust Inc E183

MILPITAS
Kla Corp A456
Devcon Construction Incorporated P187
Inspur Systems, Inc. P263

MISSION VIEJO
Mission Hospital Regional Medical Center Inc P345

MODESTO
County Of Stanislaus P170
Stan Boyett & Son, Inc. P508
Doctors Medical Center Of Modesto, Inc. P193

MONTEREY
Montage Health P351
Community Hospital Of The Monterey Peninsula P148

MOUNTAIN VIEW
Alphabet Inc A33
Intuit Inc A428
El Camino Healthcare District P201

NEWPORT BEACH
Chipotle Mexican Grill Inc A174
Hoag Memorial Hospital Presbyterian P253
American Vanguard Corp. E22

California First Leasing Corp E63

NORCO
Corona-norco Unified School District P154

NOVATO
Bank Of Marin Bancorp A97

OAKDALE
Oak Valley Bancorp (oakdale, Ca) E300

OAKLAND
Clorox Co (the) A188
Kaiser Foundation Hospitals Inc A445 P279
Kaiser Fdn Health Plan Of Colorado P279
County Of Alameda P155
Kfhp Of The Mid-atlantic States Inc. P284
City Of Oakland P130
Oakland Unified School District P392
Children's Hospital & Research Center At Oakland P115

ONTARIO
Cvb Financial Corp A230 E113

ORANGE
Orange County Health Authority, A Public Agency P398
Children's Hospital Of Orange County P116
Orange County Transportation Authority P398
St. Joseph Hospital Of Orange P502

OROVILLE
County Of Butte P157

PALO ALTO
Hp Inc A403
Vmware Inc A840
Lucile Salter Packard Children's Hospital At Stanford P306
Avidbank Holdings Inc E39

PASADENA
East West Bancorp, Inc A262 E127
Western Asset Mortgage Capital Corp A857
California Institute Of Technology P94
Schaumbond Group, Inc. P466
Pasadena Hospital Association, Ltd. P407
Huntington Hospital P257
Alexandria Real Estate Equities Inc E13
East West Bancorp, Inc A262 E127
Green Dot Corp E200

PETALUMA
Frontrow Calypso Llc P223

PITTSBURG
Uss-upi, Llc P637

PLEASANTON
Veeva Systems Inc E433
Simpson Manufacturing Co., Inc. (de) E374

PORTERVILLE
Sierra Bancorp A709 E369
R. M. Parks, Inc. P433
Sierra Bancorp A709 E369

POWAY
Cohu Inc E90

RANCHO CORDOVA
Dignity Health Medical Foundation P190

HOOVER'S HANDBOOK OF EMERGING COMPANIES 2022

467

INDEX BY HEADQUARTERS LOCATION

```
A = AMERICAN BUSINESS
E = EMERGING COMPANIES
P = PRIVATE COMPANIES
W = WORLD BUSINESS
```

RCHO STA MARG

Applied Medical Resources
  Corporation P40

REDWOOD CITY

Equinix Inc A281
Electronic Arts, Inc. A270
Dpr Construction, Inc. P194
County Of San Mateo P169
Coherus Biosciences Inc E90

RICHMOND

City Of Richmond P132

RIVERSIDE

County Of Riverside P167
Riverside Unified School
  District P447

ROCKLIN

Farm Credit West A293 P212

ROSEMEAD

Edison International A267
Southern California Edison Co. A722

ROSEVILLE

Adventist Health System/west,
  Corporation P5
Sutter Roseville Medical Center P529

SACRAMENTO

Sutter Health A750 P528
Sutter Valley Hospitals P529
County Of Sacramento P168
Sutter Health Sacramento Sierra
  Region P529
Sutter Valley Medical
  Foundation P529
Sacramento Municipal Utility
  District P455
Alston Construction Company,
  Inc. P26
California Department Of Water
  Resources P93
City Of Sacramento P132
Sacramento City Unified School
  District P455
River City Petroleum, Inc. P445
Sutter Health Plan P528

SAN BERNARDINO

County Of San Bernardino P168
San Bernardino City Unified School
  District P462
Inland Counties Regional Center,
  Inc. P262

SAN CARLOS

Rudolph And Sletten, Inc. P452

SAN CLEMENTE

Icu Medical Inc E220
Caretrust Reit Inc E68

SAN DIEGO

Qualcomm Inc A656
Sempra A704
Lpl Financial Holdings Inc. A488
County Of San Diego A224 P168
Axos Bank A89 P54
County Of San Diego A224 P168
Scripps Health P469
City Of San Diego P133
San Diego Unified School
  District P462
Sharp Healthcare P477
Rady Children's Hospital And Health
  Center P434
Sharp Memorial Hospital P478

Rady Children's Hospital-san
  Diego P434
Mercy Scripps Hospital P335
Southern Cal Schools Vol Emp
  Benefits Assoc P489
Axos Bank A89 P54
Resmed Inc. E351
Dexcom Inc E116
Realty Income Corp E346
Quidel Corp. E341
Encore Capital Group Inc E134
Neurocrine Biosciences, Inc. E290
Halozyme Therapeutics Inc E204
Franklin Wireless Corp E185
Mitek Systems, Inc. E276
Rf Industries Ltd. E354

SAN FRANCISCO

Wells Fargo & Co (new) A852
Visa Inc A839
Salesforce.com Inc A692
Pg&e Corp (holding Co) A623
The Gap Inc A777
Federal Reserve Bank Of San
  Francisco, Dist. No. 12 A300
Uber Technologies Inc A804
Block Inc A122
Williams Sonoma Inc A865
Levi Strauss & Co. A475 P297
Twitter Inc A800
First Republic Bank (san Francisco,
  Ca) A323
Federal Home Loan Bank Of San
  Francisco A298
Lendingclub Corp A473
Chinese Hospital Association A174
  P118
Dignity Health A245 P189
City & County Of San Francisco A185
  P122
Levi Strauss & Co. A475 P297
Chinese Hospital Association A174
  P118
Dignity Health A245 P189
City & County Of San Francisco A185
  P122
Levi Strauss & Co. A475 P297
Schwab Charitable Fund P468
Swinerton Incorporated P531
The Income Fund Of America
  Inc P562
American Balanced Fund, Inc. P29
Wilbur-ellis Holdings Ii, Inc. P656
Fundamental Investors, Inc. P224
Sutter Bay Hospitals P528
Ilwu-pma Welfare Trust P260
University Of California, San
  Francisco Foundation P616
University Of San Francisco Inc P628
Glu Mobile Inc. P230
Pinterest Inc E325
Dropbox Inc E123

SAN JOSE

Paypal Holdings Inc A611
Cisco Systems Inc A181
Broadcom Inc (de) A135
Western Digital Corp A857
Adobe Inc A10
Ebay Inc. A265
Sanmina Corp A693
Netapp, Inc. A549
Heritage Commerce Corp A382 E211
County Of Santa Clara P169
City Of San Jose P133
Atmel Corporation P49
Mellanox Technologies, Inc. P325
Santa Clara Valley Transportation
  Authority P464
Good Samaritan Hospital, L.p. P231
Super Micro Computer Inc E397
Cadence Design Systems Inc E61

Roku Inc E357
Zoom Video Communications
  Inc E457
Lumentum Holdings Inc E256
Xperi Holding Corp E456
Power Integrations Inc. E329
Sjw Group E375
Parade Technologies Ltd. E311
Heritage Commerce Corp A382 E211

SAN JUAN CAPISTRANO

Capistrano Unified School
  District P97
Ensign Group Inc E138

SAN LEANDRO

Regional Center Of The East Bay,
  Inc. P441
Energy Recovery Inc E136

SAN MATEO

Franklin Resources Inc A336
Tesla Energy Operations, Inc. P538
Upstart Holdings Inc E429

SAN PEDRO

Port Of Los Angeles P422

SAN RAFAEL

Westamerica Bancorporation A856
County Of Marin P163
Autodesk Inc E37
Biomarin Pharmaceutical Inc E51

SAN RAMON

Chevron Corporation A171
Cooper Companies, Inc. (the) E99

SANTA ANA

First American Financial Corp A307
Banc Of California Inc A93
Allied Universal Holdco Llc A31 P24
County Of Orange P165

SANTA BARBARA

County Of Santa Barbara P169
Sonos Inc E380
Appfolio Inc E29

SANTA CLARA

Intel Corp A420
Applied Materials, Inc. A65
Nvidia Corp A576
Advanced Micro Devices Inc A13
Agilent Technologies, Inc. A20
Servicenow Inc A706
Svb Financial Group A750
President And Board Of Trustees Of
  Santa Clara College P427
Arista Networks Inc E30
Ehealth Inc E130
Semler Scientific Inc E367

SANTA CRUZ

County Of Santa Cruz P169
Santa Cruz County Bank (ca) E360

SANTA MONICA

Activision Blizzard, Inc. A9

SANTA ROSA

Luther Burbank Corp A490 E256
Exchange Bank (santa Rosa, Ca) A285
Redwood Credit Union A667
County Of Sonoma P170
Luther Burbank Corp A490 E256
Summit State Bank (santa Rosa,
  Ca) E395

STANFORD

Leland Stanford Junior
  University A472 P295
Stanford Health Care A730 P509
Leland Stanford Junior
  University A472 P295
Stanford Health Care A730 P509

Stanford Health Services P509

STOCKTON

County Of San Joaquin P168
Coastal Pacific Food Distributors,
  Inc. P139
Stockton Unified School District P522

STUDIO CITY

Motion Picture Industry Health
  Plan P354

SUNNYVALE

Intuitive Surgical Inc A430
Hcl America Inc. P244
Trimble Inc E414
Fortinet Inc E182

SYLMAR

Tutor Perini Corp A799

TEMPLE CITY

Fulgent Genetics Inc E188

THOUSAND OAKS

Amgen Inc A56
Teledyne Technologies Inc E404

TORRANCE

American Honda Finance
  Corporation A48 P31
Torrance Health Association,
  Inc. P596
Torrance Memorial Medical
  Center P596
Harbor-ucla Medical Center P241

TUSTIN

Avid Bioservices Inc E38

VALENCIA

Sunkist Growers, Inc. P526

VENTURA

County Of Ventura P172
The Trade Desk Inc E408

VISALIA

County Of Tulare P171
Kaweah Delta Health Care District
  Guild P282

WALNUT

Shea Homes Limited Partnership, A
  California Limited Partnership P480

WALNUT CREEK

John Muir Health P273
Central Garden & Pet Co E74
United States Brent Oil Fund
  L.p. E425
United States 12 Month Oil Fund
  Lp E425
Baycom Corp E48
United States Gasoline Fund Lp E425

WEST HOLLYWOOD

Cedars-sinai Medical Center P105

WEST SACRAMENTO

Raley's P435

WESTLAKE VILLAGE

Pennymac Financial Services Inc
  (new) A614 E316
Pennymac Mortgage Investment
  Trust E317

WHITTIER

Pih Health Whittier Hospital P416
County Sanitation District No. 2 Of
  Los Angeles County P173

468   HOOVER'S HANDBOOK OF EMERGING COMPANIES 2022

INDEX BY HEADQUARTERS LOCATION

COLORADO

AURORA
University Of Colorado Health A824 P617
Children's Hospital Colorado P115
Poudre Valley Health Care, Inc. P422
Graebel Holdings, Inc. P233

BOULDER
The Regents Of The University Of Colorado P576

BRIGHTON
County Of Adams P155

BROOMFIELD
Danone Us, Inc. P181
Mwh Global, Inc. P360
Flatiron Constructors, Inc. P214
Crocs Inc E110

CASTLE ROCK
Douglas County School District P193

CENTENNIAL
Arrow Electronics, Inc. A71
Catholic Health Initiatives Colorado P102

COLORADO SPRINGS
Memorial Hospital Corporation P327
Compassion International Inc P149

DENVER
Davita Inc A237
Newmont Corp A557
Vf Corp. A835
Dcp Midstream Lp A238
Ovintiv Inc A599
M.d.c. Holdings, Inc. A492
State Of Colorado A735 P510
Colorado Housing And Finance Authority A200
State Of Colorado A735 P510
University Of Colorado P617
Pcl Construction Enterprises, Inc. P408
Modivcare Solutions, Llc P349
Denver Health And Hospitals Authority Inc P186
University Of Colorado Hospital Authority P618
University Of Denver P619
St. Joseph Hospital, Inc. P503
Saint Joseph Hospital, Inc P457
Scl Health - Front Range, Inc. P468
Summit Materials Inc E395
Advanced Energy Industries Inc E5
Simply Good Foods Company (the) E373
Antero Midstream Corp E28
Re/max Holdings Inc E345
Civitas Resources Inc E85
First Western Financial Inc E174
Farmland Partners Inc E156

DURANGO
Saddle Butte Pipeline Llc P456

ENGELWOOD
Liberty Media Corp (de) A477

ENGLEWOOD
Dish Network Corp A249
Qurate Retail Inc A660
Liberty Media Corp (de) A477
American Furniture Warehouse Co Inc P30
Kiewit Building Group Inc. P284
Ttec Holdings Inc E416
Zynex Inc E457
Liberty Broadband Corp E252

FORT COLLINS
Colorado State University P142

GLENWOOD SPRINGS
Alpine Banks Of Colorado E17

GOLDEN
Jefferson County School District No. R-1 P271
Good Times Restaurants Inc. E196

GREELEY
Pilgrims Pride Corp. A626
Banner Health A102 P56

GREENWOOD VILLAGE
National Bank Holdings Corp A544 E285
Cobank, Acb A194 P140
Air Methods Corporation P12
National Storage Affiliates Trust E286
National Bank Holdings Corp A544 E285

HENDERSON
Myr Group Inc E283

LAKEWOOD
Natural Grocers By Vitamin Cottage Inc E288
Solera National Bancorp Inc E380

LITTLETON
Thompson Creek Metals Company Usa P594

LOVELAND
Medical Center Of The Rockies P323

THORNTON
Adams 12 Five Star Schools P4

WATKINS
Pure Cycle Corp. E339

WESTMINSTER
Ball Corp A91

CONNECTICUT

BLOOMFIELD
Cigna Corp (new) A178

BRANFORD
Sachem Capital Corp E358

BRIDGEPORT
People's United Financial Inc A616 E318
Bridgeport Hospital P87
People's United Financial Inc A616 E318

BROOKFIELD
Photronics, Inc. E322

CHESHIRE
Bozzuto's, Inc. P85
Lane Industries Incorporated P292
The Lane Construction Corporation P564

DANBURY
The Danbury Hospital P554

FAIRFIELD
Save The Children Federation, Inc. P465

FARMINGTON
Otis Worldwide Corp A598

GREENWICH
Xpo Logistics, Inc. A873
Berkley (wr) Corp A111
Gxo Logistics Inc A370
Starwood Property Trust Inc. A733 E389
Interactive Brokers Group Inc E234

Starwood Property Trust Inc. A733 E389

HARTFORD
Hartford Financial Services Group Inc. A376
Hartford Healthcare Corporation P242
Hartford Hospital P243
City Of Hartford P126
Eversource Energy Service Company P209
Virtus Investment Partners Inc E441

MASHANTUCKET
Mashantucket Pequot Gaming Enterprise Inc P316

MILFORD
Doctor's Associates Inc. P192

NEW BRITAIN
Stanley Black & Decker Inc A730

NEW CANAAN
Csc Sugar, Llc P177

NEW HAVEN
Knights Of Columbus A458 P287
Yale University P660
Yale New Haven Hospital, Inc. P660
Knights Of Columbus A458 P287
City Of New Haven P129
Yale New Haven Health Services Corporation P659

NORWALK
Booking Holdings Inc A127
Emcor Group, Inc. A271
Frontier Communications Parent Inc A339
Xerox Holdings Corp A871

OLD GREENWICH
Ellington Residential Mortgaging Real Estate Investment Trust E132

ORANGE
Avangrid Inc A85
The United Illuminating Company P584

SHELTON
Prudential Annuities Life Assurance Corp A648

SOUTH WINDSOR
Gerber Scientific Products Inc P229

STAMFORD
Charter Communications Inc (new) A167
Synchrony Financial A752
United Rentals Inc A819
Equinor Marketing & Trading (us) Inc. A282 P208
Lexa International Corporation P298
Equinor Natural Gas Llc P208
Americares Foundation, Inc. P35
Tudor Investment Corporation P604
The Stamford Hospital P580
City Of Stamford P134
Tenerity, Inc. P537
World Wrestling Entertainment Inc E452
Lovesac Co E256
Dorian Lpg Ltd. E122
Cara Therapeutics Inc E67

UNCASVILLE
Mohegan Tribal Gaming Authority P349

WALLINGFORD
Amphenol Corp. A59

WATERBURY
Webster Financial Corp (waterbury, Conn) A850
City Of Waterbury P135

WESTPORT
Compass Diversified E97

WILTON
Blue Buffalo Pet Products, Inc. P76

WINDSOR
Trc Companies, L.l.c. P597

DELAWARE

DOVER
State Of Delaware A735 P511
Bayhealth Medical Center, Inc. P64

NEWARK
Slm Corp. A716 E378
University Of Delaware P618
Slm Corp. A716 E378

WILMINGTON
Dupont De Nemours Inc A260
Chemours Co (the) A168
Navient Corp A545
Wsfs Financial Corp A869 E454
The Bancorp Inc A773 E407
Barclays Bank Delaware A103 P60
Wilmington Trust Company A866 P657
Balfour Beatty, Llc P55
Barclays Bank Delaware A103 P60
Alfred I.dupont Hospital For Children P19
Wilmington Trust Company A866 P657
St. Francis Hospital, Inc. P499
Incyte Corporation E224
Wsfs Financial Corp A869 E454
The Bancorp Inc A773 E407
Founders Bay Holdings E183

DISTRICT OF COLUMBIA

WASHINGTON
Federal Reserve System A300
Fannie Mae A292
Danaher Corp A234
Carlyle Group Inc (the) A151
Federal Agricultural Mortgage Corp A296 E157
U.s. General Services Administration A803 P606
Government Of District Of Columbia A362 P232
Securities Investor Protection Corporation A702
U.s. General Services Administration A803 P606
Government Of District Of Columbia A362 P232
National Railroad Passenger Corporation P364
Wgl Holdings, Inc. P654
Aarp P2
National Association Of Letter Carriers P362
Smithsonian Institution P484
Children's Hospital P114
The Georgetown University P560
Pan American Health Organization Inc P404
The George Washington University P559
Washington Hospital Center Corporation P646

HOOVER'S HANDBOOK OF EMERGING COMPANIES 2022   469

INDEX BY HEADQUARTERS LOCATION

A = AMERICAN BUSINESS
E = EMERGING COMPANIES
P = PRIVATE COMPANIES
W = WORLD BUSINESS

Financial Industry Regulatory
Authority, Inc. P213
The Howard University P562
Childrens Hospital P117
Publishing Office, Us
Government P432
Medstar-georgetown Medical Center,
Inc. P324
District Of Columbia Water & Sewer
Authority P190
Dc Water And Sewer Authority P184
Population Services
International P421
American Chemical Society P29
Costar Group, Inc. E103
Federal Agricultural Mortgage
Corp A296 E157
Vanda Pharmaceuticals Inc E432
Easterly Government Properties
Inc E128

FLORIDA

ALTAMONTE SPRINGS
Adventist Health System/sunbelt,
Inc. A14 P5

BARTOW
Polk County School District P421
Polk County P421

BOCA RATON
Odp Corp (the) A583
Adt Inc (de) A11
Johnson Controls Fire Protection
Lp P277
Dcr Workforce, Inc. P185
Celsius Holdings Inc E74
Newtek Business Services Corp E292

BOYNTON BEACH
Bethesda Hospital, Inc. P72

BRADENTON
Beall's, Inc. P67

CLEARWATER
Morton Plant Hospital Association,
Inc. P353
Baycare Health System, Inc. P64
Marinemax Inc E260

COCOA
Southeast Petro Distributors,
Inc. P489

COCONUT CREEK
Food For The Poor, Inc. P217
Willis Lease Finance Corp. E449

CORAL GABLES
Mastec Inc. (fl) A503
Amerant Bancorp Inc A40
Professional Holding Corp E335

DANIA BEACH
Chewy Inc A173

DAVIE
Nova Southeastern University,
Inc. P390

DAYTONA BEACH
Brown & Brown Inc E57
Topbuild Corp E409
Alpine Income Property Trust Inc E17

DELAND
County Of Volusia P172

DELRAY BEACH
Morse Operations, Inc. P353

ESTERO
Hertz Global Holdings Inc
(new) A385
The Hertz Corporation A778 P561

FORT LAUDERDALE
Autonation, Inc. A82
School Board Of Broward County, The
(inc) P467
Broward County Public Schools P90
County Of Broward P157
North Broward Hospital District P379
Brandsmart Usa Of Henry County,
Llc P85
Seacor Holdings Inc. P470
Universal Insurance Holdings
Inc E426
Ocean Bio-chem, Inc. E301

FORT MYERS
Lee Memorial Health System
Foundation, Inc. P292
21st Century Oncology Holdings,
Inc P1
County Of Lee P162
Lee Memorial Hospital, Inc. P293
Finemark Holdings Inc E161

GAINESVILLE
University Of Florida P619
Shands Teaching Hospital And Clinics,
Inc. P477
Florida Clinical Practice Association,
Inc. P214

HOLLYWOOD
South Broward Hospital District P486
Nv5 Global Inc E299

JACKSONVILLE
Fidelity National Information Services
Inc A304
Csx Corp A226
Fidelity National Financial Inc A303
Landstar System, Inc. A468
Equity One, Inc. A283
Baptist Health System, Inc. P58
Crowley Maritime Corporation P175
Jacksonville Electric Authority P270
City Of Jacksonville P127
Southern Baptist Hospital Of Florida
Inc. P489
Duval County Public Schools P198
Shands Jacksonville Healthcare,
Inc. P476
Shands Jacksonville Medical Center,
Inc. P476
Frp Holdings Inc E187

JUNO BEACH
Nextera Energy Inc A559
Florida Power & Light Co. A327

KEY WEST
County Of Monroe P164

KISSIMMEE
The School District Of Osceola County
Florida P579

LAKELAND
Publix Super Markets, Inc. A651
Lakeland Regional Medical Center,
Inc. P291
Lakeland Regional Health Systems,
Inc. P291

MAITLAND
Florida Hospital Medical Group,
Inc. P215

MELBOURNE
L3harris Technologies Inc A462

MIAMI
Lennar Corp A474
World Fuel Services Corp. A868
Ryder System, Inc. A688
Watsco Inc. A849
The School Board Of Miami-dade
County P579
Baptist Hospital Of Miami, Inc. P59
Ladenburg Thalmann Financial
Services Inc. P290
The Public Health Trust Of Miami-
dade County P576
City Of Miami P128
Miami-dade Aviation
Department P341
Miami Children's Health System
Management Services, Llc P340
Aura Minerals Inc (british Virgin
Islands) E37
Evi Industries Inc E149
Veru Inc E435

MIAMI BEACH
Mount Sinai Medical Center Of
Florida, Inc. P355

MIAMI LAKES
Bankunited Inc. A100

MULBERRY
W.s. Badcock Corporation P644

NAPLES
Naples Community Hospital Inc P361

NEW PORT RICHEY
County Of Pasco P166

NORTH VENICE
Pgt Innovations Inc E321

ORLANDO
Darden Restaurants, Inc. A236
Orlando Health, Inc. P400
The Orange County Public School
District P572
County Of Orange P165
School Board Of Orange County
Florida P467
Campus Crusade For Christ Inc P96
Florida Municipal Power Agency P216
The University Of Central Florida
Board Of Trustees P584

PALM BEACH GARDENS
Carrier Global Corp A154

PANAMA CITY BEACH
St. Joe Co. (the) E385

PONTE VEDRA BEACH
Pga Tour, Inc. P414

ROCKLEDGE
Health First Shared Services,
Inc. P245

SAINT PETERSBURG
Raymond James & Associates
Inc A662 P435
Pscu Incorporated P430
Johns Hopkins All Children's Hospital,
Inc. P274

SARASOTA
Roper Technologies Inc A685
Sarasota County Public Hospital
District P465
County Of Sarasota P169
Helios Technologies Inc E209

SEMINOLE
Superior Group Of Companies
Inc E397

SOUTH MIAMI
Baptist Health South Florida,
Inc. P57
South Miami Hospital, Inc. P488

ST. PETERSBURG
Jabil Inc A433
Raymond James Financial, Inc. A663
Duke Energy Florida Llc A259
United Insurance Holdings Corp A816

STUART
Seacoast Banking Corp. Of
Florida A700 E364
Martin Memorial Medical Center,
Inc P314
Seacoast Banking Corp. Of
Florida A700 E364

SUNNY ISLES BEACH
Icahn Enterprises Lp A412

TALLAHASSEE
Capital City Bank Group, Inc. A147
E66
Florida Department Of Lottery A326
P214
Florida Housing Finance Corp A327
P215
Florida Department Of Lottery A326
P214
Florida State University P216
Florida Housing Finance Corp A327
P215
Capital City Bank Group, Inc. A147
E66

TAMPA
Mosaic Co (the) A538
Hillsborough County School
District P251
County Of Hillsborough P161
H. Lee Moffitt Cancer Center And
Research Institute, Inc. P240
Florida Health Sciences Center,
Inc. P215
Seminole Electric Cooperative,
Inc. P473
St. Joseph's Hospital, Inc. P504
University Of South Florida P629
Shriners International P481
University Community Hospital,
Inc. P612
City Of Tampa P134
Helm Fertilizer Corporation
(florida) P248
Avi-spl Holdings, Inc. P53
Pacira Biosciences Inc E310
Sila Realty Trust Inc E372

VERO BEACH
Armour Residential Reit Inc. A70
Orchid Island Capital Inc A596

VIERA
School Board Of Brevard
County P466

WEST PALM BEACH
County Of Palm Beach P166
The School District Of West Palm
Beach County P579
School Board Of Palm Beach
County P467
South Florida Water Management
District Leasing Corp. P488

WINTER HAVEN
Southstate Corp A725 E383

WINTER PARK
Anc Healthcare, Inc. P36

YULEE
County Of Nassau P165

INDEX BY HEADQUARTERS LOCATION

GEORGIA

ACWORTH
Cobb County Public Schools P141

ALPHARETTA
National Christian Charitable
  Foundation, Inc. P362
Jackson Healthcare, Llc P269
Evans General Contractors, Llc P209

ATHENS
University Of Georgia P620

ATLANTA
Home Depot Inc A394
United Parcel Service Inc A818
Coca-cola Co (the) A195
Delta Air Lines Inc (de) A241
Southern Company (the) A722
Genuine Parts Co. A349
Westrock Co A860
Pultegroup Inc A653
Norfolk Southern Corp A565
Newell Brands Inc A556
Georgia Power Co A352
Intercontinental Exchange Inc A422
Global Payments Inc A357
Federal Reserve Bank Of Atlanta, Dist.
  No. 6 A298
Graphic Packaging Holding Co A364
Veritiv Corp A832
Ncr Corp A547
Ameris Bancorp A53 E24
Atlantic Capital Bancshares Inc A78
Invesco Mortgage Capital Inc A431
State Of Georgia A735 P511
Board Of Regents Of The University
  System Of Georgia A123 P81
Georgia Housing Finance
  Authority A352
Lettie Pate Evans Foundation A475
State Of Georgia A735 P511
Board Of Regents Of The University
  System Of Georgia A123 P81
Heartland Payment Systems, Llc P247
Northside Hospital, Inc. P387
Grady Memorial Hospital
  Corporation P233
Fulton County Board Of
  Education P224
Piedmont Hospital, Inc. P416
City Of Atlanta P123
Unipro Foodservice, Inc P609
County Of Fulton P159
Altisource Solutions, Inc. P27
Emory University Hospital
  Midtown P205
Georgia Caresource Co P228
Municipal Electric Authority Of
  Georgia P358
Cooperative For Assistance And Relief
  Everywhere, Inc. (care) P153
Wells Real Estate Investment Trust
  Ii P649
Georgia Tech Applied Research
  Corporation P228
Floor & Decor Holdings Inc E178
Gray Television Inc E198
Rollins, Inc. E357
Ameris Bancorp A53 E24
Cousins Properties Inc E104
Atlanticus Holdings Corp E35
Greensky Inc E201
Dlh Holdings Corp E122

AUGUSTA
Au Health System, Inc. P51

BALL GROUND
Chart Industries Inc E80

BLAIRSVILLE
United Community Banks Inc
  (blairsville, Ga) A814 E424

BROOKHAVEN
The Salvation Army P578

BRUNSWICK
Map International (inc.) P311

BUFORD
Onewater Marine Inc E303

CALHOUN
Mohawk Industries, Inc. A532

COLUMBUS
Aflac Inc A17
Synovus Financial Corp A753 E400
City Of Columbus P125
St. Francis Hospital, Inc. P499
Synovus Financial Corp A753 E400

CONYERS
Pratt Corrugated Holdings, Inc. P424
Pratt Industries, Inc. P424

CUMMING
Forsyth County Board Of
  Education P218

DECATUR
Global Health Solutions Inc P230
County Of Dekalb P158
Dekalb County Public Library P186

DORAVILLE
Metrocity Bankshares Inc E272

DUBLIN
Morris St Bancshares Inc E281

DULUTH
Agco Corp. A19
Asbury Automotive Group Inc A73
Primerica Inc A640 E333
National Vision Holdings Inc E286
Fox Factory Holding Corp E183

FITZGERALD
Colony Bankcorp, Inc. E91

GAINESVILLE
Northeast Georgia Medical Center,
  Inc. P385

JEFFERSON
Jackson Electric Membership
  Corporation P269

JOHNS CREEK
Saia Inc E359
Ebix Inc E129

LAWRENCEVILLE
Gwinnett Hospital System, Inc. P239

MARIETTA
Cobb County School District P141
Cobb County Board Of
  Education P140
The Conlan Company P553
Kennestone Hospital Inc P283
Cobb County Medical Examiner's
  Office P140
Kennestone Hospital At Windy Hill,
  Inc. P282
Cobb Electric Membership
  Corporation P141

NORCROSS
Corecard Corp E103

PENDERGRASS
Royal Ten Cate (usa), Inc. P452

ROSWELL
Siteone Landscape Supply Inc E375

SAVANNAH
Savannah-chatham County Board Of
  Education P465
The Savannah College Of Art And
  Design Inc P578
Memorial Health, Inc. P326

STONE MOUNTAIN
Dekalb County Board Of
  Education P186

SUWANEE
Gwinnett County Board Of
  Education P239

TEMPLE
Janus International Group Inc E238

THOMASVILLE
Thomasville Bancshares, Inc. E409

TUCKER
Gms Inc E195

WEST POINT
Hyundai Transys Georgia Powertrain,
  Inc. P258

HAWAII

HILO
County Of Hawaii P160

HONOLULU
First Hawaiian Inc A317
Bank Of Hawaii Corp A96
Central Pacific Financial Corp A163
State Of Hawaii A735 P511
City & County Of Honolulu P121
Servco Pacific Inc. P474
Hawai I Pacific Health P244
The Queen's Health Systems P576
Suasin Cancer Care Inc. P523
University Of Hawai'i Of Manoa P620
University Of Hawaii System P620
Trustees Of The Estate Of Bernice
  Pauahi Bishop P603
Barnwell Industries, Inc. E47

WAILUKU
County Of Maui P163

IDAHO

BOISE
Albertsons Companies Inc A27
Micron Technology Inc. A526
Boise Cascade Co. (de) A124
Albertsons Companies, Inc. A27 P17
State Of Idaho A735 P511
Albertsons Companies, Inc. A27 P17
State Of Idaho A735 P511
Winco Holdings, Inc. P657
St. Luke's Health System, Ltd. P506
St. Luke's Regional Medical Center,
  Ltd. P507
Public Employee Retirement System,
  Idaho P430
The Amalgamated Sugar Company
  Llc P543
Saint Alphonsus Regional Medical
  Center Inc. P456
Snake River Sugar Company P485
Dbsi Inc P184
Saint Alphonsus Regional Medical
  Center, Inc. P456

COEUR D ALENE
Kootenai Hospital District P287

EAGLE
Pennant Group Inc E316

ILLINOIS

ABBOTT PARK
Abbott Laboratories A3

AURORA
Old Second Bancorp., Inc. (aurora,
  Ill.) A586 E302

BLOOMINGTON
Hbt Financial Inc A378
Growmark, Inc. A369 P236

BOLINGBROOK
Ulta Beauty Inc A807

BUFFALO GROVE
Produce Alliance, L.l.c. P429

CARBONDALE
Southern Illinois Healthcare
  Enterprises, Inc. P490
Southern Illinois University Inc P490

CARLINVILLE
Cnb Bank Shares Inc E86

CHAMPAIGN
First Busey Corp A310 E164

CHICAGO
Archer Daniels Midland Co. A68
United Airlines Holdings Inc A812
Boeing Co. (the) A123
Exelon Corp A285
Mondelez International Inc A534
Mcdonald's Corp A508
Jones Lang Lasalle Inc A442
Cna Financial Corp A191
Lkq Corp A484
Conagra Brands Inc A213
Motorola Solutions Inc A539
Old Republic International
  Corp. A586
Northern Trust Corp A566
Kemper Corp (de) A450
Federal Reserve Bank Of Chicago,
  Dist. No. 7 A299
Telephone & Data Systems Inc A763
Byline Bancorp Inc A141 E59
Commonspirit Health A207 P144
Board Of Education Of City Of
  Chicago A123 P80
Ggp, Inc. A354 P229
Hometown America Management
  Corp. A396
Commonspirit Health A207 P144
Board Of Education Of City Of
  Chicago A123 P80
The Walsh Group Ltd P590
Usg Corporation P636
University Of Chicago P616
The University Of Chicago Medical
  Center P584
Ggp, Inc. A354 P229
Rush University Medical Center P453
Walsh Construction Company P645
Brookfield Properties Retail Inc. P89
Northwestern Memorial
  Hospital P389
The Pepper Companies Inc P575
Pepper Construction Group, Llc P411
Metropolitan Water Reclamation
  District Of Greater Chicago P338
North Advocate Side Health
  Network P379
Pepper Construction Company P411
Crowe Llp P175
Central Steel And Wire
  Company P108
Ann & Robert H. Lurie Children's
  Hospital Of Chicago P37
Regional Transportation
  Authority P441

HOOVER'S HANDBOOK OF EMERGING COMPANIES 2022   471

INDEX BY HEADQUARTERS LOCATION

A = AMERICAN BUSINESS
E = EMERGING COMPANIES
P = PRIVATE COMPANIES
W = WORLD BUSINESS

Blue Cross & Blue Shield
Association P77
De Paul University P185
Chicago Community Trust P114
Loyola University Of Chicago
Inc P305
Family Health Network, Inc. P211
Newark Corporation P375
Cboe Global Markets Inc E72
Transunion E412
Littelfuse Inc E254
Morningstar Inc E279
Azek Co Inc (the) E41
Enova International Inc E137
Green Thumb Industries Inc E201
Byline Bancorp Inc A141 E59

DEERFIELD
Walgreens Boots Alliance Inc A842
Caterpillar Inc. A156
Baxter International Inc A105
Fortune Brands Home & Security,
Inc. A334
Scai Holdings, Llc P466

DES PLAINES
Brg Sports, Inc. P86

DOWNERS GROVE
Univar Solutions Inc A823
Dover Corp A255
Advocate Health And Hospitals
Corporation A15 P7
Illinois State Of Toll Highway
Authority P260
Ftd Companies, Inc. P224

EDWARDSVILLE
Prairie Farms Dairy, Inc. P423

EFFINGHAM
Midland States Bancorp Inc A529
E275

EVANSTON
Northwestern University P389
Northshore University
Healthsystem P386
North Shore University Health
System P383

FRANKLIN PARK
Hill Fire Protection, Llc A387 P251

GLENVIEW
Illinois Tool Works, Inc. A414

HARVEY
Atkore Inc E34

HINSDALE
Adventist Midwest Health P7

JOLIET
Central Grocers, Inc. P108

LAKE FOREST
Tenneco Inc A766
Grainger (w.w.) Inc. A362
Packaging Corp Of America A604

LINCOLNSHIRE
Cdw Corp A160
Zebra Technologies Corp. A876
Camping World Holdings Inc A146

MATTOON
First Mid Bancshares Inc A320 E173
Consolidated Communications
Holdings Inc E98
First Mid Bancshares Inc A320 E173

MAYWOOD
Loyola University Medical
Center P305

METTAWA
Brunswick Corp. A137

MILAN
Group O, Inc. P235

MOLINE
Deere & Co. A239
Qcr Holdings Inc A655 E339

NAPERVILLE
Edward Hospital P201

NORTH CHICAGO
Abbvie Inc A5

NORTHBROOK
Allstate Corp A31

OAK BROOK
Ace Hardware Corporation A8 P3
Federal Signal Corp. E159

PALATINE
Weber Inc E444

PARIS
North American Lighting, Inc. P379

PARK RIDGE
Advocate Health And Hospitals
Corporation A15 P7

PEORIA
Rli Corp A679 E355
Osf Healthcare System P401
Rli Corp A679 E355

RIVERWOODS
Discover Financial Services A246

ROCK ISLAND
Modern Woodmen Of America A531
P348

ROCKFORD
Mercy Health Corporation P332

ROLLING MEADOWS
Gallagher (arthur J.) & Co. A341
Kimball Hill Inc P286
Cambium Networks Corp E64

ROSEMONT
Us Foods Holding Corp A830
Wintrust Financial Corp (il) A866
E451
The Big Ten Conference Inc P545
Independent Suppliers Group,
Inc. P261
Wintrust Financial Corp (il) A866
E451

SCHAUMBURG
Paylocity Holding Corp E314

SPRINGFIELD
Horace Mann Educators Corp. A399
State Of Illinois A736 P512
Memorial Medical Center P327
Tom Lange Company, Inc. P595
City Of Springfield P133

TINLEY PARK
Panduit Corp. P404

URBANA
Carle Foundation Hospital P100

VERNON HILLS
Graham Enterprise, Inc. P233

WARRENVILLE
Edward-elmhurst Healthcare P201

WESTCHESTER
Ingredion Inc A418

WOODSTOCK
Mercy Woodstock Medical
Center P335

INDIANA

BATESVILLE
Hillenbrand Inc E214

BLOOMINGTON
Trustees Of Indiana University P602
Indiana University P261
Hoosier Energy Rural Electric
Cooperative Inc P254

BROOKVILLE
Fcn Banc Corp E157

CARMEL
Cno Financial Group Inc A193
Merchants Bancorp (indiana) A514
E267

COLUMBUS
Cummins, Inc. A228

CONVERSE
First Farmers Financial Corp E166

DANVILLE
Hendricks County Hospital P248

ELKHART
Thor Industries, Inc. A785
Lci Industries E245
Patrick Industries Inc E313

EVANSVILLE
Berry Global Group Inc A114
Onemain Holdings Inc A591
Old National Bancorp (evansville,
In) A585
Deaconess Hospital Inc P185
Atlas World Group, Inc. P48
Van Atlas Lines Inc P639
Southern Indiana Gas & Electric
Company P491
St. Mary's Health, Inc. P507
Onemain Finance Corp E303
Escalade, Inc. E145

FISHERS
First Internet Bancorp A318 E170

FORT WAYNE
Steel Dynamics Inc. A744
Do It Best Corp. P191
Petroleum Traders Corporation P414

HIGHLAND
Strack And Van Til Super Market
Inc. P522

INDIANAPOLIS
Anthem Inc A62
Lilly (eli) & Co A478
State Of Indiana A736 P512
The Finish Line Inc P556
Community Health Network,
Inc. P147
Countrymark Cooperative Holding
Corporation P155
National Collegiate Athletic
Association P363
Citizens Energy Group P121
Duke Realty Corp E124

JASPER
German American Bancorp Inc A353
E192
Kimball Electronics Inc E241
German American Bancorp Inc A353
E192

JEFFERSONVILLE
First Savings Financial Group
Inc E174

LA GRANGE
Fs Bancorp (indiana) E187

MERRILLVILLE
Northern Indiana Public Service
Company Llc P385

MICHIGAN CITY
Horizon Bancorp Inc A400 E218

MISHAWAKA
Franciscan Alliance, Inc. P219

MUNCIE
First Merchants Corp A319 E172

MUNSTER
Community Foundation Of Northwest
Indiana, Inc. P146
Munster Medical Research
Foundation, Inc. P359
Finward Bancorp E161

NOBLESVILLE
Riverview Hospital P447
County Of Hamilton P160

RICHMOND
Richmond Mutual Bancorporation
Inc E355

SOUTH BEND
1st Source Corp A1

TERRE HAUTE
First Financial Corp. (in) A316

UNION CITY
Cardinal Ethanol Llc E68

WARSAW
Zimmer Biomet Holdings Inc A878
Lakeland Financial Corp A466 E243

WEST LAFAYETTE
Inotiv Inc E229

IOWA

AMES
Danfoss Power Solutions Inc. P181
Iowa State University Of Science And
Technology P266
Ames National Corp. E25

ANKENY
Casey's General Stores, Inc. A155
Perishable Distributors Of Iowa,
Ltd. P411

CEDAR RAPIDS
United Fire Group, Inc. A815
Crst International, Inc. P176

DAVENPORT
Genesis Health System P227
Lee Enterprises, Inc. E247

DES MOINES
Principal Financial Group Inc A641
Federal Home Loan Bank Of Des
Moines A298
State Of Iowa A736 P512
Central Iowa Hospital Corp P108
Catholic Health Initiatives - Iowa,
Corp. P102
Iowa Physicians Clinic Medical
Foundation P266

DUBUQUE
Heartland Financial Usa, Inc.
(dubuque, Ia) A380 E207

472

HOOVER'S HANDBOOK OF EMERGING COMPANIES 2022

INDEX BY HEADQUARTERS LOCATION

FARNHAMVILLE
Farmers Cooperative Company P212

HILLS
Hills Bancorporation A387

IOWA CITY
Midwestone Financial Group,
Inc. A530 E276
The University Of Iowa P585
University Of Iowa Hospitals And
Clinics P621
Midwestone Financial Group,
Inc. A530 E276

JOHNSTON
Iowa Physicians Clinic Medical
Foundation P266

MASON CITY
Mercy Health Services-iowa,
Corp. P332

MONTICELLO
Innovative Ag Services Co. P262

WATERLOO
Covenant Medical Center, Inc. P174

WEST BURLINGTON
Big River Resources, Llc. P73

WEST DES MOINES
American Equity Investment Life
Holding Co A44
West Bancorporation, Inc. A855 E445
Hy-vee, Inc. A412 P258
Iowa Health System P265
Heartland Co-op P247
West Bancorporation, Inc. A855 E445

KANSAS

KANSAS CITY
Dairy Farmers Of America, Inc. A232
P178
Associated Wholesale Grocers,
Inc. A75 P46
Dairy Farmers Of America, Inc. A232
P178
Associated Wholesale Grocers,
Inc. A75 P46
The University Of Kansas Hospital
Authority P586

LEAWOOD
Crossfirst Bankshares Inc A224 E111
Amc Entertainment Inc. P28
The Sunderland Foundation P581
Tallgrass Energy, Lp P532
Crossfirst Bankshares Inc A224 E111

LENEXA
Hostess Brands Inc E219

MANHATTAN
Kansas State University P281
Landmark Bancorp Inc E245

MCPHERSON
Chs Mcpherson Refinery Inc. P119

MERRIAM
Seaboard Corp. A699

OLATHE
Tsvc, Inc. P604
Terracon Consultants, Inc. P537
D. H. Pace Company, Inc. P177
County Of Johnson P161

OVERLAND PARK
Black & Veatch Holding
Company P76
Bvh, Inc. P92
Npc Restaurant Holdings, Llc P392

Black & Veatch International
Company P76
Selectquote Inc E367

SHAWNEE MISSION
Shawnee Mission Medical Center,
Inc. P479

TOPEKA
Capitol Federal Financial Inc A149
State Of Kansas A736 P512
Kansas Department Of
Transportation P281
Stormont-vail Healthcare, Inc. P522

WICHITA
Equity Bancshares Inc A283
Unified School District 259 P609
Wesley Medical Center, Llc P650
Ascension Via Christi Hospitals
Wichita, Inc. P44

KENTUCKY

ASHLAND
King's Daughters Health System,
Inc. P286

BOWLING GREEN
Houchens Industries, Inc. P255
Commonwealth Health Corporation,
Inc. P145

EDGEWOOD
Saint Elizabeth Medical Center,
Inc. P456

FRANKFORT
Commonwealth Of Kentucky A208
P145

HENDERSON
Big Rivers Electric Corporation P73

LEXINGTON
Appalachian Regional Healthcare,
Inc. P39
Saint Joseph Health System,
Inc. P457
The Board Of Education Of Fayette
County P545
Valvoline Inc E432

LOUISVILLE
Humana Inc. A405
Yum! Brands Inc A875
Republic Bancorp, Inc. (ky) A675
E350
Stock Yards Bancorp Inc A746 E390
Baptist Healthcare System, Inc. P58
Uofl Health, Inc. P634
Norton Hospitals, Inc P390
University Health Care Inc P612
Louisville-jefferson County Metro
Government P304
Almost Family, Inc. P24
University Of Louisville P622
University Medical Center Inc P614
Turning Point Brands Inc E418
Republic Bancorp, Inc. (ky) A675
E350
Stock Yards Bancorp Inc A746 E390
Limestone Bancorp Inc E253

PIKEVILLE
Community Trust Bancorp, Inc. A211
Pikeville Medical Center, Inc. P416

LOUISIANA

ABBEVILLE
Coastal Chemical Co., L.l.c. P139

ALEXANDRIA
Red River Bancshares Inc A667 E347

BATON ROUGE
Business First Bancshares Inc A140
E58
State Of Louisiana A736 P512
Franciscan Missionaries Of Our Lady
Health System, Inc. P220
Our Lady Of The Lake Hospital,
Inc. P401
University Of Louisiana System
Foundation P622
Mmr Group, Inc. P348
Mmr Constructors, Inc. P347
Amedisys, Inc. E17
Business First Bancshares Inc A140
E58
Investar Holding Corp E235

CHALMETTE
Chalmette Refining, L.l.c. A166 P110

COVINGTON
Zen-noh Grain Corporation A877
P662
Cgb Enterprises, Inc. A166 P110
Consolidated Grain & Barge
Company A217 P151
Zen-noh Grain Corporation A877
P662
Cgb Enterprises, Inc. A166 P110
Consolidated Grain & Barge
Company A217 P151
Pool Corp E327

GRETNA
Parish Of Jefferson P406

HAMMOND
First Guaranty Bancshares, Inc. E169

HARVEY
Jefferson Parish School Board
Inc P271

JEFFERSON
Ochsner Clinic Foundation A583
P393

LAFAYETTE
Home Bancorp Inc A392 E216
Lafayette General Medical Center,
Inc. P290
Lhc Group Inc E251
Viemed Healthcare Inc E439
Home Bancorp Inc A392 E216

LAKE CHARLES
Central Crude, Inc. P107

MONROE
Lumen Technologies Inc A489
Qwest Corp A661

NEW ORLEANS
Entergy Corp A276
Ochsner Health System P394
Louisiana Childrens Medical Center,
Inc P304
Entergy Services, Llc P206
City Of New Orleans P129
The Administrators Of The Tulane
Educational Fund P542
University Medical Center
Management Corporation P615
Walton Construction - A Core
Company, Llc P646
Orleans Parish School District P400
Children's Hospital P114

RUSTON
Origin Bancorp Inc A596 E306

SCHRIEVER
Rouse's Enterprises, L.l.c. P452

MAINE

AUGUSTA
State Of Maine A737 P513
Maine Municipal Bond Bank A494
State Of Maine A737 P513
Mainegeneral Health P309

BANGOR
Eastern Maine Medical Center P200

BAR HARBOR
Bar Harbor Bankshares A102 E46

BREWER
Eastern Maine Healthcare
Systems P199

CAMDEN
Camden National Corp. (me) A144

DAMARISCOTTA
Miles Health Care, Inc P343
First Bancorp Inc (me) E162

PORTLAND
Mainehealth P309
Mainehealth Services P309
Maine Medical Center P308
Martin's Point Health Care, Inc. P315
City Of Portland P131
Northeast Bank (me) E294

WESTBROOK
Idexx Laboratories, Inc. E221

YORK
York Hospital P661

MARYLAND

ANNAPOLIS
State Of Maryland A737 P513
County Of Anne Arundel P156
Anne Arundel County Board Of
Education P38
Luminis Health Anne Arundel Medical
Center, Inc P306
Hannon Armstrong Sustainable
Infrastructure Capital Inc E205

BALTIMORE
Constellation Energy Corp A219
T Rowe Price Group Inc. A756
Under Armour Inc A810
The Johns Hopkins Health System
Corporation A778 P563
Johns Hopkins University A439 P276
The Whiting-turner Contracting
Company A783 P591
The Johns Hopkins Health System
Corporation A778 P563
Johns Hopkins University A439 P276
The Whiting-turner Contracting
Company A783 P591
University Of Maryland Medical
System Corporation P622
Johns Hopkins Hospital P276
City Of Baltimore P123
Lifebridge Health, Inc. P300
Baltimore City Public Schools P56
Mercy Health Services, Inc. P332
Sinai Hospital Of Baltimore,
Inc. P481
Maryland Transportation
Authority P316
Johns Hopkins Bayview Medical
Center, Inc. P275
Gbmc Healthcare, Inc. P225
Franklin Square Hospital Center,
Inc. P220
Mercy Medical Center, Inc. P334
Medifast Inc E266

HOOVER'S HANDBOOK OF EMERGING COMPANIES 2022

INDEX BY HEADQUARTERS LOCATION

A = AMERICAN BUSINESS
E = EMERGING COMPANIES
P = PRIVATE COMPANIES
W = WORLD BUSINESS

BEL AIR
County Of Harford P160

BETHESDA
Lockheed Martin Corp A485
Marriott International, Inc. A498
Agnc Investment Corp A22
Eagle Bancorp Inc (md) A261 E125
Walker & Dunlop Inc E443
Enviva Inc E143
Eagle Bancorp Inc (md) A261 E125

COLLEGE PARK
University Of Maryland, College Park P623

COLUMBIA
Medstar Health, Inc. A512 P324
Maxim Healthcare Services, Inc. P319

ELLICOTT CITY
Howard County Of Maryland (inc) P256

FREDERICK
County Of Frederick P159

GAITHERSBURG
Adventist Healthcare, Inc. P6
Emergent Biosolutions Inc E133

GLEN BURNIE
R. E. Michel Company, Llc P433

GREENBELT
Kbr Wyle Services, Llc P282

HAGERSTOWN
County Of Washington P172

HANOVER
Allegis Group, Inc. A30 P21
Aerotek, Inc. A16 P8
Allegis Group, Inc. A30 P21
Aerotek, Inc. A16 P8
Teksystems, Inc. P535
Maryland Department Of Transportation P316
Johns Hopkins Healthcare Llc P275

HUNT VALLEY
Mccormick & Co Inc A507
Sinclair Broadcast Group Inc A712

LARGO
Georges Prince County Government P228

LAUREL
Washington Suburban Sanitary Commission (inc) P647

OLNEY
Sandy Spring Bancorp Inc A693 E360

OWINGS MILLS
Rand Worldwide Inc. E344

ROCKVILLE
Montgomery County, Maryland P352
Supernus Pharmaceuticals Inc E398
Capital Bancorp Inc (md) E66
Bioqual Inc E51

SILVER SPRING
Holy Cross Health, Inc. P253

UPPER MARLBORO
Prince George's County Public Schools P427

WALDORF
Community Financial Corp (the) E95

MASSACHUSETTS

ACTON
Insulet Corp E232

AMESBURY
Provident Bancorp Inc (md) E338

ANDOVER
Mks Instruments Inc E277
Mercury Systems Inc E268
Vicor Corp E437

AUBURNDALE
Parexel International Corporation P405
Atrius Health, Inc. P50

BEDFORD
Ice Data Services, Inc. A413 P258
The Mitre Corporation P569
Ice Data Services, Inc. A413 P258
Irobot Corp E236
Aspen Technology Inc E33
Novanta Inc E298

BEVERLY
Axcelis Technologies Inc E39

BILLERICA
Entegris Inc E140

BOSTON
General Electric Co A345
Wayfair Inc A850
State Street Corp. A742
Santander Holdings Usa Inc. A694
American Tower Corp (new) A51
Vertex Pharmaceuticals, Inc. A834
Eastern Bankshares Inc A263
Berkshire Hills Bancorp Inc A113
Brookline Bancorp Inc (de) A136
Commonwealth Of Massachusetts A208 P146
Mass General Brigham Incorporated A503 P316
Massachusetts Housing Finance Agency A503 P317
Commonwealth Of Massachusetts A208 P146
Mass General Brigham Incorporated A503 P316
The President And Fellows Of Harvard College P575
City Of Boston P124
Massachusetts Department Of Transportation P317
Suffolk Construction Company, Inc. P523
University Of Massachusetts P623
Harvard Management Private Equity Corporation P243
The Massachusetts General Hospital P565
The Brigham And Women's Hospital Inc P546
The Children's Hospital Corporation P548
Boston University P85
Dana-farber Cancer Institute, Inc. P180
Beth Israel Deaconess Medical Center, Inc. P71
Fidelity Inv Charitable Gift Fund P213
Northeastern University P385
Commonwealth Care Alliance, Inc. P145
Boston Medical Center Corporation P84
Massachusetts School Building Authority P319
Shawmut Woodworking & Supply, Inc. P478

Massachusetts Port Authority P318
Massachusetts Water Resources Authority P319
Massachusetts Bay Transportation Authority P317
Tufts Medical Center, Inc. P604
Massachusetts Housing Finance Agency A503 P317
Ptc Inc E338
Boston Beer Co Inc (the) E55
Stag Industrial Inc E388
Cra International Inc E106
Ironwood Pharmaceuticals Inc E237

BRIGHTON
Harvard Business School Publishing Corporation P243

BROCKTON
Harborone Bancorp Inc (new) A376 E206

BURLINGTON
Keurig Dr Pepper Inc A451
Lahey Clinic Hospital, Inc. P290
Cerence Inc E76
Lemaitre Vascular Inc E249

CAMBRIDGE
Biogen Inc A117
Cambridge Bancorp A143 E64
Massachusetts Institute Of Technology P318
City Of Cambridge P124
The Charles Stark Draper Laboratory Inc P547
The Broad Institute Inc P546
Akamai Technologies Inc E10
Cargurus Inc E68
Forrester Research Inc. E181
Voyager Therapeutics Inc E442
Cambridge Bancorp A143 E64
Surface Oncology Inc E399

CHESTNUT HILL
Trustees Of Boston College P601

CHICOPEE
Consumer Product Distributors, Llc P151

CONCORD
Welch Foods Inc., A Cooperative P648

DANVERS
Abiomed, Inc. E2

FALL RIVER
Southcoast Hospitals Group, Inc. P489

FRAMINGHAM
Tjx Companies, Inc. A786
Ameresco Inc E18

HANOVER
Independent Bank Corp (ma) A416 E226

HINGHAM
Hingham Institution For Savings A389 E215

HYANNIS
Cape Cod Healthcare, Inc. P96
Cape Cod Hospital P96

LOWELL
Enterprise Bancorp, Inc. (ma) A277 E141

LYNNFIELD
New England Petroleum Limited Partnership P367

MARLBOROUGH
Boston Scientific Corp. A131
Hologic Inc A391

MIDDLEBORO
Ocean Spray Cranberries, Inc. P393

MILFORD
Consigli Construction Co Inc. P151

NATICK
Cognex Corp E88

NEWTON
Rmr Group Inc (the) E356
Industrial Logistics Properties Trust E227
Techtarget Inc E403

NORTH READING
Teradyne, Inc. E405

PITTSFIELD
Berkshire Medical Center, Inc. P70

QUINCY
Granite Telecommunications Llc P234
Randolph Bancorp Inc E344

SOMERVILLE
Allways Health Partners, Inc. P24
Trustees Of Tufts College P603

SOUTH WEYMOUTH
South Shore Hospital, Inc. P488

SPRINGFIELD
Eversource Energy A284
Baystate Health System Health Services, Inc. P66
City Of Springfield P133

STOUGHTON
Collegium Pharmaceuticals Inc E91

TAUNTON
Dennis K. Burke Inc. P186

TEWKSBURY
Covenant Health, Inc. P174

WALTHAM
Raytheon Technologies Corp A664
Thermo Fisher Scientific Inc A784
Global Partners Lp A356
Perkinelmer, Inc. E319
Dynatrace Inc E125
Repligen Corp. E349

WESTBOROUGH
Bj's Wholesale Club Holdings Inc A119

WESTFIELD
Western New England Bancorp Inc E448

WESTFORD
Kadant Inc E240

WILMINGTON
Analog Devices Inc A60
Charles River Laboratories International Inc. E78
Onto Innovation Inc E303

WORCESTER
Hanover Insurance Group Inc A375
Umass Memorial Health Care, Inc. P608
Umass Memorial Health Care Inc And Affiliates Group Return P608
Umass Memorial Medical Center, Inc. P609
City Of Worcester P135

MICHIGAN

ADA
Alticor Inc. A35 P27

474 HOOVER'S HANDBOOK OF EMERGING COMPANIES 2022

INDEX BY HEADQUARTERS LOCATION

Solstice Holdings Inc. A719 P486
Alticor Inc. A35 P27
Solstice Holdings Inc. A719 P486
Access Business Group Llc P3

ANN ARBOR
Regents Of The University Of
 Michigan A669 P440
Tecumseh Products Company
 Llc P534
Truven Holding Corp. P603
University Bancorp Inc. (mi) E427

AUBURN HILLS
Borgwarner Inc A130
Old Dura, Inc. P396

BATTLE CREEK
Kellogg Co A449

BENTON HARBOR
Whirlpool Corp A862

BLOOMFIELD HILLS
Penske Automotive Group Inc A615
Agree Realty Corp. E8

CENTER LINE
St. John Providence Physicians-
 cmg P501

COLDWATER
Southern Michigan Bancorp Inc
 (united States) E382

DEARBORN
Ford Motor Co. (de) A332
Ford Motor Credit Company Llc A334

DETROIT
General Motors Co A348
Rocket Companies Inc A683
Dte Energy Co A257
Ally Financial Inc A32
Dte Electric Company A256
American Axle & Manufacturing
 Holdings Inc A42
Henry Ford Health System A381 P249
Uaw Retiree Medical Benefits
 Trust A804 P607
Henry Ford Health System A381 P249
Uaw Retiree Medical Benefits
 Trust A804 P607
Detroit Wayne Mental Health
 Authority P187
Wayne State University P648

EAST LANSING
Greenstone Farm Credit Services
 Aca A366 P235
Michigan State University P342
Greenstone Farm Credit Services
 Aca A366 P235

FARMINGTON HILLS
Robert Bosch Llc A680 P447
Level One Bancorp Inc E251

FENTON
Fentura Financial Inc E160

FLINT
Mott, Charles Stewart Foundation
 Inc A541

GRAND RAPIDS
Spartannash Co A726
Ufp Industries Inc A805
Independent Bank Corporation (ionia,
 Mi) A417 E226
Mercantile Bank Corp. A513 E267
Spectrum Health System A727 P495
Spectrum Health Hospitals P494
Meritage Hospitality Group Inc E270
Independent Bank Corporation (ionia,
 Mi) A417 E226
Mercantile Bank Corp. A513 E267

HILLSDALE
Cnb Community Bancorp Inc E87

HOLLAND
Macatawa Bank Corp. A493

JACKSON
Cms Energy Corp A190
Consumers Energy Co. A219
Alro Steel Corporation P25

KALAMAZOO
Stryker Corp A748
Bronson Methodist Hospital Inc P88

LANSING
State Of Michigan A737 P513
Sparrow Health System P493
Housing Development Authority,
 Michigan State P255

LENOX
William Beaumont Hospital P657

LIVONIA
Masco Corp. A501
Trinity Health Corporation A793 P598
Trinity Health-michigan P599
Mercy Health Services-iowa,
 Corp. P332

MADISON HEIGHTS
Mcnaughton-mckay Electric Co. P322

MASON
Dart Financial Corp E114

MIDDLEVILLE
Hps Llc P256

MIDLAND
Dow Inc A256
Midmichigan Medical Center-
 midland P343

MOUNT CLEMENS
County Of Macomb P162

MOUNT PLEASANT
American Mitsuba Corporation P32

MUSKEGON
Mercy General Health Partners P330
Mercy Health Partners P332

NOVI
Nhk International Corporation P378
Michigan Milk Producers
 Association P342

PONTIAC
County Of Oakland P165

PORT HURON
Semco Energy, Inc. P472

ROCHESTER HILLS
Infusystem Holdings Inc E228

ROYAL OAK
Beaumont Health P68
Barrick Enterprises, Inc. P62

SAGINAW
Covenant Medical Center, Inc. P174

SOUTHFIELD
Lear Corp. A469
Sterling Bancorp Inc (mi) A745
Federal-mogul Holdings Llc A302
 P213
Metaldyne Performance Group
 Inc. P336
Barton Malow Enterprises, Inc. P63
Barton Malow Company P63
Ascension Providence Hospital P44
Sun Communities Inc E395
Credit Acceptance Corp (mi) E108

SPARTA
Choiceone Financial Services,
 Inc. E81

STURGIS
Sturgis Bancorp Inc E394

TAYLOR
Atlas Oil Company P48

TRAVERSE CITY
Munson Healthcare P358
Munson Medical Center P359

TROY
Flagstar Bancorp, Inc. A326 E177
Skyline Champion Corp E376

WARREN
St. John Hospital And Medical
 Center P500

MINNESOTA

ANOKA
Anoka-hennepin School Dist No
 11 P38

AUSTIN
Hormel Foods Corp. A400

BLOOMINGTON
Bridgewater Bancshares Inc A133 E56
Healthpartners, Inc. A380 P247
Lamex Foods Inc. P292
Toro Company (the) E410
Bridgewater Bancshares Inc A133 E56

BROOKLYN PARK
Clearfield Inc E86

BURNSVILLE
Ames Construction, Inc. P35

CIRCLE PINES
Northern Technologies International
 Corp. E295

DULUTH
Smdc Medical Center P483
County Of St Louis P170

EDEN PRAIRIE
Robinson (c.h.) Worldwide, Inc. A682
Winnebago Industries, Inc. E450

EDINA
Production Technologies, Inc. P429

FERGUS FALLS
Otter Tail Corp. E308

GRANITE FALLS
Granite Falls Energy Llc E198

HERMANTOWN
Miners Incorporated P345

HOPKINS
Digi International Inc E117

INVER GROVE HEIGHTS
Chs Inc A175

LITCHFIELD
The First District Association P557

MAPLE GROVE
Great River Energy P234

MAPLE PLAIN
Proto Labs Inc E337

MEDINA
Polaris Inc A632

MINNEAPOLIS
Target Corp A760
Us Bancorp (de) A828

General Mills Inc A346
Xcel Energy Inc A870
Ameriprise Financial Inc A52
Riversource Life Insurance Co A679
Ecmc Group, Inc. A266
Hennepin County P249
Hennepin Healthcare System,
 Inc. P249
City Of Minneapolis P128
Park Nicollet Clinic P406
Regions Hospital P441
North Memorial Health Care P382
Minneapolis Public School
 District P345
University Of Minnesota
 Physicians P624
Cliftonlarsonallen Llp P138
Datasite Global Corporation P183
Sleep Number Corp E377
Piper Sandler Companies E325
Bio-techne Corp E49
Sun Country Airlines Holdings
 Inc E396
Sps Commerce, Inc. E384

MINNETONKA
Unitedhealth Group Inc A822

MOORHEAD
American Crystal Sugar
 Company P29

NEW BRIGHTON
Api Group, Inc. P39

NEW ULM
Nuvera Communications Inc E299

RICHFIELD
Best Buy Inc A115

ROCHESTER
Saint Marys Hospital P459
Mayo Foundation For Medical
 Education And Research P321
City Of Rochester P132

SAINT CLOUD
Centracare Health System P107
Coborn's, Incorporated P141
The Saint Cloud Hospital P578

SAINT PAUL
State Of Minnesota A737 P513
Fairview Health Services A291 P210
State Of Minnesota A737 P513
Fairview Health Services A291 P210
Hmo Minnesota P252
Augustana Health Care Center Of
 Apple Valley P51
County Of Ramsey P167
Regions Hospital P441
Independent School Dist 625 P261
Regions Hospital Foundation P442

ST. LOUIS PARK
Two Harbors Investment Corp A801

ST. PAUL
3m Co A1
Ecolab Inc A266
Patterson Companies Inc A610
Fuller (hb) Company E188

STILLWATER
County Of Washington P172

WINONA
Fastenal Co. A295

MISSISSIPPI

COLUMBUS
Bankfirst Capital Corp. E46

HOOVER'S HANDBOOK OF EMERGING COMPANIES 2022   475

INDEX BY HEADQUARTERS LOCATION

A = AMERICAN BUSINESS
E = EMERGING COMPANIES
P = PRIVATE COMPANIES
W = WORLD BUSINESS

GREENVILLE
Farmers Grain Terminal, Inc. P212

GREENWOOD
Staple Cotton Cooperative
Association P509

GULFPORT
Hancock Whitney Corp A372

HATTIESBURG
First Bancshares Inc (ms) A309 E163
Cooperative Energy, A Mississippi
Electric Cooperative P153
Forrest County General Hospital
(inc) P218
First Bancshares Inc (ms) A309 E163

JACKSON
Trustmark Corp A798
State Of Mississippi A737 P513
Board Of Trustees Of State
Institutions Of Higher Learning P81
University Of Mississippi Medical
Center P624
St. Dominic Health Services,
Inc. P499

MISSISSIPPI STATE
Mississippi State University P346

RIDGELAND
Eastgroup Properties Inc E128

TUPELO
Cadence Bank A142 E61
Renasant Corp A674 E348
North Mississippi Health Services,
Inc. P382
Cadence Bank A142 E61
Renasant Corp A674 E348

MISSOURI

CARTHAGE
Leggett & Platt, Inc. A470

CHESTERFIELD
Reinsurance Group Of America,
Inc. A672
Mhm Support Services P340

CLAYTON
Olin Corp. A587
Enterprise Financial Services
Corp A278 E141

COLUMBIA
University Of Missouri System P625
Mfa Incorporated P339
Mfa Oil Company P339
University Of Missouri Health
Care P625
American Outdoor Brands Inc E22

DES PERES
Jones Financial Companies Lllp A442

FENTON
Maritz Holdings Inc. P312
Cic Group, Inc. P120

GRANDVIEW
Nasb Financial Inc E284

JEFFERSON CITY
State Of Missouri A738 P514
Missouri Department Of
Transportation P347
Hawthorn Bancshares Inc E206

JOPLIN
Freeman Health System P221
The Empire District Electric
Company P555

KANSAS CITY
Commerce Bancshares Inc A205
Umb Financial Corp A808 E421
Kansas City Life Insurance Co (kansas
City, Mo) A445
J.e. Dunn Construction Group,
Inc. P268
J.e. Dunn Construction
Company P267
Dst Systems, Inc. P195
Saint Luke's Health System,
Inc. P458
Mercy Children's Hospital P330
Missouri City Of Kansas City P347
Evergy Missouri West, Inc. P209
Saint Luke's Hospital Of Kansas
City P459
Truman Medical Center,
Incorporated P601
St Luke's Hospital Of Kansas
City P498
Umb Financial Corp A808 E421

NORTH KANSAS CITY
Cerner Corp. A164
North Kansas City Hospital P382
Maxus Realty Trust Inc E265

POPLAR BLUFF
Southern Missouri Bancorp,
Inc. A723 E383

SAINT JOSEPH
Mosaic Health System P354
Heartland Regional Medical
Center P248

SAINT LOUIS
Ascension Health Alliance A74 P43
Mercy Health A517 P330
World Wide Technology Holding Co.,
Llc A869 P659
Ssm Health Care Corporation A729
P497
Ascension Health Alliance A74 P43
Mercy Health A517 P330
World Wide Technology Holding Co.,
Llc A869 P659
Ssm Health Care Corporation A729
P497
Mccarthy Holdings, Inc. P321
Mccarthy Building Companies,
Inc. P321
The Washington University P591
Barry-wehmiller Group, Inc. P62
Barnes-jewish Hospital P62
Alberici Corporation P16
Spire Missouri Inc. P495
Mercy Hospitals East
Communities P334
City Of St. Louis P134
County Of St Louis P170
Alberici Group, Inc. P17
Alberici Constructors, Inc. P16
Saint Louis University P458
St Louis Children's Hospital P498
Missouri Baptist Medical Center P346

SIKESTON
Food Giant Supermarkets, Inc. P217

SPRINGFIELD
O'reilly Automotive, Inc. A579
Great Southern Bancorp, Inc. A366
New Prime, Inc. P368
Mercy Hospital Springfield P333
Lester E. Cox Medical Centers P296
City Of Springfield P133

Guaranty Federal Bancshares Inc
(springfield, Mo) E204

ST. LOUIS
Centene Corp A161
Emerson Electric Co. A272
Graybar Electric Co., Inc. A365
Ameren Corp A40
Post Holdings Inc A634
Stifel Financial Corp A745
Energizer Holdings Inc (new) E136
Bellring Brands Inc E48

MONTANA

BILLINGS
First Interstate Bancsystem Inc A318
E171
Billings Clinic P74
First Interstate Bancsystem Inc A318
E171

BOZEMA
Fair Isaac Corp E154

COLUMBUS
Stillwater Mining Company P522

GREAT FALLS
Benefis Hospitals, Inc P69

HELENA
State Of Montana A738 P514
Eagle Bancorp Montana, Inc. E126

KALISPELL
Glacier Bancorp, Inc. A355 E192
Cityservicevalcon, Llc P136
Glacier Bancorp, Inc. A355 E192

LEWISTOWN
Sports, Inc. P496

NEBRASKA

COLUMBUS
Nebraska Public Power District P366

DORCHESTER
Farmers Cooperative P212

KIMBALL
Risk George Industries Inc E355

LINCOLN
Nelnet Inc A548 E289
State Of Nebraska A738 P514
Union Bank And Trust Company A811
State Of Nebraska A738 P514
Board Of Regents Of The University Of
Nebraska P81
Crete Carrier Corporation P175
Bryan Medical Center P91
Nelnet Inc A548 E289

NORFOLK
Affiliated Foods Midwest Cooperative,
Inc. P9

OMAHA
Berkshire Hathaway Inc A112
Union Pacific Corp A811
First National Of Nebraska, Inc. A321
Kiewit Corporation A454 P285
Peter Kiewit Sons', Inc. A620 P412
Tmv Corp. A787 P595
Farm Credit Services Of
America A293 P211
Kiewit Corporation A454 P285
Peter Kiewit Sons', Inc. A620 P412
Tmv Corp. A787 P595
The Scoular Company P580
Kiewit Industrial Group Inc P285
Ag Processing Inc A Cooperative P9

Nebraska Medicine P366
Hdr, Inc. P244
Kiewit Infrastructure West Co. P285
Hdr Engineering, Inc. P244
The Nebraska Medical Center P570
Farm Credit Services Of
America A293 P211
Omaha Public Power District P396
Sapp Bros., Inc. P464
Kiewit Infrastructure Co. P285
Omaha Public Schools P396
City Of Omaha P130
Northern Natural Gas Company P386
Tenaska Energy, Inc. P537
Creighton Alegent Health P175
Alegent Health- Bergan Mercy Health
System P19
Creighton University P175

WAVERLY
Farmers Cooperative Company P212

NEVADA

CARSON CITY
State Of Nevada A738 P514

INCLINE VILLAGE
Tri Pointe Homes Inc E413

LAS VEGAS
Mgm Resorts International A523
Axos Financial Inc A89 E40
The Delta Academy P554
County Of Clark P157
City Center Holdings, Llc P122
City Of Las Vegas P127
Axos Financial Inc A89 E40
Sciplay Corp E362
Switch Inc E399
Sstartrade Tech Inc E385
Live Ventures Inc E256
Boomer Holdings Inc E54

RENO
Employers Holdings Inc A274
Nevada System Of Higher
Education P367
Washoe County School District P647
County Of Washoe P172
Plumas Bancorp Inc E326

SPARKS
Sierra Nevada Corporation P481

ZEPHYR COVE
Virnetx Holding Corp E440

NEW HAMPSHIRE

CONCORD
State Of New Hampshire A738 P514
University System Of New
Hampshire P633

HANOVER
Trustees Of Dartmouth College P602
Dartmouth College P182
Ledyard Financial Group Inc E247

LEBANON
Dartmouth-hitchcock Health P183
Dartmouth-hitchcock Clinic P182
Maxifacial Dental Surgery P319

MANCHESTER
Southern New Hampshire
University P492
Elliot Health System P204
Allegro Microsystems, Llc P21
Elliot Hospital Of The City Of
Manchester P204

476   HOOVER'S HANDBOOK OF EMERGING COMPANIES 2022

NEW JERSEY

ATLANTIC CITY
Marina District Development Company, Llc P311

BAYONNE
Bcb Bancorp Inc A106 E48

BEDMINSTER
Peapack-gladstone Financial Corp. A613 E315

BRANCHVILLE
Selective Insurance Group Inc A703 E366

BRIDGEWATER
Brother International Corporation P89
Amneal Pharmaceuticals Inc E26

BURLINGTON
Burlington Stores Inc A139

CAMDEN
Campbell Soup Co A145
The Cooper Health System P553
Virtua-west Jersey Health System, Inc. P643

CLINTON
Unity Bancorp, Inc. E425

EAST BRUNSWICK
Wipro, Llc P658

EAST HANOVER
Novartis Pharmaceuticals Corporation A573 P391

EDISON
Hmh Hospitals Corporation P251
Jfk Health System, Inc. P272
The Community Hospital Group Inc P552

ELIZABETH
County Of Union P171

ENGLEWOOD
Englewood Hospital And Medical Center Foundation Inc. P206

ENGLEWOOD CLIFFS
Connectone Bancorp Inc (new) A215 E97
Avio Inc. P53
Connectone Bancorp Inc (new) A215 E97

EWING
Church & Dwight Co Inc A176
New Jersey Transportation Trust Fund Authority P368
Universal Display Corp E426
Antares Pharma Inc. E28

FAIR LAWN
Columbia Financial Inc A202 E93

FAIRFIELD
Kearny Financial Corp (md) A448 E241

FOLSOM
South Jersey Industries Inc E381

FRANKLIN LAKES
Becton, Dickinson & Co A108

FREEHOLD
County Of Monmouth P163

HACKENSACK
County Of Bergen P156

HAMILTON
First Bank (williamstown, Nj) E164

HOBOKEN
Jarden Llc A436 P271

JERSEY CITY
Organon & Co A596
Provident Financial Services Inc A647
Verisk Analytics Inc E434

KEASBEY
Wakefern Food Corp. A841 P645

KENILWORTH
Merck & Co Inc A514

LINDEN
Turtle & Hughes, Inc P605

LIVINGSTON
St Barnabas Medical Center (inc) P497

LONG BRANCH
Monmouth Medical Center Inc. P350

MADISON
Realogy Holdings Corp A666
Realogy Group Llc A666

MATAWAN
Key Food Stores Co-operative, Inc. P283

MONTVALE
Berry Global Films, Llc P70

MORRISTOWN
Atlantic Health System Inc. P48
Ahs Hospital Corp. P11

NEPTUNE
Meridian Hospitals Corporation P335

NEW BRUNSWICK
Johnson & Johnson A440
Robert Wood Johnson University Hospital, Inc. P449
Johnson & Johnson Patient Assistance Foundation Inc P276
Middlesex, County Of (inc) P343

NEWARK
Prudential Financial Inc A648
Public Service Enterprise Group Inc A650
The New Jersey Transit Corporation P570
County Of Essex P159
Newark Beth Israel Medical Center Inc. P374
Genie Energy Ltd E191

OAK RIDGE
Lakeland Bancorp, Inc. A465 E242

PARSIPPANY
Pbf Energy Inc A612
Avis Budget Group Inc A86
Zoetis Inc A880
B&g Foods Inc E42
Pbf Logistics Lp E315
Lincoln Educational Services Corp E253

PATERSON
St. Joseph's Health Partners Llc P503
St. Joseph's University Medical Center Inc P505
Paterson Public School District P408

POMONA
Atlanticare Regional Medical Center P48

PRINCETON
The Trustees Of Princeton University P582
Educational Testing Service P200

Integra Lifesciences Holdings Corp E233
Essential Properties Realty Trust Inc E147
Bank Of Princeton (the) E45

RED BANK
Oceanfirst Financial Corp A582 E301

RIDGEWOOD
The Valley Hospital Inc P589

ROSELAND
Automatic Data Processing Inc. A81

SECAUCUS
Quest Diagnostics, Inc. A658

SHORT HILLS
Investors Bancorp Inc (new) A431

SOMERSET
Shi International Corp. A709 P480
Catalent Inc E70

TEANECK
Cognizant Technology Solutions Corp. A198

TRENTON
New Jersey Housing And Mortgage Finance Agency A551

UNION
Bed, Bath & Beyond, Inc. A110

WASHINGTON TOWNSHIP
Parke Bancorp Inc E312

WEST ORANGE
Barnabas Rwj Health Inc P61
A-1 Specialized Services & Supplies, Inc. P1
Barnabas Health, Inc. P60

WHIPPANY
Stephen Gould Corporation P519

WOODBRIDGE
Northfield Bancorp Inc (de) A568
Dhpc Technologies, Inc. A243 P188
New Jersey Turnpike Authority Inc P368

NEW MEXICO

ALBUQUERQUE
University Of New Mexico P625
Albuquerque Municipal School District Number 12 P18
City Of Albuquerque P122

SANTA FE
State Of New Mexico A738 P515

NEW YORK

ALBANY
State University Of New York A743 P518
Dormitory Authority - State Of New York P193
The Research Foundation For The State University Of New York P577
St. Peter's Health Partners P508
St. Peter's Health Care Services P508
Capital District Physicians' Health Plan, Inc. P97
New York State Energy Research And Development Authority P373
Albany Medical Center Hospital P16
Energy Research And Development Authority, New York State P206
Thruway Authority Of New York State P594

Albany Med Health System P15
County Of Albany P155

AMHERST
Allied Motion Technologies Inc E16

ARMONK
International Business Machines Corp A424

BALLSTON SPA
Stewart's Shops Corp. P521

BINGHAMTON
United Health Services Hospitals, Inc. P611

BRONX
Montefiore Medical Center P352
Bronxcare Health System P88
Fordham University P217
Lincoln Medical And Mental Health Center P300

BROOKLYN
Maimonides Medical Center P307
Newyork-presbyterian/brooklyn Methodist P376
Etsy Inc E148

BUFFALO
M & T Bank Corp A491
Rich Products Corporation P445
County Of Erie P159
Kaleida Health P280
Buffalo City School District P92
Erie County Medical Center Corp. P208
City Of Buffalo P124

CAMDEN
International Wire Group, Inc. P265

CANANDAIGUA
Canandaigua National Corp. A147 E65

CATSKILL
Greene County Bancorp Inc E201

COOPERSTOWN
The Mary Imogene Bassett Hospital P565

CORNING
Corning Inc A221

DEWITT
Community Bank System Inc A209 E94

EAST ELMHURST
Skanska Usa Civil Inc. P482
Skanska Usa Civil Northeast Inc. P483

EAST SYRACUSE
D/l Cooperative Inc. P178

FLUSHING
Newyork-presbyterian/queens P377

FONDA
County Of Montgomery P164

GENEVA
Lyons Bancorp Inc. E257

GLEN HEAD
First Of Long Island Corp A322

GLENS FALLS
Arrow Financial Corp. A72 E31

GLENVILLE
Trustco Bank Corp. (n.y.) A797

GOSHEN
County Of Orange P165

HOOVER'S HANDBOOK OF EMERGING COMPANIES 2022

477

INDEX BY HEADQUARTERS LOCATION

> A = AMERICAN BUSINESS
> E = EMERGING COMPANIES
> P = PRIVATE COMPANIES
> W = WORLD BUSINESS

GOUVERNEUR
Kph Healthcare Services, Inc. P288

HAUPPAUGE
Dime Community Bancshares Inc (new) A246
County Of Suffolk P171

HEMPSTEAD
Town Of Hempstead P596

HICKSVILLE
New York Community Bancorp Inc. A553

ITHACA
Tompkins Financial Corp A788
Cornell University P154

JAMAICA
St John's University, New York P498

JERICHO
1-800 Flowers.com, Inc. E1
Esquire Financial Holdings Inc E145

LIVERPOOL
Raymours Furniture Company, Inc. P436

LONG ISLAND CITY
Altice Usa Inc A35
Jetblue Airways Corp A437
New York City School Construction Authority P370

MANHASSET
North Shore University Hospital P383

MELVILLE
Schein (henry) Inc A695

MENANDS
Health Research, Inc. P246

MIDDLETOWN
Orange County Bancorp Inc E306

MINEOLA
County Of Nassau P165
Nassua County Interim Finance Authority P362

NEW CITY
County Of Rockland P167

NEW HYDE PARK
Long Island Jewish Medical Center P301

NEW YORK
Verizon Communications Inc A833
Jpmorgan Chase & Co A443
Citigroup Inc A182
Metlife Inc A520
Federal Reserve Bank Of New York, Dist. No. 2 A299
Goldman Sachs Group Inc A359
American International Group Inc A48
Morgan Stanley A537
Bristol Myers Squibb Co. A134
American Express Co. A45
Stonex Group Inc A747
Pfizer Inc A621
Travelers Companies Inc (the) A791
Philip Morris International Inc A624
Paramount Global A606
Marsh & Mclennan Companies Inc. A499
Kyndryl Holdings Inc A462
Macy's Inc A493

Colgate-palmolive Co. A199
Bank Of New York Mellon Corp A98
Lauder (estee) Cos., Inc. (the) A469
Blackrock Inc A119
Loews Corp. A485
Omnicom Group, Inc. A588
Consolidated Edison Inc A216
Fox Corp A335
Equitable Holdings Inc A283
Discovery Inc A247
Consolidated Edison Co. Of New York, Inc. A216
Interpublic Group Of Companies Inc. A427
Assurant Inc A76
News Corp (new) A558
Alleghany Corp. A29
Sirius Xm Holdings Inc A714
S&p Global Inc A691
Jefferies Financial Group Inc A436
Voya Financial Inc A841
Foot Locker, Inc. A331
Pvh Corp A654
Nielsen Holdings Plc A562 P378
Abm Industries, Inc. A6
Moody's Corp. A536
Blackstone Inc A120
Nasdaq Inc A543
Tapestry Inc A758
Warner Music Group Corp A845
Hsbc Usa, Inc. A405
International Flavors & Fragrances Inc. A425
Annaly Capital Management Inc A62
Signature Bank (new York, Ny) A710 E371
Federal Home Loan Bank New York A297 E158
Valley National Bancorp (nj) A831 E431
Chimera Investment Corp A173
Ladder Capital Corp A465
Granite Point Mortgage Trust Inc A363
Metropolitan Bank Holding Corp A522 E272
Ambac Financial Group, Inc. A38
Ares Commercial Real Estate Corp A70
City Of New York A186 P129
The Turner Corporation A781 P582
Turner Construction Company Inc A799 P604
New York City Health And Hospitals Corporation A551 P369
The New York And Presbyterian Hospital A780 P571
New York University A555 P373
Nielsen Holdings Plc A562 P378
Memorial Sloan-kettering Cancer Center A513 P328
The Trustees Of Columbia University In The City Of New York A781 P581
New York City Transit Authority A552 P370
New York University A555 P373
Signature Financial Llc A711 P481
Reckson Operating Partnership, L.p. A667 P438
Virtu Financial Llc A839 P643
The Simons Foundation Inc A781 P580
The Ford Foundation A776 P558
Brixmor Llc A135
Community Funds, Inc A210
State Of New York Mortgage Agency A739 P515
Nielsen Holdings Plc A562 P378
City Of New York A186 P129
The Turner Corporation A781 P582
Turner Construction Company Inc A799 P604

New York City Health And Hospitals Corporation A551 P369
The New York And Presbyterian Hospital A780 P571
New York University A555 P373
Nielsen Holdings Plc A562 P378
Memorial Sloan-kettering Cancer Center A513 P328
The Trustees Of Columbia University In The City Of New York A781 P581
New York City Transit Authority A552 P370
Lukoil Pan Americas, Llc P306
Metropolitan Transportation Authority P338
New York University A555 P373
Barnes & Noble, Inc. P61
Axel Johnson Inc. P53
Memorial Hospital For Cancer And Allied Diseases P327
Vns Choice P644
Trammo, Inc. P596
Signature Financial Llc A711 P481
Triborough Bridge & Tunnel Authority P598
Genpact Limited P227
St Lukes-roosevelt Institute P498
Mount Sinai St. Luke's. P356
Beth Israel Medical Center P71
The Bloomberg Family Foundation Inc P545
Lhh Corporation P299
Newmark & Company Real Estate, Inc. P375
Nfp Corp. P377
Lenox Hill Hospital P296
Guildnet, Inc. P237
Rtw Retailwinds, Inc. P452
Reckson Operating Partnership, L.p. A667 P438
Blue Tee Corp. P79
International Rescue Committee, Inc. P265
The Andrew W Mellon Foundation P544
Hunter Roberts Construction Group Llc P257
Physician Affiliate Group Of New York Pc P415
Catholic Medical Mission Board Inc P103
Virtu Financial Llc A839 P643
The Simons Foundation Inc A781 P580
Management-ila Managed Health Care Trust Fund P310
Plan International, Inc. P420
Mphasis Corporation P356
Pace University P403
Jewish Communal Fund P272
The New School P571
The Associated Press P544
New York State Housing Finance Agency P373
The Ford Foundation A776 P558
State Of New York Mortgage Agency A739 P515
New Residential Investment Corp E291
Take-two Interactive Software, Inc. E401
Iac/interactivecorp (new) E219
Virtu Financial Inc E440
Royalty Pharma Plc E358
Griffon Corp. E201
Evercore Inc E148
Msci Inc E281
Signature Bank (new York, Ny) A710 E371
Newmark Group Inc E292
Ubiquiti Inc E420

Federal Home Loan Bank New York A297 E158
Focus Financial Partners Inc E179
Cowen Inc E105
Valley National Bancorp (nj) A831 E431
Ziff Davis Inc E457
W.p. Carey Inc E442
Vici Properties Inc E437
Oppenheimer Holdings Inc E305
Pjt Partners Inc E326
Exlservice Holdings Inc E151
Moelis & Co E278
Tradeweb Markets Inc E412
Blackstone Mortgage Trust Inc E52
Stepstone Group Inc E389
Shutterstock Inc E369
Marketaxess Holdings Inc. E261
Ready Capital Corp E345
Progyny Inc E335
Global Net Lease Inc E194
Kkr Real Estate Finance Trust Inc E242
Amalgamated Financial Corp E17
Bluerock Residential Growth Reit Inc E53
Safehold Inc E359
Goldman Sachs Bdc Inc E196
Metropolitan Bank Holding Corp A522 E272
Siga Technologies Inc E370
Otc Markets Group Inc E308
Enerkon Solar International Inc E137
Exxe Group Inc E153
Mesabi Trust E271
Zedge Inc E457

NORWICH
Nbt Bancorp. Inc. A546

OCEANSIDE
South Nassau Communities Hospital P488

OSWEGO
Pathfinder Bancorp Inc. (md) E313

PEARL RIVER
Orange And Rockland Utilities Inc P397

POUGHKEEPSIE
Health Quest Systems, Inc. P246
Central Hudson Gas & Electric Corporation P108
Dutchess, County Of (inc) P198
Rhinebeck Bancorp Inc E354

PURCHASE
Pepsico Inc A618
Mastercard Inc A505
Mbia Inc. A506

REGO PARK
New York State Catholic Health Plan, Inc. A554 P372

RICHMOND HILL
The Jamaica Hospital P563

ROCHESTER
Home Properties, Limited Partnership A395
Rochester Regional Health P451
County Of Monroe P164
Rochester Gas And Electric Corporation P450
Rochester City School District P449
Rochester Institute Of Technology (inc) P450
City Of Rochester P132
Broadstone Net Lease Inc E57

478   HOOVER'S HANDBOOK OF EMERGING COMPANIES 2022

INDEX BY HEADQUARTERS LOCATION

ROSLYN
St. Francis Hospital, Roslyn, New York P499

RYE
Lict Corp E252

SCHENECTADY
General Electric International, Inc. A346 P227
The Golub Corporation P560
Mvp Health Plan, Inc. P360

STATEN ISLAND
Staten Island University Hospital P519

SYRACUSE
County Of Onondaga P165
City Of Syracuse P134
Srctec, Llc P496
St. Joseph's Hospital Health Center P504

TARRYTOWN
Regeneron Pharmaceuticals, Inc. A668
Db Us Holding Corporation P184

TROY
Rensselaer Polytechnic Institute P442

UNIONDALE
Flushing Financial Corp. A329
Long Island Power Authority P302
Arbor Realty Trust Inc E29

UTICA
County Of Oneida P165

VALHALLA
Westchester County Health Care Corporation P652

VICTOR
Constellation Brands Inc A218

WARSAW
Financial Institutions Inc. A306

WEST ISLIP
Good Samaritan Hospital Medical Center P230

WEST NYACK
The Salvation Army P578

WESTBURY
North Shore-long Island Jewish Health Care P384

WESTFIELD
National Grape Co-operative Association, Inc. P363

WHITE PLAINS
New York Power Authority P371
White Plains Hospital Medical Center P655
Turtle Beach Corp E418
Frmo Corp. E186
Northeast Community Bancorp Inc (md) E295

WILLIAMSVILLE
Evans Bancorp, Inc. E148

NORTH CAROLINA

ALBEMARLE
Uwharrie Capital Corp. E430

ASHEVILLE
Hometrust Bancshares Inc. A396 E217
Mission Hospital, Inc. P346

Hometrust Bancshares Inc. A396 E217

BOONE
Samaritan's Purse P461

BURLINGTON
Laboratory Corporation Of America Holdings A463

CARY
Ply Gem Holdings, Inc. P420
Cary Oil Co., Inc. P101
Wake County Public School System P644
Coc Properties, Inc. P142

CHAPEL HILL
University Of North Carolina Hospitals P626
University Of North Carolina At Chapel Hill P626
The University Of North Carolina P586
Investors Title Co. E235

CHARLOTTE
Bank Of America Corp A95
Duke Energy Corp A258
Honeywell International Inc A397
Truist Financial Corp A795
Nucor Corp. A575
Sonic Automotive, Inc. A719
Brighthouse Financial Inc A133
Brighthouse Life Insurance Co - Insurance Products A133
Duke Energy Carolinas Llc A258
Sealed Air Corp A701
Coca-cola Consolidated Inc A197
The Charlotte-mecklenburg Hospital Authority A774 P547
Snyder's-lance, Inc. P485
County Of Mecklenburg P163
City Of Charlotte P124
Extended Stay America, Inc. P210
Presbyterian Hospital P426
Parsons Environment & Infrastructure Group Inc. P407
Premier Healthcare Alliance, L.p. P426

CONCORD
Cardinal Logistics Holdings, Llc P98
Carolinas Medical Center Northeast P101

DURHAM
Iqvia Holdings Inc A432
Duke University P196
Duke University Health System, Inc. P197
Avaya Holdings Corp. P52
Duke University Hospital P198
The North Carolina Mutual Wholesale Drug Company P572
Research Triangle Institute Inc P443
Family Health International Inc P211

FAYETTEVILLE
Carolina Healthcare Center Of Cumberland Lp P101
Cape Fear Valley Medical Center P97

GASTONIA
Mann+hummel Filtration Technology Intermediate Holdings Inc. P310

GREENSBORO
The Fresh Market Inc P559
Guilford County School System P238
County Of Guilford P160

GREENVILLE
Pitt County Memorial Hospital, Incorporated P418

HICKORY
Commscope Holding Co Inc A209
Alex Lee, Inc. P19

HILLSBOROUGH
County Of Orange P165

HUNTERSVILLE
American Tire Distributors Holdings, Inc. P33

LEXINGTON
Wake Forest University Health Sciences P644

MONROE
County Of Union P171

MOORESVILLE
Lowe's Companies Inc A487

MORRISVILLE
Syneos Health Inc A753
Channeladvisor Corp E77
Charles & Colvard Ltd E78

MOUNT AIRY
Insteel Industries, Inc. E231

RALEIGH
Advance Auto Parts Inc A11
Martin Marietta Materials, Inc. A500
First Citizens Bancshares Inc (de) A311
State Of North Carolina A739 P515
Wake, County Of North Carolina P644
Rex Healthcare, Inc. P443
North Carolina Electric Membership Corporation P380
Suntory International P527
Duke Health Raleigh Hospital Guild P196
Biodelivery Sciences International Inc E50

SOUTHERN PINES
First Bancorp (nc) A309 E162

THOMASVILLE
Old Dominion Freight Line, Inc. A584

WILMINGTON
Live Oak Bancshares Inc A483 E255
Live Oak Banking Company A484
Live Oak Bancshares Inc A483 E255

WINSTON SALEM
Novant Health, Inc. A572 P390
North Carolina Baptist Hospital P380
North Carolina Baptist Hospital Fdn P380
Novant Medical Group Inc P391
Quality Oil Company, Llc P432

WINSTON-SALEM
Hanesbrands Inc A373

NORTH DAKOTA

BISMARCK
Mdu Resources Group Inc A511
State Of North Dakota A739 P515
North Dakota University System Foundation P381
Bnccorp Inc E53

FARGO
Sanford P463
Rdo Equipment Co. P436
North Dakota University System P381
Sanford North P464
Ni Holdings Inc E293

GRAND FORKS
Alerus Financial Corp A28 E13
Altru Health System P27

Alerus Financial Corp A28 E13

WEST FARGO
Clark Equipment Company P137

OHIO

AKRON
Goodyear Tire & Rubber Co. A360
Firstenergy Corp A324
Jersey Central Power & Light Company P271
Summa Health P524
Ohio Edison Company P394
Childrens Hospital Medical Center Of Akron P118
West Penn Power Company P651
The Cleveland Electric Illuminating Company P552
Pennsylvania Electric Company P410
Metropolitan Edison Company P337
American Transmission Systems, Incorporated P35
Summit County P524
Akron General Medical Center Inc P13

ARCHBOLD
Farmers & Merchants Bancorp Inc (oh) E155

BARBERTON
Christian Healthcare Ministries, Inc. P118

BATAVIA
Multi-color Corporation P356

BROOKLYN HEIGHTS
Graftech International Ltd E197

CANFIELD
Farmers National Banc Corp. (canfield,oh) A294 E156

CHAGRIN FALLS
Nicholas Properties & Developments, Inc. P378

CINCINNATI
Kroger Co (the) A460
Procter & Gamble Company (the) A643
Fifth Third Bancorp (cincinnati, Oh) A305
American Financial Group Inc A46
Cintas Corporation A180
Federal Home Loan Bank Of Cincinnati A297
First Financial Bancorp (oh) A314 E166
Bon Secours Mercy Health, Inc. A126 P82
Us Healthcare System P636
Uc Health, Llc. P607
Kgbo Holdings, Inc P284
University Of Cincinnati P617
Messer Construction Co. P335
County Of Hamilton P160
The Christ Hospital P550
General Electric International Operations Company, Inc. P226
Bethesda, Inc. P72
City Of Cincinnati P125
Bethesda Hospital, Inc. P72
Good Samaritan Hospital Of Cincinnati P231
Cincinnati Public Schools P121
Trihealth, Inc. P598
Scripps (ew) Company (the) E363
Medpace Holdings Inc E266
First Financial Bancorp (oh) A314 E166

HOOVER'S HANDBOOK OF EMERGING COMPANIES 2022

479

INDEX BY HEADQUARTERS LOCATION

> A = AMERICAN BUSINESS
> E = EMERGING COMPANIES
> P = PRIVATE COMPANIES
> W = WORLD BUSINESS

Phillips Edison & Co Inc E322
Meridian Bioscience Inc. E269

CLEVELAND
Cleveland-cliffs Inc (new) A187
Sherwin-williams Co (the) A707
Parker Hannifin Corp A608
Keycorp A452
Tfs Financial Corp A773
The Cleveland Clinic
   Foundation A775 P551
Eaton Corporation A264 P200
The Cleveland Clinic
   Foundation A775 P551
Eaton Corporation A264 P200
County Of Cuyahoga P158
Case Western Reserve University P102
Cleveland Municipal School
   District P138
The Metrohealth System P567
Metrohealth Medical Center P337
City Of Cleveland P125
Current Lighting Solutions, Llc P177
Crawford United Corp E107

COLUMBUS
American Electric Power Co Inc A43
Bath & Body Works Inc A104
Big Lots, Inc. A116
Huntington Bancshares Inc A408
State Auto Financial Corp. A733
State Of Ohio A740 P516
Battelle Memorial Institute P63
The Ohio State University Wexner
   Medical Center P572
Ohiohealth Corporation P394
City Of Columbus P125
Franklin County Board Of
   Commissioners P220
American Electric Power Service
   Corporation P30
Mount Carmel Health System P354
Ohiohealth Corporation Group
   Return P395
Ohiohealth Riverside Methodist
   Hospital P395
American Municipal Power, Inc. P33
Columbus City School District P144
Columbia Gas Of Ohio, Inc. P143
Ohio State University Physicians,
   Inc. P394
Jobsohio Beverage System P273
Mount Carmel Health Plan, Inc. P354
Mount Carmel Health Plan
   Medig P354
The Fishel Company P557
M/i Homes Inc E257
Mettler-toledo International,
   Inc. E272
Installed Building Products Inc E230

COLUMBUS GROVE
United Bancshares Inc. (oh) E423

DAYTON
Med America Health Systems
   Corporation P323
Miami Valley Hospital P340
The University Of Dayton P585
County Of Montgomery P164

DEFIANCE
Premier Financial Corp A639 E332
Sb Financial Group Inc E361

DELAWARE
Greif Inc A367
County Of Delaware P158

Franchise Group Inc E184

DOVER
Ffd Financial Corp E160

DUBLIN
Cardinal Health, Inc. A150

FAIRFIELD
Cincinnati Financial Corp. A178

FINDLAY
Marathon Petroleum Corp. A496
Mplx Lp A541

GROVE CITY
Mount Carmel Health System P354

HILLIARD
Advanced Drainage Systems Inc E5

HUDSON
The American Endowment
   Foundation P544

HURON
Huron Health Care Center, Inc P257

KENT
Carter-jones Companies, Inc. P101
Davey Tree Expert Co. (the) E114

KETTERING
Kettering Medical Center P283

LEBANON
Lcnb Corp E247

MARIETTA
Peoples Bancorp Inc (marietta,
   Oh) A617

MARTINS FERRY
United Bancorp, Inc. (martins Ferry,
   Oh) E422

MASON
Atricure Inc E36

MASSILLON
Fresh Mark, Inc. P221

MAUMEE
Andersons Inc A61
Dana Inc A233

MAYFIELD VILLAGE
Progressive Corp. (oh) A644
Preformed Line Products Co. E331

MEDINA
Rpm International Inc (de) A687

MIDDLEFIELD
Middlefield Banc Corp. E274

MILLERSBURG
Csb Bancorp Inc (oh) E111

MINERVA
Consumers Bancorp, Inc. (minerva,
   Oh) E99

NEWARK
Park National Corp (newark,
   Oh) A607 E312

NORTH RIDGEVILLE
Invacare Corporation (tw) P265

ORRVILLE
Smucker (j.m.) Co. A717

OXFORD
Miami University P340

PERRYSBURG
O-i Glass Inc A580
Mercy Health A517 P330

REYNOLDSBURG
Victorias Secret & Co A838

RICHFIELD
Element14 Us Holdings Inc P203

SANDUSKY
Civista Bancshares Inc A187 E84

SHAKER HEIGHTS
University Hospitals Health System,
   Inc. P614

SPRINGFIELD
County Of Clark P157

TOLEDO
Owens Corning A601
Pilkington North America, Inc. P417
Toledo Promedica Hospital P595
The University Of Toledo P587

WALBRIDGE
The Rudolph/libbe Companies
   Inc P577

WHITEHALL
Heartland Banccorp E207

WILMINGTON
Air Transport Services Group, Inc. E9

WORTHINGTON
Cf Bankshares Inc E77

OKLAHOMA

ANADARKO
Western Farmers Electric
   Cooperative P652

CATOOSA
Cherokee Nation Businesses Llc P112
Cherokee Nation Entertainment,
   Llc P113

OKLAHOMA CITY
Devon Energy Corp. A242
Continental Resources Inc. A220
Chesapeake Energy Corp. A170
Bancfirst Corp. (oklahoma City,
   Okla) A93 E44
Candid Color Systems, Inc. A147 P96
State Of Oklahoma A740 P516
Candid Color Systems, Inc. A147 P96
State Of Oklahoma A740 P516
Hobby Lobby Stores, Inc. P253
Integris Health, Inc. P263
Ou Medicine, Inc. P401
Seventy Seven Energy Llc P474
Integris Baptist Medical Center,
   Inc. P263
City Of Oklahoma City P130
Mercy Hospital Oklahoma City,
   Inc. P333
Paycom Software Inc E314
Bancfirst Corp. (oklahoma City,
   Okla) A93 E44
Bank7 Corp E46

STILLWATER
Oklahoma State University P395

TAHLEQUAH
The Cherokee Nation P548

TULSA
Oneok Inc A592
Williams Cos Inc (the) A864
Ngl Energy Partners Lp A561
Bok Financial Corp A125 E53
Oneok Partners, L.p. A593 P396
Continuum Energy Services,
   L.l.c. P152
Continuum Midstream, L.l.c. P152
St. John Health System, Inc. P500
Saint Francis Hospital, Inc. P457

Magellan Pipeline Company,
   L.p. P307
Bok Financial Corp A125 E53
Educational Development Corp. E130

OREGON

BEAVERTON
Nike Inc A562
Beaverton School District P68

BEND
St. Charles Health System, Inc. P499

CORBETT
County Of Multnomah P164

CORVALLIS
Samaritan Health Services, Inc. P461

EUGENE
Oregon University System P399
Bi-mart Acquisition Corp. P73
University Of Oregon P627

HILLSBORO
County Of Washington P172

MEDFORD
Lithia Motors Inc A481

MONMOUTH
Western Oregon University P653

PORTLAND
Pacificorp A603
Umpqua Holdings Corp A809
Precision Castparts Corp. A638 P425
Uti, (u.s.) Holdings, Inc. P638
Oregon Health & Science University
   Medical Group P399
Bonneville Power Administration P83
Legacy Health P294
City Of Portland P131
Fctg Holdings, Inc. P213
County Of Multnomah P164
Careoregon, Inc. P99
Legacy Emanuel Hospital & Health
   Center P293
Portland Public Schools P422
Blount International, Inc. P76
Fortis Construction, Inc. P218
Schnitzer Steel Industries Inc E361

ROSEBURG
Mercy Medical Center, Inc. P334

SALEM
State Of Oregon A740 P516
Oregon Department Of
   Transportation P399
Oregon State Lottery P399
Salem Health P459

WILSONVILLE
Mentor Graphics Corporation P329

PENNSYLVANIA

ABINGTON
Abington Memorial Hospital Inc P3

ALLENTOWN
Air Products & Chemicals Inc A22
Ppl Corp A637
Lehigh Valley Health Network,
   Inc. P294
Talen Energy Supply, Llc P532
Lehigh Gas Corporation P294
Computer Aid, Inc. P149
American Bank Inc (pa) E20

AUDUBON
Globus Medical Inc E194

INDEX BY HEADQUARTERS LOCATION

BALA CYNWYD
Philadelphia Consolidated Holding Corp. A623 P414

BELLEVILLE
Kish Bancorp Inc. E242

BERWYN
Ametek Inc A55

BETHLEHEM
St. Luke's Health Network, Inc. P506
Saint Luke's Hospital Of Bethlehem, Pennsylvania P459
St Luke's Hospital & Health Network Inc P498
Embassy Bancorp Inc E132

BLAIRSVILLE
Excela Health P209

BLUE BELL
Brightview Holdings Inc E56

BRYN MAWR
Main Line Hospitals, Inc. P308
Essential Utilities Inc E147

CAMP HILL
Rite Aid Corp A678

CANONSBURG
Viatris Inc A837
Centimark Corporation P106
Ansys Inc. E27
Equitrans Midstream Corp E144

CLEARFIELD
Cnb Financial Corp. (clearfield, Pa) A192 E87

CLIFTON HEIGHTS
Harlee Manor, Inc. P241

COLMAR
Dorman Products Inc E122

CONSHOHOCKEN
Amerisourcebergen Corp. A54
Allied Security Holdings Llc P23
Quaker Houghton E340

CONSHOLOCKEN
Hamilton Lane Inc E205

CORAOPOLIS
Dick's Sporting Goods, Inc A243

DANVILLE
Geisinger Health A343 P225
Geisinger Health Plan P226
The Geisinger Clinic P559
Geisinger Medical Center P226
Grandview Health Homes, Inc. P233

DENVER
Ugi Utilities, Inc. P608

DOYLESTOWN
The County Of Bucks P553
Hv Bancorp Inc E219

DUNCANSVILLE
Value Drug Company P638

DUNMORE
Fidelity D&d Bancorp Inc E160

EMLENTON
Emclaire Financial Corp. E132

EPHRATA
Enb Financial Corp E134

ERIE
County Of Erie P159
Erie Indemnity Co. E144

EXTON
West Pharmaceutical Services, Inc. E446

FORT WASHINGTON
Toll Brothers Inc. A787
Nutrisystem, Inc. P392
Ditech Holding Corporation P190

GETTYSBURG
Acnb Corp A8 E3

HARRISBURG
Commonwealth Of Pennsylvania A208 P146
Pennsylvania Housing Finance Agency A614
Psecu Services, Inc. A650
Commonwealth Of Pennsylvania A208 P146
Upmc Pinnacle Hospitals P635
Pinnacle Health Hospital P418
United Concordia Life And Health Insurance Company P610
Pennsylvania Higher Education Assistance Agency P410
Ollie's Bargain Outlet Holdings Inc E303

HERSHEY
Hershey Company (the) A383
Milton Hershey School & School Trust P344

HONESDALE
Norwood Financial Corp. E297

INDIANA
First Commonwealth Financial Corp (indiana, Pa) A313 E165
S & T Bancorp Inc (indiana, Pa) A690
First Commonwealth Financial Corp (indiana, Pa) A313 E165

JENKINTOWN
Redeemer Health Holy System P439

KENNETT SQUARE
Exelon Generation Co Llc A287

KING OF PRUSSIA
Universal Health Services, Inc. A823
Ugi Corp. A806

LANCASTER
Fulton Financial Corp. (pa) A340
The Lancaster General Hospital P564

LANSDALE
Skf Usa Inc. P483

MALVERN
Meridian Corp E270

MANHEIM
Worley & Obetz, Inc. P659

MANSFIELD
Citizens Financial Services Inc E83

MECHANICSBURG
Select Medical Holdings Corp A702
Pennsylvania - American Water Company P409

MEDIA
County Of Delaware P158

MILLERSBURG
Mid Penn Bancorp Inc A529 E274

MILTON
Kramm Healthcare Center, Inc. P288

MOON TOWNSHIP
Calgon Carbon Corporation P93
Mastech Digital Inc E263

MUNCY
Muncy Bank Financial, Inc. (muncy, Pa) E282

NEWTOWN
Epam Systems, Inc. E143

NEWTOWN SQUARE
Mercy Health System Of Southeastern Pennsylvania P333

NORRISTOWN
County Of Montgomery P164

PHILADELPHIA
Comcast Corp A202
Aramark A67
Republic First Bancorp, Inc. A676
City Of Philadelphia A186 P131
Fs Kkr Capital Corp. Ii A340 P223
City Of Philadelphia A186 P131
Thomas Jefferson University P592
Temple University-of The Commonwealth System Of Higher Education P536
The School District Of Philadelphia P579
The Children's Hospital Of Philadelphia P549
Hospital Of The University Of Pennsylvania P255
Thomas Jefferson University Hospitals, Inc. P593
Temple University Health System, Inc. P536
Community Behavioral Health P146
Health Partners Plans, Inc. P246
Fs Kkr Capital Corp. Ii A340 P223
Albert Einstein Medical Associates, Inc. P17
Five Below Inc E176
Independence Realty Trust Inc E225
Cohen & Company Inc (new) E89
Prudential Bancorp Inc (new) E338

PITTSBURGH
Kraft Heinz Co (the) A459
United States Steel Corp. A820
Pnc Financial Services Group (the) A631
Ppg Industries Inc A635
Wesco International, Inc. A853
Alcoa Corporation A28
Wabtec Corp A841
Arconic Corp A69
Fnb Corp A330 E178
Tristate Capital Holdings Inc A794 E415
Upmc A827 P634
Upmc Presbyterian Shadyside A828 P635
Upmc A827 P634
Upmc Presbyterian Shadyside A828 P635
University Of Pittsburgh P628
Smmh Practice Plan, Inc. P485
County Of Allegheny P156
Carnegie Mellon University P100
Upmc Magee-womens Hospital P635
Allegheny General Hospital Inc P20
Pittsburgh School District P419
City Of Pittsburgh P131
Board Of Public Education School District Of Pittsburgh (inc) P80
Fnb Corp A330 E178
Limbach Holdings Inc E253
Tristate Capital Holdings Inc A794 E415

PITTSTON
Benco Dental Supply Co. P69

RADNOR
Lincoln National Corp. A479

Avantor Inc A85
Airgas, Inc. A23 P12
Main Line Health System P307

READING
Reading Hospital Services Inc P438
Boscov's, Inc. P84
Redner's Markets, Inc. P439
Reading Hospital P437

SAXONBURG
Ii-vi Inc E223

SCRANTON
Peoples Financial Services Corp A618

SHIPPENSBURG
Orrstown Financial Services, Inc. A597 E307

SOUDERTON
Univest Financial Corp A825 E428

TREVOSE
Broder Bros., Co. P87

TUNKHANNOCK
County Of Wyoming A224 P172

UNIVERSITY PARK
The Pennsylvania State University A780 P574

UPPER CHICHESTER
Sunoco Pipeline L.p. P527

WARREN
Northwest Bancshares, Inc. (md) A570

WAYNE
Radian Group, Inc. A661

WELLSBORO
Citizens & Northern Corp E82

WEST CHESTER
Accesslex Institute A7

WEST READING
Customers Bancorp Inc A229 E112

WORCESTER
Allan Myers, Inc. P20

WYOMISSING
Gaming & Leisure Properties, Inc E190

YARDLEY
Crown Holdings Inc A225

YORK
York Hospital P661
Wellspan Medical Group (inc) P650
County Of York P173

PUERTO RICO

RIO GRANDE
Desarolladora Del Norte S E P187

SAN JUAN
Popular Inc. A633

TOA BAJA
Best Petroleum Corporation P71

RHODE ISLAND

LINCOLN
Narragansett Electric Comp P362

NEWPORT
Pangaea Logistics Solutions Ltd. E311

INDEX BY HEADQUARTERS LOCATION

A = AMERICAN BUSINESS
E = EMERGING COMPANIES
P = PRIVATE COMPANIES
W = WORLD BUSINESS

PAWTUCKET
Hasbro, Inc. A377
Teknor Apex Company P534

PROVIDENCE
United Natural Foods Inc. A816
Textron Inc A771
Citizens Financial Group Inc (new) A184
State Of Rhode Island And Providence Plantations A740 P516
Gilbane Building Company P229
Care New England Health System Inc P98
Rhode Island Hospital P444
City Of Providence P132
Brown University P90

WARWICK
Vanguard Charitable Endowment Program P640
Rhode Island Higher Education Savings Trust P444
Plan International, Inc. P420

WESTERLY
Washington Trust Bancorp, Inc. A847

WOONSOCKET
Cvs Health Corporation A231

SOUTH CAROLINA

AIKEN
Security Federal Corp (sc) E365

ANDERSON
Anmed Health P37

CHARLESTON
The Medical University Of South Carolina P566
Medical University Hospital Authority P324
Roper St. Francis Healthcare P451

COLUMBIA
State Of South Carolina A740 P516
Agfirst Farm Credit Bank A20 P11
State Of South Carolina A740 P516
Central Electric Power Cooperative, Inc. P107
Agfirst Farm Credit Bank A20 P11

CONWAY
Horry County School District P254

FLORENCE
Mcleod Regional Medical Center Of The Pee Dee, Inc. P322
First Reliance Bancshares Inc E174

GREENVILLE
Athene Annuity & Life Assurance Company A78 P47
Prisma Health-upstate P428
St. Francis Hospital, Inc. P499
Athene Annuity & Life Assurance Company A78 P47
Southern First Bancshares, Inc. E382

GREER
Regional Management Corp E347

HARTSVILLE
Sonoco Products Co. A720

HILTON HEAD ISLAND
Coastalsouth Bancshares Inc E88

LEXINGTON
First Community Corp (sc) E166

MONCKS CORNER
South Carolina Public Service Authority (inc) P487

MYRTLE BEACH
South Atlantic Bancshares Inc E381

SPARTANBURG
J M Smith Corporation P267
Spartanburg Regional Health Services District, Inc. P472
Security Group, Inc. P472
Security Finance Corporation Of Spartanburg P471

SUMMERVILLE
Advanced Technology International P5

WEST COLUMBIA
Lexington Medical Center P298
Lexington County Health Services District, Inc. P298

SOUTH DAKOTA

ABERDEEN
Dacotah Banks Inc. A232
Agtegra Cooperative P11

PIERRE
State Of South Dakota P517

RAPID CITY
Monument Health Rapid City Hospital, Inc. P353

SIOUX FALLS
Meta Financial Group Inc A519 E271
Sanford Health P463
The Evangelical Lutheran Good Samaritan Society P556
Meta Financial Group Inc A519 E271

TENNESSEE

BRENTWOOD
Tractor Supply Co. A790
Delek Us Holdings Inc (new) A240
Premise Health Holding Corp. P426

CHATTANOOGA
Unum Group A826
Hamilton Chattanooga County Hospital Authority P241
Emj Corporation P204
Electric Power Board Of Chattanooga P203
Memorial Health Care System, Inc. P325

CLARKSVILLE
County Of Montgomery P164

CLEVELAND
City Of Cleveland P125

COOKEVILLE
Averitt Incorporated P53
Averitt Express, Inc. P52

FARRAGUT
Educational Funding Of The South, Inc. A268

FRANKLIN
Community Health Systems, Inc. A210
Clarcor Inc. P137
Community Healthcare Trust Inc E96

GOODLETTSVILLE
Dollar General Corp A251

JACKSON
Jackson-madison County General Hospital District P270

JOHNSON CITY
Ballad Health P55

KINGSPORT
Eastman Chemical Co A263
Wellmont Health System P649

KNOXVILLE
Tennessee Valley Authority A767
Smartfinancial Inc A717 E379
Cfj Properties Llc A166 P110
Scripps Networks Interactive, Inc. P469
Regal Entertainment Group P440
Covenant Health P173
University Of Tennessee P629
Knoxville Utilities Board P287
Smartfinancial Inc A717 E379
Mountain Commerce Bancorp Inc E281

LEBANON
Wilson Bank Holding Co. A866 E450

LOUDON
Malibu Boats Inc E258

MEMPHIS
Fedex Corp A302
International Paper Co A426
Autozone, Inc. A83
First Horizon Corp A317 E169
Methodist Healthcare- Memphis Hospitals P337
American Lebanese Syrian Associated Charities, Inc. P32
St. Jude Children's Research Hospital, Inc. P505
Board Of Education-memphis City Schools P80
County Of Shelby P170
City Of Memphis P128
Monogram Food Solutions, Llc P350
Baptist Memorial Hospital P59
First Horizon Corp A317 E169
Frontdoor Inc E187

MURFREESBORO
The Middle Tennessee Electric Membership Corporation P568

NASHVILLE
Hca Healthcare Inc A378
Yellow Corp (new) A874
Pinnacle Financial Partners Inc A627 E324
Fb Financial Corp A296 E157
Capstar Financial Holdings Inc A150 E67
State Of Tennessee A741 P517
Vanderbilt University Medical Center P639
Metropolitan Government Of Nashville & Davidson County P337
The Vanderbilt University P589
Ryman Hospitality Properties, Inc. P453
Dialysis Clinic, Inc. P188
Tri Star Energy, Llc P598
Pinnacle Financial Partners Inc A627 E324
Fb Financial Corp A296 E157
Alliancebernstein Holding Lp E15
Capstar Financial Holdings Inc A150 E67

VONORE
Mastercraft Boat Holdings Inc E263

TEXAS

ABILENE
First Financial Bankshares, Inc. A315 E167

ADDISON
Guaranty Bancshares Inc A369 E203
Xmed Oxygen & Medical Equipment, Lp P659
Wingstop Inc E450
Guaranty Bancshares Inc A369 E203

AMARILLO
Affiliated Foods, Inc. P9
Bruckner Truck Sales, Inc. P91

ARLINGTON
Horton (dr) Inc A402
Texas Health Resources P541
Arlington Independent School District (inc) P43
Forestar Group Inc (new) E179

AUSTIN
Tesla Inc A768
Oracle Corp A594
National Western Life Group Inc A545
State Of Texas A741 P517
University Of Texas System A824 P630
Whole Foods Market, Inc. A863 P655
Permanent University Fund A620 P411
Texas County And District Retirement System A770 P540
Farm Credit Bank Of Texas A293 P211
State Of Texas A741 P517
University Of Texas System A824 P630
Whole Foods Market, Inc. A863 P655
Permanent University Fund A620 P411
Texas County And District Retirement System A770 P540
Workforce Commission, Texas P658
Austin Independent School District (inc) P52
City Of Austin P123
Lower Colorado River Authority P304
County Of Travis P171
Texas State University System P542
Attorney General, Texas P51
Farm Credit Bank Of Texas A293 P211
Digital Realty Trust Inc E119
Solarwinds Corp E380
Usa Compression Partners Lp E429
Digital Turbine Inc E120
Vital Farms Inc E442

BEAUMONT
Communitybank Of Texas, N.a. A212

BEDFORD
Legacy Housing Corp E249

CONROE
Spirit Of Texas Bancshares Inc A728 E384
Conroe Independent School District P150
County Of Montgomery P164
Spirit Of Texas Bancshares Inc A728 E384

COPPELL
Mr Cooper Group Inc A541 E281

CORPUS CHRISTI
Spohn Investment Corporation P496
Driscoll Childrens Health Plan P194

482   HOOVER'S HANDBOOK OF EMERGING COMPANIES 2022

INDEX BY HEADQUARTERS LOCATION

DALLAS

At&t Inc A77
Cbre Group Inc A158
Energy Transfer Lp A275
Tenet Healthcare Corp. A764
Kimberly-clark Corp. A454
Texas Instruments Inc. A770
Southwest Airlines Co A725
Jacobs Engineering Group, Inc. A435
Aecom A15
Hollyfrontier Corp A390
Sunoco Lp A750
Builders Firstsource Inc. A138
Comerica, Inc. A203
Hilltop Holdings, Inc. A387
Texas Capital Bancshares Inc A769
Triumph Bancorp Inc A795 E416
Veritex Holdings Inc A832 E435
First Foundation Inc A317 E169
Sixth Street Specialty Lending
  Inc A714
Gwg Holdings Inc A370
Baylor Scott & White Health A106
  P64
Baylor Scott & White Holdings A106
  P65
Spirit Realty Capital, Inc. A728 P496
Baylor Scott & White Health A106
  P64
Baylor Scott & White Holdings A106
  P65
Placid Refining Company Llc P419
Placid Holding Company P419
Balfour Beatty Construction Group,
  Inc. P54
Balfour Beatty Construction, Llc P55
Bearingpoint, Inc. P67
Dallas Independent School
  District P179
City Of Dallas P126
Dallas County Hospital District P179
Baylor University Medical Center P65
Steward Health Care System Llc P520
County Of Dallas P158
Southern Methodist University
  Inc P491
Children's Medical Center Of
  Dallas P117
Mv Transportation, Inc. P359
Spirit Realty Capital, Inc. A728 P496
Stevens Transport, Inc. P520
Primoris Services Corp E334
Copart Inc E101
Invitation Homes Inc E236
Cyrusone Inc E114
Crossroads Systems Inc (new) E111
Triumph Bancorp Inc A795 E416
Veritex Holdings Inc A832 E435
Texas Pacific Land Corp E407
First Foundation Inc A317 E169
Nexpoint Residential Trust Inc E293

DEER PARK

Deer Park Refining Limited
  Partnership P186

DENTON

University Of North Texas
  System P627

EDINBURG

Doctors Hospital At Renaissance,
  Ltd. P193

EL PASO

El Paso County Hospital District P202
El Paso Independent School District
  Education Foundation P202
Socorro Independent School
  District P486

FORT WORTH

American Airlines Group Inc A41

Bnsf Railway Company A122 P79
Wesco Aircraft Holdings, Inc. P650
Fort Worth Independent School
  District P218
Texla Health Harris Methodist
  Hospital Fort Worth P541
Tarrant County Texas (inc) P533
Tarrant County Hospital District P532
County Of Tarrant P171
Cook Children's Health Plan P152
Kiewit Infrastructure South Co. P285
Texas Christian University Inc P540
Firstcash Holdings Inc E175

FRISCO

The Core Group Ltd P553
Ccg Services, Inc. P103
Addus Homecare Corp E4

GAINESVILLE

Ses Holdings, Llc P474

GALVESTON

American National Group Inc A50

GRAPEVINE

Gamestop Corp A342

HOUSTON

Phillips 66 A625
Sysco Corp A754
Conocophillips A215
Hewlett Packard Enterprise Co A385
Enterprise Products Partners
  L.p. A279
Plains Gp Holdings Lp A631
Plains All American Pipeline Lp A629
Baker Hughes Company A90
Baker Hughes Holdings Llc A90
Waste Management, Inc. (de) A848
Kinder Morgan Inc. A455
Occidental Petroleum Corp A581
Halliburton Company A370
Quanta Services, Inc. A657
Eog Resources, Inc. A280
Group 1 Automotive, Inc. A368
Cheniere Energy Inc. A168
Nrg Energy Inc A574
Centerpoint Energy, Inc A162
Targa Resources Corp A759
Apa Corp A63
Westlake Corp A859
Crown Castle International Corp
  (new) A225
Cheniere Energy Partners L P A169
Kbr Inc A447
Nov Inc A571
Marathon Oil Corp. A495
Prosperity Bancshares Inc. A645 E335
Allegiance Bancshares Inc A30 E15
Cbtx Inc A159
Cameron International
  Corporation A144 P95
Memorial Hermann Health
  System A512 P326
Houston Methodist St. John
  Hospital A403 P256
The Methodist Hospital A779 P566
Cameron International
  Corporation A144 P95
Memorial Hermann Health
  System A512 P326
Houston Methodist St. John
  Hospital A403 P256
The Methodist Hospital A779 P566
Spectra Energy, Llc P494
Tauber Oil Company P533
Biourja Trading, Llc P75
County Of Harris P160
City Of Houston P126
Houston Independent School
  District P256
Texas Children's Hospital P539

Chemium International Corp. P112
Midcoast Energy Partners, L.p. P343
United Space Alliance, Llc P611
Methodist Health Care System P336
Texla Energy Management, Inc. P542
Cypress-fairbanks Independent School
  District P177
Texas Eastern Transmission, Lp P541
Technip Usa, Inc. P534
Community Health Choice Texas,
  Inc. P147
Kraton Polymers U.s. Llc P288
Cima Energy, Lp P120
Sun Coast Resources, Inc. P524
Financial Trader Corporation P214
Plains Pipeline, L.p. P420
Community Health Choice, Inc. P147
Harris County Fire Marshal P242
Ep Energy Corporation P207
Ep Energy Llc P207
Aldine Independent School
  District P18
Geokinetics Inc. P227
Anr Pipeline Company P38
Centerpoint Energy Services Retail
  Llc P106
Tmh Physician Organization P594
Natural Gas Pipeline Company Of
  America Llc P364
S & B Engineers And Constructors,
  Ltd. P454
Enterprise Te Products Pipeline
  Company Llc P207
El Paso Natural Gas Company,
  L.l.c. P202
Southern Natural Gas Company,
  L.l.c. P491
University Of Houston System P621
Enterprise Crude Pipeline Llc P206
Mid-america Pipeline Company,
  Llc P342
Texas Aromatics, Lp P539
Spring Branch Independent School
  District (inc) P496
Alief Independent School District P19
Comfort Systems Usa Inc E93
Phillips 66 Partners Lp E321
Ies Holdings Inc E222
Prosperity Bancshares Inc. A645 E335
Hess Midstream Lp E212
Magnolia Oil & Gas Corp E258
Helix Energy Solutions Group
  Inc E210
Shell Midstream Partners Lp E368
Cactus Inc E60
Allegiance Bancshares Inc A30 E15
Sharps Compliance Corp. E368

HUMBLE

Humble Independent School
  District P257

IRVING

Exxon Mobil Corp A290
Mckesson Corp A509
Fluor Corp. A328
Pioneer Natural Resources Co A628
Vistra Corp A840
Celanese Corp (de) A160
Commercial Metals Co. A206
Federal Home Loan Bank Of
  Dallas A298 E158
The Michaels Companies Inc A779
  P568
Gruma Corporation P237
Nch Corporation P365
Cec Entertainment, Inc. P104
Hms Holdings Llc P252
Finance Of America Companies
  Inc E161
Federal Home Loan Bank Of
  Dallas A298 E158

Envela Corp E142

JOHNSON CITY

Pedernales Electric Cooperative,
  Inc. P409

KATY

Academy Sports & Outdoors Inc A7
Katy Independent School
  District P282

KILGORE

Martin Resource Management
  Corporation P314
Martin Product Sales Llc P314

LAREDO

International Bancshares Corp. A423

LEWISVILLE

Kmm Telecommunications P286

LITTLE ELM

Retractable Technologies Inc E352

LONGVIEW

Friedman Industries, Inc. E185

LUBBOCK

South Plains Financial Inc A721 E382
Pro Petroleum Llc P428
Plains Cotton Cooperative
  Association P419
Covenant Health System P173
South Plains Financial Inc A721 E382

MCKINNEY

Globe Life Inc A358
Independent Bank Group Inc. A417
  E227
Encore Wire Corp. E135
Independent Bank Group Inc. A417
  E227

MIDLAND

Wtg Gas Processing, L.p. P659
Rattler Midstream Lp E345

NORTH RICHLAND HILLS

Calloway's Nursery, Inc. E64

PASADENA

Floworks International Llc P216
Pasadena Independent School
  District P408
Sunbelt Supply L.p. P525

PLANO

Toyota Motor Credit Corp. A789
Yum China Holdings Inc A875
Plano Independent School
  District P420
North Texas Tollway Authority P384
Diodes, Inc. E120
Tyler Technologies, Inc. E418
Green Brick Partners Inc E199
Ribbon Communications Inc E354

RICHARDSON

Realpage, Inc. P438

ROUND ROCK

Dell Technologies Inc A241
Round Rock Independent School
  District (inc) P451

SAN ANTONIO

Valero Energy Corp A830
Cullen/frost Bankers, Inc. A227
City Public Services Of San
  Antonio P136
City Of San Antonio P133
University Health System Services Of
  Texas, Inc. P613
Northside Independent School
  District P387
Bcfs Health And Human Services P67
County Of Bexar P156

HOOVER'S HANDBOOK OF EMERGING COMPANIES 2022

483

INDEX BY HEADQUARTERS LOCATION

```
A = AMERICAN BUSINESS
E = EMERGING COMPANIES
P = PRIVATE COMPANIES
W = WORLD BUSINESS
```

The University Of Texas Health
  Science Center At San Antonio P587
Christus Santa Rosa Health Care
  Corporation P119
Southwest Research Institute
  Inc P492
San Antonio Independent School
  District Fac P461
San Antonio Water System P461
Victory Capital Holdings Inc
  (de) E439
Xpel Inc E456
Us Global Investors Inc E429

SEGUIN
Alamo Group, Inc. E11

SPRING
Klein Independent School
  District P286

SUGAR LAND
Noble Holding (u.s.)
  Corporation P378
Meglobal Americas Inc. P325

TEMPLE
Mclane Company, Inc. A510 P322
Scott & White Memorial
  Hospital P468
Scott And White Health Plan P468

TEXARKANA
Truman Arnold Companies P600
Yates Group, Inc. P661

THE WOODLANDS
Huntsman Corp A411
Chevron Phillips Chemical Company
  Llc A173 P113
Chevron Phillips Chemical Company
  Limited Partnership A172 P113
Chevron Phillips Chemical Company
  Llc A173 P113
Chevron Phillips Chemical Company
  Limited Partnership A172 P113
H. J. Baker Sulphur, Llc P239
Championx Corp E77
Lgi Homes, Inc. E251
Western Midstream Partners Lp E447
Sterling Construction Co Inc E390
Smart Sand Inc E379

TYLER
Southside Bancshares, Inc. A724
East Texas Medical Center Regional
  Healthcare System P199
Christus Northeast Texas Health
  System Corporation P119
Trinity Mother Frances Health System
  Foundation P599

WACO
Baylor University P65
Brazos Electric Power Cooperative,
  Inc. P86

WESLACO
Idea Public Schools P259

WEST LAKE HILLS
The Drees Company P554

WESTLAKE
Schwab (charles) Corp (the) A697
Goosehead Insurance Inc E196

WICHITA FALLS
The Priddy Foundation A781 P575

WYLIE
North Texas Municipal Water
  District P384

UTAH
AMERICAN FORK
Alpine School District P25

CENTERVILLE
Management & Training
  Corporation P310

DRAPER
Comenity Bank A203 P144
Healthequity Inc E207

FARMINGTON
Davis School District P184

HURRICANE
Dats Trucking, Inc. P184

LOGAN
Utah State University P637

MIDVALE
Ally Bank A32 P24
Overstock.com Inc (de) E309

MURRAY
R1 Rcm Inc E343

NORTH SALT LAKE
Big West Oil, Llc P73

OGDEN
Big West Of California, Llc P73
Afj, Llc P9

PARK CITY
Innovative Industrial Properties
  Inc E228

SALT LAKE CITY
Zions Bancorporation, N.a. A879
State Of Utah A741 P517
Intermountain Health Care Inc A423
  P264
State Of Utah A741 P517
Intermountain Health Care Inc A423
  P264
The University Of Utah P587
Associated Food Stores, Inc. P46
C.r. England, Inc. P92
County Of Salt Lake P168
University Of Utah Health Hospitals
  And Clinics P630
Western Governors University P653
Alsco Inc. P26
Garff Enterprises, Inc. P225
Big-d Construction Corp. P74
Extra Space Storage Inc E152
Security National Financial
  Corp E365

SOUTH SALT LAKE
R.c. Willey Home Furnishings P433
Granite School District P233

ST GEORGE
Ihc Health Services, Inc. A414 P260

WEST JORDAN
Sportsman's Warehouse Holdings
  Inc E384

VERMONT
BURLINGTON
The University Of Vermont Medical
  Center Inc P588
University Of Vermont & State
  Agricultural College P630

MONTPELIER
State Of Vermont A741 P517

MORRISVILLE
Union Bankshares, Inc. (morrisville,
  Vt) E422

RUTLAND
Casella Waste Systems, Inc. E68

VIRGIN ISLANDS
CHRISTIANSTED
Limetree Bay Terminals Llc A479
  P300

VIRGINIA
ALEXANDRIA
95 Express Lanes Llc P1
City Of Alexandria P122

ARLINGTON
Aes Corp A16
County Of Arlington P156
The Nature Conservancy P569
Ceb Inc. P103
American Institutes For Research In
  The Behavioral Sciences P32
Aerovironment, Inc. E6

ASHBURN
Dxc Technology Co A261

BERRYVILLE
Eagle Financial Services, Inc. E127

BLACKSBURG
Virginia Polytechnic Institute & State
  University P642

BLUEFIELD
First Community Bankshares Inc
  (va) A313

BROADLANDS
Loudoun County Public School
  District P303

CENTREVILLE
The Parsons Corporation P573

CHARLOTTESVILLE
The University Of Virginia P589
Rector & Visitors Of The University Of
  Virginia P438
Blue Ridge Bankshares Inc (luray,
  Va) E52
Virginia National Bankshares
  Corp E439

CHESAPEAKE
Dollar Tree Inc A252
City Of Chesapeake P125

CHESTERFIELD
County Of Chesterfield P157

CHRISTIANSBURG
Carilion New River Valley Medical
  Center P99
County Of Montgomery P164

DANVILLE
American National Bankshares, Inc.
  (danville, Va) A49 E21

DULLES
National Rural Utilities Cooperative
  Finance Corp E286

FAIRFAX
Fairfax County Virginia A291 P210
Widepoint Corp E448
Fvcbankcorp Inc E190

Mainstreet Bancshares Inc E258

FALLS CHURCH
Northrop Grumman Corp A568
Inova Health Care Services P262
Inova Health System
  Foundation P262

FLOYD
Parkway Acquisition Corp E313

FREDERICKSBURG
Washington Healthcare Physicians,
  Mary P646

GLEN ALLEN
Markel Corp (holding Co) A497
Asgn Inc E31

HENRICO
County Of Henrico P161

HERNDON
Beacon Roofing Supply Inc A107
Mantech International Corp E259
Stride Inc E393
Strategic Education Inc E391

LEESBURG
County Of Loudoun, Virginia P162

LYNCHBURG
Liberty University, Inc. P299
Centra Health, Inc. P106
Bwx Technologies Inc E58

MANASSAS
Prince William County Public
  Schools P428

MARTINSVILLE
Carter Bankshares Inc A154

MC LEAN
Dyncorp International Llc P198

MCLEAN
Freddie Mac A337
Capital One Financial Corp A148
Booz Allen Hamilton Holding
  Corp. A128
Hilton Worldwide Holdings Inc A388
Primis Financial Corp A640 E333
Gladstone Commercial Corp E193

MECHANICSVILLE
Owens & Minor, Inc. A599

MIDLOTHIAN
Village Bank & Trust Financial
  Corp E439

NEWPORT NEWS
Huntington Ingalls Industries,
  Inc. A410
Riverside Healthcare Association,
  Inc. P445
Riverside Hospital, Inc. P446
City Of Newport News P129
Riverside Regional Medial
  Center P446

NORFOLK
Sentara Healthcare A706 P473
Sentara Hospitals - Norfolk P473
City Of Norfolk P130
Virginia International Terminals,
  Llc P641

PORTSMOUTH
Townebank A789 E411

RESTON
General Dynamics Corp A344
Leidos Holdings Inc A471
Nvr Inc. A577
Science Applications International
  Corp (new) A698

INDEX BY HEADQUARTERS LOCATION

Caci International Inc A141
Idemia Identity & Security Usa
  Llc P259
John Marshall Bancorp Inc E238

RICHMOND
Performance Food Group Co A619
Altria Group Inc A36
Carmax Inc. A153
Dominion Energy Inc (new) A254
Genworth Financial, Inc. (holding
  Co) A351
Virginia Electric & Power Co. A838
Atlantic Union Bankshares Corp A79
  E34
Commonwealth Of Virginia A209
  P146
Virginia Housing Development
  Authority A838 P641
Commonwealth Of Virginia A209
  P146
Vcu Health System Authority P640
Estes Express Lines P208
Virginia Department Of
  Transportation P641
Virginia Premier Health Plan,
  Inc. P642
Gpm Investments, Llc P232
City Of Richmond P132
Apple Hospitality Reit, Inc. P40
Virginia Commonwealth
  University P641
Virginia Housing Development
  Authority A838 P641
Arko Corp E30
Atlantic Union Bankshares Corp A79
  E34
Kinsale Capital Group Inc E241

ROANOKE
Carilion Medical Center P99
Carilion Services, Inc. P100

TIMBERVILLE
F & M Bank Corp. E153

TYSONS
Computer Sciences Corporation A212
  P149
Alarm.com Holdings Inc E12

VIRGINIA BEACH
Navy Exchange Service
  Command P365
City Of Virginia Beach P135
Atlantic Diving Supply, Inc. P47
Armada Hoffler Properties Inc E30

WINCHESTER
Valley Health System Group
  Return P638
County Of Frederick P159
American Woodmark Corp. E23
Trex Co Inc E412

WOODBRIDGE
County Of Prince William P167

YORKTOWN
County Of York P173

WASHINGTON

BELLEVUE
T-mobile Us Inc A757
Paccar Inc. A602
Overlake Hospital Association P402
Overlake Hospital Medical
  Center P402
Terreno Realty Corp E406

BELLINGHAM
Haggen, Inc. P240
Exp World Holdings Inc E152

BREMERTON
Harrison Medical Center P242

CASHMERE
Cashmere Valley Bank Washington
  (new) E69

EVERETT
County Of Snohomish P170
Public Utility District 1 Of Snohomish
  County P431
Coastal Financial Corp (wa) E88

HOQUIAM
Timberland Bancorp, Inc. E409

ISSAQUAH
Costco Wholesale Corp A222

KENT
Petrocard, Inc. P413

KIRKLAND
King County Public Hospital District
  2 P286
Monolithic Power Systems Inc E278

LYNNWOOD
U&i Financial Corp E419

MOUNTLAKE TERRACE
Fs Bancorp Inc (washington) E188

OLYMPIA
Heritage Financial Corp (wa) A383
  E212
State Of Washington A741 P518
Heritage Financial Corp (wa) A383
  E212

PORT ANGELES
First Northwest Bancorp E173

REDMOND
Microsoft Corporation A528
Lake Washington School
  District P291

RENTON
Providence Health & Services A647
  P429
Providence Health & Services -
  Oregon P429
Providence Health & Services-
  washington P430
Public Hospital District 1 Of King
  County P431
First Financial Northwest Inc E168

RICHLAND
Kadlec Regional Medical Center P278

SEATTLE
Amazon.com Inc A37
Starbucks Corp. A731
Nordstrom, Inc. A564
Weyerhaeuser Co A861
Expeditors International Of
  Washington, Inc. A289
Expedia Group Inc A288
Zillow Group Inc A877
Alaska Air Group, Inc. A25
Washington Federal Inc A846
Homestreet Inc A395
University Of Washington Inc A825
  P631
County Of King P161
Swedish Health Services P530
Northwest Dairy Association P388
Virginia Mason Medical Center P642
Seattle Schools District No. 1 Of King
  County Washington P471
The City Of Seattle-city Light
  Department P550
Broadmark Realty Capital Inc E56
Sound Financial Bancorp Inc E381

SPOKANE
Northwest Farm Credit Services A570
  P388
Urm Stores, Inc. P635
Northwest Farm Credit Services A570
  P388
Potlatchdeltic Corp E328

TACOMA
Columbia Banking System Inc A201
  E92
Multicare Health System P357
County Of Pierce P166
Franciscan Health System P219
Tacoma Public Schools P532
Columbia Banking System Inc A201
  E92

VANCOUVER
Peacehealth P408
Southwest Washington Health
  System P493
County Of Clark P157
Nautilus Inc E288
Northwest Pipe Co. E296

WALLA WALLA
Banner Corp. A101

WEST VIRGINIA

CHARLESTON
United Bankshares Inc A813 E423
City Holding Co. A185 E84
State Of West Virginia A741 P518
Charleston Area Medical Center,
  Inc. P110
United Bankshares Inc A813 E423
City Holding Co. A185 E84

FAIRMONT
Monongahela Power Company P351
Mvb Financial Corp E283

MOOREFIELD
Summit Financial Group Inc A749
  E394

MORGANTOWN
West Virginia United Health System,
  Inc. P651
West Virginia University Hospitals,
  Inc. P651
West Virginia University P651

WHEELING
Wesbanco Inc A853 E444

WISCONSIN

APPLETON
U.s. Venture, Inc. A804 P606
The Boldt Group Inc P546

BEAVER DAM
United Cooperative P610

BELOIT
Blackhawk Bancorp Inc E52

BROOKFIELD
Fiserv Inc A325
Cib Marine Bancshares Inc E82

EAU CLAIRE
Citizens Community Bancorp Inc
  (md) E83

FITCHBURG
Certco, Inc. P109

GLENDALE
Johnson Controls, Inc. A441 P277

Wheaton Franciscan Services,
  Inc. P654

GREEN BAY
Schneider National Inc (wi) A696
Associated Banc-corp A74
Nicolet Bankshares Inc A562 E293
Krueger International, Inc. P288
Nicolet Bankshares Inc A562 E293

JANESVILLE
Mercy Health System
  Corporation P333

LA CROSSE
Kwik Trip, Inc. P289
Gundersen Lutheran Medical Center,
  Inc. P238
Gundersen Lutheran Administrative
  Services Inc. P238

LA FARGE
Cooperative Regions Of Organic
  Producer Pools P153

MADISON
First Business Financial Services,
  Inc. A311
State Of Wisconsin A742 P518
Wisconsin Housing And Economic
  Development Authority A867
Wisconsin Alumni Research
  Foundation A867
State Of Wisconsin A742 P518
University Of Wisconsin System P632
University Of Wisconsin Hospitals And
  Clinics Authority P631
County Of Dane P158

MANITOWOC
Bank First Corp A94 E45
Orion Energy Systems Inc E306

MARSHFIELD
Security Health Plan Of Wisconsin,
  Inc. P472
Marshfield Clinic, Inc. P313
Mchs Hospitals Inc P321

MENOMONEE FALLS
Kohl's Corp. A458

MEQUON
Charter Manufacturing Company,
  Inc. P111

MIDDLETON
University Of Wisconsin Medical
  Foundation, Inc. P632

MILWAUKEE
Manpowergroup Inc A494
Wec Energy Group Inc A851
Rockwell Automation, Inc. A684
Mgic Investment Corp. (wi) A522
Aurora Health Care, Inc. A79 P52
Froedtert Memorial Lutheran
  Hospital, Inc. P223
Aurora Health Care Metro, Inc P51
The Medical College Of Wisconsin
  Inc P566
Milwaukee Public Schools (inc) P345
Wisconsin Milwaukee County P658
Rite-hite Holding Corporation P445
Robert W Baird & Co Inc P448
Marquette University P313
Froedtert Health, Inc. P222
Children's Hospital Of Wisconsin,
  Inc P116
Physicians Realty Trust E323

MOUNT HOREB
Duluth Holdings Inc E124

NEENAH
Thedacare, Inc. P592

HOOVER'S HANDBOOK OF EMERGING COMPANIES 2022

485

INDEX BY HEADQUARTERS LOCATION

> A = AMERICAN BUSINESS
> E = EMERGING COMPANIES
> P = PRIVATE COMPANIES
> W = WORLD BUSINESS

OSHKOSH
Oshkosh Corp (new) A597

RACINE
Johnson Outdoors Inc E238

RIPON
Alliance Laundry Holdings Llc P23

SUN PRAIRIE
Independent Pharmacy
  Cooperative P261

WAUKESHA
American Transmission Company,
  Llc P34
Waukesha Memorial Hospital,
  Inc. P647
Generac Holdings Inc E190

WAUSAU
Aspirus, Inc. P45
Aspirus Wausau Hospital, Inc. P45

WAUWATOSA
Waterstone Financial Inc (md) E444
Teb Bancorp Inc E402

WYOMING

GILLETTE
Cloud Peak Energy Resources
  Llc P139

Index of Executives

A

A, Juliet V Garc A776:P558
A.O, Genevieve Bell W135
Aagard, Linda P588
Aaholm, Sherry A228:A584
Aamodt, Patsy P41
Aamund, Marie-Louise W168
Aanenson, Gary P103
Aaroe, David P218
Aaron, Craig A131
Aaron, Susan A400
Aaron, Steven L P520
Aaron, Clay P520
Aaron, Todd P520
Aaron, Susan E218
Aasheim, Hilde W363
Abadin, Antonio Abril W243
Abalos, Glenda C P434
Abando, Napoleon P P335
Abani, Priya A436
Abate, Christopher A668
Abatti, Mike P261
Abbas, Fouad P300
Abbas, Syed P352
Abbasi, Faraz A466:E244
Abbey, Richard A285
Abbey, Donald E117:E220
Abbott, Henry A707
Abbott, Greg A741
Abbott, Jordan P158
Abbott, Mary J P271
Abbott, Amber P427
Abbott, Greg P517
Abbott, Michael W30
Abbott, Swati E139
Abbott, John E309
Abbott, Henry E368
Abdalla, Zein A786
Abdalla, Amy P428
Abdallah, Chaouki P228:P625
Abdel-Kerim, Ahmed P39
Abdelhafiz, Gada M P243
Abdelrahman, Emad P589
Abdool-Samad, Tasneem W6
Abdou, Nicklaus P218
Abdrabbuh, Samir A. Al W422
Abduljalil, Hala P502
Abdullah, Butool P102
Abdullah, Ahmad Sufian Che W128
Abdullah, Enick Jasani Bin W232
Abdullah, Mohd Suhail W307
Abe, Atsushi A591
Abe, Yasuyuki W459
Abe, Toshinori W491
Abel, Greg A113
Abel, Gregory E A113
Abel, Robert A529
Abel, James A549
Abel, Gregory A604
Abel, Melchiore A640
Abel, Brian Van A871
Abel, Gregory E P386
Abel, Nir W253
Abel, Robert E274
Abel, James E290
Abel, Melchiore E333

Abel, Wanda E339
Abele, Lawrence P216
Abele, Chris P658
Abelli, Donna A416:E226
Abelman, Jerome W93
Abelsen, James N P483
Abelson, David P406
Abenoja, Maureen P482
Abercrombie, Les P222
Abercrombie, Barbara P627
Abernathy, Kathleen A249
Abernethy, Matthew E290
Abeyta, Mary P154
Abgrall-Teslyk, Karine W290
Ables, Dorothy A501
Ables, Dorothy M P494
Abney, David A338:A569
Aboaf, Eric A743
Aboitiz, Jon R P427
Abou-Khalil, Nassib W359
Abou-Oaf, Ehab A455
Aboularage, Anthony P222
Aboumrad, Daniel Hajj W28
Abraham, Edward A574
Abraham, Spencer A612
Abraham, Tara A617
Abraham, Edward A801
Abraham, Karen P78
Abraham, Shema P290
Abraham, Joseph W134
Abraham, Melissa E187
Abraham, Allison E309
Abraham, Chad R E326
Abraham, Neil E347
Abraham, Silji E446
Abrahams, Gary E144
Abrahamson, Vickie P592
Abramovich, Aharon W253
Abramowitz, Bernard H P373
Abrams, Mandy P135
Abrams, Robin P244:E370
Abrams-Rivera, Carlos A460
Abramson, Andrew A832
Abramson, Steven E426
Abramson, Andrew E431
Abreg, Mart N A776:P558
Abrega, Martfn A776:P558
Abruzzo, Pat P283
Absher, Jody A207
Abston, Tyson A370:E203
Abundis, Susan A709:E370
Abutineh, Mike P60
Accogli, Giuseppe A106
Ace, Brian A209
Ace, Heather A657
Ace, Brian E95
Acebedo, Eduardo E6
Aceto, Joe P462
Acevedo, Sylvia A657
Acevedo, Dana-Lise P67
Acevedo, Elizabeth P371
Acevedo, Elizabeth P377
Acevedo, Debby P451
Aceves, Abraham P214
Ach, Heidi P159
Achard, Stephane W341
Achary, Michael A372

Achat, Catherine P161
Ache, Sean P467
Acheson, Eleanor D P364
Achten, Dominik von W222
Achtenberg, Jeff P556
Ackerman, Joel A237
Ackerman, Eileen P335
Ackerman, Melissa Melshenker P429
Ackerman, Jeffrey C P559
Ackland, Michael W485
Ackroyd, Jim A8:P4
Acord, Elizabeth L P96
Acord, Kevan E265
Acosta, Juan A838
Acosta, Philip A P486
Acosta, Juan P641
Acosta-Trant, Ivette P59
Acres, Harold R P174
Acton, Brian E197
Acut, Sabino W83
Adachi, Barbara A586
Adachi, Hiroshi P94
Adachi, Tamaki W418
Adair, Troy A294
Adair, Donald D P530
Adair, A. Jayson E101
Adair, Troy E156
Adali, Erhan W540
Adam, Mark P422
Adam, Bradley J P492
Adam, Abdulmajid Y P497
Adam, Christos W188
Adamany, Linda A437
Adamany, Stephanie A867
Adamczyk, Darius A398
Adamo, Robert A648
Adamo, Emma W45
Adams, Shirley A15
Adams, Katherine A65
Adams, Laura A251
Adams, Kevin D A166:A217
Adams, Lesley A251
Adams, Steven A308
Adams, Milburn A393
Adams, Gregory A A445
Adams, Janice A445
Adams, John A554
Adams, Ann A566
Adams, Bradley A587
Adams, Brad A602
Adams, Marty A639
Adams, Tracey A674
Adams, John A697
Adams, Richard A814
Adams, J Phillip P9
Adams, Jacob P41
Adams, Alecia P80
Adams, Kevin D P110
Adams, Korey P120
Adams, Lancing P122
Adams, Cathy P140
Adams, Kevin D P151
Adams, Susan P163
Adams, Alan P251
Adams, Patricia P271
Adams, Leah P275
Adams, Gregory A P279

Adams, Janice P279
Adams, Joe M P282
Adams, H E P285:P285
Adams, Martin P303
Adams, Martin L P303
Adams, Connie P315
Adams, Megan P347
Adams, Mary P449
Adams, Kerry P452
Adams, Jason M P457
Adams, Dan P464
Adams, Nancy P508
Adams, Heather P542
Adams, Neil J P547
Adams, Mary Jane P614
Adams, Paul W410
Adams, Robert E24
Adams, Joseph E188
Adams, Milburn E217
Adams, Joseph E297
Adams, Bradley E302
Adams, Marty E332
Adams, Tracey E348
Adams, Richard E423
Adcock, Robert A393
Adcock, Mary A461
Adcock, David B P196
Adcock, Bradley T P626
Adcock, Robert E217
Addiscott, Lynn P612
Addison, Linda A359
Addison, Ann A569
Addison, John A640
Addison, Lewis C P107
Addison, Ann P652
Addison, John E333
Adebo, Olo P184
Adebowale, Victor W132
Adefioye, Elizabeth A273
Adelgren, Paul E194
Adelman, Jeffrey D E457
Aditya, Mahesh A695
Adkerson, Richard A338
Adkins, Rodney A88:A363
Adkins, Chuck A414
Adkins, Rodney A611
Adkins, Kedrick A642
Adkins, Lewis A690
Adkins, Rodney A819
Adkins, Chuck A259
Adkins, Heather P550
Adkins, David E52
Adler, Paul A180
Adler, Steve P123
Adler, Reuven W253
Adofo-Wilson, Baye A113
Adolphsen, Nick A737:P513
Adt, Katrin W108
Advaithi, Revathi W197
Adzema, Kurt A694
Adzema, Gregg E105
Adzick, Susan A511:P322
Aeilts, Toby E53
Afable, Richard P502
Afaleq, Mohammed Al W407
Affleck-Graves, John A1
Afienko, Abbey P332

HOOVER'S HANDBOOK OF EMERGING COMPANIES 2022

COMBINED HOOVER'S HANDBOOK INDEX OF EXECUTIVES

A = AMERICAN BUSINESS
E = EMERGING COMPANIES
P = PRIVATE COMPANIES
W = WORLD BUSINESS

Aflague, Ermina P603
Afonicheva, Ludmila P596
Afzal, Zahid A639:E332
Agamanolis, Stefan P118
Agar, Rich E284
Agassi, Ronen W64
Agbaje, Segun A619
Agbamu, Omoyefe P261
Agbe-Davies, Christopher P494
Ageborg, Katarina W46
Agee, Nancy A49
Agee, Nancy Howell P99
Agee, Shannon P579
Agee, Nancy E21
Agerbo, Sussie Dvinge W515
Agg, Andy W342
Aggarwal, Rohit A411
Aggarwal, Nidhi P70
Aggarwal, Prateek P244
Aggersbjerg, Peter E273
Aggus, Gary P251
Aghili, Aziz A234
Aglialoro, Cilia P122
Agnefjaell, Peter W283
Agnew, Hugh L P560
Agogue, Christophe W184
Agoro, Kamaldeen P307
Agosto, Paula P549
Agrawal, Ajay A154
Agrawal, Vishal A406
Agrawal, Parag A801
Agrawal, Saurabh W478
Agrawal, Durga E186
Agree, Richard E8
Agree, Joel E8
Agroskin, Daniel A139
Aguero, Rocio P384
Aguila, Adrian P126
Aguilar, Victor A643
Aguilar, Edgard Corrales A723
Aguilar, Jose P303
Aguilar, Gayla P381
Aguilar, Leslie P467
Aguilera, Ernesto P499
Aguinaga, Elizabeth A192
Aguirre, Fernando A232
Aguirre, Artie A750
Aguirre, Fernando A752
Aguirre, Luz A781
Aguirre, Ramon P462
Aguirre, Artie P528
Aguirre, Luz P581
Agustin, Virgil P61
Agustin, Juan Pablo San W145
Aheran, Patrick P497
Ahern, Patrick A75
Ahern, Theresa M P97
Ahern, Paula P208
Aherrera, David P270
Ahlberg, Gregory A4
Ahlborn, Andrew E346
Ahlgrimm, Marijo P32
Ahlmann, Kaj A680:E356
Ahlstrom, Jonas W446
Ahlund, Pontus W470
Ahmad, Zubaid A702
Ahmad, Nasrin P596
Ahmad, Abdul Rahman bin W128
ahmad, Mohd Nasir W128
Ahmad, Kamaludin W307
Ahmadjian, Christina W462
Ahmaine, Mohammed W395
Ahmed, Sohail A467
Ahmed, Elizabeth A827
Ahmed, Riaz W497
Ahmed, Ajaz W533
Ahmed, Asmau A343
Ahmedfiqi, Osman P330
Ahn, John A374
Ahn, Hong P596
Ahn, Nadine W412

Ahn, Hyo Ryeol W438
Ahn, Phillip E42
Ahn, Kijun E315
Ahola, Aaron E11
Ahrens, Jere M P206
Ahrens, Chris P554
Ahtone, Caylen P113
Ahuja, Deepak A550
Ahuja, Kishore P379
Ai, Sachiko W369
Aiba, Tetsuya W255
Aichele, Stephen A208
Aichele, William A826
Aichele, Stephen P146
Aichele, William E428
Aijaz, Mufti Irshad Ahmed W64
Aiken, Robert A287
Aiken, Jason A345:A873
Aikens, Jason P258
Aila, Minna W346
Aime, Reginald Fils - A138
Aing, Melissa A512:P326
Ainsworth, Anne-Marie A390
Ainsworth, Larry K P502
Aisd, Aaron P43
Aish, Bassil P253
Aitcheson, Latoya P126
Aitken, Stuart A461:P309
Aivano, Joseph P209
Aiyar, Priya A41
Aizpiri, Arturo Gonzalo W400
Aja, Juan Carlos W525
Ajemyan, Arthur A673
Ajmani, Deep P390
Akamatsu, Yayoi P378
Akar, Joseph P661
Akash, Dave P89
Akbari, Homaira A468:W61
Akeman, Jeff P379
Aken, Mary P160
Aker, Mark P131
Akers, Jeffery P394
Akerstroem, Carina W471
Akhavan, Chris P230
Akhtar, Rizwan A666
Akimoto, Toshiya W437
Akimoto, Nobuhide W494
Akimov, Andrei W385
Akin, Richard L P454
Akins, Nicholas A44:A306
Akins, Terry A317
Akins, Nicholas K P30
Akins, Terry E170
Akita, Seiichiro W65
Akiya, Fumio W437
Akiyama, Katsusada W272
Akiyama, Satoru W272
Akiyama, Yasuji W288
Akiyama, Sakie W325:W373
Akiyoshi, Shiro P185
Akkol, Ozgur W281
Akkus, Senar W504
Akman, Jeffrey S P560
Akom, Francis P451
Akpakli, George P112
Akram, Adil P53
Akseli, Ari W275
Aksyutin, Oleg W385
Akutagawa, Tomomi W36
Al-Abdulla, Hussein Ali W134
Al-Abdulla, Hussain Ali W522
Al-Anzi, Abdullah W423
Al-Awfi, Talal W334
Al-Azzawi, Moutaz W407
Al-bayat, Isam Bin Alwan W422
Al-bilaihed, Mohammed Bin
   Abdulrahman W422
Al-dosary, Mahdi Nasser W422
Al-Fadli, Abdulla Ahmed W134
Al-Ghanoudi, Ashirf P231
Al-ghubaini, Humoud Bin Awdah W422
Al-gnoon, Khalid Bin Hamad W422
Al-Haffar, Maher W109
Al-hogail, Abdulmalik Bin
   Abdullah W422
Al-Jaber, Hessa Sultan W522
Al-jabr, Yehia Bin Ali W422

Al-Kaabi, Nasser W395
Al-khudair, Khaled Walid W407
Al-koraya, Nader W407
Al-lazzam, Faisal Bin
   Mohammed W422
Al-Mohannadi, Hamad W411
Al-Murshed, Ziad Thamer W422
Al-Nahas, Mohammed
   Talal W407:W422
Al-Naja, Mohammed Abo W407
Al-obayed, Abdulrahman Bin
   Mohammed W422
Al-Oraini, Abdullah Ali W407
Al-Otaibi, Mohammed W407
Al-Oudan, Abdulaziz W422
Al-Qudaibi, Talal W407
Al-Qurri, Walid Bin Sulaiman W64
Al-Rammah, Jamal W407
Al-sada, Ibrahim Bin Abdullah W423
Al-Sadhan, Tareq W407
Al-Saleh, Adel W95:W163
Al-Shaikh, Ahmed W422
Al-sudairi, Fahad Bin Hussein W422
Al-thani, Jassim Bin W395
Al-twaijri, Sulaiman Bin
   Abdulaziz W422
Al-Wehibi, Nader Ibrahim W422
Al-yahya, Mohammed W407
Al-zahrani, Riyadh W407
Al-zahrani, Jamaan Bin Ali W422
Al-Zamil, Riyadh Bin Fahad W422
Alabbadi, Mohammed W423
Alameddine, A.R. A629
Alaniz, Anastacio P644
Alaoudah, Emad W423
Alarcon, Juan Carlos W525
Alarid, Andy P542
Alati, Jorge Perez W110
Alba, Adriana P245
Alba, Botero P286
Albam, Amy P154
Alban, Pamela K P156
Albanese, Dominic P182
Albanese, Craig P372
Albano, Charles A7
Albataineh, Rania P59
Alber, Laura A692:A865
Alberici, John S P16:P16:P17
Albers, Martin W190
Albert, Andrew A553
Albert, Frances P15
Albert, Andrew P370
Albert, Hans P376
Albert, Barbara W190
Albert, Mario W239
Albertelli, Christine P547
Alberti, Pat P53
Albertine, John E240
Alberto, Carl P506
Alberts, Jim P209
Albi, Carlos W444
Albinson, Brock A81
Albo, Pina A672
Albrecht, Julie A721
Albrecht, Angela A740
Albrecht, Raymond P P342
Albrecht, Angela P516
Albrecht, Stan L P637
Albrecht, Felix W219
Albrectsen, Anne-Birgitte P420
Albright, Steven A741
Albright, Matt P55
Albright, Steven P517
Albright, Annetta P609
Albuquerque, Isabella Saboya De W513
Alcoser, Lisa P613
Aldabbagh, Khalid Hashim W422
Aldag, Edward E265
Aldeborgh, John E E40
Aldinger, Mike A410
Aldott, Zoltan W333
Aldred, John P251
Aldrich, Jeff A811
Aldrich, David P431
Aldrich, Angie P470
Aldridge, Bill P93
Aldridge, W. Stephen E430

Alegre, Daniel A10
Alegria, Esther E39
Alekperov, Vagit W386
Alemany, Ellen A304
Alemayehou, Mimi A801
Ales, Donna P290
Alessandrini, Evaline P607
Alessandro, Gianpaolo W509
Alexander, Angelique A7
Alexander, Keith A38
Alexander, Douglas A58
Alexander, Susan H A118
Alexander, Mark A139
Alexander, Robert A148
Alexander, Lee A185
Alexander, John A312
Alexander, Marilyn A359
Alexander, Victor A453
Alexander, Mark A502
Alexander, Keith A512
Alexander, Craig H A614
Alexander, Timothy A724
Alexander, Alica A738
Alexander, John A789
Alexander, Jackie P25
Alexander, Paul G P61
Alexander, Pamela P124
Alexander, Kenneth Cooper P130
Alexander, Kelvin P158
Alexander, Craig P179
Alexander, Allen P185
Alexander, Barbara J P228
Alexander, Barbara P228
Alexander, David P252
Alexander, Wendy P290
Alexander, Keith P327
Alexander, Sherrie P336
Alexander, Kevin P348
Alexander, Joel P387
Alexander, Jim P410
Alexander, David George A P472
Alexander, Alica P514
Alexander, Ralph P532
Alexander, Randy P598
Alexander, Tim P610
Alexander, Gordon P638
Alexander, David E64
Alexander, Paul E239
Alexander, Patrick E245
Alexander, Marcellus E364
Alexander, Robert E365
Alexander, Mark E443
Alexanderson, Marcus W402
Alfano, Jeffrey J E305
Alfaraj, Haithem W423
Alfonsi, Davide W251
Alfonso, Humberto A264
Alfonso, David P198
Alfonso, Daniel P390
Alford, Peggy A520:A611
Alford, Mack L P509
Alford, Donald E300
Alfred, Jim A724
Alfred, Ben P283
Algate, Scott P388
Alger, Eugene A289
Alger, Robert P292
Alghamdi, Ahmed W423
Algiere, Dennis A847
Ali, Mohamad A696
Ali, Saiyed A735
Ali, Mr Mushtaq P126
Ali, Saiyed P510
Ali, Frank P651
Alias, Abdul Farid W307
Alias, Patrick E89
Alicandri, John P257
Alisov, Vladimir W208
Alix, Gilles W519
Alkanhl, Abdullah Abdulrahman W423
Alkhayyal, Abdulaziz A496
Alkire, Joseph A836
Alkire, Michael P426
Allain, Bernard W90
Allaire, Bella Loykhter A663:P436
Allaire, Martin W322
Allam, Anthony P63

488

HOOVER'S HANDBOOK OF EMERGING COMPANIES 2022

COMBINED HOOVER'S HANDBOOK INDEX OF EXECUTIVES

Allan, Donald A731
Allanson, Katherine E440
Allard, Tania P15
Allard, John P167
Allard, Francis P351
Allardice, David R A299
Allardice, Robert A377:E132
Allcon, Alvin J P540
Alldian, David P P79
Alleckson, Will A24:P13
Allemand, Anita A843
Allen, Hubert A4
Allen, Quincy A7
Allen, Sharon A28:A96
Allen, Bertrand-Marc A124
Allen, James A249
Allen, Mark A302
Allen, Barbara A403
Allen, Richard A420
Allen, Robert W A423
Allen, William A436
Allen, Quincy A490
Allen, Jon A517
Allen, Analisa A523
Allen, Scott A527
Allen, Quincy A583
Allen, Stephen A593
Allen, B. Marc A643
Allen, Barry A661
Allen, Lee A736
Allen, Samuel A863
Allen, Mike P12
Allen, Sharon P18
Allen, Darrell P45
Allen, Les P73
Allen, Diane P101
Allen, Betsy P124
Allen, Jeff P147
Allen, Brenda P168
Allen, Joseph A P175
Allen, David P182
Allen, Charles P216
Allen, Herbert P216
Allen, Diane P220
Allen, Robert W P264
Allen, Daniel P P266
Allen, Stephen P P285
Allen, Thomas P291
Allen, Ellon P314
Allen, Jon P331
Allen, Erin P388
Allen, Mark P420
Allen, Karen P422
Allen, Jerold W P446
Allen, Teresa P453
Allen, Kristen P463
Allen, Meredith P509
Allen, Lee P512
Allen, Gloria P522
Allen, Elizabeth Heller P567
Allen, Richard D P578
Allen, Dee P623
Allen, Gary P625
Allen, Ken W162
Allen, Jennifer W191
Allen, Steve W405
Allen, George E30
Allen, Jeremy E78
Allen, James E122:E180
Allen, Michael E274
Allen, Joel E286
Allen, Jeffrey E395
Allen, Tonya E396
Allenbaugh, Laurel A320:E173
Allendorf, Richard A347
Allera, Marc W95
Alley, Derek P640
Allgood, Jeri P163
Allgood, Scot P637
Allison, John A393
Allison, Clyde A566
Allison, Richard A732
Allison, Amanda A779
Allison, Les P238
Allison, Amanda P568
Allison, John P609
Allison, R. Dirk E4

Allison, John E217
Allman, Keith A502
Allnutt, Lauren A567
Allocca, Lori P488
Allon, Andrea A229:E112
Alloway, Jay P281
Allred, Mark P76
Allsman, Nicole A824:P617
Allsup, Lonnie P9
Alm, Roger W523
Almaguer, Everardo Elizondo W109
Almandrez, Mary G P628
Almaraz, Jose P51
Almaraz, Frank P136
Almberg, Jeanette W446
Almeida, Jose A106
Almeida, Edmar De W206
Almeida, Flavia Buarque De W506
Almendinger, Carrie E207
Almirante, Paulo W184
Almog, Yael W63
Almon, Robert C P403
Almond, Heather E430
Almquist, Andrew P19
Almquist, Jeff P169
Alnowaiser, Turqi W219
Aloma, Angel P217
Alonazi, Riyad W423
Alonso, Joseph Anthony W70
Alonso, Mercedes W346
Alonso, Rudolfo Figueroa W381
Alonzo, Annette A227
Alonzo, Leonicio P55
Alonzo, Anne E329
Alp, Hakan W540
Alpay, John M P97
Alpen, Joachim W446
Alperin, Barry A437:A696
Alpert, Marc A486
Alpert, Robert H E111
Alpert, Henry E202
Alpert, Jordan E398
Alpert-Romm, Adria A248
Alpuche, Charles E233
Alqueres, Jose Luiz W506
Alsaad, Bader A120
Alseth, Becky E289
Alsip, Bryan P613
Alsobrooks, Angela P228
Alstead, Troy A477:P297
Alston, Cheryl A359
Alston, Littleton P175
Alston, Asia P552
Alstrom, Eric P181
Alsuwaidi, Faisal W411
Alt, Aaron A755
Altamirano, Heidi P441
Altemose, Cheryl P69
Alter, Jeffrey A63
Althann, Natica Von A637
Althofer, Eric E256
Althoff, Judson A529
Althoff, Daniel W48
Althoff, Sven W218
Altintas, N. W21
Altman, Randall A138
Altman, Samuel A288
Altman, Louis A639
Altman, Dara A714
Altman, Theresa P298
Altman, Jeffrey P335
Altman, Richard P417
Altman, Steven E117
Altman, Roger E149
Altman, Louis E332
Altmueller, Wolfgang W81
Altobello, Nancy A60
Altomare, Ronald P61
Alton, Gregg P427:E102
Altoro, Joaquin A867
Altozano, Angel Manuel
  Garcia W9:W227
Altschaefl, Michael E307
Altschuler, Steven M P549
Altshuler, David A835
Alund, Petra W446
Aluotto, Jeff P160

Aluria, Deelip A679
Alvarado, Donna A227:A608
Alvarado, Joseph A632
Alvarado, Anna A770
Alvarado, Lily P193
Alvarado, Rodrigo S P202
Alvarado, Paulina P352
Alvarado, Douglas P404
Alvarado, Donna E312
Alvarado, Janice P411
Alvarado, Rodrigo Huidobro W177
Alvarado, Rodrigo Huidobro W177
Alvarez, Raul A488
Alvarez, Ignacio A634
Alvarez, Miguel A745
Alvarez, Oscar A750
Alvarez, Jose A786
Alvarez, Cesar A849
Alvarez, Jordan P109
Alvarez, Vanessa P441
Alvarez, Yannette P521
Alvarez, Saide P533
Alvarez, Carlos P534
Alvarez, David E283
Alvarez, Cesar E387
Alvarez, Aida E393
Alvather, Jay P535
Alvera, Marco A691
Alves, Paget A76:A875
Alves, David P67
Alves, Danny P608
Alves, Herculano Anibal W309
Alves, Rodrigo W380
Alvey, John E265
Alvez, Leo W417
Alviene, Dana A439
Alviti, Paulette A535
Alymova, Natalya W424
Alzamora, Esteban P404
Alziari, Lucien A649
Amadi, Mariette Y P252
Amado, Luis Filipe Marques W172
Amado, Nuno Manuel da Silva W172
Amador, Fernando P71
Amano, Reiko W170
Amano, Hiromasa W268
Amar, Kristopher P492
Amaral, Donald A793
Amaral, Decio de Sampaio W506
Amaral, Donald E414
Amaro, Denise P255
Amatayakul, Parnsiree W441
Amato, Joseph A298
Amato, Louis P P552
Amato, Paolo W391
Amato, Elizabeth E147
Amaya, Nicolas A449
Amazan, Gaelle P322
Ambe, Kazushi W454
Amble, Joan A129
Ambrose, Annemarie P165
Ambrozie, Tony P57
Ambush, Justin P316
Amdahl, Rachel E126
Amecangelo, Dave P571
Ameen, Philip A405
Ameismeier, Donna P453
Amelio, William A691
Amen, Darrell van A396
Amend, Michael W213
America, Carmine W294
Amerson, Tim A20:P11
Ames, Johanna A546
Ames, Raymond G P36
Ames, Craig P91
Ames, Richard P207
Ametsreiter, Hannes W520
Amezcua, Rhonda P163
Amin, Bharat A410
Amirali, Ali A733:E389
Ammann, Erich W425
Amon, Cristiano A656
Amonette, Alison J P656
Amore, John W189
Amorim, Paula Fernanda Ramos W206
Amoroso, Stefano W293
Amorous, Martin P542
Amos, Daniel A18

Amos, Sister Helen P334
Amoudi, Omar Bin Abdullah Al W422
Amranand, Piyasvasti W270
Amruthur, Iyer P284
Amsden, Mark W413
Amsell, David P453
Amster, Laura F P29
Amstrong, C Micheal A778:P564
Amunategui, Domingo Cruzat W179
Amundsen, Ashley P25
Amundson, Laura P47
An, Weizhe P338
An, Zhiqiang W81
An, Cong Hui W208
An-Heid, Ling E214
Anagnost, Andrew E38
Analdo, Stephen F P410
Anami, Masaya W67
Anand, Manish P244
Anand, Sudeep P484
Anand, Dorai W395
Ananthothai, Thongchai W62
Anapa, Pinar W21
Anasenes, Nicole E27
Anata, Kazuhisa W237
Anaya, Lisa P662
Anbouba, Imad A750
Ancher-Jensen, Henrik A21
Ancheta, Mark V P596
Anchoori, Ravi A439:P276
Ancira, Carlos Eduardo Aldrete W198
Anda, Javier de A424
Andaluz, Jannette A210
Andel, Steve Van A35
Andel, Stephen Van A719
Andel, Steve Van P3:P27
Andel, Stephen Van P486
Anderman, Steven P89
Anders, Amber A739:P515
Andersen, Paul A257
Andersen, Michelle P268
Andersen, Lynn P327
Andersen, Connie P465
Andersen, Eric W35
Andersen, Jens W168
Andersen, Kim Krogh W484
Andersen, Nils W510
Andersen, Henrik W514
Andersen, Robert E456
Anderson, John A27
Anderson, David A44
Anderson, Michael A61
Anderson, Jolen A99
Anderson, Kristine A129
Anderson, Shelia A200
Anderson, Peter A228
Anderson, Gerard A258
Anderson, Steven A276
Anderson, Anthony A286
Anderson, Beverly A288
Anderson, Lars A306
Anderson, James A315
Anderson, Brian A363
Anderson, Paul A366
Anderson, Charlotte A388
Anderson, Harvey A404
Anderson, Scott A423
Anderson, Carl A A458
Anderson, Anthony A500
Anderson, Bradley A550
Anderson, Douglas A604
Anderson, John A618
Anderson, Michelle A667
Anderson, Sarah A673
Anderson, Scott A683
Anderson, Kerrii A708
Anderson, Jill A722
Anderson, Lawrence A724
Anderson, S. Elaine A724
Anderson, Adam A734
Anderson, James A745
Anderson, Barbara A773
Anderson, Crystal A825
Anderson, Helen A825
Anderson, Jennifer A866
Anderson, Lesley P44
Anderson, Erik P45

COMBINED HOOVER'S HANDBOOK INDEX OF EXECUTIVES

A = AMERICAN BUSINESS
E = EMERGING COMPANIES
P = PRIVATE COMPANIES
W = WORLD BUSINESS

Anderson, Candice P67
Anderson, Joyce P88
Anderson, Liz P91
Anderson, Matthew P96
Anderson, Jeffery P101
Anderson, Markham J J P108
Anderson, Ikaika P121
Anderson, Sharon P143
Anderson, Charles P148
Anderson, David P155
Anderson, Richard P159
Anderson, Doana P164
Anderson, Troy P170
Anderson, Jonnie P209
Anderson, Anjanette P233
Anderson, Paul P235
Anderson, Billie P236
Anderson, Derrick P240
Anderson, Derek P240
Anderson, Michael R P242
Anderson, Jason P247
Anderson, Lcpl P255
Anderson, Don P261
Anderson, Scott P264
Anderson, Kenneth W P266
Anderson, Suzanne P274
Anderson, Ronnie K P286
Anderson, Carl A P287
Anderson, Steven P292
Anderson, Teresa P310
Anderson, Gregory A P314
Anderson, Carol P349
Anderson, Richard H P364
Anderson, Darin P367
Anderson, Jill C P371
Anderson, Terry Sam P384
Anderson, Jeannette P404
Anderson, Joe Dean P417
Anderson, Carole P431
Anderson, Anita P441
Anderson, Richard A P459
Anderson, Terry D P459
Anderson, Brian B P468
Anderson, Richard A P498:P506
Anderson, Adam P510
Anderson, Charles P572
Anderson, Audrey P590
Anderson, Paul P608
Anderson, Crystal P630
Anderson, Helen P631
Anderson, Suzanne P642
Anderson, Leha P643
Anderson, Jennifer P657
Anderson, Nicholas W53
Anderson, Troy W100
Anderson, Eric W102
Anderson, Magali W229
Anderson, Jeremy W391
Anderson, William W408:W465
Anderson, Claudia W480
Anderson, Darby E4
Anderson, James E167
Anderson, Joel E176
Anderson, Carrie E234
Anderson, Ritchie E258
Anderson, Tim E457
Andersson, Johan W446
Andes, Lee A209:P146
Ando, Haruhiko W17
Ando, Hiromichi W127
Ando, Yoshiko W264
Andorfer, Ludwig W367
Andrabi, Imran P592
Andrada, Marissa A174
Andrada, Noel W83
Andrade, Cristian P503
Andrade, Miguel Stilwell de W172
Andrade, Juan W189
Andrade, Lucio de Castro W506
Andrasick, James E374
Andre, May Joe P540

Andre, Emmanuel W395
Andreadakis, Elena A298
Andree, Don E52
Andreotti, Lamberto W509
Andreski, Lynne P498
Andresky, Christa A799:P605
Andrew, Briggs P100
Andrew, Ewan W165
Andrews, David W A34
Andrews, Shaun A490
Andrews, Charles A578
Andrews, Jonathan A579
Andrews, Chris A683
Andrews, Kirkland A688
Andrews, Claudia P83
Andrews, Abigail P98
Andrews, Briggs P99
Andrews, Bob P165
Andrews, R D P224
Andrews, Stephanie P262
Andrews, Amanda P291
Andrews, Jarrett P360
Andrews, Victoria P387
Andrews, Sara P423
Andrews, Susan Mc P446
Andrews, Josh P542
Andrews, Sue P565
Andrews, Nancy E79
Andrews, Brian E100
Andrews, Pamela E188
Andreyka, Timothy A27:P15
Andrieux, Nathalie W106
Andrizzi, Flynn A P253
Andronikakis, Spyridon W27
Andronov, Sergey W503
Andrulis, Erik D P102
Andruscavage, Thomas P260
André, Axel A45
Andy, Teuber P14
Aneaknithi, Pipit W270
Anelli, Stephanie A103:P60
Anemone, Alyssa A214
Anenen, Steven E417
Ang, Pek-san W16
Ang, Janet W70
Ang, Ramon W417
Ang, John Paul W417
Angagaw, Aster A600
Angel, Stephen A636
Angel, Brent P125
Angel, David P169
Angelastro, Philip A589
Angeletti, Paola W251
Angelina, Michael A680:E356
Angelini, Laura W156
Angelini, Marisol E23
Angelle, Bryant P139
Angelo, John A491
Angelo, Philip P391
Angelo, Michael E440
Angeloro, Vincent P230
Anger, Kevin P546
Angermeier, Ingo P493
Angerthal, Michael E441
Angiolillo, Bruce A642
Angkasith, Pongsak W113
Angle, Colin E236
Angley, James P373
Angulo, Christine Stiltner P488
Angus, Derek A828
Angus, Jeff P198:P405
Angus, Derek P634
Angus, Devon E204
Anhalt, Jackie P227
Anjolras, Pierre W517
Anklam, Laura P592
Anna, Gregory E84
Annan, Angela P577
Annesser, Sue P221
Anquillare, Mark E434
Ansari, Anousheh A434
Ansay, Michael A94:E45
Anschutz, J Barron P103
Anschutz, Barron P104
Ansell, Jeff A731
Anson, Betty P499
Ansour, M. Michael E438

Anstee, Richard A299
Antebi, Yadin W63
Antes, John P346
Anthony, F. Scott A197
Anthony, Chelsea P5
Anthony, Don P85
Anthony, Douglas P90
Anthony, Tim P365
Anthony, Nicholas E124
Antin, Robert E42:E353
Antoine, Robert A147:E66
Antolik, David A690
Anton, Arthur A708
Antonello, Katherine A274
Antonio, Maria Carina W83
Antonov, Igor W208
Antonovich, Michael D A224:P162
Antonsen, Erling A442:P278
Antonsen, Lauren E69
Anuchitworawong, Chaiyarit W62
Anwar, Mariam P249
Anwar, Muhammad P533
Anwer, Muhammad P266
Anzalone, John A431
Aoki, Shuhei W339
Aoki, Shigeki W369
Aoki, John E253
Aono, Asao W491
Aoun, Joseph P385
Aoyama, Yasuhiro W314
Apanius, Nicholas P336
Apfalter, Guenther W306
Aplin, Teresa Broyles P203
Aplin, Richard P578
Aplington, David P498
Apodaca, Shawna A783:P591
Apollony, Andrew P162
Aponte, Angel P452
Apostol, Lyndon P222
Apotheker, Leo W427
Appel, David A154
Appel, Frank W162
Apperson, Kevin P320
Apperson, Eric E30
Applbaum, Hilda L P29
Apple, Robert A504:E28
Appleton, Karl P508
Appleton, William E364
Appley, Pat P595
Appleyard, Ian A743
Appling, Antoinette P501
Appold, Stacy R P160
Aquila, Richard D P660
Aquino, Dinah A734:P510
Arad, Lana P231
Aragon, Nick A739:P515
Arai, Yuko W149
Arai, Satoshi W360
Arai, Fumio W437
Arakane, Kumi W286
Arakawa, David Z P121
Arakawa, Alan P163
Arakawa, Ryuji W23
Araki, Saburo W330
Aramichi, Yasuyuki W66
Aran, Pete A457
Aran, Hakan W504
Aranda, Nancy P616
Aranguren-Trellez, Luis A418
Aranha, Brian W39
Araujo, Joleen P471
Araujo, Marcelo de W506
Arbel, Shmuel W64
Arbeloff, Jill D P24
Arboleda, Mauricio Leyva A452
Arbour, Paola A765:A770
Arbuckle, Stuart A835
Arbuckle, Barry P326
Arbulu, Amalia P263
Arcand, Alfred P99
Arce, Julio W425
Arceneaux, Randy P9
Arceo, Paul P160
Archambeau, Shellye A686
Archer, Michael A144
Archer, Dennis A417
Archer, Timothy A467

Archer, Bryan A742
Archer, Donna P282
Archer, Tim P475
Archer, Bryan P518
Archer, Brian P557
Archer, Dennis E226
Archibald, Nolan A411
Archibong, Ime A148
Arczynski, Dennis A701:E365
Ardary, Kevin P437
Ardeljan, Manny P485
Arden-Ornt, Jeanine P102
Ardenghy, Roberto W380
Ardisana, Lizabeth A409
Ardoin, Elizabeth A317:E170
Arduini, Matteo E209
Arechabala, Miguel A327:A560
Areeratchakul, Tanawong W441
Arellano, Ian W69
Arena, Brenda P496
Arenivas, Jesse A456
Arens, Arne P82
Argalas, James A90
Argalas, Lindsey W61
Argalas, James E41
Argano, Matt P559
Argasreog, Natcha W270
Argust, Annette P201
Arhebamen, Ebinehita P305
Arias, Eric P161
Arias, Fernan Ignacio Bejarano W171
Arienzo, Wendy E330
Ariffin, Wan Zulkiflee Bin Wan A291
Ariga, Akio W377
Arii, Carrie P434
Arima, Koji W158
Arima, Akira W334
Aris, Antoinette W42
Aris, Annet W397
Aristeguieta, Francisco A743
Arita, Eiji W373
Ariyoshi, Yoshinori W151
Ark, Jon A677
Arkin, Eva P387
Arline, John P563
Arlt, Tim P367
Armater, Ann P246
Armato, Carl A573:P390:P426
Armbrister, Clarence E206
Armbruster, Chris E271
Armbruster, Sara E451
Arment, Dan P86
Armer, Douglas E52
Armero, Mario W507
Armes, Roy A767
Armfield, Jeff P487
Armini, Michael P385
Armistead, Russell E P477
Armock, Greg E81
Armour, Tim P98
Armour, Meri P337
Arms, William C P499
Armstrong, Alan A126
Armstrong, Timothy A128
Armstrong, David B A366
Armstrong, Amy A428
Armstrong, Greg A571
Armstrong, Greg L A631
Armstrong, Deborah A A739
Armstrong, Austin A782
Armstrong, James A860
Armstrong, Leronne P130
Armstrong, David B P235
Armstrong, Christina P403
Armstrong, Greg L P420
Armstrong, Deborah A P515
Armstrong, Austin P583
Armstrong, Philip W213
Armstrong, Sarah W410
Armstrong, Alan E54
Armtrong, Karen P246
Arnaboldi, Nicole W308
Arnal, Gustavo A111
Arnault, Alexandre W104
Arnault, Bernard W301
Arndt, Gerald P238
Arndt, Diane P375

COMBINED HOOVER'S HANDBOOK INDEX OF EXECUTIVES

Arner, Steve P99
Arner, Eric P572
Arneson, Georgene P427
Arney, Claudia W276
Arnita, Issa P310
Arnius, Sophie W3
Arnn, Roger A291:P210
Arnold, Bradley A20
Arnold, Michael A20
Arnold, Ken A88
Arnold, Craig A264
Arnold, Dan A489
Arnold, T. L. A724
Arnold, Timothy A827
Arnold, Jennifer P14
Arnold, Sharon P135
Arnold, Judy P163
Arnold, Craig P200
Arnold, Kay K P206
Arnold, Bill P449
Arnold, Christina P572
Arnold, Greg P601
Arnold, Heiko W50
Arnoldi, Melissa A543
Arnoldussen, Jane A804:P607
Arnst, Tom A765
Arntzen, Corry P496
Arnzen, April A527
Aron, Adam P28
Aronin, Jeffrey A247
Aronis, Georgios W27
Aronne, Brian P257
Aronson, Roberta E286
Arooni, Amir A247
Aroonratana, Siripong W113
Arora, Nikesh A34
Arougheti, Michael A70
Arquette, Athan P474
Arreaga, Gabriel A461
Arreola, Fernando P424
Arriaga, Michael P133
Arriaga, Roger P462
Arriaga, Elida P658
Arriaga, Brent E210
Arrindell, Brandon E420
Arrington, Darren A385
Arrington, John E242
Arrison, Charles P48
Arroliga, Alejandro A106:P64
Arroyo, Manuel A196
Arroyo, F. Thaddeus A358
Arroyo, David P171
Arroyo, Quemuel P338
Arroyo, Isaias P530
Arsel, Semahat W281:W505
Arsenault, Matthew P57
Arterian, Hannah R A7
Arthur, Lavone A106
Arthur, Michael A A124
Arthur, Lavone P64
Arthur, Donald C P308
Arthur, Tanya P524
Artmann, Barbara W514
Artusi, Daniel E264
Artuz, Edwin A297:E158
Arvan, Peter E327
Arvanitis, Athanasios W383
Arvin, Shannon A747:E391
Arwood, Steven P255
As, Pablo J Far A776
As, Norberto Due P133
As, Pablo J Far P558
Asaad, Emad P370
Asakawa, Fumiaki W537
Asakura, Masahiro W206
Asami, Ikuju W170
Asano, Toshio W317
Asante, Ebenezer W335
Asaro, Peter P571
Asavathiratham, Chalee W441
Asbury, John A79
Asbury, Alan P131
Asbury, John E34
Ascher, Michael C P598
Aschoff, Timothy P175
Asel, Keith E206
Asgeirsdottir, Margret A258

Ash, Daniel P114
Ash, David P P156
Ash, Thomas E77
Ashaboglu, Ahmet W281:W540
Ashar, Mayank W178
Ashburn, Tom P261
Ashby, Tracy P620
Ashby, Crystal W53
Ashe, Robert E282
Asher, Andrew A162
Asher, Anthony A773
Asher, Kelly P159
Ashford, Robin A667
Ashford, Stephanie P125
Ashizawa, Toshihisa W538
Ashkenazi, Anat A478
Ashley, Marion P167
Ashley, Orozco P286
Ashley, Stanley W P546
Ashley, Euan W46
Ashloc, Mark P6
Ashmore, Alex A131
Ashmore, Terry P444
Ashtary, Mishel P32
Ashuri, Roni P325
Ashwood, George P139
Aske, Jennings P372
Askie, Bill Van P311
Askins, Benjamin P298
Aslam, Farha A627
Aslett, Bonnie P443
Aslett, Mark E268
Asmussen, Rina W267
Asp, Jim P616
Aspillaga, Marea P57
Asplund, Dale A820
Asquith, Pamella A414
Asquith, Marcia P214
Asquith, Pamella P260
Assa, Lior A89:P54
Assaf, Michal P243
Assamongkol, Pipat W62
Assante, Linda E406
Assarasakorn, Vichai W284
Asscher-Vonk, Irene W278
Assouad, Yannick W517
Astle, Angela P120
Astor, Frank P362
Astrup, Thomas P30
Atanasov, Atanas P288
Atandeyi, Kolawole P385
Atcherman, S Jeffrey P336
Athanas, Peter W27
Athanasia, Dean A96
Athorn, Max P345
Athreya, Kartik A300
Athreya, Ranganath W240
Atikul, Jamlong W65
Atiya, Sami W5
Atkins, Margaret A236:A727
Atkins, Alegna A236
Atkinson, Robert A558
Atkinson, Tracy A665
Atkinson, Mark P88
Atkinson, Kerry M P530
Atkinson, Charlene M P531
Atsumi, Naotake W34
Attaway, David A78:P47
Attinger, Per-Olof W408
Attiyah, Abdul Rahman Bin Hamad Al W134
Attiyah, Abdullah Al W517
Attolini, Gerardo Estrada W198
Attrill, Ed P188
Attrovio, Matteo W426
Attwood, Dorothy A251
Attwood, James A562:P378
Atwell, Robert A562:E293
Atwood, Denver P492
Atwood, Catherine E348
Auad, Paola Alam W56
Aubert, Brenda P422
Aubert, Christophe W184
Aubrey, William A618
Auchincloss, Murray W91
Aucoin, Renee N P50
Audette, Matthew A489

Audiffred, J Douglas P321:P321
Auerbach, Jonathan A611:A641
Auetumrongsawat, Vimlin P621
Aufman, Matt P648
Aufreiter, Nora W69
Augenstein, Mark A617
Auger, Stephen A327:P215
Augsburger, Blake A466
Augsburger, Tod P298:P298
Augsburger, Blake E244
August, Gerald A327
August, Glenn A756
August, Gerald P210
Augustin, Stanley M P601
Augustine, Cherri P316
Auld, David A403
Auman, Stan P368
Aumont, Dominique W301
Aungudomsin, Siridej W62
Auque, Francois W402
Auris, Jan-Dirk W224
Ausburn, Kevin A366
Auschel, Roland W12
Ausere, Michael J P209
Austen, William A71
Austen, Karla P360
Austin, Earl A658
Austin, Roxanne A833
Austin, Mike P25
Austin, Pam P55
Austin, Tara P392
Austin, Jennifer P467
Austin, Scott P553
Austin, Matthew S P593
Austin, Joshua P651
Austruy, Bertrand W152
Ausura, John E263
Autenried, Paul Von A134
Auzenne, Byron A502:P327
Avampato, Steven A215
Avdic, Edina A778:P564
Avedon, Marcia E191
Averette, Joseph W P452
Averill, Howard A146
Averill, Chris P411:P411
Averill, Christopher R P575
Avery, Sonja P306
Avery, Christy P367
Avery, Phyllis P452
Avery, Thomas E107
Avery, Raymond E439
Avila, Manuel O P171
Avila, Andres S P261
Avila-walker, Wendy E376
Aviles, Bernadette P305
Avilez, Bernice P119
Avitabile, Daniel A507
Avner, David W63
Avner, Iris W253
Avraham, Hava K P71
Avril, Matthew E185
Avril-Groves, Vicki A207:A367
Awada, Kaled A767
Awadi, Yousef Al W38
Axelrod, Neal A783:P583
Axtell, Todd P167
Ayada, Yujiro W237
Ayafor, Christopher P533
Ayala, John A81
Ayala, Jaime Augusto Zobel De W70
Ayala, Fernando Zobel De W70
Aydt, Timothy A541
Ayers, Don P128
Ayla, Ahmet W21
Aylouche, Mounzer M A503:P318
Aylward, George E441
Aymond, Ariel P150
Aymond, Angel P641
Aynechi, Mana P16
Ayscue, Charles F P346
Ayub, Arturo Elias W28
Ayuste, Rafael W83
Ayyappan, Ajay E151
Ayyar, Balu A199
Azagra, Juan Araluce y Martinez de W515
Azam, Asif P293

Azar, Mario P76
Azar, Amir Rahnamay- P100
Azar, Robert B P390
Azare, Monica E252
Azarela, Michael P523
Azarian, Michael A330
Azcarraga, Gina Lorenza Diez Barroso W61
Azeez, Sulaiman P300
Azevedo, Roy A665
Azevedo, Neil P160
Azinovic, Drago A625
Aziz, Raja Teh Maimunah Raja Abdul W29
Aziz, Akhtarzaite Binti Abdul W307
Aziz, Fariz bin Abdul W307
Azulay, Asaf W63
Azuma, Seiichiro W354

B

Baack, Sara A282
Baade, Arve W363
Baalmann, Richard E146
Baameur, Ahmed P161
Baatar, Bold W405:W406
Babaeva, Inna W237
Babatz, Guillermo W69
Babb, Ivy P81
Babbitt, Gary A147:E66
Babcanec, Benjamin E207
Babcock, Beverley A588
Babcock, John A613
Babcock, Calvin P59
Babcock, Linda P100
Babcock, John E316
Babeau, Emmanuel A625
Babej, Peter A183
Babiarz, Greg P22
Babikian, Shant A28:P18
Babino, Tim P623
Babot, Ron E413
Babowal, Jill A245:P189
Bacardi, Joaquin A633
Bacci, Arthur A870:E455
Bachand, Kelly A291:P210
Bachar, Amir W63
Bachelor, Alex A233:P178
Bacher, Lars A283:P208
Bachke, Tone W483
Bachman, Howard P175
Bachman, Robert J P205
Bachmann, Richard A280
Bachmann, Lisa E123
Baciarelli, Renato P119
Bacigal, Eric A381:P249
Bacigalupo, George A113
Bacigalupo, Richard J P441
Backberg, Benjamin A P77
Backes, Richard P578
Backus, Marcia A581
Bacon, Graham A280
Bacon, Ashley A444
Bacon, Renee A542
Bacon, Ken P479
Bacon, Kenneth E29
Bacungan, Ferdinand W83
Bacus, Lisa A178
Badar, Fahad W134
Badcock, Henry C P644
Badcock, Ben M P644
Baddeley, Gary E308
Badenhorst, Marissa A172
Badenoch, Alexandra W484
Baderschneider, Jean W200
Badger, Lauren P265
Badhorn, Dayna A88
Badinter, Elisabeth W395
Badlani, Sameer A292:P210
Badu, Kofi P286
Bae, Du Yong W297
Baer, Richard A781
Baer, Mark P175
Baer, Richard P582
Baerst, Peggy P97
Baetz, Cary P475

COMBINED HOOVER'S HANDBOOK INDEX OF EXECUTIVES

A = AMERICAN BUSINESS
E = EMERGING COMPANIES
P = PRIVATE COMPANIES
W = WORLD BUSINESS

Baez, Yeimy W171
Bagby, L. Douglas A723:E383
Bagel-Trah, Simone W224
Bagg, Halsey P611
Baggett, Nancy P160
Baghdadi, Zeinab P192
Bagley, Shannon A162
Bagley, Annemarie P135
Baglino, Andrew A769
Bagozzi, Sheila A215
Bagshaw, Seth P376:E277
Bague, Hugo A443
Bagwell, Norman A126:E54
Bagwell, Edward E91
Bahadur, John P356
Bahadur, Sanjay W348
Bahai, Ahmad A771
Bahensky, Donna Katen P632
Bahl, William A179
Bahri, Rajat A623
Bahtka, Tara P404
Bai, Chong'en W122
Bai, Xiaohu W321
Baier, Bill P168
Baier, Wolfgang W166
Bail, Jennifer P242
Bailey, Teresa A208
Bailey, David A315
Bailey, Holly A320
Bailey, Sallie A463
Bailey, Kathryn A617
Bailey, Anne A738
Bailey, Daniel A793
Bailey, Joe A804
Bailey, Kevin A836
Bailey, John P47
Bailey, Teresa P145
Bailey, Jacqueline P164
Bailey, Andrew P177
Bailey, Emily J P177
Bailey, Troy P213
Bailey, David P243
Bailey, Gregory P356
Bailey, Colin P381
Bailey, Jeff P420
Bailey, Kassie P509
Bailey, Anne P514
Bailey, Lara P541
Bailey, Colonel B P578
Bailey, Joe P607
Bailey, Jeffrey E51
Bailey, Elizabeth E107
Bailey, David E167
Bailey, Holly E173
Bailey, Steve E317
Bailey, Steve R E317
Bailey, Douglas E330
Bailey, Nicholas E345
Bailey, Daniel E414
Bailey-Kanelos, Courtney P168
Baileys, Kristen A828:P635
Bailliencourt, Cedric De W519
Bailly, Maud W106
Bailo, Carla A12
Bailo, Karen A645
Baily, John A680:E356
Bain, Ruthie A735:P510
Bain, Peter E441
Bainbridge, Guy W308
Baine, Edward A254
Bains, Harrison E67
Baio, Richard A112
Bair, Sheila A293
Baird, Kevin A767
Baird, W. Blake E406
Bairrington, P. E322
Baisch, Beth P132
Baitieh, Rami W104
Baivier, Meghan E396
Bakas, Michael E19
Baker, LeighAnne A7

Baker, Charles A92
Baker, Charlie A208
Baker, Kevin A366
Baker, Raymond A492
Baker, Robert A734
Baker, Adolphus A798
Baker, Abby A869
Baker, James A P9
Baker, J Craig P30
Baker, Kathryn P78
Baker, Bill John P112
Baker, Emily A P122
Baker, James P125
Baker, Donna P139
Baker, Charlie P146
Baker, Debbie P164
Baker, Michele P166
Baker, Thomas P175
Baker, Pam P203
Baker, Angie P212
Baker, Paula P221
Baker, Joselyn Butler P233
Baker, Gary P254
Baker, Ron P270
Baker, Rick P281
Baker, Caleb P292
Baker, Brenda P447
Baker, Charmaine P486
Baker, David P498
Baker, Christine P571
Baker, Abby P659
Baker, R Hal P662
Baker, Kelly W195
Baker, Graham W262
Baker, Jeff W402
Baker, Robert E68
Baker, Charles E82
Baker, Robert E111
Baker, Julian E225
Baker, William E266
Baker, Mark E309
Baker, Randy E311
Baker, Arthur E337
Baker, Gary E427
Bakhshi, Sandeep W240
Bakish, Robert A607
Bakken, Lexie A29
Bakken, A. Christopher A277
Bakken, Lexie E13
Bakker, Jaska De W391
Baklarz, Ron A512:P324
Baksaas, Jon W470
Bakun, Marek E387
Balaguer, Susan P573
Balakrishnan, Balu E330
Balandran, Adriana P486
Balbi, Arnaldo Gorziglia W177
Balbosa, Suzanne P59
Balcerak, Robert A652
Balchunas, James P644
Baldanza, B. Ben A438
Baldauf, Sari W359
Balderrama, Melissa P114
Balderson, Bill A864:P656
Balding, Elizabeth P653
Baldock, Henrietta W253:W291
Baldock, Jennifer E222
Baldridge, Don A239
Balducci, Gianmaria W511
Balduzzi, Michael A P206
Baldwin, Dennis A145
Baldwin, Robert A358
Baldwin, Mark A448
Baldwin, Lisa A673
Baldwin, Dennis P95
Baldwin, Polly P169
Baldwin, Todd P238
Baldwin, Lawanda P345
Baledge, Les A802
Bales, Brian A677
Balfour, Charles E409
Bali, Vinita A199
Baliles, Jon P132
Balish, Amanda A735:P511
Balistreri, Becky A867
Ball, James A169
Ball, Florence A224

Ball, Jeffrey A298
Ball, Vanessa P35
Ball, Florence P172
Ball, Calvin P256
Ball, Parke D P285
Ball, James P380
Ball, George L P407
Ball, Andrew P523
Ball, George L P573
Ball, Anthony Elliott W57
Ball, Frederick E6
Ball, Richard E245
Ball, Darin E329
Ballance, Robert A106
Ballance, Tom P311
Ballance, Robert E48
Ballard, J. Scott A392
Ballard, Kathy A811
Ballard, Brent P145
Ballard, Gary P212
Ballard, Dennis P461
Ballard, Joshua E137
Ballard, J. Scott E216
Ballard, Jed E296
Ballard, L. Gregory E418
Ballbach, John A688
Ballester, Alejandro A634
Ballesteros, Walter P160
Ballinas, Carlos P332
Ballinger, Chris A790
Ballintyn, Rhonda E234
Ballock, Steven P69
Ballou, Roger A826:E428
Ballout, Benjamin E137
Ballowe, Rob P251
Ballschmiede, Ronald E390
Balmann, Yves De A286
Balo, Andrew E117
Balog, Suzanne P617
Balogh, Cadd P162
Balser, Jeff P640
Baltimore, Thomas A46
Baltimore, David P546
Balushi, Ahmed bin Faqir Al W64
Bamba, Hiroyuki W279
Bambawale, Ajai W497
Bamford, William A P578
Bamfordiii, William A P578
Bamisile, Ajoke P377
Banati, Amit A335:A449
Bancroft, Trevor P493
Bancroft, Charles W210
Bancroft, Philip E348
Banda, Jose P455
Bando, Mariko W334
Bandoma, Danna P169
Bandrowczak, Steven J A872
Banducci, Bradford W531
Bandy, Cecli M P304
Banerjee, Pankaj W308
Banet, Virginie W316
Bang, Bente W154
Bang, Brian E315
Banik, Michelle W176
Banister, Gaurdie A802
Banister, Sandi P362
Banister, Guardie W178
Bankhead, Tammie P556
Banko, Frank E132
Banks, Chau A189
Banks, Bernard A229
Banks, Samuel A310
Banks, M. Katherine A371
Banks, Lee A609
Banks, Stacie L P49
Banks, Gary P103
Banks, Jeffrey P527
Banks, Diana P560
Banks, Stacie L P639
Banks, Bernard E112
Banks, Samuel E164
Banner, Jennifer A796
Bannister, David A468
Bannister, Jack A751
Banovetz, John A3
Bansal, Rishi A101
Bansal, Preeta A549:E290

Banse, Amy A11:A474
Banyard, Richard A335
Bao, Chengdi P207
Baptiste, Danielle E304
Bar, Roselyn A501
Bar-Adon, Eshel A89:A90:P54:E41
Barameeauychai, Kraisorn W62
Baran, James P131
Baratian, Jacqueline P320
Baratta, Joseph A121
Baratto, Massimo A810
Barba, James J P15:P16
Barba, Ricardo W109
Barbao, Christina P167
Barbarossa, Giovanni E224
Barbato, Angela P467
Barbato, Anthony P598
Barbeau, Patrick W250
Barbeau-Leonard, Geraldine P242
Barber, Randolph A652
Barber, Johnathan A712
Barber, Dennis P103
Barber, Cindy P134
Barber, Adena P393
Barber, Dennis P553
Barber, Johnathan A373
Barbera, Judith A741
Barbera, Charles P438
Barbera, Judith P518
Barbi, Leslie A672
Barbier, Robert P P614
Barbier, Francois W197
Barbieri, Eric P334
Barbo, William E79
Barbour, Sondra A20
Barbour, Catherine P32
Barboza, Shawn P186
Barcelon, George W83
Barcelos, Elcio Rt A829
Barchi, Daniel P372
Barclay, Kathleen E176
Bard, Benjamin A68
Bardari, Giuseppe E219
Barden, Sean T P646
Bardot, Anne W448
Bardusch, Robert A832:E431
Bardwell, Amanda W531
Bareford, Becky A300
Barela, Ed P461
Barenberg, Cheri E442
Barer, Sol W487
Barfield, Jon A219
Barfield, John A740
Barfield, Kelle J P206
Barfield, John A516
Bargabos, Sheree A745:E321
Bargamin, Stephen N P644
Barges, Demetri A147:P96
Bari, Joseph De P503
Baribeau, Nathan B P22
Barilla, Guido W152
Bariquit, Teri A565
Bark, Brian A713
Barkela, Lori P333
Barker, Kenneth A271
Barker, Stephen A372
Barker, G. Carlton A707
Barker, James P P160
Barker, Fred P323
Barker, Julie E259
Barker, G. Carlton E368
Barkhurst, Linda P355
Barkley, Michael T A602
Barkley, Pete P2
Barklow, Megan A217:P151
Barlak, Paul M P203:P375
Barleston, Karen P562
Barletta, Pierfrancesco W294
Barlow, Steven A98
Barlow, Jeff A533
Barlow, Carrolee E399
Barlows, Ted P251
Barmonde, Charles E364
Barnaba, Mark W200
Barnard, Keith P216
Barner, Sharon A228
Barnes, David A42

COMBINED HOOVER'S HANDBOOK INDEX OF EXECUTIVES

Barnes, Melody A129
Barnes, Warren A375
Barnes, David A385
Barnes, Melissa A478
Barnes, Pam A605
Barnes, John A617
Barnes, Ronald A675
Barnes, Mandela A742
Barnes, Christine P133
Barnes, C Linda P157
Barnes, Andrea P281
Barnes, David G P361
Barnes, Earl P395
Barnes, Janet P431
Barnes, Ruthe P483
Barnes, Mandela P518
Barnes, John C P625
Barnes, James M P626
Barnes, James R P640
Barnes, Chase P640
Barnes, Alan P652
Barnes, Erin P653
Barnes, Greg W30
Barnes, John E319
Barnes, Ronald E350
Barnes, Scott E388
Barnes, David E415
Barnes, Keith E436
Barnett, Joseph A217
Barnett, Mark A506
Barnett, Kimberly P113
Barnett, Tony P125
Barnett, Tonya P125
Barnett, David P127
Barnett, Joseph P151
Barnett, Blake P240
Barnett, Phillip P436
Barnett, Christin P655
Barnett, Craig E391
Barnett-Sarpalius, Jenny P304
Barnette, Kimberly P112
Barnette, Larry P493
Barnette, Steven E348
Barnette, K. E435
Barney, David A512
Barnhill, Kris P454
Barnholt, Edward A457
Barnhouse, Phillip E253
Barnhusen, Jens W190
Barnum, Jeremy A445
Barnum, Enid P238
Barnum, Katherine T P618
Barocas, Jeffrey E301
Baron, Collin A617:E319
Barone, Frank A243:P188
Baroni, Paul W69
Barouski, William A A299
Barpoulis, Sarah E381
Barr, George A310
Barr, Keith A875
Barr, Bill P304
Barr, Kenneth P384
Barr, Laurie P460
Barr, Alexis P499
Barr, Jordys P640
Barr, George E164
Barr, James E289
Barra, Ornella A55
Barra, Mary A349
Barra, Ornella A843
Barra, Melissa E378
Barrak, Khalid Al W423
Barral, Diego A189
Barranco, David A39
Barratt, Craig A430
Barre, Jerome W372
Barreda, Victor P202
Barrena, Juan Muldoon W215
Barrenechea, Mark A244
Barrera, Arturo P538
Barrera, Carlos Jimenez W22
Barrese, Stefano W251
Barreta, Anthony A445:P279
Barrett, Kayla A123
Barrett, John A180
Barrett, Katy A663
Barrett, Victor A717

Barrett, Jennifer A869
Barrett, Kayla P81
Barrett, Michael P139
Barrett, Clarissa P170
Barrett, Karin A P188
Barrett, Kevin P257
Barrett, Robert P267
Barrett, David P290
Barrett, Mark P292
Barrett, Katy P436
Barrett, Cynthia P466
Barrett, Nancy P648
Barrett, John P658
Barrett, Jennifer P659
Barrett, Deborah W213
Barrett, Peter E320
Barrett, Victor E380
Barrett, Craig E393
Barrett, Joel E409
Barrick, Robert L P62
Barrie, Andrew A448
Barrientos, Cristian W525
Barriere, Charles P209
Barril, Nove A734:P510
Barrinson, Tom P455
Barrios, Alfredo W405:W406
Barritt, Kenneth P498
Barron, Thomas A147
Barron, William A315
Barron, Eric J A780
Barron, Eric P216
Barron, Christi P335
Barron, Joe P486
Barron, Eric J P575
Barron, Pamela P600
Barron, Hal W210
Barron, Thomas E66
Barron, William E167
Barroso, Clementina Maria Damaso De
  Jesus Silva W17
Barrow-Klien, Vickie J P153
Barrows, Karen P450
Barry, Corie A115
Barry, Anthony A149
Barry, David A335
Barry, Richard A617
Barry, John M P65
Barry, Susan P657
Barry, Richard E319
Barry, David E407
Barsan, Radu E330
Barsic, Mike P579
Barsky, Carol P183
Barsky, Adam P371
Barsotti, Fabio W294
Barstow, Karen P172
Barsz, Peter A690
Barta, Michelle P114
Bartel, Ulrich E215
Bartels, Bill A737:P513
Barth, Kevin A206
Barth, Carin A368
Barth, Kevin A446
Barth, Zach P261
Barth, Dianne P522
Barthelemy, Joseph P220
Barthelemy, Nicolas E349
Bartholdson, John E254
Bartholomay, Linda P463
Bartholomew, Mindy P288
Bartholomew, Justine P392
Bartholomew, James E132
Bartl, Juergen W444
Bartlein, Robert E96
Bartlett, Thomas A51
Bartlett, Mark A756
Bartlett, Daniel A845
Bartlett, Beth P339
Bartlett, Rhian W259
Barto, Nancy A734
Barto, Nick P102
Barto, Nancy P510
Bartok, Daniel E180
Bartolini, Louis A856
Bartolome, Beatriz W509
Bartolomeo, Pasquale Di W293
Bartolone, Jason P169

Bartolotta, Joseph E257
Barton, Lisa A44:A207
Barton, Harry A317
Barton, Jacqueline A355
Barton, Denise A413
Barton, Kurt A791
Barton, Dennis P508
Barton, Harry E170
Barton, Donald E300
Bartos, Bob A24:P13
Bartschat, Michael A442:P278
Baruch, Philip W267
Baruffi, Kumi A201:E92
Barwise, Sara P200
Barwood, Marlene A P272
Barzel, Roy E439
Basara, George A690
Baschera, Pius W425
Bascunan, Felipe W110
Basden, Daniel P112
Basehore, John P201
Baselga, Jose W46
Bash, Ruth P497
Bash, Jeffrey E109
Bashaw, Walter E224
Basich, Marci A409
Basil, Jack P457
Basile, Cinzia W188
Baskerville, Bob P470
Baskerville, Donna E207
Baskin, Scott E23
Baskovic, Victoria P158
Basler, Pamela P36
Basler, Bruno W524
Basner, Kelly P385
Basolis, Elbert E164
Bason, John W45
Bass, Alexander P157
Bass, Justin P175
Bass, Adam P180
Bass, Theodore P476
Bass, Donald C P547
Bass, Mike P644
Bass, James E268
Bassanell, Melissa P463
Bassett, Lawton A54
Bassett, Tasha P551
Bassett, Lawton E25
Bassham, Terry A206
Bassham, Terry D P209
Basso, Maurizio W43
Bast, Christopher E115
Bastian, Ed A242
Bastian, R Richard E52
Bastide, Lore de la A217
Bastoni, Elizabeth W263
Bastos-Licht, Valdirene A418
Basu, Subhadeep A113
Batato, Magdi W348
Batcheler, Colleen R A214
Batchelor, Steven A848
Bateman, Christopher M P522
Bateman, Leonard E91
Bates, David A584
Bates, Mary A655
Bates, Anthony A841
Bates, Tamara P90
Bates, Melanie P130
Bates, Cathy P145
Bates, David P155
Bates, Gigi P169
Bates, Martin W P233
Bates, Jennifer P249
Bates, Ruth P334
Bates, Cera P383
Bates, Shannon P499
Bates, Mary E340
Batey, Alan A715
Batista, Alex P349
Batiste, Camille A68
Batistoni, Peter E81
Batkin, Roger A20
Batra, Sandeep W240
Batra, Nishant W359
Batra, Rajeev E277
Batres, Francisco P149
Batt, Douglas A P406

Battaglia, Silvana A55
Battaglia, Paul A789
Battaglia, Concetta W273
Battaini, Massimo W391
Battenfield, Keith P106
Battese, Betty P311
Battista, Valerio W391
Battistoni, Joseph E248
Battle, Michael E148
Battles, Julie P273
Battles, Michael E69
Battley, Todd A15
Baty, Darren A412:P258
Baty, Heather P549
Baty, Roderick E12
Bauche, Douglas A279:E142
Bauck, Bryan P107
Baucum, Carlton E A403
Baucum, Carlton A779
Baucum, Carlton E P256
Baucum, Carlton P567
Baude, Bruce A194
Baudhuin, Robert A23
Baudouin, Richard E10
Bauer, Brett A1
Bauer, Jonathan A645
Bauer, Daniel M A783
Bauer, Emily A867
Bauer, Mark P185
Bauer, Rebeka P332
Bauer, Jason P472
Bauer, Daniel M P591
Bauer, Karl-Heinz W426
Bauer, Robert E12
Bauer, Milissa E133
Bauer, Melissa E383
Bauer, Douglas E413
Bauer, Douglas F E413
Baukol, Eric E198
Baum, Richard A668
Baum, Peter A832:E431
Bauman, Larry A217:P151
Baumann, Barbara A243
Baumann, Werner W78
Baumann, Maja W524
Baumgarten, Alan S P346
Baumgartner, Kim P101
Baumgartner, Mike P109
Baumgartner, Amy P586
Baumgartner, Robert E50
Baumgartner, Mark E323
Baumscheiper, Michael W224
Bautista, Javier Velez P237
Bautista, Jeremy A445
Bauwel, Chantal Van P84
Bavazls, Marcelo P43
Baveja, Sarabjit A404
Baverov, Andrea A551
Baverso, Louis P635
Bawa, Neena P392
Bawel, Zachary A353:E192
Baxendale, Sonia W290
Baxter, Warner A40
Baxter, Greg A404
Baxter, Kathleen D A734
Baxter, Tom P42
Baxter, Amanda P281
Baxter, Kathleen D P510
Bay, Annell A64:E434
Bayardo, Jose A571
Bayarena, Marco P160
Bayer, Andrea P165
Bayes, Gina R E439
Bayh, B. Evan A306
Bayh, Evan A496
Bayless, George A225
Baylor, Jnai P29
Bayne, John A221
Baytos, David P337
Bazante, Jennifer A814:E424
Bazemore, Teresa A298
Bazile, Yamilee P374
Bazire, Nicolas W301
Bazzoli, Dan P651
Bea, Javon R P332:P333
Beach, Dawn Hudson A428
Beach, Bruce A857

COMBINED HOOVER'S HANDBOOK INDEX OF EXECUTIVES

```
A = AMERICAN BUSINESS
E = EMERGING COMPANIES
P = PRIVATE COMPANIES
W = WORLD BUSINESS
```

Beach, Quentin P169
Beach, Bruce E447
Beacher, Bob A292:P210
Beacom, Joseph A468
Beadle, Alice P11
Beaird, Robert A808:E421
Beal, Anne W210
Beall, Adam P53
Beall, Robert P67
Beam, Eric A166
Beam, S. Craig A617
Beam, Conny P11
Beam, Eric P110
Beam, Mildred P400
Beams, Mary A641
Bean, Oscar A749
Bean, Lincoln A P14
Bean, Terrina P275
Bean, James P385
Bean, Oscar E394
Beans, Ellen P91
Beard, Rob A527
Beard, Robert A807
Beard, J Anthony P123
Beard, Dave P193
Beard, Robert F P608
Beard, Grant E6
Beard, Simon E15
Beardall, Brent A846
Bearinger, David P589
Beasley, J. Barnie A44
Beasley, Scott A339
Beasley, Gary P466
Beasley, Barnie P492
Beasley, Ralph D P602
Beato, Maria Jose Garcia W57
Beattie, Arthur A637
Beattie, Richard E149
Beattie, John E229
Beatty, Vincent A846
Beatty, Paul R P529
Beaty, Beverly P542
Beauchamp, Robert P377
Beaudoin, Edward P22
Beaudoin, Pierre W389
Beaufils, Pierre-Yves W398
Beaufort, Galen P347
Beaufort, Aymar De Liedekerke W87
Beaulieu, Valerie W10
Beaune, Augustin de Romanet de W429
Beaupre, Paul P231
Beautz, Janet K P169
Beaver, Steven A18
Beaver, David A A226
Beaver, Paula A774
Beaver, David P493
Beaver, Paula P547
Beaver, Carolyn E264
Beaver, Roy E430
Beazer, Craig A480
Beazizo, Amy P529
Beazley, Eric P85
Beber, Justin W94
Beccari, Pietro W301
Bechler, Kent P154
Bechtel, Robert A652
Bechtel, John A780:P575
Beck, Andrew A20
Beck, Gregory A A166
Beck, Gregory A217
Beck, Christophe A267
Beck, Dave A300
Beck, Axel A415
Beck, Mark A600
Beck, Daniel A751
Beck, Jennifer A803
Beck, Gregory A P110
Beck, Gregory P151
Beck, Tammy P242
Beck, Teresa P569
Beck, Jennifer P606

Beck, Eric P614
Beck, Sullivan P620
Beck, Mary P627
Beck, Robert E348
Becker, Stefan A221
Becker, David A318
Becker, Christopher A322
Becker, Marc A666
Becker, Judith A670
Becker, David A700
Becker, Yin A749
Becker, Gregory A751
Becker, Russell A P39
Becker, Carl P170
Becker, Robert P252
Becker, Abbey P275
Becker, Linda P359
Becker, Martin P396
Becker, Judith P440
Becker, Bernard P522
Becker, David E170
Becker, W. Marston E283
Becker, Laurie E323
Beckerle, Mary A411:A441
Beckerle, Ken P446
Beckham, Brad A579
Beckhorn, Jay E194
Beckley, Emma L A780:P572
Beckley, Thomas E62
Beckman, David A176
Beckman, Lawrence P19
Beckman, Jason P119
Beckman, David P547
Beckman, Mitchell R P566
Beckman, Bruce E140
Beckmann, Barbara A330
Beckmann, Kai W321
Beckord, James P92
Beckton, Dana A706:P473
Beckwith, Van A371
Beckwitt, Richard A474
Bedague-Hamilius, Veronique W175
Beddingfield, Deborah A789:E411
Bedel, Vicki A828:P635
Bedessem, Michael P154
Bedessem, Mike P154
Bedient, John A1
Bedient, Patricia A26:W466
Bedingfield, Robert A698
Bednarz, Agata P382
Bedore, James A548
Bedoya, Juan P A670:P440
Bee, Michael P233
Bee, Christopher P323
Beebe, Kevin A339
Beebe, Mike A393
Beebe, Cheryl A539:A605
Beebe, Kevin A715
Beebe, Mike A802
Beebe, Calvin P321
Beebe, Mike E217
Beeber, Rich P148
Beecher, Bradley P P555
Beegle, Philip H P387
Beekhuizen, Mick A146
Beelen, Matthew J P564
Beeler, Don P119
Beeler, Jason P327
Beem, Sara P314
Beene, Delwin P147
Beer, James A26
Beer, Lori A444
Beer, Gary M P484
Beerli, Andreas W55
Beerman, Kevin E77
Beers, Marlene A637
Beery, Joseph A430
Beesley, Bradley A320:E173
Beets, Neal P128
Began, Marc E3
Begbie, Robert W345
Begemann, Brett A264
Beggs, Leland P282
Beggs, Zachary P468
Beggs, Colin W6
Begle, Curtis A114
Begleiter, Steven E262

Begley, Jody A36
Begley, Charlene A543
Begley, Christopher A878
Begnal, Joe P135
Begor, Mark A548
Beh, Hang Chwee W529
Behan, Mark A72:E31
Behar, Z. A70
Behar, Gregory W348
Behling, Kristen P181
Behling, Danielle P292
Behm, Brian W P589
Behrendt, Michael W219
Behring, Alexandre A460
Behring, Berit W154
Beia, Terrance A417:E226
Beichler, Shawn P19
Beier-Grant, Jamie P143
Beilenson, Peter P168
Beinecke, Candace A607
Beirne, Patrick E339
Beison, Jill P88
Beitel, David A877
Beitz, Tammie P546
Bekke, Nathan E248
Bektesevic, Begajeta P16
Belabbas, Karim W18
Belair, Daina A103
Belair, Sebastien W290
Belair, Daina E47
Belak, Cynthia E404
Belanoff, Joseph E102
Belardi, James R A78:P47
Belbeck, Mike P173
Belcher, Jason A314
Belcher, Tony P33
Belcher, Megan P580
Belen, Melanie W83
Belford, Keno P170
Belisle, Wendy P47
Belitsky, Lee A244
Belitz, Robert P257
Beliveau, Don P498
Beliveau-Dunn, Jeanne A268
Belk, William A719
Bell, Christopher A20
Bell, Bernice A22
Bell, James A65
Bell, Marc A70
Bell, Sandra A174
Bell, Madeline A203
Bell, Michael A222
Bell, Katherine A273
Bell, Victor A312
Bell, Thomas A566
Bell, Kevin H A702
Bell, Jean A734
Bell, Jack A866
Bell, Christopher P11
Bell, Alvin P60
Bell, Sheila P68
Bell, Michelle P125
Bell, Sergeant P127
Bell, Sara P161
Bell, Roy P246
Bell, Don P303
Bell, Deborah P345
Bell, Dave P376
Bell, Mary P427
Bell, Jean P510
Bell, Kristin P532
Bell, Arthur P539
Bell, Madeline P549
Bell, Donald P578
Bell, Charlton P598
Bell, Hans G P608
Bell, Beate W227
Bell, Colin W234
Bell, Hermann W367
Bell, Ryan E135
Bell, Katherine E239
Bell, Susan E358
Bell, Craig E439
Bell, Jack E450
Bell-Knight, Christopher W82
Bellacicco, Matthew P539
Bellamy, Don A570

Bellamy, Tania P255
Bellamy, Don P388
Belle, Beverly P612
Bellemare, Alain W18
Bellenfant, William P600
Bellens, Arnaud W389
Beller, Alan A792
Bellettini, Francesca W273
Belli, Tugrul W21
Bellini, Marina W93
Bellman, Brooke P595
Bello, Stephen P488
Belloeil-Melkin, Marie Veronique W302
Bellon, Sophie W448
Bellon-Szabo, Nathalie W448
Bellone, Steven P171
Belloni, Aldo W301
Belloni, Antonio W301
Bellos, Alexander A865
Belluzzo, Richard E436
Belman, Alex P45
Belmer, Rodolphe A551
Belo, Michael P422
Beloff, Hardie A P241
Beloff, Leland P241
Beloff, Jean P242
Belotto, Kathleen P185
Below, Peg P3
Belsky, Scott A11
Belstock, Richard E327
Belter, Paul P280
Beltran, Eduardo Navarro W177
Beltran, Francisco Camacho W198
Beltzman, Daniel P191
Bement, Lisa P233
Ben, Shenglin W541
Ben-zeev, Eti W63
Ben-Zur, Liat W507
Ben-Zvi, Shmuel W64
Bena, Pamela A331:E178
Benacci, Nancy A179
Benavides, Sarah P327
Benavidez, Martin P409
Benavidez, Janet P480
Benayoun, Marc W175
Benck, David E213
Bendapudi, Neeli A780:P575:P622
Bender, James A83
Bender, Jason A323
Bender, Michael A459
Bender, Andria A741
Bender, James A801
Bender, M. Steven A860
Bender, Traci P367
Bender, Andria P517
Bender, Kyle P601
Bender, Shannon W399
Benders, Dana A730:P509
Bendiek, Sabine W419
Bendle, Nicole P162
Bendre, Ashish E16
Bene, Robert Del A424
Beneby, Doyle A658
Benecke, William J A624:P414
Benedict, Danielle A817
Benedict, Rod P638
Benedict, Tami E39
Beneke, Andrea P625
Benevich, Eric E290
Benfield, Stephanie Stuckey P123
Benfield, Laura E P384
Benfield, James H P597
Benhamou, Eric A751
Benioff, Marc A692
Benitez, Jorge A306
Benito, Michael A382:E211
Benjamin, William A70
Benjamin, Gerald A696
Benjamin, Eric E233
Benjamin, Mark E339
Benko, Brittany A411
Benko, Cathleen A563
Benko, David P629
Benkovich, Nick A414:P259
Benn, Christine P260
Benner, Mark P308
Benner, Aimee P462

COMBINED HOOVER'S HANDBOOK INDEX OF EXECUTIVES

Bennet, Thomas P597
Bennett, Kelvin A20
Bennett, Jackie A20
Bennett, Jonathan A108
Bennett, Lynnelle A224
Bennett, James A254
Bennett, Isaac A293
Bennett, Rodney A309
Bennett, Alan A328
Bennett, James A330
Bennett, Jonathan A377
Bennett, Richard A581
Bennett, Peter A581
Bennett, Adrian A652
Bennett, Alan A786
Bennett, Jackie P11
Bennett, John P98
Bennett, Eddie P141
Bennett, Lynnelle P172
Bennett, Brett P176
Bennett, Isaac P211
Bennett, J Bradley P214
Bennett, Sarah P264
Bennett, Graham F P432
Bennett, Nancy P507
Bennett, Christopher P534
Bennett, Linda P587
Bennett, Arvilla P609
Bennett, Rhonda P662
Bennett, Ricardo W110
Bennett, David W197
Bennett, Christian W531
Bennett, Rodney E163
Bennett, Peter E448
Bennett-Martin, Pamela E174
Benning, Todd A826:E428
Benoit, Robert P347
Benoit, Garrett P348
Benoit, James L P506
Benoit, Pierre W402
Benoit, Laura E448
Benroth, Robert E423
Bensasson, Bruno W175
Bensaude, Eric A169
Bensema, David J P58
Bensen, Peter A154
Benson, P. George A20
Benson, Grant A29
Benson, David A292
Benson, Laurie A311
Benson, Jodi A347
Benson, Stanford A414
Benson, Sally A473
Benson, Molly A496:A541
Benson, Dea A666
Benson, Marta A865
Benson, Meg P120
Benson, Todd P138
Benson, Leonard P190
Benson, Stanford P260
Benson, Stephen P261
Benson, Sally P295
Benson, Rebecca P413
Benson, Chris P522:P541
Benson, Bruce P577
Benson, Nick P585
Benson, David P597
Benson, Grant E13
Benson, Beth E282
Benstock, Michael E398
Bentes, Patricia G. M. De A. W513
Bentinck, Bill E421
Bentine, John P33
Benton, Marcy A652
Benton, Patrick A805
Benton, David P292
Benton, Kelly E359
Bentsen, Tim A754:E401
Benyan, Yousef Abdullah Al W422
Benz, Hans E129
Benziger, Peter P430
Bepler, Stephen E P562
Ber, Christine P415
Ber, Bethany P452
Beracha, Barry A778:P561
Berahas, Solomon W383
Beran, Josette A775:P551

Beranek, Cheryl E86
Berard, Patrick A484
Berardi, Christina P492
Beraud, Jill A476:A477:P297
Berault, Eleanor P542
Berberian, Lance A464
Berce, Daniel E175
Berchtold, Joe A483
Berdan, Barclay P542
Berding, John A47
Beredo, Gina A601
Berendji, Sacha W311
Berenzweig, Harold P542
Beressi, Joseph W253
Beretta, Maurizio W509
Berg, Jeffrey A595
Berg, Mark A629
Berg, Hilary A807
Berg, David P30
Berg, Sarah P456
Berg, Dirk Jan van den W18
Berg, Sandra E20
Bergamo, Janet P37
Bergan, Chad A232
Bergantzel, Matthew P195
Berge, Jolyn P471
Bergen, Karen Van A589
Bergen, Bruce P171
Bergen, Jan L P564
Berger, Larry L A267
Berger, Howard A390
Berger, Anne P48
Berger, Lisa P340
Berger, Michael E10
Berger, Howard E215
Bergeron, Alain W239
Bergerson, Eric P624
Bergeson, Jan A32
Bergeson, Terry A741
Bergeson, Jan P24
Bergeson, Terry P518
Berggren, Arne W383
Bergh, Charles A404:A476:A477:P297
Berglund, Robert E271
Berglund, Steven E415
Bergman, Rick A13
Bergman, Naomi A203
Bergman, Stanley A696
Bergman, David A810
Bergman, Jason A874
Bergman, William T P536
Bergman, Chris P550
Bergmann, Chad P389
Bergmann, Theo W81
Bergonzi, Adam A507
Bergquist, Derek A770:P540
Bergquist, Leslie E198
Bergstein, Joseph A637
Bergstrm, Joakim P483
Bergstrom, Pal W470
Bergwall, Timothy A367
Berisford, John A691
Berk, Eric V P345
Berkay, H Sinan P499
Berkbigler, Marsha P172
Berke, Monique A717
Berke, Ethan M P182
Berke, Monique E379
Berkebile, Jane P395
Berkery, Rosemary A328
Berkley, William A112
Berkley, W. Robert A112
Berkley, Teresa P337
Berkowitz, David P159
Berkowitz, Martin A P579
Berkowitz, Bruce E387
Berlew, Adam A746
Berlinger, Stefanie W91
Berlinghieri, Leo E304
Berman, Walter A52
Berman, Robert A227
Berman, Ann A486
Berman, Natalie P367
Berman, Leon E97
Berman, Steven E123
Berman, Michael E377
Bermudez, Jorge A536

Bernabei, Salvatore W181
Bernacchi, Dino A719
Bernard, Edward A489
Bernard, Betsy A878
Bernard, Pamela J P196
Bernard, Michelle P205
Bernard, Karen P408
Bernardes, Ricardo P94
Bernardini, Roberto Di W152
Bernardino, Daniel W194
Bernardo, Remy A739:P515
Bernardo, Ed P596
Bernardo, Romeo W70
Bernat, Susan A775:P552
Bernd, David L W473
Berneke, Eva Soefelde W515
Berner, Kristy A617
Berner, Linda P508
Berner, Anne W446
Berner, Kristy E319
Bernhard, Robert A228
Bernica, Andrea C P76:P76
Bernick, Lea P750:P528
Bernicke, Jutta W224
Bernier, Jody P572
Bernier, Rick P605
Bernier, Jean W25
Berninger, Darren E282
Bernlohr, Timothy A860:E377
Bernritter, Tom P481
Bernstein, Dean A135
Bernstein, Luke A597
Bernstein, Lois I P357
Bernstein, Michael S P395
Bernstein, Samuel P427
Bernstein, Michael P431
Bernstein, Luke E307
Bernsten, James R A195:P140
Berquist, Carl A778:P561
Berra, Albert A709:E370
Berres, Jennifer A379
Berresford, Susan V A776:P558
Berrios, Marcelino P436
Berris, Anthony A492
Berro, Alan N P30
Berron, Diana P341
Berry, William A220
Berry, Michael A550
Berry, Thomas A647
Berry, Michael A735
Berry, William A749
Berry, Jessica A824
Berry, H Robert P57
Berry, Robert P73
Berry, Bob P112
Berry, Richard E P177
Berry, Greg P193
Berry, Hillary M P309
Berry, Beth P380
Berry, Peter P467
Berry, Michael P511
Berry, Jessica P617
Berry, Meridith P625
Berry, CJ W17
Berryhill, Tim P179
Berryman, Kevin A436
Berryman, Brad P532
Bersani, James A104
Berson, Jory A148
Bertholf, Leigh P19:P325
Bertley, Frederic A607:E312
Bertolini, Massimo W316
Bertrand, Greg P205
Bertrand, Farrah P25
Bertrand, Katy P107
Bertrand, Marc L P602
Bertrand, Maryse W322:W341
Bertsch, Leanne P310
Bertsch, Jan E59
Bertucci, Frank A372
Berube, Neil P46
Berutti, William E341
Berzin, Ann A286
Besca, Mark A497
Besga, Francisco Borja Acha W179
Besga, Francisco de Borja Acha W179
Beshar, Peter A500

Besharat, Alex W69
Beshear, Andy A208:P145
Besley, Ben P303
Besombes, Beatrice W90
Besong, John-Paul A655:A815:E340
Bess, Shay R P588
Bessant, Catherine A96
Bessette, Diane A474
Bessette, Andy A792
Bessey, Kerry A513:P328
Bessey, David P496
Best, C Munroe A108
Best, Craig A618
Best, Zia P582
Best, Eric P636
Best, Catherine W100
Bestard, Steven P336
Bestebreur, Patrick P482
Besteman, Dan A867
Bestgen, Jay P347
Bestland, Jennifer P333
Beswick, Paul A500
Betancourt, Cesar P508
Betancourt, Joseph P565
Betancourt, Jenifer P576
Bethancourt, John A243
Bethea, Paula Harper P267
Bethel, Charlie A735:P511
Bethell, Melissa W165
Betrus, Lisa P565
Bettano, Carla P24
Bettinger, Douglas A467
Bettinger, Terri A639
Bettinger, Walter A697
Bettinger, Terri E332
Bettington, Timothy A881
Betts, John A187
Betts, Debbie B P64
Betts, Craig P172
Betts, Brooks P344
Betts, John E85
Beullier, Alain W184
Beurden, Ben Van W434
Beuren, Archbold van A146
Beuret, Jean-Baptiste W514
Beyer, Robert A437
Beyer, Richard A527
Beyer, Ruth A A638
Beyer, Laurie A713
Beyer, Ruth A P426
Beyer, Gary P647
Beynon, Yan W451
Bezney, Michael P332
Bezos, Jeff A38
Bezzeccheri, Maurizio W181
Bezzecheri, Maurizio W179
Bhagat, Sarah P291
Bhagat, Vipul W82
Bhakta, Sanjay P122
Bhalla, Anant A45:A133
Bhalla, Ajay A506
Bhalla, Pavan E129
Bhalla, Vikas E151
Bhanap, Nina E343
Bhandari, Amit P75
Bhandari, Arpita P75
Bhandari, Manish P177
Bhandari, Naumit P613
Bhandari, Parul E409
Bhandarkar, Vedika W477
Bhasin, Puneet A827
Bhasin, Rachna E369
Bhathal, Alex E97
Bhatia, Vaishali A391
Bhatia, Manish A527
Bhatia, Sangeeta A835
Bhatt, Pratik A182
Bhatt, Keyur P233
Bhatt, Bankim P498
Bhatt, Om W477:W478
Bhatt, Padmanabh E399
Bhattacharya, Ashis E451
Bhatti, Hammad W476
Bhaumik, Sam E39
Bhela, Harvinder A550
Bhojwani, Gary A194
Bhuiya, Ehsanul P133

COMBINED HOOVER'S HANDBOOK INDEX OF EXECUTIVES

A = AMERICAN BUSINESS
E = EMERGING COMPANIES
P = PRIVATE COMPANIES
W = WORLD BUSINESS

Bhusri, Aneel A349
Biagas, John A640:E333
Biagini-Komas, Julianne A382:E211
Bian, Xuemei W209
Bian, Deyun W535
Bianca, Carmella P197
Biancardi, Steve P126
Bianchi, Robert J P365
Bianchi, Mirko W509
Bianchi, Stephen E83
Bianco, Lawrence A781:P580
Bibeau, Chris P242
Bibelheimer, Jason E200
Bibi, Mark E229
Bibic, Mirko W82
Bibisi, Ray E354
Bible, Daryl A796
Bible, Hannah E111
Biblo, Lee P223
Bice, R. Shawn A846
Bich, Genevieve W322
Bickford, Brian P54
Bickford, Anna P194
Bickham, W. Bradley E5
Bicking, Rachel P537
Bickley, Craig P144
Biddle, Belinda P572
Biddle, James E148
Bideaux, Patty P175
Biden, Beau A735:P511
Bidwell, Victoria P216
Bie, Richard P230
Bieber, Tammy P182
Bieber, Eric P451
Bieber, Martin A P499
Biedenkopf, Sebastian W204
Biedermann, Wynn P333
Biediger, Michael P298
Bielan, Judith A106:E48
Bieler, Ilene A743
Bienaime, Jean-Jacques E225
Bienfait, Robin W213
Bierman, James A765
Biern, Betsy P115
Biesiadecki, Brandon P572
Biesterfeld, Robert A683
Bigbee, Paul E72
Bigby, Walter E352
Bigej, Laurie P635
Bigelow, Melissa P69
Biggar, Lynne A839
Bigger, Brad P572
Biggers, Jo P155
Biggins, Lillie P541
Biggs, Brett A11
Biggs, Ray P472
Bigham, Justin A307
Bigioi, Petronel E456
Bigley, Deirdre E369
Bigos-Jaworowska, Sabina W70
Bigot, Domitille Doat-Le E273
Bihan, Sandrine Le W519
Bihuniak, Peter P61
Bilbeisi, Rana P500
Bilbrey, John A146
Bilbrey, Mary A443
Bileddo, Anthony P284
Biles, Dwayne P530
Bilgic, Murat W504
Bill, Jim P161
Billera, Patrick P638
Billes, Owen W101
Billes, Martha W101
Billiar, Tim A828:P634
Billing, Mina W3
Billings, Frank E A864
Billings, Frank A864
Billings, Tom P42
Billingsley, Lori George A629
Billingsley, Mary P428
Billingsley, Justin W395

Billington, Phillip A379
Billman, Brock P293
Billot, Thierry W106
Billotte, Mike P610
Billotti, Nicholas A799:P605
Bills, Paul P243
Bilodeau, Marc P261
Bilunas, Matthew A115
Bimmerman, Julie E358
Binbasgil, Sabri W21
Binda, Marc E13
Bindelglass, David P87
Binder, Stephanie P650
Bindra, Jagjeet A722
Binerer, David A293:P212
Binger, Benjamen M P136
Binger, James M P136
Bingham, Kim A157
Bingham, R. Dean A530
Bingham, Gwendolyn A600
Bingham, John P640
Bingham, Kim E70
Bingham, R. Dean E275
Bingham-Hall, Penny W200
Bingold, Michael A329
Binkowski, Chuck P63
Binning, Paviter W527
Binns, Justin A708
Bintz, John P247
Bintz, William E40
Biodrowski, Mark P130
Biondic, Katarina A16:P8
Biorck, Hans W470
Biraghi, Sonna A268
Birch, Jean E182
Birchmeier, Cindy A366:P235
Bird, Roger A4
Bird, Suzie A838
Bird, Anat A870
Bird, Suzie P641
Bird, Graham W213
Bird, Anat E455
Birkans, Aldis A544:E285
Birkenstock, Timothy L P116
Birkenstock, Tim P340
Birkett, Sharon E P357
Birkett, Bernard E446
Birkett-Rakow, Diana A26
Birkhimer, Harry E20
Birmingham, Melody A1
Birmingham, Martin A307
Birmingham, Scott P597
Birnbaum, Leonhard W169
Birney, Kathleen P396
Birns, Ira A869
Birrell, Gordon W91
Birx, Deborah E229
Birznieks, Gunther E432
Bisagni, Gianfranco W509
Bisaro, Paul A881
Biscardi, Joseph P1
Bischoff, Lou P44
Biscoglia, Dianna P353
Bisgaard, Chris P4
Bishar, John E29
Bisher, Jon P33
Bishop, Christopher A135
Bishop, Karen A224
Bishop, Steven A643
Bishop, Kayla A736
Bishop, Amy A770
Bishop, Deena P36
Bishop, Karen P172
Bishop, Alan P207
Bishop, John P301
Bishop, Lisa P340
Bishop, Adrianna P424
Bishop, Jake P440
Bishop, Cecelia P507
Bishop, Kayla P512
Bishop, Alison P525
Bishop, Amy P540
Bishop, Maryellen Kiley P602
Bishop, Michael P616
Bishop, Walter E376
Bisignano, Frank A325:A406
Bisio, Aldo W520

Bisio, Ronald E415
Bismarck, Nilufer Von W291
Bitner, Rachel E134
Bitter, Stephen P46
Bittner, Edward P610
Bitzer, Marc A863
Bixby, Walter A446
Bixby, R. Philip A446
Biyari, Khaled W423
Bizzarri, Marco W273
Bizzell, Sandra P158
Bjerg, Carsten W514
Bjerke, Rune W363
Bjorck, Meredith W P252
Bjorlin, Alexis E120
Bjornaas, Judith E259
Bjornholt, James A525
Bjur, Jared P213
Black, Maria A81
Black, David A176
Black, Thomas A386
Black, Steven A543
Black, Eddie P287
Black, Douglas P346
Black, Michael P528
Black, Michael E P587
Black, Andrew P630
Black, Randall P84
Black, Barton E153
Black, Archie E337:E385
Black, Laura E436
Blackburn, Katherine A306
Blackburn, Robert A731
Blackhurst, Eric A400:E218
Blackmon, Tanya A573:P390
Blackmore, Steven A638:P426
Blackstone, Gail P167
Blackstone, Becky P557
Blackstone, Kathy P557
Blackwelder, Megan P389
Blackwell, Jean A160
Blackwell, Donald K P361
Blackwood, Stephen E404
Blade, Mark A316
Blades, Alexander W383
Blagg, Tandy P253
Blahnik, Ronald E213
Blain, Keith P379
Blaine, Jennifer P496
Blair, Carolyn A32
Blair, Donald A222
Blair, Rainer A235
Blair, Kevin A754
Blair, Judith P627
Blair, W. Bradley E207
Blair, Kevin E401
Blais, Andrew A740:P516
Blais, François W239
Blaisdell, Andrew P104
Blaise, Dale P490
Blake, Katryn A33
Blake, Ryan A106
Blake, Francis A242
Blake, Vanessa P36
Blake, Joe P143
Blake, Randy P262
Blake, Joseph J P428
Blake, Ryan E48
Blake, Elizabeth E199
Blakeborough, Lawrence B P36
Blakely, Kevin A405
Blakemore, Dominic W139
Blakeslee, Christopher P87
Blakey, Richard A274
Blakey, Rachel P384
Blaku, Sherif P265
Blalock, Robert A814:E424
Blanc, Paul La P492
Blanc, Amanda W51
Blanca, Tere A101
Blancas, Monica P202
Blanch, Jodi A650
Blanchard, William P165
Blanchard, Saundra P332
Blanchard, Karl P475
Blanchard, Thomas E240
Blanchet, Paul A392

Blanchet, Lucie W341
Blanchet, Paul E216
Blanchette, Bob P204
Blanchette, Harvey P535
Blanco, Alex A610
Blanco, Monica P133
Blanco, Patricia J P465
Blanco, Arturo P499
Blangiardi, Rick P121
Blank, Donna A22
Blank, Gregory A548
Blank, Dana M A803
Blank, Dr Josef P184
Blank, Dana M P606
Blank, Bradley W E413
Blanka-Graff, Markus W286
Blankenburg, Karen A7
Blankenship, Jeffrey P270
Blanton, Caron P81
Blase, Maria E451
Blasing, Karen E38
Blasio, Bill De A186:P129
Blasquez, Tricia P430
Blaszyk, Michael A245:P189
Blatnik, Balinda P271
Blatter, Sandy P437
Blaufuss, Mark P336
Blaut, Brandon A293:P211
Blavatnik, Len A846
Blaylock, Steven P383
Blazer, Randolph E32
Blazheev, Victor W386
Blears, Hazel W132
Blegen, Bernie E279
Bleier, Ingo W187
Bleisch, N A583
Bleser, Philip A645
Blessing, William A446
Blessington, Malisa P200
Blevins, P. Rodney A254
Blevins, Robert P176
Blevins, Wade P548
Blew, Clinton A175
Bley, Daniel A851
Blickensdoerfer, Hans-Martin E388
Blickenstaff, Scott E543
Blickley, Matthew A197
Blidner, Jeffrey W94
Bliesener, Kai W522
Blin, Bruno W523
Blinn, Mark A273:A471
Blinn, Tom P529
Bliss, Lilly P443
Bliss, Ethan P519
Blissett, Julian A349
Blixt, Dianne A52
Bloch, Gilad W63
Blocher, John E184
Block, Andrew A7
Block, Joanna P204
Block, Lauren D P301
Blodgett, Rick P163
Bloemke, Nathaniel P620
Blok, Eelco W484
Blom, David P395
Blondel, Loic P537
Blondin, Leon E P55
Bloom, Mark A337
Bloom, Rick P239
Bloom, Adam P379
Bloom, Mark W13
Bloomfield, Steven F P122
Bloomquist, Cathy P261
Bloomquist, Andrea E378
Blose, Dennis R P355
Bloshtein, Eli P152
Blosser, Courtney E314
Blouin, Pedrina P402
Blouin, Pierre W341
Blount, Melba P159
Bloxam, Richard A443
Blue, Robert A254
Blue, Daniel A309
Blue, Robert A838
Blue, Dan P463
Blue, Daniel E162
Bluestone, Jeffrey A355

496

HOOVER'S HANDBOOK OF EMERGING COMPANIES 2022

COMBINED HOOVER'S HANDBOOK INDEX OF EXECUTIVES

Bluford, John F P601
Blum, Kristen A729
Blum, Audrey P120
Blum, Fred P163
Blum, John P450
Blum, Steven E38
Blum, Bradley E454
Blume, Jessica A162:A652
Blume, Oliver W522
Blumenreich, Hilary A210
Blumofe, Robert E11
Blumstein, Shelia P90
Blumstein, Jerold P579
Blunck, Thomas W337
Blunk, Maggie P587
Blunt, Ricky P161
Blunt, Matt E101
Blyer, David E149
Blythe, Douglas P161
Bo, Frode W454
Boardman, Michael A617:E319
Boasberg, Tom P467
Boatright, Nancy A98
Boattini, Jennifer A408
Boatwright, Scott A174
Boatwright, Joe A872
Bobadilla, Luis Isasi Fernandez de W61
Boban, Ivica P654
Bobb, George E404
Bobbitt, Rhodes A388
Bobbitt, Donald R P616
Bobo, Donald A269
Bobst, Wendell J A14:P5
Boccalandro, Cristina P587
Boccassino, Piero Franco Maria W252
Bochenek, David A713
Bochinsky, Michael W415
Bochnowski, David E161
Bochnowski, Benjamin E162
Bock, Sharon R P166
Bockelmann, Alexander W55
Bockius, Tom P158
Bodaken, Bruce A679
Bodenhamer, Kevin P597
Bodgs, Lynn P426
Bodhisompon, Thantika W62
Bodine, Bruce A539
Bodor, Robert E337
Boe, Casey P36
Boeck, Karel De W383
Boeckmann, Alan A122:A705:P80
Boeckstiegel, Claudia W408
Boedecker, George B P323
Boedeker, Kenneth A281
Boege, Kathleen A867:E452
Boehme, Linda P492
Boehnke, David A232
Boehnlein, Glenn A749
Boel, Nicolas W451
Boemer, Sally Mason P565
Boening, Jon Van P54
Boer, William A417
Boer, Dick W434
Boer, William E226
Boerner, Christophe A134
Boes, Charles W P542
Boettcher, Charles A848
Bogan, Marc J E439
Bogardus, James W P228
Bogart, Teresa Van De E345
Bogart, Stacy E451
Bogdanoff, Debra P173
Bogdanov, Vladimir W468
Bogdanovich, Jan W27
Boger, Richard E199
Boggess, Carrie P99
Boggs, Scott A396
Bogle, Jill P68
Bognar, Piroska W334
Boguski, Michael A642
Bohbot, Dominic A445:P279
Bohbot, Jean-Luc W529
Bohl, Howard P610
Bohle, Birgit W163
Bohlig, Tamara A90:E41
Bohm, Lori P177
Bohm, Friedrich E257

Bohman, Mark P236
Bohman, Staffan W3:W48
Bohn, Jeremiah P345
Bohn, Karen E309
Bohnert, Denise E18
Bohorquez, Carlos P201
Bohrson, Christopher E90
Bohuny, Bruce A466:E243
Bohuon, Olivier W475
Bohutinsky, Amy A877
Boid, Jonathan P121
Boigon, Aaron E327
Boillat, Pascal W135
Boise, April A264:P200
Boisvert, Gerald P242
Boisvert, Gerry J P243
Boisvert, Marc E P647
Boivin, Pierre W322:W341
Bojdak, Robert A491
Bok, Oscar De W162
Bokan, Michael A527
Boland, Sylvia P124
Bolander, Ron A736:P512
Bolash, Brian E145
Boldea, Lucian A264
Boldrini, Maura A781:P581
Boldt, Oscar C P546
Boldt, Thomas J P546
Bolduc, Guy P309
Boley, Marygen P25
Bolger, Thomas A174:P118
Bolger, T Michael P566
Bolger, Andrea W290
Bolin, Jonathan P254
Bolin, Mike P287
Boll, Jared P255
Bollesen, Michael E264
Bollin, Stacey P351
Bollinger, Kathy A102
Bollinger, Lee C A781
Bollinger, Kathy P56
Bollinger, Lee C P581
Bollore, Thierry W477
Bollore, Yannick W518
Bollore, Cyrille W518
Bolomey, Janice E425
Bolster, Jennifer P504
Bolt, Tracy A388
Bolton, Heidi P471
Boltz, William A488
Boltz, Jim P413
Boltz, Elaine E110
Bolus, Mark A210:E95
Boly, Sarah P68
Bom, Luis Manuel Pego Todo W206
Boman, Ronald P507
Boman, Paer W471
Bomboy, David A309:E163
Bommarito, Pamela P507
Bompard, Alexandre W104
Bona, Miklos P620
Bonacich, Jane P90
Bonadero, Anthony W138
Bonarti, Michael A81
Bonavita, Salvatore P284
Bonawitz, Douglas I P654
Boncariewski, Susan P186
Bond, Lisa A710
Bond, James P103
Bond, Harrison P151
Bond, Elizabeth P420
Bond, Bradley P614
Bond, Lisa E371
Bondank, Cheryl P382
Bondar, Lori A86
Bondi, Paolo W179
Bonds, Doug P87
Bondurant, Robert D P314
Bondurant, Bob P315
Bondy, Joel A552:P369
Bone, Norman W294
Boneparth, Peter A439:A459
Bonewell, Fred P136
Boney, John P45
Bonfield, Andrew A156
Bonfiglio, Joanne P55
Bonfiglio, Gregory P427

Bonga, Bradley E53
Bongiovanni, Clarice P293
Bonham, Scott W69
Boniface, William P160
Bonifas, Edward A587:E302
Bonilla, Emily P166
Bonilla, Pilar P392
Bonin, Deb P24
Bonini, John E448
Bonnafe, Jean-Laurent W87
Bonnard, Luc W425
Bonnecarrere, Celeste P503
Bonnel, Julien W402
Bonnell, William W340
Bonnell, Brian E220
Bonner, Eimear A172
Bonner, Suzanne A673
Bonner, Jo A734
Bonner, Allison P84
Bonner, Daniel P124
Bonner, Bill P157
Bonner, Sharon P221
Bonner, Yvonne P275
Bonner, Jo P510
Bonner, Dr Jim P615
Bonner, Joseph E153
Bonnevier, Pam P389
Bono, Raquel A406
Bontempo, C. Angela A491
Bontemps, Stephanie A323
Bontrager, Jeffrey A P116
Bontrager, Kimberlee E394
Bonzani, Andrew A428
Boo, Alexander A De A267
Book, Julia P73
Booker, Martin A59
Booker, Jessica A327:P214
Booker-Westerfi, Judy P72
Bookman, Dominique P336
Bookmyer, John A639:E332
Bookout, John F A779:P567
Boom, Marc
  L A403:A779:P256:P567:P594
Boondech, Prasobsook W98
Boondoungprasert, Prasit W113
Boone, Kevin A227
Boone, Cornelius A266
Boone, Jerry E P233
Boone, Jody P459
Boone, Deborah A P652
Boone, Christopher E60
Boonklum, Peangpanor W393
Boonlertvanich, Karin W270
Boonpoapichart, Kriengchai W98
Boonyanusasna, Rawin W284
Boonyawat, Nuttawit W65
Boonyoung, Pridi W98
Boor, Kathryn A426
Boor, William E72
Booth, Cynthia A315
Booth, Jane E A781
Booth, Kerri P155
Booth, Chris P314
Booth, Steve P448
Booth, Jane E P581
Booth, Richard E107
Booth, Kenneth E109
Booth, Cynthia E167
Boothe, Timothy A857:E447
Bootsma, Pieter W18
Booze, Randy P128
Boozer, Angela P131
Boozer, Leslie P217
Bopp, Mike A752
Bopp, Aric H P128
Borak, John E286
Boran, Patrick P382
Boranian, Denise P95
Boratto, Eva A819
Borba, George A230:E113
Borchers, Bradford E303
Bordelon, John A392
Bordelon, Herbie P347
Bordelon, John E216
Borden, Ian A509
Borden, Douglas E164
Bordenave, Claire W175

Borders, Lisa P123
Borders, Charlie P286
Bordovsky, Khaki P86
Borean, Cristiano W43
Borg, April M P457
Borgard, Lawrence P35
Borger, Janet P333
Borges, Steven A434
Borges, Francisco A437
Borges, Sandra Kee P126
Borges, Gary P132
Borges, Fernando W380
Borglund, Patricia P22
Borgman, Charles L A200
Borgmann, Kevin A148
Borgstrom, Marna P P660:P660
Bori, Carlos A715
Borin, Mark P323
Boring, Tricia P646
Borio, Luciana E233
Boris, David E219
Borja, Paul A326
Borja, Renato De W323
Borja, Paul E177
Borkar, Rani A66
Borkoski, Virginia P338
Borlee, Grace P142
Bornemann, Keith A388
Bornemann, Felipe Echaiz W56
Bornhoft, Barbara E299
Borninkhof, K. Michelle A84
Bornmann, David A652
Borodkin, Theresa P118
Boroughs, Timothy W126
Borowy, Don A203:P144
Borra, Barbara W397
Borras, Maria Claudia A91
Borras, Maria A802
Borrego, Miguel Angel Lopez W444
Borres, Anna P168
Borroum, Leon A362:P232
Bors, Kimberly A256
Borschuk, Richard P225
Borst, George E260
Borthwick, Alastair A96
Borup, Jens W267
Borzi, James A106
Boscak, Alexis P623
Bosch, Scott P242
Bosch, Stephan P657
Bosco, Sara A273
Boscov, Albert P84
Boshoven, Stephen A727:P495
Bosio, Chris A737:P513
Boskey, Richard S P180
Bosley, Marvenia P144
Boss, R. Daniel A280
Boss, Jane P97
Bossemeyer, Sandra W415
Boster, Gina P154
Bostian, Elizabeth A309:E162
Bostick, Thomas A227
Boston, Larris P239
Boston, Charlie P572
Boston, Carolyn P618
Bostrom, Brent A369
Bostrom, Matt P167
Bostrom, Brent P237
Bostwick, Melissa P548
Boswell, Gina A494
Boswood, Mike P603
Bosworth, Michael A724
Bosworth, Jim P101:P142
Bot, Bernard W1:W276
Botelho, Marcelo P94
Botelho, Lee P160
Botello, Yvette P171
Botta, G. Andrea A168
Bottenhofer, Alison P299
Botticelli, Anne P92
Bottiglieri, James E97
Bottom, Angela P421
Bottoms, Keisha Lance P123
Bottorff, Jim P259
Bouchard, Rhonda P521
Bouchard, Alain W25
Boucher, Richard W145

COMBINED HOOVER'S HANDBOOK INDEX OF EXECUTIVES

A = AMERICAN BUSINESS
E = EMERGING COMPANIES
P = PRIVATE COMPANIES
W = WORLD BUSINESS

Bouchiat, Pascal W488
Bouchillon, Dennis P150
Bouda, Christopher A235
Boudreau, Philip A4
Boudreau, Helen A573:P391
Boudreaux, Gail A63
Boudreaux, Chad A410
Boudreaux, Kathryn P67
Boudreaux, Mike P171
Bouet, Vivan P136
Bough, Bonin A625
Boughner, Bob P311
Bouillon, Allison P135
Boujoulian, Tara P172
Boulanger, Normand A P196
Boulanger, Bernard P567
Boulanger, Serge W322
Boulay, Joseph P64
Boulden, Melanie A11
Boulet, Jean-Francois W239
Bounds, Hank P81
Bourassa, Joel E422
Bourbulas, Mary-Kay A94:E45
Bourdeau, Jim A218
Bourdeau, Nancy P472
Bourdon, Thomas P413
Bourey, James M P129
Bourgeois, Meagan L P348
Bourget, Kristina E83
Bourke, Evelyn W311
Bourla, Albert A622
Bourne, Anedra P132
Bourne, Robert E448
Bourqui, Elisabeth W524
Bousbib, Ari A433
Boushka, Julie A760
Bousquet, Agathe W395
Boutain, Dana E96
Boutebba, Frederic W152
Boutte, Gregory W273
Bouygues, Martin W90
Bouygues, Olivier W90
Bouygues, Charlotte W90
Bouygues, Olivier W133
Bouzuk, Michael P634
Bove, Joyce M A210
Bove, V P318
Bowan, Matt P253
Bowden, Randy P55
Bowe, Patrick A61
Bowe, Monica A310:E164
Bowen, William A53
Bowen, Sharon A422
Bowen, Arthur N A838
Bowen, John A847
Bowen, Jos A P491
Bowen, William G P544
Bowen, Julie P569
Bowen, Arthur N P641
Bowen, Sharon E11
Bowen, William E25
Bowen, Julia E449
Bowen-Biggs, Tara P164
Bowens, Samuel P135
Bower, Joseph A486
Bower, Charles M P42
Bower, John P261
Bower, Vivienne W396
Bower, Huw E451
Bowers, Reveta A10
Bowers, W. Paul A18:A286
Bowers, Lee A688
Bowers, Alyssa P146
Bowers, Kirby M P162
Bowers, Alisa P417
Bowers, Thomas A E155
Bowes, Amy P586
Bowie, Paul J A16:P8
Bowie, Patrick C P358
Bowie, Peter W306
Bowker, Michael E60

Bowler, Chris A598
Bowler, E. Joseph A856
Bowles, W Bryan P184
Bowles, Connie P293
Bowles, Jack W93
Bowlin, John E191
Bowling, Ronald A750
Bowling, Kathy P40
Bowling, Ronald E394
Bowman, Michelle A301
Bowman, Stephen A319
Bowman, Lisa A352
Bowman, William A609
Bowman, Beth A760
Bowman, Maureen P68
Bowman, Jerry P98
Bowman, Azuree P122
Bowman, Jeff P153
Bowman, Jeffrey P417
Bowman, Kerry P543
Bowman, Cory P564
Bowman, Stephen E171
Bowman, Brent E245:E433
Bowser, Muriel A362
Bowser, Carmen A613
Bowser, Brad P140
Bowser, Muriel P232
Bowser, Christopher P459
Bowser, Carmen E316
Boxer, Mark A178
Boxer, Michael A784
Boxley, Abney A628
Boxley, Tracee P432
Boxley, Abney E232:E324
Boyan, George E426
Boyce, Gregory A558
Boyce, David A789
Boyce, Paula P333
Boyce, David E182
Boychuk, Jamie A227
Boychuk, Michael W290
Boyd, Martin A304
Boyd, Ralph A693
Boyd, Rebecca A717
Boyd, Kendra P31
Boyd, Terry P144
Boyd, Ken P173
Boyd, Donald P280
Boyd, Mary P330
Boyd, Vivian P498
Boyd, Randy P629
Boyd, Stephen E57
Boyd, Ralph E360
Boyd, Rebecca E380
Boydston, Cory A139
Boydston, Brent E321
Boyer, Ellen A102
Boyer, Eric P410
Boyer, Debbie P507
Boyer, Matt P580
Boyer, Geoffrey E132
Boyer, David E290
Boyes, John C A293:P212
Boyett, Dale P508
Boyington, Sheila P241
Boykin, Jennifer A410
Boykin, Haley E129
Boyko, Eric W25
Boylan, Katie M A761
Boylan, Peter C P457
Boyland, Gloria A817
Boyle, Kristoffer P175
Boyle, Theresa M P357
Boyle, Bryan P421
Boyle, Jodell J P461
Boyle, Nadine P539
Boyle, Gerry W395
Boyles, Jonathan A716
Boyles, Kevin P226
Boyles, Jonathan E379
Boyll, Ann P93
Boynton, Timothy J P291
Boynton, Lewis P319
Boysen, Doug P461
Boyt, John P107
Boza, Xavier A146:E321
Boze, Brandon A159

Bozer, Kamil W505
Bozic, Carmen A835
Bozotti, Carlo A88
Bozzoli, Carlo W181
Bozzuto, Michael A P85
Bozzuto, Jayne A P85
Braams, Conny W510
Brabec, Hannah P45
Bracey, Esi A865
Bracher, Paul A227
Bracher, Candido A506
Bracht, Berend A609
Brachtenbach, Mike P423
Brack, Dennis A296:E157
Bracken, Franklin A332
Bracken, Sam P225
Brackey, Wesley P176
Bracy, Kevin A408
Bracy, Andrew A737:P513
Bradbury, Peter A562
Bradbury, Kim A327
Bradbury, Peter P378
Bradehoft, Nancy P345
Brader, Andy P73
Bradford, Gregory A142
Bradford, Allison P218
Bradford, Michael P539
Bradicich, Kevin A375
Bradicich, Thomas E34
Bradie, Stuart A448
Bradley, Jacqueline A701
Bradley, Tom P70
Bradley, Christopher P162
Bradley, Kelly P166
Bradley, Philip C P211
Bradley, Tonya P276
Bradley, Maureen P294
Bradley, Joseph P333
Bradley, Russell P336
Bradley, Leslie P407
Bradley, James P432
Bradley, Myra James P598
Bradley, J Lindsey P600
Bradley, Bryan W100
Bradley, Catherine W276
Bradley, Michael E140
Bradley, Keith E234
Bradley, Jacqueline E365
Bradshaw, Stanley A310
Bradshaw, Richard A814
Bradshaw, Stanley E164
Bradshaw, Richard E424
Bradway, Robert A57
Bradway, Jennifer A267
Brady, Elizabeth A32
Brady, Kevin A79
Brady, Amy A260
Brady, Christopher A345
Brady, Deanna T A401
Brady, Amy A453
Brady, Robert A491
Brady, Kimberly P4
Brady, Kevin P52
Brady, Katie P357
Brady, L Keith P358
Brady, Melissa P421
Brady, Lisa P505
Brady, Patrick P529
Brady, Vicki W484
Brady, Barrett E284
Brady, Laura E284
Braeger, Matthew A74
Braemer, Richard A788
Braendlin, Daniel W75
Brafman, Lester E89
Braford, Lee E81
Braga, Rogerio Carvalho W255
Brager, David A230:E113
Bragg, Doug A579
Bragg, Sandra A770
Bragg, Lakethia P269
Bragg, Sandra P540
Bragg, Alisha P554
Bragg, Amy P627
Braham, Tor E436
Braico, Cosmo P408
Braidi, Chris P128

Brainard, Lael A301
Brainard, John P30
Brainerd, Mary A380:A749:P247
Braithwaite, Robert P253
Brajevich, Joseph A P303
Brake, Francis A870:E454
Brakefield, Sheryl P492
Brakel, Becky P379
Braker, Veronica A68
Braly, Angela A643:W94
Bram, Douglas P591
Bramble, James E152
Bramhall, Dylan A750
Bramlage, Steve A155
Bramlage, Andrew P248
Bramlett, E Chandler P262
Bramman, Anne A508:A565
Branagan, Ian W399
Brancatella, Giuseppe P192
Branch, Gregory A816
Branch, Amy P287
Branch, Matthew P345
Brand, Dennis A94
Brand, Rachel A845
Brand, Rick P212
Brand, H C W421
Brand, Dennis E44
Brandis, Karen E282
Brandley, Paul P317
Brandner, Christopher P353
Brandon, Joseph A29
Brandon, David A258
Brandt, Tim A31
Brandt, Christopher A175
Brandt, Kristi A380
Brandt, Eric A467
Brandt, Bryan A598
Brandt, Barry A869
Brandt, Tim P24
Brandt, Ken P36
Brandt, Hilde P129
Brandt, Doug P212
Brandt, Kristi P247
Brandt, Douglas P354
Brandt, Steve P463
Brandt, Barry P659
Brandt, Werner W415
Brandt, Tammy E42
Brangan, Diane E P198
Brannon, Jill A302
Brannon, Joe P380
Branstetter, Matthew E157:E422
Brantley, John P107
Brase, John A718
Brash, David P649
Brasher, Robert A468
Brasier, Barbara A534
Brass, Alan P595
Brasseux, Murray A280
Brathwaite, Nicholas E330
Bratspies, Stephen A373
Bratt, Sanida A77
Bratt, Mikael A80
Bratton, Sheryl P170
Brauchle, Gary P532
Braude, Michael A446
Braude, Katie P302
Brauer, John A203
Brauer, Bryan P256
Brauer, Lori P439
Brauer-Rieke, David P294
Braughton, Larry P60
Braun, Henrique A196
Braun, Vianei A315
Braun, James P322
Braun, Elaine P579
Braun, Joseph E123
Braun, Vianei E167
Braunagel, Pat P286
Braunegg, George A516
Brauner, Thomas P536
Brav, Angela A385
Bravata, Scott A805
Braveman, Peter E P105
Braveman, Carla P204
Braverman, Alan N A251
Bravico, Ann P171

COMBINED HOOVER'S HANDBOOK INDEX OF EXECUTIVES

Bravo, Lucy P135
Bravo, Patrick P524
Bravo, Giovanna P572
Brawley, Otis A21:E225
Braxton, Cordellia S P641
Bray, Jesse A541
Bray, Justin A713
Bray, David A802
Bray, Tana P9
Bray, Curtis P471
Bray, Dee L P522
Bray, Jesse E281
Brayboy, Regina P P642
Braziel, Rick P168
Brazier, Allan W37
Brazile, Tameka P164
Brazile, Jasmine P180
Brea, Jorge P307
Bready, Cameron A358
Breard, Linda A420:E329
Breault, Debra P188
Breaux, Randall A350
Breaux, Clayton P470
Breber, Pierre A172
Brecker, John P191
Bredesen, Governor Phil P629
Bredow, Eugene A578
Bree, Margaret Van P444
Breed, London A185:P122
Breen, Edward A203:A260
Breen, David E257
Breese, Cory P411
Breezee, Jack P529
Brega, Joao A863
Bregier, Fabrice W184:W428
Bregman, Steven E186
Breig, Geralyn A373:E2
Breighner, Robert A703
Breimann, Christoph W227
Breiner, Lindsey P308
Breit, Danny P332
Breitbard, Mark A777
Breitenbach, Matthew P156
Breitenbach, T G P323
Breithaupt, Chantelle E34
Breitschmid, Markus P642
Brekelmans, Harry W434
Brekke, Stein-Erling A283:P208
Brekke, Sigve W483
Bremer, Richard P173
Breneman, Jill P410
Brennan, Micheal A8
Brennan, Daniel A132
Brennan, Thomas A155
Brennan, Troyen A232
Brennan, Joseph A328
Brennan, Karen A443
Brennan, Katherine A500
Brennan, Murray F A513
Brennan, Micheal P4
Brennan, Anne P19
Brennan, Meagan P164
Brennan, Judy P172
Brennan, Murray F P328
Brennan, Connie P521
Brennan, Daniel P532
Brennan, Ita E62
Brennan, Alice E186
Brenner, Maxine W532
Brenner, Teresa E206
Brenoee, Lars-Erik W154
Brent, Guy W532
Bresch, Heather A837
Bresky, Jacob A700
Bresky, Ellen A700
Breslawski, James A696
Breslin, Michael P372
Breslin, Stephen E8
Bressan, Marco W509
Bressanelli, Leo A P227
Bressanutti, Irene P434
Bressette, Sharon P587
Bressler, Kathy P175
Bretches, David A64
Brethauer, Craig P504
Breton, Hugo W389
Brett, Mark P493

Brett, John W39
Breu, Nancy P141
Breuer, James A328
Breuer, Mark W156
Breuhl, James P452
Breuing, Kris P213
Breuninger, Barbara W222
Breves, Christine A821
Brew, Joseph P179
Brewer, Allen A329
Brewer, Rosalind A843
Brewer, Latonya P163
Brewer, Melanie P615
Brewer, Andrew W30
Brewer, Kevin J E40
Brewster, J. Chris E200
Brexler, James P241
Breyer, Michael K P285
Brian, Brad E60
Briant, Debbie P360
Brich, Kirsten W154
Brickey, Joe P232
Brickman, James E199
Bride, Judy P68
Brider, Connie P615
Bridge, Courtney P97
Bridgeforth, J. Scott A750:E394
Bridgers, Candice P143
Bridges, Wendy A204
Bridges, Linda A561
Bridges, S P188
Bridges, Susan A P471:P472
Bridges, Alan P604
Bridgmon, Jessica P70
Brien, Tierney P95
Brier, Bonnie S A555
Brier, Pamela P307
Brier, Bonnie S P374
Brierty, Tim P613
Brigati, Allison F A803:P606
Briggs, Xavier D A776
Briggs, Paul P254
Briggs, Craig A P285
Briggs, Xavier D P558
Briggs, Vikki E111
Brigham, Brent A804
Brigham, Margie P478
Brigham, Brent P607
Bright, W. Byron A448
Bright, Vonette Z P96
Bright, William P282
Brighton, W. Curtis A316
Brigman, Clair P590
Briks, Benjamin W261
Brilhante, William P160
Brill, Martin J P246
Brill, James E32
Brimberry, Jared A27:P15
Brimmer, Andrea E131
Brin, Sergey A34
Brinch, Brian A296:E157
Brindamour, Charles W99:W250
Briner, Michael P418
Bringhurst, Blaine R P561
Brink, Brooke P467
Brink, Martin van den W42
Brinkenfeldt-Lever, Viveca W3
Brinkley, Cynthia A41
Brinkley, Amy A686
Brinkley, Renee P420
Brinkley, Ruth P457
Brinkman, Joe E81
Brinkman, Richard E160
Brinkworth, Heather P467
Brinton, Jon E109
Brisco, Joyce P52
Brisco, John P371
Briscoe-tonic, Kimberly E95
Briskin, Jared E213
Bristow, Peter A312
Britenriker, Barbara E155
Britigan, Bradley E P366
Brito, Sylvia P174
Brito, Paulo E37
Britt, Alana P640
Britt, Douglas E209
Britt, Clair E257

Brittain, Miles E297
Britten, Will A458:P287
Brittingham, Alan P20
Britto, Mark A611
Britton, Lynn A517
Britton, William P19
Britton, Lynn P331:P334:P340
Brizan, Roseann P408
Brizard, Jean C P449
Brlas, Laurie A286:A364
Brnovich, Susan A734:P510
Broad, Matthew A236
Broadbent, Jillian W304
Broadhead, David P18
Broadsword, Joyce A735:P511
Broback, Craig P233
Brobst, Barbara A597
Brobst, Duane A826
Brobst, Barbara E307
Brobst, Duane E428
Broccard, Gary P16
Broccoli, Arthur P165
Brochick, George A615
Brock, Charisse A214
Brock, Charles A628
Brock, Joe P112
Brock, Leslie P193
Brock, Debra P314
Brock, Jane E P546
Brock, Charles E324
Brockhaus, John A228
Brockhoff, Brian E207
Brockman, Robert E286
Brockwell, Matthew A261:E126
Brodbeck, Joel T P174
Broden, Max A18
Brodhead, Richard P196
Brodian, Craig P275
Brodin, J. Per E307
Brodsky, William J P389
Brodsky, Stephen P403
Brody, Paul E235
Brody, Mark E425
Broek, Jacques van den W397
Broendell, Jane E P362
Broermann, Robert A A706:P473:P473
Brogdon, James A712
Brogdon, Jim P487
Brogdon, James E373
Brogger, Tanya P286
Brogley, Rita E392
Brokaw, George A249
Brolick, Heather E81
Bromage, Kathleen A377
Broman, Craig P578
Bromley, Andres Lehuede W33
Bron, Byron P124
Bron, Guillermo E393
Bronczek, David A802
Brondeau, Pierre W480
Bronder, Debra A548
Bronin, Luke P126
Bronkhorst, Edwin Van P554
Bronner, Philip A592
Bronner, Liliana P P570
Bronson, Dave P36
Bronstein, Sheri A96
Brook, Bruce A558
Brook, Melissa P340
Brooke, F. Dixon A754:E401
Brooker, Aaron P396
Brookman, Charles A485
Brooks, Douglas A84
Brooks, Janytra A136
Brooks, Mark A162
Brooks, Derrick A206
Brooks, Susan A320
Brooks, Alexandra A385
Brooks, Daniel A417
Brooks, David A417
Brooks, Martha A434
Brooks, Vincent A436
Brooks, Michael A484
Brooks, Raymond A496:A541
Brooks, Christopher A584
Brooks, William A719
Brooks, Rebecca A723

Brooks, Renee A725
Brooks, Brenna A741
Brooks, Robert J A841
Brooks, Jessica P37
Brooks, Marcia P123
Brooks, Notimba P128
Brooks, Joana P157
Brooks, Maggie P164
Brooks, Carrie P261
Brooks, Jody P270
Brooks, Sherr P304
Brooks, Harley P401
Brooks, Dick P401
Brooks, Gloria P450
Brooks, Dwayne P470
Brooks, Brenna P517
Brooks, Mary P533
Brooks, Roy P533
Brooks, Margaret P627
Brooks, Ruby P658
Brooks, Linda E35
Brooks, Susan E172
Brooks, Daniel E227
Brooks, David E227
Brooks, Rebecca E383
Brooks, Renee E383
Brooks, Joe E430
Brooks, Vincent E434
Brookshire, JW P454
Brookshire, William A P454
Broome, Dewayne A442:P278
Broome, Ann-Marie P566
Broome, Michael C P572
Brophy, Keith E81
Broquet, Bruce L P225
Brosam, Aaron P249
Broseta, Laurence W488
Brosig, Thomas E203
Brosius, Jessica E148
Brosnan, Sean W399
Bross, David P162
Brossoit, Jean A190
Brost, Mike P270
Brothers, Jeffrey P23
Brothers, Carl W P444
Brotman, Martin P528
Broucek, James E83
Broughman, Wade D P446:P446
Broughton, George A617
Broughton, Thomas A707
Broughton, William P262
Broughton, Thomas A368
Brouillard, Rheo A113
Brouillette, Manon W341
Brous, David A696
Broussard, Bruce A404:A406
Broussard, Bonnie P139
Broussard, Michelle P159
Broussard, Denise P220
Brower, Linda A846
Brown, Thomas A3
Brown, Gloria A20
Brown, Chad A27
Brown, Donald A32
Brown, Jeffrey J A32
Brown, Jeffrey A33
Brown, Cole A41
Brown, Adriane A41
Brown, M. Dean A79
Brown, Laura A81
Brown, Janet A102
Brown, Jennifer A106
Brown, Reginald A121
Brown, Shay A123
Brown, Mike A125
Brown, William A160
Brown, Roger A179
Brown, Jeff A185
Brown, Keith A217
Brown, Carlos A254
Brown, Darrell R A267
Brown, Lori A274
Brown, Marcus A277
Brown, David A314
Brown, Archie A315
Brown, Julie A366
Brown, Jeffrey A370

COMBINED HOOVER'S HANDBOOK INDEX OF EXECUTIVES

A = AMERICAN BUSINESS
E = EMERGING COMPANIES
P = PRIVATE COMPANIES
W = WORLD BUSINESS

Brown, Kevin A461
Brown, Bill A463
Brown, Peter A490
Brown, Tyler A497
Brown, David F M A503
Brown, Gregory A540
Brown, J. David A546
Brown, Carole A632
Brown, Marianne A697
Brown, Peter A700
Brown, Vicki A737
Brown, Kate A740
Brown, J. McCauley A747
Brown, Joy A791
Brown, William A798
Brown, Michael A841
Brown, Marianne A841
Brown, J. Powell A860
Brown, Gloria P11
Brown, Chad P15
Brown, Doug P19
Brown, Jeffrey J P24
Brown, Leah P32
Brown, Tony P34
Brown, Jennifer P64
Brown, Shay P81
Brown, Dawn P85
Brown, Jeremy P99
Brown, Carolyn P100
Brown, Jeff P122
Brown, Byron P124
Brown, Tyra P129
Brown, Michael G P130
Brown, Keith P151
Brown, Nathan P153
Brown, Charles P163
Brown, Charlie P163
Brown, Michael P169
Brown, Charlie P170
Brown, Brian P176
Brown, Nancy P186
Brown, Dhannetta P187
Brown, Jonathan P198
Brown, Blair P203
Brown, Marcus V P206
Brown, Torrey C P211
Brown, Michelle L P218
Brown, Angela P220
Brown, Marilyn P220
Brown, Eric P238
Brown, Kelsy P251
Brown, Trisha P257
Brown, Debbie P267
Brown, Cathy P270
Brown, James D P286
Brown, George J P293:P294
Brown, Julia P305
Brown, David F M P317
Brown, Diona P325
Brown, Jocelyn P351
Brown, Michael P352
Brown, Ed P354
Brown, Dan P362
Brown, Leonard P366
Brown, Jeremy P396
Brown, Kristian P401
Brown, Whitney P403
Brown, Lori P411
Brown, Shaunta P416
Brown, Karen P421
Brown, Steven P421
Brown, Dr Kenneth P427
Brown, Jordan P435
Brown, Brian P436
Brown, Carole P441
Brown, Lynn P463
Brown, Abbie P472
Brown, Chris P482
Brown, Lashawna P500
Brown, Vicki P513
Brown, Kate P516

Brown, Lisa P560
Brown, Michael W P561
Brown, Crystal P562
Brown, David F M P565
Brown, Truman R P566
Brown, Julia P579
Brown, Shea P585
Brown, Jay P607
Brown, Christopher R P608
Brown, Laurie P650
Brown, Richard H P662
Brown, Palmer W139
Brown, Derek W200
Brown, Andy W206
Brown, Jim W259
Brown, Jason W396
Brown, Celia E2
Brown, Melissa E7
Brown, Marianne E11
Brown, M. Dean E34
Brown, J. Hyatt E57
Brown, Hugh E57
Brown, J. Powell E57
Brown, P. Barrett E57
Brown, William E75
Brown, Donald E115
Brown, Lisa E129
Brown, Celeste Mellet E149
Brown, Thomas E166
Brown, Robin E166
Brown, Archie E167
Brown, David E185
Brown, Jeffrey E203
Brown, Molly Z E207
Brown, Laura E209
Brown, Nigel E229
Brown, Edward E304
Brown, Jonathan E348
Brown, Kevin E377
Brown, J. McCauley E391
Brown, Julia E426
Brown, Oscar E448
Browne, Robert A567
Browne, Colin A810
Brownie, Susan P476
Browning, Mary P545
Brownlow, Ben A663:P436
Broyles, Thomas A789
Broyles, Christine P150
Broyles, Rob P216
Broyles, Andy P470
Broyles, Thomas E411
Broz, Steven A645
Brubaker, Connie A217
Brubaker, Lisa A870
Brubaker, Connie P151
Brubaker, Terry E194
Brubaker, Lisa E455
Bruce, Timothy A135
Bruce, Kofi A347
Bruce, Carrie A667
Bruce, Donna A740:P516
Bruce, Stephanie P647
Bruce, Andrew W395
Bruck, Lori A A787:P595
Bruckner, Tim A857
Bruckner, Brian M P91
Bruckner, Chris B P91
Bruckner, Tim E447
Brudnicki, Gary P652
Bruegenhemke, Kathleen E206
Bruehlman, Ronald A433
Bruel, Franck W184
Bruff, Edward P174
Brugarolas, Catalina Minarro W9
Bruhl, Elise A187:P131
Bruhn, Michelle P463
Bruland, Peter P170
Brulard, Jean-Pierre A841
Brumback, Emerson A306
Brumbaugh, Kimberly A529
Brumbaugh, Nicole P367
Brumbaugh, Kimberly E274
Brumberg, Leonard A135
Brumfield, Chris N A293:P212
Brumley, Jessica P390
Brummer, Christopher A293

Brummer, Derek A662
Brummett, Paul P197
Brumssted, John R P588
Brumsted, John R P588
Brun, Leslie A222
Brundage, Bill W195
Brune, Catherine A40
Brunecz, Sharon E18
Brunell, Gregory P319
Brunell, Greg P319
Brunelle, David A113
Bruner, Judy A66
Brunett, Sharon P94
Brunetti, Michelle P638
Brunfield, Brian P551
Brunk, James A533
Brunk, Debbie P196
Bruno, Marc A67
Bruno, Barry A177
Bruno, John A358
Bruno, Amy A741
Bruno, James A821
Bruno, Amy P517
Bruno, Rosemary P599
Brunoehler, Jeffrey A530:E275
Bruns, Casey E68
Brunson, Don P351
Brunt, Jeff Van A804:P607
Brunts, DeAnn E43
Brusadelli, Maurizio A535
Brush, James E395
Brussow, Julie P472
Brutto, Daniel A415
Bruxelles, Henri W152
Bruxvoort, Keith P523
Bruzzano, Marco A258
Bruzzo, Christopher A271
Bryan, James A312
Bryan, Glynis A420
Bryan, Alex P6
Bryan, Amanda P135
Bryan, Douglas P335
Bryan, John P594
Bryan, Daniel P644
Bryan, Joe P644
Bryan, Tracy W69
Bryant, Jennifer A45
Bryant, Warren A252
Bryant, Hope A312
Bryant, John A598
Bryant, Pedro A675
Bryant, Todd A680
Bryant, Gregory A707
Bryant, Phil A737
Bryant, Barry A741
Bryant, Joan P96
Bryant, Kevin E P209
Bryant, Carissa P218
Bryant, Jonnie P242
Bryant, Phil P270
Bryant, Gordon P287
Bryant, Colin P315
Bryant, Jay P315
Bryant, Richard P322
Bryant, Shea P342
Bryant, Dawn P382
Bryant, Andrea P446
Bryant, Phil P513
Bryant, Barry P517
Bryant, Douglas E342
Bryant, Pedro E351
Bryant, Todd E356
Bryant, Gregory E368
Bryant, Arthur E439
Bryant, Kevin E451
Bryce, Cathy-Ann W17
Brydon, Dean E409
Brynelsen, Charles A4
Bryson, Gary P74
Brüngger, Renata Jungo W319
Bsh, Julian P134
Buberl, Thomas A424
Buccalo, Gina A804:P607
Bucciarelli, Brant P447
Buch, James E258
Buchanan, John A204
Buchanan, Michael A403

Buchanan, Edison A629
Buchanan, Ashley A779
Buchanan, Amber P147
Buchanan, Mark P171
Buchanan, Maxine P184
Buchanan, Christina P228
Buchanan, Lindsey P449
Buchanan, Ashley P568
Buchanan, Jamie P632
Buchband, Richard A494
Buchbinder, David K P116
Buchenau, Blaine P218
Buchenot, Stephen E254
Bucher, Susan P166
Buchholz, Karen A870:E454
Buchleitner, Klaus W80
Buchris, Yodfat Harel W253
Buchwald, Herbert A492
Buchwald, Emily P71
Buck, Karen A326
Buck, Michele A384
Buck, John A610
Buck, Cody P40
Buck, John P163
Buck, Brian P291
Buck, Ken E42
Buck, Karen E177
Buckingham, David C A208:P145
Buckingham, Phil P603
Buckiso, Scott A821
Buckley, Francis A30
Buckley, Neil A503
Buckley, Michael A682
Buckley, George A731
Buckley, Francis P21
Buckley, Morgan P151
Buckley, Neil P317
Buckley, John L P421
Buckley, Guy A P494
Buckley, Kim P549
Buckley, Adam P P588
Buckley, Linda P624
Buckley, John L P656
Buckley, Timothy E78
Buckley, Robert E298
Buckman, David I P23
Buckminster, Douglas A46
Buckner, W Quinn P602
Buckwalter, Marion A473:P295
Bucur, Silvana P507
Buczek, Joey P436
Budd, Wayne A612
Budde, Rex P490
Budde, Tom P646
Budden, Joan A417:A805:E226
Buddhiraju, Rajbhushan W134
Budelman, Robert P505
Buechele, Wolfgang W321
Buechler, Kenneth E342
Buehler, Ralf P203
Buehler, Christoph W514
Buehler, Alexander E137
Buehrens, Eric P71
Buellesbach, Rick P188
Buen, Maureen P157
Buenaventura, Jose W83
Buencamino, Alex P74
Buening-Griffin, Cathy A228
Bueschen, Anton P615
Buescher, John P321
Buese, Nancy A558
Buesing, Dean E198
Buesinger, Robert A860
Buettner-Schmid, Kelly P381
Buffamoyer, Ashley A78:P47
Bufferd, Allan P71
Buffett, Warren E A113
Buffington, Ronda P64
Buffington, Stephanie E407
Buffon, Beatrice W175
Bufkin, Patrick P499
Buford, Robert A229:E112
Bugarin, Tom P168
Bugh, John A366
Bugher, Mark A311
Bugher, Daniel P491
Buhrow, Jason A412:P258

COMBINED HOOVER'S HANDBOOK INDEX OF EXECUTIVES

Buhrow, Jack A P415
Bui, Tam T P170
Bui, Isabelle W184
Buick, Craig E135
Buie, Herbert A724
Bujarski, Robert E342
Bukiewicz, Ralph P578
Bukiewicz, Susan P578
Bula, Patrice W348:W425
Bulach, Matthias W187
Bulanda, Mark A273
Bulanov, Alexander W468
Bulawa, Bryan F P342
Bulcke, Paul W348
Bulgarino, Nicole E19
Bulhoes, Coralia W65
Bull, Kenneth E176
Bulla, Stacey P249
Bullard, Rodney A53
Bullard, Ketisha P132
Bullard, Linda P166
Bullard, David P416
Bullard, Rodney E25
Bullion, Diana A647:P429
Bullock, David A139
Bullock, Brian A278
Bullock, Diana P203
Bullock, Timothy P306
Bullock, Gregory P623
Bullock, Brian E141
Bulpitt, Amy P501
Bulut, Fazli W504
Bumgarner, David A186
Bumgarner, Jayne P459
Bumgarner, David E84
Bumpus, Bill P112
Bunce, John W40
Bunch, Charles A496
Bunch, C. Robert A588
Bunch, Lonnie G P484
Bunch, David P636
Bunders, Olivia P63
Bundt, Maya W514
Bunge, Katie P635
Bunger, Steven E72
Bunker, Mike P99
Bunn, Sheila A362
Bunn, James A663
Bunn, Sheila P232
Bunn, Willard E82
Bunnell, Ron A102:P56
Bunting, Theodore A375
Bunyasaranand, Boonsong W62
Bunye, Ignacio W70
Buonaiuto, Thomas A330
Buongiorno, Michael J P308
Buono, Tim P466
Burak, Mark A97
Buran, John A297:A330:E158
Buranamanit, Tanin W98
Burbach, Nicole P261
Burbach, Gerhard E59
Burby, Chris P521
Burch, Robert P165
Burchett, Ronald P417
Burchfield, Jay A579:A712:E373
Burckhardt, Andreas W55
Burckhardt, Carsten W227
Burckhart, Camille A633
Burden, Amanda P452
Burdick, Rick A83
Burdick, Kenneth A317
Burdick, Kevin A593
Burdick, Ginny R P148
Burdick, Kenneth E170
Burdiek, Ed P281
Burdine, Ivan A853:E445
Burdman, Lee A639:E332
Buretta, Sheri P120
Burfitt, Gregory P20
Burfitt, Gregory H P102
Burford, David P492
Burge, Taylor P620
Burgener, Jean P45
Burgener, Ewald W514
Burger, Bas W95
Burger, Larry E242

Burger, Edward E427
Burgess, Rosalind A735
Burgess, Kathy P81
Burgess, Michael P288
Burgess, Rosalind P510
Burgum, Doug A739:P515
Burik, Jeffrey A206
Buriko, Alexandra W424
Burk, Victor A630
Burke, William A56
Burke, Michael A68
Burke, Carolyn A173
Burke, Yvonne Brathwaite A224
Burke, Catherine A548
Burke, Courtney P15
Burke, Michael W P17
Burke, William P63
Burke, Carolyn P113
Burke, Janet P134
Burke, Yvonne Brathwaite P162
Burke, Mike P164
Burke, Edmund F P186
Burke, Wayne P200
Burke, Dan P237
Burke, James F P254
Burke, Richard P313
Burke, Cody P368
Burke, Kathleen P376
Burke, John D P602
Burke, Simon W132
Burke, Michael W301:E69:E81
Burke, James E96
Burke, Desiree E190
Burke, James E254
Burke, Kathleen E277
Burke, Robert E403
Burke, Andrew E406
Burkett, Lynn E437
Burkey, Rick A229:E112
Burkhalter, Brandy A162
Burkhard, Oliver W490
Burkhardt, Timothy E377
Burkhart, Megan A204
Burkhart, Renda A628:E324
Burkhead, Lisa Cano A738:P514
Burkholder, Edward E153
Burkholder, Eugene E156
Burklund, Brent P92
Burks, Lindsey A233:P178
Burkscoats, Thurgood P284
Burlage, David P A195:P140
Burleigh, Mary A126:P83
Burleson, Ronald E430
Burlo, Zaira W293
Burmistrova, Elena W385
Burnell, Lawrence A400
Burnell, Jody P402
Burnell, Lawrence E218
Burnett, Danielle P18
Burnett, Bonnie P19
Burnett, Joshua P88
Burnett, Don P157
Burnett, Walter P184
Burnett, Keisha P187
Burnett, Justin P525
Burnett, Kevin M P525:P581
Burnett, Sharon E52
Burnette, Kayla P100
Burnette, Don P157
Burnette, Katie P422
Burnette, Rob P644
Burns, M. A182
Burns, William A215
Burns, Stephanie A221
Burns, Jennifer A300
Burns, Mark A345
Burns, M. A360
Burns, Claire A377
Burns, M. Anthony A411
Burns, Eldridge A541
Burns, Annette A546
Burns, Gay A672
Burns, Bill A735
Burns, Steve A738
Burns, Kevin A779
Burns, Michael A819
Burns, Bill A877

Burns, Dwight P51
Burns, Glenn P55:P55
Burns, Ben P96
Burns, Joey P225
Burns, Patrick P493
Burns, Bill P511
Burns, Steve P514
Burns, Ryan P534
Burns, Kevin P567
Burns, Carrie P574
Burns, Joy P619
Burns, Susan P648
Burns, David W484
Burns, Harold E81
Burns, William E97
Burns, Eldridge E281
Burns, Richard E405
Burns, Thomas E455
Burnside, Antoinette P279
Burnside, Bill E430
Burr, Busy A541
Burr, Elizabeth A679:A751
Burr, Noman P9
Burr, Charles P158
Burr, Angel P392
Burr, Erin E188
Burr, Busy E281
Burr, Richelle E323
Burr, Ron E457
Burrell, Carol P385
Burrell, Eric P440
Burritt, David A821
Burrough, Eric E81
Burroughs, Victor P447
Burroughs, Lisa P472
Burrow, Mark P638
Burrowes, Todd A236
Burrowes, Astrid A329
Burrows, John A706
Burrows, Lori P43
Burrows, John P473
Burruano, Samuel A307
Burson, Michael L P121
Burt, Eddie A117
Burt, Carol A433
Burt, Brady A607
Burt, Tye Winston W40
Burt, Brady E312
Burton, Gregory A186
Burton, Eve A429
Burton, Lisa P134
Burton, J H P142
Burton, Carol P467
Burton, Pat P507
Burton, Christian P533
Burton, Stella P565
Burton, Richard W509
Burton, Gregory E84
Burton, Spencer E139
Burtscher, Gerhard W367
Burville, John A704:E366
Burwell, Dorothy A635
Burwick, David E55:E116
Bury, Randy P556
Burzer, Jörg W319
Busacca, Brian P271
Busch, Angela M A267
Busch, Jonathan A667
Busch, Andrea W81
Busch, Roland W443
Buser, Curtis A152
Bush, Wesley A182:A349
Bush, Tim P176
Bush, Greg P227
Bush, Stephen P468
Bush, William L P494
Bush, Chad P627
Bush, David E81
Bushey, Devon P660
Bushman, Julie E50
Bushnell, David W399
Bushong, Todd P11
Bushore, Michelle E347
Bushway, Mark A817
Busk, Douglas E109
Busquet, Alejandro Echevarria W179
Buss, Bradley A15

Bussells, Walter P270
Bussy, Jean-Franois P149
Bustany, Kelly P154
Buster, Bob P167
Busto, Ana W184
Busuioc, Monica P536
Butcher, Arthur A132
Butcher, Jeremy P418
Butcher, Benjamin E389
Buth, Jay A284
Buthman, Mark A446
Butier, Mitchell A86
Butler, Charl A20
Butler, William A147
Butler, Adrian A155
Butler, Deborah A190:A219
Butler, Gregory A284
Butler, Calvin A286
Butler, Ronald A315
Butler, Calvin A491
Butler, Gary A674
Butler, Calvin A680
Butler, Paula P9
Butler, Charl P11
Butler, Paul Edd P73
Butler, Lucretia P147
Butler, Sgt P160
Butler, Gregory B P209
Butler, Sara L P340
Butler, Mike P429
Butler, Michael P430
Butler, William P471
Butler, Jean P595
Butler, Karis P646
Butler, David P657
Butler, Monika W425
Butler, William E66
Butler, Anne E78
Butler, Ronald E167
Butler, Gary E348
Butler, Calvin E356
Butman, James A764
Butner, Geoff E39
Butsch, Margo A382:E211
Buttacavoli, Thomas E346
Buttar, Harinder P190
Butte, Grease P271
Butter, Kathleen P131
Butterfield, Virginia P169
Butterfield, Stacy M P421
Buttino, Mario P396
Button, Adrian A548
Button, Gigie P125
Button, Angie E121
Butts, Tanya E166
Butz, William P320
Butz, John P353
Butz, Stefan W166
Buzachero, Victor V P469
Buzitis, Cindi A321
Buzzard, Chuck P166
Buzzelli, Anthony A795:E416
Buzzetta, Alan P392
Buzzo, Ann A711:P481
Byers, Michael A194
Byers, Eric P73
Byford, Caroline A734:P510
Byington, Carrie A109
Byington, Mike P289
Bylund, James E349
Bynoe, Peter A339
Bynum, Richard A632
Bynum, Cherlyn P255
Bynum, Jen P414
Bynum, Trevor P648
Byrd, Daryl A317
Byrd, Carolyn A671
Byrd, Sandra P43
Byrd, William D P272
Byrd, Jacqueline P421
Byrd, Gary P424
Byrd, Tamra P620
Byrd, Vanessa Y P641
Byrd, Thomas E127
Byrd, Daryl E170
Byrne, Barbara A79:A607
Byrne, Kathryn A710

COMBINED HOOVER'S HANDBOOK INDEX OF EXECUTIVES

A = AMERICAN BUSINESS
E = EMERGING COMPANIES
P = PRIVATE COMPANIES
W = WORLD BUSINESS

Byrne, Frank A745
Byrne, David P3
Byrne, Barbara P52
Byrne, Jolene P80
Byrne, Barbara P201
Byrne, Bobbie P201:P201
Byrne, Mike P353
Byrne, Jolene P465
Byrne, Richard P569
Byrne, Darragh W156
Byrne, Kathryn E371
Byun, Donald A398:E218
Bénacin, Philippe W518

C

C, Victoria P220
Caamano, Deirdre P198
Cabalatungan, Stella W82
Caballero, Craig P610
Cabanis, Cecile W152
Cabellon, Angela L P256
Cabera, Lillian A739:P515
Cabezuela, Zaide P486
Cablik, Anna A796
Cabral, Bruce A382
Cabral, Heidi P186
Cabral, Cathie P420
Cabral, Bruce E211
Cabral, Timothy E433
Cabrales, Steven X P148
Cabrera, Ivonne A256
Cabrera, Kayla P120
Cabrera, Juan P202
Cabrera, Alfredo P352
Cabrera, Maria P488
Cacciamatta, Danilo E63
Caceci, Laura P451
Caceres, R. Louis A693
Caceres, Celia P655
Caceres, R. Louis E360
Caddell, Kari P396
Cade, Denise A626:E404
Cadet-Dantes, Pascale P228
Cadieux, Chester A126
Cadieux, Marc A751
Cadieux, Melissa P200
Cadieux, Chester E54
Cadman, George E P57
Cadoret, Frank W482
Cadwallader, Brian A442:P278
Cady, Bruce E81
Cafarella, Erika P53
Cafaro, Debra A632
Cafferty, William P456
Cafm, Francisco C P431
Caforio, Giovanni A134:A749
Cafritz, Diane A154
Cagan, Leigh A867
Cage, Christopher A472
Cagle, Mary Jo P499
Cagler, Donna P366
Cahalan, Jay E201
Cahill, John A200:A460
Cahill, Sr Helen P220
Cahill, Eileen P253
Cahill, Joseph P488
Cahill, Peter E164
Cahillane, Steven A449
Cahoj, Nicholas P44
Cai, Hongping W97
Cai, Hongbin W120
Cai, Manli W349
Cai, Jin-Yong W378
Cai, Fangfang W383
Cai, Shenglin W419
Cai, Chang W539
Cai, Manli W542
Cain, Cynthia A717

Cain, Kelli P102
Cain, Kathleen P115
Cain, Pamela P266
Cain, Pam P266
Cain, Matthew P620
Cain, Brian E85
Cain, Cynthia E380
Caine, Patrice W488
Caines, Brett A484
Caiola, Vincent P292
Cairnie, Ruth W45
Cairns, Ann A506
Cairns, Gordon W532
Cairo, Victor W39
Cairoli, Michael P505
Cairy, Rita A187:P131
Cajka, Andrew E382
Cakiroglu, Levent W281:W505:W540
Calabrese, Vincent A331
Calabrese, Gary P29
Calabrese, Vincent E178
Calabria, David A87
Calagione, Samuel E55
Calaman, Diane P179
Calantzopoulos, Andre A625
Calarco, Vincent A216
Calarco, Vincent A P660
Calari, Cesare W181
Calavia, Philippe W278
Calaway, Tonit A131:E443
Calbert, Michael A252
Calcaterra, Ronald J P107
Caldart, Gilberto A506
Caldera, Louis A518
Caldera, Leo P156
Calderini, Melinda P580
Calderon, Maria P451
Calderon, Aurora W417
Calderon, Nancy E296
Calderoni, Frank A11
Calderoni, Robert A457:E27
Caldwell, Lisa A586
Caldwell, Phyllis A592
Caldwell, Phil P122
Caldwell, Brian P154
Caldwell, Lance P233
Caldwell, Pete P255
Caldwell, Andrew P342
Caldwell, Rose P420
Caldwell, Meg P554
Caldwell, Nanci W99
Caldwell, Thomas E274
Calfee, W William P414
Calhoun, David L A124
Calhoun, Kathy P101
Calhoun, Dean E383
Cali, Brian E161
Calio, Christopher A665
Call, Valerie Mc P125
Call, Douglas P422
Call, Gregory E135
Callaghan, Brian E32
Callahan, Lisa A551
Callahan, Patrick A645
Callahan, Emily P32
Callahan, Sean P103
Callahan, Matthew P335
Callahan, Lisa P475
Callahan, Clara P593
Callahan, Karri E345
Callan, Patricia A724
Callanan, Kevin P638
Callans, Patrick A223
Callard, George A562:P378
Callas, Darcy G A531
Callas, Darcy A531
Callas, Darcy G P349
Callas, Darcy P349
Callaway, Antone A475
Calleja, Bernardo A598
Callen, Craig R P252
Callen, David E377
Callender, David A512
Callender, Robert G P206
Callender, David P326
Callery, Ed P464
Callicotte, Lisa C E429

Callicutt, Richard A628:E324
Callis, Byron P459
Callis, David C P530
Callison, Edwin A635
Callison, Tim P433
Callison, Marilyn P433
Callow, Sheri P167
Calp, Steffney P650
Calvert-Davies, Jonathan W234
Calvey, Raymond P175
Calvin, John P176
Calvin, Tim P222
Calvin, Debra P463
Calvo, Cesar P112
Calvo, Miguel Klingenberg W400
Calvosa, Lucia W185
Camacho, Alfredo P76
Camara, Fiona W428
Camargo, Jorge Marques de
  Toledo W506
Camargo, Jorge E37
Camarillo, Rene P202
Cambiaso, Enrique Ostale W525
Cambria, Christopher E269
Cameau, Rasha P128
Camelio, Chris P648
Cameron, Susan A67
Cameron, Dennis A243
Cameron, Cheryl A A825
Cameron, James A854
Cameron, Brenda P161
Cameron, Donna P290
Cameron, Steve P508
Cameron, Cheryl A P631
Camilleri, Kurt A91
Camilleri, Jessica P528
Camilli, Cecile W281
Cammarano, Terri P326
Cammisecra, Antonio W179
Camp, Christine A164
Camp, Peter Van A282
Camp, Elizabeth A754
Camp, David P354
Camp, Daniel D P487
Camp, Lynne E90
Camp, Elizabeth E103:E401
Campana, Robert A570
Campanella, Edward A72:E31
Campanello, Russell E236
Campani, Angelo W144
Campbell, Jeffrey A46
Campbell, Steven A62
Campbell, Michael A76
Campbell, Brandi A98
Campbell, Joanne A144
Campbell, George A216
Campbell, Ryan A240
Campbell, Bruce A248
Campbell, Mike A282
Campbell, David A340:A364
Campbell, Kristin A389
Campbell, Ann-Marie A394
Campbell, Patrick D A436
Campbell, Maryelizabeth A471
Campbell, Daniel A548
Campbell, Patrick A556
Campbell, Alan A591
Campbell, Cheryl A623
Campbell, Ben A683
Campbell, Sabrina V P30
Campbell, Carol P42
Campbell, Lori P44
Campbell, Susan P133
Campbell, Robert P157
Campbell, Martha P165
Campbell, Robert P203
Campbell, Patrick D P271
Campbell, Barbara P316
Campbell, Jane P351
Campbell, Jackie P363
Campbell, Belinda P392
Campbell, Christy P460
Campbell, Andy P556
Campbell, John P565
Campbell, Don P599
Campbell, Marianne P647
Campbell, Ismail P660

Campbell, Jeffrey W35
Campbell, Justine W342
Campbell, Norie W497
Campbell, Phyllis E10
Campbell, Kathleen E84
Campbell, Jaye E104
Campelli, Fabrizio W160
Campfield, Susan E297
Campion, Simon A109
Campion, Andrew A563:A732
Campori, Vittorio W316
Campos, Tony P169
Campos, Brenda P406
Campos, Melissa P449
Campos, Joselito W417
Campos, Roel E348
Campos, Kimberly E427
Campos, Timothy E436
Campos-Duffy, Rachel A562:E293
Camunez, Michael A268
Can, Charles Mc P271
Canarick, Paul A322
Canas, Cristian Toro W255
Cancelmi, Daniel A765
Cancio, Margarita P215
Candelmo, Robert A523
Candia, Serenella De W509
Candido, Alfred P165
Cang, Daqiang W220
Cangemi, Thomas A554
Canham, Rachel W95
Cannada, Charles E105
Cannady, David A126
Cannady, Ed P43
Cannady, David P83
Cannavino, James E2
Canney, Jacqui A706:W533
Cannici, Joe P339
Canning, Lori P467
Cannizzo, Mike P521
Cannon, Marc A83
Cannon, Michael A467
Cannon, Marivette P103
Cannon, Peter P184
Cannon, Maryann L P333
Cannon, M. Elizabeth W100
Cannon, Gillian E102
Cannon, Jaime E406
Cannone, Peter E277
Cano, Lorraine P257
Canose, Jeffrey L P542
Canova, Walter W171
Cantaloube, Brigitte W402
Cantera, Jose Antonio Garcia W61
Cantone, Fabienne Freymond W72
Cantor, Diana A209:P146
Cantrell, James A531
Cantrell, Christopher A738
Cantrell, Latoya P129
Cantrell, Mike P158
Cantrell, Tammy P365
Cantrell, Christopher P514
Cantrell, David P569
Cantrell, James E276
Cantu, Ernesto Torres A183
Canty, Trecia A612
Canuso, Dominic A870:E454
Cao, Thinh P240
Cao, Yong P642
Cao, Xinjian W130
Cao, Xin W154
Cao, Zhiqiang W236
Cao, Liqun W244
Cao, Min W474
Capaldi, Elizabeth P42
Caparas, Mary Mylene W323
Capasse, Thomas E346
Capasso, John A794
Capasso, Beverly P379
Capasso, John P599
Capatides, Michael W99
Cape, Shavon E126
Capek, John A4
Capek, Glen P212
Capel, Paul P302
Capel, Eddie E377
Capellas, Michael A182:W197

COMBINED HOOVER'S HANDBOOK INDEX OF EXECUTIVES

Capener, John T P530:P531
Capestany, Jaime P355
Capitani, Todd E95
Caplan, Deborah A327:A560
Caplinger, Larry E153
Capo, Brian A483
Capone, Christopher M P108
Caponi, Julie A313:E165
Capossela, Christopher A528
Capozzi, Daniel A247
Capozzi, Heidi A509
Cappareli, Peter P552
Cappello, Ramona A516
Capps, John A206
Capps, Allen A239
Capps, Kimberly A723
Capps, Stacey P169
Capps, Vickie E18
Capps, Kimberly E383
Capri, Natale W166
Captain, Brad E286
Capua, Marco Di W294
Capuano, Anthony A498
Caputo, Lisa A115
Caputo, Kenneth A702
car, Deniz Filiz A W50
Cara, Anne P396
Carandang, Christine W323
Carano, Mark E232
Carapezzi, Bill A622
Caras, Matthew A103:E47
Caravati, Martin P630
Carbajal, Salud P169
Carbajal, Francisco Javier
  Fernandez W23
Carbajal, Jose Fernandez W198
Carbajal, Francisco Javier
  Fernandez W198
Carbajal, Gabino Miguel Gomez W215
Carbone, A A346
Carbone, Ann P124
Carbone, A P227
Card, Robert A15
Card, Andrew A812
Cardenas, Ricardo A236
Cardenas, Alberto De A504
Cardenas, Ricardo A791
Cardenas, Andrea P193
Cardenas, Mitzi P601
Cardenas, Alvaro W165
Cardew, Jason A470
Cardiff, Michele A254:A838
Cardin, Robert A501
Cardinal, Tony P496
Cardinali, Sergio P390
Cardona, Anna P126
Cardona, Andres Felipe Mejia W61
Cardona, Maria Celeste Ferreira
  Lopes W172
Cardoso, Adriana P90
Cardoso, Paulo W519
Cardoso, Joao E37
Carere, Brie A302
Caret, Leanne G A124
Caret, Leanne A240
Carey, Nate A92
Carey, Matthew A174
Carey, Jennifer Craighead A340
Carey, Matthew A395
Carey, Diane P16
Carey, Russell P90
Carey, Christopher P167
Carey, Mike P555
Carfagna, Maurizio W316
Carfora, Jeffrey A613:E316
Cargill, Jon P253
Caridine, Carol P185
Cariello, Vincenzo W509
Carino, Vernice E259
Carle, Liz P399
Carleone, Joseph E39
Carletti, Elena W509
Carley, Donald A399
Carley, Beth P38
Carlile, Thomas A125
Carlile, Robert A289
Carlino, Anthony P60

Carlino, Peter E190
Carlisle, Stephen A349
Carlo, Francesca Di W181
Carlomagno, Dana P146
Carlos, Ana Dorrego de W59
Carlson, Jan A80
Carlson, Carl A136
Carlson, W. Erik A249
Carlson, Thomas A366
Carlson, Walter A764
Carlson, Prudence A764
Carlson, Leroy A764
Carlson, Letitia A764
Carlson, Michael A798
Carlson, Dean P99
Carlson, David P124
Carlson, Richard P281
Carlson, Teresa P339
Carlson, Edward P359
Carlson, Lisa P464
Carlson, Cherica P530
Carlson, Carolyn P564
Carlson, Eric P627
Carlson, LeRoy E406
Carlsson, Magnus W446
Carlton, Scott A815
Carlton, Hornung P622
Carmack, Timothy W P306
Carmichael, Gregory A306
Carmichael, Steve E135
Carmicheal, Samuel P48
Carmody, Christine A284
Carmody, John E297
Carmona, Richard A510
Carnaghi, John R P216
Carnahan, Karen A180
Carnahan, Carissa P220
Carnecchia, Scipio E277
Carnegie-brown, Bruce W61
Carneiro, Vera de Morais Pinto
  Pereira W173
Carnesecca, Allen P214
Carney, John A735
Carney, Craig A793
Carney, Lloyd A835
Carney, Mark P109
Carney, Eric P350
Carney, Patricia P406
Carney, John P511
Carney, Ray P650
Carney, Kevin E254
Carney, Craig E414
Caro, Jodi J A807
Caro, Christina P477
Carole, Hackett P594
Carollo, Chris P248
Carollo, William F P545
Carollo, Bill P545
Caron, Joseph W308
Carosi, Nicholas P262
Carotenuto, Michael A143:E65
Caroti, Stefano E116
Carpanini, Mark P421
Carpenter, Tod A56
Carpenter, Zachary A296
Carpenter, Ann A298
Carpenter, Harold A628
Carpenter, Carolyn A706
Carpenter, Amy A783
Carpenter, Carol A841
Carpenter, Mark P29
Carpenter, Ariel P133
Carpenter, Karyn P157
Carpenter, Carolyn P473
Carpenter, Leah P486
Carpenter, Amy P583
Carpenter, Zachary E157
Carpenter, Lonny E298
Carpenter, Harold E324
Carpenter, Kevin E411
Carr, J. Mcgregor A204
Carr, Ian A291
Carr, James A446
Carr, Miriam P124
Carr, Nora K P238
Carr, Robert O P247
Carr, Kay P451

Carr, Barbara P498
Carr, Sean M P507
Carr, Jon P540
Carr, Roger W53
Carr, Jeff W276
Carr, Jeffrey E84
Carr-Smith, Jennifer W531
Carrady, Robert A633
Carrasco, Jorge P551
Carraud, Lauren W428
Carraway, Barbara O P125
Carrazana, Carlos P466
Carrel, Edson A517:P331
Carrel, Michael E36
Carrera, Bill P259
Carretta, Robert P350
Carrico, Paul A364
Carrier, Patrick B P119
Carrig, John A A215
Carrigan, Gerry P384
Carrillo, Antonio A574
Carrion, Carlos P127
Carrizales, Richard P126
Carrión, Richard A633
Carrol, Tom P463
Carroll, Michael A135
Carroll, Kathleen A363
Carroll, Christopher A428
Carroll, Charles A690
Carroll, William A717
Carroll, Mary Beth P14
Carroll, Patrice P90
Carroll, Kelley P233
Carroll, Andrew W P240
Carroll, Paul P306:P317
Carroll, Bob P332
Carroll, Mary P338
Carroll, Matthew P385
Carroll, Christopher P489
Carroll, Darin P491
Carroll, Kristen L P588
Carroll, Mona P636
Carroll, Cynthia W211
Carroll, James E30
Carroll, William E379
Carrubba, Peter A552:P369
Carruthers, Wendy A132
Carruthers, Scott P12
Carson, Crystal A209
Carson, Candace A346
Carson, Benjamin A403
Carson, Lawrence A672
Carson, Russell A703
Carson, Kent P33
Carson, Gale Jones P128
Carson, Crystal P146
Carson, Lynn P152
Carson, Keith P155
Carson, Candace P227
Carson, Dawn P427
Carta, Luciano W294
Carter, J. Braxton A77
Carter, Stefani A90
Carter, Peter A242
Carter, Ashton A242
Carter, Robert A302
Carter, Ashton A346
Carter, Russell A393
Carter, Matthew A443
Carter, Maverick A483
Carter, Matthew A574
Carter, Susan A591
Carter, Charles A605
Carter, George A617
Carter, Chrystah A631
Carter, Amanda A741
Carter, Benjamin A794
Carter, Brett A871
Carter, Chase P32
Carter, Craig P184
Carter, Paul P204
Carter, Susan P274
Carter, Donald E P283
Carter, Don P283
Carter, John P315
Carter, Chris P334
Carter, Angela P396

Carter, Barry P438
Carter, Bruce P460
Carter, Shelley P462
Carter, Gregory P465
Carter, Cindy P502
Carter, Amanda P517
Carter, Alexandra P550
Carter, Ella P562
Carter, Dedric P591
Carter, Benjamin P599
Carter, Mark B P612
Carter, Debbie P651
Carter, Pamela W178
Carter, Stefani E41
Carter, Stephen P E52
Carter, Russell E217
Carter, Margot E231
Carter, William E257
Carter, George E319
Carter, Timothy L E326
Carter, George E361
Carter-Miller, Jocelyn A641
Carthew, Geoffrey P361
Carti, Vince A49:P33
Carton, John E383
Carty, Michael A316
Carty, Donald A841
Carufel, Chuck A736:P512
Carullo, Giacinto W293
Caruselle, Nicholas P519
Caruso, Joanne A436
Caruso, Thomas P79
Caruso, Lisa P126
Caruso, Joseph P126
Caruson, Kiki P629
Carvajal, Arnie P163
Carval, Christophe W175
Carvalho, Orlando E269
Carvey, Raymond P243
Casaccio, Tenee A72:E31
Casady, Mark A399
Casalou, Robert A794:P599
Casamento, Benedetta E78
Casanova, Cheryl P89
Casarez, Catrina A750:P528
Casati, Gianfranco W8
Casbon, John A317:E170
Case, Gregory A247
Case, Scott A796
Case, Kathleen P450
Case, John E124
Casella, John E69
Casella, Douglas E69
Casellas, Alberto A752
Caselli, Marilyn A216
Casely-Hayford, Margaret W132
Casey, Kathleen A337
Casey, Donald A666:A666
Casey, Nick A742
Casey, Helen A795
Casey, Lynn A871
Casey, Margaret P68
Casey, Lois P95
Casey, Brendan P166
Casey, Patrick P197
Casey, Chris P491
Casey, Nick P518
Casey, Cheryl P544
Casey, Margaret P657
Casey, Geraldine W17
Casey, Keith W110
Casey, Helen E416
Cash, Kriner P92
Cash, Susan P418
Cash, Larry E296
Cashaw, Brad A177
Cashell, Robert A355:E193
Cashion, Tana A243
Cashman, Charles E260
Cashwell, Amy P161
Casiano, Kimberly A333
Casimiro, Tracy P464
Casimiro, Didier W411
Casini, Andrea W509
Caspari, Stefan A20
Casper, Marc A784
Caspersen, Finn A647

COMBINED HOOVER'S HANDBOOK INDEX OF EXECUTIVES

A = AMERICAN BUSINESS
E = EMERGING COMPANIES
P = PRIVATE COMPANIES
W = WORLD BUSINESS

Cass, Alyce P135
Cassabaum, Michelle E26
Cassar, Alessandra P628
Cassard, David A514:E267
Cassayre, Christian W174
Casse, Roger La P390
Casseb, George A212
Cassel, Matias Jorge Domeyko W177
Cassella, Anthony E260
Casselman, Deborah P544
Cassels, Scott L A454:P285:P285:P285
Cassens, Michael A310
Cassidy, Tracy A615
Cassidy, Spring A841
Cassidy, Trevor W100
Cassidy, Ronan W434
Cassidy, Rick W474
Cassin, Brian W258
Cassmeyer, Karen A738:P514
Casso, Katie A162
Cassotis, Christina A690
Castagnetto, Michael A683
Castaigne, Robert W517
Castaldi, Alexander E321
Castaldo, Robert A503:P317
Castaneda, Hugo P119
Castaneda, Carla A P541
Casteen, John A36
Castelbuono, Anthony P300
Castellaneta, Andrew A589
Castellano, Christine A61
Castellano, Chris P40
Castellano, Lawrence P450
Castellanos, Lydia P445
Castellina, Maurizio W511
Castellon, Oscar Mehech W56
Castellvi, Betina A633
Castiglioni, Don P171
Castillo, Jim P217
Castillo, David P422
Castillo, Phina P532
Castillo, Eduardo Alberto
    Escalante W22
Castle, Don P413
Castle, Scott P508
Castle, John E383
Castleberg, David A742:P518
Castleberry, Kyla P205
Castlen, Nick P73
Castlio, Michael E395
Castor, Jane P134
Castorena, Ed A224
Castorena, Joe P94
Castorena, Ed P162
Castriotta, Kelly A497
Castro, Henrique de A325
Castro, Thomas A562
Castro, Raul Vaca A723
Castro, Craig S P148
Castro, Craig P149
Castro, Ricardo P265
Castro, Thomas P378
Castro, April P545
Castro, Henrique de W61
Castro, Maria Luisa Jorda W72
Castro, Jones W83
Castro, Maria Luisa Jorda W215
Castro, Teresita Leonardo-De W417
Castro-Corazzin, Raquel P135
Castro-Neves, Joao A460
Castro-Nicho, Carolina P415
Caswell, Rona A727
Caswell, Jim P283
Catalan, Jose A89:P54
Catalano, Anna A390
Catalano, Richard P301
Catalano, Robert P356
Catalano, Angela E305
Cataldo, Robert A815
Catanese, George A663
Catanzaro, Stephen E125

Catapano, Anthonyj P171
Cate, Richard H P631
Catena, Cornelio P145
Cates, Robert P262
Cates, Jocelyn P555
Cathell, David A9:E4
Catherman, Betty P428
Catlender, Katie P24
Catlett, Scott A875
Catlett, Cynthia E107
Catlett, Celia E253
Catoggio, Nico A635
Catoir, Christophe W10
Catolico, Michael P260
Catrini, Gianfranco P292
Catroga, Eduardo de Almeida W173
Catron, Julie E52
Catz, Safra A595
Caudell, Scott A414:P259
Caughman, S Wright P205
Caughron, Guy P548
Cauley, Robert A596
Caulfield, Thomas A858
Caulfield, Lindsay P233
Caulfield, John E29
Cauthen, Wayne P347
Cava, Courtney Della A121
Cavaliere, Joseph A373
Cavallaro, Frank A676
Cavallaro, Richard P483
Cavallo-Miller, Linda P499
Cavanagh, Michael A203
Cavanah, Michael P527
Cavanaugh, Kyle P197
Cavanaugh, Michael J P396
Cavanaugh, James P503
Cavanaugh, Kevin P640
Cavanaugh, Diane E295
Cavazos, David A Salazar P237
Cave, Michael A92
Cave, George A591
Cavell, Mike A736:P512
Caven, Jill P193
Caveney, Brian A464
Cavens, Darrell A759
Cawley, Timothy A216:A217
Caylor, Mark A569
Caywood, Marty A396:E217
Cazares, Sara L P522
Cazer, Michael A35:P27
Cazorla, Sergio P302
Cbet, Fred A P453
Cctc, Jennifer P306
Ceaser, James P296
Cebulla, Andrew J P39
Cecere, Andrew A829
Cecero, David M P533
Cecilia, Manuel Manrique W400
Cedeno, Erika P303
Ceiley, Glen E125
Ceiley, Zachary E125
Celebioglu, Levent W21
Celik, Umut P185
Celis, Arquimedes A627
Cella, Peter A172
Cella, Peter L A173
Cella, Peter P113
Cella, Peter L P113
Cella, Kevin P640
Celorio, Victor Tiburcio W198
Cen, Rn M Whelan P3
Centeno, Joseph P169
Centeno, Betsy P243
Centers, Melissa A733
Cento, Juan A76
Centrone, Jennifer W40
Centurion-Lara, Arturo A825:P631
Cepeda, BJ P658
Cepero, Monica P157
Cephas, Derrick A710:E371
Cercone, Gemma P52
Cercone, Max P155
Cerda, Alicia P18
Cerezo, Rafael Mateu De Ros W72

Cerezo, Adolfo W525
Cerise, Frederick P179
Cerkovnik, Edward E288
Cermak, Penny A106:A380:P64:P247
Cerniglia, Linda P303
Cerniglia, Kristina E215
Cernuda, Cesar A550
Cerrai, Francesco A187:P131
Cerrato, German W110
Cerulli, Joseph E314
Ceruti, Franco W251
Cervantes, Martin A48:P31
Cervantes, Arturo P133
Cerven, Leane E161
Cesaris, Ada Lucia De W185
Cesarone, Nando A819
Cesheshyan, Emelina P265
Cestat, Joe A775:P552
Cestero, Luis A633
Cha, Sam Ho P258
Chabal, Grace P585
Chabino, Doug P307
Chacon, Chanda P42
Chadaga, Smitha P293
Chadbourne, Elizabeth P315
Chadha, Rajive A592:E303
Chadsey, Deborah A570
Chadwick, David T A640
Chadwick, John A653
Chadwick, David T E333
Chae, Michael A121
Chaffin, Patrick P454
Chaffin, J. Brian E82
Chafins, Tim P118
Chagla, Dilshad F P300
Chai, Qiaolin W114
Chai, Shouping W378
Chai, Tan Kah W529
Chain, Herbert E186
Chairasmisak, Korsak W98
Chaisson, Avis P126
Chakarun, Courtney E152
Chakrabandhu, Chiradej W441
Chakravarthy, Anil A11:E27
Chalfant, Tony A383
Chalfant, Thomas E68
Chalfant, Tony E212
Chalk, Jared P130
Chalkley, Janice P209
Chalmers, Sabine W95
Chaltraw, William P638
Chalupka, Kevin P461
Chalut, Sylvain W65
Chambas, Corey A311
Chamberlin, Michael P161
Chambers, Matthew A106
Chambers, James A117
Chambers, Brian A601
Chambers, Sara A734
Chambers, Bridget A736
Chambers, George A798
Chambers, H D P19
Chambers, Matthew P64
Chambers, Phil P142
Chambers, Melissa P343
Chambers, Richard P398
Chambers, Michael J P415
Chambers, Sara P510
Chambers, Bridget P512
Chambers, Christopher V P593
Chambers, Michael P629
Chambers, Stuart W32
Chambers, M. Susan E430
Chambless, Robert A197
Chambolle, Thomas P82
Chamchuen, Kosol W285
Chammas, Emile A702
Champion, Christopher A581
Champion, Timothy P12
Champion, Bret A P286
Champion, Natalie P615
Chamroeun, Nancy P242
Chan, Leng Jin A88
Chan, Kelly A157
Chan, Edward A174
Chan, Iris A262
Chan, Simson A454

Chan, Cynthia A730
Chan, Edward P118
Chan, Howard P132
Chan, Simson P285
Chan, Jimmy P373
Chan, Cynthia P509
Chan, Mary P616
Chan, Wing-shing W16
Chan, Ka Keung W119
Chan, Peng-Hong W138
Chan, Mary W306
Chan, See Choi W393
Chan, Chew Fung W393
Chan, Kok Kwai W393
Chan, Chiew Peng W393
Chan, Ericson W543
Chan, Kelly E70
Chan, Nelson E116
Chan, Iris E127
Chan, Alan E289
Chan, Shiu Leung E397
Chance, Adrienne A727
Chance, Leonard P177
Chancellor, James P270
Chancellor, Beth P625
Chand, Gaurav A199
Chand, Sujeet A684:E337
Chandarana, Himanshu V P64
Chandarasomboon, Amorn W62
Chandler, Jodi A311
Chandler, Chris A630
Chandler, H Jody P78
Chandler, Nicole P177
Chandler, Ken P323
Chandler, Suzanne P353
Chandler, Willis P609
Chandler, Paul W132
Chandler, A. Russell E103
Chandler, Elizabeth E358
Chandoha, Marie A743
Chandor, Christopher E164
Chandra, Subodh P125
Chandrakasan, Anantha A61
Chandraraj, Girisha P87
Chandrasekaran, Suja A208:P145
Chandrasekaran,
    Natarajan W477:W478
Chandrasen, Abhijai W270
Chandrashekar, Lavanya W165
Chandrasoma, Nishka A776:P558
Chandy, Ruby A260
Chanen, Daniel P345
Chaney, Kimberly A9
Chaney, Curtis P339
Chaney, Cindy P362
Chaney, Kimberly E3
Chang, Joanne A136
Chang, Lisa A196
Chang, Chee Ling A268
Chang, Amy A644
Chang, Chee Ling A722
Chang, Anthony P29
Chang, Christopher P89
Chang, Helen P237
Chang, Florence P357
Chang, James P532
Chang, Andrew P532
Chang, Jason C P576
Chang, Ming-Chih W138
Chang, Yi-Yun W138
Chang, Fu-Chuan W138
Chang, Yung-Nan W138
Chang, Guangshen W220
Chang, Siew Yen W393
Chang, Kat Kiam W393
Chang, T. W474
Chang, Christopher W530
Chang, Kelvin W530
Chang, Herbert E279
Chang, Timothy E315
Chang, Andrew S E317
Chang-Wade, Gloria P624
Chao, Elaine A461
Chao, Albert A860
Chao, James A860
Chao, David A860
Chao, Jennie P451

COMBINED HOOVER'S HANDBOOK INDEX OF EXECUTIVES

Chao, C. Jimmy E166
Chapados, Gregory F P225
Chapados, Greg P225
Chapados, Gregory P225
Chapados, Douglas L P413
Chaparro, Andres E364
Chapek, Fred P610
Chapin, Samuel E320
Chaplain, Wayne P356
Chaplin, C. Edward A523
Chaplin, Ann A657
Chapman, Christopher P A7
Chapman, James A254
Chapman, Neil A291
Chapman, Kevin A674
Chapman, Robert H P62
Chapman, Rachel P114
Chapman, Jeffrey P309
Chapman, Archie J P323
Chapman, Carl L P491
Chapman, Rob P525
Chapman, Adrian P P654
Chapman, Robert E105
Chapman, Laurence E120
Chapman, Kevin E348
Chapoulaud-Floquet, Valerie W165
Chappell, Elizabeth A42
Chappell, Colin P363
Chappell, Robert E84
Chappell, Kathleen E127
Chappelle, John E96
Chapple, Helen P175
Chappuis, Cameron P290
Charbonneau, Brett P265
Charbonneau, Terry P477
Chard, Daniel E266
Charde, Seth P190
Charest, Yvon W341
Charette, Gary C P38
Chareyre, Pierre W184
Charles, Jamina P69
Charles, Alexandra P103
Charles, Robert M P289
Charles, David Phillip P640
Charlet, Barbara A740:P516
Charley, Ray A313:E165
Charlie, Cady P525
Charlson, Paul P26
Charlson, Jay P437
Charlton, Kevin A728:P496
Charman, Max P420
Charman, Nikki P422
Charnley, Nina A113
Charoenanusorn, Apiphan W441
Charoglu, Constantine P218
Charreton, Didier W32
Charrier, Richard P657
Charton, Jerome A267
Chartrand, Danice E383
Charvat, Peter P504:P578
Chase, Anthony A227
Chase, Sarah P67
Chase, Debra E43
Chase, Adam E364
Chassat, Sophie W302
Chatell, Cindy P535
Chatkewitz, Alexander A439
Chatlin, Bradley P507
Chatterjee, Koushik W478
Chattopadhyay, Sanat A515
Chattopadhyay, Lily P114
Chaturbedi, Ritesh P191
Chaturvedi, Chandra W240
Chaumartin, Anik W17
Chausse, Melinda A204
Chauvin, Robert P277
Chavalitcheewingul, Aree W441
Chavarria, Carla P28
Chavasse, Desmond P422
Chavers, Kevin A174
Chavez, Joann A258
Chavez, Cara P18
Chavez, Mary P169
Chavez, Jennifer P188
Chavez, Maria P464
Chavez, Francisco Medina W28
Chavira, Ron A647:P429

Chavous, Kevin E393
Chavoustie, Eric P488
Chawla, Sona A154
Cheah, Kim Teck W261
Cheah, Kim Ling W393
Chearavanont, Soopakij W98
Chearavanont, Narong W98
Chearavanont, Suphachai W98
Chearavanont, Soopakij W113
Chearavanont, Suphachai W113
Cheatham, Tim A779:P568
Cheatham, Gabriele P577
Cheatham, Alfreda P641
Cheatman, Lora C P209
Cheatum, Chris P586
Cheatwood, Chris A629
Checki, Terrence J A299
Chee, Jeffrey P577
Chee, Keng Eng W393
Chee, Johnathan E185
Cheek, Daniel W P468
Cheek, Jeffrey P577
Cheeks, George A655
Cheevanon, Tawatchai W284
Chehade, Nabil P567
Chela, Hraleen P625
Chelin, Julie A200
Chellew, Mark W30
Chemodurow, Tanya E126
Chen, Gloria A11
Chen, Xun A66
Chen, Thomas A106
Chen, Heng A157
Chen, Rosemarie A246
Chen, Wellington A639
Chen, Ping A739
Chen, Heidi A881
Chen, Dan P73
Chen, Xiaojun P498
Chen, Ping P515
Chen, Solomon P527
Chen, Robert P527
Chen, Honghui N P584
Chen, Wee Keng W29
Chen, Yanshun W88
Chen, Tsu-Pei W106
Chen, Grace W106
Chen, Kuang-Hsueh W106
Chen, Zhaohua W115
Chen, Deyou W119
Chen, Ge W120
Chen, Dayang W120
Chen, Yun W121
Chen, Hanwen W122
Chen, Zhongyue W124
Chen, Jui-Tsung W138
Chen, Hsi-Kuan W138
Chen, Kuo-Chuan W138
Chen, Bor-Heng W138
Chen, Hui Chung W195
Chen, Changchun W209
Chen, Jin W209
Chen, Bi'an W209
Chen, Liancai W223
Chen, Sanlian W223
Chen, Bin W235
Chen, Shuping W236
Chen, Hong W236
Chen, Siqing W244
Chen, Gang W265
Chen, Xingyao W349
Chen, Huanchun W349
Chen, Dexian W383
Chen, Kexiang W383
Chen, Xinying W383
Chen, Guanzhong W387
Chen, Jolene W391
Chen, Xiangyang W431
Chen, Jinzhu W432
Chen, Weili W490
Chen, Xuefeng W490
Chen, Yu-Liang W530
Chen, Dongxu W535
Chen, Shoude W535
Chen, Jianping W536
Chen, Jie E9
Chen, Heng E70

Chen, Warren E121
Chen, Hao E311
Chen, Wellington E331
Chenanda, Cariappa A228:E209
Cheney, Stephen E409
Cheng, Dunson A157
Cheng, Tony A672
Cheng, Li W24
Cheng, Pam W46
Cheng, Eva W87
Cheng, Sophia W106
Cheng, Xiaoming W116
Cheng, Yunlei W118
Cheng, Wen W120
Cheng, Hong W121
Cheng, Chih-Chuan W138
Cheng, Heng W236
Cheng, Kee Check W307
Cheng, Dunson E70
Chenoweth, Rodney A864:P656
Cheong, Yoo P646
Cheong, Kwok Leong W212
Cherecwich, Peter A567
Cherenek, Tc P341
Cheriyan, Anil A199
Cherner, Anatoly W208
Chernow, David A703
Chernow, Barbara P90
Chernyavskaya, Anna P379
Chernyshenko, Dmitry W424
Cherry, Jessica A327
Cherry, Pedro A754
Cherry, Jean P145
Cherry, Jessica P215
Cherry, Pedro E401
Chersky, Susan P80
Cherwoo, Sharda A869
Chery, Don A355:E193
Cheryl, Pietz P233
Cheshire, Marjorie A286:A632
Cheshire, Ian W95
Chesler, Randall A355:E193
Chessare, John B P225
Chestnutt, Roy W484:E120
Cheston, Sheila A569
Chetty, Indrin A381:P249
Cheung, Kenny A385
Cheung, Andy A442
Cheung, Martina A691
Cheung, Teresa P29
Cheung, Steven P171
Cheung, Andy P278
Cheung, Chris P371
Cheung, Ava P527
Cheung, Wing Lam W124
Cheunkrut, Pairote W65
Cheval, Jean W27
Cheves, Brad P491
Chevre, Claude W218
Chew, Roy P283
Chew, Lewis E62
Chhina, Ivar E258
Chiaetta, Stephen V P443
Chiang, Chih-Siung W230
Chiang, John E29
Chiaravanont, Phongthep W113
Chiarelli, Peter A463
Chiarello, Guy A325
Chiasson, Keith W111
Chickering, Mark P45
Chidekel, Aaron P19
Chidress, Andrea L P81
Chien, Teddy A445:P279
Chien, Alexander P301
Chien, S.J. W530
Chierchia, Giulia W91
Chiesa, Melanie A856
Chigateri, Pavi P288
Chih, Yu Yang W196
Chik, Ivan P183
Chikamoto, Shigeru W375
Chikan, Attila W334
Child, Paul A716
Child, William H P433
Child, Jeffrey P433
Child, Curtis K P433

Child, Curtis P433
Child, Peter W14
Child, Paul E379
Childers, Marc P525
Childers, Shelly E81
Childers, Steven E98
Childree, Robert A734:P510
Childress, Randall V P600
Childs, Jeffrey J A807
Childs, Rick L P175
Childs, Craig P339
Childs, Clinton P548
Chillura, Joseph A832:E431
Chilton, Kevin A490
Chilton, Linda E126
Chin, Dean A7
Chin, Rodney P164
Chin, Mary P165
Chin, Kenneth P441
Chin, Caroline P527
Chin, Y. W474
Chin, Eric E29
Chin, Moonhie E337
Chin, Jit E388
China, John A751
China, Bonita P157
Chinavicharana, Krisada W284
Chindemi, Craig P314
Chinea, Manuel A633
Ching, David A786
Ching, Bob P244
Ching, Patric D P474
Ching, Donny W434
Chini, Marc A459
Chinn, Carol P216
Chinnasami, Vijayan E421
Chiou, Erin P42
Chiou, Yau-De W138
Chiplock, Mark E19
Chiquoine, Ben P554
Chirachavala, Arun W62
Chirakitcharern, Paisan W113
Chirico, Emanuel A244
Chirico, James P52
Chirillo, Sarah A436:P271
Chirillo, Gary P488
Chirinos, Astor P153
Chisholm, John P658
Chisholm, Andrew W412
Chism, James P212
Chithran, Payyanadan V P206
Chittmittrapap, Weerawong W441
Chiu, Desiree P164
Chiu, Elisa P211
Chiu, Pak Yue W33
Chiu, Yi-Chiang W138
Chiu, Jingwu E311
Chivinski, Beth A340
Chlebos, Uwe W517
Chng, Kai Fong W155
Cho, Alice A319
Cho, Sunghwan A385
Cho, Alex A404
Cho, Michael A877
Cho, Bonghan W155
Cho, Vincent W530
Cho, Alice E171
Cho, Haeyoung E315
Cho, Paul E420
Choate, William A53
Choate, David P91
Choate, Mark P411
Choate, William E25
Choate, Fred E312
Chodak, Paul A44
Chofuku, Yasuhiro W317
Choi, Brian A87
Choi, Caroline A268
Choi, Jimmy A553
Choi, John P167
Choi, Eunsu P258
Choi, Jimmy P370
Choi, Mun Y P625
Choi, Koon Shum W87
Choi, Myeong Hui W271
Choi, Hyeong Seok W296
Choi, Hyeon Cheol W296

HOOVER'S HANDBOOK OF EMERGING COMPANIES 2022

COMBINED HOOVER'S HANDBOOK INDEX OF EXECUTIVES

A = AMERICAN BUSINESS
E = EMERGING COMPANIES
P = PRIVATE COMPANIES
W = WORLD BUSINESS

Choi, Yeong Geun W296
Choi, Jeong Wu W388
Choi, Yong Jun W388
Choi, Gyeong Rok W438
Choi, Dong Su W532
Chojnowski, David A845
Chojnowski, Daniel P315
Chok, Kwee Bee W232
Chombar, Francoise W507
Chong, Steven P118
Chong, Wai Sang W119
Chong, Chye Neo W232
Chong, Soo Loong W393
Chong, Yam Kiang W393
Chong, Yoke Sin W529
Choo, Nyen Fui W376
Choong, Ho Wai W232
Chopey, Stephen B A739:P515
Chopra, Daveen A269
Chopra, Naveen A607
Chopra, Arvind P244
Chopra, Deepak W465
Chorin, Jacky W175
Chosy, James L A829
Chothayaphorn, Thitivorn W65
Chou, John A55
Chou, Henry P215
Chou, Anita P416
Chou, Yen-Chia W138
Chou, James W530
Chou, Yun Hwa E311
Chouinard, Scott E182
Chow, Man Yiu W118
Chow, Chi-Leung W147
Chow, Teh-Han W199
Chow, Joan E137
Chow, Heidy E185
Chowdary, Sushma P642
Chowdary, Kosaraju W477
Choy, David P370
Choy, Wing Kay W129
Chrencik, Robert A P623
Chris, Carmello P258
Chriss, James Alexander A429
Christensen, Mylia P99
Christensen, Cindy P116
Christensen, Leslie P120
Christensen, Jesper V P181
Christensen, Larry P278
Christensen, Angela P653
Christensen, Johnny W267
Christensen, Christopher E139
Christensen, Bret E233
Christenson, Vonn A709:E370
Christian, Justin A318
Christian, Darrianne A466
Christian, David A838
Christian, Dan P2
Christian, Ronald E P491
Christian, Jeanine E122
Christian, Justin E171
Christian, Darrianne E244
Christiansen, Jason P459
Christianson, Cole P416
Christianson, Conni P633
Christie, Roderick A91
Christie, Brenda P166
Christie, Alease P291
Christie, James W101
Christie, Christopher E311
Christino, Genuino W39
Christmann, John A64
Christmas, Charles A514:E267
Christodoro, Jonathan A611
Christofer, Lyndsey W126
Christophe, Cleveland A139
Christophe, Pierrot A346:P227
Christopher, Joyce P129
Christopher, Basil P399
Christopulos, Constantine P554
Christy, James A648

Christy, Lisa P590
Christy, Jody E411
Chroffel, Bruce P618
Chronican, Philip W340:W531
Chronister, Steven P173
Chronister, Thomas E68
Chrousos, Phaedra E432
Chrysler, L. Gage A793
Chrysler, Sue P233
Chrysler, L. Gage E414
Chryssanthopoulos, Nicholas W27
Chryssikos, Georgios W188
Chu, Christie A374
Chu, Ron A790
Chu, Scott P597
Chu, Cheng-Qing W230
Chu, Victor W360
Chu, Maggie E255
Chua, Julie W82
Chua, Edgar W323
Chua, Kim Chiu W376
Chua, Sock Koong W391
Chua, Nam-Hai W529
Chuan, Lim Him W155
Chuan, John Chong Eng W307
Chuang, Hong-Jen W432
Chuaphanich, Prasan W441
Chubachi, Mitsuo W1
Chubb, Carmen A352
Chubb, Jack P612
Chuchottaworn, Paillin W441
Chuengviroj, Vichien W98
Chuenratanakul, Wirote W65
Chugg, Juliana A836
Chui, Herman P376
Chumley, Robert A542
Chumura, Thomas P624
Chun, Semin P258
Chun, Edward P402
Chun, Robyn P620
Chun, Mark R P620
Chun, Courtnee E75
Chung, Nelson A157
Chung, Harry A374
Chung, Paul A760
Chung, Alexander N P69
Chung, David P243
Chung, Mark M P326
Chung, Shui Ming W124
Chung, Nelson E70
Chung, Janice E315
Chung, Andrew E315
Church, Tracy P242
Churchill, Winston A58
Churchill, Sally J A669
Churchill, Arthur L P247
Churchill, Brian P409
Churchill, Sally J P440
Churchill, Brian P501
Churchill, Randy E39
Churchill, Laurie E250
Churchwell, Kevin P548
Chuslo, Steven E206
Chvez, Dr Jess H P451
Chwick, Jane A617:E262:E319
Chythlook, Joseph P413
Ciampa, Dominick A554
Ciampitti, Tony A56
Cianfrocca, Marguerite P651
Ciaramitaro, Paula E219
Cibik, Melanie E404
Cicarella, Tom P222
Cicerone, Keith P272
Cich, Adam W3
Cieciura, Mark E326
Ciello, Ronald Del P333
Ciesinski, David E147
Ciesla, Frank P350
Cieslak, Kimberly E250
Cieslewicz, Richard M P228
Cifrian, Roberto W198
Ciftcioglu, Ersin Onder W504
Cifu, Douglas A839:P643
Cimbri, Carlo W511
Cimen, Ismail W281
Cimenoglu, Ahmet W540
Cimino, Amy P420

Cinar, H. Cahit W504
Cintani, William A549:E290
Cioffi, Lucio Valerio W294
Ciolek, John A561
Cioli, Laura W316
Ciongoli, Adam A146
Ciorra, Anthony P302
Ciorra, Ernesto W181
Ciplak, Ufuk W281
Cirera, Carmina Ganyet W400
Ciresi, Rita L P629
Cirignano, Holly A390:E215
Cirillo, Charles E295
Ciroli, Lance A294
Ciroli, James A326
Ciroli, Lance E156
Ciroli, James E177
Ciruzzi, Vincent E13
Ciulla, John A851
Civgin, Don A32
Civil, Patricia A546
Clagett, Robert A640:E333
Claiborne, Jess P9
Clair, Joyce St. A567
Clair, Jo St P125
Clamadieu, Jean-Pierre W184
Clancy, John A278
Clancy, Brenda A815
Clancy, Kevin P246
Clancy, Makkie P340
Clancy, Brian P461
Clancy, John E141
Clancy, Paul E225
Clapper, Sarah P526
Claps, Francis X P177
Clardy, Donna P214
Clardy, David P256
Clare, Peter A152
Clare, Timothy P81
Clarey, Charles A804:P607
Clarida, Richard A301
Clariza, Ronnie E169
Clark, Suzanne A20
Clark, David A38
Clark, Gina A55
Clark, R. Kerry A63
Clark, Frank A123
Clark, Richard A221
Clark, James A232
Clark, Chris A234
Clark, Janet A281
Clark, Benjamin A289
Clark, Michael A484
Clark, Stuart A511
Clark, Maura A558
Clark, Donald A674
Clark, Bernard A697
Clark, William A712
Clark, Matthew A737
Clark, Bethany A738
Clark, John B A744
Clark, Janet A771
Clark, R. Kerry A772
Clark, Denise A817
Clark, Steve A870
Clark, Christopher A871
Clark, Kim P9
Clark, David P11
Clark, Matthew P53
Clark, Cynthia P70
Clark, Frank P80
Clark, Buster P101
Clark, Haley P119
Clark, Vonelle P150
Clark, Talisa R P158
Clark, Donald P174
Clark, Moira P183
Clark, Steve P203
Clark, Diana P269
Clark, Jeffrey P278
Clark, Crystal P282
Clark, Karri P286
Clark, Keith P311
Clark, Stuart P322
Clark, Mark T P337:P410
Clark, Edward Stuart P426

Clark, Joe P466
Clark, Alma P471
Clark, Susan P479
Clark, Meghan P498
Clark, Matthew P513
Clark, Bethany P514
Clark, John B P519
Clark, Tara P547
Clark, Mark T P552
Clark, Robert P562
Clark, Frank C P566
Clark, Michael P579
Clark, Jason P626
Clark, Lucas P629
Clark, Roy A P629
Clark, Carol P640
Clark, Caroline P640
Clark, Richard W8
Clark, Kevin W37
Clark, Ian W475
Clark, Yvette E9
Clark, Morris E85
Clark, Laura E126
Clark, Jonathan E135
Clark, Rodney E140
Clark, Theodore M E189
Clark, Matthew E326
Clark, Donald E348
Clark, Laura E353
Clark, William E373
Clark, Charles E383
Clark, Nicole E448
Clark, Donald E451
Clark, Steve E455
Clark-Sellers, Lee P421
Clarke, Teresa A51
Clarke, Michael A72
Clarke, Teresa A341
Clarke, Jeanette A P40
Clarke, Pete P166
Clarke, Christopher P252
Clarke, Stephen L P306
Clarke, David P452
Clarke, Cyril P642
Clarke, Angus W18
Clarke, David W39
Clarke, Peter W191
Clarke, Michael E31
Clarkin, Cheryl E P308
Clarkson, Daniel J P47
Clarkson, Dan P47
Clarkson, David P210
Clarno, Bev A740:P516
Classon, Rolf W203
Clatterbaugh, Carol P641
Clatterbuck, Janice A300
Clatterbuck, Michelle A429
Claude, Patrick W398
Claudia, Ontiveros P608
Claure, Marcelo A758
Claus, Gary A313
Claus, Brad P137
Claus, Mary Beth P372
Claus, Gary E165
Clausade, Josseline de W106
Clausen, Jorgen M P181
Clavel, Daniel P127
Clawson, Dan A293:P212
Claxton, Timothy E361
Clay, Reed A741
Clay, Brutus P457
Clay, Reed P517
Clay, Shaundra E234
Clay, Jeffrey E327
Claybrooks, John P176
Clayton, Norma A575
Clayton, Annette W427
Cleaf, Damian Van P311
Cleary, James A55
Cleary, John P154
Cleary, James J P202
Cleary, James P207
Cleary, Timothy J P285
Cleary, Mary Elizabeth P305
Cleary, Anne E P656
Cleary, Lisa E188
Cleaver, Chuck P314

COMBINED HOOVER'S HANDBOOK INDEX OF EXECUTIVES

Cleeland, David W P57
Clegg, Travis P244
Clegg, Catherine E197
Clegg, Don E397
Cleland, Richard C P208
Clem, Jackie E13
Clemence, Cynthia A794:P599
Clemensen, Hal A176:P11
Clement, Alden A736
Clement, Dallas A796
Clement, Scott P99
Clement, Mark P231
Clement, Alden P512
Clement, Mark P598
Clement-Holmes, Linda A179:A306
Clemente, Mario A431
Clemente, Rodney E137
Clementi, Erich W161
Clements, Carol A439
Clements, James A814
Clements, Charles P14
Clements, Hal P54
Clements, Mandy P203
Clements, David P422
Clements, James E424
Clemeson, Marry A39:P28
Clemmenson, Larry A48:P31
Clemmer, Richard A404
Clemmer, J. Harold A707
Clemmer, Richard W37
Clemmer, J. Harold E368
Clemons, James A866
Clemons, Jack W72:W166
Clemons, James E450
Clendon, Susan Mc P199
Clerc, Vincent W1
Clerico, John E130
Clermont, Ralph A544:E285
Clesceri, Shannon P99
Cleveland, Cotton A284
Cleveland, Debra P166
Cleveland, Sue P253
Cleveland, Todd E314
Clevenger, Megan P287
Clever, Xiaoqun W246
Click, Betty A253
Click, Christopher A542
Clifford, Reny P98
Clifford, Teresa P174
Clifford, Robert P594
Clifford, Deborah E38
Clift, Ruth P401
Clifton, Rita W295
Clinard, Nolan P95
Cline, Richard A396
Cline, Kimberly R A744:P519
Cline, James E413
Cline, Brenda E419
Clinton, Chelsea A288
Clinton, Stephen E160
Cloonan, Wendy A163
Cloonan, Donna P175
Clossin, Todd A853:E445
Cloues, Edward P643
Clough, Jeanette A143
Clough, Jaime P56
Clough, G Wayne P228
Clough, Jeanette E65
Clougher, John P240
Clouse, Mark A146
Clouse, Steve P462
Clulow, Christopher A228
Clutter, Robert P147
Clyburn, Frank A426
Clyburn, William E365
Clymans, Kris A614
Clymo, David W425
Cmil, Jennifer A558
Cnor, Paul A15:P7
Cns, Marcie P201
Co, Gerard Lee W83
Co, Romeo W83
Coakley, John P147
Coates, Spencer P217
Coates, Peter W211
Coatsworth, John H A781:P581
Cobarrubias, Fabiola A642

Cobb, Brent A655
Cobb, Wes P562
Cobb, Josephine P572
Cobb, James P620
Cobb, Heather E130
Cobb, Brent E340
Coben, Lawrence A574
Coben, Jerome E202
Cobert, Beth A159
Cobian, Mauricio Doehner W109
Coble, Tina P380
Coble, Paul P644
Coblentz, Julian E111
Coborn, Christopher P142
Coborn, Emily P142
Coburn, Fergal W17
Coburn, Quinn E197
Cocca, Michael P521
Coccagno, James A P93
Cocchi, Steven E381
Cochenour, David P222
Cochenour, Randy P651
Cochran, Sandra A488
Cochran, James A674
Cochran, Jeanne M A737
Cochran, Mike P307
Cochran, Karen P457
Cochran, Jeanne M P513
Cochran, Steven E60
Cochran, Edward E77
Cochran, James E348
Cochrane, Collin A668
Cochrell, Patty P242
Cock, Paul De A533
Cockerham, Bernard P212
Cockerham, Mary P439
Cockerham, Gregory E96
Cocking, Gina E82
Cockrell, Benny P423
Cockwell, Jack W94
Coco, Debbie P52
Coco, Denae P121
Cocorullo, L Mark P314
Coder, Derrick P213
Codispoti, Edward E300
Codner, Eugene P128
Cody, Kevin A233:P178
Coe, Mary A515
Coe, Scott P83
Coe, Sebastian W200
Coelho, Jose Mauricio Pereira W506
Coen, Bill P339
Cofer, Timothy E75
Cofer-Wildsmith, Marina E188
Coffey, Timothy A62
Coffey, John A126
Coffey, Mark A A401
Coffey, John E54
Coffman, Chris P155
Cofre, Daniel Alberto Rodriguez W198
Cogan, Andrew E24
Cogen, Jeff P164
Coggins, Jeff P76
Cognetti, John E161
Cogut, Charles A23
Cohan, Sean A562:P378
Cohen, Stephen A120
Cohen, Ryan A343
Cohen, Jeff A379
Cohen, Jonathan A496
Cohen, Tal A543
Cohen, Andrew A676
Cohen, David A736
Cohen, Chad M A877
Cohen, Charles F P69
Cohen, Richard S P69
Cohen, Bernard P276
Cohen, Rebecca P294
Cohen, Matthew P302
Cohen, Shai P325
Cohen, Evan P362
Cohen, Mark P416
Cohen, Nisan P440
Cohen, Andrew P444
Cohen, Gary P508
Cohen, David P512

Cohen, David W135
Cohen, Daniel E89
Cohen, Charles E150
Cohen, Robert E393
Cohn, Gary A424
Cohn, Leslie P55
Coin, Nick S A531:P349
Cok, Michael A417:E226
Coke, Michael E406
Coker, Colin A27
Coker, Key A317
Coker, Dave P492
Coker, Key E170
Col, Douglas E359
Colacchio, Thomas P182
Colalillo, Joseph A842:P645
Colanero, Stephen P28
Colangelo, Marianne P124
Colar, Patricia A387:P251
Colaruotolo, John E257
Colbert, Theodore A124
Colbert, Kit A841
Colbert, Charles A877
Colbert, Charles E A877
Colbert, Michael P164
Colbert, Charles P662
Colbert, Charles E P662
Colbert, Virgis E388
Colburn, James D P314
Coldani, Steven E327
Coldiron, Jenny P225
Coldiron, Den Ellen P614
Cole, Michel A149
Cole, Darin A217
Cole, M. Ray A309
Cole, Sue A501
Cole, Kenneth A502
Cole, Susan A613
Cole, Michael A805
Cole, Martin A858
Cole, Darin P151
Cole, Paris P184
Cole, Deborah P190
Cole, Cheryl P203
Cole, Kim Braxl P379
Cole, Bennie L P387
Cole, Debbie P499
Cole, David P566
Cole, Emma P585
Cole, Jay P652
Cole, Michael W82
Cole, David W524
Cole, M. Ray E163
Cole, Richard E248
Cole, Matthew E255
Cole, Susan E316
Cole, H. Kenneth E383
Coleal, David P650
Colella, Carmine P353
Colella, Joe P557
Colella, Gerald E277
Coleman, J. Edward A40
Coleman, Kevin A56
Coleman, Leonard A271
Coleman, Gary A359
Coleman, Denis A360
Coleman, Mary A669
Coleman, Casey A803
Coleman, Timothy A828
Coleman, Al P60
Coleman, Leigh P64
Coleman, Edward P158
Coleman, Candace P330
Coleman, Jeff P361
Coleman, Kia P365
Coleman, Mary P440
Coleman, Daniel P577
Coleman, Brandon P579
Coleman, Casey P606
Coleman, Timothy P635
Coleman, Lisa E75
Coleman, Richard K E111
Coleman, John C E129
Coleman, Glenn E234
Colenda, Christopher P651
Coles, N. Anthony A669
Coles, Pamela W409

Coletta, Edmond E69
Coletti, Julie E15
Coley, Aaron P326
Coley, Tammy E235
Colf, Richard W A454:A621:P285:P412
Colin, Chan W212
Colin, Didier W281
Colin, John E174
Collar, Gary A20
Collard, C David P114
Collawn, Patricia A168
Collazo, Jose E295
College, Eugene A293:P211
Colleran, Donald A7:A302
Colletti, Lisa A670:P440
Collier, Lisa A810
Collier, Joe P429
Collier, David E327
Collingsworth, Connie A102
Collingsworth, J M P342
Collins, James A106
Collins, Kathryn A277
Collins, Brian A278
Collins, Alvin A328
Collins, Augustus A410
Collins, Kevin A431
Collins, Arthur A447
Collins, David A474
Collins, Gary A587
Collins, Susan A768
Collins, Augustus A798
Collins, Joshua L P76
Collins, Wendy P163
Collins, Kim P165
Collins, Mark P186
Collins, Peg P193
Collins, Tim P275
Collins, Barbara P398
Collins, Gregory P403
Collins, Mindy P434
Collins, Bernadette P553
Collins, Bill P579
Collins, Henry P594
Collins, Michelle W99
Collins, James E48
Collins, Richard E117
Collins, Christine E120
Collins, Ryan M E129
Collins, Brian E141
Collins, Jeffrey E289
Collins, Gary E302
Collins, Martin E343
Collins, Craig E448
Collis, Steven A55
Collver, Ronan A134:P87
Colman, Gerard P58
Colom, Rebeca P607
Colombas, J. W249
Colombini, Jay A294:E155
Colombo, Marion A103
Colombo, William A244
Colombo, Paolo W252
Colombo, Dina E2
Colombo, Marion E47
Colon, Lina P228
Colon, Tairis P408
Colones, Robert L P322
Colonges, Guillaume De W104
Colonias, Karen A673:E374
Colonna, Jerome P68
Colonna, Suzanne P553
Colony, George E182
Colorado, Lisa P608
Colpack, Michael J P284
Colpron, Francoise A702
Colsch, Mike P260
Colson, Nathaniel A523
Colter, David A103:E47
Colton, Sam A321
Colton, Sabine P353
Colton, Cory P590
Coltrane, Scott P627
Colucci, Anthony J P208
Colucci, Nick W395
Colucciello, Michael P427
Colver, Thomas P617
Colvin, Kristie A163

HOOVER'S HANDBOOK OF EMERGING COMPANIES 2022

COMBINED HOOVER'S HANDBOOK INDEX OF EXECUTIVES

A = AMERICAN BUSINESS
E = EMERGING COMPANIES
P = PRIVATE COMPANIES
W = WORLD BUSINESS

Colvin, Garren P456
Colvin, Donald E436
Colwell, Mark P539
Colwell, Gale R P657
Colwell, Michael E240
Colyar, Michelle A387:P251
Comadran, Sol Daurella W61
Combes, Michel A625
Combs, Randy A729
Combs, Linda M A739
Combs, Robert J P414
Combs, Randy P497
Combs, Linda M P515
Combs, Bobby P533
Combs, Mark P651
Combs, Jason E364
Come, Matthew A558
Comeau, Carol P36
Comer, Diane A445
Comer, James A866
Comer, Diane P279
Comer, Jonathan B E52
Comer, Carrie E153
Comer, James E450
Comfort, Dan P128
Comfort, Cydney P149
Comin, Luciano W93
Commins-Tzoumakas, Kimberly P1
Comneno, Maurizia W316
Comnick, Terry P462
Compagna, Paolo W425
Comparato, Elena W294
Comparin, Cynthia A227
Compton, Bob A232
Compton, John A317
Compton, Jennifer A712
Compton, James M P153
Compton, Greg P167
Compton, John E170
Compton, Jennifer E373
Comstock, G P281
Comstock, Karolyn P525
Comyn, Matt W135
Conard, Diana E301
Conaway, Mary A193
Conaway, Michael P84
Conaway, Mary E87
Concannon, William A159
Concannon, Chris A839:P643
Concannon, Christopher E262
Concannon, Michael E427
Concino, Abby P146
Conde, Cesar A845
Condon, Patrick A277
Condon, Jennifer P629
Condon, Liam W78
Condra, Robert P173
Condren, Bert P85
Condrin, J. Paul A375
Condron, Robert P339
Condron, Gary D P553
Cone, C David A762
Cone, Barbara P392
Cone, David E409
Coneway, Mary P52
Confer, Jackie E242
Congcar, Congsin W65
Congdon, David A584
Congdon, John A584
Congdon, David A584
Congdon, John A584
Congdon, Chris P455
Conger, Daniel E367
Congress, Elaine P217
Conine, Bill P43
Conklin, Bret A399
Conklin, Michael A870:E455
Conley, Barbara A311
Conley, Sophie A570
Conley, Jason A686
Conley, Eric P222

Conley, Tammy P286
Conley, Melinda P288
Conley, Amber P335
Conley, Sophie P388
Conley, Karen P422
Conley, Fatimah P618
Conley, Gregory E417
Conlin, Chris P132
Conlin, Kelly E364
Conlon, Gregory A448
Connally, Stanley A147:E66
Connaughton, Bernadette E204
Connell, K. Bruce A497
Connell, Eugene E145
Connelly, Marjorie A36
Connelly, Susan A236
Connelly, James M A381:P249
Connelly, William W13
Connelly, Ryan E250
Connely, Patrick P253
Conner, Raymond A26
Conner, Peter A102
Conner, Jack A382
Conner, Brad A662
Conner, Anne A789
Conner, Thomas O P338
Conner, Isabelle W43
Conner, David W456
Conner, Marjorie E115
Conner, Jack E211
Conner, Anne E411
Connerton, John E148
Connet, James P640
Connett, Brad A696
Connly, Linda A877
Connoley, Stacy P197
Connolly, Sean M A214
Connolly, Mark A774
Connolly, Bridget P183
Connolly, Melinda P408
Connolly, Brian P657
Connolly, Patrick W102
Connolly, Michael E258
Connolly, Mark E408
Connon, Cheryl P97
Connor, Sandie O A99
Connor, Christopher A427
Connor, Jared A554
Connor, Frank A772
Connor, Martin A788
Connor, Christopher A875
Connor, Kevin P28
Connor, Jared P372
Connor, Roger W210
Connor, James E124
Connors, Nelda A131:A132
Connors, Michael P96
Connors, Michael L P97
Connors, Dan P124
Connors, Christine P588
Conoscente, Jean-Paul W429
Conrad, G. Kent A351
Conrad, Micah A592
Conrad, Jared A650
Conrad, Mary Jo P92
Conrad, Karen P143
Conrad, Angela D P257
Conrad, Scott V P530
Conrad, Melinda W30
Conrad, Diana W210
Conrad, Alexander E255
Conrad, Micah E303
Conrades, George A595
Conroy, Alexandre A109
Conroy, Kathryn A A210
Conroy, Kevin P596
Cons, Ricardo W3
Consagra, James A814:E423
Consi, Anthony A613:E316
Considine, William P118
Consigli, Anthony P151
Consigli, Anthony M P151
Consigli, Matthew D P151
Consing, Cezar W70
Constable, David A328
Constantine, Tom A89
Constantine, Thomas A90

Constantine, Tom P54
Constantine, Dow P161
Constantine, Thomas E41
Constantinides, Constantinos W395
Constantino, Ferdinand W417
Contardo, Cristian Lagos W56
Conte, Anthony E305
Conti, Jeanne Di A186
Conti, Richard P94
Conti, Jeanne Di P127
Conto, Claudio De W391
Contos, Adam E345
Contreras, Juan P207
Contreras, Sharon L P238
Contreras, Sharon P238
Contreras-Sweet, Maria A705
Contrl, Sloan Gray P493
Converse, Peter A814:E423
Conway, Mike A8
Conway, William A152
Conway, John W A226
Conway, James A278
Conway, Michael A732
Conway, James A772
Conway, Mike P4
Conway, Meagan P51
Conway, Heather W213
Conway, James E141
Conzelman, Bonnie P75
Cook, Tim A65
Cook, Rita A96
Cook, Linda A99
Cook, Dave A293
Cook, Chris A315
Cook, Robert A320
Cook, Timothy A563
Cook, W. Rand A640
Cook, Todd A667
Cook, Kenneth A693
Cook, Chris A737
Cook, Rob A803
Cook, Laura P17
Cook, Marcia P20
Cook, Laura P72
Cook, Matthew P115
Cook, Chad P158
Cook, Deborah P190
Cook, Dave P212
Cook, Robert P214
Cook, Bill P217
Cook, Carter P218
Cook, Paul P262
Cook, Kayla P278
Cook, Michelle L P313
Cook, Troy D P392
Cook, Jerry P435
Cook, Matt P461
Cook, Chris P513
Cook, Alisha P538
Cook, Jack P550
Cook, Jmaes P569
Cook, Angela P586
Cook, Rob P606
Cook, Larry N P612
Cook, Donald J P653
Cook, Sharon W340
Cook, Helen W345
Cook, Jon W533
Cook, Zerick E84
Cook, Chris E168
Cook, Robert E173
Cook, Bonnie E259
Cook, W. Rand E333
Cook, Kenneth E360
Cook, John E366
Cook, Donald General E407
Cook, Laureen E426
Cooke, Renee S P301
Cooke, Julie E290
Cookman, James A749:E394
Cooksen, Lindsey A760
Cooksey, Robert P539
Cooksey, Robert W P539
Cooley, Toni A798
Cooley, Kem P379
Cooley, Lashonda P648
Coolidge, Rhonda A775:P548

Coolidge, R. Lowell E84
Coombe, Gary A643
Coombe, Robert W128
Coombs, Dan A173:P113
Coomer, Christian A A735:P511
Cooney, Traci A738
Cooney, Anne A854
Cooney, Traci P514
Coonrod, Gregory L P62
Cooper, Angus A25
Cooper, Edith A38
Cooper, Nancy A138
Cooper, Matthew A149
Cooper, Shantella A422
Cooper, John A475
Cooper, Ellen A480
Cooper, Edith A619
Cooper, Kerry A623
Cooper, Roy A739
Cooper, Susane A740
Cooper, Stephen A846
Cooper, Cathy A846
Cooper, Justin P32
Cooper, Jay P68
Cooper, Mark P106
Cooper, Gary P112
Cooper, Dorothy P174
Cooper, Elizabeth C P252
Cooper, Troye P316
Cooper, John P337
Cooper, Roy P515
Cooper, Susane P516
Cooper, Jack P598
Cooper, Kristin P632
Cooper, Nancy W37
Cooper, Kirstine W51
Cooper, Simon W456
Cooper, Emilio E164
Cooper, Arthur E194
Cooper, H. Lee E207
Cooper, Tod E284
Cooper-Boone, Deborah P218
Cooperman, Daniel A534
Coore, Becky P642
Coorigan, Micheal P193
Cope, Cherie P124
Cope, Maureen P506
Copeland, David A315
Copeland, Rex A366
Copeland, Scott A688
Copeland, Bonnie S P56
Copeland, Lynn R P114
Copeland, Lynn P114
Copeland, Paul P330
Copeland, David E167
Copher, Ronald A355:E193
Coppa, A M P90
Coppedge, J Kenneth P274
Coppey, Pierre W517
Cora, Michael P162
Cora, Jim P502
Cora-Bramble, Denice P114
Coradi, Robert A597:E307
Coranet, Mike P257
Corasanti, Joseph E224
Corbett, John A725
Corbett, Larry P86
Corbett, Chloe P126
Corbett, Ross P207
Corbett, Brian T P308
Corbett, Alex P539
Corbett, Kevin S P571
Corbett, William P609:P609
Corbett, Alexis W65
Corbett, John E383
Corbin, Lee Anne P240
Corbino, Ralph P230
Corcoran, Anne P461
Corcos, Tommaso W251
Cordani, David A178
Cordell, Terri P594
Cordero, Daniel P67
Cordero, Glendy P392
Cordes, Rebecca H A606
Cordes, Laura P446
Cordier, Donna A208
Cordier, Emile De P84

COMBINED HOOVER'S HANDBOOK INDEX OF EXECUTIVES

Cordier, Donna P145
Cordova, Deanna P541
Cordova, Richard P550
Corielli, Emanuela P374
Corilo, Suzanne P620
Corker, Ricky W359
Corkle, Kristy P323
Corkrean, John J E189
Corlett, Glenn E332
Corley, Donna A337
Corley, Sarah T P78
Corley, Maryann P307
Corley, Robin P617
Corn, Ron A172:A173:P113:P113
Cornelius, James A808:E421
Cornell, Brian C A761
Cornell, Brian A875
Cornell, Theodore P379
Cornell, Helen E215
Cornett, Mick P130
Cornett, Maggie P262
Cornetta, Paolo W509
Cornetta, Richard E78
Cornew, Kenneth A287:A745
Cornhill, David W242
Cornils, Rhnea P45
Cornish, Thomas A101
Cornuelle, Valerie P95
Coro, Ricardo A468
Coronado, Julia A682
Coronado, Edison P259
Corr, Edwin G P311
Corr, Greg E270
Corradi, Enrico W144
Corrado, Richard E10
Correa, Chris P474
Correll, Craig P337
Correnti, Salvatore E145
Corrie, Linda P662
Corriere, John P129
Corrigan, Joanna P236
Corrigan, George M P488
Corrigan, Scott W456
Corrsin, David E19
Corry, David M P299
Corse, Brian P405
Corsini, Bryan M A606
Corson, Bradley W242
Cortes, Oswaldo A864:P656
Cortes-Vazquez, Lorraine A A186:P129
Cortesio, Jeremy P482
Cortez, Veronica P155
Corti, Robert A10
Cortina, Ignacio A598
Corum, Edward A294:E155
Corvi, Carolyn A813:P642
Corvino, Frank A P660
Corwin, Steven J A780
Corwin, Steven P372
Corwin, Steven J P572
Corzine, Chris P141
Coscia, Anthony A582:E302
Cosentino, Anthony E361
Cosenzo, Donna P240
Coslett, Jeffrey E422
Cosman, James A136
Cosner, Kelley A224:P172
Cosset, Yael A459:A461
Cossetti, Anthony A340
Cosslett, Andy W276
Cost, Mike P527
Costa, James A102
Costa, Mark A264
Costa, Roland A300
Costa, Antonio Fernando Melo Martins da W172
Costa, Jose Carlos Da Silva W206
Costa, Francisco Manuel Seixas da W263
Costa, Maurizio W316
Costa, Tabajara Bertelli W506
Costa, Donn E188
Costante, Patricia E164
Costanzo, Brian A497
Costello, Ellen A183
Costello, Beth A377
Costello, Mary P130

Costello, Larry P277
Costello, Don P316
Costello, Joseph G P441
Costello, Thomas E89
Costello, Richard E199
Costes, Yseulys W273
Costigan, Conor W156
Costonis, Michael A192
Cotarelo, Brandon P396
Cote, Joe P186
Cote, Mike P292
Cote, Jacynthe W412
Cothran, Mark E382
Cotnoir, Frederic W250
Cotoia, Michael E403
Cotran, Paul R P290
Cotten, Eugene P73
Cotter, Martin A61
Cotter, JoAnn E82
Cottington, Eric A513:P328
Cottle, Rebecca P161
Cotton, Alanna A409
Cotton, Benjamin A804
Cotton, Diana P357
Cotton, Tiffany P493
Cotton, Laurie P579
Cotton, Benjamin P607
Cotton, Leonard E52
Cottrell, Barbara A331:E178
Couch, James D P130
Couch, Laverne P508
Couchman, Glen A106:P64
Couderc, Anne-Marie W18
Coughenour, Peter E8
Coughlin, Stephen A17
Coughlin, Thomas A107
Coughlin, Brendan A185
Coughlin, Thomas E48
Coughran, Steve P205
Coull-Cicchini, Debbie W250
Coulombe, Stephen P82
Coulson, R. Cromwell E308
Coulter, Linda W434
Council, Alicia P322
Council, Chrissy P489
Countryman, Gary L P180
Counts, Adriane P175
Counts, Kenny P217
Coupet, Maylis W281
Couples, Keri A762
Courage, Catherine A420
Coureil, Herve W427
Couret, Adrien W428
Couris, John P215
Courrege, Chad P304
Coursey, Leigh A16:P8
Court, James A90
Court, David W101
Court, James E41
Courtland, Dvora B P641
Courtney, Tom A377
Courtney, Kappes P164
Courtney, Christopher E300
Courtois, Jean-Philippe A494
Courtright, Wayne E425
Coury, Robert J A837
Cousin, Ertharin A535
Cousins, Erica P332
Couto, Scott A52
Coutu, Marcel W94:W213
Coutu, Francois W322
Coutu, Michel W322
Coutu, Marcel W389
Covacevich, Teri P179
Covarrubias, Jonathan W59
Cover, Alexander A339
Covert, Stephanie E155
Covey, Susan A278
Covey, Bill A369:P237
Covey, Patrick E115
Covey, Susan E141
Covey, Michael E339
Covington, Adrienne A739
Covington, David P107
Covington, Adrienne P515
Cowan, Alister W466
Cowan, Joseph E78

Cowden, George P67
Cowe, Gordon W200
Cowen, Scott P542
Cowgill, Libby W P584
Cowin, Mark P93
Cowley, Samuel A420
Cox, Cader A147
Cox, Greg A224
Cox, Laura J A327
Cox, Richard A350
Cox, Heather A406
Cox, Robert A498
Cox, Christopher A520
Cox, Heather A574
Cox, Justin A724
Cox, David A738
Cox, Spencer J A741
Cox, Philip A751
Cox, R Mark A841
Cox, Erica A869
Cox, Chris P28
Cox, Joseph P45
Cox, Michelle P159
Cox, Carol P161
Cox, Greg P168
Cox, Colby P205
Cox, Laura J P215
Cox, Terence C P244
Cox, Terry P244
Cox, Karen P330
Cox, George P362
Cox, Russell F P390
Cox, Susan P428
Cox, David P514
Cox, Spencer J P517
Cox, Tom P528
Cox, Nancy P572
Cox, Michael E P602
Cox, Diana P647
Cox, Erica P659
Cox, Vivienne W210
Cox, Cader E66
Cox, David E132
Cox, Justin E383
Cox, Josh E395
Coy, Kim A27
Coy, Thomas P221
Coy, Rosha Mc P486
Coye, Molly E18
Coyle, Maurice A321
Coyles, Stephanie W322:W465
Coyne, Terrance E358
Coyner, Dan P636
Cozad, John A446
Cozar, Juan Pedro Perez E149
Cozart, Kevin P336
Cozens, Michelle P544
Cozza, Keith A872
Cozza, Patrick E185
Cozzi, Ray P601
Cozzone, Robert A416:E226
CPA, Tony M Astorga P78
CPA, Rick Trowbridge P466
Crabb, William P357
Crabiel, David B P343
Crabtree, Robby P533
Crabtree, Rob P540
Cracas, Teresa A179
Cracchiolo, James A52
Cracolici, Frank P356
Crady, Marc A296:E157
Craft, Joseph A126:E54
Crafton, Keith P302
Cragg, Scott E229
Craig, Pamela A3
Craig, C. A94
Craig, Pamela A222:A645
Craig, Jonathan A697
Craig, Dennis A744
Craig, Sandra A775
Craig, Julie P60
Craig, Lonnie E P125
Craig, David P160
Craig, Angie P163
Craig, C C P212
Craig, Alex P257
Craig, Deborah P421

Craig, Dennis P519
Craig, Sandra P548
Craig, Matthew P636
Craig, Andronico Luksic W56
Craig, Gregory W101
Craig, C. E44
Craig, Benjamin E296
Craighead, Martin A273:A771
Crain, Robert A20
Crain, John P622
Crain, Robert A. E407
Craker, Robin P610
Cramer, Todd P360
Cramer, Bethany P464
Cramer, David P610
Crandall, J. Taylor A388
Crandall, Steven A847
Crane, Jim A48
Crane, Chris A286
Crane, Christopher A287
Crane, Ann A409
Crane, Cindy A604
Crane, Timothy A867
Crane, Jim P31
Crane, David W478
Crane, Jennifer Ray E111
Crane, Timothy E452
Cranley, John P125
Cranor, Tim P222
Cranston, Mary A839
Crapp, Nicholas W345
Crapps, Michael E166
Crary, Charles Mc A671
Craven, Raquel P244
Craven, Katherine P319
Craven, James E P402
Craven, Raychiel P529
Crawford, Frederick A18
Crawford, Seth A20
Crawford, Gordon A39
Crawford, Victor A150
Crawford, Stephen A264
Crawford, Anne A294
Crawford, James A309
Crawford, Victor A384
Crawford, Kermit A683
Crawford, Peter A697
Crawford, Terry P28
Crawford, Gordon P28
Crawford, John P432
Crawford, Kristi P463
Crawford, Greg P569
Crawford, Beverly P643
Crawford, Millar W488
Crawford, Linda E78
Crawford, Matthew E108
Crawford, Anne E156
Crawford, James E162
Creach, Andrea A740:P516
Creamer, Eunice P48
Crean, Tim P617
Crean, Michael P647
Creary, Mike Mc A517:P331
Creasy, Ross A54:E25
Creatura, Nick A192
Creech, Dale P323
Creech, Nathan W145
Creed, Joseph A156
Creed, Greg A863
Creedon,, Mike A12
Creek, Dan P339
Creek, Phillip E257
Creekmore, John A674:E348
Creel, Diane A15
Creery, Thomas A390
Cregg, Daniel A651
Creighton, Alecia P228
Cremel, Bruno W175
Cremers, Eric E329
Cremin, Mary C A48:P31
Crenshaw, William A652
Crenshaw, Carol P114
Crenshaw, Efrem P157
Crepin, Frederic W518
Crespi, Megan A204
Crespo, Frank E246
Cress, David W P382

COMBINED HOOVER'S HANDBOOK INDEX OF EXECUTIVES

A = AMERICAN BUSINESS
E = EMERGING COMPANIES
P = PRIVATE COMPANIES
W = WORLD BUSINESS

Cresswell, Rosie P479
Cresswell, Alex W488
Creus, Jose Oliu W57
Creuzot, Cheryl A774:E408
Crevoiserat, Joanne A759
Crew, Debra A A436:P271
Crew, Debra W165
Crews, Terrel A68:A860
Crews, Kim P380
Cribb, Ashlee E329
Cribbs, Steven A789
Crilly, Sean E438
Crimmins, John A140
Criner, Elizabeth P456
Cripe, Kimberly P116
Crisci, Robert A686
Criser, Marshall A147:E66
Crisosotomo, Michele W181
Crisp, Charles A281:A760
Criss, Christopher A853:E444
Crist, Peter A867:E452
Cristina, Steven P446
Critelli, Lewis E297
Crites, John A750:E394
Crittenden, Gary E153
Croce, Michael A747
Croce, Angela P141
Croce, Kasey P633
Croce, Michael E391
Crockett, Kyle A154
Crockett, Gary P398
Crockett, June P609
Crofts, Sharon A97
Croken, Kenneth P227
Croley, Matthew P334
Cromie, William P98
Croney, Barbara P461
Cronin, Jane A708
Cronin, Christopher A738
Cronin, Annmarie P89
Cronin, Brian P392
Cronin, Christopher P514
Cronin, Kathe P603
Cronin, Mike W199
Cronin, Patrick E81
Cronin, John E263
Crooker, William E389
Crooks, James E133
Cropper, Doug P227
Cropper, Spencer E247
Crosby, Michael A869
Crosby, Nikki P5
Crosen, Kaley E127
Croson, Rachel P624
Cross, Steve A741
Cross, Jeffrey D P30
Cross, Linda P156
Cross, Mary Lou P169
Cross, Coleen P224
Cross, Stephen P228
Cross, Tamela P245
Cross, Drew P483
Cross, Steve P517
Cross, Kevin P572
Cross, Charles E P628
Cross, Raymond P633
Cross, Patricia W51
Cross, Maegan E332
Crossett, Jonathan P182
Crossland, Millie P347
Crosswhite, Mark A25
Crotts, Matthew P533
Crotty, Glenn P111
Crouch, Suzanne A736:P512
Crouse, Jerry K P537
Crouser, Mark P55
Crow, Scott A292
Crow, Michael M P42
Crow, Penny P69
Crow, Scott P211
Crowder, Heather A239

Crowder, Jason A320
Crowder, Andy A774:P547
Crowder, Antwuan P604
Crowder, Jason E173
Crowdis, Roy P603
Crowe, Ronald P428
Crowe, Terri P439
Crowell, Kimberly A147
Crowell, Eric P108
Crowell, Kimberly E66
Crowley, David J P228
Crown, Susan A415
Crown, Timothy A420
Crowther, Bruce A867
Crowther, Chip P72
Crowther, Bruce E452
Croxen, Edith P418
Croy, Jack P91
Croyle, Mike P355
Crozier, Barry P55
Crozier, Adam W95:W454
Crudele, Jeffrey P576
Cruger, William A617:E262:E319
Crum, Scott E282
Crum, Poppy E415
Crump, Rachael A420
Crutcher, Allison P139
Crutchfield, Lisa A340
Cruz, Casey A30:P21
Cruz, Marcella P167
Cruz, Chris P168
Cruz, Dimitri J P206
Cruz, Mike De P236
Cruz, Jose P449
Cruz, Markam P463
Cruz, Joseph P625
Cruz, Rosemarie W70
Cruz, Joao Manuel Verissimo Marques
  da W172
Cruz, Alex E69
Crye, Stephen P202
Cryer, Angela P129
Csabon, Robin P310
Csanyi, Sandor W333
Csapo, Peter P12
Cseplo-Adrian, Elizabeth P118
CU, Jennipher P173
Cua, Jonathan W83
Cua, Solomon W323
Cuambe, Manuel W421
Cuba, Yolanda W335
Cubba, Joseph E259
Cubbage, Lora P160
Cubbon, Henry W156
Cucchiani, Enrico W383
Cuddy, Christopher A69
Cuddy, Rhonda P625
Cuellar, Maria Angela W263
Cuenco, Ramoncito A730:P509
Cuenco, Anna Therese W323
Cuevas, Kerwin A737
Cuevas, Alex P267
Cuevas, Kerwin P513
Cuevas, Diego Gaxiola W215
Cuffe, Michael A379
Cuffee, Clarence V P125
Cuffee-Glenn, Selena P132
Cui, Shanshan W54
Cui, Jun W129
Cuiper, Olav A672
Culang, Howard A662
Culbreath, Judy A212
Culbreth, Hugh A701
Culbreth, M. Scott E24
Culbreth, Hugh E365
Culham, Harry W99
Cull, Shawn P211
Cullen, Thomas A249
Cullen, Susan A329
Cullen, Michael R P70
Cullen, Debbie P312
Cullen, Michael P488
Cullen, Tamara P609
Cullen, David P658
Cullin, David E404
Culloch, Cathy Mc P465
Culmer, George W51:W410

Culnan, Mary Beth P508
Culp, William P468
Culpepper, Karen P216
Culver, John A455
Culver, Curt A523
Culver, John A732
Cumbie, Stephen P263
Cumming, Christine A185
Cumming, Christine M A299
Cummings, Earl A163
Cummings, Robert A222
Cummings, Kevin A297
Cummings, Charles A388
Cummings, Emily P243
Cummings, Ricardo P285
Cummings, Heather P286
Cummings, Carlos Rafael
  Murrieta W381
Cummings, Kevin E158
Cummins, Robert A20
Cummins, Hugh A796
Cummins, Robert P11
Cummins, Tim P91
Cummins, Richard P165
Cummins, Diane M P556
Cummiskey, Chris A723
Cuna, Vicente W323
Cuneo, Dennis A131
Cunha, Daniel P393
Cunha, Maria da W413
Cuningham, David P522
Cunitz, Dave P247
Cunningham, Philip A133
Cunningham, T. Jefferson A491
Cunningham, Gregory G A829
Cunningham, Shirley P119
Cunningham, Carla P275
Cunningham, Kim P398
Cunningham, Ron P653
Cunningham, Susan W178
Cunningham, Peter W405:W406
Cunningham, John E13
Cunningham, Daniel E76
Cunningham, Diane E132
Cunningham, Kathleen E345
Cuomo, Andrew M P206
Cupp, Mary P256
Cupp, Scott P542
Cupp, Ronnie P553
Curadeau-grou, Patricia W340
Curatolo, Tom A396
Curci, Brian A574
Curet, Myriam A430
Cureton, Samantha P525
Curfman, Susan P541
Curia, Christopher A750:E429
Curl, Molly A54
Curl, Gregory A635:W129
Curl, Molly E203
Curley, Robert A113
Curley, Kevin A797
Curley, John P163
Curley, Catherine P553
Curley, Tim P638
Curlin, Teresa P163
Curnow, Randy P332
Currall, Steven P491
Curran, Martin A222
Curran, Teresa M A300
Curran, Michael J A512
Curran, Shawn A777
Curran, William P132
Curran, John P155
Curran, Laura P165
Curran, Brooke P309
Curran, Michael J P324
Curran, Dr Daniel J P585
Currey, Russell A860
Currey, Robert E98
Currie, Pat A106
Currie, William A805
Currie, Tina P32
Currie, Pat P64
Currie, Scott P343
Currie, Gordon W527
Currier, Rand P234
Currin, Celia E254

Curry, Jeffery A261
Curry, Mike Mc A517
Curry, Lenny P127
Curry, Mike Mc P331
Curry, Ken P367
Curry, Krista P396
Curry, Wayne P451
Curry, Robynne P643
Curry, Jeffery E126
Curtan, Grant P103
Curti, Joseph Tate P204
Curtin, Terrence A260:W480
Curtis, John M A243
Curtis, Katheryn A254
Curtis, Scott A663
Curtis, Janelle A846
Curtis, Jason P84
Curtis, Dan P98
Curtis, John M P188
Curtis, Edgar J P327
Curtis, Caroline P402
Curtis, Dana P416
Curtis, Ross W399
Cury, Jason P310
Cushing, Robert A12
Cushing, Brenda A45
Cushman, Audrey P319
Custer, Scott A484
Custer, Jami P548
Custo, Maria G P356
Cusumano, Michael W373
Cutchin, Marco P121
Cutchins, Alexis G P205
Cutifani, Mark W32
Cutijar, Anna Marie P163
Cutillo, Gian W294
Cutillo, Joseph E390
Cutler, Suzanne A299
Cutler, Paul A327
Cutler, Alexander A453
Cutler, Paul A560
Cutler, Brian P546
Cutlip, Robert E194
Cutrignelli, Raffaele W179
Cutter, Brian P152
Cuyper, Vincent De W451
Cvetich, Irene P313
Czajka, Edward A639:E331
Czajkowski, Andrew P252
Czarnezki, Joseph P658
Czebotar, Jerry A P363
Czeschin, Frank E174
Czupik, Patrick P585
Czuprynski, Vicky P260
Czyz, Annemarie W P504

D

D, Jeffrey N Joyce PH P311
D, Linda P456
D, Eric Dickson M P609
Da, Eugene P153
Dabarno, Susan W308
Dabbs, Jeremy A147:P96
Dabiri, John A577
Dabney, Cindy A709:E370
Dacus, Shannon A724
Dada, Uzair A90:E41
Daddario, Don P246
Daddona, Michael P210
Dadlani, Sunil P48
Dadyburjor, Khush W527
Dafa, Bader Omar Al W134
Daffan, Nick E434
Dafonseca, Augusto P449
Daft, Brendon P396
Dagach, Fernando Aguad W255
Daghe, Noelle A195:P140
Daglio, Michael P554
Dahan, Salvador W380
Daher, Amyra P202
Dahiya, Rakesh P491
Dahl, David P249
Dahl, Jonathan P562
Dahl, Thorbjoern Lundholm W154
Dahl, Amy E411

COMBINED HOOVER'S HANDBOOK INDEX OF EXECUTIVES

Dahlberg, Edwin P507
Dahle, Tor W454
Dahlen, Dennis A102:P56
Dahlheimer, Tim P38
Dahlin, Jonathan P74
Dahlin, P. Andrew W110
Dahlmann, David A313:E165
Dahut, Karen A129:E117
Dahya, Hanif A554
Dai, Nat P263
Dai, Shan W24
Dai, Houliang W378
Dai, Deming W387
Dai, Qinghua W419
Dai, Yiyi W535
Dai, Weili E29
Daici, Silvia P206
Daigle, Art P135
Daigle, Sandra P309
Daignault, Benoit W239
Daik, Sam P534
Dailey, Grace A183
Dailey, Jeffrey W543
Daingerfield, Richard A613:E316
Daix, Roger W488
Dajany, Adam P25
Dake, Gary A72
Dake, Gary C P521
Dake, William P P521
Dake, Gary E31
Dalal, Aruna A553:P370
Dalal, Vineet E295
Dalbey, Christopher P169
Dalboussiere, Laurence W372
Dale, Michael A4
Dale, Albert A674
Dale, Michael W P340
Dale, Kenneth P545
Dale, Christopher P638
Dale, Albert E348
Dale, Jason E442
Dalemarre, Laura A739:P515
Dalena, Taylor P347
Dalessandro, Joseph P99
Daley, Dorian A595
Daley, Pamela W91
Daley, Peggy E107
Dali, Ab. Razak Bin Md W393
Dalina, Stephen J P343
Dallara, Que Thanh A398
Dallas, H. James A162:A453
Dallas, Andrew P444
Dallas, Kevin E15
Dallas, H. James E392
Dallas, David E425
Dallas, Robert E426
Dallery, Luc W402
Dalrymple, Christopher A29
Dalton, Travis S A165
Dalton, Alexandra A241
Dalton, John A437:P200
Dalton, Willam S P240
Dalton, William P240
Dalton, Mark P590
Dalton, Karen P599
Dalton, Daniel E312
Daly, Michelle A543
Daly, Patricia P333
Daly, Jay E108
Daly, James E204
Dalzell, Richard A429
Dalziel, Jennifer C P596
Dam, Bill P209
Dam, Anders W267
Damas, Philippe W491
Dameron, Jeffrey C P111
Damewood, Tracey P73
Damgard, John E235
Damiani, Al P156
Damle, Lauren F P647
Damme, Alexandre Van A460
Damme, Niek Jan van W484
Damon, Donna E448
Damore, Joseph P346
Dampier, Charlette P115
Dan, Michael A641
Dancis, Andrew B P574

Danckers, Kathleen A773
Dancy, William L E242
Dandeneau, Ben P422
Dandridge, Edward L A124
Dandridge, Nicole A493
Danel, Salvador W56
Danella, Kate A671
Dang, Kimberly A456
Dang, Komal A679
Dangeard, Frank W345
Daniel, James A94
Daniel, Karen A206
Daniel, Larry A417
Daniel, Patricia P196
Daniel, William C P459
Daniel, Enking P539
Daniel, Alan M P540
Daniel, Chris Mc P587
Daniel, Patrick W99
Daniel, James E44
Daniel, Larry E226
Daniele, Philip A84
Daniell, Richard W487
Daniels, J. Todd A18
Daniels, Michael A142
Daniels, Jon A154
Daniels, Jennifer A200
Daniels, Robert A281
Daniels, C. Bryan A306
Daniels, Donald A339
Daniels, Ronald J A439
Daniels, Michael A562
Daniels, Mitchell A566
Daniels, Richard A751
Daniels, Ronald J P276
Daniels, Vincent C P476
Daniels, Bobbi P624
Daniels, Michael E268:E293
Danielson, David A261:E126
Danja, Franklin P627
Dankel, Roger E374
Dann, Doreen P506
Danne, Matthias W157
Dannenfeldt, Thomas W108
Danner, Cynthia P444
Dannov, David A700
Dantdler, Todd P421
Dantuono, Louis P69
Danza, Franck P299
Dao, Anthony P12
Daprile, Joseph R P203:P375
Dar, Arif A727
Darby, Ashley A224:P172
Darby, Jeff E123
Darden, J. Matthew A359
Dardenne, Jay A736:P512
Dardis, Jennifer A756
Dargan, David P418
Dargusch, Jonathan A853:E445
Darko, Alex W6
Darling, Rachel P613
Darmon, Marc W488
Darnall, Matthew A588
Darnell, Scott A739
Darnell, Aaron P142
Darnell, Scott P515
Darrah, Ryan E182
Darrenkamp, Kevin A485
Darrow, Kurt A190:A219
Dartt, William E68
Daruvala, Toos W412
Dasgupta, Satarupa P374
Dasilva, Daniel A864:P656
Daskalos, Paul P461
Dasossa, Mag P186
Dass, Chandra A P536
Dassault, Laurent W518
Dassen, Roger W42
Dastoor, Michael A434
Dastugue, Michael A373
Datar, Srikant A758
Date, Hidefumi W324
Date, Raj E200
Datesh, LuAnn E145
Datteri, Roberta W511
Daubner, Thomas P594
Dauby, D. A353:E192

Dauch, David A42
Daugherty, Sean A392
Daughtrey, William P644
Daughtry, Kevin P26
Daugiala, Alfredas P483
Daul, Richard P156
Daum, Julie A701
Daum, Martin W319
Daum, Julie E365
Daunt, James P61
Dauphinee, Aimee P393
Dauterive, Eddie P409
Dave, Rajesh P611
Davenport, Bonnie A147
Davenport, Fesia A224
Davenport, Michael A514
Davenport, J. Mays A646
Davenport, Fesia P162
Davenport, Clark P400
Davenport, Bonnie E66
Davenport, Michael E267
Davenport, J. Mays E336
Daves, Lora A723:E383
Daveu, Marie-Claire W273
Davey, Bryan P4
Davey, Brad W40
David, Danielle P92
David, Yaron P100
David, Mark P114
David, Jon P230
David, Steven P374
David, Ramon W83
David, Laurent W87
David, Tang W309
David, Ilona W334
Davidhizar, Ethan A789:E411
Davidowski, Ron J P194
Davidson, Janet A17
Davidson, Richard A296
Davidson, Wendy A317
Davidson, Carol A426
Davidson, Charles A486
Davidson, Janine A808
Davidson, Patricia P102
Davidson, Michael P114
Davidson, Julie P193
Davidson, Hollister P303
Davidson, Jack P320
Davidson, Robert G P334
Davidson, Carol W480
Davidson, Richard E157
Davidson, Wendy E170
Davidson, Janine E421
Davies, William A52
Davies, John A113
Davies, Susan A497
Davies, Pamela A721
Davies, Daniel P57
Davies, Neil P203
Davies, Christina W35
Davies, Howard W345
Davies, Mark W405:W406
Davies, Philip E438
Davila, Diana P256
Davila, Rosa P347
Davis, Tim A14
Davis, Lisa A23
Davis, Steven A28
Davis, R. Matt A36
Davis, Mark A133
Davis, J. Kimbrough A147
Davis, Zach A168:A170
Davis, George A186
Davis, Christopher A196
Davis, Laronda A208
Davis, Jeffrey A210
Davis, Gordon A216
Davis, Amy A228
Davis, Georgetta A257
Davis, Ray A276
Davis, C. William A314
Davis, Claude A315
Davis, Reginald A326
Davis, Brian A393
Davis, Steven A414
Davis, Ian A441
Davis, D. Scott A441

Davis, Charles A463
Davis, Jeffrey A464
Davis, Alicia A470
Davis, Brian A496
Davis, Steven A496
Davis, Smith A501
Davis, Robert A515
Davis, Wilbur A570
Davis, Karen A612
Davis, T. Paul A612
Davis, Lisa A615
Davis, Steven A636
Davis, Sharon A639
Davis, Charles A645
Davis, James A659
Davis, Seth A680
Davis, William A A681
Davis, Tyrell A702
Davis, Gregory A717
Davis, Martin A725
Davis, Jean A725
Davis, Austin A741
Davis, Alison A751
Davis, Thaddeus A751
Davis, Waters A760
Davis, Kern A816
Davis, Leslie A828
Davis, Jennifer A870
Davis, Derek A878
Davis, Tim P5
Davis, Steve P7
Davis, Steven P18
Davis, Andrew P27
Davis, Elizabeth P65
Davis, Tommye Lou P65
Davis, Mary P69
Davis, Kenneth L P71
Davis, Reed P83
Davis, Alden B P90
Davis, Harold P115
Davis, Scott P120
Davis, Clinton P120
Davis, Frances P124
Davis, Robin P125
Davis, George P129
Davis, Leanne P131
Davis, Lisa S P132
Davis, Charisse P141
Davis, Laronda P145
Davis, Jacqueline P159
Davis, Dennis P165
Davis, Robert P172
Davis, Bob P172
Davis, Sonya P187
Davis, Eric P196
Davis, Pamela P201
Davis, Brian P201
Davis, Sarah P210
Davis, Janet P215
Davis, Becky P220
Davis, Greg P222
Davis, Steven P260
Davis, Shirley P261
Davis, Auston P306
Davis, Jennifer P327
Davis, Martina P370
Davis, Sondra P383
Davis, Joshua P384
Davis, Mark P395
Davis, Alphonse G P400
Davis, Steven P401
Davis, Debbie P446
Davis, William A P448
Davis, Richard P497
Davis, Austin P518
Davis, Myra P540
Davis, Lisa P560
Davis, Thomas P P572
Davis, Debra A P587
Davis, John P592
Davis, Jennifer P618
Davis, Wayne P629
Davis, Josie H P631
Davis, Benjamin P633
Davis, Leslie P634
Davis, Leslie C P635
Davis, Deborah P640

HOOVER'S HANDBOOK OF EMERGING COMPANIES 2022

511

COMBINED HOOVER'S HANDBOOK INDEX OF EXECUTIVES

A = AMERICAN BUSINESS
E = EMERGING COMPANIES
P = PRIVATE COMPANIES
W = WORLD BUSINESS

Davis, Traci P647
Davis, James L P659
Davis, Darrell W25
Davis, Scott W452
Davis, Natalie W531
Davis, Julian E20
Davis, James E24
Davis, Todd E51
Davis, J. Kimbrough E66
Davis, Robert E68
Davis, Jeffrey E95
Davis, Claude E167
Davis, Diane E169
Davis, Reginald E177
Davis, Brian E217
Davis, Gregory E229
Davis, Robert E234
Davis, John E253
Davis, William E297
Davis, Sharon E332
Davis, Seth E356
Davis, Gregory E368:E379
Davis, Martin E383
Davis, Jean E383
Davis, Nathaniel E393
Davis, Jennifer E454
Davis, Paul E E456
Davisson, Katherine A703
Davoren, Peter J A782:A799:P583:P605
Dawes, Christopher P306
Dawes, Karen E349
Dawidowsky, Tim W444
Dawson, Samuel A227
Dawson, Pat A588
Dawson, Laurel A740
Dawson, Leah A874
Dawson, Haley P267
Dawson, Laurel P516
Dawson, Fiona W311
Dawson, Jonathan W342
Dawson, G. Steven E265
Dawson, Robert E354
Dawydiak, Walter P171
Daxner, Jim P537
Day, James A281
Day, Twila A411
Day, John A431
Day, Monica A798
Day, Edwin P167
Day, Terri P283
Day, Kim P334
Day, Lynn Carmen P447
Day, Jason P489
Day, James H P601
Day, Sarah P658
Day, C. Sean E97
DC, Sister Bernice Coreil A74
DC, Sister Maureen McGuire A74
DC, Sister Bernice Coreil P43
DC, Sister Maureen McGuire P43
DDS, Will Daniels P69
DDS, L Kenneth Heuler P116
DDS, Edwin Zechman P117
DDS, Rocco R Addante P182
DDS, Diane Day P351
DDS, David B Weinstein P581
De, Hector P160
Dea, Joan A697
Deacon, Mary A466:E243
Deaderick, Billy P203
Deal, Richard S E155
Dealy, Richard A629
Dealyn, Allen P80
Deambrogio, Roberto W181
Dean, Lia A148
Dean, Lloyd A208:A245
Dean, Clay A320
Dean, Lloyd A509
Dean, Robert A544
Dean, Eric A737
Dean, DOT P25

Dean, Jennifer P119
Dean, Lloyd P145:P189
Dean, Doug P204
Dean, Douglas P204
Dean, Melanie P286
Dean, Lesley P396
Dean, Anthony P427
Dean, Eric P513
Dean, Susanne P525
Dean, Eric P548
Dean, Michelle P578
Dean, Susan P588
Dean, Joey P650
Dean, Gary E13
Dean, Clay E173
Dean, Robert E285
DeAngelis, Yamynn A230:E113
Dearing, Karen E8:E396
Dearth, Jim P117
Deas, Bruce P528
Deasy, Dr John A486:P303
Deato, Alexander Francis W82
Deaton, John A395
Deaton, Chadwick A495
Deaupre, Paul P231
Debackere, Koenraad W507
Debbane, Raymond P77
Debeauvoir, Dana P171
Debel, Marlene A663
Debertin, Jay A176:P119
DeBiase, Francesca A509
Deblaere, Johan W8
DeBoer, Sidney A481
DeBoer, Bryan A481
DeBoer, Scott A527
Deboer, Steven P378
Deboer, Erica P463
Debowey, Donna E355
DeBruce, Ericka A827
Debrunner, David A33
Debs, Jody P245
Dec, Timothy E399
Decarolis, Anthony P571
Dechant, Johann W246
Decharin, Pasu W441:W441
Decherd, Robert A455
Decker, Sharon A197
Decker, Edward A394
Decker, Tina Freese A727
Decker, Daniel A736
Decker, Tina Freese P495
Decker, Daniel P512
Decker, Lynn P569
Decker, W Cody P616
DeCola, Michael A279:E142
Decolli, Debbie A187:P131
Decraene, Stefaan W87
Decrona, Bruce A285
Decubellis, Jennifer P249
Dee, Ann A318
Dee, Thomas P368
Dee, Maureen P567
Dee, Fabian W323
Dee, Ann E124:E171
Deegan, Colman W520
Deejongkit, Prasert W62
Deel, Chris P100
Deeming, Fran A624:P414
Deep, Danny A345
Deer, Aaron A201
Deer, Jill A674
Deer, Aaron E92
Deer, Jill E348
Deering, Michael P302
Deese, Willie A651
Deeter, Chris P33
Defenbaugh, Raymond E P73
DeFeo, Ron A41
DeFerie, Suzanne A309:E162
Deffenbaugh, Danny P492
Defilippis, Mike P596
Defillo, Vicente Jose Liz P89
Defosset, Donald A671
Defourny, Michel W451
DeFrancesco, Salvatore E161
DeFranco, James A249
Defreitas, Alicia P103

Defurio, Anthony A774:P547
DeGenova, Cathleen A87
Degioia, John J P560
DeGiorgio, Kenneth A308
Degrand, Robert P222
Degrandis, Leigh P548
Degregori, Amanda A730:P509
Degregorio, Nick P593
DeHaas, Deborah A256
Dehaemers, David P532
Dehahn, Erin P647
Dehaven, Michael P498
Dehaze, Alain W10
Dehner, Torsten A20
Dehring, Timothy A P386
Deible, Henry E133
Deines, Wyatt P31
Deiser, Peter P353
Deitrich, Thomas A591
Deiure, Giovannella E250
Dejaco, Lynn P241
Dejakaisaya, Voranuch W441
Dejoseph, Elizabeth P134
Dekay, Donald F P265
Deken, Paul P207
Dekker, Christopher A138
Dekker, Wout W397
Dekle, Christopher P210
Dekura, Kazuhito W151
Delabarre, Laurent W402
Delaney, Christopher A361
Delaney, Timothy A546
Delaney, Martin P12
Delaney, Kristen P141
Delaney, Emma W91
Delaney, Martin E122
Delano, David A494
Delano, Laurie A P555
Delanois, Gary P1
Delany, Jim P545
Delasotta, Fernando P48
Delatorre, Hector P662
Delattre, Francois W175
Delauder, Brad P160
Delawder, C. Daniel A608:E312
Delay, Mary G P587
Delbridge, Malinda P485
Delcourt, Ryan P575
Delellis, Ronald A P444
Deleon, Melissa P304
Deleon, Marcos P601
Delfrari, Rhona W110
Delgadillo, Rocky A186:P127
Delgadillo, Joe P387
Delgado, Mercedes P206
Delgado, Edmundo W525
Delghiaccio, Brian A677
Delgrosso, Nicole P451
Dell, Joseph A193
Dell, Michael A840
Dell, Benjamin E85
Dell, Joseph E87
Dellaquila, Frank A273:A673
Dellenback, Steve P492
DelliBovi, Alfred A330
Dellinger, Donald B P662
Dell'osso, Domenic A171
Delmas, Heather P537
Delong, Abbie P291
Delongchamps, Peter A368
DelOrefice, Christopher A109
Delorenzo, Carl P256
Delorme, Philippe W427
Deloye, Dennis A74
Delport, Dominique W518
DelSanto, Anne E6
Deltenre, Ingrid W72
Deltort, Didier A404
DeLuca, Richard A515
Deluca, Frederick A P192
Deluca, Oneida P418
Delue, Sean P468
Delventhal, Brad P578
Demahy, Anita P471
Demarco, David A72
Demarco, Nick A187:P131
Demarco, Edward P316

Demarco, David E31
Demare, Michel W46
Demarets, Pascal P23
Demarino, Shannon P118
Demaris, Shari A285
Demarsh, Steven P169
Demas, David A795:E416
Dembner, Alan P60
Demchak, William A632
Demchyk, Matthew E190
Demetriou, Steven A324:A436
Deming, Claiborne A542
Demio, Doug P24
Demir, Feray W504
Demirag, Levent W217
Demme, Kendra P90
Demmerle, Stefan A131
Demming, Peggy P613
Demmings, Keith A76
Demoleas, John P P519
Demond, Sharon P256
Demonte, Rosemarie A799:P605
Demott, Andrew E398
Demou, George E417
Dempich, Joe P109
Dempsey, Michael A94
Dempsey, Patrick A575
Dempsey, Michael E45
Demski, David E195
Denahan, Wellington A62
Denari, Aine A138
Denarvaez, Denny P649
Denault, Leo A277
Denault, Leo P P206
Denecour, Jessica A623
Denekas, Craig A144
Deneweth, Connie P358
Deng, Yunhua W130
Deng, Xiaobo W214
Deng, Jianju W220
Deng, Feng W349
Deng, Bin W383
Denges, Jim P523
Denham, Amber P614
Denham, Robert W198
Denholm, Robyn A769
Denien, Mark E124
Deninger, Matthew P319
Denis, Jean-Pierre W273
Denison, David W82:W412
Denizard-Thomps, Nancy P380
Denker, Claude A615
Denman, Kenneth A840
Dennard, Tamaya P125
Dennen, Richard A315:E167
Dennery, Charlotte W87
Denning, Shannon P230
Denninghoff, Erik P493
Dennis, Rae P309
Dennis, David P424
Dennis, Thomas St. E180
Dennison, Ann A543
Dennison, Shawn P159
Dennison, Mary P286
Dennison, Michael E184
Denny, Jessie A789
Denny, Betty P238
Denny, Jessie E411
Denomme, Linda A804:P607
Denomme, Yves W290
DeNooyer, Mary A452
Denoyel, Gilles W175
Densmore, Marianne P182
Denson, Celia A839:P643
Dent, Andrew A735:P511
Dent, Katherine E206
Dentler, Jane P173
Denton, D. Brock A180
Denton, David A488:A759
Denzel, Nora A13
Deo, Rajat P255
Deol, Jaspal P455
DePaola, Rinaldo E84
DePaolo, Joseph A710
Depaolo, Joseph J A711:P481
DePaolo, Joseph E371
Depies, Lori P159

COMBINED HOOVER'S HANDBOOK INDEX OF EXECUTIVES

Depietro, Diane P415
DePinto, Joseph W430
Depler, Thomas A187:E85
Depoortere, Michael A782:P583
DePree, Alexis A565
DePrizio, Suzy A162
Depta, Lisa P60
Deputy, Christine A565
Derbyshire, Mark W102
DeReu, William E329
Derickson, Pat P175
Derita, Nancy P500
Derksen, Brian A593
Derksen, Henk E436
Derman, Emre W21
Dermott, Frank X Mc P368
Derosa, Rebecca P65
Derosier, Pam P496
Derouche, James P309
Deroy, Sara P131
Derrick, Robert A754
Derrick, Brian P17:P524
Derrick, Robert E401
DeRuiter, Kathie A400:E218
Dery, William E160
Derylo, Maria P305
Desai, Nicholas A403
Desai, Jayshree A658
Desai, Chirantan A706
Desai, Jigisha A800
Desai, Nicholas P256
Desai, Manisha P609
DeSalva, AnnaMaria A873
Desalvo, Natalie A735:P510
Desantis, Robert A430
DeSantis, Damon E74
Descalzi, Claudio W185
Descamps, Bill P11
Deschamps, Ignacio W69
Deschamps, Isabelle W405:W406
Descheneaux, Michael A751
Desforges, Odile W194
Deshields, Taneesha A737:P513
Deshong, Leanne P103
Deshpande, Sam A406
Desiderio, Massimo W511
DeSilva, Joe A81
DeSimone, Beth A725:E384
Desjardins, Jacques P159
Desjardins, Luc W99
Desjardins, Kristi W242
Desjarlais, Roger P162
Deskins, Juanita P417
Deskus, Archana A199:A262:E127
Desmarais, Paul W213
Desmarais, Andre W213:W389
Desmarais, Paul W389
Desmarais, Olivier W389
Desmarais, Michael E104
Desmond, Laura A11
Desmond, Kenneth V A208
Desmond, John A322
Desmond, Michael A390
Desmond, Kenneth V P146
Desmond, Patrick P636
Desmond, Michael E215
Desmond, Bevin E280
Desmond-Hellmann, Susan A622
Desoer, Barbara A183:A237
Desormeaux, Joseph A346:P227
Desouza, Bryan P661
Despain, Brian P625
Despeaux, Kimberly H P206
DeSplinter, Joseph E345
Desrochers, Mark A399
Desroches, Pascal A77
Destefano, Alexa P311
DeStefano, Allison E142
Desurio, Anthony P618
Deters, Deborah A381
Deters, John E73
Deters, Deborah E208
Detherage, Mark P286
Dethlefs, Sven W487
Detoro, Karen A194
Detrick, Christine A148:E107
Detwiler, Jim P118

Deuel, Jeffrey A383:E212
Deuschle, James P445
Deutsch, Donough P87
Deutsch, Esther W253
Deutschman, Robert E120
Dev, Indraneel A490
Devaisher, Len A531:E276
Devanney, George W P171
Devanny, Earl A206
Devaraj, Tanuja P352
DeVeau, Michael A426
Deventer, Peter Van E456
Deveny, Cliff P524
Devers, Daniel P A165
Devgan, Anirudh E62
Devine, David A201
Devine, Michael A246
Devine, Denise A340
Devine, David P364
Devine, Scott P389
Devine, Cynthia W176:W412
Devine, David E92
Devine, Michael E116:E176
Devineni, Ramya P644
Devino, Terrence P602
DeVita, Betty A633
Devita, Maria V P299
DeVito, Michael A337
Devoe, Michael P48
Devoe, Andrew P598
DeVolder, Steven E81
Devoney, William P201
Devooght, Shawn P247
DeVore, Susan A63
Devore, Susan P426
Devos, Doug A35
Devos, Mr Doug L A719
Devos, Doug A727:P27
Devos, Mr Doug L P486
Devos, Doug P495
Devriendt, Wouter W509
Dew, Stephen P160
Dewald, Steven P437
Dewar, Patrick A485
Dewar, Marvin P477
Dewbrey, Diane A507
DeWeese, Steven A675:E350
Dewer, Craig P107
Dewey, Duane A798
Dewey, Susan F A838
Dewey, Chris P166
Dewey, Susan F P641
Dewhurst, Moray A327
Dewhurst, Eugene A795:E416
DeWilde, Katherine August- A323
Dewine, Mike A740:P516
DeWitt, Angie A75
Dewitt, Daniel A764
Dewitt, Rob P294
Dexter, Tracey A701
Dexter, Sara P589
Dexter, Robert W82
Dexter, Tracey E365
Dhala, Anwer P632
Dhanak, Dashyant E225
Dhanda, Anuj A28:P18
Dhandapani, Chandra A159
Dhawan, Sumit A840
Dhillon, Peter P P393
Dhimitri, Nick P523
Dholakia, Indira P162
Dhore, Prasanna A274
Diago, Miguel Angel Servin W381
Dial, Christopher E448
Dialto, Margaret P519
Diamanti, Theodhor P427
Diamond, Susan A406
Diamond, Michael A779
Diamond, Robert P280
Diamond, Margae P468
Diamond, Michael P568
Diamond, Lawrence E13
Diamond, Michael E277
Diamonte, Robin E280
Diana, Edward A P166
Diaz, Franklin Chang A228
Diaz, Joseph A243

Diaz, Diana A487
Diaz, Fred A831
Diaz, Aurora P18
Diaz, Joseph P188
Diaz, Diana P303
Diaz, Ulises E P368
Diaz, Crystal P498
Diaz, Robyn P505
Diaz, Mark P560
Diaz, Jorge E P578
Diaz, Stephanie E39
Diaz, Diana P368
Diaz-Macha, Maria P19
Diaz-Zablah, Alexandra P341
Dibadj, Ali A755
DiBella, John E375
DiBenedetto, Joseph A652
Dibkey, Brett A138
Diblasio, Alfonzo P508
Dibona, Laina P19
Dibrell, Henry P282
Dicesare, Thor P106
DiChiaro, Steven A359
Diciurcio, John A799:P214:P605
Dick, Roger E430
Dickens, Marty A628
Dickens, Zachary E153
Dickens, Marty E324
Dickenson, James P270
Dickerman, Jeffrey A289
Dickerson, Gary A66
Dickerson, Mary A662
Dickerson, Mike A783:P591
Dickey, Hal P203
Dickey, Melissa P612
Dickey, Kevin E340
Dickins, Denise E300
Dickinson, Andrew A355
Dickinson, Joan A529
Dickinson, Edward T P574
Dickinson, Jonathan E225
Dickinson, Joan E274
Dickler, Louis A846
Dickman, Susan F P272
Dickson, Ward A40
Dickson, Rebecca T P157
Dickson, Mark P451
Dickson, James W176
Dickson, Julie W308
Dicowsky, Gabriel Amos Bitran W177
Dicus, John A149
Diddee, Anu P290
DiDomenico, Vincent A106:E48
DiDonato, Thomas A470
Dieckmann, Anita P248
Dieckmann, Stephanie E219
Diede, Shannon P530
Diederich, Kirsten P381
Diederich, Michael W509
Diefenthaler, Aaron A680:E356
Diehl, Scott A374
Diehl, Valerie P102
Diehl, Walter P346
Diehm, Russell C P84
Diemant, Andreas W72
Diercksen, John A633
Dierker, Richard A177
Dierker, David A617
Diesbach, Patrice Lambert - de W372
Diesel, R Wayne A744:P519
Diess, Herbert W522
Dieter, Cory P464
Dietrich, Martin A546
Dietrich, Peter A722
Dietrich, William S A828
Dietrich, William P628
Dietrich, William S P635
Dietz, Diane A863
Dietz, Megan P173
Dietz, David W P191
Dietz, Harry W210
Dietz, Luzma E111
Dietze, Katherine E106
Dietzel, Brad P472
Diewald, Wayne P227
Diez, John A689
Diez-Canseco, Russell E442

Diezhandino, Cristina W165
Difilippo, Pasquale A A799:P605
Difuntorum, Elizabeth P120
Diganci, Todd P214
Digeronimo, Kevin E274
DiGeso, Amy A52
Digiacomo, Sam A264:P200
Digirolamo, Enrico E224
DiGrande, Sebastian A117
DiGrazia, G. Gino A652
Diiorio, Richard E228
Dijanosic, Michael W93
Dijk, Bob Van A128
Diker, Charles A486
Diliberto, Matthew J A667:P438
Dilisi, Jeffrey P451
Dill, Julie P494
Dill, David E344
Dill, Julie E390
Dilland, John P342
Dillard, Lauren A543
Dillard, Robert A721
Dillard, Ashley P53
Dillard, Allen E245
Diller, Barry A288:A524
Diller, Keeta E361
Dilley, Margarita K P108
Dilley, Michelle E388
Dillingham, Frederick E160
Dillman, Jeff P640
Dillon, David A3
Dillon, Donna A212
Dillon, Kenneth A581
Dillon, Mary Ann A794
Dillon, David A812
Dillon, Bobbi P125
Dillon, Tim P257
Dillon, Danel P321
Dillon, Mary Ann P599
Dillon, David W145
Dillow, Stacy A328
Dillow, April P646
Dilocker, Laurie P175
Diloreto, Andy P166
Dimaandal, Juliet P525
Dimagiba, Hierbert W323
DiMaio, Jack E89
Dimatteo, Lex P547
Dimauro, Vincent A P159
Dimech, John W448
Dimick, Steven A103:E47
Dimitrijevic, Marina A658
Dimmick, Ruth P18
Dimmick, Scott W P291
Dimodica, Jeffrey F A733:E389
Dimolitsas, Spiros P560
Dimon, Jamie A444
Dimotta, Jennifer A530:E275
DiMuccio, Robert A847
Din, Mohamed Ross Mohd W128
Din, Che Zakiah Binti Che W307
Dinan, Susan P403
Dincer, Suzan Sabanci W21
Dincer, Haluk W217
Dindin, Kevin P67
Dineen, James P172
DiNello, Alessandro A326:E177
Dines, Clinton W199
Ding, Huande W235
Ding, Xiongjun W287
Ding, Yi W303
Ding, Yongzhong W535
Ding, Jianzhong W542
Dingemans, Simon W533
Dinger, Stephanie A811
Dingle, Phillip S P215
Dingman, Lacey A299
Dingus, John P216
Dinis, Filipe W65
Dinkel, Thomas A316
Dinkler, Ayame P304
Dinsel, Doug P196
Dinsmoor, William S P570
Diokno, Ananias P657
Dionisio, Rommel Enrico W323
Diorio, Dena P163
Dios, Renato Vergel de W83

COMBINED HOOVER'S HANDBOOK INDEX OF EXECUTIVES

A = AMERICAN BUSINESS
E = EMERGING COMPANIES
P = PRIVATE BUSINESS
W = WORLD BUSINESS

Dioum, Serigne W335
Dipalma, Theresa Alberghini P588
DiPalma, Sheila E89
Dipaolo, Joseph A P11
Dipaolo, Mark A229
Dipietro, Dominick P98
Dipietro, Joseph A P629
Dipofi, Phil A570:P388
Dirisio, Derek A651
Dirocco, Melissa P456
Dirrane, Michael J A503:P317
Dirscherl, Dan P257
DiRusso, Lonny A688
Disalvatore, Tony P71
Disantis, Linda P123
DiSanto, Edmund A51
DiSanto, Kristen A847
DiSanzo, Deborah A115
Disarlo, Lorraine P638
Disbrow, Lisa E269
Disbrow, Joshua E457
Discello, Allison P188
Diseroad, Mark A624:P414
Dishart, Noreen A642
Dishaw, Michael F P63
Disher, Steph A228
Dishman, William A747
Dishman, Roy P353
Dishman, William E391
Dismond, Tim A159
Disney, Keri P179
Disney, Kathy P268
Dispensa, James V A123:P80
Disser, Pete P386
Dissinger, Todd E288
DiStasio, James A284
Distel, Arlene P579
Distelrath, James E160
Ditre, Cherie P574
Dittemore, Karen P354
Dittmeier, Carolyn W27
Dittus, Gina P2
Ditullio, Michael E339
Dively, Joseph A320
Dively, Mary A331
Dively, Joseph E173
Dively, Mary E178
Divincenzo, Joseph N P159
Divito, Robert A512:P324
Dixon, Robert A63
Dixon, Gregory A193
Dixon, Kimberly A764
Dixon, Anastasia P198
Dixon, April P238
Dixon, Michael P333
Dixon, Linda J P603
Dixon, Tom P648
Dixon, Gregory E87
Dizenzo, Lisa A414:P259
Dizon, Terry P550
Dizon-Scott, Marissa P530
Djebbour, Karim W173
Dmitriev, Kirill W503
Dmuchowski, Hope A317:E170
Doan, Huy A711:P481
Dobber, Ruud W46
Dobbins, John P658
Dobbs, Stephen A228
Dobbs, Stanley P462
Dobbs, Donald P P565
Dobbs, Micheal E407
Dobis, Brian A690
Dobkin, Arkadiy E144
Dobranski, Edward A323
Dobringer, Martina W515
Dobrinski, Everett A296:E157
Dobrowolski, Reginald A624
Dobrowski, Thomas E52
Dobson, Arret E312
Dobyns, Tom E96
Docherty, Alan W135

Docken, Lorie P633
Dockendorff, Charles A132
Dockery, Kimberly E91
Dockins, Cynthia P541
Dodd, Elyssa P347
Dodd, Susan P492
Dodderer, Arnold A750
Dodds, Christopher A697
Dodds, David P381
Dodds, Scott E99
Dodge, Judy P164
Dodgen, Kenneth E334
Dodig, Victor W99
Dodson, Vickie A770:P540
Dodson-Reed, Candace P256
Doeckel, Laura P99
Doehrman, Verna P191
Doer, Gary W213:W389
Doerduencue, Ahmet A427
Doerfer, Steve P22
Doerksen, Edna P530
Doerr, David M P12
Dogan, Yakup W540
Dohany, Patrick M P165
Doheny, Edward A264
Doheny, Matthew A874
Doherty, William A59
Doherty, Chris A293
Doherty, Catherine A659
Doherty, Robert A704
Doherty, Tom P29
Doherty, Chris P212
Doherty, Robert E367
Dohman, Pammie P464
Doi, Tracey A659
Doi, Nobuhiro W67
Doi, Miwako W459
Doig, John W69
Dokmecioglu, Ozan A452
Dolan, Vincent A260
Dolan, Paul A718
Dolan, Traci A745
Dolan, Janet A792
Dolan, Terrance R A829
Dolan, Amanda P16
Dolan, Patrick P62
Dolan, Jane P157
Dolan, Robert E252
Dole, Rodney P170
Dolen, James P194
Dolgin, Eliot P63
Doligale, Anne A711:P481
Doll, John P61
Doll, Cynthia P627
Dollaghan, Jim P193
Dollery, Megan P165
Dolling, David S P560
Dolloff, Jack A471
Dolman, Shael P23
Dolson, Jed E199
Dolsten, Mikael A21:A622
Dombrowski, Nadia A519:E272
Domenech, Daniel A399
Domichi, Hideaki W469
Domier, Tanya A875
Dominguez, Joseph A286
Dominguez, Carlos A377
Dominguez, Oscar P486
Dominguez, Leanna P604
Dominguez, Jose Eladio Seco W9
Dominguez, Rafael Barraza W61
Dominguez, Jaime Muguiro W109
Dominguez, Christian Tauber W255
Dominguez, Maria Victoria
  Zingoni W400
Dominissini, Ester W64
Domit, Patrick Slim W28
Domit, Carlos Slim W28
Domnisch, Michaele P284
Domont, Lawrence P7
Don, J. Andrew E286
Donadio,
  Marcela A338:A495:A566:A571
Donaghey, Elizabeth W30
Donaghue, Jason M P500
Donaghy, Stephen E427
Donahoe, John A563:A611

Donahue, Timothy J A226
Donahue, Paul A350:A612:A796
Donahue, Michael A870
Donahue, Leslie Les A P416
Donahue, Moreen O P554
Donahue, James E90
Donahue, Joseph E277
Donahue, Michael E455
Donald, James A28
Donald, Kirkland A277:A410
Donald, James A565:P18
Donald, Bruce Mc P87
Donald, Margie Mc P449
Donald, Arnold P495
Donaldson, Michael A281
Donaldson, Amy P257
Donaldson, Beverly E207
Donat, Richard P462
Donato, Leslie A55
Donavan, James P344
Donavanik, Chanin W270
Donder, Daniel J P345
Donegan, Mark A638:P426
Donegan, Lynda P601
Donelan, David P44
Dong, Xin W118
Dong, Zhonglang W194
Dong, Mingzhu W214
Dong, Yang W244
Dong, Mei W389
Donheiser, Gail P230
Doni, Puja P479
Donigan, Heyward A679
Donikowski, Tina W48
Donis, EMI A638:P426
Donkers, Wijnand W91
Donley, Jeffrey P101
Donnals, Jennifer A741:P517
Donnell, Cathy Mc P116
Donnellan, Barbara P156
Donnelly, Abby A309
Donnelly, Patricia A655
Donnelly, Michael A690
Donnelly, Patrick A714
Donnelly, Scott A772
Donnelly, Sean W39
Donnelly, Timothy E23
Donnelly, Eric E111
Donnelly, Abby E162
Donnet, Philippe W43
Donnley, Deneen A217
Donoghue, Hiranda A335
Donohoe, Bryan A70
Donohoe, Brian A856
Donohue, Elisabeth A574:A777
Donohue, Carolyn P451
Donough, Robert Mc P439
Donovan, Michael A387
Donovan, Joseph E89
Dontas, Periklis W383
Dontsop, Jean Tematio A806
Donzella, Oreste A457
Doo, Jinho A398
Doo, William W66
Doo, Lim Ah W370
Doo, Jinho E218
Doody, Christopher A795
Doody, Joseph E69
Doody, Christopher E416
Doohan, Kevin E456
Dookiesingh, Kamanie P265
Dooley, Meta P102
Dooley, Charles P170
Dooley, Susan P428
Dooley, Kevin P450
Dooley, Jill P508
Dooley, Helen W17
Dooley, Shaun W340
Dooling, Carrie P165
Doomy, Lynda P644
Doordan, Martin L P306
Dop, Kyle P247
Dopfner, Mathias A551
Doplemore, Shelia A838:P641
Doppstadt, Eric W40
Dorado, Roy P481
Doramus, Mark A712:E373

Dorchak, Glenda E27
Dorchester, Wendy P301
Dorefler, Stefan W187
Doren, Steven R Van P625
Dores, Daniel P620
Dorfler, Robert P594
Dorjee, Frank W397
Dorman, David A232
Dorn, Andrew A307
Dorn, Connie P508
Dornau, Peter E301
Dornau, Gregor E301
Dorne, Eric A817
Dornemann, Michael E402
Dorner, Irene W410
Dornetto, Mary A690
Dorothea, Mary P499
Dorph, Martin A555:P374
Dorrance, Bennett A146
Dorroh, Tina P615
Dorsey, Tracey A16:P8
Dorsey, Denicca P220
Dorto, Joseph P642
Dorton, Brett A723:E383
Dosch, Theodore A854
Dosch, Eric E169
Doser, Lynn M P81
Doss, Michael A364:A702
Doss, Richard P500
Dossantos, Emilia P498
Dotan, Ido A93
Doti, James A308
Dotson, Judith A129
Dotson, Jillian A736
Dotson, Tony P55
Dotson, Jillian P512
Dott, Edward P155
Doty, Jeff P112
Doty, Angela P160
Doty, Larry P419
Doty, William S P491
Dou, Jian W121
Doubles, Brian A752
Doucette, Elmer P200
Doucette, Mer P200
Doucette, Jami P426
Doucette, Mike J P446
Doudna, Jennifer A441
Dougan, Thomas P406
Dougher, Brendan E75
Dougherty, Lucy Clark A632
Dougherty, Michael D A632
Dougherty, Linda W465
Dougherty, Gregory E264
Doughty, Tracy P257
Doughty, Michael W308
Douglas, Stewart A56
Douglas, Gary A61
Douglas, Scott A471
Douglas, Laurie A488
Douglas, James A546
Douglas, Laurie A652
Douglas, Laura A675
Douglas, Keith A A783
Douglas, Marlis P142
Douglas, Dan P386
Douglas, Diana P536
Douglas, Keith A P591
Douglas, Blaine P649
Douglas, Paul P497
Douglas, Laura E350
Douglass, Stephen B P96
Douglass, Julie P596
Douglass, Scott R P618
Douvas, Maria W412
Douvris, Angelo A32:P24
Douwes, Art P464
Dove, Reid P1
Dow, Lisa A201
Dow, Susan P200
Dow, Robert P204
Dow, Bonnie P590
Dow, Lisa E92
Dow, Roger E345
Dow, Anne La E364
Dowdell, Robert A646:E336
Dowdle, Jeffrey A663

COMBINED HOOVER'S HANDBOOK INDEX OF EXECUTIVES

Dower, Leonard P597
Dowlin, John P160
Dowling, Michael A101
Dowling, Michael J P301:P384
Dowling, Kathleen P460
Dowling, Caroline W145:W156
Dowling, Michael E382
Down, Stephen G P476
Downard, Gary P135
Downe, William A494
Downer, Michael J A48:P31
Downes, Terry P471
Downes, Sean E427
Downey, Carolyn A70
Downey, William B P446:P446
Downey, Roger W513
Downing, Cristal A515
Downing, Walter P492
Downing, James P505
Downing, Scott E91
Downing, Philip E229
Downs, Kenneth E P509
Downs, Christina P579
Dowse, Stacey P251
Doyle, John D A74
Doyle, Joseph A115
Doyle, John A136
Doyle, Scott A163
Doyle, Donald A179
Doyle, Francis A284
Doyle, John A500
Doyle, William A867
Doyle, Kelli P26
Doyle, John D P43
Doyle, Jim P139
Doyle, John P200
Doyle, Robert P561
Doyle, Kevin P605
Doyle, Katie W283
Doyle, Daniel E76
Doyle, James E115
Doyle, Peter E186
Doyle, Jonathan J E326
Doyle, Alvaro E438
Doyle, William E452
Dozono, Elisa P399
Dozor, Donna P652
Drabble, Geoffrey W195
Drabek, Anthony E296
Dragas, Helen A254
Dragash, Mickey E72
Drago, Allyson A824:P617
Dragolovic, Goran P466
Dragovich, Dmeter P601
Drahozal, Christopher A815
Drain, Adolphus P141
Drake, Sloane A352
Drake, Bradley A370
Drake, Denny P266
Drake, Brittany P420
Drake, Matt P451
Drake, Michael V P572
Drake, Bradley E203
Drake, Angie E411
Drape, Eric W487
Draper, Daniel A691
Draper, Michelle A751
Draper, Elizabeth P422
Drass, M A512:P324
Drass, Joy P325
Draughn, James A212
Drazkowski, William A296
Drechsel, Cathy P384
Dredge, Carter A729:P497
Drees, Christopher A138
Drees, Ralph P554
Drees, David P554
Drees, Joseph D P587
Drehobl, Stephen A525
Dreiling, Richard A67
Drell, Persis A577
Drennan, Mark A724
Dresher, Carl P135
Dressen, Rich P411
Dresser, Raymond E394
Dressler, Raymond P156
Drew, J. Everitt A147

Drew, Alton A291
Drew, Theresa A721
Drew, Joel P97
Drew, Alton P210
Drew, Greg P639
Drew, J. Everitt E66
Drexler, Karen E352
Dreyer, Michael E224
Dreyfus, Maria Jelescu A629
Drezek, Maria P546
Driggers, Timothy A281
Drilling, Edward A712:E373
Drillings, Robert M P373
Driot-Argentin, Veronique W519
Driscoll, Barb P7
Driscoll, Paul P214
Driscoll, Justin E P371
Driscoll, Sharon W176
Driscoll, William E329
Driver, Darienne P345
Droege, Walter W27
Droege, Ernest-Walther W27
Droga, David W8
Drone, Nicole P240
Drosos, Virginia A332
Druckenmiller, Robert P233
Drugge, Robert E409
Druker, Brian A57
Drum, Don P430
Drumd, Don P430
Drumm, Eric P274
Drummond, David A34
Drummond, F. Ford A94
Drummond, Lance A337:A814
Drummond, Danielle P291
Drummond, David C P427
Drummond, Joseph P605
Drummond, F. Ford E44
Drummond, Lance E424
Drury, James P166
Drury, Mark E100
Dryburgh, Kerry W91
Dryer, Trevor A383:E212
Du, Michael A374
Dua, Naveen P185
Duan, Shengli W115
Duan, Chenggang W130
Duan, Rachel W234
Duan, Liangwei W378
Duan, Xiannian W434
Duane, Jon E237
Dube, Greta P200
Dube, Muriel W421
Dubin, James M P237
Dubin, Cynthia E185
Dubinsky, Jason E280
Dubis, John P456
Dubitzky, Anne P565
Dubler, Joseph M A27
Dubler, Ashley A241
Dublon, Dina A757
Dubner, Steven P647
DuBois, James A289
Dubois, Joseph P93
Dubow, Adam A134
Dubrule, Guillaume W402
Dubs, Joel W480
Dubuc, Nancy A846
Dubuche, Karl Von P602
Duc, Bernard le W82
Duce, Ronald C P285
Ducey, Doug A734
Ducey, Mark P408
Ducey, Doug P510
Ducey, John E443
DuCharme, Linda A291
Ducker, Michael A426
Duckett, Thasunda A563
Duclos, David A680:E356
Duda, Laura A361
Dudacek, Robert J P537
Dudek, Tim P162
Dudkin, Gregory A637
Dudley, William C A299
Dudley, Robert A338:W411
Dudley-Eshbach, Janet P623
Dudman, Martha A103:E47

Dudman, William E301
Dudsdeemaytha, Surasak W270
Dueck, Rodney R P406
Duenas, Juan P128
Duenas, Luis Cabra W400
Dueser, F. Scott A315:E167
Duff, Brian T P46
Duff, Molli M P304
Duff, Eugenia P321
Duffaut, Edvard P317
Duffield, Jeff P125
Dufford, Shawn P458
Duffy, Michael A677
Duffy, Julie A772
Duffy, Brendan P152
Duffy, Janet P190
Duffy, Mary P309
Duffy, Patrick P375
Dufour, Gregory A144
Dufour, Victoria P500
Dufrane, Aaron A91
Dufresne, Maryse P356
Dufresne, Richard W527
Dugan, John A183
Dugan, Patrick D A841
Dugan, Tammy P481
Dugan, Michael P536
Dugan, Richard E432
Duganier, Barbara E407
Dugenske, John A32
Duggal, Aditi P551
Duggan, Scott P559
Duggen, Bill A303
Dugger, John P10
Duggirala, Amala A671
Dugle, Lynn A448:A527:W480
Duhamel, Philippe W488
Duhaney, Patrick P125
Duijser, Machiel A267
Duke, Andrew A291:P210
Duke, Janice P340
Dukeman, Van A310:E164
Dula, Sonia A411
Dulac, Fabienne W372
Dulac, Sophie W395
Dulak, Catherine P92
Duling, Joel E59
Dulmaine, Jean P285
Dumais, Lynn A A133
Dumais, Michael A665
Dumanian, Gregory P389
Dumas, Robert A579
Dumas, Ryan P216
Dumas, Jacques W106
Dumas, Michel E197
Dumbleton, Sonia A307
Dumont, Stephanie P214
Dumora, Renaud W87
Dumurgier, Beatrice W106
Dunavant, David P351
Dunaway, William A748
Dunaway, Mike P320
Dunbar, Kent P152
Dunbar, R Reid E129
Duncan, Timothy A171
Duncan, Candace A247
Duncan, George A408
Duncan, Douglas A408
Duncan, Geoff A735
Duncan, Wayne P139
Duncan, Gary P217
Duncan, Ronald P225
Duncan, Dean R A460
Duncan, Erika P504
Duncan, Geoff P511
Duncan, George E141
Dungan, Richard W P20
Dungee, Dorothy P48
Dunham, Kara P108
Dunigan, James A648
Dunkle, Jason P193
Dunlap, Nicole A111
Dunlap, Nancy A413
Dunlap, Michael A549
Dunlap, Jay L A811
Dunlap, Edward B P106
Dunlap, Timothy M P106

Dunlap, Charles P580
Dunlap, Michael P591:P596:E290
Dunlay, Patrick P333
Dunleavy, Michael A734:P510
Dunn, Ryan A278
Dunn, Leslie A553
Dunn, Micheal A604
Dunn, Todd A728
Dunn, Sarah A759
Dunn, Dean P29
Dunn, John P47
Dunn, Cindy P233
Dunn, Stephen D P268
Dunn, Robert P P268
Dunn, Terrence P P268
Dunn, Stephen D P268
Dunn, Robert P P268
Dunn, Michelle P356
Dunn, Andrew P409
Dunn, Lauren P467
Dunn, Randy J P490
Dunn, Todd P496
Dunn, Brian P521
Dunn, Elizabeth P617
Dunn, Craig W484
Dunn, Ryan E141
Dunn, Leslie E197
Dunn, Craig E204
Dunn, Danny E280
Dunn, Alan E287
Dunn, Michael E348
Dunn, Kevin E454
Dunnahoe, Mike P454
Dunne, Gwynneth P441
Dunne, James J E326
Dunnie, Tookie P14
Dunning, Audrey A795:E416
Dunnvatanachit, Panit W62
Dunnvatanachit, Pornnit W62
Dunsmore, Stan E83
Dunton, James K A49:P33
Dunton, Robert P164
Dunton, Shirby P642
Duong, Duc Hung W232
Duplaix, Jean-Marc W273
Duplisea, Doug A621:P412
Dupont, Michael R P368
Dupont, Ty P533
Dupont, Laurent W174
Duport, Valerie W273
Duppong, Gerald P137
Duprat, Pierre-Christophe A68
Duprat, Pierre W517
Dupre, Janice A488
Dupre, David P78
Dupre, Lisa P172
Dupre, Daniel E159
Dupree, Darren E413
Dupuis, Eleanor P68
Duran, Angelita P130
Duran, Lillian P637
Duran, Mario Valcarce W110
Duran, Maria Juliana Alban W171
Durana, Cristina Aldamiz-Echevarria
  Gonzalez de W9
Durand, Patrice W184
Durban, Egon A801:A840
Durbin, Jennifer A207
Durcan, D. A13:W42
Duren, Deborah P112
Durette, Peter A860
Durham, Harold A312
Durham, Jeffrey A673
Durham, Karilee A715
Durham, Michael A778
Durham, Mikel A802
Durham, Michael P561
Durheimer, Wolfgang A615
Durkee, Robert K P582
Durkin, Brian A6
Durkin, Chris P58
Durn, Dan A11
Durnan, Jaymie E370
Durongkaveroj, Pichet W62
Durst, Linda S P344
Duryea, Tom A285
Dusek, Richard A176

COMBINED HOOVER'S HANDBOOK INDEX OF EXECUTIVES

A = AMERICAN BUSINESS
E = EMERGING COMPANIES
P = PRIVATE COMPANIES
W = WORLD BUSINESS

Dusel, Martin C P121
Dusenberry, Matthew P236
Dussault, Claude W250
Duster, Benjamin A171
Dutcher, Phillip C P361
Dutkowsky, Robert A384:A663
Dutra, Ana A318:E171
Dutto, Laurence A709:E370
Dutton, Richard A187
Dutton, Steven A285
Dutton, Chuck P423
Dutton, Richard E85
Duva, Judith P401
Duval, John P640
Duz, Cetin W21
Dvorak, Petr W281
Dvorkin, Viktar E144
Dwight, Craig A400
Dwight, John A617
Dwight, Craig E218
Dwight, John E319
Dwinell, Lauren P345
Dwork, Andrew A781:P582
Dworkin, James A400:E218
Dwozan, Michael E91
Dwyer, Jay P68
Dwyer, Hugh P265
Dwyer, Shannon P430:P502
Dy, Lucy W82
Dybal, Alexander W208
Dyck, Robert G A93
Dyck, Lonnie P636
Dyck, Mark van W139
Dye, Rebecca P524
Dyer, Gary A454
Dyer, Robert M P135
Dyer, Gary P285
Dyer, Emily P367
Dyer, Karen P608
Dyer, Joseph E32
Dyer, Corey E120
Dyhrkopp, Erik A681:P448
Dyk, Lisa P308
Dyke, Candy V A14
Dyke, Jeff A719
Dyke, Candy V P5
Dyke, David V P228
Dyke, Peter E215
Dyke, Cornelius Van E422
Dykema, John A562:E293
Dykes, Melissa P270
Dykes, Archie E29
Dykstra, Karen A841
Dykstra, David A867
Dykstra, Michele P230
Dykstra, David E452
Dymoke, Lea P399
Dymski, Michael E348
Dynysiuk, Joanna W70
Dyson, Deborah A81
Dzau, Victor P197
Dziadzio, Richard A76
Dzielak, Robert A288
Dzierzbinski, Danusia P265
Dziobek, Judy P133
Dziuk, David A A380:P247
D'Agosta, Jeffrey P361
D'Agostino, Thomas A328
D'Agostino, Teresa P133
D'Agostino, Marcelo P404
D'Alessandri, Robert P651
D'Alimonte, Christa A607
d'Amarzit, Delphine W489
D'Ambrose, Michael A124
D'Ambrosia, Steven A36
D'Ambrosio, Chris A81
D'amelio, Frank A406:A881
D'Amico, Lance A60
D'Amico, Andrew E438
D'Amours, Jacques W25
D'Antilio, Derek P376

D'apice, Leon E129
D'Aquila, Richard P660
D'Arienzo, Annette Marino P79
D'Haene, Shelley E83
D'Iorio, Steven A330
D'Souza, Francisco A346

E

E, Thomas Kevin P361
E-Newsletter, Healthy P501
Eade-Viele, Carol P19
Eads, Courtney P452
Eagle, Dustin P91
Eakle, Jason A617
Eames, Frederick P16
Eames, Andy P496
Eames, Dennis P508
Eansor, N. David E50
Earl, Nick P230
Earl, Ashlee M P546
Earl, Dustin P657
Earley, Robert P533
Earley, Franklin P P642
Earley, Michael E4
Early, Charles P365
Earnhardt, Lisa A4
Easley, Matthew A78:P47
Easley, Jeanette P121
Easley, Stephen T P209
Easley, Paul P492
Easor, J. Cliff A672
East, Stephen A788
East, Warren W42:W410
Easter, William A273
Easter, Wh A512:P326
Eastland, Woods E P509
Eastman, Stephen L A632
Eastman, A Brent P469
Eastoe, Kate W532
Eastwood, Stephanie P63
Eaton, Perry A321
Eaton, Deborah R P167
Eaton, George P464
Eaton, Rachel E251
Eatough, Chris P256
Eaves, Greg P203
Eazor, Joseph A247
Ebbe, Michael W168
Ebel, Gregory A539
Ebel, Gregory L P494
Ebel, Gregory W178
Eberhard, Michael A81
Eberhard, Sally P596
Eberhardt, Karie P366
Eberhart, H. Paulett A328
Eberhart, Ralph A436
Eberhart, H. Paulett A489:A831
Eberling, Edward P338
Ebersole, Amy P149
Ebert, John E283
Eberwein, Elise A41
Ebicioglu, Fatih W281
Ebinger, William E323
Ebner, Vicki O P608
Ebong, Francis W40
Ebror, Brian E96
Eccher, James A587:E302
Echavarria, Luis Fernando
  Restrepo W61
Echavez, Luis Hernandez W109
Echelard, Paul P379
Echelberger, Penny A511:P322
Echevarria, Joseph A99
Echevarria, Joe A872
Echevarria, Emmanuel P132
Echevarria, Sean P240
Echeverri, Juan Emilio Posada W171
Echiverri, Henry C P201
Echols, Leldon A390
Echols, Edwin P539
Eck, Joshua A740
Eck, Michael P77
Eck, Joshua P516
Eckart, Samuel E174
Eckel, Jeffrey E206

Ecker, John P327
Eckert, Robert A476:A477:A509
Eckert, Inger P177
Eckert, Matthew P278
Eckert, Robert P297
Eckert, Bret E136
Eckert, Daniel E200
Eckhart, Michael E206
Eckhoff, Heidi P577
Eckroth, Joseph A778:P561:W480
Eda, Makiko W205
Eddens, Peggy A870:E454
Eddinger, Ronnie P84
Eddington, Roderick W277
Eddy, Jodi A132
Eddy, Jan A311
Eddy, Adam P462
Edeker, Randy A412:P258
Edelman, Harriet A77:A111
Edelman, Ytzhak W64
Edelman, Martin E52
Edelson, David A486
Edelstein, Sam P134
Edelstein, Gara P230
Edelstenne, Charles W488
Edenshaw, Sidney P471
Eder, Noelle A40
Eder, Paul A512:P324
Eder, Wolfgang W246:W367:W521
Ederington, L. Benjamin A860
Edes, Beth A738:P514
Edgar, Jason A103
Edgar, Robert V A210
Edgar, Gregory P41
Edgar, Andrew P126
Edgar, Robin P333
Edgar, Jason E47
Edge, Rochelle M A298
Edgerly, Deborah P130
Edgerton, Ivis P363
Ediboglu, Ayse W505
Edison, Sheri A151:A812
Edlund, Todd E140
Edmonds-Waters, Christopher A751
Edmondson, David P420
Edmunds, Coleman A83
Edmunds, Beth P399
Edmunds, Cynthia P623
Edmunds, Wayne E282
Edone, Ryan E251
Edson, Kent A232
Edson, Pam P394
Eduardo, Marcelo A798
Edvardsen, Nina W454
Edwards, Jon A53
Edwards, Lisa A200
Edwards, Crawford A227
Edwards, Jon A251
Edwards, Maury A352
Edwards, Bruce A367
Edwards, Carladenise A381
Edwards, S. Eugene A612
Edwards, Susan A702
Edwards, John Bel A736
Edwards, Robert A814
Edwards, Joey P3
Edwards, Steven L P76
Edwards, Steve P76
Edwards, Steve L P92
Edwards, Thomas K P120
Edwards, Leslie P146
Edwards, Darnell P160
Edwards, Laurie P175
Edwards, Joe P190
Edwards, Judy P224
Edwards, Carladenise P249
Edwards, Carolyn P253
Edwards, Susan P287
Edwards, Steven D P296
Edwards, Greg P451
Edwards, C H P471
Edwards, Clarence P472
Edwards, John Bel P512
Edwards, Beverly P604
Edwards, Norman W100
Edwards, Mel W533
Edwards, Debra E23

Edwards, Jon E25
Edwards, Michael E75
Edwards, Harold E97
Edwards, Jeffrey E231
Edwards, Robert E424
Edwardson, Francesca A408
Eeckhout, Arnauld Van W133
Efendioglu, Alev P628
Effinger, Scott P136
Egan, Cynthia A375:A411
Egan, Thomas A P360
Egan, Joe P638
Egerth-Stadlhuber, Henrietta W187
Eggemeyer, John M A606
Eggemeyer, John A640:E333
Eggspuehle, Jay E207
Egidi, Kenneth P411
Ehara, George S P530
Ehinniah, Nim P389
Ehlers, Marc A293:P212
Ehlinger, Jon D P195
Ehlinger, Forrest G P242
Ehrenberg, James E271
Ehrentraut, Christian W50
Ehrlich, Craig A783
Ehrlich, Randall V P89
Ehrlich, Robert P316
Ehrlich, Craig P583
Ehrmanntraut, Dietrich A60
Eibensteiner, Herbert W521
Eichelberger, Mitch A172:P113
Eichfeld, William P490
Eichiner, Friedrich W246
Eichler, Kimberly P478
Eichmann, Matthew A367
Eichorn, Marvin P55
Eid, Joseph A134
Eid, Eric A201
Eid, Samir P370
Eid, Eric E92
Eidah, Abdullah Al W395
Eide, Ador P462
Eijsink, Jeroen A683
Eikhoff, Luanne P472
Eiler, Gary P632
Eilerman, Chris P125
Eilers, Peter E23
Einhorn, David E199
Eisele, Martin E157
Eiselstein, Shana P143
Eisen, David P648
Eisenberg, Glenn A464
Eisenberger, Mario E435
Eisenbrandt, Peter P635
Eisenhuth, Guy A867:E452
Eisenson, Michael A615
Eisenstaedt, Richard P3
Eisgruber, Christopher L P582
Eishen, Leonard E394
Eishen, Eric E394
Eisman, Robert A39
Eison, Thomas P493
Eitel, Dotti P118
Eitel, William P125
Ejel, Remy W348
Ekabut, Chaovalit W441
Ekberg, Hugh P176
Ekeji, Chika W335
Ekey, Jennifer P143
Ekholm, E. Boerje W24:E415
Ekpo, Idongesit P323
El-Erian, Mohamed W75
El-Hibri, Fuad E133
El-Khoury, Hassane A591
Elam, Anthony W307
Elamine, A K P488
Elbers, Pieter W18:W278
Elbraechter, Hanno W166
Eldar, Assaf W253
Elder, Larry P73
Elder, Richard E163
Elder, T. L. E199
Eldracher, Deborah E298
Eldred, Brian P635
Eldreth, Nathan P457
Eldridge, Michelle A514:E267
Elenio, Paul E29

COMBINED HOOVER'S HANDBOOK INDEX OF EXECUTIVES

Elez, Drazen A738:P514
Elhaj, Imad P622
Elhedery, Georges W234
Eli, Robert P304
Elia, Maryellen P251
Elias, Lindsey P343
Elias, Richard P418:E426
Eliassi-Rad, Babak P84
Elieson, Abby P630
Eliot, Courtney P642
Elizalde, Stephanie S P52
Elizalde, Raul Anaya W56
Elizondo, Carlos Jose Garcia
    Moreno W28
Elkins, David A134
Elkins, Claude A566
Elkins, Lorelei P160
Elkins, Carla P463
Ellefsen, Jacob P238
Ellehuus, Christoffer P103
Ellen, Jonathan P274
Ellenbogen, David P468
Ellenburg, Christina P321
Eller, Jay P206
Eller, Lars E155
Ellerbrook, Niel C P491
Ellert, Lisa P191
Ellinger, Deborah E236
Ellingsen, Catharine A677
Ellingson, Rachel A878
Ellington, Christopher P40
Ellington, Chris P627
Elliot, Douglas A377
Elliot, Cynthia P450
Elliot, Charles P529
Elliott, Gerri A182
Elliott, Anita A252
Elliott, Robin A310
Elliott, Christopher A370
Elliott, Steven A409
Elliott, Christine A536
Elliott, Steven A637
Elliott, Douglas G A640
Elliott, Geraldine A863
Elliott, Wayne P73
Elliott, Carla P262
Elliott, William R P313
Elliott, Brandy P418
Elliott, Robin E164
Elliott, Christopher E203
Elliott, Jay E231
Elliott, Douglas G E333
Ellis, Earl A7
Ellis, Juliet A64
Ellis, Beverly A147
Ellis, Brian A235
Ellis, James A254
Ellis, Brian A277
Ellis, Jennifer A350
Ellis, Clayton A427
Ellis, James A516
Ellis, Larry A579
Ellis, Stephen A697
Ellis, Douglas A789
Ellis, Matthew A833
Ellis, Brian P96
Ellis, Beverly P96
Ellis, Stephanie P97
Ellis, Marianne P169
Ellis, Elmer G P199
Ellis, Mark P203
Ellis, Debbie P217
Ellis, John W P225
Ellis, Ellen P248
Ellis, Suzanne P271
Ellis, Sarah P472
Ellis, Stephen P578
Ellis, David P644
Ellis, Kip E314
Ellis, Gary E411
Ellis, Douglas E411
Ellison, Marvin A302
Ellison, Seth A476:A477
Ellison, Marvin A488
Ellison, Lawrence A595
Ellison, Noni A791
Ellison, Richard P83

Ellison, Janet P296
Ellison, Seth P297
Ellison, Joel P476
Ellithorpe, Peggy P638
Ellspermann, Sue A353:E192
Elmer, Russell A706
Elmer, Katherine P192
Elmiger, Eugen E279
Elmin, Henrik W48
Elmo, Terri Di P497
Elmore, Samuel A314
Elmore, Bill P287
Elmore, Karen P342
Elmquist, Jay P455
Elmslie, Nick W346
Elorza, Jorge O P132
Elosua, Federico Toussaint W22
Elrich, Marc P352
Elsaesser, Ford A201:E92
Elsenhans, Lynn W210
Elsner, Frank A9:E4
Elste, Mark E82
Elstein, Amir W487
Elswick, Steve P157
Eltife, Kevin A447
Elting, Lauren E159
Elwell, Daniel A26
Elwell, Richard P204
Elwyn, Tashtego A663
Ely, James A703
Ely, Teresa A750
Ely, Lisa P461
Ely, Teresa E394
Emadi, Mohd Ismail Mandani Al W134
Emany, Sravan E237
Embler, Michael E294
Embree, Tracy A228
Emde, Alyson P244
Emeka, Farah P158
Emenhiser, Kip E246
Emerson, Kenneth A106
Emerson, Sarah A171
Emerson, Bertrand M A778
Emerson, Christy P107
Emerson, Bertrand M P564
Emerson, Kenneth E48
Emerson, Daniel E402
Emery, Karen P41
Emery, Douglas P242
Emery, Homer P462
Emiris, Ioannis W27
Emkes, Mark A367
Emmerc, Mark A825:P631
Emmerling, John A24:P13
Emmert, Mark A289:A862
Emmert, Mark A P363
Emmons, Diana A738
Emmons, Jennifer P471
Emmons, Diana P514
Emo, Tantri P126
Emory, Frank A573:P390
Emoto, Yasutoshi W17
Empey, Rachel W204
Emrich, Richard P87
Emswiler, Shane E27
Ende, Jack P427
Endo, Hiroshi W257
Endo, Yasuaki W288
Endo, Takaaki W334
Endo, Isao W452
Endo, Yoshinari W493
Endres, Todd P112
Endresen, William A396
Endrizzi, James A846
Engel, Robert B A195
Engel, E. Randall A558
Engel, Connie A674
Engel, John A821:A854
Engel, Christa P91
Engel, Robert B P140
Engel, Marc W1
Engel, Hans-Ulrich W76
Engel, Marc W510
Engel, Robert E16
Engel, Connie E348
Engelbert, Catherine A509
Engelbrecht, Scott P138

Engelkes, Jack A393:E217
Engels, Bob P165
Engelstoft, Morten W1
Enger, Douglas P133
Engers, Barbara P503
Engin, Eyuep W21
England, Donna M A257
England, Daniel E P92
England, Dean P92
England, Chad P92
England, Josh P92
England, Todd P92
England, Corey P92
England, Tj P92
England, Zach P92
England, Chad D P207
England, Jimmy P287
England, James W178
Englander, Daniel E20
Engle, Bridget A99
Engle, John B P469
Engle, Nic E187
Englebright, Jane A379
Englefield, F. William A608:E312
Englehart, Michael P355
Engler, John E393
Englert, Richard M E536
Engles, Gregg A174
Engles, Gregg L P182
Engles, Amanda E132
Englesson, John E132
English, James A355
English, Steven A734
English, Lori P55
English, Bob P421
English, Katrina M P607
English, James E193
English, Michela E194
Englund, Melissa P577
Engola, Paul A472
Engquist, John A533
Engstrand, Benjamin P436
Engstrom, Mike P74
Ennerfelt, P Goeran P298
Ennis, Tara P614
Enns, Peter W126
Enomoto, Hideto P378
Enomoto, Koichi W329
Enos, Deborah P24
Enos, Cassandra P93
Enrico, Carlo A506
Enrique, Castro P162
Enstad, Paul E198
Entao, Gwyneth W83
Enterline, Larry E97
Entwisle, Beverly J P602
Entwistle, David A730:P509
Enyedi, Matthew A489
Enzor, Gary E368:E430
Eppard, Amie E439
Eppinger, Frederick A162
Eppolito, Linda A112
Epps, Stacey A126:P83
Epps, JoAnne E190
Epps, Donna E359:E407
Epstein, Louis P597
Erbe, Cathi P170
Ercoline, Luke P166
Erdogan, Akif W540
Erdogmus, Mert W21
Ergen, Charles A249
Erginbilgic, Tufan W156:W505
Erhard, Karin W190
Eric, Huang A839:P643
Erickson, Randall A74
Erickson, Jon A190
Erickson, David J A300
Erickson, Andrew A743
Erickson, Rodney A A780
Erickson, Brian P30
Erickson, Rodney A P575
Erickson, Kevin P650
Erickson, Richard E417
Ericson, Per A80
Ericson, Brady A131
Ericson, Brent A369
Ericson, Amy A636

Ericson, Brent P237
Ericson, Magnus W470
Erik, John P3
Eriksen, Mary P464
Eristoff, Anne Sidamon A210
Erlich, Craig E8
Erlich, Morton E23
Erlinger, Joseph A509
Erlund, Jukka W274
Ermatinger, William A410
Ermine-Baer, Kristin A828:P635
Erminio, Courtney E274
Ernest, Douglas A814:E423
Ernst, Todd A569
Ernst, Michael A783:P591
Ernst, Elizabeth P617
Erokhin, Vladimir W468
Erpenbach, Michelle P556
Errazuriz, Blas Tomic W141
Errazuriz, Sebastian Dittborn W177
Errichettii, Ann P508
Errity, Kevin E253
Ersari, Mehmet W21
Erschen, Leslie P162
Ersteniuk, Peter P333
Ertas, Ilker A62
Ertel, Anne P615
Ertl, Rudolf W515
Eruen, Goekhan W540
Ervin, Patrick A417
Ervin, Greggory P179
Ervin, Reginald P389
Ervin, Patrick E226
Erwin, Tami A833
Erwin, Duane P45
Erwin, Michael A P186
Esamann, Douglas F A259
Esaw, Pamela A266
Escajadillo, Ricardo Ernesto
    Saldivar W198
Escandar, Pedro Samhan W255
Escarrer, Gabriel P187
Escasa-Haigh, Jo Ann P430
Escasa-Halgh, Jo Ann P502
Escobar, David P261
Escoe, Kenneth A415
Escue, Dick P60
Escuyer, Vincent P247
Eshelman, Erica P410
Eskew, Michael A32
Eslinger, Lisa E26
Esparza, Ryan P269
Esparza, Luis Bartolini W381
Espe, Matthew A854
Espel, Thomas K P437
Espeland, Curtis A264:A411
Esper, Eric A778:P561
Esperdy, Therese A536:W342
Espinola, Javier de Pedro W215
Espinoza, Carina P303
Espinoza, Jose P486
Espiritu, Octavio W70
Esposito, Carl A470
Esposito, Michael A739:P515
Esposito, Nicole M P586
Espy, Kevan P141
Esquibel, Emillo P467
Essam, Ahmed W520
Essenberg, Janice P68
Esser, Juergen W152
Essig, Stuart E234
Essman, Shon P136
Esta, Linda P579
Estby, Rebecca P142
Esteban, A Gabriel P185
Estelle, Lameisha A123:P81
Estep, Michele A582
Estep, Sandra A652
Estep, Jonathan A791
Estep, Michele E301
Esterhay, Carl E127
Esterman, Michelle P27
Estes, Joel P155
Estes, Amy P249
Estes, Christopher P334
Esteves, Irene A686
Estrada, Bernice A799

HOOVER'S HANDBOOK OF EMERGING COMPANIES 2022

COMBINED HOOVER'S HANDBOOK INDEX OF EXECUTIVES

A = AMERICAN BUSINESS
E = EMERGING COMPANIES
P = PRIVATE COMPANIES
W = WORLD BUSINESS

Estrada, Cindy A804
Estrada, Angel G P171
Estrada, Agustin P496
Estrada, Bernice P605
Estrada, Cindy P607
Estradas, J. Lorraine E29
Estrict, Ronnie P408
Etchart, Eric E12
Etheredge, James W8
Etheridge, Donell A197
Etheridge, Felicia P136
Etheridge, Don P362
Etienne, Claudine P579
Etten, David V P657
Etter, Steven A340
Ettinger, Michael A696
Ettinger, Jeffrey E411
Ettl, Robert A P243
Etzkorn, Karen E213
Etzler, Todd A400:E218
Euapiyachart, Kidsada W98
Eubanks, Richard M A598
Euchukanonchai, Krairit W284
Eugster, Dr Cris P136
Eulau, Robert A858
Eulich, John A279:E142
Eure, Hilliard E260
Eureyecko, John E20
Evangelista, Ferlou W323
Evanko, Jillian A609:E81
Evans, David A151
Evans, Charles L A299
Evans, Godfrey A396
Evans, Shad A448
Evans, Trina A453
Evans, Daniel A466
Evans, Russ A719
Evans, Mary Alice A735
Evans, Robert A760
Evans, Javier A874
Evans, Greg P3
Evans, Doug P112
Evans, Jeremy P184
Evans, Kelley P190
Evans, Robert E P199
Evans, Crystal P205
Evans, Richard T P209
Evans, Dave P226
Evans, Gemma P256
Evans, Linda P275
Evans, Dave P283
Evans, Jeremy S P287
Evans, Joshua D P305
Evans, Kari P339
Evans, Anita P353
Evans, Donnie W P408
Evans, Patricia P419
Evans, Malik P449
Evans, Russ P486
Evans, Tema P493
Evans, Mary Alice P511
Evans, Kimberly P525
Evans, Palmer P604
Evans, Brandy P637
Evans, Glenda P643
Evans, Mariah P647
Evans, J. Michael W24
Evans, Gay W456
Evans, Kirsten W525
Evans, Todd E185
Evans, Daniel E244
Evans, Jose E265
Evans, Sharlene E375
Evans-Hands, Chris P161
Evanson, Paul J P351
Evanson, Doug P462
Eveland, Scott A738:P514
Evenson, Jeffrey A222
Everett, Morgan A197
Everett, Austin P321
Everett, Kirsty W234

Everett, Jacqueline E122
Everette, James P64
Everhart, Winn A863
Evernham, Scott A585
Evers, Tony A742:P518:P633
Evers, Tami P638
Evers, Sherri W242
Everson, Carolyn A778:P561
Everson, Scott E422
Evette, Pamela S A740:P516
Evitts, Aaron A172:P113
Evoli, Lisa E234
Evrard, Sharon P220
Ewart, Thomas E174
Ewens, Peter A758
Ewert, Brian H P314
Ewert, Phil P461
Ewing, Justin A28
Ewing, Alexandra A214
Ewing, Justin P18
Ewing, Marilyn E P262
Ewing, Diane P323
Ewing, Jason P507
Exnicios, Joseph A372
Exposito, Alina P341
Eyiguen, Goekhan W217
Eyler, Phillip E377
Eyton, David W91
Eyuboglu, Yagiz W281:W505
Eyuboglu, Nurgun W540
EZ, Dino R Camu P415
Ezeigwe, Chizoba P319
Ezekiel, Laurent W533
Ezell, Antoine A109
Ezer, Dorit Ben P116
Ezra, Einav P325
Ezzell, Robert A53:E25

F

Faas, Jim P418
Fabara, Paul A839
Faber, Bob A35
Faber, Barry A713
Faber, Johanna A759
Faber, Bob P27
Faber, Lori P327
Faber, Hanneke W510
Fabisch, Gerhard W515
Fabrikant, Charles P470
Fabrikant, Eric P470
Facchini, Pier W391
Fache, Jameson Smith P102
Fache, Adrienne Palmer P321
Fache, Andrea G P542
Factourovich, Inna K P611
Faddis, Jonathan E433
Fadem, Steve P545
Fadool, Joseph A131
Faecher, Marc P597
Faella, Alfred P171
Fagan, Briana P166
Fagan, Cathlyn P384
Fagan, Chuck P430
Fagan, Tiffani P457
Fageeh, Abdul Rahman Al W422
Fagello, Juanita P89
Fagen, Catherine P301
Fagerdahl, Anders W471
Fagerholm, Jannica W275
Fagernas, Peter W275
Fagg, Kathryn W340
Fague, Philip A597:E307
Fahey, Walter P307
Fahim, Shafei P51
Fahrenkopf, Frank A323
Fahy, Michael P48
Faidley, Jeffrey P294
Fails, Karl A750
Fain, Jonathan P535
Fair, William A417
Fair, Laura J P342
Fair, William E227
Fairbairn, Carolyn W53
Fairbairn, Dame Carolyn W234

Fairbank, Richard A148
Fairbanks, Donald P347
Fairbanks, Donald W P348
Fairbanks, Bryan E413
Fairchilds, Charles A186:E84
Faircloth, Michael A373
Fairclough, Daniel W39
Fairfax, Justin E A209:P146
Fairfax, Lisa E185
Fairfield, Irene P204
Faith, Marshall P580
Faivre, Sara A296:E157
Fajardo, Jose P261
Falati, Stacie A583:P393
Falb, Derek J P120
Falcione, Ronald A390:E215
Falcon, Armando A668
Falcon, Ray P133
Falcon, Tiji P174
Falcon, Michelle P596
Falcone, Joseph C P363
Falcone, Philip P503
Falconer, Brendon A585
Faldini, Roberto W309
Falero, Xavier O P129
Falk, Michael A867
Falk, Kathleen P158
Falk, David A P375
Falkenhausen, Konstantin Von E295
Fall, Clinton P557
Falleri, Frank P207
Fallin, Wayne P647
Fallon, William A507
Fallon, Katherine Beirne A509
Fallon, Kieran A632
Fallon, Jeanne M P96
Fallon, Jeanne P97
Fallon, Lynnette C E40
Fallowfield, Tim W258
Falsey, Ann M P565
Falvey, James P392
Falwell, Trey P299
Falzon, Robert A649
Falzone, Lori P451
Fam, Yoke Fong W393
Famuyiwa, Oluyemisi O P254
Fan, David A767
Fan, Dawson P641
Fan, Luyuan W24
Fanale, James P99
Fanciulli, Francesco W391
Fandozzi, Ann E415
Fandrey, Edward A489
Fanelli, Denise P262
Fang, Li A221
Fang, Zheng A735
Fang, Joseph P392
Fang, Zheng P511
Fang, Heying W129
Fang, Xianshui W223
Fang, Mingfu W265
Fang, Sylvia W474
Fang, Rong W542
Fanjul, Oscar A500
Fanlo, Saturnino E200
Fannin, Timothy A570
Fanning, Thomas P492
Fansler, Janet P291
Fant, Suzanne P507
Fantorno, Carla P532
Farabell, Jacqueline P132
Faraci, John V A154
Faraci, John A636:A821
Farah, Roger A232:A645
Farber, Jeffrey A375
Fardan, Omar Al W134
Fardan, Hussain Ibrahim Al W134
Fardman, Emilya P350
Farhan, Faisal P6
Farinsky, Jason P455
Farkas, Chris P251
Farland, Kenn Mc P345
Farley, James A333
Farley, Joseph M P97
Farley, James P409
Farmer, Kathryn A122
Farmer, Michael A139

Farmer, Scott A180
Farmer, Curtis A204
Farmer, Kathryn P80
Farmer, Maelynn P99
Farmer, Jenifer P141
Farmer, Paul J P177
Farmer, Michael P319
Farney, Cheryl P335
Farney, Alan P644
Farnham, Linda A233:P178
Farnham, Cathrine P330
Farnsworth, David A230
Farnsworth, Thomas A628
Farnsworth, Ronald A809
Farnsworth, Diane P451
Farnsworth, David E113
Farnsworth, Thomas E324
Farnum, Michelle P124
Farnum, Allan P262
Farooqui, Duriya A422
Farquhar, Joey P659
Farr, Richard P173
Farr, David P521
Farr, Susan W93
Farrar, Jeffrey A49:E21
Farrell, Paul A131
Farrell, Matthew A177
Farrell, Michael A364
Farrell, Kathleen A549
Farrell, Thomas A838
Farrell, William J A866
Farrell, Michael A878
Farrell, Julie P7
Farrell, Lori Ann P127
Farrell, Steven P218
Farrell, Benny P339
Farrell, William J P657
Farrell, Edward E29
Farrell, Nicholas E215
Farrell, Kathleen E290
Farrell, Michael E352
Farrell, Peter E352
Farrell, Stephen E388
Farrell, Peter E443
Farren, John P544
Farren, Magda P644
Farrimond, Katherine P381
Farrington, Deborah A548
Farrington, Duane A605
Farrington, Shannon P426
Farris, Franklin A211
Farris, Judy P283
Farris, Bain P458
Farris, Bain P458:P503
Farris, Brad E204
Farris, Ray E248
Farrow, William E73
Farsi, Sheikha Yousuf Al W64
Fartaj, Vandad A614:E317:E318
Fasano, James A433
Fasano, Gerald A472
Fasching, Steven E116
Faser, Christine P332
Fasimon, Sandor W334
Fasino, Jeffrey A203:P144
Fasmer, Benedicte Schilbred W454
Fasolo, Peter A441
Fass, Maxine A780:P572
Fassbind, Renato W287
Fassino, Anthony A156
Fassio, Michelle P528
Fath, Noella P38
Fatovic, Robert A689
Fauber, Robert A536
Faubert, Richard J E40
Faught, James A874
Faul, Michelle P545
Faulds, Jason P466
Faulk, Brian A484
Faulkenberry, Barbara E430
Faulkingham, Ryan E97
Faulkner, David V P259
Faulkner, Jennifer P371
Faulkner, Mikel E175
Fauske, Daniel R A27
Faust, Megan A58
Faust, Bonnie Hartley P300

518   HOOVER'S HANDBOOK OF EMERGING COMPANIES 2022

COMBINED HOOVER'S HANDBOOK INDEX OF EXECUTIVES

Faux, Marsha P421
Fauzi, Syamsul Azuan bin Ahmad W393
Fave, John La P658
Favorite, Annette E446
Favre, Michel W193
Favre, Matthew E253
Favuzza, Steven P P584
Fawcett, Matthew A550
Fawcett, Tiffany P444
Fawcett, Dave P650
Fawcett, Mark E29
Fawcett, Robert E361
Fawzi, Tarek W395
Fay, William A73
Fay, Kay B P631
Fazio, Giulio W181
Fc, Brett P212
Fearon, Richard A264:P200:W145
Feaster, David A675:E350
Feathers, Amy P642
Federico, Peter A22
Federoff, Howard P560
Fedewa, Mary E391
Fedor, Terry A188
Fedotov, Gennady W386
Fedun, Leonid W386
Fedzhora, Liliya P641
Fee, Mariah P571
Feehan, Daniel E175
Feehery, William E446
Feeley, Andrea A866:P657
Feeney, Joe A531
Feeney, Jim P342
Feeney, Joe P349
Fees, John E59
Fegan, Jeff P P180
Fehlberg, Mark P585
Fehlman, Robert A712:E373
Fehnel, Stephen H P437
Feiccabrino, Joseph P130
Feickert, Beth P261
Feidner, Susan P116
Feiga, Tyler P535
Feiger, Mitch A306
Feight, R Preston A602
Fein, Alan P546
Fein, David W456
Feinberg, Joshua A7
Feinberg, David A44:A165
Feinberg, Melody A297
Feinberg, Sarah A553:P370
Feinberg, Melody E158
Feiner, Gary E440
Feingold, Ira A48
Feingold, Anton A70
Feingold, Halli Razon - E292
Feinknopf, Abigail A853:E444
Feintuch, Richard E321
Fejes, Balazs E144
Fekete, Frank A647
Felber, Francis E83
Feldbaum, Carl E150
Feldgreber, Rob P429
Feldkamp, Gary P555
Feldman, Greg A31
Feldman, Joshua A97
Feldman, Alan A332
Feldman, Greg P24
Feldman, Martin J P502
Feldman-Wiencek, Holly P362
Feldotte, Jonathon P63
Feldstein, Andrew E632
Felecia, Donald-Colema A640:E333
Feliciano, Javier A518
Feliciano, Lynette P169
Feliu, Juan W141
Felix, Jose Antonio Guaraldi W28
Felix, Rita W427
Fell, Rob P475
Fellenz, Sherry P63
Felli, Luis A20
Fellin, Frederick M P593
Fellner, Jennifer E219
Felsinger, Donald A69:A569
Felton, Danielle P127
Felton, Kathryn P592

Feltz, Lorianne E145
Felzien, Aidan P408
Fendel, Frederick E339
Fender, Christina A789:E411
Fenech, Ronald E246
Feng, Changli W31
Feng, Liqiong W88
Feng, Shuchen W208
Feng, Rong W235
Feng, Zhenping W235
Feng, Weidong W244
Feng, Wenhong W434
Fenimore, Christopher A669
Fenn, Richmond E37
Fennebresque, Kim A28:P18
Fennell, Laura A429
Fennell, Charles P504
Fennell, Debbie P509
Fenner, Arvie P218
Fenner, Simon P306
Fennessy, Dan P604
Fennewald, Denise P347
Fennoy, Donald P467
Fenstermaker, William A317:E170
Fenton, Jeffrey A820
Fenton, Julia P576
Fenwick, Sandra P548
Fenza, Daniel P120
Feola, Tony P132
Feragen, Jody A610
Feragne, Mark A P22
Feral-Schuhl, Christiane W106
Feransi, Toni P164
Ferderber, Fred P93
Ferdman, David E114
Ferebee, G. Maliek E122
Ferencz, Steve M P106
Ferenczy, William E342
Ferguson, Rhonda A32
Ferguson, Jeffrey A152
Ferguson, Diana A339
Ferguson, Roger A426
Ferguson, Mark A623
Ferguson, Alexis P291
Ferguson, Joel I P342
Ferguson, Troy P424
Ferguson, Stacey P499
Ferguson, Bruce P532
Ferguson, Erica P578
Ferguson, Jonathon P632
Ferjani, Ahmed W38
Ferketish, Gene B P628
Ferland, Martine A500
Ferlin, Gregg P146
Ferm, Peter W3
Fernald, Lauri A103:E47
Fernandes, Larry A418
Fernandes, Al P605
Fernandes, Ruben W32
Fernandez, Felix A157
Fernandez, Antonio A324
Fernandez, Manuel A391:A436
Fernandez, Carmen A500
Fernandez, Mario P193
Fernandez, Luz P204
Fernandez, Maria P443
Fernandez, Joe P462
Fernandez, Nuria P464
Fernandez, Aurelio M P486
Fernandez, Belinda W83
Fernandez, Philip W155
Fernandez, Felipe W172
Fernandez, Ramon W372
Fernandez, Bacil W393
Fernandez, Felix E70
Fernandez, Henry E282
Fernandez-Carbajal, Francisco A839
Fernando, Meg P544
Ferniany, Will P615
Fernkorn, Thomas W108
Fernndez-Combarro, Javier W444
Feroce, Anthony P164
Ferraby, Stephen W166
Ferrante, Sharon P552
Ferranti, Richard P445
Ferrara, Jose W493
Ferrari, Daniele A411

Ferrari, Mauro P336
Ferrari, Giorgio W144
Ferraro, Joseph A87
Ferraro, John A426:A494
Ferraro, Maria W444
Ferre, Daniele W511
Ferreira, Melissa P41
Ferreira, Deborah P434
Ferreira, Laurent W341
Ferreira, Eduardo W380
Ferrell, Tyler P91
Ferrell, Ronnie P212
Ferrer, Fernando A553
Ferrer, Javier A633
Ferrer, Fernando P338:P370
Ferrer, Antonio Garcia W9
Ferreras, Beatriz Puente W444
Ferreri, Anthony C P519
Ferrero, Jennifer A696
Ferrero, Pablo A705
Ferrier, Andrew W527
Ferris, Stephanie A304
Ferris, Samuel A779
Ferris, Richard J P414
Ferris, Samuel P567
Ferris, Jim P587
Ferriss, Stephen A695
Ferrucci, Wendy P633
Ferrufino, Jimena P112
Ferry, Thomas P19
Fesette, Neil A210:E95
Fesko, Frankie P146
Fesko, Frankie L P359
Fesko, Donald E161
Fess, Darryl A136
Fessenden, Daniel A789
Festa, Alfred A578
Fetch, Bonnie A228
Feteira, Kelly P60
Fetsko, Francis A789
Fetter, Trevor A377
Fetterman, John A208:P146
Fetterman, Jean P226
Fetterolf, Brian A795:E416
Fettig, Jeff A708
Feuer, Bradley A P61
Feuer, Michael J P560
Few, Jason A495
Feygin, Anatol A168
Fiala, Robert A773
Fichter, Darren W100
Fichuk, Karen W397
Fick, Daniel A412
Fick, Jeffrey A660
Fick, Daniel P258
Fick, Jeffrey E356
Fick, Nathaniel E392
Fiddelke, Michael J A761
Fiddler, Lori P437
Fidler, Deborah P143
Fiedelman, Cindy E120
Fiedler, Michael P175
Fiedler-kelly, Jill E375
Field, Douglas A333
Field, Darren A408
Field, James A655
Field, Aaron P22
Field, Lorne P157
Field, Scott P601
Field, Dale E126
Field, James E340
Fielder, Penny P438
Fieldly, John E74
Fields, Mark A328
Fields, Warren A416
Fields, Mark A657
Fields, Karin P211
Fields, Dana P426
Fields, Joe P489
Fields, Deborah P618
Fields, Janice W25
Fields, Warren E226
Fields, Venita E398
Fieler, Anna E343
Fieman, Richard A583
Fier, Walter A228
Fierens, Lou A794:P599

Fierro, Martha A154
Fife, Jordan P75
Fife, Heather P319
Fifer, Joseph J P494
Fighs, Charles P486
Figler, Christine P506
Figliuolo, Stephen A326:E177
Fignar, Robert A597:E307
Figoli, Darla A871
Figora, Luke P389
Figueiredo, Joao de A274
Figueiredo, Andre W513
Figueras, David Vegara W57
Figuereo, Juan A857:E116:E447
Figueroa, Domingo A210
Figueroa, Alex A647
Figueroa, John A673
Figueroa, Regina P332
Figueroa, Alex P429
Figueroa, Pablo T P505
Figueroa, Julio Santiago W56
Fijol, Emily P394
Fike, Carin A461
Fike, Andrea M P39
Filaretos, Spyros W27
File, William A186:E84
Filho, Milton Maluhy W255
Filho, Rodrigo W309
Filho, Eduardo De Oliveira Rodrigues W513
Filho, Paulo De Brito E37
Fili-Krushel, Patricia A174:A252
Filiberto, Ruth A329
Filingeri, Stephen P251
Filippin, William E96
Filipps, Frank E346
Filizetti, Gary P188
Filler, James A707:E368
Filliol, Oliver E277
Filotei, Ashley P419
Filton, Steve A824
Finale, James P99
Finberg, Robert P609
Finch, Norman A415
Finch, Bill P594
Finch, Steven W308:E16
Finchem, Timothy W P414
Fincher, Kyle P549
Findlay, D. Cameron A68
Findlay, David A466
Findlay, Michael W413
Findlay, David E244
Findley, Darren E352
Fine, Peter S A102
Fine, Marc A353
Fine, Peter S P56
Fine, David J P114
Fine, Patrick C P211
Fine, Janis P305
Fine, Michael H P447
Fine, Marc E192
Fine, Debra E197
Fine, W. Morris E235
Fine, James E235
Fine, Lauren E364
Fines, Robert E159
Finger, April P112
Fini, Salvatore De A48
Fink, Laurence A120
Fink, Nicholas A218
Fink, Anne A244
Fink, Nicholas A335
Fink, M. Kathryn A749
Fink, Marvin E354
Fink, Steven E393
Finke, Daniel A232
Finkel, Steven I P438
Finkelstein, David A62
Finkelstein, Mark A201:E92
Finley, Tammy A12:A49
Finley, John A121
Finley, Jack A126
Finley, Brett A335
Finley, Wayne P161
Finley, Lowell P247
Finley, Tammy E21
Finley, Jack E54

HOOVER'S HANDBOOK OF EMERGING COMPANIES 2022

519

COMBINED HOOVER'S HANDBOOK INDEX OF EXECUTIVES

A = AMERICAN BUSINESS
E = EMERGING COMPANIES
P = PRIVATE COMPANIES
W = WORLD BUSINESS

Finn, Christopher A152
Finn, John A367
Finn, Barry A587
Finn, Brenda P196
Finn, Chris E182
Finn, Barry E302
Finn, Gaylyn E361
Finnell, Scott E160
Finneran, John A148
Finnerty, Corinne A315:E167
Finnerty, Kevin E291
Finney, Perry E194
Finney, Elisha E273
Finnorn, Peter P262
Fino, Lisa P536
Finol, Ana P341
Finucane, Anne A865
Fiol, Maribel P356
Fioranelli, Marcelo A24:P13
Fioravanti, Mark P454
Fioravanti, Nicola W251
Fiordalice, Robert E304
Fiore, Timothy A689
Fiore, Anthony A778:P561
Fiorentino, Michele A91
Fiori, Kevin P526
Fiori, Silvia W181
Fiorile, Michael A733
Fiorini, Monica P643
Fiorito, Brittany P158
Fireman, Cassie P311
Firestone, James A361
Firestone, Fred P162
Firestone, Brooks P169
Firth, John E377
Fisackerly, Haley A277
Fisch, Harry E435
Fisch, David E456
Fischer, David A418:A520
Fischer, Mark A655
Fischer, Steve P71
Fischer, Danny P72
Fischer, Russell E P246
Fischer, Greg P304
Fischer, Robert P368
Fischer, Jennifer P402
Fischer, Stanley W63
Fischer, Sam W165
Fischer, Rudolf W425
Fischer, Tamara E124
Fischer, Jason A E282
Fischer, Jonathan E409
Fisette, Jay P156
Fish, James A848
Fish, Nick P131
Fish, Mark P360
Fish, Nate P438
Fish, John P523
Fish, Warren W200
Fishbein, Daniel W465
Fishel, Brian A453
Fisher, Daniel A92
Fisher, Tiffanie A135
Fisher, Rich A162
Fisher, E. Beauregarde A197
Fisher, Dan A266
Fisher, Michael A320
Fisher, Joe A546
Fisher, Mark A746
Fisher, Richard A765
Fisher, Robert A777
Fisher, John A777
Fisher, Mary A866
Fisher, Kyle P147
Fisher, Bill P165
Fisher, Orlan P264
Fisher, Mark P330
Fisher, Jade P400
Fisher, Michelle P416
Fisher, Caryn P455
Fisher, Michael P507

Fisher, William J P566
Fisher, Patricia P605
Fisher, Joann P616
Fisher, Jennifer P652
Fisher, Mary P657
Fisher, Stephen E101
Fisher, Helene E122
Fisher, Gregory E136
Fisher, Michael E172
Fisher, Brian E348
Fishman, Alan A465:A695
Fisk, John A22
Fisk, Jane P506
Fister, Todd A601
Fitch, Carl P650
Fitch, Laurie Lee W173
Fitt, Lawton A645
Fitterling, James A3
Fitzgerald, Joseph A132
Fitzgerald, Margaret Boles A136
Fitzgerald, Larry A244
FitzGerald, Emma A558
Fitzgerald, Michael A814
Fitzgerald, Mike P219
Fitzgerald, Michael P234:E423
Fitzgerald, Gary P448
Fitzgibbons, Michael A A594
Fitzgibbons, Carol A P262
Fitzgibbons, Carol P262
Fitzgibbons, Michael A P397
Fitzgibbons, Patrick L P506
Fitzgibbons, Timothy P P609
Fitzmaurice, Michael A503:P317
Fitzpatrick, Michael A582
Fitzpatrick, Mike P545
Fitzpatrick, Michael G P553
FitzPatrick, Mark W391
Fitzpatrick, Edward E73
Fitzpatrick, Michael E301
Fitzsimmons, Ellen A40:A796
Fitzsimmons, Robert A853
Fitzsimmons, Bill P152
Fitzsimmons, Rhiannon P276
Fitzsimmons, Katie P381
Fitzsimmons, Robert E445
Fitzsimons, Patricia Sue P660
Fix, Judy P301
Fjell, Olav E137
Flack, Shenoa P454
Flaherty, Lauren A138
Flaherty, Scott E449
Flaks, Jeffrey A P242:P243
Flament, Ashley P233
Flamholz, Sam P84
Flamini, Beth P67
Flaminia, Alinka E62
Flanagan, David A144
Flanagan, Peggy A737:P513
Flanagan, Patrick P535
Flanagan, Dennis P643
Flanagan, Timothy E197
Flanagan, Joseph E344
Flanagan, Robert E443
Flandry, Rob P493
Flanigan, John A16:P8
Flannelly, Barry E225
Flannery, Matthew A820
Flannery, Robert P632
Flannery, Mark P644
Flannery, Patrick E383
Flanscha, Janelle P278
Flatt, James W94
Flattery, Bill P100
Flattery, William J P100
Flaugher, Brett A588
Flavel, Peter W345
Flavell, David A619
Flavin, Lisa A273
Fleche, Eric La W322
Fleischer, Spencer A476:A477:P297
Fleischer, Michael R P594
Fleischut, Peter M A780:P572
Fleming, Richard A125
Fleming, Jeff A317
Fleming, William A406
Fleming, Susan A680
Fleming, Gerald P107

Fleming, Daryl P151
Fleming, Nancy P184
Fleming, Stan P361
Fleming, Dave P526
Fleming, Jeff E170
Fleming, Susan E356:E441
Flescher, Mark P373
Fleshood, John A793:E414
Flessas, Elias P298
Flessner, Kyle A771
Fletcher, Jeremy A579
Fletcher, Robert A749
Fletcher, Eric P321
Fletcher, Gary P507
Fletcher, Arlen M P619
Fletcher, John P658
Fletcher, Annette P662
Fletcher, Bruce W345
Fletcher, Thomas E184
Fletcher, Nick E246
Fletcher, Steven E248
Fletcher, Gerald E327
Fleurant, Jacques W233
Fleury, Alison J P477:P478
Fleurycurado, Frederico
  Pinheiro W506
Flexon, Robert A623
Flint, Deborah A398
Flint, Gavin T A541
Flint, Loring P263
Flitman, David A139
Flitman, David E P351
Flive, Michael P580
Flocco, Theodore A676
Floel, Martina W346:W421
Floerke, Gregory A541
Flood, Rory P426
Florance, Andrew E104
Florence, John A721
Flores, Rafael A40
Flores, Nancy A204
Flores, Sol A736
Flores, Jeanne P105
Flores, Anita M P133
Flores, Dominic P135
Flores, Leticia P202
Flores, Alison P228
Flores, Cassandra P259
Flores, Anne P387
Flores, Dr Steven P451
Flores, Sol P512
Flores, Alberto P578
Flores, Hala P647
Flores, Andre W83
Flores, Jose Antonio Gonzalez W109
Flores, Jana E69
Florey, Reinhard W371
Floriani, Kimberly A188
Florin, Daniel E36
Floris, Karla P272
Florness, Daniel A295
Flournoy, Michele A129
Flournoy, Mark A429
Flowers, Cedric A258
Flowers, Chip A735
Flowers, Dionne P134
Flowers, Andrea P418
Flowers, Chip P511
Flowers, Oscar P601
Flowers, Debbie P661
Floyd, Jennifer A393
Floyd, H. Charles A459
Floyd, Amber P128
Floyd, Kathleen P357
Floyd, Brian P418
Floyd, Jay P488
Floyd, Nancy E206
Floyd, Jennifer E217
Fluck, Michael P158
Fluhler, Stephan A320:E172
Flum, Joshua A232
Flur, Dorlisa E213
Fly, Emerson H P629
Flynn, Thomas A381
Flynn, Brian A466
Flynn, Julie M A541
Flynn, Brian A797

Flynn, James P137
Flynn, Elaine P343
Flynn, Heather P590
Flynn, Delisle P648
Flynn, Lisa P648
Flynn, Patrick W51
Flynn, Paul E117
Flynn, Thomas E208
Flynn, Peter E240
Flynn, Brian E243
Flynton, Brian P481
Foad, Jonathan P452
Foad, Keiran W61
Foellmer, Frank P530:P531
Fogarasi, Stephen P406
Fogarty, James A236
Fogarty, Ann A743
Fogel, Richard A74
Fogel, Glenn A128
Fogel, Arthur A483
Fogel, Richard A43
Fogelman, Bella P452
Fogle, Angel P135
Foglia, Lori E110
Fohey, Lisa P116
Fok, Canning W111
Fok, Winnie W446
Foletta, Mark E117
Foley, Christopher A146
Foley, William P A303
Foley, Todd A461
Foley, Brendan A508
Foley, Ursuline A648
Foley, Mike A738
Foley, Donald A866
Foley, Siobhan P129
Foley, Dan P164
Foley, M Kaye P382
Foley, Mike P514
Foley, D Sue P578
Foley, Donald P657
Foley, Isabel W145
Folgado, Nicolas P112
Folger, Sherrie P496
Folke, John R P81
Folkins, Brad P445
Folks, John P387
Folkwein, Kristy A68
Folland, Nick W311
Follens, Geert W48
Folliard, Thomas A154
Follis, Bob P247
Follmer, Cathy P332
Follten, Cathy P589
Folmar, Brett P534
Folsom, Suzanne A625
Foltz, Stephanie P410
Fong, Ivan A3
Fong, Kenny P306
Fong, Christopher W100
Fong, Kar Chun W115
Fong, David W507
Fong, Ivan E73
Fonner, Keenan A867
Fonseca, Dhiren A26
Fonseca, Lidia A622
Fonseca, Cristina W206
Fontaine, Thomas A143
Fontaine, Alyssa A789
Fontaine, Thomas E65
Fontana, Bernard W489
Fontbona, Jean Paul Luksic W56
Fontenot, Teri E252
Fonticiella, Nelson P457
Foo, Chok-Pin P311
Foo, Jixun W54
Foody, Amy P217
Foong, Seong Yew W307
Foote, James A227
Foote, Robert P69
Foras, Tanya De A418
Forbes, John E314
Ford, Robert A4
Ford, Joseph A94
Ford, William A120
Ford, Beth A120
Ford, William A333

COMBINED HOOVER'S HANDBOOK INDEX OF EXECUTIVES

Ford, Gerald A388
Ford, Jeremy A388
Ford, Monte A439
Ford, Sam A726
Ford, Kayce A726
Ford, Darrell A819
Ford, Tracy P72
Ford, Kale P107
Ford, Jeff P121
Ford, Shirley P128
Ford, Shelby P175
Ford, George P186
Ford, Michael P194
Ford, Kevin P234
Ford, Carmen P248
Ford, John P317
Ford, Gary P336
Ford, Tim P382
Ford, Michelle P569
Ford, Patrick P597
Ford, William R P654
Ford, James W210
Ford, Monte E11
Ford, Joseph E44
Forde, Terry P6
Fordham, Benjamin A211
Fordyce, L.Chris E174
Fore, Jack P55
Forese, Laura P372
Forese, James W234
Forgeur, Randy P26
Forino, Amiann P171
Forlenza, Vincent A536
Forlenza, Joseph A701:E365
Forman, Charles P261
Forman, Alan E42
Formanek, David W281
Formby, Michael D P121
Formoso, Lorenzo W417
Fornaro, Alberto A574
Fornes, Maite W400
Forney, Stephen P174
Forrest, Eric A201
Forrest, Yvette P270
Forrest, Andrew W200
Forrest, Eric E92
Forrester, Traci A188
Forrester, Meredith A754
Forrester, Raeshell P157
Forrester, Meredith E401
Forsberg, Mattias W470
Forshee, Greg P16
Forssell, Johan W48
Forst, Rita W266
Forster, Ann P472
Forsyte, Carol E9
Forsyth, John A106
Forsythe, Randy P104
Forsythe, Gerald E68
Forsythe, Patrick E191
Fort, John E352
Fortanet, Francisco A426
Forte, Andrew E297
Fortenberry, Brian P256
Forthman, Thane P218
Forthman, Michael A P225
Forti-Sciarrino, Ann P124
Fortier, Joella E A208:P146
Fortin, Richard W25
Fortin, Anne W250
Fortin, Michael E287
Fortkiewicz, Victor E381
Fortunato, Joseph A729
Fortwangler, Robert P93
Fosburgh, Bryn E415
Foschi, Marianella E85
Fosha, Joel P261
Foshee, William A707:E368
Foskett, Christopher A325
Fosler, Alan A811
Foss, David A194
Foss, Peter E207
Fossett, Mike P160
Fossett, Sheryl P315
Fossey, Emily P52
Foster, Sara A206
Foster, Byron A234

Foster, David A264
Foster, Jon A379
Foster, Vincent A658
Foster, Paul L A824
Foster, John A866
Foster, Nancy A870
Foster, Gordon K P54
Foster, Bob P127
Foster, Robert G P127
Foster, David P200
Foster, Kevin P228
Foster, Janet P298
Foster, Jennifer P321
Foster, Scott P529
Foster, Eric P530:P531
Foster, Eric M P531
Foster, Effie P627
Foster, Paul L P630
Foster, Ronald E6
Foster, James E79
Foster, Edward E409
Foster, John E450
Foster, Nancy E454
Fotheringham, John A160
Foti, Joseph C P319
Foto, Bonnie A583:P393
Fouberg, Robert A232
Fouche, Fonda P170
Foulke, Ken P608
Foulkes, David A138
Foulkes, Anne A636
Foulon, Hugues W372
Fountain, T. Heath E91
Fouque, Jorge Armando
  Andueza W33:W177
Fouquet, Christophe W42
Fournier, Shawn P162
Fournier, Dave P392
Fournier, Michele P406
Fouse, Jacqualyn E225
Fowler, Fred A238
Fowler, Bryan A257
Fowler, W. A280
Fowler, Robin A327
Fowler, Hardy A372
Fowler, Paul B A512
Fowler, William A737
Fowler, Peggy A809
Fowler, Lisa P6
Fowler, W Randall P206
Fowler, Robin P215
Fowler, Paul B P324
Fowler, Milton P330
Fowler, W Randall P342
Fowler, James C P392
Fowler, Jim P392
Fowler, Ashley P432
Fowler, William P513
Fox, George A24
Fox, Kevin A80
Fox, Matt A215
Fox, Ann A243
Fox, Len A291
Fox, James M A291
Fox, George P13
Fox, Devin P19
Fox, Hannah P52
Fox, John P68
Fox, Anthony P135
Fox, John T P205
Fox, James M P210
Fox, Rebecca P282
Fox, Jamie P368
Fox, Cary P396
Fox, Joanne P553
Fox, Kelly P577
Fox, Susan P655
Fox, Carrie E85
Fox, Richard E147
Fox, Benjamin E347
Fox, Jason E443
Foxx, Anthony A501
Foy, Douglas E19
Foye, Patrick P338
Fraccaro, Michael A506
Fraczkowski, Kurt A203:P144
Fradella, Kathleen P406

Fradin, Roger A463
Fradkin, Steven A567
Fragante, Leo W323
Fragnoli, Joseph E257
Frailey, Alton A724
Fraim, Darren P535
Frain, Diane P255
Fraioli, Edward A339
Fraley, Alton P282
Fralick, Julie P529
Frame, Catherine A266
Frame, Clark E83
Frampton, Marcus A27:P14
Franca, Adam P475
France, Robert A221
France, Gina A409
Franceschini, Luca W185
Francese, James E388
Franchini, Roberto W251
Francioli, Richard W517
Francis, Julian A108
Francis, Matt A343
Francis, Jamie P3
Francis, Jerry P102
Francis, Patricia P207
Francis, David E235
Francis, Richard E252
Francis, Cheryl E280
Francisco, Eduardo W83
Franco, Juan David Escobar W61
Franco, Jorge Elman Osorio W171
Francoeur, Bruno W466
Francois, Karen P167
Frandsen, Michele P499
Franey, Henry J P623
Frank, Kenneth A51
Frank, Edward A61
Frank, Barney A710
Frank, Elizabeth A728:P28
Frank, Brett P278
Frank, Elizabeth P496
Frank, Robert P625
Frank, Trisha E10
Frank, Thomas E235
Frank, Suzanna E248
Frank, Barney E371
Frank, Howard E387
Franke, Mary Carter A716
Franke, Carsten W3
Franke, Mary Carter E379
Frankel, Bonnie P185
Frankel, Paul P630
Frankel, Michael E353
Frankenberg, David P43
Frankenberger, Tony A511:P322
Frankiw, Allan W100
Franklin, Jerry A617
Franklin, Matthew A688
Franklin, Martin E P39
Franklin, Carol P256
Franklin, Shaun P535
Franklin, Katherine E146
Franklin, Christopher E147
Franklin, Jerry E319
Franklin, Heather E455
Frankola, James E27
Frankova, Daniela P102
Frantz, Mark E32
Franz, Arnd A484
Franz, Bob P165
Franz, Christoph W408:W543
Franzese, Yvonne A194
Franzetti, Daniel A192
Franzi, Cristiano A106
Frasch, Ronald E110
Fraschetti, Robert P506
Fraser, Liz A759
Fraser, Jason A831
Fraser, Michael P300
Fraser, James W399
Frasier, Tim A681:P448
Frater, Hugh A293
Frauenberg, James E77
Fravel, Cynthia D E52
Frawley, Rev Patrick J A554:P372
Frazell, Chad A155
Frazer, Preston A84

Frazier, Larry A366
Frazier, Kenneth A515
Frazier, Randy P124
Frazier, Karen P424
Frazier, Aletta P623
Frede, Mike P218
Frederick, Wayne A406
Frederick, Francie A A824
Frederick, Dwayne P562
Frederick, Francie A P630
Frederick, Wayne E233
Frederick, William E375
Frederick-Otool, Cecilia P408
Fredericks, Mark A465
Fredericks, Raymond P272
Fredericks, Mark E243
Frederickson, Philip A277
Fredman, Sheara A360
Fredrick, Marie P646
Fredricks, Jessica P421
Fredrickson, David W46
Fredrikson, Glen W324
Fredriksson, Marika W514
Free, Laura A552:P369
Free, Nancy P463
Freeburne, Christopher A735:P511
Freed, Robert P159
Freed, Robert L P641
Freed, Chad E391
Freedman, Paul A17
Freedman, Barry P17
Freedman, Stephen P217
Freeland, Clint A539
Freeman, Kevin A584
Freeman, Angela A683
Freeman, Bradford A722
Freeman, Randall J P85
Freeman, Dena P326
Freeman, Amy P334
Freeman, Chris P368
Freeman, Jim P609
Freeman, Dan P618
Freeman, Dave P659
Freeman, Thomas E84
Freeman, Robert E133
Freemer, Mark E133
Freer, Rudell S P302
Frei, Maye A642
Freidkin, Steven A261:E126
Freigang, Julie Scheck A400:E218
Freire, Maria E13:E150
Freitag, Randal A480
Freitag, Kristine P508
Freitas, Jorge Manuel Seabra de W206
Freixe, Laurent W348
Freleng, Andrew P171
French, Tracy A393
French, Robert W P214
French, Terry P473
French, Richard G P526
French, Hadley Mack P657
French, Reid E38
French, Tracy E217
French, Melissa E326
Freni, Charles A P108
Frenkiel, Paul A774:E408
Frenzel, Robert A610
Frenzel, Bob A871
Frerichs, Michael A736:P512
Frerichs, Robert E417
Frese, Kyle P139
Frese, Mark W219
Freshour, Kris P141
Fretwell, Betsy P127
Fretwell, Roger P222
Freudberg, Dan P337
Freund, Brin P20
Freund, Amy P540
Frew, Anita W410
Frey, Kirsten A387
Frey, Daniel A792
Frey, Jacob P128
Frey, Daniel P152
Frey, James P337
Frey, Kathy P406
Frey, Andrew E98
Freyman, Thomas A6:A767

COMBINED HOOVER'S HANDBOOK INDEX OF EXECUTIVES

```
A = AMERICAN BUSINESS
E = EMERGING COMPANIES
P = PRIVATE COMPANIES
W = WORLD BUSINESS
```

Freyne, Colm W465
Freyou, Jason A392:E216
Freytag, Svend A381:P249
Frias, James A575
Frias, Yanela C A648
Friberg, Alan P393
Friberg, Therese W3
Fribourg, Paul A486
Frick, David W348
Fricke, Craig P184
Fridriksdottir, Hafrun W487
Fried, Arthur P519
Frieden, Robert P227
Friedhoff, Gary P617
Friedlander, Eri C P304
Friedman, Alexander A336
Friedman, Brian A437
Friedman, Stacey A444
Friedman, Howard A635:A713
Friedman, Michael A739
Friedman, Amy P89
Friedman, Michael A P126
Friedman, Stephen J P403
Friedman, Michael P515
Friedman, Hanan W64
Friedman, Joel E142
Friedrich, Amy A641
Friel, Robert E446
Friend, Matthew A563:A813
Frier, Rick P537
Fries, James P182
Fries, Lloyd P283
Fries, Robert P468
Friesen, Glenda P92
Friesen, Carol P401
Frieson, Donald A488
Friestad, Jan W454
Frigerio, Dario W294
Friis, Mark A693
Friis, Morten W345
Friis, Mark E360
Frinzi, Thomas E388
Frisancho, Ariel P103
Frisch, Scott P2
Friscia, Anthony E182
Frisk, Patrik A810
Frist, William A703
Friston, Paul W311
Friton, Frederick P203
Fritz, Lance A609:A812
Fritz, Amanda P131
Fritz, George P542
Fritz, Debbie P595
Fritz, Sandra W521
Fritz, Erich E43
Fritz, Connie E69
Fritze, Steven E309
Fritzinger, Liz A638:P426
Froc, Jay W100
Frockt, Daniel P304
Frodella, Christine A824:P617
Froedge, James A273
Froehlich, Ephraim A734
Froehlich, Patti P220
Froehlich, Ephraim P510
Froehlich, Mark P640
Froetscher, Janet E73
Frogue, Barbara P296
Frohning, Andrea A611
Frol, Alan P533
Froman, Michael A506
Frome, James E385
Froment-Curtil, Alex W520
Fromm, Daniel A291:P210
Frommelt, Michele P116
Fronek, Zdenka P478
Frontz, Arlene A614
Fronzo, Pascal Di E38
Frosdal, Katarina Berner W471
Frost, Patrick A227
Frost, James A800

Frost, Sue P168
Frost, Donald E394
Fruchter, Bruce P123
Fruehauf, Richard A821
Fruhling, Julian L P254
Fruit, Molly A68
Frum, David P496
Fry, Earl A164
Fry, Stephen A478
Fry, Patrick A750
Fry, Brad A799
Fry, Kenneth P456
Fry, Patrick P528
Fry, Patrick E P529
Fry, Cynthia P599
Fry, Brad P605
Fry, Todd E231
Fry, William E284
Frye, Andrew A106
Frye, Patrick A749:E394
Frymier, Matthew E332
Frändberg, Sofia W523
Fson, Tami P479
Fu, Hai P585
Fu, Q yang W236
Fu, Bin W287
Fu, Ming W303
Fuangfu, Chansak W62
Fubasami, Seiichi W494
Fuchs, Christine A143
Fuchs, Mary Ann P197
Fuchs, Michael P507
Fuchs, Kent P619
Fuchs, Jaroslaw W70
Fuchs, Christine E65
Fuchs, Matthew E308
Fuda, Domenic W232
Fuder, Andrea W523
Fuente, Lidice La P155
Fuente, Juan Antonio Garcia W444
Fuentes, Laura A389
Fuentes, Miguel P89
Fuentes, Felipe P169
Fuentes, Domingo P180
Fuentes, Anna E152
Fugate, W. Craig A623
Fuhr, Matthew A374
Fuhrman, Stephen E P109
Fuhrman, Cathy P294
Fujibayashi, Kiyotaka W331
Fujii, Hideaki P32
Fujii, Hiroshi W52
Fujii, Ichiro W288
Fujii, Mariko W330
Fujimori, Yoshiaki A132
Fujimori, Shun W255
Fujimoto, Blenn A164
Fujimoto, Tomoko W237
Fujimoto, Junichi W288
Fujimoto, Masayoshi W450
Fujimura, Akihiko W237
Fujimura, Hiroshi W436
Fujisaki, Kazuo W272
Fujita, Motohiro W14
Fujita, Kazuko W289
Fujitani, Kazuaki W158
Fujiwara, Ichiro W68
Fujiwara, Satoru W237
Fujiwara, Kiyoshi W314
Fujiwara, Ken W324
Fujiwara, Masataka W375
Fujiwara, Takashi W491
Fujiyama, Ian A129
Fukai, Akihiko W216
Fukakusa, Janice W94
Fukasawa, Yuji W170
Fukaya, Toshinari W373
Fuks, Barb A458:P287
Fukuda, Masahito W334
Fukuda, Tomiaki W377
Fukuda, Takayuki W536
Fukui, Toshihiko W437
Fukui, Akira W536
Fukujin, Yusuke W23
Fukunaga, Carol P121
Fukunaga, Mark H P474

Fukunaga, Takehisa W52
Fukushima, Sakie W289
Fukutome, Akihiro W463
Fulgencio, Kennia P408
Fulkerson, Rick P225
Fuller, Daniel A147
Fuller, Andrew A165
Fuller, Lynn A381
Fuller, Julie A655
Fuller, Michael A707
Fuller, Rodger A721
Fuller, Jacqui A867
Fuller, Gary P195
Fuller, James E P358
Fuller, Ernie P387
Fuller, Tom P399
Fuller, Jo P473
Fuller, Shirani P565
Fuller, Debbie P569
Fuller, Will W13
Fuller, David W213
Fuller, Daniel E65
Fuller, David E98
Fuller, Samuel E180
Fuller, Robert E188
Fuller, Lynn E208
Fuller, Gilbert E366
Fuller, Michael E368
Fullerton, Clifford T A106:P64
Fullmer, Richard A P630
Fulmer, James A789
Fulton, Laura A760
Fulton, Liz P75
Fulton, Tricia E209
Fults, Dennis A512:P327
Fulwiler, Terrence A562:E293
Funaki, Ryuichiro W339
Funamoto, Kaoru W228
Funck, Robert A4
Funderburk, Terry L P155
Fung, David P616
Funk, Charles A531
Funk, Lee A837
Funk, Jane A855
Funk, Charles E276
Funk, Jane E445
Funke, Matthew A723:E383
Funo, Yuji W418
Furbee, Charles W A299
Furber, Jeffrey E388
Furey, Jessica P360
Furey, John E99
Furlong, Matt A343
Furlong, John W101
Furlow, Brenda E50
Furman, Matthew A115
Furman, Abraham P399
Furmanski, Rick P157
Furner, John A844
Furnstahl, Lawrence J P399
Furr, William A388
Furr, Joseph S A702
Furst, Branko P16
Furstenberg, Alexander von A288
Furticella, Edward E161
Furukawa, Koji W268
Furukawa, Shuntaro W351
Furumoto, Shozo W354
Furuya, Hiromichi W127
Furuya, Takayuki W313
Fusco, Jack A168:A169
Fusco, Art P107
Fusco, Vincent P440
Fusco, Vince P440
Fusco, Donald P483
Fusler, Mark E72
Futter, Ellen A216:E149
Fux, Michael P340
Fyfe, Kitty P267

G

Gabanna, Louis W133
Gabbay, Mark A443
Gabbay, Yoram W64
Gabel, Tim P443

Gabelli, Mario E253
Gabilondo, Natalia F P333
Gable, Steve A339
Gable, Davida A418
Gable, Melissa P162
Gabosch, Bradley A584
Gabow, Patricia P187
Gabriel, Jamie A278
Gabriel, Nicholas A776:P558
Gabriel, Jamie E141
Gabriele, Denise P305
Gabrielson, Sharon E368
Gachassin, Nicholas E252
Gadberry, Kirk P379
Gadberry, Shane P616
Gadd, Simon W291
Gadde, Vijaya A801
Gadiesh, Orit W426
Gadis, David L P184
Gadola, Marco W166
Gadomski, Marcin W71
Gaemperle, Chantal W301
Gaer, Steven A855:E445
Gaertner, Susan P167
Gaeta, Mary P87
Gaeta, Gillian P443
Gaffaney, Amanda P384
Gaffke, Jeanine E42
Gaffney, Paul A459
Gaffney, Sean E4
Gagan, Sohail P528
Gage, Michelle A A50
Gage, Kevin P580
Gaggini, Stefano E362
Gagle, Suzanne A496:A541
Gaglia, Philip E319:E171
Gagliardi, Theresa P53
Gagne, Paul A772
Gagne, Simon W176
Gagne-Giuffo, Alicia P644
Gagnier, Craig P85
Gagnon, Indhira P123
Gagnon, Louis W250
Gagnon, Martin W341
Gagua, Irina P231
Gahan, Kevin P146
Gahlhoff, Jerry E388
Gaibi, Maryam P644
Gaillard, Timothy P51
Gainer, Glen A741:P518
Gaines, Harold P124
Gaines, Ted P468
Gaines, Elizabeth W200
Gainor, John E359
Gaither, J Michael P34
Gaither, Shawny P147
Gaither, Chris P445
Galainena, M. David A385:A778:P561
Galante, Edward A160:A496
Galante, Joseph A628:E324
Galanti, Richard A223
Galarneau, Clayton P342
Galat, David P132
Galaviz, Paula G P223
Galaviz, Paula P223
Galbato, Chan A28:P18
Galbo, Julie W135
Galbraith, John F P103
Galbreath, Kristen P638
Galdes, Alphonse A118
Galdieri, Lou P353
Gale, Melvin P73
Gale, Ginny P354
Gales, Amy A296:E157
Galey, Robin P624
Galford, Robert E182
Galhotra, Ashwani A333
Galifi, Vincent W306
Galik, Milan E235
Galilee, Brenda E263
Galindo, Sonia A448
Galindo, Thomas A603:A603
Galindo, Norma Sierra P261
Galindo, Susan P381
Galindo, Thomas P404:E310
Galioto, Frank A187:P131

COMBINED HOOVER'S HANDBOOK INDEX OF EXECUTIVES

Galita, Gina Marie W83
Gall, A. David W340
Gall, Jeffrey E300
Gall-Robinson, Claire Le W428
Galla, Leah A837
Gallagher, Phil A88
Gallagher, Matthew A171
Gallagher, Michael A278
Gallagher, J. Patrick A341
Gallagher, Paul A348
Gallagher, Marie A619
Gallagher, Matthew A629
Gallagher, Terence A647
Gallagher, Hugh A806
Gallagher, Karen C P40
Gallagher, Sally P116
Gallagher, John J P166
Gallagher, Carol P292
Gallagher, Gerald P387
Gallagher, Paul P407
Gallagher, Dan P590
Gallagher, Candice P615
Gallagher, James W308
Gallagher, Michael E141
Gallahue, Kieran A269
Gallant, Brad P309
Galle, Jean-Loic W488
Gallego, Kate P131
Gallego, Emilio Garcia W9
Gallego, Monica Lopez-Monis W61
Gallegos, Tess P35
Gallello, Frank P364
Galler, Shelia P440
Galletti, Sarah E219
Galletti, Salvatore E219
Gallienne, Ian W12
Gallina, John A63
Gallion, Brett E111
Gallo, Anthony A864:P656
Gallo, Jose W506
Gallo, Ralph E312
Gallo-Aquino, Cristina A689
Gallopoulos, Gregory A345
Galloway, Ian A48
Galloway, Carol Mims P126
Galloway, Robert C P246
Galuchie, John E20
Galusha, Larry P26
Galvan, Roxann P441
Galvanoni, Matthew A627
Galvez, Jean-Marc A114
Galvez, Jose Damian Bogas W179
Galvez, Jose Bogas W181
Galvin, Andrea P464
Galvin, Donal W17
Galvis, Mauricio Jaramillo W171
Galyan, Deborah P261
Gamal, Bassel W395
Gamba, Aida A134:P87
Gamba, Angela W316
Gambee, Stephen A809
Gamberini, Michele W482
Gambill, Ron A268
Gambino, Frank A727
Gamble, Robert L P364
Gamble, John E114
Gamble, Scott E164
Gamboa, Ivan A867
Gamboa, Arturo Natho W177
Gambone, David M P319
Gamez, Dianna P462
Gamgort, Robert A452
Gan, David A15
Gan, Penelope W29
Gan, Kok Kim W376
Ganas, Ashley P404
Ganatra, Tanu P540
Gandhi, Natawar A362
Gandhi, Niyum A503
Gandhi, Natawar P232
Gandhi, Niyum P317
Gandre, Tom P430
Gandy, Gayleen P233
Ganeriwala, Manju A209:P146
Ganesh, Thangavel W64
Ganey, Mahogany P242
Gangeni, Bongiwe W6

Gangestad, Nick A685
Gangi, Mike P647
Gangopadhyay, Paula P427
Gann, Sherry P490
Gannfors, John A583
Gannon, Stephen A185
Gannotta, Rick P196
Gannotta, Richard J P389
Gano, Kyle E290
Ganser, Scott P610
Gansz, Kaye Stone- E257
Gant, Janet P170
Gantcher, Nathan P603
Ganti, Anita E330
Gantner, John P449
Gantt, Greg A584
Gantt, Jim P141
Gantt, Thelma P158
Gantz, Eric E133
Gao, W. A71
Gao, Jack P28
Gao, Wenbao W88
Gao, Tongqing W118
Gao, Jie W208
Gao, Dongzhang W220
Gao, Lan W292
Gao, Lang W442
Gao, Xiaosu W442
Gao, Bingxue W541
Garabedian, Barbara P253
Garafola, Rachael P467
Garber, Alan A835
Garber, Ken P32
Garber, Scott E251
Garbiso, Sandra E86
Garcetti, Eric A186:P127
Garcia, Fabian A71
Garcia, James A102
Garcia, David A106
Garcia, Alberto A145
Garcia, Claudia A770
Garcia, Paul A823
Garcia, Teri P52
Garcia, Alex P61
Garcia, Alberto P95
Garcia, Robert P127
Garcia, Lisha P128
Garcia, Jenna P130
Garcia, Jorge P173
Garcia, Joseph P193
Garcia, Ernest C P195
Garcia, Ines V P217
Garcia, Maribel P261
Garcia, Rocio P274
Garcia, Nancy P377
Garcia, Robert P455
Garcia, Ramona P486
Garcia, Victor P493
Garcia, Claudia P541
Garcia, Jason P556
Garcia, Therese P584
Garcia, Dolly P627
Garcia, Raul P657
Garcia, Antonio Botella W9
Garcia, Belen W52
Garcia, Claudia Herrera W56
Garcia, Pedro Fontana W57
Garcia, Matias Sanchez W59
Garcia, Belen Romana W61
Garcia, Francisco Javier San Felix W61
Garcia, Jacobo Diaz W72
Garcia, Begona Elices W400
Garcia, Gloria Hernandez W444
Garcia, Fabian W510
Garcia, Roberto Newell W525
Garcia, David E48
Garcia, Thomas E116
Garcia, Luis E199
Garcia, Astrid E248
Garcia-Ansorena, Ramiro Mato W61
Garden, Edward A346
Garden, Isaac A614:E317
Gardener, Jan H P159
Gardes, Frederic W90:W133
Gardiner, Warren A422
Gardner, Jeff A514
Gardner, Steven R A603:A603

Gardner, Gerald A738
Gardner, David P69
Gardner, Lydia P166
Gardner, Elizabeth P290
Gardner, Thomas R P351
Gardner, Lisa P355
Gardner, Stephen J P364
Gardner, Steven R P404
Gardner, Gerald P514
Gardner, Paul W466
Gardner, Tracy E110
Gardner, Jeff E267
Gardner, Steven R E310
Gardy, Rebecca A146
Garen, Kirsten A793:E414
Garff, Robert P225
Garff, John P225
Garff, Matthew P225
Garfinkle, Phillip E449
Garijo, Belen W321
Garland, Greg A626
Garland, Kim A734
Garland, Linda A741
Garland, Patricia A P209
Garland, Linda P518
Garland, Lisa P610
Garland, Gregory E322
Garlich, Christopher E265
Garlock, Steve P395
Garneau, Nicolas Darveau - W239
Garner, Curtis A174
Garner, Denise A189
Garner, David A712
Garner, Brenda P457
Garner, David E373
Garnett, Becky P99
Garnett, David E206
Garnick, Murray A36
Garnier, Thierry W276
Garr, Erik E98
Garrabants, Greg A89:P54
Garrabrants, Gregory A90:E41
Garratt, John A252:A406
Garrelts, James P44
Garrett, Mark A182
Garrett, Kristine A306
Garrett, Karen A393
Garrett, F. A640
Garrett, John A724
Garrett, Steven M P168
Garrett, Matina P180
Garrett, Robert Charles P252
Garrett, Amy P362
Garrett, Mathew P399
Garrett, Mark W507
Garrett, Paula E175
Garrett, Karen E217
Garrett, Michael E229
Garrett, F. E333
Garrigues, Bernard A851
Garrigues, Brad P430
Garrish, Chris P269
Garrison, Ty A207
Garrison, Karen A638
Garrison, Denise P43
Garrison, Kathryn K P77
Garrison, Ashley P224
Garrison, Larry F P246
Garrison, Karen P426
Garrison, Heather P594
Garrison, Barrett E120
Garrity, Matthew A639
Garrity, Carolyn P167
Garrity, Paul P317
Garrity, Matthew E332
Garro, George J A663:P436
Garry, Gregor A774:E408
Garske, Steven R P550
Garsys, Lucia P161
Gartee, Brandon P578
Gartelmann, Richard A587:E302
Garten, Yael A476:A477:P297
Gartner, James A212
Gartner, Melissa P101
Gartner, Anya P115
Garton, Andrea P644
Gartside, Nicholas W337

Garvell, James R P7
Garvey, Kate P96
Garvin, Robert A852
Garvin, Gene P113
Gary, Steven P208
Garza, Marty A726
Garza, Alexander A729
Garza, Jason P123
Garza, Sylvia P136
Garza, Armando P384
Garza, Ed P461
Garza, Alexander P497
Garza, Alvaro Fernandez W22
Garza, Alfonso Garza W198
Garza, Danette E162
Gasaway, Sharilyn A408
Gascho, Dwith P256
Gascoigne, Richard E332
Gasmen, Dino W70
Gaso, Berislav W334
Gasoline, Birgit W157
Gaspar, Clay A243
Gasperment, Sophie W276
Gass, Michelle A459:A619
Gass, Kevin P411
Gassel, Helmut W246
Gasselsberger, Franz W367:W521
Gasser, Michael A367
Gassner, Peter E433
Gasta, Gary P174
Gaster, R. Scott A23
Gates, Greg A489
Gates, Anne A759
Gates, Gary P396
Gathagan, Maureen A529:E274
Gati, Toby W386
Gatland-Lightne, Cheri A735:P511
Gatons, Rhonda A320:E173
Gattei, Francesco W185
Gatten, Nathan A41
Gatti, Amerino E210
Gattoni, James A468
Gatz, Ronald F P555
Gaub, Chris P367
Gaudette, Robert A574
Gaudette, Kevin P221
Gaudiosi, Monica A807
Gauer, Traci P261
Gaughen, Patrick A390
Gaughen, Robert A390
Gaughen, Kevin A390
Gaughen, Patrick E215
Gaughen, Robert E215
Gaughen, Kevin E215
Gault, Michael P345
Gault, Chris P525
Gaume, David P442
Gaumond, Mark A129
Gaurkee, Greg P249
Gauss, Mae P45
Gaustad, Mike P522
Gaut, C. Christopher A281
Gautam, Alka A672
Gautam, Pranisha P301
Gauthier, John A672
Gauthier, Joyce V P431
Gautier, Todd A463
Gavelle, Jean-Luc A59
Gavezotti, Graziella W517
Gavgani, Bernard W87
Gavigan, John A315:E167
Gavin, Kathleen P333
Gavin, Joseph H P631
Gavin, John E123
Gavinet, Andres E13
Gavish, Yuval W253
Gavitt, Jeffrey P51
Gavrielov, Moshe W474
Gawinski, Michelle M P546
Gawlinski, Edward P536
Gawne, Berc P550
Gay, Caroline P291
Gayares, Marita Socorro W70
Gaydos, John P225
Gayle, Helene P114
Gaylor, Doug E109
Gayman, Jeffrey A597

COMBINED HOOVER'S HANDBOOK INDEX OF EXECUTIVES

A = AMERICAN BUSINESS
E = EMERGING COMPANIES
P = PRIVATE COMPANIES
W = WORLD BUSINESS

Gayman, Grant P316
Gayman, Jeffrey E307
Gaymard, Clara W152
Gayner, Thomas A497
Gaynor, Coley P120
Gaytan, Ernesto E361
Gayton, Dustin P26
Gazza, Allan A734:P510
Gazzalla, Michael P489
Gdowski, Christopher E P4
Ge, Neil W155
Ge, Dawei W432
Geagea, Joseph A172
Geale, Leanne W348
Gealogo, Noravir W70
Gear, James A463
Gearhart, G David P616
Geary, Michael A346:A621
Geary, James A750
Geary, William A854
Geary, Michael P227
Geary, William P347
Geary, Michael P412
Geary, James E394
Gebhard, Robert P93
Gebhard, Bradley P384
Gebhart, Jim R P333
Gebo, Kate A813
Gebo, Alysha P521
Gebski, Christine E349
Geddes, Dana P225
Geddes, F Michael P254
Gedge, William S P660
Geduldig, Courtney A691
Gee, E Gordon P652:P652
Geelan, John W E326
Geenen, Charles A493
Geer, Charles A371
Geer, Stacey K A640:E333
Geffner, Julia P61
Gehdauer, Margaret A736:P512
Gehlmann, Gregory A793:E414
Gehring, Dean A558
Gehringer, Eric A812
Geibel-Conrad, Patricia W227
Geiger, Steven A145
Geiger, Aaron P16
Geiger, Hillary P67
Geiger, Steven P95
Geiger, Philippa P97
Geisel, Gary A491
Geisler, Heather A381
Geisler, Gina P167
Geisler, Heather P249
Geiss, Cindy P45
Geissler, Werner A625
Geist, William E50
Geist, John E55
Gelard, Yves Le W184
Geldart, Christopher T A362:P232
Gelder, Martha Van P618
Gelfand, Joel P574
Gelfand, Edward E219
Gelinas, Raymond P594
Gellart, Kathleen P208
Geller, Warren P206
Geller, Joseph E340
Gellerstedt, Lawrence E57
Gellweiler, Arno W227
Gelman, Lawrence P193
Gelter, Paul P550
Gembler, Dawn P381
Geminn, Jason P424
Gemmill, Elizabeth E426
Gempeler, Stefan W514
Gempesaw, Conrado P498
Genco, Alessandra W294
Gendell, David E222
Gendell, Jeffrey E222
Gendelman, Berry P148
Gendron, Teresa A437

Gendron, Paul E228
Gendron, Robert E438
Genereux, Scott A685
Genereux, Claude W213
Genereux, Nathalie W341
Genereux, Claude W389
Genest, Paul W389
Geng, Litang W220
Geng er, Randy P399
Genis, Olivier W174
Gennaro, Dennis De A797
Genoa, Gabriele Galateri di W43
Genovese, Anthony P89
Genrich, Stephanie A736:P512
Genshaft, Neil P222
Gensler, Christopher P172
Genster, Grit W204
Genter, Robert A698
Gentilcore, James E140
Gentile, Thomas A609
Gentile, Michael P261
Gentry, Michael A706
Gentry, Kelley P217
Gentry, Craig P316
Gentry, Michael P473
Gentzkow, Paul P682
Geoga, Douglas G P210
Geoghegan, Basil W17
George, Gary A408
George, Mark A566
George, Georgette A750
George, Brian A P19
George, Kimberly D P19
George, Richard P62
George, Dennis St P184
George, Carl St P225
George, William S P246
George, Denise P246
George, Peter P395
George, Bill P417
George, Howard P528
George, William E94:E330
George, Georgette E394
Georgelas, Theodore A814:E423
Georgeoff, Robert E19
Georges-Picot, Odile W174
Georgiadis, Margaret A509
Georgieva, Antonia E308
Geppi, John P173
Geraghty, Joanna A439
Geraghty, Sharon W213
Gerald, Aileen A224:P162
Gerard, Steven A83
Gerard, Carol P263
Gerard, Jeff P528
Gerard, Craig J P548
Gerard, Chris E18
Gerarde, Roberta P302
Gerardin, Yann W87
Gerarve, Robin A877:P662
Gerber, William A188
Gerber, Murry A821
Gerber, Robert E160
Gerberry, Amy P231
Gerberry, Robert P524
Gerb no, Anthony P642
Gerdom, Jason P243
Gere, Andrew E376
Geres, Heraldo W309
Gerhardt, Azita Saleki - E140
Gerhart, David P473
Geringer, Steven E4
Gerke, Julie P632
Gerke, Thomas E98
Gerken, R. Jay A75
Gerken, Marc P33
Gerken, Eric P193
Gerlach, James A45
Gerlach, Charles P44
Gerlin, Simon A143:E65
Gerlock, Cynthia P490
Germain, John P174
Germain, Jean-Marc E197
Germaine, Kevin P496
German, Dave E364
Germano, Donald A244
Gernandt, Karl W287

Gero, James E246
Geronimno, Mark Di P272
Geronimo, Charlotte P244
Gerrish, Steve A215
Gerry, Brett C A124
Gersbach, Chris P51
Gershwin, Stanley P318
Gerson, Gary E194
Gerst, Carl E89
Gerungan, Edwin W307
Gervais, John P251
Gervasi, Martha E327
Gerven, Wim Van W39
Gery, Laura Wade- W291
Gesing, Abbey P116
Gesten, Samuel E388
Gesualdo, Erick A780:P572
Gethers-Clark, Michelle A839
Getiso, Alemayehu P597
Getman, George A210
Getman, Beth P409
Getman, George E95
Getz, James A795:E416
Getzfrid, Lisa P246
Geus, Aart de A66
Gev, Ram W63
Geveden, Rex E59
Geyer, Guenter W515
Ghai, Rahul A598
Ghali, Wael P350
Ghan, P Mark P367
Ghani, Nik Abdul Rahim Nik Abdul W307
Ghani, Abdul Rahman Al-Abdul W395
Gharbi, Hinda W405
Ghartey-Tagoe, Kodwo A259
Ghasripoor, Farshad E137
Ghate, Sumedha P508
Gheriani, Yafit W253
Gheysens, Christopher A870:E455
Ghidorzi, Christopher A562:E293
Ghislieri, Andres Ferrero A723
Ghory, Gustavo A455
Ghoshal, Bobby E352
Ghouse, Faradina binti Mohammad W29
Ghylin, Gaylen E53
Giacalone, Annette P163
Giacobbe, Scott A7
Giacobbe, Gail A383:E212
Giacobone, Chris P232
Giamartino, Emma A159
Giamberso, John P551
Gianakos, William A329
Giancarlo, Christopher W360
Gianfagna, Charles P508
Gianforte, Greg A738:P514
Giangaspro, Barbara P108
Giangualano, Patrizia W294
Gianneschi, Stephanie P278
Giannetakis, Paola W294
Giannola, Vito A647
Gianola, John A750:E394
Giansante, Filippo W185
Giantomasi, Francis P374
Giauque, Anthony P A456
Gibber, David A713
Gibbons, Thomas A99
Gibbons, Dale A857
Gibbons, James W399
Gibbons, Michael E332
Gibbons, Dale E447
Gibbons-Peoples, Celeste P134
Gibbs, David A810
Gibbs, Lawrence A824
Gibbs, David A875
Gibbs, Michael W247
Giblin, Mike V A779:P567
Giblin, Mike P594
Gibson, Allen A28
Gibson, E. A309
Gibson, Gregory A316
Gibson, Nicole A327
Gibson, John A593
Gibson, Kurt A655
Gibson, Lee A724
Gibson, Allen P18

Gibson, Sandra Lee P78
Gibson, Donna P112
Gibson, Tom P149
Gibson, Cathy P150
Gibson, Nicole P215
Gibson, James J P443
Gibson, Valerie P524
Gibson, Brad P569
Gibson, Jeff P651
Gibson, E. E163
Gibson, Donald E201
Gibson, Kourtney E262
Gibson, Kurt E340
Gibson, Karen E342
Giddens-Reed, Anna P399
Gideon, Yu A374
Gideon, Cynthia P263
Giem, Judi A793:E414
Gier, Vanessa De P502
Giese, Cory A793:E414
Gietzen, Becky A739:P515
Giffin, Gordon W100
Gifford, William A36
Gifford, Gerard H A226
Gifford, Russell E47
Gifford, Jeffrey E297
Giger, Peter W543
Giglia, Joseph T P208
Gigliotti, Patti A828:P635
Gil, Ryan P326
Gil-Gallardo, Jose Luis de Mora W61
Gilbane, Thomas P229
Gilbert, Steven A507
Gilbert, Paul A679
Gilbert, Philippe A819
Gilbert, Mike P193
Gilbert, Ozzie P233
Gilbert, David P247
Gilbert, Karen P251
Gilbert, Deanne P286
Gilbert, Andrea P308
Gilbert, Christopher B P459
Gilbert, Susan P628
Gilbert, Martin W211
Gilbert, James E300
Gilbertson, H. John A256
Gilbertson, Roger L P464
Gilchrist, Richard A728
Gilchrist, Garlin A737
Gilchrist, Richard P496
Gilchrist, Garlin P513
Gildea, Richard W27
Gile, Elizabeth A453
Gileadi, Ido A304
Giles, John P128
Giles, Bobbi P508
Gilio, Teresa E76
Gill, Varinder P75
Gill, Baldev P127
Gill, Marcus P162
Gill, Charlotte P262
Gill, Ahmad J P460
Gill, Gurpreet P464
Gill, Jane Mc P497
Gill, Michelle P508
Gill, Terry P590
Gill, Harjit E352
Gill-Charest, Katherine A607
Gillani, Aleem A337
Gillard, Ian W62
Gilleland, Gary P653
Gillen, Laura P596
Gillespie, Brian P177
Gillespie, Aaron P375
Gillespie, Shannon P421
Gillespie, Treena P629
Gillespie, Hyrum P637
Gillette, Tom P356
Gillette, Jay P578
Gillham, Simon W518
Gilliam, Derek P146
Gillian, Cheri A321
Gillies, Crawford W75
Gillies, Claire W82
Gilligan, Thomas A708
Gilligan, J. Kevin E392
Gilliland, M. Amy A345

COMBINED HOOVER'S HANDBOOK INDEX OF EXECUTIVES

Gillis, Michelle A47
Gillis, Robert P36
Gillis, Anne D P253
Gillis, Donald P532
Gillis, Steven W475
Gillquist, Andy P292
Gilman, Dan P131
Gilmartin, MaryAnne A437
Gilmer-Pauciello, Karen A A624:P414
Gilmore, Dennis A308
Gilmore, Harry P347
Gilpin, Thomas E127
Gilrain, Kevin R P35
Gilson, Jean-Marc W324
Gilster, Megan P585
Gilstrap, Jamie K P44
Giltner, F Phillips P476
Gilyard, Reginald A159
Gim, Mark A847
Gimpiliova, Stella P31
Ginascol, John A4
Gincola, Michael P165
Ginette, Raymond P532
Gingerichboberg, Pierre A380:P247
Gingg, Ben P610
Gingras, David P332
Gingras, Joseph W P631
Ginja, Evan P243
Ginn, Donnie P76
Ginn, Scott E18
Ginn, William E115
Ginther, Andrew P125
Giocondo, Michael P459
Giordano, Anthony A582
Giordano, Francesco W509
Giordano, Michael E121
Giordano, Anthony E301
Giorgi, Diego W509
Giorgini, Gino P230
Giornelli, Lillian E105
Giovani, John Di' P505
Giovanni, Lisa P506
Giovanniello, Joseph P290
Giovinazzi, Brian A648
Giovinco, Vincent A330
Gipple, Todd A655:E340
Gipson, William A494:A684
Giraldo, Christine P525
Girard, James A463
Girard, Anita P105
Girard, Jon D P340
Girard, Mark P521
Girard, Isabelle W250
Girelli, Davide A131
Girouard, Denis W341
Giroux, Marc W322
Girre, Xavier W175
Girshick, Birgit E79
Girten, Damian P610
Girton, Tani A98
Gisel, William P445
Gist, Mark P125
Gitin, Mark E277
Gitlin, David A154
Gitlin, Mike P98
Gittleman, Sol P603
Gitzel, Timothy A539
Giuliana, Stephen P604
Given, Mark W259
Givens, Rebecca A492
Givens, Regina Horne P126
Givler, Sean A179
Giza, Helen W203
Gjanei, Elizabeth P479
Glabe, Marla A867:E452
Gladstone, David E194
Glaister, Thomas P112
Glaize, Mary E127
Glanville, Barbara P630
Glasel, Dan A243:P188
Glaser, Lisa A174
Glaser, Robert A307
Glaser, Daniel A500
Glaser, Thomas A759
Glaser, Lisa P118
Glaser, Garry P148
Glaser, Angela P171

Glaser, William D P285
Glaser, Juergen W321
Glashauser, Renate W81
Glasier, Charles N P42
Glasner, Sol P569
Glass, Lynda A9
Glass, Johnston A313
Glass, Dennis A480
Glass, Robert A682
Glass, Steven A775
Glass, Irving A842
Glass, Thomas P381
Glass, Steven P551
Glass, Irving P645
Glass, Lynda E4
Glass, Johnston E165
Glasscock, Melbern P539
Glasser, Noelle P155
Glassman, Karl A471
Glassman, Jerry P335
Glasson, Richard W533
Glastra, Matthijs E298
Glaunert, Curtis P647
Glavey, Patrick P360
Glavin, William A489
Glazer, Walter E146
Glazier, Linda P100
Glazier, Travis P165
Gleason, Thomas R A503
Gleason, John A689
Gleason, Hugh P208
Gleason, Thomas R P317
Gleason, Michael E P477
Glebikowska-Michalak, Justyna W71
Glendinning, Stewart A802
Glenn, Valerie A274
Glenn, T. Michael A490
Glenn, Ellie P498
Glenn, Shirley P615
Glenney, Chris P119
Glenning, Robert P252
Glesie, Anne P262
Glessner, Gary E422
Glick, Dave A702
Glick, Alvin P25
Glick, Randy P25
Glick, Barry P25
Glickman, Jason A623
Glickman, Dov E186
Glickman, Matthew E343
Glidden, Craig B A173
Glidden, Craig A349
Glidden, Craig B P113
Glieberman, Bernard P255
Glimcher, Laurie A61:W210
Glimcher, Michael E257
Glimco, Pete P590
Glimstrom, Anna-Karin W446
Glin, C.D. A619
Glockner, David A286
Glomnes, Einar W363
Gloor, Christoph W55
Gloria, Todd P133
Gloria, Geneva W83
Glosserman, Michael E104
Glotzbach, Edward P495
Glover, Glenda A628
Glover, Charles A702
Glover, Steve P337
Glover, John P420
Glover, Ashley P438
Glover, Chaundray P520
Glover, Chris D P540
Glover, Joseph P629
Glover, Glenda E324
Glover, Tyler E407
Gluck, Michelle A300
Gluski, Andres A848
Gluskie, Kevin W222
Glynn, Lisa P243
Glynn, Thomas P P319
Glynn, Martin W465
Gmelich, Justin E262
Gnardellis, Theodore W383
Gnyp, Natalya A243:P188
Go, Timothy A391
Go, Maria Cristina W70

Go, Jonathan W83
Go, Alvin W83
Go, Sonia Maribel W83
Go, Marilyn W83
Goar, Michael P345
Gobe, Phillip A629
Gobert, Wilfred W100
Gochman, Robert P301
Gochnauer, Richard A55
Godbold, Francis A663
Godbole, Seemantini A488
Godda, Abdul Sattar Abdul Karim Abou W395
Goddard, Terry A734:P510
Goddard, Steven P657
Goderstad, Todd P36
Godfrey, Andrea A165
Godfrey, Kerry P415
Godfrey, Donal P628
Godfrey, Ronald S P637
Godfrey, Darren W250
Godfrey, John W291
Godfrey, Weston E256
Godfrey, Curtis E343
Godina, Susie P486
Godinez, Alberto A15:P7
Goding, George P249
Godridge, Leslie A491
Godsil, Robert P260
Godwin, Janet A531:E276
Goebel, David A542
Goebel, Jeremy A630
Goebel, Maryann A701
Goebel, Sheila P623
Goebel, Maryann E365
Goeckeler, David A858
Goedecke, Nancy Collat P320
Goedecke, Glenn P320
Goel, Sanjay A51
Goelz, John E289
Goeman, Danny W200
Goenn, Elizabeth P541
Goeppinger, Kathleen P219
Goergen, Todd E109
Goering, Robert A P160
Goethals, James E394
Goette, Roland A109
Goettee, John A725:E384
Goetz, James A421
Goetz, William P381
Goff, Gregory P291
Goff, Stacey A490
Goff, John A652
Goff, Rhea E387
Goffaux, Denis W507
Goffney, Dr Latonya P18
Gogarty, Richard P596
Goggins, Colleen A433
Goggins, John A536
Goh, Hock Huat A226
Goh, An P141
Goh, Derrick W155
Goh, Shirley W307
Goh, Ti Liang W376
Goh, Chin Yee W376
Goh, Euleen W434
Goharioon, Alex P538
Goings, Maria P192
Goings, Stuart P282
Goitini, Elena W87
Gokhale, Ashutosh A410
Gokhman, Roman P438
Goland, Anthony W35
Golanowski, Marie P51
Gold, Christina A426
Gold, Amber A779
Gold, Lynn P64
Gold, Richard P192
Gold, Amber P568
Gold, Barbara P624
Gold, Barry P646
Gold-Williams, Paula P136
Goldberg, Paul A7
Goldberg, Ryan S A28
Goldberg, Scott A194
Goldberg, Carla P36
Goldberg, Elizabeth P90

Goldberg, Michael P216
Goldberg, Mark A P406
Goldberg, Neil P436
Goldberg, Michael P436
Goldberg, Steven P436
Goldberg, Craig P508
Goldberg, Ryan S E13
Goldberg, Jonathan E252
Goldberg, Joel E320
Goldblatt, Dan P493
Golden, Deborah A530
Golden, Becky S P285
Golden, Jed P377
Golden, David P439
Golden, Michael P519
Golden, John P519
Golden, Justin P519
Golden, Robert P632
Golden, Deborah E275
Golden-Epplelein, Deborah P399
Golder, Jill A7:A755
Goldfarb, Timothy P477
Goldhahn, Laura P69
Goldin, Avraham E191
Golding, John A570
Goldman, Nathan A227
Goldman, Neal P191
Goldman, Michael P377
Goldman, Lynn R P560
Goldman, Neal E78
Goldman, Kenneth E183
Goldner, Brian A607
Goldschmidt, Lawrence E P237
Goldschmidt, Ryan P325
Goldsmith, Andrea A421
Goldstein, Jeffrey A99
Goldstein, Rob A120
Goldstein, Adam A297
Goldstein, Jeffrey A304
Goldstein, Joseph A669
Goldstein, Alex A839
Goldstein, Samuel P7
Goldstein, Robert P65
Goldstein, Stacy A P220
Goldstein, Abner K P562
Goldstein, Lori P617
Goldstein, Brian P P627
Goldstein, Alex P643
Goldstein, Jennifer E13
Goldstein, Adam E158
Goldstein, Lainie E402
Goldstine, Abner E29
Goldstine, Abner D P546
Goldsworthy, Matt P54
Goldwasser, Jon P192
Goldwin, Richard P614
Goll, Shawn Cleveland E53
Golladay, Richard P218
Golodets, Olga W424
Golodryga, Zhanna A671
Golub, Todd P546
Golub, Neil M P561
Golub, Mona J P561
Golub, Jerel T P561
Golub, Aaron E305
Golubieski, John E51
Golz, Karen A61
Golz, Judy Briscoe P149
Golz, Karen E34:E236
Gomes, Maria P302
Gomes, Fernando Jorge Buso W513
Gomez, Paul A186
Gomez, Jaime A200
Gomez, Sara A825
Gomez, Aldric P76
Gomez, Paul P127
Gomez, Frank P128
Gomez, Dian P259
Gomez, Julie P441
Gomez, Gloria P550
Gomez, Mike P590
Gomez, Augusto P617
Gomez, Sara P631
Gomez, Eugenio Llorente W9
Gomez, Sylvia W61
Gomez, Frederic Mark W83
Gomez, Phillip E370

HOOVER'S HANDBOOK OF EMERGING COMPANIES 2022

525

COMBINED HOOVER'S HANDBOOK INDEX OF EXECUTIVES

A = AMERICAN BUSINESS
E = EMERGING COMPANIES
P = PRIVATE COMPANIES
W = WORLD BUSINESS

Gomo, Steven A527:E138
Gompf, Timothy P291
Gomulka, Robert P611
Goncalves, Leticia A68
Goncalves, Lourenco A188
Goncalves, Celso A188
Goncalves, Rui Paulo da Costa Cunha e Silva W206
Goncalves, Joana E67
Gonda, Alyson P236
Gonda, Barbara Garza Laguera W198
Gonda, Mariana Garza Laguera W198
Gondell, Grant P179
Gonet, Kaitlyn P244
Gong, Kevin A298
Gong, Crystal P156
Gong, Zhijie W539
Gonick, Lev P42
Gonick, Denise P360
Gonsalves, Rodney A21
Gonsalves, Glen P154
Gonsalves, Gregg E106
Gonsman, Shana P54
Gonterwitz, Kyle P281
Gonzales, Rodney P123
Gonzales, Lucy P462
Gonzales, Erika P530
Gonzales, Junius P586
Gonzalez, Richard A6
Gonzalez, Jose A192
Gonzalez, Rachel A234:A271
Gonzalez, Jose A297
Gonzalez, Maria A633
Gonzalez, Rachel A732
Gonzalez, Ana A779
Gonzalez, Colleen P115
Gonzalez, Andres P177
Gonzalez, Arthur P187
Gonzalez, Antonio P215
Gonzalez, Rene G P218
Gonzalez, Jorge P315
Gonzalez, Carlos P356
Gonzalez, Kyla P434
Gonzalez, Ana P568
Gonzalez, Lori Stewart P622
Gonzalez, Adrian Sada W22
Gonzalez, Cipriano Lopez W61
Gonzalez, Monica Jimenez W171
Gonzalez, Cristian Gonzalo Palacios W177
Gonzalez, Alberto Bailleres W198
Gonzalez, Bertha W198
Gonzalez, Carlos Crespo W243
Gonzalez, Jose E158
Gonzalez, Jorge E387
Gooch, Mark A212
Goocher, Robert P491
Good, Craig A145
Good, Jeff A251
Good, Lynn J A259
Good, Craig P95
Good, Michael P P365
Goodarzi, Sasan A429
Goode, Carol A698
Goode, Bob P222
Goode, Wilson S P642
Goodell, Drew P643
Goodfellow, Kathy P233
Goodin, David A512
Gooding, Marie A298
Goodman, Shira A159
Goodman, Adam A259
Goodman, Scott A279
Goodman, Jill A351
Goodman, Patrick A604
Goodman, Stacey A649
Goodman, Carolyn G P127
Goodman, Gary J P254
Goodman, Zach P368
Goodman, Richard H P399
Goodman, Laurie W40

Goodman, Nicholas W94
Goodman, Jesse W210
Goodman, Russell W322
Goodman, Jill E73
Goodman, Scott E142
Goodman, Vicki E150
Goodman, Leslie E164
Goodnow, John P69
Goodspeed, Linda A44:A84
Goodwin, Annie A355
Goodwin, C. Kim A633:A786
Goodwin, Sandy P163
Goodwin, Brian P310
Goodwin, Deanna P534
Goodwin, Annie E193
Goodwine, Sharon A754:E401
Goold, Alex P25
Goon, Jeremy W529
Goonan, Michael A147:E65
Goone, David A422
Goorevich, Charlie P282
Goosby, Dorothy P596
Gopakumar, K. W64
Gopal, Ajei E27
Gopalan, Srini W163
Gorbaty, Mayer P300
Gorby, John-Randall P565
Gorczynski, Ronald A717:E379
Gordeon, Tom P105
Gorder, Joseph A831
Gorder, Chris D Van P469
Gorder, Christopher Van E3
Gordillo, Rodrigo Echenique W59
Gordin, Peggy P498
Gordon, Marc A46
Gordon, Joyce A49
Gordon, Murdo A57
Gordon, Susan A142
Gordon, James A315
Gordon, George A321
Gordon, Ilene A427
Gordon, Robin A521
Gordon, Russell A688
Gordon, Joseph A737
Gordon, Ron A741
Gordon, Angela A779
Gordon, Crystal P12
Gordon, Joyce P33
Gordon, Scott R P42
Gordon, Robert P60
Gordon, Tom P105
Gordon, Eric P138
Gordon, John P180
Gordon, Alyson P196
Gordon, David P236
Gordon, Bernard P290
Gordon, Victor P400
Gordon, John P478
Gordon, Roxanne P496
Gordon, Joseph P513
Gordon, Ron P517
Gordon, Angela P568
Gordon, Sean P640
Gordon, Darin E4
Gordon, James E167
Gordon, Marlene E427
Gordon, Brooks E443
Gore, Nancy P413
Gore, Heather P562
Gore, Stephen W261
Gorelick, Joel E161
Gorgol, Karen P257
Gorgone, Linda P174
Gori, Roy W308
Gori, Francesco W391
Goris, Patrick A154
Goris, Bradley E99
Gorman, Robert A79
Gorman, Christopher A453
Gorman, James A538
Gorman, Mark J A631
Gorman, Kim P23
Gorman, Joseph C P61
Gorman, Maureen J P281
Gorman, Donna L P301
Gorman, K Chavanu P549
Gorman, Robert E34

Gorman, Kevin E291
Gorman, Louis E448
Gormley, Debra A847
Gorney, Jon A313:E165
Goron, Helen P140
Gorrie, Magnus A642
Gorrie, M Miller P85
Gorrie, M James P85
Gorriz, Michael W457
Gorsky, Alex A65:A440:A573:P391
Gosa, J. Jake A108
Gosa, Noluthando W335
Gosch, Kenneth L A232
Gosebruch, Henry A6
Gosin, Barry M P375
Gossain, Vinny P305
Gossett, Mark A567
Gossett, Dave P170
Gossett, Jeffrey P585
Gossiaux, Paul W134
Gotelli, Robert A98
Gothard, Joe P261
Goto, Teiichi W109
Goto, Yuichiro W279
Goto, Yasuhiro W418
Goto, Katsuhiro W430
Goto, Masao W450
Gottardy, Brian G P381
Gottesfeld, Stephen A558
Gottlieb, Tamar W64
Gottschalk, Sister Mary T P500
Gottschling, Helena W412
Gottscho, Richard A467
Gotuaco, Joseph W83
Goudswaard, Robert W29
Gough, Michael W P390
Goulart, Steven A521
Goulart, Alisa P168
Gould, Eric A84
Gould, Mark A A300
Gould, John A309
Gould, Andrew A581
Gould, Karen A782:A799
Gould, Howard A857
Gould, R Marcia P29
Gould, Sonya P37
Gould, Karen P583:P605
Gould, John E162
Gould, Howard E447
Goulden, David A128
Goulding, Philip L P351
Goulding, Helen E250
Goulet, Beverly W410
Goulet, Jacques W465
Goulet, Marten E198
Gourley, Samuel P28
Gover, David P529
Gowda, Meena P190
Gowder, Chris P216
Gowdy, Franklin P224
Gower, Dejanelle N P416
Gowey, Jessica P116
Gowland, Karen A125
Gowland, Glen W69
Goyal, Nitin A878
Goyal, Vijay W39
Gozzarino, Katie P502
GP, Ealmoor P659
Grab, Edward L P243
Grabill, L Kenneth P275
Grabner, Alexandra W367
Grabscheid, Erica P71
Grace, Mark A106
Grace, Ted A820
Grace, Mark P64
Grace, Marianne P158
Grace, Augie P317
Grace, William M P642
Graddick-Weir, Mirian A128:A875
Graddy, Steven P221
Grade, Joel A755
Grady, Christopher A78:P47
Grady, Jason P385
Grady, Edward E6
Graebel, David W P233
Graebel, Bill P233
Graebel, William P233

Graf, John W189
Graff, K E A293
Graff, David A549
Graff, Michael A860
Graff, Ed P36
Graff, Lindsey P45
Graff, K E P212
Graff, Jennifer P301
Graff, David E290
Gragnolati, Brian A466:P48:E243
Graham, Tracy A1
Graham, Jonathan A57
Graham, James A188
Graham, Kristiane A256
Graham, Jordan A680
Graham, Garth A698
Graham, Christopher A745
Graham, Stephen A846
Graham, Mark A A866
Graham, Shelia P158
Graham, Susan P218
Graham, John C P233
Graham, Eugene W P233
Graham, Matthew X P233
Graham, Matthew P233
Graham, Roberta P264
Graham, Randolph P363
Graham, Michelle P406
Graham, Franklin P461
Graham, Peter P493
Graham, Kim P599
Graham, David W P652
Graham, Mark A P657
Graham, Ian W195
Graham, Anthony W389
Graham, Paul W531
Graham, Peter E28
Graham, Roger E84
Graham, Tracy E246
Graham, Jordan E356
Grainger, Elizabeth P572
Grainger, Deborah P605
Gralton, Karen P116
Gram, William H A299
Gram, A D P545
Gramigna, Edward A613:E316
Gramlich, Amy P209
Grammer, Britney P316
Grams, Randy P292
Grams, Blake E411
Granata, Claudio W185
Granata, Matias W255
Granberg, Ellen P450
Grande, Bonnie P136
Grande, Maria Malaxechevarria W179
Grandi, Paolo W252
Grandia, Larry D P426
Granet, David P434
Graney, Kevin A345
Graney, Patrick A796
Grange, Pascal W90:W133
Granger, Jason P198
Granger, Harvey P489
Granger, Alberto Consuegra W171
Granger, Karine W175
Granger, Elder E122
Granger, Clarence E420
Granier, Jean-Laurent W43
Graniere, Rick P326
Granoff, David P P656
Gransee, John A867
Grant, Eric A147
Grant, William A206
Grant, Hugh A338
Grant, Daniel A501
Grant, Hugh A636
Grant, David A846
Grant, Dov P71
Grant, Ellen P124
Grant, Peter P147
Grant, Carolyn P153
Grant, Michael P167
Grant, Jack P271
Grant, Tiffany P461
Grant, Duane P485
Grant, Joi P579

COMBINED HOOVER'S HANDBOOK INDEX OF EXECUTIVES

Grant, Declan P650
Grant, Shane W152
Grant, Bruce W515
Grant, Eric E66
Grant-Snyder, Jamilah P89
Grantham, Bill A723
Grantham, Keith P174
Grantham, Helen W132
Grasby, Darren A13
Grasela, Wayne T P579
Grassi, Louis A330
Grasso, Maria A330
Grasso, Alfred P569
Grasso, Filippo W293
Grau, Dominique A21
Grau, Richard W83
Grauer, Scott A126:E54
Graupera, Carlos A340
Grava, Nancy E438
Gravallese, Julie P569
Gravelle, Michael L A303
Graves, Earl A84
Graves, John A217
Graves, Christopher A516
Graves, Mayra A647
Graves, Andrew A786
Graves, Donna P141
Graves, John P151
Graves, Carole P159
Graves, Hubert C P211
Graves, Marti P254
Graves, Matt P284
Graves, Spencer P418
Graves, Mayra P429
Graves, Gregory E140
Graves, James E175
Graves, Kris M E456
Gravino, Ronald P368
Gray, Sean A113
Gray, Jonathan A121
Gray, DeEtte A142
Gray, Andrew A332
Gray, James A418
Gray, W Todd A586
Gray, William A622
Gray, Diedre A635
Gray, Molly A741
Gray, Jim A750
Gray, Denise A767
Gray, Danielle A843
Gray, Fred P167
Gray, Joni P169
Gray, Michael P325
Gray, Alan P496
Gray, Molly P517
Gray, Tracey P522
Gray, Jim P528
Gray, Linda P530
Gray, Gina P541
Gray, Brian W399
Gray, Avrum E253
Gray, Jason E277
Gray, Charles E405
Graybeal, R P316
Grayson-Caprio, Terry E382
Graziano, Jessica A820
Greathouse, Craig E283
Greaves, Nichole P308
Grebbien, Virginia P407
Grebenc, Jane A313:E165
Grecek, Michelle P335
Greck, Sonya B P36
Greco, Tom A12
Greco, Thomas A759
Greco, Mario W543
Greco, Michele E435
Green, Anthony A62
Green, Philip A227
Green, George A238
Green, Frederec A241
Green, Steven A294
Green, Darlene A327
Green, David A358
Green, John A388
Green, Jeffrey A396
Green, Edgar A410
Green, Mark A A451

Green, Byron A463
Green, Kirsten A565
Green, William A691
Green, Jared A724
Green, Josh A735
Green, Nancy A777
Green, Paul A817
Green, Maria A852
Green, Dee P5
Green, Robert P30
Green, Debbie P57
Green, Darlene P134
Green, Judy P167
Green, Rhonda P190
Green, Darlene P214
Green, Candice P228
Green, David P253
Green, Steven P253
Green, Mart P253
Green, Kylenne P263
Green, Lance P291:P291
Green, Trent P294
Green, C Velmar P342
Green, Mike P352
Green, Marie P361
Green, Gabriella P373
Green, James P378
Green, John K P396
Green, Becky P441
Green, Christopher P462
Green, Gene E P488
Green, Josh P511
Green, Michael J P624
Green, Mary P647
Green, Gary W139
Green, John W396
Green, Michael W470
Green, Nicholas E39
Green, Matthew E104
Green, Steven E155
Green, James E248
Green, Maria E255
Green, Scott E307
Green, Eric E446
Green, Catherine E448
Green-Cheatwood, Toni P75
Greenawalt, Howard A529:E274
Greenbaum, Nathan P647
Greenberg, Lon A52:A55
Greenberg, Craig A675
Greenberg, William A801
Greenberg, Elliot P61
Greenberg, Lon R P608
Greenberg, Ian W82
Greenberg, Evan W126
Greenberg, Jordan E43
Greenberg, David E220
Greenberg, Craig E350
Greenberger, Sharon P377
Greenblatt, David E72
Greene, Jason A114
Greene, John A247
Greene, James A809
Greene, Kimberly A831
Greene, Kathie P14
Greene, Jason K P70
Greene, John P152:P152
Greene, Sonja P190
Greene, Graham F P291
Greene, Charles J P361
Greene, Toni P467
Greene, Hugh P489
Greene, Alan P577
Greene, Alexander E430
Greener, Geoffrey A96
Greener, Todd A332
Greener, Fred P73:P73
Greenfield, David A313
Greenfield, Don P374
Greenfield, Andrew E3
Greenfield, David E165
Greenleaf, Dan P349
Greenleaf, Peter E51
Greenleafe, Dan P349
Greenplate, Paul A870:E455
Greenstan, Robert P371
Greenstein, Sara A131

Greenstein, Scott A714
Greenstein, Bruce E252
Greenup, Marion A781:P580
Greenwald, Vicki P99
Greenway, Joy E215
Greenwood, Peter P544
Greer, Steven A359
Greer, Amber A739
Greer, Emily S P32
Greer, James P38
Greer, Pat P203
Greer, Dawn Loge P271
Greer, Rachel P272
Greer, James P396
Greer, Amber P515
Greeson, Audrey P620
Greever, Brian P161
Gref, Herman W424
Greff, Selene P257
Greffin, Judith A75
Greg, Perticone P276
Greger, Bradley P588
Gregg, Adam W43
Gregg, Tracy P220
Gregg, Kelly P390
Gregg, Virginia C P442
Gregg, Adam P512
Gregg, Steven W30
Gregg, Shelia E111
Gregg, Donald E457
Gregoire, Mike A13
Gregoire, Christopher A485
Gregor, Leslee Mc P506
Gregori, Nazzareno W144
Gregoriadi, Alice W188
Gregorski, Robert A94:E45
Gregory, Ginger A118
Gregory, Paul A658
Gregory, Andre A754
Gregory, Regina A760
Gregory, Karen P186
Gregory, David P256
Gregory, Karen P259
Gregory, Jim P396
Gregory, James P396
Gregory, Linsey P586
Gregory, Robert E163
Gregory, David E197
Gregory, Andre E401
Greig, Henry A752
Greiner, Joseph A414:P259
Greiner, Doris W75
Greiner, Stacy E337
Greis, Peter P550
Greiss, Hani P529
Greiss, Christine P552
Greist, Carol P14
Greninger, Claudia E266
Grensteiner, Ronald A45
Grescovich, Mark A102
Grese, Frank A368
Gresham, George E200
Greslick, Richard A193:E87
Gressett, Rex P123
Greth, Jeremy P340
Gretok, Evan P628
Gretzinger, Jerry P577
Greulich, Heidi P318
Greve, Bradley W53
Grevy, Brian W12
Grewal, Manpreet A821
Grewcock, Bruce E A454:A621:P285
Grewcock, Bruce P285:P366
Grewcock, Bruce E P412:P570
Grey, Gary P647
Greydanus, Donald P88
Gridley, Maryanne P193
Griebenow, Jill E73
Grieco, Maria Patrizia W179
Griego, Tiffany A473:P295
Grier, Stacey A189
Grier, Mark A337
Grier, Andrea P163
Griesel, Annari P552
Grieser, Angela P131
Griffeth, Jack T P385
Griffin, David A126

Griffin, Anthony H A291
Griffin, Philip A321
Griffin, Bobby A373
Griffin, John A392
Griffin, Liam A715
Griffin, Tim A734
Griffin, Bobby A854
Griffin, John D P2
Griffin, John P P49
Griffin, Caroline P193
Griffin, Anthony H P210
Griffin, April P251
Griffin, Charles P282
Griffin, Bret P358
Griffin, J Timothy P364
Griffin, Becca P393
Griffin, Marcus P428
Griffin, B R P428
Griffin, Tim P510
Griffin, Doug P532
Griffin, Judith P591
Griffin, Christopher R P636
Griffin, John P P639
Griffin, Tim W156
Griffin, David E54
Griffin, Kent E105
Griffin, Alexandra E142
Griffin, Patrick E146
Griffin, Carlyle E380
Griffith, Peter A57
Griffith, John A176
Griffith, Martin A193
Griffith, Susan A302
Griffith, James A415
Griffith, Christopher A816
Griffith, Jeri P144
Griffith, Donna H P314
Griffith, J Brian P339
Griffith, Brad W421
Griffith, Michael E75
Griffith, Martin E87
Griffith, Angie E152
Griffiths, Daniel A695
Griffiths, Dilnoza A867
Griffiths, David N P121
Griffiths, Jane W53
Griffiths, Anthony W191
Griffiths, Jane W266
Griffo, Joseph P165
Grigg, Richard R P35
Grigg, William P222
Griggs, Malcolm A185
Griggs, P.C. Nelson A543
Griggs, Kathleen M E457
Grigoriadis, Dimitri E291
Grigson, John P174
Grillo, Barbara P309
Grillo, Anthony P356
Grillot, Larry A629
Grimaldo, Aimee Sentmat de W61
Grimes, Karen P788
Grimes, Dana P151
Grimes, Howard P163
Grimet, Howard P282
Grimm, Michael A276
Grimm, Douglas P336
Grimmett, Scott P561
Grinberg, Paul A90:E41
Grinde, Jane P381
Grindle, W Harold P224
Grindstaff, Nicholas A658
Grinkevich, Elizabeth A679
Grinnan, Patrick A497
Grinnell, Elbert P161
Grinnell, David E55
Grise, Cheryl A521
Grisel, Johannes W491
Grisham, Michelle Lujan A738
Grisham, Dorothy P146
Grisham, Michelle Lujan P515
Grishanin, Maksim W502
Griska, Linda B P3
Grison, Arnaud W517
Grisoni, Constance W402
Grissett, Russell A721
Grissler, Brian P580
Grisso, Ben A841

COMBINED HOOVER'S HANDBOOK INDEX OF EXECUTIVES

A = AMERICAN BUSINESS
E = EMERGING COMPANIES
P = PRIVATE COMPANIES
W = WORLD BUSINESS

Grissom, Steven A320
Grissom, Sheri A335
Grissom, Steven E173
Griswold, Jimmy P595
Gritsenko, Valeriya P652
Gritz, Josef W521
Grobler, Fleetwood W421
Grobman, Richard P284
Grochmal, Diane P259
Grodowski, Jenie P519
Groebler, Gunnar W50
Groff, Aaron E134
Grogin, Jeffrey P E317
Groll, Jeanine P92
Gronda, Mark P174
Groneman, Joseph L P184
Groneman, William P598
Gronewold, Russell P91
Grooms, Nina E12
Groos, Holly E120
Groot, Jan de W283
Gros-Pietro, Gian Maria W251
Grose, Douglas W42
Gross, Arthur A P15
Gross, Evelyn P363
Gross, Tami P404
Gross, Daniel L P477
Gross, Jim P627:E42
Grosset, Michele W174
Grossi, Richard A491
Grossman, Eric A538
Grossman, Joe P40
Grossman, Joseph L P40
Grossman, Tracy P352
Grossman, Jeffrey P386
Grossman, Kenneth E47
Grosso, Jim P330
Grote, Debra P540
Grote, Byron W456
Groth, Jim A738:P514
Grotheer, Laurence P129
Grotkin, David P47
Grotton, Joseph A126:E54
Grove, Barry A824:P630
Grover, Surendra P371
Groves, Jeffrey A579
Groves, S Van P285
Groves, Robert M P560
Groves, Jason E266
Grow, David R P653
Groysberg, Boris A323
Grubbs, Laurie P216
Grubbs, Dale P287
Grubbs, Michael D E413
Gruber, Mark A70
Gruber, Vinzenz A535
Gruber, Julie A777
Gruber, Scott A789
Grubic, Robert A529:E274
Gruending, Colin W178
Gruenemay, Brian P218
Gruenhagen, Vinh P170
Grunau, Paul W P39
Gruner, Dean P592
Grunewald, Barbara W190
Grunst, Martin A126:E54
Gruntz, Cory P206
Grussendorf, Christi A27:P15
Grutta, Sandy P246
Grynberg, Marc W507
Gryszkiewicz, Bill P222
Gu, Yaobin A60
Gu, Wenxian W83
Gu, Feng W209
Gu, Haoliang W431
Gu, Chaoyang W432
Gu, Junying W542
Guadarrama, Belinda E395
Guaglione, Catherine P593
Guajardo, Salvador Vargas P237
Guajardo, Pablo Roberto Gonzalez W28

Gualtieri, Giuseppina W511
Guan, Bingchun W236
Guan, Xueqing W244
Guan, Shan W434
Guardino, Carl E376
Guarino, Mary P204
Guarisco, Pete P220
Guarneschelli, Philip P418
Guarrasi, Gaspare E219
Guay, Marc W322
Guba, Thomas A70
Guc, William A852
Gudgeon, Hellen P154
Guell, Miguel Montes W57
Gueltekin, Ege W21
Guenard, Jean W174
Guenter, Ismail W21
Guenthner, Steven P25
Guerci, Alan P499
Guerin, Eric A715
Guerin, Allison A730
Guerin, Vera P105
Guerin, Allison P509
Guerin, Nicolas W372
Gueronniere, Marc de la E273
Guerra, Karen W93
Guerrero, Juan A633
Guerrero, Jessica A740
Guerrero, Isabel P462
Guerrero, Jessica P516
Guerrero, Angel Alija W28
Guerrero, Pedro Guerrero W71
Guerrier, Ron A282
Guerrieri, Salvatore A147
Guerrieri, Gary A331
Guerrieri, Nick P289
Guerrieri, Salvatore E65
Guerrieri, Gary E178
Guerriero, Anne A29:E13
Guerrini, Martino A836
Guertin, Shawn A232
Guest, Robert A279:E142
Guevarra, Emma C A780:P572
Guevarra, Lazaro Jerome W83
Gueye, Gabrielle P103
Guez, Havid N Rodr P618
Guge, Brett P94
Guggenheimer, Steven W234
Gugsa, Frey P628
Gui, Sheng Yue W208
Guidi, Federica W294
Guido, Alfonso W251
Guidry, Darren A392
Guidry, Brooke A736
Guidry, Norris P290
Guidry, Brooke P512
Guidry, Darren E216
Guier, Russell A241
Guigan, John Mc P526
Guilarte, Juan Sanchez Calero W179
Guild, Deborah A632
Guilder, Greg Van A266
Guiley, Thomas E P193
Guilfoile, Mary Steele A428
Guilford, Nikki A740:P516
Guilfoyle, Jeff A737:P513
Guill, Ben A571
Guillaume, Kristen P382
Guillaume, Henri W278
Guillaume, Stephen E84
Guillaume-Grabisch, Beatrice W348
Guillemette, Larry E388
Guillemot, Philippe A721
Guillen, Federico W359
Guillin, Sergio W525
Guimaraes, Enderson A84
Guin, Timothy E430
Guinan, Mark A659
Guindani, Pietro W185
Guindo, Chirfi A118
Guion, Christopher P549
Guionnet, Francois W398
Guiony, Jean-Jacques W301
Guiot, Deann P119
Guire, Peter Mc P458
Gularte, Miguel W309
Gulbrandsen, Carl A867

Gulecki, Debbie P356
Gulich, Frank W166
Gulis, Stephen A417:E226:E377
Gull, Lorie P609
Gulling, Douglas A855:E445
Gullion, Lynn P167
Gulliver, Stuart W262
Gullixson, Renee P217
Gulyas, Diane A289
Gump, Laura A461
Gumpel, Damian A588
Gumpert, Rock P595
Gunby, Steven A71
Gunderman, Bob P658
Gundersen, Sigurd B P238
Gunderson, Kelsey W290
Gundy, Leonard E160
Gunel, Murat P661
Gunger, Dwanda P347
Gunn, Lawrence P455
Gunn, William B P602
Gunn, Robert W191
Gunnare, Chris P430
Gunning, Gina E197
Gunning, Patrick E358
Gunsalus, Robert P427
Gunsett, Daniel A367
Gunter, Jim P73
Gunter, James W P325
Gunter, Emer E23
Gunther, Conrad A246
Guo, Peng A767
Guo, Lin P633
Guo, Yimin W118
Guo, Guanghui W119
Guo, Shiqing W121
Guo, Zhaoxu W123
Guo, Shuzhan W214
Guo, Dexuan W442
Gupp, William E413
Gupta, Suren A32
Gupta, Navdeep A244
Gupta, Rohit A351
Gupta, Alka A544
Gupta, Dushyant A778
Gupta, Shivani P182
Gupta, Rishi P283
Gupta, Abhishek P317
Gupta, Dushyant P564
Gupta, Jan W10
Gupta, Rajiv W37
Gupta, Sapan W40
Gupta, Samir W128
Gupta, Piyush W155
Gupta, Sanjeev W439
Gupta, Ashok W465
Gupta, Ashwini E135
Gupta, Vivek E263
Gupta, Alka E285
Gupta, Sunil E330
Gur, Sharon W64
Gural, Jeffrey R P375
Gurander, Jan W523
Gurcak, Joseph P156
Gurdal, Hakan W222
Gurin, Patricia B P32
Gurley, Tony P644
Gurri, Mia P262
Gursoy, Ozan W504
Gurty, Thomas S Mc P603
Gurugunti, Vikas P356
Guse, Brad A867
Gusho, Mike P599
Gusinov, Alex E438
Gust, Aleksander P181
Gustafsson, Anders A427:A877
Gustas, Lisa P107
Gustavson, Timothy A666
Gutacker, Alison P36
Gutch, Matthew P521
Gutermuth, Luanne S P654
Gutgesell, Emily P261
Guth, Amy P198
Guthart, Gary A430
Guthrie, Roy A541:A592
Guthrie, Lauren A836
Guthrie, Darrin P130

Guthrie, Kevin P390
Guthrie, Roy E281
Gutierrez, Mauricio A174
Gutierrez, Carlos A286:A521
Gutierrez, Mauricio A574
Gutierrez, Carlos A581
Gutierrez, Anthony P63
Gutierrez, Berta P154
Gutierrez, Bianca P217
Gutierrez, Wanda P272
Gutierrez, Laline P326
Gutierrez, Jaime Alberto Villegas W61
Gutierrez, Pedro Fernando Manrique W171
Gutierrez, Juan W444
Gutierrez, Horacio E413
Gutierrez-Ramos, Jose-Carlos A235
Gutmann, Kathleen A819
Gutnick, Michael P A513:P328
Gutovic, Miljan W229
Gutowski, Robert E282
Gutting, Gregory E145
Guttormson, Mary P130
Guy, Kasey P55
Guy, Stephanie P68
Guy, Ronald P316
Guy, Kimberly P504
Guy, Young W529
Guyer, William E102
Guyon, Robert P521
Guyot, Jason P316
Guyton, Robert P335
Guzick, David S P477:P477:P477
Guziewicz, Andrew E29
Guzik, William A8
Guzik, Stacy A126
Guzik, William P4
Guzik, Stacy P83
Guzman, Melinda A298
Guzman, Maria P434
Guzman, David Martinez W22:W57
Guzman, Jorge Andres Saieh W255
Guzman, Douglas W412
Guzman, Enrique W525
Guzzetta, Jason P92
Guzzi, Anthony A272
Guzzone, Brandon P422
Gwartney, Amy P333
Gwillim, Ryan A138
Gwin, Andrew A74:P43
Gwon, Yeong Su W296
Gwon, Sun Hwang W297
Gyani, Mohanbir E120
Gygax, Markus W514

H

H, Hubert P2
Ha, Daisy A398
Ha, Eon Tae W238
Ha, Dae Ryong W388
Ha, Daisy E218
Haacker, Kristin P577
Haag, Natalie A149
Haag, Markus W187
Haag, William E332
Haak, Andrew P149
Haan, Ronald A493
Haas, Richard A583
Haas, George A596
Haas, Marius A860
Haas, John J P191
Haas, Nancy P365
Haas, Gerard P488
Haas, Jamie P610
Haas, Christopher P616
Haas, Herbert W218
Haase, Charlie P171
Haase, Bruce P210
Haba, Kenzo W17
Habeler-Drabek, Alexandra W187
Haber, Emily P124
Haberhauer, Regina W187
Haberl, Gary E383
Haberman, Michael E12
Habib, Reza P490

528   HOOVER'S HANDBOOK OF EMERGING COMPANIES 2022

COMBINED HOOVER'S HANDBOOK INDEX OF EXECUTIVES

Habu, Yuki W14
Hachey, Barbara G P268
Hachey, Barbara P268
Hackel, Mark P162
Hackenberg, Kim P226
Hacker, Mark A540
Hacker, Douglas A727
Hacker, Howard A765
Hacker, Doug P457
Hackerman, Nancy P482
Hackett, Ann A149
Hackett, James A328
Hackett, Ann A335
Hackett, James A571
Hackett, Steven G A638
Hackett, H. Patrick A867
Hackett, Steven G P426
Hackett, Troy M P656
Hackett, H. Patrick E452
Hackman, Jeffrey L P601
Hackney, James R P385
Haddad, Michael A75
Haddad, Ann-Marie P467
Haddad, Ghassan P488
Haddad, Louis E30
Haddock, Diane P283
Hadduck, Katy P172
Haden, Catherine P305
Haden, Dr Kent P339
Haden, Becky P506
Hadenfeldt, Cynthia P175
Haderlein, Jane P407
Hadjiliadis, Dennis P255
Hadley, David P264
Hadley, Lester P361
Haeberli, Gerard W72
Haefelfinger, John W75
Haefner, Larry A192
Haefner, Dr Jeremy P619
Haemisegger, David A227
Haendiges, Brian A351
Haenggi, Jamie E138
Haentjens, Eric W133
Haering, Paul E P108
Haertjens, Barb A531:P349
Hafeez, Kudsia A573:P391
Hafer, Greg P454
Haffajee, Charles I P97
Haffner, David A131
Hafner, Michelle A126:P83
Haft, Ian A39
Hagale, J. Tyson A471
Hagan, Nicole P48
Hagan, Timothy F P158
Hagan, Michael J P392
Hagan, Sylvia P580
Hagan, Patrick E26
Hagan, Mark E347
Hagan, James E448
Hageboeck, Charles A186:E84
Hagedorn, C. Kristopher A496
Hagedorn, Marv A735
Hagedorn, Michael A832
Hagedorn, Marv P511
Hagedorn, Michael E431
Hagel, Shawn R A638:P426
Hagemann, Robert A364:A689:A878
Hagen, Grant A410
Hagen, Thomas B A614
Hagen, Russell A862
Hagen, Colby P409
Hagen, Thomas E145
Hagen, Jonathan E145
Hagenauer, Florian W367
Hagens, Robert A220
Hager, David A243
Hager, Laurel P122
Hagerman, Melissa A351
Hagerty, James A847
Hagey, Michelle P417
Haggard, Herbert C P254
Haggen, Donald P240
Haggen, Richard P240
Haggerty, Scott P155
Haggett, Claire A7
Hagler, Mendel A552
Hagler, Tony P140

Hagler, Mendel P369
Haglund, Karl P572
Haglund, Brian E296
Hagman, Karen A48
Hagman, Martijn A655
Hagman, Karen P31
Hagood, D. Maybank A254
Hagstrom, Mikael A80
Hague, Jill P635
Hague, John E34
Hagy, Michelle P417
Hahn, Ava A467
Hahn, Diane A741
Hahn, Paul P157
Hahn, Paul J P157
Hahn, Tim P165
Hahn, Andrea P506
Hahn, Diane P518
Hahne, Christopher P333
Hai, Ling A506
Hai, Yancey W474
Haidar, Wael A126:P83
Haidlen, Thomas E300
Haight, Pat P467
Haigis, Kevin P180
Haigwood, Nancy L P399
Haile, Rick P86
Hailey, V. Ann A363:A666
Hailey, Robert P152
Haimovitz, Jules E229
Hain, Robert A70
Haines, Dennis P171
Haines, Steve P193
Haines, Robert E247
Haire, Gary P216
Haire, Melanie P644
Hairston, John A372
Hairston, Michelle A653
Hairston, John P83
Haizel, Samantha P101
Haj-Yehia, Samer W64
Hajek, Douglas A519:E272
Hajjar, Karim W451
Hajny, Mark P529
Hake, James P382
Hakim, Anat A478
Hakim, Veronique P338:P368
Hakim, Jamal P400
Hakimi, Miloud W517
Hakimzada, Ahmad P377
Hakman, Joseph E13
Haldar, Pradeep P577
Halderman, F. Howard A320:E172
Hale, Jean A211
Hale, Ted A734
Hale, Jordan A741
Hale, Q Val A741
Hale, Jeff P118
Hale, Kenneston P207
Hale, Daniel G P332
Hale, Ted P510
Hale, Jordan P517
Hale, Q Val P517
Hale, Blake P533
Hale, James E277
Hale, Karyn E422
Haley, Jeffrey A49
Haley, Michael A49
Haley, Timothy A551
Haley, John A721
Haley, Nikki A740
Haley, Charla A741
Haley, Nikki P516
Haley, Charla P517
Haley, Sean W448
Haley, Jeffrey E21
Haley, Michael E21
Haley, Patrick E150
Halfon, Jean-Michel W487
Halford, Andy W311:W456
Halford, Jeremy E197
Halkyard, Jonathan A524
Hall, O.B. Grayson A25
Hall, Mary C A39:A49
Hall, Mary A49
Hall, John A136
Hall, Patricia Hemingway A371

Hall, Greg A373
Hall, Charles A379
Hall, Patricia Hemingway A494
Hall, J. A629
Hall, Linda A652
Hall, J. Franklin A662
Hall, Michael A797
Hall, Mary C P28:P33
Hall, Mary P33
Hall, R Alan P54
Hall, Lanny P67
Hall, Jim P73
Hall, Nicole P82
Hall, Stacyee P113
Hall, Ulysha R P126
Hall, Sheila P126
Hall, Tony P158
Hall, Juree P159
Hall, Tyrell P166
Hall, Ryan P173
Hall, Dolan P206
Hall, Alex P215
Hall, Tonia P286
Hall, Kristen P319
Hall, Jodi P384
Hall, Roger P413
Hall, Charlie P416
Hall, Pj P438
Hall, Jonna P441
Hall, Joanne P497
Hall, Lauren P539
Hall, John J P556
Hall, Loretta P572
Hall, Melaina P587
Hall, Chaundra P616
Hall, Michelle W532
Hall, Douglas E115
Hall, Brian E246
Hall, Kelley E289
Hall, Amy E323
Hall-Long, Bethany A735:P511
Hallaker, Mikael W470
Hallberg, Andrea P233
Halle, Richard E288
Halleck, Hope P156
Haller, Julia A134
Halley, Chryssa A293
Halley, Mary P609
Hallgren, Wendy A800
Hallian, Terence A185:P122
Halliday, Bob A66
Halliday, Mike P166
Halliday, Matthew W30
Halligan, Donald A P316
Halligan, Catherine W195
Halligan, Dennis E368
Hallinan, Patrick A335
Halling, Jason E394
Halliwill, Donald P99
Hallman, Gary P26
Hallman, Ronald S P125
Hallmark, Jeff P151
Hallmark, Dustin P151
Hallmark, Ron P491
Halloran, Thomas A554:P372
Hallquist, Raymond D P285
Hallquist, Constance E266
Hallstead, Amanda E439
Hallum, Kathy A740:P516
Halonen, Robert P598
Halperin, Lexi P55
Halsey, Drew P205
Halsey, Casey S P268:P268
Halstead, Tammy P130
Halter, Patrick A641
Halverson, Steven A227
Halverson, Bradley A470
Halverson, John P51
Halverson, Pete P81
Halverson, Steve P286
Halverson, Sandra E122
Halvorson, Gary A104
Halvorson, Bob P345
Hamada, Michiyo W21
Hamada, Masahiro W452
Hamaguchi, James P585
Hamaguchi, Daisuke W299

Hamalainen, James A45
Hamamoto, Wataru W331
Hamann, Jennifer A812
Hamaty-Bird, Gail P217
Hamberger, Scott E127
Hamblin, Nikki E245
Hamburg, Marc D A113
Hamby, Leigh S P416
Hamel, Cathy P225
Hamel, Kristina P481
Hamer, Lynne P549
Hamic, W. Thomas A427
Hamid, Effendy W128
Hamid, Nazlee Abdul W307
Hamid, Zulkiflee Abbas bin Abdul W307
Hamil, Steven E129
Hamilton, Andrew D A555
Hamilton, Evan P26
Hamilton, Kris P168
Hamilton, Stephanie P233
Hamilton, Fredrick P254
Hamilton, Andrew D P374
Hamilton, Corey P395
Hamilton, Tiffany P403
Hamilton, John R P416
Hamilton, Adam P492
Hamilton, Jennifer P594
Hamilton, Rick P598
Hamilton, Andrew D P661
Hamilton, Jean W399
Hamlin, Pamela A143
Hamlin, George A147
Hamlin, Frank A147
Hamlin, Anne A551
Hamlin, David P139
Hamlin, Terry P427
Hamlin, Pamela E65
Hamlin, George E65
Hamlin, Frank E66
Hamlin, Stacey E383
Hamm, Harold A220
Hamm, Michele P162
Hammack, Elizabeth A360
Hammer, Douglas J A423:P264
Hammer, Glen P579
Hammers, Aaron P358
Hammes, Eric A3
Hammes, Chris P263:P264
Hammock, Sam A833
Hammond, Maryclaires A873
Hammond, John P156
Hammond, Douglas P377
Hammond, Chris P428
Hammond, Sara Beth P493
Hammond, Star P651
Hammond, Frederic E33
Hammons, Kevin A211
Hamner, R. Steven E265
Hamon, David E P194
Hamon, David P194
Hamory, Bruce H A343:P225
Hampel, Sylvia A846
Hampson, Chad P272
Hampton, Jenean A208:P145
Hampton, Monica P187
Hampton, Kelly P411
Hampton, Chris P461
Hampton, Shelly E30
Hamre, John A698:P569
Hamrock, Dave P156
Han, Sang Ki A329
Han, Joseph P473
Han, Kevin P522
Han, Huihua W125
Han, Kwee Juan W155
Han, Fangming W194
Han, Geun Tae W296
Han, Fuling W535
Han, Amy E161
Hance, James A152
Hance, Tom P120
Hancock, C. Wayne A212
Hancock, Melinda A706
Hancock, Sharon P72
Hancock, Maryjean P201
Hancock, Jim P267

COMBINED HOOVER'S HANDBOOK INDEX OF EXECUTIVES

A = AMERICAN BUSINESS
E = EMERGING COMPANIES
P = PRIVATE COMPANIES
W = WORLD BUSINESS

Hancock, Melinda P473
Hancock, David E284
Hancock, Linda E284
Hancock, Charles E409
Hand, Erik A396
Hand, Brian A750
Hand, Judi E417
Handa, Kimio W436
Handa, Tadashi W493
Handel, Michael Van A494
Handfield, Larry P576
Handjinicolaou, George W383
Handler, Richard A437
Handley, Thomas A677
Handley, Jack P286
Handline, Amra P146
Handlon, Carolyn A431
Handy, John A206
Handy, Elsie A838
Handy, Edward A847
Handy, Elsie P641
Hanebeck, Jochen W246
Haneef, Rafe W128
Hanegbi, Noam W63
Hanerkson, David P140
Haney, Cecil A345:A765
Haney, Carl P508
Haney, M.A. E322
Hanft, Adam E2
Hanick, Mel P17
Hanigan, Kevin A646:E336
Hank, Jeffrey E341
Hanke, Troy E174
Hankins, Anthony A411
Hankins, Joyce P101
Hankinson, Garth A218
Hankinson, Craig A493
Hankonen-Nybom, Raija-Leena W154
Hanks, W. Bruce A490
Hanks, Craig P543
Hankton, Furnell P347
Hanley, Michael A131
Hanley, Jeneanne A457
Hanley, Walter A484
Hanley, Patrick A584
Hanley, Matthew A729
Hanley, Joseph A764
Hanley, Kathleen P167
Hanley, Richard J P174
Hanley, Cheryl P481
Hanley, Matthew P497
Hanley, Cathy P595
Hanley, Karen P654
Hanley, Mary E376
Hanlin, Russell P526
Hanlin, Russell L P526
Hanlon, Randy A24:P13
Hanlon, Brian P588
Hanlon, Philip J P602
Hanlon, David P620
Hanly, Donna P395
Hann, Susan P7
Hanna, Randall A372
Hanna, Tania A463
Hanna, Gia P361
Hanna, David E35
Hanna, Mark E153
Hannaford, Matt P555
Hannah, David A125
Hannah, Sara P62
Hannah, Anthony P108
Hannah, Steve P176
Hannah, Brian P333
Hannam, Wendy E135
Hannan, Renee A380
Hannan, John P207
Hannan, Renee P247
Hannasch, Brian W25
Hanneman, Karl E296
Hannigan, Elizabeth P78
Hannigan, Deirdre W17

Hannon, Michael A632
Hannon, Richard M P78
Hannon, Rita P319
Hannon, Mary P595
Hannoraseth, Puntipa W65
Hanprathueangsil, Saisunee W65
Hanrahan, Paul A418
Hanratty, Paul W335
Hans, Peter P586
Hansberry, Kristin P333
Hanselman, Lisa P652
Hansen, Jon A180
Hansen, Dave A201
Hansen, Kara A251
Hansen, Marshall A293
Hansen, Steven A454
Hansen, Becky A531
Hansen, Janet A617
Hansen, Douglas A668
Hansen, Mark P38
Hansen, Rick P103
Hansen, David L P135
Hansen, Bradley P165
Hansen, Marshall P212
Hansen, Larry P247
Hansen, Steven P285
Hansen, Becky P349
Hansen, Don P398
Hansen, Douglas P433
Hansen, Dr David P447
Hansen, Jan P599
Hansen, Signhild Arnegard W446
Hansen, Dave E92
Hansen, Bruce E276
Hansen, Janet E319
Hansen, Graydon E388
Hansen, Bruce E434
Hansing, Axel E443
Hansman, Steve P195
Hanson, Diana A93
Hanson, Robert A218
Hanson, Bryan A286
Hanson, Greg A357
Hanson, James A466
Hanson, Bradley A519
Hanson, Jodee A739
Hanson, Bryan A878
Hanson, Elizabeth P102
Hanson, Dena P152
Hanson, Michael P222
Hanson, Jodee P515
Hanson, Theodore E32
Hanson, John E75
Hanson, Deborah E164
Hanson, James E243
Hanson, Bradley E272
Hanson, Doyle E286
Hanson, John E418
Hansotia, Eric A20
Hanspal, Amarpreet E34
Hantman, Perla Tabares P579
Hantson, Ludwig A392
Hanway, H. Edward A500
Hanzawa, Junichi W330
Hao, Yibin W209
Happe, Carolina Dybeck A346
Happe, Michael E451
Happell, Kathy P579
Hara, Takashi W23
Hara, Noriyuki W334
Harada, Yasuhide W127
Harada, Hiroki W356
Harada, Susumu W493
Haraf, William A697
Haraguchi, Tsunekazu W21
Haraguchi, Tetsuji W332
Harapiak, Maurice A188
Harashima, Akira W493
Harasick, Richard F P303
Harbarger, Claude P624
Harbert, Julie A277
Harbert, Joe P49
Harbert, Billy P54
Harbes, Jason P191
Harbison, Ella P132
Harbour, Ronald E254
Harbour, Austin E326

Harcum, Rick P159
Hardage, Ryan P140
Hardaker-Jones, Emma W291
Hardegg, Maximilian W187
Harden, Billy P153
Harden, M C P489
Harden, Mary E286
Harder, V. Peter W306
Hardesty, Dean A48
Hardesty, Michael A569
Hardesty, Dean P31
Hardgrove, Richard E361
Hardin, John A56
Hardin, P. Russell A350
Hardin, Scott P51
Hardin, Beverly P320
Hardin, Kimberly P616
Harding, Jonathan A8
Harding, P Russell A475
Harding, Matthew A647
Harding, Jonathan P4
Harding, Joe P658
Harding, Mark E339
Hardister, Hal P526
Hardman, Kevin A411
Hardman, Elizabeth P185
Hardman, Danny P615
Hardt, William P582
Hardtke, Brian P166
Hardwick, Mark A320
Hardwick, M Susan P491
Hardwick, Elanor W27
Hardwick, Mark E172
Hardy, Brent A414
Hardy, Cody P112
Hardy, Brent P260
Hardy, Leah P432
Hardy, Brad P521
Hardy, Eva E30
Hardy, Adrian E229
Hare, Michelle P504
Hare, Richard E199
Haren, Lexie Van P131
Harf, Peter A452
Harford, Barnaby A813
Harford, Simon P406
Hargett, Fred A573:P390
Hargis, V. Burns A126
Hargis, Burns P396
Hargis, V. Burns E54
Hargrove, Robin A535
Hariharan, Anu A87
Harik, Mario A873
Haring, Dawn P92
Harings, Roland W50
Harings, Lothar W287
Haris, Clinton E140
Harkel-Rumford, Lynne A163
Harker, Victoria A410
Harker, Patrick T P618
Harker, Victoria E393
Harkins, Kristie E308
Harkness, Shanan P242
Harkness, James E229
Harlam, Bari A679
Harlan, Clifford C A583
Harlan, Kristy A862
Harlan, Clifford C P393
Harlem, Peter P488
Harless, Samantha A877
Harless, Amanda P546
Harless, Katherine E411
Harley, Chanelle P579
Harlow, David A94
Harlow, Jo W259
Harlow, David E44
Harlow, James E304
Harman, Donna A605
Harman, Terry P169
Harmening, Andrew A75
Harmening, Jeffrey A347:E411
Harmer, Peter W135
Harmon, Eric A213
Harmon, Sarah A314
Harmon, Nicole P90
Harmon, Tom P143
Harmon, Eric P150

Harmon, Mary E204
Harmon, Richard E365
Harms, Debra P26
Harms, Gerhard von Borries W141
Harnacke, Ulrich W91
Harness, Carl P161
Harney, John P618
Harney, David W213
Harold, Gennie P196
Harp, Richard P163
Harper, Gordon E70
Harper, Troy A396
Harper, Craig A408
Harper, Hershel A804
Harper, Keith P167
Harper, Reid P170
Harper, Sarah P221
Harper, Bethany P257
Harper, Carol P452
Harper, Hershel P607
Harper, Katherine W421
Harr, Jenifer P32
Harr, Nathan P320
Harralson, Jefferson A814:E424
Harrel, Dustin P642
Harreld, Bruce P586
Harrell, Joanne A396
Harrell, James A721
Harrell, Karen P123
Harrell, Jennie P339
Harrell, Kim P501
Harrigan, Edmund E225
Harriman, Morril A734:P510
Harrington, Lauren A67
Harrington, Rich A103
Harrington, Christopher A541
Harrington, Russ P57
Harrington, Rich P60
Harrington, Wade P129
Harrington, Judy B P246
Harrington, Dale W P555
Harrington, Charles L P573
Harrington, Peter E124
Harrington, Christopher E281
Harris, Charles A49
Harris, John A182
Harris, C. Martin A200
Harris, David A243
Harris, Joi A258
Harris, John A311
Harris, Steven A320
Harris, Maria A416
Harris, Harry A463
Harris, Brian A465
Harris, Walter A486
Harris, Jonathan A507
Harris, Arno A623
Harris, Doug A652
Harris, Bernard A665
Harris, Ana A710
Harris, John A719
Harris, Michael A795
Harris, Patrice A814
Harris, Carla A845
Harris, Darrel A874
Harris, Anita P19
Harris, Joyce P20
Harris, Danny P40
Harris, Barbara P43
Harris, Patty P69
Harris, Gene T P144
Harris, Jennifer P177
Harris, Stephen P204
Harris, Emily P238
Harris, Rachel P241
Harris, Carolyn P249
Harris, Sally P251
Harris, Frances P257
Harris, Lisa P293
Harris, Mark P309
Harris, Roger P364
Harris, David P377:P413
Harris, Shawn P414
Harris, David M P472
Harris, Tom P609
Harris, Ila P624
Harris, David P625

COMBINED HOOVER'S HANDBOOK INDEX OF EXECUTIVES

Harris, Adrienne P640
Harris, Tammy P642
Harris, John W197
Harris, Jason W396
Harris, Margaret W465
Harris, Andrea W533
Harris, Charles E21
Harris, Paula E81
Harris, Gail E149
Harris, Barbara E152
Harris, Steven E172
Harris, Brian E203
Harris, Maria E226
Harris, Lawrence E235
Harris, Ana E371
Harris, Michael E416
Harris, Patrice E423
Harrison, Andrew A26
Harrison, Suzan A68
Harrison, J. Frank A197
Harrison, Alicia A417
Harrison, Marc A423
Harrison, David A571
Harrison, Tom A770
Harrison, Suzan A860
Harrison, Dayna P46
Harrison, Brandon P92
Harrison, Jeffrey P121
Harrison, Michael S P123
Harrison, Wendy P233
Harrison, Marc P264
Harrison, Saundra P305
Harrison, Carrie P334
Harrison, Dean P389
Harrison, Rebecca P399
Harrison, Anita P418
Harrison, Luther P461
Harrison, Christine P481
Harrison, Tom P540
Harrison, Hal P572
Harrison, Randi P635
Harrison, Marianne W308
Harrison, Stephen W532
Harrison, Dalen E169
Harrison, Robert E202
Harrison, Alicia E227
Harrison, Ronald E345
Harrison, Michael E377
Harrison, Tara Y E439
Harrod, William A315
Harrod, Denise E35
Harrod, William E167
Harrold, Robin P479
Harshbarger, Tim P141
Harshman, Richard A40
Harshman, Ellen A635
Harshman, Daniel E153
Hart, John A220
Hart, Eric A288
Hart, Tanya A317
Hart, Timothy D A322
Hart, Debra A366
Hart, Brooke A410
Hart, Mark A609
Hart, Gregory A813
Hart, Brett A813
Hart, Michelle P97
Hart, Sara P159
Hart, Michael P185
Hart, Richard H P301
Hart, John B P305
Hart, Charles E P353
Hart, Ann Weaver P536
Hart, Cees 't W18
Hart, Jeffrey W111
Hart, Matthew E9
Hart, Daniel E39
Hart, Eric E43
Hart, Daniel E110
Hart, Tanya E170
Hart, Alex E277
Hart, Melanie Housey E327
Hartenback, Ms Jaime P143
Hartenstein, Eddy A714
Hartfield, Nicholas P379
Hartgraves, John P86
Harthy, Said Al W64

Harthy, Nasser Bin Mohammed Al W64
Harthy, Saif Bin Salim Al W64
Hartke, Gerhardt P321
Hartke, Adam P338
Hartle, Amy P131
Hartley, Cynthia A725
Hartley, Tom P322
Hartley, Cynthia E383
Hartley, C. Keith E426
Hartman, Todd A115
Hartman, Diane P65
Hartman, Robb P143
Hartman, Scott V P290
Hartman, Amy P423
Hartman, Curtis W P570
Hartman, Matthew E429
Hartmann, Nathalie W87
Hartnett, John A415
Hartnett, Chad M P244
Hartnett, Jennifer P392
Hartnett, Mary Pat P496
Hartnett, Thomas E2
Harton, Lynn A814:E424
Hartong, Hendrik A10
Harts, Chris P7
Hartsfield, Lois P36
Hartsfield, Abigail P625
Hartsfield, Keith E236
Hartshorn, Michael A687
Hartshorn, Tanya A355
Hartsig, Joseph A111
Hartung, John A174
Hartung, Michael W197
Hartunian, Barry E304
Hartwick, Gary A285
Hartwick, Kenneth E284
Hartz, Gregory A789
Hartz, Whitt P444
Hartz, Scott W308
Hartz, C. Scott E145
Hartzband, Meryl W189
Hartzell, Jay A523
Harvey, Anne A187
Harvey, William A190:A219
Harvey, David A230
Harvey, William A570
Harvey, Meriam A621
Harvey, Robert A798
Harvey, J Dale P29
Harvey, Anne P131
Harvey, Darryl P409
Harvey, Meriam P412
Harvey, Alex W304
Harvey, David E113
Harvey, Steven E245
Harvill, Howard P220
Hasan, Aznan W307
Hasbrook, John A793:E414
Hasbrouck, Jennifer A722
Hasebe, Yoshihiro W270
Hasegawa, Nobuyoshi W68
Hasegawa, Takuro W317
Haselby, Danielle P249
Hasenberg, Amy A742:P518
Hasenfratz, Linda W193
Hash, Steven E13
Hashar, Walid Al W64
Hashim, Hasnita Binti Dato' W307
Hashimoto, Takayuki W127
Hashimoto, Hirofumi W148
Hashimoto, Kiyoshi W272
Hashimoto, Takayuki W324
Hashimoto, Takashi W339
Hashimoto, Eiji W354
Hashimoto, Yoshihiro W432
Hashimoto-Torii, Kazue P115
Hashizawa, Yuya A166:P110
Hashmi, Quazi P165
Hashmi, Aijaz P301
Hasimoglu, Ibrahim W281
Haskell, Jeanne P445
Haspel, Brad P589
Hassall, Bruce W199
Hassanein, Ahmed P290
Hassard, Charles P184
Hasse, William A P359
Hasselbarth, William C P15

Hassell, Gerald A203:A521
Hassenfeld, Alan A377
Hassett, Daniel E P625
Hassfurther, Thomas A605
Hassid, Michele A856
Hassler, Bryan P120
Hassman, Vicki P184
Hasson, Teresa S P20
Hast, Anne P466
Hasten, Vernon P43
Hasten, Laurie P P365
Hasting, Willeen P337
Hastings, Joseph A211
Hastings, Reed A551
Hastings, Douglas P565
Hasty, Atina P53
Hasuwa, Kenji W367
Hata, Hiroyuki W67
Hata, Hideo W206
Hatai, Janie P148
Hatalski, Jennifer E64
Hatch, Mike A737
Hatch, Chelsey A741
Hatch, Ed P74
Hatch, Michael P264
Hatch, Mike P513
Hatch, Chelsey P517
Hatcher, Samantha P535
Hatchoji, Takashi W312
Hatem, John E114
Hatfield, Dianne P548
Hathaway, William R P36
Hato, Hideo W461
Hatten, Terry A542
Hatter, Patricia E224
Hatto, Christopher A349
Hatton, Teresa A74:P43
Hattori, Satoru W68
Hattori, Nobumichi W192
Hattori, Rikiya W435
Hau, Robert A325
Haub, Christian W322
Haubeck, Robert P529
Hauber, Steve A546
Hauck, Andrew A315
Hauck, Kristin P607
Hauck, Andrew E167
Hauenstein, Glen A242
Haug, Laural P174
Haugetraa, Line W363
Haughaboo, Jeremy P492
Haugland, Thor-Christian W454
Haupert, John M P233
Haus, Judy P107
Hausemann, Jena P116
Hauser, Mark J P59
Hauser, Wolfhart W45
Hausladen, Douglas P129
Hausman, Rick P222
Hausmann, Dj P517
Havanec, Laurie A232
Havel, James A279:E142
Haven, Christina De A555:P374
Havens, Tom A689
Havericak, Heather P379
Haverkamp, Michael F P73
Haverty, Kevin A706
Havey, Adam E133
Havlik, Bari P214
Hawel, Thomas W2
Hawes, Frances E321
Hawig, Scott P222
Hawk, Dan P152
Hawk, Nikki P524
Hawk, Donald E403
Hawkins, Thomas A598
Hawkins, Brian A825
Hawkins, Darren A874
Hawkins, Paul P94
Hawkins, Michael P109
Hawkins, Robert P149
Hawkins, Linda P154
Hawkins, George P190
Hawkins, Linda P193
Hawkins, Ronald E P299
Hawkins, Sheri P479
Hawkins, Ilse P617

Hawkins, Mary Michael P619
Hawkins, Brian P631
Hawkins, Barbara P647
Hawkins, John E312
Hawks, Howard L A787
Hawks, Howard P81
Hawks, Howard L P537:P595
Hawley, John P9
Hawley, Sue P529
Hawley, Chad P545
Haworth, Jennifer A359
Haworth, Josh P585
Hawthorne, Douglas A126
Hawthorne, Whitnee A439
Hawthorne, Rick P216
Hawthorne, Maria E32
Hawthorne, Douglas E54
Hawthorne, Nancy E107
Hay, Lewis A63:A463
Hayafune, Kazuya W350
Hayakawa, Shigeru W501
Hayashi, Akira A877:P662
Hayashi, Noboru W17
Hayashi, Akio W17
Hayashi, Kingo W127
Hayashi, Masahiro W206
Hayashi, Nobuhide W269
Hayashi, Naomi W330
Hayashida, Peter A783:P583
Hayashida, Jon E388
Hayata, Fumiaki W459
Haycock, Sara P147
Haydar, Ziad A642
Hayden, John A672
Hayden, Dorthy P164
Hayden, Don P428
Hayden, John E364
Hayek, Matthew A531
Hayek, Andrew P466
Hayek, Matthew E276
Hayes, John A92
Hayes, William A139
Hayes, Rejji A190
Hayes, John A244
Hayes, Robin A439
Hayes, Lindsay A439
Hayes, Terry A494
Hayes, Michael A556
Hayes, Gregory A665
Hayes, Michele P56
Hayes, Lindsay P276
Hayes, Jaime P322
Hayes, George P323
Hayes, Tom P393
Hayes, Anne P409
Hayes, Paul P431
Hayes, Deborah P550
Hayes, Martha E24
Hayes, Holly E39
Hayes, William P E242
Hayes-Crosby, Ambie P200
Hayford, Michael A548
Hayles, E. Carol A266:A851
Haylon, Michael A62
Hayne, Pat P254
Hayne, Bill P553
Haynes, Jean A126
Haynes, Jana L A401
Haynes, Ernest A721
Haynes, Kenneth A774
Haynes, Jerry W P40
Haynes, Lawrence P53
Haynes, Jean P83
Haynes, Kenneth P547
Haynes, Decynthia P624
Haynes, Anthony P629
Haynes, Dennis P640
Haynesworth, Linnie A81:A527:A796
Haynie, Mark A417:E227
Hayo, Zeev W63
Hayon, Jack P201
Hays, J. Clay A798
Hays, Charles P309
Hays, James E57
Hays, Rick E126
Hayslip, Paul P14
Hayssen, Charles E86

COMBINED HOOVER'S HANDBOOK INDEX OF EXECUTIVES

A = AMERICAN BUSINESS
E = EMERGING COMPANIES
P = PRIVATE COMPANIES
W = WORLD BUSINESS

Hayutin, David L P527
Hayward, Jeffery A292
Hayward, Katie P256
Hayward, Pierre P618
Hayward, Donald E86
Haza, Rafael De la W179
Hazard, Stephen A667
Hazard, Burke P492
Hazel, Mark A306
Hazelwood, Lauris N P467
Hazen, Samuel A379
Hazen, Andrea P434
Hazleton, Christopher A242
He, Long W97
He, Zhi-qi W97
He, Qi W115
He, Biao W124
He, Ping W212
He, Zhiqiang W292
He, Hongyun W303
He, Jun W474
Heaberlin, Rhonda P286
Heacock, David A838
Heald, Jared W P209
Heald, Christopher E69
Healey, Melanie A389:A636
Health, Andrew P167
Healy, Douglas A45
Healy, Greg P82
Healy, Robert W P124
Healy, Pat P286
Heaney, Kathleen P245
Heaney, Jim P559
Heard, Michael A194
Hearn, David A327
Hearn, Peter A500
Hearn, Al P172
Hearn, David P215
Hearne, Thomas E430
Hearty, James A237
Heath, Ralph A772
Heath, Tara E55
Heaton, Michael A497
Heavner, Daniel A312
Hebard, George E129
Hebert, Kelly A212
Hebert, Maurice A534
Hebert, Kathy P441
Hebert, Chad P601
Hebert, Brigitte W340
Hechtman, Keith P57
Heck, Kristen A355
Heck, Denny A741:P518
Heck, John P580
Heck, Kristen E193
Hecker, Mark A723:E383
Heckman, Jason A775:P552
Heckman, Michael P615
Heckman, Dave P618
Heckmann, Fritz-Juergen W222
Hector, Joshua P542
Hedberg, Heidi A734:P510
Hedengran, Petra W3
Hedges, Kathleen P498
Hedin, Maria W470
Heel, Joachim A877
Heer, John P383
Heeren, Jerry P358
Hees, Bernardo A87
Heese, Lisabeth E308
Heeter, Judith A279:E142
Hefter, Marcia A246
Hegde, Beth P429
Hegde, Vinayak E109
Heglar, Robert P12
Hegstrom, Linda P255
Heib, Adam P480
Heichelheim, Judith P422
Heidari, Faye P398
Heidi, Anderson P361
Heidtbrink, Scott P209

Heil, Kevan P307
Heilborn, Andrea P160
Heilbron, Jim A25
Heilbronner, Anne-Gabrielle W372:W395
Heilbronner-Kolthoff, Lawrence A147:E66
Heilbrun, Jason P164
Heilman, Todd E P403
Heim, Christopher E118
Heimann, Ron P222
Heimes, Terry A549:E290
Heimlich, Ken A728:P496
Hein, Angela P73
Heinberg, Marshall E78
Heincl, Mark P359
Heinemann-Specht, Petra W2
Heinrich, Daniel A92
Heinrich, Kerry P6
Heinrich, Cory E198
Heinsohn, Rebecca P496
Heinz, Michael W76
Heinzel, Matthias A260:A426
Heinzen, Nancy P155
Heinzl, Thomas W524
Heinzmann, David E255
Heisey, Bradley K A787
Heisey, John L P106
Heisey, Bradley K P595
Heiskell, Steven E362
Heisler, Tom A232
Heisz, Leslie A269
Heitmann, Scott A867:E452
Heitmueller, Frauke W218
Heitz, Dan P590
Helander, Mikko W275
Helber, Andreas W81
Helberg, Tom E361
Helbig, Greg P251
Held, Gerald A550
Held, Amy A718
Held, Sascha W321
Heldman, Susan P468
Heleen, Mark A546
Helen, Xu A497
Hellemondt-Gerdingh, Marjolien van W61
Heller, Robert A98
Heller, Paul A409
Heller, Robert A719
Heller, Paul P11
Heller, Joseph P209
Heller, Cynthia P242
Heller, Andra P603
Heller, Alexandra E305
Hellfeld, Samuel E378
Helliesen, Signe W454
Hellighausen, John P532
Helling, Larry A655:E340
Hellman, Peter A106:A361
Hellmann, Elisabeth A392
Hellmich, Thomas P459
Helm, Larry A770
Helm, Roshonda P541
Helm, Dr Marlene P545
Helman, William A333
Helmer, Richard P398
Helmes, Marion W93
Helmick, Kevin A294:E156
Helmkamp, Katrina A666
Helms, Lloyd A281
Helms, Christopher A541
Helms, Larry P85
Helms, Ben P392
Helpern, Joseph A P566
Helser, Christopher A361
Helstrom, Charles P24
Helt, James A9:E4
Helten-Kindlein, Birgit W224
Helton, Sandra A641
Helvey, James A197
Hemani, Gourang W395
Hembree, Jodie P524
Heminger, Gary A636
Hemmer, Tara A848
Hemminger, Dale E257

Hemphill, Kathryn P113
Hemsley, Stephen A823
Hemstead, Louise P154
Hench, Nathan P410
Henchoz, Jean-Jacques W218:W476
Hendershot, Janeth A466:E243
Henderson, Gregory A61
Henderson, Jeffrey A109
Henderson, Steven A471
Henderson, Mike A495
Henderson, Jeffrey A656
Henderson, Jay A718
Henderson, George A724
Henderson, Deidre A741
Henderson, Michael W P43
Henderson, Sarah P264
Henderson, William P330
Henderson, Holly P334
Henderson, Deidre M P517
Henderson, Rosoloc P562
Henderson, Rebecca W398
Henderson, Jeffrey E204
Henderson, Michael E362
Hendon, Jack E81
Hendrian, Catherine A190
Hendricks, Dana A642
Hendricks, Christy P401
Hendricks, Andy P475
Hendricks, Thomas E P537
Hendricks, Bernie P572
Hendricks, Linda P629
Hendricks, James E439
Hendrickson, Keith A738:P514
Hendrix, Cody A570
Hendrix, Jawn A789
Hendrix, Cody P388
Hendrix, Anthony E23
Hendrix, Daniel E24
Hendrix, Jawn E411
Hendry, John A392
Hendry, Allenda P615
Hendry, John E216
Heneghan, Steven P565
Henerschedt, Robert A14:P5
Heng, Jiunn P539
Hengrojanasophon, Mongkol W441
Henika, Kevin P134
Henion, Bradley E81
Henkel, Herbert A3
Henkel, Robert J A74:P43
Henkel, Deanna P172
Henley, Jeffrey A595
Henley, Joseph L P123
Henn, Vicki A632
Hennah, Adrian W259:W510
Hennelly, Ben J P53
Hennelly, Patricia P301
Henneman, Pamela P118
Hennes, Duncan A183:W399
Hennessey, Michael A185:P122
Hennessey, Karen P300
Hennessey, Ruth P499
Hennessy, John A473:P295
Hennessy, Paul E369
Henney, Jane A55
Henney, Jane E P617
Hennigan, Michael A496:A541
Henning, Thomas A549
Henning, Jerry P332
Henning, Thomas E290
Henninger, Tadd A637
Hennings, Travis A666
Hennington, Christina A786
Henny, Matthias W55
Henretta, Deborah A518
Henrich, William L P587
Henrichs, Carol P19
Henrichs, Mark P621
Henricson, Stefan W470
Henrie, M. Shane A359
Henriksen, Kate W454
Henriksson, Henrik W3
Henrot, Francois W402
Henry, Kimberley A126
Henry, Peter A183
Henry, Frank M A343
Henry, Daniel A375

Henry, Maria A455
Henry, Brent L A503
Henry, Daniel A509
Henry, Jerome A585
Henry, Gary A824
Henry, Cordelia P78
Henry, Bertha P157
Henry, Mark P177
Henry, Frank M P225
Henry, Brent L P317
Henry, Lori P361
Henry, Jake P457
Henry, Ramone P584
Henry, Gary P617
Henry, Mary Anne P638
Henry, Michael W69
Henry, Simon W378:W405
Henry, Kimberley E54
Henry, Daniel E200
Henry, Gene E206
Henry, David E277
Henry, Kevin E359
Henry, George E430
Henschel, Diane P109
Henshaw, Vern P25
Hensing, John A102:P56
Henslee, Gregory A579
Hensley, Todd A723:E383
Henson, Davis P423
Henson, Thomas O P578
Hentzen, Peter P614
Hepler, Kenneth P642
Hepner, Ann P306
Heppelmann, James E339
Heppner, David A496
Hepworth, Graeme W412
Her, Duachi P249
Herbein, Robert A P20
Herbert, Christopher A337
Herbert, Greg P51
Herbold, Chris A630
Herbst, Kevin A573
Herbst, Gary P282
Herbst, Kevin P391
Herbst, Lawrence P555
Herde, Carl A747:E391
Herdener, Anthony M P385
Hereford, Daniel A717:E379
Herena, Monique A46
Herencia, Roberto A102
Herff, Jason P477
Hergan, Andrew P226
Herget, Jordan P231
Hering, Jack P574
Herlihy, J. R. E132
Herlitzka, Kristy P289
Herlyn, Jeremey E68
Herman, Alexis A228
Herman, Robert A626
Herman, CFM P27
Herman, Linda P352
Herman, Amy P482
Herman, Jeff P491
Herman, Benedikt-Richard Freiherr von W224
Herman, Robert E322
Hermance, David A56
Hermance, Frank A806
Hermandev-Lichto, Javier P488
Hermann, Chris P16
Hermann, Sandy P343
Hermann, Steve P639
Hermosillo, Juan P315
Hermus, Ben A804:P607
Hern, John F O P368
Hernadi, Zsolt W333
Hernandez, Elsa A200
Hernandez, Sandra A323
Hernandez, Catherine A445
Hernandez, Richard A496
Hernandez, Enrique A509
Hernandez, William A569
Hernandez, Carlos A648
Hernandez, Angel A727
Hernandez, Stephanie A877
Hernandez, Antonio P109
Hernandez, Manuel S P261

COMBINED HOOVER'S HANDBOOK INDEX OF EXECUTIVES

Hernandez, Mary P262
Hernandez, Raquel P274
Hernandez, Catherine P279
Hernandez, Patricia P341
Hernandez, Carol P359
Hernandez, Claudia P398
Hernandez, Bradley P441
Hernandez, Angel P450
Hernandez, Josefina P452
Hernandez, Olga M P461
Hernandez, Angel P495
Hernandez, Alex P532
Hernandez, Mavis Ann O P621
Hernandez, Enrico W83
Hernandez, Guillermo W177
Hernandez, Armando David
 Palacios W381
Hernandez, Laurie E220
Hernandez, Roland E402
Hernando, Julio A390:E215
Hernday, Natasha E455
Herndon, Lori P48
Herold, Heather P311
Herold, Florian W304
Heron, Nadine P325
Herpich, Peter M P61
Herpich, Mark E245
Herr, Robert A493
Herr, Tracy P185
Herraiz, Lizette E392
Herrera, Dennis A185:P122
Herrera, Steve P122
Herrera, Art P156
Herrera, Gina P653
Herrera, Jesus Gonzalez W109
Herrero, Fernando Maria
 Masaveu W72:W172
Herreros, Mariano Hernandez W9
Herrick, Glen A519
Herrick, Bea P169
Herrick, Glen E272
Herring, Todd A9
Herring, Joseph A696
Herring, Hayden P640
Herring, Todd E3
Herringer, Frank A697
Herrington, Matthew E153
Herriott, Simon A426
Herrman, Ernie A786
Herrmann, Ron A672
Herrmann, Mindy P261
Herrold, Jan P662
Herron, Stephen J. A139
Herron, Kevin A350
Herron, Mark A617
Herron, Dallas P136
Herron, Cherry P140
Herron, Joseph E206
Herron, Mark E319
Herrup, Karl P102
Hersacher, Christian P209
Herschenfeld, Brett A667:P438
Herscher, Penelope W194
Hersey, Thomas P159
Hershberger, Pamela A61
Hershberger, Carlo P259
Hershberger, Rodney E321
Hershey, Milton P344
Hershly, Mary Jo A825:P631
Herskovits, Thomas E185
Hertel, Janie P212
Hertel, Paula M P540
Herter, Rolf E129
Hertogh, Mark De P420
Hertz, Noreena A846
Hertz, Sandy P316
Hertz, Arthur P576
Hertzman, Brian A47
Herweck, Peter E405
Herzog, David A39
Herzog, James A204
Herzog, David A521
Herzog, Daniel E86
Heslop, James E274
Hesner, David P585
Hess, Debra A662
Hess, Lisa A662

Hess, David A726
Hess, Jason A812
Hess, Becky P226
Hess, Carol P654
Hess, Marc W2
Hess, Beat W229
Hesse, Daniel A632
Hesse, Ken P89
Hesse, Daniel E11
Hessekiel, Jeffrey E150
Hessenthaler, Leader Brian P553
Hesser, Gregory T P16
Hession, David E123
Hessius, Kerstin W471
Hessling, Rick A496:A541
Hester, Kevin A393
Hester, Randy A646
Hester, Beverly P596
Hester, Kevin E217
Hester, Randy E336
Hesterberg, Earl A368
Heston, Grant J P641
Hete, Joseph E10
Heter, Crystal P532
Hetterich, Francis A218
Hetzel, Andrew A562
Hetzel, Tyler P247
Hetzel, Andrew E293
Heuberger, Alan A240
Heuch, Cecilie W483
Heun, Judy A94:E45
Heuschel, Mary Alice A741:P518
Heutink, Chris W397
Heuvel, William A179
Hewa, John P409
Hewett, Mark A P386
Hewitt, Margaret P102
Hewitt, Kathryn P160
Hewitt, William P374
Hewitt, Martha P473
Hewitt, William P544
Hewitt, Liz W342
Hewson, Marillyn A172:A441
Hexter, David W383
Heya, Toshio W226
Heyborne, Ryan P456
Heydlauff, Dale E P30
Heyman, William A792
Heymann, Andres Ergas W56
Heyn, Markus A681:P448
Heyne, Brianna A346:P227
Heynitz, Harald Von W444
Heywood, Matthew P45
Hezlep, John A251
Hiatt, Rex P148
Hibbard, Carol J A124
Hibbard, Mike P332
Hibben, Kendra P16
Hibbs, Kelly A125
Hickam, Jerry P490
Hicker, Joe P161
Hickey, Beth A15
Hickey, David A109
Hickey, Kevin A710
Hickey, Beth P7
Hickey, Kevin P107
Hickey, John E82
Hickey, Kevin E371
Hickman, Roger P73
Hickman, Tanya P556
Hickman, Bernie W291
Hickok, Steven G P83
Hickox, Michelle A417:E227
Hicks, Lisa A324
Hicks, Bradley A408
Hicks, Sarah A741
Hicks, R Steven A824
Hicks, Gilbert P52
Hicks, Matthew P233
Hicks, Larry P380
Hicks, Holly P446
Hicks, Sarah P517
Hicks, R Steven P630
Hicks, Beverly P644
Hicks, Greg W101
Hicks, Helen W465
Hicks, Andrew W532

Hicks, Alicia E64
Hicks, J. Kennedy E105
Hicks, Randy E160
Hickson, Tracy P460
Hickson, Richard E105
Hickton, Dawne A436
Hidaka, Yoshihiro W537
Hidalgo, Celeste P452
Hiden, David A320:E173
Hieb, William A690
Hieber, Michael R P340
Hiebler, Jessica A757
Hiegl, Carol A603:A603:P404:E310
Hier, Lars A283:P208
Hietala, Kaisa A291
Higa, Ernest W439
Higaki, Connie P474
Higaki, Seiji W472
Higashi, Emiko A457
Higashi, Kazuhiro W452
Higashi, Emiko W475
Higdon, Mark P391
Higginbotham, Robert A756
Higginbotham, Michael P416
Higgins, Barbara A274
Higgins, Melina A351
Higgins, Bren A457
Higgins, John P216
Higgins, Jennifer P292
Higgins, Kelly A P294
Higgins, John E50
Higgins-Carter, Karen A851
Higginson, Michael P286
Higgs, Currie P270
High, Rob P130
High, Katherine E225
Highland, Mary Anne P499
Hightower, Kyle P636
Hightower, Caresse P644
Higley, David A112
Higuchi, Masayuki W205
Higuchi, Tetsuji W334
Higuchi, Tatsuo P375
Higuchi, Yasuyuki W378
Higuchi, Kojiro W491
Higurashi, Yutaka W356
Hikita, Sakae W148
Hilado, Maria A146:A878
Hilaire, Syndie Saint P103
Hilal, Paul A67:A227
Hilal, Said S P40
Hilal, Nabil P40
Hilburn, Beverly P570
Hilburn, Charles P615
Hildebrand, Jeffery D A824:P630
Hildebrand, Arthur K E157
Hileman, Donald A639:E332
Hilgeman, Chris P209
Hilger, Andy A30:P21
Hilgers, Berna P193
Hill, Leo A53
Hill, Richard A72
Hill, Michael A114
Hill, Grant A146
Hill, Kathryn A160
Hill, Tim A172:A173
Hill, William A388
Hill, Scott A A414
Hill, Patrick A436
Hill, Kathryn A536
Hill, Vanessa N A640
Hill, Vernon A676
Hill, Stephanie A691
Hill, Robert A721:A725
Hill, Kim P72
Hill, Angela Fenton P111
Hill, Tim P113:P113
Hill, Ashley D P117
Hill, Linda F P158
Hill, Ray P186
Hill, Chris P191
Hill, Roger P227
Hill, Scott A P259
Hill, Thomas E P283
Hill, Dan P375
Hill, Sam P420
Hill, Richard P459

Hill, Sue P599
Hill, Nigel P660
Hill, Leo E25
Hill, John E86
Hill, Edward E127
Hill, George E176
Hill, Barbara E234
Hill, Vanessa N E333
Hill, Robert E383
Hill-Milbourne, Veronica E4
Hill-Nelson, Sarah E245
Hillebrand, James A747:E391
Hillenbrand, Daniel E215
Hiller, Michael A139
Hillery, Jon P35
Hilliard, Belinda P598
Hillier, Scott A481
Hillier, Luke M P47
Hillman, Heidi P138
Hillman, James V P274
Hills, Wendy E441
Hilsheimer, Lawrence A367:E231
Hilt, Angela A189
Hilt, James E213
Hilton, Stephen A213
Hilton, Christopher A322
Hilton, Steven A518
Hilton, Michael A689
Hilton, Stephen P150
Hilton, Ronald E309
Hilzinger, Kurt A406
Hilzinger, Jeffrey E135
Himbauch, Chris P559
Himeiwa, Yasuo W432
Himes, Michael P414
Himes, Vicki P414
Himes, Vicky P414
Hinchliff, Andrew W135
Hinck, Ramona P603
Hincker, Lawrence G P100
Hinderhofer, Kathryn A143:E65
Hinds, Edmundo P349
Hinduja, Anil A337
Hine, Mark P299
Hines, Jan A266
Hines, Perry A399
Hines, George A481
Hines, Michael A786
Hines, Valerine P98
Hines, Margaret P477
Hines, Frances P496
Hines, John P532
Hines, Linda P642
Hingham, John R P565
Hingtgen, Tim A211
Hinkle, James A393
Hinkle, Allen J P360
Hinkle, James E217
Hinkleman, Jon P363
Hinman, Jacqueline A427
Hinnenkamp, Paul A277
Hinojosa, Esther P18
Hinojosa, Michael P179
Hinojosa, Guillermo Francisco
 Vogel W22
Hinojosa, Claudio Melandri W59
Hinson, Donald A383
Hinson, Michael P256
Hinson, Donald E212
Hinson, Laura E457
Hintermeyer, Mary K P116
Hinton, Jim A106:A106
Hinton, James A510
Hinton, Jim P64:P65
Hinton, Angela P123
Hinton, Don P153
Hinton, Phillip P222
Hintz, Angie P451
Hintze, Paul P334
Hipp, William E391
Hippe, Patricia A200
Hippe, Alan W408
Hippel, James E50
Hipple, Richard A453
Hippler, Kelley E182
Hirai, Yasuteru W325
Hirai, Ryutaro W450

HOOVER'S HANDBOOK OF EMERGING COMPANIES 2022

COMBINED HOOVER'S HANDBOOK INDEX OF EXECUTIVES

A = AMERICAN BUSINESS
E = EMERGING COMPANIES
P = PRIVATE COMPANIES
W = WORLD BUSINESS

Hiraizumi, Nobuyuki W268
Hiraku, Tomofumi W328
Hiramoto, Tatsuo W127
Hirano, Frank P231
Hirano, Atsuhiko W240
Hirano, Nobuyuki W326
Hirano, Nobuya W332
Hirasawa, Jun W313
Hirasawa, Akira W439
Hirata, Seiji W279
Hirawat, Samit A134
Hire, W. Jeffrey E231
Hirji, Rahim Badrudin Hassanali W308
Hirner, Beth P52
Hirner, Liane W516
Hirokawa, Yoshihiro W331
Hirose, Shinichi W493
Hirose, Takehiro W537
Hirowatari, Kiyohide W260
Hirsch, Elizabeth A211
Hirsch, Chuck A411
Hirsch, Constance P160
Hirsch, Jim P420
Hirsch, Glenn P503
Hirsl, Miroslav W281
Hirst, Alistair A449
Hirst, Martha P217
Hiscoe, Lester P479
Hise, Brent P424
Hiser, Becky P604
Hisham, Muzaffar W307
Hisham, Fauziah Binti W307
Hite, Christopher E358
Hitt, Kathy P43
Hitt, Kirby P468
Hitz, Travis P653
Hitzemann, Barbara P166
Hixon, James A740
Hixon, Chris P394
Hixon, James P516
Hjelmaker, Josef A786
Hjelmberg, Anna W471
Hjelmstad, Terry P381
Hlay, Jean E184
Ho, Hing-Yuen A23
Ho, Peter A97
Ho, Angela A582
Ho, Vivian P147
Ho, Hin Ngai W121
Ho, Tian Yee W155
Ho, Poh Wah W376
Ho, David W465
Ho, Lora W474
Ho, Angela E302
Hoaglin, Thomas A44
Hoang, Hanh H A403
Hoang, Vincent A735
Hoang, Hanh H P256
Hoang, Vincent P511
Hoar, Sherryll P460
Hobart, Lauren A244:A875
Hobbs, Franklin A33
Hobbs, Nicholas A408
Hobbs, Michael A417
Hobbs, Lee P38
Hobbs, Lee G P38
Hobbs, Charlotte A P42
Hobbs, Richard P147
Hobbs, Diane P418
Hobbs, Richard F P602
Hobbs, Michael E227
Hobby, Jean A386
Hobby, Paul A574
Hobson, Mellody A732
Hobson, David P201
Hobson, James M P325
Hobson, Kami P653
Hoch, Gordon B P439
Hochman, Rod A647
Hochman, Fredric L P114
Hochman, Rod P429

Hochman, Rodney P429
Hochman, Shalom W253
Hochschild, Roger A247:A641
Hochschwender, J. Michael A409
Hochstetler, Robert P107
Hockel, Dale P360
Hocken, Natalie A604
Hockfield, Susan A622
Hocking, Chris P620
Hockridge, Stuart E15
Hodes, Ben A700
Hodes, Harold L P368
Hodge, Michael A387
Hodge, Edmund A794
Hodge, David P340
Hodge, Edmund P599
Hodges, Julie A10
Hodges, Ernest M A293
Hodges, George A340
Hodges, Steven P133
Hodges, Ernest M P212
Hodges, Glinda P200
Hodges, Michelle E342
Hodges, Charles E409
Hodgins, Paula A840
Hodgkinson, Andrew E250
Hodnett, David P55
Hodo, Chikatomo W324:W373
Hodson, John W470
Hoechtel, Elfriede W367
Hoedl, Dean P368
Hoefinger, Peter W515
Hoefler, Brenda P262
Hoefler, Carol A P323
Hoeg, Krystyna W242
Hoekema, Dale P279
Hoeller, Heidi A546
Hoelter, Michael A61
Hoelter, Amber P45
Hoeltermand, Peter W446
Hoenig, Thomas A446
Hoepfner-leger, Isabelle W402
Hoepner, Theodore E57
Hoer, Michael E266
Hoerner, Michael P496
Hoesen, Peter Van P22
Hoesten, Mark P366
Hoetges, Timotheus W163:W224
Hoeweler, Robert E77
Hoey, Brian P317
Hoey, John Joseph P579
Hoff, Lynda A730
Hoff, Ken P62
Hoff, Lynda P509
Hoffer, Theresa A179
Hoffler, Daniel E30
Hoffman, Stephen M A300
Hoffman, Edward A662
Hoffman, James A673
Hoffman, Roy P203
Hoffman, Rany P353
Hoffman, John P449
Hoffman, Marc P456
Hoffman, Joshua E134
Hoffman, Cindy E134
Hoffman, Tom A125
Hoffmann, Charlotte W154
Hoffmann, Andre W408
Hoffmaster, Perry P439
Hoffmeister, David A160:E220
Hoffmeyer, Kevin P405
Hofheins, Todd A647:P6:P429:P429
Hofing, Gary E164
Hofmann, John P304
Hofmann, Karl P422
Hofmann, Jorg W522
Hofmann, Stephanie E2
Hofmann, Thomas E446
Hofmeister, Brandon A190
Hofmeyer, Anna Marie P219
Hofstaetter-Pobst, Gregor W367
Hofstetter, Sarah A146
Hofstetter, John E332
Hogain, Eoin O W389
Hogan, Kathleen A26
Hogan, Mark A107

Hogan, Janet L A401
Hogan, Michael A416
Hogan, Kathleen A529
Hogan, David P60
Hogan, Larry P316
Hogan, Joseph E15
Hogan, Mark E48
Hogan, Peter E201
Hogan, Michael E226
Hogan, W. Glenn E253
Hogenson, Kathleen E434
Hogg, Michael A377
Hogg, Alice P540
Hogg, Sarah P413
Hoggatt, Brian E394
Hoglund, Robert A216:A217
Hoglund, Krista P472
Hogue, Herbert L P302
Hoguet, Karen A461:A562:P378
Hohenberg, Maximilian W509
Hohlmeier, Monika W81
Hohmeister, Harry W161
Hohn, Diedrich P134
Hoidahl, Hans-Olav W25
Hoke, Kevin P164
Hoke, Doug P173
Hoke, Adriane P438
Hokenson, Christa E392
Holcomb, Michele A151
Holcomb, John A725
Holcomb, Diane A742:P518
Holcomb, John E383
Holcroft, Alexander W345
Holda, Margaret P488
Holda, Margaret M P488
Holden, Zachery A700
Holden, Angela P58
Holden, Ross J P370
Holden, Gary P374
Holden, E Wayne P443
Holden, Teresa P554
Holden, Robert E39
Holden-Baker, Sue P83
Holder, Julie A264
Holder, Sophia G P549
Holder, H. Randolph E300
Holding, Frank A312
Holdings, Midcoast P343
Holdsworth, Mark E354
Hole, Brian E449
Holecek, Nancy P61
Holladay, Mark A754:E401
Hollan, Linda P263
Holland, Christopher A434
Holland, James A456
Holland, Neal A674
Holland, David P124
Holland, Lindsey P311
Holland, John P327:P459
Holland, Julie E121
Holland, Neal E348
Holland, G. Edison E381
Hollandsworth, Dean P160
Hollandt, Andrea P184
Hollar, Jason A151
Holleaux, Didier W184
Hollen, Shawna P633
Hollenbeck, Martin A179
Hollenbeck, Margo P286
Holler, Glenn J P265
Holley, Rick A862
Holliday, Charles A240
Holliday, Susan A307
Holliday, Steven A316
Holliday, Marc A667:P438
Holliday, Keith E388
Holliger, Fredric A542
Hollihan, John A70
Hollinger, William A447
Hollingshead, James E233
Hollingshead, Jim E352
Hollingsworth, Chad A483
Hollinshead, Wayne P650
Hollis, Andrea P610
Hollman, Michael E8
Holloman, James A653
Holloway, Caitlyn A789

Holloway, Duane A821
Holloway, Caitlyn E411
Holloway, Jason E449
Hollub, Vicki A581
Holly, James A709:E370
Holm, Alan A176
Holm, Mark P107
Holman, Janet P164
Holman, Jeff P307
Holman, Cathy P522
Holman, Jonathan E32
Holmberg, Jim A292
Holmen, Kenneth P107
Holmes, Robert A94:A206
Holmes, Donald N A241
Holmes, Michael A279
Holmes, Stewart A410
Holmes, Kimberly A A451
Holmes, Ned A646
Holmes, James A655
Holmes, Rob A770
Holmes, Russell A773
Holmes, Garry P161
Holmes, Angela P270
Holmes, William P275
Holmes, Sara P291
Holmes, Kristopher P320
Holmes, Kelly W P355
Holmes, Carolyn P402
Holmes, Nicholas P434
Holmes, Norman G P491
Holmes, David W323
Holmes, Robert E45
Holmes, John E106
Holmes, Chad E107
Holmes, Michael E142
Holmes, Ned E336
Holmes, Frank E E429
Holsapple, Cindy A838:P641
Holsher, Michael P422
Holstebro, Jens P223
Holsten, Joseph A484
Holston, Michael A346
Holt, Timothy A523
Holt, Donald A529
Holt, Christopher A597
Holt, Kasha P1
Holt, Jason P101
Holt, David P130
Holt, Kara P421
Holt, Susan P624
Holt, Kevin W283
Holt, Tim Oliver W444
Holt, Alex W532
Holt, Donald E274
Holt, Christopher E307
Holt, Timothy E411
Holte, Chelsea P431
Holthaus, Michelle A421
Holtinger, Jens W523
Holtz, Timothy P553
Holtz, Clifford E252
Holtzman, James A807
Holtzman, Marc E417
Holynskyj, Oleh P519
Holzer, Sunita E381:E434
Holzer, Rhyan E442
Holzgrefe, Frederick E359
Holzmann, Thomas P112
Holzshu, Christopher A481
Hom, Donald E295
Hom-anek, Prinya W491
Homan, Jan W187
Hombach, Robert A154
Homburger, James E257
Homer, Ronald A A503:P317
Homma, Tetsuro W378
Hon, Roxanne P235
Hon, Sherry P278
Hon, Kah Cho W307
Hon, Kwee Fong W376
Honda, Keiko W330
Honda, Osamu W469
Hondal, Francis A104
Honeycutt, Jennifer A235
Honeycutt, Allison A259
Honeyman, Joel P137

534

HOOVER'S HANDBOOK OF EMERGING COMPANIES 2022

COMBINED HOOVER'S HANDBOOK INDEX OF EXECUTIVES

Hong, Arlene A111
Hong, Kean Yong W29
Hong, Bo W123
Hong, Liang W431
Honickman, Jeffery A203
Honig, Ben A621
Honig, Lyle P12
Honig, Ben P412
Honjo, Takehiro W375
Honorato, Pamela Harris W177
Hood, Amy A3
Hood, Christopher A449
Hood, Amy A529
Hood, William A816
Hood, Letha P159
Hood, Michelle P200
Hood, Mark E111
Hood, William E169
Hoogenboom, Leonard E174
Hook, Lisa A304
Hook, Richard A615
Hook, Lisa A625
Hooker, Nolan E383
Hooks, Lisa Winston P360
Hooks, Michael E258
Hooley, Joseph A291:W37
Hooper, Michele A813
Hooper, Richard P147
Hooper, Lucelia P303
Hooper, Mike P386
Hooper, Jenia P467
Hooper, Tia P492
Hooper, Tecumseh E382
Hoopes, John R P460
Hoopes, Jeffrey C P530
Hoopingarner, John E422
Hoople, Elizabeth A519:E272
Hoose, Harold E83
Hoovel, Catherine A509
Hoover, Erik A260
Hoover, Brian A679
Hoover, Jim P428
Hoover, G Michael P525
Hoover, Mike P581
Hoover, Linda M P602
Hope, Henry P452
Hopeman, Wei A128
Hopfenbeck, James P468
Hopfield, Jessica E233
Hopke, Debra P632
Hopkin, Vince A591
Hopkins, Lynn M A93
Hopkins, Jennifer A381
Hopkins, Deborah A500:A812
Hopkins, Tim P40
Hopkins, Gloria P283
Hopkins, Brendon W38
Hopkins, Jennifer E208
Hoplin, Kris P249
Hopmans, John A483
Hopp, Daniel A400:E218
Hoppe, Jessica A29
Hoppe, Robert A312
Hoppe, Jonn D P291
Hoppe, Jessica E13
Hoppenot, Herve E225
Hopper, Robert A192
Hopper, Karen P337
Hopps, Rhonda E82
Hopson, Mitch P242
Hor, Kwok Wai W232
Horak, H. Lynn A155
Horak, Jennifer P450
Horan, Mark P155
Horaszewski, Marilyn P360
Horgan, Kathryn A743
Horgan, Tanya W17
Horger, Robert A725:E383
Horiba, Atsushi W462
Horie, Nobuyuki W216
Horikami, Brian P474
Horio, Yoshiyuki W65
Horiuchi, Yosuke W429
Horiuchi, Katsumi W435
Hormaechea, Michael A355:E193
Hormell, Robert A331:E178
Horn, Bill A224

Horn, Zachary A320
Horn, Bill P168
Horn, Dennis P395
Horn, Michelle P633
Horn, Zachary E173
Hornaday, F. D. A49:E21
Hornbaker, Renee A264
Hornberger, David A597:E307
Hornbrook, Michael P319
Hornbuckle, William A524
Horne, James A372
Horne, Timothy A803
Horne, Mona P99
Horne, Timothy P606
Horne, Charles E430
Horner, Henry P361
Horner, Terry E242
Horning, Sandra A355
Horning, Brian P101
Hornish, Jo E155
Hornsby, Jessica P119
Horsman, Sarah M P357
Horstmann, Anne W337
Horstmeier, Ilka W79
Horta, Elisa P529
Hortefeux, Valerie W316
Horton, Donald A403
Horton, Chris P156
Horton, Andrew P396
Horvath, Deborah A668
Horvath, Greg P103
Horvath, Jeff P356
Horvath, Albert P484
Horvath, Ferenc W334
Horwedel, Gregory P161
Hose, Mitchell A737:P513
Hosey, Dr Ashley P141
Hoskins, Adriana A700
Hoskins, Joy P296
Hosoda, Akio W538
Hosoi, Hiroshi W182
Hosokawa, Nobuhisa W373
Hossain, Mir A439:P276
Hosseini, Abby A516
Hossle, Dwight A232
Host, Gerard A798
Host, Dennis P142
Hoster, David H E129
Hostetler, Tom P98
Hostetter, Jason P597
Hostetter, Steve P598
Hostler, Sharon L P439
Hotchkiss, Herbert E81
Hotchkiss, Richard E161
Hotsuki, Keishi A538
Hottges, Timotheus A758
Hou, Qijun W378
Hou, Cliff W474
Houbein, Patricia P163
Houchens, Steve P127
Houchins, Dion P255
Houck, Jason P446
Houde, Jean W340
Houdek, Carla P555
Hough, Louise P153
Hough, David P249
Hough, Jay P343
Hough, Laurie E377
Houghton, Keith A396
Houghton, Marella A736
Houghton, Pansy P251
Houghton, Marella P512
Houghton, Sue W396
Houghton, Amanda E207
Houghton, Keith E217
Houle, Patricia S P85
Houle, Jeff P179
Houmann, Lars D A14:P5
Hountalas, Jon W99
Hourican, Kevin A755
Hourigan, Timothy A395
House, Rebecca A684
House, Kelley P344
House, Paula P615
Houseal, Mark P164
Householder, Joseph A13
Houseknecht, Ester A E282

Housel, Morgan A497
Houser, Mark A A824
Houser, Dale P400
Houser, Mark A P630
Housman, Diane P557
Houston, Helga A409
Houston, Andrew A520
Houston, Daniel A641
Houston, Melanie A828
Houston, Steve P423
Houston, Melanie P635
Houston, Michael W533
Hout, Frits van W42
Houten, Diana Van P255
Houten, Christina Van E403
Hove, John P98
Hove, Bart P649
Hoveland, Justin P36
Hovell-Patrizi, Allegra W13
Hovey, Michael A121
Hovey, Chris W40
Hovsepian, Joe P431
Hovsepian, Ronald E27
Howard, June A18
Howard, John A363
Howard, Anne A366
Howard, Michelle A424
Howard, Julie A494
Howard, Anne A655
Howard, David A759
Howard, Brian A789
Howard, John A817
Howard, Maureen P36
Howard, Chuck P55
Howard, Tony P73
Howard, Erica O P94
Howard, Wayne P159
Howard, Anne P235
Howard, Greggory P286
Howard, Michelle P330
Howard, Christopher P477
Howard, Stephen R P657
Howard, Jeffrey E35
Howard, Ayanna E38
Howard, Anne E340
Howard, Julie E378
Howarth, Richard P55
Howe, Robert A45
Howe, Douglas A459
Howe, Jeff P658
Howe, Stephen W82
Howell, Lloyd A129
Howell, Thomas A439
Howell, Melissa A449
Howell, Lloyd A536
Howell, Heather A675
Howell, Eric A710:A711
Howell, James P104
Howell, Melita P336
Howell, James P357
Howell, Eric P481
Howell, Stephen P569
Howell, Jack W543
Howell, Laura E11:E94
Howell, Robin E199
Howell, Hilton E199
Howell, Peter E339
Howell, Heather E351
Howell, Eric E371
Howell, Brett E375
Howes, Constance A847
Howes, David P315
Howes, Richard W97
Howland, Douglas A424
Howle, Carol-Lee W91
Howorth, Derek P387
Howse, Curtis A752
Howson, David E73
Howton, Barry P151
Howze, Marc A240
Hoxit, Debbie A741:P518
Hoy, Thomas A72:A297
Hoy, Joann P90
Hoy, Thomas E31:E158
Hoyle, Amanda P55
Hoyle, Kevin P104
Hoyle, M. Eddie E91

Hoyme, Sharon P609
Hoyos, Diana W171
Hoysradt, Jean E443
Hoyt, Rebecca A64
Hoyt, Marlene A278
Hoyt, Bob W234
Hoyt, Marlene E141
Hoz, Esteban Kemp Kemp De La W56
Hrabowski, Freeman A757
Hromadko, Gary A282
Hronek, Joseph P176
Hruby, Dennis E370
Hsiao, Chiu Bin P208
Hsieh, Jackson A728:P496
Hsieh, Johnny P532
Hsieh, Tsun-Yan W308
Hsieh, Haydn W530
Hsieh, Ming E183
Hsing, Michael E279
Hsiung, Ming-Ho W106
Hsiung, Nai-Pin W195
Hsu, Hsenghung A296
Hsu, Michael A455
Hsu, Clark A639
Hsu, Johnny A639
Hsu, Michael A777
Hsu, Kevin P466
Hsu, Lai Tai Fan W66
Hsu, Judie W106
Hsu, Lai Tai Fan W119
Hsu, Chieh-Li W138
Hsu, Wen-Being W138
Hsu, Chiung-Chi W138
Hsu, Sheng-Hsiung W138
Hsu, Sheng-Chieh W138
Hsu, Chen-Chang W138
Hsu, Wen-Da W138
Hsu, David W262
Hsu, Ting-Chen W432
Hsu, Judy W456
Hsu, Clark E331
Hsu, Johnny E331
Hsu, Alex E397
Hsuan, Min Chih W138
Hu, Gary A234:A581
Hu, Brad A743
Hu, Queenie P438
Hu, Xiaolin W88
Hu, Xingguo W123
Hu, Guobin W125
Hu, Hanjie W194
Hu, Yebi W209
Hu, Yueming W220
Hu, Zuliu W244
Hu, Yuntong W265
Hu, Zaixin W387
Hu, Jean E183
Huang, Scott A174
Huang, Nick A262
Huang, Jen-hsun A577
Huang, Scott P118
Huang, Jian WEI P121
Huang, Megan P144
Huang, Zhaoran R P442
Huang, Dongling P442
Huang, Jui-Han P574
Huang, Bo P624
Huang, Tiao-Kuei W106
Huang, Ching-Lu W106
Huang, Xiumei W117
Huang, Wensheng W120
Huang, Qing W122
Huang, Hsin-Hsiung W138
Huang, Chiao-Lie W138
Huang, Shih-Hong W138
Huang, Juncan W209
Huang, De-Cai W230
Huang, Jian W236
Huang, Chaoquan W236
Huang, Lixin W236
Huang, Zhongqiang W265
Huang, Yongzhang W378
Huang, Hai W387
Huang, Jianlong W419
Huang, You W442
Huang, Wendell W474
Huang, Yu W490

COMBINED HOOVER'S HANDBOOK INDEX OF EXECUTIVES

A = AMERICAN BUSINESS
E = EMERGING COMPANIES
P = PRIVATE COMPANIES
W = WORLD BUSINESS

Huang, Wenzhou W535
Huang, Nick E127
Huang, Ta-Lun E311
Huang, Xiaoli E311
Hub, Rachel P406
Hubbard, Robert A521
Hubbard, Jean A639
Hubbard, Kym A733
Hubbard, Bryan P130
Hubbard, Lindsay P340
Hubbard, Maryann P345
Hubbard, Bart P463
Hubbard, Sonja P661
Hubbard, Linda E213
Hubbard, Jean E332
Hubbell, Jodi A319:E172
Hubble, Susan A618
Hubbs, Miranda W242
Huber, Marie A266
Huber, Jeffrey A271
Huber, Weylin P11
Huber, Johnathan P100
Huber, Lesa P261
Huber, Thomas E269
Hubert, Angela St P90
Hubler, James A700
Hubley, Denise P55
Huckaby, Hank A123:P81
Huckelberry, Chuck P418
Huckins, Bonita M A738:P514
Hudak, Carrie E85
Huddle, William E247
Hudgins, Jessie P638
Hudson, Thomas A6
Hudson, Linda A96
Hudson, Ann A285
Hudson, Nancy A446
Hudson, Brian A529
Hudson, Stephanie A762
Hudson, Sherrill A816
Hudson, Rick A825
Hudson, David A871
Hudson, Terry P65
Hudson, Larry P111
Hudson, Nicole P134
Hudson, Carol P153
Hudson, Richard P319
Hudson, Keeba P337
Hudson, Peter P346
Hudson, Jane P490
Hudson, Guy P530
Hudson, Rick P631
Hudson, Deal E35
Hudson, Brian E145
Hudson, Ian E159
Hudson, Brian E274
Hudson, Frederick E399
Hudspeth, Teneshia P160
Huebscher, Grace A337
Hueners, Jeff P112
Huerta, Christy A15:P7
Huerta, Rey P94
Huerta, Joyce L P107
Huerta, Nicolas Burr De la W56
Huerta, Miguel Mata W58
Huestis, Timothy A628
Huestis, Christine E169
Huestis, Timothy E324
Huether, Robert A551
Huey, Morris A149
Hufenbecher, Constanze W246
Huff, Brittany A741
Huff, Carrie P218
Huff, Jelada P305
Huff, Carroll W P464
Huff, Billie V P490
Huff, Brittany P517
Huff, Joe P543
Huff, Richard P571
Huffard, John A566
Huffines, James A824:P630

Huffman, Steve P34
Huffman, Abel P286
Huffman, Patty P408
Huffman, Herbert E423
Hufnagel, Charles W104
Hug, Matt C P367
Huggins, James A617
Huggins, Dan W340
Hughes, William A113
Hughes, Brian A247
Hughes, Denis A299
Hughes, Martin A375
Hughes, Emily A387
Hughes, James A523
Hughes, Melanie A536
Hughes, Jeffrey A677
Hughes, Michael A728
Hughes, Scott A736
Hughes, Kieth P11
Hughes, Diona P78
Hughes, Byron P91
Hughes, Jo P130
Hughes, Mike P159
Hughes, Wilson P225
Hughes, Stephen P262
Hughes, James P262
Hughes, David P P280
Hughes, Michael P P280
Hughes, Bill P306
Hughes, Henry P414
Hughes, Chad P476
Hughes, Michael P496
Hughes, Scott P512
Hughes, Barbara P595
Hughes, Amanda W396
Hughes, Mark E83
Hughes, Charisse E110
Hughes, Paula A E207
Hughes, James E425
Hughes, Bryan E451
Hughey, Sandy P381
Huguenard, Jackie P444
Huh, Yong Hak W438
Huhr, Eric A638:P426
Hui, Hui J P547
Hui, Ka Yan W115
Hui, Sai Tan W435
Hui, Wing Mau W436
Huie, Susan P585
Huillard, Xavier W517
Huizinga, Stuart E343
Hulet, Steven P460
Hulgrave, Shelley A615
Huling, Donna P18
Hull, John P544
Hull, Gregory E383
Huller, Kelly E195
Hullinger, Norman P87
Huls, Todd P307
Hulse, Walter A593
Hulse, Walter S A594
Hulse, Lew P246
Hulse, Walter S P397
Hulsey, Jason P222
Hulsey, Janice P610
Hulst, Michelle A97
Hulst, H. W249
Hulstein, Jeff P179
Hult, David A73
Hultberg, Arcelia P363
Hultsman, Todd P376
Humaidhi, Abdullah Al W38
Hume, Richard A32
Hume, Jeffrey A220
Hume, Richard A763
Humenik, John E248
Humphrey, Ashley A741
Humphrey, Jennifer P15
Humphrey, Jayrah P52
Humphrey, Ashley P517
Humphrey, Nikki W295
Humphrey, Scott E184
Humphreys, Odell-Jeff P212
Humphreys, Tara P621
Humphries, Brian A199
Humphries, Rosemary P184
Humphries, Mary P432

Humphries, Colin J P566
Hund-Mejean, Martina A200
Hundertmark, Johan W38
Hung, Maan-Huei A157
Hung, Jerry B P196
Hung, Jui-Reui W106
Hung, Ta-Ching W106
Hung, Benjamin W457
Hung, Maan-Huei E70
Hung, Yie-hsin E418
Hung, Priscilla E433
Hungerford, Meg E297
Hungria, Cristina P79
Hunhoff, Darin A175
Hunley, Jenny P164
Hunn, Robert P326
Hunot-Schmit, Anne-Marie W489
Hunsaker, Rebecca P623
Hunsicker, Judith E132
Hunskaker, Ron P312
Hunt, James A614
Hunt, Bruce A646
Hunt, Eugene A712
Hunt, Gordon A750
Hunt, Gary A762
Hunt, John P48
Hunt, Doris P152
Hunt, Don P172
Hunt, Robert P184
Hunt, Frank P242
Hunt, Jennifer P344
Hunt, Stephen J P373
Hunt, Gordon P528
Hunt, Briston P556
Hunt, Linda P602
Hunt, Colin W17
Hunt, Jacqueline W26
Hunt, John W531
Hunt, James E57
Hunt, Hazel E102
Hunt, Tina E221
Hunt, James E317
Hunt, Bruce E336
Hunt, Anthony E349
Hunt, Eugene E373
Hunt, Heather E376
Hunt, Tina E433
Hunter, Robert P A35
Hunter, William C A299
Hunter, Martin A414
Hunter, Shannon A584:A584
Hunter, Jerry A712
Hunter, Robert P A27
Hunter, Marvalette P126
Hunter, Donnie P203
Hunter, Martin P259
Hunter, Sandra P313
Hunter, Joan P493
Hunter, Kimberly P621
Hunter, Michael J P656
Hunter, Steven E133
Hunter, Rhonda E362
Hunter, Robert E366
Hunter, Jerry E373
Huntington, Nicholas A650
Huntington, Judith A710:E371
Huntley, David A78
Huntley, Cindy A383:E212
Hunton, Tina A215
Huntsman, Jon A172:A333
Huntsman, Peter A411
Huntzicker, James P170
Hunzeker, Fred R A787:P595
Huo, Wenxun W432
Hupp, Alicia A608
Hupp, William T P209
Hupp, Stephen E P209
Hupp, Alicia E312
Hur, Francis P165
Hurd, Laurel A556:A786
Hurley, Michael A215
Hurley, Ursula A439
Hurley, Jill A754
Hurley, Colleen P303
Hurley, Robert E131
Hurley, Jill E401
Hurlston, Michael W197

Hurrell, Miles W199
Hurst, Ron P419:P419
Hurst, Calvin E382
Hurtado, Domingo A84
Hurtado, Anna P530
Hurtado, Rami Aboukhair W61
Husain, Kamran A382:E211
Huseman, Kim P286
Hushon, Dan A213:P150
Huskins, Priya E294
Huson, Caren P422
Huss, Matthew P636
Hussar, Drew P243
Husted, Jon A740:P516
Huston, Chad A303
Huston, Amy P363
Huston, Peter W200
Huston, Danny E68
Huston, Michael E296
Hutab, Michael W166
Hutchcraft, Mitch P488
Hutcheson, Kelly A674
Hutcheson, Jennifer P454
Hutcheson, Kelly E348
Hutchings, Dane P139
Hutchings, W. Preston W40
Hutchins, Michael A337
Hutchins, Kris P223
Hutchinson, Keisha A710
Hutchinson, Asa A734
Hutchinson, Cathy P243
Hutchinson, Kirk P237
Hutchinson, Samantha P423
Hutchinson, Dixie P471
Hutchinson, Asa P510
Hutchinson, Louis J P654
Hutchinson, Keisha E371
Hutchison, Larry A359
Hutchion, John A742
Hutchison, G Duane P228
Hutchison, John P518
Hutchkin, Christine P83
Hutsell, Kathleen A233
Hutsell, Roberta A775
Hutsell, Kathleen P178
Hutsell, Roberta P548
Hutson, Allison A P204
Hutson, Richard E235
Hutt, John A52
Huttenlocher, Daniel A222
Huttle, Frank A215:E97
Hutton, William A672
Huval, Tim A406
Huval, Caroline E290
Huxley, Sarah P73
Huxtable, Kristy W135
Huynh, Toan A326
Huynh, Carolyn N A739:P515
Huynh, Toan E177
Huynh, Jamie E327
Huza, Callie P335
Hwang, Angela A819
Hwang, Seong Sik W296
Hwang, Robert W530
Hwang, Donald W530
Hwang, Gyu Mok W532
Hyatt, Thomas P40
Hyatt, Ronnie P499
Hyde, Gordon A688
Hyde, Jeffrey P148
Hyde, Kevin P233
Hyde, Randy P251
Hyde, Dwight P330
Hyder, Brent A692
Hyland, M. Elise A277
Hyland, Donna A350
Hyland, M. Elise A495
Hyland, Donna E105
Hyland, John E425
Hylander, Kenneth P364
Hyle, Kathleen A55
Hylen, Chris A381
Hylen, Theresa P190
Hylen, Chris E208
Hylton, Tracy A186:E84
Hyman, David A551
Hyman, Edward E149

536

HOOVER'S HANDBOOK OF EMERGING COMPANIES 2022

COMBINED HOOVER'S HANDBOOK INDEX OF EXECUTIVES

Hymas, Scott L P433
Hymel, Jeigh A877
Hymel, Matthew P163
Hymel, Jeigh P662
Hynes, John P99
Hynson, Lawrence P396
Hyun, Grace E435

I

Iachini, Anthony P143
Iacopetti, Dean E304
Iadanza, Thomas A832:E431
Ianieri, Linda A851
Iannacone, Nicole A279:E142
Iannarelli, Rocco P371
Iannelli, Josephine A103:E47
Ianniello, Luigi P132
Iannotti, Thomas A66
Iarlori, Simonetta W294
Ibach, Shelly E377
Ibarguen, Anthony A420
Ibnale, David E420
Ibrahim, J. Jay A448
Ibrahim, Tommy P565
Ibrahim, Shamsul Bahrom bin
    Mohamed W29
Ibrahim, Maha E116
Icahn, Brett A234
Icahn, Carl A413
Icahn, Brett A413
Icard, Laura P451
Ice, Carl R A122
Ice, Melonie A727
Ice, Carl R P80
Ice, Melonie P495
Ichikawa, Evan P323
Ichikawa, Totaro W170
Ichikawa, Tatsushi W272
Ichiki, Nobuya W151
Ichinokawa, Takashi P32
Icho, Mitsumasa W325
Ida, Shuichi W418
Ide, Akiko W492
Idehen, Francis E147
Idemitsu, Masakazu W240
Idilbi, Bashir P573
Igarashi, Makoto W1
Igarashi, Koji W327
Ige, David A735:P511
Igeta, Kazuya W255
Iglar, Kathy P608
Iglesias, Lisa A39
Iglesias, Henry A562
Iglesias, Lisa A827
Iglesias, Henry P378
Ignacio, Andrea A97
Ignatiev, Sergey W424
Ignjatovic, Dusan P102
Igoe, Paul G P196
Ihamuotila, Timo W5
Ihara, Ichiro W127
Ihara, Michiyo W237
Ihlein, Michael W30
Ihlenfeld, Jay A160
Ihler, Jon P339
Ihori, Eishin W228
Ii, Masako W326
Iijima, Masami W475
Ijima, Masaru P527
Ikebe, Kazuhiro W288
Ikeda, Kazufumi P90
Ikeda, Koji W226
Ikeda, Hajime W360
Ikeda, Kentaro W436
Ikegami, Kenji W437
Ikegawa, Yoshihiro W324
Ikemoto, Tetsuya W255
Ikeya, Koji W328
Iki, Noriko W354
Ikushima, Takahiko W328
Ilan, Haviv A771
Illa, Anisha P565
Illek, Christian A758:W163
Illgen, John E96
Ilyukhina, Elena W208

Imaeda, Tetsuro W463
Imai, Tadashi W354
Imaki, Toshiyuki W436
Imaoka, Shoichi W418
Imbault, Heather A35:P27
Imes, Cheryl P301
Imhof, Doug P217
Imhoff, Jenny P281
Imhoff, Paul P347
Immekus, Sue P545
Imperato, Donna W533
Impicciche, Joseph A74
Impicciche, Joseph R A74
Impicciche, Joseph P43
Impicciche, Joseph R P43
Imrith, Richard A7
Imsang, Kris W393
Ina, Koichi W286
Inaba, Nobuo W403
Inabnit, Christopher P327
Inacio, Cidalia E448
Inada, Koji W268
Inagaki, Seiji W68
Inal, Karen P544
Inbar, Galia W487
Incandela, Nicholas P48
Indaravijaya, Kattiya W270
Indest, John E252
Indigo, Darwin W529
Infante, Christine P85
Infantegreen, Angelica A740:P516
Infantolino, Edward E312
Ing, J Douglas P603
Ingle, Gary P335
Ingle, Jennifer P380
Ingram, Tamara A500
Ingram, Charles A519
Ingram, Sean A737
Ingram, Melissa P5
Ingram, Azia P170
Ingram, Bret P272
Ingram, Sharon P399
Ingram, Sean P513
Ingram, Tamara P311
Ingram, Von W531
Ingram, Elizabeth E257
Ingram, Charles E272
Ingrum, Jeff P468
Ingulli, Alfred E23
Ingulsrud, Brian P30
Inkley, Robert P9
Inman, Stephanie P424
Innocenti, John A828:P635
Innocenzo, Michael A286
Inoue, Shin A877:P662
Inoue, Satoru W148
Inoue, Noriyuki P335
Inoue, Tetsuo W206
Inoue, Satoshi W216
Inoue, Ryuko W356
Inoue, Makoto W373:W375
Inoue, Yukihiko W377
Inoue, Kazuyuki W436
Inoue, Osamu W462
Inoue, Atsuhiko W463
Inoue, Hisato W538
Inscho, Bill A321
Inserra, Lawrence A466
Inserra, Andre W425
Inserra, Lawrence E243
Inslee, Jay A741:P518
Insler, Todd A813
Insuasty, Jorge A625
Inukai, Akira W1
Inzana, Lugene P308
Inzina, Tommy P504
Ioannou, Stavros W188
Iordanou, Constantine E434
Ip, Ka Cheung W212
Ippolito, Peter A708
Ipsen, Laura E434
Ipser, Annice R P540
Iraka, Dana P112
Irani, Ali P263
Irby, Mark A652
Ireland, S. Leslie A183
Irie, Shuji W373

Irisawa, Hiroyuki W216
Irish, Stephen A278
Irish, Dale A737:P513
Irish, Stephen E141
Iritani, Atsushi W150
Irizarry, Alex P53
Irshad, Naveed W308
Irvine, John P177
Irving, Paul A262
Irving, Blake E38
Irving, Paul E127
Irwin, Bart P304
Irwin, Robert P449
Isa, Zamzamzairani Bin Mohd W307
Isaac, Karen P161
Isaac, Jon E256
Isaac, Antonios E256
Isaacson, Mark A539
Isaacson, Walter A813
Isaacson, Christopher E73
Isaka, Ryuichi W430
Isaza, Sergio Restrepo W171
Isbell, Corey P320
Ise, Kiyotaka W21
Ise, Katsumi W170
Isely, Kemper E288
Isely, Zephyr E288
Isely, Elizabeth E288
Isely, Heather E288
Iseman, Jay A396
Isenhour, Thomas K P171
Ishaq, Esam W64
Ishibashi, Tamio W151
Ishida, Mie W34
Ishida, Norihisa W34
Ishida, Satoshi W339
Ishida, Koichi W369
Ishiguro, Tadashi P90
Ishiguro, Shigenao W479
Ishii, Yoshimasa A790
Ishii, Yuji W377
Ishii, Toru W429
Ishii, Takayuki W491
Ishii, Yoshinori W493
Ishikawa, Keitaro W34
Ishikawa, Takatoshi W205
Ishikawa, Hiroshi W268:W279
Ishimaru, Fumio W418
Ishimoto, Hiroshi W52
Ishimura, Kazuhiko W360
Ishitani, Masahiro W338
Ishiyama, Kazuhiro W492
Ishizaki, Yuji W500
Ishizuka, Shigeki W313:W453
Ishizuki, Mutsumi W312
Ishmael, Cheryl P193
Isho, Mayyas P335
Ishrak, S. Omar A57
Ishrak, Omar A421
Isley, L Lee P586
Ismail, Khalijah Binti W307
Isobe, Tomoyasu W472
Isom, Robert A41
Isono, Hiroyuki W369
Isozaki, Yoshinori W277
Israel, Jeff P155
Israel, Michael D P652
Issa, Abdullah Bin Mohammed
    Al W407:W422
Isshiki, Toshihiro W463
Istavridis, Eleni A721
Itakura, Kazumasa W468
Itambo, Eric A195:P140
Itayem, Fadie A796
Itchon, Jesus W83
Iten-Maly, Tricia P249
Ito, Yoshihiro W17
Ito, Yukinori W17
Ito, Shintaro W21
Ito, Tomonori W36
Ito, Takeshi W36
Ito, Hisanori W127
Ito, Kenichiro W158
Ito, Motoshige W170
Ito, Tadaaki W206
Ito, Toshiyasu W237
Ito, Junichi W237

Ito, Masamichi W257
Ito, Yumiko W279
Ito, Eisaku W326
Ito, Shinichiro W331
Ito, Kenji W350
Ito, Kazuo W370
Ito, Junro W430
Ito, Kumi W452
Itoh, Atsuko W170
Itow, Marc P641
Ittard, Samuel P P487
Iturrate, Orlando Poblete W59
Iulio, David De P290
IV, Frank R Palmer P783
IV, Calvin Thomas P233
IV, Frank R Palmer P591
Iverson, Duane A442:P278
Iverson, Ellen P550
Ives, Dune A92
Ives, Louisa A322
Ives, Zachary A A739:P515
Ivey, Craig A40
Ivey, Kay A734:P510
Ivey, Bob P661
Ivie, Stanley R A606
Iwahashi, Toshiro W67
Iwai, Mutsuo W260:W479
Iwamoto, Hiroshi W317
Iwamoto, Tamotsu W436
Iwanejko, Tom P171
Iwasa, Hiromichi W331
Iwasaki, Takashi W205
Iwasaki, Masato W475
Iwase, Junichi W182
Iwata, Keiji W66
Iwata, Kikuo W67
Iwatsubo, Hiroshi W338
Iwersen, Kevin E419
Iyasu, Getachew P385
Iyengar, Jayanthi A598
Iyengar, Vijay E225
Iyer, Vijayalakshmi P281
Iyoke, Israel P43
Izadi, Azade P70
Izdebski, Marcin W71
Izsak, Alexander P284
Izumi, Yasuki W23
Izumisawa, Seiji W326
Izumiya, Naoki W367
Izurieta, Laura A751
Izzo, Ralph A99:A651

J

Jabal, Kimberly A302
Jabbar, Masood E436
Jabbari, Pina P466
Jabes, Aliza W519
Jablonski, Jack A742
Jablonski, Mark P345
Jablonski, Jeffrey P367
Jablonski, Jack P518
Jablonsky, Diane P198
Jabour, Paul P132
Jabs, Jacob P31
Jacinto, Jesus W82
Jacinto, Virgilio W417
Jackiewicz, Thomas E P585
Jackman, Worthing A658
Jackowski, Julia A155
Jackowski, Jessica P496
Jackson, Lawrence A77
Jackson, Jamere A84
Jackson, Peter A139
Jackson, Rick A149
Jackson, Brian A294
Jackson, Mike A298
Jackson, Shirley Ann A302
Jackson, Benjamin A422
Jackson, Theodore A614
Jackson, Shirley Ann A651
Jackson, Martin A703
Jackson, Yvonne A727
Jackson, Andrew A735
Jackson, Rich A735
Jackson, Stephon A756

COMBINED HOOVER'S HANDBOOK INDEX OF EXECUTIVES

A = AMERICAN BUSINESS
E = EMERGING COMPANIES
P = PRIVATE COMPANIES
W = WORLD BUSINESS

Jackson, Jamere A778
Jackson, Denise A791
Jackson, Alice A871
Jackson, Daniel P31
Jackson, Christine P81
Jackson, Loyd P86
Jackson, Frank G P125
Jackson, Patrice P128
Jackson, Typhanie P129
Jackson, Jimmy L P158
Jackson, David P160
Jackson, Rebecca P173
Jackson, Hattie P175
Jackson, Janet P193
Jackson, Rosa P P202
Jackson, Scott P216
Jackson, Brooke P230
Jackson, Kim P238
Jackson, Richard L P269
Jackson, R Shane P269
Jackson, Fred P286
Jackson, Joy P291
Jackson, Timothy P323
Jackson, Larry P332
Jackson, Melissa P334
Jackson, Rebecca P347
Jackson, Wes P351
Jackson, Ches P351
Jackson, Charles P403
Jackson, Cynthia P426
Jackson, Shirley Ann P442
Jackson, Amanda P462
Jackson, Jeramy P482
Jackson, Rosa P P491
Jackson, Crystal P499
Jackson, Andrew P511
Jackson, Rich P511
Jackson, Scott P525
Jackson, Roger P534
Jackson, Cheryl P536
Jackson, Tommy P541
Jackson, Claire P542
Jackson, Blair P556
Jackson, Jamere P561
Jackson, Barbara C P641
Jackson, Sally W210
Jackson, J. David W389
Jackson, Tony W396
Jackson, Robert E114
Jackson, Brian E156
Jackson, Teresa E257
Jackson, Daniel E392
Jackson, Harold E409
Jacob, Dianne A224
Jacob, Paul P133
Jacob, Dianne P168
Jacob, Wendy P462
Jacob, Leonard E28
Jacobowitz, Jesse P481
Jacobs, Kerry A29
Jacobs, Terry A47
Jacobs, Lew A183
Jacobs, David A253
Jacobs, Dwight A259
Jacobs, Kevin A389
Jacobs, Kathleen E A555
Jacobs, Elizabeth A655
Jacobs, Lisa A676
Jacobs, Bradley A873
Jacobs, Teresa P166
Jacobs, Ronald D P254
Jacobs, Kelly P330
Jacobs, Maria P332
Jacobs, Kathleen E P374
Jacobs, Conrad P376
Jacobs, Dennis P427
Jacobs, Bill P538
Jacobs, James K P553:P646
Jacobs, William E200
Jacobs, Elizabeth E340
Jacobsen, Rene A7

Jacobsen, Kevin A189
Jacobsen, Bell P517
Jacobsmeyer, Jay P411
Jacobson, Kenneth A88
Jacobson, Paul A349
Jacobson, Jonathon A614
Jacobson, Michael P118
Jacobson, Astrid P154
Jacobson, Cathy P222
Jacobson, James P492
Jacobson, Geraldine P651
Jacobson, Richard E169
Jacobson, Jonathon E317
Jacoby, Rebecca A691
Jacoby, Francis E388
Jacovatos, James A329
Jacquez, Erica P303
Jadlowski, Mary P177
Jadot, Maxime W87
Jaeger, Nils W523
Jaegers, Christine P226
Jafarieh, Nicolas A716:E379
Jafarnia, Korsh P336
Jaffe, Jonathan A474
Jaffe, Seth A476:A477:P297
Jafry, Syed A784:A878
Jagdfeld, Aaron E191
Jaggers, Richard P55:P55
Jagiela, Mark E405
Jagos, Ray P166
Jaha-Rashidi, Atiya P374
Jahagirdar, Balkrishna N P441
Jahanian, Farnam P100
Jahn, Timothy P58
Jahn, Andrew P378
Jahn, Barb P458:P503
Jahnke, David A319:E171:E362
Jaime, Lilia W525
Jaimes, Elsa W171
Jain, Ajit A113
Jain, Dipak A240
Jain, Manisha P300
Jain, Sunny W510
Jain, Vivek E220
Jaindl, Mark E20
Jajeh, Diana Saadeh A343
Jakins, Chip P269
Jakobsen, Niels W267
Jakosky, Donn A603:A603:P404:E310
Jakosuo-Jansson, Hannele W346
Jalali, Rahul A812
Jalbert, Elizabeth P248
Jallal, Bahija A63
Jalloh, Candra P228
Jamal, Syed P450
Jamal, Rizwan W82
Jamal, Arshil W213
Jamar, John P35
James, Esther St A16
James, Donna A132
James, Renee A183
James, Letitia A186
James, Hamilton A223
James, Alasdair A253
James, Alicia A362
James, Donna A377
James, Robert A396
James, Catherine A456
James, Renee A595
James, Brooke A617
James, Thomas A A663
James, Thomas A663
James, Deborah A772
James, Cheryl A864
James, Marie A866
James, Esther St P8
James, Becky P113
James, Letitia P129
James, Dick P143
James, Alicia P232
James, Pam P298
James, Karyl P333
James, Sly P347
James, Lark P380
James, Thomas A P436
James, Drew P496
James, David P548

James, William B P644
James, Cheryl P656
James, Marie P657
James, Todd J E52
James, Robert E217
James, Donald E359
Jameson, Steven A212
Jameson, Heidi P267
Jamieson, T J P271
Jamieson, Lee P271
Jamieson, Roberta W412
Jamieson, VeraLinn E120
Jamil, Dhiaa M A259
Jamisom, Marylin P364
Jamison, Cynthia A236:A791
Jamison, Steve P187
Jan, Barlow A598
Jandernal, Robert P343
Jandernoa, Michael A727:P495
Jandzio, Bronislao W110
Janecek, Cindy P26
Janell, Joseph E P87
Janes, Maria A847
Janese, Catherine P247
Janeway, Teresa A473
Janeway, Katherine P243
Janeway, Dean P284
Janeway, Teresa P295
Janey, Gregory E411
Jang, David P196
Jang, Yin Hwa W388
Jang, Seung Hwa W388
Jang, Simon W474
Janiga, Matthew P529
Janis, Ronald A832:E431
Janjariyakun, Vichai W98
Janki, Dan A242
Janki, Daniel A346:P227
Jankovich, Chris P175
Jankowski, Edward A143
Jankowski, Gary P314
Jankowski, Edward E65
Jannetti, Anthony E312
Janney, Karen P530
Janofsky, Christine E131
Janow, Merit A506
Jansen, James A295
Jansen, David P222
Jansen, Robert P233
Jansen, Bill P610
Jansen, Philip W95
Jansen, Rolf Habben W219
Jansky, Anita P319
Janson, Deborah K A50
Janson, Julia S A259
Jantzen, Dan P182
Jantzen, Daniel P183
Jany, Patrick W1
Janz, Jeff P313
Jara, Armando P527
Jarai, Zsigmond W334
Jaramillo, Richard P316
Jaramillo, Juan Enrique Morales W141
Jarbou, Ibrahim Bin Fahd Al W422
Jardine, Gina W145
Jared, David P139
Jared, Edmond P139
Jarel, Raquel A186:P127
Jarlegren, Magnus A80
Jarman, Samuel Y P25
Jarman, Vickie E188
Jaro, Vic P485
Jaroudi, Ismail W335
Jarrell, William P290
Jarrett, Valerie A843
Jarrett, Craig P638
Jarukornsakul, Jareeporn W441
Jarupanich, Prasert W98
Jarvis, Ernest A261
Jarvis, Patrick P63
Jarvis, Clifford P301
Jarvis, Ernest E126
Jarwaarde, Ewout Van W91
Jashinsky, Cathy P298
Jaska, James E59
Jaskolka, Norman W102
Jasper, J. A755

Jaspers, Allen P262
Jassy, Andrew A38
Jastrzebski, Ted A807
Jatou, Ross A591
Jaurequi, Pat P463
Jauron, Lisa P112
Javaid, Mohammad E95
Javellana, Jeanette W83
Javidroozi, Mazyar P206
Javier, Maria Theresa Marcial W70
Jawa, Kanwal W149
Jawa, Abdul Rahman W407
Jawaheer, Damini P115
Jay, Stefanie A266
Jay, P P300
Jay, Paul P317
Jaye, James A708
JD, Howard R Grant P290
JD, Scott Marquardt P310
JD, Mark Dalton P604
Jeanfreau, Mark A674:E348
Jearavisitkul, Pittaya W98
Jeavons, Michael W413
Jebaily, John E174
Jebens, Doug P367
Jedlicki, Anne P624
Jeffcoat, Sally P456
Jeffe, Robert A74
Jeffers, Amanda P138
Jeffers, Lewis A423
Jefferson, Elbert P128
Jefferson, Timothy P233
Jefferson, Maria P614
Jeffery, Nick A339
Jeffery, Ricardo Bartel W58
Jeffrey, Robert P156
Jeffrey, Hanks P157
Jeffrey, Chris P485
Jeffrey, David E P578
Jeffrey, David P578
Jeffrey, William W480
Jeffries, Jason P126
Jeffries, Pamela R P560
Jeffries, James A P562
Jeffs, Mike P149
Jego-laveissiere, Marie-
noelle W184:W372
Jehi, Lara A775:P533
Jejurikar, Shailesh A643
Jelenko, Jane A157:E70
Jelinek, W. Craig A223
Jelito, Ernest W222
Jellison, Douglas A575
Jelly, Maecy P637
Jemison, Mae A455
Jena, Jujudhan W425
Jenah, Susan Wolburgh W290
Jendrysik, Diane P133
Jenisch, Jan W229
Jenkins, Norman A83
Jenkins, Deborah A337
Jenkins, Decosta A628
Jenkins, Howard A652
Jenkins, Jennifer A652
Jenkins, Dorothy A860
Jenkins, Jo Ann P2
Jenkins, Melissa P25
Jenkins, Andrea P128
Jenkins, Clay P158
Jenkins, Jason P159
Jenkins, John P167
Jenkins, Decosta P203
Jenkins, John R P317
Jenkins, Jennifer P380
Jenkins, Kerri P382
Jenkins, Buddy P432
Jenkins, A Dale P443
Jenkins, Barbara M P467
Jenkins, Diane P481
Jenkins, Malinda P492
Jenkins, Barbara P572
Jenkins, John W480
Jenkins, Norman E124
Jenkins, William E191
Jenkins, David E201
Jenkins, James E245
Jenkins, Michael E307

COMBINED HOOVER'S HANDBOOK INDEX OF EXECUTIVES

Jenkins, Decosta E324
Jenkins, Frank E439
Jenks, Maria P209
Jenner, Toby W533
Jenness, Calvin P76
Jennings, Karen A227
Jennings, Michael A390
Jennings, William M P87
Jennings, Miguel P377
Jennings, Toni E57
Jensen, Karen A310
Jensen, Kirk A319
Jensen, Barry A416
Jensen, Claus Torp A513
Jensen, Derrick A658
Jensen, Jon A A737
Jensen, Karen P74
Jensen, Jerard J P321
Jensen, Claus Torp P328
Jensen, Jon A P513
Jensen, Corey E126
Jensen, Karen E164
Jensen, Kirk E171
Jensen, Keith E183
Jensen, Traci L E189
Jensen, Barry E226
Jenson, Susy P184
Jenson, Mike P602
Jentz, Alan P610
Jeon, Jung Sun W388
Jeon, Ji Pyeong W532
Jeppesen, Poul P483
Jepsen, Mary A470
Jepson, Jeff P209
Jepson, Brian D P395
Jerdan, David P553
Jerden, Evelyn E252
Jerez, Aicia P356
Jermann, Nadine W75
Jernberg, Melker W523
Jernigan, Donald L A14:P5
Jerome, Brian S P287
Jerome-Forget, Monique W65
Jesko, Danielle P140
Jesse, James P301
Jessee, William P458
Jessee, Mary P590
Jessup, Abbreyel P579
Jester, James P58
Jester, Clyde A P144
Jesus, Cathy P175
Jeter, Daniel A53:E25
Jetha, Yasmin W345
Jetley, Vivek E151
Jewell, Sally A223
Jewell, John B P598
Jewett, Ellen A129:A439
Jewett, S. Leslie E63
Jewkes, Roger A303
Jews, William A142
Ji, Chongxing W349
Ji, Guangheng W383
Jia, Jinzhong W122
Jia, Guosheng W220
Jia, Xiaoliang W442
Jia, Yimin W535
Jiamtragan, Yuttana W441
Jian, James A14:P5
Jian, Qin W118
Jiang, Joseph P488
Jiang, Enxiang P604
Jiang, Fan W24
Jiang, Yingwu W81
Jiang, Changlu W81
Jiang, Xin W87
Jiang, Yan bo W97
Jiang, Qun W114
Jiang, Jinming W154
Jiang, Hongyuan W208
Jiang, Yan W287
Jiang, Xiaoming W378
Jiang, Guizhi W535
Jiao, Yanjun W123
Jiao, Fangzheng W378
Jibson, Ronald A254
Jim, Davey P101
Jimenez, Frank A410

Jimenez, Joseph A643
Jimenez, Frank A665
Jimenez, Dianna P303
Jimenez, Barbara P341
Jimenez, Esther P398
Jimenez, Pedro Jose Lopez W9
Jimenez, Alejandro Cantu W28
Jimenez, Jorge Desormeaux W33
Jimenez, Pedro Jose Lopez W227
Jimenez, Menardo W417
Jimenez, Luis E108
Jin, Jeoung A329
Jin, Jiming P637
Jin, Shengxiang W154
Jin, Lishan W431
Jin, Qingbin W539
Jin, Ju E304
Jing, Xiandong W24
Jinks, Mark P122
Jinks, Mary P629
Jirapongphan, Siri W62
Jitjang, Krit W270
Jivanov, Iasmina P293
Jiwani, Zahra P272
Joachimczyk, Paul E24
Jobin, Luc W93
Jobin, Eric W239
Jobling, Margaret W345
Jochens, Birgit W222
Jochims, Jeffrey W600
Jockelson, Philip W233
Jocson, Ramon W70
Jodarski, Guy P154
Joerg, Ingrid W521
Joffrion, Barry P419
Jogu, Prasad P529
Johannes, Andria P36
Johanns, Michael A240
Johansen, Jakob V P205
Johansen, Terrie P570
Johansen, Judith E362
Johansson, Leif W46
Johansson, Martin W446
Johenning, Richard P59
John, Jerome F A299
John, Bozoma Saint A551
John, Jack St A803
John, Scott St. A816
John, Ryerson P162
John, Levy P366
John, Kreidler P445
John, Knochel P456
John, Meghan St P466
John, Jack St P606
John, Ryther P661
John, Scott St. W199
JohnBull, Kathryn E122
Johns, John A350:A671
Johns, Bobbie P198
Johns, Christine P282
Johns, Valerie P335
Johns, Raymond E10
Johnsen, Kjetil A283:P208
Johnsen, Richard E53
Johnson, Andrew A22
Johnson, James A40
Johnson, Stephen A41
Johnson, Johnny D A50
Johnson, Mercedes A61
Johnson, Stephen A94
Johnson, Kenneth A102
Johnson, Margaret A120
Johnson, Dannis A122
Johnson, Robert A125
Johnson, Arthur A129
Johnson, Timothy A139
Johnson, Gregory A142
Johnson, Brian A155
Johnson, Denise A156
Johnson, Gerald A156
Johnson, Cheryl A156
Johnson, James A172
Johnson, Kristina A182
Johnson, Beth A185
Johnson, Shaun A190
Johnson, Eric A194
Johnson, Heather A200

Johnson, Broderick A203
Johnson, Jason A211
Johnson, Robert A248
Johnson, William A260
Johnson, Ronald A272
Johnson, Kimberly A292
Johnson, Simon A293
Johnson, Mitchell A296
Johnson, Bart A313
Johnson, Richard A314
Johnson, Margy A321
Johnson, Julia A324
Johnson, Richard A332
Johnson, Jennifer A336
Johnson, Rupert A336
Johnson, Gregory A336
Johnson, Gerald A349
Johnson, Steven A359
Johnson, Carl A370
Johnson, Joia A373
Johnson, James A373
Johnson, Kimberly A399
Johnson, Helen A404
Johnson, Jennifer A426
Johnson, Ellen A428
Johnson, Gregory A429
Johnson, Bruce A434
Johnson, Erik S A475
Johnson, Kimberly A478
Johnson, Julia A504
Johnson, Dennis A512
Johnson, Esther A525
Johnson, Karlton A525
Johnson, Denise A539
Johnson, Felicia A554
Johnson, Jay A556
Johnson, Manuel A578
Johnson, Gregory A579
Johnson, James A598
Johnson, Belinda A611
Johnson, Rady A622
Johnson, Ryan A631
Johnson, Eric A640
Johnson, Devin A645
Johnson, Gregory A656
Johnson, Amy A665
Johnson, Joia A671
Johnson, Susan A694
Johnson, Thomas A695
Johnson, Jennifer A709
Johnson, Richard A721
Johnson, Chris A726
Johnson, Kevin A732
Johnson, Amy A734
Johnson, Carol C A737
Johnson, Wayne A739
Johnson, Tim A739
Johnson, Patricia A789
Johnson, Brintel A799
Johnson, Charles A799
Johnson, Thomas A804
Johnson, Shannon A808
Johnson, William A819
Johnson, Kathleen A819
Johnson, Jeh A821
Johnson, Janilee A828
Johnson, Marianne A857
Johnson, Netha A871
Johnson, Carleen P19
Johnson, Alan P28
Johnson, Gary P40
Johnson, Nicole Conley P52
Johnson, George P52:P53
Johnson, Gwen P53
Johnson, Antonia Axson P53
Johnson, Dannis P80
Johnson, Holly P81
Johnson, Ron P94
Johnson, Bruce P99
Johnson, Clifford P100
Johnson, Yvette P108
Johnson, Chad P112
Johnson, Kelly M P116
Johnson, Frank P123
Johnson, Toya P125
Johnson, Eric P126
Johnson, Michael P133

Johnson, Scott P P133
Johnson, Kathy P135
Johnson, Lary P P136
Johnson, Clayton P157
Johnson, Sandra P159
Johnson, Kevin P162
Johnson, Michelle P162
Johnson, Tiffany P167
Johnson, Luke P173
Johnson, Rhonda P177
Johnson, James R P179
Johnson, Neal P185
Johnson, H Keith P188
Johnson, Cristine P196
Johnson, Deborah C P200
Johnson, Tracy P214
Johnson, Brittany P215
Johnson, Jack P228
Johnson, Katherine P229
Johnson, Denise P232
Johnson, Charles L P242
Johnson, Steve P246
Johnson, Robert C P254
Johnson, Patsy P254
Johnson, Kimberly P255
Johnson, Michelle R P261
Johnson, Mark P266
Johnson, Shelley P282
Johnson, Neil P286
Johnson, Antonia Axson P298
Johnson, Carrie P306
Johnson, Melonie P311
Johnson, Colleen P316
Johnson, Kimiko P323
Johnson, Cato P337
Johnson, Barbara P340
Johnson, Colt P342
Johnson, Tyree P345
Johnson, Bernadeia P345
Johnson, Michael P349
Johnson, Philip P358
Johnson, David D P362
Johnson, Felicia P372
Johnson, Mike P380
Johnson, Darrell P398
Johnson, Tiffany P402
Johnson, Sam P421
Johnson, Joey P426
Johnson, J Keith P428
Johnson, Tracy P433
Johnson, Ilona P443
Johnson, Sandy P450
Johnson, Bret P451
Johnson, Lisa P459
Johnson, Jani L P459
Johnson, Ken P468
Johnson, Carol P471
Johnson, Lisa P473
Johnson, Warren D P502
Johnson, Amy P510
Johnson, Carol C P513
Johnson, Wayne P515
Johnson, Tim P515
Johnson, Frank P525
Johnson, Diane P P526
Johnson, Marthea P529
Johnson, Doug P532
Johnson, Bill P533
Johnson, Elizabeth P550
Johnson, Torie P580
Johnson, Anthony D P587
Johnson, Erica P593
Johnson, Krista P604
Johnson, Brintel P605
Johnson, Charles P605
Johnson, Thomas P607
Johnson, Dianne P620
Johnson, Mary P624
Johnson, Terry P634
Johnson, Janilee P634
Johnson, Diana P638
Johnson, Mary Beth P639
Johnson, Jerry N P647
Johnson, Josephine J P647
Johnson, Alan P647
Johnson, Samuel P648
Johnson, Paula E3

HOOVER'S HANDBOOK OF EMERGING COMPANIES 2022

539

COMBINED HOOVER'S HANDBOOK INDEX OF EXECUTIVES

A = AMERICAN BUSINESS
E = EMERGING COMPANIES
P = PRIVATE COMPANIES
W = WORLD BUSINESS

Johnson, Claire E19
Johnson, David E23
Johnson, B. Kristine E36
Johnson, Stephen E45
Johnson, Kenneth E60
Johnson, Edwin E69
Johnson, Willis E101
Johnson, Fred E115
Johnson, Peter E126
Johnson, Allison E138
Johnson, Jack E155
Johnson, Mitchell E157
Johnson, Robert E161
Johnson, Bart E165
Johnson, Carrie E182
Johnson, Sidney E184
Johnson, Kenton E198
Johnson, Lacy E203
Johnson, Carl E203
Johnson, Richard E229
Johnson, David E239
Johnson, Craig E247
Johnson, David E265
Johnson, Nicholas E266
Johnson, Betty E284
Johnson, M. E289
Johnson, Kathryn E309
Johnson, Jonathan E309
Johnson, Charles E322
Johnson, Eric E333
Johnson, Janice E340
Johnson, Sandra E348
Johnson, Stephen E366
Johnson, Jennifer E370
Johnson, Kristen E376
Johnson, Jerry E392
Johnson, Mercedes E405
Johnson, Shannon E421
Johnson, Marianne E447
Johnson-Leipold, Helen E239
Johnston, Lori A57
Johnston, Steven A179
Johnston, Michael A256
Johnston, Hugh A379:A619
Johnston, Jeff P102
Johnston, Christopher P132
Johnston, Matt P156
Johnston, Craig P213
Johnston, Jeffrey P334
Johnston, Laura P334
Johnston, Dean P400
Johnston, Leif P413
Johnston, Teena P650
Johnston, George W57
Johnston, David W191
Johnston, William W203
Johnston, Lori E156
Johnstone, William A94
Johnstone, Lisa P643
Johnstone, Sally P653
Johnstone, William E44
Johrendt, Michael E247
Johri, Rajive A322
Joiner, Cindy A597:E307
Jojo, Linda A286:A813
Jokinen, Tracy E12
Joko, Keiji W257
Jolkovsky, Richard P578
Jolley, James P205
Jolly, Jim P652
Jolly, Bruce W242
Joly-Pottuz, Dominique Muller W517
Jonas, Mcebisi W335
Jonas, Howard E191
Jonczyk, Kris A652
Jones, Steve A31
Jones, John A81
Jones, Regina A91
Jones, Mautra A94
Jones, Chris A155
Jones, Nicole A178

Jones, Rickee A209
Jones, David A211
Jones, Larry A211
Jones, Mary A240
Jones, Gregory A284
Jones, Jeffrey A310
Jones, Eli A315
Jones, Travis A366
Jones, Nathan A381
Jones, Robertson A382
Jones, Kevin A416
Jones, Thomas A437
Jones, Greg A453
Jones, Hal A490
Jones, René A491
Jones, Clayton A540
Jones, Jessica A541
Jones, Jessica M A541
Jones, Jay A541
Jones, Christopher A566
Jones, Thomas A569
Jones, Jeff C A603:A603
Jones, Richard A607
Jones, Douglas A614
Jones, Allen A640
Jones, Wendy A649
Jones, Randall A652
Jones, Karen A689
Jones, William A705
Jones, Robert A706
Jones, Scott A733
Jones, Gregory A737
Jones, Clarence A737
Jones, Alexandra A762
Jones, Hannah A778
Jones, Shaunna A874
Jones, Matt P15
Jones, Steve P24
Jones, Marilyn P53
Jones, Andrea P54
Jones, Greg P54
Jones, Doug P55
Jones, Theresa P56
Jones, Stephen P60
Jones, Jansen P70
Jones, Amy P81
Jones, Jim P103
Jones, Melody L P103
Jones, Michael P116
Jones, Angel P129
Jones, Bruce P139
Jones, Rickee P146
Jones, Clinton P151
Jones, Vernon P158
Jones, Yvette P158
Jones, Toni P187
Jones, Iridious P201
Jones, Ty P203
Jones, Dan P218
Jones, Chris P220
Jones, Mark P223
Jones, Jim P235
Jones, Travis P235
Jones, Jeff P247
Jones, Stephanie P249
Jones, Mark A P272
Jones, Evan C P291
Jones, Gregory P316
Jones, Jennifer P361
Jones, Donald L P366
Jones, Kevin P366
Jones, Dottie P380
Jones, Harry P387
Jones, Jeff C P404
Jones, Jacqueline P408
Jones, Janel P411
Jones, Terri P441
Jones, Marna P444
Jones, John P452
Jones, Lowry P459
Jones, Robert P473
Jones, Caroline P503
Jones, Gregory P513
Jones, Clarence P513
Jones, Lisa P537
Jones, Yvette M P542
Jones, Margaret M P549

Jones, Allan P550
Jones, Kris P556
Jones, Hannah P564
Jones, Chris P569
Jones, Alvin P578
Jones, Roberta P584
Jones, Paul T P604
Jones, Linda P609
Jones, Reed F P615
Jones, Daniel W P624
Jones, Trevor P643
Jones, J Thomas P651
Jones, Garth W16
Jones, Tim W395
Jones, Todd W396
Jones, Joann E35
Jones, Mautra E44
Jones, Russell E69
Jones, Mickey E84
Jones, Walter E86
Jones, Jeffrey E90
Jones, Daniel E136
Jones, Jeffrey E164
Jones, Ray E166
Jones, Eli E168
Jones, Nathan E208
Jones, Robertson E211
Jones, Michael E215
Jones, Kevin E226
Jones, W. Kelly E264
Jones, Jay E281
Jones, Sarah E289
Jones, James E294
Jones, Jeff C E310
Jones, Douglas E317:E317
Jones, Doug E318
Jones, Allen E333
Jones, Melody E441
Jong, Annemieke De P546
Jongsaliswang, Pichit W285
Jongsukkigparnich, Kriangsak W65
Jonietz, Michael A681:P448
Jonsson, Joanna F A49
Jonsson, Patrik A478
Jonsson, Joanna F P33
Joo, Se Don W388
Joong, Chi-Wei W106
Joos, Astrid W483
Joosub, Shameel W520
Jope, Alan W510
Joplin, Joe P384
Jopson, James A8:P4
Jordan, David A84:A317
Jordan, Lori A326
Jordan, Rhonda A418
Jordan, Gregory A632
Jordan, Rhett A717
Jordan, Robert A726
Jordan, Donna A734
Jordan, William A866
Jordan, Phyllis P2
Jordan, Steve P107
Jordan, George P107
Jordan, Patrick P183
Jordan, Denisha P198
Jordan, Arthur P198
Jordan, Barb P442
Jordan, Christopher P451
Jordan, Donna P510
Jordan, Phil W259
Jordan, Donald E166
Jordan, David E170
Jordan, Lori E177
Jordan, John E323
Jordan, Rhett E380
Jordan, William E450
Jordan-Cox, Carmen P628
Jordano, James A463
Jorden, Carolyn P555
Jorg, Cathy P530
Jorgensen, Nate A125
Jorgensen, Blake A271
Jorgensen, Lisa A742
Jorgensen, Tim A755
Jorgensen, Helge P181
Jorgensen, Lisa P518
Jorgensen, Erik P653

Josefowicz, Gregory W176
Josefsson, Lars W514
Joseph, Anthony A25
Joseph, George A516
Joseph, Victor A516
Joseph, Fred A544
Joseph, Wetteny A881
Joseph, Ronald P80
Joseph, Gloria P154
Joseph, Martin P175
Joseph, Janet P206
Joseph, Rhonda P223
Joseph, Cathy P224
Joseph, Paul E11
Joseph, Fred E285
Joseph, Celia E426
Joseph, Molly E446
Josephs, Glenn E164
Josephson, Cheryl A740:P516
Josey, Anne P267
Joshi, Nirmal P185
Joshi, Vijay P545
Joshi, Mohit W52:W247
Joskow, Paul A286
Joslin, Tim A P148
Joslin, Tim P149
Joslin, Matt P149
Joslin, Tim A P222
Joslyn, Scott P301
Jotikasthira, Charamporn W62
Joullian, Edward A126:E54
Joung, Chansoo A64
Journell, Jacqueline E174
Jouvenal, Joe P321
Jowell, Ashley A730:P509
Joy, Philip P91
Joy, Dan E115
Joyce, John A38
Joyce, Rhonda A49
Joyce, Annette A147
Joyce, Robert J A451
Joyce, Thomas A686
Joyce, Rene A760
Joyce, Tim P19
Joyce, Jonathan P146
Joyce, Rhonda E21
Joyce, Meghan E55
Joyce, Annette E66
Joyce, William E161
Joyce, Stephen E345
Joyce, Glenn E429
Joyner, Pamela A323
Joyner, Jeannie P16
Joyner, Jeff P565
Joynt, Stephen E280
Jozuka, Yumiko W436
Jr, Paul G Haaga A39
Jr, Jonathan B Lovelace A49
Jr, Alfred W Sandrock A118
Jr, John M Starcher A126
Jr, Jack E Counts A147
Jr, William C Thompson A186
Jr, Bruce L Castor A208
Jr, William L Deckelman A213
Jr, Djalma Novaes A226
Jr, Robert H Bourque A226
Jr, Douglas M Baker A267
Jr, Roby Thompson A292
Jr, John J Wixted A299
Jr, Jamie B Stewart A299
Jr, Thomas C Baxter A299
Jr, Albert Bothe A343
Jr, Ewing Werlein A403
Jr, Joseph P Lacher A451
Jr, C Thomas Evans A451
Jr, John M Conners A503
Jr, Robert E Swaney A541
Jr, Ronald J Nicolas A603:A603
Jr, Thomas Wagner A735
Jr, Lawrence J Hogan A737
Jr, John B King A744
Jr, Roy Hawkins A774
Jr, Ewing Werlein A779
Jr, Richard L Smith A782
Jr, Thomas B Gerlach A782
Jr, Leonard A Cannatelli A783
Jr, Richard L Vogel A783

540

HOOVER'S HANDBOOK OF EMERGING COMPANIES 2022

COMBINED HOOVER'S HANDBOOK INDEX OF EXECUTIVES

Jr, Len Cannatelli A783
Jr, John Pelusi A828
Jr, Daniel C Rizzo A837
Jr, Lawrence Inserra A842
Jr, Robert V A Harra A866
Jr, William F Osbourn A872
Jr, Joseph H Mancini A872
Jr, Rawle Andrews P2
Jr, Todd S Werner P7
Jr, Dennis Porter P9
Jr, Leroy J Stromberg P17
Jr, Walter Sullivan P22
Jr, William C Whitmore P23
Jr, Paul G Haaga P28:P29
Jr, Donald M Clements P30
Jr, Rick Shadyac P32
Jr, Jonathan B Lovelace P33
Jr, Richard K Trowbridge P35
Jr, John Miller P37
Jr, Donald R Breivogel P49
Jr, Robert Ownby P67
Jr, J James Pearce P72
Jr, William Bishop P77
Jr, Woodrow Myers P78
Jr, John M Starcher P83
Jr, Louis J Lavigne P94
Jr, Patrick H Nettles P94
Jr, Stanley R Rawn P94
Jr, Jack E Counts P96
Jr, George Robert Vaughan P99
Jr, Alexander C Speyer P100
Jr, John T Godwin P106
Jr, John Destefano P129
Jr, William C Thompson P129
Jr, Steven Hammond P132
Jr, Edward Augustus P135
Jr, George Woody Thompson P140
Jr, Bruce L Castor P146
Jr, Arthur C Evans P146
Jr, Jose Garcia P147
Jr, Gordon Webster P148
Jr, William L Deckelman P150
Jr, Robert Rosene P152
Jr, Robert B Rosene P152
Jr, Alphonso Jefferson P157
Jr, H Roger Zurn P162
Jr, Bruce L Castor P164
Jr, Mark H Luttrell P170
Jr, John Kennedy P171
Jr, Thomas Crowley P176
Jr, Edward J Benz P180
Jr, Alfred W Young P191
Jr, Samuel L Neal P194
Jr, Robert Willis P197
Jr, John C Fryer P198
Jr, Ed Jolley P205
Jr, Theo Bunting P206
Jr, Alan R Crain P207
Jr, Robey W Estes P209
Jr, Roby Thompson P210
Jr, Herbert H Huddleston P212
Jr, Robert P Lally P220
Jr, Albert Bothe P225
Jr, Glenn D Steele P226
Jr, Albert Bothe P226
Jr, Robert Hale P234
Jr, Robert Maloney P241
Jr, Ewing Werlein P256
Jr, Ernest J Novak P272
Jr, Howard L Barton P285
Jr, Stephen Paul Carter P285
Jr, James F McEncaney P306
Jr, John M Conners P317
Jr, Richard K Sullivan P319
Jr, John M Starcher P332
Jr, E Paul Hitter P336
Jr, C Allen Begley P336
Jr, Thomas M Dono P336
Jr, Samuel Stanley P342
Jr, David D Desper P353
Jr, Robert Blount P387
Jr, Theodore T Myre P390
Jr, Joseph Robertson P399
Jr, Griffith R Bryan P402
Jr, Ronald J Nicolas P404
Jr, Clifford Smith P406
Jr, Clyde E Ellis P407

Jr, William F Adolph P410
Jr, Bob Gernert P421
Jr, Michael Perrone P421
Jr, Glenn Steel P426
Jr, Robert J Finocchio P427
Jr, Charles D Beaman P428
Jr, Donald Anderson P430
Jr, Leonard W Sandridge P439
Jr, James L McBride P439
Jr, Billy K Cannaday P439
Jr, Thomas J McCraken P441
Jr, Dominick H Tammaro P444
Jr, Walter W Austin P446:P446
Jr, David C Munson P450
Jr, James G Slaughter P454
Jr, William Delong P459
Jr, Joseph J Devirgilio P465
Jr, Robin B Brown P469
Jr, Russell E Armistead P477
Jr, Bill McCall P487
Jr, Jerome A Benkert P491
Jr, Kenneth Bennett P492
Jr, James Labagnara P503
Jr, Dennis M Eames P508
Jr, Thomas Wagner P511
Jr, Lawrence J Hogan P513
Jr, John B King P519
Jr, Joseph Maher P521
Jr, John Tangney P523
Jr, Victor J Boschini P540
Jr, Roy Hawkins P547
Jr, William Michael Warren P549
Jr, Philip R Johnson P549
Jr, John P Sheridan P553
Jr, Glenn D Steele P559
Jr, Ewing Werlein P567
Jr, Charles Spain P567
Jr, Andres Murai P576
Jr, Kenneth O Johnson P578
Jr, William Hite P579
Jr, Richard L Smith P583
Jr, Thomas B Gerlach P583
Jr, Thomas Huddleston P584
Jr, Donald Campbell P586
Jr, Leonard A Cannatelli P591
Jr, Richard L Vogel P591
Jr, Len Cannatelli P591
Jr, L Thomas Wilburn P598
Jr, George B Hernndez P613
Jr, Jos Roberto Ju Rez P619
Jr, James Dipaula P623
Jr, Ron Cummins P623
Jr, Charlies B White P628
Jr, James W Dean P633
Jr, John Pelusi P635
Jr, William D Thompson P639
Jr, Donald R Breivogel P639
Jr, M Dwight Shelton P642
Jr, David Travis P642
Jr, William K Pou P644
Jr, Lawrence Inserra P645
Jr, Raymond K Smith P647
Jr, Roger K Mowen P649
Jr, Albert L Wright P651
Jr, David C Hardesty P651
Jr, Vincent L Ammann P654
Jr, Marcellous P Frye P654
Jr, Robert V A Harra P657
Jr, John E Pepper P661
Jr, Ronald J Nicolas E310
Jr, John B Adams E439
Ju, Tina A443
Ju, Jennifer P527
Juarez, Veronica P126
Jubb, Allison P431
Jubouri, Shams P70
Juchelka, Jan W281
Juchno, Stacy A632
Juckeland, Philip P635
Juday, Mark A32:P24
Judd, Jason A608
Judd, Wade P46
Judd, Jason E312
Jude, Justin A484
Judge, James P209
Judge, Julie P320
Judie, Kenneth A737:P513

Judiscak, Sally P353
Judlowe, Michael E8
Judy, Vickie E20
Jueckstock, Rainer A767
Juel, Carol A752
Juhl, Christian W533
Jukes, David W156
Jula, Margaret A306
Julian, Kenneth A786
Julian, James P624
Julian, Heather San P638
Juliani, Angela P135
Juliano, Dawn A710:E371
Julien, Jeffrey P A663:P436
Julien, Pierre P461
Jun, Albert P276
Jun, Sarah E315
Junck, Mary E248
Junco, Kirk P292
Junco, Kirk D P565
Juneau, Denise P471
Juneja, Girish A256
Jung, Alex A49
Jung, Andrea A65
Jung, Norman Q P506
Jung, Yannick W87
Jung, Yeon Yin W167
Jung, Gu Hwan W271
Jung, Ho Yeong W296
Jung, Chang Hwa W388
Jung, Tak W388
Jung, Mun Gi W388
Jung, Andrea W510
Jung, Seok Yeong W532
Jung, Chan Hyeong W532
Jung, Alex E22
Junglas, Steve A366:P235
Junkins, Lowell A296:E157
Junyent, Miguel Roca W9:W57
Jurczak, Joseph P414
Jurecka, Christoph W337
Jurgens, Michael A412:P258
Jurjevich, Karen W191
Juster, Kristine E413
Justice, Jim A741
Justice, Peggy Rasnick P417
Justice, Jim P518
Justice, Ronald E160
Justus, Douglas P161
Jutimitta, Auraratana W441

K

K, Sandvik Helvi P361
Ka, Denise P603
Kaar, Joel P617
Kaatz, Diane A738:P514
Kaback, Neil A294:E156
Kabaria, Vipul V P64
Kabat, Kevin A827
Kaber, Saddek Al W38
Kablawi, Hani A99
Kaboy, Sylvie P122
Kacavas, John P183
Kachelmeyer, Annette P51
Kaczmarek, Walter A382
Kaczmarek, Wade P193
Kaczmarek, Walter E211
Kaczoruk, Stanislaw W71
Kaczynski, Thomas A496:A541
Kadavy, Grant P388
Kadi, Ibrahim W423
Kado, Maki W240
Kadonaga, Sonosuke W269
Kadowaki, Ryosaku W279
Kadre, Manuel A395:A677
Kadri, Ilham W451
Kaellenius, Ola W319
Kaercher, Erica P604
Kaesemeyer, Jean P617
Kaewrathtanapattama, Taweesak W98
Kaewrungruang, Wallaya W442
Kafer, Ann A369:P237
Kaga, Atsuko W268
Kagami, Mitsuko W317
Kagan, Mariel S P242

Kagan, Michael P325
Kagawa, Ryohei W237
Kageura, Tomoko W373
Kahanu, Noelle P621
Kahkonen, Matti W346
Kahl, Cathy P316
Kahla, Vuyo W421
Kahn, Todd A759
Kahn, David P157
Kahn, Joseph P334
Kahn, Jeffrey D P549
Kahn, Brian E185
Kahramanzade, Ozgur W505
Kail, Andrew W291
Kain, Gary A22
Kainersdorfer, Franz W521
Kairis, Margaret P76
Kaiser, David A72
Kaiser, George A126
Kaiser, Laura S A423
Kaiser, Keri A719
Kaiser, Laura A729
Kaiser, Nicole P184
Kaiser, Laura S P264
Kaiser, Daphne P287
Kaiser, Rebecca P453
Kaiser, Laura P497
Kaiser, Andrea P625
Kaiser, David E31
Kaiser, George E54
Kakade, Ajitesh P636
Kakar, Rajeev W188
Kakigi, Koji W264
Kakinoki, Masumi W312
Kakiuchi, Takehiko W325
Kakizaki, Tamaki W329
Kakoullis, Panos W410
Kaku, Masatoshi W369
Kakutani, Kazuki W317
Kalambur, Ganesh P594
Kalan, Lesley A569
Kalanda, Larisa W502
Kalani, Neelesh A597:E307
Kalanihuia, Janice P576
Kalathur, Rajesh A240
Kalbaugh, J. Andrew A489
Kale, David P124
Kale, Kimberly P188
Kale, Rahul W529
Kaler, Eric W P102
Kaleta, Paul A324
Kali, Maher P111
Kalif, Guy W63
Kalif, Eliyahu W487
Kallenbach, Charles P247
Kallevik, Eivind W363
Kalmanson, Steven A684
Kalmbach, Thomas A359
Kaloski, Donald E439
Kalsbeck, Brad Van P286
Kaltenbach, Patrick E273
Kam, Keith P527
Kamada, Kazuhiko W369
Kamano, Michel P420
Kamara, Ernest T P385
Kambayashi, Hiyoo W338
Kambe, Shiro W454
Kambeitz, Stephen A608:E312
Kambich, Joseph P260
Kamenetzky, David W287
Kamezawa, Hironori A538:W330
Kamieth, Markus W76
Kamigama, Takehiro W537
Kamijo, Tsutomu W491
Kamin, John A648
Kamin, Peter E344
Kaminski, Jeff A447
Kaminski, Robert A514
Kaminski, Mark A673
Kaminski, Angel P26
Kaminski, Marcie P417
Kaminski, Robert E267
Kaminsky, Andrew E185
Kamitaki, Wayne A164
Kamiyauchi, Yuji W373
Kamke, Trent E250

COMBINED HOOVER'S HANDBOOK INDEX OF EXECUTIVES

A = AMERICAN BUSINESS
E = EMERGING COMPANIES
P = PRIVATE COMPANIES
W = WORLD BUSINESS

Kamm, Travis P128
Kampfer, Thomas E90
Kampling, Patricia A871:P35
Kamradt, Chris P496
Kamsickas, James A234
Kamsky, Virginia A234
Kan, Derek A788
Kan, Lai Kuen W436
Kanaan, Mona A851
Kanagawa, Chihiro W437
Kanamaru, Muneo W463
Kanary, Maryann P63
Kanasugi, Yasuzo W334
Kanazawa, Yugo W299
Kanda, Haruo W538
Kandt, Debbie P609
Kane, Tom A218
Kane, John A545
Kane, Julie A573
Kane, William A587
Kane, Robert A690
Kane, William A792
Kane, Margaret A793
Kane, Alisa P132
Kane, Jenny P204
Kane, Chuck P253
Kane, Kenneth P302
Kane, Julie P391
Kane, William E302
Kane, Julie E370
Kane, Margaret E414
Kane-Williams, Edna P2
Kaneb, Gary P367
Kanegae, Carole P123
Kaneko, Shingo W496
Kanema, Yuji W228
Kanemoto, Hideaki W237
Kang, Kalle P403
Kang, Dian W125
Kang, Jin E449
Kangas, Patrick P623
Kania, Don A430
Kanjanakanti, Wilaiwan W393
Kanjanapoo, Varoon W491
Kann, Ashley P463
Kanneman, Paul A712:E373
Kanouff, Yvette E140
Kanouse, Sarah P586
Kanter, Joseph P615
Kanuru, Raj E191
Kanwar, Neena P281
Kao, Ruey-Bin E236
Kao, George E397
Kapala, Norm A190
Kapffer, Daniel W157
Kapilashrami, Tanuj W259:W456
Kapito, Robert A120
Kaplan, Heather A200
Kaplan, Paul P195
Kaplan, Josh P208
Kaplan, Tamra P301
Kaplan, Betina P620
Kaplan, Alan P632:P632
Kaplan, Gary S P642
Kaplan, Richard W63
Kaplan, Beth E110
Kaplan, Seth E203
Kaplan, Ronald E413
Kaplon, Sari P350
Kapoor, Gaurav A15
Kapoor, Shumit A449
Kapoor, Deepak W478
Kapoor, Rohit E151
Kapoor, Kunal E280
Kapp, Brian P149
Kapperman, Garry A738:P514
Kappler, Ann A649
Kapples, John E233
Kapur, Vimal A398
Karaaslan, Demir W540
Karaboutis, Adriana E34

Karachun, Rita A515
Karafa, Jeffrey A640:E333
Karam, Sammy A4
Karam, Celia A148
Karam, Mary Kate M P593
Karandikar, Nitin P585
Karasawa, Yasuyoshi W334
Karaskova, Jana P233
Karavias, Fokion W188
Karawan, Gregory A351
Karczmer, Aaron A611
Kardis, Phillip A174
Kardish, Paul J E42
Karels, Gordon V P81
Karen, Ngui W155
Karhu, Piia W275
Karish, Jeffrey E120
Kariyada, Fumitsugu W226
Karl, Patricia P174
Karlin, Bridget A234
Karlsson, Arne W1
Karlstrom, Johan W145
Karmilowicz, Michael W189
Karmiol, Grace P623
Karnei, Clifton D P86
Karnik, Amogh P182
Karo, Rachel P426
Karon, Adam E11
Karp, Harold M P534
Karr, Michael A603:A603:P404:E310
Karren, Tony P299
Karrer, Joy P390
Karrip, Brian A313:E165
Karrmann, Sandra A455
Karsanbhai, Surendralal A273
Karsner, Alexander A291
Karunakaran, R. W307
Karuturi, Monica A163
Kasahara, Toshiyuki W437
Kasarda, John A584
Kasbar, Michael A868
Kasbekar, Umesh A197
Kaschke, Michael W224
Kasdin, Robert A781:P581
Kasenge, Rebecca P608
Kaser, Jeff A605
Kasey, Jay P355
Kashwagi, Yutaka W325
Kaslow, Aaron A693:E360
Kasmin, Franklin P71
Kasnet, Stephen A801
Kaspar, Kristen P158
Kaspar, Hanspeter W514
Kasparian, Mike E182
Kasper, Curt P137
Kass, Steven A613
Kass, Jordan A683
Kass, Bonnie P407
Kass, Hunter E13
Kass, Steven E316
Kassab, Leanne A193:E87
Kassel, Matt P451
Kassem, Rona P334
Kassen, Tim P307
Kasser, Mike P490
Kassim, Aj P283
Kassim, Md Hamzah Bin Md W232
Kastanis, John N P621
Kastelberg, Mary E439
Kastner, Christopher A410
Kastner, Janeen A688
Kastriner, Jared A106:P65
Kasui, Yoshitomo W461
Kasulka, Thomas A710:E371
Kasutani, Seiichi W317
Kaszynski, Michal W70
Katanozaka, Shinya W493
Kataria, Lav W395
Katayama, Hitoshi W226
Katayama, Masanori W255
Katayama, Hiroshi W324
Katayama, Yoshihiro W356
Katayama, Eiichi W378
Katch, Bob E340
Katemba, Edward L P493
Katenkamp, Erik A652
Kates, Kenneth P P621

Katinakis, Nikos W484
Kato, Kotaro W65
Kato, Yuichi W66
Kato, Kazumaro W68
Kato, Sadanori W127
Kato, Hiromichi W127
Kato, Yoshifumi W158
Kato, Toshiyuki W158
Kato, Kaoru W277
Kato, Takeharu W279
Kato, Takao W328
Kato, Wataru W329
Kato, Kaoru W330
Kato, Kikuo W338
Kato, Hiroyuki W367
Kato, Kosuke W468
Kato, Yuriko W469
Kato, Isao W491
Kato, Koki W491
Kato, Tadashi W538
Katrama, Hanne W470
Katsikogianis, Caryn W531
Katsilometes, Tom A735:P511
Katsoudas, Francine A81
Katsoyannis, George P453
Katsu, Atsushi W257
Katsukawa, Yoshihiko W279
Katsuki, Hisashi W23
Katsumi, Takeshi W268
Katsumoto, Toru W454
Katsuno, Satoru W127
Katterheinrich, Lean P144
Kattos, Andrew A707:E368
Katz, David A197
Katz, Karen A406
Katz, Robert A434
Katz, Jacob A437
Katz, Ellen P72
Katz, Paul P356
Katz, Naomi L P439
Katz, Nathalia P542
Katz, Ken P557
Katz, Louis H P560
Katz, Miriyam W253
Katz, Gary E235
Katzen, Michael E439
Katzman, Richard P105
Kau, Melanie W25
Kauchak, John E425
Kauer, Cristian Florence W59
Kauffman, Richard P206:P373
Kauffman, William R P458
Kauffman, Donna P589
Kauffman, Robert E427
Kaufman, Dave A92
Kaufman, Calvin A461
Kaufman, Brett P290
Kaufman, Irvin A P434:P434
Kaufman, Sinead W405:W406
Kaufman, Ivan E29
Kaufman, David E160
Kaufman, William E247
Kaufman, John E312
Kaufman, Michael E377
Kaufmann, Michael A150
Kaufmann, Marli P420
Kaukali, Chris T P620
Kaul, Will P235
Kaul, Priyanka E129
Kaul-Hottinger, Mary A176
Kaup, Nicholas P586
Kaur, Jaswinder P460
Kaur, Pam W234
Kaushal, Sunil W457
Kaushal, Arvind W480
Kauten, Ralph A311
Kavanaugh, James P A869:P659
Kaviratne, Nihal W370
Kavthekar, Suhas P488
Kawada, Tatsuo W149
Kawada, Junichi W436
Kawaguchi, Shingo W493
Kawahara, Kazuaki W279
Kawai, Toshiaki A790
Kawai, Shuji W150
Kawai, Eriko W331
Kawakita, Hisashi W237

Kawamoto, Hiroko W170
Kawamoto, Tetsufumi W493
Kawamura, Akihiro W34
Kawamura, Kanji W255
Kawamura, Hajime W312
Kawamura, Osamu W469
Kawan, Khaled W37
Kawanishi, David T P345
Kawano, Junko W65
Kawanobe, Osamu W491
Kawasaki, Hiroyuki A877
Kawasaki, Iris P576
Kawasaki, Hiroyuki P662
Kawasaki, Yasuyuki W463
Kawata, Hiro P231
Kawiecki, Michele A320:E172
Kay, Christopher A491
Kay, Kathleen A641
Kayano, Masayasu W268
Kaye, Mark A536
Kaygalak, Serkan W504
Kayhan, Muharrem W505
Kayser, C. Dallas A186
Kayser, Detlef W161
Kayser, C. Dallas E84
Kayton, Edward A439
Kaza, Srini E15
Kazarian, Kristina A496:A541
Kazarian, Camille E395
Kazmaier, Jessica A679
Ke, Qiubi W33
Ke, Peng W115
Keady, Robert E449
Kealey, Katie P308
Kealey, Michael E123
Kealy, Mary V P303
Kean, Steven A456
Kean, Steve P364
Keane, Margaret A32
Keane, Timothy A311
Keane, James A684
Keane, Margaret A752
Keane, John B P30
Keane, Andrea P152
Keanly, Rose W6
Keany, James P345
Kearney, Christopher A575
Kearney, Christopher J A598
Kearney, Terrence A835
Kearney, Craig P152
Kearney, Janis P317
Kearney, Jason P345
Kearns, Roger A860
Kearns, James P26
Kearns, Michael P159
Kearns, Leslie P304
Kearns, Donald B P434
Kearns, Donald P434
Kearns, Michael P479
Keathley, Wayne E P453
Keating, Francis A94
Keating, Thomas A107
Keating, Valerie A592
Keating, Mike P550
Keating, Todd P588:P608:P609
Keating, Francis E44
Keating, Thomas E48
Keatley, Travis A862
Keaton, Kevin P287
Keaton, Matthew P337
Kechot, Idris bin W307
Keck, Sharon J P12
Keck, Sharon P12
Keck, Kim A P78
Kedia, Gunjan A829
Kee, Marlow W487:P580
Keefer, Katrina P51
Keefer, Brian P149
Keeffe, Jim O' W17
Keegan, Joseph E50
Keel, Pat P505
Keeler, Thomas P165
Keeler, Tracy P256
Keeler, Brian P352
Keeler, Diane P557
Keeler, Anne E153
Keeler, Glenn E413

542

HOOVER'S HANDBOOK OF EMERGING COMPANIES 2022

COMBINED HOOVER'S HANDBOOK INDEX OF EXECUTIVES

Keeley, Michelle A45
Keeley, Brian E P57
Keeling, Tammy P498
Keels, Floyd A312
Keen, Eric L P244
Keen, Eric P245
Keenan, David A671
Keenan, Suzanne A826
Keenan, Claudia P332
Keenan, Richard P589
Keenan, Katharine E52
Keenan, Timothy J E189
Keenan, Suzanne E428
Keene, Nazzic A81:A698
Keene, Brian P60
Keene, Kristi P388
Keeney, Dianna C E52
Keenum, Mark E P346
Keesling, Rebecca A126:E54
Keetch, Chad E139
Keeton, Simon A591
Keffer, David A569
Keglevic, Paul A339
Kehaly, Pam P78
Kehl, Russell A175
Kehl, George A871
Kehl, Roxanne P261
Kehoe, Mike A738
Kehoe, James A843
Kehoe, Michael J P408
Kehoe, Mike P514
Kehrer, Bob P277
Kehrli, Todd E354
Keightley, Elizabeth P111
Keil, Richard P525
Keim, Mark A534
Keim, Michael A826
Keim, Marco W13
Keim, Michael E428
Keirns, Marylou P4
Keiser, Vicki P147
Keitel, William E418
Keith, R. Alexandra A643
Keith, Daniel A713
Keith, R. Alexandra A784
Keith, Greg P269
Keith, Stephen E37
Keizer, Henry A385:E197
Kelderman, Kim E50
Keler, Marianne A716
Keler, Sahin Alp W21
Keler, Marianne E379
Kell, James P205
Kelleher, Ann A421
Kelleher, Thomas A566
Kelleher, Kevin A666
Kelleher, Margaret Ann P353
Kelleher, Thomas E42
Kellen, Michael J P36
Keller, Christina A417
Keller, Bruno A460
Keller, Mark A597
Keller, Kimberly A811
Keller, Jonell P19
Keller, San P32
Keller, Timothy M P122
Keller, Philip P124
Keller, Glenn P155
Keller, Anne P395
Keller, Sue P652
Keller, Andreas W166
Keller, Adrian W166
Keller, Kenneth E43
Keller, Hans E129
Keller, Christina E226
Keller, Gerhard E273
Keller, Mark E307
Keller, Robert E321
Kellerhals, Patricia A206
Kellermann, Kimberly A367
Kelley, Scott A9
Kelley, Mark A A381
Kelley, Charles A593
Kelley, Angela A606
Kelley, Laurie A647
Kelley, William A785
Kelley, Michael P101

Kelley, Jennifer P249
Kelley, Mark A P249
Kelley, Jim P383
Kelley, Laurie P429
Kelley, Trenton P539
Kelley, Scott E4
Kelley, Stephen E6
Kelley, Robert E63
Kelley, Tawn E391
Kelleyfield, Alicia P98
Kelligrew, James B A829
Kellington, John A179
Kellmanson, Mary P559
Kellner, Lawrence W A124
Kellogg, Clark A320:E172
Kelly, Brian A9
Kelly, Thomas B A16
Kelly, Edmund A99
Kelly, Tom A160
Kelly, Edward A185
Kelly, Linda A208
Kelly, Thomas A A226
Kelly, Eric A271
Kelly, Theresa A330
Kelly, Jason A353
Kelly, Jack W A366
Kelly, Anastasi A410
Kelly, Douglas A448
Kelly, Edward A521
Kelly, Jeffrey A645
Kelly, L. Renee A652
Kelly, Gary A726
Kelly, Laura A736
Kelly, Robert Edward A881
Kelly, Leo P7
Kelly, Thomas B P8
Kelly, Patrick P15
Kelly, Sam P35
Kelly, Nancy P52
Kelly, William M P79
Kelly, Jhon P85
Kelly, Linda P146
Kelly, Marlena P156
Kelly, Patrick P158
Kelly, Thomas C P172
Kelly, Jack W P235
Kelly, Alan B P254
Kelly, Keven P261
Kelly, Patty P261
Kelly, Tony P304
Kelly, Stefanie P374
Kelly, Frank P388
Kelly, Angela P423
Kelly, Chere P439
Kelly, Barb P473
Kelly, Tim P476
Kelly, James J P477
Kelly, James P499
Kelly, Laura P512
Kelly, Ann P P608
Kelly, John P609
Kelly, Terri W42
Kelly, Kevin W99
Kelly, Christopher W132
Kelly, Shaun W145
Kelly, Ian W429
Kelly, Braden R E155
Kelly, Renee E163
Kelly, Jason E192
Kelly, Michael E273
Kelly, Laura E345
Kelly, Christie E347
Kelly-Ennis, Debra A36:A778:P561
Kelpy, Matthew A578
Kelroy, Jason A459
Kelsch, Kevin P282
Kelsey, Margaret A852
Kelso, John P162
Kelso, Aimee P401
Kelton, Justin P321
Kelvinton, William C P410
Kemaloglu, Ihsan W505
Kemmerly, David E18
Kemori, Nobumasa W264
Kemp, Terri A42
Kemp, Jon A260
Kemp, J. Michael A317

Kemp, Harry A470
Kemp, Ronald A638
Kemp, Brian A735
Kemp, Matthew P337
Kemp, Ronald P426
Kemp, Brian P511
Kemp, Ann P616
Kemp, Michael P630
Kemp, J. Michael E170
Kempczinski, Christopher A509
Kempen, wouter van A239
Kemper, Jonathan A206
Kemper, David A206
Kemper, John A206
Kemper, David A635
Kemper, J. Mariner A808
Kemper, Chris P36
Kemper, Charnele P363
Kemper, J. Mariner E421
Kempf, Jason P49
Kempner, Michael A215:E97
Kemps, Steven A691
Kempthorne, Dirk A682
Kendall, Sean A147:P96
Kendall, Andrew C P303
Kendrick, Megan A297
Kenerly, Margaret P646
Kenesey, Timothy A460
Keninger, Jon P262
Kenna, Robert J Mc P552
Kennah, Branden P430
Kennard, Lydia A15
Kennard, William A78:A333
Kennard, Lydia A338
Kennard, William A521
Kennard, Corey P500
Kennealy, Gesina W421
Kennedy, Kevin A98
Kennedy, Parker A308
Kennedy, Douglas A613
Kennedy, Daniel A716
Kennedy, Brian A778
Kennedy, James A813
Kennedy, Barbara A857
Kennedy, Jimmie P28
Kennedy, Patrick P168
Kennedy, Murrell P330
Kennedy, Bruce P336
Kennedy, Bridget P343
Kennedy, Pamela P360
Kennedy, Daniel P444
Kennedy, Amanda P520
Kennedy, Cheryl P522
Kennedy, Brian P561
Kennedy, Mark P577
Kennedy, Claire W65
Kennedy, Paul W147
Kennedy, John W165
Kennedy, Bryan W395
Kennedy, Melissa W395
Kennedy, Kolleen E220
Kennedy, Douglas E316
Kennedy, Daniel E379
Kennedy, Barbara E447
Kennel, Kaylan P342
Kenner, Brian A390
Kenner, Andrew A860
Kenner, Brian E215
Kennett, Ron A640:E333
Kenney, Jim A187
Kenney, Frederic A310
Kenney, Jim P131
Kenney, Frederic E164
Kenningham, Daryl A368
Kenny, David A115
Kenny, Gregory A151:A418
Kenny, David A562
Kenny, Chris A813
Kenny, David P378
Kenny, Michael P405
Kenny, Andrew P580
Kenny, John E270
Kenny, Richard E327
Kenoi, William P P160
Kent, Ahmet A3
Kent, Nevada A279
Kent, Kenneth A334

Kent, Suzette A372
Kent, James L A511
Kent, Angela P4
Kent, Cherry P37
Kent, John P165
Kent, Angel P168
Kent, Rodney D P265
Kent, Geoff P265
Kent, James L P322
Kent, Thomas P367
Kent, Nevada E142
Kenyon, Robert P48
Kenzie, Lesa Mc P458
Keo, Chamreoun P123
Keogh, John W126
Keough, Joseph A518
Keough, Shawn A735:P511
Keough, Joseph P602
Kepler, Jody P349
Keppel, Mary Ann P246
Kepple, Yann P246
Keptner, Erik A679
Kerber, Lynn A400
Kerber, Erin E109
Kerber, Lynn E218
Kereere, Suzan A325
Kereiakes, Dean P550
Keresty, Georgia E34
Keriacous, Leedia A825:P631
Kerins, Sean A72
Kern, Peter A288
Kern, Howard A706:P473
Kerner, Dave P166
Kerner, Gwen P271
Kernodle, Rex P245
Kerouani, Farida P404
Kerr, Derek A41
Kerr, Howard J P151
Kerr, Robert W P151
Kerr, Reiko A P303
Kerr, Brian C P456
Kerr, Bonnie P623
Kerr, Jason E59
Kerrigan, Dennis A375
Kerschner, Joseph E P566
Kersey, Melissa A791
Kersey, Frances P130
Kershaw, Craig P525
Kerwin, Gregory A529:E274
Keryer, Philippe W489
Kesavan, Sudhakar A7
Kess, Avrohom A792
Kessel, William A417
Kessel, Donna Van P483
Kessel, William E226
Kesseler, Brian A767
Kessiakoff, Peter W446
Kessinger, Steve P292
Kessler, Aaron A663
Kessler, George P56
Kessler, Aaron P436
Kessler, Grace P517
Kessler, Joe P598
Kessler, Denis W429
Kessler, Marla E237
Kessler, Pamela E323
Kestler, Vladimir W334
Kestner, R. Steven E332
Keswick, Benjamin W261:W262
Ketchum, John A560
Ketchum, Richard E262
Ketterling, Terry L P485
Kettle, Michelle P611
Keuer, Steve P119
Keuer, Steven P600
Keuten, John P68:P657
Kevorkian, Sarah A583:P393
Kewalramani, Reshma A835
Key, Matthew W95
Keyes, James A542
Keyler, Angela P458
Keysberg, Klaus W490
Keyser, Richard A877
Khait-Palant, Olga V P431
Khakbaznejad, Alireza P382
Khalaf, Michel A521
Khalid, Shariffuddin bin W307

HOOVER'S HANDBOOK OF EMERGING COMPANIES 2022

543

COMBINED HOOVER'S HANDBOOK INDEX OF EXECUTIVES

A = AMERICAN BUSINESS
E = EMERGING COMPANIES
P = PRIVATE COMPANIES
W = WORLD BUSINESS

Khalifa, Mazen Mohammed W407
Khambata, Farida W478
Khamseh, Ladan P398
Khan, Ahmad A457
Khan, Farina binti Farikhullah W29
Khan, Zafar W93
Khan, Parvez W134
Khan, Rehan W134
Khan, Badar W145
Khan, Nick E454
Khandpur, Ashish A3
Khanuja, Parvinderjit A703
Khanuja, Satbir E118
Khaosawas, Jiraponr W393
Khare, Anupam A598
Khasis, Lev W424
Khatibi, Alex E9
Khattar, Jack E399
Khatua, Sanjeeb P266
Khavkin, Evgeny W386
Khawandanah, Osama Bin
  Abdulwahab W422
Khayat, Clark A453
Khayat, Olivier W509
Khaykin, Oleg E436
Khehra, Raman P20
Kheradpir, Shaygan W335
Kheraj, Naguib W456
Khichi, Samrat A109
Khilnani, Vinod A1
Khir, Mohamed Fairooz
  Abdul W128:W307
Khoba, Liubov W386
Khol, Florian W521
Khomyakov, Sergey W385
Khoo, Shulamite W128
Khoo, Cheng Hoe W376
Khoo, Geok Kheng W393
Khor, Hock Seng W212
Khosla, Sanjay A881
Khosla, Suresh P1
Khosla, Ashok K P1
Khosla, Leena P1
Khouri, Frederick P217
Khouri, Mark P217
Khoury, Raymond P147
Khoury-haq, Shirine W132
Khouzami, Carim A286
Khullar, Puneet P89
Khuny, Marion W187
Khurana, Akash A854
Khuri, Zachary A597:E307
Khusakul, Wiboon W270
Khushayym, Abdulwahhab Hamza
  Bakr W423
Ki, Irena P366
Kiani, Joseph E263
Kidd, Dana A737
Kidd, Judi P317
Kidd, Dana P513
Kidd, Lindsay H P589
Kidder, Troy P34
Kidder, Amanda P135
Kiddoo, Bruce A591
Kidwell, April A738:P514
Kiefer, Donald A529:E274
Kieffer, Adam P48
Kiel, Martha P496
Kiely, W. A36
Kiely, Charles P190
Kiely, Sharon P581
Kiener, Pascal W72
Kiernan, Daniel A236
Kiesel, John L P612
Kiessling, Ralph W507
Kiffmeyer, Mary A737:P513
Kihune, Robert K U P603
Kiiskinen, Esa W274
Kijima, Tatsuo W375
Kikkawa, Takeo W240
Kiko, Richard E99

Kikuchi, Kiyomi W324
Kilaas, Liselott W363
Kilar, Jason A78
Kilbride, William A768
Kilby, Jerry A208:P145
Kilcoyne, Gerald A311
Kilcoyne, Moira W40
Kildahl, Jorgen W483
Kilemo, Pal W363
Kileman, Joel P166
Kiley, Joseph E169
Kilgore, Leslie A551
Kilgore, Krystin P525
Kilgore, Gene E29
Kilian, Gunnar W522
Kilinc, Fatih W505
Killalea, Peter A148:E11
Killebrew, Toni W402
Killefer, Nancy A520
Killian, John A216
Killian, Christopher A264
Killian, Margaret P170
Killian, Wayne P481
Killinger, Elizabeth A574
Killmer, Jonathon P252
Killmer, John E23
Kilmer, Mark A655
Kilmer, Steven P409
Kilmer, Bobbi E83
Kilmer, Mark E340
Kilpatrick, David A168
Kilpatrick, Dona P32
Kilpatrick, James T P218
Kilpatrick, C P641
Kilpatrick, Charles A P641
Kilpatrick, Deborah E378
Kilsby, Susan W165:W510
Kilty, Carolyn P525
Kim, Yup A27
Kim, James A58
Kim, Susan A58
Kim, Desir E A186
Kim, John A199
Kim, Charles A206
Kim, John A284:A336
Kim, Anthony A374
Kim, Jay A381
Kim, Kyu A398
Kim, Kevin A398
Kim, Jason A398
Kim, Joon Kyung A398
Kim, Joseph A750
Kim, Yup P15
Kim, Desir E P129
Kim, Jong Min P137
Kim, Jangyul R P142
Kim, Frank P165
Kim, Taeeuk P258
Kim, Changyoung P258
Kim, Chung P300
Kim, Jenny P389
Kim, Judy P392
Kim, Robert P476
Kim, Sue J P506
Kim, Jung-In P577
Kim, Anne P579
Kim, Nam P632
Kim, Hae W93
Kim, Dae Gi W167
Kim, Gyeong Ho W271
Kim, Jong Wu W296
Kim, Tae Seung W296
Kim, Jin Yong W297
Kim, Gyeong Ho W297
Kim, Jeong Su W388
Kim, Gwang Mu W388
Kim, Min Cheol W388
Kim, Sun Gi W388
Kim, Ji Yong W388
Kim, Hak Dong W388
Kim, Ju Hyeon W388
Kim, Seong Jin W388
Kim, Bok Tae W388
Kim, Gi Su W388
Kim, Shin Bae W388
Kim, Gyo Seong W388
Kim, James E76

Kim, O. E185
Kim, Kristina E185
Kim, Jay E208
Kim, Kyu E218
Kim, Kevin E218
Kim, Jason E218
Kim, Joon Kyung E218
Kim, Henry E315
Kim, Joo Mi E341
Kim, Kellie E449
Kimata, Masatoshi W286
Kimball, Stefanie A417
Kimball, Carly A472
Kimball, Brian P191
Kimball, Chip P291
Kimball, Stefanie E226
Kimbell, David C A807
Kimbell, Jimmy P37
Kimberly, Jack P481
Kimble, William A238
Kimble, Donald A453
Kimble, Sean E429
Kimbrough, Karin A293
Kimmel, David A446
Kimmell, Joseph E377
Kimmerle, David P193
Kimmerle, Sandra Sue P193
Kimmet, Pamela W308
Kimmitt, Robert A520
Kimoto, Kazuhiko W279
Kimura, Kazuyoshi W151
Kimura, Yasushi W357
Kimura, Shigeki W430
Kinaitis, Eric P544
Kinard, Olaf P124
Kincaid, Lisa P249
Kincaid, Cassell P494
Kindblad, Lisa P441
Kinder, Richard A456
Kinder, Richard D P364
Kindi, Majid Al W64
Kindick, Kelt A243
Kindle, John P171
Kindlick, David P643
Kindred, Jonathan A164
Kindred, Troy P160
Kindred, Deanne D P496
King, Karen A67
King, Gale A84
King, Timothy A203
King, William A235
King, Sarah A236
King, Stephen A310
King, Karen A336
King, Jerry A346
King, Gale A408
King, David A472
King, Michelle A486
King, Darren A491
King, Norma A621
King, Christine A702
King, Jeffrey A706
King, Troy A734
King, Deeanne A758
King, Kelly A796
King, Donnie A802
King, Stacy A808
King, David A865
King, Mark A876
King, Susan P7
King, Rick P40
King, Bob P46
King, Chuck P95
King, Chad P130
King, Randy P139
King, Jeff P139
King, Timothy P144
King, Yolanda P157
King, Fred P160
King, David F P162
King, Darlene P167
King, Andrea P169
King, Kevin P199
King, Terry P212
King, Jerry P227
King, Mark P232
King, Michael P260

King, Kelly P291
King, Michelle P303
King, M W P336
King, Ron P358
King, Brigitte P374
King, Norma P412
King, Jenna P447
King, Timothy P450
King, Karen P457
King, Jared P459
King, Jeffrey P473:P473
King, Kristin P490
King, Shannon P502
King, Troy P510
King, Lisa P524
King, Charles P553
King, Matthew P601
King, Angelie W70
King, Justin W311
King, Ros W395
King, Annette W395
King, Steve W395
King, Stephen E164
King, Brian E298
King, David E334
King, Silvia E382
King, Stacy E421
King, Zachary E430
Kingbury, Mike P222
Kingman, John W291
Kingsbury, Thomas A117:A791
Kingsbury, James P607
Kingsley, Scott A546
Kingsley, Lawrence D E221
Kingston, Brian W94
Kinlin, Clark A221
Kinnaird, Jeffrey A395
Kinnart, Peter W49
Kinnear, Katey P164
Kinneer, Mike P144
Kinney, Jane W111:W250
Kinney, Catherine E282
Kinoshita, Manabu W23
Kinoshita, Keishiro W356
Kinross, David E76
Kinser, Timothy A688
Kinsey, Armond P11:P48
Kinsey, Stephen P163
Kinsley, Karen W341
Kintigh, Denise P459
Kinyo, Doug P337
Kinzler, Alexander E47
Kip, Jeffrey A113
Kirac, Ipek W281
Kirby, Jefferson A29
Kirby, Brent A579
Kirby, Sarah P205
Kirby, Mary J P647
Kirby, Blaik W82
Kirby, Pamela W156
Kirchendorfer, Diane P158
Kircher, Debra P246
Kirchgraber, Paul A464
Kirchner, Jon E E456
Kirchoff, Mary P29
Kirchoff, Bob P154
Kirk, Matrice A437
Kirk, Jennifer A677
Kirk, Ron A735
Kirk, Randall A742
Kirk, Ronald A771
Kirk, Rich Van P188
Kirk, Warren J P193
Kirk, Bruce M P299
Kirk, Patrick T P332
Kirk, Ron P511
Kirk, Randall P518
Kirk, Kevin P565
Kirk, Ewan W53
Kirk, A. Russell E30
Kirk, Rose E69
Kirk, Sean E134
Kirkbride, Cheryl E111
Kirkby, Allison W95
Kirkham, Michael A617
Kirkhorn, Zachary A769
Kirkish, Mark S P445

544

HOOVER'S HANDBOOK OF EMERGING COMPANIES 2022

COMBINED HOOVER'S HANDBOOK INDEX OF EXECUTIVES

Kirkland, Scott D A267
Kirkland, Richard A485
Kirkland, James E415
Kirkley, David A392:E216
Kirkpatrick, Linda A506
Kirkwood, David W A787:P595
Kirlin, Peter E323
Kirloskar, Virendra A457
Kirrish, Abed P303
Kirsch, Eric A18
Kirsch, Sandra P114
Kirschner, Sidney E398
Kirsten, Artur W263
Kirtley, Timothy A618
Kirwan, Jeffrey A111
Kiscaden, Bradley A497
Kise, Shawn P607
Kise, Yoichi W170
Kiselick, Bill A447
Kiser, Georgette A18:A436:A548
Kiser, Dean P172
Kiser, Jennifer P187
Kiser, Terry P346
Kish, Donald A337
Kish, Mary P635
Kishida, Seiichi W23
Kishigami, Keiko W454
Kishore, Sangeeta E242
Kiss, Morgan P53
Kissam, W. A254
Kissel, Mary A873
Kissire, Deborah A160:E60
Kissner, Rita E361
Kistner, Tim P207
Kitabata, Takao W279:W312
Kitagawa, Hirokuni W228
Kitagawa, Jiro W279
Kitahara, Yoshikazu W331
Kitahara, Mutsuro W472
Kitajima, Yoshinari W148
Kitajima, Motoharu W148
Kitajima, Yoshitoshi W148
Kitamukai, Aimi Hkg A178
Kitamura, Akira W314
Kitamura, Matazaemon W339
Kitamura, Takumi W360
Kitano, Yoshihisa W264
Kitao, Yuichi W286
Kitao, Yoshihisa W350
Kitayama, Shuji W279
Kitayama, Mitchell E29
Kitazawa, Toshifumi W429
Kitazawa, Kenichi W493
Kitchell, Ryan A585
Kitchen, Carol A369:P237
Kitchens, W. James E166
Kitera, Masato W260:W312:W354
Kito, Shunichi W240
Kitowski, Nicole A75
Kitta, Masaya W494
Kittaka, Tomoya W493
Kittayarak, Kittipong W284
Kittelson, Roger P118
Kittisataporn, Karun W65
Kittrell, Marty E32
Kitts, Suzanne P542
Kitzmiller, Jason A750
Kitzmiller, Andrew E214
Kitzmiller, Jason E394
Kivisto, Nicole A512
Kivits, Patrick A860
Kiwall, Walter J P646
Kizer, Kim P188
Kizil, Oya Unlu W281
Kjos, Michael P128
Kjos, Ann P128
Klaas, Bjoern E337
Kladis, Donna P108
Klaeser, Dennis A587:E302
Klaff, Hersch A28:P18
Klaich, Daniel P367
Klane, Larry A545
Klappa, Gale A74:A852
Klapstein, Julie E18
Klaschus, Irv P96
Klasko, Stephen K P593
Klasko, Stephen P593

Klass, Cheryl P280
Klassen, Christopher P477
Klatt, Susan P586
Klaue, David A102
Klauer, Jim A223
Klaus, Jeffrey A113
Klaus, Andrew E332
Klausner, Rob P98
Klaver, Dennis P500
Klebanov, Ilya W503
Klee, Ann P523
Kleeman, Steven P73
Klees, Dee P134
Kleffel, Juliette A701:E365
Kleiman, Joel P166
Kleiman, Dr Michael P272
Kleiman, Angela E353
Klein, Barbara A418
Klein, James A655
Klein, Gerald A789
Klein, Michael A792
Klein, Luella V P211
Klein, Jane Marie A219
Klein, Robin P283
Klein, Cathy P345
Klein, Andrew A406
Klein, Christian W419
Klein, Richard E13
Klein, Michael E104
Klein, Nicholas E134
Klein, Daniel E324
Klein, James E340
Klein, Mark E361
Klein, Rebecca E376
Klein, Ronald E396
Klein-Magar, Margret W419
Kleiner, Madeleine A569
Kleinhenz, Eric P207
Kleinman, Scott A409
Kleinman, Mark A629
Kleinman, Scott A666
Kleinman, Lawrence P488
Kleinschmidt, Julie P167
Kleisterlee, Gerard W42
Klemash, Stephen A600
Klemm, Brad P187
Kley, Karl-Ludwig W169
Kleyla, John P290
Klibanski, Anne A503:P317
Klieger, Robert A607
Kliethermes, Craig A680:E356
Klika, Christine A736
Klika, Kevin A P360
Klika, Christine P512
Kliman, Gilbert E388
Klimczak, Sean A168
Klimonek, Barbara P14
Klimoski, Daniel P186
Kline, John A194
Kline, Katherine A409
Kline, Cynthia P171
Kline, Juliann P256
Kline, Douglas B P269
Kline, Mark W P540
Kline, Teresa E18
Kline, Rebecca E439
Kling, Jonathan P362
Klingenberg, Bernard W420
Klinger, James M P444
Klinken, Onno van W13
Klisura, Dean A500
Kloberdanz, Mark P411
Klock, Brian A491
Klocke, Kelly P40
Klocke, Deb P45
Klockenga, Kevin P502
Kloet, Thomas A543
Klohs, Birgit A493
Klontz, Richard P611
Klopfer, Jane A321
Klos, Mary Jo P238
Klosinski, Tom P520
Klossner, Rebecca P134
Klosson, Michael P466
Klosterman, Cole P42

Klosterman, Ronald P266
Klubert, Laura P19
Klueg, Steven P P311
Klug, Candice P566
Klugherz, Greg P442:P578
Klurfeld, Jason E149
Klusmeyer, Amy A779:P568
Kluth, Doreen P508
Kluting, Duane E270
Knabe, Don A224:P162
Knack, Monica P442
Knapp, Peter A512
Knapp, Jerry P10
Knapp, Peter P324
Knapp, Douglas P530
Knarr, Donald P119
Knaus, Ron P494
Knauss, Jeffery A210:E95
Knavish, Timothy A636
Kneale, Jennifer A760
Knecht, Julie A771
Knecht, Michael P61
Kneeland, Michael A820
Kneessy, Amy P466
Kneller, Michael A468
Knelly, Shirley J P306
Knepper, Chris P149
Knesek, Michael J P342
Knierim, Abraham P604
Knight, Gregory A163
Knight, Cecil A372
Knight, Jeffrey A585
Knight, Justin G P40
Knight, Glade M P40
Knight, Nelson G P40
Knight, Lyle R P75
Knight, Calvin P274
Knight, Reginald P565
Knight, Chris W291
Knight, Angela E135
Knight, Kenneth E374
Knighten, Benjamin E213
Knightly, Kevin A433
Knighton, Nash P212
Kniskern, Matthew P177
Knisley, Melinda P257
Knobel, Jeff A92
Knobel, Carsten W224
Knoble, Jody P51
Knobloch, George P284
Knobloch, Iris W301
Knoche, Philippe W489
Knocke, Craig A390
Knodell, Jane P81
Knoess, Christoph W412
Knoll, Thomas P222
Knoll, Allan F F437
Knoll, Josh P441
Knook, Pieter W483
Knoop, Lindsay A412:P258
Knopek, Dagmar W2
Knopf, William D P416
Knopf, Keith P435
Knopik, Stephen A652
Knott, Carolyn A719:P486
Knotts, Mike E52
Knouse-Snyder, Denise A853:E445
Knowblauch, Andy P142
Knowles, Richard P340
Knowling, Robert A679:E393
Knowlton, Suzanne A667
Knox, Kathleen A96
Knox, Cary A352
Knox, Wendell A375
Knox, J. Amanda A461
Knox, D. Bruce A853
Knox, Linda P600
Knox, D. Bruce E445
Knudsen, Jeannette A718
Knudson, Dallas A30:P21
Knudson, Kelly P468
Knuepling, Frieder W428
Knust, Susan A315:E167
Knuteson, Cory P641
Knutsen, Jerry E355
Knutson, Lisa A853
Knutson, Curtis P30

Knutson, Paul P107
Knutson, Susan M E196
Knutson, Lisa E364:E445
Ko, Alex A398
Ko, Charng-Chyi W138
Ko, Alex E218
Koanantakool, Thaweesak W441
Koay, Seok Khim W393
Kobashigawa, Wendy P163
Kobayakawa, Tomoaki W494
Kobayashi, Hidefumi W1
Kobayashi, Atsushi W1
Kobayashi, Masato W17
Kobayashi, Toshio W21
Kobayashi, Koji W21
Kobayashi, Katsuma W150
Kobayashi, Masato W206
Kobayashi, Masahiko W228
Kobayashi, Nagahisa W237
Kobayashi, Toshinori W264
Kobayashi, Tetsuya W268
Kobayashi, Noriaki W277
Kobayashi, Shinichi W312
Kobayashi, Yoshimitsu W324
Kobayashi, Shigeru W324
Kobayashi, Ken W325:W328
Kobayashi, Ayako W338
Kobayashi, Yoko W367
Kobayashi, Masayuki W375
Kobayashi, Nobuyuki W461
Kobayashi, Kazuo W491
Kobayashi, Yoshimitsu W494
Kobayashi, Koji W501
Kobayashi, Tatsuo W536
Kobayashi, Yoichi W538
Kobbeman, Robert A149
Kobe, Hiroshi W350
Kobrin, Elie P604
Kobrinsky, Shaul W253
Kobylanski, Daniel P537
Koc, Caroline W281
Koc, Omer W281
Koc, Ali W281
Koc, Rahmi W281
Koc, Omer W505
Koc, Ali W505
Koc, Rahmi W505
Koc, Ali W505:W540
Koch, Lori A260
Koch, Billy A403
Koch, Kevin J A511
Koch, Stephen A673
Koch, Jonathan A696
Koch, J Robert A779
Koch, Robert P91
Koch, Billy P256
Koch, Cheryl P275
Koch, Kevin J P322
Koch, J Robert P568
Koch, Sheryl E P617
Koch, C. James E55
Kochem, Gary P15
Kochem, Gary J P16
Kocher, Marisa P311
Kocherlakota, S. Swamy A691
Kochevar, Deborah E80
Kochuparampil, Augustine W39
Koci, Keith A188
Kociancic, Mark W189
Kocsis, Dana A775:P551
Koda, Main W260:W328
Kodachi, Cynthia P172
Kodera, Akira W127
Kodera, Tetsuya W373
Kodish, Joel A89:P54
Koduri, Raja A421
Koeberle, Yves W40
Koedam, James J P3
Koegel, J. William A142
Koehler, Michael A778
Koehler, Kevin A523
Koehler, Michael P561
Koehler, Annette W166
Koehler, Renate W321
Koehnen, Michael A793:E414
Koeings, Peg A299
Koele, Chad A16:P8
Koellner, Laurette A361:A576

COMBINED HOOVER'S HANDBOOK INDEX OF EXECUTIVES

A = AMERICAN BUSINESS
E = EMERGING COMPANIES
P = PRIVATE COMPANIES
W = WORLD BUSINESS

Koenen, Kirk P225
Koenig, Kristy A439
Koenig, Emery A539
Koenig, Dawn P128
Koenig, Kristy P276
Koenig, Carolyn L P334
Koenig, Barbara P616
Koepfer, Heike Paulmann W110
Koepfer, Peter Paulmann W110
Koeplin, David P456
Koeppel, Holly P30:W93
Koeppen, Christopher E224
Koerwer, John A806
Koester, Tilo W315
Koga, Kazutaka W288
Koga, Akira W314
Kogame, Kotaro W127
Kogan, Barry P16
Kogl, Cristen A877
Kogure, Megumi W536
Koh, Boon Hwee A21
Koh, Peter A398
Koh, Steven A398
Koh, Beng Seng W87
Koh, Yaw Hui W212
Koh, Beng Seng W212
Koh, Ching Ching W376
Koh, Beng Seng W376
Koh, Peter E218
Koh, Steven E218
Kohan, Sherry A17
Koharik, Edward E10
Kohler, Kayleen A102
Kohler, Steven A P96
Kohlpaintner, Christian W91
Kohnke, Gilbert W307
Kohno, Masaharu W463
Kohorst, W. Robert E265
Koid, Phaik Gunn W29
Koide, Masatoshi A18
Koide, Shinichi W17
Koike, Masamichi W463
Koizumi, Shinichi W367
Kok, Patrick W212
Kok, Pak Kuan W261
Kokes, Marvin A293:P212
Kokinda, John P201
Kokke, Jorgen A418
Kokologiannis, Harris W188
Kokubu, Fumiya W312
Kokuri, Lisa P603
Kolanz, Ryan P422
Kolassa, Thomas E383
Kolavo, Joe P523
Kolb, Kenneth P119
Kolb, Jeanne L P340
Kolb-Nelson, Annie P161
Kolbe, Martin W287
Kolendrander, Kirk P318
Kolesnikov, Alexander A48
Kolisch, James E301
Kolk, Wouter W283
Koller, Darwin P241
Koller, Patrick W194
Kolli, Sreelakshmi A878:E15
Kolloway, Michael R P573
Kolmsee, Ines W391:W507
Kolobkov, Pavel W208
Kolodizner, Paul P598
Kolodziej, Paul E52
Kolomentsev, Alexandre A839:P643
Kolosky, Jack P240
Kolychev, Vladimir W424
Komanduri, Chaitanya A783:P583
Komar, Michael P226
Komarov, Sergey P591
Komin, Ed P161
Komiya, Satoru W493
Komiyama, Hiroshi W437
Komoda, Masanobu W331
Komoda, Takahisa W439

Kon, Kenta W501
Kondo, Takao W68
Kondo, Jun W216
Kondo, Shiro W491
Konen, Mark A399
Konezny, Ronald E118
Kong, Garheng A464
Kong, Sooi Lin W29
Kong, Xiaokai W121
Kong, Junfeng W387
Kongkalai, Pochanee W62
Kongkasai, Yingluk W65
Kongton, Suratun W285
Konno, Shiho W299
Kono, Masaaki W279
Konold, Kyle P554
Konold, Aina E289
Konrad, Jocelyn A679
Kontogouris, Venetia W383
Kontos, Mark P569
Konyn, Mark W16
Konzelman, Sharon P284
Kooman, Kevin E253
Koonce, Paul A254:A838
Koonce, Treva P362
Koop, Alvin A719:P486
Koop, Jodi P638
Koosed, Philip E398
Kooyman, Brittany P401
Kopalek, Joseph R P608
Kopcho, Darcy P562
Kope, Dorothy A735:P511
Kopecky, Deb P481
Kopiasz, Corey S A787:P595
Koplin, Neal A618
Koplon, Norman P123
Kopp, Rochelle W334
Kopra, Panu W346
Korbelak, Stacy P38
Korde, Kishore E9
Kordelski, Michael P350
Koreny, Claudia P604
Korfu-Pedersen, Nina W446
Korkmaz, Dogan W505
Koro, Kazuyuki W435
Koroi, Boris W503
Korsch, Marija W2
Korsh, Les A610
Korsik, Aleksandr W503
Korte, Scot P176
Kortman, Kelley A174
Kortum, Joe P493
Korty, Andrew P602
Korzekwa, Christi A791
Korzekwinski, Francis A330
Kos, Dino A299
Kosa, E. Gene E84
Kosacz, Barbara E455
Kosasa, Paul A164
Koschmeder, Mark P232
Koseki, Yoshiki W369
Koselka, Helen P598
Koser, Michael P654
Koshiba, Mitsunobu W240
Koshiishi, Fusaki W279
Koshijima, Keisuke W268
Koshkawa, Kazuhiro W355
Kosidowski, Ellen P445
Kosirski, Anthony A256
Kosko, Andrew P193
Kosla, Kristen P198
Kosnitzky, Michael P576
Kosokabe, Takeshi W151
Koss, Kristen K P522
Kost, Kerry P379
Kostalnick, Charles A71
Kostas, Odysseas E229
Kostelnik, Robert A390
Koster, Christopher A162
Koster, John P170:P429
Kotagiri, Seetarama W306
Kotani, Yuichiro W496
Kotch, Noah E109
Kotcher, Peter P636
Kotek, Jim P592
Kotera, Yasuo W367
Kothandaraman, Badrinarayanan E138

Kotick, Robert A9
Kotil, Drew P91
Kotler, Dov W63
Kotler, Steven E106
Kott, Alison P123
Kottas, Jim P259
Kotte, Vijay E344
Kottman, Bill P201
Kottmann, Sherri E182
Kotwal, Shailesh M A829
Kou, Baoquan W154
Koukouvitakis, Sophia P177
Koumettis, Nikolaos A196
Kourepenis, Anthony S P547
Koury, Jaime Antonio El W215
Koutny, Lance P318
Kovac, Charles F A841
Kovach, Andrew L P11
Kovacic, Simone W304
Kovacs, Jeff P571
Koval, Erin P381
Kovalchuk, Mikhail W424
Kowal, Spencer A P118
Kowalczyk, Andrew A546
Kowalski, Suzanne P343
Kowlzan, Mark A605
Koyanagi, Stan W373
Koyano, Kenichi W536
Koyle, Cade P433
Kozaki, Takashi W17
Kozanian, Hagop A771
Kozano, Yoshiaki W439
Kozawa, Hisato W326
Kozich, Gregory A632
Kozicz, Gregory J P16:P16:P17
Kozik, Elizabeth P243
Koziol, Michael P309
Kozlak, Jodeen A447
Kozlak, Jodee A683
Kozlov, Alexey W503
Kozlowska-chyla, Beata W71
Kozlowski, Damian A774
Kozlowski, Eric P67
Kozlowski, Daniel E339
Kozlowski, Damian E408
Kozlu, Cem W281
Kozoman, Robert P185
Kozorezov, Petr A683
Kozsan, Eileen P173
Kozuchi, Kazushi W237
Kozuka, Fumiharu W463
Kozyra, William A42
Krabbenhoft, Kelby K P463
Krablin, Steven E81
Kraemmer, Rudolf W444
Kraft, Phil P162
Kraft, Joseph W454
Kraftchick, Debbra L P587
Krage, Susan A824:P617
Kragt, Jeff P154
Krajewski, David P300
Krakauer, Mary E62:E268
Krake, Cynthia P288
Krake, John P288
Kraker, Diane P529
Krakos, Greg P37
Krakowsky, Philippe A428
Kralingen, Bridget van A792:W412
Kramaric, Chuck P156
Kramer, Robin C A118
Kramer, William A315
Kramer, Kelly A355
Kramer, Richard A361
Kramer, Lewis A463
Kramer, Phil D A631
Kramer, Richard A708
Kramer, Jessica P84
Kramer, David A P92
Kramer, Frances P100
Kramer, Jill W8
Kramer, Christina W99
Kramer, Holly W199:W532
Kramer, Robert E133
Kramer, William E167
Kramer, Ronald E202
Kramer, Francis E224
Kramer, Nancy E257

Kramlich, Christine P608
Kramm, Jeffrey P288
Krammer, Lisa P389
Kran, Bob P342
Kranich, Brad A711:P481
Krantz, Donald E337
Krasnoff, Alan P P125
Krasowski, Ela A872
Kratky, Aron P357
Kratz, Owen E210
Kratze, Alexa P434
Kratzert, Niki A458:P287
Kraus, Timothy A234
Kraus, Scott A579
Krause, Brian P72
Krause, Matt P97
Krause, Melissa P119
Krause, Alan J P361
Krause, Stacy E240
Krause, Kimberly E301
Krausman, Tim P262
Krausz, Keira P392
Kravchenko, Kirill W208
Kravet, Steven J P275
Kravitz, Hal E74
Krawiec, Ronald P208
Krawitz, Natalie P625
Krayer, Anthony C P486
Krebber, Markus W415
Krebs, Donald A446
Krebsbach, David P381
Kreft, Alfred E245
Kregel, Kevin P586
Krehbiel, Anne E247
Kreidler, John P445
Kreis, Melanie W162
Kremens, Robert P450
Kremer, Wesley A665
Kremer, Melissa K A761
Kremer, Leslie P457
Kremke, Kevin L A241
Kremser, Craig W E282
Krenger, Kathy A460
Krenicki, John A243
Krenk, Chris P99
Krenke, Brian P289
Kress, Colette A577
Kress, Lynn P182
Kretzinger, Cut P354
Krewson, Lyda P134
Krhovsky, David M P494
Krieble, William A316
Krieg, Kenneth E59
Kriegner, Martin W229
Kriependorf, Bari P485
Kriesberg, Barry P243
Kriesel, Chance E250
Krift, Tom P466
Krill, Aaron P640
Krimbill, H. Michael A561
Krings, David P160
Krishna, Naveen A350
Krishna, Arvind A274
Krishnamoorthy, Shankar W184
Krishnan, Ram A619
Krishnan, Ganesh A632
Krishnan, Ramkumar A791
Krishoolndmangalam,
   Chandrashekar W65
Kriskovich, Craig P496
Krissinger, Debby P87
Kristensen, Kristian W454
Kristiansen, Thore Ernst W206
Krivo, George P198
Krivosheev, Viktor W468
Kroeger, Shadrak W480
Krohman, Barbara L P456
Krohn, Cindy P554
Krohne, Susan E258
Kroll, Werner E342
Kroloff, Mark P41
Krone, Roger A470:A472
Kroner, James A274
Krongard, Alvin A413
Krongard, Cheryl E9
Kropiunik, Frank C P16
Kroupa, Matt P4

COMBINED HOOVER'S HANDBOOK INDEX OF EXECUTIVES

Kroupa, Robert P524
Krow, Reggie P363
Krpan, Marko P335
Kruczlnicki, David A72:E31
Krueger, Daniel A852
Krueger, Shari P415
Krug, Dave P124
Kruger, James A549
Kruger, Paula A661
Kruger, Donna A736:P512
Kruger, Glen E150
Kruger, James E290
Kruk, Nadine P437
Krull, Karen A P460
Krump, Paul W126
Krupik, Ruben W63
Krupinski, Kenneth E161
Kruse, Ronia A417
Kruse, Lowell P354
Kruse, Rose P396
Kruse, Ronia E226
Krusemark, Cortni P175
Krushel, Kenneth P571
Krusmark, Christopher E378
Kruszewski, Ronald A746
Krutak, Lynn P55
Kruzner, Melinda P P298
Kruzner, Melinda P298
Krych, Ron P589
Krylova, Alexandra P306
Krystal, Andrew P616
Krystopolski, Ruth P463
Krzeminski, Laurel A71
Ksenak, Stephen A39
Kubacki, Michael A466
Kubacki, Joe A734:P510
Kubacki, Michael E244
Kubasik, Christopher A463
Kubessa, Martin W190
Kubicek, Greg A668
Kubik, Joellen P266
Kubitschek, Maria W521
Kubler, Raphael A758
Kubo, Taizo W23
Kubo, Isao W377
Kubohara, Kazunari W240
Kubota, Nina P370
Kubota, Hiroshi W356
Kubota, Shinya W435
Kuboyama, Cameron P474
Kucera, Randall A370:E203
Kuch, Logan P10
Kucharski, Kathryn P479
Kuchukov, Ilgam W411
Kucyk, Laura P379
Kuczmanski, John D P323
Kudla, Keith P211
Kudo, Lance A48:P31
Kudo, Yasumi W182
Kudo, Hideyuki W439
Kudo, Teiko W463
Kudo, Minoru W472
Kudrna, Ondrej W281
Kudumovic, Adisa P266
Kuechenmeister, Kevin P351
Kuehl, Christopher A22
Kuehn, George A778:P564
Kuehne, Klaus-Michael W287
Kuenstler, Fred P424
Kuenstler, Kevin P542
Kuether, Lynda P490
Kuffner, Michael W81
Kuffner, James W501
Kuga, Noriyuki W538
Kugel, Kevin P132
Kuhl, Shannon A639
Kuhl, Shelly E52
Kuhl, Shannon E332
Kuhlman, Russell E352
Kuhlow, John A408
Kuhn, Rebecca A102
Kuhn, Susie A332
Kuhn, Dennis A400
Kuhn, Rebecca P56
Kuhn, William P62
Kuhn, Tiffany P271
Kuhn, Sandi P335

Kuhn, James D P375
Kuhn, Dennis E218
Kuhnert, Marcus W321
Kuida, Elliot P409
Kujawa, Rebecca A560
Kukielski, Peter W363
Kuklenz, Dustin P382
Kukosky, Richard A624:P414
Kukuchka, Ronald A618
Kula, Tom P384
Kulasa, Matthew A854
Kulaszewicz, Frank A684
Kulesa, Amanda E297
Kulikowski, Lina P157
Kull, Matthew A775:P552
Kullman, Betsy P145
Kullman, Mary P495
Kullmann, Christian W190
Kulmaczewski, Leo E215
Kulper, Michael P1
Kulseth, Paul P281
Kulve, Peter Ter W510
Kumagai, Toshiyuki W272
Kumamoto, Yoshihiro W170
Kumar, Devinder A13
Kumar, Senthil A99
Kumar, Adarshna A451
Kumar, Suresh A845
Kumar, Ashok P1
Kumar, Jaya P530
Kumar, Monisha A P593
Kumar, Vinod W520
Kumar-Choudhury, Roli E250
Kumbartzki, Herbert W75
Kumbier, Michelle A767:E404
Kumihashi, Kazuhiro W237
Kummeth, Chuck E50
Kunes, Christopher E84
Kung, Ching-Yuan W106
Kung, Kuo-Chuan W230
Kung, Ming-Hsin W474
Kunibe, Takeshi W463
Kunii, Hideko W494
Kunimoto, Yoshihiko P527
Kunisch-Wolff, Christiane W2
Kunishi, Toshihiko W356
Kuniya, Hiroko W356
Kunkel, William A45
Kunkel, Thomas A792
Kunkel, Joann P463
Kunkel, Erin P574
Kunkle, Caitlin P5
Kunnary, Clifford F P136
Kunst, Michael A625
Kunstling, Ted P196
Kuntz, John A647
Kunz, John E321
Kunzler, Jacqueline A106
Kuo, Kimberly A197
Kuo, Ming-Jian W106
Kuo, Wen-Yi W196
Kuo, Tei-Wei W230
Kuok, Khoon Hong W529
Kuok, Khoon Hua W529
Kuok, Khoon Ean W529
Kuper, Susan P48
Kuperman, Jennifer A635
Kupres, Kimberley Metcalf - A598
Kurali, Andreas A625
Kuratsu, Yasuyuki W418
Kurdle, Florence B P306
Kuri, Luis Alejandro Soberon W28
Kurian, George A550
Kuribrena, Jose Antonio
  Meade W22:W234
Kurioka, Yoshinori W279
Kurisu, Duane A164
Kuriyama, Yoshifumi W288
Kuriyel, Ralf E349
Kurkowski, Arthur P422
Kurnick, Robert A615
Kurobe, Takashi W496
Kuroda, Haruhiko W67
Kurokawa, Hiroyuki W237
Kuroki, Nobuyuki P581
Kurosawa, Susumu W338
Kuroyanagi, Masafumi W148

Kurrle, Gunter P283
Kurtenbach, Anne P131
Kurth, Lauren P166
Kurtoglu, Tolga A404
Kurtz, Erin A339
Kurtz, George A386
Kurtz, Cassidy P142
Kurtz, Leslie P269
Kurtz, William P427
Kurz, Karl A243
Kurzius, Lawrence A508
Kusaki, Yoriyuki W468
Kusch, Alton P211
Kushel, J. Richard A120
Kushibiki, Toshisada W34
Kushida, Shigeki W158
Kusserow, Paul E18
Kusumi, Yuki W378
Kuta, John E344
Kutam, Sreeni A81
Kutner, Jean P618
Kutsmeda, Brian E305
Kutsumalis, Maria P571
Kutz, Stephanie P633
Kutz, Finja W509
Kuwabara, Satoko W330
Kuwano, Yukinori W151
Kuwata, Masanori W501
Kux, Barbara W224
Kuykendall, Dorthy A737:P513
Kuzma, Nathaniel P92
Kuznets, Sergei W208
Kuznets, Sergey W385
Kuznetsov, Stanislav W424
Kvidt, Scott P437
Kvisle, Harold W111
Kvistadt, Gregg P619
Kwah, Thiam Hock W529
Kwak, Jin P258
Kwan, George P125
Kwan, Savio W93
Kwan, Keen Yew W128
Kwauk, Teh-Ming W24
Kwek, Leng Hai W232
Kwiecinski, Jerzy W70
Kwietkauski, Chris P508
Kwietniak, Matthew E39
Kwilinski, Kevin P357
Kwock, Danny P82
Kwok, Amy P149
Kwok, Eva W110
Kwon, David A81
Kwon, Kenneth P345
Kwong, Raymond P546
Kwong, Connie E264
Kyle, Richard A721
Kyle, Rick P423
Kyles, David J P424
Kyles, Mable P453
Kymes, Stacy A126:E54
Kynychova, Sylva W281
Kyoya, Yutaka W329
Kyunghee, Lee D Ed P342
Kyytsonen, Matti W275
König, Thomas W169

L

L, Cynthia P2
La, Paul De P404
Laan, Remmert W278
Labarge, Kenny P259
LaBarre, Michael E204
Labarthe, Miguel Uccelli W69
Labat, Jerome A165
Labeau, Tina P165
Labelle, Tom P161
Laben, Nancy A129
Laberge, Michael A737:P513
Labeyrie, Christian W517
Labin, Karen P362
Laborde, Thierry W87
Labosky, Laura P134
Labovich, Gary A129
Labozzetta, Anthony A647
Labran, Renee E42

Labrecque, Andre G P22
Labrecque, Rachel S P40
Labrecque, Donald E383
Labrie, John P176
Labriola, Pietro W482
LaBrosse, Nicole E204
Lacaze, Alan P604
Lacaze, Claire W273
Lacek, Ryan P23
Lacerda, Francesco de W179
Lacey, William A609
Lacey, Sheila P49
Lacey, Tom E456
Lachance, Carrie E228
Lachman, M. Leanne A480
Lachs, Andreas W187
Lacker, Jeffrey M A300
Lackey, Kevin A737:P513
LaClair, Jennifer A33:A863
Lacour, Veronique W175
Lacroix, Laurent P259
Lacroix, Marc P444
Lacy, Renee A838:P641
Lacy, Paul E339
Ladany, Steven E190
Ladao, Victor P452
Ladd, Amy A430
Ladd, Kevin P217
Ladd, Steven P236
Laden-Andersen, Anker W267
Laderman, Gerald A813
Ladewig, Mary P416
Ladhani, Holli A495:A658
Ladley, Herb P55
Ladowicz, John A587:E302
Lady, Shirley S P78
Lafferty, Jane P653
Lafferty, Allison E300
Laffond, Reggie P608
Laffont, Philippe A778:P561
Lafitte, Michael A159
Lafitte, David E116
Lafon, Emily P653
Lafont, Jean-Jacques A350
Laforest, Pat P493
Lafortune, Robert P500
LaFoy, Jimmy E286
Lafranchi, Stephen P507
Lafreniere, Nora E A598
Lagano, Judith A574
Lagano, Roxanne A881
Lagarde, Michel A784
Lagatta, Loreen A79:E34
Lagazo, Michael P461
Lager, Jeffrey T P29
Lagerstrom, Timothy P242
Lageweg, Paul W93
Lagnese, Sheila A512:P324
Lagomarsino, Simone A298:E206
Lagree, Peggy A P159
Lagrene, Marc W398
Laguarta, Ramon A619:A839
Lague, Richard C P332
Lagutaine, Francesco A491
Laguzza, Toni P175
LaHaise, James A53:E25
Lahanas, Nicholas E75
Lahner, Gerhard W515
Lahti, David A738:P514
Lai, Chin Kui W376
Lai, Felix W530
Lai, Jackie W530
Lai, Quintin E446
Lai-Bitker, Ellis P155
Lai-Goldman, Myla E446
Laidlaw, Sam W405
Laing, Diana A728:P496
Laing, Ronald W100
Laing, Ian W242
Laino, Audrey P529
Laird, David A446
Laird, Fiona A498
Laird, Diane P326
Laisathit, Kirati W62
Laisathit, Niramarn W62
Laixuthai, Adit W270
Lake, Charles A18

COMBINED HOOVER'S HANDBOOK INDEX OF EXECUTIVES

A = AMERICAN BUSINESS
E = EMERGING COMPANIES
P = PRIVATE COMPANIES
W = WORLD BUSINESS

Lake, Robert A243
Lake, Marianne A444
Lake, R. Alexander A869
Lake, Robert P188
Lake, Randy W145
Lakey, Aaron A122:P80
Lakkundi, Veena A3:A684
Lakner, Stephen P6
Lakso, James L E242
Lal, Punita W155
Lalanne, Jean-Christophe W18
Lalas, Jose W P154
Lalchandani, Ajit P166
Lallathin, Larry P394
Lalley, Peter P450
Lally, James A279
Lally, Kevin P411
Lally, James E142
Lalor, Angela A235
Lalor, William P54
Lalwani, Ellen A466:E243
Lam, Christina A174:P118
Lam, Lisa P157
Lam, Chee Kin W155
Lam, Yin Shan W208
Lam, Elaine W376
Lam, Natalie W395
Lam, Ching Kam W435
Lam, Yee Mei W435
Lam, Thomas E29
Lamacchia, Timothy E150
Lamach, Michael A636
Lamancusa, Alicia P118
Lamar, William A707
Lamar, Jim P231
Lamar, Lona M P601
Lamar, William E368
Lamas, Ed A224:P162
Lamas, Felipe Rubio P237
Lamb, Jim P107
Lamb, Michael P156
Lamb, Eric P194
Lamb, John C P313
Lamb, Peter E150
Lamb, Jennifer E206
Lamb-Hale, Nicole A228
Lambdin, Rodney P587
Lambert, Phelps A585
Lambert, Megan P84
Lambert, Patrick P438
Lambert, Ellen P469
Lambert, H David P560
Lambert, Pippa W52
Lamberton, Karin T P164
Lambertz, Shelly A220
Lamble, Mark P257
Lambros, Cindy P109
Lambrugo, Lauren M P164
Lambson, T V P460
Lamel, Ira E298
Lamensdorf, Ben P509
Lamlieng, Chumpol Na W441
Lamm-Tennant, Joan A39
LaMonica, Susan A185
Lamont, Kevin E297
LaMontagne, Peter E259
Lamoreaux, Brent A414
Lamoreaux, Roy I A631
Lamoreaux, Brent P260
Lamothe, Marie-Josee W25
Lamoureux, Chad P277
Lampereur, Andrew E191
Lampkin, Andy P301
Lampkin, Patricia M P439
Lampo, Craig A59
Lampone, Salvatore W294
Lamsam, Sujitpan W270
Lamsam, Sara W270
Lamy, Mathieu W250
Lan, Sheryl P156
Lan, Jia W349

Lancaster, Ivan A315
Lancaster, Kathy A445
Lancaster, Rick P235
Lancaster, Kathy P279
Lancaster, Ivan E167
Lance, Bill A94
Lance, Ryan M A215
Lance, Jay P268
Lance, Donald W P578
Lance, Bill E44
Lance, William E297
Lanczi, Andras W334
Landahl, Mark P159
Landazuri, Pierre Perez y A418
Lande, Rashida La A460
Landel, Michel W152
Landen, Diane A542
Landen, Gordana W10
Lander, Larry P457
Lander, Eric P546
Landers, Lisa P25
Landgraf, Kurt A222
Landiribar, Javier Echenique W9:W57
Landis, Christopher E84
Landis, Gail E280
Landis, Gregory E376
Landon, Valerie W194
Landon, David E51
Landrieu, Mitchell J P129
Landrieu, Mary E419
Landrum, Julia A726
Landry, Angie A48
Landry, Robert A669
Landry, Allison A873
Landry, Sherri P104
Landry, Renee P401
Landry, Malcom P452
Landry, Dawn P650
Landsford, Gordon E P268
Landsiedel, David P137
Landsnes, Bente Avnung W154
Landy, R. Joseph E84
Lane, Andrew A4
Lane, Rita A60
Lane, H. Merritt A372
Lane, Kathleen A375
Lane, Robert A390
Lane, Rita A463:A694
Lane, Laura A819
Lane, Chris A842
Lane, Thomas A852
Lane, Claudio P155
Lane, Conan P247
Lane, Chuck P337
Lane, Debbie P396
Lane, Linda P419
Lane, Chris P645
Lane, Timothy W65
Lane, Brian E94
Lane, Robert E215
Lane, Michael J E221
Lane, John E274
Lane-Davies, Aaron P88
Laney, G. Timothy A544
Laney, Mark P248:P354
Laney, G. Timothy E285
Lang, Johann W81
Lang, James E83
Lang, Edward E239
Langan, John A208:P146
Lange, Bob De A20
Lange, Frank A30
Lange, Bob De A156
Lange, Frank P21
Lange, Donald H P120
Lange, Anne W243:W321
Lange, Thorsten W346
Langel, Craig A355:E193
Langenbach, Wilm W476
Langenbahn, Paul A548
Langevin, Eric E240
Langford, Barbara P25
Langford, Stephen P68
Langford, Mark D P285
Langham, Andrew A168:A581
Langheim, Thorsten A758:W163
Langholz, Christopher A802

Langley, W John P320
Langley, James E415
Langmead, Tim W200
Langrehr, Kristina P44
Langston, Mark P466
Lanham, Amy P156
Lanier, Nikki A639
Lanier, Gina P278
Lanier, Nikki E332
Lanigan, Susan A712:E373
Laningham, Kathy Van P616
Lankford, Damon P422
Lankler, Douglas A622
Lankswert, Bill A217:P151
Lanni, J Terrence P427
Lannie, Paul A64
Lanno, Marianne P503
Lannon, Timothy R P175
Lanoha, Richard A P285
Lansford, Gordon P268
Lansford, Gordon E P268
Lansing, William J E155
Lanter, Jennifer P572
Lantier, Meghan A133
Lantos, Phyllis R A780:P572
Lantow, Michelle A201:E92
Lantrip, Mark A723
Lantz, Brian A335
Lanza, Michael A704:E367
Lanzer, David E353
Laohasiriwong, Thanwa W284
Laokwansatit, Anucha W441
Lapham, John E369
Lapidas, Gary P609
Lapier, Russ P177
Lapierre, Justine P609
LaPlaca, Theresa A261:E126
Laplante, William A P547
Laplatney, Donald E199
LaPlume, Joseph E79
Lapointe, Greg A725:E383
Laporte, Todd P254
Laporte, Claudio Gonzalez W22
LaPrade, Frank A149
Laprade, Patricia P55
Lapuente, Christopher de W301
Lapus, Jesli W323
Lara, Gloria A727:P495
Lara, Marilyn P662
Laranjeira, Charles E311
Larbury, Dr George P390
Lardy, Eric E60
Lareau, Douglas P479
Laribee, Teresa P574
Larios, Faith P543
Larios, Michele E352
Larkin, Charles E15
Larkin, Melissa E380
Larman, Chad P333
Larnach, Fiona W396
Larner, Daniel A34
Larocca, Prue A22
Larocco, Michael A733
Laroche, Michael A688
Laroche, Jason P165
Larochelle, Steven A278:E141
Larochemorris, Renee A743
Larocque, Peter A763
LaRosa, Joseph A669
Larose, Robert C P98
LaRossa, Ralph A651
LaRouche, Michael A698
Laroyia, Varun A484
Larrabee, Steve A260
Larrabee, Laura A737:P513
Larranaga, Arantza W400
Larraz, Javier W165
Larre, Andres Bianchi W177
Larrick, Kurt P156
Larrimer, Karen A632
Larsen, Kenneth A102
Larsen, Michael A415
Larsen, Sallie A489
Larsen, Kirk A548
Larsen, Marshall A665
Larsen, Burke P184
Larsen, Ed P282

Larsen, James C P472
Larsen, Christine W99
Larsen, Kendall E440
Larson, Betty A109
Larson, Blake A569
Larson, Randall A593
Larson, Todd A672
Larson, Michael A677
Larson, Roma A736
Larson, Nils A804
Larson, Brian P113
Larson, Gaylyn P168
Larson, Jenna P266
Larson, Jody P266
Larson, Roma P512
Larson, Carol S P554
Larson, Bill P596
Larson, Nils P607
Larson, Jennifer P629
Larson, Lynette P647
Larson, Michael W198
Larson, Todd L E52
Larson, Sherry E198
Larson, Timothy E377
Larson, Victor E440
Larsson, Stefan A655
Larsson, Jan W470
Larue, Alex E186
Lasaga, Manuel P59
Lasat, Hugo W55
Lashier, Mark A172:A173
Lashier, Mark E A173
Lashier, Mark P113:P113
Lashier, Mark E P113
Lashier, Mark E322
Lashore, Adeola P157
Lashway, Heather A113
Laskawy, Philip A696
Laskey, Ryan A234
Laskey, Fred P319
Lasky, Lawrence P362
Lasonczyk, Cynthia P617
Lasota, Stephen E106
Lassere, Amy A783:P583
Lassiter, Wright A381:A659:P249
Lassner, David P621
Last, Corita P219
Laster, Dale P640
Lastra, Domingo A68
Lateef, Omar P453
Latek, Kevin E199
Latella, Robert A307
Laten, Steve P25
Laterza, Matteo W511
Laterza, Marco E352
Lathan, Christopher P180
Lathan, Grenita P256
Lathi, Dinesh E176
Latimer, Luke A313
Latimer, Maggie P168
Latimer, Luke E165
Latney, Cynthia P395
Latta, Marcia E156
Lattari, Steve A61
Lattimore, Ocea P134
Lattimore, Ray E382
Laturner, Jake A736:P512
Latwin, Anthony A224:P172
Lau, Timothy A74
Lau, Juen-Yee W130
Lau, Peng Kuee W138
Lau, Souk Huan W232
Laubacher, Pat P543
Lauber, Scott A852
Lauber, Anton W75
Laubscher, Kenton A780:P575
Lauderback, Bill P304
Lauderback, Brenda E378
Lauderdale, Meredith P572
Lauenroth-Mago, Joerg W315
Lauer, Gary A304
Lauf, Michael K P96:P97
Laughlin, John A672
Laughlin, Melinda A738
Laughlin, Jeannie P134
Laughlin, Joseph P402
Laughlin, Melinda P514

548   HOOVER'S HANDBOOK OF EMERGING COMPANIES 2022

COMBINED HOOVER'S HANDBOOK INDEX OF EXECUTIVES

Laughter, John A242
Laughton, Kim P468
Lauhon, Blaine E76
Lauk, Kurt W306
Laulis, Julia A17:E60
Launay, Romain W428
Laura, Russell P291
Lauraine, Allen P422
Laurence, Scott A439
Laurence, Jodi B P340
Laurence, Andrew E185
Laurendeau, Annie M A738:P514
Laurent, Etienne A426
Laurent, Anthony P615
Laurenzi, Cynthia P132
Laures, Karen P321
Laurito, James P108
Lauritsen, Bruce R P570
Lauritzen, Bruce R A322
Lauritzen, Bruce A322
Lauro, Jeffrey A579
Laury, Veronique W448
Laut, Steve W100
Lautenbach, Marc A146
Lauvergeon, Anne W281
Lauwers, Nicole P503
LaVange, Lisa E375
Lavares, Angelica W323
Laveck, Bill P496
Lavelle, Mark A716:E379
Lavender, Kevin A306
Lavender, Greg A421
Lavender, Sunee P615
Laver, Sue W484
Lavers, Jeffrey A3
Lavey, Richard A375
Lavigne, Bruce E198
Lavin, Pablo Jose Granifo W56
Lavinia, Robert A612
LaViolette, Paul A269
Lavizzo-Mourey, Risa A515
Law, David P38
Law, John C P105
Law, Rhea P629
Law, Chun-tak W66
Law, Yee Kwan Quinn W87
Law, Fan Chiu Fun W123:W124
Law, Song Keng W212
Law, David W391
Lawande, Sachin E89
Lawee, Ian E90
Lawer, Betsy A321
Lawer, David A321
Lawhorn, Wesley L P91
Lawing, Marty P160
Lawler, Robert A220
Lawler, John A333
Lawler, Mary A415
Lawler, Noelle S P50
Lawler, Nelda P208
Lawler, Michael A P247
Lawless, Robert A286
Lawless, Stephen T P19
Lawley, Thomas E358
Lawlor, David A449
Lawlor, Brian E364
Lawonn, Ken P478
Lawrence, Kevin A94
Lawrence, Paul A207
Lawrence, Stephen A853
Lawrence, Bruce P264
Lawrence, Sandra Aj P330
Lawrence, Melody P363
Lawrence, Joseph P426
Lawrence, Yaacov R P593
Lawrence, Paul P628
Lawrence, Jake W69
Lawrence, Kevin E44
Lawrence, Stephen E445
Lawrie, J Michael A213:P150
Laws, Christopher A274
Lawson, David A201
Lawson, Michael A545
Lawson, Ralph E P57
Lawson, Ralph P59
Lawson, T Douglas P65
Lawson, Stephen P198

Lawson, Stacey P231
Lawson, Matthew P321:P321
Lawson, Kale P337
Lawson, Deborah P471
Lawson, Sherri P496
Lawson, John D P542
Lawson, John W P641
Lawson, Brian W94
Lawson, Douglas A E40
Lawson, David E92
Lawson, John E174
Lawson, Takeitha E247
Lawson-Hall, Cathia W519
Lawton, Harry A702:A791
Laxton, Ron P179
Lay, Anne-Sophie Le W18
Layade, Nashira A666
Layden, Kelly P261
Layher, John A670:P440
Layman, Mark P55
Layne, Christopher P359
Laytart, David P332
Layton, Brent A162
Layton, Mary Jo P272
Lazar, Robert E149
Lazarakis, Spiro E118
Lazarus, Anne A187:P131
Lazat, Beatrice W273
Lazzaris, Diane A854
Lcsw, Marynne P172
Le, Christian P148
Le, Luyen P168
Le, Brian P437
Le, Huong V P506
Le, Jennifer P584
Le, Tan W396
Lea, Doretha A607
Lea, Jenny P287
Lea, Amy P296
Leach, Su P49
Leach, Mary Anne P116
Leach, Craig P596:P596
Leach, Michael E16
Leach, Jacob E117
Leader, Martin A713
Leahy, Kevin D P219
Leahy, Kathleen P308
Leal, Susan A185
Leal, Santiago P12
Leal, Susan P122
Leal, Diego P131
Leale, Erin P186
Leandro, Joao Miguel W398
Leap, Arnie E2
Leary, Robert A185
Leary, Jen P138
Leary, John P507
Leary, Matt P650
Leary, Robert W250
Leary, Dennis O E188
Leasure, Robert E229
Leatherberry, Antoinette A881
Leatherberry, Kristine W P351
Leatherberry, William E294
Leatherman, Jacob P48
Leatherman, Aaron P651
Leavell, Christopher A308
Leavell, Bill A359
Leavell, Jeff P62
Leavey, Meghan P163
Leavitt, Michael A46
Leavitt, Jesse A856
Leavy, David A248
Lebak, Kimberly A410
Lebeau, Michael E309
Lebel, Joseph A582
Lebel, Steven P206
Lebel, Joseph E302
Lebens, Michael C P537
LeBlanc, Claude A39
Leblanc, Stephen P183
Leblanc, Cara A P479
Leblanc, Thomas P560
Leblanc, Paul A P615
LeBlanc, Glen W82
LeBon, Cherylyn E101
Lech, Michael A253

Lechler, Lillian P163
Lechner, David P81
Lechusz, Joshua P51
Leclerc-Glorieux, Pauline W87
Ledakis, Peter P332
Lederer, Timothy P302
Lederer, Paul E123
Lederman, Baruch W253
Ledford, Daniel A439
Ledford, Wendy P129
Ledford, Daniel P276
Ledgett, Richard A491
LeDonne, Gary E283
Ledoux, Mark E287
Leduc, Robert A439
Lee, Debra A77
Lee, Lori A78
Lee, Danielle A104
Lee, Kewsong A152
Lee, Mark A157
Lee, Josephine A174
Lee, William A185
Lee, Edwin A185
Lee, Esther A189
Lee, Eugene A236
Lee, Lori A273
Lee, Russell A319
Lee, John A335
Lee, Brian A360
Lee, Kirk A370
Lee, Gloria A374
Lee, Bonita A374
Lee, Willard A375
Lee, Bruce A381
Lee, James A390
Lee, Rose A398
Lee, Felitia A498
Lee, Steven A533
Lee, Agnes A602
Lee, Debra A643
Lee, Bill A741
Lee, Hau A763
Lee, Joon A828
Lee, Yuchun A835
Lee, James P6
Lee, Patricia P23
Lee, David P94
Lee, Jong S P100
Lee, Judy P101
Lee, Josephine P118
Lee, William P122
Lee, Edwin P122
Lee, Helen P122
Lee, Tim P140
Lee, Robert S P170
Lee, David P171
Lee, Chris P186
Lee, Micheal P218
Lee, Parker P228
Lee, Do Hyun P228
Lee, Veronica P271
Lee, Susan P332
Lee, Irina P342
Lee, Youn P443
Lee, T H P447
Lee, Alan P449
Lee, Aline P456
Lee, Bryan P474
Lee, Bill P517
Lee, James P534
Lee, Felecia P541
Lee, Matthew P545
Lee, Kenneth P546
Lee, Benjamin P571
Lee, George P577
Lee, Joon P634
Lee, Jong E P641
Lee, Yuan Siong W16
Lee, Jiau Jiunn W29
Lee, Delman W66
Lee, Chang-Ken W106
Lee, Yu-Mei W106
Lee, Kok Kwan W128
Lee, Meng Teck W128
Lee, Lo-Chun W139
Lee, Deborah W139
Lee, Judy W155

Lee, Yan Hong W155
Lee, Susan W176
Lee, Fook Sun W212
Lee, James W212
Lee, Khai Fatt W212
Lee, Jay W230
Lee, Yun Lien W234
Lee, Sang Seung W238
Lee, Kitty W242
Lee, Yeon Mo W297
Lee, Hin Hock W307
Lee, Tih Shih W376
Lee, Seong Wuk W388
Lee, Deok Rak W388
Lee, Si Wu W388
Lee, Jae Yeol W388
Lee, Yo-hunn W393
Lee, Chin Guan W393
Lee, Kok Keong W393
Lee, Hsien Yang W409
Lee, Jill W427
Lee, Sam W530
Lee, Seok Tae W532
Lee, Janet E27
Lee, Mark E70
Lee, Joann E169
Lee, Russell E171
Lee, Yun E185
Lee, Kirk E203
Lee, Bruce E208
Lee, John E277
Lee, Victor E279
Lee, Sunggyu E295
Lee, Carter E309
Lee, Adrianne E309
Lee, Sang Young E315
Lee, Frank E323
Lee, David E406
Lee-Ebdie, Debra P114
Leech, Tony W448
Leech, Ted E188
Leeds, Mark A346
Leeds, Mark A A737
Leeds, Mark P227
Leeds, Mark A P513
Leeds, Elke P653
Leelaphantmetha, Pichit W441
Leelayouthayotin, Lackana W441
Leeming, Rosemary P226
Leenaars, Cornelis A149
Leenen, Alex W38
Leeper, Dale P339
Leer, Steven A566
Lees, Susan A32
Leetz, Tanya E162
Leeuwen, Mark Van P96
Lefeber, Marilyn Stein A541
LeFebvre, Dale A480
Lefebvre, Mojgan A792
Lefebvre, Jocelyn W389
Lefever, Willis E134
Lefever, Scott G E196
Lefevre, Deborah Hall A867
Lefevre, Deborah W25
LeFevre, Cyril E68
Lefevre, Deborah Hall E452
Leffler, Stephen P588
Lefteris, Chad T P443
Leg, Marty P384
Leger, Nicholas E292
Legg, Michael P607
Legge, Jeffrey Dale A186:E84
Leggio, Karen W480
Lego, Catherine A467
Legorburo, Jose W227
Legorreta, Pablo E358
Legrand, Jeff P216
Legrange, Brandon P348
Legras, Marc P293
Legreid, Alex P89
Legvold, Moriah P249
Lehel, Gabor W515
Lehman, John Von A47
Lehman, Daniel A149
Lehman, Gary A320
Lehman, Michael A523
Lehman, Katherine A545

COMBINED HOOVER'S HANDBOOK INDEX OF EXECUTIVES

A = AMERICAN BUSINESS
E = EMERGING COMPANIES
P = PRIVATE COMPANIES
W = WORLD BUSINESS

Lehman, Ronda P332
Lehman, Beth P620
Lehman, Samuel P638
Lehman, Gary E172
Lehman, Gregg E228
Lehmkuhl, W. Gregory E8
Lehmus, Matti W346
Lehn, Chuck A102:P56
Lehne, Kathy E P525
Lehoski, Cynthia P409
Lehoux, Becky P174
Lei, Jiangsong W125
Lei, Jihfen E404
Leibholz, Daniel A61
Leibler, Kenneth A284
Leibman, Maya A41
Leibold, Carla A229:E112
Leibowitz, Shelley A538
Leibowitz, Arthur E367
Leibson, Marie A640:E333
Leichtner, Scott J P230
Leide, Dominic E398
Leiden, Jeffrey A835
Leidle, Bruce P452
Leidwinger, Kevin A192
Leighton, Allan W132
Leighton, F. Thomson E11
Leighty, Scott P332
Leinenbach, Keith A353:E192
Leininger, G Scott A166
Leininger, Scott A166
Leininger, G Scott P110
Leininger, Scott P110
Leininger, Ina E250
Leino, Bruce P235
Leinonen, Jukka W483
Leiper, Martha A827
Leissler, Jonathan P177
Leistman, Charlene P164
Leitch, David A96
Leitch, Glenn R A401
Leite, Adam P261
Leith, Andrew P303
Leiting, Jim P73
Leitner, Lars P214
Leiva, Michele P194
Leland, D. Mark E329
Lemahieu, Kevin A94:E45
Lemaitre, Daniel E195
Lemaitre, Philippe E209
Lemarchand-Poirier, Agnes W451
Lemarie, Marie W174
Lemasters, Robb E59
Lemay, Stephane W389
Lembo, Philip A284:P209
Lemchak, Joseph A209:E95
Lemek, Brian A693:E360
Lemercier, Jean-Luc A269
Lemierre, Jean W87
Lemire, James R A208:P146
Lemke, Eric A530:E275
Lemkey, Rich P155
Lemman, Kathy A212
Lemmer, Peter A366:P235
Lemmer, Teresa P353
Lemming, Jennifer E151
Lemmo, Anneliese E221
Lemoine, David E233
Lemon, Paulette A396
Lemon, Robert P642
Lempka, Joseph R P284
Lemppenau, Joachim W521
Lempres, Elizabeth W213
Lenahan, Kevin P11
Lenard, Courtney A735:P511
Lencheck, Barbara P466
Lenehan, Pamela E291
Leness, Anthony P495
Lenhard, Felix W524
Lenhardt, Stephen W P624
Lenihan, Robert P28

Lenkheym, Martin M P211
Lenna, Robert A494
Lenner, Marc A832:E431
Lennie, William A394
Lennon, James W P23
Lennon, Carolan W17
Lennon, Gary W340
Lenny, Richard H A214
Lenny, Richard A415:A509
Lenox, Hugh P86
Lent, Jim Van A322
Lentsch, Bill A242
Lentz, Mary A416
Lentz, James A790
Lentz, Darrell P45
Lentz, Mary E226
Lenz, Denise A661:P432
Lenzi, Julianne P209
Lenzy-Jones, Delores P136
Leodler, Kathy E409
Leombruno, Todd A609
Leon, Mercedes M A210
Leon, Jonathan A600
Leon, Michael A702
Leon, Andres De P381
Leonard, James A306
Leonard, John A433
Leonard, Robert A797
Leonard, Rick P256
Leonard, Miriam A P309
Leonard, Vernon P533
Leonard, Edward F P655
Leonard, Jeffery E12
Leonard, Michael S E155
Leonardi, Thomas A792
Leonardi, Phil P384
Leone, Mike P221
Leonetti, Robert P162
Leong, Gladys W393
Leong, Justin E352
Leong-Tsan, Sue A P604
Leonhardt, Darrell P42
Leoni, Anthony P317
Leonsis, Theodore A46
Leonti, Joseph A609
Leopold, Diane A254
Leopold, Robin A444
Leopold, Diane A497
Leowarin, Sathian W441
Lepage, Nancy P162
Lepage, Mark A P314
Lepage, Philippe W184
Lepak, Vicki P45
Lepere, Kristopher P263
Lepetit, Marie-Christine W175
Lepinay, Philippe W488
Lepper, Carolyn P107
Leppert, Thomas A328
Leppert, Edward A647
Lequerique, Kristine P467
Lequient, Frederic E433
Lerch, Gail P244
Leriche, Dennis A84
Lerman, Oren P299
Lerner, Bruce A391
Lerner, Yishai A443
Lerner, J Scott P151
Lerner, Richard P206
Lerner, Teena P272
Lerner, Sara P582
Lerner, Scott E43
Leroux, Monique A691:W25:W82
Leroy, Dominique A758:W163
Lertkowit, Paisarn W62
Lerude, Robert P161
Lesar, David A163
Lesavoy, Bernard E132
Lesler, Michael A107:E48
Leslie, Nadine A647
Leslie, Brandon P63
Leslie, Paul S P179
Leslie, Timothy P284
Lesniak, Michael P132
Lester, Mike A652
Lester, Jeff P98
Lester, Bobby E152
Letelier, Mauricio Baeza W255

Letham, Dennis A767:E153
Lethbridge, Leonie W134
Letizia, John L P639
Lett, J. David A353
Lett, Rosalind K P205
Lett, J. David E192
Letta, Enrico W395
Letterio, Robbie P209
Lettieri, Richard E161
Lettman, Mike A734:P510
Letts, Joelle P256
Leu, Alfred W367
Leue, Torsten W218:W476
Leuenberger, Michael P584
Leukert, Bernd W160
Leumann, Simon W75
Leung, Sandra A134
Leung, Simon A763
Leung, Kristin P302
Leung, Kwan-Yuen W147
Leung, Oi-sie Elsie W378
Leung, Wing Han W539
Leupold, Mary P243
Leupp, Jay E207
Leusse, Paul De W372
Lev, Dalia W63
Levacher, Emmanuel W523
Levan, Bob P169
Levandoski, Karen P640
Levasseur, INA P315
Leveille, Tim D A173:P113
Leveille, Timothy W422
Levenick, Stuart A277:A363
Levens, Jerry A372
Levenson, Rodger A870
Levenson, Bruce E403
Levenson, Rodger E454
Leveque, Didier W106
Leverett, Allen P35
Levesque, Julie W341
Levesque, Paul E454
Levin, Diane A103
Levin, Joey A524
Levin, Diane P60
Levin, Jesse P103
Levin, Barry F P482
Levin, Justine P546
Levin, Richard C P661
Levin, Uri W253
Levin, Stephanie E78
Levin-Scherz, Jeffrey P50
Levine, Kyle A26
Levine, Matthew A839
Levine, Alan P55
Levine, Benjamin P284
Levine, Robert P563
Levine, Peter H P608
Levine, Peter P624
Levine, Matthew P643
Levine, Uri W247
LeVine, Suzan W395
Levingston, Charles A262:E126
Levinsky, Nik P577
Levinson, Arthur A65
Levinson, Linda A778:P561
Levitt, Brian A402
Levy, Susan Nestor A74
Levy, Paul A139
Levy, Susan A567
Levy, Susan Nestor P43
Levy, Bruce F P97
Levy, Ofer P112
Levy, Irvin P366
Levy, Judd S P373
Levy, Dina P373
Levy, Jean-Bernard W175:W193
Levy, Avraham W253
Levy, Maurice W395
Levy, Grant E9
Levy, Caroline E74
Levy, Michael E253
Levy, Tao E263
Levy, Ellen E443
Lew, Indu P61
Lewandowski, Cedric W175
Lewiner, Colette W133:W175
Lewis, Cindi A53

Lewis, Ron A92
Lewis, Raquelle A163
Lewis, Michael A260
Lewis, Holden A296
Lewis, Amanda A320
Lewis, John A326
Lewis, Sara A338
Lewis, Wilma A A362
Lewis, Scott A377
Lewis, Lee A388
Lewis, Gregory A398
Lewis, William A398
Lewis, Clinton A427
Lewis, Alison A455
Lewis, Patricia A470
Lewis, Lemuel A497
Lewis, Chrisopher A539
Lewis, Dave A619
Lewis, Michael A623
Lewis, Karla A673
Lewis, Jeffrey A713
Lewis, Timothy A734
Lewis, Patricia A823
Lewis, Derrick P32
Lewis, Glenn N P50
Lewis, Missy P57
Lewis, Donna P71
Lewis, Mary Lou P111
Lewis, Elizabeth P124
Lewis, Dawn P129
Lewis, Jim P164
Lewis, Donna P190
Lewis, Carlton P217
Lewis, Wilma A P232
Lewis, Katie P232
Lewis, Jonathan P247
Lewis, Jenny M P340
Lewis, Barry P347
Lewis, Bruce P389
Lewis, Dr Kirk P408
Lewis, Lisa P413
Lewis, Diane P422
Lewis, Carlisle KY C P477
Lewis, Carlisle C P477
Lewis, Timothy P510
Lewis, Jeanne P521
Lewis, Kathleen P528
Lewis, Kathy P529
Lewis, Kimberly P579
Lewis, Jasmine P642
Lewis, Joseph P654
Lewis, Kevin W25
Lewis, Sian W135
Lewis, Stuart W160
Lewis, Ric W291
Lewis, George W291
Lewis, Jonathan W360
Lewis, Cindi E25
Lewis, Mark E51
Lewis, Alton E169
Lewis, Amanda E173
Lewis, John E177
Lewis, Dan E206
Lewis, William E218
Lewis, Jim E245
Lewis, Joan E258
Lewis, Clunet E396
Lewis, Margaret E443
Lewnes, Ann A11
Ley, A Lily A602
Ley, James P169
Leyden, Kevin M P15
Leyden, Rob P362
Leyder, Dennis E160
Leykum, Elizabeth E222
Leyoub, Caprice P622
Leysen, Thomas W507
Leyva, Orlando E52
Lezama, Maybelline P468
Lhota, Joseph J P338
Li, Susan A26
Li, Dean A515
Li, Bin A625
LI, Tim A735
Li, Fei-Fei A801
LI, Zhuowei P197
LI, Celina P393

COMBINED HOOVER'S HANDBOOK INDEX OF EXECUTIVES

LI, Tim P511
LI, Hanna P545
LI, Heng P546
LI, Mitch P643
Li, Zhongwu W31
Li, Leyi W33
Li, Xiaobo W33
Li, Qunfeng W33
Li, Robin W54
Li, Kwok Cheung W66
Li, Kwok-sze W66
Li, Kwok Sing W66
Li, Man Bun W66
Li, Man-kiu W66
Li, Kai-cheong W66
Li, Kwok-wing W66
Li, Kwok Po W66
Li, Xuan W88
Li, Ke W97
Li, Qian W97
Li, Mingguang W117
Li, Huidi W118
Li, Ronghua W118
Li, Chaochun W118
Li, Shuhua W118
Li, Man Bun W119
Li, Ning W120
Li, Xin W121
Li, Kedong W123
Li, Qingping W129
Li, Yong W130
Li, Sheng-Hung W138
Li, Shu Fu W208
Li, Dong Hui W208
Li, Wanjun W212
Li, Maoguang W220
Li, Buhai W220
Li, Xingchun W235
Li, Pengyun W235
Li, Jianmin W236
Li, Haifeng W236
Li, Jingren W287
Li, Jianxiong W349
Li, Luguang W378
Li, Fei W387
Li, Jipeng W535
Li, Liangfu W535
Li, Yunhua W535
Li, Weiqing W539
Li, Wei W539
Li, Buqing W542
Li, Ying W542
Li, Zixue W542
Li, Xiaojia E262
Liakopoulos, Maria P109
Lian, Yu-bo W97
Liang, Douglas A329
Liang, Janet A445
Liang, Christine P45
Liang, Marcel P45
Liang, Janet P279
Liang, Lorrie P465
Liang, Susan P604
Liang, Daguang W33
Liang, Zhixiang W54
Liang, Ming-Chiao W106
Liang, Chuangshun W114
Liang, Weikang W115
Liang, Senlin W115
Liang, Yongming W116
Liang, Baojun W124
Liang, Jyh-Shyan W138
Liang, Yongpan W154
Liang, Wengen W419
Liang, Charles E397
Liao, Jun P346
Liao, Edward P488
Liao, Lin W244
Liao, Marvin W474
Liao, Daniel E323
Liaw, Y.H. W474
Liaw, Jeffrey E101
Libart, Dane A740:P516
Libbe, Allan J P578
Libbe, John A P578
Liberatore, Robert P641
Liberman, Margaret E248

Liberopoulos, Kathryn S P56
Libertino, John P290
Libiszewski, Darlene E448
Libnic, Samuel W56
Librandi, Esther P134
Libs, Gary A853:E445
Licalzi, Maria P362
Licari, Stephanie P345
Licata, Joseph A694
Liccardo, Sam P133
Licence, Stephen W291
Lich, Brad A264
Lichpenwalner, Tom P506
Licht, Russ P96
Lichtendahl, Kenneth A179
Lichtenwalner, Thomas P P459
Lichtenwalner, Rthomas P P498
Lichtman, David A323
Lickers, Eve A208:P146
Liddle, Michael A291:P210
Liebelt, Brian P163
Lieberman, Deborah P164
Lieberman, Louis P445
Lieberman, Gerald W487
Liebert, Rebecca A636
Liebowitz, Richard P377
Lied, Carol P337
Liedberg, Douglas A234
Liedel, Christopher P484
Liegeois, David P289
Lien, Clement W212
Lientz, James A431
Lies, Michel W543
Lievonen, Matti W451
Lifchez, Scott P275
Lifford, Pamela A759
Lifshitz, Yaacov W253
Liggins, Demetrus P545
Light, Darla P218
Lighte, Peter A649
Lightman, Steven E2
Lightsey, Charles A309:E163
Ligocki, Kathleen A470:A636
Liguori, Thomas A88
Like, Steven E72
Likes, Marilyn P472
Liles, Scott P468
Lillevang, Marianne W267
Lilley, David A651
Lilley, Ray P545
Lillian, Robles P243
Lillie, James E P39
Lillis, Terrance A185
Lilly, Pierre M A401
Lily, Liu W156
Lim, Luigi P204
Lim, Gabriel W83
Lim, Sim Seng W155
Lim, Weng Kin W155
Lim, Sok Hui W155
Lim, Tse Ghow W155
Lim, Hwee Hua W261
Lim, Khiang Tong W376
Lim, Chao Li W393
Lim, Say Huat W393
Lim, Then Fui W393
Lim, Yew Hui W393
Lim, TJ W509
Lim, Kim Guan W529
Lim, Siong-Guan W529
Lima, Tito A193
Lima, Marcos Eloi A460
Lima, Armando De A637
Lima, Tito E87
Limber, Joseph E455
Limcaoco, Jose Teodoro W70
Liming, Robert A740:P516
Limoges, Andrew A820
Limpiti, Tongurai W65
Lin, Sandra A44
Lin, Alice P29
Lin, Helen P126
Lin, Zhihong P228
Lin, John P532
Lin, Phyllis P625
Lin, Cheng Leo W62
Lin, Sarena W78

Lin, Jingzhen W87
Lin, William W91
Lin, Pei-Ching W106
Lin, Jen-Liang W138
Lin, Shengde W209
Lin, Chung-Cheng W230
Lin, Chong W236
Lin, J.K. W474
Lin, Horng-Dar W474
Lin, CL W530
Lin, William W530
Lin, F.C. W530
Lin, Jeff W530
Lin, Simon W530
Lin, Mao W535
Lin, Tao W535
Lin, Weiqing W541
Lin, Jennifer E415
Linares, Carlos A177
Lincoln, Blanche A277
Lincoln, Bean P14
Lincoln, David R P174
Lincoln, Dood P361
Lind, David P417
Lindahl, Richard S P103
Lindahl, Lennart P488
Lindahl, Richard E134
Lindarev, Anguel A49:E21
Lindberg, Bonita A789
Lindberg, Chuck P212
Lindberg, David W345
Lindblom, Mike P523
Lindburg, Roy E365
Linde, Tamara A651
Lindelow, Jessica P127
Lindeman, Scott P370
Lindemoen, Pam P507
Lindenbaum, Matthew A246
Lindenmuth, Gregory A113
Linder, James P366
Lindfors, Lars W346
Lindholm, Charlotta W446
Lindley, Randy P388
Lindner, Carl A47
Lindner, S. Craig A47
Lindo, Ely Roy W323
Lindow, John A502
Lindquist, Jim P272
Lindquist, Leslie P344
Lindsay, Stewart A146
Lindsay, Jeffery A573
Lindsay, Dann P38
Lindsay, Jeff P262
Lindsay, Jeffery P390
Lindsay, Donald W308
Lindsay-Wood, Elizabeth P240
Lindsey, Michele A837
Lindsey, Drennon P130
Lindsey, Steven P495
Lindsey, Shari P540
Lindsley, Dean P289
Lindstorm, Allen W P61
Lindstrom, David A531
Lindstrom, Carol E32
Lindstrom, David E276
Lindwall, Pauline W315
Lindwall, Dan W470
Linebarger, Tom A228
Ling, Jamie W29
Ling, Yiqun W120
Ling, Ke W209
Ling, Xiao W378
Ling, Curtis E264
Linger, L W A742:P518
Lingle, James E174
Lingo, Renee P2
Lingrel, Douglas A367
Liniger, Gail E345
Liniger, David E345
Link, Janet A731
Link, Denise W P138
Link, Brandi P161
Link, Wendy P166
Link, Dave P463
Link, Raymond E180
Linkel, Jacob E157
Linn, Julia P192

Linnartz, Stephanie A395:A498
Linneman, Dean A738:P514
Linnen, Edward A87
Linney, Brian P316
Linss, Roxanne P224
Linton, William W176
Liollio, Constantine A372
Liotine, Joseph A863
Liotta, Gary A330
Lipar, Jack E251
Lipar, Eric E251
Lipari, Adele P572
Lipert, John P185
Lipkin, Gerald A297:E158
Lipomi, Jack P96
Lipowsky, Ursula W218
Lippert, Jason E246
Lippoldt, Diana P650
Lippoldt, Darin E290
Lipps, Ben W203
Lipscomb, Jean P218
Lipsky, Matt P545
Lipson, Nancy A558
Lipson, Jeffrey E206
Lipstein, Steven A40
Lipton, Jeff P617
Lira, Alma P387
Liron, Eric W411
Lisa, Kenworthy A736
Lisa, Toni Jean P320
Lisa, Kenworthy P512
Lisbjerg, Michael Abildgaard W514
Lischer, David E149
Liscidini, Fabio P483
Lisenby, Jeffrey A642
Liska, Lee Ann P590:P640
Lisle, William W16
Lisowski, Sheryl A295
Lisowski, Jason A324
Lisowski, Jason J P410
Lissalde, Frederic A80:A131
Lissman, Thomas P461
List, Robin P187
Lista, George A647
Listengart, Joseph P364
Lister, Phil A411
Listerman, Randall W E157
Litak, Lisa P498
Litchfield, Caroline A515
Litchfield, Steven E264
Litchy, William P321
Litjen, Todd M A787:P595
Liton, Afroza S P508
Litsey, Jana A409
Little, Mark A61
Little, Teri A66
Little, Sonya A372
Little, R. Parrish A396
Little, Joshua A516
Little, Mitchell A526
Little, Brad A735
Little, Janet A838
Little, Craig P20
Little, Paul P26
Little, Paul David P26
Little, Bobby P33
Little, Jason P60
Little, Katherine P217
Little, George A P244
Little, George P244
Little, Robert D P415
Little, Brad P511
Little, Janet P641
Little, Thomas W82
Little, Roger W402
Little, Mark W466
Little, T. Mitchell E210
Little, R. Parrish E217
Littlefair, Andrew A388
Littlefield, Mark D A293
Littlefield, Christopher A641
Littlefield, Mark D P212
Littlejohn, Janet P67
Littlejohn, Kim P485
Littlejohn, Kimberly E430
Littleton, Stephen A291
Littleton, Sarah P43

COMBINED HOOVER'S HANDBOOK INDEX OF EXECUTIVES

A = AMERICAN BUSINESS
E = EMERGING COMPANIES
P = PRIVATE COMPANIES
W = WORLD BUSINESS

Littman, Owen E106
Litvack, Karina W185
Litwin, Jim P261
Litz, Christopher A652
Litzen, Ulla W3
Litzinger, Ronald A722
Liu, Tsu- Jae King A421
Liu, Deborah A429
Liu, Lisa A445
Liu, Don H A761
Liu, Xia A852
Liu, John A863
Liu, Ken P29
Liu, Sam P29
Liu, Jamie P29
Liu, Zhenquan P42
Liu, Xueli P126
Liu, Lisa P279
Liu, Catherine P372
Liu, Guangliang P488
Liu, Zhenqi P589
Liu, Anson P623
Liu, Yen P650
Liu, Wenyan W81
Liu, Liange W87
Liu, Jin W87
Liu, Hongfeng W88
Liu, Xiaodong W88
Liu, Huan-ming W97
Liu, Yongzhuo W115
Liu, Xuefei W115
Liu, Xianyong W119
Liu, Huiming W119
Liu, Hongbin W120
Liu, Chengjun W120
Liu, Ruchen W120
Liu, Hui W121
Liu, Xiaoyong W121
Liu, Liehong W124
Liu, Shuwei W125
Liu, Xiao W125
Liu, Zhengjun W129
Liu, Jizhen W154
Liu, Jianlong W154
Liu, Changqing W194
Liu, Shuwei W214
Liu, Yee-ru W230
Liu, Young-way W230
Liu, Ranxing W236
Liu, Jizhen W236
Liu, Wei W236
Liu, Jing W265
Liu, Xiaozhi W266
Liu, Jean W273
Liu, Jun W292
Liu, Li W321
Liu, Fuming W321
Liu, Chang W349
Liu, Yonghao W349
Liu, Yuezhen W378
Liu, Yingchuan W387
Liu, Wensheng W387
Liu, Ping W387
Liu, Yuhong W389
Liu, Fengxi W434
Liu, Mark W474
Liu, Hong W535
Liu, Jian W539
Liu, Tsu- Jae King E264
Liu, Tally E397
Liuson, Julia E62
Liuzzi, Matthew E429
Livermore, Ann A656:A819
Livingston, Julie A352
Livingston, Randall S A473
Livingston, Ian A691
Livingston, Joseph A736
Livingston, Randall S P295
Livingston, Joseph P512
Livingston, Ian W342
Livingston, Philip E344

Livingstone, David A183
Livingstone, Linda A P560
Livingstone, Catherine W135
Lizardi, Rafael A771
Lizaur, Ignacio Perez W215
Lizotte, Paul P252
Lizzari, Debbie A224:P162
Ljungqvist, Katarina W470
Llado, George E80
Llaneza, Kim A807
LLC, Wyoming Acquisition
  GP A667:P438
Lleras, Jose Antonio Vargas W179
Llewellyn, Rania W290
Llorente, Oscar Gomez W59
Lloveras, Teresa W400
Lloyd, David A367
Lloyd, Richard P306
Lloyd, Pamela P396
Lloyd, Robert E57
Lloyd, Anne E232
Lloyd, Jennifer E330
Lloyd, George E358
Lloyd-Smith, Malcolm E291
Lnp, Katy P554
Lo, Melanie P249
Lo, Yau-lai W66
Lo, Chi Lik W121
Lo, Wei-Jen W474
Loacker, Stefan W524
Loader, Enos E160
Loar, Holly P651
Lobach, David E132
Lobas, Nancy P607
Lober, Ralph E99
Lobo, Kevin A609:A749
LoCascio, Tammy A317:E170
Locatelli, Rosella W251
Loch, James E118
Lochen, Richard A618
Locher, Eric P406
Locke, Lori A248
Locke, Gary P28
Locke, Jace D P207
Locke, Dana P609
Locke, Anna E382
Locken, Dale P11
Lockhart, Dennis P A298
Lockhart, Dennis A431
Lockhart, Michael A566
Lockhart, John P492
Lockhart, Nancy W527
Lockhart, Joseph E51
Lockwood, Shannon P479
Lockwood, Charles P629
Lockwood, Kristina E200
Locoh-Donou, Francois A148
Locsin, Manuel W83
Lodge-Jarrett, Julie A244
Loeak, Wojwa P120
Loeb, David M A439:P276
Loeb, Joanne P374
Loeb, Marshall A E129
Loeblein, James A410
Loebs, Caren P137
Loeffler, Martin A59
Loeffler, Lance A371
Loeffler, Mike P386
Loeger, Julie A266
Loeger, Hartwig W515
Loehr, Donna P157
Loehr, Steve P289
Loellgen, Frank W190
Loewe, Nancy A862
Lofgren, Zoe P427
Lofgren, Beverly P463
Lofgren, Elizabeth P496
Loft, Chris P85
Loftin-Gainer, Keisha P67
Lofton, Adrienne A26
Lofton, Kevin E A245
Lofton, Kevin A355:A679
Lofton, Kevin E P189
Loftspring, Peter D P76
Loftus, John E142
Logan, Barry A849
Logan, Dwayne P339

Logan, Cheryl P396
Logan, Angie P629
Loganathan, Raghunandan S P89
Logatto, Vincent P519
Logeman, David P107
Logsdon, Jordan P25
Logsdon, Justin P255
Logue, Andrew A676
Logue, Anna P26
Loh, Sook Ling W393
Lohmann, Christopher W476
Lohr, Carolyn P467
Lohrer, Bernadette P467
Loiacono, Joseph P230
Lokeren, Mary Van P495
Lokey, James E96
Lomack, Damien P283
Lombard, Marie-Christine W517
Lombardi, Leonard A313
Lombardi, Brandon A729
Lombardi, Christy E96
Lombardi, Leonard E165
Lombardo, Gerald A P191
Lombardo, Anthony P196
Lombardozzi, Chris P493
Lombarte, Jordi A80
Lomeli, Bernardo A782:P583
Lomeo, Jody L P208:P280
Lomeo, Jody E148
Lommen, Wendy P238
London, Sarah A162
London, Eric P529
Londres, Eduardo P167
Lonegro, Frank A108
Loner, Marc P459
Lonergan, Robert A76
Lonergan, Stephen P133
Lonergan, Mike P166
Lones, Darling P529
Loney, Andrew A27:P15
Long, Michael A55
Long, Suzette A156
Long, Thomas A276
Long, David A284
Long, Gary A294
Long, Robert A455
Long, Donald A562
Long, Andrew A600
Long, Thomas A750
Long, Letitia A758
Long, Yu A759
Long, Sherry A838
Long, Tina P203
Long, Jennifer P243
Long, Amanda P464
Long, William C P470
Long, Larry P517
Long, Ronald R P542
Long, Sherry P641
Long, Matthew E134
Long, Gary E155
Long, Donald E293
Long, Gary E344
Long, Eric E429
Long, Thomas E429
Longacre, Doug A321
Longenderfer, Roger P418
Longenecker, Thomas A597:E307
Longhi, William A216
Longhi, Mario A806
Longhi, William G P397
Longhofer, T. Luke A315:E167
Longley, S. A144
Longman, Gary E82
Longo, Joseph A177
Longo, Edie M P596
Longo, Michael E213
Longobardi, Sara A617:E319
Longoria, Jennifer P528
Longstaff, Tom P100
Longstreet, Kym P323
Longstreet, Rick P493
Longsworth, Nora P587
Longwell, Char P327
Loo, Michael P603
Loo, Aaron W29
Loo, Cheau Leong W529

Looney, Bernard W91:W411
Loparco, Michael A434
Loper, D. Shane A372
Lopera, Adriana P84
Lopes, Debbie P535
Lopez, David A94
Lopez, Robert A145
Lopez, Beatriz A487
Lopez, Jorge A513
Lopez, Frank A689
Lopez, Elsie A776
Lopez, Robert P95
Lopez, Amy P119
Lopez, Jeannette P145
Lopez, Zoe P159
Lopez, Anna P224
Lopez, Barbara P255
Lopez, Natalia P265
Lopez, Anthony P283
Lopez, Beatriz P303
Lopez, Kevin P317
Lopez, Jorge P328
Lopez, Archie P409
Lopez, Nestor A Ramirez P501
Lopez, Elsie P558
Lopez, Alejandro Arango W171
Lopez, Esteban E4
Lopez, David E44
Lopez, Gerardo E347
Lopiccolo, Charles P418
Lora, Melissa A523
Loranger, Steven A269
Loranger, Joe P135
Lorberbaum, Jeffrey A533
Lorch, Nicole A318:E170
Lord, Rachel A120
Lord, Hambleton A143
Lord, Patrick A467
Lord, Phillippe A518
Lord, Hambleton E65
Lordan, John J P217
Loree, James A731:A863
Lorenson, Katie A A28:E13
Lorente, Pablo Azcoitia W179
Lorentson, Jeffrey A320
Lorentson, John C P359
Lorentson, Jeffrey E172
Lorentz, Theresa A345
Lorentz, Paul W308
Lorentzen, Oivind P470
Lorenz, W. Kent A311
Lorenzen, Jeffrey A45
Lorenzo, Jennifer Di A487
Lorenzo, Marcos F P215
Lorenzo, Jennifer Di P303
Lores, Enrique A404:A612
Loreto, Michael J Di P44
Lorey, Brandon E127
Lorig, Brian A457
Lorimer, Linda Koch P661
Lorino, Anthony P542
Lorne, Eric P349
Lorton, Donald E P99
Lortz, Andre A166:P9:P110
Losito, Bernadette P156
Losntos, Juan De P381
Lostaglia-Hosko, Andrea P396
Lostetter, Vicki A860
Lott, James A9:E4
Lotvin, Alan A232
Lotz, Jeremiah P430
Lou, Albert P539
Lou, Jianchang W223
Louder, Daryl A291:P210
Loudermilk, Robert A350
Loudon, Elizabeth A700
Loudon, Bridget W484
Louge, Michael W P395
Lough, Nicholas W232
Lougheed, James E264
Loughery, Robert E83
Loughran, Barbara A436
Loughrey, Kevin P594
Loughrey, F. Joseph E215
Loughridge, Jerome A740:P516
Louis, Harald W415
Louisma, Chantal P644

COMBINED HOOVER'S HANDBOOK INDEX OF EXECUTIVES

Lounsberry, Jackson E380
Lounsbury, Loren A321
Loureriro, Guilherme De Souza
  Macedo W525
Lousada, Max A846
Louton, Alysa P18
Louzado, Andre P135
Love, John A49
Love, Lisa A179
Love, Dan P67
Love, Ron P119
Love, Karen P147
Love, Rod A P166
Love, Dianne P171
Love, Robert P207
Love, Horace P311
Love, Karen P317
Love, John E21
Lovejoy, David A318:E170
Lovelace, Rob P98
Lovelady, Melvin A724
Loveland, Jennifer P430
Loveland-Curtze, Jennifer A780:P575
Loveless, Kathy A196
Lovell, Brigitte V P593
Loveridge, Gary F A750:P528
Lovering, Jamie A29:E13
Lovett, Laurie A562:P378
Lovett, Robert P597
Lovett, Gena E413
Lovik, Kenneth A318:E171
Loving, Richard E59
Lovingood, Preston P284
Lovins, Gregory A86
Lovoi, John E210
Low, Robert P368
Low, Melvyn W376
Low, Russell J E40
Lowber, John M P225
Lowder, Dr Steve P522
Lowder, W. Chester E430
Lowe, John A64
Lowe, Carol A71:A272
Lowe, Rebekah A396
Lowe, Roger P9
Lowe, Terrill P148
Lowe, Patricia P243
Lowe, Jennifer P283
Lowe, Heather Amick P316
Lowe, Terril P351
Lowe, Lance P529
Lowe, Mary Branigan P554
Lowe, Ken P643
Lowe, Mark A P654
Lowe, Jeffrey W212
Lowe, Eugene E159
Lowe, Rebekah E217
Lowen, Grant W37:W407
Lowenberg, John P314
Lowenthal, Albert G E305
Lower, Joseph A83
Lowery, Frederick A260
Lowery, Donna A309
Lowery, Norman A316:A316
Lowery, Christopher A600
Lowery, Donna E163
Lowman, Tim P432
Lown, Christian A337
Lowndes, Dusti P184
Lowrey, Charles A649
Lowry, Michael A600
Lowry, Katie P91
Lowry, Fred P172
Lowry, Judith P629
Lowry, Michael E63
Lowry, Robert E161
Lowry, Jennifer E284
Lowsley, Denise A375
Lowth, Simon W95
Lowther, Aaron P112
Lowthers, Bruce A304
Loy, Paul Ho Sing A466
Loy, Frank E P569
Loy, Bertrand E140
Loy, Paul Ho Sing E243
Loyo, Ann P539
Loyola, Connie P303

Lozada, Waleska P274
Lozano, Monica A65
Lozano, Rocio P38
Lozano, Tina P462
Lozano, Rogelio Zambrano W109
Lozen, Jeff P357
LP, John F Shea P480
Lu, Qun P155
Lu, Kimberly P403
Lu, John P596
Lu, Kelly P641
Lu, Wei W116
Lu, Ao W116
Lu, Xiaoqiang W120
Lu, Zhiren W122
Lu, Ching-Hsiung W138
Lu, Zhiwei W209
Lu, Fang-Ming W230
Lu, Sung-Ching W230
Lu, Fei W236
Lu, Yongzhen W244
Lu, Jinhai W287
Lu, Ming W391
Lu, Hse-Tung W432
Lu, Yi W436
Lu, Wenhan W535
Lu, Ding E311
Luallen, Eugenia A211
Luangsuwan, Nutthaporn W62
Lubarsky, Neil P593
Lubbers, Ally P89
Lubel, Kimberly A612:A860
Lubeski, Damien P308
Lubin, Richard K P180
Lubow, Stuart A246
Luburic, Danny A335
Luc, Nhon Ly W465
Luca, Guerrino De A562
Luca, Michele P53
Luca, Guerrino De P378
Lucas, Robert P292
Lucas, Bruce P355
Lucas, Philip P562
Lucas, John P652
Lucas, Hal E150
Lucas, Wonya E364
Lucas, Richard E443
Lucasbull, Wendy W6
Lucchini, Stefano W251
Luce, Charlotte P533
Lucey, Matthew A612
Lucey, Bob P172
Lucey, Kevin W156
Lucey, John E323
Luchangco, Eric Roberto W70
Luchini, David P159
Lucht, David A484
Lucia, William C P252
Lucia, Donna M P325
Lucia, Carol De P458
Luciano, Juan A68
Luciano, Melba P579
Lucido, Elizabeth Ann P162
Lucier, Jake A24:P13
Luckas, Nancy P146
Luckenbill, Patti P437:P438
Luckett, Artra P52
Luckshire, Daniel E370
Lucky, Donald E284
Lucore, Charles P501
Lucore, George E145
Lucsok, Anna E457
Ludden, Paul P491
Luddy, Frederic A706
Ludeman, Daniel A746
Ludford, Brad P458
Ludgate, Kristen A3:A404
Ludington, Bob P580
Ludkovsky, Gregory W39
Ludwig, Edward A132
Ludwig, A. Leslie A261
Ludwig, West A312
Ludwig, Logan A458
Ludwig, Jeffrey A530
Ludwig, Eric R P230
Ludwig, Logan P287
Ludwig, James P304

Ludwig, A. Leslie E126
Ludwig, Jeffrey E275
Ludwig-Beymer, Patti P201
Luedeman, Lars P63:P63
Luegering, Mark S P336
Luff, Nicholas W410
Luger, Nancy P249
Luhrmann, Klaus W177
Lui, Sai Kit W119
Luikart, John A298
Luis, Patrick E76
Luis, Victor E116
Luise, Patrizia De W511
Lujan, Audrey P123
Lukander, Jenni W359
Lukas, Brad P68
Lukaszeski, Marie P290
Lukaszewski, Michael P58
Luke, Jacquelyn R P361
Luke, Richard P362
Luke, Leslie Paul P504
Lukes, Konstantina P135
Lukesh, Kadi A738:P514
Lukish, Jeffrey P276
Lum, Anthony P169
Lum, Jonathan E109
Lummus, Dewayne A45
Luna, Wuaca P431
Luna, Joaquim Silva E W380
Lunak, Leslie A101
Lund, Randal A201
Lund, D Allen P22
Lund, David F P22
Lund, Kathleen M P22
Lund, Edward V P22
Lund, Victor P26
Lund, Per P223
Lund, Cathy N P646
Lund, Helge W91
Lund, Jens W168
Lund, Jens Hesselberg W514
Lund, Randal E92
Lund-Andersen, Sally W454
Lundberg, Gregory A589
Lundberg, Marissa P236
Lundberg, Fredrik W470
Lundequam, Michael P429
Lundergan, Dan P630
Lundgren, Terry A643
Lundgren, Tamara A689:E362
Lundmark, Pekka W359
Lundquist, Stephanie A755
Lundstedt, Martin W523
Lundstrom, Paul W197
Lung-Close, Heather P130
Luning, Christopher E147
Lunn, Eric P28
Luo, Rong W54
Luo, Hong-bin W97
Luo, Liang W119
Luo, Meijian W208
Luo, Sheng W209
Luo, Xiaoqian W235
Luo, Licheng W265
Luo, Dengwu W431
Luo, Zhipeng W480
Lupano, Carlo P589
Lupica, John W126
Lupo, Hope P255
Lupo, Anthony P519
Lupo-Adams, Linda P99
Lupoi, Alberto W316
Lupone, E. Robert A772
Luquette, Nancy A691
Lurker, Nancy A573:P391
Lusco, C. Matthew A671
Lusher, Jill P100
Lusignan, Sara P28
Lusk, C. Dale E174
Lussier, Joseph A278:E141
Luster, Alexandra E254
Lustgarten, Joyce P193
Lute, Jane A500:A812:W434
Lutero, Lu P641
Lutes, Christopher A164
Luthar, Vikram A69
Luther, Siegfried W190

Luthi, Francesca A76
Luthringer, Lifford P661
Lutoff-Perlo, Lisa A83
Lutomski, Wayne D P648
Lutsey, Meisha A142
Lutton, Lorraine P504
Lutu, Alvina P121
Lutz, Timothy P P357
Lutz, Tom P553
Lutz, Susan L P619
Lutz, Klaus W81
Lutz, Marcos Marinho W506
Luvizotto, Glauber E37
Lux, Melinda A814:E424
Luz, Maribel La P126
Lv, Xiang-yang W97
Ly, Davis A208:P146
Lyall, Wade E377
Lyash, Jeffrey A768
Lyash, Jeff P64
Lybarger, Stanley A126:E54
Lydon, Thomas A P39
Lydon, Bradford P481
Lyga, Joseph A106:E48
Lykins, Gregory A310:E164
Lyle, Dave A431
Lyle, John P594
Lyles, Lester A448
Lyles, Vanessa P34
Lyles, VI P124
Lyman, Keith P411
Lynch, Michael A42
Lynch, Robert A53
Lynch, Thomas A228
Lynch, Karen A232
Lynch, Dennis A325
Lynch, Jim A387
Lynch, Bernadette A740
Lynch, Christopher A765
Lynch, James P68
Lynch, Brian P P184
Lynch, Brian P184
Lynch, Linda P217
Lynch, Jim P251
Lynch, Donald M P272
Lynch, Jack P308:P308
Lynch, Kimberly P363
Lynch, Katie P368
Lynch, Mark S P450
Lynch, Bernadette P516
Lynch, Thomas P562
Lynch, Marlon P588
Lynch, Thomas W480
Lynch, Robert E25
Lynch, Nnenna E52
Lynch, G. Patrick E295
Lynch, James E376
Lyne, Catharine A667
Lynett, Madeline P652
Lynn, Jesse A324
Lynn, Mary P233
Lynn, Scott P454
Lynn, William W294
Lynton, Michael A846
Lynton, Carol E190
Lyon, Shawn A541
Lyon, Charles A748
Lyon, Mark P240
Lyon, Andres Lyon W33
Lyon, Joseph E102
Lyons, Martin A40
Lyons, Peter A42
Lyons, Stephanie A145
Lyons, Irving A282
Lyons, Billy A587
Lyons, Michael A632
Lyons, Thomas A648
Lyons, Stephanie P95
Lyons, Alison P194
Lyons, Addison P222
Lyons, Amy P293
Lyons, Jason P315
Lyons, Mitch P342
Lyons, Iris P624
Lyons, Daniel W242
Lyons, William E280
Lyons, Billy E302

COMBINED HOOVER'S HANDBOOK INDEX OF EXECUTIVES

A = AMERICAN BUSINESS
E = EMERGING COMPANIES
P = PRIVATE COMPANIES
W = WORLD BUSINESS

Lyski, James A154
Lysyj, Lesya E55
Lytle, Valentina P306
Lyu, Hong Bing W435
L'Esperance, Thomas P23
L'Estrange, Michael W405
L'Helias, Sophie W273
L'italien, Shawna E99

M

M, Maeona P2
M, Anna P112
M, Horst Npaulmann W110
Ma, Adrianna A66
Ma, Yongsheng W120
Ma, Zonglin W121
Ma, Li W220
Ma, Mingzhe W383
Ma, Connie W474
Maan, Malkit W232
Maas, Daren P546
Maas-Brunner, Melanie W76
Maass, Paul P580
Mabaso-koyana, Sindisiwe W335
Mabel, Richard I P438
Mabelane, Priscillah W421
Mabry, James A674:E348
Mabus, Raymond A234
Macali, Ralph A294:E156
Macaluso, Diane P22
Macaskill, Bridget A443
Macbeth, Shirley E182
Maccario, Aurelio W509
MacDiarmid, J. Hugh P23
Macdonald, Carrie A824
Macdonald, John A849
Macdonald, Walt P201
Macdonald, Alan G P317
Macdonald, Jamie P406
Macdonald, Carrie P617
Macdougall, Betty P32
Maceda, Jason E196
Macedo, Jorge Avelino Braga de W172
Macfarlane, Charles E309
Macfie, Helen P326
MacGibbon, Alan W497
Macgillivray, Diane P385
Macgregor, Catherine W184
Machen, Robert P32
Machetti, Claudio W181
Machin, Stuart W311
Machuca, Luis A809
Maciel, Antonio dos Santos W309
Macina, Robert P P564
MacInnes, Glenn A851
Macinnes, Dennis P353
Macinnes, Christina P358
Macintosh, Cynthia P469
MacIntosh, Britta E19
Mack, Michael A234
Mack, Robert P A632
Mack, John J A780
Mack, Renee P203
Mack, Jill P204
Mack, Clifford P427
Mack, John J P572
Mack, Michael P654
Mack, Dennis E150
Mack, Amy E352
Mack-Askew, Tracy A201:E92
Mack-Brooks, Pamela P255
Mackay, Leo A41
Mackay, Robert A229
Mackay, Iain W210
Mackay, Martin E80
Mackay, Robert E112
MacKay, Kimberly E446
Macke, Kevin A808:E421

Mackel, Dale E252
Mackenna, Jose Francisco Perez W56
Mackenzie, Alexander A622
Mackenzie, Bob P533
Mackenzie, Andrew W434
Mackenzie, Jonathan E266
Mackey, Edward A132
Mackey, John A285:A864
Mackey, Robin P182
Mackey, John P656
Mackey, Catherine E39
Macklem, Tiff W65
Macko, David P559
Mackzum, Errol J P168
MacLean, Elaine W17
Maclellan, Robert A757
MacLellan, Robert W306
Maclennon, John P429
Maclin, S. Todd A455
Macmillan, Stephen A392
Macmullen, Bill P129
Macnaughton, Mike P492
MacNicholas, Garry W213
Macomber, Sasha A668
Macoun, Jeffrey W213
Macphail, Winborne P466
MacPhail, Keith W111
Macpherson, Donald A363
Macpherson, DG A427
MacQuillan, Sandra A535
Macquillan, Sandra E415
MacRae, Penny W340
Macricostas, Constantine E323
Macrino, Joseph P316
MacSween, Michael W466
Macuga, Paul P588
Macyk, Irene P384
Madalena, Ralph J P373
Madamba, Charisma P243
Madani, Mohammad P51
Madden, Anne A398
Madden, Ursula P128
Madden, Christy P172
Madden, Kurt P222
Madden, Rachel P319
Madden, Donald V P597
Madden, Teresa W178:E100
Maddock, Ernest A88
Maddox, Mark P101
Maddox, Amy P127
Maddox, Mark P142
Maddox, Max P320
Maddux, Frank W203
Maddy, H. Charles A750:E394
Mader, Christoph W55
Maderd, James L P585
Madero, Ana-Maria A486:P303
Madero, Roger Saldana W109
Madhavpeddi, Kalidas W211
Madill, Justin P69
Madison, George A668
Madison, Thomas P594
Madnick, Vicki P246
Madoff, Paula W213:W389
Madon, Cyrus W94
Madonna, John A236
Madonna, Harry A676
Madonna, Elena P166
Madore, Marc A458:P287
Madre, Armelle de W488
Madrigal, Calvin P586
Madrigal, Bob P627
Madsbjerg, Saadia A196
Madsen, Mike A398
Madsen, Charles P11
Madsen, Alexandra P157
Madson, Patrick A562:E293
Maduck, Sean E102
Madyun, Adimu P392
Maeda, Kaori W226
Maeda, Masahiko W500:W501
Maertz, Tyler E391
Maes, Benoit W90
Maestas, Juan P653
Maestri, Luca A65
Maffei, Gregory A483
Maffei, Fay A624

Maffei, Gregory B A660
Maffei, Gregory A714
Maffei, Fay P414
Maffezzoni, Andrea W509
Mafi, Gabriela P224
Magana, Alejandro Ramirez W22
Maganov, Ravil W386
Magee, Michael A417
Magee, Christine W322
Magee, Brona W428
Magee, Michael E226
Magenheimer, Richard C P262
Magennis, Elizabeth A215:E97
Maggelet, Crystal Call A166:P110
Maggini, Joseph E271
Maggio, Paula A523
Maggio, Michael P261
Maggs, Thomas A797
Maggs, Everett P316
Maggy, Brad P159
Magid, Brent E248
Magier, Eugene E295
Magiera, Ann Kathleen P219
Magill, Clint P188
Maginot, Kathleen P632
Magistretti, Elisabetta W316
Maglaque, Neal A52
Magloth, Christian E273
Magness, Sue P125
Magno, Benjamin D P254
Magno, Mary P292
Magnuson, Michele A400:E218
Mago, Angela A453
Magowan, Bob P25
Magruder, Joan P498
Magstadt, Brian E374
Magturo, Roy Allan W83
Maguin, Stephen P173
Maguire, Vivian A31
Maguire, James J A624
Maguire, Vivian P24
Maguire, James J P414
Mahaffie, Alan P277
Mahajan, Puneet P523
Mahan, Lucy A321
Mahan, Chip A484
Mahan, James A484
Mahaney, Sheryl P286
Maharajh, Raja A665
Mahawongtikul, Pannalin W393
Mahbubani, Kishore W529
Mahe, Isabel Ge A732
Mahendra-Rajah, Prashanth A61:A361
Maher, Tina A316
Maher, Michael A565
Maher, Christopher A582
Maher, Christine P503
Maher, Robert L P639
Maher, Christopher E302
Maheras, Thomas A247
Mahil, Amandip P193
Mahjoub, Ali P377
Mahler, Anthony P652
Mahmood, Dawood P277
Mahmoud, Abdullatif bin Abdullah Al W395
Mahon, Kenneth A246
Mahon, Steven A698
Mahon, Paul W213
Mahon, Anita E151
Mahone, Barbara P657
Mahoney, Sean A7
Mahoney, Michael A106:A132
Mahoney, Ruth A546
Mahoney, Joanne M P165
Mahoney, P Michael P223
Mahoney, Sean W37
Mahoney, Richard E27
Mahoney, David E102
Mahoney, Daniel E107
MAI, Kevin P635
Mai, Yanzhou W124
Mai, Baowen W154
Maibach, Ryan P63
Maibach, Ben C P63
Maibach, Benjamin C P63
Maibach, Douglas L P63

Maibach, Sheryl B P63
Maida, Robert E16
Maidlow, Spencer T P174
Maier, Mike A545
Maier, Andrew W P427
Maier, Stephane E250
Mail, Ingrid M P311
Mailand, William P299
Mailer, Dee Jay P603
Mailes-Dineff, Suzanne P216:P525
Maillee, Ginette W239
Maimaitiyimin, Perhat W535
Main, Richard A278
Main, Joel P63
Main, Andy W533
Main, Timothy E57
Main, Richard E141
Main, Susan E404
Maines, Robert A296:E157
Mains, Stephanie E246
Mair, Jennifer P493
Maiuri, Louis A743
Majcher, Marian W71
Majchrowski, Don P120
Majima, Hironori W496
Majni, J Christopher P323
Major, Sean A23
Major, Cathy P253
Major, Melissa P477
Major, Leslie P611
Majoras, Deborah A644:A831
Majors, Charles A49
Majors, Michael A359
Majors, Charles E21
Majuri, Danielle P553
Makaroff, Jason P6
Makhmudova, Nigyar W152
Maki, Dana A34
Maki, Mark A P343
Maki-Kala, Jyrki W346
Makihara, Jun A625:W439
Makino, Akiji W149
Makino, Koichi W206
Makino, Jiro W354
Makino, Yuko W375
Makino, Shigenori W494
Makris, George A712:E373
Maksimow, Andre A126:P83
Malabanan, Manuel Patricio W83
Malachowski, Jeffery P146
Malady, Kyle A833:E117
Malan, Jill P498
Malana, Barbara P236
Malandra, Christy P572
Malaney, Darlene P166
Malapkowski, Bob P152
Malatesta, Brandy A736:P512
Malav, Andr S P390
Malchow, Joseph E138
Malcolm, Steven A126:A593
Malcolm, Steven J A864
Malcolm, Steven E54
Maldonado, Anjelina P96
Maldonado, Santiago Perdomo W171
Malec, Ed P601
Malee, Patrick P627
Maleh, Paul E107
Malehorn, Brad P647
Malempati, Ihari P417
Malhotra, Raghu A506
Malhotra, Kanuj P537
Malige, Matthieu W104
Malik, Aamir A622
Malik, Rajiv A837
Malik, Ajaymalik P173
Malik, M Shahbaz E189
Malin, John P212
Malinas, David A256
Malkoski, Kristine A556
Mallah, Isaac P504
Mallela, Ravi E294
Mallen, Ben P259
Mallesch, Eileen A306:W40
Mallett, Conrad A470
Mallett, Keshia P499
Malley, Peter O E47
Mallick, Imtiaz P246

COMBINED HOOVER'S HANDBOOK INDEX OF EXECUTIVES

Malliet, Jamie A867
Mallillin, Maria Corazon W83
Mallon, Liam A291
Mallon, Thomas E P3
Mallott, Anthony P471
Mallow, Betsy P373
Malloy, Marie A737
Malloy, Gary P454
Malloy, Marie P513
Malmskog, David P30
Malone, Mary A146
Malone, David A331
Malone, Michael A541
Malone, Robert A609
Malone, Evan A714
Malone, Steve P217
Malone, Richard P272
Malone, Mike P456
Malone, Thomas P458
Malone, Laura P544
Malone, Dan E12
Malone, David E178
Malone, Michael E281
Malone, Robert E404
Malone, Michael E443
Maloney, James E266
Maloney, Patrick E280
Maloy, Lisa P30
Malrieu, Francoise W184
Maltais, Nancy P587
Maltbie, John L P169
Malte, Bob P286
Maltezos, Louis E19
Maltsev, Sergey W424
Malzahn, Daniel A578
Mamik, Aneek A592
Mamilli, Wafaa A325:A881
Man, Luk Kai W232
Manabe, Masaaki W228
Manaf, Nora Abd W307
Manap, Sulaiman bin Abd W393
Manbeck, Keith A864:P656
Mancari, Mayly P118
Manchandya, Manish W422
Manchester, Jim P99
Manchur, Fred P283
Mancini, Salvatore P482
Mancini, Jessica P554
Mancini, Shawn P594
Mancuso, Salvatore A36
Mancuso, Anthony P214
Mancuso, Robert E297
Mandarich, David A492
Mandava, Surendra E62
Mandavilli, Apoorva A781:P580
Mandel, Mark A224:P168
Mandel, Lawrence P284
Mandell, Brian A239:A626
Mandell, James P548
Mandelman, Hersh P471
Mandeville, Jean F.H.P. E120
Mandinach, Barry E441
Mandine, Beatrice W372
Mandino, Matthew A447
Manditch, Douglas A330
Mandraffino, Erika W185
Mandrik, Ilya W386
Manduca, Mark A873
Manea, Dan E233
Maneker, Amy P118
Maner, William E382
Maneri, Phil P206
Mangan, Michael A508
Manganiello, Anthony A839:P643
Mangano, Rob P295
Mangione, Robert P498
Mangla, Dipty P48
Mangone, Rich A737:P513
Mangoni, John P407
Mangum, Kimberly P526
Mangurian, Christina P616
Mani, Meera P554
Manias, William G P207
Manieus, G K P533
Manifold, Stephen P64
Manifold, Albert W145
Manigan, Mark P61

Maniglia, Richard J P427
Manion, Gary P117
Manis, Dimitra A691
Manley, Mike A83
Manley, Joe A208:P145
Manley, Christine P529
Manley, Mike W410
Manley, Michael E2
Mann, Jennifer A197:A814
Mann, Chris P177
Mann, Brady P254
Mann, Lindsay K P282
Mann, Edward P283
Mann, Will P414
Mann, Aaron P604
Mann, Richard L P626
Mann, Joyce P635
Mann, Dorothy P642
Mann, Ann M E52
Mann, Theresa E204
Mann, Jennifer E424
Mannai, Khalaf Ahmad Al W134
Mannai, Saleh Abdulla Mohamed Al
   Ibrahim Al W134
Mannelly, Matthew A727
Mannen, Maryann A496:A541
Manner, Carrie E349
Manning, Joseph A4
Manning, Anna A672
Manning, Miriam P145
Manning, Christina P308
Mannis, Raymond P91
Manocha, Pooja P244
Manoharan, Arun P193
Manolamai, Poramasiri W441
Manolis, Eva E236
Manoogian, Richard A502
Manory, Joseph P P579
Manos, Kristen A453
Manos, Steven S P603
Mans, Gary P622
Manseau, James A246
Mansfield, Candy P220
Mansfield, Daniel P601
Mansfield, Michael E188
Manske, Scott P658
Mansour, Matt W396
Mansueto, Joe E280
Mansuetti, Mike A681:P448
Mantella, Philomena A727:P385:P495
Manthey, Cheryl P382
Mantia, Linda A510
Mantilla, Luis Suarez de Lezo W400
Manto, Jennifer P637
Mantovani, John P334
Mantua, Philip A693:E360
Manturov, Denis W385
Mantz, Constantine A P1
Manucy, Carter P216
Manulat, Angelita W83
Manvitz, Ted A716:E379
Manwani,
   Harish A355:A562:A657:A863:P378
Manwill, Lisa P122
Manzi, Rosina A330
Manzi, John A713
Manzo, Rose P3
Manzoni, John W165
Mao, Hsin-Kung W138
Mao, Zhihong W194
Mao, Qiwei W236
Mao, Zhanhong W303
Mao, Jianyi W431
Mao, yu Lang E137
Mapes, Michelle A293:P211
Maple, Shada P26
Maples, Phillip A94
Maples, Ricky A317
Maples, John T P485
Maples, Phillip E45
Maples, Ricky E170
Maquaire, Stéphane W104
Mar, Brett P222
Mar, Linda P529
Maraghy, Reagan E P582
Marallo, Andrew P198
Maramag, Angela Pilar W70

Maramotti, Luigi W144
Marangi, Leonard M P407
Marani, Ohad W64
Marano, Thomas F P191
Marberger, David S A214
Marbin, Jyothi N P115
Marcel, Dominique W174
Marcella, Joseph P53
Marcelo, Jeff P168
March, Jeff P430
Marchak, Margaret P242
Marchetta, Anthony L A551
Marchetti, Stephen A439:P276
Marchewka, Amber P80
Marchin, George P281
Marchiniak, Jenny P311
Marchio, Debbie P428
Marchione, Luciana Hildebrandi W255
Marchioni, Joseph A208
Marchioni, John A704
Marchioni, Joseph A146
Marchioni, John E367
Marchis, Ranieri De W509
Marchozzi, Tom P243
Marco, Lori J A401
Marcoccia, Loretta W69
Marcogliese, Richard P111
Marcon, Martha A516
Marconi, Luis G A401
Marcos, Luis R P415
Marcote, Flora Perez W243
Marcotte, Louis W250
Marcoux, Christa P174
Marcoux, Isabelle W389
Marcuccilli, James A745
Marcus, Gisele A320
Marcus, Philip P457
Marcus, Gill W211
Marcus, Joel E13
Marcus, Gisele E173
Marcus, Scott E442
Marcuse, Ivan A411
Marcy, Charles E43
Mardan, Ali P333
Marecic, Thomas A56
Marecki, Pam P541
Margalit, David L P206
Margalit-Ilovich, Ayelet P325
Margetts, Robert A411
Margol, Kanoe P576
Margolis, Daniel E132
Margolis, Joseph E153
Margulies, Anne A696
Marianacci, Alison P51
Mariani, Martin A793:E414
Maricondo, Peter E426
Marie, Caroline Gregoire Sainte W517
Marin, Jamie A133
Marin, Lina A583
Marin, Angela P637
Marin, Juan Guitard W61
Marin, Jose Casas W179
Marinelli, Grngory P69
Marinello, Anthony A797
Mariner, Jonathan A802
Marinho, Fatima W P404
Marino, Gerald P596
Marino, Ricardo Villela W255
Marion, John E283
Marisa, Howard P165
Marischen, James A746
Maritz, Steve P312
Maritz, W. Stephen P495
Mark, Richard A765
Mark, Chris P129
Mark, Christensen P168
Markee, Richard E176
Markel, Steven A497
Markell, Peter K A503:P317:P565
Markeloa, Natalia V P566
Markelov, Vitaly W208:W385
Markey, Nancy P48
Markezin, Elaine P246
Markin, Cheryl P640
Markley, Steve P191
Markoe, Lynda A111
Markov, Dimitri P593

Markov, Vladimir W385
Markovitch, Steve P395
Markowitz, Sean A168
Marks, Judith F A598
Marks, Elena P147
Marks, Timothy P438
Marks, Pauline P563
Marks, Howard W94
Marks, Thomas E150
Markstein, William E P597
Marley, Darlene P488
Marlow, Patty P642
Marlowe, Joseph P440
Marlowe, Blanche P528
Marmol, Guillermo A332
Maro, Hideharu W496
Marone, Anthony E52
Maroney, Edgar P129
Maroney, Kevin E148
Maroni, Kathy P335
Maroni, Alice C P484
Maroto, Guillermo Sabater W59
Marquardt, Jane P310
Marquardt, Dan P310
Marques, Ana Paula W173
Marques, Miguel Athayde W206
Marquette, Travis A140
Marquette, Vanessa W429
Marquez, Antonio A261
Marquez, Carl P133
Marquez, Rose P259
Marquez, Eduardo P353
Marquez, Ramon Martin Chavez W61
Marquez, Antonio E126
Marr, Christopher E389
Marr, John E419
Marracino, Roberta W509
Marraffa, John P288
Marrazzo, William A806
Marrella, John A458:P287
Marren, John A13
Marria, Mohit A174
Marriner, Kirsten A189
Marriott, David A498
Marriott, Robert P236
Marro, Peter P309
Marron, Brian A681:P448
Marroquin, Paulina Garza Laguera
   Gonda de W198
Marrs, Anna A46
Mars, Wendy W410
Marsch, Kathleen P508
Marsden, Dale P462
Marselle, Chris P456
Marsh, Martha A269
Marsh, Andrew A277:P206
Marsh, David P337
Marsh, Allen J P464
Marsh, Allen P464
Marsh, Amy K P628
Marsh, Linda E29
Marsh, William E132
Marshall, Jay A412
Marshall, Christopher A541
Marshall, Ryan A653
Marshall, Ruth A671
Marshall, Ernest A675
Marshall, Tucker A718
Marshall, Carianne A846
Marshall, David R P105
Marshall, Colin P139
Marshall, Craig P163
Marshall, Jay P258
Marshall, Ken P614
Marshall, Steven E115
Marshall, Joseph E190
Marshall, Case E257
Marshall, Christopher E281
Marshall, Ernest E350
Marshall-Provost, Tim P571
Marsolais, John P155
Marte, Mario A115
Martello, Wan Ling W24
Martello, Joseph E29
Marten, Cindy P462
Martens, Philip A364

HOOVER'S HANDBOOK OF EMERGING COMPANIES 2022

555

COMBINED HOOVER'S HANDBOOK INDEX OF EXECUTIVES

A = AMERICAN BUSINESS
E = EMERGING COMPANIES
P = PRIVATE COMPANIES
W = WORLD BUSINESS

Marter, Cyrus E86
Marthaler, Camille P187
Martin, Julian A16
Martin, Mary A47
Martin, Edward A49
Martin, Sean A106
Martin, Derek A126
Martin, Kevin A221
Martin, M. John A236
Martin, David A293
Martin, Christopher A297
Martin, Matthew A300
Martin, R. A302
Martin, Thomas A316
Martin, John A320
Martin, W. Scott A332
Martin, Doug A348
Martin, Flavius A355
Martin, Lynn A422
Martin, Thomas A456
Martin, Robert A492
Martin, Katherine A513
Martin, Antonio A552
Martin, Christopher A648
Martin, Jeffrey A705
Martin, Chrystal A741
Martin, Sue A741
Martin, Bobby A777
Martin, Robert A786
Martin, Julia P5
Martin, Julian P8
Martin, Michael P19:P43
Martin, Carole N P50
Martin, Sherry P58
Martin, Keith P91
Martin, David P134
Martin, Carl P135
Martin, Cary W P139
Martin, Michael P143
Martin, Stephen J P152
Martin, Ashton P179
Martin, Kathleen P182
Martin, Isabella P183
Martin, DEA P186
Martin, Cherie P199
Martin, Doug P205
Martin, David P211
Martin, Jennie P279
Martin, Jody P304
Martin, Ruben S P314:P315
Martin, Katherine P328
Martin, Antonio P369
Martin, Robert P379
Martin, Christopher P384
Martin, Ralph P385
Martin, Anne P508
Martin, James P508
Martin, Doug P508
Martin, Chrystal P517
Martin, Sue P518
Martin, Selina P586
Martin, Roy P603
Martin, Bill P604
Martin, David P637
Martin, Shelda P652
Martin, Nancy P660
Martin, Jose Humberto Acosta W61
Martin, Dalmacio W82
Martin, Bradley W188:W191
Martin, Jacques W239
Martin, James W405:W406
Martin, Rosemary W520
Martin, Alison W543
Martin, Edward E21
Martin, Derek E54
Martin, Jay E109:E134
Martin, Christopher E158
Martin, Dennis E159
Martin, John E172
Martin, Jackie E184
Martin, Michael E296

Martin, Ronald E300
Martin, William E361
Martin, Tami E399
Martin-Flickinger, Gerri A697
Martineau, Emily P132
Martinek, Kenneth E295
Martinek, Charles E295
Martinelli, David P349
Martines, Arnold A164
Martinet, Alain Emile Henry W309
Martinetto, Joseph A697
Martinez, Maria A182:A510
Martinez, Stacy A583
Martinez, Brett A667
Martinez, Susana A874
Martinez, Jason P18
Martinez, Benita P41
Martinez, Mike P123
Martinez, Oscar P139
Martinez, Kelly P172
Martinez, Angelica P218
Martinez, Marigold P374
Martinez, Stacy P393
Martinez, Amy P556
Martinez, Rodrigo Fernandez W22
Martinez, Armando Tamez W22
Martinez, Jose Manuel Martinez W57
Martinez, Oscar Eduardo Hasbun W219
Martinez, Carintia E279
Martinez-Mccart, Sandra P135
Martino, Chris P167
Martinovich, Robert A593
Martins, Izilda A87
Martins, Alex P584
Martinsen, Sten W363
Martinson, Eric K P576
Martire, Frank A548
Martocci, Gino A491
Martonyi, Janos W334
Martore, Gracia A860
Martucci, Pat P637
Marty, Steve P492
Marty, Rudolf W27
Marty, Thierry W273
Martyn, Derek P546
Martynov, Viktor W385
Martz, Gary A367
Martz, Walter A693
Martz, Bennett A816
Martz, Kurt P7
Martz, Sheila P114
Martz, Walter E360
Marumoto, Akira W314
Marushack, Joseph E296
Maruyama, Masatoshi W314
Maruyama, Tetsuji W377
Maruyama, Yoshimichi W430
Maruyama, Kazumasa W437
Maruyama, Heiji W537
Marvel, G. Michael A156
Marwah, Sarabjit W527
Marx, Kerstin W163
Maryasis, Elysa P87
Marzilli, Christopher A345
Marzilli, Shanna P420
Marzluf, Dirk W61
Mas, Alberto A109
Mas, Jose A504
Mas, Jorge A504
Masachs, Enric Rovira W57
Masai, Takako W324
Masanovich, Matti A767
Mascarenas, Paul A131:A591:A821
Mascaro, Daniel A645
Maschmeier, Stephanie E359
Mascia, Jonathan P243
Mashani, Saud Al W64
Mashani, Khalid Bin Mustahail Al W64
Masi, Niccolo De P230
Masiello, Wendy A448
Masih, Ashish E135
Masiyiwa, Strive A551:W510
Maslowski, Clem P445
Maslyaev, Ivan W386
Mason, Scheherazade A7
Mason, Jeanne A106
Mason, Mark A183

Mason, Jo A213
Mason, Karol A217
Mason, Thomas A276
Mason, Robert A312
Mason, Mark A396
Mason, A. Craig A446
Mason, Michael A478
Mason, Tracey A738
Mason, Steve P64
Mason, James P95
Mason, Mary P101
Mason, Jo P150
Mason, Ensen P168
Mason, Claudia P217
Mason, April P281
Mason, Debby D P337
Mason, Cheryl P378
Mason, Tracey P514
Mason, Sally P621
Mason, Barbara W69
Mason, William W290
Mason, Laura W291
Mason, John E132
Mason, Joyce E191
Mason, Caren E388
Mason, Thomas E429
Masood, Rafeh A111
Masrani, Bharat A697:W497
Masri, Maysoun D P584
Massa, Tod A209
Massa, Timothy A461
Massa, Tod P146
Massanelli, Stephen A712:E373
Massaro, Michelle P308
Massaro, Joseph W37
Massarweh, Lisa P16
Masse, William E448
Massee, Mark E91
Massengill, Matthew A858
Masser, Keith A780:P575
Massey, W Kenneth A531
Massey, Jerry L P199
Massey, W Kenneth P349
Massey, Mary P492
Massie, Easton Riley P19
Massie, John P490
Mastantuono, Gina A706
Mastella, Cláudio W380
Masters, Mary P450
Masterson, David J A706:P473
Mastioni, Marcello P27
Masto, Catherine Cortez A738:P514
Mastro, Lou P201
Mastromarino, Michael P577
Masu, Kazuyuki W325
Masuda, Ken P169
Masuda, Yoshinori W127
Masuda, Hiromu W127
Masuda, Shoji W463
Masuko, Jiro W491
Mata, Angelica P133
Mata, Jorge Pedro Jaime Sendra W215
Matak, Kristen P652
Matas, Barbara E378
Matejek, Michael P605
Matejovsky, Paul P635
Mateo, Carmen P370
Mateo, Alan E433
Matergia, Ralph E297
Mateus, Augusto Carlos Serra
    Ventura W172
Matheis, Dennis A706:P473
Matheny, Jennifer E439
Mather, Ann A551
Matherly, Laura E287
Matheson, Monique A563
Matheson, Jim A716
Matheson, Les W340
Matheson, Jim E379
Mathew, Sara A337
Mathews, Denise A456
Mathews, Rusty P198
Mathews, Krista E309
Mathias, Brooke A303
Mathias, America P43
Mathieu, Ronald P149
Mathieu, Cheryl P246

Mathis, Brandon P304
Mathis, Larry L P336
Mathis, Brian P466
Mathis, Patrick E294
Mathis, Vincent E393
Mathison, Lora P387
Mathur, Ankur A679
Matin, Tariq P503
Matis, Greg A423:P264
Matkin, Richard P420
Matlock, Stephanie P256
Matos, Nuno W234
Matosevic, Josef E209
Matson, David A102
Matson, Kenneth A359
Matsubara, Takehisa W68
Matsubara, Hiroaki W279
Matsuda, Toru W65
Matsuda, Tomoharu W269
Matsuda, Chieko W286
Matsuda, Yuzuru W286
Matsui, Yasushi W158
Matsui, Kathy W192
Matsui, Takeshi W375
Matsui, Shinobu W378
Matsui, Yukihiro W437
Matsui, Connie E204
Matsuishi, Hidetaka W403
Matsumoto, Raymond A90
Matsumoto, Colbert A164
Matsumoto, Lynette P621
Matsumoto, Masahiro W65
Matsumoto, Sachio W299
Matsumoto, Ryu W355
Matsumoto, Kazuhiro W377
Matsumoto, Masayoshi W462
Matsumoto, Masayuki W463
Matsumoto, Raymond E41
Matsumura, Takao W268
Matsuno, Masato W354
Matsuo, Yoshiro W375
Matsusaka, Hidetaka W339
Matsushita, Takashi W240
Matsuyama, Haruka W472
Matsuzaki, Takashi W149
Matsuzaki, Masatoshi W299
Matsuzaki, Satoru W373
Matt, Peter A207
Matta, Tony A189
Matta, Jason P396
Matte, James A197
Matteo, Jim P439
Mattera, Vincent E224
Mattern, Shannon P571
Matteson, Timothy A466:E243
Matthew, Anna A266
Matthews, Charles A227
Matthews, Kade A315
Matthews, Kay A751
Matthews, Charles A852
Matthews, Tenisha P7
Matthews, Lorin P65
Matthews, Martin J P87
Matthews, Jessica P127
Matthews, Jeff P261
Matthews, Lois P407
Matthews, Clint P437
Matthews, David Clint P437
Matthews, Coke P549
Matthews, Ward P578
Matthews, Phil P644
Matthews, Tanya E127
Matthews, Kade E167
Matthews, David E330
Matthews, Darryl E415
Mattimore, Karen A398
Mattingly, Jamie P390
Mattingly, Phil P595
Mattingly, Mack E35
Mattis, Archie A48
Mattison, Akanit W65
Mattke, Timothy A523
Mattlin, Julie A187:E85
Mattox, Keri A878
Mattox, Cheryl A P247
Mattox, Cheryl P247
Mattson, Eric P474

COMBINED HOOVER'S HANDBOOK INDEX OF EXECUTIVES

Matturri, Alexander E73
Matula, Alan A45
Matula, Kristopher A125
Matulis, Marc P401
Matuschka, Nikolaus W9
Matuschka, Nikolaus Graf von W227
Matuseviciene, Ausra W446
Matuszewski, Lech A734:P510
Matveev, Nikolai W468
Matyas, Lisa P429
Matytsyn, Aleksandr W386
Matyumza, Nomgando W421
Matz, R. Kevin A272
Mauad, Bruno E37
Mauch, Robert A55
Maude, Brian P147
Maudet, Amandine W518
Mauer, Ryan A846
Maughon, Bob W422
Maun, Marc A126:E54
Maung, Jenny A243:P188
Maurer, Daniel A194
Maurer, John A332
Maurer, Charles A458
Maurer, Thomas A605
Maurer, Mark A748
Maurer, Carmen P81
Maurer, Charles P287
Maurer, Matthias W227
Maurice, Laurence W543
Mauricio, Maxine A272:E298
Mauriello, Susan P169
Mauro, Ronald J Del P497
Mavian, Gregory Z P355
Maw, Scott A174
Mawakana, Tekedra A429
Maxey, Dr Rick P254
Maxfield, Sylvia A113
Maxfield, Beverly P74
Maxie, Chris P277
Maxson, Hilary W427
Maxwell, Greg G A173
Maxwell, Velma P17
Maxwell, Greg G P113
Maxwell, Shawn P132
Maxwell, Colton P225
Maxwell, Kevin P427
Maxwell, Terrance P448
Maxwell, Jamaica P554
Maxwell, Suzanne P604
May, Christopher A42
May, John A240
May, Alan A386
May, James A560
May, Keith A811
May, Holly A843
May, Lee P158
May, Brandon P353
May, Walter E P417
May, Christopher P590
May, Timothy P608
May, Gary S P616
May, Maureen P635
May, Brian W195
May, Teresa E24
Mayberry, Donnell P392
Mayer, Jessica A151
Mayer, Kevin A A251
Mayer, Michael A309
Mayer, Bethany A705
Mayer, Jean M P215
Mayer, Bradley P379
Mayer, Shawn P449
Mayer, Michael E162
Mayer, William E248
Mayer, David E282
Mayeron, John P184
Mayfield, Kelli P309
Mayfield, Thomas P375
Mayhew, Larry P376
Mayhew, Joe P557
Mayinja, Carolyn P164
Maynadier, Patrick de A177
Maynard, Easter A796
Maynard, Michael A866
Maynard, Scott P216
Maynard, Shelley P266

Maynard, Michael E450
Mayo, Marc A304
Mayo, Stephen A515
Mayo, Michael A737
Mayo, Bill A842
Mayo, Michael P58
Mayo, Michelle P200
Mayo, Michael P513
Mayo, Bill P645
Mayor, Karen P274
Mayor-Mora, Enrique A154
Mayoras, Richard E144
Mayrhofer, Siegfried W28
Mays, Randall A483
Mays, Derek P312
Mayshura, Maria E164
Mazany, Terry P114
Mazdyasni, Matthew E29
Maze, Leeann P419
Mazelsky, Jonathan J E221
Mazur-Hofsaess, Katarzyna W203
Mazza, Janice A562:P378
Mazza, Larry E283
Mazzarella, Kathleen A848
Mazzarella, Maria W252
Mazzilli, Ines W43
Mazzilli, Roberto W482
Mazzucato, Mariana W181
MBA, Stephanie Brown P157
MBA, Susan Wack P304
MBA, Gretchen Long P340
Mbanda, Laurent P149
McAbee, Chris A484
McAdams, Ben P168
McAdory, Janet P499
McAfee, Jodie P643
Mcalary, Ileana A727
McAlevey, Michael A379
McAlindon, Julie A264
McAlister, Diane P466
McAllen, Inga P193
McAllister, Nancy A617
McAllister, Marilyn P444
Mcallister, Singleton E81
McAllister, Nancy E319
McAlmont, Shaun A131:E393
McAluey, Daniel P488
Mcaneny, Deborah A443
McArthur, Kathryn P90
McArthur, Susan W213
McAtee, David A78
McAteer, Thomas E245
McAuliffe, Dorothy E30
McAvoy, John A216
McAvoy, Donald P23
McAvoy, John P397
McBrayer, Preston P595
Mcbreen, Michael E234
McBride, Joseph A30
McBride, Mary E A195
McBride, Dwight A217
McBride, Douglas A355
McBride, Kevin A706
Mcbride, Lura A815
McBride, Joseph P21
McBride, Roger L P36
McBride, Mary E P140
McBride, Kevies P159
McBride, Gary P168
McBride, Robert E P219
McBride, Dwight A P571
McBride, Renee P627
McBride, Daniel E100
Mcbride, Mary E132
McBride, Douglas E193
McCabe, Barbara A208
McCabe, John A330
McCabe, Robert A628
McCabe, Brian A724
McCabe, Barbara P146
McCabe, Thomas E59
McCabe, Robert E324
McCaffery, Michael A577
Mccahon, Jane A764
McCain, Ellis A169:A220
McCain, Linda P224
McCall, Jim A27

McCall, Jeff A474
McCall, Richard P380
McCall, Mick P389
McCall, Brian P542
McCallion, John A521
McCallion, Anne D E317
Mccallister, Michael A306:A881
McCallister, Terry E334
McCallum, Andrew H A298
McCambridge, David E296
Mccamey, William E35
McCamic, Jay A853:E445
McCanless, Ross A488
McCann, Patrick A79
McCann, Christine P333
McCann, Lauren P337
McCann, Bart P586
Mccann, James E2
McCann, Christopher E2
McCann, Patrick E34
McCanna, Pete A106:P64
McCanna, Peter P389
McCarley, Kirk P170
McCarrell, Faye P474
McCarrier, Deanna E133
McCarroll, Lisa P365
McCarthy, Margaret A44
McCarthy, Gloria A63
McCarthy, Marie A144
McCarthy, Christine M A251
McCarthy, Margaret A308
McCarthy, Mary A527
Mccarthy, Kevin A630
McCarthy, Christine A643
McCarthy, Thomas A704
McCarthy, Michael A812
McCarthy, Anne P163
McCarthy, Patricia P166
McCarthy, Jennifer P308
McCarthy, Teresa P346
McCarthy, Rhonda P494
McCarthy, Jim P524
McCarthy, John P571
Mccarthy, Aaron W306
McCarthy, Thomas E367
McCarthy, Deborah E448
Mccarthy-fry, Sarah W132
McCartney, Mary Ellen P238
Mccartney, Rob W531
McCarty, R Van A740
McCarty, Lisa P19
McCarty, Moira P300
McCarty, R Van P516
McCarty, Richard E300
McCarvel, Thomas E126
McCaskey, James E274
McCasland, Tom A94
McCasland, Kendall P659
McCasland, Tom E44
McCaslin, James A42
McCaules, Beth P467
McCaulsky, Terry P639
McCaw, Susan E9
McClain, Gretchen A56
McClain, Darren P608
McClain, David P621
McClain, James P640
McClain, Amy P646
McClanahan, David A658
McClanahan, Robert P43
McClanahan, David P106
McClean, Peter W P211
McClellan, Stephen A361
Mcclellan, Mark A441
McClellan, Amy A727
McClellan, Cynthia P564
McClellan, David P644
Mcclellan, Laurie E99
McClelland, Heather P P309
McClelland, W Kent P476
McClenahan, Tom E263
Mcclimon, David A874
Mcclincy, Christopher A289
McClintock, Douglas A330
Mcclintock, Robert E327
McClone, Dustin A562:E293
McCloy, Fiona P332

McClung, David P350
McClure, Joanne A27
McClure, Julie A30
McClure, Charles A258
McClure, Teri A328
McClure, Beverley A399
McClure, Teri A438
Mcclure, John A713
McClure, Julie P21
McClure, Robert P239
McClure, David C P288
McClure, John P367
McClure, Susan P610
Mcclure, K. W8
McClure, Lynn E206
McColgan, Michael A274
McColl, John E105
McCollam, Sharon A28:P18
McCollom, Mark A340
McCollough, Anthony P398
McCollum, Mark A860
McComas, Dave P232
McComb, Scott G E207
McCombe, Mark A120
McComish, Christopher A690
McComiskey, Mike P545
Mcconie, Jay A322
McConn, Ann M A28:E13
McConnell, Kelsey A233
McConnell, Julia A860
McConnell, Joyce E P142
McConnell, Kelsey P178
McConnell, Tracy P398
McConnell, Joe P411
McConnell, Ryan P639
McConnell, Sharyn P643
McConnell, Gregory E81
McConnell, Brian E383
McConvey, Katherine P286
McConville, Jim W52
McCool, Sherry P330
Mccormack, Pamela A465
McCormick, Christopher A117
McCormick, Michael C A267
McCormick, Andrew P329
Mccormick, Robert A797
McCormick, Ann-Marie P263
McCormick, Aimee P423
McCormick, Darryl P581
McCormick, Thomas E334
McCourt, Marion A669
McCourt, Thomas E237
Mccoy, Michael A88
McCoy, Michael A149
McCoy, Albert A246
McCoy, Dustan A338
McCoy, Sherilyn A455
McCoy, Susan A471
McCoy, Sherilyn A749
McCoy, Daniel P P155
McCoy, Julie P192
McCoy, Stephen P288
McCoy, Michelle P410
McCoy, Charles P532
McCracken, Nicola W156
McCray, Ronald A519:E272
McCrea, Marshall A276
McCreary, Lynn A325
McCreary, Michael P333
McCreary, Lynn E294
McCree, Donald A185
McCree, Jeanie P362
McCreedy, John P485:P543
McCreight, David A154
McCrury, Gerald P551
McCuen, Kyle A P207:P207
McCulloch, Tina P73
McCullough, Michael P44
McCullough, James P159
McCullough, Mark P226
McCullough, Douglas P298
McCullough, Kenneth P457
McCumber, Megan P198
McCurdy, Michael A136
McCurdy, Elizabeth P220
McCurdy, Jennifer P534
Mccurry, J. Kyle A320

COMBINED HOOVER'S HANDBOOK INDEX OF EXECUTIVES

A = AMERICAN BUSINESS
E = EMERGING COMPANIES
P = PRIVATE COMPANIES
W = WORLD BUSINESS

McCurry, Michael A517:P331:P334
Mccurry, J. Kyle E173
McCuskey, Kenneth D P181
McDanie, Linda P418
Mcdaniel, Connie A358
Mcdaniel, Jerry A530
McDaniel, Raymond A536
McDaniel, Jennifer P155
McDaniel, Alice P166
McDaniel, Reuben P193
McDaniel, Kris P220
McDaniel, Linda P418
Mcdaniel, Jerry E275
McDavid, Dan P358
McDearman, John A866:E450
McDermott, Michael A556
Mcdermott, Mike A622
McDermott, William A706
McDermott, Pat P332
McDermott, Tracey W457
McDevitt, William A98
McDevitt, Sean A108
McDevitt, Mike P549
McDevitt, Valerie P629
McDew, Darren A4
McDonagh, Brendan W17
McDonald, Rick A189
McDonald, Andrew A201
McDonald, R. Bruce A234
McDonald, Bryan A383
Mcdonald, William A406
McDonald, Scott A500
McDonald, Elizabeth A629
Mcdonald, John P28
McDonald, Mark P28
McDonald, Marcie P160
McDonald, Patricc P172
McDonald, Kris P175
McDonald, Thomas P365
McDonald, Patricia P384
McDonald, Jarred P499
McDonald, Thomas P567
McDonald, Ruth P653
McDonald, Jimmy W480
McDonald, Andrew E92
Mcdonald, Rebecca E96
McDonald, Bryan E212
McDonell, Jason A12
Mcdonie, Patrick A760
McDoniel, Kim P337
McDonnell, Padraig A21
McDonnell, Michael R A118
McDonnell, Ronald F A209
McDonnell, Eileen A824
McDonnell, Ronald F P146
Mcdonnell, Kevin E7
McDonnell, Raymond E392
McDonough, Paul A194
McDonough, Serena P492
McDonough, Erin P653
Mcdougall, Duane A125
Mcdowell, Ronda A693
McDowell, Morgan P525
McDowell, James P537
McDowell, Monte E265
Mcdowell, Ronda E360
McDowell, Charles E427
McElfresh, Jeffery A78
McElligott, Sara P275
McElreath, Tim P470
McElveen, John P196
McElwee, Darreil P170
McElyea, Dawn P144
McEndree, Lori P533
McEntee, James A774
McEntee, Christina E253
McEntee, James E408
Mcevoy, Ashley A441
Mcevoy, Robert A673
McEwan, Bill W283
McEwan, Ross W340

McFadden, Eliza E393
McFall, Thomas A579
Mcfarland, Katharina A698
McFarland, Scott A736
McFarland, J. Michael A881
McFarland, Scott P512
McFarland, R. William W191
McFatter, Dan P346
Mcfetridge, Adriane A857:E447
McGann, Tom P650
McGarrigle, Tom P158
McGarrity, Robert A652
McGarry, Michael A636
McGarry, Steven A716
McGarry, Michael A821
McGarry, Eugene P438
McGarry, Steven E379
Mcgarvie, Blythe A721
McGaughey, Tyler P122
McGeachin, Janice A735:P511
McGeary, Roderick A182:A663
Mcgee, Grant A84
McGee, Eric A408
McGee, Richard A630
McGee, Tracy A736
McGee, Freddy P37
McGee, Michael P130
McGee, Tracy P512
McGee, John P P552
McGeean, Tj P92
McGeorge, W. Scott A712:E373
McGettrick, Mark A600:A838
McGhee, James A212
McGhee, Craig P118
McGhee, Necole P141
McGill, Yvonne A66
McGill, William E260
McGimpsey, Thomas E6
McGinn, Meghan P500
Mcginnis, John A494
McGinnis, Bradley E81
McGinnis, Dana E407
McGinty, Frank G P309
McGinty, Bob P489
McGivney, Mark A500
McGlinchey, David A729
McGlothlen, Chuck P205
McGlynn, Lorelei A696
Mcglynn, Margaret A835
McGough, Thomas M A214
McGovern, Gail A258
McGovern, Jeanne A411
McGovern, Gail A611
McGowan, Christopher A125
McGowan, Paul P602
McGowan, Edward E11
McGowen, Doug P128
McGrail, Kevin M P560
McGranahan, Devin A325
McGrane, Brian J A679
McGrath, Eugene A216
McGrath, John A396
McGrath, Kieran P52
McGrath, Robert P228
McGrath, Barry P609
McGrath, Rebecca W304
McGrath, Ryan E340
McGraw, Deirdre A52
McGraw, Edward A674
McGraw, Thomas A793
McGraw, Celeste P156
McGraw, Regina P504
McGraw, Edward E348
McGraw, Thomas E414
McGreaham, David S P359
Mcgreevey, Gregory A431
Mcgregor, Scott A66
McGregor, Robert P118
McGregor, Joan P428
McGregor, George P489
McGregor, Amy P579
Mcgregor, Jay E289
McGrew, Michael A218
McGrew, Matthew A235
McGrone, Carlton P81
McGruder, Depelsha A776:P558
McGuiness, Paula P504

McGuire, Don A81
McGuire, Timothy A252
McGuire, Mark A264:P200
McGuire, Anne P396
McGuire, Tom W69
McGurk, Monica A449
McHale, Judith A607
McHale, Renee P647
McHale, Heather E303
McHargue, Rodger A316
McHenry, Daniel A368
McHugh, Margaret P22
McHugh, Mari-Len P76
McHugh, Kevin P405
McHugh, Richard E83
Mchugh, Julie E237
McIlvain, Chris P123
McIlwain, T Pinckney P P114
McIlwraith, John E270
McInerney, Thomas A351
Mcinerney, Ryan A839
Mcinnes, Ross W184
McInnis, Mary P458
McIntire, Christine P616
McIntire, Ron B P635
McIntosh, Robert A860
McIntosh, Jon P414
McIntyre, Andrew P149
McIntyre, Pamela W100
McIver, Donald P432
McIver, Jon I P441
McKain, Richard P459
McKasson, Craig P426
McKay, H. Lamar A64
McKay, Matthew A484
McKay, Linda P212
McKay, Mary P308
McKay, Tim W100
Mckay, Lamar W145
Mckay, David W412
McKay, Porter E39
McKeag, Bryan A381:E208
McKean, John P399
McKeating, Rae E449
McKee, Lynn A67
McKee, Joe M A173
McKee, Karen A291
Mckee, Michael A308
McKee, Jennifer A738
McKee, Daniel J A740
McKee, Gerard P17
McKee, Joe M P113
McKee, Jennifer P514
McKee, Daniel J P516
Mckee, Michael E347
McKeever, Robert P565
McKellar, Judsen A838:P641
McKelvy, Michael P229
McKendry, William A53:E25
McKenna, Quinn A730
McKenna, John A789
McKenna, Judith A845
McKenna, Erin P134
McKenna, Trent P144
McKenna, Tjada Doyen P153
McKenna, James C P257
McKenna, Mark P458
McKenna, Quinn P509
McKenna, Bertine P565
McKenna, Kathleen P589
Mckenna, Frank W94:W100
McKenna, Siobhan W532
McKenna, Trent E94
Mckenna, Dennis E332
Mckenney, Thomas E160
Mckenney, Michael E240
McKenzie, Diana A521:A835
McKenzie, Andr P498
McKenzie, Peter C P602
McKenzie, Jonathan W111
Mckenzie, John E295
McKeon, Timothy A371
Mckeon, Simon W340:W405
McKeon, Brian P E221
McKeough, Kathleen A847
McKernan, Thomas A308
McKernan, Stephen L P147

McKey, William P156
McKibben, Tracy A410
McKibben, Timothy E64
McKiernan, Anthony A507
McKillican, Rebecca W341
McKillips, David P104
McKim, Tony E163
McKine, Lisa P159
McKinley, Kwiniece A807
McKinley, Janet P562
Mckinney, Cassandra A204
McKinney, James J A451
McKinney, Rex A707
McKinney, Donna Kay P156
McKinney, Randall P255
McKinney, Jason P298
McKinney, Christine P446
McKinney, Marcus P457
McKinney, Myron P555
McKinney, Kim P594
McKinney, Lisa H P615
McKinney, Sean E84
McKinney, Rex E368
McKinnon, Howard P216
Mckissack, Eric A296:E157
McKnight, William A570
McKnight, Caroline P303
McKnight, Scott P368
McKnight, Craig P415
Mckoy, Philip A610
McKusick, Russ P85
Mclain, William A264
McLain, Timothy A608:E312
McLamb, Michael E260
McLaren, Reed P444
McLaren, John Bandini E396
Mclarty, Thomas A812
McLauchlin, Tracy E222
McLaughlin, Edward A506
McLaughlin, Mark A656
Mclaughlin, Theresa A743
McLaughlin, Marc A762
McLaughlin, Neal A809
McLaughlin, Steve P134
McLaughlin, Mark P163
McLaughlin, Ann P233
McLaughlin, Gary P346
McLaughlin, Rob P365
McLaughlin, Andrew W345
McLaughlin, Neil W412
McLaughlin, Michael I E155
McLay, Kathryn A845
Mclean, James A102
McLean, Kerry A429
McLean, Catherine A735
McLean, John A788
McLean, Benjamin A805
McLean, Catherine P511
McLean, Mickey P535
McLean, Christine W191
McLean, Emmett E265
McLean, Margaret E417
McLeister, Larry P485
McLellan, Richard A539
McLendon, Marna P256
McLintock,, Michael W45
Mcloughlin, Karen A115
McLoughlin, Keith A146
McLoughlin, Vin P98
McLoughlin, Dennis E311
McMahan, Marilee P316
McMahon, Robert A21
McMahon, Christine A32
McMahon, Brien A662
Mcmahon, Dirk A823
McMahon, Christine P24
McMahon, Betsy P38
McMahon, Meredith P484
McMahon, Tom P604
McMahon, Daniel E206
McMahon, Lisa E448
McMahon, Vincent E454
Mcmahon, Stephanie E454
McMaken, Carl P311
McManus, John A524
McManus, Brian M P99
McManus, Patrick P243

558   HOOVER'S HANDBOOK OF EMERGING COMPANIES 2022

COMBINED HOOVER'S HANDBOOK INDEX OF EXECUTIVES

McManus, Corin P436
McManus, Brian W322
McMaster, Henry Dargan A740
McMaster, Henry A740
McMaster, Henry Dargan P516
McMaster, Henry P516
McMillan, Lee P2
McMillan, Michael P247
McMillan, James J P403
McMillan, Ronnie G P424
McMillan, Wayde E233
McMillen, James P248
McMillen, Steve P601
McMillen, Tara P652
McMillen, Linda P652
McMillin, Nicole P247
McMillon, C. Douglas A844
McMinimee, Dan P271
McMinn, Robert S E242
McMorris, Heath P413
McMullen, Michael A21
McMullen, Elizabeth A88
McMullen, John A352
McMullen, William A461
McMullen, Marshall P111
McMullen, Michael J P522
McMurray, Kurston A561
Mcmurray, Sean A855
McMurray, James K P49:P639
Mcmurray, Sean E445
McMurry, Fred A309:E163
McNab, Sarah P286
McNab, Paul E437
Mcnabb, Frederick A424
McNabb, Forrest P74
McNair, Debora P177
McNair, Vernice P477
Mcnamara, John A367
McNamara, Robert A436
McNamara, Michael E A761
McNamara, Kevin A802
McNamara, J. Paul A814
McNamara, Patrick P151
McNamara, Meaghan P308
McNamara, Ed P426
McNamara, John P596
McNamara, Brian W210
McNamara, Simon W345
McNamara, J. Paul E423
McNamara, Michael E438
McNaney, Michael P439
McNaughton, Jarrod P283
Mcneal, Glenda A565
McNeal, Gwyn E153
McNeel, Amie A825:P631
McNeely, Joseph A61
McNeely, Bob A78
McNeely, Richard A253
McNeely, Ann A739
McNeely, Bob P47
McNeely, Ann P515
McNeil, Kami P637
McNeil, Jeffrey E138
McNeilage, Hazel A672
McNeill, Bryan A836
McNeill, Scott P203
McNeill, Elizabeth P479
McNeill, Kevin E339
McNerney, Robert A647
McNichols, Robin P266
McNiff, Mary A183
McNulty, Mary Ann P293
McPartland, James A359
McPeak, Katie P220
McPeek, Jennifer E73
Mcphail, Richard A395
McPhail, Jeff P509
Mcphaill, Kevin A709:E370
McPheely, Brian P424
McPherson, Joe A385
McPherson, Charles A725
McPherson, Cora P346
McPherson, Joe P392
McPherson, Philip E47
Mcpherson, Kevin E262
McPherson, Charles E383
McPhillips, Lindsey P652

Mcquade, Kathryn A36
McQuade, Mark A A787:P595
McQueen, Al P3
McQueen, Todd P580
McQuirk, Chris P96
Mcrae, Al A96
McRae, Lawrence A221
McRae, Dave P418
McRae, Mark P461
McRobbie, Michael E392
McRobert, Michael E265
McSain, Suzanne P132
McSally, Michael A274
McShane, Ryan P413
McSweeney, Erin W197
McTague, Emma A598
Mctear, Paul E199
McTeir, Robert H P19
McTier, Charles H A475
McTier, Michelle P162
McVaugh, Meg P72
McVay, Ashley P339
Mcvey, Richard E262
Mcwaters, Kimberly A615
McWay, Jake P296
McWhinney, Deborah A131
McWhorter, John P65
McWhorter, Dennis P86
McWhorter, John P395
McWhorter, Haden P426
McWilliams, Judith P169
Mdevivo, Michelle P353
Mdewan, Vikra P640
Mead, Judy A224
Mead, Charles A224
Mead, Christopher A341
Mead, Judy P172
Mead, Charles P172
Mead, Arthur P176
Meade, Christopher A120
Meade, Edward P321
Meador, David A258
Meador, Gary P170
Meadows, Cheryl G P141
Meagher, Laura A836
Meakins, Ian W139:W402
Meaney, Martin P165
Meaney, James W139
Means, Corey A824:P630
Means, William E125
Meany, Kathleen P338
Mears, Michael A705
Mecca, Ray P286
Mecca, John P594
Mecke, Stephen E388
Meckey, Samuel E151
Med, Wiggins P585
Medaris, Jamie A736:P512
Meddings, Kathy J P64
Medeiros, Karen P229
Medeiros, Carlos W513
Meden, Scott A565
Medhus, Tore W454
Medina, Manuel A135
Medina, Carlos P23
Medina, Erlinda P335
Medina, Marcus P604
Medina, Sergio W109
Medina, Timothy E393
Medler, Linda A632
Medline, Michael W176
Medlock, Jay P158
Medori, Rene W517
Meduski, Mary E60
Medvedev, Pavel A683
Medvedev, Alexander W208
Meehan, Thalia A143
Meehan, Ken P274
Meehan, Martin P624
Meehan, Thalia E65
Meek, Doug A742
Meek, Melinda P169
Meek, Julie P278
Meek, Doug P518
Meeker, Chris P422
Meekins, Deborah A285
Meekins, Deanna P150

Meeks, Richard P161
Meffert, Walt P349
Mefford, Amy A208
Mefford, Jeffrey A530
Mefford, Amy P145
Mefford, Jeffrey E275
Mega, Jessica A235
Megally, Michael P377
Megalou, Christos W383
Meghji, Mohsin A339
Mehan, Daniel W195
Mehl, Meghan P524
Mehler, Phillip S P187
Mehlman, Anne E110
Mehmel, Robert E203
Mehnert, Dana A463
Mehra, Jyoti A467
Mehra, Sachin A506
Mehrabian, Robert E404
Mehran, Alexander R A300
Mehrkens, Lee P167
Mehta, Siddharth A32:A443
Mehta, Apurva P152
Mehta, Shreeketa M P431
Mehta, Kashmira P648
Mehta, Tarak W5
Mehta, Harmeen W95
Mehta, Tarak W391
Mehta, Sanjiv W510
Mehta, Sanjay E405
Mei, Claire A411
Mei, Yan W194
Mei-pochtler, Antonella W43:W395
Meidinger, Adam P640
Meier, Keith A76
Meier, Cade A741
Meier, Margaret P4
Meier, Phillip P33
Meier, Charlie P254
Meier, Niklaus P325
Meier, Cade P517
Meikle, Scott A467
Meikle, Shauna P637
Meiklejohn, Mark A136
Meiler, Paula E111
Meilstrup, Eric E247
Meinolf, Michael A75
Meirovitz, Hagit Hamdani W253
Meisner, Laurie P535
Meister, Doris A491
Meister, John M A841
Meister, Paul W37
Meitz, Mary P88
Meixenberger, Christian W72
Meixner, Larry W324
Mejdell, Dag W363:W454
Mejean, Martina Hund W434
Mejia, Rosa P126
Mejia, Alberto N P131
Mejorada, Enrique Luis Castillo
   Sanchez W22
Melancon, Ben P470
Melanson, Scott P506
Melchior, Eric L P225
Meldrum, Guy W93
Meledandri, Chris W351
Melej, Cristian A390:E215
Melia, Mark P103
Melillo, Nick P5
Meline, Thierry W133
Melito, David A752
Melito, Jillian P317
Melius, Jeff P70
Melko, Charles E206
Mell, Abby P458
Mellado, Santiago P149
Mellado, Juan Maria Moreno W179
Melle, Patrice Le E291
Mellen, John A333
Mellinger, Kristin P41
Mello, Jon P535
Mellquist, Helene W523
Melnick, Gregg A111
Melnick, Paul E82
Melnkovic, A. Barry A821
Melo, Sally P477
Meloy, Mark A311

Meloy, Matthew A760
Melshenker, George P429
Melton, Danielle P11
Melton, Jasper P124
Meltzer, Neil M P300
Meltzer, Neil P482
Melucci, Jeffrey A455
Melville, Jim P25
Melville, Randolph E359
Melvin, Vincent A72
Melvin, Leland E59
Melzer, Lynn P125
Memioglu, Erol W505
Mena, David P248
Menard, Peter E121
Menassa, Roland E377
Menchel, Marc P214
Mencini, Frank A331:E178
Mencoff, Samuel A605
Mendel, John A484
Mendelsohn, Sophia A439
Mendelsohn, Nicola W165
Mendes, Paul W100
Mendez, James P37
Mendez, Alex P356
Mendez, Lincoln S P488
Mendez, Angel E377
Mendez-Andino, Jose A601
Mendicino, Thomas P308
Mendillo, Jane L P243
Mendive, Ashlee P522
Mendivil, Paulino Jose Rodriguez W23
Mendoza, Leticia P190
Mendoza, Stella P261
Mendoza, Candace P447
Mendoza, Frank P530
Mendoza, Maria Teresa Pulido W72
Mendoza, Tomas W83
Mendoza, Estelito W417
Menear, Craig A394
Menendez, Ana A849
Menendez-Cambo, Patricia A288
Menezes, Ivan W165
Meng, Amanda P641
Meng, Jinsong W31
Meng, Hsiao-Yi W196
Mengucci, John A142
Menke, Sean A848
Menke, Doug P620
Mennen, Justin A679
Menneto, Steven D A632
Menon, Ajay A627
Menon, Viju A749
Menon, Vimala W261
Menshikov, Sergey W208:W385
Mensler, Patricia P198
Mentis, Angela W340
Mento, Quince P160
Mentzer, Kevin P578
Menuau, Karl P198
Menzaghi, Frederique E67
Meo, Francesco De W204
Meoon, Alim P192
Mercado, Jhowel P302
Mercado, Pablo E94
Mercedes, Leon A210
Merchant, Susanne A737
Merchant, Art P162
Merchant, Susanne P513
Merchant, Toby E184
Mercier, John A103
Mercier, Johanna A355
Mercier, Denis W194
Mercier, Monique W239
Mercier, John E47
Mercier, Matthew E120
Mercier, Johanna E290
Merck, Peter W321
Merckle, Tobias W202
Merckle, Ludwig W222
Mercuri, Joe P578
Merdian, Charles P251
Meredith, Ian A132
Meredith, David A674
Meredith, Michael P48
Meredith, Cliff P93
Meredith, Nicole P499

COMBINED HOOVER'S HANDBOOK INDEX OF EXECUTIVES

A = AMERICAN BUSINESS
E = EMERGING COMPANIES
P = PRIVATE COMPANIES
W = WORLD BUSINESS

Meredith, David E348
Meriano, Frank V P114
Merigold, Catharine E7
Merka, Carla P408
Merkatoris, Susan A562:E293
Merkel, Michael T A166:P110
Merkel, Harold P206
Merkel, Frederick P610
Merkens, Hermann W2
Merkowitz, Justin A195:P140
Merkt, Steven W480
Merle, Denise A862
Merli, Geno J P593
Merline, John P223
Merlino, James A775:P551
Merlis, Laurence M P3
Merrera, Samantha P629
Merrick, Brent W30
Merrill, Allan A337
Merrill, Newton A491
Merrill, Mike P161
Merriman, David P334
Merrin, Patrice W211
Merritt, Sheila P325
Merritt, Jacqueline P521
Merriwether, Deidra A363
Merrywell, Christopher A201:E92
Merson, Mark W6
Merten, Jesse A32
Mertens, Blake A P555
Mertens, Peter W193
Mertz, Valerie A27:P14
Mertz, Paul P374
Mertz, Suzy P424
Mertz, Jim P556
Merz, Martina W490
Mesalam, Khalefa Al W395
Mescan, Steve P131
Mesler, Amanda W342
Meslow, Andrew A104
Mesrobian, Edmond A565
Messemer, Deborah A611
Messer, Cindy P93
Messerich, John P580
Messier, Luc W448
Messina, Carlo W252
Messina, Daniel E367
Messing, Fred M P57
Messing, Barbara E309
Messmer, Harold A682
Messner, Timothy A249
Metayer, Sylvia W448
Metcalf, James A767
Metcalf, Eric P177
Metcalf, Peter P227
Metcalfe, Tom A852
Methvin, Stacy A629
Metre, Chris Van P5
Mettala, Matti W274
Mettler, Christopher A707
Mettler, William P233
Mettler, Christopher E368
Metts, Julie P487
Metz, Adam A597
Metz, Merriann A652
Metz, Holly L P45
Metz, John P216
Metz, Adeline De W509
Metz, Christopher E75
Metz, Adam E307
Metzger, David P418
Metzger, Mick P575
Metzing, Mike P64
Meunier, John P185
Meurice, Eric W507
Meuse, David A733:E231
Meuth, Jane P490
Mewett, John W276
Mewhinney, Len A511:P322
Meyer, Barry A10
Meyer, Robert A51

Meyer, Jill A179
Meyer, Kevin S A292
Meyer, Barry M A300
Meyer, Sandy A473
Meyer, Melody A571
Meyer, James A714
Meyer, Kevin A734
Meyer, Calvin P10
Meyer, Mike P10
Meyer, Joshua P22
Meyer, Lynn P73
Meyer, David P142
Meyer, Joy P172
Meyer, Kevin S P210
Meyer, Carrie P249
Meyer, Sandy P295
Meyer, Julie A P314
Meyer, Robert P415
Meyer, Paula P416
Meyer, Cindy P421
Meyer, Todd P459
Meyer, Kevin P510
Meyer, Diane P553
Meyer, Sarah P632
Meyer, John P658
Meyer, Laurent W75
Meyer, Melody W91
Meyer, Perry E299
Meyer, John E406
Meyer-Davis, Pamela P201
Meyercord, F. Duffield A613:E316
Meyerhans, Thomas W27
Meyers, Charles A282
Meyers, Philip A A670
Meyers, Tony W P36
Meyers, Carole P182
Meyers, Philip A P440
Meyers, Audrey P589
Meyers, Brian E254
Meyrowitz, Carol A786
Meysenburg, Galen P245
Mezeul, Patricia A329
Mezger, Jeffrey A447
Mhatre, Nitin A113
Mhatre, Rohin E349
Mi, Dabin W236
Miano, Steve A414:P259
Miao, Chuanbin W88
Miao, Hua-Ben W106
Miao, Yong W287
Miastkowski, Alicia A436:P271
Miau, Feng-Chiang A763:W106
Miceli, Paul A465
Michael, Robert A6
Michael, Ralph A188
Michael, Aaron A615
Michael, Jonathan A680
Michael, Rubell P11
Michael, Mendez P85
Michael, Sam P383
Michael, Edward E342
Michael, Jonathan E356
Michaels, Shaylene P366
Michalek, Kevin P31
Michalopoulos, Georgios W27
Michalski, Gene P657
Michalsky, Bryan P282
Michas, Alexandros E320
Michaud, Brian A81
Michaud, Thomas A746
Michaud, Anik W32
Michaux, Charles P124
Michel, Todd A187
Michel, John A396:P433
Michel, John W H P433
Michel, Robert P P433
Michel, Jean-Paul W194
Michel, Bérang re W295
Michel, Todd E85
Michele, Marilyn De P602
Micheletti, Andrew A89:A90:P54:E41
Michels, David A456
Michels, Douglas E446
Michelson, Michael A878
Michiei, Robert Be A828:P634
Michihiro, Gotaro W463
Michulka, Natalie P534

Micillo, Mauro W252
Mickey, Hollis P36
Micklewright, Scott A529:E274
Miclat, Aileen P299
Micossi, Stefano W509
Middleton, Keith P598
Midgley, Clare P546
Midkiff, Mark A453
Midler, Laurence A159
Midseim, Anne-Lene W363
Miebach, Michael A506
Mielak, Gary P201:P201
Miele, Laura A271
Miele, Charles P63
Mielke, Daniela A774:E408
Mielle, Dominique E346
Miels, Luke W210
Miers, Charles P126
Migita, Akio W354
Miglani, Nalin E151
Migliorino, Robin P330
Mignone, Roberto W487
Migoya, Carlos A P576
Migoya, Alfonso Gonzalez W198
Miguel, Sergio San P341
Miguel, Josu Jon Imaz San W400
Miguelsanz, Luis W227
Mihalakos, Alysia A740:P516
Mihalik, Trevor A705
Mihaljevic, Tomislav A775:P551
Mihaylo, Steven E109
Mihok, Peter W515
Mii, Y. W474
Mijango, Manuel A P404
Mijindadi, Mohammed A346
Mikami, Yasuaki W373
Mikan, G. Mike A83
Mikati, Azim W335
Mike, Mike S P588
Mike, Kanetsugu W330
Mikells, Kathryn A291:A377
Mikes, Suzanne E99
Mikhailova, Elena W208:W385
Mikhalenko, Vyacheslav W385
Miki, Kikuo W317
Miki, Takayuki W331
Miklos, Ivan W334
Mikogami, Takashi W326
Miksad, John A216
Mikuen, Scott A463
Mikulak, Stephen P392
Milanes, Douglas A236
Milasich, Julie P220
Milauskas, Grace P100
Milavsky, Elizabeth E312
Milazzo, Joe P107
Mildenberger, Andrew P538
Mildice, Joe P411
Mildvan, Donna P71
Miles, Amy A57
Miles, Mark A114
Miles, Elizabeth A327
Miles, Rudolph A424
Miles, Amy A566:A777
Miles, Steven P22
Miles, Mark W P70
Miles, Elizabeth P214
Miles, David J P285:P285:P285
Miles, Steven P316
Miles, Carolyn P466
Miles, Samantha P577
Miles, Randall E152
Miles, Allen E448
Miles, David E451
Milewski, Frank A789
Miley, Nate P155
Miley, Jennifer P332
Milgrim, Brett A139:E321
Miliband, David P265
Milikin, Tony A452
Militar, Ramon W83
Milkie, Chris P89
Mill, Georgia P451
Millage, Timothy E248
Millan, Sheila Mc P406
Millane, Martin A143:E65
Millar, Leslie P579

Millard, Robert A463
Millard, Devin P261
Millard, Allison P304
Millard, Becca P573
Millard, Jayne P605
Millard, Robert E149
Millay, Robert H P588
Millen, Robert P P395
Miller, James A17
Miller, William A42
Miller, James A53
Miller, Elizabeth A72
Miller, Craig A102
Miller, Steve A178
Miller, Janet A188
Miller, Margaret A200
Miller, Adam A203
Miller, Joseph A216:A217
Miller, Russ A223
Miller, William A228
Miller, Charles A296
Miller, Heidi A325
Miller, Jeffrey A371
Miller, Maribess A403
Miller, DeWolfe A410
Miller, Gail A423
Miller, Jonathan A428
Miller, Neal A445
Miller, Cecil A446
Miller, Stuart A474
Miller, Tina A481
Miller, Jody A484
Miller, Dwight A530
Miller, David A542
Miller, Jonathan A562
Miller, Julie A583
Miller, D. Byrd A607
Miller, Matthew A608
Miller, Jamie A657
Miller, Ross A738
Miller, Liz A741
Miller, David A758
Miller, Susanne A773
Miller, Shane A802
Miller, Cheryl A802
Miller, Cindy A806
Miller, Michael A812
Miller, Alan A824
Miller, Marc A824
Miller, Brian P16
Miller, Carl P16
Miller, Larry P77
Miller, Debra P87
Miller, Keith P91
Miller, Catheryn P109
Miller, Tamara P133
Miller, Bruce P142
Miller, Jenifer P186
Miller, Tim P191
Miller, Darlene P206
Miller, Dean P218
Miller, Lynn P226
Miller, Dale P248
Miller, William F P252
Miller, Jennifer P254
Miller, Brad P261
Miller, Wentz J P263
Miller, Catherine P263
Miller, Gail P264
Miller, Cynthia P274
Miller, Greg P276
Miller, Neal P279
Miller, Brian P320
Miller, Allison P335
Miller, Paul P343
Miller, Stacey P344
Miller, Jonathan P378
Miller, Eddie P380
Miller, Kevin P386
Miller, Christina P392
Miller, Julie P393
Miller, Ronald D P433
Miller, Jane P451
Miller, Rena P456
Miller, Lynneia E P472
Miller, Greg P477:P477
Miller, Jessica P482

COMBINED HOOVER'S HANDBOOK INDEX OF EXECUTIVES

Miller, Ramona P500
Miller, Ross P514
Miller, Liz P517
Miller, Kurt P532
Miller, Greg P537
Miller, Randy P542
Miller, Matthew A P554
Miller, Kevin P559
Miller, Christine Z P579
Miller, Gary P585
Miller, James P594
Miller, Cynthia P607
Miller, Janet L P614
Miller, Thomas P634
Miller, Billie P641
Miller, Richard P643
Miller, Bill P647
Miller, David P650
Miller, Timothy W25
Miller, Aleksey W208
Miller, Klaus W218
Miller, Timothy W250
Miller, Stanley W335
Miller, Aleksey W385
Miller, Jonathan E11
Miller, James E25
Miller, Elizabeth E31
Miller, Kristine E60
Miller, Cheryl E74
Miller, Michael E120
Miller, David E132
Miller, Lawrence E185
Miller, Daniel E207
Miller, Michael E231
Miller, Dwight E275
Miller, Dennis E299
Miller, D. Byrd E312
Miller, Matthew E312
Miller, Kurt E383
Miller, Paul E417
Miller, Brian E419
Miller-Hobbs, Corri P640
Millerchip, Gary A461
Millett, Mark A745
Millhorn, David P629
Milligan, Michael D P53
Milligan, Mason P107
Milligan, Stephen E38
Milligan, Robert E207
Millikan, J Scott P75
Milliken, James B P81
Milliken, James P570
Millner, Thomas A115
Millones, Peter A128
Mills, Mike A145
Mills, Gary A314
Mills, Howard A351
Mills, Steven A500
Mills, Linda A546
Mills, Michael A570
Mills, Scott A641
Mills, Janet A737
Mills, Robert A791
Mills, Carrie A824
Mills, Kevin P29
Mills, Mike P95
Mills, Charlie P135
Mills, Bryan P147
Mills, Amy P164
Mills, Stephen S P377
Mills, Michael P388
Mills, Janet P513
Mills, Carrie P630
Mills, Robin W139
Mills, David W403
Mills, Robert E43
Mills, Joshua E120
Millunchick, Carol P37
Millwood, Ryan P487
Milne, Richard E53
Milne, George E79
Milner, Karen K A670:P440
Milot, Marie-Claude P388
Milowski, Nicholas B P217
Milstein, Jed A73
Milton, Mark A446
Milton, Robert E9

Milvo, Leslie P123
Mily, Elizabeth A134
Mims, Rod A78:P47
Mimura, Koichi W317
Min, Kyaw P291
Min, Chen W115
Minaka, Masatsugu W149
Minami, Shinsuke W255
Minami, Naohiro W260
Minamide, Masao W68
Minamide, Masanori W338
Minard, Marcia P500
Minardo, John E237
Minato, Alan P169
Minato, Michio W374
Minault, Pascal W90
Mineart, Beth P142
Minehan, Cathy E P565
Minemura, Yugo W468
Mineno, Yoshihiro W149
Miner, Matt A845
Miner, Stephanie P134
Mines, Linda Moss P241
Minetti, Carlos A247
Ming, Jenny A476:A477:P297
Minges, Sarah P147
Mingo, Felix de Vicente W59
Minich, Kent P337
Minich, Cassandra P414
Minick, Russell E191
Minicucci, Benito A26
Minifie, Suzanne W470
Minihan, Caileigh P503
Mink, Kim A264
Minkel, Kimberley E148
Minks, Allen P538
Minnett, Christopher E250
Minnich, George A20
Minnich, Brandt A516
Minnifield, Franky A211
Minnix, Lanesha E6
Minogue, Michael E3:E233
Minoia, Nicholas A215:E97
Minor, Donna A740
Minor, Richard P198
Minor, Donna P516
Minor, Rev Thomas Anthony P567
Minor, Glenda E362
Minter, Brian P432
Mintern, Jim W145
Minto, Emma E110
Minto, Anne E151
Mintz, Mary Theresa P3
Mintz, Susan P124
Mintz, Jack W242
Minus-Vincent, Deanna P61
Minvielle, Patrick P551
Miosi, Salvatore A523
Miquel, Chris P307
Mirabella, Mary P166
Mirabella, Alexander P171
Miramontes, Louis A679
Miranda, Raymond P160
Miranda, Rafael W94
Mirdita, Anthony P415
Mire, Michael W52
Mires, Charles E82
Miro, Mary Ann P309
Miron, Robert A248
Miron, Pierre W239
Mirro, Dr Joseph P505
Mirro, Michael J P602
Mirviss, Jeffrey A132
Mirza, Jawaid W188
Mirza, Azrul Iskandar W307
Mirzayantz, Nicolas A426
Misa, James Di E96
Misasi, Ryan A294:E155
Misawa, Naoshi P379
Misback, Ann A298
Misciasci, Katelynn A233:P178
Miscik, Judith A349:A404
Misheff, Donald A324
Mishima, Masahiko W326
Mishina, Craig P474
Mishra, Deepak A625
Miskinis, Judith P319

Miskovsky, Christopher P496
Mislan, Tim P346
Misono, Toyokazu W268
Misra, Biswa W16
Misra, Kabir W24
Misra, Sanjiv W370
Missad, Matthew A805
Missenheim, Susan A243:P188
Mistick, Kelly P131
Mistretta, Nancy A405
Mistry, Sarosh W448
Mistysyn, Allen A708
Misulis, Karl P270
Mita, Mayo W375
Mitau, Lee R E189
Mitcham, Debra P180
Mitchel, Larry P6
Mitchell, Thomas A309:A324
Mitchell, David A331
Mitchell, R. Brian A359
Mitchell, James A396
Mitchell, Rose E Kleyweg A412
Mitchell, Sara A412
Mitchell, John A546
Mitchell, Sydney L A594
Mitchell, Kevin A626
Mitchell, Royce A629
Mitchell, Pamella A670
Mitchell, H. Elizabeth A704
Mitchell, Katherine A751
Mitchell, Pleas P55
Mitchell, Laura P121
Mitchell, C Laura P121
Mitchell, Heather P130
Mitchell, Cliff P171
Mitchell, Susan P201:P201
Mitchell, Sheila P211
Mitchell, Rose E Kleyweg P258
Mitchell, Sara P258
Mitchell, Jay D P269
Mitchell, Michael R P299
Mitchell, Trish P368
Mitchell, Sydney L P397
Mitchell, Jay D P416
Mitchell, Pamella P440
Mitchell, Jenny P499
Mitchell, Adrienne P566
Mitchell, Diane P645
Mitchell, Kisha P660
Mitchell, Courtney P661
Mitchell, Arthur W463
Mitchell, Thomas E163
Mitchell, David E178
Mitchell, Kevin E322
Mitchell, H. Elizabeth E367
Mitchell, Thomas J E413
Mitchelmore, Lorraine A168
Mitchill, Neil A665
Mitola, John P260
Mitra, Subhro P381
Mitsue, Kurihara W127
Mitsunari, Miki W536
Mitsuoka, Ryuichi W338
Mitsuya, Yuko W158:W182
Mittal, Vijay P44
Mittal, Aditya W39
Mittal, Som E151
Mittelstadt, Wade A369:P237
Mitterbauer, Peter W367
Mitterway, Kathleen P302
Mitts, Heath W480
Miura, Atsunori W52
Miura, Hiroshi W66
Miura, Shigeki W67
Miura, Satoshi W226
Miura, Kunio W279
Miura, Toshiharu W429
Miwa, Etsuro W360
Mixon, Gina P269
Mixon, Jane P269
Mixon, Patti P662
Miya, Kenji W148
Miyabe, Toshihiko W350
Miyabe, Yoshiyuki W378
Miyagawa, Tadashi W375
Miyahara, Hideo W375
Miyahara, Ikuko W491

Miyajima, Tsukasa W148
Miyajima, Masaki W437
Miyakae, Tatsuyuki W537
Miyake, Seiichi W373
Miyama, Minako W148
Miyamoto, Ryuji W338
Miyamoto, Shigeru W351
Miyamoto, Yoichi W436
Miyanaga, Masato W127
Miyanaga, Shunichi W325:W326:W328
Miyanaga, Kenichi W330
Miyares, Takisha P419
Miyata, Yoshiiku W182:W279
Miyata, Yasuhiro W461
Miyauchi, Koji W418
Miyazaki, Kyoichi P120
Miyazaki, Annie P644
Miyazaki, Shoji W279
Miyazaki, Tsuyoshi W437
Miyoshi, Kenji W257
Miyoshi, Junko W257
Miyoshi, Toshiya W277
Miyoshi, Nobuhiro W354
Mize, Shawn P264
Mizel, Larry A492
Mizel, Courtney A492
Mizell, Gwen A40
Mizell, Steven A368
Miziolek, Aleksandra A767
Mizrahi, Rafael Moises Kalach W28
Mizuguchi, Makoto W279
Mizuguchi, Katsuyuki W459
Mizuno, Hiromichi A769
Mizuno, Yojiro W500
Mizushima, Toshiyuki W21
Mizuta, Hiroyuki W36
Mizutani, Hitoshi W127
Mizzi, Douglas A786
Mjoli-Mncube, Nonhlanhla W6
Mkhwanazi, Themba W32
Mleczko, Dan P552
Mlinar, Michael E271
Mlotek, Mark A696
Mlynarek, Robert W P647
Mmeje, Kenechukwu P491
Mnookin, Allison A489
MO, Weiwei P633
Moag, Anthony G A783:P591
Moates, Glenn A741:P517
Moats, Michael P588
Moazemi, Kourosh P100
Mobley, Daniel W165
Mocaby, Shawn A841
Moch, Nicolas W446
Mock, James E320
Mockabee, William P578
Mockard, Jeanne A274
Modde, Margaret Mary P174
Modelski, Maureen P261
Modeski, Michael E308
Modica, Jeffrey P351
Modise, Punki W6
Modise, Lele W335
Moe, Jeremy P546
Moebius, Scott P238
Moehlis, Jeffrey P616
Moehn, Michael A40
Moel, Howard P89
Moeller, Jon A643
Moeller, Jorgen W168
Moeller, Peter E411
Moeller-Hergt, Gustavo W27
Moerdyk, Carol E24
Moesgaard, Lars W470
Moey, Eng-kwok Seat W155
Moff, Beth P162
Moffa, Dominic A343:P225
Moffatt, Laurie A113
Moffatt, Mike P509
Moffatt, Tracey P649
Moffet, Brian L P482
Moffett, James P215
Mogefors, Svante A80
Mogg, James A593
Moglia, Peter E13
Mohamad, Amran W128
Mohamed, Mohd Hanif Bin Sher W393

COMBINED HOOVER'S HANDBOOK INDEX OF EXECUTIVES

A = AMERICAN BUSINESS
E = EMERGING COMPANIES
P = PRIVATE COMPANIES
W = WORLD BUSINESS

Mohammad, Shamim A154:A817
Mohammad, Ishrat P129
Mohammad, Shirin P264
Mohan, Janice E426
Mohanadi, Mohammed Bin Issa Al W395
Moharram, Shereef E96
Mohebbi, Afshin E120
Moheed, Ameen P154
Mohney, Jeffrey E394
Mohon, Bill P327
Mohr, Todd M A16
Mohr, Michael A A35
Mohr, Gavin A417
Mohr, Marshall A430
Mohr, Mr Michael A719
Mohr, Todd M P8
Mohr, Michael A P27
Mohr, Steven L P407
Mohr, Mr Michael P486
Mohr, Pauline van der Meer W234
Mohr, Gavin E226
Mohrman, Michael P P452
Moio, Gino P529
Moison, Franck A819
Mojica, Carmen P508
Mok, Tony W46
Mokari, Atabak E102
Mokhele, Khotso W335
Mokhtar, Mohd Kamal Bin W307
Mokoena, Charlotte W421
Molapisi, Charles W335
Moldafsky, Jamie A562:P378
Molden, Craig P170
Molden, Jim P170
Moldt, Claus E155
Molefe, Tsholofelo W335
Molepske, Michael A94:E45
Moler, William R P532
Molesevich, Patrice P226
Molewski, Michael E20
Molina, Gloria A224:P162
Molina, Luis P187
Molina, Sergio A310
Molina-Clark, Cecilia P625
Molinaro, Marcus J P198
Molinaro, Kenneth P582
Molinini, Michael A24:P13:E81
Moll, Lance A302
Moll, James E83
Moll, Sandra E245
Mollak, Leonard P244
Mollet, Chris P201:P201
Mollins, Sean A673
Molloy, Greg A727
Molloy, Lawrence A729
Molluso, Joseph A839:P643
Molmen, Dave P27
Molnar, Louis A P481
Molnar, Gary W111
Molnar, Jozsef W334
Moloko, Sello W6
Moloney, Herbert E248
Molope, Nosipho W335
Molskness, Daryl P11
Molumby, Kathleen P528
Molvar, Roger E169
Mombourquette, Arthur P97
Monaco, Jason A727
Monaco, Albert A862
Monaco, Donna P308
Monaco, Anthony P603
Monaco, Kim P614
Monaco, Albert W178
Monaco, Michael E135
Monahan, Thomas L P103
Monahan, Elizabeth F P191
Monahan, Michael P P392
Monarch, Jason P333
Moncayo, Erick A554:P372
Monday, Rachel P45

Monday, Jeff P414
Mondello, Mark A434
Mondragon, Fred P122
Mone, Brenda P167
Mones, Ann P134
Money, Laura W465
Mong, Marla P150
Mong, Tak-yeung W66
Mongar, Shane P440
Monge, Patricia P565
Mongeau, Claude A566:W111
Monger, Andrew P56
Mongiello, Simone P172
Mongillo, Stephen A413
Mongon, Thibaut A441
Monica, Esparza A486:P303
Monie, Alain A17
Monk, David P438
Monnolly, Terry P567
Monroe, Mark A220
Monroe, Sharon P347
Monserrat, Alvaro A701:E365
Monson, Kevin A531
Monson, Uri Z P164
Monson, Kevin E276
Montague, Jennifer P386
Montalbo, Joseph E311
Montalvo, Maria P168
Montalvo, Dhinora P452
Montana, Gregory A304
Montaner, Manuel Tresanchez W57
Montano, Juan A675:E350
Montaque, Michael A324
Monte, John P330
Montecalvo, David E446
Monteiro, Mallika A218
Montejo, Aurea Imelda W83
Monteleone, Joseph P415
Montemayor, Jaime A348
Montemayor, Margaret A629
Montero, Alejandro P441
Montes, Bryan P240
Montes, Alfredo Villegas W56
Montes, Rodrigo Vergara W59
Montesano, Hwa Jin Song W299
Montesi, Corliss A463
Montgomery, Thomas A56
Montgomery, William A64
Montgomery, Neela A232
Montgomery, Norman A313
Montgomery, Jacque A735
Montgomery, Richard P216
Montgomery, Nate P429
Montgomery, Jacque P511
Montgomery, Lisa P566
Montgomery, Christopher P571
Montgomery, Norman E165
Montgomery, Darrell E228
Montgomery, Michael E294
Montgomry, Andretta P138
Montiel, Ivonne W525
Montilla, Carolyn P145
Montlivault, Stephane De A598
Montoya, Jessica A89:P54
Montoya, Lorraine P187
Montplaisir, Kelly P267
Montross, Dennis A224:P172
Montross, Scott E297
Montull, Daniel Javier Servitje W215
Montupet, Jean-Paul A76
Monzon, Gilberto A634
Mood, Shawn P103
Moody, Dionta A31
Moody, Ross R A50
Moody, Dionta P24
Moody, Terry P84
Moody, Barry P304
Moody, David S P572
Moody, H. Craig E366
Moolenschot, Johannus J P496
Moolman, Ferdinand W335
Moon, Youngme A506
Moon, Lori P52
Moon, J Virgil P140
Moon, Kimberly P195
Moon, Don P299
Moon, Jacqueline P398

Moon, Christina P571
Moon, Youngme W510
Moon, Cindy E367
Moonen, Glenn P414
Mooney, Kerri A143
Mooney, Jill A266
Mooney, Beth A333
Mooney, P. Kelly A518
Mooney, John P167
Mooney, Kerri E65
Moore, Patrick A69
Moore, Christine A204
Moore, Terry A294
Moore, John F A300
Moore, Richard A309
Moore, Renee A309
Moore, Christopher A359
Moore, Thomas A410
Moore, Patrick A428
Moore, Jack A448
Moore, Betty A487
Moore, H. Phillip A562
Moore, Joe A570
Moore, Daryl A585
Moore, Pattye A593
Moore, Edward A688
Moore, Cynthia A742
Moore, Westley A810
Moore, Nancy P6
Moore, Candice P18
Moore, Antonette P25
Moore, Lena P57
Moore, Bud P68
Moore, Rob P74
Moore, Robert P74
Moore, Cory P74
Moore, Sarah P145
Moore, Gregory P168
Moore, Shirley P169
Moore, Margaret P171
Moore, John P179
Moore, Will P183
Moore, Cynthia P228
Moore, Brandon P254
Moore, Jeanette P274
Moore, William L P282
Moore, Betty P303
Moore, Robert P315
Moore, Debra L P325
Moore, David P339
Moore, T P343
Moore, Timothy P355
Moore, Joe P388
Moore, Theresaterri P415
Moore, Dana P418
Moore, Shaina P446
Moore, Cynthia P518
Moore, Lawrence P523
Moore, Lisa P525
Moore, Charles R P531
Moore, Steven P575
Moore, Christopher C P589
Moore, Carleton P621
Moore, Janissa P622
Moore, Richard H P654
Moore, Kendall P659
Moore, Daniel W69
Moore, Andrew E42
Moore, Roger E98
Moore, Terry E156
Moore, Richard E162
Moore, Renee E163
Moore, Brandon E190
Moore, Stephen E253
Moore, Clint E260
Moore, Charles E274
Moore, Maurice E284
Moore, H. Phillip E293
Moore, Jeffery E327
Moore, Thomas E365
Moore, Randall E409
Moore, H. Lynn E419
Moorfoot, Molly P535
Moorhead, Daniel E458
Moorhouse, Edward L P414
Moorleghem, Jenny Van P366
Moorsel, Guillaume V P581

Moorthy, Ganesh A526
Moorthy, Vetriselvi P494
Moorthy, Srikantan W247
Moos, Jim A472
Moose, Selina P361
Moosirilert, Somjate W491
Moot, Guy A846
Moots, Stephanie P53
Mora, Francisco P165
Morabito, Paula A596
Morafo, Nompilo W335
Morais, Diane E A32
Morais, Diane A33
Morais, Diane E P24
Moral-Niles, Christopher Del A74
Morales, Vincent A636
Morales, Howie A739
Morales, Martha A837
Morales, Adan C P19
Morales, Ron L P84
Morales, Pablo P332
Morales, Howie P515
Morales, Alex P596
Morales, David P653
Morales, Alfonso Gomez W59
Morales, Gustavo Arriagada W255
Morales, Vincent E404
Moran, James A256
Moran, Thomas A264
Moran, Robert A373
Moran, William A578
Moran, Josephine A647
Moran, Thomas P200
Moran, Linda P279
Moran, Amanda P316
Moran, Richard T P639
Moran, Kevin E432
Morandi, Brandi A282
Moranishi, Susan P155
Morant, Felicia A20:P11
Morara, Pier W511
Morato, Manuel Valls W57
Morawski, Chris P124
Morcom, George P107
Morde, Vishal A103:P60
Mordell, Mark E39
More, Ed P112
More, Daniel E376
Morea, Donna A698:A796
Morea, Ingrid P70
Moreau, Thomas W402
Morehart, Mary P498
Morehead, Jere P620
Morehead, Max E439
Morel, Gilles A863
Morel, Donald E234
Moreland, Mary A4
Moreland, Jeffrey A122:P80
Morell, Geoff W91
Morello, Angela P81
Morelock, Ruth P55
Morelock, Phillip E131
Moreno, Brian A531
Moreno, Eddie A733
Moreno, Joseph P177
Moreno, Juan A Gonzalez P237
Moreno, Homero Huerta P237
Moreno, Brian P349
Moreno, Jason P455
Moreno, Noemi P579
Moreno, Julian Acuna W255
Moreno, John E334
Moreno, Eddie E389
Moreno-Robago, Claudia P522
Moret, Blake A684:E339
Moretti, Marty P247
Morey, Carrie-Ann P154
Morfin, Annette A738:P514
Morford, Craig A291
Morgado, Robert A10
Morgado, Mario P340
Morgan, James A66
Morgan, John A243
Morgan, Sandra A379
Morgan, Emily A553
Morgan, Henry A647
Morgan, Peter A697

COMBINED HOOVER'S HANDBOOK INDEX OF EXECUTIVES

Morgan, Matt A740
Morgan, John A854:P43
Morgan, Molly P52
Morgan, Chantel P116
Morgan, Kenneth P149
Morgan, Ash P157
Morgan, Cheree P157
Morgan, Diane P164
Morgan, John P188
Morgan, Christi P216
Morgan, Mark P271
Morgan, Ashley P278
Morgan, Emily P370
Morgan, Lori J P407
Morgan, Vickie P408
Morgan, Damon P423
Morgan, Henry P429
Morgan, Sandra P444
Morgan, James I P505
Morgan, Matt P516
Morgan, Blake P538
Morgan, John P652
Morgan, Becka P653
Morgan, Bennett E191
Morgan, Jason E209
Morgante, Elizabeth P235
Morgenroth, Matthew W529
Morgenster, Ursula A199
Morgenstern, H Richard P332
Mori, Nobuchika A18
Mori, Yoshihiro W150
Mori, Simone W181
Mori, Nozomi W268
Mori, Masakatsu W277
Mori, Takahiro W354
Mori, Yasutomo W403
Mori, Kazuhiro W403
Mori, Shunzo W437
Mori, Masakatsu W538
Moriarty, Thomas A232
Moriarty, Bettyann P161
Morici, John E15
Morikawa, Noriko W326
Morikis, John A708
Morimoto, David A164
Morimoto, Takashi W268
Morin, Francois W40
Morin, Marie-lucie W465
Morin, Rene E380
Morinaka, Kanaya W472
Moris, Ricardo Aldana W33
Morisaki, Kazuto W279
Morishita, Yoshihito W494
Morissette, Dan A208:P145
Morissette, Benoit W250
Morita, Ikuo W148
Moriwaki, Yoichi W493
Moriya, Hideki W377
Moriya, Seiji W494
Moriyama, Masayuki W149
Morlacci, Laura P496
Morley, Carol P25
Moro, Masahiro W314
Morparia, Kalpana A625
Morrelli, Laura P253
Morris, Susan A28
Morris, Gregory A68
Morris, Michael A104
Morris, James A149
Morris, Rhonda A172
Morris, James A268
Morris, Michael A377
Morris, Maria A691
Morris, B. Harrison A707
Morris, Donna A845
Morris, John A848
Morris, Brad P1
Morris, Susan P18
Morris, Gerald J P77
Morris, Victor P87
Morris, Herman P128
Morris, Kenneth P152
Morris, Elizabeth S P156
Morris, Joseph M P163
Morris, Betty P175
Morris, Kenneth P196
Morris, David P225

Morris, Pamela P228
Morris, Damen P261
Morris, Sherrill P433
Morris, Bob P462
Morris, Doug P471
Morris, Mark P485
Morris, Thom P499
Morris, Robyn P507
Morris, James T P602
Morris, Jennifer W200
Morris, David W290
Morris, Dawn E20
Morris, Debra E353
Morris, B. Harrison E368
Morris, Walter E441
Morrisey, Locke J P628
Morrish, Jon W222
Morrison, Maureen A73
Morrison, Scott A92
Morrison, Patricia A106
Morrison, Daniel A143
Morrison, Lance A187
Morrison, Dale A426
Morrison, Harold A497
Morrison, Denise A521
Morrison, Julia P19
Morrison, Bethany P160
Morrison, Richard J P209
Morrison, David P238
Morrison, Bobbi P304
Morrison, Connie P333
Morrison, Tom P353
Morrison, Jeffrey P446
Morrison, Daniel E65
Morrison, Lance E85
Morrison, Ward E345
Morrison, Gregory E358
Morrisroe, Paul P535
Morrissette, Harris A798
Morrissey, Paul A121
Morrissey, John A416
Morrissey, Cassandra A512:P327
Morrissey, Joseph P444
Morrissey, Michael E150:E225
Morrissey, John E226
Morrow, John A126
Morrow, J. William A379
Morrow, Brian A687
Morrow, Sherry P16
Morrow, Terry K P88
Morrow, Diane P170
Morrow, Shawn P325
Morrow, Joseph P359
Morrow, Jason P587
Morrow, John E54
Morrow, J. Barry E254
Morrow, George E290
Morse, John A17
Morse, Robert A58
Morse, David A221
Morse, Laurence A851
Morse, Martha P67
Morse, Kristine P170
Morse, Alan R P237
Morse, Edward P353
Morshed, Bobby A442:P278
Mortensen, Brian P463
Mortimer, Brian A738:P514
Morton, James A416
Morton, Amy P133
Morton, Tina P171
Morton, Schapiro P389
Morton, Colleen P441
Morton, Randall D P638
Morton, James E226:E235
Morway, Joseph P282
Morzaria, Tushar W91
Mosbacher, Robert A243
Mosca, Andrew P261
Mosch, Peter W522
Moscho, Harold P576
Mosebrook, Jeffrey E234
Moseley, Stephen A27:P15
Mosemann, Richard P316
Moser, Scott A390
Moser, Christopher A574
Moser, Phillip G P14

Moser, Joseph D P306
Moser, Davis P337
Moser, Kathy P621
Moser, Aaron P628
Moser, Scott E215
Moses, Nancy E P135
Moses, Roxanne P144
Moses, Mark P472
Moses, Karine W82
Moses, Jon E402
Mosich, Nicholas A90:E41
Mosingo, Jerry L P534
Moskalenko, Anatoly W386
Mosko, Todd E P410
Moskowitz, Joseph A18
Moskowitz, Samuel E P220
Moskowitz, Amy P352
Mosley, Anthony P262:P615
Mosquera, Juan-Miguel P453
Moss, Kenneth A271
Moss, Patricia A512
Moss, Aaron A722
Moss, Bob A849
Moss, Erin S P194
Moss, Leah P541
Moss, John M P567
Moss, Arvid W363
Moss, Richard E451
Mosser, Kevin H P662
Mosser, Patricia P360
Mosso, Robert E84
Moster, Steven E72
Moszkowski, Neal E344
Motakef, Shahin P468
Mothner, Jonathan A752
Motl, Christopher A851
Motlagh, Katherine E114
Motley, David A331:E178:E224
Moto, Lila P413
Motoyuki, Masahiro W279
Motta, Edgar P187
Motta, Bob P479
Motta, Milena W251
Mottershead, Christopher W266
Mottola, Frank E399
Moua, Cindy P445
Moug, Kevin E308
Moukheibir, Catherine E237
Moul, Donald A560
Moulin, Emmanuel W488
Mound, Roger P62
Mount, Karen P350
Mountain, James A70
Mountford, Maria P180
Moura, Gabriel Amado de W255
Mourtzikos, Karen P648
Moutter, Simon W135
Mowat, David W290
Mowbray, Kevin E248
Mower, David P25
Mowitt, Peter A652
Mowreader, Jack P413
Mowrey, Mike P409
Mowry, Meagan E91
Moxley, James A340
Moy, Alicia A97
Moya, Andreanna E442
Moyer, Don P149
Moyer, Nancy P276
Moyer, Susan P373
Moyer, Michael P642
Moyer, Albert E264
Moynihan, Brian A96
Moyo, Dambisa A3
Mozingo, Caterina E265
Mozumdar, Subrato P356
Mozzicato, Diane P347
Mrochinski, Mary Czech - P313
Mroue, Mazen W335
Mroz, Richard A297:E158
Mrozek, Matthew A733
Mu, John A551
Mu, Yankui W529
Muawad, Riyad W423
Muchata, Jim P624
Mucic, Luka W222:W419
Mudge, Rex P523

Mudhaf, Anwar Al W38
Mudick, Stephanie A774:E408
Mudler, Gordon A P332
Muehl, Mary P391
Muehlemann, Werner W250
Muehlen, Constance von A26
Muehlhauser, Regina E294
Muehring, Gwen P578
Mueller, Andrej A117
Mueller, Meg A340
Mueller, Edward A510
Mueller, Eve A740
Mueller, Andrew P107
Mueller, Andrew T P309
Mueller, Andrea P368
Mueller, Ken P435
Mueller, Eve P516
Mueller, Udo W12
Mueller, Michael W55
Mueller, Georg W91
Mueller, Michael W290
Mueller, Juergen W419
Muenster, Silke A625
Mueting, John P575
Mugino, Hidenori W228
Muhammad, Aadam P146
Muhammad, Eqhwan Mokhzanee
  bin W29
Muhammad, Marjan W307
Muhammad, Marzimin Bin Wan W307
Muhammad, Wan Marhanim Binti
  Wan W393
Muhart, Matthew P486
Muhliesen, Angie A811
Muhsin, Bilal E263
Muina, Tomas Varela W57
Muir, Glenn E349
Mujumdar, Shveta A541:E281
Mukai, Chiaki W270
Mukand-Cerro, Ian P609
Mukherjee, Anindita A385
Mukherjee, Rupa P71
Mukherjee, Preetika P356
Mukherjee, Sanjoy W189
Mul, James J P240
Mulcahy, David A45
Mulcahy, Anne A441:A489
Mulcahy, Sean A597
Mulcahy, Anne A865
Mulcahy, Sean E307
Mulch, Angela P458
Mulder, Susan A460
Mulder, Susie A836
Mulder, Jeff P162
Mulford, Steve P551
Mulhall, Robert W17
Mulherin, Matt A410
Mulhern, Mark A260:A422
Mulhern, Candia P166
Mulhern, Anabel P167
Mulhern, Ben P345
Mulhern, Carmel W135
Mulia, Salvatore E282
Mulla, Essa Abdulfattah Kazim Al A543
Mullane, Marietta A711:P481
Mullaney, Patrick A367
Mullen, Joyce A420
Mullen, Patrick A613
Mullen, James A784
Mullen, David P112
Mullen, Renee P177
Mullen, Thomas P332
Mullen, Thomas R P334
Mullen, Charles V P428
Mullen, John W484
Mullen, Dennis E43
Mullen, Patrick E316
Muller, Betty P25
Muller, Martin W157
Muller, Frans W283
Muller, Luis E90
Mullery, Stephen A296:E157
Mullet, Matthew E188
Mulligan, Deanna A260
Mulligan, John J A761
Mulligan, Suzan P91
Mulligan, Lawrence E247

HOOVER'S HANDBOOK OF EMERGING COMPANIES 2022

563

COMBINED HOOVER'S HANDBOOK INDEX OF EXECUTIVES

A = AMERICAN BUSINESS
E = EMERGING COMPANIES
P = PRIVATE COMPANIES
W = WORLD BUSINESS

Mullin, Thomas A703
Mullings, Paul A22
Mullinix, Mark A300
Mullins, Anne A222
Mullins, Christine F A451
Mullins, James A696
Mullins, Eric A831
Mullins, Ed P424
Mullins, Karen P555
Mullis, Michael P44
Mullokandov, Izabella R P377
Mulloy, W. Patrick A675:E350
Mulloy, William E368
Mulva, J J A215
Mulvey, Kevin A414:P259
Mulvey, Amy P384
Mumford, Samantha P19
Mumford, Daniel E250
Munakata, Naoko W338
Munari, Andrea W87
Munce, Claudia A115
Munch, David P468
Muncrief, Richard A243
Mundell, W Jed P590
Mundo, Antonietta W511
Mundy, Robert A605
Muneeza, Aishath W128
Munekata, Hisako W68
Munger, Charles T A113
Munk, Christina W267
Munn, William A549
Munn, Brenda P101
Munn, Rico P278
Munn, William E290
Munnings, Roger W386
Muno, Christi P542
Munoz, George A36
Munoz, Oscar A159
Munoz, Jose A411
Munoz, Oscar A692
Munoz, Alex P336
Munoz, David Antonio Ibarra W28
Munoz, Jose W238
Munsayac, Eric P541
Munsch, Michael A186:P127
Munson, Randy P633
Muoio, Salvatore E253
Mupita, Ralph W335
Murabito, John A178:E451
Muracciole, Odile W106
Murad, Albert E305
Murakami, Ippei W36
Murakami, Kazuya W350
Murakawa, Craig P474
Murakoshi, Akira W325
Murao, Kazutoshi W375
Muraro, Robert A760
Murasawa, Atsushi W536
Murata, Tsuneo W338
Murata, Toshihiko W367
Muratoglu, Gamze W21
Murayama, Seiichi W182
Murayama, Rie W439
Murchison, Sibyl P380
Murchy, Jodie P73
Murdoch, Lachlan A559
Murdoch, Ken P466
Murdock, Daniel A203
Murdock, Trish P64
Muren, Gary A362:P232
Murga, Paul Robert W323
Murgado, Mario P340
Muri, Scott R P496
Murillo, Jorge P488
Murino, John P17
Murley, Thomas E19
Murnane, Thomas W P603
Murphey, Mike P235
Murphy, Christopher A1
Murphy, Thomas A72
Murphy, John A196

Murphy, Connie A203
Murphy, James A223
Murphy, J. Andrew A268
Murphy, Stephen A322
Murphy, Kieran A346
Murphy, Susan A381
Murphy, Diana A468
Murphy, Annette A490
Murphy, Timothy A506
Murphy, Madison A542
Murphy, Gregory A575
Murphy, Joseph A582
Murphy, John A645
Murphy, Kevin A652
Murphy, Amy A667
Murphy, Andrew A669
Murphy, Pam A684
Murphy, Kelly A696
Murphy, Gregory A704
Murphy, Michael A741
Murphy, Diana A754
Murphy, Emily W A803
Murphy, Richard A867
Murphy, John P53
Murphy, Terry P64
Murphy, David P86
Murphy, Mark P90
Murphy, Brian P91
Murphy, Edward P99
Murphy, Michael P120
Murphy, Rita P132
Murphy, Connie P144
Murphy, Karen P226
Murphy, Chris P305
Murphy, Erin P306
Murphy, Jaren P321
Murphy, Leo P335
Murphy, Michael P346
Murphy, John P444
Murphy, Michael P477
Murphy, Richard J P488
Murphy, Mark E P504
Murphy, Michael P518
Murphy, John M P554
Murphy, Celeste P563
Murphy, Brian P578
Murphy, J Pat P586
Murphy, Wendy P586
Murphy, Emily W P606
Murphy, Jeri P632
Murphy, Donal W156
Murphy, Kevin W195
Murphy, Andrew W295
Murphy, Timothy W480
Murphy, Thomas E31
Murphy, Shawn E52
Murphy, Matthew E55
Murphy, Patrick E117
Murphy, Frances E122
Murphy, Susan E208
Murphy, Raymond E234
Murphy, Joseph E302
Murphy, Gregory E366
Murphy, Thomas E387
Murphy, Diana E401
Murphy, Richard E452
Murphy-Chutorian, Douglas E367
Murray, Amy A47
Murray, Jim A162
Murray, Dennis A187
Murray, Mark A258
Murray, Kevin A298
Murray, Michael A403
Murray, Neil A443
Murray, Valerie A648
Murray, Stephen A836
Murray, Debbie P10
Murray, Douglas P387
Murray, Paul P433
Murray, Bill P535
Murray, Robert P560
Murray, Brent P640
Murray, Sheila W82
Murray, Donald W102
Murray, Eileen W234
Murray, Katie W345
Murray, Dennis E85

Murray, Joshua E102
Murrells, Steve W132
Murria, Vinodka W97
Murry, Michael P654
Murski, Mark A170
Murtagh, Nigel A697
Murthy, Rathi A288
Murthy, Ganesh P356
Muruzabal, Claudio A641
Musa, Sam P432
Musa, Shafaai W128
Musalem, Alberto A337
Musayev, Igor P272
Muschal, Thorsten W194
Muse, David A31:P24
Muse, Michael P228
Musgrove, David P542
Musil, Kevin P464
Musk, Elon A769
Musk, Kimbal A769
Musk, Elon P539
Muslah, Mansour Al W395
Musquiz, Joe P494
Mussallem, Michael A269
Musser, Eric A221
Musser, Jeffrey A289
Mussio, Alexander P573
Musslewhite, Robert E104
Musson, Samantha P103
Musto, Tammy P406
Mutairi, Hilal Al W38
Mutch, Marcy A319:E171
Mutlu, Ali P659
Mutryn, Thomas A142
Mutschink, John A274
Mutschlechner, Frenk W75
Muttaqi, Khaalid P132
Muzio, Frank A648
Muzio, Gaetano A662
Mu oz, Feliciano González W229
Mvula, Mosanda P129
Myers, Timothy A98
Myers, Catherine A315
Myers, Curtis A340
Myers, Marie A457
Myers, A Ross P20
Myers, David P32
Myers, Adam P78
Myers, Katrina P138
Myers, Rod P170
Myers, Ben P182
Myers, Jenna P191
Myers, Andrew P240
Myers, Douglas P274
Myers, Richard B P281
Myers, Dwayne P315
Myers, Michael P321
Myers, Greg P357
Myers, Jack P421
Myers, Ali P529
Myers, Amy P623
Myers, Franklin E94
Myers, Catherine E167
Myers, Larry E174
Myers, Keith E252
Myerson, Gary P387
Myles, Jenni A448
Mylod, Robert A128
Mynatt, Cynthia E430
Myong, Anne E15
Mytilinaios, Stefanos W27

N

N, Debra N Strohmaier A570:P388
Na, Wu Beng W376
Nabel, Elizabeth G P546
Nabeshima, Mika W493
Nachman, Kalfus P135
Nachmias, Stuart A217
Nachtigal, Amy P459
Nachtsheim, Jami A430
Nadamoto, Alton P474
Nadar, Shiv P244
Nadeau, Gerard A416
Nadeau, Kim P193

Nadeau, Jeanette P584
Nadeau, Marie-Jose W184
Nadeau, Gerard E226
Nadella, Satya A529
Nader, Tony P262
Nader, Anthony P263
Nadkarni, Gurudatta A216
Nadler, Michelle P498
Naef, Stephan W75
Naeger, Lorenz W222
Naftaly, Robert A804
Naftaly, Rober A804
Naftaly, Robert P607
Naftaly, Rober P607
Nagahori, Kazumasa W338
Nagai, Koji W360
Nagai, Seiko W369
Nagai, Hotaka W472
Nagai, Mikito W492
Nagamatsu, Fumihiko W430
Nagamine, Aileen P121
Nagamori, Shigenobu W350
Nagano, Satoshi W491
Nagano, Tsuyoshi W493
Nagao, Masahiko W469
Nagao, Yutaka W538
Nagaoka, Susumu W52
Nagara, Hajime W279
Nagarajan, Sundaram A721
Nagarajan, Hina W165
Nagasaki, Momoko W494
Nagasawa, Hitoshi W356
Nagashima, Yukiko W260
Nagashima, Iwao W330
Nagata, Hiroshi W257
Nagata, Mitsuhiro W472
Nagata, Jun W501
Nagel, John A867
Nagel, Alberto W316
Nagel, Willem W491
Nagel, Richard E438
Nageleisen, Christy A180
Nagi, Hamiyeh W370
Nagle, Gary W211
Naguib, Hatem E118
Nahas, Khaled Hamza A. W422
Nahhas, Mohammed Al W423
Nahmad, Albert A849
Nahmad, Aaron A849
Nahmad, Henry E149
Naidoo, Dhanasagree W6
Naidu, Tulsi W543
Naifeh, James O A741:P517
Naik, Rajan A540
Nail, Steve P212
Naim, Moises A17
Naing, Joshua W323
Nair, Biju A77
Nair, Sarita P122
Nair, A Sivaram P356
Nair, Leena W95
Nair, Radhakrishnan W240
Nair, Leena W510
Naish, Rob P31
Naito, Hiroshi P32
Naito, Fumio W268
Naito, Tadaaki W356
Naito, Kayoko W450
Najera, Luis P165
Nakabayashi, Mieko W496
Nakagawa, Roger T P90
Nakagawa, Akira W34
Nakagawa, Yutaka W432
Nakahara, Asuka A203
Nakai, Yoshihiro W429
Nakajima, Hiroaki W206
Nakajima, Norio W338
Nakajima, Yoshimi W429
Nakamori, Keitaro W279
Nakamoto, Gary A693
Nakamoto, David P127
Nakamoto, Gary E360
Nakamura, Ken W1
Nakamura, Shoji W279
Nakamura, Shinichi W327
Nakamura, Yoshihiko W328
Nakamura, Shinichi W354

COMBINED HOOVER'S HANDBOOK INDEX OF EXECUTIVES

Nakamura, Mamiko W418
Nakamura, Kuniharu W437
Nakamura, Tomomi W459
Nakane, Takeshi W350
Nakao, Mitsuhiro W496
Nakashima, Toru W463
Nakaso, Hiroshi W67
Nakata, Katsunori W403
Nakata, Takuya W537
Nakayama, Kozuru W255
Nakayama, Tsunehiro W331
Nakayama, Fujikazu W432
Nakayama, Kozue W479
Nakazawa, Hiroshi W228
Nakhata, Yaowadee W62
Nakis, Dominic A79:P52
Nalamasu, Omkaram A66
Naldi, Robert P307
Nally, Dennis A55
Nally, Michael A636
Nam, Yik Hyeon W167
Nam, Su Hui W388
Nam, Yong W480
Namatame, Masashi W493
Nambiar, Rajesh A199
Namdar, Frank A809
Namekata, Yoichi W468
Namenye, Andrew E246
Namiki, Shinichiro W65
Nanami, Shigeki W491
Nanavaty, Maulik A132
Nance, Jim P157
Nance, Jesse E174
Nance, James E430
Nangle, Barb P661
Nanthawithaya, Arthid W441
Nanty, Jerome W104
Nantz, Mark P499
Naouri, Jean-Charles W106
Naparstek, Scot P364
Napier, Joanna P40
Napier, Adam P422
Naples, Ronald J E340
Napoli, Silvio W425
Napolitano, John P159
Napp, Marc P486
Naqvi, Saiyid A337
Nara, Michihiro W369
Narang, Mahesh A228
Narayan, Ramani E295
Narayen, Shantanu A11
Nardecchia, Christopher A685
Nardelli, Robert E59
Nardi, Barak W253
Nardini, Holly G P661
Nardini, Erika E454
Narendran, Thachat W478
Narikawa, Michael E125
Narita, Susumu W34
Narita, Manabu W463
Narowski, Janice P151
Narvaez, William P159
Narwal-Shukla, Anu E152
Nasca, David A297:E148:E158
Nash, Sarah A104
Nash, William A154
Nash, Verla P610
Nash, Michael E52
Nash, Chantelle E126
Nashir, Rossaya mohd W128
Nasol, Jaime W83
Nason, Tony A653
Nason, Jennifer W405
Nasser, William P495
Nasser, Jacques W281
Nasser, Nasser Al W423
Nassetta, Christopher A389:E104
Nast, Jeff P483
Natale-Ryan, Angela P48
Natalegawa, Marty W261
Natalone, John E29
Natarajan, Prabu A698
Nathan, James A P105
Nathan, David G P180
Nathan, James R P292
Nathan, Jim P293
Nathanson, Douglas W176

Nathenson, Mike P77
Nattar, Ibrahim E137
Nauen, Andreas W444
Nauertz, Cinda P301
Naughton, Colin A80
Naughton, Marc G A165
Naumanen, Matti W275
Naumann, Susan W315
Naus, H. W249
Navarro, Eddie P223
Navarro, Ana P392
Navarro, Julio Cesar Cubillo W56
Navarro, Isabel Maria Aguilera W109
Naveda, Alfonso Botin- Sanz De
  Sautuola Y W71
Naveda, Marcelino Botin-Sanz de
  Sautola W71
Navedo, Lorena P202
Navitskas, Ted P360
Nawa, Takashi W192:W452
Nawabi, Wahid E7
Nayager, Mairéad W165
Nayak, Abhay A881
Nayak, Jay P37
Nayak, Chitra W247
Nayak, Sunil W448
Nayar, Arun A679
Nayar, Deepak E255
Naylor, Jeffrey A253
Naylor, Rachel A733
Naylor, Joseph E364
Naylor, Rachel E389
Nayyar, Nayaki A763
Nayyar, Sandeep E330
Nazar, Manoochehr A327
Nazareno, Carlo W83
Nazzaro, Frank A337
Nchez, Jos R S A552:P369
Ndamase, Kholekile W335
Ndez, Rom N Hern P399
Ndez, Salvadore M Hern P462
Ndiaye, Alioune W372
Ndoye, Fatou K P323
Neal, Stephen A577
Neal, Shana A600
Neal, J. Scott A729
Neal, John O A860
Neal, Jeff P155
Neal, Shelly P337
Neal, Melanie P493
Neal, Jeremy P590
Neal, Kecia P622
Neal, Kara E130
Neal, James E455
Neal-graves, Lisa E224
Nealis, Melanie E209
Neall, Robert P275
Nealy-Carter, Betty P228
Nearhos, Barry E269
Neate, James W69
Neatrour, Amanda P131
Neault, Gloria P309
Nebeker, Teresa A841
Necas, Kevin P625
Necastro, Timothy E145
Nedeljkovic, Milan W79
Nedell, Thomas P385
Nedorostek, Kathleen E378
Nee, Anthony M P654
Needham, Wendy A350
Needham, Daniel A575
Needham, Sabine P16
Needham, Priscilla P75
Needham, Judy P218
Neel, Lynne E132
Neeley, Amanda A315
Neeley, Paige P303
Neeley, Amanda E167
Neely, Tonya P81
Neely, Wayne P485
Neff, Douglas A206
Neff, James A400
Neff, Alexanne P35
Neff, James E218
Neff, R. Matthew E229
Nefkens, Mike A213:P150
Negron, Eduardo A633

Negron-Carballo, Edwin E74
Nehasil, Craig P289
Neidenbach, Joseph J P508
Neidorff, Michael A162
Neighbours, John A315:E167
Neike, Cedrik W443
Neikirk, Kenneth E210
Neil, Carl P213
Neil, Jennifer E328
Neill, James A350
Neill, Lance A679
Neill, Michael A683
Nelon, Jay A676
Nelson, Hannah A741:P518
Neman, Samantha P32
Nera, Carlos Volante W58
Nejade, Henri W91
Neidner, Derek W412
Neil, Steven A126:E54
Neller, Michael W35
Nelligan, Olivia A176
Nellis, Anthony A80
Nelly, Christian A280
Nelson, David A34
Nelson, Amy A64
Nelson, Georgia A92
Nelson, Chris A108
Nelson, Christopher A154
Nelson, Mark A172
Nelson, Kimberly A200
Nelson, Avery A221
Nelson, Kimberly A228
Nelson, Georgia A228
Nelson, Ronald A373
Nelson, Gregory V A403
Nelson, William A414
Nelson, Brandon A439
Nelson, Jane A558
Nelson, Jonathan A589
Nelson, Bradley A598
Nelson, Ronald A607
Nelson, William A675
Nelson, Chris A682
Nelson, Doug A738
Nelson, Mark A758
Nelson, Brian C A780
Nelson, David A855
Nelson, Ronald A856
Nelson, Mary P100
Nelson, Andy P119
Nelson, Robyn P121
Nelson, Karen P139
Nelson, W T Chip P141
Nelson, David P144
Nelson, Gary P170
Nelson, Mike P172
Nelson, Glenn P201
Nelson, Carla P203
Nelson, Deana L P215
Nelson, Bob P222
Nelson, Gregory V P256
Nelson, William P260
Nelson, Donnita P281
Nelson, Deana P291
Nelson, Vickie P296
Nelson, Patricia P384
Nelson, Tim P418
Nelson, Brock P442
Nelson, Kyle P445
Nelson, Becky P470
Nelson, Ashley P470
Nelson, Duane P494
Nelson, Doug P514
Nelson, Chris P517
Nelson, Bob H P520
Nelson, Doug P541
Nelson, Elaine P541
Nelson, Heather P548
Nelson, Brian C P572
Nelson, Sean P633
Nelson, Lauri P637
Nelson, Brendan W91
Nelson, John E26
Nelson, Dionne E105
Nelson, Cary E127
Nelson, Gary E185
Nelson, Stephen E201

Nelson, Amy E210
Nelson, William E350
Nelson, Erin E377
Nelson, Kimberly E385
Nelson, David E445
Nemat, Claudia W163
Nemerov, Jackwyn A786
Nemerson, Steven P456
Nemeth, Karla P93
Nemeth, Joseph P333
Nemeth, Stephen P396
Nemeth, Terezia E13
Nemeth, Julio E55
Nemeth, Andy E314
Nemirovsky, Julian E370
Nemser, Earl E235
Nenadyshina, Viktoriya W208
Nenzel, Andrea P409
Neoh, Anthony W129
Nepomuceno, Corazon Ma.
  Therese W323
Nerbonne, Dan A631
Nerenhausen, Frank A598
Neri, Antonio A63:A386
Neri, Leticia P147
Nerino, Alfred P337
Nesbitt, Martin A163
Nesi, Victor A746
Ness, Jon P287
Ness, Ed P358
Ness, W. Denman Van E455
Nesselbush, Robert P280
Nesselbush, Robert J P280
Nesselbush, Robert P280
Nesset, Sharon P610
Nester, Gray E57
Nestler, Timothy J P656
Nethaway, Carry P455
Neto, Roberto A A781:P581
Neto, Julio Moura W110
Neto, Jorge Novis W255
Neto, Joao W380
Neto, Otavio Lopes Castello
  Branco W506
Nettles, Cory A74
Nettles, Michelle A494
Nettles, William E309
Neu, Richard A409
Neubaur, D Ick A292:P210
Neuenschwander, Darrel P231
Neuenschwander, Darryl P231
Neuenschwander, Jean-Daniel W75
Neufeld, Ellis J P505
Neufeldt, Swen A401
Neugent, Gerard A45
Neuhaus, Joan P19
Neuhaus, Steven M P166
Neuhaus, Markus W55
Neukom, William E183
Neumann, Spencer A11:A551
Neupert, Peter A464
Nevatia, Puneet A143:E65
Neve, Jo P289
Neves, Joao Carvalho das W172
Neves, Eduardo W255
Nevils, Jacqueline A463
Nevin, Charles A146
Nevin, Zoe Mc A245
Nevin, Michael A413
Nevin, Zoe Mc P189
New, Wayne P161
New, Mitchell W16
Newallis, David A48:P31
Newbern, Thomas A84
Newberry, Darren A154
Newberry, Amanda P5
Newborn, Andrea A7
Newcomb, Robert A312
Newcomb, Daniel P451
Newcomer, Rex E P177
Newcomer, N Nelson P177
Newcomer, David E51
Newell, Donna A9
Newell, John D P622
Newell, Donna E4
Newey, Jay P638
Newfield, Richard A544:E285

COMBINED HOOVER'S HANDBOOK INDEX OF EXECUTIVES

A = AMERICAN BUSINESS
E = EMERGING COMPANIES
P = PRIVATE COMPANIES
W = WORLD BUSINESS

Newhall, Charles E399
Newhouse, Marie A172:P113
Newkirk, Russell P508
Newlands, Bill A218
Newlin, Stephen A598
Newman, Randy L A28
Newman, Jane A373
Newman, Brian A819
Newman, Diane P51
Newman, Kurt P114:P117
Newman, David P381
Newman, Cathy P600
Newman, Randy L E13
Newmyer, Joyce P6
Newpol, Jon P603
Newsom, Richard A211
Newsom, Terri P196
Newsome, Earl A108
Newsome, Kathy P111
Newsome, Jana P380
Newsome, Paul P395
Newstead, Jennifer A520
Newton, Lloyd A463
Newton, Nikki A808
Newton, Bradford P382
Newton, Louie P610
Newton, Alicia P610
Newton, Howell E199
Newton, Nikki E421
Newton-king, Nicky W253
Ney, Joe P167
Neyer, Tom P160
Neylan, Kevin A297:E158
Neyland, Stephen A239
Neyland, Stephen J P343
Nezat, David P348
Ng, Dominic A262
Ng, Keng Hooi A672
Ng, Man Wai P548
Ng, Win-kong W66
Ng, Sau Mei W118
Ng, Jimmy W155
Ng, Wai Hung W155
Ng, Chee Peng W212
Ng, Wee Lee W232
Ng, Poh Lyn W393
Ng, Cheong San W393
Ng, Dominic E127
Ngau, Jonathan E250
Ngo, Hanna P116
Ngo, Hao Q P506
Ngo, Cristina W83
Nguyen, Thong A96
Nguyen, Chao A380
Nguyen, Tuan A647
Nguyen, Xuong A748
Nguyen, Johnny P12
Nguyen, Lan Quoc P224
Nguyen, Daphne P230
Nguyen, Chao P247
Nguyen, Tuan P429
Nguyen, Albert P502
Nguyen, Mong Thi P522
Nguyen, Andy P533
Nguyen, Phuong P585
Ni, Jiayu W114
Ni, Zhen W120
Ni, Defeng W223
Ni, Shoumin W235
Ni, Mingtao W434
Niaz, Faiza P325
Niblock, Robert A632
Nibuya, Susumu W240
Nicastro, Mark A294:E156
Niccol, Brian A175:A447
Nicholas, Heidi A331
Nicholas, Polly A827
Nicholas, Jack P112
Nicholas, Richard P584
Nicholas, Susan E134
Nicholas, Heidi E178

Nicholls, Matthew A336
Nicholls, Timothy A427
Nichols, Thomas A388
Nichols, Dana A655
Nichols, George A672
Nichols, Frank P166
Nichols, Kenneth J P301
Nichols, Dave P347
Nichols, Dana E340
Nicholson, E. Allen A230
Nicholson, Robert A465
Nicholson, Larry A740
Nicholson, Brenda P423
Nicholson, Larry P516
Nicholson, Brian P559
Nicholson, E. Allen E113
Nicholson, Robert E243
Nickel, Douglas R P90
Nickel, Ellie P137
Nickels, Elizabeth A727
Nickerson, Adam P26
Nickerson, Sandy P646
Nickey, Susan E206
Nickl, Wolfgang W78
Nickle, E. Glen E309
Nickles, Allen A187
Nickles, Robert A315
Nickles, Donald A831
Nickles, Allen E85
Nickles, Robert E167
Nickol, Thomas P287
Nickolas, James A501
Nicol, Kellen P218
Nicol, Sylvie W224
Nicolas, Ernest A684
Nicolelli, Maurizio E151
Nicolet, Yaira P400
Nicoletti, Ralph E42
Nicolino, Lynda P302
Nicosia, Darlene A332
Nicosia, Santo V P240
Niebergall, Ross A463
Niederauer, Duncan A323
Niederst, Lori A645
Niedzielski, Vince E457
Niehaus, Charles A639:E332
Niehaus, Christopher E443
Niekamp, Cynthia A92:W306
Nielsen, Raymond A246
Nielsen, Mark A339
Nielsen, Steve P452
Nielsen, Cindy P556
Nielsen, Jan W154
Nielsen, T.Tod E114
Nielsen, Kelli E188
Nielsen, David E309
Nielson, Sephen P471
Niemetscheck, Amy P109
Niemi, Eric A442:P278
Nienen, Marge P116
Nierenberg, Michael E291
Nieto, Carlos Andres Santos W171
Nieves, Antonio De Jesus P71
Nieves, Gloribel P294
Niewinski, Erin P360
Niggli, Michael A623
Nightingale, Timothy A144
Nightingale, Anthony W261:W391
Nigon, Richard E295
Nigrin, Daniel P309
Nigro, Joseph A286
Nigro, James A466:E243
Nikolaev, Nikolay W386
Niland, Barbara E59
Nilekani, Nandan W247
Niljianskul, Chokechai W62
Nill, Andrew P187
Nilles, Tracy P32
Nilon, John P161
Nilsson, Gunilla P483
Nilsson, Ola W3
Nimbley, Thomas J A166
Nimbley, Thomas A612
Nimbley, Thomas J P110
Nimetz, Warren A824
Ning, Xiangdong W442
Ninivaggi, Daniel A385

Nino, Monica P168
Nino, Matthew E72
Ninomiya, James P223
Ninomiya, Hitomi W377
Nirenberg, Ron P133
Nisagornsen, Paramate W441
Nisen, Perry W487
Nish, David W234
Nishball, David P230
Nishi, Yamato W52
Nishi, Motohiro W435
Nishida, Kumpei W429
Nishida, Mitsuo W462
Nishigawa, Akihiro W435
Nishihara, Shigeru W450
Nishii, Kenichi W65
Nishikawa, Masahiro W21
Nishikawa, Kuniko W216
Nishikawa, Kazunobu W339
Nishikawa, Katsuyuki W435
Nishimura, Shingo W182
Nishimura, Keisuke W277
Nishimura, Hideki W350
Nishimura, Akira W462
Nishinomiya, Kazuo W403
Nishioka, Marcia P63
Nishioka, Seiichiro W182
Nishioka, Keiko W237
Nishisaki, Ryuji W463
Nishitani, Jumpei W377
Nishiura, Yuji W299
Nishiyama, Akihiko W325
Nishizaki, Tsuyoshi P527
Nishizawa, Keiji W452
Nissen, James A P411
Nissen, John E166
Niswonger, Jason E231
Nitanai, Takaaki W373
Nitcher, Eric W91
Nitithanprapas, Ekniti W491
Nitsch, Denise P654
Nitsche, Bruce P642
Nittoli, Rocco A437
Niu, Dongxiao W154
Niu, Yu Xin W529
Niubo, Antonio Brufau W400
Niven, Christine P335
Nix, Craig A312
Nix, D Mark P262
Nix, Josh P269
Nix, Jerry E338
Nixon, Dennis A424
Nixon, Torran A809
Nixon, Andrea P135
Nixon, George P322
Nixon, Mary P622
Nixon, Gordon W82:W527
Nizami, Null N P660
Nizzari-Mcclain, Cynthia P633
Nkeli, Mpho W421
Nkosi, Sipho W421
Noack, Dan A630
Nobel, Paul A658
Nobis, Kenneth P342
Noble, Jeremy A497
Noble, Paula P37
Noble, David P233
Noble, Walt P358
Noble, Janice P402
Noble, Jim P407
Noble, Craig W94
Nobles, Sharon P383
Noblitt, Mark A24:P13
Nocella, Andrew A813
Noda, Seiko W52
Noda, Yumiko W240
Noddle, Jeffrey A52
Noddle, Harlan J P570
Noell, Ginny P528
Noem, Kristi L P517
Noergaard, Birgit W168
Nogales, Luis A722
Nogimori, Masafumi W331
Noguchi, Naoki W351
Noguchi, Haruhiko W496
Noh, Jin Ho W532
Noji, Kunio W378

Nolan, Joseph A284
Nolan, Michael J A303
Nolan, James A370
Nolan, Bill P24
Nolan, Timothy S P164
Nolan, Christopher P165
Nolan, James E203
Nolan, Alexandra E297
Noland, William M A293
Noland, Sherry P118
Noland, William M P212
Nold, Loris W395
Nolens, Geraldine W507
Nolop, Bruce A500
Noma, Yoriko W257
Noma, Yoshinobu W496
Nomoto, Hirofumi W330
Nomura, Kazue W206
Nomura, Naoyuki W206
Nomura, Yasuhiro W356
Nomura, Katsuaki W432
Nomura, Tadashi W435
Nonka, Helena W363
Nonomura, Rikiya W360
Noonan, Thomas A422
Noonan, David L P375
Noonan-Harnsber, Helen A647:P429
Noone, John A529:E274
Noons, Mary A847
Noordende, Sander Van't A15
Noordhoek, Jeffrey A549:E290
Nopmuang, Ruchanee W62
Norberg, Kellen A332
Norcia, Gerardo A258
Norcross, Gary A304
Norcross, George E P553
Nord, David A689
Nord, Matthew A763
Nordberg, Bert W514
Nordby, Ella P291
Nordby, Roger P345
Nordenberg, Mark P628
Nordh, Hilde Vestheim W363
Nordholm, Bradford A296:E157
Nordin, Diane A641
Nordstrom, Pete A565
Nordstrom, Erik A565
Nordstrom, James A565
Noreck, Daniel E403
Noreus, Martin W470
Norgeot, Peter A277
Norgren, Lisa A803:P606
Noriega, Alfonso De Angoitia W198
Norkunas, Kathy P149
Norling, Richard A P426
Norman, William A114
Norman, Jim P25
Norman, Chris P31
Norman, Nina P292
Norman, Archie W311
Norman, Paul W335
Normington, Ann A436:P271
Normoyle, Helen W17
Norrick, Matt P155
Norrington, Lorrie E38
Norris, Brian A431
Norris, Betty A484
Norris, Cindie P556
Norris, Gina E136
Norris, John E407
Norrod, Forrest A13
North, Shannan P82
North, Dennis P217
North, Michael E18
North, John E101
North, B. E327
Northam, Ralph A209:P146
Northcutt, R. Bruce A860
Northen, Paul E358
Northland, Michelle P459
Northover, Susan P644
Norton, Larry A424
Norton, Michael F A454
Norton, Johna A478
Norton, Pierce A593
Norton, David A617
Norton, Bradley A767

COMBINED HOOVER'S HANDBOOK INDEX OF EXECUTIVES

Norton, Gale P35
Norton, Janet P58
Norton, Michael F P285
Norton, Margareta E P434
Norton, Susan E163
Norton, David E319
Norup, Keld W267
Norwalk, Leslie A162:E290
Norwick, Monica P406
Norwitt, Richard A59
Norwood, Felicia A63
Nosach, Jill P420
Noseworthy, John A823
Noseworthy, John H P321
Noshita, Emi W468
Noski, Charles A128:A386
Nostrand, Chris Van P389
Nota, Pieter W79
Notarianni, Anna W448
Notario, Dominic W65
Notaro, Julie P243
Notebaert, Richard A661
Notebaert, Nicolas W517
Nothwang, Joseph A778:P561
Noto, Anthony A336
Noto, Lucio A625
Nottoli, Don P168
Nourot, Mary P529
Nourry, Philippe W174
Novak, David A203
Novak, Christy A571
Novak, Andrew P366
Novak, Ernest P394
Novak, Trudy C P473
Novak, Alexander W385:W411:W502
Novakovic, Phebe A345:A444
Novatius, Klaus W2
Noverati, Carol P439
Noviasky, Diana P165
Novich, Neil A363:E215
Novick, Steve P131
Novicki, Kelly P459
Novo, Guillermo A636
Novoa, Cristian Peirano W59
Novoa, Francisca Riveros W177
Novogradac, Barbara A682
Novokhatski, Sasha A473:P295
Novotny, Stanley P633
Nowak, Bogdan A136
Nowakowski, Rhonda P116
Nowell, Lionel A772
Nowicki, Joseph P148
Nowlan, Kevin A131
Nowotne, Doreen W91
Noyce, James A815:A855:E445
Noyer, Christian W389
Noyes, Mark A217
Noyes, Brian P308
Noyola, Ana P172
Noznesky, Justin E36
Nuby, Angelo A503:P318
Nuckles, Brett P651
Nudi, Jon A347
Nuessel, Manfred W81
Nugent, Frances A362:P232
Nugyen, Diane P20
Nukk-Freeman, Katherin A215:E97
Numata, S. Mae A201:E92
Nunes, Adolfo W206
Nunez, Mike A215
Nunez, Diana P132
Nunez, Marisa P156
Nunez, Frank P193
Nunez, Michael P202
Nunez, Edwin P216
Nunez, Milton P300
Nunez, Eduardo P307
Nunez, Maria Eugenia de la
  Fuente W59
Nungester, Paul A639:E332
Nunn, Chalmers M P107
Nunn, Michelle P153
Nunn, Trudy P647
Nunnelly, Gary A639:E331
Nuntz, Sister Mary Ann P500
Nuriyev, Yan A330
Nusbaum, Mary Ellen P356

Nuss, Donald P478
Nusse, Roeland E50
Nusterer, Norbert A228
Nuttall, Scott A325
Nutting, Kelli P85
Nutting, Ron P437
Nuxoll, Erin A125
Nuzzo, Jessica P660
Nuzzolo, Agostino W482
Nvule, Daniel P319
Nwagbo, Chike P122
Nwamu, Chonda A41
Nyangani, Ash P540
Nyberg, Bruce A326
Nyberg, Carl W346
Nyberg, Bruce E177
Nyblad, Nels E81
Nybo, Zach P635
Nycroft, Tina P502
Nye, C. Howard A501
Nyenhuis, Michael J P311
Nygaard, Christine P403
Nyhus, Rhonda E284
Nyker, Jasandra W253
Nylander, Raye Nae P556
Nylen, Tim P148:P351
Nyman, Sven W446
Nysten, Marcus W446

O

O, Steven Herwig D P266
Oakes, John P212
Oakes, Greg E69
Oakland, Steven A332
Oakland, Pamela Witty P121
Oaklander, Peter E311
Oakley, Clark A866
Oakley, Dennis B P91
Oakley, Susan P496
Oakley, Clark E450
Oaks, Kenneth P284
Oates, Joseph A216
Oates-Forney, Tamla A848
Oatman, Russell A322
Oatman, Heather E423
Obana, William G P576
Obayashi, Hiroshi W354
Obeid, Sam P284
Ober, Gordon E115
Oberg, Kathleen A11
Oberg, Jay A204
Oberhaus, Michael A294:E156
Oberhofer, Wilhelm W81
Oberkovich, Amit W63
Oberman, Wade P531
Obermeyer, James E60
Obermiller, John A787:P595
Oberry, Greg A396
Oberst, Stephen A586
Oberton, Karleen A56:A392
Obilinovich, Paul Shiodtz W141
Oblinger, Chris A178
Oblinger, Phillip F P73
Obrand, Alexandra P263
Obrien, Lisa P124
Obrien, Julie P156
Obrien, John P609
Obryan, Megan P138
Ocampo, Marie Josephine W70
Ocampo, Frederico Rafael W83
Ocampo, Antonio W323
Ocana, Ann M P476
Ocel, Arielle P499
Ochi, Howard P168
Ochiai, Hiroyuki W350
Ochoa, Joe E42
Ochs, Rudy P332
Ochsner, Peter W72
Ockers, Thomas P230
Oconnor, Cristina A147
Oconnor, Kathy P16
Oconnor, Cristina P96
Oconnor, Scott P103
Oconnor, Christopher J P488
Odagiri, Kota A615

Odderson, IB P403
Oddleifson, Christopher A416:E226
Odean, Gerald A531:P349
Odegaard, Richard P236
Odell, Robert P480
Oderov, Pavel W208
Odgers, David A808:E421
Oditt, Alex P262
Odom, Burt P205
Oechsner, Susan P261
Oehler, Heinz W515
Oehling, James P P410
Oelrich, Stefan W78
Oesterle, Stephen A106
Oestreicher, David A757
Oetterli, Thomas W425
Oezben, Yunus W21
Oezcan, K. W21
Oezturek, Zeynep W21
of, Baltimore City P123
Off, George A764
Offer, Scott W197
Offereins, Diane A247
Offerman, Angela P393
Offers, Nathan P542
Offutt, Ronald D P437
Offutt, Christi P437
Oftedal, Brian P130
Ogania, Milagros A380:P247
Ogawa, Hiroshi W277
Ogawa, Michiko W314
Ogborn, Eric P198
Ogden, George A612
Ogi, Akira W226
Ogihara, Masayuki W538
Ogilvie, Thomas W162
Ogle, David A717
Ogle, Matt P173
Ogle, David E379
Oglesby, Stephen R P58
Oglesby, Charles E260
Ognall, Andrew A809
Ogrady, Shawn A347
Ogren, Dan P352
Ogrosky, Kori L A606
Ogura, Daisuke W279
Ogura, Yoshio W288
Ogura, Ritsuo W330
Ogura, Yoshihiro W356
Oguz, Buelent W21
Oh, Irene A262
Oh, Gyu Taek W271
Oh, Gyu Seok W388
Oh, Irene E127
Ohara, Kazuo A790
Ohara, Yoshinori A877:P662
Ohara, Hiroyuki W127
Ohashi, Casey P470
Ohashi, Yuichi W257
Ohashi, Nobuharu W377
Ohashi, Tetsuji W537
Ohba, Yasuhiro W452
Ohbayashi, Takeo W367
Ohemeng-Dapaah, Michael P299
Ohgo, Naoki W472
Ohkawabata, Fumiaki W334
Ohkubo, Hisato W257
Ohkubo, Shinichi W496
Ohkura, Koji W326
Ohl, Jamie A480
Ohlmeyer, Harm W12
Ohlssonleijon, Anna W3:W49:W427
Ohm, Seong A84
Ohmer, Adrian A804
Ohmer, Brandi P135
Ohmer, Adrian P607
Ohnishi, Yasuo W52
Ohno, Kotaro W14
Ohno, Naotake W192
Ohnuki, Tetsuo W459
Ohrn, Daniel P399
Ohrt, Tracy P633
Ohrvall, Sara W446
Ohsaki, Atsushi W459
Ohsberg, Ronald A847
Ohshima, Masahiko W463
Ohsugi, Kazuhito W216

Ohta, Katsuyuki W182
Ohta, Hiroko W182
Ohta, Jun W463
Ohtake, Takashi P379
Ohtomo, Hirotsugu W151
Ohtomo, Ken W338
Ohtsuka, Toru W360
Ohuchi, Yoshiaki W182
Ohyama, Kiichiro W237
Ohyama, Akira W403
Oikawa, Kenichiro W312
Oike, Manabu W14
Oka, Toshiko W182
Okabe, David P244
Okada, Motoya W14
Okada, Yoshifumi W52
Okada, Junji W205
Okada, Kenji W257:W493
Okada, Masamichi W501
Okamoto, Gary A P576
Okamoto, Tetsuya W356
Okane, Yuri P604
Okano, Yasushi W279
Okano, Michiyuki W439
Okanobu, Shinichi W491
Okazaki, Soichi W14
Okazaki, Takeshi W192
Okdah, Farouk El W38
Oken, Marc A500:A721
Okes, Gary D P209
Okhovat, Pejman W532
Okihara, Takamune W268
Okina, Yuri W313
Okitsu, Masahiro W432
Okolie, Patricia P254
Okomo-Okello, Francis W6
Okoro, Julie P116
Okpara, Johnbull A183
Oku, Masayuki W66
Okuda, Kentaro W360
Okumura, Mikio W452
Okun, Robert B P237
Okun, Andrew E320
Okuyama, Emiko W1
Olafson, Harlee A855:E445
Olague, Jessica A15
Olague, Michael A709
Olague, Jessica P7
Olague, Jesse P114
Olague, Michael E370
Olayan, Hutham W94
Olayiwola, Nwando A406
Olcott, George W277
Olczak, Jacek A625
Old, William A253
Oldham, Paul E6
Oldorff, Frithjof A80
Olejniczak, Dave P501
Oleksiak, Peter B A257
Olenik, John E332
Oler, Debra E327
Oleson, Cory P429
Olguin, George P462
Oliker, David P360
Olinde, Thomas A372
Oliphant, Aradhna A313
Oliphant, Jennifer P164
Oliphant, Gerald P231
Oliphant, Aradhna E165
Oliphant, Mark E245
Oliva, Sanderson P563
Olivares, Daniel P163
Oliveira, Rafael A460
Oliveira, Claudia P67
Oliveira, Flavia P182
Oliveira, Aurelio Bustilho de W179
Oliveira, Marta Claudia Ramos Amorim
  Barroca de W20
Oliver, Mary A187
Oliver, Kristin A373
Oliver, George A442
Oliver, Timothy A548
Oliver, Brad A652
Oliver, George A665
Oliver, Anne P274
Oliver, George R P277
Oliver, George P278

COMBINED HOOVER'S HANDBOOK INDEX OF EXECUTIVES

A = AMERICAN BUSINESS
E = EMERGING COMPANIES
P = PRIVATE COMPANIES
W = WORLD BUSINESS

Oliver, Bill P316
Oliver, Emily P572
Oliver, Kirk R P608
Oliver, Leigh P646
Oliver, Katherine E2
Oliver, Mary E85
Oliver, Eric E407
Olivera, Armando A216:A328
Oliverio, John D P654
Olivier, Daniel A874
Olivier, Gaelle W152
Olivieri, Fernando Angel
  Gonzalez W109
Olivo, Maria A792
Ollagnier, Jean-Marc W8
Olle, Laura E135
Olli, Amy A841
Ollmann, Michael W218
Olmes, Robin H P627
Olmstead, Diane E153
Olohan, Ryan E219
Olosky, Michael E374
Olsavsky, Brian A38
Olsen, Neil A293
Olsen, Kristin A503
Olsen, Peter A711
Olsen, Dorothy P38
Olsen, Neil P211
Olsen, Eric P235
Olsen, Kandance P235
Olsen, Kristin P318
Olsen, Peter P481
Olsen, Lloyd P600
Olsen, Kevin E123
Olson, Scott A132
Olson, Mark A294
Olson, Tagar A541
Olson, Bart R A606
Olson, Derek A733
Olson, Jeff A739
Olson, Dean P157
Olson, Jeffery P220
Olson, Greg P289
Olson, Kristin P321
Olson, Don P345
Olson, Jerry P381
Olson, Toni P431
Olson, Carrie P467
Olson, Jeff P515
Olson, Paige P517
Olson, Tim P592
Olson, Ruth P633
Olson, Jennifer E15
Olson, Timothy E83
Olson, Paul E140
Olson, Mark E155
Olson, Tagar E281
Olson, Derek E389
Olson, Richard E411
Olstad, Ellen W363
Olszewski, Daniel A311
Olszewski, Kathy P577
Oltman, Chad P396
Olvera, Jane A230:E113
Oman, Mark A308
Omar, Moanis P102
Omer, Bashir W38
Omiridis, Anastasios A451
Ommen, Nicolaas van E443
Omura, Yukiko W233
Ondik, David P209
Ondrof, Thomas A67
Oneal, Emmett P607
Oneil, James A324
Oneill, Jill P261
Onell, Lia P333
Ong, Estrellita W83
Ong, Eng Bin W376
Ong, Ming Teck W393
Ong, Laureen E454
Onge, Jenifer P4

Ongseng, Fukiat P71
Onishi, Shoichiro W494
Onishi, Akira W500
Onna, Thomas A49:P33
Ono, Caitlin P230
Ono, Mitsuru W314
Ono, Naoki W327
Ono, Akira W494
Onodera, Yoshikazu W1
Onomura, Brad P262
Onoyama, Shuhei W354
Onozawa, Yasuo W331
Ontiveros, Gregg P236
Ontiveros, Chris P236
Ontiveros, Robert P236
Onyia, Jude E290
Ooi, Sang Kuang W376
Oomi, Hideto W36
Oosterman, Wade A764:W82
Opembe, Patrick P103
Opizzi, Martina W185
Opoka, James P164
Oporto, Joseph P302
Oppel, Raymond A518
Oprescu, Sergiu-Bogdan W27
Orban, Paul A249
Orchard, Arlen P455
Orcutt, S Renee P333
Orders, James E382
Ordog, Istvan W334
Ordonez, April P477
Ordonez, Beatrice E308
Ordus, John A791
Orender, Donna G P414
Oreshkin, Maxim W411
Orgain, John B P19
Orgeron, Jerome P236
Orie, James A331:E178
Orii, Masako W367
Oringer, Jonathan E369
Orlandi, Marcia P133
Orlando, Jaime A410
Orlando, Anthony A468
Orlando, Anthony T P206
Orlando, Adolph M P578
Orlen, Gregg E448
Orlikoff, James P642
Orlowski, Lee P448
Ormanzhy, Natalya P12
Orndorf, Karen P14
Orndorff, Robert A693:E360
Ornelas, Grace P222
Ornelas, Beatriz P550
Oropeza, Anthony P161
Oroschakoff, Michelle A489
Oross, Mike P355
Orourke, Terry P102
Orozco, David P476
Orozco, Lupe P619
Orr, Mark A369
Orr, Stefahn P163
Orr, Mark P237
Orr, James P314
Orr, David P536
Orr, Lori P572
Orr, R. Jeffrey W213:W389
Orr, R. Douglas E175
Orrego, Eduardo Ebensperger W56
Orrico, Brent A102
Orris, Donna P410
Orscheln, Art A172:P113
Orsen, Melissa E381
Orsi, Christina E148
Orsini, Frank A470
Orsolino, Maria Rhoda W83
Orson, Marshall D P186
Ortberg, Robert A665:W37
Ortega, Alberto P520
Ortega-Carter, Dolores P171
Ortegon, Liisa P473:P594
Ortenzio, Robert A703
Ortenzio, Rocco A703
Orth, Bradley P138
Ortiz, Mauricio A204
Ortiz, Veronica P193
Ortiz, Marnique P284
Ortiz, Linda P327

Ortiz, Claudia P404
Ortiz, Inigo Perez E197
Ortizlugo, Lydia P371
Ortmanns, Thomas W2
Ortolano, Carrie P135
Ortolano, Frank P163
Ortolf, Tom A249
Orvos, Adam A687
Osaka, Seiji W479
Osar, Karen A851
Osborn, David A179
Osborn-Perez, Roseann P162
Osborne, Burt P128
Osborne, Tom P131
Osborne, Richard E206
Oschell, Christine A738:P514
Oscher, Ronald A56
Oseguera, Karen P406
Oses, Octavio Araneda W141
Osgood, Wendy E P309
Osgood, Steven E206
Osherova, Maria A846
Oshimi, Yoshikazu W268
Oshiro, Don A782:P583
Oshita, Hajime W264
Oskouie, Ali P339
Osman, Khidir P662
Osmonov, Asylbek A646:E336
Osono, Emi W493
Osorio, Luiz Eduardo W513
Osowick, Mark A228
Ossadnik, Victoria W169
Osswald, Oliver W229
Ostdiek, Scott P415
Ostergard, Tonn P175
Osterweil, Jody P608
Ostler, Clyde E151
Ostman, Mikael W3
Ostrander, Kevin E51
Ostrandr, Sue E P81
Ostroff, Dawn A10
Ostrover, Bruce E308
Ostrowsky, Barry A651:P60:P61
Osty, Olivier W87
Osvald, Hakan W49
Osvaldik, Peter A758
Oswald, Kathy A381
Oswald, Chris A487
Oswald, Kathy P249
Oswald, Chris P303
Oswalt, Valerie A146:P485
Ota, Saedene A164
Otabil, Tashawna P598
Otagiri, Junko W67
Otaki, Yoshio P380
Otaki, Seiichi W1
Otani, Shinya W127
Otazua, John Anthony Santa
  Maria W198
Otis, Clarence A792
Otis, Bud P159
Otis, Bill E299
Otranto, Dino W200
Otsu, Shinji W355
Otsubo, Ryan P163
Otsuka, Iwao W257
Otsuka, Norio W450
Otsuka, Yumi W501
Ott, Dusty P74
Ott, Joy P75
Ott, Michael P133
Ott, Ryan P266
Ott, Robert W480
Ottel, Robert W521
Otten, Anthony E307
Ottersgard, Lars A543:W446
Ottinger, Eric A466:E244
Oubre, Joi A186:P127
Ouchi, Atsushi W170
Ouchida, Michael P260
Outar, Gerald P365
Outland, John E194
Ouyang, Hongwu P217
Ouyang, Paul P407
Ouyang, Guoxin W119
Ovenden, James A326:E177
Overbaugh, Jason E366

Overbeck, Karin W3
Overbey, Cecil A584
Overby, Corey A133
Overgaard, Bente W267
Overlock, Willard E149
Overstreet, Linda P75
Overton, John P206
Ovesen, Jesper W446
Owen, Jeffrey A252
Owen, Terry A295
Owen, Harry P130
Owen, Debora P386
Owen, Allison C P540
Owen, Randel E175
Owen, Katherine E298
Owen, Kenneth E448
Owens, William A72
Owens, Janet P156
Owens, Russell P174
Owens, Thomas A P197
Owens, Heather P309
Owens, Steve P625
Owens, Ashley P638
Owens, J. W101
Owens, William E31
Owens, Matthew E85
Owens, William E159
Owens, James J E189
Owini, Abdullah Al W423
Owsinsky, Mike P498
Oxenreiter, Laura P56
Oxley, Stephen W266
Oyabu, Chiho W67
Oyagi, Shigeo W494
Oyler, W. Kenneth A675
Oyler, Clinton P353
Oyler, W. Kenneth E350
Ozan, Kevin A509
Ozan, Terrence W773
Ozark, Timothy A1
Ozdemir, Mehmet W540
Ozimek, Michael A797
Ozmen, Fatih P481
Ozmen, Eren P481
Ozmen, Hakan W391
Ozsuca, Ebru W504
Oztek, Durmus W504
Ozuah, Philip O P352
Ozyildiz, Recep W504
O'Boyle, Thomas A253
O'Boyle, Carolyn E55
O'brien, Shawn A79
O'Brien, Raymond A230
O'Brien, Sean A239
O'brien, James A264
O'Brien, Charles A283
O'Brien, Donna A393
O'Brien, Richard A405
O'brien, James A406
O'Brien, Daniel A416
O'Brien, Jayne A439
O'Brien, Gregory A443
O'Brien, Tom A503
O'Brien, Dana A588
O'Brien, Michael A589
O'Brien, Christopher A683
O'brien, Joseph A693
O'Brien, John A786
O'Brien, Richard A871
O'Brien, Lindsay P35
O'Brien, Charles P208
O'Brien, Charles T P208
O'Brien, Tom P317
O'Brien, Beth P409
O'Brien, John D P472
O'Brien, Ann W17
O'Brien, Susan W101
O'Brien, Eddie W156
O'Brien, Sean W239
O'brien, Shawn E34
O'Brien, Raymond E113
O'Brien, Timothy E161
O'Brien, Daniel E226
O'Brien, William E268
O'Brien, MaryJo E300
O'brien, Joseph E360
O'Brien, Dana E390

568

HOOVER'S HANDBOOK OF EMERGING COMPANIES 2022

COMBINED HOOVER'S HANDBOOK INDEX OF EXECUTIVES

O'brien, Thomas E440
O'Brien-Rice, Caitlin P32
O'Brien-Wood, Brigitte P92
O'Byrne, Kevin W259
O'Callaghan, Catherine A333
O'Connell, Patrick A52
O'connell, Diarmuid A234
O'Connell, Cynthia A327
O'connell, Katrina A777
O'Connell, Tim P134
O'Connell, Cynthia P214
O'Connell, Don E78
O'Connor, Cristina A147
O'Connor, Kevin J A154
O'Connor, Thomas A612
O'Connor, John A744
O'Connor, Timothy A871
O'Connor, Kevin P76
O'Connor, Cristina P96
O'Connor, Matt P98
O'Connor, Jack P159
O'Connor, Teri P163
O'Connor, John P519
O'Connor, Michael F P662
O'Connor, Stephen W233
O'Connor, John E250
O'connor, Shirin E284
O'Connor, Shawn E375
O'Connor, Kevin E448
O'Day, Daniel A355
O'day, Susan A416:E226
O'Dell, Timothy E77
O'Dell, Richard E359
O'Donnell, Robert G A49
O'Donnell, James A208
O'Donnell, Robert F A648
O'Donnell, Robert G P29:P33
O'Donnell, James P146
O'Donnell, Randall L P330
O'Donnell, Kevin W399
O'Donnell, Sally E160
O'Donnell, Kristin E161
O'Donoghue, Mary Jo P545
O'Donoghue, Shannon M P584
O'Donovan, James A553
O'Dowd, Kevin P553:E381
O'Dwyer, Fergal W17
O'Farrell, Linda W200
O'Farrell, Colin E47
O'Gara, Marisa P132
O'Grady, Michael A567
O'Grady, Sean P387
O'Hagan, Sarah Robb A439
O'Halloran, Brendan A103
O'Halloran, Henry P434
O'Halloran, Brendan E47
O'Hanley, Ronald A743
O'Hara, Michelle A698
O'Hara, Curt P467
O'hara, Michael E30
O'Hare, James A739:P515
O'Haver, Cort A809
O'Hayer, Matthew E442
O'Hearn, Stephen A672
O'Hearn, Patricia P133
O'Herlihy, Christopher A415:A502
O'Higgins, John W266
O'Holleran, Jennie A209:P146
O'Kane, Michael A437
O'Kane, Nicholas W304
O'Keef, Robert A363
O'Keefe, Daniel P488
O'Keefe, Dan E130
O'Keeffe, John W165
O'Kusky, Steve P309
O'Leary, James A139
O'Leary, Denis A325
O'Leary, Robert D A624
O'Leary, Christopher A764
O'Leary, Neil M P135
O'Leary, Robert D P414
O'Leary, Thomas M P575
O'Leary, Robert W493
O'Mahony, Stephen P61
O'Mahony, David W187
O'Malley, Patrick M P298

O'Malley, Edward P377
O'Malley, Kevin E295
O'Mara, Noelle A802
O'Meara, Brien A653
O'meara, Christina A693:E360
O'Moore, Paul V P3
O'Nan, Stephen B A166:P110
O'Neal, Gloria A53
O'Neal, Susan P312
O'Neal, Gloria E25
O'Neil, Mark A154
O'Neil, Claire P37
O'Neil, Patricia Steeves P453
O'Neil, Cheri P633
O'Neil, Mark E126
O'Neil, Charles E206
O'Neill, Daniel K A322
O'Neill, Tamina A381
O'Neill, Lisa A466
O'Neill, Elizabeth A476:A477
O'Neill, Myles A478
O'Neill, Heidi A563
O'Neill, Robert A608
O'Neill, Elizabeth P297
O'Neill, Anthony W32
O'Neill, James E140
O'Neill, Tamina E208
O'Neill, Lisa E244
O'Neill, Robert E312
O'Quinn, Marvin A208:A245:P145:P189
O'Reagan, Richard A502
O'Rear, Keith A862
O'Reilly, Michael A497
O'Reilly, Larry A579
O'Reilly, David A579
O'Reilly, Brian A624
O'Reilly, Charles P245
O'Reilly, Brian P414
O'Reilly, David W93
O'Rourke, James A539
O'Rourke, Robert L P94
O'Rourke, Tracy P522
O'Rourke, Tanya P542
O'Rourke, Brianne P628
O'Shaughnessy, Robert A653
O'Shaughnessy, Timothy E332
O'shea, Ana Botinsanz De
  Sautuola A196:W61
O'Sullivan, Michael A140
O'Sullivan, Stephanie A410
O'Sullivan, Margaret A665
O'Sullivan, Colleen A877
O'Toole, Timothy A268
O'Toole, Brian A517
O'Toole, Timothy A722
O'Toole, Mary P168
O'Toole, Nick P175
O'Toole, Brian P331
O'Toole, Joseph E322

P

Paasschen, Frits van A865
Paavola, Teppo W10
Pabst, Mary P418
Pacchioni, Milo W511
Pace, Cindy A521
Pace, Nicholas A600
Pace, Robert A682
Pace, Leigh P269
Pace, Gerald P345
Pace, Brandy P542
Pace, Peter E341
Pacelli, Steven E117
Pacheco, Mike A200
Pacheco, Fernando A436:P271
Pacheco, Carmita P655
Pacheco, Nilo W83
Pacheco-Clark, Ana L A750:P528
Pachman, Louis J P244
Pachman, Louis P245
Pacilio, Michael A287
Pack, Michael A598
Pack, Barry P399
Pack, William P468
Pack, Rodney P637

Packard, Julie P554
Packer, Steven J P148
Packer, Steven P351
Packer, Gayle P538
Pacyna, Michael E161
Padden, Brian A708
Paddon, Patrick E63
Paden, Frank E99
Padgett, Francine P343
Padgett, Martin E174
Padilla, Jos D P185
Padmanabhan, Srikanth A228
Padnos, Douglas A493
Padoan, Pietro W509
Padovani, Laura W75
Padovano, Nicholas A117
Padovano, Sam A782:P583
Padwa, Jeffrey P132
Paese, Joseph A529:E274
Paez, Tina P126
Paez, Rene A P488
Pagano, Vincent A169
Pagano, Renee P624
Pagano, Helena W465
Page, Gregory A3
Page, Larry A34
Page, James A144
Page, Gregory A240
Page, Andrew A332
Page, Stacey A390
Page, G. Ruffner A725
Page, Sebastien A757
Page, Crystal P99
Page, Katie P128
Page, Bob P168
Page, Lawrence P282
Page, Kiera P379
Page, Bob P586
Page, Shonaid Jemmett- W52
Page, Stephen E7
Page, Roxanne E81
Page, Stacey E215
Page, Bradley E324
Page, G. Ruffner E384
Pagels, George A P459
Pagenkopf, Julie P180
Paglia, Louis W40
Pagliaro, Renato W316
Pagliuca, Stephen E224
Pagnutti, Louis W82
Pai, Lisa A398:E302
Paiano, Robert A377
Paiboon, Nalinee W270
Paine, Tim W405
Painter, Craig P288
Painter, Jennifer E32
Painter, Jeffrey E68
Painter, Jonathan E240
Painter, Robert E415
Pairitz, Peter A400:E218
Paisar, Aaron A632
Paisley, James A253
Pak, Toni P305
Paker, Can W21
Pala, Amie A293:P211
Palacherla, Neelima P169
Palacios, Eliecer P306
Paladini, David P171
Paladino, Steven A696
Paladino, Mary E323
Paladino, Christopher E381
Paladja, Arthit W98
Palagiano, Vincent A246
Palani, Murugan P467
Palathra, Brigit P377
Palau-Hernandez, Margarita A581
Palermo, Frank A690
Palin, Carrie A550
Paliota, Armand P401
Palis, Adar P242
Palkhiwala, Akash A657
Palko, Steffen P540
Pallares, Jan P321
Pallatta, Donna P156
Pallekonda, Vinod P147
Palleschi, Pete P481
Pallin, Angel P356

Pallot, Mark A347
Palmas, Alexandre de W104
Palmberg, Dawn A736:P512
Palmberg, Kent P522
Palmer, Eric A178
Palmer, Vicki A317
Palmer, Thomas A558
Palmer, Kerri A716
Palmer, Sheryl D A762
Palmer, Steve P53
Palmer, Denitrea P60
Palmer, Matthew P90
Palmer, Thomas S P177
Palmer, Matt P291
Palmer, Douglas P443
Palmer, Kelly P445
Palmer, John W308
Palmer, Cheryl E43
Palmer, John E53
Palmer, Thomas E145
Palmer, Vicki E170
Palmer, Kerri E379
Palmieri, Jane A731
Palmieri, Christopher D P145
Palmieri, Paul E312
Palmore, Kysten P220
Palmore, Roderick E73
Palomarez, Javier A504
Palombi, Kelly A551
Palombo, Grace W213
Palomino, Jessica P228
Palou, Mario W83
Palowski, Jillian P524
Palsule, Himanshu E78
Paltrowitz, Jason E308
Paluch, John A739:P515
Palus, Jean-Francois W273
Palzer, Stefan W348
Pambianchi, Christy A421
Pamon, Steve E454
Pan, Jeffrey C P3
Pan, Junwen P589
Pan, Jinfeng W88
Pan, Nicholas Le W99
Pan, Darong W115
Pan, Zhihua W387
Pan, Richard W389
Pan, Zhaoguo W539
Pan, Wayne E367
Pana, Camelia P446
Panayiotou, Stacey A364
Panayotopoulos, Dimitri W93
Pandey, Dheeraj A11
Pandit, Sumesh P6
Pandit, Vikram E151
Pando, Antonio Cosio W28
Pandurics, Anett W334
Paneak, Raymond P41
Panetta, Leon A595
Panetta, Deborah P589
Panettieri, Christopher P246
Pangalos, Menelas W46
Pangburn, James W A50
Pangburn, Marc E206
Pangia, Bob A118
Pangrazio, Joseph A374
Paniry, Rina A733:E389
Panizari, Robert A362:E232
Panizza, Sandro W43
Panossian, Hratch W99
Panosyan, Astrid W18
Panou, Rena W188
Panozaqi, Alketa P125
Pantages, Peter E164
Pantano, Dan P87
Panthawangkun, Wirawat W270
Pantilione, Vito E312
Pantilione, Nicholas E312
Pantoya, Christine P454
Panuccio, Susan A559
Panyarachun, Disathat W393
Panzarella, Angela P38
Panzera, Chellie P503
Pao, Nicole W16
Pao, William W408
Paoli, Alberto De W179:W181
Paolillo, Regina E417

HOOVER'S HANDBOOK OF EMERGING COMPANIES 2022

569

COMBINED HOOVER'S HANDBOOK INDEX OF EXECUTIVES

A = AMERICAN BUSINESS
E = EMERGING COMPANIES
P = PRIVATE COMPANIES
W = WORLD BUSINESS

Paolucci, Jeffrey E174
Papacostas, Arthur C P536
Papadopoulo, Nicolas W40
Papadopoulos, Stelios A118:E150
Papagaryfallou, Lazaros W27
Papapostolou, Ted A413
Papdellis, Randy C P648
Pape, Kathy P410
Paperie, Fat C P165
Paperin, Stewart A70
Papermaster, Mark A13
Papincak, Terry P483
Pappagallo, Michael A135
Pappas, Christopher A324
Pappas, Natalie P539
Pappas, Peter E442
Paquette, Michael A274
Paquette, Sylvie W250
Parahus, Robert A788
Paranjpe, Nitin W510
Parapuntakul, Chakkrit W441
Paraskevopoulos, Nikolaos W227
Parasnis, Sameer E407
Paratore, Joseph P155
Paratore, Dena P450
Parcella, Gabriela E406
Parcher, Charles A187:E85
Parchinski, Kathleen P208
Parchinski, Christopher P660
Parchment, Nadia P293
Parda, David P20
Pardee, Charles A871
Pardes, Herbert A780:P572
Pardo, Holly P25
Pardo, Felipe Bayon W171
Pardo, Jaime Chico W215
Pardo, Marcela Jimenez W255
Pardun, Thomas E264
Pare, Robert W341
Paredes, Sebastian W155
Pareigat, Thomas A774:E408
Parekh, Rebecca A70
Parekh, Salil W247
Parel, Dinu A609
Parent, Louise A304:A881
Parent, Ghislain W340
Parer, Jean-Luc W281
Parfet, Donald A684
Parfitt, Colin A172
Parham, Richelle A115:A464
Parija, Soubhagya A324:P371
Parikh, Himanshu A332
Parikh, Bobby W247
Parikh, Amit E200
Parikh, Shailee E251
Parini, Michael A835
Paris, Tom Van P254
Paris, John P447
Parisi, Patricia P159
Parisi, Janet P372
Parisi, James E73
Parisot, Laurence W175
Parivash, James P163
Parivisutt, Santi W284
Park, YoungKuk A58
Park, David A90
Park, Winnie A253
Park, Anthony J A303
Park, Min A374
Park, Gary P14
Park, William P253
Park, Julie P288
Park, Hyun P351
Park, Jihye P367
Park, Gary P443
Park, Deanna P616
Park, Gary P627
Park, Jeong Guk W238
Park, Hui Jae W388
Park, Cheol W438
Park, An Sun W438

Park, Sang Yong W532
Park, David E41
Park, Kimberly E102
Park, Hong Kyun E315
Park, John E443
Parker, William A41
Parker, Paul A189
Parker, Dan A212
Parker, M Jayne A251
Parker, Ted A309
Parker, George A323
Parker, Mark A563
Parker, Teresa A567
Parker, Tom A734
Parker, Garrett P24
Parker, Erin P42
Parker, Dalton P82
Parker, Andy P188
Parker, Russell E P207
Parker, Keith P335
Parker, Terra P362
Parker, Scott P364
Parker, Mary P384
Parker, Cindy A P389
Parker, Mike P433
Parker, Cindy P473
Parker, Ryan P493
Parker, Tom P510
Parker, Dudley P579
Parker, Kellie W405:W406
Parker, Zachary E122
Parker, Ted E163
Parker, Anthony E194
Parker, Elton E235
Parker, Diane E409
Parker, Jon E409
Parkerson, Michael A774:P547
Parkhill, Karen A46
Parkins, Frederick P622
Parkinson, Scott P535
Parkinson, John E99
Parkos, Michael P43
Parks, Douglas A349
Parks, Robert A550
Parks, Kenneth A601
Parks, Delbert A713
Parks, Richard P173
Parks, Amy P384
Parmar, Manish E348
Parmenter, Darren A388
Parmentier, Jennifer A609
Parod, Daniel P507
Parod, Richard E12
Parolin, Joao Benjamin W506
Parolisi, John P55:P55
Parquette, Kacey P315
Parr, Ross A584
Parr, James P460
Parr, Jeremy W262
Parra, Christian P191
Parragh, Laszlo W334
Parrella, Andrea W294
Parrent, Dave P539
Parreott, Dawn A551
Parrett, William A595
Parrillo, Sandra A847
Parrillo, Joseph E P252
Parris, Colin W37
Parris, Julius E174
Parrish, Mark A837
Parrish, Sheriff Lori P157
Parrish, Harvey P212
Parrish, Amy P254
Parrish, Diane P507
Parsey, Merdad A355
Parshall, Joyce P589
Parsley, E. William A632
Parsley, David P362
Parsley, Elizabeth P579
Parson, Mike A738:P514
Parsons, Pat A212
Parsons, Stephen A556
Parsons, Jillian P145
Parsons, Michael P200
Parsons, Donna P456
Parsons, Suzan P638
Parsons, Dena P661

Partain, Nathan E309
Partanen, Karoliina W275
Partee, Brian A496:A541
Parthemer, Shannon P291
Partington, Marshall P403
Partipilo, Mari P7
Partridge, Laila A143
Partridge, Jack P143
Partridge, Scott P173
Partridge, Laila E65
Pas, Aaron A22
Pasard, Gail P6
Pascale, John P53:P298
Paschal, John E297
Pascual, Jose Alfredo W83
Pascuzzi, Steve P177
Pasenelli, William E96
Pashaev, Oleg W386
Pasicznyk, John G P193
Paskal, Steven P50
Paskuski, Brian P408
Paslawsky, William P459
Pasley, Brian A147:E66
Paslick, Paul A379
Pasquale, James F P371
Pasquale, Maria E225
Pasquale, Douglas E406
Pasquali, Luigi W294
Pasquariello, Maria W511
Pasquesi, John W40
Pasquier, Bernard W255
Passas, Isidoros W27
Passos, Murilo Cesar Lemos dos Santos W513
Pasterna, Asaf W253
Pasternak, Scott E413
Pastides, Harris A754:E401
Pastor, Louis J A872
Pastore, Martin J P208
Patane, Anthony P562
Patarasatienkul, Pornnapa W65
Patchett, Noni P301
Patchett, Richard B P314
Patel, Prakash A63
Patel, Bhavesh A371
Patel, Sudhir A414
Patel, Jeetendra A443
Patel, Kiran A457
Patel, Akshar A740
Patel, Dipen P143
Patel, Ayut P244
Patel, Ketul J P252
Patel, Sudhir P259
Patel, Mahendrabhai P322
Patel, Jaibala P338
Patel, Samir P370
Patel, Chintan P452
Patel, Ambar M P476
Patel, Akshar P516
Patel, Saavan P555
Patel, Nilesh P563
Patel, Chetankumar P563
Patel, Bhavana P586
Patel, Sandeep P587
Patel, Shashank E159
Patel, Raj E425
Pathak, Sumit P325
Patin, Al P290
Patiparnpreechavud, Sakchai W441
Patkotak, Crawford P41
Patolawala, Monish A3
Patonai, Nicolas P586
Patouhas, John A767
Patoux, Fiona P446
Patriarca, Michael A857:E447
Patricio, Miguel A460
Patrick, Stephen A72
Patrick, Dan A741
Patrick, Gregory P130
Patrick, Tammany P298
Patrick, Chad P346
Patrick, Morris P452
Patrick, Dan P517
Patrick, Chuck P615
Patricoff, Tracey C P488
Patrushev, Dmitry W385
Patry, Dean P38

Patsalos-Fox, Michael A199
Patsos, Theodore P608
Pattanasiri, Pisara W65
Patterson, Ryan A361
Patterson, Robert A367
Patterson, Douglas E A454
Patterson, Bill A553
Patterson, Douglas E A621
Patterson, Gavin A692
Patterson, George P28
Patterson, Emma P134
Patterson, Diane P163
Patterson, L Brooks P165
Patterson, Douglas E P285:P285
Patterson, Bill P370
Patterson, Douglas E P412
Patterson, Jason P433
Patterson, John K P550
Patterson, Jamie P594
Patterson, Roger P626
Patterson, Lynn W69
Patterson, Chad E117
Patterson, Mark E120
Pattison, Lindsay W533
Patton, Charles A44
Patton, R. David A533
Patton, Charles A796
Patton, James A866
Patton, Robin Van P148
Patton, Aaron P253
Patton, Alex P272
Patton, Brandon P503
Patton, Charles E390
Patton, James E450
Patzke, Guy P289
Pau, Melissa P51
Paul, Matthew A258
Paul, Marcia A352
Paul, Alison A755
Paul, Brenda P130
Paul, Wanda P256
Paul, Schaik P483
Paul, David P603
Paul, Stefan W286
Paul, Joseph E115
Paul, David E195
Paul, Saikat E341
Paul, Jaclyn E388
Paula, Allison P162
Paula, Jefferson de W39
Pauldine, David E343
Pauley, Katrinka P642
Pauli, Nicole W514
Paulk, Jenny P103
Paull, Matthew A23
Paull, David A294:E156
Pauls, John A808:E421
Paulsen, Frederik A625
Paulsen, Thomas W72
Paulson, Ryan A256
Paulson, Chad P76
Paulus, Ronald A A343:P36:P225:P346
Paup, Mark A570
Paus, William W446
Pavioni, Blake P604
Pavlovsky, Stan E369
Pawelski, Len P379
Pawley, Patrick P324
Pawley, Barbara P614
Pawlich, Jean P660
Pawlikowski, Ellen A665
Pawlus, Kathleen P28
Paxson, Christina P90
Paxson, Kara P283
Paxton, Ken P51
Paxton, Stuart P294
Payne, Ulice A332
Payne, Clifton A370
Payne, Lisa A502:A684
Payne, Kevin A722
Payne, David A856
Payne, Robert P73
Payne, Leslie P80
Payne, Demietre P107
Payne, John P139
Payne, Matthew P139
Payne, Phyllis P461

COMBINED HOOVER'S HANDBOOK INDEX OF EXECUTIVES

Payne, W. Joseph E10
Payne, Clifton E203
Payson, Martin D P307
Peach, Richard E362
Peacher, Stephen W465
Peacock, Christy P320
Peacock, Lynne W413
Peacor, Melissa S P167
Peacor, Melissa P167
Peak, Scott A170
Pealer, Carla P399
Peantham, Kittipat W284
Pearce, Elizabeth P84
Pearce, Zach P151
Pearce, Jim P232
Pearce, Jennifer P399
Pearce, Stephen W32:W53
Pearce, Rebecca E38
Pearison, Megan P579
Pearlman, Michael P85
Pearson, Kevin A491
Pearson, Jeffrey T P32
Pearson, Amy A322
Pearson, Beth P332
Pearson, James F P337:P394:P410
Pearson, Ronald P411
Pearson, J F P552
Pearson, Lori W94
Pearson, John W162
Pearson, David E248
Pease, Alexander A860
Peaslee, Gregory A828:P634
Peat, William P360
PEC, Mike A264:P200
Peccolo, Charles M P629
Pecente, Anthony P165
Peck, Kristin A120
Peck, Casey A387
Peck, Tom A755
Peck, Kristin A881
Peck, Cynthia P148
Peck, Kimberly P335
Peck, Cynthia P351
Peck, Jane P459
Pecor, Raymond A210:E95
Pecresse, Jerome A346
Pecsenyicki, Stephen P588
Peddy, Amy P271
Peddycoart, Nancy P501
Pedersen, John A102:P310
Pedersen, Kurt Bligaard W267
Pedersen, Bret E142
Pedersen, George E259
Pederson, Michael A4
Pedini, Claire W175
Pedonti, Patrick J P196
Pedraza, Cori P141
Pedro, Claudia San A126:E54
Pedroso, Marcio W523
Peduto, William P131
Peebles, Joel P401
Peed, R. Daniel A816
Peel, Matthew P195
Peeples, William E96
Peeters, Clare P53
Peetz, Karen A183:A780:P575
Peev, Millen P7
Pefanis, Harry A630
Pefanis, Harry N A631:P420
Pegula, Kim A677
Pehl, Vicky P199
Peiffer, Garry A541
Peigen, Seth P345
Peiler, Mark E53
Peinado, Fat P26
Peirce, Elizabeth P658
Peiros, Lawrence E329
Pekelis, Zhanna P319
Pekofske, Daniel A540
Pelasara, Rick P484
Pelavin, Sol H P32
Pelgen, Brittany P357
Pelisson, Gilles Gerard W90
Pelizzari, John P358
Pelkey, Sean A227
Pelkey, Cecelia A740:P516
Pellegrini, August A106

Pellegrini, Frank P366
Pellegrini, Mirella W181
Pellegrini, August E48
Pellegrino, Nancy A396
Pellegrino, Joseph E250
Pelletier, Liane A289
Pelletiere, Christopher V P7
Pellicciotti, William A12
Pellissier, Gervais W372
Pelowski, Alton A458:P287
Pelt, Russell Van A681
Pelt, Laurie Van P165
Pelt, Russell Van P448
Peltzman, Steven E182
Peluso, Michelle A232
Pember, Marvin A824
Pemberton, Richard S A166
Pemberton, John A723
Pemberton, Richard S P110
Pemberton, Rick P152
Pena, Arthur P133
Pena, Dena P327
Pena, Pocholo Dela W323
Pena, Mardelle E441
Penafiel, Juan Edgardo
    Goldenberg W33:W177
Penar, Eva P114
Penchienati-Bosetta, Veronique W152
Pencil, Patricia P123
Penco, Isidoro Palma W141
Penczek, Ronald A63
Pendarvis, David E352
Pendergast, Christopher A696
Pendery, Lud P152
Penegor, Todd A92
Penfield, Susan A129
Peng, Victor A457
Peng, Yi W114
Peng, Yanxiang W129
Peng, Sheng-Hua W138
Peng, Guoquan W235
Peng, Xingyu W235
Peng, Chin-Bing W530
Peng, Jiangling W535
Penido, Jose Luciano Duarte W513
Penkar, Rajan E430
Penlesky, Sherry P190
Penn, Ronda A49
Penn, Kevin P336
Penn, George H P351
Penn, Andrew W484
Penn, Ronda E21
Penn, Laurence E132
Pennekamp, Kim P160
Pennella, William P176
Penner, Greg A844
Penner, Don P159
Penner, Timothy W250
Pennes, Victor P108
Pennetti, Frank P157
Penney, Robert P106
Penning, David P38
Pennington, Hilary A776
Pennington, Chip P480
Pennington, Hilary P558
Pennington, Kelli P647
Pennoni, Celestino E312
Penny, Alfred W215
Penny, Jerome E57
Pennywell, Gwendolyn P629
Penrod, Jeremy P610
Penrose, Sheila A443:A509
Penrose, Jill A718
Penrose, Lee P506
Penske, Roger A615
Penske, Gregory A615
Pensotti, Federico A468
Pentz, Markwart von A240
Peoples, Rasheda P427
Peoples, Chanda P467
Peper, Catherine P78
Pepper, J David P411
Pepper, Dave P411
Pepper, J Stanley P575
Pepper, Richard S P575
Peppiatt-Combes, James P332
Pera, Robert E420

Peraino, Vito A47
Peram, Roja P10
Perazzo, Glory P306
Perch, Jeanmarie P427
Perda, Michael P648
Perducat, Cyril A684
Perdue, Sandra P433
Pereira, John A136
Pereira, Jaime A357
Pereira, Lincoln A368
Pereira, Lesley A380
Pereira, Justine P188
Pereira, Lesley P247
Pereira, Maria Teresa Isabel W172
Pereira, Fernando W200
Pereira, Alexandre W513
Perelman, Robert A465
Perera, Kanchana P536
Peres, Nechemia W487
Pereta, Barbara E189
Perez, Beatriz A196:A363
Perez, Sonia A372
Perez, Juan A384
Perez, Laree A501
Perez, Juan A819
Perez, Jorge P59
Perez, Cesar P167
Perez, Nicolas F P228
Perez, Dr Sylvester Syl P461
Perez, Olga P461
Perez, Jose del Valle W9
Perez, Juan Pedro Santa Maria W59
Perez, Vicente W83
Perez, Arturo Manuel Fernandez W215
Perez, Jose del Valle W227
Perez, William E239
Perez-Hickman, Fernando E292
Perez-Pineda, Federico P629
Perfetti, C. Charles A318:E171
Pergine, William P164
Perhach, Andy P81
Periago, Mirta P404
Perille, Thomas P503
Perin, Mitchell P127
Perisich, John E334
Perissinotto, Saverio W251
Perkash, Om P1
Perkes, Josh A812
Perkins, Abbey A748
Perkins, Joe A760
Perkins, Michael A853
Perkins, Elizabeth S P40
Perkins, Mike P57
Perkins, Catherine P185
Perkins, Paul P209
Perkins, James P377
Perkins, Robert P450
Perkins, Judy P471
Perkins, Scott W531
Perkins, Michael E444
Perkovich, Brian P338
Perlewitz, Kathy P222
Perlman, Dana A579
Perlman, Joel A P352
Perlmutter, Joel A842:P645
Perlowitz, Jeffrey A614:E317
Permet, Robert P354
Perna, Robert E42
Pernas, Rick P160
Pero, Joseph A553
Pero, Samuel A652
Pero, Jeffrey A668
Pero, Joseph P370
Perold, Jacques A32:E282
Perotti, William A227
Perotti, Daniel A614:E317
Perou, Jose Maria Linares W61
Peroutka, Bryan A869:P659
Perpall, Frederick A302
Perra, Alexandre W175
Perrault, Paul A136
Perreault, Roger A141
Perrelli, Kathryn A458:P287
Perrette, Jean-Briac A248
Perrin, Maria P252
Perrin, Mary P304
Perrins, Alexander P422

Perro, Richard A322
Perron, Jacques P594
Perry, Barry A72
Perry, Debra A76
Perry, Joseph A246
Perry, James A276
Perry, Jeffery A335
Perry, Debra A351
Perry, Opal A385
Perry, David A569
Perry, Mark A577
Perry, Jodi A663
Perry, Curtis A674
Perry, Kirk A718
Perry, Allegra A836
Perry, Karl E P56
Perry, Mike P60
Perry, James P188
Perry, Lee P290
Perry, Cheryl P375
Perry, Heather P479
Perry, Keith P505
Perry, Gloria P508
Perry, Carol P522
Perry, James E190
Perry, W. Wesley E191
Perry, Brian E268
Perry, Curtis E348
Persaud, Andre A679
Perschke, Daniel E364
Perselis, Anna P655
Persichetti, Chris E20
Persico, Asid P272
Person, Amanda P153
Person, Peter P483
Person, Bradley E257
Personette, Sarah A801
Persson, Fredrik W3
Perthuisot, Elodie W104
Perusse, Charles P586
Peruzzi, Enrico W293
Perzigin, Anthony P617
Pesicka, Edward A600
Pessina, Stefano A843
Pessoa, Ana W517
Pestel, Alessandro De A810
Pestello, Jack A117
Pestello, Fred P A458
Pestello, Fred P585
Petach, Ann Marie A443
Petasnick, William P223
Pete, Clint E78
Petelle, James E232
Peter, David P14
Peter, Nicolas W79
Peterffy, Thomas E235
Peterffy, William E235
Peterfreund, Robert A A503:P317
Peterjohn, William P652
Peterman, Carla A722
Peters, Susan A486
Peters, Phillip A541
Peters, Gregory A551
Peters, Len A555
Peters, Valerie A588
Peters, Scott A671
Peters, Sheila A777
Peters, Allen A805
Peters, Jim A863
Peters, Michael P35
Peters, Susan P168
Peters, Loree P357
Peters, Len P374
Peters, Robert P427
Peters, Chris P620
Peters, Richard W2
Peters, Claire W531
Peters, John E64
Peters, Joshua E130
Peters, Carter E204
Peters, Allan E341
Petersen, Paula A206
Petersen, Gary A630
Petersen, David A734
Petersen, Jeffrey P P285:P285
Petersen, Richard W P308
Petersen, Jill P366

HOOVER'S HANDBOOK OF EMERGING COMPANIES 2022

571

COMBINED HOOVER'S HANDBOOK INDEX OF EXECUTIVES

A = AMERICAN BUSINESS
E = EMERGING COMPANIES
P = PRIVATE COMPANIES
W = WORLD BUSINESS

Petersen, David P510
Petersen, John P629
Petersen, Lars Worsoee W3
Petersen, Jacob E250
Peterson, Allison A115
Peterson, Richard D A166
Peterson, Joel A193
Peterson, Kade A319
Peterson, Marissa A406
Peterson, Bradley A543
Peterson, Christopher A556
Peterson, Robert A581
Peterson, Allison A655
Peterson, Douglas A691
Peterson, Bob A739
Peterson, Ronald R A778
Peterson, Matthew A824
Peterson, Richard D P9
Peterson, Tiffani P28
Peterson, Jeannette P73
Peterson, Roger P83
Peterson, Richard D P110
Peterson, Nan P124
Peterson, Mary D P194
Peterson, Tim P252
Peterson, Ronald P276
Peterson, Michael P345
Peterson, Robin P442
Peterson, Ken P480
Peterson, Elaine P487
Peterson, Bob P515
Peterson, Randall P522
Peterson, Randy P522
Peterson, Jim P561
Peterson, Ronald R P564
Peterson, Karen P618
Peterson, Andy P640
Peterson, William W100
Peterson, Laura E10
Peterson, Joel E87
Peterson, Mary E96
Peterson, Jason E144
Peterson, Kade E171
Peterson, Chris E348
Peterson, Renee E411
Petitcolin, Philippe W175
Petko, David A727
Petkovich, Jacob E314
Petno, Douglas A444
Petracchini, Marco W185
Petrasso, Richard P318
Petrelli, Stevi A121
Petri, Mark P445
Petrie, Kim P617
Petrie, Wilfrid W184
Petrilla, Cheryl P394
Petrillo, Louis W40
Petrime, Matt P40
Petro, Randall A516
Petro, Thomas A826:E428
Petrof, Constantin P370
Petrogeorge, Michael P310
Petronchak, Jo P503
Petrosino, John P147
Petrosino, Thomas P306
Petrovic, Shacey E233
Petrucci, Angela A544:E285
Petrusky, Chuck P257
Petruzillo, Kelli Hunter A52
Petryszyn, Mary A569
Petter, Ed W95
Petters, Michael A410
Petti, Filippo P384
Pettiford, Carlos A736
Pettiford, Kathy P197
Pettiford, Carlos P512
Pettigrew, Jim W17
Pettigrew, John W342
Pettit, Thomas E191
Pettit, Baer E282
Pettiti, Gianluca A784

Pettus, Janice P346
Petty, Lora A517
Petty, Gary A717
Petty, Joseph M P135
Petty, Joseph P135
Petty, Lora P331
Petty, Brian E160
Petty, Gary E379
Petz, Carl P92
Peugeot, Robert W193
Pevenstein, Robert L P623
Peverett, Jane W99
Peverly, Francis P397
Peyrelevade, Jean W278
Pfalzgraf, David E148
Pfannenstein, Mike P142
Pfautsch, Rose Agnes P219
Pfeffer, George P194
Pfefferle, Dennis A583:P393
Pfeifer, John A598
Pfeifer, Kyle P332
Pfeifer, Mark P614
Pfeiffer, Philip A831
Pfeiffer, Wendy E341
Pfeil, Keith E195
Pfinsgraff, Martin A632
Pfister, Bruno W429
Pflanz, Robert P322
Pflederer, Kent A605
Phairatphiboon, Virat W65
Phalan, Brendan P327
Phalen, Daniel P177
Phan, Swee Kim W261
Phangaraj, Immanuel P311
Phanmanee, Chayathip W65
Pharaoh, Mazen W407
Phares, Tamara L P587
Phares, Kathryn P644
Pharmd, Geoffrey Lawton P102
Pharr, Brett A519:E272
Phatrachok, Nithi W441
PHD, Robert Sloan P65
PHD, Barry Arbuckle P301
PHD, Charles L Beaty P447
Pheffer, Susanne A322
Phegley, Richard A431
Phelan, John A387
Phelan, Kenneth A409
Phelan, David A743
Phelan, Paula P99
Phelan, Brandi P611
Phelps, Julia A607
Phelps, David E P70
Phenix, David P470
Phetcharat, Chananyarak W491
Philip, Edward A813
Philippe, Herve W518
Philippin, Charles J A807
Philippin, Charles P23
Philipps, Kate W193
Philips, Kathleen A877
Phillips, Charles A46
Phillips, Duncan A183
Phillips, Dorris A208
Phillips, Twila A293
Phillips, Randall A307
Phillips, Joyce A319
Phillips, David A361
Phillips, Terry A472
Phillips, Jeanne A542
Phillips, Nancy A607
Phillips, Charles A607
Phillips, David A652
Phillips, Ottis A717
Phillips, Ronald A755
Phillips, J David P34
Phillips, Brent P65
Phillips, Robyn P97
Phillips, Betty P101
Phillips, David P120
Phillips, Betty P142
Phillips, Dorris P145
Phillips, Erick P165
Phillips, Roya P173
Phillips, Issac P175
Phillips, Twila P211
Phillips, Jason P265

Phillips, John P267
Phillips, Dax J P313
Phillips, Brenda P316
Phillips, Jim P343
Phillips, Dave P344
Phillips, Sheila P362
Phillips, Todd P374
Phillips, Wayne P423
Phillips, Robin P441
Phillips, George W P548
Phillips, John P557
Phillips, Neil Foster P563
Phillips, William P644
Phillips, Russel Scott P659
Phillips, Elen W402
Phillips, William E39
Phillips, Joyce E171
Phillips, Kevin E259
Phillips, Ottis E380
Phillips, Christine E448
Philpot, Buddy P646
Phipps, Gilliam A729
Phipps, Chad A878
Phipps, Laura P109
Phipps, Tom P130
Phipps, David P267
Phlegar, Charles D P642
Phlipsak, Mike P561
Phocus, Rob P124
Phornprapha, Phornthep W62
Photisaro, Arawadee W393
Phr, Catherine B P123
Phyfer, Cheri A335
Pi, Nick A639:E331
Pia, Alberto Del P632
Piacenza, Bruno W224
Piacquad, David A57
Pianalto, Sandra A718
Pianka, Stephanie A555:P374
Piasecki, Nicole W53
Piat, Anita P228
Piatkowski, John P99
Piatt, Rodney L A837
Piazza, Samuel Di A443:A642:A671
Picarelli, Carmine P316
Picarelli, Sergio W10
Picaud, Geraldine W229
Picca, Bruno W251
Piccinno, Emanuele W185
Piccirilli, Ed P405
Piccirillo, Charles A749:E394
Pichai, Sundar A34
Piche, Pierre W389
Pichel, Logan A675:E351
Pichette, Patrick A801
Pichler, Barbara W187
Pichon, Emily A466:E244
Pichottka, Andrea W224
Pick, Edward A538
Pickard, Ann A448
Pickel, Michael W218
Pickerell, Blair A641
Pickett, Denise A46
Pickle, Jeri P662
Picknelly, Paul E448
Pickup, Julie P287
Piclerit, Thomas A298
Picone, Nancy P530
Piechoski, Michael
    J A621:P285:P285:P412
Pieczynski, James J A606
Piekut, Michael P637
Piepszak, Jennifer A445
Pierce, Sandra A42
Pierce, David A132
Pierce, Camille A146
Pierce, Sandra A409:A615
Pierce, Phil P53
Pierce, Tera P131
Pierce, Gen P157
Pierce, Mike P209
Pierce, Karen P218
Pierce, Roger P223
Pierce, Mark P242
Pierce, Stonish P254
Pierce, Christine P502
Pierce, Benjamin P640

Pierce, Damon P642
Pierce, Mary P657
Pierce, Edward E32
Pierce, Patrick E95
Pierce, Lacey E96
Pierce, Joseph E187
Pierce-Jones, Carolyn P220
Pierdicchi, Maria W509
Pieri, Anna W43
Pierpoint, Janice P394
Pierre, Sharon St P352
Pierre, Bryan P427
Pierre, Frantz P546
Pierschbacher, John E26
Pierson, Michael A54
Pierson, Paul A316
Pierson, Michael E25
Pierson, R. Hunter E329
Pieschel, Jim E52
Pietragallo, William A828:P635
Pietranton, Anthony A853:E445
Pietri, Antonio E33
Pietruniak, Lori P165
Piggott, Julie A A122:P80
Piggott, Robert A212
Pigott, Mark C A602
Pike, Lynn A46
Pike, Thomas A501
Pike, Drew P136
Pike, Annabelle P634
Pike, Nolan W3
Piland, Donald S P625
Pilarz, Rev Scott P313
Pileggi, Elisa A624:P414
Pilgreen, Brian P19
Pilgrim, Tony P452
Pilgrim, Trip P521
Pilmer, Donald A587:E302
Pilnick, Gary A449
Pilon, Brian A484
Pilong, Al P358
Pilz, Christine P252
Pimentel, Richard E96
Pina, Carlos Manuel Costa W206
Pinault, Francoishenri W273
Pinckney, E P65
Pineault, Ray P349
Pineda, Patricia A476:A477:P297
Pineda, Brenda P441
Pineda, Joseph Anthony W417
Pineres, Ernesto Gutierrez de W171
Pinero, Sally A216
Pines, Darryll P623
Ping, David P246
Ping, Andrew C P335
Ping, Xiaofeng W431
Pingatore, Holly E160
Pingle, Brenda P504
Pingolt, Cindy P314
Pinho, Ilidio da Costa Leite de W172
Pinkerton, Mac P683
Pinnaro, Caterina P622
Pinnaro, Maurizio W293
Pinnell, Matt P740:P516
Pinner, Ian A68
Pino, Lisette Del P130
Pinter, Jozef W187
Pinto, Daniel A444
Pinto, John A554
Pinto, Jennifer P134
Pinto, Carlos W206
Pintoff, Craig A820
Pintoff, Scott E262
Pioche, Emmanuel W194
Piper, Audrey P16
Piper, Mark P594
Pipes, Kristy E151
Pipkin, Alison P536
Pippen, Alycia P156
Pippin, William C P257
Pipsair, Sophia A736:P512
Piquemal, Thomas W106
Pires, Luciano Siani A539
Pirie, Ellen P169
Pirolli, James A61
Piros, Ryan P163
Pirro, Nicholas J P165

COMBINED HOOVER'S HANDBOOK INDEX OF EXECUTIVES

Pirthauer, Helmut E16
Pisani, James A556
Pisani, Alberto W251
Pischinger, Wolfgang W367
Pishko, Bernard A P130
Pistelli, Lapo W185
Pistorius, Clayton A583:P393
Pita, George A504
Pitayasiri, Worawat W393
Pitchford, Jim P394
Pitchford, William E229
Pitcock, Laurie P239
Pitkethly, Graeme W510
Pitkin, Jeff P206
Pitman, Elizabeth E265
Pitofsky, David A559
Pitrolo, Richard P537
Pitt, Douglas A366
Pittas, Jay P534
Pittet, Tom E81
Pittman, Steuart P156
Pittman, John E132
Pittsford, Judy P171
Pityana, Sipho W6
Piva, Gary R P657
Pizarro, Pedro A268:A722
Pizzinatto, Rodrigo de Almeida W506
Pizzo, Kristine P371
Placek, Mark P151
Placencia, Eric P27
Plache, Kim A867
Placido, Lorraine P308
Plafker, Jed A336
Plaines, Stephanie A562:P378
Plam, Kathleen P126
Plamondon, William N P195
Planas, Ramon P133
Plank, Kevin A810
Plansky, Michael E370
Planson, Steven E156
Plant, John A434:A502
Planta, Thomas von W55
Plante, Robert A613:E316
Plants, W. Jack A307
Plascencia, Gustavo A186:P127
Plater, Michael E254
Plath, Thomas A427
Platia, Edward V P646
Plato, Alexandra Von W395
Platt, Tracy L A165
Platt, Lawrence B P105
Platt, Anne P529
Platt, Gillian W145
Platteeuw, Filip W507
Plattner, Hasso W419
Platts, Karen P553
Plaza, Alvaro Alvarez-Alonso W72
Plazas, Hernando Ramirez W171
Pleas, Charlie A84
Pleasant, Dan A49:E21
Pleines, Thomas W55
Pleininger, Johann W371
Plemmons, Gregory A584
Plenborg, Thomas W168
Plenk, Bruce P135
Plesha, Scott E51
Plessis-belair, Michel W389
Plew, Daniel Van A669
Plewa, Jennifer A8:P4
Plewniak, Linda A15:P7
Plimpton, Tara A671
Pline, Jennifer A143:E65
Plisinski, Michael E304
Ploeg, Julia E153
Ploss, Ines W222
Ploss, Reinhard W246
Ploszek, Judith M P215
Plotner, Chuck P100
Plotts, Diane J P603
Plourd, Martin E96
Plourde, Donna P309
Plourde, Real W25
Plueger, John E9
Plum, Brian E52
Plum, Brian K E52
Plumart, Marc W448
Plummer, Ed A244

Plummer, William A358:A848
Plummer, Laura P73
Plummer, Shayvonne P133
Plummer, Suzy P282
Plummer, Beth P381
Plummer, James E62
Plummer, Tammy E163
Plummer, Michelle E201
Plump, Andrew W475
Plunkett, Debora A142
Plunkett, Jayne W16
Pluta, Rob A689
Plympton, Richard A147:E65
Poarch, Donald A417:E227
Poblador, Alexander W417
Pocino, Raymond M P368
Podlogar, Susan A521
Podolsky, Howard P107
Poe, Caitlin P411
Poe, Shawn K P421
Poe, Kevin P457
Poe, Alfred E43
Poelvoorde, Geert Van W39
Poenitske, Jason P P392
Poerksen, Niels A20
Poerschke, John E9
Poff, Brian E5
Pogge, Franklyn P347
Pogrebinsky, Lena P138
Pohl, Jeffery P193
Pohle, Richard A409
Pohlman, Kevin A610
Pohlman, John A P488
Pohlman, thomas E26
Pohlner, Roger E P444
Poindexter, Karen A541
Poindexter, Philip A747:E391
Poisson, Keith P225
Pojamarnpornchai, Ronnakitt W98
Pokela, Toni W274
Poladian, Avedick A581
Poland, Daniel A146
Poland, Douglas E271
Polansky, Robert B P77
Polaschek, Detlef W160
Polen, Thomas A109
Polensek, Michael D P125
Polep, Jeff P152
Polep, Eric P152
Polet, Robert A625
Polewaczyk, James F E221
Policinski, Christopher A871
Polignac, Francois Melchior De W104
Poliner, Catherine A523
Polis, Jared A735
Polis, Cindy P80
Polis, Jared P510
Polisknowski, John P489
Polito, Karyn A208:P146
Politte, Keith P334
Polius, Olivia A289
Poljak, Matt P93
Polk, James A97
Polk, Dennis A763
Polk, Hiram C P614
Polk, Dennis E406
Poll, Max P254
Pollack, Kenneth A22
Pollack, Martha A424
Pollack, Sean A702
Pollack, Martha E P154
Pollack, Stephanie P317
Pollack, Jonathan E52
Pollak, Matthew A734
Pollak, Andrea W218
Pollard, Ivan A348
Pollard, Dennis P222
Pollard, Katherine P616
Pollet, Mary Joe P554
Pollina, Lisa E137
Pollinger, Marcus W81
Pollitt, Erin P334
Pollitzer, Adam E294
Pollock, Allen P209
Pollock, Samuel W94
Pollock, Janet E12
Pollok, John A725:E383

Poloncarz, Mark P159
Poloni, Lara A15
Poloz, Stephen W178
Poludniak, Lee P222
Polyakov, Andrey W411
Polymeropoulos, Mihael E432
Polzer, Robert A881
Pomaville, David P159
Pomeroy, Brian Walter W396
Pomeroy, Bill E305
Pominski, Lisa A866:E450
Pomodoro, Livia W252
Pompa, Mark A272
Pompa, Robert N P572
Ponce, Sue P416
Ponder, Mark A279:E142
Pongritsakda, Wiwat W98
Ponnavolu, Kishore A521
Pons, Fernando Jose Frances W71
Pont, Eleuthere Du A260
Ponzanelli, Enrique W525
Pool, Dr Dennis P396
Poole, Kami A233
Poole, William A529
Poole, Dawn P150
Poole, Kami P178
Poole, Claude P198
Poole, Thomas P301
Poole, James P436
Poole, Michelle E110
Poole, William E274
Pooler, Joseph E89
Poomee, Chana W441
Poomsurakul, Yuthasak W98
Poon, Joseph A157
Poon, Christine A669:A708
Poon, Yuew Sim W393
Poon, Joseph E70
Poonpipat, Suphadej W491
Popairoj, Jiraporn W65
Popal, Ahmad P573
Popat, Dinesh E2
Pope, Lawrence A371
Pope, Mariana A403
Pope, Maria A809
Pope, John A848
Pope, Audrey P19
Pope, Brian P155
Pope, Mariana P256
Pope, Alice H P263
Pope, Linda P282
Pope, Alice P649
Pope, Richard E395
Pope, Daniel E419
Popek, Edwina J P540
Poplis, Mark P471
Popoff, Frank W437
Popour, Catherine P599
Popov, Igor P534
Popov, Anatoly W424
Popovici, Silviu A619
Poppe, Patricia A623:A863
Poppell, Jim A327:P214
Poppell, John E P619
Popper, Charles P265
Pops, Richard E291
Popwell, David A317:E170
Porat, Ruth A34:A121
Porcari, John P316
Porcella, Kelly A465
Porcile, Renee P70
Pordon, Anthony A615
Poremba, Steve P320
Porges, David A560
Pornsakulvanich, Vitoon W441
Porras, Julio Carlos W28
Porro, Stefano W509
Port, Barry E139
Portalatin, Julio A743
Porte, Susan P167
Porteous, David A409
Porter, Tracy A207
Porter, Elizabeth A472
Porter, Roger A605
Porter, Jonathan A672
Porter, Robert P11
Porter, Tom P63

Porter, Virginia P158
Porter, Lawana P179
Porter, Jody P225
Porter, Frenchie P467
Porter, Andy P546
Porter, David W3
Porter, Brian W69
Porter, Roger E153
Porter, A.Dale E174
Porter, Christopher E429
Porterfield, Clark P405
Porth, Wilfried W319
Portillo, Janice P18
Portney, Emily A99:E262
Portnoy, Dan P559
Porwal, Hemant A854
Posard, Matthew E204
Posecai, Scott A583:P393
Posey, Dan P468
Posey, Bruce E341
Poshyananda, Kovit W62
Poshyanonda, Pipatpong W270
Posner, Brian W40
Posner, Christopher E67
Posson, Denise M P442
Post, Bill P78
Post, Shelley P148
Post, Heather P172
Post, Janet P646
Poste, George E150
Postel, Gregory P587
Poster, Margaret E106
Postlethweight, Brittany P466
Postma, Richard A493
Postma, Nate P266
Postma, Sidney W P431
Potes, Kelly E81
Potier, Helene W397
Potochnic, Jennifer P622
Pototo, Dan P635
Pott, Jeffrey W46
Potter, Beth A548
Potter, Ruth P98
Potter, Roshanda P127
Potter, William P163
Potter, Silas P471
Potter, Jim P520
Potter, Shannon P521
Potter, Jason P559
Potter, Joyce P581
Potter, Kent P650
Potter, Kelly E52
Pottle, Aj P135
Pottorff, Gary W P386
Potts, Daniel A9:E4
Potts, Robert E271
Potvin, Jacques W239
Pou, William A725:E383
Poukens, Pierre A411
Poul, Mojdeh A3:A731
Poulakidas, Dean E449
Poulin, Marc W239
Poulsen, Richard P168
Poulsen, Jennifer E133
Pound, Theodore A163
Pound, Pam P353
Pounds, Don P60
Pouraghabagher, Setareh A734
Pourbaix, Alexander W111
Povlitz, David P156
Powar, Rahul W132
Powell, Ann A134
Powell, Jeffrey A193
Powell, Steven A268
Powell, Bradley A289
Powell, Jerome A301
Powell, Dennis A429
Powell, Ehren A496
Powell, Carolyn A647
Powell, Anthony A675
Powell, Aaron A708
Powell, Steven A722
Powell, Curtis A797
Powell, Aaron A876
Powell, Charlie P1
Powell, Brittney P160
Powell, Terri P347

COMBINED HOOVER'S HANDBOOK INDEX OF EXECUTIVES

A = AMERICAN BUSINESS
E = EMERGING COMPANIES
P = PRIVATE COMPANIES
W = WORLD BUSINESS

Powell, Willa P450
Powell, Larry P491
Powell, Rice W203:W204
Powell, Fred E28
Powell, Jeffrey E87:E240
Powell, Anthony E350
Power, Una W69
Power, Andrew E120
Powers, Robert A25
Powers, John A310
Powers, Roxanne P76
Powers, Kevin G P109
Powers, Glen P170
Powers, Michael P172
Powers, Donald S P359
Powers, Kevin P488
Powers, Scott W465
Powers, Brian E108
Powers, David E116
Powers, John E164
Powers, Janis E300
Powes, Hammond R P161
Powlus, Lee A617:E319
Powrie, Raymond P99
Pozen, Robert A562:P378
Pozez, Norman A261:E126
Pozzi, James E A50
Pozzo, Joseph E P172
Prabhakaran, Bharath P627
Prabhu, Krish A694
Prabhu, Vasant A839
Prada, Ariel De P612
Prado, Michael E215
Pragada, Robert A436
Pragnell, Michael W517
Prairie, Gregory P238
Prakash, Shailesh E289
Pramukti, Surjaudaja W376
Pranckevicius, John P319
Prange, Karen E36
Prasad, Vinay P294
Prasitsirigul, Sayam W65
Prater, Robert A603:A603:P404:E310
Prather, Patrise P6
Pratt, Marcel S A187
Pratt, Benjamin A539
Pratt, Frank A734
Pratt, Marcel S P131
Pratt, Charles P134
Pratt, John P193
Pratt, Brenda P382
Pratt, Dan P382
Pratt, Ramona P416
Pratt, Stephen R P508
Pratt, Frank P510
Pratt, Ronald E P534
Praw, Albert A447
Praxmarer, Marc W514
Praylo, Paul A578
Prebola, Donald A673
Precourt, Walter A539
Prehn, Ryan A736:P512
Preiser, David A578
Preisler, Donna P201
Preisser, Brenna A138
Premutico, Mauro E426
Prendergast, Thomas F A553
Prendergast, Vincent A770
Prendergast, Ed P55
Prendergast, Michael P167
Prendergast, Mark P234
Prendergast, Thomas F P370
Prendergast, Vincent P540
Prendergast, Dr E James P562
Prentace, Charles P130
Prentice, Nora P554
Pres, Thomas J La P256
Prescod, Elizabeth P164
Prescott, Gordon A113
Presecan, Anne P471

Preskenis, Donald A312
Presley, John A717
Presley, William W37
Presley, Steve W348
Presley, John E379
Presnell, Bill P525
Press, Michael B P161
Press, Dennis P626
Pressler, Paul A266
Prestidge, Corey A388
Presto, Toni A134:P87
Preston, Tracy A373
Preston, Margaret A508
Preston, Marty A552:P369
Preston, James L A410
Pretlow, Paula A865
Pretorius, Sy P406
Pretorius, Stephan W533
Pretty, Nigel A195:P140
Preusse, Mary Hogan E120
Prevost, Sgt A741:P518
Prevoznik, Michael A659
Price, Paula A135
Price, Thomas A313
Price, Harriet A314
Price, Harold A327
Price, Todd M A512
Price, Michael A514
Price, Alexandra A783
Price, Scott A819
Price, Jody P10
Price, Heather P37
Price, Aaron P39
Price, Bill P46
Price, McKinley P129
Price, John Wiley P158
Price, Lasundra P170
Price, Robert R P211
Price, Harold P215
Price, Jamie P290
Price, Todd M P326
Price, Ronald E P414
Price, Andrea P493
Price, Meredith P504
Price, Nancy P541
Price, Stuart P553
Price, Brenda P553
Price, Claudia P563
Price, Alexandra P583
Price, Richard W32
Price, Timothy W191
Price, Richard W311
Price, Thomas E165
Price, Michael E267
Price-Eastburn, Dianna P399
Prichard, J. Robert W527
Pricher, Michael P535
Pricket, Glenn P569
Prickett, Charlie P1
Prideaux, Nigel W345
Priebe, Stephen A747
Priebe, Nancy L P49:P639
Priebe, Stephen E391
Priefert, William A370:E203
Prieskorn, Laura W391
Priesman, Karen E194
Priest, Harold De P203
Priester, Joann P162
Prieto, Esther P141
Prieto, Domingo Valdes W179
Prieur, Claude A39:W308
Prigg, Becky P147
Primavera, Dianne A735:P510
Primavesi, Marco W75
Prime, Joshua A477:P297
Prince, David A381
Prince, Charles A441
Prince, Amy L P609
Prince, David E208
Principato, Giuseppe P434
Prindeze, Nick P325
Prindiville, Mark A32
Prindle, Brian P620
Pringle, Germaine P170
Pringle, Al P433
Pringle, Nisaphan P492

Prinner, John P234
Prins, Todd P588
Priscu, Daniel E137
Priselac, Thomas M P105
Prising, Jonas A494
Prisuwanna, Benjaporn W62
Pritchard, Sandy W17
Pritchett, Patricia P615
Pritzker, Penny A529
Pritzker, J B A736:P512
Privett, Stephen A P628
Privitera, Salvatore E36
Privot, John P316
Probert, Todd A142
Probst, Redgie A658
Procaskey, Alexander P609
Proch, Michel-Alain W395
Prochaska, Joseph A754:E401
Procope, Jonelle A714
Procopio, Karen P335
Proctor, H. Palmer A54
Proctor, Hawthorne A727
Proctor, Gregory A853
Proctor, Jason P119
Proctor, H. Palmer E25
Proctor, Gregory E445
Procyk, Nicholas P549
Profeta, Tommaso W294
Proffitt, Joshua E252
Profumo, Alessandro W294
Profusek, Robert A831
Progar, Michael P226
Progler, Christopher E323
Prohaska, Ron P109
Prohaska, Stefan W367
Prokopanko, James A671:A871
Proksel, Jenel P366
Pronchunas, Edward M P105
Pronger, Derk P359
Proske, Donna P519
Prosper, Charles P409
Prosser, Joseph P541
Proto, Christine P215
Prout, John P72
Prout, John S P231
Prout, John P598
Prouty, Kate E11
Provencher, Catherine P633
Provenzano, John A652
Provera, Bernardino W43
Proverbio, Massimo W251
Provoost, Rudy W397
Provost, Dawn A789:E411
Prudenti, A. Gail A101
Pruger, Robert P578
Pruis, Dirk E271
Pruit, Randy A215
Pruitt, Kristin A466
Pruitt, J. Scott A626
Pruitt, Andy P113
Pruitt, Keri P172
Pruitt, Gary P545
Pruitt, Kristin E244
Pruitt, J. Scott E322
Pruneda, Augustin P156
Pruner, Alexandra A574:A630
Pruner, Lauren P418
Prust, Robert P359
Pruzan, Jonathan A538
Pry, Russell M P524
Prybycien, Bonnie P217
Pryor, Juliette A28
Pryor, David B A74
Pryor, Felecia A131
Pryor, Juliette A350:P18
Pryor, David B P43
Pryor, Vince P201:P201
Pryor, Robert P468
Pryor, Felecia E254
Pryor, Paula E443
Prysock, Carrie P126
Psaltis, Vassilios W27
Pseli, Ghassan Dayoub W141
Psihas, Julian Lazalde A723
Pua, Seck Guan W529
Pucci, Paolo E446
Pucel, Kenneth J A632

Puckett, Lynne A160
Puckett, Karen A277
Puckett, Lynne A497
Puckett, Matt A836
Puckett, Walter P209
Puckett, Debbie P417
Pucky, Alicia P222
Pudipeddi, Raj E15
Pudloski, Sherry A881
Puebla, Juan Javier Hinojosa W381
Puech, Olivier A51
Puente, Gabriel P259
Puente, Robert R P462
Puetz, Belinda P155
Pueyo, Pilar A143:E65
Puffinburger, Darren P394
Pugh, Andrea A597
Pugh, Aaron P42
Pugh, Catherine E P123
Pugh, Randall P269
Pugh, William P418
Pugh, Sandra P634
Pugh, Michael E153
Pugh, Andrea E307
Pugliese, John A647
Pugliese, Stephanie A810
Puhy, Dorothy E P180
Puhy, Dorothy E3
Puleo, Frank A716
Puleo, Dominic J P640
Puleo, Frank E379
Puliti, Alessandro W185
Pullen, Jim P526
Pullin, Dennis E215
Pulmonologist, A Lynchburg P107
Pulomena, John A106:P343:E48
Puls, Edgar W476
Puls, H Charles E204
Pulsipher, Scott P653
Pulver, Jenny E69
Pum, Michael J P289
Puma, Mary G E40
Pumeroy, Clarence P507
Pumpian, Ann P477
Pundrich, Shari P114
Puno, Reynato W417
Punta, Stefano Del W251
Puntel, Diane A24:P13
Puntillo, Anthony E161
Punukula, Balaji A736:P512
Pupkin, Sergio A707
Purcell, Cynthia A102
Purcell, Kreg A485
Purcell, Jennifer A740
Purcell, Alfred L P248:P354
Purcell, Paul E P448
Purcell, Jennifer P516
Purcell, Cailin P565
Pureetip, Athita W62
Puri, Ajay A577
Puri, Ajai W370
Puri, Anil E109
Puripanyawanich, Suyanee W62
Purisima, Cesar W70
Purkey, Tom P569
Purrier, Paul P90
Pursell, David A64
Purtee, Pamela P355
Purves, Steve P311
Purvis, Shawn A569
Purvis, Tom A712:E373
Pushis, Glenn A745
Puskas, Sandor W334
Pusser, Brian P589
Put, Dirk Van De A535
Putin, Mikhail W385
Putnam, Nancy E422
Putney, April P161
Putz, Lasse W108
Puyfontaine, Arnaud Roy de W482
Puyfontaine, Arnaud Nicolas De W518
Pyatt, Ken P341
Pyle, Richard P23
Pyle, Thomas E239
Pyne, Christopher A827
Pötsch, Hans W522

574   HOOVER'S HANDBOOK OF EMERGING COMPANIES 2022

COMBINED HOOVER'S HANDBOOK INDEX OF EXECUTIVES

Q

Qasem, Rami A91
Qi, Dapeng W119
Qian, Zhijia W287
Qiao, Gina W292
Qin, Jeff P141
Qiu, Zhi Zhong W130
Qiu, Weiyang W209
Qiu, Yibo W223
Qu, Yang W321
Qu, Ming E311
Quade, Bradley A311
Quagliano, Michael E380
Quaid, John A541
Quaid, Maureen A P7
Qualls, Roxanne P125
Quam, Bethany A347
Quan, Nancy A196
Quan, Patrick F P29:P562
Quarles, Christa A455
Quarta, Roberto W533
Quatela, Laura W293
Quatrochi, Christopher E289
Quattlebaum, Heather P597
Quattrocchi, Robert T P387
Quay, Martha James P657
Queen, Elizabeth P395
Queenan, Daniel A159
Queener, Hugh A628:E324
Quek, Leng Chan W232
Quek, Sunny W376
Quemore, Amanda P466
Quenneville, Cathy L A32:P24
Quenon, Loretta A186:P127
Quental, Marina W513
Querubin, Linne P257
Query, K. Rex A575
Quesada-Kunkel, Ginnette P377
Quesenbery, Christy E439
Quevedo, Alexander A81
Quick, Peter A322
Quick, Janet A381:E208
Quick-Wasik, Cindy P323
Quien, Austine P169
Quigg, Andrew A645
Quigg, Diana P100
Quigley, Robert A662
Quigley, Timothy P488
Quijano-Lerma, Mariselle P408
Quillen, Michael A501
Quimpo, Jose Eduardo W83
Quin, Debra P40
Quincey, James A196:A622
Quindlen, Thomas A752
Quiniones, Gil C P371
Quinlan, Michael A186
Quinlan, Joseph A706
Quinlan, Michael E84
Quinn, Kevin A307
Quinn, Stephen A368
Quinn, Kevin A381
Quinn, Thomas A597
Quinn, Katherine A679
Quinn, Katherine B A829
Quinn, Bill P135
Quinn, Madison P165
Quinn, Joseph P175
Quinn, Brian P342
Quinn, Mary Anna P505
Quinn, Ronald N P537
Quinn, Jason W6
Quinn, Peter W156
Quinn, Noel W234
Quinn, George W543
Quinn, Kevin E208
Quinn, William E213
Quinn, Thomas E307
Quinn-Davidson, Austin P36
Quinones, Bill P179
Quinonez, Tanya A291:P210
Quintana, Julio A558
Quintana, Marie A765
Quintana-Plaza, Susana W206
Quintero-Johnson, Marie E219
Quintos, Karen A228
Quirk, Raymond R A303

Quirk, Kathleen A338:P317
Quirk, Jeanne W480
Quiroz, David P96
Quist, Scott E366
Quist, Adam E366
Quist, S. Andrew E366
Quradaghi, Ali Al W64
Qureshi, Rima A506:A833
Qureshi, Furhan P293
Qutub, Robert W399

R

R, Shereen P2
R, Bethany P136
R, Cynthia P167
R, Marek Doll P340
Raab, Lee P507
Raab, Andrew P523
Raab, Andy P523
Raabe, Christian W321
Raassina, Leevi P259
Rabatel, Christophe W104
Rabbatts, Dame Heather W45
Rabinowicz, Daniel W25
Raborn, Richard E12
Rabun, Daniel A64
Raccio, Emiliano Muratore W59
Rachev, Sharyn P371
Rachman, Sherry P173
Racioppi, Michael A696
Rackers, Eileen P347
Radano, Amy P421
Rademacher, Dennis P10
Radev, Anthony W334
Radigan, Kevin E420
Radke, Robin E271
Radloff, Diane P44
Rado, Nicholas E395
Radtke, Duane A243
Radtke, Alex P292
Radulesk, Jenny P164
Radziwill, John A748
Raehl, Deborah P632
Raets, Laurent P507
Raetz, Jeff P339
Rafael, Elizabeth E38
Raff, Robert A731
Raffa, Kathy A261:E126
Rafferty, James P70
Rafferty, Gary J P530:P531
Rafferty, William P553
Rafferty, Emily W281
Raffo, Giulia W43
Raffo, Christopher E96
Rafkin, Scott W523
Raftery, Mary P156
Ragan, Bob P650
Ragauss, Peter A64
Ragel, Larry P501
Ragen, York E191
Raghu, Chitra A485
Ragle, Jake A631
Ragni, Margaret V P635
Ragosta, Michael P589
Ragsdale, Chris P141
Rague, Vincent W335
Rahe, Maribeth A315
Rahe, Micaela P212
Rahe, Maribeth E98:E167
Rahilly, Ita A789
Rahim, Faiza P662
Rahim, Afzal Abdul W128
Rahlfs, Gary P627
Rahman, Jill A114
Rahman, Habib P345
Rahmani, Valerie W399
Rahming, Carmen M P345
Rahmstrom, Mats W48
Rahn, Joel A417
Rahn, Pete K P316
Rahn, Douglas P327
Rahn, Joel E226
Rai, Kiran P47
Raia, Christopher A260
Raifeld, Pavel E229

Raigoza, Juan P169
Raikhel, Marina P596
Raim, Ellen E289
Raina, Robin E129
Rainbolt, David A94:E44
Raine, Ed P217
Rainer, Sallie A277
Raines, Diane S P58
Raines, Lynn P493
Raines, Kelly P507
Rainey, John A543:A612
Rains, Cherie P14
Rains, Melinda P533
Rains, Darrell E365
Rainwater, Meghan P51
Raisbeck, David A264
Raiss, Sarah A207
Raj, Atul P411
Raja, Vasu A41
Raja, Praburam A66
Raja, Andaleeb H P300
Rajamannar, Raja A506
Rajamannar, Venkata A637
Rajan, Resmi P200
Rajendra, Jay W40
Rajkumar, Amanda W12
Raju, Ramanathan A552
Raju, Shubha P200
Raju, Ramanathan P369
Raju, Ryan P468
Rak, Vladimir A244
Rales, Steven A235
Raley, Mary P507
Rallsmorrison, Desiree A132:A244:A509
Ralph, Stephen A P407
Ralph, Alan W156
Ram, Jonathan A373
Ramachandran, Ramesh P325
Ramage, David A7
Ramaker, David A514:E267
Raman, Sundar W139
Raman, A Wahab bin A W393
Ramanathan, Guru E287
Ramanna, Mayura P126
Rambousek, Jasmine P137
Ramdas, Gautam E295
Ramesh, Aparna A296:E157
Ramicone, Arthur P68
Ramirez, Pamela A359
Ramirez, Antonio A602
Ramirez, Jaime A731
Ramirez, Fabiola P114
Ramirez, Aimee P114
Ramirez, Shanna P136
Ramirez, Eduardo P168
Ramirez, Amie P261
Ramirez, Luis M P317
Ramirez, Nicolas W171
Ramirez, Miguel Angel Espinoza W215
Ramji, Al-Noor W391
Ramo, Joshua A302
Ramoneda, Dorothy A312
Ramos, Denise A96
Ramos, Paula A455
Ramos, Denise A665
Ramos, Robert Kaslow- A763
Ramos, Cruz P168
Ramos, Harold P205
Ramos, Delia P217
Ramos, Rick P312
Ramos, Annette P450
Ramos, Dioscoro W83
Ramos, Bernardino W323
Ramos, Maria W456
Ramos, A. Kenneth E76
Ramos, Raul E175
Ramos, Mark K E221
Ramrath, Joseph A375
Ramsay, Michael P65
Ramsay, Norrie W110
Ramsay, Dan E340
Ramsden, Jonathan A117
Ramsden, Deanna A503
Ramsden, Peter P169
Ramsden, Deanna P318
Ramser, Mark A608:E312
Ramsey, Matthew A276

Ramsey, Samuel A716
Ramsey, Ron A741
Ramsey, Matthew A750
Ramsey, Craig P28
Ramsey, David L P111
Ramsey, Brenda P337
Ramsey, Ron P517
Ramsey, Randy P586
Ramsey, Richard E115
Ramsey, Samuel E379
Ramsey, James E385
Ramsey, Matthew E429
Ramsey-Burns, Debbie P134
Ramstad, Jennifer P172
Ramu, Raymond E359
Ramyarupa, Apichart W62
Rana, Harpreet E348
Ranalli, Tamara E342
Ranck, Angela P157
Rand, Allison A640
Rand, Edward A642
Rand, Allison E333
Randall, Catherine A25
Randall, Christopher A544
Randall, Taylor P588
Randall, Christopher E285
Randazza, Mark A196
Randhawa, Amrita W395
Rando, Anthony P177
Randolph, Amy A310:E164
Randt, Clark A656
Ranelli, John E75
Ranes, Douglas E248
Raney, Steven A663
Rangan, Kasturi P102
Ranganathan, Madhu E11
Rangel, Felicia P405
Ranger, Michael A216
Rango, Robert A457
Rangsiyopash, Roongrote W441
Ranhoff, David E138
Ranjbar, Mohammad P624
Rankin, Devina A453
Rankin, David A700
Rankin, Devina A848
Rankin, Jay P200
Rankin, Robert S P418
Rankin, Ralph P435
Rankin, Alice P468
Rankowitz, Michael E435
Ranney, Timothy P346
Ranong, Shoke Na W62
Ransom, Teran P612
Ranttila, Michael E274
Ranum, Laura P261
Ranzini, Stephen E427
Ranzini, Paul E427
Ranzini, Joseph E427
Rao, Dana A11
Rao, Venkat A190
Rao, Karthik A562:P378
RAO, Michael P640
Rao, U. B. Pravin W247
Rapanos, Vasileios W27
Raphael, Carol A696
Rapino, Michael A483:A714
Rapp, Karen A525
Rapple, Susan P546
Raquel, Thompson P132
Rardin, Laurie P182
Rasak, Jon P105
Rasche, Charlotte A646
Rasche, Steven P495
Rasche, Charlotte E336
Rasco, Craig P123
Rasco, Jane P615
Rascoff, Spencer M A877
Rash, Matthew P P40
Rashid, M A666
Rask, Jan E210
Raskas, Daniel A235
Raskin, David P336
Raskind, Peter A149
Rasmussen, Stephen A44
Rasmussen, Tiffany P233
Rasmussen, Daniel E82
Rassieur, Benjamin A206

COMBINED HOOVER'S HANDBOOK INDEX OF EXECUTIVES

A = AMERICAN BUSINESS
E = EMERGING COMPANIES
P = PRIVATE COMPANIES
W = WORLD BUSINESS

Rastetter, William E291
Ratanaprasartporn, Praralee W284
Ratatics, Peter W334
Ratcliffe, David A796
Rath, John A466
Rath, Kimberly A549
Rath, Deb P589
Rath, John E243
Rath, Kimberly E290
Rathjen, Sara A322
Rathnam, Sukumar A706
Raths, Kathy P267
Ratinoff, Edward A90:E41
Ratkin, Gary A347
Ratkovic, Gregg E131
Ratliff, Beth P426
Ratnakar, Raj A260
Ratner, Ian P470
Rattanapian, Chongrak W270
Ratterman, Joseph E73
Rattray, Sandy E282
Ratzlaff, James W A49:P33
Rau, John A869
Rauch, Douglas A729
Rauhala, Jorma W274
Raul, Wonneberger P621
Raup, Charles A384
Rausas, Christophe Pelissie du W517
Rausch, Christopher P605
Rauschenberger, Matthew P493
Rauschl, Christopher A P77
Rautenbach, Arrie W6
Rauti, Antonio A867
Ravindran, Rajeev A689
Ravine, Harris E63
Raviv, Dalit W63
Rawlings, Hunter R P154
Rawlings, Karen P308
Rawlinson, David A247:A660
Rawls, Michael A541:E281
Rawot, Billie A264:P200
Ray, Barry A531
Ray, Eric A662
Ray, Neville A758
Ray, Michael A858
Ray, James P112
Ray, Anish P152
Ray, David P153
Ray, Cindy P157
Ray, David P193
Ray, Monica P354
Ray, Bradford E253
Ray, Barry E276
Raya, Lori A727
Raya, Rogel W83
Raybon, Erine P385
Rayburn, William A652
Raymond, Philip A25
Raymond, Jade A34
Raymond, John A630
Raymond, Stephanie A637
Raymond, Mary E224
Raymund, Steven A434
Rayner, Thomas P282
Rayno, Peter A278:E141
Raynor, Linda P306
Raza, Adnan P377
Razo, Jennifer P267
Razola, Jose Francisco Doncel W61
REA, Brian A811
Read, Colin A72
Read, Nicholas A128
Read, C. Jack A185
Read, Ian A455
Read, Paul A494
Read, Vicki P637
Read, Nick W520
Read, Mark W533
Read, Colin E31
Reade, Paul A212
Reade, Philip E37

Readiness, Career A266
Ready, William A865
Reagan, Ronald A560
Ream, Deborah A8:P4
Reardon, Kathy A252
Reardon, Aaron P170
Reardon, Martine W176
Reath, Wayne A411
Reaud, Wayne A411
Reaume, Marty E385
Rebecchini, Clemente W43
Rebelez, Darren A155:A359
Rebelo, Sergio Tavares W263
Reber, Ann A738:P514
Reber, John E83
Rebsamen, C B P292
Rebsch, Gary P352
Rebstock, Russell A583:P393
Reca, Thomas P519
Recchi, Giuseppe A346:P227
Reck, Una Mae P602
Rector, Susan A617
Recupero, Mike A343
Redabaugh, Blake P577
Redae, Getachew A224:P168
Redd, Ershel A760
Redd, David A770
Redd, Mike P401
Redd, Ellis S P491
Redd, David P541
Reddin, Thomas A73
Reddin, Matthew A712:E373
Reddoch, James E358
Reddy, Christine A108
Reddy, Avinash A246
Reddy, Sundeep A692
Reddy, John Patrick P494
Reddy, Andrew P520
Reddy, Sreenath V P587
Reddy, Madhukar E264
Redetzke, Darren E411
Redfern, David W210
Rediker, Douglas E106
Reding, Douglas P314
Redlich, Rachel P272
Redman, Heather A637
Redman, Cynthia J H P305
Redmond, Andrea A32
Redmond, Katrina R A264:P200
Redmond, Velma A P410
Redner, Ryan P439
Redner, Richard E P439
Redner, Gary W P439
Redstone, Shari P607
Redwine, William A P114
Redzic, Ognjen A76
Reece, Ronald A245
Reece, H. Wade A399
Reece, Paris A492
Reece, Ronald P189
Reed, James A102
Reed, Cory A240
Reed, Colin A317
Reed, Steven A400
Reed, Tyrone A503
Reed, Suellen A736
Reed, Sam A741
Reed, Robert D A750
Reed, Michael A870
Reed, Susan P156
Reed, Betty P209
Reed, Glenn P256
Reed, Daniel C P311
Reed, Connie P311
Reed, Tyrone P318
Reed, David P318
Reed, Katie N P387
Reed, Jane P421
Reed, Colin P454
Reed, Ann P459
Reed, Stephanie P460
Reed, James P508
Reed, Suellen P512
Reed, Sam P518
Reed, Robert D P528
Reed, David P627
Reed, Dervel P647

Reed, David E6
Reed, Matthew E91
Reed, Brian E134
Reed, Colin E170
Reed, Steven E218
Reed, W. Earl E252
Reed, Robin E286
Reed, Kreighton E380
Reed, Brian E395
Reed, James E430
Reed, Michael E454
Reeder, Billy P532
Reedy, Raquel Martinez P18
Reel, Jennifer A331
Reel, Stephanie P591
Reel, Jennifer E178
Reel-Davis, Tammi P352
Reemst, Mary W304
Rees, Gary P179
Rees, Dan W69
Rees, A. W249
Rees, Andrew E110
Reese, David A57
Reese, Bruce A423
Reese, Anthony A852
Reese, Steven P25
Reese, Bruce P264
Reese, Cody P287
Reese, Cathy P359
Reese, Roger P400
Reese, Vincent P428
Reese, William P542
Reese, Amanda P632
Reese, Richard E79
Reese, J. Mitchell E346
Reeson, Terrance E327
Reeths, Lori P546
Reeve, Pamela A339
Reeve, Derek A661
Reeve, Stephene A736
Reeve, Shawn P394
Reeve, Derek P432
Reeve, Stephene P512
Reeves, Eric A62
Reeves, Kevin A617
Reeves, Tate A737
Reeves, Denise P141
Reeves, Tate P513
Reeves, Cynthia P620
Regala, Maria Nannette W83
Regalado, Tomas P128
Regalado, Antonio P486
Regan, John A328
Regan, Timothy J A783:P291
Regan, Marla P449
Regan, Timothy J P591
Regan, Barry E117
Regele, Michael B P267
Regelman, Roman A99
Regent, Aaron W69
Regev, Aviv W408
Rego, Vagner W48
Rego, Francisco Vahia de Castro Teixeira W206
Regunath, Harihoran P625
Rehder, W.M. W315
Rehder, Jeffrey E286
Reher, Penny P461
Rehm, Michael A747:E391
Rehman, Jalil A192
Rehman, Ahmed Baqar W128
Rehmel, Tina P127
Rehwinkel, Brian P651
Reic, Iskra W46
Reich, Victoria A418
Reich, Jan P450
Reichelderfer, Brenda E159
Reichenthal, Max E186
Reichert, Christopher A746
Reichert, Nicole A869
Reichert, John A P406
Reichert, James P447
Reichert, Nicole P659
Reichle, Hank P509
Reichstul, Henri W400
Reick, Angela P396
Reid, John A138

Reid, Thomas A203
Reid, Sonya A584:A584
Reid, Alan A694
Reid, Brian A711
Reid, George P37
Reid, Bob P158
Reid, Monica Nino P170
Reid, John P311
Reid, David P417
Reid, Brian P481
Reid, Bernadette P596
Reid, Richard W45
Reid, Bill W532
Reif, L Rafael P318
Reif, Rafael W474
Reifsteck, John A369:P237
Reilly, Michael A39
Reilly, Paul A76
Reilly, Brian A174
Reilly, Robert A632
Reilly, Paul A663:A663
Reilly, Katie A734
Reilly, Annemarie P103
Reilly, Christopher B P173
Reilly, Bill P232
Reilly, Bob P306
Reilly, Paul P436
Reilly, Janelle P456
Reilly, Katie P510
Reilly, Barbara G P553
Reilly, Theresa P604
Reilly, Rob W533
Reilly, Thomas E67
Reiman, Jason A384
Reimche, Brenda A P531
Reimer, Ronaldo A681
Reimer, Elizabeth P426
Reimer, Ronaldo P448
Reina, Ramon de la Riva W57
Reinauer, Greg P595
Reiner, Gary A183
Reiner, Deborah A379
Reiner, Carol P257
Reiners, Derek A561
Reinertsen, Inge W454
Reinhardt, Max E311
Reinhart, Thomas P289
Reinhart, Tom P289
Reinhart, Leslie P449
Reinhart, Charles E311
Reinsvold, Suize P301
Reis, Peter P12
Reis, Amy L P363
Reis, Cathleen P384
Reis, Danny Van Der E29
Reis, Bernard E305
Reischlein, Greg P376
Reiser, Michele W519
Reisig, Cliff P141
Reisinger, Helmut W372
Reiss, Rena A498
Reiten, R.Patrick A604
Reiter, Kara Andersen A430
Reiter, Joakim W520
Reith, Ian P222
Reitmajer, Stephanie P172
Reitsma, Raymond A514:E267
Reitz, Pamela P170
Reitzes, Mark A570
Reitzle, Wolfgang W140
Reizman, Elizabeth A98
Rekow, Elizabeth A696
Relf, Lauren P482
Relic, Zelko E15
Reller, Tami E385
Relly, J B P294
Remark, Megan P441
Rembisz, Adam P204
Remerowski, Gaia P591
Remillard, Michael P639
Remillard, Mike P639
Remnant, Philip W391
Remolana, Eli W70
Remolde, Cheryl P308
Remondi, John A546
Ren, Bing P182
Ren, Lin W97

576   HOOVER'S HANDBOOK OF EMERGING COMPANIES 2022

COMBINED HOOVER'S HANDBOOK INDEX OF EXECUTIVES

Ren, Shengjun W129
Ren, Tianbao W303
Ren, Lixin W378
Renard, Jean-Baptiste W346
Renaud, Dennis P405
Rench, Daniel P147
Rencoret, Jose Tomas Guzman W177
Renda, Larree A687
Rendle, Steven A115
Rendle, Linda A189
Rendle, Steven A836
Rendle, Linda A839
Renee, Hagen P112
Renfrew, William A321
Renk, Jerry E53
Renna, Michael E381
Renne, Louise A185:P122
Renner, Katy P161
Renner, Rob P214
Renninger, Richard A236
Renovales, Jaime Perez W61
Rensburg, Ihron W6
Rense, John P413
Renshaw, Tom P595
Rensing, Willy P152
Rensmon, P. Darryl E126
Renstroem, Lena W471
Rentfrow, Steve A P358
Rentler, Barbara A687
Rentz, Ann P421
Renuart, Gene P323
Renuart, Victor E203
Renwick, Edward P422
Reny, Luc W389
Repas, Gregory A508
Repenning, Brent E115
Repetz, Brian P459
Repo, Susan E277
Reppert, Joe P383
Rerkpiboon, Auttapol W393
Resamen, C B P292
Resch, Richard J P289
Resch, Eric W480
Resendez, Roberto A424
Resheske, Frances A216
Reshetar, Joseph P156
Reske, James A313:E165
Resnick, Andrea A759
Resnick, Alan P38
Resnick, Joseph D P215
Resta, Ferruccio W294
Restel, Anthony A317:E170
Restrepo, Robert A351:A680:E356
Retzer, Ingrid P51
Retzko, Ralf W27
Reuland, Charles P275
Reuss, Mark A349
Reuss, Herb J P285
Reuter, Debbie A382
Reuter, Heitho P653
Reuter, Debbie E211
Reutledge, Valinda P499
Revel-Muroz, Pavel W502
Revelle, Greg A459
Revels, Beverly P529
Reves, Josesph G P566
Revitsky, Steve P482
Revuelta, Alicia Reyes W57
Rewolinski, Andrew P413
Rex, Anne A61
Rex, John A823
Rex, Rock P413
Rexinger, Elwyn P345
Rexroad, Jerold A814
Rexroad, Sherry E391
Rexroad, Jerold E423
Reyes, Javier A186
Reyes, Luis A324
Reyes, Tomas N129
Reyes, Norman P133
Reyes, Marlena P154
Reyes, Emilia P159
Reyes, Isabel P190
Reyes, Marcelo P233
Reyes, Patricia P496
Reyes, James P498
Reyes, Basilio P572

Reyes, Luis W83
Reyes, Edwin Romualdo W83
Reyes, Jose Sanhueza W141
Reyes, Angelica W323
Reyes, Shirley E69
Reyes, Javier E84
Reyngoudt, Mark P437
Reynolds, Shelley A38
Reynolds, Eric A189
Reynolds, John A328
Reynolds, Douglas A617
Reynolds, Fredric A665
Reynolds, Christopher A726
Reynolds, Kim A736
Reynolds, Kathryn A738
Reynolds, Kinh P99
Reynolds, Karen P266
Reynolds, Sheila P267
Reynolds, Ronald P302
Reynolds, Walt P323
Reynolds, Julie P365
Reynolds, Dale P416
Reynolds, Yoke San L P439
Reynolds, Kimberly P502
Reynolds, Jason P507
Reynolds, Audrey P507
Reynolds, Kim P512
Reynolds, Kathryn P514
Reynolds, Paula W91:W342
Reynolds, Simone E72
Reynolds, E. Leland E166
Reynolds, Marshall E169:E395
Reynolds-Fletch, Janet A210
Reynoso, Charlie P534
Rez, Marta P P6
Reza, Tony P486
Rezet, Penny P17
Rhea, John A743
Rheaume, Lindsey A262:E126
Rhee, Don E315
Rheinheimer, Jon P286
Rhine, Richard P233
Rhinehart, Mary A364:W145
Rhoades, Ronald E82
Rhoads, Ann D P426
Rhoads, William P548
Rhoads, Ann E195:E342
Rhoden, Larry P517
Rhodes, William A84:A252
Rhodes, Ann A387
Rhodes, Jenny A614
Rhodes, Thomas A805
Rhodes, Chris P153
Rhodes, John B P206
Rhodes, Mike P259
Rhodes, Brad P384
Rhodes, Anne P395
Rhodes, Michael W497
Rhodes, Matthew E147
Rhodes, Jenny E317
Rhymer, Ernie P432
Rhyne, Anissa P163
Rhyu, James E393
Riach, Lorna P117
Rial, Sergio W61
Riano, Jewell P345
Riaz, Salma P275
Riazi, Atefeh A513:P328
Ribeiro, Fabio E37
Ricard, Corrine A539
Ricard, Denis W239
Riccardi, Daniela W273
Ricci, Jeff A386
Ricci, Giuseppe W185
Ricciardi, Christopher E89
Rice, Jill A102
Rice, Derica A134
Rice, Brian A151
Rice, Derica A152
Rice, Michael A597
Rice, David P46
Rice, April P46
Rice, David P57
Rice, Charles P129
Rice, Diane P141
Rice, Katie P163
Rice, Denise P501

Rice, Constance P534
Rice, Dame W258
Rice, Susan E140
Rice, Rex E155
Rice, John E270
Rice, Michael E307
Rich, Brian A190
Rich, Ronald A316
Rich, Melinda A491
Rich, John A602
Rich, Richard P133
Rich, Melinda P445
Rich, Robert P445
Rich, Judith F P604
Richard, Oliver A169
Richard, Mark A371
Richard, Jodi L A829
Richard, Michelle P70
Richard, Coco P75
Richard, Glenn P413
Richard, Andy P464
Richard, Stephane W372
Richard, Patrick W517
Richards, Emmet A126
Richards, Thomas A147
Richards, Mark A617
Richards, Michael A743
Richards, James J P146
Richards, Leslie P164
Richards, Catherine P220
Richards, Jeanne P315
Richards, James J P359
Richards, Tom P625
Richards, Emmet E54
Richards, Thomas E66
Richards, David E84
Richards, Mark E319
Richards, Jerald E329
Richardson, Scott A160
Richardson, John A286
Richardson, Mollie A323
Richardson, John A661
Richardson, Craig A812
Richardson, Brian A826
Richardson, Renee A839
Richardson, Chris P36
Richardson, Don P101
Richardson, Lily P120
Richardson, Ursula P135
Richardson, Leslee P139
Richardson, Don P142
Richardson, Gary P360
Richardson, Renee P643
Richardson, Xavier P646
Richardson, Karen W91
Richardson, Stephen E13
Richardson, Peter E28
Richardson, John E59
Richardson, Nina E90
Richardson, Troy E339
Richardson, Brian E428
Richcreek, M Jean P121
Richemont, Phillip P662
Richenhagen, Martin A636
Richer, Clare A641
Richerson, Michelle P490
Richey, Ellen E200
Richie, Laurel A377
Richieri, Richard E39
Richlovsky, Thomas A814:E424
Richman, Frederick A682
Richmond, Timothy A6
Richmond, Brent A853
Richmond, Estelle P146
Richmond, Olga P197
Richmond, Lynn P352
Richmond, Brent E444
Richoux, Donna P406
Richstone, Ellen E307
Richter, Glenn A426
Richter, Jeff P112
Richter, John P158
Richter, Dawn P375
Richter, Maria W402
Rick, Van M P120
Rickard, Matthew P98
Rickard, Deborah P333

Rickard, Jason E237
Ricketts, Carlton A149
Ricketts, Todd A697
Ricketts, Pete A738:P514
Rickhoff, Gerry P156
Ricks, David A11:A478
Ricks, Ron A726
Rico, Juliet P576
Ricupati, Agostino E100
Ridderbusch, Greg P235
Riddervold, Ingrid W454
Riddick, Frank E454
Riddle, Timothy A795
Riddle, Ashley P22
Riddle, Freeman E383
Riddle, Timothy E416
Rideout, Jeffrey E18
Rider, Stephanie P94
Rider, Matthew J. W13
Ridgeway, Alan A483
Ridings, Thomas E29
Ridley, Bruce A605
Ridley, Brad P84
Ridley, Marcus A P447
Riedel, Peter W222
Riedl, Melanie W246
Riedl, Georg W515
Riedman, Karol P381
Riedo, Francis X P286
Riefler, Linda E282
Rieg, James A780:P575
Riego, Henry Del P390
Rieke, Thomas P432
Riel, Susan A261:E126
Rieman, Garth A352
Riemer, Marey A867
Riemer, Julie P45
Riemer, Hans P352
Riener, Harald W515
Riesbeck, Richard E422
Riese, Ulf W470
Riester, Tom P638
Riesterer, Terry A684
Riew, John A780:P575
Riewe, Paul P557
Rifaie, Khairul W128
Rifkin, Daniel A215:E97
Rigatti, Maria A268
Rigby, Joseph A254
Rigby, Alan P71
Rigby, Joseph E381
Rigel, H. Edward E423
Rigg, Mark Knapp P121
Riggan, Mike A740:P516
Riggieri, Albert A18
Riggins, Gregory A439:P276
Riggle, Carrie A313:E165
Riggs, Kristen P384
Riggs, R. Lane A831
Riggs, Rita P489
Riggs, Jean P579
Rignac, Jean-Paul W175
Riksen, Todd A727
Riley, Kevin A319
Riley, Lynnette A735
Riley, Debbie P4
Riley, Donna P38
Riley, Blair P73
Riley, Tammy P261
Riley, Mike P362
Riley, Trent P426
Riley, Lynnette P511
Riley, Paul P561
Riley, Gillian W69
Riley, Christiana W160
Riley, Brendon W484
Riley, Bryant E42
Riley, Richard E123
Riley, Kevin E129
Rimar, Stephen P377
Rimer, Barbara A18
Rine, James A808:E421
Rineer, Tom P410
Rinehart, Charles A507
Rinehart, Doug P564
Riner, Donna P160
Riney, Stephen A64

HOOVER'S HANDBOOK OF EMERGING COMPANIES 2022

577

COMBINED HOOVER'S HANDBOOK INDEX OF EXECUTIVES

```
A = AMERICAN BUSINESS
E = EMERGING COMPANIES
P = PRIVATE COMPANIES
W = WORLD BUSINESS
```

Riney, Robert A381:P249
Ring, Nick A52
Ring, David A79
Ring, Tricia P163
Ring, David E34
Ringeisen, Berthold P217
Ringenbach, John A773
Ringgenberg, Jason A874
Ringgold, Sadie P91
Ringsted, Sean W126
Ringwald, Bradley E77
Rinker, Douglas E127
Rinn, Russell A745
Rintoul, David E197
Riopelle, Diani P467
Riordan, Kevin A102
Riordan, Michael C P428
Riordan, Christine E345
Rios, Holly A134:P87
Rios, Mabel P467
Ripley, Christopher A713
Rippe, Michelle P357
Ripple, David W P648
Rippy, John A675:E350
Riquelme, Bryant A702
Ris, Lauren A735:P511
Risberg, John F P312
Risch, Frank A629
Riseberg, David P332
Risen, Stan P170
Rishi, Girish A420
Rishi, Vibha W240
Risio, Gary De P54
Risk, Bonita E355
Risk-McElroy, Stephanie E355
Riske, Gordon W48
Riskey, Mary A801
Risley, Angie W258
Rispoli, Michael J P375
Ristuben, Steve P128
Risty, Barbara P463
Ritch, Jill A Alexander P627
Ritchey, Dean P400
Ritchey, Mike P520
Ritchie, Bradford A750:E394
Ritchotte, Alan P152
Ritenour, Jeffrey A243
Ritner, Carli P357
Ritrievi, Rory A529:E274
Rittapirom, Thaweelap W62
Rittenmeyer, Ronald A433:A765
Ritter, Thomas A9
Ritter, William A671
Ritter, Kate P564
Ritter, Ann P640
Ritter, Thomas E4
Ritter, Stephen E277
Ritter, Gordon E433
Rittershaussen, Joao W380
Ritts, Gregory J P27
Rittstieg, Andreas W91
Ritzmann, William A187:E85
Rivanis, Chris P116
Rivas, Isadore P248
Rivas, Manual P384
Rivas, Jesenia P415
Rivas, Maria E100
Rive, Ernesto Dalle W511
Rivenes, Gary P139
Rivera, Alfredo A196
Rivera, Sandra A282
Rivera, Frederick A383
Rivera, Sandra A421
Rivera, Efrain A443
Rivera, Alfredo A641
Rivera, Joseph P48
Rivera, Brandi P53
Rivera, Julie P127
Rivera, Fabian P132
Rivera, Karen P210
Rivera, Maria P377

Rivera, Paul P406
Rivera, Yesenia P467
Rivera, Cathleen M P468
Rivera, Amadeo P482
Rivera, Alma P610
Rivera, Julio P620
Rivera, Gerardo Clemente W83
Rivera, Susan Audrey W83
Rivera, Sebastian W110
Rivera, Susan W493
Rivera, Frederick E212
Rivero, Joan P253
Rivers, Marc W199
Rives, John P54
Rivet, Jeannine E3
Rivett, Phil W456
Rizk, Norman A730:P509
Rizulo, Frank G P571
Rizvi, Gowher P439
Rizza, Franco W58
Rizzardi, Russell A856
Rizzo, Mario A32
Rizzo, Bre P455
Rizzo, Renee M P632
Rizzuti, Chris P157
Rizzuti, Sergeant R P170
Rizzuti, Edward E12
Rn, Laurie B P220
Rn, Carol Bradley P294
Rn, Laura Espinosa PHD P336
Rn, Ann Cella P499
Roach, Sharon V P2
Roach, Dave P278
Roach, Mintha P287
Roach, Jill P594
Roach, David E423
Roan, Tiffany P12
Roark, Mark P598
Robaina, Ashley P612
Robb, Charles P459
Robb, Davon P545
Robb, Gary E102
Robb, Jeffery E111
Robbertz, Paul P182
Robbiati, Tarek A386
Robbins, Spencer A106
Robbins, Charles A182
Robbins, Paige A363
Robbins, Clifton S A513
Robbins, Ira A832
Robbins, Kenneth B P244
Robbins, Clifton S P328
Robbins, Claudia P467
Robbins, Larry P553
Robbins, Spencer E48
Robbins, Bradford E405
Robbins, Ira E431
Robbins-Meyer, H A224:P168
Roberson, Robin A94:E44
Roberson, Charles E244
Robert, Lucas P167
Robert, Gompf P170
Roberti, Isabel P60
Roberti, Jennifer P466
Roberto, Ann P444
Roberto, John P603
Roberts, Rebecca A6
Roberts, Daryl A44
Roberts, Diane A135
Roberts, Nolan A145
Roberts, Brian A203
Roberts, Ron A224
Roberts, Jonathan A232
Roberts, Michael A363:A405
Roberts, John A408
Roberts, Michael A490
Roberts, William R A512
Roberts, Michael A521
Roberts, Daniel A617
Roberts, Timothy A626
Roberts, Debbie A680
Roberts, Paul A683
Roberts, Sharon A733
Roberts, Jonathan A851
Roberts, Jeff P43
Roberts, Ryan P85
Roberts, Nolan P95

Roberts, Michael P98
Roberts, Anthony P141
Roberts, Alan P167
Roberts, Ron P168
Roberts, Michael P176
Roberts, Phyllis P220
Roberts, Kevin V P226
Roberts, Ben P315
Roberts, William R P324
Roberts, Charles C P330
Roberts, Jean P404
Roberts, Fred P408
Roberts, Ryan P422
Roberts, David P424
Roberts, Cory P466
Roberts, James M P477
Roberts, Charles W M P505
Roberts, Shauna R P601
Roberts, Brad P646
Roberts, Shelley W139
Roberts, Michael W234
Roberts, Simon W259
Roberts, Edwin D E157
Roberts, David E250
Roberts, Eiry E291
Roberts, Daniel E319
Roberts, Timothy E322
Roberts, Debbie E356
Robertshaw, Patricia P488
Robertson, Tammie A27
Robertson, Julie A281
Robertson, Peter A436
Robertson, Donald A577
Robertson, Euan A781
Robertson, Cliff P19
Robertson, Jake P225
Robertson, Jessica P226
Robertson, Steve P244
Robertson, William G P357
Robertson, James V P416
Robertson, Cliff A P459
Robertson, Euan P580
Robertson, Jeffrey P604
Robertson, Simon E149
Robertson-Keck, Karen P220
Robertstad, John P647
Robeson, Robin E E204
Robillard, Donald A168
Robillard, Jean P621
Robinette, Gary E P421
Robinette, Gary E377
Robins, Ronald A117
Robins, Scott A139
Robins, Christine A556
Robins, Linda P174
Robinson, Elizabeth A99
Robinson, Andy A112
Robinson, Lori A162
Robinson, Darryl A208
Robinson, Vicki A327
Robinson, Barry A331
Robinson, Kiersten A333
Robinson, William A346
Robinson, David A377
Robinson, Graham A569
Robinson, Dashiell A668
Robinson, Graham A731
Robinson, Sheila A739
Robinson, Mark A739
Robinson, Cathy A755
Robinson, Elizabeth A792
Robinson, Paul A846
Robinson, Joseph A853
Robinson, Jeff P9
Robinson, Ronnie P86
Robinson, Arthur P128
Robinson, Darryl P145
Robinson, Alva P146
Robinson, Chase P152
Robinson, Jim P155
Robinson, Cedric P160
Robinson, John P184
Robinson, Veronica P201
Robinson, Patricia P209
Robinson, Vicki P215
Robinson, John R P231
Robinson, Edmondo P240

Robinson, Mark P319
Robinson, Edward P359
Robinson, Ben P379
Robinson, Melissa P384
Robinson, John P389
Robinson, Dan P419
Robinson, Daniel P419:P419
Robinson, Allison P433
Robinson, Edwin P456
Robinson, Lisa P457
Robinson, Abby P490
Robinson, Sheila P515
Robinson, Mark P515
Robinson, David P542
Robinson, Mike P548
Robinson, Denise P565
Robinson, Carolyn P571
Robinson, Randal P613
Robinson, Linda P618
Robinson, Rayneil P620
Robinson, Samara P627
Robinson, Douglas P627
Robinson, King P632
Robinson, Dorothy P661
Robinson, Jonathan W38
Robinson, Anne W342
Robinson, Samuel W389
Robinson, Barry E178
Robinson, Donald E283
Robinson, Joseph E445
Robison, Mark A639
Robison, Kim A846
Robison, Mary P60
Robison, Randy P207
Robison, Mark E332
Robitaille, Mark P314
Robitaille, Carroll P356
Robles, Norberto A552
Robles, Ted P123
Robles, Norberto P369
Robles, Adriane P462
Robles, Monica P554
Robles, Claudia E69
Robo, James A327:A408:A560
Robusto, Dino A192
Rocap, Nisha A293:P211
Rocco, Anne W189
Roch, Lewis E68
Rocha, Oscar Gonzalez A723
Rocha, Zeb P404
Roche, Kevin A102
Roche, Talbott A271
Roche, Jean-Francois A364
Roche, John A375
Roche, Kevin P56
Roche, Brian P270
Roche, Michael W304
Roche, Robert E28
Rochelle, Anne La P101
Rochet, Lubomira A452
Rochon, Thomas A789
Rochow, Garrick A190:A219
Rock, Luke P424
Rocke, Javon P176
Rockenbach, John A738:P514
Rocker, Tchernavia A810
Rocker, Kenyatta A812
Rockett, Mike P491
Rocks, Patti A587:E302
Rockwell, Edward E144
Rocourt, Brittney P420
Rodak, Lory P161
Rodden, Lori A377
Roddenberry, Stephen A868
Roddy, Sonya P263
Rodell, Angela A27:P14
Roden, Laura A382:E211
Rodet, Vincent W175
Rodewald, Renee P38
Rodgers, Elliott A476:A477
Rodgers, Thomas A510
Rodgers, Susan P176
Rodgers, Elliott P297
Rodier, Richard E411
Rodino, Jeffrey E314
Rodis, Hallie P396
Rodkin, Gary A508

COMBINED HOOVER'S HANDBOOK INDEX OF EXECUTIVES

Rodrigue, Kathi P309
Rodrigues, Barry A103:P60
Rodrigues, Nicholas P145
Rodrigues, Henrique E37
Rodrigues, Michael E300
Rodriguez, Carlos A81
Rodriguez, Juan A204
Rodriguez, Javier A237
Rodriguez, Manuel Sanchez A293
Rodriguez, Cicely A303
Rodriguez, Javier A355
Rodriguez, Eduardo A593
Rodriguez, Jose A633
Rodriguez, Havidan A744
Rodriguez, Rudy P104
Rodriguez, Lara P156
Rodriguez, Martha P158
Rodriguez, Eliza P169
Rodriguez, Jessica P210
Rodriguez, Camille P218
Rodriguez, Yolanda P256
Rodriguez, Manuel P256
Rodriguez, Mayra P408
Rodriguez, Domingo C P488
Rodriguez, Dawn P494
Rodriguez, Barney P496
Rodriguez, Havidan P519
Rodriguez, Gabriela P520
Rodriguez, Cristella P627
Rodriguez, Florentino Perez W9
Rodriguez, Maria Soledad Perez W9
Rodriguez, Jose Mauricio W61
Rodriguez, Louisa W109
Rodriguez, Alejandro Perez W110
Rodriguez, David Ruelas W381
Rodriguez, David E24
Rodriguez-Galindo, Carlos P505
Roe, Scott A759
Roebuck, Rick P161
Roeck, Seppe De P84
Roedel, Kathryn E191
Roeder, Helene von W321
Roedler, Friedrich W187
Roehl, Kathy P592
Roemer, Dennis P505
Roemer, Aaron P654
Roer, David A237
Roest, Stan Vander P3
Roffler, Michael A323
Rogachev, Denis W386
Rogelstad, Timothy E309
Roger, Francois-Xavier W348
Rogers, Mark A58
Rogers, Carolyn A172
Rogers, James A195
Rogers, John A360
Rogers, R. Wade A411
Rogers, Amy A484
Rogers, Brian A488
Rogers, John A509
Rogers, Alex A656
Rogers, Brian A665
Rogers, William A796
Rogers, Steven A838
Rogers, Colleen A864
Rogers, Chris A869
Rogers, Carolyn P113
Rogers, Grant P122
Rogers, Jeffrey L P132
Rogers, Dennis P132
Rogers, James P140
Rogers, Harlan P153
Rogers, Mark P227
Rogers, Woody P251
Rogers, Gilbert L P298
Rogers, Greg P343
Rogers, Cleveland P365
Rogers, Rich P428
Rogers, Randy P533
Rogers, Frederick P564
Rogers, Amy P651
Rogers, Colleen P656
Rogers, Chris P659
Rogers, Mike W345
Rogers, John W533
Rogers, Michael E148
Rogers, Kristi E341

Rogerson, Craig A637
Rogge, James D P219
Rogge, Karen E304
Roggero,
   Dinorah A603:A603:P404:E310
Roggie, Brent P363
Roggin, Kevin P585
Rogier, Amy P362
Rohling, Daniel P207
Rohm, Estella P330
Rohmiller, Chelsee P381
Rohner, Urs W210
Rohr, Karl von W160
Rohrbach, Michelle E282
Rohrbacher, Markus W367
Rohrer, Katherine A18
Rohrer, Jennifer A570:P388
Rohrig, Jeff P537
Rohrs, Thomas E6
Roig, Ismael A69
Roitman, Jonathan A813
Rojas, Manuel F P71
Rojas, Jose Fernando Calderon W23
Rojas, Mauricio Rosillo W61
Rojas, Gonzalo Alberto Perez W61
Rojas, Jurgen Gerardo Loeber W171
Rojas, German Eduardo
   Quintero W171
Rojas, Hector Manosalva W171
Rojas, Rigoberto Rojo W177
Rojas, Jose Fernando Calderon W198
Rojas, Rogelio Rebolledo W215
Rojek, Kenneth J P379
Rojvatunyu, Kanchana W491
Rokach, Ronit Abramson W63
Roks, Edwin E404
Roland, Sandy P612
Rolando, Fredric V P362
Roldan, Isaac P103
Rolen, Templin P176
Rolfe, Harold A778:P561
Rolland, Marc W448
Rolle, Myron E3
Roller, David A206
Rollerson, Monica P17
Rollins, Gary E358
Rollins, Pamela E358
Rollison, Marvin L P209
Roloff, Richard P591
Rolston, Richard P175
Romain, Kenneth St. E327
Romaine, Mark A357
Romaine, Stephen A789
Roman, Michael A3
Roman, Guadalupe P180
Roman, Jose P602
Roman, Martin W334
Roman, Stephen E53
Roman, Jess E53
Roman, Eugene E144
Roman, Richard E297
Romancyk, Janet P162
Romanko, Michael E176
Romano, Kelly A806
Romano, Jenna P109
Romano, Joseph P162
Romano, Kelly E123
Romanowski, Paul A403
Romard, Ryan P539
Romberger, Scott A703
Rome, Amanda A871
Romeo, Fabio W391
Romero, Jose P129
Romero, Bethsabe P154
Romero, Ken P392
Romero, Tifinni P476
Romero, Nitza P530
Romero, Carlos P625
Romero, Axel W56
Rometty, Virginia A444
Romine, Michael P138
Rominger, Eileen A756
Romm, Sylvia P48
Rommel, Catherine T P564
Romo, Tammy A726:A765
Romo, Karen P134
Romoff, Jeffrey A A828:P634

Romojaro, Jaime Guardiola W57
Romond, Jennifer L P643
Romuld, Trine W454
Ron, Prill P409
Ronald, Mundy A737:P513
Ronan, Carey P58
Roncey, Franck W87
Rondeau, Linda P316
Rondeau, Geoffery E16
Rondinone, Ralph E436
Ronge, Catherine W133
Rongone, Bartolomeo W273
Ronkainen, Anni W275
Roobeek, Annemieke W278
Rood, Carol P144
Rood, Deb P447
Roodman, Richard D P431
Roof, Donald A820
Rooks, James V P500
Rooney, Robert A538
Rooney, Christina P133
Rooney, Jo Ann P305
Rooney, Gemma P616
Rooney, Bob W178
Rooney, David E288
Roos, Thomas A823
Roos, Andrew P233
Roosandaal, Blake Dan P74
Root, M. Darren A353
Root, Carole P30
Root, R Mark R P54
Root, Mark P54
Root, Wes P161
Root, George L P398
Root, M. Darren E192
Roozeboom, Oda P327
Roper, Ken P127
Roper, Pamela E105
Roppel, Frank A27
Rorsted, Kasper W12
Rosa, Enrica De A403
Rosa, David A430
Rosa, Dennis De P158
Rosa, James De P252
Rosa, Enrica De P256
Rosa, Mark P349
Rosado, Robert A739:P515
Rosamilia, Thomas A684
Rosano, Lawrence A554
Rosario, Angela P237
Rosario, Ramon Del W70
Rosario, Ramon Jaime Del W323
Rosario, Francisco Del W323
Rosati, Mario A694
Rosato, R. David A617:E319
Rosborough, Mark E163
Roscoe, Lauren P653
Rose, Clayton A96
Rose, Matthew K A122
Rose, M. Robert A136
Rose, Jody A143
Rose, Patricia A144
Rose, Timothy A223
Rose, Matthew A328
Rose, Michael A390
Rose, Dennis A639
Rose, Matthew K P80
Rose, Chris P128
Rose, Darlene P174
Rose, Lauren P293
Rose, Robert P308
Rose, Kathy P406
Rose, Brandon P604
Rose, Shawn W69
Rose, Alison W345
Rose, Eric E3
Rose, Jody E65
Rose, Nathaniel E206
Rose, Carlton E254
Rose, Gary E271
Rose, Dennis E332
Roseberry, Robert A372
Roseborough, Teresa A377:A395
Rosen, Roger A14
Rosen, Elaine A76
Rosen, Marc A476:A477
Rosen, Roger P5

Rosen, Marc P297
Rosen, Ronald P529
Rosen, Jodi P640
Rosen, Raymond P662
Rosen, Michel De W194
Rosen, Andrea W308
Rosen, Steven E108
Rosenbaum, Susan P68
Rosenbaum, Thomas P94
Rosenbaum, Nanette P519
Rosenberg, Steven A A713
Rosenberg, Burt P134
Rosenberg, Stuart A P243
Rosenberg, Lisa H P443
Rosenberg, Steven P554
Rosenberg, Joachim W523
Rosenberg, Bryan E219
Rosenberger, T P230
Rosenberger, Thomas P230
Rosenberger, Gwen P295
Rosenblatt, David A801
Rosenblatt, Sidney E426
Rosenblum, Jay A76
Rosenblum, David A374
Rosenbrock, Ralph P386
Rosendal, Jari W346
Rosene, Mona P182
Rosenfeld, Irene A656
Rosenfeld, Jeffrey P149
Rosenfeld, Klaus W444
Rosengren, Bjorn W5
Rosenhauer, Joan P103
Rosenkranz, David P398
Rosenstein, Beryl A778:P564
Rosensweig, Daniel A11
Rosenthal, Gary E A573:P391
Rosenthaler, Albert E A660
Rosgaard, Ole A367
Rosich, Jennifer P125
Rosier, William A578
Rosier, Micah P399
Rosiles, Adrian W69
Rosko, Thomas J P553
Roskopf, Mark A638:P426
Roskovich, Charles A652
Roslyn, Barbara A739:P515
Rosman, Adam A325
Rosner, Robert L P1
Rosowsky, David P588:P631
Ross, Cathy A92
Ross, Kendra A133
Ross, Steven A466
Ross, Susan A578
Ross, Andrew A609
Ross, Cheryl A A781
Ross, Linda A794
Ross, Ryan A865
Ross, Jeannette P18
Ross, Molly P264
Ross, James P270
Ross, Trisha P270
Ross, Yolanda P332
Ross, Katherine P379
Ross, Roger P579
Ross, Cheryl A P581
Ross, Linda P599
Ross, Amy P620
Ross, Thomas W P626
Ross, Bruce W412
Ross, Jonathan E91
Ross, Steven E244
Ross, Bridget E250
Ross, Patricia E289
Ross, Jack E346
Rosser, Carrene G P311
Rosser, Brian P445
Rosseter, Amanda A632
Rossi, James A186
Rossi, Mark P277
Rossi, Roberto Angelini W33
Rossi, Simone W175
Rossi, Roberto Angelini W177
Rossi, Salvatore W482
Rossi, Jerome E8
Rossi, James E84
Rossi, Jack E169
Rossmeissl, Jim P546

HOOVER'S HANDBOOK OF EMERGING COMPANIES 2022

COMBINED HOOVER'S HANDBOOK INDEX OF EXECUTIVES

A = AMERICAN BUSINESS
E = EMERGING COMPANIES
P = PRIVATE COMPANIES
W = WORLD BUSINESS

Rossomanno, Jennifer P120
Rossotti, Charles A129
Rostan, Richard A289
Rostrup, Jorgen Arentz W483
Roszko, Danielle P424
Roth, David A70
Roth, Kellylee A670
Roth, Robert A727
Roth, Kelsey A739
Roth, Daniel A794
Roth, Norman P87
Roth, Greg P119
Roth, Chris P149
Roth, Steven J P179
Roth, Colin P213
Roth, Kellylee P440
Roth, Robert P495
Roth, Chris P507
Roth, Kelsey P515
Roth, Daniel P599
Roth, Paul P625
Roth, Sabine W227
Roth, Ronald E86
Roth, Steven E304
Rothberger, Richard K P469
Rothermel, Daniel A229
Rothermel, Paige P78
Rothermel, Daniel E112
Rothkopf, Maximilian W219
Rothman, Thomas A128
Rothman, Irving A386
Rothschild, Jonathan P135
Rothschild, David de W106
Rothstein, Robin D P536
Rotsztain, Diego A748
Rottenberg, Julie A839
Rotter, Franz W521
Rottigni, Marco W251
Roualet, Mark A345
Rougny, Pierre P200
Roukhadze, Elena V P566
Roulet, Gary P653
Rounce, Justin A145:P95
Rounds, Bruce P23
Rountree, Arish P121
Roupie, Christophe E262
Rous, Dana P84
Rouse, Layla P126
Rouse, Jon P266
Rouse, Donald J P452
Rouse, Thomas B P452
Rouse, Bryan P466
Roush, John E6:E250
Roussat, Olivier W90:W133
Rousseau, Henri-Paul A695
Rousseau, Jean M P171
Rousseau, Jean P171
Rousseau, David P460
Rousseau, Michele W175
Rousseau, Laurent W428
Roussel, Stephane W518
Rousselin, Jorge P123
Routh, Curtiss P464
Rouvitha-panou, Irene W188
Roux, David A132
Roux, Bob A483
Roux, Roger G P434
Roverato, Jean-Francois W174
Rovey, Paul P610
Rovig, Joseph A571
Rovinescu, Calin W69:W82
Rowan, Sherry A166:P110
Rowatt, Ashley P236
Rowe, Robert Scott A145
Rowe, Sharon A186
Rowe, Zane A841
Rowe, Mike P35
Rowe, Jeanne M P45
Rowe, Robert Scott P95
Rowe, John P132
Rowe, Steve P388

Rowe, Jane W178
Rowe, Steve W311
Rowe, S. Jane W498
Rowe, Sharon E84
Rowland, Sandra A598
Rowland, Suzanne A702
Rowley, Stuart A333
Rowly, Cade P525
Roy, Michael Le A493
Roy, J Steven P1
Roy, Raja P542
Roy, Nilanjan W247
Roy, Sumit E347
Royal, Pamela A254
Royalty, James A427
Royse, Anthony P303
Rozado, Carmen Fernandez W9
Rozado, Maria del Carmen
  Fernandez W172
Rozak, Mary P155
Rozanski, Horacio A129
Rozzi, Ted P154
Ruan, Qi W117
Ruark, Jennifer P355
Rubananko, Yoram A223
Rubenstein, William A101
Rubenstein, David A152
Ruberg, David E120
Ruberti, Alexandre E74
Rubey, Wayne A P585
Rubin, Matthew A791
Rubin, Matt P209
Rubin, Bruce P595
Rubin, Elana W484
Rubin, Robert E147
Rubin, Jonathan E399
Rubini, Marina W294
Rubino, Andrew A773
Rubino, Frank P559
Rubinstein, Jerold H E429
Rubio, Teresa Martin-Retortillo W72
Rubporn, Tienchai W284
Ruby, Brian P36
Rucci, Corey E140
Rucker, Kim A160:A404:A496
Rucker, Ann A517
Rucker, Craig P72
Rucker, Kevin P76
Rucker, Craig P231
Rucker, Ann P331
Ruckphaopunt, Kukkong W62
Rudd, W. Troy A15
Rudd, Amber W112
Ruddy, David A30:P21
Ruddy, Joseph P P642
Ruddy, Benjamin E126
Rude, Brian P238
Rude, Maureen E126
Rudloff, Hans-Joerg W411
Rudnick, Ellen A610
Rudolph, Eric P151
Rudolph, Sandra P272
Rudolph, Bill P578
Rudolph, Frederick W P578
Rudolph, Philip J P578
Rudy, Christine P166
Rudy, Joseph P536
Rudy, Kazuko W430
Rudy, Thomas E83
Rue, William A704:E367
Ruediger, Michael W190
Ruedisser, Michele Sutter W187
Ruesterholz, Virginia A377
Ruff, Ellen E147
Ruffin, Marshall P263
Ruffray, Benoit De W174
Ruggeri, Rachel A732
Ruggeri, John A847:P229
Ruggieri, Raffaello W252
Ruggiero, Mark A416
Ruggiero, Nick P122
Ruggiero, Mark E226
Ruggles, Lisa E104
Ruh, William W306
Ruhig, Chris P360
Ruhlman, Barbara E332
Ruhlman, J. Ryan E332

Ruhlman, Robert E332
Rui, Yong W292
Ruisanchez, Raul Jacob A723
Ruiz, Melanie A7
Ruiz, Andrew A122
Ruiz, Jose M A661
Ruiz, Aurelio A661
Ruiz, Andrew P80
Ruiz, Nichole P82
Ruiz, Daniel P171
Ruiz, Jose P193
Ruiz, Israel P318
Ruiz, Jose M P432
Ruiz, Aurelio P432
Ruiz, Bernardo P471
Ruiz, Rosa P530
Ruiz, Maria Elena P646
Ruiz, Ignacio Herrero W173
Ruiz, Roque Velasco W525
Ruiz, Thomas E228
Rukpanich, Sunthorn W491
Rukwied, Joachim W80
Rull, Arlyn P341
Rulla, Bill P345
Rully, Rebecca P204
Rumfelt, Karen A740:P516
Rumford, Amy E78
Rumler, John P25
Rummelhoff, Irene W363
Rummelt, Andreas W46
Rumsey, Jennifer A228:E215
Runcie, Robert W P90
Rund, Doug P394
Rundatz, Frank A866:P657
Runge, Alan P347
Runger, Cindy E169
Runion, Christopher E153
Runje, Zeljko W411
Runkle, Brian A851
Ruocco, Andy P538
Rupe, Michael D P120
Rupert, Nora P467
Rupp, Christine A28
Rupp, Lorie A312
Rupp, Christine P18
Ruppert, Paul A254
Ruppert, Craig A693
Ruppert, Rob P424
Ruppert, Bradley E247
Ruppert, Michael E269
Ruppert, Craig E360
Ruscitto, Daniel P627
Rusckowski, Stephen A659
Rush, David A139:P361
Rush, Greg P406
Rush, Jean E4
Rush, Blair E83
Rushing, Rodney A707:E368
Rushton, Clifford P460
Rushton, Tim P483
Rusk, Dain A652
Rusnak, Gregory J P428
Rusniak, Sara P149
Russ, Gary P488
Russel, Kim P91
Russell, Kristin A71
Russell, John A190:A219
Russell, Kenneth A388
Russell, Paula A601
Russell, Kimberly A797
Russell, David A875
Russell, Brant P44
Russell, Howard P118
Russell, Craig P139
Russell, Martin P143
Russell, Kimberly P173
Russell, Michael P224
Russell, Audra P228
Russell, Ben P452
Russell, Mary Beth P497
Russell, Richard J P547
Russell, Melissa P562
Russell, J Calvin P570
Russell, Nancy W213
Russell, Stuart W250
Russell, Scott W419
Russell, Joyce E74

Russell, Erin E131
Russell, Cornelius E163
Russell, Erin E240
Russell, James E250
Russell, Edward E342
Russick, Andrew K P404
Russo, Michael A330
Russo, Patricia A349:A515
Russo, Marc A534
Russo, Ralph P483
Russo, Harold P660
Russon, Charles W6
Russwurm, Siegfried W490
Rust, Steven A102
Rust, Bradley A353
Rust, Michael A675
Rust, Edward A691
Rust, Rosemary P304
Rust, Bradley E192
Rust, Michael E350
Ruth, Kim A795
Ruth, Jim E142
Ruth, Jon E232
Ruth, Kim E416
Ruthenbeck, Denise P193
Rutherford, Denise A3
Rutherford, William A379
Rutherford, Boyd K A737
Rutherford, Janice P168
Rutherford, Boyd K P513
Ruths, Marina P29
Rutishauser, Lucy A713
Rutkowski, Claire P361
Rutkowski, Joseph E232
Rutland, James B P347:P348
Rutledge, Elizabeth A46
Rutledge, William L A299
Rutledge, Napoleon A350
Rutledge, Robin P323
Rutledge, Stephanie E204
Ruttanaporn, Sarut W441
Rutten, Giel A58
Rutter, Marc P96
Ruud, David A258
Ruud, Yngve W287
Ruxandra, Oana A846
Ruz, Francisco W179
Ruzzo, John N A7
Rw, Wilson P418
Ryan, Jason A163
Ryan, James A285
Ryan, Christina A353
Ryan, Sharon A427
Ryan, Kevin A453
Ryan, Lucy A569
Ryan, James A585
Ryan, Michael P A598
Ryan, Timothy A695
Ryan, Kathleen A847
Ryan, Cicely P18
Ryan, Laura P64
Ryan, William P134
Ryan, John P159
Ryan, Leslie P164
Ryan, John P180
Ryan, Kevin P267
Ryan, Philip P267
Ryan, Robert P268
Ryan, Chris P319
Ryan, Michael P327
Ryan, Lisa P346
Ryan, Casey P381
Ryan, Michael P384
Ryan, David P470
Ryan, William J P477
Ryan, Edward P565
Ryan, John M P642
Ryan, Fred M P646
Ryan, T. Timothy W213:W389
Ryan, Daniel E13
Ryan, Gavin E72
Ryan, Jennifer E129
Ryan, Patrick E164:E164
Ryan, Thomas E176
Ryan, Christina E192
Ryan, James E199
Ryan, Christopher E244

COMBINED HOOVER'S HANDBOOK INDEX OF EXECUTIVES

Ryan-Dennis, Kimberly E215
Ryback, Andrew E327
Rybar, Ronald E160
Ryburn, Nancy L P647
Rychlak, Joseph F P37
Rychlak, Lawrence E344
Ryder, John A768
Ryder, Mark P292
Ryder, David P640
Ryerkerk, Lori A160
Ryerson, Erika A742:P518
Rylander, Stephen P65
Ryman, Dave P109
Rynaski, Todd A812
Ryner, Robert P467
Ryu, Jaewon A343:P225

S

S, Jeffrey A A322
Saam, Harith P206:P373
Saari, Carolyn P305
Saari, Hannu W470
Saavedra, Aurora P454
Saba, Peter E362
Sabag, Mark W487
Sabaini, Patricio Gomez W179
Sabanci, Erol W217
Sabanci, Serra W217
Sabanovic, Ruza W483
Sabat, Joseph A294:E156
Sabater, Carlos A448
Sabatini, Gino E443
Sabatino, Thomas A767
Sabbagh, Iyad P200
Sabbatini, Brian P638
Sabeh, Christina M P20
Sabel, Myra A734:P510
Sabelhaus, Melanie E124
Sabella, Deborah P496
Sabersky, Abraham P464
Sabeti, Pardis A235
Sabia, Jim A218
Sabia, Maureen W101
Sabin, Jeff P74
Sabo, Elias E97
Sabol, Michelle P115
Sabry, James W408
Saccamano, Bob P471
Saccareccia, Angela P579
Saccaro, James A106
Sacchi, Guido A358
Sacco, Henry P90
Sacco, Barbara P290
Sacco, Frank V P486
Sacerio, Joan P476
Sachdev, Amit A835
Sachs, Andrew A229
Sachs, Bruce A835
Sachs, Andrew E112
Sachse, David A94:E45
Sackett, Neil P101
Sackett, Walter P283
Sackman, Stuart A81
Sacks, Anelise A61
Sacks, Peter A208:P146
Sacks, Ian E344
Sacristan, Carlos Ruiz A723
Sada, Armando Garza W22
Sadana, Sumit A527
Sadasivam, Shaker E224
Sadi, Ahmed Bin Hamed bin Hilal Al W64
Sadid, Hossein P102
Sadler, Robert A491
Sadler, Carole A736
Sadler, Eric P228
Sadler, Carole P512
Sadlier, Jeremy A15:P7
Sadofsky, Lynn P470
Sadolin, Annette W168
Sadoun, Arthur W395
Sadove, Stephen A67
Sadowski, Peter T A303
Sadowski, John A693:E360
Sadowsky, Allison P381

Sadro, Cheryl A P325
Sadurska, Malgorzata W70
Sadygov, Famil W208:W385
Saeed, Sultan Bin W423
Saegusa, Yukari A217
Saehler, Jeff P307
Saeki, Ichiro W257
Saeki, Kaname A257
Saeki, Yasumitsu W355
Saenz, Luis A741
Saenz, Denise P174
Saenz, Luis P517
Saether, Glenn W454
Saez, Baruc W255
Safadi, Mazen P526
Safady, Edward A646:E336
Safai, Bijan P415
Saffer, Lori Polep P152
Safyer, Steven M P89:P352
Saga, Kosuke W468
Sagalyn, Lynne E52
Sagan, Leo E448
Sagara, Kevin A705
Sagara, Akihiko W312
Sagartz, John E229
Sagehorn, David E81
Sagen, James P198
Sager, Bertrand W72
Saggau, David P235
Sah, Amit W134
Saha, Saugata A691
Sahashi, Toshiyuki W461
Sahgal, Raghav W359
Sahney, Nitin E151
Sahni, Payal A622
Saiaki, Hitoshi W170
Saich, John A703
Saideman, Susan A177
Saigh, Alexandre Teixeira de Assumpcao W506
Saik, Walker E327
Saiki, Akitaka W325
Saiki, Naoko W450
Saiki, Mitsushi W494
Saikia, Sangeeta A779:P567
Sailer, Daniel E68
Sainct, Frederique W489
Saindon, Robert P405
Saines, Ian E9
Sainsbury, Anna E283
Saint, Frederick E104
Saint-Affrique, Antoine de W152
Saint-Geours, Frederic W106
Saintil, Merline A102:A763
Saito, Steven P318
Saito, Masahiro W66
Saito, Toshihide W127
Saito, Takeshi W182
Saito, Kazuo W216
Saito, Kiyomi W268
Saito, Yasushi W272
Saito, Takahiro W435
Saito, Yasuhiko W437
Saito, Kinji W469
Saito, Noboru W479
Saito, Masanori W496
Saito, Masaaki W538
Saiyawan, Wasin W441
Sajdak, Guida E448
Sajor, Mike W195
Saka, Tamer W217
Sakach, Andrew P492
Sakaguchi, Masatoshi W68
Sakai, Akira W36
Sakai, Kiwamu W170
Sakai, Akira W228
Sakai, Noriaki W240
Sakai, Soji W312
Sakai, Ichiro W314
Sakai, Tetsuro W327
Sakai, Takako W350
Sakai, Toshiyuki W368
Sakai, Michio W491
Sakai, Kazunori W496
Sakaji, Masayuki W491
Sakakibara, Sadayuki W268
Sakakibara, Ken W377

Sakamoto, Jennifer P160
Sakamoto, Osamu W67
Sakamoto, Hideyuki W328:W357
Sakamoto, Shinji W378
Sakane, Masahiro W268:W475
Sakanushi, Tomohiro W403
Sakata, Mark P378
Sakata, Seiji W403
Sakellariou, Anastasia W27
Sakellaris, George E19
Saker, Richard A842:P645
Sakkab, Nabil A36
Saklad, Hunter E378
Sakon, Yuji W317
Saksena, Asheesh A777
Sakuntanaga, Poonnis W284
Sakurada, Kengo W452
Sakuragi, Kimie W255
Sakurai, Eriko W463
Sala, Umberto della A448
Sala, Aurora Cata W57
Salagubang, Evelyn W83
Salakas, Nikolaos W27
Salama, Khaled N P442
Salamone, Denis A491
Salanger, Matthew A546
Salanger, Atthew J P611
Salas, Hernan Arellano W56
Salas, Sergio Avila W59
Salatt, Rana W134
Salaun, Isabelle W174
Salazar, Maria P54
Salazar, Deanna P78
Salazar, Guadalupe P143
Salazar, Claudia P166
Salazar, Victor P207
Salazar, Merenda P311
Salazar, Cindy P381
Salazar, Margaret P522
Salbod, Stephen P403
Saleh, Paul N A213:P150
Salehi, Shahbaz P193
Salehpour, Ali A66
Saleki-Gerhardt, Azita A6
Salem, Paul A524
Salem, Deeb P604
Salem-Jackson, Kim E11
Salemi, Donna P128
Salen, Kristina A714
Salerno, Frederic A422
Salesky, Bryan E632
Salgado, Erica P504
Saliba, Tony E P585
Salibello, Salvatore E253
Saligram, Ravi A436
Saligram, Ravichandra A556
Saligram, Ravi P271
Salinas, Jerry A227
Salinas, Andres P349
Salinas, Erwin Kaufmann W177
Salins, Peter D A744:P519
Salisbury, John P347
Salla, Francis La A99
Salle, Charles M P47
Salley, Robert P457
Salls, Bradley P198
Salluzzo, Richard P649
Salm, Marc A652
Salmirs, Scott A7
Salmon, Thomas A114:A585
Salmon, Sandy A736
Salmon, Tom P70
Salmon, Sandy P512
Salom, Leovigildo W498
Salotti, Valentina P266
Salovey, Peter P661
Salpietro, Andrea W294
Salsberg, Eric W191
Salsbury, Jill P402
Salters, Heather P186
Saltich, Daniel J P476
Saltiel, Albert A84
Saltzman, Paul A261
Saltzman, Dan P131
Saltzman, Paul E126
Saltzman, David E291
Salus, Rae P379

Salute, Richard E292
Salvador, Scot A797
Salvador, Gary P354
Salvador, Allan P534
Salvadori, Daniel A4
Salvaggio, Anthony J P149
Salvaggio, Thomas P149
Salvati, Peter P194
Salvato, Alfred P593
Salvatore, Bryan A375
Salvatore, David P132
Salvesbergh, Fred P65
Salyer, Kelly P157
Salz, Michael E164
Salzano, Mary P236
Salzman, Marian A625
Salzwedel, Nancy P415
Samaddar, Sanjay W39
Samant, Rahul A242
Samant, Shashank A584:A584
Samarasekera, Indira W306
Samath, Jamie A30
Samet, Kenneth A A512:P324
Samet, Kent P646
Samii, Jason P59
Sammons, John A724
Samms, Caswell P503
Samper, Cristi N P569
Sample, John A147:E66
Samples, Dustin P19
Sampsell, David E118
Sampson, Heath P349
Sampson, Luke P361
Sams, Jeffrey P355
Sams, Louise E104
Samsonov, Anastasia P402
Samstag, Karl W367
Samuel, Ronald A628:E324
Samuels, Ivanetta E18
Samuelson, Scott A45
Samuelson, Errol A877
Samuelson, Bonnie M P45
Samuelson, Jonas W3
Samujh, Nishlan W253
Samz, Jeff P257
Sanada, Yukimitsu W338
Sanal, Cemal W540
Sanborn, Richard A279
Sanborn, Cynthia A566
Sanborn, Richard E E142
Sanchack, Erich E120
Sanchez, Francisco A68
Sanchez, Adalio A88
Sanchez, Robert A217
Sanchez, Pablo A405
Sanchez, Antonio A424
Sanchez, Robert A689:A771
Sanchez, Esther P71
Sanchez, Anna V P122
Sanchez, Ronda P159
Sanchez, Dana P171
Sanchez, Terry P202
Sanchez, Charlie P242
Sanchez, Alejandra P257
Sanchez, Anthony P261
Sanchez, Rolando Arias W56
Sanchez, Frederic W372
Sanchez, Julio Beraun E37
Sanchez, Perfecto E403
Sand, Jamie P212
Sand, Michael E409
Sandberg, Rebecca A801
Sandberg, Cecilia W48
Sandbrook, William E94
Sander, Ed P418
Sandercock, Brett E352
Sanders, H. Robert A162
Sanders, Scott A216
Sanders, A. Shane A235
Sanders, Robert A280
Sanders, Carol A311
Sanders, Duane A A451
Sanders, Dax A456
Sanders, Corey A524
Sanders, Dan A729
Sanders, W. Reid A801

COMBINED HOOVER'S HANDBOOK INDEX OF EXECUTIVES

A = AMERICAN BUSINESS
E = EMERGING COMPANIES
P = PRIVATE COMPANIES
W = WORLD BUSINESS

Sanders, Lezlie P46
Sanders, John P103
Sanders, Preston P132
Sanders, Michael P221
Sanders, Jeff P296
Sanders, Jeffrey D P308
Sanders, Morgan P363
Sanders, Stephanie P406
Sanders, Thomas P544
Sanders, Courtney P624
Sanders, Randy P637
Sanders, Carol W399
Sanders, E. Lawrence E96
Sanders, Dena E284
Sanders, John E297
Sanderson, Troy A285
Sanderson, La Verne P193
Sanderson, Scott P554
Sandgaard, Thomas E457
Sandgren, James A585
Sandhar, Karamjit W111
Sandifer, Marcus E74
Sandler, Debra A68:A252
Sandlin, Scott P226
Sandman, Dan A541
Sando, Gabriel P307
Sandoval, Johnny P213
Sandoz, Jonathan H A166:P110
Sandoz, Didier W448
Sandri, Marcio A601
Sandri, Fabio A627
Sands, Richard A218
Sands, Rob A218
Sands, Jeff P128
Sands, Lester P270
Sands, Rob P403
Sands, Tim P642
Sands-Caldwell, Autumn P537
Sandstrom, Alexander P40
Sandt, Susan V P245
Sandvik, Helvi P361
Sanfiel, Joaquin Cruz W177
Sanford, Linda A428
Sanford, Brent A739
Sanford, Robin P123
Sanford, Julie P467
Sanford, Brent P515
Sanford, Barbara P612
Sanford, Glenn E152
Sanghi, Steve A525
Sanghvi, Rakesh W395
Sangiambut, Manop W441
Sangiovanni-Vincente, Alberto E62
Sangkanarubordee, Sathit W113
Sanguinetti, Kevin A294:E155
Sani, Suresh A832:E431
Sanint, Gabriel Jaramillo W109
Sanjines, Javier Gerardo
  Astaburuaga W198
Sanker, Bethany E42
Sankey, Greg P580
Sanman, Randall P P235
Sanna, Bastiano A835
Sanodo, Raquel P256
Sanphasitvong, Umroong W98
Sansbury, Bryan E251
Sansone, Thomas A434
Sansone, Judith A755
Sansone, Christopher E228
Sant, R William Van E189
Santacroce, Kevin A246
Santamans, Carlos Ventura W57
Santamaria, Mary Catherine
  Elizabeth W70
Santana, Ralph A252
Santana, Rafael A792
Santana, Megan A826
Santana, Rafael A841
Santana, Megan E428
Santaniello, Daniel E161
Santarosa, Romolo A374

Santavanond, Pativate W284
Santelises, Sonja B P56
Santella, Giuseppe W511
Santelli, Jonathan A663
Santi, Ernest A363:A415
Santi, Gian Luca W511
Santiago, Karen A134
Santillan, Alfredo A P240
Santillan, Leandro W323
Santilli, Paula A619
Santilli, Ann M P303
Santino, Anthony P596
Santoki, Tsutomu P527
Santomero, Anthony W399
Santone, Angela A78
Santora, Gregory E15
Santoro, Nicola E291
Santoroski, Richard E206
Santos, Janet A15
Santos, Bernerd Da A17
Santos, Esteban A57
Santos, Daniel A735
Santos, Janet P7
Santos, Rebecca P236
Santos, Antelmo P393
Santos, Daniel P511
Santos, Montiel Delos W83
Santos, Roberto W83
Santos, Pedro Manuel de Castro Soares
  dos W263
Santos, Jose Manuel Soares dos W263
Santos, Marcos Antonio Molina
  dos W309
Santos, Marcia Aparecida Pascoal
  Marcal dos W309
Sanusi, Lamido W335
Sanyal, Dev W91
Sanz, Carlos Gustavo Cano W171
Sanz, Francisco Garcia W227
Sanzone, Virginia E220
Sanzone, ToniAnn E443
Sap, Bart W507
Saperstein, Andrew A538
Saperstein, Karen A702
Sapp, Betty A92
Sapp, Jennifer P248
Sapp, William P464
Sappington, Jonathan P37
Saptharishi, Mahesh A540
Saputo, Lino W341
Saraei, Armin A367
Saran, Atul E134
Sarandos, Theodore A551
Sarasin, Kalin W270
Sardo, Michele P165
Sargent, Angela A340
Sargent, Annie P408
Sargent, Dale P649
Sargent, Ronald E176
Sargent, Gregory E422
Sarigaphuti, Chantanida W441
Sarin, Arun A697
Sarin, Aradhana W46
Sarma, Karthik A87
Sarno, Domenic J P133
Sarnoff, Ann A612
Sarnoff, Mark P128
Sarode, Anuja P614
Sarsam, Tony A727
Sarsfield, Sally P53:P298
Sartain, Elizabeth A494
Sartain, Meg P54
Sartain, Paul P323
Sartorel, George W391
Sarver, M. Adam A314
Sarver, Billy A738
Sarver, Robert A857
Sarver, Billy P514
Sarver, Robert E447
Sarwal, Aarti P644
Sasae, Kenichiro W328
Sasagawa, Atsushi W367
Sasajima, Kazuyuki W148
Sasaki, Tomohiko W34
Sasaki, Mami W150
Sasaki, Shigeo W268
Sasaki, Hiroko W439

Sasaki, Takuo W500
Sash, Nick P259
Sasich, Keith N P285
Sass, Steven P602
Sass, Allan E191
Sassani, Manzar P563
Sassano, Carla A178
Sassano, Joseph P173
Sassenfeld, Peter-Wilhelm W227
Sasser, Bob A253
Sasser, Gary P52
Sasser, Gary D P53
Sasser, Robert P58
Sasso, Louis P343
Sastre, Maria A579
Satake, Yasumine W468
Satchi-Fainaro, Ronit W487
Satchwell, Jennifer P359
Sathvik, Bhushan P356
Sathyanarayanan, Bala A367
Sato, Lisa P402
Sato, Brandon P408
Sato, Samuel M P556
Sato, Katsuya W66
Sato, Yoshiro W127
Sato, Koji W150
Sato, Seiji W272
Sato, Kiyoshi W314
Sato, Hiroshi W327
Sato, Teiichi W350
Sato, Naoki W354
Sato, Takehito W367
Sato, Toshimi W367
Sato, Yumiko W375
Sato, Mototsugu W378
Sato, Hiroshi W461
Sato, Shigeki W479
Sato, Minoru W491
Sato, Koji W501
Satriano, Pietro A154
Satter, Muneer P569
Satterfield, Adam A584
Satterlee, Scott A296
Satterlee, Maleia P353
Satterthwaite, Livingston A228
Sattgast, Rich P517
Saucier, Grady P348
Sauder, Kevin E155
Sauer, Melissa P524
Sauer, Thomas W190
Sauer, Michael E140
Saueressig, Thomas W419
Saugier, Jean-Marc W398
Saun, Bruce Van A185:A536
Saunders, Neil A91
Saunders, Brenton A182
Saunders, Jim P364
Saunders, Jeff P366
Saunders, Steven W P473
Saunders, Rosie P524
Saunders, Donna P646
Saunders, Mark W16
Saunders, Paul E174
Saunders, F. E174
Saunier, Edwin A747
Saunier, Thomas W428
Saunier, Edwin E391
Sauvage, Edouard W184
Sauvie, Jeff P102
Savage, E. Jean A860
Savage, Jeffrey A871
Savage, Troy P P129
Savage, Brianne P163
Savage, Karen P503
Savage, Kelly P624
Savage, Sheri E420
Savard, Matt P172
Savarese, Kathleen A781:P580
Savart, Michel W106
Savastano, Albert A330
Savickas, Diana P400
Saville, Paul A578
Savitch, Lane P278
Savoff, Mark T P206
Savoie, Andree W341
Savoy, Kevin A25
Savoy, Brian D A259

Savoy, Michelle W290
Sawada, Michitaka W269:W378
Sawan, Wael W434
Sawers, John W91
Sawhney, Inderpreet W247:E215
Sawicki, Robert P401
Sawyer, Robin A144
Sawyer, Joy P139
Sawyer, Daryl P140
Sawyer, Alison P461
Sawyer, Robert W527
Sax, Jeff P170
Saxon, Laura P419
Saxon, Helena W446
Saxton, Sean P123
Saxton, Pamela L P594
Sayavedra, Laura P343
Sayer, Kevin E117
Sayles, Andy P432
Sayley, Elaine A739:P515
Saylor, Collin P284
Sayward, Shelley E69
Sazdanoff, Catherine E270
Scadina, Mark R E155
Scaff, Joe P636
Scaglione, D A583
Scagliotti, R. Michael E364
Scalia, Christopher A384
Scalzo, Bernie A224:P172
Scamihorn, Randy P140
Scaminace, Joseph A180:A609
Scanlan, Agnes A796
Scanlan, John P138
Scanlan, Agnes E344
Scanlon, Meghan A132
Scanlon, George A468
Scanlon, Donald P71
Scanlon, John P106
Scanlon, Deborah P P171
Scannell, John A491
Scannell, Timothy E233
Scantlan, Donald P467
Scarantino, Charles P443
Scarborough, Dean A151
Scarborough, Joel A359
Scarborough, Dean A364
Scarborough, Leslie P253
Scarborough, Laurie P648
Scarlett, Kamy A115
Scarlett, Catherine A546
Scarlett, Stacy P147
Scarola, James A260
Scaroni, Bruno Andrea W43
Scavilla, Daniel E195
Scavuzzo, Anthony A279:E142
Scearcy, Lynda A709:E370
Sceppaguercio, Maria A452
Sceti, Elio Leoni A460
Schaad, Jeff P378
Schaaf, Renee A641
Schaaf, Libby P130
Schach, Eric J P491
Schachinger, Joseph A507
Schacht, Jessica P476
Schacht, Horst W287
Schachtel, John E348
Schack, Wesley von E404
Schade, Christian E234
Schadler, Alletta E84
Schaedler, Barbara W408
Schaefer, Francine A15
Schaefer, Steven A232
Schaefer, Francine P7
Schaefer, Pamela P505
Schaefer, Charles E201
Schaeffer, Melissa A23
Schaeffer, Aaron P284
Schaeffer, Damon P361
Schaer, Michael P75
Schafer, Kevin A78:P47
Schafer, Amanda P116
Schafer, Curtin P120
Schafer, Dana Lee P579
Schafers, Kelley P609
Schaffer, Stewart P64
Schaffner, Jerry A388
Schale, David P54

582

HOOVER'S HANDBOOK OF EMERGING COMPANIES 2022

COMBINED HOOVER'S HANDBOOK INDEX OF EXECUTIVES

Schalekamp, William A446
Schalk, Sammy A723:E383
Schaller, Heinrich W521
Schaller, Hans-Karl W521
Schalliol, Charles A320:E172
Schalow, Laurie A174
Schalow, Monica P447
Schamach, Barry P157
Schandler, Jon B P655
Schantz, Karen P498
Schapiro, Richard A534
Schapiro, Morton P389
Schar, Gretchen A179
Schar, Dwight A578
Scharbach, Shelby P162
Schardin, Bradley E286
Scharding, Donna P156
Scharfstein, David A491
Scharman, Raegan P168
Scharmann, Steve P190
Scharwath, Tim W162
Schatz, Jacob A271
Schaub, Bryan P167
Schauffler, Todd P524
Schaumburg, Anne A574
Schaus, Philippe W302
Schechter, Lori W315
Schechter, Robert E339
Schechtman, Natalie A12
Scheel, Phillip P136
Scheffer, Henk W39
Scheid, John A704:E367
Scheidegger, Urs W425
Scheidreiter, Gerhard W521
Scheidt, Herbert W524
Scheinkestel, Nora W484
Scheiwe, Steven A541:E281
Schek, Judy P214
Schell, Christoph A404
Schell, Brian E73
Schellekens, Ronald A619
Scheller, Eric E429
Schembri, Lawrence W65
Schemm, Dennis E413
Schenck, Ginny A741
Schenck, A. William A795
Schenck, Ginny P518
Schenck, A. William E416
Schenk, John P272
Schenk, Dieter W203
Scheopner, Michael E245
Scheppke, James B P399
Scher, Peter A444
Scher, Colin P434
Scherer, Nancy P42
Scherer, Jeff P544
Scherer, Barbara E420
Scherger, Stephen A364
Scherman, Carol P82
Scherman, Golan W63
Schermeier, Olaf W203
Schermer, Gregory E248
Schermer, Robert E271
Schermerhorn, Todd A792
Scherzer, Irene P138
Scheske, Ronald E394
Schettler, David P537
Scheub, Todd E161
Scheuneman, Randall A415
Schick, Mike A203
Schick, Sue A406
Schick, Mike P144
Schieler, Keith A195:P140
Schierhorn, Joseph E296
Schifanella, Betsy P58
Schifano, Joyce P612
Schiff, Thomas A179
Schiff, Charles A179
Schifter, Richard A489
Schiller, Mark P292
Schiller, Matthew P447
Schiller, Mark P565
Schiltz, Christine P55
Schimmel, Jeffery L P639
Schindler, Tina A531:P349
Schindler, Alfred W425

Schinecker, Thomas W408
Schipani, Barbara P387
Schipper, Heiko W78
Schippers, Harrie C A M A602
Schipporeit, Erhard W218
Schiraldi, Richard A639:E333
Schirmer, Henry W397
Schirmer-Mosset, Elisabeth W75
Schisano, Giancarlo W294
Schissler, Steve P587
Schiurba, John P655
Schlapia, Jennifer P396
Schlarbaum, Jeffrey E245
Schlater, Stephen P284
Schledwitz, Karl P351
Schleidt, Peter W267
Schleifer, Leonard A669
Schleper, Denny P138
Schlesener, Neil P447
Schlesinger, Edward A221
Schlesinger, James R P569
Schlesinger, Sarah E229
Schleyer, Lorenzo Gazmuri W177
Schlichting, Nancy A106:A843
Schlifske, John A459
Schlik, Wolfgang W540
Schlitz, Lei A68:A415
Schlonsky, Michael A117
Schlosberg, Richard A722
Schloss, Howard P214
Schlosser, John A456
Schlosstein, Ralph E149
Schlotfeldt, Joachim W219
Schlotman, J. Michael A449
Schmalz, Shannon P114
Schmandt, Cheryl P342
Schmanske, Mary A472
Schmarder, Eric P124
Schmell, Eric P552
Schmid, Larry P235
Schmid, Richard J P593
Schmidl, Kurt P445
Schmidt, Paul A74
Schmidt, Darryl A94
Schmidt, Cathleen A143
Schmidt, Kurt A146
Schmidt, Barry A369
Schmidt, Timothy A649
Schmidt, John A A804
Schmidt, Thomas A A804
Schmidt, David P25
Schmidt, Barry P237
Schmidt, Marie P261
Schmidt, Rachael P366
Schmidt, Peggy P399
Schmidt, Leigh P449
Schmidt, Andrew P476
Schmidt, Joshua P478
Schmidt, John P483
Schmidt, Marlene P508
Schmidt, John A P607
Schmidt, Thomas A P607
Schmidt, Mark P615
Schmidt, David E29
Schmidt, Darryl E44
Schmidt, Cathleen E65
Schmidt, James E438
Schmidt-Trenz, Hans-Joerg W55
Schmitt, Becky A199
Schmitt, James A387
Schmitt, Betty P185
Schmitt, Erin P238
Schmitt, Peggy P382
Schmitt, Bernhard W166
Schmitt, Christophe W194
Schmitt, Thomas W195
Schmitt, Heinz W222
Schmitter, Joy A824:P617
Schmitz, Clarence A15
Schmitz, Eloise A279
Schmitz, Jeff A877
Schmitz, Doan P266
Schmitz, Vince P357
Schmitz, John D P474
Schmitz, Christoph W169
Schmitz, Eloise E142
Schmoke, Kurt A691

Schmoll, David N P421
Schmollinger, Dean P363
Schmuck, Harry E99
Schmukler, Louis A134
Schnack, Per W267
Schnapp, Jonathan P604
Schneck-Last, Vivian A716:E379
Schneden, Jim P135
Schneider, Andrea A26
Schneider, Todd A180
Schneider, Robert A605
Schneider, Ryan A666
Schneider, Barry A745
Schneider, Karen P146
Schneider, Robert P283
Schneider, John P330
Schneider, Brett P377
Schneider, Ruth P418
Schneider, Mitchell P567
Schneider, Charles P582
Schneider, Tara P596
Schneider, Julie P629
Schneider, Steve P645
Schneider, Etienne W40
Schneider, Sven W246
Schneider, Mark W348
Schneider, Terrence E118
Schneider, Louisa E308
Schneider, David E344
Schneider-Maunoury, Frederic W42
Schneiderman, Tammy A735:P511
Schneidewind, Mike A366:P235
Schnelz, Steve P345
Schnepp, Gilles W152
Schnewlin, Frank W524
Schnirman, Jack P165
Schnitzer, Alan A792
Schnoor, Anya W69
Schnuck, Todd A206
Schnur, Steven E124
Schnur, Jamie E246
Schnure, William P121
Schodde, Joseph P256
Schoderbek, Robert P451
Schoeb, Michael P23
Schoeb, Melissa W359
Schoels, Peter A326:E177
Schoemer, Richard P7
Schoen, Lawrence P247
Schoen, Anthony E174
Schoener, Timothy E83
Schoenfeld, Winston V P584
Schoenhardt, Conny W522
Schoenherr, Jay P626
Schofield, Tom A166:P110
Scholes, Jessica P550
Scholhamer, James A420
Scholl, Stephan P52
Scholten, Danielle E P299
Scholtz, Marty P585
Scholz, Philipp W224
Schomburg, Jennifer P220
Schomburger, Jeffrey A802
Schoneman, Debbra L E326
Schoner, Tina A367
Schooler, Rick P292
Schorr, Lawrence A244
Schosser, Douglas A453
Schot, Abraham W434
Schott, Stevan R P93
Schottenstein, Jay A28
Schottenstein, Robert A104
Schottenstein, Jay P18
Schottenstein, Robert E257
Schowalter, Joseph P382
Schowalter, Linda G P530
Schrader, William A285
Schrader, Michael P398
Schraeder, Werner W222
Schrag, Laura Alvarez A201:E92
Schrage, Jon M P175
Schramm, Jude A306
Schreck, Eric A797
Schreiber, Bill P179
Schreier, Richard E26
Schreiner, Linda A497
Schreiner, James E277

Schriber, Alan P35
Schrider, Daniel A693:E360
Schrieffer, Kerry P406
Schriesheim, Robert A339:A715
Schrimpf, Chris E206
Schrimsher, Neil A610
Schrock, Donald E264
Schroder, Heather A681
Schroder, John A736
Schroder, Heather P448
Schroder, John P512
Schroeder, Mark A353:A464
Schroeder, Jeffrey A516
Schroeder, Matthew A679
Schroeder, Aaron A748
Schroeder, Mark J F P124
Schroeder, Glenn P201
Schroeder, Lisa L P330
Schroeder, Alice W391
Schroeder, Gerhard W411
Schroeder, Mark E192
Schropp, Tobin A A621:P285:P412
Schrum, Roger A721
Schrum, Anita P87
Schubert, Christopher P433
Schubiger, Georg W524
Schuchard, Jeff P333
Schuck, Nicolas A410
Schueler, Kevin P557
Schueller, Joseph A387
Schueneman, Diane W75
Schuerman, Janice P339
Schuette, Stuart P34
Schugel, Jason A33
Schuh, Michele A321
Schuhle, Thomas P508
Schuler, Doug A554:P372
Schuler, Stacie E198
Schulke, Sean P177
Schull, Claudine P164
Schuller, Daniel E147
Schulman, Daniel A611
Schulte, Christie P142
Schulte, David E448
Schulte-Bockum, Jens W335
Schulten, Andre A643
Schultheis, Joab P639
Schultz, Marian A9
Schultz, Tammy A76
Schultz, John A386
Schultz, Kare A426
Schultz, John A809
Schultz, Melissa A832
Schultz, Corinne A864
Schultz, John P20
Schultz, Tim P174
Schultz, Elena P248
Schultz, David P403
Schultz, Paul L P448
Schultz, Michael P612
Schultz, Corinne P656
Schultz, Marian E4
Schultz, Wesley E299
Schultz, Melissa E431
Schulz, David A854
Schulz, Thomas W363
Schulz, Christian W426
Schulze, Corina P629
Schum, Ellen E43
Schumacher, Laura A6
Schumacher, Alan A28
Schumacher, Linda A174
Schumacher, Patrick A588
Schumacher, Alan P18
Schumacher, Stephen P114
Schumacher, Linda P118
Schumacher, INA P537
Schumacher, Dan E337
Schuman, Susan A607
Schumann, William A88
Schumann, Ellen M P472
Schumann, Mariel Von W444
Schumer, Mary P618
Schuppenhauer, Eric A185
Schurko, Allison P655
Schurr, Daniel A176
Schurz, Todd A1

COMBINED HOOVER'S HANDBOOK INDEX OF EXECUTIVES

A = AMERICAN BUSINESS
E = EMERGING COMPANIES
P = PRIVATE COMPANIES
W = WORLD BUSINESS

Schurz, Frank P569
Schussel, Wolfgang W386
Schuster, Michael P19
Schutt, Eric A742:P518
Schutt, Daniel E423
Schutte, John A747:E391
Schutter, George A362:P232
Schuyler, Matthew A389
Schuyler, Josh A711:P481
Schwab, Charles A697
Schwab, Les N P50
Schwab, Peter W521:E353
Schwab-Pomerantz, Carrie P468
Schwaerzler, Jens-Martin W224
Schwager, Charles P364
Schwager, Harald W190
Schwakopf, Terry A102:A300
Schwalb, Rolf-Dieter W42
Schwalm, Roberta A614
Schwalm, Laura P224
Schwan, Severin W408
Schwarctz, Laurie P190
Schwarts, Kin P422
Schwartz, Jennifer A352
Schwartz, Jeffery A508
Schwartz, Faith A668
Schwartz, Roberta A779
Schwartz, Raphe P116
Schwartz, James P156
Schwartz, Robert P277
Schwartz, James K P392
Schwartz, Roberta P567
Schwartz, Mel P647
Schwartz, Phillip E20
Schwartz, Elliot E29
Schwartz, Barry E190
Schwartz, Eric E234
Schwartz, Michael E292
Schwarz, Ronald A466
Schwarz, Jean-Francois W72
Schwarz, Ronald E243
Schwarzer, Axel W524
Schwarzkopf, Paul C P379
Schwarzman, Stephen A121
Schwebke, Kay P249
Schwede, Kale P496
Schweiger, Werner A284
Schweitzer, Jeffrey A826:E428
Schweizer, Kaspar W75
Schwenger, Thomas E433
Schwenn, Ellen P632
Schwieterman, Dale E68
Schwimmer, Howard E353
Schwing, Amanda P197
Schwoeble, Walt P118
Schäfer, Markus W319
Scialdone, Mike P327
Sciammas, Maurice E279
Scicluna, Martin W259
Scimeca, John V P3
Sciortino, Cathy L P154
Sciortino, John E P377
Sciuto, Joe P429
Sclama, Anthony P220
Scobie, Carolyn W396
Scofield, Audralee A824
Scofield, Melissa A832
Scofield, Audralee P630
Scofield, Melissa E431
Scoggins, Christopher A4
Scollan, Joey P204
Sconzo, Guy M P257
Scopellite, Steven A582:E302
Scott, Samuel A99
Scott, David A249
Scott, Stuart A408
Scott, Raymond A470
Scott, Richard A486
Scott, Bertram A488
Scott, Phil A741
Scott, Jill P40

Scott, Emily Allinder P64
Scott, Keith P73
Scott, Sharon P81
Scott, Brandon P123
Scott, Edward P126
Scott, Randy P134
Scott, Mychelle P147
Scott, Deb P217
Scott, Donald P259
Scott, Quentin P265
Scott, Eric M P285
Scott, Currie P343
Scott, Phil P517
Scott, Judy P533
Scott, Majeedah P579
Scott, Stephanie P638
Scott, Andrew W533
Scott, J. E174
Scott, Cochran E409
Scovill, L. E83
Scray, Mischelle P168
Screven, Edward A595
Scribner, Kent P218
Scrivanich, Luke E436
Scruggs, Frank A796
Sculley, Sheryl A523:P133
Scully, Thomas A703
Scungio, Dan P473
Scurlock, John A770
Scurto, Todd P615
Scutari, Laura P171
Sczygelski, Sidney P45
Seabury, George P508
Seadler, Einar E391
Seager, Richard A193:E87
Seagle, Brenda P471
Seah, Lim Huat W155
Seakins, Robert W425
Seale, Andre P620
Seaman, Bradley A745
Seams, Christopher E304
Sear, Steve A242
Searcy, Kathi P40
Sears, Christine A796
Sears, Andy P58
Sears, Kathrin P163
Sears, Thea E115
Seaton, Elizabeth A201
Seaton, Mark A308
Seaton, David A539
Seaton, Simon W448
Seaton, Elizabeth E92
Seaver, Derrick P169
Seaver, R. Arthur E382
Seavers, Dean A623
Seavey, Linda P631
Seay, Beverly P584
Sebastian, Teresa A17
Sebastian, Francisco W323
Sebastian, Markus E15
Sebastiano, Joanne P643
Secanky, Joseph P313
Secco, Genie Del E395
Sechin, Igor W411
Secor, Mark A400:E218
Secor, Thomas E298
Secrest, Brent A280
Security-All, Cyber A679
Sedey, Raymond P321
Sedey, Raymond J P321
Sedighi, Irina P165
Sedik, Andrew P169
Sedlak, Thomas E256
Seedorf, Herman A612
Seeger, Laureen A46
Seeger, David A673
Seeger, Britta W319
Seeger, Zvezdana W415
Seegmiller, Dwight A387
Seek, Ngee Huat W94
Seekins, Sharon P128
Seelbach, Hugh P595
Seelinger-Devey, Jeremy P301
Seeman, Chris P76
Seendripu, Kishore E264
Seeton, Eric E185
Sefzik, Peter A204

Segal, Eric A597
Segal, Ned A801
Segal, Alfredo Cutiel Ergas W56
Segal, Susan W69
Segal, Eric E307
Segalen, Loik W488
Segatto, James P211
Seger, Steve P569
Segers, Dennis E311
Segin, Robert P643
Segovia, Daisy P43
Segovia, Elizabeth E78
Segrest, Desten P212
Segulja, Tom P659
Segura, Greg P177
Sehm, Silke W218
Sehring, Robert P401
Seibel, D. Arthur A9
Seibel, Cristy P624
Seibel, D. Arthur E3
Seibert, Steven A539
Seidel, Andrew P459
Seidenberg, Martin W413
Seidenburg, J. A309:E163
Seidl, Edward C P20
Seidman, Christine A515
Seidman, Leslie A536
Seif, Margaret A61
Seifert, James E299
Seiffert, Ronald A570
Seifried, Edmond E253
Seifter, Lowell P504
Seignette, Sylvia W2
Seiler, David A311
Seiler, James P578
Seiler, Martina W224
Seiler, Joseph E253
Seim, Richard L P662
Seinfeld, Jeffrey P374
Seino, Yukiyo W127
Seinsheimer, Matthew P534
Seip, Eric A418
Seith, Douglas E36
Seitler, Dan P34
Seitz, Charles W P298
Sekaran, Palaniandy P51
Sekenski, Caren P319
Sekha, Felleng W335
Seki, Miwa W151
Seki, Jun W350
Seki, Tomomichi W494
Seki, Mitsuyoshi W537
Sekiguchi, Kenji W377
Sekimoto, Taizo W332
Sekine, Aiko W373
Seko, Yosuke W331
Seko, Tomoaki W418
Seksay, Edward A416:E226
Selanoff, Paul P112
Selberg, Jeffrey P468
Selby, Douglas A P127
Selcuk, Mustafa W504
Sele, Carol P463
Selepeo, Agnes A298
Seleznev, Kirill W208
Self, Brandt P138
Self, Dave P507
Selfridge, Michael A323
Selick, Christine P525
Seligman, Nicole A607
Seligman, Mark W345
Seligsohn, Sherwin E426
Seljeflot, Kate W276
Sellas, Susie P462
Sellers, Mary A97
Sellers, Rodney P203
Sellers, Thomas P240
Selley, Clive W95
Selman, Thomas P214
Seltz, Judith A464
Selva, Bert P480
Selvakesari, Anand A183
Selvaraj, Shelly E117
Selwood, Deborah E240
Selzer, Lawrence A862
Semach, Dustin E417
Semerjian, Dayton A489

Semmel, Cheryl P498
Semmelrock-Werzer, Gabriele W515
Semple, Heather A454:P285
Semple, Sandra A P300
Sen, Semih A775:P551
Senba, Hirohisa W257
Senge, James E129
Senger, Joe A232
Senger-Weiss, Elisabeth Krainer W187
Senisse, Alessandra P404
Senn, Hernan Somerville W179
Senner, Christopher E150
Sennesael, Kris A715
Sennikov, Julia P431
Sensel, Robert E160
Sensi, Kathryn De A486:P303
Sensing, J. Steven A689
Senty, Josh P646
Seo, Dong Hui W296
Seow, Yoo Lin W29
Seppi, Brandy E395
Sepulveda, Eli A633
Sepulveda, Ada P650
Sequeira, Ramona A269
Sequin, Donny P468
Sera, Jean A87
Serafin, Zig A536
Serafini-Lamanna, Tony E270
Serbun, Joseph A210:E95
Serdyukov, Valery W208
Sereda, Mikhail W208:W385
Seremetis, Terry W166
Sergeant, Carol W154
Serhan, Samir A23
Serim, Feyzi P473
Serinis, Karen A147:E65
Serio, Gregory A662
Serkes, Jeffrey David P351
Serna, Camilo A324
Serna, Ed P658
Serna, Edward P658
Seroka, Gene P422
Serota, Scott A696
Serra, Eileen A148
Serrano, Carla W395
Serrao, Darren C A214
Serrao, Jessica P462
Servitje, Mauricio Jorba W215
Servitje, Luis Jorba W215
Servitje, Nicolas Mariscal W215
Servitje, Raul Ignacio Obregon W215
Servitje, Andres W215
Servitje, Estibaliz W215
Seseri, Rudina A491
Seshadri, Raj A506:A663
Sesplankis, Jeffrey A556
Sessa, Matthew D P410
Sessoms, Vicki P246
Setas, Miguel Nuno Simoes Nunes
   Ferreira W172
Setchel, Frank P344
Seth, Alpna E50
Sethaudom, Thammasak W441
Sethavaravichit, Thidarat W65
Sethi, Alok A336
Sethi, Khalid P611
Sethna, Meenal E255
Setlock, Randall P582
Seto, Koichi W255
Seto, Kinya W299
Seto, Shinichiro W439
Settembri, Marco W348
Setterlund, Christian P77
Settersten, Scott M A807
Settle, John A49
Settle, Judy P390
Settle, John E21
Setzer, Nikolai W140
Sevener, Christopher P323
Severe, Constantin A740:P516
Severino, Michael A6
Severino, Jean-Michel W152
Severyn, Carol Jean A227
Sevilla, Javier P214
Sewake, Reid P160
Sewalls, Travis P457:P458

COMBINED HOOVER'S HANDBOOK INDEX OF EXECUTIVES

Sewell, Michael A179
Sewell, David A411:A860
Sewell, Collin P259
Sewing, Christian W160
Sexton, Steve P100
Sexton, Kevin P253
Sexton, John P374
Sexton, Patrick E73
Sey, Jennifer A476:A477:P297
Seyal, Adeel R P242
Seybold, Henry P382
Seydel, John R P123
Seymour, David A41
Seymour, Chris A125
Seymour, Cheyenne A740:P516
Seyrek, Nevzat W504
Seze, Amaury de W389
Sezen, Yalcin W504
Sezgin, Sitare W21
Sfamenos, Steve P75
Sferruzza, Hilla A518
Sgaglione, Lucille A112
Sgro, Gianfranco W286
Sha, Zhenquan W434
Shaar, Omar A8:P4
Shaari, Bahren W376
Shackleford, R. Mitchell A25
Shackley, Brian E7
Shackmann, Gene P247
Shackouls, Bobby A630
Shadbolt, Nicola W199
Shadel, Brooke P334
Shaeff, Julie E94
Shaevsky, Mark P657
Shafer, Charles A778:P561
Shaffer, Dennis A187
Shaffer, Timothy A294
Shaffer, Robert A306
Shaffer, Charles A701
Shaffer, Stephen P19
Shaffer, John P161
Shaffer, Shelly P257
Shaffer, Dennis E85
Shaffer, Timothy E156
Shaffer, Charles E282:E365
Shagley, Richard A316
Shah, Sachin A45
Shah, Akash A99
Shah, Prem A232
Shah, Mihir A443
Shah, Jai A471
Shah, Aarti A478
Shah, Jai A502
Shah, Aarti A577
Shah, Neal A629
Shah, Shefali P52
Shah, Paras P75
Shah, Rushi P300
Shah, Anuj P356
Shah, Arti P370
Shah, Mahesh P489
Shah, Rashmi P489
Shah, Mahesh R P489
Shah, Summit P489
Shah, Monica P489
Shah, Sachin W94
Shahar, Shai E180
Shahbaz, Shahzad W27
Shaheen, George E200
Shahid, Mohammad P476
Shail, Maureen P247
Shaked, Yuval E15
Shaker, Mark P340
Shalett, Lisa A614:E317
Sham, Lilia W239
Shamburger, Julie A724
Shamilov, Sarah P403
Shammo, David P541
Shamsaddin, Abdulrahman
   Ahmed W422
Shamsi, Khalid Al W64
Shamsi, Mohammed Issa Khalfan Al
   Huraimel Al W172
Shamsuarov, Azat W386
Shan, Helen E144
Shanahan, Kathleen P605
Shands, Hilliard A724

Shands, Mardia P530
Shane, Kathleen A639
Shane, Steven A698
Shane, Kathleen E331
Shaner, William E140
Shaneyfelt, Gwen A336
Shani, Eli W487
Shank, Suzanne A190:A219
Shankar, Ram A808
Shankar, Krishnamurthy W247
Shankar, Ram E421
Shanker, Naresh K A872
Shanker, Nick P286
Shankland, Martin W12
Shanks, Virginia A36
Shanks, Desiree P49
Shanks, Scott P527
Shanley, Michael A673
Shanley, Thomas P37
Shannon, John A29
Shannon, Margaret A658
Shannon, Robert E P127
Shannon, John P160
Shannon, Anna P430
Shannon, Nicole P451
Shannon, Jennifer P623
Shantsev, Valery W503
Shao, Ruiqing W236
Shapiola, Joe P376
Shapira, Adrianne A459
Shapiro, Glenn A32
Shapiro, Aaron A89
Shapiro, Jonathan A737
Shapiro, Paul A788
Shapiro, Aaron P54
Shapiro, Phil P154
Shapiro, Josh P164
Shapiro, Jonathan P513
Shara, Thomas A465:E243
Sharbatly, Ibrahim W407
Sharett, Anthony A519:E272
Sharff, Rich P466
Sharieff, Ghazala P469
Sharif, Muhammad Al P333
Shariff, Ahmad Shahriman Mohd W128
Sharilla, Paul P358
Sharipov, Rashid W503
Sharkey, Andrew A673
Sharkey, Allan P441
Sharma, Vivek A438
Sharma, Swati A873
Sharma, Amit P459
Sharma, Manish W378
Sharma, Vijay W478
Sharman, Scott P67
Sharman, Sandy W99
Sharon, Cagle P323
Sharp, Michael A437
Sharp, Carissa P246
Sharp, Andy P358
Sharp, Linda P411
Sharp, John W P564
Sharp, Christopher E120
Sharp, Shalini E290
Sharp, Steven E330
Sharpe, Robert A52
Sharpe, Anita A187
Sharpe, Matthew A399
Sharpe, Anita P131
Sharpe, A P215
Sharpe, Maria E251
Sharples, Brian A33
Sharpnack, David P482
Sharps, Robert A757
Sharum, Melinda P333
Shatalov, Sergey W386
Shatkus, John A673
Shato, Fred P533
Shattock, Matthew A189
Shattuck, Mayo A286
Shattuck, Kate E83
Shaughnessy, Maura A17
Shaulis, Charlie P31
Shavel, Lee E434
Shaver, Tina A639
Shaver, David A814
Shaver, Tina E332

Shaver, David E424
Shavit, Shahar P325
Shaw, Terry D A14
Shaw, Theresa A40
Shaw, Jennifer A123
Shaw, Ruth A258
Shaw, Jeffrey A274
Shaw, Angela A291
Shaw, Nzinga A500
Shaw, Alan A566
Shaw, Jeffrey A579
Shaw, Mark A726
Shaw, Terry D P5
Shaw, Jennifer P81
Shaw, Andrea P100
Shaw, James P142
Shaw, Michael P187
Shaw, Angela P210
Shaw, James P246
Shaw, Harold H P319
Shaw, David P346
Shaw, Charles P440
Shaw, Chuck P467
Shaw, Donovan P477
Shaw, Michael F P517
Shaw, Wayne W111
Shaw, JoAnne E160
Shaw, Scott E254
Shaw, Thomas E352
Shawhan, Dan P442
Shawkey, Anne P156
Shay, Scott A710:E371
Shea, Brian A52:A304
Shea, E. Stewart A317
Shea, Brian P124
Shea, Kyle P151
Shea, Kelly P182
Shea, Andrew P261
Shea, Chris P325
Shea, Agnes A P340
Shea, Mike P656
Shea, William E2
Shea, E. Stewart E170
Shea, John E209
Sheahan, Denis A143:E65
Sheahan, Richard E239
Shear, Neal A168
Shearer, Robert A581
Shearer, Carmen P225
Shearer, Tim P365
Shearer, Austin P378
Sheares, Bradley A696
Shebik, Steven A194
Shedd, Steven T P432
Shedlin, Gary A120
Shee, Tse Koon W155
Sheedy, Linda L P392
Sheehan, Daniel A351
Sheehan, Kevin A385
Sheehan, James N A401
Sheehan, John D A837
Sheehan, Arlene P306
Sheehan, Jeannine E228
Sheehan, Andrew E343
Sheehy, William A724
Sheehy, Matthew P532
Sheer, Andrea P340
Sheets, Jeffrey A860
Sheets, Roger P482
Sheets, Jeffrey E339
Sheffield, Scott A629
Sheffield, Horace A804:P607
Sheffield, Holly E100
Sheflett, George A640:E333
Shegog, Taquoya P545
Shegolev, Igor P604
Shehan, Cynthia P456
Sheidler, Jack A353:E192
Sheikh, Zeeshan A651
Sheikh, Sana P234
Sheils, Janet P38
Shekhter, Elaina E144
Sheldon, Todd A653
Sheldon, Betty P361
Sheldon, Lisa P555
Sheldon, Michael E42
Sheldon, Danley E265

Shell, Jeff A203
Shellito, Laurie P379
Shelly, Lisa P121
Shelter, Jim P455
Shelton, Afton A631
Shelton, Jean P108
Shelton, Brian P438
Shen, Dou W54
Shen, Jinjun W116
Shen, Wen-Chung W138
Shen, Chun-De W138
Shen, Bo W432
Shen, David W530
Shen, Jianlin W541
Shen, Jen-Lin E311
Shenoy, Sunil A421
Shepard, Randall A585
Shepard, Jay E237
Shepard, Julie E415
Shepardson, John E164
Sheperd, David A867
Shephard, Tom A770
Shephard, Barry P218
Shephard, Tom P540
Shepherd, Jeffrey A12
Shepherd, Joel A49
Shepherd, Brian A685
Shepherd, Nicholas A728
Shepherd, Mark B A737
Shepherd, Debbie P241
Shepherd, Mike P463
Shepherd, Nicholas P496
Shepherd, Mark B P513
Shepherd, Joel E21
Shepler, Mary P458
Sheppard, Todd P167
Sheppard, Ronald P544
Sheppard, Jack E312
Shepro, William B P27
Sher, Susan P585
Sherbet, Eric A433
Sherburne, Jane A405:E404
Shereda, Jeannette A134:P87
Sheridan, Robert A147:A390
Sheridan, Arthur A740
Sheridan, Joseph A842
Sheridan, Richard P469
Sheridan, Arthur P516
Sheridan, Joseph P645
Sheridan, Edwin E32
Sheridan, Robert E65:E215
Sheriff, Karen W82
Sherlock, Peter P569
Sherman, Merrill A136
Sherman, Patrick A320
Sherman, A. Haag A388
Sherman, Darrell C A762
Sherman, Darin P175
Sherman, Jeffrey S P252
Sherman, Kim P365
Sherman, Mark P473
Sherman, Malcolm P604
Sherman, Donald W493
Sherman, Jennifer E159
Sherman, Patrick E172
Sherman, Floyd E321
Sherrard, Roger A609
Sherrill, Gregg A32
Sherrill, Roxanne P155
Sherrill, Stephen E43
Sherrod, Shawn P125
Sherwood, Michael P127
Sherwood, Andrea P154
Shetler, Rolando Zubiran W22
Shetty, Sanjay P48
Shetty, Amrita P116
Shetzline, Michael E237
Shewmake, Donna G E439
Shey, Randolph B P301
Shi, Parker A262
Shi, Christiana A819
Shi, Junping W115
Shi, Parker E127
Shibasaki, Hiroko W314
Shibasaki, Kenichi W538
Shibata, Mitsuyoshi W255
Shibata, Koichiro W279

COMBINED HOOVER'S HANDBOOK INDEX OF EXECUTIVES

```
A = AMERICAN BUSINESS
E = EMERGING COMPANIES
P = PRIVATE COMPANIES
W = WORLD BUSINESS
```

Shibata, Makoto W327
Shibata, Satoru W351
Shibata, Masahisa W378
Shibata, Misuzu W452
Shiddi, Ameen Al W423
Shieh, Neil A186:P127
Shiel, James A112
Shields, Andre A436
Shields, Christine P121
Shields, Michael P157
Shields, Steven P198
Shields, Andre P271
Shields, Scott P281
Shields, Sabra P463
Shields, Maria E27
Shiell, Kevin E37
Shiff, Susan E67
Shiffman, Gary E396
Shigematsu, Takashi W338
Shigemori, Yutaka W151
Shigemura, Dean A97
Shigenaga, Dean E13
Shih, Elizabeth A245:P189
Shih, Stone W530
Shihara, Yoshito P527
Shikora, Stuart B P274
Shileny, Lisa A387
Shilling, Steven A193:E87
Shillingburg, Stephanie E153
Shima, Yoshihiko W493
Shimada, Koichi W23
Shimada, Takashi W205
Shimamoto, Kyoji W268
Shimamoto, Yasuji W268
Shimao, Tadashi W127
Shimauchi, Yoshikazu W147
Shimazaki, Noriaki W360
Shimberg, David A P426
Shimer, Julie E263
Shimizu, Fumio W257
Shimizu, Osamu W350
Shimizu, Keita W377
Shimizu, Motoaki W436
Shimogawa, Kristine A735:P511
Shimomura, Joby A741:P518
Shimonishi, Keisuke W151
Shin, Sookyoung A208:P146
Shin, Sungwon P637
Shin, Seiichi W21
Shin, Yo Hwan W532
Shinada, Masahiro W378
Shinault, Shawna P12
Shinbo, Katsuyoshi W463
Shindell, Richard P415
Shinder, Marcella A154
Shindo, Tetsuhiko W255
Shindo, Kosei W354
Shindo, Fumio W369
Shindo, Nakaba W537
Shingleton, Casey A738:P514
Shingleur, Rick P601
Shinichi, Takahashi W254
Shinkawa, Asa W351:W494
Shinkichi, Nakamura W147
Shinn, Mildred M P192
Shinobe, Osamu W270
Shinohara, Yukihiro W158
Shinozaki, Jun W36
Shinshi, Hirokazu W351
Shintaku, Masaaki W192
Shintaku, Yutaro W286
Shintani, Seiji W377
Shiobara, Toshio W437
Shiono, Noriko W277
Shiota, Ko W351
Shipley, Caroline A147
Shipley, Jessika A735:P511
Shipley, Caroline E65
Shipp, Earl A588:W342
Shippey, Mike P658
Shirai, Toshihiko W338

Shiraiwa, Yoshihiro W326
Shiraji, Kozo W328
Shirato, Masayoshi P32
Shirayama, Masaki W461
Shirazi, Brooke A816
Shirk, Danielle P406
Shirley, Natalie A94
Shirley, D. Ray A605
Shirley, Eric A611
Shirley, Soderman P429
Shirley, Natalie E44
Shirvani, Hamid Augustine P381
Shitgasornpongse, Supot W98
Shitoh, Atsushi W1
Shivananda, Sripada A611
Shive, Dunia A455
Shively, Stacey A111
Shivers, Aaron P129
Shlay, Judith P187
Shlomi, Irit W64
Shmal, Genadii W503
Shmerling, Michael A674:E348
Shnayder, Boris E144
Shobuda, Kiyotaka W314
Shock-Osborn, Jane P316
Shoda, Takashi W150
Shoemaker, Anthony A452
Shoemaker, Alysia P233
Shoji, Kuniko W317
Shome, Surojit W155
Shomette, Tom A172:P113
Shon, Larry De A377:A820
Shontere, Jim P480
Shook, Kevin A642
Shook, Ellyn W8
Shook, Gary R E52
Shoptaw, Robert A712:E373
Shoquist, Debora A577
Shore, David P171
Shorkey, Mike P472
Short, Andrea A1
Short, Michael A683
Short, Steve P215
Short, Gregory P319
Short, Jeffrey B P559
Shorter, Christopher J P123
Shortlands, Peter Ricketts of W184
Shorts, Kenneth P496
Shortt, Vittoria W135
Shotsky, Sergey W503
Shott, John A750:E394
Shotts, Philip A200
Shotwell, David A809
Shou, Dongua W120
Shoukry, Paul A663
Shoulders, Patrick A P602
Shoup, Scot A P315
Shoven, John E62
Showalter, Linda G P531
Showalter, Kenneth Showa P652
Shows, Susan A475
Shows, W T P153
Shrader, Ralph A129
Shrair, David A P152
Shrank, William A406
Shrewsbury, Holly A735:P511
Shrishrimal, Sumi E117
Shrock, Jason A133
Shroff, Mohak A266
Shroff, Nilufer K P582
Shropshire, Tom W165
Shrum, Kayse A740
Shrum, Ashley P458
Shrum, Kayse P516
Shryock, Steve P639
Shu, Eric P179
Shu, Standford P301
Shu, Victor P643
Shu, Lizhi W214
Shu, Ungyong W450
Shubaily, Yousef abdullah Al W128
Shuck, Aaron A663:P436
Shuck, Theresa P508
Shuda, Scott E228
Shuey, Michael P543
Shufflebarger, Thomas G P549
Shukr, Mousa P44

Shukri, Walid Bin Ibrahim W422
Shulkin, Boris W306
Shulman, Jonathan A113
Shulman, Becky A519
Shulman, Douglas A592
Shulman, Steven A843
Shulman, Mona P404
Shulman, Becky E272
Shulman, Douglas E303
Shulruff, Larry P486
Shult, Milo P616
Shumann, C R P354
Shumate, Alex A718:E114
Shumsky, Julia P7
Shumway, Jeffery A420
Shunk, Erica A257
Shunnara, Basima A208:P146
Shust, Carla P157
Shuster, Richard A775
Shuster, Matthew P50
Shuster, Rob P351
Shuster, Rob S P351
Shuster, Richard P548
Shuster, Bradley E294
Shuter, Rob W95
Shutley, R. Todd A54:E25
Shuttleworth, Julie W200
Shuv, Liat W64
Shuxian, Yang A702
Shyur, Jui-Chun W138
Si, Stephanie L P160
Si, Kanit W62
Si, Fengqi W154
Siahaan, Tigor W128
Siak, Stacey A203:P144
Sias, Aaron P530
Sibbern, Bjorn A543
Sibert, Leslie R P228
Sibinga, Erica P274
Sibiya, Philisiwe W253
Sibley, Tarrant A377
Sibley, James M A475
Sibley, Tracey Renner P85
Sibley, Don P542
Sica, Frank A459
Siciliano, F. A298
Sickler, John E427
Siddiqi, Farhan W283
Siddique, Omar P623
Siddiqui, Sonal P140
Siddiqui, Omer P184
Sideris, Harry K A259
Sidhu, Jay A229
Sidhu, Samvir A229
Sidhu, Harry P123
Sidhu, Gurdip W128
Sidhu, Jay E112
Sidhu, Samvir E112
Sidler, Sherri P185
Sidorovich, Kate E131
Siebenburgen, Christa P283
Siebers, Eric P546
Siebert, April P187
Siebert, Kevin E436
Siebold, Donna P157
Sieg, Andy A96
Siegel, Steven F A135
Siegel, Steven A135
Siegel, Michael A186
Siegel, Kenneth A192:A486
Siegel, Walter A696
Siegel, Michael P127
Siegel, Deana P532
Siegel, Judith P609
Siegel, Susan E15
Siegel, Todd E398
Sieger, Michael A645
Siegert, Shelia P278
Siegert, Nancy L P346
Siegert, Thomas P562
Siegfried, Midori P378
Siegfried, Scott P459:P506
Siegling, Dawn P167
Siegmund, Jan A199
Sielak, George P41
Siemens, Albert J P211
Siemer, Kristine A P359

Sienna, Lino P23
Sierdo, Jose W72
Sierotko, Walter A647
Sierra, Luis A745
Sierra, Claudia P161
Sierra, Andrea P408
Sierra, Jose Arnau W243
Sierra, Antonio Lorenzo W400
Sievers, Kirke P170
Sievers, Hans Christian P248
Sievert, G. Michael A758
Sievewright, Sandra A106:E48
Sieving, Charles A327:A560
Sifferlen, Mark A228
Sifferman, Eric P63
Sight, James E202
Sigismondi, Laurent W166
Sigler, Lisa P43
Sigmon, Toye P19
Signorille-browne, Julie A554
Sijbrand, Jan W17
Sik, Wan King W232
Sikka, Vishal A595
Sikorski, Ralf W415
Silagy, Eric A327:A560
Silard, Kathleen P580
Silberberg, Allison P122
Silberman, Robert E392
Silberstein, Harvey P156
Silcock, Christopher A389
Siler, Brad P233
Silguy, Yves-Thibault de W517
Silins, Andris J A503:P317
Silitch, Nicholas A649
Sill, Garrett E366
Silliman, Craig A833
Sills, James P73
Siluanov, Anton W424
Silva, Diane A278
Silva, Joe A443
Silva, Enrique A666
Silva, Paul A835
Silva, Alyson P390
Silva, Lisa P610
Silva, Claudia Almeida E W104
Silva, Luis Palha da W173
Silva, Miguel Eduardo Padilla W198
Silva, Filipe Quintin W206
Silva, Janet De W250
Silva, Diane E141
Silveira, Elvino da E304
Silver, Caroline A422
Silver, Mark A781
Silver, Alexis P306
Silver, Mark P580
Silver, Jonathan W342
Silver, Ronald E77
Silverman, David A59
Silverman, Jan P20
Silverman, Deven P379
Silverman, Daniel C P482
Silverman, Alan E161
Silverman, Louis E388
Silverman, David E422
Silvernail, Andrew A749
Silvers, J B P567
Silverstone, Bernard A334
Silverton, Michael W304
Silvi, Marcus P392
Silvio, Peter E369
Sim, Kenneth E29
Sim, Brandon E29
Sim, Judith E183
Simancas, Jose de Jesus Valdez W23
Simard, Curtis A103
Simard, Regis W210
Simard, Curtis E47
Simbul, Ma. Theresa W83
Sime, Jeff A90:E41
Simek, Jan P629
Simeus, Marie P408
Simkins, Denim P225
Simkowitz, Daniel A538
Simm, Daryl A589
Simmelink, Scott P10
Simmes, Matthew E222
Simmonds, Robert W82

COMBINED HOOVER'S HANDBOOK INDEX OF EXECUTIVES

Simmons, Kara A734
Simmons, Eileen A828:A828
Simmons, Gary A831
Simmons, Sharon P90
Simmons, Allen P168
Simmons, Carrie P237
Simmons, Laura P291
Simmons, Tj P307
Simmons, Will P473
Simmons, Iman P499
Simmons, Kara P510
Simmons, Jackie P612
Simmons, Eileen P634:P635
Simmons, Timothy E365
Simms, Joe A731
Simms, Mary P121
Simms, Susan P410
Simms, Erin P507
Simoes, Antonio W61
Simola, Jozsef W334
Simon, John F A50
Simon, Lynn A211
Simon, William A373
Simon, Pamela A736
Simon, Sam P48
Simon, Randy P109
Simon, Lola P145
Simon, Pamela P512
Simon, Edwige P617
Simon, Isabelle W489
Simon, Ronald E132
Simon, Frank E156
Simon, David E292
Simoncic, Richard A526
Simonds, Michael A827
Simone, Nicolas W380
Simonelli, Lorenzo A91
Simonelli, Charlotte A666:A666
Simonette, Peggy P660
Simonich, Brent A489
Simons, James H A781
Simons, Marilyn A781
Simons, James H P580
Simons, Marilyn P580
Simons, Nicole W227
Simons, James E343
Simonson, Richard A271
Simonte, Michael A42
Simonte, Michael K P336
Simpron, Aldrin P381
Simpson, Amanda A20
Simpson, Barry A196
Simpson, Iris A243
Simpson, Shelley A408
Simpson, Amanda P11
Simpson, Justin P43
Simpson, Sharletta P179
Simpson, Iris P188
Simpson, Diane P200
Simpson, Russell P288
Simpson, Willa P481
Simpson, Alison P612
Simrall, James P622
Sims, John A427
Sims, Gary A531
Sims, Jacob P252
Sims, J P362
Sims, Michael P467
Sims, Robert E111
Sims, Gary E276
Sims, Frank E381
Simsek, Sahismail W504
Simson, Margus W281
Simulcik, Rebecca P161
Simuro, Frank E104
Sinclair, Jack A729
Sinclair, Shannon P262
Sindelar, Michael A735:P510
Sinden, Janice A492
Sindi, Ahmed Bin Abass W422
Sine, Amy P401
Sinensky, Peter A592
Sinewgz, Larry P85
Singer, Harry A187
Singer, Arnie A266
Singer, Emily A781
Singer, Maria A824

Singer, Samantha P546
Singer, Emily P580
Singer, Lucy P631
Singer, Roger W189
Singer, Frederick W250
Singer, Aaron E83
Singer, Harry E85
Singfield, Donna P316
Singh, Rajinder A101
Singh, Manish A103
Singh, Gurmeet A117
Singh, Mohit A171
Singh, Jaspreet A258
Singh, Mala A271
Singh, Harmit A476:A477
Singh, Sumeet A623
Singh, S. Steven A846
Singh, Gurbir P44
Singh, Manish P60
Singh, Saul S P107
Singh, Sarabdeep P240
Singh, Amar P241
Singh, Harmit P297
Singh, Charan P354
Singh, Anil P415
Singh, Prabjit P529
Singh, Amandeep P573
Singh, Ranjit W17
Singh, Sanjay W87
Singh, Bijay W166
Singh, Inder W396
Singh, Manjit W465
Singh, Jesse E42
Singh, Vanila E51
Singh, Prahlad E320
Singh, Richard E326
Singh, Man Jit E454
Singh-bushell, Ekta E417
Singhal, Anchal P244
Singletary, Richard E409
Singleton, David A14
Singleton, Sean A846
Singleton, James A854
Singleton, David P5
Singleton, Kate P169
Singleton, John Knox P262:P263
Singleton, Palmer C P359
Singleton, Felicia P462
Singleton, Mark P547
Singman, Erik P127
Singmaster, Helen P435
Sinha, Bachan P538
Sink, Doug P142
Sinkin, Robert A P589
Sinsuparatn, Chanchai W284
Sinsurin, James P576
Sipes, Kevin A675:E350
Siplin, Victoria P P166
Sippel, Sandy P294
Siragusa, Daniel P477
Sire, Antoine W87
Siridej, Prachet W62
Siripokee, Than W62
Sirisumphand, Thosaporn W393
Sirk, Jasper P647
Sirpilla, John E246
Sisisky, Richard L P489
Sisitsky, Todd A433
Sisk, David A727
Sisk, Jeanene P625
Siska, Marti P127
Sisney, Brett P188
Sisney, Dan P525
Sisolak, Steve A738:P514
Sissmann, Laurent W294
Sisson, William P58
Sisson, Melissa P387
Sistine, Peter Van A94:E45
Sit, Roger A409
Sita, Veresh A87
Sites, Larry P286
Sitherwood, Suzanne P495
Sithi-Amnuai, Piti W62
Sitman, Robert E52
Sitti, Metin P100
Siu, Wing A106
Siu, Hera A361

Siu, Shawn W115
Siu, Wai Keung W129
Siu, Wing E48
Siu, Chris E420
Siva, Chokkalingam P625
Sivaram, Srinivasan A858
Siveria, Richard W P84
Sixt, Frank W110
Siy, Paul John W83
Sizemore, Vicki P55
Sizemore, Stephen P644
Sizer, Julie A312
Sj, Rev Joseph M McShane P217
Sj, Gregory R Bonfiglio P427
Sj, William P Leahy P601
Skaaden, Geir E456
Skaare, Jonathan E442
Skabelund, Nickolas P74
Skaggs, Robert A258
Skains, Thomas A796
Skala, Peter A875
Skanse, John P17
Skariah, Karuna P427
Skarjune, Dolores A359
Skaugen, Kirk W292
Skeans, Tracy A875
Skelton, Stacie P327
Skerritt, Susan A210:E95
Skiba, Leszek W71
Skidmore, Douglas A179
Skidmore, Timothy P119
Skidmore, William E274
Skiendzielewski, John P559
Skijus, Melanie A364
Skillings, Colleen E299
Skinner, Deborah A224
Skinner, Frances A617
Skinner, James A843
Skinner, Jon P65
Skinner, Jessica P240
Skinner, Anne P346
Skinner, Kelley P430
Skinner, Deborah E155
Skipper, Kathy P217
Skipworth, Michael P98
Skjerping, Dale P131
Skjorestad, Ella W454
Sklar, Joel A98
Sklare, Judy P145
Skoff, Herbert W367
Skoglund, William A587:E302
Skogman, Kyle A815
Skogsbergh, James H A15
Skogsbergh, Jim A79
Skogsbergh, James H P7
Skogsbergh, Jim P52
Skogseth, Jan W454
Skok-Vaughan, Denise-Todd P3
Skokan, Mike A412:P258
Skono, John P659
Skorkowsky, Patrick P554
Skoro, A T P286
Skory, John E P552
Skosey, Peter A122:P80
Skosnik, Dennis P156
Skou, S ren W1
Skovhus, Per W267
Skovronsky, Daniel A478
Skretting, Asbjrn P208
Skrinner, Cari P323
Skrocki, Denise P609
Skudutis, Tommy W306
Skule, Jeremy A543
Skuratovskaya, Maria A27:P15
Skvortsov, Vyacheslav W502
Skvortsova, Elena W371
Skyler, Jennifer A46
Skyler, Jay E117
Slabach, Christopher A320:E173
Slade, Rachel W340
Sladek, Joseph A708
Slager, Donald A501
Slagle, Jamie P119
Slane, Kevin A693:E360
Slate, MaryEmily A576
Slater, Pam A224
Slater, David A258

Slater, Todd A588
Slater, Pam P168
Slater, Richard W510
Slater, Austin E95
Slatoff, Karl E402
Slaton, Shawn P112:P113
Slattery, John A346
Slavensky, Jeff P651
Slavin, Kevin P505
Slavin, Peter L P565
Slavoski, William P90
Slavtcheff, Craig A146
Sledge, Charles A145:P95
Sleeth, Shaun P321
Slessor, Michael E180
Sletten, Joshua E244
Sleyster, Scott A649
Slezakova, Katarina W515
Slief, Michael P281
Slieter, Randall J A737:P513
Slifka, Eric A357
Slifka, Richard A357
Sliney, David A746
Slivinski, Bradley P185
Slivka, Alexander P36
Sloan, O. Temple A309
Sloan, Thomas A310
Sloan, Jeffrey A358
Sloan, Amy P410
Sloan, O. Temple E162
Sloan, Thomas E164
Sloan, Wayne E245
Sloane, Edward A311
Sloat, Julie A44
Slocum, Michael A149
Slocum, William E392
Slominski, Donald D P323
Slone, Reuben A12
Slotnik, Joseph A136
Sloves, Andrew E291
Slubowski, Michael A794
Slubowski, Mike P468
Slubowski, Michael P599
Slucsky, Lorie A210
Sluka, Joseph P353
Sluka, Joe P499
Slutzky, Paul E201
Slyke, Peter V P519
Smach, Thomas E110
Smail, James A294:E156
Smajer, Vojtech W281
Small, Gary A639
Small, Albert A814
Small, Tyler P164
Small, Greg P305
Small, Jeff P658
Small, Gary E333
Small, Albert E423
Smalla, Frank E55
Smalley, Gary A800
Smalley, James P242
Smalley, Carolyn P642
Smalley, Robert E127
Smallwood, Dave P651
Smart, Jill A27
Smart, Thomas A624
Smart, Jill A869
Smart, Bruce P312
Smart, Thomas P414
Smart, Jill E144
Smedegaard, Niels W168
Smedley, Maria P43:P43
Smedt, Rodney E304
Smee, Joanne A872
Smernoff, Christopher E132
Smestad, Jennifer E309
Smet, John H P29
Smet, John P562
Smiddy, Craig A586
Smile, Contessa P85
Smirl, Richard E441
Smit, Kornelis A657
Smith, David A14
Smith, Zeke A25
Smith, R. Sharon A39
Smith, Gregory A41
Smith, Stephan A48

COMBINED HOOVER'S HANDBOOK INDEX OF EXECUTIVES

A = AMERICAN BUSINESS
E = EMERGING COMPANIES
P = PRIVATE COMPANIES
W = WORLD BUSINESS

Smith, Shannon L A50
Smith, Rodney A51
Smith, Gerry A71
Smith, David A76
Smith, Chip A78
Smith, Guy H A78
Smith, Richard A84
Smith, Andrea A96
Smith, Kay A102
Smith, Kenneth A103
Smith, Cathy A106
Smith, Taylor A123
Smith, Brian A126
Smith, William A147
Smith, Phillip A163
Smith, Brandon A176
Smith, Clifford A188
Smith, Kevin A192
Smith, Brian A196
Smith, J. David A207
Smith, Barbara A207
Smith, Shelby M A208
Smith, Wayne A211
Smith, James R A213
Smith, Tom A217
Smith, Phillip A224
Smith, Mark A228
Smith, Rick A233
Smith, Sherry A240
Smith, Demica A241
Smith, Joanne A242
Smith, Carey A268
Smith, Frederick A302
Smith, John A302
Smith, Matthew A320
Smith, Lee A326
Smith, Robert A345
Smith, Ramsey A351
Smith, Andrea A379
Smith, Laura A385
Smith, Kara A390
Smith, Anna A396
Smith, David A415
Smith, Ryan A423
Smith, Daryn A434
Smith, Brian A466
Smith, Gregory A470
Smith, Elizabeth A A475
Smith, Craig A498
Smith, Michael A508
Smith, Ernest A511
Smith, Bradford A529
Smith, Jeffrey A530
Smith, Bryan A543
Smith, Mike A545
Smith, Justin A554
Smith, Oliver A562
Smith, Brad A565
Smith, David A567
Smith, Gerry A583
Smith, Richard A592
Smith, Gerald A593
Smith, Gunner A601
Smith, Daniel A601
Smith, Kent A603:A603
Smith, Gregory A613
Smith, Philip A613
Smith, Gregory A615
Smith, William A623
Smith, Reese A628
Smith, Catherine A636
Smith, Gregory A A650
Smith, Michael A652
Smith, Richard A666
Smith, Patricia K A670
Smith, Ronald A671
Smith, William A673
Smith, Abbie A689
Smith, E. Follin A689
Smith, David A713
Smith, Frederick A713

Smith, Robert A713
Smith, J. Duncan A713
Smith, David A719
Smith, Preston A724
Smith, Dwight A733
Smith, Cherie H A734
Smith, Philip A748
Smith, Salaam A777
Smith, James A782
Smith, Jocelyn A783
Smith, Carrie A783
Smith, Richard A793
Smith, Jeffrey A869
Smith, Michael A877
Smith, Kokee A877
Smith, David P5
Smith, Micah P6
Smith, H Fally P14
Smith, Stephan P31
Smith, Kelvin P45
Smith, David P47
Smith, Chip P47
Smith, Guy H P47
Smith, Lamont P51
Smith, Kay P56
Smith, Allen P57
Smith, Brad P63
Smith, Stuart P73
Smith, Benjamin P76
Smith, Taylor P81
Smith, Nate P82
Smith, Brian P83
Smith, Shane P91
Smith, Olga L P96
Smith, Marty P100
Smith, Kathleen P100
Smith, Corey P102
Smith, Rina P115
Smith, Emily P120
Smith, Durre P123
Smith, Denise P125
Smith, Merle S P126
Smith, Connie P145
Smith, Shelby M P146
Smith, James R P150
Smith, Calah P150
Smith, Tom P151
Smith, Mark P153
Smith, Charles P155
Smith, Cathi P155
Smith, Lenza P164
Smith, Margaret P166
Smith, Melanie P167
Smith, Angela P168
Smith, Phillip P168
Smith, Jeffrey V P169
Smith, Rick P178
Smith, Patricia P179
Smith, Annette P179
Smith, Sean P182
Smith, Barbara A P184
Smith, Larry P184
Smith, Andrea P187
Smith, Jim P206
Smith, Sandi P221
Smith, Phillip R P223
Smith, Amanda P249
Smith, J Steven P254
Smith, Lachlan P255
Smith, Brian P256
Smith, Ryan P264
Smith, Douglas P269
Smith, Julie P282
Smith, Steven E P286
Smith, Debbie P286
Smith, Randy Smith Randy P299
Smith, Larr P304
Smith, Quiara P306
Smith, Eugene P308
Smith, Wes P320
Smith, Jeralyn Waller P321
Smith, Ernest P322
Smith, Joann P326
Smith, Janis P330
Smith, Kathryn P355
Smith, Barbara P357
Smith, David A P361

Smith, Harold P363
Smith, Doug P367
Smith, Justin P372
Smith, Lawrence G P384
Smith, Steven P387
Smith, Charles V P398
Smith, Stanley P400
Smith, Kent P404
Smith, Rob P406
Smith, Eddie P420
Smith, Carole P422
Smith, Gary P423
Smith, Martha P429
Smith, Andrew O P431
Smith, Patricia K P440
Smith, Ward P444
Smith, Meredith P450
Smith, Mark P459
Smith, Cydni P459
Smith, Barry P461
Smith, Paulene P473
Smith, Brenda P473
Smith, Jamie P475
Smith, Tim P478
Smith, Steve P494
Smith, Franz P497
Smith, Lytton P506
Smith, Cherie H P510
Smith, Lisa L P525
Smith, Elyse P544
Smith, Chad P548
Smith, Larry T P548
Smith, Amy P556
Smith, Eric P557
Smith, Raven P562
Smith, W Stuart P566
Smith, Carey A P573
Smith, Neil P578
Smith, Julia P579
Smith, James P583
Smith, Jocelyn P583
Smith, Carrie P583
Smith, Michael P595
Smith, Rebekah P599
Smith, Bryan P603
Smith, Jason P625
Smith, Clinton P638
Smith, Andrea S P641
Smith, Amy P661
Smith, Benjamin W18
Smith, Gary W30
Smith, Eric W396
Smith, Kevin W410
Smith, Mark W457
Smith, Kristopher W466
Smith, Karen E28
Smith, Jill E33
Smith, Stacy E38
Smith, Kenneth E47
Smith, Thomas E51
Smith, Robert E59
Smith, Sherrese E60
Smith, William E66
Smith, David E79
Smith, Michael E98
Smith, Kirin E108
Smith, Arthur E109
Smith, Sally E118
Smith, Patti E132
Smith, Karen E133
Smith, Barry E139
Smith, Douglas E145
Smith, Julie E150
Smith, Donald E157
Smith, Donald R E157
Smith, Matthew E173
Smith, Lee E177
Smith, Robert E199
Smith, James E E206
Smith, Jill E206
Smith, Kara E215
Smith, Anna E217
Smith, Brian E244
Smith, Ryan E246
Smith, Julie E270
Smith, Tracey E271
Smith, Jeffrey E275

Smith, Marcus E282
Smith, Helen M E282
Smith, Oliver E293
Smith, Robert E294
Smith, William E297
Smith, Kent E310
Smith, Gregory E316
Smith, Philip E316
Smith, Reese E324
Smith, Hillary E343
Smith, Jill E344
Smith, Serene E345
Smith, Quentin E391
Smith, Gregory E405
Smith, David E409
Smith, Richard E414
Smith, Howard E443
Smith, Philip E448
Smith, Timothy E457
Smith-Calascibetta, Patricia A15:P7
Smith-Daugherty, Olivia P408
Smitherman, Christopher P125
Smithson, Michael A800
Smithwick, Michael P468
Smits, Robert P226
Smits, Hans W278
Smits-Nusteling, Carla W42
Smoak, Kara A740:P516
Smoke, Christopher P207
Smolik, Brent A495
Smorch, Matt P155
Smrz, Laurie P116
Smucker, Mark A455
Smucker, Richard A718
Smucker, Mark A718
Smucker, Timothy A718
Smullen, F W P103
Smylie, John P483
Smyth, Gerard A52
Smyth, Margaret A339
Smyth, Maureen A541
Snabe, Jim Hagemann W1:W443
Snapp, David E245
Snapper, Suzanne E139
Snee, James P A401
Snee, James A677
Sneed, Michael A441
Sneed, Paula A697
Sneed, Joel P627
Snell, Jonnie P36
Snelling, Elisa P36
Snellings, Tim P157
Sng, Miow Ching W529
Sniadecki, Matthew P658
Snider, Marcy P172
Snider, Eric P480
Snider, Steven E68
Snider, Michael E251
Snipe, Alexander E166
Snively, Joshua A725
Snively, Melissa P251
Snively, Joshua E384
Snodgres, Jon E349
Snoke, Glenn A597:E307
Snook, Carol E257
Snopud, Carolyn Beebe P431
Snow, Laura A102
Snow, Ola A151
Snow, Roderick A174
Snow, Laura P56
Snow, Roderick P118
Snow, John E30
Snowdeal, Eric P154
Snowe, Olympia A756
Snyder, Thomas G A186
Snyder, Scott A340
Snyder, Angela A340
Snyder, Barbara A453:A645
Snyder, Meredith A824
Snyder, Chandra P37
Snyder, Gerald P42
Snyder, Barbara R P102
Snyder, Thomas G P129
Snyder, Bill P156
Snyder, Alexandria P245
Snyder, Tamar P272
Snyder, Cyrus P361

588

HOOVER'S HANDBOOK OF EMERGING COMPANIES 2022

COMBINED HOOVER'S HANDBOOK INDEX OF EXECUTIVES

Snyder, William R P553
Snyder, Tim P556
Snyder, Andrew P581
Snyder, Meredith P617
Snyder, James P622
Snyder, Mark E204
So, Richard Benedict W323
So, Issei W494
Soares, Andreia P552
Soaries, DeForest A297:E158
Sobanet, Henry P143
Sobczak, Tiffany P335
Sobel, Brian A98
Sobel, Jonathan A388
Soberanis, Marco Antonio
    Murillo W381
Sobers, Patrick A544:E285
Sobey, Karl W176
Sobey, Paul W176
Sobey, Frank W176
Sobey, John W176
Sobey, Robert W176
Sobkowicz, Diane P351
Sobrepena, Aniceto W323
Sobson, Carol L A570:P388
Soccodato, Giovanni W294
Sock, Shannon A517:P331:P334
Sockwell, Darryl P348
Sodaro, Frank A586
Soderberg, Carl A144
Soderberg, John A295
Soderbery, Robert A684:A858
Soderholm, Glenn W154
Soderstrom, Johanna A802:W346
Soederberg, Jonas W446
Soejima, Naoki W472
Soh, Boon Leong W393
Soh, Gim Teik W529
Soh, Simon E169
Sohn, Sung Won A857
Sohn, Jim P330
Sohn, Young P637:E62
Sohn, Sung Won E447
Soika, Kimberly A283:P208
Soiland, Marlene A285
Soirat, Arnaud W405:W406
Soistman, Francis E131
Soito, Lois P456
Sojos, Sarah P421
Sok, Chantha P249
Soker, Jo Ann P468
Sokmen, Virma W540
Sokolich, Mark A215:E97
Sola, Jure A694
Sola, Lester P341
Sola, Matias Videla W110
Solanki, Kishore P87
Solano, Juan P576
Solanski, David P354
Solere, Henri W276
Soliday, Lance A288
Solimani, Robert P520
Solis, Grace P133
Solis, Lupe P464
Solis, Jose P594
Solis, Oscar Von Hauske W28
Solis, Marissa E98
Soliven, Philip W323
Solloway, Steven A264:P200
Soloman, Debbie P102
Solomon, David A360
Solomon, Kenneth A713
Solomon, Lesley P180
Solomon, Stuart B W271
Solomon, Jeffrey E106
Solomon, Larry E144
Solon, Kenneth A480
Soltau, Jill A84
Soltesz, James A261:E126
Soma, Siva K P20
Soma, Giovanni W281
Somaschini, Lucas W525
Somerhalder, John A324
Somerset, Gary P432
Sommers, Benjamin D P546
Son, Tae Seung W532
Sondhi, Samrat E153

Sondys, Bruce P63
Sonenreich, Steven P356
Sones, Randy A16
Sones, Randall D A30
Sones, Randy P8
Sones, Randall D P21
Sonet, Aurelien W448
Song, Karen P300
Song, Vincent P532
Song, Jie W88
Song, Kangle W129
Song, Jingshang W235
Song, Ke W265
Song, Seung Geol W297
Song, Guangju W387
Song, Hongjiong W541
Songwanich, Suwatchai W62
Soni, Deepa A377
Soni, Bhavik E214
Sonkur, Matrika P12
Sonn, Spencer W532
Sonnen, Anne W213
Sonnenberg, Steven A745
Sono, Kiyoshi W328
Sono, Mari W360
Sonoki, Hiroshi W52
Sonsteby, Charles A236
Soo, Kim Wai W29
Sood, Sapna W311
Soofe, Abdikhayr P125
Soon, Tit Koon W212
Soong, Chris A410
Sophonpanich, Chartsiri W62
Sopp, Mark A448
Sorbara, Nicole W304
Sorenes, Steffan A283:P208
Sorensen, Donna A655
Sorensen, Christopher M P281
Sorensen, Mikael W470
Sorensen, Donna E340
Sorenson, John A132
Sorenson, Charles A414:P260
Sorenson, Kory W429
Soreq, Avigal A241
Soreta, Tattika P105
Sorfleet, Diana A227
Sorg, Elaine A6
Sorgi, Vincent A637
Sori, Alfredo E P285
Soriano, Lidio A633
Soriano, Edmundo W83
Soriano, Cesar E131
Soriot, Pascal W46
Sormella, Nancy P182
Sorrentino, Frank A215
Sorrentino, Joseph A291:P210
Sorrentino, Frank E97
Sorto, Rafael A31:P24
Sortwell, Christopher T P366
Sosebee, Jane E166
Sosnowski, Scott P360
Sossen, Andrew J A733:E389
Sota, Ivan de la W26
Sotamaa, Ritva W510
Sotelo, Dan P307
Soterakis, Jack P499
Sotgia, Federica P593
Sotir, Paula P320
Soto, Myrna A190:A219
Soto, Benjamin A261
Soto, Myrna A633
Soto, Juan Alvarez De A695
Soto, Sabrina P311
Soto, Cristobal W255
Soto, Benjamin E126
Sotomayor, Julie C P478
Soucie, Keith A278:E141
Souda, Nobuyuki W237
Souder, Jeremy P574
Souders, Donald E426
Soukenik, Amber Wallace A294:E156
Soukup, Beth A P268
Soukup, Beth P268
Souleles, Thomas A605
Sounillac, Jean-Pierre W193
Sourisse, Pascale W488:W517
Sousa, Emma De A420

Soussan, Jean W90
Soutendijk, Greg A426
South, Martin A500
South, Thomas A567
South, John R P248
South, Tracy A P252
Southwick, Michael J P578
Souza, Fabian A286
Souza, Andre Nogueira de A627
Souza, Marcel P581
Souza, Alvaro Antonio Cardoso de W61
Sova, Gary E69
Sow, Ethelore C A780:P572
Sowazi, Nkululeko W335
Sowell, Joseph A379
Sowell, Ron P145
Sowinski, Janice P126
Spaashelm, Ernie E206
Spackler, John Keith P10
Spafford, Mark P36
Spage, Catherine A291:P210
Spahr, Lori A828
Spahr, Dalena P529
Spahr, Lori P634
Spain, Michael A789
Spainhour, Sterling A352:E199
Spair, Ronald A340
Spalding, William R P1
Spalding, Susan P179
Spalding, Drew P432
Spalt, Bernhard W187
Spang, Jack P602
Spangler, Sean P559
Spann, Rick A177
Spar, Debora A784
Sparby, John E344
Spark, Frances A22
Sparkman, Ricky A211
Sparks, David A529
Sparks, Monica L A606
Sparks, Terry P557
Sparks, Anne P586
Sparks, Carl E101
Sparks, Scott E210
Sparks, Daniel E265
Sparks, David E274
Spatholt, David P160
Spaude, Robin E198
Spaulding, Mark A494
Spaulding, Wynn P291
Spaziano, Greg P99
Spears, Mary A593
Spears, Stephen P52
Spears, Michael E233
Specht, William A529:E274
Specter, Eric E176
Spector, Adam A336
Spector, David A614:E317
Spector, David A E317
Spector, David E317
Speed, Stella P540
Speed, James E235
Speed, Jeffrey E454
Speer, Kevin P P248
Spees, Shane P383
Speetzen, Michael A632
Speetzen, Michael T A632
Spehar, Danielle E8
Speigner, Ehrica P549
Spellacy, Suzanne E299
Spellings, James A291
Spence, Timothy A306
Spence, Christine A734:P510
Spence, Edward F D P642
Spence, Robert E377
Spencer, Jody A54
Spencer, Matthew A357
Spencer, Octavia A414
Spencer, Barbara A553
Spencer, Terry K A594
Spencer, Elliott A723
Spencer, Ronald A750
Spencer, Larry A863
Spencer, John P25
Spencer, Rhonda P62
Spencer, Kipp P70
Spencer, Denise P87

Spencer, Lorraine P205
Spencer, Octavia P259
Spencer, Thomas P322
Spencer, Barbara P370
Spencer, Floyd P384
Spencer, Terry K P397
Spencer, J Robert P465
Spencer, Monica P544
Spencer, Marjorie P566
Spencer, Andrew P612
Spencer, Stuart W16
Spencer, Jody E25
Spencer, Ronald E394
Spera, Richard P561
Speranza, Emanuela A56
Speranzo, Anthony E344
Sperazza, Laura P237
Spergel, David A781:P580
Sperling, Scott A784
Speroni, Stefano W185
Sperry, Diane P402
Spevak, Barry A676
Sphr, Terry K P315
Sphuler, Erica A570:P388
Spiegel, Noel A662
Spiegler, Erica W75
Spieker, Marc W169
Spielman, Amanda A512:P326
Spier, Scott P332
Spier, Dr Scott P334
Spiesshofer, Ulrich W246
Spiker, Brenda P174
Spillane, Michael E55
Spiller, Scott P23
Spillers, David P257:P561
Spilman, Robert A254
Spina, Lori P230
Spina, Suzana P420
Spina, Jessica W316
Spinale, Joseph W P504
Spindle, Barbara P115
Spinelli, Anthony A613
Spinelli, Ann P452
Spinelli, Marcello W513
Spinelli, Anthony E316
Spinnato, Joseph E P371
Spinner, Debbie P128
Spinner, Janice P354
Spinosa, Frank A642
Spira, Joel E186
Spirk, Don P461
Spiro, Martin E20
Spitulnik, Aric P300
Spitz, David E78
Spitzer, Donald E180
Spivey, Jack E104
Splain, Steve A135
Splaine, Thomas A466
Splaine, Kevin R P494
Splaine, Thomas A243
Splinter, Mike A543
Spoelder, Eelco W194
Spoelman, Roger P305:P330
Spoerel, Thomas A109
Spoerry, Robert E273
Spohr, Carsten W161
Spolarich, Michael A322
Spolidoro, Laurence A251
Spong, Bernadette P400:P443
Spooner, William A P477
Spoor, Michelle A735:P510
Spradley, Scott A802
Spradlin, Jim A369
Spradlin, Shane A615
Spradlin, Jim P237
Sprague, Joseph A26
Spratt, Michael P591
Sprau, Jon A35:P27
Spraus, Joyan P224
Spray, Stephen A179
Sprecher, Jeffrey A422
Spreher, Michael P29
Sprieser, Judith A422
Spriggs, Elise A733
Spriggs, Rodney E256
Spring, Donald A530
Spring, Micho A544

COMBINED HOOVER'S HANDBOOK INDEX OF EXECUTIVES

A = AMERICAN BUSINESS
E = EMERGING COMPANIES
P = PRIVATE COMPANIES
W = WORLD BUSINESS

Spring, Kelly P158
Spring, Stevie W132
Spring, Donald E275
Spring, Micho E285
Springer, Mary E75
Springer, Noah E153
Springer, Jack E258
Springer, Jon E427
Springfield, Susan A317:E170
Sprinkle, James P551
Sprinkle, Ray P635
Sprouse, David P67
Spruill, David P542
Sprunk, Bob P358
Spuhler, Peter W190
Spurway, Robert W199
Spychall, Michael A866:P657
Spyhalsk, Anne Kocian P534
Spyrow, Flo P227
Squeri, Stephen A46
Squibb, Brian A555:P374
Squillace, Delores P439
Squires, James A566
Squires, Paul A700
Squires, Nelson A854
Squires, Christine P35
Sr, Richard M Devos A35
Sr, Albert R Zimmerli A423
Sr, Richard M Devos P27
Sr, Rex A Rock P41
Sr, George Kaleak P41
Sr, Raymond Clunie P158
Sr, Margaret Hadley P254
Sr, Linda Reedy P261
Sr, Albert R Zimmerli P264
Sr, William H Dunn P268:P268
Sr, Jesse T Williams P272
Sr, James A Miner P345
Sr, Anthony J Rouse P452
Sr, Debbie Dickie P478
Sr, John R Raymond P566
Sr, Dr John Raymond P566
Sr, Robert Curran P579
Sr, Avery B Hall P626
Srednicki, Richard E135
Sreedharan, Jay E344
Sreenan, Meghan P332
Srichai, Kobboon W113
Srichukrin, Narong W441
Sridharan, Karthik A582:E302
Srihong, Teeranun W491
Srimahunt, Pikun W441
Srinivasan, Mallika A20:W478
Srinivasan, LaVerne E402
Sripaibulya, Suteera W62
Sripaipan, Senathip W491
Sripleng, Poonpat W284
Sripratak, Adirek W98:W113
Sriram, B. W240
Srisanit, Kittiya W65
Srivanich, Payong W285
Srivastava, Ankit A214
Srivastava, Abhishek P652
Srivastava, Raman W213
Sriworasat, Rungson W113
Sroda, Rachael P375
Srur, Barbara P P465
Staats, Aaron Von E339
Stabler, D. Scott A410
Stacey, Rulon F A291:P210
Stacey, Rulon P422
Stachura, Paul A733
Stack, Edward A244
Stack, Colleen P590
Stack, John W187
Stack, David E311
Stacker, Mary P45
Stackhouse, Julie A712:E373
Stackley, Sean A463
Stacy, Leland J P50
Stacy, Donald E274

Stadelman, Chris A742:P518
Stadelmann, Douglas H P222
Stadelmann, Douglas P222
Stadigh, Kari W359
Stadler, Tammy A74
Stadler, Elisabeth W515:W521
Stadtler, Dj P364
Staehelin, Tobias W425
Staffeldt, Erik E210
Staffieri, Michael A237
Staffne, Aria A541
Stafford, Andrew A199
Stafford, William A314
Stafford, Kenneth R P619
Stafford, Ryan E255
Stagg, Kendall W100
Stagliano, Joseph A546
Staheli, Ben P14
Stahl, Stephanie A253
Stahl, Neil A669
Stahl, Jack A817
Stahl, Murray E186
Stahl, Russell E300
Stahl, Murray E407
Stahlberg, Christian W346
Stahlkopf, Deborah A182
Stainthorpe, Mark W100
Stake, James E309
Stakias, G. Michael E123
Staley, Tabitha P315
Staley, Jeanette P429
Staley, David P553
Staley, John P587
Staley, Gary E436
Stalick, Theodore A516
Stallings, Wendy A584
Stallkamp, Thomas A106
Stam, Robert P483
Stamm, K. Brad E155
Stamoulis, Christiana E225
Stanbrook, Steven A368
Stancer, Lori P126
Stancl, Craig Robert P321
Stanczyk, Russ A738:P514
Stander, Deon A86
Standeven, David A30:P21
Standing, Shannon P92
Standish, Dr Liz P396
Standley, John A843
Standridge, Brant A796
Stanek, Sharen P155
Stanek, Janet P522
Stanford, Beth P80
Stanford, Douglas P185
Stanford, Jessica P440
Stangl, Sandra A777
Stanik, John A331:E178
Stankey, John A78
Stanley, Stephen E P40
Stanley, Anthony P123
Stanley, Alicia P146
Stanley, Roger P196
Stanley, Kelly P474
Stanley, Harold P491
Stanley, Martin W304
Stansbury, Christopher A72
Stanski, Matthew E P579
Stanton, Kevin A506
Stanton, John A810
Stanton, Oliver K P597
Stanton, Katie Jacobs W519
Stanwood, Michael P216
Stanzione, Laurie A30:P21
Stanzione, Dominque P307
Stapleton, Chuck P155
Starace, Francesco W179:W181
Starheim, Gregory E286
Stark, Leah A63
Stark, Paul A187
Stark, Jack A220
Stark, Doug A293
Stark, Derek A614
Stark, Wendy A637
Stark, Doug P211
Stark, Kyle P508
Stark, David W487
Stark, Paul E85

Stark, Derek E317
Stark, Juergen E418
Starling, Curtis P112
Starnes, William A642
Starnes, Clarke A796
Starnes, Pam P58
Starns, Renee P542
Starr, Ken P65
Starr, Dan P191
Starr, Megan E185
Stars, Hauke W286
Starsia, Tim E439
Starsiak, Michael P353
Stata, Raymond A61
Staten, Jennifer A203:P144
States, Lauren A851
Staton, Daniel A70
Staub, Walter A433
Staub, Zeno W524
Stauder, Mark P263
Stauffer, Charlotte A123:P81
Stauffer, Craig P351
Stauffer, Jeffrey E134
Stausholm, Jakob W405:W406
Stauth, Scott W100
Staver, Karla E359
Stavropoulos, Nickolas A278:E141
Stawis, Allen P500
Stead, Jimmy A227
Steadman, Bevan P199
Stearns, Leah A159
Stearns, Leo P223
Steck, Brian A171
Steck, Kevin P522
Steck, Brian E85
Stecko, Paul A605
Steddum, Chris E407
Steed, Connie C P428
Steel, Robert A345
Steel, Julie P417
Steele, John A179
Steele, Gregory A285
Steele, Amber P113
Steele, Robert P141
Steele, Gail P155
Steele, Sara P194
Steele, Robert P390
Steele, Keri P529
Steele, Barbara P595
Steele, Mark T P601
Steele, Barry E228
Steelman, Tracy P413
Steen, Ida A227
Steen, Bernie P569
Steenbergen, Ewout A691
Steenbergen, Remco W161
Steenland, Douglas A41
Steenrod, Mitchell A154
Steenvoorden, Rene W397
Steer, Robert A700
Steer, Randolph E50
Steere, F William P14
Stefanie, Taylor P535
Stefanini, Pierluigi W511
Stefano, Ken De P6
Stefanowicz, Melanie P579
Stefanski, Marc A773
Steffe, Ganine P316
Steffen, Mark A P103
Steffens, Greg A723:E383
Steffes, Cathy P31
Stegmaier, James J L P157
Stegner, Jonathan P585
Stegwell, Mary Jo P40
Stehlik, Christine P230
Steichen, Jennifer L P204
Steiger, John P519
Steigerwald, Tim P336
Steigerwalt, Eric T A133
Steil, Jim P81
Steiman, Gerald S P355
Stein, Jeffrey A39
Stein, David A74
Stein, Robert A76
Stein, Clint A201
Stein, Kevin A246
Stein, Richard A306

Stein, Laurence A360
Stein, Laura A535
Stein, Sue P107
Stein, Paul P309
Stein, Clint E92
Stein, Michael E191
Stein, Steven E225
Steinbach, David P553
Steinbacher, Michele P609
Steinback, Michael A P626
Steinberg, Joseph A437
Steinberg, Darrell P132
Steinberg, Alan P159
Steinberg, Sarah P441
Steinberg, Michael P615
Steiner, Paul A206
Steiner, Jeffrey A465
Steiner, Robert A26
Steiner, Kevin P26
Steiner, Cindy P481
Steiner, Kirk P485
Steiner, Christopher P572
Steiner, Eddie E111
Steiner, Mitchell E435
Steinert, Earl A366
Steines, Ann A565
Steinfeld, Ellen A113
Steinhafel, Arthur W P421
Steinhart, Ronald A615
Steinke, Bruce A40
Steinke, Craig A139
Steinmeier, Richard A489
Steinmetz, Joann P92
Steinmetz, David P133
Steinour, Stephen A104:A409
Steinwert, Kent A294:E155
Steitz, Paul A159
Stella, Anthony A783
Stella, Mitsopoulos P184
Stella, Anthony P583
Stellar, James A744:P519
Stelling, James P A50
Stelling, Kessel A754:E401
Stemler, Steven E174
Stenberg, Melissa P203
Stendahl, Lea E523
Stengel, Scott A33
Stengel, William A350
Stenger, Thomas A398:E218
Stenman, Eric P55:P55
Stenqvist, Lars W523
Stensland, Kelly A233:P178
Stenson, Brian A744:P519
Stenzel, Mary P366
Stephens, Christopher A702
Stephens, Michael P362
Stephens, Linda P414
Stephens, Jack W315
Stephens, Gary E300
Stephens, Jeffrey P366
Stephenson, Aaron A168:A170
Stephenson, Scott A651
Stephenson, Mona A693
Stephenson, Randall A845
Stephenson, David P25
Stephenson, Craig P101
Stephenson, Don P101
Stephenson, Rick P101
Stephenson, Harry D P142
Stephenson, Don P142
Stephenson, Craig P142
Stephenson, Jim P597
Stephenson, Mona P360
Stephenson, Scott E434
Stepnowski, Amy A377
Sterett, William J P194
Sterin, Steven A260
Sterling, Choice P482
Sterling, Joan E420
Stern, Walter A39
Stern, William A53
Stern, Shoshone A668
Stern, James A801
Stern, Walter P28
Stern, Sadye P371
Stern, Rita P423
Stern, James A P603

590

HOOVER'S HANDBOOK OF EMERGING COMPANIES 2022

COMBINED HOOVER'S HANDBOOK INDEX OF EXECUTIVES

Stern, Yedidia W64
Stern, William E25
Stern, Sadie E117
Sternberg, Erich A451
Sternberg, Christina P28
Sternberg, Todd E442
Sterner, Kurtis P173
Sternhell, Rebecca K A186:P129
Sternlicht, Barry S A733:E389:E413
Sterrs, Lawrence A144
Stetelman, Andrew A309:E163
Stetson, Robert J E196
Stevanovic, Andreja E343
Steven, James A846
Stevener, Donna I P303
Stevens, Jon I A122
Stevens, Charles A264
Stevens, Melissa A306
Stevens, Daniel A381
Stevens, Gary A412
Stevens, Charles A502
Stevens, Glenn A748
Stevens, Robert A757
Stevens, Charles A767
Stevens, Wayne A798
Stevens, David P32
Stevens, Jon I P80
Stevens, Chris P185
Stevens, David P202
Stevens, Ron P240
Stevens, Clement P240
Stevens, Gary P258
Stevens, Mary Jane P269
Stevens, Sandra P309
Stevens, Ashley P375
Stevens, Matthew P437
Stevens, Gary P496
Stevens, Carla P499
Stevens, Kevin P615
Stevens, Lisa W35
Stevens, Daniel E208
Stevens, Edward E239
Stevens, Timothy E343
Stevenson, Ruth A544
Stevenson, Kimberly A715
Stevenson, Mark A784
Stevenson, Cindy P271
Stevenson, Jim P321
Stevenson, Heather P480
Stevenson, Hollie P617
Stevenson, Katharine W99
Stevenson, Brian W253
Stevenson, Robby E5
Stevenson, Tim E186
Stevenson, Kimberly E277
Stevenson, Ruth E285
Steverson, Lewis A222
Stevo, Christopher A622
Steward, David A869:P659
Steward, Randall E342
Stewart, Jeffrey A6
Stewart, William A31
Stewart, James A103
Stewart, Sue A147
Stewart, Eric A268
Stewart, Cecelia A317
Stewart, Michael A320
Stewart, John A403
Stewart, Vincent A448
Stewart, James A530
Stewart, Derrick A585
Stewart, David K A679
Stewart, Marta A708
Stewart, Karen Weldin A735
Stewart, Leanne M P1
Stewart, William P24
Stewart, James P54:P60
Stewart, Jordan P98
Stewart, David P113
Stewart, Louis P132
Stewart, Denise P249
Stewart, John P256
Stewart, C Todd P314
Stewart, Brian P433
Stewart, Karen Weldin P511
Stewart, Richard P522
Stewart, Karla P595

Stewart, Garfield P660
Stewart, Alan W165
Stewart, Sue E65
Stewart, Bonita E116
Stewart, John E120
Stewart, Cecelia E170
Stewart, Michael E172
Stewart, Samanta E203
Stewart, Michael E265
Stewart, James E275
Stewart, Lisa E448
Stheeman, Elisabeth W2
Stiber, Barri P293
Stice, J. Michael A496:A541
Stickels, Eric A210:E95
Stickney, Michael W239
Stief, Brian A442:P278
Stief, James E115
Stiefler, Jeffrey A304
Stiegmann, Gregory V P618
Stiehle, Thomas A410
Stieritz, Brian P214
Stiers, Mark A258
Stiffler, Don P145
Stigers, Mike A817
Stigers, Thomas A860
Stiles, Gaylene P333
Stiles, Dick P439
Stiles, Mitchell P P644
Still, Susan A49:E21
Stille, Goran W470
Stillwell, Kathy P239
Stilson, David P207
Stine, Douglas H P355
Stiner, Daisy P147
Stinnett, T. A747
Stinnett, Lisa P166
Stinnett, T. E391
Stinson, Kenneth E P570
Stipancich, John A686
Stiphout, Marnix Van W249
Stipp, Janice E P534
Stirdivant, David P289
Stiritz, William A635
Stirling, Lisa A476:A477:P297
Stirling, Steve P311
Stites, Jill D P116
Stith, Melvin A18
Stith, Thomas A739:P515
Stithit, Wuttikorn W393
Stitt, Kevin A740
Stitt, Jobi P401
Stitt, Donald P465
Stitt, Kevin P516
Stivers, Richard P185
Stock, Alan A9
Stock, Elane A875
Stock, Alan E4
Stockbauer, Herta W367
Stocker, Georg W157
Stockert, David E124
Stockfish, Devin A862
Stockman, Gary A213:P150
Stockmann, Bill P353
Stockton, Dmitri A240:A689
Stockton, Don P150
Stockton, Michael W P368
Stockwell, Dennis P269
Stoddard, Daniel A254
Stoddard, Jason P380
Stoddart, Richard A377
Stoddart, Paul A506
Stoehr, David A867:E452
Stoel, M D P340
Stoering, Mark A871
Stogsdill, Patricia P309
Stokely, John E127:E258:E328
Stokes, Charisse A25
Stokes, Nicole A53
Stokes, Russell A346:A819
Stokes, Melvina P121
Stokes, Michelle P579
Stokes, Nicole E25
Stokes, Eric E297
Stolicker, Melissa A366:P235
Stolinski, John P130
Stolly, Timothy E361

Stolz, Carsten W55
Stolzenberg, Eric L P534
Stone, John A58
Stone, R. Gregg A143
Stone, Alan A147
Stone, John A240
Stone, Larry A244
Stone, Jeffrey A260
Stone, Randy A260
Stone, Paul A385
Stone, Shawn A541
Stone, Andrew A668
Stone, Sarah A740
Stone, Paul A778
Stone, Jeffrey I P85
Stone, Katherine P88
Stone, Robert P126
Stone, Wade P145
Stone, Jeff P167
Stone, William C P196
Stone, Clarence P256
Stone, Mike P266
Stone, Brad P445
Stone, David L P462
Stone, Sarah P516
Stone, Paul P561
Stone, R. Gregg E65
Stone, Alan E66
Stone, Joseph E96
Stone, R. Dary E105
Stone, William E120
Stone, Shawn E281
Stoneman, Shelly W53
Stoner, Nathan A228
Stoner, Roberta B P246
Stoner, Nancy A416
Stoner, Sherry P635
Stoner, Christy E430
Stones, Charles A296:E157
Stonestreet, Dana A396:E217
Stoney, Levar M P132
Stoney, Michael E409
Stonhill, Richard P184
Stoops, John P74
Stoothoff, Anthony A32:P24
Stopyra, Jennifer P392
Storey, Jeffrey A490
Storey, Barry A754:E401
Stork, David A481
Stork, Johannes W42
Storm, Kelsie P293
Storms, Tim A770
Story, Susan A558:A663
Story, G Edward P443
Stothert, Jean P130
Stotlar, Douglas A15:A673
Stott, John A69
Stouder, Alice P141
Stough, Michael A300
Stout, David A434
Stout, Cathy A551
Stout, Mike P134
Stouvenot, Franois P396
Stovall, Dick P283
Stovall, Greg P600
Stover, Dan W145
Stovesand, Kirk E96
Stovsky, Richard E135
Stowe, Roy P269
Stowe, Jay P270
Stowell, Scott A788
Stowers, David A512
Stowers, Josh A542
Stowers, David P327
Stowers, Josh P518
Stowers, Carmen P579
Stoyles, Lyndall W484
Straber, Renee A502
Straberg, Hans W48
Strable-Soethout, Deanna A641
Strack, Jeff P523
Strack, Jeffrey P523
Straczynski, Pawel W70
Strader, John P613
Strah, Steven A324
Strain, Denise A322
Strain, Kevin W465

Straka, M. Beth A852
Straka, Ann P591
Straka, Patrick E82
Strakosch, Gregory E403
Stralen, Victor Van A804:P607
Strammello, Steve P175
Strand, Ina W25
Strange, Julia P604
Strange, James E103
Strangeway, Christine P505
Strank, Angela W410
Strapelli, David P275
Strassner, Larry P220
Strathman, Kevin A233:P178
Stratta, Guido W181
Stratton, John A345
Stratton, Julianna A736:P512
Straub, Maximiliane A681:P448
Strauch, Roger E81
Strause, Alana P438
Strauss, Mark A340
Strauss, Cindy P429:P430
Strauss, Christianne W527
Straw, Regina P220
Strazi, Brian P212
Streck, Richard J P14
Strecker, Kevin P44
Strecker, Kurt W75
Stredit-Thomas, Sukari P257
Street, Terry P446
Streeter, Stephanie A459
Strehl, Joe P170
Strei, Katherine E133
Streit, Clara Christina W263
Streit, Clara W524
Strenio, Theresa P27
Strey, Jean P167
Strickland, A. A45
Strickland, Hoyt J A50
Strickland, Jim P128
Strickland, Jill P434
Stricklen-Hilly, Brittany P394
Strimbu, William A331:E178
Stringer, Scott A186
Stringer, David A321
Stringer, Scott P129
Stringer, Mitch P153
Stringer, Ruth M P158
Stripling, Nathan P283
Strippoli, Sandra P198
Strobel, Pamela A415
Strobel, Marsha P217
Strobel, Victoria L P314
Strobel, Martin W52
Stroberg, Bob P188
Stroberg, Melanie P529
Stroh, Elizabeth P262
Strohfus, Joseph P466
Strohmeyer, Karl A282
Strom, Carrie A6
Strom, Jeff A125
Stromberg, Kristen A632
Stromberg, William A757
Stromberg, Leroy P16
Stromer, Michael A439
Stronach, Benjamin P624
Strong, Ryan A321
Strong, Dalene A366
Strong, Robert A716
Strong, John P182
Strong, Dalene P235
Strong, David P400
Strong, Matthew P404
Strong, David P443
Strong, Aaron E69
Strong, Gary E300
Strong, Robert E379
Strongwater, Steven P50
Stronks, Timothy E96
Stroud, Mark P274
Stroup, John A767
Strout, Lisa P317
Strozina, Sarah P608
Strubert, John P222
Struck, Tony P662
Strueber-Hummelt, Anke W190
Strunk, Tom A869:P659

COMBINED HOOVER'S HANDBOOK INDEX OF EXECUTIVES

A = AMERICAN BUSINESS
E = EMERGING COMPANIES
P = PRIVATE COMPANIES
W = WORLD BUSINESS

Strunk, Edward E153
Strutz, Eric W233
Strydesky, John E164
Stryker, David A411
Strzelecki, Angela A425
Stuart, Al A48
Stuart, David P172
Stuart, Cindy P251
Stuart, T. Brent E175
Stuart-Grant, Alan W30
Stubbs, Willie P206
Stubbs, Peter E153
Stuckey, Mac A154
Stuckey, Perry A264
Stucki, Aaron W480
Stucky, Duane P490
Studenmund, Jaynie E151
Studer, Michael E137
Studt, Amanda P218
Stuemper, Klaus W227
Stueve, Jo P330
Stuff, Ronald P525:P581
Stull, Brian A436:P271
Stumbaugh, Pam P22
Stumbo, Kevin A211
Stump, Kate Lucas P284
Stumpf, Nathan P52
Stuntz, Linda A268
Stupenengo, Annalisa W391
Stupp, John P495
Sturdevant, Robert P132
Sturdivant, Mike P P509
Sturges, Anthony P278
Sturgess, David E P311
Sturgill, Judie P524
Sturm, Stephan W204
Sturrock, A.Troy A276
Stutzman, Paul P234
Stuver, Douglas A604
Stwalley, Bob P398
Stylianopoulos, George P124
Stymiest, Barbara W465:W527
Stys, Richard P242
Styslinger, Lee A671
Su, Lisa A13:A182
Su, Hengxuan W117
Su, Cheng-Hui W138
Su, Yong-Ho W138
Su, Min W154
Suarez, Paul A155
Suarez, Francis X P128
Suarez, Maria P132
Suarez, Bernardo P569
Suarez-Gonzalez, Susana A426
Subandhi, Victor P94
Subasic, Stephen A731
Suber, Constance P624
Subin, Neil E89
Sublette, Bill P467
Subramaniam, Rajesh A302:A317:E170
Subramanian, Guhan A484
Subramanian, V A P299
Such, Virginia P318
Sucharitkul, Piyada W62
Sucher, Theresa P437
Suckale, Margret W222:W246
Suderman, Julie P545
Suedel, Kathleen P256
Suer, Bernard P336
Suess, Calvin A294:E155
Sufrategui, Jose Ramon Martinez W57
Sugar, Ronald A65
Sugata, Shiro W538
Sugay, Noel W83
Sugg, Laura A651
Sugg, B Alan P616
Sugg, Rebecca P624
Suggs, Sean A674
Suggs, Leo P98
Suggs, Tom P569
Suggs, Denis E314

Suggs, Sean E348
Sughrue, Timothy P353
Sugi, Hikaru W327
Sugimori, Tsutomu W182
Sugimori, Masato W314
Sugimoto, Shigeji W255
Sugita, Masahiro W1
Sugita, Naoto W68
Sugita, Koji W332
Sugiura, Masakazu W237
Sugiura, Tsuyoshi W339
Sugiyama, Yoshihiro A877:P662
Sugranes, Rosa A317:E170
Sugrue, Chiara P299
Suhm, Mary P126
Sui, Yang W87
Suit, John M P306
Suits, Duane A587:E302
Sukeno, Kenji W205
Sukey, Bibi P89
Sukhov, Gennady W208:W385
Sukpantavorn, Suchada W62
Sukvimol, Satitpong W441:W441
Sul, Thomas W166
Sulentic, Robert A159
Sulerzyski, Charles A617
Sulivan, Anne A781
Sulivan, Brian P185
Sulivan, Anne P581
Sullens, Dave P379
Sullins, Jim P171
Sullivan, Lynn A A93
Sullivan, John A143
Sullivan, Kevin A243
Sullivan, Michael A285
Sullivan, Shawn A390
Sullivan, Kathryn A427
Sullivan, Heidi A516
Sullivan, Caroline A536
Sullivan, Owen A548
Sullivan, Anne Marie A552
Sullivan, Andrew A649
Sullivan, Frank A688
Sullivan, Sean A714
Sullivan, James E A779
Sullivan, Edward P14
Sullivan, Pam P33
Sullivan, Carolyn P171
Sullivan, Kevin P188:P319
Sullivan, Teresa A P342
Sullivan, Anne Marie P369
Sullivan, Timothy F P411
Sullivan, Charles B P438
Sullivan, Teresa A P439
Sullivan, Stuart P P481
Sullivan, James E P568
Sullivan, Jeff P569
Sullivan, Timothy P575
Sullivan, George P579
Sullivan, Caryn P609
Sullivan, E Thomas P631
Sullivan, Caroline P644
Sullivan, Shannon D P646
Sullivan, Angus W135
Sullivan, Lori E12
Sullivan, John E65
Sullivan, William E114
Sullivan, Nora E148
Sullivan, Shawn E215
Sullivan, Kieran O E246
Sullivan, Lenore E329
Sullivan, Jeffrey E389
Sulpizio, Richard E352
Sulpy, Dale P571
Sult, John R P202:P491
Sultan, Fredrik P364
Sultan, Khaled Bin Saleh Al W423
Sultemeier, Chris A874:E124
Sultzbaugh, Marc P325
Sulzberger, Gabrielle A478:A506
Sumas, James J A842:P645
Sumerford, Harlow A741:P517
Sumi, Shuzo W500
Sumida, Ryoichi P90
Sumita, Makoto W479
Sumitomo, Yasuhiko W52
Summerlin, Jennifer P69

Summers, Michael A A322
Summers, Jeff P481
Summers, Angela M P566
Summit, Shah P489
Summy, Amy A464
Sumner, Randee A588
Sumner, Hall A663:P436
Sumner, Mike P627
Sumoski, David A575
Sumpter, Thomas P80
Sun, Richard A157
Sun, Angela A174
Sun, Shyan P60
Sun, Angela P118
Sun, Yu W87
Sun, Yun W88
Sun, David W106
Sun, Ruiwen W118
Sun, Patrick W120
Sun, Cui W121
Sun, Zhe W121
Sun, Fujie W130
Sun, Yongxing W154
Sun, Juyi W209
Sun, Longde W378
Sun, Richard E70
Sun, Anthony E89
Sunby, Bonnie A739:P515
Sundaram, Easwaran A854
Sundaram, Mani E11
Sunderland, Lester T P581
Sundheim, Jeremy P441
Sundy, John P197
Sung, Jae Ho W438
Sung, Christina E121
Sungur, Ahmet W504
Sunkara, Tagore P102
Sunkel, Fred Meller W59
Sunkle, David E332
Sunshine, Eugene W40:E73
Sunterapak, Todd P638
Suntrapak, Todd P638
Sununu, John A132
Sununu, Chris A738:P514
Sunwoo, Seok Ho W271
Supornpaibul, Jirawat W270
Suppasedsak, Weerapong W284
Suppiah, Iswaraan W29
Suquet, Jose A671
Surakit, Wasana W270
Suraphongchai, Vichit W441
Surdykowski, Andrew A422
Suresh, Subra P100
Surges, Monique W81
Suri, Rajeev A749
Suriano, April P536
Surjaudaja, Parwati W376
Surma, John A496:A541:A651
Surowiec, Yvonne A832:E431
Surti, Urvashi P635
Suryadevara, Madhu P578
Susan, Schmidt P429
Susca, Vito A710:E371
Susie, Lee P125
Suskind, Dennis A246
Susman, Sally A622
Sussman, Lester A262
Sussman, Elliot A824
Sussman, Elliot J P294
Sussman, Lester E127
Sustana, Mark A474
Sutaria, Saumya A765
Sutaris, Joseph A210:E95
Suter, Todd A P49:P639
Suter, Kelly E409
Sutera, Albert J P556
Sutherland, L. Frederick A216
Sutherland, Vanessa A566
Sutherland, David A821
Sutherland, Janet P282
Sutherland, David W242
Sutherlin, Michael E362
Suthumpun, Suphajee W270
Sutil, Lucia Santa Cruz W59
Sutisna, Paulus W155
Sutivong, Arak W441
Sutley, Nancy P303

Suto, Hideho W491
Sutton, George A355
Sutton, Marina A382
Sutton, Jason A410
Sutton, Mark A427
Sutton, Scott A588
Sutton, Doniel A687
Sutton, Thomas A722
Sutton, Patricia A P7
Sutton, Nathan P141
Sutton, Ellen P387
Sutton, Joseph E19
Sutton, George E193
Sutton, Marina E211
Sutula, Stanley A200:P52
Suwanprateeb, Trirat W441
Suzuki, Russell A735
Suzuki, Miyuki A858
Suzuki, Yoshihiro P22
Suzuki, Russell P511
Suzuki, Jon B P536
Suzuki, Koichi W1
Suzuki, Toshio W1
Suzuki, Toshiyuki W17
Suzuki, Kenji W21:W68
Suzuki, Nobuya W228
Suzuki, Yoichi W268
Suzuki, Teruo W299
Suzuki, Yasunobu W327
Suzuki, Yoshiteru W373
Suzuki, Kosuke W377
Suzuki, Toshihiro W469
Suzuki, Toshiaki W469
Suzuki, Junichi W536
Svanberg, Carl-Henric W523
Svasti-xuto, Wittawat W393
Svec, Laurie P45
Svec, Tamara P166
Svelto, Anna W81
Svendsen, Kurt E411
Svenson, Jennifer A103:E47
Svensson, Ake A609
Svienson, Branden P408
Svihel, Alice P51
Svoboda, Frank A359
Swaby, Jonathan P554
Swager, Karen A539
Swahn, Christian A80
Swain, Clinton A866
Swain, John P184
Swain, Stacy P345
Swain, Debra P467
Swain, Paula E225
Swain, Clinton E450
Swales, Judith W199
Swalling, John E296
Swallow, Michael F A203:P144
Swaminathan, Suresh P535
Swan, Dennis A P493
Swan, Quito P562
Swanberg, Dale P214
Swander, Robert P11
Swann, Mary A324
Swanson, Brian A89:A90
Swanson, Aloys A630
Swanson, Al A631
Swanson, Thomas A727
Swanson, Brian P54
Swanson, Angela P90
Swanson, Natalie P157
Swanson, Al P420
Swanson, Tom P430
Swanson, Brian E41
Swartz, Paul P362
Swartz, Kevin E26
Swartz, Richard E284
Swartzendruber, Kevin E374
Sweaney, Donna P631
Sweat, Tim P269
Swedjemark, Theodor W5
Sweeney, Joseph A52
Sweeney, Emily P627
Sweet, Benjamin P102
Sweet, Brett P590
Sweet, Julie W8
Sweet, Thomas E415
Sweigart, John W P439

COMBINED HOOVER'S HANDBOOK INDEX OF EXECUTIVES

Sweinberg, Sharon K P308
Sweitzer, Brandon W191
Sweklo, Julie P234
Swelheim, Erik W278
Swensen, Dawn P36
Swenson, Douglas P184
Swenson, Michael E83
Swets, Jon A493
Swett, Amy P146
Swevish, Joseph P332
Swiatkowski, Jonathan T P208
Swiecicki, Peter A589
Swieringa, John A249
Swift, Christopher A185:A377
Swift, Malcolm A508
Swift, Jamie P55
Swift, Micheal A P170
Swim, Janet A780:P575
Swinehart, Alice P335
Swinemar, Adam W290
Swinfard, Ronald P294
Swingler, Justin P52
Swinton, Matt L P286
Swinton, Carolyn P428
Switz, Robert A527
Switzer, John A396
Switzer, Matthew W640
Switzer, Julie P652
Switzer, John E217
Switzer, Matthew E333
Swoboda, Marco W224
Swofford, Connie P451
Swope, John P334
Swords, Sheridan A593
Swyers, Steven A399
Swygert, Jenny P5
Sy, Darrell P224
Sy, Teresita W83
Syal, Rajeev A409
Sydnor, Walker P107
Syed, Christine A P237
Syed, Talat P352
Syed, Arshad P464
Syed, Nadeem P653
Sykes, David P133
Sykora, Amanda P138
Sykora, Matthew P161
Sylvain, Jereme E117
Sylvester, Maryrose A848
Sylvester, Carol P275
Symancyk, James A104
Symansky, Martin P98
Symes, Jeffrey E105
Symonds, Jonathan W210
Symson, Adam E364
Syndergaard, Janyce P168
Syngal, Sonia A777
Syphax, Scott A298:A642
Syquia, Juan Carlos W70
Syta, Joseph J P450
Syvinski, Clint P572
Szablak, Chester A278:E141
Szabo, Csaba W334
Szabo, Gabriel W334
Szafranski, Sharon A415
Szczecki, Blazej W71
Szczepanski, Karen P574
Szczuk, Jason A126:P83
Szczurek, Michal W491
Szews, Charles A207:A368
Szews, Katie P45
Szkutak, Thomas A429
Szlezak, Andrzej W263
Sznewajs, Robert D A93
Sznewajs, John A190:A219:A502
Szubinski, Clint A518
Szubski, Michael P614
Szuster, Martin A877
Szybowski, Steve P536
Szyman, Catherine A269
Szymanczyk, Michael E124
Szymanski, Ken P293
Szymczak, Stephen J P286
Szymczyk, Eric P485

T

Taaveniku, Arja W470
Tabaddor, Rouz A308
Tabaka, William A405
Tabata, Takuji W1
Tabb, Kevin P71
Taber, Rodman P494
Taber, Abram P579
Taboada, Francisco Sardon de W69
Tabolt, Brian A558
Tabron, La June Montgomery A449
Tacardon, Charlie P551
Tacchetti, Gregory A733
Tachasirinugune, Sommai W113
Tachouet, Matthew P638
Tackett, Shane A26
Tad-Y, Darlene B A824:P617
Taets, Joseph A68
Taft, Kenneth P88
Taft, Jason P461
Taft, Matthias W81
Taftali, Aykut W540
Tagawa, Joji W328
Tagg, Robin P256
Taggart, Harriett A375
Tagle, Jose Manuel Manzano W59
Tago, Hideto W418
Taguchi, Sachio W66
Tahir, Sulaiman Bin Mohd W29
Tai, Luther A216
Tai, Mazie P451
Tai, Jackson W234
Tai, Jeng-Wu W432
Taipov, Marsel A683
Tait, Rachelle P249
Tait, Matthew E259
Taittinger, Anneclaire W488
Tajanlangit, Edwin W83
Takada, Yoshimasa W228
Takagi, Shuichi W375
Takahara, Ichiro W312
Takahara, Takahisa W360
Takahara, Kazuyoshi W494
Takahashi, Atsushi W66
Takahashi, Masahiro W66
Takahashi, Koichi W149
Takahashi, Yoshinori W226
Takahashi, Kyohei W313
Takahashi, Shinya W351
Takahashi, Hidetake W373
Takahashi, Toyonori W373
Takahashi, Shojiro W435
Takahashi, Hideo W435
Takahashi, Yoshimitsu W437
Takamatsu, Kazuko W268
Takamiya, Art P121
Takano, Hiromitsu W491
Takaoka, Hidenori W325
Takarsh, Jeff A742:P518
Takase, Hisashi W435
Takashima, Makoto W463
Takata, Kenji W257
Takata, Toshihisa W369
Takaura, Hideo W494
Takayanagi, Nobuhiro W327
Takeda, Becky P142:P143
Takeda, Shunsuke W36
Takegawa, Keiko W429
Takeguchi, Fumitoshi W375
Takemoto, Sue P499
Takemura, Hideaki W317
Takenaka, Heizo W373
Takeno, Ty P163
Takeoka, Yaeko W328
Takeshita, Tomio A185:P122
Takeuchi, Toshie W23
Takeuchi, Kei W150
Takeuchi, Tetsuo W257
Takeuchi, Toshiaki W269
Takeuchi, Masamichi W279
Takeuchi, Akira W327
Takeuchi, Yutaka W356
Takeuchi, Kei W375
Takeuchi, Minako W435
Takizawa, Shumpei W493
Talarico, Nick P191

Talati, Megha P640
Talavera, Alvaro P255
Talbot, Siobhan W145
Tall, Samir P40
Tallent, William W520
Tallett, Elizabeth A63:A641
Talley, Joseph P30
Talley, Jill P269
Talley, Brent P616
Talley, Michael E427
Talley, Jeffrey E430
Talley-Smith, Christy A123:P81
Talman, Lori P209
Talton, Sheila A240
Talvitie, Kristian E339
Talwalkar, Abhijit A13:A467:W480
Tam, Kam Wah W196
Tamai, Kouichi W205
Tamaka, Hideo A48:P31
Tamanaha, Charlene A735:P511
Tamayo, Arturo Condo W61
Tamberlane, John A710:E371
Tamburi, Carlo W181
Tamer, Ford E405
Tamme, Susan A675:E350
Tampo, Kuniyasu W350
Tamura, Koji W329
Tamura, Mayumi W436
Tamura, Yasuro W472
Tan, Justine A452
Tan, Irving A731
Tan, Catherine P301
Tan, Benjamin A P597
Tan, Hak Leh W16
Tan, See Dip W29
Tan, Nestor W82
Tan, Josefina W82
Tan, Edmundo W83
Tan, Cecilia Luz W83
Tan, Maria Theresa W83
Tan, Zhaohui W115
Tan, Mei Shwen W128
Tan, Chung-Hsing W138
Tan, Teck Long W155
Tan, Su Shan W155
Tan, Yew Chye W212
Tan, Jianming W214
Tan, Kong Khoon W232
Tan, Yen Yen W261
Tan, Eng Heong W261
Tan, May W308
Tan, Lita W323
Tan, Ngiap Joo W376
Tan, Yen Yen W376
Tan, Siew Peng W376
Tan, Chor Sen W376
Tan, Wing Ming W376
Tan, Shien Doon W393
Tan, Yoke Kong W393
Tan, Thomas W417
Tan, Lip-Bu W427
Tan, Mingxian W442
Tan, Soo Chay W529
Tan, Kok Liann W529
Tan, Lip-Bu E62
Tanabe, Eiichi W356
Tanabe, Kimihisa W537
Tanaka, Jo-Anne P163
Tanaka, Roger Y P656
Tanaka, Kazuhiro W127
Tanaka, Satoshi W429
Tanaka, Seiichi W450
Tanaka, Yoshihisa W472
Tanaka, Masanobu W537
Tanbara, Gregory P166
Tanchanco, Rolando W83
Tancongco, Federico W83
Tandy, Carolyn A406
Taneja, Rajat A839:E282
Tang, Michael A21
Tang, Anthony A157
Tang, Kia A519
Tang, Youhua P585
Tang, Ying-yen W66
Tang, Shoulian W88
Tang, Min W120
Tang, Yongbo W124

Tang, Shaojie W125
Tang, Jiang W129
Tang, Xiuguo W419
Tang, Fei W435
Tang, David W456
Tang, Vance E24
Tang, Anthony E70
Tang, Francis E121
Tang, Kia E272
Tango, Yasutake W260
Tangpong, Annie X P381
Tangtatswas, Singh W62
Tani, Hiroko W288
Tani, Sadafumi W403
Tanigawa, Byron P476
Taniguchi, Shinichi W127
Tanikawa, Kei W36
Tanizaki, Katsunori W463
Tanjangco, Reynaldo W83
Tanji, Kenneth A649
Tanner, Bruce A51
Tanner, Kirk A619
Tanner, Geoff A718
Tanner, Bruce A796
Tanner, Reed A853
Tanner, Bruce P172
Tanner, Hans W166
Tanner, Reed E444
Tanner, Deborah Keller E446
Tanpradith, Sasitorn P416
Tansingco, Fernand Antonio W323
Tanski, Ronald A190:A219
Tanski, Frank W27
Tantakasem, Piti W491
Tantikulanan, Thiti W270
Tantillo, Hilary P164
Tantisawetrat, Yokporn W491
Tantitemit, Kulaya W284
Tao, Kalena P630
Tao, Yun Chih W196
Tao, Yuling W349
Taparia, Siddharth A443
Tapscott, James A587:E302
Tarakji, Ahmad P586
Taranto, Joseph W189
Taranto, Eric E277
Taraporevala, Cyrus A743
Tarasi, Rocco A194
Tarbell, Terry P282
Tarbutton, Charles A352
Tarcov, Nathan P585
Tardan, Francois E300
Tardif, Francois W194
Taricani, Remo W509
Tarling, Neil P208
Tarlowe, Rochelle A589
Tarpey, John P55:P55
Tarrant, Jason A579
Tarver, Edward E166
Tarvin, Julie A424
Tarvin, Michael A703
Tasaka, Takayuki W375
Tashiro, Yuko W537
Tashma, Lauren A364
Tasman, Allan P612
Tastad, Carolyn A643
Tastard, James P228
Tata, Jasmine P37
Tata, Ratan W478
Tate, Jeffrey A471
Tate, Granville A798
Tate, Allyson P152
Tate, Amanda P337
Tate, Robert P579
Tate, Masafumi W150
Tatelbaumm, Ron P246
Tatsis, Ourania A835
Tatsuoka, Tsuneyoshi W325
Tatterson, W. Mark A814:E423
Tatum, Mark A349
Tatum, Lisa Skeete A749
Tatum, Ashley P104
Tatum, Demitrios P163
Tauber, Nancy P124
Tauber, Richard E P533
Tauber, David W P533
Taubert, Jennifer A441

COMBINED HOOVER'S HANDBOOK INDEX OF EXECUTIVES

A = AMERICAN BUSINESS
E = EMERGING COMPANIES
P = PRIVATE COMPANIES
W = WORLD BUSINESS

Tauke, Michelle A736:P512
Tauscher, Randall L P314
Taussig, Andrew P215
Tautolo, Toni P447
Tavaglinoe, John P167
Tavares, Luis P243
Tavares, Diogo Mendonca Rodrigues W206
Taw, Frederick A416:E226
Tawana, Dean P410
Taxil, Christian W175
Tay, Ah Lek W393
Tay, Kah Chye W529
Tay, Tala E96
Tayanithi, Piyapan W62
Tayano, Ken W149
Tayanukorn, Kajornvut W62
Taylor, Karin M A28
Taylor, Jason A108
Taylor, Sue A125
Taylor, Diana A183
Taylor, Douglas A188
Taylor, Andrew A206
Taylor, Lyndon A243
Taylor, Rhonda A252
Taylor, Emily A252
Taylor, Keith A282
Taylor, Frederick A309
Taylor, Beth A314
Taylor, R. Eugene A317
Taylor, Michael A320
Taylor, K. Jon A324
Taylor, Bernadette A340
Taylor, Anne A368
Taylor, Robert A388
Taylor, John A414
Taylor, Greg A463
Taylor, Daniel A524
Taylor, David A643
Taylor, Bret A692
Taylor, Jack A705
Taylor, Jodi A718
Taylor, R. Eugene A719
Taylor, Peter A722
Taylor, Darrell A741
Taylor, Teresa A758
Taylor, Bret A801
Taylor, Johnny A873
Taylor, Josh P3
Taylor, David P101
Taylor, Ivy R P133
Taylor, Larry P138
Taylor, Jeannie P162
Taylor, Celia P166
Taylor, Melissa P173
Taylor, John P260
Taylor, Nathan P267
Taylor, Mark P303
Taylor, Natalie P362
Taylor, Loren P382
Taylor, Michelle P395
Taylor, Ashly P420
Taylor, David P454
Taylor, Ren E N P455
Taylor, Mark P500
Taylor, Madeleine M P503
Taylor, Darrell P517
Taylor, Shaun P532
Taylor, Benjamin P538
Taylor, Leo P561
Taylor, Denise P561
Taylor, Liane P598
Taylor, James P612:P614
Taylor, Liya P618
Taylor, Joanne W30
Taylor, Diana W94
Taylor, Aileen W234
Taylor, Kathleen W412
Taylor, Karin M E13
Taylor, Frederick E162
Taylor, R. Eugene E170

Taylor, Michael E173:E186
Taylor, Stuart E215
Taylor, Beth E229
Taylor, John E253
Taylor, Allison E305
Taylor, Gary E346
Tazi, Omar A758
Tchoungui, Elizabeth W372
Teagle, Walter A322
Teagle, Kelly E P307
Teague, A. James A280
Teare, David W446
Teasdale, Chris W470
Techasarintr, Padoong W98
Techawiriyakul, Ekachai W284
Tecotzky, Mark E132
Tedesco, Maria A79
Tedesco, James P156
Tedesco, Jennifer P442
Tedesco, Maria E34
Tedford, Jason P470
Tee, Chui Chee W393
Teegarden, David P600
Teel, Lawrence A860
Teel, Diana P41
Teel, Michael P435
Teel, Michael J P435
Teel, Julie P435
Teeter-Balin, Jonah E7
Teets, Richard A745
Teets, J. Christopher E10
Tegan, Jennifer A789
Teglia, Karin A867:E452
Teh, Gary W212
Teichroew, Erik P203
Teig, Steve E456
Teigen, Scott P289
Teirlynck, Yves A573:P391
Teixeira, Kay P311
Teixeira, Ariel P492
Teixeira, Rui Manuel Rodrigues Lopes W172
Tejada, Omar A864:P656
Tejedor, Juan Carrillo de Albornoz W400
Tejera, Pablo Isla Alvarez De W243
Tejera, Federico Gonzalez W448
Tejwani, Uma P352
Tek, Karuna P262
Teklemichael, Chernet P459
Tekorius, Lorie E12
Tekula, Christine P48
Telesmanic, Robert A199
Telfer, Chris P399
Telleen, William F P406
Tellem, Nancy A562:P378
Telles, Linda P596
Tellock, Glen A852
Telman, Deborah E36
Temperley, Dessislava A624
Temple, Christopher A630
Temple, H Thomas P390
Temple, Larry P658
Temple-Boyer, Heloise W273
Templeton, Richard A771
Templeton, Lauren W191
Templin, Ashley A736
Templin, Mark A790
Templin, Ashley P512
Tena, Andrea P461
Tena, Ray P461
Tencate, Lee P330
Tendil, Claude W429
Teng, Chung-Yi W106
Teng, Yu W236
Teng, Chin-Chi E62
Tengel, Jeffrey A617:E319
Tengerstrom, Lindsey E P305
Tenhaeff, Ross A293:P212
Tenney, Emily P261
Tennison, Tom P211
Teno, Andrew A168:A324
Tenreiro, Sofia W206
Teo, Gary A262
Teo, Marie Elaine W370
Teo, La-Mei W529
Teo, Siong Seng W529

Teo, Gary E127
Teodosio, Tammy P430
Teofilo, Joan A372
Teoh, Su Yin W128
Teoh, Lian Ee W212
Teoh, Yih Min W232
Teplukhin, Pavel W386
Terabatake, Masamichi W260
Teraguchi, Tomoyuki W360
Terahata, Masashi W264
Terakawa, Akira W312
Teraoka, Yasuo W472
Terasaka, Koji W127
Terbsiri, Atikom W393
Tereau, Daniel E320
Teresi, Rob P236
Terracina, Roy D E429
Terrano, Janine A201:E92
Terre, Joan David Grima W9
Terrell, Frederick A99:A607
Terrell, Barrett P20
Terrell, Connie P500
Terrell, Ransom P554
Terrill, Christopher A666
Terrillion, Scott E67
Terrio, Anita A738:P514
Terry, Robert A715
Terry, Thomas A808
Terry, Hilliard A809
Terry, Mark A814
Terry, Domenica P247
Terry, Theresa P584
Terry, Alison W200
Terry, Thomas E421
Terry, Mark E424
Terryn, Kristof W543
Tersigni, Anthony E344
Teruel, Javier A562:P378
Teruel, Frank E277
Terwiesch, Peter W5
Terwindt, Steven W91
Terzariol, Giulio W26
Tese, Vincent A422
Teshima, Nobuyuki W329
Teshima, Toshihiro W452
Tesija, Kathryn W532
Teslyk, Kevin W69
Tessel, Marianna A182:A429
Tessier, Pamela P243
Tessier, Claude W25
Tessier-Lavigne, Marc A473:A669:P295
Testa, Christopher A817
Testa, S P300
Testa, Claudio W251
Testino, Edward P343
Testman, Karen P326
Teter, Timothy A577
Tetter, Joe P421
Tetu, Louis W25
Teubner, Russell A712:E373
Teves, Margarito W417
Tewes, Timothy A549:E290
Tewksbury, Theodore E264
Texier, Guillaume W402
Textor, Donald A281
Teyssen, Johannes W91
Thabet, Pierre W341
Thacher, John P P656
Thai, Beth P587
Thai-Tang, Hau A333
Thaicharoen, Yunyong W441
Thakar, Sumedh E341
Thalacker, Gail P611
Thalberg, Marisa A488
Tham, Sai Choy W155
Tham, Chai Fhong W393
Thaman, Michael A708
Thammasart, Sujint W113
Thamodaran, Dhamu A748
Than, Quang E457
Thanasorn, Phaphatsorn W98
Thanattrai, Phonganant W65
Thanawaranit, Potjanee W65
Thani, Abdullah Bin Ali Bin Jabor Al W134
Thani, Faisal bin Fahad bin Jassim Al W134

Thani, Jassim Saud Abdulaziz Hamad Al W134
Thani, Ali Al W395
Thani, Abdullah Al W395
Thansathit, Suvarn W62
Tharp, Morris A709
Tharp, William W P214
Tharp, Morris E370
Thatavakorn, Amy P612
Thatcher, Laura A686
Thaus, Kurt A764
Thavisin, Phongsthorn W393
Thayer, John A75
Thayer, Jennifer A399
Thaysen, Jacob A21
Thean, Nam Yew W212
Thebault, J. Brian A704:E367
Theberge, Angela A738:P514
Thedford, Donald A724
Theener, Ron P207
Theerarojanawong, Sa-ard W62
Theeratharathorn, Rushda W62
Theibert, Terri P355
Theiler, Jeff E323
Theilmann, Michael A28:P18
Theine, Mark E323
Theis, Ron A738
Theis, Robert P52
Theis, Ron P514
Theisen, Sonja A519
Theisen, Randall A857
Theisen, Sonja E272
Theisen, Randall E447
Theissig, Bettina W152
Thekkekara, Joe P158
Thelen, Don A322
Thelen, Simon W321
Thelen, Daniel W321
Thelen, Bruce E396
Themelis, Nicholas E262
Theobald, Neil D P536
Theobald, Stephen E443
Theodoredis, Roger A175
Theodoridis, Artemios W27
Theofilaktidis, Maria W69
Theoharides, Kathleen A P317
Theologides, Stergios A293
Theophilus, Nicole A841
Thepaut, Eric A132
Thepvanangkul, Nitima W284
Therady, Agnes P219
Theriault, Celeste P309
Therivel, Laurent A764
Theroux, Stephen A103:E47
Thiam, Tidjane W273
Thibault, Rory A741:P518
Thibault, Rene W229
Thibault, Francois W322
Thibodeau, David P117
Thibodeaux, Troy P174
Thibodeaux, Kirt P347
Thibodeaux, Wayne P541
Thiede, Jeffrey A512
Thiede, Dirk W224
Thiel, John A336
Thiele, Patricia P505
Thielman, Shane P469
Thiemann, Erin P134
Thieme, Dennis P367
Thiengwatanatham, Duangporn W393
Thierer, Mark A247
Thigpen, Mary A359:A398
Thigpen, Julie P51
Thigpen, Mary E218
Thijs, Jeroen W29
Thim, Gene P532
Thind, Aman A743
Thirring, Peter W515
Thissen, Karen A52
Thissen, Paul A737:P513
Thoma, Jeanne E39
Thomas, Rose A48
Thomas, David A258
Thomas, William A281
Thomas, Marty A335
Thomas, Deborah A377

COMBINED HOOVER'S HANDBOOK INDEX OF EXECUTIVES

Thomas, Christie A410
Thomas, David A428
Thomas, Stephen S A454
Thomas, Scott A503
Thomas, David P A554
Thomas, Geevy A565
Thomas, Shundrawn A567
Thomas, William A571
Thomas, Warner A583
Thomas, Shundrawn A672
Thomas, Daniel A703
Thomas, Rochelle A728
Thomas, John A768:A778
Thomas, Phillip A802
Thomas, Alan A803
Thomas, Charlene A819
Thomas, Cheryl A831
Thomas, Cristina Garcia A852
Thomas, Chris P20
Thomas, Amy P63
Thomas, Michael J P103
Thomas, Sylvia P128
Thomas, Doris C P145
Thomas, Doris P145
Thomas, An'dino P160
Thomas, Vanessa P170
Thomas, Dagny P170
Thomas, Scott P172
Thomas, Barry P174
Thomas, Will P186
Thomas, Stephanie P187
Thomas, Lydia P262
Thomas, Christine P271
Thomas, Michael S P274
Thomas, Stephen S P285
Thomas, Annie P305
Thomas, Scott P317
Thomas, Desiree P326
Thomas, Kevin P361
Thomas, David P P372
Thomas, Laura P379
Thomas, Warner P393
Thomas, Rochelle P496
Thomas, Suja P508
Thomas, Maggie P532
Thomas, Robin P554
Thomas, John P561
Thomas, Alan P606
Thomas, Linda L P628
Thomas, Tony P658
Thomas, Philip W69
Thomas, J. Darrell W93
Thomas, David W128
Thomas, Patrick W266
Thomas, Ralf W443
Thomas, Paul E3
Thomas, J. Darrell E123
Thomas, William E136
Thomas, Andrea E266
Thomas, Paul E284
Thomas, Kenneth E295
Thomas, Linda E296
Thomas, John E323
Thomas, Frank E365
Thomason, David A623
Thomason, Keith P569
Thomasson, Virginia A309:E162
Thoming, Christopher S P294
Thompkins, Angela A190
Thompson, James A26
Thompson, John A48
Thompson, Elizabeth A129
Thompson, Jeffrey A149
Thompson, Thomas A162
Thompson, Michael A180
Thompson, Peter A266
Thompson, Tiffany A266
Thompson, Bill A268
Thompson, Richard A294
Thompson, Larry A297
Thompson, Stephen A388
Thompson, Kirk A408
Thompson, Mark A409
Thompson, Kathleen Wilson - A510
Thompson, Craig B A513
Thompson, Erik A516
Thompson, Steven A523

Thompson, Jane A546
Thompson, Matthew A548
Thompson, John A566
Thompson, Laura A609
Thompson, H. Brian A615
Thompson, James A629
Thompson, Paul A637
Thompson, James A656
Thompson, Donald A713
Thompson, Cheryl A739
Thompson, Kathy A747
Thompson, Laura A854
Thompson, Gail P16
Thompson, Brian P18
Thompson, Bruce P23
Thompson, Doug P24
Thompson, Dwight P28
Thompson, John P31
Thompson, Jolene P33
Thompson, Carey P57
Thompson, Troy P74
Thompson, Chavela P91
Thompson, Craig P127
Thompson, Joe L P140
Thompson, Kerry P155
Thompson, Tyjuan P156
Thompson, Jennifer P166
Thompson, Linda V P180
Thompson, Liz P193
Thompson, Jerry E P207
Thompson, Michael P215
Thompson, Jeff P221
Thompson, Dashel P230
Thompson, Robert P235
Thompson, Jeff P238
Thompson, Jeffery P238
Thompson, Bryan P248
Thompson, Angela D P254
Thompson, Matt P256
Thompson, Gloria P261
Thompson, Lacey P263
Thompson, Sue P266
Thompson, Pamela P276
Thompson, Elaine C P291
Thompson, Billy P292
Thompson, Neal P312
Thompson, Jeff P323
Thompson, Craig B P327:P328
Thompson, Eric P343
Thompson, Kathleen P348
Thompson, Michael P394
Thompson, Lisa P396
Thompson, Dayna P409
Thompson, Gennifer P429
Thompson, Julie P431
Thompson, Juanita P432
Thompson, Glynn P463
Thompson, O L P487
Thompson, Nancy P505
Thompson, Cheryl P515
Thompson, Rebecca P529
Thompson, Mark P592
Thompson, Ray P600
Thompson, Nainoa P603
Thompson, Lizbeth P613
Thompson, Briana P624
Thompson, Warren E124
Thompson, Richard E156
Thompson, Larry E158
Thompson, Brandon E200
Thompson, G. Kennedy E232
Thompson, C. Reynolds E265
Thompson, Marsha E286
Thompson, Thomas E323
Thompson, Kathy E391
Thompson, Kelly E418
Thompsonas, Janice Innis - A507
Thomsen, Laurie A792
Thomsen, Kim Hvid W515
Thomson, Laurie A363
Thomson, Robert A559
Thomson, Justin A757
Thomson, Dawn P48
Thomson, Bonnie P168
Thomson, Phil W210
Thorel, Olivier W422
Thorn, Bruce A117

Thorn, Craig A321
Thornal, Kevin A392
Thornberry, Richard A662
Thornburg, Eric E376
Thornburgh, Richard A691
Thorning-Schmidt, Helle W515
Thornlow, Deirdre P197
Thornton, Robert A323
Thornton, John A333
Thornton, Matthew A708
Thornton, Kim A735
Thornton, Robert O A739
Thornton, Calvin P135
Thornton, Mark P316
Thornton, Justin P346
Thornton, Kim P511
Thornton, Robert O P515
Thornton, Tiffany P539
Thornton, Leslie T P654
Thorp, Holden P626
Thorpe, Barbara A436:P271
Thorpe, Bill P272
Thorson, John A856
Thorson, Dave P11
Thorson, Michael P235
Thorstensen, Lynnette P466
Thorud, Robert P289
Thorup, Schuyler P103
Thrappas, Peggy P608
Throener, Kevin A176
Throm, Larry P179
Throop, Darren A377
Thuestad, John W363
Thuillier, Lawrence A561
Thuran, Chris P428
Thurber, Lynn E124
Thurlow, Brenda P464
Thurman, Rhonda P365
Thurston, Muriel P343
Thurstone, Christian P187
Thwaite, Paul W345
Thway, Myint P476
Thyen, Amy P267
Thygesen, Gert A735:P511
Thygesen, Henriette Hallberg W1
Tian, Xin W220
Tian, Jinghui W378
Tian, Zhaohua W539
Tian, Hui W539
Tiarks, Roy E157
Tibbetts, Mark A737:P513
Tibbetts, Shawn E30
Tibbott, Rowland P639
Tibbs, E W P107
Tiberghien, Herve W451
Tichota, Bill P175
Tickles, Chuck P209
Tiddettes, Shawn P642
Tielke, Lori P31
Tien, Chang-Chieh W138
Tiencken, John P107
Tienghongsakul, Lawan W98
Tierney, Brian A676
Tierney, Dan A740
Tierney, Cathie P430
Tierney, Dan P516
Tiffany, Patricia A329
Tighe, Jan A360:A411:A645
Tigue, Michael Mc P497
Tilbrook, Chuck A241
Till, Mark A827
Till, Wjanand Van W423
Tillett, Ronald A79:E34
Tillman, Lee A495
Tillman, Carol P207
Tillotson, Angela P188
Tilly, Edward E73
Tilton, David A343
Tilton, Glenn A606
Tilton, David P48:P225
Tilton, Lynn P396
Tilzer, Brian A115
Timanus, H. A646:E336
Timko, Thomas A346
Timm, Jill A459
Timm, Stephen A665
Timm, Bryan A809

Timm, Terry P592
Timmerman, Douglas A33
Timmerman, Timothy P304
Timmers, Martha P429
Timmers, Michaela P441
Timmons, Darla P467
Timpano, Joseph P165
Timpe, Mark T P555
Timperman, Jurgen A154
Timuray, Serpil W152:W520
Tindal, Bruce E163
Ting, Nicholas P29
Tinga, Dante W83
Tingley, Sandy P429
Tinkle, Caleb P170
Tinsley, Janice P658
Tinsley, Dean E85
Tintsman, Robert E334
Tio, Jose Coleman A634
Tippawanich, Chawalit W393
Tippett, Leslie P44
Tippin, Jennifer W345
Tippit, James A417:E227
Tipton, John A393
Tipton, Annie P470
Tipton, John E217
Tirador, Gabriel A516
Tirawattanagool, Nopporn W65
Tirpak, Bradley E47
Tisch, Andrew A486
Tisch, Jonathan A486
Tisch, James A486
Tisch, Merryl H A744:P519
Tischendorf, Hermann W335
Tischler, Barbara L A553:P370
Tisdale, Maria P129
Tishman, Daniel A15
Tison, Stuart E140
Titapiwatanakun, Ruetima P638
Titasattavorakul, Piyawat W98
Titi, Fani W253
Titinger, Jorge E180
Tittle, Cobi P533
Titus, Martin E A787:P595
Titus, Danny E300
Titus-Johnson, Suzanne A298
Titzrath, Angela W190
Tiwari, Anoop P244
Tjernsmo, Dag W470
To, Dena P163
Toal, Sheamus P452
Toalson, Michael E439
Tobe, Tomoko W272
Tobe, Sadanobu W375
Tobias, Chris P384
Tobimatsu, Junichi W334
Tobin, Richard A256
Tobin, Daniel P554
Tobison, John E152
Tocci, Nathalie W185
Toce, Suzanne P238
Tochika, Masanori W356
Toczydlowski, Gregory A792
Todaro, Michael A491
Todd, Stephen A256
Todd, Paul A358
Todd, Amy A475
Todd, Wanda A570
Todd, Ronald C A740
Todd, Wanda P388
Todd, Peggy P479
Todd, Ronald C P516
Todd, James E52
Todd, Roderick E166
Todgham, Paul E89
Todman, Michael A535:A727:P495
Todoroki, Masahiko W437
Todorov, Pierre W175
Todt, Blair A63
Toellner, Ann P625
Toepfer, Jack A554:P372
Toeruener, S. W21
Togashi, Cheryl P462
Togawa, Masanori W149
Toh, Chong W62
Toh, Hilda W126
Toide, Iwao W325

COMBINED HOOVER'S HANDBOOK INDEX OF EXECUTIVES

```
A = AMERICAN BUSINESS
E = EMERGING COMPANIES
P = PRIVATE COMPANIES
W = WORLD BUSINESS
```

Toit, Michelle Du W421
Tojo, Noriko W375
Tokarczyk, Peter P35
Tokarev, Nikolay W502
Tokioka, Dana A97
Tokuchi, Tatsuhito W378
Tokuhira, Tsukasa W536
Tokunaga, Setsuo W326
Tokuno, Mariko W327:W538
Toland, David A736:P512
Tolbert, George P173
Toledano, Sidney W301
Toledo, Phil De P98
Toll, Robert A788
Tolla, John A90:E41
Tollackson, Susan E282
Tollefson, Adam P39
Tolleson, Amanda P85
Tolman, Sarah E163
Tolson, Aaron E131
Tomaro, Terry A750:P528
Tomasevic, Josip A20
Tomasi, Julie A807
Tomasky, Susan A496:A651:P30
Tomaszewski, Jeffrey A721
Tomazinis, Larry A403:P256
Tomazoni, Gilberto A627
Tomb, Matthew A313:E165
Tome, Carol A819
Tometich, Andrew E E189
Tomforde, Garret P188
Tomimura, Ryuichi W439
Tomina, Renee A258
Tomioka, Yasuyuki W356
Tomita, Tetsuro W170:W354
Tomizawa, Ryuichi W148
Tomkalski, Mark P292
Tomkiell, Debbie P375
Tomkins, Grant P526
Tomlin, Dervla W213
Tomlin, Laura E364
Tomlinson, Norma P587
Tomnitz, Donald E180
Tomono, Hiroshi W268
Tomova, Iva P207
Tomso, Gyorgy E200
Tondi, Francesca W509
Tondkar, Rasoul H P641
Tondreau, Pamela E137
Toney, Colin A162
Toney, Keith A247
Toney, Charles A516
Tong, Chee A174:P118
Tong, Anhtuan P596
Tong, Lowell P616
Tong, Wenhong W24
Tong, Hon-shing W66
Tong, Jimmy W212
Tong, Carlson W456
Tong, Richard E300
Tonge, Eoin W311
Tonjes, Bernd W190
Tonjum, Kurt P136
Tonnesen, Paul P76
Tonnu, Lannie P550
Tonstad, Kjetil A283:P208
Tony, Gregory P157
Tookes, Hansel A221:A689
Toole, Richard O' A851
Toole, Frampton E365
Tooley, David A724:E383
Toothaker, Scott A103
Toothaker, Bradley A466
Toothaker, Scott E47
Toothaker, Bradley E244
Topalian, Leon A575
Topete, Xavier Garcia De Quevedo A723
Topol, Deborah A P647
Topol, Eric E117
Topper, John P332

Topper, John E P334
Toppin, Bruce P383
Toprak, Yusuf W504
Topsch, Edgar W224
Torabi, Peymon E162
Toraktrakul, Somwang W65
Torbert, Ronald J P63
Torchio, Louis A570
Torell, John P604
Torento, Robert P584
Toretti, Christine A690
Torgeby, Johan W446
Torgerson, James P P584
Torgerson, William E264
Torii, Shingo W149
Toriola, Karl W335
Torkelson, Thomas E P259
Torley, Helen E204
Tornatore, Jean M P89
Tornos, Ivan A878
Toro, Rachel A245:P189
Toro, Suzan P372
Torraca, Christine P315
Torrallardona, Maria Isabel Mata W215
Torrance, Griffin P304
Torre, Ralph De La P521
Torre, Doug P544
Torrego, Agustin Batuecas W9
Torrence, Alfred P389
Torrens, Mireya Gine W57
Torres, Sherice A12
Torres, Kathryn A379
Torres, Flavio A460
Torres, Tameral P64
Torres, Brenda P175
Torres, Marilyn P338
Torres, Danny P411
Torres, Mark P486
Torres, Juan Romero W109
Torres, Rafael E420
Torrey, Ben P237
Torroella, Jose Ignacio Mariscal W215
Torstendahl, Mats W446
Tory, Jennifer W82
Torzolini, William A P23
Tosh, Jamie P69
Totemoff, Charles P112
Toth, Andras W334
Toth, Peter W406
Totoki, Hiroki W454
Totsch, Kelsey P327
Totta, DeAnn E265
Totzke, Lara C P222
Totzke, Bill P375
Tou, Janet P652
Touche, Ricardo Guajardo W198:W215
Tougas, Roger P479
Tougas, Roger C P479
Touraine, Agnes W402
Tournay, Philippe W451
Tournier, Philippe W133
Tourret, Dibrelle P160
Tousey, Angela A739:P515
Towe, Zachary E204
Towers, Kelly P561
Towery, Jennie P433
Towle, Terry A328
Towler, Thomas H P465
Townes-Whitley, Toni A543:A632
Townley, Chris A352
Towns, Douglas P315
Townsel, Beadie H P471:P472
Townsell, Donna A393:E217
Townsend, Frances A10
Townsend, Kent A149
Townsend, Frances A338
Townsend, Philippa K P97
Townsend, Tammy P222
Townsend, Bradley P429
Townsend, Adam P643
Townsend, Randy P658
Toy, Derik P179
Toya, Tomoki W468
Toyama, Ryoko W496
Toyoda, Kanshiro W21
Toyoda, Akio W158
Toyoda, Tetsuro W500

Toyoda, Akio W501
Toyoma, Makoto W288
Toyoshima, Masakazu W237
Toyoshima, Naoyuki W288
Toyota, Jun P379
Tozer, Theodore A614:E317
Tozzi, James P647
Trabalka, Mike P440
Trabaudo, John A735:P511
Trabulsi, Ann P70
Tracey, Patricia A821
Tracey, Bernard M P498
Tracey, C Lynn E187
Trachsel, Ronald W514
Tracy, Jim P455
Tracz, Robert A458:P287
Traeger, Norman E257
Traff, Rod A485
Traffas, Vincetta P219
Trager, Steven A675
Trager, A. Scott A675
Trager, Steven E350
Trager, A. Scott E350
Trager-Kusman, Andrew A675:E350
Trahan, Claude A216
Trahey, Gregg P197
Train, Michael A273
Trainor, Jennifer P420
Trainor, Christopher E215
Trairatvorakul, Prasarn W441
Trakulhoon, Kan W441:W441
Tramel, Beth P198
Tran, Nam A212
Tran, Tuan A404
Tran, Suzanna A243
Tran, An N E39
Trani, Randy P164
Trani, Eugene P P641
Transier, William E210
Tranzer, Alain W175
Trapp, Jacqueline A268
Trapp, Claude P126
Trapp, Todd E3
Trappier, Eric W488
Traquina, Perry A32
Trask, Tallman P196
Trau, Israel W63
Traugot, Amy P452
Trautman, David A608:E312
Trautz, Volker W190
Travillion, Jeff P171
Traviola, Brad P545
Traviolia, Brad P545
Travis, Nigel A12
Travis, Tracey A520
Travis, George P63
Travis, Troy P340
Travis-Brown, Deidre A208:P146
Travisano, Jacqueline A83
Trawicki, Roman A881
Traynor, Stephen A298
Treacy, Zach P177
Trease, Sandra Van A279:E142
Treasure, Jeff P286
Trecek, Mark P569
Treece, Christopher A709:E370
Treenuchagron, Chansin W393
Treewannakul, Thawat W62
Treff, Douglas E110
Trefzger, Detlef W287
Trejo, Thomas P529
Tremayne, Lisa P374
Trembulak, Frank
   J A343:P225:P226:P226:P559
Tremonti, Yvette P240
Trenbeath, Lynn V P184
Trent, Keith A268
Trent, Tammy A471
Trent, Thad A591
Trepat, Francisco Serrado W66
Treseder, Oluwadara A623
Tretiak, Gregory W213:W389
Trevino, Jan P193
Trevino, Maria Dolores Dancausa W72
Treworgy, Samantha A123:P80
Trezise, Scott A490
Triantafyllidis, Georgios W27

Tribble, J Lee A475
Tribe, Lorena P29
Tricarico, Christine P449
Trick, David A39
Trickett, Mariya W37
Trickett, Jeremy W213
Tricoire, Jean-Pascal A657:W427
Triesenberg, Ryan P553
Trieste, Maria P246
Trietsch, Gary K P242
Trietsch, Gary P242
Trigg, Donald D A165
Trigg, Blair P408
Trimble, Melody P499
Trimble, James E85
Trimbur, Nancy P521
Trimino, Humberto A554:P372
Trimmer, Mel P271
Trinchant, Javier Maldonado W61
Trinh, Trinette P551
Tripepi, Simone W179
Triplett, Timothy W P76:P76:P92
Tripp, Ann A375
Tripp, Scott P447
Trippe, Robert W P33
Triquet, John De P125
Tristan, Selena P177
Tritton, Mark A111:A565
Trius, Vincent A627
Trivedi, Dharati P193
Trivedi, Ashok E263
Trivett, Shari P293
Trivette, Theresa P612
Trochu, Cynthia A771
Trofin, Iulian P640
Trogele, Ulrich E23
Trojan, Gregory A155
Trojanowski, Matthew A778:P564
Trolli, Michele A491
Trollinger, Michael A700
Trollinger, Monica P492
Troppmann, Al E P408
Trott, Simon W405:W406
Trouche, Thomas A707:E368
Troupe, Quincy E55
Trout, J D P37
Trout, Ann M P97
Trout, John D P602
Trovo, Annamaria W511
Troxell, Bill P468
Troxell, Dean P526
Troy, Patricia P306
Troyer, Trent E160
Trubeck, William A162
Trudeau, Mark W480
Trudell, Cynthia W102:W399
Trueman, John W233
Truer, Amanda P332
Truesdale, Ken E457
Truett, Richard P73
Truex, Ronald A466:E244
Trujillo, Gary L P78
Trujillo, Jefferson P120
Trujillo, Becky P333
Trujillo, Bernie P610
Trumbull, Lesley P430
Trump, Mike P445
Trunfio, Joseph A P11
Trunkett, Camille P211
Truong, Thien A719
Truong, Danh P472
Truong, Ann P573
Trupiano, Yvonne A727
Truscott, William A52
Trust, Union Bank A811
Tryhuss, Gregg P195
Tryniski, Mark A209:E95
Trytten, Jennifer P149
Tsacalis, William A P72
Tsai, Lih-Shyng A467
Tsai, Jade P36
Tsai, Joseph W24
Tsai, Hong-Tu W106
Tsai, Cheng-Ta W106
Tsai, Cheng-Chiu W106
Tsai, Hsiang-Hsin W106
Tsai, Tsung-Hsien W106

COMBINED HOOVER'S HANDBOOK INDEX OF EXECUTIVES

Tsai, Duei W138
Tsang, Yok Sing W287
Tsarev, Kirill W424
Tschakert, Carol P381
Tscherne, Tiffany P44
Tschudin, Marie-France A573:P391
Tse, Alan A443
TSE, Conny P169
Tse, Edmund Sze-Wing W16
Tse, Hau Yin W130
Tseng, Vivian S Y P363
Tseng, Vivian P648
Tseng, Saria E279:E397
Tshabalala, Bajabulile W335
Tsien, Matthew A20:A349
Tsimbinos, John A554
Tsimbinos, Steven A582:E302
Tsingos, Christine E304
Tsitsiragos, Dimitris W27
Tsokova, Olga A323
Tsoodle, Kenton P130
Tsou, Richard P129
Tsu, Bill P503
Tsuboi, Yasuhiro W373
Tsuchiya, Michihiro W461
Tsuda, Junji W289
Tsue, Sik Yu W130
Tsui, Ying-Chun E311
Tsuji, Koichi W330
Tsuji, Shinji W452
Tsukamoto, Takashi W14
Tsukamoto, Yoichiro W65
Tsukuda, Kenji A166:P110
Tsuma, Glen E63
Tsunis, George E29
Tsushima, Yasushi W279
Tsusue, Yoichi W432
Tsutsui, Yoshinobu W463
Tsutsumi, Tomoaki W468
Tsymbalyuk, Michael P488
Tsyrkunova, Katsiaryna P70
Tu, Amy A802
Tu, Danny P532
Tu, Tu-Chuan W138
Tu, Huabin W287
Tuason, Michael P102
Tuchinda, Pornsanong W65
Tuchman, Kenneth E417
Tucker, Sara A44
Tucker, Nanci A293
Tucker, Daniel A352
Tucker, Douglas A530
Tucker, Steven A717
Tucker, Amy A741
Tucker, Timothy H P51
Tucker, Chris P120
Tucker, Thomas P193
Tucker, Nanci P211
Tucker, Melanie P268
Tucker, Kym P337
Tucker, Amy P517
Tucker, Mark W234
Tucker, David E4
Tucker, Weston E52
Tucker, Douglas E275
Tucker, Steven E380
Tucker, Allen E425
Tucker, Aaron E426
Tuckler, Domingo A327:P215
Tuder, Irma A707:E368
Tuer, David W100
Tufano, Paul E405
Tuffin, Mark A461
Tugal, Mehmet W21
Tuggle, Clyde A352
Tuggle, Deloris Simpson P225
Tuiteleleapaga, Leslie P398
Tuka, Laurie P323
Tulananda, Deja W62
Tulaney, Thomas A618
Tulenko, Stephen A536
Tulin, Stanley A672
Tulliam, Elizabeth P119
Tullier, Kelly A839
Tullis, David P483
Tulsyan, Ravi A873
Tumolo, Maureen A P350

Tumpel-Gugerell, Gertrude W515
Tumsavas, Fusun W504
Tunali, Tuerker W21
Tung, Pen-hung W24
Tung, Chee Hwa W24
Tung, Wai-Hok W87
Tung, Peter W530
Tungesvik, Geir P208
Tunis, Trisha A P220
Tunsakul, Pattarawan W441
Tuohig, Meghan E309
Tuori, Jeffery C A35:P27
Tuozzolo, Claudio E438
Turcke, Maryann W412
Turco, Kathleen M A803:P606
Turcotte, Martine W99:W176
Turcotte, Dennis E197
Turek, Zdenek A183
Turesson, John W446
Turiano, Gary A P208
Turicchi, R Scott E457
Turk, Wilhelmine Von A300
Turley, James A183:A569
Turley, Susan P193
Turley, John P240
Turlock, Kristine P311
Turnbull, Cheryl E202
Turner, Brian A28
Turner, Aprile A172
Turner, Keene A279
Turner, Leslie A324
Turner, William A366
Turner, Joseph A366
Turner, Mike A369
Turner, Michelle A463
Turner, Reginald A502
Turner, Rosemary A542
Turner, Bradford A556
Turner, Patricia A582
Turner, M. Terry A628
Turner, John A671
Turner, David A671
Turner, Christopher A876
Turner, Janet P6
Turner, Joe P17
Turner, Brian P18
Turner, Aprile P113
Turner, Sylvester P126
Turner, Sandy P159
Turner, Brooke M P200
Turner, Jeff P217
Turner, Mike P237
Turner, William P296
Turner, Jennifer P304
Turner, Hugh P311
Turner, Amy P423
Turner, Matthew P442
Turner, Angela P475
Turner, Sam P479
Turner, Pamela P489
Turner, R Gerald P491
Turner, Leagh W308
Turner, James W391
Turner, Quint E10
Turner, Robert E20
Turner, Keene E142
Turner, Kathy V E221
Turner, W. Brent E252
Turner, John E301
Turner, Patricia E302
Turner, M. Terry E324
Turney, Jeff A197
Turnipseed, Carl A299
Turoff, James A384
Turpen, Michael A126:E54
Turpin, Kevin P553
Turrentine, Rebecca J P302
Turrini, Adriano W511
Tusa, David E368
Tustin, Charlie P158
Tutas, David A805
Tutcher, Dan W178
Tuten, Steve P270
Tutkovics, Julie A409
Tutor, Ronald A800
Tutor, Rob P240
Tuttle, Lori P309

Tuttle, Barry P604
Tutton, Christopher E184
Tuuk, Mary A805
Tvaroch, Christine A331:E178
Tveit, Gro W454
Tveter, Eric A322
Twa, David P157
Twarozynski, James A417:E226
Twedt, Jill A125
Tweedall, James P482
Tweedy, Robyn P367
Twellman, Beverly P339
Twiddy, Kathryn E78
Twigge, Giovani E221
Twining, Amanda P332
Twining, Kurt P438
Twist, Krista P283
Twitchel, Sue E P531
Twitchell, Karen P288
Twite, Doug P28
Twomey, Brian A710:E371
Twumasi, Akua P18
Ty, Arthur W323
Ty, Alfred W323
Tyagi, Urvashi E352
Tyle, Craig A336
Tyler, Brian A510
Tyler, Jason A567
Tyler, Brian A677
Tyler, John P242
Tyler, Robert E P639
Tyler, Ian W32
Tyler, Staci E129
Tyler, Michele E329
Tyndal, Darlene P171
Tyree, Anthony E266
Tyrrell, Edward L A779:P567:P594
Tyson, Laura A159
Tyson, John A802:A802
Tyson, Kenneth P374
Tywater, Ty A700
Tzetzo, Nicole E16

U

Ube, Fumio W66
Ubertalli, Niccolo W509:W540
Uberuaga, Michael P133
Ubinas, Luis A78:A271
Uchibori, Tamio W299
Uchida, Kanitsu W150
Uchida, Ken W268
Uchida, Makoto A357
Uchimura, Hiroshi W272
Uchiyamada, Takeshi W501
Udell, Bob E98
Udomratchatavanich, Vasin W65
Udomsak, Suracha W441
Udpa, Satish P342
Udvar-Hazy, Steven E9
Ueberroth, Heidi A271
Uecker, Jodi A739:P515
Ueckert, Heather P468
Ueda, Takashi W331
Uehara, Hirohisa W472
Ueki, Eiji W67
Ueki, Tetsuro W496
Uemoto, Takeko A18
Ueno, Susumu W437
Ueno, Yoshitsugu W536
Ueyama, Yoshio W65
Uggla, Ane Maersk Mc-Kinney W1
Uhl, Chasity A736:P512
Uhl, Jessica W434
Uitto, Tommi W359
Ujiie, Teruhiko W1
Ukpong, Uwem A91
Ulatowski, Daniel E109
Ulbrich, Christian A443
Ulgen, Serkan W540
Ulissi, Roberto W185
Ullem, Scott A269
Ullmann, Michael A441
Ulm, Scott A7:A70
Ulrich, Frederick J P396
Ulusu, Atilla W505

Umanoff, Adam A268
Umanzor, Tara P109
Umbgrove, Johannes W27
Umeda, Hirokazu W378
Umeyama, Katsuhiro W351
Umezaki, Yuichi W332
Umpleby, D. James A172
Underberg, Sharon E E221
Underhill, Kimberly A332:A455
Underhill, Felicity W200
Underwood, Neil A484
Underwood, David M A779
Underwood, Traci P43
Underwood, Jennifer P45
Underwood, Jessica P93
Underwood, David M P567
Underwood, Baxter E396
Ung, Darith P262
Ung-Robbins, Alice P149
Ungaro, Peter A386
Unger, Laura A545
Unger, Keving P422
Unger, Laura W480
Unoura, Hiroo W326
UnRuch, Joel W8
Untalan, Myla W83
Unterborn, Craig P451
Unverferth, Steven E423
Upadhyay, Suketu A878
Upchurch, W. Howard A373
Upchurch, Kevin J A737:P513
Uperti, Christina P135
Upfold, Patrick W304
Upperman, Dorothy A658
Upson, Jill A750
Upson, Steve P42
Upson, Jill E394
Urakawa, Tatsuya W151
Urazhdin, Sergei P652
Urbain, Xavier A484
Urban, Debra A551
Urban, Philip A704
Urban, Michael A763
Urban, Sarah P112
Urban, Philip E367
Urbina, Lynne P182
Ure, Michael E448
Ureta, Fernando Concha W255
Urey, Melissa P173
Uriarte, Jessica P336
Uribe, Jorge A418
Uribe, Gonzalo A455
Uribe, Rodrigo Prieto W61
Uribe, Juan Carlos Mora W61
Uribe, Maria Cristina Arrastia W61
Uribe, Claudia Echavarria W61
Uribe, Esteban Piedrahita W171
Uribe, Jaime Caballero W171
Urist, Marshall E358
Uriu, Michiaki W288
Uriz, Charlotte W471
Urquia, Arianna P340
Urrutia, Manuel Enrique Bezanilla W33
Urry, Brent A741:P517
Ursat, Xavier W175
Urschel, Dorothy P508
Urso-Rio, Kristen A346:P227
Ursu, Raluca P374
Ushery, Candace P186
Ushijima, Arthur A P576
Ushio, Yoko W1
Usitalo, Scott A767
Utecht, Mike P345
Utermark, D. Chad A575
Utley, Mark P429
Utsumi, Tatsuro W257
Utt, Wendy P233
Utter, Lynn A560
Utterback, Cynthia E126
Utz, John A74
Uwadia, Ese P662
Uzun, Ali W281
Uzuner, Tolga A45

COMBINED HOOVER'S HANDBOOK INDEX OF EXECUTIVES

A = AMERICAN BUSINESS
E = EMERGING COMPANIES
P = PRIVATE COMPANIES
W = WORLD BUSINESS

V

V, William Matthews A725:E384
Vaart, Sandra Van Der A464
Vaccariello, Caroline E332
Vachon, Louis W340
Vachris, Ron A223
Vacy-Lyle, Mike W135
Vadala, Shawn E273
Vadera, Shriti W391
Vadlamani, Bhatt P193
Vagelos, P. Roy A669
Vaglienti, Richard P652
Vagnier, Paula P394
Vahedi, Vahid A467
Vahey, Walter E405
Vahradian, Robert E251
Vahrenholt, Fritz W50
Vaitkus, Vytas P405
Vajda, Devit P143
Valandra, Maria P75
Valavanis, Spero A400:E218
Valbuena, Abby P231
Valdes, Luis A641
Valdes, Susan L P251
Valdez, Arthur A12
Valdez, Isaac P18
Valdez, Purnima P197
Valdez, Arthur V P461
Valdivia, Raul P399
Vale, Michael A3
Valencia, Antonio A234
Valencia, Mirna P486
Valencia, Katherine P637
Valencia, Jaime Estevez W56
Valenti, Samuel A42
Valenti, Susan A789
Valenti, James N P202
Valenti, Douglas E343
Valentin, Josue P255
Valentine, Brian A62
Valerevich, Dyukov W208
Valette, Jean-Michel E55:E378
Valgiurata, Lucio Zanon di W144
Valigorsky, Maryjean A554:P372
Valkoun, Kasey P647
Valla, Natacha W428
Vallacchi, Grace A582:E301
Valladares, George P171
Vallamreddy, Kranthi P529
Valle, Alfonso Del A439
Valle, Gustavo A535
Valle, Jorge P51
Valle, Alfonso Del P276
Valle, William W203
Valle, Margherita Della W520
Vallee, Daniel P124
Vallee, Boris P243
Vallee, Laurent W104
Vallillo, Anthony J P584
Vallo, Gloria P581
Valluzzo, Charles P402
Van, Laura A750:P528
Vanacker, Peter W346
Vanamburg, Michael P452
Vanamburgh, Cindy P640
Vanaselja, Siim W213:W389
Vance, Brian A383
Vance, Katisha A642
Vance, Edward S Bubba P91
Vance, Edward Bubba P91
Vance, June P615
Vance, Brian E212
Vandal, Thierry W412
Vandekreeke, Jeff P223
Vandenberghe, James A258
Vanderhoff, Bruce P395
Vanderlaan, Meg P361
Vanderley, Betsy P166
VanderLind, Gary A361

Vanderlinden, Dick P657
Vandermeulen, Johan W93
Vandersteeg, Jim P173
Vanegas, Natalia P128
Vang, Lee P149
Vanhaelst, Bruno W448
Vanhaitsma, Jeff E271
Vanhevel, Jan W27
Vanhille, Philippe W391
Vanhuse, Venice M P384
Vanhyfte, Alyssa A737:P513
Vanikkul, Krirk W441
Vaninsky, Kirill P342
Vanlaningham, Nathan P456
Vannorman, Steven A414:P260
Vanorsdol, Rodney P169
Vanskiver, Tina P433
Vantucci, Trish P164
Vanvleck, Douglas P193
VanWees, Jason E404
Vanzo, Kendra A585
Vara, Raymond A97
Vara, Fabiola Arredondo de A146
Vara, Raymond P244
Varadarajan, Seshasayee A467
Varallo, Deborah A866:E450
Vardeman, Tracy P385
Varenne, Francois De W429
Varga, Daniel W P542
Vargas, Michelle P38
Vargas, Juan P137
Vargas, Diana P218
Vargas, David P236
Vargas, Bolgen P449
Varilek, James A588
Varischetti, Nicholas E133
Varisco, Frank P483
Varnado, Anddria A809
Varnell, John W191
Varner, Chilton E57
Varnes, Liza P470
Varnum, Daniel P332
Varona, Yanelys P650
Varona-Lukens, Violet A224:P162
Varsellona, Maria W5
Varvaro, Stephanie P69
Varwijk, Erik W278
Vasconcellos, Wallim A627
Vasel, Melissa P120
Vasella, Daniel A46
Vasilogiannaki, Athina W518
Vasiu, Peter P494
Vasos, Todd A252:A453
Vasquez, Kelly P48
Vasquez, Ivan P120
Vasquez, Anthony P193
Vasquez, Gregory P283
Vasquez, Blanca P303
Vasquez, Peter P426
Vasquez, Gus P525
Vasquez, Christann P613
Vasquez, Ricardo W340
Vassalluzzo, Scott E109
Vasseur, Denis Le W389
Vassiliadis, Michael W224
Vassiliou, Konstantinos W188
Vassoille, Jocelyne W517
Vaswani, Ashok W75
Vath, Richard R P220
Vatnick, Silvina W61
Vatulescu, Cristina P374
Vaughan, Therese A855
Vaughan, Rob P99
Vaughan, Rick P262
Vaughan, Therese E434:E445
Vaughn, Nooshin A411
Vaughn, Chad A485
Vaughn, Michael P40
Vaughn, David P95
Vaughn, Robin P255
Vaughn, D Blayne P392
Vaughn, Jacqueline P426
Vaughn, Kathleen P431
Vaughn, Mark E115
Vause, Brandy P560
Vautrain, Robert L P327
Vautrinot, Suzanne A227

Vawdrey, David K A343:P225
Vaz, Joao P525
Vaz, Nigel W395
Vazquez, Carlos A297:E158
Veal, Carol P156
Veale, Tomi P129
Veasey, Ashley W69
Vecchio, Jennifer A140
Vecchione, Kenneth A857:E447
Vedovotto, Roberto W273
Veerni, Vandhana V P395
Vega, John P128
Vega, Norlina Dela P148
Vega, Elizabeth P252
Vega, Blanca Trevino de W525
Veiel, Eric A757
Veihmeyer, John A333
Vejakul, Saranya W284
Vekich, Michael E53
Vela, Cynthia P165
Vela, Raymundo Yutani W198
Velasco, German A723
Velasco, Ernesto Vega W28
Velasco, Ignacio Garralda Ruiz
    de W179
Velasquez, Jessie A229
Velasquez, Sonia P4
Velasquez, Jessie E112
Velay-Borrini, Patricia W395
Velazquez, David A286
Vele, Oana P299
Velez, Matthew A762
Velez, Luis Guillermo Echeverri W171
Veliz, Elizabeth P642
Vella, John A P27
Vella, Ivan W406
Vellinga, David P102
Vellios, Thomas E176
Veloso, Roland Gerard W70
Vels, Michael W176
Veltmaat, Hans-Bernd A20
Veluswamy, Leslie A246
Velver, Ron P212
Vemuri, Ashok A461
Ven, Michael Van De A726
Vena, Vincenzo James A812
Venable, Jerry P280
Venable, Joshua P525
Vendemo, Shelly P102
Venderby, Christian W514
Venditto, Eileen P165
Venecia, Jose de W417
Venegas, Edmundo Miguel
    Vallejo W215
Venegas, J. Enrique E284
Venezia, Patrick A779:P568
Venhuizen, John A8:P4
Venkatakrishnan, C.S. W75
Venkataraman, Viswanathan P473
Vennam, Rajesh A236
Vennero, Thomas P131
Venosdel, Darin A579
Venrick, Kathy P323
Vento, Marc P482
Ventoza, Luis S P408
Ventre, Elizabeth P121
Ventresca, Melissa A352
Ventress, Peter W97
Ventura, Robert A313
Ventura, Joseph A406
Ventura, Robert E165
Venturini, Francesco W181
Venugopal, Dinesh P356
Vera-Vazquez, Ernest P330
Veras, Harry P371
Verdaglio, Anthony P323
Verdeaux, Gregoire A625
Verdes, Marcelino W9:W227
Verdetti, Gina P294
Verduzco, Jorge P441
Vereb, Joseph P277
Verenes, J. Chris E365
Vergara, Emerson W255
Verghese, Sunny W370
Vergis, Janet W487
Verhagen, Hendrica W249:W402
Verhoeven, Rainer W50

Verhoff, John P103:P553
Verinder, David P465
Verity, William A47
Verker, Bruce P480
Verkhov, Vyacheslav W386
Verkleeren, Ronald A221
Verma, Vic A426
Verma, Richard A757
Verma, Shashi W413
Verma, Vikas E231
Vermeer, Jennifer P586
Vermeir, Raphael Louis W185
Vermilion, Ken E42
Vermillion, Teresa A588
Vermilya, Dan P417
Verna, Tara P380
Vernet-Garnier, Claire W372
Verneuille, Janet A322
Vernon, W. Anthony A508
Verret, David E256
Verrette, Paula P407
Verrier, James A609
Verrilli, John L P530
Verschuren, Annette W100
Verslues, Ernie P339
Verst, Robert P336
Verstreken, Jan A392
Vervalin, Paul P385
Vescovi, Ana Paula Vitali Janes W506
Vesely, Liv P294
Vespertino, Danielle P655
Vespoli, Leila L P337:P410
Vespoli, L L P552
Vessey, Rupert A134
Vessey, Beth P256
Vessey, Rupert E50
Vestberg, Hans A833
Vetter, David A763
Vetter, J D P285:P286
Vetterli, Kristie P115
Vettese, Frank W412
Veurink, Jon D P386
Vezina, Dena A740
Vezina, Ann A763
Vezina, Dena P516
Vial, Martin W18:W175
Viale, Enrico W181
Viana-Baptista, Antonio Pedro de
    Carvalho W263
Viani, Giovanni W144
Vicari, Roberta P402
Vicente, Sharon Mae W83
Vick, Alfie P620
Vickers, Selwyn A25
Vickers, George M P444
Vickery, Peggy P255
Vickrey, Garrett P67
Vickrey, Kristen P475
Victor, Jeanne P571
Victor, Paul W421
Victor, Miriame E320
Vidal, Philippe W174
Vidale, Mauro P527
Vidalis, Efthymios W27
Videtto, Emily E24
Vidhani, Anand P244
Vidhayasirinun, Voraporn W62
Vieira, Bradford A707
Vieira, Donna A716
Vieira, Elaine P124
Vieira, Vasco Joaquim Rocha W172
Vieira, Bradford E368
Vieira, Donna E379
Viel, Richard W90
Vielehr, Byron A325
Vierheilig, Alexander A48
Viets, Josh A171
Vig, Ravi P22
Vigeveno, Huibert W434
Vigna, Adam P389
Vigo, Juan Manuel Cendoya Mendez
    de W61
Vijayakumar, C P244
Vijayaraghavan, Ravi E27
Vike, Jean P355
Vilagi, Oszkar W334
Vilca, Lina Vingerhoets A723

COMBINED HOOVER'S HANDBOOK INDEX OF EXECUTIVES

Vilcek, HelenBeth E161
Viljoen, Natascha W32
Villa, Laurie A439
Villa, Paula P190
Villa, Antonio P237
Villa, Norma P608
Villa, Gabriele W316
Villalobos, Hilda P109
Villalobos, Hector P483
Villalobos, Jose Vizcarra W56
Villanueva, Hazel P116
Villanueva, David P168
Villanueva, Enrique P311
Villanueva, Eleana P404
Villanueva, Evelyn W82
Villarreal, Jose A812
Villarreal, Dominick P139
Villarruel, Bonnie P58
Villasana, George A73
Villasenor, David P311
Villatoro, Jorge Eduardo Kim W381
Villeneuve, Nadia A154
Villeneuve, Costanza De W181
Villeplee, Christophe De A426
Villicana, Vicky P203
Villoch, Alexandra P57
Vimolrat, M P65
Vimooktayon, Vatchari W113
Vinals, Jose W457
Vince, Robin A99
Vincent, Mary A396
Vincent, Anton A427
Vincent, Suzanne M A442
Vincent, Mark P127
Vincent, Suzanne M P278
Vincent, Daniel L P404
Vincent, Jackie P647
Vincent, Danette P658
Vincent, Ronald E109
Vinci, Bryan A782
Vinci, Claudio P53
Vinci, Bryan P583
Vinci, Francesco W316
Vinci, Gerald E81
Vinciarelli, Patrizio E438
Vinciquerra, Anthony A657
Vinck, Karel W507
Vincze, Christopher P597
Vines, Tim P78
Vingerhoets, Cindy P193
Vinson, Ashley P52
Vinson, Julienne P56
Vinson, Sara P347
Vinyard, Justin A31:P24
Viola, Rich A125
Viola, Michael A417
Viola, Vincent A839:P643
Viola, Michael E227
Vipperman, Robert P19
Viqueira, William P571
Virani, Shailesh P333
Virella, Jose P272
Virtanen, Matti W274
Vischer, Carole W426
Visentin, Giovanni A872
Vish, Nancy P65
Viswanathan, Subramaniam A174
Viswanathan, Rajagopal W69
Vita, Charles A147
Vita, Katherine P640
Vita, Charles E65
Vitale, Robert A635
Vitale, David A813
Vitalone, Britt A510
Vitas, Heather P316
Vitayapipopskul, Santi W113
Viterbo, Edgar P420
Vithoulkas, John A P161
Vitner, Stephanie P411:P575
Vitosh, Bruce E286
Vittadini, Grazia W410
Vittal, Ireena W165
Vittavasgarnvej, Vinai W113
Vitter, Meg P304
Vivaldi, Carlo W509
Viveiros, Filomena P169
Vivek, Deepak P400

Viverito, Melissa Mark A186:P129
Viviani, Tanios A35:P27
Vlachakis, Alexandra P198
Vleck, Kathryn Van P198
Vliet, Gretchen Van P443
Vo, Thuy-Nga A68
Voegele, Michael A625
Voellmin, Dieter W75
Vogel, Carl A714
Vogel, Kimberley A793
Vogel, Scott P52
Vogel, Anita P154
Vogel, Colleen P413
Vogel, Kimberley E414
Voges, William A316
Vogler, Jane P396
Vogler, Martin W514
Vogt, Ed P92
Vogt, Susan E368
Vohra, Tajinder E320
Voigt, Diana G P415
Voigtlaender, Hans-Dietrich W2
Voigtlander, Christian E220
Voisin, Jean-Baptiste W302
Vojvodich, Lynn A333
Volas, Gerald E413
Volchyok, Leon E52
Volden, Angela A738:P514
Volent, Paula E282
Voliva, Richard A390
Volk, Becky P43
Volk, Bea P333
Volkart, Carmen E28
Volke, Robert E213
Volkmann, Irene P368
Volle, Darren P315
Voller, Chris J P14
Vollins, James E51
Vollmer, Jason A512
Vollmer, Sonya P112
Vollot, Philippe W154
Vollrath, Thomas P289
Vollrath, Dj P339
Vollucci, Maria P596
Voloch, Bill P650
Volpe, Sandra A677
Volpe, Lorraine V P206
Volpe, Michele P427
Volpetti, Stefano A625
Volz, Kim P185
Vonderfecht, Dennis P426
Vondran, Steven A51
Vonzychlin, Claus P598
Voon, Seng Chuan W29
Voorhees, Steven A796
Vora, Sanjeev P112
Voran, Nicholas P216
Vorasetsiri, Phaisarn W270
Vorobev, Vadim W386
Vorsheck, Elizabeth E145
Vos, Glen De W37
Vosburg, Craig A506
Voser, Peter W5
Voss, William A727
Voss, Susan A815
Voss, Paula P312
Voss, Zeb P338
Voss, Thomas G P542
Vounatsos, Michel A118:E320
Voyack, Frank A566
Voyadzis, Jean-Marc P325
Voyles, Janie P453
Vozos, Frank P350
Vrancken, Jennifer Van P406
Vranken, Rita Van P354
Vranos, Michael E132
Vrchakovski, Vojo A683
Vreman, Hendrik J A473:P295
Vrettou, Eleni W383
Vries, Loek De P452
Vu, Kenny P64
Vuletich, Christine P172
VunCannon, Tony A396:E217
Vyugin, Oleg W411
Vázquez, Carlos A633

W

W.Bates, Laurence W378
Waack, Roberto Silva W309
Waary, Sael Al W38
Wacha, Kim P175
Wacha, Bruce E43
Waddle, Aaron P523
Wade, Joanne E A343
Wade, Randall A561
Wade, Sharon P134
Wade, Scott P185
Wade, David P203
Wade, Joanne E P225:P226
Wade, Cynthia P344
Wade, Elizabeth P398
Wade, Rusti P542
Wade, Dana E443
Wadhanapatee, Suppawat W284
Wadhwa, Amit P604
Wadhwani, David A11
Wadhwani, Anil W308
Wadhwani, Sunil E263
Wadsworth, Jeffrey P63
Waersted, Gunn W483
Wagatsuma, Akiko A118
Wagers, Gary A102
Wagers, Thomas E284
Wagh, Girish W477
Wagler, Tyson A353
Wagler, Theresa A745
Wagler, Tyson E192
Wagnar, Jack P479
Wagner, Susan A65
Wagner, Cortney A176
Wagner, Jody A209
Wagner, Stephen A256
Wagner, Patrick A495
Wagner, Matthew P A606
Wagner, Charles A835
Wagner, Mike A867
Wagner, Christian P100
Wagner, Frederick P127
Wagner, Jody P146
Wagner, Amy P233
Wagner, Eugene D Van P286
Wagner, Harvey L P337:P394:P410
Wagner, Rebecca P411
Wagner, L D P443
Wagner, Chris P487
Wagner, Karen Van P533
Wagner, Harvey L P552
Wagner, Morgan P585
Wagner, Michael P604
Wagner, William B P612
Wagner, Hermann W2
Wagner, William E11
Wagner, Donald E125
Wagner, Mark E134
Wagner, Richard E232
Wagner, Patricia E334
Wagstaff, Nathan V P500
Waguespack, Robert L P54
Wahl, Philip E365
Wahlin, Rob P206
Waineo, Eva P648
Wainer, Andrea A4
Wainscott, James A227:A609
Wainstein, Gaston W525
Wainwright, Richard W253
Waite, G. Thomas E392
Wajner, Matthew A308
Wajsgras, David A501
Wakabayashi, Tatsuo W327
Wakamatsu, Kyosuke W257
Wakasa, Ichiro W237
Wake, Scott P414
Wakefiel, Peter D P160
Wakely, Jane A619
Walb, Terry P102
Walbaum, Joaquin W255
Walbaum, Marie-francoise W488
Walcher, Michael P207
Walchirk, Mark A611
Walcott, Dennis A186
Walcott, Wanjiku Juanita A247
Walcott, Dennis P129

Wald, Heidi P618
Waldbillig, Cathy P330
Walde, Van Der P30
Walders, William P246
Waldheim, William E429
Waldman, Adam A555
Waldman, Eyal P325
Waldman, Adam P374
Waldorf, William E202
Waldrin, Michele P638
Waldrip, Meagan P383
Waldron, John A360:A398
Waldron, Blain P144
Waldrop, Tony G P629
Walk, Belinda P92
Walkden, Pam W61
Walkenhorst, John P499
Walker, Kimberly A206
Walker, Corey A238
Walker, Kellye A264
Walker, Tristan A332
Walker, Sean A347
Walker, Karen A478
Walker, Roberto A641
Walker, Steven A647
Walker, Kevin A725
Walker, Brian A805
Walker, Lisa P42
Walker, Gordon P68
Walker, David P76
Walker, Algernon P125
Walker, William P155:P157
Walker, Larry P168
Walker, Johnnie P184
Walker, Stacy P213
Walker, Tom P217
Walker, Robert L P231
Walker, Brett P233
Walker, Crestina P242
Walker, Terry P267
Walker, Mark P287
Walker, Sarah P298
Walker, Kristen P314
Walker, Steve P333
Walker, Marsha P362
Walker, Jeanne P395
Walker, Angela P408
Walker, Gail P444
Walker, Cindi P467
Walker, Brooks P468
Walker, Annette M P502
Walker, Paul P532
Walker, Ursula P535
Walker, Chris P616
Walker, Michael P616
Walker, Robert P654
Walker, Scott P658
Walker, Andrew W48
Walker, David W532
Walker, Chris E57
Walker, John E75:E166
Walker, Lana E242
Walker, Kumi E257
Walker, Lauren E266
Walker, Burke E284
Walker, Clifford E330
Walker, Kevin E384
Walker, William E443
Walker-Lee, Robin A272
Walker-Vamos, Colleen P507
Wall, David J A147
Wall, Daniel A289
Wall, Peter A345
Wall, Aileen A436
Wall, Peter A705
Wall, David J P96
Wall, Aicp P170
Wall, Aileen P271
Wall, Heather P409
Wall, John E62
Wallace, Michael A94
Wallace, Noel A200
Wallace, Carol A224
Wallace, Richard A457
Wallace, Jason P47
Wallace, Monique P121
Wallace, Eugene P145

COMBINED HOOVER'S HANDBOOK INDEX OF EXECUTIVES

A = AMERICAN BUSINESS
E = EMERGING COMPANIES
P = PRIVATE COMPANIES
W = WORLD BUSINESS

Wallace, Delores P159
Wallace, Micah P165
Wallace, Deja P166
Wallace, Carol P168
Wallace, Phillip O P292
Wallace, Paul P292
Wallace, Chris P401
Wallace, Mark P540
Wallace, Nicole P555
Wallace, Paula P578
Wallace, Michael E44
Wallace, Carol E376
Wallach, Russell A483
Wallenberg, Jacob A543:W5
Wallenberg, Peter W48
Wallenberg, Marcus W446
Waller, Christopher A301
Waller, Robert R P459
Walley, Pete P81
Walliani, Hussain P263
Wallin, Kim A738:P514
Wallis, Tim A814
Wallis, Barbara P76
Wallis, Jackie P291
Wallis, Tim E424
Wallman, Richard E79
Walls, Todd A283
Walls, Ron A503
Walls, Todd P208
Walls, Ron P317
Walls, David E107
Walmsley, Emma W210
Walsh, David A48
Walsh, Timothy A A50
Walsh, Derrick A90
Walsh, Dennis A212
Walsh, Matthew A343
Walsh, Andrea A380
Walsh, Paul A509
Walsh, Richard A831
Walsh, Kate P84
Walsh, Greg P170
Walsh, Matthew P225
Walsh, Kate H P238
Walsh, Andrea P247
Walsh, Marshall T P471
Walsh, William P P562
Walsh, Matthew M P590
Walsh, Daniel P590
Walsh, John L P608
Walsh, Matthew M P645
Walsh, Daniel J P645
Walsh, Brian R P645
Walsh, Brian W213
Walsh, Derrick E41
Walsh, Eugene E161
Walsh, Brendan E264
Walter, W. Edward A52
Walter, Luc A59
Walter, Henry A535
Walter, Stephen P222
Walter, Kevin P333
Walter, Trisha P417
Walter, Larry P494
Waltermire, Mark P495
Walters, Judy A516
Walters, Kirk A617
Walters, Jay A804
Walters, Mark P115
Walters, Deborah D P127
Walters, H Patrick P262
Walters, Mary P449
Walters, Kelly S P555
Walters, Jay P607
Walters, Sarah W111
Walters, Marian E42
Walters, Kirk E319
Walters, Andrew E376
Walters, Elizabeth E387
Walterskirchen, Herbert W367
Walthall, Leonard E20

Walti, Beat W168
Walton, David A8
Walton, Chris A410
Walton, Michael K A602
Walton, Thomas A605
Walton, David P4
Walton, Jim P296
Walts, Steven P428
Waltz, Gwen P344
Waltz-Jaskolski, Donna A187:E85
Walz, Tim A737:P513
Walz, Pat T P662
Wampler, Kevin A253
Wampler, Dan P411
Wamsley, Patrick P566
Wamuo, Ngozi P249
Wan, David P243
Wan, Kam To W121
Wan, Chi-Wai W138
Wanblad, Duncan W32
Wandell, Keith A256
Wandelova, Petra W281
Wandke, Simon W40
Waneka, Jeffrey E284
Wang, Jane A192
Wang, Huimin A269
Wang, Chenxi A512
Wang, Shirley A639
Wang, Josephine A702
Wang, Ming-Hsien A778
Wang, Albert A851
Wang, Peter P29
Wang, Christina P133
Wang, Huilu P180
Wang, Richard P181
Wang, WEI P182
Wang, Kedong P183
Wang, Tao P276
Wang, April P338
Wang, Joy P452
Wang, Robert P496
Wang, Mian P498
Wang, Ming-Hsien P564
Wang, Zhe P615
Wang, William P643
Wang, Qin P644
Wang, Jian W18
Wang, Wanglin W31
Wang, Yidong W31
Wang, Jianhua W31
Wang, Baojun W31
Wang, Jianchao W33
Wang, Leon W46
Wang, Haifeng W54
Wang, Zhaojia W81
Wang, Bing W87
Wang, Qi W87
Wang, Huacheng W88
Wang, Zi-dong W97
Wang, Chuan-Fu W97
Wang, Chuan-fang W97
Wang, Jie W97
Wang, Li-Ling W106
Wang, Fu-Min W106
Wang, Ren W116
Wang, Yongfan W116
Wang, Xinming W116
Wang, Junhui W117
Wang, Yuhang W118
Wang, Yougui W118
Wang, Lixin W120
Wang, Jianping W120
Wang, Wenzhong W120
Wang, Xiuming W120
Wang, Huacheng W120
Wang, Xiangming W121
Wang, Xingzhong W122
Wang, Xiangxi W122
Wang, Sidong W123
Wang, Junzhi W124
Wang, Haiwu W125
Wang, Guoquan W129
Wang, Dongjin W130
Wang, Tzong-Ming W138
Wang, Ta-Chun W138
Wang, Po-Tang W138
Wang, Wei-Chia W138

Wang, Cheng-Chiang W138
Wang, Pak-Ling W147
Wang, Tianguang W209
Wang, Nan W209
Wang, Xiaohua W214
Wang, Lanyu W220
Wang, Songlin W223
Wang, Cheng-Yang W230
Wang, Yuesheng W235
Wang, Xiaobo W235
Wang, Kui W236
Wang, Xiaoqiu W236
Wang, Xueyan W236
Wang, Jingwu W249
Wang, Hongfei W265
Wang, Wei W265
Wang, Wen W265
Wang, Xiaowei W287
Wang, Qiangmin W303
Wang, Xianzhu W303
Wang, Hang W349
Wang, Pusong W349
Wang, Ke W376
Wang, Aiguo W431
Wang, Xiangdong W431
Wang, Xiaowen W434
Wang, Yijiang W434
Wang, Xiaoyan W435
Wang, Y. W474
Wang, J. W474
Wang, Kenny W530
Wang, KY W530
Wang, Zhibing W535
Wang, Qin W535
Wang, Changhui W535
Wang, Xinhua W535
Wang, Zihao W535
Wang, Yaling W535
Wang, Ruolin W539
Wang, Peng W539
Wang, Chunyao W539
Wang, Tingge W541
Wang, Lu'ning W541
Wang, Xiyu W542
Wang, Ling E286
Wang, Yu Ling E286
Wang, Judy E311
Wang, Shirley E331
Wanichthanom,
   Thumnithi W441:W441
Wanichwatphibun, Saengchart W65
Wanly, Bahaa P460
Wann, Robert A553
Wanta, Gregory A427
Wanzek, Kent W203
Ward, Beth A20
Ward, Doris M A185
Ward, Daniel A283
Ward, Jeffery A312
Ward, John A485
Ward, Matthew A531
Ward, Michael A632
Ward, Jacquelyn A694
Ward, Laysha A813
Ward, Patrick A870
Ward, Beth P11
Ward, David P25
Ward, Kathy P112
Ward, Doris M P122
Ward, Wendy P150
Ward, Daniel P208
Ward, Caroline P232
Ward, Ronnie P322
Ward, Matthew P349
Ward, Peter P371
Ward, Kevin P377
Ward, Kevin J P377
Ward, Alice P380
Ward, Stephen P424
Ward, Nicholas P444
Ward, Paul J P491
Ward, Pamela M P553
Ward, Adam P585
Ward, Betty Lou P644
Ward, Beth P649
Ward, Patrick W197
Ward, Chris W222

Ward, Greg W304
Ward, Marce E64
Ward, Janice E83
Ward, F. Stephen E163
Ward, Jeffrey E359
Ward, Susan E359
Ward, Anne E385
Ward, Philip E394
Ward, Anne E432
Ward, Patrick E454
Wardell, Lisa A46
Warden, Gail L A381
Warden, Kathy A515:A569
Warden, Gail L P249
Ware, Todd A296:E157:E286
Warfel, John E115
Wargowsky, Robert P378
Waring, Stephen P483
Waring, Wendy P609
Waring, Thomas E148
Warkomski, Denise A293:P212
Warman, Michele P544
Warmbold, Benita W69
Warne, Jen A480
Warne, Teresa P30
Warne, Robin P490
Warne, Peter W304
Warner, Douglas A A513
Warner, Brad A700
Warner, Cynthia A705
Warner, Doug A869
Warner, Ardis P53
Warner, Daniel P176
Warner, Dan P176
Warner, Charles P228
Warner, Douglas A P328
Warner, Julie P334
Warner, John P418
Warner, Jennifer P435
Warner, Jim P468
Warner, John P638
Warner, Doug P659
Warner, Stuart P660
Warner, Louise W25
Warner, Carol W82
Warner, Jerry E100
Warnica, Kimberly A495
Warnig, Matthias W411:W502
Warnke, Karl E115
Warntz, Matthew A650
Warren, Kelcy A276
Warren, Kevin A325
Warren, Jennifer A491
Warren, Burney A544
Warren, Terri A647
Warren, Kevin A819
Warren, V'Ella A825
Warren, Michael P117
Warren, Lovely A P132
Warren, Karl P158
Warren, Jim P215
Warren, Eric P359
Warren, Terri P429
Warren, Seth P447
Warren, V'Ella P631
Warren, Burney E285
Warrick, April P165
Warrier, Ammu P185
Warrington, Bernard P361
Warsh, Kevin A819
Wartman, Steven A P587
Warzala, Richard E16
Waschbichler, Werner W81
Wasden, Mitch P625
Wasechek, Wayne E329
Washburne, Ray A276
Washer, Paul W199
Washington, Justina A123
Washington, Rose A126
Washington, Delinda A380
Washington, Donald A392
Washington, Paul A417
Washington, A. Eugene A441
Washington, Herbert A491
Washington, Gregory A691
Washington, Angela A739

COMBINED HOOVER'S HANDBOOK INDEX OF EXECUTIVES

Washington, Justina P81
Washington, Aaron P100
Washington, Yolinda P130
Washington, Delinda P247
Washington, Santesia P384
Washington, Lachelle P422
Washington, Angela P515
Washington, Rose E54
Washington, Donald E216
Washington, Paul E227
Wasiuta, Robert P523
Wasiutynski, John P164
Waskey, Scott W E439
Wasley, John A298
Wass, Lisa P282
Wassenaar, Yvonne E182
Wasser, Marilyn A666:A666
Wasserman, Zachary A409
Wasserman, Frederick E122
Wassersug, Mark A422
Wassmer, Michael A149
Wassmer, Walter W83
Wasteson, Martin W470
Wasti, Rashid W527
Watabe, Nobuhiko W314
Watabiki, Mariko W299
Watanabe, Hiroyuki W14
Watanabe, Dai W286
Watanabe, Shuichi W317
Watanabe, Shinjiro W317
Watanabe, Hiroshi W327:W373
Watanabe, Nobuki W373
Watanabe, Katsuaki W462
Watanabe, Kensaku W472
Watanabe, Hayao W491
Watanabe, Katsuaki W537
Watanagase, Tarisa W441
Watanarangkun, Khobkarn W270
Watcharananan, Arunee W113
Waterhouse, Danielle P292
Waterhouse, Deborah W210
Waters, Bill A165
Waters, Andy A211
Waters, James A227
Waters, Kathleen A237
Waters, James A453
Waters, Stephen A831
Waters, Christy P522
Waters, Donald P544
Waterson, Blake A241
Waterston, Bob P159
Watjen, Thomas W40:W391
Watkin, Jared A4
Watkins, Latriece A483
Watkins, Gretchen A539
Watkins, Ron A735
Watkins, Brad A770
Watkins, William P52
Watkins, Thomas P187
Watkins, Jesse P202
Watkins, Tammy P275
Watkins, Machelle P347
Watkins, Sharon Hewitt P498
Watkins, Shana P499
Watkins, Ron P510
Watkins, Brad P540
Watkins, Jade P609
Watkins, Elizabeth P616
Watkins, Rick P659
Watkins, Tracy E83
Watkins, H. Thomas E432
Watnick, Randolph P243
Watsa, Benjamin W191
Watson, David A58
Watson, Secil A98
Watson, Mathew A115
Watson, Wendy A185
Watson, David A203
Watson, Lucas A363
Watson, Pete A367
Watson, Patricia A684
Watson, Michael A848
Watson, Patricia A P90
Watson, Wayne P130
Watson, Tonya P171
Watson, Elizabeth P172
Watson, Thomas P325

Watson, Lance P333
Watson, George E P359
Watson, Ron P362
Watson, Jackie P367
Watson, Carol P443
Watson, Bud P468
Watson, Jessica P572
Watson, John W82
Watson, Howard W95
Watson, Robert W200
Watson, Emma W273
Watson, Robert W410
Watt, John A546
Watt, Andrew E392
Wattanachai, Kasem W441
Wattenbarger, Michael E4
Watters, James A147:E65
Watters, Joseph E260
Watterson, Andrew A726
Watteville, Jacques de W72
Wattles, Alan E286
Watts, Jeffery A296
Watts, Myles A296
Watts, Russell V P157
Watts, Christella P356
Watts, Richard P410
Watts, R. Andrew E57
Watts, Myles E157
Watzinger, Gerhard E263
Waugh, Helen P489
Waugh, Ashley W199
Waunch, Gary E69
Wawrin, Stephen E146
Waxman, Herbert S P17
Way, Chrisanne P38
Way, Edward Y. W106
Waycaster, Bill A239
Waycaster, C. Mitchell A674:E348
Waylan, Alan W423
Wayland, Joseph W126
Wayman, Christine P242
Wayne, Donald A658
Wayne, John C P421
Waznowicz, Dave P316
Weadick, Paula P319
Weaner, Lisa P312
Weatherford, Benny P91
Weathers, John W A20
Weathers, Melanie A327
Weathers, Jo A P2
Weathers, John W P11
Weathers, Melanie P215
Weaver, Amy A692
Weaver, David A796
Weaver, Amy P37
Weaver, Ann P356
Weaver, Tia P643
Weaver, Susan E4
Weaver, Judith E134
Weaver, Scott E136
Weaver, Nathanial D E189
Weaving, David A666
Webb, Phillip A25
Webb, Larry A179
Webb, James A220
Webb, Carl A388
Webb, Justin A529
Webb, Jack A546
Webb, Maynard A839
Webb, David P64
Webb, Donna P99
Webb, Randi P212
Webb, Gerald P241
Webb, Kim P287
Webb, Rita P287
Webb, Steven P375
Webb, Kevin P595
Webb, Nichole P595
Webb, Helen W132
Webb, Douglas W266
Webb, Justin E274
Webb, Thomas E309
Webb-Beers, Laura P135
Webber, Paula A737:P513
Weber, Jason A9
Weber, Jennifer A68
Weber, James A204

Weber, Jennifer A512
Weber, Stephen A640
Weber, Alfred A789
Weber, Emily A824
Weber, Kyndall P121
Weber, Rosalie P175
Weber, Emily P323
Weber, Jennifer P326
Weber, Carla P334
Weber, Jeff P338
Weber, Del B P396
Weber, Tom P424
Weber, Scott P429
Weber, Joyce P522
Weber, Kathleen P617
Weber, Emily P617
Weber, John W189
Weber, Ulrich W190
Weber, Christophe W475
Weber, David E3
Weber, Jason E3
Weber, Fred E29
Weber, Mark E159
Weber, Stephen E333
Webman, Alon P325
Webster, Ranson A382
Webster, Patrick A805
Webster, Mary L P94
Webster, Cheryl P431
Webster, Karen P468
Webster, Richard P593
Webster, Ranson E211
Wechsler, George E64
Wechter, Sara A183
Weck, Pierre de A96
Weckenbrock, Michael A399
Weddington, Sharon P417
Weddle, Mary A814:E423
Wedel, Gregory A94:E44
Wee, Susie A61
Wee, Ai Ning W212
Wee, Joo Yeow W212:W376
Weed, Keith W259
Weeks, Wendell A221
Weeks, Jason A829
Weeks, Andrew A609
Weeks, Doug P57
Weeks, Harry E365
Weele, Brian P332
Weerasinghe, Rohan A183
Wegel, Michael P7
Weger, David E64
Weger, Hans E388
Wegner, Tina P162
Wegner, James P388
Wehe, Brad P28
Wehibi, Nader Al W407
Wehle, Trina P157
Wehmann, James M E155
Wehmer, Edward A867:E452
Wehner, David A520
Wehr, Alecia P116
Wehring, Brad P461
Wehrle, Richard E12
Wehrwein, Sven E36:E337
Wei, Weifeng W81
Wei, Chyou-Jui W138
Wei, Mei W208
Wei, Chuanjun W209
Wei, Jianjun W212
Wei, C.C. W474
Weiblen, Anthony A602
Weide, Ron V P610
Weideman, William A588
Weidemanis, Joakim A235
Weidemeyer, Thomas A574:A848
Weidner, Sharon P268
Weigand, David E397
Weight, Joel E309
Weightman, Peter W250
Weiglein, Laura P246
Weigley, Alycia A816
Weigley, Steven P320
Weijde, Onne Van der W145
Weikel, Mark A791
Weil, Kelley A126
Weil, Meredith A773

Weil, Stephan W522
Weil, Kelley E54
Weiland, John A151
Weiland, Ed P463
Weiler, Marc P135
Weiler, Sasha P286
Weill, Brendon P501
Weill, Morgane W104
Weill, Véronique W395
Weimer, Charles A321
Weimer, James S P254
Weinberg, John A333:E149
Weinberger, Mark A441:A521
Weiner, Russell A189
Weiner, Jeffrey A429
Weiner, David A465
Weiner, Jack P332
Weiner, Jeff P380
Weiner, Toby P403
Weiner, David S P548
Weiner, Edward G P597
Weinfurter, Daniel P185
Weingart, Saul P604
Weingarten, Steven A690
Weinraub, Michelle P652
Weinroth, George J P553
Weins, Lewis P210
Weins, Bruce P470
Weinstein, Donald A81
Weinstein, Michael Arthur P11
Weinstein, James N P182
Weinstein, James P183:P368
Weinstein, Glen E236
Weinstein, Andrew E367
Weinstock, Craig A571
Weintraub, Brad P53
Weintraub, Jonathan P158
Weir, Daniela P112
Weir, Lisa P288
Weir, David P372
Weir, Helen W283
Weirick, Cecilia C220
Weisberg, James P205
Weisbord, Robert A713
Weisel, Thomas A746
Weisenberg, Clay A866:P657
Weisenberger, Eric P394
Weiser, Cynthia A27
Weiser, Steven P27
Weishaar, Martin A724:E383
Weisickle, John A48:P31
Weiss, Jerry A337
Weiss, Daniel A853
Weiss, Richard P253
Weiss, Richard J J P292
Weiss, Howard P300
Weiss, John P355
Weiss, Mark D P653
Weiss, Amir W486
Weiss, Richard E323
Weiss, Aaron E396
Weiss, Daniel E444
Weissbeck, Ralf W10
Weissburg, Martin W523
Weissenberger-Eibl, Marion W222
Weissenfluh, Franziska von W514
Weisshaar, Egbert W426
Weissinger, Allison P186
Weissl, Josef W367
Weissman, Paul P655
Weiszhaar, Barb A404
Weitkamp, Hendrik P640
Weitz, Ron P159
Weitz, Andy W35
Weitz, Wallace E60
Weitzman, Howard E42
Weitzner, John S P453
Weixlmann, Joseph N P458
Welborn, Robert A571
Welborn, Wesley A717
Welborn, Jim P5
Welborn, Tom P347
Welborn, Thomas O P348
Welborn, Wesley E379
Welch, Michael A73
Welch, John A410
Welch, M. Scott A466

HOOVER'S HANDBOOK OF EMERGING COMPANIES 2022

601

COMBINED HOOVER'S HANDBOOK INDEX OF EXECUTIVES

A = AMERICAN BUSINESS
E = EMERGING COMPANIES
P = PRIVATE COMPANIES
W = WORLD BUSINESS

Welch, Jacob A484
Welch, Shelly P119
Welch, Brian P169
Welch, Kevin P267
Welch, H Ray P333
Welch, Alan P424
Welch, Deborah P504
Welch, Joshua E20
Welch, E. Thomas E53
Welch, M. Scott E244
Welcome, Dorothy P263
Welday, Doug P387
Weldon, Virginia V P94
Weldon, William W191
Weldy, Chris P368
Welker, Kevin P P285
Wellendorf, Don P307
Wellensiek, Brad E340
Weller, Sara W95
Wellhausen, Susan P362
Welling, Nancy P166
Wellington, Jessica A133
Wellisch, Alejandro A4
Wells, Jason A163
Wells, LeeRoy A190
Wells, Monique A258
Wells, Darren A361
Wells, James A495
Wells, Michael K A640
Wells, Jason P6
Wells, James P451
Wells, Jill P500
Wells, Ian W200
Wells, Michael W391
Wells, Michael K E333
Wells, Donna E443
Wellslager, Steven A652
Welsch, James A623
Welsh, Mark A569
Welsh, Beth A613
Welsh, Sean A727
Welsh, Charles P333
Welsh, Joan P423
Welsh, Sean P495
Welsh, W. Russell E284
Welsh, Beth E316
Welsh-Huggins, Andrew P545
Welt, Philip A112
Welter, Jason P262
Welters, Anthony A486
Weltzien, Lourdes E270
Welz, Edward A P371
Welzenbach, Mark A375
Wen, Dongfen W130
Wendel, Abigail A808:E421
Wendell, Amy A106
Wendler, Margaret A675:E350
Wendling, Brian J A660
Wendling, Sergeant P170
Wendt, Stephen C P193
Wendt, Charles P298
Wendt, Andreas W79
Weng, Volker A131
Weng, Deh-Yen W106
Weng, Min-Tung W138
Wengel, Kathryn A441:A464
Wenger, E. Philip A340
Wenick, Mark A294:E156
Wenig, Devin A349
Wenkoff, Carman A252
Wenning, Joachim W337
Wennink, Peter W42
Wente, Lisa A711
Wente, Brian D P233
Wente, Lisa P481
Wentworth, Lynn A364:E114
Wentz, Kristin A736
Wentz, Deanna P19
Wentz, Kristin P512
Wenzel, Dawn A742
Wenzel, Brian A752

Wenzel, Dawn P518
Wenzel, Dorothea W203
Weresch, Werner W522
Werk, Elliot A735:P511
Werkema, Gordon A299
Werkhoven, Jim P388
Werner, Hiltrud W522
Werner-Dietz, Stephanie W359
Wernette, Terry P174
Werochowski, Wojciech W71
Werpy, Todd A69
Wert, James E108
Werth, Clinton P48
Werthauser, Judith E176
Werthman, Ronald J A778
Werthman, Ronald P276
Werthman, Ronald J P564
Wesbrook, Dr Fredrick P472
Wesch, David E120
Wescoe, David P354
Wescott, Marsha P449
Wesley, Paul P138
Wesley-Smith, Terence P620
Wesoff, Nancy P303
Wesolowski, Karen P149
Wess, Damian P394
Wess, Mark P428
Wessel, Thomas W190
Wessel, Rick E175
Wessler, Kevin P151
Wessler, Alan P339
Wessner, David K P406
West, Mary A28
West, David A72
West, Brian J A124
West, Catherine A149
West, Robert F A195
West, Rod A252:A277
West, Nadja A441
West, Michael A536
West, Mindy A542
West, Nadja A575
West, Mindy A712
West, Nadja A765
West, Mary P18
West, Jennifer P103
West, Patrick H P127
West, Robert F P140
West, Debbie P162
West, George P224
West, Mary P332
West, James R P416
West, Robert P459
West, Carl P532
West, Mary Jo P599
West, Tereasa P602
West, Scott P605
West, Christy W P629
West, James P644
West, Mike P661
West, Bradley E321
West, Daniel E327
West, Mindy E373
West, Christopher E451
Westbroek, Carol P310
Westbrook, Kelvin A69
Westbrook, C. Hunter A396
Westbrook, Kelvin A539
Westbrook, Andy P123
Westbrook, Stacy P311
Westbrook, C. Hunter E217
Westbrook, Maureen E376
Westby, Sharon E355
Wester, K Scott P402
Westerberg,, Anna W523
Westerhold, Mary A320:E173
Westerhout, Fredrik E240
Westerlund, David A871
Westermann, Mari T A555:P374
Western, Keith A102
Westin, Fredrik A80
Westlake, Wayne P361
Westlake, Lisa W306
Westle, Marc B P36
Westman, David A517:P331
Weston, Graham A227
Weston, Marc A P181

Weston, George W45
Weston, Galen W527
Westphal, Mark A635
Westra, Richard A232
Westra, Jeff P255
Westrick, Karl J P311
Westry, Anita A737:P513
Westwell, Stephen W421
Wetherell, Russell P283
Wethington, Nadine A512:P324
Wetmore, Jonathan W242
Wetselaar, Maarten W434
Wettergren, Bjoern W524
Wetzel, Jeffrey E340
Wexler, Alan E454
Wey, Chris Van P126
Weyland, Bill P595
Weymouth, Katharine A677:E60
Whalen, Julie A288
Whalen, Kathleen A379
Whalen, Edward A485
Whalen, Julie A865
Whaley, Keith A717
Whaley, Alan A262
Whaley, Keith E379
Whaley-Smith, Teig P658
Wharton, Scott W135
Wharton, Don E42
Wheat, Bill A403
Wheat, Mary P399
Wheatley, T. Alan A406
Wheatley, Christine A461
Wheaton, Jeremy J A266
Wheaton, Kingsley W93
Wheeler, Carrie A253
Wheeler, Ted P131
Wheeler, Billie P172
Wheeler, Carmen P347
Wheeler, Jennifer P387
Wheeler, Kelsey P602
Wheeler, Charles W6
Wheeler, Michael E99
Wheeler, Scott E104
Wheeler, William E149
Wheeler-Fair, Martha P345
Whelan, Martin P610
Whelan, James W253
Whelan, Robert E34
Whelton, Pamela Daley P488
Whetstine, Michael J P285
Whetstone, Rachel A551
Whetstone, Hal P188
Whiddon, Thomas A721
Whiddon, Jeremiah P48
Whip, Jennifer A326:E177
Whipple, John A210:P430:E95
Whiskeyman, Julie P441
Whitaker, Charlie- A36
Whitaker, Michael A183
Whitaker, Jerry A702
Whitaker, Darla A771
Whitaker, Gary A866:E450
Whitbeck, Matthew P463
Whitbread, Jasmine W457
Whitby, Chris P274
Whitcomb, Joyce A78:P47
White, Teresa A18
White, Geoff A28
White, Daniel A187
White, Cris A A200
White, Charles A327
White, Richard A330
White, Steven A363
White, Duane A381
White, Bryan A414
White, James A417
White, Michael A455
White, Anne A478
White, George A489
White, Miles A509
White, William S A541
White, Katherine A585
White, Linda A585
White, Paul A621
White, Brett A666
White, Jesse A736
White, Reider A737

White, Teresa A754
White, G. Clark A760
White, Debbie A781
White, Noel A802
White, Lisa A809
White, Michael A863
White, Geoff P18
White, Kandy P27
White, William W P59
White, Tom P98
White, Robert P99
White, Eric P130
White, Esmerelda P133
White, Raymond R P158
White, Erin P159
White, Bonni L P184
White, Linda E P185
White, Charles P215
White, Joseph E P248
White, Fred P251
White, Bryan P260
White, Tom P262
White, Beth P266
White, Marietta R P281
White, Leland I P308
White, Colleen P403
White, Paul P412
White, Michael H P445
White, Van Henri P449
White, Christina P452
White, Katrina P463
White, Jesse P512
White, Reider P513
White, Debbie P575
White, Carrie P608
White, Judith S P619
White, Cecilia Velez W171
White, Sharon W295
White, Julia W419
White, Robert E36
White, Daniel E85
White, Albert E100
White, Matthew E103
White, Randall E130
White, Craig E130
White, Marvin E133
White, Duane E208
White, James E227
White, Michele E248
White, Rebecca E260
White, Thomas E390
White, Teresa E401
White-Coleman, Debra P562
Whited, Elizabeth A688
Whited, Beth A812
Whitehead, Dane A495
Whitehead, David P242
Whitehead, Shana P260
Whitehouse, Aaron E148
Whitehurst, Bradford A276
Whitehurst, Kristy A350
Whitehurst, James A813
Whitehurst, Bradford E429
Whiteing, David W456
Whitelaw, Mary W17
Whiteman, Russ P20
Whiteman, Jeffrey S P205
Whitenack, Jeanne P119
Whitesel, Thomas A331:E178
Whiteside, Debra P376
Whiteside, Darwin P384
Whiteside, Jeff E152
Whitfield, Fred A579
Whitfield, Jo W132
Whitford, Thomas A405
Whiting, Brian P172
Whiting, Donald E20
Whitley, David A741
Whitley, Shirley P111
Whitley, David P517
Whitley, B Glen P533
Whitlock, Leonard P522
Whitman, Margaret A349:A643
Whitman, Bill P533
Whitmer, Gretchen A737:P513
Whitmire, Brett E121
Whitmore, Justin A452

602

HOOVER'S HANDBOOK OF EMERGING COMPANIES 2022

COMBINED HOOVER'S HANDBOOK INDEX OF EXECUTIVES

Whitney, Anne A735
Whitney, Suzanne P29
Whitney, Marilyn P62
Whitney, Lois P163
Whitney, Anne P511
Whitson, Scott P266
Whitt, Richard A497
Whitt, Mark J A787;P595
Whitted, J. Michael E214
Whittemore, Kent A816
Whittemore, Mark P239
Whittemore, George E439
Whittick, Rob W345
Whittle, John E183
Whynot, Anita P164
Whynott, Paul A752
Whyte, Howard A796
Whyte, Maria P159
Whyte, Bruce P416
Wibergh, Johan W520;E415
Wichterich, Michael A171
Wick, Geoff P16
Wicke, Jan W476
Wicker, Dennis A309;E162
Wicker-Miurin, Jane W428
Wickert, Jonathan P266
Wickham, Kelvin W199
Wickland, David E P146;P359
Wicklund, Brian P330
Wicklund, Margaret E P485
Wicklund, Jared P555
Wickramasinghe, Mahes W102
Wicks, Kathy P23
Wicks, Bettie P26
Wicks, Tonja L P35
Wicks, Pippa W132
Widdel, Lars P323
Widder, Kenneth E342
Widener, Chris A740;P516
Widerlite, Paula P306
Widiastuti, Dini P420
Widmann, Amir E421
Wiebel, Katie P7
Wiechmann, Andrew E282
Wieder, Aron P167
Wiedman, Jim P282
Wiele, Thomas A387
Wiemeri, Kiley P18
Wiener, James A99
Wiens, Joel E355
Wierenga, Peter E271
Wierman, Heidi P308
Wierod, Morten W5
Wiersma, Lonna A514;E267
Wierzbinski, Daniel P112
Wiese, Peter A793;E414
Wieser, Lawrence A199
Wieser, Florian W108
Wieser, James E161
Wiesner, Hagen W194
Wiessmann, Robin A614
Wietharn, Rick P182
Wight, Amy P641
Wightman, Macie P445
Wigod, Mark P456
Wiinholt, Marianne W363
Wijers, Hans W249
Wijkstrom, Joakim E432
Wijnberg, Sandra A199;A756
Wike, Kevin A614
Wiker, Darren P258
Wikramanayake, Shemara W304
Wilbanks, C. David A579
Wilbanks, John F P58
Wilbanks, Johm P489
Wilbanks, John P489
Wilber, Ann A551
Wilbers, Melissa P347
Wilbur, Michael D P656
Wilbur, Cristina W408
Wilburn, Jon P65
Wilcher, Lajuana A296
Wilcher, Greta P334
Wilcher, Lajuana E157
Wilcox, Neil A325
Wilcox, Tyler A617
Wilcox, Mark A704

Wilcox, Ross W A811
Wilcox, Kevin J P27
Wilcox, Betsy P160
Wilcox, Brenda P173
Wilcox, Richard P330
Wilcox, Laura P345
Wilcox, Allison P500
Wilcox, Mark E367
Wilcox, Frank E427
Wilcoxson, Kristin P544
Wilczak, Adara P450
Wilczek, Joseph W P219
Wildberger, Karsten W108
Wilde, Frederic De A625
Wilde, Brenden P382
Wilde, Erik E191
Wilder, John S A741;P517
Wildman, Laura A614
Wilds, Eric W306
Wildstein, Harris A676
Wileke, Kina W523
Wilensky, Chandra A77
Wiley, Barbara A739
Wiley, Rusty P183
Wiley, Barbara P515
Wiley, Ronette P565
Wilhelm, Lance K P285
Wilhelm, Lura P499
Wilhelm, Edward W P556
Wilhelm, Harald W319
Wilke, Elliott A343
Wilkens, Michael A758
Wilkes, David A106
Wilkin, Janine M P569
Wilkins, Dick A20
Wilkins, C. Richard A372
Wilkins, James A496
Wilkins, David A814
Wilkins, Michael A815
Wilkins, Rayford A831
Wilkins, Charles A851
Wilkins, Dick P11
Wilkins, Carolyn W250
Wilkins, Aaron E297
Wilkins, Joseph E342
Wilkins, David E424
Wilkinski, Barbara P206
Wilkinson, Geoffrey A390
Wilkinson, Kara A410
Wilkinson, Tristram A455
Wilkinson, Mary Beth A457
Wilkinson, Peter A464
Wilkinson, Bruce P103
Wilkinson, Richard P130
Wilkinson, Anne P181
Wilkinson, Quintin P190
Wilkinson, Tali P315
Wilkinson, Wandy P421
Wilkinson, David P523
Wilkinson, Leaanne P646
Wilkinson, Walter E194
Wilkinson, Geoffrey E215
Wilkison, Bert P151
Wilkison, Rodney E198
Wilkosz, Lon P472
Wilks, Jeffery A832;E431
Will, W. Anthony A588
Will, David E340
Willard, Ann P201
Willard, L. Howard E85
Willbanks, John P58
Willbanks, Brad P322
Wille, Scott A28
Wille, Douglas A842
Wille, Scott P18
Wille, Matt P359
Wille, Douglas P645
Wille, Christoph W514
Willemse, Norman A42
Willemsen, Eugene A619
Willemsen, Jane A P274
Willett, Sean A307
Willett, Debbie P18
Willett, Robert E89
Willetts, David A413
Willey, Darro P186
Willey, Jeffrey P644

Willey, Frank E318
Willi, Rene A696
Willia, Patricia Whitley- P449
Williams, James A9
Williams, Julie A39
Williams, Anre A46
Williams, Julie F A48
Williams, Bill A52
Williams, Christopher A52
Williams, Jeffrey A65
Williams, John A74
Williams, G. Rainey A94
Williams, Maggie A106
Williams, Ashbel A147
Williams, Craig A148
Williams, Ena A155
Williams, Al A172
Williams, Christopher A189
Williams, Ronald A224
Williams, Angela A227
Williams, Valerie A243;A258
Williams, Janice A261
Williams, Randa A280
Williams, Frederica A284
Williams, Jack A291
Williams, Aaron A298
Williams, John C A300
Williams, L. Denise A304
Williams, Thomas A374
Williams, Anre A415
Williams, Ronald A441
Williams, Philip A446
Williams, Janann A511
Williams, Clay A571
Williams, Carol A588
Williams, Thomas A609
Williams, Steven A619
Williams, James P A632
Williams, Brian A636
Williams, Rick A640
Williams, Dantaya A665
Williams, Michael A666
Williams, Felicia A666
Williams, William A674
Williams, Nancy A741
Williams, William A750
Williams, Christopher A812
Williams, Darren A814
Williams, Sidney A832
Williams, Kim A862
Williams, Joseph A864
Williams, Kim A871
Williams, Stephen A877
Williams, John D A877
Williams, Jaelynn P12
Williams, Kevin P16
Williams, Edith P19
Williams, Julie P28
Williams, Steve P30
Williams, Julie F P31
Williams, Christopher P35
Williams, Katherine P36
Williams, Lakisha P54
Williams, Maggie P65
Williams, Kenneth L P76
Williams, Michael P76
Williams, Kenneth L P76
Williams, Michael P76
Williams, Nicoletta P90
Williams, Kenneth L P92
Williams, Michael P92
Williams, Steve P112
Williams, Bruce H P123
Williams, Regina V K P130
Williams, Donald P134
Williams, Ellen P158
Williams, Cindy P170
Williams, Ronald P172
Williams, Danielle P176
Williams, Kecia P177
Williams, Darlene P179
Williams, Cheryl P179
Williams, Lisa P181
Williams, Paul P185
Williams, Evelyn P199
Williams, Lucia P199
Williams, Marjorie N P211

Williams, Belinda P211
Williams, Jacob P216
Williams, Jenell P220
Williams, Wendy P238
Williams, Douglas P252
Williams, David P253
Williams, Mike P266
Williams, Brandon P271
Williams, Joan H P275
Williams, Brandy P282
Williams, Eric P303
Williams, Richard P304
Williams, Janann P322
Williams, Pipper P325
Williams, Kevin P376
Williams, Michaelle P377
Williams, Betsy P381
Williams, Steven A P390
Williams, Chris P398
Williams, Karla P409
Williams, Deberah P416
Williams, Mike P429
Williams, Amy P447
Williams, A Greg P471;P472
Williams, Pamela J P487
Williams, Sandra P496
Williams, Bonnie P501
Williams, Benjamin R P502
Williams, Nancy P518
Williams, George P530
Williams, Christopher P532
Williams, Lori P540
Williams, Lacy H P542
Williams, Dale P549
Williams, Claude P562
Williams, Robert P577
Williams, Treby P582
Williams, Jeff P598
Williams, Gregory H P617
Williams, Gordon P621
Williams, Alison P624
Williams, Paula P625
Williams, Claire P635
Williams, Debra F P648
Williams, Jack P661
Williams, John D P662
Williams, Coram W10
Williams, Nigel W135
Williams, Keith W413
Williams, Christopher W493
Williams, James E4
Williams, Paul E10
Williams, Anthony E11
Williams, Jeffrey E20
Williams, Mikel E42
Williams, G. Rainey E44
Williams, Ashbel E66
Williams, Derek E99
Williams, David E109
Williams, Janice E126
Williams, Eric E134
Williams, Edward E146
Williams, Joe E186
Williams, William B E204
Williams, Felicia E270
Williams, Kristen E311
Williams, Rick E333
Williams, William E348
Williams, Patrick E388
Williams, W. Joseph E420
Williams, Darren E423
Williams, Sidney E431
Williams, Timothy E432
Williams-Roll, Jacqueline A347
Williamson, Stephen A426
Williamson, Keith A637
Williamson, James A740
Williamson, Stephen A784
Williamson, Thad P132
Williamson, Todd P218
Williamson, Anthony P385
Williamson, Robert P392
Williamson, James P516
Williamson, Ann P621
Williamson, James W189
Williamson, Sarah E149
Williamson, Daniel E219

COMBINED HOOVER'S HANDBOOK INDEX OF EXECUTIVES

A = AMERICAN BUSINESS
E = EMERGING COMPANIES
P = PRIVATE COMPANIES
W = WORLD BUSINESS

Williamson, Mark E307
Willis, Jennifer A143
Willis, Angel A702
Willis, Renee P327
Willis, Gregory E9
Willis, Jennifer E65
Willis, Charles E449
Willis, Austin E449
Willmott, David P76
Willoughby, Dawn A718:W480
Willow, Michelle P54
Willsey, Lance E150
Wilm, Renee L A660
Wilmot, Christopher W38
Wilmott, Timothy A236
Wilroy, David P537
Wilson, Tom A32
Wilson, Mark A120
Wilson, Charles Joseph A154
Wilson, Andrew A271
Wilson, Carolyn A292
Wilson, Stephen A410
Wilson, Dwayne A418
Wilson, Kenneth A434
Wilson, David A453
Wilson, Gary A495
Wilson, Thomas A569
Wilson, Kelly A614
Wilson, Benjamin A623
Wilson, Thomas A642
Wilson, Alan A756
Wilson, Donta A796
Wilson, Alan A860
Wilson, R Lynn P91
Wilson, Steve P109
Wilson, James Michael P114
Wilson, Susan P119
Wilson, Ryan P163
Wilson, Ron P206
Wilson, Carolyn P210
Wilson, Patti P223
Wilson, John P248
Wilson, Kristin P255
Wilson, Beverly P257
Wilson, Scott P267
Wilson, Kurt P270
Wilson, Keith A P311
Wilson, Amy P347
Wilson, Kenny P349
Wilson, John P354
Wilson, San P379
Wilson, Scott P417
Wilson, Bob P445
Wilson, Mike P457
Wilson, Debbie P459
Wilson, Daniel R P477
Wilson, Nancy P496
Wilson, Edward P596
Wilson, Nicholas J P597
Wilson, Jack M P624
Wilson, Linda P635
Wilson, Sherwood G P642
Wilson, Roy P648
Wilson, Cameron W200
Wilson, Nigel W291
Wilson, Lena W345
Wilson, Michael W466
Wilson, George E32
Wilson, Joe E39
Wilson, Virginia E79
Wilson, Jeffrey E84
Wilson, James E102
Wilson, John E136
Wilson, Stephen E247
Wilson, Alexa E248
Wilson, Wayne E258
Wilson, Rachel E344
Wilson, John E358
Wilson, Erich E362
Wilson, Dwayne E390
Wilson-Edell, Kathleen P616

Wilson-Sowah, Henry P108
Wiltrout, Jeff A228
Wimberly, Marie P210
Wimbush, Michael P209
Wimpfheimer, Andrew E308
Winchester, Trisha P247
Windes, Richard A723:E383
Windhaus, Donna P73
Windhorst, Charles P249
Windmuller, Erich A213:P150
Windsor, Regina P161
Windsor, Andrew P371
Windsor, Jason W52
Winer, Sherri P472
Wines, Lynne A101
Winfrey, Teterina P211
Wing, Bill P6
Wingard, Beth P298
Wingerter, Joe A454:P285
Winges, M. Bradley A388
Wingfield, Gena G P42
Wingfield, Debbie P172
Wingo, Bill P278
Winkeljohann, Norbert W78
Winkelmann, Thomas A439
Winkelmann, Christof W2
Winkelmann, Paul W147
Winking, Kyle P183
Winkleblack, Arthur A67
Winkler, Jason A540
Winley, Amberly P283
Winn, Stephen P438
Winn, Penelope W30
Winn, James E439
Winnefeld, James A665
Winskill, Debbie P532
Winslow, Stephen P496
Winstel, John A237
Winston, Mary A174:A256
Winston, Wyman B A867
Winston, Eric P356
Winston, Roy E311
Wintemute, Eric E23
Winter, Matthew A377
Winter, P. Clinton A814
Winter, Ed P593
Winter, Gert De W55
Winter, Jaap W397
Winter, P. Clinton E423
Winterbottom, Brad A855:E445
Wintermyer, Janie P53
Winters, Kathleen A81
Winters, Nathan A877
Winters, Gene P433
Winters, William W457
Winters, Richard E184
Winters, Chad E446
Wintersteen, Wendy P266
Winzinger, Robert P167
Wippler, Luke A829
Wire, Ron P517
Wiren, Marco W346:W359
Wirick, Angela E36
Wirsbinski, Carol E86
Wirth, Robin A28
Wirth, Michael A172
Wirth, Robin E13
Wiscovitch, Zulema P46
Wisdom, Brittany P627
Wise, Andrew A72
Wise, Deanna A102
Wise, Robert G A214
Wise, Deanna P56
Wise, Bonnie P161
Wise, Wendy P166
Wise, Sarah P205
Wise, Andrew E31
Wise, R. Halsey E33
Wisecup, Reyne A295
Wiseman, Mark P282
Wiseman, Garry E289
Wisenbaker, Jamie D P286
Wishart, Ben W283
Wisidwinyoo, Wisade W98
Wisitkamthorn, Aphaporn W98
Wislar, EJ E194
Wisniewski, Leslie P132

Wisniewski, Hope P298
Wisniewski, Kim P417
Wit, Harry de W203
Witcher, Mr Craig V A719
Witcher, Kenneth P210
Witcher, Mr Craig V P486
Witczak, Eric A562:E293
Witherington, Philip W308
Withers, Dean E153
Witherspoon, Alberta P129
Withrow, Terrance E300
Witkewicz, David P452
Witkowski, Kimberly P109
Witkowski, Amy P393
Witney, Frank E320
Witoonchart, Gasinee W62
Witt, Mary A674
Witt, Marshall A763
Witt, Suann P396
Witt, Alan S P446
Witt, Dylan P529
Witt, Charles De P602
Witt, John W262
Witt, Mary E348
Witte, Blair A123:P81
Witte, Jan De E234
Wittenstein, Robin P519
Witter, Jonathan A716:E379
Wittgrove, Alan P335
Wittick, Linnea P293
Wittig, Veronica P83
Wittig, Martin W286
Wittkop, Scott P321:P321
Wittlinger, Todd P179
Wittman, Vanessa A128
Witty, Andrew A823
Witty, Monique P199
Witynski, Michael A253
Witz, Jennifer A714
Witz, Pascale W203:E320
Wix, Donya-Faye P644
Wlajnitz, Tami P275
Wo, Robert A97
Wodek, James A807
Woelfer, W. Todd A785
Woelke, Sylvia W108
Woeltjen, William P465
Woerner, John A52
Woerner, John R A679
Woerner, Liyuan P216
Woertz, Patricia A3:A643
Wohl, Richard A230
Wohl, Patrice P528
Wohl, Laurence P585
Wohl, Richard E113
Wohlgelernter, Beth P272
Wojahn, Jeffery E85
Wojnar, Theodore A291
Wojtalewicz, Jeanette P19:P175
Wojtowicz, Jean A320
Wojtowicz, Linda P604
Wojtowicz, Jean E172
Wolberg, Kirsten A716:E379
Wolcott, Daniel P649
Wold, Evie A737
Wold, Kristin P164
Wold, Evie P513
Wold, Kathleen P611
Wolf, Tom A208
Wolf, Dale A534
Wolf, William A695
Wolf, Casey A770
Wolf, Henry A778
Wolf, Christine A854
Wolf, Timothy A871
Wolf, Tom P146
Wolf, Janet P169
Wolf, Dan P358
Wolf, Jessie P463
Wolf, Jim P467
Wolf, Ginger R P472
Wolf, Casey P540
Wolf, Bryan P549
Wolf, Henry P561
Wolf, Reinhard W81
Wolf, Ute W190
Wolf, Dale E131

Wolf, Alta E242
Wolf, Kenneth E287
Wolf, Mark E390
Wolfe, Serena A62
Wolfe, Stephen A313
Wolfe, Nancy A418
Wolfe, Harriet A851
Wolfe, Brad P153
Wolfe, Alden P167
Wolfe, Richard E P243
Wolfe, Scott R P438
Wolfe, Cheryl Nester P460
Wolfe, Trevor P651
Wolfe, Stephen E165
Wolfe, Andrew E418
Wolfenbarger, Janet A15
Wolff, Jared M A93
Wolff, Armand J P87
Wolff, Nelson W P156
Wolff, Christine W227
Wolff, David E8
Wolfgeher, Barbara P382
Wolford, Joe A208:P145
Wolford, Robin P507
Wolfshohl, Candace A227
Wolfson, Larri A842:P645
Wolin, Harry A13
Wolk, Joseph A441
Wolkoff, Neal E309
Wolle, Joerg W287:W370
Wollny, Christoph W444
Woloski-Barnes, Deborah P96
Wolpert, Geoffrey A717:E379
Wolsfeld, Matthew E295
Wolt, Dave P282
Wolter, Gary P35
Wolter, Nicholas P75
Woltosz, Walter E375
Woltz, H. E232
Wolverton, David A781:P575
Womack, Chris A352
Womack, Bernard P177
Womack, Mark P580
Womack, Christopher E147
Wondafrash, Worku P322
Wondeh, Inez A856
Wonderling, Robert A826:E428
Wong, Dianson A224
Wong, Jennifer A247
Wong, Kenneth A573
Wong, Kim P24
Wong, John P29
Wong, Dianson P168
Wong, Brandon P244
Wong, Kenneth P391
Wong, Irene P554
Wong, Waikin P604
Wong, John P604
Wong, Chi-Yun W66
Wong, Wai Ming W124
Wong, Chee Kin W128
Wong, Chung-Pin W138
Wong, Tsu-Ning W146
Wong, Hon-Hing W147
Wong, Shou-Yeh W147
Wong, Wai-Nar W147
Wong, Kin Yan W196
Wong, Pakshong W212
Wong, Pik Kuen W212
Wong, Peter W234
Wong, Wai Ming W292
Wong, Daniel W304
Wong, Pik Kuen W376
Wong, Jeanette W391
Wong, Man Hoe W393
Wong, Gregory E343
Wongnongtaey, Krieng W441
Wongpanitkrit, Duangdao W65
Wongsmith, Nampung W98
Wongsuwan, Phatcharavat W98:W113
Wongtschowski, Pedro W506
Woo, Melissa P342
Woo, Tracy P576
Wood, Paul A177
Wood, Larry A269
Wood, E. Jenner A350
Wood, Phoebe A629:A637

COMBINED HOOVER'S HANDBOOK INDEX OF EXECUTIVES

Wood, Patrick A658
Wood, Adam A721
Wood, Matthew A804
Wood, William E P61
Wood, David P68
Wood, Robert H P85
Wood, Terrence P139
Wood, Richard P159
Wood, William P188
Wood, Kurt P195
Wood, Wendy P320
Wood, Amy P402
Wood, Kelly P446
Wood, Joyce P447
Wood, Christopher E P503
Wood, John P535
Wood, Matthew P607
Wood, Suzanne W195
Wood, Tony W210:W342
Wood, Leanne W520
Wood, Amy E84
Wood, Renee E99
Wood, Brent W E129
Woodall, James A304
Woodall, Niki P615
Woodard, Rita P171
Woodard, Andy P218
Woodard, Beth P423
Woodard, Carol P507
Woodard-Thompson, Charlesetta P241
Woodburn, Charles W53
Woodbury, Cory A735
Woodbury, Michael P161
Woodbury, Cory P511
Woodcock, John P55
Woodcox, Jerry E53
Woodgrift, Randel A4
Woodhouse, Hope A801
Woodhouse, Michael P456
Woodie, Joe P321
Woodliff, Dan P499
Woodring, Greig A377
Woodrow, Tracy A491
Woodruff, Robert P458
Woodrum, James A605
Woodrum, Douglas E47
Woods, Thomas A96
Woods, Eugene A115
Woods, John A185
Woods, Darren A291
Woods, Karen A315
Woods, M. Troy A358
Woods, Candace A649
Woods, Isaac A684
Woods, Gordon A709
Woods, Gina A732
Woods, Eugene A774
Woods, Lindsay P100
Woods, Frank P124
Woods, Dianne P133
Woods, Eugene A P380
Woods, Brian T P387
Woods, Rebecca P496
Woods, Eugene P547
Woods, Michael P569
Woods, Ngaire W405
Woods, Karen E167
Woods, Gordon E370
Woods, Jacqueline E451
Woodside, David A103:E47
Woodson, Genevieve P16
Woodson, R Peyton P211
Woodson, Nathaniel D P584
Woodson, Bret E451
Woodward, Skye A667
Woodward, Sarah P385
Woodward, Louann P624
Woody, Craig P619
Wooldridge, Beth P145
Woolett, Angela P496
Woolley, Kenneth E153
Woolrich, Andrew P299
Woolridge, Jack P135
Woolridge, Diane P345
Woolridge, Germaine P533
Woolsey, Michael P68
Woolson, Daniel E220

Wootton, Michael P526
Woram, Brian A447
Worden, Anita A278:E141
Worf, Heather P18
Work, Robert A665
Workman, Tamora P490
Workman, Tyler P643
Worley, Jay A24:P13
Worley, Jack P428
Worman, Douglas A192
Wormoudt, Mardi P169
Worner, John R A679
Worobel, Ryan P650
Woronoff, Michael E13
Woros, Agnes P61
Worrell, Brian A91
Worth, Philip A855:E445
Wortham, Lee E148
Worthington, Robert A514
Worthington, Scott A805
Worthington, Heather P167
Worthington, Julie P418
Worthington, Robert E267
Worthy, Delvon P646
Wortley, Michael A629
Wortman, Rand P278
Wortmann-Kool, Corien W13
Worzel, Kenneth A565
Woster, Casey M P441
Wothe, Mike E321
Woys, James A534
Wozniak, Kevin P228
Wratten, Carol P58
Wray, D. Michael A584
Wray, William A847
Wray, Peter E153
Wren, John A589
Wren, Tishya P550
Wright, Stephen A31
Wright, Kristen A84
Wright, Mary Ann A138
Wright, Deborah A183
Wright, Laura A190:A219
Wright, Bryan A287
Wright, Robert A289
Wright, Mary Ann A368
Wright, Doug A398
Wright, Randy A411
Wright, Scott A411
Wright, Mary Ann A527
Wright, Kelly A541
Wright, Lori A603:A603
Wright, John A610
Wright, Joseph A618
Wright, Adam A623
Wright, Richard A870
Wright, Rodney L P12
Wright, Stephen P24
Wright, Maria P53
Wright, Eric P69
Wright, Sharon P71
Wright, David P161
Wright, Nancy P186
Wright, Lori A P209
Wright, Roxanne P262
Wright, David H P303
Wright, Lori P404
Wright, Douglas P428
Wright, Amy P490
Wright, Judy P490
Wright, Daniel P610
Wright, Steve P633
Wright, Stacey P650
Wright, Edward P660
Wright, Cornell W82
Wright, Andrew W233
Wright, Patrick W340
Wright, Nathalie W402
Wright, Laura W480
Wright, Emory E15
Wright, Gregory E120
Wright, Jacqueline E150
Wright, Dickerson E300
Wright, Lori E310
Wright, Sharon E395
Wright, John E395
Wright, Richard E455

Wrighton, Mark A222:P591
Wrobel, Jill A138
Wrobel, Kurt P226
Wrobleski, Tammy P124
Wrobleski, Sarah P408
Wroten, Paul A203:P144
Wskeland, Oddgeir A283:P208
Wtulich, Peter C P404
Wu, Peter A157
Wu, Wayne A639
Wu, Chih-Wei A639
Wu, Shengpo A863
Wu, Sherman Z P71
Wu, Michelle P124
Wu, Jun P126
Wu, Corinna P198
Wu, Jiang P231
Wu, Dolly P263
Wu, Debbie P356
Wu, Xiaoni P441
Wu, Wei W24
Wu, Bin W33
Wu, Dong W81
Wu, Tang-Chieh W106
Wu, Shu-Ying W106
Wu, Jian-Hsing W106
Wu, Yiming W118
Wu, Jianing W120
Wu, Bingqi W121
Wu, Ting Yuk W123
Wu, Jianing W125
Wu, Xiaonan W130
Wu, Shengliang W172
Wu, Zhijie W212
Wu, Zhong W223
Wu, Senrong W236
Wu, Jianing W321
Wu, Yingjian W442
Wu, Jiang W442
Wu, Michael W474
Wu, Jiejiang W535
Wu, Xiangqian W539
Wu, Jundong W542
Wu, Peter E70
Wu, Wayne E331
Wu, Chih-Wei E331
Wunderlich, Myla P533
Wunning, Steven A708
Wurman, Richard P234
Wurster, Rick A697
Wurster, Rosemary P437
Wurtz, David P165
Wyant, Chuck P162
Wyatt, Christopher A379
Wyatt, Dale A410
Wyatt, E. Lee A428
Wyatt, Douglas A617
Wyatt, Mark P494
Wyatt, Jeff P641
Wyckoff, Virginia P396
Wye, Gretchen Van A552
Wye, John Van P346
Wye, Gretchen Van P369
Wyk, Steven Van A672
Wyk, Rene van W6
Wyles, Rick P361
Wylie, Warren P215
Wyman, Dan P125
Wyman, Eric P136
Wynn, Michael P460
Wynne, Michelle A877
Wynne, Linda P471
Wynter, Christine P644
Wyremski, Stephen A710:E371
Wyrsch, Martha A308:A658
Wyrsch, Martha B P541
Wyrsch, Martha W342
Wysk, Laura P565
Wyss, Andre A573:P391
Wyszomierski, Jack E150:E455

X

Xi, Guohua W129
Xia, Zuo-quan W97
Xia, Haijun W115

Xia, Kuanyun W116
Xia, Qinglong W130
Xia, Qing W236
Xia, Howard E224
Xian, Ming E266
Xiang, Ru'an W419
Xiang, Wenbo W419
Xiao, Xing W123
Xiao, Zheng W154
Xiao, Ji W236
Xiao, Jun W535
Xiao, Deming E279
Xie, Zhongdong W88
Xie, Hongxi W115
Xie, Ji W121
Xie, Zhichun W123
Xie, Weizhi W130
Xie, Ling W236
Xie, Mao W287
Xie, Jiren W383
Xie, Yonglin W383
Xie, Kun W436
Xie, Weiming W541
Xie, Junshi W542
Xie, Ken E183
Xie, Michael E183
Xin, Jie W125
Xing, Ziwen W214
Xing, Yi W387
Xing, Yinong E340
Xiong, Bao P159
Xolocotzi, Rafael A134:P87
Xu, Allen A48
Xu, Jeremy A418
Xu, Tony A520
Xu, Jing A735
Xu, Zi P64
Xu, Jing P511
Xu, Shishuai W31
Xu, Qian W114
Xu, Xing W116
Xu, Chongmiao W117
Xu, Feng W119
Xu, Xin W119
Xu, Wendong W119
Xu, Shancheng W122
Xu, Mingjun W122
Xu, Jinwu W129
Xu, Zuo W129
Xu, Keqiang W130
Xu, Qi W208
Xu, Jiajun W209
Xu, Bin W220
Xu, Haifeng W236
Xu, Mengzhou W236
Xu, Shouben W244
Xu, Dingbo W287
Xu, Youfang W431
Xu, Jia'na W535
Xu, Qiang W541
Xu, Ziyang W542
Xueref, Carol W174

Y

Yabe, Takeshi W52
Yabe, Nobuhiro W312
Yabokla, Erica A730:P509
Yabu, Yukiko W151
Yabuki, Jeffery W412
Yacob, Ezra A281
Yacoub, George P644
Yacuzzo, Vincent A147:E66
Yaeger, Erin P16
Yago, Natsunosuke W459
Yahes, Jarrod E369
Yahya, Didi Syafruddin W128
Yajima, Susumu W369
Yajnik, Sanjiv A149:A159
Yako, Osamu A877:P662
Yakovlev, Vadim W208
Yaku, Toshikazu W463
Yalcin, Gamze W504
Yaldo, Zaid P44
Yale, Phyllis A134:A237
Yamabe, Dayna P562

HOOVER'S HANDBOOK OF EMERGING COMPANIES 2022

COMBINED HOOVER'S HANDBOOK INDEX OF EXECUTIVES

A = AMERICAN BUSINESS
E = EMERGING COMPANIES
P = PRIVATE COMPANIES
W = WORLD BUSINESS

Yamada, Yasushi W149
Yamada, Yasuko W237
Yamada, Tatsumi W324
Yamada, Meyumi W452
Yamada, Shinnosuke W472
Yamada, Noboru W536
Yamada, Shigeaki W536
Yamadi, Asghar P196
Yamagata, Noboru W493
Yamaguchi, Brian A673
Yamaguchi, Tadaaki P94
Yamaguchi, Masato W148
Yamaguchi, Toshiaki W150
Yamaguchi, Mitsugu W279
Yamaguchi, Shogo W327
Yamaguchi, Kimiyoshi W430
Yamaguchi, Hiroyuki W494
Yamaji, Toru W436
Yamaji, Katsuhito W537
Yamakawa, Mark P576
Yamakoshi, Koji W36
Yamamoto, Glenn A48:P31
Yamamoto, Kathryn P621
Yamamoto, Katsutoshi W68
Yamamoto, Kensei W257
Yamamoto, Akira W279
Yamamoto, Yasuo W329
Yamamoto, Takashi W331
Yamamoto, Takatoshi W338
Yamamoto, Fumiaki W435
Yamamoto, Masataka W435
Yamamoto, Shunji W491
Yamamoto, Kichiichiro W493
Yamamoto, Ryutaro W494
Yamamoto, Keiji W501
Yamana, Kazuaki W329
Yamanaka, Masashi A615
Yamanaka, Norio W496
Yamane, Motoyo W257
Yamanishi, Tetsuji W479
Yamanishi, Kenichiro W500
Yamashina, Hiroko W373
Yamashita, Akinori W14
Yamashita, Masahiro W52
Yamashita, Kazuhito W260
Yamashita, Yoshinori W403
Yamashita, Takashi W463
Yamashita, Yukihiro W469
Yamashita, Mitsuhiko W477
Yamato, Shiro W52
Yamato, Satoshi W351
Yamauchi, Masaki W538
Yamaura, Masai W1
Yamazaki, Kei W237
Yamazaki, Masao W351
Yamazaki, Toru W418
Yamazaki, Shozo W463
Yan, Christine A591
Yan, Ye W118
Yan, Jianguo W119
Yan, Andrew W121
Yan, Jiarong W209
Yan, Aizhong W321
Yan, Chao W541
Yanagi, Hiroyuki W277:W537
Yanagida, Naoki W452
Yanai, Koji W192
Yanai, Kazumi W192
Yanai, Tadashi W192
Yanai, Junichi W472
Yanaranop, Cholanat W441
Yancey, Carol A350
Yancey, Shaun P P408
Yancopoulos, George A669
Yanez, Jorge Ferrando W177
Yang, Michael A374
Yang, Null Y Null P50
Yang, Andrea P125
Yang, Nha P163
Yang, Deyun P301
Yang, Teresa P434

Yang, Chih-Yuan W24
Yang, Hong W117
Yang, Qiang W118
Yang, Jie W118
Yang, Changgui W123
Yang, Xiaoping W129
Yang, Yun W130
Yang, Xiao W194
Yang, Kan W209
Yang, Liuyong W223
Yang, Baizhang W223
Yang, Xianghong W236
Yang, Chengjun W265
Yang, Liu W265
Yang, Yuanqing W292
Yang, Jigang W378
Yang, Xiaoping W383
Yang, Won Jun W388
Yang, Kevin W395
Yang, Jie W434
Yang, Jianghong W536
Yang, Zhenghong W541
Yang, Wendy E116
Yang, Emily E121
Yang, KP E311
Yang, Jackie E311
Yanisch, Stephen P35
Yankee, Colin A791
Yankevich, Alexei W208
Yannaccone, Susan A666
Yano, Yoshifumi P133
Yano, Norio W332
Yano, Hitomaro W373
Yao, Pam P481
Yao, Xiangjun W88
Yao, Xu-Jie W106
Yao, Bo W383
Yap, Bryan P563
Yap, Huey Wen W29
Yap, Anthony Paul W323
Yap, Chee Keong W370
Yapp, Alison W139
Yaqub, Beel W290
Yarak, Jamie E442
Yarashus, Valerie A A208:P146
Yardley, James A705
Yardley, William W178
Yarensky, Annie P579
Yarlagadda, Choudhary A174
Yarobough, Martin P218
Yaroslavsky, Zev A224:P162
Yarrington, Patricia E A300
Yaschik, Jeff P153
Yasinsky, John A795:E416
Yasuda, Kazuhiro W36
Yasuda, Masamichi W330
Yasuda, Yuko W338
Yasuda, Takao W377
Yasui, Mikiya W67
Yasui, Yoshikazu W327
Yasui, Hajime W435
Yasuoka, Kai W437
Yatabe, Yasushi W182
Yatch, Emily A257
Yates, Lloyd A500:A721
Yates, William A798
Yates, Michael P232
Yates, Stacy P661
Yatsurugi, Yoichiro W23
Yaudes, Jason P34
Yaudes, Jason T P34
Yawata, Haruko P596
Yazawa, Katsuyuki W17
Yazdi, Cynthia A540
Ybarbo, Sylvia P160
Ybarra, Paco A183
Ybarra, Crystal P159
Ybarra, Jesse P475
Ybarra, Jessie P496
Ye, Sulan W383
Ye, Mingjie W435
Ye, Yanliu W535
Yeager, William A328
Yeager, Rande A586
Yeager, Bill P222
Yeager, Sam P499
Yealy, Donald A828:P634

Yeaman, Eric A26
Yeaney, Jacqueline P52
Yeap, Geoffrey W474
Yearley, Douglas A788
Yearsley, William E297
Yearta, William J P358
Yeary, Frank A611
Yeatts, Susan P156
Yedla, Anupama P561
Yee, Brenda A174:P118
Yee, Gim P156
Yee, John K P326
Yee, Sheryl P455
Yee, Betty W100
Yee, Chek Toong W529
Yee, Yang Chiah E330
Yeghyayan, Silva A673
Yeh, Jason P45
Yehiav, Guy E118
Yellig, Laura P413
Yellin, Jonathan E107
Yelmanchili, Oadnaha P234
Yelmenoglu, Ibrahim W505
Yemin, Ezra Uzi A241
Yenni, Michael P406
Yeo, Albert W83
Yeoh, Ban Aik W376
Yeoh, Kim Hong W393
Yeoman, Justin P361
Yep, Gregory A426
Yerby, Jackie A740:P516
Yerks, Austin E122
Yeshaya, Sharon A538
Yeu, Elizabeth E388
Yeung, Yun Chi Kung W87
Yeung, William E137
Yezhkov, Sergey E144
Yi, Sang A878
Yi, Zuo W236
Yi, Xiaogang W419
Yih, Sng A80
Yik, Sook Ling W393
Yilmaz, Kenan W281
Yilmaz, Sezgin W504
Yim, Seung Gyu W388
Yin, Zhaojun W123
Yin, Yande W236
Yin, Peter E354
Ying, Xuejun W154
Yip, Amy W391
Yiu, Kin Wah W118
Ylagan, Victor E P554
Ynostrosa, Stephen A679
Yocham, William P422
Yocum, Arlene A188
Yocum, Deb P522
Yoda, Toshihide W317
Yoda, Makoto W493
Yoder, Emily A121
Yoder, Sheldon A387
Yoder, Ashlee P168
Yoder, Cathy P504
Yogi, Stacy P97
Yoh, Caren A329
Yohannes, Daniel A871
Yokoi, Yoshikazu W182
Yokoo, Keisuke W403
Yokota, Shinichi W68
Yokota, Noriya W277
Yokotani, Kazuya W339
Yokoyama, Yasuyuki W435
Yokoyama, Kiichi W491
Yoler, Laurie A329
Yommer, Dale P91
Yomoda, Yasuhiro A790
Yonamine, Paul A164
Yonebayashi, Akira W52
Yongpisanpop, Ampa W98
Yoo, Chung-Mok P204
Yoo, Byeong Ok W388
Yoo, C.S. W474
Yoon, Tae-Sik A70
Yoon, Chi Won W238
Yoon, Jong Gyu W271
Yoon, Yin Seop W532
Yoon, Amy E64
Yoovidhya, Saravoot W270

Yorgova, Petya P19
Yoritomi, Toshiya W237
York, Jill A587
York, Chris P65
York, Johnny P86
York, James E232
Yorke, Beth P63
Yoshida, Brian A695
Yoshida, Akio W14
Yoshida, Moritaka W21
Yoshida, Shuichi W355
Yoshida, Naoki W377
Yoshida, Kenichiro W454
Yoshifuji, Shigeru W330
Yoshihashi, Mitsuru W68
Yoshii, Keiichi W151
Yoshikawa, Eiichi W146
Yoshikawa, Nana W206
Yoshikawa, Masato W286
Yoshikawa, Masahiro W329
Yoshikawa, Hiroshi W354
Yoshimaru, Yukiko W429
Yoshimoto, Kazumi W355
Yoshimura, Yasunori W377
Yoshino, Shigehiro W494
Yost, Robert A96
Yost, Joseph A364
Yost, Robert A500
Yost, Mark E377
Yother, Alton E213
Youman, Robert E162
Young, James N A32
Young, Brent A32
Young, Ray A69
Young, Andrew A148
Young, Steven K A259
Young, John A286
Young, Terrence A294
Young, Zfrb A298
Young, Dona A332
Young, Ray A427
Young, Charles A439
Young, Christopher A507:A529
Young, Charles A612
Young, Tracie A676
Young, Dennis A694
Young, Bryan A708
Young, Jay A728
Young, Dave A735
Young, Christine L A738
Young, Tara A783
Young, James N P24
Young, Brent P24
Young, Carl P34
Young, Gary P105
Young, Wendell P125
Young, Christopher P149
Young, Rhiannon P164
Young, Anthony P164
Young, Edward P216
Young, Terrance P238
Young, Rebecca P240
Young, Barbara P253
Young, Charles P276
Young, Jeff P302
Young, Sandra P346
Young, Bill P392
Young, Svetlana P402
Young, Marty P449
Young, Mike P465
Young, Andrea P466
Young, Jay P496
Young, Dave P510
Young, Christine L P514
Young, Michael P536
Young, Tara P583
Young, Linda P585
Young, Kalbert P621
Young, Michael P635
Young, James P642
Young, Jessica P646
Young, William P250
Young, Albert E29
Young, Kenneth E42
Young, Terrence E155
Young, Micah E263

606

HOOVER'S HANDBOOK OF EMERGING COMPANIES 2022

COMBINED HOOVER'S HANDBOOK INDEX OF EXECUTIVES

Young, Nicolas E292
Young, Brian E298:E423
Young-Scrivner, Annie A875
Youngblood, Mike A511:P322
Youngblood, Tracie E91
Younger, Simon W242
Youngquist, Gene P73
Youngquist, Scott P630
Youngworth, Jacqueline A390:E215
Yousef, Tarik W38
Youso, Steve P472
Youssouf, Emily A614:E317
Yovich, Mark A483
Yow, Kuan Tuck W232
Yowan, David A545
Yowell, Adam P332
Yrarrazaval, Pedro Silva W255
Ysais, Dotti P302
Ytterberg, Jan W523
Yu, Li A639
Yu, Carrie W14
Yu, Sara W24
Yu, Shui W33
Yu, Herman W54
Yu, Jaime W82
Yu, Baocai W120
Yu, Xizhi W120
Yu, Tengqun W121
Yu, Liang W125
Yu, Yang W129
Yu, Guo-Dung W138
Yu, Vernon W178
Yu, Hongfu W419
Yu, Douglas W474
Yu, Peipei W530
Yu, Yajing W535
Yu, Gary E121
Yu, Evan E121
Yu, Li E331
Yu, K. Peony E388
Yuan, Shu W87
Yuan, Honglin W118
Yuan, Guoqiang W122
Yuan, Jingping W434
Yuasa, Yukio W216
Yuasa, Takayuki W493
Yucel, Saruhan W540
Yucoco, Liza P603
Yue, Ying W212
Yuece, Burcu Civelek W21
Yuen, Shelten G P240
Yuen, Loretta W376
Yuen, Maggie E36
Yuen, Nicole E235
Yuffa, Ilya A478
Yugala, Mongkolchaleam W62
Yuhas, George E75
Yuki, Hirakawa W438
Yultyev, Aleksandr P231
Yumiba, Yasuo W332
Yung, Mark T A606
Yung, Shun Loy W124
Yunker, Craig A789
Yurtsever, Sadrettin W504
Yusof, Noor Azam bin Mohd W29
Yusuf, Nurain A736:P512
Yuvienco, Maria Dolores W70
Yvonne, Luttschwager P522

Z

Zaas, David P196
Zaat, Steven W18
Zabaneh, Samir P247
Zabel, Steven A827
Zabetakis, Paul P299
Zabriskie, Kathryn E95
Zacarias, Fernando P42
Zacarias, Celina E96
Zacariassen, Christian P364
Zachariah, Zachariah P P390
Zacharias, Dawn P614
Zachary, Jennifer A515
Zachary, Alaine P640
Zachos, Kimon S P492
Zacur, Mark A600

Zadoks, Jeff A635
Zadrazil, Robert W509
Zaffini, AVI A740:P516
Zagajeski, Thomas P171
Zagorski, Judy A806
Zagra, Levent W505
Zahariev, Emil P604
Zaharis, Chris P205
Zahl, Brendan A544:E285
Zaid, Najm Bin Abdull Ahal W422
Zaied, Khalil P123
Zaimler, Kivanc W217
Zaitzeff, Michael A113
Zajicek, Hubert W521
Zakaria, Harussani Bin W307
Zakaria, Taswin W307
Zaks, Tal Zvi W487
Zalaznick, Lauren A562:P378
Zalesak, Emil J P293
Zallie, James A418
Zalman, David A646:E336
Zaman, Neil E62
Zamarron, Felipe P548
Zambanini, Adam E413
Zambas, Becky A789:E411
Zammit, Patrick A763
Zampini, Maria P202
Zanavich, W Marie P584
Zander, Scott P304
Zandi, Mark A523
Zane, Ellen A132:A752
Zangardi, John E341
Zanghi, Phyllis A45
Zanias, Georgios W188
Zanin, Ryan A292
Zank, Dennis W A663:P436
Zankowski, Nancy P2
Zanten, Frank van W97:W283
Zapata, Eleazar Gomez W381
Zapfe, Carl A736:P512
Zapico, David A56
Zapletal, Audrey P593
Zapolsky, David A38
Zapotocky, John A614
Zappala, Phyllis F P554
Zappala, Elizabeth P602
Zaramella, Luca A535
Zarate, Andres Eduardo Mantilla W171
Zarcone, Dominick A484:E191
Zardetto-Smith, Andrea P175
Zarin, Larry E2
Zarling, Angela P439
Zarling, Kathy P459
Zaror, Jorge Selume W255
Zarri, Francesca W185
Zaslav, David A714
Zaslav, David M P470
Zastrow, Audra P107
Zatina, Tom A511:P322
Zatyko, A.Rosamond A147:E65
Zauk, Adel M P505
Zausmer, Adam E346
Zavaglia, Joseph E188
Zavitkovski, Caroline A740:P516
Zayicek, Beth A431
Zazworsky, Leon A608:E312
Zbanek, Cathy A773
Zbaraschuk, Amy P215
Zboray, Andrew A738:P514
Zebula, Charles A44
Zecca, John A543
Zech, Gretchen A72
Zechmeister, Michael A683
Zedreck, Christina P628
Zeevi, Gary P473
Zehm, Laura P148:P351
Zehnder-Lai, Eunice W166
Zeidel, Darren W35
Zeile, Arthur A544:E285
Zeiler, Julie E236
Zeine, Elias P44
Zeisel, Karin W187
Zelenczuk, Nicholas W290
Zelinsky, Art A257
Zelkowicz, Stephen E122
Zell, Lisa P119
Zeller, Fred P134

Zeller, Joshua P422
Zeller, Pat P461
Zeller, Lyle E72
Zelnick, Strauss E402
Zeltsman, Brian P128
Zember, Dennis A640:E333
Zen-Ruffinen, Marie-Noelle W55
Zeng, Maojun P28
Zeng, Jianzhong W321
Zeng, Gang W321
Zenner, Patrick E446
Zeno, Zoraida P459
Zenty, Thomas S P614
Zepeda, Carl P119
Zeppos, Nicholas P590
Zerbe, Glenn E299
Zerbs, Michael W69
Zerilli-Marim, Mariuccia A555:P374
Zerza, Armin A10
Zettel, John P53
Zhai, Haitao W117
Zhan, Zhong W117
Zhang, Cherry A123
Zhang, John A222
Zhang, Qin P20
Zhang, Cherry P81
Zhang, Wenqin P185
Zhang, Tong P442
Zhang, Yong W24
Zhang, Jianfeng W24
Zhang, Peng W31
Zhang, Hongjun W31
Zhang, Yunyan W33
Zhang, Xiaorong W33
Zhang, Zhaohong W88
Zhang, Yu W88
Zhang, Min W97
Zhang, Chengjie W114
Zhang, Ke W114
Zhang, Jian W116
Zhang, Yi W119
Zhang, Zhichao W119
Zhang, Shaofeng W120
Zhang, Dawei W121
Zhang, Liqiang W121
Zhang, Liang W121
Zhang, Cui W123
Zhang, Ruohan W123
Zhang, Yichen W125
Zhang, Lin W129
Zhang, Dingming W172
Zhang, Ya-Qin W200
Zhang, Xiaofeng W209
Zhang, Qiusheng W214
Zhang, Jundu W214
Zhang, Wei W214
Zhang, Yuzhu W220
Zhang, Zhiqiang W235
Zhang, Xianzhi W236
Zhang, Haitao W236
Zhang, Weijiong W236
Zhang, Jun W236
Zhang, Jianping W236
Zhang, Wenwu W244
Zhang, Qiang W265
Zhang, Jingzhong W287
Zhang, Wenyang W303
Zhang, Maohan W303
Zhang, Mengxing W321
Zhang, David W348
Zhang, Minggui W349
Zhang, Wei W387
Zhang, Yanhua W387
Zhang, Yaohua W431
Zhang, Dafan W434
Zhang, Kevin W474
Zhang, Ling W535
Zhang, Chuanchang W539
Zhang, Lei W539
Zhang, Zuoxue W541
Zhang, Bo W541
Zhang, Xiang E250
Zhao, Kevin P29
Zhao, Alice P45
Zhao, Dezheng P71
Zhao, Yingnan P615

Zhao, Xin P620
Zhao, Rongzhe W114
Zhao, Dachun W118
Zhao, Wenhai W119
Zhao, Rifeng W120
Zhao, Xianguo W154
Zhao, Guoqing W212
Zhao, Donghua W223
Zhao, Ping W236
Zhao, Keyu W236
Zhao, Junwu W236
Zhao, Linghuan W292
Zhao, Zigao W387
Zhao, Xiangzhang W419
Zhao, Yong W432:W442
Zhao, Qilin W442
Zhao, Kexiong W535
Zhao, Qingchun W539
Zhao, Jin E121
Zhao, Ji E311
Zhdanov, Pavel W386
Zhen, Litao W115
Zhen, Wang W428
Zhen, Marianne E229
Zheng, Peiming A598
Zheng, Ziliang Leon P263
Zheng, Baohua P466
Zheng, Junfang W24
Zheng, Baojin W81
Zheng, Xingang W223
Zheng, Guoyu W244
Zheng, Guangqing W442
Zheng, Yongda W535
Zhiqiang, Cao W200
Zhong, Xiangqun W87
Zhong, Huifeng W88
Zhong, Wei W121
Zhong, Lixin W236
Zhong, Zhengqiang W287
Zhong, Cecelia E235
Zhou, Dongzhou W31
Zhou, Xiaochuan W33
Zhou, Ya-Lin W97
Zhou, Chengyan W115
Zhou, Jun W118
Zhou, Yingqi W236
Zhou, Da W265
Zhou, Yuanhong W287
Zhou, Jichang W321
Zhou, Dongli W387
Zhou, Jun W431
Zhou, Baocheng W490
Zhou, Yifeng W535
Zhu, Yaping P208
Zhu, Meng P263
Zhu, Keshi W31
Zhu, Jialin W115
Zhu, Dajian W123
Zhu, Xu W125
Zhu, Jiusheng W125
Zhu, Hexin W129
Zhu, Shaowen W154
Zhu, Qixin W194
Zhu, Huaming W220
Zhu, Rong'en W236
Zhu, Ning W265
Zhu, Shaofang W303
Zhu, Guangxia W321
Zhu, Liqiang W349
Zhu, Zhengfu W387
Zhu, Limin W539
Zhu, Weimin W542
Zhuang, Yong W119
Zhuang, Shangbiao W120
Zhuang, Pei W214
Zhuang, Jiansheng W542
Ziadie, Bambi P217
Ziai, Daryoush W426
Ziarno, Jeffrey P528
Zichner, Veronica P374
Zicht, J. Phillip E68
Zickefoose, John Z P154
Zidar, Thomas A867:E452
Ziebell, William A341
Ziebell, Mark E39
Ziebinski, Jarek W395
Ziecheck, Hal P353

607

HOOVER'S HANDBOOK OF EMERGING COMPANIES 2022

COMBINED HOOVER'S HANDBOOK INDEX OF EXECUTIVES

A = AMERICAN BUSINESS
E = EMERGING COMPANIES
P = PRIVATE COMPANIES
W = WORLD BUSINESS

Ziegelmeier, Lori P142
Ziegler, Marie A655
Ziegler, Richard A P35
Ziegler, Dawn P217
Ziegler, Andy P466
Ziegler, Larry P607
Ziegler, Marie E340
Zieglgansberger, J. Drew W111
Zielinski, Anita A755
Zielinski, Trudy P143
Zielinski, Matthew W292
Zielke, James K E196
Ziemba, Lawrence A630
Ziemer, James A772
Ziemianski, Karen P208
Zientara, David B P73
Zier, Dawn M P392
Zies, Ray P123
Zietlow, Don P289
Zietlow, Steve P289
Ziffer, Jack A P57
Zikalala, Nompumelelo W32
Zike, Madilyn P399
Zilberfarb, Ben-Zion W253
Zillmer, John A67:A227
Ziluca, Christopher A372
Ziman, Richard E353
Zimmer, Anthony A32
Zimmer, Jeffrey A70
Zimmer, James A320
Zimmer, Steve A486
Zimmer, Anthony P24
Zimmer, Steve P303
Zimmer, James E173
Zimmerli, Bert A414:P260
Zimmerli, Albert E344
Zimmerman, Michael A415
Zimmerman, Charles A826
Zimmerman, Jeffrey P396
Zimmerman, Barbi P500
Zimmerman, Roger E134
Zimmerman, Charles E428
Zimmermann, Deirdre P435
Zimpfer, Matthew A194
Zink, Charles L P414
Zink, Ryan E196
Zink, Gregory E292
Zinkin, Peter P55
Zinn, Judy P90
Zinn, Daniel E308
Zinni, Nicholas J P378
Zins, AMI P130
Zinsner, David A421
Zinsou-Derlin, Lionel W152
Zipf, Bruce A666
Zipfel, Liliann E239
Zipperle, Cynthia A406
Zipse, Oliver W79
Zisler, John A794:P599
Ziss, Bill P614
Zito, James A738:P514
Zitterow, David A294:E155
Zitzner, Duane A763
Ziv, Omer W64
Ziviani, Nivio W380
Ziyadeh, Omar P652
Zlatkus, Lizabeth A519:E272
Zmich, Kenneth P106
Zmitrovich, Joseph E127
Zmitrowicz, Magdalena W70
Zobel, Inigo W417
Zoeller, Johnathan A860
Zoellick, Robert A801
Zogg, Andrew A463
Zoghbi, Huda A669
Zohn, Patrick P138
Zoiss, Edward A463
Zoll, Coral P88
Zollar, Alfred A99:A424:A651
Zoncki, Stephanie P172
Zong, Wenlong W154

Zoppo, Maria Cristina W251
Zordo, Marc De A245:P189
Zoretic, Richard A534
Zorn, Rebecca A359
Zortman, Barbara P173
Zou, Hongying W321
Zuber, Maria A772
Zubkov, Viktor W385
Zubretsky, Joseph A534
Zubrow, Barry W99
Zucchero, Rocco P260
Zucker, Nehemia E457
Zuckerberg, Mark A520
Zuckerman, Steven A229
Zuckerman, Lisa A245:P189
Zuckerman, Harriet P544
Zuckerman, Steven E112
Zuckert, Michael A751
Zuehls, Dale A398:E218
Zuend, Gregor W203
Zuhl, Colleen A786
Zuhlke, Daniel L A423:P264
Zuilen, Wilfred van A878
Zukauckas, Linda A562:P378
Zulla, Caitlin P466
Zullinger, Joel A597:E307
Zumwalt, Debra A473:P295
Zuniga, Daisy P303
Zuo, Min W431
Zuraitis, Marita A185:A399
Zuraitis, Nancy P52
Zurbay, Donald A611
Zvi, Bosmat Ben W64
Zvilichovsky, David W63
Zweben, Lloyd P135
Zwergel, Ken P72
Zwonitzer, Michael P28
Zyczynski, Halina P635
Zyglocke, Hollis A497
Zygocki, Rhonda W111
Zyl, Adriaan Van A89:P54

608

HOOVER'S HANDBOOK OF EMERGING COMPANIES 2022